THE GUINNESS BOOK OF
ANSWERS

GUINNESS PUBLISHING

Editor: Clive Carpenter
Assistant Editor: Tina Persaud
Systems support: Kathy Milligan
Design: David L. Roberts
Layout: Amanda Ward
Cover design: Amanda Ward
Production Manager: Chris Lingard
Information Systems Manager: Alex Reid
Artwork, maps and diagrams: Ad Vantage Studios, Eddie
Botchway, Rhoda and Robert Burns, Peter Harper

8th Edition
First published 1991
Reprint 10 9 8 7 6 5 4 3 2 1 0

© Guinness Publishing Ltd, 1991

Published in Great Britain by Guinness Publishing Ltd,
33 London Road, Enfield, Middlesex

Printed and bound in Great Britain by the Bath Press, Bath

'Guinness' is a registered trademark of Guinness Publishing Ltd.

British Library Cataloguing in Publication Data
The Guinness Book of Answers
1. Miscellaneous facts
1. The Book of Answers
032.02

ISBN 0–85112–957–9

CONTRIBUTORS

Ronald Alley, formerly of the Tate Gallery, London
Matthew Bennett, The Royal Military Academy Sandhurst
Ephraim Borowski, University of Glasgow
Antonia Boström,
Martin Caiger-Smith, The Photographer's Gallery, London
Clive Carpenter
Gill Carpenter
Kim Chesher
Dr Dominique Collon, The British Museum
Ian Crofton
John Cunningham
Robert Dearling
Beryl Dixon
Professor Ronald Draper, University of Aberdeen
Ben Dupré
Di Ellis, S.E.E.C
Geoff Endacott
Dr David Evans, University of Exeter
Dr Mark Evans, National Museum of Wales
Peta Evelyn, The Victoria and Albert Museum
Dr Trevor Ford, formerly of the University of Leicester
Dr Peter Forey, Natural History Museum
Dr D.P. Fowler, Jesus College, Oxford
Tim Furniss
Dr Nigel Gauk-Roger
Professor Brian Gardiner, King's College, London
Professor Frank Glockling, University of Oxford
Dr Martin Godfrey, *GP* Magazine
Dr Janet Goodwyn, The Roehampton Institute, London
The late Dr Beverly Halstead
Dr Graham Handley, University of London
Richard Harding
Rosemary Harris, The Tate Gallery, London
Nigel Hawkes, of *The Times*
Dr Peter Hobson, Brunel University
Graham Holderness, The Roehampton Institute
Ingrid Holford
Robert Jameson
Ann Jones, The Tate Gallery

Dr Gareth Jones, University of Strathclyde
Dr Kim Knott, University of Leeds
Jeremy Lane, University of Sussex
Howard Loxton
Anne Marshall
Peter Matthews
Carol Michaelson
Richard Milbank
Dr D.M.P. Mingos, Keble College, Oxford
Trevor Mostyn, Editor of *The Cambridge Encyclopedia of the Middle East and North Africa*
Dr Chris Pass, University of Bradford
Tina Persaud
Dr John Pimlott, The Royal Military Academy Sandhurst
Rev. Will Pratt
Dr Jonathon Ree, Middlesex Polytechnic
Aileen Reid
Peter Reynolds, The Roehampton Institute, London
James Roberts
Samantha Roberts
Patrick Hickman Robertson
Dr Gillian Sales, King's College, London University
Denise Schulte
Andrew Scott, University College London
Dr Ian Shaw
Ian Sinclair
Dr Elizabeth Sirreyeh, University of Leeds
Dr Peter J. Smith, The Open University
Dr John Sommerville
Lesley Stevenson
Brian Stone, The Open University
Michael J.H. Taylor
Dr David Thomas, University of Sheffield
Professor Anthony K. Thorlby, University of Sussex
Dr Francis Toase, The Royal Military Academy Sandhurst
Dr Loreto Todd, University of Leeds
E.C. Tupper
Michael Vickers, The Ashmolean Museum, Oxford
David Wells
Dr Shearer West
Dr John Westwood
Alan Williams, Polytechnic of Central London
Conrad Wilson, *The Scotsman*

CONTENTS

TECHNOLOGY, INDUSTRY AND TRANSPORT 274–298

BELIEFS AND IDEAS 299–326

LANGUAGE AND LITERATURE 327–345

VISUAL ARTS 346–369

THE PERFORMING ARTS   370–406

HISTORY   407–48

THE ECONOMIC WORLD   449–80

THE INTERNATIONAL WORLD   481–640

SPACE AND TIME
THE NATURE OF THE UNIVERSE

THE UNIVERSE AND COSMOLOGY

The study of the universe, its overall structure and origin, is known as *cosmology*. In the 17th century, the universe was thought to be static, infinite and unchanging. Modern cosmology can be traced back to the 1920s, when the American astronomer Edwin Hubble, using observations made by Vesto Slipher in 1912, showed that the space between galaxies is increasing and the universe is therefore expanding.

There are several theories describing the origin and future of the universe. Among these, the *big-bang theory* is the most widely accepted. Opinions differ, however, as to the future of the universe. Some think that it will continue to expand for ever, whereas others believe that it will eventually end by collapsing in on itself in a big crunch (see below).

THE BIG BANG

The universe is thought to have originated between 15 000 and 20 000 million years ago in a cataclysmic event known as the *big bang*. Theoretical models of the big bang suggest that events in the early history of the universe occurred very rapidly.

The big bang theory suggests that, at the beginning of time, the universe comprised a mixture of different subatomic particles, including electrons, positrons, neutrinos and antineutrinos, together with photons of radiation. The temperature was 100 000 million °C (180 000 million °F) and the density of the mixture was 4000 million times that of water. One second later, the temperature had dropped to 10 000 million °C (18 000 million °F). Matter was spreading out and the density of the universe had fallen to 400 000 times that of water. Heavier particles, protons and neutrons, began to form. Fourteen seconds later the temperature had dropped to 3000 million °C (5400 million °F). Oppositely charged positrons and electrons were annihilating each other and liberating energy. Stable nuclei of helium consisting of two protons and two neutrons began to form. Three minutes after the creation of the universe, the temperature had fallen to 900 million °C (1620 million °F). This is cool enough for deuterium nuclei consisting of one proton and one neutron to form.

Thirty minutes later, the temperature was 300 million °C (540 million °F). Very few of the original particles remained, most of the electrons and protons having been annihilated by their antiparticles (positrons and antiprotons). Many of the remaining protons and neutrons had combined to form hydrogen and helium nuclei and the density of the universe was about one-tenth that of water. Expansion of the universe continued and the hydrogen and helium began to form into stars and galaxies.

The 3 K MICROWAVE BACKGROUND

Astronomers can detect an 'echo' from the big bang in the form of microwave radiation. The existence of the microwave background was predicted by George Gamow in 1948 and found by Penzias and Wilson in 1965. The radiation has a maximum intensity at a wavelength of 2.5 mm (0.1 in) and represents a temperature of 3 K (-270 °C or -454 °F). In the vicinity of the Solar System, the radiation appears to have equal intensity in all directions.

RED SHIFT

In 1868, the English amateur astronomer Sir William Huggins (1824–1910) noticed that lines in the spectra of certain stars were displaced towards the red end of the spectrum. Huggins realized that this was due to the Doppler effect, which had been discovered in 1842. Just as the noise from a moving vehicle will appear to change pitch as it passes, the colour of light from a star will change in wavelength as the star moves towards us, or away from us. Stars moving away from the Earth have their light moved towards the red end of the spectrum (*red shift*), while those moving towards us exhibit a shift towards the blue end.

HUBBLE'S LAW

In 1929, Edwin Hubble (1889–1953) – who also worked on the classification of galaxies – analysed the red shifts of a number of galaxies. He found that the speed at which a galaxy is moving away from us is proportional to its distance – i.e. the more distant a galaxy, the faster it is receding. This principle was formulated as Hubble's law, which can be written in the form: speed = H × distance, where H is the *Hubble constant*.

Various values for the Hubble constant have been proposed, but the generally accepted value is 56 km (35 mi) per second per megaparsec (a megaparsec is 3.26 million light years). Thus a galaxy that is receding from the Earth at 56 km/sec will be 326 000 light years distant.

THE FUTURE OF THE UNIVERSE

At present the universe is still expanding, but whether or not this will continue for ever depends upon the amount of matter it contains. One possible ending for the universe is the *big crunch*. The galaxies and other matter may be moving apart, but their motion is restrained by their mutual gravitational attraction. If there is sufficient matter in the universe, gravity will eventually win and begin pulling the galaxies together again, causing the universe to experience a reverse of the big bang – the big crunch.

What will follow the big crunch is hard to imagine. One possibility is that a new universe will come into being, perhaps containing completely different types of particles from our present universe. The *cyclic theory* suggests that the universe may continue alternately to expand and collapse.

However, it may be that there is not enough matter in the universe for the big crunch to happen. If this is the case, the universe will continue to expand for ever. Although this means there may never be an 'edge' to the universe, there is bound to be an end to the observable universe. Hubble's law states that the speed of recession of a galaxy is proportional to its distance. A galaxy that is far enough away to be travelling at the speed of light will no longer be visible and this will therefore mark the end of the universe we can see. At present the end of the observable universe lies at a distance of between 15 000 and 20 000 million light years.

THE STEADY-STATE THEORY

Another cosmological model, which is no longer generally accepted, is the *steady-state theory*. This supposes that the universe has always existed and will always continue to exist.

The theory was first proposed in 1948 by a group of Cambridge astronomers and popularized by Sir Fred Hoyle (1915–). However, among many other objections, the theory offers no satisfactory explanation for the 3 K microwave background radiation.

LIGHT YEARS AND PARSECS

The *light year* is a unit used to measure great distances, and is equal to the distance travelled by light in one year. Light (in a vacuum) travels at 300 000 km per second (186 000 mi per sec), and so a light year is approximately 9 461 000 million km (5 875 000 million mi).

Distances to the nearest stars can be measured by the *parallax method*. Any object, when viewed from two different vantage points, will appear to move against a background of more distant objects. This apparent change in position is called the *parallax*, and is measured as an angle. Thus if a nearby star is viewed from the Earth at intervals of six months, the Earth will have moved from one side of its orbit to the other and the star will seem to move against the background of more distant stars. The diameter of the Earth's orbit is known, so the distance of the star can be calculated.

The parallax method leads to the definition of the *parsec*, which is the distance at which an object would exhibit a parallax of one second of arc (i.e. one thirty-six thousandth of a degree). One parsec is 3.26 light years, so with the exception of the Sun, no stars are as close as one parsec.

STARS AND GALAXIES

A galaxy is a system of many thousands of millions of stars, together with interstellar gas and dust. Many galaxies are spiral in shape, while others can be spherical, elliptical or irregular. Telescopes have revealed the existence of about 1000 million galaxies, although apart from our own galaxy, only three can be clearly seen with the naked eye.

Stars – of which our Sun is an example – are accretions of gas that radiate energy produced by nuclear-fusion reactions. They range in mass from about 0.06 to 100 solar masses, one solar mass being equivalent to the mass of the Sun. The properties of a star and the manner in which it evolves depend principally on its mass.

Stars are formed within clouds of dust and gas called *nebulae*. Patches of gas and dust inside a nebula collapse under gravity, forming dark regions called protostars. As the protostars continue to collapse, they become denser and hotter. Eventually, they may become hot enough for nuclear-fusion reactions to start and thus turn into stars.

GALAXIES

The American astronomer Edwin Hubble devised a system for classifying galaxies that is still in use. He grouped galaxies into three basic categories: elliptical, spiral and irregular.

Elliptical galaxies range from the spherical E0 type to the very flattened E7.

Spiral galaxies are labelled Sa, Sb or Sc, depending upon how tightly wound the arms are. Some spirals appear to have their arms coming from the ends of a central bar and these *barred spirals* are designated SBa, SBb or SBc.

Irregular galaxies are those whose shape is neither spiral nor elliptical.

Some galaxies are extremely active and emit vast amounts of radiation. One such galaxy is the powerful radio source Centaurus A. *Quasars* are very distant and immensely bright objects, which are thought to represent the nuclei of active galaxies. They may be powered by massive central black holes (see below). The most distant quasar yet detected, PKS 2000–330, is 13 000 million light years from the Earth.

Pulsars are dense stars that emit pulses of polarized radiation as they rotate. They are believed to be neutron stars formed during supernova explosions. They were first discovered in 1967 by a team under Anthony Hewish at the Mullard Radio Astronomy Observatory. As they grow older, pulsars slow down and their flashes fade.

THE MILKY WAY

Our own galaxy is sometimes known as the *Milky Way* or 'the Galaxy'. It contains about 10 000 million stars and is an ordinary spiral galaxy. The Sun is situated in one of the spiral arms. The diameter of the Galaxy is about 100 000 light years and the Sun is some 30 000 light years from the centre. The nearest star to the Sun, Proxima Centauri, is 4.2 light years distant. The Galaxy is rotating and the Sun takes 225 million years to complete one revolution. This is sometimes called a *cosmic year*.

BINARY, MULTIPLE AND VARIABLE STARS

The majority of stars – over 75% – are members of binary or multiple star systems. *Binary stars* consist of two stars each orbiting around their common centre of gravity. An *eclipsing binary* can occur where one component of the system periodically obscures, and is obscured by, the other (as seen from Earth). This leads to a reduction in the light intensity seen from Earth – which is how binary stars were first discovered. Some stars are actually complex *multiple stars*. For example, the 'star' Castor in the constellation of Gemini has six individual components.

Most stars are of constant brightness, but some – *variable stars* – brighten and fade. The variability can be caused by a line-of-sight effect, as in eclipsing binaries (see above). In other cases, changes in the star itself cause periodic increases and reductions of energy output. Variable stars can have periods ranging from a few hours to several years.

MAGNITUDE

Magnitude is a measure of a star's 'brightness'. *Apparent magnitude* indicates how bright a star appears to the naked eye. Paradoxically, the lower the magnitude the brighter the star. Magnitude is measured on a logarithmic scale, taking as its basis the fact that a difference of 5 in magnitude is equivalent to a factor of 100 in brightness. On this basis, a star of magnitude $+1$ is 2.512 times brighter than a star of $+2$, 2.512^2 ($= 6.310$) times brighter than a star of $+3$, and 2.512^5 ($= 100$) times brighter than a star of $+6$.

The limit of naked-eye visibility depends upon how

THE BRIGHTEST STARS

Rank	Name	Bayer designation	Visual magnitude Apparent	Absolute	Brightness on scale (Sun = 1)	Distance in light years
1	Sirius	α Canis Majoris	−1·46*	+1·4	24	8·7
2	Canopus[1]	α Carinae	−0·72	−8·5	220 000	1200
3	Rigel Kentaurus[1]	α Centauri	−0·27**	+4·1**	A 1·6 B 0·5	4·3
4	Arcturus	α Bootis	−0·04	−0·1	98	34
5	Vega	α Lyrae	+0·03	+0·5	56	26
6	Capella	α Aurigae	+0·08**	−0·6**	A 87 B 69	45
7	Rigel	β Orionis	+0·12	−7·1	60 000	900
8	Procyon	α Canis Minoris	+0·38	+2·7	7·7	11·4
9	Achernar[1]	α Eridani	+0·46	−1·6	390	85
10	Betelgeuse	α Orionis	+0·50 v	−5·6 v, s	15 000	310
11	Hadar (Agena)[1]	β Centauri	+0·61	−5·1	9900	460
12	Altair	α Aquilae	+0·77	+2·3	11	16
13	Aldebaran	α Tauri	+0·85 v	−0·8 v	180	68
14	Acrux	α Crucis	+0·87**	−4·3**	A 2900 B 1900	360
15	Antares	α Scorpii	+0·96 v	−4·7 v, s	6700	330
16	Spica	α Virginis	+0·98	−3·5	2200	260
17	Pollux	β Geminorum	+1·14	+1·0	35	35
18	Fomalhaut	α Piscis Austrini	+1·16	+2·0	14	22
19	Deneb	α Cygni	+1·25	−7·5	88 000	1800
20	Mimosa	β Crucis	+1·25	−5·0 s	8900	425
21	Regulus	α Leonis	+1·35	−0·7	170	85
22	Adhara	ε Canaris Majoris	+1·50	−4·4	5000	490

* The apparent visual magnitude of Sirius will reach a maximum of −1·67 by AD 61000.
[1] Not visible from the British Isles.
** Combined magnitude for a double star system.
v Average value for very variable magnitude.
s Absolute magnitude estimated from spectroscopic data alone.

clear the sky is, but the faintest stars that can be seen on a really clear night are about magnitude +6. The world's largest telescopes can detect objects as faint as magnitude +27. Very bright objects can have negative magnitudes: the planet Venus can reach −4.4, the full Moon −12.0 and the Sun −26.8.

The nearer a star is, the brighter it will appear. Different stars lie at different distances, so apparent magnitude does not measure the true brightness of a star. *Absolute magnitude* compensates for a star's distance by calculating its apparent magnitude if it were placed at a distance of 32.6 light years (= 10 parsecs, see box). For example, Sirius is a nearby star and has an apparent magnitude of −1.46. However, its absolute magnitude is +1.4. The Sun has an absolute magnitude of +4.8.

COLOUR AND TEMPERATURE
The colour of a star gives an indication of its temperature. Hot stars are blue, while cool stars are red. Stars are grouped into *spectral types* according to their temperatures.

Type	Colour	Temperature (°C)	(°F)
O	Blue	25 000–40 000	45 000–75 000
B	Blue	11 000–25 000	20 800–45 000
A	Blue-White	7500–11 000	13 500–20 000
F	White	6000–7500	10 800–13 500
G	Yellow	5000–6000	9000–10 800
K	Orange	3500–5000	6300–9000
M	Red	3000–3500	5400–6300

Each spectral type is further subdivided on a scale 0–9. The Sun is classified as G2.

STELLAR EVOLUTION AND BLACK HOLES
The manner in which a star evolves depends upon its mass. Protostars with mass less then 0.06 of the Sun will never become hot enough for nuclear reactions to start. Those with mass between 0.06 and 1.4 solar masses quickly move on to the main sequence and can remain there for at least 10 000 million years. When the available hydrogen is used up, the core contracts, which increases its temperature to 100 million °C (180 million °F). This produces conditions in which helium can begin a fusion reaction and the star expands to become a *red giant*. Finally, the outer layers of the star are expelled, forming a *planetary nebula*. The core then shrinks to become a small *white dwarf* star.

Stars of between 1.4 and 4.2 solar masses evolve more quickly and die younger. They remain on the main sequence for about one million years before the red giant phase begins. The temperature continues to increase as even heavier elements are synthesized until iron is produced at the temperature of 700 million °C (1260 million °F). The star is then disrupted in a huge *supernova* explosion producing, a vast expanding cloud of dust and gas. At the centre of the cloud a small *neutron star* will remain. This rotates very rapidly and is incredibly dense: 1 cm³ (0.061 cu in) of neutron-star material has a mass of about 250 million tonnes (tons).

The evolution of more massive stars is stranger still. They may end their lives by producing a *black hole* – an object so dense that not even light can escape. The only means of detecting a black hole is by observing its gravitational effects on other objects. The X-ray source Cygnus X-1 may comprise a giant star and a black hole. Material would be pulled away from the star by the black hole and heated – giving off X-rays as it is pulled in.

THE NEAREST STARS

Over the next 100 000 years the nearest approach to the Sun by any stars will be to within 2·84 light years by the binary system Alpha Centauri in AD 29700 (N.B. present distance 4·35 light years).

Name	Distance in light years	Visual magnitude Apparent	Absolute	Brightness on scale Sun = 1
Proxima Centauri	4·22	11·05	15·49	0·000 056
Alpha Centauri	4·35	A −0·01 B 1·33	A 4·37 B 5·71	A 1·6 B 0·5
Barnard's Star	5·98	9·54	13·22	0·000 46
Wolf 359	7·75	13·53	16·65	0·000 019
Lalande 21185	8·22	7·50	10·49	0·0056
Luyten 726–8*	8·43	A 12·52 B 13·02	A 15·46 B 15·96	A 0·000 058 B 0·000 037
Sirius	8·65	A −1·46 B 8·68	A 1·42 B 11·56	A 24·0 B 0·0021
Ross 154	9·45	10·6	13·3	0·000 42
Ross 248	10·4	12·29	14·77	0·000 11
Epsilon Eridani	10·8	3·73	6·13	0·31
Ross 128	10·9	11·10	13·47	0·000 36
61 Cygni	11·1	A 5·22 B 6·03	A 7·56 B 8·37	A 0·084 B 0·040
Epsilon Indi	11·2	4·68	7·00	0·14
Luyten 789–6	11·2	A 12·7 B 13·4	A 15·0 B 15·7	A 0·000 089 B 0·000 047
Groombridge 34	11·2	A 8·08 B 11·06	A 10·39 B 13·37	A 0·0062 B 0·000 40
Procyon	11·4	A 0·38 B 10·7	A 2·65 B 13·0	A 7·7 B 0·000 56
Sigma 2398	11·6	A 8·90 B 9·69	A 11·15 B 11·94	A 0·0031 B 0·0015
Lacaille 9352	11·7	7·36	9·59	0·013
Giglas 51–15	11·7	14·81	17·03	0·000 014
Tau Ceti	11·8	3·50	5·71	0·46
Luyten's Star	12·3	9·82	11·94	0·0015
Luyten 725–32	12·5	12·04	14·12	0·000 20
Lacaille 8760	12·5	6·67	8·74	0·028
Kapteyn's Star	12·7	8·81	10·85	0·0041

* The B star companion is known as UV Ceti.

A GUIDE TO THE SCALE OF THE SOLAR SYSTEM AND THE UNIVERSE

The scale of the solar system is defined in terms of the *astronomical unit* (AU), which is the average distance from the Earth to the Sun. A formal definition of this unit was adopted by the International Astronomical Union in 1938 and the currently accepted value is 149 597 870 km (92 955 807 miles).

If the solar system is reduced to a scale such that the diameter of the Sun is diminished to the size of a beach ball 30·5 cm (1 ft) in diameter, then the largest planet – Jupiter – would only be a reddish-yellow plum 3·1 cm (1·2 in) in diameter, whilst the Earth would be a very small blue-green pea only 0·28 cm (0·1 in) in diameter. The distance between the Sun and the Earth would be 32·7 m (107 ft), while the edge of the solar system, defined as the farthest distance of Pluto from the Sun, would be 1·6 km (1 mile) away. The remoteness of the solar system from all other heavenly bodies is stressed by the fact that the nearest star, Proxima Centauri, would be 8760 km (5440 miles) distant on this scale (approximately the distance from London to the west coast of North America). Beyond this, distance again becomes 'astronomical' in size and in order to visualize the vastness of space use is made of the light year (see box on p. 10).

Distances measured in light years may be difficult to visualize, but an indication of these distances is that light will travel to the Earth from the following heavenly bodies (surface to surface in the case of nearby objects) in the following times:

From the Moon (at mean distance)	1·26 sec
From the Sun (at mean distance)	8 min 17 sec
From Pluto (at mean distance)	5 h 20 min
From the nearest star Proxima Centauri	4·22 years
From the centre of the Galaxy (present distance)	27 700 years
From the most distant star in our Galaxy (present distance)	62 700 years
From the nearest extra-galactic body (the Large Magellanic Cloud)	150 000 years
From the Andromeda Nebula (limit of naked eye vision)	2 150 000 years
From the most distant quasar known (QSO 0051–279)	13 000 000 000 years
From the edge of the observable Universe	15–20 000 000 000 years

THE SOLAR SYSTEM

THE AGE OF THE SOLAR SYSTEM

Meteoric evidence suggests that the solar system is 4530 ± 20 million years old, and that it was formed in less than 25 million years. It is thought that the presence of very heavy elements in both the Earth's crust and the Sun's photosphere is a result of debris from supernovae that had exploded at earlier times.

The solar system is believed to have been formed from a 'globe' of gas and dust that consisted mainly of hydrogen. Helium may have comprised 25% of the globe and about 2% was probably formed of other elements. During coalescence the globe started to rotate and flatten, with the central core rotating faster and therefore becoming more dense than the outer regions. In the outer regions, grains of dust and minute particles of water, methane and ammonia in ice form began to collide and coagulate into larger and larger units. At first they formed meteoroids, then planetesimals, and then protoplanets. The protoplanets acquired atmospheres from the reservoir of hydrogen and helium in the 'globe'. At the same time, the core of the 'globe' became much denser and eventually hot enough to trigger the fusion of hydrogen into helium to form a protostar – the Sun.

The protostar emitted large quantities of matter and radiant energy in an attempt to achieve an equilibrium state. This action removed not only the remnants of the original globe of gas and dust but also the primordial atmospheres of the inner protoplanets. Only the outer planets retained their atmospheres.

Once equilibrium is established, a star such as the Sun can continue to create energy through fusion for about 10 000 million years (i.e. for about a further 5000 million years from the present). After that time a critical amount of hydrogen will have been used up and the core will consist almost entirely of helium. It will then be unable to sustain fusion. However, energy is still being radiated from the surface and drained from the star. In an attempt to re-establish equilibrium the core contracts and releases gravitational energy. This results in the onset of fusion reactions in the hydrogen envelope immediately surrounding the core and a consequent swelling of the outer shell which, because of the reduced temperature, glows red and not white. Such a star – known as 'red giant' – can be about 40 million km (25 million mi) in diameter.

Over the next 100 million years, the Sun's central core will become denser and hotter. When its temperature has increased sufficiently it will suddenly trigger the fusion of helium into carbon. The energy released will blow away the Earth's outer atmosphere and probably destroy the rest of the solar system in the process. Only the Sun's core – about one and a half times the diameter of the Earth – will be left. It will, however, retain about half the mass of the original Sun, so its density will be about 50 000 times greater than that of the Earth. The Sun will have become a *white dwarf* star. It will still be capable of continuing to shine for several thousand million years, simply by using up the thermal energy that was stored up after the collapse of the core, but eventually it will become a burnt-out cinder.

THE SUN

Our nearest star, the Sun, is at a true distance of 1·00000102 astronomical units or 149 598 020 km (92 955 900 mi) from the Earth. The minimum distance between the Sun and the Earth – the *perihelion* – is 147 097 800 km (91 402 300 mi) – and the maximum distance – the *aphelion* – is 152 098 200 km (94 509 400 mi).

The Sun is classified as a 'yellow dwarf' star of spectral type G2. It has a diameter of 1 392 140 km (865 040 mi) – that is 109·13 times greater than that of the Earth – and a mass of $1·9889 \times 10^{27}$ tonnes ($1·9575 \times 10^{27}$ tons) – that is equivalent to 332 946·04 times the mass of the Earth.

The low density of the Sun, 1·408 g/cm^3, is consistent with its overall composition by mass of 73% hydrogen, 25% helium, and 2% of other elements. Its internal structure consists of a helium-rich core with a central temperature of 15 400 000 °C (27 720 032 °F). The core is surrounded by a radiative layer several hundred thousand kilometres thick, a convective layer several tens of thousands of kilometres thick – in which heat is transported by convection in the form of cells – and a 300 km (200 mi) outer layer – or *photosphere* – which represents the maximum depth of visibility within the Sun and reveals the convective layer cells as a patchwork of granules. The observed overall temperature of the photosphere is 5507 °C (9945 °F).

The photosphere rotates at a rate of 25·38 days (27·28 days as viewed from Earth). This value is determined from observations of *sunspots*, which occur in this layer. The production of sunspots is due to magnetic anomalies. The darkness of the sunspots is actually a contrast effect since they are still very bright, but at a temperature about 2000 °C (3600 °F) less than the overall photosphere temperature.

The Sun's atmosphere consists of a *chromosphere*, which extends about 10 000 km (6000 mi) above the photosphere. It has a low density but a sufficiently high temperature that all elements are in an ionized state – its pinkish hue is due to the presence of ionized hydrogen. The outer atmosphere – or *corona* – appears as a white halo and is an extremely thin gas at very high temperature (1 000 000 °C/1 800 000 °F).

The most spectacular features – extending from the top of the chromosphere and into the corona – are huge jets of gas flung many thousands of kilometres into space and looped back into the chromosphere by intense magnetic fields. The extremely high temperature of the corona continuously disperses the Sun's outer atmosphere into space in the form of a plasma of protons and electrons – the 'solar wind' – which permeates the whole of the solar system.

At the centre of the Sun, hydrogen undergoes nuclear fusion. In stars the size of the Sun this occurs mainly by direct proton–proton reaction, i.e. two protons react together to form a deuteron, a positron and a neutrino, then the deuteron reacts with another proton to form helium 3 and a photon, and the cycle is complete when two helium 3 nuclei react together to form helium 4 and two protons. The net result is that an extremely small amount of matter is converted to energy per cycle but the overall result for the Sun is that 4 million tonnes/ tons of matter is lost per second. However, the high temperature and luminosity of the Sun are not due directly to the nuclear reaction but to the energy generated by the extremely high internal gas pressures required to counteract the intense gravitational contraction pressure that acts on such a large mass. Acting alone, this source of energy could only supply the Sun's needs for several tens of millions of years, but this effect is extended to 10 000 million years since the nuclear fusion reaction replaces the energy lost through radiation.

THE TITIUS-BODE RULE

A theory by Titius of Wittenberg (Germany) in 1766 – publicized by Johan Bode in 1772 – suggested that the orbital distances adopted by the planets around the Sun may not be arbitrary. Titius noted that the simple series $4, 4 + (3 \times 2^0), 4 + (3 \times 2^1), 4 + (3 \times 2^2)$ etc, when divided by ten, reproduced the orbital

	Mercury	Venus	Earth	Mars	–	Jupiter	Saturn	Uranus
Sequence	0·40	0·70	1·00	1·60	2·80	5·20	10·00	19·60
Actual distance	0·39	0·72	1·00	1·52	–	5·20	9·55	19·22

distances in astronomical units of the six known planets. The discovery of Uranus in 1781 also led to a satisfactory agreement.

The gap at 2·8 astronomical units (AU) was solved by the discovery of the asteroid Ceres in 1801 and the subsequent discovery of several thousand more asteroids orbiting between 2·3 and 3·3 AU. However, the total mass of the asteroids is only two-thousandths of the Earth's mass and therefore hardly planet size, but attempts to form a planet in this region may have been disrupted by nearby Jupiter when it may have

been an even more massive protoplanet. Beyond Uranus, the Titius-Bode prediction is that the next two planets would be at 38·8 and 77·2 AU respectively, but giant Neptune is actually at 30·1 AU and small Pluto at 39·5 AU. Whilst Pluto's orbit would appear to approximate to the Titius-Bode Rule, it is actually very eccentric and highly inclined and therefore the agreement is almost coincidental. However, the fact that the two planets do not obey the prediction has been interpreted as an indication of a catastrophe that may have befallen them during the early history of the solar system.

MEAN ELEMENTS OF THE PLANETARY ORBITS

Planet	Mean distance from Sun km	miles	Orbital eccentricity	Orbital inclination	Sidereal period days	Mean orbital velocity km/s	mps
Mercury	57 909 100	35 983 000	0·205630	7° 00′ 17″	87·9693	47·87	29·75
Venus	108 208 600	67 237 700	0·006777	3° 23′ 40″	224·7008	35·02	21·76
Earth	149 598 000	92 955 900	0·016713	– – –	365·2564	29·78	18·51
Mars	227 939 200	141 634 800	0·093392	1° 50′ 59″	686·9799	24·13	14·99
Jupiter	778 298 400	483 612 200	0·048479	1° 18′ 14″	4332·59	13·06	8·12
Saturn	1 429 394 000	888 184 000	0·055543	2° 29′ 21″	10759·2	9·66	6·00
Uranus	2 875 039 000	1 786 466 000	0·046299	0° 46′ 23″	30688·5	6·81	4·23
Neptune	4 504 450 000	2 798 935 000	0·008987	1° 46′ 15″	60182·3	5·44	3·38
Pluto	5 913 490 000	3 674 490 000	0·248537	17° 09′ 00″	90777·6	4·74	2·94

The minimum (perihelion) and maximum (aphelion) distances from the Sun can be calculated from the the mean distance (a) and eccentricity (e) through the formulae: Perihelion = $a(1 - e)$ and Aphelion = $a(1 + e)$.

PHYSICAL PARAMETERS OF THE PLANETS ON THE SCALE EARTH = 1

Planet	Equatorial diameter	Volume	Mass excluding satellites	Surface gravity
Mercury	0·3825	0·0562	0·055 27	0·3769
Venus	0·9488	0·8569	0·815 00	0·9033
Earth	1·0000	1·0000	1·000 00*	1·0000
Mars	0·5326	0·1506	0·107 45	0·3795
Jupiter	11·209	1323·3	317·828	2·637
Saturn	9·449	766·3	95·161	1·136
Uranus	4·007	63·1	14·536	0·917
Neptune	3·888	57·8	17·132	1·146
Pluto	0·179	0·0058	0·0022	0·067

* The Earth–Moon system weights 1·0123 Earth masses.

THE INNER PLANETS

Mercury, Venus, Earth and Mars are traditionally grouped together as the 'Inner Planets'. The four inner members of the Sun's family are relatively small, rocky planets. As the Earth is a member of this group they are sometimes known as the *terrestrial planets*. Despite this initial similarity, the four terrestrial planets are very different worlds. Mercury and Venus are inhospitably hot, whereas for much of the year Mars is bitterly cold.

MERCURY

Mercury's proximity to the Sun makes it a difficult planet to see, as it only appears low in the west after

sunset, or low in the east before sunrise. The first telescope observations were made from Gdansk (now in Poland but then the German city, Danzig) by Johannes Hevelius (1611–87), who saw that the planet has phases like the Moon.

Although Mercury looks remarkably like the Moon, with similar craters and highlands, it lacks the large frozen lava 'seas' (or 'maria'). The most notable surface feature on Mercury is the Caloris Basin, which is 1300 km (800 mi) in diameter and is surrounded by a ring of mountains rising up to 2000 m (6500 ft). Almost all of our information about Mercury comes from *Mariner 10*, the only spacecraft to have visited the planet. The pictures it returned showed a barren, rocky world, covered in craters,

PHYSICAL PARAMETERS OF THE PLANETS

Planet		Diameter km	Diameter miles	Equatorial sidereal rotation period d	h	m	s	Equatorial inclination	Mass* kg	Mass* tons	Density g/cm³	Escape velocity km/s	Escape velocity mps	Mean surface temperature °C	Apparent magnitude**
Mercury	Equ.	4 880	3 032	58	15	30	33·9	0°	3·302 × 10²³	3·250 × 10²¹	5·428	4·25	2·64	+172	−0·42
Venus	Equ.	12 103	7 520	R 243	00	32		177° 20′	4·869 × 10²⁴	4·792 × 10²¹	5·245	10·36	6·44	+464	−4·40
Earth	Equ.	12 756	7 926		23	56	04·1	23° 26′	5·974 × 10²⁴	5·879 × 10²¹	5·515	11·19	6·95	+15	—
	Polar	12 714	7 900												
Mars	Equ.	6 794	4 221	1	00	37	22·7	25° 11′	6·419 × 10²³	6·317 × 10²	3·934	5·03	3·12	−53	−2·01
	Polar	6 752	4 196												
Jupiter	Equ.	142 984	88 846		9	50	30·0	3° 08′	1·899 × 10²⁷	1·869 × 10²⁴	1·325	60·19	37·40	−108	−2·70
	Polar	133 708	83 082												
Saturn	Equ.	120 536	74 898		10	39	22·4	26° 43′	5·685 × 10²⁶	5·595 × 10²⁶	0·685	36·07	22·41	−139	+0·67
	Polar	108 718	67 560												
Uranus	Equ.	51 118	31 763		R17	14	24·0	97° 52′	8·683 × 10²⁵	8·546 × 10²²	1·271	21·38	13·28	−197	+5·52
	Polar	49 946	31 035												
Neptune	Equ.	49 600	30 820		16	03		29° 34′	1·023 × 10²⁶	1·007 × 10²³	1·640	23·55	14·63	−193	+7·84
	Polar	48 600	30 200												
Pluto	Equ.	2 284	1 419	R 6	09	18		117° 34′	1·29 × 10²²	1·27 × 10¹⁹	2·1	1·23	0·76	−220	+15·12

R = Retrograde motion.
* Mass excluding satellites.
** The magnitudes are those at mean opposition except for Mercury and Venus, where the values have been reduced to a distance of one astronomical unit (on this scale the magnitude of the Earth is −3·86).

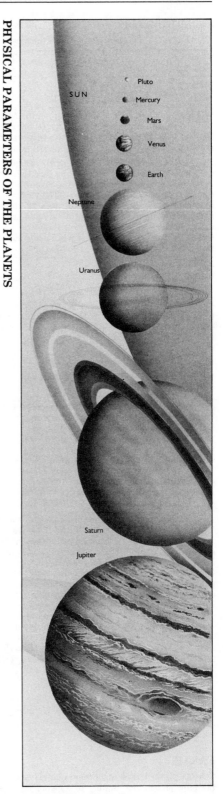

some of which are over 200 km (120 mi) in diameter.

To all intents and purposes Mercury does not have an atmosphere. It therefore experiences large temperature variations between day and night: 420 °C (788 °F) dropping to − 180 °C (− 292 °F). The latter value could not be understood until it was discovered that Mercury rotates on its axis every 59 days – that is exactly two-thirds of its orbital period. The result is that the Sun appears to 'dance about' in the Mercurian sky and a 'day' on Mercury (sunrise-to-sunrise) is equivalent to two Mercurian years or 176 Earth days.

The extraordinarily high density of the planet – compared to its size – is due to the fact that its iron-rich core is 3600 km (2200 mi) in diameter and contains 80% of the planet's mass. The relatively thin mantle or surface layer has recently been associated with the same type of 'giant impact' theory that led to the formation of the Moon (see below), but in Mercury's case the debris could not be retained to form a new moon.

Mercury has no satellites.

VENUS

Venus is similar in size to the Earth, its nearest neighbour. It is often the brightest object in the night sky, apart from the Moon. Like Mercury, Venus can only be seen with the naked eye in the morning or the evening.

Venus is an intensely hostile planet with an atmosphere consisting almost entirely of carbon dioxide at a pressure 94 times that of the Earth. Venus has an average temperature of 464 °C (867 °F) with little difference between the equator and the poles. This temperature is maintained by a runaway 'greenhouse effect' in which heat received from the Sun is trapped within the atmosphere. A thick cloud cover between 50 and 75 km (30 and 45 mi) above the surface contains a high concentration of aerosol droplets of sulphuric acid – the source of the sulphur may be due to emanations from active volcanoes. The upper clouds race around the planet once every four days – much faster than the planet itself is turning.

The first spacecraft to transmit from the surface of Venus was the Soviet *Venera 7*. The later probes *Veneras 9, 10, 13* and *14* returned pictures from the surface of the planet. Although the surface of Venus is not visible from space it has been mapped by radar. In 1978, the American *Pioneer-Venus* spacecraft was put into orbit around the planet to start making a map of the surface. This revealed a complex surface with about 60% of the planet covered by low-lying rolling plains. Upland areas, volcanoes and rift valleys were also revealed. The notable highland regions include Ishtar Terra in the north, which is 2900 km (1800 mi) in diameter and contains the Maxwell Montes mountain chain, which rises up to 8 km (5 mi) above the surrounding plateau.

Although the rotation period of Venus is longer than its year, the Venutian 'day' (sunrise-to-sunrise if it can be seen from the surface) is equivalent to 116 Earth days.

Venus has no satellites.

EARTH

The Earth is the largest of the four inner planets and the only planet that is able to support life. Its atmosphere consists mainly of nitrogen (78%) and oxygen (21%). Two-thirds of its surface is covered in water which has an average depth of 3900 m (12 900 ft). The land rises above the oceans to an average height of 880 m (2800 ft). More detailed information on the Earth's interior, atmosphere and structure will be found on pp. 54–56.

The Earth has a single satellite, the Moon.

THE MOON

The Earth's only natural satellite has an average diameter of 3475·1 km (2159·3 mi), making it larger than the planet Pluto. It has a mass of 7.343×10^{19} tonnes (7.232×10^{19} tons) or 0·0123 Earth masses.

The Moon has a mean orbital distance of 384 399·1 km (238 854·5 mi) from the Earth. Its centre of gravity is displaced from the centre by 1·8 km (1·1 mi) towards the Earth. The average minimum orbital distance – the *perigee* – is 363 295 km (225 741 mi) and the maximum orbital distance – the *apogee* – is 405 503 km (251 968 mi), but because of the perturbing effects of the Sun and nearby planets the closest and farthest approaches of the Moon in this century were 356 375 km (221 441 mi) on 4 January 1912 and 406 711 km (252 718 mi) on 2 March 1984 respectively.

The Moon orbits the Earth once every 27.3 days in *synchronous rotation* – i.e. it keeps the same face towards the Earth. Although only 59% of the Moon's surface is visible from Earth, extensive space-probe photography has now recorded the whole of the lunar surface. Surface features include craters formed by meteoritic bombardment, mountain ranges and broad plains, which in the past were mistakenly named 'seas' or 'maria'. The temperature on the lunar surface ranges from –180 °C (–292 °F) to + 110 °C (+ 200 °F).

It was not until October 1959 that the Soviet probe *Luna 3* returned the first pictures from the far side of the Moon – which turned out to be much the same as the near side, except for the absence of the maria. When men first landed on the Moon in 1969 they found rocks that were 3700 million years old – as old as some of the oldest rocks on the Earth.

As seen from the Earth, the Moon passes through a series of *phases* every 27.3 days – waxing from new Moon, through first quarter, to full Moon, then waning to last quarter and new Moon again.

The Origins of the Moon A number of theories have been put forward to explain the origin of the Moon.

As lunar surface rocks are about the same age as the Earth it has been suggested that the Earth and Moon resulted from the fission of a single molten protoplanet. The major objection to this *fission theory* is that recent calculations suggest that such a protoplanet would be too viscous to split apart in this manner.

The *co-accretion theory* suggested that the Earth and Moon were formed in a common orbit, but this cannot explain the major differences in the overall chemical composition of the two bodies (i.e. a large depletion of iron in the Moon compared to the Earth).

The *capture theory* attempted to overcome these compositional differences by suggesting that the Moon was formed in a different place in the inner solar system and then captured into Earth orbit. The major objection to this theory is that, for capture to have happened, the Moon's orbit would have to have

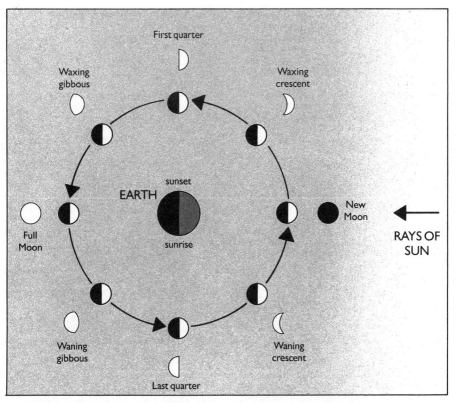

First quarter

Waxing gibbous

Waxing crescent

sunset

EARTH

New Moon

Full Moon

RAYS OF SUN

sunrise

Waning gibbous

Waning crescent

Last quarter

been highly elliptical and could not have altered into its present circular orbit in the time available.

The theory that is currently gaining acceptance is the *giant impact hypothesis*. This suggests that during the violent early history of the solar system the newly formed Earth was struck by a planetesimal – about the size of Mars – which disrupted both the mantle (surface layer) of the Earth and the planetesimal with such energy that the debris was flung into space by gas pressure. The gas remained in the vicinity of the Earth just beyond the limit of instability (the Roche limit) and within 100 years began to coalesce into a partly or fully molten Moon. Minor modifications to the theory involve whether there were several planetesimals rather than one and how much of that body was involved in forming the lunar body. Whilst this theory is not yet universally accepted it is the most plausible explanation of the Moon's origin offered so far.

MARS

Mars is the fourth planet from the Sun. It is the most hospitable planet other than the Earth, having a thin carbon-dioxide atmosphere. Early observers, including the Italian Giovanni Schiaparelli (1835–1910), believed they saw canals and vegetation on Mars, but modern observations have shown that these do not exist.

Mars has an atmospheric pressure only about one-hundredth of that of the Earth and an average temperature of about –23 °C (–9 °F). The Martian year is equivalent to 687 days.

In 1965 the American *Mariner 4* spacecraft flew by Mars and returned pictures showing a barren,

cratered surface, massive extinct volcanoes, mountain ranges, deep chasms, flat deserts and pole caps. A number of volcanoes are of an immense size. They include Olympus Mons in the Tharsis region, which is up to 600 km (370 mi) in diameter and rises 26 km (16 mi) above the surrounding plain. There are also a number of large 'channels' such as Valles Marineris, which is 4000 km (2500 miles) long, up to 200 km (125 mi) wide, and 6 km (4 mi) deep. Although there is now no direct evidence of the water that may have created these channels, it is possible that some water ice may be present at the poles under the frozen carbon-dioxide caps.

SATELLITES OF MARS

The two extremely small irregularly shaped satellites of Mars – Phobos and Deimos – were discovered by Asaph Hall in August 1877.

Phobos (Number I)
Distance from Mars 9378 km (5827 mi).
Diameter 22 km (14 mi). This is an average diameter for a highly irregularly shaped satellite.

Deimos (Number II)
Distance from Mars 23 459 km (14 577 mi).
Diameter 13 km (8 mi). This is an average diameter for a highly irregularly shaped satellite.

THE MINOR PLANETS OR ASTEROIDS

The minor planets, sometimes known as the asteroids, comprise up to 40 000 small bodies, of which only about 4000 have had their orbits determined. Most are extremely small, only a few metres in diameter and orbit mainly between Mars and

Jupiter, but one group, the Aten asteroids, discovered by the Americans E.F. Helin and I.M. Shoemaker in January 1976, has orbits smaller than that of the Earth. A single asteroid, Chiron, discovered by the American C.T. Kowal in October 1977, has been found to orbit between Saturn and Uranus.

The minor planets were once thought to be the residue of a planet broken up by the gravitational pull of Jupiter. Most astronomers now think that they represent a class of primitive objects that were 'left over' during the formation of the solar system, due to Jupiter's disruptive pull.

Three minor planets are considerably bigger than the others. Between them, Ceres, Pallas and Vesta account for over half of the total mass of the asteroids.

CERES

(Minor planet number 1). The largest minor planet, Ceres, was the first to be discovered – by the Italian Giuseppe Piazzi on 1 January 1801. Ceres has a diameter of 936 km (582 mi) and is a little under half the size of the planet Pluto. It is at a mean distance of 413.6 million km (257 million mi) from the Sun. Ceres orbits the Sun in 4.6 Earth years and has an orbital inclination of 10°. This small planet has carbon-rich surface material.

PALLAS

(Minor planet number 2). Pallas was discovered by the German Heinrich Olbers in 1802. It has a diameter of 532 km (331 mi) and is at a mean distance of 414.2 million km (257.4 million mi) from the Sun. Pallas orbits the Sun in 4.61 Earth years and has an orbital inclination of 34°. The surface layer of Pallas is a peculiar carbon.

VESTA

(Minor planet number 4). Vesta is the brightest of the minor planets and can sometimes just be seen with the naked eye – unlike Ceres, Pallas and Juno. It was discovered by Olbers in 1807 and has a diameter of 519 km (322 mi). Vesta is at a mean distance of 352.9 million km (219.3 million mi) from the Sun. Vesta orbits the Sun in 3.63 Earth years. The surface layer of Vesta is eucrite, a calcium-rich igneous rock.

OTHER MINOR PLANETS

Other well-known minor planets include:

Davida (Minor planet number 511). Davida was discovered in 1903. It has a diameter of 361 km (224 mi).

Eros (Minor planet number 433). The orbit of Eros takes it far away from the main swarm of asteroids and in 1975 it came within 24 million km (15 million mi) of the Earth. Eros is shaped like a slab with dimensions of 10 km (6 mi) × 15 km (9 mi) × 30 km (19 mi).

Euphrosyne (Minor planet number 31). Euphrosyne is one of the larger asteroids, being over 300 km (186 mi) in diameter. At one time it was listed as the fifth biggest minor planet, but it is now thought to be smaller than Davida (q.v.).

Hector (Minor planet number 624). Hector is shaped like a cylinder 110 km (68 mi) long and 40 km (25 mi) in diameter.

Hidalgo (Minor planet number 944). Hidalgo – which has a diameter of 43 km (27 mi) – is remarkable for an orbit that takes it out in the solar system almost as far as Saturn.

Hygeia (Minor planet number 10). Hygeia was discovered in 1849. It has a diameter of 414 km (257 mi) and is at a mean distance of 470.9 million km (292.6 million mi). Hygeia orbits the Sun in 5.59 Earth years.

Icarus (Minor planet number 1566). Icarus is a tiny sphere with a diameter of only 2 km (just over 1 mi). In 1968 it passed within 6.8 million km (4.2 million mi) of the Earth on its most eccentric orbit, which takes it nearer to the Sun than Mercury.

Juno (Minor planet number 3). Juno was discovered by the German Karl Harding in 1804. It has a diameter of 190 km (118 mi) and is at a mean distance of 398.8 km (247.8 million mi) from the Sun. The length of the year of Juno is equivalent to 4.36 Earth years.

THE OUTER PLANETS

The outer planets are very different from the inner planets. They are very much further away from the Sun and, with the exception of Pluto, they are much larger than the inner planets. Jupiter, Saturn, Uranus and Neptune are giant 'gas' planets without solid surfaces.

Much of our knowledge of the outer planets has been gained from the American space probes *Pioneer 10*, *Pioneer 11*, *Voyager 1* and *Voyager 2*, the last of which visited Jupiter, Saturn, Uranus and Neptune in turn from 1979 to 1989.

JUPITER

Jupiter is the largest planet in the solar system. It appears very bright to the naked eye and can outshine everything in the sky except the Sun, the Moon, Venus and (very occasionally) Mars.

Through a telescope, several belts or bands can be seen in Jupiter's atmosphere. The planet's rapid rotation rate of 9 hours 55 minutes throws the equator outwards, producing a distinct 'squashed' appearance.

The low density of Jupiter implies a composition consisting mainly of the primordial elements hydrogen and helium. A recent model suggests a structure consisting of a rock–iron–ice core about 15 000 km (9000 mi) in diameter and weighing about 15 times the mass of the Earth. This core is thought to be surrounded by a shell of metallic hydrogen (which also contains a small amount of helium). The shell is thought to extend up to 55 000 km (34 000 mi) from the centre of the planet. The outer envelope consists mainly of liquid molecular hydrogen.

Jupiter is surrounded by a gaseous atmosphere which contains helium (18% by mass) and small quantities of compounds such as water and ammonia ices and ammonium hydrosulphide. It is these compounds that impart the light and dark bands to the planet's atmosphere. The 'Great Red Spot' may have been seen as early as 1664. Modern observations of Jupiter show that the Red Spot is a whirling storm in the planet's atmosphere. This storm appears to be a swirling column rising up to 8 km (5 mi) above the surrounding clouds. Its red colour may be due to the presence of phosphorus from the decomposition of a minor atmospheric constituent, phosphine.

Jupiter radiates 69% more heat than it receives from

the Sun; this can be entirely explained by dissipation of the primordial heat available in the planet.

THE RINGS OF JUPITER

The ring system of Jupiter was discovered in March 1979. The bright central ring is 7000 km (4300 miles) in width and less than 30 km (20 mi) in thickness, with an abrupt outer boundary at 129 130 km (80 240 mi) from the centre of the planet. A faint inner ring is believed to extend to the outer edge of the planet's atmosphere and is surrounded by a 'ghost-like' halo.

SATELLITES OF JUPITER

Jupiter has 16 moons, of which the four largest, the Galilean satellites – named after their co-discoverer Galileo Galilei – are often considered 'worlds' in their own right. Jupiter's other 12 moons are all very small and are grouped into three distinct orbit bands, with four moons close to the planet, four at about 163 Jupiter radii, and four at about 314 Jupiter radii, the latter two groups probably being captured asteroids.

Metis (Number XVI)
Distance from Jupiter: 127 960 km (79 510 mi). This small satellite is embedded in the bright ring.
Diameter: 40 km (25 mi). This is an average diameter for a highly irregularly shaped satellite.

Adrastea (Number XV)
Distance from Jupiter: 128 980 km (80 140 mi). Adrastea lies at the edge of the ring.
Diameter: 20 km (12 mi).

Amalthea (Number V)
Distance from Jupiter: 181 370 km (112 700 mi).
Diameter: 166 km (103 mi). This is an average diameter for a highly irregularly shaped satellite.

Thebe (Number XIV)
Distance from Jupiter: 221 900 km (137 880 mi).
Diameter: 100 km (62 mi). This is an average diameter for a highly irregularly shaped satellite.

Io (Number I). One of the Galilean satellites, Io is continuously subject to volcanic eruptions due to gravitational interactions with Jupiter.
Distance from Jupiter: 421 800 km (262 100 mi).
Diameter: 3642 km (2263 mi).

Europa (Number II). One of the Galilean satellites, Europa has a 'billiard ball' smooth appearance, possibly owing to remelting of its icy surface.
Distance from Jupiter: 671 000 km (417 000 mi).
Diameter: 3138 km (1950 mi).

Ganymede (Number III). The Galilean satellite Ganymede is the largest and heaviest satellite in the solar system, with a mass 2·017 times greater than our own Moon.
Distance from Jupiter: 1 070 400 km (665 100 mi).
Diameter: 5262 km (3270 mi).

Callisto (Number IV). The outermost Galilean satellite, Callisto, is heavily cratered and may be showing evidence of the violent nature of the early solar system.
Distance from Jupiter: 1 882 600 km (1 169 800 mi).
Diameter: 4800 km (2983 mi).

Leda (Number XIII)
Distance from Jupiter: 11 094 000 km (6 893 000 mi).
Diameter: 15 km (9 mi).

Himalia (Number VI)
Distance from Jupiter: 11 480 000 km (7 133 000 mi).
Diameter: 170 km (106 mi).

Lysithea (Number X)
Distance from Jupiter: 11 720 000 km (7 282 000 mi).
Diameter: 35 km (22 mi).

Elara (Number VII)
Distance from Jupiter: 11 737 000 km (7 293 000 mi).
Diameter: 70 km (43 mi).

Ananke (Number XII)
Distance from Jupiter: 21 200 000 km (13 200 000 mi).
Diameter: 25 km (16 mi).

Carme (Number XI)
Distance from Jupiter: 22 600 000 km (14 000 000 mi).
Diameter: 40 km (25 mi).

Pasiphae (Number VIII)
Distance from Jupiter: 23 500 000 km (14 600 000 mi).
Diameter: 60 km (37 mi).

Sinope (Number IX)
Distance from Jupiter: 23 700 000 km (14 700 000 mi).
Diameter: 40 km (25 mi).

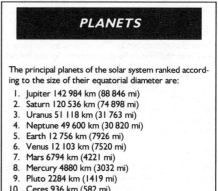

PLANETS

The principal planets of the solar system ranked according to the size of their equatorial diameter are:

1. Jupiter 142 984 km (88 846 mi)
2. Saturn 120 536 km (74 898 mi)
3. Uranus 51 118 km (31 763 mi)
4. Neptune 49 600 km (30 820 mi)
5. Earth 12 756 km (7926 mi)
6. Venus 12 103 km (7520 mi)
7. Mars 6794 km (4221 mi)
8. Mercury 4880 km (3032 mi)
9. Pluto 2284 km (1419 mi)
10. Ceres 936 km (582 mi)
11. Pallas 532 km (331 mi)
12. Vesta 519 km (322 mi)

SATURN

The next planet out from the Sun is Saturn, with its magnificent system of rings. In 1610 Galileo became the first person to look at Saturn through a telescope. He saw the rings, but could not understand what they were, at first thinking that Saturn was a 'triple planet'. It was not until 1659 that the Dutch physicist Christiaan Huygens (1629–95) realized Saturn's true nature. Most of our information about Saturn has come from three spacecraft that have flown by the planet: *Pioneer 11* in 1979, *Voyager 1* in 1980 and *Voyager 2* in 1981.

Saturn is generally considered to be like Jupiter but on a smaller scale. The planet has a similar rock–iron–ice core to Jupiter, but it has been suggested that its metallic hydrogen layer is much smaller, extending only 26 000 km (16 000 mi) from the centre of planet. Saturn radiates 76% more heat than it receives from the Sun. It is rich in helium but its outer molecular hydrogen envelope is depleted because of the presence of an intermediate zone 3000 km (1900 mi) thick in which helium is precipitating out and falling into the metallic zone. The energy from this 'precipitation' creates the extra heat within the planet.

THE RINGS OF SATURN

The distinct ring system surrounding Saturn's equator is composed of water ice or ice-covered material. Although the main ring system is 273 200 km (169 800 mi) in diameter, the overall thickness is only 10 m (33 ft). Images from the Voyager spacecraft initially

THE RINGS OF SATURN

Feature	Distance from centre km	miles	Comments
Saturn radius	60 367	*37 510*	Radius at the 100 millibar level (all values in the other tables refer to the 1000 millibar level)
D Ring inner edge	67 000	*41 600*	This ring may actually extend down to the planet surface
C ring inner edge	74 400	*46 200*	A narrow gap, the Huygens Gap, is located at
outer edge	91 900	*57 100*	87 500 km (54 400 miles)
B Ring inner edge	91 900	*57 100*	A narrow gap, the Maxwell Gap, is located at the
outer edge	117 400	*72 900*	outer edge of the ring
Cassini Division centre	119 000	*73 900*	The existence of two undiscovered moons in this 4500 km (2600 miles) wide gap (at 118 210 km/73 450 miles and 118 270 km/73 490 miles respectively) is inferred from ring perturbations
A Ring inner edge	121 900	*75 700*	
Encke Division centre	133 590	*83 010*	The existence of an unnamed moon in this 322 km (200 miles) wide gap at 133 600 km (83 020 miles) was inferred from ring perturbations
A Ring outer edge	136 600	*84 900*	A narrow gap, the Keeler Gap, is located at the outer edge of this ring
F Ring centre	140 300	*87 200*	Multiple stranded narrow eccentric ring 'shepherded' by two moons
G Ring centre	170 000	*105 600*	Fairly narrow optically thin ring
E Ring inner edge	180 000	*112 000*	Diffuse ring with maximum brightness near the orbit
outer edge	480 000	*298 000*	of Enceladus

suggested that the main A, B, and C rings consisted of many thousands of separate ringlets. However, it now appears that this may mainly be an optical effect owing to variations in reflectivity. Two extensive dusty rings (designated D and E) are present on the inside and the outside of the main rings respectively, whilst two very narrow rings (designated F and G) are present just outside of the main rings. The F ring is of particular interest since its narrowness appears to be controlled by two small 'shepherding' satellites that orbit either side of the ring, whilst another small moon, Atlas, appears to control the outer edge of the main ring system. (See also the table, the Rings of Saturn.)

SATELLITES OF SATURN

Saturn has 18 known satellites, but the existence of at least two more satellites in the Cassini ring gap is inferred from ring perturbations. The largest satellite, Titan, is big enough to have an atmosphere. The remaining satellites are only small or medium in size and appear to be composed mainly of water ice.

Atlas (Number XV)
Distance from Saturn: 137 670 km (85 540 mi). Atlas orbits in the outer edge of the main ring system of Saturn.
Diameter: 31 km (19 mi). This is an average diameter for a highly irregularly shaped satellite.

Unnamed moon (presently identified as 1981S13)
Distance from Saturn: 133 600 km (83 020 mi).
Diameter: 20 km (12 mi).

Prometheus (Number XVI)
Distance from Saturn: 139 350 km (86 590 mi). Prometheus is one of the two moons that 'shepherds' the narrow F ring.
Diameter: 102 km (63 mi). This is an average diameter for a highly irregularly shaped satellite.

Pandora (Number XVII)
Distance from Saturn: 141 700 km (88 050 mi).
Diameter: 85 km (53 mi). This is an average diameter for a highly irregularly shaped satellite.

Epimetheus (Number XI)
Distance from Saturn: 151 420 km (94 090 mi).
Diameter: 117 km (73 mi). This is an average diameter for a highly irregularly shaped satellite.

Janus (Number X)
Distance from Saturn: 151 470 km (94 120 mi).
Diameter: 188 km (117 mi). This is an average diameter for a highly irregularly shaped satellite. Janus and Epimetheus move in the same orbit and periodically approach one another.

Mimas (Number I)
Distance from Saturn: 185 530 km (115 280 mi).
Diameter: 397 km (247 mi). One huge crater on Mimas has a diameter one third that of the moon itself.

Enceladus (Number II)
Distance from Saturn: 238 030 km (147 900 mi).
Diameter: 498 km (310 mi). Enceladus is characterized by a surface that is very smooth but with large areas pitted by craters in other regions.

Tethys (Number III)
Distance from Saturn: 294 670 km (183 100 mi).
Diameter: 1028 km (639 mi). Tethys is a large moon with an icy cratered surface. Like Mimas, it has one particularly prominent crater.

Telesto (Number XIII)
Distance from Saturn: 294 670 km (183 100 mi). Telesto and Calypso are two tiny satellites that accompany Tethys on the same orbit.
Diameter: 22 km (12 mi). This is an average diameter for a highly irregularly shaped satellite.

Calypso (Number XIV)
Distance from Saturn: 294 670 km (183 100 mi).
Diameter: 24 km (15 mi).

Dione (Number IV)
Distance from Saturn: 377 410 km (234 510 mi).
Diameter: 1118 km (695 mi). A large icy cratered moon.

Helene (Number XII)
Distance from Saturn: 377 410 km (234 510 mi). This tiny moon accompanies Dione on the same orbit.
Diameter: 32 km (20 mi). This is an average diameter

for a highly irregularly shaped satellite.

Rhea (Number V)
Distance from Saturn: 527 070 km (327 510 mi).
Diameter: 1528 km (949 mi). A large icy cratered moon.

Titan (Number VI)
Distance from Saturn: 1 221 860 km (759 230 mi).
Diameter: 5150 km (3200 mi). The largest satellite in the Saturn system, Titan is the only satellite with an extensive atmosphere. This consists mainly of nitrogen with smaller amounts of methane and argon. Titan has a surface pressure about one and a half times greater than that of Earth. The surface is obscured by an orange haze, which is due to the formation of complex organic molecules in the upper atmosphere.

Hyperion (Number VII)
Distance from Saturn: 1 481 090 km (920 310 mi).
Diameter: 286 km (178 mi). This is an average diameter for a highly irregularly shaped satellite.

Iapetus (Number VIII)
Distance from Saturn: 3 561 670 km (2 213 120 mi).
Diameter: 1436 km (892 mi). Iapetus is unique in having one hemisphere that reflects light efficiently and one hemisphere that appears dull.

Phoebe (Number IX)
Distance from Saturn: 12 954 000 km (8 049 000 mi).
Diameter: 220 km (137 mi). Very little is known about Phoebe, which may be a captured asteroid.

URANUS

Uranus was discovered by William Herschel (1732–1822) on 13 March 1781. Herschel was making a routine survey of the sky when he came across an object that did not look like a star. At first he thought he had found a comet. The new object was watched carefully over the following months so that its orbit could be calculated. Once this was done, astronomers realized that Herschel had found a new planet.

When the sky is very dark and very clear, Uranus can just be seen with the naked eye. However, the planet is always extremely faint and the observer has to know exactly where to look.

Most of our information about Uranus was sent back by *Voyager 2*, which flew past the planet in January 1986. One of the strangest things about Uranus is that it orbits the Sun tipped on its side, which means that the 'calendar' on the planet must be very odd indeed. At present the planet's north pole is pointing towards the Sun and anyone above the north pole of Uranus would have been in sunlight since 1966 and will not see the Sun set until 2007. This will be followed by 42 years of darkness while the south pole points towards the Sun. Although the south pole had been in darkness for 20 years, *Voyager 2* found that it was slightly warmer than the north pole – which must give rise to very peculiar weather.

Because of its smaller size, higher density, and the fact that it does not appear to radiate more heat than it receives from the Sun, the internal structure of Uranus is thought to be different from that of Jupiter and Saturn. A recent model suggests a rocky core 15 000 km (9000 mi) in diameter surrounded by a 'sea' of water, methane, and ammonia 10 000 km (6000 mi) thick, and an outer hydrogen-rich atmosphere containing about 26% of helium by mass and a small amount of methane, which gives the planet its bland, bluish appearance.

THE RINGS OF URANUS

In 1977–78 it was discovered that Uranus had nine narrow rings in the orbital plane. Two further rings were discovered by the *Voyager 2* spacecraft in January 1986. The rings are very dark and probably rich in carbon. The ring system has been photographed from Earth. (See also the table, The Rings of Uranus.)

THE RINGS OF URANUS

Feature	Distance from centre km	miles
Uranus radius	25 559	*15 882*
1986 U2R inner edge	37 000	*23 000*
1986 U2R outer edge	39 500	*24 500*
6 centre	41 850	*26 000*
5 centre	42 240	*26 250*
4 centre	42 580	*26 460*
Alpha centre	44 730	*27 790*
Beta centre	45 670	*28 380*
Eta centre	47 180	*29 320*
Gamma centre	47 630	*29 600*
Delta centre	48 310	*30 020*
1986 U1R centre	50 040	*31 090*
Epsilon centre	51 160	*31 790*

With the exceptions of the very diffuse 1986 U2R ring and the dominant Epsilon ring, all the other rings are very narrow (widths less than 12 km (7 miles) – the Epsilon ring width varies between 22 a also has the highest eccentricity 90·0079).

SATELLITES OF URANUS

The five satellites identified from Earth are all medium sized and show the presence of water ice on the surface. Ten small satellites were discovered by the *Voyager* Imaging Team during December 1985 and January 1986. The fifteen satellites are:

Cordelia (Number VI)
Distance from Uranus: 49 750 km (30 910 mi).
Diameter: 26 km (16 mi). Cordelia and Ophelia act as shepherding satellites for the major ring (epsilon) of Uranus.

Ophelia (Number VII)
Distance from Uranus: 53 760 km (33 410 mi).
Diameter: 32 km (20 mi). (See Cordelia, above.)

Bianca (Number VIII)
Distance from Uranus: 59 170 km (36 760 mi).
Diameter: 44 km (27 mi).

Cressida (Number IX)
Distance from Uranus: 61 770 km (38 380 mi).
Diameter: 66 km (41 mi).

Desdemona (Number X)
Distance from Uranus: 62 660 km (38 930 mi).
Diameter: 58 km (36 mi).

Juliet (Number XI)
Distance from Uranus: 64 360 km (39 990 mi).
Diameter: 84 km (52 mi).

Portia (Number XII)
Distance from Uranus: 66 100 km (41 070 mi).
Diameter: 110 km (68 mi).

Rosalind (Number XIII)
Distance from Uranus: 69 930 km (43 450 mi).
Diameter: 58 km (36 mi).

Belinda (Number XIV)
Distance from Uranus: 75 260 km (46 760 mi).
Diameter: 68 km (42 mi).

Puck (Number XV)
Distance from Uranus: 86 000 km (53 440 mi).

Diameter: 154 km (96 mi).

Miranda (Number V)
Distance from Uranus: 129 780 km (80 640 mi).
Diameter: 472 km (293 mi). Miranda – the smallest of the five outer satellites that are identifiable from Earth – has a most extraordinary appearance. It is believed to have been totally disrupted and re-assembled at least once in its history.

Ariel (Number I)
Distance from Uranus: 191 240 km (118 830 mi).
Diameter: 1158 km (719 mi).

Umbriel (Number II)
Distance from Uranus: 265 970 km (165 270 mi).
Diameter: 1169 km (727 mi).

Titiania (Number III)
Distance from Uranus: 435 840 km (270 820 mi).
Diameter: 1578 km (980 mi).

Oberon (Number IV)
Distance from Uranus: 582 600 km (362 010 mi).
Diameter: 1523 km (946 mi).

NEPTUNE

Neptune is so distant that it can never be seen with the naked eye and even a small telescope will only show it as a tiny disc. Larger telescopes show that the planet is bluish-green in colour, but very few markings can be seen. Our first good look at Neptune came in August 1989, when the *Voyager 2* spacecraft flew past the planet.

The planet was discovered on 23 September 1846 thanks to mathematical predictions by Urbain Le Verrier (1811–77) and John Couch Adams (1819–92). Adams and Le Verrier had been looking at the movements of Uranus and had noticed that it was behaving in a very strange way. Sometimes it would speed up and move quickly along its orbit, whereas at other times it would slow down. The two men both thought that Uranus was being pulled by the gravity of another planet, so they set out to calculate where the 'hidden planet' must be. Both men worked on their own, but they eventually arrived at the same answer. Le Verrier sent details of his calculations to the observatory at Berlin. The German astronomers Johann Galle (1812–1910) and Heinrich d'Arrest (1822–75) looked for the planet and found it almost immediately.

Neptune is similar in size to Uranus, but it has a much more dynamic atmosphere. Neptune and Uranus may have similar internal structures but Neptune is much denser and radiates 85% more heat than it receives from the Sun (whereas the extra heat radiation from Uranus is negligible). The most prominent feature of Neptune is the Great Dark Spot, which is a huge whirlwind the size of the Earth. *Voyager* measured winds travelling at 325 m per second (700 mph) on Neptune.

Neptune has a magnetic field that is tilted at 50° to the planet's axis of rotation and offset from the centre of the planet by almost half its radius.

THE RINGS OF NEPTUNE

Neptune is now known to have a system of four rings. The two brightest rings – 1989 N2R and 1989 N1R – completely encircle the planet at 53 000 km (33 000 mi) and 63 000 km (39 000 mi) respectively. There is a third, closer 'fuzzy' ring – at 42 000 km (26 000 mi) from the planet – and a dust sheet that extends from a bright 'plateau' between the two outer rings – at 58 000 km (36 000 mi) from the planet and stretching inwards towards the planet.

SATELLITES OF NEPTUNE

Neptune is now known to have eight satellites.

Naiad (not yet numbered)
Distance from Neptune: 48 200 km (30 000 mi).
Diameter: 50 km (30 mi).

Thalassa (not yet numbered)
Distance from Neptune: 50 000 km (31 000 mi).
Diameter: 90 km (55 mi).

Despina (not yet numbered)
Distance from Neptune: 52 500 km (32 600 mi).
Diameter: 140 km (85 mi).

Galatea (not yet numbered)
Distance from Neptune: 62 000 km (38 500 mi).
Diameter: 160 km (100 mi).

Larissa (not yet numbered)
Distance from Neptune: 73 600 km (45 700 mi).
Diameter: 200 km (120 mi).

Proteus (not yet numbered)
Distance from Neptune: 117 600 km (73 100 mi).
Diameter: 400 km (250 mi).

Triton (Number I)
Distance from Neptune: 354 000 km (220 000 mi).
Diameter: 2720 km (1690 mi). As well as being the largest of Neptune's satellites Triton is also the most interesting. *Voyager* revealed that Triton has frozen pink nitrogen ice at the poles, darker ice plains, melted and refrozen basins, mysterious clefts and a range of features that have not been seen on any other object in the solar system. Triton also possesses a very thin atmosphere and has icy volcanoes erupting on its surface.

Nereid (Number II)
Distance from Neptune: 5 511 000 km (342 400 mi).
Diameter: 340 km (210 mi).

PLUTO

The discovery of the outermost planet by Clyde Tombaugh was announced on 13 March 1930, but little was known about the planet until after the discovery of its moon Charon by James Christy on 22 June 1978. The planet is now known to be quite small – a little over twice the size of Ceres – and has a low mass (see the table on p. 15). It has a thin atmosphere containing methane, and methane ice may be present on the surface. The relatively high density of the planet suggests that it may have a core consisting of partially hydrated rock surrounded by a water-ice layer up to 320 km (200 mi) thick, and an outer layer 10 km (6 mi) thick consisting mainly of methane.

Pluto has a highly eccentric orbit that sometimes carries it inside that of Neptune. This will be the relative positions of the two planets between 23 January 1979 and 15 March 1999, but Pluto and Neptune are locked in a resonance that prevents them from coming together.

SATELLITE OF PLUTO

Charon (Number I)
Distance from Pluto: 19 640 km (12 200 mi).
Diameter: 1192 km (741 mi). Pluto is a very small icy planet. Its moon, Charon, is very large by comparison, having 10% of Pluto's mass – compared with the Moon, which has only 1.2% of the Earth's mass. Together, Pluto and Charon virtually form a twin-planet system.

COMETS

Comets have long been known as apparitions in the

sky and they have entered the folklore and literature of many societies. However, their structure is mundane – they consist mainly of a central nucleus that can be regarded as a 'dirty snowball'. On approaching the Sun, the ice in a comet starts to evaporate, producing a coma around the nucleus and a tail or tails behind. The tail is the streaming of ions and dust from the coma – the ions being repelled by sunlight and the dust by the solar wind. Thus, when moving away from the Sun, the tail of the comet leads.

Comets either orbit within the solar system or adopt parabolic orbits that sweep them outside the system. The source of comets is unknown, although Jan Oort suggested that there is a reservoir or 'cloud' of comets in the outer solar system as a residue from the original accretion disc from which the solar system was formed. A recent study suggests that there is an outer 'Oort Cloud' – which has been described as a 'halo' of comets – orbiting between 20 000 and 50 000 astronomical units (1 AU = 150 000 000 km/ 93 000 000 mi) from the Sun and weighing 100 Earth masses. A denser inner concentration of comets – between 3000 and 20 000 astronomical units – is thought to weigh approximately 10 000 Earth masses and to contain about a million million (10^{12}) comets. It is suggested that periodic perturbations by giant interstellar molecular clouds, or close encounters with other stars, triggers the release of the comets into the inner solar system.

Halley's comet is the most famous and was named after Edmond Halley, who correctly predicted its return in 1758, 16 years after his death. In March 1986 this comet was visited by five spacecraft and one of them, *Giotto*, photographed the nucleus and showed it to be an elongated, very blackened iceball about 15 km (9 mi) long and 8 km (5 mi) in cross-section.

Most comets are in very eccentric orbits with periods of several hundred years. Several new comets are discovered every year. The brightest comets tend to be those with very long periods and it is therefore impossible to predict when the next bright comet will appear.

MOONS

By the beginning of 1991, 61 satellites (moons) had been discovered in the solar system orbiting the following planets: Earth (1), Mars (2), Jupiter (16), Saturn (18), Uranus (15), Neptune (8) and Pluto (1).

The diameters of the largest moons are:
1. Ganymede (Jupiter) 5262 km (3270 mi)
2. Titan (Saturn) 5150 km (3200 mi)
3. Callisto (Jupiter) 4800 km (2983 mi)
4. Io (Jupiter) 3642 km (2263 mi)
5. The Moon (Earth) 3475 km (2159 mi)
6. Europa (Jupiter) 3138 km (1950 mi)
7. Triton (Neptune) 2720 km (1690 mi)
8. Titania (Uranus) 1578 km (980 mi)
9. Rhea (Saturn) 1528 km (949 mi)
10. Oberon (Uranus) 1523 km (946 mi)
11. Iapetus (Saturn) 1436 km 892 mi)
12. Charon (Pluto) 1192 km (741 mi)
13. Umbriel (Uranus) 1169 km (727 mi)
14. Ariel (Uranus) 1158 km (719 mi)
15. Dione (Saturn) 1118 km (695 mi)
16. Tethys (Saturn) 1028 km (639 mi)

MILESTONES IN ASTRONOMY

1543
Copernicus established that the solar system is Sun-centred and not Earth-centred. This is usually considered to have been the beginning of modern astronomy. (The belief that the universe was Earth-centred had been held since the time of Ptolemy in AD 180.)

1596
Tycho Brahe published his 'pre-telescope' star catalogue, the result of 20 years' observations.

1608
The invention of the telescope by Hans Lippershey in The Netherlands.

1609
Johannes Kepler published his first two laws of planetary motion (and the third was published ten years later).

1610
Galileo Galilei and Simon Marius independently discovered the major moons of Jupiter using the newly invented telescope.

1631
The first observation of a transit of Mercury across the Sun by Gassendi. (The first observation of a transit of Venus was made eight years later by Horrocks and Crabtree.)

1638
The first identification of a variable star (Mira Ceti) by P. Holwarda.

1655
Christiaan Huygens discovered Titan, the major moon of Saturn, and correctly described Saturn's ring system.

1668
The first reflector telescope was built by Isaac Newton. (The principles of reflecting telescopes had been published five years earlier by J. Gregory.)

1675
By observations of the Jupiter moon, Io, Romer proved that light must have a definite velocity.

1687
The publication of Newton's mathematical theories of celestial mechanics. These explained the orbital motions of the planets and why the solar system is Sun-centred.

1705
Edmond Halley accurately predicted the return of Halley's comet in 1758.

1728
The discovery of the aberration of light by James Bradley.

1781
William Herschel discovered the planet Uranus. (He discovered the first four satellites of its moon system six years later.)

1801
Giovanni Piazzi discovered the first and largest of the minor planets, Ceres.

1838
The first measurement of the distance of a star (61 Cygni) by F. Bessel.

1846
Johann Galle discovered Neptune, working on the mathematical predictions of U. Le Verrier and J. Couch Adams. The major Neptune moon, Triton, was discovered in the same year by W. Lassel.

1862
The construction of the first great refractor telescopes.

1868
The discovery in the Sun's spectra independently by N. Lockyer and P. Janssen of an element that had not been previously identified on Earth (helium).

1872
H. Draper took the first photograph of the spectrum of a star (Vega).

1877
Asaph Hall discovered the two moons of Mars.

1897
A refracting telescope, 102 cm (40 in) in diameter, was built at the Yerkes Observatory, Wisconsin, USA.

1915
W. S. Adams' study of the binary companion to Sirius, Sirius B, led to the identification of white dwarf stars.

1919
J. Perrin suggested that the Sun's energy could arise from the conversion of hydrogen into helium.

1923
Eleven years after his initial discovery, V. Slipher published his findings that most galaxies have their spectra shifted towards the red end of the spectrum (red-shifted). This confirmed the prediction of W. de Sitter that such a condition existed as a requirement of an expanding universe.

1927
Abbé G. Lemaître (and, independently, A. Friedmann) formulated the 'big bang' concept to try to explain the beginning of the universe.

1929
E. Hubble's measurement of the distances of nearby galaxies led to an understanding of the relationship between distance and red shift.

1930
Clyde Tombaugh discovered the outermost planet, Pluto, by systematic photography.

1932
The first detection of extra-terrestrial radio signals (from the Sagittarius constellation) by K. G. Jansky.

1937
The first radio telescope built by G. Reber in the USA.

1948
The completion of the 508 cm (200 in) Hale reflecting telescope at the Mount Palomar Observatory, California, USA.

1957
E.M. and G.R. Burbidge, W.A. Fowler, and F. Hoyle introduced nucleocosmochronology as an independent method of estimating the age of the universe.

1961
By using radar, a number of separate research teams accurately determined the value of the astronomical unit.

1962
The existence of quasi-stellar radio sources or 'quasars' was established by Maarten Schmidt.

1964
The establishment by radar that the rotation period of Venus is very long (243 days) and retrograde.

1965
G.H. Pettengill and R.B. Dyce established by radar that the rotation period of Mercury is exactly equal to two-thirds of its orbital period. Detection of the

---

METEORITES

When a meteoroid – consisting of broken fragments originating from either comets or asteroids, and ranging in size from fine dust to bodies several kilometres in diameter – becomes visible from Earth it is referred to as a meteor. When it penetrates to the Earth's surface it is known as a meteorite.

Up to 150 meteorites – which may be either stony (aerolite) or metallic (siderite) – fall to the land surface of the Earth each year. A 'shooting star' is a tiny meteorite that burns up as it penetrates the atmosphere.

Largest known meteorites

Location	Found	Weight
Hoba West[1] (Namibia)	1920	59 tonnes
Cape York[2] (Greenland)	1897	30.9 tonnes
Bacubirito (Mexico)	1863	27 tonnes
Mbosi (Tanzania)	1930	25 tonnes
Armanty (Mongolia)	not known	20 tonnes

[1] The meteorite found at Hoba West is a block 2.75 m (9 ft) long by 2.43 m (8 ft) broad.
[2] Known as the 'Tent' meteorite – and to the Eskimos as Abnighito – this is the largest meteorite exhibited in any museum. Discovered by the expedition of Commander (later Rear-Admiral) Peary on the west coast of Greenland, this meteorite is now displayed at the Hayden Planetarium in New York City, USA.
Note: The largest of the 22 meteorites known to have fallen on the British Isles since 1653 fell at Barwell, Leicestershire, on 24 Dec 1965 and weighed at least 46.25 kg (102 lb). Its largest piece weighed 7.88 kg (17 lb 6 oz).

Meteorite showers in Europe

A meteorite shower is a 'swarm' of separate meteorites that arrive on the surface of the Earth at the same time. Such an occurrence is probably produced by the disintegration of a large meteorite at considerable altitude. Meteorite showers may contain many separate bodies – the record is held by an estimated 100 000 bodies falling at Pulutsk, Poland, in 1868. Other major meteorite showers have fallen in Europe at L'Aigle, France, in 1803 (with an estimated 2000 to 3000 bodies), and in Moravia, Czechoslovakia, in 1808 (with an estimated 200 to 300 bodies).

---

3 K background radiation by A. Penzias and R. Wilson – considered as proof that the universe was once very hot.

1967
The detection of the pulsating radio source or 'pulsar' CP 1919 by J. Bell – considered as proof of the existence of neutron stars.

1973
First close-up views of Jupiter obtained by the *Pioneer 10* spacecraft.

1974
The first details of the surface features of Mercury were obtained from *Mariner 10* spacecraft.

1976
The world's largest reflecting telescope, 600 cm (236 in) in diameter, was completed at Mount Semirodriki, Caucasus, USSR.

1977
The discovery of the rings of Uranus. C. Kowal discovered the most distant asteroid, Chiron, orbiting between Saturn and Uranus.

MAJOR OBSERVATORIES IN THE EC

Royal Greenwich Observatory
The Royal Observatory was founded in 1675 at Greenwich by King Charles II, moved to Herstmonceux Castle in East Sussex in 1957 and to Cambridge in 1990. The principal work of the Observatory is concerned with the operation of the telescopes at the Northern Hemisphere Observatory at Roque de los Muchachos on La Palma in the Canaries. On La Palma, the Observatory collaborates with Spanish and Danish astronomers in running the Carlsberg Automatic Meridian Circle; with Dutch astronomers in running the 4.2 m William Herschel telescope and the 2.5 m Isaac Newton telescope; and with Dutch and Irish astronomers in running the 1.0 m Jacobus Kapteyn telescope.

European Southern Observatory
The ESO – which is funded by Belgium, Denmark, France, Germany, Italy, the Netherlands, Sweden and Switzerland – was established in 1962. Its observatory at La Silla in Chile operates 14 telescopes, including the NTT with a diameter of 15 m.

Calar Alto
A Spanish-German joint project under construction in Spain. This observatory will have a 3.5 m diameter telescope.

CERGA
(Centre des études et de recherches en géodynamique et astronomie). Established near Grasse, France, in 1974 with an observatory on the Calern plateau.

Pic du Midi
The observatory in the French Hautes-Pyrénées was established in 1878, and was augmented by a 2.03 m telescope in 1970.

LARGEST RADIO TELESCOPES IN EUROPE

Max Planck Institute (Bonn), Effelsberger Valley, Germany
100 m (328 ft) diameter
Nançay in Sologne region, France
90 m (295 ft) diameter
Jodrell Bank Cheshire, UK
76 m (249 ft)

1978
J. W. Christy discovered Pluto's moon, Charon.

1979
Alan Guth proposed the 'inflationary' theory to explain the initial formation of the universe. The first visit to Saturn by a spacecraft, *Pioneer 11*.

1981
The *Voyager 1* and *2* observations of Saturn led to the discovery of 'shepherding' satellites that control the width of the F ring.

1983
The launch of IRAS – Infrared Astronomical Satellite – which gathers enormous amounts of data on the solar system and the universe as a whole.

1986
Voyager 2 discovers ten new moons of Uranus. Five space probes investigated Halley's comet at close quarters.

1989
Voyager 2 encountered the Neptunian system and discovered six new moons.

1990
The Hubble Space Telescope was launched. *Magellan* began radar mapping of the planet Venus.

SPACE TRAVEL

SPACEFLIGHT

MANNED SPACEFLIGHTS (to 1 January 1991)

1 USSR 1
12 April 1961
Vostok 1
Yuri Gagarin
1 hr 48 min
Landed separately from craft.

2 USA 1
5 May 1961
Freedom 7
Alan Shepard
15 min 28 sec
Suborbital; splashdown.

3 USA 2
21 July 1961
Liberty Bell 7
Gus Grissom
15 min 37 sec
Spacecraft sank.

4 USSR 2
6 August 1961
Vostok 2
Gherman Titov
1 day 1 hr 18 min
At 25, youngest person ever in space.

5 USA 3
20 February 1962
Friendship 7
John Glenn
4 hr 55 min 23 sec
First American to orbit.

6 USA 4
24 May 1962
Aurora 7
Scott Carpenter
4 hr 56 min 5 sec
Landing overshoot of 250 miles.

7 USSR 3
11 August 1962
Vostok 3
Andrian Nikolyev
3 day 22 hr 22 min

8 USSR 4
12 August 1962
Vostok 4
Pavel Popovich
2 day 22 hr 57 sec
Came to within 6·4 km (*4 miles*) of Vostok 3.

9 USA 5
3 October 1962
Sigma 7
Wally Schirra
9 hr 13 min 11 sec
Pacific splashdown.

10 USA 6
15 May 1963
Faith 7
Gordon Cooper
1 day 10 hr 19 min 49 sec
Final US one-man flight.

11 USSR 5
14 June 1963
Vostok 5
Valeri Bykovsky
4 day 23 hr 6 min
Solo flight record-holder.

12 USSR 6
16 June 1963
Vostok 6
Valentina Tereshkova
2 day 22 hr 50 min
First woman in space.

13 USSR 7
12 October 1964
Voskhod 1
Vladimir Komarov,
Konstantin Feoktistov,
Boris Yegerov
1 day 0 hr 17 min 3 sec
Riskiest flight, no
spacesuits, no ejection
seats, inside a 'Vostok'.

14 USSR 8
18 March 1965
Voskhod 2
Pavel Belyayev,
Alexei Leonov
1 day 2 hr 2 min 17 sec
Leonov makes first walk
in space.

15 USA 7
25 March 1965
Gemini 3
Gus Grissom,
John Young
4 hr 52 min 51 sec
Grissom first man in
space twice.

16 USA 8
3 June 1965
Gemini 4
James McDivitt,
Edward White
4 day 1 hr 56 min
12 sec
White walks in space.

17 USA 9
21 August 1965
Gemini 5
Gordon Cooper,
Charles Conrad
7 day 22 hr 55 min
14 sec
Breaks endurance
record.

18 USA 10
4 December 1965
Gemini 7
Frank Borman,
James Lovell
13 day 18 hr 35 min
1 sec
Acted as rendezvous
target; breaks endur-
ance record.

19 USA 11
15 December 1965
Gemini 6
Wally Schirra,
Tom Stafford
1 day 1 hr 51 min
54 sec
First rendezvous in
space.

20 USA 12
16 March 1966
Gemini 8
Neil Armstrong,

David Scott
10 hr 41 min 26 sec
Emergency landing
after first space
docking.

21 USA 13
3 June 1966
Gemini 9
Tom Stafford,
Eugene Cernan
3 day 0 hr 20 min
50 sec
Rendezvous; spacewalk;
bull's-eye splashdown.

22 USA 14
18 July 1966
Gemini 10
John Young,
Michael Collins
2 day 22 hr 46 min
39 sec
Docking; spacewalk;
record altitude of 763
km (*474 miles*).

23 USA 15
12 September 1966
Gemini 11
Charles Conrad,
Richard Gordon
2 day 23 hr 17 min
8 sec
Docking; spacewalk;
altitude of 1368 km
(*850 miles*); automatic
landing.

24 USA 16
11 November 1966
Gemini 12
James Lovell,
Edwin Aldrin
3 day 22 hr 34 min
31 sec
Docking; record
spacewalk of over 2 hr.

USA
27 January 1967
Apollo 1
Gus Grissom, Edward
White, Roger Chaffee
Killed in spacecraft fire.

25 USSR 9
23 April 1967
Soyuz 1
Vladimir Komarov
1 day 2 hr 47 min
52 sec
Komarov killed when
parachute fails; intend-
ed to dock with Soyuz 2.

USSR
24 April 1967
Soyuz 2
Valeri Bykovsky, Alexei
Yeliseyev and Yevgeny
Khrunov
Flight cancelled; was to

have docked with Soyuz
1 but this craft had
problems.

26 USA 17
11 October 1968
Apollo 7
Wally Schirra,
Donn Eisele,
Walt Cunningham
10 day 20 hr 9 min
3 sec
Earth orbit shakedown
of Command and Ser-
vice Module.

27 USSR 10
26 October 1968
Soyuz 3
Georgi Beregovoi
3 day 22 hr 50 min 45 sec
Failed to dock with
unmanned Soyuz 2.

USSR
December 1968
Zond Pavel Belyayev
Circumlunar flight
cancelled.

28 USA 18
21 December 1968
Apollo 8
Frank Borman, James
Lovell, William Anders
6 day 3hr 0 min 42 sec
Ten lunar orbits over
Christmas.

29 USSR 11
14 January 1969
Soyuz 4
Vladimir Shatalov
2 day 23 hr 20 min
47 sec
Launched with one
man, returned with
three.

30 USSR 12
15 January 1969
Soyuz 5
Boris Volynov,
Alexei Yeleseyev,
Yevgeny Khrunov
3 day 0 hr 54 min
15 sec
Yeliseyev and Khrunov
spacewalk to Soyuz 4
after docking.

31 USA 19
3 March 1969
Apollo 9
James McDivitt,
David Scott,
Russell Schweickart
10 day 1 hr 0 min
54 sec
Test of Lunar Module
in Earth orbit;
spacewalk.

32 USA 20
18 May 1969
Apollo 10
Tom Stafford, John
Young, Eugene Cernan
8 day 0 hr 3 min 23 sec
Lunar Module tested in
lunar orbit; came to 14·5
km (*9 miles*) of surface
of Moon.

33 USA 21
17 July 1969
Apollo 11
Neil Armstrong,
Michael Collins,
Edwin Aldrin
8 day 3 hr 18 min
35 sec
Armstrong and Aldrin
walk on Moon for over
2 hours.

34 USSR 13
11 October 1969
Soyuz 6
Georgi Shonin,
Valeri Kubasov
4 day 22 hr 42 min
47 sec
Welding tests.

35 USSR 14
12 October 1969
Soyuz 7
Anatoli Filipchenko,
Vladislav Volkov,
Viktor Gorbatko
4 day 22 hr 40 min
23 sec
Rendezvous to within
488 m (*1600 ft*) of Soyuz
8.

36 USSR 15
13 October 1969
Soyuz 8
Vladimir Shatalov,
Alexei Yeliseyev
4 day 22 hr 50 min
49 sec
Third flight in strange
troika mission by
Soviets.

37 USA 22
14 November 1969
Apollo 12
Charles Conrad,
Richard Gordon,
Alan Bean
10 day 4 hr 36 min
25 sec
Pinpoint landing near
Surveyor.

38 USA 23
11 April 1970
Apollo 13
James Lovell, Jack
Swigert, Fred Haise
5 day 22 hr 54 min
41 sec

Service module exploded 55 hours into mission; crew limped home using Lunar Module as lifeboat.

39 USSR 16
1 June 1970
Soyuz 9
Andiran Nikolyev,
Vitali Sevastyanov
17 day 16 hr 58 min 50 sec
Crew carried from craft on stretchers suffering acute stress of readapting to gravity after longest flight.

40 USA 24
31 January 1971
Apollo 14
Alan Shepard, Stuart Roosa, Edgar Mitchell
9 day 0 hr 1 min 57 sec
Shepard only Mercury astronaut to walk on Moon.

41 USSR 17
23 April 1971
Soyuz 10
Vladimir Shatalov,
Alexei Yeliseyev,
Nikolai Ruckavishnikov
1 day 23 hr 45 min 54 sec
Failed to enter Salyut 1 space station after soft docking.

42 USSR 18
6 June 1971
Soyuz 11
Georgi Dobrovolsky,
Vladislav Volkov,
Viktor Patsayev
23 day 18 hr 21 min 43 sec
Crew died as craft depressurized before re-entry; not wearing spacesuits.

43 USA 25
26 July 1971
Apollo 15
David Scott, Alfred Worden, James Irwin
12 day 7 hr 11 min 53 sec
First lunar rover.

44 USA 26
16 April 1972
Apollo 16
John Young, Ken Mattingly, Charles Duke
11 day 1 hr 51 min 5 sec
Space Shuttle approved

during mission; Mattingly in lunar orbit makes longest solo US flight.

45 USA 27
7 December 1972
Apollo 17
Eugene Cernan, Ron Evans, Jack Schmitt
12 day 13 hr 51 min 59 sec
Last manned expedition to Moon this century.

46 USA 28
25 May 1973
Skylab 2
Charles Conrad, Joe Kerwin, Paul Weitz
28 day 0 hr 49 min 49 sec
Spacewalk to repair severely disabled Skylab 1 space station.

47 USA 29
28 July 1973
Skylab 3
Alan Bean, Owen Garriott, Jack Lousma
59 day 11 hr 9 min 4 sec
Stranded in space temporarily as Command Module malfunctions.

48 USSR 19
27 September 1973
Soyuz 12
Vasili Lazarev,
Oleg Makarov
1 day 23 hr 15 min 32 sec
Test of space-station ferry.

49 USA 30
16 November 1973
Skylab 4
Gerry Carr, Edward Gibson, Bill Pogue
84 day 1 hr 15 min 31 sec
Longest US manned spaceflight.

50 USSR 20
18 December 1973
Soyuz 13
Pyotr Klimuk,
Valetin Lebedev
7 day 20 hr 55 min 35 sec
Soviets and Americans in space together for first time, although they don't meet.

51 USSR 21
3 July 1974
Soyuz 14
Pavel Popvich,
Yuri Artyukhin

15 day 17 hr 30 min 28 sec
First space spies, on Salyut 3.

52 USSR 22
26 August 1974
Soyuz 15
Gennadi Serafanov,
Lev Demin
2 day 0 hr 12 min 11 sec
Failed to dock with Salyut 3.

53 USSR 23
2 December 1974
Soyuz 16
Anatoli Filipchenko,
Nikolai Ruckavishnikov
5 day 22 hr 23 min 35 sec
Rehearsal for US–USSR joint flight, ASTP.

54 USSR 24
11 January 1975
Soyuz 17
Alexei Gubarev,
Georgi Grechko
29 day 13 hr 19 min 45 sec
Aboard Salyut 4.

55 USSR 25
5 April 1975
Soyuz 18-1
Vasili Lazarev,
Oleg Makarov
21 min 27 sec
Second stage failed; flight aborted.

56 USSR 26
24 May 1975
Soyuz 18
Pyotr Klimuk,
Vitali Sevastyanov
62 day 23 hr 20 min 8 sec
Aboard Salyut 4.

57 USSR 27
15 July 1975
Soyuz 19
Alexei Leonov,
Valeri Kubasov
5 day 22 hr 30 min 51 sec
Docked with Apollo 18 in joint ASTP mission.

58 USA 31
15 July 1975
Apollo 18
Tom Stafford, Vance Brand, Deke Slayton
9 day 1 hr 28 min 24 sec
Docked with Soyuz 19; flight for Mercury astronaut Slayton at 51;

crew gassed during landing, recovered.

59 USSR 28
6 July 1976
Soyuz 21
Boris Volynov,
Vitali Zholobov
49 day 6 hr 23 min 32 sec
Evacuated Salyut 5. (Soyuz 20 was Progress tanker test, unmanned.)

60 USSR 29
22 September 1976
Soyuz 22
Valeri Bykovsky,
Vladimir Aksyonov
7 day 21 hr 52 min 17 sec
Independent Earth survey flight.

61 USSR 30
14 October 1976
Soyuz 23
Vyacheslav Zudov,
Valeri Rozhdestvensky
2 day 0 hr 6 min 35 sec
Failed to dock with Salyut 5; splashed down in lake.

62 USSR 31
7 February 1977
Soyuz 24
Viktor Gorbatko,
Yuri Glazkov
17 day 17 hr 25 min 50 sec
Aboard Salyut 5.

63 USSR 32
9 October 1977
Soyuz 25
Vladimir Kovalyonok,
Valeri Ryumin
2 day 0 hr 44 min 45 sec
Failed to dock with Salyut 6.

64 USSR 33
10 December 1977
Soyuz 26
Yuri Romanenko,
Georgi Grechko
96 day 10 hr 0 min 7 sec
Aboard Salyut 6; broke endurance record.

65 USSR 34
10 January 1978
Soyuz 27
Vladimir Dzhanibekov,
Oleg Makarov
5 day 22 hr 58 min 58 sec
Visitors to Salyut 6.

66 USSR 35
2 March 1978
Soyuz 28
Alexei Gubarev,
Vladimir Remek
7 day 22 hr 16 min
Remek was from
Czechoslovakia, first
non-American, non-
Soviet in space; visit
to Salyut 6.

67 USSR 36
15 June 1978
Soyuz 29
Vladimir Kovalyonok,
Alexander Ivanchenkov
139 day 14 hr 47 min
32 sec
Aboard Salyut 6; landed
in Soyuz 31.

68 USSR 37
27 June 1978
Soyuz 30
Pyotr Klimuk,
Miroslaw Hermas-
zewski
7 day 22 hr 2 min
59 sec
Visit to Salyut 6; Her-
maszewski from Poland.

69 USSR 38
26 August 1978
Soyuz 31
Valeri Bykovsky,
Sigmund Jahn
7 day 29 hr 49 min 4 sec
Visit to Salyut 6; Jahn
from East Germany;
landed in Soyuz 29.

70 USSR 39
25 February 1979
Soyuz 32
Vladimir Lyakhov,
Valeri Ryumin
175 day 0 hr 35 min
37 sec
Visit to Salyut 6; landed
in Soyuz 34, which was
launched unmanned.

71 USSR 40
10 April 1979
Soyuz 33
Nikolai Ruckavish-
nikov,
Georgi Ivanov
1 day 23 hr 1 min 6 sec
Failed to dock with
Salyut 6; Bulgarian
Ivanov only Inter-
cosmos visitor not to
reach space station.

72 USSR 41
9 April 1980
Soyuz 35
Leonid Popov,
Valeri Ryumin
184 day 20 hr 11 min

35 sec
Salyut 6 mission takes
Ryumin to 361 days'
space experience.

73 USSR 42
26 May 1980
Soyuz 36
Valeri Kubasov,
Bertalan Farkas
7 day 20 hr 45 min
44 sec
Visit to Salyut 6; Farkas
from Hungary; landed in
Soyuz 35.

74 USSR 43
5 June 1980
Soyuz T2
Yuri Malyshev,
Vladimir Aksyonov
3 day 22 hr 19 min
30 sec
Test of new Soyuz model
to Salyut 6. (Soyuz T1
was unmanned.)

75 USSR 44
23 July 1980
Soyuz 37
Viktor Gorbatko,
Pham Tuan
7 day 20 hr 42 min
Visit to Salyut 6; Tuan
from Vietnam; landed in
Soyuz 36.

76 USSR 45
18 September 1980
Soyuz 38
Yuri Romanenko,
Arnaldo Mendez
7 day 20 hr 43 min
24 sec
Visit to Salyut 6;
Mendez from Cuba.

77 USSR 46
27 November 1980
Soyuz T3
Leonid Kizim,
Oleg Makarov,
Gennadi Strekalov
12 day 19 hr 7 min
42 sec
Maintenance crew to
Salyut 5; first three-man
Soyuz since Soyuz 11
accident.

78 USSR 47
12 March 1981
Soyuz T4
Vladimir Kovalyonok,
Viktor Savinykh
74 day 17 hr 37 min
23 sec
Final Salyut 6 long-stay
crew; Savinykh 100th
person in space.

79 USSR 48
22 March 1981

Soyuz 39
Vladimir Dzhanib-
vekov,
Jugderdemidyin
Gurragcha
7 day 20 hr 42 min
3 sec
Salyut 6 visit; Gur-
ragcha from Mongolia.

80 USA 32
12 April 1981
Columbia STS 1
John Young,
Bob Crippen
2 day 6 hr 20 min 52 sec
Maiden flight of Space
Shuttle.

81 USSR 49
15 May 1981
Soyuz 40
Leonid Popov,
Dumitru Prunariu
7 day 20 hr 41 min 52 sec
Final visiting crew to
Salyut 6; Prunariu from
Romania.

82 USA 33
12 November 1981
Columbia STS 2
Joe Engle, Dick Truly
2 day 6 hr 13 min
11 sec
First manned flight of
used vehicle.

83 USA 34
22 March 1982
Columbia STS 3
Jack Lousma,
Gordon Fullerton
8 day 0 hr 4 min 46 sec
Third test flight.

84 USSR 50
13 May 1982
Soyuz T5
Anatoli Berezevoi,
Valentin Lebedev
211 day 9 hr 4 min 32 sec
First, record-breaking,
visit to Salyut 7.

85 USSR 51
24 June 1982
Soyuz T6
Vladimir Dzhanibekov,
Alexander
Ivanchenkov,
Jean-Loup Chrétien
7 day 21 hr 50 min
52 sec
Visit to Salyut 7; Chré-
tien from France, first
Western European in
space.

86 USA 35
27 June 1982
Columbia STS 4
Ken Mattingly,

Hank Hartsfield
7 day 1 hr 9 min 31 sec
Military flight; final test
flight.

87 USSR 52
19 August 1982
Soyuz T7
Leonid Popov,
Alexander Serebrov,
Svetlana Savitskaya
7 day 21 hr 52 min
24 sec
Savitskaya second
woman in space after
20 years.

88 USA 36
11 November 1982
Columbia STS 5
Vance Brand, Robert
Overmyer, Joe Allen,
William Lenoir
5 day 2 hr 14 min 26 sec
First commercial
mission of Shuttle;
deployed two commu-
nications satellites;
first four-person flight.

89 USA 37
4 April 1983
Challenger STS 6
Paul Weitz, Karol
Bobko, Don Peterson,
Story Musgrave
5 day 0 hr 23 min
42 sec
Deployed TDRS 1;
limped into orbit after
upper stage failure; per-
formed spacewalk.

90 USSR 53
20 April 1983
Soyuz T8
Vladimir Titov,
Gennadi Strekalov,
Alexander Serebrov
2 day 0 hr 17 min
48 sec
Failed to dock with
Salyut 7; Serebrov
first person to fly
consecutive missions.

91 USA 38
18 June 1983
Challenger STS 7
Bob Crippen, Rick
Hauck, John Fabian,
Sally Ride,
Norman Thagard
6 day 2 hr 24 min
10 sec
Satellite deployment
mission is first by five
people; includes first US
woman in space.

92 USSR 54
27 June 1983
Soyuz T9

Vladimir Lyakhov,
Alexander Alexandrov
149 day 10 hr 46 min
Trouble with space
station, Salyut 7, halts
flight.

93 USA 39
30 August 1983
Challenger STS 8
Richard Truly, Dan
Brandenstein, Guoin
Bluford, Dale Gardner,
William Thornton
6 day 1 hr 8 min 40 sec
Night launch and
landing.

USSR
27 September 1983
Soyuz T10-1
Vladimir Titov,
Gennadi Strekalov
Launcher explodes on
pad; crew saved by
launch escape system.

94 USA 40
28 November 1983
Columbia STS 9
John Young, Brewster
Shaw, Owen Garriott,
Robert Parker,
Byron Lichtenberg,
Ulf Merbold
10 day 7 hr 47 min
23 sec
Flight of European
Spacelab 1; Merbold
from West Germany;
first six-up flight.

95 USA 41
3 February 1984
Challenger STS 41B
Vance Brand,
Robert Gibson,
Bruce McCandless,
Robert Stewart,
Ronald McNair
7 day 23 hr 15 min
54 sec
First independent
spacewalk using MMU
by McCandless; first
space mission to end at
launch site (Kennedy/
Canaveral).

96 USSR 55
8 February 1984
Soyuz T10
Leonid Kizim, Vladimir
Solovyov, Oleg Atkov
236 day 22 hr 49 min
Longest manned space
mission to date; Kizim
and Solovyov made
record six spacewalks.

97 USSR 56
3 April 1984
Soyuz T11

Yuri Malyshev,
Gennadi Strekalov,
Rakesh Sharma
7 day 21 hr 40 min
Visit to Salyut 7;
Sharma from India.

98 USA 42
6 April 1984
Challenger STS 41C
Bob Crippen,
Dick Scobee,
George Nelson,
Terry Hart,
James van Hoften
6 day 23 hr 40 min
5 sec
Repaired Solar Max;
with Soyuz T10 and T11
crews in space, 11 people
are up at once.

99 USSR 57
17 July 1984
Soyuz T12
Vladimir Dhzanibekov,
Svetlana Savitskaya,
Oleg Volk
11 day 19 hr 14 min
36 sec
Savitskaya becomes
first woman space-
walker, outside
Salyut 7.

100 USA 43
30 August 1984
Discovery STS 41D
Hank Hartsfield,
Michael Coats, Judy
Resnik, Steven Hawley,
Michael Mullane,
Charlie Walker
6 day 0 hr 56 min 4 sec
Launch pad abort in
June; three satellites
deployed; Walker first
industry-engineer
astronaut.

101 USA 44
5 October 1984
Challenger STS 41G
Bob Crippen, Jon
McBride, Sally Ride,
Kathy Sullivan,
David Leestma,
Marc Garneau,
Paul Scully Power.
8 day 5 hr 23 min
33 sec
First seven-up flight;
first carrying two
women; Ride first US
woman in space twice;
Sullivan first US woman
to spacewalk; Garneau
from Canada.

102 USA 45
8 November 1984
Discovery STS 51A
Rick Hauck, Dave

Walker, Joe Allen,
Dale Gardner,
Anna Fisher
7 day 23 hr 45 min
54 sec
Two spacewalks to
retrieve lost communic-
ations satellites and
return them to Earth.

103 USA 46
24 January 1985
Discovery STS 51C
Ken Mattingly, Loren
Shriver, Ellison
Onizuka, James Buchli,
Gary Payton
3 day 1 hr 33 min
13 sec
Military mission;
Payton first USAF
Manned Space Flight
Engineer.

104 USA 47
12 April 1985
Discovery STS 51D
Karol Bobko,
Don Williams,
Rhea Seddon,
Jeff Hoffman,
David Griggs,
Charlie Walker,
Jake Garn
6 day 23 hr 55 min
23 sec
Deployed three commu-
nications satellites;
unscheduled EVA
(Extra-vehicular
activity) to attempt
repair of one; Senator
Jake Garn first pas-
senger observer in
space.

105 USA 48
29 April 1985
Challenger STS 51B
Bob Overmyer, Fred
Gregory, Don Lind,
William Thornton,
Norman Thagard,
Lodewijk van den
Berg, Taylor Wang
7 day 0 hr 8 min 50 sec
Spacelab 3 research
mission.

106 USSR 58
6 June 1985
Soyuz T13
Vladimir Dzhanibekov,
Viktor Savinykh
112 day 3 hr 12 min
Complete overhaul of
Salyut 7 after systems
failures; Savinykh came
home in Soyuz T14 and
Georgi Grechko in
Soyuz T13.

107 USA 49
17 June 1985

Discovery STS 51G
Dan Brandenstein,
John Creighton,
Shannon Lucid,
Steve Nagel,
John Fabian,
Patrick Baudry,
Abdul Aziz Al-Saud
7 day 1 hr 38 min 58 sec
Satellite deployment
and research mission;
first with three nations
represented, Baudry
from France (first non-
US, non-USSR nation
to make two flights),
Abdul Aziz Al-Saud, a
Prince from Saudi
Arabia.

108 USA 50
20 July 1985
Challenger STS 51F
Gordon Fullerton, Roy
Bridges, Karl Henize,
Anthony England,
Story Musgrave,
John-David Bartoe,
Loren Acton
7 day 22 hr 45 min
27 sec
Launch pad abort on
July 12; one engine
shutdown during
launch, causing abort-
to-orbit; Henize oldest
man in space at 58;
Spacelab 2 research
mission.

109 USA 51
27 August 1985
Discovery STS 51I
Joe Engle, Dick Covey,
William Fisher,
James van Hoften,
Mike Lounge
7 day 2 hr 14 min
42 sec
Three satellites
deployed; Leasat 3
captured, repaired and
redeployed.

110 USSR 59
17 September 1985
Soyuz T14
Vladimir Vasyutin,
Georgi Grechko,
Alexander Volkov
64 day 21 hr 52 min
Mission cut short after
Vasyutin becomes men-
tally disturbed;
Grechko returned in
Soyuz T13; Savinykh
stayed with Soyuz T14
and clocked up mission
time of 168 days.

111 USA 52
3 October 1985
Atlantis STS 51J

Karol Bobko, Ron Grabe, Dale Hilmers, Bob Stewart, William Pailes
4 day 1 hr 45 min 30 sec
Military mission.

112 USA 53
30 October 1985
Challenger STS 61A
Hank Hartsfield, Steve Nagel, Bonnie Dunbar, Guion Gluford, James Buchli, Ernst Messerschmitt, Reinhard Furrer, Wubbo Ockels
7 day 0 hr 44 min 51 sec
West German-funded Spacelab D1 mission; Messerschmitt and Furrer from West Germany; Ockels from Netherlands; first eight-up mission.

113 USA 54
27 November 1985
Atlantis STS 61B
Brewster Shaw, Bryan O'Connor, Mary Cleave, Jerry Ross, Sherwood Spring, Rudolpho Neri Vela, Charlie Walker
6 day 21 hr 4 min 50 sec
Neri Vela from Mexico; Walker's third flight as Shuttle payload specialist; Ross and Spring assemble structures during EVAs.

114 USA 55
12 January 1986
Columbia STS 61C
Robert Gibson, Charles Bolden, Franklin Chang-Diaz, George Nelson, Steve Hawley, Robert Cenker, Bill Nelson
6 day 2 hr 4 min 9 sec
Much-delayed flight; Bill Nelson, a Congressman, second 'political' passenger.

USA
28 January 1986
Challenger STS 51L
Dick Scobee, Mike Smith, Judith Resnik, Ronald McNair, Ellison Onizuka, Christa McAuliffe, Gregory Jarvis
73 sec
Exploded at 14 330 m (47 000 ft); crew killed;

first flight to take off but not to reach space; first American in-flight fatalities.

115 USSR 60
13 March 1986
Soyuz T15
Leonid Kizim, Vladimir Solovyov
125 day 0 hr 1 min
First mission to new space station Mir 1; also docked with Salyut 7; Kizim clocks up over a year in space experience.

116 USSR 61
5 February 1987
Soyuz TM2
Yuro Romanenko, Alexander Laveikin
326 day 11 hr 37 min 59 sec
Record duration mission by Romanenko aboard Mir 1. Landed in Soyuz TM3 (Soyuz TM1 was unmanned). Laveikin, 200th person in space, returned after 174 days.

117 USSR 62
22 July 1987
Soyuz TM3
Alexander Viktorenko, Alexander Alexandrov, Muhammed Faris
7 day 23 hr 4 min 5 sec
Faris from Syria. Alexandrov remains on Mir for 160 days. Viktorenko and Faris land in Soyuz TM2 with Laveikin.

118 USSR 63
21 December 1987
Soyuz TM4
Vladimir Titov, Musa Manarov, Anatoli Levchenko
365 day 22 hr 39 min
Levchenko returns in Soyuz TM3 with Romanenko and Alexandrov after flight of 7 days. Titov and Manarov return in Soyuz TM6.

119 USSR 64
7 June 1988
Soyuz TM5
Anatoli Solovyov, Viktor Savinykh, Alexander Alexandrov
9 day 20 hr 10 min
Alexandrov second Bulgarian in space. Crew returns in Soyuz TM4.

120 USSR 65
31 August 1988
Soyuz TM6
Vladimir Lyakhov, Valeri Polyakov, Abdol Mohmand
8 day 20 hr 27 min
Mohmand from Afghanistan. Polyakov remains on Mir. Lyakhov and Mohmand land in Soyuz TM5 after 'stranded in space' scare.

121 USA 56
29 September 1988
Discovery STS 26
Rick Hauck, Dick Covey, Mike Lounge, David Hilmers, George Nelson
4 day 1 hr 0 min
America's return to space 32 months after Challenger disaster. Nelson first American to make successive national spaceflights.

122 USSR 66
26 November 1988
Soyuz TM7
Alexander Volkov, Sergei Krikalev, Jean-Loup Chrétien.
Visit to Mir. First non-US, non-USSR to make two spaceflights; Chrétien is also the first to make a spacewalk. Volkov and Krikalev returned April 1989.

123 USA 57
2 December 1988
Atlantis STS 27
Robert Gibson, Guy Gardner, Jerry Ross, Mike Mullane, William Shepherd
4 day 9 hr 6 min
Military mission to deploy Lacrosse spy satellite. With six cosmonauts on Mir, 11 people are in space.

124 USA 58
13 March 1989
Discovery STS 29
Michael Coats, John Blaha, James Buchli, James Bagian, Robert Springer
4 day 23 hr 39 min
Deployed TDRS satellite. STS 28 delayed.

125 USA 59
4 May 1989
Atlantis STS 30
David Walker,

Ron Grabe, Norman Thagard, Mary Cleave, Mark Lee
4 day 0 hr 57 min
Deployed *Magellan* for its journey to orbit the planet Venus. The first deployment of a planetary spacecraft from a manned spacecraft.

126 USA 60
8 August 1989
Columbia STS 28
Brewster Shaw, Richard Richards, David Leestma, James Adamson, Mark Brown
5 day 1 hr 0 min
Military mission to deploy KH-12 reconnaissance satellite.

127 USSR 67
6 September 1989
Soyuz TMB
Alexander Viktorenko, Alexander Serebrov
166 day 6 hr 58 min
Occupied Mir space station. First Soviet manned flight to operate commercial US experiments. First Soviet test of tethered MMU.

128 USA 61
18 October 1989
Atlantis STS 34
Donal Williams, Michael McCulley, Shannon Lucid, Franklin Chang-Diaz, Ellen Baker
4 day 23 hr 39 min
Deployed Jupiter orbiter *Galileo*.

129 USA 62
22 November 1989
Discovery STS 33
Frederick Gregory, John Blaha, Story Musgrave, Manley Carter, Kathryn Thornton
5 day 0 hr 6 min
Military mission to deploy Magnum elite spacecraft. First military manned spaceflight with civilian and female crew.

130 USA 63
9 January 1990
Columbia STS 32
Dan Brandenstein, James Wetherbee,

Bonnie Dunbar, Marsha Ivin, Daivid Low 10 day 21 hr 0 min Retrieved LDEF from orbit. Longest shuttle mission.

131 USSR 68
11 February 1990
Soyuz TM9
Anatoli Solovyov,
Alexander Balandin
179 day 2 hr 19 min
Occupation of Mir space station.

132 USA 64
28 February 1990
Atlantis STS 36
John Creighton, John Caspar, Mike Mullane, David Hilmers, Pierre Thuot
4 day 10 hr 18 min
Military mission to deploy KH-12 reconnaissance satellite, which broke up in orbit later.

133 USA 65
24 April 1990
Discovery STS 31
Loren Shriver, Charles Bolden, Steven Hawley, Bruce McCandless, Kathryn Sullivan
5 day 1 hr 16 min
Deployed Hubble Space Telescope. Reached record 532 km Shuttle altitude.

134 USSR 69
1 August 1990
Soyuz TM10
Gennadi Manakov, Gennadi Strekalov
130 day 19 hr 36 min
Occupation of Mir space station.

135 USA 66
6 October 1990
Discovery STS 41
Richard Richards, Robert Canbana, Thomas Akers, Bruce Melnick, William Shepherd
4 day 2 hr 10 min
Deployed *Ulysses* solar polar orbiter.

136 USA 67
15 November 1990
Atlantis STS 38
Richard Covey, Frank Culbertson, Robert Springer, Carl Meade, Sam Gemar
4 day 21 hr 54 min
Military mission.

137 USA 68
2 December 1990
Columbia STS 35
Vance Brand, Guy Gardner, Jeff Hoffman, Mike Lounge, Robert Parker, Ronald Parise, Samual Durrance
8 day 23 hr 5 min
Launch of Astro-1 observatory.

138 USSR 70
2 December 1990
Soyuz TM 11
Musa Manarov, Toyohiro Akiyama, Viktor Afanasyef.
New occupation of Mir space station. At the time of going to press Manarov and Afanasef were still in orbit. Akiyama – a Japanese journalist passenger – returned to earth with Soyuz TM10.

PLANNED FLIGHTS FOR JANUARY-MAY 1991

February 1991
Discovery STS 39
Michael Coats, Blaine Hammond, Gregory Harbaugh, Donald McMonagle, Guion Bluford, Richard Hieb, Charles Veach
Military mission.

February
Atlantis STS 37
Stephen Nagel, Jerry Ross, Jay Apt, Linda Godwin
Gamma Ray Observatory deployment mission.

March
Columbia STS 40
Bryan O'Connor, Sidney Gutierrez, Rhea Seddon, James Bagian, Tamara Jernigan, Drew Gaffney, Millie Hughes-Fulford
Spacelab Life Sciences mission.

May
Soyuz TM12
New occupation of Mir space station, with British passenger, Helen Sharman.

MMU Manned Manoeuvring Unit
EVA Extra-vehicular activity
LDEF Long Duration Exposure Facilities

MOST EXPERIENCED SPACEMEN

Name	Experience	Country	No. of Flights
Romanenko	430 day 18 hr 21 min	USSR	3
Kizim	374 day 17 hr 57 min	USSR	3
V. Titov	367 day 22 hr 56 min	USSR	2
Manarov*	365 day 22 hr 39 min	USSR	1
V. Solovyov	361 day 22 hr 50 min	USSR	2
Ryumin	361 day 21 hr 31 min	USSR	3
Lyakhov	333 day 07 hr 48 min	USSR	3
Alexandrov	309 day 18 hr 03 min	USSR	2
Savinykh	252 day 17 hr 38 min	USSR	3
Polyakov	240 day 22 hr 36 min	USSR	1
Atkov	236 day 22 hr 49 min	USSR	1
Lebedev	219 day 05 hr 59 min	USSR	2
Kovalyonok	216 day 09 hr 09 min	USSR	3
A. Volkov	216 day 09 hr 02 min	USSR	2
Berezovoi	211 day 09 hr 04 min	USSR	1
Popov	200 day 14 hr 44 min	USSR	3

* On 1 January 1991 Manarov was in orbit in Soyuz TM11. Details of this flight are not included in the total. If Soyuz TM11 remains in orbit for three months or more, as planned, Manarov will become the most experienced spaceman.

MOST EXPERIENCED SPACEWOMEN

Savitskaya	19 day 17 hr 06 min	USSR	2
Ride	17 day 21 hr 45 min	USA	2

NATIONAL MANNED SPACEFLIGHT TOTALS*

Country	Days	No. of Flights
USSR	3572*	70*
USA	548	68
France	40	3 (2 USSR, 1 USA)
Germany**	25	3 (2 USA, 1 USSR)
Bulgaria	12	2 (USSR)
Afghanistan	10	1 (USSR)
Canada	8	1 (USA)
Japan	8	1 (USSR)
Syria	8	1 (USSR)
Czechoslovakia	8	1 (USSR)
Poland	8	1 (USSR)
India	8	1 (USSR)
Hungary	8	1 (USSR)
Romania	8	1 (USSR)
Cuba	8	1 (USSR)
Mongolia	8	1 (USSR)
Vietnam	8	1 (USSR)
Saudi Arabia	7	1 (USA)
Netherlands	7	1 (USA)
Mexico	7	1 (USA)

Total 20 countries*, 4299 days**

* To nearest day up to 1 Jan 1991. Does not include uncompleted flight by Manarov and Afanasyef. ** Two flights of West Germans (17 days), one flight of an East German (8 days). *** British astronaut Helen Sharman was in space for 8 days in May 1991.

NATIONAL MAN-DAYS IN SPACE*

Country	Days
USSR	7191†
USA	2123
France	40

Rest: see National Manned Spaceflight Totals

*To 1 January 1991
†Does not include uncompleted mission by Manarov and Afanasyef.

PEOPLE WHO HAVE FLOWN INTO SPACE*

239 in total
146 USA (11 women)
70 USSR (2 women)
4 Germany (3 from W Germany; 1 from E Germany)
2 France
2 Bulgaria
1 each from: Canada, Poland, India, Hungary, Cuba, Mongolia, Vietnam, Romania, Czechoslovakia, Saudi Arabia, Mexico, The Netherlands, Afghanistan, Syria and Japan.
* To 1 January 1991; the first UK astronaut flew in May 1991.

People who have flown five missions:
John Young, USA, and Vladimir Dzhanibekov, USSR

People who have flown six missions:
John Young, USA

YOUNGEST AND OLDEST IN SPACE

Oldest: Vance Brand, 59, USA.
Oldest Soviet: Georgi Grechko, 53.
Oldest other country: Jean-Loup Chrétien, 51, France
Oldest woman: Shannon Lucid, 46, USA.
Oldest Soviet woman: Svetlana Savitskaya, 35.
Youngest: Gherman Titov, 25, USSR.
Youngest American: Sally Ride, 32.
Youngest American male: Eugene Cernan, 32.
Youngest Soviet woman: Valentina Tereshkova, 26.
Youngest other country: Dumitru Prunariu, 28, Romania.

MOON TRAVELLERS

24 Americans have travelled to the Moon.
22 Americans have orbited the Moon.
12 Americans have walked on the Moon:
Armstrong, Aldrin, Conrad, Bean, Shepard, Mitchell, Scott, Irwin, Young, Duke, Cernan, Schmitt.
3 Americans have travelled to the Moon twice: Lovell, Young, Cernan.
2 Americans have orbited the Moon twice: Young, Cernan.
Moonwalk totals: 3 days 8 hrs 22 min.
Lunar stay time total: 12 days 11 hrs 40 min.
Weight of Moon returned to Earth: 386·0 kg (850·2 lb).

FAMOUS FIRSTS IN MANNED SPACEFLIGHT

		Date of Launch
First in space:	Yuri Gagarin USSR	12 Apr 1961
First American in space:	John Glenn	20 Feb 1962
First woman in space:	Valentina Tereshkova USSR	16 Jun 1963
First non-US, non-Soviet spaceman:	Vladimir Remek Czechoslovakia	2 Mar 1978
First to make two flights:	Gus Grissom USA	25 Mar 1965
First non-US, non-Soviet to make two flights:	Jean-Loup Chrétien France	26 Nov 1988
First to make three flights:	Wally Schirra USA	11 Oct 1968
First to make four flights:	James Lovell USA	11 Apr 1970
First to make five flights:	John Young USA	12 Apr 1981
First to make six flights:	John Young USA	28 Nov 1983
First to walk in space:	Alexei Leonov USSR	18 Mar 1965
First to walk in space five times:	Leonid Kizim USSR Vladimir Solvyov USSR (Also the first to walk in space six, seven and eight times)	13 Mar 1986
First to walk in space independently:	Bruce McCandless USA	3 Feb 1984
First male–female spacewalk:	Vladimir Dzhanibekov and Svetlana Savitskaya USSR	17 July 1984
First spacewalk between Moon and Earth:	Alfred Worden USA	26 July 1971
First spacewalk by non-US, non-Soviet:	Jean-Loup Chrétien France	26 Nov 1988
First aborted ascent:	Soyuz 18-1 USSR	5 Apr 1975
First aborted launch:	Gemini 6 USA	12 Dec 1965
First spacecraft manoeuvres:	Gemini 3 USA	25 Mar 1965
First over 50 years of age in space:	Deke Slayton USA	15 July 1975
First to touch another spacecraft:	Mike Collins USA	18 July 1966
First to fly consecutive missions:	Alexander Serebrov USSR	20 Apr 1983
First crew transfer:	Alexei Yeleseyev USSR Yevgeni Khrunov USSR	15 Jan 1969
First docking:	Gemini 8 USA	16 Mar 1966
First dual flight:	Vostok 3 and 4 USSR	12 Aug 1961
First launch explosion: (crew saved by escape system)	Soyuz T10-1 USSR Vladimir Titov USSR Gennadi Strekalov USSR	27 Sept 1983
First extended mission:	Voskhod 2 USSR	18 Mar 1965
First two-crew flight:	Voskhod 2 USSR	18 Mar 1965

First three-crew flight:	Voskhod 1 USSR	12 Oct 1964
First four-crew flight:	STS 5 USA	11 Nov 1982
First five-crew flight:	STS 7 USA	18 Jun 1983
First six-crew flight:	STS 9 USA	28 Nov 1983
First seven-crew flight:	STS 41G USA	5 Oct 1984
First eight-crew flight:	STS 61A USA	30 Oct 1985
First grandfather in space:	Lev Demin USSR	24 Aug 1974
First landing at launch base:	STS 41B USA	3 Feb 1984
First military mission:	Soyuz 14 USSR	3 July 1974
First flight to the Moon:	Apollo 8 USA	21 Dec 1968
First flight to land on the Moon:	Apollo 11 USA	16 July 1969
First men on Moon:	Neil Armstrong USA Buzz Aldrin USA	16 July 1969
First mother in space:	Anna Fisher USA	8 Nov 1984
First night launch:	Soyuz 1 USSR	23 Apr 1967
First night landing:	Soyuz 10 USSR	23 Apr 1971
First rendezvous in space:	Gemini 6 and 7 USA	16 Dec 1965
First to sleep in space:	Gherman Titov USSR	6 Aug 1961
First to fly solo in lunar orbit:	John Young USA	18 May 1969
First telecast from space:	Vostok 3 USSR	11 Aug 1962
First person to fly to Moon twice:	James Lovell USA	11 Apr 1970
First woman spacewalker:	Svetlana Savitskaya USSR	17 Jul 1984
First passenger-observer:	Jake Garn USA	12 Apr 1985
First return due to illness:	Vladimir Vasyutin USSR	17 Sep 1985
First flight to take off but not reach space:	Challenger 51L USA	28 Jan 1986
First landing with each crewmember having been launched in separate spacecraft:	Yuri Romanenko USSR Alexander Alexandrov USSR Anatoli Levchenko USSR	29 Dec 1987*

* Date of landing

EURO FACTS

EUROPEAN SPACE AGENCY

The European Space Agency (8-10 rue Mario Nikis, 75738 Paris, France) was established in 1975 by the merger of two existing space organizations – the European Space Research Organization (ESRO) and the European Launcher Development Organization (ELDO).

The aims of ESA include the advancement of space technology and research, and the implementation of a European space programme through the coordination of the space programmes of individual members.

Members: Austria, Belgium, Canada (a cooperating state), Denmark, Finland (an associate member), France, Germany, Ireland (Republic of), Italy, the Netherlands, Norway, Spain, Sweden, Switzerland and the United Kingdom.

European Space Agency Spacecraft (operational and planned)

ECS Programme (European Communication Satellite)
Funded by 26 countries, the four ECS satellites (launched between 1984 and 1988) have established a European regional telecommunications network. Each satellite can simultaneously relay 12 000 telephone calls and two colour television channels.

Marecs Programme
Two satellites – launched in 1981 and 1984 – provide a maritime telecommunications network.

Hipparcos (High Precision Parallax Collecting Satellite)
This satellite – launched in 1989 – measures astronomical coordinates.

Ulysses
Launched in 1990 towards Jupiter, this satellite will collect data concerning the poles of the Sun.

ERS-1
Launched in 1990, this satellite will survey specified areas of the Earth.

IN-FLIGHT FATALITIES

Vladimir Komarov	USSR	Soyuz 1	24 April 1967
Georgi Dobrovolsky	USSR	Soyuz 11	
Vladislav Volkov	USSR	Soyuz 11	6 June 1971
Viktor Patsayev	USSR	Soyuz 11	
Dick Scobee	USA	Space Shuttle* Challenger STS 51L	
Mike Smith	USA	Space Shuttle* Challenger STS 51L	
Judith Resnik	USA	Space Shuttle* Challenger STS 51L	
Ellison Onizuka	USA	Space Shuttle* Challenger STS 51L	28 January 1986
Ronald McNair	USA	Space Shuttle* Challenger STS 51L	
Gregory Jarvis	USA	Space Shuttle* Challenger STS 51L	
Christa McAulliffe	USA	Space Shuttle* Challenger STS 51L	

* Did not reach space

TIME

TIME SYSTEMS

Time forms the basis of many scientific laws, but time itself is very difficult to define. Time, like distance, separates objects and events, and for this reason can be regarded as the fourth dimension. However, time cannot be measured directly. We must make do with measuring the way in which the passage of time affects things.

The Earth's orbit is not circular but elliptical, so the Sun does not appear to move against the stars at a constant speed. Most everyday time systems are therefore based on a hypothetical 'mean Sun', which is taken to travel at a constant speed equal to the average speed of the actual Sun.

A *day* is the time taken for the Earth to turn once on its axis. A *sidereal day* is reckoned with reference to the stars and is the time taken between successive passes of the observer's meridian by the same star. (The *meridian* is an imaginary line from due north to due south running through a point directly above the observer.) One sidereal day is 23 hours 56 minutes 4 seconds. A *solar day* is calculated with respect to the mean Sun. The mean solar day is 24 hours long.

MEASURING TIME

The earliest device for measuring time was the *sundial*, which can be traced back to the Middle East c. 3500 BC. A sundial comprises a rod or plate called a *gnomon* that casts a shadow on a disc; where the shadow points indicates the position of the Sun and hence the time of day.

Mechanical clocks, driven by falling weights, appeared in the 14th century, and the first *mechanical watches*, driven by a coiled mainspring, in the 16th century. The first *pendulum clock* was invented by Christiaan Huygens (1629–95), a Dutch physicist, in the middle of the 17th century.

Pendulum clocks could not be used on board ships owing to the vessel's motion. In 1714 the British Longitude Board offered a prize for the development of a *marine chronometer*, as the ability to tell the time accurately is vital to navigation. The English clockmaker John Harrison (1693–1776) produced his first marine chronometer in 1735 after seven years' work on the problem.

The first *quartz clock*, operated by the vibrations of a quartz crystal when an electrical voltage is applied, appeared in 1929. The quartz clock is accurate to within one second in ten years. This was followed in 1948 by the *atomic clock*, which depends on the natural vibrations of atoms. The most accurate modern atomic clocks are accurate to one second in 1.7 million years.

A *year* is the time taken for the Earth to complete one orbit of the Sun. The Earth's true revolution period is 365 days 6 hours 9 minutes 10 seconds, and this is known as a *sidereal year*. However, the direction in which the Earth's axis points is changing due to an effect known as *precession*. The north celestial pole now lies near the star Polaris in the constellation Ursa Minor, thus Polaris is also known as the Pole

Star. By the year AD 14 000, the Earth's axis will point in a different direction and the bright star Vega in Lyra will be near the pole. This effect also means that the position of the Sun's apparent path across the sky is changing with respect to the stars. A *tropical year* compensates for the effects of precession and is 365 days 5 hours 48 minutes 45 seconds long. It is the tropical year that is used as the basis for developing a calendar.

The SI unit of time is the *second*, which was originally defined as $^{1}/_{86\,400}$ of the mean solar day. However, as we have seen, the Earth is not a very good time-keeper, so scientists no longer use it to define the fundamental unit of time. The second is now defined as the duration of 9 192 631 770 periods of the radiation corresponding to the transition between the two hyperfine levels of the ground state of a caesium-133 atom.

Greenwich Mean Time (GMT) is the local time at Greenwich, England. The *Greenwich Meridian* is the line of 0° longtitude, which passes through Greenwich Observatory. The mean Sun crosses the Greenwich Meridian at midday GMT. Also known as *Universal Time* (UT), GMT is used as a standard reference time throughout the world. *Sidereal time* literally means 'star time'. It is reckoned with reference to the stars and not the Sun.

THE JULIAN AND GREGORIAN CALENDARS

By 46 BC the Roman calendar had become confused and in need of reform. On the advice of the Egyptian astronomer Sosigenes, Julius Caesar therefore introduced what became known as the Julian calendar. The year 46 BC – known as the 'Year of Confusion' – was lengthened to 445 days to bring it in line with the solar year.

Under the Julian calendar the solar year was calculated at 365 days and divided into 12 months. Each month contained 30 or 31 days except for February, which contained 28 days (or 29 days in a leap year). However, by 1582 an overestimation by Sosigenes of about 11 minutes a year had accumulated into a 10-day difference between the Julian calendar and the astronomical year. Pope Gregory XIII therefore ordered that 5 October 1582 should become 15 October, and that century years would only be leap years if divisible by 400 (i.e. 1600, 2000).

In error by 0.0005 days per year, the present Gregorian calendar will not need to be revised for many years.

SEASONS

The four seasons in the northern hemisphere are astronomically speaking:

Spring from the vernal equinox (about 21 March) to the summer solstice (21 or 22 June);

Summer from the summer solstice (21 or 22 June) to the autumnal equinox (about 21 September);

Autumn (or Fall in the USA) from the autumnal equinox (about 21 September) to the winter solstice (21 December or 22 December);

Winter from the winter solstice (21 or 22 December) to the vernal equinox (about 21 March).

In the southern hemisphere, of course, autumn corresponds to spring, winter to summer, spring to autumn and summer to winter.

The solstices (from Latin *sol*, sun; *sistere*, to stand still) are the two times in the year when the sun is farthest from the Equator and appears to be still. The equinoxes (from Latin *aequalis*, equal; *nox*, night) are the two times in the year when day and night are of equal length when the Sun crosses the equator.

The longest day has the longest interval between sunrise and sunset. It is the day on which the summer solstice falls and in the northern hemisphere occurs on 21 June, or more rarely on 22 June.

MONTHS OF THE YEAR

January	31 days; from the Roman republican calendar month Januarius, named after Janus, god of doorways and of beginnings.
February	28 days (29 in a leap year); from the Roman republican calendar month Februarius, named after Februa, the festival of purification held on the 15th.
March	31 days; from the Roman republican calendar month Martius, named after the god Mars.
April	30 days; from the Roman republican calendar month Aprilis. The Romans considered the month sacred to Venus and may have named it after her Greek equivalent Aphrodite. It may also have derived from the Latin *aperire*, 'to open', in reference to the spring blossoming.
May	31 days; from Roman republican calendar month Maius, probably named after the goddess Maia.
June	30 days; from the Roman republican calendar month Junius, probably named after the goddess Juno.
July	31 days; from the Roman republican calendar month Julius, named after Julius Caesar in 44 BC.
August	31 days; from the Roman republican calendar month Augustus named after the emperor Augustus in 8 BC.
September	30 days; seventh month of the early Roman republican calendar, from Latin *septem*, meaning 'seven'.
October	31 days; eighth month of the early Roman republican calendar, from the Latin *octo*, meaning 'eight'.
November	30 days; ninth month of the early Roman republican calendar, from the Latin *novem*, meaning 'nine'.
December	31 days; tenth month of the early Roman republican calendar, from Latin *decem*, meaning 'ten'.

LEAP YEAR

The use of leap years – years with an extra intercalary period – is common to most calendars. In the Gregorian calendar it is an extra day (29 February) that compensates for the quarter-day difference between a calendar year of 365 days and the astronomical year of 365.24219878 days. Every centennial year divisible by 400 and every other year divisible by four is a leap year.

The date when it will be necessary to suppress a further leap year, sometimes assumed to be AD 4000, AD 8000, etc., is not yet clearly definable, owing to minute variations in the Earth-Sun relationship.

The word 'leap' derives from the Old Norse *hlaupar*, indicating a leap in the sense of jump. The origin of the term probably derives from the observation that in a leap year any fixed-day festival falls on the next day of the week but one to that on which it fell in the preceding year, and not on the next day of the week as happens in common years.

THE PERPETUAL CALENDAR

There is a formula – which includes the table of values listed below – that works out the days of the week in any month in any year of the 20th century.

The method for working out the day of the week, using the table of values below, is as follows.
Using 14 June 1947 as an example:
Add together

a) the date (14)	= 14
b) the value of the month (June)	= 4
c) the year	= 47
d) the leap years already experienced that century (divide the previous line by 4 and ignore the remainder; 47 divided by 4)	= 11
Total	**76**
Divide the total by 7	= 10
	remainder 6

The remainder is the value of the day of the week in the table below. 6 = Saturday, thus 14 June 1947 was a Saturday.

Month	Value
January	0
February	3
March	3
April	6
May	1
June	4
July	6
August	2
September	5
October	0
November	3
December	5

Day	Value
Monday	1
Tuesday	2
Wednesday	3
Thursday	4
Friday	5
Saturday	6
Sunday	0

THE NEW YEAR

In early medieval times Christian Europe regarded March 25 (Annunciation Day) as New Year's Day. Anglo-Saxon England, however, used December 25 to mark the year's beginning until William the Conqueror decreed that the year should begin on 1 January. England later fell into line with the rest of Christendom, recognizing the year's commencement as March 25. The introduction of the Gregorian Calendar in 1582 confirmed 1 January as New Year's Day.

The adoption of 1 January as New Year's Day in various European countries took place in the following years:

1522	Venice and some other Italian states;
1544	Catholic states and some Protestant states of Germany;
1556	Spain, Portugal, Catholic Netherlands;
1559	Denmark, Prussia, Sweden;
1564	France;
1583	Protestant Netherlands;
1600	Scotland;
1725	Russia;
1751	England.

DAYS OF THE WEEK

English name	Named after
Sunday	The Sun
Monday	The Moon
Tuesday	Tiw, the Anglo-Saxon counterpart of the Nordic god Tyr, son of Odin
Wednesday	Woden, the Ango-Saxon counterpart of Odin, the Nordic god of war
Thursday	Thor, the Nordic god of thunder, eldest son of Odin
Friday	Frigg, the Nordic goddess of love, wife of Odin
Saturday	Saturn, Roman god of agriculture and vegetation

THE JEWISH CALENDAR

It is thought that the Jewish Calendar, as used today, was popularly in use from the 9th century BCE. It is based on the biblical calculations that place the creation in 3761 BCE. The abbreviation BCE means Before the Common Era, while CE stands for Common Era; they correspond to BC and AD, respectively. The complicated rules of the Jewish Calendar with regard to festivals and fasts have resulted in a calendar scheme in which a Jewish year may be one of the following six types:

Minimal Common (353 days);
Regular Common (354 days);
Full Common (355 days);
Minimal Leap (383 days);
Regular Leap (384 days);
Full Leap (385 days).

MONTHS OF THE JEWISH CALENDAR

1. Nisan	30 days
2. Iyyar	29 days
3. Sivan	30 days
4. Tammuz	29 days
5. Av	30 days
6. Ellul	29 days
7. Tishri	30 days
8. Marsheshvan (Heshvan)	29/30 days*
9. Kislev	29/30 days*
10. Teret	29/30 days*
11. Shevat	30 days
12. Adar	29 days (30 in a leap year)
Ve-Adar †	30 days

* can have either 29 or 30 days depending on the year.
† a 13th month is intercalated into the calendar every 3rd, 6th, 8th, 11th, 14th, 17th and 19th year of a 19-year cycle. It contains all the religious observances that usually occur in Adar.

COMPARATIVE JEWISH CALENDAR 1991–1993

Sept 1991	1 2 3 4 5 6 6 7 8	9 10 11 12 13 14 15 16 17 18 19 20 21 22 23 24 25 26 27 28 29 30
Ellul 5751	22 23 24 24 25 26 27 28 29 Tishri* 1 2 3 4 5 6 7 8 9 10 11 12 13 14 15 16 17 18 19 20 21 22	

* Jewish New Year 5752

October	1 2 3 4 5 6 7 8	9 10 11 12 13 14 15 16 17 18 19 20 21 22 23 24 25 26 27 28 29 30 31
Tishri 5752	23 24 25 26 27 28 29 30 Heshvan 1 2 3 4 5 6 7 8 9 10 11 12 13 14 15 16 17 18 19 20 21 22 23	

November	1 2 3 4 5 6 7	8 9 10 11 12 13 14 15 16 17 18 19 20 21 22 23 24 25 26 27 28 29 30
Heshvan	24 25 26 27 28 29 30 Kislev 1 2 3 4 5 6 7 8 9 10 11 12 13 14 15 16 17 18 19 20 21 22 23	

December	1 2 3 4 5 6 7	8 9 10 11 12 13 14 15 16 17 18 19 20 21 22 23 24 25 26 27 28 29 30 31
Kislev	24 25 26 27 28 29 30 Teret 1 2 3 4 5 6 7 8 9 10 11 12 13 14 15 16 17 18 19 20 21 22 23 24	

Jan 1992	1 2 3 4 5	6 7 8 9 10 11 12 13 14 15 16 17 18 19 20 21 22 23 24 25 26 27 28 29 30 31
Teret 5752	25 26 27 28 29 Shevat 1 2 3 4 5 6 7 8 9 10 11 12 13 14 15 16 17 18 19 20 21 22 23 24 25 26	

February	1 2 3 4	5 6 7 8 9 10 11 12 13 14 15 16 17 18 19 20 21 22 23 24 25 26 27 28 29
Shevat	27 28 29 30 Adar 1 2 3 4 5 6 7 8 9 10 11 12 13 14 15 16 17 18 19 20 21 22 23 24 25	

| March | 1 2 3 4 5 | 6 7 8 9 10 11 12 13 14 15 16 17 18 19 20 21 22 23 24 25 26 27 28 29 30 31 |
| Adar | 26 27 28 29 30 Ve-Adar† 1 2 3 4 5 6 7 8 9 10 11 12 13 14 15 16 17 18 19 20 21 22 23 24 25 26 |

† intercalary month; see text

| April | 1 2 3 4 5 6 7 8 9 10 11 12 13 14 15 16 17 18 19 20 21 22 23 24 25 26 27 28 29 30 |
| Ve-Adar | 27 28 29 Nisan 1 2 3 4 5 6 7 8 9 10 11 12 13 14 15 16 17 18 19 20 21 22 23 24 25 26 27 |

| May | 1 2 3 4 5 6 7 8 9 10 11 12 13 14 15 16 17 18 19 20 21 22 23 24 25 26 27 28 29 30 31 |
| Nisan | 28 29 30 Iyyar 1 2 3 4 5 6 7 8 9 10 11 12 13 14 15 16 17 18 19 20 21 22 23 24 25 26 27 28 |

| June | 1 2 3 4 5 6 7 8 9 10 11 12 13 14 15 16 17 18 19 20 21 22 23 24 25 26 27 28 29 30 |
| Iyyar | 29 Sivan 1 2 3 4 5 6 7 8 9 10 11 12 13 14 15 16 17 18 19 20 21 22 23 24 25 26 27 28 29 |

| July | 1 2 3 4 5 6 7 8 9 10 11 12 13 14 15 16 17 18 19 20 21 22 23 24 25 26 27 28 29 30 31 |
| Sivan | 30 Tammuz 1 2 3 4 5 6 7 8 9 10 11 12 13 14 15 16 17 18 19 20 21 22 23 24 25 26 27 28 29 Av 1 |

| August | 1 2 3 4 5 6 7 8 9 10 11 12 13 14 15 16 17 18 19 20 21 22 23 24 25 26 27 28 29 30 31 |
| Av | 2 3 4 5 6 7 8 9 10 11 12 13 14 15 16 17 18 19 20 21 22 23 24 25 26 27 28 29 30 Ellul 1 2 |

| September | 1 2 3 4 5 6 7 8 9 10 11 12 13 14 15 16 17 18 19 20 21 22 23 24 25 26 27 28 29 30 |
| Ellul | 3 4 5 6 7 8 9 10 11 12 13 14 15 16 17 18 19 20 21 22 23 24 25 26 27 28 29 Tishri* 1 2 3 |

* Jewish New Year 5753

| October | 1 2 3 4 5 6 7 8 9 10 11 12 13 14 15 16 17 18 19 20 21 22 23 24 25 26 27 28 29 30 31 |
| Tishri 5753 | 4 5 6 7 8 9 10 11 12 13 14 15 16 17 18 19 20 21 22 23 24 25 26 27 28 29 30 Heshvan 1 2 3 4 |

| November | 1 2 3 4 5 6 7 8 9 10 11 12 13 14 15 16 17 18 19 20 21 22 23 24 25 26 27 28 29 30 |
| Heshvan | 5 6 7 8 9 10 11 12 13 14 15 16 17 18 19 20 21 22 23 24 25 26 27 28 29 Kislev 1 2 3 4 5 |

| December | 1 2 3 4 5 6 7 8 9 10 11 12 13 14 15 16 17 18 19 20 21 22 23 24 25 26 27 28 29 30 31 |
| Kislev | 6 7 8 9 10 11 12 13 14 15 16 17 18 19 20 21 22 23 24 25 26 27 28 29 Teret 1 2 3 4 5 6 7 |

| Jan 1993 | 1 2 3 4 5 6 7 8 9 10 11 12 13 14 15 16 17 18 19 20 21 22 23 24 25 26 27 28 29 30 31 |
| Teret | 8 9 10 11 12 13 14 15 16 17 18 19 20 21 22 23 24 25 26 27 28 29 Shevat 1 2 3 4 5 6 7 8 9 |

| February | 1 2 3 4 5 6 7 8 9 10 11 12 13 14 15 16 17 18 19 20 21 22 23 24 25 26 27 28 |
| Shevat | 10 11 12 13 14 15 16 17 18 19 20 21 22 23 24 25 26 27 28 29 30 Adar 1 2 3 4 5 6 7 |

| March | 1 2 3 4 5 6 7 8 9 10 11 12 13 14 15 16 17 18 19 20 21 22 23 24 25 26 27 28 29 30 31 |
| Adar | 8 9 10 11 12 13 14 15 16 17 18 19 20 21 22 23 24 25 26 27 28 29 Nisan 1 2 3 4 5 6 7 8 9 |

| April | 1 2 3 4 5 6 7 8 9 10 11 12 13 14 15 16 17 18 19 20 21 22 23 24 25 26 27 28 29 30 |
| Nisan | 10 11 12 13 14 15 16 17 18 19 20 21 22 23 24 25 26 27 28 29 30 Iyyar 1 2 3 4 5 6 7 8 9 |

| May | 1 2 3 4 5 6 7 8 9 10 11 12 13 14 15 16 17 18 19 20 | 21 22 23 24 25 26 27 28 29 30 31 |
| Iyyar | 10 11 12 13 14 15 16 17 18 19 20 21 22 23 24 25 26 27 28 29 | Sivan 1 2 3 4 5 6 7 8 9 10 11 |

| June | 1 2 3 4 5 6 7 8 9 10 11 12 13 14 15 16 17 18 19 | 20 21 22 23 24 25 26 27 28 29 30 |
| Sivan | 12 13 14 15 16 17 18 19 20 21 22 23 24 25 26 27 28 29 30 Tammuz 1 2 3 4 5 6 7 8 9 10 11 | |

| July | 1 2 3 4 5 6 7 8 9 10 11 12 13 14 15 16 17 18 | 19 20 21 22 23 24 25 26 27 28 29 30 31 |
| Tammuz | 12 13 14 15 16 17 18 19 20 21 22 23 24 25 26 27 28 29 Av 1 2 3 4 5 6 7 8 9 10 11 12 13 | |

| August | 1 2 3 4 5 6 7 8 9 10 11 12 13 14 15 16 17 | 18 19 20 21 22 23 24 25 26 27 28 29 30 31 |
| Av | 14 15 16 17 18 19 20 21 22 23 24 25 26 27 28 29 30 Ellul 1 2 3 4 5 6 7 8 9 10 11 12 13 14 | |

| September | 1 2 3 4 5 6 7 8 9 10 11 12 13 14 15 | 16 17 18 19 20 21 22 23 24 25 26 27 28 29 30 |
| Ellul | 15 16 17 18 19 20 21 22 23 24 25 26 27 28 29 Tishri* 1 2 3 4 5 6 7 8 9 10 11 12 13 14 15 | |

* Jewish New Year 5754

THE ISLAMIC CALENDAR

The Islamic calendar is based on lunar years beginning with the year of the *Hejirah* (AD 622 of the Julian calendar), when Muhammad travelled from Mecca to Medina. It runs in cycles of 30 years, of which the 2nd, 5th, 7th, 10th, 13th, 16th, 18th, 21st, 24th, 26th and 29th are leap years. A year consists of 12 months containing alternately 30 days and 29 days, with the intercalation of one day at the end of the 12th month – Dhû'l Hijja – in a leap year. Common years have 354 days, leap years 355. The extra day is intercalated in order to reconcile the date of the first of the month with the date of the actual New Moon. Some Muslims register the first of the month on the evening that the crescent becomes visible.

Hejirah years are used principally in Iran, Turkey, Saudi Arabia and other states of the Arabian peninsula, Egypt, certain parts of India, and Malaysia.

MONTHS OF THE MUSLIM CALENDAR

1. Muharram	30 days
2. Safar	29 days
3. Rabîa I	30 days
4. Rabîa II	29 days
5. Jumâda I	30 days
6. Jumâda II	29 days
7. Rajab	30 days
8. Shaabân	29 days
9. Ramadan	30 days
10. Shawwâl	29 days
11. Dhû'l-Qa'da	30 days
12. Dhû'l Hijja	29 days (30 days in a leap year)

COMPARATIVE ISLAMIC CALENDAR 1991–1993

| Sept 1991 | 1 2 3 4 5 6 7 8 9 | 10 11 12 13 14 15 16 17 18 19 20 21 22 23 24 25 26 27 28 29 30 |
| Safar 1412 | 21 22 23 24 25 26 27 28 29 Rabîa I 1 2 3 4 5 6 7 8 9 10 11 12 13 14 15 16 17 18 19 20 21 | |

| October | 1 2 3 4 5 6 7 8 9 | 10 11 12 13 14 15 16 17 18 19 20 21 22 23 24 25 26 27 28 29 30 31 |
| Rabîa I | 22 23 24 25 26 27 28 29 30 Rabîa II 1 2 3 4 5 6 7 8 9 10 11 12 13 14 15 16 17 18 19 20 21 22 | |

| November | 1 2 3 4 5 6 7 | 8 9 10 11 12 13 14 15 16 17 18 19 20 21 22 23 24 25 26 27 28 29 30 |
| Rabîa II | 23 24 25 26 27 28 29 Jumâda I 1 2 3 4 5 6 7 8 9 10 11 12 13 14 15 16 17 18 19 20 21 22 23 | |

| December | 1 2 3 4 5 6 7 | 8 9 10 11 12 13 14 15 16 17 18 19 20 21 22 23 24 25 26 27 28 29 30 31 |
| Jumâda I | 24 25 26 27 28 29 30 Jumâda II 1 2 3 4 5 6 7 8 9 10 11 12 13 14 15 16 17 18 19 20 21 22 23 24 | |

| Jan 1992 | 1 2 3 4 5 | 6 7 8 9 10 11 12 13 14 15 16 17 18 19 20 21 22 23 24 25 26 27 28 29 30 31 |
| Jumâda II | 25 26 27 28 29 Rajab 1 2 3 4 5 6 7 8 9 10 11 12 13 14 15 16 17 18 19 20 21 22 23 24 25 26 | |

| February | 1 2 3 4 | 5 6 7 8 9 10 11 12 13 14 15 16 17 18 19 20 21 22 23 24 25 26 27 28 29 |
| Rajab | 27 28 29 30 Shaabân 1 2 3 4 5 6 7 8 9 10 11 12 13 14 15 16 17 18 19 20 21 22 23 24 25 | |

March	1 2 3 4	5 6 7 8 9 10 11 12 13 14 15 16 17 18 19 20 21 22 23 24 25 26 27 28 29 30 31
Shaabân	26 27 28 29 Ramadan	1 2 3 4 5 6 7 8 9 10 11 12 13 14 15 16 17 18 19 20 21 22 23 24 25 26 27

April	1 2 3	4 5 6 7 8 9 10 11 12 13 14 15 16 17 18 19 20 21 22 23 24 25 26 27 28 29 30
Ramadan	28 29 30 Shawwâl	1 2 3 4 5 6 7 8 9 10 11 12 13 14 15 16 17 18 19 20 21 22 23 24 25 26 27

May	1 2	3 4 5 6 7 8 9 10 11 12 13 14 15 16 17 18 19 20 21 22 23 24 25 26 27 28 29 30 31
Shawwâl	28 29 Dhû'l-Qa'da	1 2 3 4 5 6 7 8 9 10 11 12 13 14 15 16 17 18 19 20 21 22 23 24 25 26 27 28 29

June	1	2 3 4 5 6 7 8 9 10 11 12 13 14 15 16 17 18 19 20 21 22 23 24 25 26 27 28 29 30
Dhû'l-Qa'da 30	Dhû'l Hijja	1 2 3 4 5 6 7 8 9 10 11 12 13 14 15 16 17 18 19 20 21 22 23 24 25 26 27 28 29

July	1	2 3 4 5 6 7 8 9 10 11 12 13 14 15 16 17 18 19 20 21 22 23 24 25 26 27 28 29 30 31
Dhû'l Hijja 30	Muharram*	1 2 3 4 5 6 7 8 9 10 11 12 13 14 15 16 17 18 19 20 21 22 23 24 25 26 27 28 29 30

* Islamic New Year 1413

August	1 2 3 4 5 6 7 8 9 10 11 12 13 14 15 16 17 18 19 20 21 22 23 24 25 26 27 28 29	30 31
Safar	1 2 3 4 5 6 7 8 9 10 11 12 13 14 15 16 17 18 19 20 21 22 23 24 25 26 27 28 29 Rabîa I	1 2

September	1 2 3 4 5 6 7 8 9 10 11 12 13 14 15 16 17 18 19 20 21 22 23 24 25 26 27 28	29 30
Rabîa I	3 4 5 6 7 8 9 10 11 12 13 14 15 16 17 18 19 20 21 22 23 24 25 26 27 28 29 30 Rabîa II	1 2

October	1 2 3 4 5 6 7 8 9 10 11 12 13 14 15 16 17 18 19 20 21 22 23 24 25 26 27	28 29 30 31
Rabîa II	3 4 5 6 7 8 9 10 11 12 13 14 15 16 17 18 19 20 21 22 23 24 25 26 27 28 29 Jumâda I	1 2 3 4

November	1 2 3 4 5 6 7 8 9 10 11 12 13 14 15 16 17 18 19 20 21 22 23 24 25 26	27 28 29 30
Jumâda I	5 6 7 8 9 10 11 12 13 14 15 16 17 18 19 20 21 22 23 24 25 26 27 28 29 30 Jumâda II	1 2 3 4

December	1 2 3 4 5 6 7 8 9 10 11 12 13 14 15 16 17 18 19 20 21 22 23 24 25	26 27 28 29 30 31
Jumâda II	5 6 7 8 9 10 11 12 13 14 15 16 17 18 19 20 21 22 23 24 25 26 27 28 29 Rajab	1 2 3 4 5 6

Jan 1993	1 2 3 4 5 6 7 8 9 10 11 12 13 14 15 16 17 18 19 20 21 22 23 24	25 26 27 28 29 30 31
Rajab	7 8 9 10 11 12 13 14 15 16 17 18 19 20 21 22 23 24 25 26 27 28 29 30 Shaabân	1 2 3 4 5 6 7

February	1 2 3 4 5 6 7 8 9 10 11 12 13 14 15 16 17 18 19 20 21 22	23 24 25 26 27 28
Shaabân	8 9 10 11 12 13 14 15 16 17 18 19 20 21 22 23 24 25 26 27 28 29 Ramadan	1 2 3 4 5 6

March	1 2 3 4 5 6 7 8 9 10 11 12 13 14 15 16 17 18 19 20 21 22 23 24	25 26 27 28 29 30 31
Ramadan	7 8 9 10 11 12 13 14 15 16 17 18 19 20 21 22 23 24 25 26 27 28 29 30 Shawwâl	1 2 3 4 5 6 7

April	1 2 3 4 5 6 7 8 9 10 11 12 13 14 15 16 17 18 19 20 21 22	23 24 25 26 27 28 29 30
Shawwâl	8 9 10 11 12 13 14 15 16 17 18 19 20 21 22 23 24 25 26 27 28 29 Dhû'l-Qa'da	1 2 3 4 5 6 7 8

May	1 2 3 4 5 6 7 8 9 10 11 12 13 14 15 16 17 18 19 20 21 22	23 24 25 26 27 28 29 30 31
Dhû'l-Qa'da	9 10 11 12 13 14 15 16 17 18 19 20 21 22 23 24 25 26 27 28 29 30 Dhû'l Hijja	1 2 3 4 5 6 7 8 9

June	1 2 3 4 5 6 7 8 9 10 11 12 13 14 15 16 17 18 19 20	21 22 23 24 25 26 27 28 29 30
Dhû'l Hijja	10 11 12 13 14 15 16 17 18 19 20 21 22 23 24 25 26 27 28 29	Muharram* 1 2 3 4 5 6 7 8 9 10

* Islamic New Year 1414

July	1 2 3 4 5 6 7 8 9 10 11 12 13 14 15 16 17 18 19 20	21 22 23 24 25 26 27 28 29 30 31
Muharram	11 12 13 14 15 16 17 18 19 20 21 22 23 24 25 26 27 28 29 30	Safar 1 2 3 4 5 6 7 8 9 10 11

August	1 2 3 4 5 6 7 8 9 10 11 12 13 14 15 16 17 18	19 20 21 22 23 24 25 26 27 28 29 30 31
Safar	12 13 14 15 16 17 18 19 20 21 22 23 24 25 26 27 28 29	Rabîa I 1 2 3 4 5 6 7 8 9 10 11 12 13

September	1 2 3 4 5 6 7 8 9 10 11 12 13 14 15 16 17	18 19 20 21 22 23 24 25 26 27 28 29 30
Rabîa I	14 15 16 17 18 19 20 21 22 23 24 25 26 27 28 29 30	Rabîa II 1 2 3 4 5 6 7 8 9 10 11 12 13

THE CHINESE CALENDAR

The ancient Chinese calendar is based on a lunar year and consists of 12 months of alternately 29 and 30 days, making 354 days in total. To keep the calendar in step with the solar year intercalary months are inserted. The months are numbered and sometimes given one of the 12 animal names that are usually attached to years and hours in the Chinese calendar (see Chinese Zodiac). The calendar was in use until the establishment of the republic (1911) when the Gregorian calendar was introduced, and was formally banned in 1930. The calendar is, however, still used unofficially in China, and the New Year festival remains a national holiday. It is also used in Tibet, Hong Kong, Singapore, and Malaysia.

The Chinese New Year begins at the first new moon after the Sun enters Aquarius, and therefore falls between 21 January and 19 February in the Gregorian calendar.

THE JAPANESE CALENDAR

The Japanese calendar has the same structure – in terms of years, months and weeks – as the Gregorian calendar. The difference lies in the numeration of the years as the Japanese chronology is based on a series of imperial epochs. As the Gregorian calendar calculates the years from one religious date, the Japanese calendar calculates each epoch from the accession of an emperor.

The four most recent epochs are based on the reigns of the last four emperors, who are referred to by their epoch names – their personal names are never used.

Epoch Meiji   13 Oct 1868–31 July 1912
(Emperor Mutsuhito)
Epoch Taisho   1 Aug 1912–25 Dec 1926
(Emperor Yoshihito)
Epoch Showa   26 Dec 1926–7 Jan 1989
(Emperor Hirohito)
Epoch Heisei   8 Jan 1989–
(Emperor Akihito)

The months are unnamed, simply numbered. The days of the week, however, do have names:

Nichiyobi	Sun-day (Sunday)
Getsuyobi	Moon-day (Monday)
Kayobi	Fire-day (Tuesday)
Suiyobi	Water-day (Wednesday)
Mokuyobi	Wood-day (Thursday)
Kinyobi	Metal-day (Friday)
Doyobi	Earth-day (Saturday)

INDIAN CALENDARS

The principal Indian calendars reckon their epochs from historical events such as the accession or death of a ruler or a religious founder.

The Vikrama era originated in northern India and is still used in western India. It dates from 23 February 57 BC in the Gregorian calendar.

The Saka era dates from 3 March AD 78 in the Gregorian calendar. It is based on the solar year – beginning with the spring equinox. The 365 days (366 in a leap year) are divided into 12 months. The first five months are of 31 days and the remaining seven of 30 – in a leap year the first six months are of 31 days and the last six of 30. In 1957 the Saka era was declared the national calendar of India, to run concurrently with the Gregorian calendar.

The Buddhist era dates from 543 BC, the believed date of Buddha's death (Nirvana), although many Buddhist sects adopt different dates for his death. The actual date of his death was 487 BC.

The Jain era dates from the death of the founder of the Jainist religion, Vardhamana, in 527 BC.

The Parsee (Zoroastrian) era dates from 16 June AD 632 in the Gregorian calendar.

THE COPTIC CALENDAR

The Coptic calendar – which is still used in areas of Egypt and Ethiopia – dates from 29 August AD 284 of the Gregorian calendar. The Coptic year is made up of 12 months of 30 days, followed by five complementary days. In a leap year – which immediately precedes the leap year of the Julian calendar – the last month is followed by six days.

THE ANCIENT GREEK CALENDAR

The chronology of Ancient Greece was based on cycles of four years – Olympiads – corresponding with the periodic Olympic Games held on the plain of Olympia in Elis. The intervening years were simply numbered, 1st, 2nd, etc., and each Olympiad was named after the victor of the Games. The first recorded Olympiad is Choroebus, 776 BC.

THE FRENCH REPUBLICAN CALENDAR

The French republican calendar was adopted in 1793, replacing the Gregorian calendar with a secular and more regular alternative. The year was divided into 12 months of 30 days with five (in leap years, six) supplementary days at the end of the year. Weeks were replaced by decades of ten days, which were named *primidi, duodi, tridi, quartidi, quintidi, sextidi, septidi, octidi, nonidi* and *décadi*. Each month comprised three decades. The era dated from 22 September 1792 of the Gregorian calendar. The republican calendar was abolished by Napoleon I on 1 January 1806.

The months of the calendar were:

Vendémiaire (meaning 'the month of the grape harvest'). Gregorian equivalent: 23 September to 22 October.

Brumaire (meaning 'the month of mist'). Gregorian equivalent: 23 October to 21 November.

Frimaire (meaning 'the month of frost'). Gregorian equivalent: 22 November to 21 December.

Nivôse (meaning 'the month of snow'). Gregorian equivalent: 22 December to 20 January.

Pluviôse (meaning 'the month of rain'). Gregorian equivalent: 21 January to 19 February.

Ventôse (meaning 'the month of wind'). Gregorian equivalent: 20 February to 21 March.

Germinal (meaning 'the month of buds'). Gregorian equivalent: 22 March to 20 April.

Floréal (meaning 'the month of flowers'). Gregorian equivalent: 21 April to 20 May.

Prairial (meaning 'the month of meadows'). Gregorian equivalent: 21 May to 19 June.

Messidor (meaning 'the month of harvest'). Gregorian equivalent: 20 June to 19 July.

Thermidor (meaning 'the month of heat'). Gregorian equivalent: 20 July to 18 August.

Fructidor (meaning 'the month of fruit'). Gregorian equivalent: 19 August to 22 September, including the supplementary days.

TIME ZONES

Until the last quarter of the 19th century the time kept was a local affair, or in smaller countries, based on the time kept in the capital city. But the spread of railways across the larger countries caused great confusion in time-keeping as timetables could not operate without standardization.

In 1880 Greenwich Mean Time (GMT) became the legal time in the British Isles and by 1884 international time zones had been established over much of the world.

The world is divided into 24 zones, or segments, each of 15° of longitude. Twelve zones are to the east of the Greenwich meridian (0°) and are therefore in advance of GMT. Twelve are to the west of the Greenwich meridian and are therefore behind GMT. Each zone extends 7½° on either side of its central meridian.

The International Date Line runs down the 180° meridian – with some variations to include certain Pacific island nations entirely within one zone. Travelling eastward across the date line Sunday becomes Saturday; travelling westward across the date line Sunday becomes Monday.

Some large countries extend over several segments and are thus obliged to have several time zones.

THE USA

The 48 contiguous states of the USA are divided between the Eastern, Central, Mountain and Pacific time zones (respectively five, six, seven and eight hours behind GMT), while the addition of Alaska and Hawaii adds a further four time zones.

Eastern time is kept by: Connecticut, Florida (except far west), Georgia, Indiana, Kentucky (eastern part), Maine, Maryland, Massachusetts, Michigan, New Hampshire, New Jersey, New York State, North Carolina, Ohio, Pennsylvania, Rhode Island, South Carolina, Tennessee (eastern part), Vermont, Virginia, Washington DC and West Virginia.

Central time is kept in: Alabama, Arkansas, Florida (far west), Illinois, Iowa, Kansas (except far west), Kentucky (western part), Louisiana, Minnesota, Mississippi, Missouri, Nebraska (except far west), North Dakota (eastern part), Oklahoma, South Dakota (eastern part), Tennessee (western part), Texas (except far west) and Wisconsin.

Mountain time is kept in: Arizona, Colorado, Idaho (except far north), Kansas (far west), Montana, Nebraska (far west), New Mexico, North Dakota (western part), Oregon (far east), South Dakota (western part), Texas (far west), Utah and Wyoming.

Pacific time is kept in: California, Idaho (far north), Nevada, Oregon (except far east) and Washington State.

CANADA

Canada is divided into similar time zones – the Atlantic, Eastern, Central, Mountain and Pacific (respectively four, five, six, seven and eight hours behind GMT).

Atlantic time is kept in: New Brunswick, Newfoundland, Nova Scotia, Prince Edward Island, Quebec (far east), and part of the Northwest Territories.

Canadian Eastern time is kept in: Ontario (except far west), Quebec (except far east), and part of the Northwest Territories.

Canadian Central time is kept in: Manitoba, Ontario (far west), Saskatchewan (far east), and part of the Northwest Territories.

Canadian Mountain time is kept in: Alberta, Saskatchewan (except far east), and part of the Northwest Territories.

Canadian Pacific time is kept in: British Columbia and Yukon.

AUSTRALIA

Australia has three times zones. Western Australia is eight hours ahead of GMT; South Australia and the Northern Territory are nine and a half hours ahead of GMT; the rest of the country is ten hours ahead of GMT.

THE USSR

The USSR is divided into 11 time zones with all of European Russia four hours ahead of GMT. Crossing the border from Poland to the USSR, watches are advanced by two hours.

EUROPE

Europe has three time zones: GMT, mid-European time (one hour in advance of GMT) and east European time (two hours in advance of GMT).

GMT in Europe is kept by: Iceland, Ireland, Portugal, and the UK.

Mid-European time is kept by: Albania, Andorra, Austria, Belgium, Czechoslovakia, Denmark, France, Germany, Gibraltar, Hungary, Italy, Liechtenstein, Luxembourg, Monaco, Netherlands, Norway, San Marino, Spain, Sweden, Switzerland, Vatican, and Yugoslavia.

East European time is kept by: Bulgaria, Cyprus, Finland, Greece and Romania.

A very few countries, or divisions of countries, do not adhere to the Greenwich system at all. Certain other countries, such as China, do not use a zoning system, and the whole nation – despite spanning more than one of the 24 segments – elects to keep the same time. Yet a third group – including Suriname, Iran, Afghanistan and India – use differences of half an hour.

The time zones are shown on the accompanying map.

SUMMER TIME

In 1916 legal time in the UK was advanced one hour ahead of GMT as a means of extending daylight in the evening. Between 1941 and 1945 and again in 1947, 'double summer time' was introduced in the UK and legal time was advanced two hours ahead of GMT. Since then Summer Time has been in force during most years, although between 1968 and 1971 British Standard Time – in which the legal time was one hour head of GMT throughout the year – was in force.

In the UK, Summer Time is defined as 'the period beginning at two o'clock, Greenwich mean time, in the morning of the day after the third Saturday in March or, if that day is Easter Day, the day after the second Saturday in March, and ending at two o'clock, Greenwich mean time, in the morning of the day after the fourth Saturday in October'. In practice, this has been amended in most years to bring the UK closer to the beginning and ending of daylight-saving time in neighbouring EC countries.

In 1991 Summer Time began on 31 March and ended on 27 October.

WATCHES AT SEA

A watch at sea is four hours, except the period between 4 p.m. and 8 p.m. which in the Royal Navy is divided into two short watches termed the first dog watch and the last dog watch. (The word 'dog' is here a corruption of 'dodge'.)

Midnight – 4 a.m.	Middle watch
4 a.m. – 8 a.m.	Morning watch

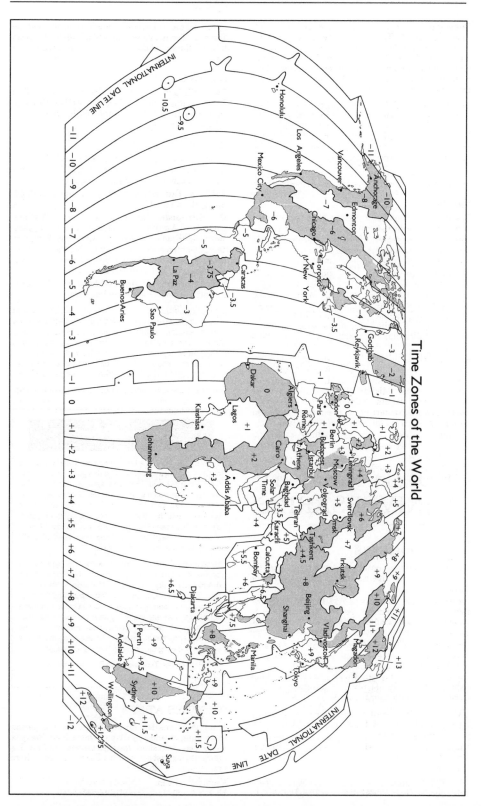

Time Zones of the World

8 a.m. – noon	Forenoon watch
noon – 4 p.m.	Afternoon watch
4 p.m. – 6 p.m.	First dog watch
6 p.m. – 8 p.m.	Last dog watch*
8 p.m. – midnight	First watch

* Called Second dog watch in the (British) Merchant Navy.

Time is marked by bells – one stroke for each half hour elapsed during a watch, which thus ends with eight bells, or four bells for a dog watch. The New Year is brought in with 16 bells.

SUNRISE AND SUNSET

The Nautical Almanac gives the GMT of sunrise and sunset for each two degrees of latitude for every third day of the year.

Sunrise is the instant when the rim of the Sun appears above the horizon.

Sunset is the instant when the last segment of the Sun disappears below the horizon.

Because of the Earth's atmosphere, the transition from day to night and vice versa is a gradual process, the length of which varies according to the declination of the Sun and the latitude of the observer. The intermediate stages are called *twilight*. There are three sorts of twilight:

Civil twilight occurs when the centre of the Sun is 6° below the horizon. Before this moment in the morning and after it in the evening ordinary outdoor activities are impossible without artificial light.

Nautical twilight occurs when the Sun is 12° below the horizon. Before this time in the morning and after it in the evening the sea horizon is invisible.

Astronomical twilight is the moment when the Sun is 18° below the horizon. Before this time in the morning and after it in the evening there is complete absence of sunlight.

HOLIDAYS AND ANNIVERSARIES

PUBLIC HOLIDAYS

The public holidays in major countries (including all member-states of the European Community) are listed below. The dates of some holidays – mainly those of a religious nature – vary from one year to the next. In such cases only the month or months in which the holiday normally falls are recorded. In many countries an additional holiday is taken when the public holiday falls upon a Sunday.

ARGENTINA

New Year (1 January), Good Friday (March or April), Labour Day (1 May), Anniversary of 1810 Revolution (*National Day*; 25 May), Occupation of Islas Malvinas/Falkland Islands (10 June), Flag Day (20 June), Independence Day (9 July), Anniversary of Death of General de San Martín (17 August), Immaculate Conception (8 December), Christmas (25 December).

AUSTRALIA

New Year (1 January), Australia Day (*National Day*; 26 January), Good Friday to Easter Monday (March

or April), Anzac Day (25 April), The Queen's Official Birthday (early June, although this holiday is celebrated in late September in Western Australia), Christmas (25–26 December; 25 December only in South Australia).

AUSTRIA

New Year (1 January), Epiphany (6 January), Easter Monday (March or April), Labour Day (1 May), Whit Monday (May or June), Corpus Christi (May or June), Assumption (15 August), *National Day* (26 October), All Saints' Day (1 November), Immaculate Conception (8 December), Christmas (25–26 December).

BELGIUM

New Year (1 January), Easter Monday (March or April), Ascension Day (April or May), Labour Day (1 May), Whit Monday (May or June), Independence Day (*National Day*; 21 July), Assumption (15 August), All Saints' Day (1 November), Armistice Day (11 November), Christmas (25 December).

BRAZIL

New Year (1 January), Tiradentes Day (21 April), Labour Day (1 May), Ascension Day (April or May), Corpus Christi (May or June), Independence Day (*National Day*; 7 September), Our Lady Aparecida (12 October), All Souls' Day (2 November), Anniversary of the Proclamation of the Republic (15 November), Christmas (25 December).

CANADA

New Year (1 January), Good Friday and Easter Monday (March or April), Victoria Day (mid-May), Canada Day (*National Day*; 1 July), Labour Day (early September), Thanksgiving Day (mid-October), Remembrance Day (11 November), Christmas (25–26 December).

CHINA

Lunar New Year (January or February), International Women's Day (8 March), Labour Day (1 May), Army Day (1 August), *National Days* (October 1–2).

CZECHOSLOVAKIA

New Year (1 January), Easter Monday (March or April), Labour Day (1 May), *National Day* (9 May), Jan Hus Day (6 July), Anniversary of the Proclamation of the Czech Republic (*National Day*; 28 October), All Saints' Day (Slovakia only; 1 November), Christmas (25–26 December).

DENMARK

New Year (1 January), Good Friday to Easter Monday (March or April), The Queen's Birthday (*National Day*; 19 April – not taken as public holiday), General Prayer Day (April or May), Ascension Day (April or May), Whit Monday (May or June), Constitution Day (5 June), Christmas (25–26 December).

FINLAND

New Year (1 January), Epiphany (beginning of January), Good Friday and Easter Monday (March or April), May Day (1 May), Ascension Day (April or May), Whit Monday (May or June), Midsummer Day (mid-June), All Saints' Day (1 November), Independence Day (*National Day*; 6 December),Christmas (25–26 December).

FRANCE

New Year (1 January), Easter Monday (March or

April), Labour Day (1 May), Liberation Day (8 May), Ascension Day (April or May), Whit Monday (May or June), Bastille Day (*National Day*; 14 July), Assumption (15 August), All Saints' Day (1 November), Armistice Day (11 November), Christmas (25 December).

GERMANY

New Year (1 January), Epiphany (mainly Catholic Länder only; 6 January), Carnival Day (February or March), Good Friday and Easter Monday (March or April), Labour Day (1 May), Ascension Day (April or May), Whit Monday (May or June), Corpus Christi (mainly Catholic Länder only; May or June), Assumption (mainly Catholic Länder only; 15 August), Unity Day (*National Day*; 3 October), All Saints' Day (mainly Catholic Länder only; 1 November), Repentance Day (mid-November), Christmas (25–26 December).

GREECE

New Year (1 January), Epiphany (6 January), Clean Monday (February or March), Independence Day (*National Day*; 25 March), Good Friday to Easter Monday (Orthodox; March or April), Labour Day (1 May), Holy Spirit Day (May or June), Assumption (15 August), Ochi Day (Anniversary of Greek defiance to the Italian ultimatum of 1940; 28 October), Christmas (25–26 December).

HUNGARY

New Year (1 January), Anniversary of 1848 Revolution (15 March), Easter Monday (March or April), Labour Day (1 May), St Stephen's Festival (20 August), Anniversary of 1956 Uprising (*National Day*; 23 October), Christmas (25–26 December).

INDIA

Pongal (January), Republic Day (*National Day*; 26 January), Maha Shrivratri (February), Holi (March), Ram Navami (April), Good Friday (March or April), Buddha Purnima (May), End of Ramadan (May), Id-uz-Zuha (July or August), Islamic New Year (August), Janmashtami (20 August), Onam (28 August), Mahatma Gandhi's Birthday (2 October), Diwali (October), Durga Puja (October or November), Guru Nanak Jayanti (1 November), Christmas (25–26 December).

INDONESIA

New Year (1 January), Ascension of the Prophet Muhammad (March), Good Friday (March or April), Ascension Day (April or May), End of Ramadan (May), Id al-Adha (July or August), *National Day* (17 August), Islamic New Year (August), Mouloud (Birthday of the Prophet Muhammad; October or November), Christmas (25 December).

IRELAND

New Year (1 January), St Patrick's Day (*National Day*; 17 March), Good Friday and Easter Monday (March or April), June Bank Holiday Monday (early June), August Bank Holiday Monday (early August), October Bank Holiday Monday (late October), Christmas (25–26 December).

ITALY

New Year (1 January), Epiphany (6 January), Easter Monday (March or April), Liberation Day (25 April), Labour Day (1 May), Festival of the Tricolour (12 May), *National Day* (2 June), Assumption (15 August), All Saints' Day (1 November), Immaculate Conception (8 December), Christmas (25–26 December).

JAPAN

New Year (1 January), Adults' Day (15 January), National Foundation Day (11 February), Vernal Equinox Day (21 March), Constitution Memorial Day (3 May), Children's Day (5 May), Respect for the Aged Day (15 September), Autumnal Equinox Day (23 September), Sports Day (10 October), Culture Day (3 November), Labour Thanksgiving Day (23 November), The Emperor's Birthday (*National Day*; 23 December).

LUXEMBOURG

New Year (1 January), Easter Monday (March or April), Labour Day (1 May), Ascension Day (April or May), Whit Monday (May or June), *National Day* (23 June), Assumption (15 August), All Saints' Day (1 November), Christmas (25–26 December).

MEXICO

New Year (1 January), Constitution Day (5 February), Birthday of Benito Juárez (21 March), Good Friday to Easter Monday (March or April), Labour Day (1 May), Anniversary of the Battle of Puebla (5 May), President's Annual Message Day (1 September), Independence Day (*National Day*; 16 September), Discovery of America Day (12 October), All Souls' Day (unofficial; 2 November), Anniversary of the Revolution (20 November), Our Lady of Guadeloupe (unofficial; 12 December), Christmas (24–25 December).

NETHERLANDS

New Year (1 January), Good Friday and Easter Monday (March or April), Queen's Day (*National Day*; 30 April), National Liberation Day (5 May), Ascension Day (April or May), Whit Monday (May or June), Christmas (25–26 December).

NEW ZEALAND

New Year (1 January), Waitangi Day (*National Day*; 6 February), Good Friday to Easter Monday (March or April), Anzac Day (25 April), The Queen's Official Birthday (early June), Labour Day (late October), Christmas (25–26 December).

NIGERIA

New Year (1 January), Good Friday to Easter Monday (March or April), End of Ramadan (May), Id al-Kabir (Feast of the Sacrifice; August), *National Day* (1 October), Mouloud (Birthday of the Prophet Muhammad; October or November), Christmas (25–26 December).

NORWAY

New Year (1 January), Maundy Thursday, Good Friday and Easter Monday (March or April), May Day (1 May), Ascension Day (April or May), Independence Day (*National Day*; 17 May), Whit Monday (May or June), Christmas (25–26 December).

PAKISTAN

Pakistan Day (*National Day*; 23 March), Beginning of Ramadan (April), End of Ramadan (May), Id al-Adha (July or August), Islamic New Year (August), Independence Day (*National Day*; 14 August), Ashoura (August or September), Defence of Pakistan Day (6 September), Anniversary of death of Quaid-i-Azam (11 September), Birthday of the Prophet (October or November), Birthday of Quaid-i-Azam and Christmas (25 December).

POLAND
New Year (1 January), Good Friday and Easter Monday (March or April), Labour Day (1 May), *National Day* (3 May), Corpus Christi (May or June), Assumption (15 August), All Saints' Day (1 November), Anniversary of the Proclamation of the Polish Republic (11 November), Christmas (25–26 December).

PORTUGAL
New Year (1 January), Carnival Day (February or March), Good Friday (March or April), Liberty Day (25 April), Labour Day (1 May), Corpus Christi (May or June), Portugal Day (*National Day*; 10 June), St Anthony's Day (Lisbon and south only; 13 June), St John the Baptist's Day (Oporto and north only; 24 June), Assumption (15 August), Anniversary of the Proclamation of the Republic (5 October), All Saints' Day (1 November), Anniversary of the Restoration of Independence (1 December), Immaculate Conception (8 December), Christmas (25 December).

SOUTH AFRICA
New Year (1 January), Good Friday to Easter Monday (March or April), Ascension Day (April or May), May Day (1 May), Republic Day (*National Day*; 31 May), Settlers' Day (5 September), Kruger Day (10 October), Covenant Day (16 December), Christmas (25–26 December).

SPAIN
New Year (1 January), Epiphany (6 January), Maundy Thursday (not a public holiday in Catalonia; March or April), Good Friday (March or April), Easter Monday (Catalonia and Balearic Islands only; March or April), St Joseph the Worker (1 May), Corpus Christi (May or June), King Juan Carlos's Saint's Day (24 June), St James (25 July), Assumption (15 August), Day of the Hispanidad (*National Day* – although not celebrated in Catalonia; 12 October), All Saints' Day (1 November), Constitution Day (6 December), Immaculate Conception (not a public holiday in Catalonia; 8 December), Christmas (25 December, plus 26 December in Catalonia and the Balearic Islands).

SWEDEN
New Year (1 January), Epiphany (6 January), Good Friday and Easter Monday (March or April), May Day (1 May), Ascension Day (April or May), Whit Monday (May or June), Day of the Swedish Flag (*National Day* – although not celebrated as a public holiday; 6 June), Midsummer Day (25 June), All Saints' Day (1 November), Christmas (25–26 December).

SWITZERLAND
New Year (1–2 January), Good Friday and Easter Monday (March or April), Labour Day (not in all cantons; 1 May), Ascension Day (April or May), Whit Monday (May or June), *National Day* (not celebrated as a public holiday in all cantons; 1 August), Christmas (25–26 December).

TURKEY
New Year (1 January), National Sovereignty and Children's Day (23 April), Spring Day (1 May), Youth and Sports Day (19 May), End of Ramadan (May), Feast of the Sacrifice (July or August), Victory Day (30 August), Republic Day (*National Day*; 29 October).

USSR
New Year (1 January), Soviet Army and Navy Day (23 February), International Women's Day (8 March), May Day (1–2 May), Victory Day (9 May), Constitution Day (7 October), Anniversary of the October Revolution (*National Day*; 7–8 November), Agricultural and Agro-Industrial Workers' Day (20 November).

UK
New Year (1 January; plus 2 January in Scotland only), St Patrick's Day (Northern Ireland only; 17 March), Good Friday (March or April), Easter Monday (March or April; not Scotland), May Day (early May; not Scotland), Liberation Day (Channel Islands only; 9 May), Spring Bank Holiday (late May in England, Wales and Northern Ireland; early May in Scotland); May Bank Holiday (Scotland only; late May), Anniversary of the Battle of the Boyne (Northern Ireland only; mid-July), Summer Bank Holiday (early August in Scotland; late August in England, Wales and Northern Ireland); Christmas (25–26 December).
NB In Scotland holidays which coincide with religious festivals are enjoyed in all areas and all industries. Other Bank holidays are often enjoyed only by banks and financial institutions. However, there are holidays specific to Scottish cities and regions (i.e. Glasgow and Edinburgh).

USA
New Year (1 January), Martin Luther King Day (mid-January), Washington-Lincoln Day (mid-February), Good Friday (March or April), Memorial Day (end of May), Independence Day (*National Day*; 4 July), Labor Day (early September), Columbus Day (mid-October), Veterans' Day (11 November), Thanksgiving Day (end of November), Christmas (25 December).

YUGOSLAVIA
New Year (1–2 January), Slovenian National Day (27 April), Labour Days (1–2 May), Fighters' Day (4 July), Serbian National Day (7 July), Montenegrin National Day (13 July), Slovenian National Day (22 July), Croatian and Bosnian National Day (27 July), Macedonian National Day (2 August), Macedonian National Day (11 October), All Saints' (Slovenia only; 1 November); *National Days* (29–30 November), Christmas (not all republics; 25 December).

NATIONAL DAYS

Afghanistan 27 April, Revolution Day, the anniversary of the Saur revolution of 1978.

Albania 11 January, Proclamation of the Republic Day (1946).

Algeria 1 November, the anniversary of the beginning of the Revolution (1954).

Andorra 8 September, National Day, the festival of the coronation of the Virgin of Meritxell.

Angola 11 November, Independence Day (1975).

Antigua and Barbuda 1 November, Independence Day (1981).

Argentina 25 May, the anniversary of the 1810 Revolution.

Australia 26 January, Australia Day, the anniversary of the raising of the British flag at Port Jackson by Captain Cook (1788).

Austria 26 October, National Day, the anniversary of the referendum establishing perpetual neutrality (1955).

Bahamas 10 July, Independence Day (1973).

Bahrain 16 December, the anniversary of the accession of the Emir, Shaikh Isa (1961).

Bangladesh 26 March, Independence Day (1971).

Barbados 30 November, Independence Day (1966).

Belgium 21 July, Independence Day, the anniversary of the presentation of the constitutional document of King Leopold I (1831).

Belize 21 September, Independence Day (1981).

Benin 30 November, National Day, the anniversary of the proclamation of the 1975 constitution.

Bhutan 17 December, National Day, the anniversary of the installation of the first king (1907).

Bolivia 6 August, Independence Day (1825).

Botswana 30 September, Botswana Day, the anniversary of independence (1966).

Brazil 7 September, Independence Day, the anniversary of the proclamation of the independence of the Empire of Brazil by Dom Pedro I in 1822.

Brunei 23 February, National Day.

Bulgaria 3 March, National Day, the anniversary of the Treaty of San Stefano (1877), which established an autonomous principality of Bulgaria.

Burkina Faso 4 August, National Day, the anniversary of the eve of independence (1960).

Burma (Myanmar) 4 January, Independence Day (1948).

Burundi 1 July, Independence Day (1962).

Cambodia 7 January (de facto), the anniversary of the fall of Phnom Penh to the forces of the (governing) State of Cambodia (1979).

Cameroon 20 May, Cameroon Day, the anniversary of the referendum that established the unitary state (1972).

Canada 1 July, Canada Day, the anniversary of the creation of the Confederation of Canada (1867).

Cape Verde 5 July, Independence Day (1975).

Central African Republic 1 December, National Day, the anniversary of the adoption of the name Central African Republic (1958).

Chad 13 April, National Day, the anniversary of the coup deposing President Tombalbaye (1975).

Chile 18 September, National Day, the anniversary of the first proclamation of independence (1810).

China 1–2 October, National Days, the anniversary of the proclamation of the People's Republic of China (1949).

China (Taiwan) 10 October, Double Tenth Day, the anniversary of the end of Japanese occupation (1945).

Colombia 20 July, Independence Day (1819).

Comoros 6 July, Independence Day (1975).

Congo 15 August, Independence Day (1960).

Costa Rica 15 September, Independence Day (1821).

Cuba 1 January, Day of Liberation, the anniversary of the revolution led by Fidel Castro (1959).

Cyprus 1 October, Independence Day – although independence was achieved on 16 August 1960.

Czechoslovakia 9 May, National Day, the anniversary of the constitution of 1948, and 28 October, the anniversary of the proclamation of the Czech Republic (1918).

Denmark 19 April, The Queen's Birthday – not taken as a public holiday.

Djibouti 27 June, Independence Day (1977).

Dominica 3 November, Independence Day (1978).

Dominican Republic 27 February, Independence Day (1844).

Ecuador 10 August, Independence (1830).

Egypt 23 July, National Day, the anniversary of the revolution of 1952.

El Salvador 15 September, Independence Day (1821).

Equatorial Guinea 12 October, Independence Day (1968).

Ethiopia 12 September, People's Revolution Day, the anniversary of the overthrow of the emperor (1974).

Fiji 10 October, Fiji Day, the anniversary of independence (1970).

Finland 6 December, Independence Day (1917).

France 14 July, National Day, the anniversary of the storming of the Bastille (1789).

Gabon 17 August, Independence Day (1960).

Gambia 18 February, Independence Day (1965).

Germany 3 October, Unity Day, the anniversary of the unification of the German Democratic Republic and the Federal Republic of Germany (1990).

Ghana 6 March, Independence Day (1957).

Greece 25 March, Independence Day, the anniversary of the start of the rising against Turkey (1821).

Grenada 7 February, Independence Day (1974).

Guatemala 15 September, Independence Day (1821).

Guinea 2 October, Independence Day (1958).

Guinea-Bissau 24 September, Independence Day – although independence was achieved on 10 September, 1974.

Guyana 26 May, Independence Day (1966) and Republic Day, the anniversary of the proclamation of the republic (1970).

Haiti 1 January, Independence Day, the anniversary of the declaration of independence by Jean-Jacques Dessalines (1804).

Honduras 15 September, Independence Day (1821).

Hungary 23 October, National Day, the anniversary of the Hungarian Uprising (1956).

Iceland 17 June, National Day, the anniversary of complete independence from Denmark (1944).

India 26 January, Republic Day, the anniversary of the declaration of the republic (1950).

Indonesia 17 August, National Day, the anniversary of the initial declaration of independence (1945).

Iran 11 February, National Day, the anniversary of the overthrow of the Shah (1979).

Iraq 17 July, Revolution Day, the anniversary of the accession to power of the Arab Socialist Renaissance (Ba'ath) Party (1968).

Ireland 17 March, St Patrick's Day.

Israel 5 Iyyar (in Jewish calendar, see pp. 36–38),

Independence Day (1948). (In the Gregorian calendar the Israeli declaration of independence took place on 14 May, 1948. The celebration of the anniversary occurs in April or May.)

Italy 2 June, National Day, the anniversary of the foundation of the republic (1946).

Ivory Coast (Côte d'Ivoire) 7 December, National Day, a combined celebration of the proclamation of the republic (4 December 1958) and independence (7 August 1960).

Jamaica First Monday in August, Independence Day (6 August 1962).

Japan 23 December, The Emperor's Birthday.

Jordan 25 May, Independence Day, the anniversary of the coronation of King Abdullah (1946).

Kenya 12 December, Independence Day (1963).

Kiribati 12 July, Independence Day (1979).

Korea (North) 15 April, the Birthday of Kim Il-Sung, and 9 September, Independence Day, the anniversary of the foundation of the People's Democratic Republic of Korea (1948).

Korea (South) 15 August, Independence Day, the anniversary of the end of Japanese occupation (1945).

Kuwait 25 February, National Day.

Laos 2 December, National Day, the anniversary of the proclamation of the republic (1975).

Lebanon 22 November, Independence Day (1943).

Lesotho 4 October, Independence Day (1966).

Liberia 26 July, Independence Day (1847).

Libya 1 September, Revolution Day, the anniversary of the overthrow of the monarchy (1969).

Liechtenstein 15 August, the Assumption (see Christian Festivals, p. 49) and the eve of the birthday of Prince Franz Joseph II (reigned 1938–89).

Luxembourg 23 June, National Day, the official birthday of the sovereign.

Madagascar 26 June, Independence Day (1960).

Malawi 6 July, Independence Day (1964).

Malaysia 31 August, National Day, the anniversary of the independence of Malaya (1957).

The Maldives 26 July, Independence Day (1965).

Mali 22 September, National Day, the anniversary of the adoption of the name Mali (1960).

Malta 21 September, Independence Day (1964).

Marshall Islands 1 May, National Day, the anniversary of the present constitution of the Marshall Islands (1979).

Mauritania 28 November, National Day, the anniversary of the establishment of the republic (1958).

Mauritius 12 March, Independence Day (1968).

Mexico 16 September, Independence Day (1821).

Micronesia 10 May, National Day (Constitution Day), the anniversary of the present constitution of the the Federated States of Micronesia (1979).

Monaco 19 November, St Devote's Day.

Mongolia 11 July, National Day, the anniversary of the recovery of independence (1921).

Morocco 3 March, the Anniversary of the Throne, the anniversary of the coronation of King Hassan II.

Mozambique 25 June, Independence Day (1975).

Namibia 21 March, Independence Day (1990).

Nauru 31 January, Independence Day (1968).

Nepal 18 February, National Democracy Day, the

birthday of King Tribhuvana (reigned 1911–55).

Netherlands 30 April, Queen's Day, the birthday of Queen Juliana (reigned 1948–80).

New Zealand 6 February, Waitangi Day, the anniversary of the signing of the Treaty of Waitangi between Britain and the Maori chiefs (1840).

Nicaragua 15 September, Independence Day (1821).

Niger 18 December, National Day, the anniversary of the proclamation of the republic (1958).

Nigeria 1 October, National Day, the anniversary of independence (1960) and the establishment of the republic (1963).

Norway 17 May, Independence Day, the anniversary of the adoption of the 1814 constitution.

Oman 18 November, National Day, the birthday of the Sultan.

Pakistan 23 March, Pakistan Day, the anniversary of the adoption of the resolution by the Muslim League to establish a Muslim state in the Indian subcontinent (1940).

Panama 3 November, Independence Day (1903).

Papua New Guinea 16 September, Independence Day and Constitution Day (1975).

Paraguay 14–15 May, Independence Day (1811).

Peru 28 July, National Day, the anniversary of independence (1826).

The Philippines 12 June, Independence Day, the anniversary of the declaration of independence during the 1896 revolution.

Poland 3 May, National Day, the anniversary of the constitution of 1791.

Portugal 10 June, Portugal Day, the anniversary of the death of the 'national poet' Camoës (1580).

Qatar 3 September, National Day, in commemoration of independence (1 September 1971).

Romania 23 August, Liberation Day, the anniversary of the arrest of Antonescu and the entry of Romania into World War II on the Allied side (1944).

Rwanda 1 July, Independence Day (1962).

St Christopher and Nevis 19 September, Independence Day (1983).

St Lucia 22 February, Independence Day (1979).

St Vincent and the Grenadines 27 October, Independence Day (1979).

San Marino 3 September, St Marino's Day.

São Tomé e Príncipe 12 July, Independence Day (1975).

Saudi Arabia 22 September 1932, the anniversary of the creation of the kingdom – not celebrated as a public holiday.

Senegal 4 April, National Day, the anniversary of the signature of the Accords of Paris (1960) that brought independence to Senegal on 20 August 1960.

Seychelles 5 June, Liberation Day, the anniversary of the revolution (1977).

Sierra Leone 27 April, Independence Day (1961).

Singapore 9 August, National Day, the anniversary of the declaration of independence (1965).

Solomon Islands 7 July, Independence Day (1978).

Somalia 26 June, National Day, the anniversary of independence (1960).

South Africa 31 May, Republic Day, the anniversary of the declaration of the republic (1961).

Spain 12 October, the Day of the Hispanidad; honours Columbus' discovery of the Western hemisphere.

Sri Lanka 4 February, National Day, the anniversary of the attainment of independence as Ceylon (1948).

Sudan 1 January, Independence Day (1956).

Suriname 25 November, Independence Day (1975).

Swaziland 6 September, Independence Day (1968).

Sweden 6 June, the Day of the Swedish Flag – although not celebrated as a public holiday.

Switzerland 1 August, National Day, the anniversary of the alliance of the 'Forest Cantons' (1291). Not celebrated as a public holiday in all cantons.

Syria 17 April, National Day, the anniversary of the departure of French troops (1946).

Tanzania 26 April, Union Day, the anniversary of the union of Tanganyika and Zanzibar (1964).

Thailand 5 December, The King's Birthday.

Togo 13 January, Liberation Day, the anniversary of the revolution of 1963.

Tonga 4 June, Independence Day (1970).

Trinidad and Tobago 31 August, Independence Day (1962).

Tunisia 20 March, Independence Day (1956).

Turkey 29 October, Republic Day, the anniversary of the election of Atatürk as the first president (1924).

Tuvalu 1 October, Independence Day (1978).

Uganda 9 October, Independence Day (1962).

USSR 7–8 November, Anniversary of the October Revolution (1917).

United Arab Emirates 2 December, National Day, the anniversary of the establishment of the federation as an independent state (1971).

UK has no national day.

USA 4 July, Independence Day, the anniversary of the declaration of independence (1776).

Uruguay 25 August, Declaration of Independence Day (1825).

Vanuatu 30 July, Independence Day (1980).

Vatican City has no national day.

Venezuela 5 July, Independence Day (1811).

Vietnam 2 September, National Day.

Western Samoa 1 January, Independence Day (1962).

Yemen 26 September and 14 October, the National Days of the former North and South Yemens.

Yugoslavia 29–30 November, National Day, the anniversary of the establishment of the Partisan government (1943).

Zaïre 24 November, National Day, the anniversary of the establishment of the government of President Mobutu (1965).

Zambia 24 October, Independence Day (1964).

Zimbabwe 18 April, Independence Day (1980).

CHRISTIAN FESTIVALS

(See also Saints' days on p. 311.)

Christian Sabbath is observed on Sunday, in accordance with the Fourth Commandment, which forbids work on the holy day. There is some debate, however, in some quarters of the Christian community as to the legitimacy of the Sabbath.

EPIPHANY

6 January. The Festival of the Epiphany commemorates the manifestation of the infant Christ to the Magi or 'wise men'. The festival was of great importance in the (Eastern) Orthodox Churches because it marked the proclamation, by the Patriarch of Alexandria, of the date of the next Easter. In western Europe, the Epiphany was a significant landmark in the Church and lay calendars, determining the dates of other festivals and activities later in the year, for example, ploughing in England began on the Monday of the first complete week after the Festival of the Epiphany. The festival is a public holiday in several European countries.

SHROVE TUESDAY

Any Tuesday between 3 February and 9 March. Shrove Tuesday is the last day before the beginning of Lent – see Ash Wednesday, below. Shrovetide – the Sunday, Monday and Tuesday before Lent – were set aside as days for the confession of sins ('shrove' is the past tense of 'shrive', meaning 'to hear confession'). Shrove Tuesday was traditionally marked by festivities before the rigours of Lent and is commemorated by carnivals in, for example, Portugal, Brazil and parts of Germany. In England, Shrove Tuesday is also known as *Pancake Day*, the day on which fats that could not be consumed during Lent were used to make pancakes.

ASH WEDNESDAY

Any Wednesday between 4 February and 10 March. The first day of Lent, Ash Wednesday takes its name from the custom of scattering ashes on the heads of penitents (in its modern form, marking the forehead with ashes in the sign of the Cross).

LENT

February to March or March to April. Lent is a period of 40 days beginning on Ash Wednesday and ending at midnight on Holy Saturday, the day before Easter Day. A reminder of the time spent by Christ in the wilderness, Lent is observed as a period of reflection, repentance and preparation for Easter. It used to be thought that the observance of Lent dated from the time of the first disciples, but it is now usually accepted that the practice probably began in the 4th century and may, originally, have been a fast of 40 hours.

Lent begins on the following days between 1991 and 2000.

1991	13 February
1992	4 March
1993	24 February
1994	16 February
1995	1 March
1996	21 February
1997	12 February
1998	25 February
1999	17 February
2000	8 March

PALM SUNDAY

Any Sunday between 15 March and 18 April. Palm Sunday is the last Sunday of Lent. It commemorates the triumphal entry of Christ into Jerusalem when His way was lined by the branches of palms.

MAUNDY THURSDAY

Any Thursday between 19 March and 22 April. Maundy Thursday – the last Thursday of Lent – takes its name from the Latin *dies mandati*, meaning 'the day of the mandate', referring to the mandate given by Christ to His disciples to love one another. It is marked in the Roman Catholic Church by the symbolic washing of feet by the priest, in commemoration of Christ washing the feet of the disciples. In England, Maundy money – specially minted coins – is distributed by the sovereign to as many elderly men and women as the sovereign's age.

GOOD FRIDAY

Any Friday between 20 March and 23 April. Good Friday is the commemoration of the Crucifixion. It is a public holiday in most Christian countries.

HOLY SATURDAY

Any Saturday between 21 March and 24 April. Holy Saturday – sometimes wrongly called 'Easter Saturday' – is the last day of Lent. Easter begins at the stroke of midnight at the end of Holy Saturday.

EASTER DAY

Any Sunday between 22 March and 25 April. Easter Day is the celebration of the Resurrection of Christ. There is no historical basis for celebrating Easter in the spring as it is not known at what time of the year these events took place.

Easter is celebrated on the first Sunday after the Full Moon that happens on or following 21 March. If the Full Moon falls upon a Sunday, Easter is celebrated upon the following Sunday. The 'Moon' used in these calculations is not the celestial Moon but a hypothetical 'calendar Moon' whose cycles alternate in periods of 30 and 29 days. (Although the Orthodox Churches calculate Easter in the same manner as other Christian Churches, their festivities take place later because Eastern Christendom still uses the Julian calendar.)

Easter falls on the following days between 1991 and 2000.
1991 31 March
1992 19 April
1993 11 April
1994 3 April
1995 16 April
1996 7 April
1997 30 March
1998 12 April
1999 4 April
2000 23 April

The day following Easter Sunday is a public holiday in most Christian countries.

ASCENSION DAY

Any Thursday between 30 April and 3 June. Ascension Day – which falls 40 days after Easter Day – is when the Ascension of Christ into Heaven is celebrated. It is a public holiday in many Christian countries.

Ascension Day falls on the following days between 1991 and 2000.
1991 9 May
1992 28 May
1993 20 May
1994 12 May
1995 25 May
1996 16 May
1997 8 May
1998 21 May
1999 13 May
2000 1 June

PENTECOST (WHIT SUNDAY)

Any Sunday between 10 May and 13 June. Pentecost – which falls seven weeks after Easter Day – commemorates the descent of the Holy Spirit upon the apostles. It marks the beginning of the activities of the Church on Earth. Its English name 'Whit' Sunday is usually said to come from 'White' Sunday in a reference to the white robes worn by the newly baptized. Whit Monday is a public holiday in many Christian countries.

Pentecost falls on the following days between 1991 and 2000.
1991 19 May
1992 7 June
1993 30 May
1994 22 May
1995 4 June
1996 26 May
1997 18 May
1998 31 May
1999 23 May
2000 11 June

TRINITY SUNDAY

Any Sunday between 17 May and 20 June. Trinity Sunday is a celebration of the Holy Trinity. In Churches of the Anglican Communion the remaining Sundays of the year are numbered 'after Trinity'.

CORPUS CHRISTI

Any Thursday between 21 May and 24 June. Corpus Christi – celebrated on the Thursday following Trinity Sunday – is a major festival of the Roman Catholic Church held in devotion to the Eucharist. Corpus Christi is a public holiday in some Roman Catholic countries.

THE ASSUMPTION

15 August. The Feast of the Assumption of the Blessed Virgin Mary is a Roman Catholic and (Eastern) Orthodox festival commemorating the doctrine of the assumption of Mary – in both body and soul – into Heaven at the end of her earthly life. It is a public holiday in most Roman Catholic countries and in Greece.

ALL SAINTS' DAY

1 November. All Saints' Day – a public holiday in some Christian (mainly Roman Catholic) countries – is a celebration of the lives of all the saints of the Church, including those whose lives are remembered on individual named saints' days (see p. 311).

ALL SOULS' DAY

2 November. All Souls' Day – a public holiday in some Latin American countries – is a major Roman Catholic festival. It is a day of prayer for the souls of the departed now in Purgatory.

ADVENT SUNDAY

The Sunday nearest to 30 November, that is any Sunday between 27 November and 3 December. Advent Sunday (Latin *adventus* meaning 'coming') is the beginning of the season of preparation for Christmas. There are usually three, and occasionally four, Sundays of Advent.

Advent begins on the following days between 1991 and 2000.
1991 1 December
1992 29 November

1993 28 November
1994 27 November
1995 3 December
1996 1 December
1997 30 November
1998 29 November
1999 28 November
2000 3 December

IMMACULATE CONCEPTION

8 December. The festival of the Immaculate Conception commemorates the (Roman Catholic) doctrine that Mary was conceived without sin. It is a public holiday in some Roman Catholic countries.

CHRISTMAS EVE

24 December. The day before the celebration of Christmas. It is a public holiday in a few Christian countries.

CHRISTMAS DAY

25 December. The celebration of the birth of Christ to Mary at Bethlehem, probably in c. 4 BC. Christmas (literally 'Christ mass') has been celebrated by Christians from the earliest times. There is, however, no reason to assume that this historical event took place on 25 December. There is some evidence to suggest that Christ was born in September.

The early Church in the East celebrated both Christmas and the Epiphany on 6 January. In the West the Feast of the Nativity has been celebrated on 25 December since AD 336 in order to take the place of the pagan Sun festival held on or near the same date. By the end of the 4th century Christmas was celebrated on 25 December throughout Christendom, except in Armenia, which still commemorates 6 January. (Although the Orthodox Churches celebrate Christmas on 25 December, their festivities take place in January in the Gregorian calendar because Eastern Christendom still uses the Julian calendar.)

BUDDHIST FESTIVALS

Different festivals and, in some cases, different dates for the same festivals, are observed in the various countries where Buddhism is practised.
Uposatha Days are fortnightly meetings of the Buddhist monastic assembly – at times of full moon and new moon – to reaffirm the rules of discipline. These meetings exclude novices and laymen. The Uposatha Day is also the name given to the more modern weekly visit to a monastery by laymen.

Other festivals

New Year is celebrated in Burma/Myanmar (16–17 April), Sri Lanka (13 April), Thailand (between 13–16 April), Tibet (in February)
The Buddha's Birth, Enlightenment and Death is celebrated in Burma/Myanmar, Sri Lanka, and Thailand (as The Buddha's Cremation) in May or June, and in Tibet in May.
The Buddha's First Sermon is celebrated in June or July in Burma/Myanmar (in conjunction with the Beginnings of the Rains Retreat Festival), and in Sri Lanka and Tibet.
The Rains Retreat is celebrated in Thailand (between July and October).
Summer Retreat is celebrated in China between June and October.
The establishment of Buddhism in Sri Lanka is celebrated in Sri Lanka in June or July.
The Procession of the Month of Asala is celebrated in Sri Lanka in July or August.
Festival of Hungry Ghosts is celebrated in China in August.
The Buddha's Birth is celebrated in China in August.
Kuan-Yin is celebrated in China in August.
The Buddha's first visit to Sri Lanka is celebrated in Sri Lanka in September.
The Buddha's Descent from Tushita is celebrated in Tibet in October.
Kathina Ceremony is celebrated in Burma/Myanmar and Thailand in November.
Festival of Lights is celebrated in Sri Lanka and Thailand in November.
The Death of Tsongkhapa is celebrated in Tibet in November.
The Arrival of Sanghamitta is celebrated in Sri Lanka in December or January.
The Conjunction of Nine Evils and the Conjunction of the Ten Virtues is celebrated in Tibet in January.
Saints' Day is celebrated in Thailand in February.

JEWISH FESTIVALS

Weekly festival Shabat (the sabbath) observed on the seventh day of the week, Saturday, in commemoration of the day of rest taken by the Almighty after the completion of the creation. It is the covenant between God and the Jewish people. On the sabbath, Jews are obliged to engage in worship and prayer at home or in the synagogue and to avoid work.

Monthly festival Rosh Hodesh, the celebration of the new moon.

Other festivals are celebrated according to the Jewish calendar (see pp. 36–38). The equivalent date in the Gregorian calendar varies from one year to another. Jewish festivals commence on the evening of the dates shown and last until sunset on the following day. Those festivals celebrated as public holidays in Israel are indicated below.

15 Shevat – *Tu B'shevat* (Festival for New Trees). In modern times this festival is associated with the planting of trees in Israel.
13 Adar – *Taanit Ester* (Fast of Ester).
14 Adar – *Purim* (Festival of Lots). Celebrated as a public holiday in Israel, Purim commemorates the deliverance of Persian Jews from persecution in the 5th century BCE (see Jewish calendar).
14 Nisan – *Taanit Behorim* (Fast of the First-born).
27 Nisan – *Pesah* (Passover). Celebrated as a public holiday in Israel, the Passover commemorates the Israelites' servitude in Egypt and the subsequent exodus from Egypt. It is called 'Passover' because on the eve of the Jewish flight from Egypt the last of the 10 plagues 'passed over' the homes of the Israelites.
27 Nisan – *Yom Ha-Shoah* (Holocaust Day). A modern commemoration of the victims of the Holocaust but not marked by a public holiday in Israel.
4 Iyyar – *Yom H'zikharon* (Remembrance Day). A modern commemoration but not marked by a public holiday in Israel.
5 Iyyar – *Yom Ha'Atzmaut* (Independence Day), an Israeli public holiday.
18 Iyyar – the 33rd Day of 'Counting the Omer'.
28 Iyyar – *Yom Yerushalayim* (Jerusalem Day). A modern festival which is not marked by a public holiday in Israel.
6–7 Sivan – *Shavuot* (the Festival of Weeks, or

Pentecost). This festival commemorates the revelation of the Torah (Law) at Sinai. It is a public holiday in Israel.

20 Sivan – the Fast of 20 Sivan.

17 Tammuz – the Fast of 17 Tammuz.

9 Av – *Tisha B'Av* (the Fast of 9 Av).

15 Av – *Tu B'Av* (the Festival of 15 Av).

1 Ellul – Festival of 1 Ellul.

1–2 Tishri – *Rosh Hashanah* (New Year). This festival celebrates the New Year of the Jewish Calendar but also begins the Ten Days of Penitence that ends on Yom Kippur (see below). These days are considered the Days of Judgement for all mankind. Many rabbinic laws govern behaviour during this time – they include the strict prohibition of work – but celebrations are also enjoyed. Rosh Hashanah is a public holiday in Israel.

3 Tishri – *Tsom Gedaliah* (the Fast of Gedaliah).

10 Tishri – *Yom Kippur* (the Day of Atonement) is the most solemn and holy day in the Jewish Calendar. A public holiday in Israel, the festival is spent in prayer and fasting. Sins are confessed in acts of reconciliation.

15 or 16–22 or 23 Tishri – *Sukkot* (the Festival of Tabernacles). Commemorated in Israel by a series of half-day public holidays, Sukkot is a remembrance of the Israelites' wanderings after the Exodus. It is named after the booths (*sukkot*, 'booth') that the Israelites lived in during this time.

22 or 23 Tishri – *Shemini Atzeret* (the Eighth Day of Conclusion). The final day of the Festival of Tabernacles is celebrated independently.

23 Tishri – *Simhat Torah* (Rejoicing in the Torah). This festival – a public holiday in Israel – is celebrated on the completion of the cycle of readings from the Torah.

25 Kislev – 2 Tevet – *Hanukah* (the Festival of the Dedication of the Temple, otherwise known as the Festival of Lights). Celebrated for eight days, the festival commemorates the revolt against the Seleucid ruler Antiochus IV Epiphanes and the rededication of the Temple in 164 BCE (see Jewish calendar). The festival is characterized by songs, candles, feasting and giving gifts to children.

10 Tevet – the Feast of 10 Tevet

ISLAMIC FESTIVALS

See also the Islamic calendar on pp. 38–40.

Many of the following festivals are public holidays in Islamic countries. As these holidays are celebrated according to the Islamic lunar calendar, the equivalent date in the Gregorian calendar varies from one year to another.

FESTIVALS

Weekly festival on Friday, the Day of Assembly.

Other festivals

1 Muharram	New Year's Day
1–10 Muharram	Muharram (New Year Festival)
12 Rabìa I	Eid Milad-un-Nabi (Festival of the Prophet's Birthday)
26 Rajab	Shab-i-Maraj (Festival of the Prophet's Night Journey and Ascension)
15 Shaabân	Night of Forgiveness
1–29/30 Ramadan	Ramadan; annual fast lasting a month observed by abstention from food, drink and sexual intercourse from dawn to dusk.

1 Shawwâl	Eid-ul-Fitr; Festival of Fast Breaking (end of Ramadan) celebrated by feasting and visiting graves.
9 Dhû'l Hijja	Day of Arafat
Dhû'l Hijja	Haj (Pilgrimage to Mecca)
10 Dhû'l Hijja	Eid-ul-Adha (Festival of Sacrifice, marking the end of the Pilgrimage to Mecca).

HINDU FESTIVALS

For information on the Hindu gods and goddesses see p. 329.

January
Makar Sankranti, Winter solstice festival.
Pongal, harvest festival in southern India.
Kumbha Mela, festival held every 12 years; worshippers bathe in the waters at the confluence of the Ganges and Jumna rivers.

January–February
Vasanta Panchami, held in honour of goddess Saraswati.
Mahashivratri, 'Great Night of Shiva', celebrated by vigils, vows, fasting and worship of goddess Shiva.

February–March
Ramakrishna utsav (20 Feb), festival for Hindu saint Ramakrishna.
Holi, a boisterous festival characterized by the throwing of red powder and by bonfires (possible origins in the celebration of the god of sexual desire, Kama).
Shivrati, main festival in honour of Shiva; spent in meditation.

March–April
Ramanavami, celebrates the birth of Shi Rama observed in sanctity and fasting.
Hanuman Jayanti, in honour of the god Hanuman.

April–May
Baisakhi, New Year festival celebrated by gift-giving, feasting, praying and bathing in sacred waters.

May–June
Ganga Dussehra, in honour of goddess Ganga; devotees bathe in the sacred waters of the River Ganges.

June–July
Jagannatha (Ratha-yatra), celebrates Krishna as the Lord of the Universe.

July–August
Naga Panchami, celebrates the birth of serpents. Worshippers empty pots of milk over snakes from the temple of Shiva.
Raksha Bandhan, an old festival in which sisters give wrist decorations to their brothers to ward off evil spirits.

August–September
Ganesh Chaturthi, in honour of the elephant-headed god, Ganesh.
Janmashtani, celebrates the birth of Krishna.

September–October
Dussehra (Durja Puja), celebrates the goddess Durga during the period of Navratri ('Nine Nights').
Gandhi Jayanti (2 October), celebrates the birth of Mahatma Gandhi.
Diwali (October), a major festival honouring Laksmi, goddess of wealth. During this time merchants open fresh accounts. Festivities include visiting, exchanging gifts, decorating houses, feasting and wearing new clothes.

WEDDING ANNIVERSARIES

A combination of traditional and commercial usage has resulted in the association of certain types of gift with specific wedding anniversaries.

British and Continental usage

First anniversary	cotton
Second anniversary	paper
Third anniversary	leather
Fourth anniversary	fruit and flowers
Fifth anniversary	wooden
Sixth anniversary	sugar
Seventh anniversary	wool or copper
Eighth anniversary	bronze or pottery
Ninth anniversary	pottery or willow
Tenth anniversary	tin
Eleventh anniversary	steel
Twelfth anniversary	silk or linen
Thirteenth anniversary	lace
Fourteenth anniversary	ivory
Fifteenth anniversary	crystal
Twentieth anniversary	porcelain
Twenty-fifth anniversary	silver
Thirtieth anniversary	pearl
Thirty-fifth anniversary	coral
Fortieth anniversary	ruby
Forty-fifth anniversary	sapphire
Fiftieth anniversary	golden
Fifty-fifth anniversary	emerald
Sixtieth anniversary	diamond
Seventieth anniversary	platinum

American usage

First anniversary	gold jewellery
Second anniversary	garnet
Third anniversary	pearls
Fourth anniversary	blue topaz
Fifth anniversary	sapphire
Sixth anniversary	amethyst
Seventh anniversary	onyx
Eighth anniversary	tourmaline
Ninth anniversary	lapis
Tenth anniversary	diamond jewellery
Eleventh anniversary	turquoise
Twelfth anniversary	jade
Thirteenth anniversary	citrine
Fourteenth anniversary	opal
Fifteenth anniversary	ruby
Sixteenth anniversary	peridot
Seventeenth anniversary	watches
Eighteenth anniversary	cat's-eye
Nineteenth anniversary	aquamarine
Twentieth anniversary	emerald
Twenty-fifth anniversary	silver jubilee
Thirtieth anniversary	pearl jubilee
Thirty-fifth anniversary	emerald jubilee
Fortieth anniversary	ruby jubilee
Forty-fifth anniversary	sapphire jubilee
Fiftieth anniversary	golden jubilee
Sixtieth anniversary	diamond jubilee

SIGNS OF THE ZODIAC

The zodiac – in astronomy – is an imaginary belt that extends 8° on either side of the annual path or *eliptic* of the Sun. The concept was devised in Mesopotamia c. 3000 BC. The orbits of the Moon and of the major planets of the solar system (except Pluto) lie entirely within the zodiac. It is divided into 12 equal areas – the *signs of the zodiac* – each of 30°. Each section is named after the constellation that at one time coincided with the sector. (A constellation is a group of stars that form an easily recognizable pattern, for example Ursa Major which is known in Britain as the Plough and in North America as the Big Dipper.) However, the signs of the zodiac no longer correspond to the constellations as proper allowance for leap days was not made in the original calculations and the constellations appear to have 'shifted' to the east. The constellation Ophiuchus is also within the astronomical zodiac but it is not considered to be a member of it.

ASTROLOGY

In astrology the zodiac is a diagram depicting the zodiac belt with symbols representing each of the 12 sections of the zodiac. The zodiac – from the Greek *zoidiakos*, circle of animals – is used by astrologers to predict the future. Some European astrologers add the 13th zodiacal sign, Ophiuchus. Although the original periods during which the Sun appears to be in each of the constellations of the zodiac no longer apply, astrology nonetheless adheres to the original dates.

Astrology is the interpretation of the influence of planets and stars upon human lives. It is based upon the concept that if an event occurred while the planets were in a particular configuration, a similar event would be likely to happen when those planetary circumstances were repeated. Astrology originated in Mesopotamia and was developed in ancient Greece, before being absorbed into the Indian, Islamic and West European cultures. In ancient times astrology was regarded as a science. In modern times it has enjoyed the support of some eminent scientists and philosophers including Carl Jung who conducted an experiment to compare the 'birth signs' of happily married and divorced couples. Although it has been condemned by various Christian councils, astrology retains great popularity through daily predictions in newspapers and specialist almanacs.

The signs of the zodiac are:

Aries (symbol: the Ram) The Sun is in the first sign of the zodiac from about March 21 to ɔril 19.

Taurus (symbol: the Bull) The Sun is in Taurus from about April 20 to May 20.

Gemini (symbol: the Twins) The Sun is in Gemini from about May 21 to June 21.

Cancer (symbol: the Crab) The Sun is in Cancer from about June 22 to July 22.

Leo (symbol: the Lion) The Sun is in Leo from about July 23 to August 22.

Virgo (symbol: the Virgin) The Sun is in Virgo from about August 23 to September 22.

Libra (symbol: the Balance) The Sun is in Libra from about September 23 to October 23.

Scorpio (symbol: the Scorpion) The Sun is in Scorpio from about October 24 to November 21. (The second half of Scorpio is sometimes referred to as Ophiuchus – symbol: the Serpent-Bearer – by some European astrologers.)

Sagittarius (symbol: the Archer) The Sun is in Sagittarius from about November 22 to December 21.

Capricorn (symbol: the Goat) The Sun is in Capricorn from about December 22 to January 19.

Aquarius (symbol: the Water Carrier) The Sun is in Aquarius from about January 20 to February 18.

Pisces (symbol: the Fishes) The Sun is in Pisces from about February 19 to March 20.

EARTH SCIENCES

THE EARTH

THE EARTH'S STRUCTURE

Moving outwards from the Earth, man has been to the Moon, landed spacecraft on planets, and sent space probes to the outermost reaches of the Solar System. But in the opposite direction the story is very different. Man's direct access to the Earth's interior is limited to the depth of the deepest mine, which is less than 4 km (2.5 mi). The Russians spent most of the 1980s drilling a hole in the crust to a target depth of 15 km (9.3 mi), but in doing so they penetrated no more than the upper 0.24% of the Earth, the average radius of which is 6371 km (3956 mi).

Unable to visit the Earth's deep interior or place instruments within it, scientists must explore in more subtle ways. One method is to measure natural phenomena – the magnetic and gravitational fields are the chief examples – at the Earth's surface and interpret the observations in terms of the planet's internal properties. A second approach is to study the Earth with non-material probes, the most important of which are the seismic waves emitted by earthquakes. As seismic waves pass through the Earth, they undergo sudden changes in direction and velocity at certain depths. These depths mark the major boundaries, or *discontinuities*, that divide the Earth into crust, mantle and core.

THE CRUST

The outermost layer of the Earth, the crust, accounts for only about 0.6% of the planet's volume. The average thickness of the *oceanic crust* is 5–9 km (3–5½ mi) and varies comparatively little throughout the world. By contrast, the *continental crust* has the much higher average thickness of 30–40 km (18½–25 mi) and varies much more. Beneath the central valley of California, for example, the crust is only about 20 km (12½ mi) thick, but beneath parts of major mountain ranges such as the Himalaya it can exceed 80 km (50 mi).

The rocks that form the continental crust are highly varied, including volcanic lava flows, huge blocks of granite, and sediments laid down in shallow water when parts of the continents were inundated by the sea. Despite the diversity of materials, the average composition is roughly that of the rock granite, and the two most common elements (in addition to oxygen) are silicon and aluminium.

The oceanic crust is much more uniform in composition and, apart from a thin covering of sediment, consists largely of the rock basalt, possibly underlain by the rock gabbro (which has the same composition as basalt but is coarser grained). Oxygen apart, the most common elements in the oceanic crust are again silicon and aluminium, but there is markedly more magnesium than in the upper continental crust. The composition of the lower crust, which cannot be sampled directly, is uncertain, but the predominant rock is probably gabbro.

THE MANTLE

The mantle extends from the base of the crust to a depth of about 2900 km (1800 mi) and accounts for about 82% of the Earth's volume. The sharp boundary between the crust and the mantle is called the *Mohorovičić discontinuity* (or *Moho* for short) after the Yugoslav seismologist Andrija Mohorovičić who discovered it in 1909.

The mantle is thought to consist largely of peridotite, a rock that contains high proportions of the elements iron, silicon and magnesium, in addition to oxygen. The mantle is inaccessible, but evidence of its composition comes from surface rocks thought to have originated there. Although mostly solid, the mantle contains a partially molten layer.

THE CORE

The core extends from the base of the mantle to the Earth's centre and accounts for about 17% of the Earth's volume. The discontinuity between the mantle and core is called the *core-mantle boundary* or, sometimes, the *Gutenberg discontinuity*, after the German-American seismologist Beno Gutenberg. The core comprises two distinct parts. The *outer core* – which extends down to a depth of about 5155 km (3200 mi) – is liquid. The *inner core* is solid.

The main constituent of the core is iron, although measurements of the Earth's rate of rotation show that the density must be slightly lower than that of pure iron. The core must therefore contain a small proportion (5–20%) of some lighter element – possibly sulphur, silicon, carbon, hydrogen or oxygen.

AN ALTERNATIVE VIEW

The division of the Earth into crust, mantle and core is based on the fact that the three zones have different chemical compositions. However, there is another way of looking at the Earth, in terms of its physical state.

In the upper mantle, at depths of 75–250 km (46½–155 mi), the velocity of seismic waves is slightly lower than in the zones just above and below. Scientists believe that this layer of the upper mantle is partially molten, and they have named it the *asthenosphere*. It is this layer that is the source of volcanic *magma* (molten rock). The rigid layer above the asthenosphere, the *lithosphere*, comprises the crust and uppermost mantle. The solid region of the mantle below the asthenosphere is called the *mesosphere*.

THE MAGNETIC FIELD

The Earth has a magnetic field, which is why a compass needle points approximately north at most places on the Earth's surface. The magnetic field has two parts. Most of it is that of a simple dipole; it is as if a giant bar magnet were placed at the centre of the Earth (although the magnet slopes at 11° to the Earth's axis of rotation). But a small proportion of it is much more complicated and changes very rapidly. This is why a compass needle points in a slightly different direction each year.

The rapid changing indicates that the magnetic field must be produced in a part of the Earth that is fluid, for no solid region could reorganize itself rapidly enough without shaking the planet to pieces. The only liquid zone inside the Earth is the outer core.

This fits in with something else. The only conceivable way in which a magnetic field could be generated within the Earth is by the flow of very large electric currents, and electric currents need a conductor. The Earth's core is the most conductive zone in the whole Earth, because it consists largely of iron. The silicates of the mantle would simply not conduct well enough.

An additional feature of the Earth's magnetic field is

MASS AND DENSITY

The Earth, including its atmosphere, has a mass of 5.974×10^{21} tonnes (5 879 000 000 000 000 000 000 tons) – the average density is 5.515 times that of water.

The Earth's atmosphere weighs 5.24×10^{15} tonnes (5 160 000 000 000 000 tons) or 0.000088 per cent of the total mass. The density of the Earth is being added to as the planet picks up cosmic dust, but estimates of this increase vary widely with 30 000 tonnes/tons a year being the upper limit.

that it has reversed from north to south and back on numerous occasions over geological time. The evidence for this has come from examining the magnetic alignment of old rocks.

CONTINENTAL DRIFT

There is ever-increasing evidence that the Earth's land surface once comprised a single primeval land mass, now called Pangaea, and that this split during the Upper Cretaceous period (100 000 000 to 65 000 000 years ago) into two super-continents, the northern one called Laurasia and the southern one Gondwanaland.

Throughout almost the whole of human history, most people have imagined the continents to be fixed in their present positions and the ocean floors to be the oldest and most primitive parts of the Earth. In the space of a few years during the early 1960s, however, both of these assumptions were overthrown in an intellectual revolution. It suddenly became possible to prove that the continents are drifting across the Earth's surface, that the ocean floors are spreading, and that none of the oceanic crust is more than about 200 million years old – less than 5% of the age of the Earth (4600 million years).

The Earth's *lithosphere* – the rigid layer that comprises the crust and the uppermost mantle – is divided into 15 *plates* of various sizes. The plates 'float' on the partially molten layer – the *asthenosphere* – below, and it is because they are floating that they have the freedom to move horizontally. A few of the plates (for example, the Pacific) are almost completely oceanic, but most include both oceanic and continental lithosphere. There are no completely continental plates. The plate boundaries are the most tectonically active parts of the Earth – they are where most mountain building, earthquakes and volcanoes occur.

HOW CONTINENTAL DRIFT WAS PROVED

Many rocks contain minute magnetic particles, usually oxides of iron and titanium. When a rock forms, these particles become magnetized in the direction of the Earth's magnetic field at the particular site. Using highly sensitive instruments, it is possible to measure this weak magnetism and from it determine the position of the north pole at the time the rock was formed.

Scientists were surprised to discover that for rocks older than a few million years the north poles determined in this way did not lie at the present north pole, and that the older the rocks the greater was the discrepancy. They were even more surprised to find that rocks of the same age from different continents gave ancient north poles in quite different positions.

There can only be one north pole at any given time, however, and that must lie close to the north end of the Earth's rotational axis. The only way of explaining the rock magnetic data, therefore, was to assume that the continents have drifted with respect to both the present north pole and each other.

THE CONTINENTS

The Earth's land surface comprises seven continents, each with their attendant islands. Europe, Africa and Asia, though politically distinct, physically form one land mass known as Afro-Eurasia, which covers 57.2 per cent of the Earth's land mass. Central America (which includes Mexico) is often included in North America (Canada, the USA and Greenland), with South America regarded as a separate continent. Europe includes all of the USSR west of the Ural Mountains. Oceania embraces Australasia (Australia and New Zealand) and the non-Asian Pacific islands. The seventh continent is Antarctica.

ASIA

Area: 44 614 000 km² (17 226 000 sq mi).
Greatest extremity* north to south: 6435 km (4000 mi).
Greatest extremity* east to west: 7560 km (4700 mi).

The USSR, which straddles the divide between Asia and Europe, does not recognize a dividing line between the two continents. However, a boundary running along the eastern foot of the Ural Mountains and following the boundary of Kazakhstan to the Caspian Sea is generally recognized internationally. The boundary between Asia and Europe in the Caucasus is disputed – some authorities recognize the crest of the Caucasus Mountains between the Caspian and Black Seas as the dividing line, while others prefer a boundary following the valley of the River Manych to the estuary of the River Don. In the East, the boundary between Asia and Oceania is also disputed. Western New Guinea – Irian Jaya – is politically part of Indonesia but is generally regarded as part of Oceania rather than part of Asia. The rest of Indonesia, the Philippines and Japan are regarded as part of Asia.

DIMENSIONS

The Earth is not a true sphere but an ellipsoid. Its equatorial diameter is $12\,756.274$ km ($7\,926.381$ miles) and its polar diameter is $12\,713.505$ km ($7\,899.806$ miles).

The Earth's equatorial circumference is $40\,075.02$ km ($24\,901.46$ miles), and its polar meridianal circumference is $40\,007.86$ km ($24\,859.73$ miles).

The volume of the Earth is $1\,083\,207\,000\,000$ km³ ($259\,875\,300\,000$ cu. miles).

The Earth has a pear-shaped asymmetry with the north polar radius being 45 m (148 ft) longer than the south polar radius and there is also a slight ellipticity of the Equator since its long axis (about longitude 37°W) is 159 m (522 ft) greater than the short axis.

AFRICA

Area: 30 216 000 km² (11 667 000 sq mi).
Greatest extremity* north to south: 7080 km (4400 mi).
Greatest extremity* east to west: 6035 km (3750 mi).

The boundary between Africa and Asia is usually

regarded as being the Suez Canal rather than the political boundary between Egypt and Israel.

NORTH AMERICA

Area: 24 230 000 km² (9 355 000 sq mi).
Greatest extremity north to south*: 7885 km (5000 mi).
Greatest extremity east to west*: 6035 km (3750 mi).

North America includes Central America (up to the Panama–Colombia border) as well as Greenland, and the Caribbean islands of the Greater Antilles, the Leeward and Windward Islands. Hawaii is often included as part of North America because it is politically part of the USA, although it is physically part of Oceania.

SOUTH AMERICA

Area: 17 814 000 km² (6 878 000 sq mi).
Greatest extremity north to south*: 7240 km (4500 mi).
Greatest extremity east to west*: 5150 km (3200 mi).

South America includes the Caribbean islands of Trinidad and Tobago, the Venezuelan Lesser Antilles, and Aruba, Bonaire and Curaçao. The northern boundary of the continent is usually taken to be the political frontier between Panama and Colombia, rather than the Panama Canal. (Until the 20th century, what is now Panama was considered to be part of South America.)

ANTARCTICA

Area 14 245 000 km² (5 500 000 sq mi).
*Greatest extremity**: 4340 km (2700 km).

Antarctica includes a relatively small number of attendant islands.

STRUCTURE

Modern theory suggests that the Earth has an outer crust on average 35 km (22 miles) thick, but varying from just 5 km (3 miles) to 80 km (50 miles). Under the crust is the mantle, with a total diameter of 2900 km (1800 miles). The mantle is however in two parts, an outer solid mantle which together with the crust forms the lithosphere, and an inner semi-molten asthenosphere, with temperature ranging from 1300 °C under the crust to 5000 °C in semi-molten parts. The earth's iron-rich core is also in two parts, an outer liquid core 2000 km (1242 miles) in diameter and an inner solid core with a diameter of 1370 km (850 miles). Core temperatures are up to 5500 °C with the density estimated in the range 12–13g/cm³, 20 per cent greater than in the surrounding liquid.

EUROPE

Area: 10 505 000 km² (4 056 000 sq mi).
Greatest extremity north to south: 2900 km (1800 mi).
Greatest extremity east to west: 4000 km (2500 mi).

Europe excludes Asiatic Turkey, thus dividing the city of Istanbul between two continents. (The boundary between Europe and Asia is described above – see Asia.) The islands of Madeira, the Azores and the Canary Islands – although strictly attendant islands to Africa – are almost always included in Europe.

OCEANIA

Area: 8 503 000 km² (3 283 000 sq mi).
*Greatest extremity** north to south*: 3000 km (1870 mi).

*Greatest extremity** east to west*: 3700 km (2300 mi).

Oceania comprises Australia, New Zealand and the entire island of New Guinea as well as the Melanesian, Micronesian and Polynesian islands. Hawaii – although physically part of Oceania – is often included in North America because it is politically part of the USA.

* excluding attendant islands.
** Australia.

GEOLOGY

THE FORMATION OF ROCKS

Rock can be one of three types – igneous, sedimentary or metamorphic. *Igneous rock* starts deep in the Earth as molten magma, which then forces its way up through the crust to cool and solidify. Sedimentary rock is mostly formed when rock of any type is weathered down into fine particles that are then re-deposited under water and later compressed. *Metamorphic rock* is igneous or sedimentary rock that has been subjected to high pressure and/or temperature, thereby changing its nature.

The Earth is perpetually recycling its rocks. Material brought to the surface is eroded, transported and ultimately returned to the Earth's interior, where it becomes available to begin the cycle all over again. This series of processes is known as the *rock cycle* or *geological cycle*. The energy to maintain it comes partly from the Sun (to fuel the erosion processes) and partly from the Earth's interior (to generate volcanic activity and uplift).

IGNEOUS ROCK

Magma – which comes from the Earth's surface via volcanic activity – comprises a mixture of oxides (compounds with oxygen) and silicates (compounds with silicon and oxygen). When it cools and solidifies, the oxides and silicates produce a complex mixture of mineral crystals. The nature and properties of the crystals in any particular igneous rock depend partly on the composition of the original magma and partly upon the physical conditions under which the magma crystallized. As compositions and conditions vary greatly, there are thousands of different igneous rock types.

Igneous rocks that form on the Earth's surface are known as *extrusive*. Those that form within the crust from magma that never reached the surface are known as *intrusive*. Intrusive rocks cool more slowly because, being surrounded by other rock rather than being open to the air, the heat cannot escape so readily. As a result, the crystals have longer to grow, and the mineral grains are larger (coarser).

Despite the many varieties of igneous rock, just six account for most of the igneous components of the crust. These are *granite*, *diorite* and *gabbro*, which are course-grained intrusive rocks, and *rhyolite*, *andesite* and *basalt*, which are fine-grained extrusive rocks.

SEDIMENTARY ROCK

At least 75% of all sedimentary rock is known as *clastic sedimentary rock*, which means that it is derived from the erosion products of other rocks. All rocks, even those in the most massive of mountain

CATEGORIES OF ROCK

Category	Example	Main constituents and formation
SEDIMENTARY – particles deposited in water or by wind or ice and subsequently cemented	SANDSTONE	Predominantly quartz grains with other minor components. May preserve bedding structures from original deposition, e.g. dune bedding, ripples, etc.
	LIMESTONE	Pure forms are totally $CaCO_3$. Comprises the remains of microscopic organisms and always deposited in water. Fine grained.
IGNEOUS – rocks formed from molten material derived from the Earth's interior	BASALT	Formed by cooling of extrusive (i.e. on land surface or under water) lava flows. Contains about 50% silica and high quantities of feldspar, pyroxine and olivine minerals.
	GRANITE	Formed by slow cooling of intrusive molten material (i.e. within the Earth's body). Has large crystals – quartz, feldspars, mica.
METAMORPHIC – rocks formed by physical and chemical changes to other rocks	MARBLE	Thermal changes to limestone cause changes to a granular crystalline rock.
	GNEISS	An older granite where the mineral content and structure has been changed through heating caused by intrusion of a new molten mass.

Other common rocks are recorded in the Geology Glossary beginning on p. 117.

ranges, are ultimately broken down into smaller and smaller fragments. When the particles become small enough they are then transported by water, wind or ice, usually ending up in the ocean. There they fall as sediment to the ocean floor where, under the pressure of subsequent deposits, they are compacted into hard rock. The most common sedimentary rock is *sandstone*.

The remaining 25% of sediment is either chemical or organic. Rivers dissolve minerals out of the rocks through which they pass, and the mineral solutions end up in the oceans. When the oceans reach their saturation limit for the particular mineral concerned, the excess mineral is precipitated out chemically as solid particles, which fall to the ocean floor. The most common chemical sedimentary rock is *limestone* (calcium carbonate: $CaCO_3$). Not all limestone is precipitated chemically, however. Many ocean organisms extract calcium carbonate from the water to build their shells, and when they die the shells sink to the ocean floor to form sediment in their own right. The most common organic sedimentary rock is again limestone, but there are other organisms that in a similar way generate silica (SiO_2) sediments.

Most sedimentary rocks are a mixture of clastic, chemical and organic, although one type usually predominates.

METAMORPHIC ROCK

When igneous or sedimentary rocks are subjected to high temperatures and pressures, especially in the presence of percolating fluids, their internal structures, and sometimes even their mineralogical compositions, may be changed. The processes involved are known collectively as *metamorphism*. The sort of temperatures and pressures required are, respectively, 300 °C (572 °F) and 100 megapascals (equivalent to almost 1000 atmospheres).

The most extreme conditions in the Earth's crust occur at plate boundaries where continents collide. Most metamorphic rocks are thus generated in the roots of mountains. Depending upon temperature and pressure, there are various grades of metamor-

phism; but in the most intense (high-grade) metamorphism, rock structures, holes and even fossils are so completely obliterated that the original rock type can no longer be identified.

As a result of the realignment of minerals under pressure, many metamorphic rocks are layered, or banded. Sometimes the layering is visible; but even when it is not, it can often be detected by the way that the rock breaks. A common example is *slate*, which easily breaks into thin sheets along the layering.

Not all metamorphic rock is layered, however. Common examples of non-layered metamorphics are *marble*, formed by the metamorphism of limestone, and *quartzite*, which is derived from sandstone.

GEOCHEMICAL ABUNDANCES OF THE ELEMENTS

Element	Lithosphere* (per cent)	Hydrosphere† (per cent)
Oxygen	46·60	85·70
Silicon	27·72	0·000 35
Aluminium	8·13	0·000 000 1
Iron	5·00	0·000 000 004
Calcium	3·63	0·042
Sodium	2·83	1·078
Potassium	2·59	0·040
Magnesium	2·09	0·128
Titanium	0·44	0·000 000 000 1
Hydrogen	0·14	10·80
Manganese	0·095	0·000 000 001
Phosphorus	0·070	0·000 006
Fluorine	0·065	0·000 13
Sulfur	0·026	0·090
Carbon	0·025	0·002 6
Zirconium	0·017	0·000 000 000 1
Chlorine	0·013	1·935
Rubidium	0·009	0·000 012
Nitrogen	0·002	0·001 7
Chromium	0·001	0·000 000 033

* Assessment based on igneous rocks.
† Mean ocean concentrations based on a salinity of 3·5%.

GEMSTONES

Gemstones are minerals that possess a rarity and usually a hardness, colour or translucency which gives them strong aesthetic appeal. Diamond, emerald, ruby and sapphire used to be classified as 'precious stones' and the others listed here as 'semi-precious stones'. This distinction is generally no longer applied. The principal gemstones are listed below in order of hardness.

Name	Hardness (Moh scale 1–10)	Chemical Composition	Colour	Major Sources	Remarks
Diamond	10.0	C	Clear (pure) often slight tinge of yellow, brown, red, black	Include: South Africa, Namibia, Australia, Brazil, USSR. From Kimberlite pipes or alluvium.	Extremely hard (name comes from Greek for 'invincible'). Largest (uncut): Cullinan 3106 carats (1 carat = 0.2 gram) Largest (cut): Star of Africa 530.2 carats. Birthstone for April.
Ruby (Red corundum)	9.0	Al_2O_3	Red (owing to chromic oxide staining)	Brazil, Burma, Sri Lanka, Thailand, India, Australia. From pegmatite and metamorphic rocks.	Largest: c. 400 carats from Burma in 1886 Birthstone for July.
Sapphire (Blue corundum)	9.0	Al_2O_3	Blue (other colours of corundum may also be called sapphire)	As for ruby but also USA	Largest: Black Star of Queensland – 1165 carat (uncut), 733 carat (after cutting). Birthstone for September.
Chrysoberyl (Alexandrite) (also known as Cats Eye when brownish colour)	8.5	$BeAl_2O_4$	Green and yellow shades, (transparent to translucent)	Brazil, USSR, Zimbabwe, Sri Lanka. From granitic rocks and pegmatite	Popular name derived from Tsar Alexander II of Russia. Alternative birthstone (from pearl) for June.
Topaz	8.0	Al_2SiO_4	Colourless, pale blue, pale yellow, greenish, rare pink	Australia, Brazil, USSR, Sri Lanka, Namibia. In granitic pegmatites, ryolites and quartz veins, and alluvial deposits	Largest stone 270 kg (596 lb) from Brazil Birthstone for November.
Spinel	7.5–8.0	$MgAl_2O_4$	Very variable, commonly red. Translucent	Burma, Sri Lanka, India, Thailand. Gem quality stones from alluvial gravels. Source is igneous rocks (e.g. gabbro) and some metamorphics	
Emerald (Green Beryl)	7.5–8.0	$Be_3Al_2Si_6O_{18}$	Green, transparent to translucent	USSR, USA, Austria, Norway, Colombia, Zambia. Found in granites	Largest: non-gem quality 61.2 kg (135 lb); gem-quality 16 200 carats. Birthstone for May.

Name	Hardness (Moh scale 1–10)	Chemical Composition	Colour	Major Sources	Remarks
Aquamarine (Blue-green Beryl)	7·5–8·0	$Be_3Al_2Si_6O_{18}$	Pale blue-green transparent to translucent	Brazil, USSR, N. Ireland	Largest: 110 kg (243 lb). Other beryls include Heliodor (yellow) and Morganite (pink). Birthstone for March.
Zircon	7·5	$ZrSiO_4$	Variable: light to reddish brown common. Transparent forms best for gems	Widely distributed: best gemstone zircons in pegmatites or concentrated in alluvial or beach gravels	Name derived from Persian meaning 'golden colour'.
Tourmaline	7·0	Na (or Mg, Fe, Li, Al, Mn)$_3$–$Al_6(BO_3)_3$$Si_6O_{18}$	Black, bluish-black. Also reds and greens	Brazil, Sri Lanka, USA, USSR	Alternative to Opal as birthstone for October.
Garnet group	6·5–7·0	Various silicates	Varies according to composition transparent to translucent	Widely distributed, metamorphic and igneous rocks	Common names and compositions: Pyrope – $Mg_3Al_2Si_3O_{12}$ Almandine – $Fe_3Al_2Si_3O_{12}$ Spessartine – $Mn_3Al_2Si_3O_{12}$ Grossular – $Ca_3Al_2Si_3O_{12}$ Uvarovite – $Ca_3Cr_2Si_3O_{12}$ Andradite – $Ca_3Fe_2Si_3O_{12}$ Garnet is birthstone for January.
Rose Quartz	7·0	SiO_2	Pink	Brazil, Sri Lanka, USA, USSR	Alternative to Opal as birthstone for October.
Smoky quartz	7·0	SiO_2	Smoky brown, red, yellow	Scotland, Switzerland, USA, USSR, Brazil	Sometimes called 'Cairngorm'.
Rock Crystal (Quartz)	7·0	SiO_2	Clear transparent	Widespread	A crystal form of common quartz. Alternative to diamond as birthstone for April.
Amethyst	7·0	SiO_2	Purple	Brazil, Sri Lanka, Germany, Madagascar, Uruguay, USSR	Purple-stained quartz. Birthstone for February.
Chrysoprase	6·5–7·0	SiO_2	Apple green	USA, Germany	Form of chalcedony (compact micro crystal quartz).
Carnelian or Cornelian	6·5–7·0	SiO_2	Red, reddish brown	Widespread, inc. U.K.	Form of chalcedony. Alternative to ruby as birthstone for July.

Name	Hardness (Moh scale 1–10)	Chemical Composition	Colour	Major Sources	Remarks
Agate	6·5–7·0	SiO_2	Striped, white-grey, blue	Brazil, India, Germany, Namibia, Madagascar, Scotland	Form of chalcedony, characterized by mixed colours in stripes.
Onyx	6·5–7·0	SiO_2	Black and white stripes	As agate	Form of agate.
Sardonyx	6·5–7·0	SiO_2	Red-brown and white stripes	As agate	Form of agate. Alternative to peridot as birthstone for August.
Jasper	6·5–7·0	SiO_2	Brown, red, yellow	Egypt, India	Form of chalcedony. Rarely uniformly coloured, often spotted or banded.
Bloodstone	6·5–7·0	SiO_2	Red spots on dark green	Various widespread	A form of chalcedony. Colour formed by spots of iron oxide. Alternative to aquamarine as birthstone for March.
Olivine (Peridot)	6·5–7·0	$(Mg,Fe)_2SiO_4$	Green	Australia, Brazil, Burma, Norway, USA	Rock-forming mineral in silica poor igneous rocks. Can be gemstone quality. Also can form through metamorphism. Birthstone for August.
Jadeite (Jade)	6·5–7·0	$NaAlSi_2O_0$	Green	Burma, China, Tibet, Canada, USA, New Zealand	Jadeite is one of two forms of jade; the other, nephrite, is softer (6·0) and is not a gemstone. Soft serpentine is sometimes sold as jade.
Moonstone	6·0–6·5	$KAlSi_3O_8$	Whitish blue with pearly sheen	Brazil, Burma, Sri Lanka	Moonstone is a potassic feldspar. Alternative to pearl as birthstone for June.
Opal	5·5–6·5	$SiO_2.nH_2O$	Milky-white, sometimes black, body with rainbow streaks	Australia, Mexico, USSR, Hungary	A solidified gel containing up to 10 per cent water. Largest: 'Desert Flame of Andamooka' (Australia) 34 215 carats.
Turquoise	5·0–6·0	$CuAl_6(PO_4)_4(OH)_8 5H_2O$	Sky blue, opaque	Egypt, Iran, Turkey, USA	A vein mineral which has undergone alteration in arid conditions. Birthstone for December.
Lapis Lazuli (Lazurite)	5·0–5·5	$(NaCa)_8(Al,Si)_{12}O_{24}(S,SO_4)$	Azure blue, opaque	Afghanistan, Chile, Tibet, USSR	A metamorphosed limestone. Alternative to sapphire as birthstone for September.

Name	Hardness (Moh scale 1–10)	Chemical Composition	Colour	Major Sources	Remarks
ORGANIC GEM MATERIAL					
Amber	2·0–2·5	$C_{40}H_{64}O_4$	Yellow, honey	Baltic and some Mediterranean coasts	Amber is fossilized plant resins, may contain small insect remains.
Coral	Varies, soft	$CaCo_3$	Various	Coasts of warm seas: India, Australia, etc	Skeletons of microscopic warm water creatures.
Pearl	Varies, soft		Pearl grey, white	Various seas	Secretions formed in molluscs, e.g. oysters and mussels. Largest: 83g (3 oz). Birthstone for June.

GEOCHRONOLOGY

Christian teaching as enunciated by Archbishop Ussher in the 17th century dated the creation of the Earth as occurring in the year 4004 BC. T. Lightfoot, Vice Chancellor of Cambridge University, dated the creation more accurately: 'Heaven and earth . . . and clouds full of water and Man were created by the Trinity on 26th October 4004 BC at nine o'clock in the morning.'

Lord Kelvin (1824–1907) calculated in 1899 that the Earth was some hundreds of millions of years old. At the beginning of the 20th century radioactive decay was used as a measurement of geochronology. In 1907 the American chemist and physicist B.B. Boltwood showed that a sample of pre-Cambrian rock dated from 1640 million years before the present (BP) measured by the uranium-lead method.

Modern dating methods, using the duration of radioisotopic half-lives, include also the contrasts obtained from thorium-lead, potassium-argon, rubidium-strontium, rhenium-osmium, helium-uranium and, in the recent range of up to 40 000 years BP, carbon-14. Modern developments, using accelerator equipment, allow carbon-14 dating to extend back beyond 100 000 years. Other methods include thermoluminescence (used since 1968) and racemization of amino acids (used since 1972) – the latter method is dependent upon the rate of change from optically active to inactive forms over a long-term period of time.

The four eras into which geological time is usually divided are: the Cenozoic (Greek *kainos* 'new'), the most recent; the Mesozoic (Greek *mesos* 'middle'); the Palaeozoic (Greek *palaios* 'ancient'); and the Proterozoic (Greek *protos* 'first') or Precambrian. The Hadean and Archaean periods – usually regarded as divisions of the Proterozoic – are sometimes added before the Proterozoic as distinct eras.

THE GEOLOGICAL TIME CHART

PROTEROZOIC or PRECAMBRIAN ERA
began 4600 million years ago

PALAEOZOIC ERA
Cambrian period began 570 million years ago
Ordovician period began 510 million years ago
Silurian period began 438 million years ago
Devonian period began 410 million years ago
Carboniferous period began 355 million years ago
divided in the USA into:
    Mississippian period (lower) and
    Pennsylvanian period (upper)
Permian period began 300 million years ago

MESOZOIC ERA
Triassic period began 250 million years ago
Jurassic period began 205 million years ago
Cretaceous period began 135 million years ago

CENOZOIC ERA
Tertiary period:
    Palaeocene epoch began 65 million years ago
    Eocene epoch began 53 million years ago
    Oligocene epoch began 34 million years ago
    Miocene epoch began 23 million years ago
    Pliocene epoch began 5.3 million years ago
Quaternary period:
    Pleistocene epoch began 1.6 million years ago
    Holocene epoch began 0.01 million years ago

PHYSICAL GEOGRAPHY

THE OCEANS

The oceans cover a greater area of the Earth than does the land – 71% or almost three quarters of the Earth's surface. The three major oceans are the Pacific, Atlantic and Indian Oceans. The Pacific is the largest ocean, and covers more than a third of the surface of the Earth. The Arctic Ocean is smaller than the other three and is covered almost entirely by ice. Seas are smaller than the four oceans.

The depth of the oceans is very small compared with their area. The deepest part – in the Western Pacific – is only about 11 000 m (36 000 ft) deep. However this is greater than the height of the highest mountain on land, Mount Everest.

SEA WATER

Sea water has solid substances dissolved in it. Sodium and chlorine (which together in their solid form make up sodium chloride – common salt) are the most abundant of these, and together with magnesium, calcium and potassium make up over 90% of the elements dissolved in sea water. Other elements are present only in very small amounts.

The saltiness, or salinity, of sea water depends on the amount of these substances dissolved in it. An average of about 3.5% of the volume of sea water consists of dissolved substances. High evaporation removes more of the pure water, leaving behind the dissolved substances, so the salinity is higher where evaporation is high, particularly if the sea water is also enclosed and cannot mix easily with the sea water in a larger ocean. This occurs, for example, in the Mediterranean and Red Seas. Low values of salinity occur in polar regions, particularly in the summer months when melting ice dilutes the sea water. Low salinity also occurs in seas such as the Baltic, which is linked to the Atlantic Ocean only by a narrow channel and which is fed by a larger number of freshwater rivers.

Most of the water on the Earth, about 94% of it, is in the oceans. More pure water is evaporated from the oceans than is returned as precipitation (rain, snow, etc), but the volume of water in the oceans remains the same because water is also returned to the oceans from the land by rivers.

WAVES

Sea water is rarely still: it is usually moving in waves, tides or currents. Waves are caused by wind blowing across the surface of the ocean. The height of a wave is determined by the wind speed, the time the wind has been blowing, and the distance the wave has travelled over the ocean. The highest wave ever recorded had a height of 34 m (116 ft), although usually they are much smaller. Waves play a very important role in the shaping of coastlines.

Water does not move along with waves. Instead the water changes shape as a wave passes, moving in a roughly circular motion, rising towards a wave crest as it arrives and falling as it passes. This motion can be seen by watching a boat: the boat bobs up and down as the waves move past it but does not move along with the waves.

There is another type of wave in the ocean, which is not generated by the winds. These are *tsunami*. They are also popularly called *tidal waves*, but this name is quite wrong because they are not caused by tides. Tsunami are due to earthquakes or the eruption of undersea volcanoes, which move a large amount of water rapidly, disturbing the sea surface and creating waves that travel away from the area of the earthquake or volcano. Tsunami travel at very high speeds, around 750 km/h (470 mph). However, in the open ocean they cause little damage because their wave height is very low, usually less than 1 m (3¼ ft), but in shallow water they slow down and their height increases to 10 m (33 ft) or more, and they can cause extensive damage when they hit a shore.

TIDES

Tides are caused by the gravitational pull of the Moon and the Sun on the Earth, causing the level of the oceans to change. The pull is greatest on the side of the Earth facing the Moon, and this produces a high tide. The pull is weakest on the side away from the Moon, where the sea water rises away from the Moon, and this also gives a high tide.

The Sun is much further away than the Moon and although it is much larger its effect on tides is less than half that of the Moon. When both the Moon and the Sun are on the same or opposite sides of the Earth, the pull is greatest, producing *spring tides*. Weaker tides, called *neap tides*, occur when the Moon and the Sun form a right angle with the Earth, because the pulls of the two are in different directions. Spring tides occur every 14 days and neap tides half-way between each spring tide.

There are two high tides and two low tides every day in most parts of the Earth, but a few areas have only one high tide and one low tide, or a mixture, with one high tide being much higher than the other. The *tidal range* (the difference between the high and the low water levels) varies from place to place, from less than a metre (3¼ ft) in the Mediterranean Sea and Gulf of Mexico to 14.5 m (47½ ft) in the Bay of Fundy on the coast of Canada.

CURRENTS

The currents near the surface of the oceans, like waves, are driven by the winds. The wind drags the water along with the wind. Currents move much more slowly than the wind, with speeds of less than 8 km/h (5 mph). They do not flow exactly in the same direction as the wind, but are deflected to one side by the Earth's spin.

FEATURES OF THE SEA BED

The region of the sea bed closest to land is the *continental margin*, which is divided into the *continental shelf*, *slope* and (sometimes) the *continental rise*. The continental shelf is the shallowest – around 130 m (430 ft) deep – and is relatively flat. It is about 100 km (60 mi) wide. The sea water over continental shelves usually has abundant marine life and most fishing is done here. About a quarter of the world's supply of oil and gas comes from the rocks beneath the continental shelves.

OCEANIC RIDGES

These are vast, rugged, undersea mountain chains often, but not always, at the centre of oceans. On average they are some 1000 km (620 mi) wide and stand up to 3000 m (10 000 ft) above the adjacent ocean basins. They form a more or less linked system about 80 000 km (50 000 mi) long, and this system enters all the major oceans. Different parts of it have different names: in the centre and south Atlantic, for example, it is called the Mid-Atlantic Ridge; in the north Atlantic to the southwest of Iceland it is the Reykjañes Ridge; in the Pacific it is known as the East Pacific Rise. On average, ridge crests lie some 2500 m (8200 ft) below the ocean surface, but there are a few places, such as Iceland, where the rocks have risen above the water surface, forming an island.

Between the ocean ridges and the continental margins there are *abyssal plains*. These are very flat and featureless parts of the sea floor, around 4000 m (13 000 ft) deep. Abyssal plains are broken in some places by *seamounts*, underwater volcanoes that have erupted from the sea floor. Seamounts may rise above the sea surface to form islands, such as Hawaii.

The deepest parts of the oceans are the *ocean trenches*. These are on average about 100 km (62 mi) wide and 7000–8000 m (23 000–26 000 ft) deep, and may be thousands of kilometres long.

COASTLINES

The country with the longest coastline is Canada, which has a total littoral (including islands) in excess of 244 000 km (151 600 mi). The USSR has a coast 106 300 km (66 050 mi) long, Australia 36 735 km (22 826 mi) and Japan 33 287 km (20 684 mi), but the coastline of Monaco is only 5.6 km (3.5 mi).

EURO FACTS

COASTLINES OF COUNTRIES IN THE EUROPEAN COMMUNITY

UK[1]	16 800 km (10 433 mi)
Greece	15 021 km (9334 mi)
Italy[2]	7500 km (4658 mi)
Denmark[3]	7314 km (4545 mi)
Spain[4]	5940 km (3691 mi)
France[5]	5500 km (3418 mi)
Ireland[6]	2669 km (1658 mi)
Germany[7]	1720 km (1068 mi)
Netherlands	1200 km (746 mi)
Portugal[8]	845 km (525 mi)
Belgium	66 km (41 mi)
Luxembourg	is landlocked

[1] including Northern Ireland but excluding the Channel Islands and the Isle of Man
[2] including Sicily and Sardinia
[3] excluding the Faeroes
[4] including the Canary and Balearic Islands
[5] 'metropolitan France', excluding overseas départements
[6] the Republic of Ireland only
[7] including the former East Germany
[8] excluding Madeira and the Azores

DEEP-SEA TRENCHES

Length (km)	Length (miles)	Name	Deepest point	Depth (m)	Depth (ft)
2250	*1400*	Mariana Trench,* W Pacific	Challenger Deep†	11 022	*36 160*
2575	*1600*	Tonga-Kermadec Trench,‡ S Pacific	Vityaz 11 (Tonga)	10 882	*35 702*
2250	*1400*	Kuril-Kamchatka Trench,* W Pacific		10 542	*34 587*
1325	*825*	Philippine Trench, W Pacific	Galathea Deep	10 497	*34 439*
		Idzu-Bonin Trench (sometimes included in the Japan Trench, see below)		9 810	*32 196*
800	*500*	Puerto Rico Trench, W Atlantic	Milwaukee Deep	9 220	*30 249*
320+	*200+*	New Hebrides Trench, S Pacific	North Trench	9 165	*30 080*
640	*400*	Solomon or New Britain Trench, S Pacific		9 140	*29 988*
560	*350*	Yap Trench,* W Pacific		8 527	*27 976*
1600	*1000*	Japan Trench,* W Pacific		8 412	*27 591*
965	*600*	South Sandwich Trench, S Atlantic	Meteor Deep	8 263	*27 112*
3200	*2000*	Aleutian Trench, N Pacific		8 100	*26 574*
3540	*2200*	Peru-Chile (Atacama) Trench E Pacific	Bartholomew Deep	8 064	*26 454*
		Palau Trench (sometimes included in the Yap Trench)		8 050	*26 420*
965	*600*	Romanche Trench, N-S Atlantic		7 864	*25 800*
2250	*1400*	Java (Sunda) Trench, Indian Ocean	Planet Deep	7 725	*25 344*
965	*600*	Cayman Trench, Caribbean		7 535	*24 720*
1040	*650*	Nansei Shotó (Ryukyu) Trench, W Pacific		7 505	*24 630*
240	*150*	Banda Trench, Banda Sea		7 360	*24 155*

* These four trenches are sometimes regarded as a single 7400 km (4600 mile) long system.
† In March 1959 the USSR research ship *Vityaz* claimed 11 022 m (36 198 ft), using echo-sounding only.
‡ Kermadec Trench is sometimes considered to be a separate feature. Depth 10 047 m (32 974 ft).

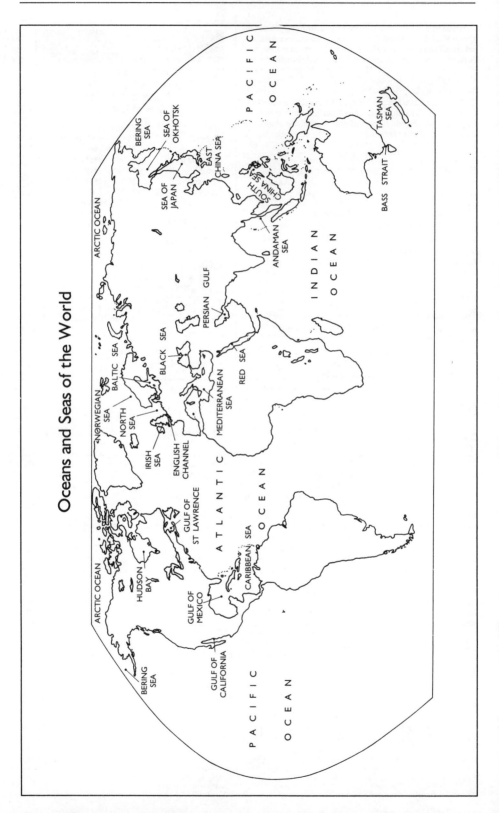

Oceans and Seas of the World

OCEANS

Ocean with adjacent seas	Area (millions km²)	Area (millions miles²)	Percentage of world area	Greatest depth (m)	Greatest depth (ft)	Greatest depth location	Average depth (m)	Average depth (ft)
Pacific	181·20	69·96	35·52	11 022	36 160	Mariana Trench	4188	13 740
Atlantic	106·48	41·11	20·88	9 460	31 037	Puerto Rico Trench	3736	12 257
Indian	74·06	28·59	14·52	7 542	24 744	Java Trench	3872	12 703
Total	361·74	139·66	70·92					

If the adjacent seas are detached and the Arctic regarded as an ocean, the oceanic areas are:

	Area (km²)	Area (m²)	Percentage of sea area
Pacific	166 240 000	64 190 000	46·0
Atlantic	86 560 000	33 420 000	23·9
Indian	73 430 000	28 350 000	20·3
Arctic	13 230 000	5 110 000	3·7
Other Seas	22 280 000	8 600 000	6·1

Ocean depths are zoned by oceanographers as *bathyl* (down to 2000 m or 6560 ft); *abyssal* (between 2000 m and 6000 m (6560 ft and 19 685 ft)) and *hadal* (below 6000 m (19 685 ft)).

SEAS

Principal seas	Average Area (km²)	Average Area (miles²)	depth (m)	depth (ft)
1. South China*	2 974 600	1 148 500	1200	4000
2. Caribbean Sea	2 753 000	1 063 000	2400	8000
3. Mediterranean Sea	2 503 000	966 750	1485	4875
4. Bering Sea	2 268 180	875 750	1400	4700
5. Gulf of Mexico	1 542 985	595 750	1500	5000
6. Sea of Okhotsk	1 527 570	589 800	840	2750
7. East China Sea	1 249 150	482 300	180	600
8. Hudson Bay	1 232 300	475 800	120	400
9. Sea of Japan	1 007 500	389 000	1370	4500
10. Andaman Sea	797 700	308 000	865	2850
11. North Sea	575 300	222 125	90	300
12. Black Sea	461 980	178 375	1100	3600
13. Red Sea	437 700	169 000	490	1610
14. Baltic Sea	422 160	163 000	55	190
15. Persian Gulf†	238 790	92 200	24	80
16. Gulf of St Lawrence	237 760	91 800	120	400
17. Gulf of California	162 000	62 530	810	2660
18. English Channel	89 900	34 700	54	177
19. Irish Sea	88 550	34 200	60	197
20. Bass Strait	75 000	28 950	70	230

* The Malayan Sea, which embraces the South China Sea and the Straits of Malacca (8 142 000 km²/3 144 000 miles²), is not now an entity accepted by the International Hydrographic Bureau.
† Also referred to as the Arabian Gulf or, popularly, 'the Gulf'.

MOUNTAINS

Mountains and mountain ranges are largely formed by the interaction of mountain-building processes (orogeny) and the subsequent erosional processes that tend to destroy them. The distribution of the world's major mountain ranges generally follows those belts of the Earth's landmasses where earthquakes and volcanoes are common. These phenomena are in turn caused by the collision of the moving plates that make up the Earth's lithosphere (see p. 54). Such collisions often result in the margin of one plate being forced upwards, and this process has resulted in the formation of many mountain ranges, although other processes may also play a part in mountain building.

The Earth's largest mountain ranges today – the Alps, Himalaya, Rockies and Andes – are all relatively young, resulting from plate collisions in the last 25 million years or so. Much older ranges include the Scottish Highlands, the Scandinavian mountains and the Appalachians in the USA, which are all around 300-400 million years old. The deeply eroded remnants of even older ranges – up to 3000 million years old – occur in many parts of Africa and Australia.

FOLDED MOUNTAINS

The world's largest and most complex continental mountain ranges are the result of the collision of tectonic plates. Mountains formed directly by plate collisions are known as *fold mountains*, because they are conspicuously folded, faulted and otherwise deformed by the hugh collision pressures. In some cases the collision is between landmasses. Thus India is pressing into the rest of Asia to form the Himalaya, and Africa is being forced into Europe, producing the Alps. In other cases the collision is between an oceanic plate and a continent. Thus the Pacific plate is spreading towards South America, forcing up the Andes. The Himalaya, the Alps and the Andes are still being formed, but some mountain ranges – for example, the Urals of the USSR and the Appalachians of the USA – are the products of older, long-ceased plate collisions.

FAULT-BLOCK AND UPWARPED MOUNTAINS

Other types of mountain exist that have not been formed by plate collisions. In *fault-block mountains* a central block of the Earth's crust has sunk and the adjacent blocks have been forced upwards. Mountains of this type define the Basin and Range Province of the western USA (Nevada and parts of Utah, New Mexico, Arizona and California) and form the Sierra Nevada of California and the Teton Range of Wyoming.

In *upwarped mountains*, on the other hand, a central block has been forced upwards. Examples are the Black Hills of Dakota and the Adirondacks of New York.

VOLCANIC MOUNTAINS

Spectacular mountains may also be built by volcanic action. Mauna Loa in Hawaii, for example, is, at 10 203 m (33 476 ft), the world's highest mountain if measured from the Pacific Ocean floor, although less than half is above sea level. Much more important than such isolated volcanoes, however, are the oceanic ridges, the undersea mountain ranges along which the bulk of the Earth's volcanism takes place (see p. 72). Intense volcanism also occurs where oceanic and continental plates collide. The Andes, for example, owe not a little of their mass to volcanic activity.

WORLD'S HIGHEST MOUNTAINS

Key to Ranges: H = Himalaya K = Karakoram.
Subsidiary peaks or tops in the same mountain massif are italicized.

Mountain	Height (m)	Height (ft)	Range	Date of First Ascent (if any)
1. Mount Everest*	8863	*29 078*	H	29 May 1953
Everest South Summit	*8750*	*28 707*	*H*	*26 May 1953*
2. K2 (Chogori)	8610	*28 250*	K	31 July 1954
3. Kangchenjunga	8598	*28 208*	H	25 May 1955
Yalung Kang (Kangchenjunga West)	*8502*	*27 894*	*H*	*14 May 1973*
Kangchenjunga South Peak	*8488*	*27 848*	*H*	*19 May 1978*
Kangchenjunga Middle Peak	*8475*	*27 806*	*H*	*22 May 1978*
4. Lhotse	8511	*27 923*	H	18 May 1956
Subsidiary Peak	*8410*	*27 591*	*H*	*unclimbed*
Lhotse Shar	*8383*	*27 504*	*H*	*12 May 1970*
5. Makalu I	8481	*27 824*	H	15 May 1955
Makalu South-East	*8010*	*26 280*	*H*	*unclimbed*
6. Dhaulagiri I	8167	*26 795*	H	13 May 1960
7. Manaslu I (Kutang I)	8156	*26 760*	H	9 May 1956
8. Cho Oyu	8153	*26 750*	H	19 Oct 1954
9. Nanga Parbat (Diamir)	8124	*26 660*	H	3 July 1953
10. Annapurna I	8091	*26 546*	H	3 June 1950
Annapurna East	*8010*	*26 280*	*H*	*29 Apr 1974*
11. Gasherbrum I (Hidden Peak)	8068	*26 470*	K	5 July 1958
12. Broad Peak I	8047	*26 400*	K	9 June 1957
Broad Peak Middle	*8016*	*26 300*	*K*	*28 July 1975*
Broad Peak Central	*8000*	*26 246*	*K*	*28 July 1975*
13. Shisham Pangma (Gosainthan)	8046	*26 398*	H	2 May 1964
14. Gasherbrum II	8034	*26 360*	K	7 July 1956

*known in Chinese as Qomolangma, in Nepalese as Sagarmatha and in Tibetan as Mi-ti gu-ti cha-pu long-na.

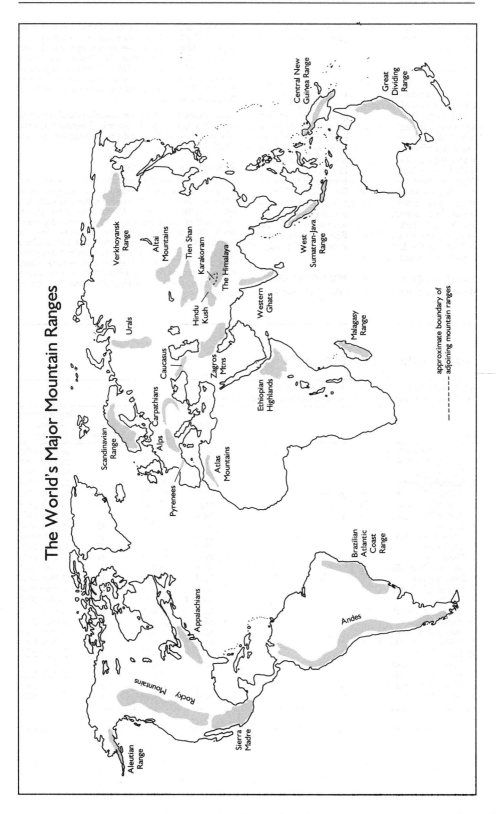

The World's Major Mountain Ranges

WORLD'S GREATEST MOUNTAIN RANGES

The greatest mountain system is the Himalaya–Karakoram–Hindu Kush–Pamir range, with 104 peaks over 7315 m (24 000 ft). The second greatest range is the Andes, with 54 peaks over 6096 m (20 000 ft).

Length (km)	Length (miles)	Name	Location	Culminating Peak	Height (m)	Height (ft)
7200	4500	Andes	W South America	Aconcagua (Argentina)	6960	22 834
4800	3000	Rocky Mountains	W North America	Mt Elbert (USA)	4400	14 433
3800	2400	Himalaya–Karakoram–Hindu Kush	S Central Asia	Mt Everest (China/Nepal)	8863	29 078
3600	2250	Great Dividing Range	E Australia	Kosciusko	2230	7 316
3500	2200	Trans-Antarctic Mts	Antarctica	Mt Vinson	5140	16 863
3000	1900	Brazilian Atlantic Coast Range	E Brazil	Pico de Bandeira	2890	9 482
2900	1800	West Sumatran–Javan Range	W Sumatra and Java	Kerintji	3805	12 484
2650*	1650*	Aleutian Range	Alaska and NW Pacific	Shishaldin	2861	9 387
2250	1400	Tien Shan	S Central Asia	Pik Pobeda	7439	24 406
2000	1250	Central New Guinea Range	Irian Jaya/Papua New Guinea	Jayakusumu or Ngga Pulut†	5030	16 503
2000	1250	Altai Mountains	Central Asia (USSR)	Gora Belukha	4505	14 783
2010	1250	Ural Mountains	Russian Federation	Gora Narodnaya	1894	6 214
1930	1200	Kamchatka Mountains**	Russian Federation	Klyuchevskaya Sopka	4850	15 910
1930	1200	Atlas Mountains	NW Africa	Jebel Toubkal (Morocco)	4165	13 665
1610	1000	Verkhoyansk Mountains	Russian Federation	Gora Mas Khaya	2959	9 708
1610	1000	Western Ghats	W India	Anai Madi	2694	8 841
1530	950	Sierra Madre Oriental	Mexico	Citlaltépetl or Orizaba	5610	18 405
1530	950	Zagros Mountains	Iran	Zard Kuh	4547	14 921
1530	950	Scandinavian Range	Norway/Sweden	Galdhopiggen (Norway)	2469	8 098
1450	900	Ethiopian Highlands	Ethiopia	Ras Dashen	4620	15 158
1450	900	Sierra Madre Occidental	Mexico	Nevado de Colima	4265	13 993
1370	850	Malagasy Range	Madagascar	Tsaratanana	2885	9 465
1290	800	Drakensberg	SE Africa	Thabana Ntlenyana (Lesotho)	3482	11 425
1290	800	Chersky Range	Russian Federation	Gora Pobeda	3147	10 325
1200	750	Caucasus	Georgia/Russian Federation, USSR	Elbrus, West Peak	5642	18 510
1130	700	Alaska Range	Alaska, USA	Mt McKinley, South Peak	6194	20 320
1130	700	Assam–Burma Range	Assam/Burma (Myanmar)	Hkakabo Razi (Burma)	5881	19 296
1130	700	Cascade Range	Northwest USA/Canada	Mt Rainier (USA)	4392	14 410
1130	700	Central Borneo Range	Central Borneo	Kinabalu (Malaysia)	4101	13 455
1130	700	Apennines	Italy	Corno Grande	2931	9 617
1130	700	Appalachians	Eastern USA/Canada	Mt Mitchell (USA)	2037	6 684
1050	650	Alps	Central Europe	Mt Blanc (France)	4807	15 771

* Continuous mainland length (excluding islands) 720 km (450 miles).
** Comprises the Sredin and Koryak Mountains.
† Formerly known as Mount Sukarno and Carstensz Pyramide.

HIGHEST MOUNTAINS OF NORTH AND CENTRAL AMERICA

Mt McKinley (known to local Indians as Denali) is the only peak in excess of 6100 m (20 000 ft) in North and Central America. It was first climbed on 7 June 1913.

Name	Height (m)	Height (ft)	Country
1. Mt McKinley, South Peak	6194	20 320	Alaska, USA
2. Mt Logan	5951	19 524	Yukon, Canada
3. Citlaltépetl (Orizaba)	5610	18 405	Mexico
4. Mt St Elias	5489	18 008	Alaska, USA/Yukon, Canada
5. Popocatépetl	5452	17 887	Mexico
6. Mt Foraker	5304	17 400	Alaska, USA
7. Ixtaccihuatl	5286	17 342	Mexico
8. Mt Lucania	5227	17 150	Yukon, Canada
9. King Peak	5221	17 130	Alaska, USA
10. Mt Blackburn	5036	16 522	Alaska, USA
11. Mt Steele	5011	16 440	Alaska, USA
12. Mt Bona	5005	16 420	Alaska, USA

Note: Mt McKinley, North Peak, is 5934 m (*19 470 ft*).

HIGHEST MOUNTAINS OF SOUTH AMERICA

The mountains of the Andes are headed by Aconcagua at 6960 m (22 834 ft) – first climbed on 14 January 1897. Aconcagua is the highest mountain in the world outside the great ranges of Central Asia.

Name	Height (m)	Height (ft)	Country
1. Cerro Aconcagua	6960	22 834	Argentina
2. Ojos de Salado	6895	22 588	Argentina/Chile
3. Nevado de Pissis	6780	22 244	Argentina/Chile
4. Huascarán Sur	6768	22 205	Peru
5. Llullaillaco	6723	22 057	Argentina/Chile
6. Mercadario	6670	21 884	Argentina/Chile
7. Huascarán Norte	6655	21 834	Peru
8. Yerupajá	6634	21 765	Peru
9. Nevados de Tres Crucées	6620	21 720	Argentina/Chile
10. Coropuna	6613	21 696	Peru
11. Nevado Incahuasi	6601	21 657	Argentina/Chile
12. Tupungato	6550	21 490	Argentina/Chile
13. Sajama	6542	21 463	Bolivia
14. Nevado Gonzalez	6500	21 326	Argentina

HIGHEST MOUNTAINS OF AFRICA

All the peaks listed in Zaïre and Uganda are in the Ruwenzori Mountains.

Name	Height (m)	Height (ft)	Location
1. Kilimanjaro[1]	5894	19 340	Tanzania
Hans Meyer Peak, Mawenzi	5148	16 890	
Shira Peak	4005	13 139	
2. Mt Kenya (Batian)	5199	17 058	Kenya
3. Mt Ngaliema[2]	5118	16 763	Zaïre/Uganda
4. Duwoni[3]	4896	16 062	Uganda
5. Mount Baker (Edward Peak)	4843	15 889	Uganda
6. Mount Emin[4]	4798	15 741	Zaïre
7. Mount Gessi[5]	4715	15 470	Uganda
8. Sella Peak[6]	4626	15 179	Uganda
9. Ras Dashen (Rasdajan)	4620	15 158	Ethiopia
10. Humphreys Peak	4578	15 021	Uganda

[1] Uhuru Point (also called Kibo and formerly called Kaiser Wilhelm Spitze).
[2] Formerly called Mt Stanley and Margherita Peak.
[3] Formerly called Mt Speke and Vittorio Emanuele Peak.
[4] Formerly called Umberto Peak.
[5] Formerly called Iolanda Peak.
[6] Formerly called Mt Luigi di Savoia.

HIGHEST MOUNTAINS OF OCEANIA

Several of the mountains of West Irian are known by more than one name. Some have changed their name since colonial days, while more than one mountain has been named Sukarno or Peak Sukarno.

The two highest mountains in Polynesia are Mauna Kea – 4205 m (13 796 ft) – and Mauna Loa – 4170 m (13 680 ft). The former is an extinct volcano; the latter is an active volcano. Both are in Hawaii, which has been politically part of the USA since 21 Aug 1959.

The highest mountain in Australia is Mt Kosciusko – 2230 m (7316 ft) – in the Snowy Mountains, New South Wales.

The highest mountain in New Zealand is Mt Cook – (3764 m (12 349 ft) – which is called Aorangi by the Maoris.

Name	Height (m)	Height (ft)	Location
1. Jayakusumu or Ngga Pulu[1]	5030	*16 503*	West Irian
2. Daam	4922	*16 250*	West Irian
3. Oost Carstensz[2]	4840	*15 879*	West Irian
4. Trikora[3]	4730	*15 518*	West Irian
5. Enggea[4]	4717	*15 475*	West Irian
6. Mandala[5]	4640	*15 223*	West Irian
7. Mt Wilhelm	4509	*14 493*	Papua New Guinea

[1] Also known as Jaya, and formerly known as Mount Sukarno, Peak Sukarno and Carstensz Pyramid.
[2] Also known as Jayakusumu Timur.
[3] Formerly known as Sukarno and Wilhelmina.
[4] Formerly Idenburg Top.
[5] Formerly Juliana.

HIGHEST MOUNTAINS OF ALPINE EUROPE

Subsidiary peaks or tops on the same massif have been omitted except in the case of Mont Blanc and Monte Rosa, where they have been indented in italic type.

Name	Height (m)	Height (ft)	Country	First Ascent
1. Mont Blanc	4807	*15 771*	France	1786
Monte Bianco di Courmayeur	4748	*15 577*	Italy[1]–France	1877
Le Mont Maudit	4465	*14 649*	Italy–France	1878
Picco Luigi Amedeo	4460	*14 632*	Italy	1878
Dôme du Goûter	4304	*14 120*	France	1784
2. Monte Rosa				
Dufourspitze	4634	*15 203*	Switzerland	1855
Nordend	4609	*15 121*	Swiss–Italian border	1861
Ostspitze	4596	*15 078*	Swiss–Italian border	1854
Zumstein Spitze	4563	*14 970*	Swiss–Italian border	1820
Signal Kuppe	4556	*14 947*	Swiss–Italian border	1842
3. Dom	4545	*14 911*	Switzerland	1858
4. Lyskamm (Liskamm)	4527	*14 853*	Swiss–Italian border	1861
5. Weisshorn	4506	*14 780*	Switzerland	1861
6. Täschhorn	4491	*14 733*	Switzerland	1862
7. Matterhorn	4476	*14 683*	Swiss–Italian border	1865
8. Dent Blanche	4357	*14 293*	Switzerland	1862
9. Nadelhorn	4327	*14 196*	Switzerland	1858
10. Grand Combin	4314	*14 153*	Switzerland	1859
11. Lenzspitze	4294	*14 087*	Switzerland	1870
12. Finsteraarhorn	4274	*14 021*	Switzerland	1829*

* Also reported climbed in 1812 but evidence lacking.

[1]The highest point in Italian territory is a shoulder of the main summit of Mont Blanc (Monte Bianco) through which a 4760 m (15 616 ft) contour passes. The highest top exclusively in Italian territory is Picco Luigi Amedeo (see above) to the south of the main Mont Blanc peak, which is itself exclusively in French territory.

HIGHEST MOUNTAINS OF CAUCASIA

One of the two traditional geographical boundaries of Europe – see The Continents (p. 55) – runs along the spine of the Caucasus Mountains, which include the following peaks higher than Mont Blanc – 4807 m (15 771 ft).

Name	Height (m)	Height (ft)
1. Elbrus, West Peak	5642	18 510
Elbrus, East Peak	*5595*	*18 356*
2. Dykh Tau	5203	17 070
3. Shkhara	5201	17 063
4. Pik Shota Rustaveli	5190	17 028
5. Koshtantau	5144	16 876
6. Pik Pushkin	5100	16 732
7. Jangi Tau, West Peak	5051	16 572
Janga, East Peak	*5038*	*16 529*
8. Dzhangi Tau	5049	16 565
9. Kazbek	5047	16 558
10. Katyn Tau (Adish)	4985	16 355
11. Pik Rustaveli	4960	16 272
12. Mishirgi, West Peak	4922	16 148
Mishirgitau, East Peak	*4917*	*16 135*
13. Kunjum Mishirgi	4880	16 011
14. Gestola	4860	15 944
15. Tetnuld	4853	15 921

HIGHEST MOUNTAINS IN THE PYRENEES

The greater part of the boundary between Spain and France runs along the crest of the Pyrenees. The range contains the following peaks over 3200 m.

Name	Height (m)	Height (ft)
1. Pico de Aneto (Spain)	3407	11 178
2. Pico de Posets (Spain)	3375	11 073
3. Monte Perdido (Spain)	3352	10 997
4. Pico de la Maladeta (Spain)	3312	10 866
5. Pic de Vignemale (France/ Spain)	3298	10 820
6. Pic de Marboré (France)	3253	10 673

HIGHEST MOUNTAINS IN SCANDINAVIA

The Scandinavian peninsula consists mainly of uplands, including the following peaks over 2200 m.

Name	Height (m)	Height (ft)
1. Galdhoppigen (Norway)	2469	8098
2. Glittertind (Norway)	2468	8097
3. Skagastolstindane (Norway)	2405	7890
4. Snohetta (Norway)	2286	7500

HIGHEST MOUNTAINS IN THE CARPATHIANS

The great arc of the Carpathians stretches from the Danube near Bratislava, in Czechoslovakia, to central Romania. The range — which passes through Slovakia, southern Poland (as the Tatra Mountains) and the western Ukraine — contains the following peaks over 2400 m.

Name	Height (m)	Height (ft)
1. Gerlachovka (Czecho- slovakia)	2655	8711
2. Moldoveanu (Romania)	2544	8346
3. Negoiu (Romania)	2543	8343
4. Mindra (Romania)	2518	8261
5. Peleanga (Romania)	2511	8238
6. Rysy (Poland)	2499	8199

HIGHEST MOUNTAINS OF ANTARCTICA

The following mountains are the highest peaks surveyed in Antarctica. Large areas of Greater Antarctica remain unsurveyed, particularly the regions inland of Wilkes Land, Enderby Land and Queen Maud Land.

Name	Height (m)	Height (ft)
1. Mt Vinson	5140	16 863
2. Mt Tyree	4965	16 289
3. Mt Shinn*	4800	15 750
4. Mt Gardner	4690	15 387
5. Mt Epperley	4602	15 098
6. Mt Kirkpatrick	4511	14 799

* *volcanic*

EURO FACTS

HIGHEST SUMMITS IN EC COUNTRIES

Belgium
Mount Botrange (Signal de Botrange) in the Ardennes 694 m (2272 ft)
Denmark[1]
Yding Skovhoj in Jutland 173 m (568 ft)
France
Mont Blanc in the Alps 4807 m (15 771 ft)
Germany
Zugspitze in the Bavarian Alps 2963 m (9721 ft)
Greece
Mount Olympus in Thessaly 2911 m (9550 ft)
Ireland
Carrauntuohill in the Macgillicuddy's Reeks 1041 m (3414 ft)
Italy
The highest point in Italy is a point just below the summit of Mont Blanc (Monte Bianco) in the Alps 4760 m (15 616 ft)
The highest peak in Italy is Mont Blanc de Courmayeur 4748 m (15 577 ft)
Luxembourg
Huldange in the Oesling plateau 550 m (1833 ft)
Netherlands
Vaalserberg in Limburg 321 m (1053 ft)
Portugal
Pico in the Azores 2315 m (67713 ft)
Spain
Pico del Tiede in the Canary Islands 3716 m (12 192 ft)
The highest peak in mainland Spain is Mulhacén in the Sierra Nevada 3478 m (11 411 ft)
United Kingdom
Ben Nevis in the Scottish Highlands 1392 m (4406 ft)

[1] 'Metropolitan' Denmark – neither the Faeroes nor Greenland is included within the EC.

VOLCANOES

A volcano is a mountain, often conical in shape, which has been built up above an opening in the Earth's crust during violent and spectacular events called *eruptions*. When these occur, molten rock, or *magma*, wells up from deep below ground and is thrown out through the opening, frequently with other rock debris.

Few spectacles in nature are more awesome or more terrifying than volcanic eruptions. In the most violent ones, tremendous explosions inside the volcano hurl large rocks, cinders and great clouds of ash, steam and gas high into the sky from the *crater*, at the top. Streams of molten rock known as *lava*, and sometimes boiling mud, pour down the surrounding slopes destroying everything in their path.

Although above 800 volcanoes have been recorded as active in historic times, 500 to 350 million years ago there were very violent periods of volcanic activity. Many thousands of volcanoes erupted constantly, and many mountain ranges today consist of the remains of long dead volcanoes. Even now, thousands of volcanoes may be erupting unseen beneath the oceans. Many volcanoes soar to great heights amid the Earth's major mountain ranges. The highest is Aconcagua, a snow-clad peak 6960 m (22 834 ft) high in the Andes of Argentina.

Because Aconcagua no longer erupts, it is said to be *extinct*. Other volcanoes that have been quiet for a very long time but may erupt again are described as *dormant*. Volcanoes that are known to have erupted in historic times are referred to as *active*, and these are always dangerous. The highest volcano regarded as active is Ojos del Salado, which rises to a height of 6895 m (22 588 ft) on the frontier between Chile and Argentina. The mountain has recently produced vents emitting hot gases and steam known as *fumaroles*.

In modern times, scientists have been able to observe and record the dramatic birth and growth of new volcanoes. A famous example is Paricutín, Mexico, which began as a plume of smoke in a farmer's field in 1943 and by 1952 had grown more than 430 m (1400 ft). Another appeared 20 years later, when the volcanic island of Surtsey emerged from the sea off southern Iceland amid loud explosions and billowing clouds of ash and steam. The new island now occupies 2.5 km² (1 sq mi).

WHAT CAUSES VOLCANIC ERUPTIONS?

Volcanoes are like gigantic safety valves that release the tremendous pressures that build up inside the Earth. These pressures are affected by the constant movement of the plates that make up the surface crust (see p. 55). As a result of this movement, molten magma in the mantle is sometimes forced upward under pressure through any breaks it can find in the surface rocks. As it rises, gases dissolved in it are released by the fall in pressure, and the magma shoots out of the volcano in explosive eruptions.

THE EARTH'S VOLCANIC ZONES

Volcanoes are found where the Earth's crust is weakest, especially along the edges of the crustal plates and most notably in the 'Ring of Fire' around the Pacific Ocean plate. Large numbers of volcanoes, known as *abyssal volcanoes*, are also scattered over the ocean floors away from the plate margins. Here the crust is only about 5 km (3 mi) thick and is easily breached by molten magma rising from the mantle below. Localized hot spots in the mantle also cause the formation of volcanoes, such as those in the Hawaiian Islands and those found on land away from the plate margins.

SOME MAJOR VOLCANIC ERUPTIONS

Santoríni (Thera)   *Height*: 584 m (1960 ft)
Location: Cyclades, Greece
Date: c. 1550 BC
A massive explosion virtually destroyed the island, and is thought by some to have contributed to the demise of Minoan civilization on nearby Crete. The disaster may also have given rise to the legend of the lost city of Atlantis.

Vesuvius   *Height*: 1280 m (4198 ft)
Location: Bay of Naples, Italy
Date: AD 79
The towns of Pompeii, Herculaneum and Stabiae were completely buried, and thousands died. In 1631 3000 people were killed, since when there have been around 20 major eruptions, the last in 1944.

Unnamed   *Height*: unknown
Location: North Island, New Zealand
Date: c. AD 130
Around 30 million tonnes (tons) of pumice were ejected, creating the vast caldera now filled by Lake Taupo. An area of c. 16 000 km² (6180 sq mi) was devastated – the most violent of all documented volcanic events.

Etna   *Height*: 3311 m (10 855 ft)
Location: Sicily, Italy
Date: 1669
20 000 people were killed, and lava overran the west part of the city of Catania, 28 km (17 mi) from the summit.

Kelud   *Height*: 1731 m (5679 ft)
Location: Java, Indonesia
Date: 1586
10 000 people killed. Another eruption in 1919 killed 5000 people.

Tambora   *Height*: 2850 m (9350 ft)
Location: Jumbawa, Indonesia
Date: 1815
An estimated 150–180 km³ (36–43 cu mi) were blasted from the cone, which dropped in height from 4100 m (13 450 ft) to 2850 m (9350 ft) in minutes. About 90 000 people were killed in the explosion and subsequent giant wave, or died later of famine.

Krakatau   *Height*: 813 m (2667 ft)
Location: Krakatau, Indonesia
Date: 1883
163 villages were wiped out and 36 380 people killed by the giant wave caused by this, the greatest volcanic explosion recorded – although possibly only one fifth of the Santoríni explosion. Rocks were thrown 55 km (34 mi) into the air, and dust fell 5330 km (3313 mi) away 10 days later. The explosion was heard over one thirteenth of the Earth's surface.

Mont Pelée   *Height*: 1397 m (4582 ft)
Location: Martinique, West Indies
Date: 1902
Within three minutes a *nuée ardente* destroyed the town of St Pierre, killing all 26 000 inhabitants – except for one, a prisoner who survived in the thick-walled prison.

Mount St Helens   *Height*: 2549 m (8360 ft)
Location: Washington State, USA
Date: 1980
66 people were presumed dead and 260 km² (100 sq mi) of forest destroyed. Smoke and ash rose to a height of 6000 m (20 000 ft), depositing ash 800 km (440 mi) away.

MAJOR VOLCANOES

Among the principal volcanoes active in recent times are:

Name	Height (m)	Height (ft)	Range or location	Country	Date of last notified eruption
Ojos del Salado	6895	22 588	Andes	Argentina/Chile	1981–steams
Llullaillaco	6723	22 057	Andes	Chile	1877
San Pedro	6199	20 325	Andes	Chile	1960
Guallatiri	6060	19 882	Andes	Chile	1960– subglacial
San José	5919	19 405	Andes	Chile	1931
Cotopaxi	5897	19 347	Andes	Ecuador	1975
El Misti	5862	19 220	Andes	Ecuador	1878
Tutupaca	5844	19 160	Andes	Ecuador	1902
Antisana	5793	18 995	Andes	Ecuador	1801 subglacial
Ubinas	5710	18 720	Andes	Peru	1969
Lascar	5641	18 507	Andes	Chile	1968
Tupungatito	5640	18 504	Andes	Chile	1964
Orizaba	5610	18 405	Altiplano de Mexico	Mexico	1687
Isluga	5566	18 250	Andes	Chile	1960
Popocatépetl	5451	17 887	Altiplano de Mexico	Mexico	1920–steams
Ruiz	5435	17 820	Andes	Colombia	1985
Tolima	5249	17 210	Andes	Colombia	1943
Sangay	5230	17 159	Andes	Ecuador	1983
Tungurahua	5048	16 550	Andes	Ecuador	1944
Guagua Pichincha	4880	16 000	Andes	Ecuador	1881
Klyuchevsk Volcano	4850	15 913	Khrebet Mountains (Kamchatka Peninsula)	USSR	1974
Cumbal	4795	15 720	Andes	Colombia	1926
Purace	4590	15 059	Andes	Colombia	1977
Cerro Negro de Mayasquer	4499	14 750	Andes	Colombia	1936
Mt Rainier	4396	14 410	Cascade Range	USA	1882
Mt Shasta	4317	14 159	Cascade Range	USA	1855
El Galeras	4294	14 080	Andes	Colombia	1947
Doña Juana	4277	14 025	Andes	Colombia	1906
Tajumulco	4220	13 881	Sierra Madre	Guatemala	rumbles
Mauna Loa	4170	13 680	Hawaii	USA	1978
Tacanáa	4078	13 379	Sierra Madre	Guatemala	rumbles
Mt Cameroon	4069	13 353	isolated mountain	Cameroon	1986
Erebus	3795	12 450	Ross Island	Antarctica	1990
Fujiyama	3776	12 388	Kanto	Japan	steams
Rindjani	3726	12 224	Lombok	Indonesia	1966
Pico de Teide	3716	12 192	Tenerife, Canary Is	Spain	1909
Semeru	3676	12 060	Java	Indonesia	1987
Nyiragongo	3470	11 385	Virunga	Zaïre	1982
Koryakskaya	3456	11 339	Kamchatka Peninsula	USSR	1957
Irazu	3452	11 325	Cordillera Central	Costa Rica	1967
Slamat	3428	11 247	Java	Indonesia	1967
Mt Spurr	3374	11 070	Alaska Range	USA	1953
Mt Etna	3311	10 855	Sicily	Italy	1987

EUROPEAN VOLCANOES (ACTIVE IN HISTORICAL TIMES)

Name	Height (m)	Height (ft)		No. eruptions since 1700	Last eruption
Iceland (18 volcanoes)					
Eldeyjar	na	na	ephemeral island	4	1926
Trölladyngja	381	1250	central Iceland	0	1390
Hekla	1501	4920	southern Iceland	67	1980
Krakatindur	na	na	eruption from a fissure	2	1913
Surtsey	174	570	island	1	1967
Eyjafallajökull	1678	5500	subglacial eruption	1	1821
Katla	1449	4750	southern Iceland	6	1955
Laki	824	2700	southern Iceland	1	1783
Grimsvötn	na	na	subglacial eruption	33	1954
Öraefajökull	c.2356	c.6900	subglacial eruption	1	1727
Kverkfjöll	c.1861	c.6100	subglacial eruption	3	1729
Askja	1520	4983	central Iceland	2	1961
Sveinagja	946	3100	eruption from a fissure	1	1875
Myvatn	na	na	major lava flow from fissure	1	1729
Krafla	824	2700	northern Iceland	1	1724
Leirhafnarskörd	244	800	northern Iceland	1	1823
Mánáreyar			submarine	1	1867
Heimaey	na	na	Vestmann Islands	1	1973
Norway (1 volcano)					
Beerenberg	2546	8347	Jan Mayen Island	2	1970
Italy (7 volcanoes)					
Monte Nuovo	140	460	Flegrean Islands	1	1538
Vesuvius	1290	4230	Campania	Many	1944
Ischia	793	2600	Flegrean Islands	0	1301
Stromboli	932	3055	Eolian Islands	Many	1986
Vulcano	503	1650	Eolian Islands	6	1975
Etna	3311	10 855	Sicily	75?	1987
Giulia Ferdinandeo			ephemeral island	3	1863
Mediterranean Sea (2 volcanoes)					
Pinne			submarine	2	1911
Foerstner			submarine	1	1891
Greece (1 volcano)					
Santoríni (Thera)	1316	4316	Santoríni, Cyclades	6	1950
Portugal – Azores (9 volcanoes)					
Faial	1049	3440	Faial Island	1	1958
Pico	2315	7713	Pico Island	3	1963
San Jorge Island	1060	3475		2	1964 ?
(unnamed) lat 38°30'N, long 27°25'W			submarine	2	1902
Santa Barbara	1029	3375	Terceira Island	2	1867
Castro Bank			submarine	1	1720
Sete Cidades	862	2825	San Miguel Island	4	1811
Agua de Pau	955	3130	San Miguel Island	0	1652
Furnas	810	2655	San Miguel Island	0	1630
Spain – Canaries (3 volcanoes)					
Caldera de Taburiente	1861	6100	La Palma	2	1971
Pico de Teide	3716	12 192	Tenerife	5	1909
Timanfaua	566	1855	Lanzarote	2	1824

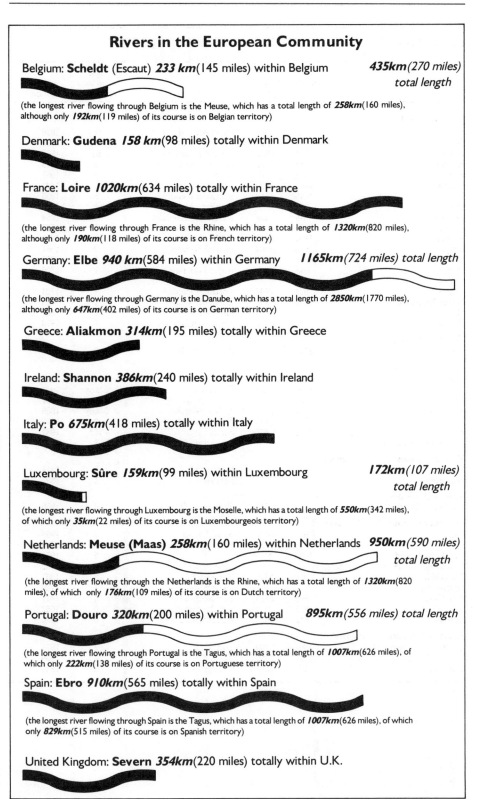

Rivers in the European Community

Belgium: Scheldt (Escaut) *233 km*(145 miles) within Belgium   *435km (270 miles)* total length

(the longest river flowing through Belgium is the Meuse, which has a total length of *258km*(160 miles), although only *192km*(119 miles) of its course is on Belgian territory)

Denmark: **Gudena** *158 km*(98 miles) totally within Denmark

France: **Loire** *1020km*(634 miles) totally within France

(the longest river flowing through France is the Rhine, which has a total length of *1320km*(820 miles), although only *190km*(118 miles) of its course is on French territory)

Germany: **Elbe** *940 km*(584 miles) within Germany   *1165km (724 miles) total length*

(the longest river flowing through Germany is the Danube, which has a total length of *2850km*(1770 miles), although only *647km*(402 miles) of its course is on German territory)

Greece: **Aliakmon** *314km*(195 miles) totally within Greece

Ireland: **Shannon** *386km*(240 miles) totally within Ireland

Italy: **Po** *675km*(418 miles) totally within Italy

Luxembourg: **Sûre** *159km*(99 miles) within Luxembourg   *172km (107 miles)* total length

(the longest river flowing through Luxembourg is the Moselle, which has a total length of *550km*(342 miles), of which only *35km*(22 miles) of its course is on Luxembourgeois territory)

Netherlands: **Meuse (Maas)** *258km*(160 miles) within Netherlands *950km (590 miles)* total length

(the longest river flowing through the Netherlands is the Rhine, which has a total length of *1320km*(820 miles), of which only *176km*(109 miles) of its course is on Dutch territory)

Portugal: **Douro** *320km*(200 miles) within Portugal   *895km (556 miles) total length*

(the longest river flowing through Portugal is the Tagus, which has a total length of *1007km*(626 miles), of which only *222km*(138 miles) of its course is on Portuguese territory)

Spain: **Ebro** *910km*(565 miles) totally within Spain

(the longest river flowing through Spain is the Tagus, which has a total length of *1007km*(626 miles), of which only *829km*(515 miles) of its course is on Spanish territory)

United Kingdom: **Severn** *354km*(220 miles) totally within U.K.

WORLD'S GREATEST RIVERS

The importance of rivers still tends to be judged on their length rather than by the more significant factors – their basin areas and volume of flow. In this compilation all the world's river systems with a watercourse of a length of 2400 km (1500 miles) or more are listed with all three criteria where ascertainable.

Length (km)	(miles)	Name of Watercourse	Source	Course and Outflow	Basin Area (km²)	(miles²)	Mean Discharge Rate (m³/s)	(ft³/s)	Notes
6670	4145	1 Nile (Bahr-el-Nil)–White Nile (Bahr el Jabel)–Albert Nile–Victoria Nile–Victoria Nyanza–Kagera–Luvironza	Burundi: Luvironza branch of the Kagera, a feeder of the Victoria Nyanza	Through Tanzania (Kagera), Uganda (Victoria Nile and Ibert Nile), Sudan (White Nile), Egypt to eastern Mediterranean	3 350 000	1 293 000	3120	110 000	Navigable length to first cataract (Aswan 1545 km 960 miles). Egyptian Irrigation Dept. states length as 6700 km (4164 miles). Discharge 2600 m³/s (93 200 ft³/s) near Aswan. Delta is 23 960 km² (9250 miles²).
6448	4007	2 Amazon (Amazonas)	Peru: Lago Villafro, head of the Apurimac branch of the Ucayali, which joins the Marañon to form the Amazonas	Through Colombia to Equatorial Brazil (Solimões) to South Atlantic (Canal do Sul)	7 050 000	2 722 000	180 000	6 350 000	Total of 15 000 tributaries, ten over 1600 km (1000 miles) including Madeira (3380 km 2100 miles). Navigable 3700 km (2300 miles) up stream. Delta extends 400 km (250 miles) inland.
6300	3915	3 Yangtze (Chang Jiang)	Western China, Kunlun Shan Mts (as Tuotuo and Tongtian)	Begins W of Tuotuohe in Qinghai, through Yunnan Sichuan, Hubei, Anhui, Jiangsu, to Yellow Sea	1 960 000	756 000	21 800	770 000	Flood rate (1931) of 85 000 m³/s (3 000 000 ft³/s). Estuary 190 km (120 miles) long.
6020	3741	4 Mississippi–Missouri–Jefferson–Beaverhead–Red Rock	Beaverhead County, southern Montana, USA	Through N. Dakota, S. Dakota, Nebraska–Iowa, Missouri–Kansas Illinois, Kentucky, Tennessee, Arkansas, Mississippi, Louisiana, South West Pass into Gulf of Mexico	3 224 000	1 245 000	18 400	650 000	Missouri is 3725 km (2315 miles) the Jefferson–Beaverhead–Red Rock is 349 km (217 miles). Lower Mississippi is 1884 km (1171 miles). Total Mississippi from Lake Itasca, Minn., is 3778 km (2348 miles) – longest river in one country. Delta is 36 000 km² (13 900 miles²).
5540	3442	5 Yenisey–Angara–Selenga	Mongolia: Ider1in branch of Selenga (Selenge)	Through Buryat ASSR (Selenga feeder) into Ozero Baykal, thence via Angara to Yenisey confluence at Strelka to Kara Sea, northern USSR	2 580 000	996 000	19 000	670 000	Estuary 386 km (240 miles) long. Yenisey is 3540 km (2200 miles) long and has a basin of 2 050 000 km² (792 000 miles²). The length of the Angara is 1850 km (1150 miles).
5464	3395	6 Huang He (Yellow River)	China: W of Bayan, Qinghai Province	Through Gansu, Inner Mongolia, Henan, Shandong to Bo Hai (Gulf of Chile), Yellow Sea, North Pacific	979 000	378 000	2 800 to 22 650	100 000 to 800 000	Changed mouth by 400 km (250 miles) in 1852. Only last 40 km (25 miles) navigable.
5409	3361	7 Ob'–Irtysh	Mongolia: Kara (Black) Irtysh via northern China (Xinjiang) feeder of Ozero Zaysan	Through Kazakhstan into Russian Federation to Ob' confluence at Khanty Mansiysk, thence Ob' to Kara Sea, northern USSR	2 978 000	1 150 000	15 600	550 000	Estuary (Obskaya Guba) is 725 km (450 miles) long. Ob' is 3679 km (2286 miles) long, Irtysh 2960 km (1840 miles) long.

Length (km)	(miles)	Name of Watercourse	Source	Course and Outflow	Basin Area (km²)	(miles²)	Mean Discharge Rate (m³/s)	(ft³/s)	Notes
8									
4880	3032	Rió de la Plata-Paraná	Brazil: as Paranáiba. Flows south to eastern Paraguay border and into eastern Argentina	Emerges into confluence with River Uruguay to form Rio de la Plata, South Atlantic	4 145 000	1 600 000	27 500	970 000	After the 120 km (75 mile) long Delta estuary, the river shares the 340 km (210 mile) long estuary of the Uruguay called Rio de la Plata (River Plate).
9									
4700	2920	Zaïre (Congo)	Zambia–Zaïre border, as Lualaba	Through Zaïre as Lualaba along to Zaïre (Congo) border to N.W. Angola mouth to S Atlantic	3 400 000	1 314 000	41 000	1 450 000	Navigable for 1730 km (1075 miles) from Kisangani to Kinshasa Estuary 96 km (60 miles) long.
10									
4400	2734	Lena–Kirenga	USSR: hinterland of W central shores of Ozero Baykal as Kirenga	Northwards through eastern Russia to Laptev Sea, Arctic Ocean	2 490 000	960 000	16 300	575 000	Lena Delta (45 000 km²/17 375 miles²) extends 177 km (110 miles) inland, frozen 15 Oct to 10 July. Second longest solely Russian river.
11									
4350	2702	Mekong (Me Nam Kong)	Central Tibet (as Lants'ang), slopes of Dza-Nag-Lung-Mong, 5000 m (16 700 ft)	Flows into China, thence south to form Burma-Laotian and most of Thai-Laotian frontiers, thence through Cambodia to Vietnam into South China Sea	987 000	381 000	11 000	388 000	Max flood discharge 48 000 m³/s (1 700 000 ft³/s).
12									
4345	2700	'Amur–Argun' (Heilongjiang)	Northern China in Khingan Ranges (as 'Argun')	North along Inner Mongolian–USSR and Manchuria–USSR border for 3743 km (2326 miles) to Tartar Strait, Sea of Okhotsk, North Pacific	2 038 000	787 000	12 400	438 000	Amur is 2824 km (1755 miles) long (711 600 basin and 388 000 flow); China Handbook claims total length to be 4670 km (2903 miles) of which only 925 km (575 miles) is exclusively in USSR territory.
13									
4241	2635	Mackenzie–Peace	Tatlatui Lake, Skeena Mts, Rockies, British Columbia, Canada (as River Finlay)	Flows as Finlay for 400 km (250 miles) to confluence with Peace; 1690 km (1050 miles) to join Slave (415 km/258 miles) which feeds Great Slave Lake, from which flows Mackenzie (1733 km/1077 miles) to Beaufort Sea	1 841 000	711 000	11 300	400 000	Peace 1923 km (1195 miles).
14									
4184	2600	Niger	Guinea: Loma Mts near Sierra Leone border	Flows through Mali, Niger and along Benin border into Nigeria and Atlantic	1 890 000	730 000	11 750	415 000	Delta extends 128 km (80 miles) inland and 200 km (130 miles) in coastal length.
15									
3750	2330	Murray–Darling	Queensland, Australia: as the Condamine, a tributary of the Culgoa, which is a tributary of the Balonne-branch of the Darling	Balonne (intermittent flow) crosses into New South Wales to join Darling, which itself joins the Murray on the New South Wales–Victoria border and flows west into Lake Alexandrina, in South Australia	1 059 000	408 000	400	14 000	Darling c. 2740 km (1700 miles) Murray 2590 km (1609 miles) or 1870 km (1160 miles).

Length (km)	(miles)	Name of Watercourse	Source	Course and Outflow	Basin Area (km²)	(miles²)	Mean Discharge Rate (m³/s)	(ft³/s)	Notes
16 3540	2200	Zambezi (Zambeze)	Zambia: north-west extremity, as Zambezi	Flows after 72 km (45 miles) across eastern Angola for 354 km (220 miles) and back into Zimbabwe (as Zambezi), later forming border with eastern end of Caprivi strip of Namibia, thence over Victoria Falls (Mosi-Oatunya) into Kariba Lake. Thereafter into Mozambique and out into southern Indian Ocean	1 330 000	514 000	7 000	250 000	Navigable 610 km (380 miles) up to Quebrabasa Rapids and thereafter in stretches totalling another 1930 km (1200 miles).
17 3530	2193	Volga	USSR: in Valdai Hills NW of Moscow	Flows south and east in a great curve and empties in a delta into the north of the Caspian Sea	1 360 000	525 000	8 200	287 000	Delta exceeds 280 km (175 miles) inland and arguably 450 km (280 miles).
18 3380	2100	Madeira–Mamoré–Grande (Guapay)	Bolivia: rises as the Beni near Illimani	Flows north and east into Brazil to join Amazon at the Ilha Tupinambaram	Tributary of No. 2		15 000	530 000	World's longest tributary, navigable for 1070 km (663 miles).
19 3283	2040	Jurua	Peru: S of Puerto Portillo	Flows east and north into Brazil to join Amazon below Fonte Boa	Tributary of No. 2		–	–	World's second longest tributary. Navigable for 965 km (600 miles). Most pronounced meanders in Amazon Basin. Descends only 453 m (1486 ft) along its entire course.
20 3211	1995	Purus (formerly Coxiuara)	Peru: as the Alto Purus	Flows north and east into Brazil to join Amazon below Beruri	Tributary of No. 2		–	–	World's third longest tributary. Navigable for 2575 km (1600 miles). Pronounced meanders.
21 3185	1979	Yukon–Teslin	North-west British Columbia, Canada, as the Teslin	Flows north into Yukon Territory and into west Alaska, USA, and thence into Bering Sea	855 000	330 000	–	–	Delta 136 km (85 miles) inland, navigable (shallow draft) for 2855 km (1775 miles).
22 3130	1945	St Lawrence	Head of St Louis River, Minn. USA	Flows into Lake Superior, thence Lakes Huron, Erie, Ontario to Gulf of St Lawrence and North Atlantic	1 378 000	532 000	10 200	360 000	Estuary 407 km (253 miles) long or 616 km (383 miles) to Anticosti Island. Discovered 1535 by Jacques Cartier.
23 3035	1885	Rio Grande (Rio Bravo del Norte)	South-western Colorado, USA; San Juan Mts	Flows south through New Mexico, USA, and along Texas–Mexico border into Gulf of Mexico, Atlantic Ocean	445 000	172 000	85	3 000	–
24 3019	1876	Syrdarya–Naryn	In Tien Shan Mountains of eastern Kirghizia	Flows west through Kirghizia then through Tadzhikistan, then north and west through Kazakhstan to the Aral Sea	462 000	178 000	–	–	Known to the ancient Greeks as the Jaxartes.

Length (km)	(miles)	Name of Watercourse	Source	Course and Outflow	Basin Area (km²)	(miles²)	Mean Discharge Rate (m³/s)	(ft³/s)	Notes
25 2989	1857	Nizhnaya Tunguska	In central Siberia, USSR	Flows east, then north and west to the Yenisey	471 000	188 000	–	–	Tributary of the Yenisey.
26 2914	1811	São Francisco	Brazil: Serra da Canastra	Flows north and east into South Atlantic	700 000	270 000	–	–	Navigable 238 km (148 miles).
27 2900	1800	Brahmaputra	South-western Tibet as Matsang (Tsangpo)	Flows east 1240 km (770 miles) south, then west through Assam, north-eastern India, joins Ganges (as Jamuna) to flow into Bay of Bengal, Indian Ocean	1 620 000	626 000	38 500	1 360 000	Joint delta with Ganges extends 360 km (225 miles) across and 330 km (205 miles) inland. Area 80 000 km² (30 800 mile²) the world's largest. Navigable 1290 km (800 miles).
28 2880	1790	Indus	Tibet: as Sengge	Flows west through Kashmir, into Pakistan and out into northern Arabian Sea	1 166 000	450 000	5 500	195 000	Delta (area 8000 km² /3100 miles²) extends 120 km (75 miles) inland.
29 2850	1770	Danube	South-western Germany: Black Forest as Breg and Brigach	Flows (as Donau) east into Austria along Czech–Hungarian border as Dunaj into Hungary (440 km /273 miles) as Duna, to Yugoslavia as Dunav along Romania–Bulgaria border and through Romania as Dunarea to Romania–USSR border as Dunay, into the Black Sea	815 000	315 000	7 000	250 000	Delta extends 96 km (60 miles) inland. Flows in territory of 8 countries.
30 2810	1750	Salween (Nu Chiang)	Tibet in Tanglha range	Flows (as Nu) east and south into western China, into eastern Burma and along Thailand border and out into Gulf of Martaban, Andaman Sea	325 000	125 000	–	–	–
31 2800	1740	Tigris–Euphrates (Shatt al-Arab)	Eastern Turkey as Murat	Flows west joining the Firat, thence into Syria as Al Furát and south and east into Iraq joining Tigris flowing into Persian Gulf at Iran–Iraq border as Shatt al-Arab	1 115 000	430 000	400 low 2 700 high	50 000	–
32 = 2740	1700	Tocantins	Brazil: near Brasilia as Paraná	Flows north to join Pará in the Estuary Báia de Marajó and the South Atlantic	905 000	350 000	10 000	360 000	Not properly regarded as an Amazon tributary. Estuary 440 km (275 miles) in length.
32 = 2740	1700	Orinoco	South-eastern Venezuela	Flows north and west to Colombia border, thence north and east to north-eastern Venezuela and the Atlantic	1 036 000	400 000	–	–	–

Length (km)	(miles)	Name of Watercourse	Source	Course and Outflow	Basin Area (km²)	(miles²)	Mean Discharge Rate (m³/s)	(ft³/s)	Notes
34 = 2650	1650	Vilyuy	Evenky region of Central	Flows east and south to join the Lena north of Yakutsk	491 000 Tributary of No.10	190 000	—	—	—
34 = 2650	1650	Xi Jiang (Si Kiang)	China: in Yunnan plateau as Nanp'an	Flows east as the Hongshui and later as the Hsün to emerge as the Hsi in the South China Sea, west of Hong Kong	602 000	232 300	—	—	Delta exceeds 145 km (90 miles) inland and includes the Pearl River or Chu.
36 2627	1632	Araguaia	In Mato Grosso, Brazil	Flows north and east to join the Tocantins	Tributary of No. 32		—	—	—
37 2600	1616	Kolyma	USSR: in Khrebet Suntarkhayata (as Kulu)	Flows north across Arctic Circle into eastern Siberian Sea	534 000	206 000	3 800	134 000	—
38 = 2575	1600	Amu-Dar'ya (Oxus)	Wakhan, Afghanistan, on the border with Xinjiang China	Flows west to form Tadzhikistan–Afghan border as Pyandzh for 680 km (420 miles) and into Turkmenistan as Amu-Dar'ya. Flows north and west into Aral Sea	465 000	179 500	—	—	—
38 = 2575	1600	Nelson–Saskatchewan	Canada: Bow Lake, British Columbia	Flows north and east through Saskatchewan and into Manitoba through Cedar Lake into Lake Winnipeg and out through northern feeder as Nelson to Hudson Bay	1 072 000	414 000	2 250	80 000	Saskatchewan 1940 km (1205 miles) in length.
40 2540	1575	Ural	USSR: South-central Urals	Flows south and west into the Caspian Sea	220 000	84 900	—	—	—
41 2510	1553	Ganges (Ganga)	In the southern Himalaya (India)	Flows south and east to join the Brahmaputra to form Jamuna	976 000	377 000	—	—	—
42 2410	1500	Paraguay	Brazil: in the Mato Grosso as Paraguai	Flows south to touch first Bolivian then Paraguayan border, then across Paraguay to form border with Argentina. Joins the Paraná south of Humaitá	1 150 000 Tributary of No. 14	440 000	—	—	—

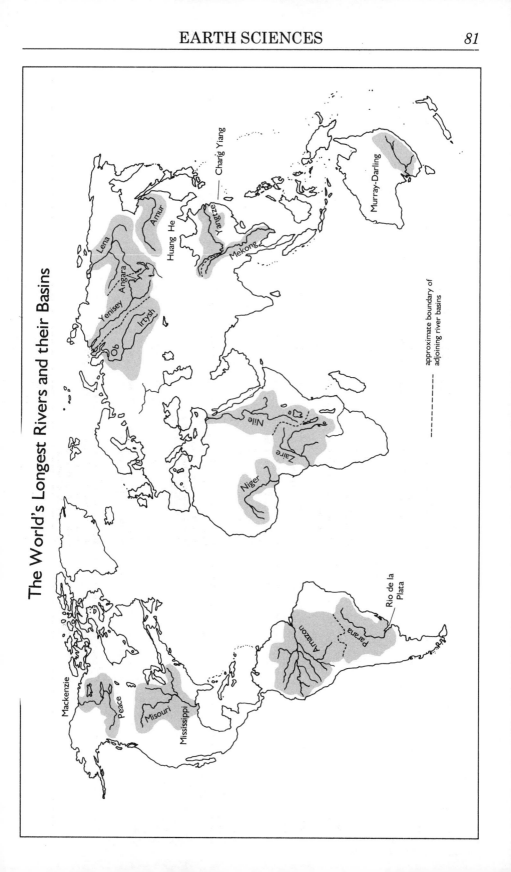

The World's Longest Rivers and their Basins

RIVERS AND LAKES

Rivers and lakes are the most important bodies of surface water on land masses. A river is a freshwater body confined in a channel which flows down a slope into another river, a lake or the sea, or sometimes into an inland desert. Small, narrow rivers may be called brooks, streams or creeks.

A lake is an inland body of water occupying a depression in the Earth's surface. Usually, lakes receive water from rivers, but sometimes only directly from springs. Lakes normally lose water into an outlet or river, but some, called *closed lakes*, have no outlet and lose water only by evaporation – for example, Lake Eyre in Australia and Great Salt Lake in Utah, USA.

WHERE DO RIVERS GET THEIR WATER FROM?

Rivers may receive their water from several sources, but all of these are indirectly or directly related to *precipitation* – a collective term for the fall of moisture onto the Earth's surface from the atmosphere. Rain falling on the ground may immediately run down slopes as *overland flow*, becoming concentrated and eventually forming a stream. This tends to occur when the ground surface is *impermeable* (i.e. water cannot pass through it, as is the case with some kinds of rock). It may also occur when the ground is already saturated with water, or when rainfall is very heavy.

Often, however, rivers receive their water from *springs*. This is because rainfall will commonly soak into the ground, to accumulate in the soil or to pass into permeable and porous rocks as *groundwater*. In *permeable* rock, water can pass right through the rock itself, whereas in *porous* rock there are holes and fissures through which water can pass. Springs occur where the top of the aquifer – a layer of rock containing water – intersects with the ground surface. Groundwater is important as a source for rivers in that it can supply water even when precipitation is not occurring, thereby constantly maintaining river flow.

A third source of water for rivers is the melting of solid precipitation (snow) or snow which has been turned to ice to form a glacier or ice sheet. This is particularly important in high-latitude and mountainous areas.

PERENNIAL, SEASONAL AND EPHEMERAL RIVERS

Rivers occur in all the world's major environments, even in polar areas and deserts. In temperate areas, such as Western Europe, northeastern USA and New Zealand, and in the wet tropics, enough precipitation tends to fall, fairly evenly throughout the year, to replenish groundwater constantly and therefore to allow rivers to flow all year round. These *perennial rivers* do, however, experience seasonal and day-to-day variations in the volume of water they carry (the *flow regime*), owing to seasonal fluctuations in precipitation and additional inputs from individual storms.

Some rivers may only flow seasonally, particularly in environments with Mediterranean-type climates, which have a very distinct wet, winter season and a dry summer. Rivers in glaciated areas may also have very seasonal flow regimes. *Glacial meltwater streams*, which receive their water directly from glaciers, usually only flow during the few months in the summer when the ice melts.

In dry desert climates, rivers may not flow for years on end, because of the infrequency of desert storms, and then only for a few days, or even hours. However, when storms do occur these *ephemeral rivers* may flow at great rates, because desert rainfall is often very heavy. This gives them considerable power and the ability to erode and transport large quantities of sediment.

Some deserts do possess perennial rivers. The Nile, for example, despite experiencing a distinctly seasonal flow regime, flows all year round through the Egyptian Desert; likewise, the Colorado River passes through desert areas of the southwestern USA. The reason that these and other rivers can successfully exist in deserts is that their *catchments* (source areas) lie in areas with wetter climates.

RIVER BASINS

Only some very short rivers are able to flow from a source to the sea without either being joined by others or becoming a *tributary* of a large river. Most rivers therefore form part of a *drainage network*, occupying a *drainage basin*. In fact, the whole of the Earth's land surface can be divided up into drainage basins, and these basins are separated by areas of relatively high ground called *watersheds*. Some drainage basins occupy only a few square kilometres, but others are enormous – the largest, the Amazon Basin, covers over 7 million sq km (2.7 million sq mi).

LONGEST RIVERS IN EUROPE

Volga (USSR) 3530 km (2193 mi)
After (nameless) headwaters of 160 km (99 mi) the Volga flows into the Rybinskoye reservoir in the Valdai Hills north of Moscow and becomes known as the Volga. It then flows south and east to the Caspian Sea.

Danube (Germany–Austria–Czechoslovakia–Hungary–Yugoslavia–Romania–Bulgaria–USSR) 2850 km (1770 mi)
Rises as the Rivers Breg and Brisach in the Black Forest in Germany and flows east through Central and South East Europe into the Black Sea.

Ural 2540 km (1575 mi)
The Ural is sometimes quoted as the third longest river in Europe, but much of its path to the Caspian Sea through Kazakhstan lies in Asia.

Dnepr (USSR) 2285 km (1420 mi)
Rises west of Moscow and flows south through Russia, Byelorussia and Ukraine to the Black Sea.

Don (USSR) 1969 km (1224 mi)
Rises in southwest Russia and flows south to the Sea of Azov.

Pechora (USSR) 1809 km (1124 mi)
Rises in the Ural Mountains and flows north through Russia to the Barents Sea.

Kama (USSR) 1805 km (1122 mi)
Rises north of Perm and flows south through Russia to join the River Volga through the Kuybyshevskoye reservoir.

Oka (USSR) 1500 km (930 mi)
Rises southwest of Moscow and flows east through Russia to join the Volga near Nizhny Novgorod (formerly Gorky).

Belaya (USSR) 1430 km (889 mi)
Rises in the south of the Ural Mountains and flows north to join the River Kama.

Dnestr (USSR) 1352 km (840 mi)

Rises near the Polish border in the western Ukraine and flows east through Moldavia into the Black Sea.

Rhine (Switzerland–Liechtenstein–Germany–France–Netherlands) 1320 km (820 mi)
Rises in the Swiss Alps and flows east then north to the North Sea.

Severnaya Dvina (USSR) 1302 km (809 mi)
Rises in northern Russia as the Sukhona and flows north to the White Sea.

Elbe (Czechoslovakia–Germany) 1165 km (724 mi)
Rises in Bohemia and flows north to the North Sea.

Vistula (Poland) 1069 km (664 mi)
Rises near the Polish–Czechoslovak border and flows north to the Baltic.

Loire (France) 1020 km (634 mi)
Rises in central France and flows north and then west to the Atlantic Ocean.

Tagus (Spain–Portugal) 1007 km (626 mi)
Rises on the border of Aragon and Castile and flows

west to the Atlantic Ocean.

Tisza (USSR–Romania–Hungary–Yugoslavia) 996 km (619 mi)
Rises in the Carpathians and flows west and then south to join the Danube north of Belgrade.

EURO FACTS

HIGHEST WATERFALLS IN THE EC

1. Gavarnie	421 m (1384 ft)	on Gave de Pau, Hautes-Pyrénées, France
2. Serio	315 m (1033 ft)	on River Serio, Lombardy, Italy
3. Cascata delle Marmore	180 m (591 ft)	on Velino River at Terni, Umbria, Italy

WATERFALLS

WORLD'S GREATEST WATERFALLS – BY HEIGHT

Name	Total Drop (m)	(ft)	River	Location
1. Angel (highest fall – 2648 ft/807 m)*	979	3212	Carrao, an upper tributary of the Caroni	Venezuela
2. Tugela (5 falls) (highest fall – 410 m/1350 ft)	947	3110	Tugela	Natal, S. Africa
3. Utigård (highest fall – 600 m/1970 ft)	800	2625	Jostedal Glacier	Nesdale, Norway
4. Mongefossen	774	2540	Monge	Mongebekk, Norway
5. Yosemite (Upper Yosemite – 435 m/1430 ft; Cascades in middle section – 205 m/675 ft; Lower Yosemite – 97 m/320 ft)	739	2425	Yosemite Creek, a tributary of the Merced	Yosemite Valley, Yosemite National Park, Cal., USA
6. Østre Mardøla Foss (highest fall – 296 m/974 ft)	656	2154	Mardals	Eikisdal, W. Norway
7. Tyssestrengane (highest fall – 289 m/948 ft)	646	2120	Tysso	Hardanger, Norway
8. Kukenaam (or Cuquenán)	610	2000	Arabopó, upper tributary of the Caroni	Venezuela
9. Sutherland (highest fall – 248 m/815 ft)	580	1904	Arthur	nr. Milford Sound, Otago, S. Island, New Zealand
10. Kile (or Kjellfossen) (highest fall – 149 m/490 ft)†	561	1841	Naerö Fjord feeder	nr. Gudvangen, Norway
11. Takkakaw (highest fall – 365 m/1200 ft)	502	1650	A tributary of the Yoho	Daly Glacier, British Columbia, Canada
12. Ribbon	491	1612	Ribbon Fall Stream	4·9 km (3 miles) west of Yosemite Falls, Yosemite National Park, Cal., USA
13. King George VI	487	1600	Utshi, upper tributary of the Mazaruni	Guyana
14. Roraima	457	1500	An upper tributary of the Mazaruni	Guyana

* There are other very high but seemingly unnamed waterfalls in this area.
† Some authorities would regard this as no more than a 'Bridal Veil' waterfall, i.e., of such low volume that the fall atomizes.

WORLD'S GREATEST WATERFALLS – BY VOLUME OF WATER

Name	Maximum Height (m)	Maximum Height (ft)	Width (m)	Width (ft)	Mean Annual Flow (m³/s)	Mean Annual Flow (ft³/s)	Location
Boyoma (formerly Stanley) (7 cataracts)	60	200 (total)	730	2400 (7th)	17 000	c. 600 000	Zaïre River, nr. Kisangani, Zaïre
Guaíra (or Salto dos Sete Quedas) ('Seven Falls')	114	374	4846	15 900	13 000	470 000*	Alto Paraná River, Brazil–Paraguay
Khône	21	70	10 670	35 000	11 000 to 12 000	400 000 to 420 000	Mekong River, Laos
Niagara:							
Horseshoe (Canadian)	48	160	760	2500	5640	199 300	Niagara River, Lake Erie to Lake Ontario
American	50	167	300	1000	360	12 700	Niagara River, Lake Erie to Lake Ontario
Paulo Afonso	58	192	–	–	2800	100 000	São Francisco River, Brazil
Urubu-punga	12	40	–	–	2700	97 000	Alto Paraná River, Brazil
Cataratas del Iguazú (Quedas do Iguaçu)	93	308	c. 4000	c. 13 000	1700	61 660	Iguazú (or Iguaçu) River, Brazil–Argentina
Patos-Maribondo	35	115	–	–	1500	53 000	Rio Grande, Brazil
Victoria (Mosi-oa-tunya):							
Leaping Water	108	355	33	108	1100	38 430	Zambezi River, Zambia
Main Fall	same height		821	2694	–		Zimbabwe
Rainbow Falls	same height		550	1800	–		
Churchill (formerly Grand)	75	245	–	–	850 to 1100	30 000 to 40 000	Churchill (formerly Hamilton) River, Canada
Kaieteur (Köituök)	225	741	90 to 105	300 to 350	660	23 400	Potaro River, Guyana

* The peak flow has reached 50 000 m³/s (1 750 000 ft³/s).

ISLANDS

An island is a body of land, smaller than a continent, that is completely surrounded by water. Islands occur in rivers, lakes, and the seas and oceans. They range in size from very small mud and sand islands of only a few square metres, to Greenland, which has an area of 2 175 600 km² (840 000 sq mi). (Note that Australia is normally considered to be a continent rather than an island.)

Islands, especially those in seas and oceans, have a range of origins. Islands can develop through constructional processes. They may also be formed by erosional processes that cause an area of land to become separated from the mainland. Rising sea levels can also lead to the development of islands, by drowning low-lying areas of land and separating higher areas from the main land mass.

VOLCANIC ISLANDS

When volcanic activity occurs beneath the oceans, it can lead to the growth of islands. This is often closely linked to the movement of the Earth's crustal plates, with island-building (e.g. Iceland) occurring both at constructive plate margins and at destructive margins. Volcanic islands (e.g. Hawaii) can also form far from any plate boundary.

Iceland, situated on the mid-Atlantic ridge, is the largest example of a volcanic island formed at a constructive plate margin. Iceland started forming about 20 million years ago – the age of the oldest rocks on the island. It is still growing in size today, as new material is periodically added, along a line of volcanic activity running from the southwest to the northeast of the island. Much of the volcanic activity responsible for Iceland's growth has not been in the form of spectacular eruptions, but rather as quiet extrusive fissure eruptions, involving the outpouring of large quantities of lava from cracks in the Earth's surface, giving rise to basaltic rocks.

Spectacular eruptions, have, however, also played their part. For example, in 1963, eruptions occurred off the south coast of Iceland. In the space of a few weeks, ash and lava built up on the sea floor and a new, small island named Surtsey was born.

ISLAND ARCHIPELAGOS

The collision of crustal plates at destructive margins can generate significant volcanic activity. If this occurs at the edge of a land mass it can cause mountain building, but when the collision zone lies beneath an ocean, island development can result. Islands which are born in this way do not occur singly, but in chains or archipelagos ('arcs') that parallel the plate boundary. This is well illustrated on the western side of the Pacific Ocean. Here thousands of islands – most of them volcanic but some formed by the folding up of the ocean floor – mark the western edge of the Pacific Plate. These islands start in the south at New Zealand, run north to the Tongan chain before heading west to New Guinea, and north again through the Philippines, Japan, the Kurile island chain and finally the Aleutian Islands, which continue to the mainland of North America. The Indonesian archipelago, which extends westwards into the Indian Ocean from the island chains of the west Pacific, is the world's largest, its 13 000 islands stretching over a distance of 5 600 km (3 500 mi).

CORAL ISLANDS

Coral islands and reefs are an important component

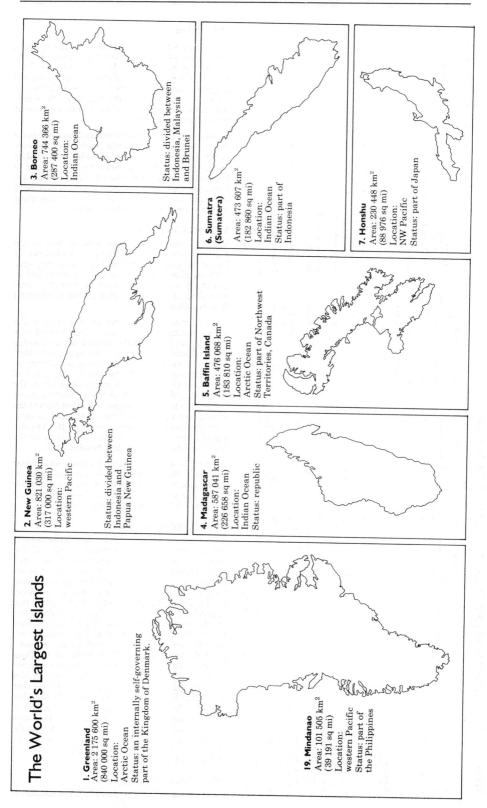

The World's Largest Islands

1. Greenland
Area: 2 175 600 km²
(840 000 sq mi)
Location:
Arctic Ocean
Status: an internally self-governing
part of the Kingdom of Denmark.

2. New Guinea
Area: 821 030 km²
(317 000 sq mi)
Location:
western Pacific
Status: divided between
Indonesia and
Papua New Guinea

3. Borneo
Area: 744 366 km²
(287 400 sq mi)
Location:
Indian Ocean
Status: divided between
Indonesia, Malaysia
and Brunei

4. Madagascar
Area: 587 041 km²
(226 658 sq mi)
Location:
Indian Ocean
Status: republic

5. Baffin Island
Area: 476 068 km²
(183 810 sq mi)
Location:
Arctic Ocean
Status: part of Northwest
Territories, Canada

6. Sumatra (Sumatera)
Area: 473 607 km²
(182 860 sq mi)
Location:
Indian Ocean
Status: part of
Indonesia

7. Honshu
Area: 230 448 km²
(88 976 sq mi)
Location:
NW Pacific
Status: part of Japan

19. Mindanao
Area: 101 505 km²
(39 191 sq mi)
Location:
western Pacific
Status: part of
the Philippines

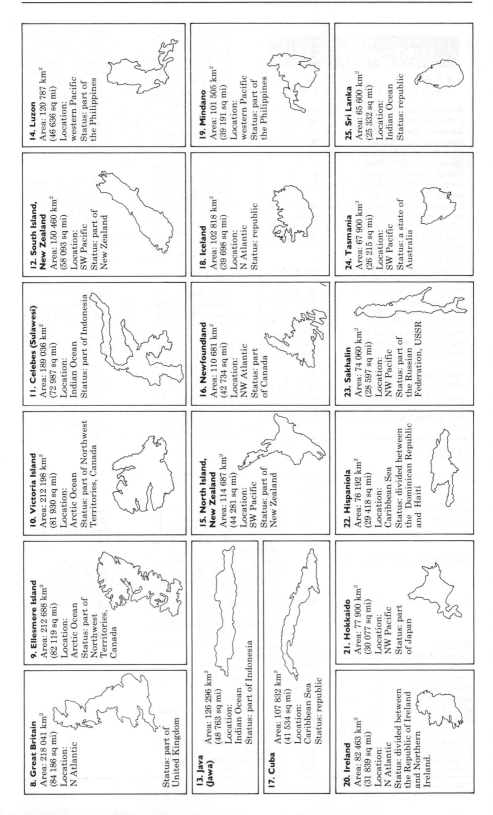

14. Luzon
Area: 120 787 km^2
(46 636 sq mi)
Location:
western Pacific
Status: part of
the Philippines

19. Mindano
Area: 101 505 km^2
(39 191 sq mi)
Location:
western Pacific
Status: part of
the Philippines

25. Sri Lanka
Area: 65 600 km^2
(25 332 sq mi)
Location:
Indian Ocean
Status: republic

**12. South Island,
New Zealand**
Area: 150 460 km^2
(58 093 sq mi)
Location:
SW Pacific
Status: part of
New Zealand

18. Iceland
Area: 102 818 km^2
(39 698 sq mi)
Location:
Status: republic

24. Tasmania
Area: 67 900 km^2
(26 215 sq mi)
Location:
SW Pacific
Status: a state of
Australia

11. Celebes (Sulawesi)
Area: 189 036 km^2
(72 987 sq mi)
Location:
Indian Ocean
Status: part of Indonesia

16. Newfoundland
Area: 110 681 km^2
(42 734 sq mi)
Location:
NW Atlantic
Status: part
of Canada

23. Sakhalin
Area: 74 060 km^2
(28 597 sq mi)
Location:
NW Pacific
Status: part of
the Russian
Federation, USSR

10. Victoria Island
Area: 212 198 km^2
(81 930 sq mi)
Location:
Arctic Ocean
Status: part of Northwest
Territories, Canada

**15. North Island,
New Zealand**
Area: 114 687 km^2
(44 281 sq mi)
Location:
SW Pacific
Status: part of
New Zealand

22. Hispaniola
Area: 76 192 km^2
(29 418 sq mi)
Location:
Caribbean Sea
Status: divided between
the Dominican Republic
and Haiti

9. Ellesmere Island
Area: 212 688 km^2
(82 119 sq mi)
Location:
Arctic Ocean
Status: part of
Northwest
Territories,
Canada

21. Hokkaido
Area: 77 900 km^2
(30 077 sq mi)
Location:
NW Pacific
Status: part
of Japan

8. Great Britain
Area: 218 041 km^2
(84 186 sq mi)
Location:
N Atlantic

Status: part of
United Kingdom

**13. Java
(Jawa)**
Area: 126 296 km^2
(48 763 sq mi)
Location:
Indian Ocean
Status: part of Indonesia

17. Cuba
Area: 107 832 km^2
(41 534 sq mi)
Location:
Caribbean Sea
Status: republic

20. Ireland
Area: 82 463 km^2
(31 839 sq mi)
Location:
N Atlantic
Status: divided between
the Republic of Ireland
and Northern
Ireland.

LARGEST ISLAND IN EACH EC COUNTRY

Belgium Apart from the small island of Outre-Meuse in the River Meuse at Liège, Belgium has no islands.
Denmark Sjaelland (Zealand) – 7016 km² (2709 sq mi).
Greenland, with an area of 2 175 600 km²/840 000 sq mi is not included within the EC although it is an integral part of the Kingdom of Denmark.
France Corsica – 8682 km² (3367 sq mi).
Germany Rügen – 926 km² (358 sq mi).
Greece Crete – 8331 km² (3216 sq mi).
Ireland The island of Ireland – of which the Republic of Ireland occupies 70 312 km² (27 148 sq mi) – has an area of 82 463 km² (31 839 sq mi). The largest island off the coast of the Republic of Ireland is Achill Island with an area of 3133 km² (1210 sq mi).
Italy Sicily – 25 460 km² (9830 sq mi).
Luxembourg is landlocked and has no lake islands.
Netherlands The former island of Walcheren – now joined to the mainland by a wide neck of land reclaimed from the sea – has an area of 212 km² (82 sq mi). The combined polders of East and West Flevoland – which could be considered to form an island surrounded by the freshwater IJsselmeer but linked to the mainland by six bridges – have an area of 958 km² (370 sq mi).
Portugal San Miguel in the Azores – 750 km² (290 sq mi).
Spain Mallorca (Majorca) – 3639 km² (1465 sq mi).
United Kingdom The mainland of Great Britain has an area of 218 041 km² (84 186 sq mi). The largest island off the coast of the British mainland is Lewis with Harris, Western Isles, Scotland, with an area of 2225 km² (859 sq mi).

of warm tropical and subtropical oceans and seas. They are formed from the skeletons of the group of primitive marine organisms known as corals. Coral islands develop where coral grows up towards the ocean surface from shallow submarine platforms – often volcanic cones. If the cone is totally submerged, then a coral atoll will develop – a circular or horseshoe-shaped coral ring which encloses a body of sea water called a lagoon. Upward growth of the coral ceases once sea level has been reached. Coral islands are therefore flat and low, unless a change in sea level has caused their elevation to change.

SEA LEVEL AND ISLANDS

Changes in sea level can cause new islands to appear or existing ones to disappear. During the last Ice Age eastern Britain was joined to mainland Europe, because sea levels were lower as much of the world's water was frozen in the ice caps and glaciers. As the ice melted, and the sea level rose, the North Sea and the Straits of Dover were re-established. By about 8500 years ago Britain was again an island.

DESERTS

Desert areas are defined in terms of aridity or the availability of water. Semi-arid areas receive on average 200–500 mm (8–20 in) of precipitation per annum, arid areas 25–200 mm (1–8 in) and hyper arid areas are those in which a continuous period of 12 months without any rainfall has been recorded. A desert may fall in any of these categories of aridity or may contain areas experiencing each of these conditions. The definitions and delineations of the desert areas listed are very approximate because deserts are advancing on many fronts and, in some places, are being reclaimed.

Globally, 13.3% of the world's land area is semi-arid, 13.7% is arid and 5.8% is hyper arid.

DESERTS

Name	Approx. area in km²	Approx. area in miles²	Territories
The Sahara	8 400 000	*3 250 000*	Algeria, Chad, Libya, Mali, Mauritania, Niger, Sudan, Tunisia, Egypt, Morocco, W. Sahara. Inc. Libyan Desert (1 550 000 km²/600 000 miles²) and Nubian Desert (260 000 km²/100 000 miles²))
Australian Desert	1 550 000	*600 000*	Australia. Embraces the Great Sandy (or Warburton) (420 000 km²/160 000 miles²), Great Victoria (325 000 km²/125 000 miles²), Simpson (Arunta) (310 000 km²/120 000 miles²), Gibson (220 000 km²/ 85 000 miles²) and Sturt Deserts
Arabian Desert	1 300 000	*500 000*	Saudi Arabia, Jordan, Oman, Yemen, UAE. Includes the Rub' al Khali or 'Empty Quarter' (647 500 km²/250 000 miles²), Syrian (325 000 km²/125 000 miles²) and An Nafud (129 500 km²/50 000 miles²) Deserts
The Gobi	1 040 000	*400 000*	Mongolia and China (Inner Mongolia)
Kalahari Desert	520 000	*200 000*	Botswana
Takla Makan	320 000	*125 000*	Xinjiang, China
Sonoran Desert	310 000	*120 000*	Arizona and California, USA and Mexico
Namib Desert	310 000	*120 000*	Namibia
Kara Kum*	270 000	*105 000*	Turkmenia, USSR
Thar Desert	260 000	*100 000*	North-western India and Pakistan
Somali Desert	260 000	*100 000*	Somalia
Atacama Desert	180 000	*70 000*	Northern Chile
Kyzyl Kum*	180 000	*70 000*	Uzbekistan-Kazakhstan, USSR
Dasht-e Lut**	52 000	*20 000*	Eastern Iran
Mojave Desert	35 000	*13 500*	Southern California, USA
Desierto de Sechura	26 000	*10 000*	Northwest Peru

* Together known as the Turkestan Desert.
** Sometimes called Iranian Desert.

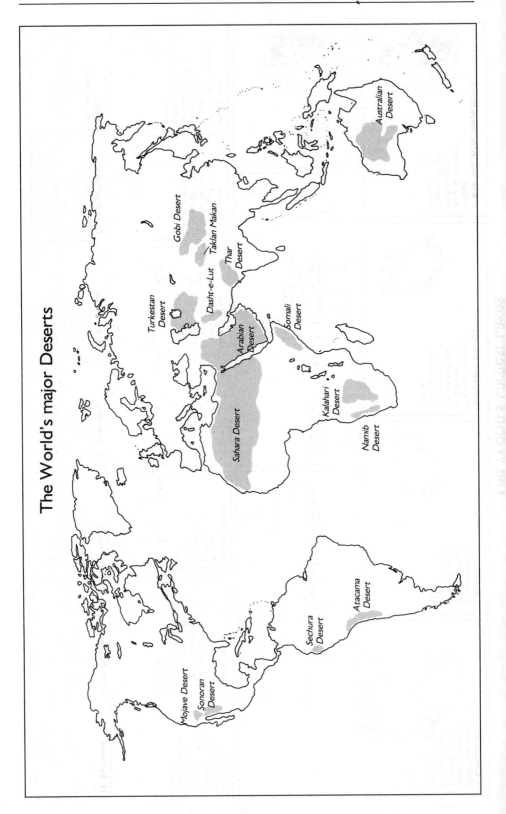

The World's major Deserts

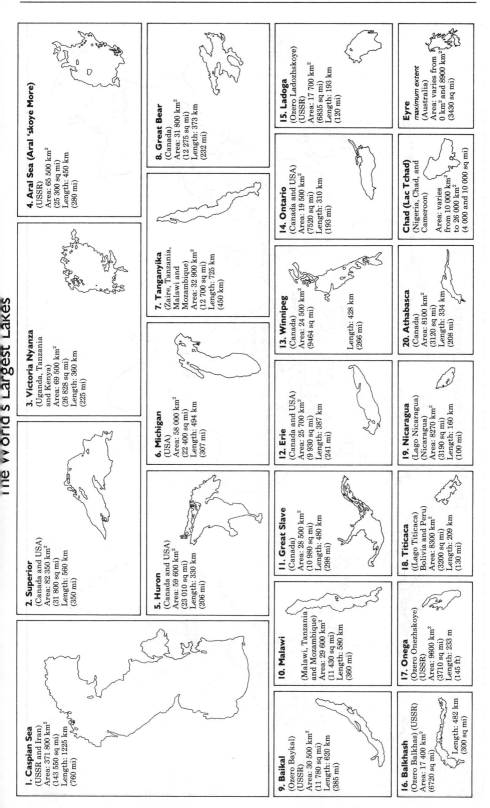

The World's Largest Lakes

1. Caspian Sea
(USSR and Iran)
Area: 371 800 km²
(143 550 sq mi)
Length: 1225 km
(760 mi)

2. Superior
(Canada and USA)
Area: 82 350 km²
(31 800 sq mi)
Length: 560 km
(350 mi)

3. Victoria Nyanza
(Uganda, Tanzania
and Kenya)
Area: 69 500 km²
(26 828 sq mi)
Length: 360 km
(225 mi)

4. Aral Sea (Aral 'skoye More)
(USSR)
Area: 65 500 km²
(25 300 sq mi)
Length: 450 km
(280 mi)

5. Huron
(Canada and USA)
Area: 59 600 km²
(23 010 sq mi)
Length: 330 km
(206 mi)

6. Michigan
(USA)
Area: 58 000 km²
(22 400 sq mi)
Length: 494 km
(307 mi)

7. Tanganyika
(Zaire, Tanzania,
Malawi and
Mozambique)
Area: 32 900 km²
(12 700 sq mi)
Length: 725 km
(450 km)

8. Great Bear
(Canada)
Area: 31 800 km²
(12 275 sq mi)
Length: 373 km
(232 mi)

9. Baikal
(Ozero Baykal)
(USSR)
Area: 30 500 km²
(11 780 sq mi)
Length: 620 km
(385 mi)

10. Malawi
(Malawi, Tanzania
and Mozambique)
Area: 29 600 km²
(11 430 sq mi)
Length: 580 km
(360 mi)

11. Great Slave
(Canada)
Area: 28 500 km²
(10 980 sq mi)
Length: 480 km
(298 mi)

12. Erie
(Canada and USA)
Area: 25 700 km²
(9 930 sq mi)
Length: 387 km
(241 mi)

13. Winnipeg
(Canada)
Area: 24 500 km²
(9464 sq mi)

Length: 428 km
(266 mi)

14. Ontario
(Canada and USA)
Area: 19 500 km²
(7520 sq mi)
Length: 310 km
(193 mi)

15. Ladoga
(Ozero Ladozhskoye)
(USSR)
Area: 17 700 km²
(6835 sq mi)
Length: 193 km
(120 mi)

16. Balkhash
(Ozero Balkhas) (USSR)
Area: 17 400 km²
(6720 sq mi)

Length: 482 km
(300 mi)

17. Onega
(Ozero Onezhskoye)
(USSR)
Area: 9600 km²
(3710 sq mi)
Length: 233 m
(145 ft)

18. Titicaca
((Lago Titicaca)
Bolivia and Peru)
Area: 8300 km²
(3200 sq mi)
Length: 209 km
(130 mi)

19. Nicaragua
(Lago Nicaragua)
(Nicaragua)
Area: 8270 km²
(3190 sq mi)
Length: 160 km
(100 mi)

20. Athabasca
(Canada)
Area: 8100 km²
(3120 sq mi)
Length: 334 km
(208 mi)

Chad (Lac Tchad)
(Nigeria, Chad, and
Cameroon)

Area: varies
from 10 000 km²
to 26 000 km²
(4 000 and 10 000 sq mi)

Eyre
maximum extent
(Australia)
Area: varies from
0 km² and 8900 km²
(3430 sq mi)

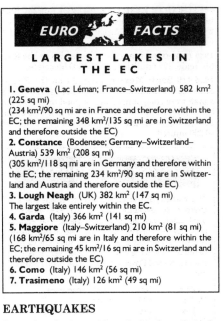

EURO FACTS

LARGEST LAKES IN THE EC

I. Geneva (Lac Léman; France–Switzerland) 582 km² (225 sq mi)
(234 km²/90 sq mi are in France and therefore within the EC; the remaining 348 km²/135 sq mi are in Switzerland and therefore outside the EC)
2. Constance (Bodensee; Germany–Switzerland–Austria) 539 km² (208 sq mi)
(305 km²/118 sq mi are in Germany and therefore within the EC; the remaining 234 km²/90 sq mi are in Switzerland and Austria and therefore outside the EC)
3. Lough Neagh (UK) 382 km² (147 sq mi)
The largest lake entirely within the EC.
4. Garda (Italy) 366 km² (141 sq mi)
5. Maggiore (Italy–Switzerland) 210 km² (81 sq mi)
(168 km²/65 sq mi are in Italy and therefore within the EC; the remaining 45 km²/16 sq mi are in Switzerland and therefore outside the EC)
6. Como (Italy) 146 km² (56 sq mi)
7. Trasimeno (Italy) 126 km² (49 sq mi)

EARTHQUAKES

An earthquake is a sudden release of energy in the Earth's crust or upper mantle. As the planet's tectonic plates jostle against each other and become distorted, tremendous strain builds up – and from time to time the strain energy is discharged in zones where the rocks are weakest. The result is a sudden violent shock that can have highly destructive effects on the Earth's surface nearby.

The damaging effects of an earthquake are due to the vibrations (*seismic waves*) emitted by the shock. For a brief moment the waves shake the ground close to the earthquake, frequently producing permanent effects. Few people are ever killed or injured directly by an earthquake; death and injury are more likely to result from the collapse of buildings caused by the earthquake.

Whether or not there are people or buildings present, earthquakes may cause fissures to appear in the ground, produce changes in the level and tilt of the ground surface, divert rivers and streams, and trigger landslides and avalanches. Undersea earthquakes may also give rise to *tsunami* – huge amounts of sea water that can travel across the oceans for thousands of kilometres, causing devastation when they hit land (see p. 62).

WHERE EARTHQUAKES OCCUR

Most earthquakes take place along the boundaries of the tectonic plates – along oceanic ridges, transform faults and subduction zones – because this is where the plates interact most intensely, and hence where distortion and strain build-up are greatest. However, not all earthquakes occur along plate margins. In North America, for example, the most damaging earthquakes of historic times have taken place not in California, through which runs a transform fault (the San Andreas fault), but in South Carolina and Missouri, both of which are far from plate margins. The reasons for this are unclear, but earthquakes within the interiors of plates may be due to deep, still active faults remaining from a much earlier phase of plate tectonics. California is still America's most

notorious seismic area, however, because it is there that earthquakes are most frequent.

The point at which an earthquake occurs is called the *focus*, or *hypocentre*. The point on the Earth's surface directly above the focus is called the *epicentre*. A world map of epicentres is largely a map of the Earth's plate boundaries.

All earthquake foci lie within about the upper 700 km (435 mi) of the Earth. Within this range, earthquakes are classified as *shallow* (focal depths of 0–70 km / 0–43 mi), *intermediate* (70–300 km / 43–186 mi), or *deep* (below 300 km / 186 mi). There are about three times as many intermediate earthquakes as there are deep ones, and about ten times as many shallow ones. It is the shallow shocks that produce most of the damage at the Earth's surface, for the obvious reason that they are closer to it. Collectively, the shallow earthquakes also release the most energy – about 75% of the total, compared to 3% for deep earthquakes.

MEASURING EARTHQUAKES

The size of an earthquake is specified by its magnitude, sometimes called the Richter magnitude after the American seismologist, Charles Richter, who devised the scale in the 1930s (see p. 121). Magnitude is actually a measure of the size (*amplitude*) of the waves emitted by the earthquake. However, the magnitude scale is logarithmic. This means that each step up the scale represents a ten-fold increase in the amplitude of the emitted waves. Thus the waves from a magnitude-7 earthquake are 10 times bigger than those from a magnitude-6 shock, 100 times bigger than those from a magnitude-5 event, and so on.

Magnitude can also be regarded as a measure of the energy released by an earthquake, because energy is related to wave size. The relationship is such that each division on the magnitude scale represents an approximately thirty-fold difference in energy. Thus a magnitude-7 earthquake releases about 30 times more energy than a magnitude-6 shock and about 30 × 30 = 900 times more energy than a magnitude-5 event. This explains why most of the energy released by earthquakes comes from the very few big shocks that occur each year rather than from the million or so smaller earthquakes.

To specify the size of an earthquake in terms of its effects, an intensity scale is used. In the West (but not in Japan or the USSR, which use slightly different systems) this is usually the *Modified Mercalli Scale* (see p. 121).

HISTORIC EARTHQUAKES

The six earthquakes in which the known loss of life has exceeded 100 000 have been:

Eastern Mediterranean In the eastern Mediterranean about 1 100 000 people were killed in an earthquake c. July 1201.

Shanxi Province, China On 2 February 1556, 830 000 were killed in an earthquake.

Calcutta, India On 11 October 1737, 300 000 died in an earthquake.

Tangshan, China An earthquake of 8.2 on the Richter Scale killed 242 000 at Tangshan on 27 July 1976. The original death toll of 655 237 was unaccountably reduced on 4 January 1977.

Gansu Province, China On 16 December 1920, 180 000 died in landslides accompanying an earthquake which registered 8·6 on the Richter Scale.

Kanto Plain, Japan An earthquake registering 8.3 on the Richter Scale killed 142 807 on the Kanto Plain, Honshu, Japan, on 1 September 1923. The material damage done in the Kanto Plain, which includes Tokyo, was estimated at £1 000 000 000.

The destructive effect of an earthquake depends not only on its size but also on the human population of the area affected, the nature of buildings and any other natural events that may be triggered. This is well indicated by the data below, which considers recent major earthquakes.

TWENTIETH-CENTURY EARTHQUAKES

Other notable earthquakes, with loss of life, during this century have included:

1906 (31 Jan): Colombian coast 8.6 on the Richter Scale.

1906 (18 Apr): San Francisco, USA 8.3 on the Richter Scale; 452 fatalities.

1908 (28 Dec): Messina, Italy 7.5 on the Richter Scale; 80 000 fatalities.

1915 (13 Jan): Avezzano, Italy 29 970 fatalities.

1920: Gansu, China (see above).

1923: Kanto Plain, Japan (see above).

1932 (26 Dec): Gansu Province, China 7.6 on the Richter Scale; 70 000 fatalities.

1935 (31 May): Quetta (which in 1935 was in India but is now in Pakistan). An earthquake registering 7.5 on the Richter Scale; 25 000 fatalities.

1939 (27 Dec): Erzincan, Turkey 7.9 on the Richter Scale; 30 000 fatalities.

1950 (15 Aug): Assam, India 8.6 on the Richter Scale; 1500 fatalities.

1952 (4 Nov): Kamchatka, USSR 8.5 on the Richter Scale.

1957 (9 Mar): Aleutian Islands, Alaska, USA 8.3 on the Richter Scale.

1960 (29 Feb): Agadir, Morocco 5.8 on the Richter Scale; 12 000 fatalities.

1960 (22 May): Lebu, Chile 8.3 on Richter Scale.

1964 (28 Mar): Anchorage, Alaska, USA 8.5 on the Richter Scale; 131 fatalities.

1970 (31 May): Northern Peru 7.7 on the Richter Scale; 66 800 fatalities.

1971 (9 Feb): Los Angeles, USA 6.5 on the Richter Scale; 64 fatalities.

1972 (23 Dec): Nicaragua 6.2 on the Richter Scale; 5000 fatalities.

1976 (4 Feb): Guatemala 7.5 on the Richter Scale; 22 700 fatalities.

1976: Tangshan, China (see above).

1977 (4 Mar): Bucharest, Romania 7.5 on the Richter Scale; 1541 fatalities.

1978 (16 Sep): Tabas, Northeast Iran 7.7 on the Richter Scale; 25 000 fatalities.

1980 (10 Oct): El Asnam, Algeria 7.5 on the Richter Scale; 2327 fatalities.

1980 (23 Nov): Potenza, Italy 6.8 on the Richter Scale; c. 3000 fatalities.

1982 (13 Dec): Yemen 6.0 on the Richter Scale; 2800 fatalities.

1983 (31 Mar): Papayan, Colombia 5.5 on the Richter Scale; 264 dead; 150 000 homeless.

1983 (26 May): North Honshu, Japan 7.7 on the Richter Scale; 58 deaths, mostly due to the effects of a tsunami.

1983 (30 Oct): Eastern Turkey 7.1 on the Richter Scale. Although there were 1233 fatalities, there was relatively little damage in this widely felt earthquake.

1985 (3 Mar): Algarroba, Chile 7.8 on the Richter Scale; 177 fatalities and 150 000 homeless.

1985 (19 Sep): Mexico City 8.1 on the Richter Scale; 20 000 fatalities. The effects of the first earthquake were compounded by a second on 20 September – 7.5 on the Richter Scale – which caused the collapse of damaged buildings. 31 000 homeless; 40 000 injured.

BRITISH EARTHQUAKES

The earliest British earthquake of which there is indisputable evidence was in AD 974 when an earthquake was felt all over England. The earliest precisely recorded was on 1 May 1048, in Worcester. British earthquakes of an intensity sufficient to have raised or moved the chair of the observer (scale 8 on the locally used Davison's scale) have been recorded on:

25 Apr	1180	Nottinghamshire
15 Apr	1185	Lincoln
1 June	1246	Canterbury, Kent
21 Dec	1246	Wells
19 Feb	1249	South Wales
11 Sept	1275	Somerset
21 May	1382	Canterbury, Kent
28 Dec	1480	Norfolk
26 Feb	1575	York to Bristol
6 Apr	1580	London[1]
30 Apr	1736	Menstrie, Clackmannan
1 May	1736	Menstrie, Clackmannan
14 Nov	1769	Inverness[2]
18 Nov	1795	Derbyshire
13 Aug	1816	Inverness[3]
23 Oct	1839	Comrie, Perth
30 July	1841	Comrie, Perth
6 Oct	1863	Hereford
22 Apr	1884	Colchester[4]
17 Dec	1896	Hereford
18 Sept	1901	Inverness
27 June	1906	Swansea[5]
30 July	1926	Jersey
15 Aug	1926	Hereford
7 June	1931	Dogger Bank (5·6R)
11 Feb	1957	Midlands
26 Dec	1979	Longtown, Cumbria
19 July	1984	W. Britain & Ireland (5·5R)
2 Apr	1990	Shropshire (5·1R)

[1] About 6 p.m. First recorded fatality – an apprentice killed by masonry falling from Christ Church.
[2] 'Several people' reported killed. Parish register indicates not more than one. Date believed to be 14th.
[3] At 10.45 p.m. Heard in Aberdeen (133 km/83 miles away), felt in Glasgow (185 km/115 miles away). Strongest ever in Scotland.
[4] At 9.18 a.m. Heard in Oxford (174 km/95 miles away), felt in Exeter and Ostend, Belgium (152 km/95 miles away). At least three, possibly five, killed. Strongest ever in British Isles at 6 on the Richter scale.
[5] At 9.45 a.m. Strongest ever in Wales. Felt over 98 000 km²/37 800 miles²).

1987 (5 Mar): Northeast Ecuador 7.0 on the Richter Scale; 2000 fatalities in a series of earthquakes over 3 days. Although they largely affected areas of low population, 75 000 people were injured.

1988 (6 Nov): Southwest China 7.6 on the Richter Scale; over 1000 fatalities and 500 000 homeless.

1988 (7 Dec): Armenia, USSR 6.9 on the Richter Scale; 25 000 fatalities. Six large cities were devastated and 500 000 people were made homeless.

1989 (22 Jan): Tadzhikistan, USSR 5.3 on the Richter Scale; 574 deaths, all due to the village of Sharora being blanketed in a mud-slide triggered by the earthquake.

1989 (17 Oct): San Francisco Bay, USA 7.1 on the Richter Scale; 67 deaths. There were relatively few deaths, probably owing to the strong building design in the major cities, but the old quarter of San Francisco was badly damaged, and the Oakland section of a raised highway collapsed. Billions of dollars' worth of damage was sustained.

GLACIATION

It has been estimated that over a tenth of the Earth's land surface – about 15 600 000 km² (6 020 000 sq mi) – is permanently covered with ice. Ice is in fact the world's biggest reservoir of fresh water, with over three quarters of the global total contained in ice sheets, ice caps and glaciers. These range in size from the huge Antarctic and Greenland ice sheets, to the small glaciers found in high-latitude and high-altitude mountain ranges.

Ice bodies develop where winter snowfall is able to accumulate and persist through the summer. Over time this snow is compressed into an ice body, and such ice bodies may grow to blanket the landscape as an *ice sheet* or *ice cap*. Alternatively, the ice body may grow to form a mass that flows down a slope – a *glacier* – often cutting a valley and eroding rock material that is eventually deposited at a lower altitude as the ice melts.

THE FORMATION OF ICE BODIES

Ice bodies develop mainly through the accumulation of snow, or sometimes by the freezing of rain as it hits an ice surface. Obviously, not all the snow that falls is turned into ice – during the northern-hemisphere winter over half the world's land surface and up to one third of the surfaces of the oceans may be blanketed by snow and ice. Most of this snow and ice is only temporary, as the Sun's warmth and energy are able to melt the cover during warm winter days or as winter passes into spring and summer.

In some places, however, the summer warmth is unable to melt all the snowfall of the previous winter. This may be because summer temperatures are rather low, or summer is very short, or because winter snowfall is very high. Where this occurs, snow lies all year round (this snow is sometimes called *firn* or *névé*) and becomes covered by the snow of the next winter. As this process continues from year to year, the snow that is buried becomes compressed and transformed into *glacier ice*.

Latitude and altitude both determine where permanent snow can accumulate. The level that separates permanent snow cover from places where the snow melts in the summer is called the *snowline* or *firnline*. The snowline increases in altitude towards the Equator: in polar regions it lies at sea level, in Norway at 1200–1500 m (4000–5000 ft) above sea level,

and in the Alps at about 2700 m (9000 ft). Permanent snow and ice can even occur in the tropics close to the equator: in East Africa, for example, the snowline lies at about 4900 m (16 000 ft), so that glaciers are found on Mount Kenya, Kilimanjaro, and the Ruwenzori Mountains.

ICE SHEETS AND ICE CAPS

Ice sheets and ice caps are ice bodies that have grown into domes that blanket an area of land, submerging valleys, hills and mountains. Occasionally, 'islands' of land, called *nunataks*, protrude through the 'sea' of ice. Ice sheets are defined as having an area over 50 000 km² (19 000 sq mi); ice caps are smaller.

SEA ICE

There is no ice sheet over the North Pole because there is no land there – however, the Arctic Ocean is always frozen and, during the winter, Arctic *sea ice* covers about 12 million km² (4.6 million sq mi).

An area of sea ice that is joined to a coast is called an *ice shelf*. Ice shelves occur in the Arctic, joined to the coasts of northern Canada and Greenland, and in the Antarctic – notably the Ross Ice Shelf, which has an area greater than France. Ocean currents and seasonal melting can cause ice sheets to break up, creating areas of *pack ice* or smaller *ice floes*.

ICE MOVEMENTS

Ice bodies move and flow under the influence of gravity. The movement of frozen water is obviously much slower than when it is in its liquid form. Most glaciers flow at a velocity between 3 and 300 m (10 and 1000 ft) per year. Glaciers on steep slopes may move much faster, and the Quarayaq Glacier, which is supplied with ice from the Greenland Ice Sheet, averages 20–24 m (65–80 ft) per day. Many glaciers experience *surges* – which may last a few days or several years – when flow is extremely rapid, often equivalent to rates of up to 10 km (6 mi) a year.

GLACIERS AND LANDSCAPE

Glacier ice is a very powerful erosional agent, smoothing rock surfaces and cutting deep valleys. *Fjords* (for example, along the coasts of Norway and Alaska) are U-shaped glacial valleys that become submerged by the sea after the melting of the ice that produced them. U-shaped valleys are classically regarded as glacial features, but they can be formed by other processes – for example, by rivers in their middle and lower reaches.

A sliding glacier erodes by *plucking* blocks of rock from its bed and by *abrading* rock surfaces, i.e. breaking off small particles and rock fragments. The rock that is eroded is transported by the ice and deposited as the glacier travels down slope and melts. Glacial deposits can form distinct landforms such as *moraines* (ridges) and *drumlins* (small hills), or they may simply be deposited as *glacial till*, a blanket of sediment covering the landscape.

RECENT GLACIAL PERIODS

The last six glacial periods (identified from ocean core evidence) have been dated as follows:

	began	*ended*
1.	72 000 years ago	10 000 years ago
2.	188 000 years ago	128 000 years ago
3.	280 000 years ago	244 000 years ago
4.	347 000 years ago	334 000 years ago
5.	475 000 years ago	421 000 years ago
6.	650 000 years ago	579 000 years ago

NAMES OF THE LAST GLACIAL PERIODS
identified from land-based evidence

Britain	N. Europe	Alps	N. America
Devensian	Weichel	Würm	Wisconsin
Wolstonian	Saale	Riss	Illinoian
Anglian	Eltser	Mindel	Kansan
Beeston			
Baventian	Menap	Günz	Nebraskan
Thurne	Eburon	Donau	
Walton	Brüggemn	Biber	

It is very difficult to correlate names derived from land-based evidence with dates derived from ocean cores, except for the most recent glacial period. These names cannot therefore automatically be assumed to relate to the last glacials identified from ocean evidence. Correlations between different regions are also difficult.

GLACIATED AREAS OF THE WORLD

It is estimated that 15 600 000 km^2 (6 020 000 miles^2) or about 10·4 per cent of the world's land surface is permanently covered with ice.

	km^2	miles^2
South polar regions	12 588 000	5 250 000
Antarctic icesheet	*12 535 000*	*4 839 000*
other Antarctic glaciers	*53 000*	*20 500*
North Polar Regions	2 070 000	799 000
Greenland ice sheet	*1 726 000*	*666 40095*
other Greenland glaciers	*76 200*	*29 400*
Canadian archipelago	*153 200*	*59 100*
Svalbard (Spitzbergen)	*58 000*	*22 400*
other Arctic islands	*55 700*	*21 500*
Asia	115 800	44 400
Alaska/Rockies	76 900	29 700
South America	26 500	10 200
Iceland	12 170	*4 699*
Alpine Europe	9 280	*3 580*
New Zealand	1015	*391*
Africa	12	*5*

WORLD'S LONGEST GLACIERS

km	miles	
515	*320*	Lambert-Fisher Ice Passage, Antarctica
418	*260*	Novaya Zemlya, North Island, USSR
362	*225*	Arctic Institute Ice Passage, Victoria Land, E Antarctica
289	*180*	Nimrod–Lennox–King Ice Passage, E Antarctica
241	*150*	Denman Glacier, E Antarctica
225	*140*	Beardmore Glacier, E Antarctica
225	*140*	Recovery Glacier, W Antarctica
200	*124*	*Petermanns Gletscher, Knud Rasmussen Land, Greenland
193	*120*	Unnamed Glacier, SW Ross Ice Shelf, W Antarctica
185	*115*	Slessor Glacier, W Antarctica

* Petermanns Gletscher is the largest in the northern hemisphere: it extends 40 km (24.8 miles) out to sea.

The largest glacier in Europe is the Aletsch Glacier (Bernese Oberland, Switzerland), which is 35 km (22 miles) long.

The longest glacier in the Himalaya-Karakoram is the Hispar-Biafo Ice Passage, which is 122 km (76 mi) long.

ICE AGES

Ice ages, more correctly called glacial periods, have been a major phenomenon of the last 2 millon years. Geological evidence, however, demonstrates that glacial periods have affected the Earth periodically over 2300 million years. It is not known why the Earth's atmosphere and surface change substantially, although it is generally thought that the causes of major ice ages relate to cyclic changes in the pattern and character of the Earth's orbit around the Sun.

Evidence for glacial periods comes from a range of sources, including studies of sediments accumulated in deep oceans and lake basins, and investigations of long cores of ice extracted from Antarctic and Greenland ice sheets. Ocean sediments are particularly valuable with their long, undisturbed sequences that can be dated using modern radiometric and palaeomagnetic methods.

It is thought that there have been between 15 and 22 glacials during the last 2 million years – they become harder to determine further back in time. At its height the most recent glacial period saw Canada and Scandinavia covered by great ice sheets. Ice caps centered on Highland Scotland, Snowdonia, the English Lake District and the Alps, with outlet and valley glaciers extending out over the lowlands.

CAVES

Caves are naturally occurring holes in the ground that can be penetrated by humans. They are often linked into complex systems of chambers and passageways, which can extend many kilometres in length, and penetrate deep into the Earth. The entrances of many caves have provided shelter for both animals and humans in the past, and their accumulated remains can tell us much about extinct animal forms and the life of prehistoric man. Some caves are also noted for their animal life today: as well as numerous invertebrates, bats, birds, snakes and even crocodiles may make their homes in caves.

By far the majority of caves occur in limestone areas. This is because of the solubility of limestone in rainwater (H_2O) containing carbon dioxide (CO_2) in solution. This solution is carbonic acid (H_2CO_3), a weak acid that can attack limestone on its own, but its effects are much greater if it is augmented by acids from soil and vegetation. Not all limestones have caves as some, such as chalk, are mechanically weak and will not support cave roofs. Others have few caves owing to their high porosity, which allows the acidic water to pass through the whole rock mass without concentrating at any particular points.

Limestone landscapes with cave systems are known as *karst landscapes*, named after an area of northern Yugoslavia. Karst landscapes are typified by a lack of surface streams, the presence of swallets (stream sinks) and collapse potholes, dry valleys (which once had streams now flowing underground), resurgences, and of bare rock pavements. These *limestone pavements* are intersected into areas known as *clints* by fissures about 50 cm (20 in) wide known as *grikes*, this process being caused by the etching out of joints and subsequent glacial smoothing. Karst landscapes may also have numerous *dolines* (funnel-shaped hollows at joint intersections) and *poljes* (enclosed valleys with internal drainage through caves). Tropical karst is typified by towers and cones formed by intense downward erosion, with "cockpits" separating cone-shaped hills.

Caves in rocks other than limestone include a variety of *sea caves* where erosion has etched out weaknesses in sea cliffs. *Lava caves* occur in many basalt volcanic areas, such as Iceland, Hawaii, Kenya and Australia. They are generally tubes within lava flows where the molten material has flowed out from beneath the solidified crust. *Fissure caves* occur in a few hard-rock areas where fault zones have been widened by erosion.

Ice caves are of two sorts. First, there are *englacial tubes* through which streams of melt water run beneath glaciers. Though entirely in ice, they show many of the features of limestone caves, although rapid changes may take place owing to glacier movement. Second, there are caves in high mountain regions where the air within the cave rarely if ever rises above freezing point, so that water percolating in from the surface during the summer freezes into icicles, often very large, and sometimes joining into ice masses underground.

WORLD'S DEEPEST CAVES

Name	Depth (m)	Depth (ft)
Réseau Jean Bernard, Haute-Savoie, France	1602	5256
Shakta Pantjukhina, Georgia, USSR	1508	4947
Sistema del Trave, Asturias, Spain	1441	4728
Aminakoateak, Navarre, Spain	1408	4630
Snezhnaya, Abkhazia, Georgia, USSR	1370	4495
Sistema Huautla, Oaxaca, Mexico	1353	4439
Réseau de la Pierre-Saint-Martin, Pyrenees, France	1342	4403
Boj-Bulok, Pamir, USSR	1315	4313
Sisterna Cuicateca, Mexico	1243	4077
Réseau Rhododendrons-Gouffre Berger, Isère, France	1242	4072
V.V. Iljukhina, Georgia, USSR	1240	4068
Scwersystem, Salzburg, Austria	1219	3999
Gouffre Mirolda, Haute-Savoie France	1211	3973
Abisso Ulivifer, Apennines, Italy	1210	3969
Veliko Fbrego, Croatia, Yugoslavia	1198	3930
Complesso Fighiera Corchia, Tuscany, Italy	1190	3986
Sistema Aranonera, Aragon, Spain	1185	3888
Dachstein-Mammuthöhle, Upper Austria, Austria	1180	3871
Jubilaümsschacht, Salzburg, Austria	1173	3848
Sima 56 de Andara, Cantabrica, Spain	1169	3835
Anou Ifflis, Djurdjura, Tunisia	1159	3802
Gouffre de la Bordure de Tourugne, Pyrenees, France	1159	3802
Abisso Vive le Donne*, Alps, Italy	1156	3792
Sistema Badalona, Pyrenees, Spain	1149	3769
Pozu del Xiyo, Picos, Spain	1148	3765

* Current dye tracing tests indicate that this cave may be over 1800 m deep

WORLD'S LONGEST CAVE SYSTEMS

Name	Length (km)	Length (mi)
Mammoth Cave, Kentucky, USA	560	348
Optimisticeskaya, Ukraine, USSR	165	103
Hölloch, Schwyz, Switzerland	133	83
Jewel Cave, South Dakota, USA	127	79
Siebenhengste-Hohganthöhlen, Bern, Switzerland	110	68
Ozernaya, Ukraine, USSR	107	66
La Coume d'Hyouernède, Haute-Garonne, France	90	56
Ojo Guareña, Castile-Leon, Spain	89	55
Wind Cave, South Dakota, USA	82	51
Zoluska, Ukraine, USSR	82	51
Fisher Ridge Cave, Kentucky, USA	77	49
Gua Airjernih, Sarawak, Malaysia	75	47
Sistema Purificacion, Mexico	72	45
Friars Hole Cave, West Virginia, USA	69	43
Lechuguilla Cave, New Mexico, USA	67	42
Ease Gill, West Yorkshire, England, UK	66	41

WORLD'S LARGEST CAVE CHAMBERS

The following list gives the surface area of the floor of the largest known cave chambers.

Name	Area (m²)	Area (sq ft)
Sarawak Chamber*, Lubang Nasib Bagus, Gunung Mulu National Park, Sarawak, Malaysia	162 700	1 751 287
Torca del Carlista, Spain	76 600	824 515
Majlis al Jinn, Oman	58 000	624 306
Belize Chamber, Belize	50 000	538 195

* Sarawak Chamber is 700 m (2300 ft) in length, with an average width of 300 m (980 ft) and is nowhere less than 70 m (230 ft) high.

DEPRESSIONS

World's deepest depressions	Maximum depth below sea level (m)	(ft)
Dead Sea, Jordan–Israel	395	*1296*
Turfan Depression, Xinjiang, China	153	*505*
Munkhafad el Qattâra (Qattâra Depression), Egypt	132	*436*
Poluostrov Mangyshlak, Kazakhstan, USSR	131	*433*
Danakil Depression, Ethiopia	116	*383*
Death Valley, California, USA	86	*282*
Salton Sink, California, USA	71	*235*
Zapadnyy Chink Ustyurta, Kazakhstan USSR	70	*230*
Prikaspiyskaya Nizmennost', Russian Federation and Kazakhstan USSR	67	*220*
Ozera Sarykamysh, Uzbekistan and Turkmenia, USSR	45	*148*
El Faiyûm, Egypt	44	*147*
Peninsula Valdiés Lago Enriquillo, Dominican Republic	40	*131*

Note: Immense areas of western Antarctica would be below sea level if stripped of their ice sheet. The deepest estimated crypto-depression is the bed rock on the Hollick–Kenyon plateau beneath the Marie Byrd Land ice cap (84° 37' S 110° W) at – 2468 m (– 8100 ft).

The bed of Lake Baykal (USSR) is 1484 m (4872 ft) below sea level, and the bed of the Dead Sea is 792 m (2600 ft) below sea level.

EURO FACTS

AREAS BELOW SEA LEVEL IN THE EC

Over one quarter of the Netherlands lies below sea level. The only other significant areas in the EC below sea level are in Cambridgeshire and Norfolk, England. These areas below sea level comprise areas of geologically recent marine and river sediments, commonly reclaimed from tidal marshland and the sea by draining and the construction of protective barriers. The level of the land often falls during reclamation owing to shrinkage as water is removed. Areas below sea level are likely to increase during the next century if global warming causes ice cap melting and sea level rise to occur.

Areas below sea level:

NETHERLANDS

Central dune barrier area (polder lands of North and South Holland) c. 6800 km² (2625 sq mi)
Friesland (Groningen area) c. 2000 km² (770 sq mi)
Wieringermeer Polder 193 km² (75 sq mi)
Noordost Polder 469 km² (181 sq mi)
Oostelijk Flevoland Polder 528 km² (204 sq mi)
Zuidelijk Flevoland Polder 430 km² (166 sq mi)

U K

Downham Market area (Norfolk/Cambridgeshire) c. 100 km² (39 mi²)
Littleport-Mildenhall (Cambridgeshire) c. 600 km² (232 mi²)
Fletton-March area (Cambridgeshire) c. 900 km² (347 mi²)

The ground surface of large areas of Central Greenland under the overburden of ice up to 341 m (11 190 ft) thick are depressed to 365 m (1200 ft) below sea level.

The world's largest exposed depression is the Prikaspiyskaya Nizmennost', which includes the northern third of the Caspian Sea – which is itself 28 m (92 ft) below sea-level – and stretches up to 400 km (250 miles) inland.

The Qattâra Depression extends for 547 km (340 miles) and is up to 128 km (80 miles) wide.

CLIMATOLOGY AND METEOROLOGY

Meteorology is the science of the atmosphere, from the Greek word '*meteorologica*', meaning 'matters of the atmosphere', and first used in a treatise by Aristotle.

Weather is the condition of the atmosphere at any one place and time, as described by air temperature and humidity, wind speed and direction, cloud amount and precipitation from cloud (drizzle, rain, snow, hail), together with atmospheric pressure, sunshine and visibility.

Climate is the normal weather condition for an area during a season or year. The climate of an area is described by means of an average of the statistics of the various weather factors over a period of time, normally 30 years. At any one time the weather may be quite different from the accepted climate.

CONSTITUENTS OF AIR

Atmospheric air consists of gases in fixed proportion, and gases in variable quantities. The most important of the fixed proportion gases are:

Nitrogen which constitutes 78% of atmospheric air.

Oxygen which constitutes 21% of atmospheric air.

The most important of the variable gases are:

Ozone which occurs at high altitudes. It provides some protection against the ultraviolet rays from the sun.

Carbon dioxide which acts like glass in a greenhouse to retain heat in the lower atmosphere.

Water vapour acquired by evaporation from oceans, rivers, and even puddles. All precipitation is produced from water vapour by condensation.

WATER IN THE ATMOSPHERE

There is one basic supply of water in the world which is continually recycled. Water evaporates from oceans; vapour condenses again as dew, fog or cloud; rain or snow falls from clouds and percolates through soil back to the oceans, or is absorbed by plants and transpired as vapour from foliage.

The warmer the air, the more vapour it can hold, although there is a maximum capacity for every

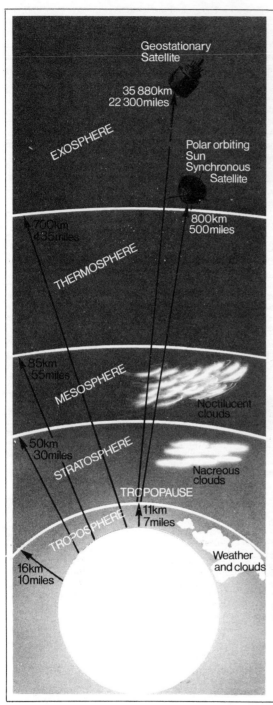

Geostationary
Satellite

35 880km
22 300miles

EXOSPHERE

Polar orbiting
Sun
Synchronous
Satellite

700km
435miles

800km
500miles

THERMOSPHERE

85km
55miles

MESOSPHERE

Noctilucent
clouds

50km
30miles

STRATOSPHERE

Nacreous
clouds

TROPOPAUSE

11km
7miles

TROPOSPHERE

16km
10miles

Weather
and clouds

THE EARTH'S ATMOSPHERIC LAYERS

In the *exosphere* – more than 700 km (435 miles) above the Earth – temperature no longer has any terrestrial meaning. Geostationary satellites at a height of 35,880 km (22,300 miles) monitor weather from fixed stations above the Equator. Sun-synchronous satellites at a lesser height orbit above both poles every two hours.

The *thermosphere* is characterized by an unremitting rise in temperature, perhaps to as much as 1480°C (2696°F) at 500 km (310 miles) high, during maximum solar activity.

The *mesosphere* is between about 50 km (30 and 55 miles) above the Earth. Temperature generally decreases with height. The boundary between the thermosphere and the mesosphere is called the mesopause.

In the *stratosphere* temperature does not decrease appreciably with height. The boundary between the mesosphere and the stratosphere – about 50 km (30 miles) above the Earth – is called the stratopause.

Cloud and precipitation form in the *troposphere*, the lowest atmospheric layer. The tropopause – the boundary between the stratosphere and the troposphere – varies from about 16 km (10 miles) above the Equator, to about 11 km (7 miles) over latitudes 50° N and S, and is only about 9 km (6 miles) above the Poles. These values are somewhat higher in summer. Air temperature generally decreases with height, although there are occasional short-term inversions when temperature increases with height.

Air temperature alters because of contact with warming or cooling surfaces or because of changes in atmospheric pressure acting upon the air. Air moving upwards into regions of lower pressure expands and thereby cools, while air subsiding into regions of higher pressure is compressed and warmed. These two methods of altering air temperature constantly battle for supremacy; e.g. air which warms by contact with a warmer ground becomes lighter and rises, and in so doing cools because of expansion.

temperature. The path followed by an air mass determines whether air is saturated with water vapour or has the capacity to hold more water vapour. For example, an air mass is moist after a long sea track, and dry after a long land track.

Relative humidity is the water vapour content of a body of air, expressed as a percentage of the maximum possible. If an air mass is saturated, its relative humidity (RH) is 100% and no more water can be evaporated into that air mass until its temperature rises again beyond its saturation temperature or *dew point*. If the temperature of the air falls below dew point, then the amount of water retained as water vapour has to be reduced by means of condensation as water drops.

All precipitation – rain, snow, hail, sleet, etc. – is the result of air cooling to dew point or below. The higher the RH when such cooling begins, the quicker condensation will occur.

CLIMATIC ZONES

There are many different climates around the world, from arctic to tropical. Climate has a crucial effect on the kinds of vegetation found in a particular region. Climate can be classified in many complex ways. The broadest and most general method is to divide each hemisphere into broad bands or climatic zones. The ancient Greeks made the earliest attempts at classifying climate. They identified a *winterless tropical region* located in the low latitudes, a *summerless polar region* where temperatures are usually very low, and an *intermediate* or *middle-latitude region*, now called the *temperate latitudes*, with cool summers and mild winters. The Greeks identified that temperature roughly follows the bands of latitude, always warm near the Equator and always cold in polar regions.

A simple classification of climates can be based on two climatic elements, namely temperature and precipitation. When both average temperature and precipitation are known it is possible to classify a particular location into a climatic type.

THE SEASONS

Apart from those locations at or very near to the Equator, all climatic regions show seasonal variation. Generally, the further away from the Equator, the greater the seasonal variation becomes.

Seasons are caused by the annual revolution of the Earth in a slightly elliptical orbit around the Sun, and by the daily rotation of the Earth on its axis. The axis of rotation is inclined at 23.5° from the vertical. The effect of the Earth's rotation and revolution around the Sun is to produce changing day length and varying angles at which the Sun's rays strike the surface of the Earth. Together these two factors cause a seasonal variation in climate.

Twice during each year, on 21 March and 23 September, the Sun's rays are directly overhead at the Equator. These two days are the *spring* and *autumn equinoxes*. On 21 June the Earth is midway between the equinoxes and the North Pole is inclined at 23.5° towards the Sun; the Sun's rays are overhead at the Tropic of Cancer (latitude 23½° N) and the *summer solstice* occurs in the northern hemisphere (and the *winter solstice* in the southern hemisphere). By 21 December the position is reversed and the Sun is overhead at the Tropic of Capricorn (23½° S) and the winter solstice occurs in the northern hemi-

sphere while the summer solstice occurs in the southern hemisphere.

CLIMATIC CONTROLS

Climate is often modified by cloud cover, the extent of which is a reflection of air pressure. Low pressure is characterized by clouds and precipitation; high pressure areas have little or no cloud. There are four major pressure belts which have a considerable influence upon world climates.

Tropical low pressure an area between 10° N and S of the Equator, where there is frequent and regular rain mainly from convection clouds. The large equatorial forests lie within this band.

Subtropical high pressure an area approximately 10–40° N and S, where there is little cloud or rain. High pressure extends across to the interior of continents in middle latitudes during the winter, but retreats into smaller cells over the relatively cold oceans during summer. The major hot deserts of the world lie within this subtropical belt.

Mid-latitude low pressure an impermanent belt of low pressure in the mid latitudes 40–70° N or S, where there is frequent but irregular rain from depressions and convection clouds, interspersed with occasional spells of high pressure with little cloud. The interiors of continents in this zone are very cold in winter (when there is high pressure) but hot in summer with some rain (low pressure). Regions bordering the oceans have a more equable climate, with much less fluctuation in temperature.

Polar high pressure an impermanent belt of high pressure between the poles and 70° N and S, where there is little precipitation at any time because the air is too cold to contain much water vapour.

The broad categories of climate are influenced by geography. Climatic controls include the proximity of land to water, and the effects of elevation, mountain barriers and ocean currents. *Climatic effects* include the seasonal and daily ranges of temperature and precipitation, together with humidity, winds, etc.

Even though two places may have similar average yearly temperature and precipitation values, or share the same latitude, they can experience different climates. If the climatic controls of the two places are not alike, then neither will be the resulting climatic effects.

As water is slower to heat up than land and slower to cool down, places in the mid-latitudes near the sea will have cooler summers and milder winters than those far from the sea. The former are said to have *maritime climates* while the latter have *continental climates*. Ocean currents can either give a location a milder climate than would be expected at that latitude (for example, the effect of the warm North Atlantic Drift on northwest Europe), or a cooler climate (for example, the effect of the cold Labrador Current on Newfoundland).

Temperature decreases with altitude. High ground may also be wetter, because warm moist air will condense as it rises over a cool land mass, so producing rain or snow. If the rain-bearing winds mostly come from one direction, the land on that side will be wetter than the land on the opposite side, which will be in a *rain shadow*. On the South Island of New Zealand, for example, there is heavy precipitation on the west side of the New Zealand Alps, but on the east side precipitation in places is as low as 330 mm (13 in). In extreme cases, where the prevailing wind is always on to the same side of high ground, a rain-shadow desert may form to leeward, e.g. Patagonia in South America.

The results of climatic controls are reflected in some of the statistics given in the accompanying table.

Rainfall increases when air is forced over high ground, and areas that lie in a rain shadow receive substantially less precipitation than similar locations on the other side of mountain ranges exposed to the prevailing winds. Compare the precipitation figures of Bergen – which lies in the path of westerly moist air masses – and Stockholm in the rain shadow to the east of the Scandinavian Mountains.

Rainfall increases with proximity to the most frequent paths of depressions (areas of low pressure). Compare the precipitation totals of Dublin – over which depressions frequently pass – and London, which is in the direct path of fewer areas of low pressure.

Rainfall is often markedly seasonal, for example when monsoon winds blow off sea on to land in the summer attracted by the deep low-pressure area over the Thar Desert on the borders of India and Pakistan – see the rainfall figures for Bombay and Darwin. Rainfall may also be seasonal because of the shift of the subtropical high-pressure belt. Beijing (Peking), China, for instance, has little rain in winter, but plenty in summer; Madrid, Spain, has little rain in summer, but experiences appreciably more in winter.

VEGETATION ZONES

Any attempt to define the world's vegetation regions is complicated by the fact that the *natural vegetation*, that is the vegetation as it was originally, has been greatly changed by human interference such as deforestation and agriculture. Elevation, slope, drainage, soil type, soil depth and climate all influence the vegetation distribution.

Climate is a major factor in determining the type and number of plants (and to a lesser extent animals) that can live in an area. Three main terrestrial ecosystems can be recognized: deserts, grasslands and forests. Precipitation is the element that determines which vegetation type will occur in an area. If the annual precipitation is less than 250 mm (10 in) then deserts usually occur. Grasslands can be found when precipitation is between 250 and 750 mm (10 and 30 in) per annum, while areas that receive more than 750 mm (30 in) rainfall a year are usually covered by forests.

The average temperature and the nature of the seasons in a region are important in that they can determine the type of desert, grassland or forest. Wherever the monthly average temperature exceeds 21°C (70°F) then hot deserts, savannah grasslands or tropical forests occur.

In the middle latitudes, the winter temperatures are low enough (one month or more below 5°C/41°F) to cause vegetation to become dormant. In autumn, growth stops, leaves are often shed and the plant survives the unfavourable winter months in a resting or dormant phase. In spring, when temperatures rise, new growth begins. In high latitudes, the winter conditions are such that between four and six months are dark and average temperature falls well below 0°C (32°F). The evergreen conifers can survive these conditions but growth is very slow and confined to the short, cool summers. In the highest latitudes, trees disappear and only small low-growing plants can survive the low temperatures.

CLOUD CLASSIFICATION

Clouds comprise water drops or ice crystals suspended in air. The water is condensed from air which rises into levels of lower atmospheric pressure, expands and cools to dew point. Air may be lifted in this manner over high ground, in thermals or at the convergence of air masses of different temperature, when cold air undercuts warm air. Water drops can remain liquid when supercooled to temperatures as low as −40° C (−40° F), but there are many ice crystals present in clouds at much lower temperatures. Water drops and crystals in clouds are transparent but take on shades between white and grey, depending upon how they are illuminated by the Sun and how thick they are. Clouds may also be coloured red by a setting Sun.

Clouds are classified according to the height of their base above the ground and whether they are rounded (cumulus) or flat (stratus).

HIGH CLOUD

Cirrus (Latin 'lock of hair'). Cirrus clouds contain ice crystals in air colder than −30° C (−22° F), and are usually higher than about 5000 m (16 500 ft). They are detached clouds forming delicate white filaments, or white, or mostly white, patches or narrow bands. They have a fibrous (hair-like) appearance or a silky sheen, or both. Cirrus are the highest of the standard cloud forms.

Cirrocumulus rounded small clouds, rather than feathery or hair-like. They appear in the form of grains or ripples, and are often more or less regularly arranged.

Cirrostratus a white veil of smooth fibrous ice crystal cloud, often seen making a halo around the Sun or Moon.

MEDIUM-LEVEL CLOUD

Medium-level clouds occur between c. 2000 m (c. 6 500 ft) and c. 7000 m (c. 23 000 ft). They are formed by water drops, either warm or supercooled.

Altocumulus are grey or white clouds having rounded shapes. Sheet or layer forms may occur. Altocumulus clouds sometimes touch.

Altostratus a flat, thick sheet cloud, often obscuring the Sun and totally hiding it when about to rain or snow. Altostratus clouds are usually greyish or bluish in colour.

LOW CLOUD

Low cloud occurs with a base below 460 m (1500 ft) and reach up to c. 2000 m (6500 ft).

Cumulus detached clouds with sharp billowing upper contours which develop upwards in thermals. They vary in appearance from small fleeces to giant cauliflowers.

Cumulonimbus the tallest of the cumulus clouds, they sometimes have an ice-crystal anvil-shaped top at the limit of convection. Cumulonimbus clouds give showers or rain, snow or hail, often with thunder and lightning.

Nimbostratus flat, relatively shapeless clouds, often seen below altostratus clouds. These grey clouds – which often merge – give rain or snow.

Stratus patches or sheets of shapeless low grey

AVERAGE RAINFALL IN SELECTED CITIES
(to the nearest 5 mm)

	J	F	M	A	M	J	J	A	S	O	N	D
In Europe												
Amsterdam	70	50	50	50	50	65	80	95	80	80	85	85
Athens	45	35	40	25	15	5	5	5	15	15	55	65
Bergen	190	145	140	110	100	115	140	180	235	245	205	195
Berlin	30	30	40	40	60	70	80	70	50	40	40	40
Bucharest	40	30	35	45	70	85	70	55	40	40	45	40
Budapest	40	40	35	45	60	75	60	55	40	40	65	50
Copenhagen	50	40	30	40	40	45	70	65	60	60	50	50
Dublin	70	50	50	45	60	55	60	75	75	70	70	80
Geneva	65	60	70	65	70	80	75	100	100	85	90	80
London	40	30	40	40	45	50	40	50	55	45	55	50
Madrid	40	40	45	45	40	30	10	10	30	50	50	45
Moscow	40	35	30	50	55	75	75	75	50	70	45	40
Paris	55	45	30	40	50	50	55	60	50	50	50	50
Prague	25	25	25	30	60	65	80	65	35	40	25	25
Rome	80	75	75	50	35	20	5	35	75	85	125	110
Stockholm	45	30	25	30	35	45	60	75	60	50	55	50
Vienna	40	45	45	45	70	65	85	70	40	55	55	45
Other Continents												
Bombay, India	5	0	5	5	15	520	710	440	300	90	20	0
Casablanca, Morocco	65	55	55	40	20	5	0	0	5	40	60	85
Dakar, Senegal	0	0	0	0	0	15	90	250	160	50	5	5
Darwin, Australia	385	310	250	95	15	5	<5	5	15	50	120	240
Douala, Cameroon	20	65	145	180	205	150	55	75	200	300	125	120
Jeddah, Saudi Arabia	30	0	0	0	0	0	0	0	0	0	40	10
New York, USA	85	80	105	90	90	85	95	130	100	8	90	85
Montreal, Canada	25	15	35	65	65	80	90	90	90	75	60	35
Peking, China	5	5	5	15	30	75	250	125	60	10	10	5
Tehran, Iran	40	25	30	25	15	0	5	0	0	5	25	25

AVERAGE TEMPERATURES IN SELECTED CITIES
(°C)

	J	F	M	A	M	J	J	A	S	O	N	D
In Europe												
Amsterdam	2	2	5	8	12	15	17	17	14	11	6	4
Athens	9	10	12	15	20	25	27	26	23	18	14	11
Bergen	1	1	3	6	10	13	14	14	12	9	4	2
Berlin	−1	1	4	8	13	17	18	17	14	8	4	1
Bucharest	−3	−1	5	11	16	20	22	22	18	11	5	0
Budapest	−1	2	6	12	16	20	21	21	17	11	6	2
Copenhagen	1	0	2	7	12	16	18	17	14	9	5	1
Dublin	5	5	6	8	11	14	15	15	13	10	7	4
Geneva	0	1	5	9	13	17	18	18	14	9	5	2
London	5	6	7	10	13	16	18	18	16	13	9	6
Madrid	5	7	10	13	16	21	24	24	20	15	9	6
Moscow	−9	−9	−4	4	12	17	18	17	11	4	−3	−8
Paris	3	4	7	10	14	17	19	18	16	11	7	4
Prague	1	2	3	8	13	16	19	17	14	8	3	1
Rome	8	9	11	14	17	22	24	24	21	17	13	9
Stockholm	−3	−3	−1	4	10	15	18	17	12	7	3	0
Vienna	−1	0	4	9	14	17	19	19	15	10	4	0
Other Continents												
Bombay, India	24	25	27	28	31	29	28	28	27	28	27	26
Casablanca, Morocco	12	13	15	16	18	20	22	23	22	19	16	13
Dakar, Senegal	21	20	21	22	23	26	27	27	27	27	26	23
Darwin, Australia	28	28	29	29	28	26	25	26	28	29	30	29
Douala, Cameroon	24	25	24	24	24	23	22	22	23	23	22	24
Jeddah, Saudi Arabia	23	25	27	29	30	32	33	31	30	28	27	25
New York, USA	0	0	5	11	16	22	25	24	20	15	8	2
Montreal, Canada	−10	−9	−3	6	13	18	21	20	15	9	2	−7
Peking, China	−5	−4	4	15	27	31	31	30	26	20	10	−5
Tehran, Iran	4	4	8	15	20	27	29	28	25	18	10	7

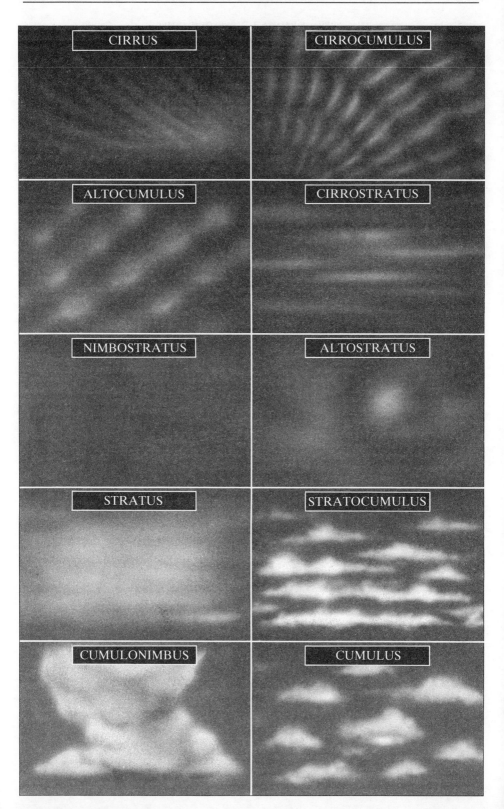

cloud, often thin enough to see the Sun through, especially when about to disperse. They often start as fog, and are later lifted by strengthening wind. Stratus clouds give drizzle and (in winter) snow grains.

Stratocumulus patches of cloud, or whole sheets, with discernible rounded shapes. They are often formed by cumulus clouds spreading out under an inversion of temperature.

WEATHER MAPS

Weather forecasting is based upon upper-air data and surface weather observations made all over the world. The material is collected and retransmitted after processing, on an international telecommunications network organized by the World Meteorological Organization (see p. 483). Information is relayed in numerical code, with five or six numerals in each group, and each observation is plotted in symbol form on a map at the position it was made.

Weather forecasters use pressure charts – popularly known as weather maps – to help them decide what the weather is going to do. From a pressure chart it is possible to find the wind direction. As a rough guide, winds blow parallel to the *isobars* – the lines that link points experiencing the same pressure. (The pressures are in millibars (mb): 1 millibar = 100 newtons per m^2 or 0.75 mm of mercury.) In the northern hemisphere, the low pressure lies to the left of the wind direction, while in the southern hemisphere it is to the right.

A pressure chart can also inform us about other aspects of the weather such as the *low-pressure area* (*depression* or *cyclone*), shown on the accompanying pressure chart. Depressions are the main areas of uplift and cloud formation in temperate latitudes.

Seen from space, depressions often possess a distinctive swirl or spiral of clouds showing where the air is rising. With depressions, the air blows anticlockwise in the northern hemisphere and clockwise in the southern. Most cloud occurs near frontal surfaces, where temperatures change rapidly. Fronts mark boundaries between air of different temperatures. When warm air is replacing cold air there is a *warm front* – shown on the chart by a thick line displaying semicircles. This front extends into the atmosphere well ahead of the surface warm front. A *cold front* – shown on the chart by a thick line displaying triangles – occurs where cold air replaces warm air. The temperature change can be quite sudden – several degrees in a few minutes. Cumulonimbus clouds often mark the line of the cold front and give a short period of heavy rain.

In a typical low-pressure system, a warm front, a cold front, an occluded front and a warm sector are found. In many depressions the cold front moves faster than the warm front, gradually squeezing out the warm sector. When this has taken place, there is an *occluded front* – shown on the chart by a thick line displaying semicircles joined to triangles. Its precise form depends on whether the air following the original cold front is warmer or cooler than the air ahead of the depression.

Weather forecasts are broadcast on a regular basis for the Shipping Forecast Areas around the British coast shown on the map on p. 104. There is as yet little international agreement concerning the names and the boundaries of shipping forecast areas. The boundaries of the areas in the Channel used by the French meteorological service are different to those used by the British.

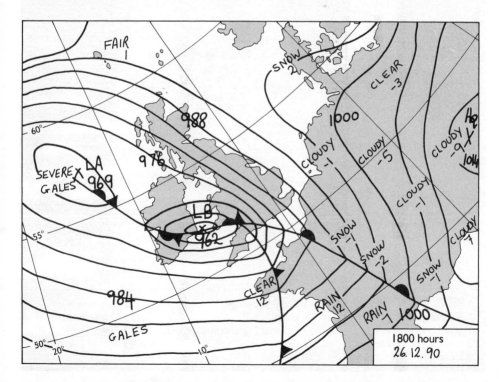

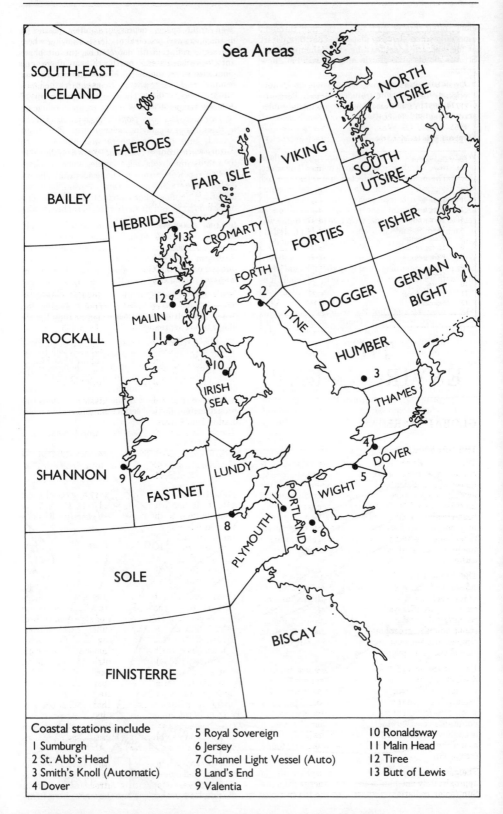

Sea Areas

SOUTH-EAST ICELAND

NORTH UTSIRE

FAEROES

1

VIKING

SOUTH UTSIRE

FAIR ISLE

BAILEY

HEBRIDES

13

CROMARTY

FORTIES

FISHER

FORTH

GERMAN BIGHT

12

2

DOGGER

MALIN

TYNE

ROCKALL

11

HUMBER

10

3

IRISH SEA

THAMES

4

DOVER

SHANNON

9

LUNDY

5

FASTNET

7

PORTLAND

WIGHT

8

PLYMOUTH

6

SOLE

BISCAY

FINISTERRE

Coastal stations include

1 Sumburgh	5 Royal Sovereign	10 Ronaldsway
2 St. Abb's Head	6 Jersey	11 Malin Head
3 Smith's Knoll (Automatic)	7 Channel Light Vessel (Auto)	12 Tiree
4 Dover	8 Land's End	13 Butt of Lewis
	9 Valentia	

BEAUFORT SCALE

A scale of numbers, designated Force 0 to Force 12, was originally devised by Commander Francis Beaufort (1774–1857) (later Rear-Admiral Sir Francis Beaufort, KCB, FRS) in 1805. (Force numbers 13 to 17 were added in 1955 by the US Weather Bureau, but are not in international use since they are regarded as impractical.)

Force No.	Descriptive term	Wind speed km/h	mph	knots
0	Calm	0–1	0–1	0–1
1	Light air	1–5	1–3	1–3
2	Light breeze	6–11	4–7	4–6
3	Gentle breeze	12–19	8–12	7–10
4	Moderate breeze	20–29	13–18	11–16
5	Fresh breeze	30–39	19–24	17–21
6	Strong breeze	40–50	25–31	22–27
7	Near gale	51–61	32–38	28–33
8	Gale	62–74	39–46	34–40
9	Strong gale	75–87	47–54	41–47
10	Storm	88–101	55–63	48–55
11	Violent storm	102–117	64–73	56–63
12	Hurricane	119	74	64

THE ENVIRONMENT

GLOBAL WARMING

THE GREENHOUSE EFFECT

The planet Earth is showing signs of gradually becoming warmer, a process known as the greenhouse effect. Scientists have discovered that the average temperature of the Earth's atmosphere has increased by 0.5 °C (0.9 °F) since accurate records began in about 1860. This may seem to be a very small increase in absolute terms, but the *rate* of temperature change – which is now faster than at any time in the past – is significant. This trend is called *global warming*.

The main reason for the greenhouse effect is a substantial increase in the so-called *greenhouse gases* such as carbon dioxide, methane, nitrous oxide, chlorofluorocarbons (CFCs) and, most recently, of benzine in the atmosphere. To understand how the greenhouse gases cause the rise in temperature we must understand the vertical structure of the atmosphere (see p. 96).

Each of the layers of the atmosphere has its own distinct chemical and physical properties. For example, in the troposphere the temperature cools rapidly. It is in the troposphere that most of our daily weather is formed and it is here too that most of the pollutants released into the atmosphere by human activities accumulate. The stratosphere is important as it is the layer in which atmospheric ozone is found (see p. 96).

The gaseous composition of the atmosphere allows approximately one half of the total energy from the Sun (solar radiation) to pass into the lower atmo-sphere, thus warming the planet. Eventually, the incoming energy – which has arrived as short-wave, intensive radiation – is reflected back into space as long-wave dissipated energy. In this way the average temperature of the Earth remains relatively constant at + 14°C. Greenhouse gases restrict the loss of the long-wave radiation and, as a result, the Earth's atmosphere is warming.

The atmosphere comprises a complex mixture of gases and water vapour.

Component gases of the lower atmosphere (by volume)
nitrogen 78.084%
oxygen 20.946%
argon 0.934%
carbon dioxide 0.033%
neon 0.00182%
helium 0.00053%
krypton 0.00012%
xenon 0.00009%
hydrogen 0.00005%
nitrous oxide 0.00005%
methane 0.00002%

Since the beginning of the Industrial Revolution (from c. 1750), the composition of the atmosphere has been gradually changing. Most significantly, carbon dioxide has increased by 28%, from 265 parts per million (p.p.m.) in 1850 to 340 p.p.m. in 1987, and is predicted to rise to 600 p.p.m. by 2050. Carbon dioxide is currently responsible for 57% of the global warming trend, with 80% of the gas originating from the burning of fossil fuels (coal, petroleum, etc.).

Global carbon-dioxide emissions The emission of carbon dioxide into the atmosphere by region/nation in 1987 was as follows:
North America 28% of the world total, incl. USA 24%
USSR and Eastern Europe 25% of world total
Western Europe 15% of world total, incl. UK 3%
China 9% of world total.

Relative contributions to the greenhouse effect It has been calculated that the relative contributions to the greenhouse effect in the 1980s were as follows:
carbon dioxide 50%
methane 18%
CFCs 14%
surface ozone 12%
nitrous oxide 6%

From about 1950, the chemical composition of the atmosphere has changed more rapidly. Industry has been responsible for the release of huge quantities of sulfur dioxide, hydrogen sulfide and nitrous oxides, all the result of burning fossil fuels. Agriculture has contributed large amounts of methane gas. Rice (paddy) fields contribute 115 million tonnes of methane every year, and 1.2 billion domesticated farm animals (particularly cattle), through the expulsion of intestinal gas, add a further 73 million tonnes. Methane comprises only 2 p.p.m. of the atmosphere, but its effectiveness as a greenhouse gas is about 30 times that of carbon dioxide, and its volume has increased by more than 400% over the last century.

The transportation systems of the world, especially aviation and motor vehicles, are responsible for the release of vast quantities of nitrous oxides, carbon dioxide, lead and benzine into the atmosphere. In the

USA, all forms of transport consume 63% of all petroleum used each year. In Western Europe, this figure is 44%. In many countries, efforts are being made to increase the energy efficiency of transportation systems, and some progress has been made to reduce the reliance on the private motor car. In California, for example, legislation is being prepared to reduce the use of private cars by 1% per annum for the next 20 years.

THE EXTENT OF GLOBAL WARMING

Using the figures for the last century as a means of predicting future temperature change, we find that an increase of between 2–3°C (3.6–5.4°F) by 2030 and at least 5°C (9°F) by 2100 are likely.

The prediction of future planetary warming is a highly controversial subject. Some experts claim that the rise in average temperature is nothing more than a natural fluctuation in the long-term history of our planet. To support this view, they claim that the existence of the Ice Age which ended about 10 000 years ago is evidence of a cooling process, whereas the current increase in temperature is merely the reverse of this trend. However, most scientists now recognize the current rate of temperature increase to be beyond the normal range and ascribe the increase to human factors rather than to natural causes.

Supporters of the global-warming theory would argue that it has been the pollution produced by domestic, agricultural and industrial activities that has caused major changes to the atmosphere. They state that unless action is taken to reduce the release of gases such as carbon dioxide, methane, nitrogen oxides, ozone and chlorofluorocarbons (CFCs) then further warming of the atmosphere will occur.

To combat the threat of global warming an agreement, known as the Montreal Protocol, was reached by representatives of the main industrialized nations meeting in Montreal, Canada, in 1987. Under the terms of the Protocol, the use of CFCs was to be halved by 1998 and the use of halon – halogenated aliphatic hydrocarbons used in fire fighting – was to be set at 1986 levels by 1992. However, by July 1990, scientific evidence had shown these targets to be insufficient to stem global warming, and an agreement was reached between the developing nations and the developed world to achieve a 50% reduction in the use of CFCs by 1995, an 85% cut by 1997 and a total ban by 2000. Halons will also be banned by 2000. Many nations wanted an even faster phasing out of these substances, but the USA, Japan and the USSR claimed that it would be impossible to meet earlier targets. A fund of $240 million has been set up to help the economies of developing countries adapt to the ban on these substances.

THE IMPACT OF GLOBAL WARMING

It is thought that the impact of global warming on the planet would be unevenly distributed. The southern hemisphere, with its extensive oceans, would suffer less increase in temperature, as the seas would be able to absorb more heat than the land masses of the northern hemisphere. The Arctic region may become, on average, 8°C (13.4°F) warmer than at present by 2100. As a result, some of the polar ice sheet would melt, causing a rise in sea levels of 20–30 cm (8–12 in) by the middle of the 21st century, with predictions of a 60–100 cm (24–40 in) rise by 2100. This would threaten many low-lying areas with inundation, including the island nations of Kiribati, Tuvalu and the Maldives, as well as much of Bangladesh and

parts of some important cities including New York, London, Leningrad, Alexandria, Rotterdam and Venice.

Profound climatic changes could also result. According to some meteorologists, the climatic belts of the northern hemisphere would be likely to move north, bringing a desert climate to the Mediterranean region and to California, Texas and Florida, and a Mediterranean-type climate to much of northwestern Europe. Storminess could also increase and rainfall totals could rise by as much as 15%, particularly in the high latitudes.

THE OZONE LAYER

The ozone layer is a naturally occurring zone found in the stratosphere, situated between 10–15 km (6–9 mi) above the Earth's surface. Ozone (O_3) is a natural component of the atmosphere. It is classified as a trace gas with a concentration of about 0.2 parts per billion (p.p.b.). A highly reactive and unstable gas, it is formed by the recombination of pairs of oxygen (O_2) atoms in the presence of intense solar radiation (mainly ultraviolet energy).

The most important function of the stratospheric ozone layer is to act as a shield against ultraviolet (UV) radiation from the Sun. In 1984, the British Antarctic Survey reported a thinning of the ozone layer over the South Pole. This depletion of ozone has been incorrectly called the *ozone hole*. It is not a hole – only a thinning of the ozone layer.

The depletion is caused by certain highly stable synthetic chemicals, which are the product of the petrochemical industry. These include chlorofluorocarbons (CFCs) used as propellants in aerosol spray cans, as refrigerant gases, solvent cleaners and in the manufacture of foam-blown plastics, and halons, used in fire-fighting equipment. These gases rise into the atmosphere, where they become partly decomposed into methyl chloroform and carbon tetrachloride. These gases become concentrated above the polar areas in the stratosphere and actively destroy the ozone molecules, thus allowing increased levels of ultraviolet light to reach the ground.

Exposure to UV light causes damage to crops, kills plankton and fish larvae, and can cause burning of the skin (sunburn) in humans. Severe sunburn produces temporary soreness, dehydration and sickness. In the longer term it can result in skin cancers, and is estimated to cause 100 000 additional eye cataracts worldwide. Epidemiologists in many hospitals in northern Europe have recorded a doubling in the incidence of skin cancers in recent years, while in Australia, doctors have claimed that a 1% decrease in the ozone layer results in a 3% increase in non-melanoma skin cancers in humans.

As a result of the Montreal Protocol (see above), CFCs and halons will be phased out by the year 2000, but so many CFCs already exist in the atmosphere that the concentration will continue to rise to 6 p.p.b. by 2000 before declining.

PHOTO-CHEMICAL SMOG

A second, and quite separate, environmental problem associated with ozone is the build-up of ground-level ozone to produce photo-chemical smog. This hazard – first recorded in Los Angeles, California – now occurs worldwide in industrial cities. A combination of oxides of nitrogen and volatile organic compounds in the presence of sunlight cause the formation of ground level ozone. These substances are almost entirely the result of human activity, for example motor-vehicle exhausts, and the chemical paint and ceramics industries.

The problem becomes most serious in summer, when stationary air masses allow the build-up of high concentrations of oxides of nitrogen and volatile organic compounds. The World Health Organization has set a safety limit of 120 p.p.b., though this figure is regularly exceeded and has reached a peak of 600 p.p.b. in California. (In Britain a maximum of 250 p.p.b. was reached in southern England in 1976.) Concentrations of 300 p.p.b. are sufficient to cause irritation to respiratory tissue and the eyes of humans, while even lower concentrations severely damage citrus fruits.

The problem of oxides of nitrogen and volatile organic compounds is a serious one, but it is at present overshadowed by the international concern with the depletion of the ozone layer.

DROUGHT AND DESERTIFICATION

A drought occurs when an area of land does not receive enough water to sustain life at the existing levels. Droughts may be due to lower than normal amounts of precipitation, to higher evaporation as a result of warmer temperatures than normal, or to a combination of these two factors.

Drought years appear to occur in cycles. From records of the Nile floods over the last 2000 years, a cycle of varying length is apparent. In the well-known Biblical story, the pharaoh of Egypt dreamed of seven ears of grain, fat and healthy, followed by seven ears of shrivelled and thin grain. This symbolized a cycle of seven damp years followed by seven years of drought. In recent decades, the years between 1968–73 were drought years, from 1973 until 1979 adequate moisture occurred, while in 1980 another cycle of drought began.

Between 1982 and 1986 much of Africa was devastated by severe drought, which resulted in widespread human deprivation. Some 10 million people were forced to leave their homes in search of food and water. China, India and North America all suffered major droughts in the 1980s. In the summer of 1988 about 43% of the central states of the USA suffered a drought of intensity equal to that of the 'Dust Bowl' years 1926–34. The grain harvest in 1988 was 31% down on that of the previous year and financial losses reached $15 billion, making the drought the costliest natural disaster in US history.

The occurrence of major droughts appears to be linked to weather changes which affect up to 66% of the globe. Changes in atmospheric pressure-patterns combine at irregular intervals of between two and seven years to produce modifications to the flow of ocean currents in the southern hemisphere. The Pacific Ocean heats up between Papua New Guinea and Micronesia, resulting in the easterly flow of a powerful warm current called El Niño ('the boy child'). It combines with other climatic changes over the southeastern Pacific to bring about the irregularity in ocean currents called the Southern Oscillation, which causes major weather disturbances lasting up to two years. On these occasions, serious droughts have occurred in India, Australia, Africa and Indonesia.

Prolonged drought in much of Western Europe in 1989–90 increased awareness of the need for proper water management. The options most frequently proposed are summarized below.

WATER MANAGEMENT APPROACHES

Input Approaches

Increase the usable supply by:

1. Building dams and creating lake reservoirs.
2. Diverting water from one region to another; draining swamps; and diverting rivers.
3. Tapping ground water.
4. Desalting seawater and purifying degraded water.
5. Towing icebergs from the Antarctic.
6. 'Controlling' the weather, for example by seeding clouds.

Control the pollution of existing supplies by preventing or limiting the addition of certain chemicals.

Redistribute population by:

1. Encouraging people to live in areas with adequate water.
2. Restricting population levels in areas with water problems (deserts or flood plains).

Decrease population growth.

Output Approaches

Decrease evaporation and plant transpiration.

Use better drainage for irrigated agriculture to minimize the salt build-up in soils.

Treat polluted waters before returning them to their sources.

Dispose of wastes by burial on land or sea or by injection into deep wells.

Reclaim waste water to allow multiple re-use.

Minimize wasteful and extravagant uses of water, and redesign industrial and other processes to use less water.

DESERTIFICATION

About 35% of the planet is classified as arid or semi-arid. True deserts – which have less than 250 mm (about 10 in) of rain a year – can be divided into cold deserts near the Earth's poles and hot deserts between about 20° and 30° latitude north and south of the Equator. Hot deserts cover about 20% of the land between the Tropics. Semi-arid areas receive up to 500 mm (about 20 in) a year. Between them, deserts and semi-arid areas account for one third of the land area of the Earth, and are home to nearly 1 billion people.

ESTIMATE OF WORLD WATER REQUIREMENTS BY AD 2000

The figures in the following table are given in cubic kilometres.

Water use	Total Requirement	Amount lost by evaporation
Irrigation	7 000	4 800
Domestic	600	4 800
Industrial	1 700	170
Dilution of wastes and effluents	9 000	–
Others	400	400
Total	18 700	10 170

AVERAGE DAILY USE OF WATER IN THE UNITED STATES (litres)

Direct personal use		Indirect agricultural use		Indirect industrial use	
Shower (5 minutes)	100	One egg	150	Cooling water for	
Shaving/washing hands	14	One ear of corn	300	electric power plants	2 700
Washing clothes	75	One loaf of bread	570	(per person per day)	
Cooking	30	One kilo of flour	625	Sunday paper	1 060
Washing dishes	38	One kilo of beef	20 800	One kilo synthetic rubber	2 500
Toilet (4 flushes)	48			One kilo aluminium	8 340
House cleaning	30			One kilo steel	300
Sprinkling lawn (800 m²)	300			One litre petrol	7–25
				One motor car	380 000

Daily average: 635 litres Daily average: 2 300 litres Daily average: 4 000 litres

Total daily average: 6 935 litres per person

Arid and semi-arid areas are increasing by about 6 million ha (over 23 000 sq mi) a year owing to a variety of reasons. Overgrazing by stock and the cultivation of poor soil are the principal causes. Poor water management (resulting in erosion, salinization and waterlogging), the cultivation of steeply sloping sites and changes in land use – particularly deforestation and strip mining – have also been important contributory factors. The process by which productive areas degenerate into land with up to 50% less productivity is called *desertification*, a term coined by the French explorer André Aubreville in 1949 to describe the deterioration of land in the Sahel.

LAND POLLUTION

Since the very earliest times all human settlements have created pollution. At first, the problem was small-scale and was easily overcome. When a location became polluted, a new area was colonized.

Human beings are gregarious animals. Gradually villages grew into towns and cities. The problem became increasingly difficult to solve as new, unpolluted sites became scarcer and dumping areas for waste and other pollutants had to found.

The Industrial Revolution, beginning in the 18th century, was responsible for creating widespread land pollution throughout Europe. An account written by a traveller to the smelting furnaces in the Swansea valley of South Wales in 1862 describes a landscape covered in 'heaps of cinders and rubbish...a horrid filthy place...it might have stood for Hell'.

Land left standing without a present use as a result of past activity and which has been physically despoiled or disfigured is called *derelict land*. Often, in the past, lower standards of pollution control were exercised. Formal land-use planning was largely unknown in Europe and North America until 1945, and industrial land use was intermingled with residential and agricultural landscapes. As a result many degraded landscapes could be found, especially in old industrial areas.

Nowadays, derelict sites have become the focal point of rehabilitation projects in which wastes are made safe by burial or by detoxification, and the land reused for a totally new purpose. Governments of the developed world now recognize that the rehabilitation of polluted land areas requires a completely integrated approach. It involves preventing further pollution at source, minimizing the risk of harm to human health, applying the most appropriate and technologically advanced solutions to restoring degraded areas, and managing them by means of sustainable land-use policies.

The principle of *integrated pollution control*, in which air, water and land pollution become the total responsibility of one environmental management body, has been adopted in many developed countries.

WASTE DISPOSAL

A major problem facing developed countries throughout the world is the disposal of domestic and industrial rubbish. In the UK, industry produces about 100 million tonnes of waste each year, of which about 27 million tonnes are recycled and valued at over £2 billion. British domestic sources produce a further 20 million tonnes, of which only 1 million tonnes is recycled. Modern waste contains a high proportion of non-degradable products – plastics, metals and chemicals. These items can cause long-term contamination if disposed of incorrectly.

Traditionally, rubbish has been burned, dumped into disused quarries, or dumped at sea. None of these methods is wholly acceptable today. Burning can generate highly toxic gases, few old quarries remain to be filled in, and dumping at sea has created major pollution of bathing waters.

National and local authorities in many countries are encouraging the recycling of materials, the prevention of waste and the conservation of new resources. Waste minimization is being achieved by better design, longer design life and improved potential for re-use. The public is also becoming more educated in environmental issues.

WATER POLLUTION

Rivers and seas have been used for the dumping of wastes since earliest times. The constant flow of rivers and the tidal movements of seas have been used as a natural sink to disperse all forms of wastes.

Clean, fresh water is vital for the very survival of the human species. The assessment of water quality depends upon its intended use. Some of the main forms of pollution are:

1. Disease-carrying agents (bacteria, viruses, parasitic worms). These kill an estimated 25 000 people each day, mainly in the less developed countries.

2. Sediment and suspended matter (soil, silt and partially treated sewage).
3. Radioactive substances (from the nuclear power industry).
4. Organic chemicals (oil, plastics, pesticides, cleaning solvents, detergents).
5. Inorganic plant nutrients (nitrates and phosphates washed from agricultural land).
6. Waste heat (in the form of cooling water from power stations and industry).

RIVER POLLUTION

Rivers can normally dilute small amounts of pollution quickly and safely. When overloaded with pollutants, or when the volume of water is reduced during summer drought, dilution becomes impossible and pollution occurs.

In Britain, the National Rivers Authority is responsible for the prevention of water pollution. It uses a five-point classification scheme to monitor pollution (see the accompanying table). Even slightly polluted water is damaging for human health, especially so if consumed over a long time span (see the accompanying table).

NATIONAL RIVERS AUTHORITY RIVER AND CANAL WATER CLASSIFICATION

Class		Current Potential Use
1A	Good	Water of high quality suitable for potable supply and with high amenity value
1B		Of lower quality than 1A but usable for substantially the same purposes
2	Fair	Waters suitable for potable supply after advanced treatment. Medium amenity quality
3	Poor	Waters polluted to an extent that fish are absent. Usable for low-grade industrial abstraction. Of considerable use if cleaned up
4	Bad	Grossly polluted waters which cause nuisance value

Because of the health risk, most developed countries have comprehensive laws and regulations concerning water quality. Fines are imposed on persons or industries found guilty of polluting water courses. Much pollution occurs accidentally from leaching of nitrates, phosphates and pesticides from agricultural land, or from leaks in underground storage tanks (petrol and oil).

In less developed countries and in Eastern Europe most rivers are severely polluted. Over 66% of India's rivers are polluted and 90% of child deaths are attributable to water-borne disease. In Poland, almost 50% of the nation's water is unfit even for industrial use – 90% of Poland's river water is too polluted to drink and it has been forecast that by the year 2000 this figure will be 100%.

POLLUTION OF THE SEAS

The oceans receive not only pollution carried in by rivers, but also direct inputs of sewage, oil spills from tankers and offshore drilling platforms, and industrial waste deliberately dumped at sea. During the 1980s ocean dumping around the world amounted to more than 172 million tonnes of solid waste each

CHEMICAL CONTAMINANTS IN DRINKING WATER AND RELATED HEALTH HAZARDS

Contaminant	Effects
Inorganic Material	
Arsenic	Cancer of the liver, kidneys and blood, and nervous system damage
Cadmium	Kidney damage, anaemia, high blood pressure
Lead	Headaches, anaemia, nervous disorders, birth abnormalities, mental retardation especially in children
Mercury	Damage to central nervous system and kidneys
Nitrates	Respiratory problems particularly to the new born and chronically sick
Synthetic Organic Substances	
Benzine	Anaemia, leukemia, chromosome damage
Carbon tetrachloride	Cancer of the liver, kidney and lung. Damage to the central nervous system
Dionysian	Skin disorders, cancer and genetic malfunction
Ethylene	Cancer and male sterility
PCBs	Liver, kidney and lung damage

year. About 80% of this was dredged materials, taken from rivers to maintain shipping channels. EC legislation will ban the dumping of this material into European waters by 1995.

About 20% of the solid waste dumped at sea is sewage sludge, a lethal mixture of toxic chemicals, infectious materials and settled solids from sewage treatment plants. In Britain, 17% of the sewage output is still discharged, untreated, to the sea. Bathing beaches have become seriously contaminated and may be unsafe to use. In 1989, for example, 24% of British bathing beaches failed to meet EC standards. Figures for beaches in Northern Ireland, Wales and Scotland which met EC guidelines were 100%, 80% and 70% respectively.

An estimated 2 million sea birds and over 100 000 marine mammals die each year by poisoning or by becoming entangled in plastic netting.

Prevention of water pollution as well as cleaning up past pollution will be expensive. Britain will spend £13·7 billion between 1989 and 1992 on new sewage plants. In the USA, greater use of technology is seen as the way to reduce water pollution. This method is called MACT (Maximum Available Control Technology). Many ecologists believe that reliance on this approach, the so-called 'technological fix', will become too expensive and has no guarantee of success. Instead, every effort should be made to use only non-polluting technology.

NUCLEAR DUMPING AT SEA

Between 1946 and 1982, 46 petabecquerels of dumped, packaged and liquid nuclear waste was dumped in more than 50 sites, mainly in the northern Atlantic and Pacific Oceans. Most waste came from civil and military power stations and reprocessing plants. In the 1980s, a moratorium on dumping nuclear wastes at sea was established by trade unions and by diplomatic concern.

COMMON DISEASES TRANSMITTED TO HUMANS THROUGH
CONTAMINATED DRINKING WATER

Type of Organism	Disease	Effects
Bacteria	Typhoid fever	Diarrhoea, severe vomiting, enlarged spleen, inflamed intestine, often fatal if untreated
	Cholera	Diarrhoea, severe vomiting, dehydration; often fatal if untreated
	Bacterial dysentery	Diarrhoea; rarely fatal except in infants without proper treatment
	Enteritis	Severe stomach pain, nausea, vomiting; rarely fatal
Viruses	Infectious hepatitis	Fever, severe headache, loss of appetite, abdominal pain, jaundice, enlarged liver; rarely fatal but may cause permanent liver damage
	Polio	High fever, severe headache, sore throat, stiff neck, deep muscle pain, severe weakness, tremors, paralysis in legs, arms, and body; can be fatal
Parasitic protozoa	Amoebic dysentery	Severe diarrhoea, headache, abdominal pain, chills, fever, if not treated can cause liver abscess, bowel perforation, and death
	Giardia	Diarrhoea, abdominal cramps, flatulence, belching, fatigue
Parasitic worms	Schistosomiasis	Abdominal pain, skin rash, anaemia, chronic fatigue, and chronic general ill health

COMPARISONS OF SOURCES OF SELECTED POLLUTANTS, EMISSIONS AND EXPOSURES

Pollutant	Major Emission Sources	Major Exposure Sources
Benzine	Industry; automobiles	Smoking
Tetrachloroethylene	Dry-cleaning shops	Dry-cleaned clothes
Chloroform	Sewage treatment plants	Showers
p-Dichlorobenzene	Chemical manufacturing	Air deodorizers
Particulates	Industry; automobiles; home heating	Smoking
Carbon monoxide	Automobiles	Driving; gas stoves
Nitrogen dioxide	Industry; automobiles	Gas stoves

AIR POLLUTION

Any particulate matter or gaseous material which accumulates in the atmosphere to such proportions that it causes harm to humans, other animals, vegetation, or damage to building materials can be described as an air pollutant. Nowadays, air pollution is primarily the result of human activity, but it is often overlooked that natural sources of air pollution can sometimes exceed the quantity of human-produced pollutants.

Pollutants from human activity have attracted notoriety because of their chemical complexity, their reactivity once released to the atmosphere and their interaction with all other living components of the biosphere.

Particulate matter is normally considered to be the simpler form of air pollution as it can be removed from the atmosphere more easily than gaseous material. (Particles can, for instance, be removed from the atmosphere by trapping on dust collectors located in chimneys.) All particulate matter, even the finest aerosols, have a mass greater than air, and thus in still air will gravitate out of the atmosphere. Large particles, over 10 micrometers in size, normally fall out of the atmosphere within 5 or 6 hours of their release from source. The finest particles, smaller than 1 micrometer, can remain in the air for several months, or even years. They are also the most damaging as they can enter the lungs of animals and cause illness. Soot, rubber and tarmac particles are known to be carcinogenic to human lung tissue. Vegetation surfaces can become coated with fine dusts, thus reducing their ability to photosynthesize.

Gaseous pollution presents a major problem for modern societies and exacts enormous health and environmental costs. Gases are usually invisible but once released can be transported hundreds of kilometres and react with many other atmospheric components to produce secondary pollutants. It is these products rather than the primary pollutants that are usually responsible for vegetation damage and respiratory illness in humans.

So severe is the damage caused by air pollution that stringent legislation has been introduced by many governments, particularly in the developed world. Overall, urban air quality has improved during the 1980s, especially for the traditional pollutants such as sulfur dioxide (SO_2) which has fallen by up to 64% throughout Europe and North America. With the exception of Milan and industrial cities in Eastern Europe, the most polluted cities are now found in the developing world, where some 625 million people breathe air which fails to meet the World Health Organization standards for SO_2.

New air pollutants are continually emerging, and for these emission-control measures must be found. For example, the increasing use of unleaded petrol, while resulting in a reduction of air-borne lead of up to 50%, has been accompanied by an increase in the amount of benzine added to petrol. The levels of benzine accumulating in the atmosphere have increased with an alarming rapidity, especially as it is a greater hazard to the atmosphere than CFCs.

ACID RAIN

Coal-fired power stations and other industrial processes emit sulfur dioxide and nitrogen oxides, which, when combined with atmospheric moisture, create *acid rain* (dilute sulfuric acid or nitric acid). Acid rain (or snow) is the main atmospheric fallout of industrial pollutants, although these may also occur as dry deposits (such as ash). Acid rain damages forests, plants and agriculture, raises the acid level in lakes and ground water, killing fish and other water-bound life, and contaminating drinking water.

Temperate forests have been seriously damaged by acid rain. The Black Forest in Germany has been steadily losing its trees through *Waldsterben* ('tree death'). The problem is also very acute in the north of Bohemia (Czechoslovakia). But Britain has the highest percentage of damaged trees in Europe – 67%. In southern Norway 80% of the lakes are devoid of fish life, and Sweden has 20 000 acidified lakes. Acid rain upsets the fine chemical balance in lakes that are home to numerous species of fish. Salmon, roach and trout are very sensitive to pH (i.e. acid)

levels in their habitat. Even a slight dip in pH levels causes heavy metals such as aluminium, mercury, lead, zinc and cadmium to become more concentrated, decreasing the amount of oxygen the fish can absorb and eventually causing their death. The absence of large fish destabilizes the ecosystem and the effects are felt throughout the food chain. The ecosystem is seriously depleted, and only some smaller creatures, such as water beetles, seem able to survive.

Acid rain also causes damage to the soil. High levels of acid rain in the soil cause lead and other heavy metals to become concentrated and interrupt the life-cycles of microorganisms. The bacteria and fungi that help break down organic matter into nutrients are disturbed and soils can lose their ability to support forests or agriculture.

There are various methods of reducing the amount of pollutants reaching the atmosphere, such as lead-free petrol, catalytic converters attached to car exhausts (which destroy some of the harmful gases), and filter systems that reduce dangerous emissions from power stations and industry.

A CLASSIFICATION OF AIR POLLUTION TYPES

Particulate Matter		Gaseous Pollution	
Human derived	*Naturally derived*	*Human derived*	*Naturally derived*
smoke	volcanic dust	Gases from	Volcanic gases and
ash	smoke + ash	combustion	water vapour
grit	sea-salt particles	SO_2	
soot		CO_2	Gases from organic
dust		H_2S	decomposition
liquid droplets		NO_X	
(acid deposition)		HF	
particles of tarmac		PANs	
and rubber		CH_4	

GLOSSARIES

CLIMATOLOGY AND METEOROLOGY GLOSSARY

adiabatic lapse rate the rate at which air cools because of expansion when rising into regions of lower atmospheric pressure: 1° C per 100 m (5·4° F per 1000 ft) in clear air, less in cloud. Similar rates apply when air subsides into higher pressure and warms.

advection fog fog that forms when air cools to dew point by travelling across a surface that is already colder, such as sea or snow.

air frost air having a temperature of 0° C (32° F) or less.

air mass a huge volume of air that has acquired temperature and humidity characteristics from its region of origin.

anabatic wind an upslope wind created when air rises from a warming hillside and is replaced by cooler air from the valley.

anemometer an instrument for measuring wind speed.

anticyclone an area of high pressure, having a

clockwise wind circulation in the northern hemisphere (anticlockwise in the southern).

aurora spectacular displays of light, mostly seen in latitudes higher than 70°. Caused by electrical solar discharges, they sometimes appear like waving curtains.

atmospheric pressure pressure due to the weight of the atmosphere. The pressure is less at higher altitudes than at sea level.

backing a change of wind direction in an anticlockwise manner, e.g. from W back to SW.

ball lightning a spherical glowing ball of electrically charged air.

banner cloud a cloud that streams downwind from a mountain peak, formed in the rising eddy behind the peak.

barometer an instrument for measuring atmospheric pressure.

barograph a barometer connected to a pen and rotating drum, so as to make a trace of changing pressure on a chart.

Beaufort scale numerals indicating the force and speed of the wind (see p. 103).

Berg wind a hot, dry wind from the interior of South Africa, blowing down the mountains and offshore.

black ice a transparent film of ice, taking the colour of the surface (e.g. a road) on which it forms.

blizzard a strong wind carrying falling snow. It gives bad visibility and causes drifting.

blood rain rain coloured with dust particles carried on upper winds; in Europe often reddish-brown with dust from the Sahara.

blue moon the moon appears blue when excessive dust in the atmosphere (e.g. after a volcanic eruption) scatters more red light than blue.

Bora a cold, usually dry, NE wind blowing from the mountains in Yugoslavia and NE Italy.

Brickfielder a very hot NE wind in SE Australia. It blows in summer, carrying dust and sand.

brockenspectre the magnified shadow of an observer cast on to cloud or fog from high ground.

buoyancy an air current is buoyant if it is warmer and therefore lighter than its surroundings.

Buys Ballot's law a convention used to locate areas of low pressure. When an observer has his back to the wind, low pressure is on the left hand in the northern hemisphere and on the right hand in the southern.

Buran a strong NE wind in the USSR and central Asia, most frequent in winter. Known as Purga when carrying snow.

calm conditions in which there is no perceptible movement of air.

cap cloud a cloud that sits above the summit of high ground, apparently stationary but in reality constantly forming on the windward edge and dispersing to leeward.

castellanus a cloud with a 'turretted' appearance, taller than it is wide. It often occurs at medium level, giving thunderstorms.

Celsius scale of temperature the temperature scale on which 0° C denotes freezing level and 100° C the boiling point of water. It is sometimes called Centigrade. See conversion tables p. 122.

Chinook a warm and dry wind that blows down the eastern side of the Rocky Mountains, USA.

climate a distinct pattern of weather found in a particular geographical zone (see p. 97).

cloud water drops or ice crytals held in suspension above the ground (see p. 98).

cloudburst a very heavy but shortlived downpour of rain.

col an area of light variable wind, between two anticyclones and two depressions.

condensation the change of state of water vapour (an invisible gas) into water drops.

conduction the transference of heat from one substance to another substance with which it is in contact. The transfer is always from the warmer surface to the colder.

contrail short for 'condensation trail'. A contrail is produced by an aircraft flying at heights above about 6000 m (20 000 ft). It may be persistent if the atmosphere is already moist.

convection the transmission of heat by movement of fluid particles, like air or water. Air which warms near the ground becomes less dense and rises, and cold air takes its place, to warm in turn.

convection rain rain that falls from convection (cumulus) clouds.

cyclone a (roughly circular) pressure pattern in which pressure is lower at the centre than on the periphery. Wind circulation around the centre is anticlockwise in the northern hemisphere and clockwise in the southern. The name 'cyclone' is more specifically used for intense storms in the Indian Ocean, Arabian Sea and Bay of Bengal. Cyclones in middle and high latitudes are called depressions or lows.

deepening a low-pressure circulation is said to deepen if the atmospheric pressure at its centre continues to fall.

depression a low-pressure circulation in middle or high latitudes. See cyclone.

deposition the change of vapour directly to ice crystals when air becomes saturated and dew point is below 0° C (32° F). Hoar frost results.

dew water drops condensed directly from air when the air temperature falls below a dew point that is warmer than 0° C (32° F).

dew point the temperature at which air becomes saturated, holding the maximum amount of vapour possible. Further cooling results in condensation.

desert an area in which rainfall is insufficient to support vegetation.

diffraction the bending of light rays around particles or water drops having the same diameter as the wavelength of light.

doldrums a belt of light variable winds near the Equator, outside the range of the trade winds. They give frequent rain storms and squalls.

drizzle precipitation consisting of very small water drops, less than 0·5 mm (0·02 in) diameter.

drought a long period of dry weather.

equatorial climate the tropical rainy climate experienced in a belt on and on either side of the Equator.

evaporation the change of state of water into invisible vapour.

eye of the storm the centre of a hurricane or cyclone. It is characterized by well-broken cloud, no rain, light wind, and wild seas.

false cirrus ice-crystal cloud at the top of a cumulonimbus cloud, which is drawn along by the wind into the shape of an anvil.

Fata Morgana a complicated mirage. It usually occurs over water, and is most frequently seen over the Strait of Messina, Italy.

Fahrenheit scale of temperature the scale of temperature in which 32° F denotes freezing level and 212° F the boiling point of water. See conversion tables p. 122.

filling a depression is said to fill when the pressure at its centre starts to rise.

flaschenblitz an unusual form of lightning that strikes upwards from the top of a cumulonimbus.

fog a layer of very small waterdrops forming upwards from the surface of the sea or ground and restricting visibility. See also advection fog, radiation fog.

fog bow a bow formed – in the same way as a rainbow – when the Sun shines on to smaller fog drops. The coloured rays overlap to form a white bow with only the faintest tinge of colour.

Föhn wind a dry, warm wind blowing down a mountain under certain conditions, and warming by compression on descent.

freezing rain rain which falls into air whose temperature is below freezing, and then freezes to ice. Also called glazed frost.

freezing the change of state of water into ice, starting at a temperature of 0° C (32° F).

front the surface boundary between air masses of different temperature and humidity, which confront each other from different directions.

frost see air frost, hoar frost.

funnel cloud a whirling, tapering cloud that descends from the main base of a storm cloud.

gale a wind in excess of force 7 on the Beaufort Scale.

geostrophic wind a wind that blows horizontally, because of pressure differences, parallel to the isobars and according to Buys Ballot's Law.

glaciation (in meteorology) the sudden change of supercooled water drops into ice crystals within a cloud.

glazed frost the coating of ice over subfreezing surfaces from freezing rain.

graupel soft, partly melted hail.

glory a ring of light, like a corona, seen around a brockenspectre.

greenhouse effect the accumulation of heat in a greenhouse because glass is more transparent to incoming solar radiation than it is to outgoing radiation from the surface beneath the glass. In the atmosphere, carbon dioxide and various other gases perform the same function as glass, trapping heat near the Earth. See p. 103.

Gregale a strong NE wind blowing in the Mediterranean in the cooler months of the year.

gust a momentary increase in wind speed.

haboob any wind strong enough to raise sand into a sand storm, particularly in the Sudan.

hail ice pellets, created in strong vertical currents within cumulonimbus. Snow flakes or water drops are tossed up and down, alternately freezing and melting, until they are heavy enough to fall to the ground.

halo a ring of light around the Sun or Moon, caused by the refraction of light through ice-crystal cloud. A halo is reddish on the inside, bluish on the outside – the reverse order of corona colours.

Harmattan a dry and cool wind, blowing from the E or NE across NW Africa. It is often dust-laden and dry enough to wither vegetation.

hectopascal a unit of pressure – the equivalent to 1 millibar of pressure.

helm wind a strong, cold, often violent wind from the NE blowing down western slopes of Cumbria (England), mainly in late winter and spring.

high an area of high pressure or anticyclone. It brings fine weather in summer, but often frost or fog in winter. Winds blow clockwise in the northern hemisphere, anticlockwise in the southern.

hill fog low cloud covering high ground.

hoar frost the deposition of ice crystals directly out of the air when dew point is at or below 0° C (32° F) and the air is saturated with vapour.

humidity See relative humidity.

hurricane an intense low-pressure storm, affecting the West Indies and Gulf of Mexico. Similar storms in the Pacific are called typhoons. Circular winds around the centre follow Buys Ballot's Law and attain wind speeds in excess of 119 km/hr (64 knots or 74 mph).

hygrometer an instrument used for measuring the humidity of air.

inversion of temperature the conditions in which temperature increases with height in the atmosphere. This is a reverse of the normal situation in which temperature decreases with height.

isobar a line on a map joining places having equal atmospheric pressure (corrected to mean sea level) at a particular time.

isohyet a line on a map joining places having equal rainfall over a given period.

isotherm a line on a map joining places having equal temperature at the same time.

jet stream a strong but narrow belt of wind near the tropopause, blowing from west to east.

Karaburan a hot dusty NE wind in central Asia.

katabatic wind a downslope wind, created on otherwise calm nights with no cloud. The air nearest to the slope cools and flows downhill, to be replaced by warmer air from above the valley.

Khamsin a hot oppressive wind over Eygpt in early summer, often laden with desert sand.

knot a unit of speed used by sailors and aviators who have no fixed points of reference with which to measure distance against time. One knot denotes a speed of one nautical mile per hour – a nautical mile is the length of a minute of latitude, standardized as 1852 m (6080 ft).

land breeze a wind blowing during the night from cooling land onto warmer sea.

latent heat heat emitted, without a change in temperature, when vapour condenses to water drops or water freezes to ice.

lenticular cloud a cloud shaped like a lens.

leeward the side opposite from the direction of the wind; the sheltered side.

Levanter a moist E wind in the eastern Mediterranean. Often strong, it is most frequent from June to October.

lightning a discharge of an electric field within a cloud, usually cumulonimbus. It may occur within the cloud, from one cloud to another, or between the cloud and the ground.

low the circulation around a centre of low pressure. See cyclone.

lull a momentary fall in wind speed.

mackerel sky a sky featuring cirrocumulus or altocumulus, arranged as a regular pattern resembling the scales of a mackerel.

mare's tails wispy cirrus clouds.

mean sea-level pressure the atmospheric pressure corrected for the height of a barometer above sea level, by adding an imaginary column of air as high as the level at which the barometer is situated.

melting the change of state from ice to water.

microclimate a climate found in a very restricted area such as a valley, garden or even a room.

millibar an international unit by which atmospheric pressure is measured. Recently it was replaced by the hectopascal. 1 millibar (mb) = 1 hectopascal (hPa) where 1000 mb is the pressure exerted by 750·06 mm/29·53 in of mercury at 0° C.

mirage an optical illusion, caused by the bending of light when passing through adjacent layers of air that have different density. An inferior mirage is seen below the real object when light passes through very hot air, shimmering like water because of convection. A superior image is seen above the real object when light bends downwards through very cold dense air.

mist very small water drops suspended in air near the ground, reducing visibilty.

Mistral a cold dry NW or N wind, funnelling down the Rhône Valley before reaching the south coast of France.

monsoon a wind that changes direction markedly according to season, akin to a sea breeze – for example the seasonal winds of south Asia that blow from the SW in summer bringing heavy rainfall. The term 'monsoon' is also applied to the rainy season during which these winds blow.

nacreous clouds clouds having the appearance of mother-of-pearl. They form in the stratosphere, often in mountainous areas, and are seen after sunset.

noctilucent clouds wispy, bluish clouds, resembling cirrus, very high in the atmosphere – usually at an altitude of 80–85 km (50–55 miles). They are probably dust or ice particles.

occlusion the surface boundary between fresh cold air and modified cool air ahead. In effect, it is a cold front that has overtaken a warm front and lifted the warm air off the ground.

orographic rain rain that is caused entirely by forced lifting of moist air over high ground.

Pampero a very cold wind which blows over the Andes across from Argentina and Uruguay to the Atlantic.

parhelion a mock sun, sometimes called a sun dog, caused by refraction of light through ice crystals that have their axes aligned vertically. There may be two parhelia, one either side of the sun and at the same elevation as the sun.

precipitation a composite term that includes rain, drizzle, snow, sleet or hail, all of which fall from clouds.

permafrost that part of the soil which remains permanently frozen in cold climates.

pressure tendency the rate of change of atmospheric pressure. A rapid fall indicates deteriorating weather, a rapid rise indicates a temporary improvement, and a slow persistent rise a developing anticyclone.

prevailing wind the most frequent wind direction to affect a particular area.

Purga a strong NE wind in the USSR and central Asia, often raising snow from the ground to give a blizzard.

radiation fog condensation within a layer of air near the ground that is cooling because of radiation heat loss from the Earth under clear skies. Light wind stirs saturated air into fog.

rain precipitation of water drops larger than 0·5 mm (0·02 in) in diameter.

rainbow a coloured arc of light in the sky, caused by refraction and internal reflection of light in raindrops. A rainbow can only be seen by an observer with his back to the Sun and facing distant rain. A primary rainbow has violet on the inside and red outside; a secondary rainbow, outside the primary, has colours in the reverse order.

rainfall the depth of all forms of precipitation for a given period as measured in a rain gauge.

rain shadow an area where rainfall is reduced because of protection by high ground from the prevailing, rain-bearing wind.

refraction the change of direction of light rays when passing through transparent media (water drops, ice crystals, air) that have different densities.

regelation the refreezing of water that has been temporarily melted because of pressure exerted on it.

relative humidity a measure of the actual vapour in air, as a percentage of the total amount that is required to saturate the air at that temperature.

ridge of high pressure isobars with exaggerated curvature extending from an anticyclone.

rime a crust of ice crystals that forms when supercooled water drops in fog make contact with solid objects whose temperature is less than 0° C (32° F). In calm air, rime builds up all around objects; in a light wind, mainly on the windward side.

Roaring Forties the region between latitudes 40° and 50° S where strong westerly winds prevail.

St Elmo's fire a discharge of static electricity from the masts of ships, wings of aircraft, etc, when the electrical field is strong. It is characterized by a bluish glow, often accompanied by a crackling noise.

scud shreds of low stratus below the main base of cloud. They appear to move very fast because they are so close to the ground.

sea breeze a daytime wind that blows from the sea to the shore, to replace air rising in thermals over the land.

sea fog an advection fog formed when warm air travels and condenses over colder sea.

secondary depression a depression that forms within the circulation of another depression, usually in a trough. It often develops at the expense of the original depression.

Seistan a strong N wind in summer in eastern Iran and Afghanistan, carrying dust and sand.

Shamal a hot, dry, dusty NW wind that blows in summer in Iraq and the Persian Gulf.

shower precipitation from a convection cloud, often heavy but usually short-lived.

Sirocco or **Scirocco** a hot dry S wind on the north coast of Africa, blowing from the Sahara.

sleet a mixture of snow and rain.

snow precipitation of ice crystals, latched together as feathery flakes.

smog (short for 'smoke-fog') fog that is heavily polluted.

Southerly Buster a sudden cold and strong S wind in southeast Australia.

squall a sudden strong wind, lasting only a few minutes. It often comes from a different direction from that which has just been experienced.

stable atmosphere the atmospheric condition in which a rising current of air soon becomes non-buoyant (i.e. colder than its surroundings) and ceases to rise. In such conditions, cumulus clouds remain small or do not form.

surface wind a wind that blows within 10 m (30 ft) of the surface of ground or sea.

sunshine the visible light received from the Sun.

sunshine recorder a glass sphere used to record hours of sunshine. It is mounted so as to focus the rays from the Sun and burn a trace upon a paper chart.

sun pillar a column of light, above or below the sun when it is low on the horizon, caused by reflection of light from the base of big storms. The intense vertical current at the centre is capable of much damage. See also funnel cloud.

trade winds are so named because as a belt of regular winds they were of benefit to sailing trading vessels. They blow on the equatorial side of the sub-tropical high-pressure belts, NE winds in the northern hemisphere, SE winds in the southern.

Tramontana a cool, dry N wind blowing across the Mediterranean coast of Spain.

tropopause the upper boundary of the troposphere. See p. 96.

tropical cyclone an intense low-pressure storm originating over tropical seas. It is called a hurricane in the Atlantic, and a typhoon in the Pacific.

trough of low pressure isobars with exaggerated curvature extending from a depression. It often brings cloud and rain.

turbulence the fluctuation of wind speed and direction. At ground level, turbulence is mainly due to surface friction.

typhoon the name given to a hurricane in the Pacific.

unstable atmosphere atmospheric conditions in which a rising current of air can remain buoyant (i.e. warmer than its surroundings) to great heights. It is characterized by the development of tall cumulonimbus.

veering a change of wind direction in a clockwise manner, e.g. from N to NE.

virga trails of precipitation falling from a cloud base but evaporating before reaching ground.

visibility the greatest distance at which an object can be seen with the naked eye.

warm front the surface boundary between a mass of warm air and cooler air ahead, over which the warm air slides.

waterspout a tornado that occurs over the sea, sucking up water from the sea.

wet-and-dry bulb thermometer a thermometer used for measuring relative humidity. Two identical thermometers are mounted alongside, one with its bulb wrapped in muslin kept moist by a wick dipping into water. Evaporation from the muslin uses up heat, so that the wet bulb thermometer reads lower than the dry, except when air is saturated and they read the same. Mathematical tables enable humidity and dew point to be obtained from the two readings.

whirlwind a local column of rotating and rising air, originating at ground level. They usually occur in hot weather when there is no cloud.

whiteout a visibility condition, in a snow storm or over extensive snow surfaces, where natural contours or landmarks are indistinguishable from each other or from cloud.

Williwaw a cold and strong downslope wind in Alaska.

wind air that is moving owing to pressure differences between places. Wind direction is desribed by the direction from which it blows, e.g. NW or 315° blows from the northwest towards the southeast.

wind vane a device for registering wind direction. The shorter arm, usually an arrow, points to the wind direction, while the broader fin blows downwind.

PHYSICAL GEOGRAPHY GLOSSARY

abyssal pertaining to the depths of the oceans.

affluent a tributary stream flowing into a larger stream or river.

aiguille (French, 'needle') a sharp point or pinnacle of rock.

alluvial fan a fan-shaped area of sediment deposited where the gradient of a stream or river is reduced and flow is slowed.

alluvium the fine sediment (sand, silt, clay) deposited by a river.

altitude height above sea level.

archipelago a group of islands.

arête a sharp ridge between two cirques.

artesian well a well that taps water held in a permeable layer of rock, sandwiched between two impermeable layers of rock in a basin. The rim of the permeable section of the basin is higher than the level of the well, so the water contained in the permeable layer pushes the water up out of the well.

atoll a ring of coral islands or coral reefs.

avalanche a mass of snow and/or ice that slides down a mountainside under its own weight.

bar shingle and sand deposited in a line or ridge across a bay or mouth of a river, or offshore, parallel to a beach.

barchan a crescent-shaped sand dune. Its shape is due to the effect of the wind from a constant direction.

bayou a swampy creek leading off a river, found in flat land.

bergschrund a gap between the upper edge of a glacier and the rock or ice wall in the back of a cirque. Also called a rimage.

bight a large bay.

bill a small peninsula.

bluff a vertical cliff, standing out prominently from the surrounding countryside.

bog an area of wet spongy ground consisting of waterlogged and partly decaying moss and other plants.

bore a tidal wave running up a river estuary.

boulder clay sediment consisting of a mix of clay

and boulders deposited by a glacier. Also called till.

bourne a stream that only flows intermittently.

bund (in the Indian subcontinent) an artificial embankment.

bush scrubland not cleared for cultivation.

butte a flat-topped hill, often with steep sides, formed in horizontal strata. A mesa is a large butte.

cairn a man-made heap of stones.

caldera a crater flanked by steep cliffs. It is usually formed when the top of a volcano has been eroded.

canal a man-made waterway, either for transport or irrigation.

canyon a river-cut gorge with steep sides, often of great depth.

cape a piece of land projecting into the sea.

cascade a small waterfall.

cataract a large waterfall.

cave an underground opening reached from the surface or from the sea.

cavern a cave.

chaparral dry scrubland, particularly in the southeastern USA.

chimney a wide vertical crack in a rock face.

cirque a rounded basin in a mountainside, formed by the action of a glacier. Also called a corrie or cwm.

cliff a steep face of rock.

col a pass or saddle between higher mountains.

coombe a short valley into the side of a hill.

confluence the point at which two rivers converge.

continent a single large landmass.

continental drift the movement of crustal plates on the molten rock that makes up the Earth's interior. See p. 55.

continental shelf the offshore seabed, down to a depth of 200 m (600 ft).

contour a line joining all points at the same height.

coral the exoskeleton of small marine animals of the same name, which live in colonies. When each animal dies the calcium-rich exoskeleton remains. As generation succeeds generation, masses of coral build up into reefs, atolls, etc.

coral reef a line of coral at or just below the surface of the sea.

cordillera parallel lines of mountains.

corrasion the mechanical erosion of rocks by the action of other rocks, gravel, etc., in a river or by wind-borne sand.

corrie a cirque.

corrosion the chemical erosion of rocks.

cove a small bay.

crater the hollow at the top of a volcanic cone, or the depression caused by the impact of a meteorite.

crevasse a vertical crack in a glacier or ice sheet.

cuesta a ridge or hill formed by sloping rock strata.

cwm a cirque.

dale an open valley, especially in northern England.

deep a marine valley or trench, considerably deeper than the surrounding seabed.

delta deposits of alluvium in a fan shape, formed where a river flows into the sea or a lake.

desert an area of arid and semi-arid climates where rainfall is low and moisture availability is scarce.

drowned valley a valley that has been submerged by a rise in sea level or by the land sinking.

drumlin a small hump-backed hill formed by the action of a glacier. Composed of boulder clay and sometimes with a rock core, swarms of drumlins are exposed as ice-sheets recede.

dune a wind-formed accumulation of sand.

dust bowl a dry region that has been badly managed agriculturally to such a degree that the topsoil has been removed by wind erosion.

dyke a vertical sheet of rock that cuts across the bedding or structural planes of the host rock.

earthquake a series of shock waves generated from a single point within the Earth's mantle or crust. See p. 90.

epicentre the point on the Earth's surface above the point at which the shock waves of an earthquake are generated.

Equator an imaginary circle around the Earth's circumference, midway between the poles.

equinox the time when the Sun appears vertically overhead at noon at the Equator – 21 March and 21 September.

erg a desert area composed of wind-blown sand and dunes.

erosion the removal or wearing away of the land surface by natural means.

estuary the mouth of a river, and the tidal stretch of that river immediately up-river of the mouth.

étang a shallow lake among coastal sand dunes.

fall line the line showing where a number of rivers leave an upland area for a lowland area, in each case passing over a waterfall or series of waterfalls.

fathom a unit of depth at sea: 1·83 m (6 ft).

fell bare hill or exposed upland area, especially in northern England.

fen marshy land in which peat is formed, especially in eastern England.

fjord a glaciated steep-sided valley that runs into the sea and is subsequently flooded. They are characterized by a great depth of water in the main body of the fjord, with a shallower bar across the mouth.

firth (known as a sea loch in Scotland) a narrow inlet in the sea coast; either an estuary or a fjord.

flood plain the plain on either side of a river formed by alluvial deposits left when the river floods and then recedes again.

fold a vertical bend in the rock strata, formed by compression within the Earth's crust.

forest a large area of land, extensively covered with trees.

frost hollow a hollow into which cold air sinks from the surrounding slopes. The hollow is therefore more liable to suffer frost than the surrounding land.

garrigue a form of scrub found in dry limestone areas around the Mediterranean.

geyser a hot spring of such depth that steam periodically forms, erupting from the mouth of the spring in a fountain of steam and hot water.

glacier a mass of ice, formed through the accumulation of snow and its transformation to ice under pressure. Glaciers slowly move down a valley towards the sea. See p. 92.

glen a long narrow steep-sided valley in Scotland.

gorge a deep, narrow, rugged valley with near-vertical walls.

grassland a large area where the rainfall is greater than that of a desert but not enough to support a forest.

great circle a circle on the Earth's surface whose centre is the Earth's centre, and hence the shortest route between two places follows the great circle on which both are situated.

gulf a large bay.

gully a narrow steep-sided channel formed by water erosion.

hammada a bare rocky desert.

hanging valley a glaciated valley entering a main valley part-way up the valley side.

headland an isolated cliff projecting into the sea.

hot spring a spring whose water is heated by hot volcanic rocks.

iceberg a massive lump of ice that has broken off the end of a glacier or ice sheet and floats in the sea or a lake.

ice floe a floating sheet of ice that has detached from an ice shelf.

ice sheet a great sheet of ice and snow covering a land mass.

ice shelf a mass of ice and snow floating on the sea.

inlet an opening into the sea or lake coast.

inselberg an isolated hill in a relatively flat area.

irrigation an artificial supply of water to a crop-producing area.

island a mass of land surrounded by water. It may occur in a river, a lake, a sea or an ocean.

islet a small island.

isthmus a narrow neck of land connecting two land masses.

jebel (in Arabic countries) a mountain range.

jungle a popular name for tropical rain forest.

karst a type of limestone scenery produced by water erosion of limestone rock. It is characterized by sinks, underground rivers and caves, and other erosion features. See p. 92.

kettle hole a hollow in the outwash plain of a glacier, formed where an ice block melts.

key or **cay** a small island or sandbank in the Caribbean.

knick point a point at which the slope of a river changes.

knoll a small rounded hill.

kyle (in Scotland) a channel of water or strait.

lagoon an expanse of water that has been separated from the sea by a narrow strip of land.

lake an expanse of water entirely surrounded by land.

landslide a mass of soil, mud and rock that slides down a mountainside or cliff-slope because of its own weight.

latitude a degree of latitude (°) is the angular distance of a point on the surface of the Earth, north or south of the Equator, taken from the centre of the Earth. A line of latitude is the line joining all points with the same degree of latitude, i.e. it is a circle with the axis of the Earth between the two poles at its centre. Compare longitude.

lava see Geology Glossary.

lava fountain a fountain of molten lava ejected from a volcano.

lava plateau a plateau formed from a flat sheet of volcanic rock.

levée a river-bank formed during flooding of the river. As the river water spreads out, alluvium is deposited, the greatest quantity being along the line of the river bank.

littoral that part of the seashore between high and low tide.

load solid material carried by a river, ranging from boulders to fine silt.

loch (in Scotland) an inlet of the sea, a fjord, or a lake.

longitude the angular distance between one of the Earth's meridians and the standard or Greenwich meridian.

longshore drift the movement of sand and shingle along the shore due to the action of the waves as they advance and retreat obliquely along the shore.

lough (in Ireland) an inlet of the sea, a fjord, or a lake.

lunar day the time between successive crossings of a meridian by the Moon – about 24 hours 50 minutes.

lunar month the time between two successive new Moons, i.e. the time the Moon takes to travel around the Earth once – $29\frac{1}{2}$ days.

maelstrom a large whirlpool.

magnetic pole the point at which the Earth's magnetic flux is strongest. The magnetic poles do not coincide with the true poles. They also move slightly with time.

mangrove swamp a tropical coastal swamp characterized by the extensive growth of mangroves, whose long tangled roots drop from the trunks and branches of the mangroves, trapping sediment.

maquis a low scrub growing on rocky soil in the Mediterranean area.

marsh low-lying soft wet land.

massif a block of mountains that only breaks up into separate peaks towards the various summits.

meander a wide curve or loop in a river. These often link up in a series of meanders.

meridian half a great circle on the Earth's surface, finishing at each pole and cutting the Equator at right-angles, i.e. a line of longitude.

mesa a tableland with steep sides. Buttes are small mesas.

meteorite a solid lump of rock that enters the atmosphere from space and is large enough not to burn up in the atmosphere but to reach the Earth's surface. See p. 24.

midnight sun the appearance of the sun throughout the day and night. This occurs in latitudes close to the poles at times around the solstices.

monadnock an isolated hill or rock, left when the surrounding rock has been eroded more rapidly.

monsoon forest tropical forest found where a monsoon climate is prevalent. Because of the dry season between monsoons, it is not so dense as tropical equatorial forest.

moor an area of high rolling land covered in grass, heather and bracken, often with marshy areas.

moraine rock and other debris transported by a glacier. Terminal moraines are formed at the ends of glaciers; lateral moraines are formed at the sides of glaciers; median moraines are formed in the middle of glaciers where two glaciers meet and unite.

mountain a mass of high land projecting well above the level of the surrounding land.

muskeg (in northern Canada) a mossy swamp.

neap tide the small tidal difference between high and low tide, caused when the Sun and Moon are out of phase.

névé granular snow, formed as snow is gradually impacted. Eventually névé forms the ice of a glacier.

nunatak a mountain peak projecting through an ice sheet.

oasis an area in a desert in which water occurs, giving rise to fertile land and allowing cultivation.

ocean a very large area of seawater, divided off by or surrounding the continents. See p. 62.

outwash alluvium carried from the end of a glacier by the melting ice.

outwash plain a plain formed by the outwash of a glacier.

oxbow lake a lake formed when a river cuts off one of its meanders, leaving a crescent-shaped or horseshoe-shaped lake.

pack ice ice floes that have been forced together to form an almost continuous sheet.

pampas grasslands between the Andes and the Atlantic in South America.

pass a gap through a mountain range that is relatively easy to traverse.

pediment a sloping plain that leads up to a mountain range.

percolation the descent of water through porous rock.

permafrost ground that is always frozen solid.

piedmont pertaining to the foot of a mountain or mountain range.

plain an extensive area of flat or gently rolling land.

plateau an extensive area of flat or gently rolling land that is raised above the level of the surrounding land.

playa a lake in an area that experiences a dry climate. It is often dry seasonally or for many years and has a saline surface.

plug a vertical core of solidified lava at the centre of a volcanic cone.

polder (in the Netherlands) an area that has been reclaimed from the sea.

pole one end of the Earth's axis; it remains stationary while all other points on Earth rotate round the axis.

pothole a hole worn down through solid rock by the swirling action of water, or water and accompanying debris.

prairie flat or rolling plains, largely grasslands, that occupy the central areas of North America east of the Rockies.

profile the profile of a river is a cross-section of its total length, showing the various slopes and changes of slope.

promontory a headland.

puy (in France) an isolated cone of a long-extinct volcano.

quagmire soft wet ground that shakes when walked on. Known as a 'shoog-bog' in some parts of Scotland.

quicksand loose sand in a dense suspension in water. Although it may look solid, its properties are those of a liquid.

race a rapid marine current caused by the tides.

ravine a small steep-sided valley, usually caused by water erosion.

reef a line of rocks just below the surface of the sea.

reg an area of the desert consisting of gravel and small rocks, but no sand.

ria an inlet of the sea, formed from a submerged river valley.

rift a valley formed by the sinking of a section of land between two parallel faults.

river capture the process by which one river erodes a larger and larger valley, eventually cutting into the valley of another river and 'capturing' its waters.

river terrace flat land on either side of a river, left when a river erodes a channel well below the level of its flood plain.

roads or **roadstead** a large area of deepwater anchorage for ships, usually well protected from bad weather.

rognon (French, 'kidney') an isolated island of rock in a glacier.

run-off rainfall that pours over the ground surface and into streams and rivers.

salt dome a mass of salt that has been forced up through layers of rock until it lies relatively close to the Earth's surface.

salt lake a lake that has only a limited outlet or no outlet at all, occurring in an area experiencing a hot dry climate. As water evaporates, the concentration of salt in the water increases.

salt marsh an area of marsh that is flooded by seawater at high tides.

salt pan an area in which salt water has evaporated completely, leaving behind a deposit of salt.

sandbank a line or bank of sand just below the surface of the sea or of a river.

savanna or **savannah** an area of grassland with few trees, found to the north and south of the equatorial areas. There is a wet and a dry season each year, limiting the growth of trees.

scarp or **escarpment** a steep slope, often forming the steeper slope of a cuesta.

scree broken rocks at the foot of a rocky slope. They are broken off by the action of weathering and tumble down the slope. Also known as talus.

sea level the mean level between high and low tides.

sea loch sea fjord.

seif a linear sand dune with a sinuous crest.

serac a tower or band of very steep ice formed when the part of the glacier below it has fallen away.

shoal an area of sandbanks.

sidereal day the interval of time for a star to describe a circle around the pole star.

sierra a long mountain range, usually very jagged.

sill a slab of igneous rock, forced when molten between two layers of sedimentary rock and subsequently exposed by erosion.

snowfield a permanent mass of snow.

snowline the level above which snow is permanently present.

solar day the interval of time between successive appearances of the Sun in the meridian of any one place.

solstice the time when the Sun appears vertically overhead at its most northerly or southerly point – 21 June and 22 December.

sound a narrow inlet of the sea.

source the point at which a river begins – a spring, lake, etc.

spit a long narrow strip of shingle or sand, attached at one end to a land mass, projecting into the sea or across an estuary.

spring a flow of water up through the ground at a particular point. It can be permanent or intermittent.

spring tide the greatest tidal difference between high and low tide, caused when the Sun and Moon are in phase.

stack an isolated pillar of rock off the coast, caused by erosion.

steppes flat grasslands stretching from central Europe to eastern Russia and on into Central Asia.

strait a narrow stretch of sea connecting two large expanses of sea or ocean.

subtropical the region between the tropics and temperate regions.

swamp low marshland that is permanently wet.

swash a flow of water up a beach after a wave has broken.

taiga a vast belt of coniferous forests in the northern hemisphere, particularly Siberia.

talus another word for scree.

tarn a mountain lake, often occupying a cirque.

temperate the region experiencing cool summers and mild winters. It lies between subtropical regions and polar circles, excluding the continental and eastern coastal regions of the northern hemisphere.

tide the rise and fall of the surface of the sea, caused by the gravitational pull of the sun.

tombolo a bar joining an island to the mainland.

trench a long deep submarine valley.

tributary a river that flows into another river rather than into a lake or the sea.

Tropic of Cancer latitude 23°N. The position at which the Sun appears vertically overhead at midday on the 21 June solstice.

Tropic of Capricorn latitude 23°S. The position at which the Sun appears vertically overhead at midday on the 22 December solstice.

tropics the region between the Tropics of Cancer and Capricorn.

truncated spur a spur that has at some time been foreshortened by the action of a glacier.

tsunami a tidal wave caused by an earthquake under the sea's surface.

tundra the area in the northern hemisphere, north of the coniferous forest belt, characterized by the absence of trees. The ground is covered by mosses, lichens and a few other plants that can survive the long harsh winters and short cool summers.

undertow the undercurrent after a wave has broken on a beach.

volcanic ash particles of lava ejected by a volcano and often falling over a wide area.

volcano a vent or fissure in the Earth's crust through which molten magma can force its way to the surface.

wadi a watercourse in the desert. It is usually dry but can contain water after the occasional rainstorms.

waterfall an abrupt fall of water in the course of a river. (See p. 83.)

water gap a gap in a ridge or line of hills, cut by a river.

watershed the dividing line, running along high land, between the tributaries feeding into two separate river systems.

water table the surface of a water-saturated part of the ground.

weir an artificial structure across a river, constructed to regulate flow.

well a hole dug from ground level to below the surface of the water table to gain access to water.

whirlpool a circular eddy of water, formed by the interaction of two or more currents.

year the time taken for the Earth to complete one revolution about the Sun.

zenith a point vertically above the ground.

GEOLOGY GLOSSARY

acid rock igneous rock with over 10% free quartz.

adobe a type of clay.

aeolian deposits particles carried and deposited by the wind.

alluvium sands and gravels carried by rivers and deposited along the course of the river.

amber a type of resin.

amorphous material having no regular arrangement.

anhedral having no crystalline structure.

anticline a fold system in the form of an arch.

aquifer a stratum of rock containing water.

arenaceous rocks sedimentary sandstones, deposited by wind or water.

argillaceous rocks sedimentary rocks deposited by water; usually marls, silts, shales, muds and clays.

ash fine material formed by volcanic explosions.

asphalt hydrocarbon, either solid or just fluid at normal temperatures.

asthenosphere a part of the Earth's mantle.

automorphic grains having a crystal structure.

ball clay reworked china clay.

banket a conglomerate of quartz.

basalt fine-grained basic igneous rock, sometimes with a glassy characteristic.

basic rock igneous rock containing little or no quartz.

batholith an intrusive mass of igneous rock.

bauxite an aluminium ore of aluminium oxide, out of which the easily leached ions have been removed.

bedding plane a surface parallel to the surface of deposition. Some rocks split along bedding planes; others have less obvious physical characteristics such as changes of particle size.

biolith rock of organic material, formed by organic processes.

bitumen a hydrocarbon mineral with a tarry texture, ranging from a viscous liquid to a solid.

black-band ironstone a sedimentary rock, formed principally from a form of coal and iron carbonate (siderite).

boghead coal coal formed from algal and fungal material.

bort anhedral diamonds in a granular mass.

boss a mass of igneous rock with steep contact surfaces with the surrounding rock.

boudinage the stretching of a rock layer to give a sausage-shaped structure.

boulder bed sedimentary rock consisting of boulders together with fine-grained material.

breccia a sedimentary rock consisting of angular material of more than 2 mm (0.08 in) diameter.

brown coal another name for lignite; a coal containing a low carbon content.

carbonate a large group of minerals, all having the carbonate group bond – CO_3 in common. They can be divided into sedimentary and non-sedimentary carbonates, limestone being the most common form of sedimentary carbonate.

carbonatite a magmatic rock consisting of calcium carbonate and occasionally other carbonates.

carstone a form of sandstone with a high proportion of limonite.

cassiterite tin oxide ore.

cataclasis the mechanical break-up of rock.

caulk barytes (barium sulphate).

celestite a strontium mineral found mainly in sedimentary rock.

ceylonite a spinel mineral.

chalcedony a silica-based mineral, found in many forms, some of which are semi-precious stones, e.g. agate, onyx, carnelian, jasper.

chalcocite copper sulfide ore.

chalcopyrite one of the principal copper ores.

chalk a fine-grained white limestone, calcium carbonate.

charnockite a granular rock, mainly consisting of quartz, feldspar and hypersthene.

chert a form of silica, found as bands and nodules in sedimentary rocks.

chiastolite a form of aluminium silicate.

china clay kaolin, formed by decomposition of feldspar in granite.

chlorite a green mineral consisting of talc units.

chondrites stony meteorites.

chromite a chromium ore, containing iron.

chrysocolla a copper ore mineral, copper silicate.

chrysoprase a green chalcedony.

chrysotile a form of asbestos.

cinnabar mercury sulfide, associated with volcanic activity.

citrine a yellow quartz.

clastic rock fragments of rock, transported to a site of deposition and built up into a conglomerate.

clay a sedimentary rock with a fine particle structure and a soft plastic texture when wet.

cleat jointing found in coal.

cleavage a flat plane of breakage, perhaps parallel to a crystal face.

cleavage plane the plane of fracture in a rock.

clint a ridge in a limestone rock surface.

coal stratified deposits of carbonaceous material, originally derived from decayed vegetable matter.

cobble a rock particle, between 125 mm (5 in) and 250 mm (10 in) in diameter.

columnar structure vertical columns or prisms, formed for example in lava and basalt, caused by the cooling of the rock.

competent the flow or flexion of a rock layer, in which it is not broken.

composite igneous bodies that have more than one material in them, e.g. due to intrusion.

concretion accumulations of sedimentary constituents in certain defined areas of rock, often around a nucleus.

conglomerate rounded pebbles cemented together in one mass.

convergence the metamorphosis of two dissimilar rocks so that they become similar.

corundum aluminium oxide, used as an abrasive and also found as gemstones, e.g. sapphire, ruby.

country rock the body of rock that encloses an intrusion by another rock, e.g. an igneous rock.

creep the gradual deformation of a rock by stress applied over a long time.

crystal a three-dimensional structure arising from the atomic structure of the substance. The symmetrical arrangement for a given substance means that the angles within the structure are constant for that substance.

culm Carboniferous rocks found in Devon and Cornwall (England).

cuprite copper oxide, an important copper ore.

deflation surface debris transported by the wind.

deformation any change in a bed or stratum after it has been formed.

dendritic branching into a many-fingered appearance.

denudation any process that results in a lowering of the land surface.

detritus particles of minerals and rocks formed by weathering and corrosion.

diamond a crystalline form of carbon. It has a cubic structure, distinguishing it from graphite.

diatomite the remains of unicellular organisms called diatoms. It is a highly-absorbent powdery material.

diorite a coarse-grained igneous rock consisting of feldspar plus ferromagnesium minerals.

dog-tooth spar calcite, crystallized into tooth-like forms.

dolerite an igneous rock similar to basalt.

dolomite calcium magnesium carbonate, or limestone with a substantial proportion of magnesium carbonate.

dyke a sheet of igneous rock that cuts across the bedding or structural planes of the host rock.

elaterite an elastic or rubbery form of bitumen.

elvan a dyke of granite.

emerald a green form of beryl.

emery fine granules of corundum and magnetite.

epidiorite a metamorphic granular rock derived from igneous rock and containing the minerals of diorite.

epidotes a group of rock-forming silicate minerals.

evaporite sediment left by the evaporation of salt water.

extrusive igneous rock that has flowed out at the Earth's surface.

fault a fracture plane in rock, along which displacement occurs.

feldspar silicate minerals, in which the silicon ions are in part replaced with aluminium ions. Calcium, sodium and potassium feldspars exist, as do the rare barium feldspars.

feldspathoid rock-forming silicates with sodium and/or potassium in the lattice structure. They never occur with quartz.

festoon bedding a type of cross-bedding.

fire clay argillaceous fossil soil found in some coal seams.

flint a type of chert.

flowage irreversible deformation, i.e. deforming a material beyond its elastic limit.

fluorite calcium fluoride, found as veins in rocks.

fold a flexing of a rock stratum.

fool's gold iron pyrites.

fossil the impression of an animal or plant, or its skeletal remains, buried by natural processes and then preserved.

fracture a break in a direction that is not a cleavage plane.

fuchsite a mica mineral containing chromium.

fulgurite a branching tube of fused silica, caused by lightning striking sandy soil.

gabbro a coarse-grained igneous rock, equivalent to basalt and dolerite. It contains feldspar, pyroxene and olivine as the major constituents.

galena lead sulfide, the most important lead ore.

gangue the material in which an ore deposit from the metal is not extracted.

gannister an arenaceous stratum found beneath coal seams.

gas cap a collection of gas above an oil deposit.

gems hard minerals, free from cleavages. Fragments are artificially cut and polished for decorative use.

garnet a semi-precious mineral with a wide range of colours, although red is the most commonly found.

geode a rock cavity containing crystals pointing inwards.

geosyncline an elongated basin, filled with sedimentary deposits. These deposits can then be deformed by orogenic forces.

gneiss banded coarse-grained rocks formed during metamorphosis.

granite a coarse-grained igneous rock, consisting essentially of quartz and feldspar and occurring as intrusive bodies in a variety of forms.

granule a rock particle of about 2–4 mm (0·08–0·16 in).

graphite a soft black form of carbon.

grike a cleft in a limestone pavement.

grit a rock in which the particle shape is angular.

gull a fissure which tapers downwards and is then filled with material from above.

gumbo a soil which, when wet, gives a sticky mud.

gypsum an evaporite calcium sulfate mineral

found in clays and limestone.

hade a fault plane's angle to the vertical.

haematite an iron-oxide iron ore.

halite common salt, left as an evaporite.

hardness the mineral property propounded by Mohs. It measures the ability of one mineral to scratch another. Corundum – number 9 – can scratch topaz – number 8 – but not diamond – number 10.

10	Diamond	5	Apatite
9	Corundum	4	Fluorite
8	Topaz	3	Calcite
7	Quartz	2	Gypsum
6	Orthoclase	1	Talc

hard-pan strongly cemented material occurring below the surface of some sediments as a result of groundwater action.

hemicrystalline rocks containing both crystalline and glassy material.

hornfels a fine-grained granular rock formed by thermal metamorphosis.

hornstone a fine-grained volcanic ash.

horst an area thrown up between two parallel faults.

humus organic material in soil.

Iceland spar a variety of calcite.

igneous one of the three major divisions of rocks. Generally they are crystalline, although glassy forms can be found. They are either extrusive, i.e. produced on the Earth's surface as a result of volcanic action, or intrusive into other rocks, in which case they only appear on the Earth's surface if the surrounding rock is eroded. See p. 56.

impervious (a rock) not allowing the passage of water.

impregnation the in-filling of pores by mineral material, e.g. oil.

inclusion a portion of one material totally enclosed within another.

incretion a cylindrical hollow concretion.

inlier an area of older rock surrounded by younger rock.

interbedded (a layer of rock) situated between two other layers.

intermediate rock rock containing no more than 10% quartz plus a feldspar.

intrusion an igneous rock structure that has forced its way into pre-existing rock.

jade a gemstone of a hard compact aggregate.

jasper a red chert-like variety of chalcedony.

jet a homogeneous form of cannel coal or black lignite.

joint a fracture in a rock structure along which no movement can be observed.

kaolin the main constituent of china clay.

kieselguhr diatomite.

kimberlite a brecciated peridotite containing mica and other minerals.

kyanite an aluminium silicate.

labradorite a type of feldspar.

landscape marble a type of limestone that, when sliced at right angles to the bedding plane, reveals patterns reminiscent of a landscape scene.

laterite an iron-oxide ore, out of which the easily leached ions have been removed.

lava molten silicates that flow out of volcanoes. In

general they are basic, although acidic lava flows are known. Acidic lavas flow readily and tend to cover much larger areas, while basic lavas are more viscous.

leaching the removal of ions from a soil or rock by the through-flow of water.

lepidolite a type of mica.

lignite brown coal, low in carbon content.

limestone a group of sedimentary rocks consisting of carbonates, principally calcium carbonate. Calcite and dolomite are the most important limestone rocks.

limonite a group of iron oxides and hydroxides.

lithifaction the formation of a large rock from small fragments.

loam sand, silt and clay in equal proportions in a soil.

loess deposits of wind-blown fine particles.

lustre the ability of minerals to reflect light.

magma the molten fluid within the Earth's interior. Igneous rocks are formed from the magma, although various constituents of the magma will be lost during this process of consolidation.

magnesite magnesium carbonate.

magnetite an iron ore consisting of ferric oxide.

malachite a carbonate ore of copper.

marble metamorphosed limestone, usually with other compounds giving marble its recognizable appearance.

marl a mudstone with a high calcium content.

metamorphism the process of heating, pressure and chemical action that causes rocks to change from one form to another in the Earth's crust.

mica a large group of silica-based minerals, characterized by the fact that the crystal structure gives cleavage into flat flexible sheets.

migmatite a form of gneiss.

mobile belt a part of the Earth's crust in which metamorphism, igneous activity and deformation occur.

monzonite coarse igneous rock with a high feldspar content.

mud wet clay soil in a near-liquid state.

mudstone a type of argillaceous rock, similar to shale, but without the property of splitting along bedding planes.

muscovite a type of mica.

natural gas gaseous hydrocarbons found together with oil deposits.

neck a volcanic plug.

nodule a rounded concretion.

obsidian a type of rhyolite with a black glassy sheen to it.

oceanite a type of basalt.

oil often called petroleum, oil is naturally occurring liquid hydrocarbon. It is invariably found in association with saline water and natural gas, and often with solid hydrocarbons.

oil shale a dark argillaceous rock. It does not contain liquid oil, but a solid organic material called kerogen, which gives oil on distillation.

olivine a group of silicates, containing ferrous iron and magnesium. They largely occur in igneous rocks.

onyx a type of banded chalcedony.

oolith a rounded lump of rock formed by accretion round a nucleus. Ooliths usually contain calcium minerals.

opal an amorphous type of silica, believed to have been derived from silica gel.

ore an aggregate of minerals from which a valued mineral is extracted.

orogeny the process or period of mountain building.

outlier a relatively small area of young rock, surrounded by older rock.

overburden soil found on top of a bed of useful mineral.

peat an early, earth-like form of coal. It is a dark-brown to black mass of partially decomposed vegetation.

pebble a rock fragment of 5–60 mm (0·2–2·3 in) diameter.

pedalfer leached soil in a region with high rainfall.

pegmatite a coarse-grained igneous rock, usually granitic. Very long crystals may be apparent.

peridot gem-quality olivine.

permeability the ability of water to percolate through a rock.

pervious rock rock through which water may pass via cracks, fissures, etc.

pitchblende uranium oxide ore.

plug the solidified lava and other material left in the neck of a volcano. Often the surrounding material is subsequently eroded away.

plutonic rock igneous material of a deep-seated origin, i.e. originating from the magma.

pudding stone a conglomerate.

pumice one of the pyroclastic rocks thrown out of a volcano. It contains a high proportion of air space.

pyrite iron sulfide.

pyroclastic rock a rock formed either by liquid lava thrown out of a volcano or solid lumps of surrounding rock broken up by volcanic action.

quartz a silica mineral with three different forms. Sand is the most common. Low quartz is a crystalline form, occurring in a variety of colours. At 573°C (1063°F) low quartz gives rise to high quartz, but its natural occurrence is rare.

red bed sedimentary rocks containing a high proportion of ferric minerals, giving them a reddish colour.

residual deposit minerals left when part of a rock is dissolved or leached away.

rhyolite a fine-grained or glassy volcanic rock, rich in quartz.

rock a mass of mineral material, usually consisting of more than one mineral type.

rock crystal a clear form of quartz.

ruby a red transparent form of corundum.

rudaceous rock sedimentary rock deposited as detritus by water or air, and divided into conglomerates and breccias.

rutile titanium oxide ore.

salt dome salt forced up through an overlying sediment as a dome. Under pressure salt behaves like a magma.

sand a type of quartz, formed of fine particles. It can also be taken to mean any fine particles of 0·0625–2 mm (0·0025–0·08 in).

sandstone arenaceous rocks, consisting of fine grains cemented together by a variety of minerals.

sapphire a blue transparent form of corundum.

schist a metamorphosed rock with the constituent minerals arranged in parallel.

scree fragments formed by the weathering of rocks.

sedimentary rock rock formed out of the material resulting from erosion and weathering, along with organic material. The principal sedimentary rocks are sandstone, limestone and shale. See p. 57.

shale a sedimentary rock composed of clay particles.

shingle gravel or pebbles found on beaches.

silica silicon dioxide, which can take a variety of forms, e.g. quartz, chalcedony, opal.

silicates the most prolific mineral group in the Earth's crust. They are based on a silicon-oxide structure, but a variety of other elements and ions can be substituted in this structure, particularly aluminium. The group includes the clays, the feldspars, the garnets, the micas, the silicas.

sill a sheet of igneous rock, lying along a bedding plane.

silt a type of argillaceous rock.

slate argillaceous rock that has been metamorphosed. The slates all show cleavage, and may have new minerals showing up as marks or even crystals.

soapstone any greasy rock, although usually applied to talc rocks.

soil the loose weathered material covering most of the Earth's land surface. It contains humus – a partially decomposed matter – which improves the fertility and water retention of the soil and so encourages plant growth.

spinels a group of minerals including magnetite and chromite.

stalactite calcium carbonate formed as a spike hanging down from the ceiling in a limestone cave.

stalagmite calcium carbonate formed as a spike standing up from the floor in a limestone cave.

stock an intrusive mass of igneous rock, smaller than a batholith.

streak a mineral's colour when in a powdered state, e.g. formed by scratching it.

subsoil partly weathered rock lying between the soil and the bedrock.

syenites a group of coarse-grained igneous rocks containing feldspars and feldspathoids.

talc magnesium silicate, the softest common mineral.

tar pit areas where asphalt or bitumen rises to the surface from an underground hydrocarbon source.

terra rossa red clayey soil formed as a result of carbonates being leached out of limestone.

topaz a clear semi-precious form of aluminium silicate.

tor piles of granite blocks, left by differential weathering of the rock around them.

touchstone a very hard fine-grained black form of basalt or chert.

tripoli a type of diatomite.

ultrabasic rock igneous ferromagnesium rock, with little or no feldspar, quartz or feldspathoid in it.

ultramarine a type of feldspathoid.

valley fill loose material filling or partly filling a valley.

vein a sheet of mineral that has intruded into a fissure or joint of a rock.

water table the upper limit of the groundwater saturation.

weathering the breaking down of stationary rocks by mechanical means, e.g. by the action of ice and the Sun, and by chemical means.

wind erosion the abrasive action of wind-driven particles of sand against stationary rocks.

wolframite a tungsten ore.

xenolith an inclusion of pre-existing rock in an igneous rock.

zeolites a group of silicates containing water of crystallization, and capable of reversible dehydration. They can act as powerful base exchangers.

zircon zirconium silicate.

THE RICHTER SCALE

The Richter scale is the scale of measurement of earthquakes that we are most familiar with. It is a measurement of an earthquake's magnitude, and as such would mean little to the layman. However, it is possible to convert these readings to a scale of intensity.

Magnitude	Probable effects
1	Detectable only by instruments.
2	Barely detectable, even near the epicentre.
4·5	Detectable within 32 km (20 miles) of the epicentre; possible slight damage within a small area.
6	Moderately destructive.
7	A major earthquake.
8	A great earthquake.

THE MODIFIED MERCALLI SCALE

I Not felt except by a few people.

II Felt by a few people at rest. Delicately suspended objects swing.

III Felt noticeably indoors. Standing cars may rock.

IV Felt generally indoors. Sleeping people are woken. Cars rocked, windows rattle.

V Felt generally. Some plaster falls and dishes and windows are broken. Pendulum clocks stop.

VI Felt by all – many frightened. Chimneys and plaster damaged. Furniture moved and objects upset.

VII Everyone runs outdoors. Felt in moving cars. Moderate structural damage.

VIII General alarm. Weak structures badly damaged. Walls and furniture fall over. Water level changes in wells.

IX Panic. Weak structures totally destroyed, extensive damage to well-built structures, foundations and underground pipes. Ground fissured and cracked.

X Panic. Only strongest buildings survive. Ground badly cracked. Rails bent. Water slopped over river banks.

XI Panic. Few buildings survive. Broad fissures in ground. Fault scarps formed. Underground pipes out of service.

XII Total destruction. Waves seen in ground, and lines of sight and level are distorted. Objects thrown in the air.

CELSIUS AND FAHRENHEIT COMPARED

The two principal temperature scales are Celsius and Fahrenheit. Temperatures in a meteorological context are given in both in this and other chapters. The Celsius scale was devised in 1743 by J. P. Christen (1683–1755) but is referred to by its present name because of the erroneous belief that it was invented by the Swedish astronomer Anders Celsius (1701–44). The Fahrenheit scale is named after Gabriel Daniel Fahrenheit (1686–1736), a German physicist.

QUICK CONVERSION

To convert ° C to ° F, multiply the ° C reading by 9, divide by 5 and add 32.

To convert ° F to ° C, subtract 32 from the ° F reading and multiply by 5, divide by 9.

KELVIN SCALE

Scientists in a non-meteorological context most frequently employ the Kelvin Scale in which one degree kelvin (K) = 1/273·16 of the triple point of water (where ice, water and water vapour are in equilibrium).

TEMPERATURE COMPARISONS

The following tables compare points on the Celsius and Fahrenheit scales.

(1) Absolute zero	=	−273·15 °C	=	−459·67 °F	=	0K
(2) Zero Fahrenheit	=	−17·8 °C	=	−0·0 °F	=	255.35K
(3) Freezing point of water	=	0·0 °C	=	32·0 °F	=	273.15K
(4) Triple point of water	=	0.01 °C	=	32.02 °F	=	273.16K
(5) Normal human blood temperature	=	36·9 °C	=	98·4 °F	=	310.05K
(6) Boiling point of water (at standard pressure)	=	100·0 °C	=	212·0 °F	=	373.15K

−40 °C = −40 °F	1 °C = 34 °F	42 °C = 108 °F
−39 °C = −38 °F	2 °C = 36 °F	43 °C = 109 °F
−38 °C = −36 °F	3 °C = 37 °F	44 °C = 111 °F
−37 °C = −35 °F	4 °C = 39 °F	45 °C = 113 °F
−36 °C = −33 °F	5 °C = 41 °F	46 °C = 115 °F
−35 °C = −31 °F	6 °C = 43 °F	47 °C = 117 °F
−34 °C = −29 °F	7 °C = 45 °F	48 °C = 118 °F
−33 °C = −27 °F	8 °C = 46 °F	49 °C = 120 °F
−32 °C = −26 °F	9 °C = 48 °F	50 °C = 122 °F
−31 °C = −24 °F	10 °C = 50 °F	51 °C = 124 °F
−30 °C = −22 °F	11 °C = 52 °F	52 °C = 126 °F
−29 °C = −20 °F	12 °C = 54 °F	53 °C = 127 °F
−28 °C = −18 °F	13 °C = 55 °F	54 °C = 129 °F
−27 °C = −17 °F	14 °C = 57 °F	55 °C = 131 °F
−26 °C = −15 °F	15 °C = 59 °F	56 °C = 133 °F
−25 °C = −13 °F	16 °C = 61 °F	57 °C = 135 °F
−24 °C = −11 °F	17 °C = 63 °F	58 °C = 136 °F
−23 °C = −9 °F	18 °C = 64 °F	59 °C = 138 °F
−22 °C = −8 °F	19 °C = 66 °F	60 °C = 140 °F
−21 °C = −6 °F	20 °C = 68 °F	61 °C = 142 °F
−20 °C = −4 °F	21 °C = 70 °F	62 °C = 144 °F
−19 °C = −2 °F	22 °C = 72 °F	63 °C = 145 °F
−18 °C = 0 °F	23 °C = 73 °F	64 °C = 147 °F
−17 °C = 1 °F	24 °C = 75 °F	65 °C = 149 °F
−16 °C = 3 °F	25 °C = 77 °F	66 °C = 151 °F
−15 °C = 5 °F	26 °C = 79 °F	67 °C = 153 °F
−14 °C = 7 °F	27 °C = 81 °F	68 °C = 154 °F
−13 °C = 9 °F	28 °C = 82 °F	69 °C = 156 °F
−12 °C = 10 °F	29 °C = 84 °F	70 °C = 158 °F
−11 °C = 12 °F	30 °C = 86 °F	71 °C = 160 °F
−10 °C = 14 °F	31 °C = 88 °F	72 °C = 162 °F
−9 °C = 16 °F	32 °C = 90 °F	73 °C = 163 °F
−8 °C = 18 °F	33 °C = 91 °F	74 °C = 165 °F
−7 °C = 19 °F	34 °C = 93 °F	75 °C = 167 °F
−6 °C = 21 °F	35 °C = 95 °F	76 °C = 169 °F
−5 °C = 23 °F	36 °C = 97 °F	77 °C = 171 °F
−4 °C = 25 °F	37 °C = 99 °F	78 °C = 172 °F
−3 °C = 27 °F	38 °C = 100 °F	79 °C = 174 °F
−2 °C = 28 °F	39 °C = 102 °F	80 °C = 176 °F
−1 °C = 30 °F	40 °C = 104 °F	81 °C = 178 °F
0 °C = 32 °F	41 °C = 106 °F	82 °C = 180 °F

LIFE SCIENCES
THE LIVING WORLD

THE BEGINNING OF LIFE

Around every star in the universe – of which the Sun is but one – there is a zone, the *ecosphere*, where water could potentially exist as a liquid. Water is the prime requisite for life as we know it. If there is a body of sufficient mass in this zone (i.e. a planet), with sufficient gravitational force to hold onto water and a gaseous atmosphere, then the conditions for life may be present.

The nature of the original conditions on the Earth can be worked out by considering our neighbouring planets, Venus and Mars, together with the gases that erupt from volcanoes. The major gases produced by volcanoes are carbon dioxide and water vapour – the principal components of the oceans and the atmosphere. On Venus it is too hot for water to be liquid, on Mars too cold – but on the Earth it is just right. Simple compounds such as ammonia and methane are known to be able to combine with carbon dioxide and water if they are subjected to ultraviolet light (as emitted by the Sun) and if an electrical spark (such as might be provided by lightning) is passed through a mixture of these gases.

From such reactions are formed simple *amino acids*. These are the building blocks of *proteins* – the essential components of living things.

PROTEIN

Proteins are chains of amino acids, and there is an almost infinite variety of forms that can be synthesized from the 20 different amino acids. They may be in the form of *enzymes*, which act as catalysts in various biochemical reactions, or they may take the form of structural materials.

DNA

One of the fundamental aspects of living things is their ability to replicate themselves and to pass on instructions for making new individuals from one generation to another. These instructions are contained in a special, complex molecule known as *deoxyribonucleic acid* or *DNA*, which is made up of various organic compounds. DNA has the capacity to replicate itself, and acts as a blueprint for making amino acids, and hence proteins.

VIRUSES

The most basic forms of life are viruses. These simply consist of a protein coat protecting a single strand of DNA. Viruses are so small (on average about 100 millionths of a mm long) that they can only be seen with an electron microscope. Viruses can only reproduce within the cells of other organisms. In this way they cause many diseases from the common cold to AIDS.

BACTERIA

Because viruses are parasitic upon more complex organisms, it is unlikely that they were the first forms of life, even though they are the simplest. The first evidence of life on Earth comes from minute globules preserved in rocks 3800 million years old. These are believed to be the fossils of primitive bacteria.

Bacteria each consist of a single *cell* – the smallest biological unit able to function independently. The largest bacteria are only a few thousandths of a mm long. A typical bacterial cell consists of a cell wall within which is contained the *protoplasm* (a jelly-like substance) and strings of DNA. A single bacterium reproduces by splitting into two new cells, each one an exact copy of the original. This process can happen as often as once every 15 minutes.

The first bacteria were probably *heterotrophic*, i.e. they fed on the organic molecules that were so abundant in the early oceans. As the 'organic soup' was used up, new types of bacteria evolved, the *autotrophs*. Some autotrophs are capable of synthesizing their food from inorganic material, while others use light energy.

About 2900 million years ago a new type of bacteria – known as *cyanobacteria* or *blue-green algae* – evolved. These bacteria had the ability to use light to photosynthesize. The waste product of photosynthesis is oxygen, and oxygen began to accumulate in the ocean waters and in the atmosphere. Whereas oxygen had previously been a poison for all living things, it was now exploited by new kinds of bacteria (described as *aerobic*) as a fuel for burning food to obtain energy. Like the most primitive bacteria, these bacteria were heterotrophic, and from them evolved all the higher animals. From the autotrophic bacteria evolved the plants, all of which use photosynthesis. In this way, animals and plants share a common ancestry.

PROTISTS

One of the most remarkable events in the history of life on Earth took place about 1500 million years ago. Suddenly the microscopic organisms – although still single-celled – became many times larger than the bacteria that preceded them. This event marked the origin of the protists, some of which are plant-like and others animal-like (the latter also being known as *protozoans*). The largest protists are about 1 mm in length.

The protists and all later, more advanced forms of life – fungi, plants and animals – are known as *eukaryotes* (meaning 'true kernel'). This is because the protoplasm in their cells is differentiated into *cytoplasm* and the *nucleus* (the 'kernel'). The nucleus is a separate part of the cell, surrounded by the cytoplasm, and contains the chromosomes, the structures into which the DNA is organized. In contrast to bacteria, the cells of protists also contain miniature organs, or *organelles*, which perform specialized tasks. One of the most important organelles is the *mitochondrion*, which contains enzymes that break up organic compounds to release energy.

LARGER ORGANISMS

The first sign of cells coming together to form large organisms is the sponges, a group of marine invertebrates that first evolved at least 570 million years ago. Sponges may grow up to 1 m (3¼ ft) across, and their structure is supported by a network of fibres or by skeletal spicules.

TAXONOMY

Taxonomy is concerned with the classification of living organisms into groups. Living organisms are named and ordered within an hierarchical classification based on various criteria such as similarity of structure or supposed evolutionary relationships.

The Swedish naturalist Carolus Linnaeus (Carl von Linné; 1707–78) formulated rules for naming organisms in 1758. He recommended that every organism be given a generic name (e.g. *Homo* – man) with a species epithet (e.g. *H. sapiens* – 'wise' man). He further suggested that species should be grouped into successively more inclusive groupings, a system that is known as a taxonomic hierarchy. The most commonly used ranks are listed below, and – as can be seen – they are slightly different when applied to animals and plants.

Animals	Plants
Kingdom	Kingdom
Subkingdom	
Division	
Subdivision	
Series	
Phylum	Phylum
Class	Class
Subclass	Subclass
Order	Order
Family	Family
Genus	Genus
Species	Species

More than one system of classification exists, but most scientists believe that the diversity of life is best expressed in terms of five kingdoms: Monera, Protista, Fungi, Plantae, Animalia.

KINGDOM MONERA

Bacteria and cyanobacteria (blue-green algae) comprise this group of about 5000 species. They are single-celled, sometimes in chains or filaments, and very small (each single cell is less than 10 micrometers – one thousandth of a mm). The genetic material floats free in the cytoplasm as a single loop of DNA (deoxyribonucleic acid). They reproduce asexually by simple binary fission and most survive in conditions of very low oxygen concentration.

About 14 phyla are usually recognized and, although they are structurally very similar, they show a great range of biochemistry. Fermenting bacteria are very important in the production of cheese and yoghurt. Chemoautotrophic bacteria – which manufacture food from simple chemicals – play a crucial role in recycling nitrites, sulfur and methane into compounds that other organisms can use. Both bacteria and cyanobacteria include forms that can fix atmospheric nitrogen and some use a primitive form of photosynthesis.

Many pathogens, such as those causing salmonella, dysentry, cholera and anthrax, also belong to this group.

All other forms of life – fungi, protista, plants and animals – are formed of eukaryote cells: the DNA is organized into chromosomes contained within a nucleus inside the cell. There are organelles such as mitochondria and, in plants, chloroplasts, which carry out specific functions such as respiration and photosynthesis.

KINGDOM FUNGI

Fungi are plant-like organisms that have no chlorophyll. The cell wall of fungi often contains chitin, and there are no motile cells at any stage of the life cycle. Fungi may be unicellular (e.g. yeasts) or, more usually, multicellular with a thread-like mycelium and distinct fruiting body. Many are parasites of plants and animals, while others are important in the process of decay and recycling. Fungi are grouped in five phyla.

Phylum Zygomycota a phylum of simple fungi producing a resistant spore after sexual reproduction (e.g. *Mucor*, bread mould).

Phylum Ascomyceta a phylum containing such fungi as yeasts, cup fungi and truffles. Following sexual reproduction they produce a characteristic sac (ascus) containing eight spores.

Phylum Basidiomycota a phylum containing mushrooms, toadstools and bracket fungi. Following sexual reproduction, the zygote produces many four-spore basidia, which are protected by fruiting bodies.

Phylum Deuteromycota a phylum containing fungi for which no reproductive stage is known. The best-known example is penicillin.

Phylum Mycophycophyta (lichens) a symbiosis of algae and sometimes cyanobacteria within a fungus.

KINGDOM PROTISTA

This kingdom consists of organisms which may be unicellular or multicellular. If the organisms are multicellular, there is no organization of cells into organs, and many only reproduce asexually. A large number of taxonomists consider that this kingdom is 'artificial': it consists of organisms that cannot be easily fitted into other kingdoms. The kingdom comprises 27 phyla, but little is known about many of them and in some cases the number of species is unknown. Phyla include:

Phylum Bacillariophyta a phylum of diatoms – small unicellular algae enclosed within a silica skeleton made of two interlocking halves. There are some 10 000 species, which are very common in both fresh and marine water. Some species can form poisonous blooms from time to time.

Phylum Chlorophyta better known as green algae. The phylum comprises approximately 7000 species of single-celled or multicellular organisms which usually live in freshwater. These organisms are green because they contain chloroplasts and have cellulose cell walls, like true plants.

Phylum Sarcodina a phylum of unicellular organisms without chlorophyll. These organisms can move and feed by pushing out pseudopodia (e.g. amoebas). Some organisms, such as foraminifera, secrete a complicated shell of calcium carbonate.

Phylum Ciliophora a phylum of unicellular organisms covered with many tiny cilia that beat in a coordinated fashion to move the organism along. Paramecium is the best-known example.

Phylum Phaeophyta better known as brown seaweeds. There are about 1500 species which are common on rocky shores. Some are commercially important for yielding alginins, commonly used in the manufacture of ice creams and sweets.

Phylum Rhodophyta better known as red algae. The 4000 or so species of this phylum are multicellular and are usually marine. They contain special pigments in addition to chlorophyll and manufacture a special kind of starch. Some species yield agar, which is commercially important.

KINGDOM PLANTAE
See The Plant World (below).

KINGDOM ANIMALIA
See The Animal World (see p. 131).

THE CLASSIFICATION OF MAN

Rank		Distinguishing features
Kingdom	Animalia	nervous system
Subkingdom	Metazoa	multicellular
Phylum	Chordata	notochord
Subphylum	Vertebrata	backbone
No rank available	Gnathostomata	jaws
	Osteichthyes	cartilage bone
	Sarcopterygii	paired appendages with muscular lobes
	Chonata	internal nares (nostrils)
Superclass	Tetrapoda	pentadactyl (five-digit) limbs
Class	Mammalia	hair, sweat and milk glands
Subclass	Eutheria	placenta
Order	Primates	fingers with sensitive pads and nails
Family	Hominidae	upright posture, flat face, large brain
Genus	*Homo*	bipedality, manual dexterity
Species	*sapiens*	double-curved spine
Subspecies	*sapiens*	well-developed chin

THE PLANT WORLD

KINGDOM PLANTAE

Plants are multicellular organisms composed of cells surrounded by a rigid cellulose wall. They contain chlorophyll *a* and *b*, amongst other pigments, and are capable of photosynthesis. The embryo, which is produced as a result of sexual reproduction, is surrounded by nutritive tissue. In the life cycle a *haploid generation* (containing one set of chromosomes) – called the gametophyte – alternates with a *diploid generation* (containing two sets of chromosomes) – the sporophyte. There are two phyla – Bryophyta and Tracheophyta.

PHYLUM BRYOPHYTA

The plants of this phylum include the mosses and liverworts. These plants have no roots or conducting

PLANT KINGDOM

Rank												
Phylum	Bryophyta	Tracheophyta										
Division		Filicophytina	Spermatophytina									
Class			Coniferopsida	Angiospermopsida								
Subclass				Dicotyledonae						Monocotyledonae		
Families inc.				Fagaceae	Labiatae	Leguminosae	Rosaceae	Compositae	Euphorbiaceae	Orchidaceae	Liliaceae	Gramineae
Examples	mosses and liverworts	ferns	conifers	oaks and beeches	mint family	pea family	rose family	daisy family	spurge family	orchids	lilies	grass family

tissue and are confined to damp places. In the life cycle, the gametophyte is the dominant phase.

PHYLUM TRACHEOPHYTA

The plants of this phylum have conducting tissue (xylem and phloem), roots, and leaves with a protective cuticle. In the life cycle, the sporophyte is the dominant generation.

Some groups such as whisk ferns (Psilophytina), lycopods (Lycophytina) and horsetails (Sphenophytina) are relatively insignificant in numbers today, but these plants formed the vast 'Coal Measure' forests of Carboniferous times. Ferns and seed plants are the most numerous existing tracheophytes.

There are two major divisions – Filicophytina and Spermatophytina.

DIVISION FILICOPHYTINA

The division Filicophytina is popularly known as the true ferns. These plants often show complex pinnate leaves that carry spore-producing sacs. The gametophyte remains free-living and requires a damp habitat.

DIVISION SPERMATOPHYTINA

The division Spermatophytina is popularly known as the seed plants. The gametophyte is very reduced and develops within cones or flowers that produce the seed on the dominant sporophyte. These plants often show secondary growth and the development of bark. Several kinds of spermatophyte are sometimes grouped as gymnosperms – plants that bear naked seeds usually in cones.

There are two classes – Coniferopsida and Angiospermopsida.

Class Coniferopsida the dominant gymnosperm group. Conifers have waxy and often needle-shaped leaves, resinous wood, and male and female cones.

Class Angiospermopsida popularly known as the flowering plants. The seeds of angiosperms develop protected within an ovary which is carried within the flower that characterizes the class.

Flowers are thought by many scientists to have been derived from highly modified leaves. The male gametes (pollen) are produced in the anthers and the egg is enclosed within the ovary, to which is attached a style to receive the pollen. Anthers, ovaries and style are surrounded by petals and sepals to form the flower. The seed develops within the ovary, and the ovary wall often thickens to form a fruit. Many angiosperms show elaborate mechanisms of pollination and dispersal of the seeds.

Angiosperms are the most conspicuous plant group today. They comprise over 250 000 species, assigned to some 300 families contained within one of two subclasses – Dicotyledonae and Monocotyledonae.

Subclass Dicotyledonae a subclass containing plants that develop as seedlings bearing two leaves (cotyledons). The flower parts often occur in fives and the leaves display a network of veins. The families of this subclass include:

Family Fagaceae A small family of 900 species whose members are conspicuous in temperate regions; e.g. beech and oak trees. The female flowers are small, while the male flowers are long catkins.

Family Rosaceae The 2000 or so species of this family are mainly temperate plants and include many of our fruit trees such as apples and pears as well as roses.

The flowers are relatively simple with free petals and sepals, and there are many anthers. The fruit is often fleshy.

Family Labiatae This relatively small family of 3500 species includes many culinary herbs such as sage, basil and thyme. The flowers are borne in whorls or spikes, and the stems are square.

Family Leguminosae The pea family – or legumes – is a very large group comprising 16 000 species. They are particularly important in the tropics where they frequently occur as trees and shrubs. The leaves are often pinnate, the flowers are bilaterally symmetrical, and the fruits are borne in pods.

Family Euphorbiaceae Examples of the 7000 species of this family are to be found worldwide. They occur as trees, shrubs or herbs. The leaves occur in alternate fashion. The flowers are simple, usually without petals. The stems contain a milky latex, best exemplified in the commercially important rubber plants.

Family Compositae This large family is represented by some 14 000 species of herb. The flowers are very small but many are crowded together into distinctive composite flower heads which look like single flowers. Within each flower head there may be some flowers with strap-like petals while others are tiny tubular flowers. Together they make up the typical daisy-like flower.

Family Ericaceae A family which includes the heathers with their needle-like leaves as well as larger trees and shrubs including rhododendrons and azaleas.

Subclass Monocotyledonae a subclass of angiosperms that develop from seedlings with only one embryonic leaf. The flower parts often occur in threes and sixes, and the leaves show parallel venation.

Family Liliaceae The 3000 species in this family include lilies, onions and garlic. The flowers have six petals which resemble one another. The ovary is always three-celled. The plant often develops from a bulb or a corm.

Family Orchidaceae The orchid family is the largest of the angiosperm families with some 17 000 species, mainly of tropical origin. The flowers are usually single but can occur in very complicated forms with elaborate pollinating mechanisms. There is usually one hanging petal. The fruit contains many extremely tiny seeds.

Family Gramineae The grass family is one of the dominant plant families of the modern world and contains many important cereal crops. The flowers are inconspicuous and are wind pollinated. The leaves are generally narrow and have a sheathing base.

Family Palmae A family of 2500 species of tropical and subtropical plants including palm trees. They range up to 60 m in height and are characterized by an unbranched trunk.

AGRICULTURAL CROPS COMMON IN EUROPE

Apples About 25 species of the genus *Malus* are cultivated for their fruit. Thousands of varieties have been bred for cooking, for dessert (eating apples) or for brewing (cider). The apple originated in Southwest Asia and is known to have been cultivated c. 450 BC.

Barley An annual temperate grass of the genus *Hordeum*, especially *H. vulgare* and *H. distichum*.

Widely grown, the grain is used in brewing and distilling, for making puddings and as animal feed. Barley probably originated in the Ethiopian highlands and was first cultivated in Ancient Egypt c. 5000 BC.

Cotton A number of subtropical shrubs, belonging to the genus *Gossypium*, are commonly referred to as cotton. Cotton fibres are grown to be made into a variety of fabrics. Members of the genus are native to most subtropical regions and the fibre has been used since early times.

Flax Flax (*Linum usitatissimum*) is a temperate plant grown for its fibre, from which linen is made, and for its seed (linseed, a source of oil). Flax fibres have been found in prehistoric settlements and in Ancient Egyptian tombs.

Maize Maize (*Zea mays*) is a tall annual grass grown for its grain, which is used for food, animal fodder and as a source of vegetable oil. In North America it is known as corn, and is sometimes referred to in Britain as Indian corn. Maize probably originated in Central America and was first cultivated in pre-colonial days in North, Central and South America.

Oats An annual temperate grass (*Avena sativa*), oats are widely grown. Its grain is mainly fed to livestock, but is also used in breakfast cereals and for biscuits. Oats originated as a weed in Western Europe and have been cultivated since early times.

Pears The pear is a temperate tree (*Pyrus communis*) related to the rose family. The second most important deciduous fruit tree, the pear is grown entirely for human consumption as a fruit or a drink (perry). Pears originated in western Asia and have been cultivated since early history.

Potatoes The potato (*Solanum tuberosum*) is a tuber-bearing plant grown for human and animal consumption. Native to the Andean region of South America, the potato has been cultivated since about AD 100 and was introduced to Europe by the Spanish in the 16th century and to England, reputedly, by Walter Raleigh.

Rapeseed A member of the mustard family, rapeseed or colza (*Brassica napus*) is grown for its seed from which an oil – used in cooking and as a fuel or a lubricant – is extracted. Colza is native to Europe.

Rice A tropical starchy cereal, rice (*Oryza sativa*) is grown almost entirely for human consumption. It is the staple crop of over one half of the world's population. The crop is produced under irrigation, and although it is largely confined to East, South and Southeast Asia, small quantities of rice have been grown in Europe since the Middle Ages. Rice is known to have been cultivated in India c. 3000 BC.

Rye Rye (*Secale cereale*) is an extensively grown temperate cereal. It is cultivated in areas in which the soil and the climate are not suitable for less hardy cereals. Rye is used to make flour and as a livestock feed. It is known to have been cultivated in Asia Minor about 6500 BC.

Soyabeans Soyabeans – known in North America as soybeans – is a subtropical legume (*Glycine soja*) grown for its beans, which are used for human consumption (for example, as a meat substitute or vegetable oil), for livestock feed, or as a source of oil for paints, fertilizers and adhesives. The plant has been cultivated in China since c. 3000 BC.

Sugar beet Sugar beet (*Beta vulgaris*) is, after sugar cane, the second most important source of sugar. A temperate crop, beet was grown for fodder long before being cultivated for sugar. Sugar was first extracted from beet in Germany in 1747.

Tobacco The leaves of many species of *Nicotiana* are cured for smoking, snuff, and chewing. Wild tobacco (*Nicotiana rustica*) is the variety grown in southern and southeast Europe. Tobacco was widely cultivated in pre-colonial America.

Tomatoes The tomato (*Lycopersicon esculentum*) is a fruit that is part of the nightshade family. Subtropical in origin, it is grown entirely for human consumption. The tomato, which is native to the Peruvian-Ecuadorian Andes, was introduced to Italy via Mexico during the 16th century.

Wheat There are thousands of varieties of this temperate cereal, although the most widespread are *Triticum vulgare* (which is used for bread), *Triticum durum* (for pasta), and *Triticum compactum* (mainly used for making cakes and biscuits). The most important cereal, wheat is usually grown in preference to other cereals where conditions allow. Wheat was cultivated in the Euphrates Valley in Iraq about 7000 BC.

EURO FACTS

AGRICULTURAL CROPS COMMON IN THE EC

Apples *Leading EC producers (in tonnes):* Germany 2 700 000, France 2 300 000, Italy 2 200 000.

Barley *Leading EC producers (in tonnes):* Germany 13 300 000, Spain 12 400 000, France 10 300 000.

Cotton *Leading EC producers (in tonnes):* Greece 200 000, Spain 100 000.

Flax *Leading EC producers (in tonnes):* France 70 000, Belgium 10 000.

Maize *Leading EC producers (in tonnes):* France 13 700 000, Italy 6 200 000, Spain 3 600 000.

Oats *Leading EC producers (in tonnes):* Germany 2 600 000, France 1 100 000, Spain 600 000.

Pears *Leading EC producers (in tonnes):* Italy 900 000, Spain 500 000, France 500 000.

Potatoes *Leading EC producers (in tonnes):* Germany 18 700 000, Netherlands 7 400 000, France 6 400 000.

Rapeseed *Leading EC producers (in tonnes):* France 2 500 000, Germany 1 600 000, UK 1 000 000.

Rice *Leading EC producer (in tonnes):* Italy 1 100 000.

Rye *Leading EC producers (in tonnes):* Germany 3 400 000, Spain 400 000, Denmark 400 000.

Soyabeans *Leading EC producer (in tonnes):* Italy 1 300 000.

Sugar beet *Leading EC producers (in tonnes):* France 26 200 000, Germany 26 100 000, Italy 13 200 000.

Tobacco *Leading EC producers (in tonnes):* Italy 150 000, Greece 150 000.

Tomatoes *Leading EC producers (in tonnes):* Italy 5 500 000, Spain 2 600 000, Greece 1 900 000.

Wheat *Leading EC producers (in tonnes):* France 29 100 000, Germany 15 900 000, UK 11 600 000.

FRUITS

Common name	Scientific name	Geographical origin	Date first described or known
Apple	*Malus pumila*	Southwestern Asia	c. 450 BC
Apricot	*Prunus armeniaca*	Central and western China	BC (Piling and Dioscorides)
Avocado (pear)	*Persea americana*	Mexico and Central America	Early Spanish explorers, Clusius 1601
Banana	*Musa sapientum*	Southern Asia	Intro: Africa 1st century AD, Canary Is 15th century
Blackcurrants	*Ribes nigrum*	Northern Europe	First recorded in Britain in 17th-century herbals
Carambola	*Averrhoa carambola*	Malaysia and Indonesia	–
Cherry	*Prunus avium*	Europe (near Dardanelles)	Prehistoric times
Coconut	*Cocus nucifera*	Pacific	Active planting since 12th century
Cranberry	*Oxycccus macrocarpus*	America	–
Custard apple	*Annona squamosa*	Peru and Ecuador	–
Date	*Phoenix dactylifera*	Unknown	Prehistoric times
Fig	*Ficus carica*	Syria westward to the Canary Is	c. 4000 BC (Egypt)
Gooseberry	*Ribes grossularia*	Europe	Fruiterer's bills from France (1276–92) of Edward I
Grape	*Vitis vinifera*	Around Caspian and Black Seas	c. 4000 BC
Grapefruit	*Citrus grandis*	Malay Archipelago and neighbouring islands	12th or 13th century
Kiwifruit	*Actinidia chinensis*	China	–
Lemon	*Citrus limon*	SE Asia	11th–13th centuries
Lime	*Citrus aurantifolia*	Northern Burma	11th–13th centuries
Lychee	*Litchi chinensis*	Southern China	–
Mandarin	*Citrus reticulata*	China	220 BC in China; Europe 1805
Mango	*Mangifera indica*	Southeastern Asia	c. 16th century; Cult. India 4th–5th century BC
Olive	*Olea europaea*	Syria to Greece	Prehistoric times
Orange	*Citrus sinensis*	China	2200 BC (Europe 15th century)
Papaya	*Carica papaya*	West Indian Islands or Mexican mainland	14th–15th centuries
Passion fruit	*Passiflora edulis*	South America	–
Peach	*Prunus persica*	China?	300 BC (Greece)
Pear	*Pyrus communis*	Western Asia	Prehistoric times
Persimmon	*Diospyros kaki*	China/Japan	Thousands of years
Pineapple	*Ananas comosus*	Guadeloupe	c. time of Columbus
Plum	*Prunus domestica*	Western Asia	Possibly AD 100
Pomegranate	*Punica granatum*	Iran	–
Pomelo	*Citrus grandis*	Java and Malaysia	17th century
Quince	*Cydonia oblonga*	Northern Iran	BC
Raspberry	*Rubus idaeus*	Europe	Turner's Herbal of 1548
Redcurrants	*Ribes* species	Europe/Northern Asia	First description in German 17th-century herbals
Rhubarb	*Rheum rhaponticum*	Eastern Mediterranean lands and Asia Minor	2700 BC (China)
Strawberry	*Fragaria* species	Europe	Rome 200 BC
Ugli	*Citrus reticulata*	Jamaica	–
Water melon	*Citrullus laratus*	Central Africa	c. 2000 BC (Egypt)

VEGETABLES

Common name	Scientific name	Geographical origin	Date first described or known
Asparagus	*Asparagus officinalis*	Eastern Mediterranean	c. 200 BC
Aubergine	*Solanum melongena*	Asia	India 4000 years ago
Beetroot	*Beta vulgaris*	Mediterranean area	2nd century BC
Broad bean	*Vicia faba*	–	Widely cultivated in prehistoric times
Broccoli	*Brassica oleracea* (variety *Italica*)	Eastern Mediterranean	1st century AD
Brussels sprout	*Brassica oleracea* (variety *gemmifera*)	Northern Europe	1587 (northern Europe)

Cabbage	Brassica oleracea (variety capitata)	Eastern Mediterranean lands and Asia Minor	c. 600 BC
Carrot	Daucus carota	Afghanistan	c. 500 BC
Cauliflower	Brassica oleracea (variety botrytis)	Eastern Mediterranean	6th century BC
Celeriac	Apium graveolens rapaceum	Mediterranean	Wild plant first used by Greeks. By 17th century garden celery distinct from wild plant
Celery	Apium graveolens	Caucasus	c. 850 BC
Chicory	Cichorium intybus	Mediterranean	Ancient Greek or Rome
Chive	Allium schoenoprasum	Eastern Mediterranean	c. 100 BC
Courgette	Cucurbita pepo	Italy	–
Cucumber	Cucumis sativus	Northern India	2nd century BC (Egypt 1300 BC)
Dasheen	Colocasia esculenta	Indo-Malaya	Important food crop in China about 100 BC
Eddoe	Colocasia antiquorum	Probably Africa	China 2000 years ago
Egg plant	Solanum melongena	India, Assam, Burma	c. 450 AD (China)
Endive	Cichorium endivia	Eastern Mediterranean lands and Asia Minor	BC
Florence fennel	Foeniculum vulgare dulce	Italy	Brought to England in Stuart times
Garden pea	Pisum sativum	Central Asia	3000–2000 BC
Garlic	Allium sativum	Middle Asia	c. 900 BC (Homer)
Gherkin (W. Indian)	Cucumis anguria	Northern India	2nd century BC
Ginger	Zingiber officinale	SE Asia	Thousands of years old
Green beans	Phaseolus vulgaris	South America	Reached England by 1594
Globe artichoke	Cynara scolymus	Western and central Mediterranean	c. 500 BC
Jerusalem artichoke	Helianthus tuberosus	Canada	1616
Kale	Brassica oleracea (variety acephala)	Eastern Mediterranean lands and Asia Minor	c. 500 BC
Kohlrabi	Brassica oleracea caulorapa	Asia	Taken from Italy to Germany mid-16th century
Lamb's tongue lettuce	Valerianella locusta	Europe	–
Leek	Allium porrum	Middle Asia	c. 1000 BC
Lettuce	Lactuca sativa	Asia Minor, Iran, Turkistan	4500 BC (Egyptian tomb)
Mange tout	Pisum sativum saccharatum	Near East	17th century
Marrow	Cucurbita pepo	America?	16th–17th century (Mexican sites 7000–5500 BC)
Mushrooms	Psalliota compestris	Unknown	Mentioned in Ancient Rome and Greece
Musk melon	Cucumis melo	Iran	2900 BC (Egypt)
Okra	Hibiscus esculentus	Tropical Africa	Egypt 13th century
Olives	Olea europaea	Eastern Mediterranean	Found on coast of Syria and dated 4th millennium BC
Onion	Allium cepa	Middle Asia	c. 3000 BC (Egypt)
Parsley	Petroselinum crispum	Southern Europe	Used by Greeks and Romans
Parsnip	Pastinaca sativa	Caucasus	1st century BC
Peas	Psium sativum	The Near East	9570 BC Burma and Thailand
Pepper	Capsicum frutescens	Peru	Early burial sites, Peru; intro. Europe 1493
Potato	Solanum tuberosum	Southern Chile	c. 1530; intro. Ireland 1565
Pumpkin	Cucurbita maxima	Northern Andean Argentina	1591
Radicchio	Cichorium intybus	Europe	Roman times
Radish	Raphanus sativus	Western Asia, Egypt	c. 3000 BC
Red cabbage	Brassica oleracea	Mediterranean area and/or Asia Minor	England 14th century
Red kidney beans	Phaseolus vulgaris	Probably South America	–
Runner beans	Phaseolus vulgaris	Central America	c. 1500 (known from Mexican sites 7000–5000 BC)
Soybean	Soja max	China	c. 2850 BC
Spinach	Spinacia oleracea	Iran	AD 647 in Nepal
Spring onion	Allium cepa	Central Asia	Collected by 19th century botanists (reference to onions can be traced to 1st Egyptian dynasty 3200 BC)
Swede	Brassica napobrassica	Europe	1620
Sweet corn	Zea mays	Andes	Cult. early times in America; intro. Europe after 1492
Sweet potato	Ipomoea batatas	Tropical America	Prehistoric Peru

Tomato (technically a fruit)	*Lycopersicon esculentum*	Bolivia–Ecuador–Peru area	Italy c. 1550
Turnip	*Brassica rapa*	Greece	2000 BC
Water chestnuts	*Eleocharis dulcis*	Southern China	Neolithic times
Watercress	*Nasturtium officinale*	–	John Gerarde's Herball of 1597
White cabbage	*Brassica oleracea capita*	Mediterranean area and/or Asia Minor	Greek kales 600 BC. Germany 1150
Yams	*Discorea rotundra*	Africa	Arrived in England in 16th century

NATIONAL PARKS

Many countries have set aside areas for the conservation of the landscape and as a protected habitat for flora and fauna.

NATIONAL PARKS IN EUROPE

Major European parks and reserves include:

Abisko National Park (Sweden) Within the Arctic Circle. Area: 75 km² (29 sq mi). Fauna includes: Arctic fox, golden eagle, lemming, lynx, reindeer, wolverine, wolf.

Abruzzi National Park (Italy) In the Apennine mountains of Abruzzi. Area: 392 km² (151 sq mi). Fauna includes: brown bear, chamois, golden eagle, lynx, polecat, wolf.

Babiogorski National Park (Poland) In the Carpathian mountains. Area: 17 km² (7 sq mi). Fauna includes: eagle owl, lynx, red deer.

Bayerischer Wald (Germany) Low mountains in eastern Bavaria. Area: 120 km² (46 sq mi). Fauna includes: European bison, lynx, otter, wildcat, wolf.

Bialowieski National Park (Poland) On plains adjoining the Byelorussian border. Area: 53 km² (20 sq mi). Fauna includes: beaver, black stork, black grouse, brown bear, elk, European bison (the main breeding centre), spotted eagle, tarpan horse.

Cévennes National Park (France) In the south of the Massif Central. Area: 844 km² (326 sq mi). Fauna includes: genet, golden eagle, mountain sheep, wild boar.

Dartmoor National Park (England, UK) Moorland in central Devon. Area: 945 km² (365 sq mi). Fauna includes: fallow, red and roe deer, wild pony.

Gran Paradiso National Park (Italy) In the Alps on the Piedmont-Valle d'Aosta border. Area: 700 km² (270 sq mi). Fauna includes: chamois, golden eagle, otter, ibex, marten, ptarmigan, white grouse.

Hansted Bird Reserve (Denmark) On the west coast of Jutland. Area: 39 km² (15 sq mi). Fauna includes: a wide variety of birds, especially cranes and plovers.

Hohe Tauern Nature Park (Austria) In the eastern Alps – the park includes the Grossglockner. Area: 2589 km² (1000 sq mi). Fauna includes: chamois, marmot.

Hortobágyi National Park (Hungary) Steppe and marshes in central Hungary. Area: 520 km² (201 sq mi). Fauna includes: many species of geese.

Lake District National Park (England, UK) In the mountains of Cumbria. Area: 2243 km² (866 sq mi). Fauna includes: fell ponies, mountain sheep, red deer.

Olímbos National Park (Greece) Around Mount Olympus in northern Greece. Area: 40 km² (15 sq mi). Fauna includes: chamois, golden eagle, roe deer, wild mountain goat, wolf.

Pallas-Ounastunturi National Park (Finland) On a plateau in Lapland. Area: 500 km² (193 sq mi). Fauna includes: brown bear, crane, elk, lemming, reindeer, whooper swan.

Pembrokeshire Coast National Park (Wales, UK) Coastal region of western Dyfed. Area: 583 km² (225 sq mi). Fauna includes: many varieties of bird, including buzzard, chough, merlin and sea birds as well as grey seal, otter, polecat.

Pfälzerwald Nature Park (Germany) The Palatinate plateau. Area: 1793 km² (692 sq mi). Fauna includes: European bison, mountain sheep, mountain goat.

Plitvicka Lakes National Park (Yugoslavia) In the Dinaric Alps of Croatia. Area: 192 km² (74 sq mi). Fauna includes: brown bear, otter, pine marten, wild cat.

Port-Cros National Park (France) Port-Cros and other islands off the Côte d'Azur. Area: 25 km² (10 sq mi) – three-quarters is submarine. Fauna: many varieties of fish and sea bird.

Pyrénées Occidentales National Park (France) On the Spanish border in the High Pyrenees. Area: 477 km² (184 sq mi). Fauna includes: civet, eagle, eagle owl, genet, ibex, lynx, otter, Pyrenean chamois, vulture.

Retezat National Park (Romania) In the western Carpathian Mountains. Area: 200 km² (77 sq mi). Fauna includes: brown bear, chamois, golden eagle, lammergeier, lynx, wild boar, wolf.

Rondane National Park (Norway) A mountainous region on the borders of Hedmark and Oppland. Area: 572 km² (221 sq mi). Fauna includes: brown bear, elk, golden eagle, lemming, lynx, reindeer, wolf.

Sarek National Park (Sweden) A mountainous area in Lapland. Area: 1940 km² (749 sq mi). Fauna includes: similar to Rondane, see above.

Skaftafell National Park (Iceland) In the south of Iceland. Area: 500 km² (193 sq mi). Fauna includes: bear, grey seal, many species of sea bird.

Snowdonia National Park (Wales, UK) The mountainous area around Snowdon in Gwynedd. Area: 2171 km² (838 sq mi). Fauna includes: otter, polecat, pine marten.

Swiss National Park (Switzerland) In the Alps of Graubünden. Area: 169 km² (65 sq mi). Fauna includes: chamois, ibex, marmot, golden eagle.

Tatra National Parks (Czechoslovakia and Poland) In the Tatra Mountains along the Polish-Slovak border. Area: 212 km² (82 sq mi) in Poland; 500 km² (193 sq mi) in Czechoslovakia. Fauna includes: brown bear, chamois, golden eagle, lynx, marmot, wolf.

Triglav National Park (Yugoslavia) In the Julian Alps of Slovenia. Area: 20 km² (8 sq mi). Fauna includes: chamois, mountain hare.

Valle de Ordesa (Spain) In the High Pyrenees on the French border. Area: 20 km² (8 sq mi). Fauna includes: brown bear, chamois, ibex, lammergeier, wild boar, wild goat.

Vanoise National Park (France) Along the Italian border in Savoy. Area: 528 km² (204 sq mi). Fauna includes: similar to Gran Paradiso which adjoins it, see above.

Veluwe National Park (Netherlands) Sandy heathlands in the eastern Netherlands. Area: 46 km² (18 sq mi). Fauna includes: fallow, red and roe deer, wild boar.

THE ANIMAL WORLD

KINGDOM ANIMALIA

One of the most important events in the evolution of life on Earth was the development of multicellular organisms – ranging from simple worms to complex insects and squids – from unicellular animal-like protists. Most groups of primitive multicellular invertebrates are found in very old fossil-bearing rocks, so it is clear that this major breakthrough occurred at least 600 million years ago.

The similarity in mineral composition of animal body fluids and sea water indicates that all groups of primitive animals arose in the sea. One of these groups (the echinoderms) is of particular interest in that they share a common ancestor with the chordates, from which all vertebrates – including man – evolved.

All animals are multicellular with some kind of interconnection – a nervous system – between the cells. Each cell is bounded by a simple flexible membrane, and, as they do not contain chloroplasts, all animals rely on an organic source of food. Sexual reproduction takes place between two different gametes, a motile sperm and non-motile egg.

Scientists group animals into approximately 28 phyla, although there is some disagreement as to whether certain small groups are distinct phyla.

SUBKINGDOM PARAZOA

The two phyla grouped in the subkingdom Parazoa comprise animals in which different cell types perform different functions – feeding, defence, reproduction, etc – although they are not grouped into tissues or organs. The sponges (Phylum Porifera) comprise some 10 000 species inhabiting both fresh and marine waters.

SUBKINGDOM EUMETAZOA

All the remaining animals are grouped under the subkingdom Eumetazoa and assigned to either the Division Radiata or the Division Bilateralia. They are characterized by discrete tissues and organs which develop from early embryonic cell layers (ectoderm and endoderm).

DIVISION RADIATA

The animals in this division all show radial symmetry – the animal may be divided along more than one

plane through the centre to give mirror-image halves. The body is organized as two layers of cells separated by a jelly-like middle layer, while the nervous system forms a diffuse net. The division comprises about 9600 species, assigned to two phyla. The Phylum Cnidaria includes jellyfishes, sea anemones and the corals – animals possessing tentacles armed with stinging cells.

DIVISION BILATERALIA

The animals contained within this division may only be divided by one plane to yield mirror halves. They possess an extra embryonic cell layer – the mesoderm – which forms most of the body and in which, in most animals, there is a body cavity – the coelom – containing the digestive tract and other visceral organs.

SUBDIVISION ACOELOMATA

The members of the four phyla comprising this subdividion do not possess a coelom. The best known are members of the Phylum Platyhelminthes, which includes the flatworms, the flukes (external and internal parasites) and the tapeworms (internal parasites). These have a recognizable head and a mouth that leads to a blind-ending gut with no anus.

SUBDIVISION PSEUDOCOELOMATA

The animals assigned to this subdivision possess a body cavity that is not developed as a true coelom. They are characterized by a through-gut with a mouth at one end and the anus at the other. Nine phyla are grouped within the subdivision, most of whose members are tiny inconspicuous animals living in sand and mud. The two most important phyla are the nematodes and the rotifers.

PHYLUM NEMATODA

The nematodes – or roundworms – comprise an extremely large group of at least 100 000 species (many undescribed). Unlike true worms they show no sign of segmentation of the body. Roundworms are found in nearly every terrestrial and aquatic environment. They include free-living forms as well as parasites, including hookworm and filaria (one of which causes elephantiasis).

PHYLUM ROTIFERA

Rotifers are minute wheel-like animals, so called because the beating of the crown of cilia resembles a spinning wheel. Most of the 2000 species live in freshwater.

SUBDIVISION COELOMATA

This vast subdivision includes all the remaining animal organisms from earthworms to man. They are characterized by possession of a true coelom and nearly all have well-developed nervous and circulatory systems. The two types of coelomate animal are distinguished by a distinction based on early embryonic development. In members of the Series Protostoma the hollow ball of cells, the blastula, which develops from the fertilized egg folds in on itself to form the gut and the resulting pore becomes the mouth. In the Series Deuterostoma the first pore becomes the anus and the mouth develops later as a second opening.

SERIES PROTOSTOMA

In most systems of classification this series includes

at least 11 phyla, some of which have very few members. Others are much more numerous – the molluscs and the arthropods are the two largest phyla in the animal kingdom. Phyla of the series Protostoma include:

PHYLUM ECTOPROCTA

The members of this phylum are sometimes called bryozoans or moss animals. There are about 5000 species which form colonies spreading over the surfaces of rocks and seaweeds. These tiny animals feed by means of tentacles.

PHYLUM ANNELIDA

The 9000 species of annelids (true worms) are characterized by an externally and internally segmented body, and a closed blood system (with discrete blood vessels). The phylum is divided into classes including:

Class Polychaeta the class containing the paddle (bristle) worms. These are mostly free-living marine animals with distinctive swimming appendages composed of many bristles on every segment. The mouth is equipped with jaws.

Class Oligochaeta the class including the familiar earthworms. In these annelids the bristles are inconspicuous.

Class Hirudinea the class containing the leeches, which are characterized by a sucker at either end. Some are free-living but many are blood-sucking parasites.

PHYLUM MOLLUSCA

This large and diverse group of animals comprises nearly 110 000 species. Most show no trace of segmentation. The body consists of a head, a foot and a hump usually covered by a shell (although sometimes the shell is contained within the body). There is an open circulation where the blood is simply pumped directly into a body cavity. There are seven classes of molluscs but only three are conspicuous in the modern world.

Class Gastropoda the class including snails, limpets and slugs. The body is coiled and is usually contained within a shell, which is reduced in slugs. There is a distinct head with eyes, and the mouth contains a rasp-like tongue – the extendable radula. The foot is particularly large.

Class Bivalvia (Lamellibranchiata) a class sometimes known as pelecypods. The body is enclosed completely within two shells covering either side of the body and hinged along one edge. The bivalves – most of which are marine – feed by filtering small particles out of a water stream that is passed over enlarged gills. Examples include clams, cockles and oysters.

Class Cephalopoda a class of molluscs in which the foot is developed into a series of tentacles. They include squids, cuttlefish and octopuses. The head is large with complex eyes, structurally very similar to our own. The shell is reduced and not externally obvious in most members of the class.

PHYLUM ARTHROPODA

The arthropods comprise by far the largest animal phylum. Over three quarters of a million species have been described, most belonging to the Class Insecta. Some scientists believe that another 10 million insects or more remain to be described. Arthropods

have segmented bodies and segmented appendages, both encased in a chitinous exoskeleton. The rather rigid exoskeleton means that growth takes place in bursts between moults. As in molluscs, there is an open circulatory system. There are nine separate classes of arthropods including such diverse animals as centipedes, millipedes and horseshoe crabs as well as members of the three dominant classes.

Class Crustacea a class characterized by hard exoskeletons and segmented appendages. Nearly every segment of the body bears appendages that are modified for sensing (antennae), eating (mandibles etc.), walking and swimming, and respiration (gills). There are two pairs of antennae. The majority of crustaceans – such as waterfleas, crabs, ostracods and copepods – are aquatic but some are terrestrial (e.g. woodlice).

Class Insecta a mainly terrestrial group, although there are important aquatic insects and many have an aquatic larval stage. Insects have a distinct head, thorax and abdomen. There is a single pair of antennae, three pairs of legs, and usually one or two pairs of wings on the thorax. Most systems of classification assign the insects to about 25 orders that may be grouped in one of two subclasses. Insects represented in the Subclass Heterometabola develop through successive stages (instars) of increasingly more 'adult' forms. Examples of this type include locusts and cockroaches (Order Orthoptera).

Many insects go through a drastic metamorphosis in their development, changing from a larva (often grub-like) through a pupal stage to emerge in fully adult form (Subclass Homometabola). Familiar examples are butterflies and moths (Order Lepidoptera), flies (Order Diptera), in which the hind pair of wings are modified as balancing organs, beetles (Order Coleoptera) and bees, ants and wasps (Order Hymenoptera), which often show very complex social organizations.

Class Arachnida the class including the scorpions and spiders. The body is divided into two parts: the head and thorax form the front part carrying four pairs of legs; the abdomen forms the hind part and in spiders often carries spinnerets to spin webs.

SERIES DEUTEROSTOMA

These are animals in which the mouth develops as a secondary opening in early ontogeny. There are four phyla, but two – beardworms and arrow worms – are very small with about 150 species of uncommon animals in total. The two remaining phyla are the echinoderms and the very numerous and diverse chordates.

PHYLUM ECHINODERMATA

The echinoderms are exclusively marine animals characterized by five rows of tiny extensible tube feet that often protrude through a calcium carbonate skeleton. There are about 6000 species arranged in five classes of which the starfishes (Class Asteroidea) and the sea urchins (Class Echinoidea) are the most conspicuous.

PHYLUM CHORDATA

All chordates have a stiffening rod – the notochord – which provides a flexible support along the back. Above the notochord is a hollow nerve cord which, in most cases, is expanded as an elaborate brain. Chordates possess a true tail developed behind the anus. The phylum includes three rather small groups of small marine animals – Subphylum Hemichordata

ANIMAL KINGDOM

Subkingdom	Division	Subdivision	Series	Phylum	Subphylum	Class	Subclass	Representative species
Parazoa				Porifera				sponges
Eumetazoa	Radiata			Cnidaria				sea anemones
	Bilateralia	Acoelomata		Platyhelminthes				flatworms
		Pseudocoelomata		Nematoda Rotifera				roundworms wheel animalcules
		Coelomata		Ectoprocta				bryozoans
			Protostoma	Annelida		Polychaeta Oligochaeta Hirudinea		paddleworms earthworms leeches
				Mollusca		Gastropoda Bivalvia Cephalopoda		snails clams squids
				Arthropoda		Crustacea Insecta Arachnida		crabs insects spiders
			Deuterostoma	Echinodermata				sea urchins
				Chordata	Hemichordata Tunicata Cephalochordata			acorn worms sea squirts lancelets
					Craniata	Agiatha Chondrichthyes Osteichthyes Amphibia Reptilia Aves Mammalia		lampreys cartilaginous fishes bony fishes amphibians reptiles birds
							Marsupialia	marsupials
							Eutheria	placental mammals

(acorn worms), Subphylum Tunicata (sea squirts) and Subphylum Cephalochordata. The remaining subphylum Craniata is by far the largest, containing birds, fishes, reptiles and mammals.

SUBPHYLUM CRANIATA

The chordates assigned to this subphylum possess a recognizable brain, eyes and nose. They include several groups that are traditionally regarded as classes, although it has become apparent that at least two of these classes (the bony fishes and the reptiles) are not natural groups because some of their members are more closely related to members of other classes. However, the traditional classes are commonly retained as convenient groups.

Class Agnatha (Cyclostomata) the lampreys and hagfishes. These animals do not have true jaws – the mouth is circular and contains a rasping tongue.

Class Chondrichthyes a class of fishes possessing cartilaginous skeletons. The body is covered with tiny toothlike scales forming a shagreen. The 5000 species include sharks and rays.

Class Osteichthyes a class of bony fishes containing approximately 22 000 species. The internal skeleton is made of bone, and the body is covered with bony scales. Bony plates on the head include large opercula protecting the gills. The dominant group of bony fishes is the teleosts, which inhabit nearly every aquatic environment and include such fishes as herring, trout, perch and cod. There is considerable evidence to suggest that some of the bony fishes such as the coelacanth and the lungfishes are genealogically nearer to the tetrapods or land-dwelling vertebrates than to other fishes.

Class Amphibia a class of about 2000 members including frogs and toads. The amphibians are the most primitive of the land-dwelling vertebrates (tetrapods). Tetrapods are animals with pentadactyl limbs (hands and feet) and other adaptations for life on land, such as a stiff vertebral column to support the body and lungs to breathe air. Amphibians have a smooth, moist skin used for gas exchange and must return to water or other moist places to lay their eggs.

Class Reptilia a class represented today by about 5000 species, including turtles, lizards, snakes, crocodiles and alligators. For 140 million years the dinosaurs, the most advanced reptiles of all time, dominated the world. Like fishes, the reptiles are not a natural group – some are more closely related to birds, while others are more closely related to mammals. Reptiles are fully terrestrial and lay an egg with a leathery shell on land in which the embryo can develop to hatch as a miniature adult. The skin is dry and scaly. Reptiles maintain their body temperature by behaviour (sitting in the sun or hiding under rocks).

Class Aves one of the more obvious vertebrate classes, the 9000 species of birds are characterized by a covering of feathers. This is an adaptation both to flight and to the regulation of their body temperature by physiological means. The arm is developed as a wing. All birds lay hard-shelled eggs.

Class Mammalia the class characterized by body hair – which in many cases completely covers the body – and by the ability of the mother to nourish the young with milk produced by mammary glands. Mammals are able to regulate their body temperature internally. Other mammalian specializations include three separate bones within the middle ear (to permit acute hearing) and – in most cases – a complex dentition (incisors, canines, premolars and molars) which occurs as two generations of teeth. One group of mammals – the monotremes (the duck-billed platypus is the most famous example) – lays eggs, but the vast majority retain the egg within the body, where it hatches.

Subclass Marsupialia (Metatheria) a group better known as marsupials. These animals bear their young at a very early stage of development and keep them in an external pouch containing the mammary glands until they are able to fend for themselves. The 300 species include wombats, opossums, kangaroos, the Tasmanian devil and the koala bear.

Subclass Eutheria a large group of truly placental mammals. The young of eutherians are retained by the mother and nourished through a placenta. There are some 3800 species of placentals traditionally divided between 16 orders. Different orders display a wide variety of tooth patterns reflecting specialized diets. The most significant orders are as follows:

Order Insectivora. Insectivores are generally small animals with long, low skulls and many teeth, which are not particularly specialized for any specific diet. Many scientists believe that the most primitive placentals must have been similar to these mammals. The order includes moles, shrews and hedgehogs.

Order Chiroptera. The bats that comprise this order are the only mammals with the ability to fly. Bats achieve flight by flapping wings developed as a membrane stretched between four fingers and the hind limbs. Most navigate and capture food by a form of sonar known as echolocation.

Order Edentata. This order includes the anteaters, armadillos and sloths – mammals that show very reduced or absent dentition. The front teeth are absent and the tongue gathers food, often a diet of insects such as ants and termites.

Order Primates. This order includes the great apes (chimpanzees and the gorilla), monkeys, lemurs, tarsiers and man. The dentition is generalized because primates have a wide diet. In most cases, primates rely heavily on binocular vision – consequently the face is characteristically short and flat. Compared with other mammals few young are produced – often a single offspring – and the young are retained within the mother for a long time and are born at a very advanced stage. Primates are characterized by a long period of parental care.

Order Rodentia. The rodents form a very large order of small mammals with a distinctive dentition. The single pair of upper and lower incisors are chisel-like; they grow continually and the enamel is confined to the front surface. The canines and front premolars are absent, and the molars are specialized for grinding, with the upper teeth biting inside the lower teeth. Rodents give birth to large numbers of young at frequent intervals, and many also look after the young in nests. Examples include beavers, mice, squirrels, porcupines and marmots.

Order Lagomorpha. The lagomorphs include rabbits and hares. Their dentition is superficially like that of rodents, but there are two pairs of upper incisors and the cheek teeth are designed for cutting with the upper teeth biting the lower teeth. The hind legs are modified for jumping.

Order Cetacea. Cetaceans include whales and dolphins – large, fully aquatic mammals in which the hair is reduced and the limbs are developed as flippers. They also possess a horizontal tail fluke. Cetaceans have a high degree of social organization, including elaborate communication.

Order Carnivora. Carnivores are primarily flesh-eating mammals and their dentition has developed large stabbing canines with special meat-shearing cheek teeth (carnassials). Many members have acute vision and hearing. The order includes the cats, bears, racoons, stoats and dogs. The seals and walruses are sometimes included in this order or placed in the separate order Pinnipedia.

Order Proboscidea. A small order confined among living creatures to the elephants. They are characterized by cheek teeth that grow continuously and keep pace with the wear caused by continual grinding of vegetation.

Order Perissodactyla. Known as the odd-toed ungulates, the members of this order include tapirs, rhinoceroses and horses. They are characterized by cropping incisors coupled with grinding cheek teeth. In many members, the legs are long and there is a central axis to both the hand and foot; in horses and zebras this is exaggerated and results in a single toe being in contact with the ground.

Order Artiodactyla. The even-toed ungulates form a large group in which the third and fourth digits have been developed into a two-toed foot. Upper incisor teeth are rarely present; instead, there is a horny pad against which the lower incisors bite. The molar cheek teeth are high-crowned and used to grind vegetation. In most members, the stomach is four-chambered, allowing plant material to be broken down by bacterial action. Artiodactyls include pigs, hippopotomuses, camels, deer, giraffes, antelope, sheep and cattle.

VELOCITY OF ANIMAL MOVEMENT

The data on this topic are notoriously unreliable because of the many inherent difficulties of timing the movement of most animals – whether running, flying, or swimming – and because of the absence of any standardization of the method of timing, of the distance over which the performance is measured, or of allowance for wind conditions.

The most that can be claimed is that a specimen of the species below has been timed to obtain the maximum speed given.

km/h	mph	Species
350	217	(a) Peregrine falcon (*Falco peregrinus*)
240+	150+	(b) Golden eagle (*Aquila chrysaetos*)
170	105.6	White-throated spine-tail swift (*Hirundapus caudacutus*)
c. 160	c. 100	Alpine swift (*Apus melba*)
154	95.7	Magnificent frigate-bird (*Fregata magnificens*)
144	89	Forked-tail swift (*Apus pacificus*)
129	80	Red-breasted merganser (*Mergus serrator*)
124	77	White-rumped swift (*Apus caffer*)
113	70	Common eider (*Somateria mollissima*)
96.5–113	60–70	(c) Racing pigeon (*Columba livia*)
109	68	Cosmopolitan sailfish (*Istiophorus platypterus*)
105	65	Mallard (*Anas platyrhynchos*)
104	65	Canvasback duck (*Aythya valisineria*)
104	65	Spur-winged goose (*Plectropterus gambensis*)
96–101	60–63	Cheetah (*Acinonyx jubatus*)
92.8–100.8	58–63	Red grouse (*Lagopus lagopus*)

(a) *45° angle of swoop in courtship display. Cannot exceed 100.5 km/h (62.5 mph) in level flight.*
(b) *Vertical dive.*
(c) *Wind-assisted speeds up to 177.1 km/h (110.07 mph) recorded.*

ANIMAL LONGEVITY

The ages given in the following table are based on ring-producing structures (e.g. teeth) or on the length of time an animal has been kept in captivity.

Maximum life span years   Species

152 +	(a)Marion's tortoise (*Testudo sumeirii*)
c.150	Quahog (*Venus mercenaria*)
120+	Man (*Homo sapiens*) – highest proven age
116+	Spur-thighed tortoise (*Testudo graeca*)
c.100	Deep-sea clam (*Tindaria callistiformis*)
>90	Killer whale (*Orcinus orca*)
80–90	Sea anemone (*Cereus pedunculatus*)
88	European eel (*Anguilla anguilla*)
82	(b)Lake sturgeon (*Acipenser fulvescens*)
70–80	Freshwater mussel (*Margaritana margaritifera*)
78	Asiatic elephant (*Elephans maximus*)
77	Tuatara (*Sphenodon punctatus*)
72 +	(a)Andean condor (*Vultur gryphus*)
c.70	African elephant (*Loxodonta africana*)
69¾	Sterlet (*Acipenser ruthenus*)
68 +	Great eagle-owl (*Bubo bubo*)
66	American alligator (*Alligator mississipiensis*)
64	Blue macaw (*Ara macao*)
62+	Siberian white crane (*Grus leucogeranus*)
62	Horse (*Equus caballus*)
62	Ostrich (*Struthio camelus*)
60+	European catfish (*Silurus glanis*)
58¾	Alligator snapping turtle (*Macrochelys temminckii*)
58 +	(d)Royal albatross (*Diomedea immutabilis*)
57 +	Orang-utan (*Pongo pygmaeus*)
56	(c)Sulphur-crested cockatoo (*Cacatua galerita*)
55½ +	Chimpanzee (*Pan troglodytes*)
55	Pike (*Esox lucius*)
54⅓	Hippopotamus (*Hippopotamus amphibius*)
54+	Slow-worm (*Anguis fragilis*)
53½ +	Gorilla (*Gorilla gorilla*)
53⅓	Stinkpot (*Sternotherus odoratus*)
51 +	Japanese giant salamander (*Andrias japonicus*)

51	White pelican (*Pelecanus onocrotalus*)
50+	Green turtle (*Chelonia mydas*)
>50	Koi carp (*Cyprinus carpio*)
c.50	North American lobster (*Homarus americanus*)
49¾	Domestic goose (*Anser a. domesticus*)
49+	Short-nosed echidna (*Tachyglossus aculeatus*)
49	(e)Grey parrot (*Psittacus erythacus*)
49	Indian rhinoceros (*Rhinoceros unicornis*)
47	European brown bear (*Ursus a. arctos*)
46+	White-throated capuchin (*Cebus capucinus*)
46+	Grey seal (*Halichoerus gypus*)
c.46	Mandrill (*Mandrillus sphinx*)
c.45	Blue whale (*Balaenoptera musculus*)
44	Herring gull (*Larus argentatus*)
42+	(d)Emu (*Dromaius novaehollandiae*)
42	Metallic wood borer (*Buprestis aurulenta*)
41	Goldfish (*Carassius auratus*)
40¼	Common boa (*Boa constrictor*)
>40	Common toad (*Bufo bufo*)
36¼	Cape giraffe (*Giraffa camelopardalis*)
35+	Bactrian camel (*Camelus ferus*)
34+	Hoffman's two-toed sloth (*Choloepus hoffmanni*)
34	Domestic cat (*Felis catus*)
34	Canary (*Severius canaria*)
33	American bison (*Bison bison*)
32⅓	Bobcat (*Lynx rufus*)
32+	Australian school shark (*Galeorhinus australis*)
31+	Indian flying fox (*Pteropus giganteus*)
30+	(d)American manatee (*Trichechus manatus*)
c.30	Red kangaroo (*Macropus rufus*)
29½	African buffalo (*Syncerus caffer*)
29½	Domestic dog (*Canis familiaris*)
29+	Budgerigar (*Melopsittacus undulatus*)
29+	Neptune crab (*Neptunus pelagines*)
c.29	Lion (*Panthera leo*)
28	African civet (*Viverra civetta*)
c.28	Theraphosid spider (*Mygalomorphae*)
27¼	Sumatran crested porcupine (*Hystrix brachyura*)
27	Medicinal leech (*Hirudo medicinalis*)
27	Domestic pig (*Sus scrofa*)
26¾	Red deer (*Cervus elephus*)
26¼	Tiger (*Panthera tigris*)
26+	(d)Giant panda (*Ailuropoda melanoleuca*)
26	Common wombat (*Vombatus ursinus*)
24¾	Vicuña (*Vicugna vicugna*)
23½	Grey squirrel (*Sciurus carolinensis*)
21+	Coyote (*Canis latrans*)
21	Canadian otter (*Lutra canadensis*)
20¾	Domestic goat (*Capra hircus domesticus*)
20¼	Blue sheep (*Pseudois nayaur*)
20+	Feather-star (*Promachocrinus kerguelensis*)
18+	Queen ant (*Myrmecina graminicola*)
18+	Common rabbit (*Oryctolagus cuniculus*)
16+	Hedgehog (*Echinops telfairi*)
15	Land snail (*Helix spiriplana*)
c.15	Brittlestar (*Amphiura chiajei*)
14⅞	Guinea pig (*Cavia porcellus*)
13½	Indian pangolin (*Manis crassicaudata*)
12	Capybara (*Hydrochoerus hydrochaeris*)
11½	Philippine tree shrew (*Urogale everetti*)
>10	Giant centipede (*Scolopendra gigantea*)
10	Golden hamster (*Mesocricetus auratus*)

9+	Purse-web spider (*Atypus affinis*)
8⅔	Fat dormouse (*Glis glis*)
8+	Greater Egyptian gerbil (*Gerbillus pyramidum*)
7+	Spiny starfish (*Marthasterias glacialis*)
7	Millipede (*Cylindroiulus londinensis*)
6	House mouse (*Mus musculus*)
5+	Segmented worm (*Allolobophora longa*)
4½	Moonrat (*Echinosorex gymnurus*)
3¾	Siberian flying squirrel (*Pteromys volans*)
2	Pygmy white-toothed shrew (*Suncus etruscus*)
1⅛	Monarch butterfly (*Danaus plexippus*)
0·5	Bedbug (*Cimex lectularius*)
0·27	(f) Black widow spider (*Latrodectus mactans*)
0·04	(f) Common housefly (*Musca domestica*)

(a) *Fully mature at time of capture*
(b) *Still actively growing when caught*
(c) *Unconfirmed claims up to 120 years*
(d) *Still alive*
(e) *Another less well substantiated record of 72 years*
(f) *Males*

GESTATION PERIODS

The figures in brackets are approximate conversions – the months have been calculated on a 30-day period.

The longest gestation period is that of the Asiatic elephant – 609 days or just over 20 months

aardvark	210 days (7 months)
alpaca	342–345 days ($11\frac{1}{4}$ months)
anteater, giant	190 days ($6\frac{1}{4}$ months)
antelope	280 days (9 months)
armadillo	from 60–120 days (2–4 mths)
ass	about $11\frac{1}{2}$ months
baboon	5–6 months
badger	$3\frac{1}{2}$–12 months incl. period of delayed implantation
bear, grizzly	210–255 days (7 months)
bear, polar	about 8 months
bear, American black	210–215 days (7 months)
beaver	about 105 days ($3\frac{1}{2}$ months)
bison, American	270–300 days (9 months)
boar, wild	115 days ($3\frac{3}{4}$ months)
bobcat	60–63 days (2 months)
buffalo, wild water	310–330 days ($10\frac{1}{4}$ months)
bush baby	110–193 days ($3\frac{1}{2}$–$6\frac{1}{4}$ mths)
capybara	150 days (5 months)
cat (domestic)	52 day (2 months)
cattle	about 283 days ($9\frac{1}{4}$ months)
cavies	from 50–90 days (3 months)
chamois	160–170 days ($5\frac{1}{4}$ months)
cheetah	91–95 days (3 months)
chimpanzee	230–240 days ($7\frac{1}{2}$ months)
civet	70 days ($2\frac{1}{4}$ months)
civet, African	80 days ($2\frac{1}{2}$ months)
civet, palm	90 days (3 months)
coati	77 days ($2\frac{1}{4}$ months)
coyote	63 days (2 months)
deer, fallow	229–240 days ($7\frac{1}{2}$ months)
deer, musk	150–180 days (5 months)
dhole	60–62 days (2 months)
dingo	63 days (2 months)

dog	53–71 days (2 months)
dog, African wild	70–73 days (2¼ months)
dolphin	10–12 months
dormouse	21–32 days
dromedary	390–410 days (13 months)
elephant, Asiatic	608 days (20 months)
ermine	about 28 days
ferret	40–76 days (1–2½ months)
fox, red	60–63 days (2 months)
gazelle	up to 188 days
gerbil	21–28 days
gibbon	7–8 months
giraffe	453–464 days (15¼ months)
goat	150 days (5 months)
gopher	12–20 days
gorilla	250–270 days (8½ months)
guinea pig	63 days (2 months)
hamster	from 15–37 days
hare	28–35 days
hare, mountain	50 days (1½ months)
hedgehog	30 days
hippo, pygmy	190–210 days (6¼ months)
hippopotamus	about 240 days (8 months)
horse	about 11½ months
hyena	93 days (3 months)
hyena, striped	about 84 days (2¾ months)
jackal	63 days (2 months)
jaguar	93–110 days (3½ months)
kangaroo	6–11 months in pouch
koala	34–36 days (1¼ months)
lemming	20–22 days
lemur	60–160 days where known
leopard	90–105 days (3¼ months)
leopard, snow	98–103 days (3¼ months)
lion	100–119 days (3½ months)
llama	348–368 days (11½–12¼ months)
lynx	60–74 days (2 months)
macaque	5–6 months
marmoset	130–170 days (2¼–5½ mths)
meerkat	77 days (2½ months)
mink	34–70 days (1½ months)
mole	28–42 days
mongoose	mostly 60 days (2 months)
moose	264 days (8½ months)
mouse	about 20–30 days
narwhal	14–15 months
ocelot	70 days (2¼ months)
opossum, American	12–13 days
orang-utan	210–270 days (8½ months)
otter	49–62 days
panda, giant	125–150 days (4½ months)
panda, Himalayan	90 days (3 months)
panda, red	150 days
peccary, collared	142 days (4¾ months)
pig	101–129 days (3¼ months)
porcupine	205–217 days (6½ months)
porcupine, North American	210 days (7 months)
porpoise	183 days (6 months)
puma	90–96 days (3 months)

rabbit	30 days
rabbit, European	28–33 days
raccoons	63 days (2 months)
rat, black	21 days
reindeer	210–240 days (7–8 months)
rhinoceros, black	15 months
seal, common	245 days (8 months)
seal, eared	12 months incl. period of delayed implantation
sea lion	330–365 days (11 months)
serval	75 days (approx.) (2½ mths)
sheep	135–160 days (4½–5 months)
shrew	13–24 days
skunks, striped	62–66 days (2 months)
sloth	from 6–11 months
squirrel	about 40 days (1⅓ months)
tapir	335–400 days (11–13 months)
tenrec	50–64 days (2¼ months)
tiger	103 days (3½ months)
vole	90 days
vicuña	330–350 days (11 months)
wallaby	40 days
walrus	15–16 months incl. 4–5 months of delayed implantation
warthog	170–175 days (5½ months)
weasel	35–45 days (1½ months)
whale	305–365 days (10–12 months)
whale, beluga	14–15 months
whale, sperm	14–15 months
wolf	61–63 days (2 months)
wolf, maned	about 65 days (2 months)
wolverine	about 9 months
yak	258 days (8½ months)
zebra	340 days (about 11½ months)
zorilla	42–44 days

Delayed implantation means that after mating the fertilized egg travels to the uterus developing as it goes into a ball of cells called the blastocyst. In most mammals the blastocyst implants into the uterus wall within a few days and development of the embryo proceeds, but in the 16 or more mustelid species (the weasel family) it floats free in the uterus for periods from a few days up to 10 months, and implants only when certain conditions are met.

COLLECTIVE NOUNS

Angel fish	Host
Animals	Menagerie, Tribe
Antelope	Herd, Troop
Ants	Army, Column, State, Swarm
Apes	Shrewdness
Asses	Herd, Pace
Baboons	Troop
Badger	Cete, Colony
Barracuda	Battery
Bass	Fleet
Bears	Sloth
Beavers	Colony
Bees	Cluster, Erst, Hive, Swarm

Birds	Congregation, Dissimulation (young), Flight, Flock, Volery, Volley
Bison	Herd
Bitterns	Sedge, Siege
Bloodhounds	Sute
Boars	Herd, Singular, Sounder
Budgerigars	Chatter
Buffalo	Herd
Bustard	Flock
Camels	Caravan, Flock
Capercaillie	Tok
Caterpillars	Army
Cats	Chowder, Clowder, Cluster
Cats, wild	Dout
Cattle	Drove, Herd
Chamois	Herd
Chickens	Brood, Clutch, Peep
Choughs	Chattering
Clams	Bed
Cockles	Bed
Colts	Race, Rag, Rake
Coots	Covert, Raft
Cormorants	Flight
Cranes	Herd, Siege
Crows	Clan, Hover, Murder
Curlews	Herd
Deer	Herd, Leash
Dogfish	Brood, Troop
Dogs	Cowardice, Kennel, Pack
Dogs (hunting)	Cry
Dolphins	Pod, School
Donkeys	Herd, Drove
Dottrel	Trip
Doves	Dole, Flight, Prettying
Ducklings in nest	Clutch
Ducklings off nest	Clatch
Ducks (diving)	Dopping, Dropping
Ducks (flying)	Flush, Plump, Team
Ducks (on land)	Flight, Flock, Leash, Mob Sail
Ducks (on water)	Badeling, Paddling, Sail
Eagles	Convocation
Eels	Swarm
Elephants	Herd
Elk (Europe)	Gang
Falcons	Cast
Ferrets	Business, Cast, Fesynes
Finches	Charm, Flight
Fish	Haul, Run, School, Shoal
Flamingos	Flurry, Regiment, Skein
Flies	Business, Cloud, Scraw, Swarm
Foxes	Earth, Lead, Skulk
Foxhounds	Pack
Frogs	Army, Colony
Geese (flying)	Flock, Gaggle, Skein
Geese (on land)	Gaggle
Geese (on water)	Gaggle, Plump
Giraffes	Corps, Herd, Troop
Gnats	Cloud, Horde, Swarm
Goats	Flock, Herd, Tribe, Trippe
Goldfinch	Charm, Chattering, Chirp, Drum
Goldfish	Troubling
Goshawks	Flight
Grasshoppers	Cloud

Greyhounds	Brace, Leash, Pack
Grouse	Brood, Covey, Pack
Guillemots	Bazaar
Gulls	Colony
Hares	Down, Drove, Husk, Lie, Trip
Hart	Herd, Stud
Hawks	Cast
Hedgehogs	Array
Hens	Brood, Flock
Heron	Scattering, Sedge, Siege
Herring	Army, Gleam, Shoal
Hippopotamuses	Herd, School
Hogs	Herd, Drove, Sounder
Horses	Harass, Herd, Stable, Stud, Troop
Horses (race)	Stable, String
Hounds	Brace, Couple, Cry, Mute, Pack, Stable
Ibis	Crowd
Insects	Swarm
Jays	Band, Party
Jellyfish	Brood, Smuck
Kangaroos	Herd, Mob, Troop
Kittens	Brood, Kindle, Litter
Lapwings	Deceit, Desert
Larks	Exultation
Lemurs	Troop
Leopards	Leap
Lice	Flock
Lions	Flock, Pride, Sawt, Souse, Troop
Locusts	Cloud, Horde, Plague, Swarm
Mackerel	School, Shoal
Magpies	Tiding, Tittering
Mallards (on land)	Bord, Flock, Flush, Suite, Sute
Mallards (on water)	Sord
Mares	Flock, Stud
Martens	Raches, Richesse
Mice	Nest
Minnows	Shoal, Steam, Swarm
Moles	Company, Labour, Movement, Mumble
Monkeys	Troop
Moose	Gang, Herd
Mules	Barren, Cartload, Pack, Span
Mussels	Bed
Nightingale	Match, Puddling, Watch
Ostrich	Flock, Troop
Otters	Bevy, Family
Owls	Parliament, Stare
Oxbirds	Fling
Oxen (domestic)	Drove, Rake, Team, Yoke
Oxen (wild)	Drove, Herd
Oyster	Bed
Parrots	Flock
Partridges	Covey
Passenger pigeons	Roost
Peacocks	Muster
Peafowl	Muster, Ostentation, Pride
Penguins	Colony, Rookery

Perch	Pack, Shoal
Pheasants	Brook, Ostentation, Pride, Nye
Pigeons	Flight, Flock
Piglets	Farrow
Pigs	Litter, Herd, Sounder
Pilchards	Shoal
Plover	Congregation, Flight, Stand, Wing
Polecats	Chine
Ponies	Herd
Porpoises	Gam, Pod, School
Poultry	Flock
Poultry (domestic)	Run
Ptarmigan	Covey
Pups	Litter
Quail	Bevy, Covey
Rabbits	Bury, Colony, Nest, Warren
Raccoons	Nursery
Racehorses	Field, String
Rats	Colony
Ravens	Unkindness
Redwings	Crowd
Rhinoceros	Crash
Roach	Shoal
Roe deer	Bevy
Rooks	Building, Clamour, Parliament
Ruffs	Hill
Sandpipers	Fling
Sardines	Family
Seals, elephant	Rookery, Team, Troop
Seals	Harem, Herd, Pod, Rookery
Sheep	Down, Drove, Flock, Hurtle, Trip
Sheldrakes	Dapping, Dropping
Smelt	Quantity
Snakes	Den, Pit
Snakes (young)	Bed
Snipe	Walk, Whisper, Wish, Wisp
Spaniels	Couple
Sparrows	Host, Surration, Quarrel
Spiders	Cluster, Clutter
Squirrels	Drey
Starlings	Chattering, Crowd, Murmuration
Sticklebacks	Shoal
Stoats	Pack
Storks	Herd, Mustering
Swallows	Flight
Swans	Bank, Bevy, Game, Herd, Squadron, Teeme, Wedge, Whiteness
Swifts	Flock
Swine	Doyet, Dryft
Swine (wild)	Sounder
Teal (on land)	Bunch, Coil, Knab, Raft
Teal (on water, rising from water)	Spring
Thrush	Mutation
Tigers	Ambush
Toads	Knab, Knot
Trout	Hover
Turkeys	Dule, Raffle, Rafter
Turtles	Bale, Dole
Turtle Doves	Pitying

Vipers	Den, Nest
Walrus	Herd, Pod
Wasps	Herd, Nest, Pladge
Weasels	Pack, Pop
Whales	Colony, Gam, Herd, Pod, School
Whiting	Pod
Widgeon	Coil, Company, Flight, Knob
Wildfowl	Plump, Sord, Sute, Trip
Wolves	Pack, Rout
Woodcocks	Covey, Fall, Flight, Plump
Woodpeckers	Descent
Wrens	Herd
Young animals	Kindle, Litter
Zebras	Herd

HIBERNATION AND AESTIVATION

While some animals avoid harsh conditions by migrating, others stay at home and hide away in burrows, caves or other safe refuges. This method of enduring winter conditions is called *hibernation* and occurs in some amphibians, reptiles and mammals.

Hibernating animals build special nests or find shelter beneath tree stumps or under leaves. Bats use crevices or may migrate to suitable caves. Hibernators become *torpid* – they enter a sleep-like state in which both heart rate and respiration are slowed, and in mammals the body temperature drops, often to within a few degrees of the environmental temperature. When the temperature of the pocket mouse's immediate surroundings approach freezing point, its body temperature drops to 2–3 °C (35.5–37.5 °F). The hedgehog may stop breathing for periods of up to an hour, separated by only a few minutes of respiration.

Many hibernators remain inactive for several months. They use very little energy, and can survive on the fat stores built up before hibernation. Some animals, such as dormice, become active at intervals, and feed on the caches of nuts and seeds they stored away in the autumn. Brown and black bears also spend most of the winter months hibernating, but do not undergo the extreme metabolic and respiratory changes found in smaller mammals.

Aestivation is the avoidance of harsh summer conditions. Earthworms hollow out chambers deep in the soil where they can remain moist. South American and African lungfish dig chambers deep in the mud when their home rivers dry up, and can survive for up to six months using air for respiration. The Californian ground squirrel remains underground from August to March, and so protects itself from summer temperatures that may reach 43 °C (110 °F).

PREHISTORIC ANIMALS

DINOSAURS

The dinosaurs, the most advanced reptiles of all time, dominated the Earth for 140 millon years – compared with the 2 million years that man has been on the planet. Unlike living reptiles – which either crawl or walk with their limbs extended out to their sides – dinosaurs walked with their limbs directly under their bodies, just like modern mammals and birds. However, like modern reptiles, most of the dinosaurs were probably cold-blooded.

Many dinosaurs were of gigantic size, some weighing up to 100 tonnes (tons). Nearly 1000 species have been identified, and although the word 'dinosaur' is from the Greek for 'terrible lizard', there were herbivores as well as carnivores. The species included:

ankylosaurus ('fused lizard'), a dinosaur whose body was covered in a thick armour of fused bony plates.

apatosaurus the original brontosaur; weighed 30 tonnes. It lived for 120 years, equally at home swimming in lakes and walking on land.

baryonyx ('heavy claw'), named 'Claws' after the massive claw on its hand, thought to have been for disembowelling dinosaurs or catching fish.

brachiosaurus ('arm lizard'), 12 m (39 ft) tall and 23 m (75 ft) long; a dinosaur that weighed 80 tonnes and had long front legs.

compsognathus a chicken-sized dinosaur that fed on lizards. It was related to birds.

deinonychus ('terrible claw'), 3 m (10 ft) long; a leaping dinosaur with a sickle-like claw on its hind feet for killing prey.

diplodocus total length 23 m (75 ft); a brontosaur with the longest known tail of all dinosaurs – 11 m (36 ft) long.

gallimimus ('chicken-mimic'), 4 m (13 ft) long; an ostrich-like dinosaur, with a large beak and no teeth.

iguanodon ('iguana tooth'), a plant-eating dinosaur with a pronounced bony spike on its 'thumb'.

kentrosaurus ('centre lizard'), a dinosaur with long sharp spikes running along the back and the tail.

maiasaurus ('mother lizard'), a duck-billed dinosaur which built nests and cared for its young in 'dinosaur nurseries'.

mamenchisaurus total length 23 m (75 ft); a brontosaur with the longest known neck of all dinosaurs – 11 m (36 ft).

megalosaurus ('giant lizard'), 9 m (30 ft) long; a flesh-eater, the first dinosaur ever discovered.

mussaurus ('mouse lizard'), 200 mm (8 in) long; the smallest known relative of the brontosaurs.

pachycephalosaurus ('thick-head lizard'), a bone-headed dinosaur with a distinctive massive bony thickening on the top of head forming a 'battering ram'.

parasaurolophus ('near ridged lizard'), a duckbilled dinosaur with a 2 m (7 m) long hollow crest – containing nasal passages – projecting behind its head.

plateosaurus ('flat lizard'), 6 m (20 m) long; a plant-eating ancestor of the brontosaurs. It had a strong claw on each hand and small serrated teeth.

polacanthus ('many spines'), 4 m (13 ft) long; a dinosaur with a large square bony 'blanket' over its hips and triangular plates along its back and tail.

protoceratops ('first horned'), 2 m (7 ft) long; the ancestor of triceratops. It possessed a similar bony frill over the neck but had no horns.

pterodactyl a flying reptile, whose membranous wings had spans of up to 11–12 m (36–39 ft).

saltasaurus ('lizard from Salta, Argentina'), a brontosaur with bony plates – each 12 cm (5 in) in diameter – embedded in the skin.

seismosaurus ('earthquake lizard'), 33 m (108 ft) long; probably the largest land animal that has ever lived.

shantungosaurus ('Shantung lizard'), 12 m (39 ft) long; the largest of the duck-billed dinosaurs.

stegosaurus ('roof lizard'), 9 m (30 ft) long, a dinosaur with two pairs of spikes on its tail, and a row of large triangular plates – 1 m high – running along its back.

supersaurus 15 m (49 ft) tall and 30 m (98 ft) long; a large dinosaur that may have weighed up to 100 tonnes.

torosaurus ('bull lizard'), a dinosaur with a bony frill extending over its shoulders. Its skull – 2.6 m (8.5 ft) long – was the largest known of any land animal.

triceratops ('three horned'), 9 m (30 ft) long; a dinosaur with a bony frill over its neck and three long horns on its forehead.

tyrannosaurus ('tyrant lizard'), 12 m (39 ft) long; a slow moving flesh-eating scavenger with relatively small two-fingered hands.

BIRDS

Birds share a common ancestry with reptiles. The first bird – archaeopteryx – had many characteristics in common with dinosaurs.

aepyornis a giant ostrich-like bird – the largest ever known. Its remains found in Mauritius gave rise to the 'Roc' of Sinbad and its fossilized eggs – the largest known eggs – were used to hold sailors' rum.

archaeopteryx (meaning 'ancient wing') the first bird, it appeared about 175 million years ago. In many respects it was indistinguishable from small carnivorous dinosaurs, but the fact that it was covered in perfect feathers indicates that it was warm-blooded and that it could fly. It had a long bony tail and teeth in its jaws.

diatryma a tall – 2 m (7 ft) – flightless bird. This flesh-eater lived at the beginning of the age of mammals, 60 million years ago.

gigantornis a bird – with an 8 m (26 ft) wingspan – dating from c. 50 million years old.

hesperornis ('western bird'), a flightless diving bird with teeth.

ichthyornis ('fish bird'), a tern-like bird with teeth in its jaws.

MAMMALS

The first reptiles that conquered the land about 295 million years ago were the mammal-like reptiles or paramammals. From detailed study of their skulls, it is presumed that the mammals orginated from them. The first true mammals appeared during the later Triassic period about 220 million years ago.

arsinoitherium a rhinoceros-like animal with a pair of horns side by side on its snout; c. 35 million years old.

basilosaurus a 20 m (66 ft) long small-headed whale with the appearance of a 'sea serpent'. It lived c. 50 million years ago.

brontotherium a large rhinoceros-like animal, 2.5 m (8 ft) at the shoulder. It had double-curved horns at the tip of the snout, and lived c. 30 million years ago.

coelodonta a thick-haired woolly rhinoceros. It lived during the last Ice Age.

diprotodon a giant rhinoceros-sized wombat; 4 m (13 ft) long.

enteledon a giant pig-like animal; 2 m (7 ft) long. With bony projections along its lower jaws and the side of its skull, it has been called the ugliest mammal ever known.

glyptodon a heavily armoured relative of the armadillo – 3.3 m (11 ft) long and 1.5 m (5 ft) high.

icaronycteris first known insect-eating bat; c. 50 million years old.

indricotherium a giant hornless rhinoceros, weighing 30 tonnes, and standing 5.5 m (18 ft) at the shoulder; c. 30 million years old.

kuehneotherium , the first true mammal, about the size of a shrew, dating from c. 220 million years ago.

mammuthus the woolly mammoth, a thick-haired elephant with spirally curved tusks inhabiting the tundra during the last Ice Age.

megaloceros a giant deer whose antlers had a 3.7 m (12 ft) span and weighed 45 kg (99 lb). It lived during the last Ice Age.

megatherium a giant ground sloth – 5.5 m (18 ft) tall – with huge clawed feet.

pakicetus the first toothed whale, c. 53 million years old. It had four paddle-like legs.

procoptodon a giant short-faced kangaroo standing 3 m (10 ft) tall.

propalaeotherium a 40 cm (16 in) high four-toed horse; c. 50 million years old.

purgatorius named after Purgatory Hill, Montana, USA, where remains of this first primate were found alongside dinosaur remains.

smilodon a sabre-tooth cat with long stabbing canine teeth.

thoatherium a one-toed horse-like litoptern, not related to true horses.

thylacoleo a marsupial lion with incisor 'stabbing' teeth at front of jaws.

thylacosmilus a pouched (marsupial) sabre-tooth cat, unrelated to true sabre-tooths; c. 15 million years old.

ENDANGERED SPECIES

Over 4500 species have been declared to be in danger. The threats to these animals include hunting, trapping, fishing, poison and pollution, the destruction of natural habitats and competition from introduced species.

Endangered species are listed in the *Red Data Book* published by the International Union for the Conservation of Nature and Natural Resources.

The numbers of endangered species vary from thousands to several hundred, and in some cases, under 100 individuals. Over the last 300 years over 100 species of mammal and some 150 species of bird have disappeared.

armadillo Although some species of this South American mammal remain relatively common, the giant, three-banded, Burmeister's and pink fairy armadillos are in danger.

aye-aye Only about 20 individuals of this small Madagascan nocturnal primate – related to lemurs – remain in the wild.

bison Millions of the American bison (or buffalo) were slaughtered by the North American Indians, settlers and hunters. Some 5000 survivors are largely confined to reserves.

Californian condor A member of the vulture family, the Californian condor may already be extinct in the wild.

European bison or wisent About 2000 European bison live in the Bialowieza Forest in Poland and in the Caucasus in the USSR.

giant anteater Hunting by man and the disappearance of much of the South American giant anteater's natural habitat have placed the species on the endangered list.

giant panda The symbol of the Worldwide Fund for Nature, the giant panda lives only in the mountains of Sichuan in China. Unlike some endangered species, it has proved especially difficult to breed in captivity and the remaining population probably does not exceed 700.

golden marmoset The Brazilian habitat of this small monkey is seriously under threat.

gorilla The loss of its habitat and illegal hunting have confined all three subspecies of gorilla to small pockets of African rain forest. Under 4000 of the Eastern lowland gorilla survive in Zaïre, while about 9000 of the Western lowland gorilla remain in Cameroon and the Central African Republic. The surviving 350 mountain gorillas are confined to the Ruwenzori Mountains on the borders of Uganda, Zaïre and Rwanda. The mountain gorillas of Rwanda received great publicity in books and on film in the 1980s but, despite government protection, they remain endangered owing to the activities of poachers.

Grevy's zebra This zebra is endangered, in part because of the increasing aridity of its habitat in Ethiopia, Kenya and Somalia.

Indian lion Under 200 Indian lions remain, guarded in the Gir Forest National Park in Gujarat.

Japanese ibis Under a dozen of these wading birds are thought to have survived the destruction of their breeding grounds.

kakapo The kakapo or parrot owl of New Zealand has been hunted almost to extinction. It is thought that less than 10 individuals remain.

Komodo dragon Although the Komodo dragon, the largest living lizard, is protected by the Indonesian authorities, the activities of collectors have reduced the population to a dangerously low level.

lemur Some 14 species of these primates – ranging in size from very small to medium – lived in Madagascar earlier this century. Owing to drought and the destruction of the forest, some of these species may already be extinct and the remainder are under threat.

mandrill The West African forest habitat of this monkey is rapidly being destroyed.

Mediterranean monk seal A European Community project aims to breed the monk seal in captivity and reintroduce it into the wild, where its numbers have been reduced to under 500 by hunting and pollution. Some countries have restrictions on fishing in the seal's breeding areas.

mountain zebra The mountain zebra is endangered because it has been pushed into more marginal areas of Namibia and South Africa by the pressure of agriculture on the land.

nene or Hawaiian goose The nene was rescued by Slimbridge Wildfowl and Wetlands Trust (Avon, UK) and successfully reintroduced to Hawaii, where some 500 nene now live in the wild.

Nile crocodile Seen as a threat by man, the Nile crocodile has become endangered owing to the activities of hunters.

orang-utan The destruction of the tropical rain forest of Borneo and Sumatra has endangered this species.

Oriental white stork The drainage of marshes has been one of the principal threats to this Asian stork of which under 5000 remain.

oryx (Arabian) The Arabian oryx was hunted almost to extinction. The species is now protected and numbers have been increased in Jordan, Oman and Saudi Arabia by releasing animals bred in captivity.

Père David's deer This deer became extinct in the wild earlier this century and has been reintroduced to China from stock bred in zoos and parks in Europe.

pygmy chimpanzee The pygmy chimpanzee is threatened by the destruction of much of its habitat in Zaïre.

rhinoceros All species of rhinoceros are under threat, mainly because of the activities of poachers seeking its horns, which are regarded as an aphrodisiac in the Far East. The numbers vary: African black rhinoceros 3000; white rhinoceros (of East and South Africa) 3500; Indian rhinoceros 1700; Sumatran rhinoceros 700; Javan rhinoceros under 60.

Tasmanian wolf or thylacine The thylacine is thought to be extinct, but the recent claims of an expedition to have found its footprints have brought hopes that this marsupial may still be alive.

tiger Less than 4000 tigers survive. Of the four remaining subspecies – Indian, Sumatran, Javanese and Siberian – the latter is under the greatest threat.

three-toed sloth A slow-moving herbivorous animal, the three-toed sloth has been a victim of deforestation in South America.

whales Commercial whaling has placed a number of species under threat. The blue whale and the fin whale, in particular, have been hunted close to extinction.

white stork The white stork – which migrates from Europe and Asia to South Africa – is threatened by the drainage of marshes, by chemical pollution, the loss of nesting sites and by electricity transmission wires.

DOMESTICATED ANIMALS

PRINCIPAL BREEDS OF CATTLE

The majority of modern breeds of cattle evolved during the 18th century when 'livestock improvers' selected stock with desired characteristics for breeding purposes.

BEEF CATTLE

The following breeds are popular in Britain and in continental western Europe.

Aberdeen Angus black hornless cattle developed as a breed in northeast Scotland at the end of the 18th century.

Blonde d'Aquitaine a popular white breed of beef cattle from southwest France.

Blue Grey a popular cross between Galloway cows and white Shorthorn bulls.

Charolais the large white Charolais was developed in the 18th and 19th centuries as a draught animal from a cross between local French cattle and the white Shorthorn.

Chianina probably the largest and heaviest cattle in common use, this white Italian breed was developed originally for draught.

Devon (or North Devon) an ancient breed, it is descended from the red cattle common in western England since the Middle Ages.

Galloway the thick-coated black Galloway is an ancient breed from southwest Scotland. The Belted Galloway is similar except that it has a 'belt' of white hair around the middle of its body.

Hereford the red Hereford, descended from ancient Welsh cattle, is easily recognized by its distinctive white 'mask'. It is often crossed with the Friesian or the Aberdeen Angus.

Highland the traditional Scottish large-horned breed has a long coat which can vary between yellow and dark red.

Limousin a red and white breed from the Massif Central of France; similar to the Hereford but larger, it lacks the Hereford's distinctive mask.

Lincoln Red a red breed whose colour can recess to black, the Lincoln Red was developed by crossing the old Lincolnshire breed with the Shorthorn.

Luing a modern red Scottish breed developed by crossing the Beef Shorthorn and Highland cattle.

Maine-Anjou a red and white breed from northwest France. Originally a dual-purpose breed, but in Britain it tends to be kept largely for beef.

Shorthorn (or Beef Shorthorn) a breed of red, roan or white horned cattle developed by the Colling brothers of County Durham at the end of the 18th century. The Shorthorn is popular in virtually all cattle-raising areas of the world and is known in North America as the Durham.

Sussex a red horned breed from the Weald of Kent and Sussex, believed to be descended from the old Celtic cattle of Britain.

DUAL-PURPOSE BREEDS OF CATTLE

The following breeds are commonly kept in Britain and in continental western Europe for both milk and beef.

Dexter the smallest of British breeds, the red or black Dexter originated in southwest Ireland. It is thought to be the closest surviving relative of the domesticated cattle of Bronze Age Britain.

Meuse-Rhine-IJssel popularly known in the UK as the MRI, this Dutch breed is widespread in Europe and increasing in popularity in the UK.

Red Poll a widely distributed breed originating in East Anglia. It is sometimes crossed with the Danish Red.

Shorthorn (Dairy) this dark red breed has lost favour in Britain to breeds that mature more quickly.

Simmental a golden red Swiss breed, developed in continental Europe mainly for beef.

South Devon a horned red breed, the largest of any British breed.

Welsh Black an uncommon breed developed from traditional Welsh varieties.

DAIRY CATTLE

The following breeds of cattle are among those more commonly kept for dairying in Britain and western continental Europe.

Ayrshire a hardy heavy breed, the red and white Ayrshire originated in southwest Scotland.

Danish Red a popular European breed from which the red British Dane has been developed.

Friesian (or Holstein-Friesian) one of the most popular breeds of cattle in the world, the Friesian is easily recognizable by its distinctive black and white markings. Originating in the Netherlands and Friesland, the Friesian was first imported into Britain in the 1890s and now outnumbers all other dairy breeds.

Guernsey the Guernsey originated in isolation on the Channel Island of the same name. It is similar in appearance to the Jersey but is larger and more yellow in colour.

Jersey the Jersey is of similar Channel Island origin to the Guernsey. This small fawn-coloured breed has distinctive black eyelashes.

Kerry a black breed, native to southwest Ireland.

PRINCIPAL BREEDS OF SHEEP

There is a greater variety of breeds of sheep than of cattle in Britain. Some 40 breeds have been developed, suitable for almost every type of rural environment from mountains to chalk downland to marshes.

LONGWOOL BREEDS

The following longwool breeds are popular in Britain and western continental Europe. These breeds are all large, with heavy fleeces and (except for the Masham) white faces. Most longwools are kept primarily for their wool, although the Romney Marsh is kept mainly for its meat.

Border Leicester developed from the Leicester in the 19th century, it is smaller and lighter than its progenitor.

Cotswold a traditional breed, from the Cotswold Hills of Oxfordshire and Gloucestershire. It is kept for meat and wool.

Devon Longwool smaller than but similar in appearance to the South Devon.

Leicester developed from a traditional Leicestershire breed in the 18th century, the Leicester has been used to improve or develop virtually all the other British longwool breeds.

Lincoln the largest of the British sheep. It has wool of great length.

Masham a popular cross between the Wensleydale and blackfaced mountain ewes. It has a curly fleece and a black and white face.

Merino one of the most widespread breeds in the world, the Merino and the many varieties developed from it are popular in Australia and North America. The Merino has been bred in Spain for its fine wool

since the 12th century.

Merino Romney a cross which is popular in Australia.

Rambouillet the largest of the European fine wool sheep, the Rambouillet was developed from the Merino in France at the end of the 18th century. The breed is widespread in the USA.

Romney Halfbred a cross between the Romney Marsh and the Cheviot which has been developed for fat lamb production.

Romney Marsh (or Kent) the smallest of the British longwools, the Romney Marsh was bred for mutton rather than for wool.

Roscommon the only significant breed of sheep native to Ireland, the Roscommon has lost favour to larger breeds.

South Devon a large hardy breed, popular in the West Country of England.

Wensleydale originating in Yorkshire, the Wensleydale is known for the fine quality of its wool.

THE DOWN BREEDS

Smaller than the longwools, the Down breeds have short wool, dark faces and wide hindquarters. The Down breeds originated in the chalk downlands of southern England and have been introduced successfully to North America, Australia and New Zealand. They are kept for both wool and meat.

Dorset Down a breed with the appearance of a smaller version of the Hampshire.

Hampshire a large hardy breed with medium wool and dark legs. It was developed by crossing the traditional Berkshire Knot and Wiltshire Horned breeds with the Southdown. It is one of the most popular meat producers in the USA.

Oxford (or Oxford Down) a large sheep developed as a cross between the Hampshire and the Cotswold.

Shropshire a cross between the Southdown and ancient breeds in the English Midlands. The Shropshire is rare in Britain although popular in the USA.

Suffolk a large breed known for its fine mutton, the Suffolk is a cross between the Southdown and the Norfolk, which is now extinct.

Southdown a sheep with a rounded body known for the quality of its meat. It was the earliest of the Down breeds to be improved and has been used to produce or to improve all the other Down breeds.

OTHER SHORTWOOL BREEDS

The shortwool breeds listed below were developed independently from the Down breeds. These sheep are kept for meat rather than for wool.

Devon closewool a shortwool sheep easily recognized by its distinctive speckled face.

Dorset Horn a medium-sized horned breed, the Dorset is widely kept in the UK, North America and Australia.

Ile-de-France one of the most popular European breeds, the Ile-de-France is an important mutton producer.

Kerry Hill a Welsh sheep resembling the Devon closewool, but with slightly longer wool and a smaller body.

EURO FACTS

PRINCIPAL ZOOS IN THE EC

Amsterdam (Netherlands)
Founded in 1836, the zoo exhibits nearly 1400 species and contains a famous animal behaviour laboratory.

Antwerp (Belgium)
A large zoo on a city centre site, Antwerp houses over 1100 species, including important exhibits of black rhinoceros and Père David's deer. The zoo is famous for the innovative nature of its animal enclosures, especially in the reptile house.

Berlin (Germany)
One of the largest zoos in the world, Berlin Zoo was opened in 1841. The best known collections include the birds of prey, wild cattle and the aquarium. The future of a smaller collection in East Berlin is in doubt.

Cologne (Germany)
One of the most famous European zoos, this sizeable collection is jointly maintained by the city and a zoological society. It houses over 700 species, specializes in primates and is known for its aquarium.

Copenhagen (Denmark)
The 2500 species in Copenhagen Zoo include a particularly comprehensive collection of birds. The zoo, founded in 1859, has bred a number of rare species, including the musk ox.

Frankfurt (Germany)
Founded in 1858, the zoo exhibits over 600 species. This major collection is known for breeding endangered species, including the lowland gorilla, okapi and black rhinoceros.

London (UK)
The Regent's Park Zoo (established in 1828) is one of the largest in the world with over 1200 species. London Zoo – which has the largest zoological library in the world – has a separate collection of some 250 species in spacious enclosures at Whipsnade in Bedfordshire.

Paris (France)
Set in the Bois de Vincennes, the Paris Zoo dates back to 1793. Its spacious natural enclosures include the famous Rocher, an artificial mountain for wild sheep. The zoo has about 300 species and is proud of its record for breeding especially rare deer, wild horses and giraffes.

Ryeland a breed similar to the Kerry Hill, but uncommon outside the Welsh Marches, where it originated.

Wiltshire Horned (or Western Horned) a traditional breed with a white face and horns.

MOUNTAIN BREEDS
The following horned, blackfaced British breeds were all developed for difficult mountainous areas. They are therefore hardy and strong-wooled.

Cheviot a widespread medium-sized breed with a white face and very little wool on the head. It originated in the Scottish Borders and is commonly crossed with the Border Leicester.

Clun Forest a popular breed in the Welsh Marches, the Clun Forest was developed from the Scottish Blackface.

Dartmoor a large coarse-wooled breed that originated in Devon.

Exmoor Horned (or Porlock) a small hardy breed, largely confined to southwest England.

Herdwick the hardiest of all the English breeds, the coarse-wooled Herdwick was developed in the Lake District.

The Lonk a sturdy breed native to the southern Pennines and the Peak District of England.

Scottish Blackface known for the strength of its wool, this breed from the Highlands of Scotland may vary in size according to its surroundings and parentage.

Swaledale a coarse-wooled sheep originating in Yorkshire.

Welsh Mountain the smallest common British breed, the Welsh Mountain sheep is coarse-wooled and very hardy.

NEW BREEDS
A number of new breeds have been developed since the 1950s, crossing British and European sheep. Of these the best known are the Cobb 101 (a cross between the Finnish Landrace and the Suffolk) and the Colbred (a cross between the Border Leicester, Clun Forest, Dorset Horn and East Friesland).

HUMAN ANATOMY AND PHYSIOLOGY

THE HUMAN BODY

BONES IN THE HUMAN BODY

Skull	Number
occipital	1
parietal – 1 pair	2
sphenoid	1
ethmoid	1
inferior nasal conchae – 1 pair	2
frontal – 1 pair, fused	1
nasal – 1 pair	2
lacrimal – 1 pair	2
temporal – 1 pair	2
macilla – 1 pair	2
zygomatic – 1 pair	2
vomer	1
palatine – 1 pair	2
mandible – 1 pair, fused	1
	22

Ears	
malleus	2
incus	2
stapes	2
	6

THE SKELETON

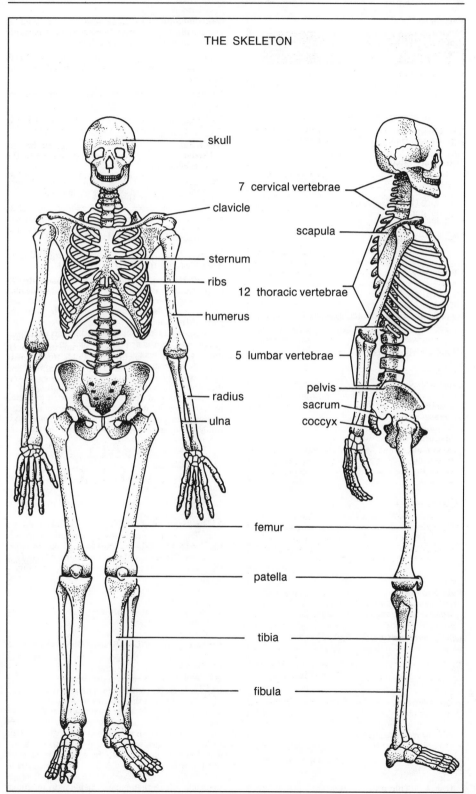

Vertebrae

cervical	7
thoracic	12
lumbar	5
sacral – 5 vertebrae fuse together to form the sacrum	1
coccyx – lowermost element of the back bone (vestigial human tail)	1
	26

Vertebral ribs

ribs, 'true' – 7 pairs	14
ribs, 'false' – 5 pairs, of which 2 pairs are floating	10
	24

Sternum (breast bone)

manubrium	1
sternebrae	1
xiphisternum	1
	3

(in the throat)	1

Pectoral girdle

clavicle – 1 pair	2
scapula (including coracoid) – 1 pair	2
	4

Upper extremity (each arm)

humerus	1
radius	1
ulna	1
carpus:	
scaphoid	1
lunate	1
triquetral	1
pisiform	1
trapezium	1
trapezoid	1
capitate	1
hamate	1
metacarpals	5
phalanges:	
first digit (thumb)	2
second digit	3
third digit	3
fourth digit	3
fifth digit	3
	30

Pelvic girdle

ilium, ischium and pubis (combined) – 1 pair of hip bones (innominate)	2

Lower extremity (each leg)

femur	1
tibia	1
fibula	1
tarsus:	
talus	1
calcaneus	1
navicular	1
cuneiform, medial	1
cuneiform, intermediate	1
cuneiform, lateral	1
cuboid	1
metatarsals	5
phalanges:	
first digit (big toe)	2

second digit	3
third digit	3
fourth digit	3
fifth digit	3
	29

Total

Skull	22
The ears	6
Vertebrae	26
Vertebral ribs	24
Sternum	3
Throat	1
Pectoral girdle	4
Upper extremity (arms): 2 × 30	60
Hip bones	2
Lower extremity (legs): 2 × 29	58
	206

ORGANS OF THE HUMAN BODY

ALIMENTARY (DIGESTIVE) SYSTEM

Food passes from the mouth and oesophagus – a 23 cm (9 in) muscular tube from the throat – to the stomach, which acts as a collecting bag and begins the process of digestion by a churning action, and by secreting hydrochloric acid and other juices (*pepsin*). Food then passes to the small intestine (small bowel) comprising the *duodenum, jejunum* and *ileum*. The duodenum is 25 cm (10 in) long, the jejunum 2.5 m (8 ft), and the ileum 4 m (13 ft) long. The liver (by means of the gall bladder) and the pancreas also secrete digestive juices into the duodenum. Both digestion and absorption of nutrients take place in the small intestine before food reaches the large intestine (colon), which is 1.5 m (5 ft) long. In the colon, body fluids are reabsorbed. Waste matter is excreted through the rectum.

THE LIVER

A vital organ – weighing about 2 kg (4 lb) – the liver has four functions:

1. The production of bile to emulsify fat in the bowel and so allow its absorption.
2. The reception of all the products of food absorption. The liver controls the storage and release of these products as energy sources. Carbohydrates are stored as glycogen, and the liver, using insulin from the pancreas, controls the body's glucose (sugar) level.
3. The purification of blood by removing toxins and worn-out red cells.
4. The production of proteins needed for blood clotting.

CIRCULATION AND RESPIRATORY SYSTEM

The ribs enclose the thoracic cavity, within which lie the heart and the two lungs. The heart weighs 250–300 g (9–11 oz) and is approximately the size of a clenched fist. It is a muscular pump, which squeezes blood out through the arteries with each beat. The arteries carry blood away from the heart through a series of branching and progressively smaller blood vessels (capillaries), which then join together again to form the veins, which return blood to the heart. The heart is divided into four compartments or chambers (*atria* and *ventricles*). The right atrium collects blood from the veins and passes it to the right ventricle, which then pumps the blood to the lungs.

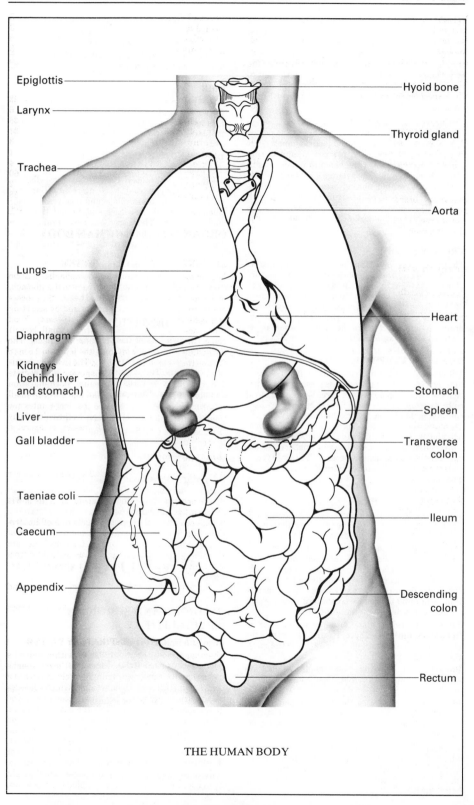

Epiglottis

Larynx

Trachea

Lungs

Diaphragm

Kidneys
(behind liver
and stomach)

Liver

Gall bladder

Taeniae coli

Caecum

Appendix

Hyoid bone

Thyroid gland

Aorta

Heart

Stomach

Spleen

Transverse
colon

Ileum

Descending
colon

Rectum

THE HUMAN BODY

In the capillaries of the lungs the process of breathing (respiration) replaces the blood's oxygen content, before the blood returns to the left side of the heart. It collects in the left atrium, then passes through the mitral valve to the left ventricle (the largest chamber of the heart), which pumps it out to the rest of the body via the aortic valve and *aorta* – the largest blood vessel of the body (2.5 cm or 1 in in diameter).

The heart beats 2500 million times in an average lifetime. At a heart rate of 70 per minute it pumps approximately 5 litres (9 pt) of blood per minute, but it can pump 20 litres (35 pt) per minute during vigorous exercise, when the heart rate increases to about 150 per minute. The average total lung volume is about 5 litres, but normal breathing only draws about 1–2 litres (4–5 pt) of air in and out with each breath. The oxygen in the air is passed into the bloodstream in exchange for carbon dioxide, which is exhaled.

URINARY SYSTEM

The two kidneys lie behind the abdominal organs, below the ribs on either side of the spine. They measure about 15 cm (6 in) in length, and each weighs 150 g (5 oz). The kidneys purify the blood in a complex system of microscopic syphons (*glomeruli* and *nephrons*), producing urine, which is then passed through drainage tubes (*ureters*) to the bladder, where urine is stored before excretion through the urethra.

BLOOD AND LYMPHATIC SYSTEM

The average blood volume is 5.5 litres (10 pt). Almost exactly 55 per cent of the blood is plasma, and 45 per cent consists of blood cells of three types. Red blood cells (*erythrocytes*) – which are biconcave discs containing the chemical *haemoglobin* – carry oxygen. There are approximately 5 million red cells per mm^3 of blood, each with a lifespan of about 120 days. The white cells (*leucocytes*) are fewer in number (8000 per mm^3) and act to combat infection. The third type of cell – platelets – helps in the normal process of blood clotting.

ENDOCRINE ORGANS

The chemicals that these glands secrete directly into the bloodstream are hormones that regulate many aspects of the body's performance.

Pituitary gland a gland situated at the base of the brain, producing hormones that control the other endocrine glands: a hormone that regulates growth; a hormone that causes the uterus to contract during childbirth; a hormone that causes the mammary glands (breasts) to produce milk; and a hormone that regulates the concentration of the urine.

Thyroid gland a gland situated in the neck in front of the windpipe. Thyroid hormone controls the rate of chemical reactions in body cells (the metabolic rate).

Parathyroid glands four glands that are embedded within the thyroid. They control calcium levels in the body.

Pancreas a gland secreting the hormone insulin, which regulates glucose levels in the body. A deficiency of insulin causes diabetes mellitus (sugar diabetes, see p. 156).

Adrenal glands glands that produce adrenalin, which prepares the body for stress ('fight or flight') by increasing heart rate and blood pressure. They also produce cortisone, which has a variety of metabolic effects.

Ovaries produce the female sexual hormones *oestrogen* and *progesterone*, and release one egg (*ovum*) per month during the woman's reproductive life.

Testes two glands that produce sperms and the male hormone *testosterone*.

SKIN

The skin can also be classed as an organ. It accounts for 16 per cent of the body's weight, and has an average surface area of 18 000 cm^2 (2800 in^2). Among its functions is the control of heat loss.

BRAIN AND NERVOUS SYSTEM

The human brain – which on average weighs about 1.4 kg (3 lb) – contains 10 000 million nerve cells, each of which has a potential 25 000 interconnections with other cells. The brain relays and receives electrical impulses through the senses, and through the nerves and spinal cord. There are 12 pairs of cranial nerves supplying the face and head. Nerves in other areas of the body can be classified as motor (which supply movement), sensory (which recognize touch, pain and temperature, and sense body position), and autonomic (which regulate the internal body activities that we are not normally aware of, e.g. bowel activity, breathing, heart rate, etc.).

HUMAN DENTITION

Man has two sets of teeth during his lifetime. The primary set (milk or deciduous teeth) number 20, and are usually acquired between the ages of six months and two years. The primary teeth are lost from about the age of six onwards when the permanent teeth begin to appear. There are 32 permanent teeth in all:

Eight incisors the central (front) teeth, four upper and four lower, which have a cutting function.

Four canine teeth the pointed fang-like teeth on either side of the incisors.

Eight pre-molars two in each quadrant of the mouth; each has two cusps.

12 molars three in each quadrant of the mouth; the upper molars have four cusps, and the lower molars five cusps, to allow efficient grinding of food. The furthest back molar in each gum is the wisdom tooth, which usually only appears at the age of 18–20 or later.

MEDICINE

MEDICAL AND SURGICAL SPECIALITIES

In most hospitals there are departments dealing with different specialities – for example, departments of neurology or paediatrics. The most important medical specialities include:

anaesthetics the study of the loss of sensation (especially pain) or consciousness by drugs: in *general anaesthetics* consciousness is lost; in *local anaesthetics* the loss of sensation applies only to a specific part of the body.

anatomy the study of the structure of the body.

audiology the assessment of hearing.

aurology the study and treatment of diseases of the ear.

bacteriology the study and treatment of bacterial (and usually also viral) infections.

bioengineering the study of the mechanical workings of the body, particularly with reference to artificial limbs and powered appliances that the body can use.

biophysics the study of electrical impulses in the body; this may be applied to an assessment of muscle disease.

cardiology the study and treatment of heart disease.

chemotherapy the treatment of diseases by drugs.

community medicine the prevention of the spread of disease and the increase of physical and mental well-being within the community.

cryosurgery the use of freezing techniques in surgery.

cytogenetics the study of chromosomes and their correlation with heredity.

cytology (medical) the microscopic study of body cells.

dentistry the treatment and extraction of teeth.

dermatology the study and treatment of skin diseases.

diabetics the study and treatment of diabetes.

embryology the study of the growth of the baby from the moment of conception to about the 20th week of pregnancy.

endocrinology the study and treatment of diseases of the glands that produce hormones.

ENT otorhinolaryngology (see below).

entomology (medical) the study of insects and moths with particular reference to the transmission of disease.

epidemiology the study of the occurrence, transmission and control of epidemics.

forensic medicine the study of injury and disease caused by criminal activity and the detection of crime by medical knowledge.

gastroenterology the study and treatment of diseases of the stomach and intestines.

genetics the study of inherited characteristics, disease and malformations.

genito-urinary medicine the study of diseases of the sexual and urine-producing organs.

geriatrics the study and treatment of the diseases and condition of elderly people.

gerontology the study of diseases of elderly people and in particular the study of the ageing process.

gynaecology the study and treatment of diseases of women, in particular the diseases of the genito-urinary tract.

haematology the study and treatment of blood diseases.

histochemistry the study of the chemical environment of the body cells.

histopathology the microscopic study of cells.

immunology the study of the immunity of the body to disease and other harmful outside influences.

laryngology the study and treatment of throat diseases.

metabolic diseases diseases of the interior workings of the body, e.g. disorders of calcium absorption, thyroid disease, or adrenal gland disease.

microbiology (medical) the study of the workings of cells.

nephrology the study and treatment of kidney disease.

neurology the study and treatment of a wide range of diseases of the brain and/or the nervous system.

neurosurgery operations on the brain or nervous system.

nuclear medicine the treatment of diseases with radioactive substances.

obstetrics the care of pregnant women and the delivery of children.

oncology the study and treatment of cancer.

ophthalmic optics (optometry) the assessment of visual disorders, the examination of eyes, and the provision of corrective treatment in the form of visual aids, e.g. spectacles or contact lenses.

optics, dispensing the dispensing of spectacles or contact lenses (cf. ophthalmic optics).

orthodontology the branch of dentistry concerned with the prevention and correction of irregularities in teeth.

orthopaedics the study and treatment of fractures and bone diseases.

orthoptics the correction of defective vision, e.g. the treatment of squints of the eye.

orthotics the provision of artificial and mechanical aids, e.g. braces to assist weakened limbs.

otology the study and treatment of diseases of the ear.

otorhinolaryngology the study and treatment of diseases of the ear, nose and throat; also known as ENT.

paediatrics the study and treatment of the diseases of children.

parasitology (medical) the study and treatment of infections of the body caused by worms, insects and other parasites.

pathology the branch of medicine concerned with the cause, origin and nature of disease.

pharmacology the use of drugs in relation to medicine.

physical medicine the treatment of injuries by exercise or electrical treatments, or the preparation of the body for surgery by similar means (see physiotherapy.)

physiology the study and understanding of the normal workings of the body.

physiotherapy the practice of physical medicine (see above).

plastic surgery the reconstruction or alteration of damaged or abnormal parts of the body by surgery.

proctology the study and treatment of diseases of the rectum.

prosthetics the making of artificial limbs and related appliances.

psychiatry the study and treatment of mental disorders.

psychoanalysis the investigation of the formation of mental illness by long-term repeated discussion between the patient and a psychoanalyst.

psychology the study of the mind, with particular reference to the measurement of intellectual activity.

psychotherapy the treatment of mental disorders by psychological methods, rather than by drugs or other physical treatments.

radiobiology the treatment or investigation of disease using radioactive substances.

radiography the taking of X-rays.

radiology the study of X-rays.

radiotherapy the treatment of diseases using X-rays.

renal diseases diseases of the kidney or urinary tract.

rheumatology the study and treatment of diseases of muscles and joints.

rhinology the study and treatment of diseases of the nose.

therapeutics curative medicine; the healing of physical and/or mental disorders.

thoracic surgery surgery on the chest or heart.

toxicology the study of poisons, their effects and antidotes.

urology the study and treatment of diseases of the kidney and the urinary tract.

vascular disease diseases of the blood vessels.

venereology the study and treatment of sexually transmitted diseases.

virology the study and treatment of virus diseases.

MAJOR COMMUNICABLE DISEASES

TRANSMISSION OF DISEASES

An infectious disease is one in which one living organism inhabits and multiplies on or within another, harming it in the process, either by the production of toxic substances or by damaging, digesting or destroying part or all of its cellular structure. Such harmful organisms are mostly microscopic – viruses, bacteria and protozoans – but also include various kinds of fungus, worms and arthropods.

Infections can be transmitted in the following ways:

Airborne transmission infection through infected droplets in the air from the nose, throat/lungs or saliva, or from dust particles from fallen skin.

Contamination infection through food or water supplies containing infected material such as faeces or urine.

Direct contact (contagion) infection from close contact with an infected person.

Sexual transmission infection through vaginal or anal intercourse, or oral sex. The use of condoms may reduce the risk of infection.

Blood-borne transmission infection through the injection of contaminated blood or blood products, or by improperly sterilized instruments. Blood-borne transmission is most common among haemophiliacs and intravenous drug users, and is occasionally the result of tattooing or acupuncture.

Animal-borne transmission infection through the injection of contaminated saliva; e.g. malaria (carried by the mosquito) and bubonic plague (transmitted by flea bites).

AIDS

Aids – acquired immune deficiency syndrome – was first identified in Los Angeles, USA, in 1981. The virus responsible for causing AIDS was isolated in 1983 and is now known as HIV (human immuno-deficiency virus). The disease is spreading rapidly throughout the Western world, and has reached epidemic proportions in the countries of eastern and central Africa.

The virus attacks one particular type of white blood cell in the body (the helper/inducer lymphocytes) and this causes immunosuppression (reduced ability to combat infection). It may also attack the nervous system and cause dementia. Acute infection with HIV after exposure leads to the production of antibodies (sero-conversion). These antibodies are detected by blood tests which become positive on average within three months of the virus being acquired, but may take up to 12 months or longer to appear. In some cases there may be no symptoms during the period of sero-conversion; in other cases a transient flu-like illness with gland swelling and muscle aches may occur.

Not all patients who sero-convert go on to experience chronic infection. In those patients who do, the infection may be without symptoms, or may give rise to illnesses of varying degrees of severity – known as PGL, ARC or AIDS itself. Current knowledge suggests that between 10 and 30 per cent of HIV-antibody-positive patients progress to AIDS within five years.

PGL – persistent generalized lymphodenopathy – is the mildest illness caused by HIV infection. It is characterized by the swelling of lymph glands at various sites of the body, but there are no other symptoms. Many patients with PGL remain well for several years.

ARC – AIDS-related complex – is the second stage of the disease, during which there is some impairment of the immune system as well as lymph gland enlargement. Symptoms may include episodes of fever, weight loss, night sweats, diarrhoea, coughing, skin rashes and profound fatigue. Blood tests may show reduced numbers of white blood cells, anaemia, or changes in blood proteins. ARC is usually only diagnosed if such symptoms or blood-test abnormalities persist over a three-month period.

AIDS itself is diagnosed once certain specific infections or types of tumour begin to appear. The most common infection is an unusual form of pneumonia (*Pneumocystis carinii*); the most common tumour is Kaposi's sarcoma – a form of skin cancer that may spread to the internal organs. The course of the disease usually involves increasingly serious episodes of infection and it is often fatal within two years. Approximately 30 per cent of subjects suffer dementia by the later stages of their disease. Recent advances in treatment have included better treatments for the episodes of infection, and the development of a drug known as AZT, which shows promise in modifying the disease itself.

By October 1990, 3798 cases of AIDS had been reported in the UK, 54 per cent of whom had died of the disease. Estimates of the numbers of people in Britain who are HIV-antibody positive vary between 20 000 and 50 000. Although about 80 per cent of the carriers of the virus are homosexual men, the AIDS virus is spreading more rapidly among heterosexuals. In January 1990 the United Nations World Health Organization (WHO) announced that the number of AIDS cases worldwide was over 215 000, a figure that is widely thought to be a considerable underestimate. In Europe and North America AIDS is at present more common in homosexual men and intravenous drug users, but in Africa heterosexual infection is much more frequent.

The only ways of acquiring HIV infection or AIDS are:

1. by having oral sex or sexual intercourse with someone who carries the virus, particularly if this is anal intercourse;
2. by sharing needles or other instruments contaminated with the blood of someone carrying the virus;
3. by receiving blood or blood products from someone with the virus (in the past some haemophiliacs have acquired the AIDS virus from treatment with blood products, but all blood products and blood transfusions in countries of the developed world are now thoroughly tested before use);
4. mothers who have the virus may pass it on to their babies.

ANTHRAX

Anthrax is a form of blood poisoning in cattle, sheep and horses that is normally fatal. It can upon rare occasions be passed to vets or butchers disposing of infected carcases or to those handling infected animal hides, wool or bone meal. The initial lesion is usually on the hand – a painful swollen boil with a black crust and surrounding redness. If untreated, blood poisoning (septicaemia) may result. It can be cured by penicillin, and a vaccine exists for those in high-risk occupations.

CHICKENPOX (VARICELLA)

Chickenpox is caused by the same virus as shingles (*Herpes zoster*). It is a mild disease, common in childhood and infectious from four days before the rash appears until seven days after the rash appears. The incubation period is usually 14 days. The rash – which may be preceded by mild headache or fever – begins as red spots, which over a few hours become raised and topped by a clear blister. Over two to three days these small blisters become opalescent and then scab over, with several crops of blisters appearing over a perod of five to seven days. The rash can occur on any part of the body – including the mouth and scalp – but tends to be most profuse on the trunk. No specific treatment is needed, except to relieve itch and prevent scratching with dirty finger nails. Complications are rare and there is no vaccine.

CHOLERA

Cholera is an acute infection of the intestine that causes profuse watery diarrhoea, vomiting and dehydration. It is caused by consuming water or food contaminated by the bacterium *Vibrio comma*, which is found in faeces. In 1854 the Englishman John Snow proved that cholera is transmitted in contaminated water when he stopped an epidemic by removing the pump handle from a well that he suspected was the source of infection. The last epidemic in Britain was in Cleethorpes in 1879. Today the disease is largely restricted to the tropics. Prevention is achieved by the availability of a clean water supply. Vaccination – two injections at an interval of two to four months – is effective for six to nine months, after which booster doses are needed.

COMMON COLD (CORYZAL)

At least 40 different viruses – either airborne or transmitted by direct contact – can cause sneezing, coughing, sore throat, running eyes and nose, headache and mild fever. Aspirin may help reduce the symptoms.

DIPHTHERIA

Diphtheria is an infection of the pharynx caused by airborne bacteria. The symptoms are an initial sore throat, obstructed breathing and inflammation of the heart. The condition is complicated by the formation of a membrane of dead tissue that can totally obstruct the airway and necessitate a tracheotomy – a surgical opening in the neck over the windpipe to allow breathing. Immunization programmes have eradicated diphtheria in the UK, where as recently as 1941 the disease caused 1622 deaths. Immunization is achieved by a series of three injections in infancy – combined with injections against tetanus and, usually, whooping cough – and booster doses at school age.

DYSENTERY

Two types of dysentery occur – *bacillary dysentery*, which is caused by the bacterium *Shigella*, and *amoebic dysentery*, caused by the amoeba *Entamoeba hystolytica*. Both types cause profuse diarrhoea (often containing blood), abdominal pain, weight loss and dehydration. Complications include liver abscesses. Amoebic dysentery is confined to the tropics. Bacillary dysentery occurs worldwide as a result of contamination of food by faecal bacteria, usually carried by water. The disease can be mild, but even after complete recovery the organism can still be excreted for several weeks. Prevention is through high standards of hygiene and the provision of a clean water supply. No immunization exists.

FOOD POISONING (GASTROENTERITIS)

Most short-lasting cases of sickness or diarrhoea are due to *viral gastroenteritis*. The commonest cause is human rotavirus, to which children under the age of three are particularly susceptible. The treatment is to stop all solid-food intake, and to concentrate instead on fluid intake to prevent dehydration. In babies, feeds of boiled water are given instead of milk. Breast-fed babies are less likely to get gastroenteritis.

Bacterial gastroenteritis may be caused by a number of bacteria, including *Salmonella*, *Listeria* and, more rarely, *Clostridium botulinum* (which causes the often fatal disease called *botulism*). Raw meat, poultry or eggs can be contaminated by the *Salmonella* bacterium, which is able to survive deep freezing. If thawing is not complete, or if the cooking time or temperature is inadequate, the cooked food remains infected. Symptoms of diarrhoea, fever and vomiting usually begin 12 to 48 hours after the food has been consumed. If complications such as septicaemia (blood poisoning) occur, the patient is treated with antibiotics. Without treatment, an infected person may become a carrier, although showing no symptoms.

Other forms of food poisoning are due to the release of a toxic chemical from the contaminating organism, rather than infection by the organism itself. Such infection usually begins within one to six hours of ingestion. Examples include *staphylococcal toxin* (often from infected cream, sometimes from meat or poultry) and the toxin of *Bacillus cereus* (from fried rice). All forms of gastroenteritis may be prevented by high standards of hygiene in food preparation and by the provision of a clean water supply.

GERMAN MEASLES (RUBELLA)

The first symptoms of German measles – a headache and sore throat – are followed by mild fever, a pink blotchy rash (first on the face, then on the body) and swelling of the lymph glands at the back of the neck. Cases are mildly infectious from five days before until five days after the rash appears. The incubation period is usually 17 to 18 days. There may be transient joint soreness, particularly in adults, but serious complications are very rare. However, German measles in a woman in the first three months of pregnancy can cause foetal damage – in the first month the risk of congenital abnormalities of eyes, ears or heart is 50 per cent. This falls to about four per cent by the fourth month.

Transmission is by direct contact with an infected person. In the UK immunization programmes were until recently aimed mainly at teenage girls. However, vaccination is now usual from the age of 14 months since the introduction in 1988 of the measles, mumps and rubella vaccine, which has been used for some years in North America.

GLANDULAR FEVER

Glandular fever – or infectious mononucleosis – is caused by the Epstein-Barr virus. Transmission is by direct contact and, because it mainly affects young adults (aged 15 to 25), a popular theory was that it was contracted by kissing. The initial symptom is a particularly sore throat, often producing a thick white coating over the area of the tonsils. Other characteristics include fever and enlargement of the lymph glands of the neck and sometimes also of the liver and spleen. This enlargement can last ten or more days and is often followed by a period of severe fatigue and mild depression before complete recovery. No treatment other than rest is available. Diagnosis can be confirmed by blood tests. No immunization is available.

GONORRHEA

Gonorrhea is a sexually transmitted (venereal) disease caused by the bacterium *Neisseria gonorrhoea*. It has an average incubation period of four days. In men it almost always causes a purulent discharge at the tip of the penis. Complications include infection of the epididymis (the tube behind the testicle) and of the prostate gland, or, in later stages, a narrowing of the urethra (urine tube). One half of the women infected by the disease may initially have no symptoms; others may suffer vaginal discharge, urinary symptoms and/or abdominal pain. The pain is due to infection spreading to the pelvic organs, including the Fallopian tubes, which may become scarred and blocked, sometimes leading to infertility. Penicillin is usually an effective cure. No immunization exists.

HEPATITIS

Hepatitis is inflammation of the liver, usually caused by a virus. It can also be caused by excessive alcohol or drug consumption. Viral hepatitis is classified as A, B, and Non A, Non B. There is no effective antiviral drug.

Hepatitis A – also called infectious hepatitis – is transmitted by close contact or faecal contamination of food or water. Following an incubation period of two to six weeks, initial symptoms include fever, nausea, weakness, discomfort and tenderness over the liver area. After about the first four days of the illness, jaundice (yellow skin) develops and the patient passes dark urine and pale faeces. Jaundice lasts one or two weeks and then appetite returns. A complete recovery is usual. An injection of human immunoglobulin gives temporary protection to travellers to those areas of the Third World where the disease is endemic.

Hepatitis B – also called serum hepatitis – is blood borne, usually transmitted by sharing contaminated needles or through sexual contact. The incubation period varies between one and five months. Symptoms identical to Hepatitis A may develop, but a high percentage of cases are 'sub-clinical', i.e. the illness is mild without evidence of jaundice. In about 19 out of 20 cases the patient becomes free of the virus within four to six months. One case in 20 becomes a chronic carrier, liable to pass on infection by blood or sexual contact, and liable to develop liver complications such as cirrhosis. Only 1 in 1000 cases dies of acute hepatitis. Immunization by a series of three injections is now available for those at high risk, e.g. nurses, doctors and dentists.

HERPES SIMPLEX

There are two common types of herpes simplex, a viral infection transmitted by direct contact.

The most common lesion produced by *Type I* of this virus is the 'cold sore' – a small crop of painful blisters that usually develop around the lips or nose and last for several days before fading. The virus may then be latent and flare up again in response to such events as another infection, trauma, emotional upset or exposure to sunlight. Other infections include blisters of the fingers (whitlow), ulceration of the cornea of the eye, and, rarely, a serious encephalitis (brain infection) to which infants are vulnerable. Those suffering from 'cold sores' should therefore avoid close contact with infants.

A variety of *Type II* of this virus causes genital herpes, a painful recurrent blistering eruption of the genitalia similar in appearance to a 'cold sore' but transmitted through sexual contact. Treatment with idoxuridine limits attacks, but does not prevent recurrence. No immunization exists.

HERPES ZOSTER

see Chickenpox and Shingles.

INFLUENZA

Influenza is an airborne viral infection. Symptoms include fever, muscle pain, sore throat, coughing, loss of appetite and general weakness. Complications include viral pneumonia, which can lead to a rapidly progressive pneumonia owing to further bacterial infection by staphylococci. Influenza may be fatal in elderly people. Pandemics can occur, such as in April–November 1918, when 21.6 million people are estimated to have died. Various types of influenza virus exist, and the virus has the capacity to change through time. Immunity from previous exposure or from vaccination is therefore never complete, and second or further attacks in the one individual can occur.

LEGIONNAIRE'S DISEASE

Legionnaire's disease is an uncommon form of pneumonia identified in 1976 and caused by the bacterium *Legionella pneumophilia*. It is transmitted airborne in water droplets from contaminated supplies, often through air-conditioning systems or showers. Symptoms include fever, coughing, chest pain and breathlessness, and the disease is sometimes fatal.

LEPROSY

Leprosy is a chronic inflammatory disease caused by the bacterium *Mycobacterium leprae*, which is transmitted by prolonged or close contact. The characteristics are very variable. Mild cases may show only a small area of altered skin pigmentation, which may heal spontaneously. Other cases progress to a thickening of superficial nerves, areas of skin without feeling, and muscle paralysis. In extreme forms there is distortion of the skin by nodule formation, thickening, fissuring and ulceration, resulting in the deformity and disfigurement that are traditionally feared. Control with sulphone drugs is possible, and some use has been made of plastic surgery.

MALARIA

Malaria is caused by a protozoa of one of four types – *Plasmodium ovale, P. malaria, P. vivax* and *P. falciparum* – and is transmitted to the bloodstream of man by the female anopheles mosquito. This mode of transmission was first proved in 1895 by the English bacteriologist Sir Ronald Ross, who discovered the protozoa in the gastrointestinal tract of the mosquito. Infection results in the destruction of red blood cells, causing intermittent fever and anaemia. The incubation period and the severity of the disease depends on the infecting species. *P. falciparum* – the most dangerous infection – causes malignant tertian malaria, in which the brain can be affected, and fits or coma – and even sudden death – may occur.

Every year in the tropics more than one million people still die of malaria and two million new cases appear, despite worldwide efforts to control the disease. All efforts at controlling malaria focus on the mosquito – the carrier – and include the destruction of the mosquito's breeding grounds, treating water with chemicals to destroy mosquito larvae, and the use of insecticides to kill adult mosquitoes. Drugs can be used to treat infected people, and measures – such as the use of nets, repellents and suitable clothing – can be taken to prevent the mosquito biting. Throughout the 1950s and 1960s the World Health Organization had considerable success in malaria eradication, particularly in the USA and Europe. The programme also led to a 500-fold decrease in malaria in India. Unfortunately resistance of mosquitoes to DDT then developed, and in many areas in the 1970s eradication began to falter.

The drugs used to prevent malaria are becoming more complex because in certain areas of the world malaria has become resistant to drugs that were previously effective. Whatever drug is used must be started one week before travel into the endemic area and should be continued for four to six weeks after leaving the area. In North Africa and the Middle East chloroquine taken once per week or proguanil taken daily are the usual preventative. For the Indian sub-continent, China, Africa and South America both drugs are advised in combination. For some parts of Southeast Asia pyrimethamine and chloroquine are advised.

MEASLES (RUBEOLA)

Measles is a viral airborne infection. An incubation period of between 8 and 14 days precedes the onset of fever and catarrhal symptoms, which last for three days before the rash appears. The rash is red and blotchy, usually starting behind the ears and spreading to the face and trunk. The inside of the cheeks may be red and Koplik's spots (little white spots – like grains of salt – in the area behind the lower back teeth) confirm the diagnosis. Other characteristics include running eyes and nose. The rash fades after three or four days. Cases are highly infectious from the onset of the fever and the catarrhal phase until

the rash fades. Bacterial infections of the ears, sinuses and chest are the most immediate complications. A rare but serious progressive brain disease known as subacute sclerosing panencephalitis can occur four or more years after infection.

Immunization is recommended from the age of 14 months and, since October 1988 in the UK, is combined with a vaccine for mumps and rubella (German measles). The intensive use of this vaccine has made measles an extremely rare condition in North America in recent years.

MENINGITIS

Meningitis is a viral or bacterial infection causing inflammation of membranes surrounding the brain.

Bacterial meningitis can be caused by a number of organisms – the most common are mengingococcal meningitis, pneumococcal meningitis and haemophilus meningitis. *E. coli* meningitis occurs mainly in new-born infants. The symptoms of bacterial meningitis are fever, severe headache, neck stiffness, intolerance of bright lights and vomiting. The speed of onset depends on the infecting organism – tubercular meningitis has a gradual onset. Meningococcal meningitis is particularly rapid and can cause sudden collapse and the rapid appearance of a rash looking like small bruises or blood blisters. Antibiotic therapy must be started with the utmost urgency.

Viral meningitis can be caused by a great number of viruses. The symptoms are similar but less severe than those of bacterial meningitis. Spontaneous recovery can be expected without specific treatment.

MUMPS

Mumps is caused by an airborne paramyxovirus. Its incubation period is usually 21 days. Initial symptoms are three to five days of mild fever and vague malaise followed by tender swelling of the parotid glands (the salivary glands on the side of the face, in front of and below the ears). Usually both sides are affected, but one side may become swollen one or two days before the other. The swelling lasts several days, and cases are infectious for one week before the swelling and until the swelling subsides. Possible complications include inflammation of the testicles (orchitis) in adult males, inflammation of the pancreas, and a mild viral meningitis. In North America, Britain and some European countries, immunization is available by means of a single injection combined with vaccination against measles and rubella (German measles).

MYALGIC ENCEPHALOMYELITIS (ME)

Myalgic encephalomyelitis is a condition probably developing as a sequel to various viral infections, most notably to Coxsackie virus infection. The symptoms are diverse, but include muscle fatigue and muscle pain provoked by minimal exercise and relieved or prevented by adequate rest. The condition is similar to the fatigue encountered after glandular fever, but may last for months – or even years. The condition is also known as post-viral syndrome and Royal Free disease, so called because of an apparent epidemic in the Royal Free Hospital, London, in the 1950s. No treatment is available.

PLAGUE

Plague is a disease of rodents that can be transmitted to man by flea bites or by airborne infection. It is caused by the bacterium *Yersinia pestis*. Symptoms include fever, weakness, delirium and painful buboes (swelling of lymph nodes). The condition is often fatal. During the 14th century – when the condition was known as the Black Death – one quarter of the population of Europe died because of plague. The Great Plague of London (1664–65) caused the death of one person in seven in the city.

PNEUMONIA

Pneumonia is a bacterial or viral infection transmitted by direct contact or by airborne infection. The principal characteristic is the inflammation of one or both lungs, in which the air sacs become filled with liquid. This causes pain and difficulty in breathing. Pneumonia can be fatal, particularly in the elderly.

POLIOMYELITIS

Polio is a viral infection of the nervous system transmitted by direct contact. It is no longer endemic in Britain, where as recently as 1948 polio caused 241 deaths in England and Wales. The majority of cases are characterized by mild fever, headache, stiffness of the neck and gastrointestinal symptoms lasting only a few days. However, other cases develop meningitis or paralysis of muscles. Paralysis may affect the breathing muscles – causing respiratory failure – or the limb muscles – resulting in permanent muscle thinning and weakness. Polio has been eradicated by immunization in the majority of developed countries. The oral vaccine Sabin is given from infancy with later booster doses. The earlier Salk vaccine was given by injection.

RABIES

Rabies is an acute viral infection endemic in warm-blooded animals in Africa and Eurasia as far west as central France. Ordinarily fatal in man, it is transmitted in the saliva of warm-blooded animals through broken skin as a result of a bite (e.g. from dogs, foxes, bats). The symptoms include spasm of the throat muscles when swallowing is attempted, aversion to water (hence the alternative name 'hydrophobia'), maniacal behaviour, and finally involvement of other muscles to cause paralysis and death. Vaccine is available for those in high-risk occupations. The last case contracted by man in the UK was in 1922.

RHEUMATIC FEVER

Rheumatic fever is caused by streptococcal bacteria and can, like scarlet fever, occur as a sequel to tonsillitis. The symptoms are fever and an arthritis that seems to move from one joint to another, causing swelling and pain. Rheumatic fever may cause damage to the heart valves, damage which only becomes apparent in later years. Occasionally it can cause chorea (St Vitus's dance), a type of involuntary movement. The disease can recur, but is today very much less common than 50 years ago. No immunization exists.

RUBELLA

See German measles.

SCARLET FEVER (SCARLATINA)

Scarlet fever is a throat infection caused by an airborne bacterium *Streptococcus pyogenus*. Symptoms include fever and a sore throat, complicated by the appearance of a uniform pink blush of the skin, which on close inspection appears as many fine red points. The cheeks are usually flushed and the area round the lips is white (circumoral pallor). The tongue has a strawberry-like colour. About a week after the rash appears there is often peeling of the skin, especially on the hands and feet. The condition is sometimes accompanied by ear and kidney infections. The incubation period is between two and five days and cases are infectious for up to ten days unless treated with penicillin. In recent years this disease seems to have become much milder in developed countries, in part because of the use of antibiotics and in part because of improved social conditions. Complications are now accordingly rare.

SCHISTOSOMIASIS (BILHARZIA)

Bilharzia is a tropical disease caused by infestation of the body with larvae of the parasitic flatworm *Schistosoma*. Eggs excreted in the faeces or urine of infected people undergo part of the larval development in freshwater snails. Larvae released by the snails penetrate the skin of people bathing in infected water and colonize blood vessels in the intestine. Symptoms include diarrhoea, and an enlargement of the spleen and liver. The condition can be fatal.

SHINGLES (HERPES ZOSTER)

Shingles is caused by a reactivation of the *Herpes zoster* virus which causes chickenpox. The virus may be present and dormant in the nerve root for years before reactivation. This painful condition is therefore not truly infectious, but it is possible to pass it on as chickenpox by close physical contact. Symptoms include groups of small blisters on a red base that appear in the skin area supplied by a particular nerve root, for example in a narrow band round one side of the chest or abdomen. The groups of blisters commonly occur in a band on one side of the face, or on one limb. Pain may precede the rash by two to three days, and may endure at the site for an average of six weeks. Sensitivity (post-herpetic neuralgia) may last for months.

SMALLPOX

The World Health Organization has declared the world free of smallpox from 1 January 1980. Vaccination is only needed for certain research scientists.

SYPHILIS

Syphilis is a sexually transmitted (venereal) disease caused by the bacterium *Treponema pallidum*. The disease has three stages. The primary stage begins after an incubation phase of (usually) two to four weeks and is characterized by a firm ulcer on the site of infection, usually the genitalia, accompanied by swelling in the nearest lymph glands (e.g. the groin). The secondary stage – six weeks later – has varying characteristics, including skin rashes, mouth ulcers, glandular swelling, and fever with muscle aches. The tertiary stage follows after a long dormant period (up to 25 years) and can affect any organ of the body but particularly the brain and nerves, possibly causing insanity, blindness and loss of balance. Syphilis may also cause localized swellings (gumma) in the skin, bones or heart. Diagnosis is by blood tests, and treatment by penicillin.

TETANUS (LOCKJAW)

The bacterium *Clostridium tetani* is widespread in nature, commonly occurring in the topsoil. Tetanus spores can gain access to the body through cuts, resulting in intense muscle spasm ('lockjaw'). Prevention is by immunization with tetanus toxoid, given as three doses in infancy with booster doses at school age and then every five years. If immunity has waned the initial three doses are repeated.

THRUSH

Thrush is a fungal disease caused by the fungus *Candida albicans*, which lives in the alimentary canal and the vagina. Thrush arises when the growth of fungus increases, in some cases following a course of broad-spectrum antibiotics. It can be passed to a baby at birth. Thrush is characterized by white patches in the mouth (particularly in infants) and by irritation of the vagina.

TUBERCULOSIS (TB)

Tuberculosis is caused by the bacterium *Mycobacterium tuberculosis*, first discovered in 1882 by the German scientist Robert Koch (1843–1910). Evidence of this disease has been found in an Egyptian mummy from the 10th century BC. The mortality rate in England and Wales in the 1850s was 60 000 per year, both adults and children dying of what was known as 'consumption'. Two strains of organism exist – human and bovine. The main source of bovine tuberculosis was infected milk, but this has been eliminated in the developed world by pasteurization. The source of the human strain is the respiratory tract of an 'open' case of pulmonary tuberculosis, i.e. the organism is coughed up or breathed out by the sufferer.

The initial infection is in the lungs and the lymph glands in the middle of the chest cavity. In the majority of cases there are no symptoms and the infection heals without treatment, but may leave a scar on the lung. During this primary infection the body develops an immunity that can be detected by means of the Mantoux test. In this test a tiny amount of dead tubercle is injected just under the skin surface and if immunity is present a raised red lump develops. In a minority of primary infections, insufficient immunity develops and the infection spreads either all through the lungs (consumption or miliary pulmonary tuberculosis) or to other organs, leading to meningitis or kidney or bone infection. In cases where the primary illness has disappeared, the infection can flare up again years later, particularly if there is undernourishment or general debility. This is known as chronic tuberculosis and most commonly affects the lungs, but can affect any organ.

Modern drug treatment is very effective for all forms of the disease, but 'open' cases are still kept in isolation until their sputum becomes free of the infecting organism. Immunization is achieved by BCG (*Bacille Calmette-Guérin*), a live attenuated vaccine (i.e. a very mild form of TB) first used in 1906. It is given by injection into the skin and results in a small ulcer that heals after several weeks, leaving a scar.

TYPHOID

Typhoid is an infection of the digestive system caused by the bacterium *Salmonella typhi*, transmitted to the body by faecally contaminated food or water. Symptoms begin with fever and progress to a rash and profuse diarrhoea with blood loss. Untreated, the mortality rate is 10 to 15 per cent; the remainder of cases recover after about three weeks, although some three per cent become chronic carriers without symptoms. The last major epidemic in the UK was in

Aberdeen in 1964, when 414 cases occurred. Immunization is achieved with two injections at an interval of one month, and immunity lasts for five years.

TYPHUS

Typhus is the name given to a group of closely related acute infectious diseases caused by *Rickettsia* parasites, which are transmitted by lice, fleas or ticks. Typhus is characterized by severe headaches, rash, high fever and delirium, and can be fatal. Typhus has been eliminated from the developed world but remains a threat to undernourished people living in unhygienic conditions in developing countries.

VARICELLA

See Chickenpox.

WHOOPING COUGH (PERTUSSIS)

Whooping cough is an acute respiratory infection caused by the bacterium *Bordetella pertussis*. It is transmitted by direct contact or by airborne infection. In developing countries, where poor nutrition exists, whooping cough has a considerable death rate. It can affect any age group, but is most common in children and is most severe in young babies. The illness begins with what seems to be an ordinary cold, but, instead of improving after a few days, the cough becomes progressively worse and is most severe at night. There are spasms of coughing, with one cough after another, until the child is forced to take in breath rapidly with a loud whooping sound. During an attack the child becomes red (or even blue) in the face, with streaming eyes. A severe coughing spasm usually ends with a bout of vomiting. These symptoms may persist for several weeks before easing, but often a cough at night may persist for several months after the infection. Complications include middle ear infection, pneumonia, and encephalitis (brain infection).

The incubation period is seven to ten days. The disease is highly infectious from seven days after exposure to three weeks after the symptoms develop. Before the introduction of vaccine in 1957 there were on average some 100 000 cases per year in the UK. By 1973, when vaccine acceptance was 80 per cent, cases had fallen to 2400. In the mid-1970s levels of vaccination fell to about 30 per cent and major epidemics followed in 1977, 1979, 1981 and 1983. Mortality from whooping cough in the UK in the 1970s remained about 1 per 1000 notified cases, with a higher death rate for infants under one year. Three vaccinations are usually given in combination with diphtheria and tetanus vaccine. Complications of vaccination are very rare, and are considerably less likely than a child dying of the disease.

NON-INFECTIOUS DISEASES

Diseases that are not transmitted have – in the developed world – replaced infections as the primary health problem. Infectious diseases such as smallpox, tuberculosis and diphtheria have been ousted from their positions as major killers by cancer, heart disease and strokes.

While factors such as an inappropriate diet, lack of exercise, excessive intake of alcohol and tobacco smoking have to take the blame for many of the diseases that afflict people today, they are not the only culprits. The genes that each of us inherits from our parents may also put us at risk from developing heart disease, schizophrenia, rheumatoid arthritis or certain types of cancer. More than 4000 genetic diseases result from the inheritance of a mutant gene.

MAJOR GENETIC DISEASES AND DISORDERS

Cystic fibrosis a hereditary mutation resulting in abnormally thick mucous secretions in the lungs and intestine. Treatment for digestive problems and lung infections can help to prolong the lives of people with cystic fibrosis, many of whom survive into their mid-twenties.

Diabetes mellitus a common and – as yet – incurable metabolic disease. In many cases the disease is genetically determined but it can also be precipitated by certain viral infections, toxins, chronic disease or pregnancy (usually temporary). In all cases, the primary defect is an absolute or relative deficiency of pancreatic insulin. Insulin deficiency results in profound metabolic derangements, the most common of which is hyperglycaemia (blood glucose levels above the normal range of 50 to 120 mg per 100 millilitres).

As blood sugar rises, glucose appears in the urine, carrying water with it and giving rise to the increased urine output and thirst that characterizes the disorder. Fat metabolism may also be enhanced leading to the accumulation of acidic by-products which, if unchecked, can result in coma or death. Diabetics can become susceptible to degenerative complications involving the nerves, eyes, kidneys and blood vessels, and it is these secondary problems that make diabetes such a devastating disease. Many diabetics are treated by dietary restrictions and the use of drugs, but some are dependent upon daily administration of insulin to control their symptoms.

Down's syndrome a chromosomal abnormality in which the affected child has an extra copy of chromosome number 21. The condition is characterized by a flat face and nose, a vertical fold of skin at the inner edge of the eye, short fingers, and mental retardation. Formerly known as mongolism, the syndrome is named after the English physician John Langdon-Down (1828–96).

Huntington's chorea a particularly distressing hereditary disease, affecting one person in 20 000. Dementia (a disorder of the mental processes) and uncontrolled movements occur, but the symptoms fail to become apparent until the affected person has reached middle age. By this time, he or she has often had children who risk suffering the same fate.

Sickle-cell disease a hereditary blood disease that mainly affects people with malarial immunity – usually people from Africa and their descendants – although it was common in malarial parts of Europe. Large numbers of red blood cells in sufferers become sickle-shaped and can cause obstructions in the blood vessels, with possible damage to organs such as the kidneys and the brain. No satisfactory treatment has yet been developed.

Thalassaemia a hereditary disease caused by a haemoglobin deficiency. Affected red blood cells cannot function normally, resulting in anaemia, enlargement of the spleen, and bone-marrow disorders. Thalassaemia – which is common in Mediterranean countries, Asia and Africa – can be treated by repeated blood transfusions.

MAJOR ENVIRONMENTAL DISEASES

Environmental hazards such as radiation and pollutants account for some types of disease. People normally encounter only small doses of radiation, from diagnostic X-rays or perhaps as a treatment for cancer. In addition, everyone is exposed to low background levels of natural radiation from the Sun and from some types of rock. However, excessive doses of radiation may follow accidents, for example at nuclear reactors.

Chemical hazards are probably more often encountered at work than at home. The list of industrial diseases is long and includes poisoning by lead, mercury and other heavy metals.

Asbestosis an industrial disease caused by inhaling fibres of asbestos. The lungs become fibrous and the affected person not only experiences increasing breathlessness, with failure of the heart and lungs, but also has an increased risk of developing lung cancer.

Lead poisoning a debilitating condition resulting from an accumulation of lead in the body, usually from water pipes or lead-based paint. Symptoms are variable and include digestive problems, irritability, severe abdominal pain, constipation, anaemia and paralysis. The illness can be acute in children, and may result in brain damage, blindness, deafness and death.

Radiation sickness a disease caused by high exposures of radiation. It is characterized by loss of cells from the bone marrow and the lining of the stomach. The person loses appetite and suffers diarrhoea, sickness, chills, fever and extreme tiredness. Death may follow because of the damage to the bowel and bone marrow, the latter resulting in loss of resistance to infection and severe anaemia. Long-term sufferers are at risk of developing cancers.

CANCER

Cancer occurs when cells grow out of control. A single cell can accumulate changes in its genes that allow it to replicate in an uncontrolled way. Such a cell can give rise to a tumour, which may manifest itself as a palpable lump or mass. Once cells become cancerous they lose the function that they once had; they simply reproduce themselves indefinitely.

A tumour is said to be *benign* if it remains localized in the place where it originated. Nevertheless, benign tumours can be life-threatening if they jeopardize normal structures, e.g. benign tumours of the brain. *Malignant* tumours have the capacity to spread around the body. Individual cells, or groups of cells, can detach themselves from the primary tumour, migrate via the blood or the lymph and become deposited on other organs. There they form secondary tumours.

In many cases the cause of the cancer is unknown. Treatment for cancer varies according to the type of tumour, the site of the primary tumour, and the extent of the spread of cancerous cells. Chemotherapy – drug therapy – can produce long remissions in some forms of cancer, but side effects occur as normal cells are damaged and white blood cells become depleted. Radiation therapy uses ionizing radiation – including X-rays and gamma rays – to destroy cancer cells. Surgery is used to remove malignant growths but is only effective if cancer cells have not migrated into other parts of the body.

Carcinoma a cancer of the skin (*melanoma*) or of the inner tissues that cover the internal cavity structures of the breast, the respiratory tracts (including lung cancer), the gastro-intestinal tract (including cancers of the stomach, colon and rectum), the endocrine glands and the genitourinary tract (including cancers of the prostate, testes, fallo-

The following countries have the highest provision of hospital beds for every 10 000 inhabitants:

Country	Number of hospital beds per 10 000 inhabitants
Nauru	257
Sweden	200
Monaco	179
Norway	160
Iceland	151
Finland	136
USSR	134
Japan	130
North Korea	130
Luxembourg	125
Mongolia	111
Germany	108
Austria	108
France	103
Australia	102
Switzerland	100

pian tubes, ovaries, bladder and kidneys).

Leukaemia a cancer of the blood-forming tissues, related to sarcoma.

Lymphoma a cancer of the lymphoid cells; either Hodgkin's disease or non-Hodgkin's disease.

Sarcoma a cancer of the connective tissues, including bones, muscles, blood vessels and fibrous tissues.

HEART DISEASES

Heart disease is the leading cause of death in developed countries. Diseases of the heart may be genetic or caused by infection or environmental factors. There are four principal types:

Congenital cardiovascular disease a heart disease affecting one person in 200. The most common conditions include abnormalities of valves, narrowing of the aorta, shunt lesions (a malformation that allows oxygen-rich blood to be pumped back to the lungs) or the tetralogy of Fallot (a defect that commonly causes 'blue babies'). Some of these conditions may be hereditary, but often the reason for a defect is unknown. In many cases surgery to correct such defects is possible.

Coronary heart disease is the most common heart disease in developed countries and the most common cause of sudden death. The coronary arteries supply blood to the heart muscle. If the lining of these arteries becomes gradually thickened by fatty tissue (atheroma), the blood supply decreases. This causes episodes of chest pain (angina) often brought on by exercise. If a blood clot then develops at one such thickened area (coronary thrombosis), the artery becomes completely blocked causing a heart attack (myocardial infarction) or even sudden death. The main factors which put an individual at risk of coronary disease are cigarette smoking, high blood pressure and high levels of cholesterol in the blood. Other risk factors include obesity, lack of exercise, diabetes, stress and genetic factors such as a family history of coronary disease. Many drug treatments

are now available and surgery can bypass a narrowed artery.

Hypertensive heart disease a condition resulting from prolonged, untreated high blood pressure (hypertension). The high pressure within the arteries forces the heart to pump against a greater resistance. This strain initially causes an increase in the thickness of the heart muscle, and then an enlargement of the heart itself. If left untreated, the heart becomes unable to cope and heart failure results.

Rheumatic heart disease is becoming less common in developed countries, but remains a major problem in the Third World. It is a delayed complication of rheumatic fever which has usually occurred in childhood. Over the years, scarring of the heart valves causes increased narrowing of the valve (sterosis), or failure of the valve to close completely, thus allowing a back-flow of blood in the wrong direction (regurgitation or incompetence). By middle age breathlessness or heart failure may result. Surgical splitting of the valve (valvotomy) or valve replacement can be dramatically beneficial.

ALLERGIES

An allergy is a hypersensitivity or an abnormal response in the body to contact with a particular substance. The term was first used in 1906 by the German paediatrician Baron Clemens von Pirquet to describe an abnormal reaction to tuberculin. The reaction may provoke illnesses such as asthma, or may be mild, producing slight discomfort and inconvenience. Many individuals have only one specific allergy (for example to a particular food or drug), but some have an inherited susceptibility to allergy in general (atopy). Examples of allergy include:

Hay fever (allergic rhinitis) is a seasonal allergy characterized by sneezing, nasal congestion and itching of the eyes, and is caused by sensitivity to pollen from grass or trees in the spring and summer months.

Hives (urticaria) an intensely itchy skin reaction characterized by raised smooth red or pale weals. In severe cases there may be swelling of the lips or the skin around the eyes. The causal allergy may be to food (e.g. fish, eggs, berries), to drugs (e.g. penicillin), or to contact with chemicals, feathers or fur. Allergy to drugs may also take the form of a red blotchy rash rather like measles.

Asthma is a respiratory disorder characterized by wheezing owing to narrowing of the airways (bronchi), partly because of spasm in the muscle of the bronchi, and partly because of swelling and congestion of the lining (mucosa) of the bronchi. Childhood asthma, unlike asthma in later life, often occurs in those who are atopic (prone to allergy), and allergy to such things as house dust, feathers, pollen, and animal fur or hair can trigger asthma attacks. There is often a family history of allergy; boys are more often affected than girls, and childhood asthma may disappear at puberty. Attacks can also be triggered by infections, by irritants such as cold air or cigarette smoke, or by stress. Many drug treatments are now available, many in the form of inhalers.

ARTHRITIS

Arthritis is a term applied to a variety of conditions which cause pain in the joints. There are two main categories.

Osteoarthritis is the most common form of arth-

PHYSICIANS

The following countries have the highest provision of
physicians for every 10 000 inhabitants:

Country	Number of doctors per 10 000 inhabitants
Czechoslovakia	35.2
Hungary	33.9
Italy	33.1
Belgium	32.1
Austria	31.6
Spain	31.1
Bulgaria	30.2
Switzerland	28.2
Germany	27.4
Greece	27.4
New Zealand	27.1
Portugal	27.0
Monaco	26.6
Netherlands	26.4
Denmark	25.7
Andorra	25.2
France	25.0

ritis. It is a degeneration caused by 'wear and tear'.
The cartilage covering the bone ends becomes eroded
and this eventually leads to roughening and swelling
of the bone itself, especially at the edges of the joint.
Surgery to replace hip and knee joints which have
been badly affected by osteoarthritis is now
commonly performed.

Inflammatory arthritis takes many different
forms but is in general due to inflammation of the
tissues lining the joints (synovium). The milder
forms are popularly known as *rheumatism*; more
severe forms can be due to rheumatoid arthritis,
gout, or bacterial infection. In rheumatoid arthritis
the body's immune system starts to react against its
own synovial tissue, damaging it, and in the process
causing pain, stiffness and swelling of the joints. Any
joint may be affected, but the fingers are often an
obvious site. In its severe forms, progressive
deformity of joints occurs. In gout, tiny crystals of
the chemical uric acid are deposited within the joint
(characteristically the joint at the base of the big
toe) causing intense pain and tenderness. Bacterial
infection causing arthritis is uncommon and results
from an open wound, or spread of infection from
another area in the body (e.g. pneumonia or venereal
disease).

DRUGS USED BEFORE 1900

Drugs – the term includes any substance that acts on
living cells – may treat or prevent a disease or
condition, or may support a stressed or failing organ.
Before this century the number of drugs available
was limited. Most were derived from plant sources,
and only a few of these (or their derivatives) remain
in use today. They include:

Digitalis an extract of foxglove leaves used to
treat heart failure by herbalists in the 16th century
and introduced into scientific medicine by William
Withering in Britain in 1785. Its derivative, digoxin,
is still widely used to treat atrial fibrillation (a rapid
and irregular heart rhythm) and cardiac failure.

Morphine an addictive narcotic analgesic (pain-

killer) derived from opium – the dried fluid exuded
from unripe poppy capsules. First recognized by
Friedrich Sertürner in Germany in 1805, but not used
in medical practice until 1821. Synthesized in 1952.

Atropine a drug derived from belladonna (deadly
nightshade) with a variety of effects on different
body tissues. Its effects include increasing the heart
rate, dilating the pupil of the eye, reducing stomach
secretions, and inducing vomiting. It is also used to
treat peptic ulcers, and biliary and renal colic.
Isolated in 1819 by Rudolph Brondes.

Ether the first general anaesthetic agent to be
administered. It was first used by Dr Crawford W.
Long, in Jefferson, Georgia (USA), on 30 Mar 1842.

Nitrous oxide (laughing gas) an anaesthetic
agent discovered in 1776 by the English chemist
Joseph Priestley, but first used as an anaesthetic in
1844 by an American dentist, Horace Wells.

Chloroform an anaesthetic agent introduced in
1847 by the English obstetrician Sir James Simpson.

Phenol (carbolic acid) a crystalline soluble
acidic derivative of benzene, used as an antiseptic
and a disinfectant. The discovery by the English
surgeon Joseph Lister in 1865 that phenol had
disinfectant properties led to the development of
antiseptic surgery and a dramatic reduction in mortality.

DRUGS INTRODUCED 1900–70

The 20th century has seen the development of vast
numbers of potent drugs. Milestones in therapeutic
advances between 1900 and the 1960s have included:

1917 Oxygen first used therapeutically.

1921 Insulin (used to treat diabetes) isolated by
Frederick Banting and C.H. Best in Toronto,
Canada.

1929 Progesterone and testosterone isolated.

1935 Tubocurarine – a muscle-relaxing drug –
isolated by Harold King.

1937 The first antibiotics – sulphonamides – introduced. Sulphapyridine (May and Baker 693) was the
most widely used of the early antibiotics, the first
effective treatments for infection.

1938 Phenytoin – an anticonvulsant used to treat
epilepsy – introduced.

1939 DDT (dichloro-diphenyl-trichloroethane) developed by the Swiss chemist Dr Paul Muller. A
powerful insecticide, DDT vastly lowered the incidence of malaria by killing malaria-carrying mosquitoes.

1940 Penicillin first used therapeutically by Sir
Howard Florey and E.B. Chain. (In 1928 the Scottish
bacteriologist Sir Alexander Fleming had discovered
that penicillin would inhibit bacterial growth.)

1943 Streptomycin introduced – the first antibiotic
effective against tuberculosis.

1948 Imipramine – an anti-depressant – introduced.

1949 Cortisone – one of a number of steroid hormones secreted by the adrenal gland – first used
therapeutically in 1949 to reduce inflammation in
rheumatoid arthritis.

1951 Halothane – a safer anaesthetic gas – introduced.

1954 Methyldopa and Reserpine – the first effective
treatments for high blood pressure – introduced.

1955 Oral contraceptives introduced. The first field
studies of a pill that could prevent ovulation were
conducted in Puerto Rico.

Early 1960s Chlordiazepoxide (Librium) and diazepan (Valium) introduced – tranquillizers for the treatment of tension and anxiety.

MODERN DRUGS

In the last few decades drugs have been discovered and developed to treat every body system and many diverse features within each system. Mentioned below are some of the most commonly prescribed drugs, classified according to their use.

The preparations listed include the vast majority of drugs currently prescribed, with the exception of antibiotics and contraceptives. Drugs are in general listed below under their 'generic names' rather than the trade names given to the preparations by the various manufacturers.

CARDIOVASCULAR SYSTEM

Beta-blockers Beta-blockers are used to slow heart rate, reduce high blood pressure and reduce anginal pain, particularly if precipitated by exercise. Examples include propanolol, atenolol, metoprolol, and pindolol.

Calcium antagonists Calcium antagonists relax the muscle layer in the walls of blood vessels. They are used in the treatment of high blood pressure, angina, and in some disorders of heart rhythm. Examples include nifedipine, verapamil, diltiazem, nicardipine.

Ace inhibitors Ace inhibitors are used in the treatment of high blood pressure, and recently also for cardiac failure. They act on the angiotensin-converting enzyme – ACE – within the kidney to modify levels of a chemical that controls blood pressure by constricting blood vessels. Examples include captopril, enalapril, and lisinopril.

Nitrates Nitrates are derived from the explosive agent nitroglycerine. They are used to dilate blood vessels and so ease anginal pain. Glyceryl trinitrate is the simplest form and is absorbed quickly if the tablet is dissolved under the tongue. Longer-acting preparations can be absorbed through the skin if worn as Elastoplast-like patches.

Digoxin See digitalis (Drugs used before 1900).

Diuretics ('water tablets') Diuretics stimulate urinary production. They are used to treat cardiac failure by removing excess fluid from the lungs, to reduce congestion in the liver, and to reduce fluid retention in the legs. Some diuretics can also be used to treat high blood pressure. Examples include frusemide, bumetanide, and bendrofluazide (which tend to encourage the excretion of potassium); amiloride, triamterene, and spironolactone (which tend to encourage the retention of potassium).

RESPIRATORY SYSTEM

Beta$_2$ agonists Beta$_2$ agonists relax the muscle in the walls of the bronchial tubes, and thus relieve the spasm occurring in these airways in asthma. At first they were mainly given orally, but in recent years they have usually been administered by inhalation, either from an aerosol or in devices designed to deliver a small amount of powder by inhalation. Examples include salbutamol, terbutaline, and rimiterol. (These have replaced older drugs such as isoprenaline, orciprenaline, and ephedrine.)

Sodium cromoglycate Sodium cromoglycate is administered by inhalation to treat asthma caused by allergy (mainly asthma in childhood). It does so by blocking the release of histamine from the mast cells and thus reducing inflammation in the bronchial tubes.

Inhaled steroids When given by inhalation, steroids can be used in very low dosage to treat asthma. The steroid reduces the sensitivity of the bronchial tubes, but it is not absorbed into the rest of the body. Examples include beclomethosone and budesonide.

GASTROINTESTINAL SYSTEM

Antacids Antacids include a large number of preparations all of which are alkaline, can neutralize gastric acids, and thus reduce indigestion. Some are combined with a seaweed derivate (alginate) to form a sticky protective layer on the lining of the upper stomach or lower gullet to reduce heartburn.

H$_2$ antagonists H$_2$ antagonists block the nerve endings in the stomach responsible for the secretion of gastric acid. These drugs have proved a very effective treatment for duodenal ulcers – a condition which until the mid-1970s frequently required surgery. The original compound cimetidine has been followed by other agents. Examples include ranitidine, and more recently nizatidine and famotidine.

PSYCHIATRIC CONDITIONS

actual neurosis a term coined by Freud to describe the physiological results of current disturbances.

affective disorder a psychosis in which disturbances of mood occur.

agitated an adjective used to describe depressions when they make the patient anxious, tense and restless.

alienation a state of feeling in which the patient feels set apart from or removed from either himself or others.

amnesia an inability to remember.

anhedonia an inability to experience pleasure.

anorexia an absence of appetite.

anxiety an irrational fear, often in response to an unrecognized stimulus.

apathy an absence of emotion.

aphanisis the fear of losing the ability to experience pleasure.

autism a childhood disorder, often persisting into adulthood, in which the patient appears to be cut off from his environment; the senses function normally, but there appears to be little perception.

behaviour disorders a group of conditions in which the behaviour of the patient is unacceptable to society.

catatonia a schizophrenic condition in which the patient suffers periods of excitement and/or stupor, during which he seems out of touch with his environment.

conversion hysteria a psychoneurosis in which the patient's symptoms are physical complaints, i.e. the symptoms are physical in their expression but psychoneurotic in their origin.

delusion a fixed idea, held by a patient, that is at variance with the beliefs and ideas held by normal people.

dementia a physical deterioration in the brain,

resulting in mental deterioration and disorder.

depersonalization a feeling of unreality.

depression a disorder of mood in which the patient suffers from low spirits (the traditional 'melancholy'), an impairment of some mental processes, and often a lack of sleep and appetite.

disassociation the existence of two or more mental processes that lack any connection.

elation a feeling of high spirits accompanying mania.

engulfment an extreme form of anxiety in which all relationships with others are seen as threatening.

exhibitionism a compulsive behaviour pattern, usually taken to mean the sexual perversion, invariably on the part of the male, in which the sex organs are exposed to a female.

extraversion an outgoing behaviour pattern. This is a component, to a greater or lesser extent, of most people's behaviour; it only becomes a problem when taken to extremes. Compare introversion.

fixation an attachment to a concept, object or person, usually appropriate to an earlier stage of development.

fugue a period of seemingly automatic behaviour which the subject subsequently cannot remember.

guilt a feeling of remorse attached to an action that has already occurred. It becomes neurotic when the action has not transgressed any value systems of the patient.

hallucination a sensation with no physical origin. Hallucinations can occur as a result of physical illness, or they can be psychotic, usually associated with schizophrenia.

hebephrenia a form of schizophrenia in which the sufferer neglects his person and appears withdrawn, often with unusual mannerisms.

hypochondriasis an imagined belief on the patient's part that he is ill, often with an incurable complaint.

hypomania a mild form of mania.

hysteria a form of neurosis, involving anxiety and physical symptoms, usually associated with a part of the body about which the patient is concerned, although there is an absence of any physical foundation for these symptoms.

illusion a misinterpretation of something that has actually occurred.

implosion the fear of being destroyed by reality.

inferiority complex a feeling of inadequacy.

inhibition the suppression of a function by the operation of another function.

introversion an introspective behaviour pattern. This is a component, to a greater or lesser extent, of most people's behaviour; it only becomes a problem when taken to extremes.

involutional melancholia a severe depression occurring at the time of the menopause.

mania a psychosis in which elation, excitement, insomnia and sometimes exhaustion eventually lead to rapid and aimless thought.

manic depressive psychosis a psychosis in which a cycle of depression and elation repeats itself. The patient is seemingly unable to control the cycle.

melancholia another term for depression.

neurasthenia an ill-defined form of tiredness that can almost be seen as a neurosis.

neurosis a mental disorder of the personality in which there is no organic damage to the nervous system. Someone suffering from a neurosis is aware that something is wrong. Compare psychosis.

obsessional neurosis a neurosis characterized by obsessions, i.e. ideas that constantly impose themselves on the patient's thinking. The resulting behaviour is repetitive, even ritualistic.

organic mental illness a mental illness resulting from damage to or a disorder of the brain.

paranoia a psychosis in which the patient suffers from delusions of persecution, often organized into a complex and coherent system that controls the patient's life.

phobia an unrealistic and excessive fear of an object or situation; a form of anxiety.

psychomotor acceleration the speeding up of thoughts and actions that occurs in mania.

psychomotor retardation the slowing down of thoughts and actions that occurs in depression.

psychopathy an antisocial, irresponsible aggressive behaviour pattern that is often impulsive.

psychosis a mental disorder that leaves the patient out of touch with reality; he is unaware of his disorder. Psychoses can either be organic, in which case disease of the brain can be shown, or functional, in which no damage to the brain can be observed.

psychosomatic illness the physiological symptoms and disturbances of function caused by the patient's personality and psychological disturbances.

regression a behaviour pattern more appropriate to an earlier stage of life, often sparked off by stress.

schizophrenia a functional psychosis characterized by disturbances of thinking, motivation and mood, coupled with hallucinations and delusions.

stupor a complete lack of movement and responsiveness, due either to organic or psychiatric causes.

traumatic neurosis a neurosis that develops shortly after an unexpected and traumatic experience. The neurosis involves the periodic reliving of the traumatic experience.

PHOBIAS

A phobia is an intense and irrational fear of an object, a situation or an organism. Terms have been coined for a wide range of phobias, including the following:

ANIMAL AND PLANT PHOBIAS

animals	zoophobia
bacteria	bacteriophobia, microphobia
bees	apiphobia, melissophobia
birds	ornithophobia
cats	ailurophobia, gatophobia
chickens	alektorophobia
dogs	cynophobia
feathers	pteronophobia
fish	ichthyophobia
flowers	anthophobia
fur	doraphobia
horses	hippophobia
insects	entomophobia
leaves	phyllophobia
lice	pediculophobia

mice	musophobia
microbes	bacilliphobia
parasites	parasitophobia
reptiles	batrachophobia
snakes	ophidiophobia,
	ophiophobia
spiders	arachnophobia
trees	dendrophobia
wasps	spheksophobia
worms	helminthophobia

ENVIRONMENTAL PHOBIAS

auroral lights	auroraphobia
clouds	nephophobia
dampness,	hygrophobia
moisture	
flood	antlophobia
fog	homichlophobia
ice, frost	cryophobia
lakes	limnophobia
lightning	astraphobia
meteors	meteorophobia
precipices	cremnophobia
rain	ombrophobia
rivers	potamophobia
sea	thalassophobia
snow	chionophobia
stars	siderophobia
sun	heliophobia
thunder	brontophobia,
	keraunophobia
water	hydrophobia
wind	ancraophobia

FOOD AND DRINK PHOBIAS

drink, alcohol	potophobia
drinking	dipsophobia
eating	phagophobia
food	sitophobia
meat	carnophobia

HEALTH AND ANATOMICAL PHOBIAS

beards	pogonophobia
blood	haematophobia
cancer	cancerophobia,
	carcinophobia
childbirth	tocophobia
cholera	cholerophobia
death, corpse	necrophobia,
	thanatophobia
deformity	dysmorphophobia
disease	nosophobia,
	pathophobia
drugs	pharmacophobia
eyes	ommatophobia
faeces	coprophobia
germs	spermophobia
hair	chaetophobia
heart conditions	cardiophobia
heredity	patroiophobia
illness	nosemaphobia
infection	mysophobia
inoculations,	trypanophobia
injections	
insanity	lyssophobia,
	maniaphobia
knees	genuphobia
leprosy	leprophobia
mind	psychophobia
physical love	erotophobia
poison	toxiphobia
pregnancy	maieusiophobia
semen	spermatophobia

sex	genophobia
sexual intercourse	coitophobia
skin	dermatophobia
skin disease	dermatosiophobia
soiling	rypophobia
surgical operations	ergasiophobia
syphilis	syphilophobia
teeth	odontophobia
tuberculosis	phthisiophobia
venereal disease	cypridophobia
vomiting	emetophobia
wounds, injury	traumatophobia

INANIMATE OBJECT PHOBIAS

books	bibliophobia
crystals, glass	crystallophobia
flutes	aulophobia
glass	nelophobia
machinery	mechanophobia
metals	metallophobia
mirrors	eisoptrophobia
missiles	ballistophobia
money	chrometophobia
needles	belonophobia
pins	enetephobia
points	aichurophobia
slime	blennophobia,
	myxophobia
string	linonophobia

MISCELLANEOUS PHOBIAS

certain names	onomatophobia
cheerfulness	cherophobia
darkness	nyctophobia
dawn	eosophobia
daylight	phengophobia
depth	bathophobia
dirt	mysophobia
disorder	ataxiophobia
dolls	pediophobia
draughts	anemophobia
dreams	oneirophobia
duration	chronophobia
dust	amathophobia,
	koniphobia
electricity	electrophobia
everything	pantophobia
failure	kakorraphiaphobia
fall of man-made	keraunothnetophobia
satellites	
fears	phobophobia
fire	pyrophobia
flashes	selaphobia
flogging	mastigophobia
freedom	eleutherophobia
ghosts	phasmophobia
graves	taphophobia
gravity	barophobia
ideas	ideophobia
imperfection	atelophobia
jealousy	zelophobia
justice	dikephobia
making false	mythophobia
statements	
many things	polyphobia
marriage	gamophobia
monsters,	teratophobia
monstrosities	
music	musicophobia
names	nomatophobia
narrowness	anginaphobia
neglect of duty	paralipophobia

new things	neophobia
night, darkness	achluophobia
novelty	cainophobia
nudity	gymnophobia
number 13	triskaidekaphobia,
	terdekaphobia
one thing	monophobia
poverty	peniaphobia
punishment	poinephobia
responsibility	hypegiaphobia
ridicule	katagelophobia
ruin	atephobia
rust	iophobia
shock	hormephobia
stealing	kleptophobia
stillness	eremophobia
strong light	photophobia
void	kenophobia
weakness	asthenophobia
words	logophobia
work	ergophobia
writing	graphophobia

PHOBIAS CONCERNING GROUPS

black people	negrophobia
children	paediphobia
human beings	anthropophobia
men	androphobia
robbers	harpaxophobia
women	gynophobia
young girls	parthenophobia

PHOBIAS CONCERNING RELIGION

churches	ecclesiaphobia
demons	demonophobia
God	theophobia
heaven	ouranophobia
hell	hadephobia,
	stygiophobia
sacred things	hierophobia
Satan	Satanophobia
sinning	peccatophobia

SENSORY PHOBIAS

being cold	frigophobia
being dirty	automysophobia
being scratched	amychophobia
being touched	haphephobia
blushing	ereuthophobia,
	eyrythrophobia
cold	cheimatophobia
colour	chromatophobia,
	chromophobia,
	psychrophobia
fatigue	kopophobia,
	ponophobia
heat	thermophobia
itching	acarophobia,
	scabiophobia
noise	phonophobia
odours	osmophobia
odours (body)	osphresiophobia
pain	algophobia,
	odynophobia
pleasure	hedonophobia
sleep	hypnophobia
smell	olfactophobia
smothering, choking	pnigerophobia
sound	akousticophobia
speaking	halophobia
speaking aloud	phonophobia
speech	lalophobia

sourness	acerophobia
stings	cnidophobia
stooping	kyphophobia
taste	geumatophobia
thinking	phronemophobia
touch	haptophobia
touching	haphephobia,
	thixophobia
trembling	tremophobia

SITUATION PHOBIAS

being alone	monophobia,
	autophobia
being beaten	rhabdophobia
being bound	merinthophobia
being buried alive	taphophobia
being looked at	scopophobia
crowds	demophobia,
	ochlophobia
enclosed spaces	claustrophobia
going to bed	clinophobia
heights	acrophobia,
	altophobia
high places	hypsophobia
home	domatophobia,
	oikophobia
home surroundings	ecophobia
infinity	apeirophobia
passing high objects	batophobia
places	topophobia
open spaces	agoraphobia
school	scholionophobia
shadows	sciophobia
sitting idle	thaasophobia
standing	stasophobia
standing upright	stasiphobia
solitude	eremitophobia,
	eremophobia

TRAVEL PHOBIAS

crossing a bridge	gephyrophobia
crossing streets	dromophobia
flying, the air	aerophobia
motion	kinesophobia,
	kinetophobia
sea swell	cymophobia
speed	tachophobia
travel	hodophobia
travelling by train	siderodromophobia
vehicles	amaxophobia,
	ochophobia
walking	basiphobia

SCHOOLS OF PSYCHOLOGY

Adlerian psychology see individual psychology.

analytical psychology a branch of psychology developed by Jung as a result of disagreements with Freud. See Jungian theory.

behavioural psychology a school of psychology largely based on the work of B.F. Skinner (see below). Its central tenet is that human behaviour can be modified by reinforcement, i.e. the provision of a 'reward' – either physical or social – or the avoidance of punishment. It assumes that the symptom is the illness and that the patient can be 'cured' by deconditioning and reconditioning.

body-centred psychology a loose grouping of therapies and ideas – rather than a school of psychology – in which work on the physical body results in an alteration in the personality or the image of self. It includes such diverse philosophies and therapies as yoga, the Alexander technique and rolfing (see Complementary medicine) and T'ai Chi.

clinical psychology a practically based area of psychology in which research findings and methods are applied to human behaviour, both normal and abnormal. It is a broadly based discipline, encompassing experimental psychology, social psychology, environmental psychology, and ethology.

developmental psychobiology the study of biological processes and systems that affect the development of behaviour. In particular, interest focuses on the behavioural characteristics enabling species to cope with environmental challenges, and the behaviour and development of the young as they relate to their environment.

ego psychology a branch of psychoanalytical theory that has developed from Freud's book *The Ego and the Id*. It is now associated with Freud's daughter, Anna Freud (see below), who developed the thinking in *The Ego and the Mechanisms of Defence*. Ego psychology concentrates on the manner in which the individual develops and acquires functions that enable him to control his impulses and his environment and to act independently.

existential analysis an area of psychology heavily influenced by existential philosophers such as Sartre and Heidegger (see Philosophy). Essentially it lays emphasis on the here and now, expecting the patient to take responsibility for his actions through which his life will take on meaning. There is little emphasis on the unconscious mental processes dwelt on by other schools of psychology.

Freudian psychoanalysis the classical psychoanalysis that can be traced back directly to teachings and writings of Freud (see below), particularly to his *An Outline of Psychoanalysis*.

humanistic psychology a branch of psychology in which the self-image of the patient (client) is paramount. The therapist is honest with the patient, but does not seek to change the patient by any approval or disapproval. This school was developed by the American psychologist Carl Ransom Rogers.

individual psychology a branch of psychoanalysis founded by Adler (see below), who regarded the individual as responsible for his own actions and able to work towards his own goals.

Jungian theory a branch of psychology contained within the ideas of Carl Gustav Jung (see below) and covering a very wide spectrum of psychology.

Kleinian theory a branch of psychology contained in the ideas of Klein (see below), who laid emphasis on the first year of a child's life as being a time rich in fantasy and a time during which the origins of neurosis occur.

learning theory a group of psychological theories that aim to explain individual behaviour and personality arising as a result of learned reactions and responses to the environment. This is in contrast to psychoanalysis, which sees behaviour and personality arising as a result of developmental processes.

neo-Freudian theory a variety of psychological thought united by the common thread that those who formulated its ideas initially espoused Freud's ideas on psychoanalysis, but subsequently broke away from, or modified, or added to, Freud's thinking. In general neo-Freudian theory emphasizes the social needs of individuals to a greater extent than Freud did.

neurolinguistics a combination of psychology, linguistics and neurology that looks at the acquisition of language, its production and processing, and its disruption or disturbances, especially those disturbances related to organic brain disease.

neuropsychiatry the study of organic brain disorders and the effects they have on behaviour and personality.

phenomenology literally, the study of phenomena, i.e. of the experiences that we have and the effect they have on personality and behaviour.

psychiatry the treatment and study of mental, emotional, personality and behavioural disorders.

psychoanalysis a method of treating mental illness, originated by Sigmund Freud. Psychoanalysis aims to bring to the surface those fears and conflicts between instinct and conscience that have been pushed into the unconscious.

psychology the study of the mind, of behaviour and of thinking.

psychopathology the study of the abnormal workings of the mind and of abnormal behaviour.

psychosynthesis a branch of psychological thinking that aims to bring together those elements of personality that are at odds with each other.

psychotherapy the treatment of mental disturbance, personality problems, behavioural difficulties, etc., by psychological means. Invariably a strong link is forged between the therapist and the patient, who often meet on a one-to-one basis.

radical therapy a relatively recent movement in psychology that calls into question society's definitions of such words as 'sane' and 'insane'. In radical therapy, 'insanity' – if there is such a thing – is seen as a social problem needing social solutions. Radical therapy – which undermines the medical model of psychology – was developed by R.D. Laing, and derives much from existentialism and humanism (see Philosophy).

social psychiatry the examination of mental disorder as a part of society. Both the social causes of such disorders and the social methods of prevention are looked at.

MAJOR PSYCHOLOGISTS

Alfred Alder (1870–1937), Austrian psychiatrist who coined the term inferiority feeling (later inaccurately called the inferiority complex). He developed a system of individual and supportive psychotherapy to help those emotionally crippled by feelings of inferiority.

Sigmund Freud (1856–1939), Austrian psychiatrist and originator of psychoanalysis. (See Ego psychology, Freudian analysis, and psychoanalysis above.)

Karen Horney (1885–1956), German-born American neo-Freudian psychologist who concentrated on the experience of childhood as the basis for neurosis, postulating that such neuroses can be avoided by good child care.

Carl Gustav Jung (1875–1961), Swiss psychologist – initially associated with Sigmund Freud in the development of psychoanalysis – who subsequently developed his own ideas. One of his most important contributions was to develop a 16-category typology of character, e.g. introversion, extraversion, thinking, feeling, etc.

Melanie Klein (1875–1961), Austrian-born British psychologist whose theories were in general within the mainstream of Freudian psychoanalysis, although there were important departures in child psychiatry. See Kleinian theory above.

Henry Stack Sullivan (1892–1949), American neo-Freudian psychiatrist whose ideas on personality were based on his observations of the patterns existing in social and interpersonal relations, and the development of personality within these patterns.

Anna Freud (1895–1952), Austrian-born British founder of child psychoanalysis. See Ego psychology above.

Erich Fromm (1900–80), German-born American neo-Freudian psychologist who was influenced by existential philosophy. He came to emphasize the part that society as a whole – its structures, expectations, etc. – has to play in determining the way in which an individual copes with basic human needs.

Jacques Lacan (1901–81), French psychoanalyst who introduced elements of structuralism and linguistics into psychoanalysis and psychology.

B(urrhus) F(rederic) Skinner (1904–), American psychologist whose work was the basis of behavioural psychology.

R(onald) D(avid) Laing (1927–), Scottish psychiatrist responsible for much pioneering work in the area of radical therapy and for bringing a more humanistic approach to psychology.

NOBEL PRIZEWINNERS IN PHYSIOLOGY OR MEDICINE

The Nobel Prize for achievement in physiology or medicine is awarded annually under the terms of the will of Alfred Nobel by the Royal Caroline Medico-Chirurgical Institute in Stockholm (Sweden).

1901 Emil von Behring, German: serum therapy
1902 Sir Ronald Ross, English: discovery of how malaria enters an organism
1903 Niels R. Finsen, Danish: light radiation treatment of skin diseases
1904 Ivan Pavlov, Russian: physiology of digestion
1905 Robert Koch, German: tuberculosis research
1906 Camillo Golgi, Italian, and S. Ramón y Cajal, Spanish: structure of nervous system
1907 Alphonse Laveran, French: discovery of the role of protozoa in diseases
1908 Paul Ehrlich, German, and Ilya Mechnikov, Russian: immunity systems research
1909 Emil Kocher, Swiss: physiology, pathology and surgery of thyroid gland
1910 Albrecht Kossel, German: cellular chemistry research
1911 Allvar Gullstrand, Swedish: dioptics of the eye
1912 Alexis Carrel, French: vascular suture and transplantation of organs
1913 Charles Richet, French: anaphylaxis research
1914 Robert Bárány, Austrian: vestibular apparatus of the inner ear
1915–18 No awards
1919 Jules Bordet, Belgian: immunity system
1920 August Krogh, Danish: discovery of the capillary motor-regulating mechanism
1921 No award
1922 Archibald Hill, English: heat production in muscles; and Otto Meyerhof, German: metabolism of lactic acid in muscles
1923 Sir Frederick Banting, Canadian, and J.J.R.

Macleod, Scottish: discovery of insulin
1924 Willem Einthoven, Dutch: discovery of electrocardiogram mechanism
1925 No award
1926 Johannes Fibiger, Danish: cancer research
1927 J. Wagner von Jauregg, Austrian: malaria inoculation in dementia paralytica
1928 Charles Nicolle, French: typhus research
1929 Christiaan Eijkman, Dutch: discovery of antineuritic vitamin; and Sir Frederick Hopkins, English: discovery of growth stimulating vitamins
1930 Karl Landsteiner, American (naturalized): grouping of human blood
1931 Otto Warburg, German: discovery of the nature and action of a respiratory enzyme
1932 Edgar D. Adrian (Lord Adrian) and Sir Charles Sherrington, English: the function of neurons
1933 Thomas Hunt Morgan, American: the role of chromosomes in transmission of heredity
1934 George R. Minot, William P. Murphy and George H. Whipple, American: liver therapy to treat anaemia
1935 Hans Spemann, German: organization in embryos
1936 Sir Henry Dale, English, and Otto Loewi, German: chemical transmission of nerve impulses
1937 Albert Szent-Györgyi, Hungarian: biological combustion
1938 Corneille Heymans, Belgian: role of sinus and aortic mechanisms in respiration regulation
1939 Gerhard Domagk, German (declined – Hitler refused to allow Germans to accept Nobel Prizes): antibacterial effect of prontosil
1940–1942 No awards
1943 Henrik Dam, Danish: discovery of Vitamin K; and Edward A. Doisy, American: discovery of chemical nature of vitamin K
1944 Joseph Erlanger, and Herbert S. Gasser, American: differentiated functions of nerve fibres
1945 Sir Alexander Fleming, Scottish, Ernst Boris Chain, British (naturalized), and Howard Florey (Lord Florey), Australian: discovery of penicillin and its curative value
1946 Hermann J. Muller, American: production of mutations by X-ray irradiation
1947 Carl F. Cori and Gerty Cori, American (naturalized): discovery of catalytic conversion of glycogen; and Bernardo Houssay, Argentinian: pituitary hormone function in sugar metabolism
1948 Paul Müller, Swiss: properties of DDT
1949 Walter Rudolf Hess, Swiss: discovery of function of the midbrain; and António Egas Moniz, Portuguese: therapeutic value of leucotomy in psychoses
1950 Philip S. Hench and Edward Kendall, American, and Tadeusz Reichstein, Swiss: adrenal cortex hormones research
1951 Max Theiler, South African: yellow fever research
1952 Selman A. Waksman, American (naturalized): discovery of streptomycin
1953 Fritz A. Lipman, American (naturalized), and Sir Hans Krebs, British (naturalized): discovery of coenzyme, a citric acid cycle in metabolism of carbohydrates
1954 John F. Enders, Thomes H. Weller and Frederick Robbins, American: tissue culture

'LEAGUE TABLE' OF EC NOBEL PRIZEWINNERS IN MEDICINE

United Kingdom	20
Germany	12
France	8
Denmark	5
Belgium	3
Italy	3
Netherlands	3
Portugal	1
Spain	1
Greece	0
Ireland	0
Luxembourg*	0

*Albert Claude, Nobel prizewinner in 1974, was a Luxembourger who became a naturalized American citizen.

of poliomyelitis viruses

1955 Axel Hugo Theorell, Swedish: nature and mode of action of oxidation enzymes

1956 Werner Forssmann, German, Dickinson Richards, American, and André F. Cournand, American (naturalized): heart catheterization and circulatory changes

1957 Daniel Bovet, Italian (naturalized): production of synthetic curare

1958 George W. Beadle and Edward L. Tatum, American: genetic regulation of chemical processes; and Joshua Lederberg, American: genetic recombination

1959 Severo Ochoa, American (naturalized), and Arthur Kornberg, American: production of artificial nucleic acids

1960 Sir MacFarlane Burnet, Australian, and Sir Peter B. Medawar, English: research into acquired immunity in tissue transplants

1961 Georg von Békésy, American (naturalized): functions of the inner ear

1962 Francis Crick, English, James D. Watson American, and Maurice Wilkins, English: molecular structure of DNA

1963 Sir John Eccles, Australian, Sir Alan Lloyd Hodgkin, English, and Sir Andrew Huxley, English: transmission of nerve impulses along a nerve fibre

1964 Konrad Bloch, American (naturalized), and Feodor Lynen, German: research into cholesterol and fatty acid metabolism

1965 François Jacob, Jacques Monod and André Lwoff, French: research into regulatory activities of body cells

1966 Charles B. Huggins, American (naturalized), and Francis Peyton Rous, American: cancer research

1967 Haldan Keffer Hartline and George Wald, American, and Ragner A. Granit, Swedish: chemical and physiological visual processes in the eye

1968 Robert W. Holley, American, H. Gobind Khorana, American (naturalized), and Marshall W. Nirenberg, American: research into deciphering the genetic code

1969 Max Delbrück, American (naturalized), Alfred D. Hershey, American, and Salvador E. Luria, American (naturalized): research into viruses and viral diseases

1970 Julius Axelrod, American, Sir Bernard Katz, British (naturalized), and Ulf von Euler, Swedish: chemistry of nerve transmission

1971 Earl W. Sutherland, American: the action of hormones

1972 Gerald M. Edelman, American, and Rodney Porter, English: research into the chemical structure of antibodies

1973 Karl von Frisch and Konrad Lorenz, Austrian, and Nikolaas Tinbergen, Dutch: animal behaviour patterns

1974 Albert Claude, American (naturalized), Christian R. de Duve, Belgian, and George E. Palade, American (naturalized): structural and functional organization of cells

1975 Renato Dulbecco, American (naturalized), Howard M. Temin and David Baltimore, American: interactions between tumour viruses and the genetic material of the cell

1976 Baruch S. Blumberg and Daniel Carleton Gajdusek, American: the origin and spread of infectious diseases

1977 Rosalyn S. Yalow, Roger Guillemin and Andrew Schally, American: development of radioimmunoassay and research on pituitary hormones

1978 Werner Arber, Swiss, Daniel Nathans and Hamilton O. Smith, American: discovery and application of enzymes that fragment DNA

1979 Allan M. Cormack, American (naturalized), and Sir Godfrey N. Hounsfield, English: development of computerized axial tomography scanning

1980 Baruj Benacerraf, American (naturalized), George D. Snell, American and Jean Dausset, French: genetic control of the immune response to foreign substances

1981 Roger W. Sperry, American: functions of the celebral hemispheres; and Torsten N. Wiesel, Swedish, and David H. Hubel, American (naturalized): visual information processing by the brain

1982 Sune K. Bergström and Bengt I. Samuelsson, Swedish, and Sir John R. Vane, English: biochemistry and physiology of prostaglandins

1983 Barbara McClintock, American: discovery of mobile plant genes which affect heredity

1984 Niels K. Jerne, British/Danish, Georges J. F. Köhler, German, and César Milstein, Argentinian: technique for producing monoclonal antibodies

1985 Michael S. Brown and Joseph L. Goldstein, American: discovery of cell receptors involved in cholesterol metabolism

1986 Stanley Cohen, American, and Rita Levi-Montalcini, Italian: discovery of chemical agents that help regulate cell growth

1987 Tonegawa Susumu, Japanese: research into genetic aspects of antibodies

1988 Sir James W. Black, Scottish, Gertrude B. Ellison and George H. Hitchings, American: development of new classes of drugs

1989 Harold Varmus and Michael Bishop, American: cancer research

1990 Joseph Murray and E. Donnall Thomas, American: transplant surgery.

COMPLEMENTARY MEDICINE

Complementary medicine includes any therapy outside orthodox Western medicine. Practitioners now prefer the term 'complementary' rather than 'alternative' medicine as they see themselves working alongside mainstream medicine. Some complementary therapies – such as yoga and acupuncture – have their roots in ancient civilizations; others, such as the Alexander technique and biofeedback, were developed recently.

In general, chronic, long-lasting illnesses have been found to respond most readily to alternative therapies. Some therapies, such as homoeopathy, also claim to be effective in many acute conditions such as burns, trauma and infections. As yet Western scientific medicine has been unable to explain fully how many of these therapies work. However, many people have undoubtedly obtained relief from them.

CHARACTERISTICS OF COMPLEMENTARY MEDICINE

The following characteristics are common to virtually every complementary therapy:
– a holistic approach, i.e. the therapist considers the state of an individual's body, mind and spirit and his environmental factors;
– an identification of the root causes of the illness;
– the provision of an opportunity for the patient's own natural healing processes to restore and maintain internal balances over time, rather than suppressing the symptoms more immediately;
– an encouragement to the patient to participate in his healing;
– a concern with diet, breathing and exercise, lifestyle and stress levels;
– taking preventive measures to avoid the need for drugs and surgery.

ACUPUNCTURE

Acupuncture – a traditional Chinese therapy – is more than 2000 years old. It is based on the belief that health depends on the individual's ability to maintain a balanced and harmonious internal environment. This is expressed through the principles of Yin and Yang, where spiritual, mental, emotional or physical blockages to the flow of vitality or 'life force' (*Chi*) may cause pain or disease. It is thought that human organs are associated with specific acupuncture 'points', which lie along 12 pairs of channels or 'meridians' where Chi is concentrated. By stimulating these points with massage or fine needles (sometimes also by warming a dried herb called *moxa* to generate heat on the skin), the flow of Chi is restored, and the imbalances that caused the illness corrected. The technique is also frequently used for anaesthesia in the East – usually following thorough psychological preparation of the patient. The stimulation of acupuncture points induces the release by the brain of morphine-like pain-relieving substances known as *endorphins*. Many Western hospitals are now using acupuncture for pain relief.

ALEXANDER TECHNIQUE

The Alexander Technique was developed by the Australian F. Matthias Alexander at the beginning of this century. It is a process of postural re-education in which the 'patient' abandons their 'natural' posture – which is the product of years of bad habits – and relearns the perfect posture possessed in childhood. It is claimed that learning the Alexander Technique leads to inner harmony and freedom of movement, as well as a sense of well-being and confidence, from which good health flows.

ANTHROPOSOPHICAL MEDICINE

Anthroposophical medicine is not so much a therapy as an alternative attitude to health and illness. It was developed by the Austrian Rudolph Steiner (1861–1925), who regarded himself as a 'spiritual scientist' and argued that the modern 'reductionist' approach to Western medicine limited the spirit. Steiner described four 'bodies' of man: the basic 'plumbing', the etheric, the astral and the 'I'. He believed it was essential for the doctor to attain the highest levels of understanding and perception, both of the spiritual nature of his patients and the plants he administered. The system uses homoeopathic medicine, prescribes a mainly vegetarian diet, eurhythmy (the art of movement), and painting therapy and movement.

AROMATHERAPY

Aromatherapy combines body and facial massage, using essential oils extracted from various parts of plants, each with specific restorative effects. The oils can also be taken internally or inhaled. Originally developed by the ancient Egyptians, aromatherapy is now used particularly in the treatment of stress-related disorders. Aromatherapy is often used with radiesthesia, when specific diagnosis is not always necessary.

AYURVEDA

Ayurveda is a metaphysical system of sacred medicine, developed in India between 3000 and 1000 BC. It is one of the historic roots of modern Western, Chinese and Japanese medicine. Ayurvedics view the Universe and the human body and mind as an intricately balanced and interacting system. As long as the seven tissues, *Dhatus*, in the human body are in balance and in context, the patient will be healthy. The patient is approached as a unique individual, and great emphasis is put on good diet and cleansing, the use of mantras, ceremonies and yogic breathing. Ayurveda also includes branches of surgery, gynaecology and psychology, especially with sexual disorders. Astrology is used for diagnosis, and an enormous pharmacopoeia of drugs is called upon.

BACH FLOWER REMEDIES

The system of 38 Bach flower herbal remedies was developed by Dr Edward Bach (1880–1936), a successful Harley Street pathologist and bacteriologist. Spring water or dew is impregnated with the properties of the different plants to produce remedies that are used mainly for emotional problems. They have no side effects and are not intended directly for a physical complaint, but are said to be particularly effective for depression, anxiety and schizophrenia. 'Rescue Remedy' – a combination of five flower herb remedies – is used by practitioners in emergencies.

BIOCHEMICS OR TISSUE SALTS

Biochemics – a branch of homoeopathy – was developed by the German chemist Dr W. H. Schuessler in the 19th century. He maintained that signs and symptoms are associated with specific imbalances in the body's 12 inorganic salts and oxides. Dr Eric Powell has since discovered 30 more essential trace elements. Combinations of these are given in homoeopathic doses, and often used for self-treatment.

BIOFEEDBACK TRAINING

Electrical equipment such as EEGs (electroencephalograms) and ECGs (electrocardiograms) are used to train patients to modify and control specific bodily responses such as blood pressure and respiration. It is said to be particularly effective for relaxation and stress-management, and there are claims from the USA that it can cure and prevent disease, even cancers, although the primary use is to treat illnesses where tension is a component.

CHIROPRACTIC

Chiropractic is a manipulative therapy which, by correcting the alignment of the bones of the spine and joints of the whole body, aims to restore nerve function, alleviate pain and promote natural health and well-being. The main method of treatment consists of 'adjustments' – manipulation of a joint using a high-velocity, low-amplitude thrust. As well as back, neck and other musculoskeletal pains, chiropractic is also used for migraine, allergies, indigestion, arthritis and emotional imbalances, especially those that are stress-related. Spinal manipulation was widely used by the ancient Egyptians, Hindus and Chinese, but the practice was only rediscovered in 1895 by the American D.D. Palmer. Today it is the most widely recognized complementary medical therapy.

COLOUR THERAPY

Colour therapy is an ancient treatment using different colours (usually in the form of light, including sunlight) to restore body, mind and spirit. It is believed that the colours' specific energies act on the cells and 'energy fields' of the patient. Some practitioners claim to see auras psychically; others use indigo Kilner screens to observe more accurately a patient's 'aura' and so determine which colours are needed to rebalance his energies. Associated with gem and rainbow therapy in the USA, colour therapy is claimed to be particularly effective for the treatment of anxiety stress, rheumatoid arthritis and arrested personality development in both children and adults.

HERBALISM

The use of plants to prevent and cure disease probably goes back to prehistoric times. Herbs are prescribed according to the individual rather than the disease, aiming to restore the body's natural balance and to stimulate its own healing mechanisms. Only small doses are needed, but the whole plant must be used to eliminate side effects that seem to be present in manufactured forms. The herbal pharmacopoeia is officially recognized by many mainstream medical institutions and is also used for the treatment of animals. Herbal remedies may be taken as a mixture orally, or occasionally rubbed into the skin as a cream or ointment. A popular method of taking a herbal cure is as an infusion or herbal tea.

HOMOEOPATHY

The homoeopathy system is based upon the principle that 'like cures like', that agents which produce the signs and symptoms of a disease in a healthy person will cure the disease. A 'minimum dose' is used as it is believed that the more diluted a drug, the more powerful or 'potentized' it becomes. The 'law of cure' states that symptoms may get worse before they get better, that they move from vital organs peripherally and disappear in the reverse order of appearance. The whole patient – rather than the disease – is looked at. Developed in Germany by Dr Samuel Hahnemann (1755–1843), homoeopathy now involves more than 2000 active substances and is recognized under law and by most medical institutions. In order to produce a homoeopathic remedy the ingredients are ground up (trituration), serially diluted (potentization) and shaken (succussion).

HYDROTHERAPY

Hydrotherapy uses water to heal by stimulating the circulation and by elimination – through sweating, excretion and relaxation. First used by the Romans, hydrotherapy remains popular in Germany. Techniques include pressure hosing, salt rubs, bathing in muds, colonic irrigation, and the drinking of mineral water as part of an elimination diet.

HYPNOTHERAPY

Hypnosis is the art of inducing an altered state of consciousness and heightened suggestibility, during which the subject is neither awake nor asleep. Popularized in the 1760s by Franz Anton Messmer as a fairground amusement, hypnosis has struggled to overcome past associations with entertainment. Today it is primarily used to treat psychosomatic and anxiety-related illnesses, but can also be used successfully for asthma, insomnia, many phobias, and to stop habits such as smoking. Its anaesthetic powers – first developed by James Braid in the 1890s – are sometimes used in dentistry and less commonly for major surgery and the control of pain at childbirth. Hypnosis is sometimes practised by doctors in conjunction with other treatments. Under hypnosis the subject can be made to regress through life – sometimes with perfect recall. This technique is widely used in psychotherapy.

IRIDOLOGY

Iridology is a diagnostic technique in which potential weaknesses and illnesses in a patient may receive early diagnosis by the examination of the iris of the eyes. It is believed that different areas of the iris are related to specific areas and systems of the body and that the lines, flecks and pigments of the iris give a detailed picture of the health (past and present) of the whole body. Carved stone representations of irises suggest that the technique was used in ancient Mesopotamia and also by Hippocrates. Iridology was rediscovered by the Hungarian neuro-surgeon Dr Ignatz von Pecezeli (1822–1911).

MACROBIOTICS

Macrobiotics is a wide (macro) view or philosophy of life (biotics) based on keeping the contrasting principles of Yin and Yang in balance, intuitively and through wholesome diet and behaviour, so as to remain happy and healthy. A diet of macrobiotic food should be grown locally, be used as fresh as possible, be carefully prepared, and include a high proportion – at least half – of grains.

MEGAVITAMIN THERAPY

Megavitamin therapy, or orthomolecular medicine, developed in the 1960s and 1970s from the work of Dr

Linus Pauling, a double Nobel Prize winner. It consists of treatment by large measured doses of Vitamin C. In the USA other vitamins are now given to patients whose poor system of digestive absorption has caused deficiencies. For example, Vitamin A is given for osteoarthritis and neuropsychiatric disorders; D for bone thinning; E for sterility and heart disease. Cures for alcoholism, hyperactivity in children, schizophrenia and depression are also claimed, but the danger of overdoses and lack of clinical trials make this therapy controversial.

NATUROPATHY

Naturopathy encourages the healing forces naturally present in everybody. A naturopath is more of a teacher than a doctor, encouraging patients to correct their diet, lifestyle and posture.

OSTEOPATHY

Osteopathy is a system of manipulation of the spine, joints and connective tissues (see also Chiropractic) developed in the USA in 1874 by Dr Andrew Still. He believed that the body cannot function properly if its 'fabric' is in bad condition or has 'lesions' (structural deviations). Although Dr Still was a devout Christian, he believed that osteopathy had a mystical and spiritual dimension. He stressed the 'Total Lesion' – a state in which the patient is disturbed biochemically and psychologically as well as structurally. This state is remedied by 'Total Adjustment'. Osteopathy also focuses on correcting diet and posture.

Cranial osteopathy was developed in the 1930s by Dr Still's disciple William Garnet Sutherland. It involves a gentle examination of the skull. The therapist feels for the very slight movements or 'pulses' of the cerebrospinal fluid – the 'involuntary mechanism'. These movements are adjusted, correcting the flow of the cerebrospinal fluid and improving the endocrine system. It is claimed that cranial osteopathy is particularly effective in the treatment of migraine, some eye conditions and general debilitation.

RADIESTHESIA, RADIONICS AND PSIONIC MEDICINE

Radiesthesia is the use of dowsing or divining to diagnose diseases and choose the appropriate remedies. Radionics is a spiritual healing at a distance – the healer has only a spot of the patient's blood, or a lock of hair or a nail. Psionics – which was developed by Dr George Laurence in England between 1904 and 1964 – combines orthodox medicine with radiesthesia to discover the fundamental causes of diseases. All of these forms of medicine acknowledge a higher level of intuition or 'etheric force' that is thought to work through energy fields and magnetic patterns beyond explanation in terms of conventional physics.

REFLEXOLOGY OR 'ZONE THERAPY'

Reflexology – an ancient Chinese and Egyptian therapy – was rediscovered in the West by Dr William H. Fitzgerald and Eunice D. Ingham in the USA earlier this century. Specific reflex points of the feet or hands are massaged to achieve early diagnosis and to prevent and cure disease. The reflex points relate to each organ and every part of the body. It is claimed that reflexology is most successful with functional disorders such as asthma, glandular problems and high blood pressure.

ROLFING

Rolfing is a deep body massage developed by Ida Rolf in the 1920s and 1930s in New York. The massage attempts to break down connective tissues that have become thickened and coarsened by bad posture and stress. Once the tissues have been freed, the patient becomes more supple, height may increase and a sense of well-being follows.

SHIATSU

Literally meaning 'finger pressure', Shiatsu is an ancient Japanese form of deep massage which is claimed to work on all levels of the body, mind and spirit by stimulating acupuncture points and meridians (see Acupuncture). Shiatsu is commonly practised among members of Japanese families – self-treatment is called *Do-in*. The therapy is used as a preventative as well as a curative treatment.

TOUCH FOR HEALING

Touch for healing – or applied kinesiology – is a diagnostic and curative technique from the USA using 'muscle testing' to identify and balance weak muscles or organs. It is frequently used with chiropractic.

YOGA

Yoga – meaning 'union of oneness' – is a Hindu system of philosophy and health care that dates back beyond 3000 BC. Breathing, posture, suppleness and meditation are essential. Hatha yoga is the branch concerned with optimum health through mastery of the body and 'controlling the waves of the mind' described by the yogi Patanjali. The chief value of yoga is in the prevention of illness.

GLOSSARIES

BOTANY GLOSSARY

abscission the shedding of a leaf, fruit, flower, etc., by a plant.

absorption the taking up of water, solutes and other substances by both active and passive mechanisms. Also, the taking up of radiant energy (from the sun) by pigments in plants.

achene a simple one-seeded indehiscent dry fruit.

active transport the transport of substances across a membrane – e.g. cell membrane – against a concentration gradient.

ADP adenine diphosphate. The conversion of ADP to ATP is of central importance in the storage of light energy absorbed during photosynthesis.

adventitious organs organs that arise in unexpected sites, e.g. leaves that grow roots.

aerial root a root that appears above soil level, usually hanging down in moist air.

aerobe an organism that can live only in the presence of oxygen.

aerobic respiration respiration involving the oxidation of organic substrates and the associated absorption of free oxygen.

alcoholic fermentation anaerobic respiration in which glucose is broken down to form ethanol and carbon dioxide. The process is carried out by yeasts.

algae a diverse group of simple plants – largely aquatic and unicellular.

alpine a regional community of plants found in high mountainous regions and on high plateaux.

alternation of generations the occurrence of an asexual and a sexual reproductive form during the life cycle of a plant.

amino acid an organic compound containing one or more amino groups. About 20 commonly occur as the basic 'building blocks' of proteins.

anaerobe an organism that can live in the absence of free oxygen.

anaerobic respiration a number of processes by which chemical energy is obtained from various substrates without the use of free oxygen.

androdioecious male and hermaphrodite flowers occurring on separate plants.

androecium the male component of a flower, consisting of several stamens.

andromonoecius male and hermaphrodite flowers carried on the same plant.

anemophily pollination by wind.

angiosperms the flowering plants.

annual any plant that germinates from seed, grows, flowers, produces seeds and then dies, all within a single year.

annual ring the ring of new wood added to the existing core of wood on a tree in a single year.

anther the tip of the stamen that produces the pollen grains.

antheridium the male sex organ in lower plants.

aphids insects that feed by sucking plant juices.

apomixis asexual reproduction.

arboretum an area in which woody plants are grown.

asexual reproduction the formation of new individuals from the parent plant without the fusion of gametes.

ATP adenosine triphosphate, a nucleotide occurring in all plants. It has one more phosphate grouping than ADP and it is the addition of this grouping that acts as an energy store.

auricle a small projection from the base of a leaf or petal.

auxin a variety of plant growth hormones that promote the elongation of shoots and roots.

axil the upper angle formed where the leaf or a similar organ joins the stem.

backcross a hybrid between an individual plant and one of its parents. Backcrossing is used to introduce desirable genes into a cultivated variety of a plant.

bacteria microscopic unicellular plants with cell nuclear material not separated from the rest of the cell contents by a nuclear membrane.

bark the protective layer of dead cells outside the vascular cambium in the stems and roots showing secondary growth.

benthos any plant living on the seabed or a lake bed.

berry any many-seeded fleshy indehiscent fruit.

biennial any plant that takes two years to complete its life cycle, growing vegetatively in the first year, then flowering, seeding and dying in the second year.

binomial nomenclature the system of naming plants using a generic name and a specific epithet. The system was developed by Linnaeus.

biochemistry the study and use of metabolism and metabolic chemicals.

biological control the control of pests by making use of their natural predators.

blight a plant disease in which leaf damage is sudden and acute.

bloom (algae) a noticeable increase in the numbers of a species in the plankton.

bolting the premature production of flowers and seeds.

bract a small leaflike structure that subtends a flower or inflorescence.

bracteole a small bract, typically on a flower stalk.

bud a short axis bearing a densely packed series of leaf or flower primordia produced by an apical meristem.

budding asexual reproduction in which a new individual is produced by an outgrowth of the parent.

bulb a fleshy underground modified shoot, made up of swollen scale leaves or leaf bases. It is a perennating organ, allowing the plant to survive for many years.

bulbil a small bulb found on an aerial bud. It functions as a means of vegetative propagation.

callus parenchymatous cells formed at the site of a wound.

calyx the sepals; the outer whorl of the perianth.

cambium a meristem that occurs parallel to the long axis of an organ. It is responsible for secondary growth.

canker a plant disease in which there is an area of necrosis which becomes surrounded by layers of callus tissue.

capillary action the process in which the effect of surface tension on a liquid in a fine tube causes that liquid to rise. The supply of water throughout a plant is largely the result of capillary action.

carbohydrates any of a large variety of organic compounds containing carbon, hydrogen and oxygen. They are energy storage molecules and form structural components.

carbon dioxide an incombustible gas that is converted to carbohydrates in plants by photosynthesis.

carpel the female reproductive organs of plants. They consist of the ovary, style and stigma, and carry and enclose the ovules in flowering plants.

catkin a hanging unisexual inflorescence, designed for wind pollination.

cellulose a carbohydrate consisting solely of glucose units. It is present in plant cell walls as highly organized microfibrils.

chlorophyll the main class of photosynthetic pigment. They absorb red and blue light and reflect green light; hence the characteristic green colour of photosynthetic plants.

chloroplast a green plastid in plant cells. It contains photosynthetic pigment molecules.

chlorosis a disorder in plants in which the chlorophyll levels drop, producing a yellow or pale unhealthy plant.

ciliate any part of the plant fringed with hairs.

circadian rhythm a cycle in which physiological responses occur at 24-hourly intervals, e.g. opening and closing of stomata, change in position of leaves.

cladode a stem structure resembling a leaf, usually produced as an adaptation to dry conditions.

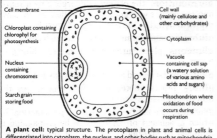

A plant cell: typical structure. The protoplasm in plant and animal cells is differentiated into cytoplasm, the nucleus, and other bodies such as mitochondria and chloroplasts.

The leaves will be reduced when a plant bears cladodes.

cleistogamy the self-pollination of flowers which do not open to reveal the reproductive organs, thus preventing cross-pollination.

climacteric the rise in respiration rate in some fruits during ripening.

club root a fungal disease in which roots become swollen and malformed, causing wilting, yellowing and stunting.

coenocarpium fruit that includes ovaries, floral parts and receptacles of a number of flowers on a fleshy axis.

collenchyma long cells with thickened but non-lignified primary cell walls; a supporting tissue.

contractile root a specialized thickened root that pulls a rhizome, bulb, corm, etc., down into the soil.

coppicing cutting trees back to ground level every 10–15 years. New shoots from the base are therefore encouraged and can be harvested when the coppice is next cut back.

cordate heart-shaped, e.g. leaves.

corm a short swollen underground stem, acting as an organ of perennation and vegetative propagation.

corolla the petals.

corolla tube the fusion of the edges of the petals.

corona a crown-like leafy outgrowth of a corolla tube.

corymb a flat-topped cluster of flowers on lateral stalks of different lengths.

cotyledon the first leaf or leaves of the embryo in seed plants. In non-endosperm seeds they are used as food storage organs.

cross-pollination pollination in which pollen from one individual is transferred to the stigma of another individual.

cultivar a variety or strain of plant produced artificially and not found in the natural population.

cuticle a layer of cutin on the surface of aerial parts of a plant, broken only by stomata and lenticels. It acts to conserve water.

cutin a waterproof substance that forms the waxy cuticle.

cutting a common form of artificial propagation whereby a portion of a living plant is detached and grown in soil or culture medium.

cymose an inflorescence in which apical tissues of the main and lateral stems differentiate into flowers.

cryptophyte any plant with perennating buds below ground or water.

damping off a disease of seedlings in which they

rot at soil level and then die. The condition is caused by crowded conditions and cold wet soil.

dark reactions part of the photosynthetic process that is not light dependent. Stored energy in ATP is used to convert carbon dioxide to carbohydrate.

deciduous woody perennial trees that shed their leaves before the winter or dry season.

decumbent a stem that lies along the ground.

deficiency disease a disease caused by the lack of an essential nutrient, especially minerals.

definite growth the maximum size beyond which the plant can grow no more.

dehiscence the bursting open of certain plant organs at maturity – especially reproductive structures – to release their contents.

denitrification the loss of nitrate from the soil owing to the action of denitrifying bacteria.

dentate a leaf margin that is toothed.

dichogamy anthers and stima maturing at different times on the same plant, thus reducing the chance of self-fertilization.

dicliny the male and female reproductive parts in different flowers.

dicotyledons those angiosperms with embryos with two cotyledons. The group includes hardwood trees, shrubs and many herbaceous plants.

diffusion the movement of ions or molecules in solution down a concentration gradient. It is involved in, for example, transpiration and the uptake of carbon dioxide.

dioecious the male and female reproductive organs on different individuals, making cross-fertilization necessary and ensuring genetic variation.

DNA the abbreviation for deoxyribonucleic acid, the chemical constituent of genes. It determines the inherited characteristics of a plant.

dormancy an inactive phase of seeds, spores and buds, often in order to survive adverse conditions.

double fertilization the process – in most flowering plants – where two male gametes participate in fertilization. One fuses with the female gamete to give the zygote which grows into the embryo, while the other fuses with the polar nuclei or definitive nucleus to give the endosperm.

double flower a flower with more than the usual number of petals.

drupe any fleshy indehiscent fruit with seed or seeds surrounded by woody tissue.

embryo a young plant after fertilization has taken place.

endocarp the innermost layer of the pericarp of an angiosperm fruit, outside the seeds. It can sometimes be woody.

endosperm the storage tissue in seeds of angiosperms.

entomophily pollination by insects.

enzyme a large protein molecule that can catalyse specific biochemical reactions.

epicalyx a calyx-like extra ring of floral appendages below the calyx, resembling a ring of sepals.

epicotyl the apical end of the axis of an embryo, immediately above the cotyledon or cotyledons. It grows into the stem.

epidermis the outer layer of cells of a plant.

epigeal the germination of the seed in which the cotyledons are raised above the surface of the ground by elongation of the hypocotl, thus forming the first leaves.

epigyny the floral parts found above the ovary.

epiphyte any plant with no roots in the soil. It is usually supported by another plant, and gets its nutrients from the air, rain and organic material on the surface of the other plant.

etiolation a disorder where plants become pale and elongated when they are grown in insufficient light and grow towards what light there is.

eukaryotic organisms with cells that have nuclei.

evergreen woody perennial plants that keep their leaves throughout the year, shedding and replacing leaves on a continuous basis.

exocarp the outermost layer of an angiosperm fruit, usually forming a skin.

F_1 generation the first filial generation obtained in breeding experiments.

F_2 generation the second filial generation, obtained by crossing the F_1 generation.

F_1 hybrid the first filial generation produced by crossing two selected parental pure lines. They do not breed true.

fermentation the anaerobic respiration of glucose and other organic substrates to obtain energy.

floral diagram a representation of flower structure. The whorls of floral parts are shown as a series of concentric circles.

floral formula the use of symbols, numbers and letters to record floral structure.

floret a small flower.

flower the sexual reproductive unit of angiosperms, consisting of perianth, androecium and gynoecium, all arising from the receptacle.

forest a plant community in which the dominant species are trees.

fragmentation asexual reproduction in which the parent splits into two or more pieces which develop into new individuals.

frond a large leaf or leaflike structure.

fruit the ripened ovary of a flower, plus any accessory parts associated with it.

fungi saprophytic, parasitic and symbiotic eukaryotic organisms, lacking chlorophyll, whose plant body is typically a mycelium.

gall an abnormal swelling or outgrowth on a plant caused by an attack by a parasite.

gamete a cell or nucleus that can undergo sexual fusion with another gamete to form a zygote, which in turn develops into a new individual.

gametophyte the generation in the life cycle of a plant that produces the gametes.

gamopetalous petals fused along their margins forming a corolla tube.

gamosepalous sepals that are fused to form a tubular calyx.

garigue scrub woodland on limestone areas with low rainfall and thin soils.

gemma a multicellular structure for vegetative reproduction found on some mosses and liverworts.

gene a unit of inheritance formed from DNA.

genotype the genetic make-up of an organism, as opposed to its physical appearance.

genus a group of obviously homologous species.

germination the changes undergone by a reproductive body, e.g. zygote, spore, pollen, grain, seed, before and during the first signs of growth.

glabrous a plant surface that has no hairs.

glaucous plant surfaces with a waxy blue-grey bloom.

gley a waterlogged soil lacking in oxygen.

glume bracts subtending each spikelet in the flowers of grasses.

grafting an artificial means of propagation by which a segment of the plant to be propagated is attached to another plant so that their vascular tissues combine.

grassland a plant community in which grasses are the dominant group.

green manure a fast-growing crop grown at the end of the season and then ploughed or dug in, thus increasing the amount of organic matter in the soil.

growth ring secondary xylem produced in a growing period in the stems and roots of many plants. When the stem or root is sliced across this ring is visible.

guard cells a pair of bow-shaped cells surrounding each stomatal pore and forming the stoma. The opening of the stoma is controlled by changes in the turgidity of the guard cells.

guttation the exudation of water in liquid form from plants.

gymnosperm any vascular plant with naked seeds borne on a sporophyll and not in an ovary.

gynandrous (flowers) stamens and styles united in a single structure.

gynodioecious plants that bear female and hermaphrodite flowers on separate individuals.

gynoecium the female part of the angiosperm flower, consisting of one or more carpels.

gynomonoecious plants that bear female and hermaphrodite flowers on the same individual.

halophyte any plant that can live in soil with a high salt concentration.

hardening the gradual exposure of plants to lower temperatures in order to increase the resistance to frost, prior to planting out.

hard seed a seed with a hard coat that is impervious to water.

hastate a leaf shaped like a three-lobed spear.

haustorium an organ produced by a parasite to absorb nutrients from the host plant.

heartwood the central part of secondary xylem in some woody plants. It is derived from the sapwood that has deteriorated with age.

helophyte any marsh plant with perennating buds in the mud at the bottom of the lake.

hemicellulose a carbohydrate found in plant cell walls, often in association with cellulose. Unlike cellulose, it can be broken down by enzymes and thus used as a nutrient reserve.

hemicryptophyte any plant with perennating buds just below the soil surface.

herbaceous perennial any plant that lives for many years, surviving each winter as an underground storage or perennating organ, the leaves and flowers dying back.

herbarium dried pressed plants kept in a collection.

herbicide any chemical that kills plants.

hermaphrodite any plant bearing both male and female reproductive parts in the same flower.

hesperidium any berry with a leathery epicarp, e.g. citrus fruit.

heteroblastic development the progressive development in the form and size of successive organs such as leaves.

heterophylly the condition of having two or more leaf types differing in morphology and function.

heterostyly the condition of having two or more different arrangements of the reproductive parts in the flowers of a single species.

hilium a scar on the seed coat at the point of abscission.

hip a type of pseudocarp fruit.

homogamy the maturation of anthers and stigmas at the same time.

honey guide dots or lines on petals that guide pollinating insects to the nectaries.

humus a soft moist organic matter in the soil, derived from rotting plant and animal matter.

hybrid an individual plant produced by genetically distinct parents.

hybrid sterility the inability of some hybrids to produce gametes.

hydrophily pollination by water transport of pollen grains.

hydrophyte any plant that is adapted to living in water or in waterlogged conditions.

hydroponics the growth of plants, for example in sand, to which nutrients are added in a liquid fertilizer.

hypha a branched filament of fungi.

hypocotl that part of the stem between the cotyledons and the radicle in the embryo.

hypogeal seed germination in which the cotyledons remain below ground owing to a lack of growth of the hypocotl.

hypogyny the floral parts inserted below the ovary.

indefinite growth unlimited growth, i.e. the plant or parts of the plant continue to grow throughout their lives.

indehiscent a fruit or fruiting body that does not open to disperse its seeds.

inflorescence a group of flowers carried on the same stalk.

insectivorous plant a plant that can obtain its nutrients by digesting insects and other tiny animals, in addition to photosynthesizing.

integument a protective envelope around the ovule of seed plants. Most gymnosperms have one integument, while most angiosperms have two.

keel the pair of fused lower petals in pea flowers.

key a list of characteristics enabling rapid identification of species.

kingdom one of the five major divisions into which all living organisms are classified.

labellum the distinct lower three petals of an orchid.

lamina the flattened bladelike section of a leaf.

lanceolate (leaves) narrow; tapering at both ends.

layering plant propagation in which runners or stolons are pegged down to the ground encouraging roots to form at that point.

leaching the washing out of minerals and other nutrients from the soil.

leaf the principal photosynthetic organ of green plants. It is formed as a lateral outgrowth from the stem, and consists of the lamina, petiole and leaf base.

leaf base the point of attachment of a leaf to the stem.

leaf spot a disease involving spots of dead tissue on the leaves.

legume a dry dehiscent fruit containing one or more seeds. It is also a general name for the plants in the family Leguminosae (the pea family).

lemma the lower of a pair of bracts beneath each flower in a grass.

lenticel a small pore containing loose cells in the periderm of plants. Gaseous exchange takes place through the lenticel.

lichen plants composed of a fungus and algae in symbiotic relationships. The lichen is distinct from either of its constituents.

life cycle the various stages an organism passes through, from fertilized egg in one generation to fertilized egg in the next generation.

light reactions those reactions in the photosynthetic chain that are dependent on light.

lignin a carbohydrate polymer making up about a quarter of the wood of a tree.

liming the addition of lime to the soil to decrease the acidity of the soil and to improve the soil structure.

linear (leaves) flat and parallel-sided leaves.

lipid water-insoluble fatty acids, consisting of carbon, hydrogen and oxygen plus some other elements. Their functions vary, but they include storage, and have structural functions.

lipoprotein an association of lipid and protein usually found in plant cell membranes.

lithophyte any plant that grows on rocky ground.

macronutrient a chemical element required by a plant in relatively large amounts.

maquis a stunted woodland in semi-arid areas that have been deforested.

meadow a moist grassland maintained by mowing.

meristem a part of a plant containing actively- or potentially actively-dividing cells.

mesocarp the middle layer of the pericarp of an angiosperm fruit – absent in some species.

mesophyte any plant with no adaptations to environmental extremes.

microflora small plants found in a given area.

micronutrient a chemical element required in small quantities, i.e. a trace element.

midrib the vein running down the middle of a leaf.

mildew a fungal disease of plants in which the fungus is seen on the plant surface.

monadelphous stamen filaments fused to form a tube.

monochasium a cymose inflorescence in which only one axillary bud develops into a lateral branch at each node.

monocotyledons angiosperms possessing one cotyledon in the embryo. The group includes palms, grasses, orchids, lilies.

monoecious female and male reproductive parts in separate floral structures on the same plant.

monopodial branching the condition in which secondary shoots or branches arise behind the main growing tip and remain subsidiary to the main stem.

morphology that branch of biology concerned with the form and structure of organisms.

mould a fungus that produces a velvety growth on the surface of its host.

multiple fruit fleshy fruit incorporating the ovaries of many flowers and derived from a complete inflorescence.

mycelium a loose mass of branching and interwoven fungal hyphae.

mycorrhiza the symbiotic relationship between a fungus and the roots of a plant.

nastic movement a plant response caused by an external stimulus. The stimulus acts merely as a trigger, and does not control the plant's response.

necrosis the death of part of a plant while the rest of the plant continues to live.

nectaries the glands at the base of a flower that secrete nectar in order to attract insect pollinators.

node the point on the plant stem at which one or more leaves develop.

offset a type of runner; a short shoot that develops from an axillary bud near the base of the stem and goes on to form a daughter plant.

ontogeny the changes that occur during the life cycle of an organism.

opposite (leaves) pairs of leaves arising at each node.

ornithophily pollination by birds.

osmosis the passage of certain molecules in a solution, down a concentration gradient and across a semipermeable membrane that prevents the passage of other molecules. In plants it is usually water molecules that pass across the membrane, equalizing solute concentrations on either side of the membrane.

ovary the swollen basal part of the carpel in angiosperms containing the ovule or ovules.

ovule the female gamete and its protective and nutritional tissues. It develops into the seed after fertilization.

palea the upper bract of the pair found beneath each floret in a grass inflorescence.

panicle an inflorescence in which the flowers are formed on stalks arising spirally or alternately from the main stem.

pappus a modified calyx consisting of a fine ring of hairs or teeth that persists after fertilization, aiding wind dispersal of the seeds.

parasitism the relationship between two organisms in which one is wholly dependent on the other for food, shelter, etc.

parenchyma unspecialized tissue in a plant, often forming a ground tissue in which other tissues are located.

parthenocarpy the production of a fruit without the process of fertilization.

pasture moist grassland maintained by grazing.

peat partially decomposed plant material, built up in poorly-drained areas.

pedicel a stalk attaching flowers to the main stem of the inflorescence.

pepo any berry with a hard exterior.

perennate any plant that is able to live from one growing season to another, usually with a period of reduced activity between seasons.

perennial any plant that lives for many years.

perianth the protective structure encircling the reproductive parts, consisting of the calyx and corolla or a ring of petals.

pericarp the wall of the fruit, derived from the ovary wall.

periderm the protective secondary tissue replacing the epidermis as the outer cellular layer of stems and roots.

perigyny floral parts inserted on the receptacle at about the same level as the ovary.

permanent wilting point the point at which the amount of water in the soil is so low that a plant wilts and will not recover unless water is added to the soil.

petal a unit of the corolla, thought to be a modified leaf.

petiole the stalk that attaches the leaf lamina to the stem.

phanerophyte any plant with perennating buds on upright stems well above soil level.

phellem the compact protective tissue replacing the epidermis as the outer layer in plants with secondary growth.

phloem the vascular tissue in plants responsible for translocation of nutrients.

photic zone the surface waters of lakes and seas, in which light penetrates and which is inhabited by plankton.

photoperiodism the alternation of day and night, controlling the physiological mechanisms of many plants.

photorespiration respiration that occurs in plants in the light.

photosynthesis a series of reactions in green plants in which light energy from the sun is used to drive reactions which convert carbon dioxide and water to carbohydrates and thence to other materials.

phycobiont an algal partner in a lichen.

phyllode a flattened petiole which performs the functions of a leaf.

phyllody the transformation of parts of a flower into leaflike structures.

pileus the cap of a mushroom or toadstool.

piliferous layer the absorbent part of the root epidermis. It is covered with root hairs.

pinna a first-order leaflet in a compound leaf.

pinnule a second-order leaflet in a compound leaf, i.e. each pinna is divided into a number of pinnules.

pistil a single carpel or group of carpels.

pith an area of parenchyma in the centre of many plant stems.

plankton microorganisms that float in surface waters of seas and lakes.

plumule an embryonic shoot derived from the epicotyl.

pollard to prune back a tree to the main trunk.

pollen the microspores, containing the male gamete, released in large numbers as a fine powder by gymnosperms and angiosperms.

pollen sac the chambers on the anther in which pollen is formed.

pollination the transfer of pollen from the male to the female parts in seed plants, i.e. from the anthers to the stigma.

pome a fleshy pseudocarp in which tissues develop from the receptacle and enclose the true fruit.

prickle a short pointed outgrowth from the epidermis.

primary growth the increase in size as a result of cell division at apical meristems.

procumbent any plant that trails loosely along the ground.

prokaryotic organisms in which the nuclear-material is not separated from the rest of the cell contents.

proteins large molecules consisting of carbon, hydrogen, nitrogen, oxygen and other elements. Plant proteins can largely be grouped as enzymes or structural and contractile proteins.

pruning cutting back some or all of the branches of woody plants, usually to promote growth in selected areas of the plant.

pseudocarp any fruit consisting of tissues other than those derived from the gynoecium.

raceme an inflorescence in which flowers are formed on individual pedicels on the main axis.

radicle an embryonic root, normally the first organ to emerge on germination.

receptacle the area at the end of the main axis of the flower, to which the floral parts are attached.

respiration the breakdown of food substances, utilizing molecular oxygen, in order to release energy.

rhizome an underground stem that acts as a means of vegetative propagation.

root a section of a plant – usually underground – that is involved with fixing the plant in position and absorbing water and nutrients. It can be used as a food storage organ.

root hair a projection from a single cell in the root epidermis. Root hairs increase the surface area for absorption.

root nodule a lumpy growth that develops on the roots of leguminous plants as a result of symbiotic infections involved with nitrogen fixation.

rosette plant any plant with leaves radiating outwards on the surface of the soil.

runner a creeping stem arising from an axillary bud, giving rise to new plants at the nodes.

rusts fungal infections causing dark rust-coloured spots on the leaves or stem.

samara an achene with the pericarp extended into a wing.

sap a liquid containing mineral salts and sugars dissolved in water, found in xylem and phloem-vessels.

saprophyte any plant that feeds on dead and decaying organic material.

sapwood the outer functional part of the secondary xylem.

scape a leafless stem of a solitary flower or inflorescence.

schizocarp a dry fruit formed from two or more one-seeded carpels that divide into one-seeded units when mature.

scion a shoot or bud cut from one plant and grafted or budded on to another.

sclerenchyma a strengthening tissue composed of dead cells.

seaweed a group of large algae found in the littoral zone and floating freely in the sea.

secondary growth the increase in diameter of a plant organ as a result of cell division in the cambium.

seed the structure that develops from the fertilized ovule in seed plants. It usually contains the embryo and a food store.

seedling a young plant.

self-incompatability the inability of gametes from the same plant to fertilize each other or form a viable embryo.

self-pollination the transfer of pollen to the stigma of the same flower or flowers on the same plant.

seminal roots roots growing from the base of the stem and taking over from the radicle during early seedling growth.

sepal an individual unit of the calyx, usually green. They may be of a different colour and take over the function of petals.

sessile unstalked.

shade plant any plant that is able to flourish in conditions of low light.

silicula a broad dry dehiscent fruit developed from the fusion of two carpels.

siliqua a structure similar to a silicula, but longer in size.

smut a fungal disease in which a black spore mass appears on the host.

soil the surface layer of the Earth's crust, consisting of water, air, living organisms, dead and decaying organisms and mineral particles.

species in the classification of plants, a single breeding group differentiated from other breeding groups by marked characteristics.

spine a modified leaf or part of a leaf, forming a pointed structure.

spore a simple asexual unicellular reproductive unit.

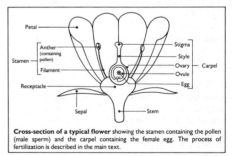

Cross-section of a typical flower showing the stamen containing the pollen (male sperm) and the carpel containing the female egg. The process of fertilization is described in the main text.

stamen the male reproductive organ in flowering plants. Together the stamens make up the androecium and produce the pollen on the anthers.

starch the most common and important food reserve carbohydrate in plants.

stele the vascular cylinder responsible for transport of water and solutes in the stems and roots of vascular plants.

stem that part of the plant above ground that carries the leaves, buds and reproductive parts.

stigma the tip of the carpel that receives the pollen

at the time of pollination and on which the pollen germinates.

stock a plant on to which shoots or buds are grafted.

stolon a long branch that bends over and touches the ground, at which point a new plant may develop.

stoma a pore in the epidermis of the aerial parts of a plant, especially the leaves, through which gaseous exchange occurs.

style that portion of the carpel between the ovary and stigma.

substrate molecules upon which enzymes act.

succulent a plant that conserves water by storing it in a swollen stem or leaves.

sucker a shoot that develops from the roots and forms its own root system.

swamp vegetation found in stagnant or slow-flowing water.

symbiosis an intimate relationship between two (or more) organisms, in which both benefit.

sympodial branching the process where the apical bud dies at the end of one season and growth continues in the next season from the lateral bud immediately below.

syncarpous a gynoecium with fused carpels.

syngenesious an androecium with fused anthers.

taproot a large tough vertical primary root, often penetrating deep into the soil. It can sometimes be a specialized food store.

taxis a directional movement of a whole plant in response to external stimuli.

tendril a modified inflorescence, branch or leaf of a climbing plant that can coil around objects to support the plant.

testa the protective outer covering of a seed.

thallus a plant body undifferentiated into leaves, stem and roots.

thorn a modified reduced branch forming a pointed woody structure. It has a vascular structure within it.

tiller a shoot that grows from the base of the stem when the main stem has been cut back, as in coppicing.

toadstool the inedible fruiting body of fungi.

transpiration the loss of water by evaporation from a plant's surfaces, especially through the stoma. This water loss sucks up water through the rest of the plant, from the roots upwards.

trifoliate a compound leaf with three leaflets.

trimerous an arrangement, especially in monocotyledons, in which the floral parts in each whorl are inserted in threes or multiples of three.

tropism the directional growth of a plant in response to an external stimulus. It can be positive or negative.

tuber the swollen underground part of a stem or root, used for food storage. It lasts for only one year.

turgor the pressure of cell contents on cell walls, swelling them out as the cell takes in water by osmosis. Turgidity is the main effect that keeps non-woody plants erect.

umbel an inflorescence in which flowers are borne on undivided stalks that arise from the main stem. The arrangement of these stalks is such that the flowers form a flat-topped plate or umbrella.

variegation streaks of different colouring in a plant organ, especially leaves and petals.

vascular bundle a strand of primary vascular tissue, consisting largely of xylem and phloem.

vegetative reproduction asexual reproduction in which specialized multicellular organs are formed and detached from the parent, generating new individuals.

vein a vascular bundle in a leaf.

venation the pattern of veins in a leaf.

vernalization the promotion of flowering by exposing young plants to cold.

vernation a pattern of rolling and folding of leaves in a bud.

vivipary young plants forming at the axils of flowers, or the germination of seeds on the parent plant before release.

weed any plant growing where it is not wanted.

wilt any plant disease causing inadequate water supply and thus wilting.

witches' broom a disorder characterized by a mass of twigs grown in response to an infection.

xylem the vascular tissue responsible for transporting water and solutes from the roots up to the leaves and other aerial parts. It constitutes the woody tissues.

zygote the product of the fusion of two gametes, before it undergoes subsequent cell division.

MEDICAL GLOSSARY

abdomen the space enclosing the digestive tract and organs, in addition to various other organs. The upper limit of the abdomen is the diaphragm; the lower limit is the pelvis.

abortion the termination of a pregnancy before the foetus can survive outside the uterus.

abscess a local infection causing inflammation and the production of pus.

accommodation the action of focusing the eye, caused by altering the thickness of a lens.

acetylsalicylic acid better known as aspirin. It relieves pain, lowers a raised temperature and reduces inflammation.

Achilles tendon the tendon in the heel, linking the muscles in the calf to the heel bone.

achondroplasia a form of dwarfism, caused by defective development of the bones of the skull and limbs.

acne an overproduction of grease by the sebaceous glands. The openings of the glands become blocked and act as foci of infection.

acromegaly an excess of growth hormone, resulting in – among other symptoms – enlargement of the hands and feet.

ACTH the usual name for adrenocorticotrophic hormone. It is produced by the pituitary gland and acts upon the adrenals.

acute the adjective used to describe a disease of rapid onset and short duration.

addiction a craving for a drug, resulting in tolerance of the drug and eventually physical dependence on it.

adenoid a lymph tissue at the back of the nose.

ADH the usual name for antidiuretic hormone. It is produced by the pituitary and affects the kidneys.

adrenalin a hormone produced by the adrenal

glands. It stimulates the heart, circulatory system and respiratory system, and inhibits digestion.

adrenals the adrenal glands. The adrenals are endocrine glands attached to the upper part of each kidney. They produce adrenalin (see above), cortisol (which affects the storage of glucose) and aldosterone (which affects the kidneys).

afterbirth the placenta.

AIDS Acquired Immune Deficiency Syndrome, a disease transmitted sexually or by exchange of blood or other body fluids.

aldosterone a hormone produced by the adrenals. It affects the kidneys, regulating the excretion of salt.

alimentary canal the mouth, oesophagus, stomach and intestines.

alveolus the air sac in the lungs where oxygen and carbon dioxide are exchanged between the air and the blood.

amenorrhoea the lack of menstrual periods.

amniocentesis taking a sample of the amniotic fluid from around the foetus in a pregnant woman. Analysis of the sample gives many indications as to the state of the foetus.

amnion the bag of membranes containing the foetus and amniotic fluid during pregnancy.

anaemia a lack of haemoglobin in the blood. This may be due to loss of blood or to defective production of haemoglobin. As haemoglobin carries oxygen in the bloodstream, anaemia gives rise to symptoms of tiredness and malaise.

anaesthetic a drug that removes sensation in a particular area or throughout the body.

analgesic a drug used to relieve pain.

anastomosis an operation joining two cut tubes, e.g. two lengths of intestine from which a diseased section has been removed.

aneurysm a bulge in an artery wall, caused by an area of weakness.

angina pain in the chest caused by insufficient supply of blood (and therefore oxygen) to the heart muscle. It is due to diseased coronary arteries.

ankylosis a loss of movement in a joint, usually caused by arthritis.

anorexia a neurosis involving loss of appetite and rejection of food.

antibiotic a naturally occurring or synthetic drug that kills bacteria. Antibiotics are used to treat bacterial infections.

antibody a chemical produced by the body's immune system in order to neutralize a specific harmful chemical or substance.

anticoagulant a drug that prevents blood from clotting.

antigen a chemical against which an antibody is formed and which the antibody 'attacks'.

antiserum serum extracted from the blood of an animal that is immune to a specific microorganism, e.g. hepatitis.

antitoxin an antibody that neutralizes a specific toxin or antigen.

arrhythmia an alteration in the natural rhythm of the heart.

arteriosclerosis a loss of elasticity in the arteries.

artery the blood vessels carrying oxygenated

blood away from the heart.

arthritis an inflammation of a joint, giving pain and restricted movement.

aspirin see acetylsalicylic acid.

asthma a contraction of the air tubes in the lungs, caused by infection, allergy or stress. It results in very difficult breathing.

athlete's foot a fungal infection of the skin between the toes.

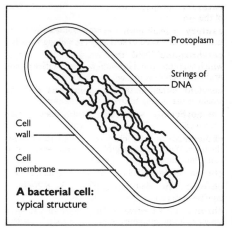

A bacterial cell:
typical structure

bacteria microorganisms – capable of being seen with a light microscope – that live off living, dead or inorganic material.

barbiturates a group of drugs used as sedatives, as anaesthetics and to promote sleep. They are potentially addictive drugs.

bedsore the common name for decubitus ulcer. Pressure of skin and tissue against bone is caused by prolonged time spent in bed. The blood supply to the area is reduced and eventually a slow-healing ulcer is formed.

benign the adjective used to decsribe a mild, usually self-limiting, form of a disease.

bile a secretion of the liver, formed by the breakdown of haemoglobin. It helps in the digestion of fats in the small intestine.

biopsy the removal of a piece of living tissue for examination.

bladder the muscular bag into which urine drains from the kidneys, before being passed out via the urethra.

blood pressure the pressure in the arteries, caused by the pumping action of the heart. It fluctuates with the heartbeat.

breech delivery the delivery of a baby at birth bottom first (instead of head first).

bronchitis an inflammation of the airways in the lungs, i.e. the bronchi and the bronchioles. The condition is often caused by infection. Overproduction of mucus is a common symptom.

bruise a bump or knock causing bleeding into the skin and surface tissues. As the blood decomposes, it gives the characteristic colours – blue and black – of a bruise.

calcitonin a hormone produced by the thyroid. It lowers the concentration of calcium in the blood.

callus a hard area of skin, formed as a result of pressure or friction.

cancer an uncontrolled cell growth, in which the body's usual checks and controls are absent for some reason.

capillary a blood vessel of one cell diameter. Capillaries form a network within the tissues and act as a link between the arteries and veins.

carcinogen a substance or drug with the potential of causing cancer.

cardiac pertaining to the heart.

cataract an opaque area that develops on the lens of the eye.

cautery a small burn – caused electrically or by use of a laser – used to seal small cut blood vessels.

cerebrospinal fluid the fluid, derived from blood, which surrounds, and is found within cavities of, the brain and spinal cord.

cervical either pertaining to the cervix of the womb or pertaining to the neck of the womb.

chemotherapy the treatment of a disease with chemicals.

cholesterol a fatty chemical, found throughout the body. When deposited in the blood vessels, it can cause blockages.

chorea uncontrolled jerky muscular contractions.

chromosome that part of a cell which contains genetic material.

chronic the adjective used to describe a disease of slow onset and long duration.

cirrhosis a disease of the liver caused by scarring. The scar tissue is hard and fibrous and eventually is liable to affect the whole liver.

clavicle the collarbone.

cold an infection – initially viral – of the mucous membranes of the nose and throat.

cold sore an infection with the herpes virus around the mouth, causing raised blisters.

colitis an inflammation of the colon or large intestine caused by infection. (The cause of ulcerative colitis is unknown.)

colon the large intestine, from the ileum to the rectum.

congenital relating to a nonhereditary condition, abnormality or disease present at birth.

conjunctivitis an inflammation of the conjunctiva of the eye, usually caused by viral or bacterial infection.

consumption traditionally an alternative name for tuberculosis.

corn a form of callus on the foot.

coronary arteries the arteries providing the blood supply to the heart muscle.

costal pertaining to the ribs.

cramp a spasm of a muscle or group of muscles.

Crohn's disease an inflammation of the final section of the small intestine (the ileum). The cause is unknown.

cystitis an inflammation of the bladder, usually due to a bacterial infection.

dandruff a condition in which flakes of skin are shed from the scalp.

diabetes in full, diabetes mellitus. A disease caused by a deficiency of – or an inability to make proper use of – insulin formed in the pancreas.

diagnosis the identification of a disease from various signs and symptoms.

dialysis the removal of harmful waste products from the blood by an osmotic process in an artificial kidney.

diaphragm the domed sheet of muscle separating the thoracic cavity from the abdominal cavity.

dilatation a process of widening, either by means of one of the body's reflexes or by mechanical means.

disc a cartilaginous pad between each vertebra, acting as a shock absorber and imparting flexibility to the spinal column as a whole.

diuretic a drug used to increase the flow of urine.

drug a chemical given to help relieve the symptoms of a disease or to modify any of the body's natural processes.

duodenum the first section of the small intestine, between the stomach and the jejunum.

dysmenorrhoea painful menstrual periods.

dyspnoea difficulty in breathing.

ECG an electrocardiogram – a measurement of the electrical changes in the heart muscle.

ECT electroconvulsive therapy. The application of an electric shock to the scalp, used to treat certain mental illnesses, especially depression.

ectopic pregnancy a pregnancy in an abnormal position, e.g. in the Fallopian tube.

eczema an inflammatory condition of the skin, often caused by an allergy.

EEG an electroencephalogram – a measurement of electrical changes in the brain.

embolism the blockage of an artery by an air bubble or, more commonly, a blood clot.

emetic a drug given to induce vomiting.

emphysema damage to the lungs where the tiny air sacs at the ends of the airways break down, leading to breathlessness.

encephalitis a viral infection of the brain.

endemic a disease that is always present in a given area.

endocrine gland a ductless gland that releases secretions (hormones) into the bloodstream, rather than into a duct for local use.

endoscopy the examination of internal organs using a tube lit from the inside; fibre-optics are invariably used now.

enteritis an inflammation of the intestine, usually caused by infection.

epilepsy a nervous disorder characterized by convulsive attacks or fits. The cause is unknown.

erythrocyte a red blood cell.

Eustachian tube a passage leading from the back of the nose to the middle ear.

expectorant a drug that loosens mucus in the respiratory tract, particularly the lungs, and aids coughing.

faeces the waste residue of food, dead and live bacteria, and water, expelled from the rectum.

farmer's lung an allergic response to fungi found in hay, straw, etc.

fibrin a protein produced in the blood during the clotting process. It forms the matrix within which the clot forms.

fibroid a lumpy benign tumour of the uterus.

fistula a passage between two parts of the body, either as a result of a wound, e.g. a stab wound, or as a result of a deliberate operation.

foetus an unborn baby, more advanced than an embryo in that it is recognizably human.

forearm the part of the arm between the elbow and the wrist.

fracture a broken bone, either completely or partially broken.

frostbite damage to the skin and deeper tissues caused by the formation of ice crystals.

fungi very simple plant forms with a parasitic or saprophytic lifestyle. Some forms cause infections, usually of the skin but sometimes internally.

gall bladder the sac under the lower side of the liver that acts as a storage organ for bile.

gall stone a solid crystalline lump precipitated from the bile in the gall bladder.

gamma globulin blood proteins responsible for immunity to specific diseases. They can be separated and given to non-immune patients, thus conferring short-term immunity.

gangrene the death and bacterial decay of tissue.

gastric pertaining to the stomach.

gastric ulcer a stomach ulcer.

gastritis an inflammation of the stomach lining.

gastroenteritis an inflammation of the stomach and intestine.

gingivitis an inflammation of the gums, caused by infection.

glaucoma a disease of the eye in which high pressure within the eyeball resulting in defects in vision.

goitre a swelling of the thyroid gland.

gout the formation of uric acid crystals around joints.

gullet the oesophagus.

haemoglobin the complex protein molecule that gives red blood cells their colour. It transports oxygen in the bloodstream.

haemolysis the breakdown of red blood cells.

haemophilia an inherited disease characterized by an inability of the blood to form clots.

haemorrhage bleeding.

halothane an anaesthetic gas.

hamstring muscles the muscles at the back of the thigh that flex the knee.

hay fever an allergy to pollen, particularly grass pollens. It causes acute irritation to the mucous membranes of the nose and to the conjunctiva of the eye.

hemiplegia a paralysis of one half of the body caused by damage or disease in the opposite half of the brain.

hepatic pertaining to the liver.

hepatitis an inflammation of the liver, usually viral.

hernia a rupture, or protrusion of an organ from one body compartment into another compartment.

herpes a group of inflammatory diseases of the skin. *Herpes simplex* causes cold sores and venereal herpes; the other group, *Herpes zoster*, causes shingles.

hiatus hernia the protrusion of a section of the stomach through the oesophageal opening in the diaphragm.

Hodgkin's disease a form of cancer of the lymph tissues, resulting in lowered resistance to infections.

hormone a chemical, released directly into the bloodstream by one organ (an endocrine gland) in order to regulate other organs or body functions.

hypertension raised blood pressure.

hyperthermia high body temperature.

hypochondria a preoccupation with or anxiety about one's health.

hypoglycaemia a condition characterized by too low a level of glucose in the blood.

hypothermia a condition characterized by a considerably lowered body temperature.

iatrogenic a disease or condition produced as a result of treatment given for another disease or condition.

ileum the latter section of the small intestine, leading into the large intestine.

ilium the haunch bone; part of the pelvis.

immunity the natural or acquired resistance of a body to invading, i.e. 'foreign', chemicals. The immune system can deal with 'invaders' larger than chemicals, e.g. microorganisms, transplants, but this is because it reacts to chemicals on the surface of the microorganism or transplant.

immunization the production of immunity to a specific disease.

incontinence the inability to control the emptying of the bladder or bowels.

incubation period the time it takes between infection by a disease-carrying microorganism and the production of symptoms of the disease.

infarct an area of dead tissue resulting from a blocked blood vessel.

infection the entry of microorganisms into the body, their subsequent multiplication and the production of disease symptoms.

inflammation heat, redness, pain and swelling produced as defensive reaction by the body to infection or damage.

inoculation a form of immunization in which a live harmless variant of the disease-causing microorganism is used to infect the body, producing immunity to both the harmless and harmful microorganisms.

insulin a hormone produced in the pancreas which regulates the metabolism of sugars by controlling the uptake of glucose from the blood by the body's cells.

intercostal muscles the muscles between the ribs.

ischaemia a lack of blood to part of the body.

islets of Langerhans the groups of cells in the pancreas responsible for the production of insulin.

IUD a intrauterine device, a form of contraception. A coil or loop implanted in the uterus prevents a fertilized ovum from embedding in the uterus wall and developing into an embryo.

jaundice a disease characterized by yellowing of skin. It is caused by a build-up of bile pigments in the blood.

jejunum the middle section of the small intestine, between the duodenum and the ileum.

jugular pertaining to the neck.

lacrimal pertaining to tears, e.g. the lacrimal gland above the eye.

laparotomy an incision in the abdominal wall, usually for purposes of examination.

large intestine the latter part of the intestine,

between the small intestine and the rectum.

larynx the voice box, at the front of the throat.

lesion an injury, wound or harmful disturbance to an organ or tissue.

leucocyte a white blood cell.

leukaemia a form of cancer characterized by overproduction of underdeveloped – and therefore useless – white blood cells.

lice insects which infest the hair of the body. Their eggs are called nits.

ligament a fibrous band of tissue holding two bones together at a joint.

linctus a syrupy medicine given to soothe coughing.

lumbar pertaining to the lower back.

lymph a fluid from the blood which leaks out of the capillaries, bathes the tissues and returns to the blood system via the lymphatic system.

lymphatic system a network of vessels and glands which collect and filter the lymph before returning it to the blood system.

malignant the adjective used to describe a severe, often fatal, form of a disease.

malnutrition a deficiency in the quality or quantity of food.

meconium a fluid consisting largely of mucus and bile, passed out of an infant's bowels soon after birth.

menarche the appearance of menstruation at puberty.

meninges the membranes enclosing the brain and spinal cord.

meningitis an inflammation of the meninges caused by viral or bacterial infection.

menopause the disappearance of menstruation, usually between the ages of about 40 and 50.

menorrhagia heavy bleeding during menstruation.

metabolism the sum total of the chemical reactions in the body by which nutrients are converted to energy, tissues are renewed, replaced and regenerated and waste products are broken down.

microorganism any organism too small to be seen with the naked eye. In medicine, usually taken to mean viruses, bacteria and some fungi and protozoans.

migraine an acute form of headache, perhaps allergic in origin, sometimes causing nausea and visual disturbances.

miscarriage an accidental abortion.

multiple sclerosis a chronic disease in which areas of the central nervous system degenerate. A variety of symptoms can be involved, depending on the areas of degeneration. These symptoms can appear and disappear at random.

myasthenia gravis a progressive form of muscle disease in which voluntary muscles become weaker.

myocardial pertaining to the heart muscle.

narcolepsy a disease characterized by periods of uncontrollable sleepiness.

narcotic a drug producing dulling or loss of consciousness.

nausea the urge to vomit.

neonatal pertaining to newborn babies.

nephritis an inflammation of the kidney, caused by infection, chemical poisoning or other reasons.

neuralgia an acute pain originating in a nerve.

neuritis an inflammation of a nerve.

nit the egg of a louse, found firmly attached to a hair or to fibres of clothing.

nystagmus a reflex rapid movement of the eyes, designed to keep moving objects in view.

obesity an excess of body fat.

oedema an excess of fluid in the tissues, either generally or locally, causing swelling.

oesophagus the section of the digestive tract between the pharynx and the stomach.

organ a distinct structure in the body designed to perform a particular function.

osteoarthritis the destruction of the cartilaginous surfaces that allow bones to move over each other.

osteoporosis a weakening of the bones in old age caused by a reduction in the calcium content of the bones.

oxytocin a hormone produced by the pituitary gland. It stimulates contractions of the uterus during labour.

palate the roof of the mouth. The hard palate is at the front, the soft palate at the back.

pancreas a gland at the back of the abdomen. It secretes digestive juices into the small intestine, and also acts as an endocrine gland, producing insulin from the islets of Langerhans.

pandemic a widespread epidemic.

paracetamol an analgesic.

paraplegia a paralysis of the lower half of the body.

parathyroids a group of small endocrine glands associated with the thyroid gland. They produce parathormone, which controls the level of calcium in the blood.

Parkinson's disease a form of paralysis in which the muscles become stiff, movement awkward, and a rhythmic twitching affects the muscles locally or generally.

patella the kneecap.

pectoral pertaining to the chest.

pelvis the ring of bone which forms the base of the abdominal cavity and which forms the hip joint on each side.

peptic ulcer an ulcer of the stomach or duodenum.

pericarditis an inflammation of the pericardium or fibrous sheath surrounding the heart.

perinatal pertaining to the period shortly before, during and shortly after birth.

peristalsis the rhythmic contractions producing flow along the digestive tract.

peritoneum the membrane lining the abdominal cavity.

peritonitis an inflammation of the peritoneum.

pharynx the part of the throat, from the back of the nose to the opening of the oesophagus, concerned with both breathing and swallowing.

phlebitis an inflammation of a vein, usually caused by a blockage of the vein by a clot.

phlegm mucus.

phrenic pertaining to the diaphragm.

piles haemorrhoids; distended varicose veins just inside the anus.

pituitary an endocrine gland on the underside of the brain. It produces a number of hormones: ACTH, which controls the adrenal glands; thyrotrophic hormone which controls the thyroid gland; gonadotrophic hormones, which control the ovaries and testes; growth hormone, controlling growth; prolactin, controlling milk production in the breasts; oxytocin, controlling contraction of the uterus during labour; and ADH, controlling loss of water from the body in the urine.

plasma the fluid component of blood.

platelet a small particle found in blood. Platelets are involved in the clotting mechanism.

pleura a double membrane surrounding the lungs.

pleurisy an inflammation of the pleura, usually caused by infection.

pneumonia an inflammation of the lungs, caused by infection. It affects the alveoli or air pockets at the ends of the airways.

pneumothorax a condition characterized by air between the lungs and chest wall, impairing breathing.

polycythaemia the opposite of anaemia; an excess of red blood cells.

polyp a tumour, usually benign, growing from a mucous membrane and attached to the membrane by a stalk.

poultice a hot dressing applied to inflamed surface areas.

prickly heat a blockage of sweat glands resulting in the production of tiny blisters and an irritating rash.

progesterone a hormone produced in the ovaries. It acts on the uterus to prepare to receive fertilized ovum.

prognosis a forecast of the course a disease will take.

prolactin a hormone produced by the pituitary that stimulates the breasts to secrete milk.

prolapse the displacement of an organ from its normal position.

prophylaxis the prevention of disease.

prostate gland a gland found only in males. It secretes part of the seminal fluid into the urethra.

prosthesis an artificial replacement for part of the body.

psoriasis scaly red blotches formed on the skin. The complaint tends to come and go, for unknown reasons.

puerperal pertaining to childbirth.

pulmonary pertaining to the lungs.

pus dead cells, dead white blood cells, dead bacteria and tissue fluid.

pyloric stenosis a constriction of the outlet from the stomach to the duodenum.

rabies a disease of certain carnivores, transmitted to humans via an animal bite. Symptoms include fever, delirium, muscle spasms and paralysis. Spasm of the throat muscles causes the inability to drink or hydrophobia.

rectum the last section of the digestive tract, between the large intestine and anus.

referred pain a pain occurring in a different part of the body from the site of injury or trauma.

reflex an automatic response to a stimulus.

remission a temporary subsidence of the symptoms of a disease.

renal pertaining to the kidneys.

rheumatic fever an acute disease – generally of children and adolescents – involving raised temperature and inflammation of various parts of the body at different times, including the joints and the valves and lining of the heart.

rheumatism pain or inflammation of the joints or muscles.

rheumatoid arthritis the formation of inflamed knots of fibrous tissue, usually around joints.

rickets faulty bone growth caused by a deficiency of vitamin D.

rodent ulcer a type of skin cancer in which a hard lump appears on the face. The centre of the lump subsequently breaks down to form an ulcer.

sciatica a pain in the region of the sciatic nerve at the back of the thigh, calf and foot.

sclerosis a thickening or hardening of a particular tissue.

scoliosis the curvature of the spine sideways.

sebum the greasy material formed by the sebaceous glands of the skin.

sedative a drug that calms or renders someone sleepy.

senility the mental, or physical, deterioration of organs – especially the brain – in old age.

sepsis an infection of tissues, causing damage.

septicaemia the spread of an infection into the blood, which carries the infecting agent throughout the body.

serum a straw-coloured fluid that separates from the blood as it clots.

shingles another name for *Herpes zoster*; a viral infection of nerves, causing painful blisters on the skin in the area that the infected nerve serves.

shock a sudden drop in blood pressure causing failure of the blood circulation system.

sign any indication of a disease observed by the doctor, nurse, etc.

sinew a tendon or ligament.

sinus a hollow cavity opening off a passageway, e.g. the nasal sinuses opening off the nose. It can also mean merely a bulge in a tube.

sinusitis an inflammation of the mucous membrane of the nasal sinuses.

spasm an uncontrolled contraction of a muscle or group of muscles.

spastic paralysis the loss or limitation of controlled movement in various muscles, caused by disease of the nervous system.

sphincter a ring of muscle around an opening to a hollow or tubular organ.

spina bifida a congenital disease in which the vertebrae do not close over the spinal column, allowing the meninges to protrude.

spleen an organ at the top of the abdominal cavity, responsible for white blood cell production, breakdown of red blood cells and some control of immunity.

spondylitis an inflammation of the vertebrae, often with loss of mobility.

sputum mucus.

squint a poor alignment of the eyes; they either turn inwards (convergent squint) or outwards (divergent squint).

stenosis a constriction or narrowing of a tube, e.g. part of the digestive tract.

stroke an interruption of blood supply to part of the brain.

subcutaneous beneath the skin.

suture the surgical stitching used to close a wound or incision.

symptom any indication of a disease observed by the patient.

syndrome a group of symptoms that frequently occur together, although they may not always be caused by the same disease.

systemic pertaining to the body as a whole.

temperature the 'normal' body temperature is between 36°C and 37·5°C (97–99.5 °F) when taken in the mouth. However, it will vary between these limits during the day and, for women, during their menstrual cycle.

tendon a fibre joining muscle to bone.

tetanus an infection of a wound with the bacterium *Clostridium tetani*. The bacteria produces a poison which causes the characteristic muscle spasms.

thorax the space enclosing the heart, lungs and oesophagus. It is bounded by the rib-cage and the diaphragm.

thrombosis a partial or complete blockage of a blood vessel by a blood clot.

thrombus a blood clot formed on the inside surface of a blood vessel.

thrush an infection by fungus of a mucous membrane, usually of the mouth or vagina.

thyroid an endocrine gland in the neck. It produces thyroxine, which controls energy production in the tissues; and calcitonin, which controls the calcium levels in the blood.

tissue a collection of cells, usually of the same type, specialized to perform a particular function.

tolerance the need to administer larger and larger doses of a drug over time, as the body gets used to it.

tomography an X-ray examination in which a 'slice' of the body is looked at.

tonsil a lymph tissue at the back of the mouth.

topical pertaining to the surface of the body.

tourniquet a constricting strap or band applied to a limb to stop arterial bleeding.

toxaemia poisoning of the blood by toxins from infecting bacteria.

toxin a poisonous substance, usually produced by bacteria.

toxoid a toxin that has been chemically modified to render it harmless. It is still able to produce an immune response when used to immunize against the original toxin.

trachea the windpipe. A tube strengthened with cartilage that runs between the larynx and the bronchi that pass into the lungs.

tranquillizer a drug used to calm the mood without inducing sleepiness.

transfusion a transfer of blood from a healthy to an ill person.

transplantation the transfer of a healthy organ to a patient to replace a diseased organ.

trauma physical damage to tissue, e.g. a wound.

tropical ulcer an ulceration of the skin, usually on the leg, commonly found in the tropics. It is very slow to heal.

tubal pregnancy a form of ectopic pregnancy occurring in the Fallopian tubes.

tumour a group of cells that starts to divide without the usual checks and controls imposed by the body. It may be malignant or benign.

ulcer a breakdown of the skin or mucous membrane that heals very slowly or not at all.

ultrasound sound waves at a frequency well above the range of human hearing, used to provide an image of internal structures.

ureter the tube leading from the kidney to the bladder.

urethra the tube leading from the bladder to the exterior.

uvula the soft projection hanging down at the back of the mouth.

vaccination the use of dead or a harmless form of a microorganism to produce artificial immunity to the harmful form of the microorganism.

vaccine the dead or harmless microorganisms used in a vaccination.

varicose veins swollen veins, usually in the legs, caused by the collapse of the valves in the veins allowing backflow of blood.

vascular pertaining to blood vessels.

vein a blood vessel returning blood from the tissues to the heart. Apart from the vein carrying blood from the lungs to the heart, all veins carry deoxygenated blood.

venereal disease a sexually transmitted disease.

vertigo a form of dizziness in which the subject feels the surroundings are spinning round.

viruses microorganisms, smaller than bacteria

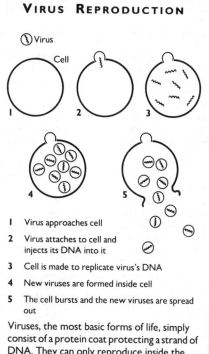

VIRUS REPRODUCTION

1 Virus approaches cell

2 Virus attaches to cell and injects its DNA into it

3 Cell is made to replicate virus's DNA

4 New viruses are formed inside cell

5 The cell bursts and the new viruses are spread out

Viruses, the most basic forms of life, simply consist of a protein coat protecting a strand of DNA. They can only reproduce inside the living cells of other organisms, and the cells are destroyed in the process. This is why viruses cause diseases.

and incapable of being seen with a light microscope. They can only reproduce inside living cells.

vitamins chemicals found in foodstuffs or synthesized by the body. They are not nutrients, but are essential for the normal functioning of growth, repair and reproduction.

wart a small tumour of the outer layer of the skin caused by a virus.

ZOOLOGY GLOSSARY

abdomen the rear section of an arthropod, often divided into segments. Alternatively, in vertebrates, the body cavity in which the principal digestive organs are found.

abomasum the fourth chamber of a ruminant's stomach.

accommodation the adjustments to the eye by which an object is brought into focus.

acetyl choline a neurotransmitter chemical found in the nervous systems of both vertebrates and invertebrates.

acoelomate an animal lacking any form of coelom.

adipose tissue a fatty tissue occurring under the skin in mammals.

adrenalin a hormone secreted in many groups of higher animals. It is said to prepare the body for 'fight and flight'. Adrenalin is also found in the nervous system acting as a neurotransmitter.

afferent a nerve that passes information back to the central nervous system, i.e. a sensory nerve.

aggression animal behaviour designed to frighten off another animal, usually of the same species, from a designated territory.

agonistic behaviour behaviour associated with aggression, but actually involving little violence.

air sac the extension of a bird's respiratory system into other parts of the body. Expansion and contraction of these sacs, with movement of the body, speed up the movement of air in and out of the bird's lungs. The air sacs also help diminish a bird's weight.

albinism an absence of pigments in the hair, skin and eyes.

alimentary canal the tube down which food passes, and in which it is broken down and digested.

alveolus an air sac at the end of a bronchiole in the lungs of reptiles and mammals. It is in the alveoli that gas exchange occurs between the air and the blood.

amino acid the constituent molecular 'building brick' of proteins.

amnion the membrane containing the embryo and the fluid in which it is bathed.

amphibia animals that can live both in water and on land. They represent the first group of animals to develop two pairs of pentadactyl limbs.

antenna a jointed appendage found on the heads of many arthropods. It is usually sensory.

anticoagulant a chemical that prevents blood from clotting.

anus the final opening of the alimentary tract.

aorta the large blood vessel that carries blood from the heart to the body. It is found in the higher four-limbed animals.

arteriole a small artery linking an artery to the capillaries.

artery a blood vessel taking blood away from the heart.

arthropod an invertebrate having an exoskeleton made of chitin, jointed limbs and a segmented body, e.g. arachnids, insects, crustaceans and centipedes.

articulation the movement of one part of a skeleton over another, often at a joint.

asexual reproduction a form of reproduction by budding that occurs only in the lower animals, e.g. the protozoa.

assimilation the incorporation of the simple molecules resulting from digestion into more complex molecules.

atlas vertebra the first vertebra; it allows free movement of the head.

autonomic nervous system the vertebrate nervous system concerned with controlling bodily functions. It consists of the sympathetic and parasympathetic nervous system.

axis vertebra the second vertebra; its articulation with the atlas vertebra allows rotational movement of the head.

barb a hair-like structure attached to the shaft of a feather.

barbule one of the 'teeth' on the barb of a feather. The barbules interlock, linking the barbs together.

bilateral symmetry the arrangement of the body and organs of an animal in only one plane of symmetry.

bile a secretion of the liver in vertebrates. It is formed from the breakdown of blood cells, and helps in digestion of fats.

bivalves a group of molluscs in which the body is enclosed within a shell consisting of two hinged halves, or valves, e.g. clams, cockles, oysters and mussels.

bladder a fluid- or gas-filled sac, often taken to mean the muscular sac into which urine drains from the kidneys.

blastula the early stage in the development of an animal embryo after fertilization.

blood the fluid that occupies the vascular system. It carries respiratory gases, digestive and excretory products and other biochemicals.

blubber a thick layer of subcutaneous fat found in many marine mammals.

bone a form of tissue, rich in calcium, that forms the endoskeleton of the higher vertebrates.

brain the forward section of the nervous system. In invertebrates it consists of ganglia; in vertebrates it consists of an enlarged part of the neural tube.

bronchiole a tube leading to the alveoli in the lungs.

bronchus one of two tubes, each tube leading to one of the lungs in vertebrates.

buccal cavity the mouth cavity.

caecum an outgrowth of the alimentary canal.

canine tooth a pointed tooth found in mammals. It is used for gripping and tearing, and is prominent in carnivores.

capillaries fine blood vessels forming a network in vertebrate tissues. They carry respiratory gases, nutrients and waste products to and from the tissues.

carapace the shell of some crustaceans, e.g. crabs, and of some reptiles, e.g. tortoise.

carnassial teeth the modified molar and premolar teeth in many carnivores. They have sharp cutting edges for dealing with meat, bones, ligaments, etc.

carnivore a meat-eating animal.

carpals bones found in the pentadactyl limb of the higher vertebrates.

cartilage a tough slippery flexible tissue, found in all vertebrates. It has skeletal functions, and some of the lower vertebrates have skeletons consisting entirely of cartilage.

central nervous system that part of the nervous system which coordinates the activities of the other parts of the nervous system. It ranges in complexity from a simple series of paired ganglia to the brain and spinal cord of vertebrates.

cephalopod a marine mollusc with well-developed head and eyes and sucker-bearing tentacles, e.g. octopuses, squids and cuttlefish.

chaeta a stiff bristle found on the body segments of worms.

chela pincers found in arthropods.

chitin the polymeric chemical that comprises the exoskeleton of arthropods.

chordates animals which have a notochord, either in the embryo or adult form.

chromatophore a cell containing pigment that is involved in colour changes.

chrysalis the pupal form of butterflies and moths.

cilium (plural **cilia**) a very fine hair, capable of independent movement. Unlike flagella, cilia are usually found in groups. They can only beat in one direction, and usually move in synchrony.

class in taxonomy, a primary grouping or classification into which a phylum or division is divided, e.g. Amphibia, Reptilia and Mammalia are three classes of phylum Chordata.

clitellum the 'saddle' of earthworms, involved in copulation.

cloaca the chamber into which the alimentary canal, the kidneys and the reproductive organs open.

coccyx a fused group of vertebrae at the base of the spine in tailless primates.

cocoon a protective covering around the eggs or larvae of many invertebrates.

coelenteron the body cavity in lower animals that functions as a digestive cavity. There is one opening, and the cavity itself is lined with two layers of cells.

coelom a body cavity in higher animals.

compound eye the simple eye found in crustaceans and insects. It is formed from hundreds of single light receptors, which build up a compound image.

cone a light-sensitive cell in the eyes of vertebrates. It detects colour and detail.

cranium the skull of vertebrates.

crop a section of the alimentary canal capable of being distended in order to store food.

crustacean a (mainly) aquatic arthropod protected by a shell-like cover, e.g. crab, lobster, shrimp, woodlice, barnacles and water flea.

deciduous teeth the first set of teeth in mammals. These are shed to make way for the adult teeth.

defaecation the discharge of waste from the body through the anus.

demersal inhabiting the sea or lake floor.

dental formula an expression of the arrangement of teeth in mammals. It indicates the number of incisors, canines, premolars and molars in one side of the upper and lower jaw.

dentine the main bulk of a tooth. It is served by blood vessels and covered with enamel.

diaphragm the dome of muscle separating the thoracic and abdominal cavities in mammals.

diastole the phase of the heart beat in which the heart muscle is relaxed.

digestion the breakdown of foodstuffs into simple molecules that can be absorbed and used by the organism.

digit a finger or toe of the vertebrate pentadactyl limb.

dorsal the surface of an animal nearest to the notochord or spinal cord.

ear a vertebrate organ, primarily of balance but subsequently adapted as an organ of hearing.

ecdysis moulting. The shedding of the exoskeleton in arthropods to allow for growth, or the shedding of the outer layer of skin in reptiles.

efferent a nerve that passes information from the central nervous system out to the tissues and organs of the body.

egg a structure containing the ovum and in which the embryo develops. It contains yolk, which nourishes the embryo during its development, and a number of membranes enclosing the contents, including an outer protective membrane, sometimes calcareous.

embryo the structure that develops from the zygote prior to birth or hatching.

enamel hard white material that encases the exposed surface of a mammalian tooth.

endocrine gland a type of gland found in vertebrates and some invertebrates, in which the secretion passes into the bloodstream and thus to the organ or organs on which it acts.

endoskeleton a rigid and often articulated structure that lies within the body tissues. It provides support and shape, and often sites of attachment for muscles.

epiglottis a cartilaginous flap that closes off the windpipe of mammals during the swallowing reflex.

excretion the elimination of waste chemicals from the body. This is not the same as defaecation.

exocrine gland a gland, found in vertebrates, in which the secretion is carried down a duct to the site of activity.

exoskeleton a rigid articulated structure that lies outside the body tissues. It provides protection, support and often sites of attachment for muscles.

faeces the remains of undigested food, bile, dead cells and bacteria, expelled through the anus.

fat body in amphibians, the fat body consists solely of fat, and provides them with food reserves during hibernation. In insects, it consists of fat, protein and other reserves, and provides nourishment during metamorphosis as well as during hibernation.

feathers light, flat epidermal structures that form the plumage of birds. There are three types of feather: contour feathers have barbs and barbules that lock together (these are the feathers on the wings and tail associated with flight); down feathers and filoplumes are fluffy feathers more important for heat retention.

fibrin a protein that forms a fibrous matrix as the basis of a blood clot.

filoplume hairlike feathers scattered over the

surface of a bird. They are important in heat retention.

fin a firm appendage forming an organ of balance or locomotion on fishes and other aquatic animals. The lateral fins of fishes are based on the pentadactyl limb, the two pectoral fins corresponding to fore limbs, the pelvic fins to the hind limbs. These, and the median and anal fin, are used for steering and balance. The caudal fin on the tail is used for propulsion.

flagellum a hairlike filament found on a cell surface. Its movement causes the cell, or the fluid around it, to move.

follicle a small sac or cavity.

gall bladder the storage organ for bile produced in the liver.

gamete a reproductive cell that can undergo fertilization.

ganglion a mass of nervous tissue, rich in nerve cell bodies. In invertebrates, ganglia form the central nervous system.

gestation the time between conception, i.e. fertilization, and birth.

gill the respiratory organ in marine and freshwater animals. Each gill has a rich blood supply, promoting gas exchange between the blood and the surrounding water.

gizzard part of the alimentary canal designed to break up hard foods.

gland an organ that secretes a specific chemical or group of chemicals, either into the bloodstream or into a specific site of activity.

glottis the opening of the larynx into the pharynx.

glycogen a storage compound in animals. It is a polymer of glucose.

gonad an organ which produces ova or sperm.

grey matter the region of the vertebrate brain that contains nerve cell bodies and synapses.

gut the alimentary canal.

haem the basis of many respiratory pigments, e.g. haemoglobin, as it can combine reversibly with oxygen.

haemocoel the body cavity containing the blood in arthropods and crustaceans.

hair cornified threads produced by follicles in the skin of mammals. The colour is due to melanin pigment. The function of hair is largely heat retention.

hallux a vestigial digit on the inside of the rear limbs of most higher terrestrial vertebrates.

haltere a modified wing of flies that provides information on stability in flight.

haw the nictitating membrane found in reptiles, birds and some domestic animals – e.g. horse and cat – that can be drawn upwards across the eye.

heart an organ found in all vertebrates and many invertebrates that drives blood around the body unidirectionally.

herbivore a plant-eating animal.

heterocercal any fish whose vertebral column extends into the tail fin. It is upturned, giving the fin a larger dorsal lobe than ventral lobe.

hibernation a period of time during winter when an animal becomes inactive and the basal metabolic rate drops, thus conserving energy.

hominid a primate in the family *Hominidae*, including early and modern man.

homiothermy the maintenance of the body temperature at a relatively constant level – this is often referred to as being 'warm-blooded'.

homocercal any fish whose tail fin does not contain the vertebral column, but is supported with fin rays.

hormone a chemical secreted by endocrine glands. Carried by the bloodstream, each hormone has a specific and often regulatory effect upon a particular organ.

ileum a section of the small intestine in mammals, immediately before the colon.

imago the sexually mature adult form of an insect.

implantation the attachment of a vertebrate fertilized ovum to the wall of the uterus.

impulse the passage of an electric current along a nerve fibre.

incisor the front teeth of mammals. They are sharp and are used for biting and gnawing of food.

instar the form adopted by an insect between moults.

insulin an important animal hormone responsible for the control of glucose levels in the blood.

intestine that part of alimentary canal in which food is digested and absorbed.

invertebrate an animal lacking a backbone or spinal column or notochord, e.g. molluscs, worms, jellyfish, coral.

iris a ring of pigmented tissue which lies over the lens of the eye in invertebrates and cephalopods. The diaphragm that controls the size of the pupil.

joint a point of contact between two body elements in invertebrates or between two bony or cartilaginous elements in vertebrates.

keel the large blade or projection from the sternum of bats and birds. It provides the surface area for the attachment of the flight muscles.

keratin the structural protein found in horn, claws, beaks, nails, hair, etc., and in the outer cells of the epidermis of vertebrates.

kidney one of two excretory organs found in vertebrates.

labrum the upper 'lip' in insects that helps in feeding.

lactation milk production. One of the chief characteristics of mammals.

lacteal lymph vessels in vertebrates, involved in the absorption of digested fats in the intestine.

larva a form taken by many animals between hatching from the egg and metamorphosing into the adult, e.g. caterpillars, tadpole.

larynx the area of the throat that controls the swallowing reflex and that contains the vocal cords.

lateral line a system of receptors for the detection of vibration (sound) and movement, arranged in a line down each side of fish and some amphibians.

lens the transparent body in the eye designed to focus light on to the retina in vertebrates.

ligament a band of fibre holding two bones together at a vertebrate joint.

liver the largest internal organ found in vertebrates. It is responsible for the major metabolic functions.

lung a respiratory organ found in vertebrates.

lung book a respiratory organ found in some insects.

lymphatic system a system of tubes containing lymph, found in vertebrates. It collects tissue fluid and returns it to the blood system, transports digested fats, and is involved in the immune system. Flow in the lymphatic system is effected by lymph hearts in some vertebrates, and by muscular and respiratory movements in mammals.

mammals a group of vertebrates characterized by being homiothermic, having hair on the skin, giving birth to well-developed young which have been nourished within the womb by a placenta and which are subsequently suckled at the mammary glands.

mammary gland a milk-producing gland found in all female mammals.

mandible the lower jaw in invertebrates.

mantles folds of skin in molluscs which secrete the shell, if present, and protect the gills.

marsupium a pouch possessed by female marsupials. The mammary glands are found within the pouch, and the young finish their development there after birth.

maxilla either a feeding appendage found in arthropods, or the upper jawbone of vertebrates.

meatus the passage leading from the outer ear to the eardrum.

median eye a third eye in the top of the head found in many invertebrates. It is formed from an outgrowth of the brain, and is represented vestigially in vertebrates by the pineal body.

medulla the central part of an organ.

melanin a pigment found in skin, hair, etc.

meninges the membranes surrounding the central nervous system of vertebrates and the spaces within it.

metacarpals bones found in the pentadactyl limb of the higher vertebrates.

metameric segmentation the division of the body into a number of similar segments along its length.

metamorphosis the change from the larval to the adult stage of an animal – a process found in insects and amphibians.

metatarsals bones found in the vertebrate pentadactyl limb. They are greatly elongated in running animals.

migration the movement of whole populations of animal species between two regions, often at roughly the same time each year.

mimicry the ability of one animal to resemble another, usually for protection.

mitral valve the heart valve of the higher vertebrates.

molar a chewing tooth occurring at the rear of the jaw in animals.

mucous membrane a surface membrane that secretes mucus.

mucus a slimy protective secretion that does not dissolve in water.

muscle a contractile tissue that produces movement in invertebrates and vertebrates.

myelin sheath a membranous sheath around nerve fibres.

nasal cavity the cavity in the head of vertebrates containing the organs of smell.

nephridium an excretory organ in invertebrates.

nerve fibre the long thin unbranched section of a nerve cell that transmits the nerve messages over long distances within the body.

nerve net a simple form of nervous system found in the invertebrates.

neurone the chief nerve cell in the nervous system. It consists of a cell body, a number of finger-like dendrites which link up with other nerve cells, and one or more nerve fibres or axons which transport impulses over relatively long distances.

nidiculous any bird that hatches in an undeveloped state and is unable to fend for itself.

nidifugous any bird that hatches in a well-developed state and is soon able to fend for itself.

notochord a form of primitive cartilaginous spinal column. It is found in adult forms of the lower vertebrates, and in embryonic forms of the higher vertebrates.

nymph an immature form of some insects, in which the wings and reproductive organs are not fully developed.

ocellus a simple form of eye, consisting of a collection of light-sensitive cells, found in some invertebrates, especially insects. It is not capable of forming an image.

oesophagus the gullet – the tube by which food passes from the mouth to the digestive tract.

oestrous cycle the reproductive cycle of female mammals.

oestrus the period of the oestrous cycle when the female mammal is 'on heat', i.e. copulation can occur.

olfactory organs organs of smell.

omasum the third chamber of a ruminant's stomach.

ommatidium a single unit in the compound eye of arthropods.

omnivore any animal that eats both plants and animals.

operculum the muscular flap covering the gills in bony fish.

optic chiasma the point at which the optic nerves cross over between the vertebrate eyes and brain.

optic nerve the nerve connecting the vertebrate eye with the brain.

orbit the socket of the vertebrate skull in which the eye lies.

order in taxonomy, a group into which a class is divided, e.g. Carnivora, Primates and Rodentia are three orders of the class Mammalia.

ossification the process by which bone is formed from cartilaginous or other tissue.

ovary the reproductive organ of female animals, producing ova and female sex hormones.

oviparous any female animal that lays eggs within which the embryo develops.

ovoviviparous any female animal in which the fertilized ova develop within the body but not receive nourishment from it (e.g. certain reptiles, fish, etc).

ovulation the release of an ovum from the ovary.

ovum (plural **ova**) an unfertilized non-motile female gamete.

pacemaker a group of cells that provides a rhythmic series of electrical impulses that drives an organ – most commonly applied to the cells in the vertebrate heart that are responsible for providing the electrical impulses for the heartbeat.

palate the roof of the mouth in vertebrates.

palp a head or mouth appendage found in many vertebrates.

parasympathetic nervous system part of the autonomic nervous system in vertebrates.

parturition the passage of the foetus out of the female's body at the end of pregnancy in mammals.

pecking order the social hierarchy found in many animals that live in groups.

pectoral fins the forward pair of lateral fins found in fishes.

pectoral girdle the ring of bones in vertebrates to which the fore limbs articulate.

pelagic any animal inhabiting the open waters of the sea or a lake.

pelvic fins the rear pair of lateral fins in fishes.

pelvic girdle the ring of bones in vertebrates to which the hind limbs articulate.

pentadactyl limb the characteristic limb of the vertebrates, with five digits or 'fingers'.

peripheral nervous system those parts of the nervous system not included in the central nervous system.

peristalsis the waves of contraction that pass down tubular organs, particularly the digestive tract.

phalange one of the types of bones of the pentadactyl limb.

pheromone a chemical produced by one animal, designed to elicit a response in another animal of the same species.

phylum the second taxonomic grouping after kingdom and before class.

pineal body a downgrowth of the vertebrate brain with endocrine functions. In some lower vertebrates it functions as the median eye.

pinna the outermost part of the outer ear in some mammals.

pituitary gland the major endocrine gland in vertebrates, occurring as downgrowth of the brain. It produces a wide range of hormones, many of them controlling other endocrine glands.

placenta the series of membranes within the uterus of viviparous animals that nourishes the developing foetus. It allows a close association of the foetal and maternal blood systems.

pleural membranes the membranes enclosing the mammalian lungs.

plexus a network of nerve cells.

poikilothermy the inability to regulate the body temperature, which therefore assumes that of the surroundings.

pollex the inner digit on the forelimbs of the higher vertebrates. It is often vestigial, or may be adapted for a variety of purposes.

polymer a naturally occurring or synthetic compound, e.g. starch.

polyp a non-motile form of those coelenterates that have the medusoid motile form.

premolar the grinding and chewing teeth occurring between the canines and molars in the jaws of mammals.

pupa a non-feeding form of an insect in which metamorphosis from a larva to an adult occurs.

pupil the opening in the iris of the eye of vertebrates and some invertebrates, through which light enters the eye.

rachis the shaft of a feather.

radial symmetry the form of symmetry found in sedentary animals, e.g. the coelenterates, in which the body is symmetrical about a number of planes passing through a central axis.

radula a strip on the tongue of molluscs that carries teeth to rasp food off rocks, etc. As the teeth are worn away they are replaced.

reflex an automatic response to a stimulus.

regeneration the regrowth or replacement of tissues and body parts lost owing to injury. Extensive regeneration is possible in many invertebrates, but regeneration is much more limited in the vertebrates.

retina a layer of sensory cells in the eyes of vertebrates and some molluscs.

rod a light-sensitive cell in the retina of vertebrate eyes.

rumen the first chamber in the stomach of ruminants.

ruminants a group of higher mammals, including cattle and sheep, in which the digestive system allows food to be swallowed and then digested later.

saliva a secretion of mucus and enzymes which moistens the food and starts off the process of digestion.

scolex the head of a tapeworm, which anchors it to the intestinal wall of the host.

sebum a greasy material produced by the sebaceous glands in the skin of mammals. It greases the hair and protects the skin.

sessile any animal which lives attached to a fixed surface or to another animal.

sibling one of a number of offspring of the same two parents.

sinus any body cavity or recess.

smooth muscle a vertebrate muscle tissue, under involuntary control, usually found around hollow organs. It can produce long-term contractions.

sperm the motile male gamete formed in the testes of male animals.

sphincter a ring of muscle around the opening to a hollow organ.

spinal cord that part of the central nervous system in vertebrates enclosed within the spinal column.

spinneret the openings on the abdomen of a spider out of which silk is produced to make webs, tie up prey, spin cocoons, etc.

spiracle a gill slit in fish, or the opening of the tracheae in insects.

striated muscle a vertebrate muscle – with a striped appearance – under voluntary control. Important in locomotion, it produces rapid powerful contractions.

stridulation the production of sound by insects, usually by rubbing body parts together.

succus entericus digestive secretions of the walls of the small intestine in vertebrates.

swim bladder an air bladder found in many fish. It is used in maintaining depth when swimming.

sympathetic nervous system part of the vertebrate autonomic nervous system.

synapse the point of contact between nerve cells at which the nerve impulse passes from one cell to another.

systole the phase of the heart beat in which the

heart muscle is contracted.

tarsals bones in the rear pentadactyl limbs of vertebrates.

telson the tail appendage found in some arthropods.

tendon a fibrous band connecting a muscle to a bone.

testis the male reproductive organ that produces sperms and male sex hormones.

tetrapod any vertebrate having four limbs.

thorax the middle section of arthropods, particularly of insects. In vertebrates, the thorax is the body cavity containing the heart and lungs.

tone the state of partial contraction of a muscle which maintains body posture.

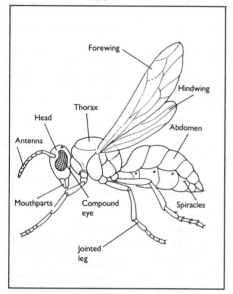

trachea in arthropods, the tracheae are tubes that take air to the tissues. In vertebrates, the trachea is the windpipe, taking air from the larynx to the lungs.

umbilical cord the connection between the embryo and the placenta in pregnant mammals.

ungulates a group of mammals that graze, that have hooves and that walk on the tips of elongated and adapted pentadactyl limbs.

urea the waste product of mammals and many other animals.

uric acid the waste product of birds and some other animals.

urine liquid produced in the kidney, containing waste products such as urea or uric acid.

uterus the womb in mammals.

vascular system the fluid-filled spaces in the body, e.g. the blood vascular system.

vasoconstriction a constriction of a blood vessel.

vasodilatation an increase in the diameter of a blood vessel.

vein a blood vessel that carries blood from the tissues to the heart.

venation the arrangement of veins in an insect's wing.

ventral the surface of an animal furthest away from the notochord or spinal column.

venule a small blood vessel linking a vein to the capillary network.

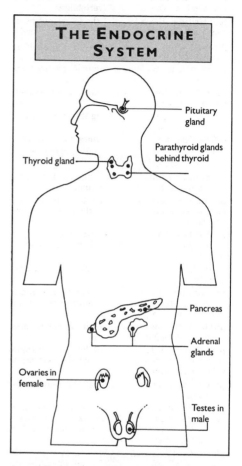

vertebra a separate bone of the vertebral column.

vertebral column bones or cartilage in close apposition, running in a line from the skull to the tail of vertebrates and enclosing the spinal cord.

vertebrate any animal having a backbone or vertebral column or notochord, e.g. fishes, amphibians, reptiles, birds, mammals.

villus a projection from a body surface – usually designed to increase the surface area of a tissue.

viviparous any animal in which embryos develop within and are nourished by the mother.

vocal cords elastic fibres in the larynx that produce sounds in vertebrates.

white matter the region of the vertebrate central nervous system consisting of nerve cell fibres.

yolk the nutrient store in eggs.

zoology the study of animals and their behaviour, including their classification, structure, physiology and history.

zoonosis any disease or infection that can be passed on from man to animals.

THE PHYSICAL SCIENCES

WEIGHTS AND MEASURES

MEASUREMENT

Measurement – in terms of length, weight or capacity – involves *comparison*. The measurement of any physical quantity entails comparing it with an agreed and clearly defined *standard*. The result is expressed in terms of agreed *units*. Each measurement is expressed in terms of the appropriate unit preceded by a number which is the *ratio* of the measured quantity of that unit. The science of measurement is called *metrology*.

Crude measurements probably date back to prehistory. The first – units of weight and length – were based upon parts of the human body. The average pace of a man was a common unit in many ancient civilizations. The length of the human thumb was another widely used measure – in England, it was the precursor of the inch. The length of ploughs and of other agricultural implements were also frequently used as early units of measurement. As civilization and trade developed the need for standardization grew. Units were fixed by local tradition or by national rulers, and many different (though sometimes related) systems developed.

THE METRIC SYSTEM

The metric system was adopted in Revolutionary France in 1799 to replace the existing traditional illogical units. It was based upon a natural physical unit to ensure that it should be unchanging. The unit selected was 1/10 000 000 of a quadrant of a great circle of the Earth, measured around the poles of the meridian that passed through Paris. This unit – equivalent to 39.37003 inches in the British Imperial system – was called the metre (from Greek *metron*, 'measure').

Several other metric units are derived from the metre. The gram – the unit of weight – is one cubic centimetre of water at its maximum density, while the litre – the unit of capacity – is one-tenth of a cubic metre. Prefixes – from Danish, Latin and Greek – are used for multiples of ten from *atto* ($\times 10^{-18}$) to *exa* ($\times 10^{18}$) – see below.

In 1875 an international conference established the International Bureau of Weights and Measures and founded a permanent laboratory at Sèvres, near Paris, where international standards of the metric units are kept and metrological research is undertaken. The prototype metre was an archive standard rather than an actual measurement upon the ground, but in 1960 the metre was redefined as 1 650 763.73 wavelengths of the red-orange light given out by the krypton-86 isotope.

The metric system is centred on a small number of *base units*. These relate to the fundamental standards of length, mass and time, together with a few others to extend the system to a wider range of physical measurements, e.g. to electrical and optical quantities. There are also two geometrical units that are sometimes referred to as *supplementary units*. These few base units can be combined to form a large number of *derived units*. For example, units of area, velocity and acceleration are formed from units of length and time. Thus very many different kinds of measurement can be made and recorded employing very few base units.

SI UNITS

A number of systems of units based upon the metric system have been in use. Initially the *cgs system* – based upon the centimetre for length, the gram for mass and the second for time – was widespread. It has, however, largely been replaced by the *mks system* in which the fundamental units are the metre for length, the kilogram for mass and the second for time. The mks system is central to the *Système International d'Unités*, which was adopted by the 11th General Conference on Weights and Measures in 1960. The SI units are now employed for all scientific and most technical purposes, and are in general use for most other purposes in the majority of countries. The SI base units are:

metre the unit of length;

kilogram the unit of mass;

second the unit of time;

ampere the unit of electric current;

kelvin degree of temperature measured on the Kelvin scale;

candela the unit of luminous intensity;

mole the unit of substance.

Details of these and supplementary and derived SI units are given in the tables below.

OTHER SYSTEMS

The most widely used remaining systems of units are the related (British) Imperial System and the US Customary Units. Although the names of most of the units of both systems are the same, the sizes of some of the units differ.

IMPERIAL SYSTEM

The two basic units are the yard (the unit of length) and the pound (the unit of mass). Subdivisions and multiples of these units are traditional in origin and do not follow the logical tenfold stages of the metric system.

The Imperial System is complicated by the existence of three different systems of measurement of weight. The *avoirdupois system* is the most widely used. The *troy system* is used to measure precious metals, while the *apothecaries' system* uses the same units as the troy system but with certain differences of name.

The use of the metric system was legalized in the United Kingdom in 1897. The intention to switch to the metric system 'within ten years' was declared on 24 May 1965 by the President of the Board of Trade, although on 23 March 1976 the Government decided not to proceed with the second reading of the Weights and Measures (Metrication) Act. However, since 1965 the metric system has replaced the Imperial System for many purposes, although loose fruit and vegetables continue to be sold by the pound, the pint and the dram will remain as the unit of capacity for alcohol, and the mile will not be replaced as the standard unit of length over long distances.

US CUSTOMARY UNITS

Some units of the Imperial system have fallen into disuse in North America. The yard, for example, is only encountered in sport. The differences between

English and American units make conversion difficult; for example, a ton in Britain is a unit of mass equivalent to 2240 pounds (or 1016.046 909 kg), while a ton in the USA and Canada is equivalent to 2000 pounds (or 907.184 kg). There are also considerable differences between the English and American gallon, and the English and American bushel.

METRIC UNITS

UNITS OF LENGTH

10 ångström	=	1 nanometre
1000 nanometres	=	1 micrometre
1000 micrometres	=	1 millimetre
10 millimetres	=	1 centimetre
10 centimetres	=	1 decimetre
1000 millimetres	=	1 metre
100 centimetres	=	1 metre
10 decimetres	=	1 metre
10 metres	=	1 dekametre
10 dekametres	=	1 hectometre
10 hectometres	=	1 kilometre
1000 metres	=	1 kilometre
1000 kilometres	=	1 megametre
Nautical		
1852 metres	=	1 int. nautical mile

UNITS OF AREA

100 sq millimetres	=	1 sq centimetre

100 sq centimetres	=	1 sq decimetre
100 sq decimetres	=	1 sq metre
100 sq metres	=	1 are
100 ares	=	1 hectare
1000 sq metres	=	1 hectare
100 hectares	=	1 sq kilometre

UNITS OF WEIGHT (MASS)

1000 milligrams	=	1 gram
10 grams	=	1 dekagram
10 dekagrams	=	1 hectogram
10 hectograms	=	1 kilogram
100 kilograms	=	1 quintal
1000 kilograms	=	1 tonne

UNITS OF VOLUME

1000 cu millimetres	=	1 cu centimetre
1000 cu centimetres	=	1 cu decimetre
1000 cu decimetres	=	1 cu metre
1000 cu metres	=	1 cu dekametre

UNITS OF CAPACITY

10 millilitres	=	1 centilitre
10 centilitres	=	1 decilitre
10 decilitres	=	1 litre
1000 millilitres	=	1 litre
1 litre	=	1 cu decimetre
10 litres	=	1 dekalitre
10 dekalitres	=	1 hectolitre
10 hectolitres	=	1 kilolitre
1 kilolitre	=	1 cu metre

THE SI UNITS

BASE UNITS

Quantity	Unit	Symbol	Definition
length	metre	m	1 650 763.73 wavelengths of the red-orange light given out by the krypton-86 isotope.
mass	kilogram	kg	the mass of the international prototype of the kilogram, which is in the custody of the Bureau International des Poids et Mésures (BIPM) at Sèvres near Paris, France.
time	second	s	the duration of 9 192 631 770 periods of the radiation corresponding to the transition between the two hyperfine levels of the ground state of the caesium-133 atom.
electric current	ampere	A	that constant current which, if maintained in two straight parallel conductors of infinite length of negligible circular cross-section, and placed 1 metre apart in a vacuum, would produce between these conductors a force equal to 2×10^{-7} newtons per metre of length.
thermodynamic temperature	kelvin	K	the fraction $1/273 \cdot 15$ of the thermodynamic temperature of the triple point of water. The triple point of water is the point where water, ice and water vapour are in equilibrium.
luminous intensity	candela	cd	the luminous intensity, in a given direction, of a source that emits monochromatic radiation of frequency 540×10^{12} Hz and has a radiant intensity in that direction of (1/683) watts per steradian.
amount of substance	mole	mol	the amount of substance of a system that contains as many elementary entities as there are atoms in $0 \cdot 012$ kilogram of carbon-12.

SUPPLEMENTARY UNITS

plane angle	radian	rad	the plane angle between two radii of a circle that cut off on the circumference an arc equal in length to the radius.
solid angle	steradian	sr	the solid angle that, having its vertex in the centre of a sphere, cuts off an area of the surface of the sphere equal to that of a square having sides of length equal to the radius of the sphere.

DERIVED UNITS

Quantity	Unit	Symbol	Other SI units
area	square metre	m^2	–
volume	cubic metre	m^3	–
velocity	metre per second	$m \cdot s^{-1}$	–
angular velocity	radian per second	$rad\ s^{-1}$	–
acceleration	metre per second squared	$m \cdot s^{-2}$	–
angular acceleration	radian per second squared	$rad\ s^{-2}$	–
frequency	hertz	Hz	s^{-1}
density	kilogram per cubic metre	$kg \cdot m^{-3}$	–
momentum	kilogram metre per second	$kg \cdot m \cdot s^{-1}$	–
angular momentum	kilogram metre squared per sec.	$kg \cdot m^2 \cdot s^{-1}$	–
moment of inertia	kilogram metre squared	$kg \cdot m^2$	–
force	newton	N	$kg \cdot m \cdot s^{-2}$
pressure, stress	pascal	Pa	$N \cdot m^{-2} = kg \cdot m^{-1} \cdot s^{-2}$
work, energy, quantity of heat	joule	J	$N \cdot m = kg \cdot m^2 \cdot s^{-2}$
power	watt	W	$J \cdot s^{-1} = kg \cdot m^2 \cdot s^{-3}$
surface tension	newton per metre	$N \cdot m^{-1}$	$kg \cdot s^{-2}$
dynamic viscosity	newton second per metre squared	$N \cdot s \cdot m^{-2}$	$kg \cdot m^{-1} \cdot s^{-1}$
kinematic viscosity	metre squared per second	$m^2 \cdot s^{-1}$	–
temperature	degree Celsius	°C	–
thermal coefficient of linear expansion	per degree Celsius, or per kelvin	$°C^{-1}, K^{-1}$	–
thermal conductivity	watt per metre degree C	$W \cdot m^{-1} \cdot °C^{-1}$	$kg \cdot m \cdot s^{-3} \cdot °C^{-1}$
heat capacity	joule per kelvin	$J \cdot K^{-1}$	$kg \cdot m^2 \cdot s^{-2} \cdot K^{-1}$
specific heat capacity	joule per kilogram kelvin	$J \cdot kg^{-1} \cdot K^{-1}$	$m^2 \cdot s^{-2} \cdot K^{-1}$
specific latent heat	joule per kilogram	$J\ kg^{-1}$	$m^2 \cdot s^{-2}$
electric charge	coulomb	C	$A \cdot s$
electromotive force, potential difference	volt	V	$W \cdot A^{-1} = kg \cdot m^2 \cdot s^{-3} \cdot A^{-1}$
electric resistance	ohm	Ω	$V \cdot A^{-1} = kg \cdot m^2 \cdot s^{-3} \cdot A^{-2}$
electric conductance	siemens	S	$A \cdot V^{-1} = kg^{-1} \cdot m^{-2} \cdot s^3 \cdot A^2$
electric capacitance	farad	F	$A \cdot s \cdot V^{-1} = kg^{-1} \cdot m^{-2} \cdot s^4 \cdot A^2$
inductance	henry	H	$V \cdot s \cdot A^{-1} = kg \cdot m^2 \cdot s^{-2} \cdot A^{-2}$
magnetic flux	weber	Wb	$V \cdot s = kg \cdot m^2 \cdot s^{-2} \cdot A^{-1}$
magnetic flux density	tesla	T	$Wb \cdot m^{-2} = kg \cdot s^{-2} \cdot A^{-1}$
magnetomotive force	ampere	A	–
luminous flux	lumen	lm	$cd \cdot sr$
illumination	lux	lx	$lm \cdot m^{-2} = cd \cdot sr \cdot m^{-2}$
radiation activity	becquerel	Bq	s^{-1}
radiation absorbed dose	gray	Gy	$J \cdot kg^{-1} = m^2 \cdot s^{-2}$

MULTIPLES AND SUBMULTIPLES

In the metric system the following decimal multiples and sub-multiples are used:

Prefix	Symbol	Value	Factor
atto- (Danish *atten* = eighteen)	a	quintillionth	$\times 10^{-18}$
femto- (Danish *femtem* = fifteen)	f	quadrillionth	$\times 10^{-15}$
pico- (L. *pico* = minuscule)	p	trillionth	$\times 10^{-12}$
nano- (L. *nanus* = dwarf)	n	thousand millionth part or billionth[1]	$\times 10^{-9}$
micro- (Gk. *mikros* = small)	*m*	millionth part	$\times 10^{-6}$
milli- (L. *mille* = thousand)	m	thousandth part	$\times 10^{-3}$
centi- (L. *centum* = hundred)	c	hundredth part	$\times 10^{-2}$
deci- (L. *decimus* = tenth)	d	tenth part	$\times 10^{-1}$
deka- (Gk. *deka* = ten)	da	tenfold	$\times 10$
hecto- (Gk. *hekaton* = hundred)	h	hundredfold	$\times 10^2$
kilo- (Gk. *chilioi* = thousand)	k	thousandfold	$\times 10^3$
mega- (Gk. *megas* = large)	M	millionfold	$\times 10^6$
giga- (Gk. *gigas* = mighty)	G	thousand millionfold or billionfold	$\times 10^9$
tera- (Gk. *teras* = monster)	T	trillion	$\times 10^{12}$
peta- (Gk. *penta* = five)	P	quadrillion	$\times 10^{15}$
exa- (Gk. *hexa* = six)	E	quintillion	$\times 10^{18}$

[1] Some confusion has existed on the nomenclature of high numbers because of differing usage in various countries. In Britain and Germany it has been customary to advance by increments of one million, while in France and the USA it is the practice to advance in increments of a thousand. Thus in Britain, one billion was originally defined as one million million – that is the American 'trillion' (see above). However, on 20 December 1974 the then Prime Minister (Harold Wilson) announced that HM Treasury would adhere to the practice of using the billion in financial statistics in the sense of £1000 million. A billion is now increasingly used in the sense of one thousand million in Britain.

THE IMPERIAL SYSTEM

DEFINITION OF UNITS

defined by the Weights and Measures Act, 1963.

yard (yd) is equal to 0·9144 metre.

pound (lb) is equal to 0·45359237 kilogram.

gallon (gal) is the space occupied by 10 pounds weight of distilled water of density 0·998859 gram per millilitre weighed in air of density 0·001217 gram per millilitre against weights of density 8·136 gram per millilitre.

OTHER BASIC UNITS OF LENGTH EMPLOYED

animal stature the hand = 4 in. *NB* – a horse of, for example, 14 hands 3 in. to the withers is often written 14·3 hands.

surveying the link = 7·92 in or one hundredth part of a chain.

approximate the span = 9 in (from the span of the hand).

biblical the cubit = 18 in.

approximate the pace = 30 in. (from the stride).

nautical the cable = 120 fathoms or 240 yd. the fathom = 6 feet.

navigation the UK nautical mile = 6080 ft (1 second of arc at the Equator).

navigation the International nautical mile (adopted also by the USA on 1 July 1954) = 6076·1 ft (0·99936 of a UK nautical mile).

METRIC AND IMPERIAL CONVERSIONS

(* = exact)

Column One	Equivalent	Column Two	To convert Col.2 to Col.1 multiply by	To convert Col.1 to Col.2 multiply by
Length				
inch (in)	–	centimetre (cm)	0·393 700 78	2·54*
foot (ft)	12 in	metre	3·280 840	0·3048*
yard (yd)	3 ft	metre	1·093 61	0·9144*
mile	1760 yd	kilometre (km)	0·621 371 1	1·609 344*
fathom	6 ft	metre	0·546 80	1·8288*
chain	22 yd	metre	0·049 70	20·1168*
UK nautical mile	6080 ft	kilometre	0·539 611 8	1·853 184*
International nautical mile	6076·1 ft	kilometre	0·539 956 8	1·852*
ångström unit (Å)	10^{-10} m	nanometre	10	10^{-1}
Area				
square inch	–	square centimetre	0·155 00	6·4516*
square foot	144 sq in	square metre	10·763 9	0·092 903*
square yard	9 sq ft	square metre	1·195 99	0·836 127*
acre	4840 sq yd	hectare (ha) (10^4 m^2)	2·471 05	0·404 686*
square mile	640 acres	square kilometre	0·386 10	2·589 988*
Volume				
cubic inch	–	cubic centimetre	0·061 024	16·387 1*
cubic foot	1728 cu in	cubic metre	35·314 67	0·028 317*
cubic yard	27 cu ft	cubic metre	1·307 95	0·764 555*
Capacity				
litre	100 centilitres	cubic centimetre or millilitre	0·001*	1000*
pint	4 gills	litre	1·759 753	0·568 261
UK gallon	8 pints or 277·4 in^3	litre	0·219 969	4·546 092
barrel (for beer)	36 gallons	hectolitre	0·611 026	1·636 59
US gallon	0·832675 UK gallons	litre or dm^3	0·264 172	3·785 412
US barrel (for petroleum)	42 US gallons	hectolitre	0·628 998	1·589 83
fluid ounce	0·05 pint	millilitre	0·035 195	28·413 074
Velocity				
feet per second (ft/s)	–	metres per second	3·280 840	0·3048
miles per hour (mph)	–	kilometres per hour	0·621 371	1·609 344
UK knot (1·00064 Int knots)	nautical mile/hour	kilometres per hour	0·539 611 8	1·853 184
Acceleration				
foot per second per second (ft/s^2)	–	metres per second per second (m s^{-2})	3·280 840	0·3048*
Mass				
grain (gr)	1/480th of an oz troy	milligram (mg)	0·015 432 4	64·798 91
dram (dr)	27·3438 gr	gram	0·564 383	1·771 85
ounce (avoirdupois)	16 drams	gram	0·035 274 0	28·349 523 125
pound (avoirdupois)	16 ounces	kilogram	2·204 62*	0·453 592 37*
stone	14 pounds	kilogram	0·157 473 04	6·350 293 18*
quarter	28 pounds	kilogram	0·078 737 5	12·700 586 36*
hundredweight (cwt)	112 pounds	kilogram	0·019 684 1	50·802 345 44*
ton (long)	2240 pounds	tonne (= 1000 kg)	0·984 206 5	1·016 046 908 8

Note: A pound troy consists of 12 ounces troy each of 480 grains

Density

| pounds per cubic inch | – | grams per cubic centimetre | 0·036 127 2 | 27·6799 |
| pounds per cubic foot | – | kilograms per cubic metre | 0·062 428 0 | 16·0185 |

Force

dyne (dyn)	10^{-5} newton	newton	10^5	10^{-5}
poundal (pdl)	–	newton	7·233 01	0·138 255
pound-force (lbf)	–	newton	0·224 809	4·448 22
tons-force	–	kilonewton (kN)	0·100 361	9·964 02
kilogram-force (kgf) (or kilopond)	–	newton	0·101 972	9·806 65

Energy (Work, Heat)

erg	10^{-7} joule	joule	10^7	10^{-7}
horse-power (hp) (550 ft/lbf/s)	–	kilowatt (kW)	1·341 02	0·745 700
therm	–	mega joule (MJ)	0·009 478 17	105·506
kilowatt hour (kWh)	–	mega Joule (MJ)	0·277 778	3·6
calorie (international)	–	joule	0·238 846*	4·1868*
British thermal unit (Btu)	–	kilo-joule (kJ)	0·947 817	1·055 06
Pressure, Stress				
millibar (mbar or mb)	1000 dynes/cm^2	Pa	0·01*	100*
standard atmosphere (atm)	760 torrs	kPa	0·009 869 2	101·325
pounds per square inch (psi)	–	Pa	0·000 145 038	6894·76
pounds per square inch (psi)	–	kilogram-force per cm^2	14·223 3	0·070 307 0

IMPERIAL UNITS

UNITS OF LENGTH

12 inches	=	1 foot
3 feet	=	1 yard
5½ yards	=	1 rod, pole or perch
4 rods	=	1 chain
10 chains	=	1 furlong
5280 feet	=	1 mile
1760 yards	=	1 mile
8 furlongs	=	1 mile

Nautical

6 feet	=	1 fathom
100 fathoms	=	1 cable length
6080 feet	=	1 nautical mile

UNITS OF AREA

144 sq inches	=	1 sq foot
9 sq feet	=	1 sq yard
304¼ sq yards	=	1 sq rod, pole or perch
40 sq rods	=	1 rood
4 roods	=	1 acre
4840 sq yards	=	1 acre
640 acres	=	1 sq mile

UNITS OF WEIGHT

avoirdupois

437½ grains	=	1 ounce
16 drams	=	1 ounce
16 ounces	=	1 pound
14 pounds	=	1 stone
28 pounds	=	1 quarter
4 quarters	=	1 hundredweight
20 hundredweights	=	1 ton

UNITS OF VOLUME

1728 cu inches	=	1 cu foot
27 cu feet	=	1 cu yard
5·8 cu feet	=	1 bulk barrel

Shipping

1 register ton	=	100 cubic feet

UNITS OF CAPACITY

8 fluid drahms	=	1 fluid ounce
5 fluid ounces	=	1 gill
4 gills	=	1 pint
2 pints	=	1 quart
4 quarts	=	1 gallon
2 gallons	=	1 peck
4 pecks	=	1 bushel
8 bushels	=	1 quarter
36 gallons	=	1 bulk barrel

MISCELLANEOUS UNITS

WATER

1 litre	weighs 1 kilogram
1 cubic metre	weighs 1 tonne
1 UK gallon	weighs 10·022 lb
1 UK gallon salt water	weighs 10·3 lb

SPEED

1 knot	=	1 nautical mph

BEER, WINES AND SPIRITS

Proof spirit contains 57·03% pure alcohol by volume (at 50 °F).
Proof strength in degrees =·% of alcohol by volume (at 50 °F) multiplied by 1·7535.

Beer

nip	=	¼ pint
small	=	½ pint
large	=	1 pint
flagon	=	1 quart
anker	=	10 gallons
tun	=	216 gallons

Wines and spirits

tot (whisky)	=	⅙, ⅕, ¼, or ⅓ gill
noggin	=	1 gill
bottle	=	1⅓ pints

Champagne

2 bottles	=	1 magnum
4 bottles	=	1 jeroboam

| 20 bottles | = | 1 nebuchadnezzar |

TYPE SIZES

Depth

| $72\tfrac{1}{4}$ points (approx) | = | 1 inch |
| 1 didot point | = | 0·376 mm |

Width

| 1 pica em | = | 12 points |

BOOK SIZES

Crown Quarto	=	246 × 189 mm
		$7\tfrac{1}{2}$ × 10 in
Crown Octavo	=	186 × 123 mm
		5 × $7\tfrac{1}{2}$ in
Demy Quarto	=	276 × 219 mm
		$8\tfrac{3}{4}$ × $11\tfrac{1}{4}$ in
Demy Octavo	=	216 × 138 mm
		$5\tfrac{5}{8}$ × $8\tfrac{3}{4}$ in
Royal Quarto	=	312 × 237 mm
		10 × $12\tfrac{1}{2}$ in
Royal Octavo	=	234 × 156 mm
		$6\tfrac{1}{4}$ × 10 in
A4	=	297 × 210 mm
		$8\tfrac{3}{4}$ × $11\tfrac{1}{4}$ in
A5	=	210 × 148 mm
		$5\tfrac{3}{4}$ × 9 in

CROPS

UK (imperial) bushel

of wheat	=	60 lb
barley	=	50 lb
oats	=	39 lb
rye	=	56 lb
rice	=	45 lb
maize	=	56 lb
linseed	=	52 lb
potatoes	=	60 lb

US bushel:

as above except

barley	=	48 lb
linseed	=	56 lb
oats	=	32 lb

bale (cotton):

| US (net) | = | 480 lb |
| Indian | = | 392 lb |

UNITS OF ENERGY

1000 British thermal units (Btu)	=	0·293 kW h
100 000 Btu	=	1 therm
1 UK horsepower	=	0·7457 kilowatt

PAPER SIZES

Large post	=	419·1 × 533·4 mm
		$16\tfrac{1}{2}$ × 21 in
Demy	=	444·5 × 571·5 mm
		$17\tfrac{1}{2}$ × $22\tfrac{1}{2}$ in
Medium	=	457·2 × 584·2 mm
		18 × 23 in
Royal	=	508 × 635 mm
		20 × 25 in
Double crown	=	508 × 762 mm
		20 × 30 in

'A' Series (metric sizes)

A0	=	841 × 1189 mm
		$33\tfrac{1}{8}$ × $46\tfrac{3}{4}$ in
A1	=	594 × 841 mm
		$23\tfrac{3}{8}$ × $33\tfrac{1}{8}$ in
A2	=	420 × 594 mm
		$16\tfrac{1}{2}$ × $23\tfrac{3}{8}$ in
A3	=	297 × 420 mm
A4	=	$11\tfrac{3}{4}$ × $16\tfrac{1}{2}$ in
		210 × 297 mm
A5	=	$8\tfrac{1}{4}$ × $11\tfrac{3}{4}$ in
		148 × 210 mm
		$5\tfrac{7}{8}$ × $8\tfrac{1}{4}$ in

PETROLEUM

1 barrel	=	42 US gallons
	=	34·97 UK gallons
	=	0·159 cubic metre

PRECIOUS METALS

24 carat implies pure metal

| 1 metric carat | = | 200 milligrams |
| 1 troy (fine) ounce | = | 480 grains |

PHYSICS

MOTION AND FORCE

Physics is the study of the basic laws that govern matter. *Mechanics* is the branch of physics that describes the movement or motion of objects, ranging in scale from a planet to the smallest particle within an atom. Sir Isaac Newton developed a theory of mechanics that has proved highly successful in describing most types of motion, and his work has been acclaimed as one of the greatest advances in the history of science.

The Newtonian approach, although valid for velocities and dimensions within normal experience, has shown to fail for velocities approaching the speed of light and for dimensions on a subatomic scale. Newton's discoveries are therefore considered to be a special case within a more general theory.

MOTION

When a body is in *motion* it can be thought of as moving in space and time. If a body moves from one position to another, the straight line joining its starting point to its finishing point is its *displacement*. This has both magnitude and direction, and is therefore said to be a *vector quantity*. The motion is *linear*.

The rate at which a body moves, in a straight line or *rectilinearly*, is its *velocity*. Again, this has magnitude and direction and is a vector quantity. In contrast, the *speed*, which has magnitude, but is not considered to be in any particular direction, is a *scalar quantity*. The *average velocity* of the body during this rectilinear motion is defined by the total time taken. Its dimensions are therefore length divided by time, and are given in metres per second (m s^{-1}). The *instantaneous velocity* (the velocity at any instant) at any point is the rate of change of velocity at that point.

If the body moves with a changing velocity, then the rate of change of the velocity is an *acceleration*. This is defined as the change in velocity in a given time interval. Its dimensions are velocity divided by time, and are given in metres per second per second (m s^2). When a body moves with uniform acceleration (uniformly accelerated motion), the displacement, velocity and acceleration are related. These relationships are described in the *kinematic equations*, sometimes called the *laws of uniformly accelerated motion*. *Kinematics* is the study of bodies in motion, ignoring masses and forces.

The Italian physicist and astronomer Galileo Galilei (1564–1642) investigated the motion of objects falling freely in air. He believed that all objects falling freely towards the Earth have the same downward acceleration. This is called the *acceleration due to gravity* or the *gravitational acceleration*. Near the surface of the Earth it is 9.80 m s^{-2}, but there are small variations in its value depending upon latitude and elevation.

When real motion is considered, both the magnitude and the direction of the velocity have to be investigated. A golf ball, hit upwards, will return to ground. During flight its velocity will change in both magnitude and direction. In this case, instead of average velocity, the *instantaneous velocities* have to be evaluated.

CIRCULAR MOTION

If a body moves in a circular path at constant speed its direction of motion (and therefore its velocity) will be changing continuously. Since the velocity is changing, the body must have acceleration, which is also changing continuously. Thus the laws of uniformly accelerated motion do not apply. The acceleration of a body moving in a circular path is called the *centripetal* ('centre-seeking') *acceleration*. This is directed inwards, towards the centre of the circle.

NEWTON'S LAWS OF MOTION

Newton's laws of motion state relationships between the acceleration of a body and the forces acting on it. A *force* is something that causes a change in the rate of change of velocity of an object.

Newton's first law: *A body will remain at rest or travelling in a straight line at constant speed unless it is acted upon by an external force.*

The force has to be an external one – in general, a body does not exert a force upon itself. The tendency of a body to remain at rest or moving with constant velocity is called the *inertia* of the body. The inertia is related to the *mass*, which is the amount of substance in the body. The unit of mass is the *kilogram* (kg).

Newton's second law: *The resultant force exerted on a body is directly proportional to the acceleration produced by the force.*

$$F = ma$$

$$F = mv_2 - mv_1$$

where F is the force exerted
  m is the mass of the body
  a is the acceleration
  v_1 is the initial velocity
  v_2 is the final velocity

The unit of force is the *newton* (N), which is defined as the force that, acting on a body of mass 1 kg, produces an acceleration on 1 m s^{-2}.

The mass of a body is often confused with its weight. The mass is the amount of matter in the body, whereas the *weight* is the gravitational force acting on the body, and varies with location. Thus a body will have the same mass on the Moon as on Earth, but its weight on the Moon will be less than on Earth because the gravitational force on the Moon is approximately one sixth of that on Earth.

Newton expressed his second law by stating that the force acting on a body is equal to the rate of change in its 'quantity of motion', which is now called

momentum. The momentum of a body is defined as the product of its mass and velocity.

Newton's third law: *To every action there is an equal and opposite reaction.*

This law states that a single isolated force cannot exist on its own: there is always a resulting 'mirror-image' force. This means that, because any two masses exert on each other a mutual gravitational attraction, the Earth is always attracted towards a ball as much as the ball is attracted towards the Earth. Because of the huge difference in their sizes, however, the observable result is the downward acceleration of the ball.

The *principle of the conservation of momentum* follows from this third law. This states that, when two bodies interact, the total momentum before impact is the same as the total momentum after impact. Thus the total of the components of the momentum in any direction before and after the interaction are equal.

GRAVITATION

Gravitational force is one of the four fundamental forces that occur in nature. The others are the electromagnetic force, the strong nuclear force, and the weak nuclear force. The electromagnetic and weak forces have recently been shown to be a part of an electro-weak force.

Gravitational force is the mutual force of attraction between masses. The gravitational force is much weaker than the other forces mentioned above. However, this long-range force should not be thought of as a weak force. An object resting on a table is acted on by the gravitational force of the whole Earth – a significant force. The almost equal force exerted by the table is the result of short-range forces exerted by molecules on its surface.

NEWTON'S LAW OF GRAVITATION

Newton's law of gravitation states:

Every particle in the universe attracts every other particle with a force that is directly proportional to the product of their masses and inversely proportional to the square of the distance between them.

$F = G$ multiplied by m_1m_2 divided by x^2

where F is the force
  G is the gravitational constant
  m_1m_2 are the masses
  x is the distance between the particles

THE KINEMATIC EQUATIONS

For a body moving in a straight line with uniformly accelerated motion:

1. $v = u + at$

2. $s = ut + \frac{1}{2}at^2$

3. $v^2 = u^2 + 2as$

4. $s = \frac{1}{2}t(u + v)$

where s = displacement
  t = time
  u = initial or starting velocity
  v = velocity after time t
  a = acceleration

SIR ISAAC NEWTON

1642 Newton was born in the small village of Woolsthorpe in Lincolnshire.
1661 He was sent to Trinity College, Cambridge.
1666 At the age of 24, Newton had made important discoveries in mathematics (the binomial theorem, differential calculus), optics (theory of colours) and mechanics.
1669 Newton became Professor of Mathematics at Cambridge.
1687 He published his *Philosophiae Naturalis Principia Mathematica*, known as the *Principia*.
1689 (and 1701) He represented Cambridge University in Parliament.
1703–27 President of the Royal Society.
1727 Newton died in London and was buried in Westminster Abbey.

Newton's law of gravitation was first described in his *Philosophiae Naturalis Principia Mathematica* ('The Mathematical Principles of Natural Philosophy'), which he wrote in 1687. Newton used the notion of a *particle*, by which he meant a body so small that its dimensions are negligible compared to other distances. The law is an 'inverse-square law', since the magnitude of the force is inversely proportional to the square of the distance between two masses.

Newtonian mechanics were so successful that a mechanistic belief developed in which it was thought that with the knowledge of Newton's laws (and later those of electromagnetism) it would be possible to predict the future of the Universe if the positions, velocities and accelerations of all particles at any one instant were known. Later the *Heisenberg Uncertainty Principle* confounded this belief by predicting the fundamental impossibility of making simultaneous measurements of the position and velocity of a particle with infinite accuracy.

THE FUNDAMENTAL PHYSICAL CONSTANTS

The constants are called 'fundamental' since they are used universally throughout all branches of science. Increasing experimental accuracy as well as advances in theory require a complete revision of the constants during each decade, the last revision being carried out in 1986. In the values recorded in the accompanying table the figures in brackets following the last digits are estimated uncertainties of those digits. Note that the speed of light is now exactly defined.

Quantity	Symbol		Value	Units
General	speed of light in vacuo	c	$2 \cdot 99792458 \times 10^8$	$\text{m} \cdot \text{s}^{-1}$
Constants	elementary charge	e	$1 \cdot 60217733(49) \times 10^{-19}$	C
	Planck constant	h	$6 \cdot 6260755(40) \times 10^{-34}$	$\text{J} \cdot \text{s}$
	gravitational constant	G	$6 \cdot 67259(85) \times 10^{-11}$	$\text{m}^3 \cdot \text{s}^{-2} \cdot \text{kg}^{-1}$
Matter in	Avogadro constant	N_A	$6 \cdot 0221367(36) \times 10^{23}$	mol^{-1}
Bulk	atomic mass constant	m_u	$1 \cdot 6605402(10) \times 10^{-27}$	kg
			$9 \cdot 3149432(28) \times 10^2$	MeV
	Faraday constant	$F = N_A e$	$9 \cdot 6485309(29) \times 10^4$	$\text{C} \cdot \text{mol}^{-1}$
	molar gas constant	R	$8 \cdot 314510(70)$	$\text{J} \cdot \text{mol}^{-1} \cdot \text{K}^{-1}$
			$8 \cdot 205783(70) \times 10^{-5}$	$\text{m}^3 \cdot \text{atm} \cdot \text{mol}^{-1} \cdot \text{K}^{-1}$
	molar volume of ideal gas	V_m	$2 \cdot 241410(19) \times 10^{-2}$	$\text{m}^3 \cdot \text{mol}^{-1}$
	(at 273·15K and 1 atm)			
	Boltzmann constant	$k = R/N_A$	$1 \cdot 380658(12) \times 10^{-23}$	$\text{J} \cdot \text{K}^{-1}$
Electron	electron rest mass	m_e	$9 \cdot 1093897(54) \times 10^{-31}$	kg
			$0 \cdot 51099906(15)$	MeV
	electron specific charge	e/m_e	$1 \cdot 75881962(53) \times 10^{11}$	$\text{C} \cdot \text{kg}^{-1}$
Proton	proton rest mass	m_p	$1 \cdot 6726231(10) \times 10^{-27}$	kg
			$9 \cdot 3827231(28) \times 10^2$	MeV
Neutron	neutron rest mass	m_n	$1 \cdot 6749286(10) \times 10^{-27}$	kg
			$9 \cdot 3956563(28) \times 10^2$	MeV
Energy	million electron volt unit	MeV	$1 \cdot 78266270(54) \times 10^{-30}$	kg
Conversion			$1 \cdot 60217733(49) \times 10^{-13}$	J

THE PARTICLES OF PHYSICS

In addition to the quanta that carry the various forces of Nature, matter is made up of leptons and quarks. These can be associated into generations or families (as described below). The existence of a fourth family is predicted from the observed amount of deuterium and helium in the Universe, while a fifth family may also exist.

Leptons have zero baryon number (B) while quarks have $B = \frac{1}{3}$ and both types of entity have half-integral spin ($J = \frac{1}{2}$). Leptons and quarks are believed to differ in the property known as 'colour' – leptons being 'colourless' while quarks exist in three 'colours'. However, both types of particle are believed to be composed of simpler entities known as 'preons'.

For each lepton and quark there is an equivalent anti-particle with opposite properties. Composites of quarks are known as 'hadrons', mesons being composed of quark and anti-quark pairs (but not necessarily of the same flavour) while baryons consist of three quarks. Hadrons may be associated into groups known as 'multiplets' which are governed by the property known as 'isospin' (I) such that there are (2I + 1) states in a multiplet. Thus the proton and neutron with $I = \frac{1}{2}$ form a two-particle multiplet, while the delta baryon resonances with $I = \frac{3}{2}$ form four-particle multiplets. While it is possible to form thousands of particles from a combination of six quarks, at the end of 1987 the existence was accepted of 71 meson multiplets and 59 baryon multiplets, representing the discovery of 238 particles and an equal number of anti-particles.

WAVE THEORY

Water waves are a phenomenon that can be seen, and the effects of sound waves are sensed directly by the ear. Some of the waves in the electromagnetic spectrum (see below) can also be sensed by the body: light waves by the eye, and the heating effect of infrared by the skin. There are other electromagnetic waves, however, that cannot be experienced directly through any of the human senses, and even infrared can generally only be observed using specialized detectors.

Wave phenomena are found in all areas of physics, and similar mathematical equations are used in each application. Some of the general principles of wave motions are explored here.

WAVE TYPES AND CHARACTERISTICS

A *travelling wave* is a disturbance that moves or *propagates* from one point to another. *Mechanical waves* are travelling waves that propagate through a material – as, for example, happens when a metal rod is tapped at one end with a hammer. An initial disturbance at a particular place in a material will cause a force to be exerted on adjacent parts of the material. An *elastic force* then acts to restore the material to its equilibrium position. In so doing, it compresses the adjacent particles and so the disturbance moves outward from the source. In attempting to return to their original positions, the particles overshoot, so that at a particular point a *rarefaction* (or stretching) follows a *compression* (or squeezing). The passage of the wave is observed as variations in the pressure about the equilibrium position or by the speed of oscillations. This change is described as *oscillatory* (like a pendulum) or *periodic*.

There are two main types of periodic oscillation – *tranverse* or *longitudinal*.

Tranverse waves In transverse waves the vibrations are perpendicular to the direction of travel.

Longitudinal waves In longitudinal waves the vibrations are parallel to the direction of travel.

Sound waves Sound waves are alternate compressions and rarefactions of whatever material through which they are travelling, and the waves are longitudinal.

Water waves Water waves may be produced by the wind or some other disturbance. The particles move in vertical circles so there are both transverse and longitudinal displacements. The motion causes the familiar wave profile with narrow peaks and broad troughs.

Wave motions transfer energy – for example, sound waves, seismic waves and water waves transfer mechanical energy. However, energy is lost as the *amplitude* – the maximum displacement from the equilibrium position – diminishes, and the wave is said to be *attenuated*. There are two distinct processes – *spreading* and *absorption*. In many cases

there is little or no absorption – electromagnetic radiation from the Sun travels through space without any absorption at all, but planets that are more distant than the Earth receive less radiation because it is spreading over a larger area and so the *intensity* (the ratio of power to area) decreases according to an inverse-square law.

The same applies to sound in the atmosphere. In some cases, however, energy is absorbed in a medium, as, for example, when light enters and exposes a photographic film, or when X-rays enter flesh. For homogeneous radiation, absorption is *exponential*; for example, if half the radiation goes through 1 mm of absorber, a quarter would go through 2 mm and an eighth through 3 mm.

The *frequency* (*f*) of the wave motion is defined as the number of complete oscillations or cycles per second. The unit of frequency is the *hertz* (Hz), named after the German physicist Heinrich Rudolf Hertz: 1 hertz = 1 cycle per second. The *wavelength* is the distance between two successive peaks or troughs in the wave. The *speed of propagation* of the compressions, or *phase speed* of the wave, is equal to the product of frequency and the wavelength.

Waves originating from a point source will propagate outwards, in all directions, forming *wavefronts*; these wavefronts will be circular or spherical if propagating through a homogeneous medium.

REFLECTION AND REFRACTION

If a wave travels from one medium to another, the direction of propagation is changed or 'bent'; the wave is said to be *refracted*. The wave will travel in the first medium with velocity v_1, and will come upon the surface of the second medium with the angle of incidence *i*. The wave will then be refracted – *r* representing the angle of refraction. The new velocity – v_2 – will be less than velocity v_1 if the second medium is more dense than the first medium, but greater than v_1 if the second medium is less dense. The velocities are related by:
$v_1/v_2 = \sin i/ \sin r$. The ratio $\sin i/\sin r$ is a constant. This relationship was formulated by the Dutch astronomer Willebrord Snell (1591–1626) and is known as *Snell's Law*.

INTERFERENCE

If several waves are travelling through a medium, the resultant at any point and time is the vector sum of the amplitudes of the individual waves. This is known as the *superposition principle*. Two or more waves combining together in this way exhibit the phenomenon of *interference*. If the resultant wave amplitude is greater than those of the individual waves then *constructive interference* is taking place; if it is less, *destructive interference* occurs. If two sound waves of slightly different frequencies and equal amplitudes are played together then the resulting sound has what is called *varying amplitude*.

AMPLITUDE AND FREQUENCY MODULATION

Radio waves can be used to carry sound waves by superimposing the pattern of the sound waves onto the radio wave. This is called *modulation*, and is one of the basic forms of radio transmission. There are two ways of modulating radio waves. In *amplitude modulation* (AM) the amplitude of the radio *carrier wave* is made to vary with the amplitude of the sound signal. For *frequency modulation* (FM) the frequency of the carrier wave is made to vary so that the variations are in step with the changes in amplitude of the sound signal.

STANDING OR STATIONARY WAVES

These are the result of confining waves in a specific region. When a travelling wave, such as a wave propagating along a guitar string towards the bridge, reaches the support, the string must be almost at rest. A force is exerted on the support that then reacts by setting up a reflected wave travelling back along the string. This wave has the same frequency and wavelength as the source wave. At certain frequencies the two waves, travelling in opposite directions, interfere to produce a stationary- or standing-wave pattern. Each pattern or mode of vibration corresponds to a particular frequency.

DIFFRACTION

Waves will usually proceed in a straight line through a uniform medium. However, when they pass through a slit with width comparable to their wavelength, they spread out, i.e. they are diffracted. Thus waves are able to bend round corners.

Huygens' principle was proposed in 1676 by the Dutch physicist Christiaan Huygens (1629–95) to explain the laws of reflection and refraction. He postulated that light was a wave motion. Each point on a wavefront becomes a new or secondary source. Diffraction describes the interference effects observed between light derived from a continuous portion of a wavefront.

STATICS, FRICTION AND ELASTICITY

In addition to the fundamental forces (described above), other forces such as frictional, elastic and viscous forces may be encountered. Because of their different natures, solids and fluids appear in some ways to react differently to similar applied forces.

Solids: When forces are applied to solids they tend to resist. Friction inhibits displacement, but is overcome after a certain limit. Bodies may be deformed by tensions.

Fluids: Fluids, although lacking definite shape, are held together by internal forces. They exert pressure on the walls of the containing vessel. Fluids – by definition – have a tendency to flow; this may be greater in some substances than in others and is governed by the viscosity of the fluid.

STATIC EQUILIBRIUM

Newton's first law (see above), stated for a single particle, can also apply to real bodies that have definite sizes and shapes and consist of many particles. Such a body may be in *equilibrium*, which means it is at rest or moving with constant velocity in a straight line. This means that it is acted on by *zero net force*, and that it has no tendency to rotate.

A body is acted on by zero force if the total or resultant of all the forces acting on it is zero – i.e. all the forces cancel each other out. If a body is at rest it is in *static equilibrium*. Studies of such conditions are important in the design of bridges, dams and buildings.

FORCES INVOLVED IN ROTATION

Torque (or *moment of a force*) measures the tendency of a force to cause the body to rotate. In this case the force causes *angular acceleration*, which is the *rate of*

change of angular momentum of the body. Torque is defined as the product of the force acting on a body and the perpendicular distance from the axis of the rotation of the body to the line of action of the force. Torque has units of force × distance, usually expressed as *newton metres* (N m).

Torque: *Torque or moment of a force = force × perpendicular distance = Fd.*

Torque is increased if either the force or the perpendicular distance is increased. If a wedge is used to keep open a door, it has maximum effect if it is placed on the floor as far from the hinge as possible.

When a body is acted upon by two equal and opposite forces, not in the same line, then the result is a *couple*, which has a constant turning moment about any axis perpendicular to the plane in which they act. When the total or net torque on a body is zero about any axis, the body is in *equilibrium*. A body is in stable equilibrium if a small linear displacement causes a force to act on the body to return it to its previous position, or an angular displacement causes a couple to act to bring it back to its previous position, called the *equilibrium position*.

CENTRE OF MASS

The *centre of mass* of a body is a point, normally within the body, such that the net resultant force produces an acceleration at this point, as though all the mass of the body were concentrated there. For bodies of certain shapes this point may lie outside the object.

If a uniform gravitational field is present, the centre of gravity coincides with the centre of mass. Thus all the weight can be considered to act at this single point. The stability of an object is helped by keeping the centre of gravity as low as possible, thus a racing car is low-slung to improve stability.

FRICTION

Sliding friction occurs when a solid body slides on a rough surface. Its progress is hindered by an interaction of the surface of the solid with the surface it is moving on. This is called *kinetic frictional force*.

Another type of friction is called *static friction*. Before the object moves, the resultant force acting on it must be zero. The frictional force acting between the object and the surface on which it rests cannot exceed its limiting value. Thus, when the other forces acting on the object, against friction, exceed this value the object is caused to accelerate. The limiting or maximum value of the frictional force occurs when the stationary object acted on by the resultant force is just about to slip.

Both these types of friction involve interaction with a solid surface. The frictional forces depend on the two contacting surfaces and in particular on the presence of any surface contaminants. The friction between metal surfaces is largely due to adhesion, shearing and deformation within and around the regions of real contact. Energy is dissipated in friction and appears as internal energy, which can be observed as heat – thus car brakes heat up when used to slow a vehicle. The results of friction may be reduced by the use of lubricants between the surfaces in contact. This is one of the functions of the oil used in car engines.

A further type of friction is *rolling friction*, which occurs when a wheel rolls. Energy is dissipated through the system, because of imperfect elasticity (see below). This effect does not depend upon surfaces and is unaffected by lubrication.

ELASTICITY

Elasticity deals with deformations that disappear when the external applied forces are removed. Most bodies may be deformed by the action of external forces and behave elastically for small deformations.

Strain is a measure of the amount of deformation. *Stress* is a quantity proportional to the force causing the deformation. Its value at any point is given by the magnitude of the force acting at that point divided by the area over which it acts.

It is found that for small stresses the stress is proportional to the strain. The constant of proportionality is called the *elastic modulus* and it varies according to the material and the type of deformation.

Young's modulus refers to changes in the length of a material under the action of an applied force.

The shear modulus relates to another type of deformation – that of planes in a solid sliding past each other.

The bulk modulus characterizes the behaviour of a substance subject to a uniform volume comparison.

HOOKE'S LAW

A special example of deformation is the extension or elongation of a spring by an applied force. *Hooke's law*, formulated by the English scientist Robert Hooke (1635–1703), states that, for small forces, the extension is proportional to the applied force. Thus a spring balance will have a uniform scale for the measurement of various weights.

In scientific terms, steel spring – which returns to its initial state readily – is almost *perfectly elastic*. In contrast, a soft rubber ball dropped on hard ground bounces to only about half its initial height, demonstrating *imperfect elasticity*.

VISCOSITY

Some bodies behave elastically for low values of stress, but above a critical level they behave in a perfectly viscous manner and 'flow' like thick treacle, with irreversible deformation. This is called *plastic flow*.

Viscosity relates to the internal friction in the flow of a fluid – how adjacent layers in the fluid exert retarding forces on each other. This arises from cohesion of the molecules in the fluid. In a solid, deformation of adjacent layers is usually elastic. In a fluid, however, there is no permanent resistance to change of shape; the layers can slide past each other, with continuous displacement of these layers.

Fluids are described as *newtonian* if they obey Newton's law that the ratio of the applied stress to the rate of shearing has a constant value. This is not true for many substances. Some paints, for example, do not have constant values for the coefficient of viscosity; as the paint is stirred it flows more easily and the coefficient is diminished. Molten lava is another non-newtonian fluid.

If adjacent layers flow smoothly past each other the steady flow is described as *laminar flow*. If the flow velocity is increased the flow may become disordered with irregular and random motions called *turbulence*. Smoke rising from a cigarette starts with smooth laminar flow but soon breaks into turbulent flow with the formation of eddies. *Reynold's number* is used to predict the onset of turbulence. It is defined as:

Re = (speed × density × dimension) divided by viscosity

or, alternatively, as the ratio is the inertial force to the viscous force:

Re = inertial force divided by the viscous force

This is a pure ratio as it has no units. It is a characteristic of the system and the dimension may be the diameter of a pipe or the radius of a ballbearing. Viscosity is relevant for small values of Reynold's number. Above a certain value, turbulence is likely to break out. Thus, for the fall of a very small raindrop, resistance is viscous and is proportional to the product of the density of air, the radius of the raindrop and its speed. For a large raindrop, the resistance is proportional to the product of the density of air, the square of the radius of the raindrop and the square of its speed.

FLUIDS AT REST

Pressure is defined as the perpendicular or normal force per unit area of a plane surface of a fluid, and its unit is the *pascal* (Pa), equivalent to 1 newton per square metre ($N m^2$). At all points in the fluid the depth of pressure is the same. The pressure depends only on depth in an enclosed fluid, and is independent of cross-sectional area.

Atmospheric pressure may be measured using a barometer. At sea level, it is equivalent to the weight of a column of mercury about 0.76 m high, which is about 1.01×10^5 Pa. It varies by up to about 5%, depending on the weather systems passing overhead.

ARCHIMEDES' PRINCIPLE

The *buoyancy force* was described by the Greek mathematician and physicist Archimedes (287–212 BC). *Archimedes' principle* states that an object placed in a fluid is buoyed up by a force equal to the weight of fluid displaced by the body.

A body with density greater than that of the fluid will sink, because the fluid it displaces weighs less than it does itself. A body with density less than that of the fluid will float.

density divided by volume = mass

A submarine varies its density by flooding ballast tanks with sea water or emptying them; this enables it to dive or rise to the surface.

SURFACE TENSION

Surface tension occurs at an interface between a liquid and either a gas or a solid. Molecules in a liquid exert forces on other molecules. At the surface there is asymmetry in these forces, resulting in surface tension. Thus falling rainwater coalesces into spherical drops.

THERMODYNAMICS

Thermodynamics is the study of heat and temperature. *Heat* is a form of energy, and the *temperature* of a substance is a measure of its internal energy. One fundamental principle in the study of thermodynamics is the *conservation of energy*. This theory was developed in the late 19th century by about a dozen scientists, including James Joule (1818–89), a brewery-owner from the north of England, and Baron Herman von Helmholtz (1821–94), a German physiologist. Although there seemed to be plenty of evidence in the world that energy was not conserved, this important principle was eventually established.

Much of the energy that seems to be lost in typical interactions – such as a box sliding across a floor – is converted into internal energy: in the case of the sliding box, this is the kinetic energy (see below) gained by the atoms and molecules within the box and the floor as they interact and are pulled from their equilibrium positions. The name given to the energy in the form of hidden motion of atoms and molecules is *thermal energy*. Strictly speaking, heat is transferred between two bodies as a result of a change in temperature, although the term 'heat' is commonly used for the thermal energy as well. Processes that turn kinetic energy, which is the organized energy of a moving body, into thermal energy, which is the disorganized energy due to the motion of atoms, include friction and viscosity.

WORK AND ENERGY

When a force (see above) acts on a body, causing acceleration in the direction of the force, *work* is done. The work done on a body by a constant force is defined as the product of the magnitude of the force and the consequent displacement of the body in the direction of the force.

The units used to measure work are *joules* (sometimes referred to as *newton metres*). A joule (J) is defined as the work done on a body when it is displaced 1 metre as the result of the action of a force of 1 newton acting in the direction of motion.

$$1\,J = 1\,N\,m$$

Energy is the capacity of a body to do work. The total energy stored in a *closed system* – one in which no external forces are experienced – remains constant, however it may be transformed. This is the principle of *conservation of energy*. It may take the form of:
mechanical energy (kinetic or potential; see below);
electrical energy;
chemical energy; or
heat energy.

There are other forms of energy including;
gravitational energy;
magnetism;
the energy of electromagnetic radiation; and
the energy of matter.

KINETIC ENERGY

The *kinetic energy* of a body is the energy it has because it is moving. Kinetic energy is equal to half the product of the mass and the square of the velocity – thus the kinetic energy of a body mass m moving at velocity v is $\frac{1}{2}\,mv^2$.

POTENTIAL ENERGY

As well as kinetic energy, which is energy of motion, a body can have *potential energy*. In contrast to the kinetic energy, which is dependent upon velocity, potential energy is dependent upon position.

The gravitational potential energy of a body of mass m at a height h above the ground is mgh, where g is the acceleration due to gravity.

This gravitational potential energy is equal to the work that the Earth's gravitational field will do on

the body as it moves to ground level. Potential energy can be converted into kinetic energy or it can be used to do work. It acts as a store of energy. If a body moves upward against the gravitational force, work is done on it and there is an increase in gravitational potential energy.

TEMPERATURE

Temperature is a measure of the internal energy or 'hotness' of a body, not the heat of the body. Thermometers are used to measure temperature. They may be based on:
the change in *volume* of a liquid (as in a mercury thermometer);
the change in *length* of a strip of metal (as used in many thermometers); or
the change in *electrical resistance* of a conductor.

Other parameters may also be involved in measuring temperature.

The *thermodynamic temperature scale* – also known as the *kelvin scale* or the *ideal gas scale* – is based on a unit called the *kelvin* (K): the scale is used in both practical and theoretical physics. An *ideal gas* is one that would obey all the gas laws (see below) perfectly. In fact no gas is ideal, but most behave sufficiently closely that the gas laws can be used in calculations. At ordinary temperatures and pressures, dry air can be considered as a very good approximation to an ideal gas.

GAS LAWS

The *ideal gas law* combines *Boyle's law* with *Charles's law*. It states that gas at low pressure (p_1) multiplied by high volume (V_1) divided by low temperature (T_1) = higher pressure (p_2) multiplied by decreased volume (V_2) divided by higher temperature (T_2).

On the Kelvin scale the freezing point of water is 273.15 K (0 °C or 32 °F) and its boiling point is 373.15 K (100 °C or 212 °F): one degree kelvin is equal in magnitude to one degree on the Celsius scale. The temperature of 0 (zero) K is known as *absolute zero*. At absolute zero (-273.15°C), for an ideal gas, the volume would be infinitely large and the pressure zero.

HEAT AND INTERNAL ENERGY

The molecular energy (kinetic and potential) within a body is called *internal energy*. When this energy is transferred from a place of high energy to one of lower energy, it is described as a flow of heat.

If two bodies of different temperatures are placed in thermal contact with each other, after a time they are found both to be at the same temperature. Energy is transferred from the warmer to the colder body, until both are at a new *equilibrium temperature*. Heat is a form of energy, and heat flow is a transfer of energy resulting from differences in temperature.

The unit of internal energy and heat is the *joule*, as defined above. Units used previously include the *calorie*, which is equivalent to 4.2 joules and is defined as the heat required to raise the temperature of 1 gram of water from 14.5 °C to 15.5 °C. (The unit used by nutritionists is referred to as the calorie but is actually the *kilocalorie*, which is equal to 1000 calories, and is equivalent to 4200 joules.)

THE KINETIC THEORY OF GASES

The kinetic theory of gases takes Newton's laws (see above) and applies them statistically to a group of molecules. It treats a gas as if it were made up of extremely small – dimensionless – particles, all in constant random movement. It is based on an ideal gas.

One conclusion is that the pressure and volume of such a gas are related to the average kinetic energy for each molecule. The kinetic theory explains that pressure in a gas is due to the impact of the molecules on the containing walls around the gas.

The temperature of an ideal gas is a measure of the average molecular kinetic energies. At a higher temperature the mean speed of the molecules is increased. For air at room temperature and atmospheric pressures the mean speed is about 500 m s^{-1} (about 1800 km/h or 1100 mph, the velocity of a rifle bullet).

The internal energy of a gas is associated with the motion of its molecules and their potential energy. For a gas that is more complex than one with monatomic molecules, account has to be taken of energies associated with the rotation and vibration of its molecules, as well as their speed.

A *thermally isolated system* is one that neither receives nor transmits transfer of heat, although the temperature within the system may vary. Such a system is called *adiabatic*. One in which the temperature remains constant is an *isothermic* system.

If mechanical or electrical work is performed on a thermally isolated system, its internal energy increases. James Joule observed the effects of doing measured amounts of work on insulated bodies (thermally isolated systems). He discovered an equivalence relation between the amount of work done *(W)* and the heat gained *(Q)*:

$$W = JQ$$

The constant *J* was described by Joule as the *mechanical equivalent of heat.*

LAWS OF THERMODYNAMICS

The first law of thermodynamics is a development of the law of conservation of energy, which states that in any interaction, energy is neither created nor destroyed. If, during an interaction, a quantity of heat (*Q*) is absorbed by a body, it is equal to the sum of the increase in internal energy *U* of the body and any external work *W* done by the body:

$$Q = U + W$$

The increase in internal energy will be made up of an increase in the kinetic energy of the molecules in the body and an increase in their potential energy, since work will have been done against intermolecular forces as the body expands.

The change in internal energy of a body thus depends only on its initial and final states. The change may be the result of an increase in energy in any form – thermal, mechanical, gravitational, etc. Another statement of this law is that it is possible to convert work totally into heat.

The second law of thermodynamics states that the converse is not true. There are several ways in which the second law may be stated but, essentially, it means that heat cannot itself flow from a cold object to a hot object. Thus the law shows that certain processes may only operate in one direction.

ENTROPY

Entropy is a parameter used in statistical mechanics to describe the disorder or *chaos* of a system. A highly disordered state is one in which molecules move haphazardly in all directions, with many different velocities. An alternative form of the second law of thermodynamics is that the entropy of the universe never decreases. It follows from this analysis that the universe is moving through increasing disorder towards thermal equilibrium. Therefore the universe cannot have existed for ever, otherwise it would have reached this equilibrium state already.

LATENT HEAT

When heat flows between a body and its surroundings there is usually a change in the temperature of the body, as well as changes in internal energies. This is not so when a change of form occurs, as from solid to liquid or from liquid to gas. This is called a *phase change* and involves a change in the internal energy of the body only.

The amount of heat needed to make the change of phase is called the *hidden* or *latent heat.* To change water at 100 °C to water vapour requires nearly seven times as much heat (*latent heat of vaporization*) as to change ice to water (*latent heat of fusion*). This varies for water at different temperatures – more heat is required to change it to water vapour at 80 °C, less at 110 °C. In each case the attractive forces binding the water molecules together must be loosened or broken. The transfer of water vapour through the Earth's atmosphere towards the poles from equatorial regions is an effective way of transferring energy. When water turns into water vapour the latent heat of vaporization is absorbed and the atmosphere cools; when the vapour turns into rain and is deposited, the latent heat is given out to the atmosphere. A similar cycle takes place in a heat pump or refrigerator.

HEAT TRANSFER

Heat conduction occurs when kinetic and molecular energy is passed from one molecule to another. Metals are good conductors of heat because of electrons that transport energy through the material. Air is a poor conductor in comparison. Thus a string vest keeps its wearer warm by trapping air and so preventing the conduction of heat outwards from the body.

Heat convection results from the motion of the heated substance. Warm air is less dense than cold air and so, according to Archimedes' principle, it rises. Convection is the main mechanism for mixing the atmosphere and diluting pollutants emitted into the air.

Radiation is the third process for heat transfer. All bodies radiate energy in the form of electromagnetic waves. This radiation may pass across a vacuum, and thus the Earth receives energy radiated from the Sun. A body remains at a constant temperature when it both radiates and receives energy at the same rate. This principle is used in the construction of the Thermos flask.

QUANTUM THEORY AND RELATIVITY

Three of the most important theories of the 20th century are the quantum theory and the theories of special and general relativity. When special relativity is combined with the full quantum theory and with electromagnetism, almost all of the physical world is described by it. The most important application is in the theory of subatomic particles. General relativity is as yet not fully combined with quantum theory and is a theory of gravity and cosmology.

The physical world is not as simple as the theories of Newton supposed, although such views are appropriate simplifications for large objects moving relatively slowly with respect to the observer. *Quantum mechanics* is the only correct description of effects on an atomic scale, and special relativity must be used when speeds approaching the speed of light, with respect to the observer, are involved.

THE DEVELOPMENT OF QUANTUM THEORY

At the very beginning of the 20th century scientists such as the German physicist Max Planck (1858–1947) discovered that the theories of classical physics were not sufficient to explain certain phenomena on the subatomic scale, particularly in the field of electromagnetic radiation and the study of light waves. Their work resulted in the development of the quantum theory, which states that *nothing can be measured or observed without disturbing it*: the observer can affect the outcome of the effect being measured.

The Scottish physicist James Clerk Maxwell (1831–79) had developed a theory about the electromagnetic-wave nature of light, and this was crucial to the development of quantum theory. Maxwell showed that at any point on a beam of light there is a magnetic field and an electric field that are perpendicular to each other and to the direction of the light beam. The fields oscillate millions of times every second, forming a wave pattern.

PHOTONS

If light is directed onto a piece of metal in a vacuum, electrons are knocked from the surface of the metal. This is the *photoelectric effect*. For light of a given wavelength, the number of electrons emitted per second increases with the intensity of the light, although the energies of the electrons are independent of the wavelength.

This discovery led the German physicist Albert Einstein (1879–1955) to deduce that the energy in a light beam exists in small discrete packets called *photons* or *quanta*. These can be detected in experiments in which light is allowed to fall on a detector, usually photographic film. This has led to the theory of the *dual nature of light*, which behaves as a wave during interference experiments but as a stream of particles during the photoelectric effect. Further work on this phenomenon has led to the acceptance of *wave-particle duality*, which is a fundamental principle in quantum physics. The way a system is described depends upon the apparatus with which it is interacting: light behaves as a wave when it passes through slits in an interference experiment, but as a stream of particles when it hits a detector.

UNCERTAINTY

Werner Karl Heisenberg (1901–76), a German physicist, interpreted wave-particle duality differently. He proposed that when a beam of light is directed at a screen with two slits, the interference pattern formed exists only if we do not know which slit the photon passed through. If we make an additional measurement and determine which slit was traversed, we destroy the interference pattern. Heisenberg showed that it was impossible to measure position and momentum simultaneously with infinite accuracy; he expressed his findings in the *uncertainty principle* named after him. This changed the thinking

about the precision with which simultaneous measurements of two physical quantities can be made.

PARTICLES

Matter is made up of vast numbers of very small particles. The behaviour of these particles cannot be described by the theories of classical physics, since there is no equivalence to subatomic particles in everyday mechanics. Thus it is not helpful to discuss the behaviour of electrons in atoms in terms of tiny 'planets' orbiting a 'sun'.

Louis Victor de Broglie (1892–1987), the French physicist, suggested that if light waves can behave like particles, then particles might in certain circumstances behave like waves. Later experiments confirmed that under appropriate conditions particles can exhibit wave phenomena.

ATOMIC ENERGY LEVELS

Quantum systems are described by a mathematical equation known as the *Schrödinger equation* after the Austrian physicist Erwin Schrödinger (1887–1961), who first formulated it. In situations such as where a negatively charged electron is bound to the positively charged nucleus of an atom, the Schrödinger equation has solutions for only *discrete* or *quantized* allowed values of the energy of the electron. The energy of an electron in an atom cannot take a lower value than the least of the allowed values – the *ground state* – so the electron cannot fall into the nucleus.

If an atom, through the interaction of forces on it, is excited into an allowed state of energy that is higher than the ground state, it can emit a photon and jump into the ground state. The energy of the photon is equal to the difference in energy levels of the two states. The energy of the photon is related to the wavelength of the light wave associated with it – thus light can be emitted by atoms only at particular wavelengths.

QUANTUM MECHANICS

Quantum mechanics is the study of the observable behaviour of particles. This includes electromagnetic radiation in all its details. In particular, it is the only appropriate theory for describing the effects that occur on an atomic scale.

Quantum mechanics deals exclusively with what can be observed, and does not attempt to describe what is happening in between measurements. This is not true of classical theories, which are essentially complete descriptions of what is occurring whether or not attempts are made to measure it.

In quantum mechanics the experimenter is directly included in the theory. Quantum mechanics predicts all the possible results of making a measurement, but it does not say which one will occur when an experiment is actually carried out. All that can be known is the probability of something being seen. In some experiments one event is very much more likely than any other, therefore most of the time this is what will be found, but sometimes one of the less probable events will occur. It is impossible to predict which will occur; the only way to find out is by making the appropriate measurement.

For example in an isotope of the element americium, 19% of the nuclei decay purely by alpha-particle emission and 81% decay by alpha emission followed by photon emission. For any individual americium nucleus it is not possible to say which decay will occur, only what will be observed on average.

In some experiments the same event can occur in different ways. What is measured depends on whether it is known which of the possible paths was taken. Thus any additional knowledge, which can only be gained by making an additional measurement, changes the outcome of the first experiment.

SPECIAL RELATIVITY

Inertial frames Physical laws such a Newton's laws of mechanics are stated with respect to some *frame of reference* that allows physical quantities such as velocity and acceleration to be defined. A frame of reference is called *inertial* if it is unaccelerated and it does not contain a gravitational field.

Einstein's relativity principle In 1905 Einstein stated that all inertial frames are equally good for carrying out experiments. This assumption, coupled with the evidence that the speed of light is the same in all frames, led Einstein to develop the theory of special relativity. This theory has been extensively tested using particle accelerators, where electrons or protons travel at speeds within a fraction of 1% of the speed of light. The masses of such particles measured by an observer in the laboratory in which the particles are travelling are higher than the masses measured by an observer at rest with respect to the particles.

Time The classical view of time is that if two events take place simultaneously with reference to one frame then they must also occur simultaneously within another frame. In terms of special relativity, however, two events that occur simultaneously in one frame may not be seen as simultaneous in another frame moving relative to the first. The sequence of cause and effect in related events is not, however, affected. Light plays a special role in synchronizing clocks in different frames because it has the same speed in all frames. In the classical view all observers have the same time scale, whereas in special relativity every inertial observer requires an individual time scale.

Space-time An important feature of special relativity is that time and space have to be considered as unified and not as two separate things. This means that time is related to the frame of reference in which it is being measured. This is a different view of space to that of Newton.

Length contraction The equations of special relativity lead to the very simple prediction that the length of a moving body in the direction of its motion measured in another frame is reduced by a factor dependent on its velocity with respect to the observer. What this means is that a car travelling very fast on a motorway would be measured by a stationary observer to be slightly shorter and heavier than usual, although the driver would not determine any difference. The length of a body is greatest when it is measured in a frame travelling *with* the body; as the speed of the body *relative to* the frame of reference approaches the speed of light the measured length approaches zero.

Time dilation A similar effect happens to moving clocks (which can be any regularly occurring phenomenon, such as the vibration of atoms – the basis of atomic clocks – or the decay of particles). A clock moving with a uniform velocity in one frame is measured as running slow in another frame. Its fastest rate is in its own frame, and at speeds – relative to the observer – approaching the speed of light the clock rate approaches zero.

Paradox of reality? Both of the above effects of length and time contraction have been the inspiration of numerous 'paradoxes' (and some science-fiction writing), and have been criticized on such grounds. But this simply goes to show that our 'common-sense' view of the world is rooted in frames that travel with respect to the observer at tiny speeds compared to that of light, and is just as inappropriate in describing these phenomena as it is in describing the quantum effects of the atomic world. Time dilation has been measured experimentally both with decaying particles and with actual macroscopic clocks. In all cases the effects predicted by special relativity were encountered.

GENERAL RELATIVITY

This is an extension of the theory of special relativity to include gravitational fields and accelerating reference frames. Gravitational fields arise because of the distortions of space-time in the vicinity of large masses, and space-time is no longer thought of as having an existence independent of the mass in the universe. Rather, space-time, mass and gravity are interdependent.

ACOUSTICS

The range of frequencies for which sound waves are audible to humans is from 20 to 20 000 Hz (i.e. vibrations or cycles per second) – the higher the frequency, the higher the pitch. In music, the A above middle C is internationally standardized at 440 Hz. For orchestral instruments, the frequencies range between 6272 Hz achieved on a handbell, and 16.4 Hz on a sub-contrabass clarinet.

Frequencies that are lower than the human audible range are referred to as *infrasonic*, and those above as *ultrasonic*. Many mammals such as dolphins and bats have sensitive hearing in the ultrasonic range, and they use high-pitched squeaks for echolocation. Large animals such as whales and elephants use frequencies in the infrasonic range to communicate over long distances.

THE VELOCITY OF SOUND

Sound shares the general characteristics of other wave forms. Sound waves are longitudinal compressions (squeezings) and rarefactions (stretchings) of the medium through which they are travelling, and are produced by a vibrating object.

If a sound wave is travelling in any medium then the pressure variations formed along its path cause strains as a result of the applied stresses. The velocity of the sound is given by the square root of the appropriate elastic modulus divided by the density.

The velocity of sound – as with the velocity of other types of wave – differs in different media. In still air at $0\,°C$, the velocity of sound is about $331\ m\ s^{-1}$ (1191.6 km/h, or 740 mph). If the air temperature rises by $1\ °C$, then the velocity of sound increases by about 0.6 m s^{-1}. The velocity of sound in a metal such as steel is about $5060\ m\ s^{-1}$. Sometimes, in a Western film, someone will put an ear to a railway line to listen for an oncoming train. This works because the sound wave travels much faster through the steel track than through the air.

The fact that the velocity of sound varies in different media is one reason why seismic techniques can be used to probe layers of rock or minerals underground. Similarly ultrasonic scanning can be used in medicine – for example, in the imaging of a baby in its mother's womb. In each case variations in materials are shown up through variations in the time it takes sound waves to travel to the detector.

REFRACTION OF SOUND

At night the air near the ground is often colder than the air higher up, as the Earth cools after sunset. Thus a sound wave moving upward will be slowly bent back towards the horizontal as it meets warmer layers of air. Eventually it will be reflected back downwards. Under these circumstances sound can be heard over long distances. This phenomenon is explained by Snell's law of refraction (see below); layers of air at different temperatures act as different media through which sound travels at different velocities.

CHARACTERISTICS OF NOTES

There are three main characteristics of the notes played by musical instruments. *Loudness* would seem to be the most simple, but it is complicated by the non-linear response of the ear. At 100 Hz and 10 000 Hz the hearing threshold is about 40 db compared to the 0 db at 2500–4000 Hz. Thus the concept of loudness is not dependent just on the energy reaching the ear, but also on frequency.

Pitch is closely related to frequency. If the frequency of vibration is doubled the pitch rises by one octave. In general, the higher the frequency the higher the pitch.

Sounds created by musical instruments are not simple waveforms, but are the result of several waves combining. This complexity results in *tone quality* or *timbre* of a note played by a particular musical instrument. Even a 'pure' note may contain many waves of different frequencies. These frequencies are *harmonics* or *multiples* of the fundamental or lowest frequency, which has 2 nodes and 1 antinode, and is called the *first harmonic*. The second harmonic has 3 nodes and 2 antinodes. The wavelength is halved and the frequency is doubled. The *third harmonic* has 4 nodes and 3 antinodes. The wavelength is one third of the original wavelength, and the frequency has tripled. Different instruments emphasize different harmonics. Musical synthesizers are able to mimic instruments by mixing the appropriate harmonics electronically at various amplitudes.

OPTICS

Optics is the branch of physics that deals with the high-frequency electromagnetic waves that we call light. Optics is concerned with the way in which light propagates from sources to detectors via intermediate lenses, mirrors and other modifying elements. The electromagnetic spectrum (see p. 208) includes a wide range of waves in addition to light, light being that small part of the spectrum that can be detected by the human eye.

This region, with wavelengths from 700 nanometres (nm; 1 nm = 10^{-9} m) in the red region to 400 nm in violet (see the prism, below), is extended for practical optical systems into the ultraviolet and the mid-infrared regions. For many purposes light can be treated as a classical wave phenomenon (see above), but some effects can only be described by using the full quantum theory (see pp. 200–201).

A *beam* of light may be considered to be made up of many *rays*, all travelling outwards from the source. This approach is used in ray diagrams. In geometric simplifications, rays of light are drawn as straight lines. The wavelength and amplitude of light waves are very short compared to the other dimensions of the systems. The basic concept is very simple: light travels in straight lines unless it is reflected by a mirror or refracted by a lens or prism (see below).

A point source of light emits rays in all directions. For an isolated point source in a vacuum the geometric wavefront will be a sphere. The variation of the speed of light in different materials must be taken into account – the speed of light (as of other electromagnetic waves) in a vacuum is 3×10^8 m s^{-1} (300 000 km or 186 000 miles per second), but it travels more slowly through other media. Light waves have transverse magnetic and electric fields.

REFLECTION AND REFRACTION

Light is reflected and refracted (i.e. bent) in the same way as other waves. In the case of a single-colour beam of light falling or *incident upon* a transparent material such as a block of glass, angle i is said to be the angle of *incidence* of the beam. Part of the beam is reflected at an angle t, the angle of *reflection*; and part is transmitted according to the law of refraction, and r is the angle of *refraction*.

Snell's law of refraction can be stated as:

$$n_1 \sin i = n_2 \sin r$$

where n_1 and n_2 are the refractive indices of the materials.

Basically, the *refractive index* of a material determines how much it will refract light.

The refractive index of a material is often expressed relative to another material. If no other material is quoted, the refractive index is assumed to be relative to air. The refractive index of a medium can also be derived as the ratio of the speed of light in a vacuum to the speed of light in the medium. The refractive index for a typical optical glass is 1.6, whereas the refractive index of diamond is about 2.4 in visible light.

THE PRISM

The refractive index of optical glasses is not constant for light of all frequencies. It is greater at the violet end and less at the red end of the spectrum. This means that a beam of light containing a mixture of different frequencies, for example sunlight, will leave a prism with the different frequencies bent by different amounts.

A *prism* is a block of glass with a triangular cross-section; it is used to deviate a beam of light by refraction. A beam of white light will be split into its component monochromatic coloured lights – from red to violet – which will form the familiar rainbow effect. Any light can be split up in this way; the display of separated wavelengths is called the *spectrum* of the original beam.

The effect of prisms on light has been well known for many centuries. Newton used this effect, called *dispersion*, to produce and study the spectrum of sunlight. Under the right conditions dispersion occurring in spherical raindrops in the atmosphere produces a rainbow.

TOTAL INTERNAL REFLECTION

When light travels from one medium to another, less dense medium it is *deviated* or turned away from the *normal* – perpendicular to the interface at the point of incidence. This means the angle of refraction (*r*) is greater than the angle of incidence (*i*). When the angle of refraction is less than 90°, some of the incident light will be refracted and some will be reflected. If the angle of incidence increases, the angle of refraction will increase more. It is possible to increase the angle of incidence to such a value that eventually the refracted ray disappears and all the light is reflected. This is known as *total internal reflection*.

THE LENS

A lens is a piece of transparent material made in a simple geometric shape. Usually at least one surface is spherical, and often both are. Under appropriate conditions a lens will produce an image of an object by refraction of light. It does this by bending rays of light from the object.

Some rays are refracted more than others, depending how they arrive at the surface of the lens. The lens affects the velocity of the rays, since light travels more slowly in a dense medium such as the lens than in a less dense medium such as air. In this way, the expanding geometric wavefront that is generated by the object is changed into a wavefront which, for a *convex* or *converging lens*, converges to a point behind the lens. If the object is located a long way from the lens (strictly an *infinite* distance, but a star is an excellent approximation for practical purposes) this point is known as the *rear focal point* or *principal focus* of the lens.

A lens has two principal foci – one on each side. The distance between the optical centre of the lens and the principal focus is the *focal length (f)*. If a point source of light is placed at the principal focus of the convex lens, the rays of light will be refracted to form a parallel beam.

MIRRORS

Mirrors are reflecting optical elements. Plane mirrors are used to deviate light beams without dispersion or to reverse or invert images. Curved mirrors, which usually have spherical or parabolic surfaces, can form images, and are often used in illumination systems such as car headlamps.

Mirrors can be coated with metals such as aluminium or silver, which have high reflectance for visible light (or gold for the infrared). Alternatively, they may be coated with many thin layers of non-metallic materials for very high reflectances over a more restricted range of frequencies. A freshly coated aluminium mirror will reflect about 90% of visible light. Special mirrors, such as those used in lasers, can reflect over 99.7% of the light at one frequency.

THE MICROSCOPE AND THE TELESCOPE

The *microscope* is a device for making very small objects visible. It was probably invented by a Dutch spectacle-maker, Zacharias Janssen (1580–1638), in 1609. Essentially, it is an elaboration of the simple magnifying glass. The *objective* – a lens with short focal length – is used to form a highly magnified image of a small object placed close to its focal point. This can be viewed directly, by means of another lens called the *eyepiece*. It can also be recorded directly on film or viewed via a video camera.

The *telescope* is used to form an enlarged image of an infinitely distant object, and the enlarged image is viewed by the observer by means of an eyepiece. The term 'infinite' is used relatively in this context: compared with the length of the telescope, the distance of the object can be considered as infinite. Telescopes are often made with reflecting mirrors instead of glass lenses, as large lenses sag under their own weight, thereby introducing distortions into the image. The primary mirror is often a large concave paraboloid.

FIBRE OPTICS

Light can be transmitted over great distances by the use of flexible glass fibres. These fibres are usually each less than 1 mm (1/25 in) in diameter, and can be used singly or in bunches. Each fibre consists of a small core surrounded by a layer of 'cladding' glass with a slightly lower refractive index. Certain rays experience total internal reflection (see above), and this, coupled with the very low absorption of modern silica glasses, allows light to travel very long distances with little reduction in intensity. Fibre optics provide the basis of endoscopy, a medical diagnostic technique, and are also used extensively in telecommunications, as light in a fibre optic cable can carry more digital (on or off) signals with less loss of intensity than a copper wire carrying electrical digital signals.

LASERS

The term 'laser' is derived from the technical name for the process – Light Amplification by Stimulated Emission of Radiation. *Stimulated emisson* is the emission of a photon – a particle of light.

When an amplifying material, such as gas, crystal or liquid, is placed between appropriate mirrors, photons from a light beam repeatedly pass through it stimulating more photons and thus increasing their number with each pass. The additional photons all have the same frequency, phase and direction. One of the mirrors is made so that a small amount of light passes through it; this is the external laser beam, which can be continuous or pulsed. This beam can be focused onto very small areas and the intensity – the ratio of power to area – can be very great, enabling some lasers to burn through thick metal plates. Lasers have a wide variety of uses, for example in surveying, communications and eye surgery.

ATOMS

Of the fundamental forces that are important in the natural world, the gravitational force is the dominant long-range force when the motion of planets and other celestial bodies is considered. When the smallest entities are investigated, the other fundamental forces – the electromagnetic force, the *strong force* (which holds together the atomic nucleus) and the *weak force* (which is involved in nuclear decay) – become important.

The word *atom* is derived from an ancient Greek word for a particle of matter so small it cannot be split up. In his atomic theory of 1803, the British chemist John Dalton (1766–1844) defined the atom as the smallest particle of an element that retained its chemical properties. Various phenomena could be explained using this hypothesis – which still holds good today.

ATOMIC STRUCTURE

However, no physical description of the atom was

available until after the discovery of the *electron* in 1897 by the British physicist J.J. Thompson (1856–1940). The nuclear atom was proposed by the English physicist Ernest Rutherford (1871–1937) in 1911. His model consists of a small but dense central *nucleus*, which is positively charged, orbited by negatively charged electrons. The nucleus contains over 99.9% of the mass of the atom, but its diameter is of the order of 10^{-15} m – compared to the much larger size (about 10^{-10} m) of the atom.

The electron was first recognized by its behaviour as a particle. In 1923 a *wave-particle duality* for atomic particles – analogous to the concept of the wave-particle duality of light proposed by the French physicist Louis Victor de Broglie (1892–1987) – was put forward. The wavelength of a particle would be equal to the Planck constant divided by its momentum.

As the wavelength is dependent on momentum it can take any value. For an electron the wavelength can be of the order of the atomic diameter. This led to the development of the *electron microscope*. At suitable energy levels the wavelength of electrons and neutrons can be equivalent to the atomic spacing in solids. Thus a crystal can be used as a *diffraction grating* (as for X-rays). This has led to a better understanding of the way in which the electrons orbit the atomic nucleus.

The Danish physicist Niels Bohr (1885–1962) had suggested that electrons were allowed to move in circular orbits or *shells* around the nucleus, but that only certain orbits were *allowable*. This theory was able to explain many of the features of the spectrum of light emitted by excited hydrogen atoms. The wavelengths of the spectral lines are related to the energy levels of the allowed orbits. The wave theory of the electron provided a reason for the allowed orbits. These would be those whose circumference was a multiple of the electron's wavelength.

When Rutherford showed experimentally that an atom must consist of a small nucleus surrounded by electrons, there was a fundamental problem. To avoid collapsing into the nucleus, the electrons would have to move in orbits – as Bohr had proposed. This means that they must have continuous acceleration towards the nucleus. But, according to the electromagnetic theory, an accelerated charge must radiate energy, so no permanent orbit could exist. Bohr therefore argued that energy could not be lost continuously but only in quanta (discrete amounts) equivalent to the difference in energies between allowed orbits. Thus light would be emitted when an electron jumps from one allowed level to another of lower energy.

NUCLEAR STRUCTURE

With the exception of the hydrogen atom, which only contains one proton, atomic nuclei contain a mixture of protons and neutrons, collectively known as *nucleons*. The *proton* carries a positive charge, equal in magnitude to that of the negatively charged electron. The *neutron* is of similar size but is electrically neutral. Each has a mass about 1836 times that of the electron (which has a rest mass of 9.11×10^{-31} kg). The protons and neutrons in the atomic nucleus are held tightly together by the *strong nuclear force*, which overcomes the much weaker electromagnetic force of repulsion between positively charged protons.

The mass of a nucleus is always less than the sum of the masses of its constituent nucleons. This is

explained using the relationship derived by Einstein. If the nucleus is to be separated into protons and neutrons then the strong nuclear force needs to be overcome and energy has to be supplied to the nucleus – from an external source – to break it up. This energy is called the *binding energy* and is related to the *mass defect* (the difference between the masses of the nucleus and its component parts). Those nuclei with large binding energies per nucleon are most stable; these have about 50–75 nucleons in the nucleus.

NUCLEAR POWER – FISSION AND FUSION

Nuclear power comes from either of two processes – *fission* and *fusion*, which are both forms of *nuclear reaction*. In the fission process a large nucleus, such as uranium-235 (^{235}U), splits to form two smaller nuclei that have greater binding energies than the original uranium. Thus energy is given out in the process. Fission is used in nuclear reactors and in atomic weapons. There are other isotopes in addition to uranium-235, such as plutonium-239, that give rise to fission.

In the fusion process, two light nuclei fuse together to form two particles, one larger and one smaller than the original nuclei. Usually one of them is sufficiently strongly bound to give a great release of energy. The fusion of hydrogen to form helium is a power source in stars such as the Sun, although the solar fusion process differs in detail from the simpler process described. Nuclear fusion is the basis of the hydrogen bomb, and research is continuing into the possible use of fusion in power generation.

RADIOACTIVITY

Radiation – either as a spontaneous emission of particles or as an electromagnetic wave – may occur from certain substances. This is *radioactivity*. The three types of radiation are from:

alpha decay,
beta decay, and
gamma decay.

Alpha (α) decay produces nuclei of helium that each contain two neutrons and two protons. They are called *alpha-particles* and are formed in spontaneous decay of the parent nucleus. Thus uranium-238 decays to thorium-234 with emission of an alpha-particle.

Beta (β) decay In beta decay the emitted particles are either electrons or *positrons* (identical to the electron but with a positive charge). The parent nucleus retains the same number of nucleons but its charge varies by plus or minus 1. In these processes another kind of particle – either a *neutrino* or *antineutrino* – is produced. The neutrino has no charge (the word means 'little neutral one') and a mass that – if it could be measured at rest – would probably be zero. The *relativistic mass* can, however, be significant, as the speed – with respect to any observer – is that of electromagnetic radiation.

Gamma (λ) decay In gamma decay high-energy photons may be produced in a process of radioactive decay if the resultant nucleus jumps from an excited energy state to a lower energy state.

The rate at which radioactive decay takes place depends only on the number of radioactive nuclei that are present. Thus the *half-life*, or the time taken for half a given number of radioactive nuclei to decay, is characteristic for that type of nucleus. The isotope carbon-14 has a half-life of 5730 years, and measurement of its decay is used in carbon-dating of organic material. Decay can result in a series of new elements being produced, each of which may in its turn decay until a stable state is achieved.

NUCLEAR PARTICLES

Over 200 elementary particles are now known. They may be divided into two types: *hadrons* and *leptons*.

Hadrons (from the Greek for 'bulky') are heavy particles that are affected by the strong force.

Leptons (from the Greek for 'small') are generally light particles, such as electrons and neutrinos (see above), that are not subject to the strong force.

A further very important distinction is that between *fermions* (Fermi-Dirac particles) and *bosons* (Bose-Einstein particles). Fermions have a permanent existence, whereas bosons can be produced and destroyed freely, provided the laws of conservation of charge and of mechanics are obeyed. Leptons are fermions.

Every type of particle is thought to have a companion *antiparticle*, that is, a particle with the same mass but opposite in some other characteristic such as charge. Thus the positron with positive charge is the antiparticle of the negatively charged electron. Some particles such as the photon may be their own antiparticles.

Whilst the leptons are thought to be fundamental particles, the hadrons are thought to be made up of *quarks* (a word borrowed from James Joyce's novel *Finnegans Wake*). Quarks may have fractional electrical charge. It is probable that free quarks do not exist.

If three quarks combine, the resulting hadron is called a *baryon*; if a quark and an antiquark combine the result is called a *meson*. A meson is a boson; it is a short-lived particle that jumps between protons and neutrons, thus holding them together. In the same way that Mendeleyev's table of chemical elements (see p. 227) predicted new elements such as gallium and germanium that were subsequently discovered, so a pattern of hadrons may be drawn up based on combinations of different types of quark. This pattern is called the *eight-fold way* – a term borrowed from Buddhism. It predicted the existence of the omega-particle (Ω-particle), the discovery of which in 1963 helped to validate the theory.

There are believed to be six types or *flavours* of quark – up, down, charmed, strange, top and bottom. Evidence for the existence of all except the top quark is now available.

Quarks carry electrical charge and another type of charge called *colour*. The force associated with the colour charge binds the quarks together and is thought to be the source of the strong force binding the hadrons together. Thus the colour force is the more fundamental force. The weak force is associated with the radioactive beta-decay of some nuclei. It has been shown – in the theory of the *electroweak* force – that the electromagnetic and weak forces are linked. This theory predicted the existence of the W and Z° particles, which were discovered at the CERN nuclear accelerator at Geneva during 1982–83.

NUCLEAR ACCELERATORS

Accelerators are large machines that accelerate particle beams to very high speeds, so enabling research into particle physics. Electric fields are used to accelerate the particles, either in a straight line (*linear accelerator*) or in a circle (*cyclotron, synchrotron* or *synchrocyclotron*). Powerful magnetic fields are used to guide the beams. Energy levels of the particles may be as high as several hundred giga electronvolts. An electronvolt (eV) is the increase in energy of an electron when it undergoes a rise in potential of 1 volt: 1 eV = 1.6 × 10^{-19} joules (J). Nuclear accelerators have provided experimental evidence for the existence of numerous subatomic particles predicted in theory.

ELECTROMAGNETISM

Electromagnetism is the study of effects caused by stationary and moving electric charges. Electricity and magnetism were originally observed separately, but in the 19th century, scientists began to investigate their interaction. This work resulted in a theory that electricity and magnetism were both manifestations of a single force, the electromagnetic force.

The electromagnetic force is one of the fundamental forces of nature, the others being gravitational force and the strong and weak nuclear forces. Recently the electromagnetic and weak forces have been shown to be manifestations of an electro-weak force. Magnetism has been known about since ancient times, but it was not until the late 18th century that the electric force was identified – by the French physicist Charles Augustin Coulomb (1736–1806).

MAGNETISM

Metallic ores with magnetic properties were being used around 500 BC as compasses. It is now known that the Earth itself has magnetic properties. Investigation of the properties of magnetic materials led to the concept of *magnetic fields*, showing the force one magnet exerts on another. These lines of force can be demonstrated by means of small plotting compasses or iron filings. An important feature of a magnet is that it has two poles, one of which is attracted to the Earth's magnetic north pole, while the other is attracted to the south pole. Conventionally, the north-seeking end of a magnet is called its *north pole*, and the other is the *south pole*. Magnets are identified by the fact that unlike or opposite poles (i.e. north and south) attract each other, while like poles (north and north, or south and south) repel each other.

Magnetic effects are now known to be caused by moving electric charges. Atomic electrons are in motion, and thus all atoms exhibit magnetic fields.

STATIC ELECTRIC CHARGES

In dry weather, a woollen sweater being pulled off over the hair of the wearer may crackle; sparks may even be seen. This is caused by an *electric charge*, which is the result of electrons being pulled from one surface to the other. Objects can gain an electric charge by being rubbed against another material.

Experiment has shown that there are two types of charge. These are now associated with the negative and positive charges on electrons and protons respectively. Similar electric charges (i.e. two positives, or two negatives) repel each other and unlike charges (i.e. a positive and a negative) attract. (Note that the terms 'positive' and 'negative' are merely conventions for opposite properties.) No smaller charge than that of the electron has been detected.

The force of repulsion or attraction is known as the *electric force*. It is described by *Coulomb's law*, an inverse-square law similar to the law for the gravitational force (see above). Coulomb's law states that the attractive or repulsive force (F) between two point (or spherically symmetrical) charges is given by:

$$F = k \frac{Q_1 Q_2}{r^2}$$

where k is a constant, Q_1 and Q_2 are the magnitudes of the charges, and r is the distance between them. The force acts along the direction of r. The unit of charge is called a *coulomb* (C) and is the quantity of electric charge carried past a given point in 1 second by a current of 1 ampere (see below).

ELECTRIC FIELD

Arrows can be plotted to show the magnitude and direction of the magnetic force that acts at points around a magnet, or the electric force that acts on a unit charge at each point. In the latter case, such a map would show the distribution of the electric field intensity. It is measured in terms of a force per unit charge, or newtons per coulomb.

In the same way that a mass may have gravitational potential energy because of its position, so a charge can have *electrical potential energy*. This potential per unit charge is measured in *volts* (V), named after the Italian physicist Alessandro Volta (1745–1827). The volt may be defined as follows: if one joule is required to move 1 coulomb of electric charge between two points, then the *potential difference* between the points is 1 joule per coulomb = 1 volt.

The electrical potential may vary with distance. This change may be measured in volts per metre (V m^{-1}). The Earth's surface is negatively charged with an average electric field over the whole of its surface of about 120 V m^{-1}. In the presence of thunderclouds or where the air is highly polluted the field may be much greater. This field is maintained partially by thunderstorms, which transfer negative charge to the Earth. Dry air can only allow an electric field of 3×10^6 V m^{-1} to build up before there is a sudden breakdown – a lightning flash. If water droplets are present, then the value is lower, perhaps 1×10^6 V m^{-1}.

ELECTRIC CURRENT, CONDUCTORS AND INSULATORS

Electric current consists of a flow of electrons, usually through a material but also through a vacuum, as in a cathode-ray tube in a TV set. Current flows when there is a *potential difference* or *voltage* (see above) between two ends of a conductor (see below). Conventional current flows from the positive terminal to the negative terminal. However, electron flow is in fact from negative to positive.

For measurement purposes, an electric current is defined as the rate of flow of charge. The unit of electric current is the *ampere* (A), often abbreviated to amp:

1 ampere = 1 coulomb per second.

The ampere is named after the French physicist André Marie Ampère (1775–1836), who pioneered work on electricity and magnetism.

A material that will allow an electric current to flow through it is a *conductor*. The best conductors are metals. A material that will not allow an electric current to flow is an *insulator*. Effective insulators include rubber, plastic and porcelain.

ELECTROMAGNETIC FIELDS

In 1820 the Danish physicist Hans Christiaan Oersted (1777–1851) discovered that a copper wire bearing an electric current caused a pivoted magnetic needle to be deflected until it was tangential to a circle drawn around the wire. This was the first connection to be established between the electrical and magnetic forces. Oersted's work was developed by the French scientists Jean-Baptiste Biot (1774–1862) and Félix Savart (1791–1841), who showed that the field strength of a current flowing in a straight wire varied with the distance from the wire. Biot and Savart were able to find a law relating the current in a small part of the conductor to the magnetic field. Ampère, at about the same time, found a more fundamental relationship between the current in a wire and the magnetic field about it.

We now believe that the Earth's magnetic field is generated by the motion of charged particles in the liquid iron part of the core. This is known as the *dynamo theory*.

From Newton's third law (see above) and Oersted's observation it might be expected that a magnetic field can exert a force on a moving charge. This is observed if a magnet is brought up close to a cathode-ray tube in a TV set. The beam of electrons moving from the cathode to the screen is deflected. The force acts in a direction perpendicular to both the magnetic field and the direction of electron flow. If the magnetic field is perpendicular to the direction of the electrons, then the force has its maximum value. This is the second way in which the electric and magnetic properties are linked.

ELECTROMAGNETIC INDUCTION

The next advance came in 1831, when the English physicist Michael Faraday (1791–1867) found that an electric current could be induced in a wire by another, changing current in a second wire. Faraday published his findings before the American physicist Joseph Henry (1797–1878), who had first made the same discovery. Faraday showed that the magnetic field at the wire had to be changing for an electric current to be produced. This may be done by changing the current in a second wire, by moving a magnet relative to the wire, or by moving the wire relative to a magnet. This last technique is that employed in a dynamo generator, which maintains an electric current when it is driven mechanically. An electric motor uses the reverse process, being driven by electricity to provide a mechanical result.

MAXWELL'S THEORY

The work of the Scottish physicist James Clerk Maxwell (1831–79) on electromagnetism is of immense importance for physics. It united the separate concepts of electricity and magnetism in terms of a new *electromagnetic force*. Maxwell extended the ideas of Ampère, when, in 1864, he proposed that a magnetic field could also be caused by a changing electric field. Thus, when either an electric or magnetic field is changing, a field of the other type is induced. Maxwell predicted that electrical oscillations would generate electromagnetic waves, and he derived a formula giving the speed in terms of electric and magnetic quantities. When these quantities were measured he calculated the speed and found that it was equal to the speed of light in a vacuum. This suggested that light might be electromagnetic in nature – a theory that was later confirmed in various ways. Thus, when an electric current in a wire changes, electromagnetic waves are generated, which will be propagated with a velocity equal to that of light.

The electric and magnetic field components in electromagnetic waves are perpendicular to each other and to the direction of propagation. The existence of electromagnetic waves was demonstrated experimentally in 1887 by the German physicist Heinrich Rudolf Hertz (1857–94) – who also gave his name to the unit of frequency. In his laboratory, Hertz transmitted and detected electromagnetic waves, and he was able to verify that their velocity was close to the speed of light.

THE ELECTROMAGNETIC SPECTRUM

Prior to Maxwell's discoveries it had been known that light was a wave motion, although the type of wave motion had not been identified. Maxwell was able to show that the oscillations were of the electric and magnetic field. Hertz's waves had a wavelength of about 60 cm; thus they were of much longer wavelength than light waves.

Nowadays we recognize a spectrum of electromagnetic radiation that extends from 'about 10^{-15} m to 10^9 m. It is subdivided into smaller, sometimes overlapping, ranges. The extension of astronomical observations from visible to other electromagnetic wavelengths has revolutionized our knowledge of the universe.

Radio waves have a large range of wavelengths – from a few millimetres up to several kilometres.

Microwaves are radio waves with shorter wavelengths, between 1 mm and 30 cm. They are used in radar and microwave ovens.

Infrared waves of different wavelengths are radiated by bodies at different temperatures. (Bodies at higher temperatures radiate either visible or ultraviolent waves.) The Earth and its atmosphere, at a mean temperature of 250 K (-23 °C or -9.4 °F) radiates infrared waves with wavelengths centred at about 10 micrometres (μ m) or 10^{-5}(1μ m $= 10^{-6}$m).

Visible waves have wavelengths of 400–700 nanometres (nm; 1 nm $= 10^{-9}$ m). The peak of the solar radiation (temperatures of about 6000 K/6270 °C/11 323 °F) is at a wavelength of about 550 nm, where the human eye is at its most sensitive.

Ultraviolet waves have wavelengths from about 380 nm down to 60 nm. The radiation from hotter stars (above 25 000 K/25 000 °C/45 000 °F) is shifted towards the violet and ultraviolet parts of the spectrum.

X-rays have wavelengths from about 10 nm down to 10^{-4} nm.

Gamma rays have wavelengths less than 10^{-11} m. They are emitted by certain radioactive nuclei and in the course of some nuclear reactions.

Note that the *cosmic rays* continually bombarding the Earth from outer space are not electromagnetic waves, but high-speed protons and x-particles (i.e. nuclei of hydrogen and helium atoms) together with some heavier nuclei.

ELECTRICITY IN ACTION

There have been several key advances in the application of electricity towards developing our civilization. The first two were the dynamo and the electric motor. The dynamo provided a way of producing electricity in large quantities, and the electric motor provided a way of converting electric current into mechanical work.

The evolution of electromagnetic theory (see above) provided the basis for the modern communications industry through radio and television, while the miniaturization of electronic components using semiconductor materials enabled powerful computers to be built for control purposes and to handle large amounts of information.

BATTERIES AND CELLS

Electric current is the flow of electrons through a conductor. The first source of a steady electric current was demonstrated by the Italian physicist Alessandro Volta (1745–1827) in 1800. His original *voltaic pile* used chemical energy to produce an electric current. The pile consisted of a series of pairs of metal plates (one of silver and one of zinc) piled on top of each other, each pair sandwiching a piece of cloth soaked in a dilute acid solution.

The same principle is still used today. The plates are called *electrodes* and must be made of dissimilar metals. Alternatively, one may be made of carbon. The positive electrode – the one from which electrons flow inside the cell – is called the *anode*. The negative electrode is the *cathode*. The acid solution is called the *electrolyte* and in a dry cell is absorbed into a paste.

A single cell can normally produce only a small voltage, but a number of them connected in a series (positive to negative) will give a higher voltage. A series of cells connected in this way is called a *battery*. Some batteries, known as *accumulators*, are designed so that they can be 'recharged' by the passage of an electric current back through them. Similar principles as those used in cells are used in electrolysis and electroplating.

CIRCUITRY

A circuit is a complete conductive path between positive and negative terminals; conventionally current flows from positive to negative, although the direction of electron flow is actually from negative to positive. When electrical components such as bulbs and switches are joined end to end the arrangement is a *series* connection. When they are connected side by side, this is called *parallel* connection.

RESISTANCE

When an electric current passes through a conductor there is a force that acts to reduce or *resist* the flow. This is called the *resistance* and is dependent upon the nature of the conductor and its dimensions. The unit of resistance is the *ohm* (Ω), named after the German physicist Georg Simon Ohm (1787–1854). He discovered a relationship between the current (I), voltage (V) and resistance (R) in a conductor:

$$V = IR.$$

This is known as Ohm's law.

POWER

Power is the rate at which a body or system does work. The power in an electric conductor is measured in *watts* (W), named after the British engineer James Watt (1736–1819). One watt is one joule per second, or the energy used per second by a current of one amp flowing between two points with a potential difference of one volt.

In an electric conductor, the power (W) is the product of the current (I) and the voltage (V).

LIGHTING, HEATING AND FUSES

A light bulb consists of a glass envelope containing an inert ('noble') gas, usually argon, at low pressure. The bulb has two electrodes connected internally by a *filament* – a fine coiled tungsten wire of high resistance. The passage of a suitable electric current through the filament will raise its temperature sufficiently to make it glow white hot (2500 °C / 4500 °F). The inert gas prevents the filament from evaporating. The efficiency of filament lamps is low. *Gas discharge lamps* are much more efficient. They consist of a glass tube with electrodes sealed into each end. The tube is filled with a gas such as neon, sodium or mercury vapour, which can be *excited* to emit light by the application of a high voltage to the electrodes.

When electrons pass through a wire they cause the atoms in it to vibrate and generate heat – the greater the resistance, the greater the heat generated. This effect is used in electric heating devices. An electric radiant heater glows red hot. The temperature reached by using a special tough resistance wire is 900 °C (1650 °F). The connecting wires are of low resistance and stay cool.

If a small resistance consisting of wire with a low melting point is connected in a circuit the amount of current that can flow will be limited by that resistance. If too much current flows the resistance will overheat and melt, breaking the circuit. This resistance is called a *fuse* and can be used as a device to protect circuits from current overload.

ALTERNATING CURRENT AND DIRECT CURRENT

There are two types of current electricity. The type produced by a battery is *direct current* (DC), in which there is a constant flow of electrons in one direction. The type used in most electrical appliances is *alternating current* (AC), in which the direction of flow of electrons alternates. The frequency of alternating current can vary over an enormous range. The electric mains operate at 50 Hz (cycles per second) in the UK and Europe, and at 60 Hz in the USA. Most of today's electricity is produced by AC generators. These were developed following Faraday's discovery of the induction of a current in a circuit as a result of a changing magnetic field.

GENERATORS AND MOTORS

A *dynamo* is an electrical current generator, consisting of a coil that is rotated in a magnetic field by some external means. The source of the rotation may be a turbine in which blades are moved by the passage through them of water, as in a hydroelectric plant, or steam, produced from a boiler heated by nuclear fission or by burning fossil fuels. Wind turbines spin as a result of the passage of air through the large rotors. Different types of generator produce either AC or DC current, while *alternators* (used to charge car batteries) produce AC current that is then rectified to DC current using semiconductor diodes.

An *electric motor* is a similar device to a generator, but works in reverse. An electric current is applied to the coil windings, causing rotation of the *armature*, which consists of a shaft on which are mounted electromagnet windings.

CONDUCTORS AND SEMICONDUCTORS

A metal consists of an array of positive ions in a 'sea'

of free electrons. The electrons move randomly with mean speeds of around 10^6 m s^{-1}. When a potential difference is applied across a metal a small drift velocity is added. The metal atoms are thought to give up one or more electrons, which can then migrate freely through the material. These electrons move in a zigzag manner along a conductor. As a result their typical velocity, called the *drift velocity*, is small, in the order of 10^{-4} m s^{-1}. Thus it would take more than an hour to move one metre. Note that the electric signals that drive the electrons travel with a speed in the order of 10^8 m s^{-1} in some circuits.

This classical picture of electron conduction explains some but not all conduction phenomena. For these a quantum mechanical model is required (see p. 201). This model explains the basis of semiconductors, which now play such an important part in electronics.

Metals are good conductors of electricity because there are always many unoccupied quantum states into which electrons can move. Non-metallic solids and liquids have nearly all their quantum states occupied by electrons, so it is difficult to produce large currents. If the numbers of unoccupied states and of electrons free to move into them are small the material is an *insulator*. If there are more free electrons and unoccupied states the substance is called a *semiconductor*.

Semiconductors have a charge-carrier density that lies between those of conductors and insulators. Two metal-like elements, silicon and germanium, are the two semiconductors used most frequently. These may be 'doped' with an impurity to modify their conduction behaviour – *n-type* doping increases the number of free electrons, *p-type* increases the number of unoccupied states. If the doping results in the charge carriers being negative electrons, then the result is an *n-type semiconductor*. If electron deficiencies or holes are the charge carriers, then the result is a *p-type semiconductor*.

Most semiconductor devices are made from materials that are partly p-type and partly n-type. The boundary between them is known as a *p-n junction*. Such a device, called a *semiconductor diode*, will act as a *rectifier*, a device used to convert alternating current to direct current.

TRANSISTORS

A transistor consists of semiconductor material in n-p-n or p-n-p form. The middle part is the *base* and the ends are the *emitter* and *collector*. An *integrated circuit* consists of many transistors, rectifiers or other components embedded in a chip of silicon.

SUPERCONDUCTIVITY

Superconductivity was discovered by the Dutch physicist Kamerlingh Onnes (1853–1926) in 1911. Below a certain critical temperature, various metals show zero resistance to current flow. Once a current is started in a closed circuit, it keeps flowing as long as the circuit is kept cold. The critical temperature for aluminium is 1.19 K (–272 °C / –457 °F), and similar values hold for other metals. Some alloys have higher critical temperatures. Up to 1986 the highest transition temperature known was about 25 K (–248 °C / –414 °F). More recently a new class of copper oxide and other materials have shown superconductivity up to at least 125 K (–148 °C / –234 °F). These developments promise enormous savings in energy.

SOLAR CELLS

The *photovoltaic effect* occurs when light is absorbed by a p-n or n-p junction. Electrons are liberated at the junction by an incident photon and diffuse through the n-type region. The hole drifts through the p-type layer until it recombines with an electron flowing round the external circuit.

The first practical photovoltaic device – called a solar cell – was made in 1954. In essence a solar cell is a light-emitting diode acting in reverse – it converts light into electric current, which is the basis of solar power.

Direct solar energy is one of the simplest sources of power. Building designs, old and new, take advantage of it for heating and lighting. Today, more active designs are becoming widespread. Each square metre (11¾ sq ft) of a solar collector in northern Europe receives roughly 1000 kilowatt-hours of solar energy in the course of a year, and can use about half of this to heat water. A similar collector in California receives twice as much energy as this.

Solar (or photovoltaic cells), which use the Sun's radiation to generate energy, are also becoming cheaper and more efficient. Earlier cells, made from large slices of crystalline silicon, were very expensive, but new materials, such as amorphous silicon and gallium arsenide, are bringing the price down towards the goal of about one dollar per watt. The latest experimental solar cells are able to convert about a third of the energy in sunlight to electricity. Solar cells are already proving the best option for producing electricity reliably in remote locations.

MILESTONES IN PHYSICS

Physics is very much concerned with fundamental particles – the building blocks out of which the Universe is constructed – and the forces which bind and regulate them. Many theories have been proposed from time to time to provide a better understanding of the vast number of facts and observations which have accumulated. The main development of physics is essentially a series of unifications of these theories.

1687 Sir Isaac Newton (1642–1727) produced the great unifying theory of gravitation which linked the falling apple with the force which keeps the stars and planets in their courses. This made available for further scientific investigation one of the basic universal forces of nature, the force of gravity (see p. 194).

1820 Hans Christian Oersted (1777–1851) of Denmark discovered that the flow of electric current in a conductor would cause a nearby compass needle to be deflected (see p. 207).

1831 Michael Faraday (1791–1867), the English physicist, published the principle of magnetic induction which led to the invention of the dynamo (see p. 207). He showed that a change in the magnetic field surrounding a conductor could cause a flow of electrical current.

1865 The unification between magnetism and electricity was brought to full flower by the Scottish physicist James Clerk Maxwell (1831–79) in his great electromagnetic theory, which described every known kind of magnetic and electric behaviour.

THE PARTICLES OF PHYSICS

Generation	Name	Electric Charge	Mass (MeV)	Quark Flavour	Electric Charge	Mass (MeV)*	Strangeness	Charm	Bottomness	Topness
		Leptons				*Quarks*				
First Family	e (electron)	-1	0.511	d (down)	$-1/3$	350	0	0	0	0
	ν_e (electron neutrino)	0	0?	u (up)	$+2/3$	350	0	0	0	0
Second Family	μ (muon)	-1	105.658	s (strange)	$-1/3$	500	-1	0	0	0
	ν_μ (muon neutrino)	0	0?	c (charm)	$+2/3$	1500	0	$+1$	0	0
Third Family	τ (tau)	-1	1784.1	b (bottom)	$-1/3$	5000	0	0	-1	0
	$\nu\tau$ (tau neutrino)	0	0?	t (top)	$+2/3$	50000	0	0	0	$+1$

* Because of the strong colour force, the masses of quarks depend on the distance over which they are measured. The approximate values given in the table are those which appear to be the sum of the masses of the hadrons (the 'long distance' masses) while the 'short distance' or Lagrangian masses are those that are required by the theory of quantum chromodynamics, i.e. for the u, d, s, and c quarks. These are approximately 6, 10, 200, and 1300 MeV respectively, whilst the masses of the bottom and top quarks are too approximately known to distinguish between the long and short distance masses.

1887 Heinrich Hertz (1857–94), the German physicist, performed a classic experiment in which electromagnetic waves were produced and transmitted across the laboratory. This laid the foundation for radio transmission and provided ample vindication for Maxwell's theory.

1895 X-rays were discovered by Wilhelm von Röntgen (1845–1923), a German physicist. When experimenting with the passage of electrical discharges through gases, he noticed that fluorescent material near his apparatus glowed.

1896 Henri Becquerel (1852–1908), the French physicist, discovered that uranium salts, even in the dark, emit a radiation similar to Röntgen's X-rays and would fog a photographic plate. This was later called radioactivity.

1897 Joseph John Thomson (1865–1940), the British physicist, discovered the first of the fundamental particles, the electron, which is the basic unit of negative electricity.

1898 Marie Curie (1867–1934) of Poland, working with her French husband, Pierre (1859–1906), announced the existence of two new chemical elements which powerfully emit radiation. She gave the name radioactivity to this active phenomena.

The New Zealand-born physicist Ernest Rutherford (1871–1937) and the English chemist Frederick Soddy (1877–1956) formulated a theory of radioactivity that forms the basis of our present understanding of the phenomenon. Three types of radioactivity were identified, a-rays, ß-rays and λ-rays.

1900 The quantum theory was proposed by the German physicist Max Planck (1858–1947). This arose out of yet another problem that had been insoluble up to that time. Calculations showed that the energy emitted from a hot body should be, at very short wavelengths, practically infinite: this was clearly not so. The calculations were satisfactory for radiation of longer wavelengths in that they agreed with the experiment. To resolve this difficulty, Planck made the very novel suggestion that energy was radiated from the body, not in a continuous flow of waves as it had been supposed up to then, but rather in distinct individual bundles. He called a bundle of energy a quantum (see p. 201).

1905 Albert Einstein (1879–1955) published his theory of the photoelectric effect. Einstein followed Planck's ideas and could see that the incident light must consist of a stream of quanta, that is, bundles of light, which came to be known as photons. A photon striking a metal surface is absorbed by an electron in it, the electron having more energy as a result. This causes it to jump from the surface, and since photons have greater energy at shorter wavelengths, so shorter wavelength light causes the emission of higher energy electrons. And, of course, the greater the intensity of the light the more quanta will be striking the surface and so more electrons will be emitted. Thus, the idea of the quantum enabled Einstein to account for the phenomena of the photoelectric effect. This was an early triumph for the new quantum theory, which was to prove fundamental in the subsequent development in physics.

1905 This year also saw the publication of Einstein's *Special (or Restricted) Theory of Relativity*. It had been said that as a child he had wondered what would happen if it were possible to travel fast enough to catch a ray of light and that this led him some years later to formulate his celebrated theory. This theory arises from an apparent contradiction between two basic postulates.

1. The velocity of light in a vacuum is a constant for all observers regardless of their state of motion relative to the light source.

2. The special principle of relativity which states that the laws of physics are the same for all observers in uniform motion relative to each other.

Imagine a train travelling with a uniform velocity v relative to the railway embankment and a ray of light transmitted with velocity c along the embankment parallel, and in the direction of the train. For an observer in the train the velocity of the light should appear to be $c-v$: obviously less than c. But this violates the special principle of relativity above: the velocity of light must be the same for an observer on the embankment and an observer on the train. The reconciliation of these two apparently contradictory conclusions is the basis for the special theory and is achieved by surrendering the concepts of absolute time, absolute distance and of the absolute significance of simultaneity. Relative theory thus confirms an important unification in physics between two of its very basic concepts: mass and energy, with the former being a congealed form of the latter with a transmission constant being the speed of light (c) squared: $E = mc^2$.

1911 Ernest Rutherford proposed a model of the atom that is the basis of our ideas of atomic structure to this day. He had from the first recognized the value of the fast-moving a-particles emitted naturally from radioactive materials as probes for discovering the nature of the atom. He arranged for a-particles to bombard a thin gold foil and found that while many passed straight through, a few were deflected at comparatively large angles, some even 'bouncing' back towards the source. He concluded from this that the mass of the atom was concentrated at its centre in a minute nucleus consisting of positively charged particles called protons. Around the nucleus and at a relatively large distance from it revolved the negatively charged electrons. The combined negative charges of the electrons exactly balanced the total positive charge of the nucleus. This important model of the atom suffered from a number of defects. One of these was that from Maxwell's electromagnetic theory the atom should produce light of all wavelengths, whereas, in fact, atoms of each element emit light consisting of a number of definite wavelengths – a spectrum – which can be measured with great accuracy. This spectrum for each element is unique.

1913 The difficulties of the Rutherford atom were overcome by the Danish physicist Niels Henrik David Bohr (1885–1962), who proposed that electrons were permitted only in certain orbits but could jump from one permitted orbit to another. In so jumping the electron would gain or lose energy in the form of photons. In this way the spectrum of light emitted, or absorbed, by an atom would relate to its individual structure. The theoretical basis to Bohr's work was confirmed by Einstein in 1917 and the Bohr theory went on successfully to explain other atomic phenomena. However, after many outstanding successes over a number of years, an increasing number of small but important discrepancies appeared with which the Bohr theory could not cope.

1919 Rutherford performed the first artificial nuclear disintegration when he bombarded nitrogen atoms with a-particles from radon-C. He demonstrated that protons were emitted as a result of the disintegration and this confirmed that the proton was, indeed, a nuclear particle.

1924 Louis-Victor de Broglie (1892–1976), a French physicist, postulated that the dual wave-particle nature of light might be shown by other particles and particularly by electrons.

Electron waves were demonstrated experimentally in 1927 by the Americans C. J. Davisson (1881–1958) and L. H. Germer (1896–1971). Subsequently, de Broglie's idea of matter waves was extended to other particles – protons, neutrons, etc. All matter has an associated wave character, but for the larger bodies of classical mechanics, the wavelengths are too small for their effects to be detectable.

1926 Erwin Schrödinger (1887–1961), a physicist from Vienna, took up the idea of de Broglie waves and applied them to the Bohr atom. The solutions to the resulting wave equation gave the allowed orbits or energy levels more accurately than the quantized orbits in the Bohr atom. Max Born (1882–1970), a German physicist, interpreted these solutions in terms of probability, i.e. they gave the probability of finding an electron in a given volume of space within the atom.

1927 The German physicist Werner Karl Heisenberg (1901–76) formulated his Uncertainty Principle. This states that there is a definite limit to the accuracy with which certain pairs of measurements can be made. The more accurately one quantity is known, the less accurate is our knowledge of the other. Position and momentum is an example of such a pair of measurements. The more exactly we know the position of, say, an electron, the less will we know about its momentum.

The uncertainty principle provides the main reason why the classical mechanics of Newton do not apply to atomic and subatomic phenomena.

1928 P.A.M. Dirac (1902–84), an English physicist and mathematician, introduced a theory of the electron that successfully brought together the ideas of quantum mechanics thus far developed with those of relativity. As a result of this, the important concept of electron spin previously advanced by Bohr became theoretically justified.

Dirac's equations revealed a negative quantity that led to the prediction of the existence of the antielectron, a particle identical to the electron, of the same mass but of opposite electric charge. This major idea, that there could exist **antimatter** in the universe composed of antiparticles, arises from Dirac's bold prediction.

1932 Ernest Orlando Lawrence (1901–58), an American physicist, developed the **cyclotron**. This was one of the first machines constructed for artificially accelerating charged particles to high velocities for research.

1932 Carl David Anderson (b. 1905), an American physicist, announced the discovery of the antielectron predicted a few years previously by Dirac. This was the first particle of antimatter to be discovered and he named it the **positron**.

1932 James Chadwick (1891–1974), an English physicist, discovered the **neutron**, a constituent of the atomic nucleus of zero charge and only slightly heavier than the proton.

1933 Wolfgang Pauli (1900–58) of Austria postulated the existence of the **neutrino**, a neutral particle of negligible mass in order to explain the fact that in β-emission in radioactivity there was a rather greater loss of energy than could be otherwise explained.

1934 Hideki Yukawa (1907–81), a Japanese physicist, sought to explain the forces that held the particles in the nucleus together – the **strong force** – and called the force-carrying particles in this case **mesons**. The meson predicted by Yukawa, the **pi meson** or **pion**, was discovered by Cecil F. Powell (1903–69) of Bristol University in 1947.

1938 Nuclear fission was discovered by Otto Hahn (1879–1968) and Fritz Strassman (b. 1902) by bombarding uranium with neutrons, when trying to produce transuranic elements. They succeeded in producing elements lighter than uranium. Enrico Fermi (1901–54) suggested that the neutrons released in fission could themselves induce further fission and that it should be possible to sustain a chain reaction.

1942 The first nuclear reactor, set up by Fermi in the University of Chicago, became critical.

1953 Murray Gell-Mann (1929–), of the USA, introduced a concept he called **strangeness**, a quality akin in some ways to electric charge, which helped to account for the increased lifetimes of the strange particles. Aided by this idea, it was found that particles could be fitted into patterns according to the amount of strangeness they possessed.

1954 In June 1954 the world's first nuclear-powered generator produced electricity (5MW) at Obnisk near Moscow, and in August 1956 the first large-scale (50MW) nuclear power generating station, Calder Hall, Cumberland (Cumbria), started up.

1953 Gell-Mann proposed the idea that hadrons – complex particles – were composed of more basic particles called 'quarks' (see p. 206).

1965 It was realized that quarks with exactly the same quantum numbers cannot exist together and therefore must possess an extra degree of freedom known as 'colour', a concept introduced by M. Y. Han and Y. Nambu (see p. 206).

1967–70 Following original concepts developed by C.N. Yang (1922–) and R. Mills (1924–) in 1954 and J. Schwinger (1918–) in 1957, the standard model to describe electro-weak interactions was introduced by S. Weinberg (1933–) and A. Salam (1926–) in 1967–68 and generalized by S.L. Glashow (1932–) in 1970. In this model both weak and electromagnetic interactions are described in a unified theory which requires the existence not only of the massless photon but also of very massive intermediate particles which are both charged (the W±) and neutral (the Z^0).

1974 A heavy meson was discovered with a lifetime that was much longer than would be expected at this mass level. Such a phenomena is usually explained in terms of the existence of a unique quantum number. The particle was named 'psi' or 'J'.

1977 The unexpected discovery in 1975 of a heavy lepton (the 'tau') led immediately to the suggestion of the existence of a tau neutrino and of two very heavy quarks in order to preserve quark-lepton symmetry. The new quarks were given the names 'bottom' and 'top' (the alternative names 'beauty' and 'truth' now appear to have been dropped). The discovery in November 1977 of two very heavy mesons with masses close to 10 000 MeV but with very long lifetimes similar to those of the psi mesons was considered as confirmation of the existence of the bottom quark, although the mesons consisted of bottom quarks and their anti-quarks and therefore showed zero net bottom.

1983 The existence of both the W± in January 1983 and the Z^0 in August 1983 were established at *Centre Européen de la Recherche Nucléaire* (CERN), Geneva, Switzerland (see 1967–70 above).

1986 Experiments in January led to a revolution in the development of superconductive materials. Superconductivity is defined as 'a complete lack of electrical resistance' and was discovered by H. Kamerlingh Onnes (1853–1926) in 1911. Over the next 75 years it was considered to be a very low-temperature effect with the maximum superconducting temperature attained being 23 K (– 250 °C), so the technique was extremely limited in use. However, in experiments by K. A. Muller and J. G. Bednorz of IBM, Zurich, in 1986, superconductivity was observed at 35 K (– 238 °C) in a mixed oxide of barium, lanthanum, and copper. In 1987 two groups in the USA and China independently reported attaining superconductive temperatures of about 90 K (– 183 °C) in a mixed oxide of yttrium, barium, and copper. Research continues and the current record holder is 125 K (– 148 °C) for a mixed oxide of thallium, barium, calcium, and copper. Such temperatures are within the range of liquid nitrogen and will dramatically reduce the cost of using superconductivity in engineering applications.

1991 A number of particles that are important in the theories of modern physics remain to be discovered: these include the tau neutrino, the top quark, and the Higgs boson (a particle suggested by Peter Higgs of the University of Edinburgh in order to explain the manifestly different behaviour of the electromagnetic and weak interaction mechanisms).

NOBEL PRIZEWINNERS IN PHYSICS

1901 Wilhelm Röntgen, German. Discovered X-rays

1902 Hendrik Antoon Lorentz, Netherlands and Pieter Zeeman, Netherlands. Investigated the influences of magnetism on radiation

1903 Antoine-Henri Becquerel, French. Discovered spontaneous radioactivity. Pierre Curie, French and Marie Curie, French (naturalized citizen). Investigated radiation phenomena (inspired by Bequerel's discovery)

1904 Lord Rayleigh, English. Discovered argon, an unreactive gas in the atmosphere

1905 Philipp Lenard, German. Research on cathode rays

1906 Sir J. J. Thomson, English. Investigated electrical conductivity of gases

1907 A. A. Michelson, USA (German-born). Established the speed of light as a constant, and other spectroscopic and metrological investigations

1908 Gabriel Lippmann, French. Photographic reproduction of colours

1909 Guglielmo Marconi, Italian and Karl Braun, German. Developed wireless telegraphy

1910 J. van der Waals, Dutch. Investigated the relationships between the states of gases and liquids

1911 Wilhelm Wien, German. Investigated the laws governing heat radiation

1912 Nils Gustav Dalén, Swedish. Invented automatic regulators for lighting buoys and beacons

1913 H. Kamerlingh Onnes, Dutch. Studied properties of matter at low temperatures; produces liquid helium

1914 Max von Laue, German. Achieved diffraction of X-rays using crystals

1915 Sir William Bragg, English and Sir Lawrence Bragg, English. Analysed crystal structure using X-rays

1916 No award

1917 Charles Barkla, English. Discovered characteristics of X-radiation of elements

1918 Max Plank, German. Formulated the first quantum theory (see p. 211)

1919 Johannes Stark, German. Discovered the Doppler effect in positive ion rays and the division of spectral lines when the source of light is subjected to strong electric force fields

1920 Charles Guillaume, Swiss. Discovered anomalies in alloys

1921 Albert Einstein, German-American Elucidated theories fundamental to theoretical physics (see p. 211)

1922 Niels Bohr, Danish. Investigated atomic structure and radiation (see p. 211)

1923 Robert Millikan, USA. Worked on elementary electric charge and the photoelectric effect

1924 Karl Siegbahn, Swedish. Worked on X-ray spectroscopy

1925 James Franck, German and Gustav Hertz, German. Defined the laws governing the impact of an electron upon an atom

1926 Jean-Baptiste Perrin, French. Worked on the discontinuous structure of matter

1927 Arthur Holly Compton, USA. Discovered wavelength change in diffused X-rays. Charles Wilson, Scottish. Invented the Cloud Chamber; made visible the paths of electrically charged particles

1928 Sir Owen Richardson, English. Discovered Richardson's Law; concerns the electron emissions by hot metals

1929 Louis de Broglie, French. Discovered the wave nature of electrons (see p. 212)

1930 Sir C. Raman, Indian. Worked on light

diffusion; discovered the Raman effect
1931 No award
1932 Werner Heisenberg, German. Formulated the indeterminacy principle of quantum mechanics (see p. 212)
1933 P.A.M Dirac, British and Erwin Schrödinger, Austrian. Introduced wave-equations in quantum mechanics (see p. 212)
1934 No award
1935 Sir James Chadwick, English. Discovered the neutron (see p. 212)
1936 Victor Hess, Austria. Discovered cosmic radiation
1937 Clinton Davisson, USA and Sir George Thomson, English. Demonstrated the interference phenomenon in crystals irradiated by electrons
1938 Enrico Fermi, Italian. Discovered radioactive elements produced by neutron irradiation
1939 Ernest Lawrence, USA. Invention of the cyclotron (see p. 212)
1940 –1942 No awards
1943 Otto Stern, USA (naturalized citizen). Discovered the magentic moment of the proton
1944 Isoder Rabi, USA (naturalized citizen). Resonance method for observing the magnetic properties of atomic nuclei
1945 Wolfgang Pauli, Austria. Discovered the exclusion principle (see p. 212 and pp. 200–1)
1946 Percy Bridgman, USA. Made discoveries in high-pressure physics
1947 Sir Edward Appleton, English. Discovered the Appleton Layer in the upper atmosphere
1948 Patrick Blackett, English. Made discoveries in nuclear physics and cosmic radiation
1949 Hudeki Yukawa, Japan. Predicted the existence of mesons (see p. 212)
1950 Cecil Powell, English. Photographic method of studying nuclear processes; discoveries about mesons (see p. 195)
1951 Sir John Cockcroft, English and Ernest Walton, Irish. Pioneered the use of accelerated particles to study atomic nuclei
1952 Felix Bloch, USA (naturalized citizen) and Edward Purcell, USA. Discovered nuclear magnetic resonance in solids
1953 Frits Zernike, Dutch. Phase-contrast microscopy method
1954 Max Born, British (German-born). Statistical studies on wave functions
Walther Bothe, German. Invention of coincidence method
1955 Willis Lamb, Jr., USA. Discoveries in the hydrogen spectrum
Polykarp Kusch, USA (naturalized citizen). Measured the magnetic moment of the electron
1956 William Shockley, USA, John Bardeen, USA and Walther Brattain, USA. Investigated semi-conductors and discovered the transistor effect
1957 Tsung-Dao Lee, Chinese and Chen Ning Yang, Chinese. Discovered violations of the principle of parity
1958 Pavel A. Cherenkov, Russian, Ilya M. Frank, Russian and Igor Y. Tamm, Russian. Investigated the effects produced by high-energy particles; the Cherenkov effect
1959 Emilio Segrè, USA (naturalized citizen) and Owen Chamberlain, USA. Confirmed the existence of the antiproton
1960 Donald Glasser, USA. Developed the bubble chamber; the device that enables the tracks of ionizing particles to be photographed
1961 Robert Hofstadter, USA. Determined shape and size of atomic nucleons
Rudolf Mössbauer, German. Discovered the Mössbauer effect; the emission of gamma rays from certain crystal substances
1962 Lev D. Landau, Russian. Contributed to the understanding of condensed states of matter
1963 J. H. D. Jensen, German and Maria Goeppert Mayer, USA (naturalized citizen). Developed shell model theory of the structure of atomic nuclei
Eugene Paul Wigner, USA (naturalized citizen). Principles governing interaction of protons and neutrons in the nucleus
1964 Charles H. Townes, USA, Nikolay G. Basov, Russian and Aleksandr M. Prokhorov, Russian. Quantum electronics leading to construction of instruments based on maser-laser principles
1965 Julian S. Schwinger, USA, Richard P. Feynman, USA, Tomonaga Shin'ichiro, Japan. Basic principles of quantum electrodynamics
1966 Alfred Kastler, French. Optical methods for studying Hertzian resonances in atoms
1967 Hans A. Bethe, USA (naturalized citizen). Discoveries concerning the energy production of stars
1968 Luis W. Alvarez, USA. Discovered resonance states as part of work with elementary particles
1969 Murray Gell-Mann, USA. Classification of elementary particles and their interactions (see p. 212)
1970 Hannes Alfvén, Swedish and Louis Néel, French. Magneto-hydrodynamics and anti-ferromagnetism and ferrimagnetism
1971 Dennis Gabor, British (Hungarian-born). Invented holography
1972 John Bardeen, USA, Leon N. Cooper, USA and John R. Schrieffer, USA. Developed the theory of superconductivity
1973 Leo Esaki, Japan, Ivar Giaever, USA (naturalized citizen) and Brian Josephson, Welsh. Tunnelling in semiconductors and superconductors
1974 Sir Martin Ryle, English and Antony Hewish, English. Radio astronomy
1975 Aage Bohr, Danish, Ben R. Mottelson, Danish (naturalized citizen) and L. James Rainwater, USA. Understanding of the atomic nucleus that paved the way for nuclear fusion
1976 Burton Richter, USA and Samuel C. C. Ting, USA. Discovered new class of elementary particles (psi, or J; see p. 213)
1977 Philip W. Anderson, USA, Sir Neville Mott, British, and John H. Van Vleck, USA. Contributed to understanding the behaviour of electrons in magnetic, non-crystalline solids
1978 Pyotr L. Kapitsa, Russian. Invented the helium liquefier, and applications
Arno A. Penzias, USA (naturalized citizen) and Robert W. Wilson, USA. Discovered cosmic microwave background radiation (support for big-bang theory; see p. 9)
1979 Sheldon Glashow, USA, Abdus Salam, Pakistani, and Steven Weinberg, USA. Established analogy between electromagnetism and the 'weak' interactions of subatomic particles (see pp. 212–13)
1980 James W. Cronin, USA and Val L. Fitch,

USA. Simultaneous violation of both charge-conjugation and parity-inversion
1981 Kai M. Siegbahn, Swedish, Nicolaas Bloembergen, USA (naturalized citizen). Electron spectroscopy for chemical analysis Arthur L. Schalow, USA. Applications of lasers in spectroscopy
1982 Kenneth G. Wilson, USA. Analysis of continuous phase transitions
1983 Subrahmanyan Chandrasekhar, USA and William A. Fowler, USA. Contributed to understanding the evolution and devolution of stars (see p. 11)
1984 Carlo Rubbia, Italian and Simon van der Meer, Dutch. Discovered subatomic particles (W;Z), supporting the electro-weak theory
1985 Klaus von Klitzing, German. Discovered the Hall effect, permitting exact measurements of electrical resistance
1986 Ernst Ruska, German, Gerd Binnig, German and Heinrich Rohrer, Swiss. Developed special electron microscopes
1987 J. Georg Bednorz, German and K. Alex Müller, Swiss. Discovered new super-conducting materials
1988 Lwon Lederman, USA, Melvin Schwartz, USA and Jack Steinberger, USA. Researched subatomic particles
1989 Norman Harvey, USA. Developed the separated field method
Hans Dehmelt, USA, and Wolfgang Paul, German. Developed and exploited the ion trap
1990 Richard E. Taylor, Canadian, Jerome Friedman, USA, and Henry Kendall, USA. Proved the existence of the quark (see p. 206)

THE FORCES OF NATURE

Four basic forces that exist in Nature are firmly established and are listed on p. 273 in ascending order of strength. They all involve the exchange of force-carrying particles or 'quanta', which are known as 'bosons' since they have integral spin, i.e. 0, 1 or 2. The strong force is explained by the theory known as 'quantum chromodynamics', which requires the existence of eight gluons, six carrying the 'colour' charge, and two that are colour neutral. The weak and electromagnetic forces have been successfully described in terms of a single 'electroweak' theory, while efforts continue to produce a unified theory of all four forces.

CHEMISTRY

WHAT IS CHEMISTRY?

Alchemy, from which modern chemistry derives its name, probably had its origins in the region of Khimi in the Nile Delta. It was here, more than 4000 years ago, that it was first discovered that the action of heat on minerals could result in the isolation of metals and glasses with useful properties – and which could therefore be sold at a profit. The practice of alchemy spread throughout the Arab world and into Asia, gaining from the Chinese the secret of making gunpowder in the process.

One of the aims of alchemy was the transmutation of metals: alchemists strove for a 'philosopher's stone' that could be used to convert 'base' metals such as iron, copper and lead into the 'noble' metal gold, which retained its lustre and its commercial value.

They thought that the philosopher's stone would also be the 'elixir' of immortality – that it would confer eternal health on those who possessed it. Much experimentation followed, which – although not leading to the desired ends – led to the development of techniques that formed the basis of modern chemistry.

Alchemy became associated with mystical practices and ideas, but from the 12th century the availability of Arab writings on alchemy gradually led to the study of chemical processes using more rational techniques and ideas – although many of the original aims were retained. Indeed, even Sir Isaac Newton experimented with the transmutation of base metals into gold – relevant research, given that he was Master of the Royal Mint!

THE AIMS OF MODERN CHEMISTRY

In modern chemistry, the philosopher's stone has been replaced by a fundamental belief in the importance of understanding the physical laws that govern the behaviour of atoms and molecules. Such an understanding has resulted in the development of methods for converting cheaply available and naturally occurring minerals, gases and oils into substances that have high commercial or social value.

During the last 150 years this approach has completely transformed our world. The discovery that iron could be made into steel by chemical means played a major part in the Industrial Revolution. In the 20th century, spectacular increases in the yields of cereals from an acre of farmland can be traced to the discovery in Germany in 1908 that nitrogen from air could be converted into ammonia fertilizers. Similarly, the greater understanding of the structures and reactions of carbon-based (organic) compounds has resulted in products such as medicines and synthetic fibres that affect all our lives.

ELEMENTS AND MOLECULES

The structure of atoms serves as a convenient starting point for discussing chemical phenomena. In chemical processes, the nuclei of atoms remain unchanged – shattering at once the alchemist's dream of transmuting elements. The great variety of known chemical compounds results from the different ways in which the electrons of atoms are able to interact either with atoms of the same kind or with atoms of a different kind. In an *element*, all the atoms are of the same kind, but the varying strengths of the interactions between the electrons in different types of atom means that elements have very different properties. For example, helium melts at -272 °C (-458 °F), whereas carbon in the form of diamond has a melting point of 3500 °C (6332 °F). This ability of electrons to interact between atoms is known as *chemical bonding* (see p. 217).

The elements nitrogen, oxygen, fluorine and chlorine form strong bonds, with two identical atoms linked together. They therefore exist at room temperature as gases, with pairs of linked atoms moving chaotically in space. Two or more atoms linked in this fashion are described as *molecules*, and a short-hand notation is used to describe their chemical identity. The atomic symbol for the element is used in conjunction with the number of atoms present to define the *chemical formula* of the molecule. The elements described above are therefore designated, respectively, by the formulae N_2, O_2, F_2 and Cl_2.

Other familiar elements, such as sulfur and phosphorus, form additional bonds to like atoms, and their formulae reflect this fact. Thus sulfur forms a ring of eight atoms and is described by the formula S_8. As the number of atoms in the fundamental unit increases, the element is no longer a gas but becomes a solid with a low melting point; thus sulfur can be extracted from the Earth as a molten fluid.

Most elements do not form discrete molecular entities such as those described above, but have structures that are held together by chemical bonds in all directions. Most of the 109 known elements are metals, such as iron and copper, and have *infinite structures* of this kind. Such elements can no longer be given distinct molecular formulae and are therefore represented by the element symbol alone; thus iron, for example, is represented simply as Fe.

CHEMICAL COMPOUNDS

In *chemical compounds*, the atoms of more than one element come together to form either molecules or infinite structures. They are described by formulae similar to those given above for elements. For example, water has a finite structure based on one oxygen atom chemically bonded to two hydrogen atoms and is denoted by the formula H_2O. Common salt (sodium chloride; NaCl) has sodium (Na) and chlorine (Cl) atoms linked together in an infinite three-dimensional lattice.

In a pure chemical compound, all the molecules have the same ratio of different atoms and behave in an identical chemical fashion. Thus a pure sample of water, for example, behaves identically to any other pure sample, however different their origins may be. Furthermore, the same ratios of atoms are retained irrespective of whether the compound is a solid, a liquid or a gas. For example, ice, water and water vapour all have molecules with the constitution H_2O. The transformation of ice into water and then into water vapour by heating is not a chemical reaction because the identities of the molecules do not change.

From the 109 chemical elements now known, more than 2 million chemical compounds have been made during the last 100 years. The chemist views chemistry as a set of molecular building blocks, constructing more and more complex and diverse molecular structures, the variety of which is limited only by his or her imagination. It is important to emphasize that the properties of a chemical compound are unique and not a sum of the properties of the individual elements from which it is made. For example, common salt does not have any properties remotely like those of metallic sodium, which catches fire on contact with water, or chlorine, which is a harmful yellow-green gas.

Although all compounds are unique, they can be classified into broad families based on common chemical properties. Acids, bases, salts, and oxidizing and reducing agents are examples of such families. Classifications reflecting the atoms present are also useful for cataloguing purposes: for example, hydrides, chlorides and oxides indicate compounds containing hydrogen, chlorine and oxygen respectively. Another particularly important classification is that of organic compounds, which contain carbon and are not only important for life processes but make up many modern industrial chemicals such as plastics, paints and artificial fibres.

MIXTURES

When elements or compounds are mixed together but not chemically bonded, they form a *chemical mixture*.

A mixture can be of two solids (e.g. salt and sand), two liquids, two gases or permutations of these. A mixture can be separated into its pure chemical constituents by either chemical or physical means. For example, adding water to the sand-salt mixture dissolves the salt, leaving the sand in a pure state. The salt and water is itself a mixture described as a *solution*, from which the pure salt can be obtained by boiling off the water.

The modern-day chemist has many other techniques for separating mixtures, such as distillation, chromatography, crystallization and electrolysis. The petrochemical industry is a prime example of how this technology can be used to convert natural gas and crude oil into a range of useful commercial and domestic products.

ELEMENTS

The world we see around us is made up of a limited number of chemical elements. In the Earth's crust, there are 82 stable elements and a few unstable (radioactive) ones. Among the stable elements, there are some, such as oxygen and silicon, that are very abundant, while others – the metals ruthenium and rhodium, for example – are extremely rare. Indeed, 98% of the Earth's crust is made up of just eight elements – in order of decreasing abundance, oxygen, silicon, aluminium, iron, calcium, sodium, magnesium and potassium.

THE PERIODIC TABLE

Each element is associated with a unique number, called its *atomic number*. This represents the number of protons – positively charged particles – in the nucleus of each atom of the element. Hydrogen has one proton, so it is the first and lightest of the elements and is placed first in the Periodic Table. Helium has two protons, and is thus the second lightest element and is placed second in the Table; and so we continue through each of the elements, establishing their order in the Table according to their atomic numbers. See p. 227.

The atomic number of bismuth is 83, and this number of protons represents the upper limit for a stable nucleus. Beyond 83, all elements are unstable, although their radioactive decay may be so slow that some of them, such a thorium and uranium, are found in large natural deposits.

The largest atomic number so far observed is 109, but only a few atoms of this element have been made artificially, so little is known about it. Its name is unnilennium, meaning 'one-zero-nine'.

THE HISTORY OF THE PERIODIC TABLE

The discovery of the Periodic Table was made possible by an Italian chemist, Stanislao Cannizzaro (1826–1910), who in 1858 published a list of fixed atomic weights (now known as relative atomic masses) for the 60 elements that were then known. By arranging the elements in order of increasing atomic weight, a curious repetition of chemical properties at regular intervals was revealed. This was noticed in 1864 by the English chemist John Newlands (1838–98), but his 'law of octaves' brought him nothing but ridicule.

It was left to the Russian chemist Dmitri Mendeleyev (1834–1907) to make essentially the same discovery five years later. What Mendeleyev did, however, was so much more impressive that he is rightly credited as the true discoverer of the Periodic Table.

Mendeleyev's genius lay in the fact that he recognized that there was an underlying order to the Periodic Table – he did not design the Periodic Table, he *discovered* it. If he was right, he knew that there should be places in his table for new elements. He was so confident in his discovery that he predicted the properties of these missing elements – and his predictions were subsequently shown to be accurate.

GROUPS AND BLOCKS

When an atom is electrically neutral, the number of electrons – negatively charged particles – circling the nucleus is the same as the number of (positive) protons in the nucleus. Thus, for example, an electrically neutral atom of calcium contains 20 protons and 20 electrons. While the atomic number identifies an atom and determines its order in the Periodic Table, it is these electrons surrounding the nucleus that determine how it behaves chemically.

Electrons can be thought of as moving around the nucleus in certain fixed orbits or 'shells', the electrons in a particular shell being associated with a particular energy level. With regard to an atom's chemical behaviour, it is the electrons in the outer shell that are most important, and it is these that fix the *group position* of the atom in the Table.

The major energy levels are numbered 1, 2, 3, etc., counting outwards from the nucleus. This number is called the *principal quantum number*, and is given the symbol n. Each energy level can hold only a certain number of electrons; the further out it is, the more it can accommodate. The maximum capacity of each shell is $2n^2$.

Each principal energy level is divided into smaller sub-levels, called s, p, d and f, which hold a maximum of 2, 6, 10 and 14 electrons respectively. It is these sub-levels that identify the main blocks of the Periodic Table: thus the s-block is made up of 2 columns or groups, the p-block of 6, the d-block of 10 and the f-block of 14. See p. 227.

GROUP POSITION AND CHEMICAL REACTIVITY

Hydrogen has one electron in the first principal energy level, while helium has two – the maximum capacity for this level. The possession of one extra electron may seem a trivial difference, but a world of difference separates hydrogen and helium: hydrogen is very reactive and forms compounds with many other elements; helium combines with nothing. These two elements are rather exceptional in all their chemical behaviour and are given a small section of their own in the Table, above groups 17 and 18 of the p-block.

The groups of the Periodic Table are numbered 1 to 18, with the f-block not included. Members of the same group have the same number of electrons in the outer shell of the atom and consequently behave in a similar manner chemically. As you go from left to right across the Table, you can see particular properties change in a regular fashion. It was this periodic rise and fall in such properties as density and atomic volume that led to the term 'Periodic Table'. In fact, however, members of the same group often bear only a superficial chemical resemblance to one another.

CHEMICAL BONDS

Although there are only 109 known elements, there are millions of chemical substances found in nature or made artificially. These substances are not simply mixtures of two or more elements: they are specifically determined chemical compounds, formed by combining two or more elements together in a chemical reaction. The chemical 'glue' that holds these compounds together is known as *chemical bonding*.

The properties of compounds vary very widely. Some are highly reactive, others inert; some are solids with high melting points, others are gases. Furthermore, the properties of a compound are generally very different from those of its constituent elements. To understand how and why these differences arise, we need to understand the different types of chemical bond.

IONIC BONDING

The atoms of the element neon have a full outer shell of electrons, with the electron configuration 2.8. This arrangement is very stable and neon is not known to form chemical bonds with any other element. An atom of the element sodium (Na) has one more electron than neon (configuration 2.8.1), while an atom of the element fluorine (F) has one electron less (configuration 2.7). If an electron is transferred from a sodium atom to a fluorine atom, two species are produced with the same stable electron configuration as neon. Unlike neon, however, the species are charged and are known as *ions*. The sodium atom, having lost a (negative) electron, has a net positive charge and is known as a *cation* (written Na^+), while the fluorine atom, having gained an electron, has a net negative charge and is called a fluoride *anion* (written F^-).

When oppositely charged ions such as Na^+ and F^- are brought together, there is a strong attraction between them; a large amount of energy is released – the same amount of energy as would have to be supplied in order to separate the ions again. This force of attraction is called an *ionic* (or *electrovalent*) *bond*. The energy released more than compensates for the energy input required to transfer the electron from the sodium atom to the fluorine atom. Overall there is a net release of energy and a solid crystalline compound – sodium fluoride (NaF) – is formed.

Atoms that have two more electrons than the nearest noble gas (such as magnesium, configuration 2.8.2) or two less (such as oxygen, 2.6) also form ions having the noble-gas configuration by transfer of

---

NOTES (for the table starting on page 218)

1. The former spelling 'sulphur' is not recommended under International Union of Pure and Applied Chemistry (I.U.P.A.C.) rules on chemical nomenclature.
2. Provisional I.U.P.A.C. names for elements 104 to 109. The names rutherfordium (Rf) and kurchatovium (Ku) have been proposed for element 104 and hahnium (Ha) and nielsbohrium (Ns) for element 105. Competing, but less substantiated, USSR claims have been made for elements 104 (G. N. Flerov et al 1964), 105 (G. N. Flerov et al 1970) and 106 (Yu. Ts. Oganessian et al 1974).
3. A value in brackets is the atomic mass of the isotope with the longest known half-life.
4. For the highly radioactive elements the density value has been calculated for the isotope with the longest known half-life.
5. This value is the minimum pressure under which liquefied helium can be solidified.
6. The melting and boiling points of carbon are based on the assumption that 'carbynes' form the stable structures above 2300 °C. This is disputed and an alternative suggestion is that graphite remains stable at high temperatures, subliming directly to vapour at 3720 °C and can only be melted at a pressure of 100 atm at 4730 °C.

TABLE OF THE 109 ELEMENTS

Atomic Number	Symbol	Element Name	Derived from	Year	Atomic Weight (Note 3)	Density at 20°C (unless otherwise stated) (g/cm³) (Note 4)	Melting Point (°C)	Boiling Point (°C)	No. of Nuclides	Discoverers
1	H	Hydrogen	Greek 'hydro genes' = water producer	1766	1·007 94	0·0871 (solid at mp) 0·000 089 89 (gas at 0°C)	−259·192	−252·753	3	H. Cavendish (UK)
2	He	Helium	Greek 'helios' = sun	1868	4·002 602	0·190 8 (solid at mp) 0·000 178 5 (gas at 0°C)	−272·375 at 24·985 atm (Note 5)	−268·928	8	J. N. Lockyer (UK) and P. J. C. Jannsen (France)
3	Li	Lithium	Greek 'lithos' = stone	1817	6·941	0·5334	180·57	1339	8	J. A. Arfwedson (Sweden)
4	Be	Beryllium	Greek 'beryllion' = beryl	1798	9·012 182	1·846	1287	2471	9	N. L. Vauquelin (France)
5	B	Boron	Persian 'burah' = borax	1808	10·811	2·333 (b Rhombahedral)	2130	3910	13	L. J. Gay Lussac and L. J. Thenard (France) and H. Davy (UK)
6	C	Carbon	Latin 'carbo' = charcoal	–	12·011	2·266 (Graphite) 3·515 (Diamond)	3530 (Note 6)	3870 (Note 6)	15	Prehistoric
7	N	Nitrogen	Greek 'nitron genes' = saltpetre producer	1772	14·006 74	0·9426 (solid at mp) 0·001 250 (gas at 0°C)	−210·004	−195·806	12	D. Rutherford (UK)
8	O	Oxygen	Greek 'oxys genes' = acid producer	1772-1774	15·9994	1·359 (solid at mp) 0·001 429 (gas at 0°C)	−218·789	−182·962	14	C. W. Scheele (Sweden) and J. Priestley (UK)
9	F	Fluorine	Latin 'fluo' = flow	1886	18·998 403	1·780 (solid at mp) 0·001 696 (gas at 0°C)	−219·669	−188·200	13	H. Moissan (France)
10	Ne	Neon	Greek 'neos' = new	1898	20·179 7	1·434 (solid at mp) 0·000 899 9 (gas at 0°C)	−248·588	−246·048	15	W. Ramsay and M. W. Travers (UK)
11	Na	Sodium	English 'soda'	1807	22·989 768	0·9688	97·819	882	17	H. Davy (UK)
12	Mg	Magnesium	Magnesia, a district of Thessaly	1808	24·3050	1·737	650	1095	15	H. Davy (UK)
13	Al	Aluminium	Latin 'alumen' = alum	1825-1827	26·981 539	2·699	660·457	2516	16	H. C. Oerstedt (Denmark) and F. Wöhler (Germany)
14	Si	Silicon	Latin 'silex' = flint	1824	28·0855	2·329	1414	3190	18	J. J. Berzelius (Sweden)
15	P	Phosphorus	Greek 'phosphorus' = light bringing	1669	30·973 762	1·825 (White) 2·361 (Violet) 2·070 (Black)	44·14 597 at 45 atm 606 at 48 atm	277 431 sublimes 453 sublimes	17	H. Brand (Germany)
16	S	Sulfur (Note 1)	Sanskrit 'solvere'; Latin 'sulfurum'	–	32·066	2·038 (solid at mp)	115·21	444·674	17	Prehistoric
17	Cl	Chlorine	Greek 'chloros' = green	1774	35·4527	2·038 (solid at mp) 0·003 214 (gas at 0°C)	−100·98	−33·99	15	C. W. Scheele (Sweden)
18	Ar	Argon	Greek 'argos' = inactive	1894	39·948	1·622 (solid at mp) 0·001 784 (gas at 0°C)	−189·352	−185·855	17	W. Ramsay and Lord Rayleigh (UK)
19	K	Potassium (Kalium)	English 'potash'	1807	39·0983	0·8591	63·60	758	20	H. Davy (UK)
20	Ca	Calcium	Latin 'calx' = lime	1808	40·078	1·526	842	1495	19	H. Davy (UK)

Atomic Number	Symbol	Element Name	Derived from	Discoverers	Year	Atomic Weight (Note 3)	Density at 20°C (unless otherwise stated) (g/cm³) (Note 4)	Melting Point (°C)	Boiling Point (°C)	No. of Nuclides
21	Sc	Scandium	Scandinavia	L. F. Nilson (Sweden)	1879	44.955 910	2.989	1541	2831	14
22	Ti	Titanium	Latin 'Titanes' = sons of the earth	M. H. Klaproth (Germany)	1795	47.88	4.504	1672	3360	17
23	V	Vanadium	Vanadis, a name given to Freyja, the Norse goddess of beauty and youth	N. G. Sefström (Sweden)	1830	50.9415	6.119	1929	3410	18
24	Cr	Chromium	Greek 'chromos' = colour	N. L. Vauquelin (France)	1798	51.9961	7.193	1860	2680	19
25	Mn	Manganese	Latin 'magnes' = magnet	J. G. Gahn (Sweden)	1774	54.938 05	7.472	1246	2051	20
26	Fe	Iron (Ferrum)	Anglo-Saxon 'iren'	Earliest smelting	c. 4000 BC	55.847	7.874	1538	2837	21
27	Co	Cobalt	German 'kobold' = goblin	G. Brandt (Sweden)	1737	58.933 20	8.834	1495	2944	21
28	Ni	Nickel	German abbreviation of 'Kupfernickel' (devil's 'copper') or niccolite	A. F. Cronstedt (Sweden)	1751	58.69	8.905	1455	2887	24
29	Cu	Copper (Cuprum)	Cyprus	Prehistoric (earliest known use)	c. 8000 BC	63.546	8.934	1084.88	2573	23
30	Zn	Zinc	German 'zink'	A. S. Marggraf (Germany)	1746	65.39	7.140	419.58	908	25
31	Ga	Gallium	Latin 'Gallia' = France	L. de Boisbaudran (France)	1875	69.723	5.912	29.772	2203	22
32	Ge	Germanium	Latin 'Germania' = Germany	C. A. Winkler (Germany)	1886	72.61	5.327	938.3	2772	22
33	As	Arsenic	Latin 'arsenicum'	Albertus Magnus (Germany)	c. 1220	74.921 59	5.781	817 at 38 atm	603 sublimes	22
34	Se	Selenium	Greek 'selene' = moon	J. J. Berzelius (Sweden)	1818	78.96	4.810 (Trigonal) 3.937 (solid at mp)	221.18	685	23
35	Br	Bromine	Greek 'bromos' = stench	A. J. Balard (France)	1826	79.904	3.119 (liquid at 20° C)	-7.25	59.76	23
36	Kr	Krypton	Greek 'kryptos' = hidden	W. Ramsay and M. W. Travers (GB)	1898	83.80	2.801 (solid at mp) 0.003 749 (gas at 0° C)	-157.386	-153.353	25
37	Rb	Rubidium	Latin 'rubidus' = red	R. W. Bunsen and G. R. Kirchhoff (Germany)	1861	85.4678	1.534	39.29	687	27
38	Sr	Strontium	Strontian, a village in Highland region, Scotland	W. Cruikshank (UK)	1787	87.62	2.582	768	1388	25
39	Y	Yttrium	Ytterby, in Sweden	J. Gadolin (Finland)	1794	88.905 85	4.468	1522	3300	23
40	Zr	Zirconium	Persian 'zargun' = gold coloured	M. H. Klaproth (Germany)	1789	91.224	6.506	1855	4360	22
41	Nb	Niobium	Latin 'Niobe' daughter of Tantalus	C. Hatchett (UK)	1801	92.906 38	8.595	2473	4860	23
42	Mo	Molybdenum	Greek 'molybdos' = lead	P. J. Hjelm (Sweden)	1781	95.94	10.22	2624	4710	22
43	Tc	Technetium	Greek 'technetos' = artificial	C. Perrier (France) and E. Segrè (Italy/USA)	1937	(97.9072)	11.40	2180	4270	21
44	Ru	Ruthenium	Ruthenia (the Ukraine, in USSR)	K. K. Klaus (Estonia/USSR)	1844	101.07	12.37	2334	4310	23

Atomic Number	Symbol	Element Name	Derived from	Discoverers	Year	Atomic Weight (Note 3)	Density at 20° C (unless otherwise stated) (g/cm³) (Note 4)	Melting Point (°C)	Boiling Point (°C)	No. of Nuclides
45	Rh	Rhodium	Greek 'rhodon' = rose	W. H. Wollaston (UK)	1804	102·905 50	12·42	1963	3700	23
46	Pd	Palladium	The asteroid Pallas (discovered 1802)	W. H. Wollaston (UK)	1803	106·42	12·01	1555·3	2975	24
47	Ag	Silver (Argentum)	Anglo-Saxon 'seolfor'	Prehistoric (earliest silversmithery)	c. 4000 BC	107·8682	10·50	961·93	2167	29
48	Cd	Cadmium	Greek 'kadmeia' = calamine	F. Stromeyer (Germany)	1817	112·411	8·648	321·108	768	33
49	In	Indium	indigo spectrum	F. Reich and H. T. Richter (Germany)	1863	114·82	7·289	156·635	2019	31
50	Sn	Tin (Stannum)	Anglo-Saxon 'tin'	Prehistoric (intentionally alloyed with copper to make bronze)	c. 3500 BC	118·710	7·288	231·968	2595	33
51	Sb	Antimony (Stibium)	Lower latin 'antimonium'	Near historic	c. 1000 BC	121·75	6·693	630·755	1635	29
52	Te	Tellurium	Latin 'tellus' = earth	F. J. Müller (Baron von Reichenstein) (Austria)	1783	127·60	6·237	449·87	989	33
53	I	Iodine	Greek 'iodes' = violet	B. Courtois (France)	1811	126·904 47	4·947	113·6	185·1	33
54	Xe	Xenon	Greek 'xenos' = stranger	W. Ramsay and M. W. Travers (UK)	1898	131·29	3·410 (solid at mp) 0·005897 (gas at 0° C)	-111·760	-108·096	36
55	Cs	Caesium	Latin 'caesius' = bluish-grey	R. W. von Bunsen and G. R. Kirchoff (Germany)	1860	132·905 43	1·896	28·47	668	36
56	Ba	Barium	Greek 'barys' = heavy	H. Davy (UK)	1808	137·327	3·595	729	1740	31
57	La	Lanthanum	Greek 'lanthano' = conceal	C. G. Mosander (Sweden)	1839	138·9055	6·145	921	3410	29
58	Ce	Cerium	The asteroid Ceres (discovered 1801)	J. J. Berzelius and W. Hisinger (Sweden) and M. H. Klaproth (Germany)	1803	140·115	6·688 (beta) 6·770 (gamma)	799	3470	30
59	Pr	Praseodymium	Greek 'prasios didymos' = green twin	C. Auer von Welsbach (Austria)	1885	140·907 65	6·772	934	3480	29
60	Nd	Neodymium	Greek 'neos didymos' = new twin	C. Auer von Welsbach (Austria)	1885	144·24	7·006	1021	3020	30
61	Pm	Promethium	Greek demi-god 'Prometheus' – the fire stealer	J. Marinsky, L. E. Glendenin, and C. D. Coryell (USA)	1945	(144·9127)	7·141	1042	3000	28
62	Sm	Samarium	The mineral Samarskite (named after Col. M. Samarski, a Russian engineer)	L. de Boisbaudran (France)	1879	150·36	7·517	1077	1794	29
63	Eu	Europium	Europe	E. A. Demarçay (France)	1901	151·965	5·243	822	1556	26
64	Gd	Gadolinium	Johan Gadolin (1760–1852)	J. C. G. de Marignac (Switzerland)	1880	157·25	7·899	1313	3270	27
65	Tb	Terbium	Ytterby, in Sweden	C. G. Mosander (Sweden)	1843	158·925 34	8·228	1356	3230	25
66	Dy	Dysprosium	Greek 'dysprositos' = hard to get at	L. de Boisbaudran (France)	1886	162·50	8·549	1412	2573	28
67	Ho	Holmium	Holmia, a Latinized form of Stockholm	J. L. Soret (France) and P. T. Cleve (Sweden)	1878–1879	164·930 32	8·794	1474	2700	26
68	Er	Erbium	Ytterby, in Sweden	C. G. Mosander (Sweden)	1843	167·26	9·064	1529	2815	27

Atomic Number	Symbol	Element Name	Derived from	Discoverers	Year	Atomic Weight (Note 3)	Density at 20°C (unless otherwise stated) (g/cm³) (Note 4)	Melting Point (°C)	Boiling Point (°C)	No. of Nuclides
69	Tm	Thulium	Latin and Greek 'Thule' = Northland	P. T. Cleve (Sweden)	1879	168·934 21	9·319	1545	1950	30
70	Yb	Ytterbium	Ytterby, in Sweden	J. C. G. de Marignac (France)	1878	173·04	6·967	817	1227	30
71	Lu	Lutetium	Lutetia, Roman name for the city of Paris	G. Urbain (France)	1907	174·967	9·839	1665	3400	34
72	Hf	Hafnium	Hafnia = Copenhagen	D. Coster (Netherlands) and G. C. de Hevesy (Hungary/Sweden)	1923	178·49	13·28	2230	4700	31
73	Ta	Tantalum	'Tantalus' – a mythical Greek king	A. G. Ekeberg (Sweden)	1802	180·9479	16·67	3020	5490	30
74	W	Tungsten (Wolfram)	Swedish 'tung sten' = heavy stone	J. J. de Elhuyar and F. de Elhuyar (Spain)	1783	183·85	19·26	3420	5860	33
75	Re	Rhenium	Latin 'Rhenus' = the river Rhine	W. Noddack, Fr. I. Tacke and O. Berg (Germany)	1925	186·207	21·01	3185	5610	32
76	Os	Osmium	Greek 'osme' = odour	S. Tennant (UK)	1804	190·2	22·59	3137	5020	34
77	Ir	Iridium	Latin 'iris' = a rainbow	S. Tennant (UK)	1804	192·22	22·56	2447	4730	33
78	Pt	Platinum	Spanish 'platina' = small silver	A. de Ulloa (Spain)	1748	195·08	21·45	1768·7	3870	34
79	Au	Gold (Aurum)	Anglo-Saxon 'gold'	Prehistoric	–	196·966 54	19·29	1064·43	2875	32
80	Hg	Mercury (Hydrargyrum)	'Hermes' ('Latin 'Mercurius'), the divine patron of the occult sciences	Near historic	c. 1600 BC	200·59	14·17 (solid at mp) 13·55 (liquid at 20° C)	-38·836	356·661	33
81	Tl	Thallium	Greek 'thallos' = a budding twig	W. Crookes (UK)	1861	204·3833	11·87	303	1468	29
82	Pb	Lead (Plumbum)	Anglo-Saxon 'lead'	Prehistoric	–	207·2	11·35	327·502	1748	33
83	Bi	Bismuth	German 'weissmuth' = white matter	C. F. Geoffroy (France)	1753	208·980 37	9·807	271·442	1566	28
84	Po	Polonium	Poland	Mme. M. S. Curie (Poland/France)	1898	(208·9824)	9·155	254	948	27
85	At	Astatine	Greek 'astos' = unstable	D. R. Corson and K. R. Mackenzie (USA) and E. Segré (Italy/USA)	1940	(209·9871)	7·0	302	377	24
86	Rn	Radon	Latin 'radius' = ray	F. E. Dorn (Germany)	1900	(222·0176)	4·7 (solid at mp) 0·010 04 (gas at 0° C)	-64·9	-61·2	30
87	Fr	Francium	France	Mlle. M. Perey (France)	1939	(223·0197)	2·8	24	650	31
88	Ra	Radium	Latin 'radius' = ray	P. Curie (France), Mme. M. S. Curie (Poland/France), and M. G. Bemont (France)	1898	(226·0254)	5·50	707	1530	28
89	Ac	Actinium	Greek 'aktinos', genitive of 'aktis' = a ray	A. Debierne (France)	1899	(227·0278)	10·04	1230	3600	26
90	Th	Thorium	'Thor', the Norse god of thunder	J. J. Berzelius (Sweden)	1829	232·0381	11·72	1760	4660	25
91	Pa	Protactinium	Greek 'protos' = first, plus actinium	O. Hahn (Germany) and Fr. L. Meitner (Austria); F. Soddy and J. A. Cranston (UK)	1917	(231·0359)	15·41	1570	4490	24
92	U	Uranium	The planet Uranus (discovered 1781)	M. H. Klaproth (Germany)	1789	238·0289	19·05	1134	4160	17

Atomic Number	Symbol	Element Name	Derived from	Discoverers	Year	Atomic Weight (Note 3)	Density at 20°C (unless otherwise stated) (g/cm³) (Note 4)	Melting Point (°C)	Boiling Point (°C)	No. of Nuclides
93	Np	Neptunium	The planet Neptune	E. M. McMillan and P. H. Abelson (USA)	1940	(237·0482)	20-47	637	4090	16
94	Pu	Plutonium	The planet Pluto	G. T. Seaborg, E. M. McMillan, J. W. Kennedy and A. C. Wahl (USA)	1940-1941	(244·0642)	20-26	640	3270	15
95	Am	Americium	America	G. T. Seaborg, R. A. James, L. O. Morgan and A. Ghiorso (USA)	1944-1945	(243·0614)	13·76	1176	2023	13
96	Cm	Curium	Pierre Curie (1859-1906) (France) and Marie Curie (1867-1934) (Poland/France)	G. T. Seaborg, R. A. James and A. Ghiorso (USA)	1944	(247·0703)	13·67	1340	3180	14
97	Bk	Berkelium	Berkeley, a town in California, USA	S. G. Thompson, A. Ghiorso and G. T. Seaborg (USA)	1949	(247·0703)	14·61	1050	2710	11
98	Cf	Californium	California	S. G. Thompson, K. Street Jr., A. Ghiorso and G. T. Seaborg (USA)	1950	(251·0796)	15-16	900	1612	18
99	Es	Einsteinium	Dr Albert Einstein (1879-1955) (USA, b. Germany)	A. Ghiorso et al (USA)	1952	(252·0829)	9·05	860	996	14
100	Fm	Fermium	Dr Enrico Fermi (1901-54) (Italy)	A. Ghiorso et al (USA)	1953	(257·0951)	–	–	–	18
101	Md	Mendelevium	Dmitry I. Mendeleyev (1834-1907) (Russia)	A. Ghiorso, B. G. Harvey, G. R. Choppin, S. G. Thompson and G. T. Seaborg (USA)	1955	(258·0986)	–	–	–	13
102	No	Nobelium	Alfred B. Nobel (1833-1896) (Sweden)	A. Ghiorso, T. Sikkeland, J. R. Walton and G. T. Seaborg (USA)	1958	(259·1009)	–	–	–	10
103	Lr	Lawrencium	Dr Ernest O. Lawrence (1901-58) (USA)	A. Ghiorso, T. Sikkeland, A. E. Larsh and R. M. Latimer (USA)	1961	(262·11)	–	–	–	9
104	Unq	Unnilquadium (Note 2)	Un-nil-quad (1-0-4)	A. Ghiorso, M. Nurmia, J. Harris, K. Eskola and P. Eskola (USA/Finland)	1969	(261·1087)	–	–	–	10
105	Unp	Unnilpentium (Note 2)	Un-nil-pent (1-0-5)	A. Ghiorso, M. Nurmia, K. Eskola, J. Harris and P. Eskola (USA/Finland)	1970	(262·1138)	–	–	–	7
106	Unh	Unnilhexium (Note 2)	Un-nil-hex (1-0-6)	A. Ghiorso et al (USA)	1974	(263·1182)	–	–	–	4
107	Uns	Unnilseptium (Note 2)	Un-nil-sept (1-0-7)	G. Münzenberg et al (Federal Republic of Germany)	1981	(262·1229)	–	–	–	2
108	Uno	Unniloctium (Note 2)	Un-nil-oct (1-0-8)	G. Münzenberg et al (Federal Republic of Germany/Finland)	1984	(265·1302)	–	–	–	2
109	Une	Unnilennium (Note 2)	Un-nil-enn (1-0-9)	G. Münzenberg et al (Federal Republic of Germany)	1982	(266·1376)	–	–	–	1

electrons – in this case Mg^{2+} and O^{2-}. The ionic compound magnesium oxide (MgO) has the same arrangement of ions as NaF, but since the ions in MgO have a greater charge, there is a stronger force between them. Thus more energy must be supplied to overcome this force of attraction, and the melting point of MgO is higher than that of NaF. Although the ions are fixed in position in the solid crystal, they become free to move when the solid is melted. As a liquid, therefore, the compound becomes electrolytic and is able to conduct electricity.

Many other more complex ionic structures are known. The formula of any ionic compound can be worked out by balancing the charges of its ions. For example, Mg^{2+} and F^- form MgF_2, while Na^+ and O^{2-} form Na_2O.

COVALENT BONDING

If we bring together two fluorine atoms, each with seven outer electrons (one less than neon), the formation of two ions with the noble-gas configuration is not possible by transfer of electrons. If, however, they share a pair of electrons – one from each atom – then both effectively achieve the noble-gas configuration and a stable molecule results.

There is a force of attraction between the shared pair of electrons and both positive nuclei, and this is what is known as a *covalent bond*. The stronger the attraction of the nuclei for the shared pair, the stronger the bond.

An atom of oxygen, having two electrons less than neon, must form two covalent bonds to attain a share in eight electrons. For example, a molecule of water (H_2O), consisting of two hydrogen atoms (H) and one oxygen atom (O), has two covalent O–H bonds. Another way for oxygen to achieve the stable noble-gas configuration is to form two bonds to the same atom. Thus two oxygen atoms bond covalently to one another by sharing two pairs of electrons. This is known as a *double bond*.

Like oxygen, sulfur (S) has six outer electrons and again needs to form two bonds to attain a share in eight electrons. There are two ways in which sulfur atoms join together – either in rings of eight atoms (S_8) or in long chains of many atoms bonded together. The different forms in which elemental sulfur exist are known as *allotropes*; other elements found in allotropic forms include carbon (graphite and diamond; see below) and oxygen (oxygen and ozone).

Atoms of nitrogen (N), containing five outer electrons, need to form three covalent bonds to attain a share in eight electrons. This may be done, for example, by forming one bond to each of three hydrogen atoms, to give ammonia (NH_3; see p. 226). Another possibility is to form all three bonds to a second nitrogen atom, which produces a nitrogen molecule (N_2; see p. 226), containing a *triple covalent bond*.

The carbon atom (C), which has four outer electrons, needs to form four bonds to attain the noble-gas configuration. Thus a carbon atom forms one bond to each of four hydrogen atoms to give methane (CH_4). Although carbon is not known to form a quadruple bond to another carbon atom, some other elements, such as the heavy metal rhenium, do form such quadruple bonds.

GIANT MOLECULES

Although two carbon atoms do not form a quadruple bond to one another, carbon atoms can combine to form a giant crystal lattice in which each atom is bonded to four others by single covalent bonds. This is the structure of diamond, one of the allotropes of elemental carbon. Many other elements and compounds exist as giant covalent crystal lattices, including quartz, which is a form of silicon dioxide (SiO_2). Crystals of these substances contain many millions of atoms held together by strong covalent bonds, so that a large amount of energy is needed to break them. Thus these substances all have high melting points and are hard solids.

INTERMOLECULAR FORCES

As we have seen, two neon atoms do not form covalent bonds with one another because of their full outer shells of electrons. There are, however, weak forces of attraction between two neon atoms. We know this because, when neon gas is compressed or cooled, it eventually turns into a liquid in which the atoms are weakly attracted to one another. These weak forces are called *van der Waals forces* and their strength depends on the size of the molecule.

Bromine (Br_2) is made up of large covalently bonded molecules that have much stronger van der Waals forces between them than exist between atoms of neon. Thus at room temperature bromine exists as a mixture of liquid and vapour. However, the forces *between* the bromine molecules are much weaker than covalent bonds, so that – while it is easy to separate the bromine molecules from one another and vaporize the liquid – it requires much more energy to separate the bromine atoms by breaking the covalent bond between them.

HYDROGEN BONDS

Some small molecules have much higher melting and boiling points than would be expected on the basis of their size. One such example is water (H_2O), which has about the same mass as a neon atom but has a much higher melting point. There must therefore be unusually strong intermolecular forces between the water molecules. Although the oxygen and hydrogen atoms share a pair of electrons in a covalent bond, the oxygen atom exerts a stronger 'pull' on these electrons and so becomes electron-rich, leaving the hydrogen atom electron-poor. As a result, there is a force of attraction between hydrogen and oxygen atoms on neighbouring molecules. This is known as *hydrogen bonding*.

As well as accounting for the surprisingly high melting point of water, hydrogen bonding is responsible for the rigid open structure of ice crystals, and is very important in influencing the structures and properties of biological molecules. Although hydrogen bonds are stronger than van der Waals forces, they are still much weaker than covalent bonds.

CHEMICAL REACTIONS

Chemical reactions are the means by which new substances are formed from old ones. Among the chemical reactions occurring everywhere around us are the changes that take place when fuels are burnt, the industrial methods by which metals are extracted from their ores, and the processes controlling life itself.

During a chemical reaction, the atomic constituents of the substances that react together (the *reactants*) are rearranged to produce different substances (the *products*). Thus, for example, in the reaction of potassium (K) with water (H_2O), potassium hydroxide (KOH) and hydrogen gas (H_2) are formed. This information can be represented as a chemical equation. By convention the reactants appear on the left-hand side and the products on the right. Letters may also be added after each chemical species to indicate its physical state – s means 'solid', l 'liquid', aq 'aqueous' (solution) and g 'gas'.

$$2K(s) + 2H_2O(l) \rightarrow 2KOH(aq) + H_2(g)$$

An essential characteristic of chemical reactions is that there is an exchange of energy between the reacting system and the surroundings. So much heat is liberated during the reaction of potassium and water that the highly flammable hydrogen gas frequently ignites above the molten metal.

STOICHIOMETRY

According to the *law of constant composition*, matter cannot be created or destroyed during a chemical reaction. Thus in the reaction described above, the number of atoms of potassium, hydrogen and oxygen (calculated by multiplying each element in the equation by the numbers placed before the chemical formula) is the same before and after the reaction, and the equation is said to be balanced. The numerical proportions in which substances combine to form the products of a chemical reaction is described as the reaction *stoichiometry*.

A balanced equation is thus a quantitative statement about the chemical reaction concerned. Such an equation (in conjunction with the mole concept; see below) enables us to predict how much product will be formed from a given mass of reactants.

THE MOLE CONCEPT

A *mole* is a measure of the amount of substance, based on the atomic theory of matter. A mole is defined as *the number of carbon atoms in 12 grams of the isotope carbon-12* and has the colossal value of 6.022×10^{23}. Every chemical compound has a fixed *relative molecular mass* or RMM (determined by the relative atomic masses of its constituent elements); so that molecular quantities (the number of moles) of any substance can be found using simple arithmetic.

REACTIONS OF ACIDS AND BASES

Acids may be defined as substances that tend to donate protons – ionized hydrogen atoms – to other molecules. For example, gaseous hydrogen chloride dissolves in water to form hydrochloric acid, by donating a proton to the water molecule. The products of the reaction are ions – electrically charged species. Many non-metal oxides form acids when dissolved in water; for example, sulfur trioxide gas (SO_3) dissolves in water to form sulfuric acid (H_2SO_4) – the reaction that occurs in the formation of acid rain.

By contrast, *bases* are defined as proton acceptors, capable of accepting protons from hydronium ions present in solution. Examples of bases include sodium and potassium hydroxides (NaOH and KOH), which generate aqueous hydroxide ions in solution. Many metal oxides are also basic, such as calcium oxide (CaO; lime). Aqueous solutions of bases are known as *alkalis*.

Acids and bases can be detected by their effects on a class of natural dyes called *indicators*. The best-known indicator is *litmus*, a dye derived from lichen,

which is turned red by acids and blue by bases.

Acids and bases react together to form compounds known as *salts*, which are neither acidic nor basic. For example, sodium hydroxide reacts with hydrochloric acid to form sodium chloride.

The end-points of such *neutralization reactions* can be determined visually by the choice of an appropriate indicator, which changes colour when acid and base are exactly neutralized, i.e. when they have completely reacted. Neutralizations are of great importance in quantitative chemical analysis.

PRECIPITATION REACTIONS

Ionic compounds that dissolve water produce *electrolyte* solutions. These consist of ions moving randomly throughout the solution; for example, sodium chloride in aqueous solution contains sodium and chloride ions. These ions are responsible for the electrical conductivity of electrolytes (see below).

Silver nitrate is another ionic solid that dissolves readily in water, producing a colourless solution of aqueous silver and nitrate ions. If solutions of silver nitrate and sodium chloride are mixed, a white turbidity (cloudiness) forms instantly. This is due to the *precipitation* of fine particles of highly insoluble silver chloride. The precipitate gradually accumulates at the bottom of the vessel, leaving colourless sodium nitrate in solution. The reaction is one in which ions are exchanged between partners. It is possible to predict the outcome of precipitation reactions from a knowledge of the solubilities of the various species involved.

OXIDATION AND REDUCTION

Magnesium metal (Mg) burns with an incandescent white flame in air because of a vigorous reaction with oxygen, forming magnesium oxide:

$$Ms(s) + O_2(g) \rightarrow 2MgO(s)$$

This is an example of the class of reactions known as *oxidations*, which include all combustion processes such as those occurring when fuels burn in air, as well as the reactions that cause metals to corrode in air.

The transfer of electrons between chemical species is a common process in many chemical reactions, so the term oxidation has come to possess a wider meaning than that implying solely the addition of oxygen atoms to an element or compound. As in the case of magnesium oxide above, oxidation means the loss of electrons by a compound. The opposite process – *reduction* – implies a gain of electrons. In the equation above, magnesium is said to be oxidized, while oxygen is reduced. The overall reaction is described as a *redox* process. Many metals are extracted from their ores by reduction reactions.

ELECTROLYSIS

If an electric current is passed through an electrolyte such as an aqueous solution of copper (II) chloride, a redox process known as *electrolysis* occurs. Positively charged Cu^2 ions are attracted to the negative electrode – the cathode – where they take up two electrons each and are thereby reduced to copper metal, which is deposited on the cathode. At the same time, the negatively charged Cl ions are attracted to the positive electrode – the anode – where they give up their extra electrons (i.e. are oxidized) to form chlorine gas. Electrolysis is the basis of *electroplat-*

ing, in which a thin layer of metal, such as copper, tin, chromium or silver, is applied as a protective or decorative finish on cheaper and less durable materials.

REACTION EQUILIBRIA

The reactions described so far have gone to completion, i.e. a fixed quantity of reactants is converted into a fixed quantity of products. However, in general such a state of affairs is more the exception than the rule. The end of a reaction occurs when there is no further change in the amount of products formed or reactants destroyed: this is the point at which the reaction is said to have reached *equilibrium*. At equilibrium, there may be appreciable amounts of reactants still present. For example, when acetic acid is dissolved in water, it forms a *weak acid*, because at equilibrium there is only a low concentration of hydronium ions.

The position of equilibrium in a chemical reaction (whether it favours reactants or products) depends in a detailed way on the thermodynamic properties of all the species involved.

RATES OF CHEMICAL REACTIONS

Very often it is important to know not only where the position of a chemical equilibrium lies but how fast it is reached. A graphic example is provided by a mixture of hydrogen gas and oxygen gas at room temperature. If undisturbed, the mixture does not react, but if a spark is passed through the gases, there is a violent explosion leading to the formation of water. Thus temperature is seen to exert a strong influence on the rate at which a reaction proceeds – the higher the temperature, the faster the reaction.

On the other hand, the same reaction can be made to proceed smoothly at room temperature by the addition of finely divided platinum metal, which acts as a catalyst. A *catalyst* is a substance that is not chemically transformed during a reaction but whose presence serves to accelerate its rate. Catalysts play an extremely important role in many industrial processes, where they allow reactions to be carried out under conditions that would otherwise have to be much more severe.

Another factor influencing the rate of reaction is the intrinsic reactivity – i.e. willingness to undergo chemical reaction – of the chemical species involved.

SMALL MOLECULES

Although the Earth's atmosphere consists almost entirely of two gases – nitrogen and oxygen – a number of other gases are present at low concentration, together with varying amounts of water vapour. With the exception of the noble gases, most other components of air form part of natural cycles, each remaining in the atmosphere only for a limited time. Not only are these gases of major importance in relation to industrial processes that dominate economies throughout the world, but cyclical processes involving water, oxygen, carbon dioxide and nitrogen – together with solar radiation – are essential to plant and animal life.

Current interest in various atmospheric gases centres on the possible global effects of changes in their atmospheric concentration due to human activities. Increase in carbon dioxide may upset the heat balance at the Earth's surface, while the use of chlorofluorocarbons (CFCs) might result in de-pletion of the ozone layer, thereby allowing destructive high-energy solar radiation to reach the Earth's surface.

Although these small molecules are simple in the sense that they are composed of few atoms, their structures and – for those with three or more atoms – their shapes vary. In most cases, their atoms are held together in the molecule by two, four or six electrons, resulting in single, double or triple covalent bonds (see p. 223).

HYDROGEN

Hydrogen (H_2) is the simplest of all stable molecules, consisting of two protons and two electrons. It is a colourless, odourless gas and is lighter than air. Most hydrogen is used on the site where it is produced, but it is also transported as compressed gas in steel cylinders and in liquid form at very low temperature.

WATER

The total amount of water (H_2O) on Earth is fixed, and most is recycled and re-used. The largest reservoirs are the oceans and open seas, followed by glaciers, ice caps and ground water. Very little is actually contained within living organisms, although water is a major constituent of most life forms.

Water is one of the most remarkable of all small molecules. On the basis of its molecular weight (18), it should be a gas; its high boiling point (100 °C / 212 °F) is due to the interaction of water molecules with each other (hydrogen bonding), which effectively increases its molecular weight. Water is also unusual in that – as ice – it is less dense than the liquid at the same temperature.

CARBON DIOXIDE AND OXYGEN

Carbon dioxide (CO_2) is a colourless gas with a slight odour and an acid taste. It is available as gas, as liquid and as the white solid known as 'dry ice'. Its cycle in nature is tied to that of oxygen, the relative levels of the two gases in the atmosphere (apart from human activity) being regulated by the photosynthetic activity of plants. It is produced on a vast scale, mostly as a by-product of other processes.

With the ever-increasing input of carbon dioxide to the atmosphere, due largely to the burning of fossil fuels and forests and the manufacture of cement, the natural 'sinks' for carbon dioxide – chiefly photosynthesis and transfer to the oceans – can no longer keep pace with the total input. If this imbalance continues, it is thought that levels will be reached where the infrared-absorbing properties of carbon dioxide will result in a progressive warming of the Earth's atmosphere, accompanied by melting of the polar ice and flooding of what is now dry land – the so-called *greenhouse effect* (see also p. 103). This is perhaps too extreme and pessimistic a view: in the past there have been many warm interglacial periods due to factors not ascribable to human activity.

Oxygen (O_2) is a highly reactive colourless, odourless and tasteless gas. At low temperature, it condenses to a pale blue liquid, slightly denser than water. Oxygen supports burning, causes rusting and is vital to both plant and animal respiration.

OZONE

Ozone (O_3) is a highly toxic, unstable, colourless gas. Its primary importance stems from its formation in the stratosphere. In this layer of the atmosphere, temperature increases with height, principally because of the reaction of high-energy ultraviolet solar radiation with oxygen.

Ozone in the stratosphere functions as a very effective filter for high-energy ultraviolet solar radiation. Radiation in this energy range is sufficiently high to break bonds between carbon and other atoms, making it lethal to all forms of life. It is currently thought that the introduction of CFCs (used in sprays and refrigerants) and the related 'halons' (used in fire extinguishers) may contribute to the partial or even total destruction of the ozone layer. These classes of compounds are highly volatile, chemically very stable and essentially insoluble in water, so that they are not washed out of the atmosphere by rain. When, by normal convection, they reach the stratosphere, they react destructively with ozone.

CARBON DIOXIDE

Carbon monoxide (CO) is a colourless, odourless, toxic gas. The input to the atmosphere due to human activity is about 360 million tonnes (tons) per year, mostly from the incomplete combustion of fossil fuels. The natural input is some 10 times this figure and results from the partial oxidation of biologically produced methane. The background level of 0.1 parts per million (ppm) can rise to 20 ppm at a busy road intersection, and a five-minute cigarette gives an intake of 400 ppm.

Since the atmospheric level of carbon monoxide is not rising significantly, there must be effective sink processes, one being its oxidation in air to carbon dioxide. In addition, there are soil microorganisms that utilize carbon monoxide in photosynthesis.

NITROGEN

Nitrogen (N_2) is a colourless, odourless gas. Although very stable and chemically unreactive, it cycles both naturally and as a result of its use in the chemical industry. The natural cycle results from the ability of some types of bacteria and blue-green algae (in the presence of sunlight) to 'fix' nitrogen – i.e. to convert it into inorganic nitrogen compounds (ammonium and nitrate salts) that can be assimilated by plants. Since 1913 human activity has increasingly contributed to the cycling of nitrogen, because of the catalytic conversion of nitrogen into ammonia (used mainly in nitrate fertilizers, see below), which ultimately reverts to nitrogen gas.

OXIDES OF NITROGEN

The presence of nitric oxide (NO) and nitrogen dioxide (NO_2) at high levels in the atmosphere is closely connected with the internal-combustion engine. At the high temperature reached when petroleum and air ignite, nitrogen and oxygen combine to form nitric oxide, which slowly reacts with more oxygen to form nitrogen dioxide. Most internal-combustion engines also produce some unburnt or partially burnt fuel: in the presence of sunlight, this reacts with nitrogen dioxide by a sequence of fast reactions, forming organic peroxides, which are the harmful constituents of photochemical smog (smoke plus fog).

AMMONIA

Ammonia (NH_3) is a colourless gas with a penetrating odour, and is less dense than air. It is highly soluble in water, giving an alkaline solution. World production is of the order of 100 million tonnes (tons) a year, most of which is converted into fertilizers (80%), plastics (9%) and explosives (4%).

OXIDES OF SULFUR

Both sulfur dioxide (SO_2) and sulfur trioxide (SO_3) are pungent-smelling acidic gases, which are produced by volcanic action and – to the extent of some 150 million tonnes (tons) a year – by the burning of fossil fuels and smelting operations.

The level of sulfur dioxide in unpolluted air is 0.002 parts per million (ppm), but in the 1952 London smog the levels rose to 1.54 ppm, accompanied by a dramatic increase in the death rate. In the atmosphere, sulfur dioxide is slowly oxidized to sulfur trioxide, water droplets and particulate matter in the air. Ultimately the latter is deposited as dilute sulfuric acid – *acid rain.*

METALS

Metals are usually defined by their physical properties, such as strength, hardness, lustre, conduction of heat and electricity, malleability and high melting point. They can also be characterized chemically as elements that dissolve (or whose oxides dissolve) in acids, usually to form positively charged ions (cations). By either definition, more than three quarters of the known elements can be classified as metals. They occupy all but the top right-hand corner of the Periodic Table (see p. 227), the remainder being non-metals. A few elements on the borderline, such as germanium, arsenic and antimony, have some of the properties of metals and are often classed as *metalloids.*

Given such a large number of metals, it is not surprising that some of them have rather untypical properties. For instance, mercury is a liquid at room temperature, and – with the exception of lithium – all the alkali metals melt below 100 °C (212 °F). The alkali metals are also quite soft – they can easily be cut with a knife – and extremely reactive – rubidium and caesium cannot be handled in air and may react explosively with water.

OCCURRENCE

Most metals occur naturally as oxides, while some – mostly the heavier ones, such as mercury and lead – occur as sulfides. Only a few – the noble and coinage metals – are found in the metallic state, being chemically the most inert metals.

A few metals do not occur naturally at all, because they are radioactive and have decayed away. Technetium and all the elements with higher atomic numbers than plutonium are made by the 'modern alchemy' of nuclear reactors or accelerators, while promethium is found only in minute amounts as a product of the spontaneous fission of uranium. The very heaviest elements have been obtained only a few atoms at a time, and are intensely radioactive.

THE DISCOVERY AND EXTRACTION OF METALS

Artificial elements have of course been known only in modern times, since the 1940s or later. The discovery of most other metals was also comparatively recent: with the exception of zinc, platinum and the handful of metals known to the Ancients, all metals have been discovered since 1735. The only metals known in antiquity were copper, silver, gold, iron, tin, mercury and lead. Of these, it was not the most abundant – iron – that was discovered first: the Bronze Age came before the Iron Age. The reason for this is that it is easier to extract the metals used in bronze – copper and tin – from their minerals than it is to extract iron from its ores. The discovery of copper is thought to have been accidental: pieces of the metal ore used in fireplaces came into contact with the hot charcoal, so releasing the metal. Essentially the same process under controlled conditions (*smelting*) is used in modern blast furnaces. Any of the metals from manganese (Mn) to zinc (Zn) in the Periodic Table can be obtained by roasting their oxides with coke at temperatures of up to about 1600° C (2912° F).

The ores of the lighter, more reactive metals cannot be reduced by carbon at practical temperatures, because their atoms are more strongly bonded in the ore. These metals are usually obtained by electrolysis or by the reaction of their compounds with an even more reactive metal. For instance, the reduction of aluminium oxide with carbon requires a temperature in excess of 2000° C (3632° F); so electrolysis of a melt of aluminium oxide in a mixture of cryolite (a double fluoride of aluminium and sodium) and calcium fluoride at about 950° C(1742° F) is used. On the other hand, titanium is obtained by converting its oxide into the chloride, which is then reduced with elemental sodium or magnesium.

CONDUCTIVITY

The conduction of heat and electricty that characterizes metals is due to their unique type of bonding. The solid metals behave as if they were composed of arrays of positively charged ions, with electrons free to move throughout the crystalline structure of the metal. This results in high electrical conductivity. The conduction of heat can also be seen in terms of the motion of electrons, which becomes faster as temperature rises. Since the electrons are mobile, the heat can be conducted readily through the solid.

The majority of metals are good conductors of electricity, but germanium and tin (in the form stable below 19°C/64°F) are semiconductors.

MECHANICAL STRENGTH

Many metals are used because of their strength. However, most pure metals are actually quite soft. In order to obtain a tough hard metal, something else has to be added. For instance, the earliest useful metal was not copper but bronze, which is copper alloyed with tin. Similarly, iron is never used in the pure state but as some form of steel.

The softness of a pure metal results from a lack of perfection in the crystal framework formed by its atoms. Even when the most rigorous conditions are employed, it is impossible to grow any material in perfect crystalline form. There will always be some atoms in the wrong place or missing from their proper place. When solidification occurs fairly rapidly, as when a molten metal is cooled in a mould, even more defects occur. Under bending or shearing, such defects can move and allow the metal to change shape easily. When the foreign atoms of an alloying element are present, they usually have a different size from those of the host and cannot easily fit into the crystal lattice. They therefore tend to site themselves where the lattice is irregular, i.e. where the defects are. The effect of this is to prevent the defects from moving, and so to increase the rigidity of the metal.

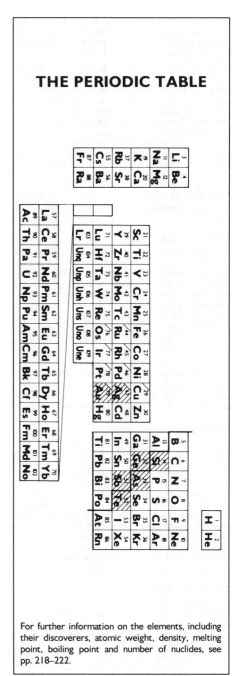

THE PERIODIC TABLE

For further information on the elements, including their discoverers, atomic weight, density, melting point, boiling point and number of nuclides, see pp. 218–222.

ORGANIC CHEMISTRY

The molecular basis for life processes, which have evolved with such remarkable elegance around carbon as the key element, is beginning to be understood, thanks to the combined triumphs of biological, chemical and physical scientists during the last hundred years.

Although the chemist can now make synthetically almost any chemical compound that nature produces, the challenge remains to achieve this objective routinely with the efficiency and precision that characterizes the chemistry of living systems.

There is something very special about the chemistry of carbon that has singled it out as the atomic building block from which all naturally occurring compounds in living systems are constructed. The subject that deals with this important area of science, nestling between biology and physics, has become so vast and significant that it has earned recognition as a separate field of scientific investigation. As it was originally thought that such carbon-based compounds could be obtained only from natural sources, this field of study became known as *organic chemistry*.

THE CARBON ATOM

Carbon's unique feature is the readiness with which it forms bonds both with other carbon atoms and with atoms of other elements. Having four electrons in its outer shell, a carbon atom requires four electrons to attain a stable noble-gas configuration. It therefore forms four covalent bonds with other atoms, each of which donates a single electron to each bond. In this way the electronic requirements are satisfied, and a three-dimensional 'tetracovalent' environment is built up around the carbon atom.

Carbon bonds are found both in pure forms of carbon (graphite and diamond) and in association with other atoms in a vast array of compounds. Compounds consisting of just carbon and hydrogen – *hydrocarbons* – are extremely important, notably as the principal constituents of fossil fuels. In addition carbon readily bonds with many other atoms, including oxygen, nitrogen, sulfur, phosphorus and the halogens, such as chlorine and bromine.

FUNCTIONAL GROUPS

Carbon combines with itself and other atoms to produce open-chain (*acyclic*) and ring (*cyclic*) skeletons, into which are built highly characteristic arrangements of atoms, known as *functional groups*. The diverse but predictable chemical behaviour of the different functional groups is a consequence of their ability either to attract or to repel electrons compared with the rest of the carbon skeleton. The overall effect of the resulting charge distribution is to create a molecule in which some regions are slightly negatively charged (*nucleophilic*), and others slightly positively charged (*electrophilic*).

Most organic reactions involve the electrophilic and nucleophilic centres of different molecules coming together as a prelude to the formation of new covalent bonds.

AMINO ACIDS

Amino acids, from which proteins are synthesized in living organisms, are characterized by their possession of two functional groups – a carboxylic-acid group (CO_2H) and an amino group (NH_2). Different amino acids, often with very different properties, are distinguished by the identity of a third group – a methyl group (CH_3) in the case of alanine.

Alanine is one of the 20 naturally occurring amino acids. A detailed examination of its structure reveals another feature of paramount importance to the modern chemist. The four groups bonded to the central carbon atom are arranged in such a way as to define a tetrahedron in three dimensions. This spatial arrangement (or *configuration*) can exist in two different forms, one the non-superimposable mirror image of the other. They differ as our right hand does to our left, so the central carbon atom is said to be *chiral* (from the Greek for 'hand') or asymmetric. The two different forms are known as *enantiomers*.

Molecular recognition – based upon chirality – is prevalent in the chemistry of the molecules of life. Nucleic acids (DNA and RNA), polysaccharides (large natural sugar molecules) and proteins, especially enzymes, all discriminate between enantiomers in their respective modes of action.

NOBEL PRIZEWINNERS IN CHEMISTRY

1901 Jacobus van't Hoff, Dutch. Laws of chemical dynamics and osmotic pressure
1902 Emil Fischer, German. Work on sugar and purine syntheses
1903 Svante Arrhenius, Swedish. Theory of electrolytic dissociation
1904 Sir William Ramsay, Scottish. Discovery and periodic system classification of inert gas elements
1905 Adolf von Baeyer, German. Work on organic dyes and hydroaromatic compounds
1906 Henri Moissan, French. The Moissan furnace; and isolation of fluorine
1907 Eduard Buchner, German. Discovery of non-cellular fermentation
1908 Lord Ernest Rutherford, British. Atomic structure and the chemistry of radioactive substance
1909 Wilhelm Ostwald, German. Pioneered catalysis, chemical equilibrium and reaction velocity work
1910 Otto Wallach, German. Pioneer work on alicyclic combinations
1911 Marie Curie, French (naturalized citizen). Discovery of radium and polonium; isolation of radium
1912 Victor Grignard, French. Grignard reagents Paul Sabatier, French. Method of hydrogenating compounds
1913 Alfred Werner, Swiss (naturalized citizen). Work on the linkage of atoms in molecules
1914 Theodore Richards, USA. Precise determination of atomic weights of many elements
1915 Richard Willstätter, German. Pioneered research on plant pigments, especially chlorophyll
1916 No award
1917 No award
1918 Fritz Haber, German. Synthesis of ammonia
1919 No award
1920 Walther Nernst, German. Work in thermochemistry
1921 Frederick Soddy, English. Studied radioactive materials; occurrence and nature of isotopes
1922 Francis Aston, English. Work on mass spectrography; whole number rule
1923 Fritz Pregl, Austrian. Method of microanalysis of organic substances
1924 No award
1925 Richard Zsigmondy, German. Elucidation of the heterogeneous nature of colloidal solutions
1926 Theodor Svedberg, Swedish. Work on disperse systems
1927 Heinrich Wieland, German. Research into the constitution of bile acids

1928 Adolf Windaus, German. Constitution of sterols and their connection with vitamins

1929 Sir Arthur Harden, English, and H. von Euler-Chelpin, Swedish (naturalized citizen). Studied sugar fermentation and the enzymes involved in the process

1930 Hans Fischer, German. Chlorophyll research, and discovery of haemoglobin in the blood

1931 Karl Bosch, German, and Friedrich Bergius, German. Invention and development of high-pressure methods

1932 Irving Langmuir, USA. Furthered understanding of surface chemistry

1933 No award

1934 Harold Urey, USA. Discovered heavy hydrogen

1935 Frédéric Joliot-Curie, French, and Irène Joliot-Curie, French. Synthesis of new radioactive elements

1936 Peter Debye, Dutch. Work on dipole moments and the diffraction of X-rays and electrons in gases

1937 Sir Walter Haworth, English. Carbohydrate and vitamin C research
Paul Karrer, Swiss. Carotenoid, flavin, and vitamin research

1938 Richard Kuhn, German. Carotenoid and vitamin research (award declined as Hitler forbade Germans to accept Nobel prizes)

1939 Adolf Butenandt, German. Work on sex hormones (award declined as Hitler forbade Germans to accept Nobel prizes)

1940–1942 No awards made

1943 George von Hevesy, Hungarian. Use of isotopes as tracers in research

1944 Otto Hahn, German. Discovery of the fusion of heavy nuclei

1945 Arturri Virtanen, Finnish. Invention of fodder preservation method

1946 James Sumner, USA. Discovery of enzyme crystallization
John Northrop, USA, and Wendell Stanley, USA. Preparation of pure enzymes and virus proteins

1947 Sir Robert Robinson, English. Research on alkaloids and plant biology

1948 Arne Tiselius, Swedish. Electrophoretic and adsorption analysis research; serum proteins

1949 William Giauque, USA. Behaviour of substances at very low temperatures

1950 Otto Diels, German, and Kurt Alder, German. Discovery and development of diene synthesis

1951 Edwin McMillan, USA, and Glenn Seaborg, USA. Discovery of and research on transuranium elements

1952 Archer Martin, English and Richard Synge, English. Development of partition chromatography

1953 Hermann Staudinger, German. Work on macromolecules

1954 Linus Pauling, USA. Studied the nature of the chemical bond

1955 Vincent Du Vigneaud, USA. First to synthesize a polypeptide hormone

1956 Nikolay Semyonov, Russian, and Sir Cyril Hinshelwood, English. Work on the kinetics of chemical reactions

1957 Sir Alexander Todd, Scottish. Work on nucleotides and nucleotide coenzymes

1958 Frederick Sanger, English. Determined the structure of the insulin molecule

1959 Jaroslav Heyrovsky, Czechoslovakian. Discovered and developed polarography

EURO FACTS

'LEAGUE TABLE' OF NOBEL PRIZEWINNERS (FOR CHEMISTRY) FROM EC COUNTRIES

Germany	22
United Kingdom	20
France	5
The Netherlands	2
Belgium	I
Italy	I
Denmark	0
Greece	0
Ireland	0
Luxembourg	0
Portugal	0
Spain	0

1960 Willard Libby, USA. Developed radio-carbon dating

1961 Melvin Calvin, USA. Studied the chemical stages that occur in photosynthesis

1962 John C. Kendrew, British, and Max F. Perutz, British (Austrian-born). Determined the structure of haemoproteins

1963 Giulio Natta, Italian, and Karl Ziegler, German. Structure and synthesis of plastics polymers

1964 Dorothy M. C. Hodgkin, English. Determined the structure of compounds essential in combating pernicious anaemia

1965 Robert B. Woodward, USA. Synthesized sterols, chlorophyll, etc. (previously produced only by living things)

1966 Robert S. Mulliken, USA. Investigated chemical bonds and electronic structure of molecules

1967 Manfred Eigen, German, Ronald G. W. Norrish, English, and George Porter, English. Studied extremely fast chemical reactions

1968 Lars Onsager, USA (naturalized citizen). Theory of the thermodynamics of irreversible processes

1969 Derek H. R. Barton, British, and Odd Hasell, Norwegian. Determined the actual 3-dimensional shape of certain organic compounds

1970 Luis F. Leloir, Argentinian (naturalized citizen). Discovered sugar nucleotides and their role in carbohydrate biosynthesis

1971 Gerhard Herzberg, Canadian. Researched the structure of molecules

1972 Christian B. Anfinsen, USA, Stanford Moore, USA, and William H. Stein, USA. Contributed to the fundamentals of enzyme chemistry

1973 Ernst Fischer, German, and Geoffrey Wilkinson, British. Organometallic chemistry

1974 Paul J. Flory, USA. Studied long-chain molecules

1975 J. W. Cornforth, British, and Vladimir Prelog, Swiss. Worked on stereochemistry

1976 William N. Lipscomb, USA. Structure of boranes

1977 Ilya Prigogine, Belgian. Advanced thermodynamics

1978 Peter D. Mitchell, British. Theory of energy transfer processes in biological systems

1979 Herbert C. Brown, USA (naturalized citizen) and Georg Wittig, German. Introduced boron and phosphorus compounds in the synthesis of organic compounds

1980 Paul Berg, USA. First preparation of a hybrid DNA.
Walter Gilbert, USA, and Frederick Sanger, English. Chemical and biological analysis of the structure of DNA

1981 Fukui Kenichi, Japanese, and Roald Hoffmann, USA (naturalized citizen). Orbital symmetry interpretation of chemical reactions

1982 Aaron Klug, British (naturalized citizen). Determined the structure of some biologically active substances

1983 Henry Taube, Canadian. Studied electron transfer reactions

1984 Bruce Merrifield, USA. Formulated method of polypeptide synthesis

1985 Herbert A. Hauptman, USA, and Jerome Karle, USA. Developed means of mapping the chemical structure of small molecules

1986 Dudley R. Herschbach, USA, Yuan T. Lee, USA, and John C. Polanyi, Canadian. Introduced methods for analysing basic chemical reactions

1987 Donald J. Cram, USA, Charles J. Pedersen and Jean-Marie Lehn, French. Developed molecules that could link with other molecules

1988 Johann Deisenhofer, German, Robert Huber, German, and Hartmut Michel, German. Studied the structure of the proteins needed in photosynthesis

1989 Tom Cech, USA, and Sidney Altman, USA. Established that RNA catalyses biochemical reactions

1990 Elias Corey, USA. Worked on synthesizing chemical compounds based on natural substances

MATHEMATICS

Many people think of mathematics in terms of rules to be learned in order to manipulate symbols or study numbers or shapes in the abstract for their own sake. Mathematical theory does develop in the abstract; it need have no dependence on anything outside itself. The truth of the theory is measured by logic rather than experiment. However, one of its most valuable uses is in describing or modelling processes in the real world, and thus there is constant interaction between pure mathematics and applied mathematics.

Mathematics may be considered as the very general study of the structure of systems. Since the study is unrelated to the physical world, rigorous formal proofs are sought, rather than experimental verifications. Theory is presented in terms of a small number of given truths (known as *axioms*) from which the entire theory can be inferred.

Thus, the aims are for generality in approach and rigour in proof, aims that explain the traditional concern of mathematicians for the unification of seemingly different branches of mathematics. As an example, Descartes (see p. 231) showed that geometrical figures could be described in terms of algebra, enabling geometric proofs to be established in terms

of arithmetic, so that both generality and rigour were advanced.

APPLIED MATHEMATICS AND MODELLING

There is no sharp boundary between the study of mathematical systems in the abstract (the field of *pure mathematics)* and the study of such systems to make inferences about certain physical systems that are described by the mathematical theory (the field of *applied mathematics).* In principle, any branch of mathematics may turn out to describe some physical, economic, biological, medical, or other system. *Modelling* a physical system consists of seeking a formal mathematical theory that conforms with the properties of the physical system. Often, as for example in computer simulations of space travel, the mathematical theories are very large and complex, but sometimes the model can be quite simple. Sometimes, known mathematics can describe and predict the behaviour of the system; at other times, modelling can give rise to completely new branches of mathematics.

Applied mathematics encompasses many specialized fields in which the relationships between the experimental findings and the mathematical theories are well established. Although the subject can include the application of statistical theory to such areas as sociology, the term is usually restricted to the application of the methods of advanced calculus, linear algebra and other branches of advanced mathematics to physical and technological processes.

NOTABLE MATHEMATICIANS

Pythagoras (c. 582–500 BC), Greek philosopher. Born in Samos, he founded a religious community at Croton in southern Italy. The Pythagorean brotherhood saw mystical significance in the idea of number. He is popularly remembered today for Pythagoras' theorem (see p. 240).

Euclid (c. 3rd century BC), Greek mathematician. Euclid devised the first axiomatic treatment of geometry and studied irrational numbers (see p. 241). Until recent times, most elementary geometry textbooks were little more than versions of Euclid's great book *The Elements.*

Archimedes (c. 287–212 BC), Greek mathematician, philosopher and engineer, born in Syracuse, Sicily. His extensions of the work of Euclid especially concerned the surface and volume of the sphere and the study of other solid shapes. His methods anticipated the fundamentals of integral calculus.

al Khwarizmi (Muhammad ibn Musa al Khwarizmi; c. 825), Iraqi mathematician who described the Hindu system of counting. His book on algebra was influential in Europe when translated into Latin in the 12th century. The name of his treatise on algebra, *Hisab al-jabr w'al-muqabalah,* or 'the science of reduction and cancellation', gave us our word 'algebra', and the modern term 'algorithm' is derived from his name.

Leonardo Pisano or **Fibonacci** (c. 1175–c. 1250), Italian mathematician. Leonardo is famous for *Liber Abaci,* an account of elementary arithmetic and algebra that popularized the Hindu system of counting in Europe. It contains the problem of the breeding rabbits, which gives rise to the famous *Fibonacci sequence,* 1, 1, 2, 3, 5, 8, 13... in which each number is the sum of the previous two. This sequence has many uses, including the design of efficient computer sorts.

Girard Desargues (1591–1661), French engineer, architect and geometrician who invented modern projective geometry. Desargues was the author of *Brouillon Project*, one of the most neglected works in the history of mathematics, lost and only rediscovered in 1845. He is remembered for *Desargues' theorem* on pairs of triangles in perspective.

René Descartes (1596–1650), French philosopher, mathematician and military scientist. Descartes sought an axiomatic treatment of all knowledge, and is known for his doctrine that all knowledge can be derived from the one certainty: *Cogito ergo sum* ('I think therefore I am'). His greatest contribution to mathematics was the creation of analytical geometry, which allows geometrical problems to be solved by algebra, and algebraic ideas to be expressed in geometrical imagery. This great invention appeared as the final Appendix to his *Discourses on Method*; the other Appendices dealt with optics and meteorological phenomena, including the rainbow.

Pierre de Fermat (1601–65), French lawyer who studied mathematics as a hobby. He contributed to the development of calculus, analytic geometry, and the study of probability (with Pascal). Fermat is regarded as the creator of the modern theory of numbers. He is most famous for his last theorem, which he claimed to have solved, without recording his proof. In 1908 a prize of 100 000 German marks was offered for a correct proof but the theorem remains unsolved to this day.

Blaise Pascal (1623–62), French mathematician who discovered what became known as *Pascal's theorem* at the age of 16, when he was writing a book on conic sections. At the age of 19, to aid his father's statistical work, he invented the first calculating machine, which performed addition and subtraction. He also investigated what became known as *Pascal's triangle*, and helped to develop the theory of probability, before abandoning mathematics and turning to theology.

Kowa Seki (1642–1708), Japanese mathematician who invented a form of calculus, and who used determinants before Leibniz. Seki suggested that an equation of the nth degree has in general n roots. He also gave 355/113 as an approximation to π, used positive and negative numbers and algebraic quantities, and studied magic squares.

Sir Isaac Newton (1643–1727), English mathematician, astronomer and physicist (see also p. 194). Newton came to be recognized as the most influential scientist of all time. He developed differential calculus and his treatments of gravity and motion form the basis of much applied mathematics.

Gottfried Wilhelm Leibniz (1646–1716), German mathematician, philosopher, logician, linguist, lawyer and diplomat. Leibniz and Newton invented calculus independently, although Leibniz's notation was superior. He was the first, in 1671, to build a calculating machine that could multiply. He was the first European mathematician to consider determinants, unaware that Kowa Seki had studied them a decade earlier. Leibniz also studied binary numbers and found mystical significance in the creation of all numbers out of nothing and unity.

Leonhard Euler (1707–83), Swiss-born mathematician, who worked mainly in Berlin and St Petersburg. He was particularly famed for being able to perform complex calculations in his head, and so

was able to go on working after he went blind. He worked in almost all branches of mathematics and made particular contributions to analytical geometry, trigonometry and calculus, and thus to the unification of mathematics. Euler was responsible for much of modern mathematical notation.

Carl Friedrich Gauss (1777–1855), German mathematician who developed the theory of complex numbers (see p. 241). He was director of the astronomical observatory at Göttingen and conducted a survey, based on trigonometric techniques, of the kingdom of Hanover. He published works in many fields, including the application of mathematics to electrostatics and electrodynamics.

Baron Augustin-Louis Cauchy (1789–1857), French mathematician and physicist who developed the modern treatment of calculus and also the theory of functions. He introduced rigour to much of mathematics. As an engineer he contributed to Napoleon's preparations to invade Britain, and he twice gave up academic posts to serve the exiled Charles X.

János Bolyai (1802–60), Hungarian mathematician who – despite being warned by his father against the attempt – investigated Euclid's parallel postulate. Bolyai eventually developed a non-Euclidean geometry, only to discover to his horror that Gauss had anticipated his work.

George Boole (1815–64), English mathematician. Despite being largely self-taught, Boole became Professor of Mathematics at University College, Cork. He laid the foundations of Boolean algebra, which was fundamental to the development of the digital electronic computer.

George Cantor (1845–1918), Russian-born mathematician who spent most of his life in Germany. His most important work was on finite and infinite sets. He was greatly interested in theology and philosophy.

Felix Christian Klein (1849–1925), German mathematician who introduced a programme for the classification of geometry in terms of group theory. His interest in *topology* (the study of geometric figures that are subjected to deformations) produced the first description of what became known as a *Klein bottle*, which has a continuous one-sided surface.

David Hilbert (1862–1943), German mathematician. In 1901, Hilbert listed 23 major unsolved problems in mathematics, many of which still remain unsolved. His work contributed to the rigour and unity of modern mathematics and to the development of the theory of *computability*.

(Jules) Henri Poincaré (1854–1912), French mathematician who is often said to have been the last mathematician to have a grasp of all the known branches of the subject. Poincaré worked on the theory of functions, differential equations, topology, celestial mechanics, mathematical physics, number theory, and non-Euclidean geometry, as well as writing on the philosophy of science and mathematics, and publishing many popular essays.

Hermann Minkowski (1864–1909), Lithuanian-born German mathematician who won the *Grand Prix des Sciences Mathématiques* of the Paris Academy of Sciences at the age of 18. (Minkowski had previously abandoned his claims to a university prize in favour of a needy colleague.) He contributed to geometry and to the theories of numbers and of relativity. Einstein said that without Minkowski's contribution, the general theory of relativity would not have been possible.

Lord Bertrand Russell (1872–1970), English philosopher and mathematician. Russell did much of the basic work on mathematical logic and the foundations of mathematics. He found the paradox, now named after him, in the theory of sets proposed by the German logician Gottlob Frege (1848–1925), and went on to develop the whole of arithmetic in terms of pure logic. He was jailed for his pacifist activities in World War 1. In 1950, he was awarded the Nobel Prize for Literature.

Emmy Noether (Amalie Noether; 1882–1935), German mathematician who was described as 'the most creative abstract algebraist of modern times'. Initially, she had difficulty in obtaining a lectureship because she was a woman. In 1933 Noether was dismissed from her post by the Nazis because she was Jewish, and went to the USA where she lectured until her death.

Srinivasa Aaiyangar Ramanujan (1887–1920), Indian mathematician. At the age of 16, Ramanujan devoted his life to mathematics after reading a book summarizing European mathematics. He had an astonishing intuition for the correct results, although many were not proved until later. He was discovered by the English mathematician G.H. Hardy, with whom he later collaborated at Cambridge.

Kurt Gödel (1906–78), Austrian-born American mathematician. Gödel stunned mathematicians in the 1930s by showing that Hilbert's dream of a general method of proving any mathematical theorem could not be realized.

Alan Turing (1912–54), English mathematician who pioneered computer theory. Turing discovered that it is impossible in general to predict if or when the Turing machine – a universal automatic machine capable of mathematical problem-solving which he designed – would stop.

John Horton Conway (1938–), English mathematician who is famous for his serious studies of mathematical recreations. Conway developed the 'Game of Life', in which an object is made up of a number of squares of an infinite chessboard. The object grows, decays and 'dies' according to very simple rules. The 'Game' can be used to simulate a general-purpose computer.

SOME MILESTONES IN GEOMETRY AND TRIGONOMETRY

From c. 3000 BC	Babylonians made early developments in geometry and measurement.
6th century BC	Pythagoras' theorem.
4th century BC	Eudoxus' geometry of irrational numbers.
330 BC	Euclid's *Elements* published.
3rd century BC	Archimedes described the relationship between the surface and volume of a sphere. Apollonius of Rhodes described conic sections.

2nd century BC	Menelaus and Ptolemy developed spherical triangles for astronomy.
AD 1637	Descartes developed analytical geometry.
1639	Desargues' Theorem.
1640	Pascal's Theorem – with Desargues' Theorem, the beginning of projective geometry.
1822	Poncelet's work on projective geometry – the principle of duality and imaginary points.
1825–32	Bolyai and Lobachevsky developed non-Euclidean geometry.
1844–61	Grassman developed the theory of n-dimensions.
1847	von Staudt's axioms – the development of planes in projective geometry.
1851	Foucault's pendulum
1854	Riemann's inaugural lecture at Göttingen gave a comprehensive view of geometry.
1867	Helmholtz investigated the properties of non-Euclidean space.
late 19th century	Dedekind and Cantor supplemented the geometrical method of analysis.
1902	Hilbert's *Foundations of Geometry*.
1911	Brouwer developed topology.
20th century	The development of transformation geometry.

MATHEMATICAL MODELS

A simple example of a mathematical model is the representation of a portion of the Earth's surface by a set of interlocking triangles, from the measurement of which maps may be constructed. The triangulation model uses the rules of geometry and trigonometry to derive angles and distances that cannot be measured directly.

Geometry establishes that two triangles each have angles of the same sizes if, and only if, corresponding pairs of sides are in the same proportions.

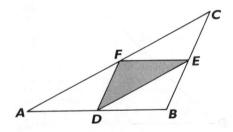

Here D, E and F are the centre-points of sides AB, BC and CA respectively. So, DE is half the length of AC, EF is half the length of AB, and FD is half the length of BC. Thus, the shaded triangle, DEF, is *similar* to the large triangle, and the angles at D, E and F are, respectively, equal to those at C, A and B. Furthermore, the triangles ADF, FEC, DBE and EFD are all *congruent*, i.e. identical in shape and size, and are thus all similar to triangle ABC.

A right-angled triangle is a triangle where one of the angles is 90°. *Pythagoras' theorem* (see p. 241) states that, in a right-angled triangle, the square of the length of the *hypotenuse* (the side opposite the right angle) equals the sum of the squares of the lengths of

the other two sides. So, in the triangle shown, below,
$AC^2 = AB^2 + BC^2$.

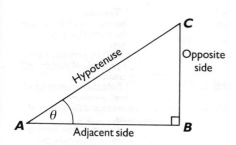

Trigonometry relies on the recognition that in a right-angled triangle the ratio of the lengths of pairs of sides depends only on the sizes of the two acute angles (i.e. angles less than 90°) of the triangle.

These ratios are given names. For example, the *sine* of an angle is the ratio of the side opposite the given angle to the hypotenuse. The Greek letters θ (*theta*) and φ (*phi*) are usually used to denote the angles; thus in the triangle shown we say that the sine of θ, usually written sin θ, is BC/AC. Similarly, since the *cosine* (cos) of the angle is the ratio of the side adjacent to the given angle to the hypotenuse, cos θ is AB/AC. The third basic ratio is the *tangent* (tan), which is the ratio of the opposite to the adjacent side, BC/AB in the example; it is easy to see that tan θ must always equal sin θ / cos θ. Pythagoras' theorem can be used to establish some very useful values for sin, cos and tan.

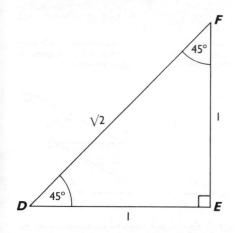

In triangle DEF, $DE = EF = 1$, so the angles at D and F are equal, that is they are each 45° (the internal angles of a triangle add up to 180°). Using Pythagoras' theorem, $DF^2 = 1^2 + 1^2 = 2$, so $DF = \sqrt{2}$. We can therefore conclude:

$$\sin 45° = \frac{1}{\sqrt{2}};$$

$$\cos 45° = \frac{1}{\sqrt{2}};$$

$$\tan 45° = 1$$

In triangle GHK, $GH = HK = KG = 2$, so the angles at G, H and K are equal, that is they are each 60°. Using Pythagoras' theorem, $KL^2 + 1^2 = 2^2$, so $KL = \sqrt{3}$. We therefore have:

$$\sin 60° = \frac{1}{2}\sqrt{3} = \cos 30°$$

$$\cos 60° = 1/2 = \sin 30°$$

$$\tan 60° = \sqrt{3}$$

$$\tan 30° = 1/\sqrt{3}$$

GEOMETRY

PLANE FIGURES

Plane figures lie entirely on one plane, i.e. they are two-dimensional. They include polygons, quadrilaterals, triangles, circles and conic sections.

POLYGONS

A polygon is a closed plane figure with three or more straight sides that meet at the same number of vertices and do not intersect other than at those vertices. (A vertex is the point at which two sides of a polygon meet.) Although we tend to think of a polygon as being a many-sided figure, it can have as few sides as three (a triangle).

Some important polygons

triangle	3 sides
quadrilateral	4 sides
pentagon	5 sides
hexagon	6 sides
heptagon	7 sides
octagon	8 sides
nonagon	9 sides
decagon	10 sides
dodecagon	12 sides

Physical properties of polygons

The sum of the interior angles = $(2n - 4) \times 90°$ where n = the number of sides.

$$\text{Each interior angle of a regular polygon} = \frac{((2n - 4) \times 90°)}{n}$$

$$\text{or} = 180° - \frac{360°}{n}$$

The sum of the exterior angles of any polygon = 360°, regardless of the number of sides. (An exterior angle of a polygon is the angle between one side extended and the adjacent side.)

The area of any regular polygon of sides $a = \frac{1}{4} na^2 \cot \frac{180°}{n}$

Where n = the number of sides; cot = cotangent, a trigonometric function.

QUADRILATERALS

A quadrilateral is a plane figure with four sides. A quadrilateral may be a rectangle, a square, a parallelogram, a rhombus or a trapezium (or trapezoid).

Rectangles

A rectangle is a quadrilateral in which all the angles are right angles, thus the opposite sides are parallel in pairs. A rectangle may be a square (see below). A rectangle that is not a square has two lines of symmetry.

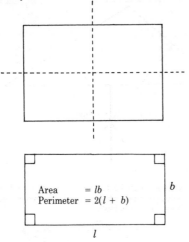

$$\begin{aligned} \text{Area} &= lb \\ \text{Perimeter} &= 2(l + b) \end{aligned}$$

Square

A square is a rectangle whose sides are all equal. It has four lines of symmetry – both diagonals and the two lines joining the middle points of pairs of opposite sides.

$$\begin{aligned} \text{Area} &= l^2 \\ \text{Perimeter} &= 4l \end{aligned}$$

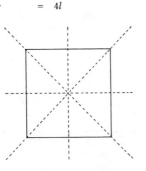

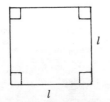

Parallelogram

A parallelogram is a quadrilateral whose opposite sides are equal in length and parallel. It has no lines of symmetry, unless it is also a rectangle, but it does have rotational symmetry about its centre, the point where the diagonals meet.

If one angle of a parallelogram is a right angle, then all the angles are right angles, and it is a rectangle. Any parallelogram can be dissected into a rectangle by cutting a right-angled triangle off one end, and sliding it to the opposite end.

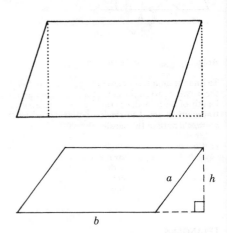

This dissection changes neither the area of the parallelogram nor the length of the sides – the area of any parallelogram is equal to the area of a rectangle with same base and the same height.

$$\begin{aligned} \text{Area} &= bh \\ \text{Perimeter} &= 2(a + b) \end{aligned}$$

Rhombus

A rhombus is a parallelogram whose sides are all equal in length. Its diagonals are both lines of symmetry, and therefore bisect each other at right angles.

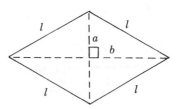

$$\begin{aligned} \text{Area} &= \tfrac{1}{2}(2a)(2b) \\ \text{i.e.} &= \tfrac{1}{2}(\text{product of the} \\ &\qquad \text{diagonals}) \\ \text{Perimeter} &= 4l \end{aligned}$$

Trapezium

A trapezium is a quadrilateral with two parallel sides of unequal length. (In North America – where such a plane figure is described as a *trapezoid* – a trapezium is a quadrilateral with no sides parallel.)

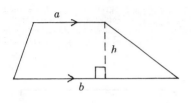

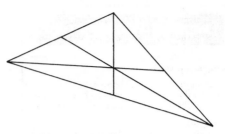

Area $= \frac{1}{2}(a + b)h$

To find the area three measurements have to taken – the *height* between the pair of parallel sides and the length of both of the parallel sides. The area of a trapezium is equal to the height multiplied by the *average* length of the parallel sides.

i.e. $= \frac{1}{2}($the sum of the parallel sides$)$
                    $\times$ the perpendicular distance between them

The three lines that bisect the sides of a triangle at right angles also meet. The point at which they meet is the centre of the circle through the vertices of the triangle.

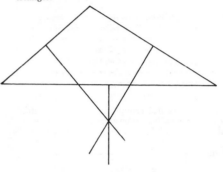

TRIANGLES

A triangle is a three-sided polygon. A *scalene* triangle has sides of three different lengths, and has no axes of symmetry. If two sides of a triangle are equal in length, the triangle is *isosceles*, and has one axis of symmetry, and a pair of equal angles.

Any triangle can be thought of as one half of a parallelogram that has been divided in two by one of its diagonals (see below).

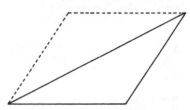

The area of a triangle is one half of the area of a parallelogram with the same base and the same height.

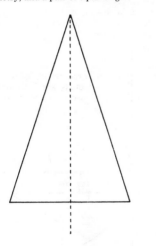

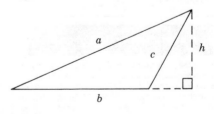

Area $= \frac{1}{2}bh$

An *equilateral* triangle has all its sides equal, and all its angles are equal to 60°.

Triangles have many curious properties. For example, the three lines that join the vertices of a triangle to the middle points of the opposite sides, meet in a point – they are said to be *concurrent*.

The area of a triangle can also be calculated from the lengths of its sides, using a formula discovered by the Greek mathematician Archimedes:

If half the sum of the sides is s, then,

Area $= \sqrt{\{s(s - a)(s - b)(s - c)\}}$

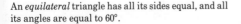

PROJECTIVE GEOMETRY

The Greek mathematician Pappus (c. AD 300) discovered the earliest theorem in *projective geometry*.

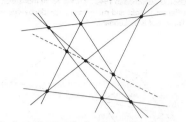

Take three points on each of two lines, and join them as in the figure with three 'X's, so that each point is joined to the points that are not directly opposite to it on the other line. The centres of the 'X's lie on a straight line.

Notice that this theorem involves no measurement at all – it is entirely about lines meeting and points lying on lines.

CIRCLES

A circle is the path of a point that moves at a constant distance – *the radius* – from a fixed point (the centre of the circle).

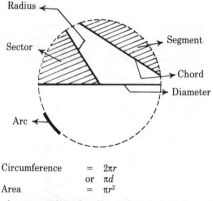

Circumference   = $2\pi r$
              or πd
Area   = πr^2

where r = radius, d = diameter, and π = pi, the ratio of the circumference of a circle to its diameter (approximately 3.141592...).

FASCINATION OF NUMBERS

Visiting the great Indian mathematician Srinivasa Ramanujan in hospital, his friend G.H. Hardy remarked that the number of his taxi had been 1729, surely a dull number. Ramanujan replied, 'No, it is a very interesting number. It is the smallest number expressible as a sum of two cubes in two different ways.'

$$1729 = 10^3 + 9^3 = 12^3 + 1^3$$

Ramanujan was fascinated by numbers, and it is no surprise that he found some weird approximations for π. You can check the following example easily with an electronic calculator.

π is the fourth root of $9^2 + 19^2/22$

CONIC SECTIONS

Conic sections are curves that are formed by the intersection of a plane and a cone. An ellipse, a parabola, a hyperbola, a rectangular hyperbola and a circle are all conic sections.

Ellipse

An ellipse is a closed conic section with the appearance of a flattened circle. It is formed by an inclined plane that does not intersect the base of the cone. An ellipse can also be thought of as a circle that has been stretched in one direction. The orbital path of each of the planets round the Sun is approximately an ellipse.

There are many ways to draw an ellipse. One of the simplest is to stretch a loop of thread round two pins, and hold it taut with a pencil. The path of the pencil will be an ellipse.

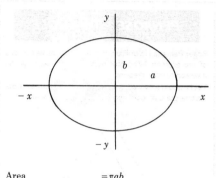

Area $= \pi ab$

Basic equation (centre at the origin)
$(x^2 / a^2 + y^2 / b^2) = 1$

Parabola

A parabola is a conic section that is formed by the intersection of cone by a plane parallel to its side.

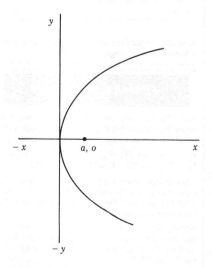

If you throw a ball in the air, then the path of the ball will be approximately a parabola with its axis vertical.

Basic equation (symmetrical about the x-axis with the focus at a, 0)
$y^2 = 4ax$

Hyperbola
A hyperbola is a conic section that is formed by a plane that cuts a cone making a larger angle with the base than the angle made by the side of the cone.

Basic equation (centre at the origin)
$(x^2 / a^2 - y^2 / b^2) = 1$

Circle The circle is a special case of an ellipse (see also above).
General equation (centre at $-g$, $-f$)
$x^2 + y^2 + 2gx + 2fy + c = 0$
Basic equation (centre at the origin)
$x^2 + y^2 = r^2$

PENROSE TRIANGLE

Roger Penrose is a brilliant mathematician as well as one of the greatest living physicists. Twenty years ago he invented twister theories.

Yet he also discovered, with his father, the Penrose tribar – a triangle that looks real but cannot actually exist.

As so often, physical and mathematical ability go together with a subtle visual imagination.

FERMAT NUMBERS

Pierre Fermat made one very famous mistake in his career. He claimed that all the numbers in this sequence, called the Fermat numbers, were prime:

$F_0 = 2^1 + 1 = 3$; $F_1 = 2^2 + 1 = 5$; $F_2 = 2^4 + 1 = 17$;
$F_3 = 2^8 + 1 = 257$; $F_4 = 2^{16} + 1 = 65\,537.....$

Unfortunately, only the first five are known to be prime. Euler showed in 1732 that $F_5 = 294\,967\,297 = 641 \times 6\,700\,417$, and every Fermat number tested since then has proved to be composite.

Actually finding the factors of a large number, even when you know that it is not prime, is very difficult. Only in 1990 did Mark Manasse and Arjen Lenstra manage to find the factors of F_9, a number of 155 digits, using a Connection machine, a massive parallel supercomputer at Florida State University. It has three prime factors, of 7, 49, and 99 digits.

PYTHAGORAS' THEOREM

Pythagoras' Theorem is the most-proved theorem in geometry, indeed in the whole of mathemetics. E.S. Loomis published in 1940 a collection of more than 370 different proofs, and more have been discovered since. This proof is by Leonardo da Vinci.

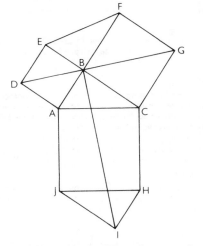

DEFG, DACG, ABJI and IHCB are all congruent (i.e. identical) shapes. The first two together make up the two smaller squares and the original triangle (ABC) twice. The second two make up the larger square and the triangle twice.

SOLIDS
Solids are three-dimensional figures, i.e. they have length, breadth and depth.

Rectangular block
A rectangular block is a solid figure, all the faces of which are rectangles.

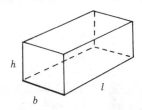

Surface area	=	$2(lb + bh + hl)$
Volume	=	lbh
		(i.e. the area of the base multiplied by the height)

The volume of any solid is always equal to the area of the base × the perpendicular height.

Prism
A prism is a solid figure whose ends are identical polygons and whose sides are parallelograms (which could be rectangles).

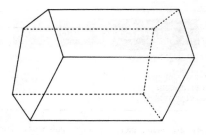

The volume of a prism equals the area of either of the ends, multiplied by the perpendicular distance between the ends.

Pyramid

A pyramid is a solid figure whose base is a polygon, and whose special vertex – the *apex* – is joined to each vertex of the base. Therefore all its faces, apart from the base, are triangles.

Any pyramid can be fitted inside a prism so that the base of the pyramid is one end of the prism, and the apex of the pyramid is on the other end of the prism.

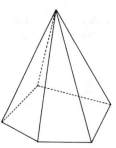

The volume of a pyramid on a rectangular base = $\frac{1}{3}(lbh)$.

Tetrahedron

A tetrahedron is a pyramid whose base is a triangle. Any of the faces of a tetrahedron can be thought of as its base.

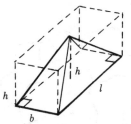

The volume of a tetrahedron = $\frac{1}{3}$ (the area of the triangular base × the height)

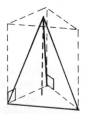

Cylinder

A cylinder is a solid figure with straight sides and a circular section.

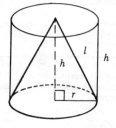

The area of the curved surface of a cylinder = $2\pi rh$. If the circles at both ends are included, then the total surface area = $2\pi rh + 2\pi r^2$.

The volume of a cylinder can be found by thinking of it as a special case of a prism. The volume equals the area of the base, multiplied by the height. The volume of a cylinder = $\pi r^2 h$

Cone

A cone is a solid figure with a circular plane base, narrowing to a point or apex.

If the slant height of the cone is 1, the area of the curved surface is $\pi r1$.

The volume of a cone can be calculated as if the cone were a special case of a pyramid. The volume is one third the volume of a cylinder with the same base and height.

The volume of a cone = $\frac{1}{3}\pi r^2 h$.

Sphere

A sphere is a solid figure every point of whose surface is equidistant from its centre.

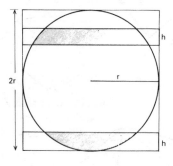

Surface area   = $4\pi r^2$
Volume   = $4/3\pi r^3$

POLYHEDRA

A polyhedron is a solid shape with all plane faces. The faces of a regular polyhedron, or regular solid, are all identical regular polygons.

There are just five regular polyhedra – the regular tetrahedron, the cube, the regular octahedron, the regular dodecahedron and the regular icosahedron.

The cube and the octahedron are dual polyhedra. The cube has six faces and eight vertices, while the

POLYHEDRA

	Faces	Type of face	Vertices	Edges
Regular Tetrahedron	4	equilateral triangles	4	6
Cube	6	squares	8	12
Regular Octahedron	8	equilateral triangles	6	12
Regular Dodecahedron	12	regular pentagons	20	30
Regular Icosahedron	20	equilateral triangles	12	30

octahedron has six vertices but eight faces. The regular dodecahedron and regular icosahedron are also dual polyhedra.

There are many more irregular polyhedra. The simplest to visualize have faces that are mixtures of two kinds of regular polygons. For example, the faces of the cuboctahedron (below) are equilateral triangles and squares.

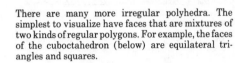

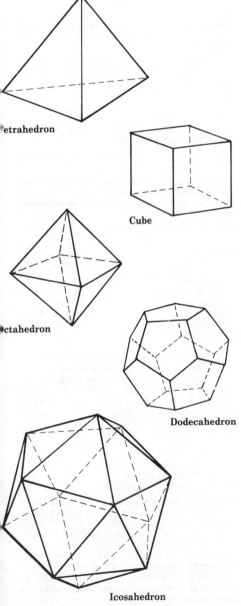

Tetrahedron

Cube

Octahedron

Dodecahedron

Icosahedron

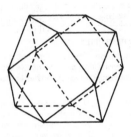

The mathematician Euler made an interesting discovery about the relationship between the number of faces (F), vertices (V) and edges (E) of polyhedra.

The equation $F + V - E = 2$ is true for all 'simple' polyhedra – the regular polyhedra listed in the table below.

The same relationship is true for an area divided into any number of regions (R) by boundaries or arcs (A) that join at nodes (N). Thus, $R + N - A = 2$.

For the area shown below:
$R = 8$ (the surrounding space
counts as a region)
$N = 12$
$A = 18$

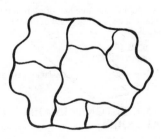

Thus $R + N - A$
$= 8 + 12 - 18$
$= 2$

Note: For such a region, or indeed any map, no more than four colours are necessary so that no two adjoining regions have the same colour.

THE SPHERE

A little-known and interesting fact about the sphere is that the area of any zone of its curved surface lying between two parallel planes is exactly equal to the curved surface of the surrounding cylinder between the same two planes. This fact was discovered by Archimedes, who requested that a sphere inscribed in a cylinder be engraved on his tomb.

This applies to any belt of the sphere, or to a cap or to the whole sphere. It thus makes the calculation of what might appear to be a difficult area quite simple.

Thus, either shaded area of the sphere on p. 238 is equal to the curved surface area of a cylinder of radius r and height h, the height of the zone.

PYTHAGORAS' THEOREM

Pythagoras (see p. 230) is the probable discoverer of the geometrical theorem that came to be named after him. (He did not, however, discover the theorem in its Euclidean form.)

The theorem states that the area of the square drawn on the *hypotenuse* of a right-angled triangle is equal to the sum of the areas of the squares drawn on the other two sides. (It is, however, also true that the area of any shape drawn on the hypotenuse is equal to the sum of the areas of similar shapes drawn on the other two sides.)

In the triangle ABC right-angled at B:
$$AC^2 = AB^2 + BC^2$$

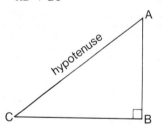

There are an infinite number of right-angled triangles whose sides are integers. Four of the smallest have the sides:

3, 4, 5   5, 12, 13
8, 15, 17   and 7, 24, 25

Such whole-number sets are sometimes called *Pythagorean triples*.

SOME MILESTONES IN ARITHMETIC AND ALGEBRA

c. 1700 BC	Babylonians developed arithmetic in the sexagesimal system (base 60).
330 BC	Euclid's *Elements* represented algebraic results in terms of lengths.
220 BC	Apollonius' *Conica*.
AD 200	Diophantus' *Arithmetica*.
630	Brahmagupta studied indeterminate equations.
1515–45	del Ferro, Tartaglia and Cardano solve the cubic equation.
1614	Napier discovered logarithms.
1637	Fermat's last theorem.
1654	The first slide rule.
1771–72	Vandermonde and Laplace developed determinant theory.
1799	Gauss proved the fundamental theory of algebra.
1801	Gauss developed groups.
1820s	Abel proved the impossibility of solving algebraically the general equation of the fifth degree.
1829	Sturm functions.
1831	Galois applied group theory to equations.
1854	Boole's *Investigation into the Laws of Thought* applied the methods of algebra to logic.
late 19th century	Weierstrasse and Dedekind developed the theory of real numbers.
1880s	Poincaré developed the concept of automorphic function.
1889–94	Peano developed a logic notation.
1906	Hilbert's work on eigenvalues.
1910–13	Russell and Whitehead published *Principia Mathematica*.
1970s	Electronic calculators came into general use.

NUMBER SYSTEMS

The *natural numbers* or *whole numbers* are those we use in counting. We learn these at an early age, perhaps pairing them with our fingers or else learning to chant their names in order: 'one, two, three, four, . . . '. Important features of our number system, these numbers can be used to count sets of objects, and form a naturally ordered progression that has a first member, the number 1, but no last member: no matter how big a number you come up with, I can always reply with a bigger one – simply by adding 1.

However, even quite simple arithmetic, as we shall see, cannot be carried out wholly within the natural numbers. Ordinarily we take the principles that govern such systems for granted, yet merely to be able to subtract and divide, for example, requires other, more complex, number systems, such as fractions and negative numbers.

NATURAL NUMBERS AND ARITHMETIC

If I have 3 sheep and you give me 4 more, I can count that I now have 7 sheep, or I can use the operation of *addition* to get the same answer: $3 + 4 = 7$. If I promise to give 5 children 4 sweets each, again I can count out 20 sweets altogether, or I can use the operation of *multiplication*: $5 \times 4 = 20$. Here, we have examples of another principle of natural numbers: any addition or multiplication of natural numbers gives another natural number. Such a system is said to be *closed* under these operations. (A closed system is one where an operation on two of its elements produces another element of that system.)

If I had 3 sheep and when you gave me your sheep I had 7, I can use the operation of *subtraction* to find how many sheep you gave to me: $7 - 3 = 4$. If I distribute 20 sweets equally to 5 children, I can use the operation of *division* to find how many I gave to each: $20 \div 5 = 4$. Subtraction is the *inverse operation* of addition; division is the inverse operation of multiplication. However, the natural numbers are not closed under the operations of subtraction and division, as we shall see later.

SIMPLE ALGEBRA

In simple algebra, we generalize arithmetic by using letters to stand for unknown numbers whose value is to be discovered, or to stand for numbers in general. Usually letters from the beginning of the alphabet are used in the latter way – for example, to express a general truth about numbers, such as $a + b = b + a$. The letters at the end of the alphabet are generally used to represent unknown numbers. For example, the information about the sheep can be expressed by the *equation*, $3 + x = 7$, where x represents the unknown number of sheep you gave to me. Since the two sides of this equation are equal, they remain equal if we treat them both the same way. If we then subtract 3 from each side we get $x = 7 - 3$, that is $x = 4$. We have *solved the equation*.

SUBTRACTION AND THE INTEGERS

The set of natural numbers is not closed under the operation of subtraction; for example, $3 - 7$ does not give a natural number as an answer. We need a system of numbers that is closed under subtraction. The smallest set of numbers that is closed under subtraction is the set of *integers*, i.e. the set $\{..., -3, -2, -1, 0, 1, 2, 3, ...\}$. Here, the positive integers can be identified with the natural numbers; zero (0) is defined as the result of subtracting any integer from itself; and the negative integers are the result of subtracting the corresponding positive integers from zero (e.g. $-3 = 0 - 3$).

Now, every subtraction has an answer within the number system of integers, that is, the integers are closed under subtraction.

DIVISION AND THE RATIONAL NUMBERS

The integers, however, are still not closed under the operation of division. We can construct a system that is by defining the result of any division, $a \div b$ to be the pair of integers, a and b, written in a notation that clearly distinguishes which divides which. Thus, we write $a \div b$ as the *ratio* or *fraction*, a/b, and we have the system of *rational numbers*.

It is important to note that rational numbers are not identical with their symbols. The same rational number may be represented by many different fractions (in fact, an infinite number of them). For example, 24/8 is the same rational number as 12/4 or 6/2. We adopt the convention of representing them, where possible, by the unique fraction in which there is no *common factor*, that can be cancelled out (thus, 14/21 becomes 2/3, where the factor, 7, has been cancelled out). It should also be noted that decimals are rational numbers, since, for example, $0.5 = 5/10 = 1/2$, and $1.61 = 161/100$.

We do have a problem, however: the rationals cannot be closed under division, because of the integer 0. We cannot give value to $a/0$ for any rational number a. This problem, however, cannot be avoided: we have to be content with the fact that the rationals, excluding the integer 0, are closed under division.

ROOTS AND IRRATIONAL NUMBERS

The figure 6^9, which we read as, '6 to the *power* 9' means 6 multiplied by itself 9 times ($6 \times 6 \times 6 \times 6 \times 6 \times 6 \times 6 \times 6 \times 6$). Generally, a^b, which we read as, 'a to the power b', means a multiplied by itself b times. These are closed operations for the systems of numbers we have so far considered. However, none of these systems guarantees the possibility of the inverse operation, the *extraction of roots*. If $b = a^n$, (where n represents an integer), then a is the nth root

of b, written $a = \sqrt[n]{b}$. For example, since $3 \times 3 = 9$, the second or *square root* of 9 (written $\sqrt[2]{9}$ or more usually $\sqrt{9}$) equals 3. To give another example, since $2 \times 2 \times 2 = 8$, the third or *cube root* of 8 (written $\sqrt[3]{8}$) is 2. But none of the systems we have considered is closed under this operation. For example, $\sqrt{2}$, $\sqrt{3}$, and $\sqrt{5}$ cannot be expressed as fractions or as terminating decimals; they are examples of what are called *irrational numbers*. They have exact meaning – for example, by Pythagoras' theorem (see p. 240), $\sqrt{2}$ is the length of the hypotenuse of a right-angled triangle whose other sides are each length 1; $\sqrt{5}$ is the length of the hypotenuse of a right-angled triangle whose other sides have lengths 1 and 2, etc. Obviously, we need to add the irrationals to our number systems to ensure closure under these calculations.

All the systems we have discussed, the natural numbers, the integers, the rational numbers and the irrationals form together the system of *real numbers*.

IMAGINARY AND COMPLEX NUMBERS

However, now we have admitted the extraction of roots, we have opened up a new gap in our number system: we have not, as yet, defined the square root of a negative number. At first sight, we may wonder why this omission should be of any great importance, but without the development of a system to include such numbers, many valuable applications to engineering and physics would not be possible. Surprisingly, we need only extend the number system by one new number. Since all negative numbers are positive multiples of -1 (for example, -6 is 6×-1, so that $\sqrt{-6} = \sqrt{6} \times \sqrt{-1}$) we are concerned only with the square root of -1. The square root of -1 is denoted by the letter i, so we have $i^2 = -1$.

Real multiples of i, such as $3i$, $2.7i$, $2i/3$, $i\sqrt{2}$, etc., are called *imaginary numbers*. The sum of a real number and an imaginary number, such as $5 + 3i$ is a *complex number*. It can be shown that every complex number can be expressed uniquely as the sum of its real and imaginary parts.

The rules for using complex numbers are the same as those for real numbers. It can be shown, for example, that

$$(a + ib)(a - ib) = a^2 + b^2.$$

The terms in brackets are thus the factors of $a^2 + b^2$. In fact it turns out that in the complex number system any algebraic expression with integer powers has exactly the same number of factors as the highest power in the expression. This result is so important that it is called the *fundamental theorem of algebra*.

OTHER NUMBER NOTATIONS

The usual notation for numbers is a *decimal place-value system*. This means that there are ten distinct digits (0, 1, 2, 3, 4, 5, 6, 7, 8, 9) and that the position of each digit determines what it contributes to the value of the number. Each position gives a value 10 times as great as the position to the right, so, for example, 7234 can be written as four units (4×10^0) on the right, plus 3 tens (3×10^1) plus 2 hundreds (2×10^2) plus 7 thousands (7×10^3). We say that ten is the *base* of the decimal place-value system.

We can easily construct systems with other bases to suit other needs.

BINARY SYSTEM

The binary system uses only the digits 0 and 1; so it

has base 2. This is used in the representation of numbers within computers, since the two numerals correspond to the on and the off positions of an electronic switch. In the binary system we count as follows: $1, 10 (= 2 + 0), 11 (= 2 + 1), 100 (= 4 + 0 + 0), 1001 (= 8 + 0 + 0 + 1)$ etc.

Binary numbers 1–20

Decimal	Binary
1	1
2	10
3	11
4	100
5	101
6	110
7	111
8	1000
9	1001
10	1010
11	1011
12	1100
13	1101
14	1110
15	1111
16	10000
17	10001
18	10010
19	10011
20	10100

This appears difficult at first sight, but is relatively easy to decipher if the following rules are remembered:
– ignore all noughts in calculation;
– count the right columns as $1 (2^0)$;
– count the second column on the right as $2 (2^1)$;
– count the third column on the right as $4 (2^2)$;
– count the fourth column on the right as $8 (2^3)$;
– count the fifth column on the right as $16 (2^4)$; and so on.

Thus 1101001 in the binary system would be the equivalent of 105 in the decimal system.

OCTAL ARITHMETIC

Sometimes, especially in computing, it is convenient to use *octal arithmetic* (with base 8) or *hexadecimal arithmetic* (base 16). In base 16, the letters A to F are used as well as the numerals 0 to 9. Obviously it is necessary to know which base is being used, so the base is indicated by a subscript, for example, $31_{10} = 1F_{16} = 37_8 = 11111_2$.

There are many other ways in which number systems vary. The following examples are taken from history.

THE EGYPTIAN NUMBER SYSTEM

The earliest example of a grouping system to represent numbers is that used by the ancient Egyptians who gave hieroglyphic symbols to $1, 10, 10^2, 10^3, 10^4, 10^5$ and 10^6. Each digit was represented by a group of the relevant hieroglyphic symbols arranged from right to left.

THE BABYLONIAN NUMBER SYSTEM

The Babylonians used a sexagesimal system, that is one with base 60. Each number up to and including 60 was represented by a grouping of only two cuneiform symbols incorporating an additional subtractive symbol for higher numbers, thus 48 was represented by 50, the subtractive symbol and two. Large numbers were represented by the grouping of cuneiform symbols for the base followed by the grouping for the remainder – thus, 607 was represented by 10

(i.e. 10 times base 60) plus seven. The system has been compared to the digital representation of time, e.g. 10.17 for 10 hours and 17 minutes.

THE GREEK NUMBER SYSTEM

The Greeks also used a grouping system on their inscriptions, but with a number of refinements. Numbers from one to 10 were represented by the initial letter of their names, thus Δ (delta) represented ten ('deka'). Similarly, 100 was represented by H (for 'hekaton'), 1000 by X (for 'chilioi') and 10 000 by M (for 'murioi'). A further refinement was the use of the symbol for five in conjunction with others to represent 50, 500 and so on. Large numbers were compiled by listing the appropriate letters from left to right, beginning with the largest element.

Because the first known description of this system was written by the grammarian Herodianus (in the

NUMERICAL TRADITIONS

Numbers have always been associated with good or bad luck, and with rhymes, folklore, colours and symbols of the zodiac.

1 The Ancient Greeks associated the number 1 with unity and reason. Both they and the Chinese believed that 1 was both an odd and an even number.

2 The Ancient Greeks thought that all even numbers were feminine and all odd numbers masculine. The Chinese held a similar belief. Two, being the first feminine number, was thought to be particularly lucky.

3 The number three is important in religion and in magic. It is significant to Christians because of the Trinity. It was equally important to the Babylonians and Ancient Egyptians because of their trinities of gods, to the Ancient Greeks because of the trinity of the Fates and to many ancient religions because of the traditional three-fold division of the world into the underworld, earth and the heavens. The number is associated with good luck in most cultures and throughout Europe oaths and spells were traditionally uttered three times. The Ancient Greeks held three to be particularly important as it was the first masculine number and the symbol of strength.

4 The number four was held to be lucky by most ancient peoples as it symbolized the four elements of earth, fire, water and air. To the Ancient Greeks it symbolized harmony.

5 The number five was held to be unlucky in the Middle Ages because it was thought to represent the five wounds inflicted at the Crucifixion and the five points of a witch's pentacle. The Ancient Greeks believed five to be lucky and held that it represented marriage (being the addition of two and three, the first male and female numbers).

6 The Ancient Greeks and the Romans believed that six was significant as it is the first perfect number (see p. 244).

7 Most ancient civilizations believed that the number seven had magical properties. There were seven days to the week and (then) seven known planets in the sky. The number seven features in the folkore of all European countries; for example, the seventh child of a seventh child was thought to possess special psychic powers.

8 The number eight is traditionally associated with wisdom.

9 The number nine frequently occurs in folklore. To the Ancient Greeks it held special significance because the numbers 1–9 make a 'magic square' (see p. 244).

2nd century BC), Greek numbers are often referred to as Herodianic numerals.

THE ROMAN NUMBER SYSTEM

Of all the early grouping systems, the Roman system is the one that has remained in regular use. It still appears on clock faces, on inscriptions on public buildings, and in some publications to indicate listings or divisions. The system uses seven of the Roman letters of the alphabet, used in isolation or in various combinations to represent numbers.

The Romans incorporated a subtractive system in which a lesser symbol appearing before a greater one altered the value of the latter, thus LX represents 60 while XL represents 40.

Arabic numeral	Roman numeral
1	I
2	II
3	III
4	IV
5	V
6	VI
7	VII
8	VIII
9	IX
10	X
11	XI
12	XII
13	XIII
14	XIV
15	XV
20	XX
25	XXV
30	XXX
40	XL
50	L
60	LX
70	LXX
80	LXXX
90	XC
100	C
200	CC
500	D
1000	M

Thus, 1991 in Roman numerals would be MCMXCI.

THE CHINESE NUMBER SYSTEM

The Chinese number system is an example of multiplicative grouping systems. In multiplicative systems, specific digits (such as the conventional 1, 2, 3, 4, 5, 6, 7, 8, 9) are combined with basic symbols to avoid the repetition involved in a simple grouping system such as the Roman number system. In the Chinese system the number 4624 would be represented by the character for four followed by the character for one thousand, the character for six followed by one hundred, two followed by 10 and, finally, the character for four. The system – in both traditional and modern Chinese script – employs twelve characters representing 1, 2, 3, 4, 5, 6, 7, 8, 9, 10, 100 and 1000.

The traditional Chinese abacus reflects this number system by using a mixture of base 5 and base 10.

The abacus has been described as a manual calculating machine. It has been used for thousands of years and may still be seen, for example, on shop counters in Russia. It consists of a frame or board containing wires upon which counters or balls are slid. Each wire represents a power of ten. The wires are sometimes divided in half by a vertical barrier to enable decimal numbers to be expressed. The Chinese abacus usually has 11 wires with two beads representing 5s on each wire above a bar, and five beads representing 1s on each wire below the bar.

POSITIONAL NUMBER SYSTEMS

Our modern system is an example of positional number systems in which the place value is predetermined. This removes the need for symbols other than the basic digits, thus – in the conventional system using base 10 – it is understood that the second place from the right represents tens, the third place from the right represents hundreds, the fourth place from the right represents thousands, and so on. The conventional system uses base 10, but it is possible to choose any number as base, e.g. the binary system (see above).

There are many other ways in which number systems can vary. Sometimes one can see vestiges of other systems in the numerical terms of a language. In French, for example, one counts up to 100 in a mixture of base 10 and base 20 – thus *quatre-vingt-dix* ('four times twenty plus ten') equals 90. Even English retains vestiges of base 12 with the words 'eleven' and 'twelve'.

PRIME NUMBERS

A prime number is a natural number that has no *proper factors* – that is, which cannot be divided by any natural numbers other than itself and 1. We can find the primes by taking a sequence of numbers such as

1, 2, 3, 4, 5, 6, 7, 8, 9, 10, 11, 12, 13, 14, 15, 16 . . .

and first deleting all the numbers divisible by 2 (excluding 2 itself, which is only divisible by itself and 1), then all those divisible by 3, then (since anything divisible by 4 has already been deleted) all those divisible by 5, and so on.

All non-prime natural numbers must by definition be divisible by other numbers apart from themselves and 1; these other numbers can in turn be repeatedly divided until one is left with a series of prime factors. Hence, all non-prime numbers can be expressed as the product of a series of primes – in fact, for each number, the expression is unique.

Prime numbers from 1 to 1000

2	3	5	7	11	13	17
19	23	29	31	37	41	43
47	53	59	61	67	71	73
79	83	89	97	101	103	107
109	113	127	131	137	139	149
151	157	163	167	173	179	181
191	193	197	199	211	223	227
229	239	241	251	257	263	269
271	277	281	283	293	307	311
313	317	331	337	347	349	353
359	367	373	379	383	389	397
401	409	419	421	431	433	439
443	449	457	461	463	467	479
487	491	499	503	509	521	523
541	547	557	563	569	571	577
587	593	599	601	607	613	617
619	631	641	643	653	659	661
673	677	683	691	701	709	719
727	733	739	743	751	757	761
769	773	787	797	809	811	821
823	827	829	839	853	857	859
863	877	881	883	887	907	911
919	929	937	941	947	953	967
971	977	983	991	997		

The prime numbers have been studied since the days of the ancient Greeks, who knew, for example, that there is no largest prime. Their proof is quite easy to understand: suppose there is a largest prime, so that all the prime numbers can be listed in order of size. Now consider the number we obtain if we multiply all these primes together, and add 1; call this number N. Clearly N cannot be divided by any of the list of primes without leaving a remainder of 1. But since these are (we are assuming) all the primes, any other number is non-prime and so has prime factors (see above). Therefore it cannot divide N unless its prime factors divide N – but no primes can divide N. Thus N must itself be prime. But it is a bigger prime than what we supposed was the biggest prime, so that supposition has led us to a contradiction and must be false. The largest known prime number (August 1989) is $391582 \times 2^{216193} - 1$, which is a number of 65087 digits.

On the other hand it is not known whether or not there are infinitely many *twin primes*. These are pairs of successive odd numbers that are both prime, like 5 and 7, 11 and 13, or 29 and 31.

Another famous conjecture about prime numbers is that of Christian Goldbach (1690–1764), who postulated that every even number is the sum of two prime numbers. It is not known whether this is true or false.

Prime numbers have recently become of great interest to cryptographers: certain codes are based on the result of multiplying two very large primes together, and because even the fastest possible computer would take years to factorize this product, the resulting code is virtually unbreakable.

PERFECT NUMBERS

FACTORS

A factor is a number that divides exactly into another number. Six divides exactly into 48 eight times – thus both six and eight are factors of 48. Similarly two divides into 6 three times – thus two and three are factors of 6 – and two divides into 8 four times – thus two and four are factors of 8.

PERFECT NUMBERS

Perfect numbers are numbers that are equal to the sum of all their factors, excluding the number itself. The first perfect number is 6 whose factors (excluding 6 itself) are one, two and three. As $1 + 2 + 3 = 6$, 6 is a perfect number.

The next perfect number is 28. The factors of 28 are one, two, four, seven and fourteen, which when added together make 28. Pythagoras knew of these first two perfect numbers in the 6th century BC. In the 3rd century BC Nichomachus of Alexandria discovered the next two perfect numbers – 496 and 8128. The fifth perfect number – 33 550 336 – was not discovered until over 1000 years later. Until the 1950s only seven perfect numbers had been discovered. Today, even with the help of computers, only thirty perfect numbers are known.

ARITHMETIC AND ALGEBRA

NUMBER BASES

Our familiar denary (base 10) system of calculating undoubtedly arose because we have 5 'digits' on each hand. Had we been created with 4 instead, we should have been just as happily working in the *octal scale* (base 8). A denary number may be easily converted to any other base simply by repeated division by the new base, the remainders being recorded at each step, thus:

8)543₁₀
  8)67 r 7
    8)8 r 3
      1 r 0

Reading from the bottom up, 543_{10} is equivalent to 1037_8 (read 'one nought three seven base eight').

MAGIC SQUARES

Magic squares are sets of figures arranged in a square in which the figures in each vertical, horizontal and diagonal line all add up to the same number. Magic squares have been known in India for over 2000 years and became popular in Europe from the 15th century.

2	9	4
7	5	3
6	1	8

Vertical lines:
2 + 7 + 6 = 15
9 + 5 + 1 = 15
4 + 3 + 8 = 15

Diagonal lines:
2 + 5 + 8 = 15
6 + 5 + 4 = 15

Horizontal lines:
2 + 9 + 4 = 15
7 + 5 + 3 = 15
6 + 1 + 8 = 15

Superstitious people used to belief that a magic square carved by the door would keep the plague from entering a building. They may also be found engraved on old charms and ornaments.

In a magic square with four digits along each side, the numbers in the smaller squares at each corner of the greater square also add up to the same number.

13	8	12	1
2	11	7	14
3	10	6	15
16	5	9	4

Vertical lines:
13 + 2 + 3 + 16 = 34
8 + 11 + 10 + 5 = 34
12 + 7 + 6 + 15 = 34
1 + 14 + 15 + 4 = 34

Horizontal lines:
13 + 8 + 12 + 1 = 34
2 + 11 + 7 + 14 = 34
3 + 10 + 6 + 15 = 34
16 + 5 + 9 + 4 = 34

Diagonal lines:
13 + 11 + 6 + 4 = 34
16 + 10 + 7 + 1 = 34

Corner squares:
13 + 8 + 11 + 2 = 34
12 + 1 + 14 + 7 = 34
15 + 4 + 6 + 9 = 34
5 + 16 + 3 + 10 = 34

To convert a number in any other base into base 10, however, each digit must be given its appropriate place-value in the given base.

Thus, 1037_8
$$= (1 \times 8^3) + (0 \times 8^2) + (3 \times 8^1) + (7 \times 8^0)$$
$$= 512 + 0 + 24 + 7$$
$$= 534_{10}$$

Base 2 or the *binary scale* is the most important non-denary base since it uses only the digits 0 and 1 (see pp. 241–42), and these can easily be related to the 'off' and 'on' of an electrical impulse and form the basis for the operation of electronic calculators and computers.

As above, a number may be converted to base 2 by repeated division. Thus, to convert 217_{10}:

2)217
2)108 r 1
2)54 r 0
2)27 r 0
2)13 r 1
2)6 r 1
2)3 r 0
1 r 1

i.e. $217_{10} = 11011001_2$

The reverse process would be 11011001_2
$$= (1 \times 2^7) + (1 \times 2^6) + (0 \times 2^5) + (1 \times 2^4) + (1 \times 2^3)$$
$$+ (0 \times 2^2) + (0 \times 2^1) + (1 \times 2^0)$$
$$= 128 + 64 + 0 + 16 + 8 + 0 + 0 + 1$$
$$= 217_{10}$$

The denary-binary conversion table on p. 242 reveals some interesting points about binary numbers. Note the repetitive patterns in the columns of the successive numbers. Since odd numbers always end in 1 and even numbers end in 0, a number is doubled simply by adding a 0 (in the same way that a denary number is multiplied by 10 by adding a nought), and divided by 2, where possible, by removing a terminal 0. Denary numbers that are powers of 2 have a binary equivalent consisting of a 1 followed by the same number of zeros as the appropriate power of 2.

The other system that is most relevant to the age of modern technology is the *hexadecimal* (base 16) system. This uses extra symbols – commonly A, B, C, D, E, F to represent 10, 11, 12, 13, 14, 15, so that: $1A5D_{16}$ represents $(1 \times 16^3) + (10 \times 16^2) + (5 \times 16^1) + (13 \times 16^0) = 6749$

PERCENTAGES

A percentage is the proportion or rate per hundred parts of a number or item.

$x\%$ of a number N
$= (x$ divided $100) \times N$

To find what percentage a quantity A is of a quantity B

$\% = (A$ divided by $B) \times 100$

To find the percentage change – increase or decrease – of a quantity

$\%$ change $=$ (actual change divided by original amount) $\times 100$

The same principle applies to profits and losses.
To find 100% given that $x\% = N$
$100\% = (N$ divided by $x) \times 100$

Percentages may not be added or subtracted unless they are percentages of the same quantity. Thus successive depreciations of 10% and 15% are not equivalent to a single depreciation of 25%.

QUICK MULTIPLICATION

The pocket calculator has made arithmetic easy. But there are times when it is handy to know short cuts in multiplication. There are several well-known short cuts that can be used in multiplying numbers by 5, 25, 50, 125, 250, and 11.

Multiplying by 5
Add one nought to the number and divide the total by two.
Example: $897 \times 5 = 8970 \div 2 = 4485$.

Multiplying by 25
Add two noughts to the number and divide the total by four.
Example: $7738 \times 25 = 773\,800 \div 4 = 193\,450$.

Multiplying by 50
Add two noughts to the number and divide the total by two.
Example: $6969 \times 50 = 696\,900 \div 2 = 348\,450$.

Multiplying by 125
Add three noughts to the number and divide the total by eight.
Example: $77 \times 125 = 77\,000 \div 8 = 9625$.

Multiplying by 250
Add three noughts to the number and divide the total by four.
Example: $39 \times 250 = 39\,000 \div 4 = 9750$.

Multiplying a two-figure number by 11
Separate the digits of the number to be multiplied. Add them together and place the result in the space between the digits.
Example: 72×11
Separate 7 and 2   7 2
Add 7 and 2   = 9
Place the total in the space   792
$72 \times 11 = 792$.
Example: 49×11
Separate 4 and 9   4 9
Add 4 and 9   = 13
Place the second digit of the total in the space   439
Add the 10 to the first digit of the answer   539
$49 \times 11 = 539$.

NINE

The number nine displays interesting properties in the nine times table. All the digits in every total add up to nine.

$1 \times 9 = 9$	$9 + 0 = 9$
$2 \times 9 = 18$	$1 + 8 = 9$
$3 \times 9 = 27$	$2 + 7 = 9$
$4 \times 9 = 36$	$3 + 6 = 9$
$5 \times 9 = 45$	$4 + 5 = 9$
$6 \times 9 = 54$	$5 + 4 = 9$
$7 \times 9 = 63$	$6 + 3 = 9$
$8 \times 9 = 72$	$7 + 2 = 9$
$9 \times 9 = 81$	$8 + 1 = 9$
$238 \times 9 = 2142$	$2 + 1 + 4 + 2 = 9$
$44349 \times 9 = 399141$	$3 + 9 + 9 + 1 + 4 + 1 = 27$
	$2 + 7 = 9$

One of the most puzzling methods of doing long multiplication is said to have been invented centuries ago by Russian peasants. The method involves division and multiplication by two.

Example: 27 x 39.

Method:

Put one of the numbers to be multiplied in one column and the other number in a second column.	27	39
Divide the first column by 2 and ignore any remainders. Multiply the second column by 2.	13	78
Continue dividing the figures in the first column – and doubling the figures in the second column – until 1 is reached in the first column.	6	156
	3	312
	1	624
List all numbers in the *second* column that are on the same line as an *odd* number in the first column.		39
		78
		312
		624
Add together these numbers.		39
		78
		312
		+624
		=1053

27 x 39 = 1053

NUMBER PATTERNS

Rectangular numbers Rectangular numbers are composite numbers, that is any number that is not prime (see p. 243). Any composite number can be represented in the form of a rectangle of dots. Thus 6 =

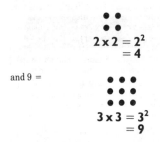

2 x 3 = 6

Square numbers
Square numbers are numbers with a pair of equal factors, and may therefore be represented as a square. Thus 4 =

• •
• •
$2 \times 2 = 2^2$
$= 4$

and 9 =

• • •
• • •
• • •
$3 \times 3 = 3^2$
$= 9$

1, 4, 9, 16, 25, 36, 49, 64, 81, 100, 121, 144, 169 are the squares of the first 13 numbers. They – and all square numbers – are positive.

Triangular numbers
Triangular numbers are numbers that can be formed into a series of equilateral triangles. Triangular

numbers – such as 3, 6, 10 and 15 – can be represented by a triangular pattern of dots. Thus 6 =

6

The differences between successive triangular numbers are the *natural* numbers.

1		3		6		10		15		21		28
	2		3		4		5		6		7		8

Fibonacci numbers were named in the 19th century after Leonardo Fibonacci of Pisa (c. 1175–c. 1250), who introduced the Arabic figures 1 to 9 plus 0 to Europe in his *Liber abaci* in 1202. He earned the title of *Stupor Mundi* (wonder of the world) from the Holy Roman Emperor. In 1225 he published a recursive sequence of his Arabic numbers 1, 1, 2, 3, 5, 8, 13, 21, 34, 55, etc., in which each number is the sum of the two preceding numbers. In the 19th century this sequence was found to occur in nature – in the arrangement of leaf buds on a stem, animal horns, the genealogy of the male bee, and spirals in sunflower heads and pine cones.

PASCAL'S TRIANGLE
Pascal's triangle is one of the most famous and most important of all number patterns.

Although it was known long before Pascal – who died in 1626 – he was the first to make ingenious and wide use of its properties. The numbers in Pascal's triangle appear in the binomial theorem, in problems about the selection of combinations of objects, and therefore in the theory of probability and statistics.

The numbers in each row are formed by adding the numbers above and to each side of it. The numbers in the rows so formed are then the coefficients of the terms in the binomial theorem. Thus the numbers in the 4th row (1 3 3 1) are the coefficients in the expansion of $(a + x)^3$, while those in the 6th row would be the expansion of $(a + x)^5$, i.e. 1 5 10 10 5 1.

```
              1
            1   1
          1   2   1
        1   3   3   1
      1   4   6   4   1
    1   5  10  10   5   1
```

Totals

First line	$1 = 2^0$
Second line	$2 = 2^1$
Third line	$4 = 2^2$
Fourth line	$8 = 2^3$
Fifth line	$16 = 2^4$
Sixth line	$32 = 2^5$

MATRICES
A matrix is an array of numbers, of rectangular shape, which presents information in a concise form. Matrices serve many purposes, and according to the circumstances they may be multiplied or added or subtracted.

Two matrices may be multiplied if there are the same number of *rows* in the second matrix as there are *columns* in the first, but they may only be added or subtracted if they have the same number of rows and columns. A 2×3 matrix is one with 2 rows and 3 columns. Thus a 2×3 matrix may be multiplied by a 3×4 or a 3×2 or a $3 \times n$ matrix where n is any number.

If $A = \begin{pmatrix} a & b \\ c & d \end{pmatrix}$ and $B = \begin{pmatrix} p & q \\ r & s \end{pmatrix}$

Then, $AB = \begin{pmatrix} a & b \\ c & d \end{pmatrix} \begin{pmatrix} p & q \\ r & s \end{pmatrix}$

$$= \begin{pmatrix} ap + br & aq + bs \\ cp + dr & cq + ds \end{pmatrix}$$

$A + B = \begin{pmatrix} a & b \\ c & d \end{pmatrix} + \begin{pmatrix} p & q \\ r & s \end{pmatrix}$

$$= \begin{pmatrix} a + p & b + q \\ c + r & d + s \end{pmatrix}$$

Transformation matrices
The transformation matrices change the position or shape of a geometrical figure, and sometimes both. The following are the principal transformation matrices:

(1) Reflection in the x-axis $\qquad \begin{pmatrix} 1 & 0 \\ 0 & -1 \end{pmatrix}$

(2) Reflection in the y-axis $\qquad \begin{pmatrix} -1 & 0 \\ 0 & 1 \end{pmatrix}$

(3) Reflection in the line $y = x$ $\quad \begin{pmatrix} 0 & 1 \\ 1 & 0 \end{pmatrix}$

(4) Reflection in the line $y = -x$ $\quad \begin{pmatrix} 0 & -1 \\ -1 & 0 \end{pmatrix}$

(5) Rotation through 90° about the origin in a $+ve$ (anticlockwise) direction $\quad \begin{pmatrix} 0 & -1 \\ 1 & 0 \end{pmatrix}$

(6) Rotation through 180° ($+ve$ or $-ve$) $\quad \begin{pmatrix} -1 & 0 \\ 0 & -1 \end{pmatrix}$

(7) $+ve$ rotation about the origin through an angle θ $\quad \begin{pmatrix} \cos\theta & -\sin\theta \\ \sin\theta & \cos\theta \end{pmatrix}$

(8) The *identity matrix* $\begin{pmatrix} a & b \\ c & d \end{pmatrix}$ leaves the elements of the multiplied matrix unchanged.

The following matrices change the shape of the figure.

(9) An enlargement, factor E $\quad \begin{pmatrix} E & 0 \\ 0 & E \end{pmatrix}$

(e.g. if $E = 3$ the figure will have its linear dimensions trebled)

(10) A stretch parallel to the x-axis, factor S $\quad \begin{pmatrix} S & 0 \\ 0 & 1 \end{pmatrix}$

(11) A stretch parallel to the y-axis, factor S $\quad \begin{pmatrix} 1 & 0 \\ 0 & S \end{pmatrix}$

(12) A shear parallel to the x-axis $\quad \begin{pmatrix} 1 & S \\ 0 & 1 \end{pmatrix}$

(13) A shear parallel to the y-axis $\quad \begin{pmatrix} 1 & 0 \\ S & 1 \end{pmatrix}$

The inverse of matrix A above (denoted by A^{-1}) is

$$\frac{1}{(ad - bc)} \begin{pmatrix} d & -b \\ -c & a \end{pmatrix}$$

The expression $(ad - bc)$ is called the determinant of the matrix.

The value of the determinant of a matrix represents the ratio by which the area of the original figure has been changed. If the determinant is zero, all the points will be moved to lie on a line, and the matrix is said to be 'singular'.

If a matrix is multiplied by its inverse the result is the identity matrix.

A transformation which does not change either the shape or the size of a figure is called an isometric transformation.

SETS

Sets can be considered simply as collections of objects. However, in the early 20th century, when attempts were made to formalize the properties of sets, contradictions were discovered that have affected mathematical thinking ever since.

A set can be specified either by stipulating some property for an object as a condition of *membership* of the set, or by listing the *members* of the set in any order.

Sets are usually indicated by the use of curly brackets { and }, known as *braces*. Consider, as an example, the Smith family that has a bicycle, a motor cycle, a van, a family car and a sports car. We could represent the vehicles ridden or driven by Mrs Smith as {bicycle, van, family car}. Sets are often shown by drawing a circle around representations of their members.

Union and intersection
We can use circles to represent the relationship between two or more sets. If Mr Smith drives the sports car and the motor cycle but also shares the use of the van with Mrs Smith, the set of vehicles used by him is {motor cycle, van, sports car}. If R is the set of vehicles used by Mr Smith and S is the set of vehicles used by Mrs Smith, R and S can be shown as two intersecting circles.

The set of all the vehicles used by the Smiths is {bicycle, motor cycle, van, family car, sports car}. This is called the *union* of the two sets and is written $R \cup S$ and spoken as 'R union S'.

The two sets have one member in common, the van. The set of members that belong to both sets are known as their *intersection*. In the example given here it is the set whose only member is the van. This is written $R \cap S = \{van\}$. This is a set even though it has only one member, the van. It is written 'van $\in$ {van}', where the symbol $\in$ means 'is a member of'.

Subsets
Formally, a set is a *subset* of another set if all the

members of the first set are members of the other set, that is, one set is contained within the other. Thus, among the Smiths' vehicles {van} is a subset of {bicycle, motor cycle, van, family car, sports car}.

If the larger set is x and the smaller set – the subset – is y, the equation $y \subset x$ means that y is a subset of x. The equation $x \supset y$ means that set x contains subset y.

Universal sets
A *universal set* groups all the items under consideration. Here that would be all the vehicles used by the Smith family.

Complements
In the universal set – the vehicles used by the Smiths – the vehicles not driven by Mrs Smith form what is known as the *relative complement* of the set of the vehicles that she uses. Thus where S is the set of vehicles used by Mrs Smith, the complement set is written $C(S)$ or S'.

Null or empty sets
An *empty* or *null* set is one containing no members. For example, the set of vehicles driven by the Smiths' young child would be a null set. It would be written {child's vehicles} ∩ {Mr Smith's vehicles} = ∅ This means that set of vehicles driven by both Mr Smith and the child is an empty set.

Disjoint set
Disjoint sets have no members *in common*. Suppose the Smith's young child has a bicycle – obviously a small one that only she can ride. The set of vehicles used by the child – C – is {child's bicycle}, a set of vehicles that does not intersect with the set of vehicles used by her mother. Thus, C and S have no members in common and their intersection is an empty set. This can be expressed by the equation
$$C \cap S = \emptyset$$

PARADOXES
Although the concept of sets outlined above is applicable for most purposes, various paradoxes came to light when *axioms* for the theory of sets were sought. Frege and Russell independently attempted to prove that all mathematics could be reduced to pure logic. In 1908 Russell discovered his axioms gave rise to important contradictions.

Russell's paradox
Some sets are members of themselves, while other sets are not members of themselves. In the set Q – a set of all sets that are not members of themselves – is Q a member of itself or not? An element of a set must have the property that defines the set – in this case Q is a member of the set of sets that are not members of themselves. Q, therefore, cannot be a member of itself – but that only means that it can't be a member of Q. But the fact that Q is not a member of itself is the property that defines Q, so Q must be a member of Q. It is therefore a member of itself. Either way, there is a contradiction. In the case of any set and any entity, either the thing is in the set or it is not.

NETWORKS
A series of nodes joined by arcs is called a network. A node is odd or even, according to the number of arcs which are drawn from it. The network may represent a road or railway system, an electricity grid and so on. Such a system will be traversable (i.e. can be drawn without covering any arc twice or taking the pencil off the paper) if there are not more than 2 odd nodes. In such a case the route must begin and end at an odd node. Two simplified networks are shown below – one is traversable and one is not. The latter was used by Euler to solve the famous Konigsberg Bridge problem.

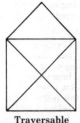

Traversable

HILBERT'S INFINITE HOTEL

The German mathematician David Hilbert dramatized the paradoxical property of infinite sets by an exercise of the imagination.

Imagine a hotel with an infinite number of rooms; then it can be full and still able to accommodate more guests. The manager simply moves the guest in room 1 to room 2, the guest in room 2 into room 3, and so on. Each guest is then in a room with a number higher than before and room 1 remains vacant for a late arrival.

Unfortunately, not one latecomer, but an infinite busload of them arrive. Instead of the moves as before, the manager puts the guest in room 1 into room 2, the guest from room 2 into room 4, the guest from room 3 into room 6, and so on. The infinite number of rooms with odd numbers are now vacant for the infinite number of latecomers.

SOME MILESTONES IN CALCULUS AND MECHANICS

1670s–80s	Leibniz and Newton independently developed calculus.
1687	Newton published his *Principia*.
1728	Bernouilli previewed Fourier series.
1748	Euler published his *Introduction to Infinitesimal Analysis*.
1788	Lagrange published his *Mécanique Analytique*.
early 19th century	Laplace published *Celestial Mechanics*.
1822	Fourier series developed.
1828	Gauss extended differential geometry.
1843	Hamilton's advances in mechanics.
late 19th century	Maxwell's equations.
1902	Lebesque integration.

CALCULUS AND MECHANICS

CALCULUS
Calculus is the branch of mathematics that studies continuous change in terms of the mathematical properties of the functions that represent it, and these results can also be interpreted in geometric

terms relating to the graph of the function. Calculus was developed independently by Newton and Leibniz in the late 17th century. Because their presentation involved paradoxical references to *infinitesimals* (infinitely small quantities), many scientists rejected their 'infidel mathematics', but at the same time there was considerable dispute about who should have the credit for its discovery.

Functions

Suppose we go out for a cycle run and keep up a speed of 15 km/h. Then our distance from home is determined by how long we have been travelling. For example, after half an hour we will have travelled 7.5 km; after an hour 15 km; after 2 hours 30 km, and so on. We can express this relationship by saying that the distance we travelled is a *function* of the time we have been travelling. Here the two quantities, time and distance, might be represented by the variables t and d, and the mathematical relationship between them means that for any number of units of time, t, we can work out the number of units of distance travelled, d, by multiplying t by 15.

In general the notation for a function is $y = f(x)$, which indicates that the value of y depends upon the value of x; in that case, y is called the *dependent variable*, and x is called the *independent variable*. The variables are thought of as running through a range of values – for example, if our journey takes a total of 3 hours, the range of t is the *interval* $(0,3)$, and the range of d is the interval $(0,45)$.

Coordinates

The real numbers can be represented geometrically by a line (an *axis*) marked off from the origin (0) using some numerical scale. Any point in a *plane*, a two-dimensional area, can similarly be represented by the pair of numbers that correspond to its respective distances from two such axes, as shown here; these numbers are the *coordinates* of the point P. Thus the coordinates of the point P in the accompanying diagram are $(1,2)$:

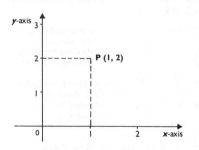

Here the independent and the dependent variables of a function are represented by the two lines at right angles (the x-axis and the y-axis) that cross at the origin. The curve representing the function is then the line that passes through the points whose coordinates satisfy the function. For example, the curve of the function $y = x^2$ is the set of pairs, (x, y), of real numbers for which y is the square of x; thus, for example, $(2,4)$, $(-1,1)$, $(-2,4)$, $(\sqrt{2},2)$, etc., are all in the graph of the function. The curve corresponding to this function is shown here:

The system of coordinates is named Cartesian coordinates after the French philosopher and mathematician René Descartes.

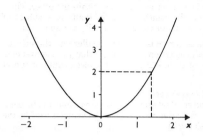

Graphs

Because a function associates elements of one set with those of another, it defines the set of all pairs of elements, (x,y), in which x is a value of the independent variable and y is the value of the function for the argument x. Another way of expressing this is that any point that *satisfies* the function $y = f(x)$ can be represented by the point $(x,f(x))$. Since a function must be a many-one relation, every such pair has a different first element, so the pairs can be listed in a unique order. The function can be thought of as moving through the values of the dependent variable as the value of the independent variable increases. This is what is represented by a graph in the Cartesian coordinate system: if we now draw a line joining the points $(x,f(x))$ as x increases, this line passes through all and only the points whose coordinates satisfy the function. Such a line is usually called a *graph*, although mathematicians prefer to use that term for the set of values of the variables, and call the diagram a *curve*. Since this way of representing change and dependency is equivalent to the function itself, curves provide us with a way of visualizing processes of change.

DIFFERENTIATION

The process of finding the derivative of a function is called *differentiation*, and this branch of mathematics is known as *differential calculus*. This process can also be interpreted geometrically. However, it is not always necessary to work out a derivative by means of a graph. Instead, certain general principles apply. The derivative of a function can itself be differentiated; for example, acceleration is the rate of change of velocity, and the derivative of the velocity function with respect to time can be worked out. This is the *second derivative* of the displacement function.

If y is any function of x, and Δy, Δx are corresponding increments of y and x, then the differential coefficient of y with respect to x

$$\left(\text{written } \frac{dy}{dx}\right) \text{ is defined as } \operatorname*{Lt}_{\Delta x \to 0} \frac{[f(x + \Delta x) - f(x)]}{\Delta x}$$

$\dfrac{dy}{dx}$ gives the gradient of a curve, i.e. it measures the rate of change of one variable with respect to another.

Thus, since velocity is the rate of change of displacement with respect to time, it may be expressed in calculus terms as $\dfrac{ds}{dt}$ where s is the displacement of a body from a fixed point and the equation of motion of the body is of the form $s = f(t)$.

Similarly, since acceleration is the rate of change of *velocity* with time, it may be expressed as $\dfrac{dv}{dt}$ or as $\dfrac{d^2s}{dt^2}$, i.e. as the second differential of s with respect to t. Acceleration may also be expressed as $v\dfrac{dv}{ds}$ i.e. as the velocity multiplied by the rate of change of velocity with distance. In general, if: $y = ax^n$

then $\dfrac{dy}{dx} = nax^{n-1}$

Since $\dfrac{dy}{dx}$ gives the gradient of a curve it may be used to find the maximum and minimum values of a function. Thus if $y = f(x)$, then when $\dfrac{dy}{dx} = 0$, the tangents to the curve will be parallel to the x axis, and will indicate the positions of the critical values (the maximum or minimum) but without distinguishing them. However,

if $\dfrac{d^2y}{dx^2}$ is $+$ ve   the critical value of x gives a *minimum* value of the function, while

if $\dfrac{d^2y}{dx^2}$ is $-$ ve   the critical value gives a *maximum* value of the function, and

if $\dfrac{d^2y}{dx^2} = 0$,   and changes sign as x increases through the point, the curve is passing through a point of inflection

Differential coefficient of a product
If $y = uv$ where u and v are functions of x, then

$$\frac{dy}{dx} = u\frac{dv}{dx} + v\frac{du}{dx}$$

Differential coefficient of a quotient
If $y = \dfrac{u}{v}$ where u and v are functions of x, then

$$\frac{dy}{dx} = \frac{v\dfrac{du}{dx} - u\dfrac{dv}{dx}}{v^2}$$

NEWTON'S LAWS OF MOTION
Newton's Laws of Motions were first published in his *Principia* in 1687. See p. 194.

The basic equations of motion with constant acceleration
$s = \tfrac{1}{2}t(u + v)$

$v = u + at$

$v^2 = u^2 + 2as$

$s = ut + \tfrac{1}{2}at^2$

where a = acceleration
s = displacement
t = time
u = initial velocity
v = final velocity

Constant velocity:
distance = velocity x time

RELATIVE VELOCITY

To find the velocity of a body A relative to a body B, combine with the velocity of A a velocity equal and opposite to that of B. The sides of the triangle represent the velocities in magnitude and direction.

Thus to a person on a ship B, the ship A would *appear* to be moving in the direction (and at the speed) represented by the double-arrowed line.

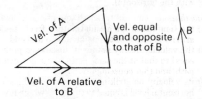

Vel. of A relative to B

Triangle of velocities
The triangle ABC shows how the track (i.e. the actual direction) and velocity relative to the ground (the ground speed) of an aircraft or boat may be found from the course set and the wind or current.

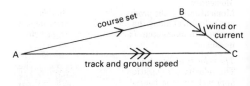

In vector terms, $\overrightarrow{AB} + \overrightarrow{BC} = \overrightarrow{AC}$

PROJECTILES
For simple cases, in which air resistance is neglected and the vertical velocity is subject only to the force of gravity, the following results may be derived from the fundamental equations of motion:

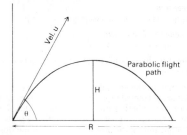

Parabolic flight path

The time of flight
$$T = \frac{2u\sin\theta}{g}$$

The time to the greatest height
$$= \frac{T}{2}$$
$$= \frac{u\sin\theta}{g}$$

The greatest height attained
$$H = \frac{u^2\sin^2\theta}{2g}$$

The range on a horizontal plane
$$R = \frac{u^2\sin 2\theta}{g}$$
For a given velocity of projection u there are, in general, two possible angles of projection to obtain a

given horizontal range. These directions will make equal angles with the vertical and horizontal respectively. For maximum range the angle makes 45° with the horizontal.

Note that:
(1) the time taken for a body moving freely under gravity is the same to rise as it is to descend.
(2) the velocity at any point on its upward path is equal to that at the same point on its downward path, and that consequently . . .
(3) its velocity on striking the ground at the same horizontal level is equal to that with which it was projected.

The impact of elastic bodies
If the bodies are smooth (e.g. two billiard balls) and only the forces between the bodies are considered, then the following equations will determine the velocities and directions of the bodies after the impact.

Momentum:
Momentum (i.e. the product of the individual masses and velocities) along the line of centres after impact is equal to momentum _in the same direction_ before impact.

The velocity of separation:
The velocity of separation is equal to the velocity of approach (also measured along the line of centres) multiplied by the coefficient of elasticity between the two bodies. If the impact is oblique (and the bodies are smooth) the velocities at right angles to the line of centres are unchanged.

If u_1 and u_2, m_1 and m_2 are the initial velocities and masses of the two spheres, and α and β are the angles these velocities make with the line of centres, and v_1 and v_2 are the components of velocities _along the line of centres_ after impact, then the above statements are represented by the following equations:

Momentum:
$m_1v_1 + m_2v_2 = m_1u_1 \cos \alpha + m_2u_2 \cos \beta$

The velocity of separation:
$v_2 \pm v_1 = e(u_1 \cos \alpha - u_2 \cos \beta)$

where e is the coefficient of elasticity between the two bodies.

Note that in the second equation v_1 and v_2 will be added or subtracted to get the 'velocity of separation' according to whether the bodies are considered to be going in the opposite or same direction respectively. The conditions of the problem will determine this for the 'velocity of approach'. In the example m_1 is 'catching up' on m_2 and therefore we take the difference in their velocities to obtain the velocity of approach.

CIRCULAR MOTION
If a body is moving in a circle with uniform speed, then its linear velocity v is given by the equation:
$v = r\omega$
where r is the radius of the circle, and ω is the angular velocity. The body will nevertheless have an acceleration (since a force is acting on it to make it move in a circle) but this will be directed _towards_ the centre.

The acceleration will be: $r\omega^2$

The force will be: $mr\omega^2$
where m is the mass of the body.

If a body is whirled round on the end of a string there

is no tendency for it to move outwards along the _radius_ of the circle. If the string breaks, it will instead move straight on along the _tangent_ to the circle.

In the case of a train going round a curve the necessary force is provided by the flanges on the wheels, while in the case of a car going round a track it is provided by the friction between the wheels and the ground. By banking the rails or road the weight of the train or car may be made to provide the necessary force.

The required angle to prevent any tendency to skid is given by the equation:
$\tan \theta = v^2$ divided by gr
where θ is the angle made with the horizontal by the banking.

WORK AND ENERGY
The work done by a force F acting on a body as it covers a displacement s is Fs.

The kinetic energy (KE) of a particle of mass m moving with velocity v is $\frac{1}{2}mv^2$.

The potential energy (PE) gained by a mass m as it is raised through a height h is mgh.

When no forces other than weight do any work on a body, then the total energy (KE + PE) remains constant.

SIMPLE HARMONIC MOTION
If a particle moves so that its acceleration is directed towards a fixed point in its path, and is proportional to its distance from that point, it is said to move with simple harmonic motion.

The fundamental equation is $\dfrac{d^2x}{dt^2} = -\omega^2x$, and by integrating the corresponding equation $v\dfrac{dv}{dx} - \omega^2x$ the velocity at any displacement x is given by

$v = \sqrt{a^2 - x^2}$ where a is the maximum value of x.
By solving the first equation we find that
$x = a \cos \omega t$ (if $t = 0$ when $x = a$) or
$x = a \sin \omega t$ (if $t = 0$ when $x = 0$)

The period of motion is given by $T = \dfrac{2\pi}{\omega}$

STATICS
Statics is the study of forces acting on bodies at rest. It can be compared with _dynamics_, which is the study of bodies in motion.

Some fundamental principles of statics include:
(1) The _moment of a force_ about a point is the product of the force and the perpendicular distance of the line of action of the force from the point.
(2) For a body to be at rest under a system of forces in one plane,
   (a) the algebraic sum of the resolved parts of the forces in any two directions which are not parallel must be zero, and
   (b) the algebraic sum of the moments of the forces about any point must be zero (i.e. clockwise moments = anticlockwise moments).

(3) For a system of particles of weights $w_1 w_2$, w_3 etc. whose distances from a fixed axis are x_1, x_2, x_3 etc.,

the position of the centre of gravity from that axis is given by $\dfrac{\Sigma wx}{\Sigma w}$ where Σwx is the sum of all the weights of the particles. From this, the centres of gravity of irregular shapes, or shapes with portions missing, can be found by the principles that: the Moment of the whole = the sum of the moments of the parts
and the Moment of the remainder = the moment of the whole − the sum of the moments of the parts removed

The positions of the centres of gravity of some important shapes are as follows:

(a) A triangle — at the intersection of the medians (i.e. the lines joining the vertices to the midpoints of the opposite sides) or at one-third of the length of the median from the base.

(b) Square, rectangle, parallelogram, rhombus — at the intersection of the diagonals.

(c) Sector of a circle of angle 2θ radians — at a distance $\frac{2}{3}\dfrac{r\sin\theta}{\theta}$ from the centre along the line bisecting the sector, where r = the radius.

For a semicircle — $\theta = \dfrac{p}{2}$ and the distance of the centre of gravity from the centre of the circle will $= \dfrac{4r}{3\pi}$

(d) A solid pyramid on any base — at a point one-quarter of the height of the pyramid above the base.

(e) A hollow cone — at a point one-third of the height from the base.

(f) A solid hemisphere — at a point along the axis distant $\dfrac{3r}{8}$ from the centre where r is the radius.

(g) A hollow hemisphere — at a point distant $\dfrac{r}{2}$ along the axis from the centre.
[Note that this is the same as for the centre of gravity of the cylinder which would surround, or contain, the hemisphere.]

(4) If a rigid body is in equilibrium under the action of three forces in a plane, the lines of action of these forces must either all be parallel, or must meet at a common point. The sum of the three forces must be zero, and therefore it must thus always be possible to draw a triangle to represent the forces.

(5) The Laws of Friction.
(a) The direction of the frictional force is opposite to that in which the body tends to move.
(b) The magnitude of the friction is, up to a certain point, exactly equal to the force tending to produce motion.
(c) Only a certain amount of friction can be called into play. This is called 'limiting friction'.
(d) The magnitude of the limiting friction for a given pair of surfaces bears a constant ratio to the normal (i.e. perpendicular) pressure between the surfaces. This ratio is denoted by m and is called the Coefficient of Friction.

(e) The amount of friction is independent of the areas and shape of the surfaces in contact provided the normal pressure remains unaltered.

(f) When motion takes place, the friction still opposes the motion. It is independent of the velocity, and is proportional to the normal pressure, but is less than the limiting friction.
If F is the limiting friction (i.e. the force of friction when motion is about to occur), and R is the normal (perpendicular) force, then

$$F = \mu R \text{ where } \mu \text{ is the coefficient of friction}$$

The resultant of the forces F and R makes an angle (usually denoted by λ) with R, and thus

$$\tan \lambda = \dfrac{F}{R}$$
$$= \mu$$

λ is called the Angle of Friction.
These relationships are illustrated in the following diagrams:

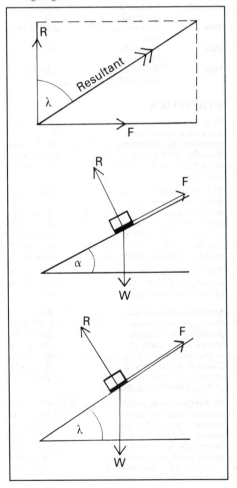

If a body is placed on an inclined plane, then if the angle of the plane (α) is less than the angle of friction, it will not slide down.
If the angle of the plane is equal to λ, the angle

of friction, the body will be just on the point of sliding. If the angle of the plane is greater than the angle of friction the body will slide.

SOME MILESTONES IN PROBABILITY AND STATISTICS

1654	Fermat and Pascal develop probability.
1713	Bernouilli's posthumous *Ars Conjectandi* combined probability theory with early statistical methods.
1763	Bayes theorem – an expression of conditional probability.
early 19th century	Laplace's probability theories.
1837	Poisson distribution – a distribution representing the number of events occurring randomly in a fixed time at an average rate.
late 19th century	Maxwell and Boltzmann separately apply probability to areas of mechanics.
1900	Pearson invented the Chi-squared test.
1922	Fisher defined maximum likelihood.
1932	Kolmogorov combined probability with set theory.

STATISTICS

Statistics is the science of gathering and analysing numerical information and of making inferences regarding the characteristics of people or of objects from that information. The numerical information is often based on a random selection of the group in question.

The 19th-century German mathematician Gauss added greatly to the application of statistics by developing the *method of least squares* while attempting to improve the accuracy of physical measurements. This method of analysing experimental data has developed into a flexible and general theory that has been adapted to most fields of statistics.

The method of least squares can also be seen as the ancestor of Fisher's *design of experiments*, a branch of statistics widely used in many disciplines.

Statistical experiments and probability

Statistical experiments rely upon a knowledge of the *probability mechanism*. Statistics applies probability theory to the data collected. Not all actions and happenings have completely predictable results. There is often only a limited range of possible outcomes, but one cannot know with certainty which of these possible outcomes to expect.

Probability theory enables us to describe with mathematical rigour the chance of an action or happening having a particular outcome. Thus, dividing the number of times an outcome of a scientific experiment falls in an event E by the number of experiments gives an estimate of the probability of event E – for instance exposing a diamond upon cutting a pack of cards.

When tossing a coin it is possible to predict which of the sides will land face upwards, which, after all, is the point of tossing coins. Assuming that the fairness of the coin is accepted – and the way that it is tossed is also fair – we know that it is just as likely to come

up heads as tails, and there is no possible other outcome. Similarly with a fair die, it is just as likely for any of its numbers – from 1 to 6 – to fall upwards, and there are no other possible outcomes. In these examples, all the possible outcomes are *equiprobable*, and that the *a priori probability* (i.e. the theoretical probability) of a coin coming up heads is 1 in 2 or 1/2, and that of throwing a 3 on a single die is 1 in 6 or 1/6.

On the other hand, *empirical probability* (often called *a posteriori probability*) is based on observation and experiment. Here, the probability of a particular outcome is calculated from the proportion of times it has been observed to have happened before under the same conditions – its *relative frequency*. If a coin is tossed 10 times, heads may only come up 3 times. The empirical probability that one of these throws came up heads is 3/10. As the number of experiments grows larger, the figure becomes closer to the true probability. Thus, if a coin is tossed 100 times and heads comes up 46 times, the empirical probability that one of these throws came up heads is 46/100 or 23/50.

There is no 'law of averages'. Experimental and theoretical probability are connected only by the *law of large numbers*, which states that as the number of trials increases, the observed empirical probability comes closer and closer to the theoretical value. If q_1, q_2,... is a sequence of outcomes and E is an event, the number of times the outcome is E in the first n experiments is expressed as

$$N(q_1, q_2, ..., q_n; E)$$

COMPUTING

COMPUTERS

Computers are machines that carry out programmed sequences of instructions to manipulate coded data. The more common digital computers – the type described here – use number codes to represent data such as letters of the alphabet, numbers, visible images, sounds and other material. The number system used is the binary system, by which all numbers (and hence number codes) can be represented by sequences of 0s and 1s (binary digits or *bits*), which on a computer can be represented by electric current being turned off and on respectively.

Each particle of data is represented by an 8-digit binary number, a *byte*. The ASCII – American Standard Code for Information Interchange (pronounced 'ass-key') – code is used for letters of the alphabet, digits 0 to 9 and punctuation marks and other signs. Other data can be coded in ways that may be specific to a type of computer or to a program and may not be easily interchangeable. Data size is measured in bytes, kilobytes (K; $1K = 2^{10}$ bytes) and megabytes (Mb; $1Mb = 2^{20}$ bytes).

HARDWARE AND SOFTWARE

The electronic and mechanical components of a computer are called the *hardware*. The hardware of a computer contains the processor, which can carry out actions of arithmetic and comparison on binary digits. The bytes of information are stored in memory, allowing the processor to process them as fast as it can read them and deal with them. Circuits called *ports* deal with the input of new data and the output of processed data (to a screen, printer or disk, for example). All of these processes are carried out under the control of a *program*, which is another set of bytes in code. The program and the data – in other words the procedures required for computer operation – are called the *software* of the system.

TYPES OF COMPUTER

Computers are now classified into the following categories:

Microcomputers use a microprocessor, which is formed on one tiny chip of silicon.

Minicomputers are computers (often used for small office networks) that are intermediate in capacity between a microcomputer and a mainframe.

Mainframes are the most powerful general-purpose computers.

Supercomputers are designed specifically for speed.

Minicomputers, large mainframe computers and supercomputers use sets of separate chips.

THE PROCESSOR AND STORAGE

The *processor* must be able to read bytes from the memory in sequence, and the bytes must be available in the correct order. Data is stored inside the computer in memory and externally in *backing stores*. Each unit of memory is a tiny semiconductor switch storing one bit of information. A memory consists of a set of such units, organized into bytes and with each set accessible by using an address number, applied in binary signal form to the chip(s). The two fundamental types of memory are *ROM* and *RAM*.

ROM is Read-Only Memory. Each byte can be read when its address number is supplied (from the microprocessor) but the contents of the memory cannot be changed nor erased.

RAM is Random-Access Memory. RAM can be read or written and is usually volatile – its contents are lost when power is cut off. CMOS (complementary metal-oxide semiconductor) RAM will retain data either with battery back-up or even without any power supply and is used for retaining small amounts of permanent data.

Backing stores are used for long-term retention. Most read-write backing stores use magnetic storage on disk or tape and it is now possible to store 1.44 Mb on a disk whose diameter is about 90 mm (3.5 in). Another form of backing store is the *CD-ROM* type. As the name suggests, this stores data in read-only form using an optical disk (like an audio compact disk); read-write versions of this are being developed. Another form is the *WORM* (Write Once Read Many) disk, which can be written by signals of higher-than-normal size and from then on used like the CD-ROM disk.

PROGRAMS

Originally, programmers worked in binary code using sets of switches in place of a keyboard. This *machine-code programming* (*first-generation language*) is feasible only for very short programs, and has been replaced by *assembly-language programming* (*second-generation language*), which uses brief instruction words like ADD. A program called an *assembler* then reads the words and associated

numbers and converts them into machine code, but such programming demands that the programmer should have a very detailed knowledge of how the hardware works.

The writing of reliable large programs is a major problem. Such programs have to be divided and each programmer writes a section. The problems start when the sections are made to work together. The development of programming has aimed to make cooperation easier and to reduce errors.

The *operating system* is an important aid. This is a program that attends to all the simple needs of the system, such as controlling the memory, keyboard, disk system, screen and other inputs and outputs. It also provides a set of standard routines that writers of programs can use with confidence. The other major aid is the use of *higher-level programming languages*, including third- or fourth-generation languages (see below).

COMPUTER LANGUAGES

A *third-generation language* uses intelligible commands that allow the program to be read more easily. In addition, good languages are *portable* – the same commands can be used for programming any type of computer. The differences between computers are dealt with by using different versions of the language program. The early third-generation languages included FORTRAN, ALGOL and COBOL, each developed for specific needs. The popular BASIC language was developed originally as a way of learning FORTRAN. More modern third-generation languages include Pascal, C and Prolog. All these languages are procedural, meaning that the programmer must write the sequence of instructions that will be used on the data. Object-oriented program languages are adaptations of familiar languages that allow for better organization when the work is split among many writers.

Fourth-generation languages (4GL) can be described as programs that write programs. The programmer writes only descriptions of the types of data and how they are to be manipulated. Most 4GLs are specialized, creating one type of program only. Typical modern 4GLs for small computers include Matrix Layout, DataBoss and SkyMaster.

SPEED AND PERFORMANCE

The 'power' of a computer is measured in terms of its processing speed, memory capacity, and backing store size. Modern microcomputers operate with four-byte units, running the timing clock at around 16 MHz, using 1Mb of memory and a backing store of 32 Mb to 640 Mb. Microcomputers can be connected together into networks to share a common backing store and printer(s).

The speed of micros is determined mainly by the speed of moving data to and from the memory and backing stores. This can be improved by using *memory caches* – small pieces of fast-acting memory. Since the same data is often needed several times, it can be reached more quickly from fast memory than from main memory or backing stores. Larger machines can use memory that operates much faster but which requires much more space and also needs cooling.

Supercomputers are used for fast real-time processing (missile tracking, weather forecasting, analysing fast reactions) and are built in circular or spherical form to minimize the length of connectors between units. The speed of electric current in cables limits such computers, and it seems likely that the use of lasers, fibre optics and light-operated switches will result in even faster machines in the late 1990s.

MILESTONES IN COMPUTING

3000 BC The abacus, using rods and beads for counting, probably developed in the Middle East and was widely used in Mediterranean countries.

1614 The Scot John Napier's logarithms allowed multiplication and division to be carried out by adding and subtracting. A device called 'Napier's bones' led to the invention of the slide rule.

1642 Blaise Pascal, in France, invented a mechanical adding machine using 10:1 gearing to represent decimal columns. The computing language Pascal is named after this pioneer of computation.

1666 The German philosopher Gottfried Wilhelm Leibniz proposed the basis of a language that would allow logical statements to be dealt with mathematically. The essence was the use of digits 0 for FALSE and 1 for TRUE. Leibniz went on to develop binary arithmetic.

1673 Leibniz improved Pascal's calculator by adding a method of shifting columns. This allowed the machine to multiply and divide as well as adding and subtracting.

1804 The French weaver J.M. Jacquard invented a loom in which changes of pattern or material could be programmed by feeding in a set of punched cards. The Jacquard loom (one of which can be seen working in the Humphries Mill at Sible Hedingham, Essex) was the first programmable device to be perfected.

1822 Charles Babbage, with support from the British Admiralty, set out to design a '*differential engine*', an advanced form of calculator for application to problems in navigation. He was assisted by Ada, Countess Lovelace, daughter of Lord Byron, who pursued the idea that the analytical engine could be made programmable, and devised some programs. The programming language ADA has been named in her memory. Babbage's machine was never built, because of escalating costs, but another version is now being constructed to prove that the design was sound.

1847 The English mathematician George Boole – working on the ideas of Leibniz – developed a mathematical system for dealing with logical problems, Boolean algebra, which is nowadays used for designing control systems and is incorporated into computer systems.

1890 Herman Hollerith in the USA combined the ideas of the Jacquard loom and the *differential engine* to construct an analyser, the *tabulator*, which used data in the form of punched cards. Using this device, which had been commissioned for working out census results, he processed the 1890 census in six weeks rather than in the six years that manual analysis would have required. The Hollerith Tabulator Corporation eventually became International Business Machines (IBM).

1898 The Dane Valdemar Poulsen devised the *telegraphone*, a pioneer magnetic recorder using steel wire. This was the ancestor of all modern tape and magnetic disk devices.

1907 Lee de Forest in the USA devised the *triode thermionic valve* (vacuum tube). This allowed an electric current between two connectors to be controlled by a voltage at a third connector and paved the way for the development of fast computers in the 1950s.

1930 Vannevar Bush, working in the USA at MIT, devised a form of *analogue computer*, a machine in which sizes of quantities are represented by electrical voltage size and actions such as addition and multiplication are represented by alterations of the voltage levels. This machine – *the differential analyser* – used the principles of calculus in electrical form and allowed differential equations such as those governing missiles, flow of liquid in pipes, and flow of air over wings to be solved much more rapidly than by using pencil and paper. The machine was only partly electrical and required mechanical gearing to be changed at frequent intervals.

1936 The mathematician Alan Turing in the UK published a paper *On Computable Numbers with an Application to the Entscheidungs problem*. This suggested that many apparently insoluble problems might become soluble if a 'universal computer' could be built which could be completely controlled by program instructions. He also devised the 'Turing test' to determine if a computer could think for itself. This was based on the principle that if a human could communicate with such a device without seeing it and never know that the device was a computer, then the device would have true intelligence.

1941 The German mathematician Konrad Zuse developed a digital computer using binary code to solve problems connected with the ballistics of rockets. The storage of bits during calculation was achieved by electromagnetic relays, but the machine had no memory.

1943 Howard Aitken working at Harvard, USA, developed the Mark I computer, using relays as bit stores and with switches to input data in binary form. The machine stood 2·5 m (8 ft) high and 15·5 m (51 ft) wide and was used to solve the ballistics problems of large naval guns.

Under Alan Turing's guidance, the decoding station at Bletchley Park (Buckinghamshire, England) developed the Colossus computer, which was used to break the German Enigma codes. The codes were thought to be unbreakable, and in some cases the information that was decoded could not be used for fear of revealing that the code was being cracked. The Colossus was the first machine to use electronic devices – *thermionic valves* – in place of mechanical or electromechanical (relay) devices. This allowed much faster processing and greater reliability, but the sheer size of the machine and number of valves meant that the time between failures was short. Neither Mark I nor Colossus had a memory, so they could not be reprogrammed by using software.

1946 The ENIAC (Electronics Number Indicator and Calculator) machine was completed in the USA. This was the first really large and fast digital computer that used thermionic valves (vacuum tubes) as storage elements. ENIAC was 5·5 m (18 ft) high, 24 m (80 ft) long and weighed 30 tons, but it worked a thousand times faster than the Harvard Mark I. Nowadays even this machine could be outperformed by a modest laptop computer. ENIAC was initially used to carry out the calculations on the feasibility of the hydrogen bomb, although it was not its original purpose. Reprogramming the machine for other purposes had to be done by reconnecting wires, because, at that time, there was no provision for using software to control a digital computer.

1948 Manchester University demonstrated a computer that used thermionic valves and had a small and simple form of memory. This allowed for some software, for easier reprogramming and for more complex calculations in which intermediate results had to be held in the memory. However, the huge number of valves resulted in low reliability – one valve had to be replaced after each eight minutes of working time.

1949 Shockley, Brittain and Bardeen, working at Bell Laboratories (USA), invented the *transistor*, and the *switching device*. These were eventually able to replace thermionic valves in computers. The transistor was small, consumed very little electrical power and could be manufactured by automated methods. Initial samples measured 13 mm (0·5 in) long, but by the time transistors could be manufactured in quantity, in 1951, much smaller sizes were achieved. The semiconductor material used initially was germanium, but by 1956 silicon was being used to make superior devices.

Konrad Zuse constructed and marketed *digital computers* in Germany. These were developments of his Z4 design and used thermionic valves.

Wilkes and Renwick at Cambridge University demonstrated the EDSAC (Electronic Delay Storage Automatic Calculator) machine. This was said to achieve a calculating speed 15 000 times faster than the human brain.

Lyons, the catering firm in the UK, developed LEO (Lyons Electronic Office), the first computer intended for commercial data processing as distinct from scientific and military engineering work. LEO was used for accounting and stock control of the Lyons Corner House tearooms. A later LEO MARK III was one of the first computers to use transistors in place of valves.

1951 The EDVAC (Electronic Digital Vacuum-tube Analysing Computer) was developed in the USA. Using thermionic valves, this was the first computer to make use of binary codes and to be programmed to create its own machine code using an assembler program.

1952 A computer was used for the first time in the USA to analyse voting patterns in a national election. It correctly predicted the outcome.

1954 IBM, the company that had developed from the Hollerith Corporation, begun the mass-production of computers. The IBM 7000 series were the first commercially obtainable computers that used transistors.

1956 The term *artificial intelligence* was coined in the USA. Artificial intelligence can be described as studies into computers – as yet unattainable – that could sense their environment and work in a way that paralleled human thought processes.

1958 The first computer dating agency was set up and led to a wedding in Hollywood (California) of the first couple matched in this way.

1959 The *microchip* – or *integrated circuit* (IC) – was developed in the USA by Robert Noyce, working with Fairchild in the USA. (An earlier proposal by G. Dummer to develop a microchip was rejected by the British Civil Service.) The manufacturing techniques for the microchip allowed a silicon transistor to be manufactured on a surface of 6·45 mm² (0·1 in²). It soon

became possible to make ten transistors, along with all the electrical connections between them, in the same space.

The microchip allowed circuits to be constructed using vastly greater numbers of transistors. This resulted in immensely improved reliability because failures arise mainly from interconnections and the use of chips greatly reduces the need for interconnections.

During the 1960s, Noyce and other engineers left Fairchild to set up their own companies, assisted by the forward-looking attitude of banks in California. Known collectively as 'the Fairchildren', these pioneers set up virtually the whole of the modern electronics and computing industries as we know them today.

1965 Digital Equipment Corporation (DEC) – making use of transistor and IC techniques – produced the first widely-marketed minicomputer, leading to the famous PDP11 and VAX machines. By this time several hundred transistors and their connections could be made on a single chip.

In Germany, print was typeset by computer for the first time.

The PROLOG language was devised to develop programs for artificial intelligence (AI) work.

The IBM 360 computers made extensive use of ICs.

1971 The microprocessor, containing several thousand transistors on one chip, was developed by Ted Hoff at Intel, the firm founded by Robert Noyce. This device, the 4004, worked with 4-bit units and provided all the processing needed for a simple computer in one chip, to which a manufacturer needed only to add memory and input/output ports.

A coin-operated computer made by Hewlett-Packard gave 2·5 minutes of computing time for 25 cents in a California public library, the first instance of easy access to a computer for the public.

1975 Altair, a small US firm later taken over by MITS, marketed the first kit for constructing a personal computer, using an Intel 8008 microprocessor and with crude input and output number indicators. US sales totalled $13 million in the first year of sales.

1977 The electronic inventiveness of Steve Wozniak combined with the marketing ability of Steve Jobs – working from the garage at Jobs' home and with a capital of $1300 – developed the Apple-1 computer, the first home computer. This was soon followed by a much more advanced design, the Apple-2, which had an extraordinary long life – many are still in use. After three years, Apple Corporation was turning over $117 million per annum.

Statistical organizations began to report health problems connected to the intensive use of VDUs, including eyestrain, back and shoulder problems, head and neck strains, and arm, wrist and leg pains.

1978 The first case of computer-related fraud by 'hacking' was reported. A hacker was charged with defrauding a Los Angeles bank of $10·2 million.

1979 Visicalc, the first spreadsheet program, was demonstrated on the Apple-2. This caused the demand for the machine to increase enormously and created a business market for microcomputers. Previously, microcomputers had been bought mainly by informed enthusiasts and students.

Loughborough University (Leicestershire, England) published its VDU manual. This has been widely used for its recommendations on the best use of VDUs so as to avoid medical problems.

1980 The Post Office Telephone service in the UK began its Prestel service using large mainframe computers to provide information to subscribers (such as travel agents) over telephone lines. The system later allowed electronic mail messages to be sent between subscribers.

New models of microcomputers proliferated as manufacturers all over the world began production. Most of the machines were totally incompatible with each other, had a limited range of uses (mainly games), and were in production for only a couple of years.

1981 IBM launched the IBM-PC microcomputer. Though the first models were less powerful than other contemporary designs, the use of an advanced form of Intel chip allowed IBM to develop the machine into a powerful unit (the PC-XT) that made the use of microcomputers acceptable for business purposes and imposed some standards on a chaotic industry. Software developed for the PC was aimed at business users rather than at computer enthusiasts, and included the famous Lotus 1-2-3 spreadsheet and Word Perfect word processor.

The MS-DOS operating system developed for the IBM PC was made available for other users who wished to develop machines that will run IBM software.

Germany introduced regulations on the design and use of VDUs in an attempt to reduce the incidence of medical problems.

1983 The IBM PC-XT was introduced, standardizing the 5·25 in floppy disk format for years to come. This machine could also be fitted with a hard disk.

1984 IBM introduced the PC-AT, a vastly faster and more advanced machine that could run the same software as their earlier models. This compatibility has been a feature of the IBM machines, allowing users to change machines without the need to scrap all of their software. The PC-AT used the Intel 80286 chip with 1Mb of memory and a 1·2Mb floppy disk drive along with a 20Mb hard disk.

The Apple Macintosh was introduced, using Motorola microprocessor chips (incompatible with IBM types) and pioneering WIMP (Window, Ikon, Mouse Programming) techniques. These ideas – developed originally at Xerox corporation – allowed computers to be used more easily. The *mouse* is a small hand-held device which can be pushed around a desk and which causes an arrow marker to move on the VDU screen. Buttons on the mouse are used to confirm selection of whatever the arrow on-screen is pointing to, and selections of menus can appear in separate windows on the screen. This type of device is now available on all microcomputers.

1985 The Transputer – a form of microprocessor that can be linked to other identical units – was developed by Iain Barron in the UK. This allowed *parallel-processing* – in which several actions can be carried out simultaneously – as distinct from the *serial* (one item at a time) action of conventional processors. When *conventional processors* appear to be carrying out several tasks at once – *multi-tasking* – they are, in fact, timesharing the tasks by carrying out portions from each task in sequence.

1986 Machines of very similar construction to the IBM machines – and which could run the same

software – were suddenly reduced in price, particularly after the introduction of the Amstrad PC 1512 in the UK. The availability of low-cost computers, along with the development of a vast library of software for the PC, led to a huge surge in the use of the PC type of machine.

The Data Protection Act in the UK required users of databases other than simple mailing lists to register so that anyone could request a copy of computer records that might affect him or her. Records held by the Government and law-enforcement agencies were excluded, but many users of home computers found that they were liable to register or face fines.

1987 IBM and other manufacturers introduced a machine using the Intel 80386 chip. This allowed older software to be run at very high speeds, and also permitted multi-tasking, so that several programs could seem to be running together.

New standards for VDU construction and use appeared from the BSI (British Standards Institute).

Laser printers, using the principle of the Xerox copier, became available, allowing the rapid printing of very high-quality material. Laser printers are extensively used along with DTP (desktop publishing) software to revolutionize the production of documents.

Laptop computers started to appear in large numbers.

1988 Acorn (UK) developed their RISC (Reduced Instruction Set Computer) microprocessor, which operates at a very high speed by using only the most common and simplest instruction steps. This led to the development of a very advanced and fast computer, the Archimedes, which is sold extensively to educational institutes in the UK, but has not been taken up widely for business use because of its incompatibility with the IBM machines.

ICL and Tender Electronic Industries jointly designed an improved laser-read optical-disk system for computers.

Wang's Freestyle computer was developed. This can work with handwritten data (using an electronic pen) and with spoken messages.

Steve Jobs, no longer associated with Apple, announced the NEXT computer.

1989 Low-price clones of the fast 80386 computers became easily available, making this type of machine a standard for business use.

Intel released the 80496 chip, a development of the 80386 that includes some on-chip memory and avoids the need for a set of supporting chips. Intel also produced their first RISC chip, the i860.

British Telecom at Martlesham Heath (Ipswich, Suffolk) developed light-operated computer circuits that promise much faster operation along with the ability to be linked over large distances by optical fibres.

The Science Museum (South Kensington, London) started a fund-raising campaign to construct Babbage's difference engine (see above). It was estimated that £250 000 would be needed by the end of 1991. Babbage's original funding was £17 000, equivalent to £435 000 in today's currency.

1990 IBM and others announced computers using the 80686 Intel chip. The price of clone machines –

using the older chips – fell sharply, particularly machines using 80386 chips. IBM also announced a machine that runs both MS-DOS (for older software) and the UNIX operating system (for software that runs on mainframe and mini computers).

Intel was reported to be working on the 80586 chip.

Several manufacturers announced multimedia systems, combining computing and video techniques.

The first laptop machine with a full-colour screen was announced by NEC.

GLOSSARIES

CHEMISTRY GLOSSARY

ablation degradation due to heat.

absolute temperature temperature measured on the absolute scale in kelvins (K), −1 K being equal to 1 °C. Zero on the absolute scale is −273·16 °C.

absorptiometer a device used to measure the absorption of light.

acetal a compound derived from an alcohol and an aldehyde or a ketone.

acetate an ester of acetic acid.

acetic acid an old name for ethanoic acid.

acetin an acetate derived from glycerol.

acetylation the introduction of one or more acetyl groups, CH_3CO, into organic compounds.

acid a substance able to form hydrogen ions when in solution, whether in water or in a non-aqueous solvent.

acid-base indicator an indicator that has a markedly different colour in acid and base solutions. The difference in colour is due to the ionized and non-ionized forms of the indicator.

acid rain pollution caused by sulphur and nitrogen oxides released into the environment by burning fuels.

actinides a series of radioactive elements, many of them artificially produced by irradiation. The series comprises actinium, thorium, protactinium, uranium, neptunium, plutonium, americium, curium, berkelium, californium, einsteinium, fermium, mendelevium and nobelium.

acyl a group left after the –OH group has been removed from carboxylic acid.

addition reaction a reaction in which unsaturated carbon bonds are saturated to give single bonds.

adhesive a substance that wets surfaces that are to be stuck together and then solidifies to form the actual joint.

adiabatic process a thermodynamic process by which heat is neither added to nor allowed to leave a system.

adsorbate a substance that is adsorbed on to an adsorbent.

adsorbent a substance that provides an adsorption surface.

adsorption the process by which free atoms or molecules become attached to a surface.

aerosol fine particles of a solid or liquid suspended in air.

alcohol an organic compound in which hydroxyl––OH group or groups are attached to carbon atoms.

aldehyde an organic compound in which a –CHO group is attached to a carbon atom.

aliphatic organic compounds with carbon atoms arranged in chains rather than rings.

alkali a substance that gives a pH of greater than 7 in water.

alkanes (formerly known as paraffins) the principal constituents of petroleum. These organic compounds have the general formula C_nH_{2n+2}.

alkenes aliphatic hydrocarbons containing one double C=C bond. They have the general formula C_nH_{2n}.

alkyd resins compounds used extensively in paints and other coatings. They are formed by condensation reactions between polybasic acids and polyhydric alcohols.

alkyls aliphatic hydrocarbons with the final hydrogen atom removed.

allotropy the existence of an element in more than one physical form in the same physical state, e.g. carbon as diamond and graphite.

alloy a combination of two or more metals, or of metallic and non-metallic elements. The physical characteristics of this combination are metallic.

alum potassium alum – $KAl(SO_4)_2.12H_2O$ – a compound used in a variety of industrial processes including dyeing, paper manufacture, and waterproofing.

alumina aluminium oxide, Al_2O_3.

aluminates compounds containing an Al^{3+} ion in anions that are hydroxide or oxide based.

amalgam compounds of a metal and mercury. They can be both liquid and solid.

amides organic compounds derived from carboxylic acids.

amines organic compounds based on ammonia. One or more of the hydrogen atoms in the ammonia molecule is substituted by alkyl groups to give primary, secondary and tertiary amines.

amino acids organic compounds containing the amino group, $–NH_2$, and the carboxyl group, –COOH. Proteins are built up from amino acids.

ammonia a pungent gas with a strong alkaline reaction.

ammonium a cation, $(NH_4)^+$, that behaves similarly to the alkali metal cations.

amphoteric having both acid and basic properties.

aniline an important organic chemical used in the dye industry. Based on the benzene ring, its formula is $C_6H_5.NH_2$. Also called phenylamine.

anion a negatively charged ion occurring in crystals, solutions and melts.

anisotropic having different properties in different directions, e.g. an anisotropic crystal has different physical properties along different crystal axes.

annealing a reduction of the stresses within a metal by heating it and then cooling it in a controlled fashion.

anode (in electrolysis) the positive electrode.

aromatic an organic compound based on the benzene ring, C_6H_6. The benzene ring is stable, even though the carbon atoms within it are unsaturated.

It therefore undergoes substitution reactions rather than addition reactions.

aryls an aromatic hydrocarbon with a hydrogen atom removed.

asbestos any of a group of silicate minerals. The SiO_4 groups are linked together into chains, giving the characteristic fibrous texture.

atom the smallest particle of a chemical element.

atomic mass unit one-twelfth of the mass of a carbon-12 atom. It is equivalent to 1.66×10^{-27} kg, approximately the mass of a proton or neutron.

atomic number the number of protons in the nucleus of an atom of an element.

atomic weight the old name for relative atomic mass.

Avogadro's number (symbol L) the number of atoms or molecules in one mole of any pure substance. $L = 6.023 \times 10^{23}$.

azo dyes a group of dyes containing the group $-N=N-$ linking two aromatic groups.

base a compound that acts as a proton acceptor and, on reaction with an acid, gives a salt and water.

benzene (C_6H_6) a colourless flammable liquid used as a solvent and an insecticide. The six carbon atoms are arranged in a ring. The bonds between the carbon atoms have characteristics between single and double bonds; they are said to resonate between the two, and as such are stable.

benzyl the $C_6H_5.CH_2-$ group.

bimolecular reaction a reaction in which only two molecular types react together, e.g.: $H_2 + I_2 \rightarrow 2HI$.

biuret reaction a test for peptides and proteins, in which the peptide linkage gives a pinkish colour with sodium hydroxide, NaOH, and copper sulphate, $CuSO_4$.

body-centred lattice a crystal structure in which atoms or molecules occur at the corners of each crystal cell and at the centre of the body of the crystal cell.

bond the link that holds atoms together in molecules and that is also the basis of crystal structure. Bonds may be covalent, ionic or hydrogen bonds.

bond energy the amount of energy that must be supplied to break a covalent bond.

borates boric acid (H_3BO_3) salts.

borax a naturally occurring source of boron, $Na_2(B_4O_5(OH)_4 \cdot 8H_2O)$.

Bordeaux mixture copper sulphate, $CuSO_4$, and calcium hydroxide, $Ca(OH)_2$, mixed in water. It is used as a fungicide.

brass an alloy of copper and zinc. Two principal forms of brass are made, one containing less than 30% zinc, the other between 30% and 40% zinc.

brine a solution of sodium chloride, NaCl.

bromates salts with bromium oxy-anions. The term is commonly taken to mean the BrO_3^- oxyanion, but BrO^- and BrO_2^- oxy-anions are also found.

bromides salts of hydrogen bromide, HBr, based on the bromide ion, Br^-.

bronze a group of alloys of copper and, originally, tin, often with smaller amounts of other elements. The term can now mean copper alloys with no tin, e.g. aluminium bronze.

buffer a mixture of acid, or alkali, and an associ-ated salt, whose pH alters only gradually with the addition of more acid or alkali. The salt acts as a supply of anions or cations that combine with hydrogen or base ions.

butane a member of the alkane series, C_4H_{10}. It is widely used in cylinders and canisters as camping gas.

carboxylic acid an organic acid containing a carboxyl group, $-COOH$.

calcite a form of naturally occurring calcium-carbonate, $CaCO_3$, found as chalk, limestone and marble.

calcium carbonate the most commonly occurring salt of calcium, $CaCO_3$. See also calcite.

camphor ($C_{10}H_{16}O$) an extract from the wood of the camphor tree. Also manufactured, it is used in medicines, as insect-repellent and in plastics.

carbohydrates naturally occurring compounds used as energy compounds, energy stores and for structural uses. The general formula for carbohydrates is $C_xH_{2y}O_y$.

carbonates salts of carbonic acid, H_2CO_3. The carbonate ion is CO_3^{2-} and forms a number of commercially important salts, including calcium carbonate.

carbon dioxide (CO_2) a product of respiration and a constituent of air. It represents the complete combustion of carbon.

carbon monoxide (CO) a toxic gas formed by the incomplete combustion of carbon.

carotene ($C_{40}H_{56}$) a precursor of vitamin A. It occurs naturally in plants as one of the chief colouring pigments, and is also found in many animal tissues.

catalyst a substance that speeds up the rate of a chemical reaction without being permanently chemically altered by the reaction.

catalytic converter a device containing platinum and rhodium metals fitted to car exhausts to reduce emissions of carbon monoxide, nitrogen oxides and hydrocarbon pollutants.

cathode (in electrolysis) the negative electrode.

cation a positively charged ion, occurring in crystals, solutions and melts.

cellulose ($C_6H_{10}O_5)_n$ the principal structural component of cell walls, formed by the polymerization of glucose.

ceramics hard non-metallic inorganic materials with high melting points, e.g. enamels, pottery, porcelain, abrasives.

CFC abbreviation for chlorofluorocarbons. Used as refrigerants and in aerosols, CFCs are now believed to damage the ozone layer.

chain reaction a process by which the product of one reaction takes part in a further reaction, the products of which take part in yet more reactions, etc.

chalk a naturally occurring form of calcium carbonate, $CaCO_3$.

charcoal a form of carbon produced by the slow burning of wood in conditions in which the supply of air is limited.

chiral a molecule that cannot be superimposed

on its mirror image.

chlorates　chlorine oxy-acid salts, formed from the ClO^-, ClO_2^-, ClO_3^- and ClO_4^- ions.

chlorides　compounds containing the Cl^- ion.

chlorofluorocarbons　see CFCs.

chlorophyll　a complex organic chemical colouring matter found in green plants. It is an essential constituent of the photosynthetic process, by which carbohydrates are produced in plants from carbon dioxide and water, using the energy of sunlight.

cholesterol　$(C_{27}H_{46}O)$　a complex organic chemical based on the sterol ring structure. It is found in animals, particularly in membranes, and also in some plants, e.g. some vegetable oils, such as coconut oil.

chromates　salts based on chromic acid, i.e. containing the CrO_4^{2-} and $Cr_2O_7^{2-}$ ions.

chromatography　a technique for separating the components of a mixture by distribution between a mobile phase, e.g. water, and a stationary phase, e.g. paper.

clay　naturally occurring aluminosilicates consisting of $AlSiO_4$, together with $Mg(OH)_2$ and $Al(OH)_3$.

coenzymes　compounds necessary for the action of enzymes. They may be altered during the course of the reaction, but will be re-formed during later reactions.

colloids　small particles, larger than atoms or molecules but too small to be seen by a light microscope, usually found in suspension or solution.

complexion　a species formed by coordination of a metal ion to other ions or molecules, e.g. Fe^{3+} and CN^- ions give $Fe(CN)_6^{3-}$.

concentration　see molarity.

condensation reaction　a reaction in which two molecules react together to give one product molecule plus a simple molecule such as water, H_2O.

conformation　the shape taken by a molecule owing to the positioning a group may have in relation to a bond. In complex organic molecules the conformation may affect physical properties.

copolymer　a polymer resulting from the combination of two or more monomers.

covalent bond　a chemical bond in which two atoms are linked by sharing two electrons – one electron originating from each atom.

crude oil　a naturally occurring mixture of hydrocarbons, often mixed with water, sulfur and other inorganic impurities.

crystal　a solid particle with a regular geometric shape caused by the regular arrangement of atoms or ions or molecules.

crystallization　the process by which crystals of a substance are removed from a solution by increasing the concentration above the saturation point.

cyanates　salts formed from the cyanate ion, NCO^-.

cyanides　salts formed from the cyanide ion, CN^-.

deliquescence　the absorption of water by a solid to give a solution.

detergent　a water-soluble surface-active agent that can wet surfaces and help to loosen oil and grease. Detergents invariably consist of a hydrophobic group that allows them to dissolve the oils and grease, and a hydrophilic group that promotes water-solubility.

dextrose　see glucose.

dialysis　the purification of a colloidal mixture by the diffusion of impurities through a semipermeable membrane.

diamond　a naturally occurring crystalline form of carbon.

dicarboxylic acids　organic acids containing two carboxyl groups –COOH.

dienes　organic chemicals with two carbon–carbon double bonds.

diffusion　the movement of a gas or liquid caused by the random movement of its atoms or molecules.

diketones　organic compounds with two keto groups – CO.

dimer　a polymer consisting of two molecules of a monomer.

distillation　the separation of two liquids or a liquid from a solid by evaporation and recondensation.

doping　the introduction of impurities into a crystal lattice, giving different electrical or other properties to the crystal.

double bond　two atoms sharing two pairs of electrons, i.e. two covalent bonds.

dry ice　solid carbon dioxide (CO_2).

EDTA　ethylenediaminetetra-acetic acid, an acid that forms complexes with most metal ions.

efflorescence　the formation of a powdery solid from crystals (by the loss of water of crystallization) or from liquids (by evaporation).

elastomer　a material with elastic properties, e.g. rubber.

electrochemical series　a series in which the elements are placed in decreasing order of oxidation potential. An element higher up the series will displace from solution an element lower down the series.

electrolysis　the decomposition of a substance in solution by the passage of an electric current.

electrolyte　a substance that – in solution – dissociates into ions. It can thus act as an electric conductor.

electronegativity　the degree to which an atom in a molecule attracts electrons to itself. In general, values of electronegativity decrease from right to left and from top to bottom of the Periodic Table of elements.

element　a substance formed of atoms all with the same atomic number.

emulsion　a dispersed colloid of one liquid in another.

enantiomers　isomers that are non-superimposable mirror images of each other in the spatial arrangement of their constituent atoms.

endothermic reaction　a reaction in which

heat is absorbed.

enthalpy (symbol: *H*) the thermodynamic function of a system equal to the sum of its internal energy and the product of its pressure and volume.

entropy (symbol *S*) a parameter used to describe the disorder or chaos of a system. The greater the disorder of a system, the greater the entropy.

enzyme a protein that catalyses one specific chemical reaction in a living organism.

epimer a type of isomer that differs in the configuration around only one of a number of atoms.

epoxy an oxygen atom joined to two different groups that are also joined to other groups.

equilibrium any state in which the properties do not change with time, e.g. in a reversible reaction it is the stage at which the rate of the forward reaction equals the rate of the reverse reaction.

ester the product of a condensation reaction between an organic acid and an alcohol.

ethane (C_2H_6) a naturally occurring constituent of natural gas; it is also extensively synthesized.

ethanoic acid (CH_3) the modern name for acetic acid. Vinegar is impure dilute ethanoic acid.

ethanol (CH_3CH_2OH) the systematic name for ethyl alcohol or alcohol. Although originally produced as result of fermentation, most ethanol is now synthesized.

ethene ($CH_2=CH_2$) the systematic name for ethylene.

ether ($C_2H_5OC_2H_5$) a volatile flammable liquid used as a solvent or as an anaesthetic. Otherwise known as diethyl ether and ethoxyethane.

ethers compounds with the general formula R^1-O-R^2, where R^1 and R^2 are alkyl or aryl groups.

ethyne the systematic name for acetylene.

eutectic a mixture of two substances having the lowest melting point of any such mixture.

evaporation the conversion of a liquid to a vapour at a temperature below its boiling point.

fats compounds of fatty acids and glycerol.

fatty acids organic acids consisting of an alkyl group attached to a carboxyl group, with the general formula $C_nH_{2n}O_2$.

Fehling's solution a solution of copper sulphate, sodium potassium tartrate and sodium hydroxide, used for testing for reducing sugars.

fermentation the use of microorganisms to break down substances and release, generally, useful products, e.g. the fermentation of sugar by yeasts, yielding alcohol and carbon dioxide.

ferrates oxy-anions of iron, incorporating the FeO_4^{2-} ion.

ferric compounds compounds incorporating Fe(III) iron.

ferrous compounds compounds incorporating Fe(II) iron.

flash point the temperature to which a substance must be heated before it can be ignited.

flocculation the coagulation of a colloid into larger particles.

fluorescein ($C_{20}H_{12}O_5$) a red crystalline substance that fluoresces bright green.

fluorides the salts of hydrogen fluoride, HF.

foam a dispersion of bubbles of gas in a liquid or solid.

fractional crystallization the separation of two or more substances by using changes in solubility with temperature. As the temperature is lowered, one substance will crystallize out first, then another, and so on.

fractional distillation the separation of two or more substances by evaporating the mixture, allowing the vapours to pass up a fractionating column. The various fractions collected are condensed at different points up the column, depending on their volatility.

free radical an atom or group of atoms with unpaired electrons. It is therefore very reactive.

gas a substance that does not resist change of shape. Gases will expand spontaneously to fill a container. The intermolecular attractions are very weak and the constituent atoms or molecules show random movement.

gasification the conversion of a solid or liquid to a gas with lower molecular weight. Gasification is usually applied to the conversion of hydrocarbon solids and liquids to fuel gases.

gasoline a mixture of various hydrocarbons used as motor fuel or aviation fuel.

gel a colloid suspension in which the particles are linked by a form of partial coagulation to form a jelly.

gelatin a protein made by boiling collagen in dilute acid.

glucose ($C_6H_{12}O_6$) the most common hexose sugar; also known as dextrose. Found in plants and animals, it is the constituent monomer of cellulose, starch, glycogen, etc.

glue a colloid mixture of proteins. It is prepared from animal waste containing collagen.

gluten a protein from wheat dough.

glycerides the esters produced from glycerol. Depending on how many of the hydroxyl groups in the glycerol molecule combine with acid radicals, the glycerides are called mono-, di- or tri-glycerides.

glycerol an odourless syrupy liquid that is also known as glycerin or 1,2,3- trihydroxypropane.

gram molecule a mole.

graphite a crystalline form of carbon, occurring naturally. It consists of flat sheets of hexagonal cells, which slip easily over each other, giving graphite its characteristic properties.

group in the Periodic Table of elements, a group is a vertical column of elements. A group will have distinct properties and characteristics in common.

haem a complex three-dimensional molecule with the formula $C_{34}H_{32}FeN_4O_4$. Haem is an important constituent of a number of active biochemicals, including haemoglobin. It has an iron atom at its centre, which can act as an electron carrier, changing from the ferrous to the ferric state and back again.

halogenation the addition or substitution of halogen atoms to a molecule.

halogens the elements making up group VII in the Periodic Table, consisting of fluorine, chlorine, bromine, iodine and astatine.

hard water water containing calcium and magnesium salts. Soft water lacks these salts.

hexanes liquid alkanes. A group of chemicals with the formula C_6H_{14}.

hexose a carbohydrate containing six carbon atoms. Glucose is the most important of the hexoses.

hydration the addition of water to a substance, particularly to ions, e.g.: $H^+ + H_2O \rightarrow H_3O^+$

hydrocarbons compounds of hydrogen and carbon only.

hydrochloric acid an aqueous solution of hydrogen chloride, HCl.

hydrogenation a form of reduction in which hydrogen gas is used to add hydrogen to a compound.

hydrogen bond a weak bond between an electronegative atom, e.g. oxygen, and a hydrogen atom covalently bonded to another electronegative atom.

hydrolysis a reaction in which water combines with a compound.

hydroxylation the introduction of a hydroxyl group, OH^-, into a molecule.

imides organic compounds containing the –CO–NH–CO–group.

imines organic compounds containing the –NH–group. The nitrogen atom is not linked to a carbonyl group or hydrogen atom.

indicator a substance that shows the presence of a particular compound or group of compounds by a characteristic colour. Indicators are used to show when the completion of a titration has occurred.

indole an organic double-ring structure based on the formula C_8H_7N.

inorganic chemistry the chemistry of all elements and molecules other than those containing carbon. Compare organic chemistry.

ion an atom or molecule that has lost or gained one or more electrons, thereby carrying a positive or negative charge. See also anion, cation.

ionic bond a chemical bond due to the electrostatic force of attraction between oppositely charged ions in a crystal lattice.

isocyanates organic compounds containing the group $-N=C=O$.

isomers compounds with the same molecular formula, but having different arrangements of atoms bonded together or existing in different three-dimensional structures due to a differing orientation about certain atoms.

isomorphism the existence of different compounds with the same crystal structure.

isonitriles organic compounds containing the group –N–C. Otherwise known as isocyanides or carbylamines.

isotonic (of two solutions) having the same osmotic pressure.

isotopes atoms of an element having the same number of protons but differing numbers of neutrons.

ketones organic compounds with the general formula R^1-CO-R^2, where R^1 and R^2 are generally alkyl groups.

lactose a disaccharide sugar with the formula $C_{12}H_{22}O_{11}$. It occurs in varying amounts in the milk of all animals.

lanthanides a series of related metallic elements with atomic numbers between 57 and 71. The series comprises lanthanum, cerium, praseodymium, neodymium, promethium, samarium, europium, gadolinium, terbium, dysprosium, holmium, erbium, thulium, ytterbium, lutetium.

lattice the regular three-dimensional arrangement of atoms in a crystal.

lime water a solution of calcium hydroxide, $Ca(OH)_2$.

liquefied petroleum gas hydrocarbon gases produced as a result of refining petroleum and liquefied under pressure. It occurs as butane and propane, although neither is a pure form of the gas.

liquid crystal a phase formed by certain substances that has the mobility of a liquid but a definite ordered structure. It is used in display units, e.g. in pocket calculators.

litmus a colouring obtained from lichens. It is used as an indicator to detect pH changes.

macromolecules large molecules with molecular weight in excess of 10 000.

magnesium alloys a group of very light alloys.

manganates salts containing the ion MnO_4^{2-}.

mercaptans a group of organic compounds containing the – SH group linked to a carbon atom. Mercaptans are otherwise known as thiols.

meta- a prefix denoting the position of groups attached to the benzene ring.

metals elements that are malleable, lustrous, and conduct heat and electricity. They tend to form cations.

methanal (HCHO) the systematic name for formaldehyde.

methane (CH_4) a gas that occurs naturally as a result of the decay of vegetable matter; othewise known as marsh gas.

methanol (CH_3OH) a volatile liquid used as a solvent and as a fuel. It is also known as methyl alcohol.

methylation the addition of a methyl group, $-CH_3$, to an organic compound.

micelle a submicroscopic aggregate of molecules.

miscibility the ability of one substance to mix with another.

molar volume the volume occupied by 1 mole of a substance in the gaseous state.

molarity the strength of a solution, usually measured by the number of moles of a substance dissolved in 1 litre of the solution; otherwise called concentration.

mole (formerly known as a gram molecule) the amount of substance that contains the same number of elementary entities (molecules, ions, atoms, etc.) as there are in 0.012 kg of carbon-12.

molecular weight the ratio of the mass per molecule of a substance to one atomic mass unit (1/12 of the mass of a carbon-12 atom).

molecule the smallest independent particle of a compound that can exist, containing two or more atoms linked by chemical bonds.

monotropy the existence of a substance in only one stable crystalline form.

naphthalene ($C_{10}H_8$) a double benzene ring structure.

natural gas a mixture of over 90% methane with other hydrocarbon gases, as well as nitrogen and carbon dioxide.

ninhydrin ($C_9H_4O_3.H_2O$) an indicator that gives

a blue colour on heating with amino acids and proteins.

nitrates salts of nitric acid, containing the ion NO_3.

nitric acid (HNO_3) a corrosive liquid that has many important industrial uses, including the manufacture of fertilizers.

nitrides compounds of nitrogen and other elements.

nitrites salts of nitrous acid, containing the ion NO_2.

nitro compounds a group of aromatic compounds with the basic formula $R-NO_2$.

noble gases a group of unreactive gases. The group comprises helium, neon, argon, krypton, xenon, and radon. Traces of all these gases are found in the atmosphere.

nylons a group of synthetic plastics and fibres, largely formed by condensation polymerization.

octanes a group of hydrocarbons with eight carbon atoms and the basic formula C_8H_{18}. The group falls in the alkane series, and the constituents are all found in crude oil.

optical activity the ability of certain substances to rotate the polarization plane of polarized light, due to the asymmetry of the molecules.

organic chemistry the chemistry of the almost infinite number of actual or potential compounds containing carbon.

ortho- a prefix denoting the position of groups attached to the benzene ring.

osmotic pressure the excess pressure that must be applied to prevent the flow of solvent through a semipermeable membrane between a solvent and solution.

oxidation the process by which a substance loses electrons, e.g. $Fe^{2+} \rightarrow Fe^{3+} + e$.

oxide a compound containing oxygen and other elements.

oximes a group of organic compounds containing $=N.OH$ linked to a carbon atom.

oxonium a positive ion with the basic formula R_3O^+, where R is hydrogen or an organic group, e.g. the hydroxonium ion H_3O^+.

ozone (O_3) an allotrope of oxygen. A layer of ozone in the upper atmosphere absorbs harmful radiation from the sun.

para- a prefix denoting the position of groups attached to the benzene ring.

patina an oxide layer formed on metals and alloys.

pentanes a group of hydrocarbons with five carbon atoms and the basic formula C_5H_{12}. The constituents are all found in crude oil.

pentose a carbohydrate containing five carbon atoms.

peptides chains of two or more amino acids linked by a peptide linkage, $-CO-NH-$. Peptide chains are arranged in three-dimensional structures to form proteins.

period a period in the Periodic Table of elements is a horizontal series of elements, from an alkali metal to a noble gas. Compare group.

Periodic Table the arrangement of elements in a table in order of increasing atomic number so that similarities between elements are emphasized (see p. 227).

permanganates a group of salts containing the MnO_4^- ion.

peroxides derivatives of hydrogen peroxide, H_2O_2, containing linked pairs of oxygen atoms.

pH the logarithm (base 10) of the reciprocal of the concentration of hydrogen ions in a solution, giving a measure of the acidity or alkalinity of a solution.

phenol ($C_6H_5 \cdot OH$) an aromatic hydroxy compound.

phenolphthalein ($C_{20}H_{14}O_4$) an aromatic compound used as an indicator.

phenyl the aromatic group C_6H_5-.

phosphates salts based on the PO_4^{3-} and $P_2O_7^{4-}$ ions.

phosphoric acid an oxy-acid of phosphorus, the best known being H_3PO_4.

phosphors substances that phosphoresce, i.e. absorb radiation and re-emit after removal of radiation source.

phosphorus acid oxy-acids of phosphorus (III), the best known being H_3PO_3.

plastics artificial organic polymers that can be moulded to shape.

polyesters polymers formed by condensation reactions between polybasic acids and polyhydric alcohols.

polymers a compound consisting of long-chain molecules made up of repeating molecular units.

polymorphism a substance existing in more than one crystalline form.

polysaccharides carbohydrates formed by condensation reactions between monosaccharides.

precipitation the production of an insoluble compound in a solution by a chemical reaction.

propane $CH_3.CH_2.CH_3$. A constituent of natural gas. An alkane.

proteins a large group of naturally occurring organic compounds consisting of chains of amino acids folded into complex three-dimensional molecules. Proteins are the basic structural materials of all living organisms.

radical an atom or molecule that has one or more free valencies.

rare earths the lanthanide series of elements.

rectification fractional distillation used to separate an organic liquid into its constituent parts.

redox simultaneous oxidation and reduction occurring in one chemical reaction.

reduction the process by which a substance gains electrons, e.g. $Cu^{2+} + 2e \rightarrow Cu$.

relative atomic mass the average mass of one atom of an element divided by one-twelfth of the mass of one atom of carbon-12.

resin a solid natural or synthetic polymer.

reversible reaction a reaction that can proceed in either direction. Such a reaction usually attains an equilibrium, depending on the concentrations of the reactants and the physical conditions.

ribose a pentose sugar, $C_5H_{10}O_5$, found in the nucleic acids.

rust a coating of impure hydrated iron (III) oxide found on iron.

salt (in popular usage) sodium chloride, NaCl; (in chemistry) the product of the reaction between a base and an acid.

sand a mixture of SiO_2 and other minerals, formed by the degradation of rocks.

saponification the hydrolysis of an ester using an alkali.

saturated compound a compound in which there are no double or triple bonds, only single bonds.

silica silicon dioxide, SiO_2, one of the most common constituents of the earth's crust.

silicates compounds containing the $SiO_4{}^{4-}$ ion. However, the term extends to cover a wide range of minerals based on the SiO_4 tetrahedral crystal structure.

silicones organic polymers that contain –Si–O–Si– linkages.

single bond a bond between two atoms involving two electrons in a single bonding orbital.

sintering the fusion of two or more substances by heating powders together under pressure at a temperature below their melting point.

soap the salt of a fatty acid.

solders alloys used to join metals together. The solder melts at a temperature below that of the metals.

solution a single-phase homogeneous mixture of two or more compounds; one of the compounds is often a liquid in which the solute is dissolved.

standard temperature and pressure (abbreviated to STP) a temperature of 273·15 K and a pressure of 101·325 kPa.

starch a naturally occurring polymer of glucose.

strength the ability of an acid or alkali to give hydroxonium ions, H_3O^+.

sublimation the change from a solid to a gaseous state without passing through a liquid state.

substitution a displacement reaction in which one atom or group in a molecule is replaced by another atom or group.

substrate the substance on which an enzyme acts.

sucrose a disaccharide carbohydrate with the formula $C_{12}H_{22}O_{11}$.

sugars carbohydrates generally based on six- or twelve-carbon atoms. They are crystalline, soluble in water and sweet to taste. They include sucrose, glucose (dextrose), lactose, and fructose.

sulfates salts based on the $SO_4{}^{2-}$ ion.

sulfides compounds of elements and sulfur, usually based on the S^{2-} ion.

sulfites salts based on the $SO_3{}^{2-}$ ion.

sulfuric acid a colourless liquid, H_2SO_4.

superconductor a substance that exhibits zero electrical resistance, usually at very low temperature.

superphosphate a mixture of calcium hydrogen phosphate, $Ca(H_2PO_4)_2$, and calcium sulphate, $CaSO_4$. It is used as a fertilizer.

surface active agents mainly organic substances that reduce surface tension when dissolved in water. They are also known as surfactants.

tellurates salts containing oxy-anions of tellurium, i.e. $TeO_6{}^{6-}$ and $TeO_3{}^{2-}$ ions.

terpenes volatile aromatic hydrocarbons with the formula $(C_5H_8)_n$. They are naturally occurring in the essential oils of many plants.

thermoplastics plastics that can be repeatedly softened by heating and hardened by cooling.

thio- containing sulfur.

titration the determination of the amount of one substance needed to react with a fixed amount of another substance. The endpoint is determined by a change in property, e.g. change in colour.

transition elements a series of elements with an incomplete inner shell of electrons. On the Periodic Table (see p. 227) they comprise scandium to zinc, yttrium to cadmium, and lanthanum to mercury.

triple bond a bond formed by three pairs of electrons shared between two atoms.

valency (also known as oxidation state) the difference between the number of electrons attached to an atom of the free element and the number of electrons associated with an atom of the element in a compound.

van der Waals' bonds weak forces between molecules due to electronic coupling.

vapour pressure the pressure of a vapour produced by a solid or liquid. In a closed system a saturated vapour pressure will eventually be established, at which the vapour will be in equilibrium with the solid or liquid.

vinegar a dilute solution of ethanoic acid.

vinyl the $CH_2=CH$ groups, otherwise known as ethenyl.

water oxygen hydride, H_2O.

zeolites aluminosilicates that have a negatively charged framework with cations present in cavities. They are used to separate mixtures, and to soften water, and as catalysts.

COMPUTING GLOSSARY

ADA a language developed for the US Defense Department to allow programming of missile-detection and similar systems with the minimum of flaws (bugs).

addressing selecting memory by using a number unique to a unit memory applied in binary form along address lines.

ALGOL a third-generation language. ALGOL was the first to concentrate on logical as distinct from mathematical processing needs.

ALU abbreviation for arithmetic and logic unit, the central part of any microprocessor.

analogue (analog) computer a computer that deals with data having physical quantity and which is constantly changing. These changes are represented by changes in voltages. The output – which may be graphed instantly by a plotting pen – can in turn drive another device. Analogue computers operate in real-time, as events occur, rather than handling previously stored and coded data as a digital computer does.

archive data stored in a form intended for long-term retention.

artificial intelligence the field of computing science involving the development of computer programs intended to simulate human learning and decision-making abilities. (See also Turing test.)

assembly language a low-level programming language that uses abbreviated commands that can easily be translated, using a program, into machine code.

backing store a storage system that is non-volatile (usually magnetic). This will retain large quantities of data when the computer is switched off.

BASIC acronym for Beginners All-Purpose Symbolic Instruction Code, a language developed originally for teaching FORTRAN but now recognized in its own right. Lack of standardization is the main drawback to use of BASIC.

binary code the representation of symbols or characters by patterns of 0s and 1s, which on a computer can be represented by electric current being turned off and on.

bit (from BInary digiT) the smallest unit of information (a 0 or a 1) that can be recognized by a computer.

bug a fault in a program. This may be minor (requiring a key to be pressed twice) or major (causing a program to 'crash').

bulletin board a computer-linked database for holding messages and information.

byte a unit of measurement for computer memory capacity. A byte usually contains eight bits. Each byte corresponds to one character of data: a single letter, number or symbol.

C a third-generation language of great power and flexibility. An object-orientated version called C++ is also available. Criticized on the grounds of obscurity ('a read-only language'), C is widely used for writing other programs.

CD-ROM a CD-type of disk that can be read by a conventional laser reader. It contains digital data from computers as distinct from digital representation of sound.

character any symbol (including numbers, letters, punctuation marks, mathematical symbols, etc.) capable of being stored and processed by a computer.

chip or **microchip** a small piece of crystal (usually silicon or other semiconductor material) printed and etched in a pattern to form a logical circuit (an integrated circuit).

circuit the complete path of an electrical current.

clock an electronic circuit that provides electrical pulses at regular intervals to produce timing for the microprocessor actions. Clock rates of 16 MHz (16 million pulses per second) are common.

clone a close copy of a machine that will run the same software. Only the PC type of machine has been extensively cloned.

COBOL acronym for Common Business Orientated Language, the first (and main) language intended for writing data-processing programs for business use.

compiler a program that will convert the statements (commands) of a programming language into machine code that can be run in one step.

conductor a substance (such as a metal) that enables the passage of electricity.

crash a total program failure. This may result in the loss of all data held in memory.

cursor a small block or arrow on the computer screen to show the position of where the next keyed instruction will be implemented.

data raw material such as characters or symbols stored in a computer from which 'information' is derived after processing.

database a structured collection of data that can be analysed and interrogated on computer to retrieve items (or combinations of items) that match selected criteria.

digital computer a computer that deals with data in binary-coded number form as distinct from the variable-voltage signals used in analogue computers.

disk a magnetic disk for storing data. See floppy disk, hard disk.

dot-matrix the method of representing characters by a set of dots either on the VDU screen or on paper when a dot-matrix printer is used.

electronic mail information directed to specific users' screens or held in 'computer mailboxes' for access by users who type in codes. Information held on a bulletin board (see above) can be accessed by any user.

fibre optics the use of thin glass fibres to carry light signals. This is now replacing the use of copper cable carrying electronic signals. Digital computers can use any medium that represents on and off signals; light is faster than electric current, and fibre optic cables can carry a far greater density of signals than can the equivalent size of electric cable.

fifth-generation language a computer language that involves the ability to make decisions and to learn. A computer using a fifth-generation language is addressed in normal language rather than in a programming language.

floppy disk a magnetic data-storage disk that is removable from the medium. Early disks were contained in cardboard envelopes and were floppy, but later versions use rigid plastic containers. Floppy disks operate at lower speeds and can handle less data than hard disks.

FORTRAN acronym for Formula Translation, one of the first programming languages for scientific and engineering uses.

fourth-generation language a computer language that requires no description of procedures, only a list of data and what is needed to be processed. The output of a 4GL is generally a set of commands in a third-generation language, usually Pascal or C.

hacker (originally) a skilled mender of faulty programs. The term now refers to a person who gains illegal access to other computers either mischievously or for criminal intent.

hard disk a magnetic data-storage disk that is not removable from the medium (except on mainframe machines). It operates at much higher speeds and with much greater amounts of data than the removable (floppy) disks.

hardware all the electronics and mechanical parts of the computer as distinct from the programs and data (the software).

hard-wired restricted functioning of a computer, limited by soldered connections and not responsive to varying software commands.

ikon a screen picture that represents a standard computer function. A typical example would be an onscreen 'wastebasket' to which a user can point to delete a file.

ink-jet a form of printer mechanism in which ink is squirted from a matrix or tiny jets on to the paper.

integrated circuit see chip.

interface an electronic circuit that converts electronic signals from one form to another or organizes the signals differently. An interface is needed to allow the computer to be connected to any other piece of equipment, including the disk system and the screen.

interpreter a program that allows the statements of a programming language to be run line-by-line.

K symbol for kilobyte.

keying in typing at a computer keyboard.

kilobyte (K) loosely one thousand bytes, although strictly 1 K = 2^{10} = 1024 bytes.

laptop a portable computer that can be battery-operated and is light enough to be used on the lap while travelling.

laser disk a disk – like an audio CD – capable of storing vast quantities of archive files in a minute area. It is prepared by focusing a narrow beam of light on to it. Its main use is archive storage of data (CD-ROM), but it can be used interactively (CDI).

machine-code the most elementary way of programming a computer by using binary codes directly.

mainframe a large computer whose stored data may be accessed by 100 or more terminals.

megabyte (Mb) loosely one million bytes, although strictly 1 Mb = 2^{20}.

memory usually refers to the currently accessible store (RAM). The term is sometimes used to refer to disk storage capabilities.

microchip see chip.

microprocessor a device capable of holding memory and instructions. A microprocessor is a basic unit of a microcomputer.

microcomputer a low-cost, independent computer unit based on the microprocessor. It requires low power and, unless linked to a network, has a limited memory.

minicomputer a small computer whose capabilities in speed, power and data handling are between those of a microcomputer and a mainframe. Minicomputers were developed during the American space research programme to meet the need for a small computer that could be moved on site.

modem a circuit that converts between digital signals and tone signals. It is used when computers need to communicate along telephone lines or radio links.

monitor see screen.

mouse a hand-held device that rolls across a table or board, its position reflecting the position of the cursor on the screen. It is used as an alternative to the computer keyboard to access a screen.

MS-DOS see operating system.

network a system of computers connected to each other through cables, by telephone, data communication technology or even by radio.

OCCAM a language developed specially for programming parallel-processing computers.

operating system a program that attends to all the routine tasks of running a computer, allowing other programs (applications programs) to make use of the disks, screen and keyboard, etc., without needing to write their own code for such operations. PC machines all use the MS-DOS operating system; many minicomputers use a system called UNIX (which requires vast amounts of memory). Mainframe machines normally use operating systems that are provided by the manufacturer.

parallel-processor a microprocessor that can be run in conjunction with another, sharing memory

and other parts of a computer system. One common example is the use of a mathematical co-processor along with the main processor in PC machines. A more complex type is the transputer.

PASCAL a programming language originally designed for academic uses by Niklaus Wirth, but now widely used for systems programming, particularly in the form of Turbo-pascal from Borland International.

port a form of interface used to connect a computer to other units such as the keyboard, printer or modem.

portable language any programming language for which a program can be written that will work on all computers for which a compiler or interpreter is available without modification to the program.

processor the central unit of a computer that carries out the actions of arithmetic and comparison. It controls all of the other units under the command of a program.

program a set of instructions that a system follows to carry out tasks.

Prestel the British Telecom videotext information service, designed to be received on home television sets and computers. The communications are carried on public telephone lines.

PROM Programmable Read-Only Memory. A chip that can be written by larger-than-normal signals and then used as a ROM, retaining its data. Data is erased by, for example, exposing the chip to ultra-violet light.

RAM Random Access Memory, memory available for current work. This is lost when the computer is switched off unless work is transferred out of the RAM on to permanent store such as a disk.

register a temporary store used in a processor to hold data while it is being used in arithmetic, logical or comparison actions.

relay switches switches controlled electromagnetically. They are typically used in analogue computers.

resistor a substance impeding the flow of a current.

ROM Read-Only Memory, a non-volatile memory (i.e. a memory that is not erased when the power is switched off) that must be present in any computer in order to make the machine usable. The ROM normally contains the commands that allow the machine to make use of its disk system so that further commands (of an operating system) can be read in.

scanner a device that transforms an image into digitally coded signals that can be stored on computer and redisplayed. Using scanners, printed text can be stored directly on to the disk without having to be keyed in.

screen the display device on a computer – also called a monitor, VDU (visual display unit) or VDT (visual display terminal). Screens basically use cathode-ray tube technology of television to create an image.

semiconductor a material, such as silicon, whose pure form has very low electrical conductivity but whose conductivity is enormously changed when traces of other elements are added – a process called *doping*. The movement of particles within the semiconductor allows its electrical conduction to be controlled by electrical signals, making it an electrically-operated switch.

silicon chip see chip, semiconductor.

software the programs that give instructions to, or run on, a computer, as opposed to the electronics and mechanical parts of a computer (the hardware).

spreadsheet a form of data-analysing program that can be used for a very wide range of applications ranging from word tables to the analysis of complex mathematical relationships. In this latter use, altering one item of data on the screen will result in the recalculation of all the other items that depend on that item. Spreadsheets are widely used for financial data and particularly in forecasting work.

terminal a device linked to a computer, comprising a keyboard or a screen, or both.

thermionic valve a device that uses metal plates to control the flow of electrons in a vacuum inside an evacuated tube. The electrons are emitted from a hot surface – the cathode – and the current between the cathode and the opposite surface – the anode – is controlled by the voltage on an intermediate grid. Thermionic valves were formerly used for electronics circuits before the invention of transistors.

transistor a device that transfers current across a resistor.

transputer a large, fast and powerful chip. When paired with another chip it enables a computer to carry out two tasks simultaneously.

Turing test a test for successful artificial intelligence that depends on a human not knowing that he or she is communicating with a computer. No computer has ever passed the Turing test.

UNIX see operating system.

user-friendly (of computer products) simple and easy-to-use.

vacuum tube the American name for the thermionic valve.

VDT see screen.

VDU see screen.

voice recognition a computer's ability to respond to spoken words.

volatile (of memory) losing all data when the power is disconnected. RAM in computers is generally volatile, making it important to save data to a backing store.

window a portion of a screen that is used as if it were an independent separate screen.

workstation the equipment used by a computer operator and, increasingly, the associated furniture, lighting and working environment.

WORM acronym for Write Once Read Many times – a form of optical disk that can be written as well as read by the computer using it.

PHYSICS GLOSSARY

A symbol for ampere.

Å symbol for Ångström.

Ar symbol for atomic weight.

absolute zero the lowest temperature theoretically possible, at which the random motion of the particles in a system is zero. It is equal to $-273 \cdot 15\,°C$ $= 0\,K = -459 \cdot 67\,°F$.

absorption spectrum a characteristic pattern of dark bands that appears in the spectrum – due to the absorption of light – when light of a continuous frequency passes through a medium into a spectroscope. The medium will absorb the wavelengths that it would normally emit if it were raised to a high enough temperature, i.e. the absorbed radiation excites atoms from the ground state to an excited state.

acceleration the rate of increase of velocity with time.

accelerator a large machine in which an electric field is used to increase the kinetic energy of charged particles such as electrons and protons by accelerating them. The stream of accelerated particles is guided into the desired path by a magnetic field.

acoustics the study and use of sound waves.

alpha (α) particle a helium nucleus that consists of two protons and two neutrons. It carries a positive charge.

alpha rays a stream of alpha particles, emitted by many radioactive substances. The alpha particles can be stopped by a piece of paper, i.e. they have a very low penetrating power.

alternating current an electric current that regularly reverses its direction in a circuit.

ammeter an instrument for measuring electric current.

amp or **ampere** (symbol A) the unit of electric current.

Ångström (symbol Å) 0.1 nanometre ($= 10^{-10}\,m$).

anion a negatively charged ion.

anode a positive electrode.

antimatter matter consisting of antiparticles, i.e. those with opposite charge but equal mass to their normal counterparts. For example, the antiparticle of an electron (negatively charged particle) is a positron (a positively charged particle). When a particle meets an antiparticle there is mutual annihilation. Anti-matter has never actually been detected but is theoretically necessary.

Archimedes' principle states that a body floating in a fluid displaces a weight of fluid equal to its own weight.

atom the smallest particle of a pure element that can take part in a chemical reaction (see p. 223).

atomic mass unit (symbol u) one-twelfth of the mass of a carbon-12 atom, which is approximately the mass of a proton or neutron.

atomic number (symbol Z) the number of protons in the nucleus of an atom of an element.

atomic weight (symbol A_r) the average mass of atoms in an element, in atomic mass units.

Avogadro's hypothesis states that equal volumes of all gases measured at the same temperature and pressure contain the same number of molecules.

background radiation low-intensity radiation resulting from bombardment of the earth by cosmic rays and from naturally occurring isotopes in soil, air, buildings, etc.

bar a unit of pressure equal to 10^5 pascals. The millibar (1/1000 bar) is used by meteorologists.

barometer a device for measuring atmospheric pressure.

becquerel (symbol Bq) a unit of radioactivity equal to one disintegration per second.

Becquerel rays alpha, beta and gamma rays emitted by uranium compounds.

beta (β) particle an electron emitted by a radioisotope during beta decay.

beta rays a stream of beta particles, emitted by nuclei of certain radioisotopes. They can penetrate thin metal foil.

betatron an accelerator producing high-energy electrons. They are accelerated by means of magnetic induction.

black body a body that absorbs all radiation falling on it.

boiling point the temperature at which the saturated vapour pressure of a liquid equals the external pressure.

boson a subatomic particle with symmetric wavefunction.

breeder reactor a nuclear reactor in which more fissile material is produced than is used.

Brownian movement the irregular movement of smoke particles, or of very small particles, e.g. pollen, in a liquid. The movement is due to molecular bombardment by moving molecules.

c the velocity of light in a vacuum, equal to $2{\cdot}99792458 \times 10^8$ m s^{-1} (approximately 300 000 km or 186 000 miles per second).

C symbol for capacitance.

calorimeter a device in which thermal measurements can be made.

candela (symbol cd) the unit of luminous intensity.

capacitance (symbol C) the ability of an isolated electrical conductor to store electrical charge.

capacitor a device containing one or more pairs of electrical conductors separated by insulators (the dielectric). It is used to store electrical charge.

capillarity the effect of surface tension on a liquid in a fine tube, causing the liquid to rise or fall in the tube.

cathode a negative electrode.

cathode ray tube a device used in TV sets, VDUs, etc. Electrons from a heated cathode are projected on to a phosphor screen. The intensity and movement of the electron beam can be controlled, and the phosphor screen converts the kinetic energy of the electrons into a bright spot of light.

Celsius scale the official name of the Centigrade temperature scale. The freezing point of water at normal atmospheric pressure is 0 °C, and the boiling point 100 °C (see p. 122).

centrifugal force the inertial force directed radially outwards, in equilibrium with the applied centripetal force.

cf symbol for candela.

centripetal force a lateral force that makes a body move in a circular path. It is directed towards the centre of the circle.

CGS the system of units based on the centimetre, gram and second. It has now been superseded by the more coherent SI system. See p. 189.

charge (symbol Q) the ability of some elementary particles, such as electrons and protons, to exert forces on one another. Like charges repel, unlike forces attract.

Ci symbol for curie.

concave curving inwards. Concave mirrors converge rays of light, concave lenses diverge them.

conductor any substance (such as a metal) that offers a relatively low resistance to an electric current. (See insulator.)

conservation of mass and energy the principle that, in any system, the sum of the mass and energy is always constant.

conservation of momentum the principle that, in any system, the linear or angular momentum remains the same unless there is an external force acting on the system.

convection the transfer of heat in a fluid by movement of the fluid.

convex curving outwards. A convex mirror diverges rays of light, a convex lens converges them.

cosmic rays particle radiation reaching the earth from space.

cryogenics the study and production of very low temperatures.

curie (symbol Ci) the unit of activity of a radioactive substance. It corresponds to $3{\cdot}7 \times 10^{10}$ disintegrations per second, and is about equal to the activity of 1 g of radium.

current (symbol I) the rate of flow of electricity. The unit is the ampere.

cyclotron an accelerator in which the beam of charged particles follows a spiral path.

decay the breakdown of a radioactive nuclide into a daughter product by disintegration.

decibel one-tenth of a bel. (A bel is a logarithmic unit for comparing two amounts of power.) One decibel represents an increase in intensity of about 26 per cent – about the smallest increase that the ear can detect. (The decibel is *not* a measure of loudness, as the sensitivity of the ear varies with frequency.)

densitometer an instrument for measuring the density of a substance.

density (symbol r) the mass per unit volume of a substance, usually measured in kilograms per cubic metre.

dielectric an insulator that has very low electrical conductivity.

diffraction the phenomenon of waves appearing to travel round corners. It occurs when a wavefront meets a narrow slit or obstacle (see p. 197).

diffractometer an instrument used to measure the intensities of diffracted X-rays or neutron beams at different angles to each other.

diffusion the process by which substances – atoms, molecules, or groups of molecules – mix due to the kinetic motions of the particles.

diode an electronic device with only two electrodes.

direct current an electric current that flows in one direction only and is reasonably constant in magnitude.

discharge the passage of electric current through a gas-discharge tube, usually with luminous effects.

disintegration the emission of particles by a nucleus, either after a collision or spontaneously.

dispersion the process by which a beam of white light is spread out to produce spectra.

Döppler effect the apparent change in frequency of a harmonic wave (e.g. light or sound) when there is relative motion along a line between the source and the observer.

dynamo a machine that converts mechanical energy into electrical energy; a generator.

e the charge on an electron.

earth a connection between an electrical circuit and the earth, which has an electronic potential of zero.

efficiency (symbol h) the ratio of the useful energy output of a machine to the energy input. A perfect machine would have an efficiency of 1.

Einstein's law ($E = mc^2$) the law of equivalence of mass and energy, whereby the product of a mass m and the square of the speed of light c has energy E, and vice versa.

elasticity the ability of a substance to return to its original size and shape after being deformed.

electric field strength (symbol E) the strength of an electric field at a given point, measured in volts per metre.

electric flux (symbol c) the quantity of electricity displaced across a given area in a dielectric, measured in coulombs.

electric potential (symbol V) the work done in bringing a unit positive charge from infinity to a point. (See also potential difference.)

electrolyte a substance that conducts electricity in solution because of the presence of ions.

electron a negatively charged elementary particle, found spinning around the nuclei of atoms. As free electrons they are responsible for electrical conduction.

electronics the study and use of electricity in semiconductors.

electronvolt (symbol eV) the energy acquired by an electron in falling freely through a potential difference of 1 volt.

elementary particle any particle of matter that cannot be subdivided into smaller particles.

energy (symbol E) a measure of the capacity of a system to do work, measured in joules.

enthalpy (symbol H) the thermodynamic function of a system equal to the sum of its internal energy and the product of its pressure and volume.

entropy (symbol S) the disorder of a system. The greater the disorder of a system, the greater the entropy.

evaporation the conversion of a liquid to a vapour at a temperature below the boiling point.

Fahrenheit scale temperature scale on which the freezing point of water at normal atmospheric pressure is 32 °F, and the boiling point 212 °F (see p. 122).

fallout radioactive material that falls to earth after a nuclear explosion.

farad (symbol F) the unit of capacitance, in which a charge of 1 coulomb is acquired when 1 volt is applied.

fermion a particle with anti-symmetric wave function.

ferromagnetism the phenomenon by which certain solids (e.g. iron, cobalt, nickel) can be magnetized by weak magnetic fields.

fibre optics the study and use of the transmission of light by very fine flexible glass rods.

fission a type of nuclear reaction in which a heavy nucleus is split into two or more fragments, normally accompanied by the emission of neutrons or gamma rays.

fluid a liquid or gas.

fluidics the study and use of jets of fluid in circuits to perform tasks usually carried out by electronic circuits.

fluorescence the emission of light or radiation. When electromagnetic radiation, e.g. X-rays, ultra-violet light, etc., strikes a fluorescent substance, radiation of a longer wavelength, e.g. visible light, is emitted.

flux the strength of a field of force through a specified area.

force (symbol F) any action that tends to alter a body's state of rest or uniform motion.

free fall the downward motion in a gravitational field, unimpeded by any buoyancy effects.

freezing point the temperature at which both the solid and liquid phases of a substance can exist in equilibrium, e.g. the temperature at which water freezes and ice melts.

frequency (symbol v or f) the number of complete cycles or oscillations that occur in a unit of time, normally measured in hertz.

fusion (1) the change of state from liquid to solid at the melting point. (2) **nuclear fusion** type of nuclear reaction in which light atomic nuclei combine to form a heavier atomic nucleus with the release of energy (see fission).

g the symbol for the acceleration due to free fall. On the earth it is approximately $9{\cdot}81$ m s^{-2}.

gain the efficiency of an electronic system.

galvanometer an instrument for measuring or detecting electrical currents.

gamma (γ) rays electromagnetic radiation emitted by certain radioactive substances. Gamma rays can penetrate much greater distances than alpha and beta rays, and form the extreme short-wave end of the electromagnetic spectrum.

Geiger counter a device for detecting ionizing radiation, especially alpha particles. Because a Geiger counter can count the particles it can measure the strength of radioactivity.

gravitation the attraction that all bodies have for one another.

ground the US term for earth.

h the symbol for Planck's constant.

hadron a subatomic particle that interacts through the strong force. It is made up of quarks.

half-life the time in which a radioactive substance decays to half its original quantity or half its original activity.

harmonic a simple multiple of a fundamental frequency.

heat the form of energy transferred between bodies as a result of differences in their temperature.

heat pump a device for extracting heat from large quantities of a substance, e.g. water, air, at a low temperature and supplying it at a higher temperature, e.g. to a building.

hertz (symbol Hz) the unit of frequency, equal to 1 cycle or oscillation per second.

holography a laser technique for producing stereoscopic images without cameras.

hydrodynamics the study and use of the motion of fluids.

hysteresis the lagging of an effect behind the cause when the cause varies in amount, e.g. magnetic induction lagging behind an applied cycle of magnetic changes.

Hz symbol for hertz.

I symbol for current.

ice point the temperature at which ice and water are in equilibrium at standard pressure.

induction the process by which electricity is passed from one circuit to another without the need for physical contact between them. When an electrical conductor is moved so that it cuts the flux of a magnetic field, a potential difference is induced between the ends of the conductor. This is the basis of the way dynamos generate electricity.

inertia the tendency for a body to remain at rest or in a state of uniform motion in a straight line.

infrared rays electromagnetic radiation (heat) emitted by hot bodies. It consists of radiation of longer wavelengths than the red end of the visible spectrum.

insulator any substance (such as rubber, plastic, ceramic) that offers a high resistance to electric current. (See conductor).

integrated circuit a complete circuit in a single package, usually in or on a single chip of silicon.

interference the combination of two or more coherent waves from different sources by which areas of minimum and maximum intensity occur where the waves are superimposed on each other.

ion an atom, group of atoms, molecule or group of molecules that is electrically charged by the presence or absence of one or more electrons than normal.

isobar a line joining places with the same atmospheric pressure.

isotopes atoms of an element having the same number of protons but different numbers of neutrons.

joule (symbol J) the unit of energy or work; the work done by a constant force of 1 newton when moving an object 1 metre in the direction of the applied force.

kelvin (symbol K) the unit of thermodynamic temperature, equivalent to 1 °C.

kinetic energy (symbol T) the energy possessed by virtue of a body's motion.

laminar flow a steady flow in which a fluid moves in parallel layers (laminae), although the velocities of the fluid particles in each lamina are not necessarily equal.

laser (abbreviation for Light Amplification by Stimulated Emission of Radiation) a source of intense coherent radiation of a single wavelength in the infrared, visible and ultraviolet regions of the spectrum.

latent heat the quantity of heat released or absorbed when a substance changes phase at a fixed temperature.

lattice a regularly repeated three-dimensional array of points that determines the positions of atoms or molecules in a crystalline structure.

lens a piece of transparent material, bounded by two regularly curved surfaces and designed to focus light to a fixed point (see also concave, convex).

lepton a subatomic particle that interacts through the weak or electromagnetic interaction.

light a narrow section of the electromagnetic spectrum that is visible to the human eye.

longitudinal waves waves in which displacement of the transmitting medium is in the same plane as the direction of travel, e.g. sound waves.

lumen (symbol lm) the unit of luminous flux, i.e. the rate of flow of radiant energy.

lux (symbol lx) the unit of illumination.

machine a device for doing work, in which a small effort is used to overcome a larger force or load.

Mach number (symbol M) the ratio of the relative velocity of a body in a fluid to the velocity of sound in the fluid. Mach 1 thus indicates the speed of sound.

magnetic bottle an arrangement of magnetic fields designed to contain a plasma.

magnetic field a field of force containing magnetic flux.

magnetism attractive and repulsive forces due to the motion of electrons around the atoms in a substance.

magnifying power the ratio of the size of an image produced by an instrument to the size of the image as seen by the naked eye.

maser (abbreviation for Microwave Amplification by Stimulated Emission of Radiation) the microwave equivalent of a laser.

mass the quantity of matter in a body; the reluctance of a body to accelerate when acted on by a force. It is measured in kilograms in the SI system (see p. 189).

mass number (symbol A) the number of nucleons in a nucleus.

mass spectrometer an instrument for measuring atomic masses of elements that can be formed into a beam of ions.

mechanics the study of motion and the equilibrium of bodies.

metrology the study of the accurate measurement of mass, length and time.

microscope an instrument, containing converging lenses, that produces an enlarged image of small objects.

microwaves electromagnetic waves with a wavelength between infrared radiation and radio waves.

mm HG (abbreviation for millimetres of mercury) a unit of pressure measured by the height in mm of a column of mercury supported by the pressure.

mole (symbol mol) the amount of substance that contains the same number of elementary entities (molecules, ions, atoms, etc.) as there are in 0·012 kg of carbon-12.

moment a turning effect, equal to the magnitude of the force and the perpendicular distance from the line of action of the force to the axis.

momentum (symbol p) the product of the mass and the velocity of a body.

monochromatic radiation radiation of one wavelength or of a very narrow band of wavelengths.

motor a machine that converts electrical energy into mechanical energy.

neutrino a lepton with little or no rest mass and zero electric charge.

neutron a constituent of the atomic nucleus, with zero charge and about the same mass as the proton.

neutron number (symbol N) the number of neutrons present in the nucleus of an atom.

neutron star a massive star consisting largely of neutrons.

newton (symbol N) the unit of force that gives a mass of 1 kilogram an acceleration of 1 metre per second per second.

Newton's laws see p. 194.

Newton's rings circular interference fringes formed between a lens and a glass plate with which the lens is in contact.

NTP abbreviation for normal temperature and pressure.

nuclear fusion see fusion.

nuclear isomers nuclei with the same mass number and atomic number but different radioactive properties.

nuclear magnetic resonance an effect observed when radio-frequency radiation is absorbed by matter. It is due to the spin of atomic nuclei developing characteristic magnetic moments. The effect is exploited in, for example, medical imaging devices.

nucleon the collective name for the constituents of the atomic nucleus, i.e. protons and neutrons.

nucleus the most massive part of an atom, consisting of neutrons and protons held together by binding forces.

ohm (symbol Ω) the unit of resistance; the resistance between two points if an applied potential difference of 1 volt produces a current of 1 amp.

optics the study and use of light.

orbit a curved path described, for example, by a planet or comet around the sun or a particle such as an electron in a field of force such as that encountered around an atomic nucleus.

oscillation a vibration (i.e. a movement backwards and forwards between two points) with a regular frequency.

osmosis the use of a semipermeable membrane that allows certain kinds of molecule in a liquid to pass through it but that prevents the passage of other molecules.

parallax the apparent displacement of an object caused by an actual change of point of observation.

parity (symbol P) a physical property characterized by the behaviour of wave functions when reflected. Parity invariance states that no distinction can be made between laws of physics for a right-handed system of coordinates and for a left-handed system of coordinates.

pascal (symbol Pa) the unit of pressure; the pressure resulting from 1 newton acting uniformly over 1 m^2.

Pascal's principle states that pressure applied at any point to a fluid at rest is transmitted without loss to all other parts of the fluid.

Pauli exclusion principle states that no two fermions can exist in identical quantum states, e.g. no two electrons in an atom can have the same quantum number.

pendulum a mass suspended from a fixed point that oscillates with a known and fixed period.

period (symbol T) the time occupied by one complete vibration or oscillation.

permeability (symbol m) the ratio of magnetic flux density in a body to the external magnetic field strength inducing it.

phase (1) the proportion of a period that has elapsed, taken from a fixed point in the cycle. (2) any of three physical states – solid, liquid, gas – in which a substance can exist.

photoemission the release or emission of electrons due to bombardment of the substance by electromagnetic radiation, e.g. light.

piezoelectric effect the production of an electrical potential difference across a piece of crystal, e.g. quartz, when subjected to pressure.

pitch the frequency of a sound.

Planck's constant a universal constant equal to the energy of any quantum of radiation divided by its frequency: $h = 6.626 \times 10^{-34}$ J s.

Planck's law states that electromagnetic radiation consists of small indivisible packets called photons or quanta whose energy equals hf, where h is Planck's constant and f is the frequency of the radiation.

plasma a gas of positive ions and free electrons with roughly equal positive and negative charges.

polarization the restriction of particle displacement to a single plane. It can only occur in transverse waves, e.g. electromagnetic radiation.

pole a point towards which lines of magnetic flux converge.

positron a positive electron, the antiparticle of the electron.

potential difference the difference in electric potential between two points in an electric field. The potential difference between two points is the work done per coulomb of positive electrical charge taken from one point to the other, measured in volts.

power (symbol P) the work done per second, measured in watts.

pressure (symbol p) the force per unit area, measured in pascals.

prism a refracting substance, such as glass, with two plane intersecting surfaces. It deviates a beam of light and disperses it into its constituent colours.

proton a positively charged elementary particle with about 1836 times the mass of an electron (which is negatively charged) and the same mass as a neutron (which has no charge). With the exception of hydrogen, all atomic nuclei contain protons and neutrons; the hydrogen nucleus consists solely of one proton.

Q symbol for charge.

quantum mechanics a mathematical physical theory based on Planck's quantum theory and the probability of finding an elementary particle at any particular point.

quantum theory the theory based on Planck's idea of discrete quanta of electromagnetic radiation.

quark a fundamental constituent of hadrons.

r symbol for density.

rad the unit of absorbed radiation, equal to 0.01 joule per kilogram of absorbing material.

radiation any energy propagated as rays, streams of particles or waves.

radioactivity the spontaneous disintegration of the nuclei of some isotopes in certain elements, with the emission of alpha or beta particles, sometimes together with gamma rays.

radiopaque the property of being opaque to radiation, especially gamma rays and X-rays, e.g. bones are radiopaque to X-rays but other body tissues are not.

radio waves electromagnetic radiation of radio frequency.

rectifier an electrical device that allows current to flow in only one direction and thus converts alternating to direct current.

reflection the process by which some of the light or sound striking a surface between two different media is thrown back into the original medium.

refraction the change of direction a ray of light or

sound wave undergoes when it passes from one medium to another.

relativity a theory developed by Einstein, confirming the unification of mass and energy, the former being a 'congealed' form of the latter.

resistance (symbol R) the ratio between the potential difference across a conductor and the current passing through it, measured in ohms.

resistivity (symbol r) the resistance per unit length of unit cross-sectional area of a conductor, measured in ohm-metres.

resonance the maximum response that occurs when a driving frequency applied to a system is equal to the natural frequency of the system.

rheology the study and use of the deformation and flow of matter.

saturated vapour a vapour in dynamic equilibrium with its liquid at a given temperature. Saturated vapour can hold no more substance in the gaseous phase at that temperature.

scalar a quantity – such as speed – that has magnitude but not direction (see vector).

scattering the deflection of radiation by interaction with nuclei or electrons, the deflection of sound waves by a reflecting surface, or the deflection of light waves by fine particles.

Snell's law see p. 196.

Schrödinger wave equation the basic equation of wave mechanics. It shows the behaviour of a particle moving in force field.

scintillation the emission of small flashes of light when radiation strikes certain substances.

second (symbol s) the basic SI unit of time.

semiconductor a substance – such as silicon or germanium – with a resistivity between that of conductors and insulators. Junctions between semiconductors form the basis of the modern electronics industry.

semipermeable membrane a membrane that allows the passage of certain molecules in a fluid while preventing the passage of other molecules (see osmosis).

shell any of various energy states in which electrons move round the atomic nucleus.

simple harmonic motion the periodic motion of a body subjected to a restoring force proportional to the displacement from the centre. The period of oscillation is independent of amplitude and the displacement varies sinusoidally with time.

sinusoidal the condition of having a waveform the same as that of a sine function.

SI (abbreviation for *Système International d'Unités*) an internationally agreed coherent system of units based on the metre, kilogram and second (see p. 189).

solenoid a coil of wire with a greater length than diameter. When an electric current is passed through the wire it forms an electromagnet.

specific (when applied to an extensive physical property) a restriction on the meaning of 'per unit mass' of the substance.

spectrometer an instrument for producing, recording or examining a spectrum of radiation.

spectrum a distribution of electromagnetic radiation. It is usually applied to the visible display of colours, but can be applied to any part of the range of electromagnetic radiation.

speed the rate of increase of distance travelled with time.

standard atmosphere (symbol atm) a unit of pressure equal to 101 325 pascals.

standard temperature and pressure a standard condition for the reduction of gas pressures and temperatures. It is equal to 0 °C and 101 325 pascals.

steam point the temperature at which the liquid and vapour phases of water are in equilibrium at standard pressure, i.e. 100 °C.

strain the change of shape and/or volume of a body due to applied forces.

strange particle a subatomic particle with an exceptionally long lifetime.

stress forces in equilibrium acting on a body and tending to produce strain.

superconductivity the property of a substance that has virtually no electrical resistance at a low temperature. When many metals and alloys are cooled to near absolute zero (0 K, -273 °C), their electrical resistance almost vanishes.

supercooling the slow and continuous cooling of liquids to below their normal freezing point.

superfluid a fluid, at a very low temperature, that has very high thermal conductivity and can flow through very fine channels without friction.

telescope an instrument for producing a magnified or intensified image of a distant object. Optical telescopes use lenses or lenses and mirrors; radio telescopes use electronic circuitry to amplify radio signals from distant sources.

temperature (symbol T) the hotness of a body that determines which direction heat flows when the body is in contact with other bodies.

thermodynamics the study and use of the interrelationships between heat and other forms of energy.

tone the quality of a musical sound, caused by the presence of harmonics.

transducer a device for converting a non-electrical variable into a proportionately variable electrical signal.

transformer a device, consisting of two electrical circuits magnetically coupled together, that either steps up voltage and steps down current, or vice versa.

transistor a semiconductor device in which a small base current or voltage can control or modulate a larger collector current or voltage.

transverse waves waves in which displacement of the transmitting medium is perpendicular to the direction of travel, e.g. electromagnetic waves.

tribology the study of friction, lubrication and wear of surfaces.

triple point the temperature at which, for any substance, the three physical states of the substance can exist at equilibrium. For water this occurs at 0.01 °C and b10Pa.

u symbol for atomic mass unit.

ultrasonics the study and use of frequencies beyond the limits of human hearing, i.e. above about 20 kHz.

ultraviolet radiation electromagnetic radiation lying beyond the violet end of the visible spectrum and before the X-ray region.

unified field theory a theory – yet to be developed – that seeks to link together the properties of gravitational, nuclear and electromagnetic fields.

vacuum a space or vessel devoid of matter or from

To the amazement of those who don't like mathematics, mathematicians actually find mathematics enjoyable! They also find a sense of form and beauty an aid when they are doing mathematics.

G. H. Hardy claimed that many popular puzzles are really bits of mathematics in disguise and that everyone enjoys getting a 'kick' out of solving them.

Serge Lang was asked, 'Why do you do this kind of work?' 'Because it gives me chills in the spine.'

Roger Penrose writes that 'It is a mysterious thing how something which looks attractive may have a better chance of being true than something which looks ugly.'

which all air has been removed.

valence electrons those electrons in the outermost shell of an atom that are involved in chemical changes.

vapour a substance in gaseous form but below its critical temperature. It can thus be liquefied merely by pressure, without the need for cooling.

vector a quantity – such as velocity – that has direction as well as magnitude (see scalar).

velocity (symbol v) the rate of increase of distance travelled by a body in a particular direction.

viscosity the ability of fluids to offer resistance to flow.

visible spectrum visible electromagnetic radiation between 380 and 780 nm.

volt (symbol V) the potential difference between two points such that 1 joule of work is done by every coulomb of positive charge moved from one point to the other.

watt (symbol W) the unit of power resulting from the dissipation of 1 joule in 1 second.

wave a curve of an alternating quantity plotted against time, giving rise to a disturbance travelling through a medium.

wavelength (symbol l) the distance between one vibrating particle in a wave train and the next particle that is vibrating in the same phase.

wave mechanics a form of quantum mechanics.

weight the pull of gravity on a body, measured in newtons (see mass).

work (symbol w or W) a transfer of energy. Work is carried out when a force moves its point of application. It is measured in joules (1 joule = 1 newton moved through 1 metre).

X-rays electromagnetic radiation lying between ultraviolet radiation and gamma rays.

Z symbol for atomic number.

'LEAGUE TABLE' OF NOBEL PRIZE WINNERS (PHYSICS) FROM EC COUNTRIES

Germany	17
United Kingdom	17
France	6
The Netherlands	5
Italy	3
Denmark	2
Ireland	1
Belgium	0
Greece	0
Luxembourg	0
Portugal	0
Spain	0

Some ancient units of measurement literally used whatever was at hand. The *palm* – which measured about 75 mm (3 in) – was simply the distance between the base of the fingers and the beginning of the wrist of the human hand. Because no two hands are exactly the same size, standardization became necessary.

The *hand* – which measures about 100 mm (4 in) – is still used for measuring the height of horses. It is the distance between the tip of the thumb and the tip of the little finger when all the fingers are fully extended.

The *cubit*, a measure that is mentioned frequently in the Bible, was about 450 mm (18 in). It was the distance from the tip of the middle finger to the elbow.

FORCES OF NATURE

Force	Range	Quanta	Mass (GeV)	Spin	Notes
gravity	very long	graviton	0 ?	2	acts on all matter, weak within the atom
weak	less than 10^{-16} cm	charged $W^{\pm}$ neutral Z^0	80.5 91.1	1 1	acts on all the basic particles, leptons and quarks, involved in radioactive processes
electromagnetic	very long	photon (γ)	0	1	acts on all charged particles; provides the basis to the reactions of chemistry and hence biology
strong	less than 10^{-13} cm	Gluon (g)	0 ?	1	acts on the quarks allowing them free movement within the hadrons, i.e. the mesons and baryons, but confines them within these particles

TECHNOLOGY, INDUSTRY AND TRANSPORT

TECHNOLOGY AND INDUSTRY

AIRCRAFT

The term 'aircraft' includes every man-made device that flies in the atmosphere. The most important group of aircraft, called *aerodynes*, are not naturally buoyant but heavier than air. Aerodynes obtain their lift in a variety of ways: by jet thrust; by means of rotating blades; or by means of fixed wings, with a separate propulsion system to make the wings move through the air. A smaller group is the *aerostats*, which are naturally buoyant (lighter than air). Those without power are called balloons (gas-filled or hot-air), while those with propulsion and some means of steering are called airships or dirigibles.

THE PRINCIPLE OF FLIGHT

When the *weight* of an aircraft (due to the force of gravity) is exceeded by the *lift* (the upward force created by the wings or by hot air or lighter-than-air gases), the aircraft will rise in the air. In the case of aeroplanes and gliders, lift is produced as a result of the characteristic profile – the *aerofoil section* – of the wing. The wing is rounded and thicker at the front (the *leading edge*), and tapers away to a sharp edge at the back (the *trailing edge*).

Lift is created as the wings move through the air at speed and relies on the fact that air pressure drops as air speed increases. As air passes over the wing, it has to move further, and thus faster, over the more curved upper surface than the lower surface. This causes a considerable reduction in pressure above the wing, especially at the front, where the wing is thickest and the upper surface most sharply curved. Lift can be increased both by increasing the speed of airflow over the wing and by increasing the curvature of the upper wing surface.

Any aircraft with propulsion also experiences *thrust* – the resultant force pulling or pushing it through the air; and *drag* – the equal and opposite force caused by the resistance of the air to the frontal surfaces of the aircraft. Drag is effectively wasted energy, so the aim of aircraft designers is to reduce drag without sacrificing lift.

Gliders, lacking an independent source of propulsion, have to fly downhill from the moment they are cast off after take-off. The pilot thus seeks columns of rising warmer air, called *thermals*. Modern gliders are so efficient that they have climbed to nearly 15 000 m (49 200 ft) and flown 1460 km (907 mi).

AIRCRAFT STABILITY

In the absence of other forces, an aircraft's centre of gravity would have to be at the same point as its centre of lift for the craft to remain in equilibrium. In practice, however, because of thrust and drag, nearly all aeroplanes are designed to be naturally stable in the longitudinal plane, but with the centre of gravity ahead of the centre of lift. This causes a downward movement of the nose, which is counteracted by a constant download on the horizontal tail. Any disturbance tending to tilt the aircraft nose-up or nose-down is countered automatically by the change in the angle of the wings and of the horizontal tail.

Today, thanks to extremely fast computers, fighter planes can be deliberately made naturally unstable. This has two advantages: instead of a download the tailplane imparts an upload, thus helping the wing instead of fighting it; and as the fighter is always trying to depart from straight flight (restrained by computers that apply restoring forces 40 or more times per second), the aircraft can be made exceptionally agile.

AIRCRAFT CONTROLS

Aeroplanes and gliders are controlled in the longitudinal (*pitch*) axis by *elevators* on the tailplane, or by having a fully powered pivoted tailplane. A few modern designs have a foreplane instead of a tailplane, and a very few have both. Directional control is provided by a vertical *rudder*, which is usually located on the tailplane as well. The rudder is also an important control surface if a multi-engined aircraft should suffer failure of an engine mounted far out on a wing.

Lateral (*roll*) control was formerly provided only by *ailerons* – pivoted portions of the trailing edge near the tips of the wings – but today roll control can be effected by asymmetric use of the tailplanes or by asymmetric deflection of *spoilers*. The spoilers are door-like surfaces hinged along the top of the wing. Differentially they control roll, and symmetrically they serve as airbrakes by increasing drag. Spoilers can also be used in *direct lift control* to enable the aircraft trajectory to be varied up or down without changing the attitude of the fuselage. On landing, spoilers act as 'lift dumpers', instantly killing wing lift and thus increasing the weight on the wheels and the effectiveness of the brakes.

All early aircraft used cables in tension or push/pull pivoted rods to convey pilot commands to the control surfaces. From about 1950 powered controls were widely introduced, in which the surfaces were moved by hydraulic actuators, the pilot's controls being provided with some form of artificial 'feel' so that he could sense what was happening. By 1970 *fly by wire* was rapidly becoming common, in which the pilot's controls send out small electrical signals, which are carried through multiple wires to the surface power units. Today *fly by light* is being introduced: pilot signals are conveyed as variable light output along optical fibres, thus offering colossal bandwidth and data-handling capacity.

THE HIGH-LIFT SYSTEM

An aircraft has to work hardest during take-off and landing, when airspeed is at its lowest and yet maximum lift is required. To facilitate these manoeuvres, most aircraft have a *high-lift system*, brought into action for the approach and landing, and usually also for take-off.

Along the leading edge of the wing there may be *slats*, slender portions of the wing moved out and away on parallel arms, or alternatively *Krüger flaps*, which swing down and around from underneath the leading edge. These full-span devices greatly increase the available lift, especially from a thin wing suitable for fast jets.

Along the trailing edge are fitted *flaps*. These again come in many forms, but all swing back and down from the wing. When selected to a take-off setting, such as 15°, they increase lift and slightly increase drag; when fully down, at the landing setting of perhaps 40°, they increase lift even more but also greatly increase drag.

AIRCRAFT PROPULSION

Until 1939 virtually all aeroplanes were powered by piston engines driving a *propeller*, which provides thrust by accelerating air through aerodynamic rotating blades. Almost all modern propellers are of the variable-pitch type – the angle at which the blades attack the air can be altered. The blades are set to fine pitch for take-off to match high engine speed with low aircraft speed, and then automatically adjusted to coarse pitch for cruising flight, to match economical low engine speed to high forward speed. After landing, some propellers can be set to reverse pitch to help brake the aircraft.

During and after World War II, the propeller gave way to the turbojet for most purposes. The turbojet itself was largely eclipsed by the turbofan, which offers better fuel economy and reduced noise levels.

MILESTONES IN AVIATION

1783 First manned balloon flight by the Montgolfier brothers in hot-air balloon in Paris.

1783 First hydrogen-balloon flight by the French physicist Jacques A.C. Charles. He travelled 26 km (16 miles), beginning in Paris.

1797 First parachute jump by André-Jacques Garenerin. He dropped 1981 m (6500 ft) over Paris in a parachute made of white canvas with a basket attached.

1852 Henri Giffard of France manned the first flight of a mechanically-propelled airship – a *dirigible*. It measured 43 m (144 ft) long and 12 m (39 ft) wide.

1891 Otto Lilienthal of Germany began his controlled glider flight experiments.

1900 Count Ferdinand von Zeppelin of Germany flew the first of his rigid-frame airships. With an internal combustion engine and aluminium frame, it reached a speed of 29 kph (18 mph).

1903 The first successful flight by a 'heavier-than-air machine' by Orville and Wilbur Wright near Kitty Hawk, North Carolina, USA. During a later flight that day Wilbur Wright sustained flight for 59 seconds.

1907 Paul Cornu of France manned the first free vertical flight of a twin-rotor helicopter.

1908 The first cross-country flight of a 'heavier-than-air machine' by Henry Farman, from Mourmelons to Reims in France, in a machine using ailerons.

1909 Louis Blériot made the first cross-Channel flight, from Calais to Dover in 37 minutes.

1910 The Zeppelin airship entered commercial service in Germany.

1912 Construction of the monocoque introduced for the Deperdussin racer.

The leading woman aviator of the day, Harriet Quimby, became the first woman to fly across the Channel.

1915 Start of the Zeppelin bomb raids over Great Britain.

The first all-metal cantilever-wing aircraft, the German Junker J1, was built.

1919 Britons John Alcock and Arthur Brown made the first direct non-stop transatlantic crossing in 16 hours 27 minutes.

1923 The Spanish aviator Juan de la Cierva designed and flew the first autogyro.

1927 The American Charles Lindbergh made the first solo transatlantic flight, from New York to Paris.

1930 The jet engine was patented by Frank Whittle in Britain. It used a gas turbine for jet propulsion.

1935 The Douglas DC-3 'Dakota' – conceived as an airliner – made its maiden flight.

1936 The first entirely successful helicopter, Heinrich Focke's Fa-61, made its maiden flight.

1937 The world's largest airship, the *Hindenburg*, burst into flames in New Jersey, USA, ending the age of airship travel.

The first flight of the US Lockheed XC-35, the first fully pressurized aircraft.

1939 The German Heinkel He-178 was the first aircraft to fly solely on the power of a turbojet engine.

Igor Sikorsky designed the prototype modern helicopter, with a single main rotor and a small tail rotor.

1947 The American Bell X-1 exceeded the speed of sound in level flight.

1949 The De Havilland Comet became the first jet airliner. It entered service in 1952.

1954 The first experimental flight of vertical take-off aircraft.

1958 The first US jet airliner – the Boeing 707 – entered commercial service.

1967 Computer guidance systems were fitted into aircraft for the first time. The Autoland blind landing system was introduced into service in Britain.

1968 The first flight of the Soviet supersonic airliner, the Tupolev Tu-144.

1969 The Anglo-French supersonic airliner, Concorde, made its maiden flight.

The first operational V/STOL (vertical/short take-off and landing) aircraft – the Harrier – entered service with the Royal Air Force.

1970 The Boeing 747 became the first wide-bodied 'jumbo' jet to enter service.

1976 The supersonic airliner Concorde entered commercial service.

1977 The American *Gossamer Condor* became the first successful heavier-than-air human-powered aircraft.

1979 The first man-powered flight across the Channel is made by *Gossamer Albatross*.

1981 At the average speed of 48 kph (30 mph), Stephen Ptacek flew the *Solar Challenger* across the Channel, powered only by solar cells.

1987 Richard Branson and Per Lindstrand made the first transatlantic hot-air balloon flight.

1989 The Bell-Boeing V-22 Osprey flew for the first time. Its tilt rotor concept combines the advantages of the aeroplane with those of the helicopter.

MOTOR VEHICLES

The engine is the power unit of a car, providing the motion that is ultimately transmitted to the driven wheels. However, a series of interconnected mechanisms, including the clutch, the gearbox and the

Clutch-and-gearbox assembly. The clutch consists of the flywheel (driven round by the crankshaft), a clutch (or friction) plate and a pressure plate. When the clutch is engaged (i.e. with the pedal released), powerful springs force the clutch plate against the flywheel, thereby linking the flywheel to the shaft transmitting power to the gearbox. When the clutch is disengaged, levers work against the springs to separate the clutch plate from the flywheel, so disconnecting the transmission. The friction linings on the clutch plate allow the plate to slip before becoming fully engaged, so preventing a shuddering jerk on starting.

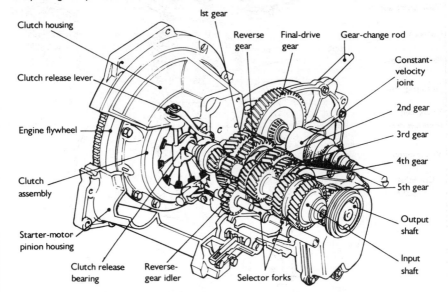

Clutch housing
1st gear
Reverse gear
Final-drive gear
Gear-change rod
Constant-velocity joint
Clutch release lever
2nd gear
Engine flywheel
3rd gear
4th gear
Clutch assembly
5th gear
Starter-motor pinion housing
Output shaft
Clutch release bearing
Reverse-gear idler
Selector forks
Input shaft

The gearbox allows optimum (i.e. high) engine speed to be matched to a wide variety of driving conditions. By means of selector forks actuated by the gearstick, different-sized gears linked to the input shaft can be engaged with different-sized gears on the shaft transmitting power to the differential. A (relatively) small gear on the input shaft engaged with a large gear on the transmission shaft produces low speed but high power; high speed and low power are achieved by reversing the gear ratios on the input and output shafts. In top gear, no gears are engaged and transmission passes directly through the gearbox to the differential.

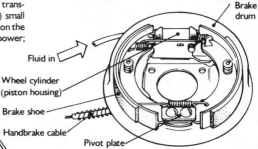

Brake drum
Fluid in
Wheel cylinder (piston housing)
Disc
Brake shoe
Handbrake cable
Pivot plate

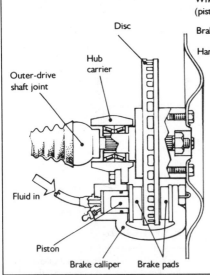

Hub carrier
Outer-drive shaft joint
Fluid in
Piston
Brake calliper
Brake pads

Brakes. A *drum brake* (fitted here to rear) consists of a drum, which is attached to the bub and therefore rotates at wheel speed. Within the drum are two shoes covered in a friction lining, which are attached to the axle and do not rotate. Depression of the brake pedal operates a hydraulic system that actuates a piston, which forces the shoes outwards and thus against the inner surface of the drum.

A *disc brake* (fitted here to front) consists of a steel disc, which is attached to the wheel and rotates at wheel speed. A hydraulic system operated by the brake pedal actuates a piston housed in a stationary calliper that straddles the disc, causing two brake pads to be forced onto each side of the disc. As with the drum brake, the resulting friction causes the car to slow down.

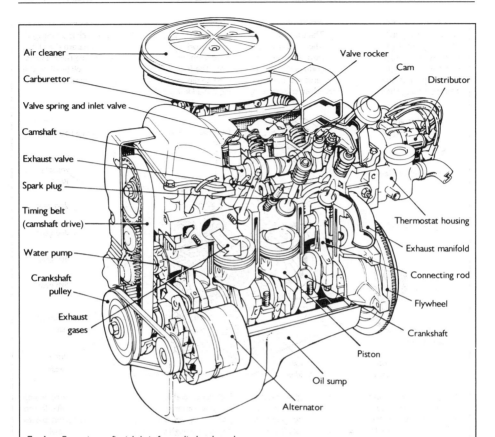

Air cleaner
Carburettor
Valve spring and inlet valve
Camshaft
Exhaust valve
Spark plug
Timing belt (camshaft drive)
Water pump
Crankshaft pulley
Exhaust gases

Valve rocker
Cam
Distributor
Thermostat housing
Exhaust manifold
Connecting rod
Flywheel
Crankshaft
Piston
Oil sump
Alternator

Engine. Four pistons fit tightly in four cylinders bored into the cylinder block. Each piston is driven downwards in a fixed sequence on the power stroke of the four-stroke cycle. A *connecting rod* from each cylinder is attached to a cranked (dog-legged) shaft (*the crankshaft*), which is turned a half-revolution by each successive power stroke. To one end of the crankshaft is bolted a heavy disc called *the flywheel*, which provides the drive to the gearbox via the clutch; at the other end, a belt-and-pulley system causes *the camshaft* to rotate at half the speed of the crankshaft. Pear-shaped lobes (*cams*) along the length of the camshaft act on a series of rocker mechanisms that cause the inlet and exhaust valves on each cylinder to open and close in exact timing with the four strokes of the piston.

Rack-and-pinion steering is a simple and effective system used in many cars. A toothed pinion at the base of the steering column acts on a toothed rack, moving it to left or right and thus converting the rotary motion of the steering wheel into linear motion. At each end of the rack, track rods act on pivoted steering arms, so altering the angle of the front wheels.

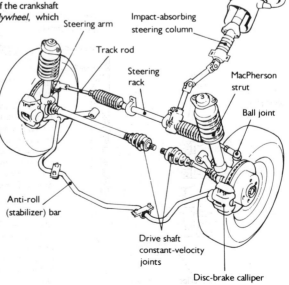

Steering arm
Impact-absorbing steering column
Track rod
Steering rack
MacPherson strut
Ball joint
Anti-roll (stabilizer) bar
Drive shaft constant-velocity joints
Disc-brake calliper

Suspension. The *Mac-Pherson strut* is a very common suspension arrangement, consisting of a spring mounted on an arm that runs from the wheel to a secure place on the bodyframe. The arm moves up and down with road irregularities, so compressing the spring and absorbing bumps.

To counteract the compressed spring's tendency to rebound, a *shock absorber* is fitted (within the spring, in the case of the MacPherson strut). This is essentially a fluid-filled piston-and-cylinder assembly. The piston moves in and out to the same extent as the spring, so forcing the thick fluid back and forth through channels in the piston and thus deadening the bounce of the spring.

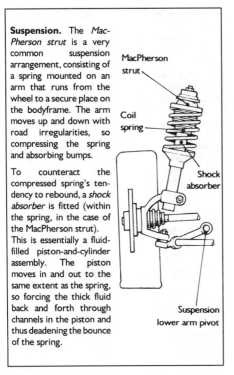

MacPherson strut

Coil spring

Shock absorber

Suspension lower arm pivot

engine, the precise proportions of petrol and air in the fuel mixture entering the cylinders must be carefully regulated. This is generally achieved by a *carburettor*. Although different types of carburettor exist, nearly all are in the form of a tube into which air is drawn by the downward movement of the pistons on their successive induction strokes. As the air accelerates through the narrowed middle section of the carburettor, its pressure falls, so causing a jet of fuel to be drawn through a nozzle from a reservoir, which is itself fed by a pump from the petrol tank. Within the carburettor, on the engine-side of the fuel jet, a circular flap (known as a butterfly valve) is actuated by the accelerator pedal in such a way as to control the volume of air–fuel mixture drawn into the engine, thus regulating engine speed. In most designs, a similar valve (the *choke*) on the air-intake side of the fuel jet regulates the amount of air entering the carburettor and thus the richness of the fuel mix.

Increasingly, direct *fuel-injection* is being used in place of the carburettor. This is more efficient and economical than the carburettor, since accurately metered and appropriate amounts of fuel can be delivered to each cylinder's combustion chamber. There are several systems – both mechanical and electrical – but the basic principle is that fuel is injected at high pressure into the combustion chamber from a point behind the inlet valve.

TRANSMISSION

The term 'transmission' embraces all the components that are responsible for transferring the engine's power from the flywheel to the driven wheels. The spinning motion of the flywheel is transmitted to the *gearbox* via the *clutch* (see diagram). When the clutch pedal is depressed, the spinning flywheel is disconnected from the shaft transmitting power to the gearbox, so allowing the car to move off gently and smooth gear-changes to be made.

A gearbox is necessary because – unlike (say) an electric motor – most internal-combustion engines develop their full power and torque (turning effort) within a relatively narrow band of engine speeds (usually between 3000 and 5000 revolutions per minute). By means of the gearbox (and partly by the differential; see below), the engine speed is kept within these limits while allowing the car to operate at widely varying speeds and in a wide range of driving conditions.

For example, a steep hill requires a low gear, because it is only at high engine speeds that the engine is able to deliver enough torque to keep the wheels turning. On the other hand, where little torque is required, as when travelling at speed on a level road, a high gear may be used, thus matching high road speed with (relatively) low engine speed. In this way engine life is prolonged, passenger comfort enhanced and fuel consumption kept to a minimum.

After passing through the gearbox-and-clutch assembly, the drive is transferred to the *differential*. In front-wheel-drive cars, transmission from gearbox to differential is direct; in rear-wheel-drive cars, if the engine is mounted at the front of the car, the differential is driven by a crown wheel and pinion at the end of a propeller shaft.

The rotation rate of the shaft from the gearbox is further stepped down by the differential (normally to about a quarter of the gearbox speed). However, the

differential, is required to transmit the power of the engine to the wheels in a usable form. At the same time, a number of subsidiary systems, including steering and brakes, are necessary in order to give adequate control over the movement of the car.

Most cars today are fitted with an overhead-valve, four-stroke petrol engine, with four or six cylinders linked to the crankshaft. The crankshaft also drives a camshaft, which opens and closes the valves at the top of each cylinder in the correct sequence. The four cylinders fire in turn so there is a power stroke for every half-revolution of the crankshaft.

Although the primary function of the engine is to spin the flywheel – the first link in the chain that transmits the engine's power to the wheels – the rotary motion of the crankshaft is also used to turn the *alternator*, which generates the current for the car's electrical systems. At the same time, the rotation of the camshaft drives both the oil pump and the distributor.

THE IGNITION SYSTEM

The purpose of the ignition system is to produce a spark of sufficient strength to ignite the petrol–air mixture at the exact moment when each piston in turn is nearly at the top of the compression stroke. The spark is produced as an electric current jumps (arcs) between the two electrodes of a spark plug; however, the voltage supplied by the battery is insufficient for this purpose. The voltage from the battery is first boosted by the *coil* to around 15 000 volts before passing to the *distributor*, in which a spinning rotor (driven by the camshaft) directs the current to each spark plug in turn.

THE FUEL SYSTEM

For efficient and economical combustion within the

differential's distinctive function is to allow power to be divided between the driven wheels in whatever proportion is required. Such a mechanism is necessary when cornering, because the outside driven wheel needs to be turned more rapidly than the inside wheel.

MOTORING MILESTONES

1885 Karl Benz produced the prototype of the automobile using an internal combustion motor.

1885–1886 Gottlieb Daimler patented his gas engine, using it first on a motorcycle and then on a four-wheeled vehicle.

1895 Pneumatic tyres – invented in 1888 – were adapted for use on motor vehicles.
The first motor car race was held, from Paris to Bordeaux and back.

1896 Henry Ford built his first car.

1903 The Ford Motor Company was founded by Henry Ford.

1906 Rolls-Royce began the production of the 'Silver Ghost'. A seven-litre, six-cylinder luxury tourer, it was capable of travelling considerable distances with complete reliability.

1908 The Ford Motor Company introduced the first production-line car – the Model T Ford.

1922 Independent front suspension was introduced in the Lambda, but was not in general use until after 1945.

1920s Mercedes pioneered supercharging.

1934 Citroën made the first car with front-wheel drive and independent front-wheel suspension.

1936 The first diesel-engined production car, the Mercedes-Benz 260D, was launched.

1940 The Jeep, the first vehicle to realize the potential of four-wheel drive, was launched.

1959 Austin Morris launched the Mini Minor, which profoundly influenced the design of all subsequent small cars.

1966 Electronic fuel-injection systems were developed in Britain.

1980 The Audi Quattro, the first mass-produced saloon car with four-wheel drive, was launched.

1980s Many countries introduced legislation to enforce or encourage the use of catalytic converters in cars to detoxify some of the harmful substances in the exhaust gases.

CAR GLOSSARY

air cleaner filter, usually of paper, to remove dust from air and protect engine.

alternator generates electricity to recharge battery.

anti-roll bar device to limit roll on cornering.

cam eccentric shape on camshaft which operates rockers as the shaft rotates.

camshaft shaft which operates valves through a series of cams along its length.

carburettor device for mixing air and fuel in correct proportions.

connecting rod link which transmits force of burning fuel from piston to crankshaft.

constant-velocity joints used on front-wheel-drive cars to provide smooth power when cornering.

crankshaft reciprocal motion of pistons is converted to rotary motion through cranks (dog-legs) on shaft.

distributor device for directing high voltage to spark plugs.

exhaust manifold tubes which gather exhaust from cylinders and direct it into exhaust pipe.

flywheel smooths out uneven operation of engine.

oil sump reservoir of oil which flows through main bearings.

piston fits tight in cylinder and transmits pressure of burning fuel mixture.

spark plug source of the spark which ignites the fuel mixture inside the cylinder.

thermostat closes off radiator when engine cold, to reduce warming-up time.

timing belt link between crankshaft and camshaft, to ensure valves open at right moment.

valve rocker lever arrangement for transmitting force from camshaft to valves.

valve spring used to close valve through which fuel enters engine, or exhaust gases leave it.

water pump circulates cooling water through radiator and cylinder block.

MILESTONES IN TEXTILES

Paleolithic (c. 30 000 years ago)
Bone awls and later bone needles were used to sew animal skins together.

Neolithic (3200 years ago)
The spindle, used for spinning animal and vegetable fibres into yarn, and the loom, used for weaving cloth, were invented. No textiles from this period have survived.

1000 BC
Elaborate fabrics woven in silk were being produced on hand looms in China.

c. AD 1300
The spinning wheel came into use, doubling the speed at which yarn could be made. Its origins are obscure, some scholars believing it may have originated in India much earlier. The horizontal frame loom, set on legs and with treadles to raise and lower the threads, also came into use at about the same time.

1589
The stocking-frame, a device for increasing the speed of knitting, invented by a Nottinghamshire clergyman, William Lee. For fear of unemployment, its use was discouraged by Queen Elizabeth I.

1733
John Kay, a weaver from Lancashire, invented the flying shuttle, a device which could carry the threads through a piece of cloth much wider than the span of a weaver's arms. It doubled the productivity of the loom.

1764
James Hargreaves, a weaver and carpenter, invented the spinning jenny which allowed several strands of yarn to be spun at once.

1769
Richard Arkwright of Preston, an early industrialist, produced the first truly mechanical spinning machine, the water frame, so called because it was powered by water wheels. This vital invention, requiring power beyond that of a single human being, began the factory system and led to a huge expansion of cotton production in England.

1779
Samuel Crompton, a yeoman from Bolton, devised a machine that combined the merits of the jenny and the water frame. Because of its mixed parentage it became known as the spinning mule. It produced a yarn both fine and strong, and finally solved the problems of mechanical spinning.

1785
The power loom was invented by Edmund Cartwright, a Leicestershire clergyman, bringing mechanization to the weaving of cloth. Early designs, made of wood, were not very satisfactory, and only the arrival of cast iron frames in the 19th century solved the problems.

1801
Joseph-Marie Jacquard devised a method for the automatic weaving of the complex silks, using a series of punched cards to control the lifting of the warp threads in the correct sequence. This was the first use of punched cards, later important in computers.

1823
Collier and Magnan, of Paris, introduced heavy duty, wide looms capable of weaving draperies and tarpaulins. Similar machines were produced in England (Sharpe and Roberts, 1830) and in Saxony (Schonherr, 1845).

1824
Charles Mackintosh, a Glasgow chemist, produced the first waterproof garments, using rubber, hence the mackintosh.

1851
Isaac M. Singer, of Boston, Massachusetts, produced the first practical domestic sewing machine.

1856
In Leicester, Matthew Townsend invented the latch needle, which increased the possibilities of knitting machines. In 1864 William Cotton, also of Leicester, produced a powered machine capable of knitting a dozen socks or stockings at once.

1892
The first artificial fibre, rayon, was made from cellulose by the chemists C. F. Cross and E. J. Bevan.

1893
The zip fastener was invented by the American engineer Whitcomb Judson. It finally became a huge success in 1918, after improvements made by the Swedish engineer Gideon Sundback.

1937
The American chemist Wallace Carothers, working for Du Pont, discovered nylon, the product of mixing adipic acid with hexamethylinediamine.

1941
J. T. Dickinson and J. R. Whinfield produced terylene (dacron in the USA) from terephthalic acid and ethylene glycol.

1948
The Swiss engineer Georges de Mestral invented Velcro, a form of woven nylon that consists of hooks and loops that link together to create a fastener.

1960
Open-end spinning, a faster system capable of producing high-quality yarn, developed in Czechoslovakia.

1970s
Lasers introduced for cutting out cloth into the shapes needed to make clothes.

TEXTILE GLOSSARY

carding the process of teasing out the mass of natural fibres and lining them up for spinning.

cashmere a fine wool from the coat of the Kashmir goat.

chintz fabric printed with patterns rather than woven, originally from the Hindi word 'tchint', meaning mottled.

combing alternative to carding for untangling and straightening fibres before spinning.

damask form of satin weave in which areas where warp threads lie on top are alternated with areas where weft threads do, producing variations of shading.

dry cleaning method of cleaning using solvents rather than water, thereby avoiding shrinkage. The solvent used today is perchlorethylene.

flax plant which produces from its stem the natural fibre flax, used to make linen.

fulling process for thickening woollen cloth, using alkalis like Fuller's Earth.

heddle fine wire with an eyelet through which a warp thread passes. Used for raising and lowering the warp threads to allow passage of the shuttle.

hemp Fibre from hemp plant, used for canvas and sailcloth.

jute plant fibre used for making sacks and carpet backings.

loom framework for holding parallel warp threads through which the weft threads are carried by the shuttle.

mohair luxury fibre produced from the hair of the Angora goat.

satin weave in which the warp threads are interwoven not with every weft thread but with every third or fourth. This means that they lie on top, producing a glossy finish.

shuttle boat-shaped object attached to the weft thread and used to carry it to and fro through the warp threads.

twill form of weave used to produce gaberdine, serge and whipcord.

warp the set of threads running lengthwise along the loom, and hence along the length of the finished cloth.

weft the set of threads running across the loom, weaving in and out of the warp threads.

velvet a pile weave in which some of the threads are cut after weaving so that they stand up to produce a carpet-like effect. Corduroy, plush and velour are also pile weaves.

MILESTONES IN SHIPBUILDING

8th millennium BC Reed and dugout boats were used.

3rd millennium BC Sailing boats were used in Egypt.

c. 1200 BC The Phoenicians developed ocean-going 'roundships'.

5th century BC The Greek trireme, the fastest of the Mediterranean galleys, was widely used.

8th century AD The Vikings of Scandinavia developed the longship with a hinged sternpost rudder and mast. It was sturdy enough to enable the Vikings to cross the Atlantic.

SPECIAL SHIPS

A number of special types of ship have been developed either to meet a new demand or to utilize technological advances. *Twin hulls* provide a large deck area and great stability. This is useful for helicopter operation from both naval and merchant vessels, for towing a variety of hydrographic equipment, or as a base for operating small submersibles or diving bells. Where a large part of the hull is kept well below the sea surface, the ship is known as a *semi-submersible*. The hulls of such vessels are much less affected by waves than conventional hulls and are therefore suitable for oil exploration. The *small water-plane area twin hull* (SWATH) ship is a variant of the semi-submersible. It experiences little motion because it has a much reduced response to surface waves.

The *hydrofoil* uses fins to create sufficient hydrodynamic lift to raise the hull clear of the water. Hydrofoils are suitable for small high-speed ferries, as they provide a comfortable ride in moderate sea conditions. The *hover-craft* is also used for ferries. The hull is carried on an air cushion, and in some variants there are no elements of the ship in the water. A hovercraft can run over flat areas of land such as mudbanks and beaches as easily as it can over water. In other variants the craft has an underwater propulsor and sidewalls that remain partly submerged.

15th–16th centuries The Mediterranean *carrack* – with as many as four masts – became the standard large ship. The smaller version of the carrack, the *caravel*, was widely used by the Spanish and Portuguese for the voyages of discovery.

16th century The galleon became the standard fighting ship in western Europe.

18th century The ships of the line evolved from galleons. They had heavier timbers to allow bigger and more numerous guns to be carried.

18th to 19th centuries Clipper cargo ships developed. The clipper sacrificed cargo space for a more streamlined design, increasing speed.

1802 The launch of the first commercially successful paddle-steamer, the *Charlotte Dundas*, in Scotland. (A small paddle-steamer had briefly sailed in 1783 in France but had proved impractical.)

1816 A steam-paddle service ran across the English Channel.

1821 The Royal Navy ordered its first paddle steamers for auxiliary missions (such as towing ships of the line over short distances).

The first iron-hulled merchant ship, the *Aaron Manby*, was launched.

1836 The Swedish-American John Ericsson and Englishman Francis Pettit-Smith developed the screw propeller.

1838 The *Great Western* (designed by Brunel) and the *Sirius* crossed the Atlantic, proving that steam power was suitable for long voyages.

1840 The Royal Navy ordered its first screw steamer, HMS *Rattler*. Brunel redesigned the passenger liner SS *Great Britain* for screw propulsion.

1858–1859 Construction began on the first ironclad, the French *Gloire*, a wooden warship covered with armoured plate. However, the British HMS *Warrior*, which had an iron hull and armoured plate, was the first ironclad to be launched (1859).

The *Great Eastern*, five times as large as the largest ship then afloat, was launched. Of revolutionary length (to give it greater speed), the ship was divided into 22 compartments to make it more resistant to damage.

1886 The first custom-built oil tanker, the German ship *Gluckauf*, was launched.

1890s Battleships were designed to an all-metal (steel) construction.

1897 The first turbine-driven steamship, the *Turbinia*, was built by C. Parsons.

1898 The Italian Enrico Forlanini developed the first true hydrofoil.

1902 The first marine diesel engine was installed, on a French canal boat.

1905 The Royal Navy adopted the steam-turbine for the revolutionary battleship HMS *Dreadnought*.

1902–1914 The diesel engine was widely adopted as a cheap propulsion unit for merchant ships and minor naval craft.

1920–39 The heyday of ocean liners. Their ever-increasing size, speed and standards of comfort culminated in the *Queen Mary* and the *Queen Elizabeth*.

1957–58 The first nuclear-powered ship, the Soviet naval icebreaker *Lenin*, was launched. The American merchant ship *Savannah* was the first commercial nuclear-powered ship.

1960s Container ships – carrying standardized containers for transporting cargo – were increasingly used by the world's merchant navies.

Roll-on, roll-off vessels were developed from the design of naval landing-ships for ferry traffic.

1970s Larger oil tankers were launched, such as the Japanese Universe class of 326 000 tonnes (tons) deadweight.

Hydrofoils entered commercial service as passenger ferries.

SHIPPING TONNAGES

Tonnage is the capacity of a ship expressed in terms of tonnes (tons). In the UK, four tonnage systems are in use – gross registered tonnage (GRT), net registered tonnage (NRT), deadweight tonnage (DWT) and displacement tonnage.

Gross registered tonnage is used for merchant shipping. It is the sum in cubic feet of all the enclosed spaces divided by 100, i.e. 1 grt = 100 ft^3 of enclosed space.

Net registered tonnage is also used for merchant shipping. It is the gross registered tonnage (see above) less deductions for crew spaces, engine rooms and ballast, which cannot be utilized for paying passengers or cargo.

Deadweight tonnage is used mainly for tramp ships and oil tankers. It is the number of UK long tons (2240 lb; 1.016 tonnes) of cargo, stores, bunkers and passengers that is required to bring down a ship from her height line to her load-water line, i.e. the carrying capacity of a ship.

Displacement tonnage is used for warships and US merchant shipping. It is the number of tons (tonnes) of sea water displaced by a vessel charged to its load-water line, i.e. the weight of the vessel and its contents in tons.

WORLD'S LARGEST SHIPS

The largest passenger vessel ever launched was the

liner *Queen Elizabeth* (UK), which was 314 m (1031 ft) long and had a gross tonnage of 82 998 tons (tonnes). Completed in 1940, she was used as a troop ship before entering regular service on the transatlantic run with the Cunard Line in 1946. The ship was retired in 1968 and sold for conversion as a seagoing college, *Seawise University*, which was destroyed by fire in Hong Kong on 9 Jan 1972. The largest active liner is the *Norway*, which was built as the *France* and served on the transatlantic route from 1961 to 1975. In June 1979 she was bought by the Norwegian Knut Kloster, renamed *Norway*, and recommissioned as a cruise ship in August 1979. *Norway* is 70 202·19 GRT and 315·66 m (1035 ft 7 in) in length.

IRON AND STEEL

The Iron Age began in the Near East in the 2nd millennium BC, and we still live in it today. Iron and steel account for almost 95% of the total tonnage of all metal production. Ships and trains, cars and trucks, bridges and buildings – all these and thousands of things besides depend on the strength, flexibility and toughness of steel.

Iron is extracted industrially from naturally occurring ores. The two most important of these are iron oxides – hematite (Fe_2O_3) and magnetite (Fe_3O_4). Mixed with carbon and heated to 1500 °C (2730 °F), iron oxides are reduced to metallic iron, the carbon combining with the oxygen to form carbon dioxide. This process is called *smelting*. In the Middle Ages charcoal was used to provide the carbon, but in 1709 Abraham Darby (1677–1717) of Coalbrookdale in Shropshire, England, succeeded in smelting iron with coke, which could readily be produced from coal. This made possible a huge increase in iron production during the Industrial Revolution.

The first link in the production of iron is the *blast furnace*, in which iron ore is reduced to iron. The biggest modern blast furnaces are huge constructions up to 30 m (100 ft) tall, with walls more than 3 m (10 ft) thick, and capable of making more than 10 000 tonnes (tons) of iron a day. The iron produced in the blast furnace is still contaminated with some residual impurities. Depending on the ore, it usually contains some 3 to 5% carbon, 1% manganese and 3% silicon.

FROM IRON TO STEEL

The iron tapped from a blast furnace is a raw material, not a finished product. To be useful, it must be converted either into cast iron or into steel. *Cast iron* is produced by remelting pig iron (iron that has been cast into moulds and allowed to cool) and carefully adjusting the proportions of carbon, silicon and other alloying elements. Strong and resistant to wear, cast iron can be machined and is easily cast into quite complex shapes. The moulds into which it is cast are made of sand contained in moulding boxes. The shape to be cast is impressed into the sand, and the molten iron poured into it. When solid, the casting is removed and the sand re-used to make a fresh mould.

The great bulk of the iron produced in a blast furnace is converted into steel, by greatly reducing the carbon content. A way of removing carbon economically from pig iron was discovered in 1857 by the English engineer Henry Bessemer (1813–98). In the *Bessemer process*, air blown through the molten iron combined with some of the carbon, carrying it away as carbon monoxide and carbon dioxide. It also

oxidized some of the iron, which then combined with the silicon and manganese to form a slag. After just 15 minutes, several hundred tonnes (tons) of iron had been converted into steel. The entire converter rotated on an axle like a cement mixer to pour out the molten steel.

A much slower and more controllable process was invented in the 1860s by a number of engineers – the *open-hearth process*. In this process gas from low-grade coal was used to heat pig iron in a shallow furnace. The chemical changes were the same as in the Bessemer converter, but the process had the advantage that scrap steel could be added to the mixture. The process took up to 12 hours to produce steel, allowing very careful control of the final composition.

Today both the Bessemer and the open-hearth processes have been superseded in most countries by a process that combines the merits of both. In the *L-D process* (short for Linz-Donawitz), a jet of almost pure oxygen is blown through a lance onto the surface of molten iron. The process is quick and can absorb up to 20% scrap, while producing steel of very high quality. The addition of lime to the oxygen enables iron of higher phosphorus content to be converted, and in this form the process is known as the *basic oxygen furnace*.

For the more expensive steels, including alloy and stainless steels, *electric-arc furnaces* are used. Heat is provided by three carbon electrodes, which are lowered into a mixture of scrap and alloying additions. Silicon, manganese and phosphorus are removed as slag, and carbon is removed by adding some iron ore, which reacts just as in the blast furnace. The fact that an electric-arc furnace can melt a charge consisting entirely of scrap is a big advantage in developed countries, where recycled steel makes up a large proportion of total production.

TYPES OF STEEL

Steel is sold in the form of cast slabs, or rolled into plates, strips, rods (for nails, screws and wire) or beams (for buildings, bridges and other constructional uses). To make it suitable for a particular use, the characteristics of a steel can be altered by a number of processes, including heat treatment and alloying.

The most important factor in any steel is the carbon content. High-carbon steels are harder and stronger, but they are also more brittle and cannot be welded. For adequate weldability, carbon contents below 0.2% are needed. The precise characteristics of any steel also depend on heat treatment, which determines the microstructure of the steel. Steel can be hardened by heating it to red heat – around 850 °C (1560 °F) – and then quenching it in water, but such a steel is also brittle. The hardness can largely be retained and the brittleness reduced by a second heating to a lower temperature – to around 250 °C (480 °F). The steel is then allowed to cool in air. Such steel is said to be *tempered*.

Alloying steel with other elements in addition to carbon is also important. A steel containing 3% nickel, for example, is immensely tough, and is used for gears and shafts that have to take a lot of strain. Steels containing up to 13% manganese have very hard edges, and are used for items such as rock-breaking machinery. The metal molybdenum is added to alloy steels to reduce brittleness. *Stainless steels*, containing around 14% chromium and sometimes nickel as well, do not rust because of the formation of an impermeable oxide layer on their surface. Such steels are now widely used for cutlery, kitchen sinks and the cladding of buildings.

TYPES OF STEEL

Type of steel	Carbon content (%)	Typical uses
Mild steel	0.08	Car bodies, tin cans
	0.2	Buildings, bridges, ships
Medium-carbon	0.25–0.45	Gun barrels, railway wheels
High-carbon	0.45–1.5	Tools, scissors, cutlery
Cast iron	2.5–4.5	Machine tools, engine blocks, ironmongery

MILESTONES IN PHOTOGRAPHY

1725 J. Schulze discovered that in the presence of nitric acid silver was darkened by the action of light, but more discoveries were needed to transform images cast by a lens into records that were positive (that is, without the reversal of black and white), and permanent.

c. 1800 Thomas Wedgewood was making short-lived silhouette images with silver nitrate.

1826 Joseph Niepce made his first successful picture, with the image projected by a lens on to a metal plate covered with bitumen of judea, which hardens under the influence of light. Washing away the unhardened parts produced a printing plate.

1835 The first successful silver image, on a copper plate, was produced by Louis Daguerre, who discovered that there was a second ('latent') image that could be developed with mercury vapour.

1837 Daguerre made permanent pictures using a salt 'fixer'. Positive and permanent, his 'Daguerreotype' was the first popular photographic system.

1839 Sir John Herschel suggested sodium thiosulphate ('hypo') as the best fixing agent. Hippolyte Bayard invented a method of making positive pictures on paper. Joseph Reade discovered that gallic acid is a powerful developer.

1840 A mathematically calculated portrait lens designed by Josef Petzval, providing a large aperture and therefore shorter exposures, was put into production by Voigtlander & Sohn.

1841 William Fox Talbot patented his 'Calotype' process. This used a paper-base negative image from which unlimited numbers of positive prints could be made. The use of gallic acid reduced his average exposure time to five minutes.

1847 Niepce de Saint-Victor made binder for silver iodide from white of egg (albumen). This made fine-detail glass negatives possible. Louis Blanquart-Evrard improved the Calotype process by impregnating rather than coating paper with the light-sensitive mixture.

1851 Gustave le Gray introduced his waxed-paper process, which produced a negative almost as good as a glass plate.

Frederick Scott Archer introduced the 'wet-plate' process. This used collodion (guncotton and ether) as a binding agent poured on a glass plate, which was then dipped in silver nitrate and exposed in the camera and developed before it was dry. Using this method, exposures for portraits could be reduced to ten seconds or less.

Fox Talbot took the first high-speed flash photograph, using the spark discharge of a battery.

1854 Fox Talbot, who had been reluctant to share his knowledge, lost his legal claim to exclusive rights to the wet-plate process. Rapid progress in photography in England followed.

1861 James Clerk Maxwell demonstrated the possibility of producing colour pictures by superimposing red, green and blue negatives of the same subject (the 'additive' process). Each negative was exposed through the corresponding colour filter. Practical application of the process was delayed by the lack of red-sensitive emulsions.

1868 Louis du Hauron suggested that colour pictures could be made with a single plate, through a screen covered with tiny transparent dots or lines of red, blue and yellow.

1871 Richard Maddox, following previous experimenters, devised a method of producing dry plates, with gelatine replacing collodion.

1873 John Burgess introduced commercially viable gelatine dry plates. Hermann Vögel discovered that silver particles dyed orange had greater sensitivity to green light.

1874 Edmond Becquerel's discovery that green dyes increase sensitivity to red made 'panchromatic' (red-sensitive) emulsion possible.

1878 Charles Bennett discovered that prolonged heating during the manufacture of emulsions greatly increases their sensitivity.

1880s Flash powder, a mixture of magnesium powder and potassium chlorate, was introduced.

1888 George Eastman introduced his roll-film box camera, bringing photography to the masses. (His Eastman Kodak Company was successfully sued for infringement of the roll-film patent.)

1890 Carl Zeiss's 'Protar' lens utilized a wide range of different barium glasses to reduce distortions.

1893 The 'kinetoscope', a peep-box for viewing moving pictures on a 35 mm perforated film strip, was marketed by Thomas Edison.

1895 Auguste and Louis Lumière introduced their cinematograph for moving pictures. This apparatus – which advanced and held the film by a claw device – became the basis of the movie film industry.

1904 The Lumière brothers marketed colourplates, with an outer coating of green, red and blue starch grains. The developed image was re-exposed and redeveloped ('reversed') to produce a positive colour transparency.

1924 The Leica miniature camera, utilizing 35 mm movie film, was introduced.

1925 The first flashbulb was introduced.

1935 Kodachrome, the first successful colour film utilizing three emulsion layers of differing colour response, was introduced for the production of positive transparencies.

1940 The modern electronic, or speed, flash was introduced.

1947 The Polaroid-Land 'instant picture' camera was demonstrated. Processing agents were incorporated in the film and activated within the camera after exposure.

1963 'Instant print' colour films were introduced.

1977 Polaroid introduced an 8 mm colour movie film.

1981 The first commercial video camera, the Sony Mavica, was demonstrated.

1982 Polaroid introduced still transparency films that can be processed rapidly outside the camera.

MISCELLANEOUS INVENTIONS

Inventions and discoveries in the fields of music, chemistry, medicine and physics are treated in the relevant chapters. The following list covers significant inventions that are not included in those chapters or on the preceding pages of this chapter.

Object	Year	Inventor	Notes
adding machine	1623	Wilhelm Schickard (Ger)	Earliest commercial machine devised by William Burroughs (US) in St Louis, Missouri, in 1885.
bakelite	1909	Leo H. Baekeland (Belg/US; 1863–1944)	First use, electrical insulation by Loando & Co, Boonton, New Jersey.
ball-point pen	1888	John J. Loud (US)	First practical and low cost writing pens by Lazlo and Georg Biro (Hungary) in 1938.
barbed wire	1867	Lucien B. Smith (patentee)	Introduced to Britain in 1880 by 5th Earl Spencer in Leicestershire.
barometer	1644	Evangelista Torricelli (1608–47)	
battery (electric)	1800	Alessandro Volta (1745–1827)	Demonstrated to Napoleon I in 1801.
bicycle	1839–40	Kirkpatrick Macmillan (Scot; 1810–78)	Pedal-driven cranks. First direct drive in March 1861 by Ernest Michaux (Fr).
bicycle tyres (pneumatic)	1888	John Boyd Dunlop (Scot; 1840–1921)	Principle patented but undeveloped by Robert William Thomson (Eng), 1845. First motor car pneumatic tyres adapted by André and Edouard Michelin (Fr) 1895 (see rubber tyres).
Bifocal lens	1780	Benjamin Franklin (US; 1706–90)	His earliest experiments began c. 1760.
Bunsen burner	1855	Robert Wilhelm von Bunsen (Ger; 1811–99) at Heidelberg	Michael Faraday (Eng; 1791–1867) had previously designed an adjustable burner.
burglar alarm	1858	Edwin T. Holmes (US)	Electric, installed at Boston, Mass, USA.
car (steam gun tug)	1769	Nicolas Cugnot (Fr; 1725–1804)	Three-wheeled military tractor. Earliest for passengers was Richard Trevithick's eight-seater in Camborne, Cornwall, in 1801.
(internal combustion)	1826	Samuel Brown (Eng)	First powered with internal combustion engine was gas-powered carriage on Shooter's Hill, Blackheath, SE London.
(petrol)	1885	Karl Benz (Ger; 1844–1929)	First successful run Mannheim Nov or Dec. Patented 29 Jan 1886.
carburettor	1876	Gottlieb Daimler (Ger; 1834–1900)	Carburettor spray: Charles E. Duryea (US) (1892).
carpet sweeper	1876	Melville R. Bissell (US)	Grand Rapids, Mich., USA.
cash register	1879	James Ritty (US)	Built in Dayton, Ohio. Taken over by National Cash Register Co 1884.
cellophane	1908	Dr Jacques Brandenberger (Switz), Zurich	Machine production not before 1911.
celluloid	1861	Alexander Parkes (Eng) (1813–90)	Invented in Birmingham, England; developed and trade marked by J. W. Hyatt (US) in 1870.
cement (portland)	1824	Joseph Aspdin (Eng; 1779–1885)	Wakefield, Yorkshire.
chronometer	1735	John Harrison (Eng; 1693–1776)	Received in 1772 a prize of £20 000 on offer by the government since 1714.
clock (mechanical)	725	I-Hsing and Liang-Tsan (China)	Earliest escapement. Clockwork known in Greece by 80 BC.
(pendulum)	1656	Christiaan Huygens (Neths; 1629–95)	
compact disc	1978	Philips (Netherlands) and Sony (Japan)	Needleless laser beam-read discs. First marketed in October 1982.
dental plate	1817	Anthony A. Plantson (US; 1774–1837)	

Object	Year	Inventor	Notes
dental plate (rubber)	1855	Charles Goodyear (US; 1800–60)	
diesel engine	1895	Rudolf Diesel (Ger; 1858–1913)	Diesel's first commercial success, Augsburg, 1897.
disc brake	1902	Dr F. Lanchester (Eng; 1868–1946)	First used on aircraft 1953 (Dunlop Rubber Co).
dynamo	1832	Hyppolite Pixii (Fr), demonstrated in Paris	Rotative dynamo, demonstrated by Joseph Saxton, Cambridge, England, in 1833.
electric blanket	1883	Exhibited Vienna, Austria Exhibition	
electric flat iron	1882	H. W. Seeley (US)	New York City, USA (Patent 6 June).
electric lamp	1879	Thomas Alva Edison (US; 1847–1931)	First practical demonstration at Menlo Park, New Jersey, USA. Pioneer work on carbon filaments, Sir Joseph Swan (Eng; 1828–1914), 1860.
electric motor (DC)	1873	Zénobe Gramme (Belg; 1826–1901)	Exhibited in Vienna.
electric motor (AC)	1888	Nikola Tesla (Serbian-born, US; 1856–1943)	
electromagnet	1824	William Sturgeon (Eng; 1783–1850)	Improved by Joseph Henry (US; 1797–1878).
fountain pen	1884	Lewis E. Waterman (US; 1837–1901)	Patented by D. Hyde (US), 1830, undeveloped.
galvanometer	1834	André-Marie Ampère (1755–1836)	First measurement of flow of electricity with a free-moving needle.
gas lighting	1792	William Murdoch (GB; 1754–1839)	Private house in Cornwall, 1792; factory Birmingham, 1798; London streets, 1807
glass (stained)	ante 850		Earliest complete window Augsburg, Germany, c. 1080.
glassware	c. 2600 BC	in Mesopotamia	Glass blowing, Sidon, Syria, c. 50 BC.
glider	1853	Sir George Cayley (GB; 1773–1857)	Near Brompton Hall, Yorks. Passenger possibly John Appleby. Emmanuel Swedenborg (1688–1772) sketches dated 1716.
gramophone	1878	Thomas Alva Edison (US; 1847–1931)	Hand-cranked cylinder at Menlo Park, NJ. First described in 1877 by Charles Cros (Fr; 1842–88).
gyro-compass	1911	Elmer A. Sperry (US; 1860–1930)	Tested on USS Delaware. Gyroscope devised 1852 by Jean Foucault (Fr; 1819–68).
hovercraft	1953	Sir Christopher Cockerell (Eng; b. 1910)	Earliest air-cushion vehicle patent was in 1877 by J. I. Thornycroft (Eng; 1843–1928). First 'flight' Saunders Roe SRN-1 at Cowes, England, 1959.
integrated circuit	1952	Concept by Geoffrey Dummer (Eng; b. 1909)	First practical circuit by Harwick Johnson (US), Princeton, NY, 1953.
laser	1960	Dr Charles H. Townes (US; b. 1915). First construction by Theodore Maiman (US; b. 1927)	Demonstrated at Hughes Research, Malibu, California. Abbreviation for Light Amplification by Stimulated Emission of Radiation.
lift	1852	Elisha G. Otis (US; 1811–61)	Earliest elevator at Yonkers, NY.
lightning conductor	1752	Benjamin Franklin (US; 1706–90)	Philadelphia, Pennsylvania, USA.
linoleum	1860	Frederick Walton (Eng)	
loudspeaker	1900	Horace Short (Eng) patentee	A compressed air Auxetophone. First used on the Eiffel Tower, summer 1900. Earliest open-air electric public address system used by Bell Telephone on Staten Island, NY, USA, June 1916.
machine gun	1718	James Puckle; in use 1721	Richard Gatling (US; 1818–1903) model dates from 1861.
maps	c. 2250 BC	Sumerian (clay tablets of river Euphrates)	Earliest measurement by Eratosthenes c. 220 BC. Earliest printed map printed in Bologna, Italy, 1477.
margarine	1869	Hippolyte Mège-Mouriès (Fr)	
match, safety	1845	Anton von Schrötter (Austrian)	François Devosne developed the first phosphorus (unsafe) match in 1816.

Object	Year	Inventor	Notes
microphone	1876	Alexander Graham Bell (US; 1847–1922)	Name coined 1878 by Prof David Hughes, who gave demonstration in London in January 1878.
microprocessor	1971	Marcian E. Hoff (US; b. 1937)	Launched by US company Intel in the same year.
microscope	1590	Zacharias Janssen (Neth)	Compound convex-concave lens.
motor cycle	1885	Gottlieb Daimler (1834–1900) of Cannstatt, Germany	First rider Paul Daimler (10 Nov 1885).
neon lamp	1910	Georges Claude (Fr; 1871–1960)	First installation at Paris Motor Show.
parking meter	1935	Carlton C. Magee (US)	Oklahoma City, USA.
pasteurization	1867	Louis Pasteur (1822–95)	Destruction of pathogenic micro-organisms by heat. Effective against tuberculous milk.
pocket calculator	1971	Jack St Clair Kilby (b. 1924); James van Tassell and Jerry D. Merryman (US; b. 1932)	The 'Pocketronic', manufactured by Texas Instruments Inc., Dallas.
porcelain	851	Earliest report from China	Reached Baghdad in 9th century.
potter's wheel	c. 6500 BC	Asia Minor	Used in Eridu, Mesopotamia.
printing press	c. 1455	Johann Gutenberg (Ger; c. 1400–68)	
printing (rotary)	1846	Richard Hoe (US; 1812–86)	Philadelphia Public Ledger rotary printed, 1847.
propeller (ship)	1837	Francis Smith (Eng; 1808–74)	Hand propeller screw used in 1776 submarine (q.v.).
pyramid	2856 BC	Imhotep (Egypt)	Earliest was Djoser step pyramid, Sakkara, Egypt.
radar	1922	Dr Albert H. Taylor and Leo C. Young	Radio reflection effect first noted. First harnessed by Dr Rudolph Kühnold, Kiel, Germany, in 1934. Word coined in 1940 by Cdr S. M. Tucker USN.
razor			
(electric)	1931	Col. Jacob Schick (US)	First manufactured Stamford, Conn.
(safety)	1895	King C. Gillette (US); patented 1901	First disposable blades. Earliest fixed safety razor by Kampfe.
record (long-playing)	1948	Dr Peter Goldmark (US)	Micro-groove developed in the CBS Research Laboratories.
refrigerator	1850	James Harrison (Austral) and Alexander Catlin Twining (US)	Simultaneous development at Rodey Point, Victoria, Australia, and in Cleveland, Ohio. Earliest domestic refrigerator 1913 in Chicago, Illinois.
rubber			
(latex foam)	1928	Dunlop Rubber Co (UK)	Team led by E.A. Murphy at Fort Dunlop, Birmingham.
(tyres)	1846	Thomas Hancock (Eng; 1786–1865)	Introduced solid rubber tyres for vehicles (1847) (*see also* bicycle).
(vulcanized)	1841	Charles Goodyear (US; 1800–60)	
(waterproof)	1824	Charles Macintosh (Scot; 1766–1843)	First experiments in Glasgow with James Syme. G. Fox in 1821 had marketed a Gambroon cloth, but no detail has survived.
safety pin	1849	Walter Hunt (US)	First manufactured New York City, NY.
Scotch tape	1930	Richard Drew (US; 1899–1980)	Developed from opaque masking tape.
self-starter	1911	Charles F. Kettering (US; 1876–1958)	Developed at Dayton, Ohio; sold to Cadillac.
sewing machine	1829	Barthélemy Thimmonnier (Fr; 1793–1854)	A patent by Thomas Saint (Eng) dated 17 July 1790 for an apparently undeveloped machine was found in 1874. Earliest practical domestic machine by Isaac M. Singer (US; 1811–75).
silk manufacture	c. 50 BC	Reeling machines devised, China	Silk mills in Italy c. 1250.
skyscraper	1882	William Le Baron Jenny (US)	Home Insurance Co. Building, Chicago, Ill, 10 storey (top four with steel beams).
slide rule	1621	William Oughtred (Eng; 1575–1660)	Earliest slide between fixed stock by Robert Bissaker, 1654.
spectacles	c. 1286	in Pisa, Italy (convex)	Concave lens for myopia. Nicholas of Cusa (1401–64) c. 1450.
steam engine	1698	Thomas Savery (GB; c. 1650–1715)	Denis Papin (Fr; 1647–1712) had invented the pressure cooker 1679.
steam engine (condenser)	1769	James Watt (Scot; 1736–1819)	

Object	Year	Inventor	Notes
steam engine (piston)	1712	Thomas Newcomen (Eng; 1663–1729)	Hero of Alexandria (*fl.* AD 62) had devised a toy-like aeropile.
submarine	1776	David Bushnell (US), Saybrook, Conn	Hand-propelled screw, one man crew, used off New York. A 12- man wooden and leather submersible devised by Cornelius Drebbel (Neth) demonstrated in Thames in 1624.
tank	1914	Sir Ernest Swinton (Eng; 1868–1951)	Built at Lincoln, designed by William Tritton. Tested 1915.
telegraph (mechanical)	1787	M. Lammond (Fr) demonstrated a working model, Paris	
telegraph code	1837	Samuel F.B. Morse (US; 1791–1872)	The real credit belonged largely to his assistant Alfred Vail (US), who first transmitted at Morristown, NJ on 8 Jan 1838.
telephone	1849	Antonio Meucci (It) in Havana, Cuba	Instrument worked imperfectly by electrical impulses.
	1876	Alexander Graham Bell (US; 1847–1922).	First exchange at Boston, Mass, 1878.
telescope (refractor)	1608	Hans Lippershey (Neth)	
thermometer	1593	Galileo Galilei (It; 1564–1642)	Clinical. Santorio Santorio developed the mercury thermometer c. 1615.
transistor	1948	John Bardeen, William Shockley and Walter Brattain (US)	Researched at Bell Telephone Laboratories. First application for a patent was by Dr Julius E. Lilienfeld in Canada on October 1925 (*see* Electronic Computer).
typewriter	1867	Christopher Sholes (US)	Manufactured by the gunsmith Philo Remington in 1874.
washing machine	1907	Hurley Machine Co (US)	Marketed under the name of 'Thor' in Chicago, Illinois, USA.
watch	1462	Bartholomew Manfredi (It)	Earliest mention of a named watchmaker (November), but in reference to an earlier unnamed watchmaker.
water closet	1589	Designed by Sir John Harington (Eng)	Installed at Kelston, near Bath.
welder (electric)	1877	Elisha Thomson (US; 1853–1937)	
wheel	c.3580 BC	Sumerian civilization, Uruk, Iraq	Pottery cup with 3 four-wheeled waggons; Brónócice, Poland c. 3500 BC.
windmill	c. 600	in Iran for corn grinding	
writing	c. 3600 BC	Sumerian civilization (pictographs)	Earliest evidence found in SE Iran, 1970
zip fastener	1891	Whitcomb L. Judson (US); exhibited 1893 at Chicago Exposition	First practical fastener invented in USA by Gideon Sundback (Sweden) in 1913.

MILESTONES IN RADIO AND TELEVISION

1861 James Clerk Maxwell, Scottish physicist and mathematician, predicted the existence of an invisible form of electromagnetic wave travelling at the speed of light.

1887 Heinrich Hertz, German physicist, demonstrated the reality of Maxwell's waves, by allowing a small spark to jump across an air gap, and detecting the waves at the other side of a room with a similar air gap.

1894 Guglielmo Marconi, a young Italian inventor, made a bell ring in the attic of his parents' house in Bologna by sending a radio message across the room.

1901 Marconi succeeded in sending a radio message in Morse Code across the Atlantic, from Cornwall to Newfoundland.

1906 Music and speech was broadcast for the first time, by the American physicist Reginald Fessenden. The sounds were carried on radio waves by 'modulating' them, superimposing the sound waves on to the radio waves. The amplitude of the radio wave was altered to carry the sound – giving rise to the term *amplitude modulation*, or AM.

1907 Lee De Forest, an American inventor, used a triode valve to amplify radio signals.

1917 Lucien Lévy, in France, and Edwin Armstrong, in the USA, devised 'superheterodyne' circuits that made tuning much easier, reduced power requirements and simplified the construction of receivers.

1921 The first radio station, KDKA, began broadcasting in Pittsburgh, USA. The British Broadcasting Company (BBC) began daily transmissions the following year.

1925 Using a mechanical scanning system, the Scot John Logie Baird transmitted the first recognizable pictures of human faces.

1931 Vladimir Zworykin, a Russian-born inventor living in the USA, demonstrated the first practical electronic television camera.

1933 Edwin Armstrong devised frequency modulation (FM), in which the frequency rather than the amplitude of the carrier wave is modulated by the signal. This reduced the problem of random noise caused by static.

1936 The BBC television service was inaugurated at Alexandra Palace in London. It utilized two systems: Logie Baird's mechanical system, and an electronic system developed by an EMI research team under Isaac Schoenberg.

1945 Arthur C. Clarke, British science-fiction writer, described in *Wireless World* the possible use of a satellite in geostationary orbit for broadcasting radio and TV signals.

1951 Regular television broadcasting in colour was begun by Columbia Broadcasting System in New York.

1952 The first transistor radio, small enough to carry in the pocket, was made by Sony in Japan.

1953 The Federal Communications Commission in the USA adopted the NTSC (National Television Systems Committee) system for colour broadcasting.

1956 Improved colour TV became available using a system called SECAM (*Sequential Couleur à Memoire*) developed in France.

1958 The first video recording device, in which TV signals were recorded on magnetic tape, was installed in a US TV studio by the Ampex Corporation. A key invention, by Alexander Poniatoff of Ampex, was the rotating playback head, which enabled more information to be packed on to the tape.

1962 A third colour TV System PAL (Phase Alternance Line) was developed in Germany. (All three colour systems are incompatible.)

1962 The first transatlantic pictures are carried live, bounced off the communications satellite Telstar.

1963 The first geostationary satellites, the Syncom series built by Hughes Aircraft Corporation, were placed in orbit.

1965 Intelsat-1, Early Bird, went into geostationary orbit. It had the capacity for a single TV channel between Europe and North America.

1967 A colour TV service began in Britain, using the PAL system.

1970s Rival VCR systems emerged from Philips, Sony and JVC. The JVC system, known as VHS (video home system) proved the most successful and by the mid-80s millions of VCRs were installed in homes.

1974 Information systems, using the spare lines on a 625-line TV system, were broadcast in Britain. The BBC version is called Ceefax, the ITV system Oracle.

1974 ATS-6, an experimental direct broadcasting satellite, was launched by NASA and used to broadcast to Indian villages equipped with a receiver dish.

1979 The first regular direct broadcasting system, beaming pictures directly to people's houses (rather than through a ground station), was launched in Canada. The ANIK-B, requiring only a small rooftop dish, was the forerunner of many direct broadcasting systems.

1989 Commercial satellite broadcasting began in Britain with Sky Television, followed in 1990 by British Satellite Broadcasting (now merged).

TRANSPORT

RAIL

If a railway is defined as a track that guides vehicles

travelling along it, the Babylonians could be said to have invented this system of transport (2245 BC) when they used tracks formed of parallel lines of stone blocks with grooves in the centre to guide wagons.

The first positive record of the use of steam power on a railway was in 1804 when a locomotive built by Richard Trevithick hauled a train at Penydarren Ironworks in South Wales. The first railway to be operated entirely by steam engines from its opening was the Liverpool and Manchester, on 15 September 1830.

The 'standard gauge' of 1435 mm (4 ft 8½ in) was first established on the Willington Colliery wagonway near Newcastle-upon-Tyne in 1764–5. Today this gauge is standard in Great Britain, Canada, the USA, Mexico, Europe (except Ireland, Spain, Portugal, Finland and the USSR), North Africa, the Near Eastern countries, China, South Korea and parts of Australia (served by the Australian National Railways). In South America it is found in Paraguay, Uruguay, the Argentine Urquiza system, Central and Southern Railways of Peru, Venezuela, and short lines in Brazil. It is also used by some lines in Japan.

The modern standard system of railway electrification at 25 kV 50 Hz was first used in France in 1950, and in Britain, on the Colchester–Clacton–Walton lines, on 16 March 1959.

The world's first railway tunnel was an underground line at Newcastle-upon-Tyne, England, which was built in 1770. The first underwater public railway tunnel was the Thames Tunnel on the East London Railway, opened in 1843. The Channel Tunnel's twin-bore railway will be 7·6 m (25 ft) diameter and 49·4 km (30·7 miles) long of which 38 km (23·6 miles) will be under the sea (see UK Transport section).

PRINCIPAL RAILWAY SYSTEMS OF THE WORLD

Railway system	Year of first railway	mm	Gauge ft in	Route km	length miles
Argentina	1857	1676	5　6	22 101	13 733
		1435	4 8½	3 088	1 919
		1000	3 3⅜	11 844	7 359
		750	2 5½	285	177
				37 318	23 188
Australia	1854	1600	5　3	8 396	5 217
		1435	4 8½	14 243	8 850
		1067	3　6	16 749	10 407
				39 388	24 474
Brazil	1854	1600	5　3	1 736	1 079
		1000	3 3⅜	21 711	12 286
		762	2　6	202	125
				23 649	13 490
Canada	1836	1435	4 8½	68 023	42 267
		1067	3　6	1 146	712
		915	3　0	178	111
				69 347	43 090
Chile	1851	1676	5　6	4 282	2 661
		1435	4 8½	370	230
		1000	3 3⅜	3 300	2 050
				7 952	4 941

China	1880	1435	*4 8½*	c. 50 000	c. 31 000
Czecho-slovakia	1839	1520	*4 11*	101	*63*
		1435	*4 8½*	13 039	*8 102*
		1000	*3 3⅜* ⎫	177	*110*
		600	*1 11½* ⎭		
				13 317	*8 275*
France	1832	1435	*4 8½*	34 362	*21 351*
Germany	1835	1435	*4 8½*	42 665	26 511
United Kingdom	1830	1435	*4 8½*	17 248	*10 718*
		600	*1 11½*	19	*12*
				17 267	*10 730*
India	1853	1676	*5 6*	31 789	*19 753*
		1000	*3 3⅜*	25 209	*15 664*
		762	*2 6*	3 521	*2 188*
		610	*2 0*	390	*242*
				60 909	*37 847*
Italy	1839	1435	*4 8½*	16 133	*10 024*
Japan	1872	1435	*4 8½*	1 177	*731*
		1067	*3 6*	20 145	*12 517*
				21 322	*13 248*
Mexico	1850	1435	*4 8½*	14 151	*8 793*
		914	*3 0*	457	*280*
		mixed		72	*45*
				14 680	*9 118*

Pakistan	1861	1676	*5 6*	7 754	*4 818*
		1000	*3 3⅜*	444	*276*
		762	*2 6*	610	*379*
				8 808	*5 473*
Poland	1842	1435	*4 8½*	23 855	*14 822*
Romania	1869	1435	*4 8½*	10 515	*6 534*
		762	*2 6* ⎫	568	*353*
		610	*2 0* ⎭		
				11 083	*6 887*
South Africa	1860	1065	*3 6*	22 891	*14 223*
		610	*2 0*	706	*439*
				23 597	*14 662*
Spain	1848	1676	*5 6*	13 531	*8 407*
Sweden	1856	1435	*4 8½*	11 158	*6 933*
		891	*2 11*	182	*113*
				11 340	*7 046*
Turkey	1896	1435	*4 8½*	8 140	*5 847*
USA	1830	1435	*4 8½*	294 625	*183 077*
		1520	*4 11⅞*	c. 141 800	c. *88 110*
		1435	*4 8½*	73	*45*
		1067	*3 6*	761	*473*
		up to 1 m		2 571	*1 598*
				c. 439 830	c. *273 303*
USSR	1837	1524	*5 0*	145 292	*90 283*

MAJOR 'METROS'

Railway systems partly or wholly underground

City	System begun	Total length of route	Number of lines	Number of stations
London (UK)	1863	408 km (254 mi)	10	273
New York (USA)	1868	373 km (232 mi)	23	466
Paris (France)	1900	307 km (191 mi)	18	430
Moscow (USSR)[1]	1935	225 km (140 mi)	8	123
Tokyo (Japan)	1927	217 km (135 mi)	10	192
Berlin (Germany)[2]	1902	168 km (104 mi)	8	134
Chicago (USA)	1892	156 km (97 mi)	6	142
Copenhagen (Denmark)	1934	135 km (84 mi)	7	61
Mexico City (Mexico)	1969	125 km (78 mi)	5	57
Washington DC (USA)[3]	1976	118 km (73 mi)	3	47
Seoul (South Korea)[4]	1974	117 km (72 mi)	2	20
San Francisco (USA)	1972	115 km (71 mi)	1	34
Madrid (Spain)[5]	1919	112 km (70 mi)	11	141
Stockholm (Sweden)[6]	1950	108 km (67 mi)	3	94
Osaka (Japan)	1933	91 km (57 mi)	6	88

Hamburg (Germany)	1912	90 km (56 mi)	3	80
Bucharest (Romania)	1979	87 km (54 mi)	2	21
Leningrad (USSR)	1955	83 km (52 mi)	3	43
Nagoya (Japan)	1957	69 km (43 mi)	4	56
Barcelona (Spain)[7]	1924	69 km (43 mi)	4	7
Milan (Italy)	1964	66 km (41 mi)	2	57
Toronto (Canada)	1954	64 km (40 mi)	2	58
Philadelphia (USA)	1907	63 km (39 mi)	3	68
Montreal (Canada)[8]	1966	61 km (38 mi)	3	51
Boston (USA)	1897	61 km (38 mi)	3	51

[1] an additional 17 km under construction
[2] an additional 8 km under construction
[3] an additional 434 km under construction and projection
[4] an additional 34 km under construction
[5] an additional 4 km under construction
[6] an additional 6 km under construction
[7] an additional 21 km under construction
[8] an additional 13 km under construction

OTHER 'METRO' SYSTEMS (with the year in which the first section was opened)

Amsterdam, Netherlands (1977), Athens, Greece (1925), Atlanta, USA (1979), Baku, USSR (1967), Baltimore, USA (1983), Beijing (Peking), China (1971), Brussels, Belgium (1976), Budapest, Hungary (1896), Buenos Aires, Argentina (1913), Cairo, Egypt (1987), Calcutta, India (1984), Caracas, Venezuela (1983), Cleveland, USA (1955), Detroit, USA (1986), Dneipropetrovsk, USSR (1984), Frankfurt, Germany (1968), Fukuoka, Japan (1981), Glasgow, UK (1896; reopened 1979), Helsinki, Finland (1982), Hong Kong (1979), Kharkov, USSR (1975), Kiev, USSR (1960), Kobe, Japan (1977), Kubyshev, USSR (1986), Kyoto, Japan (1981), Lille, France (1983), Lisbon, Portugal (1959), Lyon, France (1978), Marseille, France (1977), Miami, USA (1984), Minsk, USSR (1984), Munich, Germany (1971), Naples, Italy (1987), Newcastle-upon-Tyne, UK (1980), Nizhny Novgorod (Gorky) USSR (1985), Novosibirsk, USSR (1985), Nürnberg, Germany (1972), Oslo, Norway (1966), Prague, Czechoslovakia (1974), Pusan, South Korea (1984), Pyongyang, North Korea (1973), Rio de Janeiro, Brazil (1979), Rome, Italy (1955), Rotterdam, Netherlands (1968), Santiago, Chile (1975), São Paulo, Brazil (1974), Sapporo, Japan (1971), Sendai, Japan (1985), Singapore (1986), Seville, Spain (1987), Sofia, Bulgaria (1985), Tashkent, USSR (1977), Tbilisi, USSR (1966), Tianjin, China (1980), Toulouse, France (1985), Vancouver, Canada (1985), Vienna, Austria (1976), Wuppertal, Germany (1902), Yerevan, USSR (1981), Yokohana, Japan (1972).

'Metros' are also under construction in Buffalo (USA), Sverdlovsk (USSR) and Tehran (Iran).

LARGEST MERCHANT SHIPS

The largest oil tanker and ship of any kind in service is the 550 051 tonnes (tons) deadweight *Helias Fos*, a steam turbine tanker built in 1979. She has a gross registered tonnage of 254 583 tonnes (tons) and a net registered tonnage of 227 801 tonnes (tons). *Helias Fos* is Greek-owned by the Bilinder Marine Corporation of Athens.

The largest ship afloat was the *Happy Giant*, formerly the *Seawise Giant*, which had a deadweight tonnage of 564 763 tonnes (tons). She was attacked by Iraqi planes in the Gulf in December 1987 and was severely damaged in another attack in May 1988. The ship was bought by a Norwegian company and is being refitted in South Korea, but changes to the structure of the oil tanker, including the replacement of her steam turbines by a diesel engine, will reduce her tonnage to approximately 420 000 tonnes (tons).

A French tanker fleet includes, in order of size, the *Pierre Guillaumat*, *Prairial*, *Bellamya*, and *Batillus*, not all of which were in service early in 1991. They range in deadweight tonnage from 555 051 tonnes (tons) to 553 662 tonnes (tons).

FLAGS OF CONVENIENCE

A large proportion of the world's merchant shipping flies flags of convenience. Ships are registered by their owners in other countries that offer financial, legal or other incentives to fly their flag. The first countries to offer such advantages were Liberia and Panama, which now have the world's largest registered merchant fleets, although almost all of the vessels involved are owned by European and North American companies.

The largest merchant fleets in 1988 were those of:

Country	Registered tonnage
Liberia	49 500 000
Panama	43 600 000
Japan	29 200 000
Greece	21 400 000
USSR	18 900 000
Cyprus	18 300 000
USA	17 700 000
China	12 400 000

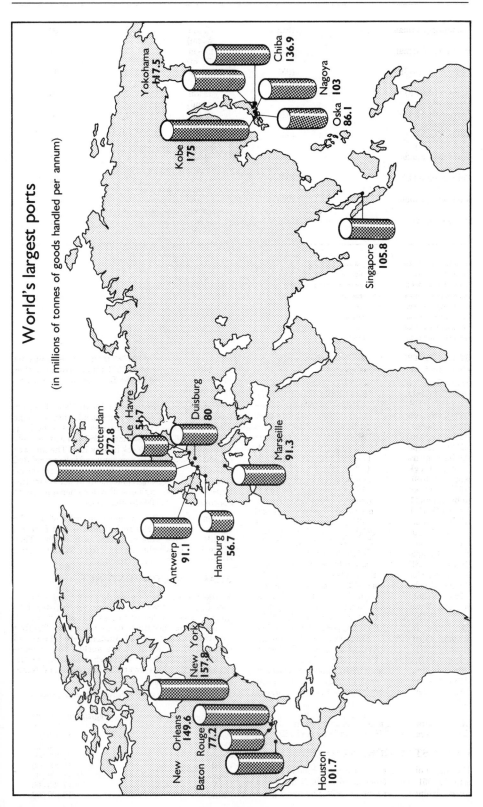

World's largest ports

(in millions of tonnes of goods handled per annum)

Yokohama 117.5

Chiba 136.9

Nagoya 103

Oska 86.1

Kobe 175

Singapore 105.8

Rotterdam 272.8

Le Havre 54.7

Duisburg 80

Marseille 91.3

Antwerp 91.1

Hamburg 56.7

New York 157.8

New Orleans 149.6

Baton Rouge 77.2

Houston 101.7

MARITIME PORTS

The figures in this list of the world's busiest ports are in millions of tonnes of goods handled per year.

Port	
Rotterdam (Netherlands)	272.8
Kobe (Japan)	175
New York	157.8
New Orleans (USA)	149.6
Chiba (Japan)	136.9
Yokohama (Japan)	117.5
Singapore (Singapore)	105.8
Nagoya (Japan)	103
Houston (USA)	101.7
Marseille (France)	91.3
Antwerp (Belgium)	91.1
Osaka (Japan)	86.1
Duisburg* (Germany)	80
Baton Rouge (USA)	77.2
Hamburg (Germany)	56.7
Le Havre (France)	51.7

* an inland port

EURO FACTS

OTHER LEADING EC PORTS

(millions of tonnes of goods handled per year)

Port	
London (UK)	48
Genoa (Italy)	46.1
Dunkerque (France)	35.7
Bremen–Bremerhaven (Germany)	29.8
Amsterdam (Netherlands)	29.4
Forth Estuary ports (UK) (Grangemouth–Leith)	28.8
Bilbao (Spain)	28.6
Tees Estuary ports (UK) (Middlesbrough–Teesport–Hartlepool)	28.2
Milford Haven (UK)	26.8
Ghent (Belgium)	26.6
Venice (Italy)	25.2
Trieste (Italy)	23.2

MAJOR SHIP CANALS

The following canals can be used by ocean-going shipping.

Canal	Route	Year opened	Length
St Lawrence Seaway (Canada – USA)	Montreal to Lake Ontario	1959	304 km[1] (189 mi)
Suez Canal (Egypt)	Mediterranean Sea to Red Sea	1869	162 km (101 mi)
Albert Canal (Belgium)	River Meuse (Maes) to River Scheld	1939	129 km (80 mi)
Kiel Canal (Germany)	North Sea to Baltic Sea	1895	99 km (62 mi)
Alfonso XIII Canal (Spain)	Seville to Gulf of Cadiz	1926	85 km (53 mi)
Panama Canal (Panama)	Pacific Ocean to Caribbean Sea	1914	81 km (50 mi)
Sabine–Neches Waterway (USA)[2]	Beaumont to Gulf of Mexico	1916	72 km (45 mi)
Houston Ship Canal (USA)[2]	Houston to Gulf of Mexico	1914	69 km (43 mi)
Manchester Ship Canal (UK)	Manchester to the Mersey estuary	1894	58 km (36 mi)
Welland Canal (Canada)	Lake Ontario to Lake Erie	1933	44 km (28 mi)
North Sea Canal (Noordzeekanaal) (Netherlands)	Amsterdam to Ijmuiden on the North Sea	1876	27 km (17 mi)
Chesapeake and Delaware Canal[3] (USA)	Chesapeake Bay to Delaware River	1829	22 km (14 mi)

[1] The canalized section of the St Lawrence Seaway that enables shipping to sail 3769 km (2342 mi) from the North Atlantic up the St Lawrence estuary and through the Great Lakes to Duluth, Minnesota.

[2] Part of a series of artificial and natural channels providing a discontinuous navigation, linking the Texan Gulf coast ports with the Mississippi Delta and Florida. Total length: 1770 km (1100 mi).

[3] Part of the Atlantic Intracoastal Waterway, a series of artificial and natural channels providing a discontinuous navigation of 1900 km (3057 mi) between Massachusetts and Florida.

OTHER MAJOR NAVIGATION CANALS

The following canals are suitable for barges rather than for ocean-going shipping.

Canal	Route	Year opened	Length
Volga–Baltic Waterway (USSR)	Astrakhan to Leningrad	1965	2300 km (1850 mi)
Grand Canal (China)	Beijing (Peking) to Harchon	540 BC – AD 1327	1781 km (1107 mi)
Karakumsky Canal (USSR)	Amu-Dar'ya (Oxus) to Khrebet Kopet Dag	1980	1069 km (664 mi)
New York State Barge Canal (USA)	Hudson River to Lake Erie	1918	837 km (520 mi)
Rajasthan Canal (India)	Bamgarh to Western Haryana	1955	649 km (403 mi)
Trent Canal (Canada)	Lake Huron to Lake Ontario	1833 – 1918	443 km (275 mi)
Irtysh–Karaganda Canal (USSR)	Karaganda to River Irtysh	1971	451 km (280 mi)

WORLD'S MAJOR AIRPORTS

Airport name and location	Terminal passengers (000)	International passengers (000)	Air transport movements (000)	Cargo (000 tonnes)
O'Hare International, Chicago, USA	56 679	3 152*	763.7	662.3
Hartsfield International, Atlanta, USA	45 900	n.a.	751.0	400.1
Los Angeles International, USA	44 399	8 065	565.3	960.4
Dallas/Fort Worth Regional, USA	44 271	n.a.	653·9	400·0
Heathrow Airport, London, UK	37 510	30 659	330·4	642·1
Tokyo International (Haneda), Japan	32 177	13 893	100.8	431·1
Stapleton International, Denver, USA	31 798	n.a.	460·5	n.a.
John F. Kennedy International, NY, USA	31 166	18 021	279·9	1179·9
San Francisco International, USA	30 507	3 579	419.1	466·3
Miami International, USA	24 525	9 446	311·8	686·8
Frankfurt International, Germany	24 344	18 398	279·1	894·6
La Guardia Airport, NY, USA	24 159	n.a.	334·7	n.a.
Logan International, Boston, USA	23 369	2 772	373·1	265·2
Newark, NY, USA	22 496	n.a	342·5	408·0
Orly, Paris, France	22 206	8 704	184·3	236·2
Gatwick, London, UK	20 745	19 619	182·5	192·0
Lambert International, St Louis, USA	20 170	n.a.	379·8	n.a.
Honolulu International, Oahu, USA	20 156	4 192	245·9	283·8
Osaka International, Japan	20 061	n.a.	n.a.	384·4
Metropolitan, Detroit, USA	19 708	n.a.	336·1*	83·1*
Toronto International (Pearson), Canada	19 300	8 903*	284·4	241·5*
Pittsburgh International, USA	17 987	n.a.	357·1	n.a.
Charles de Gaulle, Paris, France	17 887	16 172	178·5	575·5
Minneapolis–St Paul International, USA	17 734	n.a.	293·7	n.a.
Washington National, USA	15 440	n.a.	n.a.	n.a.
Orlando International, USA	16 354	n.a.	n.a.	n.a.
Hong Kong International	15 277	15 277	87.4	694.1
Dulles International, Washington DC, USA	14 713*	n.a.	192·4*	15.7*
Philadelphia International, USA	14 673*	1 056*	n.a.	140.9*
New Tokyo International, Japan	14 657	13 893	100.8	1202.7
Schiphol, Amsterdam, Netherlands	14 482	14 397	186.8	575.3
Seattle–Tacoma, USA	14 445*	n.a.	274.9*	193.3*
Fiumicino, Rome, Italy	13 638*	6 912*	144.0*	192.3*
Barajas, Madrid, Spain	13 243	6 007	128.7	178.9
Arlanda, Stockholm, Sweden	13 145	5 567	224.8	72.1

The figures given (for 1988) are the latest available.
* 1987 figures.

MAIN COMMERCIAL AIRCRAFT IN AIRLINE SERVICE*

Name of Aircraft**	Nationality	Wingspan	Length	Max. cruising speed	Range with max. payload	Max. takeoff weight	Max. seating capacity
Yakolev YAK-40	USSR	25·00 m (82 ft 0 in)	20·36 m (66 ft 9 in)	550 kph (297 knots)	1450 km (782 naut miles)	16 000 kg (35 275 lb)	32
Boeing 727 (200)	USA	32·92 m (108 ft 0 in)	46·69 m (153 ft 2 in)	964 kph (520 knots)	3966 km (2140 naut miles)	95 025 kg (209 500 lb)	189
McDonnell Douglas DC9 (Super 81)	USA	32·87 m (107 ft 10 in)	45·06 m (147 ft 10 in)	902 kph (487 knots)	4925 km[1] (2657 naut miles)	63 500 kg (140 000 lb)	172
Boeing 737 (200)	USA	28·35 m (93 ft 0 in)	30·53 m (100 ft 2 in)	927 kph (500 knots)	4262 km (2300 naut miles)	56 472 kg (124 500 lb)	130
Boeing 747 (200)	USA	59·46 m (195 ft 8 in)	70·66 m (231 ft 10 in)	964 kph (520 knots)	10 562 km[2] (5700 naut miles)	377 840 kg (833 000 lb)	516
Fokker F27 (Mk 500)	Netherlands	29·00 m (95 ft 2 in)	25·06 m (82 ft 2 in)	480 kph (259 knots)	1741 km (935 naut miles)	20 410 kg (45 000 lb)	60
McDonnell Douglas DC8 (Srs 63)	USA	45·23 m (148 ft 5 in)	57·12 m (187 ft 5 in)	965 kph (521 knots)	7240 km (3907 naut miles)	158 000 kg (350 000 lb)	259
McDonnell Douglas DC10 (Srs 40)	USA	50·41 m (165 ft 5 in)	55·50 m (182 ft 1 in)	992 kph (498 knots)	7505 km (4050 naut miles)	259 450 kg (572 000 lb)	380
Boeing 707/720 (707-320)	USA	44·42 m (145 ft 9 in)	46·61 m (152 ft 11 in)	973 kph (525 knots)	9265 km[3] (5000 naut miles)	151 315 kg (333 600 lb)	219
Lockheed L-1011 Tristar (500)	USA	47·34 m (155 ft 4 in)	50·05 m (164 ft 2 in)	973 kph (525 knots)	9653 km (5209 naut miles)	224 980 kg (496 000 lb)	400
Airbus A300B (A300B4-200)	International	44·84 m (147 ft 1 in)	53·62 m (175 ft 11 in)	911 kph (492 knots)	5095 km[4] (2750 naut miles)	165 000 kg (363 760 lb)	336
BAC One-eleven (Srs 500)	UK	28·50 m (93 ft 6 in)	32·61 m (107 ft 0 in)	871 kph (470 knots)	2744 km (1480 naut miles)	47 400 kg (104 500 lb)	119
Antonov AN 24/-26 (An 26)	USSR	29·20 m (95 ft 10 in)	23·80 m (78 ft 1 in)	440 kph (237 knots)	1100 km (594 naut miles)	24 000 kg (52 911 lb)	40
Tupolev Tu-154 (154B)	USSR	37·55 m (123 ft 3 in)	47·90 m (157 ft 1 in)	950 kph (513 knots)	2750 km (1485 naut miles)	96 000 kg (211 650 lb)	169
Ilyushin IL-18 (11-18D)	USSR	37·40 m (122 ft 9 in)	35·90 m (117 ft 9 in)	675 kph (364 knots)	3700 km (1997 naut miles)	64 000 kg (141 095 lb)	128
BAC/Aérospatiale Concorde	UK/France	25·56 m (83 ft 10 in)	62·10 m (203 ft 9 in)	2179 kph (1176 knots)	6230 km (3360 naut miles)	185 065 kg (408 000 lb)	110[5]

* No details available for Fokker F28.
**Scheduled and non-circulated services including all-freight. Specifications apply to version in brackets.
1 Range quoted with max. fuel.
2 With 442 passengers.
3 With 147 passengers.
4 With 269 passengers.
5 122 seats in summer with wardrobes deleted.

DISTANCE IN KILOMETRES BETWEEN AIRPORTS

Where there are no regular scheduled flights, no figure is given.

	Athens	Bahrain	Bangkok	Bombay	Buenos Aires	Cairo	Chicago	Copenhagen	Frankfurt	Hong Kong	Johannesburg	Karachi	Lagos	Lima	London	Madrid	Manila	Mexico City	Montreal	Moscow	Nairobi	New York	Paris	Peking (Beijing)	Rio de Janeiro	Rome	San Francisco	Singapore	Sydney	Tehran	Tokyo	Vancouver
Athens	–	2829	7916	5164	11699	1117	8758	2136	1807	8541	7131	4320	4043	11762	2414	2359	9637	11274	7616	2251	4564	7914	2093	7617	9704	1047	10918	9053	15315	2458	9543	9792
Bahrain	2829	–	5358	2411	13293	1929	12934	4461	4437	6389	6297	1661	5457	14333	5090	5185	7364	13963	7530	3467	3399	10614	4822	6182	11460	3862	13730	6326	12504	1048	8314	11782
Bangkok	7916	5358	–	3008	16877	7249	13062	8601	8963	1719	8989	3701	10604	19676	9540	10157	2199	15717	13378	7069	7207	13912	9433	3296	16073	8814	12730	1443	7538	5457	4642	11782
Bombay	5164	2411	3008	–	14935	4339	12953	6849	6564	4298	8109	876	7617	15716	7207	7512	5132	15132	12069	5047	4529	12523	6999	4763	13771	6160	13516	3917	10152	2803	6782	11297
Buenos Aires	11699	13293	16877	14935	–	11844	9043	12086	11494	18443	8109	15716	7932	3151	11129	10079	9162	7391	9051	13488	10411	8528	11062	19277	1996	11170	10395	15867	11760	13781	18285	11297
Cairo	1117	1929	7249	4339	11844	–	9866	3197	2922	8123	6258	3556	3927	12435	3540	3349	9162	12363	8722	2913	3540	9009	3204	7530	9893	2125	11994	8255	14395	1955	10067	10835
Chicago	8758	12934	13062	12953	9043	9866	–	6849	6966	12425	14009	12363	10975	5851	6312	6185	13686	2718	1198	8073	12822	1187	6665	10554	9893	7734	2983	15039	14857	11003	10067	2828
Copenhagen	2136	4461	8601	6849	12086	3197	6849	–	678	8662	9204	5537	5511	11086	982	2058	9780	9545	5799	1539	6699	6184	1035	7191	10178	1535	8801	9959	16031	3657	8706	7657
Frankfurt	1807	4437	8963	6564	11494	2922	6966	678	–	9165	8684	5690	4853	10717	654	1420	10290	9545	5851	2021	6312	6185	471	7783	9560	966	9142	10270	16484	3765	9360	8057
Hong Kong	8541	6389	1719	4298	18443	8123	12425	8662	9165	–	10694	4775	11835	18344	9640	10519	1125	14122	12956	7149	8750	12956	9627	1985	17687	9271	15446	2576	7374	6186	2936	10245
Johannesburg	7131	6297	8989	8109	8109	6258	14009	9204	8684	10694	–	7041	4522	10901	9068	8097	10975	14588	11699	9164	2910	12822	8707	11699	7146	5303	15446	8649	11019	7283	16966	11706
Karachi	4320	1661	3701	876	15716	3556	12363	5537	5690	4775	7041	–	7041		6334	6658	5716	14588	11241	4202	4367	11675	6128	4910		5303		4736	11003	1930	6969	11706
Lagos	4043	5457	10604	7617	7932	3927	10975	5511	4853	11835	4522	7041	–		4853	3827	11455	11526	9219	6251	3828	8498	4685		6022	4018		11455			13506	11938
Lima	11762	14333	19676	15716	3151	12435	5851	11086	10717	18344	10901			–	10143	9520	16605		6419	12620		6419	10248			10834	7255	18812	12978	12812	15413	8154
London	2414	5090	9540	7207	11129	3540	6312	982	654	9640	9068	6334	4853	10143	–	1244	10759	8901	5213	2506	6830	5536	341	8148	9245	1460	8610	10873	17008	4411	9585	7574
Madrid	2359	5185	10157	7512	10079	3349	6185	2058	1420	10519	8097	6658	3827	9520	1244	–	11644	9063	5550	3418	6189	5758	1031	9199	8140	1360	8610	11373	17661	4753	10764	8422
Manila	9637	7364	2199	5132	9162	9162	13686	9780	10290	1125	10975	5716	11455	16605	10759	11644	–	14218	13886	10752	9401	13686	9195	2873	18107	10390	14149	2373	6258	7247	2993	3926
Mexico City	11274	13963	15717	15132	7391	12363	2718	9545	9545	14122	14588	14588	11526		8901	9063	14218	–	3712	10683	11701	3712	9195	17302	7661	10390	3027	15738	12978	14218	11247	3940
Montreal	7616	7530	13378	12069	9051	8722	1198	5799	5851	12956	11699	11241	9219	6419	5213	5550	13886	3712	–	7036	11526	536	5523	10440	8189	6605	4072	14794	16011	9433	10384	3679
Moscow	2251	3467	7069	5047	13488	2913	8073	1539	2021	7149	9164	4202	6251	12620	2506	3418	10752	10683	7036	–	6366	7477	2479	5802	11526	2397	7477	8443	14794	2486	7502	8180
Nairobi	4564	3399	7207	4529	10411	3540	12822	6699	6312	8750	2910	4367	3828		6830	6189	9401	11701	11526	6366	–	11828	6475	9219	8937	5380	15446	7456	12128	4374	11296	
New York	7914	10614	13912	12523	8528	9009	1187	6184	6185	12956	12822	11675	8498	6419	5536	5758	13686	3712	536	7477	11828	–	5829	10971	7723	6886	4149	15329	16002	9839	10824	3926
Paris	2093	4822	9433	6999	11062	3204	6665	1035	471	9627	8707	6128	4685	10248	341	1031	9195	9195	5523	2479	6475	5829	–	8214	9144	1100	8971	10728	16954	4198	9736	7938
Peking (Beijing)	7617	6182	3296	4763	19277	7530	10554	7191	7783	1985	11699	4910			8148	9199	2873	17302	10440	5802	9219	10971	8214	–	17302	9186	8120	4486		5617	2132	8487
Rio de Janeiro	9704	11460	16073	13771	1996	9893	9893	10178	9560	17687	7146		6022		9245	8140	18107	7661	8189	11526	8937	7723	9144	17302	–	9186	10633	15738	13516		18519	11206
Rome	1047	3862	8814	6160	11170	2125	7734	1535	966	9271	5303	5303	4018	10834	1460	1360	10390	10390	6605	2397	5380	6886	1100	9186	9186	–	10052	10010	16302	3396	9880	9007
San Francisco	10918	13730	12730	13516	10395	11994	2983	8801	9142	15446	15446			7255	8610	8610	14149	3027	4072	7477	15446	4149	8971	8120		10052	–	13579	11829		8222	1286
Singapore	9053	6326	1443	3917	15867	8255	15039	9959	10270	2576	8649	4736	11455	18812	10873	11373	2373	15738	14794	8443	7456	15329	10728	4486	15738	10010	13579	–	6296	6615	5361	12811
Sydney	15315	12504	7538	10152	11760	14395	14857	16031	16484	7374	11019	11003		12978	17008	17661	6258	12978	16011	14794	12128	16002	16954		13516	16302	11829	6296	–	12909	7826	12492
Tehran	2458	1048	5457	2803	13781	1955	11003	3657	3765	6186	7283	1930		12812	4411	4753	7247	11247	9433	2486	4374	9839	4198	5617		3396		6615	12909	–	7713	10556
Tokyo	9543	8314	4642	6782	18285	10067	10067	8706	9360	2936	16966	6969	13506	15413	9585	10764	2993	11247	10384	7502	11296	10824	9736	2132	18519	9880	8222	5361	7826	7713	–	7500
Vancouver	9792	11782	11782	11297	11297	10835	2828	7657	8057	10245	11706	11706	11938	8154	7574	8422	3926	3940	3679	8180		3926	7938	8487	11206	9007	1286	12811	12492	10556	7500	–

To convert kilometres to miles multiply by 0·62137

MAJOR WORLD AIRLINES

Airline	Passenger km (000)	Aircraft km (000)	Passengers carried	Total no. of aircraft
Aeroflot, USSR	213 169 200	132 600 (est.)	124 219 300	102
United Airlines, USA	111 077 500	872 500	56 657 000	407
American Airlines, USA	104 114 500	942 200	64 327 400	466
Delta Airlines, USA	83 122 900	837 700	60 303 000	393
Continental Airlines, USA	65 186 500	670 500	37 044 300	384
Northwest Orient Airlines, USA	63 655 800	573 200	37 367 400	321
Transworld Airlines (TWA), USA	55 842 400	433 700	25 160 500	212
British Airways, UK	54 089 400	320 600	21 733 400	200
Japan Air Lines (JAL), Japan	49 327 700	227 500	19 988 800	95
Pan American World Airways, USA	47 053 900	260 700	16 890 500	140
Eastern Airlines, USA	46 330 900	451 800	35 935 400	259
Air France, France	34 334 700	242 700	14 764 000	129
Lufthansa, Germany	34 006 300	307 200	17 727 500	131
Singapore Airlines, Singapore	28 062 000	104 800	6 046 900	39
US Airlines, USA	27 860 600	366 900	32 810 900	235
Qantas, Australia	26 208 200	104 900	3 938 700	36
KLM Royal Dutch Airlines, Netherlands	23 303 400	135 000	6 229 000	78
Air Canada, Canada	22 812 200	209 900	11 337 200	113
Iberia, Spain	20 496 900	152 700	14 955 000	86
Cathay Pacific Airways, Hong Kong	19 666 300	76 200	6 031 300	30
Canadian Airlines, Canada	18 017 200	171 900	8 734 200	88
Thai Airways International, Thailand	16 394 500	82 200	5 723 400	41
Alitalia, Italy	15 634 100	114 200	9 154 500	121
Korean Air, Korea	14 681 900	94 300	9 826 000	59
Swissair, Switzerland	14 324 100	117 500	7 033 400	53
SAS, Scandinavia	14 026 800	152 900	13 319 900	119
Varig International, Brazil	13 663 800	112 100	6 300 000	74
Garuda Indonesian Airlines, Indonesia	13 295 106	106 400	6 980 000	75
All Nippon Airways (ANA), Japan	11 694 000	67 300	12 777 100	105
America West, USA	11 184 200	139 500	12 651 000	70
Mexicana, Mexico	10 763 300	91 200	8 115 100	42
Air New Zealand, New Zealand	10 728 400	66 800	4 631 900	37
South African Airways, South Africa	9 117 000	n/a	5 400 000	39
Air India, India	9 106 500	50 400	2 162 000	21
Indian Airlines, India	8 743 100	66 700	10 271 100	58
Pakistan International, Pakistan	8 743 100	58 900	4 889 400	42
Malaysia Airlines, Malaysia	8 657 600	57 000	7 683 600	43
Olympic Airways, Greece	7 530 800	52 000	6 659 700	55
Saudia Airlines, Saudi Arabia	7 379 300	49 700	4 865 400	84
Aerolineas, Argentina	7 347 700*	62 400*	3 818 200*	31
Sabena, Belgium	6 528 300	60 700	2 604 600	28
Braniff Airways, USA	6 513 000	66 800	4 321 600	35
Philippine Airlines, Philippines	6 289 300	35 000	3 355 700	45
TAP-Air, Portugal	5 639 900	47 400	2 796 000	28
UTA, France	5 435 100	31 800	828 800	11
Aeromexico, Mexico	4 101 300	40 800	3 137 300	32
Japan Air System	3 803 900	36 700	5 705 100	78

The figures given (for 1988) are the latest available.
* 1987 figures.

MOTORWAYS

The first dual carriageway was constructed in 1909 near Berlin in Germany. In 1924 the world's first motorway was opened between Milan and Varese in northern Italy. This was the beginning of a 500 km (275 mi) network of motorways constructed in Piedmont and Lombardy between 1925 and 1939. In 1933 the German autobahn network was begun.

The following countries had the greatest length of motorways in 1987 (the latest year for which comparable figures are available).

Country	Length in km (miles)
USA	80 530 (50 039)
Australia	16 100 (10 004)
Germany	9930* (6170)
France	6085 (3781)
Italy	5901 (3667)

Canada	5848
	(3634)
Japan	3435
	(2134)

* Combined figure for the former East Germany and West Germany.

WHERE CARS ARE MADE

The table on page 473 lists the major automobile manufacturing countries. The following list gives the percentages of a country's output represented by particular companies in 1987, the last year for which comparable figures are available.

Argentina Renault 26%, Fiat 14%, Volkswagen 11%, Peugeot 10%.

Australia Ford 37%, Holden-Bedford 28%, Toyota 16%, Nissan 12%.

Brazil Autolina 47%, Volkswagen 39%, Fiat 16%.

Canada Ford 52%, General Motors 40%.

France Peugeot 48%, Renault 38%, Citroën 10%.

Germany Volkswagen-Audi 40%, Opel 19%, Ford-Werke 18%, Daimler-Benz 12%, BMW 9%, Porsche 1%. (This excludes car production in the former East Germany where the manufacture of Trabant and Wartburg cars ceased early in 1991.)

Italy Fiat 95%.

Japan Toyota 34%, Nissan 22%, Honda 12%, Toyo–Kogyo (Mazda) 10%, Mitsubishi 7%, Suzuki 4%, Fuji (Subaru) 4%.

Spain Seat 27%, Opel 21%, Ford–España 19%, Fasa–Renault 17%, Talbot (España) 7%, Citroën–Hispania 5%.

Sweden Volvo 68%, Saab 26%.

USSR Lada 62%, Moskvitch 16%.

USA Ford 26%, Chevrolet 24%, Oldsmobile 16%, Chrysler 15%, Buick 14%.

UK British–Leyland/Rover 50%, Ford 18%.

CAR OWNERSHIP

EC countries are listed separately.

	Persons per car	Total no. of cars
USA	1.7	139 041 000
Japan	4.1	29 478 342
USSR	24.0	11 750 000
Canada	2.2	11 477 314
Brazil	13.5	10 025 000
Australia	2.2	7 072 800
Mexico	15.0	5 200 000
Argentina	7.9	3 928 000
Poland	10.2	3 650 000
Sweden	2.5	3 366 570
South Africa	10.5	3 078 635
Yugoslavia	7.8	2 972 807
Switzerland	2.3	2 732 720
Czechoslovakia	5.7	2 700 000
Austria	2.8	2 684 780
Venezuela	11.0	1 800 000
Finland	2.9	1 698 671
Hungary	8.4	1 660 300
Norway	2.6	1 623 137
Iran	28.0	1 575 000
New Zealand	2.1	1 550 000
India	500.0	1 506 000
Saudi Arabia	8.7	1 325 000

Malaysia	14.0	1 125 000
Puerto Rico	3.1	1 125 000
Turkey	45.3	1 087 815

The figures given (for 1987) are the latest available.

EURO FACTS

CAR OWNERSHIP IN THE EC

	Persons per car	Total no. of cars
Germany*	2.5	31 766 368
Italy	2.5	22 500 000
France	2.5	21 970 000
United Kingdom	2.7	20 605 514
Spain	4.0	9 750 000
The Netherlands	2.8	5 117 748
Belgium	2.8	3 497 818
Denmark	3.2	1 587 641
Greece	7.2	1 378 493
Portugal	7.9	1 290 000
Ireland	4.8	736 595
Luxembourg	2.3	162 481

The figures given (for 1987) are the latest figures available.
* Combined figure for the former East Germany and West Germany.

INTERNATIONAL VEHICLE REGISTRATION LETTERS

A	Austria
AFG	Afghanistan
AL	Albania
AND	Andorra
AUS	Australia
B	Belgium
BD	Bangladesh
BDS	Barbados
BG	Bulgaria
BH	Belize
BR	Brazil
BRN	Bahrain
BRU	Brunei
BS	Bahamas
BUR	Burma (Myanmar)
C	Cuba
CDN	Canada
CH	Switzerland
CI	Ivory Coast (Côte d'Ivoire)
CL	Sri Lanka
CO	Colombia
CR	Costa Rica
CS	Czechoslovakia
CY	Cyprus
D	Germany
DK	Denmark
DOM	Dominican Republic
DY	Benin
DZ	Algeria
E	Spain
EAK	Kenya

EAT	Tanzania	RCA	Central African Republic
EAU	Uganda	RCB	Congo
EAZ	Zanzibar (Tanzania)	RCH	Chile
EC	Ecuador	RH	Haiti
ES	El Salvador	RI	Indonesia
ET	Egypt	RIM	Mauritania
ETH	Ethiopia	RL	Lebanon
		RM	Madagascar
F	France and territories	RMM	Mali
FJI	Fiji	RN	Niger
FL	Liechtenstein	RO	Romania
FR	Faeroe Islands	ROK	Korea
		ROU	Uruguay
GB	United Kingdom	RP	Philippines
GBA	Alderney	RSM	San Marino
GBG	Guernsey	RU	Burundi
GBJ	Jersey	RWA	Rwanda
GBM	Isle of Man		
GBZ	Gibraltar	S	Sweden
GCA	Guatemala	SD	Swaziland
GH	Ghana	SF	Finland
GR	Greece	SGP	Singapore
GUY	Guyana	SME	Suriname
		SN	Senegal
H	Hungary	SU	Union of Soviet Socialist Republics
HK	Hong Kong	SWA	Namibia
HKJ	Jordan	SY	Seychelles
		SYR	Syria
I	Italy		
IL	Israel	T	Thailand
IND	India	TG	Togo
IR	Iran	TN	Tunisia
IRL	Republic of Ireland	TR	Turkey
IRQ	Iraq	TT	Trinidad and Tobago
IS	Iceland		
		USA	United States of America
J	Japan		
JA	Jamaica	V	Vatican City
		VN	Vietnam
K	Cambodia		
KWT	Kuwait	WAG	Gambia
		WAL	Sierra Leone
L	Luxembourg	WAN	Nigeria
LAO	Laos	WD	Dominica
LAR	Libya	WG	Grenada
LB	Liberia	WL	St Lucia
LS	Lesotho	WS	Western Samoa
		WV	St Vincent and the Grenadines
M	Malta		
MA	Morocco	YU	Yugoslavia
MAL	Malaysia	YV	Venezuela
MC	Monaco		
MEX	Mexico	Z	Zambia
MS	Mauritius	ZA	South Africa
MW	Malawi	ZRE	Zaïre
		ZW	Zimbabwe
N	Norway		
NA	Netherlands Antilles		
NIC	Nicaragua		
NL	Netherlands		
NZ	New Zealand		

Other countries either do not have registration letters or use letters that are not internationally recognized.

RIGHT- AND LEFT-HAND DRIVING

Of the 221 separately administered countries and territories in the world 58 drive on the left and 163 on the right. In Britain it is believed that left-hand driving is a legacy of the preference of passing an approaching horseman or carriage right side to right side to facilitate right-armed defence against sudden attack. On the Continent postillions were mounted on the rearmost left horse in a team and thus preferred to pass left side to left side. While some countries have transferred from left to right the only case recorded of a transfer from right to left is in Okinawa, Japan, on 30 July 1978.

P	Portugal
PA	Panama
PAK	Pakistan
PE	Peru
PL	Poland
PNG	Papua New Guinea
PY	Paraguay
RA	Argentina
RB	Botswana
RC	Taiwan

BELIEFS AND IDEAS

PHILOSOPHY

CLASSICAL PHILOSOPHY

The word 'philosophy' is derived from the Greek, meaning 'love of wisdom'. Broadly speaking, 'philosophy' can be taken to mean any questioning of or reflection upon those principles underlying all knowledge and existence.

Philosophy differs from religion since its quest for underlying causes and principles does not depend on dogma and faith; and it differs from science, since it does not depend solely on fact. Its interrelation with both science and religion can be seen in the large number of philosophers who were also either theologians or scientists, and the few, such as Blaise Pascal and Roger Bacon, who were all three. Philosophy developed from religion, but became distinct when thinkers sought truth independent of theological considerations.

Until the 19th century the term 'philosophy' was used to include what we now distinguish as 'science' (from the Latin for 'knowledge'), and this terminology persists in some university courses such as 'natural philosophy' for physics and 'moral sciences' for what we now call philosophy. Eventually all the branches of science, from physics to psychology, broke away – psychology being the last to do so in the 20th century.

Philosophy is traditionally divided into three sectors: ethics, metaphysics and epistemology.

ETHICS

Ethics is the study of how we decide how people ought to live and act. Philosophers' opinions about ethics tend to resolve into an opposition between two main schools: the Idealists and the Utilitarians. The *Idealists* consider that the goodness or badness of a course of action must be judged by standards derived from outside the everyday world: from God, or heaven, or perhaps from a human higher self. The *Utilitarians* hold that the effects that a course of action produces in this world are all that is relevant to its ethical value.

The Idealist school began with the Greek philosopher Plato, who wrote in the 4th century BC. Plato, in a series of dialogues, depicts his former teacher Socrates discussing the problems of philosophy with friends and opponents. In the dialogues, Socrates' procedure is to draw out wisdom from those with whom he is discussing the question. He rarely makes a statement of his own – rather he asks questions which compel others either to discover the truth for themselves or else to appear foolish.

In these dialogues, especially the *Protagoras*, the *Phaedo* and the *Gorgias*, Plato developed a system of ethics that is essentially idealistic. Socrates argues that the good comes from the realm of 'ideas' or 'forms'. This is a perfect world of which the world of ordinary experience is only a pale replica. For Plato, individual conduct is good in so far as it is governed by the form or idea of the good, which is to be discovered only after a thorough philosophical education.

Another important work that has to be classed as Idealist is Aristotle's *Nicomachean Ethics*. Aristotle was a pupil of Plato and he also thought of the good as divine, but his ethics had a more 'practical' bent.

He equated happiness with the good and was responsible for the doctrine of the *golden mean*. This stated that every virtue is a middle-point between two vices. Generosity, for instance, is the mean between prodigality and stinginess. The same tendency to give Idealism a practical turn is found in the works of the 18th-century philosopher Immanuel Kant. The most famous part of Kant's ethics is that connected with the phrase 'categorical imperative'. In Kant's own words: 'Act only according to a maxim of which you can at the same time will that it shall become a general law.' In other words, before acting in a certain way, the individual must ask himself: 'Would I be happy if everyone behaved like this?'

The Utilitarians are more directly concerned than the Idealists with earthly welfare. The earliest Western philosopher in this tradition was Epicurus, a Greek of the 4th century BC. Instead of deriving ideas of right and wrong from above, Epicurus maintained that 'we call pleasure the beginning and end of the blessed life'. The term *Epicurean* is often used to describe one who indulges in excessive pleasure, but this usage is not just. Epicurus did not condone excesses. On the contrary, he said that pleasure was only good when moderate and calm.

The Utilitarian tradition has on the whole had more adherents than the Idealistic tradition in modern philosophy. Jeremy Bentham, for example, writing in the 18th century, acknowledged his debt to Epicurus in his *Principles of Morals and Legislation*. Bentham agreed that pain and pleasure were the 'sovereign masters' governing man's conduct. He added to this a doctrine of *utility*, which argued that 'the greatest happiness of the greatest number is the measure of right and wrong'. John Stuart Mill is perhaps the most famous of the Utilitarians. He extended Bentham's doctrines by arguing that 'some kinds of pleasure are more valuable than others'. This doctrine is explained in his essay *Utilitarianism* (1863).

METAPHYSICS

The term 'metaphysics' originated as the title of one of Aristotle's treatises. It probably meant only that he wrote it after his treatise *Physics*, but the term is usually employed to describe speculation as to the ultimate nature of reality.

EPISTEMOLOGY

Epistemology is the study of the nature, grounds and validity of human knowledge – how we come to know; how far we can rely on different kinds of belief; how science can be separated from superstition; and how conflicts between rival scientific theories can be resolved. Those epistemologists who are usually called *Rationalists* assert that knowledge is born in the individual and has only to be drawn forth. The other point of view – *Empiricism* – is that at birth the mind is a passive blank sheet on which knowledge is then imprinted.

Rationalists This school is represented classically by Plato, who discussed various theories of knowledge and discarded those built on the shifting sands of sense perception. The senses are, he thought, too fallible. True knowledge comes from those general notions that are derived from the realm of the ideas, which the soul possesses prior to birth.

The 17th-century French philosopher-scientist René Descartes, although not a Platonist, was a Rationalist in that he regarded sensory knowledge as a bad foundation for science. Its certainty, he argued, could never equal that of mathematics or of our own knowledge of our thoughts. This inalienable certainty is expressed in his famous statement 'I think; therefore I am': however deep my doubt, I must exist in order to doubt.

Empiricism The classic representative of Empiricism was John Locke, a 17th-century English philosopher. In his *Essay Concerning Human Understanding*, Locke defined an opposite point of view to Plato and Descartes. He regarded the mind at birth as comparable to an empty cabinet. As we live, 'experience' fills it with 'ideas' either of our inner states (*ideas of reflection*) or of external objects (*ideas of sensation*). He argued that human knowledge could never get beyond the limits of such ideas.

MODERN PHILOSOPHY

The classical description of philosophy is in terms of the three fields of metaphysics, ethics and epistemology. The main movements of modern philosophy – Hegelianism, Analytic Philosophy, and Phenomenology – would regard such a division of the subject as outmoded.

Hegelianism At the beginning of the 19th century, Georg Wilhelm Friedrich Hegel criticized all previous conceptions of philosophy as being lifeless, one-sided and unhistorical. Hegel proposed that philosophy must always be rooted in history, but at the same time always striving for a conception of reality as a single developing whole, every part of which is animated by all the others.

Analytical Philosophy This movement was founded at the beginning of the 20th century by Bertrand Russell, building on the work of the mathematician Gottlob Frege. Analytical philosophy – which is no less critical of philosophical tradition – is based on the idea that authentic philosophy is essentially the study of logic, that is to say of formal patterns of reasoning abstracted from their metaphysical, ethical, epistemological or historical contexts.

Phenomenology This movement – which was founded at the same time as analytic philosophy – has come to dominate 20th-century European philosophy just as the analytic school has dominated philosophy in the English-speaking world. This movement claims that philosophers always tend to miss the one fundamental question – why our experience should be framed in terms of a distinction between an objective world and our subjective experience of it. Heidegger and Derrida have developed this line of thought by arguing that, so far from trying to build on past philosophy, we should attempt to 'destroy' or 'deconstruct' it.

PHILOSOPHICAL TERMS

a posteriori knowledge knowledge that comes from experience.

a priori knowledge knowledge that can be derived from pure reasoning, without reference to experience, i.e. by reasoning (as in mathematics and logic).

aesthetics the study of the nature of beauty and taste, especially in art.

analytic truths truths that can be proved by analysing the concepts they involve.

axiom a necessary and self-evident proposition requiring no proof.

causality the relationship between a cause and its effect.

deduction reaching a conclusion by purely *a priori* means.

dialectic literally, debate; by extension, the technique of proceeding from a thesis, through its negation or antithesis, to a synthesis in which both are reconciled on a higher level.

empirical knowledge knowledge derived from experience rather than reason.

epistemology a branch of philosophy that attempts to answer questions about the nature of knowledge and especially the nature of science.

ethics a branch of inquiry that attempts to answer questions about right and wrong, good and evil; and how we decide how human life should be lived.

induction the process of drawing general conclusions from particular instances.

logic the study of the structure or form of valid arguments, disregarding their content.

metaphysics a branch of philosophy concerned with systems of ideas that attempt to explain the nature of reality.

paradox a statement whose truth implies its falsehood, e.g. the Cretan philosopher Epimenides said 'All Cretans are liars'. As he was Cretan himself, is his statement true or false?

sophistry a fallacious argument.

synthesis the outcome of the confrontation of two arguments by which a truth is discovered.

teleology the practice of explaining processes in terms of what they achieve rather than what preceded them.

PHILOSOPHICAL SCHOOLS AND THEORIES

Since the days of the early Greeks, philosophers have been divided into different schools and have advanced opposing theories. Among the many basic outlooks and theories are the following:

altruism the principle of living and acting in the interest of others rather than for oneself.

analytical philosophy (see Modern Philosophy above)

asceticism the belief that withdrawal from the physical world into the inner world of the spirit is the highest good attainable.

atomism the belief that the entire universe is ultimately composed of interchangeable indivisible units.

critical theory a philosophical version of Marxism associated with the *Frankfurt School* (founded 1921).

criticism the theory that the path to knowledge lies midway between dogmatism and scepticism.

determinism the belief that the universe and everything in it (including individual lives) follows a fixed or pre-determined pattern. This belief has often been used to deny free will.

dialectical materialism the theory – often attributed to Marx – that reality is strictly material and is based on an economic struggle between opposing forces, with occasional interludes of harmony.

dogmatism the assertion of a belief without arguments in its support.

dualism the belief that the world consists of two radically independent and absolute elements, e.g. good and evil, or (especially) spirit and matter.

egoism the belief that the serving of one's own interests is the highest end.

empiricism the doctrine that there is no knowledge except that which is derived from experience.

existentialism the doctrine that the human self and human values are fictions, but inevitable ones, and that it is bad faith to deny one's own free will, even in a deterministic universe.

fatalism the doctrine that what will happen will happen and nothing we do will make any difference.

hedonism the doctrine that pleasure is the highest good.

humanism any system that regards human interests and the human mind as paramount in the universe.

idealism any system that regards thought or the idea as the basis either of knowledge or existence.

interactionism the theory that physical events can cause mental events, and vice versa.

materialism the doctrine that asserts the existence of only one substance – matter – thus denying the existence of spirit.

monism a belief in only one ultimate reality, whatever its nature.

naturalism a position that seeks to explain all phenomena by means of strictly natural (as opposed to supernatural) categories.

nominalism the doctrine that general terms are, in effect, nothing more than words. (Compare realism.)

operationalism the doctrine that scientific concepts are tools for prediction rather than descriptions of hidden realities.

pantheism the belief that God is identical with the universe.

personalism the theory that ultimate reality consists of a plurality of spiritual beings or independent persons.

phenomenology (see Modern Philosophy above)

pluralism the belief that there are more than two irreducible kinds of reality.

positivism the doctrine that man can have no knowledge outside science.

pragmatism a philosophical method that makes practical consequences the test of truth.

predestination the doctrine that the events of a human's life are determined beforehand.

rationalism the theory that reason alone, without the aid of experience, can arrive at the basic reality of the universe.

realism the doctrine that general terms have a real existence.

relativism the rejection of the concept of absolute and invariable truths.

scepticism the doctrine that nothing can be known with certainty.

sensationalism the theory that sensations are the ultimate and real components of the world.

stoicism a philosophical school that believed that reason (God) was the basis of the universe and that humanity should live in harmony with nature.

structuralism the doctrine that language is essentially a system of rules; or the extension of this idea to culture as a whole.

theism the belief in a God.

transcendentalism the belief in an ultimate reality that transcends human experience.

voluntarism the theory that will is a determining factor in the universe.

PHILOSOPHERS AND THEIR THEORIES

PRE-SOCRATIC GREEKS

Thales of Miletus (624–550 BC). Thales – an exponent of monism – is regarded as the first Western philosopher.

Anaximander of Miletus (611–547 BC). Anaximander continued Thales' quest for universal substance, but reasoned that universal substance need not resemble any known substances.

Heraclitus of Ephesus (533–475 BC). Heraclitus opposed the concept of a single ultimate reality and held that the only permanent thing is change.

Empedocles of Acragas (c. 495–435 BC). Empedocles believed that there were four irreducible substances (water, fire, earth and air) and two forces (love and hate).

Parmenides of Elea (c. 495 BC). A member of the Eleatic school, Parmenides formulated the basic doctrine of idealism.

Zeno of Elea (c. 495–430 BC). Zeno argued that plurality and change are appearances, not realities.

Protagoras of Abdera (481–411 BC). An early relativist and humanist who doubted human ability to attain absolute truth.

CLASSICAL GREEK PHILOSOPHERS

Socrates (c. 470–399 BC). Socrates developed the Socratic method of enquiry (see Ethics, above). Socrates was the teacher of Plato, through whose writings his idealistic philosophy was disseminated.

Democritus of Abdera (460–370 BC). Democritus began the tradition in Western thought of explaining the universe in mechanistic terms.

Antisthenes (c. 450–c. 360 BC). The chief of the group known as the Cynics, Antisthenes stressed discipline and work as the essential good.

Plato (c. 428–347 BC). The founder of the Academy at Athens, Plato developed the idealism of his teacher Socrates and was the teacher of Aristotle.

Aristotle (384–322 BC). Greek philosopher and scientist, whose works have influenced the whole of Western philosophy. Aristotle taught that there are four factors in causation: form; matter; motive cause, which produces change; and the end, for which a process of change occurs.

HELLENISTIC PERIOD

Pyrrho of Elis (c. 365–275 BC). Pyrrho – who initiated the Sceptical school of philosophy – believed that man could not know anything for certain.

Epicurus (341–270 BC). A proponent of atomism and hedonism, Epicurus taught that the test of truth is in sensation.

Zeno of Citium (c. 335–263 BC). Chief of the Stoics – so called because they met in the *Stoa Poikile* or Painted Porch at Athens – Zeno taught that man's role is to accept nature and all it offers, good or bad.

Plotinus (AD 205–270). Plotinus was the chief exponent of Neo-Platonism, a combination of the teachings of Plato and Oriental concepts.

Augustine of Hippo (AD 354–430). St Augustine of Hippo was an exponent of optimism. One of the greatest influences on medieval Christian thought, Augustine believed that God transcends human comprehension.

Boethius (c. AD 480–524). Late Roman statesman. In *The Consolations of Philosophy* Boethius proposed that virtue alone is constant.

MEDIEVAL PERIOD

Avicenna (980–1037). Arabic follower of Aristotle and Neo-Platonism. Avicenna's works revived interest in Aristotle in 13th-century Europe.

Anselm (1033–1109). Italian Augustinian and realist. Anselm is famous for his examination of the proof of God's existence.

Peter Abelard (1079–1142). French theologian and philosopher. Abelard's nominalism caused him to be declared a heretic by the Church.

Averroës (1126–98). A great philosopher of Muslim Spain, and a leading commentator on Aristotle. Averroës regarded religion as allegory for the common man and philosophy as the path to truth.

Maimonides (1135–1204). Jewish student of Aristotle. Maimonides sought to combine Aristotelian teaching with that of the Bible.

St Thomas Aquinas (1225–74). Italian scholastic philosopher. Aquinas evolved a compromise between Aristotle and Scripture, based on the belief that faith and reason are in agreement. His philosophical system is known as Thomism.

THE RENAISSANCE

Desiderius Erasmus (1466–1536). Dutch. The greatest of the humanists, Erasmus helped spread the ideas of the Renaissance throughout northern Europe.

Niccolò Machiavelli (1469–1527). Italian. Machiavelli placed the state as the paramount power in human affairs. His book *The Prince* brought him a reputation for amoral cynicism.

TRANSITION TO MODERN THOUGHT

Francis Bacon (1561–1626). English statesman and philosopher of science. In his major work, *Novum Organum*, Bacon sought to revive the inductive system of deductive logic in interpreting nature.

Thomas Hobbes (1588–1679). English materialist. Hobbes believed the natural state of man is war. In *Leviathan* Hobbes outlined a theory of human government whereby the state and man's subordination to it form the sole solution to human selfishness.

René Descartes (1596–1650). French dualist, rationalist and theist. The Cartesian system of Descartes is at the base of all modern philosophy. Descartes evolved a theory of knowledge that underlies modern science and philosophy based on the certainty of the proposition 'I think, therefore I am'.

Blaise Pascal (1623–62). French theist. Pascal held that sense and reason are mutually deceptive, that truth lies between dogmatism and scepticism.

Benedict de Spinoza (1632–77). Dutch rationalist metaphysician. Spinoza developed the ideas of Descartes while rejecting his dualism.

John Locke (1632–1704). English empiricist. Locke's influence in political, religious, educational and philosophical thought was wide and deep. In his great *Essay Concerning Human Understanding* he sought to refute the rationalist view that knowledge derives from first principles.

EIGHTEENTH CENTURY

Gottfried Wilhelm von Leibniz (1646–1716). German idealist and absolutist. Leibniz's optimistic view was ridiculed by Voltaire in *Candide*. Leibniz held that reality consisted of units of force called monads.

George Berkeley (1685–1753). Anglo-Irish idealist and theist. Berkeley taught that things exist only in being perceived and that the very idea of matter is contradictory.

David Hume (1711–76). Scottish empiricist, philosopher and historian. Hume developed the ideas of Locke into a system of scepticism according to which human knowledge is limited to the experience of ideas and sensations whose truth cannot be verified.

Jean-Jacques Rousseau (1712–78). French social and political philosopher. Rousseau advocated a 'return to nature' to counteract the inequality among men brought about by civilized society.

Immanuel Kant (1724–1804). German founder of critical philosophy. At first influenced by Leibniz, then by Hume, Kant sought to find an alternative approach to the rationalism of the former and the scepticism of the latter. In ethics, he formulated the *Categorical Imperative*, which states that what applies to oneself must apply to everyone else unconditionally.

Jeremy Bentham (1748–1832). English utilitarian. Bentham believed, like Kant, that the interests of the individual are at one with those of society. He regarded pleasure and pain rather than basic principle as the motivation for right action.

Johann Gottlieb Fichte (1762–1814). German. Fichte formulated a philosophy of absolute idealism based on Kant's ethical concepts.

NINETEENTH CENTURY

Georg Wilhelm Friedrich Hegel (1770–1831). German. Hegel's metaphysical system was rationalist and absolutist, based on the belief that thought and being are one, and nature is the manifestation of an Absolute Idea.

Arthur Schopenhauer (1788–1860). German idealist. Schopenhauer gave the will a leading place in his metaphysics. The foremost expounder of pessimism, expressed in *The World as Will and Idea*, he rejected absolute idealism as wishful thinking, and taught that the only tenable attitude lay in utter indifference to an irrational world. He held that the highest ideal was nothingness.

Auguste Comte (1798–1857). French. Comte was the founder of positivism, a system which denied transcendent metaphysics and stated that the Divinity and man were one, that altruism is man's highest duty, and that scientific principles explain all phenomena.

Ludwig Feuerbach (1804–72). German. Feuerbach argued that religion was no more than a projection of human nature. He was an important influence on Marx.

John Stuart Mill (1806–73). English exponent of utilitarianism. Mill differed from Bentham by recognizing differences in quality as well as quantity in pleasure. His most famous work is *On Liberty* (1859).

Søren Kierkegaard (1813–55). Danish religious existentialist. Kierkegaard's thought is the basis of modern (atheistic) existentialism. He taught that only existence has reality, and the individual has a unique value.

Karl Marx (1818–83). German revolutionary thinker who, with Friedrich Engels, was the founder of modern Communism. Marx was a critical follower of Hegel.

Herbert Spencer (1820–1903). English evolutionist. Spencer's 'synthetic philosophy' interpreted all phenomena according to the principle of evolutionary progress.

Charles S. Peirce (1839–1914). American physicist, mathematician and founder of the philosophical school called pragmatism. Peirce regarded logic as the basis of philosophy and taught that the test of an idea is whether it works.

William James (1842–1910). American psychologist and pragmatist. James held that reality is always in the making and that each man should choose the philosophy best suited to him.

Friedrich Wilhelm Nietzsche (1844–1900). German. Nietzsche held that the 'will to power' is basic in life and that the spontaneous is to be preferred to the orderly. He attacked Christianity as a system that fostered the weak, whereas the function of evolution is to evolve 'supermen'.

TWENTIETH CENTURY

Gottlob Frege (1848–1925). German mathematician. Frege revolutionized formal logic and thus paved the way for analytic philosophy.

Henri Bergson (1859–1941). French evolutionist. Bergson asserted the existence of a 'vital impulse' that carries the universe forward, with no fixed beginning and no fixed end. He believed that the future is determined by the choice of alternatives made in the present.

John Dewey (1859–1952). American pragmatist. Dewey developed a system known as instrumentalism. He saw man as continuous with, but distinct from, nature.

Edmund Husserl (1859–1938). German. Husserl developed a system called phenomenology, which sought to ground knowledge in pure experience without presuppositions.

Alfred North Whitehead (1861–1947). British evolutionist and mathematician. Whitehead held that reality must not be interpreted in atomistic terms, but in terms of events. He held that God is intimately present in the universe, yet distinct from it – a view called pantheism.

Benedetto Croce (1866–1952). Italian. Croce was noted for his role in the revival of historical realism.

Bertrand Russell (1872–1970). British agnostic. Russell adhered to many systems of philosophy before becoming a major expounder of logical positivism – the view that scientific knowledge is the only factual knowledge.

George Edward Moore (1873–1958). British moral philosopher. Moore developed the doctrine of ideal utilitarianism in *Principia Ethica*, 1903.

Martin Heidegger (1889–1976). German student of Husserl. Heidegger furthered the development of

phenomenology and greatly influenced atheistic existentialists.

Gabriel Marcel (1889–1973). French. Initially a student of the English-speaking idealists, Marcel was preoccupied with the Cartesian problem of the relation of mind and matter.

Ludwig Wittgenstein (1889–1951). Austrian. The most influential philosopher of the 20th century, Wittgenstein developed two highly original but incompatible systems of philosophy, both dominated by a concern with the relations between language and the world.

Herbert Marcuse (1898–1979). A German-American philosopher who attempted to combine existentialism and psychoanalysis with a libertarian Marxism which was critical of Communism.

Gilbert Ryle (1900–76). British. Ryle studied the nature of philosophy and the concept of mind as well as the nature of meaning and the philosophy of logic.

Sir Karl Popper (1902–90). British critical rationalist. He held that scientific laws can never be proved to be true and that the most that can be claimed is that they have survived attempts to disprove them.

Theodor Adorno (1903–69). A German philosopher who combined Marxism with avant-garde aesthetics.

Jean-Paul Sartre (1905–80). French. An influential philosopher who developed the existentialist thought of Heidegger. An atheistic supporter of a subjective, irrational human existence, he was opposed to an orderly overall reality. His slogan was 'existence before essence'.

Maurice Merleau-Ponty (1907–61). French phenomenologist. Merleau-Ponty was famous for insisting on the role of the human body in our experience of the world.

Simone de Beauvoir (1908–86). French existentialist. The founder of modern feminist philosophy.

Claude Lévi-Strauss (1908–). A French anthropologist and proponent of structuralism. His writings investigate the relationship between culture (exclusively an attribute of humanity) and nature, based on the distinguishing characteristics of man – the ability to communicate in a language.

Willard van Orman Quine (1908–). An American philosopher who combined pragmatism with logical positivism and destroyed many of the dogmas of early analytic philosophy.

Sir Isaiah Berlin (1909–90). British moral and political philosopher and historian. Berlin argued against determinist philosophies of history. He emphasized the importance of moral values, and the necessity of rejecting determinism if the ideas of human responsibility and freedom are to be retained.

Alfred J. Ayer (1910–89). British philosopher. Ayer was the principal advocate of logical positivism, developed from Russell.

Donald Davidson (1917–). American. A leading philosopher of language, and follower of Quine.

Jurgen Habermas (1929–). German. Habermas is a critical Marxist with strong Kantian and liberal affinities.

Jacques Derrida (1930–). French. The founder of deconstruction, a development of Heidegger's technique of interpreting traditional philosophers with great care in order to reveal their constant incoherence.

RELIGION

WHAT IS RELIGION?

Religion is one of the most universal activities known to humankind, being practised across virtually all cultures, and from the very earliest times to the present day. Although various writers have attempted a wide and general definition, none of these definitions has been universally accepted.

Religion appears to have arisen from the human desire to find an ultimate meaning and purpose in life, and this is usually centred around belief in a supernatural being (or beings). In most religions the devotees attempt to honour and/or to influence their god or gods – commonly through such practices as prayer, sacrifice or right behaviour.

MAJOR RELIGIONS OF THE WORLD

It is difficult to obtain figures for the number of practising – rather than nominal – adherents of the world's major religions. In the case of religions practised in China – Daoism, Confucianism and Buddhism – no figures are available and the totals given for these religions should be treated with caution. The following figures are estimates based upon United Nations statistics and figures released by individual religious bodies.

CHRISTIANS 1 670 000 000

This total includes:
Roman Catholics c. 925 000 000
Orthodox Christians 160 000 000
Anglicans 70 000 000
Lutherans 55 000 000
Methodists 55 000 000
Calvinists, Reformed Churches and Presbyterians 47 000 000
Baptists 35 000 000
(excluding independent African churches of a Baptist persuasion).

ISLAM c. 900 000 000

This total includes:
Sunnis over 800 000 000
Shiite sects over 80 000 000
Some Islamic authorities estimate that there are over 1 000 000 000 followers of Islam.

HINDUS c. 655 000 000

Some authorities estimate the number of practising adherents of Hinduism as under 500 000 000.

BUDDHISTS c. 310 000 000

The majority of Buddhists are thought to follow the *Mahayana ('Great Vehicle')*.

CONFUCIANS 200 000 000–300 000 000

The number of Confucians in China is not known. Most estimates of the number of practising adherents of Confucianism outside China range between 5 500 000 and 6 000 000.

FOLLOWERS OF ASIAN PRIMAL RELIGIONS c. 180 000 000

FOLLOWERS OF AFRICAN PRIMAL RELIGIONS c. 100 000 000

SHINTOISTS 20 000 000–30 000 000

Estimates of the number of practising adherents of Shinto range between 3 400 000 and 35 000 000. Over

90 000 000 Japanese are said to belong to the Shinto 'community' but have no active allegiance to the religion.

DAOISTS c. 20 000 000

JEWS 18 000 000

The majority of Jews belong to Liberal, Reform and other traditions rather than Orthodox.

SIKHS 17 000 000

BAHA'IS 4 500 000

JAINS 3 300 000

CHRISTIANITY

The Western calendar, shaped and determined by Christianity, sees the birth of Jesus of Nazareth, known as the Christ, as the turning point of history. In dating the modern era from the supposed date of his birth (it seems likely Jesus was actually born c. 4 BC), Christianity was making a profound statement about the significance of Jesus Christ.

Jesus means the Saviour, taken from the Hebrew root '*yasha*', to save; Christ means the anointed one, from the Greek verb *chrio*, to anoint.

For Christians, the Jewish child born in Bethlehem was no ordinary human. He was and is both human and divine, the Son of God. While it is possible to say that a historical person named Jesus lived between c. 4 BC and c. AD 29, it is only faith that can claim that he was the Christ, the anointed one of God, the long-awaited Messiah of the Jews.

THE NATURE OF GOD

Christians believe that God is the creator of the universe and all life. They believe that Jesus Christ is the only Son of God, who has existed with God the Father from before time began. Jesus was incarnated (given human form), when by the power of the Holy Spirit, his human mother, Mary, gave birth to him. (The subsequent husband of the Virgin Mary – Joseph of Nazareth – was 27 generations descended from King David.) Christians believe that the purpose of Christ's incarnation was to reconcile humanity with God, as human sinfulness had broken the relationship with God. Through the death of Jesus upon the Cross at Calvary, God broke the power of sin and evil, and through the Resurrection (the rising) of Jesus from the dead on the third day God showed the triumph of life over death, and gave the promise of everlasting life to those who believe in Jesus.

In the doctrine of the Trinity, Christians believe that God is one but has three co-equal 'persons' – God the Father, God the Son (Jesus Christ) and the Holy Spirit.

CHRISTIAN TEACHING

The life and teaching of Christ are recorded in the four Gospels and in several quotations and stories found in other books of the New Testament of the Bible. These were all written by Christians who believed Jesus to be in some way both human and divine. Our knowledge of Jesus therefore comes from the pens of believers.

Jesus taught that God is like a father who cares for every person on Earth. He taught that through repentance and forgiveness, God calls all humanity to him in love and seeks every individual to do his will on Earth. Jesus taught that through living as God wishes, the Kingdom of God – justice, love, mercy and peace – could come upon Earth, either in individual lives or possibly to the world as a whole.

THE APOSTLES AND THE CHURCH

The Church holds that through the 12 key disciples of Jesus, the apostles, authority on Earth was given to the Church, which is seen to be the body of Christ on Earth. The Church is therefore held to be essential to salvation – to being freed from sin and to the possibility of everlasting life.

Jesus appointed 12 disciples. The following are common to the lists in the books of Matthew, Mark, Luke and the Acts.

Peter (martyred in Rome c. AD 64). A fisherman from Galilee called to be a disciple by Jesus at the beginning of his ministry, St Peter was recognized in the early Church as the leader of the disciples and is recognized by the Roman Catholic Church as the first of the popes. Peter – originally called Simon – was the brother of Andrew (see below).

Andrew (traditionally said to have been crucified at Patras in Greece c. AD 65). The brother of Peter, St Andrew was a fisherman called by Jesus to be a fisher of men. He was previously a disciple of John the Baptist.

James the son of Zebedee (beheaded in the Holy Land c. AD 44). St James the Great – like his brother John and the apostles Peter and Andrew – was a fisherman, and was one of the first disciples to be called by Jesus.

John the Apostle (fate unknown). St John the Apostle (also known as St John the Divine) was a fisherman and the brother of James (see above). He wrote the Gospel according to St John, the Revelation and three letters in the New Testament.

Philip (fate unknown). St Philip came from Bethsaida and was called at the same time as Nathaniel (see Bartholomew).

Bartholomew (traditionally said to have been martyred by the Babylonians). St Bartholomew is thought to have been called Nathaniel, the disciple whose calling is mentioned in St John, as Bartholomew is a family name – meaning son of Tolmai – rather than a given name.

Thomas (traditionally said to have died in India). Known as 'Doubting Thomas', St Thomas was the apostle who requested physical proof of the Resurrection.

Matthew (fate unknown). St Matthew – who is believed to have been a tax collector – is traditionally said to have been the author of the first Gospel.

James the son of Alphaeus (fate unknown, although traditionally said to have been martyred in Persia). Also known as St James the Less.

Simon the Canaanite (or Simon Zelotes) (fate unknown). St Simon is thought to have been a member of the Jewish nationalist group, the Zealots.

Thaddeus (or Jude) (fate unknown). Called Judas (not Iscariot) in St Luke, Thaddeus in St Mark and St Matthew and referred to as Judas of James in some versions of the Bible, this apostle is (like Simon) believed to have been a Zealot. He is better known as St Jude, patron of the desperate.

Judas Iscariot (traditionally said to have hanged himself after the Crucifixion.) The treasurer of the apostles, Judas betrayed Jesus to the chief priests for 30 pieces of silver. The name Iscariot is thought to derive from the Latin word *sicarius*, meaning murderer. Matthias was elected by the apostles to take the place of Judas.

FORMS OF CHRISTIANITY

Christianity has three major forms: Roman Catholic, with the pope as head of the Church; Orthodox, with the patriarch of Constantinople (Istanbul) as the first amongst equals of the various patriarchs of the different Orthodox Churches, such as the Russian Church; and the Protestant movement, made up of denominations such as the Lutheran, Methodist, Baptist and Anglican Churches, and so on.

ROMAN CATHOLICISM

Rome was the only Western Church founded by an apostle (St Peter). From Ireland to the Carpathians, Christians came to acknowledge the bishop of Rome as pope (from the Vulgar Latin *papa*, 'father'), and used Latin for worship, scripture-reading and theology. Roman Catholics recognize the pope as the lawful successor of St Peter, who was appointed by Christ to be head of the Church.

In the 16th century most of northern Europe broke the link with Rome to form reformed Protestant Churches. This division of Western Christianity led to the terms 'Protestant' for these northern Churches and 'Roman Catholic' (though to its members it was simply 'the Church') for Latin Christianity.

Supreme in southern Europe, Catholic Christianity was extended to the Americas and parts of Asia and Africa. Since the Second Vatican Council (1962–66) Latin has for most purposes given way to local languages.

The Roman Catholic Church claims catholicity inasmuch as it was charged (*de jure*) by Christ to 'teach all nations' and *de facto* since it is by far the largest Christian Church. The Roman Catholic Church claims infallibility in interpreting both the written and unwritten word of God. The pope has delegated certain administrative powers to the Curia, the work of which is done by 11 permanent departments or congregations, but the Church's strong centralized authority is focused on the papacy.

POPES

The pope – otherwise known as the bishop of Rome – is the chief bishop of the Roman Catholic Church and is considered by Catholics to be the Vicar of Christ on Earth and the successor of St Peter, the first bishop of Rome. He is elected by the College of Cardinals in the Vatican, meeting in secret conclave. The College consists of those cardinals aged under 80; in May 1991, 101 of the 141 cardinals were eligible as electors.

There have been over 30 antipopes, rivals to the papacy elected in opposition to the one who has been chosen canonically. In the 11th and 12th centuries the Holy Roman Emperors chose over a dozen antipopes; in the 14th century several antipopes were elected following the Great Schism. Unity was restored at the Council of Constance in 1415.

St Peter c. 33–67
St Linus 67–76
St Cletus (also called Anacletus) 76–88
St Clement I 88–97

Clement II 1046–47
Benedict IX (restored) 1047–48
Damasus II (Poppo) 1048
St Leo IX 1048–54
Victor II 1055–57
Stephen IX or X 1057–58
Nicholas II 1058–61
Alexander II 1061–73
St Gregory VII (Hildebrand de Soana) 1064–85
Victor III (Desiderius, Prince of Benevento) 1086–87
Urban II (Odon de Lagery) 1088–99
Paschal II (Ranieri) 1099–1118
Gelasius II (Giovanni Gaetani) 1118–19
Callistus II (Gui de Bourgogne) 1119–24
Honorius II (Lamberto Scannabecchi) 1124–30
Innocent II (Gregorio Papareschi) 1130–43
Celestine II (Guido di Castello) 1143–44
Lucius II (Gerardo Caccianemici) 1144–45
Eugenius III (Bernardo Paganelli) 1145–53
Anastasius IV (Corrado) 1153–54
Adrian IV (Nicholas Breakspeare*) 1154–59
Alexander III (Rolando Bandinelli) 1159–81
Lucius III (Ubaldo Allucingoli) 1181–85
Urban III (Uberto Crivelli) 1185–87
Gregory VIII (Alberto di Morra) 1187
Clement III (Paolo Scolari) 1187–91
Celestine III (Giacinto Buboni) 1191–98
Innocent III (Lothario, Count of Segni) 1198–1216
Honorius III (Cencio Savelli) 1216–27
Gregory IX (Ugolino, Count of Segni) 1227–41
Celestine IV (Goffredo Castiglioni) 1241
Innocent IV (Sinibaldo Fieschi) 1243–54
Alexander IV (Rainaldo, Count of Segni) 1254–61
Urban IV (Jacques Pantaléon) 1261–64
Clement IV (Gui Faucois) 1265–68
Gregory X (Theobaldo Visconti) 1271–76
Innocent V (Pierre de Tarentaise) 1276
Adrian V (Ottobono dei Fieschi) 1276
John XXI (Pedro Juliani) 1276–77
Nicholas III (Giovanni Gaetano Orsini) 1277–80
Martin IV (Simon de Brion) 1281–85
Honorius IV (Giacomo Savelli) 1285–87
Nicholas IV (Girolamo Moschi) 1288–92
St Celestine V (Pietro del Morrone) 1294
Boniface VIII (Benedetto Gaetani) 1294–1303
Benedict XI (Nicola Boccasini) 1303–04
Clement V (Bertrand de Got) 1305–14
John XXII (Jacques Duèse) 1316–34
Benedict XII (Jacques Fournier) 1334–42
Clement VI (Pierre Roger) 1342–52
Innocent VI (Etienne Aubert) 1352–62
Urban V (Guillaume Grimoard) 1362–70
Gregory XI (Pierre Roger de Beaufort) 1370–78
Urban VI (Bartolommeo Prignano) 1378–89
Boniface IX (Pietro Tomacelli) 1389–1404
Innocent VII (Cosimo dei Migliorati) 1404–06
Gregory XII (Angelo Corrari) 1406–15
Martin V (Odo Colonna) 1417–31
Eugenius IV (Gabriele Condolmieri) 1431–47
Nicholas V (Tommaso Parentucelli) 1447–55
Callistus III (Alonso Borgia) 1455–58
Pius II (Aeneas Piccolomini) 1458–64
Paul II (Pietro Barbo) 1464–71
Sixtus IV (Francesco della Rovere) 1471–84
Innocent VIII (Giovanni Battista) 1484–92
Alexander VI (Roderigo Borgia) 1492–1503
Pius III (Francesco Todeschini) 1503
Julius II (Giuliano della Rovere) 1503–13
Leo X (Giovanni de Medici) 1513–21
Adrian VI (Adrian Florensz Boeyens**) 1522–23
Clement VII (Giulio de Medici) 1523–34
Paul III (Alessandro Farnese) 1534–49

Julius III (Giovanni Maria Ciocchi del Monte) 1550–55
Marcellus II (Marcello Cervini) 1555
Paul IV (Giovanni Pietro Carafa) 1555–59
Pius IV (Gianangelo de Medici) 1559–65
St Pius V (Antonio Michele Ghislieri) 1566–72
Gregory XIII (Ugo Buoncompagni) 1572–85
Sixtus V (Felice Perretti) 1585–90
Urban VII (Giovanni Battista Castagna) 1590
Gregory XIV (Niccolo Sfondrati) 1590–91
Innocent IX (Giovanni Antonio Facchinetti) 1591
Clement VIII (Ipollito Aldobrandini) 1592–1605
Leo XI (Alessandro Ottaviano de Medici) 1605
Paul V (Camillo Borghese) 1605–21
Gregory XV (Alessandro Ludovisi) 1621–23
Urban VIII (Maffeo Barberini) 1623–44
Innocent X (Giovanni Battista Pamfili) 1644–55
Alexander VII (Fabio Chigi) 1655–67
Clement IX (Giulio Rospigliosi) 1667–69
Clement X (Emilio Altieri) 1670–76
Innocent XI (Benedetto Odescalchi) 1676–89
Alexander VIII (Pietro Ottoboni) 1689–91
Innocent XII (Antonio Pignatelli) 1691–1700
Clement XI (Gianfrancesco Albani) 1700–21
Innocent XIII (Michelangelo de Conti) 1721–24
Benedict XIII (Pietro Francesco Orsini) 1724–30
Clement XII (Lorenzo Corsini) 1730–40
Benedict XIV (Prospero Lambertini) 1740–58
Clement XIII (Carlo della Torre Rezzonico) 1758–69
Clement XIV (Giovanni Vincenzo Antonio Ganganelli) 1769–74
Pius VI (Giovanni Angelo Braschi) 1775–99
Pius VII (Barnabo Chiaramonti) 1800–23
Leo XII (Annibale della Genga) 1823–29
Pius VIII (Francesco Xaverio Castiglioni) 1829–30
Gregory XVI (Bartolomeo Cappellari) 1831–46
Pius IX (Giovanni Maria Mastai-Ferretti) 1846–78
Leo XIII (Vincenzo Gioaccchino Pecci) 1878–1903
St Pius X (Giuseppe Sarto) 1903–14
Benedict XV (Giacomo della Chiesa) 1914–22
Pius XI (Achille Ratti) 1922–39
Pius XII (Eugenio Pacelli) 1939–58
John XXIII (Angelo Giuseppe Roncalli) 1958–63
Paul VI (Giovanni Battista Montini) 1963–78
John Paul I (Albino Luciani) 1978
John Paul II (Karol Wojtyla) 1978–

Key: * Adrian IV was the only English Pope.
** A Dutchman, Adrian VI was the last non-Italian to be elected to the papacy until the Pole, Karol Wojtyla, was elected in 1978.

UNIAT CHURCHES

Some smaller non-Latin Churches owe allegiance to the pope. They are called the Uniat Churches. Although these Churches are in full communion with the Roman Catholic Church, they retain their own organization and liturgies. Apart from the Malankara Orthodox Syrian (Jacobite) Church in southern India – which has 1 600 000 adherents – most of the Uniat Churches are in the Middle East and Eastern Europe. The largest of these Churches – with nearly 4 000 000 adherents – is the Ukrainian Uniat Church, which until 1990 was illegal in the USSR.

Apart from the Ukrainians, the (Roman) Catholic Christians of the Uniat Churches belong to congregations owing allegiance to:
  – the (Armenian rite) patriarch of Cilicia (based in Beirut, Lebanon);

– the (Chaldean rite) patriarch of Babylon (based in Baghdad, Iraq);
– the (Coptic rite) patriarch of Alexandria (based in Cairo, Egypt);
– the (Maronite rite) patriarch of Antioch (based in Bkerke, Lebanon);
– the (Melchite rite) patriarch of Antioch (based in Damascus, Syria);
– the (Syrian rite) patriarch of Antioch (based in Beirut, Lebanon).

PATRONS OF GROUPS AND PROFESSIONS

Patron saints of groups and of professions include the following:

Group/profession	Saint(s)	Feast day(s)
Academics	Albert the Great	Nov 15
Accountants	Matthew	Sep 21
Actors	Genesius	Aug 26
Advertising executives	Bernardine of Siena	May 20
Air pilots	Joseph of Copertino	Sep 18
Announcers	John Chrysostom	Sep 13
Archers	Sebastian	Jan 20
Architects	Benedict and	Mar 21
	Thomas	Dec 21
Artillerymen	Barbara	Dec 4
Bakers	Michael and	Sep 29
	Honorius of Amiens	May 16
Bankers	Matthew	Sep 21
Basket makers	Paul the Hermit	Jan 25
Bellfounders	Agatha	Feb 5
Biologists	Albert the Great	Nov 15
Blind people	Clair	Jan 2
Boatmen	Nicholas	Dec 6
Boilermakers	Maurus	Jan 15
Bookbinders	Celestine the Fifth and	May 19
	John of God	Mar 8
Booksellers	John of the Latin Gate	May 6
Business executives	Expeditus	Apr 19
Butchers	Nicholas	Dec 6
Carpenters	Joseph	Mar 19
Cavalrymen	George	Apr 23
Charity	Vincent de Paul and	Jul 19
	Louise de Marillac	Mar 15
Chemists	Albert the Great	Nov 15
Children	Nicholas	Dec 6
Choirboys	Nicholas	Dec 6
Circus performers	Julian the Hospitaller	Jan 29
Clockmakers	Eligius	Dec 1
Cooks	Martha	Jul 29
Coopers	John the Baptist and	Jun 24
	Michael	Sep 29
Cripples	Giles	Sep 1
Customs officers	Matthew	Sep 21
Cutlers	John the Baptist	Jun 24
Deaf people	Francis de Sales	Jan 29

Delicatessens	Anthony	Jan 17
Dentists	Appollonia	Feb 9
Diplomats	Gabriel	Mar 24
Disabled ex-servicemen	Raphael	Oct 24
Doctors	Luke and	Oct 18
	Pantaleon	Jul 27
Domestic servants	Zita	Jul 5
Down-and-outs	Alexis and	Jul 17
	Giles	Sep 1
Drinkers	Bibiana	Dec 2
Drivers	Christopher and	Jul 25
	Frances of Rome	Mar 9
Dry cleaners/Dyers	Maurice	Sep 22
Editors	John Bosco	Jan 31
Electricians	Lucy	Dec 13
Emigrants	Frances Cabrini	Dec 22
Engineers	Dominic (La Caussade)	May 12
Farmers	Benedict	Mar 21
Farm workers	Isidore the Labourer	May 15
Ferrymen	Julian the Hospitaller	Jan 29
Firemen	Lawrence	Aug 10
Fishermen	Peter	Jun 29
Forestry workers	Hubert	Nov 3
Furnishers	Louis of France	Aug 25
Gardeners	Fiacre and	Aug 30
	Dorothy	Feb 2
Glaziers	Luke	Oct 18
Glassworkers	Clair	Jan 2
Glove makers	Mary Magdalene	Jul 22
Gravediggers	Maurus	Dec 15
Hairdressers	Louis of France	Aug 25
Hatters	James the Less	May 1
Hermits	Anthony the Hermit	Jan 17
Hired hands	Notburga	Sep 13
Hospital staff	John of God	Mar 8
Housekeepers	Martha	Jul 29
Hunters	Hubert	Nov 3
Immigrants	Frances Cabrini	Dec 22
Innkeepers	Julian and	Jan 29
	Vincent	Jan 28
Insurance agents	Yves	May 19
Interior decorators	Genevieve	Jan 3
Jewellers	Eligius	Dec 1
Joiners	Joseph	Mar 19
Journalists	Francis de Sales and	Jan 29
	Bernardine of Siena	May 20
Labourers	Isidore the Labourer	May 10
Lacemakers	Anne	Jul 26
Laundry workers	Clare	Aug 12
Lawyers	Yves and	May 19
	Raymund of Penafort	Jan 23
Learner drivers	Expeditus	Apr 19
Leatherworkers	Bartholomew and Crispin and Crispinian	Aug 24 / Oct 25

Category	Patron	Date
Locksmiths	Peter	Apr 29
Lost objects	Anthony of Padua	Jun 13
Lovers	Valentine	Feb 14
Machine workers	Benedict	Mar 21
Managers	Thomas	Dec 21
Market gardeners	Phocas	Sep 22
	and Fiacre	Aug 30
Merchants	Nicholas	Dec 6
Messengers	Adrian	Sep 8
Metalworkers	Stephen	Dec 26
Midwives	Raymund Nonnatus	Aug 31
Millers	Blaise	Feb 3
	and Winnoc	Nov 6
Miners	Barbara	Dec 4
Missionaries	Teresa of Avila	Oct 3
	and Francis Xavier	Dec 3
Musicians	Cecilia	Nov 22
	and Blaise	Feb 3
	and Dunstan	May 19
Naturalists	Albert the Great	Nov 15
Navigators	Nicholas of Bari	May 7
	and Cuthbert	Mar 20
	and Elmo	Jun 2
Needlewomen	Clare	Aug 12
Nurses	Camillus	Jul 14
Opticians	Clair	Jan 2
Orphans	Jerome Emiliani	Feb 8
Painters	Luke	Oct 18
Parachutists	Michael	Sep 29
Pawnbrokers	Nicholas	Dec 6
Pedestrians	Martin of Tours	Nov 11
People in desperate straits	Jude	Oct 28
Perfumers	Mary Magdalene	Jul 22
Pharmacists	James the Great	Jul 25
Philosophers	Catherine	Jul 25
Photographers	Veronica	Aug 6
Physicians	Luke	Oct 18
	and Cosmas and Damian	Sep 27
Physicists	Albert the Great	Nov 15
Pilgrims	James the Great	Jul 25
Plumbers	Eligius	Dec 1
Police	Genevieve	Jan 3
	and Sebastian	Jan 20
Poor people	Lawrence	Aug 10
Porters	Christopher	Jul 25
Potholers	Benedict	Mar 21
Preachers	John Chrysostom	Sep 13
Pregnant women	Anne	Jun 26
Priests	John Vianney	Aug 4
Printers	Augustine	Aug 28
Prisoners	Leonard	Nov 6
Prison officers	Hippolytus	Aug 13
Quarry workers	Rock	Aug 16
Race relations	Martin de Porres	Nov 3
Radiologists	Michael	Sep 29
Radio workers	Gabriel	Mar 24
Refugees	Benedict Labre	Apr 16
Roofers	Vincent Ferrer	Apr 5
Ropemakers	Paul	Jun 29
Sacristans	Guy	Jun 12
Sailors	Nicholas of Bari	May 7
Scouts	George	Apr 23
Sculptors	Luke	Oct 18
Secretaries	John Cassian	Jul 23
Servants	Blandina	Jun 2
Shepherds	Germaine of Pibrac	Jan 19
Shepherdesses	Genevieve	Jan 3
Shipwrights	Julian the Hospitaller	Jan 29
Shoemakers/repairers	Crispin and Crispinian	Oct 25
Shopkeepers	Francis of Assisi	Oct 4
Shorthand typists	Genesius	Aug 25
Sick people	Camillus	Jul 14
Soldiers	Maurice	Sep 22
	and Martin of Tours	Nov 11
	and George	Apr 23
Spokesmen/women	John Chrysostom	Sep 13
Students	Catherine	Nov 11
Surgeons	Luke	Oct 18
Tanners	Bartholomew	Aug 24
Tax collectors	Matthew	Sep 21
Taxi drivers	Fiacre	Aug 30
	and Christopher	Jul 25
Teachers	Cassian of Imola	Aug 13
Television workers	Gabriel	Mar 24
	and Clare	Aug 12
Tourists	Christopher	Jul 25
Tour operators	Francis Xavier	Dec 3
Tradesmen	Francis of Assisi	Oct 4
Translators	Jerome	Sep 30
Travellers	Julian the Hospitaller and	Jan 29
	Christopher	Jul 25
Underwriters	Yves	May 19
University academics	Thomas Aquinas	Jan 28
Upholsterers	Genevieve	Jan 3
Virgins	Maria Goretti	Jul 6
Weavers	Blaise	Feb 3
	and Barnabas	Jun 11
Wine growers	Vincent and	Jan 22
	John of the Latin Gate	May 6
Wine merchants	Nicholas	Dec 6
Workers	Joseph	Mar 19
Writers	Francis de Sales	Jan 29
Young people	Casimir	Mar 4
	and Louis Gonzaga	Jun 21

RELIGIOUS ORDERS

Largest Roman Catholic religious orders for men

Order	Founded	Number of priests and brothers
Jesuits (Society of Jesus; priests only)	1540 (by St Ignatius Loyola)	26 600
Franciscans (Order of Friars Minor)	1209 (by St Francis of Assisi)	20 000
Salesians (Society of St Francis de Sales; an educational order)	1864 (by St John Bosco)	17 200
Capuchins (Order of Friars Minor Capuchin)	1525 (by Matteo de Basci)	11 900
Benedictines (Order of St Benedict)	about 530 (by St Benedict)	9 300
Christian Brothers (Institute of the Brothers of Christian Schools)	1684 (by St Jean-Baptiste de la Salle)	9 100
Dominicans (Order of Friars Preachers)	1215 (by St Dominic)	6 700
Redemptorists (Congregation of the Most Holy Redeemer)	1732 (by St Alfonso de Liguori)	6 500
Marists (Society of Mary; priests only)	1824 (by Jean-Claude Colin)	6 300
Oblates of Mary Immaculate (a missionary order)	1816 (by Charles-Joseph-Eugene de Mazenod)	5 700
Divine World Missionaries	1875 (by Arnold Janssen)	5 500
Franciscans Conventual (Order of Friars Minor Coventual)	1209 (by St Francis of Assisi)	4 100
Vincentians (sometimes known as Lazarists; Congregation of the Mission)	1625 (by St Vincent de Paul)	3 900

Largest Roman Catholic religious orders for women

Order	Founded	Number of members
Daughters of Charity of St Vincent de Paul	1633 (by St Vincent de Paul)	33 000
Carmelites	1451 (re-formed 1562 by St Teresa of Avila)	24 500
Benedictines	6th century (by St Scholastica)	24 400
Sisters of Mercy	1831 (by Catherine Elizabeth McAuley)	23 000
Sisters of Divine Providence	1762 (by Jean Martin Moye)	21 000
Salesians	1872 (by St John Bosco)	17 100
Poor Clares	about 1215 (by St Clare)	16 400
Sisters of the Immaculate Conception	1863 (by Louis Peydessus)	11 400

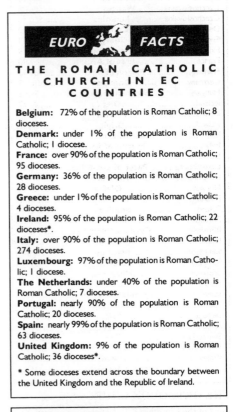

EURO FACTS

THE ROMAN CATHOLIC CHURCH IN EC COUNTRIES

Belgium: 72% of the population is Roman Catholic; 8 dioceses.

Denmark: under 1% of the population is Roman Catholic; 1 diocese.

France: over 90% of the population is Roman Catholic; 95 dioceses.

Germany: 36% of the population is Roman Catholic; 28 dioceses.

Greece: under 1% of the population is Roman Catholic; 4 dioceses.

Ireland: 95% of the population is Roman Catholic; 22 dioceses*.

Italy: over 90% of the population is Roman Catholic; 274 dioceses.

Luxembourg: 97% of the population is Roman Catholic; 1 diocese.

The Netherlands: under 40% of the population is Roman Catholic; 7 dioceses.

Portugal: nearly 90% of the population is Roman Catholic; 20 dioceses.

Spain: nearly 99% of the population is Roman Catholic; 63 dioceses.

United Kingdom: 9% of the population is Roman Catholic; 36 dioceses*.

* Some dioceses extend across the boundary between the United Kingdom and the Republic of Ireland.

EURO FACTS

ST BENEDICT – PATRON SAINT OF EUROPE

The Italian St Benedict of Nursia (c. 480–c. 550) withdrew from the world c. 500 to live as a hermit. He established 12 monasteries, including Monte Cassino, of which he became abbot. Benedict's monastic rule is regarded as the basis of Western monasticism. The Greek brothers St Cyril (c. 827–69) and St Methodius (c. 825–84), who evangelized the Slavs, are co-patrons of Europe.

PATRON SAINTS

Patrons of European countries include:

Country	Saint(s)	Feast day(s)
Austria	Leopold	Nov 15
Austria	Florian	Dec 14
Belgium	Joseph	Mar 19
Belgium	Charles the Good	Mar 2
Bulgaria	Cyril and Methodius	Jul 7
Cyprus	Barnabas	Jun 11
Czechoslovakia	Wenceslaus	Sep 28
Czechoslovakia	Ludmilla	Sep 16
Denmark	Canute	Jan 19/June 10
England	George	Apr 23
Finland	Henry of Uppsala	Jan 19
France	Joan of Arc	May 30
France	Martin of Tours	Nov 11
Germany	Boniface	Jun 5
Hungary	Stephen of Hungary	Sep 2
Iceland	Olaf	July 29
Ireland	Patrick	Mar 17
Ireland	Brigit	Feb 2
Italy	Catherine of Siena	Apr 24
Italy	Francis of Assisi	Oct 4
Lithuania	Casimir	Mar 4
Luxembourg	Peter of Luxembourg	Jul 5
Luxembourg	Willibrord	Nov 7
Norway	Olaf	Jul 29
Poland	Casimir	Mar 4
Poland	Stanislas	May 7
Portugal	Anthony of Padua	Jan 13
Romania	Cyril and Methodius	Jul 7
Russia	Nicholas	Dec 6
San Marino	Marinus	Sep 4
Scotland	Andrew	Jun 16
Scotland	Margaret	Jun 16
Serbia	Sava	Jan 14
Spain	James the Great	Jul 25
Spain	Ferdinand	May 30
Sweden	Eric	May 18
Sweden	Bridget	Oct 8
Switzerland	Gall	Oct 16
Switzerland	Nicholas von Flue	Sep 25
Wales	David	Mar 1

Yugoslavia (see Serbia)

THE ORTHODOX CHURCHES

Most of the Churches called Orthodox derived from the ancient Greek Christianity of the Eastern Mediterranean. The direct link with Churches founded by apostles and the memory of a Christian Roman Empire (the Byzantine Empire) that lasted until 1453 heighten the importance of tradition as a guide of the Church. Tradition includes the scriptures, the first seven Church councils and the writings of the Church fathers (the early medieval writers on Christian doctrine), the liturgy and the veneration of holy pictures (icons).

The Orthodox Church maintains that it is the 'one true Church of Christ which is not and has not been divided' and it regards the Roman Catholic Church as schismatic. The Ecumenical Patriarch of Constantinople (Istanbul) is the senior figure, but each autonomous Church has its own patriarch and is self-governing.

PRINCIPAL ORTHODOX CHURCHES

Russian Orthodox Church 50 000 000 members
Ethiopian Orthodox Church 22 000 000 members
Romanian Orthodox Church 18 900 000 members
Greek Orthodox Church (in Greece) 9 700 000 members
Serbian Orthodox Church 9 000 000 members
Bulgarian Orthodox Church 7 200 000 members
Georgian Orthodox Church 5 000 000 members
Greek Orthodox Archdiocese of North and South America 5 000 000 members
Armenian Apostolic Church 4 000 000 members
Macedonian Orthodox Church 1 000 000 members
Polish Autocephalous Orthodox Church 1 000 000 members

PROTESTANTISM

In 16th-century Europe, movements to reform the Church accompanied fresh interpretations of the Bible and the use of everyday language in place of Latin. These movements rejected Roman authority and established reformed national forms of Christianity in the various states of northern Europe, such as Lutheranism in Sweden and parts of Germany, Calvinism in Switzerland and Scotland, and Anglicanism in England. This process is known as the *Reformation*.

The majority Protestant movement aimed to reform the Church within each state while keeping the idea that the Church embraced the whole community. The Radical (or Anabaptist) movement insisted that the Church consisted only of those who made a commitment to Christ, and broke the link with the state. A minority in Europe, this movement produced the dominant Christian forms in North America.

The 18th century saw movements for spiritual reform in Protestant countries – Pietism in Germany and the Evangelical Revival in Britain, North America and elsewhere. These brought the majority and radical streams closer together. European emigration brought all the Protestant traditions to America, Canada and Australia. In the USA they took new life and new shapes in a huge community – largely Christian, but multi-ethnic and with no national Church. Some completely new forms of Christianity also arose, such as Pentacostalism. Today the American scene is characterized by a large number of denominations.

New expressions of Christianity are appearing in the southern continents as Christians there meet situations not encountered in the West. There are some signs that a tradition of Christianity is developing that may be as distinctly African as Catholicism or Protestantism have been Western, in that African Independent Churches reflect African ways of worship and address issues of African life. In India, united Churches of South India and North India have developed, and these replace the denominational Churches of Western origin.

ECUMENISM

One characteristic of Christianity today is the increased understanding and co-operation both between Christians in different parts of the world and between Christians of different traditions and backgrounds. The word *ecumenical* is used to describe such spirit and action. Though sometimes used in a narrower sense to refer to the movement associated with the World Council of Churches, the word simply means 'worldwide' (from the Greek *oikumene*, 'inhabited world').

WORLD COUNCIL OF CHURCHES

The World Council of Churches (founded in 1948) has its headquarters in Geneva, Switzerland. The Council – whose membership includes most of the main Christian Churches, except the Roman Catholic – promotes ecumenical Christian action and study. There are similar organizations in many countries. In the United Kingdom the Council of Churches for Britain and Ireland includes the Roman Catholic Church in membership.

THE ANGLICAN COMMUNION

THE CHURCH OF ENGLAND

Henry VIII renounced the supremacy of the pope in 1534, founding the Church of England with the monarch as its head. Protestant reforms were instituted during the reign of Edward VI (1547–53). After the reign of the Catholic Mary I, the independent Church of England was re-established in 1558. The Church of England retains the episcopal form of government and has preserved many of the Catholic traditions of liturgy. However, it holds most of the basic tenets of the reformed faith of Protestantism. Its doctrine is based upon the Thirty-Nine Articles; its liturgy is based upon *The Book of Common Prayer* (1549 and 1662) and its successors. The 18th-century Evangelical Movement emphasized the Protestant tradition, while the 19th-century Oxford Movement emphasized the Catholic tradition. These two movements continue in the Church of England as the Low Church and the High Church.

The Church in England is divided into two provinces – Canterbury and York – each headed by an archbishop. The archbishop of Canterbury is recognized as first among equals by the leaders of the provinces of the Anglican Communion. (The dioceses of the Anglican Communion in Britain are detailed in the UK chapter.) Each of the Churches of the Anglican Communion is self-governing. Some Churches, including the Church of the Province of New Zealand and the Episcopal Church in the USA, ordain women priests and elect women bishops. The Church of Ireland also has women priests.

THE ANGLICAN DIOCESE OF EUROPE

The diocese of Gibraltar in Europe – which covers all of continental Europe – was founded in 1970 as the newest see in the Province of Canterbury. Although the bishop is based in London, the diocesan cathedral is in Gibraltar, and there are pro-cathedrals in Valletta (Malta) and Brussels (Belgium).

PRINCIPAL ANGLICAN CHURCHES

Church of England 26 000 000 members (1 900 000 practising)
Church of the Province of Uganda 4 000 000 members
Anglican Church of Australia 3 700 000 members
Episcopal Church in the USA 2 500 000 members
Church of the Province of Southern Africa 2 000 000 members

Church of the Province of Kenya 1 000 000 members
Anglican Church of Canada 900 000 members
Church of the Province of New Zealand 900 000 members
Church of the Province of Nigeria 800 000 members

Other provinces include the Anglican Church of Papua New Guinea, the Anglican Church of the Southern Cone of America, the Church in Wales, the Church of Ireland, the Church of the Province of Burma, the Church of the Province of Burundi, Rwanda and Zaïre, the Church of the Province of Central Africa, the Church of the Province of the Indian Ocean, the Church of the Province of Kenya, the Church of the Province of Melanesia, the Church of the Province of the Sudan, the Church of the Province of Tanzania, the Church of the Province of West Africa, the Church of the Province of the West Indies, the Episcopal Church in Jerusalem and the Middle East, the Episcopal Church of Brazil, the Episcopal Church of Scotland, the Holy Catholic Church in Japan.

BAPTISTS

Baptist Churches, which take their name from the practice of baptism by immersion of adult believers, developed within the English and American Puritan movements in the 17th century. Individual Baptist churches are self-governing. There are more than 35 000 000 Baptists, the majority of whom live in the USA. The Baptist Church in the USSR is growing rapidly.

PRINCIPAL BAPTIST CHURCHES

Southern Baptist Convention (USA) 14 750 000 members
National Baptist Convention (USA) 6 300 000 members
American Baptist Churches in the USA 1 600 000 members
All-Union Council of Evangelical Christian Baptists (USSR) 550 000 members
Nigerian Baptist Convention 500 000 members
Burma Baptist Convention 400 000 members
Telegu Baptist Church (India) 340 000 members
General Association of Regular Baptist Churches (USA) 300 000 members
Conservative Baptist Association of America 250 000 members
American Baptist Association 250 000 members
Baptist Union of Great Britain 170 000 members

CONGREGATIONALISTS

The liberal Protestant Congregationalist churches developed from the Independents in England in the 16th and 17th centuries. Each congregation is independent in the organization of its own affairs. In England, Australia, Canada, India and the USA the majority of Congregationalist churches have joined United Churches (see p. 314).

CHRISTIAN SCIENTISTS

The Church of Christ, Scientist, is a liberal Protestant denomination founded in the USA by Mary Baker Eddy in 1879. Christian Scientists – who deny the deity but not the divinity of Jesus – emphasize the practice of spiritual healing. Christian Scientists claim their own sources of knowledge supplementary to the Scriptures.

DISCIPLES OF CHRIST

The Disciples of Christ were founded during a period of religious revival on the American frontier in the first half of the 19th century. They attempted to unite the divisions of Protestantism through a return to New Testament practice.

PRINCIPAL CHURCHES OF THE DISCIPLES

Christian Church (Disciples of Christ; USA) 1 100 000 disciples

Christian Churches of Christ (USA)   1 100 000 disciples

INDEPENDENT AFRICAN CHURCHES

Dissatisfaction with Western forms of worship has encouraged the emergence of a number of African Churches. The Kimbanguist Church of Zaïre began in the 1920s when followers were attracted by the preaching and miraculous healings of Simon Kimbangui, a Baptist catechist. Various Zion Churches in South Africa emphasize adult baptism by immersion, divine healing and preparation for a Second Coming. Aladura ('Owners of Prayer') Churches in West Africa emphasize prophets and divine healing. The incorporation of traditional African beliefs and values is a feature of a number of Churches.

PRINCIPAL AFRICAN CHURCHES

Church of Jesus Christ on Earth through the Prophet Simon Kimbangui (Zaïre)   5 000 000 members

Zion Christian Church (South Africa)   4 000 000 members

Church of the Lord – Aladura (Nigeria)   1 000 000 members

African Israel Nineveh Church (Kenya)   350 000 members

LUTHERANS

The beliefs of the Lutheran Churches are derived from the teaching of the German Martin Luther (1483–1546) and were formulated in the Augsburg Confession of 1530. Luther taught that redemption could only be achieved through faith in Christ (justification by faith), and that Scripture is the sole rule of faith. Over 55 000 000 people belong to Lutheran Churches, whose greatest influence is in Germany and in Scandinavia.

PRINCIPAL LUTHERAN CHURCHES

United Churches (Germany) 13 500 000 members

United Lutheran Protestant Church of Germany 9 400 000 members

Evangelical Lutheran Church of Denmark 4 700 000 members

Evangelical Lutheran Church of Finland 4 360 000 members

Federation of Evangelical Churches (Germany) 4 000 000 members

Lutheran Church in America 2 900 000 members

Lutheran Church – Missouri Synod (USA) 2 600 000 members

American Lutheran Church 2 300 000 members

United Evangelical Lutheran Churches in India 1 500 000 members

Evangelical Church of the Lutheran Confession in Brazil 870 000 members

Lutheran Church in Hungary 430 000 members

METHODISM

Methodism developed out of the religious revival within the Church of England led by John Wesley (1703–91) and his brother Charles (1707–88). The differences between the early Methodists and contemporary Anglicans were largely of emphasis rather than doctrine. All Methodist Churches have a strong central authority, and those of the American tradition are episcopal. Over 55 000 000 people belong to Methodist Churches, whose greatest influence is in the USA and Africa.

PRINCIPAL METHODIST CHURCHES

United Methodist Church (USA) 9 700 000 members

African Methodist Episcopal Zion Church (USA) 3 500 000 members

African Methodist Episcopal Church (USA) 2 200 000 members

Korean Methodist Church 1 030 000 members

Methodist Church Nigeria 480 000 members

Methodist Church in India 470 000 members

Methodist Church (UK) 450 000 members

Methodist Church of Southern Africa 400 000 members

OLD CATHOLICS

The Old Catholics comprise congregations that have separated from the Roman Catholic Church since the 18th century. The Dutch Church of Utrecht was formed in 1724 in support of Jansenism, a movement based on the teachings of Cornelius Jansen, who held that the efficacy of the sacraments depended upon the state of grace of the recipient. Various Central European Old Catholic congregations seceded because of their opposition to the doctrine of papal infallibility.

PENTECOSTALISTS

Pentecostalism grew out of the charismatic movement in a number of Protestant Churches in the USA in the last 150 years. Pentecostalists emphasize 'baptism by the Holy Spirit', a post-conversion religious experience, which may be accompanied by divine healing and 'speaking in tongues'. The Pentecostalists' largest Church is the United Pentecostal Church International (USA), which has 1 000 000 adherents.

PLYMOUTH BRETHREN

The Plymouth Brethren were founded in 1831 by J.N. Darby in Plymouth (England). They have no clergy and no formal creed, and emphasize biblical prophecy and an imminent Second Coming.

REFORMED CHRISTIANS AND PRESBYTERIANS

The Reformed Churches are Calvinistic rather than Lutheran in doctrine. They trace their origins to the teaching of the French Protestant John Calvin (1509–64), a leader of the Reformation in France and Switzerland. While believing that faith is dependent upon Scripture alone, Calvinists insist that, as man lacks free will, only the elect are predestined to be saved. The Reformed Churches include the Presbyterians, whose name is derived from their form of government by lay leaders — known as presbyters or elders — and by pastors.

THE CHURCH OF SCOTLAND

The established Church of Scotland is Presbyterian in constitution. It is presided over by a Moderator who is chosen annually by the elected General Assembly, at which the British sovereign (as head of the Church) is represented by a Lord High Commissioner. Scotland is divided into 12 synods for administrative purposes.

PRINCIPAL REFORMED AND PRESBYTERIAN CHURCHES

Dutch Reformed Church (South Africa) 3 000 000 members
Presbyterian Church (USA) 2 900 000 members
Reformed Churches (Switzerland) 2 900 000 members
Netherlands Reformed Church 2 700 000 members
Protestant Church in Indonesia 2 300 000 members
Reformed Church in Hungary 2 000 000 members
Presbyterian Church of Korea 1 540 000 members
Church of Jesus Christ (Madagascar) 1 250 000 members
United Church of Zambia 1 000 000 members
Church of Scotland 840 000 members
Reformed Churches in the Netherlands 830 000 members
Reformed (Calvinist) Church (Romania) 700 000 members
Church of Central Africa (Malawi) 700 000 members

SEVENTH-DAY ADVENTISTS

Adventist Churches emphasize the imminence of the Second Coming. The Seventh-day Adventist Church was established in the 19th century in the USA, where there are 5 600 000 members.

SOCIETY OF FRIENDS (QUAKERS)

The Society of Friends was founded in the 17th century by the English Puritan George Fox. Quakerism emphasizes the immediate application of Christ's teaching to everyday life, while rejecting the need for formalized services, creeds or clergy. Worship is spontaneous. Friends' meetings wait in silence for the 'inward light'. Quakers are pacifists.

UNITARIANS

Unitarians deny the doctrine of the Trinity. The belief that God is one person was held by some in the early Church (Arianism), but modern Unitarianism dates in Europe from the 16th century, and in the English-speaking world from the foundation of a Unitarian chapel in London by Theophilus Lindsey (1774).

UNITED CHURCHES

The ecumenical movement among Christian Churches has resulted in the union of a number of Protestant Churches. The pressure for unity has been particularly strong in countries without a Christian tradition where the historic differences between denominations appear meaningless.

PRINCIPAL UNITED CHURCHES

United Church of Christ (USA) 1 700 000 members
(formed 1957 from the union of Congregational, Evangelical and Reformed Churches)
Church of South India 1 500 000 members
(formed 1947 with the union of Anglican, Congregational, Methodist, Presbyterian and Reformed Churches)

Uniting Church in Australia 1 100 000 members
(formed 1977 with the union of Congregational, Methodist and Presbyterian Churches)
Church of North India 1 000 000 members
(formed 1970 with the union of Anglican, Baptist, Congregational, Methodist and Presbyterian Churches)
United Church of Canada 860 000 members
(formed 1925 with the union of Congregational, Methodist and Presbyterian Churches)

MARGINAL GROUPS

Various movements related to Christianity stand apart from the forms mentioned above by not giving ultimate significance to Christ. Western examples include some forms of Unitarianism (which deny Christ's divinity); the Watchtower Movement or Jehovah's Witnesses (who also deny Christ's divinity, and condemn all Churches) and Mormonism (which claims its own sources of knowledge supplementary to the Scriptures.)

JEHOVAH'S WITNESSES

The Jehovah's Witnesses – or the Watchtower Movement as they are officially known – grew out of the International Bible Studies Association, founded in Pittsburgh, Pennsylvania (USA) by Charles Taze Russell (1872). This movement is known for its literal interpretation of the Bible and its concern with Armageddon, the imminent final battle in which Witnesses will be saved. Although Witnesses deny Christ's divinity, they recognize Jesus as God's agent. They believe that the Theocracy (God's Kingdom) will be established on Earth after Armageddon and the Second Coming. The Witnesses have faced persecution in a number of countries because they refuse to acknowledge many of the claims made on the individual by secular governments. They are renowned for not accepting blood transfusions.

MORMONS

The Mormons – or the Church of Jesus Christ of Latter-Day Saints as they are officially known – are active missionaries. They were founded in the USA in 1830 by Joseph Smith. Smith claimed to have received from an angel the Book of Mormon, which is accepted by the Latter-Day Saints as an addition to Scripture. Mormons hold the belief that God evolved from man and that man himself has the potential to attain deity. Mormonism denies the Trinity in favour of a polytheistic belief in three independent persons. It teaches that after death there is a full resurrection of the body and a reuniting of families. Dead relatives can be baptized or married in the faith to ensure their salvation.

The Mormons were led to their current centre in Salt Lake City, Utah, by Brigham Young. There are over 7 000 000 Mormons, the majority in North America.

UNIFICATION CHURCH

Sometimes known as 'the Moonies', the Unification Church was founded in the 1950s by a Korean, Sun Myung Moon. It is thought to have over 2 000 000 members, the majority in South Korea and Japan. The Church teaches the 'Divine Principle' which holds that, following humanity's fall from grace, a restoration to perfection can be achieved through the first messiah, Jesus, and the second, the Reverend Moon. Love of creation and family life are of central importance to members.

THE BIBLE

THE HEBREW BIBLE

The 24 books of the Hebrew Bible are grouped into three divisions – *Torah* (The Law), *Nevi'im* (Prophets) and *Ketuvim* (Writings).

The Torah. The Torah was traditionally ascribed to Moses and is known to Christians as the Pentateuch. It has five books – Genesis, Exodus, Leviticus, Numbers and Deuteronomy.

The Nevi'im. The Nevi'im has eight books – Joshua, Judges, Samuel, Kings, Isaiah, Jeremiah, Ezekiel, and the Book of the Twelve (the Minor Prophets).

The Ketuvim. The Ketuvim comprises religious poetry and 'wisdom literature'. It has 11 books – Psalms, Proverbs, Job, the Song of Songs, Ruth, Lamentations, Ecclesiastes, Esther, Daniel, Ezra and Nehemiah, and Chronicles.

THE OLD TESTAMENT

The Christian Church received the Old Testament from Greek-speaking Jews. This version contained additional books, and parts of books, not found in Hebrew. These writings, which later became known as the *Apocrypha*, are regarded as part of Holy Scripture by the Roman Catholic Church, but at the Reformation they were denied this status by Protestants. The Authorized Version of 1611 included these books between the Old and New Testaments.

The Old Testament reorders and divides some of the books of the Hebrew Bible. Samuel, Kings and Chronicles are each divided into two, while Ezra and Nehemiah and each of the 12 Minor Prophets are counted as separate books. The English Authorized Version has 39 Old Testament books, and the Roman Catholic Vulgate (including books regarded by Protestant Churches as Apocryphal) has 46.

BOOKS OF THE OLD TESTAMENT

The 1611 Authorized Version	*The Roman Catholic Vulgate*
Genesis	Genesis
Exodus	Exodus
Leviticus	Leviticus
Numbers	Numbers
Deuteronomy	Deuteronomy
Joshua	Josue
Judges	Judges
Ruth	Ruth
First Book of Samuel	First Book of Kings
Second Book of Samuel	Second Book of Kings
First Book of Kings	Third Book of Kings
Second Book of Kings	Fourth Book of Kings
First Book of Chronicles	First Book of Paralipomenon
Second Book of Chronicles	Second Book of Paralipomenon
Ezra	First Book of Esdras
Nehemiah	Second Book of Esdras
	Tobias
	Judith
Esther	Esther
Job	Job
Psalms	Psalms
Proverbs	Proverbs
Ecclesiastes	Ecclesiastes
Song of Solomon	Canticle of Canticles
	Wisdom of Solomon
	Sirach
Isaiah	Isaias
Jeremiah	Jeremias
Lamentations	Lamentations
	Baruch
Ezekiel	Ezechiel
Daniel	Daniel
Hosea	Osea
Joel	Joel
Amos	Amos
Obadiah	Abdias
Jonah	Jonas
Micah	Micheas
Nahum	Nahum
Habakkuk	Habacuc
Zephaniah	Sophonias
Haggai	Aggeus
Zechariah	Zacharias
Malachi	Malachias
	First Book of Machabees
	Second Book of Machabees

THE NEW TESTAMENT

The 27 books of the New Testament were written between AD 50 and 100. Covering the period from the birth of Christ to the spread of Christianity through the Roman Empire, these books are grouped into four divisions – the Gospels, the Acts of the Apostles, the Epistles and the Apocalypse.

The Gospels are the four books that describe the life and works of Jesus Christ. They are traditionally attributed to Matthew, Mark, Luke and John the Divine.

The Acts of the Apostles is a single book, traditionally ascribed to Luke. It describes the spread of Christianity from Jerusalem to Rome.

The Epistles are 21 books written as letters to early churches and Christian individuals. They are the Letters of Paul to the Romans, Corinthians (1 and 2), Galatians, Ephesians, Philippians, Colossians, Thessalonians (1 and 2), Timothy (1 and 2), Titus and Philemon, the anonymous Letter to the Hebrews, the Letter of James, the two Letters of Peter, the three Letters of John, and the Letter of Jude.

The Apocalypse is also known as the Book of Revelation. It contains a prophetic description of the end of the world.

ISLAM

Islam is the world's second largest religion. The Arabic term *islam* means 'the act of resignation' to God. It is derived from the root letters *slm*, from which come the noun *salam* (which means 'peace') and the verb *aslama* (which means 'he submitted'). Islam emphasizes an uncompromising monotheism and a strict adherence to religious practices. Muslims believe that Islam is the religion that brings peace to mankind when man commits himself to God and submits himself to His will, and that God's will was made known through the Qur'an (Koran), the book revealed to his messenger, the Prophet Muhammad (570–632).

Muhammad was a member of the Quraysh tribe, which guarded the sacred shrine known as the Kaaba in the Arab trading city of Mecca (Makka). In 610 Muhammad received his first revelations, which commissioned him to preach against the idolatry and polytheism of the Arab tribes. In 622, he led his followers to Medina (al-Madina), where political power was added to his spiritual authority. Before Muhammad died in 632, the whole of Arabia had embraced Islam or entered into a peace treaty with the Prophet.

Muslims believe that – over a period of 20 years – Muhammad received revelations from God (Allah) via the Archangel Gabriel. These revelations form the Qur'an (literally 'The Recitation'), Islam's scripture. Muhammad also accepted the inspiration of the Jewish and Christian scriptures. The collections of Muhammad's sayings and doings – the *Hadith* – are next in importance, for the Prophet is regarded as the best model of obedience to God's will. Muslims teach that Islam was the religion of Adam and the main prophet sent by God to call man back to his path. Muslims revere Abraham, Moses and Jesus amongst other prophets, but Muhammad is the final prophet, because the Qur'an completed and superseded earlier revelations.

THE PILLARS OF FAITH

Certain essential religious duties, described as the 'Five Pillars', are intended to develop the spirit of submission to God. They are:

Profession of the faith The basic belief of Islam is expressed in the *Shahada*, the Muslim confession of faith: 'There is no God but Allah and Muhammad is his Prophet.' From this fundamental belief are derived beliefs in angels (particularly Gabriel), the revealed Books (of the Jewish and Christian faiths in addition to the Qur'an), a series of prophets, and the Last Day, the Day of Judgement.

Prayer The act of worship is performed five times a day – at dawn, midday, mid-afternoon, sunset and before bed. After washing themselves, Muslims face in the direction of Mecca and pray communally at the mosque or individually in any place that is ritually clean, often using a prayer rug. Each prayer consists of a set number of 'bowings', for example two at dawn, four at midday. The 'bowing' is composed of a prescribed succession of movements, in which the worshipper stands, bows, kneels with forehead to the ground, and sits back on the haunches. Recitations in Arabic, mostly words of praise and verses from the Qur'an, accompany each movement. Attendance at the mosque is not compulsory, but men are required to go to the special congregational prayers held every Friday at noon. (The mosque also has an educational role and teaching ranges from advanced theology to religious instruction for children.)

Alsmgiving An offering, known as *zakat*, is given by Muslims with sufficient means as an annual charitable donation.

Fasting Muslims fast from shortly before sunrise until sunset every day during the Islamic month of Ramadan, the month in which they believe the Qur'an was first revealed. The person fasting may not eat, drink or smoke. However, the sick, the elderly and children are exempt from fasting.

Pilgrimage Pilgrimage to Mecca (the *hajj*) is to be undertaken at least once in a lifetime by every Muslim who can afford it. The pilgrimage takes place during the Islamic month of Dhu'l-Hijja. See Holy Places of Islam, below.

Jihad Jihad is sometimes regarded as another pillar of the faith. It means 'striving' and is commonly used to describe the duty of waging 'holy wars' to spread Islam and to defend Islamic lands.

SECTS OF ISLAM

Sunnism and Shiism (or Shiah Islam) are the two main forms of Islam. Although the majority of Muslims are Sunnis, the Shiites are dominant in Iran, which is about 93 per cent Shiite. The main difference between Sunni and Shiah Islam lies in the latter's belief that the charisma of the Prophet was inherited by his descendants, in whom they invest supreme spiritual and political authority. The Sunnis believe that orthodoxy is determined by the consensus of the community. Sunni caliphs exercised political but not spiritual authority – the historic caliphate ceased to exist in 1924 in Turkey.

Shiism has produced a variety of sects, including the Ismailis and Zaidis, though the majority are known as 'Twelvers' (*Ithna 'Ashariyya*). They believe that the 12th Imam or successor to Muhammad in linear descent disappeared and is now the Hidden Imam, who will return as the Mahdi before the end of the world. Senior religious lawyers, known as *mujtahids*, interpret the Hidden Imam and share his infallibility. The Ayatollah (literally 'sign of God') Khomeini was regarded, in Iran, as such a mujtahid. Other Shiites revere living Imams, such as the Aga Khan Khojas, whose leader (the Aga Khan) claims to be a descendant of Muhammad through Ismail, the 7th Imam.

Islam's mystical or Sufi tradition has both Sunni and Shiite adherents. Many of its orders or circles have appointed or hereditary *pirs* (spiritual guides) and venerate their predecessors as saints. Sufi missionaries played an important role in Islam's expansion into Africa and Asia.

Though the sheer variety of races and cultures embraced by Islam has produced differences, all segments of Muslim society are bound by a common faith and a sense of belonging to a single community. With the loss of political power during the period of Western colonialism in the 19th and early 20th centuries, the concept of the Islamic community, instead of weakening, became stronger. This, in harness with the discovery of immense oil reserves, helped various Muslim peoples in their struggle to gain political freedom and sovereignty in the mid-20th century.

Islam as a total way of life is a missionary religion committed to bringing all men into the Household of Faith (*Dar-al-Islam*). However, it affords special status to followers of its sister faiths, Judaism and Christianity, which have existed as protected minority communities in many Muslim lands.

HOLY PLACES OF ISLAM

Mecca. Mecca is the most holy city of Islam and was the birthplace of the Prophet Muhammad. Every Muslim with sufficient means attempts a pilgrimage (or *hajj*) to Mecca at least once. The main goal of pilgrims is the al-Haram Mosque. In the mosque's central courtyard is the Kaaba, a cube-shaped building that is believed to have been built by Abraham at the place on earth immediately below God's house in heaven. The city is forbidden to non-Muslims.

Medina In Arabic the city's name is al-Madina or, more fully, Madinat Rasul Allah (meaning City of the Messenger of God). Medina contains many Islamic holy places, including the Prophet's Mosque (within which is the tomb of Muhammad), the Mosque of Quba (the first in Islam), and a number of sites connected with the Prophet's participation in the Battle of Uhud and the Battle of the Ditch. The city is forbidden to non-Muslims.

Jerusalem Jerusalem is the third most holy city of Islam. In the area of Solomon's Temple is the Dome of the Rock, a golden-domed mosque containing the rock on which it is believed Abraham prepared to sacrifice his son and from which the Prophet Muhammad made his ascent into heaven.

Shiite holy places While Mecca, Medina and Jerusalem are places of pilgrimage for all Muslims, Shiite Muslims have their own additional holy places. Najaf (in Iraq) contains the tomb of Ali ibn

Abi Talib, the founder of Shiah Islam and cousin and son-in-law to the Prophet Muhammad. Karbala (in Iraq) is the site of the death in battle of Ali's son Husayn. Meshhed (in Iran) is the burial place of the eighth Shiite Imam.

EURO FACTS

ISLAM IN THE EUROPEAN COMMUNITY

The followers of Islam in EC countries include:

France	2 500 000
(mainly of North African origin)	
Germany	1 800 000
(mainly Turkish)	
United Kingdom	1 000 000
(mainly of Pakistani, Bangladeshi and Indian origin)	

GLOSSARY OF ISLAMIC TERMS

Adhan	Call to prayer
Ahl al-Kitab	'The People of the Book', i.e. those who have received divine revelation, especially Jews and Christians
Ahmadis	Sect founded in 19th-century Punjab by Mirza Ghulam Ahmad
Allah	God
Aya	Sign; verse of Qur'an
Ayatollah	Senior religious scholar in Iran
Caliph	Former title of the head of the Muslims
Dajjal	Antichrist
Dar al-Harb	'House of War', territory outside Muslim control
Dar al-Islam	'House of Islam', territory under Muslim control
Dervish	Member of a Sufi brotherhood
Din	Religion
Fatiha	Opening chapter of Qur'an
Fatwa	Authoritative opinion of a jurisconsult (see Mufti, below)
Fiqh	Islamic jurisprudence
Hadith	Report of a saying or act of Muhammad or one of his Companions
Hajj	Pilgrimage to Mecca
Halal	Permitted by Islamic law
Hanafi madhhab	System of jurisprudence ascribed to Abu Hanifa (d. 767)
Hanbali madhhab	System of jurisprudence ascribed to Ahmad ibn Hanbal (d. 855)
Haram	Sacred area of Mecca, Medina, Jerusalem
Harām (haraam)	Forbidden by Islamic law
ᶜId al-Adha	'Feast of the sacrifices', celebrated on 10 Dhu'l-Hijja, one of the days of pilgrimage
ᶜId al-Fitr	'Feast of the 'fast-breaking', celebrated at the end of the Ramadan fast
Ijmaᶜ	Unanimous opinion of the religious authorities, used in formulating law
Ijtihad	Creative interpretation of the law
Imam	(1) Prayer leader
	(2) Spiritual leader of the Muslims
	(3) Head of the Shiite community
Ismailis	Shiite sect with several subdivisions
Jahiliyya	Period of religious ignorance among pre-Islamic Arabs
Jamiᶜ	Mosque
Jihad	Duty to spread the message of Islam; holy war
Kaᶜba or Kaaba	Cube-shaped building in al-Haram Mosque, Mecca
Kafir	Unbeliever
Kalam	Theology
Khutba	Sermon
Madhhab	System of jurisprudence
Madrasa	College for Islamic sciences
Mahdi	Restorer of religion and justice before the end of the world
Maliki madhhab	System of jurisprudence ascribed to Malik ibn Anas (d. 796)
Masjid	Mosque
Mihrab	Semicircular recess in mosque marking direction of Mecca
Mirza	Persian title of prince; gentleman
Muezzin	One who calls Muslims to prayer

Mufti	Religious lawyer, jurisconsult
Mujtahid	Senior religious lawyer using ijtihad (see above)
Mulla	Cleric
Murshid/pir	Sufi master
Nabi	Prophet
Qadar	Belief that events happen by God's will
Qadi	Judge
Qibla	Direction faced in prayer
Qiyas	Reasoning by analogy, used in formulating law
Qur'an	Sacred book of Islam
Ramadan	Month of fasting
Rasul Allah	God's messenger, prophet
Ridda	Apostasy
Salat	Ritual prayer
Sanusis	Mystical brotherhood founded by Muhammad al-Sanusi in 19th-century Libya
Sayyid/sharif	Descendant of Muhammad
Shafi^ci madhhab	System of jurisprudence ascribed to Muhammad al-Shafi^ci (d. 819)
Shahada	Profession of faith
Shaikh	(1) Tribal leader
	(2) Man of religion
	(3) Sufi master
Shari^ca	Islamic law
Shirk	Associating other beings with God; polytheism
Sira	Traditional biography of Muhammad
Sufism	Islamic mysticism
Sunna	Practice of Muhammad and his Companions
Sunnis	Muslim majority claiming to follow sunna
Sura	Chapter of Qur'an
Tawhid	Belief in the unity of God
^cUlama'	Religious scholars
Umma	The Islamic community
Wahhabis	Followers of 18th-century Arabian reformer, Muhammad ibn ^cAbd al-Wahhab
Wali	Saint
Wudu'	Ritual ablution
Zaidis	Shiite sect
Zakat	Alms-tax

MAJOR PROPHETS

Major Prophets in the Qur'an	*Biblical Equivalents*
Adam	Adam
Nuh	Noah
Ibrahim	Abraham
Musa	Moses
^cIsa	Jesus
Muhammad	

HINDUISM

The word Hindu was first used by Arab invaders in the 8th century AD to describe those who lived beyond the Sind or Indus Valley. The term Hinduism is now used to describe the religion and social institutions of the great majority of the people of India, though strictly speaking it is an English word. The origins of Hinduism (or *Sanatan-Dharma*, meaning 'ancient way of life') lie in the *Arya-Dharma* (Aryan way of life) of the Indo-Europeans who invaded the Indus Valley from Asia Minor and Iran c. 1500 BC. They wrote the *Vedas* (Rig-Veda, Yajur-Veda, Sama-Veda, Atharva-Veda), which are collections of prayers, hymns and formulas for worship. The Aryans worshipped nature-deities, including *Agni* (fire) and *Surya* (Sun).

The Aryans absorbed some of the traditions of the indigenous inhabitants. This process of assimilation resulted in the great epic poems composed between 200 BC and AD 200, the *Ramayana* and the *Mahabharata*, which includes the famous *Bhagavadagita*.

Three deities dominate these epics: Brahma, Vishnu and Shiva, representing creation, preservation and destruction. There are other gods and demi-gods, and also important *avatars* (incarnations), such as Krishna (a form of Vishnu; see below). Some gods (such as the goddess of smallpox) are renowned for particular activities; others are local deities operating only in a particular area.

Philosophical Hinduism developed in the 5th century BC with a core of 18 *Upanishads* (philosophical scriptures). The laws of Manu (written during the first two centuries AD) contain the concept that God created distinct orders of men; priests (*Brahmans*); soldiers and rulers (*Kshatriyas*); farmers and traders (*Vaisyas*); and artisans and labourers (*Sudras*). The so-called caste system thus developed.

Hinduism tolerates a great variety of beliefs and practices and there is absolute freedom with regard to the choice and mode of one's philosophy. The Brahmans recognize six schools as orthodox. The best known are yoga, sankhya and vedanta, of which the great philosopher Shankara (Sankara; AD 788–820) was an exponent. The Brahmans regard Buddhism and Jainism as heterodox.

The aim of most Hindus is to be reunited with the absolute and thereby to escape the wheel of existence (*Samsara*), which is determined by *Karma* (literally 'deeds' or 'actions'). *Moksa* (release) may be gained through yoga, through *Jnana* (knowledge) or through *Bhakti* (devotion to one's God).

Hinduism traditionally divides life into four ideal periods: *Brahmacharya* (celibate period), *Grihastha* (householder), *Vanaprastha* (retired stage), and *Sannyasa* (renunciation). Hinduism embraces many local as well as national traditions and has numerous pilgrim centres, temples, ashrams (religious retreats) and orders of monks. A Hindu temple (*mandir*) may be a huge, ornate building dedicated to the worship of a major deity – visited particularly during festivals and pilgrimages – or it may be a small shrine at the roadside at which offerings to a local spirit are made. The concept of the spiritual teacher, or guru, is important, and many contemporary gurus attract European as well as Indian devotees.

Several reform movements began in the 19th century, including the Ramakrishna Mission, founded by Swami Vivekananda (1862–1902), the Arya Samaj of Dayananda Saraswati (1824–83), and the Brahmo Samaj of Ram Mohan Roy (1772–1833). Gandhian '*Ahimsa*' (non-violence) was inspired by Hindu philosophy. The International Society of Krishna Consciousness founded by Swami Prabhupada (1896–1977) in 1966 has attracted Western attention (see below).

HINDU GODS AND GODDESSES

Gods of the Vedas
Indra Thunder god, god of battle.
Varuna Guardian of order; divine overseer.
Agni God of fire.
Surya God associated with the sun.

Major gods of Hinduism
Brahma The creator; linked with the goddess Saraswati.
Vishnu The preserver; with Shiva, one of Hinduism's greatest gods. Vishnu has ten incarnations or avatars, and is married to Lakshmi.
Shiva A great god, associated with destruction. In Hindu mythology, Shiva is married to Parvati and is the father of Ganesh.
Ganesh The elephant-headed god, worshipped as the remover of obstacles and god of good luck.
Hanuman The monkey warrior-god associated with the god Rana.

Vishnu's ten avatars (incarnations)
Matsya The fish.
Kurma The tortoise.
Varaha The boar.
Narasimha The man-lion.
Vamana The dwarf.
Ramachandra or *Rama* The god of the *Ramayana* epic, identified by his bow and quiver of arrows.
Parasurama Rama bearing an axe.
Krishna The important god featured in the *Bhagavadagita*. He is worshipped particularly as a baby and as a flute-playing cowherd.
The Buddha The great teacher from the 6th–5th

centuries BC and founder of Buddhism.
Kalki 'The one to come'; a future *avatar*.

Major goddessess of Hinduism
The goddesses are manifestations of the great creative spirit or *Shakti*. The most popular are:
Parvati Wife of Shiva; also known as *Uma*.
Durga All-powerful warrior goddess, also known as *Amba*, and linked with Shiva.
Kali Goddess associated with destruction.
Lakshmi Goddess of beauty, wealth and good fortune; wife of Vishnu.
Sarawati Goddess of learning, arts and music; wife of Brahma.

HARE KRISHNA
The International Society for Krishna Consciousness was started in 1966 in the USA by a *sannyasi* or monk from India, Bhaktivedanta Swami, known to his Western and Indian followers as 'Prabhupada'. It is a neo-Hindu movement based on a philosophy from northern India that focuses on love of the God *Krishna*. Service to God and humanity takes the form of temple worship, chanting and singing God's name, active missionary work through the sale of the movement's publications and distribution of food.

BUDDHISM
Buddhism is based on the teaching of Siddhartha Gautama (c. 563–483 BC) of the Gautama clan of the Sakyas in India. He was later named the Buddha, meaning 'the enlightened one'.

After an early life of pleasure, Gautama became deeply dissatisfied, and he experimented with asceticism and yoga before experiencing *bodhi* or awakening during a long period of meditation under a tree in Gaya. For the rest of his long life, Gautama taught about the impermanence and suffering of human life and the way to escape such suffering.

The Buddha is said to have taught the four noble truths. These are:
(1) All forms of existence are subject to suffering (*dukkha*);
(2) The origin of suffering is craving;
(3) The cure for suffering is the cessation of craving;
(4) There is a 'Way' to end suffering. The 'Way' differs with the type of Buddhism. Zen Buddhists rely upon meditation, while Therevada Buddhists believe that craving ceases by means of the Eightfold Path of right view, right thought, right speech, right action, right livelihood, right effort, right mindfulness and right concentration. This is represented in the Wheel of Law (*dharma chakra*), which has eight spokes for the eight steps towards enlightenment (*nirvana*).

The Buddha taught that since impermanence (*anicca*) is an unalterable fact of life, we can be truly happy only by becoming detached from the delusive notions of 'me' and 'mine'. This detachment is called the not-self (*anatta*). His teaching made no provision for God or the soul. He taught the law (*dharma*) of cause and effect, and encouraged his disciples to take refuge in the *sangha*, the monastic way of celibacy, non-violence, poverty and vegetarianism.

SCHOOLS OF BUDDHISM
Buddhism, as it developed, separated into three broad schools.

Therevada Buddhism. Therevada Buddhism ('the school of the elders') is practised in Sri Lanka, Burma (Myanmar) and Thailand. It is said to have been the original Buddhism of India. This school remains non-theistic and emphasizes the importance of the celibate life to gain *nirvana*. In 1956, Dr Bhimrao Ramji Ambedkar (1891–1956), the leader of India's untouchables, converted to Buddhism, and approximately four million of his disciples followed his example.

Mahayana Buddhism Mahayana Buddhism (which refers to itself as the 'Greater Vehicle') is practised in Vietnam, Cambodia, Laos, China and Japan. It has several sub-divisions, including Zen and Pure Land Buddhism. In Mahayana, the concept of the *Bodhisattva* (literally 'one bound for enlightenment who delays entry into nirvana in order to help others') developed to include many such heavenly beings alongside, but subordinate to, the Buddha, who was regarded as having three bodies (*kaya*), the historical body, the bliss body, and the absolute body.

Vajrayana or **Tantric Buddhism** Vajrayana (the 'Diamond Vehicle') developed in Tibet. This makes much use of *mantras* (sacred chants) and also of images, which depict the Bodhisattvas as very active in the world, opposing evil. The male quality of compassion is often united with the female quality of wisdom.

In the West, Buddhism in all forms has attracted a significant following. The Friends of the Western Buddhist Order was formed in 1969 and seeks to find forms of expression amenable to the West, which some call *Navayana* (a 'New Vehicle').

FOLLOWERS OF BUDDHISM

Over 310 000 000 people follow Buddhism, with the majority in the Mahayana ('Great Vehicle') school. Buddhism is a major religion in the following countries:

Bhutan (state religion; almost 100%)
Burma or Myanmar (85%)
Cambodia (majority)
China (c. 15%)
China – Taiwan (majority)
Japan (nearly 60%; overlaps with Shintoism)
Korea, North
Korea, South (over 35%)
Laos (over 90%)
Malaysia
Mongolia
Nepal (16%)
Singapore (majority)
Sri Lanka (70%)
Thailand (state religion; 95%)
Vietnam (majority)

CONFUCIANISM

Confucianism is an approach to life and way of thinking based on the teachings of Kongfuzi (Confucius; 551–479 BC). Kongfuzi was not the sole founder of Confucianism, but was rather a member of the founding group of *Ju* or meek ones. He was a scholar-official, a keeper of accounts from the province of Lu in China.

Kongfuzi taught that the main ethic is *jen* (benevolence), and that truth involves the knowledge of one's own faults. He believed in altruism and restraint, and insisted on filial piety. He believed that people could be led by example, and encouraged the rulers of his own time to imitate those in former periods whose leadership had brought about prosperity. Kongfuzi hoped for a true king (*wang*) who would rule by moral example rather than constraint. He stressed *li*, the rules of proper conduct in ritual, etiquette and social behaviour. Kongfuzi is considered to represent the Confucian 'Ideal Person', a model of sincerity, modesty and rightmindedness. Gradually, through diligent training and study ('self-cultivation'), he re-moulded his character to conform to the Will of Heaven.

Confucianism is better described as a philosophy or code of social behaviour than a religion in the accepted sense since it has no church or clergy and is not a formal institution. Kongfuzi's teachings were developed by Mengzi (Mencius; 372–289 BC) and became the basis of Chinese ethics and behaviour, in which there is an emphasis on the preservation of the family and the state, and the performance of proper rites for the ancestors. As its object was to emphasize the development of human nature and the person, Confucianism had a great hold over Chinese education for many years. During the early 19th century, attempts were made by its followers to promote Confucianism to a state religion and, though this failed, a good deal of Confucian teaching remained alongside other aspects of Chinese philosophy and practice despite the onslaught of Communist ideology in the traditional area of its influence. Rural people in mainland (Communist) China tend to be more religious than Chinese living in capitalist countries such as Hong Kong and Taiwan, but in China itself practising any religion has been difficult since Marxism became the official belief system in 1949. A more liberal policy towards religion emerged in the late 1970s and Confucianism is still followed in China, although estimates vary.

PRIMAL RELIGIONS

The word 'primal' is used to convey the idea that these religions came first in human history, and underlie all the major religions of the world. By studying the religious beliefs and customs of primal peoples we can learn much about the religious heritage that we share. It is wrong to think of these religions as primitive. They often contain beliefs and ideas about the world that achieve high levels of sophistication.

The primal religions that survive today are the religions of non-literate, usually tribal societies. Unlike the universal religions such as Christianity, Islam, Hinduism and Buddhism – which have a wealth of written records and scriptures – the primal religions have no written sources. This does not mean, however, that primal religions are without history or are in some way 'fossilized' remnants of a past age. Like the universal religions, they have long and complex histories.

AFRICAN TRADITIONAL RELIGIONS

Christianity and Islam are popular in Africa, but there are also many traditional religions practised there by different tribal groups, such as the Nuer, Dinka, Dogon, Yoruba, Zande and Shona. These religions developed in pre-literate communities and environments that were often independent of one another and far apart. In African traditional religions – as in most primal religions – there is a conception of a supreme being, sometimes prominent in religious life, sometimes remote and uninterested in human affairs. The Ashanti of Ghana call their god Nyame, and other West African peoples have similar names for their deity. The supreme god of the Yoruba people of Nigeria is known as Olorun, 'Owner of the Sky'. He is the creator of all things, the giver of life and breath, and the final judge of all people. In many parts of Africa the supreme being is considered so great and so remote that he is not worshipped. Divinities and ancestors, who act as intermediaries between people and the supreme god, are worshipped instead. Only in times of extreme distress is the god directly approached by the people.

Divinities are powerful named spirits, each with their own specific characteristics. Most African peoples believe in a multitude of divinities other than the supreme god. Common themes in African primal religions include divination, cults of affliction and possession, ancestor veneration, and secret societies.

OTHER MODERN PRIMAL RELIGIONS

In the Americas, Asia and Oceania, there is widespread belief in many deities. As well as powerful divinities and ancestor spirits, most primal peoples believe in numerous minor spirits, who may be good, malevolent or capricious. They may be the souls of the forgotten dead, who haunt the living, or the spirits of places such as rivers, mountains, bridges, rocks or trees. Among Arctic hunting peoples, spirits commonly take animal form.

In Oceania and in some other societies *mana* is a spiritual power or life force that is believed to permeate the universe. Originally a Melanesian word, it is now applied by anthropologists to spiritual power in other primal religions. Mana is not a spirit, and it has no will or purpose – it is impersonal and flows from one thing to another, and can be manipulated to achieve certain ends. Charms, amulets and medicines contain this power for the benefit of the wearer and user.

There is a whole range of religious specialists, including the medicine men of North America and the shamans of Siberia and the Arctic. Shamanism is generally found in hunting and gathering societies among peoples living in scattered, often migratory, groups. It is the dominant religious element among the Inuit (Eskimo) from Greenland to Alaska, and among the reindeer herders and fishers of northeastern Asia. The shaman is a religious specialist – either a man or a woman – who, in times of trouble, mediates with the spirit world on behalf of his people. The shaman's power lies in his ability to enter an ecstatic trance. During ecstasy he sends out his soul to communicate with the spirit world, to ensure a favourable result for the hunt or to diagnose or cure disease.

MODERN FORMS OF PRIMAL RELIGION

Most primal peoples today are profoundly influenced by contact with more powerful societies and their religions. This has led to the development of new movements within primal religions, and in some cases to new religions. Most of these movements have developed out of interaction with Christianity. In Latin America and the Caribbean, for example, a mixture of African religion and rites involving Latin words and the crucifix has produced new cults such as voodoo, while in Papua New Guinea and Vanuatu primal and Christian elements have combined in movements known as 'cargo cults'.

SHINTO

Shinto ('the way of the gods') is the native religion of Japan. The religion gained the name Shinto during the 6th century AD to distinguish it from Buddhism, which was then reaching Japan from the Chinese mainland. The earliest surviving Shinto texts include semi-mythological genealogies of the emperors, tracing their divine descent from Amaterasu, the sun-goddess.

Early Shinto consisted of ritual practices directed at agriculture rather than philosophical or moral beliefs. The help of the deities (*kami*) was sought for the physical and spiritual needs of the people, and there was great stress laid upon purification by

Shinto priests, and upon offerings and prayer. The more important national shrines were dedicated to well-known national figures, but other shrines were set up for the worship of deities of mountain and forest.

In the 19th century, the religion was divided into Shrine Shinto (*jinja*) and Sect Shinto (*kyoha*). A number of denominations were formed and these were dependent on private support for their teaching and organization. Different denominations had very little in common and varied widely in belief and practice. Some adhered to the traditional Shinto deities while others did not. Of the 13 denominations, *Tenrikyo* is the best known.

In 1871, Shinto became the Japanese national religion. State Shinto taught that a citizen's religious duty was obedience to the divine emperor. In 1946 Emperor Hirohito renounced all claims to divinity, and the new postwar constitution safeguards religious freedom and prohibits any association between religion and state. Estimates of the number of practising adherents of Shinto range between 3 400 000 and 35 000 000. Over 90 000 000 Japanese are said to belong to the Shinto 'community' but have no active allegiance to the religion. However, interest in Shinto is increasing and in 1990 Emperor Akihito was enthroned according to Shinto rites.

DAOISM (TAOISM)

Daoism, the Chinese teachings of the Way or Dao, is grounded in the works of Lao Tzu (6th–5th century BC) and Chuang-Tzu (4th century BC). It teaches that the Dao is the source of all things. The Dao works within the world, bringing about harmonious development. It acts as a model for rulers and leaders who allow their people to live spontaneously according to their own conditions and needs. The Dao is symbolized by water and by female rather than male imagery. The goal of the Way is immortality, which can only be achieved by the return to a properly balanced body composed of *yin* (the quiescent, feminine side) and *yang* (the active, male side).

Unlike Confucianism, Daoism advocates spontaneity and naturalness, abandoning oneself to the current of the Dao. Everything, good or bad, is the sublime operation of the Dao and should not be interfered with. Daoists naturally tend to solitude, meditation and simple living. Their techniques of quiet contemplation are similar to Buddhist meditation.

In China, Daoism, like Buddhism, periodically received imperial support. It developed many schools and texts until the 16th century, and continued to have some impact on popular religion after that time in synthesis with other philosophical ideas and religious practices.

The aspects of Daoism most well known in the West are yin and yang (in macrobiotic cooking, for example), the book of divination – the *I Ching* – and a meditative form of exercise, *T'ai Chi*.

JUDAISM

The biblical account of the origin of the Jewish religion traces its history back to Abraham's revolt against the idol-worship of his native Mesopotamia (now Iraq), when he smashed his father's idols and fled to Canaan (present-day Israel). Judaism is the oldest of the monotheistic religions. The word Jew is derived from the Latin *Judaeus*, that in turn is derived from the Hebrew *Yehudhi*, signifying a descendant of Jacob, Abraham's grandson.

The Exodus of the Jews from Egypt is believed to have occurred c. 1290 BC and was the decisive event or watershed in Israel's history. The Exodus resulted in the emergence of Israel as a distinct nation. The observance of the Passover (*Pesach*) makes every believing Jew a participant in the event that delivered their ancestors from bondage and established a special relationship between themselves and the One True God (the God of Abraham, Isaac and Jacob). The special relationship with the One God consists of an undertaking by the Jewish people to keep God's laws faithfully. Although Judaism expects non-Jews to observe certain basic ethical laws, it does not regard Jewish ritual as obligatory and does not seek converts. In fact, God promises the righteous of all people a place in the world to come, and the eventual re-establishment of the royal house of David; the *Messiah* (meaning the 'anointed') will inaugurate an age of universal peace and security.

Jewish scripture comprises the same books as the Christian Old Testament (see above). The *Torah* is the Hebrew name for the Law of Moses (the Pentateuch) which was divinely revealed to Moses on Mount Sinai, soon after the Exodus. The Hebrew scriptures also contain the books of the prophets, the wisdom literature (e.g. Solomon) and the historical writings (e.g. Kings). The *Talmud* contains civic and religious laws and is a collection of originally oral traditions. The two main versions were completed in Jerusalem in the 5th century BC and in Babylon at the end of the 6th century. The *Mishnah* is the oral law dating from between the 1st century BC to the 3rd century AD.

At the beginning of the Christian era, Judaism was divided into several sects, including the Pharisees, the Sadducees and the Essenes. The fall of Jerusalem (AD 70) resulted in the diaspora, which led to Jews settling throughout Europe, Africa and Asia Minor, often under severe discrimination and disabilities. During this period, the Yiddish language evolved in Central Europe from German and Hebrew elements. Jewish philosophy also developed, as did *Cabala* (mysticism), especially in Spain, where under the tolerant Muslim Moors there was much interaction between Jewish, Muslim and Christian scholars.

Jewish emancipation began with the enfranchisement of Jews in France in September 1791. The new climate stimulated the growth of the Reform movement, founded by David Friedlander (1756–1834), which accepted for Judaism the status of a religious sect within the European nations, loyal to their countries of adoption. Orthodox Judaism regards all religious authority as deriving from the Torah, and the beliefs of Orthodox Judaism were codified as the Thirteen Principles of Faith by the Spanish court physician and philosopher Rabbi Moses Maimonides (1135–1204). Conservative Judaism – which is strongest in the USA – stands midway between Orthodoxy and Reformed Judaism. Associated with the name of Solomon Schechter (1830–1915), it teaches that the faith must find its place in the contemporary world. There are also Liberal and Progressive Jews who reject the divinity of the Torah and rabbinic authority, and believe, to varying degrees, that Jewish practice must adapt to changing circumstances. They have introduced changes such as holding services partly in the vernacular (rather than Hebrew).

RITUAL AND WORSHIP

Jewish law lays down a complex set of laws of *kashrut*, which distinguishes permitted (*kosher* or *kasher*) from prohibited (*treifa*) foods. Only mammals that have both cloven hoofs and chew the cud, such as cows and sheep, are permitted as food, and they must be killed by a skilled *shochet* in a way that minimizes pain to the animal and drains as much blood as possible. Fish must have scales and fins (so that eels and sturgeon are forbidden), and shellfish and birds of prey are prohibited. In addition, milk and meat and their derivatives must be strictly separated and must not be cooked or prepared together, nor eaten at the same meal.

The Jewish day starts at sunset, and the week on Sunday, so that the *Shabbat*, the day of rest ordained by the Torah, is observed from dusk on Friday to nightfall on Saturday. This day of rest derives from the account of the creation in the Bible, where God rested on the seventh day. During Shabbat – the Sabbath – productive work and kindling fire are prohibited; other prohibitions include carrying, writing, cooking and travelling (except short distances by foot).

Synagogues were first built to serve as temporary places of worship after the destruction of the Temple in Jerusalem by the Babylonians in 586 BC, but although the Jews did rebuild the Temple, the practice of local houses of prayer continued. However, the second Temple was also destroyed and never rebuilt, and to this day the synagogue service is modelled upon, and refers to, the Temple service. The central role of the synagogue in Jewish religion is attested by its Hebrew name, which translates as 'house of meeting' and 'house of study', as well as 'house of prayer'.

Although there are no requirements for a specially constructed building, many synagogues incorporate such ancient Jewish symbols as the Star of David, the *Menorah* (the seven-branched Temple candlestick), and the two tablets containing the Ten Commandments in their decoration. The congregation usually faces the Ark, a cupboard containing the Torah scrolls, which are handwritten on parchment by a specially trained scribe. Above the Ark, which is usually in the wall facing Jerusalem, a light is kept burning as a sign of God's eternal presence.

Services are held in the evening, morning and afternoon. Each service has as its centre a period of silent prayer. For a formal service to take place, a quorum of ten men – a *minyan* – must be present, otherwise the Torah cannot be read. Any of the minyan can read the Torah or lead prayers. The function of the rabbi is as a teacher and interpreter of the Law.

Judaism as a total way of life revolves around the family as its main institution. Jews cannot surrender their religion. You are a Jew if your mother was Jewish. A boy becomes a man for religious purposes at his bar mitzvah at the age of 13, but is circumcised eight days after birth. Festivals include the Passover, Shavuot (Pentecost), Rosh Hashanah (New Year) and Yom Kippur (Day of Atonement).

The majority of Jews still live in the diaspora, but the state of Israel (although officially secular) is important to most Jews as a symbol of the hope and pride that sustained their faith during centuries of persecution. Israeli Judaism is very cosmopolitan. Different groups from the diaspora preserve their distinctive traditions – including the Sephardim (from Portuguese, Spanish and North African communities), the Ashkenazim (from Central Europe), and most recently the Falasha (from Ethiopia).

SIKHISM

Sikhism originated in the Punjab (India), where it is still the majority religion. It was founded by Guru Nanak (1479–1539), who taught how to lead a good life and seek final union with God. Sikhism is based on the concept of the guru: that God is the true Guru; the Sikh spiritual teachers were called gurus; and the scriptures, the *Granth* are said to be the guru. Sikhs believe in the existence of only one true God and that through worship and meditation the most devoted Sikhs can experience and know him. They believe that each person is trapped in his own failings and weaknesses and the only hope is found in the mercy of the true Guru.

THE TEN GURUS

Sikhism was developed under Nanak and the nine successive Sikh orthodox gurus, each chosen by his predecessor on the basis of his spiritual enlightenment. The succession of gurus is as follows:

Nanak	1469–1539
Angad	1504–52
Amar Das	1479–1534
Ram Das	1534–81
Arjan	1563–1606
Har Govind	1595–1644
Har Rai	1630–61
Har Krishan	1656–64
Tegh Bahadur	1621–75
Gobind Singh	1666–1708

THE FIVE Ks

The first five gurus developed the majority of the Sikh doctrines. The final guru, Gobind Singh, established the Sikh community with its shared symbols and the names 'Singh' and 'Kaur' for men and women respectively. The shared symbols are the so-called *five Ks*:

Kesh uncut hair worn in a turban and uncut beard.

Kangha a comb, to keep the hair clean.

Kara a metal bracelet.

Kaccha knee-length undershorts.

Kirpan a dagger.

WORSHIP AND SOCIETY

The holy scripture, the *Guru Granth*, is the central document for all Sikh rituals and ceremonies. It contains the teachings of the first five gurus. The Sikhs worship in temples known as *gurdwara* (the guru's door). The most important temple is the Golden Temple at Amritsar, built in the 16th century. There are no priests to conduct the services – anyone can lead the worship, although some are specially trained to read the *Granth*.

The Sikh community in the Punjab has called for the establishment of a separate Sikh homeland, *Khalistan*, and in the 1980s, a minority of extremist Sikhs began a campaign of terrorism to achieve this aim. Sikhism has spread outside the Punjab during the 20th century to Britain, the USA, Canada and parts of Southern and East Africa. It is an ethnic religion in that it attempts to keep the community intact and does not aim to convert members from outside. It does not deny the existence of other faiths but strives for its members to be devoted to God.

BAHA'ISM

Baha'ism evolved from the teachings of two 19th-century Persian visionaries – Mirza Ali Muhammad (1820–50), who called himself the Bab ('gateway'); and Mirza Husain Ali (1817–92), who called himself Baha'ullah ('Glory of God'). In 1863 Baha'ullah announced that he was the manifestation of God sent to redeem the world, as earlier prophesied by the Bab. He was imprisoned and exiled many times. He developed his teachings into a religion based on a new scripture, the *Kitab Akdas*.

After his death the followers of this faith grew in number until, today, it is present in over 70 countries in various parts of the world, predominantly in south-west Asia. About two-thirds of its followers are converts from Islam or their descendants. The remainder are mostly west Europeans and Americans.

Baha'ullah's followers see him as a divine healer, relieving human suffering and uniting mankind. The Baha'i faith does not predict an end to this world, or any intervention by God, but declares that there will be a change within humanity and society by which the world will return to peace and recover from the deterioration of moral values.

Baha'ism is not a minor sect but a universal religion that emphasizes the value of all religion and the spiritual unity of all humanity. The Baha'i faith has been persecuted in Iran since 1979 and all Baha'i institutions were banned in that country in 1983.

JAINISM

Jainism (from Hindi *jaina*, meaning 'saint') is an ancient religion that probably evolved during the first millennium BC. It spread from east to west across India, but with the rise of Hinduism declined and became restricted to two different regions, where it still exists today – Gujarat and Rajasthan in western India, and the Deccan in southern India.

Jainism has its own scriptures passed down orally from Mahavira (born c. 540 BC), one of the religion's great teachers. Jainism holds that the material world is eternal, moving on in a never-ending series of vast cycles. Like all Indian religions, it upholds the universal law of *karma*, which states that all actions, thoughts and words produce results that affect future deeds, forming a chain of cause and effect.

Jains do not believe in God – or gods – but in the perfectibility of the individual soul. In practice, the faith of Jainism seems very pessimistic as it sees the world as full of misery. However, prayer and worship can lead to liberation and salvation (*moksha*), when the individual soul is freed from matter and the suffering it brings. Jains practise non-violence (*ahimsa*), respect for all creatures, and vegetarianism.

ZOROASTRIANISM AND PARSIISM

The origins of Zoroastrianism are attributed to the Persian (Iranian) prophet Zoroaster or Zarathustra (c. 1200 BC). It was the Persian state religion from the 6th century BC to the 6th century AD. Following the expansion of Islam in Iran, the Zoroastrians were persecuted and retreated to the cities of Yazd and Kerman. In the 10th century AD, some fled to India. Bombay has become the centre for these Zoroastrians, known as Parsis.

Zoroastrianism acknowledges the existence of a good god, *Ahura Mazda*, and an evil spirit, *Angra Mainyu*. Ahura Mazda is assisted by angelic beings and it is believed that through their efforts good will finally triumph. The main scripture is the *Avesta*, which stresses the importance of worship based on fire. Zoroastrians are also known for the towers of silence (*daxma*) they use for the disposal of the dead.

Zoroastrianism is a small religion, but its followers are spread throughout the world. Intermarriage and conversion are not encouraged.

ANCIENT RELIGIONS

ANCIENT GREEK AND ROMAN RELIGION

Written evidence about religion in Europe begins with the Linear B texts of the Mycenaean civilization in Greece (c. 1450 BC). These show the importance of Poseidon the sea god and of 'the Lady' of various locations (presumably a mother goddess). Some other divine names occur, including Zeus and Hera, which later appear in the epic poetry of Homer. Homer's gods lived ageless and immortal on Mount Olympus, but acted like humans – and not the best-behaved humans. They could change shape, intervene in human life, and might respond to gifts and prayers to change human destiny, but they did not change human nature. By the 6th century BC the Olympian gods were part of the official worship of the Greek city-states. But ancient Greek religion had little to do with morality, and the moral, metaphysical and scientific concerns of the Athenian philosophers of the 5th and 4th centuries led to very different ideas of God. These ideas challenged popular religion, and in 399 BC the philosopher Socrates was condemned for atheism and corrupting youth by undermining the gods of the state.

Early Roman religion was probably shaped by the Bronze Age culture of the Etruscans and was concerned with the agricultural cycle. Two forms of religious expression developed. Domestic piety recognized household gods (*lares* and *penates*), while the state cult ensured corporate well-being. As Rome encountered Greek culture, the state deities were identified with Olympian equivalents. As the Roman Empire expanded, its armies brought back foreign cults and religious ideas. The most important of these cults – until Christianity became the state religion in the 4th century AD – was Mithraism, a male-only mystery cult based on the worship of Mithras, the Persian god of light, truth and justice. Generally speaking, however, Roman official religion resisted innovations, or admitted them only when of proven worth. Divine honours were accorded to Julius Caesar after his assassination, and to Augustus, most of his successors, and various members of the imperial family at death. In the Eastern provinces of the Roman Empire living emperors were saluted as divine.

The twelve Olympian gods

Zeus	The overlord of the Olympian gods and goddesses; God of the sky and all its properties (Roman: Jupiter)
Hera	Protector of women and marriage, and goddess of the sky; wife of Zeus (Roman: Juno)
Poseidon	God of the sea and earthquakes (Roman: Neptune)
Demeter	Goddess of the harvest (Roman: Ceres)
Apollo	God of prophecy, music and medicine (No direct Roman equivalent)
Artemis	Goddess of chastity, childbirth and the young (Roman: Diana)
Ares	God of war (Roman: Mars)
Aphrodite	Goddess of love and beauty (Roman: Venus)
Hermes	God of trade and travellers (Roman: Mercury)
Athene (or Athena)	Goddess of prudence and wise council; the protectress of Athens (Roman: Minerva)
Hephaestus (or Hephaestos)	God of fire and metalcraft (Roman: Vulcan)
Hestia	Goddess of fire (Roman: Vesta)

Other important gods and goddesses:

Adonis	God of vegetation and rebirth
Aeolus	God of the winds
Alphito	Barley goddess of Argos
Arethusa	Goddess of springs and fountains
Asclepius	God of healing
Atlas	A Titan who carries the earth
Attis	God of vegetation
Boreas	God of the northern wind
Cronus	Father of the god Zeus
Cybele	Goddess of the earth
Dionysus	God of wine and the 'good life' (Roman: Bacchus)
Eos	Goddess of the dawn (Roman: Aurora)
Erebus	God of darkness
Eros	God of love (Roman: Cupid)
Gaia (Gaea)	Goddess of the earth
Ganymede	Beautiful youth who became cupbearer to Zeus
Hades	(see Pluto)

Hebe	Goddess of youth
Hecate	Goddess of witchcraft, magic and the moon
Helios	God of the sun (Roman: Sol)
Hygiea	Goddess of health (Roman: Salus)
Hypnos	God of sleep (Roman: Somnus)
Irene	Goddess of peace (Roman: Pax)
Iris	Goddess of the rainbow
Morpheus	God of sleep and dreams
Nemesis	God of retribution
Nereus	God of the sea
Nike	Goddess of victory (Roman: Victoria)
Oceanus	Titan with divinity of the rivers and seas
Pan	God of flocks and herds (and associated with fertility) (Roman: Sylvanus)
Persephone	Goddess of the underworld and of corn (Roman: Proserpina)
Pluto (or Hades)	God of the underworld
Prometheus	Titan; god of fire and the creation of man
Rhea	Titaness; mother of many gods, wife of Cronus
Selene	Goddess of the moon (Roman: Luna)
Thanatos	Goddess of night and death (Roman: Mors)
Triton	A merman sea god
Uranus	Sky god responsible for the sun and rain

ANCIENT EGYPTIAN RELIGION

The pharaohs of ancient Egypt were regarded as divine, and were called 'Horus' or 'Son of Re'. The autocratic rule of the pharaohs was legitimized by the mythology of Re as the Sun god and ruler of the gods; as 'Son of Re' the pharaoh embodied the life-giving power of the sun. Horus was the son of Isis, the Divine Mother, and of Osiris, the god of inundation, vegetation and the dead. As Horus, the pharaoh embodied the periodic renewal of life and fertility borne on the annual flooding of the land by the River Nile. Local deities were often linked with national ones. The most significant was Amun, the god of invisibility, one of the characteristic elements of chaos out of which the Earth emerged. From c. 2000 BC he was combined with Amun to become Amun-Re, whose temple at Thebes was to become the most powerful and wealthiest in Egypt.

Principal gods and goddesses of Ancient Egypt

Amun	God of Thebes; often represented as a man, sometimes with an erect penis
Anubis	The jackal-headed god of the necropolis; patron of the embalmers
Aten	Creator god manifest in the sun disc
Atum	The original sun god of Heliopolis
Bastet	Cat goddess
Bes	Domestic god, usually depicted as a dwarf
Edjo	Cobra goddess who appears as the pharaoh's protector on the royal diadem
Geb	God of the Earth; the physical support of the world
Hathor	Often represented as a cow, a cow-headed woman, or a woman with a cow's headdress. Recognized as the suckler of the pharaoh
Horus	Falcon god, identified with the pharaoh during his reign. The son of Osiris and Isis, Horus grew up to avenge his father's murder by Seth
Imhotep	Architect of the Step Pyramid, chief minister of Djoser (c. 2700 BC) Later venerated as the god of learning and medicine
Isis	Wife of Osiris and mother of Horus
Khepri	The scarab-beetle god, identified with the sun god Re as creator god
Maat	Goddess of truth, justice and order; depicted as a woman with an ostrich feather on her head
Min	God of fertility and harvest; protector of desert travellers and god of the road
Mut	Vulture goddess of Thebes; a mighty divine mother
Nekhbet	Vulture goddess, who sometimes appears beside Edjo on the royal diadem
Nephthys	Sister of Isis
Nut	Goddess of the sky
Osiris	God of the dead. Identified with the dead king and depicted as a mummified king. Also god of the inundation of the Nile and of vegetation
Ptah	Creator god of Memphis and patron of craftsmen. Represented as a mummified man
Ptah-Soker-Osiris	God combining the principal gods of creation, death and the afterlife Represented as a mummified king
Re or Ra	The sun god of Heliopolis and the supreme judge. Other gods aspiring to universal recognition would often link their name to his, e.g. Amun-Re
Re-Harakhti	Falcon god, incorporating the characteristics of Re and Horus
Sebek	A protector of reptiles and patron of kings
Sekhmet	Lion-headed goddess, wife of Ptah, venerated in the area of Memphis. Regarded as the bringer of sickness and destruction to the enemies of Re

Seth	God of violence and storms. Brother and murderer of Osiris, represented as an animal of unidentified type
Shu	God of light and air
Sobek	Crocodile god
Thoueris	Hippopotamus goddess, the patron of women in childbirth
Thoth	The ibis-headed god of Hermopolis; scribe to the gods and inventor of writing

GERMANIC (NORSE) RELIGION

The religions of the Germanic peoples survived into the Middle Ages: Denmark, Norway and Iceland did not become Christian until the 10th and 11th centuries, and Sweden not until the 12th century. Germanic religion had many deities. In early times, three in particular were worshipped: Wotan or Woden (Norse: Odin), father of the gods and the slain; Tiw or Tiwaz (Norse: Tyr), the giver of law; and Thor, the thunder deity. In Norse literature, Tyr plays little part. Odin and Thor belong to the Aesir, the gods of Asgard, who defeated the Vanir, another race of gods. Aesir and Vanir became reconciled, and the Vanir Frey and his female counterpart Freya, closely associated with fertility, are major figures. There was no supreme deity, only a chaos of divine energy. The worshipper chose the divinity thought most likely to serve him.

People and places in Germanic (Norse) religion

Aesir	The race of gods including Odin and Thor; defeated the Vanir
Asgard	Home of the Gods
Balder	'The Beautiful', son of Odin, tragically slain by Loki
Fenrir	'Great Wolf', son of Loki; bound by Tyr, but will break free at Ragnarok
Frey	Fertility god, one of the Vanir
Freya	Frey's sister, consort of Odin
Frigg	Odin's wife. Her name is preserved in 'Friday'
Hel	Kingdom of the dead; also personified as Loki's daughter
Loki	The trickster god of Asgard. Imprisoned in a cave for the murder of Balder, he will break loose at Ragnarok
Midgard	The world of men. It is held by a coiled serpent, who will show himself at Ragnarok
Njord	Father of Frey and Freya, associated with ships and sailing
Norns	Three maidens who rule the fates of men and daily water the world tree Yggdrasil
Odin (Old Germanic: Wotan, Anglo-Saxon: Woden)	Chief of the Aesir; god of battle, poetry and death
Ragnarok (German: Götterdämmerung)	'The twilight of the gods', the coming day of destruction for Asgard and Midgard and their inhabitants in a battle with the forces of evil
Thor	God of Thunder
Tyr (Old Germanic: Tiwaz)	A war god who has bound Fenrir
Valhalla	Odin's great hall for warriors
Valkyries	Spirit maidens who guide in battle and conduct the chosen slain to Valhalla
Vanir	The race of gods associated with fertility; defeated by the Aesir
Yggdrasil	The self-renewing world tree, which forms the centre of the worlds of gods, giants and men

CELTIC RELIGION

Little is known about the Celtic deities owing to a lack of written material. Celtic religious beliefs were centred on the relationship between the divine spirit world with the land and the waters. Hills, rocks, springs, rivers and many other features were thought to be the homes of guardian spirits. Trees were also inhabited by spirits and certain species – such as the oak and the yew – had a ritualistic role. The druids – the priest-poets of the Celts – took their name from an ancient Indo-European word meaning 'knowing the oak'.

Celtic gods and festivals

Belenus	The god of war
Beltane	The festival of Bel's fire (May 1); marks the beginning of hunting and wooing
The Brigits	Three Irish mother-goddesses; presided over poetry, metalwork and healing
Cernunnos	The stag-horned Lord of the Animals; appears on many surviving artifacts
Imbolc	The festival of springtime (February 1)
Lug	The sun god, Lug was also the patron of music
Lugnasag	The festival of harvest and the marriage of Lug
Macha	Known in Britain as Rhiannon, Macha was the mare goddess
Manannan	The god of the oceans
Morrígan	The powerful crow goddess associated with death and battle
Samain	The festival of the dead (November 1) and the end of summer

LANGUAGE AND LITERATURE
LANGUAGE

LANGUAGES OF THE WORLD

No one is certain how many living languages there are in the world, but it is likely that the number exceeds 5000. Each language is unique in that it has its own system of sounds, words and structures, and yet almost all are related either closely or distantly to other languages found in the same part of the world.

LANGUAGE FAMILIES

Languages are classed in families containing related tongues. The languages of the largest family — Indo-European – are spoken by about half the world's population. Based in South Asia and Europe, these languages have been taken to many parts of the world by European colonists. The group includes all the languages of Europe (except Finnish, Estonian, Lappish, Magyar and Basque) as well as the Iranian group of languages and the Indic languages, including Gujarati, Marathi, Hindi, Urdu, Bengali, Sindhi, Sinhalese, Rajasthani and Punjabi.

WORLD'S PRINCIPAL LANGUAGES

1. Guoyo (Chinese) Guoyo is standardized Northern Chinese and is also known as Mandarin. Alphabetized into Zhuyin fuhao (37 letters) in 1918, it was converted to the Pinyin system of phonetic pronunciation in 1958. Spoken in China and by Chinese communities throughout Southeast Asia, including those in Singapore and Malaysia. Language family: Indo-Chinese. 845 000 000 speakers.

2. English English evolved from Anglo-Saxon, and shows strong Norman-French and Latin influences. It is spoken as the first language in Australia, Canada, Caribbean Commonwealth countries, Ireland, New Zealand, UK and the USA. English is widely understood or has an official status in Commonwealth and former Commonwealth nations, including Nigeria, India, South Africa, Kenya, Tanzania, Malaysia, Ghana and Zimbabwe. Language family: Indo-European. 435 000 000 speakers.

3. Hindustani (Hindi) Hindi is the foremost of the 845 languages of India. Language family: Indo-European. 338 000 000 speakers.

4. Spanish (Castilian) Castilian evolved as a separate Romance language in the 10th century and has been the most widely used literary language of Spain since the 13th century. It is spoken as the first language in Spain (except the Basque Country, Catalonia and Galicia) and in the Latin American countries except Brazil. Language family: Indo-European. 331 000 000 speakers.

5. Great Russian Great Russian is the foremost of the official languages of the Soviet Union and is spoken as a first language by over one half of the population of the USSR. Language family: Indo-European. 291 000 000 speakers.

6. Arabic Arabic dates from the 6th century, when it originated in the Arabian peninsula. It is spoken throughout North Africa and southwest Asia. Language family: Semitic-Hamitic. 192 000 000 speakers.

7. Bengali Bengali is the official language of Bangladesh and of the Indian state of West Bengal. Language family: Indo-European. 181 000 000 speakers.

8. Portuguese Portuguese became a language distinct from Spanish in the 14th century. It is spoken in Portugal, Brazil and in former Portuguese territories in Africa, including Angola and Mozambique. Language family: Indo-European. 171 000 000 speakers.

9. Malay-Indonesian Malay-Indonesian originated in northern Sumatra, although the dialect of the southern part of the Malay peninsula is recognized as the standard form of the language. It is spoken in Malaysia, Indonesia (where it is called Bahasa) and southernmost Thailand. Language family: Malayo-Polynesian. 138 000 000 speakers.

10. Japanese The earliest inscription of Japanese (in Chinese characters) dates from the 5th century. It is spoken in Japan with minorities in former Japanese territories. Language family: Japanese is unrelated to any other language. 124 000 000 speakers.

11. German German has been known in a written form since the 8th century. It is spoken in Germany, Switzerland and Austria, and by minorities throughout central and southeast Europe. There are considerable variations between spoken dialects. Language family: Indo-European. 118 000 000 speakers.

12. French French developed in the 9th century from a mixture of Frankish and Gaulish. It is spoken in France, Belgium, Québec (Canada), Switzerland, Luxembourg, Haiti, French possessions (including Polynesia, Martinique and Guadeloupe) and former French and Belgian territories in western and central Africa. Language family: Indo-European. 117 000 000 speakers.

13. Urdu Urdu, which is related closely to Hindustani, is written in Arabic script. It is the official language of Pakistan and one of the 15 official languages of India. Language family: Indo-European. 90 000 000 speakers.

14. Punjabi Punjabi is considered by some linguists to be a variety of Hindustani. One of the 15 official languages of India, Punjabi is spoken in the Indian Punjab and in adjoining parts of Pakistan. Language family: Indo-European. 81 000 000 speakers.

15. Korean Korean has been a written language since the 5th century, initially using Chinese characters and since the 15th century using its own alphabet. It is spoken in North and South Korea. Language family: Korean is not known to be related to any other tongue. 70 000 000 speakers.

16. Telugu Telugu has been known in a written form since the 11th century. It is spoken in the state of Andhra Pradesh in southern India. Language family: Dravidian. 66 000 000 speakers.

17. Tamil Tamil, which is the second oldest written Indian language, has its own distinctive script. It is spoken in the state of Tamil Nadu in southern India, in northern Sri Lanka and in parts of Malaysia. Language family: Dravidian. 64 000 000.

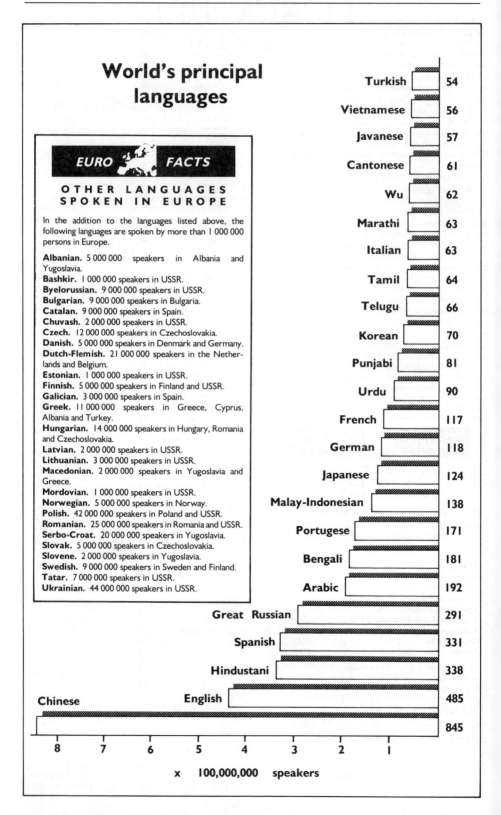

World's principal languages

EURO FACTS

OTHER LANGUAGES SPOKEN IN EUROPE

In the addition to the languages listed above, the following languages are spoken by more than 1 000 000 persons in Europe.

Albanian. 5 000 000 speakers in Albania and Yugoslavia.
Bashkir. 1 000 000 speakers in USSR.
Byelorussian. 9 000 000 speakers in USSR.
Bulgarian. 9 000 000 speakers in Bulgaria.
Catalan. 9 000 000 speakers in Spain.
Chuvash. 2 000 000 speakers in USSR.
Czech. 12 000 000 speakers in Czechoslovakia.
Danish. 5 000 000 speakers in Denmark and Germany.
Dutch-Flemish. 21 000 000 speakers in the Netherlands and Belgium.
Estonian. 1 000 000 speakers in USSR.
Finnish. 5 000 000 speakers in Finland and USSR.
Galician. 3 000 000 speakers in Spain.
Greek. 11 000 000 speakers in Greece, Cyprus, Albania and Turkey.
Hungarian. 14 000 000 speakers in Hungary, Romania and Czechoslovakia.
Latvian. 2 000 000 speakers in USSR.
Lithuanian. 3 000 000 speakers in USSR.
Macedonian. 2 000 000 speakers in Yugoslavia and Greece.
Mordovian. 1 000 000 speakers in USSR.
Norwegian. 5 000 000 speakers in Norway.
Polish. 42 000 000 speakers in Poland and USSR.
Romanian. 25 000 000 speakers in Romania and USSR.
Serbo-Croat. 20 000 000 speakers in Yugoslavia.
Slovak. 5 000 000 speakers in Czechoslovakia.
Slovene. 2 000 000 speakers in Yugoslavia.
Swedish. 9 000 000 speakers in Sweden and Finland.
Tatar. 7 000 000 speakers in USSR.
Ukrainian. 44 000 000 speakers in USSR.

Language	Speakers
Turkish	54
Vietnamese	56
Javanese	57
Cantonese	61
Wu	62
Marathi	63
Italian	63
Tamil	64
Telugu	66
Korean	70
Punjabi	81
Urdu	90
French	117
German	118
Japanese	124
Malay-Indonesian	138
Portugese	171
Bengali	181
Arabic	192
Great Russian	291
Spanish	331
Hindustani	338
English	485
Chinese	845

8   7   6   5   4   3   2   1

x   100,000,000   speakers

=18. Italian Italian had developed as a distinct language from Latin by the 10th century. It is spoken in Italy, Ticino (southern Switzerland) and in Italian communities abroad in e.g. USA. Language family: Indo-European. 63 000 000 speakers.

=18. Marathi. Marathi has been known as a written language since the 6th century. It is spoken in Maharashtra state in western central India. Language family: Indo-European. 63 000 000 speakers.

20. Wu Wu is a dialect spoken, but not officially encouraged, in the Chiang Jiang delta region of China. Language family: Indo-Chinese. 62 000 000 speakers.

21. Cantonese Cantonese is a distinctive dialect of Chinese spoken in Guangdong province in southern China. Language family: Indo-Chinese. 61 000 000 speakers.

22. Javanese Javanese, which is closely related to Malay, is spoken by about one half of the population of Indonesia. Language family: Malayo-Polynesian. 57 000 000 speakers.

23. Vietnamese Vietnamese is of uncertain origin but has certain tonal similarities to Chinese and Thai. It is spoken in Vietnam and adjoining parts of Indo-China. Language family: Vietnamese is probably a Mon-Khmer language, although it is sometimes classed as a Thai language. 56 000 000 speakers.

24. Turkish Turkish is closely related to a variety of Altaic languages spoken in central Asia, including Turkmen and Jagatai Turkish (Uzbek). Turkish – the national language of Turkey – has been written in a Latin script rather than the Arab script since 1928. Language family: Altaic. 54 000 000 speakers.

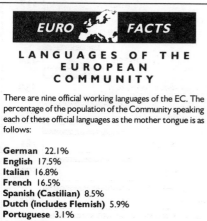

THE ORIGINS OF ENGLISH

The West Germanic group of Indo-European languages includes English, Dutch, Frisian, Afrikaans and German. English also includes a very large proportion of Romance words that are derived from Latin and related to modern languages such as French and Italian.

OLD ENGLISH

Various Celtic languages were spoken in England before the 5th century when invaders speaking West Germanic languages (Frisian, Saxon and Jutish) arrived from across the North Sea. It is from these languages that Old English (the language of the Anglo-Saxons) developed. Although Old English is as different from Modern English as a foreign language, it provided the basis of modern English both in the way sentences are formed and in most of the short, non-abstract words that are used in ordinary vocabulary.

The 7th-century Christian missions to Britain brought learning and literacy. At first this was entirely Latin, but an Old English written language did emerge, initially in the northeast and later, and most notably, in the West Saxon kingdom of Alfred the Great in the second half of the 9th century. From the late 8th century to the 10th century, the vocabulary was added to by the Norse language of further invaders from Scandinavia (the Vikings).

MIDDLE ENGLISH

The Norman Conquest of 1066 not only changed the government of England, it also changed the way in which the English language developed. English now became the language of a conquered people and ceased to be the 'national language'. A Romance language, Norman French, was the language of the court, and a Normanized Latin the language of government, learning and the Church. Nevertheless, literature was still written in English, with dialect forms in different parts of the country. For 300 years after the Conquest, English and French slowly merged. By the end of the 14th century, English was being used for official purposes. By 1400 a language had developed that, despite its many dialect variations, was recognizably the beginnings of the English we know today.

Middle English was different in two ways from Old English. Its vocabulary no longer came from a single source but showed an inextricable mixture of Germanic and Romance words. Often the more basic word today is Germanic and the derived word Romance; for example, things connected with *moon* (Germanic) are *lunar* (Romance). The other important difference relates to the simplification of grammar; for example, grammatical gender was lost and so adjectives ceased to 'agree'.

RENAISSANCE ENGLISH

By 1500 English was not very far removed from the language we use today. The establishment of a strong central government confirmed the acceptance of English as the national language for all public purposes, despite the revival of classical languages during the Renaissance when it was a common view that Latin was the only suitable language for serious writing. The introduction of printing into England by William Caxton in the 15th century brought more books into English and printers began to regularize spelling and punctuation. Although regional dialects continued to be spoken, the idea of a standard form of written English was now accepted.

MODERN ENGLISH

From the late 17th century, English usage became more regular and consistent. Standards of spelling and meaning were supported by dictionaries, the most famous being that of Samuel Johnson in 1755. Grammarians made recommendations for correct English usage based on Latin and regarded as a prescriptive set of rules for all to follow. The grammar of English did not greatly change after the middle of the 17th century.

The main recent development has been the growth of vocabulary. In the late 19th century new discoveries, inventions and ideas brought further expansion of the vocabulary. Colonialism also added words to English from the languages of India, Africa, the Far East and the Middle East. The 20th century has witnessed continuing growth. Technical advances have brought still more new words such as the large vocabulary of computing. Some words have become obsolete or changed their meanings (for example *quick* formerly meant *alive*). There have been few changes in grammar, although there has been a tendency to drop some forms now regarded as old-fashioned.

ARTIFICIAL LANGUAGES

Over 500 artificial languages have been devised, the majority since the middle of the 19th century. The following are among the best known:

Esperanto Esperanto was devised by Luwik Lejzer Zamenhof, a Polish oculist, in 1887. It is a phonetic language using 28 letters, each letter representing a single sound. The language is written as it sounds and sounds as it is written. There are 16 simple rules of grammar to which there are no exceptions. A vocabulary of over 12 000 words is constructed from 2629 'roots', the majority of which are Romance. Esperanto is spoken by several million people and taught at over 150 universities and other institutes of higher education. Over 160 Esperanto dictionaries and nearly 135 000 books in the language have been published. A world Esperanto congress has been held in most years since 1905 – the most recent conference attracted delegates from over 70 countries.

Ido Ido was devised by the French linguists Louis Couturat and Louis de Beaufront in 1908. It is a simplified version of Esperanto, but is not nearly so widely used or studied as its 'parent' language.

Novial Novial is a simplification of Ido. Devised by the Danish linguist Otto Jespersen in 1924, Novial attempts to balance ease of speech with regularity of grammar.

Volapük Volapük was devised by Johann Martin Schleyer, a German priest, in 1879. It is based on a simplified Germanic vocabulary and has a regular grammar. The language is now almost extinct, but it enjoyed considerable popularity in academic German circles in the 1880s, when up to half a million people were reported to be learning it.

Interlingua Interlingua was devised by Giuseppe Peano, an Italian mathematician, in 1908. Originally known as Latino sine flexione, it is based on a synthesis of Latin, English, French and German vocabulary with a simplified regular grammar derived from Latin. Interlingua enjoyed a brief vogue and there is still an Academia pro Interlingua.

Other artificial languages Other artificial languages that have enjoyed a brief period of popularity included *Sol-Ré-Sol* (patronized by Napoleon III and Victor Hugo), *Anglo-latin* (a 19th-century cross between English and Latin vocabulary and grammar) and *Timiero* (a 'numerical' language).

LITERATURE

LITERARY FORMS AND TERMS

acrostic a number of lines of writing, eg a poem, in which certain letters, especially the first letters of each line, make a word or words.

act a major division of a dramatic work.

alexandrine a line of verse with six iambic feet.

allegory a poem, novel, drama, etc., in which the events and characters symbolize a deeper meaning beyond their apparent literal meaning.

alliteration a figure of speech in which the same consonant or vowel is repeated at the beginning of each or some of the words or stressed syllables in a line of poetry (eg the stuttering rifle's rapid rattle).

anagram a word made from another word by changing the order of the letters (eg god – dog).

anecdote a short amusing story about a person or event.

antonym a word that means the opposite of another word.

aphorism a short statement expressing a general truth in witty fashion (eg necessity is the mother of invention).

assonance the repetition of the same vowel sound in a line of verse.

autobiography an account of a person's life written by himself or herself.

ballad a song or poem that tells a story.

ballade a verse form consisting of three stanzas and an envoi, each ending with the same line.

biography an account of a person's life written by someone else.

blank verse unrhymed verse, often in iambic pentameters.

canto a division of a long poem.

clerihew a comic poem consisting of two couplets each with an irregular meter.

cliché an expression that has lost its force by being used too much (eg time flies).

colloquialism a word or phrase used in everyday informal speech rather than in a formal or literary context.

couplet two successive lines of poetry, usually rhyming and having the same meter.

dialogue speech of the characters in a novel or play.

doggerel comic verse of poor quality, usually with an irregular meter.

drama a work to be performed on stage, radio or television by actors.

dramatis personae (a list of) all the characters in a play or story.

eclogue a short pastoral poem in the form of a conversation or soliloquy.

elegy a serious meditative poem, esp. a lament for the dead.

envoi a brief dedicatory stanza at the end of certain forms of poetry, esp. ballads.

epic a long narrative poem recounting in an elevated style the deeds of a legendary hero.

epigram a short witty statement in verse or prose.

epithet a descriptive word or phrase added to or substituted for a person's name (eg Charles the Bold).

euphemism an inoffensive word or phrase substituted for an unpleasant or hurtful one.

fable a short tale in prose or verse that points a moral.

farce a humorous play characterized by absurd or improbable situations.

fiction literary works invented by the imagination, such as novels and short stories.

foot a metrical division or unit of verse, consisting of two or more syllables, one of which has a strong stress, the other or others a weak stress (eg for mén/may cóme/ and mén/ may gó).

free verse unrhymed verse without a regular rhythm.

heroic couplet two lines of rhyming verse in iambic pentameters.

hyperbole deliberate use of exaggeration for emphasis.

iambic pentameter a line of verse consisting of five feet, each of which consists of a short syllable followed by a long one.

idiom an expression or group of words whose meaning cannot be worked out from the literal meaning of its constituent words.

idyll a work in verse or prose describing an idealized country life.

legend a popular story passed down from earlier times, the truth of which has not been established.

limerick a short humorous poem five lines in length.

litotes ironic understatement, especially the use of a negative to express the contrary (eg *I won't be sorry when it's over* = *I will be extremely glad when it's over*).

lyric poetry verse expressing the personal thoughts and feelings of the writer.

maxim a short phrase or statement expressing a general truth or principle or rule of conduct.

melodrama a dramatic work characterized by exciting and sensational events and usually having a happy ending.

metaphor a figure of speech in which one person or thing is described in terms of another (eg he is a cunning fox).

metonym a word used in metonymy (eg *the bottle* used to stand for alcoholic drink).

metonymy a figure of speech in which the name of an attribute or adjunct is substituted for that of the thing that is being referred to (eg *crown* used to refer to a monarch).

meter the rhythmic arrangement of syllables in poetry, according to the number and type of feet in a line.

monologue a long speech for a single performer in a drama.

myth a story about superhuman beings, regarded by ancient societies as being a true explanation of certain natural phenomena, how the world came into existence, etc.

novel an extended prose narrative recounting the story of fictional characters within a recognizable social context.

novella a short novel.

octave group of eight lines of verse.

ode a lyric poem in which the poet directly addresses the subject, with lines of differing lengths and a complex rhythm.

onomatopoeia formation of words whose sound imitates the sound of the noise or action described (eg *bang, buzz, hiss*).

oxymoron a figure of speech in which apparently contradictory terms are used together to achieve an epigrammatic effect (eg *precious bane*).

paradox a statement that appears to be self-contradictory, but on closer examination can be seen to contain a truth.

parody a literary work which imitates the style of a particular writer in a humorous or satirical way.

plot the story line of a novel or play.

poem a literary work in verse, characterized by concentrated or striking language used for its suggestive power as well as its literal meaning and often making use of rhyme, meter, alliteration, etc.

prose written language as in ordinary usage, as distinct from poetry.

pun the humorous use of a word to suggest different meanings, or of words of the same sound with different meanings; a play on words.

quatrain group of four lines of verse, often with alternate rhymes.

rhyme identity or similarity of sound between the endings of words or lines of verse.

rhyme royal verse form consisting of stanzas of seven lines of iambic pentameters with a complex rhyme scheme.

rondeau verse form consisting of ten or thirteen lines using only two rhymes throughout and repeating the opening words twice as a refrain.

saga a long story recounting heroic deeds, especially a medieval tale of Scandinavian heroes; series of connected books about several generations of a family or other social group.

satire a literary work using ridicule, irony or sarcasm to expose folly or vice.

scene a subdivision of a play, smaller than an act, in which the action is continuous.

sestet a group of six lines of verse.

short story a prose narrative of shorter length than a novel.

soliloquy a speech in a drama in which a character expresses his or her thoughts aloud without addressing a particular person.

sonnet a poem consisting of 14 lines of iambic pentameters with rhymes arranged according to a fixed scheme, and divided into an octave and a sestet (Petrarchan sonnet), or three quatrains and a couplet (Elizabethan sonnet).

stanza a group of lines in a poem, arranged in a particular metrical pattern.

synecdoche figure of speech in which a part is used to indicate a whole, or a whole used to indicate a part.

synonym a word identical or similar in meaning to another one.

tautology the use of words that repeat a meaning that has already been conveyed.

tercet group of three lines of verse.

tragedy a drama in which the protagonist, usually a man of outstanding personal qualities, falls from grace through a combination of personal failing and circumstances that he cannot control; any dramatic or literary work dealing with sad or serious events and ending in disaster.

verse written language with a metrical structure; poetry.

villanelle a verse form usually consisting of five stanzas of three lines (tercets) and one stanza of four lines (quatrain), using only two rhymes throughout according to a fixed scheme.

CLASSICAL LITERATURE

Western literature began with the literature of Greece and Rome, and the literatures of Europe have constantly imitated, adapted, reacted against and returned to this inescapable Classical inheritance. The 1500 years from Homer to the early Middle Ages saw the birth of almost all the major forms of prose and poetry, and the very concept of literature itself as a separate activity first made its appearance. The term 'Classical literature' may give the impression of order and a uniformity of style, but on closer inspection the literatures of Greece and Rome present a more varied scene.

Early Greek literature began with the epics of Homer. The first personal poetry appeared in the middle of the 7th century BC, while philosophical and historical writing in the 6th century BC marked the beginning of Greek literary prose. Tragedy – which is thought to have its roots in primitive rituals – began with the plays of Aeschylus, while comedy first appeared about the same time in the works of Aristophanes. The 4th century BC was an age of prose, but the chief writers of this Hellenistic age – Plato and Aristotle – worked in a genre (philosophy) sometimes now excluded from the category of literature.

From its beginning early Roman literature was heavily influenced by Greek, and it was not until the middle years of the 1st century BC that Latin really began to rival Greek for literary creativity. The greatest period of Roman literature was under the emperor Augustus, when Virgil and Horace flourished. Later genres range from imperial histories and elegant love poems to satire and low comedy.

MAJOR GREEK WRITERS

Homer (?8th century BC), epic poet: *Iliad, Odyssey* (These may not in fact be the work of the same man.)

Hesiod (?8th–7th centuries BC), epic poet: *Theogony*.

Archilochus (mid-7th century BC), soldier-poet.

Alcaeus (7th–6th centuries BC), lyric poet.

Sappho (b. mid-7th century BC), lyric poetess, the pioneer of the brief subjective love poem.

Pindar (c. 520–445 BC), lyric poet: *Epinician Odes.*

Bacchylides (6th–5th centuries BC), lyric poet of choral songs for victorious athletes.

Aeschylus (c. 525–456 BC), tragic poet and dramatist: *Oresteia*, a trilogy of plays.

Sophocles (c. 497–405 BC), dramatist and tragic poet: *Oedipus Rex* (c. 430 BC), *Antigone* (441 BC).

Herodotus (c. 490–c. 425 BC), historian and prose writer, known as the 'father of history'.

Euripides (c. 485–406 BC), tragic dramatist: *Medea* (431).

Thucydides (c. 455–399 BC), Athenian historian.

Aristophanes (c. 445–385 BC), comic dramatist: *Peace* (421 BC) and *Lysistrata* (411 BC).

Isocrates (436–338 BC), orator and speechwriter.

Plato (c. 428–347 BC), philosopher: *The Republic* and *The Laws.*

Aristotle (384–322 BC), philosopher: treatises on logic, metaphysics, politics, biology, etc.

Demosthenes (384–322 BC), orator and statesman.

Menander (342–292 BC), comic dramatist.

Callimachus (c. 310–240 BC), poet and epigrammatist.

Theocritus (c. 3rd century BC), pastoral poet: *Idylls.*

Plutarch (c. AD 46–120), biographer: *Parallel Lives*, a biography of 50 lives of famous Greeks and Romans.

MAJOR ROMAN WRITERS

Plautus (c. 250–184 BC), comic dramatist and writer.

Ennius (239–169 BC), poet: the *Annals*, an historical epic.

Cicero (106–43 BC), orator, statesman and writer.

Lucretius (c. 98–c. 55 BC), poet and philosopher.

Sallust (86–35 BC), historian.

Catullus (c. 84–c. 55 BC), love poet.

Virgil (70–19 BC), poet: *Eclogues, Georgics* and the *Aeneid* (a national epic).

Horace (65–8 BC), poet: *Odes, Satires* and *Epistles.*

Livy (59 BC–AD 17), historian: *History of Rome.*

Propertius (c. 50–after 16 BC), elegiac poet.

Ovid (43 BC–AD 17), poet: *Art of Love.*

Seneca (AD 4–65), philosopher-playwright and essayist.

Petronius (d. AD 65), satirical writer: *Satyricon*, comic novel.

Lucan (AD 39–65), epic poet: *Pharsalia.*

Martial (c. AD 40–104), epigrammatist.

Tacitus (c. AD 56–117), historian.

Juvenal (?AD 60–?140), satirical poet.

Pliny the Younger (AD ?62–c.113), orator and statesman, remembered for his letters.

Apuleius (active AD 155), philosopher and author: *The Golden Ass*, a romance.

ASIAN LITERATURE

The diverse cultures of the Middle East, India, China, and Japan produced bodies of writing which, while relatively unknown in the wider world, nonetheless offer a richness and scope equal to any other.

Literature written in Arabic owes much of its inspiration to the emergence of Islam. Persia possessed a literature more varied in its forms and content than that written in classical Arabic, and was to enrich the Arabic literary tradition with new genres such as the epic poem. Indian literature appeared extensively only in the 16th century when classical Sanskrit literature (c. 200 BC–AD c. 1100) became popular. Key Sanskrit texts include the epic poems *Ramayana* and *Mahabharata* (from the 3rd century BC). Popular prose in all Indian languages appeared in the 19th century and there is now a large literature in English.

China's literary heritage is particularly distinguished by its poetry, which was generally sung to musical accompaniment. The earliest and most famous work to survive is the *Shi jing* (Book of Songs), which includes love songs, folk songs, ritual hymns, and political songs. Chinese literature exerted a major influence on that of Japan, which, despite its briefer history, boasts high achievement in poetry, drama (particularly the *No* plays) and the novel. The *haiku* – a 17-syllable verse usually in lines of seven, five and seven syllables – is the best known of the characteristic forms of Japanese poem.

MAJOR ARABIC WRITERS

Abu Nuwas (c. AD 762–c. 813), major court poet.

Mutanabbi (915–965), a leading classical poet.

Abu Muhammad al-Kasim al-Hariri (1054–1122), writer of tales: *The Assemblies of al-Hariri.*

Masudi (d. 956), historian, geographer and philosopher.

Ghazali (1058–1111), theologian and Islamic philosopher: *Restoration of the Sciences of Religion.*

Ahmad Shawqi (1868–1932), neoclassical poet.

Hafiz Ibrahim (1870–1932), neoclassical poet.

Tawfiq al-Hakim (1898?–1987), novelist and playwright: *The Return of the Spirit* (1933), *People of the Cave* (1933), and *Sheherazade* (1934).

Naguib Mahfouz (1911–), Egyptian novelist and short-story writer: *Midaq Alley* and *Miramar.*

Badr Shakir al-Sayyab (1929–64), free verse poet.

MAJOR PERSIAN WRITERS

Rudaki (d. 940–41), poet.

Firdausi (933–1031), epic poet: *Book of Kings.*

Omar Khayyám (?1048–?1122), poet: *Rubáiyát,* well known in the West through its translation by Edward Fitzgerald.

Nizami (1140–1202), epic poet: *Five Treasures.*

Farid ad-Din Attar (d. c. 1229), mystic poet: *Conference of the Birds.*

Jalal ed-Din Rumi (d. 1273), classical poet.

Sa'di (c. 1213–1291), classical poet: *Gulistan* and *Bustan.*

Hafiz (1325–89), classical poet: *Diwan.*

MAJOR CHINESE WRITERS

Qu Yuan (4th–3rd century BC), allegorical poet.

Du Fu (Tu Fu; 712–770), poet whose works commented on social conditions: *The Army Carts.*

Li Bo (Li Po; 701–762), widely regarded as the greatest Chinese poet.

Wang Shifu (c. 1250–?1337), dramatist: *Romance of the Western Chamber.*

Luo Guan-zhong (active 14th century), novelist: *The Water Margin.*

Cao Zhan (1715–63), novelist: *The Dream of the Red Chamber.*

Lu Xun (1881–1936), essayist and short-story writer.

Mao Dun (1896–1985), short-story writer and novelist: *Zi ye* (*Midnight*, 1933).

Lao She (1899–1966), novelist and playwright.

Ding Ling (1904–86), novelist and short-story writer.

Ba Jin (1904–), novelist, essayist and short-story writer: *Jia* (*Family*, 1931).

MAJOR INDIAN WRITERS

Kālidsa (?c. 4–5th centuries), Sanskrit poet and dramatist: *Meghadūla* and *Sakuntalā and the token of recognition.*

Jayadeva (12th century), poet: *Gitagovinda.*

Bankim Chandra Chatterjee (1838–94), nationalist writer: *Anandamath* (1882).

Rabindranath Tagore (1861–1941), poet, novelist, playwright and essayist: *Gitanjali* (1912).

R.K. Narayan (1906–), novelist writing in English: *The Financial Expert* (1952), *The Vendor of Sweets* (1967), and *Malgudi Days* (1982).

Raja Rao (1909–), novelist writing in English: *Kanthapura* and *The Serpent and the Rope.*

Bhabhani Bhattacharya (1906–), writer of social novels in English.

MAJOR JAPANESE WRITERS

Murasaki Shikibu (973–1014), novelist: *The Tale of Genji.*

Sei Shonagon (966/7–1013), prose writer: *The Pillow Book.*

Matsuo Basho (1644–94), haiku poet: *The Narrow Road to the Deep North* (1694).

Ihara Saikaku (1642–93), novelist: *The Life of an Amorous Man* (1682).

Ueda Akinari (1734–1809), novelist: *Tales of Rain and Moon* (1776).

Kawabata Yasunari (1899–1972), novelist.

Mishima Yukio (1925–70), novelist: *The Temple of the Golden Pavilion* (1956) and *The Sea of Fertility* (1965–70).

MEDIEVAL LITERATURE

Epic and *Romance* are loose terms used to describe the narrative literature of medieval Western Europe, most of which was in the form of long poems about mythical heroes. In epic and romance, national languages replaced the old universal literary language, Latin. This literature retains its vividness and immediacy and continues to spawn new creations in all the arts.

Perhaps the chief glory of medieval European literature lies in its stories, which were composed in poetry or prose for reciting, or in the form of plays for acting. They covered the known world, both its past and its present. Stories were the main source of popular and aristocratic entertainment and education. Since few people outside the Church and the nobility could read and write, the stories that have survived were written down and preserved within religious or noble communities. The most famous European collections of stories are Boccaccio's *Decameron* and Chaucer's *Canterbury Tales.* However, the chief subject of medieval literature was religion, alliterative religious poetry and mystery plays (based on the Christian story from the Creation to the Last Judgement) being among the most prominent genres. In the 15th century dramatized sermons called *moralities* first appeared, and throughout the medieval period *fables* (short tales or poems with a moral) were popular.

CANTERBURY TALES

The English poet Geoffrey Chaucer (?1343–1400) was one of the most outstanding contributors to Medieval literature. His *Canterbury Tales* – which drew on the *Decameron* – was an unfinished collection of 24 stories extending to 17 000 lines of verse and prose. In the *Canterbury Tales*, 30 pilgrims – representing the most diverse trades and social classes – gather at an inn in Southwark and agree to engage in a storytelling contest as they ride to the shrine of St Thomas Beckett in Canterbury. The tales they tell are preceded by a prologue presenting vivid and humorous character sketches of the pilgrims, and are linked together by vigorous exchanges between them.

The *Canterbury Tales* presents a highly varied collection of different types of story: courtly romance (in the classical *Knight's Tale*, a shortened version of Boccaccio's epic, the *Teseida*), allegorical tale, the devotional tale, beast tale and racy fabliau – a short verse tale usually in couplets with lines of eight syllables. Prologue, tales and 'links' combine to present a unified whole – a profound and satisfying portrayal of medieval England – from which Chaucer's genius for characterization and understanding of social relationships shines forth.

MEDIEVAL WRITERS

Geoffrey of Monmouth (d. 1155), Welsh chronicler: *History of the Kings of Britain* and *Vita Merlini.*

Wace (b. c. 1100), Anglo-Norman poet: *Roman de Brut* and *Roman de Rou.*

Chrétien de Troyes (active 1170–90), French poet: *Érec et Énide, Cligès* and *Perceval.*

Gottfried von Strassburg (active 1210), German poet: *Tristan and Isolde.*

Wolfram von Eschenbach (?1170–1220), German poet: *Parzival.*

Guillaume de Lorris (d. 1237), French poet: *Roman de la Rose* (the first 4058 lines of the poem).

Jean de Meun (?1250–?1305), French poet: *Roman de la Rose* (the last 17 722 lines; see Guillaume de Lorris).

Dante Alighieri (1265–1321), Italian poet: *Divine Comedy.*

Francesco Petrarch (1304–74), Italian sonnet writer.

Giovanni Boccaccio (1313–75), Italian poet and storyteller: *Decameron*, a collection of a hundred often earthy tales.

John Gower (?1330–1408), English poet: *Confessio Amantis* ('The Lover's Confession').

William Langland (c. 1330–c. 1386), English alliterative poet: *Piers Plowman.*

François Villon (b. 1431), French poet: *Le Lais* and *Le Testament.*

Geoffrey Chaucer (?1343–1400), English poet: *Canterbury Tales* (see box), and *Troilus and Criseyde.*

John Skelton (c. 1460–1529): English colloquial poet.

Sir Thomas Malory (d. 1471), English writer of Arthurian romance in prose: *Morte D'Arthur.*

RENAISSANCE LITERATURE

The Renaissance drama of the 16th century is a secular theatre of human activity rather than the religious drama of the Middle Ages. The stage no longer represents Heaven and Hell, but the world of history and the material present. In the 16th century a flowering of the professional theatre in England produced the plays of Marlowe, Kyd and Shakespeare. Their plays are largely dramatic reworkings of traditional stories. Ben Jonson, however, dealt with bourgeois characters in a contemporary English setting. The late 16th and early 17th centuries were also a 'golden age' for Spanish drama. Lope de Vega and Calderon achieved popularity through their prolific output of dramas. The English Jacobean theatre was dominated by revenge tragedies and court entertainments comprising expensive and elaborate masques.

Renaissance poetry, while less often celebrated than Renaissance painting, sculpture, architecture, or drama, flourished from the late 15th to the mid-17th century throughout Western Europe. The period saw a reawakening of interest in Classical learning that is reflected in the work of poets who showed a deep and imaginative interest in antiquity, its civilizations and especially its literature. Renaissance poetry is richly diverse in form and style and includes romantic epic, narrative verse and varieties of lyric (of which the most celebrated form was the sonnet).

MAJOR RENAISSANCE WRITERS

Lodovico Ariosto (1474–1533), Italian epic poet: *Orlando Furioso.*

Sir David Lindsay (c. 1486–1555), Scottish poet: *Ane Pleasant Satyre of the Thrie Estaitis.*

François Rabelais (c. 1494–c. 1553), French humanist and physician: *Gargantua and Pantagruel,* a comic prose satire.

Hans Sachs (1494–1576), German comic poet and dramatist.

Joachim Du Bellay (?1522–1560), French poet.

Pierre de Ronsard (?1524–1585), French poet: *Sonnets pour Hélène.*

Luis de Camoëns (1524–80), Portuguese poet: *The Lusiads* (1572), an epic of Portuguese exploration.

Guillaume du Bartas (1544–1590), French religious poet: *La Semaine.*

Torquato Tasso (1544–95), major Italian epic poet: *Aminta* (1573) and *Jerusalem Delivered* (1575).

Edmund Spenser (1552–99), English poet: *The Fairie Queene* (1590 and 1596), a moral allegory.

Sir Philip Sidney (1554–86), English pastoral poet: *Arcadia* (1590).

Thomas Kyd (1558–94), English dramatist: *The Spanish Tragedy* (1592), a revenge tragedy.

Felix Lope de Vega (1562–1635), prolific Spanish playwright and poet, who claimed to have written 1500 plays, of which only 500 survive.

William Shakespeare (see box).

Christopher Marlowe (1564–93), English dramatist and poet: *Tamburlaine the Great* (c. 1587), *Dr Faustus* (c. 1588), *The Jew of Malta* (1589), and *Edward II* (c. 1592).

John Donne (1572–1631), English metaphysical poet: *Divine Sonnets.*

Ben Jonson (1572–1637), English dramatist and poet: *Volpone* (1606), *The Alchemist* (1610) and *Bartholomew Fair* (1614).

John Webster (c. 1578–c. 1632), English tragic dramatist: *The White Devil* (1612) and *The Duchess of Malfi* (1613–14).

John Fletcher (1579–1625), English dramatist who wrote romantic tragi-comedies, in collaboration with Beaumont (see below).

Thomas Middleton (1580–1627), English tragic dramatist: *Women Beware Women* (1621) and *The Changeling* (1622; with William Rowley).

Francis Beaumont (1584–1616), English dramatist who wrote romantic tragi-comedies in collabor-ation with Fletcher (see above).

John Ford (1586–?1639), English dramatist: *'Tis Pity She's a Whore*.

George Herbert (1593–1633), English meta-physical poet: *The Temple*.

John Davies (1596–1626), English poet: *Orchestra* (1596).

Pedro Calderon de la Barca (1600–81), Spanish dramatist: *El Alcalde de Zalamea*.

John Milton (1608–74), English poet: the Christian epics *Paradise Lost* (1667) and *Paradise Regained* (1677).

WILLIAM SHAKESPEARE

The dramatic achievement of William Shake-speare (1564–1616), the elder surviving child of a Stratford-upon-Avon alderman and trader, is without parallel in English literature. No other dramatist has had such success in so many different genres. His 37 plays – written between 1594 and 1611 – include comedies, history plays, tragedies and tragi-comedies.

In comedies such as *Twelfth Night* and *As You Like It*, Shakespeare excelled in a particular type of romantic festive drama depicting the maturing of a romantic hero with the help of an assertive and powerful woman. In his huge cycle of history plays, Shakespeare covers the period of English history from 1399 to 1485. In tragedy, Shakespeare began with melodrama but went on to produce such mature masterpieces as *Hamlet, King Lear* and *Macbeth*. Later in his career, as popular fashion veered towards romantic tragi-comedy, Shakespeare wrote some extraordinary and complex plays, notably *The Tempest* and *The Winter's Tale*, which re-examine, within a framework of romance, the conventions of comedy, history and tragedy.

Although some works were published indi-vidually, Shakespeare's plays were not collected together for publication during his lifetime. Thanks to the efforts of Shakespeare's fellow-actors John Heminges and Henry Condell, the majority of the plays appeared in collected form in the First Folio in 1623.

As well as being considered the greatest English dramatist, Shakespeare was also a notable poet – the *Sonnets* (1609), variously addressed to a fair young man and a dark lady, deal with the themes of time, death, love and art.

SHAKESPEARE'S PLAYS	Publication date
Titus Andronicus (early tragedy)	1594
*Henry VI Part 2** (early history)	1594
The Taming of the Shrew (see also 1623, First Folio; early comedy)	1594
*Henry VI Part 3** (early history)	1595
Romeo and Juliet (early tragedy)	1597
Richard II (history)	1597
Richard III (history)	1597
Henry VI Part I (early history)	1598
Love's Labour's Lost (early comedy; revised version; original (?1596) probably lost)	1598
Henry IV Part 2 (history)	1600
A Midsummer Night's Dream (comedy)	1600
The Merchant of Venice (comedy)	1600
Much Ado About Nothing (comedy)	1600
Henry V (history; first 'true' text published 1623 in First Folio) (history; first performed 1599)	1600
*Sir John Falstaff and the Merry Wives of Windsor** (comedy; first 'true' text published in 1623 in First Folio)	1602
(*Hamlet**	1603)
Hamlet (tragedy; 'according to the true and perfect copy')	1604
King Lear (tragedy)	1608
Pericles, Prince of Tyre (late tragi-comedy or 'romance')	1609
Troilus and Cressida (tragi-comedy)	1609

Posthumously Published

Othello (tragedy)	1622
First Folio – 36 plays in all, including the first publication of *The Taming of the Shrew* (Shakespeare's revised version of the 1594 version)	1623

Henry IV Part I (history)
The Two Gentlemen of Verona (early romantic comedy)
The Comedy of Errors (comedy)
King John (history)
As You Like It (comedy)
Julius Caesar (Roman play)
Twelfth Night (comedy)
Measure for Measure (tragi-comedy)
All's Well That Ends Well (tragi-comedy)
Macbeth (tragedy)
Timon of Athens (tragedy)
Antony and Cleopatra (Roman play)
Coriolanus (Roman play)
Cymbeline (late tragi-comedy or 'romance')
The Winter's Tale (late tragi-comedy or 'romance')
The Tempest (late tragi-comedy or 'romance')
Henry VIII (late tragi-comedy or 'romance')

*Bad quartos or unauthorized editions.

SHAKESPEARIAN ROLES

Hamlet is widely considered to be the greatest role in English drama. It is also the longest in the Shakespearian canon. In Shakespeare's plays the following characters present the greatest challenge to actors in terms of the number of lines to learn.

Hamlet (Hamlet)	1569
Richard III (Richard III)	1161
Iago (Othello)	1117
Othello (Othello)	888
Coriolanus (Coriolanus)	886
Timon (Timon of Athens)	863
Antony (Antony and Cleopatra)	820
Lear (King Lear)	770
Richard II (Richard II)	755
Brutus (Julius Caesar)	727
Macbeth (Macbeth)	705
Cleopatra (Antony and Cleopatra)	670
Prospero (The Tempest)	665
Romeo (Romeo and Juliet)	618
Petruchio (Taming of the Shrew)	585
Imogen (Cymbeline)	541

CLASSICISM IN LITERATURE

Knowledge of and interest in the works of ancient Greek and Roman authors was a key aspect of the Renaissance. After that explosive fusion of old and new ideas came a period when *Neoclassical* writers tried to imitate in modern languages what they thought was the spirit and style of the classics. *Neoclassicism* was especially strong in the French theatre during the 17th century and in England from the Restoration of 1660 to the end of the 18th century. In poetry, a taste for natural description and meditation became popular in the 18th century. Pastoral verse began with Pope and achieved perfection with Gray.

MAJOR NEOCLASSICAL WRITERS

Pierre Corneille (1606–84), French classical tragic dramatist: *Le Cid* (1637), *Horace* (1640), *Cinna* (1640), *Polyeucte* (1643) and *Le Menteur* (1643).

Molière (Jean-Baptiste Poquelin; 1622–73), French actor and classical comic dramatist of comedy: *Tartuffe* (1664), *Le Misanthrope* (1666), and *L'Avare* (1668; 'The Miser').

John Dryden (1631–1700), English satirical poet and tragic dramatist: *All for Love* (1677; a reworking of Shakespeare's *Antony and Cleopatra*) and *Absalom and Achitophel*, an allegorical poem.

Nicolas Boileau (1636–1711), French poet and critic: *L'Art Poétique*, a statement of classical aesthetics.

Jean Racine (1639–99), French classical tragic dramatist: *Andromaque* (1667), *Britannicus* (1669), *Bérénice* (1670), *Bajazet* (1672), *Mithridate* (1673) and *Phèdre* (1677).

William Wycherley (1641–1715), English comic dramatist: *The Country Wife* (1675), a Restoration comedy.

Sir John Vanbrugh (1664–1726), English comic dramatist: *The Relapse* (1696) and *The Provoked Wife* (1697), Restoration comedies.

William Congreve (1670–1729), English comic dramatist: *The Way of the World* (1700) and *Love for Love* (1695), Restoration comedies.

George Farquhar (1678–1707), English comic dramatist: *The Beaux' Stratagem* (1707).

Pierre Marivaux (1688–1763), French comic dramatist and novelist: *The Game of Love and Chance* (1730) and *The False Confidences* (1737).

Gotthold Ephraim Lessing (1728–81), German dramatist and critic: *Miss Sara Sampson* (1755), *Minna von Barnhelm* (1767) and *Nathan the Wise* (1779).

Alexander Pope (1688–1744), English satirical poet: *The Rape of the Lock* (1714), *The Dunciad* (1728–43), *Epistle to Arbuthnot* (1735) and *An Essay on Man* (1733–34).

Thomas Gray (1716–71), English poet: *Ode on a Distant Prospect of Eton College* and *Elegy Written in a Country Churchyard* (1751).

Oliver Goldsmith (?1730–74), Irish poet, dramatist and novelist: *The Deserted Village* (1771), a poem, *The Vicar of Wakefield* (1766), a novel, and *She Stoops to Conquer* (1773), a comedy.

Pierre-Augustin Caron de Beaumarchais (1732–99), French comic dramatist: *Le Barbier de Seville* (1775) and *The Marriage of Figaro* (1784).

Richard Sheridan (1751–1816), English dramatist; *The Rivals* (1775) and *School for Scandal* (1777).

THE BEGINNINGS OF THE NOVEL

One of the most dramatic shifts in literary fashion occurred in the early 18th century, when a relatively new form, the *novel* – an extended prose narrative treating in a realistic manner the story of fictional individuals within a recognizable social context – achieved popularity with a wide audience. The novel soon came to be seen as a vehicle for serious literary expression.

Up to the 16th century the dominant literary form had been verse. There had been earlier examples of prose fiction, notably the *Satyricon* of Petronius, and *The Golden Ass* of Apuleius. The Italian *novella* – a type of short story of a humorous nature (found in Boccaccio's *Decameron* – lent its name to the extended prose fictions of Defoe, Richardson and others. A number of important strands can be seen in the early novel. Some novels had a strong emphasis on *realism* – the representation of life as it is. The use of the *first person narrative* was often used to increase the realism. The *epistolary novel* written in the form of letters was also common. The *picaresque novel* – from the Spanish word *picaro*, meaning a wily rogue – enjoyed a vogue in the 17th century and is probably best represented by *Don Quixote*.

MAJOR EARLY NOVELISTS

Miguel de Cervantes (1547–1616), Spanish poet and prose writer: *Don Quixote* (1615), a parody of chivalric literature – regarded by many as the first true novel.

J.J.C. von Grimmelshausen (c. 1621–76), German novelist: *Simplicissimus* (1669), a picaresque novel set during the Thirty Years War.

Madame de la Fayette (Marie-Madeleine, Countess de la Fayette; 1634–93), French novelist: *The Princess of Cleves* (1678).

Daniel Defoe (1660–1731), English novelist: *Robinson Crusoe* (1719) and *Moll Flanders* (1722).

Jonathan Swift (1667–1745), Anglo-Irish satirist: *Gulliver's Travels* (1726), a satirical fantasy.

Pierre Marivaux (1688–1763), French dramatist and novelist (see also Neoclassical writers): *The Life of Marianne* (1731–41) and *The Fortunate Peasant* (1735).

Samuel Richardson (1689–1761), English novelist: *Pamela* (1740–41) and *Clarissa* (1747–48), epistolary novels.

Voltaire (François-Marie Arouet; 1694–1778), French philosopher, dramatist and prose-writer: *Candide* (1759), a philosophical tale.

Antoine-François Prévost (L'Abbé Prévost; 1697–1763), French novelist: *Manon Lescaut* (1731).

Henry Fielding (1707–54), English novelist and dramatist: *Joseph Andrews* (1742), *Shamela* (1741; a parody of Richardson's *Pamela*), *Jonathan Wild* and *Tom Jones* (1749).

Laurence Sterne (1713–68), Irish-born English novelist: *The Life and Opinions of Tristam Shandy* (1759–68).

Tobias Smollett (1721–71), Scottish novelist: *The Expedition of Humphry Clinker* (1741).

Bernardin de Saint Pierre (1737–1814), French novelist: *Paul and Virginie* (1787).

Choderlos de Laclos (1741–1803), French novelist: *Dangerous Liaisons* (1782).

ROMANTICISM

The word 'Romantic' was first used to describe a genre of literature around 1800 by the brothers Schlegel, August Wilhelm (1767–1845) and Friedrich (1772–1829). These German intellectuals idealized the era of classical antiquity, especially the culture of ancient Greece, and then contrasted it with the literature of the Christian era from the Middle Ages up to their own time. This second era they called modern – as distinct from ancient – and defined as Romantic.

Romanticism in British literature emerged, in the 1780s, in parallel with the revolutionary struggles of the French people. In a reaction against the rigidity of Classicism the Romantics believed in imagination, nature and the free expression of emotion. These traits are evident in the works of the English 'Lake poets' – Wordsworth, Coleridge and Southey.

Whereas in Europe Romanticism tended to seek a home in the novel and the drama, in Britain the movement was largely a poetic one; but it also manifested itself in certain types of prose. Among these were Gothic novels, tales of the macabre and the fantastic set in wild landscapes of rugged mountains, and ruined castles.

MAJOR ROMANTIC WRITERS

Horace Walpole (1717–97), English Gothic novelist: *The Castle of Otranto* (1765).

Johann Wolfgang von Goethe (1749–1832), German poet, dramatist, and novelist: the Romantic novella, *Die Leiden des jungen Werthers* (1774), the classical verse dramas *Iphigenia* (1787) and *Torquato Tasso* (1790) and his masterpiece *Faust* (1808).

William Blake (1757–1827), English poet: *Songs of Innocence* (1789) and *Songs of Experience* (1794).

Friedrich Schiller (1759–1805), German dramatist and poet: *The Robbers* (1781), the historical dramas *Wallenstein* (1798–9), and *Maria Stuart* (1800).

Robert Burns (1759–96), Scottish poet: notable for his use of the Scottish dialect: '*Tam o'Shanter*'.

Mrs Ann Radcliffe (1764–1823), English Gothic novelist: *The Mysteries of Udolpho* (1794).

François René de Chateaubriand (1768–1848), French novelist and prose-writer: *Le Génie du Christianisme* (1802), *Atala* (1801) and *René* (1805).

William Wordsworth (1770–1850), English poet: *Lyrical Ballads* (1798; a collection of poems written with Coleridge) and *The Prelude* (1798–1805).

Sir Walter Scott (1771–1832), Scottish novelist and poet: *Minstrelsy of the Scottish Border* (1802–3), a collection of ballads, *Ivanhoe* (1819), and *The Heart of Midlothian* (1818).

Samuel Taylor Coleridge (1772–1834), English poet: *Lyrical Ballads* (see Wordsworth), including *The Rime of the Ancient Mariner* and *Kubla Khan*.

Thomas De Quincey (1785–1859), English essayist: *Confessions of an English Opium Eater* (1821).

Lord Byron (George Gordon Byron; 1788–1824) English poet: *Childe Harold's Pilgrimage* (1812–18), and *Don Juan* (1819–24), a satirical epic.

Alphonse de Lamartine (1790–1869), French poet: *Méditations poétiques* (1820).

Percy Bysshe Shelley (1792–1822), English poet: *Queen Mab*, a poem, *The Cenci* and *Prometheus Unbound*, (1820), verse dramas, *Adonais* (1821), an elegy on the death of Keats, and *The Mask of Anarchy* (1832).

John Keats (1795–1821), English poet: *Odes* (*To a Nightingale*, *On a Grecian Urn*, *To Autumn*).

Heinrich Heine (1797–1856), German poet and essayist: *Reisebilder* (1826) and *Das Buch der Lieder* (1827).

Mary Wollstonecraft Shelley (1797–1851), English Gothic novelist: *Frankenstein* (1818).

Giacomo Leopardi (1798–1837), Italian lyric poet: *I Canti* (1816–36).

Alexander Pushkin (1799–1837), Russian poet and novelist: *Eugene Onegin* (1833), a verse novel.

Victor Hugo (1802–85), French poet, dramatist and novelist: the verse collections *Autumn Leaves* (1831) and *Les Contemplations* (1856), and the novels *The Hunchback of Nôtre Dame* (1831) and *Les Misérables* (1862).

Alexandre Dumas (1802–70), French novelist: *The Three Musketeers* (1844).

George Sand (Amandine Aurore Lucie Dupin; 1804–76), French novelist: *The Haunted Pool* (1841) and *Fanchon the Cricket* (1850).

Elizabeth Barrett Browning (1806–61), English poet: *Sonnets from the Portuguese* (1847) and *Aurora Leigh* (1857).

Alfred, Lord Tennyson (1809–92), English poet: the poems *The Lady of Shalott* (1832) and *The Lotus Eaters* (1833), the collections *In Memorium* (1850) and the *Idylls of the King* (1855).

Alfred de Musset (1810–57), French poet and dramatist: *Les Nuits* (1835–37), a collection of lyric poems, and *Lorenzaccio* (1834), a drama.

Robert Browning (1812–89), English poet: the poems *The Pied Piper of Hamelin* (1842) and *Home Thoughts from Abroad* (1845), the play *Pippa Passes* and *The Ring and the Book* (1868–69), a long poem in the form of a series of dramatic monologues.

Mikhail Lermontov (1814–41), Russian poet and novelist: the poems *The Angel* (1832) and *The Demon* (1841) and the novel *A Hero of Our Time* (1840).

LATER 19TH-CENTURY LITERATURE

The novel became the dominant literary form in 19th-century Britain. At its best it is both popular and literary. The world that most 19th-century British novelists were writing about was one characterized by increasing urbanization and industrialization – a world dominated by the owners of capital.

In the 19th century American literature took on a specifically national character in its treatment of certain themes and ideas. Uncontaminated by history or tradition, the New World presented exciting possibilities for the creative writer. The writing of a native literature was a key factor in this process. Torn apart by the Civil War there was an even deeper need for literature to unite the nation and re-establish a national consciousness.

REALISM

The term Realism is commonly used to describe works of art that appear to represent the world as it is, not as it might or should be. It can be applied to literature from almost any period but is especially associated with those 19th-century novelists and dramatists who claimed to be giving detailed, accurate and objective descriptions of life, in sharp contrast to what they saw as the idealizing of their 18th-century predecessors.

NATURALISM

Towards the end of the 19th century prose fiction assumed a new focus with the appearance of Naturalism, a specialized form of Realism based on the philosophical doctrines of materialism and determinism. For the novelist it amounts to a belief that everything in the world – including human behaviour – has observable physical causes; and that the individual is therefore shaped by society.

MAJOR REALIST AND NATURALIST WRITERS

Honoré de Balzac (1799–1850), French novelist: *La Comédie humaine*, a sequence of 94 novels, including *Old Goriot* (1835) and *Lost Illusions* (1837–43).

Stendhal (Marie Henri Beyle; 1783–1842), French novelist: *Scarlet and Black* (1830) and *The Charterhouse of Parma* (1839).

Nikolai Gogol (1809–52), Russian novelist and dramatist: *Dead Souls* (1842), a novel, and *The Government Inspector* (1836), a comic drama.

Georg Büchner (1813–37), German dramatist: *Danton's Death* (1835) and *Woyzeck* (1837).

Ivan Turgenev (1818–83), Russian novelist, short-story writer and dramatist: *A Month in the Country* (1850), a play, and *Fathers and Sons* (1861), a novel.

Gustave Flaubert (1821–80), French novelist: *Madame Bovary* (1857) and *Sentimental Education* (1869).

Fyodor Dostoevski (1821–81), Russian novelist: *Crime and Punishment* (1866) and *The Brothers Karamazov* (1880).

Henrik Ibsen (1828–1906), Norwegian dramatist: *Ghosts* (1881), *Hedda Gabler* (1890), and *The Master Builder* (1892).

Leo Tolstoy (1828–1910), Russian novelist: *War and Peace* (1869) and *Anna Karenina* (1877).

Émile Zola (1840–1902), French novelist: *The Dram Shop* (1877), *Nana* (1880), the novel cycle *The Rougon-Macquart*, including *Germinal* (1885) and *La Débâcle* (1892), and *J'accuse*, a letter criticizing the accusers of Dreyfus.

August Strindberg (1849–1912), Swedish dramatist: *Miss Julie* (1888) and *The Dance of Death* (1901).

Guy de Maupassant (1850–93), French novelist and short-story writer: *Boule de suif* (1881), a short story, and *Bel-Ami* (1885).

Anton Chekhov (1860–1904), Russian dramatist: *Uncle Vanya* (1899), *The Three Sisters* (1901), and *The Cherry Orchard* (1904).

Maxim Gorki (1868–1936), Russian novelist: *Mother* and an autobiographical trilogy (1913–23).

MAJOR 19TH-CENTURY BRITISH WRITERS

Jane Austen (1775–1817), novelist: *Sense and Sensibility* (1811), *Pride and Prejudice* (1813), *Mansfield Park* (1814), *Emma* (1815), and *Persuasion* (1818).

Benjamin Disraeli (1804–81), novelist and politician: the trilogy *Coningsby* (1844), *Sybil* (1845) and *Tancred* (1847).

Elizabeth Gaskel (1810–65), novelist: *Mary Barton* (1848), *Ruth* (1853), and *Cranford* (1853).

William Makepeace Thackeray (1811–63); novelist: *Vanity Fair* (1846–8) and *Pendennis* (1848–50).

Charles Dickens (1812–70), novelist: *Oliver Twist* (1838), *Nicholas Nickleby* (1839), *The Old Curiosity Shop* (1841), *Barnaby Rudge* (1841), *David Copperfield* (1850), *Bleak House* (1853), *Hard Times* (1854), *Little Dorrit* (1857), *A Tale of Two Cities* (1859), and *Great Expectations* (1861).

Anthony Trollope (1815–82), novelist: *Barsetshire Chronicles* (1857–67), a sequence of six novels, including *The Warden* and *Barchester Towers*.

Charlotte Brontë (1816–55), novelist: *Jane Eyre* (1847), *Shirley* (1849) and *Villette* (1853).

Emily Brontë (1818–48), novelist: *Wuthering Heights* (1847).

Charles Kingsley (1819–75), novelist: *Westward Ho!* (1855) and *The Water Babies* (1863), a children's story.

George Eliot (Mary Ann Evans; 1819–80), novelist: *Adam Bede* (1859), *The Mill on the Floss* (1860), *Silas Marner* (1861) and *Middlemarch* (1871–2).

Anne Brontë (1820–49), novelist: *The Tenant of Wildfell Hall* (1847).

Matthew Arnold (1822–88), English poet, essayist and critic: *The Forsaken Merman*, *Thyrsis*, *Dover Beach*, and *Essays in Criticism*.

William Wilkie Collins (1824–89), novelist: the mystery novels *The Woman in White* (1860) and *The Moonstone* (1868).

William Morris (1834–96), novelist, poet, and artist: *News from Nowhere* (1891).

Thomas Hardy (1840–1928), novelist and poet: *Far from the Madding Crowd* (1874), *The Return of the Native* (1878), *The Mayor of Casterbridge* (1886), *The Woodlanders* (1887), *Tess of the D'Urbervilles* (1891), and *Jude the Obscure* (1895) – all set in Dorset (part of Hardy's fictional 'Wessex').

Robert Louis Stevenson (1850–94), Scottish novelist: *Treasure Island* (1883) and *The Strange Case of Dr Jekyll and Mr Hyde* (1886).

Oscar Wilde (Fingal O'Flahertie Wills; 1854–1900), Irish dramatist, poet and novelist, famous for his witty epigrams: *The Picture of Dorian Gray* (1891), a novel, *The Importance of Being Earnest* (1895), a play, and *Ballad of Reading Goal* (1898), a poem.

George Bernard Shaw (1856–1950), Irish dramatist and critic. *Pygmalion* (1913) and *Saint Joan* (1923).

Joseph Conrad (Teodor Jozef Konrad Korzeniowski; 1857–1924), Polish-born English writer. *Lord Jim* (1900), *Heart of Darkness* (1902), *Nostromo* (1904), and *The Secret Agent* (1907).

Sir Arthur Conan Doyle (1859–1930), detective novelist: *The Memoirs of Sherlock Holmes* (1894) and *The Hound of the Baskervilles* (1902).

Rudyard Kipling (1865–1936), novelist, poet and short-story writer: *Plain Tales from the Hills* (1888), *Kim* (1902), and the children's stories *Jungle Book* (1894), and *Just So Stories* (1902).

H(erbert) G(eorge) Wells (1866–1946), novelist: the science-fiction stories *The Time Machine* (1895) and *War of the Worlds* (1898), *The Invisible Man* (1897), and the humorous novel *Kipps* (1904).

Arnold Bennett (1867–1931), novelist and critic: the trilogy *Clayhanger, Hilda Lessways*, and *These Twain* (1910–15).

J(ohn) M(illington) Synge (1871–1909), Irish dramatist: *Playboy of the Western World* (1907).

MAJOR 19TH-CENTURY AMERICAN WRITERS

Washington Irving (1783–1859), essayist and short-story writer: *Sketch Book of Geoffrey Crayon* (1820), including the stories *Rip Van Winkle* and *The Legend of the Sleepy Hollow*.

James Fenimore Cooper (1789–1851), novelist: *The Spy* (1821), *The Last of the Mohicans* (1826), and *The Pathfinder* (1840).

Ralph Waldo Emerson (1803–82), poet and essayist.

Nathaniel Hawthorne (1804–64), novelist and short-story writer: *The Scarlet Letter* (1850), *The Blithedale Romance* (1852) and *The Marble Faun* (1860).

Edgar Allan Poe (1809–49), poet, critic and short-story writer: *Tales of the Grotesque and Arabesque* (1840), including the macabre tale *The Fall of the House of Usher*.

Henry David Thoreau (1817–62), writer and essayist: *A Life in the Woods* (1854) and the influential essay *Civil Disobedience* (1849).

Herman Melville (1819–91), short-story writer and novelist: *Moby-Dick* (1851) and *Billy Budd* (1924).

Emily Dickinson (1830–86), poet.

Mark Twain (Samuel Langhorne Clemens; 1835–1910), novelist and short-story writer: *The Adventures of Tom Sawyer* (1876), *Life on the Mississippi* (1883), and *The Adventures of Huckleberry Finn* (1884).

Henry James (1843–1916), novelist: *The Wings of the Dove* (1902), *The Ambassadors* (1903), and *The Golden Bowl* (1904).

MODERN LITERATURE

The literary movements of the late 19th- and early 20th century – Symbolism, Aestheticism and Modernism – shared a belief in the absolute value of art, reinforced by various forms of contempt for the everyday world, and especially for people who served its interests. There resulted a rift between writers and the public at large, who were seen as 'bourgeois' in a disparaging sense. Artists lived for their art alone, sometimes flaunting their difference from the rest of society by affected or deliberately shocking behaviour.

Towards the end of the 19th century and in the early years of the 20th, the great Realist consensus on the modern novel began to exhibit signs of strain, and finally broke up altogether. This development did not, of course, happen overnight, though there are signs of its origin in the later writings of Hardy, Conrad, James, Dostoevski, and even in those of the Realist novelist *par excellence*, Tolstoy himself.

Modern drama in Britain and America is distinctive for its concern with issues. These may, amongst other things, relate to politics, morality, racism, and/or religion. Equally, the main concerns of modern theatre may be to do with theatre itself – how it works; what it means; the nature of its conventions, and the kind of language it uses. The ideas explored in modern drama may be those specifically associated with Modernism. Foremost among these are the workings of time and memory; the problems surrounding communication, and a sense that life is meaningless. European theatre of the 20th century witnessed enormous expansion in experiment and innovation. Radical developments fundamentally challenged the basic relationship between performers and spectators established in the 19th century. Movements such as German Expressionism, Epic Theatre, the Theatre of Cruelty and the Theatre of the Absurd were designed to break away from the dominant theatrical convention of Naturalism.

Modern poetry includes both 'difficult' poetry and poetry that is more directly accessible to the reader. The difficult poetry is obscure and highly allusive in the Modernist manner exemplified by T.S. Eliot's *The Waste Land* and Ezra Pound's *Cantos*. The more accessible poetry – though not necessarily easy to understand – belongs to a tradition which does not break so abruptly with previous poetry.

MAJOR MODERN WRITERS

Luigi Pirandello (1867–1936), Italian dramatist: *Six Characters in Search of an Author* (1921).

André Gide (1869–1951), French novelist: *The Immoralist* (1902), *Strait is the Gate* (1909), and *The Vatican Cellars* (1914).

Marcel Proust (1871–1922), French novelist: *Remembrance of Things Past* (1913–27).

W. Somerset Maugham (1874–1965), English novelist and short-story writer: *Of Human Bondage* (1915), *The Moon and Sixpence* (1919), *Cakes and Ale* (1930) and the play *The Circle* (1921).

Thomas Mann (1875–1955), German novelist: *Death in Venice* (1912), a short story, and the novels *Buddenbrooks* (1900), *The Magic Mountain* (1924), and *Doctor Faustus* (1947).

Herman Hesse (1877–1962), German novelist (from 1923 a Swiss citizen): *Siddhartha* (1922) and *Steppenwolf* (1927).

E(dward) M(organ) Forster (1879–1970), English novelist: *A Room with a View* (1908), *Howard's End* (1910) and *A Passage to India* (1924).

P(elham) G(renville) Wodehouse (1881–1975), English comic novelist: the *Psmith* and *Jeeves* novels.

James Joyce (1882–1941), Irish writer: *Dubliners* (1914), a collection of short stories, and the novels

Portrait of the Artist as a Young Man (1914–15), *Ulysses* (1922), and *Finnegan's Wake* (1939).

Virginia Woolf (1882–1941), English novelist: *Mrs Dalloway* (1925) and *To the Lighthouse* (1927).

Franz Kafka (1883–1924), Czech novelist writing in German: *The Trial* (1925) and *The Castle* (1926).

D(avid) H(erbert) Lawrence (1885–1930), English novelist, short-story writer and poet: *Sons and Lovers* (1913), *The Rainbow* (1915), *Women in Love*, and *Lady Chatterley's Lover* (1928).

Eugene O'Neill (1888–1953): American dramatist: *The Iceman Cometh* (1946) and *A Long Day's Journey Into Night* (1956).

Jean Cocteau (1889–1963): French poet, novelist and dramatist: *Les Enfants terribles* (1929) and the play *La Machine Infernale* (1934).

Boris Pasternak (1890–1960), Russian novelist: *Dr Zhivago* (1957).

Aldous Huxley (1894–1963), English novelist: *Brave New World* (1932).

J(ohn) B(oynton) Priestley (1894–1984), English novelist and dramatist: the novel *The Good Companions* (1929) and the play *Laburnum Grove*.

Robert Graves (1895–1985), English poet and novelist: *Goodbye to all that* (1929), his World War I autobiography, and *I, Claudius* (1934), a historical novel.

F. Scott Fitzgerald (1896–1940), American novelist: *The Beautiful and Damned* (1922), *The Great Gatsby* (1925), and *Tender is the Night* (1934).

William Faulkner (1897–1962), American novelist: *The Sound and the Fury* (1929).

Bertolt Brecht (1898–1956), German dramatist: *The Threepenny Opera* (1928), a musical drama, and the plays *Mother Courage* (1941), *The Good Woman of Setzuan* and *The Caucasian Chalk Circle*.

Ernest Hemingway (1899–1961), American novelist: *A Farewell to Arms* (1929) and *For Whom the Bell Tolls* (1940).

Noel Coward (1899–1973), English comic dramatist: *Private Lives* (1930) and *Blithe Spirit* (1941).

Vladimir Nabokov (1899–1977), Russian-born American writer: *Lolita* (1958) and *Pale Fire* (1962).

Jorge Luis Borges (1899–1986), Argentinian poet and short-story writer: *Fictions* (1944).

John Steinbeck (1902–68), American novelist: *Of Mice and Men* (1937) and *Grapes of Wrath* (1939).

Evelyn Waugh (1903–66), English novelist: *Decline and Fall* (1928), *A Handful of Dust* (1934), and *Brideshead Revisited* (1945).

George Orwell (1903–50), English novelist and essayist: *Animal Farm* (1945), a political allegory, and *Nineteen Eighty-Four* (1949), a nightmarish fable of the future.

Christopher Isherwood (1904–86), English novelist and dramatist: *Mr Norris Changes Trains* (1935) and *Goodbye to Berlin* (1939).

Graham Greene (1904–91), English novelist: *Brighton Rock* (1938), *The Power and the Glory* (1940), *The Heart of the Matter* (1948), *Our Man in Havana* (1958) and *The Honorary Consul* (1973).

Jean-Paul Sartre (1905–80), French philosopher, dramatist and novelist: the novel *Nausea* (1937), the philosophical essay *Being and Nothingness* (1943), and the trilogy *Les Chemins de la liberté* (1945–49).

Mikhail Sholokhov (1905–84), Soviet novelist: *And Quiet Flows the Don* (1934).

Samuel Beckett (1906–89), Irish dramatist and novelist: the plays *Waiting for Godot* (1952), *Endgame* (1957) and *Happy Days* (1961), and the novel *Malone Dies* (1951).

Alberto Moravia (Alberto Pincherle; 1907–90), Italian novelist: *The Time of Indifference* (1929) and *The Conformist* (1952).

Christopher Fry (1907–), English dramatist: *The Lady's Not for Burning* (1948), a verse drama.

Tennessee Williams (1911–83), American dramatist: *The Glass Menagerie* (1944), *A Street Car Named Desire* (1947), and *Cat On A Hot Tin Roof* (1955).

William Golding (1911–), English novelist: *Lord of the Flies* (1954), *Pincher Martin* (1956), and *The Spire* (1964).

Eugène Ionescu (1912–), Romanian-born French dramatist: the absurd dramas *The Bald Prima Donna* and *The Rhinoceros*.

Patrick White (1912–1990), Australian novelist: *The Tree of Man* (1955), *Voss* (1957) and *Riders in the Chariot*.

Albert Camus (1913–60), French novelist, dramatist and essayist: the novels *The Outsider* (1942) and *The Plague* (1947), and the essay *The Myth of Sisyphus*.

Arthur Miller (1915–), American dramatist: *Death of a Salesman* (1949) and *The Crucible* (1952).

Saul Bellow (1915–); American novelist: *Henderson the Rain King* (1959) and *Herzog* (1964).

Anthony Burgess (1917–), English novelist and critic: *Clockwork Orange* (1962) and *Earthly Powers* (1980).

Alexander Solzhenitsyn (1918–), Russian novelist: *One Day in the Life of Ivan Denisovitch* (1962), *First Circle* (1964), and *Cancer Ward* (1966).

Doris Lessing (1919–), English novelist: *The Golden Notebook* (1962) and *The Good Terrorist* (1985).

Iris Murdoch (1919–), English novelist: *The Bell* (1958), *A World Child* (1975) and *The Sea, The Sea* (1978).

Alain Robbe-Grillet (1922–), French novelist: *The Voyeur* (1955) and *Jealousy* (1957).

Norman Mailer (1923–), American novelist: *The Naked and the Dead* (1948).

James Baldwin (1924–), American novelist: *Go Tell It On the Mountain* (1954).

John Fowles (1926–), English novelist: *The Magus* (1966) and *The French Lieutenant's Woman* (1969).

Günter Grass (1927–), German novelist: *The Tin Drum* (1959) and *Dog Years* (1965).

Edward Albee (1928–), American dramatist: *Who's Afraid of Virginia Woolf?* (1962).

Gabriel Garcia Marquez (1928–), Colombian novelist: *One Hundred Years of Solitude* (1967).

John Osborne (1929–), English dramatist: *Look Back in Anger* (1956).

Harold Pinter (1930–), English playwright: *The Birthday Party* (1958) and *The Caretaker* (1960).

John Updike (1932–), American novelist: *Rabbit, Run* and *Couples*.

Joe Orton (1934–67), English dramatist: *Loot* (1965) and *What the Butler Saw* (1969).

Thomas Pynchon (1937–), American novelist: *V*

(1963) and *Gravity's Rainbow* (1973).

Tom Stoppard (1937–), English dramatist: *Rosencrantz and Guildenstern are Dead* (1966) and *The Real Inspector Hound* (1968).

Alan Ayckbourn (1939–), English playwright: *Relatively Speaking* (1967) and *The Norman Conquests* (1974).

Salman Rushdie (1947–), Indian-born British novelist: *Midnight's Children* (1981) and *Satanic Verses* (1988).

MAJOR MODERN POETS

Charles Baudelaire (1821–67), French poet: *Les fleurs du mal* (1857; The Flowers of Evil).

Stéphane Mallarmé (1842–98), French poet: *L'après-midi d'un faune* (1876; The Afternoon of a Faun) and *Vers et Prose*.

Gerard Manley Hopkins (1844–89), English poet: the poems *Pied Beauty* and *The Windhover* (1918).

W(illiam) B(utler) Yeats (1865–1939), Irish poet and dramatist: the poems *Sailing to Byzantium*, *Among School Children*, and *Lapis Lazuli*.

Walter De La Mare (1873–1956), English poet noted for his children's verse: the collection *The Listeners and Other Poems* (1912).

Robert Frost (1874–1963), American poet: *North of Boston* (1914) and *New Hampshire* (1923).

Rainer Maria Rilke (1875–1926), Austrian poet: *Duino Elegies* (1922) and *Sonnets to Orpheus* (1923).

Edward Thomas (1878–1917), English poet: *Collected Poems*, including the poem *Adlestrop*.

Wallace Stevens (1879–1955), American poet: *Harmonium* (1923) and *The Man with the Blue Guitar* (1937).

Ezra Pound (1885–1972), American poet: *Cantos* (1925–69).

Siegfried Sassoon (1886–1967), English war poet.

Rupert Brooke (1887–1915), English war poet: the sonnet *The Soldier* (1915).

Edith Sitwell (1887–1965), English poet: *Façade* (1922).

T(homas) S(tearns) Eliot (1888–1965), English poet, dramatist and critic: *The Waste Land* (1922), *Four Quartets* (1943), and the plays *Murder in the Cathedral* (1935) and *The Cocktail Party* (1950).

Isaac Rosenberg (1890–1918), English war poet: the poem *Dead Man's Dump*.

Hugh MacDiarmid (1892–1978), Scottish poet: *A Drunk Man Looks at the Thistle* (1926).

Wilfred Owen (1893–1918), English war poet: the poems *Anthem for Doomed Youth* and *Strange Meeting*.

John Betjeman (1906–84), English poet: *Collected Poems* (1968).

W(ystan) H(ugh) Auden (1907–73), Anglo-American poet, dramatist and critic: *On the Frontier* (1938), *New Year Letter* (1941), *The Age of Anxiety* (1948), *Nones* (1951), and *About the House* (1965).

Louis MacNeice (1907–63), Irish poet: *Blind Fireworks* (1929) and *Autumn Journal* (1939).

Dylan Thomas (1914–53), Welsh poet: *Deaths and Entrances* (1946), and the play for voices *Under Milk Wood* (1954).

Robert Lowell (1917–77), American poet: *Lord Weary's Castle* (1946) and *For the Union Dead* (1964).

Philip Larkin (1922–85), English poet: *The North Ship* (1945), *The Less Deceived* (1955) and *The Whitsun Weddings* (1964).

Ted Hughes (1930–), English poet: *The Hawk in the Rain* (1975) and *Crow* (1970).

Sylvia Plath (1932–63), American poet: the verse collections *The Colossus* (1960) and *Ariel* (1965), and the novel *The Bell Jar* (1971).

Seamus Heaney (1939–), Irish poet: *North* (1975), *Field Work* (1979), and *Station Island* (1984).

POPULAR MODERN WRITERS

John Buchan (1875–1940), English adventure novelist: *The Thirty-Nine Steps*.

Raymond Chandler (1888–1969), American detective novelist: *The Big Step* (1939) and *The Long Goodbye* (1953).

Agatha Christie (1890–1976), English detective novelist, the creator of the detectives Hercule Poirot and Miss Marple.

J(ohn) R(onald) R(euel) Tolkien (1892–1973), English novelist: *The Hobbit* and *The Lord of the Rings*.

Dorothy L. Sayers (1893–1957), English detective novelist: *The Nine Tailors* (1934) and *Gaudy Night* (1935).

Dashiell Hammett (1894–1961), American detective novelist: *The Maltese Falcon* (1930).

Dennis Wheatley (1897–1977), English horror novelist.

Barbara Cartland (1901–), English writer of romantic fiction.

Georgette Heyer (1902–74), English writer of historical romance.

Georges Simenon (1903–89), Belgian detective novelist, creator of the detective Maigret.

Catherine Cookson (1906–), English writer of romantic fiction.

Victoria Holt (1906–), English writer of historical romances.

Ian Fleming (1908–64), English suspense novelist, creator of James Bond: *Casino Royale* (1953) and *Diamonds are Forever* (1956).

Harold Robbins (1912–), American novelist: *The Carpetbaggers* (1961).

Arthur C. Clarke (1917–), English science fiction novelist: *2001: A Space Odyssey*.

Isaac Asimov (1920–), American science fiction novelist: *I, Robot* (1950).

Alistair Maclean (1922–87), Scottish adventure novelist: *HMS Ulysses* (1955), *The Guns of Navarone* (1957) and *Where Eagles Dare* (1967).

John Le Carré (1931–), English spy novelist: *The Spy Who Came in from the Cold* (1963) and *Tinker, Tailor, Soldier, Spy* (1974).

Barbara Bradford Taylor (1933–), English novelist: *A Woman of Substance* and *Hold the Dream*.

Frederick Forsyth (1938–), English adventure novelist: *The Day of the Jackal* (1971) and *The Fourth Protocol* (1984).

Stephen King (1946–), American horror novelist: *Carrie* and *Salem's Lot*.

POPULAR CHILDREN'S WRITERS

Johann Rudolph Wyss (1782–1830), Swiss novelist: *Swiss Family Robinson* (1827).

Jakob Grimm (1785–1863), German philologist and, with his brother Wilhelm (see below), collector of German folktales.

Wilhelm Grimm (1786–1859), German philologist and collector of folktales (see Jakob Grimm).

Captain Marryat (Frederick Marryat; 1792–1848), English novelist and children's story writer: *The Children of the New Forest* (1847).

Hans Christian Andersen (1805–75), Danish novelist, dramatist and fairy tale writer: *The Ugly Duckling, The Snow Queen* and *The Little Mermaid.*

Edward Lear (1812–88), English artist, poet and writer of children's verse: *The Book of Nonsense* (1846).

Charles Kingsley (1819–75), English novelist (see also Major 19th-century British Writers): *The Water Babies* (1863).

Thomas Hughes (1822–96), English politician, novelist and children's story writer: *Tom Brown's Schooldays* (1857).

C. Collodi (Carlo Lorenzini; 1826–90), Italian novelist, journalist and writer of children's stories: *Pinocchio* (1880).

Louisa May Alcott (1832–88), American novelist: *Little Women* (1868).

Lewis Carroll (Charles Lutwidge Dodgson; 1832–98), English mathematician and children's story writer: *Alice's Adventures in Wonderland* (1865) and *Through the Looking-Glass* (1872).

Frances Hodgson Burnett (1849–1924), Anglo-American children's story writer: *Little Lord Fauntleroy* (1885) and *The Secret Garden* (1911).

Robert Louis Stevenson (1850–94), Scottish novelist (see also Major 19th-century British Writers): *Treasure Island* (1883).

L. Frank Baum (1856–1919), American novelist and children's story writer: *The Wonderful Wizard of Oz* (1900).

Selma Lagerlöf (1858–1940), Swedish novelist (see also Nobel Prizewinners in Literature): *The Wonderful Adventures of Nils* (1907).

E(dith) Nesbit (1858–1924), English children's story writer: *The Railway Children* (1906).

Kenneth Grahame (1859–1932), Scottish children's story writer: *The Wind in the Willows* (1908).

James Barrie (1860–1937), Scottish novelist, dramatist and children's story writer: *Peter Pan* (1904).

Rudyard Kipling (1865–1936), English novelist, poet and short-story writer (see also Major 19th-century British Writers): *Jungle Book* (1894) and *Just So Stories* (1902).

Beatrix Potter (1866–1943), English illustrator and children's story writer: *The Tale of Peter Rabbit* (1900).

Hilaire Belloc (1870–1955), French-born English poet, essayist, historian and writer of verse for children: *The Bad Child's Book of Beasts* (1896) and *Cautionary Tales* (1907).

Walter De La Mare (1873–1956), English poet (see also Major Modern Poets): *Songs for Childhood* (1902).

A(lan) A(lexander) Milne (1882–1956), English novelist, dramatist and children's story writer: *Winnie-the-Pooh* (1926) and *The House at Pooh Corner* (1928).

Arthur Ransome (1884–1967), English journalist and children's story writer: *Swallows and Amazons* (1931).

Enid Blyton (1892–1968), English children's story writer, the creator of Noddy.

J(ohn) R(onald) R(euel) Tolkien (1892–1973), English novelist (see also Popular Modern Writers): *The Hobbit* (1937).

C(live) S(taples) Lewis (1898–1963), English scholar, science fiction novelist and children's story writer: *The Lion, the Witch and the Wardrobe* (1950) and *The Last Battle* (1956).

Erich Kästner (1899–1974), German novelist, poet and children's story writer: *Emil and the Detectives* (1929).

Antoine de Saint-Exupéry (1900–44), French aviator, novelist and children's story writer: *Le Petit Prince* (1943).

(Georges Rémi) Hergé (1907–83), Belgian illustrator and children's story writer, the creator of Tintin.

Roald Dahl (1916–91), English novelist and children's story writer: *Charlie and the Chocolate Factory* (1964).

Rosemary Sutcliff (1920–), English novelist and writer of historical novels for children: *Warrior Scarlet* (1958).

René Goscinny (1926–77), French writer of children's stories, the creator of Asterix.

Raymond Briggs (1934–), English illustrator and writer of children's stories: *The Snowman* (1978).

POETS LAUREATE

The title of poet laureate has been bestowed upon a contemporary poet by the British monarch since the reign of Charles II. The laureate writes commemorative verses to celebrate major public occasions.

John Dryden (1631–1700; laureate 1668–88)

Thomas Shadwell (1642?–92; laureate 1688–92)

Nahum Tate (1652–1715; laureate 1692–1715)

Nicholas Rowe (1674–1718; laureate 1715–18)

Laurence Eusden (1688–1730; laureate 1718–30)

Colley Cibber (1671–1757; laureate 1730–57)

William Whitehead (1715–85; laureate 1757–85; appointed after Thomas Gray declined the offer)

Thomas Warton (1728–90; laureate 1785–90)

Henry James Pye (1745–1813; laureate 1790–1813)

Robert Southey (1774–1843; laureate 1813–43)

William Wordsworth (1770–1850; laureate 1843–50)

Alfred, Lord Tennyson (1809–92; laureate 1850–92; appointed after Samuel Rogers declined the offer)

Alfred Austin (1835–1913; laureate 1896–1913)

Robert Bridges (1844–1930; laureate 1913–30)

John Masefield (1878–1967; laureate 1930–67)

Cecil Day-Lewis (1904–72; laureate 1968–72)

Sir John Betjeman (1906–84; laureate 1972–84)

Ted Hughes (b. 1930; laureate 1984–)

NOBEL PRIZEWINNERS IN LITERATURE

ORIGIN OF THE NOBEL PRIZES

The five original Nobel Prizes are awarded for outstanding achievement in the fields of physics, chemistry, medicine, literature and peace. The prizes were established by the chemist and inventor of dynamite, Alfred Nobel (1833–96). Concerned about the destructive uses of dynamite, he left a fortune in trust for the foundation and administration of the prizes which he hoped would encourage international co-operation and world peace. A sixth Nobel prize, the Nobel Memorial Prize in Economic Science, was introduced in 1968 by the Swedish national bank (see relevant chapters for other Nobel prizewinners).

The literature prize was first given in 1901 and is judged by the Swedish Academy.

1901 Sully-Prudhomme, French poet, noted for his later philosophical poetry.

1902 Theodor Mommsen, German historian: *History of Rome* (1854–56, 1885).

1903 Bjornstjerne Bjornsen, Norwegian novelist, poet and dramatist: helped revive Norwegian as a literary language.

1904 Frédéric Mistral, French poet: promoted Provençal as a literary language.
Juan Echegaray, Spanish dramatist: *The World and his Wife* (1881)

1905 Henryk Sienkiewicz, Polish novelist: *Quo Vadis?* (1895).

1906 Giosue Carducci, Italian Classical poet.

1907 Rudyard Kipling, British novelist and poet (see later 19th-century literature).

1908 Rudolf Eucken, German Idealist philosopher.

1909 Selma Lagerlöf, Swedish novelist: well-known for novels based on legends and sagas (see Popular Children's writers).

1910 Paul von Heyse, German poet, novelist and dramatist.

1911 Maurice Maeterlinck, Belgian Symbolist poet and dramatist: *Pelléas et Mélisande* (1892) and *The Blue Bird* (1908)

1912 Gerhart Hauptmann, German dramatist, novelist and poet: introduced Naturalism to German theatre.

1913 R. Tagore, Indian playwright and poet (see Indian literature).

1914 No award

1915 Romain Rolland, French novelist and biographer: the 10-volume *Jean-Christophe* (1904–12).

1916 Verner von Heidenstam, Swedish lyric poet.

1917 Karl Gjellerup, Danish novelist
Henrik Pontoppidan, Danish novelist: *Lucky Peter* (1898–1904).

1918 No award

1919 Carl Spitteler, Swiss poet and novelist: *The Olympic Spring* (1900–05).

1920 Knut Hamsun, Norwegian novelist: *Pan* (1894) and *The Growth of the Soil* (1917).

1921 Anatole France, French novelist; his work is noted for its elegance and scepticism.

1922 Jacinto Benavente y Martinez, Spanish dramatist of social satires.

1923 William Butler Yeats, Irish poet (see Modern poets).

1924 Wladyslaw Stanislaw Reymont, Polish novelist: *The Promised Land* (1895)
and *The Peasants* (1904–05).

1925 George Bernard Shaw, Irish dramatist (see Modern writers).

1926 Grazia Deledda, Italian Naturalist novelist.

1927 Henri Bergson, French dualist philosopher.

1928 Sigrid Undset, Norwegian novelist; her novels are about women and religion.

1929 Thomas Mann, German novelist (see Modern writers).

1930 Sinclair Lewis, American satirical novelist: *Babbitt* (1922).

1931 Erik Axel Karlfeldt, Swedish lyric poet; wrote about love, nature and peasant life.

1932 John Galsworthy, British novelist and dramatist: *The Forsyte Saga* (1906–28).

1933 Ivan Bunin, Russian émigré novelist, best known for his short stories.

1934 Luigi Pirandello, Italian dramatist (see Modern writers).

1935 No award

1936 Eugene O'Neill, American dramatist (see Modern writers).

1937 Roger Martin du Gard, French novelist: the *Les Thibaults* (1922–40).

1938 Pearl Buck, American novelist; famous for her novels about China.

1939 Frans Eemil Sillanpää, Finnish novelist: *Meek Heritage* (1919) and *People of the Summer Night* (1934).

1940–43 No award

1944 Johannes V. Jensen, Danish writer of essays and travel books.

1945 Gabriela Mistral, Chilean lyric poet.

1946 Hermann Hesse, German-born Swiss novelist (see Modern writers).

1947 André Gide, French novelist and essayist (see Modern writers).

1948 T.S. Eliot, American-born English poet (see Modern poets).

1949 William Faulkner, American novelist (see Modern writers).

1950 Bertrand Russell, British philosopher and mathematician: *A History of Western Philosophy* (1945).

1951 Pär Lagerkvist, Swedish novelist whose work was concerned with good and evil and man's search for God.

1952 François Mauriac, French poet, novelist and dramatist, well known for his Catholic novels.

1953 Sir Winston Churchill, British statesman, historian and orator.

1954 Ernest Hemingway, American novelist (see Modern writers).

1955 Halldór Laxness, Icelandic novelist who wrote about Icelandic life in the style of the sagas.

1956 Juan Ramón Jiménez, Spanish lyric poet.

1957 Albert Camus, French novelist and dramatist (see Modern writers).

1958 Boris Pasternak, Russian novelist and poet; declined award (see Modern writers).

1959 Salvatore Quasimodo, Italian poet.

1960 Saint-John Perse, French lyric poet.

1961 Ivo Andrić, Yugoslav novelist; best known for his Bosnian historical trilogy.

1962 John Steinbeck, American novelist (see Modern writers).

1963 George Seferis, Greek poet and essayist; introduced Symbolism to Greek literature.

1964 Jean-Paul Sartre, French philosopher-writer; declined award (see Modern writers).

1965 Mikhail Sholokhov, Russian novelist (see Modern writers).

1966 Shmuel Yosef Agnon, Israeli novelist, considered the leading writer in Hebrew. Nelly Sachs, German-born Swedish Jewish poet; her works concentrate on the persecution of Jews.

1967 Miguel Angel Asturias, Guatemalan novelist and poet, his work ranges from Guatemalan legends to international politics.

1968 Kawabata Yasunari, Japanese novelist (see Japanese writers).

1969 Samuel Beckett, Irish novelist, dramatist (see Modern writers).

1970 Aleksandr Solzhenitsyn, Russian novelist (see Modern writers).

1971 Pablo Neruda, Chilean poet who champions the cause of the working class.

1972 Heinrich Böll, German novelist, critical of Germany's political past.

1973 Patrick White, Australian novelist (see Modern writers).

EURO FACTS

'LEAGUE TABLE' OF NOBEL PRIZEWINNERS (FOR LITERATURE) FOR EC COUNTRIES

France	12
Germany	6
UK	6
Italy	5
Spain	5
Denmark	3
Ireland	3
Greece	2
Belgium	1
Luxembourg	0
Netherlands	0
Portugal	0

1974 Eyvind Johnson, Swedish novelist, well known for his 4 autobiographical novels. Harry Martinson, Swedish novelist and poet: the poem *Aniara* (1956) and the novel *The Road* (1948).

1975 Eugenio Montale, Italian poet, well known for his complexity and pessimism.

1976 Saul Bellow, American novelist (see Modern writers).

1977 Vicente Aleixandre, Spanish lyric poet, whose work sympathized with the Republican cause.

1978 Isaac Bashevis Singer, American author who wrote in Yiddish: described Jewish life in Poland.

1979 Odysseus Elytis, Greek poet: distinguished by his joyful and sensuous poetry.

1980 Czeslaw Milosz, Polish-American poet and novelist: *The Captive Mind* (1953).

1981 Elias Canetti, Bulgarian-born German writer: *Auto da fé* (1935) and *Crowds and Power* (1960).

1982 Gabriel García Márquez, Colombian novelist (see Modern writers).

1983 William Golding, British novelist (see Modern writers).

1984 Jaroslav Seifert, Czech poet: *Switch off the Lights* (1938).

1985 Claude Simon, French novelist; exponent of the *nouveau Roman*.

1986 Wole Soyinka, Nigerian playwright and poet whose work merges Nigerian and Western traditions.

1987 Joseph Brodsky, American (Russian émigré) poet and essayist; much of his work deals with loss and exile.

1988 Naguib Mahfouz, Egyptian novelist (see Arabic writers).

1989 Camilo José Cela, Spanish novelist, well known for his brutally realistic novels.

1990 Octavio Paz, Mexican poet, exponent of Magic Realism, noted for his international perspective.

BOOKER PRIZEWINNERS

The Booker McConnell Prize is an annual award for a novel by a citizen of the United Kingdom, a Commonwealth country, the Republic of Ireland or South Africa and first published in Britain. It was established in 1968 by the trading company Booker McConnell in collaboration with the Publishers' Association.

1969 P.H. Newby, *Something to Answer For*
1970 Bernice Rubens, *The Elected Member*
1971 V.S. Naipaul, *In a Free State*
1972 John Berger, *G*
1973 J.G. Farrell, *The Siege of Krishnapur*
1974 (joint prizewinners)
     Nadine Gordimer, *The Conservationist*
     Stanley Middleton, *Holiday*
1975 Ruth Prawer Jhabvala, *Heat and Dust*
1976 David Storey, *Saville*
1977 Paul Scott, *Staying On*
1978 Iris Murdoch, *The Sea, The Sea*
1979 Penelope Fitzgerald, *Offshore*
1980 William Golding, *Rites of Passage*
1981 Salman Rushdie, *Midnight's Children*
1982 Thomas Keneally, *Schindler's Ark*
1983 J.M. Coetzee, *Life and Times of Michael K.*
1984 Anita Brookner, *Hôtel du Lac*
1985 Keri Hulme, *The Bone People*
1986 Kingsley Amis, *The Old Devils*
1987 Penelope Lively, *Moon Tiger*
1988 Peter Carey, *Oscar and Lucinda*
1989 Kazuo Ishiguro, *The Remains of the Day*
1990 A.S. Byatt, *Possession*

PULITZER FICTION AWARD-WINNERS

The Pulitzer prizes are annual awards endowed by the American publisher Joseph Pulitzer in 1917. They are given for achievements in American journalism and literature. Awards are made for the best reporting of national news and of international news, the most distinguished editorial, the best local reporting and the best news photograph as well as for achievement in fiction.

1918 Ernest Poole, *His Family*
1919 Booth Tarkington, *The Magnificent Ambersons*
1920 No award
1921 Edith Wharton, *The Age of Innocence*
1922 Booth Tarkington, *Alice Adams*
1923 Willa Cather, *One of Ours*
1924 Margaret Wilson, *The Able McLaughlins*
1925 Edna Ferber, *So Big*

1926 Sinclair Lewis, *Arrowsmith*
1927 Louis Bromfield, *Early Autumn*
1928 Thornton Wilder, *The Bridge at San Luis Rey*
1929 Julia Peterkin, *Scarlet Sister Mary*
1930 Oliver LaFarge, *Laughing Boy*
1931 Margaret Ayer Barnes, *Years of Grace*
1932 Pearl S. Buck, *The Good Earth*
1933 T.S. Stribling, *The Store*
1934 Caroline Miller, *Lamb in His Bosom*
1935 Josephine Winslow Johnson, *Now in November*
1936 Harold L. Davis, *Honey in the Horn*
1937 Margaret Mitchell, *Gone With the Wind*
1938 John Phillips Marquand, *The Late George Apley*
1939 Marjorie Kinnan Rawlings, *The Yearling*
1940 John Steinbeck, *The Grapes of Wrath*
1941 No award
1942 Ellen Glasgow, *In This Our Life*
1943 Upton Sinclair, *Dragon's Teeth*
1944 Martin Flavin, *Journey in the Dark*
1945 John Hersey, *A Bell for Adano*
1946 No award
1947 Robert Penn Warren, *All the King's Men*
1948 James A. Michener, *Tales of the South Pacific*
1949 James Gould Cozzens, *Guard of Honor*
1950 A.B. Guthrie, Jr *The Way West*
1951 Conrad Richter, *The Town*
1952 Herman Wouk, *The Caine Mutiny*
1953 Ernest Hemingway, *The Old Man and the Sea*
1954 No award
1955 William Faulkner, *A Fable*
1956 Mackinley Kantor, *Andersonville*
1957 No award
1958 James Agee, *A Death in the Family*
1959 Robert Lewis Taylor, *The Travels of Jamie McPheeters*
1960 Allen Drury, *Advise and Consent*
1961 Harper Lee, *To Kill a Mockingbird*
1962 Edwin O'Connor, *The Edge of Sadness*
1963 William Faulkner, *The Reivers*
1964 No award
1965 Shirley Ann Grau, *The Keepers of the House*
1966 Katherine Anne Porter, *The Collected Stories of Katherine Anne Porter*
1967 Bernard Malamud, *The Fixer*
1968 William Styron, *The Confessions of Nat Turner*
1969 N. Scott Momaday, *House Made of Dawn*
1970 Jean Stafford, *Collected Stories*
1971 No award
1972 Wallace Stegner, *Angle of Repose*
1973 Eudora Welty, *The Optimist's Daughter*
1974 No award
1975 Michael Shaara, *The Killer Angels*
1976 Saul Bellow, *Humboldt's Gift*
1977 No award
1978 James Alan McPherson, *Elbow Room*
1979 John Cheever, *The Stories of John Cheever*
1980 Norman Mailer, *The Executioner's Song*
1981 John Kennedy Toole, *A Confederacy of Dunces*
1982 John Updike, *Rabbit is Rich*
1983 Alice Walker, *The Color Purple*
1984 William Kennedy, *Ironweed*
1985 Alison Lurie, *Foreign Affairs*
1986 Larry McMurtry, *Lonesome Dove*
1987 Peter Taylor, *A Summons to Memphis*
1988 Toni Morrison, *Beloved*

1989 Anne Tyler, *Breathing Lessons*
1990 Oscar Hijuelos, *The Mambo Kings Play Songs of Love*
1991 John Updike, *Rabbit at Rest*

EURO FACTS

MAJOR EUROPEAN LITERARY PRIZES

France

The Goncourt Prize – *Prix Goncourt* – is the most prestigious French literary prize. Founded in 1903, it is awarded annually by the Académie Goncourt for the best French novel of the year. The prize money, however, is nominal at 50 F.

Notable winners of the Goncourt Prize include:

1919 Marcel Proust, *A l'ombre des jeunes filles en fleurs*
1933 André Malraux, *La condition humaine*
1948 Maurice Druon, *Les Grandes Familles*
1954 Simone de Beauvoir, *Les Mandarins*
1968 Bernard Clavel, *Les Fruits d'hiver*
1975 Emile Ajar, *La Vie devant soi*

Other notable French literary prizes include the *Prix Femina*, founded in 1904 by the magazine *Vie heureuse*, the forerunner of the magazine *Femina* and the *Prix Interallié*, founded in 1930.

Notable winners of the Femina Prize include:

1931 Antoine de Saint-Exupéry, *Vol de nuit*
1968 Marguerite Yourcenar, *L'OEuvre au noir*
1977 Régis Debray, *La neige brûle*

Germany

Founded in 1927, the Goethe Prize is the most eminent German annual literary prize.

Notable winners of the Goethe Prize include:

1928 Albert Schweitzer
1930 Sigmund Freud
1946 Herman Hesse
1949 Thomas Mann
1976 Ingmar Bergman

Italy

Major literary prizes in Italy include the Bagutta Prize (founded in 1927), the Bancarella Prize (founded in 1952), the Campiello Prize (founded in 1963) and the Antonio Feltrenelli International Prize.

United Kingdom

The Whitbread Literary Awards are given annually in six classes: novel, first novel, children's novel, poetry, biography and book of the year.

Notable winners of the Whitbread Literary Award for a novel include:

1974 Iris Murdoch, *The Sacred and Profane Love Machine*
1977 Beryl Bainbridge, *Injury Time*
1978 Paul Theroux, *Picture Palace*
1985 Peter Ackroyd, *Hawksmoor*
1986 Kazuo Ishiguro, *An Artist of the Floating World*
1988 Salman Rushdie, *The Satanic Verses*

VISUAL ARTS
PAINTING AND SCULPTURE

ART TECHNIQUES AND MEDIA

DRAWING

Drawing is the process of artistic depiction of objects or abstractions on a two-dimensional surface by linear (and sometimes tonal) means. The result may be a cartoon – a full size preparatory drawing for a painting or a work in another medium – or a finished work.

Drawing tools and media include:

chalk Black chalk (black stone) and red chalk (mineral) were used extensively from the 16th century for preparatory drawings. Chalk is also used for finished works.

charcoal charred wood, used extensively from the 16th century in preparatory drawings.

ink liquids for drawing or painting. Generally the colours are a suspension or are present in a dye. Sometimes, as with Indian ink or white ink, there may be opaque pigments in suspension. Ink may be applied with a pen or a brush for a preparatory drawing or a finished work.

pencil The graphite pencil – developed in the 17th century – replaced the silverpoint in preparing the surface to be painted on. Pencils are manufactured in varying degrees of softness and darkness. The graphite pencil is not only used to produce preliminary sketches but also for finished works.

silverpoint a metal point used mainly in the 15th century on prepared paper to make rough outlines that will be covered over by other media or to achieve a delicate effect through the tiny (and eventually tarnished) particles of silver left behind.

PAINTING

Painting is the visual and aesthetic expression of ideas and emotions primarily in two dimensions, using colour, line, shapes, texture and tones. The great variety of painting techniques reflects the range of surfaces that are painted on; for instance, tempera technique is used for painting on wood panels, and fresco technique for painting on walls.

Painting tools and media include:

airbrush technique a system of spraying colour with an airbrush, an implement that resembles a fountain pen. It has a small container near the nozzle. Air pressure is applied via a mechanical compressor and can be controlled to create fine, delicate lines or a wide sweep.

acrylic an opaque, water-soluble quick-drying paint. It can be applied with heavy knife-laid impasto (see below) or diluted with water to wash-like consistency. Acrylic paint is manufactured from pigment bound in a synthetic resin, normally acrylic or PVA. It is a 20th-century development, initially used in wall painting. The colour, unlike that of oil paint, does not alter with time.

fresco (Italian, 'fresh') a wall-painting technique in which powdered pigments are mixed in water and applied to a wet lime-plaster.

gouache a painting technique, similar to watercolour, in which the binding medium is glue. White pigment is added to give some opacity. Used by French painters since the 18th century, gouache is widely used in commercial illustration.

impasto the laying on of paint so thickly on a canvas that it protrudes from the surface.

oils the most widely used painting technique. Oil paint is based on a mixture of dry pigment and vegetable oil, commonly linseed, poppy or walnut oil. It is slow drying, so the artist is able to make revisions and build up layers of colour. The composition is built up in layers of thicker or thinner paint, and variety in brushwork can have significant visual effect.

pastels sticks of pigment made by mixing powdered pigment with gum or resin binder. Pastels give soft colours which retain their freshness.

pigments colours derived from earths, natural dyes and minerals or chemically synthesized. The earliest pigments, used by prehistoric man, included burnt wood, bone, chalk and earth colours. In addition to these, medieval painters used *verdigris* (copper resinate; green), *ultramarine* (lapis lazuli; blue), *white lead*, *azurite* (copper carbonate; blue), *madder* (red), *lead-tin yellow*, and *vermilion* (cinnabar; red). Later came *Prussian blue* (1705) and *Naples yellow*, but during the 19th century the range of colours expanded to include new chemical colours.

tempera a technique – used for painting on wood panels – based on a mixture of a water-based liquid with an oily or waxy medium. Traditionally egg white and egg yolk are used together with an oil such as linseed oil, but egg (which acts as a binder) may also be used with water alone. Its quick-drying properties and luminosity of colour account for the attraction of tempera.

watercolour painting a technique in which pigment is bound in a gum arabic medium and thinned with water for use. It was used as a paint in Egyptian painting, but most fully exploited by 18th- and 19th-century British landscape artists. Distinguished by its translucent quality, watercolour is extremely versatile. Some watercolours are *monochrome* – painted in only one colour.

SCULPTURE

Sculpture describes the processes of carving, engraving, modelling, casting or assembling so as to produce representations or abstractions of an artistic nature in relief, in intaglio, or in the round. The two main sculpture techniques are *carving* and *modelling*.

Carving The carved image is created by cutting unwanted material away from a block of hard material, usually stone or wood. *Stone carving* can be done from granite, limestone, sandstone, alabaster and a variety of marbles. Other materials that have been commonly carved for small-scale sculpture include ivory, amber and semi-precious stones.

Modelling Modelling involves manipulating some soft and yielding material such as wax, clay or plaster until the desired image is achieved. A three-dimensional shape is built up around an *armature* (framework) in metal or wood. Models are generally turned into a more lasting form, either by heating, as with clay, or by *casting* them in bronze or some other metal. The two principal techniques of casting are the *lost-wax process* and *sand casting*.

Assemblage Assemblage is the term used for all works of art constructed from everyday objects. It refers to works of three-dimensional and planar construction, including collage.

PRINTMAKING

Images were first printed from engraved wooden blocks onto parchment some 3000 to 4000 years ago. In the West, the development of printing coincided with the invention of movable type in the 15th century. Since then, a great variety of different printing techniques have evolved, including *relief techniques*, *intaglio techniques* (where the image is printed from lines cut into a metal plate) and *planographic techniques* (which are characterized by surface-printing methods). The principal techniques include:

aquatint an intaglio technique used to imitate the effect of watercolours. A copper plate is coated with powdered resin. Repeated immersions in an acid bath produce a tonal effect as small areas of copper between the particles of dust are exposed.

engraving an intaglio technique that originated from the carving of gems and armour. A zinc or copper plate is engraved with a sharp tool. The plate is then inked with a tacky ink and all the uncut surfaces are wiped clean – leaving the ink only in the recessed furrows.

etching an intaglio technique used during the 17th and 18th centuries and revived in the late 19th century by James Whistler (1834–1903). The design is etched onto a copper plate coated in a blackened acid-resistant material, using a steel needle, which exposes the metal. Before being inked and printed – using the same method as for engraving – the plate is immersed in acid, which bites into the exposed lines. To accentuate areas of light and shade, parts of the plate are protected with a varnish, and the plate is then re-immersed in the acid.

linocuts a relief technique using the floor-covering material linoleum, a cheap and easily carved surface. Although it does not allow great subtlety of detail, it was favoured by artists in the 1920s, including Picasso.

lithography a planographic technique depending upon the mutual incompatibility of water and grease. A design is drawn or painted onto a grained alloy plate – originally a thin limestone slab – using a greasy material such as crayon or lithographic ink. A solution of nitric acid and gum arabic is applied to the unmarked areas which repels the lithographic ink wiped onto the plate before printing. The drawn surfaces attract the ink and the moist surfaces repel it. The method was invented by the Bavarian Aloys Senefelder, in 1776.

mezzotint an intaglio technique used for reproductions after oil paintings in the 18th and 19th centuries. A serrated rocker is passed over the plate, leaving a varying number of indentations in which ink will collect and produce tonal effects. The tone engraving is then produced by scraping away for darker tones and burnishing for highlights.

screen printing a 20th-century planographic method where a screen of silk or gauze is tautly stretched over a wooden or metal frame. The design is applied to the screen in the form of a stencil so that areas not to be coloured are blocked out. Ink is wiped across the screen and forced through the mesh onto paper.

woodcuts a relief technique used as early as the 14th century and used extensively by Albrecht Dürer (1471–1528). The design is drawn onto wood and cut away – along the grain – leaving only the raised lines of the image ready to be inked. The woodcut is printed by laying paper onto the inked block.

wood engraving a relief technique – thought to have been invented by Thomas Bewick (1753–1828) – that differs from woodcutting in that normally a hard, fine-grained wood is cut into across the grain. The resulting image is usually much finer than a woodcut. The technique was commonly used for fine book illustrations during the 19th century.

PREHISTORIC ART

The world's most ancient works of art date from 30 000 BC. This is vastly earlier than the first written records and means that the greater part of art history is, in fact, prehistoric. It was during the prehistoric period that virtually all the major artistic media evolved, including drawing, painting, sculpture, ceramics and, arguably, architecture.

PALAEOLITHIC ART FROM 30 000 BC

Figurines Figurines shaped out of clay, bone, stone, wood and ivory have been found scattered over a wide area from Spain to Siberia. They depict both animals and humans. They depict, typified by the famous 'Venus' of Willendorf in Austria, portray women with exaggerated breasts and buttocks, and have been linked to a supposed fertility cult. Others, such as the female head from Brassempouy in France, are more elegant and naturalistic.

Cave painting Painting, engraving and relief on the walls of caves began later than figurine sculpture, and flourished soon after 16 000 BC. The hunters who created them were inspired by the animals around them, particularly by large mammals such as deer, horses, wild cattle, bison, woolly rhinoceroses and mammoths. The first examples rediscovered were at Chaffaud (Vienne), France, in 1834. The famous Lascaux cave paintings in France were discovered in 1940. Cave art has been found mostly in southern France and northeastern Spain (Altamira), although notable examples have also been discovered in Czechoslovakia, the Urals (USSR), India, Australia – the cave art at Mootwingie dates from c. 1500 BC – and the Sahara, where the earliest cave art dates from *post* 5400 BC.

NEOLITHIC ART

In the Neolithic (New Stone Age) period, farming and settled village life spread across Europe (c. 6500–4000 BC). This encouraged both the use of pottery and the development of architecture. Shaped and decorated vessels were produced almost everywhere, but the most inventive and prolific potters lived in eastern Europe. The Vinca culture produced thousands of fired-clay figurines, including some dramatically stylized heads found at Predionica in Serbia. Related cultures produced pots shaped like human figures, animals or even houses. Neolithic houses, tombs and temples have also produced many examples of prehistoric art. At the Maltese temple complex of Tarxien (c. 3000–2000 BC) there are animal friezes and the surviving half of a monumental sculpture depicting a monumentally corpulent diety.

BRONZE AND IRON AGE ART

During later European prehistory, despite advances in pottery and architecture, the most exciting artistic innovations arose from the development of metalwork. In the 2nd millennium BC in eastern Europe, early cast bronze weapons and jewellery were delicately engraved with curved-line designs. Similar decoration appears on Scandinavian metalwork: a remarkable ritual object found at Trundholm in Denmark consists of a cast bronze horse pulling an engraved gold-covered sun. Duirng the 1st millennium BC many more bronze figures were cast, notably in Scandinavia, central Europe and Sardinia. Engraving remained common, but the beating or embossing of metalwork grew in importance. Embossed friezes on *situlae* (buckets) from northern Italy and Yugoslavia illustrate religious processions. The early Celts decorated weapons, vessels and pieces of jewellery in such a fluid style that it is often impossible to separate the stylized Celtic heads and animals from the surrounding plant-like ornament.

THE ART OF THE ANCIENT NEAR EAST AND EGYPT

Early civilizations flourished along the great river valleys of the Nile in Egypt, and the Tigris and Euphrates from Anatolia (present-day Turkey), through Syria into Mesopotamia (present-day Iraq). The rivers linked these regions in an extensive trade network that also encompassed Persia (present-day Iran) to the east, but variations in climate, geography, natural resources and population resulted in corresponding variations in artistic traditions.

MESOPOTAMIAN ART 6000–3600 BC

Covering the Sumerian, Assyrian and Babylonian epochs, Mesopotamian art is represented by many styles, although most incorporate figures, animals (both real and mythical) and plants. It is now seen mainly in the sculptural works on palaces (e.g. Nineveh) and on tiles.

EGYPTIAN ART 3100–341 BC

Egyptian art is essentially a decorative tomb art, based on the notion of immortality; the deceased were recorded and equipped for the afterlife in writing (hieroglyphs), pictures and material wealth and goods.

GREEK AND ROMAN ART

The arts of Greece and Rome are characterized by a sense of proportion, harmony and balance. Since the Renaissance, Classical decoration, whether ornate or simple, has frequently provided architects with a fruitful source of ideas, and Classical imagery has enriched the work of poets, painters and sculptors. In general, Classical form has exerted a largely civilizing influence over the past two and a half millennia.

GREEK ART 2000–27 BC

Minoan and Mycenaean art (2000–1100 BC) consists mainly of sculptured engravings, decorated pottery and some frescos. The Archaic period (800–500 BC) saw the development of sculpture, especially human figures. This tendency was developed in the Classical period (500–323 BC), where the body was glorified and drapery carved to imitate movement. The Hellenistic period (323–27 BC) was characterized by greater emotional expression, and is notable for its portraits. Throughout the period pottery was decorated with figures and scenes from story and legend.

ROMAN ART 100 BC–AD 400

Roman art excelled in copying Greek sculpture and relief carving to a very high quality. Portrait busts were popular, and Roman painting was mainly executed in fresco in a naturalistic style (e.g. at Pompeii). Mosaic floors were also highly decorative.

The concentration on what has survived, and the elevation of some of it to the first rank of artistic excellence in modern eyes, have tended to obscure the fact that we now possess very little of what ancient Greeks and Romans might have considered to be artistically important. The Greeks and Romans themselves tended rather to appreciate highly wrought works in gold and silver. Since articles of precious metal were the first to be seized or melted down in times of war or hardship, such works have virtually all vanished, but contemporary accounts of shrines and individuals speak of great amounts of sculpture and vases made of gold and silver, and it was in these media that eminent craftsmen preferred to work.

ISLAMIC ART: 7TH–17TH CENTURY

Geographically Islamic art extends from Indonesia in the east to Morocco and Spain in the west. The word 'Islamic' reflects a culture and society united by Islam, but as artistic influences from Arabia (the birthplace of Islam) were minimal, Islam can in some ways also be seen as a catalyst for the development of existing Byzantine, Persian and later Indian styles that prevailed when the conquering Muslim armies arrived.

Originally based on superb Koranic calligraphy, it is a highly decorative art form which reaches its apotheosis in the miniature painting, the ceramic tile, and carpetmaking, in which floral and geometric motives reach a high peak of formal perfection. Although by no means absolute, traditionally there is a ban on the representation of living figures in a religious context, which accounts for the often semi-abstract nature of Islamic ornament and for the virtual absence of sculpture.

SOUTH ASIAN ART

India's earliest civilization flourished in the Indus Valley between 2300–1700 BC, centred on the cities of Harappa and Mohenjo-Daro. Its architecture was utilitarian, but some fine statues in sandstone and slate were produced. Little survives between the time of the Harappa civilization and that of the Mauryas (321–185 BC), during whose rule Persian and Greek influences are apparent, notably in architecture.

Essentially traditional and religious, Buddhist and Hindu works of art are symbols and manifestations of gods. One of the most distinctive Buddhist architectural forms is the *stupa* – an ornate burial mound. The Mauryas popularized man-made caves and initiated a revival in sculpture. Temples for both religions became increasingly ornate and complex. In the 7th century fresco painting and rock sculpture in India had reached a peak and by the 13th century erotic carvings had become popular.

CHINESE AND JAPANESE ART

China is the longest surviving civilization in the world, with an art history stretching back at least

4000 years. Because it was the most advanced country in eastern Asia, China influenced many of its neighbours, and later also the Islamic world and western Europe. The distinctiveness of Chinese art has been complemented by very high technical skills, and for many centuries ceramics, bronzes, jade carvings, silk and lacquer were produced to standards surpassing those of all other cultures.

The advent of Buddhism (1st century AD) encouraged religious art in China, in particular sculptures of Buddha. Landscape painting became popular under the Tang Dynasty (618–907) and Chinese pottery reached perfection under the Sung (960–1279), becoming much more elaborate under the Ming (1368–1644). Japan was heavily influenced by Chinese art, but later indigenous Japanese art forms include *netsuke* (miniature sculptures), painted screens, and *Ukiyo-e* woodblock colour prints.

MAJOR ARTISTS

Gu Kaizhi (Ku K'ai-Chih; c. 345–405), a leading Chinese painter, considered to be the founder of landscape painting.

Hui Zong (1082–1135), an emperor and major painter of the flower-and-bird category of painting.

Huang Gong-Wang (1269–1354), major Chinese landscape painter of his time, celebrated for the introduction of dry ink and slanting brush technique.

Suzuki Harunobu (1725–70), Japanese colour-print artist.

Toshusai Sharaku (d. 1801), Japanese *Ukiyo-e* printer. Unpopular in his day, but his work is now highly prized in the West.

Kitagawa Utamaro (1753–1806), Japanese colour-print artist (*Ukiyo-e* school): *Insects* (1788).

Katsushika Hokusai (1760–1849), Japanese painter, draughtsman and wood engraver (a major *Ukiyo-e* print designer): *Mangwa* (1814–78) and *Views of Mt Fuji.*

Ando Hiroshige (1797–1858), Japanese painter and colour-print artist: *Fifty-three Stages of the Tokaido Highway* (1833).

AUSTRALASIAN AND OCEANIC ART

Pottery and metalwork were unknown in Australasia and Oceania before the arrival of Europeans. However, other art forms were flourishing. Cave paintings – both representational and abstract – and tree bark paintings have been found in Australia. Melanesia boasts highly decorated tools and utensils, bark drawings and 'Uli' statues – statues with huge heads, small bodies, and tiny legs. The art of bark painting, plaiting, weaving, tattooing, wood carving and personal adornment reached a degree of perfection in Polynesia, particularly New Zealand and Samoa. The Easter Island Heads are remarkable statue heads carved from soft volcanic stone, some of them standing 12 m (40 ft) high and weighing up to 50 tonnes (tons). They were erected between AD 1000 and 1600, but their meaning is still not fully understood.

NATIVE AMERICAN ART

The greatest architecture and stone sculpture of the Americas is divided between the ancient civilizations of Mesoamerica and the Central Andes. Before and after the arrival of Europeans, tribal North America excelled in wooden sculpture, textiles and pottery.

The Aztec altars were covered with detailed sculpted stone images of gods and animals. Other notable Aztec art includes worked gold, cut stone, featherwork and intricate weaving. The Olmec and Maya were also sculptors; the latter inscribed their *stelae* (stone columns) with writing and animal motifs, and adorned their temples with carved friezes.

AFRICAN ART

The finest African art, excluding the products of Egypt and the Muslim north, is largely concentrated in the rain forests and savannah woodland of central western Africa. Far to the north and south lies the ancient rock art of the Sahara and southern Africa.

The earliest known sculptural tradition of sub-Saharan Africa emerged c. 500 BC in northern Nigeria. Its products are grouped together as the 'Nok culture', and consist of naturalistic terracottas of animals and more stylized terracottas of human figures; the figures often have simplified bodies, disproportionately large heads and distinctive eyes. It may have influenced the realistic, if idealized, terracottas and bronzes of the Ife Kingdom (11th–16th century). Superb metalworkers, the Benin Kingdom (1500–1700) produced plaques decorated in high and low relief with scenes of warriors, chiefs and Portuguese traders.

African art is probably best known for its carved wooden masks and sculptures. Both masks and figures tend to face forward, are symmetrically arranged around a vertical axis, and are carved from a single piece of wood. Masks often have beads, feathers, hair or fibre as added decoration.

EARLY MEDIEVAL ART

The period between the Classical Age and the Renaissance has sometimes been described dismissively as the 'Dark Ages'. This is both inaccurate and misleading. These centuries formed an essential artistic bridgehead, when new approaches to pictorial form were worked out and deeper spiritual values attached to works of art. The major patron became the Christian Church, and most of the greatest monuments are related to churches and monasteries.

BYZANTINE ART

At first an admixture of Hellenic, Roman, Middle Eastern and Oriental styles, Byzantine art dates from and has its first centre in the establishment of Constantinople as capital of the Roman Empire in the East. The First Golden Age was in the 6th century, when Hagia Sophia (St Sophia) was built in the city. The Second Golden Age occurred between 1051 and 1185, when Western Europe was influenced by the severe, spiritually uplifted style of the Byzantines. These two Ages are dominated by the use of mosaic work, but by the Third Golden Age (1261–1450) this expensive medium was being replaced by fresco painting.

ROMANESQUE ART

A widespread western European style in the 11th and 12th centuries was mainly architectural, distinguished by the use of rounded arches. The sculpture is mainly church work intended to inspire awe of the divine power by depicting scenes of heaven and hell, demons and angels, and the omnipotent deity. Illuminated manuscripts of high quality include the Winchester Bible.

GOTHIC ART

Gothic painting and sculpture flourished alongside architecture. The Romanesque world of fantastic beasts is largely left behind and a new emphasis is placed on nature and humanity's place within its hierarchy. This is shown in a more human relationship between God and the individual, and in the greater expression of human emotions.

Gothic sculpture is narrative and realistic, particularly the friezes. In painting the style evolved more slowly and is seen in manuscript illumination and frescos.

INTERNATIONAL GOTHIC

A later mixture of styles of painting and sculpture in Europe due to the movements of notable peripatetic artists and the increase in trade, travel and court rivalry. The main influences were northern France, the Netherlands and Italy, and its main features are rich and decorative colouring and detail, and flowing line.

MAJOR ARTISTS

Giovanni Pisano (active 1265–1314), Pisan sculptor: the pulpit in S Andrea, Pistoia (1301), particularly the panel of the *Massacre of the Innocents*.

Giotto di Bondone (c. 1267–1337), influential Florentine painter, who introduced a new naturalism: *Ognissanti Madonna* (c. 1310–15).

Cimabue (active 1272–1302), Florentine painter who introduced more realistic painting: *The S. Trinità Madonna*.

Duccio di Buoninsegna (active 1278–1319), Sienese painter; influential in his introduction of two-dimensional decorative surface art in Siena.

Ambrogio and Pietro Lorenzetti (active c. 1319–48), Sienese sculptors and painters: Ambrogio's early realistic landscapes and Pietro's *Descent from the Cross*.

Gentile da Fabriano (c. 1370–1427), Italian painter of the International Gothic style: *Adoration of the Magi* (1423).

Lorenzo Monaco (c. 1370/2–1422/5), Sienese International Gothic painter and miniaturist: *Adoration* (c. 1424).

Claus Sluter (active c. 1380–d. 1405/6), Flemish International Gothic sculptor: monumental figures at Chartreuse de Champmol, Dijon (1390s–1403).

Antonio Pisanello (c. 1395–1455/6), Veronese painter: *St George and the Princess* and *Vision of St Eustace* (1435–38).

Limbourg Brothers (Paul, Jean, Herman; d. c. 1416), Franco-Flemish manuscript illuminators: *Très Riches Heures*.

THE EARLY RENAISSANCE

The term *renaissance* ('rebirth') was first coined in the 19th century to describe a period of intellectual and artistic renewal that lasted from about 1350 to about 1550. The dominant theme of this period is the revival of interest in classical literature and art by 14th- and 15th-century humanists and the rediscovery by artists of their cultural past. Florence was the first centre of such rediscovery, with Padua, Venice and finally Rome rivalling Florence in the pursuit of antiquarian learning and artistic excellence. After 1500, the movement also spread to northern Europe.

Architecture, painting and sculpture, deriving from Greek and Roman models and using classical motifs, moved into unparalleled prominence. Advances were made in the realistic depiction of figures. Other artistic inventions included perspective and painting with oil. Religious art continued into the 15th century, but painters were also able to decorate private palaces with secular narratives of historical or mythological subjects.

MAJOR ARTISTS

Lorenzo Ghiberti (1378–1455), Florentine sculptor and goldsmith: bronze doors for the Florence Baptistery, the second set, so-called 'Gates of Paradise', includes highly sophisticated representations of space and form.

Donatello (c. 1386–1466), highly influential Florentine sculptor: equestrian statue of *Gattemalata* (1443–47) and the high altar for the church of St Anthony.

Paolo Uccello (c. 1397–1475), Florentine painter: fresco *Deluge* and the panels depicting the *Rout of Romano*, which experiment with perspectives.

Fra Angelico (c. 1399–1455), Florentine religious painter: cycle of frescos in San Marco, Florence.

Masaccio (1401–c. 1428), influential Florentine painter: *Trinity* fresco (1428), in Santa Maria Novella, Florence, and the fresco paintings in the Brancacci Chapel, Florence (c. 1425–28).

Fra Filippo Lippi (c. 1406–69), Florentine painter: fresco paintings of the lives of St Stephen and St John the Baptist, Prato Cathedral (1452–65).

Piero della Francesca (c. 1420–92), Italian painter: *The Flagellation of Christ* (c. 1456) and the cycle *The Story of the True Cross* at the Church of San Francesco, Arezzo (1452–66).

Giovanni Bellini (c. 1430–1516), member of a notable artistic Venetian family: the altarpieces of the Frari (1488), San Zaccaria (c. 1505) and other mythological scenes.

Andrea Mantegna (c. 1431–1506), northern Italian painter, celebrated for his perfectionist work on perspective.

Sandro Botticelli (c. 1445–1510), Florentine painter: *Primavera* ('Spring'; 1477–78) and *Birth of Venus*.

Leonardo da Vinci (1452–1519), one of the greatest Italian painters and sculptors (also architect, musician, engineer, and scientist): the unfinished *Adoration of the Magi*, *Madonna of the Rocks* (two versions: 1483–c. 1486 and 1483–1508), *The Last Supper* (c. 1495–98), and *Mona Lisa* (c. 1503).

EARLY NETHERLANDISH AND GERMAN ART

The Netherlandish and German art of the period from around 1400 to 1570 is often described under the blanket term 'Northern Renaissance'. While this label recognizes the originality and vitality of the northern contemporaries of the Italian Renaissance masters, it obscures the very important divide between the 15th and 16th centuries. In the earlier century the rediscoveries of the Italians aroused little interest north of the Alps, but in the 16th century Netherlandish and German artists became increasingly fascinated by classical antiquity.

As in Italy, Flemish and German painters moved towards more realistic figure work, and their experimentations led to the development of portraiture, nudes, meticulously accurate details, distant landscapes, spatial illusionism and careful depiction of light and shadow. Oil painting was introduced and woodcuts and engravings achieved a new depth of expression.

MAJOR ARTISTS

Rogier van der Weyden (c. 1399–1464), influential Flemish painter: *The Deposition* (pre-1443) and the altarpiece of the *Last Judgement* (c. 1450).

Jan van Eyck (active 1422–41), Flemish painter, celebrated for the realistic detail of his portraits: the Ghent altarpiece (1432; in collaboration with his brother Hubert; d. 1426).

Petrus Christus (active 1444–72/3), Flemish painter: noted for the use of geometric perspective in *Lamentation* (c. 1448) and *St Eligius and Two Lovers* (1449).

Dierick Bouts (active 1448–75), early Flemish painter, distinguished by his calm, reflective and elongated figures.

Quentin Massys (1464/5–1530), Flemish painter: portrait of *Erasmus* (1517).

Hugo van der Goes (active 1467–82), Flemish painter: Portinari altarpiece (c. 1474–76) and Monforte altarpiece (c. 1472).

Martin Schongauer (active 1469–91), early German engraver: celebrated for his subtle description of light and texture.

Albrecht Dürer (1471–1528), German painter, engraver and theoretician: *Knight, Death and the Devil, St Jerome in his Cell*, and *Melancholia*.

Joachim Patenir (c. 1480–1524), Flemish landscape and religious painter: *Flight into Egypt*.

Albrecht Altdorfer (c. 1480–1538), German painter and engraver, distinguished by his development of the landscape genre: *The Battle of Alexander and Darius on the Issus* (1529).

Hieronymous Bosch (active 1480/1–1516), Flemish painter, celebrated for his fantastic and grotesque imagery: *Garden of Earthly Delights* (c. 1505–10).

Hans Baldung Grien (1484/5–1545), German religious and mythological painter: *Death and the Maiden*.

Lucas van Leyden (c. 1489–1533), Dutch painter and engraver of historical and domestic scenes: *Last Judgement* (1526–27).

Hans the Younger Holbein (1497/8–1543), German portrait and religious painter: *Dead Christ* (1521) and *Erasmus* (1517).

Mathias Grünewald (c. 1470–1528), German religious painter: crucifixion of Christ on the Isenheim altarpiece.

Pieter the Elder Bruegel (c. 1525–69), foremost of a Flemish family of painters: *Peasant Wedding Dance* (1566), series of landscape paintings depicting the months of the year such as *Hunters in the Snow* (1565) and the proverb series including *The Blind Leading the Blind* (1568).

THE HIGH RENAISSANCE AND MANNERISM

The focus of artistic activity in Italy shifted during the early 16th century from Florence to Rome. One of the most concentrated groups of artistic genius ever known was gathered in the papal city. The role of the artist changed even more dramatically than in the previous century, and a number of academies were established, confirming the professional status of the artist. At the same time, the artistic innovations of the Italian Renaissance began to spread to northern Europe.

Artistic innovation later led to the superficial elegance of Mannerism. A style that became popular all over Catholic Europe, Mannerism displayed exaggerated sophistication and virtuosity – sometimes combined with a heightened emotionalism and religiosity. However, the Counter-Reformation brought in restrictions on both subject matter and treatment in religious art, and by the end of the 16th century Mannerism had lost much of its vigour.

MAJOR ARTISTS

Michelangelo Buonarroti (1475–1564), foremost Italian sculptor, painter, and architect: the sculpture *David* (1501–4), the ceiling of the Sistine Chapel (1508–12), statues *Moses and the Slaves* (1513–16) and the fresco *Last Judgement* (Sistine Chapel; 1536–41).

Raphael (1483–1520), highly successful Italian painter: wall paintings in the Vatican, including *School of Athens, Triumph of Religion, The Miracle of Bolsena* and *The Deliverance of St Peter*.

Fra Bartolommeo (c. 1474–c. 1517), Florentine High Renaissance painter: *Last Judgement* in the Santa Maria Nuova.

Giorgione (c. 1476/8–1510), Venetian painter who introduced pastoral subjects to paintings.

Andrea del Sarto (1486–1530), Italian High Renaissance painter of frescos and altarpieces: *The Madonna of the Harpies* (1517).

Titian (Tiziano Vecellio; c. 1487/90–1576), Venetian Renaissance painter, notable for his dream-like pastorals, colour, and free handling of paint: *Venus and Adonis* (1554) and the altarpiece of the *Assumption of the Virgin* (Church of Santa Maria Gloriosa dei Frari, Venice).

Jacopo da Pontormo (1494–1556), Florentine painter, one of the creators of Mannerism: *Deposition* (c. 1526).

Giulio Romano (1492–1546), Italian painter, architect, decorator and one of the founders of Mannerism: the decoration of the Palazzo del Tè.

Antonio Correggio (c. 1495–1534), influential Italian High Renaissance painter: *Jupiter and Io*.

Parmigianino (1503–40), Italian Mannerist painter and etcher: *The Vision of St Jerome* and *Madonna of the Long Neck* (c. 1535).

Agnolo Bronzino (1507–72), Florentine Mannerist painter, well known for his portraits: *Venus, Cupid, Folly* and *Time*.

Jacopo Tintoretto (1518–94), Venetian Mannerist painter: *Last Judgement*.

Paolo Veronese (1528–88), Venetian painter: frescos in the Villa Maser near Treviso, a series of religious feast scenes, including *Marriage at Cana* (1562) and *The Feast in the House of Levi* (1573).

Jean Goujon (active 1540–62), French Mannerist sculptor and architect: *Fountain of the Innocents* (1547–49) and the *Tribune of Caryatids*.

Giambologna (1529–1608), Flemish Mannerist sculptor: the influential sculpture *The Rape of the Sabines* (1579–83).

El Greco (Domenikos Theotocopoulos; 1541–1614), Greek Mannerist painter and sculptor (working in Spain): *The Burial of Count Orgaz* (1586) and *Christ Stripped of his Garments* (1577–79).

THE BAROQUE AND CLASSICISM

Classicism and the Baroque were the two dominant trends in the visual arts of the 17th century, particularly in Catholic countries and most importantly in Italy and France. Although frequently divergent and opposed, they both originated in the reaction in Italy against the aridity of Late Mannerism. A return to the naturalism, harmonious equilibrium and compositional coherence of the High Renaissance was combined with a new physical realism, emotional immediacy and dynamic vigour.

The Baroque style combined the dramatic effects of energetic movement, vivid colour and decorative detail with expressive originality and freedom. Classicism deployed more restrained qualities of directness and precision to enliven traditional ideas of balance and decorum.

MAJOR ARTISTS

Annibale Carracci (1560–1609), member of a notable family of Italian painters: decoration of the gallery ceiling in the Farnese Palace, Rome.

Michelangelo Merisis da Caravaggio (1573–1610), early Italian Baroque painter notable for the dramatic use of light and shade: *The Beheading of St John the Baptist*.

Guido Reni (1575–1642), Italian Classical painter: ceiling fresco *Aurora* (1613).

Peter Paul Rubens (1577–1640), foremost Flemish painter, celebrated for the epic grandeur of his work: *The Raising of the Cross* (1610–11) and *Descent from the Cross* (1611–14; Antwerp Cathedral).

Domenichino (1581–1641), Bolognese painter, noted for his landscapes.

Nicolas Poussin (1594–1665), French Classical painter, notable for the mathematical precision of his landscapes: *Landscape with Diogenes*.

Pietro da Cortona (1596–1669), Italian Baroque painter: *Allegory of Divine Providence and Barberini Power* (1633–39), a ceiling fresco.

Gianlorenzo Bernini (1598–1680), Italian High Baroque sculptor and painter: the sculptures *Apollo and Daphne* (1625) and *Ecstasy of Saint Theresa* (1645–52).

Anthony van Dyck (1599–1641), Flemish painter and etcher, known for his elegant portraits.

Diego Velásquez (1599–1660), Spanish painter: *Las Meninas* (1656), *Pope Innocent X* (1650), and *The Surrender of Breda* (1634–35).

Claude Lorraine (1600–82), French Classical landscape painter, notable for his rendering of light and atmosphere in his paintings.

Salvator Rosa (1615–73), Italian Baroque painter and etcher noted for his tempestuous landscapes.

THE DUTCH SCHOOL

In the 17th century a sudden flowering of the art of painting in the Netherlands coincided with the overthrow of Spanish rule and Dutch mercantile success throughout the world. The stubborn tenacity that enabled them to triumph over apparently superior forces at home and abroad was reflected in the solid sobriety with which the Dutch viewed their surroundings. Dutch artists concentrated on the types of painting in which they had long specialized – still life, genre (scenes of everyday life), landscape and portraiture.

MAJOR ARTISTS

Frans Hals (1580/85–1666), genre and portrait painter: *The Merry Drinker*, *The Laughing Cavalier*, *The Governors of the Almshouse*, and *Lady Regents of the Almshouse*.

Hendrick Terbrugghen (1588–1629), painter specializing in genre painting: *The Flute Player* (1621).

Gerard von Honthorst (1590–1656), painter specializing in portraits and genre painting: *The Merry Fiddler* (1623).

Pieter Saenredam (1597–1665), painter of church interiors: *View in the Nieuwe Kert at Haarlem* (1652).

Adriaen Brouwer (1605/6–38), painter specializing in scenes of peasant revelry: *The Smokers* (c. 1637).

Rembrandt van Rijn (1606–69), painter, etcher and draughtsman, particularly celebrated for his portraits: *The Anatomy Lesson* (1632), *The Night Watch* (1642), and his series of self-portraits.

Gerard Terborch (1617–81), portrait and genre painter of genteel interiors: *Parental Admonition* (c. 1654/55).

Willem Kalf (1619–93), still-life painter: *Still Life with a Nautilus Cup* (1642–46).

Aelbert Cuyp (1620–91), landscape painter, noted for his views of rivers and towns in evening and morning light: *View of the Dordrecht*.

Jan Steen (1626–79), prolific genre painter, notable for his scenes of merry-making: *St Nicholas' Feast*.

Jacob van Ruisdael (1628/9–82), landscape painter and etcher, distinguished by his dramatic scenes: *Jewish Cemetery* (c. 1660).

Pieter de Hooch (1629–84), genre painter celebrated for his use of light in garden and courtyard scenes: *Courtyard in Delft* (1658).

Jan Vermeer (1632–75), genre painter noted for his domestic interiors with subtle lighting and geometrical shapes: *Allegory of the Faith* (1669–70), *Allegory of Painting* (c. 1665), and *Girl with a Pearl Earring*.

Meindert Hobbema (1638–1709), landscape painter: *Avenue at Middelharnis* (1689).

ROCOCO AND NEOCLASSICISM

The synthesis in later 17th-century Italy of Classicist idealization and Baroque vigour was taken up in France and spread throughout Europe as the accepted courtly 'Grand Manner'. It was soon diluted by the 18th-century desire for the informal and undemanding, which found its artistic expression in the style known as Rococo. For perhaps the first time the prime function of art was perceived as decorative rather than illustrative or didactic.

Neither the attitude nor the style were fully accepted in England, where Baroque licence had already been challenged early in the new century by the more 'rational' concept of Palladianism. By the 1750s a reaction to the still freer and more exotic forms of the Rococo appeared not only in England but in France, cradle of the style. Archaeological discoveries in Italy and Greece prompted a re-examination of the origins of European civilization. French intellectualism developed this into international Neoclassicism.

MAJOR ARTISTS

Antoine Watteau (1684–1721), French Rococo painter who introduced romantic figures in a park or garden setting to the Rococo style: *Embarkation for Cythera* (1717).

Giambattista Tiepolo (1696–1770), Italian Rococo painter: noted for the ceiling paintings and frescos in the Labia Palace and Palacio Real, Madrid.

Antonio Canaletto (1697–1768), Venetian view painter of the period, noted for the topographical quality in his art.

François Boucher (1703–70), French Rococo painter: *The Rising of the Sun, The Setting of the Sun* (1753), and *Reclining Girl* (1751), a famous female nude.

Francesco Guardi (1712–93), member of a family of notable Venetian painters; celebrated for his view paintings and architectural scenes.

Thomas Gainsborough (1727–88), English portrait and landscape painter: *Mr and Mrs Andrews* (c.1750), *The Blue Boy* (c. 1770), and *The Harvest Wagon* (c. 1770).

Jean-Honoré Fragonard (1732–1806), French Rococo painter: four *Progress of Love* paintings (1771–73) and *The Swing* (1769).

Jacques-Louis David (1748–1825), French Neoclassical painter: *Death of Marat* (1793), *View of the Luxembourg Gardens* (1794), and *Mme de Verninac* (1799).

Antonio Canova (1757–1822), Italian Neoclassical sculptor: *Daedalus and Icarus* (1779).

ROMANTICISM

Romanticism was a movement in art that emerged in the late 18th century, and that flourished until the middle of the 19th. The movement was a reaction both against the aesthetic and ethical values of Classical and Neoclassical art, and against the ugliness and materialism of the Industrial Revolution. The influence of Romantic writers such as Rousseau, Schiller, Goethe, Scott and Byron was particularly important in providing both subject matter and a philosophy for the Romantic painters. The values of the wider Romantic movement (see p. 357) are central to an understanding of the visual art of the period. Indeed it is the *content* of Romantic painting and the attitude of the artists themselves that give the movement coherence, as in terms of style and technique there are enormous variations.

MAJOR ARTISTS

John Constable (1776–1837), English landscape painter: *The Hay Wain* (1821).

Eugène Delacroix (1798–1863), French painter: *The Massacre at Chios* (1823) and *The Death of Sardanapalus* (1827).

Caspar David Friedrich (1774–1840), German landscape painter, noted for his evocative scenes of mountain peaks and moonlit shores.

Henry Fuseli (1741–1825), Swiss painter living in England, notable for his explorations of the darker side of human nature: *The Nightmare* (1782).

Théodore Géricault (1791–1824), French painter and one of the founders of Romanticism: *Charging Chasseur* and *The Raft of the Medusa* (1819).

Francisco de Goya y Lucientes (1746–1848), Spanish painter and etcher: *Maja Nude* and *Maja Clothed* (1797–1800), *The Third of May* (1814), and *The Disasters of War* (etchings, 1810–20).

John Martin (1789–1854), British painter and engraver, noted for his sensationalist apocalyptic scenes: *The Deluge* (1834).

Samuel Palmer (1805–81), English painter and etcher of pastoral scenes.

Joseph Mallord William Turner (1775–1851), foremost English landscape painter: *The Fighting Téméraire* (1838), and *Rain, Steam and Speed* (1844).

REALISM

Realism was a movement that flourished between 1840 and 1880, originating in France, and soon spreading throughout Europe and to America. The Realists reacted against the subjectivity, individualism and historical obsessions of many of the Romantics, adopting instead a naturalistic style of art based on truth to nature. The grand, heroic subject matter of the Romantic movement was replaced by simple views of everyday life, and Romantic emotionalism was abandoned in favour of detached, objective observation. The term 'Realism' applies to both style and subject matter. Usually Realists avoided the vivid, dramatic brushstrokes favoured by Romantic artists, preferring to make their paintings distinct and precise, with straight forward subjects.

THE BARBIZON SCHOOL

During the 1840s, the village of Barbizon, on the outskirts of the Fontainebleau forest, became the centre for a group of French landscape painters. They began the direct study of nature, aiming to create a naturalistic depiction of landscape without the restrictions of academic conventions. Their work encouraged the emergence of Impressionism.

THE PRE-RAPHAELITE BROTHERHOOD

A brotherhood of seven London artists (1848–56) formed to make a return to the style of Italian painting before Raphael (hence the name) as a protest against the frivolity of the prevailing English School of the day. The founders and most important exponents of the movement were William Holman Hunt, John Everett Millais and Dante Gabriel Rossetti. Their subject matter was often drawn from religion and legend, and their style minutely detailed.

THE ARTS AND CRAFTS MOVEMENT c. 1870–1900

Based on the revival of interest in the medieval craft system, and led by William Morris (1834–96), the aims of the movement were to fuse the functional and the decorative, and to restore the worth of handmade crafts in the face of the growing mass-produced wares of the late 19th century.

MAJOR ARTISTS

Eugène Boudin (1824–98), French painter of seascapes and beach scenes: *Women on the Beach at Trouville* (1872).

Ford Madox Brown (1821–93), English painter, whose style was similar to that of the Pre-Raphaelites: his social beliefs were reflected in his famous painting *Work* (1852–65).

Edward Burne-Jones (1833–98), English Symbolist painter, illustrator, and designer. Strongly influenced by the Pre-Raphaelites, he is noted for his ethereal aesthetic and dreamlike style.

Camille Corot (1796–1875), French landscape and figure painter, an important precursor of the Impressionists: *The Studio* (1870), *Ponte de Mantes* (1870), and *Sens Cathedral* (1874).

Gustav Courbet (1819–77), French painter and foremost Realist artist: *The Peasants of Flagey, The Stonebreakers* and *A Burial at Ornans.*

Charles-François Daubigny (1817–78), French landscape painter of the Barbizon school.

Honoré Daumier (1808–79), French caricaturist, whose works contain bitter satires on political and social subjects.

Thomas Eakins (1844–1916), American Realist painter: *The Biglen Brothers Racing* (1873) and *The Writing Master* (1881).

William Powell Frith (1819–1909), English narrative painter: *Derby Day* (1858) and *The Railway Station* (1862).

Winslow Homer (1836–1910), American landscape, seascape and genre painter: *The Northeaster, Cannon Rock* (1895), and *Saguenay River* (1899).

William Holman Hunt (1827–1910), English painter and one of the founders of the Pre-Raphaelite Brotherhood, noted for the detail and symbolism in his paintings: *The Awakening Conscience* (1853–54).

Sir John Everett Millais (1829–96), English portrait, genre, landscape and history painter and co-founder of the Pre-Raphaelite Brotherhood. Best-known for *Bubbles* (1886), which was subsequently used in a soap advertisement.

Jean-François Millet (1814–75), French Realist painter, celebrated for his dignified depiction of French peasants: *The Gleaners* (1857) and *The Angelus* (1859).

Dante Gabriel Rossetti (1828–82), English painter, poet and co-founder of the Pre-Raphaelite Brotherhood. He later worked in watercolours before returning to oils.

Théodore Rousseau (1812–67), French landscape painter of the Barbizon School: *Descent of the Cattle* (1835).

IMPRESSIONISM AND NEOIMPRESSIONISM

Although often regarded as the first of the modern movements, Impressionism was neither a school nor a movement with a clearly defined programme. Instead it is better regarded as an ill-defined association of artists who joined together for the purpose of mounting independent group exhibitions, rather than compromise their art in order to be included in the Paris Salon, the official state-sponsored exhibition. In all there were eight Impressionist exhibitions, held from 1874 to 1886. While they had no stated aims or manifesto their work shared some techniques and certain subjects. Their approach was naturalistic, and their two main subjects were landscape and modern (often city) life. Often painted in the open air, their paintings show a concern with capturing the fleeting moment, particularly the effects of light, which they attempted to capture with a free handling of paint.

NEOIMPRESSIONISM

At the final Impressionist exhibition, Seurat, Signac and Pissarro all showed canvases using the latest *divisionist* (or *pointillist*) techniques. This involved the use of pure colours applied in such small patches (often dots) that they appeared to fuse to form an intermediary tone when viewed from an appropriate distance. Hence grass might be composed of touches

of blue alongside areas of yellow. These ideas were not new, but had been used in a much less systematic way by the Impressionist painters. However, the static quality of works such as Seurat's *Bathers at Asnières* (1884) and its large format marked a departure from the aims of orthodox Impressionism.

MAJOR ARTISTS

Mary Cassatt (1844–1926), American Impressionist painter, noted for her paintings of mothers and children and her graphics based on Japanese prints.

Edgar Degas (1834–1917), French Impressionist painter and sculptor, whose favourite subjects were dancers and race horses: the bronze *The Little Dancer of Fourteen* (1880–81), *The Rehearsal* (1882), and *Two Laundresses* (1882).

Edouard Manet (1832–83), French painter, considered the father of modern painting: *Déjeuner sur l'herbe* ('Picnic on the grass'; 1863) and *Olympia* (1863).

Claude Monet (1840–1926), French Impressionist painter, particularly of landscapes: *Women in the Garden* (1867) and the series *Waterlilies* (1899–1926).

Berthe Morisot (1841–95), French painter notable for her paintings of women and children.

Camille Pissarro (1831–1903), French Impressionist painter, briefly flirted with pointillism during the 1880s.

Auguste Renoir (1841–1919), French Impressionist painter: *Umbrellas* (1883), *The Bathers* (1884–87), and *The Theatre Box* (1874).

Georges Seurat (1859–91), French painter, founder and leading exponent of Neoimpressionism: *Bathers at Asnières* (1884).

Paul Signac (1863–1935), French Neoimpressionist painter, theoretician of Neoimpressionism.

Alfred Sisley (1839–99), French Impressionist painter born of English parents, well known for his landscapes.

James McNeill Whistler (1834–1903), American painter and graphic artist, who worked in England. Briefly with the Realist school, his later, more Impressionist work became abstract: *Nocturne* series.

POST-IMPRESSIONISM AND FAUVISM

Just as the Impressionists reacted against the established art of their day, a succession of artists later reacted against Impressionism itself. The Post-Impressionists, as they became known, were active mainly in France between about 1880 and 1905. They included artists who painted in a wide variety of styles but who shared a desire to go beyond pure naturalism and to give more emphasis to colour, emotions and imagination. From these individuals the major art movements of the 20th century emerged.

Fauvism (c. 1905–7) was a short-lived but highly influential French movement of artists surrounding Matisse. It is summarized by the daring and spontaneous handling of paint in bold, brilliant, sometimes non-representational colour, in a subjective, joyous response to the visual world.

MAJOR ARTISTS

Pierre Bonnard (1864–1947), French painter, noted for his middle-class interiors and nudes.

Paul Cézanne (1839–1906), French painter, briefly painted with the Impressionist group. Many of his works had a crucial influence on the Cubists.

André Derain (1880–1954), French painter, one of the founders of Fauvism.

Kees van Dongen (1877–1968), Dutch painter. His work developed along Fauvist lines, but his later works were principally of Parisian society.

Raoul Dufy (1877–1953), French painter. Briefly connected with the Fauves but celebrated for his colourful scenes of racecourses and the seaside.

Paul Gauguin (1848–1903), French painter, sculptor and printmaker, celebrated for his brightly coloured, mystical paintings of Brittany and the South Seas: *Where Do We Come From? What Are We? Where Are We Going?* (1897).

Vincent van Gogh (1853–90), Dutch painter, a major influence on 20th-century art: *The Potato Eaters* (1885), *Les Souliers, A Cornfield of Cypresses, The Yellow Chair* and *Sunflowers* (1888–89).

Albert Marquet (1875–1947), French painter, noted for his bright Fauve colours in his early paintings.

Henri Matisse (1869–1954), influential 20th-century artist and founder of Fauvism: *Dance* and *Music* (1909–10), and the series of *Odalisques*.

George Rouault (1871–1958), French painter, noted for his expressionist religious work.

Henri Rousseau (1844–1910), French painter, noted for his naïve, stylized jungle paintings (1900–10).

Walter Sickert (1860–1942), English painter who concentrated on paintings of lower-class London life: *Ennui* (c. 1913).

Henri de Toulouse-Lautrec (1864–1901), French painter and draughtsman, famous for his lithographs and posters of dance halls and cabarets: *Le Moulin Rouge* (1891).

Maurice de Vlaminck (1876–1958), French Fauvist painter: *The Bridge at Chatou* (1906).

Edouard Vuillard (1868–1940), French painter, noted for his domestic paintings: *Mother and Sister of the Artist* (c. 1893).

SYMBOLISM, SECESSION AND EXPRESSIONISM

The Symbolist movement emerged in the 1880s as a reaction against the naturalist movement (the idea that art was an imitation of nature) and against modern industrialism and materialistic values. The Symbolists sought to escape into the past or into the world of fantasy, including dreams. They believed that art existed alongside, not in direct relation to, the real world, and that it had its own rules. Symbolism foreshadowed Surrealism.

Anti-naturalism was also shared by many of the German and Austrian Secessions of the 1890s – breakaway groups who revolted against the academicism of conventional painting. Similarly, a diverse group of later artists, known as the Expressionists, wished to emphasize – often through unnaturalistic distortion – the importance of emotion and the artist's inner vision. A group of German Expressionist artists, known as *Die Brücke* ('The Bridge'), aimed to integrate art and life by using art as a means of communication. Though to some extent the German equivalent of Fauvism, their work was

deliberately rougher and cruder, with broken, unnaturalistic colours and heavily expressive, stylized forms. Another independent German Expressionist group was *Der Blaue Reiter* ('The Blue Rider'). Rather than promoting one particular tendency, its aim was for each artist to achieve an individual style. They did, however, share a use of bold colours and a tendency towards abstraction.

MAJOR ARTISTS

Aubrey Beardsley (1872–98), English Symbolist artist and illustrator, noted for his decadent illustrations.

Max Beckman (1884–1950), German Expressionist painter: *The Night* (1918–19).

Edward Burne-Jones (see Realism); his work became increasingly Symbolist.

James Ensor (1860–1949), Belgian painter, a major influence on Expressionism and Surrealism: *Entry of Christ into Brussels* (1880).

George Grosz (1893–1959), German illustrator, painter and satirical caricaturist.

Erich Heckel (1883–1970), German Expressionist painter, graphic artist and co-founder of *Die Brücke*.

Alexej Jawlensky (1864–1941), Russian painter loosely associated with *Der Blaue Reiter*: *Head of a Young Girl* and *Night* (1933).

Wassily Kandinsky (1866–1944), Russian-born painter, pioneer of abstract art and member of *Der Blaue Reiter*.

Ernst Ludwig Kirchner (1880–1938), German Expressionist painter, graphic artist and co-founder of *Die Brücke*.

Gustave Klimt (1863–1918), Austrian painter, and founder of the Vienna Secession, distinguished by his highly decorative paintings: *The Kiss* (1908).

Oskar Kokoschka (1886–1980), Austrian Expressionist painter: *The Tempest* (1914).

Max Liebermann (1847–1935), German painter and founder of the Berlin Secession.

Auguste Macke (1887–1914), German painter, founder of *Der Blaue Reiter*.

Franz Marc (1880–1916), German Expressionist painter, member of *Der Blaue Reiter*: *The Blue Horse* (1911) and *Fighting Forms* (1913).

Gustave Moreau (1826–98), French painter and one of the leading Symbolists, noted for his *femme fatale* paintings: *The Apparition* (1876) and *Sâlomé Dancing* (1876).

Edvard Munch (1863–1944), Norwegian painter, a forerunner of Expressionism: *The Scream* (1893).

Emil Nolde (1867–1956), German Expressionist and member of *Die Brücke*, well known for his landscapes and religious pictures.

Odilon Redon (1840–1916), French Symbolist painter and lithographer: *The Cyclops* (1898).

Egon Schiele (1890–1918), Austrian Expressionist draughtsman and painter, famous for his explicit and angular nudes.

ABSTRACTION

In the first half of the 20th century a revolution occurred in the practice of art. From 1910 artists in different countries began to produce abstract or non-figurative art, sometimes abstracting from a landscape or still life until the subject disappeared.

CUBISM

From around 1907 artists such as Picasso and Braque began to analyse objects, breaking them down into geometrical shapes and restructuring them in order to show each form's many facets in a single image. Continuing into the 1920s, Cubism never became completely abstract.

FUTURISM, VORTICISM AND RAYONISM

Futurism was founded in Italy in 1909 by the poet Filippo Marinetti. He urged artists to turn their backs on the art of the past and to seek inspiration from industrial society and the dynamism of modern life. Futurism aimed to incorporate the thrust of modern technology (particularly the sense of speed) into art. Vorticism in Britain and Rayonism in Russia shared some of the aims of Futurism, and also employed crisp geometrical forms and jagged lines.

DE STIJL, SUPREMATISM AND CONSTRUCTIVISM

These slightly later movements – the first Dutch and the other two Russian – restricted themselves to pure geometrical abstraction. Constructivism was a sculptural movement using man-made materials.

MAJOR ARTISTS

Giacomo Balla (1871–1958), Italian Futurist painter and sculptor: the painting *Dynamism of a Dog on a Leash* (1912).

Umberto Boccioni (1882–1916), Italian Futurist painter and sculptor: the sculpture *Unique Forms of Continuity in Space* (1913).

Constantin Brancusi (1876–1957), highly influential Romanian-French abstract sculptor, famous for his concentration of form and the qualities of his materials: *Endless Column* (1937).

Georges Braque (1882–1963), French painter and co-founder of Cubism: *Grand Nu* ('Great Nude'; 1907–08) and the *Atelier* series (1948 onwards).

Carlo Carra (1881–1966), Italian Futurist painter.

Robert Delaunay (1885–1941), French painter, influenced by Cubism: *Circular Forms* (from 1912).

Jacob Epstein (1880–1959), American-born English sculptor. Early Vorticist works include *The Rock-Drill* (1913–14); later work was more representational.

Naum Gabo (1890–1977), Russian sculptor and co-founder of Constructivism.

Henri Gaudier-Brzeska (1891–1915), influential French Vorticist sculptor.

Natalia Goncharova (1881–1962), Russian Rayonist painter.

Juan Gris (1887–1955), Spanish painter, noted for his development of the Cubist style: *Homage to Picasso* (1911–12).

Barbara Hepworth (1903–75), British abstract sculptress.

Wassily Kandinsky (see Expressionism); his work developed from Expressionism to Abstraction.

Paul Klee (1879–1940), Swiss painter, graphic artist and an influential 20th-century artist. His works range from Symbolist to Abstract.

Fernand Léger (1881–1955), French painter, famous for his distinctive semi-abstract monumental style, often depicting people and machines.

Wyndham Lewis (1882–1957), British painter, writer and leader of the Vorticists: *Workshop* (1914).

Kasimir Malevich (1878–1935), Russian painter, founder of Suprematism: *White on White* series (c. 1918).

Amedeo Modigliani (1884–1920), 20th-century Italian painter and sculptor, famous for his elongated figures and erotic nudes: *Reclining Nude* (c. 1919).

Piet Mondrian (1872–1944), Dutch painter who developed from Symbolism to the pure abstraction of De Stijl: *Composition with Red, Yellow and Blue* (1939–42).

Henry Moore (1898–1986), British sculptor, draughtsman and graphic artist, well known for his rounded forms: *Two Forms* (1934) and *Reclining Figure* (1938).

Ben Nicholson (1894–1982), British abstract painter, some of whose works involve carved relief.

Antoine Pevsner (1886–1962), Russian-born French painter, abstract sculptor and co-founder of Constructivism.

Pablo Picasso (1881–1973), Spanish painter, sculptor, graphic artist, founder of Cubism and the most outstanding artist of the 20th century: *The Old Guitarist* (1904), the Cubist *Les Demoiselles d'Avignon* (1907), *Guernica* (1937).

DADA AND SURREALISM

The aftermath of World War I brought a crisis of faith in a society whose intellectual and moral values were held responsible for the appalling destruction of the war. There already existed a growing revolt against traditional values, derived from the writings of Darwin, Marx and Freud. Two art movements that grew out of this climate were Dada and Surrealism. Although they were essentially different in purpose and character, some common ground existed, and a number of Dada artists later joined the Surrealist movement.

Dada, which first emerged in 1916, was an international movement that rejected existing social values and its art. Instead it aimed to be anarchic, anti-aesthetic and anti-rational; simultaneously art and anti-art. Surrealism, founded in 1924, was a French avant-garde movement of literary origin inspired by Dadaism, and greatly influenced by Freud's theories of psychoanalysis. Irrational association, spontaneous techniques and an elimination of premeditation to free the workings of the unconscious mind, as well as an interest in dreams, were the main motivations of its practitioners.

MAJOR ARTISTS

Jean (Hans) Arp (1887–1966), French Dadaist artist, celebrated for his rounded abstract sculptures.

Marc Chagall (1887–1985), Russian-born French painter; although not a Surrealist his work has a dreamlike style with irrational juxtapositions: *I and the Village* (c. 1911).

Giorgio de Chirico (1888–1928), Italian painter and forerunner of the Surrealists, notable for his haunting city-scapes.

Salvador Dali (1904–89), Spanish Surrealist artist, famous for his hallucinatory paintings (and Surrealist film-making): *The Persistence of Memory* (1931).

Marcel Duchamp (1887–1968), highly influential French Dadaist artist: *The Bride Stripped Bare by her Bachelors, Even* (1915–23).

Max Ernst (1891–1976), German Dadaist painter,

sculptor and collagist, initially a Dadaist, then a Surrealist: *Here Everything is Still Floating* (1920).

George Grosz (see Expressionism); member of the Berlin Dada group.

Raoul Hausmann (1886–1971), Austrian Dadaist, well known for his photomontages.

John Heartfield (Helmut Herzfelde; 1891–1968), German artist, notable for his political photomontages: *Hurrah, the butter is finished* (1935).

René Magritte (1898–1967), Belgian Surrealist, famous for his conventional paintings made bizarre by the unexpected juxtaposition of objects: *The Key of Dreams* (1930) and *Time Transfixed* (1938).

André Masson (1896–1987), French Surrealist painter, notable for his spontaneous drawings undertaken while in a trance.

Joan Miró (1893–1983), Spanish Surrealist painter: *Still Life with an Old Shoe* and *Dog Barking at the Moon*.

Paul Nash (1889–1946), British painter, whose visionary landscapes and war paintings show Surrealist influences.

Francis Picabia (1879–1953), French painter of the Dada school: *I see again in memory my dear Udnie* (1914).

Man Ray (1890–1976), American painter, photographer and film-maker, involved both with Dada and Surrealism, and famous for his technical experimentation (see Photography).

Kurt Schwitters (1887–1948), German Dadaist painter and sculptor, famous for his Merz pieces (haphazard combinations of materials).

Graham Sutherland (1903–80), British painter whose early landscapes had a dreamlike Surreal quality; his later works include well-known portraits.

MOVEMENTS IN ART SINCE 1945

The postwar period has been characterized by extremely varied approaches to the problems of art. Although much of the best work has been abstract, some artists have continued to work in more traditional styles.

Abstract Expressionism emerged in New York soon after World War II. It places emphasis on spontaneous personal expression, rejecting contemporary, social and aesthetic values. It was the first movement in the USA to develop independently of and actually influence Europe. Some exponents practised action painting.

Action Painting was a technique used by some of the Abstract Expressionists. It involved spattering the canvas in a semi-random fashion, so recording the action of the painter at the moment of painting as well as his emotional state.

Conceptual Art grew partly out of Minimal Art as artists started to make works of a temporary character utilizing different types of process and system, e.g. inscribing imaginary geometric patterns on the landscape, and working with photographs and texts.

Environmental Art is an art movement in which the artist aims to create not just an object but an entire environment. In order to involve all the senses of the spectator it can include sight and sound effects combined with painted or sculptured work.

Kinetic Art is all art that incorporates movement – real or apparent – generated by motors, artificial light or optical illusion.

Minimal Art emerged in the mid-1960s from the rejection of the aesthetic qualities of art in favour of the physical reality of the art object. The material used is important, as are their strictly geometrical formats and placings within settings.

Neoexpressionism is primarily, although not exclusively, a German movement that became prominent in the 1980s. Paintings are executed with great vigour in styles sometimes reminiscent of German Expressionism. It marks a return to myths, religion and mysterious symbolism as subject matter.

Op Art (optical art) is an abstract art form based on creating optical effects which appear to move on a flat surface. It reached its peak in the 1960s.

Pop Art was an almost simultaneous reaction against Abstract Expressionism in the UK and USA in the late 1950s. It uses the images of mass media, advertising and pop culture, presenting the common, everyday object as art.

Performance Art (also known as **Happenings**) began in the late 1950s, and involves the artist in directing and/or performing an entertainment (intended to be spontaneous) that involves a strong visual element and that may also include theatre, music, film, and the participation of the audience.

Photo-Realism a mainly American movement, beginning in the late 1960s, in which the artist meticulously copies from a photograph.

MAJOR ARTISTS

Francis Bacon (1909–), British painter (born in Dublin), noted for the disturbing quality of his twisted figures: *Three Studies at the Base of a Crucifixion* (1944) and *Study after Velazquez*, a series of portraits of Pope Innocent X.

Joseph Beuys (1921–86), influential German Performance artist: *Coyote* (1974), a week-long dialogue with a live coyote.

Alexander Calder (1898–1976), American Kinetic sculptor, best known for his metal mobiles.

César (1921–), French sculptor, notable for his use of plastics and used materials: *The Yellow Buick* made from crushed car bodies.

Christo (1935–), Bulgarian-born Belgian artist, who has embarked on such projects as wrapping up sections of the Australian coastline in plastic.

Willem De Kooning (1904–), American Abstract Expressionist: *Woman* series.

Alberto Giacometti (1901–66), Swiss sculptor, well known for his elongated bronze human figures.

Gilbert and George (Gilbert Proesch, 1943– , and George Passmore, 1942–), English avant-garde artists involved in various art forms, including Performance Art; noted for the presentation of themselves as works of art.

Richard Hamilton (1922–), English Pop artist, his work reflects his interest in marketing styles: *$he* (1958–61).

David Hockney (1937–), English painter and draughtsman, initially prominent in Pop Art, but notable for his innovations in many styles: *A Bigger Splash*.

Jasper Johns (1930–), American painter, printmaker and sculptor, best known as the founder of Pop Art: *Target* and *Flags* paintings.

Donald Judd (1928–), American Minimalist sculptor. His work concentrates on rows of geometric units (often boxes).

Anselm Kiefer (1945–), German Neoexpressionist painter, his work concentrates on Germany's history.

Franz Kline (1910–62), American Abstract Expressionist painter, distinguished by his black strokes on white backgrounds.

Sol LeWitt (1928–), American Minimalist sculptor, noted for his displays of white and black cubes.

Roy Lichtenstein (1923–), American Pop artist, best known for his enlarged paintings of comic strip images: *Whaam!* (1963).

Robert Motherwell (1915–), American Abstract Expressionist painter, also notable for his collages.

Barnett Newman (1905–70), American Abstract Expressionist painter, noted for his large, coloured canvases broken by 'zips' (bands) of colour.

Jackson Pollock (1912–56), American Abstract Expressionist painter, a notable exponent of Action Painting.

Robert Rauschenberg (1925–), American artist best known for his combination of Pop Art and Abstract Expressionism: *Combine* paintings and *Monogram* (1959).

Bridget Riley (1931–), foremost British Op artist: *Fall* (1963).

Mark Rothko (1903–70), American Abstract Expressionist, noted for his vast expanses of colour that fill the canvas.

Nicolas de Stäel (1914–55), French-Russian abstract painter, whose works are characterized by broad patches of paint: *The Roofs* (1952).

Jean Tinguely (1925–), Swiss Kinetic artist, celebrated for his machines: *Homage to New York* (1960), a machine from assorted junk materials that blew itself up before an audience.

Victor Vasarély (1908–), French painter (born in Hungary). Considered the pioneer of Op art, he is well known for his grid-like compositions.

Andy Warhol (1928–87), American painter and graphic designer, celebrated as one of the foremost Pop artists: prints of Campbell soup cans, Coca-cola bottles and Marilyn Monroe.

HIGHEST PRICES FOR PAINTINGS

This list shows the highest prices for paintings fetched at auction (to October 1990).

Artist	Painting	Price
Van Gogh	*Docteur Gachet*	£49,100,000
Renoir	*Au Moulin de la Galette*	£46,488,095
Van Gogh	*Irises*	£30,187,623
Picasso	*Self-portrait: Yo Picasso*	£28,825,301
Picasso	*Au Lapin Agile*	£25,710,675
Picasso	*The Mirror*	£16,677,195
Manet	*Rue Mosnier*	£16,600,000
Van Gogh	*Self-portrait*	£15,714,000
Gauguin	*Mata Mua (In Olden Times)*	£14,478,313
Monet	*Dans la prairie*	£14,300,000
Picasso	*Les Tuileries*	£13,750,000
de Kooning	*Interchange*	£13,039,092
Van Gogh	*le Vieil If*	£12,790,000
Kandinsky	*Fugue*	£12,440,476
Picasso	*Mère et Enfant*	£11,813,013
Cézanne	*Pommes et Serviette*	£11,000,000
Renoir	*Jeune fille au char*	£10,803,571

MAJOR ART GALLERIES IN EC COUNTRIES

BELGIUM
Antwerp *Royal Museum of Fine Arts:* Old Masters (van Eyck, Titian, Rubens); 19th- and 20th-century Belgian art (Ensor, Leys).

Bruges *Stedelijk Museum Voor Schone Kunsten:* Netherlandish and Flemish 15th- to 17th-century (van Eyck, Memling) and Belgian 20th-century art (Ensor, Magritte).

Brussels *Royal Belgian Museums of Fine Arts:* Old Masters (Pieter Bruegel the Elder, Rubens, Goya); 19th- and 20th-century Belgian and French art (Delacroix, Vuillard, Magritte, Ensor, Delvaux).

DENMARK
Copenhagen *Statens Museum for Kunst:* Old Masters (Mantegna, Rubens, Hals); 19th-century Danish and 20th-century international art.

FRANCE
Paris *Musée du Louvre:* Italian 15th- to 17th-century Old Masters (Uccello, Leonardo, Caravaggio); French 17th- to 19th-century (Poussin, Watteau, Delacroix); Northern Renaissance and Baroque (van Eyck, Dürer, Rubens); and Spanish art (Velásquez, Murillo, Goya).
Musée d'Orsay: French 19th-century art (Salon painting; Courbet, Corot); Impressionists (Monet, Degas, Renoir); Post-Impressionists (Cézanne, Gauguin, Van Gogh).
Centre Georges Pompidou: 20th-century and contemporary French and international art.
Musée Picasso: Collection of Picasso paintings.

GERMANY
Berlin *Gemälde Galerie (Dahlem):* Renaissance (Bellini, Raphael, Giorgione, Dürer, van Eyck, Bosch); Dutch and Flemish 17th-century (Rembrandt, Rubens, Vermeer); and Baroque and Rococo art (Velásquez, Carracci, Watteau).
Bode Museum: Italian Renaissance and Baroque (Ghirlandaio, Giorgione, Giordano); and Northern 15th- to 17th-century art (Cranach, van Eyck, Rembrandt; German Romantics (Friedrich, Menzel).

Cologne *Wallraf-Richartz-Museum/Ludwig Museum:* Renaissance and Baroque (Lochner, Van Dyck, Claude Lorraine, Murillo); 19th-century French (Corot, Monet); 19th-century German (Friedrich, Menzel, Böcklin); and 20th-century Pop and American Conceptual art.

Dresden *Gemälde Galerie:* Old Masters (Holbein, Titian, Watteau).

Frankfurt *Stadelsches:* German and Flemish 14th- to 19th-century (van Eyck, Dürer, Elsheimer, Corinth); Italian and Spanish (Botticelli, Tiepolo, Velasquez); German Romantic and Expressionist; 19th-century French (Delacroix, Courbet, Degas); and 20th-century art (Picasso, Ernst, Bacon).

Munich *Alte Pinakothek:* Renaissance (Dürer, Altdorfer, van der Weyden, Bouts, van Leyden); 17th-century Flemish and Dutch (Rubens, Rembrandt, van Goyen); Italian Renaissance and Baroque (Leonardo, Titian, Reni); French Baroque and Rococo (Poussin, Boucher); and Spanish art (El Greco, Goya).
Neue Pinakothek: 18th- and 19th-century European art (Nazarenes, Romantics, Secessionists).

GREECE
Athens *National Picture Gallery and Alexander Soutzos Museum*: 17th- to 20th-century Greek; and 14th- to 20th-century European art (El Greco, Caravaggio, Picasso).

IRELAND
Dublin *National Gallery of Ireland*: Italian Renaissance and Baroque (Fra Angelico, Titian, Lanfranco); and Dutch and Flemish Baroque art (Jordaens, Rembrandt, Ruisdael); portraiture (Reynolds).

ITALY
Florence *Uffizi Gallery*: 13th- and 14th-century Italian (Cimabue, Duccio, Giotto); Florentine Renaissance (Uccello, Botticelli, Michelangelo); 16th-century Venetian (Titian, Tintoretto); Northern Renaissance (van der Goes, van der Weyden); and Italian and Northern Baroque art (Caravaggio, Rubens, Claude Lorraine).
Pitti Palace: 16th- and 17th-century art (Raphael, Van Dyck, Velásquez).

Milan *Brera Gallery*: Italian 15th- to 19th-century art (Mantegna, Veronese, Appiani).

Naples *Capodimonte*: 14th- to 17th-century Italian (Simone Martini, Titian, Caravaggio); Northern Renaissance (Bruegel, Witz); and Neapolitan Baroque art (Caracciolo, Ribera, Solimena).

Rome *Pinacoteca*: Byzantine to 18th-century Italian art (Leonardo, Raphael, Caravaggio).
National Gallery of Rome: Palazzo Barberine: 13th- to 18th-century Italian art (Raphael, Tintoretto, Sacchi).
Palazzo Corsini: 18th-century Italian art (Canaletto, Cortona, Strozzi).
Borghese Gallery: 16th- to 18th-century Italian art (Raphael, Titian, Caravaggio).
The Vatican (technically in the sovereign Vatican City State; i.e. outside the EC): Raphael's Loggie in the papal apartments; the Sistine Chapel (works by Botticelli, Perugino and Michelangelo).

Venice *Galleria dell'Accademia*: 14th- to 18th-century Venetian art (Bellini, Titian, Veronese).
Peggy Guggenheim Collection: 20th-century international art (Cubism, Futurism, Dada, Abstractionism).

LUXEMBOURG
Luxembourg *Musée de l'Etat de Luxembourg*: 15th- to 18th-century European art (Steen).

NETHERLANDS
Amsterdam *Rijksmuseum*: 15th- and 16th-century Dutch (tot Sint Jans, van Leyden, Cornelis van Haarlem); 17th-century Dutch (Rembrandt, Hals, Vermeer, Steen); and Italian art (Veronese, Tiepolo).
Stedelijk Museum: International art from c. 1860 (Van Gogh, Mondrian, Cobra school, Pop Art, Conceptual Art).

Haarlem *Frans Hals Museum*: Collection of Hals paintings.

The Hague *Mauritshuis*: Netherlandish and German 15th- and 16th-century (van der Weyden, Cranach, Holbein); Flemish and Dutch 17th- and 18th-century (Rembrandt, Vermeer, Ruisdael); and Italian 16th- and 17th-century art (Raphael, Titian, Carracci).

Otterlo *Kröller Muller*: modern painting (Van Gogh).

PORTUGAL
Lisbon *Calouste Gulbenkian Museum*: Old Masters (Rembrandt, Rubens, Guardi); 18th- and 19th-century

French art (Boucher, Fragonard, Manet).
National Museum of Ancient Art: Portuguese 15th- to 18th-century; Northern Renaissance (Bosch, Dürer, Holbein); Italian 16th- to 18th-century (Raphael, del Sarto, Giordano); and French 17th- and 18th-century art (Poussin, Rigaud).

SPAIN
Barcelona *Museum of Catalan Art*: Gothic 13th- to 15th-century; Catalan (Bermejo, Huguet); and Spanish Baroque art (El Greco, Zurbarán, Velásquez).

Madrid *The Prado*: Spanish (Velásquez, Zurbarán, Goya); Italian Renaissance (Titian, Tintoretto, Veronese); Northern Renaissance and Baroque (Bosch, Bruegel, Rubens); French and British art (Poussin, Gainsborough).
The Escorial: Northern 15th- to 17th-century (van der Weyden, Bosch, Dürer, Rubens); Italian 16th-century (Titian, Tintoretto); and Spanish 17th- and 18th-century art (Velásquez, Ribera, Goya).

Seville *Museum of Fine Arts of Seville*: Sevillian 17th-century art (Zurbarán, Murillo).

UNITED KINGDOM
Cambridge *Fitzwilliam Museum*: Italian Renaissance (Domenico Veneziano, Titian, Veronese); Italian Baroque (Carracci, Reni, Claude Lorraine); Dutch and Flemish 17th-century (Rembrandt, Rubens, Ruisdael); French 18th- and 19th-century (Boucher, Barbizon school, Cézanne); and British 19th- and 20th-century art (Hogarth, Gainsborough, Spencer).

Edinburgh *National Gallery of Scotland*: Italian Renaissance (Verrocchio, Titian, Raphael); Baroque (Guercino, Velásquez, Zurbarán); French 17th- and 18th-century (Poussin, Claude Lorraine, Chardin, Watteau); Flemish and Dutch Baroque (Rubens, van Dyck, Vermeer); and British 18th- and 19th-century artists (Gainsborough, Constable).

Glasgow *Burrell Collection*: Old Masters (Memling, Hals, Rembrandt); 19th-century French art (Delacroix, Cézanne, Degas).

London *National Gallery*: Italian medieval and Renaissance (Duccio, Masaccio, Piero della Francesca); Italian 16th- to 18th-century (Leonardo, Titian, Caravaggio, Canaletto); Northern Renaissance (van Eyck, Christus, Bosch); Dutch and Flemish 16th-century (Rubens, Rembrandt, de Hooch); Spanish 17th- and 18th-century (Velásquez, Murillo, Goya); and French 17th- to 20th-century art (Claude Lorraine, Poussin, Degas, Monet, Cézanne).
Tate Gallery: British 17th- to 19th-century (Turner, Hogarth, Reynolds, Blake, Pre-Raphaelites); Modern and 20th-century British (Sickert, Spencer, Sutherland, Hockney), European (Fauvism, Cubism, Abstractionism) and international art (Op Art, Pop Art, Abstract Expressionism).
Victoria and Albert Museum: British watercolours and miniatures (Blake, Constable, Hilliard, Oliver); European art (Boucher, Rembrandt); Raphael cartoons.
Wallace Collection: Dutch and Flemish (Rembrandt, Van Dyck, Rubens); Italian 16th- and 17th-century (del Sarto, Titian, Rosa); French 18th- and 19th-century (Watteau, Boucher, Fragonard, Vernet, Delacroix); and British art (Gainsborough, Reynolds, Bonington).
Courtauld Gallery: French Impressionist and Post-Impressionist art; French and English early 20th-century collection.
Wellington Museum: Continental painting (Correggio, Elsheimer, Velásquez, Goya).

PHOTOGRAPHY

When Louis Daguerre announced his discovery of a process for making photographic images (or *daguerreotypes*) in 1839, the French painter Paul Delaroche declared, 'From today painting is dead!' Delaroche voiced the expectations of many: that the camera's ability to capture in an instant every detail of the real world would spell the end of painting and drawing, and that photography was the art form of the future. An equally vocal opposing camp claimed that photography was a science, not an art – a purely mechanical process that could never rival in feeling or expression the sensitive hand of the painter or draughtsman.

Since 1839, photography has assumed a vast range of forms and uses – in science and medicine, geographic exploration, anthropology, journalism and advertising – but its close relationship with art has continued throughout.

NINETEENTH-CENTURY PHOTOGRAPHERS: THE PIONEERS

Many early photographers attempted to gain status and approval by self-consciously adopting the high moral themes – and even copying the forms of – 19th-century painters; others favoured the deep tones and soft focus that suggested the delicate sweep of brushstrokes. Despite this, and with gradual improvements in photographic technology, photographers came to respect the photograph for its unique immediacy, its ability to capture a real sense of life.

Julia Margaret Cameron (1815–79), British photographer; pioneer of portrait photography.

Roger Fenton (1819–69), English pioneer war photographer, noted for his Crimean War pictures.

William Henry Fox Talbot (1800–77), English chemist, linguist and photographer who in 1839 invented the photographic negative.

Eadweard Muybridge (Edward James Muggeridge; 1830–1904), English photographer, famous for his early experiments in capturing motion in photographic images, and for his landscape photographs of the American West.

EARLY MODERNISTS

Photography began to gain new status as an independent medium in the early 20th century. Early modernist photographers advocated 'pure' photograph, with aesthetic value beyond its descriptive or utilitarian function.

Alfred Stieglitz (1864–1946), American photographer, publisher and gallery owner whose work turned from pictorialism to a search for abstract form and a specifically photographic way of seeing.

Paul Strand (1890–1976), American photographer who abandoned pictorialism for a pure, objective photographic approach to his subjects.

Edward Weston (1886–1958), American photographer. His precise photographs of natural and human forms combine a formal beauty with the reality of the object.

DOCUMENTARY PHOTOGRAPHERS

Many photographers now regarded as great masters would never have regarded themselves as artists at all, but they detected surreal qualities in everyday life. They documented the life they saw around them, and so fit into a broad documentary approach that encompasses a vast span of attitudes and subject matter.

Bill Brandt (1904–83), English photographer who mixed grim realism with the surreal, creating an evocative record of the British social scene.

Henri Cartier Bresson (1908–), French photographer; combined an artist's genius for perfect composition with a photojournalist's insistence on capturing the 'decisive moment'.

Walker Evans (1903–75), American photographer; produced a powerful record of the faces, homes and lives of America's 1930s rural poor.

Lewis Hine (1874–1940), American photographer, noted for his campaigning pictures of New York's poor and immigrant population from the turn of the century.

Erich Salomon (1886–1944), German photojournalist. Master of the candid shot, he caught politicians and celebrities off guard for the new magazines of the 1920s.

Eugene Smith (1918–78), American photojournalist, notable for his impassioned documentary photographs from around the world (seen mostly in *Life* magazine in the 1940s and 50s).

THE AVANT-GARDE

Photographers continued to innovate and to find new ground. Photomontage – the technique of combining several photographs into one photograph – became popular, while some photographers experimented with 'new objectivity' and Pop Art.

John Heartfield (1891–1968), German pioneer of the photomontage (see p. 357).

Laszlo Moholy Nagy (1894–1946), Hungarian-born American photographer, celebrated for his constructivist-inspired, semi-abstract images, and his inspiring teaching at the Bauhaus.

Alexander Rodchenko (1891–1956), Soviet photographer and photomontagist; introduced 'New Photography' to post-revolutionary Russia.

August Sander (1876–1964), German photographer; celebrated for his ambitious project *Man of the Twentieth Century*, a picture of a society – the doomed Weimar Republic – through the faces of its people.

Andy Warhol (1928–1987), American Pop artist who used photographic images from the media (see p. 358).

THE SURREAL AND THE EVERYDAY

Since the 1950s photography and art have become more closely aligned. At the same time in the USA, a new, seemingly informal approach to urban or 'street' photography evolved.

Diane Arbus (1923–71), American photographer, well known for her intense portraits of American social outcasts.

Eugene Atget (1857–1927), French photographer, recording the streets and scenes of old Paris; his unusual images of the commonplace inspired the Surrealists.

Brassai (Gyula Halasz; 1899–1984), Hungarian-born French photographer. His pictures of bohemian Paris and his eye for the bizarre and the taboo was much appreciated by the Surrealists.

Andre Kertesz (1894–1985), Hungarian-born American photographer, noted for his pioneering use of the small hand-held camera, the well-observed social scene, the surreal figure study, still life, and later the fashion image.

Man Ray (Emanuel Rabinovitch; 1890–1976), American photographer who produced poetic and bizarre surreal images (see p. 357).

Garry Winogrand (1928–84), American photographer who created a highly influential brand of urban street photography, fusing the 'snapshot' approach with a sense of energy and crowded events in his images.

MAJOR PHOTOGRAPHY FESTIVALS

Arles (France) *Rencontres Internationales de la Photographie.* Biennial, held since 1980; a gala of exhibitions, workshops and audiovisual presentations at a number of locations in and around Arles.

Barcelona (Spain) *Primavera Photografica de Catalunya.* Biennial, held since 1982; a large number of photographic exhibitions, discussions and related events in Barcelona and other Catalan towns.

Cologne (Germany) *Photokina.* Annual, held since 1950; an industrial showcase for camera and photographic equipment manufacturers, with concurrent exhibitions of photographs at other locations in the city.

Houston (USA) *Fotofest* Biennial, held since 1986; the major photographic event in the USA, with scores of exhibitions from around the world, mainly under one roof.

Paris (France) *Mois de la Photo.* Biennial, held since 1978; a month of exhibitions (loosely based on a changing series of themes) and photography-related events in over 100 public spaces, museums and private galleries.

Rotterdam (Netherlands) *Fotografie Bienale.* Biennial, held since 1980; a major international exhibition on a changing theme, with a concurrent conference and exhibitions in public and private galleries.

ARCHITECTURE

Architecture is the art and science of designing and erecting buildings that are both suitable for an intended purpose and aesthetically pleasing. The design of a particular building will depend upon many factors, including the technology and materials available, the cost of those materials, the function of the building, and the taste of the building's architect, its owner and its users.

In ancient times buildings were monumental in scale, constructed to the greater glory of a deity or the dead. Secular architecture developed more slowly with an emphasis upon grandeur and security rather than comfort. Not until the Greeks developed the Classical orders of architecture did ideas of proportion and harmony evolve. Succeeding architectural styles have both reflected and influenced contemporary technology and artistic taste.

EGYPTIAN ARCHITECTURE

The appearance of Egyptian buildings was influenced by climatic features such as fierce heat and bright sunshine – which meant only small windows were required – and by a plentiful local supply of building stone. At the time of the Third Dynasty – during the Ancient Kingdom (2575–2134 BC) – *mastabas* or tomb houses were built, and from these small, flat-topped buildings with sloping sides the pyramids developed. The 4th-dynasty Great Pyramids at Giza are the largest and best preserved, but the oldest pyramid still in existence, and the world's first large-scale monument in stone, is the Djoser step pyramid at Saqqara, built c. 2620 BC by Imhotep, who is considered to be the first architect in history.

During the Middle Kingdom (2040–1640 BC) monolithic buildings were increasingly replaced by a system of construction consisting of series of stone columns and horizontal beams; e.g. the mortuary temples of Mentuhetep at Deir el-Bahari (11th Dynasty). The most imposing buildings were tombs and temples, reflecting the importance of religion, the priesthood and the afterlife to the Egyptians. Temples, such as the great temple of Amun at Karnak (12th Dynasty), were vast sprawling complexes of courtyards, halls and avenues built of stone. Stone was used only sparingly for secular buildings – even the Pharaohs' palaces were built principally of sun-dried brick.

Notable New Kingdom buildings (1552–1070 BC) include the great Hypostyle Hall – a vast columned hall with 134 columns – built at Karnak by Rameses I, the mortuary temple of Rameses III at Medinet Habu in Thebes, and the funerary temple at Deir el-Bahari for Queen Hatshepsut.

NEAR EASTERN ARCHITECTURE

The use of mud-brick rather than stone and the increasing importance of vast palace complexes characterize Near Eastern architecture. In the 5th millennium BC huge circular buildings occur alongside T-shaped units with elaborately niched and buttressed façades. These temples display a monumentality only paralleled by *ziggurats*, stepped pyramid-shaped temple towers. The largest surviving example is the Ziggurat of Ur (c. 2113–2096 BC) – built to three stories surmounted by a summit temple – with a base of 61 m by 45.7 m (200 by 150 ft). The public buildings of the city of Babylon were of vast dimensions, but only mounds now show where the original city stood because its mud-bricks had little resistance to weathering.

The major buildings of the Assyrian period were the palaces in Nineveh of kings such as Ashurbanipal. These enormous palaces were raised on platforms of mud-bricks and reached by broad stairs and ramps. Planned around inner courtyards, with numerous rooms connected by corridors, they were faced with stone and decorated with bas-reliefs of sculptured monsters, painting on plaster, and coloured glazed bricks. Structurally the buildings were quite sophisticated with some use of arches, vaults and domes.

Persian architecture made greater use of stone and wooden columns and flat roofs. The palace of Persepolis (6th–4th centuries BC) displays some Assyrian features – raised platforms, bas-relief sculptures and coloured glazed bricks – but is distinguished by its halls of tall columns.

GREEK ARCHITECTURE

Buildings of the Early Greek period (before c. 700 BC) are characterized by the distinct appearance of the masonry wall in their construction. There are three types: *cyclopean*, which is constructed of large stone piles, the gaps between which are filled with smaller stones held together by clay; *stone blocks* laid in a regular course with joints that are not always vertical; and *polygonal*, where many-sided blocks are worked together to form a strong structure.

Doric **Ionic** **Corinthian**

The architecture of the later (Hellenic) period is distinguished by the use of the column. Columns gave Classical Greek buildings an uncomplicated appearance. The most important buildings were temples, usually located on a prominent site, e.g. the 5th-century Parthenon on the Acropolis in Athens (designed by Praxiteles). The typical temple was a simple rectangle. Its low-pitched roof was supported by a colonnade of columns. The three *orders* of column were Doric (c. 640–c. 300 BC), Ionic (c. 560–c. 200 BC) and Corinthian (c. 420–c. 100 BC). An order is the design of an entire column consisting of base, shaft and capital with an entablature over the top as the horizontal element. The Doric order is the simplest of the three orders, the capital being a simple flattened cushion of stone (e.g. the columns of the Parthenon). The more slender and ornamental columns of the Ionic order are topped by a capital that is ornamented with four spiral motifs called *volutes* (e.g. the temple of Artemis in Ephesus and the Erechtheion in Athens). The Corinthian order is the lightest and least-used of the three Greek orders. The capital displays acanthus-leaf decoration combined with volutes that are smaller and more open than the Ionic (e.g. the Olympeion in Athens).

ROMAN ARCHITECTURE

The character of Roman architecture derives from the fusion of the Etruscan and Greek cultures on the Italian peninsula between the 8th and 6th centuries BC. The Romans adopted the central concept of Greek architecture – the three orders – but changed the manner in which the orders were expressed through adopting arches and vaults, both Etruscan technical innovations not used by the Greeks. The Romans also added two new orders – the rarely used Tuscan (which is similar to the Doric but with a plain entablature) and the Composite (which displays Ionic volutes and Corinthian leaves). The new techniques and orders were applied to an array of new building types and shapes, including circular temples, triumphal arches, baths, aqueducts, basilicas and amphitheatres. Roman architects used a wider variety of building materials than the Greeks. The introduction by the Romans of tufa, limestone, brick and especially concrete allowed structural innovations that were employed most successfully in vast structures such as the Baths of Caracalla (AD 211–17).

The major public buildings of Imperial Rome were characterized by flamboyant luxury, but only the husks of a few great buildings remain. The Pantheon (AD 120–24) in Rome is one of the most impressive survivors. A large circular temple dedicated to all the gods, the Pantheon has a height and a diameter of 43.2 m (142 ft). Its huge hemispherical dome is partly concealed on the outside by the massive walls which rise up in counterthrust to the dome, and an opening at the centre of the dome's apex reduces its weight and allows in natural light.

MAJOR ARCHITECTS

Vitruvius (fl. first century BC), Roman architect, engineer and writer: *De architectura*, 10 books covering building materials, city planning and the design and construction of public and private buildings.

Apollodorus of Damascus (fl. first century AD), Greek engineer and architect: Trajan's Forum in Rome.

BYZANTINE ARCHITECTURE

With the demise of the Roman Empire in the West, the power base shifted to the East, to Constantinople (formerly Byzantium). From the 5th century AD Byzantine emperors provided lavish patronage for architects, who inherited and developed the structural innovations of the Romans, and combined them with a variety of decorative influences from both Greece and Asia. Byzantine architecture is characterized by the construction of domes over square bases. The Romans had always built domes over cylindrical or polygonal bases, but the Byzantines effected the transition of the circular dome to the square base, usually composed of four arches, by inserting *pendentives*. The advantage of a square base over a circular or polygonal base was that vaulted aisles, semi-domed apses and other domes could be easily erected adjacent to a central dome. The most famous example of this type of structure is Hagia Sophia (begun AD 537) in Constantinople (now Istanbul), designed by Anthemius of Tralles and Isidorus of Miletus. A former cathedral – it became a mosque when Constantinople fell to the Ottoman Turks in 1453 – Hagia Sophia is a vast rectangle 76 m (250 ft) by 67 m (220 ft), with a large central dome 33 m (108 ft) in diameter.

Byzantine architecture spread throughout Asia Minor and as far north as the Ukraine and Russia. Russian architects initially followed the Byzantine pattern, but a distinct Russian personality soon emerged in the buildings of Novgorod and Kiev. The wide Byzantine windows were narrowed and roofs steepened to cope with the heavy snow of Russian winters, and in time domes were constructed in the bulbous shape that became a distinguishing feature of Russian architecture. To the west Venice was the only major state in direct contact with the Byzantine Empire. St Mark's in Venice was begun in 1063 and is essentially a Byzantine church.

EARLY MEDIEVAL ARCHITECTURE

In the West, the fall of the Roman Empire in the 5th century brought fragmentation and a power vacuum. Barbarian tribes overran Europe, producing a climate hardly conducive to ambitious building. The products of these (largely nomadic) civilizations were mostly portable and their buildings were in general constructed of wood. Where stone was used many of the features of Roman building persisted, but often in a much simplified or debased form.

ANGLO-SAXON ARCHITECTURE

In England, much of the architecture of the Anglo-Saxons, from the 6th century until the Norman Conquest of 1066, was timber-framed. Surviving stone buildings, such as the 10th- or early 11th-century tower at Earl's Barton, in Northamptonshire, reflect this in the application of long strips of stone, called 'long-and-short work', to wall-surfaces as non-structural decoration. Ecclesiastical and private buildings were generally small in scale, with small spaces or rooms opening into one another through narrow doorways.

CAROLINGIAN ARCHITECTURE

Charlemagne, crowned Holy Roman Emperor in 800, consciously evoked the grandeur of Imperial Rome at his court at Aachen (Germany). For his Palatine Chapel there he closely followed late Roman prototypes and even reused Roman materials. The chapel (792–805) has an octagonal interior, showing the influence of Byzantine domed structures. Its massive sturdy piers are typical of the solidity of all Carolingian architecture.

ROMANESQUE ARCHITECTURE

In the decades following the year 1000 a huge increase in church building took place and all the most important buildings and developments until the 16th century can be traced in church architecture. These new churches swept away the older, smaller structures, and over the years, new building techniques developed, such as the barrel-and-rib vault seen for the first time at Durham Cathedral in northern England.

The typical Romanesque church grew from the simple groundplan of a Roman basilica – the addition of *transepts*, a *chancel* and an *apse* at the east end produced the cross-shaped groundplan followed with innumerable variations throughout the Middle Ages. The *nave* was often of considerable height. The interior elevations of the nave were often divided into two or three storeys with the *clerestory* at the top, *arcades* of columns at the bottom (opening into aisles parallel to but lower than the nave) and a *triforium* in the middle storey opening into the roofspace of the aisles. High towers were often built over the *crossing* of transepts and nave, and at the west end. These innovations were made possible by the development of simple stone vaulting systems. In earlier buildings vaults were usually either barrel vaults or *groin vaults*. Romanesque builders reversed

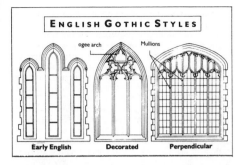

ENGLISH GOTHIC STYLES

ogee arch — Mullions

Early English — Decorated — Perpendicular

previous practice by constructing the vaults before the arches. This meant that the arches could be made much lighter as the stonework between the groins (or ribs) was not load-bearing.

The Romanesque style was disseminated throughout Europe quickly because of the network of related monasteries ruled over by a single great house. The most influential of these was Cluny in Burgundy, whose church was – until it was demolished in the 19th century – the largest Romanesque building. Typically Romanesque architecture is massive and simple. Piers are large and where there are attached columns or mouldings these are large in scale. Local variations – or schools – are most noticeable in building materials and decoration. In Romanesque buildings in England and France special attention was paid to the embellishment of capitals surmounting columns and to doorways – the *tympanum* was usually elaborately carved, often with a figure of Christ in Majesty. Fine surviving Romanesque buildings include Peterborough Cathedral in England (1117–93), St Etienne, Caen (c. 1068–1115), St Sernin, Toulouse (1077–1119 and later), Angouleme Cathedral (c. 1105–28 and later) and Notre Dame la Grande, Poitiers (c. 1130–45), all in France, and Trier Cathedral in Germany (1016–47).

GOTHIC ARCHITECTURE

The Gothic style emerged in the 12th century and survived in some areas of northern Europe until the 16th. In Gothic architecture a transcendental quality is evoked by pointed arches, vaulted ceilings and an emphasis on light through large pointed windows. Although pointed arches and windows are perhaps the most obvious features of Gothic building, what characterizes Gothic architecture is a method of building and a sense of structure and space that pervades the whole building, rather than any specific design feature.

Rib-vaulting was begun by Romanesque builders, but the idea of building 'skeletons of stone' was not fully developed until Gothic buildings were designed. Walls became just infill between supporting piers as by big windows for stained glass, and the thick walls with passages typical of Romanesque were replaced with thin walls.

It is generally accepted that the first Gothic structure is the choir of St Denis in Paris rebuilt by Abbot Suger (1140–44). In the following 80 years Gothic cathedrals were built in the region around Paris; e.g. Laon (1160–1225), Noyon (1145–1228), and Notre Dame de Paris (1168–c. 1250), all of which had four-storey elevations to the nave, with massive round piers at the aisle level. Later examples include Chartres (1194–1260), Reims (1211–90), Amiens (1220–88), and Beauvais (1247–1568). Chartres was the first important example of an emphasis on *tracery*. Tracery gradually became lighter and more complex and decorative, leaving even larger areas of stained glass. The interiors of Gothic cathedrals became increasingly vast, with naves of great height. The interior surfaces are articulated by ribs beginning at the ceiling vaults of the nave and running down the piers of the clerestory, triforium and nave arcades. This vertical thrust emphasizes the great height of the buildings, and as the clusters of ribs become increasingly narrow in diameter the whole interior seems lighter. The divisions between the aisles, nave, transepts, apse and chapels are less emphatic, creating a sense of spaces flowing into one another, quite different from the solid division and massiveness of the Romanesque. Although the walls of great Gothic churches were lighter they still required support and *buttresses* – and sometimes *flying buttresses* – were added to the exterior of the building to carry the structural thrust from the vaults.

Gothic architecture is found, with various regional variations, throughout western and central Europe. The earliest Gothic work in England is probably the choir of Canterbury Cathedral (1174–85), begun by the French architect William of Sens. English Gothic is generally divided into three stylistic periods, characterized by their window styles.

The English style which corresponds to the early Gothic of Laon and Noyon in France is the *Early English* (c. 1190–1250). Typically, Early English buildings – such as the choir (1192–1200) and Angel Choir (1256–80) of Lincoln Cathedral – have simple pointed *lancet* windows, without tracery, and clear horizontal divisions between the internal storey or wall divisions.

The *Decorated* style (c. 1250–1360) is exemplified by the nave of Exeter Cathedral (early 14th century), where the vaults have additional ribs, the main piers are made up of clusters of small columns, and window tracery is used in a variety of flowing patterns. Decorated style is characterized by the *ogee arch* and decorated wall surfaces. During this period the tracery changed from geometric to flowing.

The *Perpendicular* style (c. 1360–c. 1550), as its name implies, emphasized vertical features. Perpendicular tracery is made up of many geometrically arranged narrow stone bars, and arches and vaults are much flatter. Whereas the Decorated style added extra ribs to the vaulting, the Perpendicular was distinguished by many subordinate ribs in the vaults curving round to form a fan shape, often with additional carved decoration (e.g. the south transept and cloisters of Gloucester Cathedral). The primary examples of English Gothic can be seen at Westminster Abbey and the cathedrals of Canterbury, Lincoln, Salisbury, Ely and Wells.

Gothic in Germany and the rest of central Europe seems to have been imported from France, rather than to have developed from the indigenous Romanesque. A particular feature of German Gothic is the *hall church* (e.g. St Elizabeth, Marburg). In Italy the Classical, Romanesque and Byzantine traditions persisted much longer than in northern Europe and Italian Gothic, with the exception of Milan Cathedral (c. 1385–1485) in the north, has none of the structural and spatial daring of northern Gothic. Roofs are often flat or open timber, as at S. Croce, Florence (1294–1442), with an absence of pinnacles and flying buttresses.

RENAISSANCE ARCHITECTURE

The Renaissance was a period of intellectual and artistic renewal that lasted from c. 1350 to c. 1550. The dominant theme of the period was the revival of interest in the arts and literature of Classical Greece and Rome. The Renaissance began in Italy because the physical remains of Classical Rome were more plentiful there than elsewhere in Europe, and also because the Gothic had never taken hold in Italy as it had in northern Europe. The most important figure of the Early Renaissance is the Florentine Filippo Brunelleschi, who studied Roman remains at first hand. Another Florentine, Leon Battista Alberti, was the theorist of the Renaissance style in its early years. In his book *De Re Aedificatoria* (1485) he attempted to define the Renaissance aesthetic. Alberti studied classical geometry as well as architecture and applied this to his buildings whose parts relate to each other and to the whole construction according to mathematical laws.

The Early Renaissance style is found in various forms throughout Italy, but the High Renaissance style, which flourished first in Rome, is found with much less regional variation. High Renaissance buildings are generally bolder than Early Renaissance ones, reflecting the architects' greater familiarity with the Classical precedents, and the variety of uses to which they could put the orders of columns and pilasters.

The Renaissance in France and England developed principally in palaces and large country houses rather than in church architecture. It also differed in character from Italian Renaissance architecture because the Gothic had flourished in northern Europe much longer. In English and French Renaissance architecture, Classical features such as columns, pilasters and pediments were mixed with Gothic features and decoration to form picturesque buildings quite different from those of Brunelleschi and Alberti. France's geographical proximity to Italy meant that Renaissance features first appeared there before the end of the 15th century, but the style dominated from the mid-16th century. The Palais du Louvre (1546–1878) in Paris shows French Renaissance architecture at every stage of its development. Renaissance architecture did not appear in England until the 16th century. Although houses such as Longleat (1567–80), in Wiltshire, and Wollaton Hall (1580–88), in Nottinghamshire, have symmetrical façades and Renaissance details such as pilasters and balustrades, the rooms are frequently distributed asymmetrically throughout the groundplan and the houses retain such medieval features as the great hall. Their rooflines are made lively by the addition of elaborate chimneys and carving, and window bays break forward from the line of the façade, so that the character of the buildings is as much Gothic as Renaissance.

MAJOR ARCHITECTS

Filippo Brunelleschi (1377–1446), Florentine architect and engineer: the dome of Florence Cathedral (1420–36), a double shell of brickwork supported on ribs.

Leon Battista Alberti (1404–72), Florentine architect, writer and principal founder of Renaissance architectural theory.

Donato Bramante (1444–1514), Italian architect: the Tempietto at S. Pietro in Montorio, Rome – one of the finest High Renaissance buildings, although it is only 4.5 m (15 ft) in diameter.

Philibert Delorme (1510–1570), French architect: the châteaux of Anet and Saint-Germain-en-Laye, and the palace at Fontainebleau.

Pierre Lescot (c. 1515–78), French architect: rebuilding of the Louvre.

Jean Bullant (c. 1520–1578), French architect: Petit-Château (Chantilly).

Robert Smythson (c. 1536–1614), English architect: Wollaton Hall (Nottinghamshire) and Longleat House (Wiltshire) with Sir John Thynne.

MANNERISM

Mannerism followed hard on the heels of the High Renaissance in Italy. When Italian architects had thoroughly studied the way Classical architects used the basic elements of columns, pilasters and entablatures, they felt able to use these elements in new ways, for example greatly exaggerating the proportion of one element or adding features such as *consoles* for decoration rather than support. Although such typically Mannerist features are found in buildings elsewhere in Europe, it is a particularly Italian phenomenon and flourished in Italy at a time when other European countries were just beginning to discover the Renaissance.

EARLY PALLADIAN ARCHITECTURE

A different kind of Mannerism was practised by Andrea Palladio, who built many villas and palaces around Vicenza, near Venice. Palladio followed the Mannerist practice of using Classical elements in ways that the Romans would never have done. However, he always followed a strict system of proportional rules, and the effect is always harmonious. The Palladian style became highly influential in England, where Inigo Jones was an early but isolated follower. Jones travelled to Italy and studied Classical remains, as well as Palladio's thesis *The Four Books on Architecture*, which describes both his theories of proportion and his own buildings which exemplified them. Palladianism did not take root in England until the 18th century, although Jones' ideas encouraged a new compactness in the groundplans of 17th-century English country houses.

MAJOR ARCHITECTS

Michelangelo Buonarrotti (1475–1564), Italian painter, sculptor, poet and architect (see also Painting): the Biblioteca Laurentiana (1526), Florence, and the Dome of St Peter's in Rome.

Giulio Romano (Giulio Pippi; 1492–1546), Roman architect and principal founder of the Mannerist style: Palazzo del Tè (1525–35) in Mantua.

Giacomo da Vignola (1507–73), Italian architect: church of Il Gèsu (1568–84), in Rome.

Andrea Palladio (1508–80), Italian architect and founder of the Palladian style: the Palazzo Chiericati (1550–c. 1580) and the Villa Capra (Rotonda) (c. 1550–54), Vicenza.

Giorgio Vasari (1511–1574), Florentine painter, writer and court architect: the Uffizi (Florence).

Inigo Jones (1573–1652), English designer and architect: the Queen's House at Greenwich (begun 1616), whose entrance hall is a perfect cube.

BAROQUE AND ROCOCO

The Baroque style – one of the dominant trends in the visual arts in the 17th century – has been described as work that utilized movement, whether actual (e.g. curving walls) or implied (e.g. figures portrayed in vigorous action). It produced striking visual effects in buildings and decoration, although it could occasionally be over-ornate and theatrical. The Baroque style began in Italy, where its leading exponents were Bernini, Borromini and Maderna. In Spain, Germany and Austria, Baroque architecture attained and even exceeded the exuberance of Italian Baroque. The Neumünster-Stiftskirche (façade, 1710–19), at Würzburg (Germany), is truly Baroque with its concave modelling, clustered and variously disposed orders, and vigorous dramatic effect. In England – where the chief proponents of the style were Wren and Vanbrugh – and also in France, Baroque exteriors are much more restrained and traditionally Classical. Only interior decoration attains levels of lively and theatrical exuberance. At the end of the 17th century Baroque reached Russia, where a clearly national variation – Naryshkin Baroque – developed.

ROCOCO

In the 18th century the desire for the informal in architecture found expression in the highly decorative Rococo style. The origins of Rococo can be seen in the later works commissioned by Louis XIV of France, such as the châteaux of Marly and La Ménagerie, and under Louis XV, the Rococo style dominated. Rooms became wholly or partly elliptical and decoration was derived from foliage, grotesques and shells. In Germany and Austria Rococo became more even lavish, and an emphasis on whimsical decoration and oval and circular spaces created a sense of fluidity. Rococo was not fully accepted in England, where Baroque licence had already been challenged by the more 'rational' Palladian style.

MAJOR ARCHITECTS

Carlo Maderna (1556–1629), Italian architect who largely determined the style of early Baroque.

François Mansart (1598–1666), French Baroque architect who replaced the traditional steep pitch roof with the lower-angled form of the *mansard roof*.

Giovanni Lorenzo Bernini (1598–1680), Italian Baroque architect and sculptor: the colonnade of St Peter's in Rome.

Francesco Borromini (1599–1667), Italian Baroque architect: the facade of the church of S. Carlo alle Quattro Fontane (1665–67) in Rome.

Pieter Post (1608–65), Dutch Baroque architect: (with Jacob van Campen) Mauritshuis (the Dutch Parliament) in the Hague.

Louis Le Vau (1612–70), French Baroque architect: the plan of Versailles.

Sir Christopher Wren (1632–1723), English Baroque architect: St Paul's Cathedral (1675–1710) and numerous London churches.

Jules Hardouin-Mansart (1646–1708), French Baroque architect who completed the design of Versailles.

Johann Fischer von Erlach (1656–1723), Austrian Baroque and Rococo architect and influential architectural historian.

Nicholas Hawksmoor (1661–1736), English Baroque architect famous for his London churches.

Sir John Vanbrugh (1664–1726), English architect who developed a particularly personal and English Baroque: Blenheim Palace and Castle Howard.

José de Churriguera (1665–1725), member of a prominent family of architects who developed a distinctly Spanish Baroque.

Germain Boffrand (1667–1754), French Rococo architect.

Johann Lucas von Hildebrandt (1668–1745), Austrian Baroque architect: the Belvedere Palace (Vienna) and the Mirabell Palace (Salzburg).

Nicolas Pineau (1684–1754), French woodcarver, interior designer and architect who was influential in introducing Rococo to St Petersburg (now Leningrad), Russia.

Dominikus Zimmerman (1685–1766), Bavarian architect whose church at Wies (1746–54) in Bavaria is widely considered to be the finest example of German Baroque.

Balthasar Neumann (1687–1753), German Baroque and Rococo architect: The Residenz in Würzburg (Germany).

Johann Michael Fischer (1692–1766), Bavarian architect of late Baroque and Rococo churches.

PALLADIANISM AND NEOCLASSICISM

The influence of Palladio and his English interpreter Inigo Jones was not reflected in British architecture in general until around 1710, when a group of aristocrats 'rediscovered' Palladio, and began to build themselves country mansions and suburban villas, often very closely following Palladio's work. This fascination with Palladio was not reflected elsewhere in Europe: in Spain and Italy the Baroque persisted well into the 18th century. In France a grander classicism, more decorative and 'muscular' than Palladio's, prevailed. Typical is the monumental façade of St Sulpice, Paris (1733–49), composed of superimposed Doric and Ionic screens of columns, flanked by towers, but both in France and in Germany restrained Classical exteriors contrasted with lavish Rococo interiors.

Around the middle of the 18th century British architecture became more consciously 'Antiquarian' or Neoclassical in character. Architects travelled to Italy to study not just Renaissance architecture and Palladio, but also their Classical precedents. There was also a great proliferation of books of Classical, Renaissance and Neoclassical buildings for architects to study. Until 1762 – and the publication of *The Antiquities of Athens* by Nicholas Revett and James Stewart – the term 'Neoclassical' meant 'Neo-Roman', for Greece was, in the 18th century, still a wild and little-known country. Although Stuart and Revett designed several monuments and churches in the Greek style from the 1760s, the Greek Revival reached its height in Britain between 1805 and 1830. It was especially popular with those architects – such as William Wilkins – who favoured simple, bold forms, over the more elegant decorative Roman style.

Although there was not the same Greek Revival in France, the designs of Etienne-Louis Boullée and Claude-Nicolas Ledoux share some of the same fascination with simplified forms. Ledoux designed buildings whose plans reflect their functions, and whose forms are massive and undecorated, presaging both the modern movement and Fascist architecture of the 20th century (see below). Contrasting with the purism of the Greek Revival is the Picturesque movement, which affected all the arts, including architecture. The architect John Nash – whose

celebrated works are Neoclassical – was equally at home designing 'picturesque' buildings such as the Royal Pavilion (1815–21) in Brighton, mixing exotic styles such as Indian and Chinese.

MAJOR ARCHITECTS

William Kent (1685–1748), English Palladian architect and the pioneer of the English informal garden: Horse Guards Building, Whitehall, London (1750–58).

Richard Boyle, Earl of Burlington (1694–1753), English architect and patron of Palladian architecture: Chiswick House (begun 1725), west London, (designed with William Kent).

Giovanni Nicolò Servandoni (1695–1766), Italian theatre designer and architect: façade of St Sulpice, Paris.

Jacques-Germain Soufflot (1713–80), French Neoclassical architect: the Panthéon (1757–90).

Giambattista Piranesi (1720–78), Italian architect, artist and draughtsman whose prints of Classical Rome were an important influence on the early Neoclassical movement.

Sir William Chambers (1723–96), pioneer English Neoclassical architect: Somerset House (1776–1856) in London.

Etienne-Louis Boullée (1728–99), French architect, teacher and co-founder of the Revolutionary Neoclassical movement.

Robert Adam (1728–92), Scottish furniture and interior designer and Palladian architect: the south front and interior of Kedleston Hall, Derbyshire.

Claude-Nicolas Ledoux (1736–1806), French architect and co-founder of the Revolutionary Neoclassical movement.

Jean-François-Thérèse Chalgrin (1739–1811), French Neoclassical architect: arc de Triomphe (1806–35).

Giacomo Quarenghi (1744–1817), Italian architect who designed many important Neoclassical and Palladian buildings in Russia.

John Nash (1752–1835), English Neoclassical architect and planner: Regent's Park and Regent Street, London.

Sir John Soane (1753–1837), English Neoclassical architect: the Bank of England (1792–1833) in London.

Benjamin Latrobe (1764–1810), British-born American architect who pioneered Neoclassicism in the USA.

William Wilkins (1778–1839), English Neoclassical architect: Downing College, Cambridge (designed 1804).

Karl Friedrich Schinkel (1781–1841), German Neoclassical pioneer and state architect of Prussia: Altes Museum (1822–30) in Berlin.

Leo von Klenze (1784–1864), German architect: many Greek Revival public buildings, including the Glyptothek (1816–34) in Munich.

William Strickland (1788–1854), American Neoclassical architect and engineer: Second Bank of the United States.

THE AGE OF REVIVALS

Although the Greek Revival remained strong in Scotland and in Germany until the 1850s, it was past its peak in England by about 1830 when the Gothic

Revival began. Architects had used Gothic details in their buildings sporadically throughout the 18th century, usually in the spirit of the Picturesque movement. Features such as fan vaults were used purely for decoration, often in materials such as plaster rather than the stone of the medieval originals. Arbury Hall (1776) in Warwickshire and Fonthill Abbey (1796–1807) are early examples of this style.

As scholars studied medieval buildings and began to classify the different styles within the Gothic, so architects became more serious about building in a consistent and authentic manner. By the time the new Palace of Westminster came to be designed by Barry and Pugin in the 1830s and 1840s, the Gothic had been appropriated as a particularly British style, and thus especially suitable for the British Houses of Parliament. Pugin, along with the art critic John Ruskin, did not see the Gothic as just another style to be adopted and adapted – they believed that the Gothic was the only Christian style (Classical buildings being 'pagan'). From the late 1840s Gothic Revival buildings appeared all over Britain, and to a lesser extent Europe and the English-speaking world, at first favouring the Perpendicular style (e.g. the Houses of Parliament in London) and later a much bolder 12th-century French Gothic style (e.g. St Finbar's Cathedral, Cork).

The Arts and Crafts movement in Britain is often seen as a secular and domestic equivalent to the Gothic Revival. It was begun in the late 1850s by William Morris, who hated the mechanical quality of machine-made goods and wished to revive traditional craftsmanship. Arts and Crafts is reflected in architecture in the revived use of traditional British building techniques and styles such as tile-hung walls, windows with small panes, and half-timbering.

New building materials and new building types were developed during the 19th century. The most important technological advance was the use of iron for construction. Iron could be used with glass to create great new structures such as the Crystal Palace, built by Joseph Paxton for the Great Exhibition of 1851, or with more conventional brick or stone supports for such purposes as roofing railway stations. It also began to be used structurally for buildings which would otherwise have been built only of stone or brick; e.g. the interior of the National Library in Paris (1860–62), by Henri Labrouste, is composed entirely of a framework of iron columns and floors. Later in the century, buildings entirely supported by a steel framework – often concealed within masonry walls – began to be built, (e.g. the Reliance Building, Chicago, by Burnham and Root), but the full potential of this system was not realized until the 20th century.

Outside Britain 19th-century architects used a tremendous variety of architectural styles, although none predominates. At the end of the 19th century Art Nouveau appeared – a style that affected not only architecture but also the decorative and graphic arts. It is characterized by undulating curves and extreme forms of decoration derived from burgeoning vegetation.

MAJOR ARCHITECTS

Horace Walpole (1717–97), English writer: Strawberry Hill at Twickenham near London (1749, with William Robinson), the first Gothic Revival building.

James Wyatt (1746–1813), English architect: the extravagant early Gothic Fonthill Abbey in Wiltshire.

Karl Friedrich von Schinkel (1781–1841), German (see Neoclassical Architects): Werdersche Kirche (1821–30) in Berlin, one of the first Gothic Revival buildings in Europe.

Sir Charles Barry (1795–1860), English architect: Houses of Parliament (1840–60) in London.

Henri Labrouste (1801–75), French architect and pioneer of iron-frame construction.

Sir George Gilbert Scott (1811–78), English Gothic Revival architect: the Albert Memorial (1863–72) in London.

Augustus Welby Northmore Pugin (1812–52), English Gothic Revival church architect.

William Butterfield (1814–1900), English architect of Gothic Revival churches characterized by their horizontal lines and strong use of colour.

Eugène-Emmanuel Viollet-le-Duc (1814–79), the leading French Gothic Revival architect.

James Renwick (1818–95), American Gothic Revival architect: St Patrick's Cathedral, New York.

George Edmund Street (1824–81), English architect of Gothic Revival churches: the Law Courts (begun 1874) in London.

William Burges (1827–81), English Gothic Revival architect: St Finbar's Cathedral, Cork (1863–76).

Richard Norman Shaw (1831–1912), Scottish architect and urban designer: noted for his domestic architecture.

Antonio Gaudi (1852–1926), Spanish (Catalan) architect of extraordinary organic-looking Art Nouveau façades which rise up to an undulating roofline: Casa Batlló, Barcelona (1905–07).

(Baron) Victor Horta (1861–1946), Belgian Art Nouveau architect: town houses including the Hotel Tassel (1892–93) with its sinuous iron that flows down from the ceilings to form the banisters.

Hector Guimard (1867–1942), French architect: Art Nouveau stations on the Paris Metro.

Charles Rennie Mackintosh (1868–1928), Scottish Art Nouveau architect whose designs had a sparseness and economy: Glasgow School of Art (1897–1909).

Sir Edwin Lutyens (1869–1941), English architect and town planner: the plan and principal buildings of New Delhi, India.

20th-CENTURY ARCHITECTURE

INTERNATIONAL MODERNISM

Structural advances such as steel framing, pioneered in the 19th century, have revolutionized architectural design in the 20th century. Buildings supported by a steel frame can be built much higher than those relying upon a traditional load-bearing wall. The steel frame also allows the construction of buildings whose walls are little more than a skin of steel and glass. When concrete came into general use this principle was further extended by the use of cantilevers, where floors can be internally supported by columns, thus making the outer walls a separate structural element. One of the earliest examples of this is the Fagus factory (1914) at Alfeld-an-der-Leine, Germany, by Walter Gropius. Gropius founded the Bauhaus school, where architects and designers were taught to be aware of the needs of modern-day living and to design functionally according to this understanding.

Le Corbusier popularized the use of reinforced concrete (concrete with steel frame set within it for strength), flat roofs and buildings raised on stilts ('pilotis'). He also designed whole cities (e.g. Chandigarh in India), dividing them up logically into areas for living and working, with green spaces and vast blocks of flats. His theories greatly influenced town planning and were much practised in the post-war rebuilding of Europe.

The style of buildings popularized by the Bauhaus, Le Corbusier and others is known as International Modernism, for the simple reason that the simplicity of the designs meant that similar buildings were found throughout the world. It remained the principal style for large-scale projects until the 1960s, when High-Tech architecture appeared. High-tech began as student drawing-board exercises in the 1960s, and is a logical extension of the Modernist thesis that a building's structure should be evident from its appearance. High-Tech buildings such as the Lloyds' Building in London and the Centre Beaubourg (the Pompidou Centre) in Paris express a building's machine-like functionalism by having its heating, electrical and water piping, and aircon-ditioning, on the exterior.

POST-MODERNISM

Post-Modernism literally means any style of architecture that is not Modernist but has been used since the advent of Modernism. It has been particularly associated with architecture that uses such Classical details as columns and pediments in a decorative manner. Michael Graves in his Portland Public Building (1982) in Portland, Oregon, used brightly coloured and simplified columns, pediments and garlands on a grand scale. This use of bright colours, simplified details, plastics, reflective glass and other shiny materials such as chromium is typical of Post-Modernism.

Although International Modernism has been the most influential style in the 20th century, it has not been the only one. Classical buildings continued to be built in different variations and in the 1930s a particularly simplified and monumental Classicism was used in Nazi Germany and Fascist Italy as a way of suggesting to the people that these were régimes comparable in grandeur and durability to the Roman Empire. In the 1970s and 1980s a more traditional form of Classicism developed when, for example, Quinlan Terry and his teacher Raymond Erith built Classical-style houses that were archaeologically correct in their detailing. This style became very popular in the mid-1980s in Britain, partly as a reaction against the all-pervasive concrete of Modernism, and Terry was called upon to build on a larger, more public scale, as at Richmond Riverside (London). This style has won some important patrons, including the Prince of Wales, who proposes to build an entire new village, with Classically arcaded shops and a town square, in Dorset to the designs of the Luxembourg-born American architect Leon Krier.

MAJOR ARCHITECTS

Louis Sullivan (1856–1924), American architect and pioneer of skyscrapers: Wainwright Building, St Louis, Missouri.

Frank Lloyd Wright (1869–1959), American International Modernist architect: Guggenheim Museum, New York (designed 1943).

Walter Gropius (1883–1969), German architect, architectural theorist, teacher and founder of the Bauhaus,

Le Corbusier (Charles-Édouard Jeanneret; 1887–1965), Swiss-born French International Modernist architect and town planner: Notre-Dame-du-Haut (1950–55), Roncamp (France).

Ludwig Mies van der Rohe (1888–1969), German-born American architect who popularized the rectilinear forms of International Modernism.

Alvar Aalto (1898–1976), Finnish architect, city planner and furniture designer: Säynätsalo town hall (1950–52).

Richard Rogers (1933–), English High-Tech architect: the Lloyds' Building (1981–86) in London.

Quinlan Terry (1937–), English Post-Modernist architect of Classical buildings.

GLOSSARY OF TERMS

abacus the flat upper part of the capital of a column.

apse a semicircular termination or recess at the end of a chapel or the chancel of a church.

arcade a set of arches and its supporting columns.

architrave a beam extending across the top of the columns in Classical architecture.

baptistry a building used for baptisms; sometimes merely a bay or chapel reserved for baptisms.

barrel vault a continuous vault, either semi-circular or pointed in section; also called tunnel vault.

bay a compartment or unit of division of an interior or of a façade – usually between one window or pillar and the next.

belvedere an open-sided structure designed to offer extensive views, usually in a formal garden.

boss a projection, usually carved, at the intersection of stone ribs of Gothic vaults and ceilings.

buttress a vertical mass of masonry built against a wall to strengthen it and to resist the outward pressure of a vault.

campanile a bell tower.

capital the top of a column, usually carved.

caryatid a sculptured female figure serving as a supporting column.

chancel that part of a church containing the altar, sanctuary and choir.

clerestory a row of windows in the upper part of the wall of a church.

console an ornamental Classical bracket supporting part of a wall.

cornice the projecting upper part of the entablature in Classical architecture; also decorative plasterwork between the wall and ceiling.

cross vault see groin vault.

crossing the intersection of the nave and transepts in a church.

dado the lower part of an interior wall when panelled or painted separately from the main part.

drum the cylindrical lower part of a dome or cupola.

entablature in Classical architecture, the beam-like division above the columns, comprising architrave, frieze and cornice.

flying buttress an arch conveying the thrust of a vault towards an isolated buttress.

frieze the decorated central division of an entablature, between the architrave and the cornice.

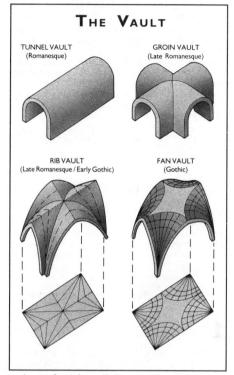

THE VAULT

TUNNEL VAULT
(Romanesque)

GROIN VAULT
(Late Romanesque)

RIB VAULT
(Late Romanesque / Early Gothic)

FAN VAULT
(Gothic)

groin vault (also called a cross vault) the intersection of two barrel vaults. Where barrel vaults require support along both edges, a groin vault only requires support at its four corners, thus allowing windows to be inserted between the supports.

hall church a church where the aisles are more or less the same height as the nave.

keystone the central, wedge-shaped stone of an arch, so called because the arch cannot stand up until it is in position.

lancet window a window with a single, sharply pointed arch. The style is associated with the Early English period of Gothic architecture.

mezzanine a low storey introduced between two loftier ones, usually the ground and first floors.

nave the main body of a church.

ogee arch a pointed arch with an S-shaped curve on both sides.

order any of several Classical styles of architecture. Each order is distinguished by its design of column. (See Greek Architecture.)

oriel a bay window on an upper floor, supported by projecting stonework.

pediment in Classical architecture, the low-pitched gable above the entablature, usually filled with sculpture.

pendentive a triangular section of vaulting with concave sides supporting a circular dome over a square or polygonal base.

pier the vertical masonry support for a wall arch.

rustication heavy stonework with the surface left rough, or with deeply channelled joints, used principally on Renaissance buildings.

spandrel a triangular space between the curves of two adjacent arches and the horizontal moulding above them.

tracery ornamental stonework dividing Gothic windows up into smaller areas of glass.

triforium an arcade of arches, forming a gallery, above the arches of the nave or chancel of a church.

tunnel vault see barrel vault.

tympanum the triangular space bounded by the mouldings of a pediment; also, the semicircular space, often carved, between the lintel and arch of a Gothic doorway.

vault an arched structure – usually of stone, brick or concrete – forming a roof or ceiling.

THE SEVEN WONDERS OF THE WORLD

In the 2nd century BC the writer Antipater of Sidon described the following seven buildings as the pre-eminent sights of the ancient world:

The Pyramids of Giza the only one of the seven wonders in still existence. (See Egyptian architecture.)

The Hanging Gardens of Babylon a series of landscaped terraces, probably 7th century BC.

The Statue of Zeus at Olympia a large figure of Zeus enthroned, c. 420 BC.

The Temple of Artemis at Ephesus a structure famous for its great size.

The Mausoleum of Halicarnassus the huge tomb of the Anatolian king, Mausolus.

The Colossus of Rhodes a vast bronze statue commemorating the siege of Rhodes (305–04 BC).

The Pharos of Alexandria a huge lighthouse constructed c. 280 BC.

WORLD'S TALLEST BUILDING

The tallest office building in the world is the Sears Tower, the national headquarters of Sears, Roebuck and Co. in Wacker Drive, Chicago Illinois, USA. It has 110 storeys and rises to 443 m (1454 ft). Begun in August 1970, it was 'topped out' on 4 May 1973. The addition of two TV antennae brought the total height to 520.29 m (1707 ft). The building's working population of 16 700 is served by 103 elevators and 18 escalators. It has 16 000 windows.

BRITAIN'S TALLEST BUILDING

The tallest office building in the UK is Canary Wharf Tower in London Docklands. It attained its full height of 243.5 m (800 ft) in November 1990. The original development plan for Canary Wharf included three 50-storey office blocks rising to a height of 259 m (850 ft).

Before November 1990 the tallest office building in the UK was the National Westminster Tower in Bishopsgate in the City of London. At 183 m (600 ft 4 in) tall, it is still the tallest cantilevered building in the world.

The highest structure in the UK is the IBA television mast at Belmont in Lincolnshire. Completed in September 1967, it rises to a height of 387.1 m (1272 ft).

THE PERFORMING ARTS
MUSIC

THE ORIGINS OF MUSIC

In its most primitive form, music may evoke the sound of the elements – earth, air, fire, water. Since humans have always been imitative animals, it seems natural that nature itself should have provided the scope for the earliest music and the materials for the earliest musical instruments. Where these materials – sticks, stones, bones, bells, reed pipes or whatever – were not available, the human voice was a more than adequate substitute, relieving loneliness, making contact with other people, reflecting the rhythms of manual labour or simply of walking, celebrating victories, or paying tribute to primitive deities – often in combination with dancing.

The sophisticated evolution of music – even the notes of a simple scale or chord – took place over a period of centuries. There was certainly a rich musical tradition in the years before Christ – for example in India, China, Egypt and Greece, much of it tantalizing because it was passed on orally, not written down. Even today, in Asia particularly, this tradition persists, because music is regarded as improvisatory and contemplative, ceaselessly changing, rather than something perfected and fixed on paper.

In Europe, much of what we today call music emerged through the spread of Christianity and of Judaism, particularly through medieval *plainsong* chants, which were single lines of notated vocal melody in free rhythm (i.e. not divided into bar lengths) sung in churches, and through *Gregorian chant*, named after Pope Gregory I, in whose time (around AD 600) it was systematized. This still forms part of Roman Catholic musical ritual. However, its *modes* (or 'scales') gradually gave way to the modern scale.

THE COMPONENTS OF MUSIC

A musical *note*, therefore, is more than just a 'noise'. It is a single sound of definite pitch and duration, which can be identified in writing. The *pitch* of a note is its height or depth in relation to other notes, or in relation to an absolute pitch. This absolute pitch has internationally been set at A = 440 Hz (hertz); that is, the A above middle C has a frequency of 440 cycles or vibrations per second.

A *scale* is a progression of notes in ascending or descending order, while a *melody* (or tune) assembles a series of notes into a recognizable musical shape. However, to suggest, as some people do, that modern music lacks 'melody' may merely mean that the listener has failed to identify, or come to terms with, the melodies it contains – even Beethoven and Verdi, to some ears, once seemed unmelodic.

A melody usually, though not necessarily, possesses *rhythm*, which listeners often assume to mean *beat*. In fact, the beat of a piece of music is simply its regular pulse, determined by the *bar lines* by which music is metrically divided (two beats in the bar and so forth). Rhythm can be an infinitely more complex arrangement of notes into a mixture of short and long durations within a single bar or across a series of bars. The *time* in which a piece of music (or section of a piece) is written is identified by a *time signature* at the beginning of the piece or section. Thus 3/4 time (three-four time), which is waltz time, represents three crotchets to the bar. This means that the main beat comes every three crotchets: *1* 2 3, *1* 2 3, etc.; 4/4 time, which is march time, has four crotchets: *1* 2 3 4, *1*

2 3 4, etc.; 3/8 and 6/8 represent three and six quavers, respectively. There are also many more complex time signatures.

A melody may have *harmony*. This means that it is accompanied by *chords*, which are combinations of notes, simultaneously sounded. It may also have *counterpoint*, whereby another melody, or succession of notes with musical shape, is simultaneously combined with it. 'Rules' of harmony and counterpoint, stating which notes could be acceptably combined and which could not, have been matters of concern to scholars, teachers and pupils in the course of musical history. But as with any other grammar, progressive composers have known when to break or bend the rules to the benefit of their own music.

TONALITY

The old modes, or scales, employed in the Middle Ages gradually gave way in the 17th century to a modern *tonality* – scales laid out in 12 major and minor *keys*, each consisting of a sequence of seven notes, divided into tones and semitones. Each of the 12 major and minor scales starts on one of the 12 semitones into which an octave is divided. Melodies in a specific key use the notes of that scale, and the order in which the notes are used determines the nature of the melody. On a piano the scale of C major consists entirely of white notes, starting on C.

The notes from C to the next C, either above or below, form an *octave*. A note and another note an octave above sound 'the same' because the higher note has double the frequency. For example, the A above middle C is 440 cycles per second, and the A above that is 880 cycles. From C to D (the first 'white' note above) represents an interval of a tone, from C to C sharp (the first 'black' note) an interval of a semitone, so called because it represents half a tone. But from E to F, and from B to C, also forms a semitone (on a piano there is no black note between them). A scale therefore consists of a mixture of tone and semitone intervals.

A *chromatic scale*, on the other hand, employs nothing but semitones, and thus requires all 12 of the white and black notes to be used. The *whole-tone scale* – used, for example, by Debussy – moves entirely in tones. Starting on C, it would consist of the notes C–D–E–F sharp–G sharp–A sharp.

In musical terminology, a sharp indicates a semitone rise in pitch, and a flat a semitone fall. A natural is a note that is neither sharp nor flat, though the indication sign needs only to be used in special circumstances.

The first note of a scale is known as the *tonic*, or 'keynote'. The tonic of the scale of C is therefore the note C. All other scales require one or more black notes to be played in order to produce the same sequence of intervals.

It is important to remember that scales are conventions – conventions to which our ears are attuned through familiarity. The modes of ancient Greece and medieval Europe employed different sequences of tones and semitones, and the scales used in Indian music and some modern jazz, for example, may use quarter tones.

The development of tonality was celebrated by Johann Sebastian Bach (1685–1750) in 24 keyboard preludes and fugues, one in each key, known as the *Well-tempered Clavier*. These displayed the advantages of the (at the time) novel system of *equal temperament*, whereby all of the notes of a keyboard instrument were 'tempered' to be precisely a semitone apart. The notes C sharp and D flat thus became identical, which was not (and still is not) the case with other instruments. On a string instrument, where the notes are not pre-set, C sharp and D flat are slightly different from each other – imperceptibly so to the ears of most listeners.

In the course of a piece of music, a composer may often *modulate*, or change key, in order to avoid monotony. In Bach's time, an established and logical change was to the key based on the fifth note of the scale, known as the *dominant*. But modulations to harmonically more 'distant' keys were found to be a source of dramatic effects, as also was the sudden contrast between a minor key and a major, exploited by composers such as Beethoven with increasing freedom. By the time Wagner composed *Tristan and Isolde* (1865), modulation had become so fluid that it was only a step away from *atonality*, or the composition of music in no fixed key at all. Atonality was systematized by Schoenberg in what he described as *dodecaphonic* or 'twelve-note' music. In this method of composition, one of the major influences on 20th-century music, the twelve notes within an octave were employed in such a way that there was no home key and no reliance on modulation in the old sense, though key relationships did often remain implied, even if not specifically stated.

MUSICAL FORMS, STRUCTURES AND TERMS

absolute music music in which no extra-musical (i.e. descriptive) element is intended or should be inferred.

a cappella term to describe a vocal work without instrumental accompaniment.

aleatory music music in which each performance is dictated by chance elements.

anthem a short sacred vocal work.

aria a sung solo in opera or oratorio.

arietta a short aria.

atonal (of music) using all 12 notes of the scale.

aubade or **alborda** a morning song.

barcarolle a piece suggesting the song of a Venetian gondolier.

Baroque a period of music, c. 1650 to the death of Bach (1750).

boléro a Spanish dance in three-time.

bourrée an old French dance in common time (4/4).

cadence musical phrase used for ending phrases, sections or complete works.

cadenza a solo virtuoso piece before the final cadence in an aria, or at appropriate places in a concerto.

canon a work or section in which successive entries of the same melody overlap.

cantata a vocal work – sacred or secular – for one or more voices with instruments, sometimes short and light, sometimes extensive and with large forces, but always in several movements.

capriccio or **caprice** a fanciful work in free style.

cassation a divertimento-like work, probably intended for performance in the street.

catch a witty vocal piece for several voices in which the singers 'catch up' each other's words, often making puns with scatalogical or obscene results.

chaconne a graceful Spanish dance in three-time, its melody varied over a repeated bass phrase. Originally it was always in a major key.

chord a group of notes played simultaneously.

chromatic scale a scale including semitones so that all 12 notes within the octave are sounded.

classical strictly: a musical period of c. 1750 to c. 1800; loosely: 'serious' music as opposed to pop, jazz and light.

clef ('key') an indication of the 'register' in which the piece is to be performed. It takes the form of a medieval letter (C, F, or G) placed upon the relevant line of the stave. C = middle C; G = the fifth above; F = the fifth below. See Music Symbols.

coda ('tail') an ending piece designed to close a composition.

concertino a small concerto; also, the soloists in a concerto grosso.

concerto a work, usually in three movements, for one or more solo instruments with orchestra.

concerto grosso a Baroque form in which several soloists (the concertino) play against an orchestra; *cf* the later symphonie concertante.

concertstück ('concert piece') piece for soloist(s) and orchestra, usually in one movement.

continuo (often preceded by 'basso'), up to c. 1800, a keyboard instrument together with viol-/double bass/cello/bassoon/archlute (in various combinations). Both instruments 'continued' the sound, i.e. they 'filled in' any missing harmonies not actually written down by the composer.

contrapuntal using counterpoint.

counterpoint two or more tunes played simultaneously without violating the rules of harmony.

descriptive music see programme music.

development see sonata form.

diatonic relating to the notes of the given key.

divertimento a multi-movement work of a diverting nature.

dodecaphony another term for twelve-note music.

dominant the keynote a fifth above the tonic.

duet a piece for two musicians.

ecossaise a piece in 'Scottish style'.

electronic music music consisting entirely of electronically produced sounds.

elegy a piece of a sad or funereal nature.

ensemble a group of musicians, smaller than an orchestra.

étude or **study** an exercise.

exposition see sonata form.

fantasia a piece whose imaginative course follows no formal rules.

finale the last movement of a multi-movement work; also, the ending of a movement.

fugato in fugal style. See fugue.

fugue a polyphonic composition in which the first statement of a tune is in the tonic; the second statement overlaps the first, and is in the dominant; and so on.

gavotte a lively dance in two-time.

gigue a jig, a sprightly dance in 6/8 or 12/8 time.

glee an 18th-century English piece for three or more voices unaccompanied.

harmony the art of combining notes into chords according to strict rules in a way that is pleasing.

hymn a song of praise to God.

impromptu a form originated by Chopin, supposedly extemporized.

incidental music music for a stage work.

intermezzo ('in the middle') a piece lying between two sections, whether in a piece of music, a play or an opera, etc.

introduction a piece which begins a work, often with material unrelated to the main work.

libretto ('little book') the text of an oratorio or opera. The 'big book' is the musical score.

lied a type of German Romantic song introduced in the late 18th century.

madrigal a secular song for several voices unaccompanied.

mass the Roman Catholic sung service of communion.

minimalism a modern American style of composition involving the extensive repetition of the simplest of melodies or rhythms, sometimes over slowly changing harmonies.

minuet an 18th-century dance in three-time.

modern a musical period from c. 1900 to the present day.

motet a part song, usually sacred in nature and usually unaccompanied.

movement a division of a musical work. The term derives from the various dance movements of the original suite.

musique concrète a French invention in which recorded sounds (usually from everyday life) are manipulated on tape into a composition.

nocturne a night piece.

obligato or **obbligato** ('obligatory' meaning 'indispensable') a vocal or instrumental part which plays an important, but not necessarily solo, role.

occasional music music written for a specific occasion.

opera drama set to music, in which most, or all, of the words are sung.

operetta light opera, often with spoken dialogue.

opus ('work') an individual work or group of works of a composer; each opus is given a number either by the composer or by a subsequent cataloguer. Opus numbers do not always reflect the chronology of composition.

oratorio the religious equivalent of opera but without action, costumes or scenery.

ornaments embellishments of a note or phrase, such as a trill (a rapid alternation of a written note with the one above or below), a gracenote (a subsidiary note appended to a written note), a mordent (a quick touching of the note below during the playing of a written note), etc.

overture the orchestral introduction to an opera or oratorio. A concert overture has no connection with a staged work.

passacaglia ('passing along the street') a form akin to the chaconne, but originally always in a minor key.

pentatonic scale a scale only using five notes (such as the black notes on a piano); often used in folk music.

pitch the precise height or depth of a note, according to its vibrations (cycles) per second. Today, A above middle C = 440 cycles per second.

polka a lively dance of Bohemian or Polish origin in three-time.

polonaise a slow or moderately-paced Polish dance in three-time.

polyphony ('many voiced') a style combining independent but interconnected melodic lines, i.e. using counterpoint.

prelude or **praeludium** an introductory movement.

programme music music which describes a place, event, person, etc. Compare absolute music.

recapitulation see sonata form.

recitative a vocal linking passage in an opera or oratorio imitating speech patterns; often declamatory, and less florid than an aria.

register the compass (lowest to highest notes) of a voice or instrument.

requiem a mass for the dead.

rhapsody a multi-sectioned piece akin to the capriccio, often with a nationalistic content.

ricercare ('research'), a learned piece written in the 16th and 17th centuries to explore obscure avenues of polyphony.

romance a vocal piece which sets a lyric tale to music; also, an instrumental work or movement in a graceful vein with a more agitated central section.

Romantic a period of music, c. 1800–c. 1900.

rondo a work in which the main section alternates with different sections ('episodes').

saltarello an Italian dance, quick, exciting, and involving jumping steps.

sarabande a stately Spanish dance in three-time.

scherzo ('joke') usually a rapid and light-hearted piece.

serenade a work for evening performance.

serial music music in which a sequence of notes are used equally and in strict rotation; the usual form is twelve-note music (see below).

siciliano a graceful dance in three-time, originating in Sicily.

singspiel a play with alternating musical pieces.

solo a work for one musician. In the 18th century solos were often accompanied.

sonata a (usually) multi-movement chamber work for one to four instrumentalists.

sonata form an 18th-century invention in which the first part ('exposition') states the musical material, modulating from tonic to dominant, the second part ('development') develops it (or other material), and the third part ('recapitulation') repeats it often with modifications in the tonic key. There is sometimes a coda.

song a sung melody, with or without accompaniment.

study see étude.

suite a work comprising several separate sections, or 'movements'; each section was originally a different dance.

symphonic poem or **tone** a 19th-century orchestral form, descriptive or evocative in character.

symphonie concertante a showy French invention (often wrongly termed 'sinfonia concertante') in which several soloists play against an orchestra; cf the earlier concerto grosso.

symphony a major orchestral work, usually of four movements.

tempo the pace at which a work is performed.

toccata a fantasia-like piece requiring brilliant execution.

tone poem see symphonic poem.

tonic term relating to the first degree of a minor or major scale.

trio a piece for three musicians. Larger groupings are equally self-explanatory: quartet, quintet, sextet, septet, octet, nonet, dectet.

trio sonata a Baroque and Classical chamber work for two melody instruments and continuo.

twelve-note music system of musical composition devised by Arnold Schoenberg (1874–1951) in which all 12 notes of the scale are used in sequence and in strict rotation.

variations a work which subjects a theme to a series of variations.

MUSICAL DIRECTIONS

accelerando becoming faster.

adagietto the diminutive of adagio, i.e. slightly quicker than adagio.

adagio ('at ease') a slow, comfortable pace.

allegretto the diminutive of allegro, i.e. a little slower than allegro.

allegro ('cheerful' or 'sprightly') a lively but not too fast a pace.

andante ('walking pace') moving along unhurriedly but regularly.

andantino the diminutive of andante. Originally this meant a little slower but today is taken to mean a little faster than andante.

arpeggio notes of a chord played upward or downward in quick succession, in imitation of a harp.

crescendo getting louder.

diminuendo getting quieter.

forte loudly.

fortissimo very loudly.

largo ('spacious') a broad, slow tempo.

lento slow.

mezza voce ('middle voice'), a subdued tone, between piano and forte.

mezzo moderately.

moderato moderate pace. Often used in conjunction with allegro, andante, etc, to moderate that pace.

pianissimo very quietly.

piano quietly.

pizzicato plucking the strings of a bowed instrument.

prestissimo very fast.

presto fast.

ralentando, ritardando or **ritenuto** getting slower.

sotto voce ('under the voice' or 'secretly') between forte and piano but nearer the latter.

vibrato rapid alteration of pitch or intensity of a note intended to impart 'expression'.

vivace lively. In old music, brightly but not too fast.

MUSIC SYMBOLS

CLEFS

Clef symbols denote the register in which a work is to be performed.

Treble: 𝄞 = **G clef.** A representation of a medieval letter G, the focal point of which indicates the line G.

Bass: 𝄢 = **F clef.** A relic of the medieval letter F, centred on the F line.

INDICATIONS OF PITCH

♭ = **Flat.** This sign flattens all the notes of the pitch indicated which follow it in the bar.

♯ = **Sharp.** This sign sharpens all the notes of the pitch indicated which follow it in the bar.

♮ = **Natural.** This sign indicates that a previously flattened or sharpened note is to return to its natural pitch.

REPEAT SIGNS

Repeat (or da capo). Two vertical lines preceded by a colon instruct the player(s) to return to the beginning of the movement or piece, or to the previous repeat sign.

NOTE LENGTHS

Early notation employed four note lengths: double long, long, short ('breve'), and half-short ('semibreve'). Today, the longest note used – the breve – equals the early 'short', but it is uncommon.

Note	Names	Meaning
𝅝	semibreve (whole note)	half-short
𝅗𝅥	minim (half-note)	shortest (i.e. minimum)
𝅘𝅥	crotchet (quarter-note)	hook or crook (from its old appearance)
𝅘𝅥𝅮	quaver (eighth-note)	to trill, or quaver (quiver) in very short notes
𝅘𝅥𝅯	semiquaver (sixteenth-note)	half-quaver
𝅘𝅥𝅰	demisemiquaver (thirty-second-note)	half of half a quaver

The hemidemisemiquaver has one half of the duration or time value of the demisemiquaver. The semihemidemisemiquaver, in turn, has one half of the duration or time value of the hemidemisemiquaver.

American notation In the USA, the semibreve is known as the whole note, the minim as the half note, the crochet as the quarter note, the quaver as the eighth note and so on.

TIME SIGNATURES

Examples of time signatures:

¾ = three quarter-notes (crotchets) to the bar

⅜ = three eighth-notes (quavers) to the bar

Other time signature meanings may be inferred from these examples.

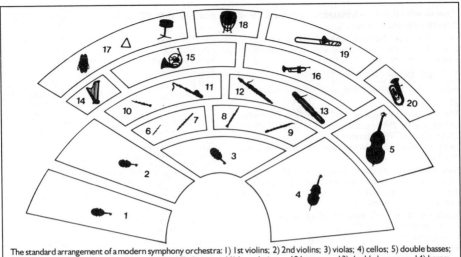

The standard arrangement of a modern symphony orchestra: 1) 1st violins; 2) 2nd violins; 3) violas; 4) cellos; 5) double basses; 6) piccolos; 7) flutes; 8) oboes; 9) cor anglais; 10) clarinets; 11) bass clarinets; 12 bassoons; 13) double bassoons; 14) harps; 15) horns; 16) trumpets; 17/18) percussions; 19) trombones; 20) tubas.

POPULAR INSTRUMENTS

accordion and **concertina** The accordion, invented in Germany in 1822, is box-like, with studs and, sometimes, a keyboard for note selection. The concertina, an English invention of 1829, is hexagonal and never boasts a keyboard.

bongos The bongos are small single-headed paired drums played with the hands. They are popular in Latin American music.

comb and paper Although this impromptu noise-maker is primitive, the membrane and reed principle is widespread and ancient in music. See kazoo.

guitar The guitar is a six-stringed development of the lute, possibly Moorish. It became the dominant instrument in Spanish music as early as the 8th century. The earliest surviving printed music for the guitar dates from 1546, while the first concerto for guitar dates from 1808.

hurdy-gurdy The hurdy-gurdy was a European import from the East in the 9th century. It is roughly violin-shaped. The strings are activated by a resined wheel turned by a crank, and a keyboard stops the strings. The first 'art' use of the instrument was in 1733.

Jew's harp The Jew's harp is a metal frame holding a metal tongue which is plucked with the finger. The resulting vibrations are amplified by the player's mouth cavity. The first concerto was written for the instrument c. 1750, and sophisticated multi-instrument versions appeared later.

kazoo The kazoo is a membrane-vibrating instrument popular with children. The player hums through the instrument, modifying the voice with a hand over the membrane. It was first made in America c. 1850, probably based on ethnic African models.

keyboards 'Keyboards' is a generic term for keyboard instrument(s). The tone is often extensively varied electronically.

mirliton Mirliton is another name for kazoo.

mouth organ or **harmonica** The harmonica was invented in Germany in 1821, but the first concerto was not written for the instrument until 1951. Different notes are produced according to whether the instrument is blown or sucked; the chromatic version can reach four octaves by the use of a slide.

ocarina The ocarina (Italian 'little goose') is a goose-egg-shaped wind instrument, originally clay but now made from plastic. It originated in Egypt c. 3000 BC.

synthesizer A synthesizer is an electronic sound-generator, created c. 1950 to imitate natural instruments, although it also creates its own tones. It is now common in popular music and commercialized jazz, where it is often attached to a keyboard.

tom tom The tom tom is a Western imitation of African drums, used since the 1920s in dance and jazz bands. The first 'art' use of the instrument was in 1943.

ukelele The ukelele (Hawaiian 'jumping flea') was developed in Hawaii from a version of the Portuguese machada in the 1870s. It is popular in America, and has been widely used in jazz and light music.

zither The zither is a horizontal stringed instrument associated with Central Europe but widespread elsewhere in different varieties. The strings are plucked.

ORCHESTRAL INSTRUMENTS

WOODWIND

piccolo or **octave flute** *Earliest concerto:* c. 1735, by Vivaldi. *Earliest orchestral use:* 1717, Handel's Water Music. *History:* The name 'piccolo' (Italian 'small') dates from 1856, but the instrument goes back to prehistory with the flute and sopranino recorder as its more immediate parents.

flute (transverse or cross-blown). *Earliest concerto:* 1725, A. Scarlatti. *Earliest orchestral use:* 1681, Lully. *History:* Prehistoric (c. 18 000 BC); the modern Boehm flute dates from 1832.

oboe *Earliest concerto:* 1708, Marcheselli. *Earliest orchestral use:* 1657, Lully's L'amour malade. *History:* The oboe – the name comes from French *hautbois*, 'high wood' (1511) – originated in the Middle Ages from the schalmey family.

cor anglais *Earliest extant concerto:* 1817, Donizetti. *Earliest orchestral use:* 1722, Volckmar cantata. *History:* Purcell wrote for 'tenor oboe' c. 1690; this may have become the English horn. Alternatively, the name may come from 'angled horn', referring to its crooked shape.

clarinet *Earliest concerto:* c. 1740?, Vivaldi (concerto for two clarinets); c. 1747, Molter (concerto for one clarinet). *Earliest orchestral use:* 1726, Faber's *Mass. History:* The clarinet was developed by J. C. Denner (1655–1707) from the recorder and schalmey families.

bass clarinet *Earliest orchestral use:* 1838, Meyerbeer's *Les Huguenots. History:* The prototype was made in 1772 by Gilles Lot of Paris; the modern Boehm form originated in 1838.

bassoon *Earliest concerto:* c. 1730?, Vivaldi. *Earliest orchestral use:* c. 1619. *History:* The bassoon was introduced in Italy c. 1540 as the lowest of the double-reed group.

double bassoon *Earliest orchestral use:* c. 1730, Handel. *History:* The instrument was 'borrowed' from military bands for elemental effects in opera.

saxophone *Earliest concerto:* 1903, Debussy's *Rhapsody. Earliest orchestral use:* 1844, Kastner's *Last King of Judah. History:* The saxophone was invented by Adolphe Sax, c. 1840.

BRASS

trumpet *Earliest concerto:* before 1700, Torelli; 1796, Haydn (keyed trumpet). *Earliest orchestral use:* c. 1800, keyed; 1835 valved, in Halévy's *La Juive. History:* The natural trumpet is of prehistoric origin: it formed the basis of the earliest orchestras.

horn *Earliest concerto:* 1717–21, Bach or Vivaldi (two horns); before 1721, Telemann (one horn). *Earliest orchestral use:* 1639, Cavalli. *History:* The horn was a prehistoric hunting instrument. The earliest music horns were the German helical horns of the mid-16th century; the rotary valve horn patented in 1832.

trombone *Earliest concerto:* c. 1760, Wagenseil. *Earliest orchestral use:* c. 1600, as part of bass-line. *History:* The Roman *buccina* or slide-trumpet developed into the medieval sackbut, which became the modern trombone c. 1500.

tuba *Earliest concerto:* 1954, Vaughan Williams. *Earliest orchestral use:* 1830, Berlioz's *Symphonie Fantastique. History:* The tuba was patented by W. Wieprecht and Moritz, in Berlin in 1835.

PERCUSSION

anvil *History:* The anvil has been used for musical effect since 1528.

bass drum *Earliest Western use:* 1680, Freschi's opera *Berenice vendicativa. Earliest orchestral use:* 1725, Finger's *Concerto alla Turchesa. History:* The bass drum originated in the ancient Orient.

bells *History:* Bells have been used since ancient Egypt c. 3500 BC, but were first used in 'art' music in a funeral cantata by G. M. Hoffman, c. 1730.

castanets *History:* Castanets were known to the Egyptians by 730 BC. The name comes from the material from which they were made – chestnut wood (Spanish *castaña*).

Chinese blocks or **temple blocks** *Earliest orches-* tral use: 1923, Walton's *Façade. History:* Chinese blocks originated in the ancient Far East and entered European music via jazz bands, c. 1920.

cymbals *Earliest orchestral use:* 1680, Strungk's *Esther. History:* Cymbals originated in Ottoman Turkish military bands.

gong or **tam tam** *Earliest orchestral use:* 1791, Gossec's *Funeral March. History:* The gong originated in Indonesia by or before 300 BC.

marimba *Earliest orchestral use:* before 1914, Grainger's *In a Nutshell. History:* The marimba is an African form of the xylophone.

side or **snare drum** *Earliest orchestral use:* 1749, Handel's *Fireworks Music. History:* The small drums of prehistory were the direct ancestor of the medieval tabor, which developed into its modern form in the 18th century.

tambourine *Earliest orchestral use:* 1820. *History:* The tambourine was used by Arabs in the Middle Ages, but the prototype came from ancient Assyria or Egypt. The word 'tambourine' was first used in 1579.

tenor drum *Earliest orchestral use:* 1842. *History:* The tenor drum was originally developed for military use.

timpani or **kettle drum** *Earliest concerto:* c. 1780, J.C.C. Fischer. *Earliest orchestral use:* in an anonymous intermedia of 1565. *History:* The kettle drum originated in the ancient Orient.

triangle *Earliest orchestral use:* 1774, Glantz's *Turkish Symphony*, but used in opera from 1680. *History:* The triangle was used in Ottoman Turkish military bands.

vibraphone *Earliest orchestral use:* 1932. *History:* The instrument was first used in dance bands in the 1920s.

xylophone *Earliest orchestral use:* 1852, Kastner's *Livre-Partition. History:* The xylophone dates back to ancient times, probably originating in Africa. The earliest known use in Western music was in 1511.

STRINGS

violin *Earliest concerto:* 1698, Torelli. *Earliest orchestral use:* c. 1600. *History:* The violin family is descended from the lyre, although its more direct ancestors were the 6th-century crwth, rebec and fiddle. The first modern instruments, of Lombardic origin, appeared c. 1545. The words violin and fiddle derive ultimately from Latin *vitulari* ('to skip like a calf').

viola *Earliest concerto:* before 1721, Telemann. *Earliest orchestral use:* c. 1600. *History:* See the violin, above.

violoncello or **cello** *Earliest concerto:* 1701, Jacchini. *Earliest orchestral use:* c. 1600. *History:* See the violin, above.

double bass *Earliest extant concerto:* c. 1765, Vanhal. *Earliest orchestral use:* c. 1600. *History:* The double bass developed alongside the violin family, but is a closer relative to the bass viol or violone.

harp *Earliest concerto:* 1738, Handel. *Earliest orchestral use:* c. 1600. *History:* The harp is possibly prehistoric, but it did not attain its modern form until 1792.

KEYBOARD INSTRUMENTS

celesta Instead of strings, as in the piano, the celesta's hammers strike metal plates to give a bell-like effect. The celesta was invented by Mustel in Paris, in 1880; it was first used by an orchestra in Widor's ballet *Der Korrigane*, in the same year. The related **glockenspiel** (German 'bell-play') is sometimes equipped with a keyboard but more usually the plates are struck by hand-held hammers.

clavichord In the clavichord, metal tangents (blades) strike upward to activate the string partway along its length and to 'stop' (damp) the rest. Therefore, one string may serve for many notes but not simultaneously. The clavichord – which dates from the Middle Ages – has an exceedingly intimate voice, making it ideal for domestic use.

harmonium This portable reed-organ was invented by Grenié in Paris, c. 1835. Usually heard as accompaniment for hymns in church, its first 'art' use was by César Franck about 1858.

harpsichord The harpsichord evolved from the psaltery during the 14th century – the earliest surviving example is dated 1521. It usually has two manuals which control sets of strings that are plucked by plectra. Mainly a domestic instrument, it also supported the bass line in early orchestras. The first solo concerto for harpsichord was written c. 1720, but by c. 1800 it was eclipsed by the pianoforte, although it has been reintroduced since 1903.

organ The organ ultimately derives from the antique panpipes, but subsequent developments have made it the biggest and most powerful of all instruments. The first organ concerto was by Handel, c. 1730, while Saint-Saëns first used it in a symphony in 1886.

pianoforte The first piano was built by Cristofori in Florence before 1700, working on the dulcimer principle of hammers hitting strings, and seeking a keyboard instrument which, unlike the harpsichord, could play both loud and soft (hence, its early name, 'fortepiano'). The earliest printed music for piano was by Giustini (1732); first concerto for piano was probably by J. B. Schmidt in 1763. The instrument attained its current name about 1776 and its modern iron-framed form about 1850.

spinet The spinet is the same shape as a harpsichord but it is smaller. The name may come from the Latin *spina* ('spines' or 'quills' – the plucking agent). It developed early in the 15th century.

virginals A table harpsichord, the virginals are rectangular in shape. The English first printed music for the instrument was *Parthenia*, published in London in 1611.

PLAINSONG AND POLYPHONY

Two of the crucial developments in the early history of Western music were *plainsong* and *polyphony*, both of which came about through the spread of the Christian religion, and whose musical foundations lay partly in Jewish chant, partly in Greece and Rome, and almost anywhere else where Christianity had taken root.

PLAINSONG

Plainsong, consisting of a single line of vocal melody in 'free' rhythm (i.e. not divided into metred bar lengths), gained ground during the early years of Christianity and reached its peak in Gregorian chant, still used in the Roman Catholic Church today. Other parts of Europe produced their own ritual music of similar type. In *antiphons*, two separate bodies of singers performed plainsong chants in response to one another.

MONOPHONY AND POLYPHONY

Plainsong, being confined to a single line of unaccompanied melody, falls into the category of *monophonic* music – Greek for 'single sound', implying absence of harmonic support or other melodies performed simultaneously with the original. *Polyphony*, conversely, means 'many sounds', and indicates the simultaneous sounding of two or more independent melodic lines to produce a coherent musical texture. The melodies in polyphony are described as being in *counterpoint* to each other, and the resulting music as *contrapuntal*. The art of polyphony began to emerge in Europe in the 12th and 13th centuries.

ARS ANTIQUA AND ARS NOVA

The most influential centre of musical activity in the 12th and 13th centuries was the church of Notre Dame in Paris. Here there developed a musical style based on plainsong and *organum*, an early form of polyphony involving the addition of parts to a plainsong melody. Such music was described by writers of the early 14th century as 'Ars Antiqua' (Latin for 'old art') to distinguish it from its successor 'Ars Nova' (Latin for 'new art'). Ars Nova, which flourished in France and Italy in the 14th century, incorporated significant innovations in the areas of rhythm and harmony. The polyphonic setting of poetry to music began in this period in the form of the *ballade, rondeau* and *virelai*, collectively known as *chansons*. In France the *troubadours* – itinerant poet-musicians, often of aristocratic birth – were active in Provence in the 11th and 12th centuries. Their German equivalents were the *Minnesinger* (German 'love singers'), whose successors, the guilds of *Meistersinger* ('Mastersingers'), established themselves in some German cities in the 15th and 16th centuries.

MAJOR COMPOSERS

Léonin (active 12th century), French choirmaster of Notre Dame in Paris.

Pérotin (c. 1160–1240), French choirmaster of Notre Dame in Paris.

Walther von der Vogelweide (active late 12th century, early 13th century), the most notable of the German Minnesinger.

Guillaume de Machaut (c. 1300–77), French composer who championed *isorhythms*, whereby rhythm and melody followed strictly repeated patterns that were not in synchronization, and was a pioneer of chansons.

Hans Sachs (1494–1576), the most famous of the Meistersinger. He is the hero of Wagner's opera of that name.

THE RENAISSANCE

Generally, the beginning of the Renaissance in music is reckoned to be found in the increasing secularization of music that took place at the court of Burgundy in the early years of the 15th century. During this period significant developments occurred both in religious and secular musical forms. In the domain of religious music, composers concentrated their efforts on the forms of the mass and the motet. Different types of mass setting developed, especially where the Reformation had established Protestant worship. In Germany the Lutheran chorale (later to exercise a deep influence on the music of J.S. Bach) took root, while in England the anthem (the Protestant equivalent of the Latin motet) took its place in the liturgy of the Church of

England. But as the 16th century progressed, it was Italy that emerged as the crucially important musical centre. The polyphonic mass reached its apogee in the work of three great composers: Palestrina, Victoria and Lassus.

The art of the madrigal – a secular polyphonic composition for several voices, usually based on poems of some literary merit – had its roots in Italy, where early forms of the madrigal first appeared in the 14th century. Early madrigal composers were Flemish composers resident in Italy, and their madrigals were written for three or four voices. A larger number of voices and a more consistently polyphonic style became the norm as the century progressed. Madrigals began to appear in England in the late 16th century. A native English tradition of madrigal composition incorporating features of the secular song as exemplified by Byrd and Gibbons was quickly established by composers such as Morley and Weelkes.

In the Middle Ages instruments were principally used to double voices in vocal polyphony or to provide music for dancing. A burgeoning of instrumental music took place in the 16th century when dance forms such as the stately *pavane* and vigorous *galliard* emerged. Non-dance forms of instrumental music included the *canzona*, the *ricercare* and the *fantasia*. Instrumental music in the 16th century was performed principally on the lute, the organ, the virginal and other stringed keyboard instruments, and by ensembles of viols and other instruments.

MAJOR COMPOSERS

John Dunstable (c. 1385–1453), English composer active in France.

Guillaume Dufay (c. 1400–74), Franco-Flemish composer active at the Burgundian court.

Gilles Binchois (c. 1400–60), Franco-Flemish composer active at the Burgundian court.

Johannes Ockeghem (c. 1425–c. 1495), Flemish composer of sacred and secular music.

Josquin Desprès (1440–1521), Flemish composer of masses, motets and chansons.

Thomas Tallis (c. 1505–85), English composer who introduced the European polyphonic tradition to England: masses, two settings of the Magnificat, and the extraordinary 40-part motet, *Spem in alium*.

Andrea Gabrieli (c. 1510–86), Venetian composer in a flamboyant polychoral (multi-choir) style.

Giovanni Palestrina (c. 1525–84), Italian composer of over 100 masses and 250 motets.

Roland de Lassus (1532–94), Flemish composer of nearly 2000 works.

William Byrd (1543–1623), English composer of sacred music, in particular for the Roman liturgy, and of fantasias for viol consort.

Luis de Victoria (c. 1548–1611), Spanish composer of church music characterized by intense dramatic feeling.

Luca Marenzio (c. 1553–99), Italian composer of madrigals.

Giovanni Gabrieli (1557–1612), Venetian composer of motets featuring a rich instrumental accompaniment. He was the nephew and pupil of Andrea Gabrieli (see above).

Thomas Morley (1557–c. 1602), English organist and composer of madrigals.

Carlo Gesualdo (c. 1560–1613), Italian composer of madrigals.

John Bull (c. 1562–1628), English composer of keyboard music, especially for the virginals.

John Dowland (1563–1626), English composer of songs with lute accompaniment.

Claudio Monteverdi (1567–1643), Italian composer of three innovative operas and the *Vespro della Beata Vergine* ('Vespers of the Blessed Virgin'; 1610), which runs the entire gamut of contemporary types of sacred music.

Thomas Tomkins (1572–1656), Welsh composer of polyphonic madrigals.

John Wilbye (1574–1638), English composer of madrigals.

Thomas Weelkes (c. 1576–1623), English organist and composer of madrigals.

Gregorio Allegri (1582–1652), Italian composer: *Miserere*.

Girolamo Frescobaldi (1583–1643), Italian organist and composer of toccatas, fugues and capriccios.

Orlando Gibbons (1583–1625), English composer of sacred and secular music, including anthems.

Heinrich Schütz (1585–1672), German composer of choral music whose style was to prove an influence on German composers up until the time of Bach and Handel.

MUSIC OF THE BAROQUE

Baroque, Classical and *Romantic* are the categories to which most music performed in the concert hall or opera house are assigned. But the boundaries of each are hazy, and the word Baroque is particularly difficult to define. A word of obscure origin, by the 17th and 18th centuries Baroque had become a term for the ornate, particularly ecclesiastical, architecture of the period. Other than defining a particular period between 1650 and 1750, Baroque has little meaning in application to music, though in its suggestion of ornateness of style it is obviously descriptive of certain types of 17th- and 18th-century composition. A distinction is generally made between composers of the 'early Baroque' (such as Monteverdi, Frescobaldi and Schütz; see above) and those of the 'late Baroque' (most notably Bach and Handel).

The vocabulary and techniques of instrumental and vocal composition underwent a massive expansion in the 17th century. Revolutionary change took place also in the formal organization of music: the medieval modes that had been the basis of polyphonic composition in the 16th century giving way during the 17th century to a system involving the exclusive use of modern scales. In addition, innovations such as the *concertato* style – in which specific instrumental or vocal parts were accompanied by a *basso continuo*, or 'thorough bass' (involving a low-pitched instrument such as a cello or bass viol combined with a harpsichord, organ or lute) – distinguish the Baroque from the Renaissance that preceded it. The development of the two major new instrumental genres of the Baroque – the sonata and the concerto – was largely the work of Italian composers. As well as providing the emerging vocal genres of opera, cantata and oratorio, Italy was the principal source of instrumental ensemble music throughout the 17th century.

In France, as in England and Germany, composers were strongly influenced by Italian models of instrumental music. However, the greatest achievements of the French Baroque were in the domain of harpsichord music and opera. The overtures and dance movements from Lully's operas enjoyed a flourishing life outside the operatic context. So-called French overtures on the Lullian model were used by Handel in some of his operas and oratorios, and became an integral part of the Baroque orchestral suite.

Opera is the Italian word for 'work'. but as an abbreviation of *opera in musica* (a 'musical work'), it began to be used in 17th-century Italy for music dramas in which singers in costume enacted a story with instrumental accompaniment. The first true masterpieces in the form were by the Venetian composer Monteverdi (see above), and many of the most prominent opera composers of the late 17th century and early 18th century came from Naples, giving rise to the term the *Neapolitan School*. The greatest operas of the early 18th century were written in England by Handel.

MAJOR COMPOSERS

Louis Couperin (c. 1626–61), French composer of harpsichord and organ music.

Jean-Baptiste Lully (1632–87), Italian-born French composer who established the form of the French opera, which was to reach its peak in the operas of Rameau.

Arcangelo Corelli (1653–1713), Italian pioneer composer of concertos and sonatas: the 12 *Concerti Grossi* (1714) established the form of the concerto grosso.

Johann Pachelbel (1653–1706), German composer of canons, airs and 78 choral preludes.

Henry Purcell (1659–95), English composer of theatre music, church music, string fantasias and sonatas: the miniature opera *Dido and Aeneas* (1689), the incidental music for *The Fairy Queen* (1692) and *Queen Mary's Funeral Music* (1695).

Alessandro Scarlatti (1660–1725), Neapolitan composer of operas (of which 115 survive). One of Scarlatti's important innovations was the three-movement form of the Italian opera overture or *sinfonia*, regarded by many as being the earliest forerunner of the Classical symphony.

François Couperin (*'Le Grand'*; 1668–1733), French composer – nephew of Louis (see above). He composed in a wider range of genres than his uncle, but is best known for his elegant harpsichord pieces.

Tommaso Albinoni (1671–1750), Italian composer who wrote prodigious amounts of instrumental and vocal music, including 42 operas.

Reinhardt Keiser (1674–1739), German composer of over 100 operas.

Antonio Vivaldi (1678–1741), Italian priest, violinist and composer: sacred music, 94 operas (of which 50 survive), sonatas, cantatas and more than 460 concertos, including *The Four Seasons* (1725).

Georg Phillipp Telemann (1681–1767), German composer of concertos and orchestral suites who, in his lifetime, enjoyed a greater reputation than his friends Bach and Handel.

Jean-Philippe Rameau (1683–1764), French composer of operas: *Hippolyte et Aricie* (1733) and *Castor et Pollux* (1737).

Domenico Scarlatti (1685–1757), Neapolitan composer – son of Alessandro (see above). His 550 single-movement sonatas for harpsichord considerably extended the technical and musical possibilities of keyboard writing.

George Frideric Handel (1685–1759), German-born British composer, impresario, musical director, virtuoso keyboard player and teacher. In his operas, oratorios, concertos and suites, he created a highly individual style of writing, best seen in: *Water Music* (1717), *Music for the Royal Fireworks* (1749), 14 operas, anthems including *Zadok the Priest* (1727), the *Concerti Grossi* (1734–40) and numerous oratorios, including *Saul* and *Israel in Egypt* (1739), *Messiah* (1741), *Solomon* (1748) and *Jephtha* (1751).

Johann Sebastian Bach (1685–1750), German composer of concertos, sonatas, over 250 cantatas and keyboard music. He is held by many to be the greatest of all Baroque composers: *Brandenburg Concertos* (1721), a collection of 48 preludes and fugues *The Well-Tempered Clavier* (1722–44), *St John Passion* (1723), *St Matthew Passion* (1729), the *Mass in B minor* (1733–38), and the *Goldberg Variations* (1742).

Wilhelm Friedemann Bach (1710–84), German organist and composer – eldest son of Johann Sebastian (see above).

Carl Philipp Emmanuel Bach (1714–88), German composer of over 200 sonatas – 3rd son of Johann Sebastian.

Johann Christian Bach ('The English Bach'; 1735–82), German composer of concertos, symphonies, sacred music and 13 operas – 11th son of Johann Sebastian (see above).

THE CLASSICAL PERIOD

If the music of J.S. Bach represents the summit of the Baroque era, that of his sons, particularly Carl Philip Emanuel and Johann Christian (see above), provides a link with the period loosely known as Classical. It was a time of new developments in the art of the symphony and concerto, of the birth of the string quartet and piano sonata, and of the humanizing of opera.

Vienna, the capital of the Austrian Habsburg Empire, now became the centre of musical progress, with Haydn, Mozart, and, before long, Beethoven as its principal representatives. In the next generation Schubert was to sustain Vienna's musical pre-eminence. Both Beethoven and Schubert were to extend the Classical forms and infuse them with a Romantic sensibility. All four composers collectively became known as the First Viennese School. Classicism, in musical terms, has been defined as a style accepting certain basic conventions of form and structure (notably the sonata form; see under Musical Forms, Structures and Terms above), and using these as a natural framework for the expression of ideas. Unlike Romantic music (see below), which developed out of Classicism, it saw no need to break the set boundaries, although in a discreet way its greatest practitioners did so more often than not.

MAJOR COMPOSERS

Giovanni Battista Sammartini (c. 1698–75), Italian composer of about 2000 works in many genres.

Christoph Willibald von Gluck (1714–87), German composer who made opera more genuinely dramatic: the operas *Orpheus and Eurydice* (1762) and *Alceste* (1767).

Johann Stamitz (1717–57), German composer of the Mannheim School, whose works are characterized by 'Mannheim rockets' (brilliant scale passages).

Jiři Benda (1722–95), Czech composer who pioneered melodrama: *Ariadne auf Naxos* (1774).

Giuseppe Sarti (1729–1802), Italian composer of over 70 operas.

Franz Joseph Haydn (1732–1809), Austrian composer of piano sonatas and trios, concertos, operas, masses, string quartets (a form he established) and 104 symphonies: the *London Symphonies* (Nos. 92–104; 1789–95), and the oratorios *The Creation* (1798) and *The Seasons* (1801).

Karl Stamitz (1745–1801), German composer of the Mannheim School – son of Johann (see above).

Luigi Boccherini (1747–1805), Italian composer of operas, 20 symphonies and 91 string quartets.

Antonio Salieri (1750–1825), Italian composer of over 40 operas. His hostility to Mozart led to (groundless) rumours that he poisoned Mozart.

Wolfgang Amadeus Mozart (1756–91), Austrian composer of 49 symphonies, over 40 concertos, 26 string quartets, 21 operas, 7 string quintets and sonatas: the operas *Le nozze di Figaro* (The Marriage of Figaro; 1786), *Don Giovanni* (1787), *Così fan tutte* (1790) and *Die Zauberflöte* (The Magic Flute; 1791), the symphonies *Paris* (1778), *Prague* (1786) and *Jupiter* (1790), and the orchestral piece *Eine kleine Nachtmusik* (1787).

Luigi Cherubini (1760–1842), Italian composer of masses and 30 operas: the operas *Médée* (1797) and *les Deux Journées* (adapted in English as The Water Carrier; 1800).

Ludwig van Beethoven (1770–1827), German composer of chamber music, 9 symphonies, 5 piano concertos, violin concerto, triple concertos, 32 piano sonatas, 16 string quartets and over 200 song settings: the opera *Fidelio* (1805), the symphonies *Eroica* (No. 3; 1803–04), *Pastoral* (No. 6; 1807–08) and *Choral* (No. 9; 1817–23), the piano sonatas *Pathétique* (1799), *Moonlight* (1800–01) and *Hammerklavier* (1817–19), the *Emperor* piano concerto (1809), and the *Missa Solemnis* (1818–23). See also the Music of the Romantics, below.

Niccoló Paganini (1782–1840), Italian virtuoso violinist and composer of violin concertos and 24 caprices.

Franz Schubert (1797–1828), Austrian composer of 9 symphonies, string quartets, piano sonatas and 600 *Lieder*: the symphonies *Unfinished* (No. 8; 1822) and *Great* (No. 9; 1825), the piano quintet *Die Forelle* (The Trout; 1819), a string quartet in C major (1828), the piano sonata *Grand Duo* (1824), the song cycles *Die schöne Müllerin* (1823) and *Winterreise* (1827), and the song settings *Erlkönig* (1815) and *Die Forelle* (The Trout; 1817).

MUSIC OF THE ROMANTICS

Romanticism in music was not necessarily born in 1800. But the first year of the 19th century, when Beethoven had just produced the first of his nine symphonies, is as good a time as any by which to commemorate the establishment of composers as individual artists – rather than as servants of rich patrons, which had been the case throughout the Baroque and Classical periods.

Beethoven, in his third symphony, the *Eroica* (1803–4), finally shattered the bounds of Classicism. It was not only the biggest symphony ever written until that time (though Beethoven himself was to surpass it in his ninth), it was also recognized to be a personal testament in music, the first of its kind, symbolizing Beethoven's battle with the growing deafness that was to destroy his career as a public performer, but which intensified his inspiration as a composer. The crucial role played by Beethoven in the progress of symphonic form, and of the art of the string quartet and piano sonata, was something no later composer could ignore. In his last quartets in particular, Beethoven explored the most profound emotional and spiritual tensions with a musical daring not seen again for another century.

The composer as artist was attracted to representational or *programme music* – music that evokes pictorial scenes or finds some way to tell a story in purely musical terms. Berlioz, Mendelssohn and Liszt were notable proponents of this genre. Liszt coined the term 'symphonic poem' for his descriptive orchestral works. In opera, Wagner expanded and transformed the art of opera into what he preferred to describe as 'music drama'. In Italy, Verdi followed a parallel if more cautious path.

The rise of nationalist feeling all over Europe inspired many composers. Although Liszt's Hungarian Rhapsodies lacked Hungarian authenticity (in that Liszt mistook gypsy music for Hungarian folk music), nationalism in music was becoming a major force. Folk rhythms, folk dances, folk songs, folk legends and folk harmonies served as important sources of inspiration to such composers as Smetana, Dvořák, Grieg and Tchaikovsky.

MAJOR COMPOSERS

Ludwig van Beethoven (1770–1827), see above and The Classical Period.

Niccolo Paganini (1782–1840), see The Classical Period.

Daniel Auber (1782–1871), French composer of 42 operas: *La Muette de Portici* (1828).

Carl Maria von Weber (1786–1826), German composer of operas, symphonies, chamber and piano music: the operas *Der Freischütz* (1821) and *Oberon* (1826).

Gioacchino Rossini (1792–1868), Italian composer of 36 operas: *Tancredi* (1813), *The Barber of Seville* (1816), *La Cenerentola* (Cinderella; 1817), *La gazza ladra* (The Thieving Magpie; 1817) and *William Tell* (1829).

Gaetano Donizetti (1797–1848), Italian composer: the operas *Maria Stuarda* (1834) and *Lucia di Lammermoor* (1835).

Franz Schubert (1797–1828), see The Classical Period.

Vincenzo Bellini (1801–35), Italian composer: the opera *Norma* (1825).

Hector Berlioz (1803–69), French composer: the symphonies *Symphonie Fantastique* (1830) and *Harold in Italy* (1833), the choral symphony *Roméo et Juliette* (1839), the operas *Benvenuto Cellini* (1838) and *Les Troyens* (The Trojans; 1856–59), and the cantata *La Damnation de Faust* (1846).

Johann Strauss the elder (1804–49), Austrian composer of waltz music and *Radetzky March* (1848).

Mikhail Glinka (1804–57), Russian composer: the operas *A Life for the Tsar* (1836) and *Ruslan and Ludmilla* (1842).

Felix Mendelssohn (1809–47), German composer: the overtures *A Midsummer Night's Dream* (1826) and *Hebrides* (or *Fingal's Cave*; 1830), and the oratorios *St Paul* (1836) and *Elijah* (1846).

Frédéric Chopin (1810–49), Polish composer of nocturnes, ballades, mazurkas, polonaises, studies, waltzes and scherzos, all for the piano.

Robert Schumann (1810–56), German composer of songs, piano music and symphonies: the song cycles *Dichterliebe* (Poet's Love; 1840) and *Frauen-liebe und -Leben* (1840).

(Ferencz) Franz Liszt (1811–86), Hungarian composer of a series of 13 descriptive orchestral works ('symphonic poems') and of piano pieces: the symphonies *Faust* (1853–61) and *Dante* (1856), the symphonic poem *Les Préludes* (1856), and the piano piece *Liebesträume* (1850).

Giuseppe Verdi (1813–1901), Italian composer of opera: *Nabucco* (1842), *Il Trovatore* (1853), *La Traviata* (1853), *Aida* (1871), *Otello* (1887) and *Falstaff* (1893).

Richard Wagner (1813–83), German composer of opera: *The Flying Dutchman* (1843), *Tannhäuser* (1845), *Lohengrin* (1846–48), *Tristan and Isolde* (1857–59), *The Mastersingers of Nuremberg* (1862–67), *Parsifal* (1877–82) and the opera cycle *The Ring* (*Das Rheingold*, *Die Walküre*, *Siegfried* and *Götterdämmerung*; 1852–74).

Charles François Gounod (1818–93), French composer: the opera *Faust* (1859).

Jacques Offenbach (1819–80), French composer of operetta: the opera *The Tales of Hoffmann* (1881).

César Franck (1822–90), Belgian composer: *Symphonic Variations* (1885).

Bedřich Smetana (1824–84), Czech composer of operas, chamber music and symphonic poems: the opera *The Bartered Bride* (1866).

Anton Bruckner (1824–96), Austrian composer: *Te Deum* (1881–84) and nine symphonies.

Johann Strauss the younger (1825–99), Austrian composer: the operetta *Die Fledermaus* (1874), and the waltzes *An der schönen blauen Donau* (Blue Danube) and *Kaiser-Walzer* (Emperor Waltz).

Johannes Brahms (1833–97), German composer of symphonies, choral works and a large canon of chamber music: the choral works *A German Requiem* (1868) and *Alto Rhapsody* (1869).

Camille Saint-Saëns (1835–1921), French composer: the opera *Samson et Dalila* (1877) and the orchestral pieces *Danse macabre* (1874) and *Carnaval des animaux* (1886).

Léo Delibes (1836–91), French composer: the opera *Lakmé* (1883) and the ballet *Coppélia* (1870).

Mily Balakirev (1837–1910), Russian composer who made an important contribution to the national school of Russian music.

Georges Bizet (1838–75), French composer: the opera *Carmen* (1875).

Modest Musorgsky (1839–81), Russian composer: the opera *Boris Godunov* (1868–72) and the piano piece *Pictures at an Exhibition* (1874).

Pyotr Ilyich Tchaikovsky (1840–93), Russian composer: the symphony *Pathétique* (1893), the opera *Eugène Onegin* (1877–78), and the ballets *Swan Lake* (1875–76), *The Sleeping Beauty* (1888–89) and *Nutcracker* (1891–92).

Antonin Dvořák (1841–1904), Czech composer: *Slavonic Dances* (1878–86) and the symphony *From the New World* (No. 9; 1893).

Jules Massenet (1842–1912), French composer: the operas *Manon* (1884) and *Don Quichotte* (1910).

Sir Arthur Sullivan (1842–1900), English composer of operetta and oratorios, the former to libretti by W.S. Gilbert.

Edvard Hagerup Grieg (1843–1907), Norwegian composer: the incidental music for the play *Peer Gynt* (1876).

Nikolay Rimsky-Korsakov (1844–1908), Russian composer of operas including *The Snow Maiden* (1881–82) and *The Golden Cockerel* (1906–07), and of orchestral pieces including *Scheherazade* (1888).

Gabriel Fauré (1845–1924), French composer: the opera *Pénélope* (1913) and the *Requiem* (1884).

Hubert Parry (1848–1918), English composer of songs and choral music: *Songs of Farewell* (1916) and *Jerusalem* (1916).

Vincent D'Indy (1851–1931), French composer: *Symphonie Cévenole* (1886).

Charles Villiers Stanford (1852–1924), Irish composer: *Irish Symphony* (No. 3; 1886) and *Songs of the Sea* (1904).

Leoš Janáček (1854–1928), Czech composer of operas: *Jenufa* (1904), *Katya Kabanova* (1921), *The Cunning Little Vixen* (1924), *The Makropoulos Case* (1926) and *From the House of the Dead* (1930).

Engelbert Humperdinck (1854–1921), German composer: the opera *Hansel und Gretel* (1893).

Ruggero Leoncavallo (1858–1919), Italian composer: the opera *Pagliacci* (1892).

Giacomo Puccini (1858–1924), Italian composer of operas: *La Bohème* (1896), *Madama Butterfly* (1904) and *Tosca* (1904).

Isaac Albéniz (1860–1909), Spanish composer whose works are characterized by traditional Spanish rhythms: *Iberia* (1906–09).

Gustav Mahler (1860–1911), Austrian composer of nine large-scale symphonies: the symphonies *Resurrection* (No. 2; 1884–94) and *Symphony of a Thousand* (No. 8; 1906–07).

Pietro Mascagni (1863–1945), Italian composer: the opera *Cavalleria rusticana* (1890).

Richard Strauss (1864–1949), German composer of operas and symphonic poems: the operas *Salome* (1905), *Elektra* (1909) and *Der Rosenkavalier* (1911).

Enrique Granados (1867–1916), Spanish composer of operas and piano music: *Goyescas* (1914).

MODERNISTS AND NEW MUSIC

The years around 1900 marked the beginnings of Modernism. Wagner's *Tristan and Isolde* (1865) – see above – was the German figurehead, with Debussy's *Pelléas and Mélisande* (1902) as its French counterpart. From these two operas, the major trends in 20th-century music all flowed.

Modernism in music – as in the visual arts and literature – involved a radical break with existing conventions. It also involved what often appears as a greater distancing between the composer and the audience – audiences have tended to find Modernist works 'difficult'. However, although Modernism has been in the intellectual forefront of music in the 20th century, many composers have followed more accessible paths.

Music since 1945 has evolved in many different ways. for many composers – especially in the 1950s – the once revolutionary twelve-note technique of Schoenberg became the new orthodoxy, while the avant-garde of the 1960s and 1970s enthusiastically embraced the novel sound possibilities offered by the development of electronic music.

MAJOR COMPOSERS

Edward Elgar (1857–1934), English composer:

Enigma Variations (1898–99) and the oratorio *The Dream of Gerontius* (1899–1900).

Hugo Wolf (1860–1903), Austrian composer, notably of songs: *Italian Serenade* (1892).

Frederick Delius (1862–1934), English composer: the orchestral piece *On hearing the first cuckoo in spring.*

Claude Debussy (1862–1918), French composer whose works are characterized by a 'dream-like' quality sometimes called 'musical impressionism': numerous works for piano, the orchestral pieces *Prélude à l'après-midi d'une faune* (1892–4), *Nocturnes* (1893–99) and *La Mer* (1903–05), and the opera *Pelléas et Mélisande* (1902).

Carl Nielsen (1865–1931), Danish composer whose work is characterized by 'progressive tonality': six symphonies including *The Inextinguishable* (No. 4; 1915–16).

Jean Sibelius (1865–1951), Finnish composer: seven symphonies, the symphonic poems *Kullervo* (1892) and *Finlandia* (1899), and the suite *Karelia* (1893).

Alexander Glazunov (1865–1936), Russian composer: the ballet *The Seasons* (1901).

Ferruccio Busoni (1866–1924), Italian composer: the piano piece *Fantasia contrappuntistica* (1910–12).

Erik Satie (1866–1925), French composer for piano: the ballet *Parade* (1917), and the piano pieces *Trois Gymnopédies* (1888) and *Trois morceaux en forme de poire* (1903).

Franz Lehár (1870–1948), Hungarian composer of operetta: *The Merry Widow* (1905).

Alexander Skryabin (1872–1915), Russian composer of symphonies and piano sonatas: the symphony *Prometheus* (No. 5; 1909–10).

Ralph Vaughan Williams (1872–1958), English composer: *Sea Symphony* (1906–09), the opera *The Pilgrim's Progress* (1951) and songs based upon folk-songs.

Sergey Rakhmaninov (1873–1943), Russian composer whose works – notably for piano – are characterized by Romantic nostalgia.

Gustav Holst (1874–1934), English composer: the suite *The Planets* (1914–16) and *Egdon Heath* (1927).

Charles Ives (1874–1954), American composer of highly individualistic works: the orchestral set *Three Places in New England* (1903–14).

Arnold Schoenberg (1874–1951), Austrian composer whose later works are characterized by atonality, particularly the twelve-note system which he devised: the string sextet *Verklarte Nacht* (1899), the orchestral piece for soprano and five instruments *Pierrot Lunaire* , and the unfinished opera *Moses und Aron* (1932–51).

Maurice Ravel (1875–1937), French composer: the orchestral pieces *Rapsodie espagnole* (1907), *Pavane pour une infante défunte* (1910) and *La Valse* (1919–20), and the ballet score *Boléro* (1928).

Manuel de Falla (1876–1946), Spanish composer whose works echo Andalusian folk music: the ballet *The Three-Cornered Hat* (1917–19).

Ottorino Respighi (1879–1936), Italian composer: the ballet *The Fantastic Toyshop* (1919) and the orchestral suites *Fountains of Rome* (1914–16), *Old Airs and Dances for Lute* (1917) and *Pines of Rome* (1924).

John Ireland (1879–1962), English composer of chamber music and songs.

Ernst Bloch (1880–1959), Swiss composer who became a naturalized American citizen: *Israel Symphony* (1912–16).

Béla Bartók (1881–1945), Hungarian composer of fiercely modernist music based on folk music: *Music for Strings, Percussion and Celesta* (1936) and *Concerto for Orchestra* (1943).

Karol Szymanowski (1882–1937), Polish composer: the ballet *Harnasie* (1926).

Igor Stravinsky (1882–1971), Russian-born composer: the ballets *The Firebird* (1910), *Petrushka* (1911) and *The Rite of Spring* (1913).

Zoltán Kodály (1882–1967), Hungarian composer whose works are characterized by a strong national flavour: the opera *Háry János* (1925–27).

Percy Grainger (1882–1961), Australian composer who became a naturalized American citizen: folk songs and lighter works often based upon traditional tunes.

Edgard Varèse (1883–1965), French-born American composer, who made early experiments in electronic music.

Anton Webern (1883–1945), Austrian composer whose works are characterized by serialism: chamber symphony (1924) and chamber concerto (1934).

Alban Berg (1885–1935), Austrian composer: the operas *Wozzeck* (1914–20) and *Lulu* (1928–35), and the *Lyric Suite* (1928).

Heitor Villa-Lobos (1887–1959), Brazilian composer: the orchestral works *Bachianas Brasileiras* (1930–44).

Frank Martin (1890–1974), Swiss composer: *Petite Symphonie Concertante* (1946).

Sergey Prokofiev (1891–1953), Russian composer: the ballet *Romeo and Juliet* (1935), the operas *The Love for Three Oranges* (1921) and *War and Peace* (1941–52), and the piece for orchestra and narrator *Peter and the Wolf* (1936).

Arthur Honegger (1892–1955), Swiss composer: the orchestral piece *Pacific 231* and the oratorio *Jeanne d'Arc au bûcher.*

Darius Milhaud (1892–1974), French composer whose works are characterized by polytonality.

Paul Hindemith (1895–1963), German composer who is associated with the term 'utility music': the opera *Mathis der Maler* (1938).

Carl Orff (1895–1982), German composer: the oratorio *Carmina Burana* (1935–36).

Henry Cowell (1897–1965), American composer of 20 symphonies.

Ernst Křenek (1900–), Austrian composer who became a naturalized American citizen: the opera *Jonny spielt auf* (1925–26).

Kurt Weill (1900–50), German composer: *Die Dreigroschenoper* (The Threepenny Opera; 1927).

Aaron Copland (1900–90), American composer of works based on American folk idioms: the ballets *Billy the Kid* (1938) and *Appalachian Spring* (1944).

William Walton (1902–83), English composer: *Façade* (1921) and the cantata *Belshazzar's Feast* (1931).

Joaquin Rodrigo (1902–), Spanish composer of music for guitar and orchestra in a traditional Spanish style: *Aranquez Concerto* (1940).

Luigi Dallapiccola (1902–75), Italian composer whose works were the first in Italy to use the twelve-note method.

Aram Khachaturian (1903–1978), Armenian composer: the ballet *Spartacus* (1956).

Michael Tippett (1905–), English composer: the operas *The Midsummer Marriage* (1955), *The Knot*

Garden (1970) and *New Year* (1989).

Dmitri Shostakovitch (1906–75), Russian composer of 15 symphonies and string quartets: the opera *The Lady Macbeth of the Mtsensk District*.

Olivier Messiaen (1908–), French composer of organ, piano and religious works: the piano work *Catalogue d'oiseaux*.

Elliott Carter (1908–), American composer: *Symphony of Three Orchestras* (1977).

Samuel Barber (1910–81), American composer: *Adagio for Strings* (1938) and the opera *Vanessa* (1958).

John Cage (1912–), American composer: the percussion and electronic pieces *Imaginary Landscapes* (1939–62).

Benjamin Britten (1913–76), English composer: operas *Peter Grimes* (1945), *Billy Budd* (1951), *The Turn of the Screw* (1954) and *Death in Venice* (1973).

Witold Lutoslawski (1913–), Polish composer of works incorporating modern techniques: *String Quartet* (1964).

Iannis Xenakis (1922–), Romanian-born Greek composer of works which, although mostly scored for conventional instruments, are often written with the aid of a computer.

Gyorgy Ligeti (1923–), Hungarian composer: *Requiem* (1965) and the opera *Le Grand Macabre* (1975).

Luigi Nono (1924–), Italian composer of works characterized by their uncompromising severity: the opera *Intolleranza* (1960).

Luciano Berio (1925–), Italian composer of electronic and other modern music.

Pierre Boulez (1925–), French composer of works using the twelve-note technique: *Le Marteau sans maître* (1953–55) and *Pli selon pli* (1957–62).

Hans Werner Henze (1926–), German composer: the oratorio *The Raft of Medusa* (1968) and the war opera *We Come to the River* (1976).

Karlheinz Stockhausen (1928–), German composer: the seven-part opera cycle *Licht* (1984–), the piece for three orchestras *Gruppen* (1957), and *Hymnen* (1967), *Prozession* (1967), *Stimmung* (1968) and *Jubilaeum* (1977).

Edison Denisov (1929–), Soviet composer of highly original music which draws upon electronic techniques and folk music.

Krzysztof Penderecki (1933–), Polish composer of works characterized by the use of sensational effects: *Threnody for the Victims of Hiroshima* (1960) and the opera *The Devils of Loudon* (1969).

Harrison Birtwhistle (1934–), English composer: the opera *Punch and Judy* (1966–67).

Peter Maxwell Davies (1934–), English composer: the opera *Taverner* (1970), the theatre pieces *Vesalii Icones* (1969) and *Eight Songs for a Mad King* (1969).

Alfred Shnitke (1934–), Soviet composer of works that often include a humorous element, for example a 'silent' cadenza in which the performer has to go through the motions of playing.

Terry Riley (1935–), American composer of minimalist music characterized by the extensive repetition of simple melodies in changing harmonies.

Philip Glass (1937–), American minimalist composer of avant-garde operas.

FAMOUS CONDUCTORS

Gasparo Spontini (1774–1851), Italian composer: held important conducting posts in Paris and Berlin.

Louis Spöhr (1784–1859), German violinist and composer: court music director at Cassel 1822–59, he was the first conductor to use a baton.

Hector Berlioz (1803–69), French conductor known for grandiose and exotic effects; better remembered as a composer.

Felix Mendelssohn (1809–47), German composer: conductor of the Leipzig Gewandhaus Orchestra.

Louis Jullien (1812–60), French conductor and composer whose showy manner delighted London audiences for many years.

Hans von Bülow (1830–94), German conductor, pianist and composer: based in Munich and Berlin, but travelled widely.

Arthur Nikisch (1855–1922), Hungarian-born German violinist: conductor at Leipzig Opera and Gewandhaus, Boston SO, etc.

Gustav Mahler (1860–1911), Austrian composer and conductor: noted for his work in Hamburg (1891–7), the Vienna Imperial Opera (1897–1907) and the Metropolitan Opera, New York (1908–11).

Felix Weingartner (1863–1942), Austrian composer and conductor of many European, English and American orchestras.

Richard Strauss (1864–1949), German composer: conductor of the Berlin Royal Court Orchestra, Munich PO and Berlin PO.

Arturo Toscanini (1867–1957), Italian cellist and conductor, noted for his severely disciplined approach and phenomenal memory: founded and conducted the NBC SO.

Sir Henry Wood (1869–1944), English conductor who founded the London Promenade concerts.

Pierre Monteux (1875–1964), French-born American conductor: he gave the riotous première of Stravinsky's *The Rite of Spring* in Paris in 1913, founded the Paris SO (1929) and worked with the San Francisco and Boston SOs. Chief conductor of the LSO in 1961 (signing a 25-year contract at the age of 86).

Bruno Walter (1876–1962), German pianist and conductor: after appointments in Vienna, Berlin, Leipzig, Salzburg and Amsterdam, he emigrated to the USA, there conducting the Los Angeles, NBC and New York orchestras and recording with the Columbia SO.

Sir Thomas Beecham (1879–1961), English conductor and founder of the Beecham SO (1909), Beecham Opera Co (1915), LPO (1932) and RPO (1946).

Leopold Stokowski (1882–1977), American organist and conductor of Polish/Irish parentage: conducted widely but is associated with Cincinnati, Philadelphia, NBC, Hollywood Bowl, New York and Houston orchestras.

Vaclav Talich (1883–1961), Czech conductor: chief conductor of the Czech PO (1919–41) and after the war.

Ernest Ansermet (1883–1969), Swiss conductor: founder of L'Orchestre de la Suisse Romande.

Otto Klemperer (1885–1973), German conductor and composer, noted for his work late in life with the Philharmonia Orchestra in the UK.

Wilhelm Furtwängler (1886–1954), German conductor, composer and author remembered chiefly for his work with the Berlin PO.

Sir Adrian Boult (1889–1983), English conductor of the BBC SO, LPO and many others in the UK and abroad.

Erich Kleiber (1890–1956), Austrian conductor of the Berlin Staatsoper: also conducted in South America, London, Amsterdam, etc.

Sir John Barbirolli (1890–1970), English conductor and cellist particularly remembered for his association with the Hallé Orchestra.

Karl Böhm (1894–1981), Austrian conductor best remembered for his work with Viennese and Berlin orchestras.

Sir Malcolm Sargent (1895–1967), English organist, composer and chief conductor of the Royal Choral Society and the BBC SO: associated especially with the 'Proms' from 1921 until his death.

Dmitri Mitropoulos (1896–1960), Greek conductor and composer: worked with the Minneapolis SO and New York PO.

Hans Schmidt-Isserstedt (1900–73), German composer: conductor of the North German Radio and Vienna SOs.

Franz Konwitschny (1901–62), German conductor, notably of the Leipzig Gewandhaus Orchestra.

Antal Dorati (1906–88), Hungarian-born American conductor and composer: worked with many orchestras in the Old and New Worlds, latterly with the Philharmonia Hungarica.

Karel Ancerl (1908–73), Czech conductor, principally of the Czech PO: director of the Toronto SO.

Herbert von Karajan (1908–89), Austrian conductor particularly remembered for his work with the Philharmonia and Berlin Philharmonic Orchestras.

Sir Georg Solti (1912–), Hungarian conductor and pianist, director of many orchestras, including Royal Opera House, London, Chicago SO and LPO: director of Salzburg Easter Festival from 1992.

Leonard Bernstein (1918–90), American conductor, pianist and composer: laureate conductor for life of the New York PO.

Sir John Pritchard (1921–89), English conductor: director of Royal Liverpool PO, LPO, Huddersfield Choral Society and BBC SO.

Sir Neville Marriner (1924–), English violinist and conductor: founder of the Academy of St Martin-in-the-Fields (1959) and of the Los Angeles Chamber Orchestra (1969) and music director of both the Minneapolis and Stuttgart Radio SOs since 1979.

Sir Charles Mackerras (1925–), Australian conductor, director and chief guest conductor of many orchestras in Australia, America and Europe: recently working with the Orchestra of the Age of Enlightenment and the National Welsh Opera Company.

Sir Colin Davis (1927–), English conductor: chief of the Bavarian Radio SO and guest conductor of the Boston SO, LSO, etc.

Kurt Masur (1927–), German conductor, working with the Dresden Philharmonic and, since 1969, with the Leipzig Gewandhaus: honorary conductor of Yomiuri Nippon SO, Tokyo and director of New York PO from 1992/3 season.

Bernard Haitink (1929–), Dutch violinist and conductor: music director of Royal Opera House, London, and previously at Glyndebourne, Amsterdam Concertgebouw, LPO, etc.

André Previn (1929–), American jazz pianist and music director at MGM studios: turned increasingly to serious music as conductor at Houston and

Pittsburgh, then with the LSO, RPO, and Los Angeles PO, and currently principal conductor of the RPO.

Gennadi Rozhdestvensky (1931–), Russian conductor who, after important posts in Russia and Stockholm, became conductor of the BBC SO.

Claudio Abbado (1933–), Italian conductor and pianist: resident or principal conductor of La Scala, Milan, Vienna PO, London SO, director of the Chamber Orchestra of Europe and artistic director of the Berlin PO.

Seiji Ozawa (1935–), Japanese conductor: musical director of Toronto SO, San Francisco SO, Boston SO, and principal conductor of the New Japan PO.

Simon Rattle (1955–), English conductor: principal conductor of the City of Birmingham SO.

Other prominent conductors are mentioned in the list of Orchestras of the European Community.

MAJOR ORCHESTRAS OF THE EUROPEAN COMMUNITY

Belgium

Baroque Orchestre 'La Petite Bande', conductor Sigiswald Kuijken

Orchestre National de Belgique (National Orkest van Belgié), conductor Mendi Rodan

Orchestre Philharmonique de Liège, conductor Pierre Bartholomée

Orchestre Symphonique de la RTBF, conductor Alfred Walter

Denmark

Arhus Symphony Orchestra, principal conductor Norman del Mar

Royal Danish Orchestra, joint conductors Mikael Schonwandt and Peter Ernst Lassen

Radio Symphony Orchestra, Denmark: guest conductors

France

Ensemble Intercontemporain, director Peter Eötvös

Orchestre de Lyon, conductor Serge Baudo

Orchestre de Paris, musical director Daniel Barenboim

Orchestre du Capitole de Toulouse, music director Michael Plasson

Orchestre du Philharmonique de Strasbourg, music director Theodor Guschlbauer

Germany

Berlin Symphony Orchestra, chief conductor Claus Peter Flor

Bamberg Symphony Orchestra, conductor Horst Stein

Berlin Philharmonic Orchestra, director Claudio Abbado

Leipzig Gewandhaus Orchestra, conductor Kurt Masur

Munich Philharmonic Orchestra, director Sergiu Celibidache

Musica Antiqua Köln, director Reinhard Goebel

Radio Symphony Orchestra (RIAS), Berlin, conductor Riccardo Chailly

Symphonie Orchester des Hessischen Rundfunks, conductor Eliahu Inbal

Symphonie-Orchester des Norddeutschen Rundfunks, conductor Günter Wand

Ireland

New Irish Chamber Orchestra, director Nicholas Kraemer
Radio Telefis Eireann Symphony Orchestra, principal conductor János Fürst

Italy

I Solisti Veneti, conductor Claudio Scimone
Orchestra Sinfonica dell'Accademia Nazionale di Santa Cecilia, conductor Giuseppe Sinopoli

Luxembourg

Luxembourg Radio and TV Symphony Orchestra

Netherlands

Hague Residentie Orchestra, conductor Hans Vonk
Rotterdam Philharmonic Orchestra, conductor James Conlon
Royal Concertgebouw Orchestra, Amsterdam, conductor Bernard Haitink

Portugal

Gulbenkian Chamber Orchestra, conductor Renato Ruotolo
Gulbenkian Foundation Orchestra, conductor Michel Corboz

Spain

Barcelona City Orchestra, director Antoni Ros Marba
National Orchestra of Spain, director Jesús López Cobos
Symphony Orchestra of Spanish Radio and Television, director Miguel Angel Gómez Martinez.

United Kingdom

Academy of Ancient Music, director Christopher Hogwood
Academy of St Martin-in-the-Fields, director Iona Brown
BBC Philharmonic Orchestra, conductor Edward Downes
BBC Scottish Symphony Orchestra, principal conductor Jerzy Maksymiuk
BBC Symphony Orchestra, principal conductor Andrew Davis
BBC Welsh Symphony Orchestra, conductor Erich Bergel
Bournemouth Symphony Orchestra, conductor Rudolph Barshai
Chamber Orchestra of Europe, director Claudio Abbado
City of Birmingham Symphony Orchestra, conductor Simon Rattle
English Chamber Orchestra, principal conductor Jeffrey Tate
English Concert, director Trevor Pinnock
Hallé Orchestra, principal conductor Stanislaw Skrowaczewski
London Mozart Players, director Jane Glover
London Philharmonic Orchestra, principal conductor Klaus Tennstedt; musical director Franz Welser-Möst
London Symphony Orchestra, director Michael Tilson Thomas
Philharmonia Orchestra, principal conductor Giuseppe Sinopoli
Royal Liverpool Philharmonic Orchestra, principal conductor Marek Janowski
Royal Philharmonic Orchestra, principal conductor André Previn
Scottish National Orchestra, principal conductor Neeme Järvi
Ulster Orchestra, principal conductor Vernon Handley

MAJOR EC OPERA COMPANIES

Belgium

Antwerp: Koninklijke Vlaamse Opera
Brussels: Koninklijke Muntschouwburg (Théâtre Royal de la Monnaie/Opéra National)
Ghent: Opera voor Vlaanderen (Flanders Opera)
Liège: Opéra Royal de Wallonie

Denmark

Arhus: Den Jyske Opera (Jutland Opera)
Copenhagen: Royal Danish Opera

France

Lyon: Opéra de Lyon
Nice: Opéra de Nice
Paris: Opéra de Paris
Strasbourg: Opéra du Rhin

Germany

Berlin: Deutsche Oper
  Deutsche Staatsoper
  Komische Oper
Bonn: Oper der Stadt Bonn
Cologne: Oper der Stadt Köln
Dresden: Staatsoper
Düsseldorf: Deutsche Oper am Rhein
Frankfurt-am-Main: Oper Frankfurt
Hamburg: Hamburgische Staatsoper
Karlsruhe: Badisches Staatstheater
Munich: Bayerische Staatsoper
Rostock: Volkstheater
Schwerin: Staatstheater
Stuttgart: Staatstheater

Greece

Athens: Ethniki Lyriki Skini (National Opera)

Ireland

Cork: Cork City Opera
Dublin: Dublin Grand Opera Society
  Irish National Opera
Wexford: Wexford Festival Opera

Italy

Bologna: Teatro Communale di Bologna
Florence: Teatro Communale Firenze
Milan: Teatro alla Scala
Venice: Teatro la Fenice (Teatro Malibran)

Netherlands

Amsterdam: De Nederlandse Operastichting (Netherlands Opera)

Portugal

Lisbon: São Carlos Theatre

Spain

Barcelona: Gran Teatro del Liceo
Madrid: Compañia Lirica del Teatro de la Zarzuela

United Kingdom

Cardiff: Welsh National Opera
Glasgow: Scottish Opera
London: English National Opera
  Royal Opera House (Covent Garden)

NOTABLE OPERA SINGERS

Adreana Basile (c. 1580–c. 1640), Italian contralto
Luigi Lablanche (1794–1858), Italian bass
Henriette Sontag (1806–54), German soprano
Osip Petrov (1806–78), Russian bass
Maria Malibran (1808–36), Spanish mezzo-soprano
Jenny Lind (1820–87), Swedish soprano, the 'Swedish nightingale'
Pauline Viardot Garcia (1821–1910), French mezzo-soprano
Teresa Stolz (1834–1902), Bohemian soprano
Christine Nilsson (1843–1921), Swedish soprano
Victor Maurel (1848–1923), French baritone
Dame Nellie Melba (Helen Porter Mitchell; 1861–1931), Australian soprano
Enrico Caruso (1873–1921), Italian tenor
Feodor Chaliapin (1873–1938), Russian bass
Amelita Galli-Curci (1882–1963), Italian soprano
Giovanni Martinelli (1885–1969), Italian tenor
Maggie Teyte (Maggie Tate; 1886–1976), English soprano
Beniamino Gigli (1890–1957), Italian tenor
Toti dal Monte (1893–1975), Italian soprano
Kirsten Flagstad (1895–1962), Norwegian soprano
Rosa Ponselle (1897–1981), American soprano
Marian Anderson (1902–), American contralto
Zinka Milanov (1906–89), Yugoslav soprano
Sir Peter Pears (1910–86), English tenor
Jussi Bjorling (1911–60), Swedish tenor
Kathleen Ferrier (1912–53), English contralto
Licia Albanese (1913–), Italian-born American soprano
Mario del Monaco (1915–82), Italian tenor
Elisabeth Schwarzkopf (1915–), German soprano
Tito Gobbi (1915–84), Italian baritone
Boris Christoff (1918–), Bulgarian bass
Birgit Nilsson (1918–), Swedish soprano
Nicola Rossi-Lemeni (1920–), Italian bass
Franco Corelli (1921–), Italian tenor
Giuseppe di Stefano (1921–), Italian tenor
Renata Tebaldi (1922–), Italian soprano
Maria Callas (1923–77), Greek soprano
Victoria de los Angeles (1923–), Spanish soprano
Carlo Bergonzi (1924–), Italian tenor
Dietrich Fischer-Dieskau (1925–), German baritone
Nicolai Gedda (1925–), Swedish tenor
Dame Joan Sutherland (1926–), Australian soprano
Leontyne Price (1927–), American soprano
Dame Janet Baker (1933–), English mezzo-soprano
Montserrat Caballé (1933–), Spanish soprano
Teresa Berganza (1935–), Spanish mezzo-soprano
Luciano Pavarotti (1935–), Italian tenor
Placido Domingo (1941–), Spanish tenor
Dame Kiri te Kanawa (1944–), New Zealand soprano
Frederica von Stade (1945–), American mezzo-soprano
José Carreras (1946–), Spanish tenor

JAZZ

JAZZ SINGERS AND PERFORMERS

William Christopher Handy (1873–1958), American blues musician and songwriter: the song *St Louis Blues*.
Buddy Bolden (Charles Bolden; 1878–1931), American jazz cornetist.
'Jelly Roll' Morton (Ferdinand la Menthe Morton; 1885–1941), American jazz pianist, singer and songwriter.
Joe 'King' Oliver (1885–1938), American jazz cornetist.
Sidney Bechet (1897–1959), American jazz clarinetist and soprano saxophonist.
Bessie Smith (1898–1937), American blues singer.
Duke Ellington (Edward Kennedy Ellington; 1899–1974), American jazz composer, bandleader and pianist: the song *Mood Indigo*.
Louis 'Satchmo' Armstrong (1900–71), American jazz trumpeter and bandleader.
Bix Beiderbecke (Leon Beiderbecke; 1903–31), American jazz cornetist, pianist and composer: the piano piece *In a Mist*.
Glenn Miller (1904–44), American jazz trombonist, composer and bandleader: the songs *Moonlight Serenade* and *In the Mood*.
Count Basie (William Basie; 1904–84), American jazz pianist and bandleader who was famous for his 'big band' style.
Jimmy Dorsey (James Dorsey; 1904–57), American jazz alto saxophonist, clarinetist and bandleader.
Earl Hines (1905–83), American jazz pianist, composer and bandleader.
Tommy Dorsey (Thomas Dorsey; 1905–56), American jazz trombonist and bandleader.
Stéphane Grappelli (1908–), French jazz violinist and pianist.
Benny Goodman (Benjamin David Goodman; 1909–86), American jazz clarinetist and bandleader.
Art Tatum (Arthur Tatum; 1910–56), American jazz pianist.
Django Reinhardt (1910–53), Belgian jazz guitarist.
Artie Shaw (Arthus Arshewsky; 1910–), American jazz clarinetist and bandleader.
Gil Evans (1912–88), American jazz pianist and composer.
Woody Herman (Woodrow Herman; 1913–87), American clarinetist and bandleader.
Nat King Cole (Nathanial Coles; 1919–65), American jazz pianist and singer.
Billie Holiday (1915–59), American blues singer.
Theolonius Monk (1917–82), American jazz pianist.
Dizzy Gillespie (John Birks Gillespie; 1917–), American jazz trumpeter.
Ella Fitzgerald (1918–), American jazz singer.
Dave Brubeck (1920–), American jazz pianist.
Charles Brown (1920–), American jazz guitarist.
Charlie 'Bird' Parker (1920–55), American jazz saxophonist.
Erroll Garner (1923–), American jazz pianist.
Sarah Vaughan (1924–90), American jazz singer.
Oscar Peterson (1925–), American jazz pianist.

Max Roach (1925–), American jazz drummer.

John Coltrane (1926–67), American jazz saxophonist.

Miles Davis (1926–), American jazz composer and trumpeter.

Fats Domino (Antoine Domino; 1928–), American jazz and blues pianist, singer and composer: the song *Blueberry Hill.*

Carl Perkins (1928–58), American jazz pianist.

Ray Charles (1932–), American jazz singer, pianist and composer.

Ornette Coleman (1930–), American jazz alto saxophonist.

Wayne Shorter (1933–), American tenor saxophonist.

DANCE

Forms of dance vary from those that employ the whole body in free and open movement to those in which movement is restricted to certain parts – just to the eyes in the case of one Samoan courtship dance. Dance is usually rhythmic, often with an element of repetition, and forms a pattern in both time and space. Dance can be a simple expression of pleasure in movement of the body or an art form of complex patterns and significant gestures.

Folk dances, the traditional dances of particular areas, are dances that have evolved rather than have been invented. They often retain features that once had magical and ritual significance. Emphasis is usually on the group, although pairs or individuals may be featured or encouraged to give bravura displays. More modern social dances developed from courtship dances and, although some may involve unison dancing by the group, the emphasis is usually placed on couples.

HISTORY OF DANCE

PREHISTORY AND ANCIENT TIMES
In prehistory, unorganized or loosely organized dances took place for warlike or communal purposes – courtship, harvest, rain or religion. The origins of theatrical dance in Greece date from c. 500 BC. Folk dances in Europe gradually became divorced from magic and ritual, but their origins are often still clear to see (e.g. the *horn dance* performed annually at Abbot's Bromley in England, the *hora* of eastern Europe, and the *sardanas* of Catalonia).

THE MIDDLE AGES
In the 12th century, court dancing began to develop, particularly in Provence. Processional or winding chain dances began to give way to couples dancing together. By the 14th century two main forms of dance had emerged. The basic medieval dance – the *basse danse* – used small gliding steps, the feet scarcely losing contact with the floor. The *haute danse* was a high leaping dance, mainly for men. Popular dances in the Middle Ages included:

pavane a stately processional dance, derived from instrumental music in Padua, and possibly the first stylized dance.

galliard a sprightly jigging dance from Italy. Its name implies 'gaiety'.

THE 15th CENTURY
In 1416, Domenico de Piacenza published the first European dance manual *De Arte Saltandi et Choreas Ducendi* (On the Art of Dancing and Directing Choruses). The first true ballet, with settings by Leonardo da Vinci, was danced at Tortona, in Piedmont, Italy, in 1489. Ballet was introduced to the court of Henry VIII of England as masque. Popular dances in the 15th century included:

branle an English clog dance with circular figures.

allemande (French 'from Germany') a stately processional dance.

courante (Italian 'current', that is 'running'), a stately Italian dance which included the elegant bending of the knees.

volta (Italian 'vault') a twirling dance in which the woman is lifted from the floor and bounced upon the man's knees.

THE 16th CENTURY
The first printed account of a ballet – dated 15 October 1581 – described the dance held to celebrate the marriage of the duc de Joyeuse and Marguerite de Lorraine. During the 16th century, brighter social dances appeared with faster livelier steps. Popular dances in the 16th century included:

morisca (Spanish 'Moorish') a Spanish dance derived from dances of Moorish Spain and first recorded in 1446 in Burgos.

sarabande a slow and graceful dance, involving advances and retreats and couples passing between rows of dancers. It was introduced to Spain probably from Morocco c. 1588.

THE 17th CENTURY
In 1661 the French king, Louis XIV, established a group of dancing instructors, the *Académie Royale de Danse*, to codify court dances. Its director, Charles Louis Beauchamp (1636–1705), is credited with inventing the 'five positions'. After the founding of the *Académie Royale de Musique et de Danse* under the composer Lully in 1672 there was a permanent demand for professional dancers. Ballet masques, often with hideous and elaborate masks, became popular.

In Britain lively longways (facing rows) and circle dances became very popular. They involved simple walks, runs, and skipping and hopping steps, often with couples changing positions within a set. In 1651 John Playford's *English Dancing Master*, a collection of tunes and steps, was published.

The first waltz was developed from the minuet and the Ländler in 1660, but the dance did not gain popularity until considerably later. Popular dances in the 17th century included:

mazurka a Polish round dance for eight couples with the second beat accentuated.

gigue a lively dance based on the traditional English jig.

bourée a lively dance starting on the upbeat.

chaconne a graceful dance introduced into Spain from Peru c. 1580 and then spread through western Europe.

gavotte (Provençal dialect *gavoto*, 'a native of the Alps') a lively dance in which each couple had the chance to dance on their own. It reached its greatest popularity at the court of the French king Louis XIV.

minuet (from the French *pas menu*, 'small steps') a favourite at the French court, this delicate dance was often followed by the boisterous gavotte as a contrast. It was recorded by Lully in 1663.

passacaglia a popular Italian dance, resembling the chaconne, but in a minor key.

rigaudon a lively French dance, known in England as the rigadoon.

Ländler (German 'small country') a traditional Austrian dance in which the partners turned in each other's arms with a hop and a step.

matelot a Dutch sailor's clog dance.

contredanse a dance for opposing groups. A mistranslation of 'country dance', contredanse developed in France and was reintroduced into England.

cotillion (French 'petticoat') a dance for two groups of four pairs each. The quadrille developed from the cotillion in the 19th century.

THE 18th CENTURY

The movement towards dance as a form of artistic expression is often said to have begun with the publication of Jean-Georges Noverre's *Lettres sur la danse er sur les ballets* (1760). In ballet, Gaetano Vestris perfected the *grand jeté* at the Paris Opera. Pirouettes and leaps pushed forward the physical frontiers of ballet, and Vestris's abandonment of the customary masks in *Medée et Jason* (1770) opened ballet to the possibility of showing emotion through movement.

In social dance the waltz developed in Austria – the first recorded use of the word 'waltz' was in 1754. The gavotte and the minuet continued to be popular.

THE 19th CENTURY

By the 19th century court dances had been superseded by professional dancers. La Sylphide (1832) – choreographed by Filippo Taglione – is said to have ushered in the era of true European ballet, abandoning the more rigid portrayal of Greek myths. Sometime after 1800 ballerinas began to dance 'on point' (on the tips of the toes), stiffening the ends of their dancing slippers to give more support. Pointwork became a key feature of choreography for women.

In social dance improvisation was allowed by the two most popular dances of the age, the waltz and the polka. In these dances contact was made in the embrace that dancers used for much of the 20th century. Dance styles were also developed for the popular theatre, including the cancan, a high-kicking exhibitionist female dance that originated on the Paris stage c. 1835. Popular dances in the 19th century included:

waltz an Austrian dance that developed from the Ländler – see above.

quadrille a French derivation of the 17th-century contredanse. It comprises a series of five 'figure' dances for four couples.

polka a bouncing dance which was introduced to Paris in 1843. It developed from a Bohemian courtship dance.

cakewalk a graceful walking dance which takes its name from the cakes offered as prizes for competitive performances held in the southern states of USA from c. 1872. It was introduced into ballrooms from c. 1900.

Paul Jones a group dance in which partners are exchanged.

the lancers a quadrille for eight or 16 couples.

THE 20th CENTURY

In ballet, the *Ballets Russes* was established in Paris by Diaghilev in 1909. His dazzling dancers and stunning stagings attracted wild enthusiasm, and brought Russian ballet to the West. Offshoots from the *Ballets Russes* established companies in the Russian classical tradition in the USA, UK, Australia and other countries. New free dance forms emerged as dancers such as Isadora Duncan and Ruth St Denis incorporated elements from other cultures – particularly Greek and Far Eastern – into abstract dance. Rudolf Laban and his disciples greatly extended the range of dance movement, while Emile Jacques-Dalcroze developed a system of musical rhythm in movement. Later in the century younger choreographers such as Twyla Tharp and Alvin Ailey incorporated rock, African, West Indian and jazz music into their work.

In social dance, most of the new dances of the 20th century originated in the Americas, and had their origins in the offbeat syncopated rhythms originally brought by black slaves from Africa. Other influences included the jigs and clog dances of Irish immigrants and the mixing of African, Spanish and Portuguese styles in Latin American dance. Other dances have been invented for particular shows or films, or to promote sheet music or record sales. The ballroom dance craze, which began in the 1920s, involved mostly couples dancing to the music of small instrumental groups. From 1939, dancing became increasingly energetic as jazz and pseudo-jazz groups provided the musical accompaniment. The modern discothèque style – that is the use of recorded music for dancing – originated in Paris c. 1951.

Popular 20th-century dances include:

samba a lively Latin American dance in double time. It originated in Brazil c. 1885 and was introduced to ballrooms c. 1920 as the maxixe. The name 'samba' was renamed c. 1940.

quickstep a dance in rapid quadruple time. It was invented in the USA in 1900 and reached a peak of popularity in the 1920s.

tango a lively syncopated Latin American dance characterized by gliding steps and dramatic pauses. It was introduced to the USA from Argentina, but its origins may have been the Cuban *habañera*.

barn dance a traditional American form of dancing associated with festivities held on the completion of a new barn.

one-step an early 20th-century dance characterized by long quick steps. It was a precursor of the foxtrot.

Boston a slow dance derived from the waltz.

turkey trot a ragtime variation of the one-step. It gained considerable popularity during World War I.

foxtrot a dance in quadruple time, alternating long and short steps. There are both slow and quick variations. It was introduced in 1912 in the USA and was, allegedly, named after Harry Fox. The slow foxtrot evolved c. 1927 into the 'blues dance'.

Charleston one of the most popular dances of the 1920s, named after a Mack and Johnson song of 1923 about the town Charleston, South Carolina. The dance is characterized by a side kick from the knee.

pasodoble a Spanish-style two-step.

rumba a Cuban dance popularized in 1923.

black bottom a type of jerky athletic foxtrot first mentioned in the *New York Times* in December 1926.

conga a single-file dance developed in 1935 from the rumba and African dances.

jitterbug a fast American dance to jazz accompaniment. It gained great popularity during World War II.

jive a jerky improvised variation of the jitterbug.

mambo an off-beat rumba of Cuban origin. It was introduced into the USA in 1948.

rock'n'roll an energetic free dance, in part evolved from the jive and in part improvised. Characterized by a heavy beat and simple melody, it was introduced by Bill Haley and his Comets in 1953.

cha cha cha a variation of the mambo in which couples dance with lightly linked hands. It was introduced in 1954.

twist a lively dance – characterized by body torsion and knee-flexing – in which partners rarely touch. It was introduced in 1961.

bossa nova a variation of the samba, originating in Brazil.

go-go a repetitious dance of verve, usually exhibitionist. It dates from 1965.

reggae a dance introduced from Jamaica in 1969. It is characterized by the strong accentuation of the upbeat.

pogo a dance invented by punk rockers in 1976. Dancers jump vertically from the ground in imitation of a pogo stick.

disco dancing a flamboyant freestyle modern dance accompanied by exaggerated hand movement. It was popularized by the film *Saturday Night Fever* (1977).

break dancing a modern style of dance in which dancers perform acrobatic feats. It was introduced c. 1980.

robotics a style of dance in which dancers imitate clockwork dolls with rigid limb movements.

BALLET

Ballet is a theatrical form of dance based upon a set of positions, steps and expressive gestures that demand considerable skill and training. Ballet may tell a story or offer abstract patterns of movement. Though generally aiming at an appearance of effortless grace, it can also be highly dramatic. Balletic entertainments were first developed in the French court in the 16th century, but ballet companies in many countries have created their own distinctive national styles.

There are several ways in which ballet differs from other forms of dance. Most obvious is the 90° 'turned-out' position of the feet, which permits a remarkable degree of balance in all positions. Ballet also requires a tension and arching of the foot and Achilles tendon to provide a powerful jump and to cushion landing. Dancers begin training at an early age to achieve the positions required, and must continue to exercise every day.

The history of ballet is summarized in the History of Dance (above).

BALLET TERMS

à terre steps which do not entail high jumps. They include the *glissade, pas balloné* and *pas brisé*.

battement ballet exercises.

batterie or battu a jump during which a dancer beats the calves sharply together.

corps de ballet a group of dancers supporting the principal dancers.

divertissement a self-contained dance within a ballet, designed purely as an entertainment or to show off a dancer's technique.

elevation any high jump in ballet. Elevations include the *entrechat, rivoltade, pas de chat,* and *cabriole.*

enchaînement a sequence of steps linked to make a harmonious whole.

entrechat a vertical jump during which the dancer changes the position of the legs after beating the calves together.

fouetté a spectacular pirouette in which the dancer throws his raised leg to the front and side in order to achieve momentum for another turn.

jeté a jump from one leg to the other, basic to many ballet steps. These include the *grand jeté en avant,* in which the dancer leaps forward as if clearing an obstacle, and the *jeté fouetté* where the dancer performs a complete turn in mid-air.

pas a basic ballet step in which weight is transferred from one leg to another. The term is also used in combination to indicate the number of performers in a dance; a *pas seul* is a solo and a *pas de deux* a dance for two dancers.

pirouette a complete turn on one leg, performed either on the ball of the foot or on the toes.

plié bending the legs from a standing position. *Demi-plié* involves bending the knees as far as possible while keeping the heels on the floor.

relevé bending the body from the waist to one side or the other during a turn or a pirouette.

rivoltade or revoltade a step in which a dancer raises one leg in front, jumps from the other and turns in the air, landing in the original position but facing the other way.

saut a plain jump in the air without embellishment.

soutenu a movement executed at a slower tempo than usual.

sur les pointes on the toes.

variation a solo by a male dancer in a *pas de deux*.

MAJOR CHOREOGRAPHERS

Pierre Beauchamps (1636–?1705), French choreographer and theorist who is credited with inventing the 'five positions'.

John Weaver (1673–1760), English choreographer of 'pantomime-ballets'.

Marie Sallé (1707–56), French choreographer who placed emphasis on plot and interpretation.

Jean-Georges Noverre (1727–1810), French choreographer: the inventor of the 'ballet d'action'.

Charles-Louis Didelot (1767–1837), Swedish choreographer and ballet master at St Petersburg.

Salvatore Vigagno (1769–1821), Neapolitan classical choreographer.

Filippo Taglioni (1777–1871), Italian Romantic choreographer.

Auguste Bournonville (1805–79), Danish Romantic choreographer who developed a free, more lyrical technique.

Jules Perot (1810–92), French Romantic choreographer.

François Delsarte (1811–71), French ballet theorist and choreographer who influenced Dalcroze and Shawn.

Christian Johansson (1817–1903), Danish teacher who was influential in the flowering of Russian ballet in the second half of the 19th century.

Marius Petipa (1818–1910), French choreographer and ballet master at St Petersburg: the founder of the Russian classical style.

Arthur Sainte-Leon (1821–70), French Romantic choreographer: *Coppelia*.

Lev Ivanov (1834–1901), Russian classical choreographer who worked with Petipa: *Nutcracker*.

Emile Jacques-Dalcroze (Jacob Dalkes; 1865–1950), Austrian ballet theorist who trained Rambert and Wigman.

Rudolph von Laban (1879–1958), Polish ballet theorist and notator.

Michel Fokine (1880–1942), Russian classical choreographer.

Adolph Bolm (1884–1951), Russian classical choreographer.

Fyodor Lopokov (1886–1973), Russian classical choreographer.

Mary Wigman (1886–1973), German modern choreographer.

Oskar Schlemmer (1888–1943), German choreographer who pioneered the Bauhaus style.

Bronislav Nijinska (1891–1972), Russian choreographer for Diaghilev's *Ballets Russes*.

Hanya Holm (1893–), German ballet teacher of modern dance.

*Martha Graham (1894–91), American founder of a distinctive style of modern dance.

Doris Humphrey (1895–1958), American modern choreographer.

Leonide Massine (1895–1979), Russian classical choreographer.

*Kurt Joos (1901–79), German classical and modern choreographer.

Frederick Ashton (1904–88), English classical choreographer.

George Balanchine (1904–83), Russian classical choreographer: founder-choreographer of the New York City Ballet.

Leonid Lavrovsky (1905–67), Russian classical choreographer.

Serge Lifar (1905–67), Russian classical choreographer.

Birgit Cullberg (1908–), Swedish classical amd modern choreographer.

*José Limon (1908–72), Mexican modern choreographer.

Anthony Tudor (1908–87), English modern choreographer.

Agnes de Mille (1909–), American classical and modern choreographer.

*Alwin Nikolais (1912–), American modern choreographer.

Anna Sokolow (1915–), American pioneer of modern dance.

Jerome Robbins (1918–), American classical and contemporary choreography.

*Merce Cunningham (1919–), American postmodern pioneer.

Roland Petit (1924–), French dramatic classical choreographer.

Robert Cohan (1925–), American contemporary choreographer.

Glen Tetley (1926–), American modern choreographer.

Yuri Grigorovich (1927–), Soviet classical choreographer whose work is characterized by its spectacular quality.

*Maurice Bejart (1927–), French choreographer of dance theatre.

John Cranko (1927–73), South African classical choreographer.

Erik Bruhn (1928–), Danish classical choreographer.

Kenneth MacMillan (1929–), Scottish classical and modern choreographer.

*Paul Taylor (1930–), American contemporary choreographer.

*Alvin Ailey (1931–), American modern and contemporary choreographer.

*Twyla Tharp (1941–), American choreographer in a variety of genres.

John Neumeier (1942–), American classical choreographer.

Jiri Kylian (1947–), Czech classical choreographer.

*Mark Morris (1956–), American classical and post-modern choreographer.

David Bintley (1957–), English classical choreographer.

[*Choreographers with their own companies, often bearing their names.]

MAJOR DANCERS

Marie Sallé (1707–56), see Major Choreographers.

Marie Camargo (Marie-Anne de Cupis; 1710–70), Belgian dancer – *La Camargo* – acclaimed for her jumps, especially the entrechat.

Auguste Vestris (1760–1842), French dancer who developed the execution of ballet technique.

Marie Taglioni (1804–84), Italian dancer whose dancing typified the early Romantic ballet.

Fanny Cerrito (1817–1909), Neapolitan dancer.

Fanny Esler (1818–84), Austrian dancer.

Carlotta Grisi (1819–99), Italian dancer.

Virginia Zucchi (1849–1930), Italian dancer who performed mainly in Russia.

Isadora Duncan (1877–1927), American pioneer of modern dance.

Adeline Genee (Anita Jensen; 1878–1970), Danish dancer who was influential in maintaining standards of British dancing.

Anna Pavlova (1881–1931), Russian classical dancer who was a member of Diaghilev's *Ballets Russes*: She created the chief role of *Les Sylphides*.

Tamara Karsavina (1885–1978), Russian classical dancer.

Vaslav Nijinsky (?1888–1950), Russian classical dancer who was a member of Diaghilev's *Ballets*

Russes. The ballets *Petrushka* and *Scheherazade* were created for him.

Olga Spessivtseva (1895–), Russian classical dancer.

Alexandra Danilova (1903–), Russian classical dancer and teacher.

Anton Dolin (Sydney Healey-Kay; 1904–83), English classical dancer who danced with the *Ballets Russes.*

Robert Helpmann (1909–1986), Australian classical and modern dancer and actor.

Alicia Markova (Lilian Alicia Marks; 1910–), English classical dancer.

Galina Ulanova (1910–), Russian classical dancer.

Margot Fonteyn (Margaret Hookham; 1918–91), English classical dancer who is widely recognized as the greatest British dancer.

Rosella Hightower (1920–), American classical dancer.

Maya Plisetskaya (1925–), Russian classical dancer who gained acclaim for her ability to integrate acting and dancing.

Maria Tallchief (1925–), American classical dancer.

Margorie Tallchief (1927–), American classical dancer – sister of Maria.

Rudolph Nureyev (1938–), Russian classical dancer acclaimed for the power and athleticism of his dancing.

Lynn Seymour (1939–), Canadian classical dancer.

Antoinette Sibley (1939–), English classical dancer.

Natalia Makarova (1940–), Russian classical dancer.

Suzanne Farrell (1945–), American classical dancer.

Peter Martins (1946–), Danish classical dancer.

Mikhail Baryshnikov (1948–), Latvian-born classical dancer based in North America.

Wayne Sleep (1948–), English classical, modern and show dancer.

Peter Schaufuss (1949–), Danish classical dancer.

Gelsey Kirkland (1952–), American classical dancer.

Patrick Dupond (1959–), French classical and modern dancer (and pop singer).

Michael Clark (1962–), English innovative contemporary dancer.

Sylvie Guillem (1966–), French classical dancer.

CINEMA

THE SILENT CINEMA

Long before the invention of the kinematograph – or cinema as it is now called – the *camera obscura* and the magic lantern had been used to project images upon a screen. Although lantern slides sometimes had mechanical parts that made the image move, 'films' make use of the phenomenon known as 'persistence of vision' to give an optical simulation of movement, and their development only became possible with the invention of photographic films.

There are several claims to the invention of cinema. The American Thomas Edison (1847–1931) was the first to market a successful film machine, but it was in Europe that the potential of cinema was first recognized. Then came World War I and the American film industry, uninterrupted by the conflict that held back development in Europe, began its long dominance.

The early American cinemas, known as 'nickelodeons', attracted only the working classes, who paid 5 cents to see a 20-minute programme of short films. A little later, French films of successful plays running an hour or more, featuring stage actors, brought in patrons who would pay a dollar a ticket. For a time Italy took the lead in film-making with a series of spectacular productions of historical subjects including *The Last Days of Pompeii, Quo Vadis!* (1913) and the two-hour long *Cabiria* (1914), about the Punic Wars. In the years after World War I the European cinema could not compete with Hollywood commercially but led in terms of experiment.

Early feature films were often tinted with a colour appropriate to the scene, or even with several colours applied by stencil for parts of a major film. *Kinemacolor*, invented in Britain in 1906, used two colour filters in the camera and projector, and two reels of film exposed alternately. It was the first 'natural' colour. *Technicolor*, developed in the USA about 1915, at first used a prism to split colour to two film reels. It was replaced by a variety of different processes until, in 1941, a three-colour system on a single film was introduced. *Eastmancolor* – a negative three-colour movie – was introduced in 1951.

In silent films, dialogue or any information that could not be presented as part of the action had to be conveyed by text inserted between the pictures. Additional atmosphere was supplied by live music, usually a honkytonk piano. Separate sound recordings were used with film in Berlin as early as 1896, and a sound-on-movie process was patented by Lauste in 1906 (see below). In 1926 Warner Brothers presented a synchronized music track on disc to accompany their film *Don Juan.* This was followed by *The Jazz Singer* (1927), which included songs and a snatch of dialogue and is generally accepted as the first 'talkie'.

PIONEERS OF THE CINEMA

Etienne Marey (1830–1904), French physiologist who invented a photographic 'gun' (1882) that took a sequence of pictures on a revolving photographic plate.

Thomas Edison (1847–1931), American inventor – see above. His first film *Fred Ott's Sneeze*, showed a laboratory assistant sneezing and was less than a minute long. His later films featured vaudeville and circus acts, but made no attempt to tell a story.

George Eastman (1854–1932), American inventor of flexible film.

William Friese-Greene (1855–1921), British inventor who outlined designs for a camera and projector.

Eugene Lauste (1856–1935), French inventor who

patented a sound-on-movie process in 1906, though it was not at first effective for speech.

W.K.L. Dickson (1860–1935), American inventor of a camera (the *Kinetograph*, patented 1891) and a viewer (the *Kinetoscope*). This system was launched commercially in 1894 as a slot machine for solo viewing.

Georges Méliès (1861–1938), French impresario who turned his theatre into a cinema and developed trick photography through the use of stop action and double exposure: the fantasy film *Voyage to the Moon* (1902).

August Lumière (1862–1954), with his brother Louis (see below), French inventor of a *cinematographe*, a camera and projector in one. It was first demonstrated in public in Paris on 28 December 1895. The portable camera developed by the Lumière brothers enabled them to film real life and not to be restricted by their equipment to filming in a studio.

Louis Lumière (1864–1948), French inventor – see August Lumière above.

Thomas Armat (1866–1948), American inventor of the *Vitascope* projector.

Edwin Porter (1869–1941), American film maker: the 12-minute *The Great Train Robbery* (1903), which was shot on outside locations.

Adolphe Zukor (1873–1976), Hungarian-born American film maker and founder of the Famous Players-Paramount studios for which Edwin Porter directed *The Count of Monte Cristo* and *The Prisoner of Zenda*.

Cecil Hepworth (1874–1956), English film maker: *Rescued by Rover* (1905), shot on outside location.

D.W. Griffith (1875–1948), American pioneer film maker who experimented with lighting, long-shots and close-ups, takes of different lengths, and different camera set-ups and angles within a scene. He built up a team of actors including Mary Pickford, Dorothy and Lilian Gish, and Lionel Barrymore. Griffith was probably the first American director to make a film lasting more than one reel (12 minutes) and, in 1910, one of the earliest to take his crew to California. Griffith's epic *The Birth of a Nation* (1915) was a landmark in early cinema.

Robert Weine (1881–1938), German film director: *Cabinet of Dr Cagliari* (1919), a film using expressionist settings.

Jack Warner (1882–1978), American film producer who founded – with his brothers Harry (1881–1958), Albert (1884–1967), and Samuel (1888–1927) – the Warner Brothers studios.

Mack Sennett (1884–1960), American director of slapstick comedy films: the cleverly edited and speeded-up antics of the Keystone Cops, and films featuring such actors as Roscoe 'Fatty' Arbuckle, Charlie Chaplin and Buster Keaton.

Georg Pabst (1887–1967), German film director: *Pandora's Box* (1928).

F.W. Murnau (1888–1931), German film maker: *Nosferatu* (1921), an early Dracula film.

Jean Cocteau (1889–1963), French writer, critic and film director who experimented with film as a serious art form: *Blood of a Poet* (1930).

Fritz Lang (1890–1976), Austrian film director: *Metropolis* (1931).

René Clair (1898–1981), French film director: early comedies including *An Italian Straw Hat* (1927), films experimenting with sound including *Sous les*

toits de Paris (1930) and notable later films including *Les Belles de Nuit* (1952).

Sergei Eisenstein (1898–1948), Russian director who used symbols to reinforce ideas and edited shots to make a 'collision' of images: *Battleship Potemkin* (1925).

Abel Gance (1899–1981), French film director: the epic *Napoléon* (1927), which used a wide screen with three overlapping images.

Luis Buñuel (1900–83), Spanish film director who collaborated with Salvador Dali in the first surreal films: *Un Chien Andalou* (1928), and notable later films including *Belle de jour* (1966) and *The Discreet Charm of the Bourgeoisie* (1972).

HOLLYWOOD

Hollywood is not so much a place as a whole style of films and film-making. Within a year of the Nestor Studio opening in this suburb of Los Angeles, California, in 1911 there were 15 other studios close by, and Hollywood rapidly became the centre of the industry and the film community. For 40 years, the 'majors' – the handful of big production companies – dominated world cinema.

In the early years of cinema, films were made all over the USA, but three factors led to the development of Hollywood as a film centre. The first was the weather – sunshine almost throughout the year allowed virtually unrestricted outside shooting. The second was the great variety of scenic location. The third was the Motion Picture Patents Company (established 1909) which tried to restrict film-making in America to its nine member companies.

Hollywood became an efficient production machine. Top directors were capable of turning out as many as six productions a year.

MAJOR HOLLYWOOD DIRECTORS

Cecil B. De Mille (1881–1959), American film producer and director: *The Ten Commandments* (1923), *King of Kings* (1927) and *The Greatest Show on Earth* (1952).

Ernst Lubitsch (1892–1947), German-born American director of comedies: *Heaven Can Wait* (1943).

King Vidor (1894–1982), American film director and producer who directed films for 66 years: *The Big Parade* (1925), *Hallelujah!* (1929) and *The Citadel* (1938).

Josef von Sternberg (1894–1969), Austrian-born American film director: *Blue Angel* (1930).

Busby Berkeley (William Berkeley Enos; 1895–1976), American film director whose films were characterized by spectacular dancing sequences: *Gold Diggers of 1933* (1933).

John Ford (Sean O'Feeney; 1895–1973), American film director: *The Grapes of Wrath* (1940), *How Green Was My Valley* (1941), *The Quiet Man* (1952), and Western films including *Stagecoach* (1939).

Frank Capra (1897–), American film director of gently satirical comedy films: *It Happened One Night* (1934), *Mr Deeds Goes To Town* (1936) and *You Can't Take It with You* (1938).

Alfred Hitchcock (1899–1980), English film director who worked in Hollywood from 1939: *Rebecca* (1940), *Psycho* (1960) and *The Birds* (1963).

George Cukor (1899–), American film director: *Little Women* (1933), *A Star Is Born* (1954) and *My*

Fair Lady (1964).

Walt Disney (1901–66), American film producer and director who created the cartoon characters Mickey Mouse and Donald Duck.

William Wyler (1902–81), American film director: *The Best Years of Our Lives* (1946).

Elia Kazan (Elia Kazanjoglou; 1909–), Greek-born American film director: *A Streetcar Named Desire* (1951) and *On the Waterfront* (1954).

Billy Wilder (Samuel Wilder; 1906–), Austrian-born American film director: *Double Indemnity* (1944) and *Sunset Boulevard* (1950).

Otto Preminger (1906–86), Austrian-born American film director: *Exodus* (1961).

John Huston (1906–), American film director: *The Maltese Falcon* (1941), *The African Queen* (1951) and *The Night of the Iguana* (1964).

Fred Zinneman (1907–), Austrian-born American film director: *High Noon* (1952), *A Man For All Seasons* (1966) and *The Day of the Jackal* (1973).

Edward Dmytryk (1908–), American film director: *Crossfire* (1947).

Joseph Losey (1909–84), American film director who worked mainly in Britain: *The Servant* (1963) and *The Go-Between* (1971).

Jules Dassin (1911–), American film director: *Never on Sunday* (1959).

Orson Welles (1915–85), American film director: *Citizen Kane* (1940).

Bob Fosse (1925–88), American film director: *All That Jazz* (1979).

Sam Peckinpah (1926–84), American director of Western films: *The Wild Bunch* (1969).

Stanley Kubrick (1928–), American film director and writer: *Paths of Glory* (1957), *Lolita* (1962), *2001: A Space Odyssey* (1968) and *A Clockwork Orange* (1971).

Woody Allen (1935–), see also Notable Film Actors. As a director his films include: *Annie Hall* (1977) and *Hannah and her Sisters* (1986).

Francis Ford Coppola (1939–), American film director: *Patton* (1969), *The Godfather* (1972) and *Apocalypse Now* (1979).

Steven Spielberg (1947–), American film director and producer: *E.T.* (1982) and *The Color Purple* (1986).

WORLD CINEMA

Despite Hollywood's long dominance in world cinema, the country producing the highest number of films per annum has long been India, apart from a period in the 1950s when there was a boom in production in Japan. Hong Kong also produces large numbers of films and even France often exceeds the USA in the number made each year.

MAJOR DIRECTORS

Jean Cocteau (1889–1963), French writer, critic and film director: *Beauty and the Beast* (1946) – see also Pioneers of the Cinema.

Jean Renoir (1894–1979), French film director: *La Grande Illusion* (1937) and *La Règle du Jeu* (1939).

Alfred Hitchcock (1899–1980), British film director who worked in Hollywood from 1939 – see above.

Luis Buñuel (1900–83), Spanish film director – see Pioneers of the Cinema.

Vittorio De Sica (1902–74), Italian director: *Bicycle Thieves* (1948).

Leni Riefenstahl (1902–), German film director: the propagandist films *Triumph of the Will* (1934) and *Olympia* (1938).

Grigori Kozintsev (1905–73), Soviet film director: *Hamlet* (1964).

Luchino Visconti (1906–76), Italian film director: *Ossessione* (1942) and *Death in Venice* (1970).

Roberto Rossellini (1906–77), Italian film director: *Rome, Open City* (1945).

Carol Reed (1906–76), English film director: *The Third Man* (1949).

Robert Bresson (1907–), French film director: *Les Anges du péché* (1943) and *Un condamné à mort s'est echappé* (1956).

Laurence Olivier (1907–89), English actor and director: *Henry V* (1944).

Jacques Tati (1908–82), French actor and director of comedy films: *Monsieur Hulot's Holiday* (1951).

David Lean (1908–91), English film director: *Oliver Twist* (1948), *The Bridge on the River Kwai* (1957) and *Lawrence of Arabia* (1962).

Marcel Carné (1909–), French film director: *Le Jour se Lève* (1939) and *Les Enfants du Paradis* (1945).

Akira Kurosawa (1910–), Japanese film director: *Seven Samurai* (1954) and *Rann* (1986).

Masaki Kobayashi (1916–), Japanese film director: *The Human Condition* (1959–61).

Ingmar Bergman (1918–), Swedish film writer, producer and director: *The Seventh Seal* (1957), *Through a Glass Darkly* (1961) and *Cries and Whispers* (1972).

Federico Fellini (1920–), Italian film director: *La Dolce Vita* (1959) and *8½* (1963).

Sergei Bondarchuk (1920–), Soviet film director: *Boris Godunov* (1986).

Satyajit Ray (1921–), Indian film director: *Pather Panchali* (1955).

Grigori Chukrai (1921–), Soviet film director: *The Forty-First* (1956).

Michael Cacoyannis (1922–), Greek film director: *Stella* (1955) and *Electra* (1961).

Pier Paolo Pasolini (1922–75), Italian film director: *Gospel According to St Matthew* (1963).

Alain Resnais (1922–), French film director: *Hiroshima Mon Amour* (1959).

Richard Attenborough (1923–), English actor, producer and director: *Gandhi* (1982).

Lindsay Anderson (1923–), English film director: *This Sporting Life* (1963).

Franco Zeffirelli (Franco Zeffirelli Corsi; 1923–), Italian film director: *Romeo and Juliet* (1968).

Andrzej Wajda (1926–), Polish film director: *Ashes and Diamonds* (1958).

Karel Reisz (1926–), Czech-born British film director: *Saturday Night and Sunday Morning* (1960) and *The French Lieutenant's Woman* (1984).

John Schlesinger (1926–), British film director: *Midnight Cowboy* (1969).

Ken Russell (1927–), English film director: *Women in Love* (1969) and *Tommy* (1975).

Nicholas Roeg (1928–), British director: *Performance* (1970) and *Bad Timing* (1980).

Claud Chabrol (1930–), French film director: *Le Boucher* (1969).

Jean-Luc Godard (1930–), French film director: *A Bout de Souffle* (1960).

Louis Malle (1932–), French film director: *Les Amants* (1958) and *Au revoir les enfants* (1987).

Andrei Tarkovsky (1932–88), Soviet film director: *Andrei Rublev* (1966) and *Solaris* (1971).

Milos Forman (1932–), Czech film director: *The Fireman's Ball* (1967).

François Truffaut (1932–84), French film director: *Les Quatre-cent Coups* (1959) and *Day for Night* (1973).

Ken Loach (1936–), English film director: *Kes* (1970).

Yilmaz Güney (1937–84), Turkish film director: *Yol* (1981).

Werner Hertzog (1942–), German film director: *Aguirre, Wrath of God* (1973) and *Fitzcarraldo* (1982).

Bernardo Bertolucci (1940–), Italian film director: *Last Tango in Paris* (1972) and *The Last Emperor* (1988).

Peter Weir (1944–), Australian film director: *Picnic at Hanging Rock* (1975) and *Green Card* (1991).

Rainer Werner Fassbinder (1946–82), German film director: *Despair* (1977).

Bill Forsyth (1947–), Scottish film director: *Gregory's Girl* (1980) and *Local Hero* (1983).

Claude Berri (1954–), French film director: *Jean de Florette* and *Manon des Sources* (1986).

MOTION PICTURE ACADEMY AWARDS (OSCARS)

1929
Actor: Emil Jannings, *The Way of All Flesh*.
Actress: Janet Gaynor, *Seventh Heaven*.
Director: Frank Borzage, *Seventh Heaven*; Lewis Milestone, *Two Arabian Knights*.
Picture: *Wings*, Paramount.

1930
Actor: Warner Baxter, *In Old Arizona*.
Actress: Mary Pickford, *Coquette*.
Director: Frank Lloyd, *The Divine Lady*.
Picture: *Broadway Melody*, MGM.

1931
Actor: George Arliss, *Disraeli*.
Actress: Norma Shearer, *The Divorcee*.
Director: Lewis Milestone, *All Quiet on the Western Front*.
Picture: *All Quiet on the Western Front*, Universal.

1932
Actor: Lionel Barrymore, *Free Soul*
Actress: Marie Dressler, *Min and Bill*
Director: Norman Taurog, *Skippy*
Picture: *Cimarron*, RKO.

1933
Actor: Fredric March, *Dr Jekyll and Mr Hyde*; Wallace Beery, *The Champ* (tie).
Actress: Helen Hayes, *Sin of Madelon Claudet*.
Director: Frank Borzage, *Bad Girl*.
Picture: *Grand Hotel*, MGM.
Special: Walt Disney, *Mickey Mouse*.

1934
Actor: Charles Laughton, *Private Life of Henry VIII*.
Actress: Katharine Hepburn, *Morning Glory*.
Director: Frank Lloyd, *Cavalcade*.
Picture: *Cavalcade*, Fox.

1935
Actor: Clark Gable, *It Happened One Night*.
Actress: Claudette Colbert, *It Happened One Night*.
Director: Frank Capra, *It Happened One Night*.
Picture: *It Happened One Night*, Columbia.

1936
Actor: Victor McLaglen, *The Informer*.
Actress: Bette Davis, *Dangerous*.
Director: John Ford, *The Informer*.
Picture: *Mutiny on the Bounty*, MGM.

1937
Actor: Paul Muni, *Story of Louis Pasteur*.
Actress: Luise Rainer, *The Great Ziegfeld*.
Sup. Actor: Walter Brennan, *Come and Get It*.
Sup. Actress: Gale Sondergaard, *Anthony Adverse*.
Director: Frank Capra, *Mr Deeds Goes to Town*.
Picture: *The Great Ziegfeld*, MGM.

1938
Actor: Spencer Tracy, *Captains Courageous*.
Actress: Luise Rainer, *The Good Earth*.
Sup. Actor: Joseph Schildkraut, *Life of Emile Zola*.
Sup. Actress: Alice Brady, *In Old Chicago*.
Director: Leo McCarey, *The Awful Truth*.
Picture: *Life of Emile Zola*, Warner Bros.

1939
Actor: Spencer Tracy, *Boys Town*.
Actress: Bette Davis, *Jezebel*.
Sup. Actor: Walter Brennan, *Kentucky*.
Sup. Actress: Fay Bainter, *Jezebel*.
Director: Frank Capra, *You Can't Take It With You*.
Picture: *You Can't Take It With You*, Columbia.

1940
Actor: Robert Donat, *Goodbye, Mr Chips*.
Actress: Vivien Leigh, *Gone With the Wind*.
Sup. Actor: Thomas Mitchell, *Stage Coach*.
Sup. Actress: Hattie McDaniel, *Gone With the Wind*.
Director: Victor Fleming, *Gone With the Wind*.
Picture: *Gone With the Wind*, Selznick International, MGM.

1941
Actor: James Stewart, *The Philadelphia Story*.
Actress: Ginger Rogers, *Kitty Foyle*.
Sup. Actor: Walter Brennan, *The Westerner*.
Sup. Actress: Jane Darwell, *The Grapes of Wrath*.
Director: John Ford, *The Grapes of Wrath*.
Picture: *Rebecca*, Selznick International, UA.

1942
Actor: Gary Cooper, *Sergeant York*.
Actress: Joan Fontaine, *Suspicion*.
Sup. Actor: Donald Crisp, *How Green Was My Valley*.
Sup. Actress: Mary Astor, *The Great Lie*.
Director: John Ford, *How Green Was My Valley*.
Picture: *How Green Was My Valley*, 20th Century Fox.

1943
Actor: James Cagney, *Yankee Doodle Dandy*.
Actress: Greer Garson, *Mrs Miniver*.
Sup. Actor: Van Heflin, *Johnny Eager*.
Sup. Actress: Teresa Wright, *Mrs Miniver*.
Director: William Wyler, *Mrs Miniver*.
Picture: *Mrs Miniver*, MGM.

1944
Actor: Paul Lukas, *Watch on the Rhine*.
Actress: Jennifer Jones, *The Song of Bernadette*.
Sup. Actor: Charles Coburn, *The More the Merrier*.
Sup. Actress: Katina Paxinou, *For Whom the Bell*

Tolls.
Director: Michael Curtiz, *Casablanca.*
Picture: *Casablanca,* Warner.

1945
Actor: Bing Crosby, *Going My Way.*
Actress: Ingrid Bergman, *Gaslight.*
Sup. Actor: Barry Fitzgerald, *Going My Way.*
Sup. Actress: Ethel Barrymore, *None But the Lonely Heart.*
Director: Leo McCarey, *Going My Way.*
Picture: *Going My Way,* Paramount.

1946
Actor: Ray Milland: *The Lost Weekend.*
Actress: Joan Crawford, *Mildred Pierce.*
Sup. Actor: James Dunn, *A Tree Grows in Brooklyn.*
Sup. Actress: Anne Revere, *National Velvet.*
Director: Billy Wilder, *The Lost Weekend.*
Picture: *The Lost Weekend,* Paramount.

1947
Actor: Frederic March, *The Best Years of Our Lives.*
Actress: Olivia de Havilland, *To Each His Own.*
Sup. Actor: Harold Russell, *The Best Years of Our Lives.*
Sup. Actress: Anne Baxter, *The Razor's Edge.*
Director: William Wyler, *The Best Years of Our Lives.*
Picture: *The Best Years of Our Lives,* Goldwyn, RKO.

1948
Actor: Ronald Colman, *A Double Life.*
Actress: Loretta Young, *The Farmer's Daughter.*
Sup. Actor: Edmund Gwenn, *Miracle on 34th Street.*
Sup. Actress: Celeste Holm, *Gentleman's Agreement.*
Director: Elia Kazan, *Gentleman's Agreement.*
Picture: *Gentleman's Agreement,* 20th Century Fox.

1949
Actor: Laurence Olivier, *Hamlet.*
Actress: Jane Wyman, *Johnny Belinda.*
Sup. Actor: Walter Huston, *Treasure of Sierra Madre.*
Sup. Actress: Claire Trevor, *Key Largo.*
Director: John Huston, *Treasure of Sierra Madre.*
Picture: *Hamlet,* Two Cities Film, Universal International.

1950
Actor: Broderick Crawford, *All the King's Men.*
Actress: Olivia de Havilland, *The Heiress.*
Sup. Actor: Dean Jagger, *Twelve O'Clock High.*
Sup. Actress: Mercedes McCambridge, *All the King's Men.*
Director: Joseph L. Mankiewicz, *Letter to Three Wives.*
Picture: *All the King's Men.* Columbia.

1951
Actor: Jose Ferrer, *Cyrano de Bergerac.*
Actress: Judy Holliday, *Born Yesterday.*
Sup. Actor: George Sanders, *All About Eve.*
Sup. Actress: Josephine Hull, *Harvey.*
Director: Joseph L. Mankiewicz, *All About Eve.*
Picture: *All About Eve,* 20th Century Fox.

1952
Actor: Humphrey Bogart, *The African Queen.*
Actress: Vivien Leigh, *A Streetcar Named Desire.*
Sup. Actor: Karl Malden, *A Streetcar Named Desire.*
Sup. Actress: Kim Hunter, *A Streetcar Named Desire.*
Director: George Stevens, *A Place in the Sun.*
Picture: *An American in Paris,* MGM.

1953
Actor: Gary Cooper, *High Noon.*
Actress: Shirley Booth, *Come Back, Little Sheba.*

Sup. Actor: Anthony Quinn, *Viva Zapata!*
Sup. Actress: Gloria Grahame, *The Bad and the Beautiful.*
Director: John Ford, *The Quiet Man.*
Picture: *Greatest Show on Earth,* C.B. DeMille, Paramount.

1954
Actor: William Holden, *Stalag 17.*
Actress: Audrey Hepburn, *Roman Holiday.*
Sup. Actor: Frank Sinatra, *From Here to Eternity.*
Sup. Actress: Donna Reed, *From Here to Eternity.*
Director: Fred Zinnemann, *From Here to Eternity.*
Picture: *From Here to Eternity,* Columbia.

1955
Actor: Marlon Brando, *On the Waterfront.*
Actress: Grace Kelly, *The Country Girl.*
Sup. Actor: Edmond O'Brien, *The Barefoot Contessa.*
Sup. Actress: Eve Marie Saint, *On the Waterfront.*
Director: Elia Kazan, *On the Waterfront.*
Picture: *On the Waterfront,* Horizon-American, Columbia.

1956
Actor: Ernest Borgnine, *Marty.*
Actress: Anna Magnani, *The Rose Tattoo.*
Sup. Actor: Jack Lemmon, *Mister Roberts.*
Sup. Actress: Jo Van Fleet, *East of Eden.*
Director: Delbert Mann, *Marty.*
Picture: *Marty,* Hecht and Lancaster's Steven Prods., UA.

1957
Actor: Yul Brynner, *The King and I.*
Actress: Ingrid Bergman, *Anastasia.*
Sup. Actor: Anthony Quinn, *Lust for Life.*
Sup. Actress: Dorothy Malone, *Written on the Wind.*
Director: George Stevens, *Giant*
Picture: *Around the World in 80 Days,* Michael Todd, UA.

1958
Actor: Alec Guinness, *The Bridge on the River Kwai.*
Actress: Joanne Woodward, *The Three Faces of Eve.*
Sup. Actor: Red Buttons, *Sayonara.*
Sup. Actress: Miyoshi Umeki, *Sayonara.*
Director: David Lean, *The Bridge on the River Kwai.*
Picture: *The Bridge on the River Kwai,* Columbia.

1959
Actor: David Niven, *Separate Tables.*
Actress: Susan Hayward, *I Want to Live.*
Sup. Actor: Burl Ives, *The Big Country.*
Sup. Actress: Wendy Hiller, *Separate Tables.*
Director: Vincente Minnelli, *Gigi.*
Picture: *Gigi,* Arthur Freed Production, MGM.

1960
Actor: Charlton Heston, *Ben Hur.*
Actress: Simone Signoret, *Room at the Top.*
Sup. Actor: Hugh Griffith, *Ben Hur.*
Sup. Actress: Shelley Winters, *Diary of Anne Frank.*
Director: William Wyler, *Ben Hur.*
Picture: *Ben Hur,* MGM.

1961
Actor: Burt Lancaster, *Elmer Gantry.*
Actress: Elizabeth Taylor, *Butterfield 8.*
Sup. Actor: Peter Ustinov, *Spartacus.*
Sup. Actress: Shirley Jones, *Elmer Gantry.*
Director: Billy Wilder, *The Apartment.*
Picture: *The Apartment,* Mirisch Co., UA.

1962
Actor: Maximilian Schell, *Judgement at Nuremberg.*
Actress: Sophia Loren, *Two Women.*

Sup. Actor: George Chakiris, *West Side Story.*
Sup. Actress: Rita Moreno, *West Side Story.*
Director: Jerome Robbins, Robert Wise, *West Side Story.*
Picture: *West Side Story*, UA.

1963
Actor: Gregory Peck, *To Kill a Mockingbird.*
Actress: Anne Bancroft, *The Miracle Worker.*
Sup. Actor: Ed Begley, *Sweet Bird of Youth.*
Sup. Actress: Patty Duke, *The Miracle Worker.*
Director: David Lean, *Lawrence of Arabia.*
Picture: *Lawrence of Arabia*, Columbia.

1964
Actor: Sidney Poitier, *Lilies of the Field.*
Actress: Patricia Neal, *Hud.*
Sup. Actor: Melvyn Douglas, *Hud.*
Sup. Actress: Margaret Rutherford, *The VIPs.*
Director: Tony Richardson, *Tom Jones.*
Picture: *Tom Jones*, Woodfall Prod., UA-Lopert Pictures.

1965
Actor: Rex Harrison, *My Fair Lady.*
Actress: Julie Andrews, *Mary Poppins.*
Sup. Actor: Peter Ustinov, *Topkapi.*
Sup. Actress: Lila Kedrova, *Zorba the Greek.*
Director: George Cukor, *My Fair Lady.*
Picture: *My Fair Lady*, Warner Bros.

1966
Actor: Lee Marvin, *Cat Ballou.*
Actress: Julie Christie, *Darling.*
Sup. Actor: Martin Balsam, *A Thousand Clowns.*
Sup. Actress: Shelley Winters, *A Patch of Blue.*
Director: Robert Wise, *The Sound of Music.*
Picture: *The Sound of Music*, 20th Century Fox.

1967
Actor: Paul Scofield, *A Man for All Seasons.*
Actress: Elizabeth Taylor, *Who's Afraid of Virginia Woolf?*
Sup. Actor: Walter Matthau, *The Fortune Cookie.*
Sup. Actress: Sandy Dennis, *Who's Afraid of Virginia Woolf?*
Director: Fred Zinnemann, *A Man for All Seasons.*
Picture: *A Man for All Seasons*, Columbia.

1968
Actor: Rod Steiger, *In the Heat of the Night.*
Actress: Katharine Hepburn, *Guess Who's Coming to Dinner*
Sup. Actor: George Kennedy, *Cool Hand Luke.*
Sup Actress: Estelle Parsons, *Bonnie and Clyde.*
Director: Mike Nichols, *The Graduate.*
Picture: *In the Heat of the Night*, Mirisch Co., UA.

1969
Actor: Cliff Robertson, *Charly.*
Actress: Katharine Hepburn, *The Lion in Winter*; Barbra Streisand, *Funny Girl* (tie).
Sup. Actor: Jack Albertson, *The Subject Was Roses.*
Sup. Actress: Ruth Gordon, *Rosemary's Baby.*
Director: Sir Carol Reed, *Oliver!*
Picture: *Oliver!* Romulus, Columbia.

1970
Actor: John Wayne, *True Grit.*
Actress: Maggie Smith, *The Prime of Miss Jean Brodie.*
Sup. Actor: Gig Young, *They Shoot Horses Don't They?*
Sup. Actress: Goldie Hawn, *Cactus Flower.*
Director: John Schlesinger, *Midnight Cowboy.*
Picture: *Midnight Cowboy*, Hellman-Schlesinger, UA.

1971
Actor: George C. Scott, *Patton.* (refused)
Actress: Glenda Jackson, *Women in Love.*
Sup. Actor: John Mills, *Ryan's Daughter.*
Sup. Actress: Helen Hayes, *Airport.*
Director: Franklin Schaffner, *Patton.*
Picture: *Patton*, 20th Century Fox.

1972
Actor: Gene Hackman, *The French Connection.*
Actress: Jane Fonda, *Klute.*
Sup. Actor: Ben Johnson, *The Last Picture Show.*
Sup. Actress: Cloris Leachman, *The Last Picture Show.*
Director: William Friedkin, *The French Connection.*
Picture: *The French Connection*, D'Antoni-Schine-Moore 20th Century Fox.

1973
Actor: Marlon Brando, *The Godfather.*
Actress: Liza Minnelli, *Cabaret.*
Sup. Actor: Joel Grey, *Cabaret.*
Sup. Actress: Eileen Heckart, *Butterflies Are Free.*
Director: Bob Fosse, *Cabaret.*
Picture: *The Godfather*, Ruddy, Paramount.

1974
Actor: Jack Lemmon, *Save the Tiger.*
Actress: Glenda Jackson, *A Touch of Class.*
Sup. Actor: John Houseman, *The Paper Chase.*
Sup. Actress: Tatum O'Neal, *Paper Moon.*
Director: George Roy Hill, *The Sting.*
Picture: *The Sting*, Bill/Phillips-Hill, Zanuck/Brown, Universal.

1975
Actor: Art Carney, *Harry and Tonto.*
Actress: Ellen Burstyn, *Alice Doesn't Live Here Anymore.*
Sup. Actor: Robert DeNiro, *The Godfather, Part II*
Sup. Actress: Ingrid Bergman, *Murder on the Orient Express.*
Director: Francis Ford Coppola, *The Godfather, Part II*
Picture: *The Godfather, Part II*, Coppola Co., Paramount.

1976
Actor: Jack Nicholson, *One Flew Over the Cuckoo's Nest.*
Actress: Louise Fletcher, *One Flew Over the Cuckoo's Nest.*
Sup. Actor: George Burns, *The Sunshine Boys.*
Sup. Actress; Lee Grant, *Shampoo.*
Director: Milos Forman, *One Flew Over the Cuckoo's Nest.*
Picture: *One Flew Over the Cuckoo's Nest*, Fantasy Films, UA.

1977
Actor: Peter Finch, *Network.*
Actress: Faye Dunaway, *Network.*
Sup. Actor: Jason Robards, *All the President's Men.*
Sup. Actress: Beatrice Straight, *Network.*
Director: John G Avildsen, *Rocky.*
Picture: *Rocky*, Chartoff-Winkler, UA.

1978
Actor: Richard Dreyfuss, *The Goodbye Girl.*
Actress: Diane Keaton, *Annie Hall.*
Sup. Actor: Jason Robards, *Julia.*
Sup. Actress: Vanessa Redgrave, *Julia.*
Director: Woody Allen, *Annie Hall.*
Picture: *Annie Hall*, Rollins-Joffe, UA.

1979
Actor: John Voight, *Coming Home.*

Actress: Jane Fonda, *Coming Home.*
Sup. Actor: Christopher Walken, *The Deer Hunter.*
Sup. Actress: Maggie Smith, *California Suite.*
Director: Michael Cimino, *The Deer Hunter.*
Picture: *The Deer Hunter,* EMI Films/Cimino, Universal.

1980
Actor: Dustin Hoffman, *Kramer vs Kramer.*
Actress: Sally Field, *Norma Rae.*
Sup. Actor: Melvyn Douglas, *Being There.*
Sup. Actress: Meryl Streep, *Kramer vs Kramer.*
Director: Robert Benton, *Kramer vs Kramer.*
Picture: *Kramer vs Kramer,* Joffe, Columbia.

1981
Actor: Robert DeNiro, *Raging Bull.*
Actress: Sissy Spacek, *Coal Miner's Daughter.*
Sup. Actor: Timothy Hutton, *Ordinary People.*
Sup. Actress: Mary Steenburgen, *Melvin and Howard.*
Director: Robert Redford, *Ordinary People.*
Picture: *Ordinary People,* Wildwood, Paramount.

1982
Actor: Henry Fonda, *On Golden Pond.*
Actress: Katharine Hepburn, *On Golden Pond.*
Sup. Actor: John Gielgud, *Arthur.*
Sup. Actress: Maureen Stepleton, *Reds.*
Director: Warren Beatty, *Reds.*
Picture: *Chariots of Fire,* Enigma, The Ladd Co., Warner Bros.

1983
Actor: Ben Kingsley, *Gandhi.*
Actress: Meryl Streep, *Sophie's Choice.*
Sup. Actor: Louis Gossett, Jr, *An Officer and a Gentleman.*
Sup. Actress: Jessica Lange, *Tootsie.*
Director: Richard Attenborough, *Gandhi.*
Picture: *Gandhi,* Indo-British Films, Columbia.

1984
Actor: Robert Duvall, *Tender Mercies.*
Actress: Shirley MacLaine, *Terms of Endearment.*
Sup. Actor: Jack Nicholson, *Terms of Endearment.*
Sup. Actress: Linda Hunt, *The Year of Living Dangerously.*
Director: James L. Brooks, *Terms of Endearment.*
Picture: *Terms of Endearment,* Brooks, Paramount.

1985
Actor: F. Murray Abraham, *Amadeus.*
Actress: Sally Field, *Places in the Heart.*
Sup. Actor: Haing S Ngor, *The Killing Fields.*
Sup. Actress: Peggy Ashcroft, *A Passage to India.*
Director: Milos Forman, *Amadeus.*
Picture: *Amadeus,* Zaintz, Orion.

1986
Actor: William Hurt, *Kiss of the Spider Woman.*
Actress: Geraldine Page, *The Trip to Bountiful.*
Sup. Actor: Don Ameche, *Cocoon.*
Sup. Actress: Anjelica Huston, *Prizzi's Honor.*
Director: Sydney Pollack, *Out of Africa.*
Picture: *Out of Africa,* Universal.

1987
Actor: Paul Newman, *The Color of Money.*
Actress: Marlee Matlin, *Children of a Lesser God.*
Sup. Actor: Michael Caine, *Hannah and Her Sisters.*
Sup. Actress: Dianne West, *Hannah and Her Sisters.*
Director: Oliver Stone, *Platoon.*
Picture: *Platoon,* Herndale, Orion.

1988
Actor: Michael Douglas, *Wall Street.*
Actress: Cher, *Moonstruck.*

Sup. Actor: Sean Connery, *The Untouchables.*
Sup. Actress: Olympia Dukakais, *Moonstruck.*
Director: Bernardo Bertolucci, *The Last Emperor.*
Picture: *The Last Emperor,* Herndale, Columbia.

1989
Actor: Dustin Hoffman, *Rain Man.*
Actress: Jodie Foster, *The Accused.*
Sup. Actor: Kevin Kline, *A Fish Called Wanda.*
Sup. Actress: Geena Davis, *The Accidental Tourist.*
Director: Barry Levinson, *Rain Man.*
Picture: *Rain Man,* Guber-Peters, UA.

1990
Actor: Daniel Day Lewis, *My Left Foot.*
Actress: Jessica Tandy, *Driving Miss Daisy.*
Sup. Actor: Denzel Washington, *Glory.*
Sup. Actress: Brenda Fricker, *My Left Foot.*
Picture: *Driving Miss Daisy,* Zanuck Co., Warner Bros.

1991
Actor: Jeremy Irons, *Reversal of Fortune.*
Actress: Kathy Bates, *Misery.*
Sup. Actor: Joe Pesci, *Goodfellas.*
Sup. Actress: Whoopi Goldberg, *Ghosts.*
Picture: *Dances with Wolves,* Majestic Films.

NOTABLE FILM ACTORS

Woody Allen (Allen Stewart Konigsberg; 1935–), American: *What's New Pussycat* (1965), *Annie Hall* (1977; **AA**), *Hannah and Her Sisters* (1986), *Crimes and Misdemeanours* (1990)

Julie Andrews (Julia Wells; 1934–), English: *Mary Poppins* (1964; **AA**), *The Sound of Music* (1965)

Lauren Bacall (Betty Jean Perske; 1924–), American: *To Have and Have Not* (1944), *The Big Sleep* (1946), *Key Largo* (1948)

Brigitte Bardot (Camille Javal; 1933–), French: *And God Created Woman* (1956), *En Cas de Malheur* (1957), *Babette Goes to War* (1959), *Vie Privée* (1961), *Viva Maria* (1965), *The Novices* (1970)

Warren Beatty (1937–), American: *Splendour in the Grass* (1961), *Bonnie and Clyde* (1967), *Shampoo* (1975), *Reds* (1981), *Dick Tracy* (1990)

Ingrid Bergman (1915–1982), Swedish: *Intermezzo* (1936), *Casablanca* (1943), *For Whom the Bell Tolls* (1943), *Gaslight* (1944; **AA**), *Spellbound* (1945), *Joan of Arc* (1948), *Anastasia* (1956; **AA**), *The Inn of the Sixth Happiness* (1958)

Dirk Bogarde (Derek Van Den Bogaerd; 1921–), English: *Doctor in the House* (1953), *A Tale of Two Cities* (1958), *The Servant* (1963), *The Damned* (1969), *Death in Venice* (1970)

Humphrey Bogart (1899–1957), American: *A Devil With Women* (1930), *The Maltese Falcon* (1941), *Casablanca* (1942), *To Have and Have Not* (1943), *The Big Sleep* (1946), *Key Largo* (1948), *The African Queen* (1952; **AA**), *The Caine Mutiny* (1954)

Clara Bow (1905–1965), American: *Mantrap* (1926), *It* (1927), *Wings* (1927)

Marlon Brando (1924–), American: *A Streetcar Named Desire* (1951), *The Wild One* (1953), *On the Waterfront* (1954; **AA**), *The Teahouse of the August Moon* (1956), *The Young Lions* (1958), *The Godfather* (1972; **AA**), *Last Tango in Paris* (1972)

Yul Brynner (Youl Bryner; 1915–1985), Russian-born: *The King and I* (1956; **AA**), *The Brothers Karamazov* (1958), *The Magnificent Seven* (1960), *Invitation to a Gunfighter* (1964)

Richard Burton (Richard Jenkins; 1925–1984), Welsh: *Look Back in Anger* (1959), *Cleopatra* (1962),

The VIPs (1963), Becket (1964), The Night of the Iguana (1964), Who's Afraid of Virginia Woolf? (1966), Anne of a Thousand Days (1970)

James Cagney (1899–1986), American: The Public Enemy (1931), Angels With Dirty Faces (1938), Yankee Doodle Dandy (1942; **AA**)

Michael Caine (Maurice Micklewhite; 1933–), English: Zulu (1963), Ipcress File (1965), Educating Rita (1983), Hannah and Her Sisters (1985)

Lon Chaney (Alonzo Chaney; 1883–1930), American: The Hunchback of Notre Dame (1923), The Phantom of the Opera (1925)

Sir Charles Chaplin (1889–1977), English: The Tramp (1915), The Kid (1920), The Gold Rush (1924), The Circus (1928; **AA**), City Lights (1931), Modern Times (1936), The Great Dictator (1940), Limelight (1952)

Maurice Chevalier (1888–1972), French: Love Me Tonight (1932), Gigi (1958), Fanny (1961)

Julie Christie (1940–), English: Darling (1965; **AA**), Doctor Zhivago (1965), The Go-Between (1971), Heat and Dust (1983)

Montgomery Clift (1920–66), American: Red River (1948), A Place in the Sun (1951), From Here to Eternity (1953), The Misfits (1960) Freud (1963)

Claudette Colbert (Lily Claudette Chauchoin; 1905–), French: It Happened One Night (1934; **AA**), I Met Him in Paris (1937), Three Came Home (1950)

Ronald Colman (1891–1958), English: Raffles (1930), A Tale of Two Cities (1935), The Prisoner of Zenda (1937), Random Harvest (1942), A Double Life (1948; **AA**)

Sean Connery (Thomas Connery; 1929–), Scottish: Doctor No (1962), From Russia With Love (1963), Goldfinger (1964), The Untouchables(1987; **AA**)

Gary Cooper (Frank J. Cooper; 1901–61), American: Mr Deeds Goes to Town (1936), Sergeant York (1941; **AA**), For Whom the Bell Tolls (1943), High Noon (1952; **AA**), Vera Cruz (1954)

Sir Noel Coward (1899–1973), English: In Which We Serve (1941; **AA**) Our Man in Havana (1959)

Joan Crawford (Lucille le Sueur; 1906–77), American: Grand Hotel (1932), The Women (1939), Mildred Pierce (1945; **AA**), Whatever Happened to Baby Jane? (1962)

Bing Crosby (Harry Lillis Crosby; 1901–77), American: Road to Singapore (1940), Going My Way (1944; **AA**), The Bells of St Mary's (1945), White Christmas (1954)

Tom Cruise (1962–), American: Top Gun (1985), Rain Man (1988), Born on the Fourth of July (1989)

Tony Curtis (Bernard Schwarz; 1925–), American: Some Like it Hot (1959), Spartacus (1960)

Bette Davis (Ruth Elizabeth Davis; 1908–89), American: Dangerous (1935; **AA**), The Private Lives of Elizabeth and Essex (1939), The Little Foxes (1941), All About Eve (1950), Whatever Happened to Baby Jane? (1962)

Doris Day (Doris Kappelhoff; 1924–), American: Calamity Jane (1953), The Pyjama Game (1957), Pillow Talk (1959)

Olivia de Havilland (1916–), American: Gone With the Wind (1939), To Each His Own (1946; **AA**), The Heiress (1949; **AA**)

Robert De Niro (1943–), American: The Godfather Part Two (1974; **AA**), The Deer Hunter (1978), Raging Bull (1980; **AA**), The Mission (1986)

James Dean (1931–55), American: East of Eden (1955), Rebel Without a Cause (1955)

Catherine Deneuve (Catherine Dorleac; 1943–), French: Les Parapluies de Cherbourg (1964), Belle de Jour (1967), Mayerling (1968)

Gerard Depardieu (1948–), French: Le Dernier Metro (1980), Jean de Florette (1985), Trop Belle Pour Toi (1989), Cyrano de Bergerac (1991)

Marlene Dietrich (Maria Magdalena von Losch; 1901–), German: The Blue Angel (1930), Shanghai Express (1932), Destry Rides Again (1939), A Foreign Affair (1948)

Robert Donat (1905–58), English: The Thirty-Nine Steps (1935), The Citadel (1938), Goodbye Mr Chips (1939; **AA**), The Winslow Boy (1948)

Kirk Douglas (Issur Danielovitch Demsky; 1916–), American: Gunfight at the OK Corral (1957), Paths of Glory (1957), Spartacus (1960), Lonely Are the Brave (1962)

Faye Dunaway (1941–), American: Bonnie and Clyde (1967), Network (1976; **AA**)

Clint Eastwood (1930–), American: A Fistful of Dollars (1964), For a Few Dollars More (1965), The Good The Bad and the Ugly (1966), Dirty Harry (1971), Every Which Way But Loose (1978)

Douglas Fairbanks (Douglas Ullman; 1883–1939), American: The Mark of Zorro (1920), The Three Musketeers (1921), Robin Hood (1921), The Thief of Baghdad (1923), Don Q Son of Zorro (1925)

W.C. Fields (Claude Dukinfield; 1879–1946), American: David Copperfield (1934), My Little Chickadee (1940), The Bank Dick (1940)

Peter Finch (William Mitchell; 1916–77), English: A Town Like Alice (1956), The Trials of Oscar Wilde (1960), Sunday Bloody Sunday (1971), Network (1976; **AA**)

Errol Flynn (1909–59), Irish-born American: Captain Blood (1935), The Adventures of Robin Hood (1938), The Sea Hawk (1940), They Died With Their Boots On (1941), Too Much Too Soon (1958)

Henry Fonda (1905–82), American: Young Mr Lincoln (1939), The Grapes of Wrath (1940), Twelve Angry Men (1957), On Golden Pond (1981; **AA**)

Jane Fonda (1937–), American: They Shoot Horses Don't They? (1969), Klute (1971; **AA**), Coming Home (1978; **AA**), On Golden Pond (1981)

Harrison Ford (1942–), American: Star Wars (1977), Raiders of the Lost Ark (1981), Indiana Jones and the Temple of Doom (1984), The Witness (1985)

Jean Gabin (Alexis Moncourge; 1904–76), French: Pepe le Moko (1937), La Grande Illusion (1937), La Bete Humaine (1938), Le Jour se Leve (1939), Le Chat (1972)

Clark Gable (1901–60), American: It Happened One Night (1934; **AA**), Mutiny On the Bounty (1935), Gone With the Wind (1939), The Misfits (1961)

Greta Garbo (Greta Gustafson; 1905–90), Swedish: Grand Hotel (1932), Queen Christina (1933), Anna Karenina (1935), Camille (1936), Ninotchka (1939)

Ava Gardner (1922–89), American: Show Boat (1951), The Barefoot Contessa (1954), The Night of the Iguana (1964)

Judy Garland (Frances Gumm; 1922–69), American: The Wizard of Oz (1939), Meet Me in St Louis (1944), A Star is Born (1954)

Richard Gere (1949–), American: Yanks (1979), An Officer and a Gentleman (1982), Pretty Woman (1990)

Mel Gibson (1956–), Australian: *Mad Max Beyond the Thunderdome* (1985), *Lethal Weapon* (1987)

Lillian Gish (Lillian de Guiche; 1896–), American: *Birth of a Nation* (1914), *Intolerance* (1916), *The Wind* (1928), *A Wedding* (1978), *The Whales of August* (1987)

Paulette Goddard (Marion Levee; 1905–90), American: *Modern Times* (1936), *The Great Dictator* (1940)

Cary Grant (Archibald Leach; 1904–86), English-born American: *She Done Him Wrong* (1933), *Bringing Up Baby* (1938), *The Philadelphia Story* (1940), *Arsenic and Old Lace* (1944), *North by Northwest* (1959), *Charade* (1963)

Sir Alec Guinness (1914–), English: *Oliver Twist* (1948), *Kind Hearts and Coronets* (1949), *The Lavender Hill Mob* (1951), *The Bridge on the River Kwai* (1957; **AA**), *Tunes of Glory* (1960), *Lawrence of Arabia* (1962)

Gene Hackman (1930–), American: *Bonnie and Clyde* (1967), *The French Connection* (1971; **AA**), *Mississippi Burning* (1989)

Oliver Hardy (1892–1957), American, and **Stan Laurel** (Arthur Stanley Jefferson; 1890–1965), English-born: *The Music Box* (1932; **AA**), *Sons of the Desert* (1933), *Way Out West* (1936), *A Chump at Oxford* (1940)

Jean Harlow (Harlean Carpentier; 1911–37), American: *Hell's Angels* (1930)

Rex Harrison (Reginald Carey; 1908–90), English: *Blithe Spirit* (1945), *My Fair Lady* (1964; **AA**), *The Yellow Rolls-Royce* (1964), *Doctor Dolittle* (1967)

Rita Hayworth (Margarita Carmen Cansino; 1918–87), American: *The Strawberry Blonde* (1941), *Cover Girl* (1944), *Miss Sadie Thompson* (1953), *Pal Joey* (1957)

Audrey Hepburn (Audrey Hepburn-Ruston; 1929–), Belgian-born American: *Roman Holiday* (1953; **AA**), *The Nun's Story* (1959), *Breakfast at Tiffany's* (1961), *Charade* (1963)

Katharine Hepburn (1907–), American: *Morning Glory* (1932; **AA**), *Little Women* (1933), *The Philadelphia Story* (1940), *The African Queen* (1951), *Guess Who's Coming to Dinner?* (1967; **AA**), *The Lion in Winter* (1968; **AA**), *On Golden Pond* (1981; **AA**)

Charlton Heston (John Charlton Carter; 1924–), American: *The Ten Commandments* (1956), *Ben Hur* (1959; **AA**), *El Cid* (1961), *55 Days at Peking* (1963), *The Agony and the Ecstasy* (1965), *Khartoum* (1966)

Dustin Hoffman (1937–), American: *The Graduate* (1967), *Midnight Cowboy* (1969), *All the President's Men* (1976), *Kramer vs Kramer* (1980; **AA**), *Tootsie* (1983), *Rain Man* (1988; **AA**)

William Holden (1918–81): *Sunset Boulevard* (1950), *Stalag 17* (1953; **AA**), *The Bridge on the River Kwai* (1957), *The Wild Bunch* (1969)

Bob Hope (Leslie Townes Hope; 1903–), English-born American: *Thanks For the Memory* (1938), *Road to Singapore* (1940), *Road to Morocco* (1942)

Leslie Howard (Leslie Stainer; 1890–1943), English: *The Scarlet Pimpernel* (1935), *Pygmalion* (1938), *Gone With the Wind* (1939)

Trevor Howard (1916–88), English: *Brief Encounter* (1946), *The Third Man* (1949), *Mutiny on the Bounty* (1962), *The Charge of the Light Brigade* (1968)

Rock Hudson (1925–85), American: *Magnificent Obsession* (1954), *Pillow Talk* (1959)

Glenda Jackson (1937–), English: *Women in Love* (1969; **AA**), *Sunday Bloody Sunday* (1971), *A Touch of Class* (1972; **AA**)

Al Jolson (Asa Yoelson; 1886–1950), Lithuanian-born American: *The Jazz Singer* (1927), *The Singing Fool* (1928), *Sonny Boy* (1929)

Boris Karloff (William Henry Pratt; 1887–1969), English: *Frankenstein* (1931), *The Mask of Fu Manchu* (1932)

Danny Kaye (David Daniel Kaminsky; 1913–87), American: *The Secret Life of Walter Mitty* (1947), *Hans Christian Andersen* (1952)

Buster Keaton (1895–1966), American: *The Butcher Boy* (1917), *The Paleface* (1922.

Gene Kelly (Eugene Curran Kelly; 1912–), American: *For Me and My Gal* (1942), *An American in Paris* (1951), *Singin' in the Rain* (1952), *Invitation to the Dance* (1956)

Grace Kelly (from 1956 HSH Princess Grace of Monaco; USA 1928–82), American: *The Country Girl* (1954; **AA**), *High Society* (1956)

Deborah Kerr (Deborah Kerr-Trimmer; 1921–), Scottish: *Love on the Dole* (1941), *From Here to Eternity* (1953), *The King and I* (1956), *The Sundowners* (1960)

Alan Ladd (1913–64), American: *This Gun For Hire* (1942), *The Great Gatsby* (1949), *Shane* (1953)

Dorothy Lamour (Dorothy Kaumeyer; 1914–), American: *Road to Singapore* (1940), *Road to Morocco* (1942)

Burt Lancaster (1913–), American: *Elmer Gantry* (1960; **AA**), *Birdman of Alcatraz* (1962)

Charles Laughton (1899–1962), English: *The Private Life of Henry VIII* (1933; **AA**), *Mutiny on the Bounty* (1935), *The Hunchback of Notre Dame* (1939), *Hobson's Choice* (1954)

Vivien Leigh (Vivien Hartley; 1913–67), English: *Gone With The Wind* (1939; **AA**), *Lady Hamilton* (1941), *A Streetcar Named Desire* (1951; **AA**)

Jack Lemmon (1925–), American: *Mister Roberts* (1955; **AA**), *Some Like it Hot* (1959), *Irma La Douce* (1963), *The Odd Couple* (1968), *Save the Tiger* (1973; **AA**)

Gina Lollobrigida (1927–), Italian: *Belles de Nuit* (1952), *Solomon and Sheba* (1959)

Sophia Loren (Sophia Scicoloni; 1934–), Italian: *Boy on a Dolphin* (1957), *Two Women* (1961; **AA**), *The Millionairess* (1960)

Myrna Loy (Myrna Williams; 1905–), American: *The Jazz Singer* (1927), *The Mask of Fu Manchu* (1932), *The Rains Came* (1939), *The Best Years of our Lives* (1946)

Shirley Maclaine (Shirley Maclean Beaty; 1934–), American: *Irma La Douce* (1963), *Sweet Charity* (1968), *Terms of Endearment* (1983; **AA**)

Steve McQueen (1930–80), American: *The Magnificent Seven* (1956), *The Great Escape* (1963), *The Cincinnati Kid* (1965), *Bullitt* (1968)

James Mason (1909–84), English: *The Wicked Lady* (1946), *The Desert Fox* (1951), *A Star is Born* (1954), *The Shooting Party* (1984)

Marcello Mastroianni (1923–), Italian: *La Dolce Vita* (1959), *Divorce Italian Style* (1962)

Walter Matthau (Walther Matasschanskayasky; 1920–), American: *The Fortune Cookie* (1966; **AA**), *The Odd Couple* (1968), *Hello Dolly* (1969), *The Sunshine Boys* (1975)

Sir John Mills (1908–), English: *Waterloo Road* (1944), *Great Expectations* (1946), *Hobson's Choice* (1954), *Tunes of Glory* (1960), *Ryan's Daughter* (1971; **AA**)

Robert Mitchum (1917–), American: *Night of the Hunter* (1955), *The Sundowners* (1960), *Ryan's Daughter* (1971)

Marilyn Monroe (Norma Jean Baker; 1926–62), American: *All About Eve* (1950), *Gentlemen Prefer Blondes* (1953), *The Seven Year Itch* (1955), *Some Like it Hot* (1959), *The Misfits* (1961)

Jeanne Moreau (1928–), French: *The Lovers* (1959), *Jules et Jim* (1961), *Diary of a Chambermaid* (1964)

Anna Neagle (Marjorie Robertson; 1904–86), English: *Nell Gwyn* (1934), *Victoria the Great* (1937), *Nurse Edith Cavell* (1939)

Paul Newman (1925–), American: *The Hustler* (1961), *Butch Cassidy and the Sundance Kid* (1969)

Jack Nicholson (1937–), American: *Easy Rider* (1969), *Five Easy Pieces* (1970), *One Flew Over the Cuckoo's Nest* (1976; **AA**), *Terms of Endearment* (1983; **AA**), *Prizzi's Honor* (1985)

David Niven (1909–83), Scottish: *Raffles* (1940), *Around the World in Eighty Days* (1956), *Separate Tables* (1958; **AA**)

Merle Oberon (Estelle O'Brien Merle Thompson; 1911–79), English: *The Scarlet Pimpernel* (1934), *Wuthering Heights* (1939)

Laurence Olivier (Lord Olivier; 1907–89), English: *Wuthering Heights* (1939), *Pride and Prejudice* (1940), *Henry V* (1944; **special AA**), *Hamlet* (1948; **AA**), *Richard III* (1956), *The Entertainer* (1960)

Peter O'Toole (1932–), Irish: *Lawrence of Arabia* (1962), *Becket* (1964), *The Lion in Winter* (1968), *Goodbye Mr Chips* (1969)

Al Pacino (Alfredo Pacino; 1939–), American: *The Godfather* (1972)

Gregory Peck (1916–), American: *The Gunfighter* (1950), *The Big Country* (1958), *Beloved Infidel* (1959), *To Kill a Mockingbird* (1963; **AA**)

Mary Pickford (Gladys Smith; 1893–1979), Canadian: *Pollyanna* (1919), *Little Lord Fauntleroy* (1921), *Coquette* (1929; **AA**)

Walter Pidgeon (1897–1984), Canadian: *How Green Was My Valley* (1941), *Mrs Miniver* (1942)

Sidney Poitier (1924–), American: *The Blackboard Jungle* (1955), *Porgy and Bess* (1959), *Lilies of the Field* (1963; **AA**), *In the Heat of the Night* (1967), *Guess Who's Coming to Dinner?* (1967)

Anthony Quinn (1915–90), American: *Viva Zapata* (1952; **AA**), *Lust for Life* (1956; **AA**), *Zorba the Greek* (1964)

Robert Redford (1936–), American: *Butch Cassidy and the Sundance Kid* (1969), *The Candidate* (1972), *The Sting* (1973), *All the President's Men* (1976)

Vanessa Redgrave (1937–), English: *Camelot* (1967), *Isadora* (1968), *Julia* (1977; **AA**), *The Ballad of the Sad Cafe* (1991)

Edward G. Robinson (Emanuel Goldenberg; 1893–1973), Romanian-born American: *Little Caesar* (1930), *Double Indemnity* (1944), *Key Largo* (1948)

Ginger Rogers (Virginia McMath; 1911–), American: *Flying Down to Rio* (1933), *Top Hat* (1935),

Follow the Fleet (1936), *Kitty Foyle* (1940; **AA**)

Mickey Rooney (Joe Yule Jnr; 1920–), American: *Boys' Town* (1938; **special AA**), *Babes in Arms* (1939), *The Bold and the Brave* (1956)

Jane Russell (1921–), American: *The Paleface* (1948), *Gentlemen Prefer Blondes* (1953)

George Sanders (1906–72), American: *The Moon and Sixpence* (1942), *The Picture of Dorian Gray* (1944), *All About Eve* (1952; **AA**)

George Segal (1934–), American: *The Owl and the Pussycat* (1970), *A Touch of Class* (1973)

Peter Sellers (1925–80), English: *I'm All Right Jack* (1959), *Only Two Can Play* (1962), *The Pink Panther* (1963), *Dr Strangelove* (1963), *Being There* (1979)

Jean Simmons (1929–), English: *Great Expectations* (1946), *Black Narcissus* (1946), *Elmer Gantry* (1960)

Frank Sinatra (1915–), American: *From Here to Eternity* (1953; **AA**), *The Man With the Golden Arm* (1956), *High Society* (1956), *Pal Joey* (1957), *The Manchurian Candidate* (1962)

Maggie Smith (1934–), English: *The VIPs* (1963), *The Prime of Miss Jean Brodie* (1969; **AA**), *California Suite* (1978; **AA**)

Sylvester Stallone (1946–), American: *Rocky* (1976), *Rambo* (1985)

Rod Steiger (1925–), American: *On the Waterfront* (1954), *Al Capone* (1958), *In the Heat of the Night* (1967; **AA**)

James Stewart (1908–), American: *Mr Smith Goes to Washington* (1939), *Destry Rides Again* (1939), *The Philadelphia Story* (1940; **AA**), *It's a Wonderful Life* (1946), *Harvey* (1950)

Meryl Streep (Mary Louise Streep; 1951–), American: *Kramer vs Kramer* (1979; **AA**), *The French Lieutenant's Woman* (1981), *Sophie's Choice* (1982; **AA**), *Silkwood* (1983), *Out of Africa* (1986)

Barbra Streisand (1942–), American: *Funny Girl* (1968; **AA**), *Hello Dolly* (1969), *Funny Lady* (1975), *A Star is Born* (1976)

Donald Sutherland (1935–), Canadian: *M*A*S*H* (1970), *Kelly's Heroes* (1970), *Klute* (1971).

Gloria Swanson (G. Svensson; 1897–1983), American: *Sadie Thompson* (1928), *Queen Kelly* (1928), *Sunset Boulevard* (1950)

Elizabeth Taylor (1932–), English: *National Velvet* (1944), *Cat on a Hot Tin Roof* (1958), *Butterfield 8* (1960; **AA**), *Cleopatra* (1962), *Who's Afraid of Virginia Woolf?* (1967; **AA**)

Shirley Temple (1928–), American

Spencer Tracy (1900–67), American: *The Power and the Glory* (1933), *Captains Courageous* (1937; **AA**), *Northwest Passage* (1940), *Pat and Mike* (1952), *Guess Who's Coming to Dinner?* (1967)

Rudolph Valentino (Rodolpho d'Antonguolla; 1895–1926), Italian-born: *The Four Horsemen of the Apocalypse* (1921), *The Sheik* (1921), *Blood and Sand* (1922), *Son of the Sheik* (1926)

Orson Welles (1915–85), American: *Citizen Kane* (1941), *The Third Man* (1949), *The Trial* (1962)

Natalie Wood (Natasha Gurdin; 1938–81): *Rebel Without a Cause* (1955), *West Side Story* (1961), *Bob and Carol and Ted and Alice* (1969)

THEATRE

THE ORIGINS OF THEATRE

The origins of drama were in the rituals that hunters enacted to ensure success or to placate the spirit of their prey and in the ceremonies through which farmers sought to ensure the renewal of the seasons. The religious rituals in which the Egyptian pharaohs re-enacted the murder and resurrection of the god Osiris may have been one of the first 'plays'.

GREEK AND ROMAN THEATRE

Western drama had its first flowering in ancient Greece in the festival that honoured Dionysus, the god of fertility and wine. From the orgiastic celebrations of his cult developed a form of choral performance – the *dithyramb* – in which a tale of gods and heroes was recounted in song and dance. To this, in the 6th century BC, Thespis, a priest, is credited with adding a solo performer who engaged in dialogue with the leader of the chorus, resulting in the first Greek play.

These early plays were known as *tragedies*, a word originally meaning 'goat-song', perhaps because the song was offered at the same time that a goat was sacrificed. Thespis is believed to have taken a troupe of actors around Greece performing plays, and modern actors are sometimes referred to as *thespians* after him.

Within a century, serious tragedies had been joined by bawdy *satyrs* – the satyrs were horse-tailed goat-eared men who were supposed to be Dionysus's followers. These plays often made fun of the scandalous love-life of the gods.

The actors – all male – increased in number from a single speaker (the first actor) to three men. In a single play, the three actors might each play several roles, each character clearly identified by its costume and face mask, but no more than three characters could appear in any one scene.

Touring troupes may have performed in market places, but most Hellenic cities had a hillside theatre where people could stand or sit on a semicircle of wooden or stone benches to watch the actors perform on a flattened circle called the *orchestra* ('threshing floor'). Later a row of buildings across the back of the orchestra provided a narrow raised platform which the actors could sometimes use, although eventually all of the action took place upon this stage. Large theatres, such as the one at Epidavros, could hold up to 14 000 spectators, and performances could last all day.

Roman theatre followed the style of the Greek in staging and performance, although Roman theatre buildings were considerably more elaborate than their Hellenic counterparts. However, a preference for scabrous plots drew the disapproval of the Christian Church with the result that the Byzantine Emperor Justinian I ordered the closure of all theatres in the 6th century AD.

Greek and Roman dramatists and their works are summarized under Classical Literature (see p. 332).

MEDIEVAL AND RENAISSANCE THEATRE

Travelling entertainers probably preserved the elements of theatre, but it was in the Church itself that formal drama reappeared as parts of Christian teaching and liturgy began to be given dramatic form. The performance of plays retelling Bible stories – *miracle* or *mystery plays* – developed, to be followed by moral secular tales. These were staged in a variety of ways. Sometimes there were settings – or *mansions* – side by side on a wide outdoor stage; sometimes the plays were performed within a ring of platforms. In Britain and Iberia, each scene was often acted on a separate cart – or *pageant* – which was pulled through the streets for the play to be performed at a number of locations.

Medieval actors – again all male – were usually members of various craft guilds, the 'mysteries' being not those of religion but of trades and professions. Individual craft guilds became responsible for the performance of an appropriate play.

With the renewed interest in classical ideas during the Renaissance, schools and universities began to perform Roman plays in Latin texts. Some attempts were even made to re-create theatres like those of ancient Rome, for example, the Teatro Olimpico (1585) in Vincenza, Italy, which unlike ancient Roman theatres was roofed over.

The flowering of drama in Elizabethan England was accompanied by the construction of the first modern public theatres in northern Europe. London's first public playhouse opened in 1576. It was built in the fields to the north of the city walls because the city fathers had forbidden the performance of plays within 'the Square Mile'. It was soon followed by a group of theatres south of the River Thames – again outside the City of London – and these included the Rose, the Swan and the Globe. Their circular, galleried design was based upon the courtyards of inns. The stage jutted out into the centre of the yard which was open to the sky. Although some scenic elements were used, and there were colourful costumes and effects, most of the scene-setting was built into the text.

This was the type of theatre for which Shakespeare wrote. It allowed for rapidly moving dramas in which one scene followed straight on from another. The actors were in close contact with the audience, members of which either stood in the yard or sat in the galleries and even on the stage itself. Even in the largest London Elizabethan theatre – which could accommodate up to 3000 spectators – no one was more than about 10 m (30 ft) from the stage.

Indoor performances were largely restricted to court *masques*, an entertainment that emphasized music, dance and elaborate effects. Masques – which originated at the French and Italian courts – were enacted by nobles and were not intended for viewing by a wider public. Masques were, however, the direct ancestor of both ballet and opera.

Renaissance dramatists and their works are summarized under Renaissance Literature (see p. 334) and Shakespeare (see p. 335).

THEATRE IN THE 17th AND 18th CENTURIES

In the middle of the 16th century, some Italian court masques were performed behind a frame separating the stage from the spectators. Originally scenic elements had been arranged around the performance space, but the retreat behind this frame (originally a temporary structure) marked the birth of the *proscenium* and the beginning of the modern theatre. Although these temporary proscenium arches did support curtains they were erected to provide atmosphere and spectacle rather than to hide changes of scene. The first permanent proscenium to be installed in a theatre was at the Teatro Farnese in Parma, Italy (1618–19), but scenery was not usually changed behind curtains until the 18th century.

European theatres in the 17th century were almost invariably roofed, and English open courtyard theatres did not survive the ban on stage plays during the Civil War and Commonwealth (1642–60).

During the 18th century, important changes in stage design were introduced by the Bibiena family of Bologna in Italy. Previously stage sets were based upon one-point perspective using a single vanishing point. Ferdinando Bibiena developed angle perspective, that is perspective with two vanishing points. The Bibienas created sets that gave the impression of great size. Late in the 18th century new styles of scenery appeared. Classical ruins became popular and stage designers strove to create a 'mood', emphasizing light and dark.

In France the Italian designer Giacomo Torelli mystified audiences by changing scenery while the opera or ballet continued rather than at the end of scenes. To celebrate the wedding of Louis XIV in 1660, Gaspare Vigarani built the Salle des Machines, a large theatre equipped with many machines and special effects, including a platform that could 'fly' the French royal family on to the stage. The Comédie Française, by contrast, made its home in a stark converted tennis court, although the Opéra enjoyed a lavish Baroque building well equipped with scenery and machines.

Italian models were used for most theatrical and stage designs in Europe in the 18th century. The stage was enlarged and, initially, the forestage – the area in front of the proscenium – was fairly deep with doors opening on to it for the entrances and exits of performers, and some members of the public sat in 'boxes' on either side. By the end of the 18th century the standing pit had been abolished and the audience was all seated. However, permanent theatres were uncommon. Most plays were staged by travelling troupes who had many plays in their repertoire. This prevented sufficient rehearsals and discouraged the development of acting skills.

Neoclassical and Romantic dramatists and their works are summarized on pp. 336–37.

THEATRE IN THE 19th and 20th CENTURIES

Many theatres retained close proximity between actors and audience well into the 19th century, but as stronger lighting was developed, eventually using gas and electricity, it became possible to light up both actors and scenery more brilliantly, even well upstage. The proscenium advanced further and further until it became a 'picture frame' for the whole action of the play.

In the 19th century, theatres increased in number and different types of theatre evolved for different genres – plays, opera, ballet, music hall and so on. There were also major innovations in acting and staging. The design of theatres with improved acoustics encouraged players to forsake the traditional declamatory style of acting in favour of a more natural manner. Scenery, however, remained elaborate. Wagner's opera house at Bayreuth (opened in 1876) introduced the orchestra pit, and he is thought to be the first person to darken the house lights during a performance. A bigger long-term impact was

made by the Meiningen troupe founded and directed by the German prince Georg II of Saxe-Meiningen, who emphasized the importance of research and rehearsal, and introduced the split stage, historical accuracy in scenery and the concept that scenery, lighting, costumes, properties, actors, text and actions formed an interwoven whole, every part of which must fit.

From c. 1850 to c. 1945 the picture-frame stage was the kind of theatre most people expected. Improved lighting techniques allowed the side walls of a 'room' to be constructed and the ceiling to be lowered above the stage so that the audience appeared to be looking into a room with one wall removed – the 'fourth wall', as the division between the actors and audience came to be known. This box proved the ideal setting for the theatrical revival at the end of the 19th century in Europe, which has been seen as the final flowering of Realism (see p. 338). Plays emphasized the lives and concerns of ordinary people. Scenes became shorter and sometimes abrupt, while settings became more intimate and less monumental and spectacular.

At the end of the 19th century André Antoine revolutionized staging by removing the 'fourth wall' and establishing the concept that every play requires its own distinct setting. Realism in acting triumphed while scenery and settings became simpler, often stark. Settings often became a shorthand indication of locale or mood. Skeleton tracery, primitive masonry, sometimes cloth, paper or even light rather than structures have all enjoyed favour as settings for performances. This revolution reached its climax in Jerzy Grotowski's Lab Theatre in Poland, in which every performance is seen as an independent entity requiring a unique playing space and arrangement of the audience and actors.

Theatres with picture frame prosceniums and tiered seating are still in the majority, but all kinds of arrangements are now used, including the projecting apron stage and 'theatre in the round'. Many performance settings can be arranged to suit a particular production, sometimes with no seats and no stage as such, but with the action moving from place to place among the audience, as for example in street theatre.

Dramatists of the 19th and 20th centuries, and their works, are summarized on pp. 338–41.

NOTABLE STAGE ACTORS AND DIRECTORS

Lope de Rueda (?1509–65), Spanish actor-manager.

Andre Calmo (1509/10–71), Venetian actor-dramatist.

Richard Tarlton (d. 1588), English clown.

Will Kempe (c. 1550–c. 1607), English actor-clown.

Edward Alleyn (1566–1626), English actor who played leading roles in Marlowe's plays.

Richard Burbage (1567–1619), English actor who played leading roles in many first performances of Shakespeare's plays.

Molière (Jean-Baptiste Poquelin; 1622–73), French actor-dramatist – see Literature (p. 336).

Thomas Betterton (c. 1635–1710), English actor who played leading roles in many Restoration and Shakespearean plays.

Nell Gwyn (Eleanor Gwyn; ?1642–87), English actress.

Michel Baron (Michel Boyron; 1653–1729), French actor who created the leading roles in many of Racine's plays.

Colley Cibber (1671–1757), English actor-manager, dramatist and Poet Laureate.

Adrienne Lecouvreur (1692–1730), French actress who was noted for the natural style of her acting.

James Quin (1692–1766), English actor.

Charles Macklin (1699–1797), Irish actor and dramatist.

David Garrick (1717–79), English Shakespearean actor and manager whose natural style of acting had a major effect upon the tastes and standards of the time.

Konrad Ekhof (1720–78), German actor.

Friedrich Ludwig Schröder (1744–1816), German actor-manager and dramatist who introduced Shakespeare to the German stage.

Sarah Siddons (1755–1831), English tragic actress who became famous for her interpretation of Lady Macbeth.

John Philip Kemble (1757–1823), English tragic actor and theatre manager – the brother of Sarah Siddons.

François Joseph Talma (1763–1826), French actor and manager who developed realism in acting and staging.

Edmund Kean (1787–1833), English Shakespearean actor.

Mikhail Semyonovich Shchepkin (1788–1863), Russian actor whose performances were characterized by understatement.

William Macready (1793–1873), English actor who developed the techniques of acting.

Frédérick Lemaître (1800–76), French actor.

Johann Nepomuck Nestroy (1801–62), Austrian dramatist and character actor.

Ira Aldridge (1805–67), Afro-American tragic actor who worked mainly in Europe.

Edwin Forrest (1806–72), American actor.

Charles Kean (1811–68), English actor-manager who revived the Shakespearean canon.

Charlotte Cushman (1816–76), the first American actress to achieve an international reputation.

Rachel (Elisa Félix; 1820–58), Swiss-born French tragic actress who became famous for her interpretation of Phèdre.

Adelaide Ristori (1922–06), Italian tragic actress.

Georg II (1826–1914), sovereign duke of the German state of Saxe-Meiningen. He founded and directed an influential acting company.

Tommasso Salvini (1829–1915), Italian actor.

Joseph Jefferson (1829–1905), American actor who became famous for his creation of the role of Rip Van Winkle.

Edwin Booth (1833–93), American tragic actor who became famous for his interpretation of Hamlet. He was the brother of the assassin of President Lincoln.

Henry Irving (John Henry Brodribb; 1838–1905), English director and Shakespearean actor.

Helena Modjeska (1840–1909), Polish-born American actress who achieved great success on the British and American stage in Shakespearean roles despite her poor English.

Constant-Benoît Coquelin (1841–1909), French actor who was renowned for his versatility.

Sarah Bernhardt (1844–1923), French actress who gained international acclaim for her tragic roles in *Phèdre*, *La Dame aux camélias* and *L'Aiglon*.

James O'Neill (1846–1920), Irish-born American actor.

Ellen Terry (1847–1928), English actress who was the leading lady in many of Henry Irving's Shakespearean productions.

Herbert Beerbohm Tree (1853–1917), English actor-manager.

Réjane (Gabrielle Réju; 1856–1920), French actress.

Eleanora Duse (1858–1924), Italian actress who became famous for her portrayal of heroines in the plays of D'Annunzio and Ibsen.

André Antoine (1858–1943), French actor, director, critic and film producer.

Vladimir Nemirovich-Danchenko (1858–1943), Russian director, drama teacher and co-founder of the Moscow Art Theatre.

Annie Horniman (1860–1937), English theatre manager who started the repertory theatre movement in the UK.

Constantin Stanislavsky (1863–1938), Russian actor and director who developed the Stanislavsky method of acting, better known as 'the method'.

Mrs Patrick Campbell (Beatrice Stella Tanner; 1865–1940), English actress who created the role of Eliza Doolittle and who enjoyed great success in Ibsen and Shakespeare.

Olga Knipper (1868–1959), Russian actress who gained great acclaim in leading roles in the plays of her husband, Chekhov.

Max Reinhardt (Max Goldman; 1873–1943), Austrian director who was instrumental in the foundation of the Salzburg Festival.

Lillian Baylis (1874–1937), English theatre manager who founded the Old Vic.

Vsevolod Emilievich Meyerhold (1874–1940), Russian actor, director and producer who experimented in 'nonrealistic' theatre.

Ivan Mikhailovich Moskvin (1874–1946), Russian actor.

Harley Granville Barker (1877–1946), English-born director and producer who worked mainly in France.

Lionel Barrymore (1878–1954), American character actor and director.

Jacques Copeau (1878–1949), French actor-director.

Ethel Barrymore (Ethel Blythe; 1878–1959), American stage and film actress.

Sybil Thorndyke (1882–1976), English Shakespearean actress who created the title role in Shaw's *Saint Joan*.

John Barrymore (1882–1942), American actor who played romantic leading men and Shakespearean roles.

Laurette Taylor (Loretta Cooney; 1884–1946), American actress.

Charles Dullin (1885–1949), French actor-director.

Lyn Fontanne (Lillie Louise Fontanne; 1887–1983), English-born American actress who usually played opposite her husband Alfred Lunt.

Louis Jouvet (1887–1951), French actor, director and designer who had a great influence on 20th-century French theatre.

Edith Evans (1888–1976), English actress who won acclaim in a wide variety of dramatic roles.

Alfred Lunt (1892–1977), American actor-director who was particularly associated with the plays of Noel Coward – see also Lyn Fontanne, above.

Margaret Rutherford (1892–1972), English stage and film actress who specialized in playing eccentrics.

Erwin Piscator (1893–1966), innovative German producer and director, who, with Brecht, developed 'epic theatre'.

Paul Scofield (1922–), English Shakespearean actor.

Franco Zeffirelli (Franco Zeffirelli Corsi; 1923–), Italian stage and film director and designer.

Marlon Brando (1924–), American actor. See Notable Film Actors (p. 396).

Geraldine Page (1924–87), American stage actress.

Julian Beck (1925–85), American producer, director and actor.

Peter Brook (1925–), English director, noted for innovative productions of international theatre.

Richard Burton (Richard Jenkins; 1925–84), Welsh actor, who gained initial success on stage, mainly in Shakespearean roles, but who worked almost exclusively in films from the 1950s.

John Dexter (1925–90), English director.

John Neville (1925–), English actor and director, who has been particularly associated with the Stratford Festival in Ontario, Canada.

Dario Fo (1926–), Italian actor, writer and director of popular political theatre.

Judith Malina (1926–), German-born American producer and director.

George C. Scott (1927–), American stage and film actor and director.

Eric Porter (1928–), English actor.

William Gaskill (1930–), English director.

Peter Hall (1930–), English director. Founder of the Royal Shakespeare Company.

Anne Bancroft (Anna Maria Italiano; 1931–), American stage and film actress.

Dorothy Tutin (1931–), English stage and film actress.

Ian Holm (1931–), English actor.

Mike Nichols (1931–), American director.

Roger Planchon (1931–), French director of the Theatre National Populaire since 1972.

Jerzy Grotowski (1933–), Polish director of the innovative Lab Theatre.

Alan Bates (1934–), English actor.

Jonathan Miller (1934–), English director of plays for stage and television, and of opera.

Ariane Mnouchkine (1934–), French director.

Joseph Chaikin (1935–), American director.

Judi Dench (Judith Dench; 1935–), English actress.

Albert Finney (1936–), English actor.

Nuria Espert (1936–), Spanish actress.

Glenda Jackson (1936–), English stage and film actress. See Notable Film Actors.

Carmelo Bene (1937–), Italian actor, director and dramatist.

Dustin Hoffman (1937–), American stage and film actor. See Notable Film Actors (see p. 398).

Anthony Hopkins (1937–), Welsh actor.

Alan Howard (1937–), English actor who is particularly associated with the Royal Shakespeare Company.

Vanessa Redgrave (1937–), English stage and film actress – daughter of Michael Redgrave (see above). See also Notable Film Actors (p. 399).

Peter Stein (1937–), German director.

Derek Jacobi (1938–), English actor.

Nicol Williamson (1938–), Scottish actor.

Ian McKellan (1939–), English actor.

Michael Gambon (1940–), English actor.

Trevor Nunn (1940–), English director who is particularly associated with the Royal Shakespeare Company.

Robert Wilson (1941–), American director.

Patrice Chereau (1944–), French director.

Anthony Sher (1949–), South African-born British actor.

John Malkovich (1953–), American actor-director.

Kenneth Branagh (1961–), Irish-born British actor-director.

THEATRE GLOSSARY

Absurd, Theatre of the the description applied to the work of Ionesco, Adamov, Beckett and some other writers of the 1950s because it presented the absurdity of the human condition.

act a major division of a play. An interval normally separates two acts.

alienation the effect that Bertolt Brecht sought to create by means of his theory of performance designed to help audiences to look critically at social issues. In order to achieve this he wanted to distance audiences emotionally from the action and characters on the stage in order that they might more clearly see and understand the social and political contexts in which characters acted.

anti-pros the American equivalent of front of the house lights.

apron an extension of the stage in front of a proscenium.

arena theatre theatre-in-the-round; also originally used to describe an open stage.

auditorium the area of the theatre occupied by the audience.

bar a pipe from which lamps are hung behind borders. They are numbered from the front of the stage.

barn doors hinged flaps at the sides of lamps to restrict the beam.

batten a horizontal wooden bar or metal pipe from which scenery or lights are suspended; or a row of lamps in joined compartments that give diffused light over a long area – these are called ground-rows when on the stage floor.

boat truck a wheeled platform on which scenery

and furniture can be preset and pushed on-stage.

blocking fixing actors' movements in rehearsal and recording those movements in the prompt copy.

boom a vertical pipe for lighting.

border horizontal masking to hide lights and anything else above stage.

box a separate compartment in the auditorium for seating several people, often either side of the proscenium. In some old theatres whole tiers are divided into boxes.

box office the office at which tickets are purchased (originally only boxes could be reserved).

bring in to fade in lights quickly.

bring up to increase the intensity of the lights.

Broadway the fashionable theatre area of New York, not just a section of the street of that name but defined by American Equity as extending between 5th and 9th Avenues from 34th Street to 56th Street, and from 5th to the Hudson River bounded by 56th and 72nd Streets.

bump in/out the Australian term for 'get in/out' (q.v.).

call a message to actors or stage crew that they are needed; also, notice of rehearsals, costume fittings, etc.

cabaret a show comprising dancing, singing or other forms of light entertainment, usually performed in a nightclub or restaurant.

circle a tier of seating in the auditorium.

cleat line a rope used for lashing flats together. Nailed to the upper part of one flat, it is flicked around a projection on another, then wrapped round projections lower down and tied-off with a slip knot, so providing a rapid way of erecting and dismantling scenery.

cloth an item of hanging canvas scenery. A backcloth is at the rear of the stage; a cut cloth is one with areas cut out so that the audience can see through them.

comedy a light and amusing play.

Commedia dell'Arte Italian farce popular between the 16th and 18th centuries. It relied upon a cast of stock characters including Harlequin, Pantaloon and Columbine. The genre influenced contemporary dramatists such as Molière.

community theatre a term used in Britain to describe plays and performances performed in a geographic location by its residents, or imported from theatres and performed by professionals, or addressed to a community formed either by geography or a common interest. This form of theatre may include community drama-documentaries (for example the Black Theatre Co-operative, Gay Sweatshop Theatre, the Solent People's Theatre of Hampshire). Linking this diversity is usually a concern for social improvement, and the resulting work can be analytical, critical or celebratory.

corpse to come out of character and laugh at something not part of the play.

cruelty, theatre of the form of theatre defined by Antonin Artaud as his ideal. Artaud felt that in such a theatre an audience would be continually confronted with their real selves, and such a confrontation would inevitably lead to deep feelings akin to physical pain and discomfort.

cue words or actions to which an actor answers or which indicate the moment for an effect or scenic or lighting change. The term is also used to mean the sound or lighting change itself.

curtain call the line-up of actors before the applauding audience at the end of a performance.

cut cloth see cloth.

cyclorama a curved cloth or other backing at the rear of the stage which is lit to give the impression of the sky or of continuing space.

director the person who rehearses actors and decides and coordinates artistic aspects of a production.

dimmer a control device for increasing or decreasing light levels. The earliest types were simple hand-operated electrical resistances; now they are often electronic and computerized.

dip a light plug in the stage floor, covered by a small trap.

downstage the area of the stage nearer the audience.

dramatis personnae a list of the characters in a play.

dress circle the first balcony or tier of auditorium seating.

dress rehearsal a rehearsal with full scenery, costumes and effects.

dry to forget one's lines.

effects any sounds, special lighting devices, etc., required by the play.

ensemble a group of actors performing together.

epic theatre the concept of theatre developed by Bertolt Brecht.

Equity the name of the actors' union in both the UK and the USA.

Expressionism a style of theatre popular in Germany c. 1900–30. It embraced a wide variety of moods but was always antinaturalistic.

fade in/out to bring in/take out lights or sounds slowly.

false pros(cenium) the inner frame of a narrow proscenium arch.

farce a humorous play in which characters usually represent basic types. The structure of the play usually relies on mishaps, coincidence, embarrassing disclosures and on visual jokes, including chases.

flat a scenic unit of canvas stretched on a wooden frame. It may have openings to take doors, windows or a fireplace.

flies the space above the stage where lights and scenery can be hung out of the view of the audience.

float see boat truck.

floats the footlights (they were originally wicks floating in bowls of oil).

flood a lamp with a reflector giving a wide beam. A flood cannot be focused.

fly to move a person, object or piece of scenery from the stage by means of a line, rope or wire, usually vertically into the flies.

FOH See front of house.

follow spot a bright spotlight that is moved to keep an actor lit irrespective of the general stage lighting.

footlights a lighting batten at the front of the stage. The lights, which shine upwards, were originally needed to counteract strong shadows from overhead lamps. Footlights are now infrequently used.

forestage the area in front of the house curtain in proscenium theatres.

free theatre see fringe.

fringe a term first used in the 1950s for performances and companies that were not an official part of the Edinburgh International Festival. The use of the term developed to include any unofficial or unconventional work, but since this implies a disconnection from the mainstream of theatre development, many fringe groups now prefer the word 'alternative'. In the USA 'Off-Broadway' and in Europe 'free theatre' are used in a similar manner to 'fringe'.

front of house the areas of the theatre used by the audience. The term usually applies only to the auditorium but it can include foyers, etc. (The front-of-house staff are the box office and ushers.)

gallery the highest tier or balcony of seats, traditionally known as 'the gods'.

gauze a cloth of fine weave, transparent when lit from behind, so that any front-lit scene painted on it seems to disappear.

get-in/out the process of moving scenery and all equipment in or out of a theatre.

go the instruction to operate cues.

gods the gallery or gallery spectators.

grand guignol a French genre that piles horror on horror.

grid a framework or scaffold above the stage or acting area from which scenery and lights are suspended.

ground row cut-out scenery on the stage floor representing walls, the skyline, etc. The ground row usually masks lighting. Also, a lighting batten used to light a cyclorama or backcloth.

house the auditorium, or the audience (as in 'the house is in', i.e. the audience is in the theatre).

kill to switch off sound or lights, or to remove something from the set.

legs hanging cloth wings.

lime(light) bright spotlights used to follow actors – limelights originally used a piece of lime to create bright incandescence.

lines the words of an actor's part. Also the ropes used for raising and lowering scenery from the flies.

Living Newspaper the term associated with the US Federal Theatre Project of the 1930s. Unemployed newspaper and theatre people used documentary presentation methods to focus attention on current social problems and possible solutions, eg. *Power* (1937), suggesting the need for public ownership of utilities.

lose to remove from the stage.

mask to hide equipment or space behind scenes from the audience. Also for one actor to block another from the audience. Also a covering worn to hide the face or to represent a different face.

melodrama a sensational romantic drama characterized by extremes of character.

Method, The an acting technique developed by Lee Strasberg at the New York Actors' Studio from the teachings of Stanislavsky.

mime acting through gesture and without words.

miracle play medieval religious drama based on miraculous incidents from the lives and works of the saints and performed on the days dedicated to them.

morality play medieval allegorical drama showing ordinary humans exposed to temptation.

mystery play medieval religious drama originally presented by members of craft guilds (mysteries).

Noh Theatre classic Japanese theatre – probably the oldest form of theatre which has been continuously performed in the same traditional manner.

Off-Broadway small theatres, usually converted from other spaces, created to provide an opportunity for productions unable to find a home in Broadway commercial theatre. The use of the term dates from c. 1952. As Off-Broadway became more commercial, avant garde and experimental work was driven to other performing spaces referred to as 'Off-off Broadway'.

OP opposite-prompt – the right-hand side of the stage facing the audience (the left in the USA).

open stage a stage or performing space surrounded by an arc of the audience.

orchestra the circular floor in ancient Greek theatre where most of the play took place.

pantomime originally, an all-mime performance, but now generally the popular Christmas entertainments based on fairy stories which originally incorporated the Harlequinade from the Commedia dell'Arte. They traditionally feature transvestite performers in the male romantic roles and the leading comic female part.

pipe a hollow metal bar from which scenery and lighting are suspended.

pit the lower floor of the auditorium, traditionally covered by open benches. The pit is now usually called the stalls.

playbill a poster or leaflet advertising a play. The term is also sometimes used for the programme.

plot the story line of a play. Also a list of requirements and cues for each technical department, as in 'lighting plot', etc.

'Poor' Theatre the term coined by Jerzy Grotowski for a style of theatre which rejects superfluous technical means (lighting, sound, make-up, props) and works directly with the actor's body and the audience relationship, as in the work in his Laboratory Theatre in Poland.

practical a prop or piece of a set that can be used, e.g. food that has to be eaten, a door that has to open.

producer the person who presents the show, raises the money, and employs the cast and the production team. Until the 1960s the term was used for what is now called the director – formerly the producer would have been known as the manager.

promenade a performance in which actors and audience share a space, and the action (and audience) move within it; or a performance in which the action moves through several spaces.

prompt to help an actor by whispering the lines that he has forgotten.

prop(erty) anything used on the stage which does not form part of the scenery, costumes or technical equipment. **Hand props** are those carried or handled by the actors.

prompt copy or **prompt book** a copy of the script in which the positions and moves of scenery, furniture and actors and all the cues for changes and effects are recorded.

prompt corner the control centre from which stage management give all cues and prompts.

prompt side stage left facing the audience (right in the USA). It is usually, but not always, the side on which the prompt corner is placed.

proscenium originally the shallow platform in front of the skene, or rear building, of the Greek theatre. Now the name is applied to the wall dividing the auditorium from the stage where the proscenium arch is located. The proscenium arch is the frame through which the audience views the stage.

PS prompt side.

read through the first reading of the whole play by the cast – often the first rehearsal.

rehearsal a practice or trial performance of a play.

repertory theatre originally a theatre having a repertoire of plays for presentation. The term more generally implies a theatre that presents a succession of plays, usually with the same company, rather than presenting a single play as long as it draws an audience.

return a flat joined at right angles to another. Also a ticket brought back for resale.

reveal a small return by an arch, window or doorway to show the thickness of a wall.

revue an entertainment of songs, sketches, dances, etc, usually unconnected.

rostrum a movable stage platform, usually a flat surface set on a collapsible, hinged supporting frame.

round, in the see theatre in the round.

SM the stage manager.

soliloquy a speech, supposedly unheard by others on the stage, in which a character speaks his or her thoughts.

spot(light) a lamp that can be focused and whose angle and size of beam can be controlled. **Fresnel spots** throw a soft-edged beam, **profile** or **mirror spots** produce a hard-edged beam of more intense light.

stage manager the person responsible for the organization and conduct of rehearsals, the co-ordination of all technical departments, the making and updating of the prompt copy, and the running of performances. There may be more than one stage manager, together with assistant stage managers (ASMs). In a large theatre running plays in repertoire, a production manager may head the team. Sometimes the term 'stage director' is used.

stock company the American term for a repertory company.

strobe a lamp that produces short flashes of light, giving the impression of freezing movement.

stalls the lowest part of the auditorium.

strike to dismantle a stage set.

tabs curtains – originally tableau curtains because they were opened and closed on tableaux (moments when the actors froze). **House tabs** are those between the stage and the audience.

theatre in the round a theatre in which the audience sits on all sides of the acting area. The term is commonly used even where the shape of the stage is rectangular or polygonal.

thrust stage a stage projecting into the audience.

tormentor a narrow curtain or flat used to mask wings behind the proscenium.

tragedy a serious drama in which the downfall of the principal character is brought about by a personal failing, or by social and psychological circumstances.

trap an opening in the stage floor, covered either by hinged or sliding panels. A **grave-trap** is the size and shape of a grave and a **star trap** has triangular hinged panels forming a circular hole just big enough for an actor to push through – star traps are used for sudden appearances, especially of the demon king in pantomime.

trough a lighting ground row, usually with circular filters to give a wide beam spread. Troughs are used to light a cyclorama.

traverse tabs drawn across the stage.

traverse staging a rectangular acting area with audience seated on both its long sides.

unities the three principles of dramatic structure by which a play was limited to a single plot (unity of action), taking place at a single location (unity of place), on a single day (unity of time). Classical French drama was characterized by the unities.

up stage the area of the stage further back from the audience. For one actor to 'upstage' another means that they draw attention away from the other and on to themselves for selfish reasons.

wings the areas backstage at the side of the acting area. Also flats or curtains hung facing the audience at the sides of the stage to mask these areas.

wardrobe the costumes and the staff and premises handling them.

warn to give instructions to the actors or technicians to stand by for a cue.

ARTS FESTIVALS IN THE EC

Belgium Festival of Flanders, a music festival held in several Flemish towns (Apr–Oct); Festival of Wallonia, a music festival held in several Walloon towns (Sep–Nov).

Denmark Copenhagen – dance (May).

France Aix-en-Provence – music (Jul–Aug); Arles – music, dance and folklore (Jul); Avignon – drama and dance (Jul–Aug); Cannes – film (May); Lille – music, dance, dance and folklore (Oct–Nov); Lyon – Berlioz festival (Sept); Mulhouse – Bach festival (Jun); Paris – music (Jan), dance (Sep–Dec); Strasbourg – choral (Mar–Apr).

Germany Ansbach – Bach festival (Jul–Aug); Bayreuth – Wagner festival (Jul–Aug); Berlin – film (Feb–Mar), music, dance and drama (Sept–Oct); Bonn – Beethoven festival (May–Sep); Halle – Handel festival (Jun); Leipzig – Bach festival (Sep); Wiesbaden – music, ballet and drama (May).

Greece Athens – international music and drama festival (summer); Epidavros – music and drama (summer).

Ireland Wexford – opera (Oct–Nov).

Italy Bergamo/Brescia – music (Apr–May); Florence – music, particularly opera (May–Jun); Perugia – sacred music (Sep–Oct); Spoleto – music, dance and drama (Jun–Jul); Venice – contemporary music (Sep – every other year), film (Aug–Sep).

Netherlands Festival of Holland – music, dance and drama festival in Amsterdam, The Hague and Rotterdam (Jun).

Portugal Estoril – music, dance and drama (Jul–Aug).

Spain Barcelona – music, dance and drama (Oct); Cuenca – religious music (Easter); Granada – music, dance and folklore (Jun–Jul).

United Kingdom Aldeburgh – opera (Jun); Brighton – music, dance and drama (May); Cheltenham – music and literature (Jul); Chichester – drama (May–Oct); Edinburgh – drama, music and dance (Aug–Sep); Glasgow Mayfest – drama, dance and music (May); Glyndebourne – opera (May–Aug); Promenade Concerts – music festival held in London (Jun–Sep); Three Choirs – choral festival held alternately in Gloucester, Hereford and Worcester (Aug–Sep); Welsh National Eisteddfod – music, dance, drama and folklore festival held alternately in north and south Wales (Aug).

HISTORY
TIME CHARTS

────────────**PREHISTORY TO 3000 BC**────────────

c. 70 million First primates appear.

c. 6–4 million *Australopithecus* genus appears in southern and eastern Africa with perfect erect posture.

c. 2·5 million Probable appearance of *Homo habilis* and first tools in Africa.

c. 1·7 million First structured habitat is built by *Homo habilis* in southern and eastern Africa.

c. 1.6 million Emergence of *Homo erectus* in eastern Africa.

c. 1·5 million More sophisticated Acheulian bifacial tools are in use in Africa.

c. 1 million Beginning of lower Palaeolithic Culture in Europe and the Near East. *Homo erectus* controls fire.

c. 700 000 Acheulian bifacial tools are used in Europe.

c. 300 000 *Homo erectus* develops strategies for hunting large mammals.

c. 250 000 Development of the Levalloisian method of cutting stone; flakes of a predetermined form are produced.

c. 200 000 Emergence of *Homo sapiens*.

c. 100 000 Rise of stone flake industries; beginning of Middle Palaeolithic Culture in Europe and the Near East.

c. 130 000 *Homo sapiens* splits into two lines, *Homo sapiens neanderthalensis* and *Homo sapiens sapiens* (modern humans) in Africa and possibly the Near East.

c. 80 000 Appearance of *Homo sapiens sapiens* in western Asia and Near East. First burials and religious thought.

c. 40 000 Probable arrival of *Homo sapiens sapiens* (modern humans) in Australia.

c. 35 000 *Homo sapiens sapiens* (modern man) in Europe.

c. 30 000 Beginning of Upper Palaeolithic Age. Appearance of figurative art. Neanderthals extinct.

c. 23 000 Modern humans probably arrive in America.

c. 18 000 Development of arrowhead industry influenced by Eastern cultures. Height of Palaeolithic art.

c. 15 500–10 000 Development of cave art and more sophisticated mural art.

c. 15 000 Cave wall paintings at Lascaux. Cave art begins in South America.

c. 14 000–11 000 Free standing round cabins are built for the first time.

c. 11 000 First permanent settlements in Middle East. Systematic gathering, storing of wild cereal and hunting.

c. 9 000–4 000 Beginning of the Neolithic period.

c. 8 500–8 000 Wheat and barley – the first cereals – grown in Jordan.

c. 8 000 First systematic harvesting of pulses in France.

c. 8 000–7 000 Beginning of art in northern Europe.

c. 7 600 First agriculture in southwest Asia.

c. 7 500–7 000 The domestication of goats and sheep in Near East.

c. 6 000 The first farming communities of southeast Europe appear.

c. 5 000 Domestication of llamas in South America and some agricultural development in Mexico.

c. 4 500 Megalithic menhirs in Brittany and Portugal.

c. 4 000 Rice cultivation in China.

c. 3 000–2 500 Gradual progression to Bronze Age in central-western Asia, Europe, Egypt and China.

THE ANCIENT WORLD

Europe

c. 3000 BC Development of the Minoan civilization in Crete: foundation of Knossos and Phaestus.

c. 2500–2400 Simple henges erected in England.

c. 2200–1450 Middle Minoan Age: control of the sea ensures Minoan prosperity.

c. 1700 Bronze Age in Western Europe.

c. 1600 Linear B script in use in Minoan civilization.

1500–1150 Mycenaean civilization begins its domination in mainland Greece.

c. 1500 Beginning of Urnfield cultures in Hungary and Romania.

c. 1450 The Minoan city of Knossos falls to invaders (possibly Mycenaeans).

c. 1300 First Celts appear in the Upper Danube area.

c. 1200 Sack of Troy (possibly by Mycenaeans).

1200–1100 Dorians overthrow the Mycenaean civilization and usher in period of Greek 'Dark Ages'.

900–500 Celtic Hallstatt culture (iron-using) supersedes Urnfield cultures.

850 Foundation of Carthage by Phoenicians from Tyre.

c. 800 Emergence of polis – Greek city-states.

753 Traditional date of foundation of Rome.

750 Greeks settle southern Italy.

c. 750–600 Increase in the number of city-states; the political rights of the citizen restricts the power of the aristocracy.

594 Solon introduces reforms in Athens.

509 Last Roman king expelled; establishment of Republic.

499–479 Greek–Persian Wars: Greek city-states revolt against Persian rule; Persians eventually routed and Athens and Sparta emerge as the dominant forces in Greece.

c. 450 Celtic La Têne culture: Celtic, Greek and Etruscan civilizations come into contact; culture characterized by abstract and figurative patterned art and ironwork with Greek influences.

Egypt

c. 3100–2700 BC Menes conquers the Delta, unites Upper and Lower Egypt and becomes pharaoh of the first unified dynasty; foundation of Memphis.

c. 3000 Hieroglyphic and Elamite pictographic scripts in use.

c. 2575–2134 Old Kingdom. Building of Great Pyramids at Giza.

c. 2134–2040 First Intermediate Period: era of anarchy and political fragmentation.

c. 2040 Unity of Egypt is restored under Mentuhotep of Thebes: start of the Middle Kingdom: administrative reforms, co-regencies and the conquest of Nubia.

c. 1640–1550 Hyksos invade and rule Egypt; Thebans remain independent; Hebrews enter Egypt.

c. 1550 Ahmose, Prince of Thebes, expels Hyksos and reunites Egypt.

1540–1479 Tutmosis begins period of Egyptian expansion: foundation of empire in Palestine and Syria extending to the Euphrates.

1360 Amenhotep IV (Akhenaton) rejects all gods except Aton, the Sun disc; imperial neglect leads to loss of Asian empire.

c. 1300 Oppression of Jews under Rameses II; Jewish exodus from Egypt.

1200–1100 Attempts by the Sea People to invade Egypt thwarted by Rameses III.

1070–1000 Egypt divided: priesthood of Amun rule in Thebes, while pharaohs rule in Tanis.

750 Nubians conquer Egypt.

525 Egyptian attempt to regain independence fails; Persians take control.

332 Egypt conquered by Alexander the Great; on his death Ptolemy founds the Hellenistic Kingdom of Egypt.

THE ANCIENT WORLD

Near East	Southern and Eastern Asia

Near East

c. 3000 BC Beginnings of the Sumerian civilization; foundation of city states Uruk, Eridu and Ur.

c. 2334–2279 Sargon the Great founds Akkad and Akkadian Empire; conquers all Mesopotamia.

c. 2200 Guti tribesmen from Iran destroy Akkadian Empire.

c. 2113 Third dynasty of Ur founded by Ur-Nammu; a period of prosperity follows.

c. 2006 Sack of Ur by Elamites (a people of ancient Iran).

c. 1792–1750 Hammurabi of Babylon reunites Mesopotamia.

c. 1650 Foundation of Hittite Old Kingdom by King Mursilis.

c. 1500 Migration of Phrygians into Asia Minor: establishment of Phrygia.

1380–1350 Hittite Empire reaches greatest extent under Suppiluliumas I.

1313–1283 Unsuccessful Hittite invasions of Egypt.

c. 1230 Jews occupy Israel.

c. 1200 Overthrow of Hittite Empire by Phrygians and allied tribes.

1200–1100 'Sea People' raid Syria and Palestine.

c. 1100 Assyrian Empire set up in Mesopotamia.

c. 1000 Israelite Kingdom founded by Saul and David.

911–824 Period of Assyrian expansion.

c. 935 Israelite Kingdom divided into Israel and Judah.

c. 850 Chaldea (now Armenia) attacked by Assyrians.

722 Palestine annexed by Assyrians; many Jews exiled to Babylon.

670 Assyrians destroy Memphis and Thebes but fail to hold Egypt.

626 Nabopolassar establishes the Chaldean dynasty of Babylon.

612 Medes, Babylonians and Scythians bring down Assyrian Empire.

600 Assyrian Empire divided amongst its conquerors.

605–562 Nebuchadnezzar II of Babylon extends the empire to include Syria and Palestine; extensive building programme (including the Hanging Gardens).

539 Cyrus the Great conquers Babylonian Empire and founds Achaemenid Persian Empire that dominates the Middle East.

536 Return of Jews from Babylon to Judah.

Southern and Eastern Asia

2850 BC Legendary Golden Age of China begins.

c. 2300 Indus Valley civilization: development of the cities of Harappa and Mohenjo-daro.

c. 1500 Aryan invasion of India: fall of Indus Civilization; intermingling of Aryan and indigenous Dravidian cultures produces Hinduism.

c. 1500–1050 Shang dynasty in China; Bronze Age in China; first evidence of Chinese script.

1500–400 Ganges civilization in India.

1122–256 Zhou dynasty in China.

c. 800–700 Growth of Chinese cities and merchant class; iron industry develops; flourishing of literature and philosophy: Kongfuzi (Confucius), Mengzi (Mencius) and Taoism.

771 Nomad attacks on China cause removal of capital to Luoyang: start of Later Zhou period: imperial power diminished.

c. 500 Emergence of Buddhist and Jain religions.

c. 481–221 'Warring States' in China – a period of anarchy during which power devolved to smaller states.

CLASSICAL WORLD (to fall of Rome)

Hellenic World

499 BC Ionian Greeks revolt against Persian rule: beginning of the Greek-Persian wars.

480 Battle of Salamis: Athenians defeat Persian fleet.

479 Greek army defeat Persians at Plataea and Mycale and liberate Greece.

478 Athenian empire; Athens assumes leadership of the Delian League.

462–429 Pericles dominates Athens as the city-state's leading politician.

431 Outbreak of Peloponnesian War between Athens and Sparta.

413 Athenian fleet destroyed.

404 Athenian surrender to Sparta: beginning of Spartan domination of Greece.

399 Execution of Socrates.

378–7 Athens founds the Aegean Confederacy.

371 Thebans defeat Spartans and begin Theban hegemony in Greece.

338 Philip II of Macedon conquers Greek city-states (at Battle of Chaironeia).

336 Philip II assassinated: accession of Alexander (the Great).

334–326 Alexander's invasion and conquer of the Persian Empire: Granikos (334), Issos (333), Gaugamela (332) and Hydaspes (326).

326–323 Spread of Greek Civilization: Alexander occupies Egypt, Syria and invades the Punjab.

323 Alexander the Great dies at Babylon: the Hellenistic Age in Middle East and Eastern Mediterranean begins.

323–301 Power-struggle between Alexander's generals for control of the empire. By 301 BC Ptolemy gains Egypt, Seleucus most of the Asiatic provinces (the Seleucid Empire).

c. 240 Greece dominated by two federations of city-states: Aitolia and Achaia.

238 Foundation of kingdom of Pergamon.

c. 211–148 Macedonian Wars: Rome finally defeats Macedonia which becomes a Roman province.

148–146 Rome annexes Greece.

133 Attalos III of Pergamon bequeaths his kingdom to Rome.

64 Seleucid Empire falls to Rome.

AD 330 Constantine the Great shifts seat of power to Byzantium, which he renamed Constantinople.

395 Byzantine Empire results from division of Roman Empire into East and West.

Roman World

509 BC Foundation of Roman republic.

390 Gauls occupy Rome.

290 End of Third Samnite War; Rome dominates central Italy.

272 Rome completes conquest of peninsular Italy after the defeat of Pyrrhus and southern Italian Greek cities.

264–241 First Punic War between Rome and Carthage: Sicily becomes first Roman province.

218–202 Second Punic War: Hannibal initially inflicts crushing blows on Roman forces but is finally defeated at Zama. Rome gains Carthaginian provinces in Spain.

149–146 Third Punic War: Carthage destroyed and Africa becomes a Roman province.

133–96 Expansion of Roman Empire to include Asia (W. Turkey; 133), southern Gaul (121), Cilicia (101) and Cyrenaica (96).

91 Social War: Italian cities revolt against Rome. Roman franchise granted to most Italians.

73 Spartacus leads Third Servile War (suppressed 71).

60 First Triumvirate: Pompey, Caesar and Crassus.

58 Caesar begins his conquest of Gaul.

49 Caesar at war with Pompey and Senate.

48 Caesar takes Rome and becomes dictator.

44 Caesar assassinated by Brutus and Cassius.

43–42 Second Triumvirate: Antony, Octavian and Lepidus formed.

31 Octavian defeats Antony and Cleopatra, annexes Egypt and becomes dictator of Rome.

27 Octavian is proclaimed emperor – 'Augustus'.

AD 43 Roman invasion of Britain.

66 First Jewish revolt.

68–69 Anarchy following death of Nero; order restored by Vespasian.

70 Titus destroys Jerusalem.

98–180 Period of peace and prosperity under Antonine emperors.

122 Beginning of Hadrian's Wall.

193–197 Civil war in Rome; order restored by Severus.

212 All free inhabitants of Empire gain Roman citizenship.

260 Persians overrun Syria and capture Emperor Valerian.

284–305 Diocletian reforms Roman Empire; establishes 'college' of emperors.

313 Edict of Milan: Christianity tolerated in Roman Empire.

395 Empire divided into East and West.

410 Visigoths sack Rome; Romans withdraw from Britain.

476 Final Western Roman Empire overthrown: fall of the Roman Empire.

AFRICA (c. 900 to the Colonial Age)

Northern and Eastern Africa

973–1171 Fatimid dynasty in Egypt.

1050–1140 Almoravid Empire flourishes in Morocco.

1147–1269 Almohad Empire controls coast of North Africa from western Sahara to Egyptian border.

1171–1250 Ayyubid dynasty in Egypt.

c. 1200 Christian kingdoms in the Sudan fall to Muslim invaders.

1250–1517 Mamelukes rule Egypt.

1448 First European fort on African coast established by the Portuguese at Arguin (Mauritania).

c. 1450 Sultanate of Agadès (in modern Niger) becomes powerful in southern Sahara.

1498–c. 1600 Portuguese active on Kenyan coast.

1516 Corsair (pirate) cities of North African coast accept authority of Ottoman Empire.

1517 Egypt comes under Ottoman rule.

1553 Beginning of Sharifian dynasties in Morocco.

1591 Songhay Empire (modern Mali) destroyed by Morocco.

c. 1600–c. 1800 Kingdom of Gondar flourishes in Ethiopia.

1798–1801 French invasion of Egypt.

1805–40 Reign of Mehemet Ali in Egypt.

1820 Mehemet Ali takes northern Sudan.

1830 French invasion of Algeria.

1841 Egypt achieves virtual independence from Ottoman Empire.

1850–68 Emperor Theodore consolidates independent Ethiopia.

1861 Zanzibar becomes independent from Oman.

1862 France acquires Djibouti.

1867 British expedition to Ethiopia.

1869 Suez Canal opens.

1881 France establishes a protectorate over Tunisia.

1882 Britain occupies Egypt.

1885 The Mahdists take Khartoum, kill General Gordon and create a theocratic state in the Sudan.

1890 Germany colonizes modern Rwanda, Burundi and mainland Tanzania. Zanzibar becomes a British protectorate.

1894 British protectorate established in Uganda.

1896 Ethiopia successfully counters attempted invasion by Italian forces.

1899 Joint Anglo-Egyptian rule established in the Sudan. Southern Somalia becomes an Italian colony.

1904 French and Spanish rule established in Morocco.

1905–06 First Moroccan Crisis: French interests in Morocco disputed by Germany.

Southern and Western Africa

c. 800–1000 Takrur state controls modern Senegal.

c. 1000 Rise of the Kanem Empire (northern Nigeria).

c. 1200–1400 Great Zimbabwe Empire.

c. 1400 Kanem-Borno Empire powerful in northern Nigeria and Chad.

c. 1400 Rise to power of Mossi states in modern Burkina Faso.

1441 Portuguese arrive in Guinea-Bissau.

1482 Portuguese establish trading base on Gold Coast (Ghana).

c. 1450–1550 Powerful Kongo and Ndongo kingdoms in Angola and Zaïre.

c. 1500 Portuguese slaving bases established along West coast of Africa.

1531 Portuguese establish trading posts in Mozambique.

1638 The Dutch take Mauritius. France establishes fort of Saint-Louis in Senegal.

1652 Cape settlement established by Dutch East India Company.

c. 1700–1830 Kingdom of Dahomey (modern Benin) flourishes as one of the principal slave trading states.

c. 1700 Rise of Asante kingdom to power in modern Ghana.

1713 Britain becomes dominant in Nigerian slave trade.

1798 Britain occupies the Cape.

1813 British missionaries become active in Bechuanaland (modern Botswana).

1821–22 American Colonization Society establishes Liberia for freed slaves.

1835–37 The Great Trek: Boers leave the Cape to found the republics of the Transvaal and Orange Free State.

1843 Britain annexes the Gambia and Natal.

1847 Liberia becomes independent.

1850 Britain ousts Danes from Gold Coast (Ghana).

1861 Britain acquires Lagos (Nigeria).

1880s Brazza establishes French protectorate over the Congo.

1884 German protectorates of Kamerun (Cameroon) and South West Africa (Namibia) proclaimed.

1885 Congo Free State (Zaïre) becomes a personal possession of King Léopold II of the Belgians. British colonization of Nigeria.

1889–90 French rule in Central Africa and Chad begins.

1890s French take Mossi kingdom (modern Burkina Faso). British South Africa Company establishes control in modern Zambia and Zimbabwe.

1896 French take Madagascar, overthrowing the Merina monarchy.

1899 Beginning of Boer War in South Africa.

THE EARLY MIDDLE AGES

Britain and Northern Europe

400–500 Saxons, Jutes and Angles (Germanic tribes) invade and settle in Britain.
519 Kingdom of Wessex founded.
c. 595 Kingdom of Mercia founded.

654 Kingdom of Northumbria formed.

787 Viking raids on Britain begin: pillage of Lindisfarne.
757–796 Construction of Offa's Dyke separates England and Wales during the reign of Offa of Mercia.
795 Norwegians settle in Ireland.

844 Kenneth MacAlpin becomes king of Picts and Scots: forms Kingdom of Alban, unifying Scotland.
866 Danes conquer Northumbria, East Anglia and Mercia.
874 Danes and Norwegians settle Iceland.

937 Battle of Brunanburh: Athelstan of Wessex defeats north Welsh, Scots and Norse.
954 England united by Wessex.
991 Renewed Viking raids on England.

1013 The Dane Swegn overthrows King Aethelred and becomes King of England.
1016 Cnut, son of Swegn, becomes king of England after succession dispute with Aethelred.
1027 Cnut becomes king of Norway.
1035 Death of Cnut: division of the Danish Empire (Denmark, England and Norway).
1042 Edward the Confessor succeeds Cnut's son Harthacnut to the English throne.
1066 Harold, Earl of Wessex succeeds Edward; William of Normandy challenges succession and defeats Harold at the Battle of Hastings.
1070 Rebellion in northern England crushed by William the Conqueror.

Byzantine Empire

527 Accession of Justinian I to Byzantine throne: beginning of military expansion and administrative reform.
534 Byzantines under General Belisarius conquer Vandal kingdom in North Africa.
551 Belisarius recovers Italy from Ostrogoths.

c. 650 Byzantine empire overrun by Persians, Slavs, Bulgars and Arabs: Constantinople besieged by Arabs in 673–77 and 718.

726 Emperor Leo III introduces Iconoclastic Decree banning use of religious images: leads to religious disunity.
c. 750 The Byzantine Empire retains only Greece and Asia Minor.
751 Foundation of Carolingian dynasty ends Byzantine power in the west.

811 Bulgars defeat Byzantines.
843 Restoration of images as an aid to worship; end of period of religious disunity.

961 Byzantines recover Crete.
965 Byzantines recover Cyprus.
971 Eastern Bulgaria conquered by Byzantines.

1018 Byzantines finally conquer the Bulgarians under Basil II ('the Bulgar-Slayer').
1048 Seljuk Turks begin expansion into Byzantine Empire and attack Armenia.
1055 Seljuk Turks take Baghdad.
1060 Normans invade and annex Sicily.
c. 1070 Byzantines lose southern Italy to the Normans.
1071 Byzantine army destroyed by Seljuk Turks at Manzikert: Turks overrun Anatolia (present-day Asian Turkey).

Western Europe

c. 486 Clovis defeats last Roman governor in Western Europe and founds the Frankish kingdom and the Merovingian dynasty.

c. 496 Franks acquire Rhineland.

c. 500 Franks conquer Visigoths and extend their empire to the Pyrenees.

638 Death of King Dagobert I: power passes to 'mayors of the palace'.

711 Successful Muslim invasion of Spain.

718 Foundation of Christian kingdom of Asturias in northern Spain.

732 Battle of Poitiers: Arabs defeated by Franks under Charles Martel.

751 Pepin I founds Carolingian dynasty after usurping the Merovingian throne.

771 Charlemagne (Carolingian king) begins military campaign of conquest: Saxony (772), Lombard Kingdom (773), Bavaria (788), Avar Kingdom (795–6).

792–793 Revolts in Benevento and Saxony against Carolingian rule; attacks by Muslims; famine.

800 Charlemagne crowned Emperor of what became known as Holy Roman Empire.

c. 840 Viking raids on Carolingian Empire begin.

843 Treaty of Verdun divides Carolingian Empire.

845 Viking attack on Paris.

846 Arabs attack Rome.

884–887 Temporary reunion of Carolingian Empire under Charles the Fat.

885–886 Viking siege of Paris.

929 Umayyad caliphatē established in Córdoba, Spain.

955 Battle of Lechfeld: Germans halt westward expansion of Magyars.

962 Coronation of Emperor Otto: Holy Roman Empire becomes largely German.

987 Hugh Capet, King of France, founds Capetian dynasty.

1031 Fragmentation of Muslim Spain: northern Spain dominates Iberian Peninsula.

1032 Kingdom of Burgundy becomes part of German Empire.

1092 Almoravids dominate most of Muslim Spain.

1094 Christian soldier, El Cid, takes Valencia.

The Church

563 Foundation of Iona monastery by St Columba: Celtic Christianity established in northern Britain.

590 Gregory the Great becomes pope.

597 St Augustine of Canterbury travels to Kent to convert English to Christianity; becomes first Archbishop of Canterbury. Conversion of King Ethelbert.

653 Lombards convert to Christianity.

663 Synod of Whitby establishes the domination of Roman Christianity over Celtic Christianity.

726 Beginning of the Iconoclast Movement (the abolition of the veneration of icons).

754 Pope gains temporal powers in central Italy.

843 Restoration of the veneration of icons in the Eastern Christian Church.

864–5 Bulgars and Serbs converted to Orthodox Christianity.

910 Abbey of Cluny founded in France: spreads monastic reforms.

955 Magyars accept Christianity.

965–966 Danish and Polish sovereigns accept Christianity.

1053 Pope defeated and captured by the Normans at Melfi.

1054 East-West Schism: Eastern (Orthodox) Church and Western (Roman) Church finally split.

1059 Pope Nicholas II decrees that only cardinals have the right to elect the pope.

1073 Gregory VII becomes pope and enforces papal authority and Church discipline.

1099 Godfrey of Bouillon leads First Crusade: takes Jerusalem.

THE LATER MIDDLE AGES ──────────

British Isles

1100 William Rufus killed in New Forest.

1135 Stephen of Blois seizes English throne.

1138–46 Civil war between adherents of Stephen and Matilda.

1141 Matilda becomes 'Lady of England' for 7 months.

1144 Geoffrey Plantagenet, Count of Anjou, conquers Normandy.

1152 Henry Plantagenet, Duke of Normandy and Count of Anjou, marries Eleanor, Duchess of Aquitaine: gains half of France.

1154 Henry Plantagenet inherits English throne.

1169 Beginning of the Anglo-Norman invasion of Ireland.

1170 Subjugation of Ireland.

1179 Grand Assize: judicial reform.

1204 King John loses Normandy to France.

1215 King John forced to concede Magna Carta (charter of rights for Clergy, Barons and Commoners).

1258 Simon de Montfort forces reforms on Henry III.

1277–83 Conquest of Wales by Edward I.

1290 Scottish throne disputed by 13 claimants. Jews expelled from England.

1296 Annexation of Scotland by Edward I.

1298 Scottish hero, William Wallace, defeated by Edward I.

1298 Robert Bruce continues struggle for Scottish independence.

1306 Robert Bruce crowned King Robert I of Scotland.

1314 Battle of Bannockburn: Edward II of England disastrously defeated by Robert the Bruce and his army.

1338 Beginning of the Hundred Years War: series of Anglo-French conflicts originating from English claims on the French throne.

1346 English victory at Battle of Crécy. Scottish King captured at Battle of Neville's Cross.

Northern and Eastern Europe

1138 Beginning of Hohenstaufen dynasty (Holy Roman Emperors). Poland fragments into independent principalities.

1139 Division of Russian state into independent principalities.

1174 Coast of Finland settled by Swedes.

1176 Byzantine Emperor suffers major defeat by the Seljuk Turks: end of Byzantine revival.

1177 Peace of Venice between Pope and Emperor.

1198 Bohemia becomes a kingdom.

1223 Byzantines recover Salonika.

1227 Danes defeated by Germans: cede Holstein to German Empire.

1237 Volga Bulgars conquered by Mongols.

1238 Mongols conquer principality of Vladimir, the Georgians and the Cumans.

1240 Kiev falls to Mongols.

1241 Mongols invade Poland and Hungary but withdraw shortly after.

1261 Byzantine Emperor recaptures Constantinople.

1291 The Swiss cantons of Uri, Schwyz and Unterwalden declare themselves independent of the Habsburgs.

1300 Foundation of the Islamic Ottoman Empire in northern Anatolia by Osman I.

1320 Golden Horde (Mongols) lose Kiev to Lithuanians.

1336 Ottomans take Bergama.

1346 Estonia is sold to Teutonic Knights by Danes. The Black Death enters Europe and spreads to western and southern Europe.

THE LATER MIDDLE AGES

Western and Southern Europe

1110 Saragossa (last independent emirate of Muslim Spain) taken over by the Almoravid Berber dynasty.

1118 King of Aragon captures Saragossa.

1137 Union of Catalonia and Aragon through marriage.

1144 Alfonso of Portugal annexes Lisbon.

1155 Frederick Barbarossa, a bitter rival of Pope Alexander III, becomes Emperor.

1158 Imperial authority in northern Italy is restored by Frederick Barbarossa.

1160 Henry the Lion, Duke of Saxony and Bavaria, conquers the Wends of the Lower Elbe.

1180 Frederick Barbarossa banishes Henry the Lion.

1191 Richard I of England captures Cyprus.

1209–28 Simon de Montfort leads crusades against the Albigensian sect (European followers of the Cathar heresy).

1212 Christian kings defeat Almohades in southern Spain.

1218 Frederick II succeeds Otto IV and becomes master of the Empire and Kingdom of Sicily.

1229 Albigensian heretics crushed; territory ceded to France and Inquisition established in Toulouse.

1248 Moors lose Seville to Ferdinand III of Castile.

1250 Death of Emperor Frederick II.

1256–73 Interregnum in Holy Roman Empire: period of political anarchy in Germany.

1266–68 Charles of Anjou takes Sicilian crown and defeats Conradin of the Hohenstaufen.

1282 'Sicilian Vespers': rule of Charles of Anjou overthrown in successful Sicilian rebellion: Peter III of Aragon takes crown though Charles of Anjou remains King of Naples.

1306 Jews expelled from France.

1330 Moors reconquer Gibraltar.

1347 Calais is taken by Edward III. Popular revolt in Rome led by Cola di Rienzi.

The Church

1100 Foundation of the Latin Kingdom of Jerusalem: becomes a Crusader state along with Antioch and Edessa.

1109 Capture of Tripoli by Crusaders: becomes fourth Crusader state.

1122 Concordat of Worms: reaffirms papal spiritual, and imperial temporal, power over bishops.

1147 Second Crusade: prompted by the fall of Edessa.

1170 Murder of Thomas Becket, Archbishop of Canterbury: later canonized by Pope.

1184 Creation of the Inquisition.

1189–92 Third Crusade prompted by Saladin's capture of Jerusalem: led by Richard Lionheart, Frederick Barbarossa and Philip Augustus of France; only Acre retained.

1199 Foundation of the Order of Teutonic Knights by Emperor Frederick II to overcome and convert pagans in the north-east of Europe.

1202–4 Fourth Crusade: sack of Constantinople.

1209 St Francis of Assisi founds Franciscan Order.

1217–21 Fifth Crusade: Damietta, Egypt taken.

1221 Crusades surrender Damietta on assurances of safe conduct from Egypt.

1228 Crusade of Frederick II: by negotiation adds Jerusalem to the Kingdom of Acre.

1229 Teutonic Knights begin conversions in Prussia.

1244 Jerusalem falls to band of fugitive Turks.

1248 Seventh Crusade led by Louis IX of France takes Damietta, Egypt.

1270 Eighth Crusade; Louis IX dies on Crusade against Tunis.

1274 Death of Thomas Aquinas.

1291 Fall of Acre: end of Crusades in Holy Land.

1307–14 Destruction of the Order of Knights Templar.

1309 Teutonic Knights take Danzig. Papal court moves to Avignon and is dominated by French interests.

THE LATER MIDDLE AGES

British Isles

1360 Edward II of England and King John of France make peace: England renounces claim to French throne and gains Aquitaine, Calais and Ponthieu.

1369 Renewal of Hundred Years War.

1375 Truce in Hundred Years War.

1381 Peasants' Revolt against the Poll Tax led by Wat Tyler and John Ball.

1400–1408 National Welsh rebellion led by Owen Glendower fails.

1406 Prince James of Scotland captured by the English.

1415 Henry V again claims the French throne; invades France and wins battle of Agincourt.

1420 Henry V marries daughter of Charles VI and becomes heir to French throne.

1424 James I of Scotland finally released by English.

1455 Beginning of War of the Roses (civil war): House of York (white rose), and House of Lancaster (red rose) go to war over the succession to the throne.

1460 Yorkist victory in Battle of Northampton, but Richard of York is later killed at Wakefield.

1461 Yorkists defeated at Battle of St Albans, but son of Richard of York crowned Edward IV.

1469 Orkney and Shetland incorporated into Scotland.

1470 Lancastrian invasion restores Henry VI to throne.

1471 Edward regains throne after Battles of Barnet and Tewkesbury.

1485 Henry Tudor finally defeats Richard III at Bosworth field; his marriage to Edward IV's eldest daughter ends war: beginning of Tudor dynasty.

Northern and Eastern Europe

1354 Ottomans take Ankara.

1356 Ottoman Turks enter Europe.

1361 Ottomans capture of Adrianople, which becomes their European capital.

1363 Ottomans defeat Bosnians, Serbs and Hungarians.

1380 Supremacy of Ottoman Sultan recognized by Byzantine Emperor John Palaeologus. Union of Norway and Denmark.

1389–90 Ottoman annexation of Serbia and five Turkish emirates in Anatolia.

1393 Ottoman annexation of Bulgaria and last emirate of Anatolia.

1395 Tamerlane defeats the Golden Horde.

1397 Norway, Sweden and Denmark come under one sovereign.

1399 Lithuanians defeated by Golden Horde.

1404 Four sons of Beyazit, Ottoman Sultan, fight for the succession to the Ottoman Empire.

1417 Followers of John Huss begin Hussite movement in Bohemia.

1419 Hussites reject Emperor Sigismund's claim to Bohemian crown: beginning of Hussite War (till 1436).

1453 Constantinople falls to Ottoman Turks; end of Byzantine Empire.

1466 Restoration of western Prussia to Poland by Teutonic Knights.

1475–77 War between Swiss and Charles the Bold of Burgundy: Charles defeated and killed at Nancy.

1477 Habsburg Emperor Frederick III driven out of Austria by King of Hungary.

1478 Hungary gains Lusatia, Moravia and Silesia through treaty with the Bohemians.

THE LATER MIDDLE AGES

Western and Southern Europe

1356 Black Prince of England captures French King John at Poitiers.

1358 Jacquerie French peasant uprising: ends with the massacre of peasants at Meaux.

1366–67 War in Castile: the Black Prince invades and restores King Pedro to the throne.

1369 Renewal of Hundred Years War.

1384 Philip of Burgundy gains Flanders through marriage: beginning of Burgundian Empire.

1396 Peace of Paris: 28-year truce in the Hundred Years War.

1410 France weakened by Civil War between Burgundy and Orléans.

1411 Sigismund of Hungary is elected German Emperor.

1417 Normandy falls to Henry V.

1419 Anglo-Burgundian alliance.

1422 Death of Henry V and Charles VI: France divided between English Duke of Bedford and French Charles VII.

1428 English lay siege to Orléans.

1429 French inspired to retake Orléans by Joan of Arc: Charles VII crowned King of France.

1430 Joan of Arc captured by Burgundians and burnt at stake (1431).

1434 Cosimo di Medici dominates Florence and begins Medici dynasty.

1435 Burgundians abandon alliance with England and ally with Charles VII.

1436 Charles VII recaptures Paris.

1450–53 France regains Normandy (1450), Guienne (1451) and Bordeaux (1453).

1453 England ceases attempts to conquer France (retains only Calais): end of Hundred Years War.

1477 Burgundy is annexed by French crown.

The Church

1377 Papacy returns to Rome.

1378 Death of Pope Gregory XI: The Great Schism: two Popes elected; Pope Urban VI in Rome recognized by England, Italy and Germany, and Clement VII in Avignon recognized by France, Scotland, Spain and Sicily; the split reflects the political split of the Hundred Years War.

1409 Attempt by General Council of Pisa to end Schism fails.

1412 John Huss excommunicated for speaking out against sale of indulgences.

1415–17 Council of Constance finally ends Great Schism; election of new Pope, Martin V. John Huss burnt at stake.

1478 Establishment of the Spanish Inquisition.

1492 Jews expelled from Spain.

RENAISSANCE AND THE REFORMATION ————

Spanish possessions	Britain and Ireland	France
1492 Granada, the last Muslim emirate in Iberia, falls to Spain. Jews are expelled from Spain. **1494** Treaty of Tordesillas: Spain and Portugal agree to divide the New World.	**1494** Irish Parliament made subservient to English Parliament (Poynings' Laws).	**1491** Charles VIII of France acquires Brittany through marriage. **1494** Charles VIII invades Italy to claim the crown of Naples: start of Franco-Italian wars.
1516 Charles I of Spain (Emperor Charles V) succeeds. **1518–23** Revolt in Spain by comunero movement.	**1513** Battle of Flodden: English defeat Scots and kill James IV. **1514** Anglo-French alliance. **1515** Thomas Wolsey becomes a cardinal and Lord Chancellor of England.	**1515** Francis I invades Italy and defeats the Swiss and Milanese. **1520** Abortive Anglo-French alliance: Field of the Cloth of Gold.
1550 Duke of Alba sent to restore order in rebellious Spanish Netherlands.	**1533** Henry VIII divorces Catherine of Aragon: under Act of Supremacy Henry VIII breaks with Rome to become Supreme Head of the English Church. **1535** Sir Thomas More and John Fisher executed for refusing to accept Succession Oath. **1536–39** Dissolution of the monasteries by Henry VIII. **1536** Union of England and Wales.	**1536** Emperor Charles V invades Provence.
1556 Charles V abdicates Spain and Netherlands in favour of his son, Philip II.	**1552** Cranmer's Prayer Book: Protestant in character. **1553** England becomes Catholic again under Queen Mary: persecution of Protestants. **1558** Elizabeth I comes to the throne. **1559–63** Protestantism re-established in England by Acts of Supremacy and Uniformity, and the 39 Articles.	**1552** Annexation of Metz, Toul and Verdun by King Henry II of France. **1558** France gains Calais, England's last possession in France. **1559** Treaty of Cateau – Cambrésis ends Franco-Italian wars.
1568 Protestant Dutch revolt against Spanish Habsburg rule begins. **1576** Sack of Antwerp by Spanish soldiers. **1579** Dutch northern provinces form Union of Utrecht.	**1560s** Beginning of Anglo-Spanish maritime feud. **1567** Mary Queen of Scots forced to abdicate. **1568** Flight of Mary Queen of Scots to England, where she is imprisoned by Elizabeth I.	**1560–74** Regency of Catherine de Medici. **1562** Beginning of the Wars of Religion in France between Huguenots (Protestants) and the Catholic League. **1572** Massacre of St Bartholomew: slaughter of Huguenots in France.
1580 Philip II of Spain takes throne of Portugal. **1581** United Provinces – the northern Protestant Netherlands – proclaim independence from Spain.	**1587** Execution of Mary Queen of Scots after implication in plot to assassinate Elizabeth I. **1588** Defeat of Spanish Armada by English fleet. **1594** Irish rebellion against English rule led by Earl of Tyrone.	**1593** Henry, King of Navarre, becomes Henry IV of France and converts to Catholicism. **1598** Edict of Nantes guarantees freedom of worship for Protestants; end of French Wars of Religion.

RENAISSANCE AND THE REFORMATION

The Empire and Eastern Europe	Italy	The Church
1496 Philip of Habsburg marries Joan (the Mad), heiress to Castile and Aragon.	**1494** French forces drive the Medici out of Florence and invade Rome. **1495** French retreat from Italy.	**1478** Establishment of Spanish Inquisition. **1492** Rodrigo Borgia becomes Pope Alexander VI.
1504 Philip of Habsburg becomes King of Castile, as Philip I. **1519** Charles I of Spain inherits Austrian Habsburg lands; elected Holy Roman Emperor as Charles V.	**1501** France and Spain agree to divide the Kingdom of Naples between them. **1503** Ferdinand V of Spain becomes King of Naples. **1512** France expelled from Italy by joint Venetian, Spanish and Papal forces.	**1517** Martin Luther nails his 95 Theses criticizing the Church to the Wittenberg Church door: beginning of the Reformation. **1519** Luther renounces papal supremacy. **1520** Luther declared a heretic: accepts the protection of the Elector of Saxony.
1522 Charles V divides his dominions between Austrian and Spanish Habsburgs: his brother Ferdinand I succeeds to Austria. **1524–25** Peasants' War in Germany. **1526** Ferdinand I gains Hungarian and Bohemian crowns through marriage. Hungary defeated by Ottoman Turks at Battle of Mohács.	**1527** Italy falls under the control of Charles V. Expulsion of the Medici. **1530** The Medici family return to Florence. **1531** Alessandro de Medici becomes duke of Tuscany. **1535** Death of the last Sforza ruler of Milan. **1540** Milan becomes Spanish.	**1523** Ulrich Zwingli presents his Theses in Zurich: precipitates the spread of Protestantism in Switzerland. **1525–27** Spread of Lutheranism: Teutonic Knights (1525), Sweden (1527) and parts of Switzerland. **1529** Luther and Zwingli divided on the nature of the Eucharist.
1547 Ivan the Terrible becomes Tsar. **1555** Peace of Augsburg: every prince of the Empire allowed to choose the faith of his territory. **1556** Charles V abdicates: his brother Ferdinand I becomes emperor.	**1545** Beginning of Farnese dynasty in Parma. **1556** Charles V abdicates: Naples in favour of his son, Philip II as successor.	**1536** Denmark becomes Lutheran. **1545–63** Council of Trent: the Roman Catholic Church reforms in a response to the Reformation. **1551–2** Council of Trent rejects Lutheran and Zwinglian beliefs.
1571 Battle of Lepanto between Ottoman Turks and Holy League (forces of Venice, Spain, Genoa and Papacy): Ottomans defeated. **1564** Ivan the Terrible embarks on reign of terror.		**1562–63** Council of Trent ends any hope of reconciliation with the Protestants.
1584 Death of Ivan the Terrible: his successor, Theodore I, is challenged by the aristocratic boyar families.	**1580** Carlo Emmanuele I begins territorial expansion of duchy of Savoy. **1597** Death of last Este duke of Ferrara.	**1582** Pope Gregory XIII introduces Gregorian Calendar.

ASIA: 500 BC TO THE COLONIAL AGE

China

1100–256 BC Zhou dynasty.

800–300 China beset by warring states.

551–479 Development of Confucian social thought.

221 The State of Qin unites China: abolition of feudalism and the building of the Great Wall.

206 BC–AD 220 Han dynasty assumes power: conquest of Korea, invention of paper and the introduction of Buddhism.

220 Fall of Han dynasty.

220–280 North China succumbs to warlordism and invasions from non-Chinese people.

581 Sui dynasty reunites China: major government reforms.

618 Expensive military ventures contribute to the fall of the Sui dynasty: succeeded by the Tang.

618–907 Tang dynasty: empire extended; invention of printing and gunpowder and increase in international trade.

755 Abortive rebellion of An Lushan: nomad invasions and revolts further weaken the empire.

907 Last Tang emperor abdicates: China fragments; period of military dictators and warfare.

960 Sung dynasty reunites much of northern China and restores peace.

1126 Northern invasion by Jin horsemen forces the removal of the Sung dynasty to the south.

1279 Mongols conquer all of China: beginning of harsh Mongol rule.

1275–1292/5 Marco Polo enters the service of Kublai Khan and travels widely within the empire.

1368 Overthrow of the Mongols in China by the native Ming dynasty.

1403–24 Emperor Yongle extends empire, moves capital to Beijing and encourages Confucianism.

1424 Death of Yongle; expansionist policies abandoned; 150 years of relative peace.

1517 European traders and missionaries given limited access to the empire.

1592 Unsuccessful Japanese incursions into China.

1644 Ming dynasty collapses after rebellions and attacks by the Manchus; foundation of Qing dynasty.

1683 Taiwan is incorporated into China.

1693 Kangxi leads invasion of Mongolia.

1692 Catholic missionaries are allowed to make conversions.

1735–95 Expansion of Empire into Turkistan, Annam (Vietnam), Burma and Nepal.

1757 Foreign traders are restricted to Guangzhou.

1793 British delegations denied diplomatic relations.

c. 1800–1900 Western involvement in China increases; imperial power diminished.

Japan

c. AD 400 The Yamamoto clan dominate their rivals and establish imperial rule.

594–622 Under Prince Shotoku Taishi the study of Buddhism and Chinese writing is encouraged; the Chinese administrative system and calendar is copied.

c. 800–900 Imperial power is undermined by the Fujiwara family. Decline in Chinese influence.

c. 1000–1100 The Fujiwara effectively hold power. Development of a military class – the Samurai – in the provinces.

1100–1192 Civil war between military rivals.

1192 Samurai Minamoto Yaritomo conquers rivals; establishes first shogunate (military government), usurping the power of the emperor.

1192–1333 Under the Kamakura Shogunate Zen Buddhism becomes popular. Feudalism is introduced.

1333 Takanju Ashikaya defeats the Hojos (regents), overthrows the emperor and installs Koyo on throne.

1339 Emperor Koyo appoints Ashikaya as Shogun.

1339–1400 Fighting between daimyo (feudal lords) and their Samurai armies leads to political chaos.

1542 Portuguese introduce muskets into Japan.

1573 The Japanese warrior Oda Nobunaga ousts the Shogun from Kyoto and establishes firm rule.

1582 Oda Nobunaga is assassinated; his successor, Hideyoshi, continues to unify country.

1591 Hideyoshi breaks power of daimyo and disarms peasants.

1592 Invasion of Korea; Seoul is captured, but the Chinese armies force a retreat.

1603 Hideyoshi dies. Establishment of Tokugawa shogunate; further curbs on the freedom of daimyo.

1641 Christianity and travel abroad is proscribed and foreigners discouraged: Japan becomes isolated from the rest of the world.

1650–1800 Period of economic growth: emergence of merchant class and rising educational standards.

1853–4 US commodore Perry enters two Japanese ports: US trade and technology ends Japanese isolation.

1868 Popular support for the Tokugawa shogunate declines and imperial power (Meiji restoration) is restored.

ASIA: 500 BC TO THE COLONIAL AGE

India

c. 500–400 BC Emergence of Buddhism and Jainism: leads to a succession of Hindu and later Buddhist dynasties.

321–185 BC The Maurya dynasty becomes the first all India Hindu empire (excluding the southern tip).

185 BC–AD 320 Disintegration of Maurya dynasty: India dissolves into small kingdoms with local power struggles.

AD 320–480 Northern India is reunited by the Gupta dynasty.

600–650 Harsha dynasty: Buddhist empire in the north.

c. 700–800 First Muslim invasion of India; Sind (southern Pakistan) is made a province of the Caliphate.

1000–1200 Beginning of the main Muslim invasions from Afghanistan; collapse of Hindu kingdoms.

1526 Mogul invasions; Mogul Empire established by Babur; conquers all India except extreme south.

1530 Hamayun succeeds Babur as Mogul Emperor.

1540 Unable to assert his authority Hamayun is exiled to Persia.

1554–5 Hamayun recovers the throne: Persian culture influences the administration, architecture and Court language.

1555 Akbar, the greatest Mogul ruler, succeeds. Military conquest of Rajasthan, Gujarat, Bengal, Kashmir and North Deccan; introduction of centralized administration and religious tolerance.

1605–27 Encouragement of the arts under the rule of Jahangir.

1628–56 Reign of Shah Jahan: building of the Taj Mahal.

1657 Shah Jahan falls ill; struggle for succession by his four sons; Aurangzeb kills his brothers, imprisons his father and becomes emperor.

1659–1707 Aurangzeb continues expansionist policies and ends religious tolerance: increase in opposition to Mogul rule and decline of Empire.

1674 Sivaji defeats Moguls; Maratha kingdom established in west central India.

c. 1700 British East India Company secures the important ports in India.

1707–61 Aurangzeb dies: regional dynasties assert their independence, leading to a power vaccum.

1761 Battle of Panipat: Maratha defeated in their attempt to dominate all India.

c. 1760s British East India Company has become the dominant force in India.

Southeast Asia

c. AD 400–500 The Mon Kingdom in Burma established.

c. 800 Arrival of the Burmans from China; hostilities break out with indigenous people.

c. 800 Jayavarman II expels Javanese invaders from Khmer (Cambodia), re-unites country and founds Khmer Kingdom: introduction of cult of god-king and foundation of Angkor.

c. 800–900 Migration of people from southern China: foundation of Lao people.

c. 849–1287 Burma unified by the people of Pagan; revolts by Mon and Shan people; spread of Buddhism.

c. 900–1000 People of southern and western China migrate to and settle Siam (Thailand).

939 Annamese (of central Vietnam) overthrow Chinese and set up independent kingdom.

1220–96 Overthrow of Khmer control in Siam: the kingdoms of Sukhothai and Chiangmai dominate.

1287–1301 Pagan falls to Mongols.

1350–1400 The Ayuthia succeeds the Sukhothai kingdom; Siamese devastate declining Khmer kingdom and unite Siam.

1354 Foundation of kingdom of Lanxang in Laos.

1431 Khmer rulers abandon Angkor for Phnom Penh: decline of Khmer empire.

1471 Annamese conquer the Champa (part of Vietnam).

1539 Burma reunited under the Toungoo.

1550–1700 Siamese–Burmese Wars.

1558 Rebellion in Annam: kingdom divides into two.

1701 Kingdom of Lanxang divides into two.

1752 Toungoo dynasty falls in Burma.

1757 The Burmese dynasty of Konbaung is established; series of wars with Siam begins.

1767 Burma overthrows Ayuthia Kingdom and occupies Siam.

1770 Burma repels a Chinese invasion.

1777 Burmese expelled from Siam under leadership of General Taksin.

1784 Burma conquers kingdom of Arakan, bringing Burmese territory to the border of British India.

c. 1800–50 Laos fragments into several states.

1802 Reunion of Annam under Nguyen Anh (with French assistance).

1824–51 General Chakri of Siam (later Rana I) founds new dynasty; Bangkok becomes new capital and Thai empire extended into Laos and northern Malaya.

1864 Cambodia becomes a French protectorate.

THE AMERICAS TO THE COLONIAL AGE ———

Caribbean and North America

10 000 BC Temporary landbridge during Ice Age connects Asia and Alaska: a few Siberian families reach North America. Population spreads from Alaska over North America; their descendants become American Indian hunters.

c. 8000 Ciboney (hunter-gatherer-fishing people) of South America reach Hispaniola.

c. 5000 First centres of population in Mexico.

5000–4000 Arrival of Inuit (Eskimo) in North America.

c. 1500–400 Olmec culture in Mesoamerica (Mexico and Northern Central America).

c. 100 Development of first true city, Teotihuacán; dominates central Mexico for 600 years.

AD 200–1000 Migration of Arawak Indians from NE South America to Caribbean.

300 Rise of Maya civilization in Central America (Mexico, Guatemala and Yucatán peninsula).

500 Beginning of maize cultivation in North America.

500–1600 American Indians in the Mississippi Basin become farmers with small settlements.

c. 900 Toltecs establish a military state in Tula, northern Mexico, and by 985 control Mexico.

c. 1000 Arawak culture in the Caribbean destroyed by migrating Caribs from South America.

c. 1180 Toltec state overrun by nomadic tribes.

c. 1200–50 Migration of Aztec people into North Mexico; foundation of Aztec Empire.

c. 1200–1450 Mayapán becomes a powerful city.

1400–1500 Expansion of Aztec Empire to cover most of modern Mexico.

1441 Sack of Mayapán by rival cities; several smaller Maya states are formed.

1519 The Spaniard Cortés reaches the Aztec Empire; Montezuma welcomes him believing him to be a demi-god.

1520 Aztec revolt; Montezuma is killed.

1521 Aztec Empire defeated by Spaniards.

Andean America

9000 BC South America settled from Central America.

2500 Development of agriculture in Indian communities.

1000–200 Chavin culture flourishes on Peruvian coast; improved agriculture (maize) and metallurgy.

AD 600–1000 Rise of Ayamará Indians in Bolivia.

1000 Chimú state formed on north coast of Peru.

c. 1200 Foundation of Inca dynasty by Manco Capac; foundation of capital, Cuzco.

1438 Emperor Pachacuti rebuilds Cuzco and embarks on period of expansion.

1471–74 Emperor Topa Inca extends empire (Tahuantinsuyu) into southern Peru; begins road-building programme.

1476 Chimú state (Ecuador) conquered by Topa Inca.

1480 Bolivia succumbs to Inca rule.

1484 North and central Chile and north-west Argentina conquered by Incas.

1493 Huayna Capac becomes Inca emperor; founds second capital, Quito.

1498 Inca territory extends to Colombia.

1525 Disputed Inca succession leads to civil war: empire partitioned between the brothers Huascar and Atahualpa.

1532 Spaniards, under Pizarro reach the coast and Atahualpa is taken prisoner.

1533 Spanish execute Atahualpa and take Cuzco.

1535 Inca Empire completely dominated by the Spanish.

COLONIAL AMERICA TO 1850

North America

1497 Cabot discovers Newfoundland.

1605 French settle Nova Scotia.

1607 Jamestown, Virginia, is founded by the English.

1620 English Pilgrim Fathers settle Plymouth, Massachusetts.

1650s Colonization of Canada by the French.

1664 English gain New York from the Dutch.

1670 Foundation of Hudson's Bay Company.

1699–1702 French colonization of Louisiana.

1744–54 Britain and France go to war over control of North America.

1763 France ousted from Canada by British.

1765 British impose the Stamp Act on American colonies.

1773 Boston Tea Party.

1774 Continental Congress issues Declaration of Rights.

1775 War of American Independence breaks out at Lexington.

1776 US Declaration of Independence.

1778 France, Holland and Spain (1779) join war against Britain.

1781 British surrender at Yorktown; American loyalists emigrate to Canada.

1787 US Constitution.

1803 Louisiana Purchase: Mississippi Valley sold to US by France.

1819 USA gains Florida from Spain.

1837 Papineau and MacKenzie Rebellions in Canada.

Caribbean

1492 Columbus discovers Bahamas, Cuba and Hispaniola.

1493 Hispaniola settled by Spanish. Columbus discovers Jamaica and Puerto Rico.

1498 Columbus discovers Trinidad.

1505 Discovery of Bermuda by Juan Bermudez. First black slaves brought to Hispaniola. Puerto Rico conquered by Spanish.

1536–1609 Beginning of French and British penetration into Spanish Caribbean.

1612 English colonization of Bermuda.

1630–40 First English and French claims to West Indian islands.

1655 English capture Jamaica from Spanish and begin colonization.

1697 Spain loses Haiti (half of Hispaniola) to the French.

1761 British dominate the West Indies.

1763 Britain gains Grenada from France.

1791 Toussaint L'Ouverture leads successful Black slave revolt in Haiti.

1796 British capture Guyana.

1801 Haiti becomes a republic.

1833–80 Abolition of slavery in colonies by Britain 1833; France 1848; Holland 1863; Spain (Puerto Rico) 1873, (Cuba) 1880.

Latin America

1494 Spain and Portugal agree to divide New World colonies.

1498 Third journey by Columbus; discovers Venezuela.

1500 Pedro Alvares Cabral lands in Brazil and claims territory for Portugal.

1501 Portuguese exploration of Brazil.

1502 Columbus explores Central American coastline.

1519 Cortés begins expedition to Mexico.

1520 Last emperor of Aztecs surrenders to Cortés; foundation of Spanish Mexico.

c. 1520 Missionaries arrive in Spanish colonies: forced conversions begin.

1523–35 Spanish conquest of Central America.

1532 Portuguese begin to settle Brazil.

1532–33 Pizarro conquers Incas in Peru.

c. 1549 Silver found in Peru and Mexico: wealth sent to Spain.

1717 Spanish reorganization of South American colonies.

1780–81 Peruvian Indians revolt against Spanish rule.

1808–20 Nationalist uprisings in Spanish colonies; Simon Bolívar emerges as nationalist leader.

1811–30 Full independence in South American colonies: Paraguay and Venezuela (1811), Argentina (1816), Chile (1818), Colombia (1819), Mexico, Central America and Peru (1821), Brazil (1822), Uruguay (1828).

THE 17TH CENTURY

Britain and Ireland

1600 Irish Rebellion ends when Earl Tyrone surrenders to English Governor.

1603 James VI of Scotland succeeds to English throne as James I, uniting the two crowns.

1605 Failure of Catholic Gunpowder Plot to blow up Parliament; conspirators executed (1606).

1629 Charles I begins personal rule.

1638–39 First Bishops' War: Charles unsuccessfully attempts to impose Anglicanism on Scots.

1640 Second Bishops' War: Charles defeated by Scots; forced to call Long Parliament.

1642 Outbreak of Civil War between supporters of the King (Cavaliers) and Parliamentarians (Roundheads); King flees London.

1644 Battle of Marston Moor: a decisive victory for the Roundheads and Scots.

1645 Formation of the Roundhead New Model Army; Oliver Cromwell becomes second in Command; victory in Battle of Naseby.

1646–47 Scots sell Charles to Parliament.

1649 Charles executed; England becomes a Commonwealth.

1649–50 Irish and Scottish rebels defeated by Cromwell.

1653 Cromwell becomes Lord Protector and effective dictator.

1658 Death of Cromwell; succeeded by son Richard.

1660 Richard Cromwell loses political control and retires; Restoration of Charles II (after agreeing to an amnesty and religious toleration).

1665 Great Plague of London; 60 000 killed.

1666 Great Fire of London.

1677 Mary, daughter of Duke of York and eventual heir to the throne, marries the Dutch William III of Orange.

1678 'Popish Plot': wave of anti-Catholicism.

1679 Exclusion Crisis: Parliament attempts to prevent the succession of Catholic James, Duke of York.

1685 Death of Charles II; Catholic James I succeeds; countrywide revolts.

1688 'Glorious Revolution': William III of Orange arrives in England to take throne (with Parliamentary backing); James I flees to France.

1689 William III and Mary become joint sovereigns; Bill of Rights establishes a constitutional monarchy.

1690 Battle of the Boyne (in Ireland): William III defeats James and retains crown.

1694 Death of Queen Mary: William III becomes sole sovereign.

France

1610 Marie de Medici becomes Regent for the child Louis XIII.

1627–28 La Rochelle, a Huguenot port, is attacked and besieged by Chief Minister Richelieu; Huguenots surrender and lose political power.

1635 France declares war on Spain, entering the Thirty Years War.

1643 French defeat Spanish at Rocroi. Louis XIV 'The Sun King' succeeds to French throne.

1648 Fronde (a period of civil disorder) begins with riots in Paris.

1652 France paralysed by Fronde; Dunkirk falls to Spain.

1658 Battle of the Dunes: French and British defeat Spanish; England regains Dunkirk.

1659 Treaty of Pyrenees ends Franco-Spanish War; France replaces Spain as major western European power.

1661 Louis XIV takes control of government.

1662 Charles II sells Dunkirk to Louis XIV.

1665 Colbert becomes Controller-General of Finance: heralds period of economic prosperity.

1669 Protestant worship further restricted.

1672 France declares war on Dutch, who are joined by the Holy Roman Empire, Brandenburg and finally Spain and Lorraine. Third Anglo-Dutch War (1672–74).

1678 Treaty of Nijmegen ends war between France and the Netherlands (and Spain); Peace of Nijmegen (1679) ends war between France and Empire.

1683 Death of Colbert: end of economic prosperity.

1685 Edict of Nantes revoked: Protestantism banned; thousands of Huguenots flee France.

1688 France invades Rhineland; precipitates Nine Years War (or War of the Grand Alliance).

1689 Formation of the Grand Alliance of England, the United Provinces, Austria, Spain and Savoy against France.

1697 France finally defeated by Grand Alliance: Peace of Ryswick.

Spain

1604 General Spinola of Spain captures Ostend.

1607 Spanish fleet defeated by Dutch.

1609 Spain agrees to a nine-year truce in the war with the Netherlands.

1621–48 Spain wages an unsuccessful war against the United Provinces.

1635 Spain at war with France, entering the Thirty Years War.

1640 Catalans and Portuguese rebel against Spanish rule.

1643 Spain defeated by French at Rocroi.

1659 Treaty of Pyrenees ends Franco-Spanish War; Spain loses its place as principal western European power to France.

1665 Spanish defeated by British and Portuguese forces: Portugal regains independence.

1668 Spain recognizes independence of Portugal in Treaty of Lisbon.

1692 Spanish crown declares bankruptcy.

1698 Spanish Empire partitioned. Charles II of Spain leaves territories to Infant Elector Prince of Bavaria in his will.

1699 Death of Infant Elector Prince of Bavaria; re-opens question of Spanish Succession.

1700 Philip of Anjou, grandson of Louis XII, becomes heir.

Rest of Europe

1600 Failure of coup against Geneva by Carlo Emmanuele I (of Savoy).

1613 Beginning of Romanov Dynasty in Russia.

1618 Protestant Bohemian revolt against future Habsburg Emperor Ferdinand II sparks off Thirty Years War.

1625 Protestant Danes renew war against the Catholic Habsburg Emperor, Ferdinand II.

1629 Danes suffer a series of defeats and withdraw from war; Swedes – led by Gustavus Adolphus – declare war on Habsburg Emperor.

1632 Gustavus Adolphus defeats Habsburgs at Lützen but is killed in battle.

1635 France goes to war with Habsburgs in alliance with Sweden and United Provinces.

1648 Treaty of Westphalia settles most of the issues of the Thirty Years War except the Franco-Spanish War; full Dutch independence.

1649 Establishment of serfdom in Russia.

1652–54 Anglo-Dutch sea war; Dutch finally recognize English Navigation Acts.

1654 Abdication of Queen Christina of Sweden.

1658 Danes finally expelled from southern Sweden: Peace of Roskilde.

1665–67 Second Anglo–Dutch Naval War.

1667 Truce of Andrusovo ends 13-year war between Russia and Poland; Kiev ceded to Russia.

1671 Turks declare war on Poland.

1672 Poland invaded by Turks and Cossacks; Poles surrender Podolia and Ukraine.

1673 Battle of Khorzim: Turks defeated by Poles led by Jan Sobieski.

1674 Jan Sobieski elected King of Poland.

1681 Treaty of Radzin: Russia gains most of Ukraine from Turkey.

1682 Accession of Peter the Great in Russia.

1683 Sobieski expels Turks from Vienna.

THE 18TH CENTURY

Britain

1701 Act of Settlement excludes Roman Catholic Stuarts from throne and recognizes the Hanoverian claim.

1707 Act of Union unites Scotland and England.

1712 Last execution for witchcraft in Britain.

1714 George the Elector of Hanover becomes George I.

1715 First Jacobite uprising in Scotland defeated.

1720 South Sea Bubble: failure of South Sea Company causes financial panic.

1721 Walpole becomes first Prime Minister.

1730 Methodists founded by John and Charles Wesley. Introduction of four-year crop rotation by Lord Townshend.

1736 Porteous riots in Edinburgh.

1742 Fall of Walpole.

1745–46 Last Jacobite rebellion in Britain fails.

c. 1750 Development of manufacturing industry; beginning of the Industrial Revolution.

1750 Britain joins Austro-Russian alliance against Prussia.

1755 Joint French and Indian War against Britain in North America.

1756 Outbreak of the Seven Years War.

Western and Southern Europe

1701 War of the Spanish Succession begins.

1704 British defeat French at Blenheim; British fleet captures Gibraltar from Spain.

1713 Treaty of Utrecht: end of War of Spanish Succession.

1715 Death of Louis XIV.

1719 France declares war on Spain.

1720 'Mississippi Bubble' in France. Treaty of Hague ends hostilities between Spain and Quadruple Alliance (Britain, France, Holy Roman Empire and the Netherlands).

1725 Treaty of Vienna: alliance between Spanish Bourbons and Austrian Habsburgs.

1727–29 War between Britain and Spain and France: Spain besieges Gibraltar (until 1728).

1739 Britain and Spain at war over British trade with South American colonies; merges with War of the Austrian Succession in 1740.

1740 War of the Austrian Succession: Maria Theresa succeeds to the thrones of Austria, Bohemia and Hungary: Frederick the Great seizes Silesia for Prussia.

1744–48 Britain and France at war over the colonies in North America.

1748 End of the War of the Austrian Succession.

1753 France faces national bankruptcy.

1755 Lisbon destroyed by earthquake.

1756 Diplomatic revolution: alliance between Britain and Prussia and alliance between France and Austria. Beginning of Seven Years War sparked off by British and French colonial rivalry and European struggle between Prussia and Austria.

Northern and Eastern Europe

1700 Great Northern War breaks out between Sweden and Russia, Denmark and Poland over supremacy in the Baltic.

1701 Charles XII of Sweden invades Poland.

1703–12 Hungarian revolt against Austria.

1706 Sweden imposes Stanislaus on the Polish throne.

1708 Sweden invades Russia.

1709 Peter (the Great) of Russia defeats Charles XII of Sweden at Battle of Poltava.

1711 Turkey declares war on Russia.

1720 Treaty of Nystadt ends Great Northern War: Sweden loses an empire and Russia becomes a major Baltic power.

1725 Death of Peter the Great.

1733–35 War of the Polish Succession: France and Spain fight Austria and Russia.

1734–35 War between Turkey and Persia.

c. 1740s Danubian principalities (Moldavia and Walachia) increasingly independent under Greek 'princes'.

1756 Outbreak of the Seven Years War.

1757 Sweden joins Seven Years War against Britain and Prussia.

THE 18TH CENTURY

Britain

1760 Enclosure Act changes farming practice: beginning of the Agricultural Revolution.

1762 Britain declares war on Spain.

1763 End of Seven Years War. MP and journalist John Wilkes is imprisoned for attacking the government in his paper.

1764 Wilkes is expelled from the House of Commons.

1765 Stamp Act imposes a tax on the American colonies: anti-British feeling increases campaign for independence.

1771 Richard Arkwright establishes first factory system for cotton spinning.

1775 War of American Independence breaks out at Lexington.

1776 American Declaration of Independence.

1780 Anti-Catholic riots in London.

1781 British troops surrender in America: end of War of Independence.

1782 Irish Parliament made independent of British parliament.

1791 Birmingham riots: fear of the spread of revolution in France leads to repressive rule.

1793 Britain joins continental powers against Revolutionary France.

Western and Southern Europe

1761 Influenza epidemic spreads across Europe.

1763 Peace of Paris: end of Seven Years War.

1770 Smallpox epidemic in Europe.

1778 Holland and France join American colonies in War of Independence.

1779–83 Spain enters War of Independence against Britain and lays siege to Gibraltar.

1781 Joseph I of Austria introduces religious toleration and abolishes serfdom.

1789 French Revolution: overthrow of Bourbon monarchy; abolition of feudal rights and privileges.

1792 France declares war on Austria and Prussia; beginning of Revolutionary Wars; National Convention formed to rule France; France becomes a Republic.

1793 Louis XVI executed; Reign of Terror begins under Robespierre.

1794 Robespierre executed: end of Reign of Terror.

1795 Napoleon leads army into renewed Revolutionary Wars.

1799 Napoleon seizes power in France.

Northern and Eastern Europe

1762 Accession of Catherine II (the Great); Russia changes sides in Seven Years War and allies with Prussia against Austria. Russian noblemen gain economic and social rights that free them from service obligations.

1766 Catherine II grants freedom of worship in Russia.

1772 First partition of Poland between Russia, Prussia and Austria.

1773–74 The Cossack leader Pugachev leads popular revolt against rule of Catherine II: uprising crushed.

1775 Reforms of provincial government carried out by Catherine II.

1784 Convention of Constantinople: Turkey accepts Russian annexation of Crimea.

1787 Russia and Turkey at war.

1788 Famine in Hungary.

1793 Second partition of Poland.

1795 Third partition of Poland.

THE 19TH CENTURY

Britain and Ireland

1801 Act of Union joins Britain and Ireland, abolishing Irish Parliament.

1807 Slave trade abolished in British Empire.

1810 Durham miners strike.

1811 Prince of Wales becomes regent (future George IV), owing to insanity of George III.

1812 Assassination of PM Spencer Percival. Anglo-American War (until 1814).

1815 Britain gains the Cape, Mauritius, Ascension Island, Heligoland, Ceylon, Trinidad, Tobago, St Lucia in postwar settlement.

1819 Peterloo Massacre of peaceful radical demonstrators in Manchester.

1820 Cato Street conspiracy: plot to assassinate Cabinet uncovered.

1828 Nonconformists allowed to hold office.

1829 Catholic Emancipation Act: Catholics can hold office.

1832 First Reform Bill extends vote.

1833 Slavery abolished in British Empire.

1834 Tamworth Manifesto.

1836 Chartist Movement begins.

1838 Foundation of the Anti-Corn Law League.

1839 First Chartist Petition.

Western Europe

1802 Peace of Amiens ends war between Britain and France.

1803 Britain declares war on France in renewal of Napoleonic Wars.

1804 Napoleon becomes Emperor; Code Napoleon adopted in France.

1805 Nelson defeats the French and Spanish fleets at Trafalgar. Napoleon defeats Austro-Russian forces at Austerlitz.

1806 Napoleon abolishes Holy Roman Empire; creation of the Confederation of the Rhine; beginning of economic warfare between France and Britain; French invade Portugal.

1808 Peninsular War begins.

1810 Napoleon marries Marie Louise of Austria.

1811 French finally driven out of Portugal.

1812 Napoleon invades Russia.

1813 Battle of Vittoria: French driven from Spain. Napoleon defeated at Battle of Leipzig.

1814 Napoleon abdicates and is exiled to Elba; Congress of Vienna.

1815 Napoleon's 100 Days end in defeat at Waterloo; Congress of Vienna resumes; Confederation of Germany formed.

1822 End of Congress System of diplomatic alliances. Civil war in Spain.

1823 Spanish Liberals defeated in civil war with help of French troops.

1830 July Revolution in France; revolution in Belgium leads to independence.

Southern and Eastern Europe

1801 France defeats Turks at Heliopolis, Egypt.

1804 Persia and Russia at war over Russian annexation of Georgia.

1805 Napoleon crowns himself king of Italy.

1811 Russia fails to force Japan to trade with West.

1815 Kingdom of Poland re-established (under Russian rule).

1820–32 Greek war of independence against Turks.

1825 Decembrist uprising in Russia leads to repressive rule by Tsar Nicholas I.

1826 Russia and Persia at war.

1827 Russians win war and annex Armenia.

1830 Polish uprising against Russia. Revolution in northern Italy against Austrian occupation.

1831 Italian nationalist movement founded by Mazzini.

1832 Poland becomes a Russian province.

THE 19TH CENTURY

The Americas	Africa and Middle East	Asia and Australasia
1803 USA makes 'Louisiana Purchase' from France.	**1806** Britain seizes Cape Colony from Dutch.	**1803–5** First Maratha War in India.
1804 Haiti proclaims its independence from France.	**1807** Sierra Leone and Gambia become British colonies.	**1804** Castle Hill Rising in New South Wales.
1807 Colombian independence movement begins.		**1806** Sepoy mutiny against British at Vellore, India.
1808 Uprisings in Spain's South American colonies.		**1808** Overthrow of Governor Bligh in Rum Rebellion, Australia.
1810 Simon Bolivár becomes popular nationalist leader in South America.	**1810** Mauritius and Seychelles annexed by Britain.	**1811** British occupy Java.
1812–14 Anglo-American War.	**1818** Zulu Kingdom formed by Shaka.	**1817** Revolt against British rule in Ceylon repressed.
1810–20 Independence for Paraguay and Venezuela (1811), Argentina (1816), Chile (1818), Colombia (1819).		**1819** Singapore is founded as British colony.
1813 USA seizes West Florida from Spain.		
1817 Independent government of Venezuela formed by Bolivár.		
1819 Spain cedes Florida to USA.		
1820 Missouri Compromise: slave-owning states allowed to join union.	**1820** Gold Coast becomes a British colony.	**1824** Britain gains Assam. First Anglo-Burmese War (until 1826).
1820–30 Independence for Mexico and Peru (1821), Brazil (1822), Uruguay (1828).	**1821–22** Foundation of Liberia.	**1825–30** Java War: Dutch defeat Javanese anti-colonial forces.
1823 Monroe Doctrine.	**1824–31** First Ashanti War in Gold Coast.	**1828** Western Australia founded.
1830 Large-scale removal of Indians to reservations begins.	**1830** Algeria becomes a French colony.	**1834** South Australia founded.
1836 Battles of the Alamo and San Jacinto; Texas gains independence from Mexico.	**1834** Kaffir War between Bantu people and white settlers.	**1837** Colonization of New Zealand begins.
1837 Papineau and Mackenzie Rebellions in Canada.	**1836** Great Trek begins: Boers settle Orange Free State and Transvaal.	**1838–42** First Anglo-Afghan War.
1838 Foundation of Central American republics.	**1838** Massacre of Zulus at Battle of Blood River.	**1839** First Opium War between Britain and China.

THE 19TH CENTURY ──────────────────

Britain and Ireland

1843 Agitation in Ireland for repeal of Act of Union.
1846 Repeal of Corn Laws. Potato famine in Ireland.
1847 Young Ireland Movement founded.

1850 Palmerston intervenes in Don Pacifico Affair.
1851 Great Exhibition of London.
1853 Gladstone's first Budget.

1866 Second major Reform Act adds one million to electorate.
1867 Trade Unions declared illegal.
1868 First Trades Union Congress.
1869 Disestablishment of Church of Ireland.

1870 Gladstone's Irish Land Act.
1871 Trade Unions declared legal.
1872 Ballot Act introduces secret ballot in elections.
1877 Parnell leads Irish Nationalist MPs in policy of obstruction in House of Commons.

1881–82 Parnell imprisoned.
1882 Phoenix Park Murders spark off Anglo-Irish Crisis.
1884 Third Reform Act.
1886 First Irish Home Rule Bill fails.

1890 Divorce scandal ends Parnell's political career.
1891 Keir Hardie becomes first Independent Labour Party MP.
1893 Second Irish Home Rule Bill fails.

Western Europe

1848 Revolutions in Paris and Berlin suppressed by 1849; universal suffrage introduced in France.
1849 Second French Republic established; Louis Philippe abdicates.

1850 France abolishes universal suffrage.
1852 Fall of Second Republic in France; Louis Napoleon becomes Emperor Napoleon III.

1862 Bismarck becomes Chancellor of Prussia. Prussia gains Schleswig Holstein after war with Denmark.
1866 Austro-Prussian War.
1867 Formation of North German Confederation. Austro-Hungarian 'Dual Monarchy' founded.

1871 France defeated in Franco-Prussian War: Alsace ceded to Germany; German unification under Kaiser Wilhelm I: Bismarck becomes Chancellor of Germany. Paris Commune is crushed.

1882 Italy, Germany and Austria form the Triple Alliance.
1884 Berlin Conference sparks off 'Scramble for Africa' – race by European powers for African colonies.

1890 Fall of Bismarck. Anglo-German agreement over colonies.
1894 Dreyfus Affair begins in France; splits nation.
1897 First Zionist Congress meets in Basel, Switzerland.

Southern and Eastern Europe

1848 Revolution against Austrian Empire in Italian states, Prague and Budapest suppressed by 1849.

1854 Crimean War starts: France, Britain, Austria and Turkey against Russia.
1856 End of Crimean War: Treaty of Paris guarantees Turkey's integrity.

1861 Italian unification led by Garibaldi and Cavour.
1863 Polish revolt against Russian rule.
1868 Liberal uprising in Spain.
1869 Carlist uprising in Spain crushed.

1870 Italy annexes Rome.
1873 First Spanish Republic.
1877 Massacre of Bulgarians by Turks: Russo–Turkish War.
1878 End of Russo–Turkish War; Romania, Serbia and Montenegro independent.

1891 Launch of the Young Turk Movement.
1894 and **1896** Massacres of Armenians by Turks.

THE 19TH CENTURY

The Americas	Africa and Middle East	Asia and Australasia
1840 Act of Union joins Upper and Lower Canada.	**1841** Mehemet Ali recognized as hereditary ruler of Egypt.	**1840** New Zealand becomes a British colony.
1845 US–Mexican War starts.	**1846–53** Xhosa War: Xhosa resist expansion of Dutch and British colonists in Cape Colony.	**1841** Britain occupies Hong Kong.
1847 Mormons settle Salt Lake City.		**1842** Massacre in Khyber Pass as British retreat from Afghanistan.
1848 End of US–Mexican War. USA gains California and New Mexico. Californian gold rush.		**1845** Maori rising against British in New Zealand.
		1845–49 Sikh Wars: British annexation of the Punjab.
1850 Compromise over slavery in new US states.	**1851** British occupy Lagos. End of slave trade.	**1850** Taiping Rebellion starts in China.
	1854 Livingstone begins exploration of central Africa.	**1857–58** Indian Mutiny suppressed; Crown government of India begins.
		1857 Second Opium War.
		1859 Cambodia becomes a French protectorate.
1860–1 Southern US states secede to form Confederacy.	**1866** Livingstone's third expedition in Africa.	**c. 1860s** Gold rushes in New Zealand.
1861 American Civil War begins.	**1868** Britain annexes Basutoland.	**1860** Second Maori War in New Zealand. Chinese ports forced to trade with West.
1863 Emancipation of slaves in USA.	**1869** Opening of Suez Canal.	**1864** Qing Dynasty finally crushes Taiping Rebellion; 20 million dead.
1865 Confederacy surrenders; Lincoln assassinated.		**1867** End of transportation of convicts to Australia.
1866 Civil Rights Bill for US Blacks passed.		
1867 USA purchases Alaska from Russia.		
1876 Battle of Little Big Horn Custer's US cavalry wiped out by Sioux.	**1873** Second Ashanti War.	**1877** Queen Victoria becomes Empress of India.
1879 War of the Pacific: Chile defeats Peru and Bolivia; Bolivia loses Pacific coast.	**1877** Britain annexes the Transvaal.	**1878** Second Anglo–Afghan War.
	1879 Britain and France gain control of Egypt. Zulu Wars.	
1889 Panama Canal Scandal. Brazil becomes a republic.	**1881** First Boer War. Nationalist revolt in Egypt.	**1885** Indian National Congress meets for first time.
	1883 Kruger becomes President of the Transvaal.	
	1885 Khartoum falls to Mahdi: death of General Gordon.	
1890 Battle of Wounded Knee: final defeat of Sioux.	**1890** Establishment of Rhodesia by Cecil Rhodes.	**1894** War between China and Japan begins.
1893 USA overthrows Hawaiian government.	**1895** Rhodes resigns after Jameson Raid.	**1895** End of war between China and Japan: Japan gains Formosa (Taiwan) and Korea.
1898 Spanish-American War: Spain cedes Puerto Rico, Guam, Philippines and Cuba to USA.	**1896** Italy fails to take Ethiopia.	
	1898 Fashoda Incident.	
	1899 Second Boer War starts.	

THE 20TH CENTURY TO 1939

Britain and Ireland

Western Europe

Southern and Eastern Europe

1900 Labour Representative Committee formed.

1902 End of Boer War.

1906 British Labour Party founded after election.

1909 Lloyd George's 'People's Budget' introduces social security measures: leads to constitutional crisis (1910–11).

1904 Entente Cordiale between Britain and France established.

1906 End of Dreyfus affair.

1905 Norway becomes independent from Sweden.

1907 Triple Entente of France, Britain and Russia formed.

1903 Formation of Bolshevik Party in Russia.

1905 'Bloody Sunday' Revolution in Russia: Duma (Parliament) set up with limited powers.

1911 Parliament Act reduces powers of House of Lords.

1913 House of Lords rejects Third Irish Home Rule Bill. Militant suffragette demonstrations held in London.

1914 Britain declares war on Germany: outbreak of World War I.

1915 Coalition government formed.

1916 Easter Rising in Ireland suppressed.

1918 Civil war in Ireland.

1914 Austrian heir Archduke Franz Ferdinand assassinated: Austria declares war on Serbia; Germany declares war on Russia and France: outbreak of WWI.

1914 Beginning of trench warfare on Western Front.

1916 One million dead at Battle of the Somme.

1918 Austria–Hungary and Germany surrender.

1919 Treaty of Versailles; Spartacist Rising in Berlin crushed.

1910 Portugal becomes a republic.

1915 Italy joins Allies and Bulgaria joins Central Powers.

1916 Portugal and Romania join war against Germany.

1917 October Revolution: Bolsheviks take control.

1918 Russia withdraws from war; Russian Civil War.

1919 End of Habsburg Empire: independence for Czechoslovakia, Poland, Yugoslavia and Hungary.

1921 Irish Free State established in southern Ireland: civil war continues (until 1923).

1924 First Labour Government.

1926 General Strike.

1929 Hunger march from Glasgow to London.

1920 Weimar Republic established in Germany.

1923 Kapp Putsch fails: Hitler arrested.

1927 German economy collapses on Black Friday.

1921 Greece and Turkey at war.

1921 End of Russian Civil War.

1922 Fascists march on Rome: Mussolini becomes PM.

1924 Death of Lenin: Stalin emerges as successor.

1925 Mussolini establishes dictatorship.

1929 Lateran Treaties recognize sovereignty of Vatican City.

1931 Dominion states gain full independence. National government formed after fall of Labour government.

1932 Great Hunger March.

1936 Abdication of Edward VIII.

1937 PM Chamberlain adopts policy of appeasement of Germany.

1939 Britain declares war on Germany: outbreak of World War II.

1930 107 Nazis are elected to Reichstag.

1933 Hitler becomes Chancellor of Germany.

1935 Nuremberg laws legalize anti-Semitism in Germany.

1936 Rome-Berlin Axis formed.

1936 Germany and Japan sign Anti-Comintern Pact.

1938 German annexation of Austria – *Anschluss* – and Czech Sudetenland.

1939 Germany signs non-aggression pact with USSR; invades Czechoslovakia and Poland: outbreak of WWII.

1930 Beginning of the extermination of Kulaks (wealthy peasants) in USSR.

1933 Stalinist purges begin.

1935 Soviet 'Show Trials' of ex-Party members.

1936 Outbreak of Spanish Civil War.

1937 Italy joins Anti-Comintern Pact.

1939 Nationalists win Spanish Civil War. German-Soviet pact assigns Baltic States to USSR. USSR invades Finland.

————————————THE 20TH CENTURY TO 1939

The Americas	Africa and Middle East	Asia and Australia
1901 US President McKinley assassinated: T. Roosevelt succeeds him. **1902** Cuba becomes fully independent.	**1900** North and South Nigeria become British protectorates. **1902** End of Boer War. **1904** Massacres of Herero rebels by Germans in South West Africa. **1906** Revolution in Iran forces the establishment of a constitution. **1907** Belgian government takes over control of Congo from Léopold III following atrocities. **1910** South Africa becomes independent dominion.	**1900** Anti-Western Boxer Rebellion in China ends after foreign intervention. **1901** Australian Commonwealth established. **1904** Russo–Japanese War. **1907** New Zealand becomes an independent dominion.
1910 Mexican Civil War begins. **1916** US troops occupy Dominican Republic. **1917** USA declares war on Germany. **1919** US President Wilson instrumental in the establishment of the League of Nations.	**1911** Agadir Crisis: Germany sends gunboat to Morocco to force territorial concessions from France. **1917** Britain supports idea of Jewish state in Palestine in Balfour Declaration. **1919** Ottoman Empire dismantled: Britain gains mandate over Palestine and Iraq; France gains mandate over Syria.	**1911–12** Revolution in China ends imperial rule: republic established. **1919** Punjab riots; Amritsar Massacre by British troops fuels Indian nationalist sentiment.
1920 Beginning of Prohibition in USA (until 1933). **1921** US women are given the vote. **1928** Outbreak of Chaco War between Paraguay and Bolivia. **1929** Wall St Crash precipitates Great Depression worldwide.	**1920** Kenya becomes a British colony. **1921** Reza Khan seizes power in Iran (becomes Shah in 1925). **1922** British protectorate over Egypt ends. **1923** Turkish republic formed with Mustapha Kemal as president. **1929** Arab–Jewish clashes and anti-British riots in Palestine.	**1921** Gandhi begins civil disobedience campaign in India. **1921** Chinese Communist Party formed. **1927–28** Civil War in China: Nationalists defeat Communists and form government.
1930 Vargas comes to power in Brazil. **1933** President F.D. Roosevelt launches New Deal policy to counter effects of Depression.	**1930** Haile Selassie crowned emperor of Ethiopia. **1932** Saudi Arabia established. **1935–36** Italians invade and occupy Ethiopia.	**1931** Mukden Incident: Japan seizes Manchuria. **1932** Indian Congress is declared illegal: Gandhi is arrested. **1934–35** 'Long March' by defeated Chinese Communists. **1935** Burma separated from India. **1937** Japan invades China. **1938** Japan gains effective control over China.

THE 20TH CENTURY SINCE 1939 ———————

Britain and Ireland

1940 National government formed under Churchill following Dunkirk evacuation. Battle of Britain.
1940–41 London Blitz.
1945 End of WWII. Labour government comes to power: establishment of welfare state.
1948 British Citizenship Act: all Commonwealth citizens qualify for British passports.
1949 Irish Republic leaves Commonwealth.

1956 Suez Crisis leads to resignation of PM Eden.
1958 Race riots in London and Nottingham.

1963 France vetoes Britain's application to join EEC.
1968 Britain withdraws from East of Suez. Immigration control introduced.
1969 Troops sent to Northern Ireland to restore order.

1972 Direct rule introduced in Northern Ireland.
1973 Britain and Ireland join EEC.
1974 Power-sharing experiment in Northern Ireland abandoned.
1979 Winter of industrial action.

1982 Falklands War.
1984–85 Year-long miners' strike.
1985 Anglo-Irish Accord on Northern Ireland.
1987 Third Thatcher government formed.
1990 Thatcher resigns; John Major becomes PM.

Western Europe

1940 Germany invades France.
1941 First extermination camps set up in Germany.
1944 D-Day Allied landings.
1945 Germany surrenders; Germany and Austria occupied; United Nations founded.
1945–46 Nuremburg Trials.
1948 Communists blockade Berlin: Allied Berlin Airlift.
1949 NATO is formed. Germany is divided into East and West Germany.

1952 End of Allied occupation of West Germany.
1957 EEC (later EC) established.
1958 Fifth Republic of France established under Charles De Gaulle.
1959 EFTA founded.

1961 Berlin Wall is built.
1968 Anti-government student demonstrations and strikes in France.
1969 Beginning of Ostpolitik in West Germany.

1973 Denmark joins EC.
1974 Overthrow of Portuguese dictatorship.
1975 Death of Franco: restoration of democracy in Spain.

1981 Mitterand becomes first socialist president of French Fifth Republic.
1986 Spain and Portugal join EC.
1989 Berlin Wall opened.
1990 German reunification.

Southern and Eastern Europe

1940 Italy joins war against Allies.
1941 Germany invades Yugoslavia, Greece and USSR.
1941 Bulgaria and Romania join the Axis Powers.
1943 Invasion of Sicily by Allies; Italy surrenders.
1944 Soviet offensive in East.
1945–48 Communist takeover in Eastern Europe.
1946 Civil War in Greece.

1953 Death of Stalin.
1955 Warsaw Pact formed.
1956 De-Stalinization in Eastern Europe; Soviet troops crush anti-Soviet uprising in Hungary.

1964 Clashes between Greeks and Turks break out in Cyprus.
1967 Military coup in Greece.
1968 'Prague Spring' in Czechoslovakia; reform ended when Soviet troops invade.

1974 Turkish invasion of Cyprus leads to partition. Democracy restored in Greece.

1981 Greece joins EC.
1985 Gorbachov comes to power: begins policy of reform.
1989 Free elections in Poland; Romanian revolution; hardline Communist regimes fall in Eastern Europe.
1990 Free elections in Hungary, Romania, Bulgaria, Czechoslovakia. Baltic States try to secede. German reunification.

THE 20TH CENTURY SINCE 1939

The Americas

Africa and Middle East

Asia and Australasia

1941 Lend Lease Act passed. USA enters war on Allied side.

1947 Truman Doctrine: containment of Communism.

1948 Marshall Plan adopted to provide US aid for Europe.

1941 War extends to North Africa.

1943 Germans and Italians withdraw from North Africa.

1948 State of Israel established; first Arab–Israeli War.

1948 Nationalists in power in South Africa: policy of apartheid begins.

1941 Japan bombs Pearl Harbor: USA enters World War II.

1945 US atomic bombs dropped on Hiroshima and Nagasaki; Japan surrenders.

1946–49 Nationalists defeated in Chinese Civil War: Mao Zedong and Communists come to power.

1947 India gains independence; Pakistan becomes separate state.

1948 Gandhi assassinated.

1950–54 McCarthy witch-hunt of suspected Communists in USA.

1956–58 Cuban Civil War: Fidel Castro comes to power.

1957 US Civil Rights Act passed; race riots in southern states.

1960 Bay of Pigs: attempt by US-backed exiles to invade Cuba fails.

1952 Moroccan uprising against French. Mau Mau rebellion starts in Kenya.

1954 Nasser takes full control of Egypt. Beginning of Algerian War of Independence.

1956 Suez Crisis. Independence for Morocco, Sudan and Tunisia.

1957–75 Decolonization in Black Africa.

1950–53 Korean War.

1954 Vietnam gains independence from French; divided into Communist North and Western-backed South Vietnam.

1959 Uprising in Tibet crushed by China.

1961 Cuban Missile Crisis.

1963 President Kennedy is assassinated; Civil Rights Campaign led by Martin Luther King.

1967 Race riots in the USA.

1968 Martin Luther King and Robert Kennedy assassinated. Growing opposition to US role in Vietnam.

1962 Algeria achieves independence after bitter struggle.

1965 White Rhodesian government unilaterally declares independence: guerrilla fighting follows.

1967 Six Day Arab–Israeli War: Arabs defeated; PLO formed.

1962 A US military command is set up in South Vietnam.

1965 US marines sent to Vietnam.

1966–76 Cultural Revolution throws China into political chaos.

1968 Tet Offensive by North Vietnamese forces.

1969 USA begins talks with North Vietnamese.

1972 Civil War breaks out in El Salvador.

1973 Peace of Paris: US troops withdraw from Vietnam.

1974 Watergate scandal forces Nixon to resign.

1979 Somoza overthrown by Sandinistas in Nicaragua.

1972 Lebanese civil war begins.

1973 Third Arab–Israeli War.

1974–75 Portuguese African colonies gain independence.

1977 Crackdown on anti-apartheid activity in South Africa.

1979 Islamic Revolution in Iran.

1971 Bangladesh becomes an independent state.

1973 US troops leave Vietnam.

1975 South Vietnam surrenders: end of Vietnam War. Khmer Rouge come to power in Kampuchea (Cambodia).

1976 Mao Zedong dies: end of era in Chinese history. Pol Pot becomes PM of Cambodia and embarks on bloody purge.

1979 Soviet forces back coup in Afghanistan: civil war breaks out. Vietnam invades Cambodia.

1980 Cold War heats up following invasion of Afghanistan.

1986 'Iran-gate' scandal.

1987 INF Treaty signed by USA and USSR.

1990 Chile and Brazil hold free elections: return to civilian government. American troops sent to the Gulf.

1980 Rhodesia becomes independent; renamed Zimbabwe.

1980–88 Iran–Iraq War.

1982 Israel invades Lebanon.

1986 Palestinians intensify violent anti-Israeli campaign.

1990 Namibia gains independence; South Africa begins to dismantle apartheid: Nelson Mandela is set free. Iraq invades Kuwait.

1986 Overthrow of President Marcos of the Philippines.

1988 Vietnamese forces withdraw from Cambodia.

1989 Soviet troops are gradually withdrawn from Afghanistan. Peaceful pro-democracy demonstrations are violently crushed in Tiananmen Square, China.

KINGS, RULERS AND STATESMEN

The following tables list heads of state and/or recent heads of government for selected countries. Further information on the recent history and present constitution of these and other states will be found in the Countries of the World section, starting on p. 492.

ARGENTINA

PRESIDENTS

(since 1946)
Gen. Juan Domingo Perón *Peronist* 1946–55
Gen. Eduardo Lonardi *military* 1955
Gen. Pedro Eugenio Aramburu *military* 1955–58
Arturo Frondizi *Radical* 1958–62
Dr José Maria Guido *np* 1962–63
Dr Arturo Umberto Illia *Radical* 1963–66
Gen. Juan Carlos Ongania *military* 1966–70
Gen. Roberto Levingston *military* 1970–71
Gen. Alejandro Agustin Lanusse *military* 1971–73
Héctor Cámpora *Peronist* 1973
Raúl Lastiri *Coalition* 1973
Gen. Juan Domingo Perón *Peronist* 1973–74
Maria Estela Martinez de Perón *Peronist* 1974–76
(the first woman president in the world)
Gen. Jorge Rafael Videla *military* 1976–81
Gen. Roberto Viola *military* 1981
Gen. Leopoldo Fortunato Galtieri *military* 1981–82
Gen. Reynaldo Bignone *military* 1982–83
Dr Raúl Alfonsin *Radical* 1983–88
Carlos Saul Menem *Peronist* 1988–

Key: *np* = non-party

AUSTRIA

EMPERORS

(before 1804, see Holy Roman Empire)
Franz I 1804–35
Ferdinand I 1835–48
Franz Joseph I 1848–1916
Karl I 1916–18

PRESIDENTS

Dr Karl Seitz 1918–20
Dr Michael Hainisch 1920–28
Dr Wilhelm Miklas 1928–1938 when Austria was included within the German Reich
Dr Karl Renner 1945–50
Dr Theodor Körner 1951–57
Dr Adolf Schärf 1957–65
Dr Franz Jonas 1965–74
Dr Rudolf Kirchschläger 1974–86
Dr Kurt Waldheim 1986–

CHANCELLORS

(since 1945)
Dr Karl Renner *Coalition* 1945
Dr Leopold Figl *PP* 1945–53
Dr Julius Raab *PP* 1953–61
Dr Alfons Gorbach *PP* 1961–74
Dr Josef Klaus *PP* 1974–70
Dr Bruno Kreisky *Soc* 1970–83
Dr Fred Sinowatz *Soc-PP* 1983–86
Dr Franz Vranitzky *Soc-PP* 1986–

Key: *PP* = People's Party (conservative)
Soc = Social Democrat

AUSTRALIA

PRIME MINISTERS

Sir Edmund Barton *Coalition* 1901–03
Alfred Deakin *Lib-Lab* 1903–04
John Christian Watson *Lab* 1904
Sir George Houston Reid *Coalition* 1904–05
Alfred Deakin *Lib-Lab* 1905–08
Andrew Fisher *Lab* 1908–09
Alfred Deakin *Lib-Con* 1909–10
Andrew Fisher *Lab* 1910–13
Sir Joseph Cook *Lib* 1913–14
Andrew Fisher *Lab* 1914–15
William Morris Hughes *Lab-Nat* 1915–23
Stanley Melbourne Bruce *Nat-Co* 1923–29
James Henry Scullin *Lab* 1929–32
Joseph Aloysius Lyons *UA* 1932–39
Sir Earle Christmas Grafton Page *Co-UA* 1939
Sir Robert Gordon Menzies *UA-Co* 1939–41
Sir Arthur William Fadden *Co-UA* 1941
John Joseph Curtin *Lab* 1941–45
Francis Michael Forde *Lab* 1945
Joseph Benedict Chifley *Lab* 1945–49
Sir Robert Gordon Menzies *Lib-Co* 1949–66
Harold Edward Holt *Lib-Co* 1966–67
Sir John McEwen *Lib-Co* 1967–68
John Grey Gorton *Lib-Co* 1968–71
William McMahon *Lib-Co* 1971–72
Edward Gough Whitlam *Lab* 1972–75
John Malcolm Fraser *Lib-Co* 1975–83
Robert (Bob) James Lee Hawke *Lab* 1983–

Key: *Co* = Country Party (now National Party)
Lab = Labor Party
Lib = Liberal Party
Nat = Nationalist (succeeded by United Australia Party 1931)
UA = United Australia Party (succeeded by Liberal Party 1944)

BANGLADESH

PRESIDENTS

Syed Nazrul Islam *Awami* 1971–72
Shaikh Mujib-ur-Rahman *Awami* 1972
(Shaikh Mujib-ur-Rahman was also PM 1972–75; the post of premier was revived in 1991)
Abu Sayed Choudhury *Awami* 1972–73
Muhammad Ullah *Awami* 1973–75
Shaikh Mujib-ur-Rahman *Awami* 1975 (assassinated)
Khandaker Moshtaque Ahmed *caretaker* 1975
Justice Abusadat Muhammad Sayem *np* 1975–77
Maj. Gen. Zia-ur-Rahman *BNP* 1977–81 (assassinated)
Justice Abdus Sattar *BNP* 1981–82
Gen. Hossian Muhammad Ershad *JD* 1982–90
Justice Shahabuddin Ahmed *np* 1990–

Key: *Awami* = Awami League
BNP = Bangladesh Nationalist Party
JD = Jatiya Party
np = non-party

BELGIUM

KINGS

Léopold I 1831–65
Léopold II 1865–1909
Albert I 1909–34
Léopold III 1934–51
Baudouin I 1951–

PRIME MINISTERS

(since 1958)
Gaston Eyskens *SC* 1958–61
Théo Lefèvre *SC* 1961–65
Pierre Harmel *SC* 1965–66
Paul vanden Boeynants *SC* 1966–68
Gaston Eyskens *SC* 1968–72
Edmond Leburton *Soc* 1972–74
Léo Tindemans *SC* 1974–78
Paul vanden Boeynants *SC* 1978–79
Wilfried Martens *SC* 1979–81
Mark Eyskens *SC* 1981
Wilfried Martens *SC* 1981–

Key: *SC* = Social Christian (conservative)
Soc = Socialist

BRAZIL

PRESIDENTS

(since 1930)
Dr Getúlio Dornelles Vargas *New State* 1930–45
Chief Justice Dr José Linhares *caretaker* 1945–46
Marshal Eurico Gaspar Dutra *military* 1946–51
Dr Getúlio Dornelles Vargas *PTB* 1951–54
Dr João Café Filho *PTB* 1954–55
Carlos Coimbra de Luz *caretaker* 1955
Nereu de Oliveira Ramos *caretaker* 1955–56
Juscelino Kubitschek de Oliveira *Coalition* 1956–61
Jânio de Silva Quadros *np-UDN* 1961
Pascoal Ranieri Mazzilli *caretaker* 1961
João Belchior Goulart *PTB* 1961–64
Pascoal Ranieri Mazzilli *caretaker* 1964
Marshal Humberto de Alencar Castelo *military* 1964–67
Marshal Artur da Costa e Silva *military* 1967–69
Gen. Emilio Garrastazu Medici *military* 1969–74
Gen. Ernesto Geisel *military* 1974–79
Gen. João Baptista de Oliveira Figueiredo *military* 1979–85
Tancredo Neves *PFL* 1985
José Sarney *PFL* 1985–90
Fernando Collor de Mellor *PRN* 1990–

Key: *np* = non-party
PFL = Liberal Front
PRN = National Reconstruction Party
PTB = Brazilian Labour Party
UDN = National Democratic Union

BULGARIA

PRINCES

Alexander I 1879–86
Ferdinand I 1886–1908 when he became king

KINGS

Ferdinand I 1908–1918
Boris III 1918–43
Simeon II 1943–46

PRESIDENTS

Vassil Kolarov *Comm* 1946–47
Mintso Neitsev *Comm* 1947–50
Georgi Damyanov *Comm* 1950–58
Dimiter Ganev *Comm* 1958–64
Georgi Traikov *Comm* 1964–71
Todor Zhivkov *Comm* 1971–89
Petar Mladenov *Comm* 1989–90
Zhelo Zhelev *UDF* 1990–

Key: *Comm* = Communist
UDF = Union of Democratic Forces

CANADA

PRIME MINISTERS

Sir John Alexander MacDonald *Lib-Con* 1867–73
Alexander MacKenzie *Lib* 1873–78
Sir John Alexander MacDonald *Lib-Con* 1878–91
Sir John Joseph Caldwell Abbott *Lib-Con* 1891–92
Sir John Sparrow David Thompson *Lib-Con* 1892–94
Sir Mackenzie Bowell *Lib-Con* 1894–96
Sir Charles Tupper *Lib-Con* 1896
Sir Wilfred Laurier *Lib* 1896–1911
Sir Robert Laird Borden *Con* 1911–20
Arthur Meighen *Con* 1920–21
William Lyon MacKenzie King *Lib* 1921–26
Arthur Meighen *Con* 1926
William Lyon MacKenzie King *Lib* 1926–30
Richard Bedford Bennett *Con* 1930–35
William Lyon Mackenzie King *Lib* 1935–48
Louis Stephen St Laurent *Lib* 1948–57
John George Diefenbaker *PCon* 1957–63
Lester Bowles Pearson *Lib* 1963–68
Pierre Elliott Trudeau *Lib* 1968–79
Charles Joseph Clark *PCon* 1979–80
Pierre Elliot Trudeau *Lib* 1980–84
John Napier Turner *Lib* 1984
Brian Mulroney *PCon* 1984–

Key: *Con* = Conservative (succeeded by Progressive Conservative Party in 1942)
Lib = Liberal
PCon = Progressive Conservative

CHINA

MANCHU EMPERORS

Shun-Chih 1644–61
Kangxi 1661–1722
Yangzheng 1722–35
Qian-long 1735–96
Jiajiang 1796–1820
Daoguang 1821–50
Xian Feng 1851–61
Tongzhi 1862–75
Guangxu 1875–1908
Xuan Zong (better known in the West by his personal name *Puyi*) 1908–12

PRESIDENTS (REPUBLIC OF CHINA)

In all there were 15 presidents or claimants to the presidency of China between 1912 and 1949; the more notable included:
Sun Yixian (*Sun Yat-sen*) 1912, 1917–25
Gen. Yuan Shikai 1912–16
Jiang Jie Shi (*Chiang Kai-shek*) 1928–31, 1943–49

PRESIDENTS (PEOPLE'S REPUBLIC OF CHINA)

Mao Zedong 1949–58
Marshal Zhu De 1958–59
Liu Shaoqui 1959–68
Dung Pi Wu 1968–75
(No president 1975–83)
Li Xiannian* 1983–88
Yang Shangkun 1988–

PRIME MINISTERS

Zhou Enlai 1949–76
Hua Guofeng* 1976–80
Zhao Ziyang 1980–87
Li Peng 1987–

LEADERS OF THE COMMUNIST PARTY

Mao Zedong 1949–76
Hua Guofeng* 1976–81
Hu Yaobang 1981–87
Zhao Ziyang 1987–89
Jiang Zemin 1989–

Key: * Since 1977 Deng Xiaoping has been the effective ruler of China although he has not held any of the three major offices of state.

CZECHOSLOVAKIA

PRESIDENTS

Tomás Garrigue Masaryk 1918–35
Edvard Beneš 1935–38
Gen. Jan Sirovy 1938
Dr Emil Hacha 1938–39 when Czechoslovakia was overrun by German forces
(German occupation 1939–45)
Edvard Beneš *np* 1940–45 (in exile); 1945–48
Klemens Gottwald *Comm* 1945–53
Antonín Zapotocky *Comm* 1953–57
Antonín Novotny *Comm* 1957–68
Gen. Ludvik Svoboda *Comm* 1968–75
Dr Gustáv Husák *Comm* 1975–89
Vaclav Havel *CF* 1989–

PRIME MINISTERS

(since 1946)
Klemens Gottwald *Comm* 1946–48
Antonín Zapotocky *Comm* 1948–53
Viliam Siroky *Comm* 1953–63
Josef Lenart *Comm* 1963–68
Oldrich Cernik *Comm* 1968–70
Lubomir Strougal *Comm* 1970–88
Ladislav Adamec *Comm* 1988–89
Marian Calfa *CF-PAV coalition* 1989–

LEADERS OF THE COMMUNIST PARTY

From 1948 to 1989 the effective ruler of Czechoslovakia was the leader of the Communist Party; the more notable included:
Rudolf Slánský 1948–52
Antonín Novotny 1953–68
Alexander Dubček 1968–69
Gustáv Husák 1969–87

Key: *CF* = Civic Forum
Comm = Communist
np = non-party
PAV = Public Against Violence

DENMARK

KINGS

Christian I 1448–81
Hans 1481–1513
Christian II 1513–23
Frederik I 1523–33
Christian III 1533–59
Frederik II 1559–88
Christian IV 1588–1648
Frederik III 1648–70
Christian V 1670–99
Frederik IV 1699–1730
Christian VI 1730–46
Frederik V 1746–66
Christian VII 1766–1808
Frederik VI 1808–39
Christian VIII 1839–48
Frederik VII 1848–63

Christian IX 1863–1906
Frederik VIII 1906–1912
Christian X 1912–1947
Frederik IX 1947–1972
Margrethe II 1972–

PRIME MINISTERS

(since 1945)
Vilhelm Buhl *Coalition* 1945
Knud Kristensen *Lib* 1945–47
Hans Hedtoft *Soc Dem* 1947–50
Erik Eriksen *Lib-Con* 1950–53
Hans Hedtoft *Soc Dem* 1953–55
Hans Christian Hansen *Soc Dem* 1955–60
Viggo Kampmann *Soc Dem* 1960
Jens Otto Krag *Soc Dem* 1960–68
Hilmar Baunsgaard *Radical* 1968–71
Jens Otto Krag *Soc Dem* 1971–72
Anker Jorgensen *Soc Dem* 1972–73
Poul Hartling *Lib* 1973–75
Anker Jorgensen *Soc Dem* 1975–82
Poul Schlüter *Lib-Con* 1982–

Key: *Con* = Conservative
Lib = Liberal
Soc Dem = Social Democrat

EGYPT

KINGS

Fuad I 1922–36
Faruq 1936–52
Fuad II 1952–53

PRESIDENTS

Gen. Muhammad Neguib *military* 1952–54
Col. Gamal Abdel Nasser *military* 1954–70
Anwar Sadat *NDP* 1970–81 (assassinated)
Gen. Muhammad Hosni Mubarak *NDP* 1981–

Key: *NDP* = National Democratic Party

FINLAND

PRESIDENTS

Dr Kaarlo Juho Stahlberg *NPP* 1919–25
Lauri Relander *AP* 1925–31
Dr Pehr Svinhufvud *Coalition* 1931–37
Kyösti Kallio *Coalition* 1937–40
Risto Ryti *Coalition* 1940–44
Marshal Carl Gustav Mannerheim *Coalition* 1944–46
Juhi Kusti Paasikiva *Coalition* 1946–56
Dr Urho Kaleva Kekkonen *AP* 1956–82
Mauno Henrik Koïvisto *Soc Dem* 1982–

Key: *AP* = Rural Party
NPP = National Progressive Party
Soc Dem = Social Democrat

FRANCE

KINGS

(since 987)
Hugues 987–996
Robert II 996–1031
Henri I 1031–60
Philippe I 1060–1108
Louis VI 1108–37
Louis VII 1137–80
Philippe II 1180–1223
Louis VIII 1223–26
Louis IX (St Louis) 1226–70

Philippe III 1270–85
Philippe IV 1285–1314
Louis X 1314–16
Jean I 1316
Philippe V 1316–22
Charles IV 1322–28
Philippe VI 1328–50
Jean II 1350–64
Charles V 1364–80
Charles VI 1380–1422
Charles VII 1422–61
Louis XI 1461–83
Charles VIII 1483–98
Louis XII 1498–1515
François I 1515–47
Henri II 1547–59
François II 1559–60
Charles IX 1560–74
Henri III 1574–89
Henri IV 1589–1610
Louis XIII 1610–43
Louis XIV 1643–1715
Louis XV 1715–74
Louis XVI 1774–92
(Louis XVII nominally 1793–95)

FIRST REPUBLIC
The Convention 1792–1795
Directorate 1795–99
Consulate (three consuls) 1799–1804

EMPEROR (FIRST EMPIRE)
Napoleon I (Bonaparte) 1804–14

KING
Louis XVIII 1814–15

EMPERORS (FIRST EMPIRE)
Napoleon I (restored) 1815
(Napoleon II nominally 1815, for 16 days)

KINGS
Louis XVIII (restored) 1815–24
Charles X 1824–30
(Louis XIX nominally 1830, for 1 day)
(Henri V nominally 1830, for 8 days)
Louis-Philippe 1830–48

PRESIDENT OF SECOND REPUBLIC
Louis-Napoleon Bonaparte 1848–52

EMPEROR (SECOND EMPIRE)
Napoleon III (Louis-Napoleon Bonaparte) 1852–70

PRESIDENTS OF THIRD REPUBLIC
Adolphe Thiers 1871–73
Patrice Mac-Mahon, duc de Magenta 1873–79
Jules Grévy 1879–87
Sadi Carnot 1887–94 (assassinated)
Jean Casimir-Périer 1894–95
Félix Faure 1895–99
Émile Loubet 1899–1906
Armand Fallières 1906–13
Raymond Poincaré 1913–20
Paul Deschanel 1920
Alexandre Millerand 1920–24
Gaston Doumergue 1924–31
Paul Doumer 1931–32 (assassinated)
Albert Lebrun 1932–40

FRENCH STATE (at Vichy)
Philippe Pétain 1940–44

HEADS OF PROVISIONAL GOVERNMENT
General Charles de Gaulle 1944–46
Félix Gouin 1946

Georges Bidault 1946
Vincent Auriol 1946
Léon Blum 1946–47

PRESIDENTS OF FOURTH REPUBLIC
Vincent Auriol 1947–54
René Coty 1954–58

PRESIDENTS OF FIFTH REPUBLIC
General Charles de Gaulle 1959–69
Georges Pompidou 1969–74
Valéry Giscard d'Estaing 1974–81
François Mitterand 1981–

PRIME MINISTERS OF THIRD REPUBLIC
In all there were 88 PMs of the Third Republic; the more notable included:
Léon Gambetta 1881–82
Georges Clemenceau 1906–09, 1917–20
Aristide Briand 1909–11, 1913, 1915–17, 1921–22, 1925–26, 1929
Raymond Poincaré 1912–13, 1922–24, 1926–29
Édouard Herriot 1924–25, 1926, 1932
Pierre Laval 1931–32, 1935–36
Édouard Daladier 1933, 1934, 1938–40
Léon Blum 1936–37, 1938

HEADS OF GOVERNMENT OF FRENCH STATE
The head of the Vichy government was the Vice President of the Council; occupants of the post included:
Pierre Laval 1940; 1942–44

PRIME MINISTERS OF FOURTH REPUBLIC
In all there were 24 PMs of the Fourth Republic; the more notable included:
Robert Schuman 1947–1948; 1948
Pierre Mendès-France 1954–55
General Charles de Gaulle 1958–59

PRIME MINISTERS OF FIFTH REPUBLIC
Michel Debré *Gaullist* 1959–62
Georges Pompidou *Gaullist* 1962–68
Maurice Couve de Murville *Gaullist* 1968–69
Jacques Chaban-Delmas *Gaullist* 1969–72
Pierre Messmer *Gaullist* 1972–74
Jacques Chirac *Gaullist* 1974–76
Raymond Barre *np* 1976–81
Pierre Mauroy *Soc* 1981–84
Laurent Fabius *Soc* 1984–86
Jacques Chirac *Gaullist* 1986–88
Michel Rocard *Soc* 1988–91
Edith Cresson *Soc* 1991–

Key: *np* = non-party
Soc = Socialist

GERMANY
KINGS OF PRUSSIA
Friedrich I 1701–13
Friedrich Wilhelm I 1713–40
Friedrich II (*Frederick the Great*) 1740–86
Friedrich Wilhelm II 1786–97
Friedrich Wilhelm III 1797–1840
Friedrich Wilhelm IV 1840–61
Wilhelm I 1861–71 when he also became Emperor of Germany

EMPERORS OF GERMANY
Wilhelm I 1871–88
Friedrich III 1888
Wilhelm II 1888–1918

PROVISIONAL GOVERNMENT
Six-man ruling council 1918–19

PRESIDENTS
Friedrich Ebert 1919–25
Marshal Paul von Beneckendorff und von
Hindenburg 1925–34

**LEADERS OF THE THIRD GERMAN
REICH**
Adolf Hitler 1934–45
Admiral Karl Dönitz 1945 (6 days)

ALLIED OCCUPATION
1945–49

PRESIDENTS OF FEDERAL REPUBLIC
Prof. Theodor Heuss 1949–59
Dr Heinrich Lübke 1959–69
Dr Gustav Heinemann 1969–74
Walter Scheel 1974–79
Karl Carstens 1979–84
Richard von Weizsaecker 1984–

CHANCELLORS OF THE GERMAN EMPIRE
Otto, Prince von Bismarck-Schönhausen 1871–90
Count Leo von Caprivi 1890–94
Prince Chlodwig von Hohenlohe-Schillingsfürst
1894–1900
Prince Bernhard von Bülow 1900–09
Theobald von Bethmann-Hollweg 1909–17
Dr George Michaelis 1917
Count Georg von Hertling 1917
Prince Maximilian of Baden 1918
Friedrich Ebert 1918

CHANCELLORS OF THE REPUBLIC
Six man ruling council 1918–19
Philipp Scheidemann *SPD* 1919
Gustav Bauer *SPD* 1919–20
Hermann Müller *SPD* 1920
Konstantin Fehrenbach *Centre-Cath* 1920–21
Dr Joseph Wirth *Centre* 1921–22
Dr Wilhelm Cuno *np* 1922–23
Dr Gustav Stresemann *DVolk* 1923
Dr Wilhelm Marx *Centre* 1923–25
Dr Hans Luther *np* 1925–26
Dr Wilhelm Marx *Centre* 1926–28
Hermann Müller *SPD* 1928–30
Dr Heinrich Brüning *Centre* 1930–32
Franz von Papen *Nat* 1932
General Curt von Schleider *np* 1932–33
Adolf Hitler *Nazi* 1933–34

THE THIRD GERMAN REICH
1934–45 (see above)

ALLIED OCCUPATION
1945–49 (see above)

FEDERAL GERMAN CHANCELLORS
Konrad Adenauer *CDU* 1949–63
Prof Ludwig Erhard *CDU* 1963–1966
Dr Kurt Georg Kiesinger *CDU* 1966–1969
Dr Willy Brandt *SPD* 1969–1974
Walter Scheel *FDP* 1974
Helmut Schmidt *SPD* 1974–82
Helmut Kohl *CDU* 1982–

Key: *Cath* = Catholic
CDU = Christian Democrat (conservative)
DVolk = German People's Party
Nat = National Party
np = non-party
SPD = Social Democrat
FDP = Free Democratic Party

EAST GERMANY
The German Democratic Republic (East Germany),
which was established in the Soviet zone of occupation in 1949, united with the Federal Republic of
Germany in October 1990. Effective power was held
by the leader of the Socialist Unity Party (the
Communist Party); the more notable included:

Walter Ulbricht 1950–71
Erich Honecker 1971–89

GREECE

KINGS
Othon 1832–62
Giorgios I 1863–1913
Konstantinos I 1913–17
Alexandros 1917–20
Konstantinos I (restored) 1920–22
Giorgios II 1922–24

PRESIDENTS OF THE HELLENIC REPUBLIC
Admiral Pavlos Kondoriotis 1924–26
Gen. Theodoros Pangalos 1926
Admiral Pavlos Kondoriotis 1926–29
Alexandros Zaimis 1929–35

KINGS
Giorgios II (restored) 1935–47
Pavlos 1947–64
Konstantinos II 1964–73

PRESIDENTS OF THE HELLENIC REPUBLIC
Giorgios Papadopoulos 1973
Gen Phaedon Gizikis 1973–74
Mikael Stassinopoulos 1974–75
Konstantinos Tsatos 1975–85
Christos Sartzetakis 1985–90
Konstantinos Karamanlis 1990–

PRIME MINISTERS OF GREECE
(since 1967)
Giorgios Papadopoulos *military* 1967–73
Spyros Markezinis *military* 1973
Adamantios Androutsopoulos *military* 1973–74
Konstantinos Karamanlis *NDP* 1974–80
Giorgios Rallis *NDP* 1980–84
Andreas Papandreou *PASOK* 1984–89
Tzannis Tzannetakis *caretaker* 1989
Yannis Grivas *caretaker* 1989–90
Xenefon Zolotas *caretaker* 1990
Konstantinos Mitsotakis *NDP* 1990–

Key: *NDP* = New Democracy Party
(conservative)
PASOK = Panhellic Socialist Movement

THE HOLY ROMAN EMPIRE

EMPERORS
Karl I (*Charlemagne*) 800–814
Ludwig I (*Louis I*) 814–840
Lothar I 840–855
Ludwig II (*Louis II*) 855–875
Karl II (*Charles II*) 875–877
Karl III (*Charles III*) 877–887
Arnulf 887–898
Ludwig III* (*Louis III*) 899–911
Konrad I* 911–918
Heinrich I* (*Henry I*) 919–936
Otto I 936–973
Otto II 973–983
Otto III 983–1002

Heinrich II (*Henry II*) 1002–24
Konrad II 1024–39
Heinrich III (*Henry III*) 1039–56
Heinrich IV (*Henry IV*) 1056–1105
Heinrich V (*Henry V*) 1105–25
Lothar II 1125–37
Konrad III* 1138–52
Friedrich I (*Frederick Barbarossa*) 1152–90
Heinrich VI (*Henry VI*) 1190–97
Philipp* 1198–1208
Otto IV 1198–1215
Friedrich II (*Frederick II*) 1215–50
Konrad IV* 1250–54
Konrad V 1254 (claimant)
Richard* 1257
Alfons* 1267
Rudolf I* 1273–91
Adolf* 1292–98
Albrecht I (*Albert I*) 1298–1308
Heinrich VII (*Henry VII*) 1308–13
Ludwig IV (*Louis IV*) 1314–47
Karl IV (*Charles IV*) 1347–78
Wenzel 1378–1400
Rupprecht Klem* 1400–10
Sigismund 1410–37
Albrecht II* (*Albert II*) 1438–39
Friedrich III (*Frederick III*) 1440–93
Maximilian I 1493–1519
Karl V (*Charles V*) 1519–55
Ferdinand I 1556–64
Maximilian II 1564–76
Rudolf II 1576–1612
Matthias 1612–19
Ferdinand II 1619–37
Ferdinand III 1637–57
Leopold I 1658–1705
Joseph I 1705–11
Karl VI (*Charles*) 1711–40
Karl III (*Charles*) 1742–45
Franz I Stephan (*Francis I*) 1745–65
Joseph II 1765–90
Leopold II 1790–92
Franz II (*Francis II*) 1792–1806 when he abdicated
  and abolished the Holy Roman Empire; see Austria

Key: * = emperor-elect. Frederick III was the last emperor to go to Rome for coronation; all succeeding emperors assumed the imperial title upon election.

HUNGARY

PRESIDENTS
Zoltan Tildy *SP* 1946–48
Arpad Szakasits *Comm* 1948–50
Sándor Rónai *Comm* 1950–52
István Dobi *Comm* 1952–67
Pál Losonczi *Comm* 1967–87
Károly Németh *Comm* 1987–88
Bruno Straub *Comm* 1988–89
Mátyás Szuros *caretaker* 1989–90
Arpad Goncz *AFD* 1990–

PRIME MINISTERS
(since 1948)
István Dobi *Comm* 1948–52
Mátyás Rákosi *Comm* 1952–53
Imre Nagy *Comm* 1953–55
Andras Hegedus *Comm* 1955–56
Imre Nagy *Comm* 1956
Janos Kadar *Comm* 1956–58
Dr Ferenc Münnich *Comm* 1958–61
Janos Kadar *Comm* 1961–65
Gyula Kallai *Comm* 1965–67

Jenö Fock *Comm* 1967–75
György Lázár *Comm* 1975–87
Károly Grocz *Comm* 1987–88
Miklos Németh *Comm* 1988–90
Joszef Antall *DF* 1990–

LEADERS OF THE COMMUNIST PARTY
From 1948 to 1989 the effective ruler of Hungary was the leader of Socialist Workers' (Communist) Party; the more notable included:
Mátyás Rákosi 1949–53 and 1953–56
Janos Kadar 1956–88

Key: *AFD* = Alliance of Free Democrats (liberal)
Comm = Communist
DF = Democratic Forum (conservative)
SP = Smallholders' Party

INDIA

MOGUL EMPERORS
Babur 1526–30
Humayan 1530–39
(Interregnum – usurpers 1539–55)
Humayan (restored) 1555–56
Akbar 1556–1605
Jahangir 1605–27
Dawar Bakhsh 1627–28
Shah Jahan 1628–58
Aurangzeb Alamgir I 1658–1707
Bahadur Shah I (*also known as Shah Alam I*) 1707–12
Farrukhsiyar 1713–19 (assassinated)
Rafi-ud-Daulat 1719
Shah Jahan II 1719 (assassinated)
Nikusiyar 1719 (assassinated)
Muhammad Shah 1719–20
Muhammad Ibrahim 1720
Muhammad Shah (restored) 1720–48
Ahmad Shah 1748–54
Alamgir II 1754–59 (assassinated)
Shah Jahan III 1759–60
Shah Alam II 1759–1802 when he became King of Delhi

PRESIDENTS
Dr Rajendra Prasad 1949–62
Dr Sarvapalli Radhakrishnan 1962–67
Dr Zahir Hussain 1967–69
Varahgiri Venkata Giri 1969–74
Fakhruddin Ali Ahmed 1974–77
Basappa Danappa Jatti 1977
Neelam Sanjiva Reddy 1977–82
Giani Zail Singh 1982–87
Ramaswamy Venkataraman 1987–

PRIME MINISTERS
Jawaharlal Nehru *Congress* 1949–64
Gulzarilal Nanda *Congress* 1964
Lal Bahadur Shastri *Congress* 1964–66
Gulzarilal Nanda *Congress* 1966
Indira Gandhi *Congress (I)* 1966–77
Morarji Desai *Janata* 1977–79
Charan Singh *Janata* 1979–80
Indira Gandhi *Congress (I)* 1980–84
  (assassinated)
Rajiv Gandhi *Congress (I)* 1984–89
Vishwanath Pratap Singh *Coalition* 1989–90
Chandra Shekhar *Coalition* 1990–91

INDONESIA

PRESIDENTS
Dr Muhammad Achmed Sukarno *np* 1949–67
Gen Raden Suharto *Golkar* 1967–
Key: *np* = non-party

THE REPUBLIC OF IRELAND

PRESIDENTS

Dr Douglas Hyde 1938–45
Sean Thomas O'Kelly 1945–59
Eamon de Valera 1959–73
Erskine Childers 1973–74
Cearbhall O'Dalaigh 1974–76
Dr Patrick Hillery 1976–90
Mary Robinson 1990–

EXECUTIVE PRESIDENTS

(Heads of government)
Arthur Griffith *Rep* 1922
Michael Collins *Rep* 1922
William Thomas Cosgrave *FG* 1922–32
Eamon de Valera *FF* 1932–37

PRIME MINISTERS (Taoiseach)

Eamon de Valera *FF* 1937–48
John Costello *FG* 1948–51
Eamon de Valera *FF* 1951–54
John Costello *FG* 1954–57
Eamon de Valera *FF* 1957–59
Sean Lemass *FF* 1959–66
John Mary (Jack) Lynch *FF* 1966–73
Liam Cosgrave *FG-Lab* 1973–77
John Mary (Jack) Lynch *FF* 1977–79
Charles Haughey *FF* 1979–81
Garret Fitzgerald *FG-Lab* 1981–82
Charles Haughey *FF* 1982
Garret Fitzgerald *FG-Lab* 1982–87
Charles Haughey *FF* 1987–

Key: *FF* = Fianna Fail
FG = Fine Gael
Lab = Labour
Rep = Republican

ISRAEL

PRIME MINISTERS

David Ben Gurion *Mapai* 1948–53
Moshe Sharett *Mapai* 1953–55
David Ben Gurion *Mapai* 1955–63
Levi Eshkol *Mapai* 1963–69
Gen. Yigal Allon *Lab* 1969
Golda Meir *Lab* 1969–74
Itzhak Rabin *Lab* 1974–77
Menahem Begin *Likud* 1977–83
Itzhak Shamir *Likud* 1983–84
Shimon Peres *Coalition* 1984–86
Itzhak Shamir *Coalition** 1986–

Key: *Lab* = Labour (formed from Mapai in 1968)
* from 1990 *Likud*

ITALY

KINGS

Vittorio Emanuele II 1861–78
Umberto I 1878–1900 (assassinated)
Vittorio Emanuele III 1900–46
Umberto II 1946

PRESIDENTS

Alcide de Gasperi 1946
Enrico de Nicola 1946–48
Luigi Einaudi 1948–55
Giovanni Gronchi 1955–62
Antonio Segni 1962–64
Giuseppe Saragat 1964–71
Giovanni Leone 1971–78
Amintore Fanfani (acting) 1978

Alessandro Pertini 1978–85
Francesco Cossiga 1985–

PRIME MINISTERS OF THE KINGDOM OF ITALY

In all there were 42 PMs of the Kingdom of Italy; the more notable included:
Camillo Benso, Count Cavour 1861
Francesco Crispi 1879–81, 1893–96
Giovanni Giolitti 1892–93, 1903–05, 1911–14, 1920–21
Francesco Nitti 1919–20
Benito Mussolini 1922–43
Marshal Pietro Badoglio 1943–44
Alcide de Gasperi 1945–46

PRIME MINISTERS OF THE REPUBLIC

Alcide de Gasperi *CD Coalition* 1946–53
Giuseppe Pella *CD* 1953–54
Amintore Fanfani *CD* 1954
Mario Scelba *CD* 1954–55
Antonio Segni *CD* 1955–57
Adone Zoli *CD* 1957–58
Amintore Fanfani *CD Coalition* 1958–59
Antonio Segni *CD* 1959–60
Fernando Tambroni *CD* 1960
Amintore Fanfani *CD Coalition* 1960–63
Giovanni Leone *CD Coalition* 1963
Aldo Moro *CD Coalition* 1963–68
Giovanni Leone *CD* 1968
Mariano Rumor *CD Coalition* 1968–70
Emilio Colombo *CD* 1970–72
Giulio Andreotti *CD Coalition* 1972–73
Mariano Rumor *CD Coalition* 1973–74
Aldo Moro *CD Coalition* 1974–76
Giulio Andreotti *CD Coalition* 1976–79
Ugo La Malfa *Rep Coalition* 1979
Giulio Andreotti *CD Coalition* 1979
Francesco Cossiga *CD Coalition* 1979–80
Arnaldo Forlani *CD Coalition* 1980–81
Giovanni Spaldolini *Coalition* 1981–82
Amintore Fanfani *CD Coalition* 1982–83
Bettino Craxi *Soc Coalition* 1983–87
Amintore Fanfani *CD Coalition* 1987
Giovanni Goria *CD Coalition* 1987–88
Ciriaco De Mita *CD Coalition* 1988–90
Giulio Andreotti *CD Coalition* 1990–

Key: *CD* = Christian Democrat
Coalition = some of the periods indicated as government by coalition included more than one coalition
Rep = Republican
Soc = Socialist

JAPAN

EMPERORS

(since 1763)
Gosakuramachi 1763–71
Gomomozono 1771–79
Kokaku 1779–1817
Ninko 1817–46
Komei (*personal name* Osahito) 1846–66
Meiji (*personal name* Mutsuhito) 1867–1912
Taisho (*personal name* Yoshihito) 1912–26
Showa (*personal name* Hirohito) 1926–89
Heisei (*personal name* Akihito) 1989–

PRIME MINISTERS OF JAPAN

(since 1945)
Kijuro Shidehara *np* 1945–46
Ichiro Hatayma *Lib* 1946
Shigeru Yoshida *np* 1946–47
Tetsu Katayama *Soc* 1947–48

Hitoshi Ashida *Coalition* 1948
Shigeru Yoshida *Lib* 1948–55
Ichiro Hatoyama *Lib-Dem* 1955–56
Tanzan Ishibashi *Lib-Dem* 1956–1957
Nobusuke Kishi *Lib-Dem* 1957–60
Hayeto Ikeda *Lib-Dem* 1960–64
Eisaku Sato *Lib-Dem* 1964–72
Kakeui Tanaka *Lib-Dem* 1972–74
Takeo Miki *Lib-Dem* 1974–76
Takeo Fukuda *Lib-Dem* 1976–78
Masayoshi Ohira *Lib-Dem* 1978–80
Zenko Suzuki *Lib-Dem* 1980–82
Yasuhiro Nakasone *Lib-Dem* 1982–87
Noboru Takeshita *Lib-Dem* 1987–89
Sosuke Uno *Lib-Dem* 1989
Toshiki Kaifu *Lib-Dem* 1989–

Key: *Lib* = Liberal
Lib-Dem = Liberal Democrat
np = non-party
Soc = Socialist

KOREA

PRESIDENTS OF SOUTH KOREA

Dr Syngman Rhee *Lib* 1948–60
Huh Chung *acting* 1960
Yun Po Sun *Dem* 1960–62
Gen. Park Chung Hi *military-DRP* 1962–1980
  (assassinated)
Choi Kyu Hah *DRP* 1980
Gen. Chun Doo Hwan *military-DJP* 1980–87
Roh Tae Woo *DJP/DLP* 1987–

Key: *Lib* = Liberal
DJP = Democratic Justice Party
DLP = Democratic Liberal Party
DRP = Democratic Reunification Party
Dem = Democrat

LUXEMBOURG

GRAND DUKES

Guillaume I 1815–40
Guillaume II 1840–49
Guillaume III 1849–90
Adolphe I 1890–1905
Guillaume IV 1905–12
Marie-Adélaïde 1912–19
Charlotte 1919–64
Jean I 1964–

PRIME MINISTERS

(since 1945)
Pierre Dupong *SC* 1945–54
Joseph Bech *SC* 1954–58
Pierre Frieden *SC* 1958–69
Pierre Werner *SC* 1969–74
Gaston Thorn *Dem* 1974–79
Pierre Werner *SC* 1979–84
Jacques Santer *SC* 1984–

Key: *Dem* = Democratic Party (liberal)
SC = Social Christian Party (conservative)

MEXICO

PRESIDENTS

There have been over 80 presidents of Mexico; the
more notable before 1924 included:
Gen. Antonio López de Santa Anna 1833–35, 1839,
  1842, 1843, 1844
Gen. Benito Juárez 1858, 1859–61, 1867–72
Gen. Porfirio Díaz 1877–80, 1884–1911

Presidents since 1924
Gen. Plutarco Elías Calles *PRI* 1924–28
Emilio Portes Gil *PRI* 1928–30
Pascual Ortiz Rubio *PRI* 1930–32
Gen. Abelardo Rodríguez *PRI* 1932–34
Gen. Lázardo Cárdenas *PRI* 1934–40
Gen. Manuel Ávila Camacho *PRI* 1940–46
Miguel Alemán Valdès *PRI* 1946–52
Adolfo Ruiz Cortines *PRI* 1952–58
Adolfo López Mateos *PRI* 1958–64
Dr Gustavo Díaz Ordaz *PRI* 1964–70
Luis Echeverría Alvárez *PRI* 1970–76
José López Portillo *PRI* 1976–82
Miguel de la Madrid Hurtado *PRI* 1982–88
Carlos Salinas de Gortari *PRI* 1988–

Key: *PRI* = Institutional Revolutionary Party
  (so-named since 1929)

NETHERLANDS

KINGS AND QUEENS

Willem I 1815–40
Willem II 1840–49
Willem III 1849–90
Wilhelmina 1890–1948
Juliana 1948–80
Beatrix 1980–

PRIME MINISTERS

(since 1945)
Prof. Willem Schermerhorn *Lab-Cath* 1945–46
Dr Louis Beel *Cath-Lab* 1946–48
Dr Willem Drees *Lab-Cath* 1948–58
Dr Louis Beel *Cath-led coalition* 1958–59
Prof. Jan de Quay *Cath-led coalition* 1959
Dr Louis Beel *Cath-led coalition* 1959
Prof. Jan de Quay *Cath-led coalition* 1959–63
Dr Victor Marijnen *Cath-led coalition* 1963–65
Dr Joseph Cals *Cath-led coalition* 1965–66
Prof. Jelle Zijstra *Cath-led coalition* 1966–67
Petrus de Jong *Cath-led coalition* 1967–71
Barend Biesheuvel *Cath-led coalition* 1971–73
Dr Johannes den Uyl *Lab-led coalition* 1973–77
Andreas van Agt *CDA-led coalition* 1977–82
Rudolph Lubbers *CDA-led coalition* 1982–

Key: *Cath* = Catholic (merged with another confessional party to form Christian Democratic Appeal
in 1980)
CD = Christian Democratic Appeal
Lab = Labour

NEW ZEALAND

PRIME MINISTERS OF THE DOMINION

Sir Joseph Ward *Lib* 1907–12
William Fergusson Massey *Ref* 1912–25
Sir Francis Bell *Ref* 1925
Joseph Gordon Coates *Ref* 1925–28
Sir Joseph Ward *UP* 1928–30
George Forbes *Ref-UP* 1930–35
Michael Joseph Savage *Lab* 1935–40
Peter Fraser *Lab* 1940–49
Sir Sidney George Holland *Nat* 1949–57
Sir Keith Jacka Holyoake *Nat* 1957
Sir Walter Nash *Lab* 1957–60
Sir Keith Jacka Holyoake *Lab* 1960–72
Sir John Ross Marshall *Nat* 1972
Norman Eric Kirk *Lab* 1972–74
Hugh Watt (acting PM) *Lab* 1974

Wallace Rowling *Lab* 1974–75
Sir Robert David Muldoon *Nat* 1975–84
David Lange *Lab* 1984–89
Geoffrey Palmer *Lab* 1989–90
Michael Moore *Lab* 1990
Jim Bolger *Nat* 1990–

Key: *Lab* = Labour
Lib = Liberal (succeeded by the United Party in 1927)
Nat = National Party (formed from a merger of the Reform Party and the United Party in 1936)
Ref = Reform Party
UP = United Party

NIGERIA

PRESIDENTS

Dr Nnamdi Azikiwe *NCNC* 1963–66
Dr Nwafor Orizu *caretaker* 1966
Gen Johnson Aguiyi-Ironsi* *military* 1966 (assassinated)
Gen Yakubu Gowon* *military* 1966–75
Brig Murtala Ramat Muhammad* *military* 1975–76 (assassinated)
Lieut-Gen Olusegun Obasanjo* *military* 1976–79
Alhaji Shehu Shagari *NPN* 1979–83
Gen Muhammadu Buhari *military* 1983–85
Gen Ibrahim Babangida *military* 1985–

Key: *NCNC* = National Council for Nigeria and the Cameroons
NPN = National Party of Nigeria
*Heads of state who did not assume the presidency.

NORWAY

KINGS

(since the restoration of independence)
Haakon VII 1905–51
Olav V 1951–91
Harald V 1991–

PRIME MINISTERS

(since 1945)
Einar Gerhardsen *Lab* 1945–51
Oscar Torp *Lab* 1951–55
Einar Gerhardsen *Lab* 1955–63
Johan Lyng *Lib-CP-CPP* 1963
Einar Gerhardsen *Lab* 1963–65
Per Borten *CP-led coalition* 1965–71
Trygve Bratteli *Lab* 1971–72
Lars Korvald *Coalition* 1972–73
Trygve Bratteli *Lab* 1973–76
Odvar Nordli *Lab* 1976–81
Gro Harlem Bruntland *Lab* 1981
Kare Willoch *Con (from 1983 coalition)* 1981–86
Gro Harlem Bruntland *Lab* 1986–89
Jan Syse *Con-led coalition* 1989–90
Gro Harlem Brundtland *Lab* 1990–

Key: *CP* = Centre Party
CPP = Christian People's Party
Lab = Labour
Lib = Liberal

PAKISTAN

PRESIDENTS

Maj. Gen. Iskander Mirza 1956–58
Gen. Muhammad Ayub Khan 1958–69
Gen. Agha Muhammad Yahya Khan 1969–71
Zulfiqar Ali Bhutto 1971–73
Fazal Elahi Chaudhri 1973–78

Gen. Muhammad Zia ul-Haq 1978–88
Ghulam Ishaq Khan 1988–

PRIME MINISTERS OF PAKISTAN

Liaquat Ali Khan *ML* 1947–51
Khwaja Nazimuddin *ML* 1951–53
Mohammed Ali *ML* 1953–55
Chaudhri Muhammad Ali *ML* 1955–56
Hussein Shaheed Suhrawardy *AL* 1956–57
Ismael Ibrahim Chundrigar *AL* 1957
Malik Firoz Khan Noon *AL* 1957–58
Gen. Muhammad Ayub Khan *military* 1958–69
Gen. Agha Muhammad Yahya Khan *military* 1969–71
Nural Amin *caretaker* 1971
Zulfiqar Ali Bhutto *PPP* 1971–77
Gen. Muhammad Zia ul-Haq *military* 1977–85
Muhammad Khan Junejo *ML* 1985–88
Gen. Muhammad Zia ul-Haq *military* 1988
(Period without a PM 1988)
Benazir Bhutto *PPP* 1988–90
Ghulam Mustafa Jatoi *IDA* 1990
Nawaz Sharif *IDA* 1990–

Key: *AL* = Awami League
IDA = Islamic Democratic Alliance
ML = Muslim League
PPP = Pakistan People's Party

THE PHILIPPINES

PRESIDENTS

Manuel Roxas *Lib* 1946–48
Elphino Quirino *Lib* 1948–53
Rámon Magsayay *Nat* 1953–1957
Carlos Polestico Garcia *Nat* 1957–61
Diosdado Macapagal *Lib* 1961–65
Ferdinand Marcos *Nat* 1965–86
Corazón Aquino *UNIDO* 1986–

Key: *Lib* = Liberal
Nat = Nacionalista
UNIDO = Nacionalista Party

POLAND

PRESIDENTS

Marshal Jósef Pilsudski* *PPS* 1918–22
Gabriel Narutowicz *caretaker* 1922
Stanislaw Wojciechowski *np* 1922–26
Prof Ignacy Móscicki *np* 1926–39
(Poland under German occupation 1939–44)
Boleslaw Bierut *Comm* 1944–52
Aleksander Zawadski *Comm* 1952–64
Edward Ochab *Comm* 1964–68
Marshal Marian Spychalski *Comm* 1968–70
Józef Cyrankiewicz *Comm* 1970–72
Prof Henryk Jablonski *Comm* 1972–85
Gen Wojciech Jaruzelski *Comm* 1985–1990
Lech Walesa *Solidarity* 1990–

LEADERS OF THE COMMUNIST PARTY

From 1945 to 1989 the effective ruler of Poland was the leader of the Communist Party; the more notable included:
Boleslaw Bierut 1945–56
Wladyslaw Gomulka 1956–70
Edward Gierek 1970–89

Key: *Comm* = Communist
np = non-party
PPS = Polish Socialist Party
* Pilsudski was military dictator of Poland 1926–35

PORTUGAL

PRESIDENTS

Dr Téofilo Braga 1910–11
Dr Manuel da Arriaga 1911–15
Dr Téofilo Braga 1915
Dr Bernardino Luis Machado 1915–17
Major Cardoso da Silva Pais 1917–18
Admiral João da Canto e Castro 1918–19
Dr Antonio José de Almeida 1919–23
Manoel Teixeira Gomes 1923–25
Dr Bernardino Luis Machado 1925–26
Commander José Mendes Cabecadas 1926
Gen. Manoel Gomes de Costa 1926
Gen. Oscar de Carmona 1926–51
Marshal Francisco Craveiro Lopes 1951–58
Admiral Américo Tomás 1958–74
Gen. Antonio de Spinola 1974
Gen. Francisco da Costa Gomes 1974–76
Gen. Antonio Ramalho Eanes 1976–86
Dr Mário Lopés Soares 1986–

PRIME MINISTERS

(since 1932)
Dr Antonio de Oliveira Salazar *NU* 1932–68
Prof. Marcelo Caetano *NU* 1968–74
Gen. Antônio de Spinola *MFA* 1974
Prof. Adelino da Palma Carlos *MFA-Soc-Comm* 1974
Col. Vasco dos Santos Goncalves *Soc-Comm* 1974–75
Admiral José Pinheiro de Azevedo *Soc-Comm* 1975–1976
Commander Vasco Almeida e Costa *Coalition* 1976
Dr Mário Lopés Soares *Soc* 1976–78
Prof. Carlos Mota Pinto *Coalition* 1978–79
Dr Maria de Lourdes Pintasilgo *caretaker* 1979–80
Dr Francisco sá Carneiro *AD* 1980
Dr Francisco Pinto Balsemão *AD* 1980–82
Prof. Diogo Freitas do Amaral *Coalition* 1982–83
Dr Mário Lopés Soares *Soc* 1983–85
Anibal Cavaco Silva *PSD* 1985–

Key: *AD* = Democratic Alliance
Comm = Communist
MFA = Armed Forces Movement
NU = National Union
PSD = Social Democrat
Soc = Socialist

ROMAN EMPIRE

CLAUDIAN EMPERORS

Augustus (Octavianus) 27 BC–AD 14
Tiberius AD 14–37
Gaius Caesar (*better known as Caligula*) 37–41 (assassinated)
Claudius I 41–54
Nero 54–68

LATER CLAUDIAN EMPERORS

Galba 68–69 (assassinated)
Otho 69
Vitellius 69 (assassinated)

FLAVIAN EMPERORS

Vespasianus 69–79
Titus 79–81
Domitianus 81–96 (assassinated)

ANTONINE EMPERORS

Nerva 96–98
Trajanus 98–117
Hadrianus 117–38
Antoninus Pius 138–61

Lucius Verus 161–69
Marcus Aurelius 169–180
Commodus 180–192 (assassinated)

EMPERORS OF AFRICAN AND ASIAN ORIGIN

(including co-emperors)
Pertinax 193 (assassinated)
Didius Julianus 193 (assassinated)
Septimus Severus 193–211
Marcus Aurelius Antoninus I (*better known as Caracalla*) 211–217 (assassinated)
Geta 209–12 (assassinated)
Macrinus 217–19 (assassinated)
Marcus Aurelius Antoninus II (*better known as Elagabalus*) 218–22 (assassinated)
Severus Alexander 222–35 (assassinated)
Maximinus 235–38 (assassinated)
Gordianus I 238
Gordianus II 238 (assassinated)
Pupienus Maximus 238 (assassinated)
Balbinus 238 (assassinated)
Gordianus III 238–44 (assassinated)
Philippus 244–49 (assassinated)
Decius 249–51 (assassinated)
Gallius 251–53 (assassinated)
Hostilianus 251
Aemilianus 253 (assassinated)
Valerianus 253–60
Gallienus 260–68 (assassinated)

ILLYRIAN EMPERORS

Claudius II 268–70
Quintillus 270
Aurelianus 270–75 (assassinated)
Ulpia Severina (Empress) 275
Tacitus 275–76 (assassinated)
Florianus 276 (assassinated)
Probus 276–82 (assassinated)
Carus 282–83
Carinus 283–85
Numerianus 283–84 (assassinated)

COLLEGIATE EMPERORS

(More than one emperor ruled at a time in a 'collegiate' system.)
Diocletianus 284–305
Maximianus 286–305
Constantius I (*better known as Chlorus*) 305–06
Galerius 305–11
Severus 306–07
Maximianus (restored) 307–08
Maximinus Daia 308–13
Constantinus I (*Constantine the Great*) 312–37
Maxentius 306–12 (assassinated)
Licinius 308–24
Constantinus II 337–40
Constans I 337–50 (assassinated)
Constantius II 337–61
Magnus Magnentius 350–53
Julianus (*Julian the Apostate*) 361–63
Jovianus 363–64

COLLEGIATE EMPERORS

(ruling part of the Roman Empire)
Valentinianus I 364–75 (Emperor in the West)
Gratianus 367–83 (Emperor in the West; assassinated).
Valens 364–78 (Emperor in the East)
Procopius 365–66 (Emperor in the East)
Valentinianus II 375–85 (Emperor in the West)
Magnus Maximus 383–88 (Emperor in the West)
Flavius Victor 386–88 (Emperor in the West)
Theodosius I 379–95 (Emperor in the East 379–88; in the East and in the West 388–95)

Valentinianus II (restored) 388–92 (Emperor in the West)
Eugenius 392–94 (Emperor in the West)
Honorius 393–95 (Emperor in the West; in 395 he became emperor of the Western Roman Empire)

EMPERORS OF THE WESTERN EMPIRE

Honorius 395–423
Constantius III 421
Valentinianus III 425–55 (assassinated)
Petronius Maximus 455 (assassinated)
Avitus 455–56
Majorianus 457–61
Libius Severus 461–65
Anthemius 467–72
Olybrius 472
Glycerius 473–74
Julius Nepos 474–75
Romulus Augustus 475–76 when he was expelled from Rome by the Vandals

ROMANIA

KINGS

Carol I 1881–1914
Ferdinand I 1914–27
Mihai I 1927–30
Carol II 1930–40
Mihai I (restored) 1940–47

PRESIDENTS

Prof. Constantin Parhon *Comm* 1948–52
Dr Petru Groza *Comm* 1952–58
Ion Gheorghe Maurer *Comm* 1958–61
Gheorghe Gheorghiu-Dej *Comm* 1961–65
Chivu Stoica *Comm* 1965–67
Nicolae Ceausescu *Comm* 1967–89
Ion Iliescu *NSF* 1989–

Key: *Comm* = Communist
NSF = National Salvation Front

RUSSIA AND USSR

TSARS

(from 1533; after 1721 the tsar was officially styled emperor)
Ivan IV (*Ivan the Terrible*) 1533–84
Fyodor I (*Theodore I*) 1584–98
Boris (*Boris Godunov*) 1598–1605
Fyodor II (*Theodore II*) 1605
Dmitri 1605–06
Vasily IV 1606–10
Mikhail (*Michael*) 1613–45
Aleksey (*Alexei*) 1645–76
Fyodor III (*Theodore III*) 1676–82
Ivan V (co-Tsar) 1682–96
Piotr I (*Peter I; the Great*) 1682–1725
Ekaterina I (*Catherine I*) 1725–27
Piotr II (*Peter II*) 1727–30
Anna 1730–40
Ivan VI 1740–41
Elisaveta (*Elizabeth*) 1741–62
Piotr III (*Peter III*) 1762
Ekaterina II (*Catherine II; the Great*) 1762–96
Pavel (*Paul*) 1796–1801
Aleksandr I (*Alexander I*) 1801–25
Nikolai I (*Nicholas I*) 1825–55
Aleksandr II (*Alexander II*) 1855–81
Aleksandr III (*Alexander III*) 1881–94
Nikolai II (*Nicholas II*) 1894–1917

PRESIDENTS OF THE RUSSIAN FEDERATION

Yakov Sverdlov 1917–19
Mikhail Kalinin 1919–22

PRESIDENTS OF THE USSR

Mikhail Kalinin 1922–46
Nikolai Shvernik 1946–53
Marshal Kliment Voroshilov 1953–60
Leonid Ilich Brezhnev 1960–64
Anastas Mikoyan 1964–65
Nikolai Podgorny 1965–77
Leonid Ilich Brezhnev 1977–82
Vassili Kuznetsov (acting President) 1982–83
Yuri Andropov 1983–84
Konstantin Chernenko 1984–85
Andrei Gromyko 1985–88
Mikhail Gorbachov 1988–

PRIME MINISTERS

Vladymir Ilich Lenin (*b. Ulyanov*) 1917–24
Aleksey Rykov 1924–30
Genrikh Yagoda 1930–31
Vyacheslav Molotov 1931–41
Marshal Josif Djugashvili Stalin 1941–53
Georgy Malenkov 1953–55
Marshal Nikolai Bulganin 1955–58
Nikita Khruschev 1958–64
Alexei Kosygin 1964–80
Nikolai Tikhonov 1980–85
Nikolai Ryzhkov 1985–1990
Valentin Pavlov 1990–

USSR COMMUNIST PARTY LEADERS

Marshal Josif Djugashvili Stalin 1922–53
Nikita Khruschev 1953–64
Leonid Brezhnev 1964–82
Yuri Andropov 1982–84
Konstantin Chernenko 1984–85
Mikhail Gorbachov 1985–

SOUTH AFRICA

PRESIDENTS

Charles Robberts Swart *Nat* 1961–67
Jozua François Naudé *Nat* 1967–68
Jacobus Johannes Fouché *Nat* 1968–75
Dr Nicolaas Diederich *Nat* 1975–78
Balthazar John Vorster *Nat* 1978–79
Marais Viljoen *Nat* 1979–84
Pieter Willem Botha *Nat* 1984–89
Frederick Willem de Klerk *Nat* 1989–

PRIME MINISTERS

(the post of Prime Minister was abolished in 1984)
Gen Louis Botha *SA* 1910–19
Field Marshal Jan Christiaan Smuts *SA* 1919–24
Gen James Barry Munnik Hertzog *Nat* 1924–39
Field Marshal Jan Christiaan Smuts *UP* 1939–48
Daniel François Malan *Nat* 1948–54
Johannes Gerhardhus Strijdom *Nat* 1954–58
Charles Robberts Swart *Nat* 1958
Hendrik Verwoerd *Nat* 1958–66 (assassinated)
Balthazar John Vorster *Nat* 1966–78
Pieter Willem Botha *Nat* 1978–84

Key: *Nat* = Nationalist Party
SA = South African Party
UP = United Party

SPAIN

KINGS

(including joint sovereigns)

Fernando V (*Ferdinand V*) 1474–1516
Isabel I (*Isabella I*) 1474–1504
Juana 1504–55
Felipe I (*Philip I*) 1504–06
Carlos I (*Emperor Charles V*) 1516–56
Felipe II (*Philip II*) 1556–98
Felipe III (*Philip III*) 1598–1621
Felipe IV (*Philip IV*) 1621–65
Carlos II (*Charles II*) 1665–1700
Felipe V (*Philip V*) 1700–24
Luis 1724
Felipe V (restored) 1724–46
Fernando VI (*Ferdinand VI*) 1746–59
Carlos III (*Charles III*) 1759–88
Carlos IV (*Charles IV*) 1788–1808
Fernando VII (*Ferdinand VII*) 1808
Carlos IV (restored) 1808
José (*Joseph Bonaparte*) 1808–13
Fernando VII (restored) 1813–33
Isabel II (*Isabella II*) 1833–68
(Regency 1868–70)
Amadeo 1870–73

PRESIDENTS OF THE FIRST REPUBLIC

Estanislao Figueras y Moragas 1873
Francisco José Pi y Margall 1873
Nicolás Salmerón 1873
Emilio Castelar y Ripoli 1873–74
Marshal Francisco Serrano y Domínguez 1874

KINGS

Alfonso XII 1874–85
Maria Cristina 1885–86
Alfonso XIII 1886–1931

PRESIDENTS OF THE SECOND REPUBLIC

Niceto Alcalá Zamora y Torres 1931–36
Manuel Azaña y Diaz 1936

LEADER (Caudillo) OF THE SPANISH STATE

Gen. Francisco Franco y Bahamonde 1936–75

KING

Juan Carlos I 1975–

PRIME MINISTERS

(since 1936)

Gen. Francisco Franco y Bahamonde (Head of
   government) *Falange* 1936–73
Admiral Luis Carrero Blanco *Falange* 1973
Carlos Arias Navarro *np* 1973–75
Adolfo Suárez González *UCD* 1975–81
Leopoldo Calvo Sotelo *UCD* 1981–82
Felipe González *PSOE* 1982–

Key: *np* = non-party
PSOE = Socialist Workers' Party
UCD = Centre Democrat

SWEDEN

KINGS

(since 1523)
Gustaf I Adolf 1523–60
Eric XIV 1560–68
Johan III 1568–92
Sigismund 1592–99
Carl IX 1599–1611
Gustaf II Adolf (*Gustavus Adolphus*) 1611–32

Christina 1632–54
Carl X Gustaf 1654–60
Carl XI 1660–97
Carl XII 1697–1718
Ulrika Eleonora 1718–26
Fredrik 1726–51
Adolf Fredrik 1751–71
Gustaf III 1771–92 (assassinated)
Gusfaf IV Adolf 1792–1809
Carl XIII 1809–18
Carl XIV Johan 1818–44
Oscar I 1844–59
Carl XV 1859–72
Oscar II 1872–1907
Gustaf V 1907–50
Gustaf VI 1950–73
Carl XVI Gustaf 1973–

PRIME MINISTERS

(since 1932)
Per Albin Hansson *Soc Dem* 1932–46
Tage Erlander *Soc Dem* 1946–69
Olof Palme *Soc Dem* 1969–76
Nils Olof Thorbjörn Fälldin *Centre* 1976–78
Ola Ullsten *Lib* 1978–79
Nils Olof Thorbjörn Fälldin *Centre* 1979–82
Olof Palme *Soc Dem* 1982–86 (assassinated)
Ingvar Carlsson *Soc Dem* 1986–

Key: *Lib* = Liberal
Soc Dem = Social Democrat

TURKEY

PRESIDENTS

Kemal Atatürk (*b. Mustafa Kemal*) *RPP* 1923–38
Gen Ismet Inönü *RPP* 1938–50
Gen Celal Bayer *DP* 1950–60
Gen Cemal Gürsel *military* 1960–66
Gen Cevdet Sunay *np* 1966–73
Admiral Fahri Korutürk *np* 1973–80
Gen Kenan Evren *military* 1980–89
Turgat Özal *MP* 1989–

Key: *DP* = Democrat
MP = Motherland Party
np = non-party
RPP = Republican People's Party

UNITED STATES OF AMERICA

PRESIDENTS

George Washington *Fed* 1789–97
John Adams *Fed* 1797–1801
Thomas Jefferson *Dem Rep* 1801–09
James Madison *Dem Rep* 1809–17
James Monroe *Dem Rep* 1817–25
John Quincy Adams *Dem Rep* 1825–29
Andrew Jackson *Dem* 1829–37
Martin Van Buren *Dem* 1837–41
William H. Harrison *Whig* 1841
John Tyler *Whig* 1841–45
James K. Polk *Dem* 1845–49
Zachary Taylor *Whig* 1849–50
Millard Fillmore *Whig* 1850–53
Franklin Pierce *Dem* 1853–57
James Buchanan *Dem* 1857–61
Abraham Lincoln *Rep* 1861–65 (assassinated)
Andrew Johnson *Dem U* 1865–69
Ulysses Simpson Grant (*b. Hiram Grant*)
   Rep 1869–77

UNITED KINGDOM

KINGS AND QUEENS
(1066–1603 of England, 1603–1707 of England and Scotland, 1707–1801 of Great Britain, from 1801 of the United Kingdom)
William I 1066–87
William II 1087–1100
Henry I 1100–35
Stephen 1135–41 and 1141–54
Matilda 1141 (April–Nov)
Henry II 1154–89
Richard I 1189–99
John 1199–1216
Henry III 1216–72
Edward I 1272–1307
Edward II 1307–27
Edward III 1327–77
Richard II 1377–99
Henry IV 1399–1413
Henry V 1413–22
Henry VI 1422–61 and 1470–71
Edward IV 1461–70 and 1471–83
Edward V 1483 (April–June)
Richard III 1483–85
Henry VII 1485–1509
Henry VIII 1509–47
Edward 1547–53
Jane 1553 (July; 9 days)
Mary I 1553–58
Elizabeth I 1558–1603
James I (VI of Scotland) 1603–25
Charles I 1625–49
Charles II 1660–1685 (*de jure* from 1649)
James II 1685–88
William III 1689–1702 with
Mary II 1689–94

Anne 1702–14
George I 1714–27
George II 1727–60
George III 1760–1820
George IV 1820–30
William IV 1830–37
Victoria 1837–1901
Edward VII 1901–10
George V 1910–36
Edward VIII 1936 (Jan–Dec)
George VI 1936–52
Elizabeth II 1952–

PRIME MINISTERS (since 1902)
Arthur James Balfour (Conservative) 1902–05
Sir Henry Campbell-Bannerman (Liberal) 1905–08
Herbert Henry Asquith (Liberal) 1908–16
David Lloyd George (Liberal-led coalition) 1916–22
Andrew Bonar Law (Conservative) 1922–23
Stanley Baldwin (Conservative) 1923–24
Ramsay MacDonald (Labour) 1924 (Jan–Nov)
Stanley Baldwin (Conservative) 1924–29
Ramsay MacDonald (Labour) 1929–35
Stanley Baldwin (National government) 1935–37
Neville Chamberlain (National government) 1937–40
Winston Churchill (Coalition) 1940–45
Clement Atlee (Labour) 1945–51
Sir Winston Churchill (Conservative) 1951–55
Sir Anthony Eden (Conservative) 1955–57
Harold MacMillan (Conservative) 1957–63
Sir Alexander Douglas-Home (Conservative) 1963–64
Harold Wilson (Labour) 1964–70
Edward Heath (Conservative) 1970–74
Harold Wilson (Labour) 1974–76
James Callaghan (Labour) 1976–79
Margaret Thatcher (Conservative) 1979–90
John Major (Conservative) 1990–

See History Section of United Kingdom Chapter

Rutherford B. Hayes *Rep* 1877–81
James A. Garfield *Rep* 1881 (assassinated)
Chester A. Arthur *Rep* 1881–85
Grover Cleveland *Dem* 1885–89
Benjamin Harrison *Rep* 1889–93
Grover Cleveland *Dem* 1893–97
William McKinley *Rep* 1897–1901 (assassinated)
Theodore Roosevelt *Rep* 1901–09
William H. Taft *Rep* 1909–13
Woodrow Wilson *Dem* 1913–21
Warren Gamaliel Harding *Rep* 1921–23
Calvin Coolidge *Rep* 1923–29
Herbert C. Hoover *Rep* 1929–33
Franklin Delano Roosevelt *Dem* 1933–45
Harry S. Truman *Dem* 1945–53
Dwight D. Eisenhower *Rep* 1953–61
John Fitzgerald Kennedy *Dem* 1961–63 (assassinated)
Lyndon B. Johnson *Dem* 1963–69
Richard M. Nixon *Rep* 1969–74
Gerald R. Ford (*b. Leslie Lynch King*) *Rep* 1974–77
Jimmy Carter *Dem* 1977–81
Ronald Reagan *Rep* 1981–89
George Bush *Rep* 1989–

Key: *Dem* = Democrat
Dem Rep = Democratic Republican
Dem U = Democrat (Union)
Fed = Federalist
Rep = Republican

YUGOSLAVIA

KINGS
Peter I 1918–21
Alexander I 1921–34 (assassinated)
Peter II 1934–41(–45 in exile)

PRESIDENTS
Dr Ivan Ribar 1945–53
Marshal Josip Broz Tito 1953–1980
Collective presidency* 1980–

PRIME MINISTERS
(since 1963 when the post of premier was reintroduced)
Petar Stambolic *LC* 1963–67
Mika Spiljak *LC* 1967–69
Mitja Ribicic *LC* 1969–71
Dzemal Bijedic *LC* 1971–77
Veselin Djuranovic *LC* 1977–82
Milka Planinc *LC* 1982–86
Branko Mikulic *LC* 1986–89
Ante Markovic *LC/ARF* 1989–

Key: *ARF* = Alliance of Reform Forces
LC = League of Communists

*The president of the collective presidency holds office for one year according to a fixed sequence of republics and provinces.

THE ECONOMIC WORLD

NATIONAL ECONOMIES

GROSS NATIONAL PRODUCT

The best means of measuring the economic power of a country is its gross national product. Gross national product (GNP) comprises the *gross domestic product* (GDP) plus income received from abroad, less payments made abroad. Gross domestic product is the sum of all output produced domestically. It is usually stated to be equal to total domestic expenditure plus the value of exports, less the value of imports. There are, however, three ways of estimating GDP in use by different countries:
– *the expenditure basis* estimates GDP on the basis of how much money has been spent in a country;
– *the output basis* estimates GDP on the basis of value of goods that have been sold in a country;
– *the income basis* estimates GDP on the basis of how much income has been earned in a country.

National income is the sum of all income received in an economy during a particular period of time, usually one financial year. It is equal to GNP less depreciation.

NATIONAL ECONOMIES

The following entries list the sovereign states of the world, and their major dependencies. The gross national product and the gross national product per head of population is given for each state. Figures are also given for total imports and total exports and for the major contributors to each category. In most cases the figures given are for 1988, the most recent year for which official figures are available. (* = estimated figure.)

Afghanistan
Gross national product ($ million): 3860 (1986)*
Gross national product per head ($): 234 (1986)
Total imports ($ million): 851 (1986) of which wheat (1983/84) 4.5%, vegetable oil (1983/84) 3.6%.
Principal trading partner: USSR.
Total exports ($ million): 536 (1986) of which natural gas (1983/84) 41.9%, dried fruit (1983/84) 26.3%.
Principal trading partner: USSR.

Albania
Gross national product ($ million): 2800 (1986)
Gross national product per head ($): 930 (1986)
Total imports ($ million): 441 (1987) of which machinery and equipment (1988) 28.5%, fuels, minerals and metals (1988) 25.2%.
Principal trading partners: Greece, Yugoslavia, Germany.
Total exports ($ million): 441 (1987) of which minerals and metals (1988) 39.8%, raw materials (1988) 16.1%.
Principal trading partners: Italy, Greece, Yugoslavia.

Algeria
Gross national product ($ million): 63 560 (1987)
Gross national product per head ($): 2760 (1987)
Total imports ($ million): 9177 (1986) of which cereals (1985) 10.5%, industrial machinery and equipment (1985) 7.5%.
Principal trading partners: France, Germany, Italy.
Total exports ($ million): 7831 (1986) of which

refined petroleum products (1985) 37.8%, gas (1985) 34.7%.
Principal trading partners: France, Italy, USA.

Andorra
Gross national product ($ million): 340 (1982)
Gross national product per head ($): 9000 (1982)
Total imports ($ million): 624 (1986).
Total exports ($ million): 19 (1986)
No breakdown of these figures is available.
Principal trading partners: France, Spain.

Angola
Gross national product ($ million): 1665 (1988)*
Gross national product per head ($): 190 (1988)
Total imports ($ million): 682 (1983) of which transport equipment (1985) 15.8%, electrical equipment (1985) 13.0%.
Principal trading partners: USA, Portugal, Brazil.
Total exports ($ million): 1840 (1983) of which mineral products (1985) 93.0%, pearls, gemstones, precious metals (1985) 3.3%.
Principal trading partners: USA, Spain, Portugal.

Antigua and Barbuda
Gross national product ($ million): 230 (1988)
Gross national product per head ($): 2800 (1988)
Total imports ($ million): 199 (1986) of which minerals, fuels, lubricants, etc. (1984) 25.0%, machinery and transport equipment (1984) 21.8%.
Principal trading partners: USA, UK.
Total exports ($ million): 25 (1986) of which manufactured articles (1984) 37.9%, machinery and transport equipment (1984) 30.1%.
Principal trading partners: Trinidad, USA, Barbados.

Argentina
Gross national product ($ million): 83 040 (1988)
Gross national product per head ($): 2640 (1988)
Total imports ($ million): 5819 (1987) of which electrical machinery 1987 (11.5%), minerals, fuels and oils, and bituminous substances (1987) 11.4%.
Principal trading partners: USA, Brazil, Germany.
Total exports ($ million): 6360 (1987) of which residues and waste from food industry (1987) 13.8%, cereals (1987) 11.7%.
Principal trading partners: USA, USSR, Netherlands, Brazil.

Australia
Gross national product ($ million): 204 446 (1988)
Gross national product per head ($): 12 390 (1988)
Total imports ($ million): 26 980 (1987) of which road vehicles and parts (1988/89) 10.2%, petroleum and petroleum products (1988/89) 7.5%.
Principal trading partners: USA, Japan, UK, Germany.
Total exports ($ million): 26 455 (1987) of which textile fibres and waste (1987/88) 13.7%, ores and metal scrap (1987/88) 12.9%.
Principal trading partners: Japan, USA, New Zealand.

Austria
Gross national product ($ million): 117 644 (1988)
Gross national product per head ($): 15 560 (1988)

Total imports ($ million): 32 679 (1987) of which road vehicles and parts (1988) 10.9%, electrical machinery (1988) 6.8%.
Principal trading partners: Germany, Italy, Switzerland.
Total exports ($ million): 27 171 (1987) of which iron and steel (1988) 7.5%, electrical machinery (1988) 7.4%.
Principal trading partners: Germany, Italy, Switzerland.

Bahamas
Gross national product ($ million): 2611 (1988)
Gross national product per head ($): 10 570 (1988)
Total imports ($ million): 3289 (1986) of which crude petroleum (1985) 55.4%, petroleum products (1985) 18.1%.
Principal trading partners: Iran, Nigeria, USA.
Total exports ($ million): 2702 (1986) of which crude petroleum (1985) 68.0%, petroleum products (1985) 20.1%.
Principal trading partners: USA, UK.

Bahrain
Gross national product ($ million): 3027 (1987)
Gross national product per head ($): 6610 (1987)
Total imports ($ million): 2613 (1987) of which non-petroleum products (1987) 53.8%, petroleum products (1987) 46.2%.
Principal trading partners: Japan, UK, USA.
Total exports ($ million): 2244 (1987) of which petroleum products (1987) 82.6%, aluminium products (1987) 6.8%.
Principal trading partners: Saudi Arabia, Iran, Kuwait.

Bangladesh
Gross national product ($ million): 18 310 (1988)
Gross national product per head ($): 170 (1988)
Total imports ($ million): 2665 (1987) of which basic manufactures (1987/88) 24.4%, food and live animals (1987/88) 19.1%.
Principal trading partners: Japan, USA, Singapore.
Total exports ($ million): 1075 (1987) of which jute goods (1987/88) 22.6%, fish and fish preparations (1987/88) 12.3%.
Principal trading partners: USA, Iran, Pakistan.

Barbados
Gross national product ($ million): 1530 (1988)
Gross national product per head ($): 5990 (1988)
Total imports ($ million): 515 (1987) of which machinery and transport equipment (1988) 23.1%, basic manufactures (1988) 19.2%.
Principal trading partners: USA, Japan.
Total exports ($ million): 156 (1987) of which basic manufactures (1988) 24.3%, sugar (1988) 17.8%.
Principal trading partners: USA, UK.

Belgium
Gross national product ($ million): 143 560 (1988)
Gross national product per head ($): 14 550 (1988)
Total imports ($ million): 78 780 (1987) of which road vehicles and parts (1987) 13.5%, chemicals and chemical products (1987) 10.4%.
Principal trading partners: Germany, Netherlands, France, UK.
Total exports ($ million): 78 624 (1987) of which chemicals and chemical products (1987) 12.6%, cars (1987) 11.5.
Principal trading partners: France, Germany, Netherlands, UK.

Belize
Gross national product ($ million): 264 (1988)
Gross national product per head ($): 1460 (1988)
Total imports ($ million): 143 (1987) of which manufactured goods (1987) 29.3%, food (1987) 22.1%.
Principal trading partners: USA, UK, Netherlands Antilles.
Total exports ($ million): 99 (1987) of which sugar (1987) 31.5%, garments (1987) 15.7%.
Principal trading partners: USA, UK, Trinidad.

Benin
Gross national product ($ million): 1530 (1988)
Gross national product per head ($): 340 (1988)
Total imports ($ million): 294 (1983) of which beverages and tobacco (1984) 14.8%, refined petroleum products (1984) 11.0%.
Principal trading partners: France, Netherlands, Japan.
Total exports ($ million): 67 (1983) of which fuels (1984) 44.7%, raw cotton (1984) 19.9%.
Principal trading partners: Germany, France, Netherlands.

Bhutan
Gross national product ($ million): 202 (1987)
Gross national product per head ($): 150 (1987)
Total imports ($ million): 48 (1986) of which aircraft (1983) 10.8%, diesel fuel (1983) 10.3%.
Principal trading partner: India.
Total exports ($ million): 22 (1986) of which cement (1983) 25.3%, talcum powder (1983) 10.3%
Principal trading partner: India.

Bolivia
Gross national product ($ million): 3930 (1988)
Gross national product per head ($): 570 (1988)
Total imports ($ million): 767 (1987) of which raw materials for industry (1987) 31.6%, industrial goods (1987) 23.2%.
Principal trading partners: USA, Argentina, Brazil.
Total exports ($ million): 569 (1987) of which metallic minerals (1988) 45.5%, natural gas (1988) 35.8%.
Principal trading partners: Argentina, USA, Netherlands.

Botswana
Gross national product ($ million): 1191 (1987)
Gross national product per head ($): 1050 (1987)
Total imports ($ million): 944 (1988) of which food, beverages and tobacco (1987) 16.7%, machinery and electrical goods (1987) 16.2%.
Principal trading partners: South Africa, UK.
Total exports ($ million): 1351 (1988) of which diamonds (1987) 84.5%; copper-nickel matte (1987) 4.4%.
Principal trading partners: Switzerland, USA, South Africa.

Brazil
Gross national product ($ million): 328 860 (1988)
Gross national product per head ($): 2280 (1988)
Total imports ($ million): 16 299 (1987) of which mineral products (1988) 31.5%, chemicals (1988) 14.7%.
Principal trading partners: USA, Argentina, Germany, Iraq.
Total exports ($ million): 26 225 (1987) of which processed foods (1987) 17.2%, metals (1987) 11.8%.
Principal trading partners: USA, Japan, Netherlands, Germany.

Brunei
Gross national product ($ million): 3317 (1987)
Gross national product per head ($): 14 120 (1987)
Total imports ($ million): 615 (1985) of which
machinery and transport equipment (1986) 38.0%,
basic manufactures (1986) 21.1%.
Principal trading partners: Singapore, Japan, USA.
Total exports ($ million): 2972 (1985) of which
natural gas (1986) 52.9%, crude petroleum (1986)
40.6%.
Principal trading partners: Japan, Thailand.

Bulgaria
Gross national product ($ million): 67 590 (1988)
Gross national product per head ($): 7510 (1988)
Total imports ($ million): 16 095 (1987) of which
machinery and equipment (1987) 43.5%, fuels, min-
erals, raw materials and metals (1987) 32.4%.
Principal trading partners: USSR, Germany,
Czechoslovakia.
Total exports ($ million): 15 921 (1987) of which
foodstuffs, beverages and tobacco products (1987)
25.1%, hoisting and hauling equipment (1987) 10.5%.
Principal trading partners: USSR, Germany,
Czechoslovakia.

Burkina Faso
Gross national product ($ million): 1960 (1988)
Gross national product per head ($): 230 (1988)
Total imports ($ million): 405 (1986) of which
manufactured goods (1987) 26.1%, chemicals (1987)
13.5%.
Principal trading partners: France, Ivory Coast,
USA.
Total exports ($ million): 83 (1986) of which
cotton (ginned) (1987) 43.2%, manufactured goods
(1987) 31.7%.
Principal trading partners: Ivory Coast, Taiwan,
France.

Burma (Myanmar)
Gross national product ($ million): 7450 (1986)
Gross national product per head ($): 200 (1986)
Total imports ($ million): 306 (1987) of which
raw materials for industry (1988) 29.7%, machinery
and equipment (1988) 27.8%.
Principal trading partners: Japan, Singapore.
Total exports ($ million): 222 (1987) of which
rice and rice products (1983/84) 40.8%, teak (1983/84)
24.5%.
Principal trading partners: Singapore, China.

Burundi
Gross national product ($ million): 1200 (1988)
Gross national product per head ($): 230 (1988)
Total imports ($ million): 212 (1987) of which
petroleum and vehicles (1987) 37.3%; food and tex-
tiles (1987) 35.6%.
Principal trading partners: Belgium, Germany.
Total exports ($ million): 86 (1987) of which
coffee (1987) 80.9%, tea (1987) 6.9%.
Principal trading partners: Germany, Belgium.

Cambodia
Gross national product ($ million): 585* (1985)
Gross national product per head ($): 80 (1985)
Total imports ($ million): 118 (1985) of which
road vehicles and parts (1985) 17.4%, iron and steel
(1985) 9.2%.
Principal trading partners: USSR, Vietnam.
Total exports ($ million): 12 (1985) of which
iron and steel manufactures (1985) 36.7%, clothing

and accessories (1985) 14.9%.
Principal trading partners: USSR, Vietnam.

Cameroon
Gross national product ($ million): 11 270 (1988)
Gross national product per head ($): 1010 (1988)
Total imports ($ million): 1749 (1987) of which
road transport equipment (1986) 11.3%, iron and
steel (1986) 6.0%.
Principal trading partners: France, Germany,
Japan.
Total exports ($ million): 829 (1987) of which
crude petroleum (1986) 35.6%; coffee (1986) 16.3%.
Principal trading partners: Netherlands, France,
USA.

Canada
Gross national product ($ million): 437 471 (1988)
Gross national product per head ($): 16 760 (1988)
Total imports ($ million): 87 578 (1987) of which
motor vehicle parts (1988) 10.9%, automobiles and
chassis (1988) 9.3%.
Principal trading partners: USA, Japan, UK,
Germany.
Total exports ($ million): 94 402 (1987) of which
automobiles and chassis (1988) 12.6%, motor vehicle
parts (1988) 6.1%.
Principal trading partners: USA, Japan, UK,
Germany.

Cape Verde
Gross national product ($ million): 170 (1987)
Gross national product per head ($): 500 (1987)
Total imports ($ million): 82 (1987) of which
foodstuffs and beverages (1988) 27.2%, machinery
(1988) 16.0%.
Principal trading partners: Portugal, Germany.
Total exports ($ million): 5.6 (1987) of which
bananas (1988) 36.7%, frozen tuna (1988) 30.5%.
Principal trading partners: Portugal, Central Afri-
can Republic, Guinea-Bissau.

Central African Republic
Gross national product ($ million): 1080 (1988)
Gross national product per head ($): 390 (1988)
Total imports ($ million): 252 (1986) of which
food (1988/89) 20.5%, chemicals and plastics
(1988/89) 15.6%.
Principal trading partners: France, Japan.
Total exports ($ million): 131 (1986) of which
coffee (1988/89) 47.9%, diamonds (1988/89) 25.2%.
Principal trading partners: France, Belgium.

Chad
Gross national product ($ million): 850 (1988)
Gross national product per head ($): 160 (1988)
Total imports ($ million): 162 (1984) of which
petroleum products (1983) 16.8%, cereal products
(1983) 16.8%.
Principal trading partners: France, Nigeria.
Total exports ($ million): 138 (1984) of which
raw cotton (1983) 91.1%, live cattle (1983) 1.2%.
Principal trading partners: France, Cameroon,
Nigeria.

Chile
Gross national product ($ million): 19 220 (1988)
Gross national product per head ($): 1510 (1988)
Total imports ($ million): 4023 (1987) of which
technical and electrical equipment (1985) 23.8%,
mineral products (1985) 20.2%.

Principal trading partners: USA, Japan, Brazil.
Total exports ($ million): 5102 (1987) of which
copper (1985) 41.2%, meat and fish meal (1985) 7.2%.
Principal trading partners: USA, Japan, Germany.

China, People's Republic
Gross national product ($ million): 356 490 (1988)
Gross national product per head ($): 330 (1988)
Total imports ($ million): 43 393 (1987) of which
machinery and transport equipment (1988) 30.2%,
basic manufactures (1988) 18.8%.
Principal trading partners: Japan, USA, Hong Kong,
Germany.
Total exports ($ million): 39 542 (1987) of which
basic manufactures (1988) 22.1%, light industrial
products (1988) 15.9%.
Principal trading partners: Hong Kong, Japan, USA.

China (Taiwan)
Gross national product ($ million): 125 360 (1988)
Gross national product per head ($): 6335 (1988)
Total imports ($ million): 55 734 (1987) of which
electronic components (1988) 7.9%, thermoplastic
resins (1988) 1.4%.
Principal trading partners: Japan, USA.
Total exports ($ million): 67 755 (1987) of which
calculating machines (1988) 8.9%, plastic articles
(1988) 8.3%.
Principal trading partners: USA, Japan, Hong Kong.

Colombia
Gross national product ($ million): 37 210 (1988)
Gross national product per head ($): 1240 (1988)
Total imports ($ million): 3907 (1987) of which
machinery (1988) 24.0%, chemicals (1988) 11.8%.
Principal trading partners: USA, Brazil, Venezuela.
Total exports ($ million): 4642 (1987) of which
coffee (1988) 32.7%, petroleum and products (1988)
25.7%.
Principal trading partners: USA, Japan, Nether-
lands.

Comoros
Gross national product ($ million): 200 (1988)
Gross national product per head ($): 440 (1988)
Total imports ($ million): 52 (1987) of which
rice (1988) 15.6%, vehicles (1988) 7.9%.
Principal trading partner: France.
Total exports ($ million): 12 (1987) of which
vanilla (1988) 77.7%, ylang-ylang (1988) 11.6%.
Principal trading partners: USA, France.

Congo
Gross national product ($ million): 1950 (1988)
Gross national product per head ($): 930 (1988)
Total imports ($ million): 751 (1985) of which
machinery (1985) 20.4%, food, beverages and
tobacco (1985) 15.4.
Principal trading partners: France, Italy, USA.
Total exports ($ million): 1077 (1985) of which
petroleum and products (1985) 93.3%, wood (1985)
2.5%.
Principal trading partners: USA, Spain, France.

Costa Rica
Gross national product ($ million): 4690 (1988)
Gross national product per head ($): 1760 (1988)
Total imports ($ million): 1130 (1986) of which
primary and intermediate goods, including petrol-
eum (1988) 48.9%, consumer goods (1988) 22.3%.
Principal trading partners: USA, Japan, Guatemala.

Total exports ($ million): 1026 (1986) of which
coffee (1988) 26.0%, bananas (1988) 20.5%.
Principal trading partners: USA, Germany,
Guatemala.

Cuba
Gross national product ($ million): 15 152 (1985)
Gross national product per head ($): 1509 (1985)
Total imports ($ million): 7600 (1986) of which
minerals, fuels and lubricants (1987) 34.7%,
machinery and transport equipment (1988) 30.7%.
Principal trading partners: USSR, Germany, Japan.
Total exports ($ million): 5401 (1986) of which
sugar (1987) 73.8%, petroleum products (1987) 6.7%.
Principal trading partners: USSR, Germany,
Bulgaria.

Cyprus
Gross national product ($ million): 4320 (1988)
Gross national product per head ($): 6260 (1988)
Total imports ($ million): 1484 (1987) of which
textile and textile articles (1988) 10.7%, road vehicle
parts (1988) 10.6%.
Principal trading partners: Turkey, UK, Germany.
Total exports ($ million): 608 (1987) of which
clothing (1988) 32.1%, footwear (1988) 6.9%.
Principal trading partners: UK, Turkey, Italy.

Czechoslovakia
Gross national product ($ million): 158 168 (1988)
Gross national product per head ($): 10 140 (1988)
Total imports ($ million): 23 284 (1987) of which
machinery and transport equipment (1987) 35.7%,
fuels (1987) 27.9%.
Principal trading partners: USSR, Germany, Poland.
Total exports ($ million): 23 016 (1987) of which
machinery and transport equipment (1987) 58.1%,
consumer goods (1987) 15.8%.
Principal trading partners: USSR, Germany, Poland.

Denmark
Gross national product ($ million): 94 792 (1988)
Gross national product per head ($): 18 470 (1988)
Total imports ($ million): 25 345 (1987) of which
consumer goods (1988) 24.1%, machinery and capital
equipment (1988) 11.5%.
Principal trading partners: USA, Germany, Nether-
lands, Sweden.
Total exports ($ million): 25 499 (1987) of which
meat (1988) 10.0%, industrial machinery (1988)
7.6%.
Principal trading partners: USA, Germany, Norway,
Sweden.

Faeroe Islands
Gross national product ($ million): 686 (1987); *Gross
national product per head ($):* 14 600 (1987); *Total
imports ($ million):* 334 (1986) of which transport
equipment (1988) 22.4%, household goods for consumption (1988) 25.1%. Principal trading partners:
Denmark, Norway. *Total exports ($ million):* 245
(1986) of which frozen fish fillets (1987) 21.7%, ships
(1987) 19.9%. Principal trading partners: Denmark,
Germany.

Greenland
Gross national product ($ million): 465 (1988); *Gross
national product per head ($):* 8780 (1988); *Total
imports ($ million):* 363 (1986) of which household
consumption goods (1988) 35.8%, construction
industry goods (1988) 13.6%. Principal trading partners: Denmark, Norway. *Total exports ($ million):*

238 (1986) of which shrimps, prawns and molluscs (1988) 63.8%, zinc (1988) 14.9%. Principal trading partners: Denmark, Germany.

Djibouti
Gross national product ($ million): 407* (1988)
Gross national product per head ($): 1118 (1985)
Total imports ($ million): 225 (1984) of which food and beverages (1986) 27.9%, machinery and electrical machinery (1986) 10.8%.
Principal trading partners: France, Ethiopia, Japan.
Total exports ($ million): 13 (1984) of which live animals (1983) 30.8%, food and food products (1983) 18.6%.
Principal trading partners: France, Somalia.

Dominica
Gross national product ($ million): 130 (1988)
Gross national product per head ($): 1650 (1988)
Total imports ($ million): 56 (1986) of which machinery and transport equipment (1985) 22.5%, food (1985) 19.3%.
Principal trading partners: Canada, Trinidad, St Lucia.
Total exports ($ million): 42 (1986) of which bananas (1985) 48.2%, coconut-based soaps (1985) 25.0%.
Principal trading partners: UK, Jamaica, Trinidad.

Dominican Republic
Gross national product ($ million): 4690 (1988)
Gross national product per head ($): 680 (1988)
Total imports ($ million): 1512 (1987) of which crude petroleum and petroleum products (1985) 33.2%, foodstuffs (1985) 13.4%.
Principal trading partners: USA, Venezuela, Mexico.
Total exports ($ million): 718 (1987) of which raw sugar (1985) 21.5%, ferronickel (1985) 16.3%.
Principal trading partners: USA, Netherlands.

Ecuador
Gross national product ($ million): 10 920 (1988)
Gross national product per head ($): 1080 (1988)
Total imports ($ million): 2052 (1987) of which industrial raw materials (1988) 41.3%, industrial capital goods (1988) 23.6%.
Principal trading partners: USA, Japan, Germany, Brazil.
Total exports ($ million): 1989 (1987) crude petroleum (1988) 39.9%, shrimp (1988) 17.7%.
Principal trading partners: USA, Germany, Panama.

Egypt
Gross national product ($ million): 33 250 (1988)
Gross national product per head ($): 650 (1988)
Total imports ($ million): 11 941 (1987) of which foodstuffs (1986/87) 30.2%, machinery and transport equipment (1986/87) 25.2%.
Principal trading partners: USA, Germany, Italy.
Total exports ($ million): 4352 (1987) of which petroleum and petroleum products (1986/87) 50.7%, raw cotton (1986/87) 15.0%.
Principal trading partners: Italy, France, Romania.

El Salvador
Gross national product ($ million): 4780 (1988)
Gross national product per head ($): 950 (1988)
Total imports ($ million): 885 (1986) of which chemical products (1988) 16.1%, transport equipment (1988) 10.8%.

Principal trading partners: USA, Guatemala.
Total exports ($ million): 713 (1986) of which coffee (1988) 58.4%, raw sugar (1988) 3.2%.
Principal trading partners: USA, Germany.

Equatorial Guinea
Gross national product ($ million): 140 (1988)
Gross national product per head ($): 350 (1988)
Total imports ($ million): 39 (1987) of which machinery and transport equipment (1984) 25.4%, fuels and lubricants (1984) 20.1%.
Principal trading partners: Spain, Gabon, Cameroon.
Total exports ($ million): 50 (1987) of which cocoa (1984) 42.4%, fuels and lubricants (1984) 19.5%.
Principal trading partners: Spain, Netherlands, Germany.

Ethiopia
Gross national product ($ million): 5760 (1988)
Gross national product per head ($): 120 (1988)
Total imports ($ million): 1097 (1986) of which food and beverages (1985/86) 24.0%, road transport equipment (1985/86) 13.0%.
Principal trading partners: USSR, USA, Germany, Italy.
Total exports ($ million): 477 (1986) of which coffee (1985/86) 72.0%, animal hides (1985/86) 11.9%.
Principal trading partners: USA, Germany, Djibouti.

Fiji
Gross national product ($ million): 1130 (1988)
Gross national product per head ($): 1540 (1988)
Total imports ($ million): 379 (1987) of which machinery and transport equipment (1988) 21.1%, food, beverages and tobacco (1988) 17.6%.
Principal trading partners: USA, New Zealand, Australia.
Total exports ($ million): 307 (1987) of which sugar (1988) 45.6%, gold (1988) 18.7%.
Principal trading partners: UK, Australia.

Finland
Gross national product ($ million): 92 015 (1988)
Gross national product per head ($): 18 610 (1988)
Total imports ($ million): 19 862 (1987) of which raw materials (1988) 54.4%, consumer goods (1988) 22.8%.
Principal trading partners: Germany, USSR, Sweden, Japan.
Total exports ($ million): 20 061 (1987) of which paper and paper products (1988) 33.4%, metal products and machinery (1988) 31.0%.
Principal trading partners: USSR, Sweden, UK, Germany.

France
Gross national product ($ million): 898 671 (1988)
Gross national product per head ($): 16 080 (1988)
Total imports ($ million): 157 913 (1987) of which machinery (1988) 26.3%, chemicals and chemical products (1988) 16.0%.
Principal trading partners: Germany, Italy, Belgium, USA.
Total exports ($ million): 143 490 (1987) of which machinery (1988) 24.5%, agricultural products (1988) 17.5%.
Principal trading partners: Germany, Italy, Belgium, UK.

French Guiana or Guyane
Gross national product ($ million): 186* (1985).
Gross national product per head ($): 2268 (1985).
Total imports ($ million): 394 (1987) of which food
products (1987) 22.3%, electrical and non-electrical
machinery (1987) 20.9%. Principal trading partners:
France, Trinidad. *Total exports ($ million)*: of which
54 (1987) shrimps, prawns and rice (1987) 70.2%,
wood (1987) 12.7%. Principal trading partners:
France, Trinidad.

French Polynesia
Gross national product ($ million): 1370 (1985). *Gross
national product per head ($)*: 7840 (1985). *Total
imports ($ million)*: 394 (1987) of which machinery
and appliances (1988) 23.5%, food products (1988)
18.6%. Principal trading partners: France, USA,
Australia. *Total exports ($ million)*: 83 (1987) of
which petroleum re-exports (1988) 44.8%, black cul-
tured pearls (1988) 22.2%. Principal trading partners: France, USA, Japan.

Guadeloupe
Gross national product ($ million): 1100 (1985). *Gross
national product per head ($)*: 3300 (1985). *Total
imports ($ million)*: 1040 (1987) of which food (1987)
22.8%, electrical machinery and apparatus (1987)
14.7%. Principal trading partners: France, Martinique. *Total exports ($ million)*: 93 (1987) bananas
(1987) 50.2%, wheat flour (1987) 8.2%. France, Martinique.

Martinique
Gross national product ($ million): 1400 (1985). *Gross
national product per head ($)*: 4280 (1985). *Total
imports ($ million)*: 1119 (1987) of which transport
equipment (1987) 22.2%, food products (1987) 19.0%.
Principal trading partners: France, Venezuela. *Total
exports ($ million)*: 193 (1987) of which bananas
(1987) 48.0%, petroleum products (1987) 14.0%. Principal trading partners: France, Guadeloupe.

Mayotte
Gross national product ($ million): na. *Gross national
product per head ($)*: na. *Total imports ($ million)*:
38.5 (1985) of which food (1985) 23.9%, metals (1985)
15.9%. Principal trading partners: France, South
Africa. *Total exports ($ million)*: 3 (1986) of which
ylang-ylang 18.0%. Principal trading partners:
France, Comoros.

New Caledonia
Gross national product ($ million): 860 (1988). *Gross
national product per head ($)*: 5760 (1988). *Total
imports ($ million)*: 626 (1987) of which food (1988)
20.1%, transportation equipment 1988 (18.1%). Principal trading partners: France, Australia, Japan.
Total exports ($ million): 225 (1987) of which ferro-
nickel and nickel matte (1988) 83.5%. Principal
trading partners: France, USA.

Réunion
Gross national product ($ million): 2120 (1986). *Gross
national product per head ($)*: 3940 (1986). *Total
imports ($ million)*: 1465 (1987) of which food and
agricultural products (1987) 20.7%, electrical and
non-electrical machinery (1987) 15.5%. Principal
trading partners: France, Italy, Bahrain. *Total
exports ($ million)*: 148 (1987) of which sugar (1987)
74.9%; rum (1987) 3.2%. Principal trading partners:
France, Portugal.

St Pierre et Miquelon
Gross national product : na. *Gross national product
per head ($)*: na. *Total imports ($ million)*: 60 (1986).
Principal trading partners: Canada, France. *Total
exports ($ million)*: 8 (1986) of which fish

(1986) 99%. Principal trading partners: USA, France.

Wallis and Futuna Islands
Gross national product ($ million): na. *Gross national
product per head ($)*: na. *Total imports ($ million)*: 13
(1983). Principal trading partner: France. *Total
exports ($ million)*: 0.02 (1983) of which ylang-ylang
18.0%. Principal trading partner: France.

Gabon
Gross national product ($ million): 3200 (1988)
Gross national product per head ($): 2970 (1988)
Total imports ($ million): 976 (1987) of which
machinery and mechanical equipment (1987) 22.2%,
food and agricultural products (1987) 21.4%.
Principal trading partners: France, USA, Japan.
Total exports ($ million): 1974 (1985) of which
crude petroleum and petroleum products (1987)
68.9%, wood (1987) 12.1%.
Principal trading partners: France, USA, Spain.

Gambia
Gross national product ($ million): 180 (1988)
Gross national product per head ($): 220 (1988)
Total imports ($ million): 100 (1986) of which
food (1987) 28.1%, machinery and transport equip-
ment (1987) 22.4%.
Principal trading partners: UK, China, France.
Total exports ($ million): 35 (1986) of which
peanut oil (1987) 16.8%, shelled peanuts (1987)
14.3%.
Principal trading partners: Ghana, Netherlands.

Germany
(Combined figures are given for the former East and
West Germany – import and export figures exclude
inter-German trade.)
Gross national product ($ million): 1 252 205 (1988)
Gross national product per head ($): 25 710 (1988)
Total imports ($ million): 256 882 (1987) of which
road vehicles and parts (1988) 7.1%, petroleum and
products (1988) 5.8%.
Principal trading partners: France, Netherlands,
Italy, UK.
Total exports ($ million): 323 713 (1987) of which
general industrial machinery and equipment (1988)
6.5%, electrical machinery, apparatus and appli-
ances (1988) 6.5%.
Principal trading partners: France, UK, USA,
Netherlands.

Ghana
Gross national product ($ million): 5610 (1988)
Gross national product per head ($): 400 (1988)
Total imports ($ million): 783 (1986) of which
mineral fuels and lubricants (1985) 29.1%;
machinery and transport equipment (1985) 26.4%.
Principal trading partners: UK, Germany, USA.
Total exports ($ million): 862 (1986) of which
cocoa (1985) 59.4%, gold (1985) 15.0%.
Principal trading partners: UK, Netherlands, Japan.

Greece
Gross national product ($ million): 48 040 (1988)
Gross national product per head ($): 4790 (1988)
Total imports ($ million): 13 154 (1987) of which
machinery and transport equipment (1988) 23.0%;
food, beverages and tobacco (1988) 16.8%.
Principal trading partners: Germany, Italy, France,
Netherlands.
Total exports ($ million): 6509 (1987) of which
food, beverages and tobacco (1988) 27.8%, textiles

(1988) 23.0%.
Principal trading partners: Germany, Italy, France, USA.

Grenada
Gross national product ($ million): 139 (1988)
Gross national product per head ($): 1370 (1988)
Total imports ($ million): 83 (1986) of which
basic manufactures (1983) 25.4%, food (1983) 22.9%.
Principal trading partners: UK, Trinidad.
Total exports ($ million): 29 (1986) of which
fresh fruit (1983) 21.9%, cocoa beans (1983) 21.4%.
Principal trading partners: UK, Trinidad.

Guatemala
Gross national product ($ million): 7620 (1988)
Gross national product per head ($): 880 (1988)
Total imports ($ million): 592 (1987) of which
machinery, equipment and tools (1988) 22.2%,
consumer goods (1988) 18.1%.
Principal trading partners: USA, Germany, Mexico.
Total exports ($ million): 419 (1987) of which
coffee (1988) 36.0%, sugar (1988) 7.3%.
Principal trading partners: USA, El Salvador, Germany.

Guinea
Gross national product ($ million): 2300 (1988)
Gross national product per head ($): 350 (1988)
Total imports ($ million): 468 (1987) of which
semi-manufactured goods (1988) 43.9%, capital
goods (1988) 17.0%.
Principal trading partners: France, USA.
Total exports ($ million): 584 (1987) of which
bauxite and alumina (1988) 78.1%, diamonds (1988)
10.8%.
Principal trading partners: USA, France.

Guinea-Bissau
Gross national product ($ million): 145 (1987)
Gross national product per head ($): 160 (1987)
Total imports ($ million): 50 (1982) of which
food, beverages and tobacco (1985) 23.3%, crude
petroleum and products (1985) 12.5%.
Principal trading partners: Portugal, USSR.
Total exports ($ million): 12 (1982) of which
cashews (1985) 41.4%, fish and crustaceans (1985)
27.6%.
Principal trading partners: Portugal, Spain.

Guyana
Gross national product ($ million): 327 (1988)
Gross national product per head ($): 410 (1988)
Total imports ($ million): 255 (1985) of which
fuels and lubricants (1985) 44.3%, capital goods
(1985) 17.8%.
Principal trading partners: Trinidad, USA, UK.
Total exports ($ million): 231 (1986) of which
bauxite (1985) 34.4%, sugar (1985) 31.2%.
Principal trading partners: UK, USA, Canada.

Haiti
Gross national product ($ million): 2240 (1988)
Gross national product per head ($): 360 (1988)
Total imports ($ million): 442 (1985) of which
food and live animals (1988/89) 20.2%, machinery
and transport equipment (1988/89) 19.0%.
Principal trading partners: USA, Japan.
Total exports ($ million): 170 (1986) of which
manufactured goods (1988/89) 54.5%, coffee
(1988/89) 17.2%.
Principal trading partners: USA, France, Germany.

Honduras
Gross national product ($ million): 4110 (1988)
Gross national product per head ($): 850 (1988)
Total imports ($ million): 875 (1986) of which
machinery and transport equipment (1987) 23.1%,
chemical products (1987) 22.6%.
Principal trading partners: USA, Venezuela,
Mexico.
Total exports ($ million): 854 (1986) of which
coffee (1987) 39.8%, bananas (1987) 24.7%.
Principal trading partners: USA, Germany, Japan.

Hungary
Gross national product ($ million): 26 030 (1988)
Gross national product per head ($): 2460 (1988)
Total imports ($ million): 9858 (1987) of which
machinery and transport equipment (1988) 28.8%;
semifinished products (1988) 25.5%.
Principal trading partners: Germany, USSR,
Austria.
Total exports ($ million): 9582 (1987) of which
machinery and transport equipment (1988) 33.4%,
food and agricultural products (1988) 20.7%.
Principal trading partners: USSR, Germany,
Czechoslovakia.

Iceland
Gross national product ($ million): 5019 (1988)
Gross national product per head ($): 20 160 (1988)
Total imports ($ million): 1589 (1987) of which
ships and aircraft (1988) 8.5%, motor vehicles (1988)
8.4%.
Principal trading partners: Germany, UK, Denmark.
Total exports ($ million): 1376 (1987) of which
frozen fish (1988) 26.3%, salted fish (1988) 16.4%.
Principal trading partners: USA, UK, Germany.

India
Gross national product ($ million): 271 440 (1988)
Gross national product per head ($): 330 (1988)
Total imports ($ million): 16 370 (1987) of which
crude petroleum and products (1987/88) 18.2%, non-
electrical machinery (1987/88) 12.9%.
Principal trading partners: Japan, Germany, USA,
UK.
Total exports ($ million): 11 087 (1987) of which
pearls, stones and jewellery (1987/88) 16.6%, ready-
made garments (1987/88) 11.4%.
Principal trading partners: USA, USSR, Japan,
Germany.

Indonesia
Gross national product ($ million): 76 060 (1988)
Gross national product per head ($): 580 (1988)
Total imports ($ million): 10 718 (1986) of which
machinery and transport equipment (1988) 38.5%,
chemicals (1988) 19.2%.
Principal trading partners: Japan, USA, Singapore,
Germany.
Total exports ($ million): 14 805 (1986) of which
crude petroleum (1988) 21.3%, natural gas (1988)
13.7%.
Principal trading partners: Japan, USA, Singapore,
South Korea.

Iran
Gross national product ($ million): 93 500 (1987)
Gross national product per head ($): 1800 (1987)
Total imports ($ million): 18 296 (1983) of which
machinery and transport equipment (1985/86) 32.5%,
iron and steel (1985/86) 14.7%.
Principal trading partners: Germany, Japan, UK.

Total exports ($ million): 12 378 (1985) of which petroleum and products (1987) 98.4%, agricultural products (1987) 1.3%.
Principal trading partners: Japan, Germany, UK.

Iraq
Gross national product ($ million): 40 700 (1987)
Gross national product per head ($): 2420 (1987)
Total imports ($ million): 6636 (1983) of which machinery and transport equipment (1987) 39.8%, manufactured goods (1987) 27.1%.
Principal trading partners: Turkey, USA, Germany.
Total exports ($ million): 9785 (1983) of which fuels and other energy (1987) 99.0%, food and agricultural raw materials (1987) 1.0%.
Principal trading partners: Brazil, Italy, Turkey.

Ireland
Gross national product ($ million): 26 750 (1988)
Gross national product per head ($): 7480 (1988)
Total imports ($ million): 13 626 (1987) of which machinery and transport equipment (1987) 33.5%; chemicals (1987) 12.3%.
Principal trading partners: UK, USA, Germany, France.
Total exports ($ million): 15 997 (1987) of which office machinery (1987) 20.9%, food (1987) 15.8%.
Principal trading partners: UK, Germany, France, USA.

Israel
Gross national product ($ million): 38 440 (1988)
Gross national product per head ($): 8650 (1988)
Total imports ($ million): 11 910 (1987) of which diamonds (1988) 20.3%, investment goods (1988) 15.2%.
Principal trading partners: USA, Belgium, Germany.
Total exports ($ million): 8415 (1987) of which machinery (1988) 29.1%, diamonds (1988) 29.0%.
Principal trading partners: USA, UK, Germany.

Italy
Gross national product ($ million): 765 282 (1988)
Gross national product per head ($): 13 320 (1988)
Total imports ($ million): 125 004 (1987) of which machinery and transport equipment (1987) 29.4%, chemicals and chemical products (1987) 16.1%.
Principal trading partners: Germany, France, Netherlands, USA.
Total exports ($ million): 116 595 (1987) of which non-transport machinery (1987) 28.6%, textiles (1987) 10.9%.
Principal trading partners: Germany, France, UK, USA.

Ivory Coast (Côte d'Ivoire)
Gross national product ($ million): 8590 (1988)
Gross national product per head ($): 740 (1988)
Total imports ($ million): 2054 (1986) of which machinery and transport equipment (1987) 21.3%, fuels (1987) 15.0%.
Principal trading partners: France, Nigeria, Germany.
Total exports ($ million): 3325 (1986) of which cocoa beans (1987) 33.6%, coffee (1987) 12.7%.
Principal trading partners: France, Netherlands, Italy.

Jamaica
Gross national product ($ million): 2610 (1988)
Gross national product per head ($): 1080 (1988)

Total imports ($ million): 1208 (1987) of which fuels (1988) 13.5%, machinery (1988) 13.6%.
Principal trading partners: USA, Netherlands Antilles, Venezuela.
Total exports ($ million): 657 (1987) of which aluminium/bauxite (1988) 37.8%, garments (1988) 15.4%.
Principal trading partners: USA, UK, Canada.

Japan
Gross national product ($ million): 2 576 541 (1988)
Gross national product per head ($): 21 040 (1988)
Total imports ($ million): 149 515 (1987) of which food (1988) 15.5%, machinery and equipment (1988) 14.2%.
Principal trading partners: USA, Indonesia, South Korea, Australia.
Total exports ($ million): 229 224 (1987) of which motor vehicles (1988) 18.4%, office machinery (1988) 6.9%.
Principal trading partners: USA, South Korea, Germany, Taiwan.

Jordan
Gross national product ($ million): 4420 (1988)
Gross national product per head ($): 1500 (1988)
Total imports ($ million): 2703 (1987) of which machinery and transport (1987) 20.3%, basic manufactures (1987) 18.5%.
Principal trading partners: Iraq, USA, Saudi Arabia.
Total exports ($ million): 734 (1987) of which chemicals (1987) 28.1%, phosphate fertilizers (1987) 24.5%.
Principal trading partners: Iraq, Saudi Arabia, India.

Kenya
Gross national product ($ million): 8310 (1988)
Gross national product per head ($): 360 (1988)
Total imports ($ million): 1756 (1987) of which machinery and transport equipment (1987) 34.4%, crude petroleum (1987) 19.8%.
Principal trading partners: UK, Japan, UAE.
Total exports ($ million): 961 (1987) of which coffee (1987) 25.8%, tea (1987) 21.7%.
Principal trading partners: UK, USA, Germany.

Kiribati
Gross national product ($ million): 40 (1988)
Gross national product per head ($): 650 (1988)
Total imports ($ million): 21 (1984) of which food (1988) 28.7%, machinery and transport equipment (1988) 27.2%.
Principal trading partners: Australia, Japan, New Zealand.
Total exports ($ million): 4 (1985) of which copra (1988) 63.0%, fish and fish preparations (1988) 24.3%.
Principal trading partners: Marshall Islands, USA.

Korea, Democratic People's Republic
Gross national product ($ million): 15 640* (1988)
Gross national product per head ($): 767 (1988)
Total imports ($ million): 2425 (1987).
Principal trading partners: USSR, Japan, China.
Total exports ($ million): 1856 (1987).
Principal trading partners: USSR, China, Japan.
No recent breakdown of these figures is available.

Korea, Republic
Gross national product ($ million): 150 270 (1988)

Gross national product per head ($): 3530 (1988)
Total imports ($ million): 40 799 (1987) of which
petroleum and products (1987) 11.3%, electronic
components (1987) 6.2%.
Principal trading partners: Japan, USA, Germany.
Total exports ($ million): 47 213 (1987) of which
transport equipment (1987) 10.8%, electrical
machinery (1987) 8.9%.
Principal trading partners: USA, Japan, Hong Kong,
Germany.

Kuwait
Gross national product ($ million): 26 250 (1988)
Gross national product per head ($): 13 680 (1988)
Total imports ($ million): 7699 (1984) of which
transport equipment (1984) 15.4%, electrical
machinery (1984) 12.3%.
Principal trading partners: Japan, USA, Germany.
Total exports ($ million): 7512 (1986) of which
petroleum and products (1984) 87.5%.
Principal trading partners: Japan, Italy, Germany.
(Kuwait's international trade was disrupted by the
Iraqi occupation, August 1990 – February 1991.)

Laos
Gross national product ($ million): 710 (1988)
Gross national product per head ($): 180 (1988)
Total imports ($ million): 48 (1984).
Principal trading partners: USSR, Thailand, Japan.
No recent breakdown is available for imports.
Total exports ($ million): 12 (1984) of which
electricity (1985) 50.1%, wood (1985) 29.3%.
Principal trading partners: China, USSR, Thailand.

Lebanon
Gross national product ($ million): 643* (1985)
Gross national product per head ($): 241 (1985)
Total imports ($ million): 3615 (1981) of which
consumer goods (1982) 40.0%, machinery and
transport equipment (1982) 35.0%.
Principal trading partners: Italy, France, USA.
Total exports ($ million): 886 (1981) of which
jewellery (1985) 10.2%, clothing (1985) 5.2%.
Principal trading partners: Saudi Arabia, Syria.

Lesotho
Gross national product ($ million): 690 (1988)
Gross national product per head ($): 410 (1988)
Total imports ($ million): 392 (1987) of which
manufactured goods (1981) 37.4%, food and live
animals (1981) 18.9%.
Principal trading partners: South Africa, UK.
Total exports ($ million): 35 (1987) of which
diamonds (1981) 42.1%, food and live animals (1981)
10.3%.
Principal trading partner: South Africa.

Liberia
Gross national product ($ million): 1051 (1987)
Gross national product per head ($): 450 (1987)
Total imports ($ million): 259 (1986) of which
petroleum and products (1987) 17.3%, basic manufac-
tures (1987) 17.0%.
Principal trading partners: USA, Germany, Japan.
Total exports ($ million): 408 (1986) of which
iron ore (1987) 58.1%, rubber (1987) 23.8%.
Principal trading partners: Germany, USA, Italy.

Libya
Gross national product ($ million): 23 000 (1988)
Gross national product per head ($): 5410 (1988)

Total imports ($ million): 7175 (1982) of which
machinery and transport equipment (1982) 36.8%,
consumer goods (1982) 27.1%.
Principal trading partners: Italy, USSR, Germany.
Total exports ($ million): 10 841 (1985) of which
crude petroleum (1987) 95.8%.
Principal trading partners: Italy, USSR, Germany.

Liechtenstein
Gross national product ($ million): 450 (1985)
Gross national product per head ($): 16 500 (1985)
Total imports ($ million): 314 (1987) of which
machinery and transport (1987) 32.2%, metal pro-
ducts (1987) 14.5%.
Principal trading partners: Switzerland, Austria.
Total exports ($ million): 770 (1987) of which
machinery and transport equipment (1987) 48.3%,
metal products (1987) 19.9%.
Principal trading partners: Switzerland, Austria.

Luxembourg
Gross national product ($ million): 8372 (1988)
Gross national product per head ($): 22 600 (1988)
Total imports ($ million): 5259 (1988) of which
electrical machinery (1988) 17.2%, transport equip-
ment (1988) 10.1%.
Principal trading partners: Belgium, Germany,
France.
Total exports ($ million): 4737 (1988) of which
plastic materials and rubber manufactures (1988)
13.9%, electrical machinery (1988) 10.8%.
Principal trading partners: Germany, Belgium,
France.

Madagascar
Gross national product ($ million): 2080 (1988)
Gross national product per head ($): 180 (1988)
Total imports ($ million): 353 (1986) of which
chemical products (1987) 14.9%, machinery (1987)
14.2%.
Principal trading partners: France, Germany, Qatar.
Total exports ($ million): 332 (1987) of which
coffee (1987) 27.9%, vanilla (1987) 25.6%.
Principal trading partners: France, USA, Japan.

Malawi
Gross national product ($ million): 1320 (1988)
Gross national product per head ($): 160 (1988)
Total imports ($ million): 296 (1987) of which
basic manufactures (1987) 41.0%, machinery and
equipment (1987) 18.9%.
Principal trading partners: South Africa, Japan,
Germany.
Total exports ($ million): 276 (1987) of which
tobacco (1987) 62.1%, sugar (1987) 10.5%.
Principal trading partners: UK, USA, Germany.

Malaysia
Gross national product ($ million): 31 620 (1988)
Gross national product per head ($): 1870 (1988)
Total imports ($ million): 12 699 (1987) of which
thermionic valves and tubes (1987) 17.8%, petroleum
products (1987) 5.0%.
Principal trading partners: Japan, Singapore,
Germany.
Total exports ($ million): 17 935 (1987) of which
thermionic valves and tubes (1987) 15.3%, crude
petroleum (1987) 13.9%.
Principal trading partners: Japan, Singapore, USA.

Maldives
Gross national product ($ million): 80 (1988)
Gross national product per head ($): 410 (1988)

Total imports ($ million): 87 (1987) of which food, beverages and tobacco (1987) 14.3%, basic manufactures (1987) 9.7%.
Principal trading partners: Japan, Thailand.
Total exports ($ million): 31 (1987) of which fresh skipjack tuna (1987) 32.3%, dried skipjack tuna (1987) 7.4%.
Principal trading partners: Thailand, Sri Lanka.

Mali
Gross national product ($ million): 1800 (1988)
Gross national product per head ($): 230 (1988)
Total imports ($ million): 476 (1987) of which machinery and transport equipment (1986) 26.8%, petroleum products (1986) 16.5%.
Principal trading partners: Ivory Coast, France.
Total exports ($ million): 260 (1987) of which raw cotton and cotton products (1986) 36.8%, live animals (1986) 25.0%.
Principal trading partners: France, Ivory Coast.

Malta
Gross national product ($ million): 1740 (1988)
Gross national product per head ($): 5050 (1988)
Total imports ($ million): 1138 (1987) of which machinery and transport equipment (1988) 37.2%, semi-manufactured goods (1988) 23.4%.
Principal trading partners: Germany, Italy, UK
Total exports ($ million): 603 (1987) of which machinery and transport equipment (1988) 35.5%, semi-manufactured goods (1988) 10.6%.
Principal trading partners: Germany, UK, Italy.

Marshall Islands
Total imports ($ million): 44 (1986)
Principal trading partner: USA.
Total exports ($ million): 11 (1986)
Principal trading partner: USA.
No figure for the gross national product is available.

Mauritania
Gross national product ($ million): 910 (1988)
Gross national product per head ($): 480 (1988)
Total imports ($ million): 382 (1987) of which food (1983) 22.9%, crude petroleum and products (1983) 18.7%.
Principal trading partners: France, Spain, Senegal.
Total exports ($ million): 428 (1987) of which fish (1986) 59.2%, iron ore (1986) 40.8%
Principal trading partners: France, Japan, Spain.

Mauritius
Gross national product ($ million): 1890 (1988)
Gross national product per head ($): 1810 (1988)
Total imports ($ million): 675 (1986) of which manufactured goods – material (1987) 40.0%, machinery and transport equipment (1987) 22.1%.
Principal trading partners: France, Japan, South Africa.
Total exports ($ million): 675 (1986) of which clothing (1987) 48.1%, sugar (1987) 37.1%.
Principal trading partners: UK, France, USA.

Mexico
Gross national product ($ million): 151 870 (1988)
Gross national product per head ($): 1820 (1988)
Total imports ($ million): 12 742 (1987) of which chemical products (1988) 9.7%, automobile equipment (1988) 8.6%.
Principal trading partners: USA, Japan, Germany.
Total exports ($ million): 20 628 (1987) of which

crude petroleum (1988) 28.5%, automobile parts (1988) 9.5%.
Principal trading partners: USA, Japan, Spain.

Micronesia
Gross national product ($ million): 130 (1988)
Gross national product per head ($): 1500 (1988)
Principal trading partner: USA.
No figures for imports or exports are available.

Monaco
Principal trading partners: France, Italy. No separate figures are available for Monaco whose imports and exports are included in the French total.

Mongolia
Gross national product ($ million): 1161* (1988)
Gross national product per head ($): 608 (1988)
Total imports ($ million): 655 (1981) of which machinery and equipment (1987) 32.2%, fuels, minerals and metals (1987) 30.8%.
Principal trading partner: USSR.
Total exports ($ million): 436 (1981) of which raw materials and food products (1987) 40.2%, minerals and metals (1987) 39.5%.
Principal trading partner: USSR.

Morocco
Gross national product ($ million): 17 830 (1988)
Gross national product per head ($): 750 (1988)
Total imports ($ million): 4230 (1987) of which capital goods (1987) 20.9%, crude oil (1987) 15.1%.
Principal trading partners: France, Spain, Germany.
Total exports ($ million): 2827 (1987) of which food, beverages and tobacco (1987) 27.1%, phosphates (1987) 13.2%.
Principal trading partners: France, USA, Spain.

Mozambique
Gross national product ($ million): 1550 (1988)
Gross national product per head ($): 100 (1988)
Total imports ($ million): 482 (1984) of which foodstuffs (1987) 37.6%, capital equipment (1987) 18.9%.
Principal trading partners: USSR, South Africa, Germany.
Total exports ($ million): 86 (1984) of which shrimps (1987) 38.7%, cashew nuts (1987) 32.0%.
Principal trading partners: USA, Germany, Japan.

Namibia
Gross national product ($ million): 1150 (1986)
Gross national product per head ($): 1020 (1986)
Total imports ($ million): 671 (1987).
Total exports ($ million): 710 (1987).
Principal trading partner: South Africa.
No recent breakdown of these figures is available.

Nauru
Gross national product ($ million): 160 (1986)
Gross national product per head ($): 20 000 (1986)
Total imports ($ million): 11 (1976/77)
Principal trading partners: Australia, New Zealand.
Total exports ($ million): 0.7 (1976/77) of which phosphates 99%.
Principal trading partners: Australia, New Zealand.

Nepal
Gross national product ($ million): 3150 (1988)
Gross national product per head ($): 170 (1988)
Total imports ($ million): 535 (1987) of which

manufactured goods (1985/86) 29.5%, machinery and transport equipment (1985/86) 22.9%. Principal trading partners: India, Japan, South Korea. *Total exports ($ million):* 155 (1987) of which basic manufactures (1986/87) 34.5%, food and live animals (1986/87) 22.7%. Principal trading partners: India, USA, UK.

Netherlands
Gross national product ($ million): 214 458 (1988) *Gross national product per head ($):* 14 530 (1988) *Total imports ($ million):* 91 314 (1987) of which machinery and transport equipment (1988) 27.8%, foodstuffs, beverages and tobacco (1988) 13.6%. Principal trading partners: Germany, Belgium, France, UK. *Total exports ($ million):* 92 876 (1987) of which machinery and transport equipment (1988) 20.9%, foodstuffs, beverages and tobacco (1988) 20.0%. Principal trading partners: Germany, Belgium, France, UK.

Aruba
Gross national product ($ million): 1610 (1985). *Gross national product per head ($):* 6810 (1985). *Total imports ($ million):* 236 (1987) of which food and agriculture products (1987) 52.5%, machinery and transport equipment (1987) 28.0%. Principal trading partner: USA. *Total exports ($ million):* 26 (1987) of which beverages and tobacco (1987) 50.3%, machinery and transport equipment (1987) 13.1%. Principal trading partner: Netherlands.

Netherlands Antilles
Gross national product ($ million): 1610 (1985). *Gross national product per head ($):* 6110 (1985). *Total imports ($ million):* 1502 (1987) of which crude petroleum and products (1987) 69.9%, machinery and transport equipment (1987) 8.1%. Principal trading partners: Venezuela, USA. *Total exports ($ million):* 1308 (1987) of which crude petroleum and products (1987) 95.2%, machinery and transport equipment (1987) 0.9%. Principal trading partner: Netherlands.

New Zealand
Gross national product ($ million): 32 109 (1988) *Gross national product per head ($):* 9620 (1988) *Total imports ($ million):* 7209 (1987) of which machinery (1988/89) 29.8%, transport equipment (1988/89) 9.9%. Principal trading partners: Japan, Australia, USA, UK. *Total exports ($ million):* 7189 (1987) of which food and live animals (1988/89) 40.4%, wool (1988/89) 13.0%. Principal trading partners: USA, Japan, Australia, UK.

Cook Islands
Gross national product ($ million): 11 (1984). *Total imports ($ million):* 21. *Total exports ($ million):* 4 (1984) of which clothing (1984) 41.7%. Principal trading partner: New Zealand. No other recent figures are available.

Niue
Total imports ($ million): 2 (1985). *Total exports ($ million):* 0.1 (1985). Principal trading partner: New Zealand. No other recent figures are available.

Tokelau
Total imports ($ million): 0.06 (1983/84). *Total exports ($ million):* 0.03 (1983/84) of which copra (1983/84) 80.8%. Principal trading partner: New Zealand. No other recent figures are available.

Nicaragua
Gross national product ($ million): 2911 (1987) *Gross national product per head ($):* 830 (1987) *Total imports ($ million):* 770 (1986) of which primary and intermediate goods for industry (1988) 20.1%, crude petroleum and products (1988) 15.0%. Principal trading partners: Mexico, USA. *Total exports ($ million):* 247 (1986) of which coffee (1988) 35.9%, cotton (1988) 22.5%. Principal trading partners: USA, Germany.

Niger
Gross national product ($ million): 2190 (1988) *Gross national product per head ($):* 310 (1988) *Total imports ($ million):* 285 (1984) of which cereals (1985) 23.3%, petroleum products (1985) 10.9%. Principal trading partners: France, Nigeria, Algeria. *Total exports ($ million):* 274 (1984) of which uranium (1985) 78.9%, foodstuffs (1985) 14.5%. Principal trading partners: France, Japan, Nigeria.

Nigeria
Gross national product ($ million): 31 770 (1988) *Gross national product per head ($):* 290 (1988) *Total imports ($ million):* 3917 (1987) of which machinery and transport equipment (1986) 46.0%, manufactured goods (1986) 19.3%. Principal trading partners: UK, Germany, France, Japan. *Total exports ($ million):* 7383 (1987) of which crude petroleum (1987) 95.3%, food and live animals (1987) 2.9%. Principal trading partners: USA, Germany, France, Italy.

Norway
Gross national product ($ million): 84 165 (1988) *Gross national product per head ($):* 20 020 (1988) *Total imports ($ million):* 22 576 (1987) of which machinery and transport equipment (1988) 28.3%, metals and metal products (1988) 11.8%. Principal trading partners: Sweden, Germany, UK, Denmark. *Total exports ($ million):* 21 432 (1987) of which crude petroleum (1988) 22.7%, metals and metal products (1988) 18.1%. Principal trading partners: UK, Germany, Sweden, Netherlands.

Oman
Gross national product ($ million): 7110 (1988) *Gross national product per head ($):* 5070 (1988) *Total imports ($ million):* 2384 (1986) of which machinery and transport equipment (1988) 33.5%, manufactured goods (1988) 21.6%. Principal trading partners: Japan, UAE, UK. *Total exports ($ million):* 2526 (1986) of which crude petroleum (1988) 88.0%, fish (1988) 1.5%. Principal trading partners: Japan, South Korea, Thailand.

Pakistan
Gross national product ($ million): 37 153 (1988) *Gross national product per head ($):* 350 (1988) *Total imports ($ million):* 5825 (1987) of which non-electric machinery (1987/88) 17.6%, mineral oils (1987/88) 16.2%. Principal trading partners: Japan, Canada, USA, Germany. *Total exports ($ million):* 4090 (1987) of which raw cotton (1987/88) 13.7%, cotton yarn (1987/88)

12.2%.
Principal trading partners: USA, Japan, Germany,
Sri Lanka.

Panama
Gross national product ($ million): 5091 (1987)
Gross national product per head ($): 2240 (1987)
Total imports ($ million): 1275 (1986) of which
capital goods (1987) 16.3%, crude petroleum (1987)
14.4%.
Principal trading partners: USA, Japan, Mexico.
Total exports ($ million): 335 (1987) of which
bananas (1987) 25.3%, shrimps (1987) 19.2%.
Principal trading partners: USA, Costa Rica,
Germany.

Papua New Guinea
Gross national product ($ million): 2920 (1988)
Gross national product per head ($): 770 (1988)
Total imports ($ million): 931 (1986) of which
machinery and transport equipment (1986) 34.1%,
food and live animals (1986) 18.0%.
Principal trading partners: Australia, Singapore,
Japan.
Total exports ($ million): 1171 (1987) of which
gold (1986) 39.8%, copper ore and concentrates
(1986) 15.6%.
Principal trading partners: Japan, Germany, South
Korea.

Paraguay
Gross national product ($ million): 4780 (1988)
Gross national product per head ($): 1180 (1988)
Total imports ($ million): 517 (1987) of which
machinery and transport equipment (1988) 40.4%,
fuels and lubricants (1988) 18.6%.
Principal trading partners: Brazil, Argentina,
Japan.
Total exports ($ million): 275 (1986) of which
cotton fibres (1988) 41.1%, soya beans (1988) 30.2%.
Principal trading partners: Brazil, Argentina,
Netherlands.

Peru
Gross national product ($ million): 29 185 (1987)
Gross national product per head ($): 1440 (1987)
Total imports ($ million): 2886 (1987) of which
raw and intermediate materials (1987) 45.9%,
industrial capital goods (1987) 19.8%.
Principal trading partners: USA, Japan, Germany.
Total exports ($ million): 2577 (1987) of which
copper (1987) 19.8%, petroleum and products (1987)
10.5%.
Principal trading partners: USA, Japan, Germany.

Philippines
Gross national product ($ million): 37 710 (1988)
Gross national product per head ($): 630 (1988)
Total imports ($ million): 6811 (1987) of which
mineral fuels and lubricants (1987) 18.5%, materials
and accessories for manufacture of electrical equipment (1987) 11.4%.
Principal trading partners: USA, Japan, Taiwan.
Total exports ($ million): 5565 (1987) of which
semiconductor devices (1987) 10.2%, ready-made
garments (1987) 9.9%.
Principal trading partners: USA, Japan, Netherlands.

Poland
Gross national product ($ million): 69 970 (1988)
Gross national product per head ($): 1850 (1988)

Total imports ($ million): 9961 (1987) of which
machinery and transport equipment (1988) 35.7%,
chemicals (1988) 15.9%.
Principal trading partners: USSR, Germany,
Czechoslovakia.
Total exports ($ million): 11 185 (1987) of which
machinery and transport equipment (1988) 39.2%,
chemicals (1988) 10.9%.
Principal trading partners: USSR, Germany,
Czechoslovakia.

Portugal
Gross national product ($ million): 37 260 (1988)
Gross national product per head ($): 3670 (1988)
Total imports ($ million): 13 443 (1987) of which
machinery and transport equipment (1988) 37.0%,
crude petroleum (1988) 8.5%.
Principal trading partners: Germany, Spain, France,
Italy.
Total exports ($ million): 9169 (1987) of which
clothing (1988) 26.3%, machinery and transport
equipment (1988) 20.1%.
Principal trading partners: France, Germany, UK,
USA.

Macau
Gross national product ($ million): 810 (1982) *Gross
national product per head ($)*: 2710 (1982) *Total
imports ($ million)*: 1120 (1987) of which industrial
raw materials (1987) 66.8%, non-edible consumer
goods (1987) 12.4%. Principal trading partners: Hong
Kong, China. *Total exports ($ million)*: 1395 (1987) of
which textiles and garments (1987) 73.5%, toys
(1987) 9.9%. Principal trading partners: USA, Hong
Kong.

Qatar
Gross national product ($ million): 4060 (1988)
Gross national product per head ($): 11 610 (1988)
Total imports ($ million): 1099 (1986) of which
machinery and transport equipment (1987) 40.4%,
manufactured goods (1987) 17.2%.
Principal trading partners: Japan, UK, Germany.
Total exports ($ million): 3541 (1985) of which
crude petroleum (1987) 91.1%, liquefied gas and
others (1987) 8.9%.
Principal trading partners: Japan, Italy, France.

Romania
Gross national product ($ million): 148 048 (1988)
Gross national product per head ($): 6400 (1988)
Total imports ($ million): 10 590 (1986) of which
mineral fuels (1987) 53.5%, machinery (1987) 28.4%.
Principal trading partners: USSR, Egypt, Iran.
Total exports ($ million): 12 543 (1986) of which
machinery and transport equipment (1987) 37.6%,
fuels (1987) 23.2%.
Principal trading partners: USSR, Germany, Italy.

Rwanda
Gross national product ($ million): 2064 (1988)
Gross national product per head ($): 310 (1988)
Total imports ($ million): 441 (1987) of which
machinery and transport equipment (1985) 21.6%,
electrical equipment (1985) 4.8%.
Principal trading partners: USA, Kenya, Belgium.
Total exports ($ million): 118 (1986) of which
coffee (1988) 78.9%, tea (1988) 13.1%.
Principal trading partners: Germany, Belgium,
Uganda.

St Christopher and Nevis
Gross national product ($ million): 120 (1988)

Gross national product per head ($): 2770 (1988)
Total imports ($ million): 54 (1985) of which
food (1984) 19.7%, crude petroleum and products
(1984) 9.9%.
Principal trading partners: USA, UK, Trinidad.
Total exports ($ million): 22 (1985) of which
sugar (1984) 56.8%, electrical machinery and
apparatus (1984) 10.9%.
Principal trading partners: USA, UK, Trinidad.

St Lucia
Gross national product ($ million): 220 (1988)
Gross national product per head ($): 1540 (1988)
Total imports ($ million): 155 (1986) of which
basic manufactures (1987) 35.4%, food products
(1987) 20.3%.
Principal trading partners: USA, UK.
Total exports ($ million): 83 (1986) of which
bananas (1987) 71.2%, clothing (1987) 14.0%.
Principal trading partners: UK, USA, Jamaica.

St Vincent and the Grenadines
Gross national product ($ million): 130 (1988)
Gross national product per head ($): 1100 (1988)
Total imports ($ million): 87 (1986) of which
basic manufactures (1987) 35.3%, machinery and
transport equipment (1987) 19.7%.
Principal trading partners: USA, UK, Trinidad.
Total exports ($ million): 64 (1986) of which
bananas (1987) 38.0%, flour (1987) 12.0%.
Principal trading partners: UK, Trinidad, USA.

San Marino
Gross national product ($ million): 188 (1987)
Gross national product per head ($): 8590 (1987)
Principal trading partner: Italy.
No other figures are available.

São Tomé and Príncipe
Gross national product ($ million): 32 (1987)
Gross national product per head ($): 280 (1987)
Total imports ($ million): 14 (1977) of which
machinery and electrical equipment (1987) 59.0%,
food and other agricultural products (1987) 32.0%.
Principal trading partners: Germany, Portugal.
Total exports ($ million): 23 (1977) of which
cocoa (1984) 80.0%, copra (1984) 15.0%.
Principal trading partners: Germany, Netherlands,
Portugal.

Saudi Arabia
Gross national product ($ million): 86 527 (1988)
Gross national product per head ($): 6170 (1988)
Total imports ($ million): 19 113 (1986) of which
machinery and appliances (1987) 19.1%, foodstuffs
and tobacco (1987) 16.5%.
Principal trading partners: USA, Japan, UK, Italy.
Total exports ($ million): 20 085 (1986) of which
crude petroleum (1987) 94.3%.
Principal trading partners: Japan, USA, Italy,
France.

Senegal
Gross national product ($ million): 4520 (1988)
Gross national product per head ($): 630 (1988)
Total imports ($ million): 620 (1985) of which
crude petroleum and products (1986) 18.1%, agri-
cultural and industrial equipment (1986) 16.3%.
Principal trading partners: France, Nigeria, Algeria.
Total exports ($ million): 402 (1985) of which
petroleum products (1986) 16.8%, crustaceans, mol-

luscs and shellfish (1986) 10.5%.
Principal trading partners: USA, France, Ivory
Coast.

Seychelles
Gross national product ($ million): 260 (1988)
Gross national product per head ($): 3800 (1988)
Total imports ($ million): 143 (1988) of which
machinery and transport equipment (1988) 32.0%,
manufactured goods (1988) 27.3%.
Principal trading partners: UK, South Africa,
Bahrain.
Total exports ($ million): 29 (1988) of which
petroleum products (1988) 43.1%, canned tuna
(1988) 33.4%.
Principal trading partners: Pakistan, France.

Sierra Leone
Gross national product ($ million): 930 (1988)
Gross national product per head ($): 240 (1988)
Total imports ($ million): 137 (1987) of which
food and live animals (1985) 29.8%, machinery and
transport equipment (1985) 23.3%.
Principal trading partners: USA, UK, Germany.
Total exports ($ million): 132 (1987) of which
rutile (1985) 21.8%, coffee (1985) 20.3%.
Principal trading partners: USA, UK, Netherlands.

Singapore
Gross national product ($ million): 24 010 (1988)
Gross national product per head ($): 9100 (1988)
Total imports ($ million): 32 559 (1987) of which
crude petroleum (1988) 9.4%, office machines (1988)
5.4%.
Principal trading partners: Japan, USA, Malaysia.
Total exports ($ million): 28 686 (1987) of which
office machines (1988) 13.8%, petroleum products
(1988) 12.2%.
Principal trading partners: USA, Malaysia, Japan.

Solomon Islands
Gross national product ($ million): 130 (1988)
Gross national product per head ($): 430 (1988)
Total imports ($ million): 63 (1986) of which
machinery and transport equipment (1987) 29.1%,
manufactured goods (1987) 20.5%.
Principal trading partners: Japan, USA.
Total exports ($ million): 67 (1986) of which
fish products (1987) 41.0%, wood products (1987)
29.0%.
Principal trading partners: Japan, UK, Netherlands.

Somalia
Gross national product ($ million): 970 (1988)
Gross national product per head ($): 170 (1988)
Total imports ($ million): 112 (1985) of which
food (1984) 25.5%, machinery and transport equip-
ment (1984) 22.0%.
Principal trading partners: USA, Italy, Germany.
Total exports ($ million): 91 (1985) of which
live animals (1987) 67.0%, bananas (1987) 22.6%.
Principal trading partners: Saudi Arabia, Italy.

South Africa
Gross national product ($ million): 77 720 (1988)
Gross national product per head ($): 2290 (1988)
Total imports ($ million): 14 126 (1987) of which
motor vehicles (1988) 14.2%, chemicals (1988) 10.6%.
Principal trading partners: Germany, UK, USA,
Japan.
Total exports ($ million): 10 861 (1986) of which

gold (1988) 39.2%, metals and products (1988) 13.8%.
Principal trading partners: USA, Japan, UK,
Netherlands.

Spain
Gross national product ($ million): 301 829 (1988)
Gross national product per head ($): 7740 (1988)
Total imports ($ million): 49 058 (1987) of which
transport equipment (1988) 11.7%, agricultural and
food products (1988) 10.1%.
Principal trading partners: USA, Germany, France,
UK.
Total exports ($ million): 34 154 (1987) of which
transport equipment (1988) 17.2%, agricultural and
food products (1988) 15.6%.
Principal trading partners: France, USA, Germany,
UK.

Sri Lanka
Gross national product ($ million): 7020 (1988)
Gross national product per head ($): 420 (1988)
Total imports ($ million): 2029 (1987) of which
petroleum (1987) 14.5%, machinery and transport
equipment (1987) 13.4%.
Principal trading partners: Japan, Saudi Arabia,
USA.
Total exports ($ million): 1302 (1987) of which
tea (1987) 26.6%, rubber (1987) 7.4%.
Principal trading partners: USA, UK, Iraq.

Sudan
Gross national product ($ million): 8070 (1988)
Gross national product per head ($): 340 (1988)
Total imports ($ million): 961 (1986) of which
machinery and transport equipment (1987) 32.7%,
manufactured goods (1987) 19.2%.
Principal trading partners: UK, USA, Germany.
Total exports ($ million): 333 (1986) of which
cotton (1987) 30.4%, gum arabic (1987) 17.8%.
Principal trading partners: Italy, China, Germany.

Suriname
Gross national product ($ million): 1050 (1988)
Gross national product per head ($): 2450 (1988)
Total imports ($ million): 338 (1985) of which
fuels and lubricants (1987) 21.5%, machinery and
transport equipment (1987) 17.4%.
Principal trading partners: USA, Netherlands,
Trinidad.
Total exports ($ million): 364 (1984) of which
aluminium/bauxite (1987) 62.4%, shrimps (1987)
14.6%.
Principal trading partners: Netherlands, Norway,
USA.

Swaziland
Gross national product ($ million): 580 (1988)
Gross national product per head ($): 790 (1988)
Total imports ($ million): 301 (1986) of which
machinery and transport equipment (1986) 15.4%,
minerals, fuels and lubricants (1986) 15.4%.
Principal trading partners: South Africa, USA.
Total exports ($ million): 227 (1986) of which
sugar (1986) 33.7%, wood and products (1986) 20.0%.
Principal trading partners: South Africa, UK.

Sweden
Gross national product ($ million): 160 029 (1988)
Gross national product per head ($): 19 150 (1988)
Total imports ($ million): 40 995 (1987) of which
transport equipment (1988) 12.8%, chemicals (1988)
10.2%.

Principal trading partners: Germany, UK, Finland,
USA.
Total exports ($ million): 44 839 (1987) of which
transport equipment (1988) 15.8%, paper products
(1988) 11.1%.
Principal trading partners: Germany, Norway, UK,
USA.

Switzerland
Gross national product ($ million): 178 442 (1988)
Gross national product per head ($): 27 260 (1988)
Total imports ($ million): 50 915 (1987) of which
machinery (1987) 20.3%, chemical products (1987)
11.0%.
Principal trading partners: Germany, France, Italy,
UK.
Total exports ($ million): 45 742 (1987) of which
non-electrical machinery (1987) 20.3%, electrical
machinery (1987) 11.9%.
Principal trading partners: Germany, France, USA,
Italy.

Syria
Gross national product ($ million): 19 540 (1988)
Gross national product per head ($): 1670 (1988)
Total imports ($ million): 2487 (1987) of which
machinery and equipment (1987) 30.2%, chemicals
and products (1987) 21.2%.
Principal trading partners: USSR, Iran, Germany.
Total exports ($ million): 1353 (1987) of which
crude petroleum and natural gas (1987) 33.2%,
chemicals and products (1987) 29.4%.
Principal trading partners: USSR, Italy, Romania.

Tanzania
Gross national product ($ million): 3780 (1988)
Gross national product per head ($): 160 (1988)
Total imports ($ million): 780 (1986) of which
transport equipment (1988) 36.3%, intermediate
goods (1988) 32.2%.
Principal trading partners: Germany, Japan, UK.
Total exports ($ million): 346 (1986) of which
coffee (1988) 25.9%, cotton (1988) 23.6%.
Principal trading partners: Germany, UK.

Thailand
Gross national product ($ million): 54 550 (1988)
Gross national product per head ($): 1000 (1988)
Total imports ($ million): 12 849 (1987) of which
machinery and transport equipment (1987) 32.4%,
basic manufactures (1987) 19.6%.
Principal trading partners: Japan, USA, Singapore.
Total exports ($ million): 11 546 (1987) of which
food and live animals (1987) 36.5%, basic manufac-
tures (1987) 19.6%.
Principal trading partners: USA, Japan, Singapore.

Togo
Gross national product ($ million): 1240 (1988)
Gross national product per head ($): 370 (1988)
Total imports ($ million): 288 (1985) of which
food products (1986) 15.6%, cotton yarn and fabrics
(1986) 15.4%.
Principal trading partners: France, Germany,
Netherlands.
Total exports ($ million): 190 (1985) of which
calcium phosphates (1986) 48.3%, food products
(1986) 26.6%.
Principal trading partners: France, Germany, Italy.

Tonga
Gross national product ($ million): 80 (1988)

Gross national product per head ($): 800 (1988)
Total imports ($ million): 40 (1986) of which
basic manufactures (1987) 18.3%, food and live
animals (1987) 21.6%.
Principal trading partners: New Zealand, Australia,
Japan.
Total exports ($ million): 6 (1986) of which
coconut oil products (1988) 16.9%, bananas (1988)
15.4%.
Principal trading partners: New Zealand, Australia,
USA.

Trinidad and Tobago
Gross national product ($ million): 4160 (1988)
Gross national product per head ($): 3350 (1988)
Total imports ($ million): 1219 (1987) of which
machinery and transport equipment (1987) 29.2%,
food (1987) 19.0%.
Principal trading partners: USA, Japan, Canada.
Total exports ($ million): 1462 (1987) of which
crude petroleum (1987) 35.5%, petroleum products
(1987) 35.3%.
Principal trading partners: USA, Puerto Rico, UK.

Tunisia
Gross national product ($ million): 9610 (1988)
Gross national product per head ($): 1230 (1988)
Total imports ($ million): 3047 (1987) of which
textiles (1988) 8.2%, wheat (1988) 5.4%.
Principal trading partners: France, Germany, Italy.
Total exports ($ million): 2171 (1987) of which
clothing and accessories (1988) 16.8%, petroleum
and products (1988) 16.1%.
Principal trading partners: France, Germany, Italy.

Turkey
Gross national product ($ million): 68 600 (1988)
Gross national product per head ($): 1280 (1988)
Total imports ($ million): 14 149 (1987) of which
fuels (1988) 18.9%, machinery (1988) 16.7%.
Principal trading partners: Germany, USA, Italy,
Iraq.
Total exports ($ million): 10 153 (1987) of which
textiles (1988) 27.4%, agricultural products (1988)
20.1%.
Principal trading partners: Germany, USA, Italy,
Iran.

Tuvalu
Gross national product ($ million): 5 (1981)
Gross national product per head ($): 680 (1981)
Total imports ($ million): 3 (1986) of which
food and live animals (1986) 29.5%, manufactured
goods (1986) 25.2%.
Principal trading partners: Fiji, Australia.
Total exports ($ million): 0.02 (1986) of which
copra (1986) 86.4%.
Principal trading partners: Fiji, Australia.

Uganda
Gross national product ($ million): 4480 (1988)
Gross national product per head ($): 280 (1988)
Total imports ($ million): 293 (1980) of which
machinery and transport equipment (1979) 48.4%,
metals and products (1979) 4.6%.
Principal trading partners: Kenya, UK, Japan.
Total exports ($ million): 399 (1984) of which
unroasted coffee (1979) 96.7%, raw cotton (1979)
1.0%.
Principal trading partners: USA, UK, Japan.

USSR
Gross national product ($ million): 2 310 000 (1987)
Gross national product per head ($): 8160 (1987)
Total imports ($ million): 96 061 (1987) of which
machines and equipment (1988) 40.9%, chemical
products (1988) 2.5%.
Principal trading partners: Germany, Czechoslovakia, Bulgaria, Poland.
Total exports ($ million): 107 874 (1987) of which
petroleum and products (1988) 29.4%, machines and
equipment (1988) 16.2%.
Principal trading partners: Germany, Czechoslovakia, Bulgaria, Poland.

United Arab Emirates
Gross national product ($ million): 23 580 (1988)
Gross national product per head ($): 15 720 (1988)
Total imports ($ million): 6791 (1985) of which
machinery and transport equipment (1986) 31.0%,
basic manufactures (1986) 21.1%.
Principal trading partners: Japan, USA, UK.
Total exports ($ million): 13 124 (1985) of which
crude petroleum (1982) 92.0%, basic manufactures
(1982) 1.2%.
Principal trading partners: Saudi Arabia, Japan,
Qatar.

United Kingdom
Gross national product ($ million): 730 038 (1987)
Gross national product per head ($): 12 800 (1987)
Total imports ($ million): 154 392 (1987) of which
road vehicles and parts (1988) 10.6%, office
machines and automatic data processing (1988)
5.9%.
Principal trading partners: Germany, USA, France,
Netherlands.
Total exports ($ million): 131 210 (1987) of which
petroleum and products (1988) 6.8%, office machines
and automatic data processing equipment (1988)
6.5%.
Principal trading partners: USA, Germany, France,
Netherlands.
Anguilla
Total imports ($ million): 2* (1986). Total exports
($ million): 2* (1986) of which lobsters (1985) 50%*.
Principal trading partner: UK. No other figures are
available.
Bermuda
Gross national product ($ million): 1262. Gross
national product per head ($): 22 540. Total imports
($ million): 402 (1985) of which food (1985) 16.0%,
petroleum and products (1985) 14.1%. Principal
trading partners: USA, Japan. Total exports ($ mil-
lion): 23 (1985) of which drugs and medicine (1985)
57.1%. Principal trading partners: Jamaica, USA.
British Virgin Islands
Gross national product ($ million): 75 (1985). Total
imports ($ million): 105 (1987). Principal trading
partners: USA, UK, Trinidad. Total exports ($ mil-
lion): 2.5 (1987). Principal trading partner: American Virgin Islands.
Cayman Islands
Total imports ($ million): 116* (1984). Total exports
($ million): 1* (1984). Principal trading partners:
UK, Jamaica, USA. No other figures are available.
Channel Islands (Guernsey and Jersey)
Gross national product ($ million): 1350 (1985).
Gross national product per head ($): 10 390 (1985).
Total imports and total exports ($ million): figures
included in the UK total. Principal trading partners:

UK, France.

Falkland Islands
Total exports ($ million): 3 (1983) of which wool 40% (1983). Principal trading partner: UK. No other recent figures are available.

Gibraltar
Gross national product ($ million): 130 (1985). *Gross national product per head ($)*: 4370 (1985). *Total imports ($ million)*: 147 (1985) of which fuels (1988) 20.7%, foodstuffs (1988) 14.3%. Principal trading partners: UK, Spain, Japan. *Total exports ($ million)*: 62 (1985) of which petroleum products (1988) 51.5%, manufactured goods (1988) 40.8%. Principal trading partners: UK, Spain, Morocco.

Hong Kong
Gross national product ($ million): 52 380 (1988). *Gross national product per head ($)*: 9230 (1988). *Total imports ($ million)*: 48 463 (1987) of which machinery and transport equipment (1988) 28.8%, textile yarn and fabrics (1988) 12.6%. Principal trading partners: China, Japan, Taiwan. *Total exports ($ million)*: 48 474 (1987) of which clothing (1988) 30.9%, machinery and transport equipment (1988) 25.3%. Principal trading partners: USA, China, Germany.

Isle of Man
Gross national product ($ million): 380 (1985). *Gross national product per head ($)*: 5910 (1985). *Total imports and exports ($ million)*: included in the UK total. Principal trading partner: UK.

Montserrat
Gross national product ($ million): 13 (1985) *Total imports ($ million)*: 6 (1985). Principal trading partners: UK, USA, Trinidad. *Total exports ($ million)*: 1 (1985). Principal trading partners: Guadeloupe, UK, Antigua.

St Helena and dependencies
Total imports ($ million): 6 (1987) of which fuels (1984) 31.2%. Principal trading partners: UK, South Africa. *Total exports ($ million)*: 0.06 (1984). Principal trading partners: UK, South Africa. No other figures are available.

Turks and Caicos Islands
Total imports ($ million): 26 (1985). *Total exports ($ million)*: 3 (1985). Principal trading partner: USA.

USA
Gross national product ($ million): 4 863 674 (1988) *Gross national product per head ($)*: 19 780 (1988) *Total imports ($ million)*: 424 082 (1987) of which transport equipment (1988) 18.9%, non-electric machinery (1988) 14.2%.
Principal trading partners: Japan, Canada, Germany, Taiwan.
Total exports ($ million): 252 866 (1987) of which non-electric machinery (1988) 18.8%, transport equipment (1988) 14.6%.
Principal trading partners: Canada, Japan, Mexico, UK.

American Samoa
Gross national product ($ million): 190 (1985). *Gross national product per head ($)*: 5410 (1985). *Total imports ($ million)*: 284 (1984). *Total exports ($ million)*: 212 (1984) of which tuna (1984) 98.0%. Principal trading partners: USA, Western Samoa.

Belau (Palau)
Total imports ($ million): 5* (1987). *Total exports ($ million)*: 1* (1987). Principal trading partner: USA.

Guam
Gross national product ($ million): 670 (1985). *Gross national product per head ($)*: 5470 (1985). *Total imports ($ million)*: 355 (1981) of which crude petroleum (1983) 28.8%, machinery and transport equipment (1983) 19.1%. Principal trading partners: USA, Japan. *Total exports ($ million)*: 77 (1981) of which clothing (1983) 16.9%, beverages and tobacco (1983) 12.0%. Principal trading partner: USA.

North Mariana Islands
Total imports ($ million): 149 (1987) of which construction materials (1987) 26.7%, food (1987) 15.5%. Principal trading partner: USA. No other figures are available.

Puerto Rico
Gross national product ($ million): 18 520 (1987). *Gross national product per head ($)*: 5540 (1987). *Total imports ($ million)*: 11 859 (1988) of which metals and products (1988) 20.3%, food (1988) 13.2%. Principal trading partners: USA, Japan, Ecuador. *Total exports ($ million)*: 13 186 (1988) of which chemicals and products (1988) 36.7%, metal and products (1988) 17.7%. Principal trading partners: USA, Dominican Republic, American Virgin Islands.

Virgin Islands
Gross national product ($ million): 1074 (1986). *Gross national product per head ($)*: 9760 (1986). *Total imports ($ million)*: 2643 (1987) of which crude petroleum (1986) 66.8%, food (1986) 8.2%. Principal trading partners: USA, Puerto Rico. *Total exports ($ million)*: 2119 (1987) of which petroleum products (1986) 88.2%, chemical products (1986) 8.8%. Principal trading partners: USA, Puerto Rico.

Uruguay
Gross national product ($ million): 7430 (1988) *Gross national product per head ($)*: 2470 (1988) *Total imports ($ million)*: 1130 (1987) of which machinery and appliances (1988) 17.1%, chemical products (1988) 16.1%.
Principal trading partners: Brazil, Argentina, USA.
Total exports ($ million): 1189 (1987) of which textiles and products (1988) 35.1, live animals and animal products (1988) 19.5%.
Principal trading partners: Brazil, USA, Germany.

Vanuatu
Gross national product ($ million): 120 (1988) *Gross national product per head ($)*: 820 (1988) *Total imports ($ million)*: 70 (1987) of which basic manufactures (1988) 31.0%, machinery and transport equipment (1988) 24.4%.
Principal trading partners: Australia, Japan, New Zealand.
Total exports ($ million): 18 (1987) of which copra (1988) 45.1%, beef and veal (1988) 11.4%.
Principal trading partners: Netherlands, Japan, Belgium.

Venezuela
Gross national product ($ million): 59 390 (1988) *Gross national product per head ($)*: 3170 (1988) *Total imports ($ million)*: 7951 (1987) of which machinery and transport equipment (1987) 43.7%, chemicals (1987) 16.6%.
Principal trading partners: USA, Germany, Japan.
Total exports ($ million): 8402 (1987) of which crude petroleum and products (1987) 82.3%, base metals (1987) 10.4%.
Principal trading partners: USA, Germany, Japan.

Vietnam
Gross national product ($ million): 6500* (1988)
Gross national product per head ($): 109 (1988)
Total imports ($ million): 421 (1987) of which
fuel and raw materials (1985) 44.7%, machinery
(1985) 23.2%.
Principal trading partners: USSR, Japan, Australia.
Total exports ($ million): 169 (1987) of which
raw materials (1985) 46.0%, handicrafts (1985)
24.1%.
Principal trading partners: USSR, Singapore, Hong
Kong.

Western Samoa
Gross national product ($ million): 100 (1988)
Gross national product per head ($): 580 (1988)
Total imports ($ million): 62 (1987) of which
food (1983) 21.3%, machinery (1983) 21.0%.
Principal trading partners: New Zealand, Australia,
Japan.
Total exports ($ million): 11 (1987) of which
coconut oil (1986) 29.3%, taro (1986) 19.4%.
Principal trading partners: New Zealand, Australia,
USA.

Yemen
(Combined figures are given for the former North
and South Yemen – import and export figures exclude
inter-Yemeni trade.)
Gross national product ($ million): 6700 (1988)
Gross national product per head ($): 575* (1988)
Total imports ($ million): 441 (1986) of which food
and live animals (1987) 31.8%*, machinery and
transport equipment (1987) 20%*.
Principal trading partners: Saudi Arabia, Italy,
Japan.
Total exports ($ million): 82 (1987) of which food and
live animals (1987) 16.7%*, coffee (1987)
9.4%*.
Principal trading partners: USA, Japan, Pakistan.

Yugoslavia
Gross national product ($ million): 63 070 (1988)
Gross national product per head ($): 2680 (1988)
Total imports ($ million): 12 603 (1987) of which
machinery and transport equipment (1988) 27.2%,
mineral fuels (1988) 17.6%.
Principal trading partners: Germany, USSR, Italy,
USA.
Total exports ($ million): 11 425 (1988) of which
machinery and transport equipment (1988) 30.8%,
manufactured goods (1988) 28.6%.
Principal trading partners: USSR, Germany, Italy,
Czechoslovakia.

Zaïre
Gross national product ($ million): 5740 (1988)
Gross national product per head ($): 170 (1988)
Total imports ($ million): 884 (1986) of which
mining equipment (1987) 32.0%, food, beverages and
tobacco (1987) 14.6%.
Principal trading partners: Belgium, France,
Germany.
Total exports ($ million): 1092 (1986) of which
copper (1987) 51.5%, coffee (1987) 16.0%.
Principal trading partners: Belgium, USA, France.

Zambia
Gross national product ($ million): 2160 (1988)
Gross national product per head ($): 290 (1988)
Total imports ($ million): 581 (1986) of which

machinery and transport equipment (1984) 28.7%,
basic manufactures (1984) 16.3%.
Principal trading partners: Japan, South Africa,
UK.
Total exports ($ million): 461 (1986) of which
copper (1984) 86.8%, zinc (1984) 4.3%.
Principal trading partners: Japan, UK, USA.

Zimbabwe
Gross national product ($ million): 6070 (1988)
Gross national product per head ($): 660 (1988)
Total imports ($ million): 985 (1986) of which
machinery and transport equipment (1987) 34.7%,
chemicals (1987) 17.8%.
Principal trading partners: South Africa, Germany,
UK.
Total exports ($ million): 1018 (1986) of which
tobacco (1987) 19.0%, gold (1987) 18.9%.
Principal trading partners: South Africa, UK,
Germany.

UNEMPLOYMENT

The average rate of unemployment as a percentage of the
total workforce during 1989 for the G7 countries (see p.
487) was as follows:

Italy	11.3%
France	10.5%
Canada	7.8%
UK	7.8%
Germany	7.8%
USA	5.5%
Japan	2.5%

CURRENCIES OF THE WORLD
As at 7 January 1991
On the financial markets, currencies are most
commonly quoted in US dollars, as given here.

Afghanistan 1 afghani = 100 puls (puli);
1$US = AF 52.0724.

Albania 1 new lek = 100 qindarka (qintars);
1$US = 5.1817 leks.

Algeria 1 dinar = 100 centimes;
1$US = DA 11.9884.

Andorra uses French and Spanish currency (qv).

Angola 1 kwanza = 100 1wei; 1$US = Kz 30.9501.

Antigua and Barbuda 1 East Caribbean dollar[1]
= 100 cents; 1$US = EC$ 2.6951.

Argentina 1 austral = 100 centavos;
1$US = A 5831.85.

Australia 1 Australian dollar = 100 cents;
A$ 1.2883.

Austria 1 Schilling = 100 Groschen;
1$US = S 10.7686.

Bahamas 1 Bahamian dollar = 100 cents;
1$US = US$ 2.

Bahrain 1 Bahrain dinar = 1000 fils;
1$US = BD 0.3698.

Bangladesh 1 taka = 100 poisha;
1$US = Tk 35.1521.

Barbados 1 Barbados dollar = 100 cents;
1$US = BD$ 2.0076.

Belgium 1 Belgian franc (frank) = 100 centimes
(centiemen); 1$US = BF 31.5582.

Belize 1 Belizean dollar = 100 cents; 1$US = BZ$ 1.9963.

Benin 1 CFA franc^2 = 100 centimes; 1$US = CFAF 260.1.

Bhutan 1 ngultrum = 100 chetrums; 1$US = Nu 18.363. The ngultrum is fixed at a par with the Indian rupee which is also legal tender in Bhutan.

Bolivia 1 boliviano = 100 centavos; 1$US = Bs 3.4037.

Botswana 1 pula = 100 thebe; 1$US = P 1.853

Brazil 1 new cruzado = 100 centavos; 1$US = NCz$ 174.357.

Brunei 1 Brunei dollar = 100 cents; 1$US = B$ 1.7536.

Bulgaria 1 leva = 100 stotinki (stotinka); 1$US = 2.8155 leva.

Burkina Faso 1 CFA franc^2 = 100 centimes; 1$US = CFAF 260.1.

Burma (Myanmar) 1 kyat = 100 pyas; 1$US = K 6.0745.

Burundi 1 Burundi franc = 100 centimes; 1$US = FBu 163.431.

Cambodia 1 new riel = 100 sen; 1$US = 459.155 riels.

Cameroon 1 CFA franc^2 = 100 centimes; 1$US = CFAF 260.1.

Canada 1 Canadian dollar = 100 cents; 1$US = Can$ 1.1529.

Cape Verde 1 Cape Verde escudo = 100 centavos; 1$US = CV Esc 65.2151.

Central African Republic 1 CFA franc^2 = 100 centimes; 1$US = CFAF 260.1.

Chad 1 CFA franc^2 = 100 centimes; 1$US = CFAF 260.1.

Chile 1 Chilean peso = 100 centavos; 1$US = Ch$ 336.306.

China, People's Republic 1 yuan (or renminbiao) = 10 jiao (chiao) = 100 fen; 1$US = Y 5.2809.

China (Taiwan) 1 new Taiwan dollar = 100 cents; 1$US = NT$ 27.0724.

Colombia 1 Colombian peso = 100 centavos; Col$ 530.981.

Comoros 1 CFA franc^2 = 100 centimes; 1$US = CFAF 260.1.

Congo 1 CFA franc^2 = 100 centimes; 1$US = CFAF 260.1

Costa Rica 1 Costa Rican colon = 100 centimos; 1$US = ¢ 104.092.

Cuba 1 Cuban peso = 100 centavos; 1$US = 0.7951 pesos.

Cyprus 1 Cyprus pound = 100 cents; 1$US = £C 0.4333. Turkish currency is used in northern Cyprus.

Czechoslovakia 1 koruna = 100 haléřu (halér); 1$US = Kčs 27.6232.

Denmark 1 Danish krone = 100 ore; 1$US = Dkr 5.8945. Danish currency is also used in the Faeroe Islands and Greenland.

Djibouti 1 Djibouti franc = 100 centimes; 1$US = DF 176.417.

Dominica 1 East Caribbean dollar^1 = 100 cents; 1$US = EC$ 2.6951

Dominican Republic 1 Dominican peso = 100 centavos; 1$US = RD$ 11.1794.

INFLATION

The average rate of inflation for the calendar year 1989 for the G7 countries (see p. 487) was as follows:

Canada	11.5%
UK	7.9%
Italy	5.7%
USA	5.1%
France	3.1%
Germany	3.0%
Japan	1.0%

Ecuador 1 sucre = 100 centavos; 1$US = 1 S 889.402.

Egypt 1 Egyptian pound = 100 piastres = 1000 millièmes; 1$US = LE 2.8793.

El Salvador 1 Salvadorian colón = centavos; 1$US = ¢ 6.4323.

Equatorial Guinea 1 CFA franc^2 = 100 centimes; 1$US = CFAF 260.1.

Ethiopia 1 birr = 100 cents; 1$US = Br 2.0443.

Fiji 1 Fiji dollar = 100 cents; 1$US = F$ 1.4519.

Finland 1 markka (Finnmark) = 100 penniä (penni); 1$US = Fmk 3.6728.

France 1 French franc = 100 centimes; 1$US = F 5.2019.
French currency is also used in overseas départements and collectivités territoriales – Guadeloupe, Guyane, Martinique, Réunion, Mayotte, and St Pierre et Miquelon. The French overseas territories of French Polynesia, New Caledonia, and the Wallis and Futuna Islands use the CFP franc. 1 CFP franc = 100 centimes; 1$US = CFPF 93.8352

Gabon 1 CFA franc^2 = 100 centimes; 1$US = CFAF 260.1

Gambia 1 dalasi = 100 butut; 1$US = D 7.3347.

Germany 1 Deutschmark = 100 Pfennige; 1$US = DM 1.532.

Ghana 1 new cedi = 100 pesewas; 1$US = 345.986 cedis.

Greece 1 drachma = 100 leptae (lepta); 1$US = Dr 160.467.

Grenada 1 East Caribbean dollar^1 = 100 cents; 1$US = EC$ 2.6951.

Guatemala 1 quetzal = 100 centavos; 1$US = Q 5.1891.

Guinea 1 franc guineén = 100 centimes; 1$US = GF 618.861.

Guinea-Bissau 1 Guinea peso = 100 centavos; 1$US = PG 648.793.

Guyana 1 Guyanese dollar = 100 cents; 1$US = G$ 44.2025.

Haiti 1 gourde = 100 centimes; 1$US = G 5.

Honduras 1 lempira = 100 centavos; 1$US = L 5.3302.

Hungary 1 forint = 100 fillér; 1$US = Ft 71.406.

Iceland 1 new Icelandic krona = 100 aurar (eyrir); 1$US = ISK 55.9286.

India 1 Indian rupee = 100 paisa (paise); 1$US = Rs 18.363.

Indonesia 1 rupiah = 100 sen; 1$US = Rp 1929.01.

Iran 1 Iranian rial = 100 dinars; 1$US = Rls 65.9496.

Iraq 1 Iraqi dinar = 5 riyals = 20 dirhams = 1000 fils; 1$US = ID 0.3155.

Ireland 1 Irish pound (punt) = 100 pence; 1$US = I£ 0.5724.

Israel 1 new Israel shekel = 100 agorot (agora); 1$US = NIS 2.0278.

Italy 1 Italian lira (lire) = 100 centesimi; 1$US = 1152.02 lire.

Ivory Coast 1 CFA franc[2] = 100 centimes; 1$US = CFAF 260.1.

Jamaica 1 Jamaican dollar = 100 cents; 1$US = J$ 7.7059.

Japan 1 yen = 100 sen; 1$US = Y 136.674.

Jordan 1 Jordanian dinar = 1000 fils; 1$US = JD 0.6497.

Kenya 1 Kenya shilling = 100 cents; 1$US = K Sh 23.767.

Kiribati uses Australian currency (qv).

Korea, Democratic People's Republic (North Korea) 1 won = 100 chon (jun); 1$US = 0.9682 won.

Korea, Republic of 1 won = 100 chun (jeon); 1$US = W 724.029.

Kuwait 1 Kuwaiti dinar = 1000 fils; 1$US = KD 0.2875[3].

Laos 1 new kip = 100 at; 1$US = KN 683.736.

Lebanon 1 Lebanese pound = 100 piastres; 1$US = LL 873.19.

Lesotho 1 loti (maloti) = 100 lisente; 1$US = M 2.5658. The Lesothan loti is kept on a par with the South African rand.

THE ERM

The ERM (the Exchange Rate Mechanism) is an agreement between 10 of the 12 members of the EC to limit movement in the value of their currencies. The ERM is not a totally fixed system. ERM members agree a set of exchange rates against each other's currencies and a margin on either side of these *central rates* to allow for some daily movement in the markets. Most members maintain their exchange rates within 2.25% of the central rates, but Spain and the UK allow a wider degree of fluctuation and allow their currencies to move within 6% of the central rate. The Greek drachma and the Portuguese escudo are not yet members of the ERM.

The pivot of the system is the German mark, against which all other ERM currencies have an agreed central rate. The British pound has a central rate of DM 2.95 and is allowed to float in daily trading between DM 2.77 and DM 3.13.

Sterling's target exchange rates

The pound sterling has the following target exchange rates (central rates) within the ERM system.

Belgian franc	60.84
Danish crown	11.25
German mark	2.95
French franc	9.89
Irish punt	1.10
Italian lira	2207.25
Luxembourg franc	60.84
Dutch guilder	3.32
Spanish peseta	191.75

Liberia 1 Liberian dollar = 100 cents; 1$US = L$ 1. The Liberian dollar is fixed on a par with the US dollar which is also legal tender in Liberia.

Libya 1 Libyan dinar = 1000 dirhams; 1$US = LD 0.2681.

Liechtenstein uses Swiss currency (qv).

Luxembourg 1 Luxembourg franc = 100 centimes; 1$US = Lux F 31.5582. The Luxembourg franc is fixed on a par with the Belgian franc which is also legal tender in Luxembourg.

Madagascar 1 Malagasy franc (franc malgache) = 100 centimes; 1$US = FMG 1351.52.

Malawi 1 Malawi kwacha = 100 tambala; 1$US = MK 2.5708.

Malaysia 1 ringgit or Malaysian dollar = 100 sen; 1$US = M$ 2.7101.

Maldives 1 rufiyaa (Maldivian rupee) = 100 laaris (larees); 1$US = Rf 9.6702.

Mali 1 CFA franc[2] = 100 centimes; 1$US = CFAF 260.1.

Malta 1 Maltese lira (Maltese pound) = 100 cents = 1000 mils; 1$US = Lm 0.2974.

Marshall Islands uses US currency (qv).

Mauritania 1 ouguiya = 5 khoums; 1$US = UM 77.256.

Mauritius 1 Mauritian rupee = 100 cents; 1$US = Mau Rs 13.8247.

Mexico 1 Mexican peso = 100 centavos; 1$US = Mex$ 2935.6.

Micronesia uses US currency (qv).

Monaco uses French currency (qv).

Mongolia 1 tugrik = 100 möngös; 1$US = 3.3494 tugriks.

Morocco 1 dirham = 100 francs (centimes); 1$US = DH 7.8958.

Mozambique 1 metical (meticais) = 100 centavos; 1$US = Mt 1025.13.

Namibia uses South African currency (qv).

Nauru uses Australian currency (qv).

Nepal 1 Nepalese rupee = 100 paisa; 1$US = NRs 30.2534.

Netherlands 1 Netherlands gulden (guilder) or florin = 100 cents; 1$US = F 1.7287.
The Netherlands overseas dependencies have their own currencies on a par with the Dutch guilder. In Aruba, 1 Aruban florin = 100 cents; 1$US = AF 1.7867. In the Netherlands Antilles, 1 Antillean guilder = 100 cents; 1$US = NA F 1.7867.

New Zealand 1 New Zealand dollar = 100 cents; 1$US = $NZ 1.688.

Nicaragua 1 new córdoba = 100 centavos; 1$US = C$ 29944.91.

Niger 1 CFA franc[2] = 100 centimes; 1$US = CFAF 260.1.

Nigeria 1 naira = 100 kobo; 1$US = N 8.7838.

Norway 1 Norwegian krone (kroner) = 100 ore; 1$US = NKr 5.9876.

Oman 1 rial Omani = 1000 baiza; 1$US = RO 0.3856.

Pakistan 1 Pakistani rupee = 100 paisa; 1$US = PRs 21.5634.

Panama 1 balboa = 100 centésimos; 1$US = B 1. The Panamanian balboa is kept on a par with the US dollar which is also legal tender in Panama. The only notes circulating in Panama are in US denominations; Panamanian currency circulates in coins.

Papua New Guinea 1 Kina = 100 toea; 1$US = K 0.9527.

Paraguay 1 guarani = 100 céntimos; 1$US = G 1253.02.

Peru 1 new sol = 100 céntimos; 1$US = NS 0.5191.

Philippines 1 Philippine peso = 100 centavos; 1$US = P 26.7576.

Poland 1 zloty = 100 groszy; 1$US = Zl 9708.29.

Portugal 1 Portuguese escudo = 100 centavos; 1$US = Esc 137.041.
The Portuguese overseas territory of Macau has its own currency, the pataca. 1 pataca = 100 avos; 1$US = 8.028 patacas.

THE ECU

The ecu is a unit of account, based upon a basket of European currencies, used as a reserve asset in the *European Monetary System*, the system that enables member states of the EC to coordinate their exchange rates through the ERM (see p. 467). ECU is an abbreviation for European Currency Unit; the *écu* was also a late medieval French coin.

The ERM is the first stage of the plan for monetary union within the EC. The ecu is widely envisaged as the eventual European currency, and a limited issue of ecu coins has already been made in Belgium, where they are legal tender. Commemorative ecu coins have been issued in France, Ireland and Spain.

Qatar 1 Qatar riyal = 100 dirhams; 1$US = QR 3.6482.

Romania 1 leu (lei) = 100 bani; 1$US = 34.853 lei.

Rwanda 1 Rwanda franc (Franc rwandais) = 100 centimes; 1$US = RF 120.383.

St Christopher and Nevis 1 East Caribbean dollar[1] = 100 cents; 1$US = EC$ 2.6951

St Lucia 1 East Caribbean dollar[1] = 100 cents; 1$US = EC$ 2.6951

St Vincent and the Grenadines 1 East Caribbean dollar[1] = 100 cents; 1$US = EC$ 2.6951

San Marino uses Italian currency (qv).

São Tomé and Príncipe 1 dobra = 100 centavos; 1$US = Db 150.42.

Saudi Arabia 1 Saudi riyal = 100 halalah; 1$US = SRls 3.7578.

Senegal 1 CFA franc[2] = 100 centimes; 1$US = CFAF 260.1.

Seychelles 1 Seychelles rupee = 100 cents; 1$US = SR 5.0367.

Sierra Leone 1 leone = 100 cents; 1$US = Le 182.791.

Singapore 1 Singapore dollar = 100 cents; 1$US = S$ 1.7536.

Solomon Islands 1 Solomon Islands dollar = 100 cents; 1$US = SI$ 2.6002.

Somalia 1 Somali shilling = 100 centesimi; 1$US = So Sh 2615.19.

South Africa 1 rand = 100 cents; 1$US = R 2.5658.

Spain 1 Spanish peseta = 100 céntimos; 1$US = Ptas 97.0094.

Sri Lanka 1 Sri Lanka rupee = 100 cents; 1$US = SL Rs 39.6117.

Sudan 1 Sudanese pound = 100 piastres; 1$US = LSd 4.4918.

Suriname 1 Suriname gulden (guilder) or florin = 100 cents; 1$US = Sf 1.7817. The Suriname guilder is kept on a par with the Dutch guilder.

Swaziland 1 lilangeni (emalangeni) = 100 cents; South African (qv); 1$US = E 2.5658. The Swazi lilangeni is kept on a par with the South African rand.

Sweden 1 Swedish krona (kronor) = 100 öre; 1$US = SKr 5.7069.

Switzerland 1 Swiss franc (Schweizer Franken) = 100 Rappen (centimes); 1$US = Sw F 1.2919.

Syria 1 Syrian pound = 100 piastres; 1$US = LS 20.9614.

Tanzania 1 Tanzanian shilling = 100 cents; 1$US = T Sh 194.832.

Thailand 1 baht = 100 satangs; 1$US = B 24.9737.

Togo 1 CFA franc[2] = 100 centimes; 1$US = CFAF 260.1.

Tonga 1 pa'anga = 100 seniti; 1$US = T$ 1.2883. The Tongan pa'angal is kept on a par with the Australian dollar.

Trinidad and Tobago 1 Trinidad and Tobago dollar = 100 cents; 1$US = TT$ 4.2421.

Tunisia 1 Tunisian dinar = 1000 millimes; 1$US = D 0.8483.

Turkey 1 Turkish lira = 100 kurus; 1$US = LT 2991.47.

Tuvalu uses Australian currency (qv).

Uganda 1 Uganda new shilling = 100 cents; 1$US = U Sh 538.484.

USSR 1 rouble (rubl') = 100 kopeks; 1$US = 0.5582 roubles.

United Arab Emirates 1 UAE dirham = 100 fils; 1$US = Dh 3.6807.

United Kingdom 1 pound sterling = 100 new pence (pennies); 1$US = £ 0.5246.
The Channel Islands, Gibraltar and the Isle of Man use British currency. A number of other British dependencies and overseas territories have their own currencies.
Anguilla and Montserrat use the East Caribbean dollar.
Bermuda, the Cayman Islands and Hong Kong have their own dollars. The Bermuda dollar is kept on a par with the US dollar. In the Cayman Islands, 1$US = 0.835 Caymanian $. In Hong Kong, 1$US = HK$ 7.7696.
The pound sterling and the US dollar are legal tender in the British Indian Ocean Territory.
The US dollar is legal tender in the British Virgin Islands and the Turks and Caicos Islands.
The Falkland Islands £ and the St Helena £ are kept on a par with the pound sterling.

USA 1 US dollar = 100 cents; 1$US = US$1. US currency is also used in American Samoa, Guam, North Mariana Islands, Palau (Belau), Puerto Rico, and the US Virgin Islands.

Uruguay 1 new Uruguayan peso = 100 centésimos; 1$US = NUr$ 1598.71.

Vanuatu 1 vatu = 100 centimes; 1$US = VT 107.293.

Vatican City uses Italian currency (qv).

Venezuela 1 bolívar = 100 céntimos; 1$US = Bs 52.8856.

Vietnam 1 dông = 10 hào = 100 xu; 1$US = D 6498.03.

Western Samoa 1 tala = 100 sene; 1$US = WS$ 2.2426.

Yemen 1 Yemeni riyal = 100 rials; 1$US = YRls 12.0278. The riyal – the currency of the former People's Democratic Republic of Yemen (South Yemen) – is also is circulation.

Yugoslavia 1 dinar = 100 para; 1$US = Din 13.6739.

Zaïre 1 Zaïre = 100 makuta (likuta) = 10 000 sengi; 1$US = Z 1899.9.

Zambia 1 Zambian kwacha = 100 ngwee; 1$US = K 45.8027.

Zimbabwe 1 Zimbabwe dollar = 100 cents; 1$US = Z$ 2.6337.

[1] The East Caribbean dollar is the common currency of Anguilla, Antigua and Barbuda, Dominica, Grenada, Montserrat, St Christopher and Nevis, St Lucia, and St Vincent and the Grenadines.

[2] The CFA Franc is the common currency of Benin, Burkina Faso, Cameroon, Central African Republic, Chad, Congo, Equatorial Guinea, Gabon, Ivory Coast, Mali, Niger, Senegal, and Togo.

[3] The Kuwaiti dinar was not quoted on the international money market on 7 January 1991. Latest available figure for this currency – included above – was on 3 August 1990.

PRODUCTION AND CONSUMER FIGURES

The annual production figures given below are for 1988, the last year for which comparable data is available for the majority of commodities.

ANNUAL PRODUCTION OF MAJOR MINERAL ORES

BAUXITE

Country	Production (in tonnes)
Australia	34 200 000
Guinea	16 300 000
Jamaica	7 700 000
Brazil	6 600 000
USSR	4 900 000
Yugoslavia	3 400 000
Hungary	3 100 000

COAL

Country	Production (in tonnes)
China	885 000 000
USSR	610 000 000
USA	607 000 000
Poland	192 000 000
India	180 000 000
South Africa	177 000 000
Australia	134 000 000
UK	104 000 000
Germany	79 000 000

COPPER

Country	Production (in tonnes)
Chile	1 420 000
USA	1 260 000
USSR	1 000 000
Canada	770 000
Zambia	530 000
Zaïre	500 000
Poland	440 000
Peru	400 000

CRUDE PETROLEUM

Country	Production (in tonnes)
USSR	624 000 000
USA	409 000 000
Saudi Arabia	227 000 000
China	137 000 000
Mexico	135 000 000
Iraq	131 000 000
Iran	113 000 000
UK	111 000 000
Venezuela	103 000 000
Canada	78 000 000
Kuwait	76 000 000
UAE	71 000 000
Nigeria	69 000 000

(Note: Following the Iraqi invasion of Kuwait on 2 August 1990, Kuwaiti oil production ceased and Iraqi oil production was greatly reduced, particularly after the start of the Gulf War on 16 January 1991. Saudi Arabian production has increased to compensate for the disappeareance of Kuwaiti oil on the world market.)

DIAMONDS

Country	Production (in carats)
Australia	35 000 000
Zaïre	23 000 000
Botswana	15 000 000
USSR	12 000 000
South Africa	9 000 000
Angola	1 000 000
China	1 000 000
Namibia	900 000

GOLD

Country	Production (in tonnes)
South Africa	621
USSR	280
USA	205
Australia	152
Canada	129
Brazil	100
China	65

IRON ORE

Country	Production (in tonnes)
USSR	150 000 000
China	75 200 000
Australia	64 800 000
Brazil	46 400 000
USA	35 600 000
India	33 200 000
Canada	24 300 000
Sierra Leone	15 600 000
Sweden	13 300 000

NATURAL GAS

Country	Production (in terajoules)

USSR	27 700 000
USA	16 600 000
Canada	3 800 000
Netherlands	2 100 000
UK	1 600 000
Romania	1 600 000
Algeria	1 600 000
Norway	1 200 000

(Note: a terajoule is a measure of energy equivalent to 34.13 tonnes of coal.)

SILVER

Country	Production (in tonnes)
Mexico	2400
Peru	2000
USSR	1550
Canada	1250
USA	1200
Australia	1100
Poland	830
Chile	500

TIN

Country	Production (in tonnes)
Malaysia	30 400
China	28 000
Brazil	28 500
Indonesia	26 200
USSR	15 000
Thailand	15 000

URANIUM

Country	Production (in tonnes)
Canada	12 400
USA	5 200
South Africa	3 800
Australia	3 600
Namibia	3 500
France	3 400
Niger	3 000

ZINC

Country	Production (in tonnes)
Canada	1 500 000
USSR	950 000
Australia	760 000
Peru	590 000
China	340 000
Mexico	280 000
Spain	270 000

ANNUAL PRODUCTION OF MAJOR CROPS

APPLES

Country	Production (in tonnes)
USSR	5 700 000
China	5 000 000
USA	3 700 000
Germany	2 700 000
France	2 300 000
Italy	2 200 000

BARLEY

Country	Production (in tonnes)
Germany	13 300 000
Spain	12 400 000
France	10 300 000

Canada	10 100 000
UK	8 900 000
Turkey	7 500 000
USA	6 300 000

MAIZE (CORN)

Country	Production (in tonnes)
USA	125 000 000
China	74 000 000
Brazil	24 700 000
Romania	19 500 000
USSR	16 000 000
France	13 700 000
Mexico	12 000 000

RICE

Country	Production (in tonnes)
China	173 400 000
India	102 000 000
Indonesia	41 600 000
Bangladesh	21 900 000
Thailand	20 500 000
Vietnam	15 400 000
Burma	14 100 000

WHEAT

Country	Production (in tonnes)
China	87 500 000
USSR	84 500 000
USA	49 300 000
India	44 600 000
France	29 100 000
Turkey	20 500 000
Germany	15 900 000
Canada	15 700 000
Australia	14 100 000

BANANAS

Country	Production (in tonnes)
Brazil	5 200 000
India	4 600 000
China	2 800 000
Philippines	2 300 000
Ecuador	2 200 000
Indonesia	1 900 000
Thailand	1 600 000
Vietnam	1 500 000
Burundi	1 500 000

CASSAVA

Country	Production (in tonnes)
Brazil	24 700 000
Thailand	19 600 000
Zaïre	16 100 000
Nigeria	14 000 000
Indonesia	13 700 000

COCOA BEANS

Country	Production (in tonnes)
Ivory Coast	720 000
Brazil	347 000
Ghana	255 000
Malaysia	215 000
Cameroon	130 000
Nigeria	125 000

COFFEE

Country	Production (in tonnes)
Brazil	1 330 000

Colombia	780 000
Indonesia	350 000
Mexico	283 000
India	210 000
Uganda	210 000
Ivory Coast	210 000
Ethiopia	180 000

COTTON LINT

Country	Production (in tonnes)
China	4 100 000
USA	3 400 000
India	1 500 000
Pakistan	1 400 000
Brazil	700 000
Egypt	350 000

JUTE

Country	Production (in tonnes)
India	1 200 000
Bangladesh	730 000
China	590 000

POTATOES

Country	Production (in tonnes)
USSR	62 700 000
Poland	34 300 000
China	29 600 000
Germany	18 800 000
USA	14 500 000
India	13 000 000
Romania	8 000 000
Netherlands	7 400 000
France	6 400 000

RUBBER

Country	Production (in tonnes)
Malaysia	1 600 000
Indonesia	1 100 000
Thailand	1 100 000

SUGAR BEET

Country	Production (in tonnes)
USSR	87 800 000
France	26 200 000
Germany	26 100 000
USA	22 800 000
Poland	13 300 000
Italy	13 200 000
Turkey	12 500 000

SUGAR CANE

Country	Production (in tonnes)
Brazil	277 000 000
India	165 000 000
Cuba	73 000 000
China	57 000 000
Mexico	42 000 000
Pakistan	35 000 000
USA	28 000 000
Australia	28 000 000

TEA

Country	Production (in tonnes)
India	690 000

China	560 000
Sri Lanka	225 000
Kenya	160 000
USSR	160 000
Turkey	152 000
Japan	100 000

TOBACCO

Country	Production (in tonnes)
China	2 400 000
USA	600 000
Brazil	450 000
USSR	340 000
India	320 000
Turkey	180 000

LIVESTOCK

CATTLE

Country	Number
India	201 000 000
Brazil	134 000 000
USSR	118 800 000
USA	99 000 000
China	74 000 000
Argentina	51 000 000
Mexico	31 000 000
Ethiopia	31 000 000
Colombia	24 000 000
Bangladesh	23 500 000
Australia	23 500 000
Sudan	22 500 000
France	21 000 000
Germany	21 000 000

SHEEP

Country	Number
Australia	164 000 000
USSR	140 800 000
China	103 000 000
India	57 000 000
New Zealand	64 800 000
Turkey	40 000 000
Iran	35 000 000
South Africa	30 000 000
Argentina	29 000 000
UK	28 000 000

PIGS

Country	Number
China	335 000 000
USSR	77 400 000
USA	43 000 000
Germany	36 200 000
Brazil	32 700 000
Poland	19 600 000
Mexico	18 800 000

GOATS

Country	Number
India	107 000 000
China	78 000 000
Pakistan	33 000 000
Nigeria	26 000 000
Somalia	18 000 000
Ethiopia	17 500 000

ANNUAL PRODUCTION OF AGRICULTURAL, FORESTRY AND FISHING PRODUCTS

BEEF AND VEAL

Country	Production (in tonnes)
USA	10 900 000
USSR	8 600 000
Brazil	2 600 000
Argentina	2 500 000
Germany	2 000 000
France	1 800 000
Australia	1 600 000
Italy	1 200 000
Mexico	1 100 000
UK	1 000 000

BEER

Country	Production (in hectolitres)
USA	229 000 000
Germany	112 100 000
USSR	65 700 000
UK	60 000 000
Japan	48 500 000
Brazil	30 000 000
Mexico	27 200 000
Canada	23 200 000
Czechoslovakia	22 400 000
Spain	21 000 000

BUTTER (AND GHEE)

Country	Production (in tonnes)
USSR	1 800 000
India	800 000
Germany	750 000
USA	540 000
France	500 000
Pakistan	310 000
New Zealand	280 000
Poland	270 000

COW'S MILK

Country	Production (in tonnes)
USSR	106 000 000
USA	65 100 000
Germany	33 100 000
France	31 400 000
India	22 500 000
Poland	15 000 000
UK	15 000 000
Brazil	13 200 000

EGGS

Country	Production (in tonnes)
China	6 700 000
USSR	4 700 000
USA	4 100 000
Japan	2 400 000
Brazil	1 300 000
Germany	1 000 000
India	1 000 000

FISHING CATCH
(Maritime and Freshwater)

Country	Catch (in tonnes)
Japan	11 900 000
USSR	11 200 000
China	9 300 000
USA	5 700 000
Chile	4 800 000
Peru	4 600 000
India	2 900 000
South Korea	2 900 000
Thailand	2 200 000
Philippines	2 000 000
Norway	1 900 000
Denmark	1 700 000
North Korea	1 700 000
Iceland	1 600 000
Spain	1 400 000

PAPER

Country	Production (in tonnes)
USA	68 000 000
Japan	23 000 000
Canada	16 000 000
China	13 000 000
Germany	11 000 000
USSR	10 000 000
Finland	8 000 000
Sweden	8 000 000

ROUNDWOOD – CONIFEROUS

Country	Production (in cubic metres)
USA	340 000 000
USSR	315 000 000
Canada	180 000 000
China	135 000 000
Sweden	45 000 000
Brazil	40 000 000
Finland	34 000 000
Germany	32 000 000
France	21 000 000
Japan	20 000 000

ROUNDWOOD – NON-CONIFEROUS

Country	Production (in cubic metres)
India	235 000 000
USA	180 000 000
Brazil	165 000 000
Indonesia	160 000 000
China	140 000 000
Nigeria	93 000 000
USSR	63 000 000
Malaysia	42 000 000
Philippines	37 000 000
Thailand	34 000 000
Zaïre	32 000 000

SHEEP MEAT

Country	Production (in tonnes)
USSR	830 000
New Zealand	610 000
Australia	580 000
China	380 000
UK	330 000
Turkey	320 000
Iran	230 000
Spain	220 000

SUGAR

Country	Production (in tonnes)
India	9 100 000

Brazil	8 500 000
USSR	8 350 000
Cuba	7 500 000
China	6 200 000
USA	6 100 000
France	4 400 000
Mexico	3 800 000
Germany	3 600 000
Australia	3 500 000

WINE

Country	Production (in tonnes)
Italy	6 900 000
France	6 400 000
Spain	2 300 000
Argentina	1 800 000
USA	1 700 000
USSR	1 500 000
Germany	1 000 000
Romania	1 000 000
Portugal	1 000 000
South Africa	800 000

WOOL

Country	Production (in tonnes)
Australia	920 000
USSR	475 000
New Zealand	350 000
China	220 000
Argentina	140 000
South Africa	90 000
UK	65 000
Turkey	60 000

ANNUAL PRODUCTION OF MANUFACTURED GOODS

ALUMINIUM

Country	Production (in tonnes)
USA	5 300 000
USSR	2 400 000
Canada	1 600 000
Germany	1 300 000
Japan	1 100 000
Australia	1 100 000
Brazil	850 000

CARS

Country	Number
Japan	8 200 000
USA	7 100 000
Germany	4 500 000
France	3 100 000
Italy	1 800 000
Spain	1 400 000
USSR	1 300 000
UK	1 200 000
Belgium	1 100 000
South Korea	800 000
Canada	800 000
Sweden	400 000
Brazil	400 000

CEMENT

Country	Production (in tonnes)
China	186 000 000
USSR	136 000 000
Japan	72 000 000

USA	67 000 000
Germany	38 000 000
India	37 000 000
Italy	36 000 000
South Korea	26 000 000
Brazil	25 000 000
France	24 000 000
Spain	23 000 000
Mexico	22 000 000
Turkey	22 000 000

COMMERCIAL VEHICLES

Country	Number
Japan	4 500 000
USA	3 900 000
Canada	830 000
France	550 000
Brazil	550 000
UK	300 000

CRUDE STEEL

Country	Production (in tonnes)
USSR	162 000 000
Japan	107 000 000
USA	90 000 000
China	59 000 000
Germany	49 000 000
Brazil	25 000 000
Italy	24 000 000
France	19 000 000
UK	19 000 000

SHIPPING (MERCHANT)

Country	Launched (tonnes)
Japan	4 600 000
South Korea	3 400 000
Germany	730 000
Italy	430 000
Yugoslavia	330 000
Denmark	280 000
China	270 000
Brazil	260 000
Finland	250 000

TELEVISION SETS

Country	Number
Japan	17 700 000
China	16 700 000
USA	13 700 000
USSR	9 400 000
South Korea	7 800 000
Germany	4 400 000
Taiwan	3 900 000
UK	3 000 000
Brazil	2 200 000
France	1 900 000
Italy	1 700 000
Singapore	1 500 000

ENERGY CAPACITY

The following figures record the total installed capacity of major producers of electricity.

Country	Capacity (kilowatt-hours)	
USA	720 000 000	(76% thermal)
USSR	321 700 000	(71% thermal)
Japan	173 300 000	(65% thermal)
Germany	104 300 000	(73% thermal)

Canada	98 400 000	(58% hydroelectric)
France	92 100 000	(48% nuclear)
China	87 000 000	(69% thermal)
UK	66 500 000	(83% thermal)
Italy	56 200 000	(65% thermal)
India	54 700 000	(69% thermal)
Brazil	44 800 000	(84% hydroelectric)
Spain	35 100 000	(43% thermal)
Australia	33 500 000	(78% thermal)
Sweden	33 100 000	(48% hydroelectric)
Poland	29 800 000	(93% thermal)
South Africa	24 700 000	(94% thermal)
Mexico	24 100 000	(71% thermal)
Norway	23 700 000	(99% hydroelectric)
Czechoslovakia	20 400 000	(72% thermal)
Romania	19 700 000	(77% thermal)
South Korea	19 600 000	(64% thermal)
Netherlands	17 200 000	(97% thermal)
Taiwan	16 600 000	(54% thermal)
Argentina	16 300 000	(56% thermal)
Yugoslavia	16 100 000	(49% thermal)
Austria	15 800 000	(66% hydroelectric)
Switzerland	15 200 000	(76% hydroelectric)
Belgium	14 200 000	(52% thermal)
Saudi Arabia	14 100 000	(100% thermal)
Iran	13 400 000	(87% thermal)
Venezuela	12 500 000	(65% thermal)
Finland	11 500 000	(58% thermal)
Bulgaria	10 200 000	(64% thermal)
Turkey	10 100 000	(62% thermal)

ECONOMICS

ECONOMIC SCARCITY

Economics is concerned with the problem of using the available resources of a country as efficiently as possible to achieve the maximum fulfilment of society's unlimited demands for goods and services. The ultimate purpose of economic endeavour is to satisfy human wants for products. The problem is that although wants are virtually without limit, the resources – natural resources, labour and capital – available to produce goods and services are limited in supply. Since resources are scarce – relative to the demands they are called upon to satisfy – mechanisms are required in order to allocate resources between individual end uses (see microeconomics, below) and to ensure that all the available resources are fully employed (see macroeconomics, below).

ECONOMIC SYSTEMS

An economy can be 'organized' in a number of ways.

Market economies

In a *private enterprise* or *market economy* the means of production are privately held by individuals and businesses. Economic decision-making is highly decentralized, and resources are allocated through a large number of individual markets for goods and services. The *market* brings together buyers and producers. By establishing prices for products and suitable profit rewards for suppliers, the market will determine how much of a product will be produced and sold. Proponents of enterprise systems highlight the inefficiencies and rigidities usually associated with state bureaucracies (see Command economies, below), and suggest that competition, far from being wasteful, acts as an important spur to efficiency and

encourages enterprise, leading to lower prices and better goods and services.

Command economies

In a *command, centrally planned* or *state economy,* economic decision-making is centralized in the hands of the state. The means of production – except labour – are under collective ownership. The state bureaucracy decides which products – and how many of each – are to be produced in accordance with some centralized national plan. Resources are allocated between producing units by quotas. Advocates of this system emphasize the benefits of synchronizing and coordinating the allocation of resources as a unified whole, avoiding the 'wastes' of duplication inherent in competition.

Mixed economies

In a *mixed economy* the state provides some goods and services (for example, electricity, postal services, medical care, education, etc), while others are provided by private enterprise. The precise 'mix' of private enterprise and state activities to be found in particular countries varies substantially and is very much influenced by the political philosophies of the government concerned.

The formation of the European Community, programmes of 'privatization' in Britain, France and a number of Latin American countries, and the collapse of the command economies of the countries of eastern and central Europe bear testimony to the current ascendancy of the 'free' market economies.

MICROECONOMICS

THE PRICE SYSTEM

Microeconomics is concerned with how resources that are scarce are allocated to produce a multitude of goods and services to meet the demands of consumers for these products. In a market economy, the *price system* operates to synchronize the actions of buyers and sellers of products, and so determining the underlying pattern of resource allocation. The following simple example explains how the price system 'works' to this end.

Let us assume two products, coffee and tea, and that initially prices are such as to equate supply and demand for these products in their respective markets. If there is a change in consumer demand away from tea and towards coffee, the increased demand for coffee – coupled with an unchanged coffee supply in the short-run – results in an *excess demand* for coffee at the prevailing price. This extra demand causes the price of coffee to rise. By the same token, the fall in demand for tea – coupled with an unchanged tea supply in the short-run – results initially in an *excess supply* of tea at the prevailing price and a fall in the price of tea as suppliers seek to clear unsold stocks.

These changes in prices will affect the profits of coffee and tea suppliers. The rising price of coffee will increase the profitability of supplying coffee and the falling price of tea will decrease the profitability of supplying tea. Over the longer term, existing coffee producers will expand production and new producers will enter the market, causing the price of coffee to fall until a new *equilibrium price* – at which supply will again equal demand – is reached. Similarly, the falling price of tea will drive less efficient suppliers out of the market, while other suppliers will curtail their output. The resulting decline in tea supply will continue until tea supply adjusts to the lower level of demand and prices stabilize, restoring the equality of supply and demand.

Changes in product markets will have repercussions in the resource markets. In order to expand coffee supply, extra labour and capital resources must be drawn into coffee production and this can only be achieved by offering them a higher return than they receive elsewhere. By contrast, the tea industry will release resources as firms leave the market, and the remaining resources will earn lower returns. The 'price' of a product acts as a resource 'signaller', serving to reallocate resources away from products where the demand is falling (as reflected in lower prices) to be redeployed in the production of products where demand is increasing (as reflected in higher prices).

However, the response of supply within the price system to changes in consumer demand may be very slow and painful, because less efficient firms are not eliminated quickly but linger on making low profits or losses. Also, resources cannot always be easily 'switched' from one activity to another. For example, in the case of labour, a significant amount of retraining may be required or workers may be required to move from one area of the country to another. Thus, occupational and geographical immobilities may inhibit effective resource redeployment.

The market may also be distorted by monopolies. Monopoly suppliers of products may deliberately restrict supply in order to force up prices; similarly, powerful labour unions may force up wage rates.

MICROECONOMIC POLICY

Because of the problems noted above, governments often attempt to improve the allocation of resources by using a variety of industrial, competition, regional and labour policies. *Industrial policy*, for example, can be used to reorganize industries beset by excess capacity, by compensating firms for leaving the industry or encouraging firms to merge and close down redundant plant. Industrial policy can also be used to foster innovation by providing grants and tax benefits to firms investing in research and development and to provide retraining facilities to improve occupational mobility. *Competition policy* can be used to prevent dominant firms from profiteering at the expense of consumers and to outlaw price-fixing agreements between firms. Similarly, competition policy can be used to prevent mergers and takeovers likely to have anti-competitive consequences. *Regional policies* can be used alongside macroeconomic policies to stimulate employment opportunities by encouraging new firms and industries to invest in areas of high unemployment to replace declining industries. Finally, it is possible for a government to improve the functioning of resource markets by adopting *labour policies* – for example, attacking restrictive labour practices and reducing the monopoly power of trade unions.

MACROECONOMICS AND THE MARKET ECONOMY

Macroeconomics is concerned with how the economy as a whole 'works'. It seeks to identify determinants of the levels of national income, output and spending, employment and prices, and the balance of payments.

The premise of macroeconomics – and the rationale for governments 'managing the economy' – is that there are certain 'forces' at work in the economy that transcend individual markets. The level of spending in the economy affects all markets to a greater or lesser degree as well as affecting the overall levels of employment and prices in the economy. Thus, if total spending (i.e. *aggregate demand*) is too low relative to the output potential of the economy (i.e. *aggregate supply*) the result is likely to be rising unemployment. If total spending is too high, causing the economy to 'overheat', the result may be inflation and/or rising levels of imports, leading to balance-of-payments problems.

THE CIRCULAR FLOW OF NATIONAL INCOME AND EXPENDITURE

'Households' purchase goods and services from 'businesses', using income received from supplying economic resources (their labour and/or capital) to businesses. Businesses produce goods and services using resources supplied to them by households.

This basic model can be developed to incorporate a number of 'injections' to and 'withdrawals' from the income flow. For example, not all of the income received by households is spent – some is saved. Saving is a withdrawal from the income flow. Businesses not only produce *consumer goods*, they also produce *investment* or *capital goods* (factories, machines, etc). Investment injects funds back into the income flow. Part of the income received by households is taxed by the government and serves to reduce the amount of income consumers have available to spend. Taxation is a withdrawal from the income flow. However, when governments spend their taxation receipts by providing public goods (schools, roads, etc.) and benefits such as old-age pensions and unemployment benefit, they inject income back into the 'flow'. Households spend some of their income on goods and services produced abroad. Imports are a withdrawal from the income flow. On the other hand, some output is sold to overseas customers. Exports represent spending by foreigners on domestically produced goods and services and so constitute an injection into the income flow.

MACROECONOMIC POLICY

Governments attempt to 'manage' or control income and spending flows in the economy in order to ensure that they are consistent with their overall economic objectives. Typically, governments are concerned to secure four main macroeconomic objectives: *full employment* (unemployment is to be avoided because it results in 'lost' output to the economy); *price stability* (inflation is to be avoided because it produces harmful effects, for example people on fixed incomes – such as pensioners – suffer a fall in their standard of living); *economic growth* (growth is desirable because it enables the economy to produce more goods and services over time, serving to increase living standards); and a *balance of payments equilibrium* (a persistent excess of imports over exports is to be avoided since this is likely to lower domestic incomes and lead to job losses).

Governments use four main methods – *fiscal policy, monetary policy, prices and incomes policies* and *management of the exchange rate* – to control the level and distribution of spending in the economy.

Fiscal policy involves the use of various taxation measures to control spending. If spending needs to be reduced, the authorities can, for example, increase 'direct taxes' on individuals (raising income tax rates) and companies (raising corporation tax rates). Spending can also be reduced by increasing 'indirect taxes' – an increase in value-added taxes on products in general, or an increase in excise duties on particular products such as petrol and beer, will, by increasing their prices, lead to a reduction in purchasing power. Alternatively, the government can use changes in its own expenditure to affect spending levels; a cut in current purchases of products or capital investment by the government, for example, will reduce total spending in the economy.

Taxation and government expenditure are linked together in terms of the government's overall fiscal or budget position. A *budget surplus* (with government taxation and other receipts exceeding expenditure) serves to decrease total spending, while a *budget deficit* (where expenditure is greater than taxation receipts) serves to increase total spending in the economy.

Monetary policy involves the regulation of the money supply (notes and coins, bank deposits, etc.), and of credit and interest rates in the economy. If, for example, the authorities wish to reduce the level of spending they can seek to reduce the money supply by an *open market operation* such as selling government securities to the general public. Buyers pay for these securities by running down their bank deposits – an important component of the money supply. This forces the banks in turn to reduce the amount of bank loans to personal and business customers.

The authorities can also seek to reduce spending by making borrowing more expensive, i.e. by the increasing interest rates on loans used to buy cars, televisions, houses, etc. This is done by direct government intervention in the money markets to reduce the availability of monetary assets relative to the demand for them, and so forcing up base lending rates. Occasionally, the authorities use more direct methods to limit credit by, for example, 'instructing' the banks to limit or reduce the amount of loans they make available.

Prices and incomes policies are statutory controls on costs and prices.

The management of the exchange rate influences the country's external trade and payments position.

NOBEL PRIZEWINNERS IN ECONOMICS

Established in 1969.
1969 Ragnar Frisch, Norwegian, and Jan Tinbergen, Dutch: for work in econometrics.
1970 Paul A. Samuelson, USA: for scientific analysis of economic theory.
1971 Simon Kuznets, USA (naturalized citizen): for research on the economic growth of nations.
1972 Sir John Hicks, English, and Kenneth J. Arrow, USA: for contributions to the general economic equilibrium theory.
1973 Wassily Leontief, USA (naturalized citizen): for work on input analysis.
1974 Gunnar Myrdal, Swedish, and Friedrich von Hayek, British: for analysis of the interdependence of economic, social and institutional phenomena.
1975 Leonid V. Kantorovich, Russian, and Tjalling C. Koopmans, USA (naturalized citizen): for contributions to the theory of optimum allocation of resources.

1976 Milton Friedman, USA: for consumption analysis, monetary theory and economic stabilization.
1977 Bertil Ohlin, Swedish, and James Meade, English: for contributions to theory of international trade.
1978 Herbert A. Simon, USA: for decision-making processes in economic organization.
1979 W. Arthur Lewis, English, and Theodore W. Schultz, USA: for analysis of economic processes in developing nations.
1980 Lawrence R. Klein, USA: for development and analysis of empirical models of business fluctuations.
1981 James Tobin, USA: for empirical macroeconomic theories.
1982 George Stigler, USA: for work on the economic effects of governmental regulation.
1983 Gerard Debrau, USA: for mathematical proof of supply and demand theory.
1984 Sir Richard Stone, English: for the development of a national income accounting system.
1985 Franco Modigliani, USA: for analysis of household savings and financial markets.
1986 James McGill Buchanan, USA: for political theories advocating limited government role in the economy.
1987 Robert M. Solow, USA: for contributions to the theory of economic growth.
1988 Maurice Allais, French: for contributions to the theory of markets and efficient use of resources.
1989 Trygve Haavelmo, Norwegian: for testing fundamental econometric theories.
1990 Harry Markowitz, Merton Miller and William Sharpe, USA: for pioneering theories on managing investment portfolios and corporate finances.

GLOSSARY

ECONOMIC TERMS

accelerator the impetus to increase new investment in an economy as rising demand puts pressure on existing supply capacities.

advertising the use of the media (commercial, television, newspapers, posters) to promote the sales of products and services.

aggregate demand the total amount of spending on goods and services in an economy.

aggregate supply the total amount of goods and services produced by an economy. (See gross national product.)

agricultural policy a policy aimed at improving the efficiency of the farm sector and protecting farmers' incomes by the use of grants and price and income support.

appreciation an increase in the price of an asset, or value (exchange rate) of a country's currency that makes imports cheaper and exports more expensive. (See depreciation, and floating exchange rate.)

arbitrage the buying and selling of products, etc., between separate markets (e.g. two countries) in order to take advantage of any price differences in these markets.

asset an item of property (a house, shares, money owed by debtors, etc.) that has a money value.

balance of payments the balance of a country's imports and exports; a financial statement of a country's transactions with other countries in goods and services ('the current account') and capital flows (investment, loans, etc.).

balance of trade a financial statement of a country's transactions with other countries in *goods*.

balance sheet a financial statement of a firm's assets and liabilities on the last day of a trading period.

bank a financial institution that accepts deposits from persons and businesses, and provides them with various facilities (money transmission via cheques, loans and overdrafts, etc.).

bank deposit a sum of money held on deposit with a bank either as a 'current account' (from which withdrawals can be made, subject to notice being given) or an 'investment account'. (See cheque.)

barriers to entry obstacles in the way of new firms attempting to enter a market, such as customer brand loyalty to established firm's products.

barter the exchange of one product for another product. (See money.)

base rate the lowest or 'floor' interest rate charged by the banks on loans and overdrafts. This usually applies only to their most credit-worthy customers, others being charged higher rates.

bill of exchange a financial security representing an amount of credit extended by one firm to another, usually for three months.

black economy economic activities that go 'unrecorded', in particular, work performed by people who wish to avoid disclosing their income to the tax authorities.

black market an 'unofficial' market in a product which is either prohibited by law (e.g. narcotics) or which is in short supply.

bond a financial security issued by a company or the government as a means of raising long-term loan finance.

budget (government) a financial review of a government's receipts (from taxes, etc.) and expenditures (social security, etc.).

budget deficit an excess of expenditure over receipts in a government's budget.

budget surplus an excess of receipts over expenditures in a government's budget.

building society a financial institution that accepts deposits from persons and businesses and makes mortgages available for house purchase (and limited banking facilities).

business cycle the tendency for industrial production to swing upwards ('recovery' to 'boom') and downwards ('recession' to 'slump') as demand in the economy rises and falls.

capital physical assets, such as factories used to produce products, and financial assets, such as shares used to finance physical investment.

capital formation additions to the capital stock of an economy.

capital goods products such as machinery and equipment that are purchased by businesses as opposed to consumers. (See consumer.)

capital stock a country's accumulated stock of productive assets such as factories, machinery and equipment.

cartel a group of producers (e.g. the OPEC oil cartel) who act together to fix uniform prices, limit production, etc.

central bank: the premier bank of a country (usually owned by the state). It is responsible for regulating the state's internal and external monetary affairs. (See monetary policy, and exchange rate.)

centrally planned economy an economy in which all or most of the country's productive assets are owned by the state as opposed to individuals and firms. (See nationalization, and p. 474.)

cheque a written order drawn upon a bank. It is a means of purchasing products or withdrawing cash from a bank deposit.

collusion a market situation where suppliers act together to suppress competition. (See cartel.)

commodity market a market that is engaged in the buying and selling of commodities such as tin, copper, wheat, cattle, etc., and the determination of market prices for these products.

common market a group of countries that have entered a formal agreement to provide for the free movement of products, capital and labour across national boundaries.

comparative advantage the advantage possessed by a country engaged in international trade if it can produce a given good at a lower resource cost than other countries.

competition a market situation where suppliers compete against one another in terms of price, quality, advertising, etc.

competition policy a policy aimed at improving market efficiency and protecting consumers by controlling monopolies, mergers, cartels and anti-competitive practices such as refusals to supply, exclusive dealing, etc.

concentration a measure of the extent to which the supply of a particular product is controlled by the leading suppliers.

consumer goods products such as toys, bread, etc., which are purchased by consumers as opposed to businesses. (See capital goods.)

consumption the proportion of current income that is used to purchase goods and services. (See savings.)

convertibility the ability to exchange one foreign currency (e.g. the UK £) for another currency (e.g. the US $).

corporation tax a levy by the government on the income (profits) earned by businesses.

cost the payment (wages, materials, etc.) incurred by a firm in producing its products.

cost of living the general level of prices in an economy as measured by a price index. (See retail price index.)

credit an amount of money made available in the form of a loan, overdraft, mortgage, etc., to persons or businesses.

currency bank notes and coins issued by the monetary authorities of a country. They form part of a country's money supply.

debt an amount of money owing to a person or business that has advanced credit in the form of a loan, overdraft, or mortgage.

deflation a reduction in the level of demand and a fall in the rate of growth of the general price level (disinflation). (See inflation.)

deindustrialization a relative decline in the industrial sector of the economy compared to other sectors, particularly services.

demand the want, need or desire for a product backed by the money to purchase it.

demand curve a line depicting the total amount of a product buyers are prepared to purchase over a range of prices. (See equilibrium market price.)

depreciation a fall in the value of an asset due to wear and tear, or in the value (exchange rate) of a country's currency; the latter makes imports more expensive and exports cheaper. (See appreciation and floating exchange rate.)

devaluation an administered reduction in the value (exchange rate) of a country's currency under a fixed exchange rate system; this makes imports more expensive and exports cheaper. (See revaluation.)

discount market a market engaged in the buying and selling of bills of exchange and Treasury bills.

disposable income the income remaining to households after the payment of all taxes on income.

diversification the combination in one firm of a number of unrelated productive activities, e.g. brewing and publishing.

dividend income received from the ownership of shares.

dumping the sale of a product in an export market at a price that is *lower* than its domestic price.

economic growth an increase in the amount of goods and services produced in an economy over time.

economics the study of the allocation of *limited* resources of capital, labour, etc., to meet the (*unlimited*) demands of society for goods and services.

economies of scale a fall in the average cost of producing a product as the volume of output is increased.

elasticity of demand the extent to which the demand for a product is affected by changes in its *own* price, consumer's income and the prices of *other* products.

embargo a ban on international trade with a particular country or in particular products.

equilibrium market price the price at which the total demand for a product is exactly equal to the total quantity supplied so that the market price 'stabilizes' for the present. (See excess demand, and excess supply.)

eurocurrency a currency that is used to finance trade and investment outside its country of origin, in Western Europe.

European Community (EC) an alliance of 12 countries that seeks to establish free trade between members (the 'Common Market'; see p. 483).

European Currency Unit (ECU) the monetary asset used by the European Community to settle payments imbalances between members and to value intra-EC government transactions (see p. 468).

European Monetary System (EMS) the mechanism that co-ordinates the exchange rates of member countries of the European Community and facilitates the settlement of payments imbalances. (See European Currency Unit and fixed exchange rates; p. 467.)

excess demand demand for a product that is greater than supply at the prevailing price which causes the price to rise. (See equilibrium market price.)

excess supply supply of a product that is greater than demand at the prevailing price. Excess supply

causes the price to fall. (See equilibrium market price.)

exchange rate the price of one foreign currency expressed in terms of another. Exchange rates between currencies may be left to 'float' upwards or downwards day-by-day according to market forces, or the authorities may intervene to stabilize or 'fix' the exchange rate at a particular value. (For the exchange rates of all currencies against the US$, see table on pp. 465–69.)

export a produce (or asset) that is sold in an overseas market. (See balance of payments.)

factors of production natural resources (tin, wheat, etc.), labour and capital that are used as inputs in the production of goods and services.

fiscal policy the manipulation by the government of taxes, tax rates and government expenditure as a means of controlling the level of spending in the economy.

fixed exchange rate an exchange rate for a currency that is 'pegged' at a particular value by the authorities as opposed to being allowed to 'float' according to market forces.

floating exchange rate an exchange rate for a currency that is free to fluctuate according to market forces as opposed to being 'fixed' by the authorities.

foreign exchange market a market that is engaged in the buying and selling of foreign currencies and the determination of exchange rates between currencies.

free trade international trade that takes place without barriers such as tariffs being placed on the free movement of products between countries. (See common market.)

futures market a market in which financial securities and commodities are transacted for delivery at some specified future date. (See spot market.)

General Agreement on Tariffs and Trade (GATT) a negotiating forum for the removal of tariffs and other obstacles to free trade. (See p. 483.)

gross domestic product (GDP) the money value of the total amount of goods and services produced by an economy over a one-year period.

gross national product (GNP) GDP plus net property income (profits, interest, dividends) from abroad.

hedging the buying and selling of commodities and financial securities on the futures market in order to counteract price fluctuations.

horizontal integration the specialization by a firm in a *particular* line (or 'stage') of production.

import a product (or asset) that is bought from an overseas supplier. (See balance of payments.)

income wages, profits, interest, rents, etc., that are received for performing work, or supplying an asset.

income tax a levy by the government on the income received by individuals.

index-linking the linking of incomes (wages, pensions, etc.) and assets to the general price level so that their values are not eroded by inflation.

industrial policy a policy aimed at improving market efficiency by supporting innovation and promoting rationalization schemes to remove excess capacity.

inflation a persistent tendency for the general price level of goods to rise over a period of time.

insurance company a financial institution that specializes in collecting premiums from policy holders, to provide them with cover against various risks, including loss of life, fire and theft.

interest income received from lending out money in the form of loans, mortgages, etc.

interest rate the (percentage) rate at which charges are made for borrowing money in the form of loans, overdrafts, mortgages, etc.

International Monetary Fund (IMF) an institution that oversees the exchange-rate policies of member countries and provides financial support for countries in balance-of-payments difficulties.

international trade the import and export of goods and services between countries. (See free trade, and comparative advantage.)

investment the creation of *physical* assets such as factories and the acquisition of *financial* assets such as stocks and shares.

investment trust company a financial institution that issues shares and uses its capital to invest in other companies' stocks and shares.

invisible trade imports and exports of *services*, transfers of interest, profit etc. as opposed to goods. (See visible trade, and balance of payments.)

legal tender that part of the money supply which is issued by the government (typically, notes and coins).

loan a sum of money advanced by a lender (creditor) to a borrower (debtor). (See interest rate.)

M0 a UK money supply definition comprising bank notes and coins plus banks' till money and operational balances at the Bank of England.

M3 a UK money supply definition comprising M0 (see above) plus private sector bank deposits and public sector sterling deposits.

market an exchange mechanism that brings together the buyers and sellers of a product, thereby establishing product prices. (See equilibrium market price.)

merger a combination of two or more firms by the mutual agreement of the firm's management and shareholders. (See takeover.)

mixed economy an economy in which a country's productive resources are owned both by the state (the public sector) and by individuals and firms (the private sector). (See private enterprise economy, and centrally planned economy.)

monetarism an economic doctrine that emphasizes the influence of money on the functioning of the economy, in particular its role in causing inflation.

monetary policy the manipulation by the government of the money supply, credit and interest rates as a means of controlling the level of spending in the economy.

money a financial asset such as notes and coins issued by the government, which is generally acceptable as a 'medium of exchange' and can be used to pay for goods and services.

money market a market dealing in the short-run lending and borrowing of money to finance bills of exchange and Treasury bills.

money supply the total amount of money (principally, notes, coins, and bank deposits) in an economy that can be used to finance the purchase of goods, services and assets.

Monopolies and Mergers Commission a UK body that investigates monopolies, mergers and take-overs to determine whether or not they are in 'the public interest'.

monopoly a market situation where one producer controls the entire supply of a good or service.

mortgage a sum of money advanced by a lender (e.g. a building society) to a borrower, usually as a means of financing the purchase of an asset (a house, or a factory).

multinational company a business that owns productive assets (factories, offices, etc.) in a number of countries.

multiplier the process whereby some initial increase in income in an economy leads to further increases in income as that income is spent and re-spent.

national debt the money owed by the government to domestic and overseas lenders arising from accumulated budget deficits.

national income the total money value of the income resulting from a country's economic activities over a one-year period.

nationalization the taking into public ownership of a business or resource previously in the private sector.

Office of Fair Trading the UK body charged with administering British competition policy.

oligopoly a market situation where the supply of a product is controlled by a few large producers.

OPEC a group of major oil-producing countries. OPEC acts as a cartel in regulating oil prices. (See p. 487.)

option the right to sell or buy a commodity or financial asset at an agreed price on the futures market.

overdraft a facility provided by a bank, etc., that enables a customer to take out more money than they have deposited with the bank up to a specified limit.

pension fund a financial institution that specializes in collecting superannuation contributions from members during their working lives, and providing them with a pension income when they retire.

price the money value of a product or asset.

price level the general level of prices in an economy as measured by a price index. (See retail price index.)

prices and incomes policy the control of prices and incomes (particularly wages) in order to stop or slow inflation in an economy.

price system an allocative mechanism in which the interaction of buyers and sellers in markets establishes product prices and determines which and how many products are required.

private enterprise economy an economy in which all or most of a country's productive assets are owned by individuals and firms as opposed to the state.

privatization the sale of a nationalized (publicly owned) business, etc., to the private sector by issuing share capital.

productivity a measure of the efficiency of a given resource input (labour, capital) in producing output.

profit the income received from selling a product or asset at a price higher than it cost to produce or buy.

protectionism the erection of barriers to trade, such as tariffs, to protect domestic producers from the competition of low-priced imports.

public sector borrowing requirement (PSBR) the money borrowed by the government to cover a budget deficit.

quantity theory of money the proposition that inflation is caused by an 'excessive' increase in the money supply.

quota a limitation on the production of, or trade in, a product. Quotas are imposed by suppliers or by the government.

regional policy a policy aimed at removing regional imbalances in income and unemployment levels by e.g. providing financial support to firms located in 'depressed' areas.

rent income received from the ownership of property.

Restrictive Practices Court a UK body that investigates trade practices such as price-fixing agreements between firms to determine whether they are in 'the public interest'.

retail price index (RPI) a measure of the average prices of a 'basket' of goods and services bought by consumers over time. (See inflation.)

revaluation an administered increase in the value of an asset, or value (exchange rate) of a country's currency under a fixed exchange-rate system.

savings that proportion of current income that is not immediately spent, but is invested and used to finance future consumption.

share a financial security issued by a joint-stock company as a means of raising capital, which in the case of an ordinary share carries voting and dividend rights.

specialization a form of division of labour whereby each individual or business concentrates their productive efforts on a single or limited number of activities.

speculation the buying and selling of a commodity or financial asset in order to make a capital gain.

spot market a market in which financial securities, commodities, etc., are transacted for *immediate* delivery. (See futures market.)

standard of living the general level of economic prosperity in an economy.

stock a fixed-interest financial security issued by a company or the government as a means of raising capital.

stock exchange or **capital market** a market engaged in the buying and selling of existing stocks and shares and in raising capital by the issue of new securities.

supply the amount of a product offered for sale by suppliers (see p. 474).

supply curve a line depicting the total amount of a product that producers are prepared to supply over a range of prices. (See equilibrium market price.)

takeover the acquisition by one firm of another firm by purchasing its capital share. (See merger.)

tariff a tax levied by the government on imported goods, often as a means of protecting domestic producers from foreign competition.

tax a levy by the government on the income of individuals and businesses (e.g. income tax and corporation tax), spending (e.g. value added tax), wealth (e.g. inheritance tax), imported goods (e.g. customs duty), etc.

terms of trade an index of the relative prices of a country's imports and exports, indicating that if export prices go up faster than import prices the country is better off.

Treasury bill a British financial security (with a life of three months) issued by the government as a means of borrowing money.

unemployment rate the percentage of the available labour force in an economy currently out of work.

unit trust a financial institution that sells 'units' to savers, using the moneys received to invest in stocks and shares, etc.

value added tax (VAT) a levy by the government on the value added to a good or service at each separate 'stage' in its production.

vertical integration the combination in one firm of a number of sequentially linked activities in the production of a good or service, e.g. oil extraction, refining and petrol retailing.

visible trade imports and exports of *goods* that are recorded by the customs authorities as they enter or leave a country. (See invisible trade, and balance of payments.)

wage income received by persons for undertaking employment.

wealth the stock of assets owned by an individual or a country.

wealth tax a tax (called an inheritance tax in the UK) levied on a person's assets when those assets are transferred to others.

World Bank an institution that provides economic and financial assistance to less developed countries. (See p. 482.)

THE INTERNATIONAL WORLD

INTERNATIONAL ORGANIZATIONS

THE UNITED NATIONS

'A general international organization...for the maintenance of international peace and security' was encapsulated in Clause 4 of the proposals of the Four-Nation Conference of Foreign Ministers signed in Moscow on 30 October 1943 by Anthony Eden, later the Earl of Avon (for the UK), Cordell Hull (USA), Vyacheslav Skryabin Molotov (USSR) and Foo Ping-sheung (China).

Proposals to found such an organization were agreed between the four powers at Dumbarton Oaks, Washington DC, USA, between 21 August and 7 October 1944. These proposals were laid before the United Nations Conference at San Francisco beginning on 25 April 1945. On 26 June 1945 – the final day of the conference – delegates of the 50 participating countries signed the United Nations Charter, which came into force on 24 October 1945. The first United Nations General Assembly had 51 members – the 50 original signatories plus Poland, which signed the Charter on 15 October 1945.

There are 158 members of the United Nations – 156 of the 171 de facto sovereign states of the world plus Byelorussia and the Ukraine (which are Union republics of the USSR in separate membership of the UN).

The following 14 sovereign states are not members of the UN:

Andorra
China, Republic of (Taiwan)
Kiribati
Korea, People's Democratic Republic of (North Korea)
Korea, Republic of (South Korea)
Marshall Islands
Micronesia, Federated States of
Monaco
Nauru
San Marino
Switzerland
Tonga
Tuvalu
Vatican City (the Holy See)

However, North and South Korea, Monaco, San Marino, Switzerland and the Vatican City have observer status at the UN, with the right to be present at sessions of the General Assembly but without the privilege of being able to participate.

MEMBERS OF THE UNITED NATIONS

Original members (October 1945)
Argentina, Australia, Belgium, Bolivia, Brazil, Byelorussia[1], Canada, Chile, China[2], Colombia, Costa Rica, Cuba, Czechoslovakia, Denmark, the Dominican Republic, Ecuador, Egypt, El Salvador, Ethiopia, France, Greece, Guatemala, Haiti, Honduras, India[3], Iran, Iraq, Lebanon, Liberia, Luxembourg, Mexico, the Netherlands, New Zealand, Nicaragua, Norway, Panama, Paraguay, Peru, the Philippines, Poland, Saudi Arabia, South Africa, Syria, Turkey, the Ukraine[1], USSR, UK, USA, Uruguay, Venezuela and Yugoslavia.

[1]Byelorussia and the Ukraine are not independent countries but Union republics of the USSR with separate membership of the UN.

[2]From 1945 until 1971 the seat for China at the UN was occupied by the Republic of China (Taiwan). In 1971 the UN withdrew recognition of the Republic of China in favour of the People's Republic of China.
[3]Although India did not gain independence until 1947, an Indian delegation signed the UN Charter in 1945.

Members elected in 1946 Afghanistan, Iceland, Sweden, Thailand.

Members elected in 1947 Pakistan, Yemen. (From 1962 Yemen was officially known as the Yemen Arab Republic and popularly known as North Yemen. In 1990 North Yemen merged with the People's Democratic Republic of Yemen – popularly known as South Yemen – which had been a UN member since 1967.)

Member elected in 1948 Myanmar (elected as Burma).

Member elected in 1949 Israel.

Member elected in 1950 Indonesia.

Members elected in 1955 Albania, Austria, Bulgaria, Cambodia[1], Finland, Hungary, Ireland, Italy, Jordan, Laos, Libya, Nepal, Portugal, Romania, Spain, Sri Lanka[2].

[1]The Cambodian seat at the UN is held by the government-in-exile, which was overthrown in 1979. The de facto government of Cambodia is not recognized by the UN.
[2]Elected as Ceylon.

Members elected in 1956 Japan, Morocco, Sudan, Tunisia.

Members elected in 1957 Ghana, Malaysia (elected as Malaya).

Member elected in 1958 Guinea.

Members elected in 1960 Benin[1], Burkina Faso[2], Cameroon, Central African Republic, Chad, Congo, Cyprus, Gabon, Ivory Coast, Madagascar, Mali, Niger, Nigeria, Senegal, Somalia, Togo, Zaïre[3].

[1]Elected as Dahomey.
[2]Elected as Upper Volta.
[3]Elected as the Republic of the Congo.

Members elected in 1961 Mauritania, Mongolia, Sierra Leone, Tanzania[1].

[1]Tanganyika and Zanzibar – a UN member since 1963 – merged to form Tanzania in 1964.

Members elected in 1962 Algeria, Burundi, Jamaica, Rwanda, Trinidad and Tobago, Uganda.

Members elected in 1963 Kenya, Kuwait.

Members elected in 1964 Malawi, Malta, Zambia.

Members elected in 1965 The Gambia, the Maldives, Singapore.

Members elected in 1966 Barbados, Botswana, Guyana, Lesotho.

Members elected in 1968 Equatorial Guinea, Mauritius, Swaziland.

Member elected in 1970 Fiji.

Members elected in 1971 Bahrain, Bhutan, Oman, Qatar, United Arab Emirates.

Members elected in 1973 The Bahamas, Germany[1].

[1]From 1973 to 1990 both the German Democratic

Republic – East Germany – and the Federal Republic of Germany – West Germany – were members of the UN.

Members elected in 1974 Bangladesh, Grenada, Guinea-Bissau.

Members elected in 1975 Cape Verde, the Comoros, Mozambique, São Tomé e Principe, Papua New Guinea, Suriname.

Members elected in 1976 Angola, the Seychelles, Western Samoa.

Members elected in 1977 Djibouti, Vietnam.

Members elected in 1978 Dominica, the Solomon Islands.

Member elected in 1979 St Lucia.

Members elected in 1980 St Vincent and the Grenadines, Zimbabwe.

Members elected in 1981 Antigua and Barbuda, Belize, Vanuatu.

Member elected in 1983 St Christopher and Nevis.

Member elected in 1984 Brunei.

Members elected in 1990 Liechtenstein, Namibia.

THE ORGANIZATION OF THE UN

The UN has six principal organs (see below). All are based in New York, with the exception of the International Court of Justice, which is based in The Hague (Netherlands).

THE GENERAL ASSEMBLY

The Assembly is composed of all member states and can discuss anything within the scope of the Charter. Each member state has up to five delegates but only one vote. The annual session of the General Assembly begins on the third Tuesday of September. The Charter also has provision for special sessions. A President is elected by the General Assembly each September for a single term.

Decisions of the General Assembly are made by a qualified majority of those present (two thirds) on 'important' questions, and by a simple majority on other issues.

THE SECURITY COUNCIL

The Charter of the UN identifies the Security Council as the main organ for maintaining international peace and security. It has 5 permanent members – China, France, the USSR, the UK and the USA (the 'great powers' at the end of World War II) – and 10 other members who are elected by the General Assembly for a term of two years. (From 1945 to 1971, China was represented by the Republic of China – Taiwan. Since 1971, China has been represented by the People's Republic of China.)

Decisions of the Security Council are reached by a majority vote of at least 9 of the 15 members. However, any one of the permanent members of the Security Council can exercise its right of veto.

THE ECONOMIC AND SOCIAL COUNCIL

The Economic and Social Council acts as a coordinating body for the numerous specialized agencies created by the UN. The Council – which has 54 members elected for a term of three years – aims to promote international cooperation in the economic, social and related fields.

THE TRUSTEESHIP COUNCIL

The Trusteeship Council was established to supervise the progress to independence of trust territories – former German, Italian and Japanese possessions. In 1991 the only trust territory was Palau (or Belau) – part of the Trust Territory of the Pacific Islands administered by the USA. (The Council formally terminated the remainder of the trusteeship – over the Marshall Islands and Micronesia – in 1990.)

THE INTERNATIONAL COURT OF JUSTICE

The International Court of Justice (the 'World Court') is available to offer legal rulings on any case brought before it by UN members. (All member states plus San Marino and Switzerland are parties to the Statute of the Court.) In the event of a party failing to adhere to a judgement of the Court, the other party may have recourse to the Security Council.

The World Court comprises 15 judges elected by the Security Council and the General Assembly for a term of nine years.

THE SECRETARIAT

The Secretariat performs the role of a civil service for the UN. Its head is the Secretary General, who combines the tasks of chief administrative officer of the organization with that of international mediator. (See box for a list of incumbents.)

THE SPECIALIZED AGENCIES

The specialized agencies attached to the UN are listed below. They all report to the Economic and Social Council with the exception of IAEA, which reports to the General Assembly, and GATT:

International Labour Organization (ILO), concerned with social justice for workers. It was established in 1946 and is seated in Geneva with 150 members.

Food and Agriculture Organization (FAO), set up in 1945 to improve the production of agricultural products worldwide, protect the welfare of rural workers and promote conservation. The 158 members have their headquarters in Rome.

United Nations Educational, Scientific and Cultural Organization (UNESCO), established in 1946 to stimulate education, science and culture. It has 158 members including non-UN countries and is seated in Paris.

International Civil Aviation Organization (ICAO), founded to encourage safety measures and coordinate facilities for international flight in 1947. It is situated in Montreal with 158 members.

International Bank for Reconstruction and Development (IBRD), set up in 1945 to aid development – particularly in poorer member countries – through capital investment (also known as The World Bank). It has 151 members and headquarters are in Washington.

International Monetary Fund (IMF), founded in 1946 to promote international monetary cooperation, currency stabilization, and trade expansion. Headquarters are in Washington and it has 151 members.

Universal Postal Union (UPU), set up in 1947 (it had been the General Postal Union, an independent body, since 1875). The Union aids and advises on improvements to postal services. It has 159 members and is situated in Bern.

World Health Organization (WHO), established in 1948 and situated in Geneva. It aims to promote the attainment – by all peoples – of the highest possible standards of health. It has 166 members.

International Telecommunication Union (ITU), created in 1947 to encourage international cooperation in all forms of telecommunication. It has its origins in the International Telegraph Union established in 1865. It has 154 members and is based in Geneva.

World Meteorological Organization (WMO), created in 1950 (with its antecedents in the International Meteorological Organization founded in 1873). It aims to standardize meteorological observations and apply the information to the greatest international benefit. It has 155 members and is situated in Geneva.

International Finance Corporation (IFC), set up in 1957 to promote the flow of private capital for investment in less-developed member countries and to stimulate the capital markets. It has 133 members and its main offices are in Washington.

International Maritime Organization (IMO), set up to co-ordinate safety at sea, and encourages anti-pollution measures. It was set up in 1948 and has its base in London. It has 131 members.

International Development Association (IDA), assists less-developed countries (unable to qualify for IBRD loans; see p. 482) by providing credit on special terms. It was established in 1960 and now has 135 members. Its headquarters are in Washington.

World Intellectual Property Organization (WIPO), set up in 1970 (a specialized UN agency only in 1974). It promotes the protection of intellectual properties (artistic work), inventions, copyright, and access to technology. It has 121 members and is based in Geneva.

International Fund for Agricultural Development (IFAD), mobilizes additional funds for agricultural and rural development in developing countries. It was set up in 1977 and has its headquarters in Rome. It has 130 members.

General Agreement on Tariffs and Trade (GATT), set up in 1957, lays down a common code of practice in international trade and trade relations. It has 96 members and is based in Geneva.

International Atomic Energy Agency (IAEA). The Agency, established in 1957, encourages the use of atomic energy for peaceful aims, and ensures that it is not used for military purposes. It is situated in Vienna and has 113 members.

In addition to the specialized agencies there are other important subsidiary organs set up by the UN. These include:

United Nations High Commissioner for Refugees (UNHCR), provides legal and political protection for refugees until they can acquire citizenship in a new country. Its predecessor was the International Refugee Organization founded in 1951.

United Nations International Children's Fund (UNICEF), created in 1946, to improve the health, education and general welfare of children all over the world.

United Nations Relief and Works Agency for Palestinian Refugees in the Near East (UNRWA), provides food, health services, education and vocational training for the displaced Palestinian refugees.

United Nations Industrial Development Organization (UNIDO), assists developing countries with financial, design, technological and market research advice.

UN PEACEKEEPING

In the event of an armed dispute between member states of the UN, the Security Council or, in special circumstances, the General Assembly, may offer to mediate or negotiate a ceasefire. If requested, armed forces may be provided, under the control of the Secretary General, to supervise the ceasefire or monitor the disengagement. These peacekeeping units – drawn from member states who volunteer their services and are acceptable to the states in conflict – have only limited powers.

Only once, during the Korean War (1950–53), did the UN provide forces to fight, although during the Congo (Zaïre) troubles (1960–64) UN forces were used to intervene to put down an illegal revolt. Except in the case of the UN forces in Korea and the Congo (Zaïre), UN troops have been entrusted only with a peacekeeping role. They cannot do more than defend themselves in the event of fighting breaking out and must be withdrawn if requested to do so by the host country.

The multinational force dispatched to the Gulf after August 1990 to evict Iraqi troops from occupied Kuwait acted in response to a UN resolution but was not a UN force. Major current UN peacekeeping operations:

UN Force in Cyprus 1964–
UN Emergency Force on the Syrian–Israeli border 1973–
UN Interim Force in Lebanon 1978–
UN Force on Iraqi–Kuwaiti border 1991–

SECRETARY GENERALS

Trygve Lie (Norway)	1946–53
Dag Hammarskjöld (Sweden)	1953–61
U Thant (Burma)	1961–72
Kurt Waldheim (Austria)	1972–81
Javier Perez de Cuellar (Peru)	1982–

THE EUROPEAN COMMUNITY

In 1950 the governments of Belgium, France, the Federal Republic of Germany, Italy, Luxembourg and the Netherlands began negotiations to integrate their interests in specific fields. The result was the Treaty of Paris (1951) under which the European Coal and Steel Community was created. Attempts to establish a community concerned with cooperation in foreign affairs and defence proved abortive, but in 1957 the European Economic Community (the EEC) and the European Atomic Energy Community (Euratom) – with memberships identical to the European Coal and Steel Community – came into being under the terms of the Treaty of Rome.

The three Communities were distinct entities until 1967, when they merged their executives and decision-making bodies into a single European Community (the EC). The Community has been enlarged through the accession of Denmark, Greece, Ireland, Portugal, Spain and the UK.

EC plans for economic and monetary union have been discussed and there has been increased co-ordination in foreign policies and research and development. Since 1975 the EC has had its own revenue independent of national contributions.

The Single European Market
In 1992 the EC will achieve a Single European Market in which all duties, tariffs and quotas will have been removed on trade between member states and all obstacles to the free movement of people, money and goods will have been abolished within the Community.

INSTITUTIONS OF THE EUROPEAN COMMUNITY

The Commission of the European Community consists of 17 members appointed by their national governments for a term of four years. The Commissioners elect from their number a President and six Vice Presidents. The Commission – which acts independently of national governments – makes proposals to the Council of Ministers and executes the decisions of the Council.
President: Jacques Delors (France)
Vice Presidents: Frans Andriessen (Netherlands), Henning Christophersen (Denmark), Manuel Marin (Spain), Filippo Maria Pandolfi (Italy), Martin Bangemann (Germany), Sir Leon Brittan (UK).
Members: Antonio Cardoso E. Cunha (Portugal), Carlo Ripa Di Meana (Italy), Jean Dondelanger (Luxembourg), Ray MacSharry (Ireland), Abel Matutes (Spain), Bruce Millan (UK), Vasso Papandreou (Greece), Peter Schmidhuber (Germany), Christiane Scrivener (France), Karel Van Miert (Belgium).
The Commission meets in Brussels, Belgium.

The Council of Ministers is the main decision-making body of the EC. The Council consists of the foreign ministers of each of the member states. Specialist councils – for example, of the 12 ministers of agriculture – also meet, while heads of government meet three times a year as the **European Council**.

Ministers represent national interests. The decisions of the Council are normally unanimous although there is provision for majority voting in certain areas. The Presidency of the Council of Ministers rotates, with each member state taking the chair for a period of six months (see the table below).

The Council of Ministers and the European Council meet in the nation currently holding the Presidency.

The European Parliament consists of 434 members directly elected for five years (since 1979) by universal adult suffrage according to the local practice of each member state. Members have the right to be consulted on legislative proposals submitted by the Council of Ministers or the Commission and the power to reject or amend the budget of the EC.

The Parliament meets in Strasbourg (France), its committees meet in Brussels (Belgium), and its Secretariat is based in Luxembourg.

The European Court of Justice consists of 13 judges and six advocates-general appointed for six years by the governments of member states acting in concert. At least one representative is appointed from each member state. The Court is responsible for deciding upon the legality of the decisions of the Council of Ministers and the Commission and for adjudicating between states in the event of disputes. The Court, whose decisions are binding on member states, meets in Luxembourg.

CMEA (COMECON)

The Council for Mutual Economic Assistance (CMEA) was founded in 1949 to coordinate the economic development of the socialist countries of Eastern Europe. The upheavals of 1989–90 undermined the principles upon which CMEA had been established, and with the introduction of free market economies in East European countries the organization was disbanded in March 1991.

MEMBERS OF THE EUROPEAN COMMUNITY

	Date of accession	No. of European Commissioners	No. of Members of European Parliament	Next period as President of the Council of Ministers
Belgium	(founder member)	1	24	Jan–Jun 93
Denmark	1 Jan 1973	1	16	Jul–Dec 93
France	(founder member)	2	81	Jul–Dec 95
Germany	(founder member)	2	81	Jan–Jun 94
Greece	1 Jan 1981	1	24	Jul–Dec 94
Ireland	1 Jan 1973	1	15	Jan–Jun 96
Italy	(founder member)	2	81	Jul–Dec 96
Luxembourg	(founder member)	1	6	Jan–Jul 97
The Netherlands	(founder member)	1	25	Jul–Dec 91
Portugal	1 Jan 1986	1	24	Jan–Jun 92
Spain	1 Jan 1986	2	60	Jan–Jun 95
United Kingdom	1 Jan 1973	2	81	Jul–Dec 92

Candidates for membership of the EC
Turkey, Austria, Cyprus and Malta have applied for full membership of the EC. Sweden has indicated that it will make an application, possibly in concert with Norway and Finland. (Norway signed a Treaty of Accession on 22 January 1972 but was unable to join the EC following the rejection of membership in a national referendum in November 1972.) Switzerland is considering an eventual application for membership, and the governments of Czechoslovakia, Hungary and Poland have indicated that EC membership is a long-term aim. Morocco applied for membership in 1986 but was not accepted as a candidate as the whole of the Moroccan national territory lies outside the continent of Europe.

Council of Europe

The Council of Europe was founded in London on 5 May 1949. It aims to achieve a greater unity between its members to safeguard their common European heritage and to facilitate their economic and social progress. Membership is restricted to European democracies, that is those states which 'accept the principles of the rule of law and of the enjoyment by all persons within their jurisdiction of human rights and fundamental freedoms'.

The Council of Ministers, consisting of the foreign minister of each member state, meets twice each year; their deputies – the permanent representative appointed to the Council by each member state – meet once a month. Agreements by the Council members or their deputies are either formalized as European Conventions or take the form of recommendations to individual governments.

The Parliamentary Assembly of the Council of Europe meets three times a year for about one week to debate reports on social, economic, political, agricultural, cultural, educational, environmental, legal, regional and other matters. These reports are drawn up by the 13 permanent parliamentary committees. The Council of Europe has achieved some 140 conventions and other agreements, including the European Convention for the Protection of Human Rights in 1950.

Headquarters: Strasbourg, France

Member	Year of accession	No. of members in Assembly
Austria	1956	6
Belgium	1949 (founder)	7
Cyprus	1961	3
Czechoslovakia	1991	7
Denmark	1949 (founder)	5
Finland	1989	5
France	1949 (founder)	18
Germany	1951	18
Greece	1949	7
(withdrew 1969-74)		
Hungary	1990	7
Iceland	1950	3
Ireland	1949 (founder)	4
Italy	1949 (founder)	18
Liechtenstein	1978	2
Luxembourg	1949 (founder)	3
Malta	1965	3
Netherlands	1949 (founder)	7
Norway	1949 (founder)	5
Portugal	1976	7
San Marino	1988	2
Spain	1977	12
Sweden	1949 (founder)	6
Switzerland	1963	6
Turkey	1949	12
UK	1949 (founder)	18

Poland and Yugoslavia have applied for full membership of the Council of Europe.

'Special guest status'
Special guest status of the Council of Europe has been accorded to Bulgaria, Poland, Romania, the USSR and Yugoslavia.

Western European Union

The WEU was founded on 17 March 1948 with the original intention of collaborating 'in economic, social and cultural matters and for collective self-defence'. These functions have been gradually transferred to the EC, the Council of Europe and NATO. However, in 1984 the WEU was reactivated to improve military cooperation between members and to help them strengthen their contributions to NATO.

Headquarters: London, UK.

Membership:
Belgium, France, Germany, Italy, Luxembourg, Netherlands, Portugal, Spain, UK.

EFTA: European Free Trade Association

The European Free Trade Association aims to achieve free trade in industrial goods between member states, to help create a single West European market and to encourage an expansion in world trade. The first aim was met in December 1966 when nearly all internal tariffs on industrial goods were abolished. Considerable progress was made towards the second aim in April 1984 when trade agreements with the EC abolished tariffs on industrial goods between EFTA and EC countries. The EC and EFTA are currently discussing the creation of a single European trading area, which would not, however, replace either of the two existing trade groupings, although certain EFTA members have applied or are considering applications to join the EC.

EFTA was founded on 3 May 1960 in Stockholm, Sweden.

Each full member state maintains a permanent delegation in Geneva. The heads of these delegations meet once a fortnight, while ministers of EFTA governments meet twice a year.

Headquarters: Geneva, Switzerland

Current membership:
Austria, Finland, Iceland, Liechtenstein (associate), Norway, Sweden and Switzerland.

CSCE: Conference on Security and Cooperation in Europe

The Conference on Security and Cooperation in Europe was established in 1975 under the Final Act of a security conference held in Helsinki, Finland. The aims of CSCE were formulated in the Charter of Paris, which was signed by the 34 member nations on 21 November 1990. Members affirmed a 'commitment to settle disputes by peaceful means' and a 'common adherence to democratic values and to human rights and fundamental freedoms'. Members pledged to 'cooperate and suport each other with the aim of making democratic gains irreversible', to frame common objectives in protecting the environment, and to protect national minorities.

The Charter – which was described as formally ending the Cold War – envisaged a CSCE parliamentary assembly with members of parliament drawn from all 34 states. It was agreed that CSCE foreign ministers should meet at least once a year. The Charter established the following CSCE institutions:

CSCE Secretariat A small secretariat was established to be based in Prague, Czechoslovakia.

CSCE Conflict Prevention Centre The Centre – which has been charged with reducing the risk of conflict in Europe – was formed. It will be based in Vienna, Austria.

CSCE Office of Free Elections The Office was established to monitor the conduct of elections throughout Europe. It will be based in Warsaw, Poland.

Membership
Austria, Belgium, Bulgaria, Canada, Cyprus, Czechoslovakia, Denmark, Finland, France, Germany, Greece, Hungary, Iceland, Ireland, Italy, Liechtenstein, Luxembourg, Malta, Monaco, Netherlands, Norway, Poland, Portugal, Romania, San Marino, Spain, Sweden, Switzerland, Turkey, UK, USA, USSR, Vatican City and Yugoslavia. Albania has observer status.

OTHER MAJOR INTERNATIONAL ORGANIZATIONS

ASEAN

The Association of South East Asian Nations was founded in Bangkok, Thailand, on 8 August 1967. It aims to accelerate the economic, social and cultural development of member states, to maintain stability in the region, and to encourage cooperation between members.

Headquarters: Djakarta, Indonesia.

Membership: Brunei, Indonesia, Malaysia, Philippines, Singapore, and Thailand.

CACM

The Central American Common Market was founded in Managua, Nicaragua, on 15 December 1960. It aims to liberalize trade between member states and to establish a free-trade area in Central America.

Headquarters: Guatemala City, Guatemala.

Membership: Costa Rica, El Salvador, Guatemala, Honduras, and Nicaragua.

CARICOM

The Caribbean Community and Common Market was founded 4 July 1973 at Chaguaramas, Trinidad. The aims of the Caribbean Community are to promote cooperation in cultural, educational, health, scientific and technological matters, and to co-ordinate foreign policy. The associated Caribbean Common Market aims to promote economic cooperation.

Headquarters: Georgetown, Guyana.

Membership: Antigua and Barbuda, Bahamas (Community only), Barbados, Belize, Dominica, Grenada, Guyana, Jamaica, St Christopher and Nevis, St Lucia, St Vincent and the Grenadines, Trinidad and Tobago. Montserrat – a British colony – is also a full member of Caricom. The Dominican Republic, Haiti and Suriname are observer members.

COLOMBO PLAN

The Colombo Plan for Cooperative Economic and Social Development in Asia and the Pacific was founded in 1950 to promote economic and social development within the region and to encourage training programmes, capital aid and technical co-operation.

Headquarters: Colombo, Sri Lanka.

Membership: Afghanistan, Australia, Bangladesh, Bhutan, Burma (Myanmar), Cambodia, Canada, Fiji, India, Indonesia, Iran, Japan, Korea (South), Laos, Malaysia, Maldives, Nepal, New Zealand, Pakistan, Papua New Guinea, Philippines, Singapore, Sri Lanka, Thailand, UK, and USA.

THE COMMONWEALTH

The Commonwealth may be said to have its foundations in the 1926 Imperial Conference, which defined the position of the dominions of the British Empire as 'freely associated...members of the British Commonwealth of Nations'. The modern Commonwealth dates from 1949, when India became a republic but remained a member of the British Commonwealth recognizing 'the King as the symbol of the free association of...independent member nations'. The majority of Commonwealth members are republics and some have their own sovereign, but all recognize the British sovereign as Head of the Commonwealth.

The Commonwealth is an informal grouping of the UK and the majority of its former dependencies. It has no written constitution. It aims to encourage international, scientific and technical, educational and economic cooperation between members.

Commonwealth heads of government meet every two years, and other ministers meet at irregular intervals. The Commonwealth Secretariat was established in 1965 as the main agency for multilateral communications between the governments of members.

Secretary Generals of the Commonwealth:
Sir Shridath ('Sonny') Ramphal (*Guyana*) 1965–90
Chief Emeka Anyaoku (*Nigeria*) 1990–

Headquarters: London, UK.

Membership: Antigua and Barbuda, Australia, Bahamas, Bangladesh, Barbados, Belize, Botswana, Brunei, Canada, Cyprus, Dominica, The Gambia, Ghana, Grenada, Guyana, India, Jamaica, Kenya, Kiribati, Lesotho, Malawi, Malaysia, Maldives, Malta, Mauritius, Namibia, Nauru (special member), New Zealand, Nigeria, Pakistan, Papua New Guinea, St Christopher and Nevis, St Lucia, St Vincent and the Grenadines, Seychelles, Sierra Leone, Singapore, Solomon Islands, Sri Lanka, Swaziland, Tanzania, Tonga, Trinidad and Tobago, Tuvalu (special member), Uganda, UK, Vanuatu, Western Samoa, Zambia, and Zimbabwe. (Special members do not participate in ministerial meetings.)

ECOWAS

The Economic Community of West African States was founded in Lagos, Nigeria, in May 1975. It aims to promote trade and cooperation between member states and to increase self-reliance within West Africa. An ECOWAS force intervened in an attempt to stop the civil war in Liberia in 1990.

Headquarters: Lagos, Nigeria.

Membership: Benin, Burkina Faso, Cape Verde, The Gambia, Ghana, Guinea, Guinea-Bissau, Ivory

Coast, Liberia, Mali, Mauritania, Niger, Nigeria, Senegal, Sierra Leone, and Togo.

'GROUP OF SEVEN' (G7)
G7 is an informal grouping of the leading Western economic powers. Since 1975 the heads of government of these states have met for regular summits concerning major economic, monetary and political problems.
Membership: Canada, France, Germany, Japan, Italy, UK, and USA. The EC has observer status.

GULF COOPERATION COUNCIL (GCC)
The Council was established in 1981 to promote economic, cultural and social cooperation between the Arab states of the Gulf. It has since also taken on a security role.
Headquarters: Riyadh, Saudi Arabia.
Membership: Bahrain, Kuwait, Oman, Qatar, Saudi Arabia, UAE.

INTERNATIONAL RED CROSS AND RED CRESCENT
The International Red Cross and Red Crescent movement is a neutral organization founded to negotiate between warring parties, to protect casualties of armed conflict, to develop the activities of individual societies, to protect prisoners of war (through the terms of the *Geneva Convention*) and to coordinate relief for the victims of natural and other disasters. The Conference of the International Red Cross and Red Crescent meets every four years.
Headquarters: Geneva, Switzerland.
Membership: the Red Cross or Red Crescent Societies of 150 countries.

LAIA
The Latin American Integration Association – also known as ALADI (Asociación Latinoamericana de Integración) – was established on 31 December 1980 as a replacement for the Latin American Free Trade Area, which was formed in 1961. It aims to encourage trade and to remove tariffs between member states.
Headquarters: Montevideo, Uruguay.
Membership: Argentina, Bolivia, Brazil, Chile, Colombia, Ecuador, Mexico, Paraguay, Peru, Uruguay, and Venezuela.

Costa Rica, Cuba, Dominican Republic, El Salvador, Guatemala, Honduras, Italy, Nicaragua, Panama, Portugal and Spain have observer membership.

LEAGUE OF ARAB STATES
The League of Arab States, which is popularly known as the *Arab League*, was founded in Cairo, Egypt, on 22 March 1945. It aims to protect the independence and sovereignty of member states, to strengthen ties between them, and to encourage coordination of their social, economic, political, cultural and legal policies.
Headquarters: Cairo, Egypt.
Membership: Algeria, Bahrain, Djibouti, Egypt, Iraq, Jordan, Kuwait, Lebanon, Libya, Mauritania, Morocco, Oman, Palestine Liberaton Organization, Qatar, Saudi Arabia, Somalia, Sudan, Syria, Tunisia, United Arab Emirates, and Yemen.

NON-ALIGNED MOVEMENT
The nonaligned movement is not a formal organization but a conference that usually meets every three years. The aims of the movement are to promote world peace, to reject the system of world power blocs

and to help bring about a more even distribution of the world's wealth. Over 100 countries attended the last two conferences of the non-aligned movement, membership of which varies from one conference to another.

OAS
The Organization of American States was founded in Bogotá, Colombia, on 30 April 1948 as a successor to the International Union of American Republics (later the Pan American Union) founded on 14 April 1890. Its aims are to maintain the independence and territorial integrity of member states, to achieve peace and justice on the continent, and to encourage collaboration and inter-American solidarity.
Headquarters: Washington DC, USA
Membership: Antigua and Barbuda, Argentina, Bahamas, Barbados, Belize, Bolivia, Brazil, Canada, Chile, Colombia, Costa Rica, Cuba (suspended since 1962), Dominica, Dominican Republic, Ecuador, El Salvador, Grenada, Guatemala, Guyana, Haiti, Honduras, Jamaica, Mexico, Nicaragua, Panama, Paraguay, Peru, St Christopher and Nevis, St Lucia, St Vincent and the Grenadines, Suriname, Trinidad and Tobago, USA, Uruguay, and Venezuela.

OAU
The Organization of African Unity was founded on 25 May 1963 in Addis Ababa, Ethiopia. It aims to promote African unity and collaboration in economic, social, cultural, political, defence, scientific, health and other matters, and to eliminate colonialism and apartheid from Africa.
Headquarters: Addis Ababa, Ethiopia.
Membership: Algeria, Angola, Benin, Botswana, Burkina Faso, Burundi, Cameroon, Cape Verde, Central African Republic, Chad, Comoros, Congo, Djibouti, Egypt, Equatorial Guinea, Ethiopia, Gabon, The Gambia, Ghana, Guinea, Guinea-Bissau, Ivory Coast, Kenya, Lesotho, Liberia, Libya, Madagascar, Malawi, Mali, Mauritania, Mauritius, Mozambique, Namibia, Niger, Nigeria, Rwanda, São Tomé e Principe, Senegal, Seychelles, Sierra Leone, Somalia, Sudan, Swaziland, Tanzania, Togo, Tunisia, Uganda, Zaïre, Zambia, and Zimbabwe. In 1982 the Sahrawi Arab Democratic Republic (Western Sahara) was admitted to membership; Morocco, which claims the Western Sahara, withdrew from the OAU in protest.

OECD
The Organization for Economic Cooperation and Development was founded on 30 September 1961 to replace the Organization for European Economic Cooperation which had been established in connection with the Marshall Aid Plan in 1948. It aims to encourage economic and social welfare in member states and to stimulate aid to developing countries.
Headquarters: Paris, France.
Membership: Australia, Austria, Belgium, Canada, Denmark, France, Finland, Germany, Greece, Iceland, Ireland, Italy, Japan, Luxembourg, the Netherlands, New Zealand, Norway, Portugal, Spain, Sweden, Switzerland, Turkey, UK, and USA. The EC has observer status.

OPEC
The Organization of the Petroleum Exporting Countries was founded in Baghdad, Iraq, in 1960. It aims to coordinate the petroleum-producing and exporting policies of its member states.
Headquarters: Vienna, Austria.

Membership: Algeria, Ecuador, Gabon, Indonesia, Iran, Iraq, Kuwait, Libya, Nigeria, Qatar, Saudi Arabia, United Arab Emirates, and Venezuela.

SAARC

The South Asian Association for Economic Co-operation was founded in December 1985. It aims to encourage trade and economic development in South Asia.

Headquarters: Delhi, India.

Membership: Bangladesh, Bhutan, India, Maldives, Nepal, Pakistan, and Sri Lanka.

SADCC

The Southern African Development Coordination Conference was founded in Arusha, Tanzania, in July 1979. It aims to harmonize the development plans of member states and reduce their dependence on South Africa.

Headquarters: Gaborone, Botswana.

Membership: Angola, Botswana, Lesotho, Malawi, Mozambique, Namibia, Swaziland, Tanzania, Zambia, and Zimbabwe.

SOUTH PACIFIC FORUM

The South Pacific Forum was founded on 5 August 1971 in Wellington, New Zealand. It has no formal constitution but exists to further cooperation in a wide range of issues of mutual interest. The membership and the organization of the Forum is common with the South Pacific Bureau for Economic Cooperation (SPEC), established in 1973 to encourage trade, economic and transport matters.

Headquarters: Suva, Fiji.

Membership: Australia, Cook Islands (a self-governing New Zealand territory), Fiji, Kiribati, Marshall Islands, Federated States of Micronesia, Nauru, New Zealand, Niue (a self-governing New Zealand territory), Papua New Guinea, Solomon Islands, Tonga, Tuvalu, Vanuatu, and Western Samoa.

DEFENCE

NUCLEAR WARFARE

For more than four decades, direct conflict between the major powers has been avoided largely through deterrence – the prevention of aggression by means of threats of such overwhelming destruction that potential aggressors can see no worthwhile gains to be had from their actions. Deterrence has been based on the existence of nuclear weapons of proven capability, backed by a belief that, in certain mutually understood circumstances, such weapons would be used. Recent events in Europe – the reunification of Germany, anti-communist revolutions and the spread of *glasnost* (greater openness) in the USSR eased the strain of the Cold War confrontation between power blocs dominated by the USA and USSR. The signature of the Charter of Paris in November 1990 has been said to have formally ended the Cold War, but large nuclear stockpiles remain.

Since the atom-bomb attacks on Japan by the USA in August 1945, a further four countries have openly joined the 'nuclear club' – the USSR (1949), Britain (1952), France (1960) and China (1964). (Other countries also possess or are thought to possess a nuclear capability – see below.)

The members of the 'nuclear club' deploy weapons that may be used on the battlefield (*tactical*), in a theatre of war (*intermediate* or *medium range*) or between continents (*strategic*). The USA and the USSR – the principal possessors of strategic nuclear weapons – operate a system of deterrence known as Mutual Assured Destruction (MAD): if one side should attack the other using nuclear weapons, the victim has the ability to absorb such a ' first strike' and to hit back using 'second-strike' retaliatory weapons invulnerable to surprise attack – chiefly in submarines, hiding in deep-ocean areas of the world. Despite improved relations between the USA and USSR, both countries continue to deploy their nuclear forces with such a scenario in mind.

NUCLEAR WEAPONS

Eight major systems of nuclear delivery exist:

Intercontinental ballistic missiles (ICBMs) with ranges up to 14 800 km (9200 miles). These are strategic nuclear weapons.

Submarine-launched ballistic missiles (SLBMs) on board sub-surface ballistic nuclear (SSBN) submarines, with ranges up to 9100 km (5650 miles). These are also strategic nuclear weapons.

Long-range bombers with ranges up to 12 800 km (7450 miles). These are both strategic and theatre nuclear weapons.

Intermediate/medium-range ballistic missiles (I/MRBMs) with ranges up to 5000 km (3100 miles). These are theatre nuclear weapons.

Medium-range bombers with ranges up to 11 000 km (6800 miles) are also theatre nuclear weapons.

Short-range ballistic missiles (SRBMs) with ranges up to 900 km (570 miles) are both tactical and theatre weapons.

Short-range aircraft with ranges up to 3800 km (2360 miles) are also both tactical and theatre.

Artillery with ranges up to 21.6 km (13.2 miles) are tactical.

Warheads fitted to such weapons may produce explosions ranging between 1 megaton (MT) in the Soviet SS–11 Sego ICMB, with its range of 13,000 km (8000 miles), to 0.5 kiloton (KT) in the American M–110 203 mm self-propelled howitzer artillery, with a range of 18 km (11 miles). One KT is equivalent to 1000 tons of TNT and one MT to one million tons of TNT. ICMBs and SLBMs are fitted with multiple warheads known as MIRVs (multiple independently targetable re-entry vehicles): the Soviet SS–18 Satan – subject to projected cuts in the latest round of Superpower arms talks – has 10 MIRV warheads on each missile.

'STAR WARS' AND ARMS CONTROL

Until 1989–90, a major fear was that the delicate balance of deterrence could be easily upset, particularly if one side created an ability to defend itself against attack while retaining the capability to inflict damage on the enemy. In March 1983 President Ronald Reagan of the USA announced an intention to deploy a space-based defensive system – the Strategic Defense Initiative (SDI or 'Star Wars') – using laser and charged particle beam weapons designed to destroy incoming enemy warheads as they followed an orbital trajectory towards the USA. SDI would have required enormous research and funds, but the project has been halted because of the improved relationship between the superpowers. Some experimental work on SDI has continued, but the US Congress has reduced the money available and Reagan's successor, George Bush, has used the possibility of SDI cancellation or delay to gain nuclear arms-control concessions from the USSR.

Fears of an imbalance leading to the possibility of one side 'winning' a nuclear exchange have also produced arms-control negotiations and agreements in the past. Between 1969 and 1972, the superpowers conducted Strategic Arms Limitation Talks (SALT), producing a package known as SALT I (1972), which placed a common 'ceiling' on the number of weapons deployed by both sides. SALT II (1979) attempted to reduce that ceiling, but was not accepted by the USA after Soviet troops had invaded Afghanistan (December 1979). Further negotiations initially failed to reach agreement, although in December 1987 the superpowers did sign an Intermediate Nuclear Forces (INF) agreement, cutting the number of theatre weapons in Europe. A Strategic Arms Reduction Treaty (START), initiating substantial cuts to ICBMs, was signed in late 1990.

THE SPREAD OF NUCLEAR POWER
The fear of superpower imbalance has been replaced by fear of 'proliferation' – the spread of nuclear capability to powers outside the major blocs. Some countries are known to possess the ability to create nuclear explosions – India, for example, test-exploded a device in 1974 – and few people would doubt that both Israel and South Africa have developed nuclear weapons. The greatest concern is currently centred on states such as Pakistan, Libya and Iraq, chiefly because of the unstable nature of their relations with other powers.

CONVENTIONAL WAR
Military conflict conducted without access or recourse to nuclear weapons is known as conventional war, if fought between the armed forces of recognized states. Conventional war in the 20th century has taken a number of forms:

Total wars are fought for the complete destruction of the enemy, using all available weapons against both military and civilian targets, wherever they may be found. World War I (1914–18) had elements of totality, but World War II (1939–45) was the closest to total war yet fought. With the advent of nuclear weapons, total war has become equated with complete nuclear devastation, although it is still possible for non-nuclear powers to fight such conflicts.

Limited wars are fought under conscious restraint, usually by nuclear-capable powers choosing not to use their nuclear arsenals. Other limitations may include geography, force levels and targetting. Examples are the Korean War (1950–53), the American war in Vietnam (1965–73) and the Falklands/Malvinas War (1982).

Local wars (regional wars) are fought between non-nuclear countries. Examples are the various Arab–Israeli Wars (1948, 1956, 1967, 1973 and 1982) and the Iran–Iraq (First Gulf) War (1980–88). Despite a lack of nuclear weapons, such wars can be devastating for the countries involved, which may be fighting to the full capability of their forces.

There is always a danger of conventional wars escalating into nuclear confrontations, either because nuclear-capable countries are directly involved or because they are dragged in by non-nuclear allies. Until the end of the 1980s, the greatest danger seemed to lie in Europe, where forces of the North Atlantic Treaty Organisation (NATO) and the Warsaw Pact faced each other, each centred upon a rival Superpower. Since the political changes in Eastern Europe (1989–90), this threat has appeared to recede.

In November 1990 a treaty on Conventional Forces in Europe (CFE) was signed between the 16 member states of NATO and the 6 member states of the Warsaw Pact. The treaty outlined an agreement to limit conventional forces in Europe, defined by the treaty as the area between the Atlantic Ocean and the Ural Mountains. The treaty stipulated that – within 40 months of the signature of the document – the aggregate number of items of conventional warfare possessed by each defence pact within the area covered by the treaty should not exceed:

20 000 battle tanks, of which no more than 16 500 should be active units;

30 000 armoured combat vehicles, of which no more than 27 300 should be active units (and of the 30 000 vehicles no more than 18 000 should be armoured infantry fighting vehicles);

20 000 pieces of artillery;

6800 combat aircraft;

2000 attack helicopters.

Early in 1991 the treaty had not been ratified, and doubts had been expressed whether the transfer of equipment by the USSR to bases east of the Urals was a breach of the spirit of the treaty.

NATO
The North Atlantic Treaty Organization, an idea first broached by the Secretary of State for External Affairs for Canada on 28 April 1948, came into existence on 4 April 1949 and into force on 24 August 1949. NATO is often popularly referred to as the Western Alliance.

North Atlantic Council
The North Atlantic Council is the highest authority of the alliance. It comprises 16 permanent representatives – one from each member state – and is chaired by the Secretary General of NATO. The foreign ministers of the member states meet at least twice a year.

Defence Planning Committee
The defence of the NATO area is the responsibility of the Defence Planning Committee. France is not a member of the DPC, which meets regularly at ambassadorial level and twice a year at ministerial level.

Headquarters: Brussels, Belgium.

Secretary General: Manfred Wörner (*Germany*).

Members:
Belgium (founder member)
Canada (founder member)
Denmark (founder member)
France (founder member). France left the military command structure of NATO on 1 July 1966 but remains a member of the alliance. The headquarters of the organization were subsequently removed from Paris to Brussels.
Germany (admitted on 5 May 1955). The reunification of Germany on 3 October 1990 extended the boundary of the NATO alliance to the Polish border.
Greece (admitted 18 February 1952). Greece left the military command structure on 14 August 1974, but Greece was reintegrated into NATO's Defence Planning Committee on 20 October 1980.
Iceland (founder member)
Italy (founder member)
Luxembourg (founder member)
Netherlands (founder member)
Norway (founder member)

Portugal (founder member)
Spain (admitted on 30 May 1982)
Turkey (admitted on 18 February 1952)
United Kingdom (founder member)
USA (founder member)

THE WARSAW PACT

The Warsaw Pact refers to a treaty of friendship and non-aggression signed between the USSR and its former eastern European satellite states on 14 May 1955. The aim was to set up a joint military command structure and to ensure that all members of the Pact would come to the defence of any one member in the event of aggression. The original members were Albania, Bulgaria, Czechoslovakia, Hungary, Poland, Romania and the USSR. The Democratic Republic of Germany (East Germany) was initially only an observer, but achieved full membership in late 1955. From 1962 Albania began to distance itself from the Pact, and withdrew completely in 1968.

Political changes in eastern Europe in 1989–90 weakened the Pact. East Germany ceased to exist when German reunification was achieved (October 1990). Hungary ceased to participate in the military command structure of the alliance in June 1990. The Warsaw Pact was formally disbanded in March 1991.

GULF COOPERATION COUNCIL

The GCC – originally an economic and social organization – has assumed a security role. The GCC played an important role in the Second Gulf War. See p. 487.

ANZUS

ANZUS was set up in 1951 to form a collective defence policy for the preservation of peace in the Pacific. Partners share in defence and technical intelligence, the supply of equipment, and combine exercises.

Headquarters: Canberra, Australia.
Membership: Australia, New Zealand, USA.

INSURGENCY AND 'TERRORISM'

Insurgency and 'terrorism' force many countries to react to levels of violence but do not constitute full-scale war. Insurgency involves politico-military actions (including guerrilla warfare) within a country by groups intent on the overthrow of the established government. It has often been associated with the fight against colonial regimes, but it has been used equally effectively against established domestic governments regarded by the groups involved as denying the territorial, political or socio-economic rights of the people.

'Terrorism' is far more difficult to define, for it depends almost entirely on perception. To a threatened government, it is the use of indiscriminate violence by a minority group to instil fear into the majority of the people, preparatory to political demands. To sympathizers of the groups involved, however, it is often a case of fighting for freedom and justice. International 'terrorism' arises when groups from different countries cooperate to increase the level and nature of the threat, using techniques such as bomb attacks, kidnaps and hijacks.

THE NUCLEAR BALANCE

Country	ICBMs	SLBMs	Long-Range Aircraft	I/MRBMs	Medium-Range Aircraft
USA	1000	900	291	207	62
Britain	–	64	–	–	–
France	–	96	–	18	–
USSR	1451	960	195	383	791
China	8	12	–	60	120

SHORT-RANGE NUCLEAR WEAPONS
Numbers of nuclear-armed short-range aircraft and artillery pieces are difficult to gauge because of the recent turmoil in Eastern Europe, so the following figures can only be guidelines:

Country/Bloc	Short-Range Aircraft	Nuclear-Armed Artillery
USA/NATO	4467	9047
France	170	–
USSR/Warsaw Pact	3405	9917

CONVENTIONAL ARMED FORCE COMPARISON: SELECTED POWERS

Country	Manpower (excl. Reserves)	Main Battle Tanks	Artillery Pieces	Armed Helicopters	Combat Aircraft	Warships (incl Submarines)
USSR	4 258 000	53 350	31 500	2 050	5 334	632
China	3 030 000	8 000	14 500	400	5 949	149
USA	2 124 900	15 992	6 442	2 322	5 634	362
Vietnam	1 249 000	1 950	N/A	–	441	69
Iraq[1]	1 000 000	5 500	3 500	160	513	43
France	466 300	1 340	764	610	726	64
Britain	311 600	1 290	550	313	748	77
Israel	141 000	3 794	1 360	77	574	64

[1]before 15 January 1991

WINNERS OF THE NOBEL PEACE PRIZE

1901 Jean Henri Dunant, Swiss philanthropist: founder of the Red Cross.
Frédéric Passy, French economist: advocate of international arbitration and peace.
1902 Elie Ducommun, Swiss writer, and Charles Albert Gobat, Swiss: for their work for peace within the International Peace Bureau.
1903 Sir William Cremer, English trade unionist; an advocate of international arbitration.
1904 Institute of International Law (founded 1873).
1905 Bertha von Suttner, Austrian novelist: for her influential peace novels.
1906 Theodore Roosevelt, US President: for mediation at the end of the Russo-Japanese War (1904).
1907 Ernesto Teodoro Moneta, Italian journalist: founder of the International League for Peace and president of the International Peace Conference (1906).
Louis Renault, French jurist: for his international arbitration.
1908 Klas Pontus Arnoldson, Swedish politician: for mediation in the problems of the Norwegian-Swedish Union.
Fredrik Bajer, Danish politician: for his work for female emancipation, the peace movement and Scandinavian cooperation.
1909 Baron d'Estournelles de Constant, French diplomat.
Auguste Beernaert, Belgian politician: for work at the Hague Peace Conferences.
1910 International Peace Bureau (founded 1891).
1911 Tobias Asser, Dutch jurist: for his part in forming the Permanent Court of Justice (1899 Hague Peace Conference).
Alfred Fried, Austrian pacifist: co-founder of the German peace movement.
1912 Elihu Root, US politician: for his international arbitration.
1913 Henri Lafontaine, Belgian international lawyer: for his work as president of the International Peace Bureau.
1914–1916 No award.
1917 International Red Cross Committee, worldwide humanitarian agency working for the prevention and relief of human suffering.
1918 No award.
1919 Woodrow Wilson, US president.
1920 Léon Bourgeois, French politician: an advocate of the League of Nations and all international cooperation.
1921 Karl Branting, Swedish politician: for his conciliatory international diplomacy.
Christian Lous Lange, Norwegian peace advocate: for his work as secretary general of the Inter-Parliamentary Union.
1922 Fridtjof Nansen, Norwegian explorer and statesman: for his relief work after World War I.
1923–24 No award.
1925 Sir Austen Chamberlain, English politician: for work on the Locarno Pact (1925).
Charles G. Dawes, US politician: for the reorganization of Germany's reparation payments.
1926 Aristide Briand, French politician.
Gustav Stresemann, German politician: for his work for European reconciliation.

1927 Ferdinand Buisson, French educationalist: co-founder of the League of Human Rights (1898).
Ludwig Quidde, German historian and politician: for his work for peace in Germany.
1928 No award.
1929 Frank B. Kellogg, US politician: for the Kellogg-Briand Pact (1928).
1930 Nathan Söderblom. Swedish Lutheran archbishop: for his efforts for peace through church unity.
1931 Jane Addams, US social reformer and pacifist: for her social work, support of women's suffrage, and peace.
Nicholas Murray Butler, US educationalist: for his work in forming the Carnegie Endowment for International Peace.
1932 No award.
1933 Sir Norman Angell, English economist: for his work on the economic futility of war.
1934 Arthur Henderson, English politician: for his work for disarmament.
1935 Carl von Ossietzky, German journalist who spoke out against Nazi rearmament.
1936 Carlos Saavedra Lamas, Argentinian jurist: for his efforts to end the Chaco War (1932–35).
1937 Viscount Cecil of Chelwood, English politician who was a principal draftsman of the League of Nations Covenant 1919.
1938 Nansen International Office for Refugees (founded 1931).
1939–1943 No awards.
1944 International Red Cross Committee (see 1917).
1945 Cordell Hull, US politician: for his part in organizing the United Nations.
1946 Emily Greene Balch, US sociologist and political scientist: leader of the women's movement for peace during and after World War I.
John R. Mott, US Methodist evangelist: for his work in international church and missionary movements.
1947 American Friends Service Committee, a US Quaker organization that promotes peace through programmes of social service.
Friends Service Council, the British counterpart of the American Friends Service Committee (see above).
1948 No award.
1949 Lord Boyd-Orr, Scottish scientist: for his work on nutritional requirements.
1950 Ralph Bunche, US diplomat: for negotiating the Arab–Israeli truce in 1949.
1951 Léon Jouhaux, French trade unionist: co-founder of the International Confederation of Free Trade Unions.
1952 Albert Schweitzer, German missionary, doctor and philosopher: for his medical and other work in Africa.
1953 George C. Marshall, US politician: for his European recovery programme – the Marshall Plan – after World War II.
1954 Office of the United Nations High Commissioner for Refugees (see United Nations).
1955–1956 No award.
1957 Lester B. Pearson, Canadian politician: for his efforts to solve the Suez Crisis (1956).
1958 Dominique Georges Pire, Belgian cleric and educationalist: for his aid to displaced Europeans after World War II.

1959 Philip Noel-Baker, English politician: an advocate of world disarmament.
1960 Albert Lutuli, president of the African National Congress: for his non-violent struggle against apartheid.
1961 Dag Hammarskjöld, Swedish Secretary General of the UN (posthumously awarded).
1962 Linus Pauling, US chemist: for his campaigns for the control of nuclear weapons and nuclear testing.
1963 International Red Cross Committee (see 1917).
      League of Red Cross Societies: for their relief work after natural disasters.
1964 Martin Luther King, Jr., US Black civil rights leader.
1965 United Nations Children's Fund (see UN).
1966–67 No award.
1968 René Cassin, French jurist: principal author of the UN Declaration of Human Rights.
1969 International Labour Organization (see UN).
1970 Norman E. Borlaug, US agricultural scientist: for technological advances in agriculture.
1971 Willy Brandt, German politician: for reconciliation between West and East Germany.
1972 No award.
1973 Henry Kissinger, US politician, and Le Duc Tho, North Vietnamese politician: for the peace settlement of the Vietnam War. (Le Duc Tho declined the award.)
1974 Eisaku Satō, prime minister of Japan: for his anti-nuclear policies.
      Sean MacBride, Irish statesman: for his campaign for human rights.
1975 Andrei D. Sakharov, Russian nuclear physicist: for his advocacy of human rights and disarmament.
1976 Mairead Corrigan, Northern Irish, and Betty Williams, Northern Irish: founders of the Peace People Organization dedicated to ending sectarian strife in Northern Ireland.
1977 Amnesty International: for work to secure the release of political prisoners.
1978 Menachem Begin, Israeli prime minister, and Anwar el-Sadat, president of Egypt: for the Israel–Egypt peace treaty (1979).
1979 Mother Teresa of Calcutta, Yugoslav-born Indian charity worker: for her help with the destitute in India.
1980 Adolfo Pérez Esquivel, Argentinian sculptor and architect: for work for human rights in Latin America.
1981 United Nations High Commissioner for Refugees (see UN).
1982 Alva Myrdal, Swedish diplomat: for advocacy of nuclear disarmament.
      Alfonso García Robles, Mexican diplomat: for advocacy of nuclear disarmament.
1983 Lech Walesa, Polish politician and trade unionist: for work for the Solidarity movement.
1984 Desmond Tutu, Anglican Archbishop of Johannesburg: for his campaign for the abolition of apartheid through peaceful means.
1985 International Physicians for the Prevention of Nuclear War.
1986 Elie Wiesel, French writer and human rights activist.
1987 Oscar Arias Sánchez, president of Costa Rica: for promoting a peace plan for Central America.

1988 United Nations Peacekeeping Forces.
1989 The Dalai Lama, spiritual and exiled temporal leader of Tibet.
1990 Mikhail Gorbachev, Soviet president: for promoting greater openness in the Soviet Union, and helping to end the Cold War.

COUNTRIES OF THE WORLD

SOVEREIGN STATES

A country may variously be described as an area that is distinguished by its people, its geography or its culture, or as a land that enjoys political autonomy, more usually referred to as 'sovereignty'. This section describes the sovereign states of the world, that is the independent states that, in theory, exercise unrestricted power over their own destinies.

However, in some ways the concept of sovereignty is of limited value in the closing years of the 20th century. It could be argued that there is no such thing as a truly independent state. The overwhelming majority of sovereign states are members of one or more of the various economic and military alliances described on pp. 481–90. Most states have come to recognize that the demands of security and trade bring agreed limits upon the freedom of action of individual countries. Countries rely upon their neighbours and other states, at least economically, and are therefore restricted in their independence.

There is some disagreement about the number of sovereign states in the world. Certain authorities do not accept the Vatican City as a country and some of the countries listed in this section have considerable restrictions to their independence. Monaco, for example, is obliged by treaty to act 'in complete conformity' with French interests and has a French civil servant as its head of government. Andorra has experienced difficulties in obtaining international recognition owing to perceived limitations on its sovereignty. The Marshall Islands and Micronesia – former US trust territories – are described in their constitutions as 'sovereign' and both enjoy diplomatic relations with foreign governments even though the USA maintains complete control of their defence and security. There is, however, a distinctive and intangible characteristic by which we may recognize a country.

Individual entries in this chapter detail:
Official name: Each sovereign state's official name in its principal language(s).
Member of: Its membership of major international organizations (see pp. 481–90).
Area: Its de facto area in square kilometres (and in square miles). In the case of some countries, more than one figure is given for the area of the state where the country's area may be disputed, not defined or because the country may lay claim to part of a neighbouring territory.
Population: Its population according to figures given in the latest census or official estimate. Where there is no recent or reliable official estimate, an estimate of the national population from UN sources is given.
Capital and major cities: In many cases the names of cities in their local languages are given in brackets.

Except where noted, the population figure given for a city relates to the agglomeration or urban area: that is the city, its suburbs and surrounding built-up areas rather than for local government districts. *Languages*: The principal languages only are indicated. *Religion*: The principal religions only are indicated. As most censuses do not question respondents concerning their religious affiliation, the percentages given are an approximation. *Life expectancy*: The most recent figure is given from UN sources. *Labour force*: The total labour force, or numbers employed, are given for each country. In many Third World countries, the labour force is defined as those in employment, and the actual size of the working population is considerably larger. *Government*: The constitutional provisions of each state are summarized. In some cases, the provisions recorded may not in practice be adhered to owing to dictatorship, the role of the military, etc. The names of the main political parties and the heads of state and of government are given. *Federal states*: The area, population, capital and largest city of each state, province or other unit within all federal and quasi-federal systems are given. *Education*: The literacy rate, the years in which schooling is compulsory and the number of universities and/or equivalent institutions are given. *Defence*: The total armed strength and details of the length and nature of military service are given. *Geography*: The main geographical features are described, including the principal rivers, highest point and a summary of the climate. *Economy*: The most important economic activities, resources and trends are summarized. Details of each country's international trade, imports and exports are given on pp. 449–65. Details of each country's currency and its value in terms of the US dollar are given on pp. 465–69. *Recent history*: Summaries of the principal events of each country's 19th- and 20th-century history are given. (See also the History chapter beginning on p. 407.) *Dependent Territories*: The area, population, capital and largest city of each country's dependent territories are given.

AFGHANISTAN

Official name: Jamhuria Afghanistan (Republic of Afghanistan).

Member of: UN.

Population: 18 614 000 (1986 est), plus over 5 000 000 refugees (1988 est) in Pakistan and Iran.

Capital and major cities: Kabul 1 425 000 (1987; including suburbs), Kandahar (Qandahar) 191 000, Herat 151 000, Mazar-i-Sharif 110 000, Jalalabad 58 000, Kunduz 58 000, Baghlan 42 000 (1982 est).

Languages: Pushto (50%), Dari (30%).

Religions: Sunni Islam (80%), Shia Islam (20%).

Life expectancy: 39 years.

Labour force: (1979 census) 3 868 000; agriculture and forestry 2 369 500, manufacturing 423 373, wholesale and retail trade 137 900.

GOVERNMENT

The constitution provides for a two-chamber National Assembly, elected by universal adult suffrage. The Loya Jirgha (the supreme state body)

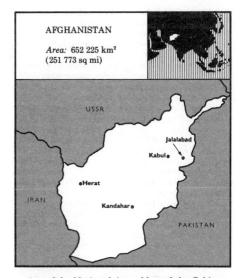

AFGHANISTAN
Area: 652 225 km²
(251 773 sq mi)

USSR

Jalalabad
Kabul
Herat
IRAN
Kandahar
PAKISTAN

consists of the National Assembly and the Cabinet, and provincial, legal and tribal representatives. The Loya Jirgha elects the President, who appoints a Prime Minster, who, in turn, appoints the Council of Ministers. The People's Democratic Party of Afghanistan is the sole legal party although the government has agreed in principle that the party should relinquish its monopoly on power.

President: Dr Sayid Muhammad Najibullah.

Prime Minister: Fazel-Haq Khailiqyar.

EDUCATION

Literacy rate: 25% (1985 est). *Years of compulsory schooling:* 7–15. *Universities:* 5.

DEFENCE

Total armed strength: 55 000 (1989 est). *Military service:* 3+ years.

GEOGRAPHY

The central highlands, dominated by the Hindu Kush, cover over three quarters of the country and contain several peaks over 6400 m (21 000 ft). North of the highlands are plains, an important agricultural region, while the southwest of the country is desert and semidesert. *Principal rivers:* Helmand, Bandihala-Khoulm, Kabul, Murghab. *Highest point:* Noshaq 7499 m (24 581 ft).

CLIMATE

The central highlands have very cold winters and short cool summers, while the desert regions have cold winters and hot summers. Except in parts of the highlands, it is dry.

ECONOMY

Most of the usable land is pasture, mainly for sheep, but cereal crops, particularly wheat and maize, are also important. Principal exports include fresh and dried fruit, wool and cotton. Natural gas, found in the northern plains, is also exported, but rich deposits of coal and iron ore are comparatively underdeveloped.

RECENT HISTORY

Afghanistan secured its independence in 1921 after three wars with the British. A period of unrest followed until a more stable monarchy was established in 1933. A coup in 1973 overthrew the monarchy. A close relationship with the USSR resulted from the 1978 Saur Revolution, but the Soviet invasion (1979) led to civil war. In 1989 the Soviets withdrew, leaving the cities in the hands of the government and Muslim fundamentalist guerrillas controlling the countryside. A fundamentalist administration was formed in exile in Pakistan, but attempts to effect a reconciliation between the government in Kabul and fundamentalist and other leaders both in Afghanistan and in exile have been unsuccessful.

ALBANIA

Official name: Republika Shqipërisë (Republic of Albania).

Member of: UN, CSCE (observer).

Population: 3 143 000 (1988 est).

Capital and major cities: Tirana (Tiranë) 225 700, Durrës 78 700, Elbasan 78 300, Shkodër (Scutari) 76 300, Vlorë (Vlonë or Valona) 67 700, Korçë (Koritsa) 61 500 (1987 est).

Languages: Albanian (Gheg and Tosk dialects).

Religions: Before the freedom to practise religion was forbidden in 1967, 70% of the population followed Sunni Islam, and there were small Greek Orthodox and Roman Catholic minorities. In 1990, the freedom to practise religion was restored and a small number of mosques and churches reopened.

Life expectancy: 72.1 years.

Labour force: (1988 est) 1 200 000; agriculture 700 000, industry 300 000, services 200 000.

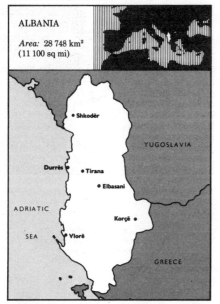

ALBANIA

Area: 28 748 km²
(11 100 sq mi)

GOVERNMENT

The 250-member People's Assembly is elected by universal adult suffrage every four years. The Assembly elects a Council of Ministers, but power is effectively held by a 15-man presidium (whose chairman is State President) elected from the Assembly. Until the end of 1990, the only political party was the (Communist) Albanian Party of Labour. Political reforms in 1990–91 allowed the registration of other

parties, including the Democratic Party.
President: Ramiz Alia.
Prime Minister: Fatos Nano.

EDUCATION
Literacy rate: no figure available. **Years of compulsory schooling:** 7–15. **Universities:** 1.

DEFENCE
Total armed strength: 40 700 (1989 est). **Military service:** 2 years army; 3 years airforce, navy and paramilitary units.

GEOGRAPHY
Coastal lowlands support most of the country's agriculture. Mountain ranges cover the greater part of Albania. **Principal rivers:** Semani, Drini, Vjosa. **Highest point:** Mount Korab 2751 m (9025 ft).
Climate: Hot, dry summers with mild, wet winters along the coast; equally hot summers but with very cold winters in the mountains.

ECONOMY
Albania is poor by European standards. The state-owned economy is mainly based on agriculture and the export of chromium and iron ore. Until the end of 1990, Albania refused financial and technical help from abroad, but technical and financial aid agreements are now being negotiated with several West European countries.

RECENT HISTORY
Independence from the Ottoman (Turkish) Empire was declared in 1912. The country was occupied in both the Balkan Wars and World War I, and the formation of a stable government within recognized frontiers did not occur until the 1920s. Interwar Albania was dominated by Ahmed Zogu (1895–1961), who made himself king (as Zog I) in 1928 and used Italian loans to develop his impoverished country. He fled when Mussolini invaded in 1939. Communist-led partisans took power when the Germans withdrew (1944). Under Enver Hoxha (1908–85), the regime pursued rapid modernization on Stalinist lines, allied, in turn, to Yugoslavia, the USSR and China, before opting (in 1978) for self-sufficiency and isolation. In 1990, a power struggle within the ruling Communist Party was won by the more liberal wing led by President Alia, who instituted a programme of economic, political and social reforms. The Communist Party retained a majority in multi-party elections held in April 1991.

ALGERIA
Official name: El Djemhouria El Djazaïria Demokratia Echaabia (the Democratic and Popular Republic of Algeria).
Member of: UN, OAU, Arab League, OPEC.
Population: 24 579 000 (1989 est).
Capital and major cities: Algiers (El Djazaïr or Alger) 1 722 000, Oran (Ouahran) 664 000, Constantine (Qacentina) 449 000 (1987) Annaba 348 300, Blida (el-Boulaïda) 191 300, Sétif (Stif) 187 000 (1983 est).
Languages: Arabic (official), French, Berber.
Religion: Sunni Islam (official).
Life expectancy: 62.5 years.
Labour force: (1985) 3 884 000; financing, insur-

ALGERIA

Area: 2 381 741 km²
(919 595 sq mi)

ance, business services and community and social services 1 107 000, agriculture, forestry and fishing 999 000, construction 670 000.

GOVERNMENT

The 281-member National Assembly is elected by universal adult suffrage every five years. The executive President – who appoints the Prime Minister – is also elected for a 5-year term. Following a revision to the constitution in 1990, Algeria became a multi-party state. The principal party is the FLN (the Socialist Front de Libération Nationale), which was formerly the only legal party.
President: Col. Bendjedid Chadli.
Prime Minister: Mouloud Hamrouche.

EDUCATION

Literacy rate: 45% (est). *Years of compulsory schooling:* 6–15. *Universities:* 16.

DEFENCE

Total armed strength: 138 500 (1989 est). *Military service:* selective.

GEOGRAPHY

Over 85% of Algeria is covered by the Sahara Desert. To the north lie the Atlas Mountains, which enclose a dry plateau. In the southeast are the Hoggar mountains. Along the Mediterranean coast are plains and lower mountain ranges. *Principal river:* Chéliff. *Highest point:* Mont Tahat 2918 m (9573 ft).

Climate: Mediterranean climate along the coastline with hot summers, mild winters and adequate rainfall. In the Sahara, it is hot and arid.

ECONOMY

Petroleum and natural gas are the main exports. Industry has traditionally been concerned with oil and gas, but light industry is being encouraged. Tourism has become an important source of foreign currency. Nearly one quarter of the adult population is involved in agriculture, but lack of rain and suitable land mean that Algeria has to import two thirds of its food. The small amount of arable land mainly produces wheat, barley, fruit and vegetables, while arid pasturelands support sheep, goats and cattle.

RECENT HISTORY

Nationalist riots against French colonial rule were ruthlessly suppressed in 1945, and in 1954 the FLN initiated a revolt that became a bitter war. A rising by French settlers, in favour of the integration of Algeria with France, led to the crisis that returned de Gaulle to power in France (1958). Despite two further risings by the settlers, and the activities of the colonists' terrorist organization, the OAS, Algeria gained independence in 1962. The first president, Ahmed Ben Bella (1916–), was overthrown in 1965 by Colonel Houari Boumédienne (1932–78), who aimed to re-establish the principles of the 1963 socialist constitution. His successor, Colonel Benjedid Chadli (1929–), began to steer Algeria towards democracy in the late 1980s. Multi-party local elections in 1990 were won by the newly-formed fundamentalist FIS (Islamic Salvation Front).

ANDORRA

Official name: Les Valls d'Andorrà (The Valleys of Andorra).
Population: 50 000 (1989).
Capital: Andorra la Vella 18 500 (1986).
Languages: Catalan (official), French and Spanish.
Religion: Roman Catholic.
Life expectancy: 70 years.
Labour force: (1989 est) 25 000; tourism 10 000, service industries 5000, agriculture and forestry 5000.

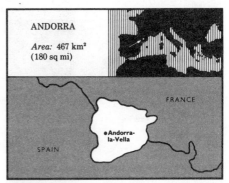

ANDORRA

Area: 467 km²
(180 sq mi)

GOVERNMENT

Andorra has joint heads of state (co-princes) – the president of France and the Spanish bishop of Urgel – who delegate their powers to permanent representatives who retain certain rights of veto. The 28-member General Council – four councillors from each parish – is elected for four years by universal adult suffrage, and (since 1981) chooses an Executive Council (government).
Head of government (President of the Executive Council): Óscar Ribas Reig.

EDUCATION

Literacy rate: 95% (1989 est). *Years of compulsory schooling:* 6–14. *Universities:* none.

DEFENCE

Total armed strength: there are no armed forces.

GEOGRAPHY

Situated in the eastern Pyrenees, Andorra is surrounded by mountains. *Principal river:* Valira. *High-*

est point: Pla del'Estany 3011 m (9678 ft).
Climate: Mild in spring and summer, but cold for six months, with snow in the winter.

ECONOMY
The economy used to be based mainly on sheep and timber. Tourism has been encouraged by the development of ski resorts and by the duty-free status of consumer goods.

RECENT HISTORY
Andorra's joint allegiance to the French head of state and to the Spanish bishop of Urgel has made difficulties for Andorra in obtaining international recognition. In the 1970s and 1980s, however, it has achieved some constitutional and financial reform.

ANGOLA
Official name: A República Popular de Angola (The People's Republic of Angola).
Member of: UN, OAU, SADCC.
Population: 9 739 000 (1989 est).
Capital and major cities: Luanda 1 134 000 (1988; including suburbs), Huambo 203 000, Benguela 155 000, Lobito 150 000 (1982–3 est).
Languages: Portuguese (official), Ovimbundu, Kimbundu, Bakongo, Chokwe.
Religions: Roman Catholic (45%), animist (45%).
Life expectancy: 44 years.
Labour force: (1988 est) 3 918 000; agriculture and forestry 2 766 000, services 600 000, industry 327 000.

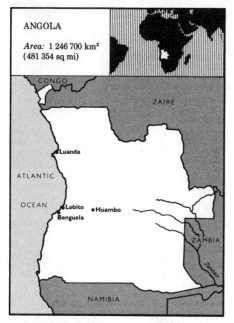

ANGOLA

Area: 1 246 700 km²
(481 354 sq mi)

CONGO

ZAIRE

Luanda

ATLANTIC

OCEAN   Lobito ●Huambo
         Benguela

ZAMBIA

NAMIBIA

GOVERNMENT
In April 1991, the MPLA party renounced its leading role and Marxist-Leninism. The chairman of the party's Central Committee remains State President, and the Council of Ministers is responsible to the party's 13-member Politburo, but, in future, multi-

party elections will be held every five years for a 318-member National Assembly.
President: José Eduardo dos Santos.

EDUCATION
Literacy rate: 59% (1985 est). *Years of compulsory schooling*: 7–15. *Universities*: 1 federal university.

DEFENCE
Total armed strength: 100 000 (1989 est). *Military service*: selective.

GEOGRAPHY
Plateaux, over 1000 m (3300 ft), cover 90% of Angola. In the west is a narrow coastal plain and in the southwest is desert. *Principal rivers*: Cunene (Kunene), Cuanza (Kwanza), Congo (Zaïre), Cuando (Kwando), Zambezi. *Highest point*: Serra Môco 2610 m (8563 ft).
Climate: Angola is tropical, with slightly lower temperatures in the uplands. October to May is the rainy season, but the southwest is dry all year.

ECONOMY
The development of Angola has been hampered by war. The country is, however, rich in minerals, particularly diamonds, iron ore and petroleum. Although less than 5% of the land is arable, over half the adult population is engaged in agriculture, mainly producing food crops. The main export crop is coffee.

RECENT HISTORY
Angola was a Portuguese colony from the late 15th century. In the 20th century, forced labour, heavy taxation and discrimination from white settlers helped to stimulate nationalism. Portugal's repression of all political protest led to the outbreak of guerrilla wars in 1961. When independence was finally conceded (1975), three rival guerrilla movements fought for control of the country. With Soviet and Cuban support, the MPLA, under Dr Agostinho Neto (1922–79), gained the upper hand and also managed to repulse an invasion from South Africa. In the 1980s, Cuban troops continued to support the MPLA government against Jonas Savimbi's South African-aided UNITA movement in the South. The withdrawal of foreign forces encouraged several attempts to end the civil war. A cease-fire was agreed in May 1991.

ANTIGUA AND BARBUDA
Member of: UN, Commonwealth, CARICOM, OAS.
Population: 78 400 (1989 est).
Capital: St John's 36 000 (1986 est).
Language: English.
Religion: mainly Anglican.
Life expectancy: 72 years.
Labour force: (1985 est) 32 300; agriculture and forestry 8000, tourism and service industries 12 000, industry 9000.

GOVERNMENT
The 17-member House of Representatives is elected by universal adult suffrage for five years. The Senate, which also has 17 members, is appointed. Government is by a Cabinet of Ministers. A Prime Minister, commanding a majority in the lower house,

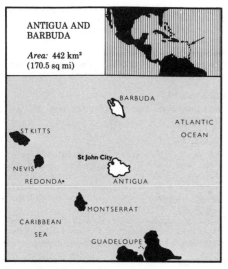

ANTIGUA AND
BARBUDA

Area: 442 km²
(170.5 sq mi)

San Miguel de Tucumán 498 600, Mar del Plata
414 700, Santa Fé 292 000 (1980).
Languages: Spanish (official), Guarani (3%).
Religion: Roman Catholic (nearly 93%).
Life expectancy: 70.6 years.
Labour force: (1987 est) 11 793 000; community
and social work 2 400 000, manufacturing 2 000 000,
agriculture and forestry 1 202 000.

ARGENTINA

Area: 2 766 889 km² (1 068 302 sq mi),
excluding territories claimed by Argentina: the Falkland Islands (Islas Malvi-
nas), S. Georgia, S. Sandwich Islands,
and parts of the Antarctic

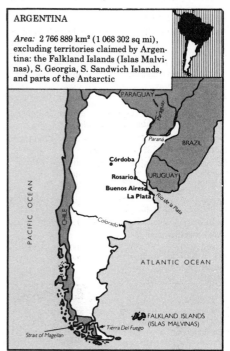

is appointed by the Governor General, the representative of the British Queen as sovereign of Antigua. The main political party is the Antigua Labour
Party.
Prime Minister: Vere C. Bird.

EDUCATION
Literacy rate: 90%. *Years of compulsory schooling:*
5–16. *Universities:* a department of the University of
the West Indies.

DEFENCE
Total armed strength: 700 (1989). *Military service:*
none.

GEOGRAPHY
Antigua is a low limestone island, rising in the west.
Barbuda – 45 km / 25 mi to the north – is a flat wooded
coral island. Redonda is a rocky outcrop. There are
no significant rivers. *Highest point:* Boggy Peak 402
m (1319 ft).
Climate: The tropical climate is moderated by sea
breezes. Rainfall is low for the West Indies, and
Antigua island suffers from drought.

ECONOMY
Tourism is the mainstay of the country. In an attempt
to diversify the economy, the government has encouraged agriculture, but the lack of water on Antigua
island is a problem.

RECENT HISTORY
The British colonies of Antigua and Barbuda were
united in 1860. Britain granted Antigua complete
internal self-government in 1967 and independence
in 1981.

ARGENTINA

Official name: República Argentina (the Argen-
tine Republic).
Member of: UN, OAS, LAIA.
Population: 31 929 000 (1989 est).
Capital and major cities: Buenos Aires 10 880 000
(1989 est; including suburbs), Córdoba 984 000,
Rosario 957 000, Mendoza 606 000, La Plata 565 000,

GOVERNMENT
The President and Vice-President are elected for a
six-year term of office by an electoral college of 600
members who are chosen by universal adult suffrage.
The lower house of Congress (the Chamber of
Deputies) has 254 members elected by universal
suffrage for four years, with one half of its members
retiring every two years. The 46 members of the
upper house (the Senate) are chosen by provincial
legislatures to serve for nine years, with 18 members
retiring every three years. The main political parties
are the UCR (radicals), the Partido Justicialista
(Peronist), and the Partido Intransigente.
President: Carlos Saul Menem.

EDUCATION
Literacy rate: 95.5% (1985 est). *Years of compulsory
schooling:* 6–14. *Universities:* 29 state and 23 private
universities.

DEFENCE
Total armed strength: 95 000 (1989). *Military service:*
6–12 months army; 12 months airforce; 14 months
navy.

GEOGRAPHY
The Andes extend as a rugged barrier along the
border with Chile. South of the Colorado River is
Patagonia, an important pastureland – although

much of it is semidesert. Nearly 80% of the population lives in the pampas, whose prairies form one of the world's most productive agricultural regions. The subtropical plains of northeast Argentina contain part of the Gran Chaco prairie and rain forests. *Principal rivers*: Paraná, Colorado, Negro, Salado, Chubut. *Highest point*: Cerro Aconcagua 6960 m (22 834 ft).

Climate: Most of Argentina has a mild temperate climate, although the south is cooler and the northeast is subtropical. The higher parts of the Andes have a subpolar climate. Rainfall is heavy in the Andes and the far northeast, but generally decreases towards the dry south and southwest.

ECONOMY

Argentina is one of the world's leading producers of beef, wool, mutton, wheat and wine. The pampas produce cereals, while fruit and vines are important in the northwest. Pasturelands cover over 50% of Argentina – for beef cattle in the pampas and for sheep in Patagonia. However, manufacturing (including chemicals, steel, cement, paper, pulp and textiles) now makes the greatest contribution to the economy. The country is rich in natural resources, including petroleum, natural gas, iron ore and precious metals, and has great potential for hydroelectric power. Argentina is remarkably self-sufficient, although its status as an economic power has declined owing to political instability and massive inflation.

RECENT HISTORY

From 1880, large-scale European immigration and British investment helped Argentina, a former Spanish colony, to develop a flourishing economy. Prosperity was ended by the Depression, and, in 1930, the long period of constitutional rule was interrupted by a military coup. In 1946, a populist leader, Juan Perón (1895–1974), came to power with the support of the unions. His wife Eva was a powerful and popular figure, and after her death (1952), Perón was deposed (1955) because of his unsuccessful economic policies, and his anticlericalism. Succeeding civilian governments were unable to conquer rampant inflation, and the military took power again (1966–73). An unstable period of civilian rule (1973–76) included Perón's brief second presidency. In the early 1970s, urban terrorism grew and the economic crisis deepened, prompting another coup. The military junta that seized control in 1976 received international condemnation when thousands of opponents of the regime were arrested or disappeared. In April 1982, President Galtieri ordered the invasion of the Falkland Islands and its dependencies, which had long been claimed by Argentina. A British task force recaptured the islands in June 1982, and Galtieri resigned. Constitutional rule was restored in 1983 under President Raul Alfonsin. Argentina faces grave economic problems and in January and February 1991, the value of the Argentine currency, the austral, collapsed.

ARGENTINIAN EXTERNAL TERRITORY

Argentine Antarctic Territory see p. 638.

AUSTRALIA

Official name: The Commonwealth of Australia.
Member of: UN, Commonwealth, ANZUS, OECD, South Pacific Forum.

Population: 16 807 000 (1989 est).

Capital and major cities: Canberra 273 600, Sydney 3 391 600, Melbourne 2 916 600, Brisbane 1 157 200, Perth 1 001 000, Adelaide 987 100, Newcastle 423 300, Wollongong 236 800, Gold Coast 208 100, Hobart 178 100, Geelong 147 100, Townsville 101 700, Launceston 88 500, Ballarat 75 200, Cairns 69 500, Darwin 68 500, Bendigo 62 400 (including suburbs; 1986).

Language: English.

Religions: Anglican (26%), Roman Catholic (26%), Uniting Church in Australia, Orthodox.

Life expectancy: 75.7 years.

Labour force: (1987) 7 675 100; wholesale and retail 1 408 000, manufacturing 1 151 400, transport and communications 512 300.

GOVERNMENT

The Federal Parliament consists of two chambers elected by compulsory universal adult suffrage. The Senate has 76 members elected by proportional representation – 12 senators elected from each state for six years, 2 from both territories elected for three years. The House of Representatives has 148 members elected for three years. A Prime Minister, who commands a majority in the House of Representatives, is appointed by the Governor General, who is the representative of the British Queen as sovereign of Australia. The Prime Minister chairs the Federal Executive Council (or Cabinet), which is responsible to Parliament. Each state has its own government. The main political parties are the Australian Labor Party, the Australian Democrats (liberal), the Liberal Party of Australia (conservative), and the National Party of Australia (conservative). *Prime Minister*: Bob (Robert) Hawke.

STATES AND TERRITORIES

New South Wales *Area*: 801 600 km² (309 500 sq mi). *Population*: 5 762 000 (1989 est). *Capital*: Sydney 3 391 600.

Queensland *Area*: 1 727 200 km² (666 875 sq mi). *Population*: 2 830 000 (1989 est). *Capital*: Brisbane 1 157 200.

South Australia *Area*: 984 000 km² (379 925 sq mi). *Population*: 1 423 000 (1989 est). *Capital*: Adelaide 987 100.

Tasmania *Area*: 67 800 km² (26 175 sq mi). *Population*: 451 000 (1989 est). *Capital*: Hobart 178 100.

Victoria *Area*: 227 600 km² (87 875 sq mi). *Population*: 4 315 000 (1989 est). *Capital*: Melbourne. 2 916 600.

Western Australia *Area*: 2 525 500 km² (975 100 sq mi). *Population*: 1 591 000 (1989 est). *Capital*: Perth 1 001 000.

Australian Capital Territory *Area*: 2400 km² (925 sq mi). *Population*: 278 000 (1989 est). *Capital*: Canberra 273 600.

Northern Territory *Area*: 1 346 200 km² (519 750 sq mi). *Population*: 156 000 (1989 est). *Capital*: Darwin 68 500.

EDUCATION

Literacy rate: over 95%. *Years of compulsory schooling*: 6–15. *Universities*: 19.

DEFENCE

Total armed strength: 69 600 (1989). *Military service*: none.

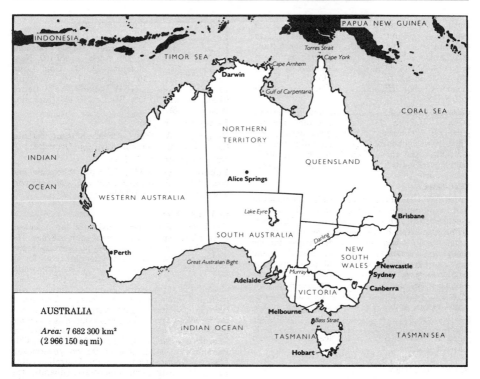

AUSTRALIA

Area: 7 682 300 km²
(2 966 150 sq mi)

GEOGRAPHY

Vast areas of desert cover most of the land in central and western Australia, a region of plateaux between 400 and 600 m (1300–2000 ft) with occasional higher regions, such as the Kimberley Plateau. In contrast to this arid, scarcely populated area – which covers more than 50% of the country – are the narrow coastal plains of the fertile, well-watered east coast where the majority of Australians live. Behind the plains – which range from temperate forest in the south, through subtropical woodland to tropical rain forest in Queensland – rise the Eastern Uplands, or Great Dividing Range. This is a line of ridges and plateaux, interrupted by basins, stretching from Cape York Peninsula in the north to the island of Tasmania. West of the uplands is the Great Artesian Basin extending from the Gulf of Carpentaria to the Murray River and Eyre Basins. Landforms in the basin include rolling plains, plateaux, salt lakes and river valleys, while the natural vegetation ranges from savannah and mixed forest to arid steppe and desert. Between the Murray River and Eyre Basins are the Flinders and Mount Lofty Ranges. Many of Australia's rivers flow intermittently. *Principal rivers*: Murray, Darling, Lachlan, Flinders, Diamentina, Ashburton, Fitzroy. *Highest point*: Mount Kosciusko 2230 m (7316 ft).

Climate: The north is tropical with wet summers (January to March) and dry winters. The north coast of Western Australia and the Northern Territory are subject to summer monsoons. The Queensland coast, which experiences tropical cyclones, has the heaviest rainfall, over 2500 mm (100 in) near Cairns. The interior is extremely hot and dry – over one third of Australia has less than 255 mm (10 in) of rain a year. The coastal fringes in the south are either temperate or subtropical, with winter rainfall, hot or warm summers and moderate winter temperatures. Winter snowfall is common in the highlands of the southeast and Tasmania.

ECONOMY

Since World War II, Australia's economy has been dominated by mining, and minerals now account for about 40% of the country's exports. Australia has major reserves of coal, petroleum and natural gas, uranium, iron ore, copper, nickel, bauxite, gold and diamonds. Manufacturing and processing are largely based upon these resources: iron and steel, construction, oil refining and petrochemicals, vehicle manufacturing and engineering are all prominent. The food-processing and textile industries are based upon agriculture. Australia's reliance on the agricultural sector has fallen considerably and in 1990 government plans for the reduction of the sheep population were announced. However, the country is still the world's leading producer of wool. Major interests include sheep, cattle, cereals (in particular wheat), sugar (in Queensland) and fruit. A strong commercial sector, with banks and finance houses, adds to the diversity of the economy.

RECENT HISTORY

In 1901, the Commonwealth of Australia was founded when the six British colonies of New South Wales, Queensland, South Australia, Tasmania, Victoria, and Western Australia came together in a federation. Australia made an important contribution in World War I – one fifth of its servicemen were killed in action. The heroic landing at Gallipoli in the Dardenelles is commemorated with a day of remembrance in Australia. The Depression hit the country badly, but the interwar years did see international recognition of Australia's independence. World War II, during which the north was threatened by Japan, strengthened links with America.

Australian troops fought in Vietnam and important trading partnerships have been formed with Asian countries. Since 1945, migrants from all over Europe have gained assisted passage to Australia, further diluting the British connection. Australia now has a close relationship with the USA and is a regional power in the South Pacific region.

AUSTRALIAN EXTERNAL TERRITORIES

Ashmore and Cartier Islands are located in the Timor Sea, respectively 850 km (527 mi) and 790 km (490 mi) west of Darwin. *Area*: 5 km^2 (2 sq mi). *Population*: uninhabited.

Australian Antarctic Territory see p. 638.

Christmas Island is located in the Indian Ocean 360 km (223 mi) south of Java Head. *Area*: 135 km^2 (52 sq mi). *Population*: 1300 (1990 est). *Capital*: Flying Fish Cove.

Cocos (Keeling) Islands are located in the Indian Ocean, about 2768 km (1720 mi) northwest of Perth. The territory contains 27 islands. *Area*: 14 km^2 (5.5 sq mi). *Population*: 670 (1989). *Capital*: Bantam Village (on Home Island).

Coral Sea Islands Territory lies east of Queensland, between the Great Barrier Reef and 157° 10′ E. *Area*: 8 km^2 (5 sq mi) of land in a sea area of 780 000 km^2 (300 000 sq mi). *Population*: no permanent inhabitants. A meteorological station is staffed by 3 officers.

Heard and MacDonald Islands are located in the southern Indian Ocean, southeast of the Kerguelen Islands and about 4023 km (2500 mi) southwest of Fremantle. *Area*: 292 km^2 (113 sq mi). *Population*: no permanent inhabitants.

Norfolk Island is located in the southwest Pacific Ocean, 1676 km (1042 mi) from Sydney and about 643 km (400 mi) from New Zealand. *Area*: 34.5 km^2 (13.3 sq mi). *Population*: 1980 (1986). *Capital*: Kingston.

AUSTRIA

Official name: Republik Österreich (Republic of Austria)

Member of: UN, EFTA, OECD, CSCE, Council of Europe.

Population: 7 603 000 (1989 est).

Capital and major cities: Vienna (Wien) 1 479 800 (1987 est), Graz 243 200, Linz 199 900, Salzburg 139 400, Innsbruck 117 300, Klagenfurt 87 300, Villach 53 000, Wels 51 000 (1981).

Language: German.

Religion: Roman Catholic (89%).

Life expectancy: 73.9 years.

Labour force: (1988) 3 433 000; services 1 163 000, manufacturing 945 000, commerce 460 000.

GOVERNMENT

Executive power is shared by the Federal President – who is elected by universal adult suffrage for a six-year term – and the Council of Ministers (Cabinet), led by the Federal Chancellor. The President appoints a Chancellor who commands a majority in the Federal Assembly's lower chamber, the Nationalrat, whose 183 members are elected by universal adult suffrage according to proportional representation for a term of four years. The 63 members of the upper chamber – the Bundesrat – are elected by the assemblies of the nine provinces of the

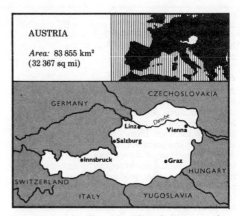

AUSTRIA

Area: 83 855 km^2
(32 367 sq mi)

Federal Republic. The main political parties are the Social Democrats (socialist), the People's Party (conservative), and the Freedom Party (liberal). *Federal President*: Kurt Waldheim. *Federal Chancellor*: Franz Vranitzky.

AUSTRIAN STATES (Länder)

Burgenland *Area*: 3966 km^2 (1531 sq mi). *Population*: 270 000 (1981). *Capital*: Eisenstadt 10 000.

Carinthia (Kärnten) *Area*: 9533 km^2 (3681 sq mi). *Population*: 536 000 (1981). *Capital*: Klagenfurt 87 300.

Lower Austria (Niederösterreich) *Area*: 19 171 km^2 (7402 sq mi). *Population*: 1 428 000. *Capital*: the state administration is in Vienna, i.e. outside the state. *Largest city*: St Pölten 50 400.

Salzburg *Area*: 7154 km^2 (2762 sq mi). *Population*: 442 000. *Capital*: Salzburg 139 400.

Styria (Steiermark) *Area*: 16 387 km^2 (6327 sq mi). *Population*: 1 187 000. *Capital*: Graz 243 200.

Tirol *Area*: 12 647 km^2 (4883 sq mi). *Population*: 587 000. *Capital*: Innsbruck 117 300.

Upper Austria (Oberösterreich) *Area*: 11 979 km^2 (4625 sq mi). *Population*: 1 270 000. *Capital*: Linz 199 900.

Vienna (Wien) *Area*: 415 km^2 (160 sq mi). *Population*: 1 531 000. *Capital*: Vienna 1 479 800.

Vorarlberg *Area*: 2601 km^2 (1004 sq mi). *Population*: 305 000. *Capital*: Bregenz 24 600. *Largest city*: Dornbirn 38 600.

EDUCATION

Literacy rate: over 98%. *Years of compulsory schooling*: 6–15. *Universities*: 6.

DEFENCE

Total armed strength: 42 500 (1989). *Military service*: 6 months' training; up to 60 days' reservist training.

GEOGRAPHY

The Alps – much of which are covered by pastures and forests – occupy nearly two thirds of Austria. Lowland Austria – in the east – consists of low hills, the Vienna Basin and a flat marshy area beside the Neusiedler See on the Hungarian border. Along the Czech border is a forested massif rising to 1200 m (4000 ft). *Principal rivers*: Danube (Donau), Inn, Mur. *Highest point*: Grossglockner 3798 m (12 462 ft). **Climate:** There are many local variations in climate owing to altitude and aspect. The east is drier than the west, and is, in general, colder than the Alpine region in the winter and hotter, but more humid, in the summer. Areas over 3000 m (10 000 ft) are snow-covered all year.

ECONOMY

Although Austria produces about 90% of its own food requirements, agriculture employs only 8% of the labour force. The arable land in the east has fertile soils producing good yields of cereals, as well as grapes for wine. Dairy produce is an important export from the pasturelands in the east and in the Alps. The mainstay of the economy is manufacturing industry, including machinery and transport equipment, iron and steel products, refined petroleum products, cement and paper. Natural resources include magnesite and iron ore, as well as hydroelectric power potential and the most considerable forests in central Europe. The Alps attract both winter and summer visitors, making tourism a major earner of foreign currency. Austria retains economic links with countries in central Europe that were once part of the Habsburg empire.

RECENT HISTORY

In 1918–19, the Austro-Hungarian Habsburg empire was dismembered. An Austrian republic was established as a separate state, despite considerable support for union with Germany. Unstable throughout the 1920s and 1930s, Austria was annexed by Germany in 1938 (the Anschluss). Austria was liberated in 1945, but Allied occupation forces remained until 1955 when the independence of a neutral republican Austria was recognized. The upheavals in central Europe in 1989–90 encouraged Austria to strengthen links with newly democratic Hungary and Czechoslovakia and the Yugoslav republic of Slovenia. Austria is a candidate for membership of the EC.

BAHAMAS

Official name: The Commonwealth of the Bahamas.
Member of: UN, Commonwealth, OAS, CARICOM (Community only).
Population: 249 000 (1989 est).
Capital: Nassau 140 000 (1986).
Language: English.
Religions: Baptist (29%), Anglican (23%), Roman Catholic (22%).
Life expectancy: 70.5 years.
Labour force: (1986) 110 900; services and tourism 31 550, social and community work 30 000, agriculture 5000.

GOVERNMENT

The Senate (the upper house of Parliament) has 16 appointed members. The House of Assembly (the lower house) has 49 members elected by universal adult suffrage for five years. A Prime Minister, who commands a majority in the House, is appointed by the Governor General, who is the representative of the British Queen as sovereign of the Bahamas. The Prime Minister chairs the Cabinet, which is responsible to the House. The main political parties are the Progressive Liberal Party and the Free National Movement.
Prime Minister: Sir Lynden Pindling.

EDUCATION

Literacy rate: 95%. *Years of compulsory schooling:* 5–14. *Universities:* 2 university colleges.

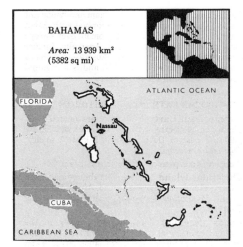

BAHAMAS
Area: 13 939 km²
(5382 sq mi)

ATLANTIC OCEAN
FLORIDA
Nassau
CUBA
CARIBBEAN SEA

DEFENCE

Total armed strength: 750 (1989). *Military service:* none.

GEOGRAPHY

The Bahamas comprises some 700 long, flat, narrow islands, and over 2000 barren rocky islets. There are no significant rivers. *Highest point:* Mount Alvernia, Cat Island 63 m (206 ft).

Climate: The climate is mild and subtropical, with no great seasonal variation in temperature. Rainfall averages just over 1000 mm (39 in). The islands are liable to hurricanes.

ECONOMY

Tourism – mainly from the USA – is the major source of income, and, with related industries, it employs the majority of the labour force. The islands have become a tax haven and financial centre.

RECENT HISTORY

Britain granted internal self-government to the Bahamas in 1964. Since independence in 1973, the Bahamas have developed close ties with the USA, although the relationship has been strained at times owing to an illegal drug trade through the islands.

BAHRAIN

Official name: Daulat al-Bahrain (The State of Bahrain).
Member of: UN, Arab League, OPEC, GCC.
Population: 488 500 (1989 est).
Capital: Manama 147 000 (1987).
Language: Arabic.
Religions: Sunni Islam 40%, Shia Islam 60%.
Life expectancy: 70.6 years.
Labour force: (1981) 138 150; community and social work 48 000, construction 29 000, trade and leisure industry 19 000, business services 5000.

GOVERNMENT

Bahrain is ruled directly by an Amir (a hereditary monarch), who appoints a Cabinet of Ministers. The 1973 Constitution provides for a National Assembly consisting of Cabinet plus 30 other members elected by popular vote. However, the Assembly was dis-

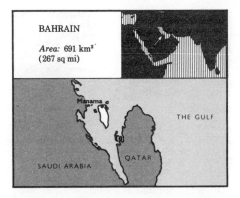

Labour force: (1985) 29 510 000; agriculture and forestry 16 712 000, trade and leisure industry 3 610 000, manufacturing 2 700 000.

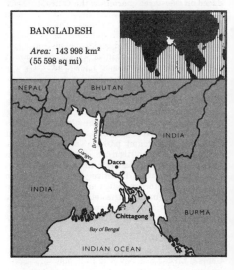

solved in 1975 and has not been reconvened.
Amir: HH Shaikh Isa II bin Sulman Al-Khalifa (succeeded upon the death of his father, 2 November 1961).

EDUCATION
Literacy rate: 70% (1985 est). *Years of compulsory schooling*: schooling is not compulsory. *Universities*: 2.

DEFENCE
Total armed strength: 3350 (1989). *Military service*: none.

GEOGRAPHY
Bahrain Island, the largest of the 35 small islands in the archipelago, consists mainly of sandy plains and salt marshes. There are no rivers. *Highest point*: Jabal al-Dukhan 134 m (440 ft).
Climate: The climate is very hot. The annual average rainfall is 75 mm (3 in).

ECONOMY
The wealth of Bahrain is due to its petroleum and natural gas resources, and the oil-refining industry. As reserves began to wane in the 1970s, the government encouraged diversification. As a result, Bahrain is now one of the Gulf's major banking and communication centres.

RECENT HISTORY
Bahrain – a British protectorate from the end of the 19th century – was the first state in the region to develop its petroleum industry. Since independence in 1971, there has been tension between the Sunni and Shiite communities. Responding to threats from revolutionary Shiite Iran, Bahrain entered defence agreements with Saudi Arabia and other Gulf states, and joined the coalition forces against Iraq after the invasion of Kuwait (August 1990).

BANGLADESH

Official name: Gana Praja Tantri Bangla Desh (People's Republic of Bangladesh).
Member of: UN, Commonwealth, SAARC.
Population: 110 290 000 (1989 est).
Capital and major cities: Dhaka 4 770 000, Chittagong 1 840 000, Khulna 860 000, Rajshahi 430 000 (1987), Comilla 185 000, Barisal 174 000 (1984 est).
Languages: Bengali (95%), tribal dialects.
Religion: Sunni Islam (over 85%).
Life expectancy: 49.6 years.

GOVERNMENT
Bangladesh is governed by a President, who is elected for a maximum of two five-year terms by universal adult suffrage. The President appoints a Council of Ministers from the Parliament (Jatiya Sangsad), which comprises 300 members elected for five years by universal suffrage and 30 women chosen by the elected members. The main political parties include the Jatiya Party, the Awami League, Jamit-i-Islami and the BNP (Bangladesh Nationalist Party). *President (acting)*: Justice Shahabuddin Ahmed. *Prime Minister*: Khalida Zia.

EDUCATION
Literacy rate: 25% (1986). *Years of compulsory schooling*: schooling is not compulsory. *Universities*: 7.

DEFENCE
Total armed strength: 103 000 (1989). *Military service*: none.

GEOGRAPHY
Most of Bangladesh comprises alluvial plains in the deltas of the rivers Ganges and Brahmaputra, which combine as the Padma. The swampy plains – generally less than 9 m (30 ft) above sea level – are dissected by rivers dividing into numerous distributaries with raised banks. The south and southeast coastal regions contain mangrove forests (the Sundarbans). The only uplands are the Sylhet Hills in the northeast and the Chittagong hill country in the east. *Principal rivers*: Ganges, Brahmaputra. *Highest point*: Keokradong 1230 m (4034 ft).
Climate: The climate is tropical with the highest temperatures between April and September. Most of the country's rainfall comes during the annual monsoon (June to October) when intense storms accompanied by high winds bring serious flooding. Rainfall totals range from 1000 mm (40 in) in the west to 5000 mm (200 in) in the Sylhet Hills.

ECONOMY
With a rapidly increasing population, Bangladesh is

among the world's poorest countries and is heavily dependent on foreign aid. About 80% of the population is involved in agriculture. Rice is produced on over three quarters of the cultivated land, but although the land is fertile, crops are often destroyed by floods and cyclones. The main cash crops are jute – Bangladesh yields 90% of the world's production – and tea. Industries include those processing agricultural products – jute, cotton and sugar. Mineral resources are few, but there are reserves of natural gas.

RECENT HISTORY

On the partition of British India in 1947, as the majority of its inhabitants were Muslim, the area became the eastern province of an independent Pakistan. Separated by 1600 km (1000 mi) from the Urdu-speaking, politically dominant western province, East Pakistan saw itself as a victim of economic and ethnic injustice. Resentment led to civil war in 1971 when Indian aid to Bengali irregulars gave birth to an independent People's Republic of Bangladesh ('Free Bengal') under Sheik Mujib-ur-Rahman. The Sheik's assassination in 1975 led eventually to a takeover by General Zia-ur-Rahman, who amended the constitution to create an 'Islamic state'. The General in turn was assassinated in 1981, and General Ershad took power in 1982. Martial law was lifted in 1986 when the constitution was amended and a civilian government took office. Following a period of unrest, President Ershad was deposed in 1990 and charged with corruption. In March 1991, the BNP, led by Zia's widow, won multi-party elections.

BARBADOS

Member of: UN, Commonwealth, CARICOM, OAS.

Population: 255 200 (1988 est).

Capital: Bridgetown 102 000 (1989 est).

Language: English.

Religions: Anglican (70%), Methodist (9%).

Life expectancy: 73.5 years.

Labour force: (1987) 121 200, tourism and services 24 300, manufacturing 12 400, agriculture and forestry 6900.

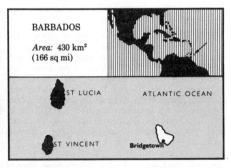

BARBADOS

Area: 430 km²
(166 sq mi)

ST LUCIA   ATLANTIC OCEAN

ST VINCENT   Bridgetown

GOVERNMENT

The 21 members of the Senate are appointed; the 27 members of the House of Assembly are elected by universal adult suffrage for five years. The Governor General, the representative of the British Queen as sovereign of Barbados, appoints a Prime Minister who commands a majority in the House. The PM appoints a Cabinet responsible to the House. The main political parties are the Democratic Labour Party and the Barbados Labour Party. *Prime Minister:* L. Erskine Sandiford.

EDUCATION

Literacy rate: 98% (1985). *Years of compulsory schooling:* 5–16. *Universities:* 1 university campus (part of the University of the West Indies).

DEFENCE

Total armed strength: 154 plus volunteers and reservists. *Military service:* none.

GEOGRAPHY

Barbados is generally flat and low, except in the north. There are no significant rivers. *Highest point:* Mount Hillaby (340 m/1115 ft).

Climate: Barbados has a tropical climate. Rainfall is heavy, with totals everywhere above 1000 mm (40 in). The island is subject to hurricanes.

ECONOMY

Tourism – which employs about one third of the labour force – is the main source of income. The government has encouraged diversification, and there has been a growth in banking and insurance. Sugar – once the mainstay of Barbados – remains the main crop.

RECENT HISTORY

In the British colony of Barbados in the 1930s, economic and social conditions for black Barbadians were miserable. Riots in 1937 led to reforms and also greatly increased black political consciousness. As a result, Barbadians, such as Grantley Adams and Errol Barrow, became prominent in Caribbean politics. Barbados gained independence in 1966 and has become an important influence among the smaller islands of the Lesser Antilles.

BELGIUM

Official name: Royaume de Belgique or Koninkrijk België (Kingdom of Belgium).

Member of: UN, NATO, EC, CSCE, WEU, Council of Europe, OECD.

Population: 9 878 000 (1989 est).

Capital and major cities: Brussels (Bruxelles or Brussel) 973 500, Antwerp (Antwerpen or Anvers) 919 453, Liège (Luik) 591 500, Ghent (Gent or Gand) 484 900, Charleroi 429 200, Malines (Mechelen) 293 200, Courtrai (Kortrijk) 274 500, Namur (Namen) 264 600, Bruges (Brugge) 260 100 (all including suburbs; 1987).

Languages: Flemish (a dialect of Dutch; 57%), French (42%).

Religion: Roman Catholic (72%).

Life expectancy: 74.3 years.

Labour force: (1987) 4 216 800; manufacturing 781 800, trade and tourism 730 100, transport and communications 257 400.

GOVERNMENT

Belgium is a constitutional monarchy. The Chamber of Deputies (the lower house of Parliament) comprises 212 members elected by universal adult suffrage for four years under a system of proportional representation. The Senate (the upper house) has 182 members: 106 directly elected, 50 chosen by provincial councils, 25 co-opted, plus the heir to the

throne. The King appoints a Prime Minister, who commands a majority in the Chamber, and, upon the PM's advice, other members of the Cabinet. The main political parties are the (Flemish) CVP (Christelijke Volkspartei) and its French-speaking equivalent the Parti social chrétien, the two Socialist parties – Socialistische Partei and the Parti socialiste belge, two liberal parties – the (Flemish) PVV and the (French-speaking) PRL, and Flemish and Walloon regional parties. The regional councils of Flanders, Wallonia and Brussels are composed of the deputies and elected senators from each region.
King: HM Baudouin I, King of the Belgians (succeeded 15 July 1951 upon the abdication of his father).
Prime Minister: Wilfried Martens.

BELGIUM

Area: 30 519 km²
(11 783 sq mi)

EDUCATION
Literacy: 98%. *Years of compulsory schooling*: 6–16. *Universities*: 19 (including colleges of university status).

DEFENCE
Total armed strength: 92 400 (1989). *Military service*: 10 months or 1 year.

GEOGRAPHY
The forested Ardennes plateau occupies the south-east of the country. The plains of central Belgium, an important agricultural region, are covered in fertile loess. The north, which is flat and low-lying, contains the sandy Kempenland plateau in the east and the plain of Flanders in the west. Enclosed by dykes behind coastal sand dunes are polders – former marshes and lagoons reclaimed from the sea. *Principal rivers*: Scheldt (Schelde or Escaut), Meuse (Maes), Sambre. *Highest point*: Botrange 694 m (2272 ft).

Climate: Belgium experiences relatively cool summers and mild winters, with ample rainfall throughout the year. Summers are hotter and winters colder inland.

ECONOMY
Belgium is a small, densely populated industrial country with few natural resources. In the centre and the north, soils are generally fertile and the climate

encourages high yields of wheat, sugar beet, grass and fodder crops. Metalworking – originally based on small mineral deposits in the Ardennes – is the most important industry. Textiles, chemicals, ceramics, glass and rubber are also important, but, apart from coal, almost all the raw materials required by industry now have to be imported. Economic problems in the 1970s and 1980s have mirrored Belgium's linguistic divide, with high unemployment largely confined to the French-speaking (Walloon) south, while the industries of the Flemish north have prospered. Banking, commerce and, in particular, administration employ increasing numbers, and Brussels has benefited from its role as the unofficial EC 'capital'.

RECENT HISTORY
Belgium's neutrality was broken by the German invasion in 1914 (which led to Britain's declaration of war against Germany). The brave resistance of King Albert in 1914–18 earned international admiration; the capitulation of Leopold III when Belgium was again occupied by Germany (1940–45) was severely criticized. The Belgian Congo (Zaïre), acquired as a personal possession by Leopold II (1879), was relinquished amidst scenes of chaos in 1960. Belgium is now the main centre of administration of the EC and of NATO, but the country is troubled by the acute rivalry between its Flemish and French speakers and is gradually moving towards a federal system.

BELIZE
Member of: UN, Commonwealth, CARICOM, OAS.
Population: 185 000 (1989 est).
Capital and major cities: Belmopan 3700, Belize City 49 700, Orange Walk 10 500, Corozal 8500, Dangriga 8100 (1988).
Languages: English (official), Creole, Spanish.
Religion: Roman Catholic majority.
Life expectancy: 68.5 years.
Labour force: (1980) 47 327; agriculture and forestry 14 745, community and social work 8956, trade and tourism 5646.

BELIZE

Area: 22 965 km²
(8867 sq mi)

GOVERNMENT
The eight members of the Senate (the upper house of the National Assembly) are appointed by the Gover-

nor General, the representative of the British Queen as sovereign of Belize. The 28 members of the House of Representatives (the lower house) are elected by universal adult suffrage for five years. The Governor General appoints a Prime Minister, who commands a majority in the House, and – on the PM's advice – a Cabinet, which is responsible to the House. The main political parties are the People's United Party and the United Democratic Party.
Prime Minister: George Price.

EDUCATION
Literacy rate: 90% (1988 est). *Years of compulsory schooling*: 6–14. *Universities*: 1.

DEFENCE
Total armed strength: 700 (1989). *Military service*: none.

GEOGRAPHY
Tropical jungle covers much of Belize. The south contains the Maya Mountains. The north is mainly swampy lowlands. *Principal rivers*: Hondo, Belize, New River. *Highest point*: Victoria Peak 1122 m (3681 ft).
Climate: The subtropical climate is tempered by trade winds. Rainfall is heavy, but there is a dry season between February and May.

ECONOMY
The production of sugar, bananas and citrus fruit for export dominates the economy.

RECENT HISTORY
The colony of British Honduras was renamed Belize in 1973 and gained independence in 1981. Following a severe hurricane in 1961, the capital was moved inland from Belize City to a purpose-built new town, Belmopan. Guatemala continues to claim Belize as part of her territory, despite international efforts to achieve a settlement.

BENIN

Official name: La République du Bénin (the Republic of Benin).
Member of: UN, OAU, ECOWAS.
Population: 4 592 000 (1989 est).
Capital and major cities: Porto-Novo 208 000, Cotonou 487 000 (1982).
Languages: French (official), Fon (43%).
Religions: Animist (65%), Sunni Islam (15%).
Life expectancy: 46 years.
Labour force: (1988 est) 2 097 000; agriculture 1 326 000, industry 100 000, services 500 000.

GOVERNMENT
The National Assembly comprises 206 Commissioners elected by universal adult suffrage every five years. The Assembly, in turn, elects the President for a five-year term to head the National Executive Council, whose Permanent Committee comprises the Cabinet of Ministers led by a Prime Minister. Reforms in 1989–90 removed the monopoly of power formerly enjoyed by the Parti de la Révolution Populaire du Bénin, and permitted the establishment of other political parties. Multi-party presidential elections were held in 1991.
President: Nicephore Soglo.
Prime Minister: to be announced.

BENIN
Area: 112 622 km²
(43 484 sq mi)

NIGER
BURKINA FASO
NIGERIA
GHANA
TOGO
Porto-Novo
Cotonou *Bight of Benin*
ATLANTIC OCEAN

EDUCATION
Literacy rate: 25% (1985 est). *Years of compulsory schooling*: 5–12. *Universities*: 1.

DEFENCE
Total armed strength: 7800. *Military service*: selective.

GEOGRAPHY
In the northwest lies the Atacora Massif; in the northeast, plains slope down to the Niger Valley. The plateaux of central Benin fall in the south to a low fertile region. A narrow coastal plain is backed by lagoons. *Principal rivers*: Ouémé, Niger. *Highest point*: Atacora Massif 635 m (2083 ft).
Climate: The north is tropical; the south is equatorial.

ECONOMY
The economy is based on agriculture, which occupies the majority of the labour force. The main food crops are cassava (manioc), yams and maize; the principal cash crop is palm oil. In the late 1980s, this centrally planned socialist state looked for increased Western assistance, and in 1989 the command economy was abandoned.

RECENT HISTORY
Benin was known as Dahomey until 1975. Political turmoil followed independence from France in 1960, and five army coups took place between 1963 and 1972. The regime established by Colonel Kerekou in 1972 brought some stability, and after 1987, experiments with state socialism were moderated. In 1989 President Kerekou disavowed Marxist-Leninism, and appointed a civilian administration to guide Benin towards becoming a market economy. Kerekou was defeated in multi-party elections in 1991.

BHUTAN

Official name: Druk-yul (Realm of the Dragon).
Member of: UN, SAARC.
Population: 1 408 000 (1989 est).

Capital: Thimphu 15 000 (1987 est).
Language: Dzongkha (Tibetan; official).
Religion: Buddhist.
Life expectancy: 47.9 years.
Labour force: (1982 est) 650 000; agriculture and forestry 613 000, public services 22 000, trade 9000.

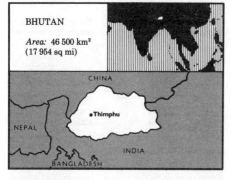

BHUTAN

Area: 46 500 km²
(17 954 sq mi)

CHINA

•Thimphu

NEPAL

INDIA

BANGLADESH

GOVERNMENT
Bhutan is a hereditary monarchy without a written constitution. The King shares power with a Council of Ministers, the National Assembly and the head of Bhutan's 5000 Buddhist monks. Of the 151 members of the National Assembly, 106 are directly elected by universal adult suffrage for a three-year term; the remainder include the Royal Advisory Council, the Ministers and 10 religious representatives. There are no political parties.
King: HM the *Druk Gyalpo* Jigme Singhye Wangchuk, King of Bhutan (succeeded 24 July 1972 on the death of his father).

EDUCATION
Literacy rate: no figure available. *Years of compulsory education*: education is free but not compulsory. *Universities*: none.

DEFENCE
Total armed strength: no figure is released. *Military service*: part-time militia training.

GEOGRAPHY
The Himalaya make up most of the country. The valleys of central Bhutan are wide and fertile. The narrow Duars Plain – a subtropical jungle – lies along the Indian border. *Principal rivers*: Amo-chu, Wang-chu, Machu. *Highest point*: Khula Kangri 7554 m (24 784 ft).
Climate: Hot and very wet in the Duars Plain, temperatures get progressively lower with altitude resulting in glaciers and permanent snow cover in the north. Precipitation is heavy.

ECONOMY
Bhutan is one of the poorest and least developed countries in the world. About 90% of the labour force is involved in producing food crops.

RECENT HISTORY
Bhutan's contact with British-dominated India led to border friction and partial annexation in 1865. In 1949 India returned this territory but assumed influence over Bhutan's external affairs. In 1907 the governor of Tongsa became the first king of Bhutan.

BOLIVIA
Official name: Républica de Bolivia (Republic of Bolivia).
Member of: UN, OAS, LAIA.
Population: 7 193 000 (1989 est).
Capital and major cities: La Paz (administrative capital) 1 050 000, Sucre (legal capital) 96 000, Santa Cruz 615 000, Cochabamba 377 000, Oruro 195 000, Potosí 114 000, Tarija 68 500 (1988 est).
Languages: Spanish (official; 55%), Quéchua.
Religion: Roman Catholic (official; 95%).
Life expectancy: 53.1 years.
Labour force: (1987 est) 2 101 100, agriculture and forestry 791 300, community and social work 391 500, trade and tourism 136 000.

BOLíVIA

Area: 1 098 581 km²
(424 164 sq mi)

BRAZIL

PERU

Lake Titicaca
•La Paz

•Santa Cruz

PACIFIC
OCEAN

•Sucre

CHILE   ARGENTINA

PARAGUAY

GOVERNMENT
The President (who appoints a Cabinet), the 27-member Senate and the 130-member Chamber of Deputies are elected for four-year terms by universal adult suffrage. The main political parties are the Movimiento Nacionalista Revolucionario and Acción Democrática Nacionalista.
President: Jaime Paz Zamora.

EDUCATION
Literacy rate: 75% (1985 est). *Years of compulsory schooling*: 6–13. *Universities*: 8 state and 2 private universities.

DEFENCE
Total armed strength: 28 000 (1989). *Military service*: selective.

GEOGRAPHY
The Andes divide into two parallel chains between which is an extensive undulating depression (the Altiplano), containing Lake Titicaca, the highest navigable lake in the world. In the east and northeast, a vast lowland includes tropical rain forests (the Llanos), subtropical plains and semiarid grasslands (the Chaco). *Principal rivers*: Beni, Mamoré, Pilcomayo, Paraguay. *Highest point*: Sajama 6542 m (21 463 ft).
Climate: Rainfall is negligible in the southwest,

and heavy in the northeast. Temperature varies with altitude from the cold Andean summits and cool, windy Altiplano to the tropical northeast.

ECONOMY
Bolivia is a relatively poor country, despite being rich in natural resources such as petroleum and tin. Lack of investment, political instability and the high cost of extraction have retarded development. Agriculture, which is labour intensive, produces domestic foodstuffs (potatoes and maize), as well as export crops (sugar cane and cotton). The cultivation of coca (the source of cocaine) is causing concern.

RECENT HISTORY
In the 19th century, Bolivia – a former Spanish colony – was characterized by political instability. In three devastating wars – the War of the Pacific (1879–83), alongside Peru against Chile, and the Chaco Wars (1928–30 and 1933–35) against Paraguay – Bolivia sustained great human and territorial losses. After 1935, political instability continued with a succession of military and civilian governments. Since 1982, however, Bolivia has had democratically elected governments.

BOTSWANA
Official name: The Republic of Botswana.
Member of: UN, OAU, Commonwealth, SADCC.
Population: 1 212 000 (1988 est).
Capital and major cities: Gaborone 111 000, Francistown 49 000, Selibi-Pikwe 46 500, Molepolole 29 000, Serowe 28 000, Mochudi 26 500 (1988).
Languages: English (official), Setswana.
Religions: Animist (over 50%), Anglican.
Life expectancy: 56.5 years.
Labour force: (1988 est) 403 000; agriculture and forestry 260 000, community and social work 70 000, trade and tourism 16 000.

BOTSWANA

Area: 582 000 km²
(224 711 sq mi)

ANGOLA ZAMBIA
ZIMBABWE
NAMIBIA
Gaborone
SOUTH AFRICA

GOVERNMENT
Thirty of the 36 members of the National Assembly are elected by universal adult suffrage for five years. Of the remainder, four are nominated by the President and specially elected; the Speaker and Attorney General are non-voting members. The President, who chairs and appoints a Cabinet, is elected for five

years by the Assembly. (There is also a 15-member House of Chiefs whose sole brief is to deal with tribal, constitutional and chieftancy matters.) The main political parties are the Botswana Democratic Party and the Botswana National Front.
President: Dr Quett Masire.

EDUCATION
Literacy rate: 70% (1985 est). *Years of compulsory schooling:* schooling is not compulsory. *Universities:* 1.

DEFENCE
Total armed strength: 4500. *Military service:* none.

GEOGRAPHY
A central plateau divides a flat near-desert in the east of Botswana from the Kalahari Desert and Okavango Swamps in the west. *Principal rivers:* Chobe, Shashi. *Highest point:* Tsodilo Hill 1375 m (4511 ft).
Climate: The climate is subtropical with extremes of heat and occasionally temperatures below freezing. Most of Botswana is periodically subject to drought.

ECONOMY
Nomadic cattle herding and the cultivation of subsistence crops occupies the majority of the labour force. The mainstay of the economy is mining for diamonds, copper-nickel and coal.

RECENT HISTORY
The area became the British protectorate of Bechuanaland in 1885. Development was slow, and many Africans had to seek work in South Africa. Nationalism was late to develop, and independence – as Botswana – was granted without a struggle in 1966. Under the first president, Sir Seretse Khama, and his successor, Botswana has succeeded in remaining a democracy.

BRAZIL
Official name: A República Federativa do Brasil (the Federative Republic of Brazil).
Member of: UN, OAS, LAIA.
Population: 147 404 000 (1989 est).
Capital and major cities: Brasília 1 577 000, São Paulo 10 099 000 (15 900 000 agglomeration), Rio de Janeiro 5 615 000 (9 019 000 agglomeration), Belo Horizonte 2 122 000, Salvador 1 811 000, Fortaleza 1 589 000, Nova Iguaçu 1 325 000 (part of Rio de Janeiro agglomeration), Recife 1 290 000, Curitiba 1 285 000, Pôrto Alegre 1 275 000, Bélem 1 121 000 (1985 est).
Language: Portuguese.
Religion: Roman Catholic (91%).
Life expectancy: 64.9 years.
Labour force: (1986) 56 816 000; service industries 16 338 000, agriculture and forestry 14 331 000, mining and manufacturing 8 987 000.

GOVERNMENT
Under the constitution of October 1988, the President – who appoints and chairs a Cabinet – is elected for a five-year term by universal adult suffrage. The lower house of the National Congress (the Chamber of Deputies) has 487 members elected for four years by compulsory universal adult suffrage. The 72

members of the upper house (the Federal Senate) are elected directly for an eight-year term – one third and two thirds of the senators retiring alternately every four years. Each of the 25 states and the Federal District of Brasília has its own legislature. The principal political parties are the (moderate) PMDB (Brazilian Democratic Movement), the (moderate) PFL (Liberal Front), the (conservative) National Reconstruction Party, the (socialist) PT (Worker's Party) and the Democratic Labour Party. A referendum in 1993 will decide whether Brazil will retain its present constitution or restore the monarchy.
President: Fernando Collor de Mello.

BRAZIL

Area: 8 511 965 km²
(3 286 488 sq mi)

BRAZILIAN STATES AND TERRITORIES

Population figures are for 1985.

Acre *Area*: 152 589 km² (58 915 sq mi). *Population*: 385 000. *Capital*: Rio Branco 146 000.

Alagoas *Area*: 27 731 km² (10 707 sq mi). *Population*: 2 381 000. *Capital*: Maceió 484 000.

Amazonas *Area*: 1 564 445 km² (604 032 sq mi). *Population*: 1 887 000. *Capital*: Manaus 834 000.

Bahia *Area*: 561 026 km² (216 612 sq mi). *Population*: 11 386 000. *Capital*: Salvador 1 811 000.

Ceará *Area*: 150 630 km² (58 158 sq mi). *Population*: 6 207 000. *Capital*: Fortaleza 1 589 000.

Espirito Santo *Area*: 45 597 km² (17 605 sq mi). *Population*: 2 429 000. *Capital*: Vitória 254 000.

Goiás *Area*: 642 092 km² (247 912 sq mi). *Population*: 4 765 000. *Capital*: Goiânia 928 000.

Maranhão *Area*: 328 663 km² (126 897 sq mi). *Population*: 4 978 000. *Capital*: São Luis 564 000.

Mato Grosso *Area*: 881 001 km² (340 154 sq mi). *Population*: 1 660 000. *Capital*: Cuiaba 283 000.

Mato Grosso do Sul *Area*: 350 548 km² (135 347 sq mi). *Population*: 1 729 000. *Capital*: Campo Grande 387 000.

Minas Gerais *Area*: 587 172 km² (226 707 sq mi). *Population*: 15 239 000. *Capital*: Belo Horizonte 2 122 000.

Pará *Area*: 1 250 722 km² (482 904 sq mi). *Population*: 4 617 000. *Capital*: Bélem 1 121 000.

Paraiba *Area*: 56 372 km² (21 765 sq mi). *Population*: 3 146 000. *Capital*: João Pessoa 398 000.

Paraná *Area*: 199 554 km² (77 048 sq mi). *Population*: 8 308 000. *Capital*: Curitiba 1 285 000.

Pernambuco *Area*: 98 281 km² (37 946 sq mi). *Population*: 7 106 000. *Capital*: Recife 1 290 000.

Piaui *Area*: 250 934 km² (96 886 sq mi). *Population*: 2 584 000. *Capital*: Teresina 476 000.

Rio de Janeiro *Area*: 44 268 km² (17 092 sq mi). *Population*: 13 351 000. *Capital*: Rio de Janeiro 9 019 000.

Rio Grande do Norte *Area*: 53 015 km² (20 469 sq mi). *Population*: 2 244 000. *Capital*: Natal 513 000.

Rio Grande do Sul *Area*: 282 184 km² (108 951 sq mi). *Population*: 8 859 000. *Capital*: Pôrto Alegre 1 275 000.

Rondônia *Area*: 243 044 km² (93 839 sq mi). *Population*: 862 000. *Capital*: Pôrto Velho 202 000.

Santa Catarina *Area*: 95 985 km² (37 060 sq mi). *Population*: 4 339 000. *Capital*: Florianópolis 219 000. Largest city: Joinville 260 000.

São Paulo *Area*: 247 898 km² (95 714 sq mi). *Population*: 32 091 000. *Capital*: São Paulo 15 900 000.

Sergipe *Area*: 21 994 km² (84 919 sq mi). *Population*: 1 366 000. *Capital*: Aracaju 362 000.

Amapá (territory) *Area*: 140 276 km² (54 161 sq mi). *Capital*: Macapá 170 000.

Federal District (Distrito Federal) *Area*: 5814 km² (2245 sq mi). *Population*: 1 792 000. *Capital*: Brasília 1 577 000.

Fernando de Noronha (territory) *Area*: 26 km² (10 sq mi). *Population*: 1300. The island territory is administered from the mainland.

Roraima (territory) *Area*: 230 104 km² (88 843 sq mi). *Capital*: Boa Vista 66 000.

EDUCATION

Literacy rate: 78% (1985). *Years of compulsory schooling*: 7–14. *Universities*: 74.

DEFENCE

Total armed strength: 324 000. *Military service*: 1 year.

GEOGRAPHY

Nearly one half of Brazil is drained by the world's largest river system, the Amazon, whose wide, low-lying basin is still largely covered by tropical rain forest, although pressure on land has led to extensive deforestation. North of the Amazon Basin, the Guiana Highlands contain Brazil's highest peak. A central plateau of savannah grasslands lies south of the Basin. The east and south of the country contain the Brazilian Highlands – a vast plateau divided by fertile valleys and mountain ranges. A densely populated narrow coastal plain lies at the foot of the Highlands. *Principal rivers*: Amazon, Paraná, São Francisco, Madeira, Juruá, Purus. *Highest point*: Pico da Neblina 3014 m (9888 ft).

Climate: The Amazon Basin and the southeast coast are tropical with heavy rainfall. The rest of Brazil is either subtropical or temperate (in the savannah). Only the northeast has inadequate rainfall.

ECONOMY

Agriculture employs about one quarter of the labour force. The principal agricultural exports include coffee, sugar cane, soyabeans, oranges, beef cattle and cocoa. Timber was important, but environmental concern is restricting its trade. Rapid industrialization since 1945 has made Brazil a major manufacturing country. While textiles, clothing and food processing are still the biggest industries, the iron and steel, chemical, petroleum-refining, cement, electrical, motor-vehicle and fertilizer industries have all attained international stature. Brazil has enormous – and, in part, unexploited – natural resources, including iron ore, phosphates, uranium, copper, manganese, bauxite, coal and vast hydroelectric-power potential. In the last two decades, rampant inflation has hindered development.

RECENT HISTORY

A former Portuguese possession, Brazil became independent in 1822 with the head of a branch of the Portuguese royal family as emperor. The long reign of the liberal Emperor Pedro II brought stability and economic growth. Opposition from landowners (angered by the abolition of slavery in 1888) and from the military (who were excluded from political power) led to a coup in 1889. Pedro II was forced to abdicate and a federal republic was established. The republic was initially stable, but social unrest mounted and, in 1930, Getúlio Vargas seized power. Vargas attempted to model Brazil on Mussolini's Italy, but was overthrown by the military in 1945. In 1950, Vargas was elected president again, but he committed suicide rather than face impeachment (1954). Short-lived civilian governments preceded a further period of military rule (1964–85), during which the economy expanded rapidly, but political and social rights were restricted. Brazil returned to civilian rule in 1985 and in 1990 Brazilians were able to vote for a president for the first time in 29 years. The country faces problems concerning the development of the Amazon Basin and in balancing the needs of developers and landless peasants on the one hand and the advice of conservationists and the interests of tribal peoples on the other.

BRUNEI

Official name: Negara Brunei Darussalam (Sultanate of Brunei).

Member of: UN, Commonwealth, ASEAN.

Population: 251 000 (1989 est).

Capital: Bandar Seri Begawan 52 000 (1988 est).

Languages: Malay (official), Chinese, English.

Religion: Sunni Islam (official).

Life expectancy: no figure available.

Labour force: (1986 est) 81 000; community and social work 30 000, construction 13 000, trade and tourism 8000.

BRUNEI

Area: 5765 km²
(2226 sq mi)

SOUTH CHINA SEA

Bandar Seri Begawan

SABAH

SARAWAK   BORNEO

GOVERNMENT

The Sultan, a hereditary monarch, rules by decree,

assisted by a Council of Ministers whom he appoints. There are no political parties. *Sultan*: HM Haji Hassanal Bolkiah, Sultan of Brunei (succeeded upon the abdication of his father, 5 October 1967).

EDUCATION

Literacy rate: 71% (1981 est). *Years of compulsory schooling*: schooling is not compulsory. *Universities*: 1.

DEFENCE

Total armed strength: 4200 (1989). *Military service*: none.

GEOGRAPHY

Brunei consists of two coastal enclaves. The (larger) western part is hilly; the eastern enclave is more mountainous and forested. *Principal river*: Brunei River. *Highest point*: Bukit Pagon (on the border with Malaysia) 1850 m (6070 ft).

Climate: Brunei has a tropical monsoon climate with rainfall totals in excess of 2500 mm (100 in).

ECONOMY

Exploitation of substantial deposits of petroleum and natural gas has given Brunei one of the world's highest per capita incomes. Most of the country's food has to be imported.

RECENT HISTORY

In the 19th century the sultans of Brunei ruled a fraction of their former territory. The British restored order to what had become a pirates' paradise and established a protectorate from 1888 to 1971. Oil was discovered in 1929. Full independence was restored in 1984 under the absolute rule of Sultan Hassanal Bolkiah, allegedly the world's richest man.

BULGARIA

Official name: Republika Bulgariya (Republic of Bulgaria).

Member of: UN, CSCE, Council of Europe (guest).

Population: 8 987 000 (1989 est).

Capital and major cities: Sofia (Sofiya) 1 129 000, Plovdiv 357 000, Varna 305 000, Ruse 190 500, Burgas 197 000, Stara Zagora 156 500, Pleven 134 000, Tolbukhin 111 000, Sliven 107 000 (1987 est).

Languages: Bulgarian (official; over 90%), Turkish (under 8%).

Religions: Orthodox (80%), Sunni Islam (8%).

Life expectancy: 72.6 years.

Labour force: (1985) 4 686 140; heavy industry 1 778 000, community and social work 993 000, agriculture and hunting 772 000.

GOVERNMENT

The 400-member National Assembly is elected every five years by universal adult suffrage. The Assembly, in turn, elects the Council of Ministers and the State Council (whose President is head of state). The Bulgarian Communist Party renounced its leading role in 1989 and re-formed as the Bulgarian Socialist Party. The other main political movement is the coalition Union of Democratic Forces. *President*: Zhelo Zhelev. *Prime Minister*: Dimitar Popov.

BULGARIA

Area: 110 912 km²
(42 823 sq mi)

ROMANIA

Danube — Ruse
Varna

YUGOSLAVIA

• Sofia

BLACK SEA

• Plovdiv

TURKEY

GREECE

five wars to win the lands they had been promised in the earlier Treaty of San Stefano (1877). Victorious in the first two wars (1885 and 1912), Bulgaria was on the losing side in the final Balkan War (1913) and in World Wars I and II (1915–1918 and 1941–1944), and forfeited territory. After the Red Army invaded (1944), a Communist regime, tied closely to the USSR, was established and the king was exiled (1946). Following popular demonstrations in 1989, the hardline leader Todor Zhivkov (1911–) was replaced by reformers who promised free elections and renounced the leading role of the Communist Party. Free elections were held in June 1990, when the Bulgarian Socialist Party (BSP) – formerly the Bulgarian Communist Party – was returned to power. Faced by severe economic problems, the BSP was unable to govern alone and a coalition government with a non-party premier took office in 1991.

EDUCATION

Literacy rate: no figure available. *Years of compulsory schooling*: 6–16. *Universities*: 3 (plus 30 institutes of higher education).

DEFENCE

Total armed strength: 117 500 (1989 est). *Military service*: 2 years army and airforce; 3 years navy.

GEOGRAPHY

The Balkan Mountains run from east to west across central Bulgaria. To the north, low-lying hills slope down to the River Danube. To the south, a belt of lowland separates the Balkan Mountains from a high, rugged massif, which includes Bulgaria's highest peak. *Principal rivers*: Danube, Iskur, Maritsa, Tundzha. *Highest point*: Musala 2925 m (9596 ft).

Climate: The continental north has warm summers and cold winters, while the southeast has a more Mediterranean climate.

ECONOMY

With fertile soils, and few other natural resources, Bulgaria's has a strong agricultural base. Production is centred on large-scale, mechanized cooperatives. The principal crops include: cereals (wheat, maize, barley), fruit (grapes) and, increasingly, tobacco. Agricultural products are the basis of the food-processing, wine and tobacco industries. CMEA grants helped develop industry including engineering, fertilizers and chemicals. Trade patterns were disrupted in Eastern Europe in 1990 and 1991 following the social, economic and political upheavals that had swept the region. Bulgaria – whose trade links with the USSR had been particularly close – suffered more than most CMEA countries, with severe shortages of many commodities including oil. At the beginning of 1991 industrial production was declining and little progress had been made towards the privatization of industry and agriculture.

RECENT HISTORY

Russian intervention in the Ottoman (Turkish) Empire in the Balkans at the end of the 19th century produced an autonomous Bulgarian state (1878). Bulgaria was a principality until 1908, and an independent kingdom until 1946. However, the boundaries, established at the Congress of Berlin (1878), failed to satisfy the Bulgarians, who waged

BURKINA FASO

Official name: Burkina Faso or République de Burkina (previously Upper Volta).

Member of: UN, OAS, ECOWAS.

Population: 8 714 000 (1989 est).

Capital and major cities: Ouagadougou 442 000, Bobo-Dioulasso 229 000, Koudougou 52 000, Ouahigouya 39 000, Banfora 35 500 (1985).

Languages: French (official), Mossi.

Religions: Animist (53%), Sunni Islam (36%).

Life expectancy: 47.2 years.

Labour force: (1988 est) 4 565 000; agriculture and forestry 3 874 000, services 320 000, industry 140 000.

BURKINA FASO

Area: 274 200 km²
(105 869 sq mi)

MALI

NIGER

• Ouagadougou

BENIN

GHANA

TOGO

IVORY COAST

GOVERNMENT

The Popular Front, which took power in a coup in 1987, holds power. The Chairman of the Front is head of state and appoints a Council of Ministers. It was announced in 1990 that a commission would be appointed to draft a new constitution and that presidential and legislative elections would be held and multi-party politics would be resumed in 1991. *Head of state*: Capt Blaise Campaore.

EDUCATION

Literacy rate: 13% (1985 est). *Years of compulsory schooling*: 7–13. *Universities*: 1.

DEFENCE

Total armed strength: 8700 plus 1750 paramilitary (1989). *Military service*: none.

GEOGRAPHY

The country consists of plateaux about 500 m (1640 ft) high. *Principal rivers*: Mouhoun (Black Volta), Nakambe (White Volta), Nazinon (Red Volta). *Highest point*: Mt Tema 749 m (2457 ft).

Climate: The country is hot and dry, with adequate rainfall – 1000 mm (40 in) – only in the savannah of the south. The north is semidesert.

ECONOMY

Burkina Faso, one of the world's poorest states, has been severely stricken by drought in the last two decades. Nomadic herdsmen and subsistence farmers – producing mainly sorghum, sugar cane and millet – form the bulk of the population. Cotton, manganese and zinc are exported.

RECENT HISTORY

Burkina Faso was the French colony of Upper Volta. During the colonial era, the country acted as a labour reservoir for more developed colonies to the south. Since independence in 1960, the country – which changed its name to Burkina Faso in 1984 – has had a turbulent political history, with a succession of military coups. In 1990 and 1991, pressure for liberalization and civilian rule came from local students and from foreign-aid donors, upon whom the country is heavily dependent.

BURMA (MYANMAR)

Official name: Myanmar Naingngandaw (The Union of Myanmar). The name Burma was officially dropped in May 1989.

Member of: UN.

Population: 40 810 000 (1989 est).

Capital and major cities: Rangoon 2 459 000, Mandalay 533 000, Moulmein 220 000, Bago 151 000, Pathein 144 000, Taunggyi 108 000 (1983).

Languages: Burmese (official; 80%), Karen, Mon, Shan, Kachin.

Religion: Buddhist (85%).

Life expectancy: 60 years.

Labour force: 17 000 000 (1989 official employment figures); agriculture 10 042 000, trade 1 622 000, manufacturing 1 384 000.

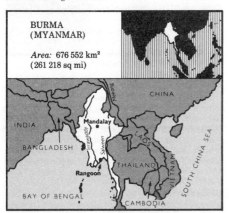

BURMA (MYANMAR)

Area: 676 552 km²
(261 218 sq mi)

GOVERNMENT

Power is held by a 19-member State Law-and-Order Restoration Council whose Chairman is head of state. There is constitutional provision for a 489-member Assembly which is empowered to elect a Council of Ministers and a Council of State, whose Chairman will be head of state. Multi-party elections were held in May 1990 but the military State Law-and-Order Restoration Council refused to transfer power to the majority National League for Democracy. The other main political party is the military-backed National Unity Party.

President: Gen. Saw Maung.

Prime Minister: Maj.-Gen. Phone Myint.

EDUCATION

Literacy rate: 66% (1980 est). *Years of compulsory schooling:* schooling is not compulsory. *Universities:* 3.

DEFENCE

Total armed strength: 200 000 (1989). *Military service* none.

GEOGRAPHY

The north and west of Burma are mountainous. In the east is the Shan Plateau along the Thai border. Central and south Burma consists of tropical lowlands. *Principal rivers:* Irrawaddy, Sittang, Mekong. *Highest point:* Hkakado Razi 5881 m (19 296 ft).

Climate: Burma is tropical, experiencing monsoon rains – up to 5000 mm (200 in) in the south – from May to October.

ECONOMY

Burma is rich in agriculture, timber and minerals, but because of poor communications, lack of development and serious rebellions by a number of ethnic minorities, the country has been unable to realize its potential. Subsistence farming involves the majority of the labour force.

RECENT HISTORY

Separated from British India in 1937, Burma became a battleground for British and Japanese forces in World War II. In 1948, Burma left the Commonwealth as an independent republic, keeping outside contacts to a minimum, particularly following the coup of General Ne Win in 1962. Continuing armed attempts to gain autonomy by non-Burman minorities have strengthened the army's role. In 1988–89, demonstrations for democracy appeared to threaten military rule, but were repressed. The military retained power following multi-party elections in 1990, and detained or restricted the principal members of the National League for Democracy, including the party leader, Aung San Suu Kyi.

BURUNDI

Official name: La République du Burundi or Republika y'Uburundi (The Republic of Burundi).

Member of: UN, OAU.

Population: 5 149 000 (1988 est).

Capital and major city: Bujumbura 273 000 (1986), Gitega 95 000 (1982).

Languages: Kirundi, French, Kiswahili.

Religion: Roman Catholic (65%).

Life expectancy: 48.5 years.

Labour force: (1983 est) 2 480 800; agriculture 2 320 000, public sector 95 000, private sector 38 000.

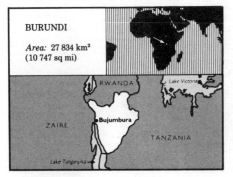

BURUNDI

Area: 27 834 km²
(10 747 sq mi)

RWANDA — Lake Victoria

ZAIRE ●Bujumbura

TANZANIA

Lake Tanganyika

GOVERNMENT
Power is held by a 31-member military committee, whose Chairman is President. The Committee has appointed a civilian Council of Ministers. Party politics has been suspended.
President: Maj. Pierre Buyoya.
Prime Minister: Adrien Sibomana.

EDUCATION
Literacy rate: 40% (1982 est). *Years of compulsory schooling*: 7–13. *Universities*: 1.

DEFENCE
Total armed strength: 7200 (1989). *Military service*: none.

GEOGRAPHY
Burundi is a high plateau, rising from Lake Tanganyika in the west. *Principal rivers*: Kagera, Ruzizi. *Highest point*: Mt Hela 2685 m (8809 ft).
Climate: The lowlands are hot and humid. Temperatures are cooler in the mountains.

ECONOMY
Over 92% of the labour force is involved in agriculture, producing both subsistence crops and crops for export, such as coffee.

RECENT HISTORY
Burundi was a semi-feudal kingdom in which the minority Tutsi tribe of pastoralists dominated the Hutu majority of agriculturalists. Colonized by Germany in 1890, it was taken over by Belgium after World War I under a League of Nations mandate. Independence came in 1962, after much conflict throughout the country. Following a military coup in 1966, a republic was established. The killing of the deposed king in 1972 led to a massacre of the Hutu. There have since been further coups. Serious ethnic unrest in 1988 led to an exodus of Hutu refugees to Rwanda.

CAMBODIA

Official name: Roat Kampuchea (The State of Cambodia) – previously known as the Khmer Republic and Kampuchea.
Population: 8 055 000 (1989 est).
Capital and major cities: Phnom-Penh 700 000 (1986 est), Battambang 66 000 (1983 est).
Languages: Khmer (official), French.

Religion: Buddhist majority.
Life expectancy: 48.4 years.
Labour force: (1988 est) 3 707 000; agriculture 2 629 000, services 630 000, industry 220 000.

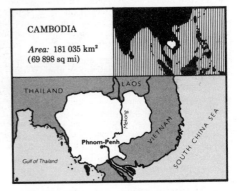

CAMBODIA

Area: 181 035 km²
(69 898 sq mi)

LAOS

THAILAND

Mekong

VIETNAM

Phnom-Penh

SOUTH CHINA SEA

Gulf of Thailand

GOVERNMENT
The sole legal party is the (Communist) People's Revolutionary Party, whose Politburo exercises effective power. The 123 members of the National Assembly are elected for five years by universal adult suffrage. The life of the Assembly elected in 1981 has been extended until 1991 to allow a commission to draft a new constitution. The Assembly elects a Council of State, whose Chairman is head of state. Executive power is exercised by the Council of Ministers appointed by, and responsible to, the National Assembly.
Head of state: Heng Samrin.
Prime Minister: Hun Sen.

EDUCATION
Literacy rate: 75% (1988 est). *Years of compulsory schooling*: 5–14. *Universities*: 1.

DEFENCE
Total armed strength: 99 300 (1989 est). *Military service*: 5 years.

GEOGRAPHY
Central Cambodia consists of fertile plains in the Mekong River valley and surrounding the Tonle Sap (Great Lake). To the north and east are plateaux covered by forests and savannah. The southern Phnom Kravanh mountains run parallel to the coast. *Principal river*: Mekong. *Highest point*: Phnum Aoral 1813 m (5947 ft).
Climate: Cambodia is tropical and humid. The monsoon season (June–November) brings heavy rain to the whole country, with annual totals as high as 5000 mm (200 in) in the mountains.

ECONOMY
Invasion, civil wars, massacres of the civilian population (1976–79) and the (temporary) abolition of currency (in 1978) all but destroyed the economy. Aided by the Vietnamese since 1979, agriculture and – to a lesser extent – industry have been slowly rebuilt, but Cambodia remains one of the world's poorest nations. Rice yields – formerly exported – still fall short of Cambodia's own basic needs.

HISTORY
A French protectorate was established in 1863 and

continued, apart from Japanese occupation during World War II, until independence was regained in 1953. Throughout the colonial period, Cambodia's monarchy remained in nominal control. In 1955, King (now Prince) Norodom Sihanouk abdicated to lead a broad coalition government, but he could not prevent Cambodia's involvement in the Vietnam War or allay US fears of his sympathies for the Communists. In 1970 he was overthrown in a pro-US military coup. The military regime was attacked by Communist Khmer Rouge guerrillas, who sought to create a self-sufficient workers' utopia. The Khmer Rouge were finally victorious in 1975. Under Pol Pot, they forcibly evacuated the towns and massacred up to 2 000 000 of their compatriots. In 1978 Vietnam – Cambodia's traditional foe – invaded, overthrowing the Khmer Rouge. The hostility between the two countries had been sharpened by the Sino-Soviet split in which they took different sides. After Vietnamese troops withdrew in 1989, resistance forces of the exiled tripartite coalition government – led by Prince Sihanouk and including the Khmer Rouge – became active in much of western and southern Cambodia. International efforts to mediate between the opposing sides in the civil war resulted in a peace conference in 1990, which agreed, in general terms, to end the civil war, to exclude foreign troops and to hold multi-party elections under the supervision of the UN. The peace plan remains to be implemented, largely because of objections to the participation of the Khmer Rouge.

CAMEROON

Official name: La République unie du Cameroun (The United Republic of Cameroon).

Member of: UN, OAU.

Population: 11 407 000 (1989 est).

Capital and major cities: Yaoundé 654 000, Douala 1 030 000 (1986 est), Nkongsamba 71 000, Maroua 67 000, Garoua 64 000 (1976).

Languages: French, English (both official).

Religions: Animist (40%), Sunni Islam (20%), Roman Catholic (20%).

Life expectancy: 52.9 years.

Labour force: (1985 est) 3 918 000; agriculture and forestry 3 000 000, manufacturing 175 000, trade and tourism 154 000.

GOVERNMENT

The 180 members of the National Assembly are elected for a five-year term by universal adult suffrage. The sole legal party is the Union National Camerounaise. The President – who is also directly elected for a five-year term – appoints a Council of Ministers.
President: Paul Biya.

EDUCATION

Literacy rate: 56% (1985 est). *Years of compulsory schooling*: 6–12 (East Cameroon; 6–13 in West Cameroon but not compulsory). *Universities*: 1.

DEFENCE

Total armed strength: 11 600 (400 paramilitary, 700 navy, 300 airforce). *Military service*: none.

GEOGRAPHY

In the west, a chain of highlands rises to the volcanic Mont Cameroun. In the north, savannah plains dip towards Lake Chad. The coastal plains and plateaus

in the south and the centre are covered with tropical forest. *Principal rivers*: Sanaga, Nyong. *Highest point*: Mont Cameroun 4069 m (13 353 ft).

Climate: Cameroon is tropical, with hot, rainy conditions on the coast, but drier inland.

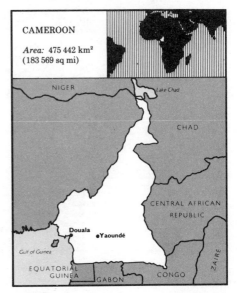

CAMEROON

Area: 475 442 km² (183 569 sq mi)

ECONOMY

Cameroon is a major producer of cocoa, and other export crops include bananas, coffee, cotton, rubber and palm oil. The diversity of Cameroon's agriculture, and the rapid development of the petroleum industry, have given the country one of the highest standards of living in tropical Africa.

RECENT HISTORY

Germany declared a protectorate over Kamerun in 1884. After World War I, Cameroon was divided between the UK and France. The French Cameroons became independent in 1960. Following a plebiscite (1961), the north of the British Cameroons merged with Nigeria; the south federated with the former French territory. A unitary state replaced the federation in 1972. A number of arrests followed attempts to establish an opposition political party in April 1990, but in June 1990 the President hinted at the future acceptance of a multi-party system.

CANADA

Member of: UN, Commonwealth, OAS, NATO, CSCE, G7.

Population: 26 219 000 (1989 est).

Capital and major cities: Ottawa 819 300, Toronto 3 427 200, Montréal 2 921 400, Vancouver 1 380 700, Edmonton 785 500, Calgary 671 300, Winnipeg 625 300, Québec 603 300, Hamilton 557 000, St Catharine's–Niagara 343 300, London 342 300, Kitchener 311 000 (1986).

Languages: English (63% as a first language; official), French (25% as a first language; official).

Religions: Roman Catholic (47%), United Church of Canada (15%), Anglican (10%).

Life expectancy: 76.3 years.

Labour force: (1988) 13 275 000; trade 2 328 000,

CANADA

Area: 9 970 610 km²
(3 849 674 sq mi)

manufacturing 2 271 000, transport and communications 960 000.

GOVERNMENT

The Canadian Federal Parliament has two houses – a Senate of 104 members appointed by the Governor General to represent the provinces, and the House of Commons, whose 295 members are elected for five years by universal adult suffrage. A Prime Minister, commanding a majority in the House of Commons, is appointed by the Governor General, who is the representative of the British Queen as sovereign of Canada. The PM, in turn, appoints a Cabinet of Ministers which is responsible to the House. Each province has its own government and legislature. The main political parties are the Liberal Party, the Progressive Conservative Party and the (socialist) New Democratic Party.
Prime Minister: Brian Mulroney.

CANADIAN PROVINCES AND TERRITORIES

Population figures are for 1986.
Alberta *Area:* 661 199 km² (255 285 sq mi). *Population:* 2 366 000. *Capital:* Edmonton 785 500.
British Columbia *Area:* 948 596 km² (366 255 sq mi). *Population:* 2 889 000. *Capital:* Victoria 264 600. *Largest city:* Vancouver 1 380 700.
Manitoba *Area:* 650 087 km² (251 000 sq mi). *Population:* 1 063 000. *Capital:* Winnipeg 625 300.
New Brunswick *Area:* 73 437 km² (28 354 sq mi). *Population:* 709 000. *Capital:* Fredericton 44 300. *Largest city:* St John 120 900.
Newfoundland and Labrador *Area:* 404 517 km² (156 185 sq mi). *Population:* 568 000. *Capital:* St John's 161 900.
Nova Scotia *Area:* 55 490 km² (21 425 sq mi). *Population:* 873 000. *Capital:* Halifax 296 000.
Ontario *Area:* 1 068 582 km² (412 582 sq mi). *Population:* 9 102 000. *Capital:* Toronto 3 427 200.
Prince Edward Island *Area:* 5657 km² (2184 sq mi). *Population:* 127 000. *Capital:* Charlottetown 15 800.

Québec *Area:* 1 540 680 km² (594 860 sq mi). *Population:* 6 533 000. *Capital:* Québec 603 300. *Largest city:* Montréal 2 921 400.
Saskatchewan *Area:* 651 900 km² (251 700 sq mi). *Population:* 1 010 000. *Capital:* Regina 175 200. *Largest city:* Saskatoon 175 900.

Northwest Territories *Area:* 3 379 285 km² (1 304 903 sq mi). *Population:* 56 000. *Capital:* Yellowknife 10 900. In April 1990 it was announced that agreement had been reached to divide the Northwest Territories into two separate territories – Nunavut Territory with an Inuit (Eskimo) majority in the east and Nenedeh Territory with a native Canadian (Indian) majority in the west.
(**Nunavut** *Area:* c. 2 000 000 km² (c. 772 000 sq mi). *Population:* c. 24 000. *Capital:* the capital has not been chosen; Yellowknife in Nenedeh is likely to be the administrative centre for a transitionary period. *Largest town:* Frobisher Bay on Baffin Island 2 900.)
(**Nenedeh** *Area:* c. 1 380 000 km² (c. 533 000 sq mi). *Population:* c. 28 000. *Capital:* Yellowknife 10 900.)
Yukon Territory *Area:* 482 515 km² (186 299 sq mi). *Population:* 29 200. *Capital:* Whitehorse 17 800.

EDUCATION

Literacy rate: over 97% (est). *Years of compulsory schooling:* varies from province to province, generally 5–16. *Universities:* 66.

DEFENCE

Total armed strength: 89 000. *Military service:* none.

GEOGRAPHY

Nearly one half of Canada is covered by the Laurentian (or Canadian) Shield, a relatively flat region of hard rocks stretching round Hudson's Bay and penetrating deep into the interior. Inland, the Shield ends in a scarp that is pronounced in the east, beside the lowlands around the St Lawrence River and the Great Lakes. To the west, a line of major lakes (including Lake Winnipeg) marks the boundary with the interior plains, the Prairies. A broad belt of mountains – over 800 km (500 mi) wide – lies west of the plains. This western cordillera comprises the Rocky, Mackenzie, Coast and St Elias Mountains – which include Canada's highest point. A lower, more discontinuous, chain of highlands borders the east of Canada, running from Baffin Island, through Labrador and into New Brunswick and Nova Scotia. *Principal rivers*: Mackenzie, Slave, Peace, St Lawrence, Yukon, Nisutlin, Nelson, Saskatchewan. *Highest point*: Mount Logan 5951 m (19 524 ft).

Climate: Much of Canada experiences extreme temperatures, with mild summers and long, cold winters. The climate in the far north is polar. Average winter temperatures only remain above freezing point on the Pacific coast. In most of British Columbia precipitation is heavy. In the rest of the country, rainfall totals are moderate or light. Nearly all of Canada experiences heavy winter snowfalls.

ECONOMY

Canada enjoys one of the highest standards of living in the world, due, in part, to great mineral resources. There are substantial deposits of zinc, nickel, gold, silver, iron ore, uranium, copper, cobalt and lead, as well as major reserves of petroleum and natural gas, and enormous hydroelectric-power potential. These resources are the basis of such industries as petroleum refining, motor vehicles, metal refining, chemicals, and iron and steel. Canada is one of the world's leading exporters of cereals – in particular, wheat from the Prairie provinces. Other agricultural interests include fruit (mainly apples), beef cattle and potatoes. Vast coniferous forests have given rise to large lumber, wood-pulp and paper industries. Rich Atlantic and Pacific fishing grounds have made Canada the world's leading exporter of fish and seafood. The country has an important banking and insurance sector, and the economy is closely linked with that of the USA – tariff agreements exist between them.

RECENT HISTORY

Britain, anxious to be rid of responsibility for Canada, encouraged confederation, and in 1867 Ontario, Québec, New Brunswick and Nova Scotia formed the Dominion of Canada. Other provinces joined between 1870 and 1905, but Newfoundland did not become part of Canada until 1949. The late 19th century saw important mineral finds, such as the Klondike gold rush, and the western provinces developed rapidly. The nation was linked by the Canadian Pacific Railway, which was used to bring troops to quell a French Canadian rebellion in the Prairies (1885). In World War I, Canadian forces distinguished themselves at Vimy Ridge, and Canada won itself a place as a separate nation at the peace conferences after the war. The Statute of Westminster (1931) recognized Canadian independence. The Depression of the 1930s had a severe impact on Canada – Newfoundland, for example, went bankrupt. Canada played an important role in World War II and the Korean War, and was a founder member of NATO. Throughout the 1970s and 1980s, there was friction over the use and status of the French language, and separatism became an issue in Québec. The Canadian constitution was redefined in 1982, but Québec refused to ratify it. A series of constitutional amendments – the Meech Lake accord – was formulated to persuade Québec to adhere to the constitution, but a number of English-speaking provinces would not agree to Québec being declared 'a distinct society' with additional powers. The failure of the Meech Lake accord (June 1990) encouraged the nationalist party in Québec (the Parti Québecois) to call for 'sovereignty association' (a politically independent Québec in economic association with Canada).

CAPE VERDE

Official name: A República de Cabo Verde (The Republic of Cape Verde).

Member of: UN, OAU, ECOWAS.

Population: 337 000 (1989 est).

Capital: Praia 57 700 (1980).

Languages: Portuguese (official), Crioulu.

Religion: Roman Catholic (over 95%).

Life expectancy: 61.5 years.

Labour force: (1980) 66 600; agriculture and forestry 22 000, construction 19 000, trade and tourism 4000.

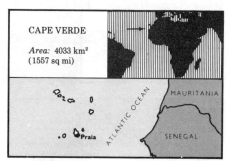

CAPE VERDE

Area: 4033 km² (1557 sq mi)

GOVERNMENT

The 83 members of the National People's Assembly are elected for five years by universal adult suffrage. The Assembly elects a President – also for a five-year term – who appoints a Council of Ministers. Until the end of 1990, the (socialist) PAICV party was the only legal political organization. However, Cape Verde now has a multi-party system. *President*: Antonio Mascarenhas. *Prime Minister*: Carlos Viega.

EDUCATION

Literacy rate: 48% (1985 est). *Years of compulsory schooling*: 7–14. *Universities*: none.

DEFENCE

Total armed strength: 1300 (1989). *Military service*: none.

GEOGRAPHY

Cape Verde consists of ten volcanic, semi-arid islands. There are no significant rivers. *Highest point*: Monte Fogo 2829 m (9281 ft).

Climate: Cooled by northeast winds, temperatures seldom exceed 27 °C (80 °F). Rainfall is low.

ECONOMY

Lack of surface water hinders agriculture, and over 90% of Cape Verde's food has to be imported. Money sent back by over 600 000 Cape Verdeans living abroad is vital to the economy.

RECENT HISTORY

Cape Verde – a former Portuguese colony – was

linked with Guinea-Bissau in the struggle against colonial rule, but gained independence separately in 1975. The PAICV party offended Catholics by decriminalizing abortion and unrest grew in 1987–88. Social and political reforms were agreed in 1990, and in 1991 the PAICV was overwhelmingly defeated in elections by a newly legalized opposition group – the Movement for Democracy.

CENTRAL AFRICAN REPUBLIC

Official name: La République Centrafricaine (The Central African Republic).
Member of: UN, OAU.
Population: 2 813 000 (1989 est).
Capital and major cities: Bangui 598 000 (1988 est), Bambari 52 000, Bouar 50 000 (1987 est).
Languages: French (official), Sangho (national).
Religions: Animist (60%), Roman Catholic (20%).
Life expectancy: 50 years.
Labour force: (1988 est) 1 341 000; agriculture 868 000, services 300 000, industry 77 000.

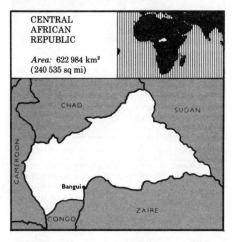

CENTRAL AFRICAN REPUBLIC
Area: 622 984 km²
(240 535 sq mi)

GOVERNMENT

The President – who appoints a Council of Ministers – is elected for a six-year term by universal adult suffrage. The Congress consists of a 52-member National Assembly (elected directly for a five-year term) and an Economic and Regional Council (half of whose members are elected by the Assembly; the remainder are appointed by the President). Until April 1991 the sole legal political party was the Rassemblement démocratique centrafricain.
President: Gen. André-Dieudonné Kolingba.

EDUCATION

Literacy rate: 40% (1985 est). *Years of compulsory schooling:* 6–14. *Universities:* 1.

DEFENCE

Total armed strength: 3800 (1989). *Military service:* 2 years' selective service.

GEOGRAPHY

The country is a low plateau, rising along the border with Sudan to the Bongos Mountains and in the west to the Monts Karre. *Principal rivers:* Oubangui, Zaïre, Chari. *Highest point:* Mt Gaou 1420 m (4659 ft).

Climate: The north is savannah, with little rain between November and March. The south is equatorial with high temperatures and heavy rainfall.

ECONOMY

Subsistence farming dominates, although cotton and coffee are produced for export. Diamonds contribute over one third of the country's foreign earnings. The country is one of the poorest in the world, and – largely owing to mismanagement during Bokassa's rule – its economy has declined since independence.

RECENT HISTORY

French influence began in 1889, and the region became the French colony of Oubangi-Chari in 1903. It suffered greatly from the activities of companies that were granted exclusive rights to large areas of the colony. Independence – as the Central African Republic – was gained in 1960. Jean-Bédel Bokassa took power in a coup in 1965. In 1976 he declared himself emperor and was crowned in an extravagantly expensive ceremony. Revolts by students and schoolchildren helped to end his murderous regime in 1979. Moves towards democratization began in 1986. Political pluralism has been allowed since 1991.

CHAD

Official name: La République du Tchad (The Republic of Chad).
Member of: UN, OAU.
Population: 5 538 000 (1989 est).
Capital and major cities: N'Djamena 512 000, Sarh 100 000, Moundou 90 000 (1986 est).
Languages: French and Arabic (both official).
Religions: Sunni Islam (45%), animist (25%).
Life expectancy: 50 years.
Labour force: (1988 est) 1 896 000; agriculture 1 361 000, services 197 000, industry 76 000.

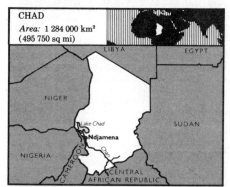

CHAD
Area: 1 284 000 km²
(495 750 sq mi)

GOVERNMENT

A referendum in 1989 approved a new constitution which upholds single-party government and creates an elected National Assembly with a maximum term of office of five years. This constitution is in abeyance following a coup in 1990.
President: Idriss Deby.

EDUCATION

Literacy rate: 25% (1985 est). *Years of compulsory schooling:* 8–14. *Universities:* 1.

DEFENCE

Total armed strength: 17 200 (1989 est). *Military service:* 3 years.

GEOGRAPHY

Deserts in the north include the Tibesti Mountains, the highest part of the country. Savannah and semidesert in the centre slope down to Lake Chad. The Oubangui Plateau in the south is covered by tropical rain forest. *Principal river*: Chari. *Highest point*: Emi Koussi 3415 m (11 204 ft).

Climate: Chad is hot and dry in the north, and tropical in the south.

ECONOMY

Chad – one of the poorest countries in the world – has been wracked by civil war and drought. With few natural resources, it relies on subsistence farming, exports of cotton and on foreign aid.

RECENT HISTORY

The area around Lake Chad became French in the late 19th century. The French conquest of the north was not completed until 1916. Since independence in 1960, Chad has been torn apart by a bitter civil war between the Muslim Arab north and the Christian and animist Black African south. Libya and France intervened forcefully on several occasions, but neither was able to achieve its aims. In October 1988, the civil war was formally ended. However, from March 1989 the former Chadian army chief, Idriss Deby, led a rebel force from bases in Sudan against the government in N'Djamena and took control of the whole country late in 1990.

CHILE

Official name: República de Chile (The Republic of Chile).

Member of: UN, OAS, LAIA.

Population: 12 961 000 (1989 est).

Capital and major cities: Santiago (capital) 4 858 000 (1987 est), Valparaiso (legislative capital) 280 000, Viña del Mar 286 000, Concepción 240 000, Talcahuano 210 000 (1986), Antofagasta 176 000, Temuno 172 000, Rancagua 152 000 (1985).

Language: Spanish.

Religion: Roman Catholic (90%).

Life expectancy: 70.7 years.

Labour force: (1988) 4 552 000; community and social work 1 155 200, agriculture and forestry 865 000, trade and tourism 732 000.

GOVERNMENT

Executive power is held by the President, who appoints a Cabinet of Ministers. Under the constitution introduced in 1990, the President is elected by universal adult suffrage for a single eight-year term. The National Congress has an upper chamber – of 26 senators directly elected for eight years and nine senators appointed by the President – and a lower chamber of 120 deputies elected for a four-year term by universal adult suffrage. Since 1990, the National Congress has met in Valparaiso. The principal political parties include the (conservative) Christian Democrat Party, the (centrist) National Renovation Party, the Socialist Party, and the (right-wing) Independent Democratic Union. *President*: Patricio Aylwin.

EDUCATION

Literacy rate: 95% (1983 est). *Years of compulsory schooling*: 6–14 or 15. *Universities*: 8.

CHILE
Area: 756 945 km² (292 258 sq mi)

DEFENCE

Total armed strength: 128 000. *Military service*: 2 years.

GEOGRAPHY

For almost 4000 km (2500 mi), the Andes form the eastern boundary of Chile. Parallel to the Andes is a depression, in which lies the Atacama Desert in the north and fertile plains in the centre. A mountain chain runs between the depression and the coast, and, in the south, forms a string of islands. *Principal rivers*: Loa, Maule, Bio-Bio. *Highest point*: Ojos del Salado 6895 m (22 588 ft).

Climate: The temperate climate is influenced by the cool Humboldt Current. Rainfall ranges from being negligible in the Atacama Desert in the north to heavy – over 2300 mm (90 in) – in the south.

ECONOMY

In 1973, the military junta took over a country in economic collapse. Strong measures cured rampant inflation, but unemployment is high, wages are low and Chile's economic decline has been spectacular. The main agricultural region is the central plains, where cereals (mainly wheat and maize) and fruit (in particular grapes) are important. Excellent fishing grounds yield one of the world's largest catches of fish. There are considerable mineral resources and great hydroelectric-power potential. Chile is the world's largest exporter of copper, and has major reserves of iron ore, coal, petroleum, natural gas, molybdenum, lithium and iodine.

RECENT HISTORY

Chile gained independence from Spain in 1818. For the next century – during which Chile gained territory in two wars against Peru and Bolivia – conservative landowners held power. Between the late 1920s and the 1940s, Chile was governed by liberal and radical regimes, but social and economic change was slow. The election of the Christian Democrats (1964) brought some reforms, but not until Salvador Allende's Marxist government was elected in 1970 were major changes – including land reform – realized. Chile was polarized between right and left, and political chaos resulted in an American-backed military coup led by General Augusto Pinochet in 1973. Tens of thousands of leftists were killed, imprisoned or exiled by the junta. Pinochet reversed Allende's reforms, restructuring the economy in favour of landowners and exporters. Pressure on the dictatorship from within Chile and abroad encouraged the junta to return the country to democratic rule in 1990.

CHILEAN EXTERNAL TERRITORY

Chilean Antarctic Territory see p. 638.

CHINA

Official name: Zhonghua Renmin Gongheguo (The People's Republic of China).

Member of: UN.

Population: 1 096 140 000 (1988 est), Han (Chinese) 93%, with Mongol, Tibetan, Uighur, Manchu and other minorities.

Capital and major cities: Beijing (Peking) 10 880 000, Shanghai 12 620 000, Tianjin 5 620 000, Shenyang 4 440 000, Wuhan 3 640 000, Guangzhou (Canton) 3 490 000 (1988 est), Chongquin 2 830 000, Harbin 2 670 000, Chengdu 2 640 000, Xian 2 390 000, Zibo 2 330 000, Nanjing (Nanking) 2 290 000, Nanchang 2 290 000, Lupanshui 2 240 000, Taiyuan 1 930 000, Changchun 1 910 000, Dalian (Darien) 1 680 000, Zhaozhuang 1 610 000, Zhengzhou 1 610 000, Kunming 1 520 000, Jinan 1 460 000, Tangshan 1 410 000, Guiyang (Kweiyang), 1 400 000, Lanzhou (Lanchow) 1 390 000, Linyi 1 390 000, Pingxiang 1 310 000, Qiqihar (Tsitsihar) 1 300 000, Anshan 1 300 000, Fushun 1 270 000, Qingdao (Tsingtao) 1 270 000, Xintao 1 270 000, Yancheng 1 270 000, Hangzhou 1 270 000, Yulin 1 260 000, Chao'an 1 230 000, Dongguang 1 230 000, Xiaogan 1 220 000, Fushu (Foochow) 1 210 000, Suining 1 200 000, Shijiazhuang (Shihkiachwang) 1 190 000, Changsha 1 190 000, Xintai 1 170 000, Puyang 1 130 000, Baotou (Paotow) 1 120 000, Bozhou 1 110 000, Jilin (Kirin) 1 070 000, Zhongshan 1 070 000, Luoyang 1 060 000, Laiwu 1 050 000, Urümqi 1 040 000, Leshan 1 040 000, Ningbo 1 030 000, Datong 1 020 000, Heze 1 020 000, Huainan 1 020 000, Handan 1 010 000, Linhai 1 010 000, Macheng 1 010 000, Changshu 1 000 000 (1986).

Languages: Chinese (Guoyo or 'Mandarin' dialect in the majority, with local dialects in south and southeast, e.g. Cantonese), with small Mongol, Tibetan and other minorites.

Religions: Officially atheist but those religions and philosophies practised include Confucianism, Daoism, Buddhism (c. 15%).

Life expectancy: 69.4 years.

Labour force: (1987 est) 527 833 000; agriculture and forestry 317 200 000, industry 93 430 000, construction 25 000 000.

GOVERNMENT

The 2978 deputies of the National People's Congress are elected for a five-year term by the People's

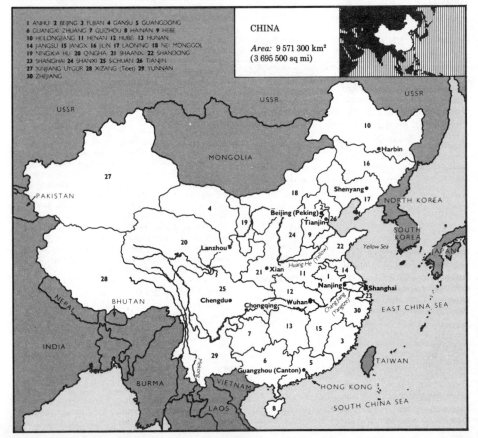

I ANHUI 2 BEIJING 3 FUJIAN 4 GANSU 5 GUANGDONG 6 GUANGXI ZHUANG 7 GUIZHOU 8 HAINAN 9 HEBEI 10 HEILONGJIANG 11 HENAN 12 HUBEI 13 HUNAN 14 JIANGSU 15 JIANGXI 16 JILIN 17 LAONING 18 NEI MONGGOL 19 NINGXIA HUI 20 QINGHA 21 SHAANXI 22 SHANDONG 23 SHANGHAI 24 SHANXI 25 SICHUAN 26 TIANJIN 27 XINJIANG UYGUR 28 XIZANG (Tibet) 29 YUNNAN 30 ZHEJIANG

CHINA

Area: 9 571 300 km² (3 695 500 sq mi)

Congresses of the 22 provinces, five autonomous provinces and three municipal provinces, and by the People's Liberation Army. The Congress elects a Standing Committee, a President (for a five-year term), a Prime Minister and a State Council (or Cabinet) – all of whom are responsible to the Congress. The only legal party is the Chinese Communist Party, which holds a Congress every five years. The Party Congress elects a Central Committee, which in turn elects a Politburo, and it is these two bodies that hold effective power.

President: Yang Shangkun.
Prime Minister: Li Peng.
General Secretary of the Communist Party: Jiang Zemin.

CHINESE PROVINCES

Populations are for 1986 unless otherwise stated.

Guangxi Zhuang (autonomous province) *Area*: 220 400 km^2 (85 100 sq mi). *Population*: 38 730 000. *Capital*: Nanning 963 000.

Nei Monggol (Inner Mongolia; autonomous province) *Area*: 450 000 km^2 (173 700 sq mi). *Population*: 20 070 000. *Capital*: Hohhot (Huhehot) 810 000.

Ningxia Hui (autonomous province) *Area*: 170 000 km^2 (65 600 sq mi). *Population*: 4 150 000. *Capital*: Yinchuan 410 000.

Xinjiang Uygur (Sinkiang; autonomous province) *Area*: 1 646 900 km^2 (635 870 sq mi). *Capital*: Urümqi 1 040 000.

Xizang (Tibet; autonomous province) *Area*: 1 221 600 km^2 (471 660 sq mi). *Population*: 1 990 000. *Capital*: Lhasa 108 000.

Anhui *Area*: 139 900 km^2 (54 020 sq mi). *Population*: 51 560 000. *Capital*: Hefei 900 000.

Fujian *Area*: 123 100 km^2 (47 530 sq mi). *Population*: 27 130 000. *Capital*: Fushu 1 210 000.

Gansu *Area*: 530 000 km^2 (204 600 sq mi). *Population*: 20 410 000. *Capital*: Lanzhou 1 390 000.

Guangdong *Area*: 197 900 km^2 (76 400 sq mi). *Population*: 56 200 000. *Capital*: Guangzhou (Canton) 3 490 000 (1988 est).

Guizhou *Area*: 174 000 km^2 (67 200 sq mi). *Population*: 29 690 000. *Capital*: Guiyang 1 400 000.

Hainan *Area*: 33 570 km^2 (12 960 sq mi). *Population*: 6 200 000. *Capital*: Haikou 300 000.

Hebei *Area*: 202 700 km^2 (78 260 sq mi). *Population*: 55 480 000. *Capital*: Shijiazhuang (Shihkiachwang) 1 190 000.

Heilongjiang *Area*: 463 600 km^2 (179 000 sq mi). *Population*: 33 110 000. *Capital*: Harbin 2 670 000.

Henan *Area*: 167 000 km^2 (64 480 sq mi). *Population*: 77 130 000. *Capital*: Zhengzhou 1 610 000.

Hubei *Area*: 187 500 km^2 (72 400 sq mi). *Population*: 49 310 000. *Capital*: Wuhan 3 640 000.

Hunan *Area*: 210 500 km^2 (81 270 sq mi). *Population*: 56 220 000. *Capital*: Changsha 1 190 000.

Jiangsu *Area*: 102 200 km^2 (39 460 sq mi). *Population*: 62 130 000. *Capital*: Nanjing (Nanking) 2 290 000.

Jiangxi *Area*: 164 800 km^2 (63 630 sq mi). *Population*: 34 600 000. *Capital*: Nanchang 2 290 000.

Jilin *Area*: 187 000 km^2 (72 200 sq mi). *Population*: 22 980 000. *Capital*: Changchun 1 910 000.

Liaoning *Area*: 151 000 km^2 (58 300 sq mi). *Population*: 36 860 000. *Capital*: Shenyang 4 440 000.

Qinghai *Area*: 721 000 km^2 (278 400 sq mi). *Population*: 4 070 000. *Capital*: Xining 610 000.

Shaanxi *Area*: 195 800 km^2 (75 600). *Population*: 30 020 000. *Capital*: Xian 2 390 000.

Shandong *Area*: 153 300 km^2 (59 190 sq mi). *Capital*: Jinan 1 460 000.

Shanxi *Area*: 157 100 km^2 (60 660 sq mi). *Population*: 26 270 000. *Capital*: Taiyuan 1 930 000.

Sichuan *Area*: 569 000 km^2 (219 700 sq mi). *Population*: 101 180 000. *Capital*: Chengdu 2 640 000.

Yunnan *Area*: 436 200 km^2 (168 420 sq mi). *Capital*: Kunming 1 520 000.

Zhejiang *Area*: 101 800 km^2 (39 300 sq mi). *Population*: Hangzhou 1 270 000.

Beijing (Peking) (municipal province) *Area*: 17 800 km^2 (6870 sq mi). *Population*: 10 810 000 (1988 est). *Capital*: Beijing 10 810 000.

Shanghai (municipal province) *Area*: 5800 km^2 (2240 sq mi). *Population*: 12 620 000 (1988 est). *Capital*: Shanghai 12 620 000.

Tianjin (municipal province) *Area*: 4000 km^2 (1540 sq mi). *Population*: 8 080 000. *Capital*: Tianjin 5 620 000 (1988 est).

EDUCATION

Literacy rate: 65% (1982 est). *Years of compulsory schooling*: education is not compulsory but is available from 7–17. There are plans to introduce 9 years of compulsory schooling by 1995. *Universities*: 37 plus over 1000 institutions of higher education.

DEFENCE

Total armed strength: 3 030 000 (1989 est). *Military service*: selective – 3 years for the army and naval infantry; 4 years for the air force and navy.

GEOGRAPHY

China is the third largest country in the world in area and the largest in population. Almost half of China comprises mountain chains, mainly in the west, including the Altaï and Tien Shan Mountains in Xinjiang Uygur, and the Kun Lun Mountains to the north of Tibet. The Tibetan Plateau – at an altitude of 3000 m (10 000 ft) – is arid. In the south of Tibet is the Himalaya, containing 40 peaks over 7000 m (23 000 ft). In the far south, the Yunnan Plateau rises to nearly 3700 m (12 000 ft), while in the far northeast, ranges of hills and mountains almost enclose the Northeast Plain, more usually known as Manchuria. Crossing central China – and separating the basins of the Yellow (Huang He) and Yangtze (Chang Jiang) rivers – is the Nan Ling Range of hills and mountains. In east and central China, three great lowlands support intensive agriculture and dense populations – the plains of central China, the Sichuan Basin and the flat North China Plain. A vast loess plateau, deeply dissected by ravines, lies between the Mongolian Plateau – which contains the Gobi Desert – and the deserts of the Tarim and Dzungarian Basins in the northwest. *Principal rivers*: Yangtze (Chang Jiang), Huang He (Yellow River), Xijiang (Sikiang or Pearl River), Heilongjiang (Amur). *Highest point*: Mount Everest 8863 m (29 078 ft).

Climate: In general, temperatures increase from north to south, and rainfall increases from northwest to southeast. Northeast China has a continental climate with warm and humid summers, long cold winters, and rainfall of less than 750 mm (30 in). The central lowlands contain the hottest areas of China, and have 750 to 1100 mm (30 to 40 in) of rainfall. The south is wetter, while the extreme subtropical south experiences the monsoon. The continental loess plateau is cold in the winter, warm in summer and has under 500 mm (20 in) of rain. The northwest is arid, continental and experiences cold winters. The west – Tibet, Xinjiang Uygur, Gansu and Nei Monggol – experiences an extreme climate owing to its altitude and distance from the sea; rainfall is low and most of Tibet has less than two months free of frost.

ECONOMY

Agriculture occupies three quarters of the labour force. All large-scale production is on collective farms, but traditional and inefficient practices remain. Nearly two thirds of the arable land is irrigated, and China is the world's largest producer of rice. Other major crops include wheat, maize, sweet potatoes, sugar cane and soyabeans. Livestock, fruit, vegetables and fishing are also important, but China is still unable to supply all its own food. The country's mineral and fuel resources are considerable and, for the most part, underdeveloped. They include coal, petroleum, natural gas, iron ore, bauxite, tin, antimony and manganese in major reserves, as well as huge hydroelectric power potential. The economy is centrally planned, with all industrial plant owned by the state. Petrochemical products account for nearly one quarter of China's exports. Other major industries include iron and steel, cement, vehicles, fertilizers, food processing, clothing and textiles. The most recent five-year plans have promoted modernization and reform, including an 'open-door' policy under which joint ventures with other countries and foreign loans have been encouraged, together with a degree of small-scale private enterprise. Most of this investment went into light industry and textiles. Special Economic Zones were created to encourage industrial links with the west, but progress was halted when foreign investment diminished after the 1989 pro-democracy movement was suppressed.

RECENT HISTORY

At the beginning of the 20th century China was in turmoil. The authority of the emperor had been weakened in the 19th century by outside powers greedy for trade and by huge rebellions which had left large areas of the country beyond the control of the central government. In 1911 a revolution, led by the Guomintang (Kuomintang or Nationalists) under Sun Zhong Shan (Sun Yat-sen; 1866–1925), overthrew the last of the Manchu emperors. Strong in the south (where Sun had established a republic in 1916), the Nationalists faced problems in the north, which was ruled by independent warlords. Sun's successor, Jiang Jie Shi (Chiang Kai-shek; 1887–1975), made some inroads in the north, only to be undermined by the emergent Communist Party.

After a series of disastrous urban risings, the Communist Mao Zedong (Mao Tse-tung; 1893–1976) concentrated on rural areas. After being forced to retreat from Jiangxi in 1934, Mao led his followers for 12 months on a 9000 km (5600 mi) trek, the 'Long March', to the remote province of Shaanxi. In 1931 the Japanese seized Manchuria and established a puppet regime. After the Japanese occupied Beijing (Peking) and most of coastal China in 1937, Jiang and Mao combined against the invaders but were able to achieve little against superior forces. After World War II, the Soviets tried to ensure that Mao's Communists took over China. In 1946 Mao marched into Manchuria, beginning a civil war that lasted until 1949 when Mao declared a People's Republic in Beijing and Jiang fled to the offshore island of Taiwan, where a Nationalist government was set up (see below).

In 1950 Chinese forces invaded Tibet – an independent state since 1916. Repressive Communist rule alienated the Tibetans, who, loyal to their religious leader the Dalai Lama, unsuccessfully rose in revolt in 1959. Chinese 'volunteers' were active in the Korean War on behalf of the Communist North Koreans (1950–53). China has been involved in a number of border disputes and conflicts, including clashes with the USSR in the late 1950s, with India in 1962 and with Vietnam in 1979. Relations with the USSR deteriorated in the 1950s, triggered by ideological clashes over the true nature of Communism. The Sino-Soviet rift led to the acceleration of Chinese research into atomic weapons – the first Chinese bomb was tested in 1964 – and a rapprochement with the USA in the early 1970s.

The 'Great Leap Forward', an ambitious programme of radicalization in the 1950s, largely failed. In the 1960s Mao tried again to spread more radical revolutionary ideas in the so-called Cultural Revolution. Militant students formed groups of 'Red Guards' to attack the existing hierarchy. Thousands died as the students went out of control, and the army had to restore order. Since Mao's death (1976), China has effectively been under the leadership of Deng Xiaoping (1904–), although he holds none of the major state or party offices. A more careful path has been followed both at home and abroad; a rapprochement with the USSR was achieved in 1989, and agreement has been reached with the UK for the return of Hong Kong to Chinese rule in 1997. China was opened to foreign technology and investment, together with a degree of free enterprise, but this led to internal pressures for political change, culminating in massive pro-democracy demonstrations by students and workers early in 1989. These were brutally suppressed in the massacre of students in Tiananmen Square (June 1989) and hardline leaders such as President Yang Shangkun have gained in influence.

CHINA, REPUBLIC OF (TAIWAN)

Official name: Chung-hua Min Kuo (The Republic of China).

Population: 19 904 000 (1988 est).

Capital and major cities: Taipei 2 682 000, Kaohsiung 1 362 000, Taichung 730 500, Tainan 668 000, Panchiao 520 000, Shanchung 367 000, Chungho 355 500 (1988 est).

Language: Chinese (northern or Amoy dialect).

Religions: Buddhist, Daoist, Christian minority.

Life expectancy: 73 years.

Labour force: (1988) 8 247 000; manufacturing 2 798 000, commerce 1 539 000, agriculture and forestry 1 112 000.

GOVERNMENT

The Legislative Yuan submits proposals to the National Assembly. In both bodies, the majority of members are Guomindang (Kuomintang) Nationalist Party 'life members' elected in 1947–48 to represent constituencies on the Chinese mainland.

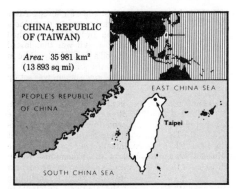

CHINA, REPUBLIC OF (TAIWAN)

Area: 35 981 km²
(13 893 sq mi)

From February 1988, these 'life members' began to be retired, and there will eventually be no seats reserved for mainland representatives. Constitutional changes were promised in 1991. In the meantime, elections are held in Taiwan by universal adult suffrage for 73 of the 274 members of the Legislative Yuan for a three-year term, and 84 of the 752 members of the National Assembly for a six-year term. The Assembly elects a President for a six-year term. The Council of Ministers is responsible to the Legislative Yuan. The principal political parties are the (Nationalist) Guomintang (Kuomintang) and the (Taiwanese) National Democratic Progressive Party.
President: Lee Teng-hui.
Prime Minister: Hao Po-ts'un.

EDUCATION

Literacy rate: 94% (1988). *Years of compulsory schooling:* 6–15. *Universities:* 16.

DEFENCE

Total armed strength: 405 500. *Military service:* 2 years.

GEOGRAPHY

Taiwan is an island 160 km (100 mi) off the southeast coast of mainland China with a mountainous interior. Most of the inhabitants live on the coastal plain in the west. The Republic of China also includes the small islands of Quemoy and Matsu close to the Chinese mainland. *Principal rivers:* Hsia-tan-shui Chi, Chosui Chi. *Highest point:* Yu Shan 3997 m (13 113 ft).

Climate: Taiwan – which is subtropical in the north, and tropical in the south – has rainy summers and mild winters. Tropical cyclones (typhoons) may occur between July and September.

ECONOMY

Despite Taiwan's diplomatic isolation, the island is a major international trading nation, exporting machinery, electronics, and textiles. Taiwan is the world's leading shipbreaker. Mineral resources include coal, marble, gold, petroleum and natural gas. Despite the fertility of the soil, agriculture has declined in relative importance.

RECENT HISTORY

In 1895, the Chinese province of Taiwan – which used to be called Formosa – was taken by the Japanese, who began the modernization of agriculture, transport and education. In 1949, the Nationalist forces of Jiang Jie Shi (Chiang Kai-shek) were driven onto

Taiwan by the Communist victory on the mainland (see China above). Under US protection, the resulting authoritarian regime on Taiwan declared itself the Republic of China, and claimed to be the legitimate government of all China. America's rapprochement with the mainland People's Republic of China lost Taiwan its UN seat in 1971 and US recognition in 1978. By the late 1980s Taiwan was moving cautiously towards democracy, although its international status remained problematic. In 1988 a native Taiwanese became president. Since 1990 the retirement of 'life members' from Taiwan's political bodies has accelerated and in May 1991 Taiwan effectively recognized Communist China.

COLOMBIA

Official name: La República de Colombia (The Republic of Colombia).
Member of: UN, OAS, LAIA.
Population: 32 317 000 (1989 est).
Capital and major cities: Bogotá 3 983 000, Medellín 1 468 100, Cali 1 350 600, Barranquilla 899 800, Cartagena 531 400, Cúcuta 379 500, Bucaramanga 352 300, Manizales 299 400, Ibagué 293 000 (1985).
Languages: Spanish, over 150 Indian languages.
Religions: Roman Catholic (official; over 95%).
Life expectancy: 64.8 years.
Labour force: (1985) 9 558 000; agriculture and forestry 2 414 413, community and social services 1 998 500, trade and tourism 1 262 000.

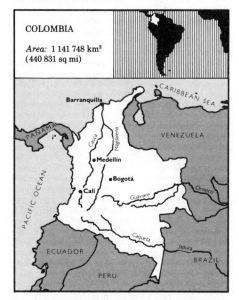

COLOMBIA

Area: 1 141 748 km²
(440 831 sq mi)

GOVERNMENT

A President (who appoints a Cabinet of 13 members), a Senate of 112 members and a House of Representatives of 199 members are elected for a four-year term by universal adult suffrage. The main political parties are the Liberal Party, the Social Conservative Party, the (leftist) M-19 (April 19th Movement) and the (leftist) UP (Patriotic Union).
President: Cesar Gaviria.

EDUCATION

Literacy rate: 88% (1985 est). *Years of compulsory*

schooling: 6–12. *Universities*: 98 state and private institutions offering degree courses.

DEFENCE
Total armed strength: 130 400 (plus 80 000 paramilitary). *Military service*: 1–2 years.

GEOGRAPHY
The Andes run north to south through Colombia with the greater part of the country lying to the east of the mountains in the mainly treeless grassland plains of the Llanos and the tropical Amazonian rain forest. A coastal plain lies to the west of the Andes. *Principal rivers*: Magdalena, Cauca, Amazon (Amazonas). *Highest point*: Pico Cristóbal Colón 5775 m (18 947 ft).
Climate: The lower Andes are temperate; the mountains over 4000 m (13 100 ft) experience perpetual snow. The rest of the country is tropical. The coasts and the Amazonian Basin are hot and humid, with heavy rainfall. The Llanos have a savannah climate.

ECONOMY
Colombian coffee is the backbone of the country's exports; other cash crops include bananas, sugar cane, flowers and tobacco. However, profits from the illegal cultivation and export of marijuana and cocaine probably produce the greatest revenue. Mineral resources include iron ore, silver and platinum as well as coal, petroleum and natural gas. The main industries are food processing, petroleum refining, fertilizers, cement, textiles and clothing, and iron and steel.

RECENT HISTORY
The struggle for independence from Spain (1809–1819) was fierce and bloody. Almost from Colombia's inception, the centralizing pro-clerical Conservatives and the federalizing anti-clerical Liberals have struggled for control, leading to civil wars (1899–1902 and 1948–1957) in which 400 000 people died. Since 1957 there have been agreements between the Liberals and Conservatives to protect a fragile democracy threatened by left-wing guerrillas, right-wing death squads and powerful drug-trafficking cartels. The 1990 presidential and legislative elections were disrupted by the assassination of several candidates, but by early 1991 the uncomprising stand taken against the drug cartels by President Virgilio Barco and his successor Cesar Gaviria was beginning to pay dividends. Violence was decreasing and a number of leading drug-traffickers had been arrested. In a separate development, left-wing former guerrillas – such as M-19 – had abandoned their armed struggle in favour of legitimate political activity.

COMOROS

Official name: La République fédérale islamique des Comores (The Federal Islamic Republic of the Comoros).

Member of: UN, OAU.

Population: 412 000 (1987 est; excluding Mayotte, which is administered by France).

Capital and main towns: Moroni 60 000 (1987), Mutsamudu 13 000, Fomboni 5400 (1980).

Languages: French and Arabic (official languages), Comoran (a blend of Swahili and Arabic).

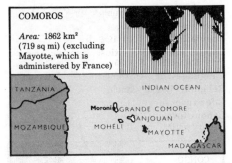

COMOROS

Area: 1862 km²
(719 sq mi) (excluding Mayotte, which is administered by France)

Religion: Sunni Islam (official).
Life expectancy: 52 years.
Labour force: 140 000 (economically active).

GOVERNMENT
The President – who is elected for a six-year term by universal adult suffrage – appoints a Council of Ministers. The 42 members of the Federal Assembly are directly elected for five years. From 1978 to 1990 only candidates of the Udzima party could stand for election, but other parties are now allowed to operate.
President: Siad Mohamed Djohar.

EDUCATION
Literacy rate: 15% (1985 est). *Years of compulsory schooling*: 7–15. *Universities*: none.

DEFENCE
Total armed strength: 750. *Military service*: none.

GEOGRAPHY
Ngazidja (Grande Comore) – the largest island – is dry and rocky, rising to an active volcano. Ndzouani (Anjouan) is a heavily eroded volcanic massif. Moili (Mohéli) is a forested plateau with fertile valleys. There are no significant rivers. *Highest point*: Mont Kartala (active volcano; 2361 m/7746 ft).
Climate: The tropical climate of the Comoros is dry from May to October, but with heavy rain for the rest of the year.

ECONOMY
Poor and eroded soils, overpopulation and few resources combine to make these underdeveloped islands one of the world's poorest countries. Subsistence farming occupies the majority of the population, although vanilla, cloves and ylang-ylang are produced for export.

RECENT HISTORY
The four Comoran islands became a French colony in 1912. In a referendum in 1974, three islands voted to become independent, which they declared themselves without French agreement. The fourth island, Mayotte, voted against independence, and remains under French rule. Following a coup in 1978, an Islamic republic was proclaimed, and a single-party state established. In 1989, the third attempted coup in a decade resulted in the assassination of the president and a brief period of rule by European mercenaries. Civilian rule was restored in December 1989.

CONGO

Official name: La République populaire du

Congo (The People's Republic of the Congo).
Member of: UN, OAU.
Population: 2 245 000 (1989 est).
Capital and major cities: Brazzaville 596 000, Pointe-Noire 298 000 (1985).
Languages: French (official), Lingala (50%).
Religion: Roman Catholic (over 50%).
Life expectancy: 48.5 years.
Labour force: (1988 est) 750 000; agriculture and forestry 450 000, industry 78 000, services 168 000.

CONGO

Area: 342 000 km²
(132 047 sq mi)

CAMEROON

CENTRAL AFRICAN REPUBLIC

EQUATORIAL GUINEA

Oubangui

Zaïre

GABON

ZAIRE

Brazzaville

Pointe-Noire

CABINDA

GOVERNMENT

The 153-member National People's Assembly is elected for a five-year term by universal adult suffrage. Until 1991 candidates were chosen by the sole legal party, the (Marxist-Leninist) Parti congolais du travail (PCT), but other political parties are now allowed to operate. The PCT congress elects a 75-member Central Committee, whose Chairman is head of state and who, as head of government, appoints a Council of Ministers and a Prime Minister. In 1991 it was announced that major constitutional changes would be made.
President: Col. Denis Sassou-Nguesso.
Prime Minister: to be appointed.

EDUCATION

Literacy rate: 62% (1985 est). *Years of compulsory schooling:* 6–16. *Universities:* 1.

DEFENCE

Total armed strength: 8800 (plus 6100 paramilitary).
Military service: none.

GEOGRAPHY

Behind a narrow coastal plain, the plateaux of the interior are covered by tropical rain forests and rise to over 700 m (2300 ft). *Principal rivers:* Zaïre (Congo), Oubangui. *Highest point:* Mont de la Lékéti 1040 m (3412 ft).
Climate: Congo's tropical climate is hot and humid. Rainfall exceeds 1200 mm (47 in) a year.

ECONOMY

Petroleum and timber are the mainstays of the centrally planned economy. Subsistence agriculture – chiefly for cassava – occupies over a third of the labour force.

RECENT HISTORY

In the 1880s, the explorer Brazza placed the kingdom of the Teke people under French protection, and in 1905 the region became the colony of Moyen-Congo. Independence was gained in 1960. In 1963, following industrial unrest, a Marxist-Leninist state was established. Since then, ethnic tensions have led to political unrest and military coups. In 1990 it was announced that Congo would adopt a multi-party system.

COSTA RICA

Official name: República de Costa Rica (The Republic of Costa Rica).
Member of: UN, OAS, CACM, LAIA (observer).
Population: 2 941 000 (1987 est).
Capital and major cities: San José 692 000, Limón 34 000, Alajuela 29 000, (1988 est).
Language: Spanish.
Religions: Roman Catholic (official).
Life expectancy: 73.7 years.
Labour force: (1988) 1 006 137; agriculture and forestry 275 500, community and social work 242 000, mining and manufacturing 170 000.

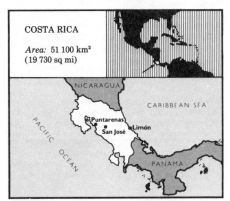

COSTA RICA

Area: 51 100 km²
(19 730 sq mi)

NICARAGUA

CARIBBEAN SEA

PACIFIC OCEAN

Puntarenas

San José

Limón

PANAMA

GOVERNMENT

Executive power is vested in the President, who is assisted by two Vice-Presidents and by a Cabinet of Ministers that he appoints. The President, Vice-Presidents and the 57-member Legislative Assembly are elected for four-year terms by compulsory universal adult suffrage. The principal political parties are the PUSC (Social Christian Unity Party) and the PLN (National Liberation Party).
President: Rafael Angel Calderón Fournier.

EDUCATION

Literacy rate: 94%. *Years of compulsory schooling:* 6–13. *Universities:* 4.

DEFENCE

Total armed strength: none, although there are 750 civil guards.

GEOGRAPHY

Between a narrow plain on the Pacific coast and a wider plain along the Caribbean coast rise a central plateau and mountain ranges. *Principal river:* Rio Grande. *Highest point:* Chirripó Grande 3820 m (12 533 ft).

Climate: Rainfall is heavy along the Caribbean coast, but the Pacific coast is drier. Temperatures are warm in the lowlands, cooler in the highlands.

ECONOMY

Coffee is Costa Rica's major export. Bananas, sugar cane, beef cattle, cocoa and timber are also important.

RECENT HISTORY

The area was under Spanish rule – as part of Guatemala – until 1821. Although it was part of the Central American Federation (1823–38), Costa Rica developed largely in isolation from its neighbours. Dominated by small farms, Costa Rica prospered, attracted European immigrants, and developed a stable democracy. Following a brief civil war in 1948, the army was disbanded. Costa Rica has since adopted the role of peacemaker in Central America.

CUBA

Official name: La República de Cuba (The Republic of Cuba).

Member of: UN, OAS (suspended), LAIA (observer).

Population: 10 402 000 (1988 est).

Capital and major cities: Havana (La Habana) 2 059 000, Santiago de Cuba 390 000, Camagüey 275 000, Holguín 218 000, Guantánamo 193 000, Santa Clara 188 500, Bayamo 119 000 (1988).

Language: Spanish.

Religion: Roman Catholic (40%).

Life expectancy: 74 years.

Labour force: (1981) 3 540 700; business services 1 086 000, agriculture and forestry 791 000, mining and manufacturing 668 000.

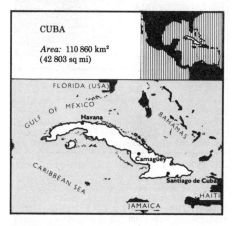

CUBA

Area: 110 860 km² (42 803 sq mi)

FLORIDA (USA)

GULF OF MEXICO

Havana

BAHAMAS

Camagüey

CARIBBEAN SEA

Santiago de Cuba

JAMAICA

HAITI

GOVERNMENT

The Communist Party is the only legal political party. The Party Congress elects a Central Committee, which elects the Politburo. Municipal councils are elected for a term of two and a half years by citizens aged 16 and over. The municipal authorities, in turn, elect 499 Deputies for a five-year term to the National Assembly of People's Power. The Assembly elects 31 of its members to form the Council of State, whose President – as head of state and government – appoints a Council of Ministers. *President:* Fidel Castro Ruz.

EDUCATION

Literacy rate: 98% (1981 est). *Years of compulsory schooling:* 6–12. *Universities:* 4.

DEFENCE

Total armed strength: 180 500 (plus 119 000 paramilitary forces). *Military service:* 3 years.

GEOGRAPHY

Three ranges of hills and mountains run east to west across Cuba. *Principal river:* Cauto. *Highest point:* Pico Turquino 1971 m (6467 ft).

Climate: The climate is semitropical. Temperatures average 26 °C (78 °F), and rainfall is heavy. The island is subject to hurricanes.

ECONOMY

Sugar (the leading export), tobacco and coffee are the main crops. State-controlled farms occupy most of the land but are unable to meet Cuba's food needs. Production of nickel – Cuba's second most important export – is increasing. Trade is overwhelmingly with the USSR and the countries of Eastern Europe, but the disruption of trading patterns that has followed the adoption of market economies in Eastern Europe has badly affected Cuba. The end of Soviet subsidies has severely damaged the Cuban economy which – at the beginning of 1991 – was on the verge of collapse.

RECENT HISTORY

The first war for independence from Spain (1868–78) was unsuccessful. The USA intervened in a second uprising (1895–98), forcing Spain to relinquish the island, but independence was not confirmed until after two periods of American administration (1899–1901 and 1906–09). Under a succession of corrupt governments, the majority of Cubans suffered abject poverty. In 1959, the dictatorship of Fulgencio Batista was overthrown by the guerrilla leader Fidel Castro (1926–), whose revolutionary movement merged with the Communist Party to remodel Cuba on Soviet lines. In 1961, US-backed Cuban exiles attempted to invade at the Bay of Pigs, and relations with America deteriorated further in 1962 when the installation of Soviet missiles on Cuba almost led to world war. Castro has encouraged revolutionary movements throughout Latin America, and his troops have bolstered Marxist governments in Ethiopia and Angola. Despite being a close ally of the USSR, Cuba became a leading Third World power, but the upheavals in the USSR and Eastern Europe in 1989–90 left the Cuban government increasingly isolated as a hardline Marxist state.

CYPRUS

Official name: Kypriaki Dimokratia (in Greek) or Kibris Cumhuriyeti (in Turkish) (The Republic of Cyprus).

Member of: UN, Commonwealth, CSCE, Council of Europe.

Population: 733 000 (1989 est).

Capital and major cities: Nicosia 205 000, Limassol 120 000, Larnaca 54 000 (1989 est).

Languages: Greek (75%), Turkish (24%).

Religions: Orthodox (75%), Sunni Islam (24%).

Life expectancy: 74.6 years.

Labour force: (1988; Greek Cypriot area) 233 000, agriculture and forestry 56 000, trade and tourism 60 000, community and social work 63 000. In 1986, the labour force of the Turkish Cypriot area was 64 000.

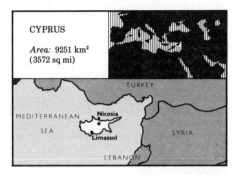

CYPRUS

Area: 9251 km²
(3572 sq mi)

MEDITERRANEAN SEA
TURKEY
Nicosia
Limassol
SYRIA
LEBANON

GOVERNMENT

A 56-member House of Representatives is elected by universal adult suffrage in the Greek Cypriot community for five years – an additional 24 seats for the Turkish Cypriot community remain unfilled. The President – who appoints a Council of Ministers – is elected from the Greek Cypriot community by universal adult suffrage for a five-year term. There is provision in the constitution for a Vice President to be similarly elected from the Turkish Cypriot community. In 1975, the administration of the Turkish Cypriot community unilaterally established the 'Turkish Republic of Northern Cyprus', which is unrecognized internationally except by Turkey.
President: Giorgios Vassiliou.

EDUCATION

Literacy rate: no figure available. *Years of compulsory schooling*: 5½–12 in the Greek Cypriot area; in the Turkish Cypriot area, nursery, primary, secondary and adult education is available but not compulsory. *Universities*: a university is to be established in the Greek Cypriot area in 1991.

DEFENCE

Total armed strength: 13 000 (1989). *Military service*: 29 months.

GEOGRAPHY

The south of the island is covered by the Troodos Mountains. Running east to west across the centre of Cyprus is a fertile plain, north of which are the Kyrenian Mountains and the Karpas Peninsula. *Principal rivers*: Seranhis, Pedieas. *Highest point*: Mount Olympus 1951 m (6399 ft).

Climate: Cyprus has a Mediterranean climate with hot dry summers and mild, variable winters, during which snow falls in the Troodos Mountains.

ECONOMY

Potatoes, fruit, wine, clothing and textiles are exported from the Greek Cypriot area, in which ports, resorts and an international airport have been constructed to replace facilities lost since partition. The Turkish Cypriot area – which exports fruit, potatoes and tobacco – relies heavily on aid from Turkey. Tourism is important in both zones.

RECENT HISTORY

British administration in Cyprus – formerly an Ottoman (Turkish) possession – was established in 1878. During the 1950s, Greek Cypriots – led by Archbishop (later President) Makarios III (1913–77) – campaigned for Enosis (union with Greece). The Turkish Cypriots advocated partition, but following a terrorist campaign by the Greek Cypriot EOKA movement, a compromise was agreed. In 1960, Cyprus became an independent republic. Power was shared by the two communities, but the agreement broke down in 1963, and UN forces intervened to stop intercommunal fighting. The Turkish Cypriots set up their own administration. When pro-Enosis officers staged a coup in 1974, Turkey invaded the north. Cyprus was effectively partitioned. Over 200 000 Greek Cypriots were displaced from the north, into which settlers arrived from Turkey. Since then, UN forces have manned the 'Attila Line' between the Greek south and Turkish north, but attempts to reunite Cyprus as a federal state have been unsuccessful.

CZECHOSLOVAKIA

Official name: Ceskoslovensko (Czechoslovakia) or Ceská a Slovenská Federativní Republika (Czech and Slovak Federative Republic).
Member of: UN, CSCE, Council of Europe.
Population: 15 636 000 (1989).
Capital and major cities: Prague (Praha) 1 212 000, Bratislava 436 000, Brno 390 000, Ostrava 330 000, Košice 232 000, Plzen 175 000, Olomouc 106 753, Liberec 104 000 (1989 est).
Languages: Czech (64%), Slovak (31%), Hungarian.
Religions: Roman Catholic (77%), Protestant.
Life expectancy: 72 years.
Labour force: (1988) 8 161 000; mining and manufacturing 2 950 000, agriculture and forestry 933 000, construction 797 000.

CZECHOSLOVAKIA

Area: 127 905 km²
(49 371 sq mi)

POLAND
GERMANY
Prague
Elbe
Ostrava
Vltava (Moldau)
Brno
USSR
Bratislava
Danube
AUSTRIA
HUNGARY

GOVERNMENT

The Federal Assembly is elected by universal adult suffrage for five years – 200 members to the Chamber of the People and 150 members to the Chamber of Nations. The Assembly elects a President, who appoints a Federal Prime Minister and Government responsible to the Assembly. The main political parties are Civic Forum, Public Against Violence (Civic Forum's Slovak equivalent), the (conservative) Christian Democratic Union, and the Communist Party. In the 1991, Civic Forum split into two – the Democratic Right Wing and the Liberal Club. The two republics – Czech and Slovak – have their own governments and PMs.
President: Vaclav Havel.
Prime Minister: Marián Calfa.

CZECHOSLOVAK REPUBLICS

Czech Lands (Ceské Zemé) *Area*: 78 880 km²

(30 456 sq mi). *Population*: 10 450 000. *Capital*: Prague 1 212 000.

Slovakia (Slovensko) *Area*: 49 025 km² (18 930 sq mi). *Population*: 5 175 000. *Capital*: Bratislava 436 000.

EDUCATION

Literacy rate: 99%. *Years of compulsory schooling*: 6–16. *Universities*: 5.

DEFENCE

Total armed strength: (1989 est) 210 700. *Military service*: 2 years (army); 3 years (air force).

GEOGRAPHY

The Carpathian uplands of the east (Slovakia) include the Tatra Mountains. In the west (Bohemia), the Elbe basin is ringed on three sides by uplands. The Moravian plain lies to the east of Bohemia. *Principal rivers*: Danube (Dunaj), Elbe (Labe), Vltava (Moldau), Morava. *Highest point*: Gerlachovka 2655 m (8737 ft).

Climate: The climate is continental with cold winters and warm summers.

ECONOMY

Apart from coal and brown coal, there are few mineral resources, but the country is heavily industrialized. Manufactures include industrial machinery, motor vehicles and consumer goods. Czechoslovakia is switching from a centrally planned to a free-market economy. Most large businesses are still state-controlled, but the majority of the smaller enterprises have been privatized. Efforts are being made to attract foreign investment and buyers for the heavy industrial concerns. The timber industry is important. The main crops include wheat, maize, potatoes, barley and sugar beet.

RECENT HISTORY

Within the Habsburg Austro-Hungarian Empire, the Czech Lands (Bohemia and Moravia) were part of Austria, and Slovakia was part of Hungary. Nationalism grew in the 19th century, and on the collapse of the Habsburg Empire, the Czechs and Slovaks united in an independent state (1918) – largely due to the efforts of Thomas Masaryk, who became Czechoslovakia's first president. In 1938, Hitler demanded that Germany be granted the Sudetenland, where Germans predominated. Lacking allies, Czechoslovakia was dismembered – Bohemia and Moravia became German 'protectorates' and a puppet state was established in Slovakia. The Nazi occupation included the massacre of the inhabitants of Lidice (1942) and the Slovak Uprising (1944). Following liberation (1945), a coalition government was formed, but the Communists staged a takeover in 1948. In 1968, moves by Party Secretary Alexander Dubček to introduce political reforms met with Soviet disapproval, and invasion by Czechoslovakia's Warsaw Pact allies. The conservative wing of the Communist party regained control until 1989, when student demonstrations developed into a peaceful revolution led by the Civic Forum movement. Faced by overwhelming public opposition, the Communist Party renounced its leading role and hardline leaders were replaced by reformers. A new government, in which Communists were in a minority, was appointed and Civic Forum's leader – the playwright Vaclav Havel – was elected president. In 1990 free multi-party elections were held, Soviet troops were withdrawn and the foundations of a

market economy were laid. The new Czechoslovak democracy faces economic and environmental problems (particularly acid rain), and the possible threat of Slovak separatism.

DENMARK

Official name: Kongeriget Danmark (Kingdom of Denmark).

Member of: UN, EC, NATO, Council of Europe, CSCE, OECD.

Population: 5 135 000 (metropolitan Denmark, excluding dependencies; 1989 est).

Capital and major cities: Copenhagen (København) 1 352 000, Aarhus (Århus) 195 200, Odense 137 300, Aalborg (Ålborg) 113 700, Esbjerg 71 000, Randers 55 500, Horsens 47 000 (1986).

Language: Danish.

Religion: Lutheran (over 90%).

Life expectancy: 76 years.

Labour force: (1989; excluding unemployment figures) 2 608 000; manufacturing 509 000, community and social services 951 000, trade and tourism 346 000.

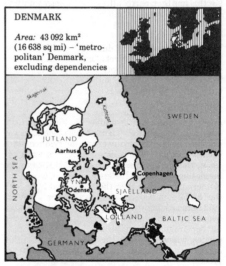

DENMARK

Area: 43 092 km² (16 638 sq mi) – 'metropolitan' Denmark, excluding dependencies

GOVERNMENT

Denmark is a constitutional monarchy. The 179 members of Parliament (the Folketing) are elected by universal adult suffrage under a system of proportional representation for a four-year term. Two members are elected from both of the autonomous dependencies. The Monarch appoints a Prime Minister, who commands a majority in the Folketing. The PM, in turn, appoints a State Council (Cabinet), which is responsible to the Folketing. The main political parties are the Liberal Party, the Conservative People's Party, the Social Democratic Party, the Socialist People's Party, and the Radical Liberals.

Queen: HM Queen Margrethe II (succeeded upon the death of her father, 14 January 1972).

Prime Minister: Poul Schluter.

EDUCATION

Literacy rate: nearly 100%. *Years of compulsory schooling:* 7–16. *Universities:* 3, plus 3 technical universities.

DEFENCE
Total armed strength: 31 600 (1989). *Military service:* 9–12 months.

GEOGRAPHY
Denmark is a lowland of glacial moraine – only Bornholm, in the Baltic, has ancient hard surface rocks. The islands to the east of Jutland make up nearly one third of the country. *Principal river:* Gudená. *Highest point:* Yding Skovhøj 173 m (568 ft).
Climate: The climate is temperate and moist, with mild summers and cold winters. Bornholm – to the east – is more extreme.

ECONOMY
Denmark has a high standard of living, but few natural resources. Danish agriculture is organized on a cooperative basis, and produces cheese and other dairy products, bacon and beef – all mainly for export. About one fifth of the labour force is involved in manufacturing, with iron and metal working, food processing and brewing, engineering and chemicals as the most important industries. The high cost of imported fuel has been a problem for the economy, but this has been partly alleviated by petroleum and natural gas from the North Sea.

RECENT HISTORY
In the 1860s, the Danish duchies of Schleswig and Holstein became the subject of a complicated dispute with Prussia. After a short war with Prussia and Austria (1864), Denmark surrendered the duchies, but northern Schleswig was returned to Denmark in 1920. In the 20th century, Denmark's last colonial possessions were either sold (Virgin Islands) or given independence (Iceland) or autonomy (Greenland and the Faeroe Islands). The country was occupied by Nazi Germany (1940–45), and has since been a member of the Western Alliance. From the 1960s, Denmark's economic and political ties have increasingly been with Germany, the UK and the Netherlands, rather than the traditional links with the Nordic countries (Norway and Sweden). Thus, in 1973 Denmark joined the EC, but the political consequence of joining the Common Market has been a further fragmentation of the country's political parties, which has made the formation of coalition and minority governments a protracted and difficult process.

DANISH AUTONOMOUS DEPENDENCIES
Faeroe Islands (Faeroerne) *Area:* 1399 km² (540 sq mi). *Population:* 47 300 (1989 est). *Capital:* Tórshavn 14 600 (1988 est).
Greenland (Gronland or **Kalaallit)** *Area:* 2 175 600 km² (840 000 sq mi). *Population:* 55 400 (1989 est). *Capital:* Nuuk (formerly Godthab) 11 200 (1987 est).

DJIBOUTI
Official name: Jumhuriya Jibuti (The Republic of Djibouti).
Member of: UN, OAU, Arab League.
Population: 512 000 (1989 est).
Capital: Djibouti 220 000 (1987).
Languages: Arabic and French (both official).
Religion: Sunni Islam.
Life expectancy: 47 years.

Labour force: (1987 est) 400 000; no breakdown of this figure is available.

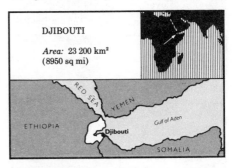

DJIBOUTI

Area: 23 200 km² (8950 sq mi)

GOVERNMENT
Every five years the 65-member Chamber of Deputies is elected by universal adult suffrage from candidates of the only legal party – the Rassemblement populaire pour le progrès. The President – who is directly elected every six years – appoints a Prime Minister and Council of Ministers who are responsible to him.
President: Hassan Gouled Aptidon.
Prime Minister: Barkat Gourad Hamadou.

EDUCATION
Literacy rate: no figure available. *Years of compulsory schooling:* education is available from 7 to 13 but is not compulsory. *Universities:* none.

DEFENCE
Total armed strength: 2870 (1989). *Military service:* none.

GEOGRAPHY
Djibouti is a low-lying desert – below sea level in two basins, but rising to mountains in the north. There are no significant rivers. *Highest point:* Musa Ali Terara 2062 m (6768 ft).
Climate: Djibouti is extremely hot and dry, with rainfall under 125 mm (5 in) on the coast.

ECONOMY
Lack of water largely restricts agriculture to grazing sheep and goats. The economy depends on the expanding seaport and railway, which both serve Ethiopia.

RECENT HISTORY
France acquired a port in 1862 and established the colony of French Somaliland in 1888. In the 1950s and 1970s, the Afar tribe and Europeans voted to remain French, while the Issas (Somalis) opted for independence. In 1977, the territory became the Republic of Djibouti, but the new state has suffered ethnic unrest and drought.

DOMINICA
Official name: Commonwealth of Dominica.
Member of: UN, Commonwealth, CARICOM, OAS.
Population: 82 800 (1989 est).
Capital: Roseau 22 000 (including suburbs), Portsmouth 3000 (1987).
Languages: English (official), French patois.

Religion: Roman Catholic (80%).

Life expectancy: 74 years.

Labour force: (1981) 25 300; agriculture and forestry 8000, construction 2300, trade and tourism 1700.

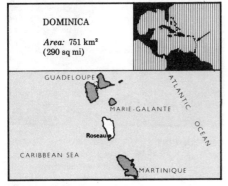

DOMINICA

Area: 751 km²
(290 sq mi)

GUADELOUPE

MARIE-GALANTE

Roseau

CARIBBEAN SEA

MARTINIQUE

ATLANTIC OCEAN

GOVERNMENT

Every five years, 21 members of the House of Assembly are elected by universal adult suffrage and nine are appointed by the President, who is elected for a five-year term by the House. The President appoints a Prime Minister and Cabinet. The main political parties are the (conservative) Dominica Freedom Party, the United Workers' Party, and the Dominica Labour Party.
President: Clarence Seignoret.
Prime Minister: Eugenia Charles.

EDUCATION

Literacy rate: 80% (1985). *Years of compulsory schooling*: 5–15. *Universities*: 1 university college (part of the University of the West Indies).

DEFENCE

Total armed strength: there are no armed forces.

GEOGRAPHY

Dominica is surrounded by steep cliffs with a forested mountainous interior. *Principal river*: Layou. *Highest point*: Morne Diablotin 1447 m (4747 ft).

Climate: Dominica has a tropical climate with little seasonal variation and very heavy rainfall. The island is subject to hurricanes.

ECONOMY

Dominica is a poor island. It produces bananas, timber and coconuts, and exports water to drier neighbours. Tourism is increasing in importance.

RECENT HISTORY

A former British colony, Dominica was a member of the West Indies Federation (1958–62), gained autonomy in 1967 and independence in 1978.

DOMINICAN REPUBLIC

Official name: República Dominicana (The Dominican Republic).

Member of: UN, OAS, LAIA (observer), CARICOM (observer).

Population: 7 012 000 (1989 est).

Capital and major cities: Santo Domingo 1 600 000, Santiago 308 000, La Romana 101 000, San Pedro 87 000 (1986).

Language: Spanish.

Religions: Roman Catholic (official; 95%).

Life expectancy: 64.6 years.

Labour force: (1981) 1 784 000; agriculture and forestry 420 500, community and social services 363 000, manufacturing 224 000.

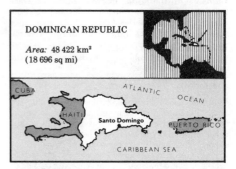

DOMINICAN REPUBLIC

Area: 48 422 km²
(18 696 sq mi)

CUBA

HAITI

Santo Domingo

ATLANTIC OCEAN

PUERTO RICO

CARIBBEAN SEA

GOVERNMENT

The President and the National Congress – a 30-member Senate and a 120-member Chamber of Deputies – are elected for four years by universal adult suffrage. The President appoints a Cabinet. The main political parties are the (conservative) PR (Partido Reformista) and the (left-wing) PRD (Partido Revolucionario Dominicano).
President: Joaquin Balaguer.

EDUCATION

Literacy rate: 78% (1985 est). *Years of compulsory schooling:* 7–14. *Universities:* 8.

DEFENCE

Total armed strength: 20 800 (1989). *Military service:* none.

GEOGRAPHY

The republic consists of the eastern two thirds of the island of Hispaniola. The fertile Cibao Valley in the north is an important agricultural region. Most of the rest of the country is mountainous. *Principal river:* Yaque del Norte. *Highest point:* Pico Duarte 3175 m (10 417 ft).

Climate: The climate is largely subtropical, but it is cooler in the mountains. Rainfall is heavy, but the west and southwest are arid. Hurricanes are a hazard.

ECONOMY

Sugar is the country's traditional mainstay and major export. Mineral deposits include bauxite, gold and ferro-nickel. Tourism is now the greatest foreign-currency earner.

RECENT HISTORY

A former Spanish colony, the country declared independence as the Dominican Republic in 1821, but was annexed by Haiti (1822–44). The 19th century witnessed a succession of tyrants, and by 1900 the republic was bankrupt and in chaos. The USA intervened (1916–24). Rafael Trujillo (1891–1961) became president in 1930 and ruthlessly suppressed opposition. He was assassinated in 1961. Civil war in 1965 ended after intervention by US and Latin American troops. Since then, an infant democracy has survived violent elections. The country faces grave economic problems.

ECUADOR

Official name: República del Ecuador (The Republic of Ecuador).

Member of: UN, OAS, OPEC, LAIA.

Population: 10 490 000 (1989 est).

Capital and major cities: Quito 1 234 000, Guayaquil 1 699 000, Cuenca 218 000, Machala 159 000, Portoviejo 156 000 (1989).

Language: Spanish (official; 93%).

Religion: Roman Catholic (94%).

Life expectancy: 66 years.

Labour force: (1988 est) 3 344 368; agriculture and forestry 787 000, community and social work 555 000, manufacturing 287 000.

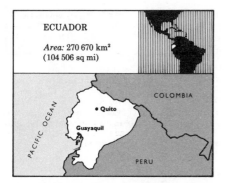

ECUADOR

Area: 270 670 km²
(104 506 sq mi)

The President is elected by compulsory universal adult suffrage for a single term of 4 years. The 72-member Chamber of Representatives is also directly elected; 12 members are elected for four years and 60 members for a single term of 2 years. The President appoints a Cabinet of Ministers. The principal political parties include the (conservative coalition) FRN (National Reconstruction Front), the (left-wing coalition) Social Democratic Left, and the Christian Democrat coalition.
President: Rodrigo Borja.

EDUCATION

Literacy rate: 80% (1982 est). *Years of compulsory schooling:* 6–14. *Universities:* 8, plus 8 technical universities.

DEFENCE

Total armed strength: 42 000 (1989). *Military service:* 2 years (selective).

GEOGRAPHY

The Andes divide the Pacific coastal plain in the west from the Amazonian tropical rain forest in the east.
Principal rivers: Napo, Pastaza, Curaray, Daule.
Highest point: Chimborazo 6267 m (20 561 ft).

Climate: The Amazonian Basin has a wet tropical climate. The tropical coastal plain is humid in the north, arid in the south. The highland valleys are mild, but the highest peaks have permanent snow.

ECONOMY

Agriculture is the largest single employer, and major export crops include cocoa, coffee and, in particular, bananas. Petroleum is the major foreign-currency earner. High inflation and foreign debt are severe problems.

RECENT HISTORY

In 1822 Ecuador was liberated from Spanish rule by the armies of Antonio José de Sucre (1795–1830) and Simón Bolívar (1783–1830). Initially federated with Colombia and Venezuela, Ecuador became completely independent in 1830. Throughout the 19th century there were struggles between liberals and conservatives. Since 1895 there have been long periods of military rule, but democratically elected governments have been in power since 1978. Relations with neighbouring Peru have long been tense – war broke out in 1941, when Ecuador lost most of its Amazonian territory, and there were border skirmishes in 1981. Emergency economic measures in 1988 led to a wave of strikes and unrest.

EGYPT

Official name: Jumhuriyat Misr al-'Arabiya (Arab Republic of Egypt).

Member of: UN, OAU, Arab League.

Population: 52 000 000 (1988 est).

Capital and major cities: Cairo (El-Qahira) 13 300 000 (including suburbs; 1987 est), Alexandria (El-Iskandariyah) 5 000 000, El-Giza 1 671 000 and Shubrâ El-Kheima 553 000 are both part of the Cairo agglomeration, Port Said (Bur Sa'id) 364 000, El Mahalla El Kubra 355 000 (1986 est).

Language: Arabic.

Religion: Sunni Islam (92%), Christian (8%).

Life expectancy: 60.6 years.

Labour force: (1985 est) 12 891 000; trade 1 215 000, government services 2 577 000, agriculture and forestry 4 465 000.

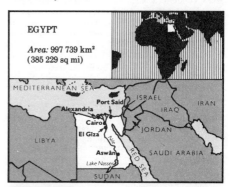

EGYPT

Area: 997 739 km²
(385 229 sq mi)

GOVERNMENT

Every five years, 448 members are elected by universal adult suffrage to the Majlis ash-Sha'ab (People's Assembly); the remaining 10 members are appointed by the President, who is nominated by the Assembly and confirmed by referendum for a six-year term. The President appoints a Prime Minister, Ministers and Vice-President(s). The principal political parties include the (socialist) National Democratic Party, the (traditional) New Wafd Party, and the Socialist Labour Party.
President: Mohammed Hosni Mubarak.
Prime Minister: Atef Sedki.

EDUCATION

Literacy rate: 51% (1986 est). *Years of compulsory schooling:* 6–12. *Universities:* 13.

DEFENCE

Total armed strength: 448 000 (1989). *Military service:* 3 years (selective).

GEOGRAPHY

Desert covers more than 90% of Egypt. The Western Desert – which stretches into Libya and Sudan – is low-lying. The Eastern Desert is divided by wadis and ends in the southeast in mountains beside the Red Sea. The vast majority of the population lives in the Nile River valley and delta, intensively cultivated lands that rely on irrigation by the annual flood of the Nile. East of the Suez Canal is the Sinai Peninsula. *Principal river:* Nile. *Highest point:* Mount Catherine (Jabal Katrina) 2642 m (8668 ft).

Climate: Egyptian winters are mild and summers are hot and arid. Alexandria has the highest rainfall total – 200 mm/8 in – while the area beside the Red Sea receives virtually no rain.

ECONOMY

Over a third of the labour force is involved in agriculture, producing maize, wheat, rice and vegetables for the domestic market, and cotton and dates mainly for export. Petroleum reserves (small by Middle Eastern standards), canal tolls and tourism are major foreign-currency earners. The economy is held back by the demands of a large public sector and food subsidies.

RECENT HISTORY

In the 19th century, Egypt was nominally part of the Ottoman (Turkish) Empire, although it was effectively ruled by a local dynasty. The construction of the Suez Canal bankrupted Egypt, and the UK – a major creditor – occupied Egypt (1882) and established a protectorate (1914–22). The corrupt regime of King Farouk was toppled in a military coup (1952) and a republic was established (1953). The radical Gamal Abdel Nasser (1918–70) became president in 1954. He nationalized the Suez Canal and made Egypt the leader of Arab nationalism. Nasser was twice defeated by Israel in Middle East wars (1967 and 1973), but his successor, President Anwar Sadat, made peace with Israel (1979) and was ostracized by the Arab world. Since Sadat's assassination (1981), Egypt has regained its place in the Arab fold, and the prominent role played by Egypt in the coalition against Saddam Hussein's Iraq (1991) confirmed Egypt as one of the leaders of the Arab world. The country is faced by severe economic problems, and there is a growth in Islamic fundamentalism.

EL SALVADOR

Official name: La República de El Salvador (The Republic of El Salvador).

Member of: UN, OAS, CACM, LAIA (observer).

Population: 5 107 000 (1988 est).

Capital and major cities: San Salvador 1 058 000, Santa Ana 477 000, San Miguel 155 000 (all including suburbs) (1985 est).

Language: Spanish (official).

Religion: Roman Catholic (over 95%).

Life expectancy: 67.1 years.

Labour force: (1980) 1 566 000; agriculture and forestry 637 000, trade and tourism 256 000, manufacturing 248 000.

GOVERNMENT

The President – who appoints a Cabinet of Ministers – is elected by universal adult suffrage for a single five-year term. Every three years, direct elections are also held for the 60-member National Assembly.

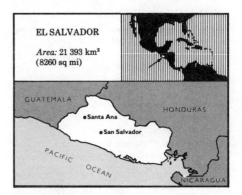

EL SALVADOR

Area: 21 393 km² (8260 sq mi)

Nationwide elections have been disrupted since 1981 owing to guerrilla action. The main political parties are (right-wing) ARENA (the Nationalist Republican Alliance), the (left-wing) Democratic Convergence, the PCN (National Reconstruction Party), and the PDC (Christian Democratic Party). *President:* Alfredo Cristiani.

EDUCATION

Literacy rate: 72% (1985 est). *Years of compulsory schooling:* 7–16. *Universities:* 1 national, 33 private.

DEFENCE

Total armed strength: 43 500 (plus 12 600 paramilitary forces). *Military service:* 2 years (selective).

GEOGRAPHY

The country is mountainous, with ranges along the border with Honduras and a higher volcanic chain in the south. *Principal rivers:* Lempa, San Miguel. *Highest point:* Volcán de Santa Ana 2381 m (7812 ft). **Climate:** The tropical coast is hot and humid, while the interior is temperate.

ECONOMY

Agricultural products – in particular coffee and sugar cane – account for nearly two thirds of the country's exports. The economy has declined owing to the state of near civil war.

RECENT HISTORY

El Salvador was liberated from Spanish rule in 1821, but remained in the Central American Federation until 1838. The country has suffered frequent coups and political violence. In 1932 a peasant uprising – led by Agustín Farabundo Martí – was harshly suppressed. El Salvador's overpopulation has been partially relieved by migration to neighbouring countries. Following a football match between El Salvador and Honduras in 1969, war broke out because of illegal immigration by Salvadoreans into Honduras. Political and economic power is concentrated into the hands of a few families, and this has led to social tension. The country has been in a state of virtual civil war since the late 1970s with the US-backed military, assisted by extreme right-wing death squads, combating left-wing guerrillas – the FMLN-FDR (Farabundo Martí National Liberation Movement). The Christian Democrat President José Napoleón Duarte (in office 1984–89) attempted a negotiated peace, but his successor, Alfredo Cristiani of the ARENA party, has stated his opposition to negotiation in favour of a military solution.

EQUATORIAL GUINEA

Official name: La República de Guinea Ecuatorial (The Republic of Equatorial Guinea).
Member of: UN, OAU.
Population: 343 000 (1989 est).
Capital and major cities: Malabo 15 000, Bata 24 000 (1983).
Languages: Spanish (official), Fang, Bubi.
Religions: Roman Catholic majority.
Life expectancy: 44 years.
Labour force: (1980 est) 159 000; agriculture and forestry 104 000, services 36 000, industry 18 000.

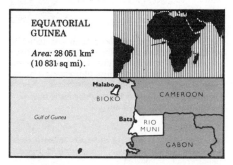

EQUATORIAL GUINEA

Area: 28 051 km²
(10 831 sq mi).

Malabo
BIOKO
CAMEROON
Gulf of Guinea
Bata
RIO MUNI
GABON

GOVERNMENT
The constitution provides for the election of a President for a seven-year term. However, effective power is in the hands of the Supreme Military Council, whose President is head of state and of government. A 41-member House of Representatives is directly elected for a five-year term. All candidates for election are nominated by the President and since 1987 all are members of the single party of government, the PDGE (Partido Democratico de Guinea Ecuatorial).
President: Brig. Gen. Teodoro Obiang.

EDUCATION
Literacy rate: 37% (1980 est). *Years of compulsory schooling:* 6–14. *Universities:* none.

DEFENCE
Total armed strength: 1300 (1989) plus 2000 paramilitary forces. *Military service:* none.

GEOGRAPHY
The republic consists of the fertile island of Bioko (formerly Fernando Póo), the much smaller islands of Pagalu (formerly Annobón) and the Corisco Group, and the district of Mbini (formerly Río Muni) on the African mainland. *Principal rivers:* Campo, Benito, Muni. *Highest point:* Pico de Moca (Moka) 2850 m (9350 ft).
Climate: The tropical climate is hot and humid with heavy rainfall.

ECONOMY
Mbini exports coffee and timber, but cocoa production on Bioko slumped after the departure of Nigerian workers (1976). The economy relies heavily upon foreign aid.

RECENT HISTORY
The colony of Spanish Guinea was created in 1856. The harsh plantation system practised during the colonial era attracted much international criticism. Independence in 1968 began under the dictatorship of Francisco Nguema, who was overthrown by his nephew Teodoro Obiang in a military coup in 1979. One-party rule has been in force since 1987, but coups were attempted in 1981, 1983, 1986 and 1988.

ETHIOPIA

Official name: Hebretasebawit Ityopia (People's Democratic Republic of Ethiopia). Previously known as Abyssinia.
Member of: UN, OAU.
Population: 48 898 000 (1989 est).
Capital and major cities: Addis Ababa 1 413 000, Asmara 275 000, Dire Dawa 98 000, Gondar 81 000, Nazret 76 000, Dessie 69 000 (1984).
Languages: Amharic (official), Arabic.
Religions: Sunni Islam (45%), Ethiopian Orthodox (40%).
Life expectancy: 48 years.
Labour force: (1984) 18 492 300; agriculture and forestry 14 000 000, services 2 200 000, industry 1 400 000.

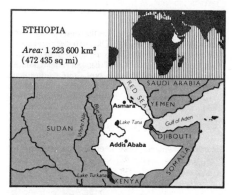

ETHIOPIA

Area: 1 223 600 km²
(472 435 sq mi)

SAUDI ARABIA
RED SEA
Asmara
YEMEN
White Nile
Blue Nile
Lake Tana
Gulf of Aden
SUDAN
DJIBOUTI
Addis Ababa
SOMALIA
Lake Turkana
KENYA

GOVERNMENT
The constitution provides for elections every five years by universal adult suffrage for the 835-member National Assembly (Shengo), which elects the President and appoints the Cabinet. Following the takeover by the Ethiopian People's Revolutionary Democratic Front (May 1991), the constitution was suspended and an interim administration established. It was announced that a broad-based provisional government would be appointed and that free multi-party elections would be held by 1993.
Head of interim government: Meles Zenawi.

EDUCATION
Literacy rate: 71% (1987 est). *Years of compulsory schooling:* education is free 6–19 but not compulsory. *Universities:* 3.

DEFENCE
Total armed strength: 321 600 (1989). *Military service:* 30 months.

GEOGRAPHY
The Western Highlands – including Eritrea, the Tigré Plateau and the Semien Mountains – are separated from the lower Eastern Highlands by a wide rift valley. *Principal rivers:* Blue Nile (Abay

Wenz), Tekeze, Awash, Omo, Sagan. *Highest point:* Ras Dashen 4620 m (15 158 ft).

Climate: Very hot and dry in the north and east, with a temperate climate in the highlands.

ECONOMY

Secessionist wars have damaged an impoverished, underdeveloped economy. The majority of the population is involved in subsistence farming, but drought and overgrazing have led to desertification. Coffee is the main foreign-currency earner. The economy is in serious difficulties owing to the diminution of aid from the USSR.

RECENT HISTORY

Under Emperor Menelik II, Ethiopia survived the European scramble for empire and defeated an Italian invasion (1896). However, the Italians occupied Ethiopia from 1936 to 1941. Emperor Haile Selassie (1892–1975) played a prominent part in African affairs, but – failing to modernize Ethiopia or overcome its extreme poverty – he was overthrown in 1974. Allied to the USSR, a Marxist military regime instituted revolutionary change, but, even with Cuban help, it was unable to overcome secessionist guerrilla movements in Eritrea, Tigré and the east. Drought, soil erosion and civil war brought severe famine in the 1980s. By April 1991, the government had lost control of most of Eritrea, all of Tigré and parts of six other provinces. The entire country faced a recurrence of severe famine. Following Mengistu's flight from Ethiopia in May, Tigrayan rebels took the capital, set up an interim government and announced a national constitutional conference (for June 1991).

FIJI

Official name: Matanitu Ko Viti (Republic of Fiji).

Member of: UN, South Pacific Forum.

Population: 734 000 (1989 est), Indians 48%, Fijians 44%.

Capital: Suva 69 700 (1986).

Languages: English, Fijian, Hindi.

Religions: Methodist (40%), Hindu (over 40%).

Life expectancy: 70.4 years.

Labour force: (1986) 242 000; agriculture and forestry 106 000, trade and tourism 26 000, manufacturing 18 000.

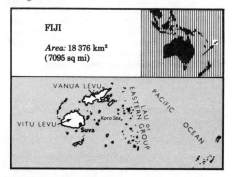

FIJI

Area: 18 376 km²
(7095 sq mi)

VANUA LEVU

VITU LEVU

Koro Sea

Suva

PACIFIC OCEAN

EASTERN LAU GROUP

GOVERNMENT

The 70-seat House of Representatives is elected by universal adult suffrage for five years – 37 members by Fijians, 27 by Indians, 1 by Rotumans, 5 by others. The 34-member Senate comprises 24 members chosen

by the traditional Council of Chiefs, 1 to represent Rotuma, 9 appointed by the President. The Council of Chiefs appoints the President for a five-year term. The President, in turn, appoints a PM who commands a majority in the House. Political parties include the Alliance Party and the National Federation Party. *President:* Penaia Ganilau. *Prime Minister:* Sir Mara Kamisese.

EDUCATION

Literacy rate: 87% (1986). *Years of compulsory schooling:* schooling is not compulsory. *Universities:* 1.

DEFENCE

Total armed strength: 3500 (1989). *Military service:* none.

GEOGRAPHY

The mountainous larger islands are volcanic in origin. The smaller islands are mainly coral reefs. *Principal rivers:* Rewa, Sigatoka, Navva, Nodi, Ba. *Highest point:* Tomaniivi (Mount Victoria) 1323 m (4341 ft).

Climate: Fiji experiences high temperatures and heavy rainfall with local variations.

ECONOMY

Fiji's economy depends on agriculture, with sugar cane as the main cash crop. Copra, ginger, fish and timber are also exported.

RECENT HISTORY

During a period of great unrest, outside interests supported rival factions until Chief Cakobau, who controlled the west, requested British assistance and ceded Fiji to Britain (1874). Indian labourers arrived to work on sugar plantations, reducing the Fijians, who retained ownership of most of the land, to a minority. Since independence (1970), racial tension and land disputes have brought instability. A military takeover in 1987 overthrew an Indian-led government and established a Fijian-dominated republic outside the Commonwealth. Fiji returned to civilian rule in January 1990, with the resignation of the military officers from the cabinet. The new constitution guarantees political power for the native Melanese (Fijian) population and elections are scheduled for 1992.

FINLAND

Official name: Suomen Tasavalta (Republic of Finland).

Member of: UN, EFTA, CSCE, Council of Europe, OECD.

Population: 4 955 000 (1988 est).

Capital and major cities: Helsinki (Helsingfors) 990 000 (1989; including suburbs), Turku (Åbo) 261 000, Tampere (Tammerfors) 256 000, Espoo (Esbo) 168 000 and Vantaa (Vanda) 151 000 are both suburbs of Helsinki, Oulu (Uleaborg) 99 000, Lahti 95 000, Pori (Björneborg) 79 000, Kuopio 78 000 (1986; including suburbs).

Languages: Finnish (94%), Swedish (6%).

Religion: Lutheran (91%).

Life expectancy: 76 years.

Labour force: (1988) 2 548 000; community and social work 724 000, services 519 000, agriculture and forestry 238 000.

GOVERNMENT

The 200-member Parliament (Eduskunta) is elected

FINLAND

Area: 338 145 km²
(130 557 sq mi)

for four years under a system of proportional representation by universal adult suffrage. Executive power is vested in a President elected for six years by direct popular vote. The President appoints a Council of State (Cabinet) – headed by a Prime Minister – responsible to the Parliament. The main political parties include the Centre Party, the (conservative) National Coalition Party, the Social Democratic Party, the (left-wing) People's Democratic League, the Rural Party, and the Communist Party.
President: Mauno Koivisto.
Prime Minister: Esko Aho.

FINNISH AUTONOMOUS COUNTY

Åland Islands (Ahvenanmaa) *Area:* 1527 km² (590 sq mi). *Population:* 24 000 (1988 est). *Capital:* Mariehamn 10 000 (1988 est).

EDUCATION
Literacy rate: almost 100% (1988). *Years of compulsory schooling:* 7–16. *Universities:* 23.

DEFENCE
Total armed strength: 31 000 (1989) – the size of Finnish forces are restricted by a treaty with the USSR. *Military service:* 11 months (residents of the Åland Islands are exempt).

GEOGRAPHY
Nearly one third of Finland lies north of the Arctic Circle and one tenth of the country is covered by lakes, some 50 000 in all. Saimaa – the largest lake – has an area of over 4400 km² (1700 sq mi). During the winter months the Gulfs of Bothnia (to the west) and of Finland (to the south) freeze, and ports have to be kept open by icebreakers. The land has been heavily glaciated, and except for mountains in the northwest most of the country is lowland. *Principal rivers:* Paatsjoki, Torniojoki, Kemijoki, Kokemäenjoki. *Highest point:* Haltiatunturi 1342 m (4344 ft).

Climate: Warm summers with long, extremely cold winters, particularly in the north.

ECONOMY
Forests cover about two thirds of the country and wood products provide over one third of Finland's foreign earnings. Metalworking and engineering – in particular shipbuilding – are among the most important of Finland's industries, which have a reputation for quality and good design. Finland enjoys a high

standard of living, although – apart from forests, copper and rivers suitable for hydroelectric power – the country has few natural resources. There is a large fishing industry, and the agricultural sector produces enough cereals and dairy products for export.

RECENT HISTORY
Throughout the 19th century Finland was a grand duchy ruled by the Russian Tzar. Tension grew as Russia sought to strengthen its political and cultural leverage. In 1906 Finland was allowed to call its own Duma (Parliament), but repression followed again in 1910. After the Russian Revolution of 1917, civil war broke out in Finland. The pro-Russian party was defeated and an independent republican constitution (still in force today) was established (1919). Finland's territorial integrity lasted until the Soviet invasion in 1939, after which land was ceded to the USSR. The failure of a brief alliance with Germany led to further cession of territory to the Soviet Union in 1944. Finland has, since 1945, retained its neutrality and independence. Finland has achieved some influence through the careful exercise of its neutrality, for example hosting the initial sessions of CSCE (the 'Helsinki accords'). Government in Finland is characterized by multi-party coalitions, and since 1987 parties of the left have lost favour. Economically, Finland is integrated into Western Europe through membership of EFTA and OECD.

FRANCE

Official name: La République Française (The French Republic).

Member of: UN, EC, NATO, WEU, G7, OECD, CSCE, Council of Europe.

Population: 56 107 000 (1989 est) – 'metropolitan' France.

Capital and major cities: Paris 8 707 000, Lyon 1 221 000, Marseille 1 111 000, Lille 936 000, Bordeaux 640 000, Toulouse 541 000, Nantes 465 000, Nice 449 000, Toulon 410 000, Grenoble 392 000, Rouen 380 000, Strasbourg 373 000, Valenciennes 350 000, Lens 323 000, Saint-Etienne 317 000, Cannes 296 000, Nancy 278 000, Tours 263 000, Clermont-Ferrand 256 000, Le Havre 255 000, Caen 182 000, Avignon 173 000, Montpellier 221 000, Orléans 220 000, Mulhouse 220 000, Dijon 209 000, Douai 202 000, Reims 199 000, Dunkerque 196 000, Angers 196 000, Le Mans 191 000, Brest 187 000, Metz 185 000, Caen 182 000, Avignon 173 000, Limoges 172 000, Mantes-la-Jolie 168 000, Amiens 153 000, Béthune 147 000, Trappes 142 000 (all including suburbs; 1982).

Languages: French, with Breton and Basque minorities.

Religions: Roman Catholic (over 90%).

Life expectancy: 77 years.

Labour force: (1987) 23 973 000; community and social work 6 686 000, manufacturing 4 648 000, agriculture and forestry 1 595 000.

GOVERNMENT
Executive power is vested in the President, who is elected for a 7-year term by universal adult suffrage. The President appoints a Prime Minister and a Council of Ministers – both responsible to Parliament – but it is the President, rather than the PM, who presides over the Council of Ministers. Parliament has two chambers. The Senate (the upper house) comprises 321 members – 296 of whom repre-

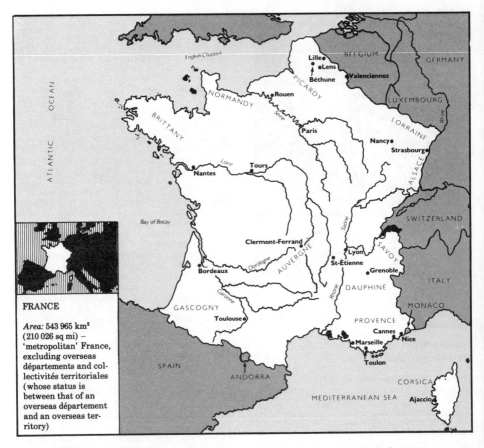

FRANCE

Area: 543 965 km²
(210 026 sq mi) –
'metropolitan' France,
excluding overseas
départements and col-
lectivités territoriales
(whose status is
between that of an
overseas département
and an overseas ter-
ritory)

sent individual départements and 13 of whom represent overseas départements and territories – elected
by members of municipal, local and regional
councils. The remaining 12 senators are elected by
French citizens resident abroad. Senators serve for
nine years, with one third of the Senate retiring every
three years. The National Assembly (the lower
house) comprises 577 deputies – including 22 for
overseas départements and territories – elected for a
five-year term by universal adult suffrage from
single-member constituencies, with a second ballot
for the leading candidates if no candidate obtains an
absolute majority in the first round. The main political parties include the PS (Socialist Party), the
(conservative Gaullist) RPR (Rally for the
Republic), the (centrist) UDF (Union for French
Democracy), the PC (Communist Party), and the
(right-wing) FN (National Front). Since 1982, the 96
metropolitan French départements have been
grouped into 22 regions which have increased powers
of local government.
President: François Mitterrand.
Prime Minister: Edith Cresson.

FRENCH REGIONS

Population figures for the regions and the cities are
for 1987 and 1982 respectively.

Alsace *Area:* 8280 km² (3197 sq mi). *Population:*
1 605 000. *Capital:* Strasbourg 373 000.

Aquitaine *Area:* 41 308 km² (15 949 sq mi).
Population: 2 708 000. *Capital:* Bordeaux 640 000.

Auvergne *Area:* 26 013 km² (10 044 sq mi).
Population: 1 329 000. *Capital:* Clermont-Ferrand
256 000.

Brittany (Bretagne) *Area:* 27 208 km² (10 505 sq
mi). *Population:* 1 374 000. *Capital:* Rennes 234 000.

Burgundy (Bourgogne) *Area:* 31 582 km² (12 194
sq mi). *Population:* 1 604 000. *Capital:* Dijon 209 000.

Centre *Area:* 39 151 km² (15 116 sq mi). *Population:*
2 333 000. *Capital:* Orléans 220 000. *Largest city:* Tours
263 000.

Champagne-Ardenne *Area:* 25 606 km² (9886 sq
mi). *Population:* 1 359 000. *Capital:* Reims 199 000.

Corsica (Corse) *Area:* 8680 km² (3351 sq mi).
Population: 243 000. *Capital:* Ajaccio 54 000.

Franche-Comté *Area:* 16 202 km² (6256 sq mi).
Population: 1 099 000. *Capital:* Besançon 121 000.
Largest city: Montbéliard 128 000.

Ile-de-France *Area:* 12 012 km² (4638 sq mi).
Population: 10 290 000. *Capital:* Paris 8 707 000.

Languedoc-Roussillon *Area:* 27 376 km² (10 570
sq mi). *Population:* 2 072 000. *Capital:* Montpellier
221 000.

Limousin *Area:* 16 942 km² (6541 sq mi).
Population: 735 000. *Capital:* Limoges 172 000.

Lorraine *Area:* 23 547 km² (9091 sq mi).
Population: 2 320 000. *Capital:* Nancy 278 000.

Lower Normandy (Basse-Normandie) *Area:*
17 589 km² (6791 sq mi). *Population:* 1 374 000. *Capital:*
Caen 182 000.

Midi-Pyrénées *Area*: 45 348 km² (17 509 sq mi). *Population*: 2 370 000. *Capital*: Toulouse 541 000.

Nord-Pas-de-Calais *Area*: 12 414 km² (4793 sq mi). *Population*: 3 923 000. *Capital*: Lille 936 000.

Pays de la Loire *Area*: 32 082 km² (12 387 sq mi). *Population*: 3 013 000. *Capital*: Nantes 465 000.

Picardy (Picardie) *Area*: 19 399 km² (7490 sq mi). *Population*: 1 787 000. *Capital*: Amiens 153 000.

Poitou-Charentes *Area*: 25 810 km² (9965 sq mi). *Population*: 1 601 000. *Capital*: Poitiers 103 000. *Largest city*: Angoulême 104 000.

Provence-Côte d'Azur *Area*: 31 400 km² (12 124 sq mi). *Population*: 4 116 000. *Capital*: Marseille 1 111 000.

Rhône-Alpes *Area*: 43 698 km² (16 872 sq mi). *Population*: 5 177 000. *Capital*: Lyon 1 221 000.

Upper Normandy (Haute-Normandie) *Area*: 12 317 km² (4756 sq mi). *Population*: 1 685 000. *Capital*: Rouen 380 000.

EDUCATION
Literacy rate: no figure available. *Years of compulsory schooling:* 6–16. *Universities:* 69, plus 2 national polytechnics with university status.

DEFENCE
Total armed strength: 466 300 (1989). *Military service:* 12–18 months.

GEOGRAPHY
The Massif Central – a plateau of old hard rocks, rising to almost 2000 m (6500 ft) – occupies the middle of France. The Massif is surrounded by four major lowlands, which together make up almost two thirds of the total area of the country. The Paris Basin – the largest of these lowlands – is divided by low ridges and fertile plains and plateaux, but is united by the river system of the Seine and its tributaries. To the east of the Massif Central is the long narrow Rhône-Saône Valley, while to the west the Loire Valley stretches to the Atlantic. Southwest of the Massif Central lies the Aquitaine Basin, a large fertile region drained by the River Garonne and its tributaries. A discontinuous ring of highlands surrounds France. In the northwest the Armorican Massif (Brittany) rises to 411 m (1350 ft). In the southwest the Pyrenees form a high natural boundary with Spain. The Alps in the southeast divide France from Italy and contain the highest peak in Europe (outside the Caucasus). The lower Jura – in the east – form a barrier between France and Switzerland, while the Vosges Mountains separate the Paris Basin from the Rhine Valley. In the northeast, the Ardennes extend into France from Belgium. The Mediterranean island of Corsica is an ancient massif rising to 2710 m (8891 ft). *Principal rivers*: Rhine (Rhin), Loire, Rhône, Seine, Garonne, Saône. *Highest point*: Mont Blanc 4807 m (15 771 ft).

Climate: The south is Mediterranean with warm summers and mild winters. The rest of France has a temperate climate, although the more continental east experiences warmer summers and colder winters. Rainfall is moderate, with highest falls in the mountains and lowest falls in the Paris Basin.

ECONOMY
Nearly two thirds of France is farmed. The principal products include cereals (wheat, maize, barley and even rice), meat and dairy products, sugar beet, and grapes for wine. France is remarkably self-sufficient in agriculture, with tropical fruit and animal feeds being the only major imports. However, the small size of land holdings remains a problem, despite consolidation and the efforts of cooperatives. Reafforestation is helping to safeguard the future of the important timber industry. Natural resources include coal, iron ore, copper, bauxite and tungsten, as well as petroleum and natural gas, and plentiful sites for hydroelectric power plants. The major French industries include: textiles, chemicals, steel, food processing, motor vehicles, aircraft, and mechanical and electrical engineering. Traditionally French firms have been small, but mergers have resulted in larger corporations able to compete internationally. France is now the West's fourth industrial power after the USA, Japan and Germany. During the later 1980s many of the state-owned corporations were privatized. Over one half of the labour force is involved in service industries, in particular administration, banking, finance, and tourism.

RECENT HISTORY
The Second Empire (1852–70) of Napoleon III (nephew of Napoleon I) was brought to an end by defeat in the Franco-Prussian war of 1870–1. After this defeat, the Third Republic (1871–1940) was established, and immediately faced the revolt of the Paris Commune, when radical republicans and socialists set up a self-governing commune in the capital. It was bloodily suppressed by French troops in May 1871, and 20 000 communards were killed or executed. Continuing controversy over the role of religion in the state – particularly the question of religious-based or secular education – did not end until Church and state were finally separated in 1905. At the end of the 19th century the French colonial empire reached its greatest extent, in particular in Africa, SE Asia and the Pacific. The Third Republic also saw continuing conflict over France's own boundaries – Alsace-Lorraine was lost in 1870 but recovered in 1918 at the end of World War I (1914–18), during which trench warfare in northern France claimed countless lives. Georges Clemenceau (1841–1929) – who had led France as prime minister during the war – lost power in 1919 when the French electorate perceived the harsh peace terms as being too lenient to Germany.

Between 1919 and 1939 French government was characterized by instability and frequent changes of administration. In 1936 Léon Blum (1872–1950) led a Popular Front (Socialist-Communist-Radical) coalition to power and instituted many important social reforms. In World War II (1939–45), Germany rapidly defeated the French in 1940 and completely occupied the country in 1942. Marshal Philippe Pétain (1856–1951) led a collaborationist regime in the city of Vichy, while General Charles de Gaulle (1890–1970) headed the Free French in exile in London from 1940. France was liberated following the Allied landings in Normandy in 1944. After the war, the Fourth Republic (1946–58) was marked by instability and the Suez Crisis of 1956 – when France and the UK sought to prevent Egypt's nationalization of the canal. The end of the colonial era was marked by nationalist revolts in some of the colonies, notably Vietnam – where the Communists defeated French colonial forces at Dien Bien Phu in 1954 – and Algeria. The troubles in Algeria – including the revolt of the French colonists and the campaign of their terrorist organization, the OAS – led to the end of the Fourth Republic and to the accession to power of General de Gaulle in 1959.

As first president of the Fifth Republic, de Gaulle granted Algerian independence in 1962. While the French colonial empire – with a few minor exceptions – was being disbanded, France's position within Western Europe was being strengthened, especially by vigorous participation in the European Community. At the same time, de Gaulle sought to pursue a foreign policy independent of the USA, building up France's nuclear capability and withdrawing French forces from NATO's integrated command structure. Although restoring political and economic stability to France, domestic dissatisfaction – including the student revolt of May 1968 – led de Gaulle to resign in 1969. De Gaulle's policies were broadly pursued by his successors as president, Georges Pompidou (in office 1969–74) and Valéry Giscard d'Estaing (1974–81). The modernization of France continued apace under the country's first Socialist president, François Mitterand (1916–   ), who was elected in 1981.

FRENCH OVERSEAS DEPARTEMENTS

The overseas départements are integral parts of the French Republic.

Guadeloupe (a group of islands in the Caribbean including Guadeloupe, the immediate dependencies of La Désirade, Les Saintes, Marie-Galante, and the more distant islands of Saint-Barthélemy and Saint-Martin). *Area*: 1780 km² (687 sq mi) – Guadeloupe and immediate dependencies 1706 km² (659 sq mi), Saint-Barthélemy 21 km² (8 sq mi), Saint-Martin 53 km² (20.5 sq mi). *Population*: 341 000 (1989 est) – Guadeloupe and immediate dependencies 330 000, Saint-Barthélemy 3100, Saint-Martin 8100. *Capital*: Basse-Terre 38 000 (1982). (The capital of Saint-Barthélemy is Gustavia; the capital of Saint-Martin is Marigot.) *Largest town*: Pointe-à-Pitre 122 000 (1982).

Guyane (French Guiana) (a territory situated between Brazil and Suriname) *Area*: 90 000 km² (34 750 sq mi). *Population*: 95 000 (1989 est). *Capital*: Cayenne 45 000 (1982).

Martinique (an island in the Caribbean) *Area*: 1100 km² (425 sq mi). *Population*: 332 000 (1989 est). *Capital*: Fort-de-France 101 000 (1982).

Réunion (an island in the southern Indian Ocean) *Area*: 2512 km² (970 sq mi). *Population*: 566 000 (1989 est). *Capital*: Saint-Denis 120 000 (1982).

FRENCH COLLECTIVITES TERRITORIALES

The collectivités territoriales – a status between that of an overseas département and an overseas territory – are integral parts of the French Republic.

Mayotte (an island in the Comoros group) *Area*: 376 km² (145 sq mi). *Population*: 69 000 (1988 est). *Capital*: Dzaoudzi 5900 (1982).

Saint-Pierre-et-Miquelon (two main islands and six small islets south of the Newfoundland coast) *Area*: 242 km² (93 sq mi). *Population*: 6300 (1989 est). *Capital*: Saint-Pierre 5400 (1982).

FRENCH OVERSEAS TERRITORIES

French Polynesia (five archipelagos in the Pacific Ocean including the Australes, Marquises and Gambier islands). *Area*: 4200 km² (1622 sq mi). *Population*: 196 000 (1989 est). *Capital*: Papeete (on Tahiti) 23 400 (1983).

New Caledonia (New Caledonia and its dependencies – the Loyalty Islands, Ile des Pins and the Bélep archipelago – are situated in the south Pacific Ocean.) *Area*: 19 103 km² (7376 sq mi). *Population*: 152 000. *Capital*: Nouméa 60 000 (1983).

Southern and Antarctic Territories (Southern Territories only – two archipelagos and two small islands situated in the extreme south of the Indian Ocean.) *Area*: Kerguelen Archipelago 18 130 km² (7000 sq mi); Crozet Archipelago 1295 km² (500 sq mi), Amsterdam Island 155 km² (60 sq mi), St Paul Island 18 km² (7 sq mi). *Population*: there is a fluctuating population of scientific missions of c. 140. *Principal settlement*: Port-aux-Français (on Kerguelen) 100. (See p. 638.)

Wallis and Futuna Islands (two small archipelagos in the Pacific Ocean) *Area*: 274 km² (106 sq mi) – kingdom of Uvéa 159 km² (61 sq mi), kingdom of Sigave 64 km² (25 sq mi), kingdom of Alo 51 km² (20 sq mi). *Population*: 14 600 (1989 est) – Uvéa 8100, Sigave 4200, Alo 4200 (1982). *Capital*: Mata-Utu (in Uvéa) 800 (1982).

GABON

Official name: La République Gabonaise (The Gabonese Republic).

Member of: UN, OAU, OPEC.

Population: 1 245 000 (1989 est).

Capital and major cities: Libreville 352 000, Port-Gentil 164 000, Franceville 75 000 (1987).

Languages: French (official), 40 local languages.

Religions: Animist (50%), Roman Catholic (40%).

Life expectancy: 53 years.

Labour force: (1988 est) 485 000, agriculture and forestry 337 000, industry 50 000, services 65 000.

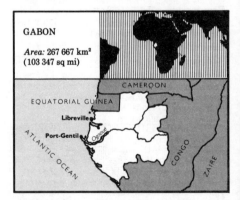

GABON

Area: 267 667 km²
(103 347 sq mi)

GOVERNMENT

The President – who is elected by compulsory universal adult suffrage for a seven-year term – appoints a Council of Ministers (over which he presides) and a Prime Minister. The National Assembly has 120 members – 111 directly elected for five years, the remaining 9 appointed by the President. Until 1990 the PDG (Parti démocratique gabonais) was the only legal political party. Other parties – including the main opposition group, the PGP (Parti gabonais de progrès) – are now allowed to operate.
President: Omar Bongo.
Prime Minister: Casimir Oye Mba.

EDUCATION

Literacy rate: 62% (1985 est). *Years of compulsory schooling*: 6–16. *Universities*: 2.

DEFENCE

Total armed strength: 3200 (1989). *Military service:* none.

GEOGRAPHY

Apart from the narrow coastal plain, low plateaux make up most of the country. *Principal river:* Ogooué. *Highest point:* Mont Iboundji 1580 m (5185 ft). **Climate:** The equatorial climate is hot and humid with little seasonal variation.

ECONOMY

Petroleum, natural gas, manganese, uranium and iron ore – and a relatively small population – make Gabon the richest Black African country, although most Gabonese are subsistence farmers.

RECENT HISTORY

Gabon was colonized by the French in the late 19th century. Pro-French Léon M'Ba (1902–67) led the country to independence in 1960. Deposed in a coup (1964), he was restored to power by French troops. Under his successor, Omar Bongo, Gabon has continued its pro-Western policies. Pro-democracy demonstrations and strikes, followed by anti-government riots in 1990, prompted France to dispatch troops to Gabon to restore order. President Bongo appointed a transitional government and permitted the establishment of a multi-party system.

GAMBIA

Official name: The Gambia.

Member of: UN, OAU, ECOWAS, Commonwealth.

Population: 835 000 (1989 est).

Capital and major cities: Banjul 147 000 (with suburbs), Brikama 24 000 (1986).

Language: English (official).

Religions: Sunni Islam (85%), Protestant (10%).

Life expectancy: 43 years.

Labour force: (1988 est) 374 000; agriculture and forestry 306 000, manufacturing 8500, construction 4000.

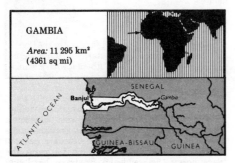

GAMBIA

Area: 11 295 km²
(4361 sq mi)

GOVERNMENT

The President and 36 of the 50 members of the House of Representatives are elected by universal adult suffrage every five years. The remaining members of the House are appointed. The President appoints a Vice-President – to lead the government in the House – and a Cabinet of Ministers. The main political parties are the People's Progressive Party and the National Convention Party.

President: Sir Dawda Kairaba Jawara.

EDUCATION

Literacy rate: 25% (1985 est). *Years of compulsory schooling:* schooling is not compulsory. *Universities* none.

DEFENCE

Total armed strength: 900 (1989). *Military service:* normally voluntary, but compulsory in certain circumstances.

GEOGRAPHY

The Gambia is a narrow low-lying country on either bank of the River Gambia. *Principal river:* Gambia. *Highest point:* an unnamed point on the Senegalese border 43 m (141 ft). **Climate:** The climate is tropical, with a dry season from November to May.

ECONOMY

The economy is largely based on the cultivation of groundnuts. Tourism is increasing in importance.

RECENT HISTORY

A British colony was established in 1843. The Gambia achieved independence in 1965 under Sir Dawda K. Jawara. In 1981 an attempted coup against his rule encouraged efforts to merge with the neighbouring French-speaking country of Senegal, but the confederation was dissolved in 1989. The Gambia remains a democracy.

GERMANY

Official name: Bundesrepublik Deutschland (The Federal Republic of Germany).

Member of: UN, EC, NATO, CSCE, WEU, G7, OECD, Council of Europe.

Population: 77 643 000 (1988).

Capital and major cities: Berlin (capital in name only) 3 300 000, Bonn (capital de facto) 278 000, Hamburg 1 571 000, Munich (München) 1 202 000, Cologne (Köln) 931 000, Essen 622 000, Frankfurt 621 000, Dortmund 584 000, Düsseldorf 566 000, Stuttgart 556 000, Leipzig 547 000, Bremen 533 000, Duisburg 525 000, Dresden 520 000, Hannover 495 000, Nuremberg (Nürnberg) 475 000, Bochum 386 600, Wuppertal 374 000, Chemnitz 313 000, Bielefeld 299 000, Mannheim 295 000, Magdeburg 289 000, Gelsenkirchen 284 000, Münster 268 000, Karlsruhe 268 000, Wiesbaden 267 000, Mönchengladbach 255 000, Brunswick (Braunschweig) 248 000, Augsburg 246 000, Rostock 246 000, Kiel 244 000, Aachen 239 000, Halle 235 000, Oberhausen 222 000, Krefeld 217 000, Erfurt 217 000, Lübeck 209 000, Hagen 206 000, Mainz 189 000, Freiburg 186 000, Kassel 185 000, Saarbrücken 184 000, Herne 171 000, Mülheim 170 000, Hamm 166 000, Solingen 158 000, Leverkusen 155 000, Osnabrück 154 000, Ludwigshafen 152 000, Neuss 144 000, Potsdam 140 000 (1987/88 est).

Language: German.

Religions: Protestant (41% – mainly Lutheran), Roman Catholic (36%).

Life expectancy: 73.5 years.

Labour force: (1988 est; combined figures for the former East and West Germanies) 35 435 400; industry and manufacturing 12 144 500, agriculture and forestry 2 083 200, commerce 2 940 200.

GOVERNMENT

Each of the 16 states (Länder; singular Länd) is

GERMANY

Area: 357 050 km²
(137 857 sq mi)

represented in the 68-member upper house of Parliament – the Federal Council (Bundesrat) – by three, four or six members of the state government (depending on population). These members are appointed for a limited period. The lower house – the Federal Assembly (Bundestag) – has 662 members elected for four years by universal adult suffrage under a mixed system of single-member constituencies and proportional representation. Executive power rests with the Federal Government, led by the Federal Chancellor – who is elected by the Bundestag. The Federal President is elected for a five-year term by a combined sitting of the Bundesrat and an equal number of representatives of the states. The Parliament, Government, ministries and the Federal Chancellor and President are based in Bonn, although Berlin was named as capital in August 1990. The main political parties include the (socialist) SPD (Social Democratic Party), the (conservative) CDU (Christian Democratic Union) and CSU (Christian Social Union, its Bavarian equivalent), the (liberal) FDP (Free Democratic Party), Die Grünen (the Green Party), and the PDS (Party of Democratic Socialism; the former East German Communist Party). Each state has its own Parliament and Government.
Federal President: Dr Richard von Weizsäcker.
Federal Chancellor: Dr Helmut Kohl.

GERMAN LÄNDER
Population figures are for 1987/88.
Baden-Württemberg *Area:* 35 752 km² (13 803 sq mi). *Population:* 9 327 000. *Capital:* Stuttgart 556 000.

Bavaria (Bayern) *Area:* 70 546 km² (27 238 sq mi). *Population:* 11 026 000. *Capital:* Munich (München) 1 202 000.

Berlin *Area:* 883 km² (341 sq mi). *Population:* 3 300 000. *Capital:* Berlin 3 300 000.

Brandenburg *Area:* 28 016 km² (10 817 sq mi). *Population:* 2 712 000. *Capital:* Potsdam 140 000.
Bremen *Area:* 404 km² (156 sq mi). *Population:* 654 000. *Capital:* Bremen 533 000.
Hamburg *Area:* 755 km² (292 sq mi). *Population:* 1 571 000. *Capital:* Hamburg 1 571 000.
Hesse (Hessen) *Area:* 21 114 km² (8152 sq mi). *Population:* 5 544 000. *Capital:* Wiesbaden 267 000. *Largest city:* Frankfurt 621 000.
Lower Saxony (Niedersachsen) *Area:* 47 431 km² (18 313 sq mi). *Population:* 7 196 000. *Capital:* Hannover 495 000.
Mecklenburg-West Pomerania (Mecklenburg-Vorpommern) *Area:* 26 694 km² (10 307 sq mi). *Population:* 2 110 000. *Capital:* Schwerin 128 000. *Largest city:* Rostock 246 000.
North Rhine-Westphalia (Nordrhein-Westfalen) *Area:* 34 066 km² (13 153 sq mi). *Population:* 16 677 000. *Capital:* Düsseldorf 566 000. *Largest city:* Cologne (Köln) 931 000.
Rhineland-Palatinate (Rheinland-Pfalz) *Area:* 19 848 km² (7663 sq mi). *Population:* 3 611 000. *Capital:* Mainz 189 000.
Saarland *Area:* 2571 km² (993 sq mi). *Population:* 1 042 000. *Capital:* Saarbrücken 184 000.
Saxony (Sachsen) *Area:* 17 713 km² (6839 sq mi). *Population:* 5 056 000. *Capital:* Dresden 520 000. *Largest city:* Leipzig 547 000.
Saxony-Anhalt (Sachsen-Anhalt) *Area:* 20 297 km² (7837 sq mi). *Population:* 3 056 000. *Capital:* Magdeburg 289 000.
Schleswig-Holstein *Area:* 15 720 km² (6069 sq mi). *Population:* 2 613 000. *Capital:* Kiel 244 000.
Thuringia (Thüringen) *Area:* 15 209 km² (5872 sq mi). *Capital:* Erfurt 217 000.

EDUCATION
Literacy rate: no figure available. *Years of compulsory schooling:* 6–18. *Universities:* 70 institutions with university status.

DEFENCE
Total armed strength: 667 400. *Military service:* 12–15 months.

GEOGRAPHY
The North German Plain – a region of fertile farmlands and sandy heaths – is drained by the Rivers Elbe and Weser and their tributaries. In the west, the plain merges with the North Rhine lowlands which contain the Ruhr coalfield and over one fifth of the country's population. A belt of plateaux, formed of old hard rocks, crosses the country from east to west and includes the Hunsrück and Eifel highlands in the Rhineland, the Taunus and Westerwald uplands in Hesse, and extends into the Harz and Erz Mountains in Thuringia. The Rhine cuts through these central plateaux in a deep gorge. In southern Germany, the Black Forest (Schwarzwald) separates the Rhine valley from the fertile valleys and scarplands of Swabia. The forested edge of the Bohemian uplands marks the border with Czechoslovakia, while the Bavarian Alps form the frontier with Austria. *Principal rivers:* Rhine (Rhein), Elbe, Danube (Donau), Oder, Moselle (Mosel), Neckar, Havel, Leine, Weser. *Highest point:* Zugspitze 2963 m (9721 ft).

Climate: The climate is temperate, but with considerable variations between the generally mild north coastal plain and the Bavarian Alps in the south, which have cool summers and cold winters. The eastern part of the country has warm summers and cold winters.

ECONOMY

Germany is the West's third industrial power after the USA and Japan. The country's recovery after World War II has been called the 'German economic miracle'. The principal industries include mechanical and electrical engineering, chemicals, textiles, food processing and vehicles, with heavy industry and engineering concentrated in the Ruhr, chemicals in cities on the Rhine, and motor vehicles in large provincial centres such as Stuttgart. From the 1980s, there has been a spectacular growth in high-technology industries. Apart from coal and brown coal, and relatively small deposits of iron ore, bauxite, copper ore, nickel, tin, silver, potash and salt, Germany has relatively few natural resources, and the country relies heavily upon imports. Labour has also been in short supply, and large numbers of 'guest workers' (Gastarbeiter) – particularly from Turkey and Yugoslavia – have been recruited. Since 1990 the labour shortage in the western part of the country has also been met by migration from the east, the former German Democratic Republic. Service industries employ almost twice as many people as manufacturing industry. Banking and finance are major foreign-currency earners, and Frankfurt is one of the world's leading financial and business centres.

The unification of Germany in October 1990 presented a major problem for the German economy. The GDR's economy had previously been the most successful in CMEA (Comecon), but, compared with West Germany, it lagged in terms of production, quality, design, profitability and standards of living. A trust – the Treuhandanstalt – was established to oversee the privatization of the 8000 state-run firms in eastern Germany. The main industries of the former GDR include machinery and transportation equipment, steel, cement, chemicals, fertilizers and plastics, but many of these have been unable to compete with their western counterparts. The Trabant and Wartburg car firms, for example, ceased production in 1991, and, bought by West German firms, began production of western models. However, many other East German firms have gone bankrupt, and by April 1991 unemployment in the former GDR stood at nearly 12%, and was rising sharply.

The main German agricultural products include hops (for beer), grapes (for wine), sugar beet, wheat, barley, and dairy products. The collectivized farms of the former GDR – which provided that country's basic food needs – were privatized in 1990–91. Forests cover almost one third of the country and support a flourishing timber industry.

RECENT HISTORY

In 1871, a German Empire – of four kingdoms, six grand duchies, five duchies and seven principalities – was proclaimed with the King of Prussia as Emperor of Germany (Kaiser). From 1871 to 1918, an expansionist unified Germany attempted to extend its influence throughout Europe, engaged in naval and commercial rivalry with Britain, and built a colonial empire. Under the mercurial Kaiser Wilhelm (reigned 1888–1918), Germany was a destabilizing force in world politics.

In June 1914, the heir to the throne of Austria-Hungary was assassinated in Sarajevo. The Austrians – supported by the Germans, who feared for the disintegration of their ally – blamed Serbia and threatened to attack. The Serbs in turn appealed for aid from their fellow Slavs in Russia, who began to mobilize their vast army. Fearing attack, Germany put into action a strategy known as the Schlieffen Plan, and declared war on both Russia and France. The plan was designed to knock out France (Russia's ally) before the Russians completed mobilization. As German troops crossed into neutral Belgium, as a preliminary to attacking France, the UK – as a guarantor of Belgium's independence – declared war on Germany. The war lasted from 1914 to 1918, with Germany, Austria and Turkey ranged against a worldwide alliance. The Western Front quickly became bogged down in trench warfare, and the balance of power between the two sides only shifted in favour of the Allies when the USA entered the war against Germany in 1917. On the Eastern Front Russia dissolved into revolutionary chaos (1917) and the Germans took the opportunity to attack with decisive results. By August 1918, Austrian and Turkish power was broken and the Germans were isolated. With public confidence at home evaporating, Germany surrendered in November 1918.

Defeat in World War I led to the loss of much territory in Europe and the colonies overseas, the end of the German monarchies, the imposition of a substantial sum for reparations, and the occupation of the Rhineland by Allied forces until 1930. The liberal Weimar republic (1919–33) could not bring economic or political stability. In the early 1930s the National Socialist German Workers', or Nazi, Party increased in popularity, urging the establishment of a strong centralized government, an aggressive foreign policy, 'Germanic character' and the overturn of the postwar settlement. In 1933, the Nazi leader, Adolf Hitler (1889–1945) became Chancellor and in 1934 President. His Third Reich (empire) annexed Austria (1938), dismembered Czechoslovakia (1939), and embarked on the extermination of the Jews and others that the Nazis regarded as 'inferior'. In furtherance of territorial claims in Poland, Hitler concluded the Nazi-Soviet Non-Aggression Pact (24 August), which allowed the USSR to annex the Baltic republics (Estonia, Latvia and Lithuania) and agreed to divide Poland between the Soviets and the Nazis. Invading Poland on 1 September 1939, Hitler launched Germany into war.

Britain and France declared war on Germany two days later but could do nothing to help the Poles. After a pause known as the 'Phoney War', Hitler turned towards the west (1940) and invaded Denmark, Norway, Belgium, the Netherlands, Luxembourg and France. After Italy entered the war against the UK and France (1941), the Balkan Front opened up, when Italy invaded Albania and Greece. The German invasion of the USSR (1941) opened the Eastern Front. Also in 1941 Japan joined the Axis powers (Germany and Italy) by attacking the US naval base at Pearl Harbor, Hawaii. At the height of Axis power in 1942, Germany controlled – directly or through allies – virtually the whole of Europe except the British Isles, and neutral Switzerland, Sweden, Spain and Portugal. The tide against the Axis countries turned in North Africa late in 1942. In 1943, Italy surrendered, and Soviet forces started to push back the Germans. In 1944 the Allied landings in Normandy began the liberation of Western Europe, and advances into the Balkans cleared the Germans from Soviet territory. After massive Allied bombing attacks, the end came swiftly for Germany. Hitler committed suicide in April 1945 and Berlin fell to the Soviets early in May.

In 1945, Germany lost substantial territories to Poland, and was divided – as was its capital, Berlin – into four zones of occupation by the Allies (Britain, France, the USA and the USSR). Their intention was a united, disarmed Germany, but cooperation between the Allies rapidly broke down, and in 1948–49 the USSR blockaded West Berlin. The western zones of Germany were merged economically in 1948. After the merger of the western zones to form the Federal Republic of Germany, the German Democratic Republic was proclaimed in the Soviet zone (October 1949). The GDR's economic progress suffered by comparison with that of the Federal Republic. Food shortages and repressive Communist rule led to an uprising in 1953. West Germany gained sovereignty – as a member of the Western alliance – in 1955.

The division of Germany was only grudgingly accepted in West Germany. Chancellor Konrad Adenauer (1876–1967) refused to recognize East Germany as a separate state and relations with the Soviet Union remained uncertain. Major problems with the Eastern bloc included the undefined status of the areas taken over by Poland in 1945 and the difficult position of West Berlin – a part of the Federal Republic isolated within Communist East Germany. Relations between the two Germanys were soured as large numbers of East Germans fled to the West, and this outflow was stemmed only when Walter Ulbricht (East German Communist Party leader 1950–71) ordered the building of the Berlin Wall (1961).

Adenauer strove to gain the acceptance of West Germany back into Western Europe through reconciliation with France and participation in the European Community. The economic revival of Germany begun by Adenauer continued under his Christian Democrat (conservative) successors as Chancellor – Ludwig Erhard (1963–66) and Georg Kiesinger (1966–69). Under the Social Democrat Chancellors – Willy Brandt (1969–74) and Helmut Schmidt (1974–82) – treaties were signed with the Soviet Union (1970) and Poland (recognizing the Oder-Neisse line as Poland's western frontier), and relations with the GDR were normalized (1972). Under Helmut Kohl – Christian Democrat Chancellor from 1982 – West Germany has continued its impressive economic development and enthusiastic membership of the EC.

In the late 1980s, West Germany acted as an economic and cultural magnet for much of Eastern Europe. The root causes of the GDR's problems remained, however, and resurfaced in the late 1980s. The ageing Communist leadership led by Erich Honecker proved unresponsive to the mood of greater freedom emanating from Gorbachev's USSR. In 1989 fresh floods of East Germans left the GDR for the West by way of Poland, Czechoslovakia and Hungary. Massive public demonstrations in favour of reform – led by the New Forum opposition movement – resulted in the appointment of a new leader, Egon Krenz. The Berlin Wall was reopened (November 1989) allowing free movement between the two Germanys, but demonstrations in favour of more radical change continued, and, in a further change of leadership, Krenz was replaced. A non-Communist president, a new Prime Minister (Hans Modrow) and a government including members of opposition groups were appointed.

Free elections were held in East Germany in March 1990 when the Communist Party was reduced to a minority. When the East German economy collapsed, West German Chancellor Helmut Kohl proposed the monetary union of the two Germanys. The call for German reunification became unstoppable. 'Two-plus-four' negotiations between the two Germanys and the four major wartime allies began in February 1990. Despite the initial opposition of the USSR, the reunification of Germany as a full EC and NATO member was agreed. German reunification took place on 3 October 1990 and all-German elections took place in December 1990. Soviet troops are scheduled to withdraw from the former GDR by 1994. Reunited Germany is the greatest economic power in Europe, and, after the USSR, the most populous state.

GHANA

Official name: The Republic of Ghana.

Member of: UN, OAU, ECOWAS, Commonwealth.

Population: 14 566 000 (1989).

Capital and major cities: Accra 1 105 000, Kumasi 490 000, Sekondi-Takoradi 175 000, Tamale 170 000, Tema 131 500, Cape Coast 57 000 (1987 est).

Languages: English (official), Asante, Ewe.

Religions: Animist (40%), Protestant (30%).

Life expectancy: 54 years.

Labour force: (1984) 5 580 100; agriculture and forestry 3 311 000, trade and tourism 792 000, manufacturing 589 000.

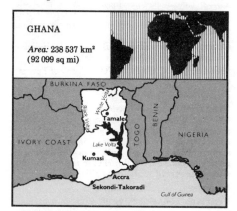

GHANA

Area: 238 537 km² (92 099 sq mi)

GOVERNMENT

Power is vested in the Provisional National Defence Council, which rules by decree. There are no political parties. Elections for the 110 administrative districts of local government were held in 1989. However, despite the election of a chairman and committee in each district, the PNDC have appointed District Secretaries responsible for administration and finance.

Chairman of the Council: Flight. Lt. Jerry Rawlings.

EDUCATION

Literacy rate: 53% (1985 est). *Years of compulsory schooling:* 6–15. *Universities:* 3.

DEFENCE

Total armed strength: 11 600 (1989). *Military service:* voluntary.

GEOGRAPHY

Most of the country comprises low-lying plains and plateaux. In the centre, the Volta Basin – which ends in steep escarpments – contains the large Lake Volta reservoir. *Principal river:* Volta. *Highest point:* Afadjato 872 m (2860 ft).

Climate: The climate is tropical with 2000 mm (80 in) of rainfall on the coast, decreasing markedly inland. The north is subject to the hot, dry Harmattan wind from the Sahara.

ECONOMY

Political instability and mismanagement have damaged the economy of Ghana. Nearly two thirds of the labour force is involved in agriculture, with cocoa being the main cash crop. Forestry and mining for bauxite, gold and manganese are also important activities.

RECENT HISTORY

Britain ousted the Danes (1850) and the Dutch (1872) to establish the Gold Coast colony in 1874. The great inland kingdom of Ashanti was not finally conquered until 1898. After World War II, the prosperity of the cocoa industry, increasing literacy and the dynamism of Dr Kwame Nkrumah (1909–72) helped the Gold Coast set the pace for decolonization in Black Africa. After independence in 1957 – as Ghana – Nkrumah's grandiose policies and increasingly dictatorial rule led to his overthrow in a military coup in 1966. Ghana has since struggled to overcome its economic and political problems. There were six coups in 20 years, including two by Flight Lieutenant Jerry Rawlings (1979 and 1982).

GREECE

Official name: Ellenikí Dimokrátia (Hellenic Republic) or Ellás (Greece).

Member of: UN, EC, NATO, Council of Europe, CSCE, OECD.

Population: 10 096 000 (1989).

Capital and major cities: Athens (Athínai) 3 027 000, Thessaloníki (formerly known as Salonika) 406 000, Piraeus (Piraiévs) 196 000 (part of the Athens agglomeration), Patras (Pátrai) 142 000, Lárisa 102 000, Heraklion (Iráklion, formerly known as Candia) 102 000, Volos 71 000, Kavalla 57 000, Canea (Khania) 47 000 (1981).

Language: Greek (official).

Religion: Orthodox (97%; official).

Life expectancy: 76 years.

Labour force: (1987) 3 760 000; agriculture and forestry 976 000, manufacturing 750 000, community and social services 648 000.

GOVERNMENT

The 300-member Parliament is elected for four years by universal adult suffrage under a system of proportional representation. The President – who is elected for a five-year term by Parliament – appoints a Prime Minister (who commands a majority in Parliament) and other Ministers. The main political parties include the (conservative) NDP (New Democracy Party), PASOK (the Pan-Hellenic Socialist Party), the (centre) Democratic Renewal Party, and the (Communist-led) Left Alliance.
President: Konstantinos Karamanlis.
Prime Minister: Konstantinos Mitsotakis.

GREECE

Area: 131 957 km²
(50 949 sq mi)

GREEK SELF-GOVERNING COMMUNITY

Mount Athos (Ayion Oros) (an autonomous monks' republic). *Area:* 336 km² (130 sq mi). *Population:* 1470 (1981). *Capital:* Karyai 235 (1981).

EDUCATION

Literacy rate: 93% (1985). *Years of compulsory schooling:* 6–15. *Universities:* 16.

DEFENCE

Total armed strength: 208 500 (1989). *Military service:* 20–24 months.

GEOGRAPHY

Over 80% of Greece is mountainous. The mainland is dominated by the Pindus Mountains, which extend from Albania south into the Peloponnese Peninsula. The Rhodope Mountains lie along the Bulgarian border. Greece has some 2000 islands, of which only 154 are inhabited. *Principal rivers:* Aliákmon, Piniós, Akhelóös. *Highest point:* Mount Olympus 2911 m (9550 ft).

Climate: Greece has a Mediterranean climate with hot dry summers and mild wet winters. The north and the mountains are colder.

ECONOMY

Agriculture involves over one quarter of the labour force. Much of the land is marginal – in particular the extensive sheep pastures. Greece is largely self-sufficient in wheat, barley, maize, sugar beet, fruit, vegetables and cheese, and produces enough wine, olives (and olive oil) and tobacco for export. The industrial sector is expanding rapidly and includes the processing of natural resources such as petroleum and natural gas, lignite, uranium and bauxite. Tourism, the large merchant fleet, and money sent back by Greeks working abroad are all important foreign-currency earners. Greece receives special economic assistance from the EC.

RECENT HISTORY

In the 18th century, various European powers,

especially Russia, sought to use the Greeks in their quarrels with the Turks, who had ruled Greece since the early 15th century. The outbreak of revolution against Turkish rule in 1821 attracted support throughout Europe. The leaders of the Greek state established in 1830 brought Western European constitutional institutions to Greece, but the monarchy established under a Bavarian prince in 1832 was swept away by revolution in 1862. Under a Danish prince – who became King George I in 1863 – Greece gained extra territory in 1863, 1881 and 1913, as Turkish power declined.

The 20th century has been marked by great instability. Eleuthérios Venizélos (1864–1936) dominated Greek politics from 1910 to 1935, a period of rivalry between republicans and royalists. An attempt by his rival King Constantine I to seize Anatolia from Turkey (1921–22) ended in military defeat and the establishment of a republic in 1924. The monarchy was restored in 1935, but it depended upon a military leader, General Ioannis Metaxas (1871–1941), who, claiming the threat from Communism as justification, ruled as virtual dictator. The nation was deeply divided. The German invasion of 1941 was met by rival resistance groups of Communists and monarchists, and the subsequent civil war between these factions lasted from 1945 to 1949, when, with British and US aid, the monarchists emerged victorious. Continued instability in the 1960s led to a military coup in 1967. King Constantine II, who had not initially opposed the coup, unsuccessfully appealed for the overthrow of the junta and went into exile. The dictatorship of the colonels ended in 1974 when their encouragement of a Greek Cypriot coup brought Greece to the verge of war with Turkey. Civilian government was restored, and a new republican constitution was adopted in 1975. Greece has since forged closer links with Western Europe, in particular through membership of the EC (1981). In 1988 a major financial scandal – the Koskotas affair – implicated several government ministers in massive fraud. The Koskotas affair – and the controversial divorce of the Prime Minister, Andreas Papandreou – brought down the PASOK government. A period of instability, coalition and temporary governments, and two indecisive general elections followed (June 1989–April 1990), until the (conservative) NDP came to power under Konstantinos Mitsotakis.

GRENADA

Official name: The State of Grenada.

Member of: UN, OAS, CARICOM, Commonwealth.

Population: 98 000 (1987 est).

Capital: St George's 7500 (1980 est).

Language: English.

Religions: Roman Catholic (over 60%), Anglican.

Life expectancy: 67 years.

Labour force: 45 000 (1986).

GOVERNMENT

The Governor General – the representative of the British Queen as sovereign of Grenada – appoints a Prime Minister (who commands a majority in the House of Representatives), other members of the Cabinet and the 13-member Senate (the upper house of Parliament). The 15-member House of Representatives is elected for five years by universal adult

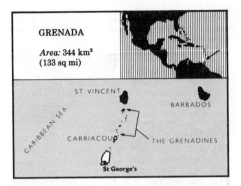

GRENADA
Area: 344 km²
(133 sq mi)

ST VINCENT
BARBADOS
CARRIACOU
THE GRENADINES
CARIBBEAN SEA
St George's

suffrage. The main political parties include the National Democratic Congress, the National Party, the United Labour Party and the New National Party.

Prime Minister: Nicholas Braithwaite.

EDUCATION

Literacy rate: 85%. *Years of compulsory schooling:* 6–14 (in urban areas). *Universities:* none, but there is a department of the University of the West Indies.

DEFENCE

Total armed strength: small paramilitary Special Service Unit. *Military service:* none.

GEOGRAPHY

A forested mountain ridge covers much of this well-watered island. The island of Carriacou forms part of Grenada. *Principal rivers:* there are no significant rivers. *Highest point:* Mount St Catherine 840 m (2706 ft).

Climate: Grenada has a tropical maritime climate with a dry season from January to May.

ECONOMY

The production of spices, in particular nutmeg, is the mainstay of a largely agricultural economy. Tourism is increasing in importance.

RECENT HISTORY

Grenada became British in 1783. Independence was gained in 1974. The left-wing New Jewel Movement seized power in a coup in 1979. In 1983 the PM Maurice Bishop was killed in a further coup in which more extreme members of the government seized power. Acting upon a request from East Caribbean islands to intervene, US and Caribbean forces landed in Grenada. After several days' fighting, the coup leaders were detained. Constitutional rule was restored in 1984.

GUATEMALA

Official name: República de Guatemala (Republic of Guatemala).

Member of: UN, OAS, CACM, LAIA (observer).

Population: 8 935 000 (1989).

Capital and major cities: Guatemala City 1 800 000 (including suburbs), Quezaltenango 88 000, Escuintla 61 000, Mázatenango 38 000 (1989).

Language: Spanish (official).

Religions: Roman Catholic (official; 75%).

Life expectancy: 62 years.

Labour force: (1988 est) 2 652 000; agriculture and forestry 1 541 000; manufacturing 361 000; services 318 000.

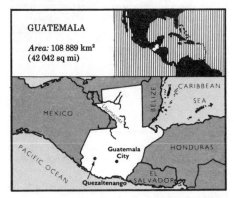

GUATEMALA

Area: 108 889 km² (42 042 sq mi)

GOVERNMENT

A President – who appoints a Cabinet – and a Vice President are elected for a five-year term by universal adult suffrage. The 100-member National Congress is also directly elected for five years – 75 members are directly elected; the remaining 25 members are returned under a system of proportional representation. The main political parties include the (rightwing) Christian Democratic Party, the National Centre Union, the National Party of Democratic Cooperation, and the (democratic left) FUR (an electoral pact of three parties).
President: Jorge Antonio Serrano.

EDUCATION

Literacy rate: 55% (1985 est). *Years of compulsory schooling:* 7–14 (in urban areas). *Universities:* 5.

DEFENCE

Total armed strength: 42 200 (1989). *Military service:* 2 years.

GEOGRAPHY

Pacific and Atlantic coastal lowlands are separated by a mountain chain containing over 30 volcanoes. *Principal river:* Usumacinta, Montagua. *Highest point:* Tajumulco 4220 m (13 881 ft)
Climate: The coastal plains have a tropical climate; the mountains are more temperate.

ECONOMY

More than one half of the labour force is involved in agriculture. Coffee is the major export, while the other main crops include sugar cane and bananas.

RECENT HISTORY

Guatemala was the administrative centre of Spanish Central America. Independence was proclaimed in 1821, but the country was part of Mexico (1821–23) and the Central American Federation (1823–39). Guatemala has a history of being ruled by dictators allied to landowners. However, in the 1950s President Jacobo Arbenz expropriated large estates, dividing them among the peasantry. Accused of being a Communist, he was deposed by the army with US military aid (1954). For over 30 years, the left was suppressed, leading to the emergence of guerrilla armies. Thousands of dissidents were killed or dis-

appeared. Civilian government was restored in 1986, but unrest continues and there have been serious abuses of human rights by the military.

GUINEA

Official name: La République de Guinée (The Republic of Guinea).
Member of: UN, OAU, ECOWAS.
Population: 6 705 000 (1989 est).
Capital and major cities: Conakry 705 000, Kankan 89 000, Kindia 56 000 (1983).
Languages: French (official), Soussou, Manika.
Religion: Sunni Islam (85%).
Life expectancy: 42 years.
Labour force: (1988 est) 2 991 000; agriculture and forestry 2 260 000, industry 237 000, services 270 000.

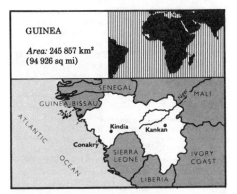

GUINEA

Area: 245 857 km² (94 926 sq mi)

GOVERNMENT

Power is exercised by the Military Committee for National Recovery, whose President is head of state and of government. There are no political parties.
President: Gen. Lansana Conte.

EDUCATION

Literacy rate: 21% (1985 est). *Years of compulsory schooling:* 7–13. *Universities:* 2.

DEFENCE

Total armed strength: 9700, plus 9600 paramilitary. *Military service:* 2 years.

GEOGRAPHY

Tropical rain forests cover the coastal plain. The interior highlands and plains are covered by grass and scrubland. There are mountains in the southwest. *Principal river:* Niger, Bafing, Konkouré, Kogon. *Highest point:* Mont Nimba 1752 m (5748 ft).
Climate: The climate is tropical with heavy rainfall. Temperatures are cooler in the highlands.

ECONOMY

Bauxite accounts for nearly 80% of Guinea's exports. However, over 75% of the labour force is involved in agriculture, producing bananas, oil palm and citrus fruits for export, and maize, rice and cassava as subsistence crops. Despite mineral wealth, Guinea is one of the world's poorest countries and relies heavily on aid.

RECENT HISTORY

Increasing French influence in the 19th century led

to the establishment of the colony of French Guinea (1890). Unlike the rest of French Africa, Guinea voted for a complete separation from France in 1958, suffering severe French reprisals as a result. The authoritarian radical leader Sékou Touré (1922–84) isolated Guinea, but he became reconciled with France in 1978. The leaders of a military coup (1984) have achieved some economic reforms.

GUINEA-BISSAU

Official name: Republica da Guiné-Bissau (Republic of Guinea-Bissau).

Member of: UN, OAU, ECOWAS.

Population: 943 000 (1989 est).

Capital and major towns: Bissau 125 000 (1988 est), Bafatá 13 500 (1980 est).

Languages: Portuguese (official), Crioulo.

Religions: Animist majority, Sunni Islam (30%).

Life expectancy: 45 years.

Labour force: (1980 est) 403 000; agriculture and forestry 332 000, services 57 000, industry 14 000.

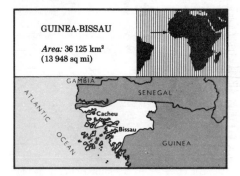

GUINEA-BISSAU

Area: 36 125 km²
(13 948 sq mi)

GAMBIA
SENEGAL
ATLANTIC OCEAN
Cacheu
Bissau
GUINEA

GOVERNMENT

Until 1991, the PAIGC was the only legal party, and the 150-member National Assembly was indirectly elected. Future multi-party direct elections will be held by universal adult suffrage. The Assembly elects a President, who appoints Ministers.

President: Brig. Gen. João Bernardo Vieira.

EDUCATION

Literacy rate: 32% (1985 est). *Years of compulsory schooling:* 7–12. *Universities:* none.

DEFENCE

Total armed strength: 9200 (1989). *Military service:* none.

GEOGRAPHY

Most of the country is low-lying, with swampy coastal lowlands and a flat forested interior plain. The northeast is mountainous. *Principal rivers:* Cacheu, Mansôa, Géba, Corubel. *Highest point:* an unnamed point in the Fouta Djallon plateau 180 m (591 ft).

Climate: The climate is tropical with a dry season from December to May.

ECONOMY

The country has one of the lowest standards of living in the world. Its subsistence economy is based mainly on rice. Timber is exported.

RECENT HISTORY

The colony of Portuguese Guinea was created in 1879. Failing to secure reform by peaceful means, the PAIGC movement mounted a liberation war (1961–1974). Independence was declared in 1973 and recognized by Portugal in 1974. After a military coup (1980), the aim of union with Cape Verde was dropped. Democratic reforms were introduced in 1991.

GUYANA

Official name: The Cooperative Republic of Guyana.

Member of: UN, Commonwealth, CARICOM, OAS.

Population: 754 000 (1989 est).

Capital: Georgetown 187 000 (1986 est).

Languages: English (official), Hindu, Urdu.

Religions: Hinduism (nearly 40%), with Anglican, Sunni Islam and Roman Catholic minorities.

Life expectancy: 69.8 years.

Labour force: (1980) 239 000; community and social services 57 500, agriculture and forestry 49 000, trade and tourism 15 000.

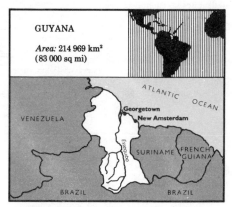

GUYANA

Area: 214 969 km²
(83 000 sq mi)

ATLANTIC OCEAN
VENEZUELA
Georgetown
New Amsterdam
Essequibo
SURINAME
FRENCH GUIANA
BRAZIL
BRAZIL

GOVERNMENT

The 65-member National Assembly consists of 53 members elected for five years under a system of proportional representation by universal adult suffrage and 12 appointed regional representatives. The President – the leader of the majority in the Assembly – appoints a Cabinet led by the First Vice-President. The main political parties are the (left-wing) People's National Congress, the (left-wing) People's Progressive Party, the (conservative) United Force, and the (left-wing) Working People's Alliance.

President: Hugh Hoyte.

First Vice-President and Prime Minister: Hamilton Green.

EDUCATION

Literacy rate: 96% (1985 est). *Years of compulsory schooling:* 6–14. *Universities:* 1

DEFENCE

Total armed strength: 5450 (1988). *Military service:* none.

GEOGRAPHY

A coastal plain is protected from the sea by dykes. Tropical rain forest covers much of the interior.

Principal rivers: Essequibo, Courantyne, Mazaruni, Demarara. *Highest point:* Mt Roraima 2772 m (9094 ft).

Climate: The interior is tropical, while the coastal plain is more moderate.

ECONOMY
Guyana depends on mining bauxite and growing sugar cane and rice. Nationalization and emigration have caused economic problems.

RECENT HISTORY
Guyana is the former colony of British Guiana. From the 1840s large numbers of Indian and Chinese labourers were imported from Asia to work on sugar plantations. Racial tension between their descendants – now the majority – and the black community (descended from imported African slaves) led to violence in 1964 and 1978. Guyana has been independent since 1966. Since 1987–88 President Hoyte has begun liberal economic reforms, but austerity measures have been in force since the end of 1988. There have been growing opposition allegations of electoral malpractice.

HAITI
Official name: La République d'Haïti (Republic of Haiti).

Member of: UN, OAS, CARICOM (observer).

Population: 5 523 000 (1988 est).

Capital and major cities: Port-au-Prince 738 000 (1984 est), Cap Haïtien 72 000 (1982 est).

Languages: Creole, French (both official).

Religions: Voodoo (majority), Roman Catholic (official).

Life expectancy: 54.7 years.

Labour force: (1988 est) 2 350 000; agriculture and forestry 1 185 000, trade and tourism 261 000, manufacturing 115 500.

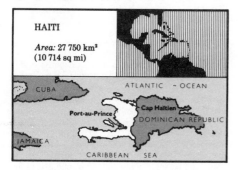

HAITI

Area: 27 750 km²
(10 714 sq mi)

ATLANTIC · OCEAN

CUBA

Cap Haïtien

Port-au-Prince

DOMINICAN REPUBLIC

JAMAICA

CARIBBEAN   SEA

GOVERNMENT
The 1987 constitution provides for elections by universal adult suffrage for a 27-member Senate, a 77-member Chamber of Deputies and a President, all to serve a five-year term. A large number of new political parties were formed during the period 1987–90; 12 of the main parties are associated in the so-called Group of 12.
President: Fr. Jean-Baptiste Aristide.
Prime Minister: René Préval.

EDUCATION
Literacy rate: 38% (1985 est). *Years of compulsory schooling:* 6–12. *Universities:* 1.

DEFENCE
Total armed strength: 7400 (1989). *Military service:* none.

GEOGRAPHY
Haiti is the western part of the island of Hispaniola. Mountain ranges run from E to W, alternating with densely populated valleys and plains. *Principal river:* Artibonite. *Highest point:* Pic La Selle 2680 m (8793 ft).

Climate: Haiti's tropical climate is moderated by altitude and by the sea.

ECONOMY
Two thirds of the labour force is involved in agriculture, mainly growing crops for domestic consumption. Coffee is the principal cash crop. With few resources, overpopulated Haiti is the poorest country in the western hemisphere.

RECENT HISTORY
Independence from France was proclaimed in 1804 during a revolt led by Jean-Jacques Dessalines and Henri Christophe, both of whom reigned as monarchs of Haiti. A united republic was achieved in 1820. Coups, instability and tension between blacks and mulattos wracked Haiti until the US intervened (1915–35). President François Duvalier ('Papa Doc'; in office 1956–71) and his son Jean-Claude ('Baby Doc'; 1971–86) cowed the country into submission by means of their infamous private militia, the Tontons Macoutes. The military took control after the younger Duvalier fled during a period of violent popular unrest. A civilian government – elected in 1988 – was almost immediately toppled by Gen. Namphy, who was in turn overturned by another military coup within three months. A Supreme Court judge served as interim president (March 1990–February 1991) until she was replaced in multi-party elections by a radical priest, Fr. Aristide, who promised sweeping economic reforms. Violence and intimidation by the Tontons Macoutes remains endemic.

HONDURAS
Official name: La República de Honduras (Republic of Honduras).

Member of: UN, OAS, CACM, LAIA (observer).

Population: 4 530 000 (1989 est).

Capital and major cities: Tegucigalpa 679 000, San Pedro Sula 461 000, La Ceiba 68 000, Choluteca 68 000, Progreso 65 000, Puerto Cortés 43 000 (1987 est).

Language: Spanish.

Religion: Roman Catholic (90%).

Life expectancy: 62.6 years.

Labour force 1 218 200 (employment figure 1988); agriculture and forestry 640 500, manufacturing 161 000.

GOVERNMENT
The President and the 134-member National Assembly are elected by universal adult suffrage for four years. The main political parties are the PLH (Liberal Party of Honduras) and the (right-wing) PN (National Party).
President: Rafael Callejas.

EDUCATION
Literacy rate: 60% (1985). *Years of compulsory school-*

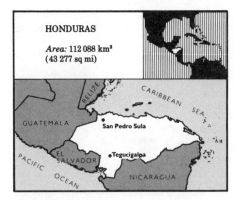

HONDURAS

Area: 112 088 km²
(43 277 sq mi)

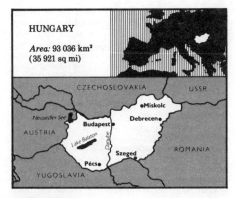

HUNGARY

Area: 93 036 km²
(35 921 sq mi)

ing: 7–12. *Universities:* 1 state, 2 private.

DEFENCE
Total armed strength: 19 200 (1989). *Military service:* 8 months.

GEOGRAPHY
Over three quarters of Honduras is mountainous, and there are small coastal plains. *Principal rivers:* Patuca, Ulúa. *Highest point:* Cerio las Minas 2849 m (9347 ft).
Climate: The tropical lowlands experience high rainfall (1500–2000 mm / 60–80 in). The more temperate highlands are drier.

ECONOMY
The majority of Hondurans work in agriculture, but despite agrarian reform, living standards remain low. Bananas are the leading export, although coffee, timber and meat are increasingly important. There are few natural resources.

RECENT HISTORY
Honduras gained freedom from Spain in 1821, but was part of Mexico until 1823 and the Central American Federation until 1839. Between independence and the early 20th century, Honduras experienced constant political upheaval and wars with neighbouring countries. US influence was immense, largely owing to the substantial investments of the powerful United Fruit Company in banana production. After a short civil war in 1925, a succession of military dictators governed Honduras until 1980. Since then the country has had democratically elected pro-US centre-right civilian governments.

HUNGARY

Official name: Magyarország (Hungary) or Magyar Köztársásag (The Hungarian Republic)
Member of: UN, CSCE, Council of Europe.
Population: 10 589 000 (1989 est).
Capital and major cities: Budapest 2 114 000, Debrecen 219 000, Miskolc 210 000, Szeged 189 000, Pécs 183 000, Györ 132 000, Nyíregyháza 120 000, Székesfehérvár 114 000, Kecskemét 105 000 (1989).
Language: Magyar (Hungarian).
Religions: Roman Catholic (54%), Calvinist and Lutheran (22%).
Life expectancy: 71.3 years.
Labour force: (1989) 4 814 000; manufacturing 1 541 000, services 1 129 000, agriculture and forestry 885 000.

GOVERNMENT
The 386-member National Assembly is elected for five years by universal adult suffrage. It comprises 58 members elected from a national list under a system of proportional representation, 152 members elected on a county basis and 176 elected from single-member constituencies. An executive President – who is elected by the Assembly – appoints a Cabinet and a Prime Minister from the majority in the Assembly. The main political parties include the (centre right) Democratic Forum, the (liberal) Alliance of Free Democrats, the Socialist Party (formerly the Communist Party), the Smallholders' Party, and the Christian Democratic People's Party.
President: Arpad Goncz.
Prime Minister: Jozsef Antall.

EDUCATION
Literacy rate: no figure available. *Years of compulsory schooling:* 6–14. *Universities:* 10, plus 9 technical universities

DEFENCE
Total armed strength: 91 000 (1989). *Military service:* 12 months.

GEOGRAPHY
Hungary west of the River Danube is an undulating lowland. There are thickly wooded highlands in the northeast. The southeast is a great expanse of flat plain. *Principal rivers:* Danube (Duna), Tisza, Drava. *Highest point:* Kékes 1015 m (3330 ft).
Climate: The climate is continental, with long, hot, dry summers, and cold winters.

ECONOMY
Nearly one fifth of the labour force is involved in agriculture. Major crops include cereals (maize, wheat and barley), sugar beet, fruit, and grapes for wine. Despite considerable reserves of coal, Hungary imports more than half of its energy needs. The steel, chemical fertilizer, pharmaceutical, machinery and vehicle industries are important. Since the early 1980s, private enterprise and foreign investment have been encouraged, and between 1989 and 1991 most of the large state enterprises were privatized.

RECENT HISTORY
In the 19th century Hungarian resentment against Austrian rule grew. Lajos Kossuth (1802–94) led a nationalist revolt against Austrian rule (1848–49), but fled when Austria regained control with Russian aid. Austria granted Hungary considerable auton-

omy in the Dual Monarchy (1867) – the Austro-Hungarian Empire. Defeat in World War I led to a brief period of Communist rule under Béla Kun (1919), then occupation by Romania. In the postwar settlement, Hungary lost two thirds of its territory. The Regent, Admiral Miklás Horthy (1868–1957), cooperated with Hitler during World War II in an attempt to regain territory, but defeat in 1945 resulted in occupation by the Red Army, and a Communist People's Republic was established in 1949. The Hungarian Uprising in 1956 was a heroic attempt to overthrow Communist rule, but was quickly suppressed by Soviet forces, and its leader, Imre Nagy, was executed. János Kadar – Party Secretary 1956–88 – tried to win support with economic progress. However, in the late 1980s reformers in the Communist Party gained the upper hand, and talks with opposition groups led to agreement on a transition to a fully democratic, multi-party state. The (Communist) Hungarian Socialist Workers' Party transformed itself into the Socialist Party but was heavily defeated in the first free elections in May 1990 when conservative and liberal parties won most seats. Soviet troops left Hungary in 1990, and the country has taken rapid steps to join Western European organizations and establish a free-market economy.

ICELAND

Official name: Lýdveldid Island (The Republic of Iceland).

Member of: UN, NATO, EFTA, Council of Europe, CSCE, OECD.

Population: 252 000 (1988 est).

Capital and major cities: Reykjavik 140 000 (with suburbs), Akureyri 14 000, Keflavik 7300 (1988).

Language: Icelandic.

Religion: Lutheran (97%).

Life expectancy: 77.1 years.

Labour force (employment figures): (1987) 132 000; mining and manufacturing 28 500, community and social services 37 000, trade and tourism 21 000.

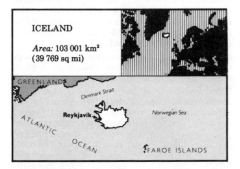

ICELAND

Area: 103 001 km²
(39 769 sq mi)

GREENLAND
Denmark Strait
ATLANTIC OCEAN
Reykjavik
Norwegian Sea
FAROE ISLANDS

GOVERNMENT

The 63-member Althing (Parliament) is elected under a system of proportional representation by universal adult suffrage for a four-year term. The Althing elects 20 of its members to sit as the Upper House and the remaining 43 members to sit as the Lower House. The President – who is also directly elected for four years – appoints a Prime Minister and a Cabinet who are responsible to the Althing. The main political parties include the (conservative)

Independence Party, the Progressive Party, the (socialist) People's Alliance, the Social Democratic Party, and the Women's Alliance.
President: Vigdis Finnbogadottir.
Prime Minister: Steingrimur Hermannsson.

EDUCATION

Literacy rate: 100%. *Years of compulsory schooling:* 7–16. *Universities:* 1, plus institutions of higher education.

DEFENCE

Total armed strength: There are no armed forces except for a coastal defence force.

GEOGRAPHY

The greater part of Iceland has a volcanic landscape with hot springs, geysers and some 200 volcanoes – some of them active. Much of the country is tundra. The south and centre are covered by glacial icefields. *Principal rivers:* Thjórsá, Skjalfanda Fljót. *Highest point:* Hvannadalshnúkur 2119 m (6952 ft).
Climate: The cool temperate climate is warmed by the Gulf Stream, which keeps Iceland milder than most places at the same latitude.

ECONOMY

The fishing industry provides the majority of Iceland's exports. Hydroelectric power is used in the aluminium-smelting industry, while geothermal power warms extensive greenhouses. Ample grazing land makes the country self-sufficient in meat and dairy products.

RECENT HISTORY

Icelandic nationalism grew in the 19th century, and in 1918 Iceland gained independence from Denmark. However, the two countries remained linked by their shared monarchy. In World War II the Danish link was severed and a republic was declared (1944). Disputes over fishing rights in Icelandic territorial waters led to clashes with British naval vessels in the 1950s and 1970s.

INDIA

Official name: Bharat (Republic of India).

Member of: UN, Commonwealth, SAARC.

Population: 796 600 000 (1987 est) – including the Indian-held part of Jammu and Kashmir.

Capital and major cities: Delhi 5 729 000, Calcutta 9 194 000, Bombay 8 243 000, Madras 4 289 000, Bangalore 2 922 000, Ahmedabad 2 548 000, Hyderabad 2 546 000, Poona (Pune) 1 686 000, Kanpur 1 639 000, Nagpur 1 302 000, Jaipur 1 015 000, Lucknow 1 008 000, Coimbatore 920 000, Patna 919 000, Surat 914 000, Madurai 909 000, Indore 829 000, Varanasi 797 000, Jabalpur 757 000, Agra 747 000, Vadodara 744 000, Cochin 686 000, Dhanbad 678 000, Bhopal 671 000, Jamshedpur 670 000, Allahabad 650 000 (all including suburbs; 1981)

Languages: Hindi (30%; official), English (official), Bengali (8%), Telugu (8%), Marathi (8%), Tamil (7%), Urdu (5%), Gujarati (5%), with over 1600 other languages.

Religions: Hindu (83%), Sunni Islam (11%), Christian (mainly Roman Catholic) (nearly 3%).

Life expectancy: 57.5 years.

Labour force: (1981) 244 605 000; agriculture and

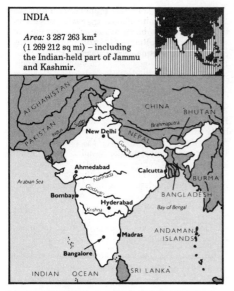

INDIA

Area: 3 287 263 km²
(1 269 212 sq mi) – including
the Indian-held part of Jammu
and Kashmir.

forestry 153 015 000, manufacturing 25 143 000, community and social services 18 557 000.

GOVERNMENT

India is a federal republic in which each of the 25 states has its own legislature. The upper house of the federal parliament – the 250-member Council of States (Rajya Sabha) – consists of 12 members nominated by the President and 238 members elected by the assemblies of individual states. One third of the Council retires every two years. The lower house – the House of the People (Lok Sabha) – consists of 542 members elected for a five-year term by universal adult suffrage, plus two nominated members. The President – who serves for five years – is chosen by an electoral college consisting of the federal parliament and the state assemblies. The President appoints a Prime Minister – who commands a majority in the House – and a Council of Ministers, who are responsible to the House. The main political parties include the Congress (I) Party, the Janata Dal (People's Party), the (right-wing Hindu) Bharatiya Janata Party (Indian People's Party), the Communist Party of India – Marxist, the Communist Party of India, and a number of regional groupings.
President: Ramaswamy Venkataraman.
Prime Minister: Chandra Shekhar.

INDIAN STATES

The population figures are for 1981.
Andhra Pradesh *Area*: 276 814 km² (106 878 sq mi). *Population*: 53 404 000. *Capital*: Hyderabad 2 546 000.

Arunachal Pradesh *Area*: 83 587 km² (32 269 sq mi). *Population*: 628 000. *Capital*: Itanagar 50 000.

Assam *Area*: 78 523 km² (30 310 sq mi). *Population*: 19 903 000. *Capital*: Gauhati 125 000.

Bihar *Area*: 173 876 km² (67 134 sq mi). *Population*: 69 823 000. *Capital*: Patna 919 000.

Goa *Area*: 3701 km² (1429 sq mi). *Population*: 1 082 000. *Capital*: Panaji 77 000.

Gujarat *Area*: 195 984 km² (75 669 sq mi). *Population*: 33 961 000. *Capital*: Gandhinagar 62 000. *Largest city*: Allahabad 650 000.

Haryana *Area*: 44 222 km² (17 074 sq mi). *Population*: 12 851 000. *Capital*: Chandigarh (i.e. outside the state) 450 000. *Largest city*: Rohtak 166 000.

Himachal Pradesh *Area*: 55 673 km² (21 495 sq mi). *Population*: 4 238 000. *Capital*: Simla 71 000.

Jammu and Kashmir *Area*: 101 283 km² (39 105 sq mi) – the Indian-held part of the state only. *Population*: 5 982 000. *Capital (summer only)*: Srinagar 520 000. *Capital (winter only)*: Jammu 223 000.

Karnataka *Area*: 191 773 km² (74 044 sq mi). *Population*: 37 043 000. *Capital*: Bangalore 2 922 000.

Kerala *Area*: 38 864 km² (15 005 sq mi). *Population*: 25 403 000. *Capital*: Cochin 686 000.

Madhya Pradesh *Area*: 442 841 km² (170 981 sq mi). *Population*: 52 139 000. *Capital*: Bhopal 671 000. *Largest city*: Indore 829 000.

Maharashtra *Area*: 307 762 km² (118 827 sq mi). *Population*: 62 694 000. *Capital*: Bombay 8 243 000.

Manipur *Area*: 22 356 km² (8632 sq mi). *Population*: 1 434 000. *Capital*: Imphal 157 000.

Meghalaya *Area*: 22 429 km² (8660 sq mi). *Population*: 1 336 000. *Capital*: Shillong 175 000.

Mizoram *Area*: 21 090 km² (8143 sq mi). *Population*: 488 000. *Capital*: Aizawl 74 000.

Nagaland *Area*: 16 527 km² (6381 sq mi). *Population*: 773 000. *Capital*: Kohima 34 000.

Orissa *Area*: 155 707 km² (60 118 sq mi). *Population*: 26 370 000. *Capital*: Bhubaneshwar 219 000. *Largest city*: Cuttack 327 000.

Punjab *Area*: 50 376 km² (19 450 sq mi). *Population*: 16 670 000. *Capital*: Chandigarh (i.e. outside the state) 450 000. *Largest city*: Ludhiana 606 000.

Rajasthan *Area*: 342 239 km² (132 138 sq mi). *Population*: 34 262 000. *Capital*: Jaipur 1 015 000.

Sikkim *Area*: 7298 km² (2818 sq mi). *Population*: 315 000. *Capital*: Gangtok 37 000.

Tamil Nadu *Area*: 130 357 km² (50 331 sq mi). *Population*: 48 298 000. *Capital*: Madras 4 289 000.

Tripura *Area*: 10 477 km² (4045 sq mi). *Population*: 2 060 000. *Capital*: Agartala 132 000.

Uttar Pradesh *Area*: 294 413 km² (113 673 sq mi). *Population*: 110 862 000. *Capital*: Lucknow 1 008 000. *Largest city*: Kanpur 1 639 000.

West Bengal *Area*: 87 853 km² (33 920 sq mi). *Population*: 54 581 000. *Capital*: Calcutta 9 194 000.

INDIAN UNION TERRITORIES

Andaman and Nicobar Islands (Territory) *Area*: 8293 km² (3202 sq mi). *Population*: 188 000. *Capital*: Port Blair 50 000.

Chandigarh *Area*: 114 km² (44 sq mi). *Population*: 450 000. *Capital*: Chandigarh 450 000.

Dadra and Nagar Haveli *Area*: 491 km² (190 sq mi). *Population*: 104 000. *Capital*: Silvassa 15 000.

Daman and Diu *Area*: 112 km² (43 sq mi). *Population*: 52 000. *Capital*: Daman 21 000.

Delhi *Area*: 1485 km² (573 sq mi). *Population*: 5 729 000. *Capital*: Delhi 5 729 000.

Lakshadweep *Area*: 32 km² (12 sq mi). *Population*: 42 000. *Capital*: Kavaratti 10 000.

Pondicherry *Area*: 492 km² (190 sq mi). *Population*: 605 000. *Capital*: Pondicherry 251 000.

EDUCATION

Literacy rate: 64% (1981). *Years of compulsory schooling*: 6–14, except in Nagaland and Himachal Pradesh. *Universities*: 132.

DEFENCE

Total armed strength: 1 260 000 (1989). *Military service:* none.

GEOGRAPHY

The Himalaya cut the Indian subcontinent off from the rest of Asia. Several Himalayan peaks in India rise to over 7000 m (23 000 ft). South of the Himalaya, the basins of the Rivers Ganges and Brahmaputra and their tributaries are intensively farmed and densely populated. The Thar Desert stretches along the border with Pakistan. In south India, the Deccan – a large plateau of hard rocks – is bordered in the east and west by the Ghats, discontinuous ranges of hills descending in steps to coastal plains. Natural vegetation ranges from tropical rain forest on the west coast and monsoon forest in the northeast and far south, through dry tropical scrub and thorn forest in much of the Deccan to Alpine and temperate vegetation in the Himalaya. *Principal rivers:* Ganges (Ganga), Brahmaputra, Sutlej, Yamuna, Tapti, Godavari, Krishna. *Highest point:* Kangchenjunga 8598 m (28 208 ft).

Climate: India has three distinct seasons: the hot season from March to June, the wet season – when the southwest monsoon brings heavy rain – from June to October, and a cooler drier season from November to March. Temperatures range from the cool of the Himalaya to the tropical heat of the southern states.

ECONOMY

Two thirds of the labour force are involved in subsistence farming, with rice and wheat as the principal crops. Cash crops tend to come from large plantations and include tea, cotton, jute and sugar cane – all grown for export. The monsoon rains and irrigation make cultivation possible in many areas, but drought and floods are common. India is one of the ten largest industrial powers in the world. Major coal reserves provide the power base for industry. Other mineral deposits include diamonds, bauxite, and titanium, copper and iron ore, as well as substantial reserves of natural gas and petroleum. The textile, vehicle, iron and steel, pharmaceutical and electrical industries make important contributions to the economy, but India has balance-of-payment difficulties and relies upon foreign aid for development. Over one third of the population is below the official poverty line.

RECENT HISTORY

The British Indian Empire included present-day Pakistan and Bangladesh, and comprised the Crown Territories of British India and over 620 Indian protected states. The Indian states covered about 40% of India, and enjoyed varying degrees of autonomy under the rule of their traditional princes. From the middle of the 19th century the British cautiously encouraged Indian participation in the administration of British India. British institutions, the railways and the English language – all imposed upon India by a modernizing imperial power – fostered the growth of an Indian sense of identity beyond the divisions of caste and language. However, ultimately the divisions of religion proved stronger. The Indian National Congress – the forerunner of the Congress Party – was first convened in 1885, and the Muslim League first met in 1906. Political and nationalist demands grew after British troops fired without warning on a nationalist protest meeting – the

Amritsar Massacre (1919). The India Acts (1919 and 1935) granted limited autonomy and created an Indian federation, but the pace of reform did not satisfy Indian expectations. In 1920 Congress – led by Mohandas (Mahatma) Karamchand Gandhi (1869–1948) – began a campaign of non-violence and non-cooperation with the British authorities. However relations between Hindus and Muslims steadily deteriorated, and by 1940 the Muslim League was demanding a separate sovereign state.

By 1945, war-weary Britain had accepted the inevitability of Indian independence. However, religious discord forced the partition of the subcontinent in 1947 into predominantly Hindu India – under Jawaharlal (Pandit) Nehru (1889–1964) of the Congress Party – and Muslim Pakistan (including what is now Bangladesh) – under Mohammed Ali Jinnah (1876–1948) of the Muslim League. Over 70 million Hindus and Muslims became refugees and crossed the new boundaries, and thousands were killed in communal violence. The frontiers remained disputed. India and Pakistan fought border wars in 1947–49, 1965 (over Kashmir) and 1971 – when Bangladesh gained independence from Pakistan with Indian assistance. Kashmir is still divided along a cease-fire line. In 1962 there were also border clashes with China.

Under Nehru (PM 1947–64) India became one of the leaders of the nonaligned movement of Third World states. Under the premiership (1966–77 and 1980–84) of his daughter Indira Gandhi (1917–84) India continued to assert itself as the dominant regional power. Although India remained the world's largest democracy – despite Mrs Gandhi's brief imposition of emergency rule (1975–77) – local separatism and communal unrest have threatened unity. The Sikhs have conducted an often violent campaign for an independent homeland – Khalistan – in the Punjab. In 1984 Mrs Gandhi ordered the storming of the Golden Temple of Amritsar, a Sikh holy place that extremists had turned into an arsenal. In the same year Mrs Gandhi was assassinated by her Sikh bodyguard and was succeeded as PM by her son Rajiv Gandhi. From 1986, his government lost popularity because of charges of corruption and inefficiency, and he was defeated in a general election in November 1989. V.P. Singh formed a coalition government. In 1990, a proposal to build a Hindu temple on the site of a mosque in the holy city of Ayodha led to violence between Hindus and Muslims. In November 1990, the government fell. Chandra Shekhar formed a minority government with the support of the Congress (I) Party, but his resignation in March 1991 forced an election. Fierce intercommunal fighting broke out during campaigning, and in May Rajiv Gandhi was assassinated in a bomb explosion.

INDONESIA

Official name: Republik Indonesia (Republic of Indonesia).

Member of: UN, OPEC, ASEAN.

Population: 177 046 000 (1989 est).

Capital and major cities: Jakarta 7 829 000, Surabaya 2 345 000, Medan 2 110 000, Bandung 1 613 000, Semarang 1 208 000, Palembang 875 000, Ujung Pandang (Makassar) 842 000 (1985 est).

Languages: Bahasa Indonesia (official), Javanese, Madurese, Sundanese and about 25 other main languages.

Religions: Sunni Islam (80%), Roman Catholic (3%), other Christians (7%), Hindu (2%).

INDONESIA

Area: 1 919 443 km²
(741 101 sq mi) –
including East
Timor

Life expectancy: 61 years.

Labour force: (1986) 70 193 000; agriculture and forestry 35 000 000, trade and tourism 10 000 000, community and social services 8 000 000.

GOVERNMENT

Every five years elections are held by universal adult suffrage for 400 members of the House of Representatives; the remaining 100 members are chosen by the President. The People's Consultative Assembly – which consists of the members of the House plus 500 representatives of provincial governments, occupational and special interests – meets once every five years to oversee broad principles of state policy and to elect the President, who appoints a Cabinet. The principal political parties are (government alliance) Golkar, the Muslim Development Party, and the (Christian and nationalist) Indonesian Democratic Party.
President: Gen. T.N.I. Suharto.

EDUCATION

Literacy rate: 74% (1985 est). *Years of compulsory schooling:* 7–12. *Universities:* 48 state, 25 private.

DEFENCE

Total armed strength: 284 000. *Military service:* none.

GEOGRAPHY

Indonesia consists of nearly 3700 islands, of which about 3000 are inhabited. The southern chain of mountainous, volcanic islands comprises Sumatra, Java with Madura, Bali, and the Lesser Sunda Islands (including Lombok, Flores and Timor). Java and its smaller neighbour Madura are fertile and densely populated, containing nearly two thirds of Indonesia's people. The northern chain comprises Kalimantan (the Indonesian sector of Borneo), the irregular mountainous island of Sulawesi (Celebes), the Moluccas group, and Irian Jaya (the western half of New Guinea). Over two thirds of the country is covered by tropical rain forests. *Principal rivers:* Kapuas, Digul, Barito. *Highest point:* Ngga Pulu (Carstenz Pyramid) 5030 m (16 503 ft) (on Irian Jaya).

Climate: The climate is tropical with heavy rainfall throughout the year.

ECONOMY

Indonesia has great mineral wealth – petroleum, natural gas, tin, nickel, coal, bauxite and copper – but is relatively poor because of its great population. Most Indonesians are subsistence farmers with rice

being the major crop, but both estate and peasant farmers produce important quantities of rubber, tea, coffee, tobacco and spices for export. Industry is largely concerned with processing mineral and agricultural products.

RECENT HISTORY

From the 17th century, the East Indies became the major and most profitable part of the Dutch Empire. Except for a brief period of British occupation (1811–14) and occasional local risings, the Netherlands retained control until 1942 when the Japanese invaded and were welcomed by most Indonesians as liberators from colonial rule. Upon Japan's surrender in 1945, Achmed Sukarno (1901–70) – the founder of the nationalist party in 1927 – declared the Dutch East Indies to be the independent republic of Indonesia. Under international pressure, the Dutch accepted Indonesian independence (1949) after four years of intermittent but brutal fighting. Sukarno's rule became increasingly authoritarian and the country sank into economic chaos. In 1962 he seized Netherlands New Guinea, which was formally annexed as Irian Jaya in 1969, although a separatist movement persists. Between 1963 and 1966 Sukarno tried to destabilize the newly-created Federation of Malaysia by armed incursions into north Borneo.

General T.N.I. Suharto's suppression of a Communist uprising in 1965–66 enabled him to reverse Sukarno's anti-Americanism and eventually to displace him with both student and army support. Around 80 000 members of the Communist Party were killed in this period. The annexation of Portuguese East Timor by Indonesia in 1976 is unrecognized by the international community, and guerrilla action by local nationalists continues. An ambitious programme of resettlement has been attempted to relieve overcrowded Java, but the Javanese settlers have been resented in the outlying, underdeveloped islands.

IRAN

Official name: Jomhori-e-Islami-e-Irân (Islamic Republic of Iran). Until 1935 Iran was known as Persia.

Member of: UN, OPEC.

Population: 54 333 000 (1989 est).

Capital and major cities: Tehran 6 022 000, Mashad 1 500 000, Isfahan 1 000 000, Tabriz 971 000, Shiraz 848 000, Ahvaz 580 000, Bakhtaran 561 000, Qom 543 000 (all including suburbs; 1986).

Languages: Farsi or Persian (official; 50%), Azerbaijani (27%), with Kurdish, Luri, Baluchi and Arabic minorities.

Religion: Shia Islam (official; 93%).

Life expectancy: 63 years.

Labour force: (1976) 9 796 000; agriculture and forestry 2 992 000, manufacturing 1 672 000, services 1 621 000.

GOVERNMENT

A Council of Experts – 83 Shiite clerics – is elected by universal adult suffrage to appoint the Wali Faqih (religious leader), who exercises supreme authority over the executive, legislature, judiciary and military. There is no fixed term for the Wali Faqih, whose role may be taken by a joint leadership of three or five persons. The 270-member Islamic Consultative Assembly (Majlis) and the President are directly

IRAN
Area: 1 648 000 km²
(636 296 sq mi)

elected for four years. The President appoints a Cabinet which is responsible to the Majlis. Iran is effectively a single-party state with most members of the Majlis belonging to the Islamic Republican Party. However, the Liberation Movement of Iran is also allowed to operate.

Supreme Religious Leader: Ayatollah Mohammad Khamenei.

President: Hojatolislam Rafsanjani.

EDUCATION

Literacy rate: 62% (1986). *Years of compulsory schooling:* 6–14. *Universities:* 21.

DEFENCE

Total armed strength: 604 500 (1989). *Military service:* 24–30 months.

GEOGRAPHY

Apart from restricted lowlands along the Gulf, the Caspian Sea and the Iraqi border, Iran is a high plateau, surrounded by mountains. The Elburz Mountains lie in the north; the Zagros Mountains form a barrier running parallel to the Gulf. In the east, lower areas of the plateau are covered by salt deserts. *Principal rivers:* Kàrùn, Safid, Atrak, Karkheh. *Highest point:* Demavend 5604 m (18 386 ft).

Climate: Iran has an extreme climate ranging from very hot on the Gulf to sub-zero temperatures in winter in the northwest. The Caspian Sea coast has a subtropical climate with rainfall totals around 1000 mm (40 in) a year. Most of Iran, however, has little rain.

ECONOMY

Petroleum is Iran's main source of foreign currency. The principal industries are petrochemicals, carpet-weaving, textiles, vehicles and cement, but the war with Iraq and the country's international isolation have severely interrupted trade. Over a quarter of the labour force is involved in agriculture, mainly producing cereals (wheat, maize and barley) and keeping livestock, but lack of water, land ownership problems and manpower shortages have restricted yields.

RECENT HISTORY

In the 19th century, Russia and Britain became rivals for influence in the region. In 1921 an Iranian

Cossack officer, Reza Khan Pahlavi (1877–1944), took power. Deposing the Qajar dynasty in 1925, he became Shah (emperor) himself as Reza I and modernized and secularized Iran. However, because of his pro-German sentiments, he was forced to abdicate by Britain and the USSR (1941) and was replaced by his son Mohammed Reza (1919–80). The radical nationalist prime minister Muhammad Mussadiq briefly toppled the monarchy (1953). On regaining his throne, the Shah tightened his grip through oppression and sought popularity through land reform and rapid development with US backing. However, the policy of Westernization offended the clergy, and a combination of students, the bourgeoisie and religious leaders eventually combined against him, overthrowing the monarchy in 1979 and replacing it with a fundamentalist Islamic Republic inspired by the Ayatollah Ruhollah Khomeini (1900–89). The Western-educated classes fled Iran as the clergy tightened control. Radical anti-Western students seized the US embassy and held 66 American hostages (1979–81). In 1980 Iraq invaded Iran, beginning the bitter First Gulf War, which lasted until 1988 and resulted in great losses of manpower for Iran. Following the death of Khomeini in 1989, economic necessity brought about a less militant phase of the Islamic revolution. The new president, Rafsanjani, emphasized pragmatic rather than radical policies and attempted to heal the diplomatic rift with Western powers. President Saddam Hussein of Iraq returned occupied Iranian territory following his invasion of Kuwait (1990).

IRAQ

Official name: Al-Jumhuriya al-'Iraqiya (The Republic of Iraq).

Member of: UN, Arab League, OPEC.

Population: 17 215 000 (1989 est).

Capital and major cities: Baghdad 4 649 000, Basrah (Al Basrah) 617 000, Mosul (Al Mawsil) 571 000, Irbil 334 000, As Sulaymaniyah 279 000, An Najaf 243 000 (1985).

Languages: Arabic (official; 80%), Kurdish (15%).

Religions: Sunni Islam (40%), Shia Islam (50%), with a small Christian minority.

Life expectancy: 64 years.

Labour force: (1977) 3 134 000; community and social services 958 000, agriculture and forestry 944 000, construction 322 000.

GOVERNMENT

The 250-member National Assembly is elected for a four-year term by universal adult suffrage. The non-elected Revolutionary Command Council appoints the President, who – in turn – appoints the Council of Ministers. The only effective legal party is the Arab Ba'ath Socialist Party, which is part of the National Progressive Front coalition. In 1989 it was announced that a new constitution would allow political pluralism, but this has not been implemented.

President: Saddam Hussein.

Prime Minister: Sadoun Hammadi.

EDUCATION

Literacy rate: no figure available. *Years of compulsory schooling:* 6–12. *Universities:* 6.

DEFENCE

Total armed strength: 1 000 000 (1989); 300 000

IRAQ
Area: 441 839 km²
(170 595 sq mi)

effective force, March 1991. *Military service:* 21–24 months.

GEOGRAPHY
The basins of the Rivers Tigris and Euphrates contain most of the arable land and most of the population. Desert in the southwest occupies nearly one half of Iraq. *Principal rivers:* Tigris (Dijlah), Euphrates (al Furat). *Highest point:* Rawanduz 3658 m (12 001 ft).

Climate: Summers are hot and dry with temperatures over 40 °C (104 °F). Most of the rainfall – ranging from 100 mm (4 in) in the desert to 1000 mm (40 in) in the mountains – comes in winter.

ECONOMY
Agriculture involves one third of the labour force. Irrigated land in the Tigris and Euphrates basins produces cereals, fruit and vegetables for domestic consumption, and dates for export. Iraq depends upon its substantial reserves of petroleum, but exports were halted by international sanctions (1990) and the Second Gulf War (1991). The Iraqi economy was badly damaged during the First Gulf War against Iran, and devastated by the Second Gulf War.

RECENT HISTORY
Iraq was absorbed by the Turkish Ottoman Empire in the 16th century. In World War I the British occupied the area, but Iraqi nationalists were disappointed when Iraq became a British mandate with virtual colonial status (1920). In 1921 the Amir Faisal ibn Husain became King and in 1932 Iraq became fully independent. Following a military coup that brought pro-German officers to power in 1941, the British occupied Iraq until 1945. The royal family and the premier were murdered in the 'Free Officers' coup in 1958. Differences in the leadership led to a further coup in 1963 and a reign of terror against the left. In 1968 Ba'athist (pan-Arab nationalist) officers carried out another coup. Embittered by the Arabs' humiliation in the 1967 war and by US support for the Israelis, the regime turned to the Soviets.

In 1980 President Saddam Hussein attacked a weakened Iran, responding to Iran's threat to export Islamic revolution. What had been intended as a quick victory became the costly First Gulf War

(1980–88), resulting in many casualties and the virtual bankruptcy of the country. In an attempt to restore Iraq's economic fortunes, Saddam Hussein invaded oil-rich Kuwait (2 August 1990). The international community was almost unanimous in its condemnation of the invasion and UN sanctions against Iraq were imposed. Forces from the USA, the UK and over 20 other countries (including Egypt and Syria) were dispatched to the Gulf to prevent an Iraqi invasion of Saudi Arabia. Following Saddam Hussein's failure to respond to repeated UN demands to withdraw from Kuwait, the Second Gulf War began on 16 January 1991 with an American and British air bombardment of Baghdad. On 24 February, coalition forces entered Kuwaiti and Iraqi territory to liberate Kuwait. Coalition forces routed the Iraqi army which sustained heavy casualties. Iraq accepted all the UN resolutions regarding Kuwait and agreed to a ceasefire after a campaign that lasted only 100 hours. During March and April – with coalition forces in occupation of southern Iraq – Saddam Hussein suppressed revolts by Shiites in the south and Kurds in the north. International efforts were made to feed and protect over 1 000 000 Shiite and Kurdish refugees, many of whom fled to Iran and Turkey.

IRELAND
Official name: Poblacht na h'Éireann (Republic of Ireland).

Member of: UN, EC, CSCE, Council of Europe, OECD.

Population: 3 515 000 (1989 est).

Capital and major cities: Dublin 921 000, Cork 173 700, Limerick 76 600, Dún Laoghaire 54 700 (part of the Dublin agglomeration), Galway 47 100, Waterford 41 100 (all including suburbs; 1986).

Languages: Irish (official), English.

Religion: Roman Catholic (95%).

Life expectancy: 74 years.

Labour force: (1989) 1 090 000; commerce 223 000, construction 215 000, agriculture and forestry 163 000.

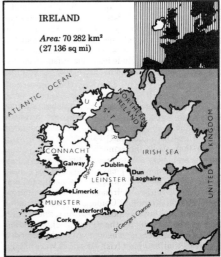

IRELAND
Area: 70 282 km²
(27 136 sq mi)

GOVERNMENT
The Seanad (Senate) comprises 60 members – 11 nominated by the Taoiseach (Prime Minister), six elected by the universities and 43 indirectly elected

for a five-year term to represent vocational and special interests. The Dáil (House) comprises 166 members elected for five years by universal adult suffrage under a system of proportional representation. The President is directly elected for a seven-year term. The Taoiseach and a Cabinet of Ministers are appointed by the President upon the nomination of the Dáil, to whom they are responsible. The main political parties include Fianna Fáil, Fine Gael, the Labour Party, the Worker's Party and the Progressive Democrats.
President: Mary Robinson.
Prime Minister: Charles Haughey.

EDUCATION

Literacy rate: 99%. *Years of compulsory schooling:* 6–15. *Universities:* 7 university colleges.

DEFENCE

Total armed strength: 13 000 (1989). *Military service:* none.

GEOGRAPHY

Central Ireland is a lowland crossed by slight ridges and broad valleys, bogs and large lakes, including Loughs Derg and Ree. Except on the east coast north of Dublin, the lowland is surrounded by coastal hills and mountains including the Wicklow Mountains (south of Dublin), the Comeragh Mountains (Co. Waterford) and the Ox Mountains and the hills of Connemara and Donegal in the west. The highest uplands are the Macgillicuddy's Reeks in the southwest. The rugged Atlantic Coast is highly indented. *Principal rivers:* Shannon, Suir, Boyne, Barrow, Erne. *Highest point:* Carrauntuohill 1041 m (3414 ft).
Climate: Ireland has a mild temperate climate. Rainfall is high, ranging from over 2500 mm (100 in) in the west and southwest to 750 mm (30 in) in the east.

ECONOMY

Manufactured goods – in particular machinery, metals and engineering, electronics and chemical products – now account for over 80% of Ireland's exports. Agriculture – which was the traditional mainstay of the economy – concentrates upon the production of livestock, meat and dairy products. Food processing and brewing are major industries. Natural resources include lead-zinc, offshore petroleum and natural gas, and hydroelectric power sites.

RECENT HISTORY

In 1798 the failure of a nationalist revolt against British rule was followed by the amalgamation of the British and Irish parliaments and the establishment of the United Kingdom of Great Britain and Ireland (1801). In the 1840s thousands died in the Irish potato famine, and many more were evicted by Anglo-Irish landowners and joined à mass emigration, especially to the USA. The result was that between 1845 and 1851 the population of Ireland declined by almost three million. Daniel O'Connell (1775–1847) led a movement seeking to repeal the Union, and to gain land and civil rights for the Roman Catholic majority. His campaign helped lead to Catholic Emancipation (1829), after which Irish Catholics were able to become MPs in the British Parliament at Westminster. However, relations between the Protestant and Catholic communities deteriorated, in part owing to the increasingly violent actions of the nationalist Fenians, whose goal was Irish independence. British

policy on Ireland vacillated between conciliation and coercion – Gladstone, recognizing the need for reform, disestablished the (Anglican) Church of Ireland and granted greater security of tenure to peasant farmers. In the 1880s Charles Stewart Parnell (1846–91) led a sizeable bloc of Irish MPs in a campaign to secure Irish Home Rule (i.e. self-government). Home Rule Bills were introduced in 1883 and 1893, but after their rejection by Parliament, more revolutionary nationalist groups gained support in Ireland.

Fearing Catholic domination, Protestant Unionists in Ulster strongly opposed the Third Home Rule Bill in 1912. Nationalists declared an independent Irish state in the Dublin Easter Rising of 1916, which was put down by the British. After World War I, Irish nationalist MPs formed a provisional government in Dublin led by Eamon de Valera (later PM and President; 1882–1975). Except in the northeast, British administration in Ireland crumbled and most of the Irish police resigned to be replaced by British officers – the 'Black and Tans'. Fighting broke out between nationalists and British troops and police, and by 1919 Ireland had collapsed into violence. The British response in 1920 was to offer Ireland two Parliaments – one in Protestant Ulster, another in the Catholic south. Partition was initially rejected by the south, but by the Anglo-Irish Treaty (1921) dominion status was granted, although six (mainly Protestant) counties in Ulster – Northern Ireland – opted to remain British. The Irish Free State was proclaimed in 1922 but de Valera and the Republicans refused to accept it. Civil war broke out between the provisional government – led by Arthur Griffith and Michael Collins – and the Republicans. Although fighting ended in 1923, de Valera's campaign for a republic continued and in 1937 the Irish Free State became the Republic of Eire. The country remained neutral in World War II and left the Commonwealth – as the Republic of Ireland – in 1949. Relations between south and north – and between the Republic and the UK – have often been tense during the 'troubles' in Northern Ireland (1968–). However, the Anglo-Irish Agreement (1985) provided for the participation of the Republic in political, legal and security matters in Northern Ireland. Irish political life has been characterized by the alternation of the two main parties – Fine Gael and Fianna Fáil – in government.

ISRAEL

Official name: Medinat Israel (The State of Israel).
Member of: UN.
Population: 4 563 000 (1989) – Jewish (85%), Arab (15%), including East Jerusalem.
Capital and major cities: Jerusalem (not recognized internationally as capital) 506 000, Tel-Aviv 1 624 000, Haifa 393 000, Beersheba (Be'er Sheva) 116 000 (all including suburbs; 1985).
Languages: Hebrew (official; 85%), Arabic (15%).
Religions: Judaism (official; 85%), Sunni Islam (13%), various Christian denominations.
Life expectancy: 75.1 years.
Labour force: (1988) 1 464 000; services 580 000, mining and manufacturing 324 000, trade and tourism 216 000.

GOVERNMENT

The 120-member Knesset (Assembly) is elected by

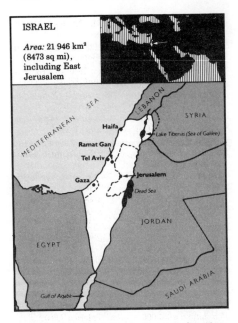

ISRAEL

Area: 21 946 km²
(8473 sq mi),
including East
Jerusalem

RECENT HISTORY

The Turkish Ottoman Empire ruled the area from the early 16th century until 1917–18, when Palestine was captured by British forces. The Zionists had hoped to establish a Jewish state, and this hope was intensified following the Balfour Declaration by the British foreign secretary in favour of a homeland (1917). However, Palestine came under British administration and it was not until 1948–9 – after the murder of some 6 million Jews in concentration camps by the Nazis – that an explicitly Jewish state emerged. The establishment of a Jewish state met with hostility from Israel's neighbours and indigenous Palestinians (many of whom left the country), leading to a series of Arab-Israeli wars. In 1956, while the UK and France were in conflict with Egypt over the Suez Canal, Israel attacked Gaza – from which the Palestinians had raided Israel – and overran Sinai, but withdrew following UN condemnation. After an uneasy peace, the UN emergency force between Israel and Egypt was expelled in 1967. Egypt imposed a sea blockade on Israel, which responded by invading Sinai. In six days, an Arab coalition of Egypt, Jordan and Syria was defeated, and Israel occupied Sinai, Gaza, the West Bank and the Golan Heights. In 1973, Egypt attacked Israel across the Suez Canal, but a ceasefire was arranged within three weeks. In 1979 Israel and Egypt signed a peace treaty; Egypt recognized Israel's right to exist and Israel withdrew from Sinai in stages. In 1982 Israeli forces invaded Lebanon, intent on destroying bases of the PLO (Palestinian Liberation Organization), and became involved in the complex civil war there. Eventually Israeli forces withdrew in 1985. In 1987 the intifada (Palestinian uprising) against continued Israeli rule in Gaza and the West Bank began. The harsh reaction of Israeli security forces attracted international condemnation. The intifada continued sporadically and was given extra impetus by the large-scale influx of Soviet Jews into Israel (from 1990) and the encouragement given to the Palestinians and their leader Yasser Arafat by President Saddam Hussein of Iraq. Israeli politics in the 1980s and 1990s have been dominated by Itzhak Shamir (the leader of Likud) and Simon Peres (the leader of Labour), and characterized by political instability owing to the system of proportional representation and the large number of very small parties.

Information concerning the occupied territories – Gaza and the West Bank (Judaea and Samaria) – can be found on pp. 638–39.

proportional representation for four years by universal adult suffrage. A Prime Minister and Cabinet take office after receiving a vote of confidence from the Knesset. The President is elected for a five-year term by the Knesset. Over ten political parties are represented in the Knesset – the largest are the (right wing) Likud Party and the (centre-left) Labour Alignment.
President: Chaim Herzog.
Prime Minister: Itzhak Shamir.

EDUCATION

Literacy rate: 88% Jews; 70% Arabs. *Years of compulsory schooling:* 5–15. *Universities:* 6.

DEFENCE

Total armed strength: 141 000 (1989). *Military service:* 36 and 24 months for men and women respectively.

GEOGRAPHY

Israel – within the boundaries established by the 1949 cease-fire line – consists of a fertile thin coastal plain beside the Mediterranean, parts of the arid mountains of Judaea in the centre, the Negev Desert in the south, and part of the Jordan Valley in the northeast. *Principal rivers:* Jordan (Yarden), Qishon. *Highest point:* Har Meron (Mt Atzmon) 1208 m (3963 ft).

Climate: Israel's climate is Mediterranean with hot, dry summers and mild, wetter winters. The greater part of Israel receives less than 200 mm (8 in) of rain a year.

ECONOMY

Severe economic problems stem, in part, from Israel's large defence budget and political circumstances, which prevent trade with neighbouring countries. Israel is a major producer and exporter of citrus fruit. Much land is irrigated and over 75% of Israel's arable land is farmed by collectives (kibbutzim) and cooperatives. Mineral resources are few, but processing imported diamonds is a major source of foreign currency. Tourism – to biblical sites – is important.

ITALY

Official name: Italia (Italy) or Repubblica Italiana (Republic of Italy).

Member of: UN, EC, NATO, WEU, G7, Council of Europe, OECD, CSCE.

Population: 57 436 000 (1989).

Capital and major cities: Rome (Roma) 2 817 000, Milan (Milano) 1 479 000, Naples (Napoli) 1 201 000, Turin (Torino) 1 025 000, Palermo 729 000, Genoa (Genova) 722 000, Bologna 427 000, Florence (Firenze) 421 000, Catania 372 000, Bari 359 000, Venice (Venezia) 328 000, Messina 271 000, Verona 259 000, Taranto 245 000, Trieste 237 000, Padua (Padova) 224 000, Caligari 222 000, Brescia 198 000, Reggio di Calabria 178 000, Modena 177 000, Parma 175 000, Livorno 173 000, Prato 165 000, Foggia 159 000, Salerno 154 000, Perugia 148 000 (1988).

Languages: Italian (official), with small minori-

ties speaking German, French and Albanian.
Religion: Roman Catholic (over 90%).
Life expectancy: 77 years.
Labour force: (1988) 24 000 000; community and social services 5 729 000, manufacturing 4 723 000, trade and tourism 4 528 000.

ITALY

Area: 301 277 km²
(116 324 sq mi)

GOVERNMENT

The two houses of Parliament are elected for a five-year term under a system of proportional representation. The Senate has 315 members elected by citizens aged 25 and over to represent the regions, plus two former Presidents and five life senators chosen by the President. The Chamber of Deputies has 630 members elected by citizens aged 18 and over. The President is elected for a seven-year term by an electoral college consisting of Parliament and 58 regional representatives. The President appoints a Prime Minister – who commands a majority in Parliament – and a Council of Ministers (Cabinet) who are responsible to Parliament. The main political parties include the (conservative) Christian Democrat Party, the Democratic Party of the Left (formerly the Communist Party), the PSI (Socialist Party), the RPI (Republican Party), the Radical Party, the Liberal Party, the Social Democratic Party, and the (right-wing) MSI-DN. The 20 regions of Italy have their own regional governments.
President: Francesco Cossiga.
Prime Minister: Giulio Andreotti.

ITALIAN REGIONS

The population figures for the regions and the cities are for 1984 and 1988 respectively.

Abruzzi *Area:* 10 794 km² (4168 sq mi). *Population:* 1 244 000. *Capital:* L'Aquila 66 000. *Largest city:* Pescara (which shares some of the functions of capital with L'Aquila) 131 000.

Basilicata *Area:* 9992 km² (3858 sq mi). *Population:* 617 000. *Capital:* Potenza 65 000.

Calabria *Area:* 15 080 km² (5822 sq mi). *Population:* 2 117 000. *Capital:* Catanzaro 102 000. *Largest city:* Reggio di Calabria 178 000.

Campania *Area:* 13 595 km² (5249 sq mi).

Population: 5 608 000. *Capital:* Naples (Napoli) 1 201 000.

Emilia Romagna *Area:* 22 123 km² (8542 sq mi). *Population:* 3 947 000. *Capital:* Bologna 427 000.

Fruili-Venezia Giulia *Area:* 7846 km² (3029 sq mi). *Population:* 1 224 000. *Capital:* Trieste 237 000.

Lazio *Area:* 17 203 km² (6642 sq mi). *Population:* 5 080 000. *Capital:* Rome (Roma) 2 817 000.

Liguria *Area:* 5413 km² (2090 sq mi). *Population:* 1 778 000. *Capital:* Genoa (Genova) 722 000.

Lombardy (Lombardia) *Area:* 23 834 km² (9202 sq mi). *Population:* 8 885 000. *Capital:* Milan (Milano) 1 479 000.

Marche *Area:* 9692 km² (3742 sq mi). *Population:* 1 424 000. *Capital:* Ancona 104 000.

Molise *Area:* 4438 km² (1714 sq mi). *Population:* 333 000. *Capital:* Campobasso 49 000.

Piedmont (Piemonte) *Area:* 25 399 km² (9807 sq mi). *Population:* 4 412 000. *Capital:* Turin (Torino) 1 025 000.

Puglia *Area:* 19 347 km² (7470 sq mi). *Population:* 3 978 000. *Capital:* Bari 359 000.

Sardinia (Sardegna) *Area:* 24 090 km² (9301 sq mi). *Population:* 1 629 000. *Capital:* Cagliari 222 000.

Sicily (Sicilia) *Area:* 25 708 km² (9926 sq mi). *Population:* 5 051 000. *Capital:* Palermo 729 000.

Tuscany (Toscana) *Area:* 22 992 km² (8877 sq mi). *Population:* 3 581 000. *Capital:* Florence (Firenze) 421 000.

Trentino-Alto Adige *Area:* 13 613 km² (5256 sq mi). *Population:* 877 000. *Capital:* Trento 101 000.

Umbria *Area:* 8456 km² (3265 sq mi). *Population:* 815 000. *Capital:* Perugia 148 000.

Valle d'Aosta *Area:* 3262 km² (1259 sq mi). *Population:* 114 000. *Capital:* Aosta 38 000.

Veneto *Area:* 18 368 km² (7092 sq mi). *Population:* 4 366 000. *Capital:* Venice (Venezia) 328 000.

EDUCATION

Literacy rate: 97% (1985 est). *Years of compulsory schooling:* 6–14. *Universities:* 59.

DEFENCE

Total armed strength: 390 000 (1989). *Military service:* 1 year.

GEOGRAPHY

The Alps form a natural boundary between Italy and its western and northern neighbours. A string of lakes – where the mountains meet the foothills – include Lakes Maggiore, Lugano and Como. The fertile Po Valley – the great lowland of northern Italy – lies between the Alpine foothills in the north, the foothills of the Apennine Mountains in the south, the Alps in the west and the Adriatic Sea in the east. The narrow ridge of the Ligurian Alps joins the Maritime Alps to the Apennines, which form a backbone down the entire length of the Italian peninsula. Coastal lowlands are few and relatively restricted but include the Arno Basin in Tuscany, the Tiber Basin around Rome, the Campania lowlands around Naples, and plains beside the Gulf of Taranto and in Puglia (the 'heel' of Italy). The two major islands of Italy – Sardinia and Sicily – are both largely mountainous. Much of Italy is geologically unstable and liable to earthquakes. The country has four active volcanoes, including Etna on Sicily and Vesuvius near Naples. *Principal rivers:* Po, Tiber

(Tevere), Arno, Volturno, Garigliano. *Highest point:* a point just below the summit of Monte Bianco (Mont Blanc) 4760 m (15 616 ft).
Climate: Italy enjoys a Mediterranean climate with warm, dry summers and mild winters. Sicily and Sardinia tend to be warmer and drier than the mainland. The Alps and the Po Valley experience colder, wetter winters.

ECONOMY
Northern Italy, with its easy access to the rest of Europe, is the main centre of Italian industry. The south, in contrast, remains mainly agricultural, producing grapes, sugar beet, wheat, maize, tomatoes and soya beans. The majority of farms are small – and many farmers in the south are resistant to change – thus incomes in southern Italy (the 'Mezzogiorno') are on average substantially lower than in the north. Agriculture in the north is more mechanized and major crops include wheat, maize, rice, grapes (for the important wine industry), fruit and fodder crops for dairy herds. Industrialization in the south is being actively promoted. The industries of the north are well developed and include electrical and electronic goods, motor vehicles and bicycles, textiles, clothing, leather goods, cement, glass, china and ceramics. The north is also an important financial and banking area, and Milan is the commercial capital of Italy. Apart from stone – in particular marble – and Alpine rivers that have been harnessed for hydroelectric power, Italy has few natural resources. Tourism and money sent back by Italians living abroad are important sources of foreign currency.

RECENT HISTORY
The kingdom of Italy – uniting most of the peninsula – was proclaimed in March 1861. Venetia (1866) and Rome (1870) were subsequently included. Political development after unification was unsteady. Overseas ventures – such as the attempt to annex parts of Ethiopia (1895–96) – were often frustrated. Parliament was held in low esteem and the end of the 19th century saw a series of assassinations – including King Umberto I in 1900. Italy entered World War I on the Allied side in the expectation of territorial gains from Austria. However, Italy won far less territory than anticipated in the peace treaties after the war, when fear of Communist revolution led to an upsurge of Fascism. The Fascist Benito Mussolini (1883–1945) became Prime Minister in 1922 with a programme of extensive domestic modernization and an aggressive foreign policy. In 1936 Italy allied with Germany in the Rome-Berlin Axis, and declared war on Britain and France in 1940. When Italy was invaded by Allied troops in 1943, Mussolini was dismissed by the king and Italy joined the Allies.

In 1946 a republic was proclaimed. Communist influence increased, both at local and national level – in 1976, for example, the Communists controlled the local administration in Rome, Naples, Florence and Bologna. However, the dominance of the (conservative) Christian Democrat Party has kept the Communists out of the succeeding coalitions that have ruled Italy. Particularly in the 1970s, terrorist movements – of both the left and the right – have been active, kidnapping and assassinating senior political and industrial figures, including the former PM Aldo Moro in 1978. Considerable attempts have been made to effect a true unification of the country by encouraging the economic development of the south.

However, the political structure of Italy remains unstable and coalitions have often been short-lived – between 1945 and 1991, 49 governments came to and fell from power.

IVORY COAST/CÔTE D'IVOIRE
Official name: La République de la Côte d'Ivoire (The Republic of the Ivory Coast). Since 1986 Côte d'Ivoire has been the only official name.
Member of: UN, OAU, ECOWAS.
Population: 12 135 000 (1989 est).
Capital and major cities: Yamoussoukro (de jure and administrative capital) 120 000, Abidjan (de facto and legislative capital) 1 850 000, Bouaké 220 000 (1987 est).
Languages: French (official), Dioula, Baoulé.
Religions: Animist (65%), Sunni Islam (nearly 25%), Roman Catholic (over 10%).
Life expectancy: 52.9 years.
Labour force: (1980 est) 3 547 000; agriculture and forestry 2 314 000, services 940 000, industry 293 000.

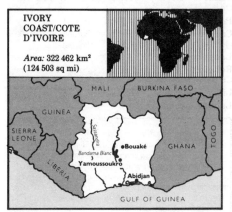

IVORY COAST/COTE D'IVOIRE

Area: 322 462 km² (124 503 sq mi)

GOVERNMENT
The President – who is elected for a five-year term by universal adult suffrage – appoints a Council of Ministers who are responsible to him. The 175-member National Assembly is also directly elected for five years. Until 1990, the Democratic Party was the only legal party, but the Ivorian Popular Front, the Workers' Party, the Socialist Party and the Social Democratic Party are now allowed to operate. *President:* Felix Houphouët-Boigny.

EDUCATION
Literacy rate: 43% (1985 est). *Years of compulsory schooling:* education is free at all levels but not compulsory. *Universities:* 4.

DEFENCE
Total armed strength: 7100 (1989). *Military service:* none.

GEOGRAPHY
The north is a savannah-covered plateau. In the south, tropical rain forest – increasingly cleared for plantations – ends at the narrow coastal plain. *Principal rivers:* Sassandra, Bandama, Komoé. *Highest point:* Mont Nimba 1752 m (5748 ft).

Climate: The south is equatorial with high temperatures and heavy rainfall; the north has similar temperatures but is drier.

ECONOMY

The country depends on exports of cocoa, coffee and timber, and suffered in the 1980s when prices for these commodities fell. Natural resources include petroleum, natural gas and iron ore. Political stability has helped economic growth.

RECENT HISTORY

Colonized by France in the 19th century, the Ivory Coast became a relatively prosperous part of French West Africa. Independence was achieved in 1960 under the presidency of Félix Houphouët-Boigny (1905–), who has kept close links with France in return for aid and military assistance, and is Africa's longest-serving president. Multi-party elections were held in 1990, but the opposition parties made claims of electoral fraud.

JAMAICA

Member of: UN, Commonwealth, CARICOM, OAS.

Population: 2 376 000 (1989).

Capital and major cities: Kingston 642 000 (1986 est), Spanish Town 81 000 (1982 est).

Language: English.

Religions: Anglican (20%), various Protestant Churches (over 50%).

Life expectancy: 73.8 years.

Labour force: 728 700.

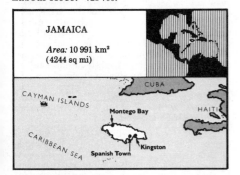

JAMAICA

Area: 10 991 km²
(4244 sq mi)

CAYMAN ISLANDS

CUBA

Montego Bay

HAITI

CARIBBEAN SEA

Spanish Town   Kingston

GOVERNMENT

The 60-member House of Representatives (the lower house of Parliament) is elected for five years by universal adult suffrage. The 21-member Senate is appointed on the advice of the Prime Minister and the Leader of the Opposition. The Governor General – the representative of the British Queen as sovereign of Jamaica – appoints a Prime Minister who commands a majority in the House. The PM, in turn, appoints a Cabinet of Ministers who are responsible to the House. The main political parties are the (radical) People's National Party and the (centre) Jamaican Labour Party.
Prime Minister: Michael Manley.

EDUCATION

Literacy rate: 85%. *Years of compulsory schooling:* 6–16. *Universities:* 1.

DEFENCE

Total armed strength: 2800 (1989). *Military service:* none.

GEOGRAPHY

Coastal lowlands surround the interior limestone plateaux (the 'Cockpit Country') and mountains. *Principal river:* Black River. *Highest point:* Blue Mountain Peak 2256 m (7402 ft).

Climate: The lowlands are tropical and rainy; the highlands are cooler and wetter. Jamaica is subject to hurricanes.

ECONOMY

Agriculture is the mainstay of the economy, with sugar cane and bananas as the main crops. Jamaica is one of the world's leading exporters of bauxite. Tourism is a major foreign-currency earner.

RECENT HISTORY

Jamaica became a British colony in the 17th century. By the 1930s, severe social and economic problems led to rioting and the birth of political awareness. Since independence in 1962, power has alternated between the radical People's National Party – led by Michael Manley – and the more conservative Jamaican Labour Party – whose leaders have included Sir Alexander Bustamente and Edward Seaga.

JAPAN

Official name: Nippon or Nihon ('The Land of the Rising Sun').

Member of: UN, G7, OECD.

Population: 123 120 000 (1989).

Capital and major cities: Tokyo 11 680 000, Yokohama 3 121 000, Osaka 2 544 000, Nagoya 2 100 000, Sapporo 1 582 000, Kobe 1 427 000, Kyoto 1 419 000, Fukuoka 1 157 000, Kawasaki 1 114 000, Hiroshima 1 043 000, Kitakyushu 1 035 000, Sendai 865 000, Sakai 808 000, Chiba 800 000 (including suburbs) (1988). The Keihin metropolitan area – Tokyo-Yokohama – had 29 272 000 inhabitants in 1985.

Language: Japanese.

Religions: Shintoism (about 75%) overlaps with Buddhism (nearly 60%), Soka Gakkai (7%), various Christian denominations (under 3%).

Life expectancy: 77.2 years.

Labour force: (1988) 61 660 000; services 17 140 000, trade and tourism 14 000 000, electricity, gas and water 14 500 000.

GOVERNMENT

The head of state is the Emperor who has no executive power. The 252-member House of Councillors – the upper house of the Diet (Parliament) – is elected for six years by universal adult suffrage. One half of the councillors retire every three years. A system of proportional representation is used to elect 50 of the councillors. The 512-member House of Representatives is elected for four years, also by universal adult suffrage. The Diet chooses a Prime Minister who commands a majority in the lower house. The PM in turn appoints a Cabinet of Ministers who are responsible to the Diet. The main political parties are the Liberal Democratic Party, the Socialist Party, Komeito (Clean Government Party), the Communist Party, and the Democratic Socialist Party.
Emperor: HIM the Heisei Emperor – known outside Japan as Emperor Akihito (who succeeded upon the death of his father, 7 January 1989).
Prime Minister: Toshiki Kaifu.

EDUCATION

Literacy rate: almost 100%. *Years of compulsory*

schooling: 6–15. *Universities:* 400 (public and private).

DEFENCE

Total armed strength: 247 000 (1989). *Military service:* none.

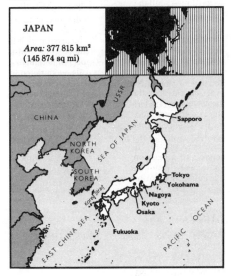

JAPAN

Area: 377 815 km²
(145 874 sq mi)

GEOGRAPHY

Japan consists of over 3900 islands, of which Hokkaido in the north occupies 22% of the total land area, and Shikoku and Kyushu in the south respectively occupy 5% and 11% of the area. The central island of Honshu occupies 61% of the total land area and contains 80% of the population. To the south of the four main islands, the Ryukyu Islands – including Okinawa – stretch almost to Taiwan. Nearly three quarters of Japan is mountainous. Coastal plains – where the population is concentrated – are limited. The principal lowlands are Kanto (around Tokyo), Nobi (around Nagoya) and the Sendai Plain in the north of Honshu. There are also over 60 active volcanoes in Japan, and the country is prone to severe earthquakes. *Principal rivers:* Tone, Ishikarai, Shinano, Kitakami. *Highest point:* Fujiyama (Mount Fuji) 3776 m (12 388 ft).

Climate: Japan experiences great variations in climate. Although the whole country is temperate, the north has long cold snowy winters, while the south has hot summers and mild winters. Rainfall totals are generally high, with heavy rain and typhoons being common in the summer months.

ECONOMY

Despite the generally crowded living conditions in the cities, the Japanese enjoy a high standard of living. The country has the second largest industrial economy in the world, despite having very few natural resources. Japanese industry is heavily dependent on imported raw materials – about 90% of the country's energy requirements come from abroad and petroleum is the single largest import. There is, therefore, considerable interest in offshore petroleum exploration, particularly in the Korean Straits. Japan's economic success is based on manufacturing industry, which – with construction – employs nearly one third of the labour force. Japan is the world's

leading manufacturer of motor vehicles, and one of the major producers of ships, steel, synthetic fibres, chemicals, cement, electrical goods and electronic equipment. Rapid advances in Japanese research and technology have helped the expanding export-led economy. The banking and financial sectors have prospered in line with the manufacturing sector, and Tokyo is one of the world's principal stock exchanges and commercial centres. Agriculture is labour intensive. Although Japan is self-sufficient in rice, agriculture is not a priority and a high percentage of its food requirements – particularly cereals and fodder crops – have to be imported. The traditional Japanese diet is sea-based and the fishing industry is a large one, both for export and for domestic consumption.

RECENT HISTORY

At the end of the 19th century, the Meiji Emperor overthrew the last shogun and restored power to the throne. He encouraged Western institutions and a Western-style economy, so that by the beginning of the 20th century Japan was rapidly industrializing and on the brink of becoming a world power. By the time of the death of the Meiji Emperor in 1912, the Japanese had established an empire. Japan had defeated China (1894–95) – taking Port Arthur and Taiwan – and startled Europe by beating Russia (1904–5) by land and at sea. Korea was annexed in 1910. Allied with Britain from 1902, Japan entered World War I against Germany in 1914, in part to gain acceptance as an imperial world power. However, Japan gained little except some of the German island territories in the Pacific and became disillusioned that the country did not seem to be treated as an equal by the Great Powers. The rise of militarism and collapse of world trade in the 1930s led to the rise of totalitarianism and a phase of aggressive Japanese expansion. In 1931 the Japanese army seized Chinese Manchuria, and in 1937 mounted an all-out attack on China itself, occupying large areas. Japan became allied to Nazi Germany and in 1941 Japanese aircraft struck Pearl Harbor in Hawaii, bringing the USA into World War II. An initial rapid Japanese military expansion across SE Asia and the Pacific was halted, and the war ended for Japan in disastrous defeat and the horrors of atomic warfare.

Emperor Hirohito (reigned 1926–89) surrendered in September 1945. Shintoism – which had come to be identified with aggressive nationalism – ceased to be the state religion, and in 1946 the emperor renounced his divinity. The Allied occupation (1945–52) both democratized politics and began an astonishing economic recovery based on an aggressive export policy. The economy was jolted by major rises in petroleum prices in 1973 and 1979, but Japan nevertheless maintained its advance to become a technological front-runner. By 1988 Japan surpassed the USA as the world's largest aid-donor. The Japanese political world is dominated by the Liberal Democrats, who have held office since 1955 despite a number of financial scandals in the 1980s.

JORDAN

Official name: Al-Mamlaka al-Urduniya al-Hashemiyah (The Hashemite Kingdom of Jordan).

Member of: UN, Arab League.

Population: 3 059 000 (1989) – East Bank only.

Capital and major cities: Amman 972 000, Zarqa 392 000, Irbid 271 000, Salt 134 000 (1986 est).

Language: Arabic (official).

Religion: Sunni Islam (over 90%).
Life expectancy: 66 years.
Labour force: (1986) 535 440; services 247 000, trade 54 000, transport 46 000.

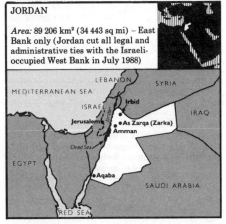

JORDAN

Area: 89 206 km² (34 443 sq mi) – East Bank only (Jordan cut all legal and administrative ties with the Israeli-occupied West Bank in July 1988)

GOVERNMENT

Jordan is a constitutional monarchy. The King appoints the 30 members of the Senate – the upper house of the National Assembly – and names a Prime Minister and Cabinet. The senators serve an eight-year term, with one half of their number retiring every four years. The 80 members of the House of Representatives are elected every four years by universal adult suffrage. Although political parties are technically banned, a number of parties are allowed to operate, including the Muslim Brotherhood.
King: HM King Hussein I (succeeded upon the deposition of his father, on grounds of illness, 11 August 1952).
Prime Minister: Mudar Badran.

EDUCATION

Literacy rate: 71% (1988 est). *Years of compulsory schooling:* 5–14. *Universities:* 9.

DEFENCE

Total armed strength: 82 250 (1989). *Military service:* none.

GEOGRAPHY

The steep escarpment of the East Bank Uplands borders the Jordan Valley and the Dead Sea. Deserts cover over 80% of the country. *Principal river:* Jordan (Urdun). *Highest point:* Jabal Ramm 1754 m (5755 ft).

Climate: The summers are hot and dry; the winters are cooler and wetter, although much of Jordan experiences very low rainfall.

ECONOMY

Apart from potash – the principal export – Jordan has few resources. Arable land accounts for only about 5% of the total area. Foreign aid and money sent back by Jordanians working abroad are major sources of foreign currency.

RECENT HISTORY

The area was conquered by the (Turkish) Ottoman Empire in the 16th century. In World War I the British aided an Arab revolt against Ottoman rule. The League of Nations awarded the area east of the River Jordan – Transjordan – to Britain as part of Palestine (1920), but in 1923 Transjordan became a separate emirate. In 1946 the country gained complete independence as the Kingdom of Jordan with Amir Abdullah (1880–1951) as its sovereign.

The Jordanian army fought with distinction in the 1948 Arab-Israeli War, and occupied the West Bank territories which were formally incorporated into Jordan in April 1950. In 1951 Abdullah was assassinated. His grandson King Hussein (reigned 1952–) was initially threatened by radicals encouraged by Egypt's President Nasser. In the 1967 Arab-Israeli War, Jordan lost the West Bank, including Arab Jerusalem, to the Israelis. In the 1970s the power of the Palestinian guerrillas in Jordan challenged the very existence of the Jordanian state. After a short but bloody civil war in September 1979 the Palestinian leadership fled abroad. King Hussein renounced all responsibility for the West Bank in 1988. The Palestinians – who form the majority of the Jordanian population – supported Iraq in the Gulf Crisis of 1990–91, although King Hussein adopted a position of neutrality.

KENYA

Official name: Jamhuri ya Kenya (Republic of Kenya).
Member of: UN, OAU, Commonwealth.
Population: 23 883 000 (1989).
Capital and major cities: Nairobi 1 429 000, Mombasa 426 000, Kisumu 167 000, Nakuru 48 000 (1985 est).
Languages: Swahili (official), English, Kikuyu, Luo, with over 200 tribal languages.
Religions: Animist (under 50%), Roman Catholic (over 15%), other Christians (10%).
Life expectancy: 56 years.
Labour force: (1988 est) 9 274 000; agriculture and forestry 7 200 000, industry 485 000, services 1 000 000.

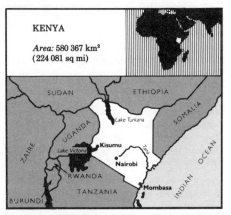

KENYA

Area: 580 367 km² (224 081 sq mi)

GOVERNMENT

The President and 188 members of the 202-member National Assembly are elected by universal adult suffrage every five years. The remaining 14 Assembly members, the Vice President and the Cabinet of Ministers are appointed by the President. KANU (Kenya African National Union) is the only legal

political party.
President: Daniel arap Moi.

EDUCATION

Literacy rate: 40% (1985 est). *Years of compulsory schooling:* education is available at all levels but schooling is not compulsory. *Universities:* 4.

DEFENCE

Total armed strength: 23 600 (1989). *Military service:* none.

GEOGRAPHY

The steep-sided Rift Valley divides the highlands that run from north to south through central Kenya. Plateaux extend in the west to Lake Victoria and in the east to coastal lowlands. *Principal rivers:* Tana, Umba, Athi, Mathioya. *Highest point:* Mount Kenya 5199 m (17 058 ft).

Climate: The coastal areas have a hot and humid equatorial climate. The highlands – which are cooler – experience high rainfall. The north is very hot and arid.

ECONOMY

Over 75% of the labour force is involved in agriculture. The main crops include wheat and maize for domestic consumption, and tea, coffee, sisal, sugar cane and cotton for export. Large numbers of beef cattle are reared, and Kenya is one of the few states in

black Africa to have a major dairy industry. Tourism is an important source of foreign currency.

RECENT HISTORY

The peoples of the area were forcibly brought under British rule in 1895 in the East African Protectorate, which became the colony of Kenya in 1920. White settlement in the highlands was bitterly resented by the Africans – particularly the Kikuyu – whose land was taken. Racial discrimination and attacks on African customs also created discontent. Black protest movements emerged in the 1920s, and after World War II these had developed into nationalism. From the 1920s, black protest was led by Jomo Kenyatta (c. 1893–1978), who in 1947 became the first president of the Kenya African Union. When the violent Mau Mau rising – which involved mainly Kikuyu people – broke out (1952–56), Kenyatta was held responsible and was imprisoned on doubtful evidence (1953–61). After the British had crushed the Mau Mau revolt in a bloody campaign, they negotiated with Kenyatta and the other African nationalists. Independence, under Kenyatta's KANU party, followed in 1963. His moderate leadership and pro-capitalist policies earned him British support and the gratitude of the remaining whites. His policies were continued by his successor, Daniel arap Moi, but considerable restrictions on political activity followed an attempted military coup in 1982. Violent demonstrations in favour of a multi-party state were suppressed in 1990.

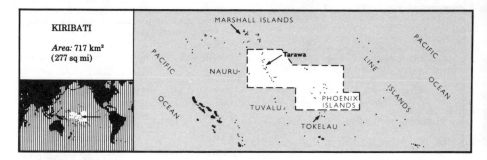

KIRIBATI

Area: 717 km² (277 sq mi)

MARSHALL ISLANDS

PACIFIC

NAURU

PACIFIC

OCEAN

Tarawa

LINE

TUVALU

PHOENIX ISLANDS

ISLANDS

PACIFIC

OCEAN

TOKELAU

KIRIBATI

Official name: Republic of Kiribati.

Member of: Commonwealth, South Pacific Forum.

Population: 68 000 (1988 est).

Capital: Tarawa 23 000 (1988).

Languages: English (official), I-Kiribati.

Religions: Roman Catholic, Kiribati Protestant.

Life expectancy: no figure available.

Labour force: (1985) 25 400; agriculture and fishing 15 000, trade and tourism 3 000, services 3 000.

GOVERNMENT

The President and 39 members of the Assembly are elected by universal adult suffrage every four years. An additional member for Banaba is appointed to the Assembly, whose members nominate three or four of their number as presidential candidates. The President appoints a Cabinet of Ministers, which is responsible to the Assembly. All the members of the Assembly are independents, although a political party has been formed in opposition.
President: Ieremia Tabai.

EDUCATION

Literacy rate: 90%. *Years of compulsory schooling:* 6–14. *Universities:* none, but Kiribati participates in the University of the South Pacific.

DEFENCE

Total armed strength: Kiribati has no armed forces.

GEOGRAPHY

With the exception of the island of Banaba – which is composed of phosphate rock – Kiribati comprises three groups of small coral atolls. There are no significant rivers. *Highest point:* 81 m (265 ft) on Banaba.

Climate: Kiribati has a maritime equatorial climate with high rainfall.

ECONOMY

Most islanders are involved in subsistence farming and fishing. The only significant export is copra.

RECENT HISTORY

In the 18th century, the atolls were discovered by British sea captains, including Thomas Gilbert. The

Gilbert Islands – which became British in 1892 – were occupied by Japan (1942–43). British nuclear weapons were tested on Christmas Island (1957–64). In 1979 the islands gained independence as Kiribati (pronounced Kiri-Bass).

KOREA, DEMOCRATIC PEOPLE'S REPUBLIC OF

Official name: Chosun Minchu-chui Inmin Konghwa-guk (Democratic People's Republic of Korea). Popularly known as North Korea.

Member of: UN (observer).

Population: 22 418 000 (1989 est).

Capital and major cities: Pyongyang 2 000 000, Hamhung 670 000, Chongjin 530 000, Sinuiju 330 000, Kaesong 310 000 (1986 est).

Language: Korean.

Religions: Buddhism, Confucianism, Daoism.

Life expectancy: 70 years.

Labour force: (1988 est) 9 891 000; agriculture and forestry 3 494 000, industry 2 373 000, services 2 111 000.

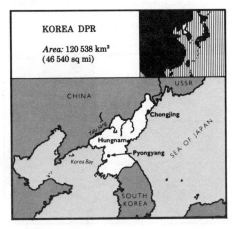

KOREA DPR

Area: 120 538 km²
(46 540 sq mi)

GOVERNMENT

The Party Congress of the (Communist) Korean Worker's Party elects a Central Committee, which in turn elects a Politburo, the seat of effective power. Citizens aged 17 and over vote in unopposed elections every four years for the 615-member Supreme People's Assembly. The Assembly elects the President, Prime Minister and Central People's Committee, which nominates Ministers.
President: Kim Il-Sung.
Prime Minister: Yon Hyong Muk.

EDUCATION

Literacy rate: no figure is available. *Years of compulsory schooling:* 5–16. *Universities:* 1.

DEFENCE

Total armed strength: 1 040 000 (1989). *Military service:* selective.

GEOGRAPHY

Over three quarters of the country consists of mountains. *Principal rivers:* Imjin, Ch'ongch'ŏn, Yalu. *Highest point:* Paek-tu 2744 m (9003 ft).

Climate: The country has long cold dry winters and hot wet summers.

ECONOMY

Almost 40% of the labour force work on cooperative farms, mainly growing rice. Natural resources include coal, zinc, magnetite, iron ore and lead. Great emphasis has been placed on industrial development, with the metallurgical, machine-building, chemical and cement industries being the most important.

RECENT HISTORY

Korea – a Japanese possession from 1910 to 1945 – was divided into zones of occupation in 1945. The USSR established a Communist republic in their zone north of the 38th parallel (1948). North Korea launched a surprise attack on the South in June 1950, hoping to achieve reunification by force. The Korean War devastated the peninsula. At the ceasefire in 1953 the frontier was re-established close to the 38th parallel. North Korea has the world's first Communist dynasty, whose personality cult has surpassed even that of Stalin. President Kim Il-Sung (1912–) and his son and anticipated successor, Kim Jong-Il, have rejected the reforms of perestroika.

KOREA, REPUBLIC OF

Official name: Daehan-Minkuk (Republic of Korea). Popularly known as South Korea.

Member of: UN (observer).

Population: 42 380 000 (1988 est).

Capital and major cities: Seoul (Soul) 10 513 000, Pusan 3 754 000, Taegu 2 206 000, Inchon 1 604 000, Kwangju 1 165 000 (1989), Taejon 866 000, Ulsan 551 000, Masan 449 000 (1985).

Language: Korean (official).

Religions: Buddhist (over 35%), various Christian Churches (nearly 25%).

Life expectancy: 69 years.

Labour force: (1988) 17 305 000; manufacturing 4 667 000, trade and tourism 3 647 000, agriculture and forestry 3 484 000.

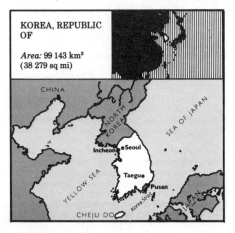

KOREA, REPUBLIC OF

Area: 99 143 km²
(38 279 sq mi)

GOVERNMENT

The 299-member National Assembly is elected by universal adult suffrage every four years – 224 members are directly elected to represent constituencies; the remaining 75 members are chosen under a system of proportional representation. The President – who appoints a State Council (Cabinet)

and a Prime Minister – is directly elected for a single five-year term. The main political parties include the Democratic Liberal Party (a merger of the Democratic Justice Party, the Reunification Democratic Party and the New Democratic Republican Party) and the Party for Peace and Democracy.
President: Roh Tae Woo.
Prime Minister: Ro Jaibong.

EDUCATION
Literacy rate: 95% (1985 est). *Years of compulsory schooling:* 6–12. *Universities:* 104 degree-awarding institutions and 251 graduate schools.

DEFENCE
Total armed strength: 650 000 (1989). *Military service:* 30–36 months.

GEOGRAPHY
Apart from restricted coastal lowlands and the densely-populated river basins, most of the country is mountainous. *Principal rivers:* Han, Kum, Naktong, Somjin, Yongsan. *Highest point:* Halla-san 1950 m (6398 ft) on Cheju Island.

Climate: Korea experiences cold dry winters and hot summers during which the monsoon brings heavy rainfall.

ECONOMY
About 20% of the labour force is involved in agriculture. The principal crops are rice, wheat and barley. A flourishing manufacturing sector is dominated by a small number of large family conglomerates. The important textile industry was the original manufacturing base, but South Korea is now the world's leading producer of ships and footwear, and a major producer of electronic equipment, electrical goods, steel, petrochemicals, motor vehicles (Hyundai) and toys. Banking and finance are expanding.

RECENT HISTORY
The Yi dynasty (1392–1910) gave Korea a long period of cultural continuity, but in 1910 Korea was annexed by the Japanese, who instituted a harsh colonial rule. After World War II, the peninsula was divided into Soviet and US zones of occupation. In 1948 the Republic of Korea was established in the American (southern) zone. The surprise invasion of the South by the Communist North precipitated the Korean War (1950–53). The war cost a million lives and ended in stalemate with the division of Korea confirmed. Closely allied to the USA, an astonishing economic transformation took place in South Korea. However, the country has experienced long periods of authoritarian rule including the presidencies of Syngman Rhee and Park Chung-Hee, but the ruler of ex-General Roh Tae Woo – amid political unrest in 1987 – introduced a more open regime. Much prestige was gained through the successful Seoul Olympic Games, and trading and diplomatic contacts have been established with the USSR and all the former Communist countries of Eastern Europe. This has left North Korea increasingly isolated. In 1990 North and South Korea tentatively began talks at prime ministerial level.

KUWAIT

Official name: Daulat al-Kuwait (State of Kuwait).

Member of: UN, Arab League, OPEC, GCC.

Population: 2 014 000 (1989 est). Immediately prior to the Iraqi invasion (August 1990), there were 800 000 Kuwaiti nationals. When Kuwait was liberated in February 1991, only 300 000 Kuwaitis remained inside the emirate. It was announced in February 1991 that most of the exiles would not be allowed to return until the infrastructure of the state had been restored. Almost one half of the 1 200 000 foreign workers before the invasion were Palestinian, the majority of whom fled. It was indicated in February 1991 that many of the foreign workers previously resident in Kuwait would not be allowed to return to the emirate.

Capital: Kuwait City 1 111 000 (including agglomeration; 1985).

Language: Arabic (official).

Religions: Sunni Islam (official; about 70%), Shia Islam (30%).

Life expectancy: no figure available.

Labour force: (Kuwaiti nationals only; 1985) 123 500; services 93 000, transport and communications 8000, trade and restaurants 6000. *Labour force including foreign nationals:* 662 588; services 326 729, construction 124 156 (including 1462 Kuwaitis), trade and restaurants 75 931, transport and communications 37 205.

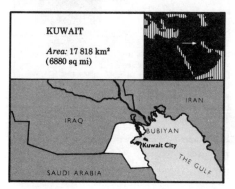

KUWAIT

Area: 17 818 km² (6880 sq mi)

GOVERNMENT
Kuwait is a monarchy ruled by an Amir, who is chosen from and by the adult male members of the ruling dynasty. The Amir appoints a Prime Minister and a Council of Ministers. There is constitutional provision for a 50-member National Assembly elected for four years by literate adult male Kuwaiti nationals whose families fulfil stringent residence qualifications. In 1986 the Amir suspended the constitution and has since ruled by decree. There are no political parties.
Amir: HH Shaikh Jabir III bin Ahmad as-Sabah (succeeded upon the death of his cousin, 31 December 1977).
Prime Minister: HH Shaikh Saad al-Abdullah as-Sabah, Crown Prince of Kuwait.

EDUCATION
Literacy rate: 75% (1985 est). *Years of compulsory schooling:* education is free 4–18 but not compulsory. *Universities:* 1.

DEFENCE
Total armed strength: 20 300 (1989). *Military service:* 2 years.

GEOGRAPHY
Most of the country is desert, relatively flat and low lying. There are no permanent rivers. *Highest point:* 289 m (951 ft) at Ash Shaqaya.

Climate: Kuwait experiences extremely high temperatures in summer. Almost all the annual rainfall of 100 mm (4 in) comes during the cooler winter.

ECONOMY
The Kuwaiti economy was devastated by the Iraqi invasion and the Second Gulf War. Large reserves of petroleum and natural gas were the mainstay of Kuwait's economy. However, the retreating Iraqis set some 500 wells ablaze. It was indicated in February 1991, that commercial oil production would not be possible until November 1991 at the earliest. Before the invasion, industry, based mainly on these resources, included petrochemicals and fertilizers. Owing to lack of water, little agriculture is possible.

RECENT HISTORY
In 1760 the Sabah family created the emirate that has lasted to today, although from 1899 to 1961 Kuwait was a British-protected state. Oil was discovered in 1938 and was produced commercially from 1946. Iraq attempted to take over Kuwait in 1961, but the dispatch of British troops to the Gulf discouraged an Iraqi invasion. On 2 August 1990 – despite having recognized the emirate's sovereignty in 1963 – Iraq invaded Kuwait. On 8 August, the Iraqi president, Saddam Hussein, declared that Kuwait was Iraq's 19th province. Iraq refused to withdraw despite repeated UN demands and on 16 January 1991 the war to remove Iraqi forces from Kuwait – the Second Gulf War – began. On 24 February, coalition forces entered the emirate to liberate Kuwait from Iraqi rule. The emirate was freed within 100 hours in a campaign during which the Iraqi forces were routed. The country was found to have been devastated by the occupying Iraqi forces. After the liberation of Kuwait, pressure for constitutional reform grew.

LAOS
Official name: Saathiaranagroat Prachhathippatay Prachhachhon Lao (The Lao People's Democratic Republic).

Member of: UN.

Population: 3 936 000 (1989).

Capital and major cities: Vientiane (Viengchane) 377 000 (1985), Savannakhet 51 000, Pakse 45 000, Luang Prabang 44 000 (1980 est).

Language: Lao (official).

Religion: Buddhism (over 90%).

Life expectancy: 49 years.

Labour force: (1988 est) 1 851 000; agriculture and forestry 1 341 000, industry 130 000, services 315 000.

GOVERNMENT
Effective power is exercised by the Central Committee of the (Communist) Lao People's Revolutionary Party. Pending the implementation of a new constitution, representatives of directly elected local authorities have met as the National Congress to appoint the President, the Prime Minister and the Council of Ministers. There is constitutional provision for a 79-member Supreme People's Assembly to be elected for five years by universal adult suffrage.
Acting President: Phoumi Vongvichit.
Prime Minister: Kaysone Phomvihan.

LAOS
Area: 236 800 km² (91 400 sq mi)

EDUCATION
Literacy rate: 74% (1985 est). *Years of compulsory schooling:* education is available but not compulsory. *Universities:* 1 medical university, plus 8 institutions of university level.

DEFENCE
Total armed strength: 55 150 (1989). *Military service:* 18 months.

GEOGRAPHY
Except for the Plain of Jars in the north and the Mekong Valley and low plateaux in the south, Laos is largely mountainous. *Principal river:* Mekong. *Highest point:* Phou Bia 2820 m (9252 ft).

Climate: Laos has a tropical climate with heavy monsoon rains between May and October.

ECONOMY
War, floods and drought have retarded the development of Laos, one of the poorest countries in the world. The majority of Laotians work on collective farms, mainly growing rice. Since 1990, the Laotian government has attempted to encourage Western investment.

RECENT HISTORY
A French protectorate was established in 1893. Japanese occupation in World War II led to a declaration of independence, which the French finally accepted in 1954. However, the kingdom was wracked by civil war, with royalist forces fighting the Communist Pathet Lao. The Viet Cong used Laos as a supply route in the Vietnam War, and US withdrawal from Vietnam allowed the Pathet Lao to take over Laos (1975). Since 1990, the government has begun to introduce reforms, but there is no suggestion that a multi-party system will be tolerated.

LEBANON
Official name: Al-Lubnan (The Lebanon).

Member of: UN, Arab League.

Population: 2 828 000 (1988 est).

Capital and major cities: Beirut (Bayrūt) 200 000, Tripoli (Tarabulus) 500 000, Zahleh 200 000, Saida 100 000 (1989 est; following considerable movement of population during the civil war).

Languages: Arabic (official).

Religions: Islam (57%; Shiite majority, Sunni and Druze minorities), Christian (43%; Maronite majority, with Armenian, Greek Orthodox, Syrian and other minorities).

Life expectancy: 67 years.

Labour force: (employment figures; 1985 est) 453 000; services 171 000, agriculture and forestry 104 000, trade, hotels and restaurants 78 000.

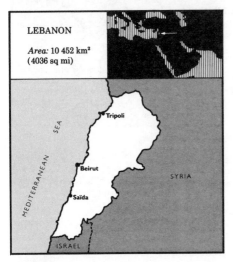

LEBANON

Area: 10 452 km²
(4036 sq mi)

Tripoli

SEA

Beirut

SYRIA

MEDITERRANEAN

Saïda

ISRAEL

GOVERNMENT

The constitution was amended in 1991 to provide for the election by universal adult suffrage of an 108-member National Assembly (comprising 54 deputies elected by Muslims and 54 deputies elected by Christians). The Assembly elects a (Maronite) President, who appoints a (Sunni Muslim) Prime Minister, who, in turn, appoints a Council of Ministers (six Christians and five Muslims).
President: Elias Hrawi.
Prime Minister: Umar Karami.

EDUCATION

Literacy rate: 77% (1985 est). *Years of compulsory schooling:* education is free 5–17 but not compulsory.
Universities: 5.

DEFENCE

Total armed strength: 22 300 (Christian and Muslim sectors; 1989). *Military service:* none.

GEOGRAPHY

A narrow coastal plain is separated from the fertile Beka'a Valley by the mountains of Lebanon. To the east are the Anti-Lebanese range and Hermon Mountains. *Principal rivers:* Nahr al-Litāni. *Highest point:* Qurnat as-Sawdā 3088 m (10 131 ft).

Climate: The lowlands have a Mediterranean climate. The cooler highlands experience heavy snowfall in winter.

ECONOMY

Civil war has devastated the economy. Unemployment is high and the basic infrastructure has broken down.

RECENT HISTORY

Intercommunal friction was never far from the sur-

face when the Ottomamn Turks ruled Lebanon. A massacre of thousands of Maronites by the Druzes (1860) brought French intervention. After World War I, France received Syria as a League of Nations mandate, and created a separate Lebanese territory to protect Christian interests. The constitution under which Lebanon became independent in 1943 enshrined power-sharing between Christians and Muslims. The relative toleration between the various religious groups in Lebanon began to break down in the late 1950s when Muslim numerical superiority failed to be matched by corresponding constitutional changes. Radical Muslim supporters of the union of Syria and Egypt in 1958 clashed with the pro-Western party of Camille Chamoun (President 1952–58). Civil war ensued, and US marines landed in Beirut to restore order. The 1967 Arab-Israeli war and the exile of the Palestinian leadership to Beirut (1970–71) destabilized Lebanon. Civil war broke out in 1975, with subsequent Syrian and Israeli interventions. The war continued, plunging the country into ungovernable chaos, with Maronites, various Sunni and Shia Lebanese groups (including Iranian-backed fundamentalists), Syrian troops, Druze militia and UN peace-keeping forces all occupying zones of the fragmented country. In 1990, the Christian militia of Michel Aoun was crushed by the Syrians and the Lebanese government was able to reassert its authority over the whole of Beirut. However, Israeli-sponsored forces continue to occupy the south and the (Islamic fundamentalist) Hizbollah forces control the Beka'a Valley.

LESOTHO

Official name: The Kingdom of Lesotho.

Member of: UN, Commonwealth, OAU, SADCC.

Population: 1 715 000 (1989).

Capital: Maseru 106 000 (1986).

Languages: Sesotho and English (official).

Religions: Roman Catholic (40%), with Lesotho Evangelical and Anglican minorities.

Life expectancy: 56 years.

Labour force: (1988 est) 784 000; agriculture and forestry 636 000, services 65 000, industry 28 000.

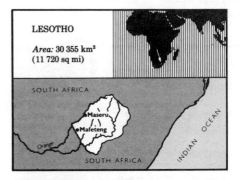

LESOTHO

Area: 30 355 km²
(11 720 sq mi)

SOUTH AFRICA

Maseru
Mafeteng

OCEAN

Orange

INDIAN

SOUTH AFRICA

GOVERNMENT

Since a military coup in 1986, Lesotho has been ruled by a six-man Military Council and a Council of Ministers. There are no political parties.
King: HM King Letsie III (succeeded upon the exile and deposition of his father, 12 November 1990).
Head of government (Chair of the Military Council): Col. Elias Ramaema.

EDUCATION

Literacy rate: 74% (1985 est). *Years of compulsory schooling:* 6–13. *Universities:* 1.

DEFENCE

Total armed strength: 2000 (1989). *Military service:* none.

GEOGRAPHY

Most of Lesotho is mountainous. *Principal rivers:* Orange, Caledon. *Highest point:* Thabana Ntlenyana 3482 m (11 425 ft).

Climate: Lesotho has a mild subtropical climate with lower temperatures in the highlands.

ECONOMY

Livestock – cattle, sheep and goats (for mohair) – are the mainstay of the economy. Natural resources include diamonds and abundant water, which is exported to South Africa.

RECENT HISTORY

Lesotho was founded in the 1820s by the Sotho leader, Moshoeshoe I (c. 1790–1870). The kingdom escaped incorporation into South Africa by becoming a British protectorate (known as Basutoland) in 1868. Although independence was achieved in 1966, the land-locked state remained dependent on South Africa. Chief Jonathan (Prime Minister 1966–86) – who curbed the monarchy's powers and attempted to limit South African influence – was deposed in a military coup. In 1990, the Military Council exiled King Moshoeshoe II and placed his son on the throne.

LIBERIA

Official name: The Republic of Liberia.
Member of: UN, OAU, ECOWAS.
Population: 2 508 000 (1989).
Capital: Monrovia 465 000 (1987 est).
Language: English (official).
Religions: Animist majority, with Sunni Islam and various Christian minorities.
Life expectancy: 54 years.
Labour force: (1980) 549 000; agriculture and forestry 393 000, services 55 000, mining 28 000.

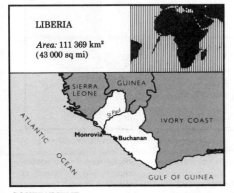

LIBERIA

Area: 111 369 km²
(43 000 sq mi)

SIERRA LEONE
GUINEA
ATLANTIC OCEAN
St Paul
Monrovia
Buchanan
IVORY COAST
GULF OF GUINEA

GOVERNMENT

The constitution provides for a President, Vice President, 26-member Senate and 64-member House of Representatives to be elected for six years by universal adult suffrage. The President appoints a Cabinet of Ministers. The Liberian political system broke down in 1990 owing to civil war.
Head of state: (acting president): Amos Sawyer. Two rebel leaders also claim to be president.

EDUCATION

Literacy rate: 35% (1985 est). *Years of compulsory schooling:* 6–16. *Universities:* 1.

DEFENCE

Total armed strength: 5800 (1989). *Military service:* none.

GEOGRAPHY

A low swampy coastal belt borders a higher zone of tropical forest. *Principal rivers:* St Paul, St John, Cess. *Highest point:* Mount Nimba 1380 m (4540 ft).

Climate: Liberia has a tropical climate with a wet season in the summer and a dry season in winter.

ECONOMY

Three quarters of the labour force is involved in agriculture, producing cassava and rice as subsistence crops, and rubber, coffee and cocoa for export. Liberia is a major exporter of iron ore, but the economy has been shattered by civil war.

RECENT HISTORY

Founded by the American Colonization Society in 1821–22 as a settlement for freed slaves, Liberia was declared a republic in 1847. Black American settlers dominated the local Africans and extended their control inland. From 1878 to 1980 power was held by presidents from the True Whig Party, including William Tubman (President 1944–71). His successor, William Tolbert, was assassinated during a military coup led by Samuel Doe, the first Liberian of local ancestry to rule. Doe was overthrown in a coup in 1990. Troops from several West African countries were dispatched by ECOWAS to restore order but civil war between the rebel forces of Charles Taylor and Prince Yormie Johnson continued until a ceasefire was signed early in 1991.

LIBYA

Official name: Daulat Libiya al-'Arabiya al-Ishtrakiya al-Jumhuriya (The Great Socialist People's Libyan Arab Jamahiriya).
Member of: UN, Arab League, OPEC.
Population: 4 232 000 (1988 est).
Capital and major cities: Tripoli (Tarabulus) 991 000, Benghazi (Banghazi) 485 000, Misurata (Misratah) 178 000 (1984). In 1988 government functions were decentralized to Sirte (Surt) and Al Jofrah as well as Tripoli and Benghazi.
Language: Arabic (official).
Religion: Sunni Islam (over 97%).
Life expectancy: 66 years.
Labour force: (1981 est) 800 000; construction 165 000, services 191 000, agriculture and forestry 147 000.

GOVERNMENT

Over 1000 delegates from directly elected local Basic People's Congresses, trade unions, 'popular committees' and professional organizations meet as the Great People's Congress, which chooses a Revolutionary Leader – head of state – and the General

LIBYA

Area: 1 759 540 km²
(679 363 sq mi)

international terrorism provoked US air raids on
Tripoli and Benghazi in 1986, since when Gaddafi has
kept a lower international profile.

LIECHTENSTEIN

Official name: Fürstentum Liechtenstein (The
Principality of Liechtenstein).

Member of: UN, Council of Europe, CSCE.

Population: 28 000 (1988 est).

Capital and major settlements: Vaduz 4900,
Schaan 4800 (1989).

Language: German (official).

Religion: Roman Catholic (over 85%).

Life expectancy: no figure available.

Labour force: (employment figures; 1987 est)
13 000; services 7000, industry and commerce 6000,
agriculture and forestry 400.

People's Committee (which is equivalent to a
Council of Ministers). The appointed General Secret-
ariat assists the Congress. There are no political
parties.
Head of state: Moamar al Gaddafi.
*Head of government (Secretary-General of the General
People's Committee):* Omar al-Muntasser.

EDUCATION
Literacy rate: 67% (1985 est). *Years of compulsory
schooling:* 6–15. *Universities:* 4.

DEFENCE
Total armed strength: 87 500 (including 2500 in the
'Islamic pan-African legion'; 1989). *Military service:*
3 years army, 4 years navy and air force.

GEOGRAPHY
The Sahara Desert covers most of Libya. In the
northwest – Tripolitania – coastal oases and a low
plain form the country's main agricultural region. In
the northeast (Cyrenaica) a coastal plain and mountain ranges support Mediterranean vegetation. *Principal river:* Wādi al-Fārigh. *Highest point:* Pico Bette
2286 m (7500 ft).

Climate: Libya is hot and dry, with lower temperatures and higher rainfall near the coast.

ECONOMY
Libya is one of the world's largest producers of
petroleum. Liquefied gas is also exported. Coastal
oases produce wheat, barley, nuts, dates and grapes.

RECENT HISTORY
In 1911 the Italians took Libya, which had been under
Ottoman (Turkish) rule since the 16th century. The
British Eighth Army defeated the Italians in the
Libyan Desert (1942), and after World War II the
country was divided between British and French
administrations. Libya gained independence in 1951
under King Idris, formerly Amir of Cyrenaica.
Although oil revenues made Libya prosperous, the
pro-Western monarchy became increasingly unpopular. In 1969 junior army officers led by Col.
Moamar al Gaddafi (1942–) took power. Gaddafi
nationalized the oil industry, but his various
attempts to federate with other Arab countries
proved abortive. In the 1970s he began a cultural
revolution, dismantled formal government, collectivized economic activity, limited personal wealth and
suppressed opposition. Libya's alleged support of

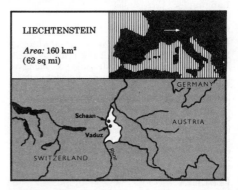

LIECHTENSTEIN

Area: 160 km²
(62 sq mi)

GOVERNMENT
The country is a constitutional monarchy ruled by a
Prince. The 25-member Landstag (Parliament) is
elected under a system of proportional represen-
tation by universal adult suffrage for four years. The
Landstag elects a 5-member National Committee
(Cabinet) including a Prime Minister, who is for-
mally appointed by the Prince. The main political
parties are the VU (Fatherland Union) and the FBP
(Progressive Citizens' Party).
Prince: HSH Prince Hans Adam II (succeeded upon
the death of his father, 13 November 1989).
Prime Minister: Hans Brunhart.

EDUCATION
Literacy rate: 100%. *Years of compulsory schooling:*
7–15. *Universities:* none.

DEFENCE
Total armed strength: defence is the responsibility of
Switzerland.

GEOGRAPHY
The Alps stand in the east of the principality. The
west comprises the floodplain of the River Rhine.
Principal rivers: Rhine (Rhein), Samina. *Highest
point:* Grauspitze 2599 m (8326 ft).

Climate: The country has a mild Alpine climate.

ECONOMY
Liechtenstein has one of the highest standards of
living in the world. Tourism, banking and manufacturing (precision goods) are all important.

RECENT HISTORY

Separated from Germany by Austrian territory, Liechtenstein was the only German principality not to join the German Empire in 1871. Since 1924 the country has enjoyed a customs and monetary union with Switzerland, although since 1989 the country has taken a more active role internationally, for instance joining the UN.

LUXEMBOURG

Official name: Grand-Duché de Luxembourg (Grand Duchy of Luxembourg).

Member of: UN, EC, NATO, WEU, CSCE, OECD, Council of Europe.

Population: 377 000 (1989).

Capital: Luxembourg 120 000 (including suburbs), Esch-sur-Alzette 24 000, Differdange 16 000, Dudelange 14 000, Petange 12 000 (1988).

Languages: Letzeburgish (national), French (official), German.

Religions: Roman Catholic (97%).

Life expectancy: 74 years.

Labour force: (1988 est) 175 000; trade and tourism 64 000, mining and manufacturing 37 000, community and social services 24 000.

LUXEMBOURG

Area: 2586 km² (999 sq mi)

GOVERNMENT

Luxembourg is a constitutional monarchy with a Grand Duke or Duchess as sovereign. The 60-member Chamber of Deputies is elected under a system of proportional representation by universal adult suffrage for five years. A Council of Ministers and a President of the Council (Premier) – commanding a majority in the Chamber – are appointed by the sovereign. The main political parties are the (centre-right) Social Christian Party, the Socialist Party, and the (liberal) Democratic Party.
Grand Duke: HRH Grand Duke Jean I (succeeded upon the abdication of his mother, 12 November 1964).
Prime Minister: Jacques Santer.

EDUCATION

Literacy rate: 100%. *Years of compulsory schooling:* 6–15. *Universities:* 1.

DEFENCE

Total armed strength: 800, plus 500 gendarmes. *Military service:* none.

GEOGRAPHY

The Oesling is a wooded plateau in the north. The Gutland in the south is a lowland region of valleys and ridges. *Principal rivers:* Moselle, Sûre, Our, Alzette. *Highest point:* Huldange 550 m (1833 ft).

Climate: Luxembourg has cool summers and mild winters.

ECONOMY

The iron and steel industry – originally based on local ore – is important. Luxembourg has become a major banking centre. The north grows potatoes and fodder crops; the south produces wheat and fruit, including grapes.

RECENT HISTORY

In 1815 Luxembourg became a Grand Duchy with the Dutch king as sovereign, but in 1890 it was inherited by a junior branch of the House of Orange. Occupied by the Germans during both World Wars, Luxembourg concluded an economic union with Belgium in 1922 and has enthusiastically supported European unity.

MADAGASCAR

Official name: Repoblika Demokratika n'i Madagaskar (The Democratic Republic of Madagascar).

Member of: UN, OAU.

Population: 11 602 000 (1989 est).

Capital and major cities: Antananarivo (Tananarive) 663 000 (1985 est), Toamasina 83 000 (1982), Antsirabé 79 000, Fianarantsoa 68 000, Mahajanga 66 000 (1975).

Languages: Malagasy and French (official).

Religions: Animist majority, Roman Catholic (20%), various Protestant Churches (20%).

Life expectancy: 51.5 years.

Labour force: (1988 est) 4 920 000; agriculture and forestry 3 800 000, services 540 000, industry 245 000.

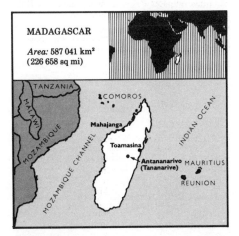

MADAGASCAR

Area: 587 041 km² (226 658 sq mi)

GOVERNMENT

The President is elected by universal adult suffrage for a seven-year term. He and the Supreme Revolutionary Council together appoint a Prime Minister and a Council of Ministers. The 137-member National Assembly is directly elected for five years. A ban on political parties was lifted in March 1990,

since when several parties have been formed.
President: Admiral Didier Ratsiraka.
Prime Minister: Col. Victor Ramahatra.

EDUCATION

Literacy rate: 68% (1985 est). *Years of compulsory schooling:* 6–13. *Universities:* 1.

DEFENCE

Total armed strength: 21 000 (1989). *Military service:* none.

GEOGRAPHY

Massifs form a spine running from north to south through the island. To the east is a narrow coastal plain; to the west are fertile plains. *Principal rivers:* Ikopa, Mania, Mangoky. *Highest point:* Maromokotro Tsaratanana Massif 2885 m (9465 ft).

Climate: The climate is tropical, although the highlands are cooler. The north receives monsoon rains, but the south is dry.

ECONOMY

Three quarters of the labour force are involved in agriculture. The main crops are coffee and vanilla for export, and rice and cassava for domestic consumption. The island also produces chromite.

RECENT HISTORY

In the early 19th century, the island was united by the Merina kingdom. The Merina sovereigns attempted to modernize Madagascar but the island was annexed by France in 1896, although resistance continued until 1904. Strong nationalist feeling found expression in a major rising (1947–48) that was only suppressed with heavy loss of life. Independence was finally achieved in 1960, but the pro-Western rule of President Philibert Tsirana became increasingly unpopular. Since a military coup in 1972, Madagascar has had left-wing governments, but political and economic liberalization began in 1990.

MALAWI

Official name: The Republic of Malawi.

Member of: UN, Commonwealth, OAU, SADCC.

Population: 8 515 000 (1989).

Capital and major cities: Lilongwe 220 000, Blantyre 500 000, Mzuzu 115 000 (1987 est).

Languages: English (official), Chichewa.

Religions: Animist majority, Roman Catholic (10%), Presbyterian (under 10%).

Life expectancy: 46 years.

Labour force: (1988 est) 3 410 000; agriculture and forestry 2 623 000, manufacturing 85 000, community and social services 83 000.

GOVERNMENT

Under the constitution the President is directly elected, but in 1971 Dr Hastings Kamuzu Banda was declared President for life. Elections are held by universal adult suffrage every five years for 112 members of the National Assembly. The President appoints additional members as well as a Cabinet of Ministers. The Malawi Congress Party is the only legal party.
President: Dr Hastings Kamuzu Banda.

EDUCATION

Literacy rate: 42% (1985 est). *Years of compulsory schooling:* education is not compulsory. *Universities:* 1.

DEFENCE

Total armed strength: 7250 (1989). *Military service:* none.

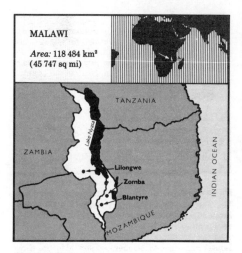

MALAWI

Area: 118 484 km²
(45 747 sq mi)

GEOGRAPHY

Plateaux cover the north and centre. The Rift Valley contains Lake Malawi and the Shire Valley. The Shire Highlands lie on the Mozambique border. *Principal river:* Shire. *Highest point:* Mount Sapitawa 3002 m (9849 ft).

Climate: Malawi has an equatorial climate with heavy rainfall from November to April.

ECONOMY

Agriculture is the mainstay of the economy, providing most of Malawi's exports. Tobacco, maize, tea and sugar cane are the main crops.

RECENT HISTORY

David Livingstone and other British missionaries became active in the area from the 1860s. A British protectorate, later called Nyasaland, was declared in 1891. In 1915 the Rev. John Chilembwe led a violent rising in the fertile south where Africans had lost much land to white settlers. Dr Hastings Kamuzu Banda (c. 1902–) led the country's opposition to the resented union with the white-dominated Central African Federation (1953–63). Since independence as Malawi in 1964, Banda has provided strong rule and – despite criticism – maintained close relations with South Africa.

MALAYSIA

Official name: Persekutuan Tanah Melaysiu (The Federation of Malaysia).

Member of: UN, Commonwealth, ASEAN.

Population: 17 421 000 (1989 est).

Capital and major cities: Kuala Lumpur 938 000, Ipoh 301 000, George Town 251 000, Johor Baharu 250 000, Petaling Jaya 208 000, Kelang 192 000, Kuala Trengganu 187 000, Kota Baharu 171 000, Kuantan 137 000, Seramban 136 000, Kuching 120 000 (1981).

Languages: Bahasa Malaysia (Malay; official; over 57%), English, Chinese (33%), Tamil.

Religions: Sunni Islam (official; over 55%), with Buddhist, Daoist and various Christian minorities.

Life expectancy: 70 years (west Malaysia only).

Labour force: (1988 est) 6 600 000; agriculture and forestry 1 908 000, trade and tourism 1 070 000, manufacturing 1 013 000.

MALAYSIA

Area: 329 758 km²
(127 320 sq mi)

GOVERNMENT

The Yang di-Pertuan Agong (the King of Malaysia) holds office for five years. He is elected – from their own number – by the hereditary sultans who reign in 9 of the 13 states. The 69-member Senate (upper house) comprises 43 members appointed by the King and two members elected by each of the state assemblies for a three-year term. The 177-member House of Representatives is elected by universal adult suffrage for five years. The King appoints a Prime Minister and a Cabinet commanding a majority in the House, to which they are responsible. The main political parties include the National Front (a coalition of parties including UMNO – the United Malays National Organization) and Spirit of '46. Each state has its own parliament and government.
King of Malaysia: HM Azlan Shah (ibni Sultan Yusof Izzudin), Raja of Perak, Yang di-Pertuan Agong.
Prime Minister: Mohamad Mahathir.

MALAYSIAN STATES

Population figures are for 1981.

Johore (Johor) (sultanate) *Area:* 18 985 km² (7330 sq mi). *Population:* 1 602 000. *Capital:* Johor Baharu 250 000.

Kedah (sultanate) *Area:* 9425 km² (3639 sq mi). *Population:* 1 102 000. *Capital:* Alor Star (Alur Setar) 72 000.

Kelantan (sultanate) *Area:* 14 931 km² (5765 sq mi). *Population:* 787 000. *Capital:* Kota Baharu 171 000.

Malacca *Area:* 1650 km² (637 sq mi). *Population:* 453 000. *Capital:* Malacca 88 000.

Negeri Sembilan (sultanate) *Area:* 6643 km² (2565 sq mi). *Population:* 564 000. *Capital:* Seremban 136 000.

Pahang (sultanate) *Area:* 35 965 km² (13 886 sq mi). *Population:* 771 000. *Capital:* Kuantan 137 000.

Penang (Pinang) *Area:* 1033 km² (399 sq mi). *Population:* 912 000. *Capital:* George Town 251 000.

Perak (sultanate) *Area:* 21 005 km² (8110 sq mi). *Population:* 1 762 000. *Capital:* Ipoh 301 000.

Perlis (sultanate) *Area:* 795 km² (307 sq mi). *Population:* 148 000. *Capital:* Kangar 13 000.

Sabah *Area:* 80 520 km² (29 388 sq mi). *Population:* 982 000. *Capital:* Kota Kinabalu 60 000. *Largest city:* Sandakan 74 000.

Sarawak *Area:* 121 449 km² (48 250 sq mi). *Population:* 1 295 000. *Capital:* Kuching 120 000.

Selangor (sultanate) *Area:* 7962 km² (3074 sq mi). *Population:* 1 468 000. *Capital:* Shah Alam 24 000. *Largest city:* Port Kelang 192 000.

Trengganu (sultanate) *Area:* 12 955 km² (5002 sq

mi). *Population:* 542 000. *Capital:* Kuala Trengganu 187 000.

Federal Territory *Area:* 243 km² (94 sq mi). *Population:* 938 000. *Capital:* Kuala Lumpur 938 000.

EDUCATION

Literacy rate: 65% (1989). *Years of compulsory schooling:* education is free but not compulsory. *Universities:* 7.

DEFENCE

Total armed strength: 129 500 (1989). *Military service:* none.

GEOGRAPHY

Western (peninsular) Malaysia consists of mountain ranges – including the Trengganu Highlands and Cameron Highlands – running north to south and bordered by densely populated coastal lowlands. Tropical rainforest covers the hills and mountains of Eastern Malaysia – Sabah and Sarawak, the northern part of the island of Borneo. *Principal rivers:* Pahang, Kelantan. *Highest point:* Kinabalu (in Sabah) 4101 m (13 455 ft).
Climate: Malaysia has a tropical climate with heavy rainfall (up to 2500 mm / 100 in in the west). There is more seasonal variation in precipitation than temperature, with the northeast monsoon (from October to February) and the southwest monsoon (from May to September) bringing increased rainfall, particularly to peninsular Malaysia.

ECONOMY

Rubber, petroleum and tin are the traditional mainstays of the Malaysian economy, but all three suffered drops in price on the world market in the 1980s. Pepper (mainly from Sarawak), cocoa and timber are also important. Nearly one third of the labour force is involved in agriculture, with large numbers of Malays growing rice as a subsistence crop. Manufacturing industry is now the largest exporter; major industries include rubber, tin, timber, textiles, machinery and cement. The government has greatly encouraged industrialization, investment and a more active role for the ethnic Malay population in industry, which – along with commerce and finance – has been largely the preserve of Chinese Malaysians. A growing tourist industry is being very actively promoted.

RECENT HISTORY

Malaysia's ethnic diversity reflects its complex history and the lure of its natural wealth and prime trading position. The British established themselves on the island of Penang in 1786, founded Singapore in 1819, and in 1867 established an administration for the Straits Settlements – Malacca, Penang and Singapore. Ignoring Thai claims to overlordship in the peninsula, the British took over the small sultanates as protected states. The British suppressed piracy, developed tin mining with Chinese labour and rubber plantations with Indian workers. Sarawak became a separate state under Sir James Brooke – the 'White Raja' – and his family from 1841, and was ceded to the British Crown in 1946. Sabah became British – as British North Borneo – from 1881. The Japanese occupied the whole of Malaysia during World War II. A Federation of Malaya – the peninsula – was established in 1948, but was threatened by Communist insurgency until 1960.

Malaya became independent in 1957 with a constitution protecting the interests of the Malays, who were fearful of the energy and acumen of the Chinese. Sabah, Sarawak and Singapore joined the Federation – renamed Malaysia – in 1963. Singapore left in 1965, but the unity of the Federation was maintained, with British armed support, in the face of an Indonesian 'confrontation' in Borneo (1965–66). Tension between Chinese and Malays led to riots and the suspension of parliamentary government (1969–71), but scarcely hindered the rapid development of a resource-rich economy. During the 1980s and early 1990s, the growth of Islamic fundamentalism led to a defensive re-assertion of Islamic values and practices among the Muslim Malay ruling elite. In 1990, the dominant position of UMNO was seriously challenged for the first time by the new Spirit of '46 party.

THE MALDIVES

Official name: Dhivehi Jumhuriya (Republic of Maldives).

Member of: UN, Commonwealth, SAARC.

Population: 206 000 (1989 est).

Capital: Malé 46 300 (1985).

Languages: Dhivehi (Maldivian; official).

Religion: Sunni Islam (official).

Life expectancy: 61 years.

Labour force: (1985) 52 500; agriculture and forestry 15 000, manufacturing 12 000, trade and tourism 5500.

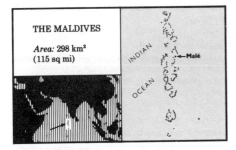

THE MALDIVES

Area: 298 km²
(115 sq mi)

GOVERNMENT

The Majilis (Assembly) consists of 8 members appointed by the President, and 40 elected by universal adult suffrage for five years. The President – who is directly elected for five years – appoints a Cabinet. There are no political parties.
President: Abdul Maumoon Gayoom.

EDUCATION

Literacy rate: 93% (1986). *Years of compulsory schooling:* schooling is not compulsory. *Universities:* none.

DEFENCE

Total armed strength: there are no armed forces.

GEOGRAPHY

The country is a chain of over 1190 small low-lying coral islands, of which 203 are inhabited. There are no significant rivers. *Highest point:* 3 m (10 ft).

Climate: The Maldives have a tropical climate with heavy rainfall brought by the monsoon between May and August.

ECONOMY

The growing tourist industry has displaced fishing as the mainstay of the economy. However, most Maldivians subsist on fish and coconuts.

RECENT HISTORY

From 1887 until independence in 1965 the Maldives were a British protectorate, but the ad-Din sultanate, established in the 14th century, was only abolished in 1968.

MALI

Official name: La République du Mali (The Republic of Mali).

Member of: UN, OAU, ECOWAS.

Population: 7 911 000 (1989).

Capital: Bamako 650 000, Ségou 89 000, Mopti 74 000 (1987).

Languages: French (official), Bambara (60%).

Religions: Sunni Islam (nearly 70%), animist.

Life expectancy: 44 years.

Labour force: (1988 est) 2 809 000; agriculture and forestry 2 300 000, services 290 000, industry 47 000.

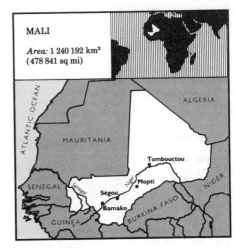

MALI

Area: 1 240 192 km²
(478 841 sq mi)

GOVERNMENT

The constitution was suspended following a military coup in March 1991. Government is in the hands of a 17-member National Reconciliation Council. The Council has pledged to hold multi-party elections for an 82-member National Assembly (to serve for three years) and a President (to serve for six years).
President: Lt.-Col. Amadou Toumani Toure.

EDUCATION

Literacy rate: 17% (1985 est). *Years of compulsory schooling:* 8–15. *Universities:* none.

DEFENCE

Total armed strength: 7300 (1989). *Military service:* selective (2 years).

GEOGRAPHY

Mali comprises low-lying plains but rises in the Adrar des Iforas range in the northeast. The south is savannah; the Sahara Desert is in the north. *Principal rivers:* Niger, Sénégal, Falémé. *Highest point:* Hombori Tondo 1155 m (3789 ft).

Climate: Mali is hot and largely dry, although the south has a wet season from June to October.

ECONOMY

Drought in the 1970s and 1980s devastated Mali's livestock herds. Only one fifth of Mali can be cultivated, producing mainly rice, millet and cassava for domestic use, and cotton for export.

RECENT HISTORY

Conquered by France (1880–95), Mali became the territory of French Sudan. Mali became independent in 1960. A radical socialist government was toppled in 1968 by the military regime of General Moussa Traore, whose government faced severe economic problems. Pressure from students for a multi-party system led to a military coup in March 1991.

MALTA

Official name: Repubblika Ta'Malta (Republic of Malta).

Member of: UN, Commonwealth, CSCE, Council of Europe.

Population: 349 000 (1988 est).

Capital and principal towns: Valletta 213 600 (agglomeration; 9200 city), Birkirkara 21 000, Qormi 19 000 and Sliema 14 000 are part of the Valletta agglomeration (1988).

Languages: Maltese and English (official).

Religions: Roman Catholic (official; 98%).

Life expectancy: 73 years.

Labour force: (1988) 130 000; manufacturing 28 000, commerce 13 000, public sector 56 000.

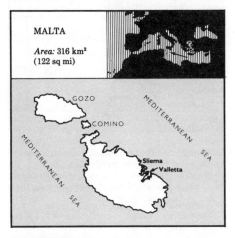

MALTA

Area: 316 km²
(122 sq mi)

GOVERNMENT

The 65-member House of Representatives is elected by universal adult suffrage under a system of proportional representation for five years. The President – who is elected for five years by the House – appoints a Prime Minister and a Cabinet who command a majority in the House. The main political parties are the (conservative) National Party and the Malta Labour Party.
President: Vincent Tabone.
Prime Minister: Eddie Fenech Adami.

EDUCATION

Literacy rate: 88% (1986). *Years of compulsory schooling:* 5–16. *Universities:* 1.

DEFENCE

Total armed strength: 1500 (1989), plus 700 reserves.
Military service: none.

GEOGRAPHY

The three inhabited islands of Malta, Gozo and Comino consist of low limestone plateaux with little surface water. There are no significant rivers. *Highest point:* an unnamed point, 249 m (816 ft).

Climate: The climate is Mediterranean with hot dry summers, and cooler wetter winters.

ECONOMY

The main industries are shipbuilding and repairing, tourism and light industry. Malta is virtually self-sufficient in agricultural products.

RECENT HISTORY

The French held Malta from 1798 to 1800, provoking the Maltese to request British protection (1802). As a British colony (from 1814), Malta became a vital naval base, and the island received the George Cross for its valour in World War II. Malta gained independence in 1964. Maltese political life has been polarized between the National Party and the Maltese Labour Party. Dom Mintoff – Labour PM 1971–84 – developed close links with Communist and Arab states, notably Libya.

MARSHALL ISLANDS

Official name: The Republic of the Marshall Islands.

Member of: South Pacific Forum.

Population: 42 000 (1989 est).

Capital and principal towns: Majuro 20 000 (1989 est).

Languages: Marshallese and English (official).

Religions: Roman Catholic and various Protestant denominations.

Life expectancy: no figure is available.

Labour force: no figures are available.

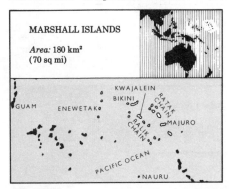

MARSHALL ISLANDS

Area: 180 km²
(70 sq mi)

GOVERNMENT

The 33-member Nitijela (Parliament) and the President are elected by universal adult suffrage for four years. The traditional Council of Chiefs is a consultative body. There are no political parties.
President: Amata Kabua.

EDUCATION

Literacy rate: over 95% (1989 est). *Years of compul-*

sory schooling: 6–14. *Universities:* none.

DEFENCE
Total armed strength: there are no armed forces. The USA has full responsibility for the country's defence.

GEOGRAPHY
The Marshall Islands comprise two chains of small coral atolls and islands, with over 1150 islands in total. There are no significant rivers. *Highest point:* unnamed, 6 m (20 ft).

Climate: The climate is tropical with heavy rainfall.

ECONOMY
The islands have practically no resources and depend upon subsistence agriculture, tourism and US grants.

RECENT HISTORY
The Marshall Islands were under Spanish (1875–85), German (1885–1914), and Japanese administration (1914–1945) before becoming part of the US Pacific Islands Trust Territory. They became internally self-governing in 1979. In 1986 US administration in the islands was formally terminated and the Marshall Islands became a sovereign republic, able to conduct its own foreign affairs, although under a Compact of Free Association the USA retains complete responsibility for the republic's defence and security until 2001. The UN did not recognize this new status of the Marshall Islands until December 1990, when the trusteeship was finally dissolved.

MAURITANIA

Official name: Jumhuriyat Muritaniya al-Islamiya (Islamic Republic of Mauritania).

Member of: UN, OAU, Arab League.

Population: 1 916 000 (1988 est).

Capital: Nouakchott 600 000 (with suburbs), Kaédi 32 000, Nouadhibou (Port Etienne) 30 000 (1987).

Languages: Arabic (official); French.

Religion: Sunni Islam (official).

Life expectancy: 46 years.

Labour force: (1988 est) 615 000; agriculture 403 000, services 115 000, industry 47 000.

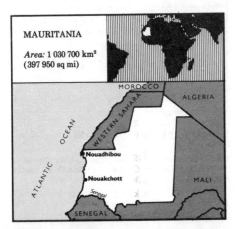

MAURITANIA

Area: 1 030 700 km²
(397 950 sq mi)

GOVERNMENT
The 24-member Military Committee for National Salvation – which came to power in a military coup in 1979 – is headed by the President, who appoints a Council of Ministers. Political parties are banned but elections give a choice of candidates.
President: Col. Maaouiya Ould Taya.

EDUCATION
Literacy rate: 17%. *Years of compulsory schooling:* 6–12. *Universities:* 1.

DEFENCE
Total armed strength: 11 000 (1989). *Military service:* none.

GEOGRAPHY
Isolated peaks rise above the plateaux of the Sahara Desert that cover most of Mauritania. *Principal river:* Sénégal. *Highest point:* Kediet Ijill 915 m (3050 ft).

Climate: The climate is hot and dry, with adequate rainfall only in the south.

ECONOMY
Persistent drought has devastated the nomads' herds of cattle and sheep. Fish from the Atlantic and iron ore are virtually the only exports.

RECENT HISTORY
The French arrived on the coast in the 17th century, but did not annex the Arab emirates inland until 1903. Mauritania became independent in 1960. When Spain withdrew from the Western Sahara in 1976, Morocco and Mauritania divided the territory between them, but Mauritania could not defeat the Polisario guerrillas fighting for West Saharan independence and gave up its claim (1979). Tension between the dominant Arab north and Black African south led to violence in 1989.

MAURITIUS

Member of: OAU, Commonwealth.

Population: 1 061 000 (1989).

Capital: Port Louis 136 000, Beau Bassin/Rose Hill 92 000, Quatre Bornes 65 000, Curepipe 63 000 (1985 est).

Languages: English (official), Creole (French; nearly 30%), Hindi (over 20%), Bhojpuri.

Religions: Hindu (51%), Roman Catholic (30%), Sunni Islam (16%), with Protestant minorities.

Life expectancy: 67 years.

Labour force: (employment figures for the island of Mauritius only; 1988) 271 000; manufacturing 106 000, community and social services 65 000, agriculture and forestry 50 000.

GOVERNMENT
Elections are held by universal adult suffrage every five years for 62 members of the Assembly; up to 8 additional members may be appointed. The Governor General – the representative of the British Queen as sovereign of Mauritius – appoints a Prime Minister who commands a majority in the Assembly. The PM, in turn, appoints a Cabinet responsible to the Assembly. A republican constitution is planned. The main political parties are the Mouvement Socialiste Mauricien, the Labour Party, the Parti Mauricien

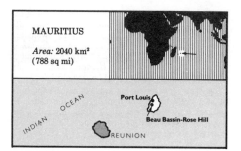

MAURITIUS

Area: 2040 km²
(788 sq mi)

INDIAN OCEAN

Port Louis
Beau Bassin-Rose Hill
REUNION

Social Democrate and the Mouvement Militant Mauricien.
Prime Minister: Aneerood Jugnauth.

EDUCATION
Literacy rate: 83% (1985 est). *Years of compulsory schooling:* schooling is free but not compulsory. *Universities:* 1.

DEFENCE
Total armed strength: 0. *Military service:* none.

GEOGRAPHY
The central plateau of Mauritius is surrounded by mountains. Other islands in the group include Rodrigues and the Agalega Islands. There are no significant rivers. *Highest point:* Piton de la Rivière Noire 826 m (2711 ft).
Climate: The climate is subtropical, although it can be very hot from December to April. Rainfall is high in the uplands.

ECONOMY
The export of sugar cane dominates the economy. Diversification is being encouraged, and light industry – in particular clothing – and tourism are of increasing importance.

RECENT HISTORY
Mauritius was French from 1715 until 1814, when it became British. Black slaves were imported, followed in the 19th century by Indian labourers whose descendants are the majority community. Independence was gained in 1968.

MEXICO
Official name: Estados Unidos Mexicanos (United Mexican States).
Member of: UN, OAS, LAIA.
Population: 84 275 000 (1989 est).
Capital and major cities: Mexico City 18 748 000, Guadalajara 3 256 000, Monterrey 2 335 000, Netzahualcóyotl 2 331 000 (part of the Mexico City agglomeration), Puebla 1 218 000, León 947 000, Tijuana 932 000, Ciudad Juárez 786 000, Mérida 580 000 (with suburbs; 1985).
Languages: Spanish (90%; official), various Indian languages.
Religion: Roman Catholic (96%).
Life expectancy: 70 years.
Labour force: (1980) 21 942 000; agriculture and forestry 5 701 000, manufacturing 2 693 000, services 2 451 000.

GOVERNMENT
The 64-member Senate and the President – who may serve only once – are elected by universal adult suffrage for six years. The 400-member Chamber of Deputies is directly elected for three years – 100 of the members are elected under a system of proportional representation; the remaining 300 represent single-member constituencies. The President appoints a Cabinet. The principal political parties are the PRI (Institutional Revolutionary Party), the PAN (National Action Party) and the PRD (Democratic Revolutionary Party). Each of the 31 states has its own Chamber of Deputies.
President: Carlos Salinas de Gortari.

MEXICO

Area: 1 958 201 km²
(756 066 sq mi)

USA

PACIFIC OCEAN

Gulf of California

Rio Grande

Monterrey

Guadalajara
León
Mexico City
Puebla

GULF OF MEXICO

GUATEMALA

EDUCATION
Literacy rate: 91% (1985 est). *Years of compulsory schooling:* 6–12. *Universities:* 82.

DEFENCE
Total armed strength: 141 500 (1989). *Military service:* part-time, compulsory.

MEXICAN STATES
Population figures for the states are for 1981.
Aguascalientes *Area:* 5471 km² (2112 sq mi). *Population:* 503 000. *Capital:* Aguascalientes 359 000 (1981).
Baja California *Area:* 69 921 km² (26 996 sq mi). *Population:* 1 225 000. *Capital:* Mexicali 511 000 (1981).
Baja California Sur *Area:* 73 475 km² (28 369 sq mi). *Population:* 221 000. *Capital:* La Paz 130 000 (1981).
Campeche *Area:* 50 812 km² (19 619 sq mi). *Population:* 372 000. *Capital:* Campeche 152 000 (1981).
Chiapas *Area:* 74 211 km² (28 653 sq mi). *Population:* 2 097 000. *Capital:* Tuxtla Gutiérrez 166 000 (1981).
Chihuahua *Area:* 244 938 km² (94 571 sq mi). *Population:* 1 934 000. *Capital:* Ciudad Juárez 786 000 (1985).
Coahuila *Area:* 149 982 km² (57 908 sq mi). *Population:* 1 558 000. *Capital:* Saltillo 322 000 (1981). *Largest city:* Torreón 364 000.
Colima *Area:* 5191 km² (2004 sq mi). *Population:* 339 000. *Capital:* Colima 85 000 (1981).
Durango *Area:* 123 181 km² (47 560 sq mi).

Population: 1 160 000. *Capital*: (Victoria de) Durango 321 000 (1981).

Guanajuato *Area*: 30 491 km² (11 773 sq mi). *Population*: 3 044 000. *Capital*: Guanajuato 48 000. *Largest city*: León 947 000 (1985).

Guerrero *Area*: 64 281 km² (24 819 sq mi). *Population*: 2 174 000. *Capital*: Chilpancingo 39 000 (1981). *Largest city*: Acapulco 462 000 (1981).

Hidalgo *Area*: 20 813 km² (8036 sq mi). *Population*: 1 517 000. *Capital*: Pachuca de Soto 135 000 (1981).

Jalisco *Area*: 80 836 km² (31 211 sq mi). *Population*: 4 294 000. *Capital*: Guadalajara 3 256 000 (1985).

México *Area*: 21 355 km² (8245 sq mi). *Population*: 7 546 000. *Capital*: Toluca de Lerdo 357 000 (1981). *Largest city*: Netzahuacóyotl (part of the Mexico City agglomeration) 2 331 000 (1985).

Michoacán *Area*: 59 928 km² (23 138 sq mi). *Population*: 3 049 000. *Capital*: Morelia 353 000.

Morelos *Area*: 4950 km² (1911 sq mi). *Population*: 932 000. *Capital*: Cuernavaca 232 000.

Nayarit *Area*: 26 979 km² (10 417 sq mi). *Population*: 730 000. *Capital*: Tepic 177 000.

Nuevo León *Area*: 64 924 km² (25 067 sq mi). *Population*: 2 658 000. *Capital*: Monterrey 2 335 000 (1985).

Oaxaca *Area*: 93 952 km² (36 275 sq mi). *Population*: 2 518 000. *Capital*: Oaxaca 157 000.

Puebla *Area*: 33 902 km² (11 493 sq mi). *Population*: 3 280 000. *Capital*: Puebla 1 218 000 (1985).

Querétaro *Area*: 11 449 km² (4420 sq mi). *Population*: 726 000. *Capital*: Querétaro 294 000.

Quintana Roo *Area*: 50 212 km² (19 387 sq mi). *Population*: 210 000. *Capital*: Chetumal 25 000 (1981).

San Luis Potosí *Area*: 63 068 km² (24 351 sq mi). *Population*: 1 671 000. *Capital*: San Luis Potosí 407 000 (1981).

Sinaloa *Area*: 58 328 km² (22 520 sq mi). *Population*: 1 880 000. *Capital*: Culiacán Rosales 560 000 (1981).

Sonora *Area*: 182 052 km² (70 290 sq mi). *Population*: 1 499 000. *Capital*: Hermosillo 341 000 (1981).

Tabasco *Area*: 25 267 km² (9756 sq mi). *Population*: 1 150 000. *Capital*: Villahermosa 251 000 (1981).

Tamaulipa *Area*: 79 304 km² (30 619 sq mi). *Population*: 1 925 000. *Capital*: Ciudad Victoria 153 000 (1981). *Largest city*: Matamoros 239 000 (1981).

Tlaxcala *Area*: 4016 km² (1551 sq mi). *Population*: 547 000. *Capital*: Apizaco 23 000.

Veracruz *Area*: 71 699 km² (27 683 sq mi). *Population*: 5 265 000. *Capital*: Jalapa Enrique 213 000. *Largest city*: Veracruz 305 000.

Yucatán *Area*: 38 402 km² (14 827 sq mi). *Population*: 1 035 000. *Capital*: Mérida 580 000 (1985).

Zacatecas *Area*: 73 252 km² (28 283 sq mi). *Population*: 1 145 000. *Capital*: Zacatecas 81 000.

Federal District *Area*: 1479 km² (570 sq mi). *Population*: 9 373 000. *Capital*: Mexico City 18 748 000 (1985; including suburbs and parts of the agglomeration beyond the Federal District).

GEOGRAPHY

Between the Sierra Madre Oriental mountains in the east and the Sierra Madre Occidental in the west is a large high central plateau with several volcanoes. The coastal plains are generally narrow in the west, but wider in the east. The Yucatán Peninsula in the southeast is a broad limestone lowland; Baja California in the northwest is a long narrow mountainous peninsula. Mexico is prone to earthquakes. *Principal rivers:* Río Bravo de Norte (Rio Grande), Balsas, Grijalva, Pánuco. *Highest point:* Volcán Citlaltepetl (Pico de Orizaba) 5610 m (18 405 ft).

Climate: There is considerable climatic variation, in part reflecting the complexity of the relief. In general, the south and the coastal lowlands are tropical, while the central plateau and the mountains are cooler and drier.

ECONOMY

One quarter of the labour force is involved in agriculture and many Mexicans are still subsistence farmers growing maize, wheat, kidney beans and rice. Coffee, cotton, fruit and vegetables are the most important export crops. Mexico is the world's leading producer of silver. The exploitation of large reserves of natural gas and petroleum enabled the country's spectacular economic development in the 1970s and 1980s. An expanding industrial base includes important petrochemical, textile, motor-vehicle and food-processing industries. Economic problems remain, and high unemployment has stimulated immigration – often illegal – to the US.

RECENT HISTORY

The first revolt against Spanish rule broke out in 1810, but Mexican independence was not gained until 1821 after a guerrilla war led by Vicente Guerrero. Initially an empire – under Agustín Itúrbide – Mexico became a republic in 1823, but conflict between federalists and centralists erupted, developing into civil war. In 1836 Texas rebelled against Mexico, declaring independence. When the USA annexed Texas in 1845, war broke out, resulting in the loss of half Mexico's territory – Texas, New Mexico and California. A period of reform began in 1857, with a new liberal constitution. A civil war (1858–61) between reformists and conservatives was won by the reformists under Benito Juárez (1806–72), but the economy was shattered. After Mexico failed to repay debts, Spain, Britain and France invaded in 1863. Although Spain and Britain soon withdrew, France remained, appointing Archduke Maximilian of Austria (1832–67) as Emperor (1864). Under US pressure and Mexican resistance, the French withdrew in 1867. Maximilian remained in Mexico City and was captured and executed. Juárez reestablished the republic.

The authoritarian rule of General Porfirio Díaz (President 1876–80 and 1888–1910) brought peace, but wealth was concentrated into a few hands. Revolution against the power of the landowners erupted in 1910. The reformist policies of President Francisco Madero (1873–1913) were supported by the outlaw Pancho Villa (1877–1923), but revolutionary violence continued, and in 1916–17 a US expeditionary force was sent against Villa. From 1924 the revolution became anticlerical and the Church was persecuted. Order was restored when the Institutional Revolutionary Party came to power in 1929. In the 1930s the large estates were divided and much of the economy was nationalized. Political opposition has been tolerated, although the ruling party is virtually guaranteed perpetual power. In 1989, the first non-PRI state governor was elected, and in 1989–90 opposition claims of electoral fraud were made in several state and city elections.

MICRONESIA

Official name: The Federated States of Micronesia.

Member of: South Pacific Forum.

Population 109 000 (1989).

Capital: Kolonia 7000 (1989 est).

Languages: English, Trukese, Ponapean, Yapese, Kosraean.

Religions: Roman Catholic and various Protestant denominations.

Life expectancy: 66 years.

Labour force: no figures are available.

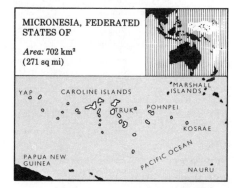

MICRONESIA, FEDERATED STATES OF

Area: 702 km²
(271 sq mi)

GOVERNMENT

The President (who serves for four years) and the 14-member National Congress are elected by universal adult suffrage. The Congress comprises one senator elected by each of the four states for four years, and ten senators representing constituencies elected for two years. There are no national political parties. Each state has its own government and parliament.
President: John Hagelelgam.

MICRONESIAN STATES

Population figures are for 1980.

Kosrae *Area:* 109 km² (42 sq mi). *Population:* 5500. *Capital:* Kosrae 5000.

Pohnpei (formerly Ponape) *Area:* 373 km² (144 sq mi). *Capital:* Kolonia 7000.

Truk *Area:* 116 km² (45 sq mi). *Population:* 37 700. *Capital:* Moen 5000.

Yap *Area:* 101 km² (39 sq mi). *Population:* 8172. *Capital:* Colonia 3000.

EDUCATION

Literacy rate: over 95% (1989 est). *Years of compulsory schooling:* 6–14. *Universities:* none.

DEFENCE

Total armed strength: there are no armed forces. The USA has full responsibility for the country's defence.

GEOGRAPHY

The Micronesian islands comprise over 600 islands in two main groups. The majority of the islands are low coral atolls, but Kosrae and Pohnpei are mountainous. There are no significant rivers. *Highest point:* Mt Totolom 791 m (2595 ft).

Climate: The climate is tropical with heavy rainfall.

ECONOMY

Apart from phosphate, the islands have practically no resources and depend upon subsistence agriculture, fishing and US grants.

RECENT HISTORY

Previously known as the Caroline Islands, the islands were under Spanish (1874–99), German (1899–1914), and Japanese administration (1914–45) before becoming part of the US Pacific Islands Trust Territory. They became internally self-governing in 1979. In 1986 US administration in the islands was formally terminated and the Federated States became a sovereign republic, able to conduct its own foreign affairs, although under a Compact of Free Association the USA retains complete responsibility for the republic's defence and security until 2001. The UN did not recognize this new status of the Federated States until December 1990, when the trusteeship was finally dissolved.

MONACO

Official name: Principauté de Monaco (Principality of Monaco).

Member of: CSCE, UN (observer).

Population: 30 000 (1983 est).

Capital and major cities: Monaco 1200, Monte-Carlo 13 200 (1982).

Languages: French (official), Monegasque.

Religion: Roman Catholic.

Life expectancy: no figure available.

Labour force: no figures available.

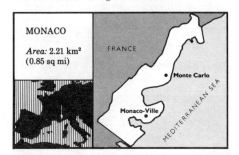

MONACO

Area: 2.21 km²
(0.85 sq mi)

GOVERNMENT

Monaco is a constitutional monarchy. Legislative power is jointly held by the Prince and the 18-member National Council, which is elected by universal adult suffrage for five years. Executive power is held by the Prince, who appoints a four-member Council of Government headed by the Minister of State, a French civil servant chosen by the sovereign.
Prince: HSH Prince Rainier III (succeeded upon the death of his grandfather, 9 May 1949).
Minister of State: Jean Ausseil.

EDUCATION

Literacy rate: 99%. *Years of compulsory schooling:* 6–16. *Universities:* none.

DEFENCE

Total armed strength: there are no armed forces except for a small palace guard.

GEOGRAPHY

Monaco consists of a rocky peninsula and a narrow

stretch of coast. Since 1958 the area of the principality has increased by one fifth through reclamation of land from the sea. *Principal river:* Vésubie. *Highest point:* on Chemin de Révoirés 162 m (533 ft).

Climate: Monaco has a Mediterranean climate.

ECONOMY
Monaco depends upon real estate, banking, insurance, light industry and tourism.

RECENT HISTORY
Monaco was annexed by France in 1793 but restored in 1814, under the protection of the king of Sardinia. The greater part of the principality was lost – and eventually annexed by France – in 1848. Since 1861 Monaco has been under French protection. Prince Rainier III granted a liberal constitution in 1962.

MONGOLIA

Official name: Bugd Nairamdakh Mongol Ard Uls (Mongolian People's Republic).

Member of: UN.

Population: 2 094 000 (1990 est).

Capital and main cities: Ulan Bator (Ulaan Baatar) 548 000, Darhan 86 000, Erdenet 56 000 (1989), Baganuur 25 000 (1984).

Languages: Khalkh Mongolian (official; 78%), Kazakh.

Religions: Religion has been suppressed, but pockets of Buddhism remain.

Life expectancy: 65 years.

Labour force: (1980) 772 000; agriculture and forestry 308 000, services 303 000, industry 162 000.

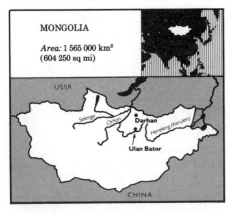

MONGOLIA
Area: 1 565 000 km²
(604 250 sq mi)
USSR
Selenge
Orhon
Darhan
Hereleng (Kerulen)
Ulan Bator
CHINA

GOVERNMENT
The 430-member People's Great Hural is elected by universal adult suffrage for a five-year term. The Hural – which appoints a Council of Ministers headed by a Prime Minister – devolves its powers to an eight-member Presidium, whose Chairman is head of state. The main political parties are the Mongolian People's Revolutionary (Communist) Party and the Mongolian Democratic Party.
Head of state (Chairman of the Presidium): Punsalmaagiyn Ochirbat.
Prime Minister: Dash Byambasuren.

EDUCATION
Literacy rate: 80% (est). *Years of compulsory schooling:* 6–16. *Universities:* 1.

DEFENCE
Total armed strength: 21 500 (1989 est). *Military service:* 2 years.

GEOGRAPHY
Mongolia comprises mountains in the north, a series of basins in the centre, and the Gobi Desert and Altai Mountains in the south. *Principal rivers:* Selenga, Orhon, Hereleng. *Highest point:* Mönh Hayrhan Uul 4362 m (14 311 ft).

Climate: Mongolia has a dry climate with generally mild summers and severely cold winters.

ECONOMY
Mongolia depends on collectivized animal herding (cattle, sheep, goats and camels). Cereals (including fodder crops) are grown on a large scale on state farms. The industrial sector is dominated by food processing, hides and wool. Copper is a major export.

RECENT HISTORY
In 1921, Outer Mongolia broke away from China with Soviet assistance, and in 1924 the Mongolian People's Republic was established. Pro-democracy demonstrations early in 1990 led to a liberalization of the regime. The first multi-party elections were held in July 1990 when the Communists were returned to power.

MOROCCO

Official name: Al-Mamlaka al-Maghribiya (The Kingdom of Morocco).

Member of: UN, Arab League.

Population: 24 530 000 (1989 est) excluding the Western Sahara.

Capital and major cities: Rabat (incl. Salé) 929 000, Casablanca 2 505 000, Fez (Fès) 590 000, Marrakech 511 000, Oujda 531 000 (all including suburbs; 1985).

Languages: Arabic (official; 65%), Berber, French.

Religion: Sunni Islam (official).

Life expectancy: 63 years.

Labour force: (1982) 5 999 000; agriculture and forestry 2 352 000, services 1 007 000, manufacturing 931 000.

GOVERNMENT
Morocco is a constitutional monarchy. The 306-member Chamber of Representatives consists of 206 members elected by universal adult suffrage for six years and 100 members chosen by an electoral college representing municipal authorities and professional bodies. The King appoints a Prime Minister and Cabinet. The main political parties include the Union Constitutionnelle, the Rassemblement National des Indépendents, the Mouvement Populaire, Istiqlal, the Union Socialiste des Forces Populaires and the Parti National Démocrate.
Head of state: HM King Hassan II (succeeded upon the death of his father, 26 February 1961).
Prime Minister: Azzedine Laraki.

EDUCATION
Literacy rate: 33% (1985 est). *Years of compulsory schooling:* 7–13. *Universities:* 6.

DEFENCE
Total armed strength: 192 500 (1989). *Military service:* 18 months.

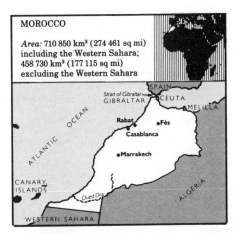

MOROCCO

Area: 710 850 km² (274 461 sq mi)
including the Western Sahara;
458 730 km² (177 115 sq mi)
excluding the Western Sahara

GEOGRAPHY

Over one third of Morocco is mountainous. The principal uplands are the Grand, Middle and Anti Atlas Mountains in the west and north and a plateau in the east. Much of the country – including the disputed Western Sahara territory – is desert. *Principal rivers:* Oued Dra, Oued Moulouya, Sebov. *Highest point:* Jebel Toubkal 4165 m (13 665 ft).

Climate: The north has a Mediterranean climate with hot dry summers and warm wetter winters. The south and much of the interior have semiarid and tropical desert climates.

ECONOMY

Nearly one half of the labour force is involved in agriculture, producing mainly citrus fruits, grapes (for wine) and vegetables for export, and wheat and barley for domestic consumption. Morocco is the world's leading exporter of phosphates. Other resources include iron ore, lead and zinc. Since independence many important industries and services have come into state ownership. Tourism is growing.

RECENT HISTORY

In the 19th century Spain confirmed control of several long-claimed coastal settlements. In the 'Moroccan Crises' (1905–6 and 1911), French interests in Morocco were disputed by Germany. Under the Treaty of Fez in 1912 France established a protectorate over Morocco, although the Spanish enclaves remained. The 1925 Rif rebellion stirred nationalist feelings, but independence was not gained until 1956. King Hassan II (reigned 1961–) has survived left-wing challenges through strong rule and vigorous nationalism – as in his 1975 'Green March' of unarmed peasants into the then-Spanish (Western) Sahara. Morocco continues to hold the Western Sahara despite international pressure and the activities of the Algerian-backed Polisario guerrillas fighting for the territory's independence.

For informaton on the disputed Western Sahara, see p. 639.

MOZAMBIQUE

Official name: A República de Moçambique (Republic of Mozambique).
Member of: UN, OAU, SADCC.
Population: 15 293 000 (1989).

Capital and main cities: Maputo 1 007 000, Beira 292 000, Nampula 197 000 (1989).
Languages: Portuguese (official).
Religions: Animist majority, with Roman Catholic and Sunni Islam minorities.
Life expectancy: 45 years.
Labour force: (1980) 5 671 000; agriculture and forestry 4 755 000, mining and manufacturing 347 000, services 243 000.

MOZAMBIQUE

Area: 799 380 km²
(308 641 sq mi)

GOVERNMENT

Until November 1990, effective power was held by Frelimo, which was the only legal political party. The party's president was head of state. In November 1990, a new constitution was introduced, under which multi-party elections will be held for a 250-member Assembly of the Republic. The President – who will appoint a Council of Ministers – will be elected by the Assembly.
President: Joaquim Alberto Chissano.

EDUCATION

Literacy rate: 38% (1985 est). *Years of compulsory schooling:* 7–14. *Universities:* 1.

DEFENCE

Total armed strength: 71 000 (1989). *Military service:* 2 years.

GEOGRAPHY

The Zambezi River separates high plateaus in northern Mozambique from lowlands in the south. *Principal rivers:* Limpopo, Zambezi, Shire. *Highest point:* Mount Bingo 2436 m (7992 ft).

Climate: Mozambique has a tropical climate, with maximum rainfall and temperatures from November to March.

ECONOMY

Over 80% of the labour force is involved in farming, mainly growing cassava and maize as subsistence crops. Fishing is a major employer – prawns and shrimps make up nearly one half of Mozambique's exports. The economy has been devastated by civil war.

RECENT HISTORY

The Portuguese established coastal trading posts from 1531, but did not control the whole country until the end of the 19th century. Forced labour and minimal development helped to fuel nationalist feelings, and in 1964 the Frelimo movement launched a guerrilla war against Portuguese rule. Independence was achieved in 1975, and a Marxist-Leninist state was established. The pressures of poverty and the destabilization of the country by South Africa – through support for the Renamo guerrilla movement – led to renewed ties with the West, and Marxism was abandoned by Frelimo in 1989. At the beginning of 1991, the country faced severe famine.

MYANMAR

See Burma.

NAMIBIA

Official name: The Republic of Namibia or Republiek van Namibie.

Member of: UN, Commonwealth, SADCC, OAU.

Population: 1 252 000 (1988 est).

Capital: Windhoek 115 000 (1988 est).

Languages: Afrikaans and English (official).

Religions: Lutheran (30%), Roman Catholic (20%), other Christian Churches (30%).

Life expectancy: 57 years.

Labour force: No figures available.

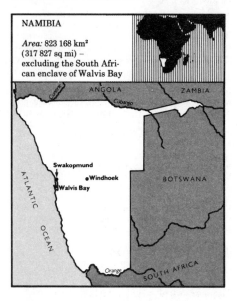

NAMIBIA

Area: 823 168 km² (317 827 sq mi) – excluding the South African enclave of Walvis Bay

GOVERNMENT

A 72-member Assembly is elected by universal adult suffrage every five years. The President – who appoints the Prime Minister – is also directly elected for a term of five years and can nominate up to six non-voting members of the National Assembly. The main political parties include the (left wing) SWAPO (South West African People's Organization), the (centre) Democratic Turnhalle Alliance, and Action Christian National.
President: Sam Nujoma.
Prime Minister: Hage Geingob.

EDUCATION

Literacy rate: 75% (1985 est). *Years of compulsory schooling:* 7–14. *Universities:* none.

DEFENCE

Total armed strength: no figure available.

GEOGRAPHY

The coastal Namib Desert stretches up to 160 km (100 mi) inland. Beyond the Central Plateau, the Kalahari Desert occupies the eastern part of the country. *Principal river:* Orange. *Highest point:* Brandberg 2579 m (8461 ft).

Climate: Namibia has a hot dry tropical climate. Rainfall on the coast averages under 100 mm (4 in).

ECONOMY

Over 60% of the labour force is involved in agriculture, mainly raising cattle and sheep. The economy depends upon exports of diamonds and uranium, and is closely tied to South Africa.

RECENT HISTORY

A German protectorate of South West Africa – excluding Walvis Bay, which had been British since 1878 – was declared in 1884. Seeking land for white settlement, the Germans established their rule only after great bloodshed – over three quarters of the Herero people were killed in 1903–4. South Africa conquered the territory during World War I, and (after 1919) administered it under a League of Nations mandate. In 1966, the UN cancelled the mandate, but South Africa – which had refused to grant the territory independence – ignored the ruling. The main nationalist movement, SWAPO, began guerrilla warfare to free Namibia, the name adopted by the UN for the country. South Africa unsuccessfully attempted to exclude SWAPO's influence. After a cease-fire agreement in 1989, UN-supervised elections were held in November 1989 for a constituent assembly. Independence – under the presidency of SWAPO leader Sam Nujoma – was achieved in March 1990.

NAURU

Official name: The Republic of Nauru.

Member of: Commonwealth (special member), South Pacific Forum.

Population: 8040 (1983).

Capital: Yaren.

Languages: Nauruan (official), English.

Religions: Nauruan Protestant Church, Roman Catholic.

Life expectancy: no figure available.

Labour force: no recent figures available.

GOVERNMENT

The 18-member Parliament is elected by universal adult suffrage for three years. Parliament elects the President, who in turn appoints a Cabinet of Ministers. There are no political parties.
President: Bernard Dowiyogo.

EDUCATION

Literacy rate: 99%. *Years of compulsory schooling:* 6–16. *Universities:* there is a university extension centre of the University of the South Pacific.

DEFENCE

Total armed strength: there are no armed forces.

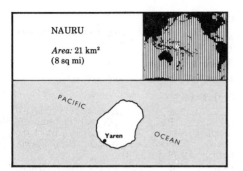

NAURU

Area: 21 km²
(8 sq mi)

PACIFIC

Yaren

OCEAN

GEOGRAPHY

Nauru is a low-lying coral atoll. There are no rivers. *Highest point:* 68 m (225 ft) on the central plateau.

Climate: Nauru has a tropical climate with heavy rainfall, particularly between November and February.

ECONOMY

Nauru depends almost entirely upon the export of phosphate rock, stocks of which are expected to run out by 1995. Shipping and air services and 'tax haven' facilities are planned to provide revenue when the phosphate is exhausted.

RECENT HISTORY

Germany annexed Nauru in 1888 following a request from German settlers on the island for protection during unrest between Nauru's 12 clans. Australia captured Nauru in 1914 and administered it – except for a period of Japanese occupation (1942–45) – until independence was granted in 1968.

NEPAL

Official name: Nepal Adhirajya (Kingdom of Nepal).

Member of: UN, SAARC.

Population: 18 452 000 (1989 est).

Capital: Kathmandu 235 000 (1981).

Languages: Nepali (official; 51%), Maithir (12%).

Religions: Hindu (official; 82%), Buddhist (16%).

Life expectancy: 49 years.

Labour force: (1981) 6 851 000; agriculture and forestry 6 244 000, services 313 500, trade and tourism 109 000.

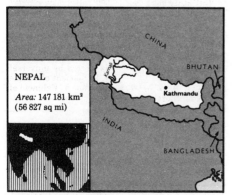

NEPAL

Area: 147 181 km²
(56 827 sq mi)

CHINA

Karnali

BHUTAN

Kathmandu

INDIA

BANGLADESH

GOVERNMENT

Nepal is a constitutional monarchy. Since 1990, Nepal has had a two-chamber Parliament. The Lower House consists of 205 members elected for five years by universal adult suffrage. The Upper House consists of 60 appointed and indirectly elected members, including six members appointed by the King. Political parties have been allowed since 1990 – the largest are the (liberal) Nepali Congress Party, the Unified Marxist-Leninists and the Communist Party.
King: HM King Birendra (succeeded upon the death of his father, 31 January 1972).
Prime Minister: Girija Prasad Koirala.

EDUCATION

Literacy rate: 25% (1985). *Years of compulsory schooling:* 6–11. *Universities:* 1.

DEFENCE

Total armed strength: 35 000 (1989). *Military service:* none.

GEOGRAPHY

In the south are densely populated subtropical lowlands. A hilly central belt is divided by fertile valleys. The Himalaya dominate the north. *Principal rivers:* Karnali, Naryani, Kosi. *Highest point:* Mount Everest 8863 m (29 078 ft).

Climate: The climate varies between the subtropical south and the glacial Himalayan peaks. All of Nepal experiences the monsoon.

ECONOMY

Nepal is one of the least developed countries in the world, with most of the labour force involved in subsistence farming, mainly growing rice, beans and maize. Forestry is important, but increased farming has led to serious deforestation.

RECENT HISTORY

In 1768 the ruler of the principality of Gurkha in the west conquered the Kathmandu Valley, and began a phase of expansion that ended in defeat by the Chinese in Tibet (1792) and the British in India (1816). From 1846 to 1950 the Rana family held sway as hereditary chief ministers of a powerless monarchy. Their isolationist policy preserved Nepal's independence at the expense of its development. A brief experiment with democracy was followed by a re-assertion of royal autocracy (1960) by King Mahendra (reigned 1952–72). Mass unrest and violent pro-democracy demonstrations in 1990 forced the King to concede a democratic constitution. Multi-party elections were held in May 1991.

THE NETHERLANDS

Official name: Koninkrijk der Nederlanden (The Kingdom of the Netherlands).

Member of: UN, EC, NATO, CSCE, WEU, Council of Europe, OECD.

Population: 14 864 000 (1988 est).

Capital and major cities: Amsterdam – capital in name only – 1 031 000, The Hague ('s Gravenhage) – the seat of government and administration – 680 000, Rotterdam 1 036 000, Utrecht 521 000, Eindhoven 381 000, Arnhem 297 000, Heerlen-Kerkrade 267 000, Enschede 250 000, Nijmegen 241 000, Tilburg 226 000, Haarlem 214 000, Groningen 207 000, Dordrecht 203 000, 's Hertogenbosch 193 000, Leiden 183 000 (all including suburbs; 1988).

Language: Dutch (official).
Religions: Roman Catholic (under 40%), Netherlands Reformed Church (20%), Reformed Churches (Calvinistic; under 10%).
Life expectancy: 77 years.
Labour force: (1987) 4 741 000; manufacturing and mining 922 000, trade and tourism 855 000, agriculture 267 000.

THE NETHERLANDS

Area: 41 785 km² (16 140 sq mi), or 33 937 km² (13 103 sq mi) excluding fresh-water

GOVERNMENT

The Netherlands is a constitutional monarchy. The 75-member First Chamber of the States-General is elected for a six-year term by the 12 provincial councils – with one half of the members retiring every three years. The 150-member Second Chamber is elected for a four-year term by universal adult suffrage under a system of proportional representation. The monarch appoints a Prime Minister who commands a majority in the States-General. The PM, in turn, appoints a Council of Ministers (Cabinet) who are responsible to the States-General. The main political parties include the (conservative) CDA (Christian Democratic Appeal Party), PvdA (the Labour Party), the (liberal) VVD (People's Party for Freedom and Democracy), D66 (Democracy 66), the (Calvinist) SGP (Political Reformed Party), and the PPR (Political Party of Reformed Democrats).
Queen: HM Queen Beatrix (succeeded on the abdication of her mother, 30 April 1980).
Prime Minister: Ruud Lubbers.

EDUCATION

Literacy rate: 99%. *Years of compulsory schooling:* 5–16. *Universities:* 21.

DEFENCE

Total armed strength: 103 700 (1989). *Military service:* 14–17 months.

GEOGRAPHY

Over one quarter of the Netherlands – one of the world's most densely populated countries – lies below sea level. A network of canals and canalized rivers cross the west of the country where sand dunes and man-made dykes protect low-lying areas and polders (land reclaimed from the sea). The coast has been straightened by sea walls protecting Zeeland in the southwest and enclosing a freshwater lake, the IJsselmeer, in the north. The east comprises low sandy plains. *Principal rivers:* Rhine (Rijn) –

dividing into branches including the Lek, Waal and Oude Rijn, Maas (Meuse). *Highest point:* Vaalserberg 321 m (1053 ft).
Climate: The country has a maritime temperate climate, with cool summers and mild winters.

ECONOMY

Despite having few natural resources – except natural gas – the Netherlands has a high standard of living. Agriculture and horticulture are highly mechanized with a concentration on dairying and glasshouse crops, particularly flowers. Food processing is a major industry, and the country is a leading exporter of cheese. Manufacturing includes chemicals, machinery, petroleum refining, metallurgical and electrical engineering industries. Raw materials are imported through Rotterdam, which is the largest port in the world and serves much of Western Europe. Banking and finance are well developed.

RECENT HISTORY

The Congress of Vienna (1815) united all three Low Countries in the Kingdom of the Netherlands under the House of Orange, but Belgium broke away in 1830 and Luxembourg in 1890. The Dutch were neutral in World War I, but suffered occupation by the Germans 1940 to 1945. Following a bitter colonial war, the Dutch accepted that they could not reassert control over Indonesia after World War II. The Netherlands has shown enthusiasm for European unity, and, with the other Low Countries, founded Benelux, the core of the EC. Dutch politics has been characterized by a large number of small parties, some of a confessional nature, and a system of proportional representation has prevented any of these parties attaining a parliamentary majority. The formation of a new coalition government after each general election has been difficult and time-consuming.

DUTCH EXTERNAL TERRITORIES

Aruba (an island off the coast of Venezuela) *Area:* 193 km² (75 sq mi). *Population:* 63 000 (1989 est). *Capital:* Oranjestad 16 000 (1985).
Netherlands Antilles (also called **The Antilles of the Five**; Curaçao and Bonaire are off the coast of Venezuela; the other three islands are in the Leeward Islands in the eastern Caribbean.) *Area:* 800 km² (309 sq mi) – Curaçao 444 km² (171 sq mi), Bonaire 288 km² (111 sq mi), St Maarten 34 km² (13 sq mi), St Eustatius – popularly known as Statia – 21 km² (8 sq mi), Saba 13 km² (5 sq mi). *Population:* 183 000 (1989) – Curaçao 147 000, Bonaire 8800, St Maarten 13 200, St Eustatius 1400, Saba 1000 (all 1981). *Capital:* Willemstad 50 000 (1981). (Kralendijk is the capital of Bonaire, Philipsburg of St Maarten, Oranjestad of St Eustatius, and Bottom of Saba.)

NEW ZEALAND

Official name: Dominion of New Zealand.
Member of: UN, Commonwealth, ANZUS, South Pacific Forum, OECD.
Population: 3 359 000 (1989 est).
Capital and major cities: Wellington 351 000, Auckland 899 000, Christchurch 333 000, Hamilton 169 000, Napier with Hastings 116 000, Dunedin 113 000, Palmerston North 94 000, Invercargill 54 000, Rotorua 51 000, New Plymouth 46 000, Nelson 44 000, Whangarei 43 000, Wanganui 40 000 (all including suburbs; 1988 est).

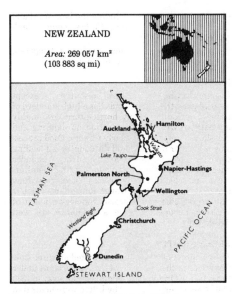

NEW ZEALAND

Area: 269 057 km²
(103 883 sq mi)

Languages: English (official), Maori.

Religions: Anglican (25%), Presbyterian (nearly 20%), Roman Catholic (over 15%).

Life expectancy: 74.5 years.

Labour force: (1988) 1 591 000; services 397 000, trade and tourism 299 000, agriculture and forestry 156 000.

GOVERNMENT

The 97-member House of Representatives is elected by universal adult suffrage for three years to represent single-member constituencies, four of which have a Maori electorate and representative. The Governor General – the representative of the British Queen as sovereign of New Zealand – appoints a Prime Minister who commands a majority in the House. The PM, in turn, appoints a Cabinet, which is responsible to the House. The main political parties are the Labour Party and the (conservative) National Party. Tokelau is an autonomous island territory.
Prime Minister: Jim Bolger.

ISLAND TERRITORY

Tokelau *Area:* 13 km² (5 sq mi). *Population:* 1700 (1986). *Capital:* there is no capital; each atoll has its own administrative centre.

EDUCATION

Literacy rate: no figure available. *Years of compulsory schooling:* 6–15. *Universities:* 6, plus an agricultural college with university status.

DEFENCE

Total armed strength: 12 400 (1989). *Military service:* none.

GEOGRAPHY

On South Island, the Southern Alps run from north to south, and in the southwest reach the sea in the deeply indented coast of Fjordland. The Canterbury Plains lie to the east of the mountains. North Island is mainly hilly with isolated mountains, including volcanoes – two of which are active. Lowlands on

North Island are largely restricted to coastal areas and the Waikato Valley. *Principal rivers:* Waikato, Clutha, Waihou, Rangitaiki, Mokau, Wanganui, Manawatu. *Highest point:* Mount Cook 3764 m (12 349 ft).

Climate: The climate is temperate, although the north is warmer. Rainfall is abundant almost everywhere, but totals vary considerably with altitude and aspect, rising to over 6350 mm (250 in) on the west coast of South Island.

ECONOMY

The majority of New Zealand's export earnings come from agriculture, in particular meat, wool and dairy products. Forestry is expanding and supports an important pulp and paper industry. Apart from coal, lignite, natural gas and gold, the country has few natural resources, although its considerable hydroelectric-power potential has been exploited to produce plentiful cheap electricity – an important basis of New Zealand's manufacturing industry. Natural gas – from the Kapuni Field on North Island and the Maui Field off the Taranaki coast – is converted to liquid fuel. Despite having only a small domestic market and being remote from the world's major industrial powers, New Zealand has a high standard of living.

RECENT HISTORY

North Island was ceded to the British Crown by Maori chiefs under the Treaty of Waitangi (1840), while South Island was claimed by right of discovery. New Zealand was governed as a part of New South Wales until a separate colonial government was established in 1841. The 1840s were marked by fierce armed resistance to British settlement by the Maoris, the majority of whom live in North Island. Relations between the Maoris and the white settlers deteriorated further during the 1850s as the colonists sought more land and Maori chiefs increasingly refused to sell it. When troops were used to evict Maoris from disputed lands in Waitara, war broke out (1860). Fighting continued for most of the decade in North Island, and guerrilla action in the King Country – the centre of North Island – was not suppressed until 1870. The Maori Wars retarded the European settlement of North Island, while – in the last quarter of the 19th century – the discovery of gold and the introduction of refrigerated ships to export meat and dairy products greatly stimulated the colonization and economy of South Island. However, by the beginning of the 20th century, North Island was dominant again, and by 1911 migrants from Britain had boosted the country's population to one million. Subsequent immigration has remained overwhelmingly British, although there are sizeable communities of Samoans, Cook Islanders, Yugoslavs and Dutch.

Liberal governments (1891–1912) pioneered many reforms and social measures, including votes for women (1893) and the world's first old-age pensions (1898). Dominion status was granted in 1907, although the country did not formally acknowledge its independent status until 1947. In World War I, New Zealand fought as a British ally in Europe, achieving distinction in the disastrous Allied expedition to the Gallipoli peninsula during the campaign against Turkey (1915). When Japan entered World War II in 1941, New Zealand's more immediate security was threatened. The major role played by the USA in the Pacific War led to New Zealand's postwar alliance with Australia and America in the ANZUS pact, and the country sent troops to support the Americans in Vietnam.

The entry of Britain into the EC in 1973 restricted the access of New Zealand's agricultural products to what had been their principal market. Since then New Zealand has been forced to seek new markets, particularly in the Far and Middle East. Under Labour governments (1972–75 and 1984–90), the country adopted an independent foreign and defence policy. A ban on vessels powered by nuclear energy or carrying nuclear weapons in New Zealand's waters placed a question mark over the country's role as a full ANZUS member.

NEW ZEALAND'S DEPENDENT TERRITORIES

Ross Dependency See p. 638.

NEW ZEALAND'S ASSOCIATED TERRITORIES

Cook Islands (a group of 15 islands in the southern Pacific Ocean). *Area*: 234 km² (90 sq mi). *Population*: 18 000 (1989 est). *Capital*: Avarua 5000 (1985 est).

Niue (an island in the southern Pacific Ocean). *Area*: 259 km² (100 sq mi). *Population*: 2100 (1989). *Capital*: Alofi 1000 (1989 est).

NICARAGUA

Official name: República de Nicaragua (Republic of Nicaragua).

Member of: UN, OAS, CACM, LAIA (observer).

Population: 3 745 000 (1989 est).

Capital and main cities: Managua 1 000 000, León 101 000, Granada 89 000 (1986 est).

Languages: Spanish (official), Miskito.

Religion: Roman Catholic (90%).

Life expectancy: 62 years.

Labour force: (1980) 864 000; agriculture and forestry 392 000, services 175 500, commerce 105 000.

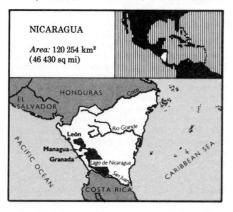

NICARAGUA

Area: 120 254 km²
(46 430 sq mi)

GOVERNMENT

The 92-member National Assembly is elected by proportional representation for six years by universal adult suffrage. The President – who appoints a Cabinet – is also directly elected for a six-year term. The main political parties include the (left-wing) FSLN (Sandinista National Liberation Front) and the (14-party coalition) UNO (National Opposition Union).
President: Violetta Chamorro.

EDUCATION

Literacy rate: 88% (est). *Years of compulsory schooling:* 7–12. *Universities:* 4.

DEFENCE

Total armed strength: 80 000 (1989). *Military service:* none.

GEOGRAPHY

A fertile plain on the Pacific coast contains the majority of the population. Mountain ranges rise in the centre of the country. Tropical jungle covers the Atlantic coastal plain. *Principal rivers:* Coco, Rio Grande, San Juan, Escondido. *Highest point:* Pico Mogotón 2107 m (6913 ft).
Climate: The climate is tropical and humid with a rainy season from May to October.

ECONOMY

A largely agricultural economy has been devastated by guerrilla warfare, a US trade embargo and hurricanes. Coffee, cotton and sugar cane are the main export crops.

RECENT HISTORY

Nicaragua remained a Spanish possession until independence was gained in 1821. Independent Nicaragua witnessed strife between conservatives and liberals. Early in the 20th century, the political situation deteriorated, provoking American intervention – US marines were based in Nicaragua from 1912 to 1925, and again from 1927 until 1933. General Anastasio Somoza became president in 1937. Employing dictatorial methods, members of the Somoza family, or their supporters, remained in power until overthrown by a popular uprising led by the Sandinista guerrilla army in 1979. Accusing the Sandinistas of introducing Communism, the USA imposed a trade embargo on Nicaragua, making it increasingly dependent on Cuba and the USSR. Right-wing Contra guerrillas, financed by the USA, fought the Sandinistas from bases in Honduras. A ceasefire between the Contras and Sandinistas was agreed in 1989. In free presidential elections in February 1990, the Sandinista incumbent Daniel Ortega was defeated by Violetta Chamorro of the opposition coalition.

NIGER

Official name: La République du Niger (The Republic of Niger).

Member of: UN, OAU, ECOWAS.

Population: 7 523 000 (1989 est).

Capital and main cities: Niamey 399 000, Zinder 83 000, Maradi 65 000 (1983 est).

Languages: French (official), Hausa (60%).

Religion: Sunni Islam (85%).

Life expectancy: 44.5 years.

Labour force: (1988 est) 3 444 000; agriculture and forestry 3 034 000, services 210 000, industry 47 000.

GOVERNMENT

The 1989 constitution provides for a 93-member National Assembly to be indirectly elected by regional and local meetings of the sole legal political party – the MNSD (Mouvement National pour la Sociétié de Développement). The President – who appoints a

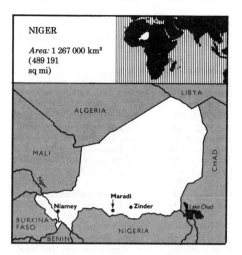

NIGER

Area: 1 267 000 km²
(489 191
sq mi)

Prime Minister – is elected for seven years.
President: Brig. Gen. Ali Saibou.
Prime Minister: Aliou Mahamidou.

EDUCATION

Literacy rate: 14% (1985 est). *Years of compulsory schooling:* 7–15. *Universities:* 2.

DEFENCE

Total armed strength: 3200 (1989). *Military service:* 2 years (selective).

GEOGRAPHY

Most of Niger lies in the Sahara Desert; the south and the Niger Valley are savannah. The central Aïr Mountains rise to just over 2000 m (6562 ft). *Principal rivers:* Niger, Dillia. *Highest point:* Mont Gréboun 2022 m (6634 ft).
Climate: Niger is dry and hot. The south has a rainy season from June to October.

ECONOMY

Livestock herds and harvests of subsistence crops – millet, sorghum, cassava and rice – have been reduced by desertification. Uranium is mined.

RECENT HISTORY

The French territory of Niger was proclaimed in 1901, but much of the country was not brought under French control until 1920. Independence was achieved in 1960 under President Hamani Diori. After the economy was wracked by a prolonged drought, Diori was overthrown in a military coup (1974). In 1989, civilian rule was restored – although the military head of state retained power. Following student demonstrations against austerity measures and in favour of a multi-party system (1990–91), it was announced that a conference would be convened in May 1991 to usher in political changes.

NIGERIA

Official name: The Federal Republic of Nigeria.
Member of: UN, OAU, Commonwealth, OPEC, ECOWAS.
Population: 117 000 000 (1990 est).
Capital and major cities: Abuja (new federal

capital, still under construction) 289 000, Lagos (existing capital) 3 000 000 (1990 est), Ibadan 1 200 000, Ogbomosho 620 000, Kano 565 000, Oshogbo 400 000, Ilorin 400 000 (1989 est), Abeokuta 309 000, Port Harcourt 296 000, Ilesha 273 000, Onitsha 269 000 (1983).
Languages: English (official), with over 150 local languages, of which Hausa, Yoruba and Ibo are the most widely spoken.
Religions: Sunni Islam (nearly 45%), various Christian Churches including Anglican, Roman Catholic, Methodist, Lutheran, Baptist and Presbyterian (nearly 35%).
Life expectancy: 50.5 years.
Labour force: (1983) 29 453 000; agriculture and forestry 9 296 000, trade and tourism 6 534 000, services 7 081 000.

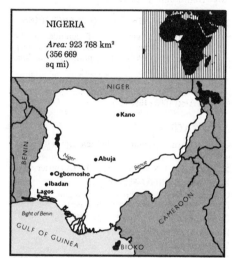

NIGERIA

Area: 923 768 km²
(356 669
sq mi)

GOVERNMENT

Since 1983 Nigeria has been ruled by the Armed Forces Ruling Council whose President is head of state and of government. Elections by universal adult suffrage are scheduled to be held before the end of 1992 for the 21 state administrations, a 450-member Federal Assembly and a President to serve a six-year term. Two political parties – the Social Democratic Party and the National Republican Convention – were legalized in 1989.
President: Gen. Ibrahim Babangida.

NIGERIAN STATES

The population figures for the states are 1989 estimates.
Akwa Ibom *Area:* 8381 km² (3236 sq mi). *Population:* 5 215 000. *Capital:* Uyo 48 000 (1983).
Anambra *Area:* 17 675 km² (6824 sq mi). *Population:* 7 404 000. *Capital:* Enugu 228 000 (1983).
Bauchi *Area:* 64 605 km² (24 944 sq mi). *Population:* 5 005 000. *Capital:* Bauchi 62 000 (1983).
Bendel *Area:* 35 500 km² (13 707 sq mi). *Population:* 5 066 000. *Capital:* Benin City 166 000 (1983).
Benue *Area:* 45 174 km² (17 442 sq mi). *Population:* 4 996 000. *Capital:* Makurdi 89 000 (1983).
Borno *Area:* 116 400 km² (44 942 sq mi). *Population:* 6 170 000. *Capital:* Maiduguri 231 000 (1983).

Cross River *Area*: 18 856 km² (7280 sq mi). *Population*: 1 945 000. *Capital*: Calabar 126 000 (1983).

Gongola *Area*: 91 390 km² (35 286 sq mi).*Population*: 5 363 000. *Capital*: Yola 10 000 (1983).

Imo *Area*: 11 850 km² (4575 sq mi). *Population*: 7 560 000. *Capital*: Owerri 35 000 (1983).

Kaduna *Area*: 45 745 km² (17 662 sq mi). *Population*: 3 403 000. *Capital*: Kaduna 247 000 (1983).

Kano *Area*: 43 285 km² (16 712 sq mi). *Population*: 11 888 000. *Capital*: Kano 565 000 (1989).

Katsina *Area*: 24 500 km² (9460 sq mi). *Population*: 5 033 000. *Capital*: Katsina 149 000 (1983).

Kwara *Area*: 66 896 km² (25 818 sq mi). *Population*: 3 513 000. *Capital*: Ilorin 400 000 (1989).

Lagos *Area*: 3345 km² (1292 sq mi). *Population*: 4 345 000. *Capital*: Ikeja 60 000 (1983). *Largest city*: Lagos 3 000 000 (1989 est).

Niger *Area*: 65 037 km² (25 111 km²). *Population*: 2 223 000. *Capital*: Minna 99 000 (1983).

Ogun *Area*: 16 762 km² (6472 sq mi). *Population*: 3 193 000. *Capital*: Abeokuta 309 000 (1983).

Ondo *Area*: 20 959 km² (8092 sq mi). *Population*: 5 619 000. *Capital*: Akure 117 000 (1983).

Oyo *Area*: 37 705 km² (14 558 sq mi). *Population*: 10 723 000. *Capital*: Ibadan 1 200 000 (1989).

Plateau *Area*: 58 030 km² (22 405 sq mi). *Population*: 4 145 000. *Capital*: Jos 149 000 (1983).

Rivers *Area*: 21 850 km² (8436 sq mi). *Population*: 3 541 000. *Capital*: Port-Harcourt 296 000 (1983).

Sokoto *Area*: 102 535 km² (39 589 sq mi). *Population*: 9 343 000. *Capital*: Sokoto 148 000 (1983).

Federal Capital Territory *Area*: 7315 km² (2824 sq mi). *Population*: 280 000. *Capital*: Abuja 280 000 (1989).

EDUCATION

Literacy rate: 35% (1984). *Years of compulsory schooling*: 6–12. *Universities*: 24 (18 federal and 6 state).

DEFENCE

Total armed strength: 94 500 (1989). *Military service*: none.

GEOGRAPHY

Inland from the swampy forest and tropical jungles of the coastal plains, Nigeria comprises a series of plateaux covered – for the most part – by open woodland or savannah. The far north is semi-desert. Isolated ranges of hills rise above the plateaux, the highest of which are the central Jos Plateau and the Biu Plateau in the northeast. *Principal rivers*: Niger, Benue, Cross River, Yobe, Osse. *Highest point*: Vogel Peak (Dimlany) 2042 m (6700 ft).

Climate: The coastal areas are very humid and hot, with an average temperature of 32 ° C (90 ° F). Rainfall is heavy on the coast but decreases gradually inland – although there is a rainy season from April to October. The dry far north experiences the Harmattan, a hot wind blowing out of the Sahara.

ECONOMY

Nigeria is the major economic power in West Africa. The country depends upon revenue from petroleum exports, but a combination of falling petroleum prices and OPEC quotas has resulted in major economic problems, although it has also encouraged diversification. Natural gas is to be exported in liquid form to Europe. Major industries include petrochemicals, textiles and food processing. Over 50% of the labour force is involved in agriculture, mainly producing maize, sorghum, cassava, yams and rice as subsistence crops. Cocoa is an important export.

RECENT HISTORY

In 1861, Britain acquired Lagos, and in 1885 a British protectorate was established on the coast. In the scramble for empire, the commercial Royal Niger Company colonized the interior from 1886, and in 1900 its territories were surrendered to the British Crown as the protectorate of Northern Nigeria. In 1914 the coast and the interior were united to form Britain's largest African colony. An unwieldy federal structure introduced in 1954 was unable to contain regional rivalries after independence (1960). In 1966, the first Prime Minister, Sir Abubakar Tafawa Balewa (1912–66), and other prominent politicians were assassinated in a military coup. After a counter-coup brought General Yakubu Gowon to power, a bitter civil war took place (1967–70) when the Eastern Region – the homeland of the Ibo – attempted to secede as Biafra. Although the East was quickly re-integrated once Biafra was defeated, Nigeria remained politically unstable. The number of states was gradually increased from 3 to 21 in an attempt to prevent any one region becoming dominant. A military coup overthrew Gowon in 1975, and an attempt at civilian rule (1979–83) also ended in a coup. Another coup brought General Ibrahim Babangida to power in 1985. It is planned to reintroduce civilian rule before the end of 1992.

NORWAY

Official name: Kongeriket Norge (Kingdom of Norway).

Member of: UN, EFTA, NATO, CSCE, Council of Europe, OECD.

Population: 4 233 000 (1990 est).

Capital and major cities: Oslo 456 000, Bergen 211 000, Trondheim 136 000, Stavanger 97 000, Kristiansand 64 000, Drammen 52 000 (1989).

Languages: Two official forms of Norwegian – Bokmaal (80%), Nynorsk (or Landsmaal; 20%); Lappish.

Religion: Lutheran (official; nearly 90%).

Life expectancy: 77 years.

Labour force: 2 114 000 (1988 employment figure); civil and business services 739 000, commerce 390 000, manufacturing 337 000.

GOVERNMENT

Norway is a constitutional monarchy. The 165-member Parliament (Storting) is elected under a system of proportional representation by universal adult suffrage for a four-year term. In order to legislate, the Storting divides itself into two houses – the Lagting (containing one quarter of the members) and the Odelsting (containing the remaining three quarters of the members). The King appoints a Prime Minister who commands a majority in the Storting. The PM, in turn, appoints a Council of Ministers who are responsible to the Storting. The main political parties include the Labour Party, the Conservative Party, the Christian Democratic Party, the Centre Party, the Socialist Left Party, the Progress Party and the Liberal Party.

NORWAY

Area: 323 878 km² (125 050 sq mi), or 386 958 km² (149 469 sq mi) including the Arctic island territories of Svalbard (formerly known as Spitzbergen) and Jan Mayen

King: HM King Harald V (succeeded upon the death of his father, 17 January 1991).
Prime Minister: Gro Harlem Bruntland.

EDUCATION
Literacy rate: no figure available. *Years of compulsory schooling:* 7–16. *Universities:* 4, plus 11 institutions of higher education.

DEFENCE
Total armed strength: 34 100 (1989). *Military service:* 12 months army, 15 months navy and air force. Conscripts are liable to recall.

GEOGRAPHY
Norway's coastline is characterized by fjords, a series of long, deep, narrow inlets formed by glacial action. The greater part of Norway comprises highlands of hard rock. The principal lowlands are along the Skagerrak coast and around Oslofjord and Trondheimsfjord. Svalbard (Spitsbergen) is a bleak archipelago in the Arctic. *Principal rivers*: Glomma (Glama), Lågen, Tanaelv. *Highest point*: Galdhøpiggen 2469 m (8098 ft).
Climate: Norway's temperate climate is the result of the warming Gulf Stream. Summers are remarkably mild for the latitude, while winters are long and very cold. Precipitation is heavy – over 2000 mm (80 in) in the west, with marked rain shadows inland.

ECONOMY
Norway enjoys a high standard of living. Only a small proportion of the land can be cultivated, and agriculture – which is heavily subsidized – is chiefly concerned with dairying and fodder crops. Timber is a major export of Norway, over one half of which is forested. The fishing industry is an important foreign-currency earner, and fish farming – which has been encouraged by government development schemes – is taking the place of whaling and deep-sea fishing. Manufacturing – which has traditionally been concerned with processing fish, timber and iron ore – is now dominated by petrochemicals and allied industries, based upon large reserves of petroleum and natural gas in Norway's sector of the North Sea. Petroleum and natural gas supply over one third of the country's export earnings. The development of industries such as electrical engineering has been helped by cheap hydroelectric power.

RECENT HISTORY
Danish kings ruled Norway as a part of their own realm from the 14th century until 1814. At the end of the Napoleonic Wars, Norway attempted to regain autonomy, but the country came under the rule of the kings of Sweden, although a separate Norwegian Parliament was allowed a considerable degree of independence. Growing nationalism in Norway placed great strains upon the union with Sweden, and in 1905 – following a vote by the Norwegians to repeal the union – King Oscar II of Sweden gave up his claims to the Norwegian crown to allow a peaceful separation of the two countries. After a Swedish prince declined the Norwegian throne, Prince Carl of Denmark was confirmed as King of Norway – as Haakon VII – by a plebiscite. Norway was neutral in World War I, and declared neutrality in World War II, but was occupied by German forces (1940) who set up a puppet government under Vidkun Quisling. After the war, Norway joined NATO and agreed in 1972 to enter the EC, but a national referendum rejected membership.

NORWEGIAN EXTERNAL TERRITORIES
Norwegian Antarctic Territories (Bouvet Island, Peter I Island, Queen Maud Land): see p. 638.

OMAN
Official name: Sultanat 'Uman (Sultanate of Oman).
Member of: UN, Arab League, GCC.
Population: 1 422 000 (1989 est).
Capital: Muscat 85 000 (with suburbs; 1982 est).
Languages: Arabic (official), Baluchi.
Religions: Ibadi Islam (75%), Sunni Islam (25%).
Life expectancy: 55.4 years.
Labour force: (1988 est) 393 000; agriculture and forestry 165 000, services 85 000, industry 65 000.

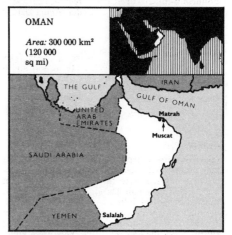

OMAN

Area: 300 000 km² (120 000 sq mi)

GOVERNMENT
Oman is an absolute monarchy in which the Sultan – who rules by decree – is advised by an appointed Cabinet. The Sultan appoints the 52 members of the State Consultative Council. In 1990 it was announced that an elected consultative assembly would be established. There are no political parties.
Sultan: HM Qaboos bin Said (succeeded upon the deposition of his father, 23 July 1970).

EDUCATION
Literacy rate: 20% (1988). *Years of compulsory schooling:* schooling is not compulsory. *Universities:* 1.

DEFENCE

Total armed strength: 25 500 (1989). *Military service*: none.

GEOGRAPHY

A barren range of hills rises sharply behind a narrow coastal plain. Desert extends inland into the Rub' al Khali ('The Empty Quarter'). A small detached portion of Oman lies north of the United Arab Emirates. There are no significant rivers. *Highest point*: Jabal ash Sham 3170 m (10 400 ft).

Climate: Oman is very hot in the summer, but milder in the winter and the mountains. The country is extremely arid with an average annual rainfall of 50 to 100 mm (2 to 4 in).

ECONOMY

Oman depends almost entirely upon exports of petroleum and natural gas. Owing to aridity, less than 1% of Oman is cultivated.

RECENT HISTORY

Ahmad ibn Sa'id, who became Imam in 1749, founded the dynasty that still rules Oman. His successors built an empire including the Kenyan coast and Zanzibar, but in 1861 Zanzibar and Oman separated. A British presence was established in the 19th century and Oman did not regain complete independence until 1951. Sultan Qaboos – who came to power in a palace coup in 1970 – has modernized and developed Oman. In the 1970s South Yemen supported left-wing separatist guerrillas in the southern province of Dhofar, but the revolt was suppressed with military assistance from the UK.

PAKISTAN

Official name: Islami Jamhuria-e-Pakistan (Islamic Republic of Pakistan).

Member of: UN, Commonwealth, SAARC.

Population: 118 820 000 (1989 est; including the Pakistani-held areas of Kashmir – Azad Kashmir – and the disputed Northern Areas – Gilgit, Baltistan and Diamir).

Capital and major cities: Islamabad 201 000, Karachi 5 103 000, Lahore 2 922 000, Faisalabad 1 092 000, Rawalpindi 806 000, Hyderabad 795 000, Multan 730 000, Gujranwala 597 000, Peshawar 555 000, Sialkot 302 000, Sargodha 291 000, Quetta 286 000 (1981).

Languages: Urdu (national; 20%), Punjabi (60%), Sindhi (12%), English, Pushto, Baluchi.

Religions: Sunni Islam (official; 92%), Shia Islam (5%), with small Ismaili Muslim and Ahmadi minorities.

Life expectancy: 54.5 years.

Labour force: (1985) 29 000 000; agriculture and forestry 14 000 000, manufacturing 4 000 000, trade and tourism 3 000 000.

GOVERNMENT

The 87-member Senate (the upper house of the Federal Legislature) comprises 19 senators elected for six years by each of the four provinces, plus 8 senators elected from the federally administered Tribal Areas and 3 senators chosen to represent the federal capital. The 237-member National Assembly comprises 207 members elected by universal adult suffrage for five years, 20 seats reserved for women, and 10 members representing non-Islamic minorities. The President – who is chosen by the Federal

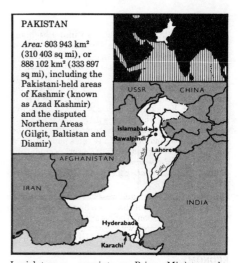

PAKISTAN

Area: 803 943 km² (310 403 sq mi), or 888 102 km² (333 897 sq mi), including the Pakistani-held areas of Kashmir (known as Azad Kashmir) and the disputed Northern Areas (Gilgit, Baltistan and Diamir)

Legislature – appoints a Prime Minister who commands a majority in the National Assembly. The PM, in turn, appoints a Cabinet of Ministers, responsible to the Assembly. The President has the power to dismiss the current government and dissolve the national and provincial assemblies. The main political parties include the PPP (Pakistan People's Party) and the (coalition) Islamic Democratic Alliance. The four provinces, Azad Kashmir and the Northern Areas have their own legislatures.
President: Ghulam Ishaq Khan.
Prime Minister: Nawaz Sharif.

PAKISTANI PROVINCES

Population figures for the provinces are for 1983.

Baluchistan *Area*: 347 188 km² (134 050 sq mi). *Population*: 4 611 000. *Capital*: Quetta 286 000.

North-West Frontier *Area*: 74 522 km² (28 773 sq mi). *Population*: 11 658 000. *Capital*: Peshawar 555 000.

Punjab *Area*: 205 345 km² (79 284 sq mi). *Population*: 50 460 000. *Capital*: Lahore 2 922 000.

Sind *Area*: 140 913 km² (54 407 sq mi). *Population*: 20 312 000. *Capital*: Karachi 5 103 000.

Federal Capital Territory *Area*: 907 km² (350 sq mi). *Population*: 204 000. *Capital*: Islamabad 201 000.

DISPUTED TERRITORIES

The disputed territories – the 'state' of Azad Kashmir and the agencies of Baltistan, Gilgit and Diamir – are held by Pakistan but are disputed by India. *Combined area*: 83 806 km² (32 358 sq mi). *Combined population*: 2 300 000.

Azad Kashmir *Capital*: Muzaffarabad.

Baltistan *Capital*: Skardu.

Diamir *Capital*: Chilas.

Gilgit *Capital*: Gilgit.

EDUCATION

Literacy rate: 30% (1985 est). *Years of compulsory schooling*: schooling is not compulsory. *Universities*: 22.

DEFENCE

Total armed strength: 520 000 (1989). *Military service*: none.

GEOGRAPHY

The Indus Valley divides Pakistan into a highland region in the west and a lowland region in the east. In Baluchistan – in the south – the highlands consist of ridges of hills and low mountains running northeast to southwest. In the north – in the North-West Frontier Province and the disputed territories – the mountain chains rise to over 7000 m (21 300 ft) and include the Karakoram, and parts of the Himalaya and Hindu Kush. The Indus Valley – and the valleys of its tributaries – form a major agricultural region and contain the majority of Pakistan's population. A continuation of the Indian Thar Desert occupies the east. *Principal rivers:* Indus, Sutlej, Chenab, Ravi, Jhelum. *Highest point:* K2 (Mount Godwin Austen) 8607 m (28 238 ft).

Climate: The north and west of Pakistan are arid; the south and much of the east experience a form of the tropical monsoon. Temperatures vary dramatically by season and with altitude, from the hot tropical coast to the cold mountains of the far north.

ECONOMY

Nearly one half of the labour force is involved in subsistence farming, with wheat and rice as the main crops. Cotton is the main foreign-currency earner. The government is encouraging irrigation schemes, but over one half of the cultivated land is subject to either waterlogging or salinity. Although there is a wide range of mineral reserves – including coal, gold, graphite, copper and manganese – these resources have not been extensively developed. Manufacturing is dominated by food processing, textiles and consumer goods. Unemployment and underemployment are major problems, and the country relies heavily upon foreign aid and money sent back by Pakistanis working abroad.

RECENT HISTORY

From the 18th century the region came under British rule. Pakistan as a nation was born in August 1947 when British India was partitioned as a result of demands by the Muslim League for an Islamic state in which Hindus would not be in a majority. Large numbers of Muslims moved to the new state and up to 1 000 000 people died in the bloodshed that accompanied partition. Pakistan had two 'wings' – West Pakistan (the present country) and East Pakistan (now Bangladesh) – separated by 1600 km (1000 mi) of Indian territory. A number of areas were disputed with India. Kashmir – the principal bone of contention – was effectively partitioned between the two nations, and in 1947–49 and 1965 tension over Kashmir led to war between India and Pakistan. The problem of Kashmir remains unsolved, with fighting continuing intermittently along parts of the cease-fire line.

The Muslim League leader Muhammad Ali Jinnah (1876–1949) was the first Governor General, but Jinnah, who was regarded as 'father of the nation', died soon after independence. Pakistan – which became a republic in 1956 – suffered political instability and periods of military rule, including the administrations of General Muhammad Ayub Khan (from 1958 to 1969) and General Muhammad Yahya Khan (from 1969 to 1971). Although East Pakistan contained the majority of the population, from the beginning West Pakistan held political and military dominance. In elections in 1970, Shaikh Mujibur Rahman's Awami League won an overwhelming majority in East Pakistan, while the Pakistan

People's Party (PPP) won most of the seats in West Pakistan. Mujibur Rahman seemed less interested in leading a new Pakistani government than in winning autonomy for the East. In March 1971, after abortive negotiations, the Pakistani army was sent from the West to East Pakistan, which promptly declared its independence as Bangladesh. Civil war broke out and India supported the new state, forcing the Pakistani army to surrender by the end of the year.

The leader of the PPP, Zulfiqar Ali Bhutto (PM 1972–77), was deposed in a military coup led by the Army Chief of Staff, Muhammad Zia al-Haq. Bhutto was imprisoned (1977) for allegedly ordering the murder of the father of a former political opponent, sentenced to death (1978) and, despite international protests, hanged (1979). In 1985 Zia lifted martial law and began to return Pakistan to civilian life. In 1986 Bhutto's daughter and the PPP's new leader, Benazir, was allowed to return to Pakistan, where her political rallies attracted enormous crowds. In 1988 Zia was killed in a plane crash. In scheduled elections a few months later the PPP became the largest party, and Benazir Bhutto became the first woman prime minister of an Islamic state. In August 1990, she was accused of nepotism and corruption by the president and dismissed. The following elections were won by the Islamic Democratic Alliance.

PANAMA

Official name: La República de Panamá (The Republic of Panama).

Member of: UN, OAS, LAIA (observer).

Population: 2 370 000 (1989 est).

Capital and major cities: Panama City 688 000 (including suburbs), San Miguelito 252 000 (part of the Panama City agglomeration), Colón 59 000, David 50 000 (1989).

Languages: Spanish (official).

Religions: Roman Catholic (over 90%).

Life expectancy: 73 years.

Labour force: 689 000 (1989 employment figure); agriculture and forestry 203 000, services 202 000, trade and tourism 103 000.

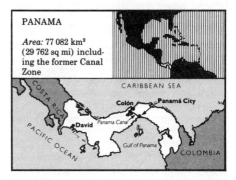

PANAMA

Area: 77 082 km² (29 762 sq mi) including the former Canal Zone

CARIBBEAN SEA

COSTA RICA   Colón   Panamá City

PACIFIC OCEAN   David   *Panama Canal*   Gulf of Panama   COLOMBIA

GOVERNMENT

The constitution provides for the election by compulsory universal adult suffrage of a 67-member Legislative Assembly, a President and two Vice Presidents for five years. The President appoints a Cabinet of Ministers. The main political parties include the Authentic Liberal Party, the Christian Democratic Party and the Nationalist Republican Liberation

Movement (who cooperated in the 1989 elections as the Democratic Alliance), the Authentic Panamenista Party, and the (coalition) Colina. *President*: Guillermo Endara.

EDUCATION

Literacy rate: 89% (1985). *Years of compulsory schooling*: 6–15. *Universities*: 3.

DEFENCE

Total armed strength: 4400 (1989). *Military service*: none.

GEOGRAPHY

Panama is a heavily forested mountainous isthmus joining Central America to South America. *Principal rivers*: Tuira (with Chucunaque), Bayano, Santa Maria. *Highest point*: Chiriqui 3475 m (11 467 ft).
Climate: Panama has a tropical climate with little seasonal change in temperature.

ECONOMY

Income from the Panama Canal is a major foreign-currency earner. Panama has a higher standard of living than its neighbours, although the political crisis of 1989 damaged the economy. Major exports include bananas, shrimps and mahogany.

RECENT HISTORY

Panama was part of Spanish New Granada (Colombia). In the 1880s a French attempt to construct a canal through Panama linking the Atlantic and Pacific Oceans proved unsuccessful. After Colombia rejected US proposals for completing the canal, Panama became independent (1903), sponsored by the USA. The canal eventually opened in 1914. The USA was given land extending 8 km (5 mi) on either side of the canal – the Canal Zone – complete control of which will be handed to Panama in 2000. From 1983 to 1989 effective power was in the hands of General Manuel Noriega, who was deposed by a US invasion and taken to stand trial in the USA, accused of criminal activities.

PAPUA NEW GUINEA

Official name: The Independent State of Papua New Guinea.

Member of: UN, Commonwealth, South Pacific Forum.

Population: 3 592 000 (1989 est).

Capital and main cities: Port Moresby 152 000, Lae 80 000, Madang 25 000 (1987 est).

Languages: English (official), Pidgin English, Motu, and over 700 other local languages.

Religions: Roman Catholic (over 30%), various Protestant Churches (nearly 30%).

Life expectancy: 54 years.

Labour force: (1980) 733 000; agriculture and forestry 564 500; services 77 000, trade and tourism 25 000.

GOVERNMENT

A 109-member Parliament is elected for five years by universal adult suffrage. The Governor General – the representative of the British Queen as sovereign of Papua New Guinea – appoints a Prime Minister who commands a majority in Parliament. The PM, in turn, appoints a Cabinet, which is responsible to Parlia-

PAPUA NEW GUINEA

Area: 462 840 km² (178 704 sq mi)

ment. The main political parties are the People's Democratic Movement, the People's Progress Party, the Melanesian Alliance, the National Party, and the United Party.
Prime Minister: Rabbie Namaliu.

EDUCATION

Literacy rate: 32%. *Years of compulsory schooling:* schooling is not compulsory. *Universities:* 2.

DEFENCE

Total armed strength: 3200 (1989). *Military service:* to be introduced 1991–92.

GEOGRAPHY

Broad swampy plains surround New Guinea's mountainous interior. *Principal rivers:* Fly (with Strickland), Sepik. *Highest point:* Mount Wilhelm 4509 m (14 493 ft).
Climate: The country experiences a tropical climate with high temperatures and heavy monsoonal rainfall.

ECONOMY

Over 80% of the labour force is involved in agriculture – mainly subsistence farming – although agricultural exports include palm oil, copra and cocoa. The mainstay of the economy is minerals, including large reserves of copper, gold, silver and petroleum.

RECENT HISTORY

European colonization was not attempted until 1828 when the Dutch claimed western New Guinea. A British protectorate, established in the southeast in 1884, was transferred to Australia (1906) and renamed Papua. Northeast New Guinea came under German administration in 1884, but was occupied by Australian forces in 1914. From 1942 to 1945 Japanese forces occupied New Guinea and part of Papua. In 1949 Australia combined the administration of the territories, which achieved independence as Papua New Guinea in 1975. Bougainville island attempted to secede (1990–91).

PARAGUAY

Official name: La República del Paraguay (The Republic of Paraguay).

Member of: UN, OAS, LAIA.

Population: 4 157 000 (1989 est).

Capital and major cities: Asunción 729 000 (including suburbs), San Lorenzo, 124 000, is a part of the Ascunción agglomeration, Ciudad del Este 117 000, Encarnación 64 000, Conceptión 63 000 (1985).

Languages: Spanish (official), Guaraní (90%).

Religion: Roman Catholic (97%).

Life expectancy: 66.1 years.

Labour force: (1982) 1 032 000; agriculture and forestry 445 500, services 174 000, manufacturing 125 000.

PARAGUAY

Area: 406 752 km²
(157 048 sq mi)

BOLIVA

Paraguay

BRAZIL

ARGENTINA

Asunción

Parana

Encarnación

GOVERNMENT

The President (who appoints a Council of Ministers), a 36-member Senate and a 72-member Chamber of Deputies are elected by universal adult suffrage for five years. The political party gaining the largest number of votes receives two thirds of the seats in each House; the remaining seats are allocated proportionately. The main political parties are the Colorado Party and the Authentic Radical Liberal Party.

President: Gen. Andres Rodriguez Pedotti.

EDUCATION

Literacy rate: 88% (1985). *Years of compulsory schooling:* 7–14. *Universities:* 1 state, 1 Catholic.

DEFENCE

Total armed strength: 16 000 (1989). *Military service:* 18 months army, 24 months navy.

GEOGRAPHY

The country west of the Paraguay River – the Chaco – is a flat semiarid plain. The region east of the river is a partly forested undulating plateau. *Principal rivers:* Paraguay, Paraná, Pilcomayo. *Highest point:* Cerro Tatug 700 m (2297 ft).

Climate: The climate is subtropical, with considerable variation in rainfall between the wet southeast and the dry west.

ECONOMY

Agriculture – the main economic activity – is dominated by cattle ranching, cotton and soya beans. Cheap hydroelectric power from the Yacyreta-Apipe dam – the world's longest – has greatly stimulated industry.

RECENT HISTORY

The Jesuits controlled the country from 1609 until 1767, when they were expelled. Since independence

from Spain in 1811, Paraguay has suffered many dictators, including General José Francia, who totally isolated Paraguay (1814–40). War against Argentina, Brazil and Uruguay (1865–70) cost Paraguay over one half of its people and much territory. The Chaco Wars with Bolivia (1929–35) further weakened Paraguay. General Alfredo Stroessner gained power in 1954, ruling with increasing disregard for human rights until his overthrow in a military coup in 1989.

PERU

Official name: República del Perú (Republic of Peru).

Member of: UN, OAS, LAIA.

Population: 21 792 000 (1989 est).

Capital and major cities: Lima 5 494 000, Arequipa 592 000, Callao 560 000, Trujillo 491 000, Chiclayo 395 000, Piura 297 000 (1989 est).

Languages: Spanish, Quechua and Aymara (all official).

Religion: Roman Catholic (official; 95%).

Life expectancy: 61.4 years.

Labour force: (1985) 6 555 500; (1981) 5 314 000, agriculture and forestry 1 934 000, services 1 808 000, trade and tourism 637 000.

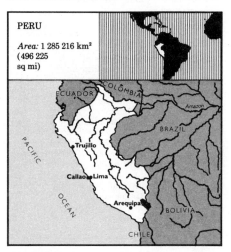

PERU

Area: 1 285 216 km²
(496 225 sq mi)

COLOMBIA

ECUADOR

Amazon

BRAZIL

PACIFIC

Trujillo

OCEAN

Callao **Lima**

Arequipa

BOLIVIA

CHILE

GOVERNMENT

The President and the National Congress – comprising a 60-member Senate and a 180-member Chamber of Deputies – are elected by universal adult suffrage for five years. The President appoints a Council of Ministers headed by a Prime Minister. The main political parties include the (left-wing) APRA (American Popular Revolutionary Alliance), the (centre-right) Democratic Front, the IU (Izquierda Unida – Unified Left), the (liberal) Acción Popular, and Cambio 90.

President: Alberto Fujimori.

Prime Minister: to be announced.

EDUCATION

Literacy rate: 75% (1985 est). *Years of compulsory schooling:* 6–15. *Universities:* 27 national, 19 private (2 of which are Catholic).

DEFENCE

Total armed strength: 120 000 (1989). *Military service:* 2 years selective.

GEOGRAPHY

The coastal plain is narrow and arid. The Andes – which are prone to earthquakes – run in three high parallel ridges from north to south. Nearly two thirds of Peru is tropical forest (the Selva) in the Amazon Basin. *Principal rivers:* Amazon, Ucayali, Napo, Marañón. *Highest point:* Huascarán 6768 m (22 205 ft).

Climate: A wide climatic variety includes semitropical desert – cooled by the Humboldt Current – on the coast, the very cold Alpine High Andes, and the tropical Selva with heavy rainfall.

ECONOMY

About one third of the labour force is involved in agriculture. Subsistence farming dominates in the interior; crops for export are more important near the coast. Major crops include coffee, sugar cane, cotton and potatoes, as well as coca for cocaine. Sheep, llamas, vicuñas and alpacas are kept for wool. Rich natural resources include silver, copper, coal, gold, iron ore, petroleum and phosphates. The fishing industry – once the world's largest – has declined since 1971. A combination of natural disasters, a very high birth rate, guerrilla warfare and the declining value of exports has severely damaged the economy. Peru is very heavily in debt.

RECENT HISTORY

Much of South America was governed from Lima as the Spanish Viceroyalty of Peru. Independence was proclaimed in 1821 after the Argentine San Martín took Lima, but Spanish forces did not leave until 1824. Independent Peru saw political domination by large landowners. Progress was made under General Ramon Castilla (1844–62) and civilian constitutional governments at the beginning of the 20th century, but instability and military coups have been common. War (1879–83) in alliance with Bolivia against Chile resulted in the loss of nitrate deposits in the south, while victory against Ecuador (1941) added Amazonian territory. From 1968 a reformist military government instituted a programme of land reform, attempting to benefit workers and the Indians, but faced with mounting economic problems the military swung to the right in 1975. Since 1980 elections have been held regularly, but owing to the economic crisis and the growth of an extreme left-wing guerrilla movement – the Sendero Luminoso ('Shining Path') – Peru's democracy remains fragile.

THE PHILIPPINES

Official name: República ñg Pilipinas (Republic of the Philippines).

Member of: UN, ASEAN.

Population: 60 097 000 (1989 est).

Capital and major cities: Manila 5 926 000, Quezon City 1 166 000 (part of the Manila agglomeration), Davao City 610 000, Cebu City 490 000, Zamboango City 344 000, Bacolod City 262 000, Iloilo City 245 000 (1980).

Languages: Pilipino (based on Tagalog; national), Tagalog (over 20%), English (40%), Spanish, Cebuano (over 20%), Iloco (10%), with many local languages.

Religions: Roman Catholic (85%), Aglipayan Church (4%), Sunni Islam (4%).

Life expectancy: 64 years.

Labour force: (1988) 22 937 000; agriculture and

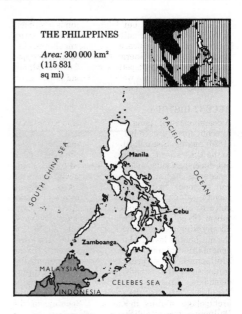

THE PHILIPPINES

Area: 300 000 km²
(115 831 sq mi)

forestry 10 163 000, wholesale and retail trade 3 000 000, manufacturing 2 000 000.

GOVERNMENT

The President and the 24-member Senate – the upper House of Congress – are elected by universal adult suffrage for six years. The House of Representatives – the lower House of Congress – comprises 200 directly elected members and no more than 50 members appointed by the President from minority groups. The President appoints a Cabinet of Ministers. The main political parties include the Liberal Party, PDP–Laban (Pilipino Democratic Party–People's Power Movement), and the Nacionalista Party. *President:* Corazon Aquino.

EDUCATION

Literacy rate: 73% (1980). *Years of compulsory schooling:* 7–13. *Universities:* 52.

DEFENCE

Total armed strength: 112 000 (1989). *Military service:* none.

GEOGRAPHY

Some 2770 of the Philippines' 7000 islands are named. The two largest islands, Luzon and Mindanao, make up over two thirds of the country's area. Most of the archipelago is mountainous with restricted coastal plains, although Luzon has a large, densely populated central plain. Earthquakes are common. *Principal rivers:* Cagayan, Pampanga, Abra, Agusan, Magat, Laoang, Agno. *Highest point:* Mount Apo 2954 m (9692 ft).

Climate: The climate is tropical maritime with high humidity, high temperatures and heavy rainfall. Typhoons are frequent.

ECONOMY

Almost one half of the labour force is involved in agriculture. Rice and maize are the principal subsistence crops, while coconuts, sugar cane, pineapples and bananas are grown for export. The timber industry is important, but deforestation is a problem as land is cleared for cultivation. Major industries include textiles, food processing, chemicals and electrical engineering. Mineral resources include copper (a major export), gold, petroleum and nickel. Money sent back by Filipinos working abroad is an important source of foreign currency.

RECENT HISTORY

A combination of rising nationalism and resentment at economic injustice led to an unsuccessful revolt (1896) against Spanish rule. The islands were ceded to the USA after the Spanish-American War (1898), but American rule had to be imposed by force and resistance continued until 1906. A powerful American presence had a profound effect on Filipino society, which bears the triple imprint of Asian culture, Spanish Catholicism and American capitalism. US policy in the Philippines wavered between accelerating and delaying Filipino self-rule. In 1935 the nationalist leader Manuel Quezon became president of the semi-independent 'Commonwealth' of the Philippines. The surprise Japanese invasion of 1941 traumatized the islands' American and Filipino defenders. Japan set up a puppet 'Philippine Republic', but, after the American recapture of the archipelago, a fully independent Republic of the Philippines was established in 1946.

Between 1953 and 1957 the charismatic President Ramon Magsaysay crushed and conciliated Communist-dominated Hukbalahap guerrillas, but his death ended a programme of land reforms. Coming to power in 1965, Ferdinand Marcos (1917–89) inaugurated flamboyant development projects, but his administration presided over corruption on an unprecedented scale. Marcos used the continuing guerrilla activity as a justification for his increasingly repressive rule. When he attempted to rig the result of presidential elections in 1986, Marcos was overthrown in a popular revolution in favour of Corazon Aquino. President Aquino is the widow of a leading opposition politician who had allegedly been murdered on Marcos' orders. Her government has faced several attempted military coups and groups of insurgents including the (Islamic) Moro National Liberation Front and the (Communist) New People's Army.

POLAND

Official name: Polska Rzecpospolita (Republic of Poland).

Member of: UN, CSCE, Council of Europe (guest).

Population: 37 931 000 (1989 est).

Capital and major cities: Warsaw (Warszawa) 1 671 000, Lódź 845 000, Kraków 745 000, Wroclaw 640 000, Poznań 586 000, Gdańsk 469 000, Szczecin 409 500, Bydgoszcz 378 000, Katowice 366 000 (1988 est).

Language: Polish.

Religion: Roman Catholic (94%).

Life expectancy: 72 years.

Labour force: (1978) 17 962 000; agriculture and forestry 5 419 000, manufacturing 5 370 000, services 3 097 000.

GOVERNMENT

The 100-member Senate – the upper house – and the 460-member Sejm – the lower house – are elected for four years by universal adult suffrage. (Only 161 of

POLAND

Area: 312 683 km² (120 727 sq mi)

the members of the Sejm were elected on a multiparty basis in 1989. The remaining 299 seats in the Sejm were reserved for candidates representing the Communists and two allied parties.) The President – who is directly elected – appoints a Prime Minister who commands a majority in the Sejm. The PM, in turn, appoints a Council of Ministers. The main political parties are Solidarity Citizen's Committee (according to its constitution, a trade union and not formally a political party), the Liberal Democratic Congress (an offshoot of Solidarity, formed in support of Lech Walesa's presidential candidacy), ZSL (the United Peasants' Party), SD (the Democratic Party), and the Social Democracy Party (the former Communist Party).
President: Lech Walesa.
Prime Minister: Jan Krzysztof Bielecki.

EDUCATION

Literacy rate: 98%. *Years of compulsory schooling:* 7–14. *Universities:* 11.

DEFENCE

Total armed strength: 412 000 (1989 est). *Military service:* 18 months army and airforce, 2 years navy.

GEOGRAPHY

Most of Poland consists of lowlands. In the north are the Baltic lowlands and the Pomeranian and Mazurian lake districts. Central Poland is a region of plains. In the south are the hills of Little Poland and the Tatra Mountains, part of the Carpathian chain. *Principal rivers:* Vistula (Wisa), Oder (Odra), Narew. *Highest point:* Rysy 2499 m (8199 ft).
Climate: Poland's climate tends towards continental with short warm summers and longer cold winters.

ECONOMY

Polish agriculture remains predominantly small-scale and privately owned. Over one quarter of the labour force is still involved in agriculture, growing potatoes, wheat, barley, sugar beet and a range of fodder crops. The industrial sector is large-scale and, until the switch to a free-market economy began in 1990, centrally planned. Poland has major deposits of coal, as well as reserves of natural gas, copper and silver. Engineering, food processing, and the chemical, metallurgical and paper industries are important, but the economic situation has steadily deteriorated since the 1960s. To add to inflation and a rampant black market, Poland has crippling foreign debts. The USA and EC began considerable aid programmes in 1989, and some progress has been made towards privatization.

RECENT HISTORY

In the 19th century the greater part of Poland was within Imperial Russia, against which the Poles revolted unsuccessfully in 1830, 1848 and 1863. National feeling also grew in the areas ruled by Austria and Prussia. After World War I, Poland was restored to statehood (1919), but the country was unstable. Marshal Józef Pilsudski (1867–1935) staged a coup in 1926, and became a virtual dictator. During the 1930s relations with Hitler's Germany – which made territorial claims on parts of Poland – became strained. An alliance with Britain was not enough to deter Hitler from attacking Poland, and thus precipitating World War II (1939). Poland was partitioned once again, this time between Nazi Germany and the USSR. Occupied Poland lost one sixth of its population, including almost all the Jews, and casualties were high after the ill-fated Warsaw Rising (1944). Poland was liberated by the Red Army (1945), and a Communist state was established. The new Poland lost almost one half its territory in the east to the USSR, but was compensated in the north and west at the expense of Germany.

A political crisis in 1956 led to the emergence of a Communist leader who enjoyed a measure of popular support, Wladyslaw Gomulka. In 1980, following the downfall of Gomulka's successor, Edward Gierek, a period of unrest led to the birth of the independent trade union Solidarity (Solidarność), led by Lech Walesa (1943–). Martial law was declared by General Wojciech Jaruzelski in 1981 in an attempt to restore Communist authority. Solidarity was banned and its leaders were detained, but public unrest and economic difficulties continued. In 1989 Solidarity was legalized and agreement was reached on political reform. Solidarity won free elections to the new Senate, and with the support of former allies of the Communists won enough seats to gain a majority in the Sejm, and Tadeusz Mazowiecki of Solidarity became PM. Disagreements concerning the speed at which market reforms were advancing and personality clashes during the presidential election split Solidarity in 1990. Walesa became president in December 1990, and it was announced that multi-party elections for the Sejm would be held in 1991.

PORTUGAL

Official name: A República Portuguesa (The Portuguese Republic).

Member of: UN, EC, NATO, Council of Europe, CSCE, WEU, OECD.

Population: 10 372 000 (1989 est) including Madeira and the Azores.

Capital and major cities: Lisbon (Lisboa) 1 612 000, Oporto (Porto) 1 315 000, Amadora (part of the Lisbon agglomeration) 96 000, Setúbal 77 000, Coímbra 72 000, Braga 64 000, Vila Nova de Gaia 62 500 (part of the Oporto agglomeration), Barreiro 51 000 (part of the Lisbon agglomeration), Funchal 44 000 (1981; all including suburbs).

Language: Portuguese (official).

Religion: Roman Catholic (nearly 90%).

Life expectancy: 73 years.

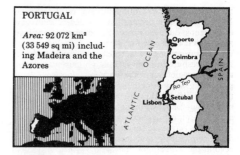

PORTUGAL

Area: 92 072 km² (33 549 sq mi) including Madeira and the Azores

Labour force: (1987) 4 732 000; manufacturing 1 081 000, services 976 000, agriculture and forestry 975 500.

GOVERNMENT

An executive President is elected for a five-year term by universal adult suffrage. The 250-member Assembly is directly elected for four years. The President appoints a Prime Minister who commands a majority in the Assembly. The PM, in turn, appoints a Council of Ministers (Cabinet), responsible to the Assembly. The main political parties include PSD (the Social Democratic Party), PS (the Socialist Party), the (centre-left) PRD (Democratic Renewal Party), the (centre-right) CDS (the Centre Democratic Party), and PCP (the Communist Party). Madeira and the Azores have their own autonomous governments.
President: Mario Alberto Soares.
Prime Minister: Anibal Cavaco Silva.

PORTUGUESE AUTONOMOUS REGIONS

Azores (Açores) *Area:* 2247 km² (868 sq mi). *Population:* 254 000 (1988). *Capital:* Ponta Delgada 22 000 (1981).
Madeira (includes Porto Santo) *Area:* 794 km² (306 sq mi). *Population:* 272 000 (1988). *Capital:* Funchal 44 000 (1981).

EDUCATION

Literacy rate: 86% (1988). *Years of compulsory schooling:* 6–15. *Universities:* 13.

DEFENCE

Total armed strength: 75 300 (1989). *Military service:* 12–15 months army, 18–20 months navy and air force.

GEOGRAPHY

Behind a coastal plain, Portugal north of the River Tagus is a highland region, at the centre of which is the country's principal mountain range, the Serra da Estrela. A wide plateau in the northeast is a continuation of the Spanish Meseta. Portugal south of the Tagus is mainly an undulating lowland. The Atlantic islands of Madeira and the Azores are respectively nearly 1000 km (620 mi) and 1200 km (745 mi) southwest of the mainland. *Principal rivers:* Tagus (Rio Tejo), Douro, Guadiana. *Highest point:* Pico 2315 m (7713 ft) in the Azores. Malhao de Estrela, at 1993 m (6537 ft), is the highest point on the mainland.
Climate: Portugal has a mild and temperate climate which is wetter and more Atlantic in the north, and drier, hotter and more Mediterranean inland and in the south.

ECONOMY

Agriculture involves about 20% of the labour force,

but lacks investment following land reforms in the 1970s, since when production has fallen. The principal crops include wheat and maize, as well as grapes (for wines such as port and Madeira), tomatoes, potatoes and cork trees. The country lacks natural resources. Manufacturing industry includes textiles and clothing (major exports), footwear, food processing, cork products, and, increasingly, electrical appliances and petrochemicals. Tourism and money sent back by Portuguese working abroad are major foreign-currency earners. Despite recent impressive economic development – following severe disruption during and immediately after the 1974 revolution – Portugal remains Western Europe's poorest country.

RECENT HISTORY

Portugal experienced political instability for much of the 19th century. Portugal's African empire was confirmed, although the country lacked the power to gain more territory in the scramble for Africa. The monarchy was violently overthrown in 1910, but the Portuguese republic proved unstable and the military took power in 1926. From 1932 to 1968, under the dictatorship of Premier Antonio Salazar (1889–1970), stability was achieved but at great cost. Portugal became a one-party state, and expensive colonial wars dragged on as Portugal attempted to check independence movements in Angola and Mozambique. In 1974 there was a left-wing military coup whose leaders granted independence to the African colonies (1974–75), and initially attempted to impose a Marxist system on the country. However, elections in 1976 decisively rejected the far left. Civilian rule was restored as Portugal effected a transition from dictatorship to democracy, and simultaneously – through the loss of empire and membership of the EC (from 1986) – became more closely integrated with the rest of Europe.

PORTUGUESE OVERSEAS TERRITORY

Macau (an enclave on the southern Chinese coast) *Area*: 17 km² (6.5 sq mi). *Population*: 484 000 (1989). *Capital*: Macau 484 000.

QATAR

Official name: Dawlat Qatar (State of Qatar).
Member of: UN, Arab League, OPEC, GCC.
Population: 427 000 (1989 est).
Capital: Doha 217 000 (1986).
Language: Arabic.
Religion: Wahhabi Sunni Islam (official; 98%).
Life expectancy: 70 years.
Labour force: (1986) 200 000; services 96 500, building and construction 40 500, trade and tourism 22 000, agriculture and forestry 6000.

GOVERNMENT

Qatar is an absolute monarchy. The Amir – who is head of state and of government – appoints a Council of Ministers. There is a 30-member nominated Advisory Council, but there are neither formal elected institutions nor political parties.
Amir and head of government: HH Shaikh Khalifa bin Hamad Al-Thani (succeeded upon the deposition of his cousin, 22 February 1972).

EDUCATION

Literacy rate: 40%. *Years of compulsory schooling:* schooling is not compulsory. *Universities:* 1.

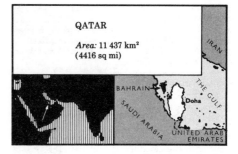

QATAR

Area: 11 437 km²
(4416 sq mi)

DEFENCE

Total armed strength: 7000 (1989). *Military service:* none.

GEOGRAPHY

Qatar is a low barren peninsula projecting into the Gulf. There are no rivers. *Highest point:* 73 m (240 ft) in the Dukhan Heights.

Climate: Qatar is very hot in summer, but milder in winter. Rainfall averages between 50 and 75 mm (2 to 4 in).

ECONOMY

Qatar's high standard of living is due almost entirely to the export of petroleum and natural gas. The steel and cement industries have been developed in an attempt to diversify.

RECENT HISTORY

In the 1860s Britain intervened in a dispute between Qatar and its Bahraini rulers, installing a member of the Qatari Al-Thani family as shaikh. Qatar was part of the Ottoman Empire from 1872 until 1914. Its ruler signed protection treaties with Britain in 1916 and 1934, and did not regain complete independence until 1971. Qatar joined the coalition against Saddam Hussein's Iraq in the Second Gulf War (1991).

ROMANIA

Official name: Rômania.
Member of: UN, CSCE, Council of Europe (guest).
Population: 23 200 000 (1989 est)
Capital and major cities: Bucharest (Bucuresti) 2 014 000, Brasov 352 000, Constanta 333 000, Timisoara 325 000, Iasi 313 000, Cluj-Napoca 310 000, Galati 295 000, Craiova 281 000 (1986 est).
Languages: Romanian (official; over 90%), Hungarian (under 8%), German.
Religions: Orthodox (85%), Roman Catholic.
Life expectancy: 70 years.
Labour force: (1977) 10 794 000; agriculture and forestry 3 976 000, industry 3 503 000, services 1 324 000.

GOVERNMENT

The President, directly elected by universal adult suffrage for a 30-month term, may hold office for a maximum of two terms. A 396-seat National Assembly and 119-seat Senate also serve 30-month terms of office, and are elected on a modified system of proportional representation. The main political parties include the National Salvation Front, the Magyar Democratic Union of Romania, the National

ROMANIA

Area: 237 500 km²
(91 699
sq mi)

Liberal Party, and the National Peasants' Party.
President: Ion Iliescu.
Prime Minister: Petre Roman.

EDUCATION

Literacy rate: 98%. *Years of compulsory schooling*:
6–16. *Universities*: 7.

DEFENCE

Total armed strength: 171 000 (1989 est). *Military
service*: 16 months army and air force, 24 months
navy.

GEOGRAPHY

The Carpathian Mountains run through the north,
east and centre of Romania. To the west of the
Carpathians is the tableland of Transylvania and the
Banat lowland. In the south the Danube Plain ends in
a delta on the Black Sea. *Principal rivers*: Danube
(Dunăria), Mures, Prut. *Highest point*: Moldoveanu
2544 m (8346 ft).
Climate: Romania experiences cold snowy winters
and hot summers. Rainfall is moderate in the lowlands but heavier in the Carpathians.

ECONOMY

State-owned industry – which employs nearly 40% of
the labour force – includes mining, metallurgy,
mechanical engineering and chemicals. Natural resources include petroleum and natural gas. Considerable forests support a timber and furniture
industry. Major crops include maize, sugar beet,
wheat, potatoes and grapes for wine, but agriculture
has been neglected, and – because of exports – food
supplies have fallen short of the country's needs.
Economic mismanagement under Ceausescu decreased already low living standards.

RECENT HISTORY

Romania's independence from the (Turkish)
Ottoman Empire was internationally recognized in
1878. When both the Russian and Austro-Hungarian
Empires collapsed at the end of World War I,
Romania won additional territory with substantial
Romanian populations from both. 'Greater Romania'
was beset with deep social and ethnic divisions,
which found expression in the rise of the Fascist Iron
Guard in the 1930s. King Carol II suppressed the
Guard and substituted his own dictatorship, but he

was forced by Germany to cede lands back to
Hungary (1940), while the USSR retook considerable
territories, including the present Moldavian Soviet
Republic. Carol fled and Romania – under Marshal
Ion Antonescu – joined the Axis powers (1941),
fighting the USSR to regain lost territories. King
Michael dismissed Antonescu and declared war on
Germany as the Red Army invaded (1944), and a
Soviet-dominated government was installed (1945).
The monarchy was abolished in 1947. From 1952,
under Gheorghe Gheorghiu-Dej (1901–65) and then
under Nicolae Ceausescu (1918–89), Romania dis-
tanced itself from Soviet foreign policy while main-
taining strict Communist orthodoxy at home.
Ceausescu – and his wife Elena – impoverished
Romania by their harsh, corrupt and nepotistic rule.
When the secret police – the Securitate – put down
demonstrations in Timisoara (1989), a national
revolt (backed by the army) broke out. A National
Salvation Front (NSF) was formed (22 December
1989) and a military tribunal executed Nicolae and
Elena Ceausescu on charges of genocide and corruption (25 December 1989). The Communist Party was
dissolved and much of Ceausescu's oppressive social
and economic legislation was annulled. However,
opposition groups expressed doubts concerning the
NSF's commitment to democracy and were unable to
gain access to the media. In May 1990, Ion Iliescu was
elected president, and the National Salvation Front,
of which he was leader, was confirmed in power by a
huge majority. An international team of monitors
judged Romania's first post-war multi-party elections to be 'flawed' but not fraudulent. Romania has
sought to obtain Western aid and investment to
overcome severe social and economic problems.

RWANDA

Official name: La République Rwandaise
(French) or Republika y'u Rwanda (Kinyarwanda)
(Republic of Rwanda).
Member of: UN, OAU.
Population: 6 990 000 (1989 est).
Capital and main cities: Kigali 157 000, Butare
22 000, Ruhengeri 16 000 (1981).
Languages: French and Kinyarwanda (both
official).
Religions: Animist, Roman Catholic.
Life expectancy: 48.5 years.
Labour force: (1988 est) 3 320 000; agriculture
and forestry 3 041 000, services 73 603, trade and
tourism 26 000.

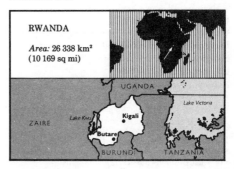

RWANDA

Area: 26 338 km²
(10 169 sq mi)

GOVERNMENT

The President (who appoints a Council of Ministers)
and the 70-member National Development Council

are elected for five years by compulsory universal adult suffrage. The MRND party (Mouvement Révolutionnaire National pour le Développement) was the only legal political party until February 1991, when it was announced that other parties would be allowed to operate.
President: Maj. Gen. Juvenal Habyarimana.

EDUCATION
Literacy rate: 47% (1985 est). *Years of compulsory schooling:* 7–15. *Universities:* 1.

DEFENCE
Total armed strength: 5200 (1989). *Military service:* none.

GEOGRAPHY
Rwanda is a mountainous country. Most of the western boundary is formed by Lake Kivu. *Principal river:* Luvironza. *Highest point:* Mont Karisimbi 4507 m (14 787 ft).
Climate: The climate is tropical with cooler temperatures in the mountains.

ECONOMY
Subsistence farming dominates Rwanda's economy. Coffee and tin are the main exports. There are major (largely unexploited) reserves of natural gas under Lake Kivu.

RECENT HISTORY
The feudal kingdom of Rwanda was a German possession from 1890 until it was taken over by Belgium after World War I. The monarchy – of the dominant minority Tutsi people – was overthrown by the majority Hutu population shortly before independence in 1962. Tribal violence followed an unsuccessful Tutsi attempt to regain power in 1963, and strife between the Hutu and Tutsi has continued intermittently. In 1990–91 an army of Tutsi refugees invaded Rwanda, occupying much of the north. In February 1991, in an attempt to solve the problem, Rwanda's neighbours agreed to grant citizenship to Tutsi refugees, and Rwanda conceded the principle of multi-party elections.

SAINT CHRISTOPHER AND NEVIS
Official name: The Federation of Saint Christopher and Nevis. St Christopher is popularly known as St Kitts.
Member of: UN, Commonwealth, CARICOM, OAS.
Population: 44 000 (1989 est).
Capital: Basseterre 18 500 (1986 est).
Language: English (official).
Religion: Anglican majority.
Life expectancy: 67 years.
Labour force: (1984 est) 14 800; agriculture and forestry 4000, manufacturing 2000, public utilities 1000.

GOVERNMENT
The National Assembly consists of 11 members elected by universal adult suffrage for five years and 3 or 4 appointed members. The Governor General – the representative of the British Queen as sovereign of St Kitts – appoints a Prime Minister who commands a majority in the Assembly. The PM appoints a Cabinet responsible to the Assembly. The

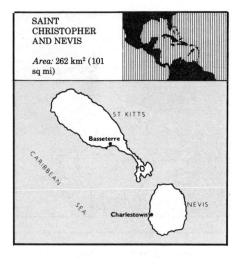

SAINT CHRISTOPHER AND NEVIS

Area: 262 km² (101 sq mi)

main political parties are the People's Action Movement, the Labour Party, and the Nevis Reformation Party. Nevis has its own legislature.
Prime Minister: Kennedy Simmonds.

AUTONOMOUS ISLAND
Nevis *Area:* 93 km² (36 sq mi). *Population:* 9600 (1986). *Capital:* Charlestown 1700 (1986).

EDUCATION
Literacy rate: 91% (1980). *Years of compulsory schooling:* 5–14. *Universities:* an extra-mural department of the University of the West Indies.

DEFENCE
Total armed strength: there are no armed forces.

GEOGRAPHY
St Kitts and Nevis are two well-watered mountainous islands, set 3 km (2 mi) apart. There are no significant rivers. *Highest point:* Nevis Peak 985 m (3232 ft).
Climate: The moist tropical climate is cooled by sea breezes.

ECONOMY
The economy is based on agriculture (mainly sugar cane) and tourism.

RECENT HISTORY
St Kitts was united with Nevis and the more distant small island of Anguilla in a single British colony, which gained internal self-government in 1967. When Anguilla – a reluctant partner – proclaimed independence in 1967, the British intervened, eventually restoring Anguilla to colonial rule while St Kitts-Nevis progressed to independence in 1983.

SAINT LUCIA
Member of: UN, Commonwealth, CARICOM, OAS.
Population: 150 000 (1989).
Capital and main towns: Castries 53 000, Vieux Fort 13 500 (1986 est).
Languages: English (official), French patois (majority).

Religion: Roman Catholic (over 80%).
Life expectancy: 70 years.
Labour force: (1980) 49 500 (no other figures are available).

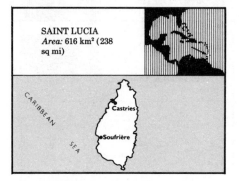

SAINT LUCIA
Area: 616 km² (238 sq mi)

Castries
Soufrière
CARIBBEAN SEA

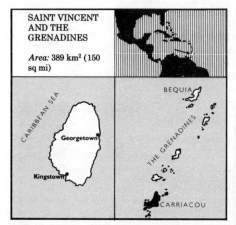

SAINT VINCENT AND THE GRENADINES
Area: 389 km² (150 sq mi)

CARIBBEAN SEA
Georgetown
Kingstown
BEQUIA
THE GRENADINES
CARRIACOU

GOVERNMENT

The 11-member Senate is appointed. The 17-member House of Assembly is elected by universal adult suffrage for five years. The Governor General – as representative of the British Queen as sovereign of St Lucia – appoints a Prime Minister who commands a majority in the House. The PM, in turn, appoints a Cabinet which is responsible to the House. The main political parties are the United Workers' Party, the Labour Party, and the Progressive Labour Party.
Prime Minister: John Compton.

EDUCATION

Literacy rate: 78%. *Years of compulsory schooling:* 5–15. *Universities:* 1 (extra-mural branch of the University of the West Indies).

DEFENCE

Total armed strength: there are no armed forces.

GEOGRAPHY

St Lucia is a forested mountainous island. There are no significant rivers. *Highest point:* Mount Gimie 959 m (3145 ft).
Climate: St Lucia has a wet tropical climate. There is a dry season from January to April.

ECONOMY

The economy depends on agriculture, with bananas and coconuts as the main crops. Tourism is increasingly important.

RECENT HISTORY

After being disputed by England and France, St Lucia finally became a British colony in 1814. Internal self-government was achieved in 1967 and independence in 1979.

SAINT VINCENT AND THE GRENADINES

Member of: UN, OAS, CARICOM, Commonwealth.
Population: 114 000 (1989 est).
Capital: Kingstown 19 000 (1987 est).
Language: English (official).
Religions: Anglican, Methodist, Roman Catholic.
Life expectancy: 71 years.

Labour force: (1980) 35 000; agriculture and forestry 9000, services 7500, trade and tourism 2500.

GOVERNMENT

The single-chamber House of Assembly consists of 6 nominated senators and 15 representatives elected for five years by universal adult suffrage. The Governor General – who is the representative of the British Queen as sovereign of St Vincent – appoints a Prime Minister who commands a majority of the representatives. The PM in turn appoints a Cabinet responsible to the House. The main political parties are the New Democratic Party and the Labour Party.
Prime Minister: David Jack.

EDUCATION

Literacy rate: 85% (1983). *Years of compulsory schooling:* schooling is not compulsory. *Universities:* none.

DEFENCE

Total armed strength: there are no armed forces.

GEOGRAPHY

St Vincent is a mountainous wooded island. The Grenadines – which include Bequia and Mustique – are a chain of small islands to the south of St Vincent. There are no significant rivers. *Highest point:* Mount Soufrière, an active volcano, 1234 m (4048 ft).
Climate: The country experiences a tropical climate with very heavy rainfall in the mountains.

ECONOMY

Bananas and arrowroot are the main crops of a largely agricultural economy.

RECENT HISTORY

The island became a British colony in 1763, gained internal self-government in 1969, and achieved independence in 1979.

SAN MARINO

Official name: Serenissima Repubblica di San Marino (Most Serene Republic of San Marino).
Member of: CSCE, Council of Europe, UN (observer).
Population: 22 900 (1989).
Capital and main towns: San Marino 4500

(including Borgo Maggiore 2100), Seravalle 4600 (1989 est).
Language: Italian.
Religion: Roman Catholic (official).
Life expectancy: 77 years.
Labour force: (1987) 12 000; manufacturing 4000, civil service 2000, commerce 2000.

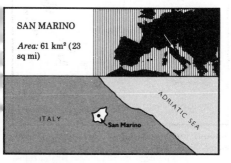

SAN MARINO

Area: 61 km² (23 sq mi)

ITALY · San Marino · ADRIATIC SEA

GOVERNMENT

The 60-member Great and General Council is elected by universal adult suffrage for five years. The Council elects two of its members to be Captains-Regent, who jointly hold office as heads of state and of government for six months. The Captains-Regent preside over a 10-member Congress of State – the equivalent of a Cabinet – which is elected by the Council for five years. The main political parties are the (conservative) Christian Democratic Party, the Socialist Party, and the Communist Party.

EDUCATION

Literacy rate: 98% (1987). *Years of compulsory schooling:* 6–14. *Universities:* none.

DEFENCE

Total armed strength: there are no armed forces.

GEOGRAPHY

The country is dominated by the triple limestone peaks of Monte Titano, the highest point at 739 m (2424 ft). There are no significant rivers.
Climate: San Marino has a mild Mediterranean climate.

ECONOMY

Manufacturing and tourism – in particular visitors on excursions – are the mainstays of the economy.

RECENT HISTORY

San Marino has retained its autonomy because of its isolation and by playing off powerful neighbours against each other. Its independence was recognized by Napoleon (1797), the Congress of Vienna (1815) and the new Kingdom of Italy (1862). In 1957 a bloodless 'revolution' replaced the Communist-Socialist administration that had been in power since 1945.

SÃO TOMÉ E PRÍNCIPE

Official name: A República Democrática de São Tomé e Príncipe (The Democratic Republic of São Tomé and Príncipe).
Member of: UN, OAU.
Population: 118 000 (1989 est).

Capital: São Tomé 35 000 (1984 est).
Language: Portuguese (official).
Religion: Roman Catholic majority.
Life expectancy: 65 years.
Labour force: (1981) 31 000; agriculture and forestry 16 000, trade and tourism 2000, mining 2000.

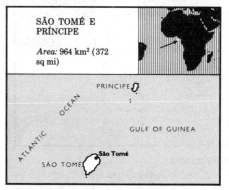

SÃO TOMÉ E PRÍNCIPE

Area: 964 km² (372 sq mi)

PRINCIPE · OCEAN · GULF OF GUINEA · ATLANTIC · SÃO TOMÉ · São Tomé

GOVERNMENT

The 40-member National People's Assembly is elected by universal adult suffrage for five years. Political parties include the (left-wing) MLSTP (the sole legal political party until 1990) and the (moderate) PCD. The President – who appoints a Prime Minister and Council of Ministers – is also directly elected.
President: Daniel Daio.
Prime Minister: Miguel Trovoava.

EDUCATION

Literacy rate: 53% (1981). *Years of compulsory schooling:* schooling is not compulsory. *Universities:* none.

DEFENCE

Total armed strength: 500 (1989). *Military service:* none.

GEOGRAPHY

The republic consists of two mountainous islands about 144 km (90 mi) apart. There are no significant rivers. *Highest point:* Pico Gago Coutinho (Pico de São Tomé) 2024 m (6640 ft).
Climate: The climate is tropical. A wet season – with heavy rainfall – lasts from October to May.

ECONOMY

Cocoa is the mainstay of a largely agricultural economy. Most of the land is nationalized.

HISTORY

Early in the 20th century, the islands' plantations were notorious for forced labour. Independence from Portugal was gained in 1975 as a one-party socialist state. An invasion and coup attempt failed in 1988. Economic difficulties have since led the country to lessen its dependence on the USSR, and in 1990 the MLSTP abandoned Marxism. The opposition PCD won multi-party elections in January 1991.

SAUDI ARABIA

Official name: Al-Mamlaka al-'Arabiya as-Sa'udiya (The Kingdom of Saudi Arabia).

Member of: UN, Arab League, OPEC, GCC.

Population: 14 016 000 (1988 est).

Capital and major cities: Riyadh (Ar Riyad) – the royal capital – 1 308 000, Jeddah (Jiddah) – the administrative capital – 1 500 000, Mecca (Makkah) 550 000, Ta'if 300 000 (1981), Medina (Al-Madinah) 198 000, Dammam 128 000, Hufuf 101 000 (1974).

Language: Arabic (official).

Religion: Islam (official) – Sunni (mainly Wahhabi) 85%, Shia 15%.

Life expectancy: 64 years.

Labour force: (1988 est) 3 802 000; agriculture and forestry 1 555 000, services 1 123 000, industry 495 000.

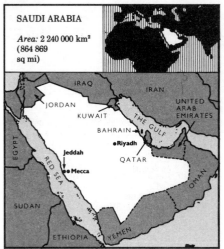

SAUDI ARABIA

Area: 2 240 000 km²
(864 869 sq mi)

GOVERNMENT

Saudi Arabia is an absolute monarchy with neither formal political institutions nor parties. The King – appoints a Council of Ministers. In April 1991 it was announced that an 80-member consultative body would be appointed.

King: HM King Fahd ibn Abdul Aziz Al Saud (succeeded upon the death of his brother, 13 May 1982).

EDUCATION

Literacy rate: 25% (1980 est). *Years of compulsory schooling:* schooling is not compulsory. *Universities:* 7.

DEFENCE

Total armed strength: 65 700 (1989). *Military service:* none.

GEOGRAPHY

Over 95% of the country is desert, including the Rub 'al-Khali ('The Empty Quarter') – the largest expanse of sand in the world. The Arabian plateau ends in the west in a steep escarpment overlooking a coastal plain beside the Red Sea. There are no permanent streams. *Highest point:* Jebel Razikh 3658 m (12 002 ft).

Climate: The country is very hot – with temperatures up to 54 °C (129 °F). The average rainfall is 100 mm (4 in), but many areas receive far less and may not experience any precipitation for years.

ECONOMY

Saudi Arabia's spectacular development and present prosperity are based almost entirely upon exploiting vast reserves of petroleum and natural gas. Industries include petroleum refining, petrochemicals and fertilizers. The country has developed major banking and commercial interests. Less than 1% of the land can be cultivated.

RECENT HISTORY

In the 20th century the Wahhabis – a Sunni Islamic sect – united most of Arabia under Ibn Saud (1882–1953). In 1902 Ibn Saud took Riyadh and in 1906 defeated his rivals to control central Arabia (Nejd). Between 1912 and 1927 he added the east, the southwest (Asir) and Hejaz (the area around Mecca). In 1932 these lands became the kingdom of Saudi Arabia. Although the country has been pro-Western, after the 1973 Arab-Israeli War, Saudi Arabia put pressure on the USA to encourage Israel to withdraw from the occupied territories by cutting oil production. Saudi Arabia has not escaped problems caused by religious fundamentalism and the rivalry between Sunni and Shia Islam. In 1980 Saudi Arabia found itself bound to support Iraq in its war with Shiite Iran. Influenced by the Iranian revolution and the First Gulf War, Saudi Arabia formed the defensive Gulf Cooperation Council (GCC) with its neighbouring emirates. Saudi Arabia was threatened by Iraq following the invasion of Kuwait (August 1990), and played a major role in the coalition against Saddam Hussein in the Second Gulf War (1991).

SENEGAL

Official name: La République du Sénégal (The Republic of Senegal).

Member of: UN, OAU, ECOWAS.

Population: 7 400 000 (1989 est).

Capital and major cities: Dakar 1 382 000, Thies 156 000, Kaolack 132 000, Ziguinchor 107 000, St Louis 92 000 (1985 est).

Languages: French (official), various local languages including Wolof, Serer and Fulani.

Religions: Sunni Islam (90%), Roman Catholic.

Life expectancy: 45.3 years.

Labour force: (1988 est) 3 062 000; agriculture and forestry 2 416 000, services 349 000, industry 170 000.

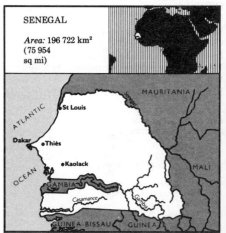

SENEGAL

Area: 196 722 km²
(75 954 sq mi)

GOVERNMENT
Every five years the President and the 120-member National Assembly are elected by universal adult suffrage. The President appoints and leads a Cabinet. Since 1983 there has been no Prime Minister. The number of political parties is constitutionally limited to three – the PS (Parti Socialiste), the (liberal) PDS, and the (Marxist) PAI.
President: Abdou Diouf.

EDUCATION
Literacy rate: 28% (1985 est). *Years of compulsory schooling*: 6–12. *Universities*: 1.

DEFENCE
Total armed strength: 8500 (1989). *Military service*: 2 years (selective).

GEOGRAPHY
Senegal is mostly low-lying and covered by savannah. The Fouta Djalon mountains are in the south. *Principal rivers*: Sénégal, Gambia, Casamance. *Highest point*: Mont Gounou 1515 m (4970 ft).

Climate: Senegal has a tropical climate with a dry season from October to June.

ECONOMY
Over three quarters of the labour force is involved in agriculture, growing groundnuts and cotton as cash crops, and rice, maize, millet and sorghum as subsistence crops. The manufacturing sector is one of the largest in West Africa, but unemployment is a major problem.

RECENT HISTORY
Senegal gradually came under French control from the 17th century. A national political awareness developed early in the 20th century, and the country contributed substantially to the nationalist awakening throughout French Africa. After independence in 1960, under the poet, Léopold Sedar Senghor (1906–), Senegal maintained close relations with France, and received substantial aid. Attempted federations with Mali (1959–60) and Gambia (1981–89) were unsuccessful. Senghor retired in 1980, having re-introduced party politics.

SEYCHELLES
Official name: The Republic of Seychelles.
Member of: UN, OAU, Commonwealth.
Population: 67 000 (1989 est).
Capital: Victoria 23 000 (1983 est).
Languages: Creole (official), English, French.
Religion: Roman Catholic (92%).
Life expectancy: 72 years.
Labour force: (1980) 27 700 (no other figures are available).

GOVERNMENT
The President – who appoints a Council of Ministers – is elected for five years by universal adult suffrage. The National Assembly comprises 23 directly elected members and 2 members appointed by the President. The Seychelles People's Progressive Front is the only legal political party.
President: France Albert René.

EDUCATION
Literacy rate: 60% (1983). *Years of compulsory*

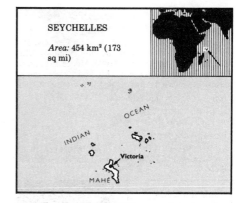

SEYCHELLES
Area: 454 km² (173 sq mi)

schooling: 6–15. *Universities:* none, but there is a polytechnic.

DEFENCE
Total armed strength: 1300. *Military service:* 2 years.

GEOGRAPHY
The Seychelles consist of 40 mountainous granitic islands and just over 50 smaller coral islands. There are no significant rivers. *Highest point:* Morne Seychellois 906 m (2972 ft) on the island of Mahé.

Climate: The islands have a pleasant tropical maritime climate with heavy rainfall.

ECONOMY
The economy depends heavily on tourism, which employs about one third of the labour force.

RECENT HISTORY
The islands became a French colony in the middle of the 18th century, were ceded to Britain in 1814 and gained independence in 1976. The Prime Minister – France Albert René – led a coup against President James Mancham in 1977, and established a one-party socialist state seeking nonalignment. Attempts to overthrow René, including one involving South African mercenaries (1981), have been unsuccessful.

SIERRA LEONE
Official name: The Republic of Sierra Leone.
Member of: UN, OAU, ECOWAS, Commonwealth.
Population: 3 946 000 (1989 est).
Capital and main cities: Freetown 550 000 (including suburbs), Koidu 80 000 (part of the Freetown agglomeration), Bo 26 000 (1985).
Languages: English (official), Krio, Mende.
Religions: Animist majority, Sunni Islam and Christian minorities.
Life expectancy: 40.5 years.
Labour force: (1988 est) 1 380 000; agriculture and forestry 880 000, services 220 000, industry 200 000.

GOVERNMENT
The President – who appoints a Cabinet – is elected for seven years by universal adult suffrage. The 127-member House of Representatives comprises 105 members directly elected for five years, 10 members appointed by the President and 12 Paramount Chiefs.

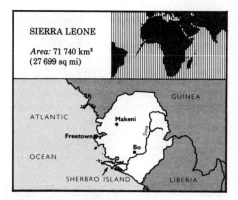

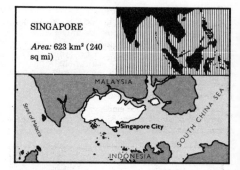

The All-People's Congress is the only legal political party.
President: Joseph Momoh.

EDUCATION

Literacy rate: 30% (1985 est). *Years of compulsory schooling*: schooling is not compulsory. *Universities*: 1.

DEFENCE

Total armed strength: 3150 (1989). *Military service*: none.

GEOGRAPHY

The savannah interior comprises plateaux and mountain ranges. The swampy coastal plain is forested. *Principal rivers*: Siwa, Jong, Rokel. *Highest point*: Bintimani Peak 1948 m (6390 ft).

Climate: The climate is tropical with a dry season from November to June.

ECONOMY

Subsistence farming – mainly rice – involves the majority of the labour force. The decline of diamond mining has added to economic problems, and since 1987 a state of 'economic emergency' has been in operation.

RECENT HISTORY

The coast – an 18th-century settlement for former slaves – became a British colony in 1808; the interior was added in 1896. Independence was gained in 1961. A disputed election led to army intervention (1967), and Dr Siaka Stevens – who came to power in a coup in 1968 – introduced a one-party state. An invasion by Liberian rebels (April-May 1991) disrupted the south and threatened the government.

SINGAPORE

Official name: Hsing-chia p'o Kung-ho Kuo (Chinese) or Republik Singapura (Malay) or Republic of Singapore.

Member of: UN, ASEAN, Commonwealth.

Population: 2 685 000 (1989 est).

Capital: Singapore 2 685 000 (1989 est).

Languages: Malay, Chinese, English and Tamil (all official).

Religions: Buddhist (majority), with Sunni Islam, Christian, Daoist and Hindu minorities.

Life expectancy: 73 years.

Labour force: (1988) 1 281 000; manufacturing 352 500, trade and tourism 283 500, services 271 500, agriculture and forestry 5000.

GOVERNMENT

The 81 members of Parliament are elected from single- and multi-member constituencies by universal adult suffrage for five years. There is constitutional provision for a small number of 'non-constituency' seats for non-elected members of the opposition. The President – who is elected by Parliament for four years – appoints a Prime Minister who commands a parliamentary majority. The PM, in turn, appoints a Cabinet which is responsible to Parliament. It has been announced that the constitution is to be revised to create an executive presidency. The main political party is the People's Action Party; other parties include the Singapore Democratic Party and the Workers' Party.
President: Wee Kim Wee.
Prime Minister: Goh Chok Tong.

EDUCATION

Literacy rate: 87% (1989). *Years of compulsory schooling:* education is not compulsory. *Universities:* 6.

DEFENCE

Total armed strength: 55 500 (1989 est). *Military service:* 30 months enlisted men, 24 months officers.

GEOGRAPHY

Singapore is a low-lying island – with 56 islets – joined to the Malay peninsula by causeway. *Principal river:* Sungei Seletar. *Highest point:* Bukit Timah 177 m (581 ft).

Climate: The climate is tropical with monsoon rains from December to March.

ECONOMY

Singapore relies on imports for its flourishing manufacturing industries and entrepôt trade. Finance and tourism are important. Singapore has the second highest standard of living in Asia, after Japan.

RECENT HISTORY

Singapore was revived by Sir Stamford Raffles for the British East India Company (1819), and developed rapidly as a port for shipping Malaya's tin and rubber. It acquired a cosmopolitan population and became a strategic British base. Occupied by the Japanese (1942–45), it achieved self-government (1959), and joined (1963) and left (1965) the Federation of Malaysia. Since independence it has become wealthy under the strong rule of Prime Minister Lee Kuan Yew (1923– ; PM 1965–91).

SOLOMON ISLANDS

Member of: UN, Commonwealth, South Pacific Forum.

Population: 308 000 (1989 est).

Capital and main cities: Honiara 30 500, Gizo 3700 (1986).

Languages: English (official), Pidgin English, over 85 local (mainly Melanesian) languages.

Religions: Anglican (35%), Roman Catholic (20%), other Christian Churches.

Life expectancy: 69 years.

Labour force: (1986 employment figures) 24 000; agriculture and forestry 8500, services 7000, trade and tourism 2500.

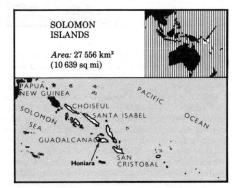

SOLOMON ISLANDS

Area: 27 556 km² (10 639 sq mi)

SOMALIA

Official name: Jamhuuriyadda Dimuqraadiga Soomaaliya (Somali Democratic Republic).

Member of: UN, Arab League, OAU.

Population: 7 339 000 (1989 est).

Capital: Mogadishu 800 000 (1985 est), Hargeisa 70 000, Kismayu 70 000, Berbera 65 000 (1981 est).

Languages: Somali (national), Arabic (official).

Religion: Sunni Islam (official).

Life expectancy: 47 years.

Labour force: (1988 est) 2 842 000; agriculture and forestry 2 048 000, services 300 000, industry 155 000.

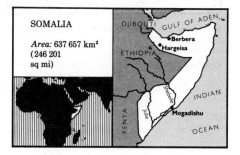

SOMALIA

Area: 637 657 km² (246 201 sq mi)

GOVERNMENT

The 38-member National Parliament – which is elected by universal adult suffrage for four years – elects a Prime Minister who appoints a Cabinet. A Governor General is the representative of the British Queen as sovereign of the islands. The main political parties are the Solomon Islands United Party and the People's Alliance Party. It is expected that a federal republican system will be introduced during the 1990s.

Prime Minister: Solomon Mamaloni.

EDUCATION

Literacy rate: 60%. *Years of compulsory schooling:* schooling is not compulsory. *Universities:* 1 (part of the University of the South Pacific).

DEFENCE

Total armed strength: there are no armed forces.

GEOGRAPHY

The mountainous volcanic Solomons comprise six main islands and several hundred small islands. There are no significant rivers. *Highest point:* Mount Makarakomburu 2447 m (8028 ft).

Climate: The climate is tropical, with temperature and rainfall maximums from November to April.

ECONOMY

One third of the labour force is involved in subsistence farming, although copra, cocoa and coconuts are exported. Lumbering is the main industry.

RECENT HISTORY

The Solomon islanders were exploited as a workforce for plantations in other Pacific islands before Britain established a protectorate in 1893. Occupied by the Japanese (1942–45), the Solomons were the scene of fierce fighting, including a major battle for Guadalcanal. Independence was gained in 1978.

GOVERNMENT

The constitution provides for an Assembly comprising 171 members – 165 elected by universal adult suffrage for five years and 6 appointed by the President, who is elected by direct universal suffrage for a seven-year term. Until 1991, the Somali Revolutionary Socialist Party was the only legal political party. Following the overthrow of President Siad Barre (January 1991) multi-party elections were promised.

Acting President: Ali Madahi Mohamed.

EDUCATION

Literacy rate: 12% (1985 est). *Years of compulsory schooling:* 6–14. *Universities:* 1.

DEFENCE

Total armed strength: 65 000 plus 29 500 paramilitary (1989). *Military service:* 18 months selective.

GEOGRAPHY

Somalia occupies the 'Horn of Africa'. Low-lying plains cover most of the south, while semi-arid mountains rise in the north. *Principal rivers:* Juba, Shebelle. *Highest point:* Surud Ad 2408 m (7900 ft).

Climate: Somalia is hot and largely dry with rainfall totals in the north as low as 330 mm (13 in).

ECONOMY

Nearly two thirds of the labour force are nomadic herdsmen or subsistence farmers. Bananas are grown for export in the south, but much of the country suffers from drought.

RECENT HISTORY

In 1886 Britain established a protectorate in the north of the region, while the Italians took the south. In World War II the Italians briefly occupied British Somaliland. In 1960 the British and Italian territories were united as an independent Somalia. In

1969 the president was assassinated and the army – under Major-General Muhammad Siad Barre – seized control. Barre's socialist Islamic Somalia became an ally of the USSR. In 1977 Somali guerrillas – with Somali military support – drove the Ethiopians out of the largely Somali-inhabited Ogaden. Somalia's Soviet alliance was ended when the USSR supported Ethiopia to regain the Ogaden. In the late 1980s dissident groups within Somalia challenged Barre. In January 1991 they overran the capital and deposed Barre, but rival groups controlled districts in the north and south.

SOUTH AFRICA

Official name: Republic of South Africa or Republiek van Suid-Afrika.

Member of: UN.

Population: 30 193 000 (1989 est) including Walvis Bay – 21 000 (1981) – and the 'independent' homelands – 5 954 000 (1985).

Capital and major cities: Pretoria (administrative capital) 823 000, Cape Town (Kaapstadt) (legislative capital) 1 912 000, Bloemfontein (judicial capital) 233 000, Johannesburg 1 609 000, Durban 982 000, Port Elizabeth 652 000, Vereeniging 540 000, East London 194 000, Pietermaritzburg 193 000, Kimberley 150 000 (all including suburbs; 1985).

Languages: Afrikaans and English (both official), Xhosa, Zulu, Sesotho.

Religions: Dutch Reformed Church, independent African Churches, with Anglican, Methodist, Roman Catholic, Hindu and Sunni Islam minorities.

Life expectancy: 61 years.

Labour force: (1985; excluding the 'independent' homelands) 7 615 500; services 1 965 000, manufacturing 1 379 500, agriculture and forestry 1 179 500.

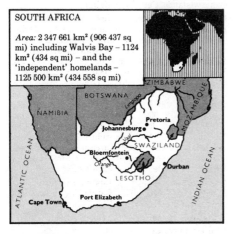

SOUTH AFRICA

Area: 2 347 661 km² (906 437 sq mi) including Walvis Bay – 1124 km² (434 sq mi) – and the 'independent' homelands – 1125 500 km² (434 558 sq mi)

GOVERNMENT

Parliament consists of three chambers elected for five years. The House of Assembly has 166 members elected by adult white suffrage plus 4 members nominated by the President and 8 elected by the House. The House of Representatives has 80 members directly elected by coloured (mixed race) voters, and the House of Delegates has 40 members directly elected by Indian voters – these two Houses also have 2 members nominated by the President and 3 members elected by the House. The State President – who appoints a Cabinet – is chosen by an electoral college

in which members of the (white) House of Assembly form a majority. Blacks have no parliamentary vote, but elect the Legislative Assemblies of the ten homelands. Four homelands – Bophuthatswana, Ciskei, Transkei and Venda – have been granted 'independence' by South Africa, but this status is unrecognized internationally. The main black political parties are the (mainly Xhosa) African National Congress and the (mainly Zulu) Inkatha movement. The main white political parties include the (conservative) National Party, the (centre) Democratic Party, and the (right-wing) Conservative Party. *President:* Frederik Willem De Klerk.

SOUTH AFRICAN PROVINCES

Cape (Kaap) (includes Walvis Bay) *Area:* 641 379 km² (247 638 sq mi). *Population:* 5 041 000. *Capital:* Cape Town (Kaapstadt) 1 912 000.

Natal *Area:* 55 281 km² (21 344 sq mi). *Population:* 2 145 000. *Capital:* Pietermaritzburg 193 000.

Orange Free State (Oranje Vrystaat) *Area:* 127 338 km² (49 166 sq mi). *Population:* 1 777 000. *Capital:* Bloemfontein 233 000.

Transvaal *Area:* 227 034 km² (87 658 sq mi). *Population:* 7 532 000. *Capital:* Pretoria 823 000.

HOMELANDS

Population figures are not available for the capital cities of the homelands.

Bophuthatswana (an 'independent' homeland) *Area:* 44 000 km² (16 988 sq mi). *Population:* 1 433 000 (1983). *Capital:* Mmabatho.

Ciskei (an 'independent' homeland) *Area:* 8500 km² (3280 sq mi). *Population:* 660 000 (1981). *Capital:* Bisho.

Gazankulu *Area:* 6565 km² (2535 sq mi). *Population:* 497 000 (1985). *Capital:* Giyani.

KaNgwane *Area:* 3823 km² (1476 sq mi). *Population:* 393 000 (1985). *Capital:* Louieville.

KwaNdebele *Area:* 3244 km² (1253 sq mi). *Population:* 236 000 (1985). *Capital:* Siyabuswa.

Kwazulu *Area:* 36 074 km² (13 928 sq mi). *Population:* 3 747 000 (1985). *Capital:* Ulundi.

Lebowa *Area:* 21 833 km² (8430 sq mi). *Population:* 1 836 000 (1985). *Capital:* Lebowakgomo.

Qwaqwa *Area:* 655 km² (253 sq mi). *Population:* 182 000 (1985). *Capital:* Phuthadithaba.

Transkei (an 'independent' homeland) *Area:* 41 002 km² (15 831 sq mi). *Population:* 2 524 000 (1983). *Capital:* Umtata.

Venda (an 'independent' homeland) *Area:* 6677 km² (2578 sq mi). *Population:* 377 000 (1983). *Capital:* Thohoyandou.

EDUCATION

Literacy rate: whites 93%, Asians 71%, coloureds 62%, blacks 32%. *Years of compulsory schooling:* 7–16 (7–11 for black children). *Universities:* 17 including 10 white only, 4 black only, 1 mixed race, 1 Indian and 1 'open' university (degrees by correspondence – no colour bar).

DEFENCE

Total armed strength: 103 000 (1989). *Military service:* 1 year (whites).

GEOGRAPHY

The Great Escarpment rises behind a discontinuous

coastal plain and includes the Drakensberg Mountains. A vast plateau occupies the interior, undulating in the west and rising to over 2400 m (about 8000 ft) in the east. Much of the west is semi-desert, while the east is predominantly savannah grassland (veld). Walvis Bay is an enclave on the Namibian coast. *Principal rivers:* Orange (Oranje), Limpopo, Vaal. *Highest point:* Injasuti 3408 m (11 182 ft).

Climate: South Africa has a subtropical climate with considerable regional variations. The hottest period is between December and February. Rainfall is highest on the east coast, but much of the country is dry.

ECONOMY

The country is the world's leading exporter of gold – which normally forms about 40% of South African exports – and a major producer of uranium, diamonds, chromite, antimony, platinum and coal (which meets three quarters of the country's energy needs). Industry includes chemicals, food processing, textiles, motor vehicles and electrical engineering. Agriculture supplies one third of South Africa's exports, including fruit, wine, wool and maize. The highest standard of living in Africa is very unevenly distributed between whites and non-whites. The withdrawal of some foreign investors has increased the drive towards self-sufficiency.

RECENT HISTORY

Black African peoples were long established in what is now South Africa when white settlement began in the Dutch colony of Cape Town (1652). The conquest of the local African societies was only completed late in the 19th century. Britain acquired the Cape (1814), abolished slavery (1833), and annexed Natal (1843). The Boers (or Afrikaners) – of Dutch and French Huguenot descent – moved inland on the Great Trek (1835–37) to found the republics of the Transvaal and Orange Free State. After the discovery of diamonds (1867) and gold (1886), the Boers (Afrikaners) – led by Paul Kruger (1825–1904), president of the Transvaal – resisted British attempts to annex their republics, in which British settlers were denied political rights. This culminated in the Boer War (1899–1902). Although they lost the war, the Afrikaners were politically dominant when the Union of South Africa was formed (1910).

The creation of the African National Congress (ANC) in 1912 was a protest against white supremacy, and by the 1920s black industrial protest was widespread. South Africa entered World War I as a British ally, taking German South West Africa (Namibia) after a short campaign (1914–15); after the war, the territory came under South African administration. Despite strong Afrikaner opposition, South Africa – under General Jan Christiaan Smuts (1870–1950; PM 1919–24 and 1939–48) – joined the Allied cause in World War II. After the Afrikaner National Party came to power (1948), racial segregation was increased by the policy of apartheid ('separate development'), which deprived blacks of civil rights, segregated facilities and areas of residence by race, and confined black political rights to restricted homelands ('Bantustans'). Black opposition was crushed following a massacre of demonstrators at Sharpeville, and the ANC was banned (1960) by the government of Hendrik Verwoerd (1901–66; PM from 1958 to 1966, when he was assassinated). International pressure against apartheid increased. In 1961 South Africa left the Commonwealth, the majority of

whose members continue to press for economic sanctions against South Africa. In 1966 the UN cancelled South Africa's trusteeship of South West Africa (Namibia), but South Africa continued to block the territory's progress to independence.

Black opposition revived in the 1970s and 1980s and found expression in strikes, the Soweto uprising of 1976, sabotage and the rise of the black consciousness movement. South African troops intervened in the Angolan civil war against the Marxist-Leninist government (1981) and were active in Namibia against SWAPO black nationalist guerrillas. P.W. Botha (1916– ; PM 1978–1984 and president 1984–89) granted political rights to the coloured and Indian communities, and implemented minor reforms for blacks. However, in 1986 – in the face of continuing unrest – Botha introduced a state of emergency, under which the press was strictly censored, the meetings of many organizations were banned and the number of political detainees – including children – rose sharply. His successor F.W. de Klerk released some ANC prisoners, and agreed to UN-supervised elections in Namibia leading to independence for that territory. In 1990 de Klerk lifted the ban on the ANC and released its imprisoned leader Nelson Mandela (1918–). In 1990–91, negotiations between the government and black leaders has led to the dismantling of the legal structures of apartheid. Fighting between ANC and Inkatha supporters in black townships has caused concern.

SPAIN

Official name: España (Spain).

Member of: UN, NATO, EC, WEU, CSCE, Council of Europe, OECD.

Population: 39 159 000 (1989 est) including Canary Islands, Ceuta and Melilla.

Capital and major cities: Madrid 3 101 000, Barcelona 1 704 000, Valencia 732 000, Seville (Sevilla) 655 000, Zaragoza 575 000, Málaga 566 000, Bilbao 382 000, Las Palmas de Gran Canaria 358 000, Valladolid 329 000, Palma de Mallorca 307 000, Murcia 305 000, Córdoba 298 000, Hospitalet 278 000, Vigo 263 000, Gijón 259 000, Granada 257 000, La Coruña 242 000, Badalona 224 000, Santa Cruz de Tenerife 211 000, Vitoria 201 000, Sabadell 188 000, Santander 187 000, Oviedo 186 000, Pamplona 179 000, Jérez de la Frontera 179 000, Elche 178 000, Mostoles 177 000, San Sebastián 177 000, Cartagena 169 000, Leganés 168 000, Tarrasa 160 000, Burgos 159 000, Salamanca 156 000, Cádiz 156 000, Almería 155 000, Alcalá de Henares 145 000 (1987 est).

Languages: Spanish or Castilian (official; as a first language over 70%), Catalan (as a first language over 20%), Basque (3%), Galician (4%).

Religion: Roman Catholic (nearly 99%).

Life expectancy: 77 years.

Labour force: (1987) 11 369 000; services 2 562 000, manufacturing 2 589 000, trade and tourism 2 238 000, agriculture and forestry 1 722 000.

GOVERNMENT

Spain is a constitutional monarchy. The Cortes (Parliament) comprises a Senate (Upper House) and a Chamber of Deputies (Lower House). The Senate consists of 208 senators – 4 from each province, 5 from the Balearic Islands, 6 from the Canary Islands and 2 each from Ceuta and Melilla – elected by universal adult suffrage for four years, plus 49

SPAIN

Area: 504 782 km² (194 897 sq mi) including the Canary Islands, Ceuta and Melilla

senators indirectly elected by the autonomous communities. The Congress of Deputies has 350 members directly elected for four years under a system of proportional representation. The King appoints a Prime Minister (President of the Council) who commands a majority in the Cortes. The PM, in turn, appoints a Council of Ministers (Cabinet) responsible to the Chamber of Deputies. The main political parties include the PSOE (Socialist Workers' Party), the (conservative) AP (Popular Alliance), the (left-wing coalition) Izquierda Unida (United Left, which includes the Communist Party), the (centre) CDS (Democratic and Social Centre), the (Catalan) Convergencia i Unio, and the (Basque) Herri Batasuna. Each of the 17 autonomous communities (regions) has its own legislature.
King: HM King Juan Carlos I (succeeded upon the restoration of the monarchy, 22 November 1975).
Prime Minister: Felipe Gonzalez Marquez.

SPANISH AUTONOMOUS COMMUNITIES

Population figures for the autonomous communities and the cities are for 1988 and 1987 respectively.
Andalusia (Andalucia) *Area:* 87 268 km² (33 694 sq mi). *Population:* 6 824 000. *Capital:* Sevilla (Seville) 655 000.
Aragón *Area:* 47 669 km² (18 405 sq mi). *Population:* 1 208 000. *Capital:* Zaragoza 575 000.
Asturias *Area:* 10 565 km² (4079 sq mi). *Population:* 1 135 000. *Capital:* Oviedo 186 000.
Balearic Islands (Islas Baleares) *Area:* 5014 km² (1936 sq mi). *Population:* 673 000. *Capital:* Palma de Mallorca 307 000.
Basque Country (Euzkadi or Pais Vasco) *Area:* 7 261 km² (2803 sq mi). *Population:* 2 196 000. *Capital:* Vitoria 201 000. *Largest city:* Bilbao 382 000.
Canary Islands (Islas Canarias) *Area:* 7273 km² (2808 sq mi). *Population:* 1 453 000. *Equal and alternative capitals:* Las Palmas 358 000 and Santa Cruz de Tenerife 211 000.
Cantabria *Area:* 5289 km² (2042 sq mi). *Population:* 528 000. *Capital:* Santander 187 000.
Castile–La Mancha (Castilla–La Mancha) *Area:* 79 226 km² (30 589 sq mi). *Population:* 1 693 000. *Capital (provisional):* Toledo 62 000. *Largest city:* Albacete 126 000.
Castile–Leon (Castilla–León) *Area:* 94 147 km² (36 350 sq mi). *Population:* 2 625 000. *Capital:* Valladolid 329 000.

Catalonia (Catalunya) *Area:* 31 930 km² (12 328 sq mi). *Population:* 6 099 000. *Capital:* Barcelona 1 704 000.
Extremadura *Area:* 41 602 km² (16 063 sq mi). *Population:* 1 098 000. *Capital:* Mérida 42 000. *Largest city:* Badajoz 120 000.
Galicia (Galiza) *Area:* 29 434 km² (11 364 sq mi). *Population:* 2 848 000. *Capital:* Santiago de Compostela 95 000. *Largest city:* La Coruña 242 000.
Madrid *Area:* 7995 km² (3087 sq mi). *Population:* 4 925 000. *Capital:* Madrid 3 101 000.
Murcia *Area:* 11 317 km² (4369 sq mi). *Population:* 1 015 000. *Capital:* Murcia 305 000 (although the regional parliament meets at Cartagena 169 000).
Navarre (Navarra) *Area:* 10 421 km² (4024 sq mi). *Population:* 520 000. *Capital:* Pamplona 179 000.
La Rioja *Area:* 5034 km² (1853 sq mi). *Population:* 259 000. *Capital:* Logroño 116 000.
Valencia *Area:* 23 305 km² (8998 sq mi). *Population:* 3 647 000. *Capital:* Valencia 732 000.

SPANISH ENCLAVES IN NORTH AFRICA

Ceuta *Area:* 19 km² (7 sq mi). *Population:* 71 000. *Capital:* Ceuta 71 000.
Melilla *Area:* 14 km² (5.5 sq mi). *Population:* 56 000. *Capital:* Melilla 56 000.

EDUCATION

Literacy rate: 97%. *Years of compulsory schooling:* 6–14. *Universities:* 20 state, 1 open, 2 independent, 2 autonomous, 8 technical.

DEFENCE

Total armed strength: 285 000 (1989). *Military service:* 12 months (to be reduced to 9 months between 1991 and 1993).

GEOGRAPHY

In the north of Spain a mountainous region stretches from the Pyrenees – dividing Spain from France – through the Cantabrian mountains to Galicia on the Atlantic coast. Much of the country is occupied by the central plateau, the Meseta. This is around 600 m (2000 ft) high, but rises to the higher Sistema Central in Castile, and ends in the south at the Sierra Morena. The Sierra Nevada range in Andalusia in the south contains Mulhacén, mainland Spain's highest peak at 3478 m (11 411 ft). The principal lowlands include the Ebro Valley in the northeast, a coastal plain around Valencia in the east, and the valley of the Guadalquivir River in the south. The Balearic Islands in the Mediterranean comprise four main islands – Mallorca (Majorca), Menorca (Minorca), Ibiza and Formentera – with seven much smaller islands. The Canary Islands, off the coast of Morocco and the Western Sahara, comprise five large islands – Tenerife, Fuerteventura, Gran Canaria, Lanzarote and La Palma – plus two smaller islands and six islets. The cities of Ceuta and Melilla are enclaves on the north coast of Morocco. *Principal rivers:* Tagus (Tajo), Ebro, Douro (Duero), Guadiana, Guadalquivir. *Highest point:* Pico del Tiede 3716 m (12 192 ft) in the Canaries.
Climate: The southeast has a Mediterranean climate with hot summers and mild winters. The dry interior has a continental climate with warm summers and cold winters. The high Pyrenees have a cold Alpine climate, while the northeast (Galicia) has a wet Atlantic climate with cool summers.

ECONOMY

Over 15% of the labour force is involved in agriculture. The principal crops include barley, wheat, sugar beet, potatoes, citrus fruit and grapes (for wine). Pastures for livestock occupy some 20% of the land. Manufacturing developed rapidly from the 1960s, and there are now major motor-vehicle, textile, plastics, metallurgical, shipbuilding, chemical and engineering industries, as well as growing interests in telecommunications and electronics. Foreign investors have been encouraged to promote new industry, but unemployment remains high. Banking and commerce are important, and tourism is a major foreign-currency earner with around 50 000 000 foreign visitors a year, mainly staying at beach resorts on the Mediterranean, Balearic Islands and the Canaries.

RECENT HISTORY

During the first half of the 19th century, Spain saw a series of struggles between liberal and monarchist elements, with radical republicans poised to intervene from the left and army officers from the right. In the Carlist Wars (1833–39, 1849 and 1872–76) the supporters of Queen Isabella II (1830 – 1904) – Ferdinand VII's daughter – countered the rival claims of her uncle Don Carlos and his descendants. Isabella was deposed in the revolution of 1868, which was followed by a short-lived liberal monarchy under an Italian prince (1870–73) and a brief republican experiment in 1873–4. In the last decades of the 19th century, the political situation became increasingly unstable, with anarchist violence, the turmoil of labour disturbances, pressure for provincial independence, and growing anti-clericalism. As a result of the Spanish-American War of 1898 the last significant colonial possessions – Cuba, the Philippines, Guam and Puerto Rico – were lost. The end of Spain's empire inflicted a severe wound to Spanish pride and led to doubts as to whether the constitutional monarchy of Alfonso XIII (1886–1941) was capable of delivering the dynamic leadership that Spain was thought to require.

Spain remained neutral in World War I, during which social tensions increased. A growing disillusionment with parliamentary government and political parties led to a military coup in 1923 led by General Miguel Primo de Rivera (1870–1930). Primo was initially supported by Alfonso XIII, but in 1930 the King withdrew that support. However, the range of forces arrayed against the monarchy and the threat of civil war led Alfonso to abdicate (1931). The peace of the succeeding republic was short-lived. Neither of the political extremes – left nor right – was prepared to tolerate the perceived inefficiency and lack of authority of the Second Spanish Republic. In 1936, nationalist army generals rose against a newly elected republican government. Led by General Francisco Franco (1892–1975) and supported by Germany and Italy, the nationalists fought the republicans in the bitter Spanish Civil War. Franco triumphed in 1939 to become ruler – Caudillo – of the neo-Fascist Spanish State. Political expression was restricted, and from 1942 to 1967 the Cortes (Parliament) was not directly elected. Spain remained neutral in World War II, although it was beholden to Germany. After 1945, Franco emphasized Spain's anti-Communism – a policy that brought his regime some international acceptance from the West during the Cold War.

In 1969, Franco named Alfonso XIII's grandson Juan Carlos (1938–) as his successor. The monarchy was restored on Franco's death (1975) and the King eased the transition to democracy through the establishment of a new liberal constitution in 1978. In 1981 Juan Carlos played an important role in putting down an attempted army coup. In 1982 Spain joined NATO and elected a socialist government, and since 1986 the country has been a member of the EC. Despite the granting of some regional autonomy since 1978, Spain continues to be troubled by campaigns for provincial independence – for example in Catalonia – and by the violence of the Basque separatist movement ETA.

SRI LANKA

Official name: Sri Lanka Prajatantrika Samajawadi Janarajaya (Democratic Socialist Republic of Sri Lanka). Known as Ceylon until 1970.

Member of: UN, Commonwealth, SAARC.

Population: 16 855 000 (1989 est).

Capital and major cities: Colombo (current capital) 683 000, Sri Jayawardenepura Kotte (legislative capital and capital designate) 104 000, Dehiwala-Lavinia 191 000, Jaffna 143 000, Moratuwa 162 000, Kandy 102 000, Galle 82 000 (1986).

Languages: Sinhala (official; 72%), Tamil (official; 21%), English (official).

Religions: Buddhist (70%), Hindu (15%), with Roman Catholic and Sunni Islam minorities.

Life expectancy: 69 years.

Labour force: (1985) 5 972 000; agriculture and forestry 2 531 000, manufacturing 650 000, services 632 000.

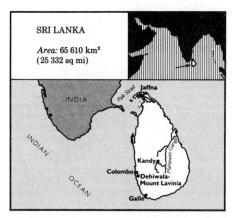

SRI LANKA

Area: 65 610 km²
(25 332 sq mi)

GOVERNMENT

The 168-member Parliament is elected for six years under a system of proportional representation by universal adult suffrage. The President – who is also directly elected for six years – appoints a Cabinet and a Prime Minister who are responsible to Parliament. The main political parties are the UNP (United National Party), the SLFP (Sri Lanka Freedom Party), the LSSP (Lanka Sama Samaja Party), the Communist Party, and several Tamil parties. There is constitutional provision for an autonomous Tamil state in the northeast of the island.
President: Ranasinghe Premadasa.
Prime Minister: D.B. Wijetunge.

AUTONOMOUS AREA

North Eastern Province *Area*: 18 833 km² (7271

sq mi). *Population:* 2 800 000 (1981). *Capital:* Jaffna 143 000 (1986).

EDUCATION
Literacy rate: 85% (1985 est). *Years of compulsory schooling:* 5–15. *Universities:* 6, plus 2 university colleges, 1 open university.

DEFENCE
Total armed strength: 49 200, plus 48 500 paramilitary (1989). *Military service:* none.

GEOGRAPHY
Central Sri Lanka is occupied by highlands. Most of the rest of the island consists of forested lowlands, which in the north are flat and fertile. *Principal rivers:* Mahaweli Ganga, Kelani Ganga. *Highest point:* Pidurutalagala 2527 m (8292 ft).
Climate: The island has a tropical climate modified by the monsoon. Rainfall totals vary between 500 mm (20 in) in the southwest and 1000 mm (40 in) in the northeast.

ECONOMY
About 50% of the labour force is involved in agriculture, growing rice for domestic consumption, and rubber, tea and coconuts for export. Major irrigation and hydroelectric installations on the Mahaweli Ganga river are being constructed. Industries include food processing, cement, textiles and petroleum refining, but the economy – in particular tourism – has been damaged by guerrilla activity.

RECENT HISTORY
From 1796 British rule replaced the Dutch in Ceylon, uniting the entire island for the first time. Nationalist feeling grew from the beginning of the 20th century, leading to independence in 1948, and a republican constitution in 1972. The country has been bedevilled by Tamil-Sinhalese ethnic rivalry, which led to major disorders in 1958, 1961 and since 1977. In 1971 a Marxist rebellion was crushed after heavy fighting. Sri Lanka elected the world's first woman Prime Minister, Sirimavo Bandaranaike (1916– ; PM 1960–65 and 1970–77). In the 1980s separatist Tamil guerrillas fought for an independent homeland (Eelam). Fighting between rival Tamil guerrilla groups, Sinhalese extremists and government forces reduced the northeast to near civil war. An Indian 'peace-keeping' force intervened (1987), but this aggravated an already complex situation. Indian forces were completely withdrawn in 1990. The Tamil Northeast Province is scheduled to achieve autonomy under the dominant Tamil Tigers guerrillas, who registered as a political party in 1989. However, Tamil guerrilla activity continues in the northeast, and (Maoist) JVP guerrillas are active in the south.

SUDAN

Official name: Al Jumhuriyat al-Sudan (The Republic of Sudan).
Member of: UN, Arab League, OAU.
Population: 27 268 000 (1989 est).
Capital and main cities: Khartoum 1 334 000 (comprising Omdurman 526 000, Khartoum 476 000, Khartoum North 341 000), Port Sudan 207 000, Wadi Medani 141 000, El Obeid 140 000 (1983).
Language: Arabic (over 50%; official).

Religions: Sunni Islam (70%), animist (nearly 20%), with various Christian Churches.
Life expectancy: 50.3 years.
Labour force: (1988 est) 7 716 000; agriculture and forestry 4 824 000, services 460 000, trade and tourism 250 000.

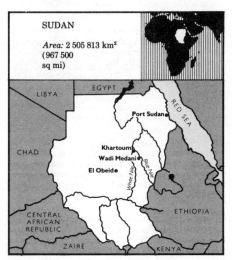

SUDAN
Area: 2 505 813 km²
(967 500 sq mi)

GOVERNMENT
Since the military coup in June 1989, the country has been ruled by the 15-member Command Council of the Revolution of National Salvation, whose chairman is head of state and of government. Political activity has been suspended, although in 1991 a federal system comprising nine regions was instituted.
Head of state and government: Lt. Gen. Omar Hassan Ahmed al-Bashir.

SUDANESE REGIONS
Population figures are for 1983.
Bahr el Ghazal *Area:* 200 894 km² (77 566 sq mi). *Population:* 2 266 000. *Capital:* Wau (Waw) 55 000.
Central Region (al-Wasta) *Area:* 139 017 km² (53 675 sq mi). *Population:* 4 013 000. *Capital:* Wadi Medani 141 000.
Dafur *Area:* 508 684 km² (196 404 sq mi). *Population:* 3 094 000. *Capital:* El Fasher 60 000.
Eastern Region (ash-Sharqiyah) *Area:* 334 074 km² (129 086 sq mi). *Population:* 2 208 000. *Capital:* Kassala 100 000.
Equatoria (al-Istiwaiyah) *Area:* 197 969 km² (76 436 sq mi). *Population:* 1 406 000. *Capital:* Juba 60 000.
Khartoum *Area:* 28 165 km² (10 875 sq mi). *Population:* 1 803 000. *Capital:* Khartoum 1 334 000.
Kurdufan *Area:* 380 255 km² (146 817 sq mi). *Population:* 3 093 000. *Capital:* El Obeid 140 000.
Northern Region (ash-Shamiliyah) *Area:* 476 040 km² (183 941 sq mi). *Population:* 1 083 000. *Capital:* ad-Damir 20 000.
Upper Nile (A'ali an-Nil) *Area:* 238 792 km² (92 198 sq mi). *Population:* 1 600 000. *Capital:* Malakal 35 000.

EDUCATION
Literacy rate: 20% (1975). *Years of compulsory*

schooling: schooling is free but not compulsory.
Universities: 4.

DEFENCE
Total armed strength: 72 800 (1989). *Military service:* none.

GEOGRAPHY
The Sahara Desert covers much of the north and west, but is crossed by the fertile Nile Valley. The southern plains are swampy. Highlands are confined to hill country beside the Red Sea and mountains on the Ugandan border. *Principal rivers:* Nile (Nil), Nil el Azraq (Blue Nile), Nil el Abyad (White Nile). *Highest point:* Kinyeti 3187 m (10 456 ft).
Climate: The south is equatorial, but the north is dry with some areas receiving negligible rainfall.

ECONOMY
Almost two thirds of the labour force is involved in agriculture, growing cotton for export, and sorghum, cassava and millet for domestic consumption. Since the early 1980s Sudan has been severely affected by drought and famine.

RECENT HISTORY
In 1820–21 Sudan was conquered by the Egyptians, who were challenged in the 1880s by an Islamic leader who claimed to be the Mahdi. The Mahdists took Khartoum, killed Sudan's Egyptian-appointed governor, General Charles George Gordon (1885), and created a theocratic state. Britain intervened, and from 1899 Sudan was administered jointly by Britain and Egypt. Nationalism developed strongly after World War I, but independence was only achieved in 1956. Sudan remains politically unstable, alternating between civilian and military regimes, the most recent gaining power in a coup in June 1989. The civil war between the Muslim north and the animist–Christian south that began in 1955 remains unresolved.

SURINAME
Official name: Republiek Suriname (Republic of Suriname).
Member of: UN, OAS.
Population: 405 000 (1989 est).
Capital: Paramaribo 246 000 (including suburbs; 1988 est).
Languages: Dutch (official; 30%), Sranang Togo (majority), Hindi (30%), Javanese (15%), Chinese, English, Spanish (official – designate).
Religions: Hinduism (28%), Roman Catholic (22%), Sunni Islam (20%), Moravian (15%).
Life expectancy: 67 years.
Labour force: (1985) 99 000; civil service 40 000, agriculture and forestry 17 000, manufacturing 11 000.

GOVERNMENT
There is constitutional provision for a 51-member National Assembly elected for five years by universal adult suffrage, a President and a Vice-President – who is also the Prime Minister – to be elected by the Assembly, and a Cabinet, appointed by the President. The constitution and political activity have been suspended following a military coup in December 1990.

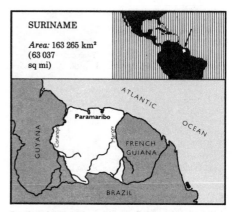

SURINAME

Area: 163 265 km² (63 037 sq mi)

Paramaribo

GUYANA   Corantijn   Maroni   FRENCH GUIANA

ATLANTIC OCEAN

BRAZIL

Leader of the military council: Col. Ivan Graanoogst.
President: Johan Kraag.
Prime Minister: to be announced.

EDUCATION
Literacy rate: 90% (1985 est). *Years of compulsory schooling:* 6–12. *Universities:* 1.

DEFENCE
Total armed strength: 3050 (1989). *Military service:* none.

GEOGRAPHY
Suriname comprises a swampy coastal plain, a forested central plateau, and southern mountains. *Principal rivers:* Corantijn, Nickerie, Coppename, Saramacca, Suriname, Commewijne, Maroni. *Highest point:* Julianatop 1286 m (4218 ft).
Climate: Suriname has a tropical climate with heavy rainfall.

ECONOMY
The extraction and refining of bauxite is the mainstay of the economy. Other exports include shrimps, sugar and oranges. Economic development is hampered by political instability and emigration.

RECENT HISTORY
Dutch settlement began in 1602 and the area was confirmed as a Dutch colony in 1667. Suriname has a mixed population, including American Indians, and the descendants of African slaves and of Javanese, Chinese and Indian plantation workers. Since independence in 1975, racial tension has contributed to instability, and there have been several coups in which Col. Desi Bouterse played an important role. Following a further coup in December 1990, it was announced that elections would take place in May 1991.

SWAZILAND
Official name: Umbuso Weswatini (The Kingdom of Swaziland).
Member of: UN, Commonwealth, OAU, SADCC.
Population: 746 000 (1989 est).
Capital and major cities: Mbabane – administrative capital – 39 000 (1986), Lobamba – legislative and royal capital – 6000 (1980 est), Manzini 52 000 (1986).
Languages: siSwati and English (both official).

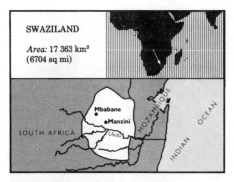

SWAZILAND

Area: 17 363 km²
(6704 sq mi)

Mbabane
Manzini

SOUTH AFRICA

MOZAMBIQUE

INDIAN OCEAN

Usutu

Religions: Various Christian Churches (over 60%), animist minority.

Life expectancy: 56 years.

Labour force: (1988 est) 297 000; agriculture and forestry 202 000.

GOVERNMENT

Swaziland is a monarchy in which the King appoints a Prime Minister and Cabinet. The King is advised by the 20-member Senate and the 50-member House of Assembly, and appoints 10 members to both. Each of the 40 traditional tribal communities elects 2 members to the Electoral College, which chooses 10 of its members to sit in the Senate and 40 in the House. No political parties are permitted.

King: HM King Mswati III (succeeded upon the resignation of his mother as Queen Regent, 25 April 1986).

Prime Minister: Obed Dlamini.

EDUCATION

Literacy rate: 68% (1985 est). *Years of compulsory schooling:* schooling is not compulsory. *Universities:* 1, plus 1 university centre.

DEFENCE

Total armed strength: 2657 (1983). *Military service:* 2 years.

GEOGRAPHY

From the mountains of the west, Swaziland descends in steps of savannah (veld) towards hill country in the east. *Principal rivers:* Usutu, Komati, Umbuluzi, Ingwavuma. *Highest point:* Emlembe 1863 m (6113 ft).

Climate: The veld is subtropical, while the highlands are temperate.

ECONOMY

The majority of Swazis are subsistence farmers. Cash crops include sugar cane (the main export).

RECENT HISTORY

The Swazi kingdom came under British rule in 1904. The country resisted annexation by the Boers in the 1890s and by South Africa during the colonial period. Following independence (1968), King Sobhuza II suspended the constitution in 1973 and restored much of the traditional royal authority. A bitter power struggle after his death (1982) lasted until King Mswati III was invested in 1986.

SWEDEN

Official name: Konungariket Sverige (Kingdom of Sweden).

Member of: UN, EFTA, CSCE, Council of Europe, OECD.

Population: 8 527 000 (1989 est).

Capital and major cities: Stockholm 1 471 000, Göteborg 720 000, Malmö 466 000, Uppsala 162 000, Orebro 120 000, Linköping 120 000, Norrköping 120 000, Västeras 118 000, Jönköping 110 000, Helsingborg 107 000, Boras 101 000 (all including suburbs; 1988).

Languages: Swedish (official), small Lappish minority.

Religion: Evangelical Lutheran Church of Sweden (over 90%).

Life expectancy: 77 years.

Labour force: (1989 employment figures) 4 466 000; services 1 653 000, trade and tourism 652 000, agriculture and forestry 159 000.

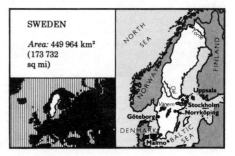

SWEDEN

Area: 449 964 km²
(173 732 sq mi)

NORTH SEA

NORWAY

FINLAND

Uppsala

Vänern

Stockholm

Göteborg

Norrköping

DENMARK

BALTIC SEA

Malmö

GOVERNMENT

Sweden is a constitutional monarchy in which the King is ceremonial and representative head of state without any executive role. The 349-member Riksdag (Parliament) is elected for three years by universal adult suffrage under a system of proportional representation. The Speaker of the Riksdag nominates a Prime Minister who commands a parliamentary majority. The PM, in turn, appoints a Cabinet of Ministers who are responsible to the Riksdag. The main political parties are the Social Democratic Labour Party, the (conservative) Moderate Party, the Liberal Party, the Centre Party, and the Communist Party.

King: HM King Carl XVI Gustaf (succeeded upon the death of his grandfather, 15 September 1973).

Prime Minister: Ingvar Carlsson.

EDUCATION

Literacy rate: 100%. *Years of compulsory schooling:* 7–16. *Universities:* 34.

DEFENCE

Total armed strength: 64 500 (1989). *Military service:* 7½–15 months army and navy, 8–12 months air force.

GEOGRAPHY

The mountains of Norrland – along the border with Norway and in the north of Sweden – cover two thirds of the country. Svealand – in the centre – is characterized by a large number of lakes. In the south are the low Smaland Highlands and the fertile lowland of Skane. *Principal rivers:* Ume, Torne, Angerman, Klar, Dal. *Highest point:* Kebnekaise 2123 m (6965 ft).

Climate: Sweden experiences long cold winters and warm summers, although the north – where snow remains on the mountains for eight months – is more severe than the south, where Skane has a relatively mild winter.

ECONOMY

Sweden's high standard of living has been based upon its neutrality in the two World Wars, its cheap and plentiful hydroelectric power, and its mineral riches. The country has about 15% of the world's uranium deposits, and large reserves of iron ore that provide the basis of domestic heavy industry and important exports to Western Europe. Agriculture – like the bulk of the population – is concentrated in the south. The principal products include dairy produce, meat (including reindeer), barley, sugar beet and potatoes. Vast coniferous forests are the basis of the paper, board and furniture industries, and large exports of timber. Heavy industries include motor vehicles (Saab and Volvo), aerospace and machinery, although the shipbuilding industry – in the 1970s the world's second largest – has ceased to exist.

RECENT HISTORY

The founder of the present Swedish dynasty, the French marshal Jean-Baptiste Bernadotte, was elected crown prince to the childless king (1810), and succeeded in 1818. In 1814 Sweden lost Finland and the last possessions south of the Baltic, but gained Norway from Denmark in compensation. The union of Norway and Sweden was dissolved in 1905 when King Oscar II (reigned 1872–1907) gave up the Norwegian throne upon Norway's vote for separation. In the 20th century neutral Sweden has developed a comprehensive welfare state under social democratic governments. The country assumed a moral leadership on world issues but was jolted by the (unclaimed) assassination of PM Olof Palme (1986).

SWITZERLAND

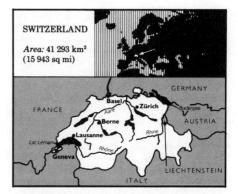

SWITZERLAND

Area: 41 293 km² (15 943 sq mi)

Official name: Schweizerische Eidgenossenschaft (German) or Confédération suisse (French) or Confederazione Svizzera (Italian) or Confederaziun Helvetica (Romansch); (Swiss Confederation).

Member of: EFTA, CSCE, OECD, Council of Europe, UN (observer).

Population: 6 689 000 (1989 est).

Capital and major cities: Berne (Bern) 301 000, Zürich 840 000, Geneva (Genève) 385 000, Basel 363 000, Lausanne 262 000, Lucerne (Luzern) 161 000, St Gallen 126 000, Winterthur 108 000, Biel/Bienne 83 000, Thun 78 000, Lugano 69 000, Neuchâtel 66 000, Fribourg (Freiburg) 57 000, Schaffhausen 54 000, Zug 52 000 (all including suburbs; 1986).

Languages: German (74%), French 20%, Italian (5%), Romansch (under 1%) – all official.

Religions: Roman Catholic (48%), various Protestant Churches (44%).

Life expectancy: 76.5 years.

Labour force: (1986) 3 219 000, manufacturing 961 000, trade and tourism 603 000, agriculture and forestry 209 000.

GOVERNMENT

Switzerland is a federal republic in which each of the 20 cantons and 6 half cantons has its own government with very considerable powers. Federal matters are entrusted to the Federal Assembly comprising the 46-member Council of States and the 200-member National Council. The Council of States is directly elected for three or four years with two members from each canton and one from each half canton. The National Council is elected for four years by univer-sal adult suffrage under a system of proportional representation. The Federal Assembly elects a seven-member Federal Council – the equivalent of a Cabinet – for four years. The Federal Council appoints one of its members to be President for one year. All federal and cantonal constitutional amendments must be approved by a referendum. The main political parties include the (liberal) Radical Democratic Party, the Social Democratic Party, the (conservative) Christian Democratic Party, the (centre) People's Party, and the Liberal Party.
President: Flavio Cotti (President for 1991). (René Felber will be President in 1992.).

SWISS CANTONS

Population figures for the cantons are for 1988.

Aargau (Argovie) *Area:* 1404 km² (542 sq mi). *Population:* 479 000. *Capital:* Aarau 16 000 (1980).

Appenzell: Ausser Rhoden (a half canton). *Area:* 243 km² (94 sq mi). *Population:* 50 000. *Capital:* Herisau 14 000 (1980).

Appenzell: Inner Rhoden (a half canton). *Area:* 172 km² (66 sq mi). *Population:* 13 000. *Capital:* Appenzell 5300 (1980).

Basel-Land (a half canton). *Area:* 428 km² (165 sq mi). *Population:* 227 000. *Capital:* Liestal 12 000 (1980).

Basel-Stadt (a half canton). *Area:* 37 km² (14 sq mi). *Population:* 193 000. *Capital:* Basel (Basle) 363 000 (including parts of the agglomeration outside the half canton; 1986).

Berne (Bern) *Area:* 6049 km² (2336 sq mi). *Population:* 929 000. *Capital:* Berne (Bern) 301 000 (1986).

Fribourg (Freiburg) *Area:* 1670 km² (645 sq mi). *Population:* 197 000. *Capital:* Fribourg (Freiburg) 57 000 (1986).

Geneva (Genève) *Area:* 282 km² (109 sq mi). *Population:* 366 000. *Capital:* Geneva (Genève) 385 000 (including parts of the agglomeration outside the canton; 1986).

Glarus *Area:* 684 km² (264 sq mi). *Population:* 37 000. *Capital:* Glarus 6000 (1980).

Graubünden (Grisons). *Area:* 7109 km² (2745 sq mi). *Population:* 167 000. *Capital:* Chur 31 000 (1980).

Jura *Area:* 838 km² (324 sq mi). *Population:* 65 000. *Capital:* Delémont 12 000 (1980).

Lucerne (Luzern) *Area:* 1494 km² (577 sq mi). *Population:* 309 000. *Capital:* Lucerne (Luzern) 161 000 (1980).

Neuchâtel *Area:* 797 km² (308 sq mi). *Population:* 157 000. *Capital:* Neuchâtel 66 000 (1986).

St Gallen *Area*: 2016 km² (778 sq mi). *Population:* 407 000. *Capital*: St Gallen 126 000 (1986).

Schaffhausen *Area*: 298 km² (115 sq mi). *Population*: 70 000. *Capital*: Schaffhausen 54 000 (1986).

Schwyz *Area*: 908 km² (351 sq mi). *Population*: 105 000. *Capital*: Schwyz 12 000 (1980).

Solothurn *Area*: 791 km² (305 sq mi). *Population*: 220 000. *Capital*: Solothurn 16 000 (1980).

Thurgau (Thurgovie) *Area*: 1006 km² (388 sq mi). *Population*: 195 000. *Capital*: Frauenfeld 19 000 (1980).

Ticino (Tessin) *Area*: 2811 km² (1085 sq mi). *Population*: 279 000. *Capital*: Bellinzona 17 000 (1980). *Largest city*: Lugano 69 000 (1986).

Unterwalden: Nidwalden (a half canton). *Area:* 274 km² (106 sq mi). *Population*: 31 000. *Capital*: Stans 6000 (1980).

Unterwalden: Obwalden (a half canton). *Area*: 492 km² (190 sq mi). *Population*: 28 000. *Capital*: Sarnen 7000 (1980).

Uri *Area*: 1075 km² (415 sq mi). *Population*: 33 000. *Capital*: Altdorf 8000 (1980).

Valais (Wallis) *Area*: 5231 km² (2020 sq mi). *Population*: 235 000. *Capital*: Sion 23 000 (1980).

Vaud *Area*: 3211 km² (1240 sq mi). *Population*: 557 000. *Capital*: Lausanne 262 000 (1986).

Zug *Area*: 239 km² (92 sq mi). *Population*: 83 000. *Capital*: Zug 52 000 (1986).

Zürich *Area*: 1729 km² (668 sq mi). *Population*: 1 137 000. *Capital*: Zürich 840 000 (1986).

EDUCATION

Literacy rate: 99%. *Years of compulsory schooling*: 7–16. *Universities*: 7, plus 2 technical institutes with university status.

DEFENCE

Total armed strength: 1 100 000 (when mobilized; there is no standing army). *Military service*: 1 year between ages 20–50, with recall for training.

GEOGRAPHY

The parallel ridges of the Jura Mountains lie in the northwest on the French border. The south of the country is occupied by the Alps. Between the two mountain ranges is a central plateau that contains the greater part of Switzerland's population, agriculture and industry. *Principal rivers*: Rhine (Rhein), Rhône, Aare, Inn, Ticino. *Highest point*: Dufourspitze (Monte Rosa) 4634 m (15 203 ft).

Climate: Altitude and aspect modify Switzerland's temperate climate. Considerable differences in temperature and rainfall are experienced over relatively short distances; for instance, the cold Alpine climate around the St Gotthard Pass is only 50 km (just over 30 miles) from the Mediterranean climate of Lugano.

ECONOMY

Nearly two centuries of neutrality have allowed Switzerland to build a reputation as a secure financial centre. Zürich is one of the world's leading banking and commercial cities. The country enjoys one of the highest standards of living in the world. Industry – in part based upon cheap hydroelectric power – includes engineering (from turbines to watches), textiles, food processing (including cheese and chocolate), pharmaceuticals and chemicals.

Dairying, grapes (for wine) and fodder crops are important in the agricultural sector, and there is a significant timber industry. Tourism and the international organizations based in Switzerland are major foreign-currency earners. Foreign workers – in particular Italians and Yugoslavs – help alleviate the country's labour shortage.

RECENT HISTORY

Switzerland occupies a strategic position, but the Swiss have used their remarkable position to withdraw from, rather than participate in, European power politics. The French Revolutionary Wars saw the creation of a Helvetian Republic in 1798, but in 1803 Napoleon dismantled this unitary state and returned the country to a confederation. At the Congress of Vienna (1815) Swiss neutrality was recognized and the country gained its present boundaries. Continuing tensions in the early 19th century saw attempts by some cantons to secede and set up a new federation, but the compromises of a new constitution in 1848 – which is still the basis of Swiss government – balanced cantonal and central power. As a neutral country Switzerland proved the ideal base for the Red Cross (1863), the League of Nations (1920) and other world organizations, but Switzerland itself avoids membership of any body it considers might compromise its neutrality – a referendum in 1986 confirmed that Switzerland should not seek membership of the United Nations.

SYRIA

Official name: Al-Jumhuriya al-'Arabiya as-Suriya (The Syrian Arab Republic).

Member of: UN, Arab League.

Population: 11 719 000 (1989 est).

Capital and major cities: Damascus (Dimashq) 1 361 000, Halab (formerly Aleppo) 1 308 000, Homs 464 000, Latakia 258 000, Hama 214 000 (1989).

Languages: Arabic (over 90%; official), with Armenian and Kurdish minorities.

Religions: Islam (official; Sunni 75%, Shia 10%, with Druze minority), with various Orthodox and Roman Catholic minorities.

Life expectancy: 65 years.

Labour force: (1984) 2 356 000; agriculture and forestry 571 700, services 536 500, manufacturing 337 000.

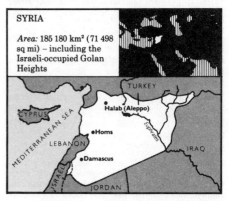

SYRIA

Area: 185 180 km² (71 498 sq mi) – including the Israeli-occupied Golan Heights

GOVERNMENT

The 250-member National People's Assembly is elected by universal adult suffrage for four years. The

President – who is directly elected for seven years – appoints a Prime Minister (to assist him in government) and a Council of Ministers. The National Progressive Front – including the ruling Ba'ath Arab Socialist Party, the Arab Socialist Union Party, the Syrian Arab Socialist Party, the Arab Socialist Party and the Communist Party – has a leading role.
President: Hafez al-Assad.
Prime Minister: Mahmoud Zubi.

EDUCATION
Literacy rate: 60% (1985 est). *Years of compulsory schooling*: 6–12. *Universities*: 4.

DEFENCE
Total armed strength: 404 000 (1989). *Military service*: 30 months.

GEOGRAPHY
Behind a well-watered coastal plain, mountains run from north to south. Inland, much of the country is occupied by the Syrian Desert. *Principal river*: Euphrates (Al Furat), Asi (Orontes). *Highest point*: Jabal ash Shaik (Mount Hermon) 2814 m (9232 ft).
Climate: The coast has a Mediterranean climate. The arid interior has hot summers and cool winters.

ECONOMY
Petroleum is the main export although Syria's petroleum reserves are small by Middle Eastern standards. Agriculture involves nearly one quarter of the labour force, with cultivation concentrated in the coastal plain and irrigated land in the Euphrates Valley. Major crops include cotton, wheat and barley.

RECENT HISTORY
Ottoman rule in Syria lasted from 1516 until 1917, when a combined British-Arab army was led into Damascus by Prince Faisal ibn Husain. In 1920 independence was declared with Faisal as king, but the victors of World War I handed Syria to France (1920) as a trust territory. Since independence in 1946 Syria has suffered political instability. The pan-Arab, secular, socialist Ba'ath Party engineered Syria's unsuccessful union with Egypt (1958–61). Syria fought wars with Israel in 1948–49, 1967 and 1973, and in the 1967 Arab-Israeli War Israel captured the strategic Golan Heights from Syria. A pragmatic Ba'athist leader Hafiz al-Assad came to power in 1970 and allied Syria to the USSR. Assad's popularity has been challenged by Syria's increasing involvement in Lebanese affairs since 1976 and by Shiite fundamentalism. In 1990 Syria defeated the Lebanese Christian militia of Michel Aoun and restored the authority of the Lebanese government to the whole of Beirut. Since 1989–90, economic pressures have lessened Syria's dependence upon the USSR. Syria's participation in the coalition against its old rival Iraq in 1990 gained greater international acceptance for Syria, which had attracted criticism for its sponsorship of terrorism.

TANZANIA

Official name: Jamhuri ya Muungano wa Tanzania (Swahili) or The United Republic of Tanzania.
Member of: UN, Commonwealth, OAU.
Population: 23 997 000 (1988 est).
Capital and major cities: Dodoma (legislative and de jure capital) 204 000, Dar es Salaam (administrative capital) 1 096 000, Mwanza 252 000, Tabora 214 000, Mbeya 194 000, Tanga 172 000, Zanzibar 157 000 (1985 est).
Languages: English and Swahili.
Religions: Sunni Islam (about 65%), Roman Catholic (20%), Hindu, Anglican.
Life expectancy: 53 years.
Labour force: (1988 est) 12 070 000; agriculture and forestry 9 884 000, services 309 000, manufacturing 99 000.

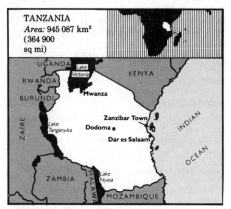

TANZANIA
Area: 945 087 km² (364 900 sq mi)

GOVERNMENT
The President is nominated by the CCM (Chama Cha Mapinduzi – the Revolutionary Party), the sole legal party, and confirmed in office by universal adult suffrage for a five-year term. The President appoints a Cabinet of Ministers and two Vice Presidents – one President of Zanzibar, the other concurrently Prime Minister. The 243-member National Assembly comprises 118 members directly elected from the mainland, 50 members directly elected from Zanzibar, plus appointed and indirectly elected members. Zanzibar has its own legislature.
President: Ali Hassan Mwinyi.
Prime Minister: John Malecela.

AUTONOMOUS STATE
Zanzibar *Area*: 1660 km² (641 sq mi). *Population*: 605 000 (1987). *Capital*: Zanzibar 157 000 (1985).

EDUCATION
Literacy rate: 85% (1983). *Years of compulsory schooling*: 7–14. *Universities*: 2 (incl. 1 agricultural).

DEFENCE
Total armed strength: 46 700, plus 101 400 paramilitary (1989). *Military service*: 2 years.

GEOGRAPHY
Zanzibar comprises three small islands. The mainland – formerly Tanganyika – comprises savannah plateaux divided by rift valleys and a north–south mountain chain. *Principal rivers*: Pangani (Ruvu), Rufiji, Rovuma. *Highest point*: Kilimanjaro 5894 m (19 340 ft), the highest point in Africa.
Climate: Tanzania has a tropical climate, although the mountains are cooler.

ECONOMY
Subsistence agriculture involves over 70% of the

labour force. Cash crops include coffee, tea, cotton and tobacco. Mineral resources include diamonds and gold. Tanzania had a centrally planned economy, but more pragmatic policies have been implemented since 1985–87.

RECENT HISTORY

In 1964 Tanganyika and Zanzibar united to form Tanzania. Zanzibar – formerly an Omani possession – became an independent sultanate in 1856 and then a British protectorate (1890–1963). After independence in 1963 the sultan of Zanzibar was deposed in a radical left-wing coup. The mainland became the colony of German East Africa in 1884, the British trust territory of Tanganyika in 1919 and an independent state in 1961. President Julius Nyerere's policies of self-reliance and egalitarian socialism were widely admired, but proved difficult to implement and were largely abandoned by the time he retired as President in 1985.

THAILAND

Official name: Prathet Thai (Kingdom of Thailand).

Member of: UN, ASEAN.

Population: 55 448 000 (1989 est).

Capital and major cities: Bangkok 5 845 000 (1989 est), Nakhon Ratchasima (Khorat) 191 000, Songkhla 173 000, Chiang Mai 150 000, Chon Buri 115 000, Nakhon Si Thammarat 102 000 (1983–85 est).

Language: Thai (official).

Religions: Buddhism (95%), Sunni Islam (4%).

Life expectancy: 65 years.

Labour force: (1988 employment figures) 29 464 000; agriculture and forestry 19 576 500, services 3 017 000, commerce 2 897 000.

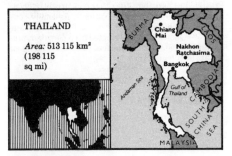

GOVERNMENT

Thailand is a constitutional monarchy. The constitution provides for a National Assembly, which comprises a non-political Senate – whose 261 members are appointed by the King – and a 347-member House of Representatives elected by universal adult suffrage for four years. The King appoints a Prime Minister who commands a majority in the House. The PM in turn appoints a Cabinet of Ministers responsible to the House. Following a military coup in February 1991 the constitution and political activity have been suspended. Executive power is in the hands of a National Peacekeeping Council whose leader is effective head of government.

King: HM King Bhumibol Adulyadej (Rama IX) (succeeded upon the death of his brother, 9 June 1946).

Head of military junta: Gen. Sunthorn Kongsompong.

Prime Minister: Anand Panyarachun.

EDUCATION

Literacy rate: 91% (1985). *Years of compulsory schooling:* 7–14. *Universities:* 16 (including technical institutes of university status).

DEFENCE

Total armed strength: 283 000, plus 141 700 paramilitary (1989). *Military service:* 2 years.

GEOGRAPHY

Central Thailand is a densely populated fertile plain. The north is mountainous. The infertile Khorat Plateau occupies the northeast, while the mountainous Isthmus of Kra joins southern Thailand to Malaysia. *Principal rivers:* Mekong, Chao Pyha, Mae Nam Mun. *Highest point:* Doi Inthanon 2595 m (8514 ft).

Climate: Thailand has a subtropical climate with heavy monsoon rains from June to October, a cool season from October to March, and a hot season from March to June.

ECONOMY

Two thirds of the labour force is involved in agriculture, mainly growing rice – Thailand is the world's largest exporter of rice. Other important crops include tapioca and rubber. Tin and natural gas are the main natural resources. Manufacturing – based on cheap labour – is expanding and includes textiles, clothes, electrical and electronic engineering, and food processing. Tourism has become a major foreign-currency earner.

RECENT HISTORY

Thailand was known as Siam before 1939. Rama I (reigned 1782–1809), founder of the present Chakkri dynasty, moved the capital to Bangkok. His successors were forced to cede their claims over neighbouring lands to Britain and France. A constitutional monarchy was established by a bloodless coup (1932), whose Westernized leaders – Pibul Songgram and Pridi Phanomyang – struggled for political dominance for the next quarter of a century. During World War II Thailand was forced into an alliance with Japan. Since then Thailand has made a decisive commitment to the US political camp, which has brought major benefits in military and technical aid. Despite continuing army interventions in politics – in February 1991 the military took over the government for the 17th time in 50 years – Thailand has prospered. However, the stability of the country was compromised by the wars in Vietnam and is still threatened with unwilling involvement in the continuing Cambodian conflict as Cambodian refugees and guerrillas remain in Thai border regions.

TOGO

Official name: La République Togolaise (The Togolese Republic).

Member of: UN, OAU, ECOWAS.

Population: 3 622 000 (1989 est).

Capital and main cities: Lomé 366 000, Sokodé 33 500, Kpalimé 25 500 (1983 est).

Languages: French, Ewe and Kabiye (all official).

Religions: Animist (50%), Roman Catholic (nearly 30%), Sunni Islam (nearly 20%).

Life expectancy: 52.5 years.

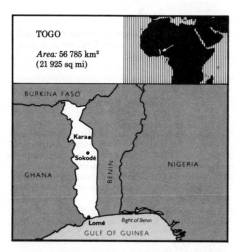

TOGO

Area: **56 785 km²**
(21 925 sq mi)

Labour force: (1988 est) 1 336 000; agriculture and forestry 939 000, trade and tourism 106 000, services 70 000.

GOVERNMENT
The President – who appoints a Council of Ministers – is elected by universal adult suffrage for seven years. The 77-member National Assembly is directly elected for five years. Until 1991 the Rassemblement du peuple togolais was the sole legal political party. *President:* Gen. Gnassingbe Eyadema.

EDUCATION
Literacy rate: 32% (1981). *Years of compulsory schooling:* 6–12. *Universities:* 1.

DEFENCE
Total armed strength: 5900 (1989). *Military service:* 2 years (selective).

GEOGRAPHY
Inland from a narrow coastal plain is a series of plateaux rising in the north to the Chaine du Togo. *Principal rivers:* Moni, Oti. *Highest point:* Pic Baumann 983 m (3225 ft).
Climate: Togo has a hot and humid tropical climate, although the north is drier.

ECONOMY
The majority of the labour force is involved in subsistence farming, with yams and millet as the principal crops. Phosphates are the main export.

RECENT HISTORY
Colonized by Germany in 1884, Togoland was occupied by Franco-British forces in World War I, after which it was divided between them as trust territories. British Togoland became part of Ghana; the French section gained independence as Togo in 1960. Togo has experienced great political instability and several coups. Following anti-government protests, the principle of multi-party elections was conceded in March 1991.

TONGA
Official name: Pule'anga Fakatu'i'o Tonga (The Kingdom of Tonga).
Member of: Commonwealth, South Pacific Forum.

Population: 96 000 (1989 est).
Capital: Nuku'alofa 28 900 (1986).
Languages: Tongan, English.
Religions: Methodist (78%), Roman Catholic.
Life expectancy: 72 years.
Labour force: (1986) 24 500; agriculture and forestry 10 500, services 5500, trade and tourism 2000.

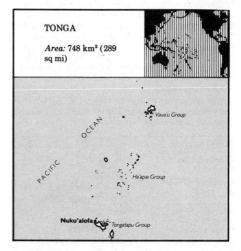

TONGA

Area: **748 km² (289 sq mi)**

GOVERNMENT
Tonga is a constitutional monarchy. The King appoints a Prime Minister and other Ministers to the Privy Council, which acts as a Cabinet. The 31-member Legislative Assembly comprises the King, the Privy Council, 9 hereditary nobles (chosen by their peers) and 9 representatives of the people elected for three years by universal adult suffrage. There are no political parties.
King: HM King Taufa'ahau Tupou IV (succeeded upon the death of his mother, 15 December 1965).
Prime Minister: HRH Prince Fatafehi Tu'ipelehake.

EDUCATION
Literacy rate: 90–95%. *Years of compulsory schooling:* 5–14. *Universities:* none.

DEFENCE
Total armed strength: a small land and marine force is maintained but its size is not published. *Military service:* none.

GEOGRAPHY
The 172 Tongan islands – 36 of which are inhabited – comprise a low limestone chain in the east and a higher volcanic chain in the west. There are no significant rivers. *Highest point:* Kao 1030 m (3380 ft).
Climate: The climate is warm with heavy rainfall.

ECONOMY
Agriculture involves most Tongans, with yams, cassava and taro being grown as subsistence crops. Coconut products are the main exports.

RECENT HISTORY
Civil war in the first half of the 19th century was ended by King George Tupou I (reigned 1845–93), who reunited Tonga, preserved its independence and

gave it a modern constitution. From 1900 to 1970 Tonga was a British protectorate. Since 1987 pressure for constitutional reform has increased.

TRINIDAD AND TOBAGO

Official name: Republic of Trinidad and Tobago.
Member of: UN, Commonwealth, CARICOM, OAS.
Population: 1 285 000 (1989 est).
Capital and main towns: Port of Spain 59 000, San Fernando 34 000, Arima 29 000 (1988).
Languages: English (official), Hindi minority.
Religions: Roman Catholic (34%), Hinduism (25%), Anglican (15%), Sunni Islam (6%).
Life expectancy: 70 years.
Labour force: (1988) 372 000; trade and tourism 191 000, agriculture and forestry 48 000, mining and manufacturing 55 000.

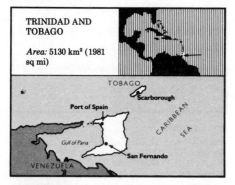

TRINIDAD AND TOBAGO

Area: 5130 km² (1981 sq mi)

GOVERNMENT

The 31-member Senate – the Upper House of Parliament – is appointed by the President, who is elected by a joint sitting of Parliament. The 36-member House of Representatives is elected for five years by universal adult suffrage. The President appoints a Prime Minister who commands a majority in the House. The PM, in turn, appoints a Cabinet, which is responsible to the House. The main political parties include the (socialist coalition) National Alliance for Reconstruction, the (centre) People's National Movement, and the (socialist) United National Congress. Tobago has full internal self-government.
President: Noor Mohammed Hassanali.
Prime Minister: Arthur Robinson.

AUTONOMOUS ISLAND

Tobago *Area*: 301 km² (116 sq mi). *Population*: 44 000 (1987). *Capital*: Scarborough 6100 (1980).

EDUCATION

Literacy rate: 96% (1985 est). *Years of compulsory schooling*: 6–12. *Universities*: 1.

DEFENCE

Total armed strength: 2650 (1989). *Military service*: none.

GEOGRAPHY

Trinidad is generally undulating. Tobago is more mountainous. *Principal rivers*: Caroni, Orotoire, Oropuche. *Highest point*: Cerro Aripo 940 m (3085 ft) in Trinidad.

Climate: Trinidad has a humid tropical climate, with a dry season from January to May.

ECONOMY

Petroleum and petrochemicals are the mainstay of the economy. Trinidad also has important reserves of natural gas and asphalt. Tourism is a major foreign-currency earner.

RECENT HISTORY

Trinidad became British in 1797; Tobago was ceded to Britain in 1802. African slaves were imported to work sugar plantations, but after the abolition of slavery in the 1830s, labourers came from India. The islands merged as a single colony in 1899 and gained independence in 1962 under Dr Eric Williams. His moderate policies brought economic benefits but provoked a Black Power revolt and an army mutiny in 1970. The country has been a republic since 1976. In July 1990, a small group of Islamic fundamentalists held the PM and several government ministers and parliamentarians hostage during an attempted coup.

TUNISIA

Official name: Al-Jumhuriya at-Tunisiya (Republic of Tunisia).
Member of: UN, Arab League, OAU.
Population: 7 973 000 (1989 est).
Capital and major cities: Tunis 1 150 000 (including suburbs), Sfax 232 000, Bizerta 95 000, Djerba 92 000, Gabès 92 000, Sousse 83 500 (1984).
Languages: Arabic (official), Berber minority.
Religion: Sunni Islam (official; 99%).
Life expectancy: 69 years.
Labour force: (1984) 2 137 000; agriculture and forestry 475 000, manufacturing 318 000, services 307 000.

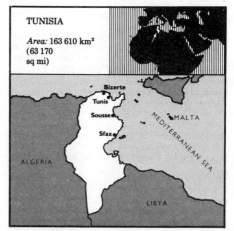

TUNISIA

Area: 163 610 km² (63 170 sq mi)

GOVERNMENT

The President and the 141-member National Assembly are elected by universal adult suffrage for a five-year term. The President appoints a Cabinet, headed by a Prime Minister. The main political parties are the (socialist) RCD (Democratic Constitutional Rally), the MDS (Movement of Democratic Socialists), and independents standing for the (banned Islamic) Renaissance Party.
President: Zine el-Abidine Ben Ali.
Prime Minister: Hamed Karoui.

EDUCATION

Literacy rate: 55% (1985 est). *Years of compulsory schooling*: 6–12. *Universities*: 3.

DEFENCE

Total armed strength: 38 000 (1989). *Military service*: 12 months (selective).

GEOGRAPHY

The north is occupied by the Northern Tell and High Tell mountains. Wide plateaux cover central Tunisia. The Sahara Desert lies south of a zone of shallow salt lakes. *Principal river*: Medjerda. *Highest point*: Jabal ash-Shanabi 1544 m (5066 ft).

Climate: The north has a Mediterranean climate with adequate rainfall. The south has a hot dry climate.

ECONOMY

Phosphates and petroleum are the mainstay of the economy, normally providing over 40% of Tunisia's exports. The principal crops are wheat, barley and vegetables, as well as olives and citrus fruit for export. Tourism is a major foreign-currency earner.

RECENT HISTORY

In 1881 France established a protectorate, although the bey (monarch) remained the nominal ruler. Nationalist sentiments grew in the 20th century. Tunisia was occupied by the Germans from 1942 to 1943, but French rule was restored until 1956, when independence was gained under Habib Bourguiba (1903–). In 1957 the monarchy was abolished. In the late 1980s the regime became increasingly unpopular and intolerant of opposition. Since Bourguiba was deposed by his PM (1988) – because of 'incapacity' – multi-party politics have been permitted.

TURKEY

Official name: Türkiye Cumhuriyeti (Republic of Turkey).
Member of: UN, NATO, OECD, CSCE, Council of Europe.
Population: 55 541 000 (1989).
Capital and major cities: Ankara 2 252 000, Istanbul 5 476 000, Izmir 1 490 000, Adana 778 000, Bursa 614 000 , Gaziantep 479 000, Konya 439 000, Kayseri 378 000, Eskisehir 367 000, Mersin 314 000, Diyarbakir 305 000 (all including suburbs; 1985).
Languages: Turkish (official); Kurdish (7%).
Religion: Sunni Islam (99%).
Life expectancy: 64 years.
Labour force: (1985) 18 423 000; agriculture and forestry 7 272 000, services 2 584 000, manufacturing 2 353 000.

GOVERNMENT

The 450-member National Assembly is elected by universal adult suffrage for five years. The President – who is elected by the Assembly for seven years – appoints a Prime Minister and a Cabinet commanding a majority in the Assembly. The main political parties are the (conservative) Motherland Party, the Social Democratic Populist Party, and the Correct Way Party.
President: Turgut Ozal.
Prime Minister: Yildirim Akbulut.

EDUCATION

Literacy rate: 90% (1989). *Years of compulsory schooling*: 6–14. *Universities*: 29.

TURKEY

Area: 779 452 km² (300 948 sq mi)

DEFENCE

Total armed strength: 650 900 (1989). *Military service*: 18 months.

GEOGRAPHY

Turkey west of the Dardenelles – 5% of the total area – is part of Europe. Asiatic Turkey consists of the central Anatolian Plateau and its basins, bordered to the north by the Pontic Mountains, to the south by the Taurus Mountains, and to the east in high ranges bordering the Caucasus. *Principal rivers:* Euphrates (Firat), Tigris (Dicle), Kizilirmak (Halys), Sakarya. *Highest point*: Büyük Ağridaği (Mount Ararat) 5185 m (17 011 ft).

Climate: The coastal regions have a Mediterranean climate. The interior is continental with hot, dry summers and cold, snowy winters.

ECONOMY

Agriculture involves just under one half of the labour force. Major crops include wheat, rice, tobacco, and cotton. Both tobacco and cotton have given rise to important processing industries, and textiles account for one quarter of Turkey's exports. Manufacturing – in particular the chemical and steel industries – has grown rapidly. Natural resources include copper, coal and chromium. Unemployment is severe. Money sent back by the large number of Turks working in Western Europe is a major source of foreign currency. Tourism is increasingly important.

RECENT HISTORY

At the beginning of the 19th century, the (Turkish) Ottoman Empire extended from the Danube to Aden, and from the Euphrates to Algiers. The empire was, however, suffering a long decline in military and political might and in extent. The Ottoman Empire came to be regarded as 'the sick man of Europe', and the future of the empire and its Balkan territories troubled the 19th century as 'the Eastern Question'. In 1908 the Young Turks revolt attempted to stop the decline, but defeat in the Balkan Wars (1912–13) virtually expelled Turkey from Europe.

Alliance with Germany in World War I ended in defeat and the loss of all non-Turkish areas. The future of Turkey in Asia itself seemed in doubt when Greece took the area around Izmir and the Allies defined zones of influence. General Mustafa Kemal (1881–1938) – later known as Atatürk ('father of the Turks') – led forces of resistance in a civil war and went on to defeat Greece. Turkey's present boundaries were established in 1923 by the Treaty of

Lausanne. With the abolition of the sultanate (1922) Turkey became a republic, which Atatürk transformed into a secular Westernized state. Islam was disestablished, Arabic script was replaced by the Latin alphabet, the Turkish language was revived, and women's veils were banned.

Soviet claims on Turkish territory in 1945 encouraged a pro-Western outlook, and in 1952 Turkey joined NATO. PM Adnan Menderes was overthrown by a military coup in 1960 and hanged on charges of corruption and unconstitutional rule. Civilian government was restored in 1961, but a pattern of violence and ineffective government led to a further army takeover in 1980. In 1974, after President Makarios was overthrown in Cyprus by a Greek-sponsored coup, Turkey invaded the island and set up a Turkish administration in the north (1975). Differences with Greece over Cyprus have damaged the country's attempts to join the EC, as has the country's record on human rights. In 1983 civilian rule replaced the military government. Since then Turkey has drawn as close as possible to Western Europe, although the emergence of Islamic fundamentalism in the late 1980s has raised doubts concerning Turkey's European identity.

TUVALU

Member of: Commonwealth (special member), South Pacific Forum.

Population: 8900 (1989).

Capital: Funafuti 2800 (1985).

Languages: Tuvaluan and English.

Religion: Protestant Church of Tuvalu (98%).

Life expectancy: 62 years.

Labour force: (1980) 936; government service 468, phosphates 114, merchant marine 255.

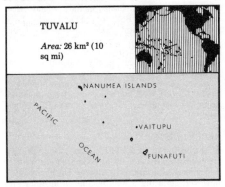

TUVALU

Area: 26 km² (10 sq mi)

NANUMEA ISLANDS

PACIFIC OCEAN

•VAITUPU

FUNAFUTI

GOVERNMENT

The 12-member Parliament – which is elected by universal adult suffrage for four years – chooses a Prime Minister who appoints other Ministers. A Governor General represents the British Queen as sovereign of Tuvalu. There are no political parties. *Prime Minister*: Bikenibeu Paeniu.

EDUCATION

Literacy rate: 45%. *Years of compulsory schooling*: 6–12. *Universities*: 1 extension centre of the University of the South Pacific.

DEFENCE

Total armed strength: there are no armed forces.

GEOGRAPHY

Tuvalu comprises nine small islands. There are no rivers. *Highest point*: an unnamed point, 6 m (20 ft).

Climate: Tuvalu experiences high temperatures and heavy rainfall of 3000–4000 mm (120–160 in) per year.

ECONOMY

Subsistence farming – based on coconuts, pigs and poultry – involves the majority of the population. The only export is copra from coconuts.

RECENT HISTORY

Tuvalu was claimed for Britain in 1892 as the Ellice Islands, which became linked administratively with the Gilbert Islands. A referendum in 1974 showed a majority of Polynesians in the Ellice Islands in favour of separation from the Micronesians of the Gilbert Islands (Kiribati). Independence was achieved as Tuvalu in 1978.

UGANDA

Official name: The Republic of Uganda.

Member of: UN, Commonwealth, OAU.

Population: 16 789 000 (1987 est).

Capital and main towns: Kampala 455 000 (1981), Jinja 45 000, Masaka 29 000, Mbale 28 000 (1980).

Languages: English and Swahili (both official), with local languages including Luganda.

Religions: Roman Catholic (over 40%), Protestant Churches (30%), animist (15%), Sunni Islam.

Life expectancy: 51 years.

Labour force: (1988 est) 7 695 000; agriculture and forestry 6 306 000, services 700 000, industry 372 000.

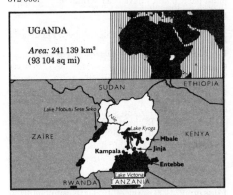

UGANDA

Area: 241 139 km² (93 104 sq mi)

SUDAN   ETHIOPIA

Lake Mobutu Sese Seko

Nile

ZAÏRE   Lake Kyoga   Mbale   KENYA

Kampala   Jinja

Entebbe

Lake Victoria

RWANDA   TANZANIA

GOVERNMENT

The commander of the National Resistance Army – which took power in 1986 – is President. He appoints a Prime Minister and other Ministers. The advisory 278-member National Resistance Council comprises 210 indirectly elected members and 68 members appointed by the President. Political activity has been suspended.

President: Yoweri Museveni.

Prime Minister: George Adyebo.

EDUCATION

Literacy rate: 52%. *Years of compulsory schooling*: schooling is not compulsory. *Universities*: 3.

DEFENCE

Total armed strength: 70 000 (1989). *Military service*: none.

GEOGRAPHY

Most of Uganda is a plateau that ends in the west at the Great Rift Valley and the Ruwenzori Mountains. Lake Victoria covers southeast Uganda. *Principal rivers*: Nile, Semliki. *Highest point*: Ngaliema 5118 m (16 763 ft).

Climate: Uganda's tropical climate is moderated by its altitude.

ECONOMY

Agriculture involves over three quarters of the labour force. Coffee normally accounts for 90% of Uganda's exports. Subsistence crops include plantains, cassava and sweet potatoes.

RECENT HISTORY

The British protectorate of Uganda – established in 1894 – was built around the powerful African kingdom of Buganda, whose continuing special status contributed to the disunity that has plagued the country since independence in 1962. Dr Milton Obote, who suppressed the Buganda monarchy in 1966, was overthrown in a coup by General Idi Amin in 1971. Amin earned international criticism when political and human rights were curtailed, opponents of the regime were murdered and the Asian population was expelled. The army took over in 1979, supported by Tanzanian troops. Obote was restored but was ousted in a military coup in 1985, since when instability and guerrilla action have continued.

UNION OF SOVIET SOCIALIST REPUBLICS†

Official name: Soyuz Sovyetskikh Sotsialisticheskikh Respublik (The Union of Soviet Socialist Republics†). Popularly known as the Soviet Union.

Member of: UN, CSCE. The Ukraine and Byelorussia have separate membership of the UN.

Population: 288 800 000 (1990 est).

Capital and major cities: Moscow (Moskva) 8 967 000, Leningrad 5 020 000†, Kiev (Kiyev) 2 587 000, Tashkent 2 073 000, Baku 1 757 000, Kharkov 1 611 000, Minsk 1 589 000, Nizhny Novgorod (formerly Gorky) 1 438 000, Novosibirsk 1 436 000, Sverdlovsk 1 367 000, Tbilisi 1 260 000, Kuybyshev 1 257 000, Yerevan 1 199 000, Dnepropetrovsk 1 179 000, Omsk 1 148 000, Chelyabinsk 1 143 000, Alma-Ata 1 128 000, Donetsk 1 110 000, Kazan 1 094 000, Perm 1 091 000, Ufa 1 083 000, Rostov (Don) 1 020 000, Volgograd 999 000, Riga 915 000, Krasnoyarsk 912 000, Saratov 905 000 (1989 est).
† It is proposed to change the name of the country to the Union of Soviet Sovereign Republics and of the city of Leningrad to St Petersburg.

Languages: 112 languages are recognized. Russian is the first language of about 53% of the population. Other major languages include Ukrainian (16%), Uzbek, Byelorussian, Kazakh, Tartar, Azeri, Armenian, Georgian, Moldavian (Romanian), Tadzhik, Lithuanian, Bashkir, Kirghiz, Udmurt, Chuvash, Latvian, Estonian.

Religions: Over 40 religions are officially recognized. Russian Orthodox (18%), Sunni Islam (16%), Shia Islam (2%), Roman Catholic (2%).

Life expectancy: 69 years.

Labour force: (1979) 135 424 000; (1979 est) industry 60 000 000, agriculture and forestry 40 000 000, education and research 18 000 000.

GOVERNMENT

The 2250-member Congress of People's Deputies is elected for five years, and comprises 750 members from constituencies elected by universal adult suffrage, 750 directly elected members representing the 15 Union Republics, the 25 Autonomous Republics, the 8 Autonomous Regions, and the 10 Autonomous Areas, plus 750 members elected by 32 official organizations.

Members of the Congress of People's Deputies elect the bicameral Supreme Soviet (Parliament) – comprising the Soviet of the Union and the Soviet of Nationalities. The Soviet of the Union consists of 271 deputies elected from the 750 constituency members of the Congress of People's Deputies. The Soviet of Nationalities consists of 271 deputies elected from the 1500 members representing republics, regions and official organizations. Congress reviews the membership of 20% of the Supreme Soviet every year. The Prime Minister and Council of Ministers are appointed by the Supreme Soviet and are responsible to it. The executive State President was chosen by the Congress in 1990, but will, in future, be elected by universal adult suffrage for a term of five years. The President is assisted by a Presidential Council comprising one representative from each of the 15 Union republics.

In 1990, the Communist Party – which had been the only legal political body – renounced its leading role. Nationalist, reformist and independent groups took part in elections in the Union republics and cities, taking control in some areas. The Communist Party Congress meets every five years to elect the Central Committee, which in 1989 comprised 287 full members and 170 candidate (non-voting) members. The Congress elects the Politburo, which – until the creation of the executive Presidency and Presidential Council – exercised effective power.

The USSR is a federal state of 15 Union Republics each of which has – in theory – considerable autonomy, including the right to secede.
President: Mikhail Gorbachev.
Prime Minister: Valentin Pavlov.

UNION REPUBLICS

Population figures are for 1989.

Armenia (Haikakan or Armenija) *Area*: 29 800 km² (11 500 sq mi). *Population*: 3 283 000. *Capital*: Yerevan 1 199 000.

Azerbaijan (Azarbaijchan) *Area*: 86 600 km² (33 400 sq mi). *Population*: 7 029 000. *Capital*: Baku 1 757 000. (Azerbaijan includes the autonomous republic of Nakichevan.)

Byelorussia (Belorossiya) *Area*: 207 600 km² (80 200 sq mi). *Population*: 10 200 000. *Capital*: Minsk 1 589 000.

Estonia* (Eesti) *Area*: 45 100 km² (17 400 sq mi). *Population*: 1 573 000. *Capital*: Tallinn 478 000.

Georgia (Sakartvelo or Gruziya) *Area*: 69 700 km² (26 900 sq mi). *Population*: 5 449 000. *Capital*: Tbilisi 1 260 000. (Georgia includes three autonomous republics – Abkhazia, Adjaria and South Ossetia.)

Kazakhstan *Area*: 2 717 300 km² (1 049 200 sq mi). *Population*: 16 538 000. *Capital*: Alma-Ata 1 128 000.

Kirghizia (Kirgiziya) *Area*: 198 500 km² (76 600 sq mi). *Population*: 4 291 000. *Capital*: Frunze 632 000.

Latvia* (Latvija) *Area*: 64 500 km² (24 900 sq mi). *Population*: 2 681 000. *Capital*: Riga 915 000.

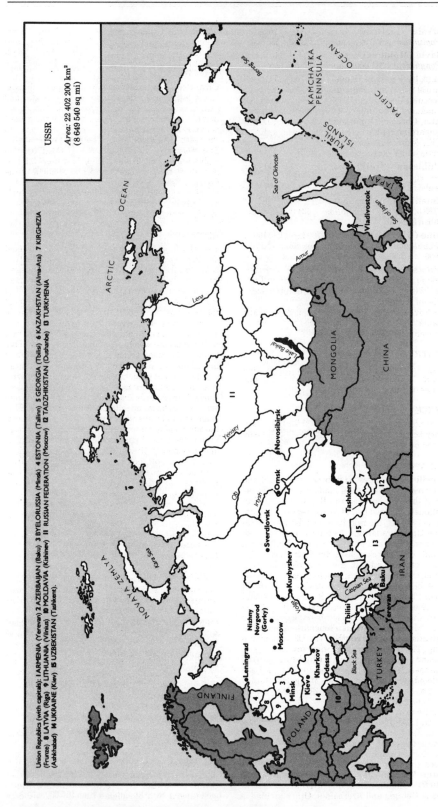

USSR

Area: 22 402 200 km²
(8 649 540 sq mi)

Union Republics (with capitals): 1 ARMENIA (Yerevan) 2 AZERBAIJAN (Baku) 3 BYELORUSSIA (Minsk) 4 ESTONIA (Tallinn) 5 GEORGIA (Tbilisi) 6 KAZAKHSTAN (Alma-Ata) 7 KIRGHIZIA (Frunze) 8 LATVIA (Riga) 9 LITHUANIA (Vilnius) 10 MOLDAVIA (Kishinev) 11 RUSSIAN FEDERATION (Moscow) 12 TADZHIKISTAN (Dushanbe) 13 TURKMENIA (Ashkhabad) 14 UKRAINE (Kiev) 15 UZBEKISTAN (Tashkent).

Lithuania* (Lietuva) *Area*: 65 200 km² (25 200 sq mi). *Population*: 3 690 000. *Capital*: Vilnius 566 000.

Moldavia (Moldova) *Area*: 33 700 km² (13 000 sq mi). *Population*: 4 341 000. *Capital*: Kishinev 663 000.

Russian Federation (Rossiya) *Area*: 17 075 400 km² (6 592 800 sq mi). *Population*: 147 386 000. *Capital*: Moscow (Moskva) 8 967 000. (The Russian Federation includes 16 autonomous republics – Bashkiria, Buryatia, Checheno-Ingushetia, Chuvashia, Dagestan, Kabardino-Balkaria, Kalmykia, Karelia, Komi, Mari El, Mordova, North Ossetia, Tataria, Tuva, Udmurtia and Yakutia.)

Tadzhikistan (Tojikiston) *Area*: 143 100 km² (55 300 sq mi). *Population*: 5 112 000. *Capital*: Dushanbe 582 000.

Turkmenia (Tiurkmenostan) *Area*: 488 100 km² (188 500 sq mi). *Population*: 3 534 000. *Capital*: Ashkabad 382 000.

Ukraine (Ukraina) *Area*: 603 700 km² (233 100 sq mi). *Population*: 51 704 000. *Capital*: Kiev (Kiyev) 2 587 000.

Uzbekistan (Ozbekiston) *Area*: 447 400 km² (172 700 sq mi). *Population*: 19 906 000. *Capital*: Tashkent 2 073 000. (Uzbekistan includes the autonomous republic of Karakalpakia.)

* The Soviet annexation of Estonia, Latvia and Lithuania (1940) is not recognized by Western governments.

EDUCATION

Literacy rate: 99% (1979). *Years of compulsory schooling:* 7–17. *Universities:* 904 universities and institutes of university status.

DEFENCE

Total armed strength: 4 258 000 (1989 Western est). *Military service:* 2 years army/air force; 2–3 years navy and border force.

GEOGRAPHY

The USSR is the largest country in the world and covers over 15% of the total land area of the globe. Much of the area between the Baltic and the Ural Mountains is covered by the North European Plain, south of which the relatively low-lying Central Russian Uplands stretch from the Ukraine to north of Moscow. The Urals run north–south for 2000 km (1250 mi), dividing European Russia from Asia. To the east of the Urals is the vast West Siberian Lowland, the greater part of which is occupied by the basin of the River Ob and its tributaries. The Central Siberian Plateau – between the Rivers Yenisey and Lena – rises to around 1700 m (5500 ft). Beyond the Lena are the mountains of east Siberia, including the Chersky Mountains and the Kamchatka Peninsula. The greater part of the south of the USSR is mountainous. The Yablonovy and Stanovoy Mountains rise inland from the Amur Basin, which drains to the Pacific coast. The Altai Mountains lie south of Lake Baikal and along the border with Mongolia. Most of Kirghizia lies within the Tien Shan Mountains, while Tadzhikistan includes part of the Pamirs, which rise to over 7000 m (23 000 ft). A great lowland in Central Asia drains to the Aral Sea and to the Caspian Sea (which is below sea level). The Kara Kum desert lies in the south of Central Asia and ends at the Koppeh Dagh range on the Iranian border. Between the Caspian and Black Seas are the high Caucasus Mountains – containing Elbrus at 5642 m (18 510 ft) – and the mountains of Transcaucasia in Armenia, Georgia and Azerbaijan. Other highlands include the Crimean Mountains and the Carpathians in the southwest of the USSR. *Principal rivers*: Yenisey, Ob (with Irytsh), Amur (with Argun), Lena, Volga. *Highest point*: Pik Kommunizma 7495 m (24 590 ft).

Climate: The USSR has a wide range of climatic types, but most of the country is continental and experiences extremes of temperature. The Arctic north is a severe tundra region in which the subsoil is nearly always frozen. The forested taiga zone – to the south – has long hard winters and short summers. The steppes of Kazakhstan, the central Russian Uplands and the Ukraine have cold winters but hot, dry summers. The semi-desert zone – north of the Caspian Sea – and the desert area – east of the Caspian – have cold winters, hot summers and little to negligible rainfall. The Crimean coast has a Mediterranean climate.

ECONOMY

The USSR has the third largest gross national product in the world, and is the largest producer of coal, iron ore, steel, petroleum and cement. However, its centrally planned economy is in crisis and under Gorbachov the system is being decentralized. Lack of motivation in the labour force affects all sectors of the economy. In 1990–91 production was falling in many sectors and severe shortages of food and consumer goods – in part, the result of a poor system of distribution – was experienced in most parts of the country. Manufacturing involves over one third of the labour force and includes the steel, chemical, textile and heavy machinery industries. The production of consumer goods is not highly developed. Agriculture is large scale and organized either into state-owned farms or collective farms. Despite mechanization and the world's largest fertilizer industry, the USSR cannot produce enough grain for its needs, in part because of poor harvests, and poor storage and transport facilities. Major crops include wheat, barley, oats, potatoes, sugar beet, fruit, and cotton. Natural resources include the world's largest coal reserves, one third of the world's natural gas reserves, one third of the world's forests, major deposits of manganese, gold, potash, bauxite, nickel, lead, zinc and copper, as well as plentiful sites for hydroelectric power installations. Petroleum and petroleum products normally account for almost one third and machinery for about one sixth of the USSR's exports.

RECENT HISTORY

Throughout the 19th century, the Russian Empire's frontiers were extended into Central Asia, the Caucasus and the Far East, and at the same time Russia attempted to increase its influence in southeast Europe at the expense of the declining Turkish Empire. These imperial tendencies sometimes led to confrontation with Western European powers. Tsar Alexander III (reigned 1881–94) combined repression at home with restraint abroad. Under Nicholas II (reigned 1894–1917), Russia saw rapid industrialization, rising prosperity, and – following the failed revolution of 1905 – limited constitutional reform, but this progress was cut short by World War I.

Following the revolution of February 1917 – largely brought about by the catastrophic conduct of the war – the Tsar abdicated and a provisional government was established. On 7 November 1917 the Bolsheviks (Communists) – led by Vladymir Ilich Lenin (1870–1924) – overthrew the provisional government in a bloodless coup. Russia withdrew from the war by the Treaty of Brest-Litovsk (March 1918), by which Russia ceded Poland to Germany and Austria and recognized the independence of Estonia, Finland, Georgia, Latvia, Lithuania and the Ukraine. Other parts of the former empire soon declared independence, including Armenia, Azerbaijan and Central Asia. A civil war between the Bolsheviks and the White Russians (led by former Tsarists) lasted until 1922.

The Communists gradually reconquered most of the former Russian empire and in December 1922 formed the Union of Soviet Socialist Republics. The economy was reorganized under central control, but shortages – and, in some regions, famine – were soon experienced. After Lenin's death (1924), a power struggle took place between the supporters of Joseph Stalin (1879–1953) and Leon Trotsky (1879–1940). Stalin expelled his opponents from the Communist Party in 1927 and forced Trotsky into exile in 1929 (and had him murdered in 1940). Stalin ordered the rapid industrialization of the country. In 1929–30 he liquidated the kulaks (the richer peasants who were generally hostile to the government). Severe repression continued until Stalin's death in 1953 – opponents were subjected to 'show trials' and summary execution, and millions died as a result of starvation or political execution.

In World War II – in which up to 20 million Soviet citizens may have died – the USSR at first concluded a pact with Hitler (1939), and invaded Poland, Finland, Romania and the Baltic states, annexing considerable territory. However, in 1941 the Germans invaded the USSR, precipitating the Soviet Union's entry into the war on the Allied side. In victory the Soviet Union was confirmed as a world power, controlling a cordon of satellite states in Eastern Europe and challenging the West in the Cold War. However, the economy stagnated and the country was drained by the burdens of an impoverished and overstretched empire. Leonid Brezhnev (1964–82) reversed the brief thaw that had been experienced under Nikita Khrushchev (1956–64), and far-reaching reform had to await the policies of Mikhail Gorbachev after 1985.

Faced with severe economic problems, Gorbachev attempted to introduce reconstruction (*perestroika*) and greater openness (*glasnost*) by implementing social, economic and industrial reforms. The state of the economy also influenced the desire to reduce military spending by reaching agreements on arms reduction with the West. Dissent was tolerated, a major reform of the constitution led to more open elections, and the Communist Party gave up its leading role. Many hardliners in the Communist Party were defeated by reformers (many of them non-Communists) in elections to the new Congress of People's Deputies in 1989. The abandonment of the Brezhnev Doctrine – the right of the USSR to intervene in the affairs of Warsaw Pact countries (as it had done militarily in Hungary and Czechoslovakia) – prompted rapid change in Eastern Europe, where one after another the satellite states renounced Communism and began to implement multi-party rule. From 1989 there were increased nationalist stirrings within the USSR. In the Baltic republics, popular movements called for a restoration of the independence they had enjoyed from 1919 to 1940, and Lithuania openly attempted to secede. Disturbances in the Caucasus – initially over the status of the Nagorno Karabakh region, which was disputed by Armenia and Azerbaijan – erupted into

serious violence between the Orthodox Christian Armenians and the Shiite Muslim Azeris in 1990, when Gorbachov sent troops to restore Soviet power in Baku, the Azeri capital.

Gorbachov redrafted the constitution, instituting a strong executive presidency and assuming emergency powers, including the right to rule by decree. In the Russian Federation, Gorbachov was increasingly challenged by the populist leader Boris Yeltsin (President of the Russian Federation since 1990). By the beginning of 1991, reform was overshadowed by the priority of preventing the USSR from breaking up. Army units tightened control in the Baltic republics, suppressing demonstrations in Latvia and Lithuania with bloodshed. The army and conservative elements within the Communist Party were in the ascendant as press freedom was gradually restricted and the Foreign Minister, Edvard Shevadnadze, resigned, warning of the dangers of a new dictatorship. Gorbachov attempted to gain approval for a new Union Treaty, but was opposed by the majority of the Union republics – which had declared their law to take precedence over that of the USSR. A dangerous contest between the centre and the republics seemed imminent, with Gorbachov, the military and the Communist Party on one side and the disparate supporters of Yeltsin, the radicals and reformers, and the republics on the other. Some republics were intent upon secession – in 1990-91, Estonia, Georgia, Latvia and Lithuania declared independence.

UNITED ARAB EMIRATES

Official name: Al-Imarat Al'Arabiya Al-Muttahida (The United Arab Emirates).

Member of: UN, Arab League, OPEC, GCC.

Population: 1 856 000 (1987 est.)

Capital and main cities: Abu Dhabi 243 000, Dubai 266 000, Sharjah 125 000, al'Ayn 102 000 (1984).

Languages: Arabic (official); English (commercial).

Religion: Sunni Islam (official).

Life expectancy: 71 years.

Labour force: (1980) 558 000; services 188 000, construction 155 000, trade and tourism 75 000, agriculture and forestry 26 000.

GOVERNMENT

The hereditary rulers of the seven emirates – who are absolute monarchs – form the Supreme Council of Rulers, which elects one of its members as President. The Prime Minister and Council of Ministers are appointed by the President. The Supreme Council appoints a 40-member advisory Federal National Council. There are no political parties.
President: HH Shaikh Zayid bin Sultan Al Nihayyan.
Prime Minister: HH Shaikh Maktum bin Rashid Al Maktum.

EMIRATES

Population figures for the emirates are for 1985.

Abu Dhabi *Area*: 67 350 km² (26 000 sq mi). *Population*: 670 000. *Capital*: Abu Dhabi 243 000 (1985).

Ajman *Area*: 250 km² (100 sq mi). *Population*: 64 000. *Capital*: Ajman 30 000 (1980).

Dubai *Area*: 3900 km² (1510 sq mi). *Population*: 419 000. *Capital*: Dubai 266 000 (1984).

Fujairah *Area*: 1150 km² (440 sq mi). *Population*: 54 000. *Capital*: Fujairah 32 000 (1980).

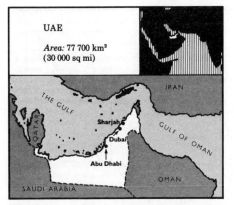

UAE

Area: 77 700 km²
(30 000 sq mi)

Ras al-Khaimah Area: 1700 km² (660 sq mi). Population: 117 000. Capital: Ras al-Khaimah 74 000 (1980).

Sharjah Area: 2600 km² (1000 sq mi). Population: 269 000. Capital: Sharjah 125 000 (1984).

Umm al-Qaiwain Area: 750 km² (290 sq mi). Population: 29 000. Capital: Umm al-Qaiwain 12 000 (1980).

EDUCATION

Literacy rate: 54% (1975). Years of compulsory schooling: 6–12. Universities: 1.

DEFENCE

Total armed strength: 43 000 (1989). Military service: none.

GEOGRAPHY

The country is a low-lying desert except in the Jajar Mountains in the east. There are no permanent streams. Highest point: Al-Hajar 1189 m (3901 ft).

Climate: Summer temperatures may rise to over 40° C (104° F); winter temperatures are milder. Rainfall totals are very low.

ECONOMY

Based upon the export of offshore and onshore reserves of petroleum and natural gas, the country has one of the highest standards of living in the world. Dry docks, fertilizer factories, commercial banking interests, international airports and an entrepôt trade have been developed. Immigrants from the Indian subcontinent and Iran form the majority of the labour force. Agriculture is confined to oases and a few coastal sites irrigated by desalinated water.

RECENT HISTORY

A political vacuum in the mid-18th century was filled by the British, who saw the region as a link in the trade route to India. Treaties ('truces') were signed with local rulers during the 19th century, bringing the Trucial States under British protection. In 1958 oil was discovered in Abu Dhabi. In 1968 the Trucial States, Bahrain and Qatar laid the foundations of a federation, but when the British withdrew in 1971 only six states formed the United Arab Emirates. Bahrain and Qatar gained separate independent statehood, while Ras al-Khaimah joined the federation in 1972. The UAE – as members of the GCC – joined the coalition against Saddam Hussein's Iraq (1990–91).

UNITED KINGDOM

Official name: The United Kingdom of Great Britain and Northern Ireland.

Member of: UN, EC, NATO, Commonwealth, G7, OECD, CSCE, Council of Europe.

Population: 57 065 000 (1988 est).

Capital and major cities: London 7 680 000 (London Urban Area – Greater London 6 731 000), Birmingham 2 355 000 (West Midlands Urban Area; city 993 700), Manchester 2 340 000 (Greater Manchester Urban Area; city 445 900), Glasgow 1 660 000 (Central Clydeside Urban Area; city 715 600), Leeds-Bradford 1 480 000 (West Yorkshire Urban Area; Leeds city 709 600, Bradford city 464 100), Newcastle-upon-Tyne 780 000 (Tyneside Urban Area; city 279 600), Liverpool 750 000 (Urban Area; city 469 600), Sheffield 645 000 (Urban Area; city 528 300), Nottingham 600 000 (Urban Area; city 273 500), Bristol 525 000 (Urban Area; city 377 700), Edinburgh 460 000 (Urban Area; city 438 200), Brighton 440 000 (Brighton-Worthing Urban Area; borough 149 200), Belfast 435 000 (Urban Area; city 296 900), Portsmouth 415 000 (Urban Area; city 183 800), Leicester 410 000 (Urban Area; city 278 500), Middlesbrough 380 000 (Teesside Urban Area; borough 143 200), Stoke-on-Trent 375 000 (The Potteries Urban Area; city 246 800), Coventry 350 000 (Coventry-Bedworth Urban Area; city 306 200), Bournemouth 335 000 (Urban Area; borough 154 800), Hull 325 000 (Kingston-upon-Hull Urban Area; city), Cardiff 284 000 (Urban Area and city), Swansea 280 000 (Urban Area; city 186 900), Birkenhead 280 000 (Urban Area; former borough 99 000), Southend 275 000 (Urban Area; borough 165 400), Southampton 270 000 (Southampton-Eastleigh Urban Area; city 196 700), Blackpool 265 000 (Urban Area; borough 143 800), Plymouth 258 000 (Urban Area and city), Preston 250 000 (Urban Area; borough 128 100), Rochester (Medway Towns Urban Area; city 146 600), Aldershot 230 000 (Urban Area; former borough 55 000), Luton 217 000 (Luton-Dunstable Urban Area; borough 167 600), Derby 215 000 (Urban Area and city), Aberdeen (Urban Area and city) 214 000, Reading (Urban Area; borough 132 400), Sunderland 200 000 (Urban Area; the borough has a population of 296 600 and covers a wider area than the Urban Area), Norwich 190 000 (Urban Area; city 117 300), Northampton 185 000 (Urban Area; borough 182 100). (The population figures for the Urban Areas – the cities and their agglomerations – and for the local government areas are for 1981 and 1988 respectively.)

Languages: English, Welsh (21% of the population of Wales, though only 1% of the population of Wales speak Welsh as their first language), Gaelic (under 1% of the population of Scotland).

Religions: Anglican (55% nominal, 4% practising), Roman Catholic (9%), Presbyterian (3%, including Church of Scotland), Methodist (2%), various other Christian Churches (4%), Sunni Islam (2%), Judaism (under 1%).

Life expectancy: 75 years.

Labour force: (1987) 24 989 000; services 7 455 000, manufacturing 5 398 000, trade and tourism 5 061 000, agriculture and forestry 592 000.

GOVERNMENT

The UK is a constitutional monarchy without a written constitution. The House of Lords – the Upper

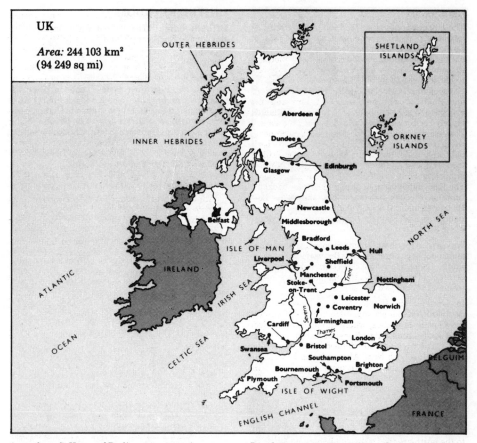

UK

Area: 244 103 km²
(94 249 sq mi)

(non-elected) House of Parliament – comprises over 750 hereditary peers and peeresses, over 20 Lords of Appeal (non-hereditary peers), over 370 life peers, and 2 archbishops and 24 bishops of the Church of England. The House of Commons consists of 650 members elected for five years by universal adult suffrage. The sovereign appoints a Prime Minister who commands a majority in the Commons. The main political parties include the Conservative Party, the Labour Party, the Liberal Democrats and regional parties including the Scottish National Party, the (Welsh Nationalist) Plaid Cymru, the Ulster Unionists, the Democratic Unionist Party and the (Northern Ireland) Social Democratic and Labour Party. The UK comprises four countries – England, Scotland, Wales and Northern Ireland; there is constitutional provision for devolved government for the latter.
Queen: HM Queen Elizabeth II (succeeded upon the death of her father, 6 February 1952).
Prime Minister: John Major.

COUNTRIES OF THE UNITED KINGDOM

England *Area*: 130 441 km² (50 363 sq mi). *Population*: 47 563 000 (1988). *Capital*: London 7 680 000 (London Urban Area – Greater London 6 731 000).

Northern Ireland *Area*: 14 120 km² (5452 sq mi). *Population*: 1 578 000. *Capital*: Belfast 435 000 (Urban Area; city 296 900).

Scotland *Area*: 78 775 km² (30 415 sq mi).

Population: 5 094 000 (1988). *Capital*: Edinburgh 460 000 (Urban Area; city 438 200). *Largest city*: Glasgow 1 660 000 (Central Clydeside Urban Area; city 715 600).

Wales *Area*: 20 768 km² (8019 sq mi). *Population*: 2 857 000 (1988). *Capital*: Cardiff 284 000 (Urban Area and city).

CROWN DEPENDENCIES

The Crown Dependencies are associated with but not part of the UK.

Guernsey (includes Alderney, Sark and smaller dependencies) *Area*: 75 km² (29 sq mi). Guernsey (island) has an area of 63.3 km² (24.5 sq mi). Alderney has an area of 7.9 km² (3.07 sq mi); Sark has an area of 5.1 km² (1.99 sq mi). *Population*: 54 400 (Guernsey island; 1988). Alderney has a population of 2000 (1986) and Sark has a population of 600 (1986). *Capital*: St Peter Port 18 000 (1986). The capital of Alderney is St Anne's. There are no towns or villages on Sark, on which settlement is scattered.

Isle of Man *Area*: 572 km² (221 sq mi). *Population*: 64 300 (1986). *Capital*: Douglas 20 400 (1986).

Jersey *Area*: 116.2 km² (44.8 sq mi). *Population*: 80 200 (1986). *Capital*: St Helier 30 000 (1986).

EDUCATION
Literacy rate: 96%. *Years of compulsory schooling*: 5–16. *Universities*: 48 (including 1 private).

DEFENCE
Total armed strength: 311 600. *Military service*: none.

GEOGRAPHY

The UK comprises the island of Great Britain, the northeast part of Ireland plus over 4000 other islands. Lowland Britain occupies the south, east and centre of England. Clay valleys and river basins – including those of the Thames and the Trent – separate relatively low ridges of hills, including the limestone Cotswolds and Cleveland Hills, and the chalk North and South Downs and the Yorkshire and Lincolnshire Wolds. In the east, low-lying Fenland is largely reclaimed marshland. The flat landscape of East Anglia is covered by glacial soils. The northwest coastal plain of Lancashire and Cheshire is the only other major lowland in England. A peninsula in the southwest – Devon and Cornwall – contains granitic uplands, including Dartmoor and Exmoor. The limestone Pennines form a moorland backbone running through northern England. The Lake District (Cumbria) is an isolated mountainous dome rising to Scafell Pike, the highest point in England at 978 m (3210 ft).

Wales is a highland block, formed by a series of plateaux above which rise the Brecon Beacons in the south, Cader Idris and the Berwyn range in the centre, and Snowdonia in the north, where Snowdon reaches 1085 m (3560 ft).

In Scotland, the Highlands in the north and the Southern Uplands are separated by the rift valley of the Central Lowlands, where the majority of Scotland's population, agriculture and industry are to be found. The Highlands are divided by the Great Glen in which lies Loch Ness. Although Ben Nevis is the highest point, the most prominent range of the Highlands is the Cairngorm Mountains. The Southern Uplands lie below 853 m (2800 ft). Other Scottish lowlands include Buchan in the northeast, Caithness in the north, and a coastal plain around the Moray Firth. To the west of Scotland are the many islands of the Inner and Outer Hebrides, while to the north are the Orkney and Shetland Islands.

Northern Ireland includes several hilly areas, including the Sperrin Mountains in the northwest, the uplands in County Antrim, and the Mourne Mountains rising to Slieve Donard at 852 m (2796 ft). Lough Neagh – at the centre of Northern Ireland – is the UK's largest lake.
Principal rivers: Severn, Thames (with Churn), Trent-Humber, Aire (with Ouse), (Great or Bedford) Ouse, Wye, Tay (with Tummel), Nene, Clyde. *Highest point*: Ben Nevis 1392 m (4406 ft).
Climate: The temperate climate of the UK is warmed by the North Atlantic Drift. There is considerable local variety, particularly in rainfall totals, which range from just over 500 mm (20 in) in the southeast to 5000 mm (200 in) in northwest Scotland.

ECONOMY

Over one fifth of the British labour force is involved in manufacturing. The principal industries include iron and steel, motor vehicles, electronics and electrical engineering, textiles and clothing, aircraft, and consumer goods. British industry relies heavily upon imports of raw materials. The country is self-sufficient in petroleum (from the North Sea) and has important reserves of natural gas and coal – although the coal industry is declining as seams in traditional mining areas become uneconomic. As Britain is a major trading nation, London is one of the world's leading banking, financial and insurance centres, and the 'invisible earnings' from these services make an important contribution to exports.

Tourism is another major foreign-currency earner. Agriculture (with forestry) involves about 2% of the labour force and is principally concerned with raising sheep and cattle. Arable farming is widespread in the east, where the main crops are barley, wheat, potatoes and sugar beet. In the 1970s and 1980s the UK did not experience the same rate of economic growth as most other West European countries. Economic problems have included repeated crises of confidence in the value of the pound, credit squeezes and high (regional) rates of unemployment. Since 1980 most major nationalized industries have been privatized.

RECENT HISTORY

The United Kingdom – formed in 1801 through the union of Great Britain and Ireland – fought almost continuous wars against Revolutionary and Napoleonic France (1789–1815), and emerged from the wars with colonial gains. The reign of Queen Victoria (1837–1901) witnessed the height of British power. Britain – the first country to undergo an industrial revolution – dominated world trade. British statesmen – including PMs Sir Robert Peel (1788–1850), Lord Palmerston (1784–1865), William Ewart Gladstone (1809–98) and Benjamin Disraeli (1804–81) – dominated the world stage. The British Empire included much of Africa, the Indian subcontinent, Canada and Australasia. Parliamentary democracy increased with the gradual extension of the right to vote, starting with the Reform Act of 1832. Representative government was granted to distant colonies, beginning with Canada and Australia, but was denied to Ireland, where nationalist sentiment was stirring. By the end of the 19th century Britain's economic dominance was beginning to be challenged by the USA and, more particularly, by Germany. Rivalry with Imperial Germany was but one factor contributing to the causes of World War I. PM Herbert Asquith (1852–1928) led a reforming Liberal Government from 1908 to 1916 but – after criticism of his conduct of the war – he was replaced by David Lloyd George (1863–1945), who as Chancellor of the Exchequer had introduced health and unemployment insurance.

The 'old dominions' – Canada, Australia, New Zealand and South Africa – emerged from the war as autonomous countries, and their independent status was confirmed by the Statute of Westminster (1931). The Easter Rising in Ireland (1916) led to the partition of the island in 1922. Only Northern Ireland – the area with a Protestant majority – stayed within the United Kingdom, but in the 1970s and 1980s bitter conflict resurfaced in the province as Roman Catholic republicans – seeking unity with the Republic of Ireland – clashed with Protestant Loyalists intent upon preserving the link with Britain. British troops were stationed in Northern Ireland to keep order and to defeat the terrorist violence of the IRA.

In World War II Britain – led by PM Sir Winston Churchill (1874–1965), who had strenuously opposed appeasement in the 1930s – played a major role in the defeat of the Axis powers, and from 1940 to 1941 the UK stood alone against an apparently invincible Germany. Following the war, the Labour government of Clement Attlee (1883–1967) established the 'welfare state'. At the same time, the British Empire began its transformation into a Commonwealth of some 50 independent states, starting with the independence of India in 1947. By the late 1980s decolonization was practically complete and Britain was no longer a world power, although a British nuclear deterrent was retained. By the 1970s the United Kingdom was involved in restructuring its domestic economy and, consequently, its welfare state – from 1979 to 1990 under the Conservative premiership of Margaret Thatcher (1925–). The country has also joined (1973) and has attempted to come to terms with the European Community. Under John Major (1943–) – Prime Minister since 1990 – the UK participated in the coalition against Iraq in the Second Gulf War (1991).

UK DEPENDENCIES

Anguilla (a small island in the Leeward Islands in the eastern Caribbean. The colony includes Sombrero, 48 km (30 mi) north of Anguilla.) *Area*: 96 km² (37 sq mi) – Anguilla 91 km² (35 sq mi); Sombrero 5 km² (2 sq mi). *Population*: 6900 (1989 est); Sombrero has no permanent population. *Capital*: The Valley 500 (1988 est).

Bermuda (a group of 100 small islands in the western Atlantic) *Area*: 54 km² (21 sq mi). *Population*: 58 800 (1989). *Capital*: Hamilton 3000 (1987).

British Antarctic Territory see p. 638.

British Indian Ocean Territory (the Chagos archipelago in the Indian Ocean) *Area*: 60 km² (23 sq mi). *Population*: the islands are used as US and British defence bases. There is no permanent civilian population.

British Virgin Islands (the eastern part of the Virgin Islands group in the Caribbean) *Area*: 153 km² (59 sq mi). *Population*: 14 000 (1988). *Capital*: Road Town 2500 (1988).

Cayman Islands (a group of three islands 290 km (180 mi) west of Jamaica) *Area*: 259 km² (100 sq mi). *Population*: 25 500 (1989). *Capital*: George Town 13 000 (1989).

Falkland Islands (a group of two main and over 100 small islands in the southern Atlantic, about 770 km (480 mi) northeast of Cape Horn) *Area*: 12 170 km² (4698 sq mi). *Population*: 1940 (1989). *Capital*: Port Stanley 1230 (1986).

Gibraltar (a small peninsula on the south coast of Spain, commanding the north side of the Atlantic entrance to the Mediterranean Sea) *Area*: 6.5 km² (2.5 sq mi). *Population*: 29 500 (1989 est). *Capital*: Gibraltar 29 500 (1989 est).

Hong Kong (Kowloon peninsula on the coast of the Chinese province of Guangdong, Hong Kong Island, some 235 other small islands and the New Territories, adjoining the Kowloon peninsula. China will recover sovereignty over Hong Kong and the New Territories on 1 July 1997.) *Area*: 1045 km² (403 sq mi) – Hong Kong Island 79 km² (30.4 sq mi), Kowloon peninsula 42 km² (16.3 sq mi), New Territories 924 km² (356.6 sq mi). *Population*: 5 754 000 (1989). *Capital*: Victoria, part of the Hong Kong agglomeration.

Montserrat (a small island north of Guadeloupe in the Caribbean) *Area*: 98 km² (38 sq mi). *Population*: 12 400 (1989). *Capital*: Plymouth 3000 (1985).

Pitcairn Islands (four islands in the South Pacific about 4800 km (3000 mi) east of New Zealand) *Area*: 48 km² (18.5 sq mi) – Pitcairn 4.5 km² (1.75 sq mi), Henderson, Ducie and Oeno 43.5 km² (16.75 sq mi). *Population*: 65 (all on Pitcairn; 1990). *Capital*: Adamstown 65 (1990).

St Helena and Dependencies (St Helena is an island in the South Atlantic, 1930 km (1200 mi) west of Africa. The dependencies are Ascension, an island 1130 km (700 mi) to the northwest of St Helena, and Tristan da Cunha, a group of six islands 2120 km (1320 mi) southwest of St Helena.) *Area*: 419 km² (162 sq mi) – St Helena 122 km² (47.3 sq mi), Ascension 88 km² (34 sq mi), Tristan da Cunha group 200 km² (78 sq mi). (Tristan da Cunha has an area of 98 km² (38 sq mi), Gough 90 km² (35 sq mi), Inaccessible 10 km² (4 sq mi) and the Nightingale Islands 2 km² (0.8 sq mi)). *Population*: 7200 (1990) – St Helena 6880, Ascension 1030, Tristan da Cunha 290 (Gough, Inaccessible and the Nightingale Islands are uninhabited). *Capital*: Jamestown (on St Helena) 1330 (1987) – the capital of Ascension is Georgetown 1030 (1990); the capital of Tristan da Cunha is Edinburgh 290 (1990).

South Georgia and South Sandwich Islands (South Georgia is an island 1290 km (800 km) east of the Falkland Islands. The South Sandwich Islands are 760 km (470 mi) southeast of South Georgia.) *Area*: 4091 km² (1580 sq mi) – South Georgia 3755 km² (1450 sq mi), South Sandwich Islands 336 km² (130 sq mi). *Population*: there is no permanent population, although a scientific settlement is maintained at Grytviken on South Georgia.

Turks and Caicos Islands (two groups of islands – 30 in all – southeast of the Bahamas) *Area*: 430 km² (166 sq mi). *Population*: 9500 (1989). *Capital*: Cockburn Town 2900 (1985 est) on Grand Turk.

UNITED STATES OF AMERICA

Member of: UN, NATO, OAS, CSCE, G7.

Population: 248 709 000 (1990).

Capital and major cities: Washington D.C. 3 924 000 (D.C.-Va-Md; city 623 000), New York 18 087 000 (NY-NJ; city 7 165 000), Los Angeles 14 532 000 (Cal; city 3 097 000), Chicago 8 066 000 (Ill-Ind; city 2 922 000), San Francisco 6 253 000 (Cal; city 713 000), Philadelphia 5 899 000 (Pa-NJ-Del; city 1 647 000), Detroit 4 665 000 (Mich; city 1 089 000), Boston 4 172 000 (Mass; city 571 000), Dallas 3 885 000 (Texas; city 974 000), Houston 3 711 000 (Texas; city 1 706 000), Miami 3 193 000 (Fla; city 373 000), Atlanta 2 834 000 (Ga; city 426 000), Cleveland 2 760 000 (Ohio; city 546 000), Seattle 2 559 000 (Wash; city 488 000), San Diego 2 498 000 (Calif; city 960 000), Minneapolis–St Paul 2 464 000 (Minn; Minneapolis city 358 000, St Paul city 266 000), St Louis 2 444 000 (Mo-Ill; city 429 000), Baltimore 2 382 000 (Md; city 764 000), Pittsburgh 2 243 000 (Pa; city 402 000), Phoenix 2 122 000 (Ariz; city 853 000), Tampa 2 068 000 (Fla; city 275 000), Denver 1 848 000 (Colo; city 505 000), Cincinnati 1 744 000 (Ohio-Ky-Ind; city 370 000), Milwaukee 1 607 000 (Wis; city 621 000), Kansas City 1 566 000 (Mo-Kan; city 160 000), Sacramento 1 481 000 (Calif; city 304 000), Portland 1 478 000 (Ore-Wash; city 366 000), Norfolk 1 396 000 (Va; city 280 000), Columbus 1 377 000 (Ohio; city 566 000), San Antonio 1 302 000 (Texas; city 843 000), Indianapolis 1 250 000 (Ind; city 710 000), New Orleans 1 239 000 (La; city 559 000), Buffalo 1 189 000 (NY; city 339 000), Charlotte 1 162 000 (NC; city 331 000), Providence 1 142 000 (RI-Mass; city 154 000), Hartford 1 086 000 (Conn; city 136 000), Orlando 1 073 000 (Fla; city 137 000), Salt Lake City 1 072 000 (Utah; city 165 000), Rochester 1 002 000 (NY; city 243 000), Oklahoma City 963 000 (Okla; city 443 000), Louisville 963 000 (Ky-Ind; city 290 000), Memphis 935 000 (Tenn-Ark-Miss; 648 000), Dayton 930 000 (Ohio; city 181 000), Birmingham 895 000 (Ala; city 280 000), Nashville

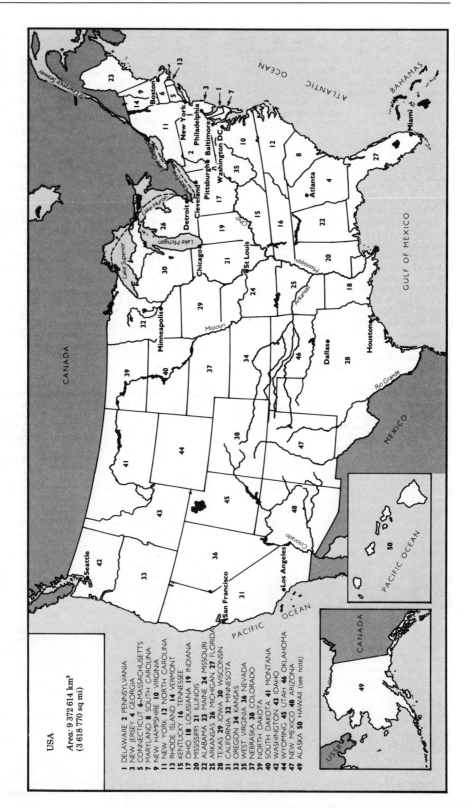

USA

Area: 9 372 614 km²
(3 618 770 sq mi)

1 DELAWARE 2 PENNSYLVANIA
3 NEW JERSEY 4 GEORGIA
5 CONNECTICUT 6 MASSACHUSETTS
7 MARYLAND 8 SOUTH CAROLINA
9 NEW HAMPSHIRE 10 VIRGINIA
11 NEW YORK 12 NORTH CAROLINA
13 RHODE ISLAND 14 VERMONT
15 KENTUCKY 16 TENNESSEE
17 OHIO 18 LOUISIANA 19 INDIANA
20 MISSISSIPPI 21 ILLINOIS
22 ALABAMA 23 MAINE 24 MISSOURI
25 ARKANSAS 26 MICHIGAN 27 FLORIDA
28 TEXAS 29 IOWA 30 WISCONSIN
31 CALIFORNIA 32 MINNESOTA
33 OREGON 34 KANSAS
35 WEST VIRGINIA 36 NEVADA
37 NEBRASKA 38 COLORADO
39 NORTH DAKOTA
40 SOUTH DAKOTA 41 MONTANA
42 WASHINGTON 43 IDAHO
44 WYOMING 45 UTAH 46 OKLAHOMA
47 NEW MEXICO 48 ARIZONA
49 ALASKA 50 HAWAII (see note)

890 000 (Tenn; city 462 000), Greensboro 883 000 (NC; city 159 000), Albany 843 000 (NY; city 99 000), Honolulu 805 000 (Hawaii; city 373 000), Richmond 796 000 (Va; city 219 000), Jacksonville 795 000 (Fla; city 578 000), Scranton 727 000 (Pa; city 84 000), Tulsa 726 000 (Okla; city 374 000), West Palm Beach 692 000 (Fla; city 68 000), Syracuse 650 000 (NY; city 164 000), Austin 645 000 (Texas; city 397 000), Allentown 635 000 (Pa; city 104 000), Grand Rapids 626 000 (Mich; city 183 000), Toledo 611 000 (Ohio-Mich; city 344 000), Raleigh 609 000 (NC; city 169 000), Omaha 607 000 (Neb-Iowa; city 334 000), Greenville 593 000 (SC; city 57 000), Knoxville 589 000 (Tenn; city 174 000), Fresno 565 000 (Calif; city 267 000), Baton Rouge 538 000 (La; city 239 000), Las Vegas 536 000 (Nev; city 183 000), Tucson 531 000 (Ariz; city 365 000), El Paso 526 000 (Texas-NM; city 464 000), Youngstown 518 000 (Ohio-Pa; city 108 000), Springfield 516 000 (Mass-Conn; city 150 000).

The population figures given for the standard metropolitan areas with over 1 000 000 inhabitants are for 1990; the figures for the smaller metropolitan areas – and for the cities – the local government units – are for 1984. Where an agglomeration stretches over more than one state, the state in which the major part of the urban area is situated is given first. The standard abbreviations for the states are given below in the list of US states.

Languages: English (official), Spanish (6%, as a first language).

Religions: Roman Catholic (27%), Baptist (12%), Methodist (6%), Lutheran (4%), Judaism (3%), Orthodox (2%), Presbyterian (2%).

Life expectancy: 75 years.

Labour force: (1989) 125 557 000; financial services 24 230 000, manufacturing 21 652 000, medical services 9 000 000, agriculture and forestry 3 500 000.

GOVERNMENT

Congress comprises the Senate (the Upper House) and the House of Representatives (the Lower House). The Senate has 100 members – two from each state – elected by universal adult suffrage for six years, with one third of the senators retiring every two years. The 435-member House of Representatives is directly elected for a two-year term from single-member constituencies. Additional non-voting members of the House are returned by the District of Columbia, Guam, Puerto Rico, United States Virgin Islands and American Samoa. Executive federal power is vested in the President, who serves a maximum of two four-year terms. Presidential candidates submit to a series of 'state primary' elections to enable individual parties to select a preferred candidate. The President and Vice President are elected by an electoral college of delegates pledged to support individual presidential candidates – the college itself is elected by universal adult suffrage. Upon the approval of the Senate, the President appoints a Cabinet of Secretaries. Each of the 50 states has a separate constitution and legislature with wide-ranging powers. Executive power in each state is held by a Governor who is elected by direct popular vote. The main political parties are the Democratic Party and the Republican Party.
President: George Bush.

AMERICAN STATES

Population figures for the states and larger cities are for 1990. Figures for the smaller cities are for 1984.

Alabama (abbreviation Ala; joined the Union on 14 December 1819 as the 22nd state). *Area:* 133 915 km² (51 705 sq mi). *Population:* 4 041 000. *Capital:* Montgomery 285 000 (city 185 000). *Largest city:* Birmingham 895 000 (city 280 000).

Alaska (no abbreviation; 3 January 1959 as the 49th state). *Area:* 1 530 693 km² (591 004 sq mi). *Population:* 550 000. *Capital:* Juneau 20 000. (In 1976, Alaskan voters approved a proposal to move the state capital to Willow South at some future date.) *Largest city:* Anchorage 227 000 (city and metropolitan area).

Arizona (Ariz; 14 February 1912 as the 48th state). *Area:* 295 259 km² (114 000 sq mi). *Population:* 3 665 000. *Capital:* Phoenix 2 122 000 (city 853 000).

Arkansas (Ark; 15 June 1836 as the 25th state). *Area:* 137 754 km² (53 187 sq mi). *Population:* 2 351 000. *Capital:* Little Rock 493 000 (city 170 000).

California (Calif; 9 September 1850 as the 31st state). *Area:* 411 047 km² (158 706 sq mi). *Population:* 29 760 000. *Capital:* Sacramento 1 481 000 (city 304 000). *Largest city:* Los Angeles 14 532 000 (city 3 097 000).

Colorado (Colo; 1 August 1876 as the 38th state). *Area:* 269 594 km² (104 091 sq mi). *Population:* 3 294 000. *Capital:* Denver 1 848 000 (city 505 000).

Connecticut (Conn; 9 January 1788 as the 5th state). *Area:* 12 997 km² (5018 sq mi). *Population:* 3 287 000. *Capital:* Hartford 1 086 000 (city 136 000).

Delaware (Del; 7 December 1787 as the 1st state). *Area:* 5292 km² (2044 sq mi). *Population:* 666 000. *Capital:* Dover 24 000. *Largest city:* Wilmington 464 000 (city 70 000).

Florida (Fla; 3 March 1845 as the 27th state). *Area:* 151 939 km² (58 664 sq mi). *Population:* 12 938 000. *Capital:* Tallahassee 208 000 (city 112 000). *Largest city:* Miami 3 193 000 (city 373 000).

Georgia (Ga; 2 January 1788 as the 4th state). *Area:* 152 576 km² (58 910 sq mi). *Population:* 6 478 000. *Capital:* Atlanta 2 834 000 (city 426 000).

Hawaii (21 August 1959 as the 50th state). *Area:* 16 760 km² (6471 sq mi). *Population:* 1 108 000. *Capital:* Honolulu 805 000 (city 373 000).

Idaho (3 July 1890 as the 43rd state). *Area:* 216 430 km² (83 564 sq mi). *Population:* 1 008 000. *Capital:* Boise City 189 000 (city 107 000).

Illinois (Ill; 3 December 1818 as the 21st state). *Area:* 149 885 km² (57 871 sq mi). *Population:* 11 431 000. *Capital:* Springfield 190 000 (city 102 000). *Largest city:* Chicago 8 066 000 (city 2 922 000) – the agglomeration extends into Indiana.

Indiana (Ind; 11 December 1816 as the 19th state). *Area:* 94 309 km² (36 413 sq mi). *Population:* 5 544 000. *Capital:* Indianapolis 1 250 000 (city 710 000).

Iowa (Ia; 28 December 1846 as the 29th state). *Area:* 145 752 km² (56 275 sq mi). *Population:* 2 777 000. *Capital:* Des Moines 377 000 (city 191 000). *Largest city:* Davenport 381 000 (city 102 000).

Kansas (Kan; 29 January 1861 as the 34th state). *Area:* 213 096 km² (82 277 sq mi). *Population:* 2 478 000. *Capital:* Topeka 159 000 (city 119 000). *Largest city:* Wichita 429 000 (city 283 000). Part of Kansas City agglomeration extends into Kansas.

Kentucky (Ky; 1 June 1792 as the 15th state). Area: 104 659 km² (40 409 sq mi). *Population:* 3 685 000. *Capital:* Frankfort 26 000. *Largest city:* Louisville 963 000 (city 290 000).

Louisiana (La; 30 April 1812 as the 18th state). *Area:* 123 677 km² (47 752 sq mi). *Population:* 4 220 000. *Capital:* Baton Rouge 538 000 (city 239 000). *Largest city:* New Orleans 1 239 000 (city 559 000).

Maine (Me; 15 March 1820 as the 23rd state). *Area:* 86 156 km² (33 265 sq mi). *Population:* 1 228 000. *Capital:* Augusta 22 000. *Largest city:* Portland 201 000 (city 62 000).

Maryland (Md; 28 April 1788 as the 7th state). *Area:* 27 091 km² (10 460 sq mi). *Population:* 4 781 000. *Capital:* Annapolis 32 000. *Largest city:* Baltimore 2 382 000 (city 764 000).

Massachusetts (Mass; 6 February 1788 as the 6th state). *Area:* 21 455 km² (8284 sq mi). *Population:* 6 016 000. *Capital:* Boston 4 172 000 (city 571 000).

Michigan (Mich; 26 January 1837 as the 26th state). *Area:* 251 493 km² (97 102 sq mi). *Population:* 9 295 000. *Capital:* Lansing 416 000 (city 128 000). *Largest city:* Detroit 4 665 000 (city 1 089 000).

Minnesota (Minn; 11 May 1858 as the 32nd state). *Area:* 224 329 km² (86 614 sq mi). *Population:* 4 375 000. *Capital:* St Paul 266 000. *Largest city:* Minneapolis–St Paul 2 464 000 (Minneapolis city 358 000).

Mississippi (Miss; 10 December 1817 as the 20th state). *Area:* 123 514 km² (47 689 sq mi). *Population:* 2 573 000. *Capital:* Jackson 382 000 (city 209 000).

Missouri (Mo; 10th August 1821 as the 24th state). *Area:* 180 514 km² (69 697 sq mi). *Population:* 5 117 000. *Capital:* Jefferson City 34 000. *Largest city:* St Louis 2 444 000 (429 000) – the agglomeration extends into Illinois.

Montana (Mont; 8 November 1889 as the 41st state). *Area:* 380 847 km² (147 046 sq mi). *Population:* 799 000. *Capital:* Helena 24 000. *Largest city:* Billings 119 000 (city 70 000).

Nebraska (Nebr; 1 March 1867 as the 37th state). *Area:* 200 349 km² (77 355 sq mi). *Population:* 1 578 000. *Capital:* Lincoln 203 000 (city 180 000). *Largest city:* Omaha 607 000 (city 334 000).

Nevada (Nev; 31 October 1864 as the 36th state). *Area:* 286 352 km² (110 561 sq mi). *Population:* 1 202 000. *Capital:* Carson City 32 000. *Largest city:* Las Vegas 536 000 (city 183 000).

New Hampshire (NH; 21 June 1788 as the 9th state). *Area:* 24 023 km² (9279 sq mi). *Population:* 1 109 000. *Capital:* Concord 30 000. *Largest city:* Manchester 136 000 (city 95 000).

New Jersey (NJ; 18 December 1787 as the 3rd state). *Area:* 20 168 km² (7787 sq mi). *Population:* 7 730 000. *Capital:* Trenton 92 000. *Largest city:* Newark 1 871 000 (city 329 000) – part of the New York agglomeration.

New Mexico (NM; 6 January 1912 as the 47th state). *Area:* 314 924 km² (121 593 sq mi). *Population:* 1 515 000. *Capital:* Santa Fe 100 000 (city 52 000). *Largest city:* Albuquerque 449 000 (city 351 000).

New York (NY; 26 July 1788 as the 11th state). *Area:* 136 583 km² (52 735 sq mi). *Population:* 17 990 000. *Capital:* Albany 843 000 (city 99 000). *Largest city:* New York 18 087 000 (city 7 165 000) – much of the New York agglomeration extends into New Jersey.

North Carolina (NC; 21 November 1789 as the 12th state). *Area:* 136 412 km² (52 669 sq mi). *Population:* 6 629 000. *Capital:* Raleigh 609 000 (city 169 000). *Largest city:* Charlotte 1 162 000 (city 331 000).

North Dakota (ND; 2 November 1889 as the 39th state). *Area:* 183 117 km² (70 702 sq mi). *Population:* 639 000. *Capital:* Bismarck 45 000. *Largest city:* Fargo 143 000 (city 66 000).

Ohio (no abbreviation; 1 March 1803 as the 17th state). *Area:* 115 998 km² (44 787 sq mi). *Population:* 10 847 000. *Capital:* Columbus 1 377 000 (city 566 000). *Largest city:* Cleveland 2 760 000 (city 546 000).

Oklahoma (Okla; 16 November 1907 as the 46th state). *Area:* 181 185 km² (69 956 sq mi). *Population:* 3 146 000. *Capital:* Oklahoma City 963 000 (city 443 000).

Oregon (Ore; 14 February 1859 as the 33rd state). *Area:* 251 418 km² (97 073 sq mi). *Population:* 2 842 000. *Capital:* Salem 89 000. *Largest city:* Portland 1 478 000 (city 366 000) – the agglomeration extends into Washington.

Pennsylvania (Pa; 12 December 1787 as the 2nd state). *Area:* 119 251 km² (46 043 sq mi). *Population:* 11 882 000. *Capital:* Harrisburg 447 000 (city 52 000). *Largest city:* Philadelphia 5 899 000 (city 1 647 000) – the agglomeration extends into New Jersey and Delaware.

Rhode Island (RI; 29 May 1790 as the 13th state). *Area:* 3139 km² (1212 sq mi). *Population:* 1 003 000. *Capital:* Providence 1 142 000 (city 154 000) – the agglomeration extends into Massachusetts.

South Carolina (SC; 23 May 1788 as the 8th state). *Area:* 80 582 km² (31 113 sq mi). *Population:* 3 487 000. *Capital:* Columbia 433 000 (city 99 000). *Largest city:* Greenville 593 000 (city 57 000).

South Dakota (SD; 2 November 1889 as the 40th state). *Area:* 199 730 km² (77 116 sq mi). *Population:* 696 000. *Capital:* Pierre 12 000. *Largest city:* Sioux Falls 118 000 (city 81 000).

Tennessee (Tenn; 1 June 1796 as the 16th state). *Area:* 109 152 km² (42 144 sq mi). *Population:* 4 877 000. *Capital:* Nashville 890 000 (city 462 000). *Largest city:* Memphis 935 000 (city 648 000) – the agglomeration extends into Arkansas and Mississippi.

Texas (no abbreviation; 29 December 1845). *Area:* 691 027 km² (266 807 sq mi). *Population:* 16 987 000. *Capital:* Austin 645 000 (city 397 000). *Largest city:* Dallas 3 885 000 (city 974 000).

Utah (no abbreviation; 4 January 1896 as the 45th state). *Area:* 219 887 km² (84 899 sq mi). *Population:* 1 723 000. *Capital:* Salt Lake City 1 072 000 (city 165 000).

Vermont (Vt; 4 March 1791 as the 14th state). *Area:* 24 900 km² (9614 sq mi). *Population:* 563 000. *Capital:* Montpelier 8000. *Largest city:* Burlington 121 000 (city 37 000).

Virginia (Va; 26 June 1788 as the 10th state). *Area:* 105 586 km² (40 767 sq mi). *Population:* 6 187 000. *Capital:* Richmond 796 000 (city 219 000). *Largest city:* Norfolk 1 396 000 (city 280 000).

Washington (Wash; 11 November 1889 as the 42nd state). *Area:* 176 479 km² (68 139 sq mi). *Population:* 4 867 000. *Capital:* Olympia 27 000. *Largest city:* Seattle 2 559 000 (city 488 000).

West Virginia (W Va; 20 June 1863 as the 35th state). *Area:* 62 758 km² (24 231 sq mi). *Population:* 1 793 000. *Capital:* Charleston 267 000 (city 59 000). *Largest city:* Huntington 334 000 (city 61 000).

Wisconsin (Wisc; 29 May 1848 as the 30th state). *Area:* 171 496 km² (66 215 sq mi). *Population:* 4 892 000. *Capital:* Madison 333 000 (city 171 000). *Largest city:* Milwaukee 1 607 000 (city 621 000).

Wyoming (Wyo; 10 July 1890 as the 44th state). *Area:* 253 324 km² (97 809 sq mi). *Population:* 454 000. *Capital:* Cheyenne 47 000. *Largest city:* Casper 51 000.

FEDERAL DISTRICT

District of Columbia (DC). *Area:* 179 km² (69 sq mi). *Population:* 607 000. *Capital:* Washington 3 924 000 (city 607 000) – the greater part of the agglomeration is in Virginia and Maryland.

EDUCATION

Literacy rate: 97%. *Years of compulsory schooling:* 7–16 (most states). *Universities:* approximately 3600 universities and degree-awarding colleges.

DEFENCE

Total armed strength: 2 124 900 (1989). *Military service:* none, although there is a selective call-up in time of war.

GEOGRAPHY

The Atlantic coastal plain stretches along the entire east coast, including the lowland peninsula of Florida, and along the coast of the Gulf of Mexico, where it reaches up to 800 km (500 mi) inland. The Blue Ridge escarpment rises sharply to the west of the plain. This is the most easterly part of the forested Appalachian Mountains, which stretch north–south for some 2400 km (1500 mi) and reach 2037 m (6684 ft) at Mount Mitchell. The largest physical region of the USA is a vast interior plain drained by the Mississippi and major tributaries, including the Missouri, Arkansas, Nebraska, Ohio and Red River. This lowland stretches from the Great Lakes in the north to the coastal plain in the south, and from the Rocky Mountains in the west to the Appalachians in the east. The Central Lowlands – the eastern part of the lowland – comprise the Cotton Belt in the south and the Corn (maize) Belt in the north. The Great Plains – the drier western part of the lowland – begin some 480 km (300 mi) west of the Mississippi. The west of the USA is the country's highest region and includes the Rocky Mountains in the east and the Cascades, the Sierra Nevada and the Coastal Ranges in the west. The mountains continue north through Canada into Alaska. The western mountainous belt is prone to earthquakes, in particular along the line of the San Andreas Fault in California. Within the mountains are deserts – including the Mojave and the Arizona Deserts – and the large Intermontane Plateau containing the Great Basin, an area of internal drainage around the Great Salt Lake. The 20 islands of Hawaii – in the Pacific – are volcanic in origin and contain active volcanoes. The USA's natural vegetation ranges from tundra in Alaska to the tropical vegetation of Hawaii, and includes coniferous forest in the northwest, Mediterranean scrub in southern California, steppe and desert in the Intermontane Plateau, and prairie grasslands on the Great Plains. *Principal rivers:* Mississippi (with Missouri and Red Rock), Rio Grande, Yukon (with Nisutlin), Arkansas, Colorado, Ohio (with Allegheny), Red River, Columbia. *Highest point:* Mount McKinley 6194 m (20 320 ft) in Alaska.

Climate: Within the USA there are great regional differences in climate. The mountains behind the Pacific northwest coast are the wettest region of the USA. Coastal California has a warm Mediterranean climate. Desert or semidesert conditions prevail in mountain basins. The continental Great Plains receive 250–750 mm (10–30 in) of rain a year, while the Central Lowlands to the east are generally wetter. Extremes of temperature are experienced in the north of the continental interior. The east is generally temperate. The Appalachians and the east-

ern coastal plain are humid, with temperatures rising in the south where Florida is subtropical. Coastal Alaska has a cold maritime climate while the north and interior is polar. Hawaii has a Pacific climate with high temperatures and little seasonal variation.

ECONOMY

The position of the USA as the world's leading economic power is threatened by Japan. The USA is self-sufficient in most products apart from petroleum, chemicals, certain metals and manufactured machinery, and newsprint. Agriculture is heavily mechanized and produces considerable surpluses for export. The main crops include maize, wheat, soya beans, sugar cane, barley, cotton, potatoes and a wide variety of fruit (including citrus fruit in Florida and California). More than one quarter of the USA is pastureland, and cattle and sheep are important in the Great Plains. Forests cover over 30% of the country and are the basis of the world's second largest timber industry. The USA has great natural resources, including coal (mainly in the Appalachians), iron ore, petroleum and natural gas (mainly in Texas, Alaska and California), copper, bauxite, lead, silver, zinc, molybdenum, tungsten, mercury and phosphates, and major rivers that have proved suitable for hydroelectric power plants. The industrial base of the USA is diverse. Principal industries include iron and steel, motor vehicles, electrical and electronic engineering, food processing, chemicals, cement, aluminium, aerospace industries, telecommunications, textiles and clothing, and a wide range of consumer goods. Tourism is a major foreign-currency earner. Service industries involve over three quarters of the labour force. Finance, insurance and banking are important, and Wall Street (New York) is one of the world's major stock exchanges. US economic policy exerts an influence throughout the world; thus a revival of pressure for trade protectionism in the late 1980s and the early 1990s caused international concern.

RECENT HISTORY

At the beginning of the 19th century, the USA doubled in size with the Louisiana Purchase (1803). This acquisition took the US frontier deep into the Central Lowlands. The expansion of the USA to the west was part of the transformation of the country from an underdeveloped rural nation into a world power stretching from the Atlantic to the Pacific. As a result of wars against Mexico in the 1840s vast new territories were added to the Union – Texas, California, Arizona and New Mexico. Strains appeared between the increasingly industrial North and the plantation South over the issue of slavery. This led to the Civil War under the presidency of Abraham Lincoln (1809–65). The North was victorious, but after federal troops were withdrawn from the South in 1877 racial segregation returned to the South until after World War II.

Between 1880 and 1900 the USA emerged as an industrial giant. At the same time, the population increased dramatically, as immigrants flocked to the New World, in particular from Germany, Eastern Europe and Russia. Interest in world trade increased American involvement abroad. The Cuban revolt against Spanish rule led the USA into a war against Spain (1898) and brought US rule to the Philippines, Puerto Rico and Guam. American participation in World War I from 1917 hastened the Allied victory, but the idealistic principles favoured by President Woodrow Wilson (1856–1924) were compromised in the post-war settlement.

After the war the USA retreated into isolationism and protectionism in trade. The imposition of Prohibition (1919–33) increased smuggling and the activities of criminal gangs, but the 1920s were prosperous until the Depression began in 1929 with the collapse of the stock market. Federal investment and intervention brought relief through the New Deal programme of President Franklin Roosevelt (1882–1945). The Japanese attack on Pearl Harbor brought the USA into World War II (1941). American involvement in the European and Pacific theatres of war was decisive and committed the USA to a world role as a superpower in 1945. US assistance was instrumental in rebuilding Europe (through the Marshall Plan) and Japan.

From the late 1940s to the end of the 1980s, the USA confronted the Soviet Union's perceived global threat in the Cold War. As the leader of the Western alliance, the USA established bases in Europe, the Far East and the Indian and Pacific Oceans, so encircling the Soviet bloc. The USA was involved in the Korean War (1950–53) against Chinese and North Korean forces, and in direct military intervention in Guatemala (1954), Lebanon (1958 and 1983–85), the Dominican Republic (1965), Panama (1968 and 1989) and Grenada (1983). The greatest commitment, however, was in Vietnam, where from 1964 to 1973 US forces attempted to hold back a Communist takeover of Indochina, but a growing disenchantment with the war forced an American withdrawal.

From the 1950s the civil rights movement – led by Martin Luther King (1929–68) – campaigned for full political rights for blacks and for desegregation of schools, hospitals, buses, etc. In the early 1960s President John F. Kennedy (1917–63) made racial discrimination illegal. Kennedy supported the unsuccessful invasion of Cuba by right-wing exiles (1961), successfully pressured the USSR to withdraw its missiles from Cuba (1962), and was assassinated in 1963. Growing economic problems in the 1970s led to the election of a monetarist President, Ronald Reagan (1911–   ), in 1981. The USA continued to support movements and governments perceived as being in the Western interest – for example, backing Israel in the Middle East and providing weapons to the UNITA guerrillas in Angola and the Contra guerrillas in Nicaragua. However, the increasing economic challenge from Japan, and the collapse of Soviet power in Eastern Europe in 1989, raised questions about the USA's future world role. Early in 1990 President George Bush (1924–   ) announced plans to close certain overseas bases, but later in the same year he organized the international coalition against Iraq after the invasion of Kuwait (2 August 1990). American forces played a major role in the massive but short air and ground war (January to February 1991) that liberated Kuwait.

US DEPENDENCIES

Commonwealth Territories in Association with the USA

North Mariana Islands (an archipelago in the North Pacific) *Area*: 471 km² (184 sq mi). *Population*: 19 600 (1985 est). *Capital*: Chalan Kanoa (on Saipan). (Saipan had a population of 17 200 in 1985.)

Puerto Rico *Area*: 9104 km² (3515 sq mi). *Population*: 3 308 000 (1989). *Capital*: San Juan 1 086 000 (1980).

US External Territories

American Samoa (a group of six islands to the east of Western Samoa) *Area*: 197 km² (76 sq mi). *Population*: 32 400 (1986 est). *Capital*: Pago Pago 3000 (1980).

Guam (the largest of the Mariana Islands in the north Pacific) *Area*: 541 km² (209 sq mi). *Population*: 129 0000 (1989). *Capital*: Agaña 5500 (1989). *Largest city*: Tamuning 16 600 (1989).

Palau (Belau) (an island group between the Philippines and the Federated States of Micronesia) *Area*: 497 km² (192 sq mi). *Population*: 15 000 (1987 est). *Capital*: Koror 8100 (1987).

Virgin Islands of the United States *Area*: 352 km² (136 sq mi). *Population*: 109 500 (1986). *Capital*: Charlotte Amalie 11 800 (1980).

Territories administered by US Department of Defense
(These unincorporated territories of the USA are all small Pacific islands.)

Johnston Atoll *Area*: under 1 km² (0.5 sq mi). *Population*: 327 (1980).

Kingman Reef *Area*: 0.03 km² (0.01 sq mi). Uninhabited.

Midway Islands *Area*: 5 km² (2 sq mi). *Population*: 453 (1980).

Wake Island *Area*: 8 km² (3 sq mi). *Population*: 300 (1980).

URUGUAY

Official name: La República Oriental del Uruguay (The Eastern Republic of Uruguay).

Member of: UN, OAS, LAIA.

Population: 3 060 000 (1988 est).

Capital and major cities: Montevideo 1 246 000, Salto 77 000, Paysandú 75 000, Las Piedras 61 000 (1985).

Language: Spanish (official).

Religions: Roman Catholic (majority), Protestant.

Life expectancy: 71 years.

Labour force: (1985) 1 153 000; services 362 000, manufacturing 212 000, agriculture and forestry 179 000.

URUGUAY

Area: 176 215 km² (68 037 sq mi)

BRAZIL

Salto

Paysandú

ARGENTINA

Lago Merín

Montevideo

Río de la Plata

ATLANTIC OCEAN

GOVERNMENT

The President and Congress – consisting of a 30-member Senate and a 99-member Chamber of Deputies – are elected for four years by universal adult suffrage. The President appoints a Council of

Ministers. The main political parties are the (conservative) National Blanco Party, the (centre) Colorado Party, and the (left-wing coalition) Broad Front.
President: Luis Alberto Lacalle.

EDUCATION
Literacy rate: 97% (1978). *Years of compulsory schooling:* 6–15. *Universities:* 1.

DEFENCE
Total armed strength: 24 700 (1989). *Military service:* none.

GEOGRAPHY
Uruguay consists mainly of low undulating plains and plateaux. The only significant ranges of hills are in the southeast. *Principal rivers:* Río Negro, Uruguay, Yi. *Highest point:* Cerro de las Animas 500 m (1643 ft).
Climate: Uruguay has a temperate climate with warm summers and mild winters. Rainfall averages around 900 mm (35 in).

ECONOMY
Pastureland – for sheep and beef cattle – covers about 80% of the land. Meat, wool and hides are the leading exports. Despite a lack of natural resources, Uruguay has a high standard of living.

RECENT HISTORY
In 1808 independence was declared from Spain, but Uruguay had to repulse successive Brazilian and Argentinian armies (1811–27) before independence was achieved (1828). Until 1903 Uruguay was ruled by dictators and wracked by civil war. However, prosperity from cattle and wool, and the presidencies of the reformer José Battle (1903–7 and 1911–15), turned Uruguay into a democracy and an advanced welfare state. A military dictatorship held power during the Depression. By the late 1960s severe economic problems had ushered in a period of social and political turmoil, and urban guerrillas became active. In 1973 a coup installed a military dictatorship that made Uruguay notorious for abuses of human rights. In 1985 the country returned to democratic rule.

VANUATU

Official name: The Republic of Vanuatu or La République de Vanuatu.
Member of: UN, Commonwealth, South Pacific Forum.
Population: 145 000 (1989).
Capital: Port-Vila 19 000 (1989).
Languages: English (official; 60%), French (official; 40%), Bislama (national language), and 130 other local dialects.
Religions: Protestant (mainly Presbyterian and Anglican; nearly 70%), Roman Catholic, animist.
Life expectancy: 69 years.
Labour force: (1979) 51 000; agriculture and forestry 39 000, services 5500, trade and tourism 2000.

GOVERNMENT
The 46-member Parliament is elected for four years by universal adult suffrage. It elects a Prime Minister who appoints a Council of Ministers. The President is elected for five years by Parliament and the

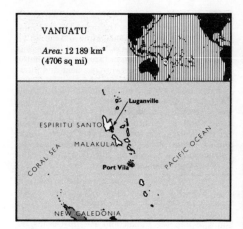

VANUATU
Area: 12 189 km²
(4706 sq mi)

Luganville
ESPIRITU SANTO
CORAL SEA
MALAKULA
Port Vila
PACIFIC OCEAN
NEW CALEDONIA

Presidents of Regional Councils. The main political parties include the (socialist) Vanuaaku Pati, the Union of Moderate Parties, and a number of regional parties.
President: Fred Timakata.
Prime Minister: Father Walter Lini.

EDUCATION
Literacy rate: 10–20%. *Years of compulsory schooling:* schooling is not compulsory. *Universities:* none.

DEFENCE
Total armed strength: There are no armed forces.

GEOGRAPHY
Vanuatu comprises over 75 islands, some of which are mountainous and include active volcanoes. There are no significant rivers. *Highest point:* Mt Tabwebesana 1888 m (6195 ft).
Climate: Vanuatu's tropical climate is moderated by southeast trade winds from May to October.

ECONOMY
Subsistence farming occupies the majority of the labour force. The main exports include copra, fish and cocoa. Tourism is increasingly important.

RECENT HISTORY
British and French commercial interests in the 19th century resulted in joint control over the islands – then known as the New Hebrides – and the establishment of a condominium in 1906. The islands gained independence as Vanuatu in 1980, but have been troubled by attempted secession and political unrest.

VATICAN CITY

Official name: Stato della Cittá del Vaticano (State of the Vatican City). Also known as the Holy See.
Membership of: CSCE, UN (observer).
Population: 830 (1980 est).
Languages: Italian and Latin (both official).
Religion: The Vatican is the headquarters of the Roman Catholic Church.
Life expectancy: no figure available.

GOVERNMENT
The Pope is elected Bishop of Rome and head of the

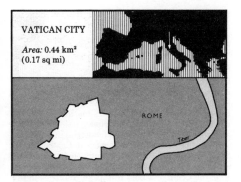

VATICAN CITY

Area: 0.44 km²
(0.17 sq mi)

ROME

Tiber

VENEZUELA

Area: 912 050 km²
(352 144 sq mi)

CARIBBEAN SEA

TRINIDAD AND TOBAGO

Valencia Caracas

Maracaibo Orinoco

GUYANA

COLOMBIA

BRAZIL

Roman Catholic Church for life by the Sacred College of Cardinals. The administration of the Vatican City is in the hands of a Pontifical Commission appointed by the Pope.
Pope: HH (His Holiness) Pope John Paul II (elected 16 October 1978).

EDUCATION
Universities: 5 pontifical universities.

DEFENCE
Total armed strength: Swiss Guard.

GEOGRAPHY
The state consists of the Vatican City, a walled enclave on the west bank of the River Tiber in Rome, plus a number of churches in Rome (including the cathedral of St John Lateran) and the papal villa at Castelgandolfo.

RECENT HISTORY
The tiny Vatican City state is all that remains of the once extensive Papal States. During the Revolutionary and Napoleonic Wars, the Papal States were variously annexed to countries created by Napoleon and absorbed into the French Empire (1798–1815). The Papal States were restored in 1815, but all except Rome and Latium were lost during Italian unification (1859–60). When the French troops protecting the Pope were withdrawn in 1870, Italian forces entered Rome, which became the capital of the new kingdom of Italy. Pope Pius IX (reigned 1846–78) protested at the loss of his temporal power and retreated into the Vatican, from which no Pope emerged until 1929, when the Lateran Treaties provided for Italian recognition of the Vatican City as an independent state. Since the 1960s the Papacy has again played an important role in international diplomacy, particularly under Popes Paul VI (reigned 1963–78) and John Paul II (1978–).

VENEZUELA

Official name: La República de Venezuela (Republic of Venezuela).
Member of: UN, OAS, LAIA.
Population: 19 245 500 (1989 est).
Capital and major cities: Caracas 3 373 000, Maracaibo 1 365 000, Valencia 1 227 000, Maracay 924 000, Barquisimeto 764 000, Cuidad Guayana 517 000 (1989).
Language: Spanish.
Religion: Roman Catholic (nearly 95%).
Life expectancy: 70 years.

Labour force: (1989) 6 643 000; services 1 781 000, trade and tourism 1 301 500, manufacturing 1 159 000, agriculture and forestry 847 500.

GOVERNMENT
The President and both Houses of the National Congress are elected for five years by universal adult suffrage. The Senate – the upper House – comprises 49 elected senators, plus former Presidents and additional senators to represent minority parties. The Chamber of the Deputies has 201 directly elected members. The President appoints a Council of Ministers. The main political parties are AD (Democratic Action), COPEI (the Social Christian Party), and the (left-wing) Radical Cause Party.
President: Carlos Perez.

EDUCATION
Literacy rate: 87% (1985). *Years of compulsory schooling:* 7–14. *Universities:* 11.

DEFENCE
Total armed strength: 70 500 (1989). *Military service:* 2 years (selective).

GEOGRAPHY
Mountains in the north include the north-south Eastern Andes and the Maritime Andes, which run parallel to the Caribbean coast. Central Venezuela comprises low-lying grassland plains (the Llanos). The Guiana Highlands in the southeast include many high steep-sided plateaux. *Principal rivers:* Orinoco, Rio Meta, Coroni, Apure. *Highest point:* Pico Bolivar 5007 m (16 423 ft).
Climate: The tropical coast is arid. The cooler mountains and the tropical Llanos are wet, although the latter has a dry season from December to March.

ECONOMY
Petroleum and natural gas normally account for almost 95% of export earnings. Agriculture is mainly concerned with raising beef cattle, and growing sugar cane and coffee for export; bananas, maize and rice are grown as subsistence crops.

RECENT HISTORY
Spain began to develop Venezuela in the 17th

century. In 1806 Francisco Miranda (1752–1816) led a war of independence that was successfully concluded by Simon Bolívar (1783–1830) in 1823. Initially united with Colombia and Ecuador, Venezuela seceded in 1830. Independence was followed by a series of military coups, revolts and dictators, including Juan Vicente Gómez, whose harsh rule lasted from 1909 to 1935. Since General Marcos Peréz Jiménez was overthrown in 1958, Venezuela has been a civilian democracy.

VIETNAM

Official name: Công hoa xâ hôi chu nghia Viêt (The Socialist Republic of Vietnam).

Member of: UN.

Population: 64 747 000 (1989).

Capital and major cities: Hanoi 3 000 000, Ho Chi Minh City (formerly Saigon) 3 900 000, Haiphong 1 280 000, Da Nang 500 000 (1989 est).

Language: Vietnamese (official).

Religions: Buddhist (the major religion), with Daoist, Roman Catholic and Cao Dai minorities.

Life expectancy: 64 years.

Labour force: (1987 est) 27 968 000; agriculture and forestry 20 246 000, administration and commerce 3 206 000, manufacturing 3 047 000.

VIETNAM

Area: 329 566 km²
(127 246 sq mi)

GOVERNMENT

The 496-member National Assembly is elected by universal adult suffrage for five years. The Assembly elects, from its own members, a Council of State – whose Chairman is head of state – and a Council of Ministers, headed by a Prime Minister. Effective power is in the hands of the Communist Party of Vietnam, which is the only legal party.
President: Vo Chi Cong.
Prime Minister: Do Muoi.

EDUCATION

Literacy rate: 84% (1979). *Years of compulsory schooling:* 6–16. *Universities:* 94 institutions of university status.

DEFENCE

Total armed strength: 1 249 000 (1989). *Military service:* 3 years.

GEOGRAPHY

Plateaux, hill country and chains of mountains in Annam (central Vietnam) lie between the Mekong River delta in the south and the Red River (Hongha) delta in the north. *Principal rivers:* Mekong, Song-koi, Songbo, Ma, Hongha. *Highest point:* Fan si Pan 3142 m (10 308 ft).

Climate: Vietnam has a hot humid climate, although winters are cool in the north. Heavy rainfall comes mainly during the monsoon season from April to October.

ECONOMY

Over three quarters of the labour force is involved in agriculture, mainly cultivating rice. Other crops include cassava, maize and sweet potatoes for domestic consumption, and rubber, tea and coffee for export. Natural resources include coal, phosphates and tin, which are the basis of industries in the north. The wars in Vietnam, involvement in Cambodia and the loss of skilled workers through emigration have all had a serious effect on the economy. Despite aid from the USSR and East European countries in the 1980s, Vietnam remains underdeveloped, and lacks the investment to overcome basic problems such as food shortages. By 1990, this aid had considerably diminished, adding to Vietnam's problems.

RECENT HISTORY

In 1802 Nguyen Anh united Tonkin (the north), Annam (the centre) and Cochin-China (the south), and made himself emperor of Vietnam. The French intervened in the area from the 1860s, established a protectorate in Vietnam in 1883 and formed the Union of Indochina – including Cambodia and Laos – in 1887. Revolts against colonial rule in the 1930s marked the start of a period of war and occupation that lasted for over 40 years. The Japanese occupied Vietnam in 1940 and eventually set up a puppet government under the Emperor Bao Dai. In 1941 the Communist leader Ho Chi Minh established the Viet Minh as a nationalist guerrilla army to fight the Japanese. In the closing months of the war, the Viet Minh received US aid, and – after the Japanese surrender – a Democratic Republic of Vietnam was established in Hanoi with Ho as president. French rule was not re-established until 1946, with Ho's republic initially recognized as a 'free state' within French Indochina. After clashes between the Hanoi government and the French, Ho left Hanoi and began a guerrilla war against the colonial authorities and the restored Emperor Bao Dai.

The Viet Minh gradually gained all of Tonkin and in 1954 forced the French to surrender at Dien Bien Phu after a siege of 55 days. The Geneva Peace Agreement (July 1954) partitioned Vietnam between a Communist zone in the north and a zone ruled by Boa Dai in the south. Elections for the entire country were scheduled for 1956, but the north refused to participate. In 1955 Bao Din was deposed and Ngo Dinh Diem proclaimed a republic in South Vietnam. Diem's oppressive regime encouraged Communist guerrilla activity in the south and in 1960 the (Communist) Viet Cong was formed in South Vietnam with the aim of overthrowing the pro-Western government.

In 1961 US President John F. Kennedy sent American military advisers to help South Vietnam. By 1964 the 'advisers' had grown into an army of regular US troops. After the North Vietnamese allegedly attacked US naval patrols (1964), the Americans began regular aerial bombardment of the north. By the end of 1964 nearly 200 000 US combat troops were in action in Vietnam. The 1968 (Communist) Tet offensive was withstood but the weakness of South Vietnam became evident. Opposition to the war increased in the USA. Peace talks began in 1969 but in 1970 US forces were active against the Viet Cong in both Laos and Cambodia. The war was formally ended by the Paris Peace Agreements (1973), but continued after the withdrawal of US troops. Since the Communist takeover of the south (1975) and the reunification of Vietnam, reconstruction has been hindered by a border war with China (1979) and the occupation of Cambodia (1979–89) by Vietnamese forces. Lack of Western aid and investment has hindered economic development, and this, combined with political repression, has led to large numbers of refugees (the 'Boat People') fleeing the country. Since 1989–90 more pragmatic policies have been adopted in an attempt to attract Western capital.

WESTERN SAMOA

Official name: The Independent State of Western Samoa.

Member of: UN, Commonwealth, South Pacific Forum.

Population: 168 000 (1988).

Capital: Apia 33 200 (1981).

Languages: English and Samoan (official).

Religions: Protestant (70%).

Life expectancy: 67 years.

Labour force: (1981) 41 500; agriculture and forestry 25 000, services 8000, trade and tourism 2000.

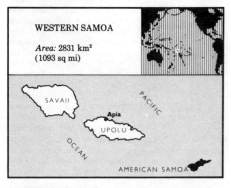

WESTERN SAMOA

Area: 2831 km²
(1093 sq mi)

SAVAII

Apia

UPOLU

PACIFIC

OCEAN

AMERICAN SAMOA

GOVERNMENT

The Legislative Assembly comprises 45 members elected for three years by the elected heads of extended families, and 2 members directly elected by non-Samoan citizens. A referendum in 1990 approved the eventual introduction of universal adult suffrage. The current head of state is analogous to a constitutional monarch, but future heads of state will be elected for a five-year term by the Assembly. The head of state appoints a Prime Minister who commands a majority in the Assembly. The PM, in turn, appoints a Council of Ministers, who are responsible to the Assembly. The main political parties include the Human Rights Protection Party and the Christian Democratic Party.
Head of state: Malietoa Tanumafili II.
Prime Minister: Eti Tofilau.

EDUCATION

Literacy rate: 97% (1990). *Years of compulsory schooling:* 6–15. *Universities:* 1.

DEFENCE

There are no armed forces. Defence remains the responsibility of New Zealand.

GEOGRAPHY

The country consists of seven small islands and two larger and higher volcanic islands. There are no significant rivers. *Highest point:* Mauga Silisli 1857 m (6094 ft).

Climate: The islands have a tropical climate with high temperatures and very heavy rainfall.

ECONOMY

The majority of Samoans are involved in subsistence agriculture. Copra (from coconuts), cocoa and bananas are the main exports.

RECENT HISTORY

From the 1870s the USA, Britain and Germany became active in Samoa, and in 1899 the three rival powers divided the group, giving the nine western islands to Germany. New Zealand occupied the German islands in 1914, and administered Western Samoa until independence was granted in 1962.

YEMEN

Official name: Al-Jamhuriya al-Yamaniya (The Republic of Yemen).

Member of: UN, Arab League.

Population: 11 250 000 (1989 est).

Capital and cities: Sana'a 427 000 (1986), Aden 318 000 (1984), Taiz 178 000, Hodeida 155 000 (1986).

Language: Arabic (official).

Religions: Sunni Islam 53%, Zaidist Shia Islam 47%.

Life expectancy: no figure available.

Labour force: (1985–86 est) 1 640 500; agriculture and forestry 1 050 000, services 200 000 (combined figure for the former North and South Yemen).

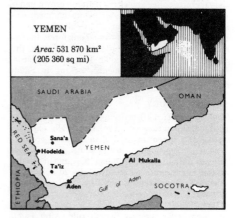

YEMEN

Area: 531 870 km²
(205 360 sq mi)

SAUDI ARABIA

OMAN

RED SEA

Sana'a
Hodeida
Ta'iz
YEMEN
Al Mukalla
Aden
Gulf of Aden
SOCOTRA

ETHIOPIA

GOVERNMENT

Following the union of the Yemen Arab Republic (North Yemen) and the People's Democratic Republic of Yemen (South Yemen) on 22 May 1990, a five-member Presidential Council was formed to hold office for 30 months. A 309-member transitional House of Representatives was formed comprising the 159 members of the former North Yemeni Consultative Council, the 111 members of the former South Yemeni Supreme People's Council and 39 additional members chosen from both countries by the Presidential Council. For the transitional period, the President of North Yemen is President and the President of South Yemen is Prime Minister of the united country. A new constitution is to be drafted and the first all-Yemeni elections are to be held at the end of 1992. There are no national political parties, although the Yemeni Socialist Party had a leading role in South Yemen from 1967 until unification. In 1989 it was announced that, in principle, other parties would be allowed to operate in South Yemen. *President*: Col. Ali Abdullah Saleh. *Prime Minister*: Hayder Abu Bakr al-Attas.

EDUCATION
Literacy rate: 10.5% (1985 est). *Years of compulsory schooling:* schooling is not compulsory in the former North Yemen, but was, in theory, compulsory in the former South Yemen from 7 to 15. *Universities:* 2.

DEFENCE
Total armed strength: 64 000 (1990 est). *Military service:* 3 years in the former North Yemen, 2 years in the former South Yemen.

GEOGRAPHY
In the west, the Yemen Highlands rise from a narrow coastal plain. In the south, an arid plateau – 3200 m (10 500 ft) high – extends from the coastal plain into the Arabian Desert that occupies most of the north and east. *Principal river:* Bana (almost the only significant permanent river). *Highest point:* Jebel Hadhar 3760 m (12 336 ft).
Climate: Most of the highlands in the north and west have a temperate climate. The rest of the country is very hot and dry, although the mountains are cooler in winter.

ECONOMY
Cereal crops, coffee and citrus fruit are grown under irrigation in the fertile highlands in the north and west. In the south, subsistence agriculture and fishing occupy the majority of the labour force. Petroleum is becoming a major export, although the reserves are small by Middle Eastern standards. Money sent back by Yemenis working in Saudi Arabia is an important source of revenue.

RECENT HISTORY
The Ottoman Turks first occupied the north and west in the 16th century and were not finally expelled until 1911, when Imam Yahya secured (North) Yemen's independence. In the south, Britain took Aden as a staging post to India (1839) and gradually established a protectorate over the 20 sultanates inland. Tension grew in the Aden Protectorate in 1959 when Britain created a federation of the feudal sultanates and the city of Aden. In 1963 an armed rebellion began against British rule. After much bloodshed – and a civil war between two rival liberation movements – independence was gained in 1967 as South Yemen. In (North) Yemen, a republican revolution broke out in 1962, and from 1963 until 1970 a bloody civil war was fought, with President Nasser's Egypt supporting the victorious republicans and Saudi Arabia supporting the royalists. Marxist South Yemen became an ally of the USSR and was frequently in conflict with North Yemen, although eventual union of the two Yemens was the objective of both states. The collapse of the Communist regimes in Eastern Europe and the end of considerable Soviet aid (1989–90) hastened the collapse of South Yemen's weak economy, and the two countries merged in May 1990.

YUGOSLAVIA
Official name: Socijalistička Federativna Republika Jugoslavija (The Socialist Federal Republic of Yugoslavia).
Member of: UN, CSCE, Council of Europe (guest).
Population: 23 710 000 (1989 est).
Capital and major cities: Belgrade (Beograd) 1 470 000, Zagreb 1 175 000, Skopje 507 000, Sarajevo 449 000, Ljubljana 305 000, Novi Sad 258 000, Split 236 000, Nis 231 000, Pristina 216 000, Rijeka 193 000, Maribor 186 000, Banja Luka 184 000, Kragujevac 165 000, Tetovo 162 000, Leskovac 159 000, Osijek 159 000, Subotica 155 000 (1981).
Languages: Serbo-Croat – a single language with two written forms, Serbian (47%) and Croatian (20%). Minorities include Slovene (8%), Albanian (8%), Macedonian (6%) and Hungarian (2%).
Religions: Orthodox (over 35%), Roman Catholic (nearly 30%), Sunni Islam (nearly 15%).
Life expectancy: 72 years.
Labour force: (1981) 9 359 000; agriculture and forestry 2 683 000, industry and manufacturing 2 210 000, services 1 585 000.

YUGOSLAVIA
Area: 255 804 km² (98 766 sq mi)

GOVERNMENT
Local 'self-managing organizations' are elected by universal adult suffrage. Delegates from these bodies are elected for four years to the 220-member Federal Chamber – 30 from each of the 6 republics and 20 from each of Serbia's 2 autonomous provinces. The Chamber of Republics and Provinces has 12 members from each republican assembly and 8 from each of Serbia's autonomous provinces. The Presidency is held for one year by members of an eight-person Collective Presidency, comprising one representative from each republic and one from each of Serbia's autonomous provinces. The Federal Executive (Cabinet) – headed by a Prime Minister – is responsible to the Federal Chamber. The republics have their own legislatures with considerable powers.

The only party to compete on a national basis is the (socialist) Alliance of Reform Forces. The main political parties in the republics are: in Bosnia-Herzegovina, the (Muslim) Democratic Action Party, the (ethnic Serbian) Democratic Party, and the (ethnic Croatian) Democratic Community; in Croatia, the (nationalist centre-right) Croatian

Democratic Union and the Party for Democratic Change (formerly the League of Communists); in Macedonia, the (nationalist) Internal Macedonian Revolutionary Organization, the Macedonian League of Communists, the (ethnic Albanian) Party for Democratic Prosperity, the (Yugoslav national) Alliance for Reform Forces, the Young Democratic Progressive Party, and the Socialist Party; in Montenegro, the Montenegrin League of Communists, the (ethnic Albanian and Muslim) Democratic Coalition, and the (Yugoslav national) Alliance for Reform Forces; in Serbia, the Serbian Socialist Party (the former Communist Party), the (Serbian nationalist) Serbian Renewal Movement, and the (Yugoslav national) Alliance for Reform Forces; in Slovenia, the (Slovene nationalist coalition) Demos (which includes the Christian Democratic Party), the Democratic Renewal Party (the former Communist Party), and the Liberal Party.
President: at the time of going to press the Collective Presidency was not functioning.
Prime Minister: Ante Markovic.

YUGOSLAV REPUBLICS

Population figures for the republics and the cities are for 1988 and 1981 respectively.
Bosnia-Herzegovina (Bosna i Hercegovina) *Area*: 51 129 km² (19 741 sq mi). *Population*: 4 441 000. *Capital*: Sarajevo 449 000.
Croatia (Hrvatska) *Area*: 56 538 km² (21 829 sq mi). *Population*: 4 679 000. *Capital*: Zagreb 1 175 000.
Macedonia (Makedonija) *Area*: 25 713 km² (9928 sq mi). *Population*: 2 088 000. *Capital*: Skopje 507 000.
Montenegro (Crna Gora) *Area*: 13 812 km² (5333 sq mi). *Population*: 632 000. *Capital*: Titograd 132 000.
Serbia (Srbija) (including the autonomous provinces of Kosovo and Vojvodina) *Area*: 88 361 km² (34 116 sq mi). *Population*: 9 776 000. *Capital*: Belgrade (Beograd) 1 470 000.
Slovenia (Slovenija) *Area*: 20 251 km² (7819 sq mi). *Population*: 1 943 000. *Capital*: Ljubljana 305 000.

EDUCATION

Literacy rate: 91% (1985 est). *Years of compulsory schooling*: 7–15 (Croatia 6–15). *Universities*: 19.

DEFENCE

Total armed strength: 180 000 (1989 est). *Military service*: 12 months.

GEOGRAPHY

The indented Adriatic coast is lined by many small islands. Ridges of mountains occupy the greater part of the country. They include the Julian Alps, the Dinaric Mountains, and parts of the Rhodope, Pindus, Balkan and Carpathian Mountains. The north and northeast is occupied by plains drained by the rivers Danube, Sava and Drava. *Principal rivers:* Danube (Dunav), Drava, Slava, Morava, Vardar. *Highest point*: Triglav 2864 m (9396 ft).
Climate: The coast has a Mediterranean climate; the interior has a moderate continental climate.

ECONOMY

Agriculture involves about one quarter of the labour force. Most of the land is privately owned. Major crops include maize, wheat, sugar beet, grapes, potatoes, citrus fruit and fodder crops for sheep.

Industry – which is mainly concentrated in Slovenia, Croatia and around Belgrade – includes food processing, textiles, metallurgy, motor vehicles and consumer goods. Natural resources include uranium, coal, petroleum and natural gas. The republics are moving towards a market economy at unequal rates (Slovenia and Croatia having made the greatest progress), but Yugoslavia suffers rampant inflation. There is a wide difference in standards of living between the more advanced and westernized northern republics and the underdeveloped southern ones (in particular, Macedonia). Tourism and money sent home by Yugoslavs working abroad are important sources of foreign currency.

RECENT HISTORY

At the beginning of the 19th century, Slovenia was part of Austria and Croatia was part of Hungary within the Habsburg Empire. Mountainous Montenegro was effectively autonomous, and the rest of the country was under (Turkish) Ottoman rule. Led by Karadjordje, the Serbs rose against Turkish rule between 1804 and 1813. Under his rival Miloš Obrenović, the Serbs rose again in 1815 and became an autonomous principality, but the country was destabilized by rivalry between the Karadjordje and Obrenović dynasties. Both Serbia and Montenegro were recognized as independent in 1878. By the start of the 20th century a Croat national revival within the Habsburg Empire looked increasingly to Serbia to create a South ('Yugo') Slav state. After Serbia gained Macedonia in the Balkan Wars (1912–13), Austria grew wary of Serbian ambitions. The assassination of the Habsburg heir (1914) by a Serb student in Sarajevo provided Austria with an excuse to try to quash Serbian independence. This led directly to World War I and the subsequent dissolution of the Habsburg Empire, whose South Slav peoples united with Serbia and Montenegro in 1918.

The interwar Kingdom of Serbs, Croats and Slovenes – renamed Yugoslavia in 1929 – was run as a highly centralized 'Greater Serbia'. The country was wracked by nationalist tensions, and Croat separatists murdered King Alexander in 1934. Attacked and dismembered by Hitler in 1941, Yugoslavs fought the Nazis and each other. The Communist-led partisans of Josip Broz Tito (1892–1980) emerged victorious in 1945, and re-formed Yugoslavia on Soviet lines. Expelled from the Soviet bloc in 1948 for failing to toe the Moscow line, the Yugoslav Communists rejected the Soviet model, and pursued policies of decentralization, workers' self-management and non-alignment. However, after Tito's death in 1980, the Yugoslav experiment faltered in economic and nationalist crises. The wealthier northern republics of Slovenia and Croatia led the movement towards democracy and Western Europe, while Serbia forcefully resisted the separatist aspirations of Albanian nationalists in Kosovo province.

In 1990 the Communists conceded the principle of free elections. By the end of the year, the League of Communists of Yugoslavia had ceased to exist as a national entity, and elections in the republics were won by various centre-right, nationalist and regional socialist parties in all the republics except Serbia and Montenegro, where Communist parties won. The Alliance of Reform Forces – a new national political party formed by Premier Ante Markovic – fared poorly in elections in most republics. By the beginning of 1991 the future of Yugoslavia was in doubt. Serbia exacerbated ethnic unrest by the legal removal of most of the autonomous powers of Kosovo and Vojvodina. Croatian demands for greater independence led to conflict between Serbia and Croatia, and in April and May 1991 violence erupted between Croats and Serb minority communities in Croatia. Referenda in Slovenia and Croatia produced majorities in favour of secession, with Slovenia threatening secession by 26 June 1991. In May 1991 Serbia and Montenegro blocked the accession of a Croat to the presidency and a constitutional crisis threatened the continued existence of Yugoslavia.

ZAÏRE

Official name: La République du Zaïre (Republic of Zaïre).

Member of: UN, OAU.

Population: 33 336 000 (1987 est).

Capital and major cities: Kinshasa 2 778 000 (1985), Kananga 704 000, Lubumbashi 451 000, Mbuji-Mayi 383 000, Kisangani 339 000, Bukavu 209 000, Kikwit 172 000, Matadi 162 000 (1976).

Languages: French (official), with over 400 local languages including Kiswahili, Kiluba, Kikongo and Lingala.

Religions: Roman Catholic (48%), animist, various Protestant churches (13%).

Life expectancy: 53 years.

Labour force: (1988 est) 12 686 000; agriculture and forestry 8 358 000, services 2 500 000, industry 2 000 000.

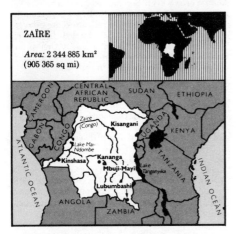

ZAÏRE

Area: 2 344 885 km²
(905 365 sq mi)

GOVERNMENT

The 210-member National Legislative Council is elected by compulsory universal suffrage for five years. The President – who is directly elected for seven years – appoints the National Executive Council of Commissioners (Ministers). The Mouvement populaire de la révolution is the only legal political party. However in March 1990 it was announced that after March 1991 a three-party system would be allowed to operate and a new constitution would be drawn up.
President: Marshal Mobutu Sese Seko.
Prime Minister: Mulumba Lukoji.

EDUCATION

Literacy rate: 61% (1985 est). *Years of compulsory schooling:* 6–12. *Universities:* 3.

DEFENCE

Total armed strength: 26 000, plus 25 000 paramilitary (1989). *Military service:* compulsory; length varies.

GEOGRAPHY

Over 60% of the country comprises a basin of tropical rain forest, drained by the River Zaïre (Congo) and its tributaries. Plateaux and mountain ranges surrounding the basin include the Ruwenzori Massif in the east. *Principal rivers:* Zaïre, Lualaba, Lomami, Oubangui, Uganbi, Kasai. *Highest point:* Mont Ngaliema 5109 m (16 763 ft).

Climate: Zaïre has a humid, tropical climate with little seasonal variation, although the north is drier from December to February.

ECONOMY

Over two thirds of the labour force is involved in agriculture. Although subsistence farming predominates, coffee, tea, cocoa, rubber and palm products are exported. Minerals are the mainstay of the economy, with copper, cobalt, zinc and diamonds normally accounting for about 60% of Zaïre's exports. Zaïre suffers rampant inflation and one of the lowest standards of living in Africa.

RECENT HISTORY

The region – now Zaïre – was ravaged by the slave trade, and in 1885 became the personal possession of King Leopold II of the Belgians. However, international outrage at the brutality of the regime in the Congo Free State forced the king to grant the region to Belgium as a colony in 1908. As the Belgian Congo, the colony became a major exporter of minerals. The provision of social services, especially primary education, was relatively advanced, but the administration curbed almost all African political activity. As a result, the country was inadequately prepared when Belgium suddenly decolonized the Congo in 1960. Within days of independence, the army mutinied and the richest region – Katanga, under Moïse Tshombe – attempted to secede. The Congo invited the United Nations to intervene, but the UN force was only partly successful in overcoming continuing civil wars. Colonel Mobutu twice intervened and in 1965 made himself head of state. Pursuing 'authenticity', he renamed the country Zaïre and himself Mobuto Sése Séko. He gradually restored the authority of the central government and introduced a one-party state (1967). Mobutu's strong rule has attracted international criticism, but he has maintained the support of Western countries that value Zaïre as a source of strategic minerals. In 1990, popular discontent won some reforms and it was announced that free elections would be held under a new constitution in the summer of 1991.

ZAMBIA

Official name: The Republic of Zambia.

Member of: UN, Commonwealth, OAU, SADCC.

Population: 8 148 000 (1989 est).

Capital and major cities: Lusaka 870 000, Kitwe 472 000, Ndola 443 000, Kabwe 200 000, Mufulira 199 000, Chingola 195 000 (1988 est).

Languages: English (official), with local languages including Nyanja, Bemba, and Tonga.

Religions: Christian majority (Roman Catholic and various Protestant churches), animist.

Life expectancy: 54 years.

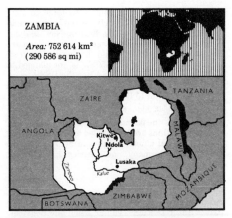

ZAMBIA

Area: 752 614 km²
(290 586 sq mi)

Labour force: (1986) 360 500; industry and manufacturing 106 000; agriculture and forestry 35 000, trade and tourism 29 000.

GOVERNMENT

The 135-member National Assembly consists of 125 members elected by universal adult suffrage for five years and 10 members nominated by the President. The President – who is directly elected for five years – appoints a Cabinet headed by a Prime Minister. The 27-member House of Chiefs has advisory powers. From 1972–73 until 1990, Zambia was a one-party state under the United National Independence Party. In December 1990, a constitutional amendment permitted the formation of opposition parties. New parties formed subsequently include the Movement for Multiparty Democracy.
President: Kenneth Kaunda.
Prime Minister: Gen. Malimba Masheke.

EDUCATION

Literacy rate: 75% (1985 est). *Years of compulsory schooling:* 7–14. *Universities:* 2.

DEFENCE

Total armed strength: 16 200 (1989). *Military service:* none.

GEOGRAPHY

Zambia comprises plateaux some 1000 to 1500 m (3300 to 5000 ft) high, above which rise the Muchinga Mountains and the Mufinga Hills. *Principal rivers:* Zambezi, Kafue, Luapula. *Highest point:* an unnamed peak in the Muchinga Mountains, 2164 m (7100 ft).
Climate: Zambia has a tropical climate with a wet season from November to April.

ECONOMY

Zambia's economy depends upon the mining and processing of copper, lead, zinc and cobalt. Agriculture is underdeveloped and many basic foodstuffs have to be imported. Maize, groundnuts and tobacco are the main crops.

RECENT HISTORY

The area was brought under the control of the British South Africa Company of Cecil Rhodes in the 1890s. In 1924 Britain took over the administration from the Company, but development of the colony (known as Northern Rhodesia) was initially slow. Skilled

mining jobs were reserved for white immigrants, and, fearing increased discrimination, Africans unsuccessfully opposed inclusion in the Central African Federation – with Nyasaland (Malawi) and Southern Rhodesia (Zimbabwe) – in 1953. Against strong opposition from white settlers, Kenneth Kaunda (1924–) led Northern Rhodesia, renamed Zambia, to independence in 1964. A one-party state was introduced in 1972–73. Popular discontent at the lack of a democratic alternative erupted in mid-1990 after the doubling of the price of cornmeal (the staple food). Following riots, a government commission conceded the legalization of opposition parties and announced that free elections would be held (provisionally) in October 1991.

ZIMBABWE

Official name: The Republic of Zimbabwe.
Member of: UN, Commonwealth, OAU, SADCC.
Population: 9 122 000 (1987 est).
Capital and major cities: Harare (formerly Salisbury) 863 000, Bulawayo 495 000, Chitungwiza 229 000 (1983), Gweru 79 000, Mutare 69 000 (1982).
Languages: English (official), Chishona, Sindebele.
Religions: Anglican (over 30%), Roman Catholic (about 15%), Presbyterian, Methodist, animist
Life expectancy: 63 years.
Labour force: (1988 est) 3 611 000; agriculture and forestry 2 497 000 (1985), services 1 043 000, manufacturing 164 000.

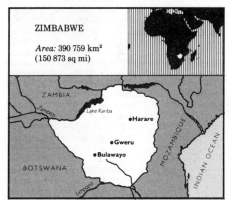

ZIMBABWE

Area: 390 759 km²
(150 873 sq mi)

GOVERNMENT

The 150-member House of Assembly comprises 120 members directly elected by universal adult suffrage for six years, 12 nominated members, 10 traditional chiefs and 8 appointed provincial governors. The House elects a President for a six-year term of office. The ZANU-PF (Zimbabwe African National Union) party has a leading role, although other parties – including ZUM (Zimbabwe Unity Movement) – are permitted.
President: Robert Mugabe.

EDUCATION

Literacy rate: 45–55%. *Years of compulsory schooling:* 7–14. *Universities:* 1.

DEFENCE

Total armed strength: 49 500 (1989). *Military service:* 1 year.

GEOGRAPHY

Central Zimbabwe comprises the ridge of the Highveld, rising to between 1200 and 1500 m (about 4000 to 5000 ft). The Highveld is bounded on the southwest and northeast by the Middle Veld and the Lowveld plateaux. *Principal rivers*: Zambezi, Limpopo, Sabi. *Highest point*: Mount Inyangani 2592 m (8504 ft).

Climate: The climate is tropical in the lowlands and subtropical at altitude. There is a pronounced dry season from June to September.

ECONOMY

Agriculture involves about two thirds of the labour force. Tobacco, sugar cane, cotton, wheat and maize are exported as well as being the basis of processing industries. Natural resources include coal, gold, asbestos and nickel.

RECENT HISTORY

The area was gradually penetrated by British and Boer hunters, missionaries and prospectors from the 1830s, and was occupied by the British South Africa Company of Cecil Rhodes in the 1890s. The highlands of what became Southern Rhodesia were settled by white farmers, who deprived Africans of land and reduced them to a cheap labour force. Britain took over the administration from the Company in 1923 and granted self-government to the white colonists. Immigration from Britain and South Africa increased after World War II, but the whites remained outnumbered by the Africans by more than 20 to 1. Racial discrimination stimulated African nationalism, initially led by Joshua Nkomo (1917–). Southern Rhodesia – with Northern Rhodesia (Zambia) and Nyasaland (Malawi) – formed the Central African Federation in 1953. When the Federation was dissolved (1963), Britain refused the white Southern Rhodesian administration independence without progress to majority rule. The white government led by Ian Smith (1919–) unilaterally declared independence in 1965, renaming the country Rhodesia. Internal opposition was crushed and international economic sanctions were overcome, but guerrilla wars, mounted by African nationalists during the 1970s, became increasingly effective. In 1979 Smith had to accept majority rule, but the constitution he introduced was unacceptable either to the Zimbabwe African People's Union (ZAPU) of Joshua Nkomo or to the Zimbabwe African National Union (ZANU) of Robert Mugabe (1928–). All parties agreed to the brief reimposition of British rule to achieve a settlement. ZANU under Mugabe took the country to independence in 1980. In 1987 ZANU and ZAPU finally agreed to unite, effectively introducing a one-party state, although proposals for an official one-party system have been shelved. On 25 July 1990 the State of Emergency, first imposed by the Smith government in 1965, was allowed to lapse and a general amnesty was announced.

OTHER TERRITORIES

ANTARCTICA

All territorial claims south of latitude 60° S are in abeyance under the terms of the Antarctic Treaty (signed in 1959), which came into force in 1961. Territorial claims in Antarctica have been made by Argentina, Australia, Chile, France, New Zealand, Norway, and the UK. The Argentinian, Chilean and British claims overlap, while that part of the continent between 90° W and 150° W is not claimed by any country. Neither the USA nor the USSR recognize any territorial claim in Antarctica, except for Norwegian claims to Bouvet Island.

Area: 14 245 000 km² (5 500 000 sq mi).

Population: no permanent population, but over 40 scientific stations are maintained by those countries with territorial claims in the continent and by the USA, USSR, Germany, South Africa, India, Japan, Poland and Brazil.

TERRITORIAL CLAIMS

Adélie Land (Terre Adélie) France claims that part of Antarctica between 136° E and 142° E, extending to the South Pole. *Area*: 432 000 km² (166 800 sq mi). Adélie Land is part of the French Southern and Antarctic Territories (Terres Australes et Antarctiques Françaises), created in 1955 and administered from Paris (see also p. 536).

Argentinian Antarctic Territory (Antárdida Argentina) Argentina claims that part of Antarctica between 74° W and 25° W, extending to the South Pole, a claim that overlaps with the British territorial claim.

Australian Antarctic Territory Australia claims that part of Antarctica between 160° E and 45° E, except for Adélie Land. *Area*: 6 120 000 km² (2 320 000 sq mi).

Bouvet Island (Bouvetøya) A Norwegian Antarctic territory (54° 25 S and 3° 21 E). *Area*: 50 km² (19 sq mi). The island is uninhabited. As Bouvet Island is north of 60° S, the provisions of the Antarctic Treaty do not apply and Norway's claim to the island is uncontested.

British Antarctic Territory The UK claims that part of Antarctica between 20° W and 80° W, extending to the South Pole, a claim that overlaps with Argentinian and Chilean claims. *Area*: 1 810 000 km² (700 000 sq mi).

Chilean Antarctic Territory (Antárdida Chilena) Chile claims that part of Antarctica between 90° W and and 53° W, extending to the South Pole, a claim that overlaps with the British and Argentinian territorial claims.

Peter I Island (Peter I Oy) Norway claims the island, which is 68° 48 S and 90° 35 W. *Area*: 180 km² (69 sq mi).

Queen Maud Land (Dronning Maud Land) Norway claims that part of Antarctica between 20° W and 45° E. *Area*: as no inland limit has been made to the Norwegian claim, no estimate of the area of the territory can be made.

Ross Dependency New Zealand claims that part of Antarctica between 160° E and 150° W, extending to the South Pole. *Area*: 450 000 km² (175 000 sq mi).

GAZA AND THE WEST BANK

Area: 6257 km² (2416 sq mi) – Gaza 378 km² (146 sq mi), the West Bank 5879 km² (2270 sq mi).

Population: 1 800 000 (1990 est) – Gaza 545 000 (1985 est), West Bank 836 000 (1985 est).

Main cities: Gaza (Ghazzah) 120 000 (1980), Nablus (Nabulus) 80 000 (1984), Hebron (Al-Khalil) 75 000 (1984).

Language: Arabic.
Religions: Sunni Islam majority, Christian and small Jewish minorities.

GOVERNMENT
Gaza and the West Bank are under Israeli occupation.

EDUCATION
Literacy rate: no figure available. *Years of compulsory schooling:* education is free and where possible compulsory 6–14. *Universities:* 1.

GEOGRAPHY
The Gaza Strip is a small lowland area, between Israel and Egypt, beside the Mediterranean. The West Bank is a mountainous and arid area between the Israeli border in the west and the River Jordan and the Dead Sea in the east. *Principal river:* Jordan. *Highest point:* an unnamed point north of Hebron, 1013 m (3323 ft).
Climate: Gaza and the West Bank have a dry Mediterranean climate, with hot dry summers and cooler wetter winters.

ECONOMY
The overpopulated Gaza Strip has little industry and a little agriculture. Only the Jordan Valley in the West Bank can support arable farming. Both areas rely heavily upon foreign (largely Arab) aid and money sent back by Palestinians working abroad. Many Gaza and West Bank Palestinians commute daily into Israel to work.

RECENT HISTORY
The Gaza Strip, formerly under Egyptian rule, was occupied by Israeli forces in June 1967. The West Bank, formerly under Jordanian administration, was occupied by Israeli forces from 6–11 June 1967. In 1988, Jordan severed all legal ties with the West Bank. Beginning in 1988, an uprising (*intifada*) by Palestinians living in Gaza and the West Bank increased tension in these territories. On 15 November 1988, the Palestinian Liberation Organization issued a declaration of Palestinian independence in Gaza and the West Bank. This declaration has received recognition by over 30 countries.

SOVEREIGN MILITARY ORDER OF MALTA, TERRITORY OF

Area: 1.2 ha (3 acres) – Villa del Priorato di Malta (on the Aventine Hill in Rome) and 68 via Condotti (in the same city).

GOVERNMENT
The Knights are a charitable, monastic Roman Catholic order whose Knights of Justice live as a religious community in two buildings in Rome. They elect for life one of their number to be Prince and Grand Master, who is recognized as a sovereign by over 40 countries, excluding the UK. The military order, which issues its own passports, has many of the trappings of a state and is frequently said to be the 'smallest country in the world'.
Head of State: HEH (His Eminent Highness) Fra' (Brother) Andrew Bartie, Prince and Grand Master (elected on 8 April 1988; a Scot until he took a Knights' passport).

RECENT HISTORY
The 'Knights of Malta' were rulers of Rhodes until

expelled by the Turks (1523), and then of Malta until expelled by Napoleon I (1798). Since the 1830s, their sovereignty has been confined to their two properties in Rome.

WESTERN SAHARA

Area: 266 000 km² (102 676 sq mi).
Population: 186 000 (1989 est) – including many Moroccan settlers in El-Aaiun (Laayoune).
Capital: El-Aaiun (Laayoune) 97 000 (1982).
Language: Arabic.
Religion: Sunni Islam.
Life expectancy: 40 years.

GOVERNMENT
Most of the Western Sahara is under Moroccan administration. In 27 February 1976 Sahrawi exiles in Algeria proclaimed the Saharan Arab Democratic Republic, which has been recognized by over 70 countries and admitted to membership of the OAU. *President:* Mohammed Abdulaziz.

GEOGRAPHY
The Western Sahara is a low flat desert region with hills in the northeast. There are no permanent streams.

ECONOMY
All trade is controlled by the Moroccan government. The territory has few resources except for phosphate deposits. A fishing port has been developed at El-Aaiun.

RECENT HISTORY
Western Sahara is a former Spanish possession on the coast of northwest Africa. Spain, Morocco and Mauritania reached an agreement to end Spanish rule (on 31 December 1975) and to divide the territory between Morocco and Mauritania (on 28 February 1976). Morocco organized its sector into three provinces and upon the withdrawal of Mauritania from its sector (August 1979), organized that area into a fourth province. The Polisario liberation movement – which had been fighting Spanish rule since 1973 – declared the territory independent. They control part of the east of the Western Sahara and continued guerrilla activity against the Moroccans until informal UN talks between the Sahrawis (the indigenous population) and the Moroccans (1988–89). Agreement was reached to implement a ceasefire and to hold a referendum on the future of the territory. At the beginning of 1991, no date had been agreed for that referendum.

FORMER STATES

Ceased during World War II
Danzig was a free city under the League of Nations from 1919 until September 1939 when it was annexed by Germany. Danzig is now the Polish city of Gdansk, see p. 591.
Estonia was an independent Baltic republic which was incorporated into the USSR in August 1940. The annexation of Estonia is not recognized by Western governments. (See Estonia under USSR p. 617.)

Latvia was an independent Baltic republic which was incorporated into the USSR in August 1940. The annexation of Latvia is not recognized by Western governments. (See Latvia under USSR p. 617.)

Lithuania was an independent Baltic republic which was incorporated into the USSR in August 1940. The annexation of Lithuania is not recognized by Western governments. Pre-war Lithuania was smaller than the present republic – its capital was Kaunas. Before World War II Vilnius, the capital of the Union republic of Lithuania, was a Polish city. (See Lithuania under USSR p. 619.)

Tannu Tuva was a central Asian republic covering an area of 170 500 km² (68 850 sq mi) on the borders of China and the USSR. In 1911, Tannu Tuva was taken from China by Russia in 1911. Independence was granted in 1921, but the country was annexed by the USSR in October 1944. It is now the autonomous republic of Tuva in the Russian Federation. It has a population of 280 000 (1985) and its capital is Kyzyl (71 000).

Ceased since World War II

German Democratic Republic (East Germany) was formed out of the Soviet zone of occupation in Germany in October 1949 (see German recent history, p. 540). The GDR reunited with the Federal Republic of Germany on 3 October 1990. East Germany had an area of 108 333 km² (41 827 sq mi) and a population of 16 641 000 (1987). Its capital was East Berlin. The area of the GDR now comprises the German states (Länder) of Berlin, Brandenburg, Mecklenburg-West Pomerania, Saxony, Saxony-Anhalt and Thuringia (see p. 538).

Hyderabad was a large Indian princely state that opted to resume independence when India was partitioned in 1947 (see p. 549). Indian troops were withdrawn in November 1947 and the state was effectively sovereign until September 1948 when Indian forces invaded. The former Hyderabad state is now divided between the Indian states of Andhra Pradesh, Madhya Pradesh and Maharashtra.

Ras al-Khaimah is one of seven emirates of the former Trucial Coast. Ras al-Khaimah did not join the United Arab Emirates (see p. 620) when it was formed in December 1971 and was sovereign until it adhered to the federation in February 1972.

Sikkim was an independent Himalayan kingdom protected by India from 1950 until 1974 when it became a state associated with the Indian Union. Sikkim became an Indian state in 1975 (see p. 548).

Somaliland was an independent state from 26 June to 1 July 1960 – the period between gaining independence from the UK and merging with the former Italian colony Somalia (see p. 601).

Tanganiyka was an independent state from May 1961 until April 1964 when it combined with Zanzibar to form Tanzania (see p. 611).

Tibet was, in practice, an independent country from 1911 until May 1951. It was invaded by Chinese troops in October 1950 and is now the Chinese autonomous province of Xizang (see p. 519).

Vietnam (South) was an independent empire from 1954 to 1955, then a republic from 1955 until July 1976 when it united with (Communist) North Vietnam (see p. 632). It had an area of 163 170 km² (63 000 sq mi). The capital was Saigon.

Yemen (North) united with South Yemen in May 1990 (see p. 633). It had an area of 195 000 km² and a population of 9 274 000 (1986). The capital was Sana'a.

Yemen (South) united with North Yemen in May 1990 (see p. 633). It had an area of 336 869 km² (130 066 sq mi) and a population of 2 345 000 (1986). The capital was Aden.

Zanzibar was an independent sultanate from December 1963 until April 1964 when it combined with Tanganiyka to form Tanzania (see p. 611). Zanzibar remains an autonomous state.

THE WORLD'S MAJOR CITIES

Urbanization – the increased migration of rural dwellers into cities – has been a particular feature of the second half of the 20th century. In 1950 under 30% of the population of the world lived in urban regions, but by 1990 almost 44% lived in cities, towns or their suburbs. The greatest proportion of urban dwellers is to found in countries of the developed world.

The growth of the largest cities in the world has been impressive, especially those in the Third World. In 1900 only 16 cities (including suburbs) had over one million inhabitants – London (England, UK) 6 400 000, New York (USA) 4 200 000, Paris (France) 3 900 000, Berlin (Germany) 2 400 000, Chicago (USA) 1 700 000, Vienna (Austria) 1 600 000, Tokyo (Japan) 1 400 000, St Petersburg (now Leningrad; Russia) 1 400 000, Philadelphia (USA) 1 400 000, Manchester (England, UK) 1 200 000, Birmingham (England, UK) 1 200 000, Moscow (Russia) 1 200 000, Peking (China) 1 100 000, Calcutta (India) 1 000 000, Boston (USA) 1 000 000, and Glasgow (Scotland, UK) 1 000 000.

In time, the term 'millionaire city' came to be coined for a city possessing at least one million inhabitants. At the beginning of 1991 it was estimated that there were 269 'millionaire cities', of which 130 were in Asia, 46 in North or Central America, 45 in Europe (including Istanbul which is physically half in Europe and half in Asia), 24 in South America, 20 in Africa and 4 in Oceania.

NB In the list of the world's major cities (below) the population figure given relates to the agglomeration or urban area; that is the city, its suburbs and surrounding built-up area rather than for local government districts.

City	Country	Date of Census or Estimate	Population
Mexico City	Mexico	(1985)	18 748 000
New York	USA	(1990)	18 087 000
São Paulo	Brazil	(1985)	15 900 000
Los Angeles	USA	(1990)	14 531 000
Cairo	Egypt	(1987)	13 300 000
Shanghai	China	(1988)	12 620 000
Tokyo	Japan	(1988)	11 680 000
Beijing (Peking)	China	(1988)	10 880 000
Buenos Aires	Argentina	(1989)	10 880 000
Seoul	South Korea	(1989)	10 513 000
Calcutta	India	(1981)	9 194 000
Rio de Janeiro	Brazil	(1985)	9 019 000
Moscow	USSR	(1989)	8 967 000
Paris	France	(1982)	8 707 000
Bombay	India	(1981)	8 243 000
Chicago	USA	(1990)	8 066 000
Jakarta	Indonesia	(1985)	7 829 000
London	UK	(1981)	7 678 000
Tehran	Iran	(1986)	6 022 000
Manila	Philippines	(1980)	5 926 000
Philadelphia	USA	(1990)	5 899 000
Bangkok	Thailand	(1989)	5 845 000
Hong Kong	Hong Kong	(1989)	5 754 000
Delhi	India	(1981)	5 729 000

SPORT
A – Z
OF SPORTS

AMERICAN FOOTBALL

American football evolved in American universities in the second half of the 19th century as a descendant from soccer and rugby in Britain. The first professional game was played in 1895 at Latrobe, Pennsylvania. The American Professional Football Association was formed in 1920 and twelve teams contested the first league season. The association became the National Football League (NFL) in 1922. The American Football League (AFL) was formed in 1960. The two leagues merged in 1970, and under the NFL were reorganized into the National Football Conference (NFC) and the American Football Conference (AFC).

The major trophy is the Super Bowl, held annually since 1967 as a competition between firstly champions of the NFL and AFL, and since 1970 between the champions of the NFC and AFC.

The game is 11-a-side (12-a-side in Canada) with substitutes freely used. Pitch dimensions (NFL): 109·7 × 47·8 m (360 × 160 ft). Ball length 280–286 mm (11–11¼ in), weighing 397–425 g (14–15 oz).

Super Bowl winners
1967 Green Bay Packers
1968 Green Bay Packers
1969 New York Jets
1970 Kansas City Chiefs
1971 Baltimore Colts
1972 Dallas Cowboys
1973 Miami Dolphins
1974 Miami Dolphins
1975 Pittsburgh Steelers
1976 Pittsburgh Steelers
1977 Oakland Raiders
1978 Dallas Cowboys
1979 Pittsburgh Steelers
1980 Pittsburgh Steelers
1981 Oakland Raiders
1982 San Francisco 49ers
1983 Washington Redskins
1984 Los Angeles Raiders
1985 San Francisco 49ers
1986 Chicago Bears
1987 New York Giants
1988 Washington Redskins
1989 San Francisco 49ers
1990 San Francisco 49ers
1991 New York Giants

ARCHERY

Although developed as an organized sport from the 3rd century AD, archery is portrayed much earlier as a skill in Mesolithic cave paintings. Archery became firmly established as an international sport in 1931 with the founding of the governing body, *Federation Internationale de Tir à l'Arc* (FITA). The most popular form of archery is termed target archery. Other forms are field archery, shooting at animal figures, and flight shooting, which has the sole object of achieving distance.

The World Target Championships were first held in Poland in 1931 and have been biennial since 1957. The sport was included in the Olympic Games from 1900 to 1908, then again in 1920 (the Belgian style of shooting) and was re-introduced in 1972. Olympic archery is now contested at double FITA rounds, and as for the World Championships there is a final round of 36 arrows for the leading contestants. The 1988 Olympic champions were: (men) *team* South Korea, *individual* Jay Barrs (USA); (women) *team* South Korea, *individual* Kim Soo-nyung (S. Korea).

ATHLETICS (TRACK AND FIELD)

There is evidence that competitive running was involved in early Egyptian rituals at Memphis c. 3800 BC, but organized athletics is usually dated to the ancient Olympic Games c. 1370 BC. The earliest known Olympiad was in July 776 BC, when Coroibos of Elis is recorded as winning the foot race over a distance of about 180–185 m (164–169 yd).

The sport is administered internationally by the International Amateur Athletic Federation (IAAF), formed in 1912, initially with 17 members. It ratified the first list of world records in 1914. The IAAF now has 184 nations affiliated to it, more than any other international organization, sporting or otherwise. The major championships are the quadrennial Olympic Games and World Championships. The modern Olympics were revived in 1896 (see p. 663) and separate World Championships were introduced in 1983, when they were held in Helsinki, Finland. Subsequent championships have been held in 1987 in Rome, Italy, and in 1991 in Tokyo, Japan.

Marathon events, held since 1896, commemorate the legendary run of an unknown Greek courier, possibly Pheidippides, who in 490 BC ran some 38·6 km (24 miles) from the Plain of Marathon to Athens with news of a Greek victory over the numerically superior Persian army. Delivering his message – 'Rejoice! We have won' – he collapsed and died. Since 1908 the distance has been standardized as 42 195 m (26 miles 385 yd).

Dimensions in field events:
Shot (men) – weight 7·26 kg (16 lb), diameter 110–130 mm (4·33–5·12 in)
Shot (women) – weight 4 kg (8 lb 13 oz), diameter 95–110 mm (3·74–4·33 in)
Discus (men) – weight 2 kg (4·409 lb), diameter 219–221 mm (8·622–8·701 in)
Discus (women) – weight 1 kg (2·204 lb), diameter 180–182 mm (7·086–7·165 in)
Hammer – weight 7·26 kg (16 lb), length 117·5–121·5 cm (46·259–47·835 in), diameter of head 110–130 mm (4·33–5·12 in)
Javelin (men) – weight 800 g (28·219 oz), length 260–270 cm (102·362–106·299 in)
Javelin (women) – weight 600 g (21·164 oz), length 220–230 cm (86·61–90·55 in).

TRACK & FIELD ATHLETICS WORLD RECORDS
Men

	min:sec	
100 m	9.92	Carl Lewis (USA) 1988*
200 m	19.72	Pietro Mennea (Ita) 1979
400 m	43.29	Butch Reynolds (USA) 1988
800 m	1:41·73	Sebastian Coe (UK) 1981
1000 m	2:12·18	Sebastian Coe (UK) 1981
1500 m	3:29·46	Saïd Aouita (Mor) 1985

1 mile	3:46·32	Steve Cram (UK) 1985
2000 m	4:50·81	Saïd Aouita (Mor) 1987
3000 m	7:29·45	Saïd Aouita (Mor) 1989
5000 m	12:58·39	Saïd Aouita (Mor) 1987
10 000 m	27:08·23	Arturo Barrios (Mex) 1984
20 km	57:18·40	Dionisio Castro (Por) 1990
1 hour	20944 m	Jos Hermens (Hol) 1976
25 000 m	1hr 13:55·80	Toshihiko Seko (Jap) 1981
30 000 m	1hr 29:18·80	Toshihiko Seko (Jap) 1981
Marathon	2hr 06:50·00	Belayneh Dinsamo (Eth) 1988
3000 m steeple	8:05·35	Peter Koech (Ken) 1989
110 m hurdles	12·92	Roger Kingdom (USA) 1989
400 m hurdles	47·02	Edwin Moses (USA) 1983
4×100 m relay	37·79	France 1990
4×400 m relay	2:56·16	United States 1968 & 1988

metres

High jump	2·44	Javier Sotomayor (Cub) 1989
Pole vault	6.06	Sergey Bubka (USSR) 1988
Long jump	8.90	Bob Beamon (USA) 1968
Triple jump	17·97	Willie Banks (USA) 1985
Shot	23·12	Randy Barnes (USA) 1990
Discus	74·08	Jürgen Schult (GDR) 1986
Hammer	86·74	Yuriy Sedykh (USSR) 1986
Javelin	90·98	Steve Backley (UK) 1990
Decathlon	8847 pts	Daley Thompson (UK) 1984

Track walking
min:sec

20 km	1hr 18:40·00	Ernesto Canto (Mex) 1984
50 km	3hr 41:38·40	Raúl González (Mex) 1979

Road walking – fastest recorded times

20 km	1hr 18:13·00	Pavol Blazek (Cz) 1990
50 km	3hr 37:41·00	Andrey Perlov (USSR) 1989

* Ben Johnson's 9.83 in 1987 was nullified as a record following his admission of drug taking

Women
min:sec

100 m	10·49	Florence Griffith-Joyner (USA) 1988
200 m	21·34	Florence Griffith-Joyner (USA) 1988
400 m	47·60	Marita Koch (GDR) 1985
800 m	1:53·28	Jarmila Kratochvilová (Cz) 1983
1000 m	2:30·60	Tatyana Providokhina (USSR) 1978
1500 m	3:52·47	Tatyana Kazankina (USSR) 1980
1 mile	4:15·61	Paula Ivan (Rom) 1989
2000 m	5:28·69	Maricica Puica (Rom) 1986
3000 m	8:22·62	Tatyana Kazankina (USSR) 1984
5000 m	14:37·33	Ingrid Kristiansen (Nor) 1986
10 000 m	30:13·74	Ingrid Kristiansen (Nor) 1986
Marathon	2hr 21:06	Ingrid Kristiansen (Nor) 1985
100 m hurdles	12·21	Yordanka Donkova (Bul) 1988
400 m hurdles	52·94	Marina Stepanova (USSR) 1986
4 × 100 m	41·37	GDR 1985
4 × 400 m	3:15·17	USSR 1988

metres

High jump	2·09	Stefka Kostadinova (Bul) 1986
Long jump	7·52	Galina Chistyakova (USSR) 1988
Triple Jump	14.54	Li Huirong (Chn) 1990
Shot	22·63	Natalya Lisovskaya (USSR) 1987
Discus	76·80	Gabrielle Reinsch (GDR) 1988
Javelin	80·00	Petra Felke (GDR) 1988
Heptathlon	7291 pts	Jackie Joyner-Kersee (USA) 1988

Track walking
min:sec

5000 m	20:07·52	Beate Anders (GDR) 1990
10 km	41:56·21	Nadezhda Ryashkina (USSR) 1990

Road walking – fastest recorded time

10 km	41:30	Kerry Saxby (Aus) 1988

OLYMPIC GAMES RECORDS (1988)

Men
min:sec

100 m	9·92	Carl Lewis (USA) 1988
200 m	19·75	Joe DeLoach (USA) 1988
400 m	(A)43·86	Lee Evans (USA) 1968
800 m	1:43·00	Joaquim Cruz (Bra) 1984
1500 m	3:32·53	Sebastian Coe (UK) 1984
5000 m	13:05·59	Saïd Aouita (Mor) 1984
10 000 m	27:21·46	Brahim Boutayeb (Mor) 1988
Marathon	2hr 09:21	Carlos Lopes (Por) 1984
3000 m steeple	8:05·51	Julius Kariuki (Ken) 1988
110 m hurdles	12·98	Roger Kingdom (USA) 1988
400 m hurdles	47·19	Andre Phillips (USA) 1988
4 × 100 m	37·83	USA 1984
4 × 400 m	2:56·16	USA 1968 (A) & 1988
20 km walk	1hr 19:57	Jozef Pribilinec (Cz) 1988
50 km walk	3hr 38:29	Vyacheslav Ivenenko (USSR) 1988

metres

High jump	2·38	Gennadiy Avdeyenko (USSR) 1988
Pole vault	5.90	Sergey Bubka (USSR) 1988
Long jump (A)	8·90	Bob Beamon (USA) 1968
Triple jump	17·61	Khristo Markov (Bul) 1988
Shot	22·47	Ulf Timmermann (GDR) 1988
Discus	68·82	Jürgen Schult (GDR) 1988
Hammer	84·80	Sergey Litvinov (USSR) 1988
Javelin	*85·90	Jan Zelezný (Cz) 1988
Old javelin	94·58	Miklos Nemeth (Hun) 1976
Decathlon	8847 pts	Daley Thompson (UK) 1984

Women
min:sec

100 m	10·54	Florence Griffith-Joyner (USA) 1988
200 m	21·34	Florence Griffith-Joyner (USA) 1988
400 m	48·65	Olga Bryzgina (USSR) 1988
800 m	1:53·43	Nadezhda Olizarenko (USSR) 1980
1500 m	3:53·96	Paula Ivan (Rom) 1988
3000 m	8:26·53	Tatyana Samolenko (USSR) 1988
10 000 m	31:05·21	Olga Bondarenko (USSR) 1988
Marathon	2hr 24:52	Joan Benoit (USA) 1984
100 m hurdles	12·38	Yordanka Donkova (Bul) 1988
400 m hurdles	53·17	Debbie Flintoff-King (Aus) 1988
4 × 100 m	41·60	GDR 1980
4 × 400 m	3:15·18	USSR 1988

metres

High jump	2·03	Louise Ritter (USA) 1988
Long jump	7·40	Jackie Joyner-Kersee (USA) 1988
Shot	22·41	Ilona Slupianek (GDR) 1980
Discus	72·30	Martina Hellmann (GDR) 1988
Javelin	74·68	Petra Felke (GDR) 1988
Heptathlon	7291 pts	Jackie Joyner-Kersee (USA) 1988

* performance made in qualifying round.
(A) at high altitude, Mexico City 2240 m.

EUROPEAN CHAMPIONSHIPS

European Championships are held every four years.
They were first staged in Turin in 1934 for men only.
Women's championships were held separately in
1938, but men's and women's events were combined
at one venue from 1946.

1990 EUROPEAN CHAMPIONS
Men

	min:sec	
100 m	10·00	Linford Christie (UK)
200 m	20·11	John Regis (UK)
400 m	45.08	Roger Black (UK)
800 m	1:44·76	Tom McKean (UK)
1500 m	3:38·25	Jens-Peter Herold (GDR)
5000 m	13:22·00	Salvatore Antibo (Ita)
10 000 m	27:41·27	Salvatore Antibo (Ita)
Marathon	2:14:02	Gelindo Bordin (Ita)
3000 m steeple	8:12·66	Francesco Panetta (Ita)
110 m hurdles	13·18	Colin Jackson (UK)
400 m hurdles	47·92	Kriss Akabusi (UK)
4 x 100 m	37·79	France
4 x 400 m	2:58·22	United Kingdom
20 km walk	1:22:05	Pavol Blazek (Cz)
50 km walk	3:54:36	Andrey Perlov (USSR)
	metres	
High jump	2·34	Dragutin Topic (Yug)
Pole vault	5·85	Rodion Gataullin (USSR)
Long jump	8·25	Dietmar Haaf (FRG)
Triple Jump	17·74	Leonid Voloshin (USSR)
Shot	21·32	Ulf Timmermann (GDR)
Discus	64·58	Jürgen Schult (GDR)
Hammer	84·14	Igor Astapkovich (USSR)
Javelin	87·30	Steve Backley (UK)
Decathlon	8574 pts	Christian Plaziat (Fra)

Women

	min:sec	
100 m	10·89	Katrin Krabbe (GDR)
200 m	21·95	Katrin Krabbe (GDR)
400 m	49·50	Grit Breuer (GDR)
800 m	1:55·87	Sigrun Wodars (GDR)
1500 m	4:08·12	Snezana Pajkic (Yug)
3000 m	8:43·06	Yvonne Murray (UK)
10 000 m	31:46·83	Yelena Romanova (USSR)
Marathon	2:31:27	Rosa Mota (Por)
100 m hurdles	12·79	Monique Ewanje-Épée (Fra)
400 m hurdles	53·62	Tatyana Ledovskaya (USSR)
4 x 100 m	41·68	GDR
4 x 400 m	3:21·02	GDR
10 km walk	44:00	Anna Rita Sidoti (Ita)
	metres	
High jump	1·99	Heike Henkel (FRG)
Long jump	7·30	Heike Drechsler (GDR)
Shot	20·38	Astrid Kumbernuss (GDR)
Discus	68·46	Ilke Wyludda (GDR)
Javelin	67·68	Päivi Alafranti (Fin)
Heptathlon	6688 pts	Sabine Braun (FRG)

AUSTRALIAN FOOTBALL

Originally a hybrid of soccer, Gaelic football and
rugby, Australian football laws were codified in 1866
in Melbourne, with the oval (rather than round) ball
in use by 1867. In 1877 the Victorian Football
Association was founded, from which eight clubs
broke away to form the Victorian Football League
(VFL). Four more teams had been admitted by 1925,
and in 1987 teams from Queensland and Western
Australia joined the league to now make it the
Australian Football League. The VFL (now AFL)
Grand Final is played annually at the Melbourne
Cricket Ground.

Teams are 18-a-side. Pitch dimensions are: width
110–155 m (120–170 yd), length 135–185 m (150–200
yd), encompassing an oval boundary line. The oval
ball measures 736 mm (29½ in) in length, 572 mm
(22¾ in) in diameter and weighs 452–482 g (16–17
oz).

BADMINTON

The modern game is believed to have evolved from
Badminton Hall, Avon, England, c. 1870, or from a
game played in India at about the same time. Modern
rules were first codified in Poona, India, in 1876. A
similar game was played in China 2000 years earlier.

The International Badminton Federation was
founded in 1934, with 94 affiliated member nations.
The main centres of the sport are Canada, China,
Denmark, India, Indonesia, Japan, Malaysia, New
Zealand, South Africa, USA, and the UK.

The World Championships were instituted in 1977
and initially held every three years, but are now
staged biennially, as are the international team
competitions – the Thomas Cup (for men; first held
1949) and the Uber Cup (for women; first held 1957).
China won both competitions in 1986, 1988 and 1990.
The major tournament prior to the introduction of
World Championships was the annual All England
Championships, initially held in 1899. Court dimensions: 13·41 × 6·1 m (44 × 20 ft; singles game 3ft
narrower). The net is 1·5 m (5 ft) high at the centre;
two or four players.

Badminton has been added to the Olympic programme for 1992, with medals contested at singles
and doubles for both men and women

BASEBALL

The modern, or Cartwright, rules were introduced
in New Jersey on 19 June 1846, although a game of
the same name had been played in England prior to
1700. Baseball is mainly played in America, where
there are two leagues, the National (NL) and the
American (AL), founded in 1876 and 1901
respectively. It is also very popular in Japan. The
winners of each US league meet annually in a best of
seven series of games – the World Series – established
permanently in 1905. Baseball has been added to the
Olympic programme for 1992.

Recent World Series winners

1980 Philadelphia Phillies (NL)
1981 Los Angeles Dodgers (NL)
1982 St Louis Cardinals (NL)
1983 Baltimore Orioles (AL)
1984 Detroit Tigers (AL)
1985 Kansas City Royals (AL)
1986 New York Mets (NL)
1987 Minnesota Twins (AL)

1988 Los Angeles Dodgers (NL)
1989 Oakland Athletics (AL)
1990 Cincinnati Reds (NL)

The game is 9-a-side. A standard ball weighs 148 g (5–5¼ oz) and is 23 cm (9–9½ in) in circumference. Bats are up to 7 cm (2¾ in) in diameter and up to 1·07 m (42 in) in length.

BASKETBALL

A game not dissimilar to basketball was played by the Olmecs in Mexico in the 10th century BC, but the modern game was devised by (Canadian-born) Dr James Naismith in Massachusetts, in December 1891.

The governing body is the *Fédération Internationale de Basketball Amateur* (FIBA), formed in 1932. The game is played worldwide and by 1989, 178 national federations were members of FIBA. An Olympic sport for men since 1936, and for women since 1976, the 1988 titles were won by the USSR (men) and USA (women). The World championships, first held for men in 1950 and for women in 1953, are staged every four years.

Teams are 5-a-side, with seven substitutes allowed. The rectangular court is 26·0 m (85 ft) in length, and 14·0 m (46 ft) wide, and the ball is 75–78 cm (30 in) in circumference and weighs 600–650 g (21–23 oz).

OLYMPIC CHAMPIONS
Men
USA: 1936, 1948, 1952, 1956, 1960, 1964, 1968, 1976, 1984
USSR: 1972, 1988
Yugoslavia: 1980
Women
USSR: 1976, 1980
USA: 1984, 1988

WORLD CHAMPIONS
Men
Argentina: 1950
USA: 1954, 1986
Brazil: 1959, 1963
USSR: 1967, 1974, 1982
Yugoslavia: 1970, 1978, 1990
Women
USA: 1953, 1957, 1979, 1986, 1990
USSR: 1959, 1964, 1967, 1971, 1975, 1983

BIATHLON

A combination of cross-country skiing and rifle shooting, in which competitors ski over prepared courses carrying a small-bore rifle, the biathlon has been an Olympic event for men since 1960. A women's competition will be introduced in 1992. Men compete individually over 10 km or 20 km distances. There are two shooting competitions at a target 50 metres away over the 10 km distance and four – both prone and standing – over the 20 km distance. The relay event is four by 7·5 km, each member shooting once prone and once standing. Penalties are imposed for missing the target. The women's equivalent distances are 7·5 km, 15 km and 3 by 7.5 km relay.

The sport's governing body is *L'Union Internationale de Pentathlon Moderne et Biatholon* (UIPMB), which took on the administration of biathlon in 1957, and staged the first World Championships in 1958.

BILLIARDS

Probably deriving from the old French word *billiard*

(a stick with a curved end), a reference as early as 1429 suggests the game was originally played on grass. Louis XI of France (1461–83) is believed to be the first to have played billiards on a table. Rubber cushions were introduced in 1835, and slate beds in 1836.

The World Professional and Amateur Championships have been held since 1870 and 1926 respectively.

Dimensions of table: 3·66 × 1·87 m (12 × 6 ft).

BOARDSAILING (WINDSURFING)

Following a High Court decision, Peter Chilvers has been credited with devising the prototype boardsail in 1958. As a sport, it was pioneered by Henry Hoyle Schweitzer and Jim Drake in California in 1968. The World Championships were first held in 1973 and boardsailing was added to the Olympic Games in 1984.

BOBSLEIGH AND TOBOGGANING

Although the first known sledge dates back to c. 6500 BC in Heinola, Finland, organized bobsleighing began in Davos, Switzerland, in 1889.

The International Federation of Bobsleigh and Tobogganing was formed in 1923, followed by the International Bobsleigh Federation in 1957.

The World and Olympic Championships began in 1924, and competition is for crews of two or four. The driver steers while the rear man operates brakes and corrects skidding. With the four-man, the middle two riders alter weight transference for cornering.

The oldest tobogganing club is the St Moritz in Switzerland, founded in 1887, and home of the Cresta Run, which dates from 1884. The course is 1212·25 m (3977 ft) long with a drop of 157 m (514 ft). Solo speeds reach 145 km/h (90 mph). In lugeing, the rider sits or lies back, as opposed to lying face down in tobogganing.

BOWLING (TEN-PIN)

The ancient German game of nine-pins was banned in Connecticut in 1847, and subsequently in other US states. Ten-pin bowling was introduced to beat the ban. Rules were first standardized by the American Bowling Congress (ABC), formed in September 1895.

Concentrated in the USA, the game is also very popular in Japan and Europe. The World Championships were introduced for men in 1954 and women in 1963, under the *Fédération Internationale des Quilleurs* (FIQ), which governs a number of bowling games.

The ten pins are placed in a triangle at the end of a lane of total length 19·16 m (62 ft 10¾ in) and width 1·06 m (42 in).

BOWLS

The known history of outdoor bowls goes back as far as the 13th century in England, but it was forbidden by Edward III because its popularity threatened the practice of archery. The modern rules were not framed until 1848–9 in Scotland by William Mitchell. There are two types of greens, the crown and the level, the former being played almost exclusively in northern England and the Midland counties.

Lawn bowls is played mostly in the UK and Commonwealth countries. The International Bowling Board was formed in July 1905. The Men's and Women's World Championships are held every four years, with singles, pairs, triples and fours events. The World Championships for Indoor Bowls were introduced in 1979.

BOXING

Competitively, boxing began in ancient Greece as one of the first Olympic sports. Boxing with gloves was first depicted on a fresco from the isle of Thera, c. 1520 BC. Prize-fighting rules were formed in England in 1743 by Jack Broughton, but modern day boxing was regularized in 1867 when the 8th Marquess of Queensberry gave his name to the new rules. Boxing only became a legal sport in 1901.

Professional boxing has several world governing bodies, the two oldest being the World Boxing Council (WBC) and the World Boxing Association (WBA), based in Mexico City and Manila respectively. Neither body has been able to agree on fight regulations, and the situation has been further complicated by the formation of the International Boxing Federation (IBF) in the USA in 1983 and the World Boxing Organization (WBO) in 1988. Recognized weight categories are:

Limit in lb (kg)	Weight category
105 (48)	strawweight (WBC), mini-flyweight (WBA, IBF, WBO)
108 (49)	light-flyweight (WBC), junior flyweight (WBA, IBF, WBO)
112 (51)	flyweight
115 (52)	super-flyweight (WBC), junior bantamweight (WBA, IBF, WBO)
118 (54)	bantamweight
122 (55)	super bantamweight (WBC), junior featherweight (WBA, IBF, WBO)
126 (57)	featherweight
130 (59)	super featherweight (WBC) junior lightweight (WBA, IBF, WBO)
135 (61)	lightweight
140 (64)	super lightweight (WBC), junior welterweight (WBA, IBF, WBO)
147 (67)	welterweight
154 (70)	super lightweight (WBC), junior middleweight (WBA, IBF, WBO)
160 (73)	middleweight
168 (76)	super middleweight
175 (79)	light heavyweight
190 (86)	junior heavyweight (WBO), cruiser-weight (WBC, WBA, IBF)
190 (86) +	heavyweight

Weight categories in amateur boxing are:

Limit in kg (lb)	Weight category
48 (106)	light flyweight
51 (112)	flyweight
54 (119)	bantamweight
57 (126)	featherweight
60 (132)	lightweight
63.5 (140)	light welterweight
67 (148)	welterweight
71 (157)	light middleweight
75 (165)	middleweight
81 (179)	light heavyweight
91 (201)	heavyweight
91 (201) +	super heavyweight

CANOEING

Modern canoes and kayaks originated among the Indians and Inuit (Eskimos) of North America, but canoeing as a sport is attributed to an English barrister, James MacGregor, who founded the Royal Canoe Club in 1866.

With a kayak, the paddler sits in a forward-facing position and uses a double-bladed paddle, whereas in a canoe the paddler kneels in a forward-facing position and propels with a single-bladed paddle. An Olympic sport since 1936, competitions for Olympic titles are now held in nine events for men at 500 m and 1000 m, and three for women each at 500 m.

CHESS

Derived from the Persian word *Shah*, meaning a king or ruler, the game itself originated in India under the name *Caturanga*, a military game (literally 'four corps'). The earliest surviving chessmen are an ivory set found in Russia and dated c. AD 200. By the 10th century, chess was played in most European countries and there are today some 40 million enthusiasts in the USSR alone. The governing body, founded in 1922, is the *Fédération Internationale des Echecs* (FIDE), which has been responsible for the World Chess Championship competitions since 1946, although official champions date from 1886 and there were unofficial champions before then.

Players are graded by FIDE according to competitive results on the ELO scoring system, with results issued twice yearly. Grandmaster level is 2500, a rating currently attained by about 100 players. The highest rating ever achieved is 2800 by the current world champion Gary Kasparov, reached in January 1990, when he surpassed the previous best, 2785 of Bobby Fischer. The highest rated woman player is Judit Polgar (Hungary) at 2550.

WORLD CHAMPIONS

1851–8 Adolf Anderssen (Ger)
1858–62 Paul Morphy (USA)
1862–6 Adolf Anderssen (Ger)
1866–94 Wilhelm Steinitz (Aut)
1894–1921 Emanuel Lasker (Ger)
1921–7 José Capablanca (Cub)
1927–35 Alexandre Alekhine (Fra)
1935–7 Max Euwe (Hol)
1937–46 Alexandre Alekhine* (Fra)
1948–57 Mikhail Botvinnik (USSR)
1957–8 Vasiliy Smyslov (USSR)
1958–60 Mikhail Botvinnik (USSR)
1960–1 Mikhail Tal (USSR)
1961–3 Mikhail Botvinnik (USSR)
1963–9 Tigran Petrosian (USSR)
1969–72 Boris Spassky (USSR)
1972–5 Bobby Fischer (USA)
1975–85 Anatoliy Karpov (USSR)
1985– Gary Kasparov (USSR)

WOMEN'S WORLD CHAMPIONS

1927–44 Vera Menchik* (UK)
1950–3 Lyudmila Rudenko (USSR)
1953–6 Yelizaveta Bykova (USSR)
1956–8 Olga Rubtsova (USSR)
1958–62 Yelizaveta Bykova (USSR)
1962–78 Nona Gaprindashvili (USSR)
1978– Maya Chiburdanidze (USSR)

* The reorganization of the sport after 1946, and the death of Alekhine in 1946 and Menchik in 1944 left the sport without a world or women's champion in 1947 and 1945–49 respectively.

CRICKET

SUMMARY OF TEST MATCH RESULTS
(as at 5 Sept 1990)

The first figure is the number of wins by the team on the left, over the team in that column, the second figure is the number of draws. Thus in England v Australia Tests, England have won 88, Australia 101, with 80 Tests left drawn.

	A	E	I	NZ	P	SA	SL	WI	Wins	Tests
Australia	–	104/80	20/16*	10/10	12/13	29/13	3/1	28/16*	205	503
England	88/80	–	31/36	31/34	13/29	46/38	2/1	22/36	233	672
India	8/16*	11/36	–	12/13	4/37	–	2/4	6/30	44	272
New Zealand	8/16*	11/36	–	12/13	4/37	–	2/4	6/30	43	208
Pakistan	9/13	5/29	7/37	13/16	–	–	5/3	7/10	46	198
South Africa	11/13	18/38	–	9/6	–	–	–	–	38	172
Sri Lanka	0/1	0/1	1/4	0/2	1/3	–	–	–	2	33
West Indies	22/16*	41/36	26/30	8/12	10/10	–	–	–	107	280

* plus one tie. There have been two tied Tests: Australia v West Indies 1960 and Australia v India 1986

A drawing dated c. 1250 shows a bat and ball game resembling cricket, although the formal origins are early 18th century. The formation of the MCC (Marylebone Cricket Club) in 1787 resulted in codified laws by 1835.

The International Cricket Conference (ICC), so called since 1965, has allowed membership from non-Commonwealth countries. There are seven full members, 18 associate members and five affiliated members. The seven Test-playing full members are: Australia, England, India, New Zealand, Pakistan, Sri Lanka and West Indies.

There are four English domestic competitions. The County Championship, a league of the 18 first-class counties with matches over three or four days; the one-day knockouts of the Nat. West (previously Gillette) Trophy of 60-over matches and the Benson & Hedges of 55; and the one-day Refuge Assurance League (formerly John Player League) of 40-over matches played on Sundays. The first-class domestic competitions of Australia, New Zealand, India and the West Indies are the Sheffield Shield, the Shell Trophy, the Ranji Trophy and the Red Stripe Cup (formerly Shell Shield) respectively.

The World Cup, the international one-day tournament, is held every four years, with the seven Test-playing countries plus the winner of the ICC Trophy, which is competed for by non-Test playing countries. The West Indies won the first two World Cup competitions in 1975 and 1979; India won the 1983 tournament and Australia won in 1987.

The first Women's World Cup was held in 1988, with Australia the winners.

Dimensions: Ball circumference 20·79–22·8 cm (8³/₁₆–9 in), weight 155–163 g (5½–5¾ oz); pitch 20·11 m (22 yd) from stump to stump.

CURLING

Similar to bowls on ice, curling dates from the 15th century, although organized administration of the sport only began in 1838 with the Grand (later Royal) Caledonian Curling Club in Edinburgh. The sport is traditionally popular in Scotland and Canada. The International Curling Federation was formed in 1966, and curling was included in the 1988 Olympic Games as a demonstration sport, as it had been also in 1924, 1932 and 1964, and will be again in 1992.

CYCLING

The first known cycling race was held over 2 km (1·2 mi) in Paris on 31 May 1868. The Road Record

Association in Britain was formed in 1888, and F. T. Bidlake devised the time trial (1890) as a means of avoiding traffic congestion caused by ordinary mass road racing.

Competitive racing, popular worldwide, is now conducted both on road and track. The Tour de France (founded in 1903) is the longest-lasting non-motorized sporting event in the world, taking 21 days to stage annually. The yellow jersey, to distinguish the leading rider, was introduced in 1919. The World Championships were first held in 1893 at two events, the sprint and motor-paced over 100 km. A range of road and track events are now contested annually for amateur and professional men and for women.

TOUR DE FRANCE WINNERS (from 1947)

1947 Jean Robic (Fra)
1948 Gino Bartali (Ita)
1949 Fausto Coppi (Ita)
1950 Ferdinand Kübler (Swi)
1951 Hugo Koblet (Swi)
1952 Fausto Coppi (Ita)
1953–5 Louison Bobet (Fra)
1956 Roger Walkowiak (Fra)
1957 Jacques Anquetil (Fra)
1958 Charly Gaul (Lux)
1959 Frederico Bahamontès (Spa)
1960 Gastone Nencini (Ita)
1961–4 Jacques Anquetil (Fra)
1965 Felice Gimondi (Ita)
1966 Lucien Aimar (Fra)
1967 Roger Pingeon (Fra)
1968 Jan Janssen (Hol)
1969–72 Eddy Merckx (Bel)
1973 Luis Ocana (Spa)
1974 Eddy Merckx (Bel)
1975 Bernard Thevenet (Fra)
1976 Lucien van Impe (Bel)
1977 Bernard Thevenet (Fra)
1978–9 Bernard Hinault (Fra)
1980 Joop Zoetemelk (Hol)
1981–2 Bernard Hinault (Fra)
1983–4 Laurent Fignon (Fra)
1985 Bernard Hinault (Fra)
1986 Greg LeMond (USA)
1987 Stephen Roche (Ire)
1988 Pedro Delgado (Spa)
1989–90 Greg LeMond (USA)

Cycling has been included in the modern Olympic Games since 1896. There are currently seven men's and two women's events on the Olympic programme.

1988 OLYMPIC CHAMPIONS
Men Sprint: Lutz Hesslich (GDR)

1000 m time trial: Aleksandr Kirichenko (USSR) 1:04·499

4000 m individual pursuit: Gintautas Umaras (USSR)

Points: Dan Frost (Den)

Road race: Olaf Ludwig (GDR)

100 km road team time trial: GDR

Team pursuit: USSR

Women

Sprint: Erika Salumyae (USSR)

Road race: Monique Knol (Hol)

A 3000 m pursuit for women has been added to the programme for 1992.

DARTS

Brian Gamlin of Bury, Lancashire, is credited with devising the present numbering system on the darts board, although in non-sporting form darts began with the heavily weighted throwing arrows used in Roman and Greek warfare. Immensely popular in the UK – there are today some 6 000 000 players – the sport is rapidly spreading in America and parts of Europe. The World championships were first held in 1978.

WORLD CHAMPIONS

1978 Leighton Rees (Wal)

1979 John Lowe (Eng)

1980 Eric Bristow (Eng)

1981 Eric Bristow (Eng)

1982 Jocky Wilson (Sco)

1983 Keith Deller (Eng)

1984 Eric Bristow (Eng)

1985 Eric Bristow (Eng)

1986 Eric Bristow (Eng)

1987 John Lowe (Eng)

1988 Bob Anderson (Eng)

1989 Jocky Wilson (Sco)

1990 Phil Taylor (Eng)

1991 Dennis Priestley (Eng)

EQUESTRIANISM

Horse riding is some 5000 years old, but schools of horsemanship, or equitation, were not established until the 16th century, primarily in Italy and then in France. The earliest known jumping competition was in Islington, London in 1869.

An Olympic event since 1912, events are held in dressage, show jumping and three-day event, with team and individual titles for each. Dressage (the French term for the training of horses) is a test of a rider's ability to control a horse through various manoeuvres within an area of 60 × 20 m (66× 22 yd). In show jumping, riders jump a set course of fences, incurring four faults for knocking a fence down or landing (one or more feet) in the water, three faults for a first refusal, six faults then elimination for 2nd and 3rd, and eight faults for a fall. The three-day event encompasses dressage, cross country and jumping. The governing body is the *Fédération Equestre Internationale*, founded in May 1921.

1988 OLYMPIC CHAMPIONS

	Individual	Team
Show Jumping	Pierre Durand (Fra) on Jappeloup	FRG
Three-day event	Mark Todd (NZ) on Charisma	FRG
Dressage	Nicole Uphof (FRG) on Rembrandt	FRG

FENCING

Fencing (fighting with single sticks) was practised as a sport, or as part of a religious ceremony, in Egypt as early as 1360 BC. The modern sport developed directly from the duelling of the Middle Ages.

There are three types of sword used today. With the foil (introduced in the 17th century), only the trunk of the body is acceptable as a target. The épée (a mid-19th century introduction) is marginally heavier and more rigid, and the whole body is a valid target. The sabre (a late 19th-century introduction) has cutting edges on both sides of the blade, and scores on the whole body from the waist upwards. Only with the sabre can points be scored with the edge of the blade rather than the tip.

Women compete in foil only at the Olympic Games, but the women's épée was added to the annual World Championships from 1989. For men, there are individual and team events for each type of sword in the Olympics. The world governing body is the *Fédération Internationale d'Escrime*, founded in 1913.

OLYMPIC CHAMPIONS 1988

Men

	Individual	Team
Foil	Stefano Cerioni (Ita)	USSR
Épée	Arndt Schmidt (FRG)	France
Sabre	Jean-François Lamour (Fra)	Hungary

Women

	Individual	Team
Foil	Anja Fichtel (FRG)	FRG

FIVES

Eton Fives originate from a handball game first recorded as being played against the buttress of Eton College Chapel in 1825. The rules were codified in 1877, and last amended in 1981.

Rugby Fives, a variation, dates from c. 1850. Both are more or less confined to the UK.

FOOTBALL (Association)

A game resembling football, *Tsu-Chu-Tsu*, meaning 'to kick the ball with feet' (*chu* meaning 'leather') – was played in China around 400 BC. Calcio, closer to the modern game, existed in Italy in 1410. Official references to football date to Edward II's reign in England – he banned the game in London in 1314; later monarchs issued similar edicts. The first soccer rules were formulated at Cambridge University in 1846; previously football was brutal and lawless. The Football Association (FA) was founded in England on 26 October 1863. Eleven per side became standard in 1870.

The governing body, *the Fédération Internationale de Football Association* (FIFA), was founded in Paris on 21 May 1904 and football is now played throughout the world.

Domestic competitions in England are dominated by the professional League game – the Football League was formed in 1888 with 12 teams and now has four divisions totalling 93 teams. The FA Challenge Cup was introduced in 1871, and the Rumbelows (previously League, Milk and Littlewoods) Cup was instituted in 1960. 'Non-League' or semi-professional football is also widespread in England and Wales with the semi-professional GM Vauxhall Conference as the major competition. In Scotland, the Scottish Cup was

EURO FACTS

EUROPEAN CHAMPIONSHIPS

1960 USSR
1964 Spain
1968 Italy
1972 Germany (W)
1976 Czechoslovakia
1980 Germany (W)
1984 France
1988 Netherlands

EUROPEAN CHAMPION CLUBS CUP

1956–60 Real Madrid
1961–2 Benfica (Lisbon)
1963 AC Milan
1964–5 Internazionale Milan
1966 Real Madrid
1967 Glasgow Celtic
1968 Manchester United
1969 AC Milan
1970 Feyenoord (Rotterdam)
1971–3 Ajax Amsterdam
1974–6 Bayern Munich
1977–8 Liverpool
1979–80 Nottingham Forest
1981 Liverpool
1982 Aston Villa
1983 SV Hamburg
1984 Liverpool
1985 Juventus (Turin)
1986 Steaua Bucharest
1987 FC Porto
1988 PSV Eindhoven
1989–90 AC Milan
1991 Red Star Belgrade

started in 1873 and the Scottish League – now comprising 38 teams in three divisions – was formed in 1890.

Internationally, the World Cup has been held every four years since 1930 (except in 1942 and 1946). The European Championship, instituted in 1958 as the Nations Cup, is held every four years. The European Champions Club Cup, instituted in 1955 as the European Cup, is contested annually by the League Champions of the member countries of the Union of European Football Associations (UEFA). The European Cup Winners Cup was instituted in 1960 for national cup winners (or runners-up if the winners are in the European Cup). The UEFA Cup was instituted in 1955 as the Inter-City Fairs Cup, and has been held annually since 1960. The European Super Cup (instituted in 1972) is played between the winners of the European Champions Club Cup and the Cup Winners Cup; and the World Club Championship (instituted in 1960) is a contest between the winners of the European Cup and the Copa Libertadores (the South American championship).

Football is an 11-a-side game; the ball's circumference is 68–71 cm (27–28 in) and weight 396–453 g (14–16 oz). Pitch length 91–120 m (100–130 yd), width 45–91 m (50–100 yd).

THE WORLD CUP

Year	Winner	Venue
1930	Uruguay	Uruguay
1934	Italy	Italy
1938	Italy	France
1950	Uruguay	Brazil
1954	Germany (W)	Switzerland
1958	Brazil	Sweden
1962	Brazil	Chile
1966	England	England
1970	Brazil	Mexico
1974	Germany (W)	Germany (W)
1978	Argentina	Argentina
1982	Italy	Spain
1986	Argentina	Mexico
1990	Germany (W)	Italy

THE FA CUP (ENGLAND AND WALES)

The FA Cup, or Football Association Challenge Cup, was instituted in 1871, 17 years before the birth of the Football League. The first final was played at Kennington Oval, London, in 1872, when the Wanderers defeated Royal Engineers 1–0. Southern amateur clubs dominated the early years and the Cup did not 'go north' until Blackburn Olympic won in 1883. The final has been played at Wembley Stadium since 1923, when Bolton Wanderers defeated West Ham.

1872 Wanderers
1873 Wanderers
1874 Oxford University
1875 Royal Engineers
1876 Wanderers
1877 Wanderers
1878 Wanderers
1879 Old Etonians
1880 Clapham Rovers
1881 Old Carthusians
1882 Old Etonians
1883 Blackburn Olympic
1884 Blackburn Rovers
1885 Blackburn Rovers
1886 Blackburn Rovers
1887 Aston Villa
1888 West Bromwich Albion
1889 Preston North End
1890 Blackburn Rovers
1891 Blackburn Rovers
1892 West Bromwich Albion
1893 Wolverhampton Wanderers
1894 Notts County
1895 Aston Villa
1896 Sheffield Wednesday
1897 Aston Villa
1898 Nottingham Forest
1899 Sheffield United
1900 Bury
1901 Tottenham Hotspur
1902 Sheffield United
1903 Bury
1904 Manchester City
1905 Aston Villa
1906 Everton
1907 Sheffield Wednesday
1908 Wolverhampton Wanderers
1909 Manchester United
1910 Newcastle United
1911 Bradford City
1912 Barnsley
1913 Aston Villa

EURO FACTS

EUROPEAN CUP WINNER'S CUP

1961 Fiorentina
1962 Atletico Madrid
1963 Tottenham Hotspur
1964 Sporting Lisbon
1965 West Ham United
1966 Borussia Dortmund
1967 Bayern Munich
1968 AC Milan
1969 Slovan Bratislava
1970 Manchester City
1971 Chelsea
1972 Glasgow Rangers
1973 AC Milan
1974 FC Magdeburg
1975 Dynamo Kiev
1976 Anderlecht
1977 SV Hamburg
1978 Anderlecht
1979 Barcelona
1980 Valencia
1981 Dynamo Tbilisi
1982 Barcelona
1983 Aberdeen
1984 Juventus (Turin)
1985 Everton
1986 Dynamo Kiev
1987 Ajax Amsterdam
1988 Mechelen
1989 Barcelona
1990 Sampdoria (Genoa)
1991 Manchester United

EURO FACTS

UEFA CUP

1958 Barcelona
1960 Barcelona
1961 AS Roma
1962–3 Valencia
1964 Real Zaragoza
1965 Ferencvaros (Budapest)
1966 Barcelona
1967 Dynamo Zagreb
1968 Leeds United
1969 Newcastle United
1970 Arsenal
1971 Leeds United
1972 Tottenham Hotspur
1973 Liverpool
1974 Feyenoord (Rotterdam)
1975 Borussia Mönchengladbach
1976 Liverpool
1977 Juventus (Turin)
1978 PSV Eindhoven
1979 Borussia Mönchengladbach
1980 Eintracht Frankfurt
1981 Ipswich Town
1982 IFK Göteborg
1983 Anderlecht
1984 Tottenham Hotspur
1985–6 Real Madrid
1987 IFK Göteborg
1988 Bayer Leverkusen
1989 Napoli
1990 Juventus (Turin)
1991 Internazionale Milan

1914 Burnley
1915 Sheffield United
1920 Aston Villa
1921 Tottenham Hotspur
1922 Huddersfield Town
1923 Bolton Wanderers
1924 Newcastle United
1925 Sheffield United
1926 Bolton Wanderers
1927 Cardiff City
1928 Blackburn Rovers
1929 Bolton Wanderers
1930 Arsenal
1931 West Bromwich Albion
1932 Newcastle United
1933 Everton
1934 Manchester City
1935 Sheffield Wednesday
1936 Arsenal
1937 Sunderland
1938 Preston North End
1939 Portsmouth
1946 Derby County
1947 Charlton Athletic
1948 Manchester United
1949 Wolverhampton Wanderers
1950 Arsenal
1951 Newcastle United
1952 Newcastle United
1953 Blackpool
1954 West Bromwich Albion
1955 Newcastle United
1956 Manchester City
1957 Aston Villa

1958 Bolton Wanderers
1959 Nottingham Forest
1960 Wolverhampton Wanderers
1961 Tottenham Hotspur
1962 Tottenham Hotspur
1963 Manchester United
1964 West Ham United
1965 Liverpool
1966 Everton
1967 Tottenham Hotspur
1968 West Bromwich Albion
1969 Manchester City
1970 Chelsea
1971 Arsenal
1972 Leeds United
1973 Sunderland
1974 Liverpool
1975 West Ham United
1976 Southampton
1977 Manchester United
1978 Ipswich Town
1979 Arsenal
1980 West Ham United
1981 Tottenham Hotspur
1982 Tottenham Hotspur
1983 Manchester United
1984 Everton
1985 Manchester United
1986 Liverpool
1987 Coventry City
1988 Wimbledon
1989 Liverpool
1990 Manchester United
1991 Tottenham Hotspur

GAELIC FOOTBALL

Gaelic football developed from a traditional inter-parish 'football free for all' with no time limit, no defined playing area nor specific rules. The Gaelic Athletic Association established the game in its present form in 1884; teams are 15-a-side. Played throughout Ireland, the All-Ireland Championship, first held in 1887, is contested annually by Irish counties; the final is played at Croke Park, Dublin, each September.

GLIDING

Around AD 1500 Leonardo da Vinci defined the difference between gliding and powered flight in some drawings. However, the first authenticated man-carrying glider was designed by Sir George Cayley in 1853.

In competitive terms, gliders contest various events – pure distance, distance to a declared goal, to a declared goal and back, height gain and absolute altitude. The World Championships were first held in 1937 and have been biennial since 1948.

Hang gliding has flourished in recent years, boosted by the invention of the flexible 'wing' by Professor Francis Rogallo in the early 1960s. The first official World Championships were held in 1976.

GOLF

A prohibiting law passed by the Scottish Parliament in 1457 declared 'goff be utterly cryit doune and not usit'. This is the earliest mention of golf, although games of similar principle date as far back as AD 400. Golf is played worldwide today.

Competition is either 'match play', contested by individuals or pairs and decided by the number of holes won, or 'stroke play', decided by the total number of strokes for a round. The modern golf course measures an average total distance of between 5500 and 6400 metres, and is divided into 18 holes of varying lengths. Clubs are currently limited to a maximum of 14, comprising 'irons' Nos. 1–10 (with the face of the club at increasingly acute angles), and 'woods' for driving. Golf balls in the UK and North America have the minimum diameter of 42·62 mm (1·68 in).

Professionally, the four major tournaments are the British Open, the US Open, the US Masters and the US Professional Golfers' Association (USPGA).

THE BRITISH OPEN GOLF CHAMPIONSHIP

The oldest open championship in the world, 'The Open', was first held on 17 October 1860 at the Prestwick Club, Ayrshire, Scotland. It was then over 36 holes; since 1892 it has been over 72 holes of stroke play. Since 1920, the Royal and Ancient Golf Club has managed the event.

Winners	*Score*
(UK unless specified)	
1860 Willie Park, Sr	174
1861 Tom Morris, Sr	163
1862 Tom Morris, Sr	163
1863 Willie Park, Sr	168
1864 Tom Morris, Sr	167
1865 Andrew Strath	162
1866 Willie Park, Sr	169
1867 Tom Morris, Sr	170
1868 Tom Morris, Jr	170
1869 Tom Morris, Jr	154
1870 Tom Morris, Jr	149
1871 Not held	
1872 Tom Morris, Jr	166
1873 Tom Kidd	179
1874 Mungo Park	159
1875 Willie Park, Sr	166
1876 Robert Martin	176
1877 Jamie Anderson	160
1878 Jamie Anderson	170
1879 Jamie Anderson	170
1880 Robert Ferguson	162
1881 Robert Ferguson	170
1882 Robert Ferguson	171
1883 Willie Fernie	159
1884 Jack Simpson	160
1885 Bob Martin	171
1886 David Brown	157
1887 Willie Park, Jr	161
1888 Jack Burns	171
1889 Willie Park, Jr	155
1890 John Ball	164
1891 Hugh Kirkcaldy	169
1892 Harold Hilton	305
1893 William Auchterlonie	322
1894 John Taylor	326
1895 John Taylor	322
1896 Harry Vardon	316
1897 Harry Hilton	314
1898 Harry Vardon	307
1899 Harry Vardon	310
1900 John Taylor	309
1901 James Braid	309
1902 Alexander Herd	307
1903 Harry Vardon	300
1904 Jack White	296
1905 James Braid	318
1906 James Braid	300
1907 Arnaud Massy (Fra)	312
1908 James Braid	291
1909 John Taylor	295
1910 James Braid	299
1911 Harry Vardon	303
1912 Edward (Ted) Ray	295
1913 John Taylor	304
1914 Harry Vardon	306
1920 George Duncan	303
1921 Jock Hutchinson (USA)	296
1922 Walter Hagen (USA)	300
1923 Arthur Havers	295
1924 Walter Hagen (USA)	301
1925 James Barnes (USA)	300
1926 Robert T. Jones, Jr (USA)	291
1927 Robert T. Jones, Jr (USA)	285
1928 Walter Hagen (USA)	292
1929 Walter Hagen (USA)	292
1930 Robert T. Jones, Jr (USA)	291
1931 Tommy Armour (USA)	296
1932 Gene Sarazen (USA)	283
1933 Denny Shute (USA)	292
1934 Henry Cotton	283
1935 Alfred Perry	283
1936 Alfred Padgham	287
1937 Henry Cotton	283
1938 Reg Whitcombe	295
1939 Richard Burton	290
1946 Sam Snead (USA)	290
1947 Fred Daly	293
1948 Henry Cotton	284
1949 Bobby Locke (SAf)	283
1950 Bobby Locke (SAf)	279
1951 Max Faulkner	285
1952 Bobby Locke (SAf)	287
1953 Ben Hogan (USA)	282

1954 Peter Thomson (Aus)	283
1955 Peter Thomson (Aus)	281
1956 Peter Thomson (Aus)	286
1957 Bobby Locke (SAf)	279
1958 Peter Thomson (Aus)	278
1959 Gary Player (SAf)	284
1960 Kel Nagle (Aus)	278
1961 Arnold Palmer (USA)	284
1962 Arnold Palmer (USA)	276
1963 Bob Charles (NZ)	277
1964 Tony Lema (USA)	279
1965 Peter Thomson (Aus)	285
1966 Jack Nicklaus (USA)	282
1967 Robert de Vicenzo (Arg)	278
1968 Gary Player (SAf)	299
1969 Tony Jacklin	280
1970 Jack Nicklaus (USA)	283
1971 Lee Trevino (USA)	278
1972 Lee Trevino (USA)	278
1973 Tom Weiskopf (USA)	276
1974 Gary Player (SAf)	282
1975 Tom Watson (USA)	279
1976 Johnny Miller (USA)	279
1977 Tom Watson (USA)	268
1978 Jack Nicklaus (USA)	281
1979 Severiano Ballesteros (Spa)	283
1980 Tom Watson (USA)	271
1981 Bill Rogers (USA)	276
1982 Tom Watson (USA)	284
1983 Tom Watson (USA)	275
1984 Severiano Ballesteros (Spa)	276
1985 Sandy Lyle (USA)	282
1986 Greg Norman (Aus)	280
1987 Nick Faldo	279
1988 Severiano Ballesteros (Spa)	273
1989 Mark Calcavecchia (USA)	275
1990 Nick Faldo	270

US OPEN

First played on a 9-hole course at Newport, Rhode Island, on 4 October 1895, and annually – over 72 holes of stroke play – at a variety of venues from 1898.

Winners	*Score*
(since 1946; US unless specified)	
1946 Lloyd Mangrum	284
1947 Lew Worsham	282
1948 Ben Hogan	287
1949 Cary Middlecoff	286
1950 Ben Hogan	287
1951 Ben Hogan	287
1952 Julius Boros	281
1953 Ben Hogan	283
1954 Ed Furgol	284
1955 Jack Fleck	287
1956 Cary Middlecoff	281
1957 Dick Mayer	282
1958 Tommy Bolt	283
1959 Billy Casper	282
1960 Arnold Palmer	280
1961 Gene Littler	281
1962 Jack Nicklaus	283
1963 Julius Boros	293
1964 Ken Venturi	278
1965 Gary Player (SAf)	282
1966 Billy Casper	278
1967 Jack Nicklaus	275
1968 Lee Trevino	275
1969 Orville Moody	281
1970 Tony Jacklin (UK)	281
1971 Lee Trevino	280
1972 Jack Nicklaus	290
1973 Johnny Miller	279

1974 Hale Irwin	287
1975 Lou Graham	287
1976 Jerry Pate	277
1977 Hubert Green	278
1978 Andy North	285
1979 Hale Irwin	284
1980 Jack Nicklaus	272
1981 David Graham (Aus)	273
1982 Tom Watson	282
1983 Larry Nelson	280
1984 Fuzzy Zoeller	276
1985 Andy North	279
1986 Raymond Floyd	279
1987 Scott Simpson	277
1988 Curtis Strange	278
1989 Curtis Strange	278
1990 Hale Irwin	280

US MASTERS

Held annually at the Augusta National course in Georgia, the Masters was introduced in 1934. Both the course and the tournament were the idea of the legendary golfer Bobby Jones. Entry to the Masters is by invitation only and the eventual winner is presented with the coveted green jacket. It is contested over 72 holes of stroke play.

Winners	*Score*
(since 1946; US unless specified)	
1946 Herman Keiser	282
1947 Jimmy Demaret	281
1948 Claude Harmon	279
1949 Sam Snead	282
1950 Jimmy Demaret	283
1951 Ben Hogan	280
1952 Sam Snead	286
1953 Ben Hogan	274
1954 Sam Snead	289
1955 Cary Middlecoff	279
1956 Jack Burke, Jr	289
1957 Doug Ford	282
1958 Arnold Palmer	284
1959 Art Wall, Jr	284
1960 Arnold Palmer	282
1961 Gary Player (SAf)	280
1962 Arnold Palmer	280
1963 Jack Nicklaus	286
1964 Arnold Palmer	276
1965 Jack Nicklaus	271
1966 Jack Nicklaus	288
1967 Gay Brewer	280
1968 Bob Goalby	277
1969 George Archer	281
1970 Billy Casper	279
1971 Charles Coody	279
1972 Jack Nicklaus	286
1973 Tommy Aaron	283
1974 Gary Player (SAf)	278
1975 Jack Nicklaus	276
1976 Raymond Floyd	271
1977 Tom Watson	276
1978 Gary Player (SAf)	277
1979 Fuzzy Zoeller	280
1980 Severiano Ballesteros (Spa)	275
1981 Tom Watson	280
1982 Craig Stadler	284
1983 Severiano Ballesteros (Spa)	280
1984 Ben Crenshaw	277
1985 Bernhard Langer (FRG)	282
1986 Jack Nicklaus	279
1987 Larry Mize	285
1988 Sandy Lyle (UK)	281
1989 Nick Faldo (UK)	283
1990 Nick Faldo (UK)	278
1991 Ian Woosnam (UK)	277

GREYHOUND RACING

Greyhounds were first used in sport at coursing – chasing of hares by pairs of dogs – and brought to England by the Normans in 1067. The use of mechanical devices was first practised in England, but the sport was popularized in the USA. The first regular track was opened at Emeryville, California, in 1919.

Races are usually conducted over distances of between 210 m (230 yd) for the sprint and 1096 m (1200 yd) for the marathon. The Derby, the major race in Britain, was instituted in 1927.

GYMNASTICS

Tumbling and similar exercises were performed c. 2600 BC as religious rituals in China, but it was the ancient Greeks who coined the word gymnastics, which encompassed various athletic contests including boxing, weightlifting and wrestling. A primitive form was practised in the ancient Olympic Games, but the foundations of the modern sport were laid by the German Johann Friedrich Simon in 1776, and the first national federation was formed in Germany in 1860.

The International Gymnastics Federation was founded in Belgium in 1881, and gymnastics was included in the first modern Olympic Games in 1896. Current events for men are: floor exercises, horse vaults, rings, pommel horse, parallel bars and horizontal bar. The events for women are: floor exercises, horse vault, asymmetrical bars and balance beam. Rhythmic gymnastics for women was introduced for the first time at the 1984 Los Angeles Games. The USSR, USA, Romania, China and Japan are now the strongest nations.

At the 1988 Olympics the USSR won both men's and women's team events. The combined exercises individual champions were Vladimir Artemov (men; USSR) and Yelena Shushunova (women; USSR).

HANDBALL

Handball, similar to soccer only using the hands rather than the feet, was first played at the end of the 19th century. It is a growing sport; by 1989 there were 101 countries affiliated to the International Handball Federation.

Handball was introduced into the Olympic Games at Berlin in 1936 as an 11-a-side outdoor game, but on its reintroduction in 1972, it was an indoor 7-a-side sport (the standard size of the team was reduced to its present level in 1952, although in Britain handball is often played with teams of five). At the 1988 Olympics the winners were the USSR (men) and South Korea (women).

HARNESS RACING

Trotting races were held in Valkenburg, in the Netherlands, in 1554, but harness racing was developed, and is most popular in North America. The sulky, the lightweight vehicle, first appeared in 1829. Horses may trot, moving their legs in diagonal pairs, or pace, moving fore and hind legs on one side simultaneously.

HOCKEY

Early Greek wall carvings c. 500 BC show hockey-like games, while curved-stick games appear on Egyptian tomb paintings c. 2050 BC. Hockey in its modern form, however, developed in England in the second half of the 19th century, with Teddington HC (formed 1871) standardizing the rules. The English Hockey Association was founded in 1886. Hockey was included in the 1908 and 1920 Olympic Games, with England the winners on both occasions. It has been held at every Games from 1928 and the tournaments were dominated for many years by India, winners at all six Games 1928–1956, and also in 1964 and 1980, and by Pakistan, winners in 1960, 1968 and 1984. However their supremacy has been successfully challenged by nations from Europe and Australasia in recent years. Women's hockey was introduced to the Olympics in 1980. The 1988 Olympic champions were Great Britain (men) and Australia (women). The governing body, the *Fédération Internationale de Hockey* (FIH), was formed in 1924 and had 103 member nations in 1990.

Dimensions: ball circumference 223–224 cm ($8^1/_5$–$9^1/_2$ in) and weight 155–163 g ($5^1/_2$–$5^3/_4$ oz); pitch length 91·44 m (100 yd); width 50–55 m (55–60 yd).

FIH (IHF) WORLD CUP

First contested in 1971 for men and 1974 for women. Winners:

Men

Pakistan	1971, 1978, 1982
Netherlands	1973, 1990
India	1975
Australia	1986

Women

Netherlands	1974, 1978, 1983, 1986, 1990
Germany (W)	1976, 1981

HORSE RACING

Early organized racing appears to have been confined to chariots – Roman riders had a foot on each of two horses. The first horse-back races were staged by the Greeks in the 33rd Ancient Olympiad in 648 BC. The first recognizable modern race meeting was held at Smithfield, London, in 1174, while the first known prize money was a purse of gold presented by the English king Richard I in 1195.

In Britain the Jockey Club is now the governing body of flat racing, steeplechasing and hurdle racing, having merged with the National Hunt Committee in 1968. The flat racing season in Britain takes place between late March and early November. Thoroughbreds may not run until they are two years old. The five classic races are the Two Thousand Guineas and the One Thousand Guineas (held at Newmarket over 1600 m / 1 mile), the Derby and the Oaks (held at Epsom over 2400 m / 1$^1/_2$ miles) and the St Leger (held at Doncaster over 2800 m / 1$^3/_4$ miles).

Steeplechase and hurdle races are run over distances of 2 or more miles, with at least one ditch and six birch fences for every mile. The UK National Hunt season can last from early August to 1st June, and the two most important steeplechases are the Grand National, first run in 1839, at Aintree over a course of 7220 m (4 miles 856 yd) with 30 jumps, and the Gold Cup run over 5·2 km (3$^1/_4$ miles) at Cheltenham.

The premier British hurdle race is the Champion Hurdle, held annually over 3·2 km (2 miles) at Cheltenham. Recent winners of major races are listed below. (The name of the jockey is given in brackets.)

THE DERBY (winners since 1980)
1980 Henbit (Willie Carson)
1981 Shergar (Walter Swinburn)
1982 Golden Fleece (Pat Eddery)
1983 Teenoso (Lester Piggott)
1984 Secreto (Christy Roche)
1985 Slip Anchor (Steve Cauthen)
1986 Shahrastani (Walter Swinburn)
1987 Reference Point (Steve Cauthen)
1988 Kahyasi (Ray Cochrane)
1989 Nashwan (Willie Carson)
1990 Quest for Fame (Pat Eddery)

GRAND NATIONAL (winners since 1980)
1980 Ben Nevis (Charlie Fenwick)
1981 Aldaniti (Bob Champion)
1982 Grittar (Dick Saunders)
1983 Corbiere (Ben De Haan)
1984 Hallo Dandy (Neale Doughty)
1985 Last Suspect (Hywel Davies)
1986 West Tip (Richard Dunwoody)
1987 Maori Venture (Steve Knight)
1988 Rhyme N'Reason (Brendan Powell)
1989 Little Polveir (Jimmy Frost)
1990 Mr Frisk (Marcus Armytage)
1991 Seagram (Nigel Hawke)

CHELTENHAM GOLD CUP (winners since 1980)
1980 Master Smudge (Richard Hoare)
1981 Little Owl (Jim Wilson)
1982 Silver Buck (Robert Earnshaw)
1983 Bregawn (Graham Bradley)
1984 Burrough Hill Lad (Phil Tuck)
1985 Forgive 'N' Forget (Martin Dwyer)
1986 Dawn Run (Jonjo O'Neill)
1987 The Thinker (Ridley Lamb)
1988 Charter Party (Richard Dunwoody)
1989 Desert Orchid (Simon Sherwood)
1990 Norton's Coin (Graham McCourt)
1991 Garrison Savannah (Mark Pitman)

PRIX DE L'ARC DE TRIOMPHE
Europe's most prestigious race was first run in 1920. It is run over 2400 metres (c. 1 mile 4 furlongs) at Longchamp on the first Sunday in October. Winners since 1980.

1980 Detroit (Pat Eddery)
1981 Gold River (Gary Moore)
1982 Akiyda (Yves Saint-Martin)
1983 All Along (Walter Swinburn)
1984 Sagace (Yves Saint-Martin)
1985 Rainbow Quest (Pat Eddery)
1986 Dancing Brave (Pat Eddery)
1987 Trempolino (Pat Eddery)
1988 Tony Bin (John Reid)
1989 Carroll House (Michael Kinane)
1990 Saumarez (Gerald Mossé)

HURLING

Hurling is an ancient game that has been played in Ireland since pre-Christian times, but has been standardized only since the founding of the Gaelic Athletic Association in 1884. The hurl, or stick, is similar to a hockey stick only flat on both sides. The All-Ireland Championship, first held in 1887, is contested annually by Irish counties; the final is played at Croke Park, Dublin, each September.

ICE HOCKEY

A game similar to hockey on ice was played in Holland in the early 16th century, but the birth of modern ice hockey took place in Canada, probably at Kingston, Ontario, in 1855. Rules were first formulated by students of McGill University in Montreal, who formed a club in 1880.

The International Ice Hockey Federation was formed in 1908, and the World and Olympic Championships inaugurated in 1920. The USSR have won seven of the last eight Olympic titles. The major professional competition is the National Hockey League (NHL) in North America, founded in 1917, whose teams contest the Stanley Cup.

Teams are 6-a-side; the ideal rink size is 61 m (200 ft) long and 26 m (85 ft) wide.

ICE AND SAND YACHTING

Ice, sand and land yachting require, in basic form, a wheeled chassis beneath a sailing dinghy. Dutch ice yachts are thought to date back to 1768, but ice yachting today is mainly confined to North America. Land and sand yachts of Dutch construction go back even further to 1595. The sports are governed by the International Federation of Sand and Land Yacht which recognizes speed records. International championships were first staged in 1914.

ICE SKATING

Second-century Scandinavian literature refers to ice skating, although archaeological evidence points to origins ten centuries earlier. The first English account of the sport is dated 1180, while the first British club, the Edinburgh Skating Club, was formed around 1742. Steel blades, allowing precision skating, were invented in America in 1850. The International Skating Union was founded in the Netherlands in 1892.

Ice skating competition is divided into figure skating, speed skating and ice dancing. Figure skating has been an Olympic event since the Winter Games were first organized in 1924, but there were also events at the 1908 and 1920 Games. Ice dancing was not included until 1976.

The first international speed skating competition was in Hamburg, Germany, in 1885, with World Championships officially dated from 1893. Speed skating for men was first included in the 1924 Olympics; women's events were included in 1960.

OLYMPIC FIGURE SKATING CHAMPIONS

Singles

	Men	Women
1980	Robin Cousins (UK)	Anett Pötzsch (GDR)
1984	Scott Hamilton (USA)	Katarina Witt (GDR)
1988	Brian Boitano (USA)	Katarina Witt (GDR)

Pairs
1980 Irina Rodnina and Aleksandr Zaitsev (USSR)
1984 Yelena Valova and Oleg Vasilyev (USSR)
1988 Yekaterina Gordeyeva and Sergey Grinkov (USSR)

Ice Dance
1980 Natalya Linichuk and Gennadiy Karponosov (USSR)
1984 Jayne Torvill and Christopher Dean (UK)
1988 Natalya Bestemianova and Andrey Bukin (USSR)

JUDO

Judo developed from a mixture of pre-Christian

Japanese fighting arts, the most popular of which was ju-jitsu – thought to be of ancient Chinese origin. 'Ju' means 'soft', i.e. the reliance on speed and skill as opposed to 'hard' brute force. Judo as a modern combat sport was devised in 1882 by Dr Jigoro Kano. Points are scored by throws, locks on joints, certain pressures on the neck, and immobilizations. Today, students are graded by belt colours from white to black, the 'master' belts. Grades of black belts are 'Dans', the highest attainable being Tenth Dan.

The International Judo Federation was founded in 1951 and the World Championships were first held in Tokyo in 1956, with women competing from 1980. Judo has been included in the Olympics since 1964 (except 1968), and there are currently eight weight divisions. Women's judo was held as a demonstration sport at the 1988 Olympic Games.

OLYMPIC CHAMPIONS OF 1988

Men

Weight	Winner
Over 95 kg	Hitoshi Saito (Jap)
95 kg	Aurelio Miguel (Bra)
86 kg	Peter Seisenbacher (Aut)
78 kg	Waldemar Legien (Pol)
71 kg	Marc Alexandre (Fra)
65 kg	Lee Kyung-keun (SKo)
60 kg	Kim Jae-yup (SKo)

KARATE

Literally meaning 'empty hand' fighting, karate is based on techniques devised from the 6th-century Chinese art of Shaolin boxing (*Kempo*), and was developed by an unarmed populace in Okinawa as a weapon against Japanese forces c. 1500. Transmitted to Japan in the 1920s by Funakoshi Gichin, the sport was refined and organized with competitive rules.

There are five major styles in Japan: shotokan, wado-ryu, goju-ryu, shito-ryu and kyokushinkai, each placing different emphases on speed and power. The military form of taekwondo is the Korean martial art (see p. 659). Wu shu is a comprehensive term embracing all Chinese martial arts. Kung fu is one aspect of these arts popularized by the cinema. Many forms of the martial arts have gained devotees in Europe and the Americas.

LACROSSE

North American Indians played the ancestor of the sport *baggataway*, and a French clergyman, likening the curved stick to a bishop's crozier, called it *la crosse*. The French may also have named it after their game *Chouler à la crosse*, known in 1381. Certainly in its recognizable form the game had reached Europe by the 1830s, and was introduced into Britain in 1867.

The International Federation of Amateur Lacrosse (IFAL) was founded in 1928. The men's World Championships were held in 1967 and every four years from 1974, with the USA winning on each occasion to 1990, except against Canada in 1978. Lacrosse was played in the 1904 and 1908 Olympic Games, and as a demonstration sport in 1928, 1932 and 1948. The women's World Championships were held in 1969, 1974 and 1978, and a World Cup in 1982, 1986 and 1989, when the winners were the USA.

The game is 10-a-side (12-a-side for women at international level). Pitch dimensions: 100×64 m (100×70 yd). Ball weight in England 142 g (5 oz), circum-

ference 184–203·2 mm ($7\frac{1}{4}$–8 in), colour yellow; in USA weight 142–149 g (5–5$\frac{1}{4}$ oz), circumference 196·9–203·2 mm ($7\frac{3}{4}$–8 in), colour orange or white.

MODERN PENTATHLON AND BIATHLON

In the ancient Olympic Games, the pentathlon was the most prestigious event. It then consisted of discus, javelin, running, jumping and wrestling. The modern pentathlon, introduced into the Olympics in 1912, consists of riding (an 800 m course with 15 fences; riders do not choose their mounts); fencing (épée), shooting, swimming (300 m freestyle) and finally a cross-country run of 4000 m. Each event is held on a different day, with scaled points awarded for each activity.

The sport's governing body is *L'Union Internationale de Pentathlon Moderne et Biathlon*, the UIPMB. It was founded in 1948 as the UIPM, taking on the administration of biathlon in 1957 (see Biathlon). Hungary won the 1988 Olympic team title and provided the individual champion in János Martinek. The World Championships have been held annually for men from 1949 and for women from 1981.

MOTORCYCLE RACING

The earliest motorcycle race – which also included motorcars – was held at Sheen House, Richmond, Surrey, UK, in 1897 over a 1·6 km (1 mile) oval course. The first international race for motorcycles only was held in 1905. The *Fédération Internationale des Clubs Motocyclystes* (FICM) organized the 1905 event, but it has since been succeeded as the governing body by the *Fédération Internationale Motocycliste* (FIM).

The World Championships were started in 1949 by the FIM and competitors gain points from a series of grand prix races. Races are currently held for the following classes of bike: 50 cc, 125 cc, 250 cc, 500 cc and sidecars.

In road racing the Isle of Man TT races (Auto-Cycle Union Tourist Trophy), first held in 1907, are the most important series. The 60·72 km (37·73 miles) 'Mountain' course, with 264 corners and curves, has been in use since 1911.

In moto-cross, or scrambling, competitors race over rough country including steep climbs and drops, sharp turns, sand, mud and water.

MOTOR RACING

The first known race between automobiles was over 323 km (201 miles) in Wisconsin in 1878, but it is generally accepted that the first 'real' race was the Paris–Bordeaux–Paris run of 1178 km (732 miles) in 1895. Emile Levassor (Fra), the winner, averaged 24·15 kph (15·01 mph). The first closed circuit race was in Rhode Island (USA), 1896, while the oldest grand prix is the French, inaugurated in 1906.

Competition at the highest level, the Formula One, is over the series of grand prix races (each usually about 656 km/200 miles in length) held worldwide, points scored according to placing. The first World Championships were held in 1950, with the Manufacturers' Championships starting in 1958. Formula Two and Three Championships are held for cars with lesser cubic capacities.

Other forms of competition include the Le Mans circuit, a 24-hour race for touring cars; 'rallying' over public roads through several thousands miles; and drag racing, a test of sheer acceleration, most firmly established in the USA.

WORLD DRIVER CHAMPIONS

1950 Giuseppe Farina (Ita)
1951 Juan Manuel Fangio (Arg)
1952 Alberto Ascari (Ita)
1953 Alberto Ascari (Ita)
1954 Juan Manuel Fangio (Arg)
1955 Juan Manuel Fangio (Arg)
1956 Juan Manuel Fangio (Arg)
1957 Juan Manuel Fangio (Arg)
1958 Mike Hawthorn (UK)
1959 Jack Brabham (Aus)
1960 Jack Brabham (Aus)
1961 Phil Hill (USA)
1962 Graham Hill (UK)
1963 Jim Clark (UK)
1964 John Surtees (UK)
1965 Jim Clark (UK)
1966 Jack Brabham (Aus)
1967 Denny Hulme (NZ)
1968 Graham Hill (UK)
1969 Jackie Stewart (UK)
1970 Jochen Rindt (Aut)
1971 Jackie Stewart (UK)
1972 Emerson Fittipaldi (Bra)
1973 Jackie Stewart (UK)
1974 Emerson Fittipaldi (Bra)
1975 Niki Lauda (Aut)
1976 James Hunt (UK)
1977 Niki Lauda (Aut)
1978 Mario Andretti (USA)
1979 Jody Scheckter (SAf)
1980 Alan Jones (Aus)
1981 Nelson Piquet (Bra)
1982 Keke Rosberg (Fin)
1983 Nelson Piquet (Bra)
1984 Niki Lauda (Aut)
1985 Alain Prost (Fra)
1986 Alain Prost (Fra)
1987 Nelson Piquet (Bra)
1988 Ayrton Senna (Bra)
1989 Alain Prost (Fra)
1990 Ayrton Senna (Bra)

NETBALL

Modern netball – which grew out of basketball – was invented in the USA in 1891. The use of rings instead of baskets dates from 1897, and the term netball was coined in 1901 in England, where the sport was introduced in 1895. National Associations date from 1924 and 1926 in New Zealand and England, but the International Federation was not formed until 1960. The World Championships have been held every four years, since 1963, with the most recent winners being Australia in 1983 and New Zealand in 1987.

Netball is a no-contact, 7-a-side sport played almost exclusively by females. The court measures 30·48 × 15·24 m (100 × 50 ft); ball circumference 68–71 cm (27–28 in), weight 397–454 g (14–16 oz).

ORIENTEERING

'Orienteering' was first used to describe an event held in Oslo (Norway) in 1900, based on military exercises, but the founding of the modern sport is credited to a Swede Major Ernst Killander in 1918.

Basically a combination of cross-country running and map-reading, the sport is very popular in Scandi-

navia and has a keen band of followers in Britain. The International Orienteering Federation was founded in 1961, and the World Championships have been held since 1966, largely dominated by Sweden and Norway.

PELOTA VASCA (Jaï Alaï)

The sport, which originated in Italy as *longue paume*, was introduced into France in the 13th century. Said to be the fastest of all ball games, various forms of pelota are played according to national character or local custom throughout the world. 'Gloves' and 'chisteras' (curved frames attached to a glove) are of varying sizes, and courts can be open or enclosed with wide differences in dimensions and detail. The *Federacion Internacional de Pelota Vasca* has staged the World Championships every four years since 1952.

PÉTANQUE

Pétanque, or *boules*, originated in France from its parent game *jeu provençal*. Its origins go back over 2000 years, but it was not until 1945 that the *Fédération Française de Pétanque et Jeu Provençal* was formed, and subsequently the *Fédération Internationale* (FIPJP).

POLO

The game, played by teams of four on horseback, has its origins in Manipur state, India, c. 3100 BC, when it was played as *Sagol Kangjei*. It is also claimed to be of Persian origin, having been played as *Pulu* c. 525 BC. Polo was introduced to England from India in 1869, and now has a keen following in the USA and Argentina. Polo is played on the largest pitch of any game, with maximum length of 274 m (300 yds) and width of 182 m (200 yds) without boards, or 146 m (160 yds) with boards. Polo games are often contested on a handicap basis, each player being awarded a handicap measured in goals up to a maximum of ten, attained by the world's best players.

POWERBOAT RACING

Steamboat races date from 1827, petrol engines from 1865, but powerboat racing started in about 1900. International racing was largely established by the presentation of a Challenge Trophy in 1903, by Sir Alfred Harmsworth, which has been won most often by the USA. Races are also held for 'circuit' or shorter course competition, and offshore events began in 1958. Speed records are recognized in various categories by the various governing bodies.

RACKETBALL

Two versions of the game exist: (American) racquetball and (British) racketball. The original game was invented in 1949 by the American Joe Sobek when he sawed half the handle off a tennis racquet. In the USA the International Racquetball Association – founded in 1968 – changed its name in 1980 to the American Amateur Racquetball Association (AARA). The sport now has more than ten million players in the USA. The international governing body is the International Racquetball Federation (IRF). British racketball – introduced in 1976 – uses squash courts 9.75 m by 6.4 m (32 ft by 21 ft) and a less bouncy ball than that used in the larger American courts.

RACKETS

Rackets is a racket and ball game for two or four players, derived – as other forms of handball – from games played in the Middle Ages. In England it was often played against walls of buildings, especially those of the Fleet Prison, London, in the 18th century. An inmate, Robert Mackay, claimed the first world title in 1820. The World Championship, currently held by James Male (GB), is now determined on a challenge basis.

REAL TENNIS

Real tennis evolved from the game *jeu de paume* ('game of the palm') played in French monasteries in the 11th century, in which the hand, rather than a racket, was used. The long-handled racket was not invented until about 1500. The World Championship at real tennis is the oldest world championship of any sport, dating to approximately 1740. Today, real tennis is only played in five countries – England, Scotland, USA, France and Australia and the total number of courts in use throughout the world has dwindled to approximately 30.

ROLLER SKATING

The first roller skate was devised by Jean-Joseph Merlin of Belgium in 1760, but proved disastrous in demonstration. The present four-wheeled type was patented by New Yorker James L. Plimpton in 1863. Competition is along similar lines to ice skating – speed, figure and dance.

ROWING

A literary reference to rowing is made by the Roman poet Virgil in the *Aeneid* (published after his death in 19 BC). Regattas were held in Venice c. AD 300. The earliest established sculling race is the Doggett's Coat and Badge, first rowed in August 1716 from London Bridge to Chelsea on the River Thames, and still contested annually.

The governing body, the *Fédération Internationale de Sociétés d'Aviron*, was founded in 1892, and the first major international meeting, the European Championships, was held a year later.

Olympic Championships were first held in 1900 for men and in 1976 for women. Current events are held for: (men) single, double and coxless quadruple sculls, coxless and coxed pairs, coxless and coxed fours and eights; (women) single and double sculls, coxless pairs, coxless quadruple sculls, coxed fours and eights. With sculling, the sculler has a smaller oar in each hand rather than pulling one oar with both hands. In the 1992 Olympics, the women's coxed fours are to be replaced by the coxless fours.

The Oxford-Cambridge Boat Race was first held in 1829, from Hambledon Lock to Henley Bridge, and won by Oxford. The current course, used continuously since 1864, is from Putney to Mortlake and measures 6·779 km (4 miles 374 yd). In the 136 races to 1991 Cambridge have won 69 times, Oxford 67 and a dead heat was declared in 1877.

RUGBY LEAGUE

The game originated as a breakaway from rugby union on 29 August 1895, on account of the English governing body forbidding northern rugby clubs paying players, who thus lost Saturday wages. Three years later full professionalism came into being. In 1906 the major change from 15-a-side to 13 was made, and the title 'rugby league' was adopted in 1922.

Rugby league is played principally in Great Britain, Australia, New Zealand, France and Papua New Guinea. Major trophies in England are the Challenge Cup (instituted 1897), the League Championship (instituted 1907), the Premiership Trophy (instituted 1975) and the John Player Trophy (instituted 1972). Australia won the World Cup in 1988.

Dimensions: Pitch length maximum 100·58 m (110 yd), width maximum 68·58 m (75 yd). Ball length 27·3–29·2 cm ($10^{3}/4$–$11^{1}/2$ in), circumference at widest point 584–610 mm (23–24 in).

CHALLENGE CUP WINNERS (from 1980)

1980	Hull Kingston Rovers
1981	Widnes
1982	Hull
1983	Featherstone Rovers
1984	Widnes
1985	Wigan
1986	Castleford
1987	Halifax
1988–90	Wigan

RUGBY UNION

Rugby union was developed at Rugby School, England. A traditional yarn tells of William Webb Ellis illegally picking up the ball and running with it during a football game, although this may be apocryphal. Certainly the game was known to have been played at Cambridge University by 1839. The Rugby Football Union was formed on 27 January 1871.

The International Rugby Football Board was formed in 1890. Teams representing the British Isles have toured Australia, New Zealand and South Africa since 1888, although they were not composed of players from all the Home Countries until 1924, when the term 'British Lions' was first coined.

The International Championship – between England, Ireland, Scotland, and Wales – was first held in 1884, with France included from 1910. Now also known as the Five Nations tournament, the 'Grand Slam' – winning all four matches – is prized. The 'Triple Crown' is achieved when a Home Country side defeats the other three.

The first World Cup was contested by 16 national teams in Australia and New Zealand in 1987. In the final New Zealand beat France 29–9. The second World Cup will be in Britain in 1991, with the final at Twickenham.

The game is 15-a-side. Dimensions: pitch of maximum 68·58 m (75 yd) width, and 91·44 m (100 yd) goal lines. Ball length 27·9–28·5 cm ($10^{3}/4$– $11^{1}/2$ in) and weight 382–439 g ($13^{1}/2$–$15^{1}/2$ oz).

INTERNATIONAL CHAMPIONSHIP

Winners (outright/shared wins)

Wales (21/11)	1893, 1900, 1902, 1905, 1906*, 1908–9, 1911, 1920*, 1922, 1931, 1932*, 1936, 1939*, 1947*, 1950, 1952, 1954*–5*, 1956, 1964*, 1965–6, 1969, 1970*, 1971, 1973*, 1975–6, 1978–9, 1988*
England (19/9)	1883–4, 1886*, 1890*, 1892, 1910, 1912*, 1913–4, 1921, 1923–4, 1928, 1930, 1932*, 1934, 1937, 1939*, 1947*, 1953, 1954*, 1957–8, 1960*, 1963, 1973*, 1980, 1991

Scotland (13/8) 1886*, 1887, 1890*, 1891, 1895, 1901, 1903–4, 1907, 1920*, 1925, 1926*–7*, 1929, 1933, 1938, 1964*, 1973*, 1984, 1986*, 1990

Ireland (10/8) 1894, 1896, 1899, 1906*, 1912*, 1926*–7*, 1932*, 1935, 1939*, 1948–9, 1951, 1973*, 1974, 1982, 1983*, 1985

France (9/8) 1954*, 1955*, 1959*, 1960*, 1961–2, 1967–8, 1970*, 1973*, 1977, 1981, 1983*, 1986*, 1987, 1988*, 1989

* denotes shared win (there was a quintuple tie in 1973)

The championships of 1885, 1888–9, 1897–8 and 1972 were not completed for various reasons.

Grand Slam

A Five Nations country has defeated the other four countries during one season as follows:

Wales (8) 1908–9†, 1911, 1950, 1952, 1971, 1976, 1978

England (8) 1913–14, 1921, 1923–4, 1928, 1957, 1980, 1991

France (4) 1968, 1977, 1981, 1987

Scotland (3) 1925, 1984, 1990

Ireland (1) 1948

†not including France at that time

SHINTY

Shinty (from the Gaelic *sinteag*, a bound) goes back some 2000 years in Celtic history and legend, to the ancient game of *camanachd*, the sport of the curved stick. Having been introduced by the invading Irish Gaels it kept close associations with hurling but is essentially native to Scotland. The governing body, the Camanachd Association, was set up in 1893.

SHOOTING

The first recorded club for gun enthusiasts was the Lucerne Shooting Guild in Switzerland, dating from c. 1466, and the first known shooting match took place in Zürich in 1472. The National Rifle Association in Britain was founded in 1860. The Clay Pigeon Shooting Association developed from trap shooting in the USA. Skeet shooting is a form of clay pigeon designed to simulate a range of bird game and was invented in the USA in 1915. Pistol events, like air rifle, are judged by accuracy in scoring on a fixed target, from various distances and positions.

Shooting events for men were held in the first modern Olympic Games in 1896, but the 1984 Games included two mixed events (men and women) for the first time. Only two other Olympic sports have mixed competition, equestrianism and yachting.

At the 1988 Olympics there were seven men's, four women's and two mixed events.

SKIING

A well-preserved ski found in Sweden is thought to be 4500 years old, and various other evidence from Russia and Scandinavia chronicles primitive skiing, but the modern sport did not develop until 1843 with a competition in Tromsø, Norway. The first modern slalom was held at Mürren, Switzerland, in 1922 and the International Ski Federation (FIS) was founded in 1924.

Alpine skiing is racing on prepared slopes, against the clock, whereas Nordic skiing is either cross-country or ski jumping. The Alpine World Championships date from 1931, and Alpine skiing has been included in the Olympics since 1936 as a combination event. Events are now split into downhill, slalom, giant slalom, super giant slalom and Alpine combination (slalom and downhill). Nordic events were included in the Olympic Games from 1924 and comprise cross-country, ski jumping, and the combination of the two disciplines.

The world's best skiers contest a series of events each winter for the World Cups in Alpine skiing and the Nordic events of cross-country and ski jumping.

OVERALL ALPINE WORLD CUP CHAMPIONS
(from 1980)

Men

1980 Andreas Wenzel (Lie)
1981–3 Phil Mahre (USA)
1984 Pirmin Zurbriggen (Swi)
1985–6 Marc Girardelli (Lux)
1987 Pirmin Zurbriggen (Swi)
1988 Pirmin Zurbriggen (Swi)
1989 Marc Girardelli (Lux)
1990 Pirmin Zurbriggen (Swi)
1991 Marc Girardelli (Lux)

Women

1980 Hanni Wenzel (Lie)
1981 Marie-Thérèse Nadig (Swi)
1982 Erika Hess (Swi)
1983 Tamara McKinney (USA)
1984 Erika Hess (Swi)
1985 Michela Figini (Swi)
1986–7 Maria Walliser (Swi)
1988 Michela Figini (Swi)
1989 Vreni Schneider (Swi)
1990 Petra Kronberger (Aut)
1991 Petra Kronberger (Aut)

SNOOKER

Colonel Sir Neville Chamberlain concocted the game of snooker as a cross between 'black pool', 'pyramids' and billiards, in 1875 at Madras, India. The term 'snooker' came from the nickname given to first-year cadets at the Royal Military Academy, Woolwich. The game reached England in 1885, when the world billiards champion, John Roberts, who had been introduced to snooker in India, demonstrated the new sport.

Rules were codified in 1919, and the World Professional Championship was instituted in 1927. Since 1970 the professional game has been controlled by the World Professional Billiards and Snooker Association.

A full size table measures 3.66×1.87 m (12×6 ft); ball values are: red (1), yellow (2), green (3), brown (4), blue (5), pink (6) and black (7).

Recent world champions:

1980 Cliff Thorburn (Can)
1981 Steve Davis (Eng)
1982 Alex Higgins (NI)
1983 Steve Davis (Eng)
1984 Steve Davis (Eng)
1985 Dennis Taylor (NI)
1986 Joe Johnson (Eng)
1987 Steve Davis (Eng)
1988 Steve Davis (Eng)
1989 Steve Davis (Eng)
1990 Stephen Hendry (Sco)

SOFTBALL

Softball, the indoor derivative of baseball, was invented by George Hancock in Chicago, USA, in 1887, and rules were first codified in Minnesota in 1895. The name softball was not adopted until 1930. A 9-a-side game (except in the USA), softball is played in Canada, Japan, the Philippines, most of Latin America, New Zealand and Australia. The ball is as hard as a baseball, but as distinct from baseball must be pitched underarm and released below hip level. The pitching distance is 14 m (45 ft 11 in) for men, 11·11 m (36 ft 5½ in) for women and 18·3 m (60 ft) in between bases for both. 'Slow pitch' softball is a modern variation.

SPEEDWAY

Motorcycle racing on dust track surfaces has been traced back to 1902 in the USA, but the first 'short track' races were in Australia in 1923. Evolving in Britain in the 1920s, the National League was instituted in 1932. The first World Championships were held in September 1936 at Wembley (London) under the auspices of the *Fédération Internationale Motocycliste* (FIM). A team competition was inaugurated only as late as 1960. Each race is contested by four riders (six in Australia) over four laps; the bikes have no brakes, one gear and are limited to 500 cc.

SQUASH

Squash developed at Harrow School, England, in 1817 from a game used for practising rackets but with a softer, 'squashy' ball. The first national championship was held in the USA in 1907. The British Open Championships, for women and men were first contested in 1922 and 1930 respectively. However, the World Amateur Championships were introduced decades later in 1967 (after the foundation of the International Squash Rackets Federation that year). The first World Championships for both men and women followed in 1976.

Court dimensions: 9·75 m (31 ft 11¾ in) long and 6·40 m (21 ft) wide, with front wall height 4·75 m (15 ft 7 in) up to the boundary line. The 'tin' runs along the bottom of the front wall, above which the ball must be hit.

SURFING

Originating in Polynesia, the first reference to surfing on a board dates from 1779 in an account written in Hawaii. Revived in the early 20th century in Australia, hollow boards were introduced in 1929. The World Amateur Championships began in 1964.

SWIMMING

Competitive swimming dates from 36 BC in Japan, which was the first country to seriously adopt the sport – Emperor Goyozei decreed its introduction in schools. In Britain, organized competitive swimming was only introduced in 1837 when the National Swimming Society was formed. Australia led modern developments with an unofficial world 100 yd championship in 1858 at Melbourne.

The first widely used technique (possibly excepting the 'doggy paddle') was the breaststroke. From this developed the side-stroke, a similar action performed sideways, last used by an Olympic champion, Emil Rausch (of Germany), to win the 1904 one-mile event.

A style resembling the front crawl had been seen in various parts of the world by travellers in the mid-19th century. Backstroke developed as inverted breaststroke, which modified towards inverted crawl. Butterfly began as an exploitation of a loophole in the rules for breaststroke allowing the recovery of arms from the water, and was recognized as a separate stroke in 1952. The medley event, using all four strokes in turn, originated in the USA in the 1930s.

The world-governing body for swimming, diving, water polo and synchronized swimming is the *Fédération Internationale de Natation Amateur* (FINA), founded in 1908. The World Championships in swimming were first held in 1973, and are now held quadrennially.

Swimming has been an integral part of the Olympics since 1896, the first modern Olympic Games, with 100 m, 400 m, 1500 m and 100 m freestyle events for men. Women first competed in 1912. Diving was introduced in 1904 (1912 for women), and water polo in 1900.

Synchronized swimming, a form of water ballet, was first recognized internationally in 1952 and was included in the first World Championships in 1973. It appeared in the Olympics for the first time in 1984.

SWIMMING WORLD RECORDS

Men
50 m freestyle: 21·81 Tom Jager (USA) 1990
100 m freestyle: 48·42 Matt Biondi (USA) 1988
200 m freestyle: 1:46·69 Giorgio Lamberti (Ita) 1989
400 m freestyle: 3:46·95 Uwe Dassler (GDR) 1988
800 m freestyle: 7:50·64 Vladimir Salnikov (USSR) 1986
1500 m freestyle: 14:50·36 Jörg Hoffman (Ger) 1991
4 × 100 m freestyle: 3:16·53 USA 1988
(Chris Jacobs, Troy Dalbey, Tom Jager, Matt Biondi)
4 × 200 m freestyle: 7:12·51 USA 1988
(Troy Dalbey, Matt Cetlinski, Doug Gjertsen, Matt Biondi)
100 m backstroke: 54·51 David Berkoff (USA) 1988
200 m backstroke: 1:58·14 Igor Polyanskiy (USSR) 1985
100 m breaststroke: 1:01·45 Norbert Rosza (Hun) 1991
200 m breaststroke: 2:11·23 Mike Barrowman (USA) 1991
100 m butterfly: 52·84 Pablo Morales (USA) 1986
200 m butterfly: 1:55·69 Melim Stewart (USA) 1991
200 m individual medley: 1:59·36 Tamás Darnyi (Hun) 1991
400 m individual medley: 4:12·36 Tamás Darnyi (Hun) 1991
4 × 100 m medley: 3:36·93 USA 1988
(David Berkoff, Richard Schroeder, Matt Biondi, Chris Jacobs)

Women
50 m freestyle: 24·98 Yang Wenyi (Chn) 1988
100 m freestyle: 54·73 Kristin Otto (GDR) 1986
200 m freestyle: 1:57·55 Heike Friedrich (GDR) 1986
400 m freestyle: 4:03·85 Janet Evans (USA) 1988
800 m freestyle: 8:16·22 Janet Evans (USA) 1989
1500 m freestyle: 15:52·10 Janet Evans (USA) 1988
4 × 100 m freestyle: 3:40·57 GDR 1986
(Kristin Otto, Manuela Stellmach, Sabina Schulz, Heike Friedrich)
4 × 200 m freestyle: 7:55·47 GDR 1987
(Manuela Stellmach, Astrid Strauss, Anke Möhring, Heike Friedrich)

100 m backstroke: 1:00·59 Ines Kleber (GDR) 1984
200 m backstroke: 2:08·60 Betsy Mitchell (USA) 1986
100 m breaststroke: 1:07·91 Silke Hörner (GDR) 1987
200 m breaststroke: 2:26·71 Silke Hörner (GDR) 1988
100 m butterfly: 57·93 Mary T. Meagher (USA) 1981
200 m butterfly: 2:05·96 Mary T. Meagher (USA) 1981
200 m individual medley: 2:11·73 Ute Geweniger (GDR) 1981
400 m individual medley: 4:36·10 Petra Schneider (GDR) 1982
4 × 100 m medley: 4:03·69 GDR 1984 (Ina Kleber, Sylvia Gerasch, Ines Geissler, Birgit Meineke)

SWIMMING OLYMPIC RECORDS

Men

50 m freestyle: 22·14 Matt Biondi (USA) 1988
100 m freestyle: 48·63 Matt Biondi (USA) 1988
200 m freestyle: 1:47·25 Duncan Armstrong (Aus) 1988
400 m freestyle: 3:46·95 Uwe Dassler (GDR) 1988
1500 m freestyle: 14:58·27 Vladimir Salnikov (USSR) 1980
4 × 100 m freestyle: 3:16·53 (USA) 1988
4 × 200 m freestyle: 7:12·51 (USA) 1988
100 m backstroke: 54·51 David Berkoff (USA) 1988*
200 m backstroke: 1:58·99 Rick Carey (USA) 1984
100 m breaststroke: 1:01·65 Steven Lundquist (USA) 1984
200 m breaststroke: 2:13·34 Victor Davis (Can) 1984
100 m butterfly: 53·00 Anthony Nesty (Suriname) 1988
200 m butterfly: 1:56·94 Michael Gross (FRG) 1988
200 m individual medley: 2:00·17 Tamás Darnyi (Hun) 1988
400 m individual medley: 4:14·75 Tamás Darnyi (Hun) 1988
4 × 100 m medley: 3:36·93 (USA) 1988
* in heat

Women

50 m freestyle: 25·49 Kristin Otto (GDR) 1988
100 m freestyle: 54·79 Barbara Krause (GDR) 1980
200 m freestyle: 1:57·65 Heike Friedrich (GDR) 1988
400 m freestyle: 4:03·85 Janet Evans (USA) 1988
800 m freestyle: 8:20·20 Janet Evans (USA) 1988
4 × 100 m freestyle: 3:40·63 (GDR) 1988
100 m backstroke: 1:00·89 Kristin Otto (GDR) 1988
200 m backstroke: 2:09·29 Krisztina Egerszegi (Hun) 1988
100 m breaststroke: 1:07·95 Tania Dangalakova (Bul) 1988
200 m breaststroke: 2:26·71 Silke Hörner (GDR) 1988
100 m butterfly: 59·00 Kristin Otto (GDR) 1988
200 m butterfly: 2:06·90 Mary T. Meagher (USA) 1984
200 m individual medley: 2:12·64 Tracy Caulkins (USA) 1984
400 m individual medley: 4:36·29 Petra Schneider (GDR) 1980
4 × 100 m medley: 4:03·74 (GDR) 1988

EUROPEAN CHAMPIONSHIPS

First held in Budapest in 1926, and subsequently in 1927, 1931, 1934, 1938, 1947, at four-yearly intervals 1950–74, in 1977, and biennially from 1981.

1989 winners

50 m freestyle: Vladimir Tkachenko (USSR) 22·64
100 m freestyle: Giorgio Lamberti (Ita) 49·24
200 m freestyle: Giorgio Lamberti (Ita) 1:46·69
400 m freestyle: Artur Wojdat (Pol) 3:47·78
1500 m freestyle: Jörg Hoffmann (GDR) 15:01·52
4 × 100 m freestyle: Germany (W) 3:19·68
4 × 200 m freestyle: Italy 7:15·39

100 m backstroke: Martin Lopez-Zubero (Spa) 56·44
200 m backstroke: Stefano Battistelli (Ita) 1:59·96
100 m breaststroke: Adrian Moorhouse (UK) 1:01·71
200 m breaststroke: Nick Gillingham (UK) 2:12·90
100 m butterfly: Rafal Szukala (Pol) 54·47
200 m butterfly: Tamás Darnyi (Hun) 1:58·87
200 m individual medley: Tamás Darnyi (Hun) 2:01·03
400 m individual medley: Tamás Darnyi (Hun) 4:15·25
4 × 100 m medley relay: USSR 3:41·44
Springboard diving: Albin Killat (Germany (W))
1 m springboard diving Edwin Jongejans (Hol)
Highboard diving Georgiy Chogovadze (USSR)

Women

50 m freestyle: Catherine Plewinski (Fra) 25·63
100 m freestyle: Katrin Meissner (GDR) 55·38
200 m freestyle: Manuela Stellmach (GDR) 1:58·93
400 m freestyle: Anke Möhring (GDR) 4:05·84
800 m freestyle: Anke Möhring (GDR) 8:23·99
4 × 100 m freestyle relay: (GDR) 3:42·46
4 × 200 m freestyle relay: (GDR) 7:58·54
100 m backstroke: Kristin Otto (GDR) 1:01·86
200 m backstroke: Dagmar Hase (GDR) 2:12·46
100 m breaststroke: Silke Börnicke (GDR) 1:09·55
200 m breaststroke: Susanne Börnicke (GDR) 2:27·7
100 m butterfly: Catherine Plewinski (Fra) 59·08
200 m butterfly: Kathleen Nord (GDR) 2:09·33
200 m individual medley: Daniela Hunger (GDR) 2:13·2
400 m individual medley: Daniela Hunger (GDR) 4:41·82
4 × 100 m medley relay: (GDR) 4:07·40
Springboard diving: Marina Babkova (USSR)
1 m springboard diving: Irina Lachko (USSR)
Highboard diving: Ute Wetzig (GDR)
Synchronized (solo): Khristina Falasinidi (USSR)
Synchronized (duet): Karine Schuler and Marianne Aeschbacher (Fra)
Synchronized (team): France

TAEKWONDO

Taekwondo is a martial art developed over 20 centuries in Korea. All its activities are based on a defensive spirit and it was officially recognized as part of Korean tradition and culture in 1955. The sport has spread internationally and there are now an estimated 22 million practitioners in the 115 member-states of the World Taekwondo Federation. Taekwondo was a demonstration sport at the 1988 Olympic Games in Seoul and will be again in 1992.

TABLE TENNIS

The earliest evidence of a game resembling table tennis goes back to London sports goods manufacturers in the 1880s. Known as *gossima*, it was the introduction of the celluloid ball and the noise it made when it hit that brought the name 'ping pong' and the Ping Pong Association in 1902. Interest declined until the use of attached rubber mats to the wooden bats (allowing spin) in the early 1920s. The International Table Tennis Association was founded in 1926, and the World Championships have been held since 1927. The Swaythling and Corbillon Cups are held as world team championships, instituted in 1927 and 1934 for men and women respectively. China has been particularly dominant in recent years. Dimensions: ball diameter 37·2–38·2 mm (1·46–1·5 in), weight 2·4–2·53 g (0·08 oz), table length 2·74 m (9 ft), 1·525 m (5 ft) wide.

TENNIS

Lawn tennis evolved from the indoor game of real tennis (see p. 656) and 'field tennis' is mentioned in a 1793 magazine. Major Harry Gem founded the first club in Leamington Spa, Warwickshire (UK), in 1872. The All England Croquet Club added Lawn Tennis to their title in 1877 when they held their first Championships. The United States Lawn Tennis Association (now USLTA) was founded in 1881, the English association was founded in 1888. The International (Lawn) Tennis Federation was formed in Paris in March 1913.

The Wimbledon, or All England, Championships have been regarded since 1877 as the most important in the world, alongside the US, French and Australian Opens. Together these four make up the 'Grand Slam', the elusive distinction of holding all four titles at once. The US Open (instituted 1881) is now held at Flushing Meadows, New York, and the French at Roland Garros, Paris. The Australian Championships, now held at Flinders Park, Melbourne, were instituted in 1905.

Men and women today compete in various 'circuits' in the second richest sport in the world to golf. 'Grand prix' tournaments are scaled according to a standard, with points accumulated to decide world rankings. The international team competition for men is the Davis Cup, won most times by the USA (30), Australia (Australasia 1907–19; 26), and Great Britain (9).

DAVIS CUP WINNERS
(since 1983)
1983 Australia
1984–5 Sweden
1986 Australia
1987 Sweden
1988–9 Germany (W)
1990 USA

The women's international team competition for the Federation Cup has been held annually since 1963. The USA have a record 14 wins, including 1986 and 1989–90, with Australia achieving seven wins and Czechoslovakia five, including 1983–5 and 1988. The Wightman Cup was an annual USA–GB women's contest. Begun in 1923 the USA has won on 51 occasions to Great Britain's 10 (the last time being 1978). However, with the decline of British tennis standards, the decision was taken to suspend the event.

Tennis was reintroduced to the Olympic Games in 1988, when the winners were: men's singles, Miloslav Mecir (Cz); men's doubles, Ken Flach & Robert Seguso (USA); women's singles, Steffi Graf (W. Germany); women's doubles, Pam Shriver & Zina Garrison (USA). Tennis had last been held as an official sport in 1924, although it had been a demonstration sport in 1968 and 1984.

THE WIMBLEDON CHAMPIONSHIPS

Wimbledon, 'The All England Championships', dates back to 1877 when it comprised just one event, the men's singles. Women's singles and men's doubles were introduced in 1884, with women's doubles and mixed doubles becoming full Championship events in 1913.

Men's Singles (since 1947)
1947 Jack Kramer (USA)
1948 Bob Falkenburg (USA)
1949 Ted Schroeder (USA)
1950 Budge Patty (USA)
1951 Dick Savitt (USA)
1952 Frank Sedgman (Aus)
1953 Vic Seixas (USA)
1954 Jaroslav Drobny (Cz)
1955 Tony Trabert (USA)
1956 Lew Hoad (Aus)
1957 Lew Hoad (Aus)
1958 Ashley Cooper (Aus)
1959 Alex Olmedo (USA)
1960 Neale Fraser Aus)
1961 Rod Laver (Aus)
1962 Rod Laver (Aus)
1963 Chuck McKinley (USA)
1964 Roy Emerson (Aus)
1965 Roy Emerson (Aus)
1966 Manuel Santana (Spa)
1967 John Newcombe (Aus)
1968 Rod Laver (Aus)
1969 Rod Laver (Aus)
1970 John Newcombe (Aus)
1971 John Newcombe (Aus)
1972 Stan Smith (USA)
1973 Jan Kodes (Cz)
1974 Jimmy Connors (USA)
1975 Arthur Ashe (USA)
1976 Bjorn Borg (Swe)
1977 Bjorn Borg (Swe)
1978 Bjorn Borg (Swe)
1979 Bjorn Borg (Swe)
1980 Bjorn Borg (Swe)
1981 John McEnroe (USA)
1982 Jimmy Connors (USA)
1983 John McEnroe (USA)
1984 John McEnroe (USA)
1985 Boris Becker (Germany (W))
1986 Boris Becker (Germany (W))
1987 Pat Cash (Aus)
1988 Stefan Edberg (Swe)
1989 Boris Becker (Germany (W))
1990 Stefan Edberg (Swe)

Women's Singles (since 1947)
1947 Margaret Osborne (USA)
1948 Louise Brough (USA)
1949 Louise Brough (USA)
1950 Louise Brough (USA)
1951 Doris Hart (USA)
1952 Maureen Connolly (USA)
1953 Maureen Connolly (USA)
1954 Maureen Connolly (USA)
1955 Louise Brough (USA)
1956 Shirley Fry (USA)
1957 Althea Gibson (USA)
1958 Althea Gibson (USA)
1959 Maria Bueno (Bra)
1960 Maria Bueno (Bra)
1961 Angela Mortimer (UK)
1962 Karen Susman (USA)
1963 Margaret Smith (Aus)
1964 Maria Bueno (Bra)
1965 Margaret Smith (Aus)
1966 Billie Jean King née Moffitt (USA)
1967 Billie Jean King (USA)
1968 Billie Jean King (USA)
1969 Ann Jones (UK)
1970 Margaret Smith-Court (Aus)
1971 Evonne Goolagong (Aus)
1972 Billie Jean King (USA)
1973 Billie Jean King (USA)
1974 Chris Evert (USA)
1975 Billie Jean King (USA)
1976 Christ Evert (USA)

1977 Virginia Wade (UK)
1978 Martina Navratilova (Cz)
1979 Martina Navratilova (Cz)
1980 Evonne Goolagong-Cawley (Aus)
1981 Chris Evert-Lloyd (USA)
1982 Martina Navratilova (USA)
1983 Martina Navratilova (USA)
1984 Martina Navratilova (USA)
1985 Martina Navratilova (USA)
1986 Martina Navratilova (USA)
1987 Martina Navratilova (USA)
1988 Steffi Graf (Germany (W))
1989 Steffi Graf (Germany (W))
1990 Martina Navratilova (USA)

Women's Doubles
1947 Pat Todd & Doris Hart (USA)
1948 Louise Brough & Margaret Osborne-du Pont (USA)
1949 Louise Brough & Margaret Osborne-du Pont (USA)
1950 Louise Brough & Margaret Osborne-du Pont (USA)
1951 Doris Hart & Shirley Fry (USA)
1952 Doris Hart & Shirley Fry (USA)
1953 Doris Hart & Shirley Fry (USA)
1954 Louise Brough & Margaret Osborne-du Pont (USA)
1955 Angela Mortimer & Anne Shilcock (UK)
1956 Angela Buxton (UK) & Althea Gibson (USA)
1957 Althea Gibson & Darlene Hard (USA)
1958 Maria Bueno (Bra) & Althea Gibson (USA)
1959 Jean Arth & Darlene Hard (USA)
1960 Maria Bueno (Bra) & Darlene Hard (USA)
1961 Karen Hantze & Billie Jean Moffitt (USA)
1962 Karen Hantze-Susman & Billie Jean Moffitt (USA)
1963 Maria Bueno (Bra) & Darlene Hard (USA)
1964 Margaret Smith & Lesley Turner (Aus)
1965 Maria Bueno (Bra) & Billie Jean Moffitt (USA)
1966 Maria Bueno (Bra) & Nancy Richey (USA)
1967 Rosemary Casals & Billie Jean King née Moffitt (USA)
1968 Billie Jean King & Rosemary Casals (USA)
1969 Margaret Smith-Court & Judy Tegart (Aus)
1970 Billie Jean King & Rosemary Casals (USA)
1972 Billie Jean King & Rosemary Casals (USA)
1972 Billie Jean King (USA) & Betty Stove (Hol)
1973 Billie Jean King & Rosemary Casals (USA)
1974 Evonne Goolagong (Aus) & Peggy Michel (USA)
1975 Ann Kiyomura (USA) & Kazuko Sawamatsu (Jap)
1976 Chris Evert (USA) & Martina Navratilova (Cz)
1977 Helen Cawley (Aus) & Joanne Russell (USA)
1978 Kerry Reid & Wendy Turnbull (Aus)
1979 Billie Jean King (USA) & Martina Navratilova (Cz)
1980 Kathy Jordan & Anne Smith (USA)
1981 Martina Navratilova (Cz) & Pam Shriver (USA)
1982 Martina Navratilova & Pam Shriver (USA)
1983 Martina Navratilova & Pam Shriver (USA)
1984 Martina Navratilova & Pam Shriver (USA)
1985 Kathy Jordan (USA) & Liz Smylie (Aus)
1986 Martina Navratilova & Pam Shriver (USA)
1987 Claudia Kohde-Kilsch (Germany (W)) & Helena Sukova (Cz)
1988 Steffi Graf (Germany (W)) & Gabriella Sabatini (Arg)
1989–90 Jana Novotná and Helena Suková (Cz)

Men's Doubles
1947 Bob Falkenburg & Jack Kramer (USA)

1948 John Bromwich & Frank Sedgman (Aus)
1949 Ricardo Gonzales & Frank Parker (USA)
1950 John Bromwich & Adrian Quist (Aus)
1951 Ken McGregor & Frank Sedgman (Aus)
1952 Ken McGregor & Frank Sedgman (Aus)
1953 Lew Hoad & Ken Rosewall (Aus)
1954 Rex Hartwig & Mervyn Rose (Aus)
1955 Rex Hartwig & Lew Hoad (Aus)
1956 Lew Hoad & Ken Rosewall (Aus)
1957 Budge Patty & Gardnar Mulloy (USA)
1958 Sven Davidson & Ulf Schmidt (Swe)
1959 Roy Emerson & Neale Fraser (Aus)
1960 Rafael Osuna (Mex) & Dennis Ralston (USA)
1961 Roy Emerson & Neale Fraser (Aus)
1962 Bob Hewitt & Fred Stolle (Aus)
1963 Rafael Osuna & Antonio Palafox (Mex)
1964 Bob Hewitt & Fred Stolle (Aus)
1965 John Newcombe & Tony Roche (Aus)
1966 Ken Fletcher & John Newcombe (Aus)
1967 Bob Hewitt & Frew McMillan (SAf)
1968 John Newcombe & Tony Roche (Aus)
1969 John Newcombe & Tony Roche (Aus)
1970 John Newcombe & Tony Roche (Aus)
1971 Roy Emerson & Rod Laver (Aus)
1972 Bob Hewitt & Frew McMillan (SAf)
1973 Jimmy Connors (USA) & Ilie Nastase (Rom)
1974 John Newcombe & Tony Roche (Aus)
1975 Vitas Gerulaitis & Sandy Mayer (USA)
1976 Brian Gottfried (USA) & Raul Ramirez (Mex)
1977 Ross Case & Geoff Masters (Aus)
1978 Bob Hewitt & Frew McMillan (SAf)
1979 John McEnroe & Peter Fleming (USA)
1980 Peter McNamara & Paul McNamee (Aus)
1981 John McEnroe & Peter Fleming (USA)
1982 Peter McNamara & Paul McNamee (Aus)
1983 John McEnroe & Peter Fleming (USA)
1984 John McEnroe & Peter Fleming (USA)
1985 Balazs Taroczy (Hun) & Heinz Gunthardt (Switz)
1986 Joachim Nystrom & Mats Wilander (Swe)
1987 Ken Flach & Robert Seguso (USA)
1988 Ken Flach & Robert Seguso (USA)
1989 John Fitzgerald (Aus) and Anders Järryd (Swe)
1990 Rick Leach and Jim Pugh (USA)

Mixed Doubles
1947 Louise Brough (USA) & John Bromwich (Aus)
1948 Louise Brough (USA) & John Bromwich (Aus)
1949 Sheila Summers & Eric Sturgess (SAf)
1950 Louise Brough (USA) & Eric Sturgess (SAf)
1951 Doris Hart (USA) & Frank Sedgman (Aus)
1952 Doris Hart (USA) & Frank Sedgman (Aus)
1953 Doris Hart & Vic Seixas (USA)
1954 Doris Hart & Vic Seixas (USA)
1955 Doris Hart & Vic Seixas (USA)
1956 Shirley Fry & Vic Seixas (USA)
1957 Darlene Hard (USA) & Mervyn Rose (Aus)
1958 Lorraine Coghlan & Bob Howe (Aus)
1959 Darlene Hard (USA) & Rod Laver (Aus)
1960 Darlene Hard (USA) & Rod Laver (Aus)
1961 Lesley Turner & Fred Stolle (Aus)
1962 Margaret Osborne-du Pont (USA) & Neale Fraser (Aus)
1963 Margaret Smith & Ken Fletcher (Aus)
1964 Lesley Turner & Fred Stolle (Aus)
1965 Margaret Smith & Ken Fletcher (Aus)
1966 Margaret Smith & Ken Fletcher (Aus)
1967 Billie Jean King (USA) & Owen Davidson (Aus)
1968 Margaret Smith-Court & Ken Fletcher (Aus)
1969 Ann Jones (UK) & Fred Stolle (Aus)
1970 Rosemary Casals (USA) & Ilie Nastase (Rom)
1971 Billie Jean King (USA) & Owen Davidson (Aus)

1972 Rosemary Casals (USA) & Ilie Nastase (Rom)
1973 Billie Jean King (USA) & Owen Davidson (Aus)
1974 Billie Jean King (USA) & Owen Davidson (Aus)
1975 Margaret Smith-Court (Aus) & Marty Riessen (USA)
1976 Françoise Durr (Fra) & Tony Roche (Aus)
1977 Greer Stevens & Bob Hewitt (SAf)
1978 Betty Stove (Hol) & Frew McMillan (SAf)
1979 Greer Stevens & Bob Hewitt (SAf)
1980 Tracey Austin & John Austin (USA)
1981 Betty Stove (Hol) & Frew McMillan (SAf)
1982 Anne Smith (USA) & Kevin Curren (SAf)
1983 Wendy Turnbull (Aus) & John Lloyd (UK)
1984 Wendy Turnbull (Aus) & John Lloyd (UK)
1985 Martina Navratilova (USA) & Paul McNamee (Aus)
1986 Kathy Jordan & Ken Flach (USA)
1987 Jo Durie & Jeremy Bates (UK)
1988 Zina Garrison & Sherwood Stewart (USA)
1989 Jana Novotná (Cz) & Jim Pugh (USA)
1990 Zina Garrison & Rick Leach (USA)

TRAMPOLINING

Equipment similar to today's trampoline was used by a show business group, 'The Walloons', just prior to World War I. The word originates from the Spanish *trampolin*, a springboard, and indeed springboards date to circus acrobats of the Middle Ages. The birth of the sport follows the invention of the prototype 'T' trampoline by the American George Nissen in 1936. The World Championships, administered by the International Trampolining Association, were instituted in 1964 and held biennially since 1968.

VOLLEYBALL

Although an Italian game *pallone*, similar to volleyball, was played in the 16th century, the modern game was invented as *minnonette* in 1895 by William Morgan at Massachusetts, USA, as a game for those who found basketball too strenuous. The name volleyball came a year later. The game spread rapidly worldwide and reached Britain in 1914. The first international tournament was the inaugural European Championship in 1948, the year after the founding of the International Volleyball Federation.

Although proposed for the 1924 Games by the USA, volleyball was not included in the Olympics until 1964. The USA won the 1984 and 1988 men's titles as well as the 1986 world title, and the USSR won the 1988 Olympic title for women, after China had won the 1984 Olympic and 1986 world titles. The USSR also holds the 1990 women's world title.

Court dimensions are 18 × 9 m (89 ft × 29 ft 6⅜ in); ball circumference 65–67 cm (25½–26½ in), 250–260 g (8·85–9·9 oz) in weight. Net height is 2·43 m (7 ft 11¾ in) for men and 2·24 m (7 ft 4¼ in) for women.

WALKING

Walking races have been included in the Olympic events since 1906 but walking matches have been known since 1859. Walking as a sport is defined as 'progression by steps so that unbroken contact with the ground is maintained'. Road walking has become more prevalent than track walking, and the Olympic distances are currently 20 km and 50 km.

WATER SKIING

Water skiing as we now know it was pioneered by Ralph Samuelson (USA) on Lake Pepin, Minnesota, in 1922. Having tried and failed with snow skis, he gave exhibitions with pine board skis culminating in the first jump, off a greased ramp, in 1925. The *Union Internationale de Ski Nautique* was set up in July 1946 and the British Water Ski Federation was formed in 1954.

Competitively, the sport is divided into trick skiing, slalom and ski jumping. (Trick skiing, performed at lower speeds, involves gymnastic feats rewarded according to difficulty.) The World Championships, begun in 1947 and held biennially, include an overall title, in which the USA have figured prominently in recent years, both for men and women.

Skiing barefoot brought a new element to the sport and competitions are held for straight speed records.

WEIGHTLIFTING

In China during the Zhou dynasty, which ended in 256 BC, weightlifting became a compulsory military test. Competitions for lifting weights of stone were held in the ancient Olympic Games. The amateur sport, however, is of modern vintage with competitions dating from c. 1850, and the first championships termed 'world' from 1891. The International Weightlifting Federation was established in 1920 in Estonia.

Weightlifting was included in the first modern Olympics in 1896, and then from 1920. In 1988 there were ten weight divisions, from up to 52 kg (115 lbs) to over 110 kg (243 lbs). Competition is decided by the aggregate of two forms of lifting, the snatch and the clean and jerk. A third form, the press, was dropped in 1976 because of the difficulty in judging it. Eastern European countries, especially the USSR and Bulgaria, have dominated the sport in which world records have, in recent years, been broken more frequently than in any other. Women's weightlifting world championships were held in 1987.

Powerlifting involves different techniques which perhaps have greater emphasis on sheer strength rather than technique. The three basic lifts are the squat (or deep knee bend), bench press and dead lift. The International Powerlifting Federation was founded in 1972, with the USA recently dominant with American world record holders in nine of the 11 weight divisions for men stretching to 125 + kg (276 + lbs) and seven of the 10 women's weight divisions to 90 + kg (198 + lbs).

WRESTLING

One of the oldest sports in the world, organized wrestling may date to c. 2750–2600 BC. It was the most popular sport in the ancient Olympic Games, and victors were recorded from 708 BC. Wrestling developed in varying forms in different countries, with the classical Greco-Roman style popular in Europe, and free style more to the liking of countries in the East and the Americas. The main distinction is that in Greco-Roman the wrestler cannot seize his opponent below the hips nor grip with the legs. The International Amateur Wrestling Federation (FILA) also recognizes sambo wrestling, akin to judo and popular in the USSR. FILA was founded in 1912, although the sport was in the first modern Olympics in 1896. There are currently ten weight divisions in both free style and Greco-Roman events at the Games.

Sumo wrestling is a traditional form in Japan dating

to 23 BC. Conducted with ceremony and mysticism, weight and bulk are vital since the object is to force the opponent out of the circular ring, using any hold.

YACHTING

Yachting dates to the race for a £100 wager between Charles II and his brother James, Duke of York, on the Thames in 1661 from Greenwich to Gravesend and back. The first recorded regatta was held in 1720 by the Cork Harbour Water Club (later Royal Cork Yacht Club), the oldest yacht club, but the sport did not prosper until the seas became safe after the Napoleonic Wars in 1815. That year the Yacht Club (later the Royal Yacht Squadron) was formed and organized races at Cowes, Isle of Wight, the beginning of modern yacht racing. The International Yacht Racing Union (IYRU) was established in 1907.

There were seven classes of boat at the 1988 Olympic Games, one of which, the 470, had separate competitions for men and women. Other major competitions include the Admiral's Cup – a biennial inter-nation, Channel and inshore race from Cowes to Fastnet Rock, Ireland, and back to Plymouth – and the quadrennial Whitbread Round the World Race, instituted in 1973. The America's Cup was originally won as an outright prize by the schooner *America* on 22 August 1851 at Cowes and later offered by the New York Yacht Club as a challenge trophy. Since 1870 the Cup has been challenged by the UK in 16 contests, by Canada in two, Australia eight and New Zealand one, but the USA were undefeated until 1983, when *Australia II* defeated the American boat *Liberty*. However Denis Conner in *Stars & Stripes* regained the Cup over *Kookaburra III* (Australia) in 1987 and defended it against New Zealand in 1988.

THE OLYMPIC GAMES

Celebration of the Modern Olympic Games

	Year	Venue	Date	Countries	Competitors Male	Female
I	1896	Athens, Greece	6–15 Apr	13	311	–
II	1900	Paris, France	20 May–28 Oct	22	1319	11
III	1904	St Louis, USA	1 July–23 Nov	13[1]	617	8
*	1906	Athens, Greece	22 Apr–2 May	20	877	7
IV	1908	London, England	27 Apr–31 Oct	22	2013	43
V	1912	Stockholm, Sweden	5 May–22 July	28	2491	55
VI	1916	Berlin, Germany	Not held due to war	–	–	–
VII	1920	Antwerp, Belgium	20 Apr–12 Sept	29	2618	74
VIII	1924	Paris, France	4 May–27 July	44	2956	136
IX	1928	Amsterdam, Netherlands	17 May–12 Aug	46	2724	290
X	1932	Los Angeles, USA	30 July–14 Aug	37	1281	127
XI	1936	Berlin, Germany	1–16 Aug	49	3738	328
XII	1940	Tokyo, then Helsinki	Not held due to war	–	–	–
XIII	1944	London, England	Not held due to war	–	–	–
XIV	1948	London, England	29 July–14 Aug	59	3714	385
XV	1952	Helsinki, Finland	19 July–3 Aug	69	4407	518
XVI	1956[2]	Melbourne, Australia	22 Nov–8 Dec	67	2958	384
XVII	1960	Rome, Italy	25 Aug–11 Sept	83	4738	610
XVIII	1964	Tokyo, Japan	10–24 Oct	93	4457	683
XIX	1968	Mexico City, Mexico	12–27 Oct	112	4749	781
XX	1972	Munich, Germany	26 Aug–10 Sept	122	6086	1070
XXI	1976	Montreal, Canada	17 July–1 Aug	92	4834	1251
XXII	1980	Moscow, USSR	19 July–3 Aug	81	4238	1088
XXIII	1984	Los Angeles, USA	28 July–12 Aug	140	5458	1620
XXIV	1988	Seoul, South Korea	20 Sept–5 Oct	159	6279	2186
XXV	1992	Barcelona, Spain	25 July–8 Aug			
XXVI	1996	Atlanta, USA	20 July–4 Aug			

* This celebration to mark the tenth anniversary of the Modern Games was officially intercalated but is not numbered.
[1] Including newly discovered French national.
[2] The equestrian events were held in Stockholm, Sweden, 10–17 June with 158 competitors from 29 countries.

The ancient Olympic Games were staged every four years at Olympia, 120 miles west of Athens. The earliest celebration of which there is a certain record is that of July 776 BC, from which all subsequent Games are dated. However, earlier Games were certainly held, perhaps dating back to 1370 BC. The early Games had considerable religious significance. The Games grew in size and importance to the height of their fame in the 5th and 4th centuries BC. Events

included running, jumping, wrestling, throwing the discus, boxing and chariot racing. As well as being sporting contests, the Olympics were great artistic festivals upholding the Greek ideal of perfection of mind and body. Winners were awarded a branch of wild olive, the Greeks' sacred tree.

The final Olympic Games of the ancient era were held in AD 393 before the Roman Emperor, Theodosius I, decreed the prohibition of the Games, which were not favoured by the early Christians and which were then long past their great days.

The first modern Games, in Athens in 1896, were at the instigation of Pierre de Fredi, Baron de Coubertin (1863–1937). A far cry from today's huge organization, just 311 competitors (from 13 countries) took part, of whom 230 were from Greece and others were foreign tourists. By contrast, 159 countries were represented by a total of 8465 athletes at the 1988 Games in Seoul, Korea.

Celebrations of the Winter Games

	Year	Venue	Date	Countries	Competitors Male	Female
I*	1924	Chamonix, France	25 Jan–4 Feb	16	281	13
II	1928	St Moritz, Switzerland	11–19 Feb	25	468	27
III	1932	Lake Placid, USA	4–15 Feb	17	274	32
IV	1936	Garmisch-Partenkirchen, Germ.	6–16 Feb	28	675	80
V	1948	St Moritz, Switzerland	30 Jan–8 Feb	28	636	77
VI	1952	Oslo, Norway	14–25 Feb	22	623	109
VII	1956	Cortina d'Ampezzo, Italy	26 Jan–5 Feb	32	687	132
VIII	1960	Squaw Valley, USA	18–28 Feb	30	521	144
IX	1964	Innsbruck, Austria	29 Jan–9 Feb	36	893	200
X	1968	Grenoble, France	6–18 Feb	37	1065	228
XI	1972	Sapporo, Japan	3–13 Feb	35	1015	217
XII	1976	Innsbruck, Austria	4–15 Feb	37	900	228
XIII	1980	Lake Placid, USA	13–24 Feb	37	833	234
XIV	1984	Sarajevo, Yugoslavia	7–19 Feb	49	1287	223
XV	1988	Calgary, Canada	23 Feb–6 Mar	57	1226	336
XVI	1992	Albertville, France				
XVII	1994	Lillehammer, Norway				

* There were Winter Games events included in the Summer Games of 1908 (London) and 1920 (Antwerp) which attracted six countries, 14 males and seven females for the first, and 10 countries, 73 males and 12 females for the latter.

Table of Olympic medal winners – Summer Games, 1896–1988

		Gold	Silver	Bronze	Total
1.	USA	746	560	475	1781
2.	USSR	395	323	299	1017
3.	Great Britain	174	223	207	604
4.	Germany[1]	157	207	207	571
5.	France	153	167	177	497
6.	Sweden	131	139	169	439
7.	GDR[2]	153	129	127	409
8.	Italy	147	121	124	392
9.	Hungary	124	112	136	372
10.	Finland	97	75	110	282
11.	Japan	87	75	82	244
12.	Australia	71	67	87	225
13.	Romania	55	64	82	201
14.	Poland	40	56	95	191
15.	Canada	39	62	73	174
16.	Switzerland	40	66	57	163
17.	Netherlands	43	47	63	153
18.	Bulgaria	37	62	52	151
19.	Denmark	33	58	53	144
20.	Czechoslovakia	45	48	49	142
21.	Belgium	35	48	42	125
22.	Norway	42	33	33	108
23.	Greece	22	39	39	100
24.	Yugoslavia	26	29	28	83
25.	Austria	19	26	34	79
26.	South Korea	19	22	29	70
27.	China	20	19	21	60
28.	Cuba	23	21	15	59
29.	New Zealand	26	6	23	55
30.	South Africa[3]	16	15	21	52
31.	Turkey	24	13	10	47
32.	Argentina	13	18	13	44
33.	Mexico	9	12	18	39
34.	Brazil	7	9	20	36
35.	Kenya	11	9	11	31
36.	Iran	4	11	15	30
37.	Spain	4	12	8	24
38.	Jamaica	4	10	8	22
39.	Estonia[4]	6	6	9	21
40.	Egypt	6	6	6	18
41.	India	8	3	3	14
42.	Ireland	4	4	5	13
43.	Portugal	2	4	7	13
44.	North Korea[5]	2	5	5	12
45.	Mongolia	0	5	6	11
46.	Ethiopia	5	1	4	10
47.	Pakistan	3	3	3	9
48.	Uruguay	2	1	6	9
49.	Venezuela	1	2	5	8
50.	Chile	0	6	2	8
51.	Trinidad	1	2	4	7
52.	Philippines	0	1	6	7
53.	Morocco	3	1	2	6
54.	Uganda	1	3	1	5
55.	Tunisia	1	2	2	5
56.	Colombia	0	2	3	5
57.	Lebanon	0	2	2	4
=58.	Puerto Rico	0	1	3	4
=58.	Nigeria	0	1	3	4
60.	Peru	1	2	0	3
61.	Latvia[4]	0	2	1	3
=62.	Taipei (Taiwan)	0	1	2	3
=62.	Ghana	0	1	2	3
=62.	Thailand	0	1	2	3
65.	Luxembourg	1	1	0	2
66.	Bahamas	1	0	1	2
67.	Tanzania	0	2	0	2
=68.	Cameroun	0	1	1	2
=68.	Haiti	0	1	1	2
=68.	Iceland	0	1	1	2
=71.	Algeria	0	0	2	2
=71.	Panama	0	0	2	2
=73.	Zimbabwe	1	0	0	1
=73.	Suriname	1	0	0	1

		Gold	Silver	Bronze	Total
=75.	Ivory Coast	0	1	0	1
=75.	Singapore	0	1	0	1
=75.	Sri Lanka	0	1	0	1
=75.	Syria	0	1	0	1
=75.	Costa Rica	0	1	0	1
=75.	Indonesia	0	1	0	1
=75.	Netherlands Antilles	0	1	0	1
=75.	Senegal	0	1	0	1
=75.	Virgin Islands	0	1	0	1
=84.	Bermuda	0	0	1	1
=84.	Dominican Rep.	0	0	1	1
=84.	Guyana	0	0	1	1
=84.	Iraq	0	0	1	1
=84.	Niger	0	0	1	1
=84.	Zambia	0	0	1	1
=84.	Djibouti	0	0	1	1

[1] Germany 1896–1964 and from 1992, West Germany 1968–88.
[2] GDR, East Germany, 1968–88.
[3] South Africa, up to 1960.
[4] Estonia and Latvia, up to 1936.
[5] North Korea, from 1964.

Table of Olympic medal winners – Winter Games, 1924–88

		Gold	Silver	Bronze	Total
1.	USSR	79	57	59	195
2.	Norway	54	60	54	168
3.	USA	42	47	34	123
4.	GDR[1]	39	36	35	110
5.	Finland	33	43	34	110
6.	Austria	28	38	32	98
7.	Sweden	36	25	31	92
8.	Germany[2]	26	26	23	75
9.	Switzerland	23	25	25	73
10.	Canada	14	13	17	44
11.	Netherlands	13	17	12	42
12.	France	13	10	16	39
13.	Italy	14	10	9	33
14.	Czechoslovakia	2	8	13	23
15.	Great Britain	7	4	10	21
16.	Liechtenstein	2	2	5	9
17.	Japan	1	4	2	7
18.	Hungary	0	2	4	6
=19.	Belgium	1	1	2	4
=19.	Poland	1	1	2	4
21.	Yugoslavia	0	3	1	4
22.	Spain	1	0	0	1
23.	North Korea[3]	0	1	0	1
=24.	Bulgaria	0	0	1	1
=24.	Romania	0	0	1	1

Totals include all first, second and third places, including those events not on the current schedule.
[1] GDR, East Germany, 1968–88.
[2] Germany, 1924–64 and from 1992, West Germany, 1968–88.
[3] From 1964.

MISCELLANEOUS GAMES

ALL AFRICAN GAMES

The All African Games are multi-sport competitions open to athletes from African nations. The Games were held at irregular intervals between 1965 and 1987. Since 1987 they have been held every four years.

1965	Brazzaville, Congo
1973	Lagos, Nigeria
1978	Algiers, Algeria
1987	Nairobi, Kenya
1991	Cairo, Egypt
1995	Harare, Zimbabwe

ASIAN GAMES

First held in 1951, the Asian Games are multi-sport competitions open to athletes from Asian nations. Since 1954 the Games have been held every four years.

1951	New Delhi, India
1954	Manila, Philippines
1958	Tokyo, Japan
1962	Djakarta, Indonesia
1966	Bangkok, Thailand
1970	Bangkok, Thailand
1974	Tehran, Iran
1978	Bangkok, Thailand
1982	New Delhi, India
1986	Seoul, South Korea
1990	Beijing (Peking), China

THE COMMONWEALTH GAMES

The Commonwealth Games are multi-sport competitions, held every four years, and contested by representatives of the nations of the Commonwealth. They were first staged as the British Empire Games in 1930, when 11 nations competed. The Games became the British Empire and Commonwealth Games in 1954, and the British Commonwealth Games in 1970, although in practice the word 'British' has been dropped from the title.

England, Northern Ireland, Scotland, Wales, the Isle of Man, Guernsey and Jersey are represented separately in the Commonwealth Games.

1930	Hamilton, Canada
1934	London, England
1938	Sydney, Australia
1950	Auckland, New Zealand
1954	Vancouver, Canada
1958	Cardiff, Wales
1962	Perth, Australia
1966	Kingston, Jamaica
1970	Edinburgh, Scotland
1974	Christchurch, New Zealand
1978	Edmonton, Canada
1982	Brisbane, Australia
1986	Edinburgh, Scotland
1990	Auckland, New Zealand
1994	Victoria, Canada

PAN-AMERICAN GAMES

The Pan-American Games are multi-sport competitions open to athletes from North, Central and South American nations and the island nations of the Caribbean. They have been held every four years since 1951.

1951	Buenos Aires, Argentina
1955	Mexico City, Mexico
1959	Chicago, USA
1963	São Paulo, Brazil
1967	Winnipeg, Canada
1971	Cali, Colombia
1975	Mexico City, Mexico
1979	San Juan, Puerto Rico
1983	Caracas, Venezuela
1987	Indianapolis, USA
1991	Havana, Cuba

UNITED KINGDOM

PHYSICAL AND POLITICAL GEOGRAPHY

Various names are used for the islands geographically known as the British Isles. Geographical, political, legal and popular usages differ, making definition necessary.

THE BRITISH ISLES
The British Isles is a convenient but purely *geographical* term to describe that group of islands lying off the northwest coast of Europe, comprising principally the island of Great Britain and the island of Ireland. The British Isles comprises four political units: the United Kingdom of Great Britain and Northern Ireland; the Republic of Ireland; the Crown dependency of the Isle of Man and – by convention and for convenience – the Crown dependencies of the Channel Islands.
Area: 314 798 km² (121 544 miles²).

THE UNITED KINGDOM (of Great Britain and Northern Ireland)
The term United Kingdom first came into use officially on 1 Jan 1801. Initially it referred to Great Britain and the whole island of Ireland. With the establishment of the constitution of the Irish Free State as a dominion on 6 Dec 1922, the term 'United Kingdom of Great Britain and Ireland' became inappropriate, and in May 1927 the Westminster Parliament adopted as its style 'Parliament of the United Kingdom of Great Britain and Northern Ireland'. The sovereign did not adopt the new style until 29 May 1953 – Ireland having ceased to be a dominion within the Commonwealth on 18 April 1949.
Area: 244 103 km² (94 249 miles²).
Population: 57 065 400 (1988 estimate).

GREAT BRITAIN
Great Britain is the geographical and political name of the main or principal island of the British Isles group. In a strict geographical sense, off-shore islands, for example the Isle of Wight, Anglesey or Shetland, are not part of Great Britain. The name Great Britain – for the union of England and Wales with Scotland – came into popular (but unofficial) use when James VI of Scotland succeeded Queen Elizabeth I of England (24 March 1603). With the Union of the parliaments of England and Scotland, on 1 May 1707, the style 'Great Britain' was formally adopted.
Area: (of the island of Great Britain) 218 041 km² (84 186 km²); (of the union of England and Wales with Scotland) 229 984 km² (88 797 miles²).
Population (of the union of England and Wales with Scotland): 55 487 300 (1988 estimate).

ENGLAND
England is geographically the southern and larger part of the island of Great Britain. It borders Scotland to the north and Wales to the west. The islands off the English coast, such as the Isle of Wight and the Isles of Scilly, are administratively part of England. Politically and geographically England – historically a separate kingdom until 1707 – is that part of Great Britain governed by English law

(which also pertains in Wales). The last significant changes in the border of England were the inclusion of Berwick-upon-Tweed (from Scotland) in 1746 and the formal transfer of the former county of Monmouthshire back to Wales in 1974.
Area: 130 441 km² (50 363 miles²).
Population: 47 536 300 (1988 estimate).

WALES
The area now recognized as the Principality of Wales was incorporated into England by Act of Parliament in 1536. The former county of Monmouthshire was legally part of England from 1536 until 1 April 1974, although it remained administratively part of Wales for most purposes during that period. The other county boundaries between England and Wales expressly cannot be altered by the ordinary processes of local government reorganization. By statute, Wales may not be represented by fewer than 35 MPs at Westminster.
Area: 20 768 km² (8019 miles²).
Population: 2 857 000 (1988 estimate).

SCOTLAND
Scotland consists of the northern and smaller part of the island of Great Britain. The Kingdom of Scotland effectively lost much of its independence on 24 March 1603 when King James VI of Scotland also became King James I of England. From 1603 to 1707 Scotland remained (for part of the time only nominally) an independent nation. Scotland and England continued to have separate parliaments until the Union of the Parliaments at Westminster on 1 May 1707. Scotland continues, however, to have its own distinctive legal system. By statute, Scotland may not be represented by less than 71 MPs at Westminster.
Area: 78 775 km² (30 415 miles²).
Population: 5 094 000 (1988 estimate).

IRELAND
Ireland is the second largest island of the (geographical) British Isles. Henry VIII assumed the style 'King of Ireland' in 1542, although Governors of Ireland (the exact title varied) ruled on behalf of the Kings of England from 1172. The viceroyalty did not disappear until 1937. The Union of the Parliaments of Great Britain and Ireland occurred on 1 January 1801. (See the Republic of Ireland p. 552.)

NORTHERN IRELAND
Northern Ireland consists of six of the nine counties of the ancient Irish province of Ulster in the northeastern corner of the island. From 1921 until 1973 Northern Ireland had a federal relationship with the Parliament of the United Kingdom in Westminster. The Northern Ireland Parliament – established in 1921 and popularly known as Stormont – enjoyed autonomy, although certain major powers were reserved by the Union Parliament in Westminster, whose sovereignty was unimpaired. The Northern Ireland Parliament was abolished by the Northern Ireland Constitution Act 1973, although some legislative functions were transferred to the new Northern Ireland Assembly and Executive. However,

the collapse of the Executive led to the discontinuance of Assembly meetings in 1974, and the British Secretary of State for Northern Ireland became responsible for the government of Northern Ireland. This measure was intended to be temporary but direct rule has continued. A constitutional convention, established under the Northern Ireland Constitution Act 1974, collapsed in February 1976. Northern Ireland is represented by the fixed number of 12 MPs at Westminster.
Area: 14 120 km² (5452 miles²).
Population: 1 578 100 (1988 estimate).

THE CROWN DEPENDENCIES

The Crown dependencies are territories associated with but not part of the United Kingdom.

THE ISLE OF MAN

The Isle of Man (Manx, *Ellan Vannin*) is a Crown dependency.

Area: 572 km² (221 sq mi).
Highest point above sea level: Snaefell 619 m (2034 ft).
Population: 64 282 (1986 census).
Capital: Douglas (with a population of 20 368 in 1986). The ancient capital was Castletown (3019), although the Manx parliament – the Tynwald – continues to hold a traditional open-air session at Tynwald Hill, near Peel.

Administration: In the middle of the 9th century the Isle of Man was settled by Norse invaders, who established the Tynwald as the national Parliament. It is now the oldest continuously existing national parliament in the world and celebrated its millennium in 1979. In 1266 the island was sold by Norway to Scotland, but the island alternated between English and Scottish rule until 1333, when it was ceded to the English crown but did not become part of England. The Isle of Man was then held by a succession of English noblemen until 1405, when Henry IV granted it to the Stanley family. The Stanleys – who became the earls of Derby in 1485 – adopted the title Lord of Mann and the Isles. Apart from the period 1651 to 1660, when the island was governed by the English Commonwealth, the earls of Derby ruled the Isle of Man until 1736, when they were succeeded by the Scottish dukes of Atholl. In 1765 the Duke of Atholl sold the Lordship of Mann to the British Crown and the island became a Crown dependency.

The Queen – as Lord of Mann – appoints a Lieutenant Governor as the representative of the Crown. The island is governed by a Council of Ministers – the Chief Minister and nine ministers – who enjoy a majority in the Tynwald. The Tynwald comprises the Legislative Council (the upper house) and the House of Keys (the lower house). The two houses sit separately to consider legislation, but sit jointly – as Tynwald Court – for other purposes. The Legislative Council comprises the Bishop of Sodor and Man, the non-voting Attorney-General, and eight members chosen by the House of Keys. The 24 members of the House of Keys have been elected by universal male adult suffrage since 1866 and by universal adult suffrage since 1881. There are 13 political constituencies on the island. In the past two or three decades the Isle of Man has assumed increasing independence from the United Kingdom. The island is not part of the European Community, but enjoys a special relationship with it.

THE CHANNEL ISLANDS

The Channel Islands (French *Iles Anglo-Normandes*) comprise the Crown dependencies of the two Bailiwicks of Jersey and Guernsey. The Bailiwick of Guernsey includes the dependencies of Alderney and Sark, and the small islands of Herm, Brechou, Jethou and Lihou. The tiny uninhabited islets of Ortach, Burhou, the Casquets, Les Minquiers (including Maîtresse Ile) and the Ecrehou Islands (including Marmaoutier, Blanche Ile, and Maître Ile) also form part of the Channel Islands group.

The second duke of Normandy – William I 'Longsword' – annexed the Channel Islands in 933. Duke William II of Normandy became King of England – as William I – in 1066. His son, Henry I, transferred Jethou from Normandy to England in 1091, and the other islands were annexed by the English crown in 1106. In 1204 Normandy was conquered by France and King John of England was declared to have forfeited all his titles to the duchy. The islanders, however, remained loyal to John. France recognized the islands' allegiance to the English crown under the terms of the Treaty of Paris (1258).

The Channel Islands maintained a considerable degree of home rule and – until 1689 – neutrality. Before the Reformation the islands formed part of the diocese of Coutances in Normandy, but were later placed under the (Anglican) bishops of Winchester. The people of the islands traditionally spoke Norman French, but English became dominant by the mid-19th century. The Channel Islands were occupied by German forces on 30 June–1 July 1940, and fortified for defence. They were relieved by British forces on 9 May 1945.

The British Government is responsible for the defence and international relations of the Channel Islands, which have – in the last two or three decades – assumed increased independence. There is a Channel Islands department in the British Home Office in London. Neither Jersey nor Guernsey is part of the European Community, although the islands have a special relationship with it.

JERSEY

Area: 116.2 km² (44.8 sq mi).
Highest point above sea level: 138 m (453 ft).
Population: 80 200 (1986 census).
Capital: St Helier 30 000 (1986).
Administration: The Queen – as Duke of Normandy – appoints a Lieutenant Governor as the representative of the Crown. The government of the island is conducted by committees elected by the States, the parliament of Jersey. The Crown appoints a Bailiff as President of the Assembly of the States. The members of the Assembly of the States are elected by universal adult suffrage and comprise 12 senators (chosen for six years), 12 *connétables* (constables; three years) and 29 deputies (three years). The Lieutenant Governor, the Dean of Jersey, the Attorney General and the Solicitor General are non-voting members.

GUERNSEY

(French *Guernesey*)
Area: of the Bailiwick 75 km² (29 sq mi); of the island 63.3 km² (24.5 sq mi).
Highest point above sea level: 106 m (349 ft).
Population: (island) 54 380 (1986).
Capital: St Peter Port 18 000 (1986).
Administration: The Queen – as Duke of Normandy –

appoints a Lieutenant Governor as the representative of the Crown. The government of the island is conducted by committees elected by the States, the parliament of Guernsey. The Crown appoints a Bailiff as President of the Assembly of the States. The members of the Assembly of the States are elected by universal adult suffrage and comprise 12 jurats, 12 conseillers, 33 people's representatives, and 10 douzaine (parish) representatives, plus two representatives of Alderney. The Lieutenant Governor, the Procureur (Attorney General) and Comptrolleur (Solicitor General) are non-voting members.

Dependencies of Guernsey:

Alderney

(French *Aurigny*)
Area: 7.9 km² (3.07 sq mi).
Highest point above sea level: 85.5 m (281 ft).
Population: 2000 (1986).
Capital: St Anne's.
Administration: The Bailiwick of Guernsey is responsible for providing education, health and police services to Alderney. In other respects the island is governed by its own parliament – the States – which comprises a President of the States and 12 members elected by universal adult suffrage.

Sark

(French *Sercq*)
Area: 5.1 km² (1.99 sq mi). Great Sark has an area of 4.2 km²; Little Sark has an area of 0.9 km².
Highest point above sea level: 114 m (375 ft).
Population: 600 (1986).
Capital: There are no towns or villages on Sark, on which settlement is scattered.
Administration: Sark is part of the Bailiwick of Guernsey but enjoys considerable autonomy. It is governed by its own parliament – the Chief Pleas – which comprises 40 tenants and 12 deputies, who are elected by universal suffrage. The hereditary seigneur of Sark retains the right of veto over decisions of the Chief Pleas and appoints its president, the seneschal.
The Seigneur of Sark: Michael Beaumont, 22nd Seigneur of Sark, who succeeded his mother Sybil Hathaway in 1974.

Other Dependencies of Guernsey:

Herm has an area of 1.29 km² (0.8 sq mi). The island is leased by the States of Guernsey to a tenant who is charged with carrying out the day-to-day administration of Herm.
Brechou has an area of 0.3 km² (0.1 sq mi).
Jethou has an area of 18 ha (44 acres).
Lihou has an area of 15 ha (38 acres).

HIGHEST PEAKS IN THE BRITISH ISLES

The British Isles do not possess any mountains of great height. In only two Scottish regions – Grampian and Highland – does the terrain surpass a height of 1219 m (4000 ft). In Great Britain there are seven mountains and five subsidiary summits (tops) above 1219 m (4000 ft), all in Scotland, and a further 283 mountains and 271 tops between 914 m and 1219 m (3000 and 4000 ft), of which only 21 (see below) are in England or Wales. South of the Scottish border, 914 m (3000 ft) is only surpassed in Gwynedd and Cumbria. Scotland possesses 54 mountains higher than Snowdon and 165 higher than Scafell Pike. Ben Nevis was probably first climbed about 1720, and Ben Macdhui was thought to be Great Britain's highest mountain until as late as 1847.

SCOTLAND'S TEN HIGHEST PEAKS

	m	ft
1. Ben Nevis, Highland	1392	*4406*
2. Ben Macdhui, Grampian	1310	*4300*
3. Braeriach, Grampian-Highland border	1294	*4248*
North Top (Ben Macdhui)	*1293*	4244
4. Cairn Toul, Grampian	1292	*4241*
South Plateau (Braeriach)	*1264*	4149
Sgor an Lochan Uaine (Cairn Toul)	*1254*	4116
Coire Sputan Dearg (Ben Macdhui)	*1248*	4095
5. Cairngorm, Grampian–Highland border	1244	*4084*
6. Aonach Beag, Highland	1237	*4060*
Coire an Lochain (Braeriach)	*1230*	4036
7. Càrn Mor Dearg, Highland	1222	*4012*
8. Aonach Mor, Highland	1218	*3999*
Carn Dearg (Ben Nevis)	*1216*	3990
Coire an t'Saighdeir (Cairn Toul)	*1215*	3989
9. Ben Lawers, Tayside	1214	*3984*
Cairn Lochan (Cairngorm)	*1214*	3983
10. Beinn a'Bhùird (North Top), Grampian	1196	*3924*

WALES' TEN HIGHEST PEAKS

(all in Gwynedd)

	m	ft
1. Snowdon (Yr Wyddfa)	1085	*3560*
Garnedd Ugain or Crib Y Ddisg (Yr Wyddfa)	*1065*	3493
2. Carnedd Llewelyn	1062	*3484*
3. Carnedd Dafydd	1044	*3426*
4. Glyder Fawr	999	*3279*
5. Glyder Fâch	994	*3262*
Pen Yr Oleu-wen (Carnedd Dafydd)	*978*	3210
Foel Grach (Carnedd Llewelyn)	*974*	3195
Yr Elen (Carnedd Llewelyn)	*960*	3151
6. Y Garn	946	*3104*
7. Foel Fras	942	*3091*
8. Elidir Fawr	923	*3029*
Crib Goch (Yr Wyddfa)	*921*	3023
9. Tryfan	917	*3010*
10. Aran Fawddwy	905	*2970*

IRELAND'S TEN HIGHEST PEAKS

	m	ft
1. Carrauntuohill (or Carrauntual), Kerry	1041	*3414*
2. Beenkeragh, Kerry	1010	*3314*
3. Caher, Kerry	975	*3200*
4. Ridge of the Reeks (*two* other tops of the same height, a *third* of 957 m (*3141 ft*), and a *fourth* of c. 930 m (*3050 ft*)), Kerry	c. 975	c. *3200*
5. Brandon, Kerry	953	*3127*
Knocknapeasta (Ridge of the Reeks)	*933*	3062
6. Lugnaquillia, Wicklow	926	*3039*
7. Galtymore, Tipperary	920	*3018*
8. Slieve Donard, County Down	*852	2796
9. Baurtregaum, Kerry	852	*2796*
10. Mullaghcleevaun, Wicklow	849	*2788*

* Highest peak in Northern Ireland

ENGLAND'S TEN HIGHEST PEAKS
(all in Cumbria)

		m	ft
1.	Scafell Pike	978	*3210*
2.	Sca Fell	963	*3162*
3.	Helvellyn	950	*3116*
	Broad Crag (Scafell Pikes)	*930*	3054
4.	Skiddaw	930	*3053*
	Lower Man (Helvellyn)	*922*	3033
	Ill Crags (Scafell Pikes)	*c. 922*	*c.* 3025
	Great End (Scafell Pikes)	*909*	2984
5.	Bow Fell	902	*2960*
6.	Great Gable	898	*2949*
7.	Cross Fell	893	*2930*
8.	Pillar Fell	892	*2927*
	Catstye Cam (Helvellyn)	*889*	2917
9.	Esk Pike	884	*2903*
	Raise (Helvellyn)	*880*	2889
10.	Fairfield	872	*2863*

NATIONAL PARKS

The National Parks of England and Wales were established under the 1949 National Park and Access to the Countryside Act. The Act made provisions for the protection and conservation of these areas, and provides access to the land for public enjoyment. The Act also registers Areas of Outstanding Natural Beauty, which are similarly protected by law. The Act did not, however, register any areas in Scotland and Northern Ireland as National Parks. Discussion for such provision is presently in progress.

The National Parks are (with area, designation date, location and distinguishing features):

Brecon Beacons (1344 sq km/519 sq mi), 1957, Powys, Dyfed, Gwent and Mid Glamorgan; includes the valley of the Usk and the Black Mountains.

Dartmoor (945 sq km/365 sq mi), 1951, Devon; consists of rocky moorland and contains many prehistoric remains.

Exmoor (686 sq km/265 sq mi), 1954, Somerset and Devon; a moorland plateau supporting wild ponies and red deer, and including many ancient remains.

Lake District (2280 sq km/880 sq mi), 1951, Cumbria; includes glaciated lakes and England's highest mountains: Scafell Pike, Helvellyn and Skiddaw.

Northumberland (1031 sq km/398 sq mi), 1956, Northumberland; comprises an area of hill country from Hadrian's Wall to the Scottish border.

North York Moors (1433 sq km/553 sq mi), 1952, North Yorkshire and Cleveland; contains woodland and moorland and includes Hambleton Hills and Cleveland Way.

Peak District (1404 sq km/542 sq mi), 1951, Derbyshire, Staffordshire, South Yorkshire, Cheshire, West Yorkshire and Greater Manchester; an area of gritstone moors and limestone dales.

Pembrokeshire Coast (583 sq km/225 sq mi), 1952, Dyfed; consists of open moorland, cliffs and Skomer Island.

Snowdonia (2171 sq km/838 sq mi), 1951, Gwynedd; it comprises the deep valleys and rugged mountains – including Snowdon – in northern Wales.

Yorkshire Dales (1762 sq km/680 sq mi), 1954, North Yorks., and Cumbria; composed mainly of limestone and millstone grit, it contains the summits of Ingleborough, Whernside and Pen-y-Ghent.

MOUNTAIN AND HILL RANGES OF THE UNITED KINGDOM

Range	Length (km)	Length (miles)	Culminating peak	Height (m)	Height (ft)
Scotland					
Grampian Mountains	250	*155*	Ben Macdhui, Grampian	1310	*4300*
North West Highlands	225	*140*	Càrn Eige, Highland	1181	*3877*
*Southern Uplands	200	*125*	Merrick, Dumfries & Galloway	842	*2764*
Monadh Liath Mountains	*55*	*35*	Càrn Dearg, Highland	942	*3093*
England					
Pennines	195	*120*	Cross Fell, Cumbria	893	*2930*
North Downs	135	*85*	Leith Hill, Surrey	294	*965*
Cotswold Hills	95	*60*	Cleeve Hill, Gloucestershire	330	*1083*
South Downs	85	*55*	Butser Hill, Hampshire	271	*888*
Cheviot Hills	70	*45*	The Cheviot, Northumberland	815	*2676*
Chiltern Hills	70	*45*	Coombe Hill, Buckinghamshire	259	*852*
Berkshire Downs	55	*35*	Walbury Hill, Berkshire	296	*974*
Cumbrian Mountains	*50*	*30*	Scafell Pike, Cumbria	978	*3210*
Exmoor	50	*30*	Dunkery Beacon, Somerset	519	*1706*
North Yorkshire Moors	50	*30*	Urra Moor, Bottom Head	454	*1491*
Hampshire Downs	*40*	*25*	Pilot Hill, Hampshire	285	*938*
Yorkshire Wolds	35	*22*	Garrowby Hill, Humberside	246	*808*
Wales					
Cambrian Mountains	175	*110*	Snowdon (Yr Wyddfa), Gwynedd	1085	*3560*
Berwyn Mountains	65	*40*	Aran Fawddwy, Gwynedd	905	*2972*
Northern Ireland					
Sperrin Mountains	65	*40*	Sawel Mt, Londonderry-Tyrone	682	*2240*
Mountains of Mourne	50	*30*	Slieve Donard, County Down	852	*2796*
Antrim Hills	40	*25*	Trostan, Antrim	553	*1817*

* Includes: Lammermuir Hills (Lammer Law, Lothian 528 m/1733 ft); Lowther Hills (Green Lowther, Strathclyde, 732 m/2403 ft); Pentland Hills (Scald Law, Lothian, 578 m/1898 ft) and the Tweedsmuir Hills (Broad Law, Border, 839 m/2754 ft).

LONGEST RIVERS IN THE UNITED KINGDOM

Specially compiled maps issued by the Ordnance Survey in the second half of the last century are still the authority for the length of the rivers of the United Kingdom. It should, however, be noted that these measurements are strictly for the course of a river bearing the one name; thus, for example, where the principal headstream has a different name its additional length is ignored – unless otherwise indicated.

Length (km)	Length (miles)	Names	Remotest source	Mouth	Area of basin (km²)	Area of basin (miles²)*	Extreme discharge (cusecs)†
354	220	Severn (for 254 km)	Lake on E side of Plinlimmon, Powys	Bristol Channel	11 421	4409·7	23 100 (1937)
346	215	Thames (for 178 km) – Isis (69 km) – Churn	Severn Springs, Gloucestershire	North Sea (The Nore)	9 948	3841·6	27 900 (1894)
297	185	Trent (236 km) – Humber (61 km)	Biddulph Moor, Staffs	North Sea (as Humber)	10 436	4029·2	5 510
259	161	Aire (126 km) – (Yorkshire) Ouse (72 km) and Humber (61 km)	NW of North Yorks	North Sea (as Humber)	11 366	4388·4	4 580 (Aire only)
230	143	Ouse (Great or Bedford)	nr Brackley, Northamptonshire	The Wash	8 582	3313·6	11 000
215	135	Wye (or Gwy)	Plinlimmon, Powys	Into Severn 4 km (2·5 miles) S of Chepstow, Gwent	4 184	1615·3	32 000
188	117	Tay (150 km) – Tummel	(Tay) Beinn Oss, Tayside	North Sea	5 080	1961·6	49 000
161	100	Nene (formerly Nen)	nr Naseby, Northants	The Wash	2 369	914·5	13 500
158	98·5	Clyde (inc. Daer Water)	nr Earncraig Hill, extreme S Strathclyde	Firth of Clyde (measured to Port Glasgow)	3 040	1173·8	20 200
157·5	98·0	Spey	Loch Spey, Highland	North Sea	2 988	1153·5	34 200
155·3	96·5	Tweed	Tweed's Well, Borders	North Sea	5 160	1992·3	21 400
137·1	85·2	Dee (Aberdeenshire)	W of Cairn Toul, Grampian	North Sea	2 116	817·2	40 000
136·7	85	Avon (Warwickshire or Upper)	nr Naseby, Northants	Into Severn at Tewkesbury	(part of Severn Basin)		8 560
129·5	80·5	Don (Aberdeenshire)	Carn Cuilchathaidh, Grampian	North Sea	1 336	515·7	
127	79	Tees	Cross Fell, Cumbria	North Sea	2 237	863·6	13 600
122	76	Bann (Upper Bann – Lough Neagh – Lower Bann)	Mountains of Mourne, SW Down	Atlantic Ocean	–	–	–
118·5	73	Tyne (55 km) – North Tyne (63 km)	Cheviots between Peel Fell and Carter Fell	North Sea	2 917	1126·4	42 000
112·5	70	Dee (Cheshire)	Bala Lake, Gwynedd	Irish Sea	2 119	818·1	16 000
111	69	Eden (Cumberland)	Pennines, SE of Kirby Stephen	Solway Firth, Irish Sea	2 400	926·7	–
104·5	65	Usk	Talsarn Mt, Powys	Bristol Channel	1 740	672·0	23 700
104·5	65	Wear	W of Wearhead, Northumberland	North Sea	1 198	462·6	6 130
104·5	65	Wharfe	12 km (7·5 miles) S of Hawes, North Yorks	Into York Ouse, nr Cawood	(part of Ouse Basin)		15 300
103·5	64·5	Forth	Duchray Water, Ben Lomond	Firth of Forth, North Sea	1 626	627·9	–

* This column gives the hydrometric area of the whole river system as per *The Surface Water Survey*.
† This column gives the highest recorded discharge in cubic feet per second (note: 1 cusec = 0·0283168 m³/sec or 538 170 gallons per day) taken at the lowest sited gauging on the river.

UK LOCHS AND LAKES

Area (km²)	Area (miles²)	Name	Max. Length (km)	Max. Length (miles)	Max. Breadth (km)	Max. Breadth (miles)	Max. Depth (m)	Max. Depth (ft)
Northern Ireland								
381·7	147·39	Lough Neagh, Antrim, Down, Armagh, Tyrone, Londonderry	28	18	17	11	31	102
105·0	40·57	Lower Lough Erne, Fermanagh	28	18	8·8	5·5	68	226
31·7	12·25	Upper Lough Erne, Fermanagh – Cavan	16	10	5·6	3·5	27	89
Scotland (fresh-water lochs)								
71·2	27·5	Loch Lomond, Strathclyde-Central	36·4	22·64	8	5	189	623
56·6	21·87	Loch Ness, Highland	36·6	22·75	3·2	2	228	751
38·7	14·95	Loch Awe, Strathclyde	41·0	25·5	3·2	2	93	307
28·4	11·0	Loch Maree, Highland	21·7	13·5	3·2	2	111	367
26·6	10·3	Loch Morar, Highland	18·5	11·5	2·4	1·5	309	1017
26·3	10·19	Loch Tay, Tayside	23·4	14·55	1·7	1·07	154	508
22·5	8·70	Loch Shin, Highland	27·7	17·35	1·6	1	49	162
19·5	7·56	Loch Shiel, Highland	28·1	17·5	1·4	0·9	128	420
19·0	7·34	Loch Rannoch, Tayside	15·6	9·75	1·7	1·1	134	440
18·5	7·18	Loch Ericht, Highland–Tayside	23·4	14·6	1·7	1·1	156	512
16·1	6·25	Loch Arkaig, Highland	19·3	12·0	1·4	0·9	109	359
15·2	5·9	Loch Lochy, Highland	15·9	9·9	2·0	1·25	161	531

England (all in Cumbria)

Area (km²)	Area (miles²)	Name	Max. Length (km)	Max. Length (miles)	Max. Breadth (km)	Max Breadth (yd)	Max. Depth (m)	Max. Depth (ft)
14·7	5·69	Windermere	16·8	10·50	1·47	1610	66	219
8·9	3·44	Ullswater	11·8	7·35	1·0	1100	62	205
5·3	2·06	Bassenthwaite Water	6·1	3·83	1·18	1300	21	70
5·3	2·06	Derwentwater	4·6	2·87	1·94	2130	21	72
4·8	1·89	Coniston Water	8·7	5·41	0·79	870	56	184
2·9	1·12	Ennerdale Water	3·8	2·40	0·9	1000	45	148
2·9	1·12	Wastwater	4·8	3·00	0·8	880	78	258
2·5	0·97	Crummock Water	4·0	2·50	0·9	1000	43	144
1·3	0·54	Haweswater	3·7	2·33	0·54	600	31	103
0·9	0·36	Buttermere	2·0	1·26	0·61	670	28	94
Wales								
8·2	3·18	Lake Vyrnwy (dammed), Powys	7·5	4·7	0·06	1000	36	120
4·3	1·69	Bala Lake (Llyn Tegid), Gwynedd	6·1	3·8	0·53	850	38	125

* Rutland Water with a surface area of 12.54 km² (4.84 sq mi) is the largest reservoir in the UK in terms of surface water.

WATERFALLS

The principal waterfalls of the British Isles are:

Height (m)	Height (ft)	Name
200	658	Eas-Coul-Aulin, Highland
112	370	Falls of Glomach, Highland
106	350	Powerscourt Falls, County Wicklow
>90	>300	Pistyll-y-Llyn, Powys–Dyfed
73	240	Pistyll Rhaiadr, Clwyd
62	205	Foyers, Highland
62*	204	Falls of Clyde, Strathclyde
60	200	Falls of Bruar, Tayside (upper fall)
60	200	Cauldron (or Caldron) Snout, Cumbria
60	200	Grey Mare's Tail, Dumfries & Galloway

* Total height; the falls comprise Bonnington Linn (9m/ 30 ft), Cora Linn (25 m/84 ft), Dunbaff Linn (3 m/10 ft) and Stonebyres Linn (24 m/80 ft)

CAVES

Large or deep caves are few in Great Britain. Great Britain's deepest cave is Ogof Ffynnon Ddu (308 m/1010 ft) in Powys, Wales. The largest system is the Ease Gill system with 66 km (41 mi) of surveyed passages. England's deepest cave is Giant's Hole, Oxlow Caverns, Derbyshire, which descends 214 m (702 ft). Scotland's deepest cave is Cnoc nan Uamh, which is 76 m (249 ft) deep. The Republic of Ireland's deepest is Carrowmore Cavern, County Sligo, being 140 m (459 ft) deep. Northern Ireland's deepest is Reyfad Pot, Fermanagh, being 179 m (587 ft) deep.

EXTREMITIES OF THE BRITISH ISLES

Island of Great Britain

Great Britain has the following extreme (mainland) dimensions:

Most northerly point	Easter Head, Dunnet Head, Highland	Lat	58°	40′	24″ N
Most westerly point	Corrachadh Mor, Ardnamurchan, Highland	Long	6°	14′	12″ W
Most southerly point	Lizard Point, Cornwall	Lat	49°	57′	33″ N
Most easterly point	Lowestoft Ness, Lowestoft, Suffolk	Long	1°	46′	20″ E

Other extreme points (mainland) in its 3 constituent countries are:

Most southerly point in Scotland	Gallie Craig, Mull of Galloway, Dumfries & Galloway	Lat	54°	38′	27″ N
Most easterly point in Scotland	Keith Inch, Peterhead, Grampian	Long	1°	45′	49″ W
Most northerly point in England	Meg's Dub, Northumberland	Lat	55°	48′	37″ N
Most westerly point in England	Dr Syntax's Head, Land's End, Cornwall	Long	5°	42′	15″ W
Most northerly point in Wales	Point of Air, Clwyd	Lat	53°	21′	08″ N
Most westerly point in Wales	Porthtaflod, Dyfed	Long	5°	19′	43″ W
Most southerly point in Wales	Rhoose Point, South Glamorgan	Lat	51°	22′	40″ N
Most easterly point in Wales	Lady Park Wood, Gwent	Long	2°	38′	49″ W

Island of Ireland

Most northerly point in Ireland	Malin Head, Donegal	Lat	55°	22′	30″ N
Most northerly point in Northern Ireland	Benbane Head, Moyle, Antrim	Lat	55°	15′	0″ N
Most westerly point in Ireland	Dunmore Head, Kerry	Long	10°	28′	55″ W
Most westerly point in Northern Ireland	Cornaglah, Fermanagh	Long	8°	10′	30″ W
Most southerly point in Ireland	Brow Head, Cork	Lat	51°	26′	30″ N
Most southerly point in Northern Ireland	Cranfield Point, Newry and Mourne, Down	Lat	54°	01′	20″ N
Most easterly point in Ireland (Northern)	Townhead, Ards Peninsula, Down	Long	5°	26′	52″ W
Most easterly point in Republic of Ireland	Wicklow Head, Wicklow	Long	5°	59′	40″ W

UNITED KINGDOM'S LARGEST ISLANDS

	km²	miles²
Yell, Shetland	214·16	*82·69*
Hoy, Orkney	136·85	*52·84*

England (12 largest)

	km²	miles²
Isle of Wight	380·99	*147·09*
*Sheppey (Kent)	94·04	*36·31*
*Hayling (Hampshire)	26·84	*10·36*
*Foulness (Essex)	26·14	*10·09*
*Portsea (Hampshire)	24·25	*9·36*
*Canvey (Essex)	18·45	*7·12*
*Mersea (Essex)	18·04	*6·96*
*Walney (Cumbria)	12·99	*5·01*
*Isle of Grain (Kent)	12·85	*4·96*
*Wallasea (Essex)	10·65	*4·11*
St Mary's, Isles of Scilly	6·29	*2·43*
*Thorney (West Sussex)	4·96	*1·91*

Scotland (12 largest)

	km²	miles²
Lewis with Harris (Wn. Isles)	2225·30	*859·19*
Skye (Highland)	1666·08	*643·28*
Mainland, Shetland	967·00	*373·36*
Mull (Strathclyde)	899·25	*347·21*
Islay (Strathclyde)	614·52	*246·64*
Mainland, Orkney	536·10	*206·99*
Arran (Strathclyde)	435·32	*168·08*
Jura (Strathclyde)	370·35	*142·99*
North Uist (Western Isles)	351·49	*135·71*
South Uist (Western Isles)	332·45	*128·36*

Wales (12 largest)

	km²	miles²
*Anglesey (*Ynys Mon*; Gwynedd)	713·80	*275·60*
Holy I (Gwynedd)	39·44	*15·22*
Skomer (Dyfed)	2·90	*1·12*
Ramsey (Dyfed)	2·58	*0·99*
Caldey (Dyfed)	2·79	*0·84*
Bardsey (Gwynedd)	1·99	*0·76*
Skokholm (Dyfed)	1·06	*0·41*
Flat Holm (South Glamorgan)	0·33	*0·13*
*Llanddwyn I (Gwynedd)	0·31	*0·12*
Puffin Island (Gwynedd)	0·28	*0·11*
The Skerries (Gwynedd)	0·15	*0·06*
Cardigan Island (Dyfed)	0·15	*0·06*

Northern Ireland's principal offshore island is Rathlin Island 14·41 km² (5·56 miles²)

* Bridged or linked by causeway to the mainland

COUNTIES, REGIONS AND ISLAND AUTHORITIES

The boundaries of the UK's traditional counties were redrawn in 1974 and 1975 for administrative purposes. The maps on pp. 684–85 show the names and the boundaries of the traditional counties and of the new administrative areas. The 'new counties' are regarded as artificial by many people and the traditional names continue to be widely used. Moreover, the 1974 Act stated 'The new county councils are solely for the purpose of defining areas of first-level government of the future; they are administration areas and will not alter the traditional boundaries.'

In England the 40 traditional counties were replaced as administrative units by 45 administrative counties, but the six metropolitan county councils – and the Greater London Council – were abolished in 1986.

In Scotland the 33 traditional counties were replaced as administrative units by nine regions and three island authorities.

In Wales the 12 traditional counties were replaced as administrative units by eight new counties.

In Northern Ireland the six traditional counties were replaced as administrative units by 26 districts.

Population figures A mid-1988 estimate is given.

Districts The population and administrative head-quarters of the districts within each county or region are given. Many districts are named after their administrative centre. The headquarters of those districts named after a geographical feature or an historic area are given in brackets.

Metropolitan Counties The councils of the metropolitan counties were abolished on 31 March 1986. These names are marked by an asterisk.

ADMINISTRATIVE COUNTIES OF ENGLAND

AVON

First recorded use of the name 1973 – from the River Avon – Welsh *afon*, meaning 'river'. It is argued that Avon is a pre-Celtic word later adopted into Celtic language.

Area 1345 km² (519 miles²)

Population 954 300

Density 709 per km² (1839 per mile²)

Administrative HQ Avon House, The Haymarket, Bristol.

Highest point above sea level Nett Wood, East Harptree 251 m (825 ft).

Districts Bath (city) 84 800; Bristol (city) 377 700; Kingswood 89 700; Northavon (HQ: Thornbury) 130 800; Wansdyke (HQ: Keynsham) 82 200; Woodspring (HQ: Weston-super-Mare) 189 100.

Road lengths	km	miles
motorway and trunk	122.3	76
principal	402.3	250
other	4153.7	2581

Schools and colleges nursery 16; primary 373; secondary 61; special 32; colleges of FE and HE 9; polytechnic 1.

BEDFORDSHIRE

First recorded use of name 1011– Anglo-Saxon *Bedanfordscir*, meaning 'the shire of Beda's ford or river crossing'.

Area 1235 km² (477 miles²).

Population 530 700.

Density 430 per km² (1113 per mile²).

Administrative HQ County Hall, Cauldwell St, Bedford.

Highest point above sea level Dunstable Downs 243 m (798 ft).

Districts Luton 167 600; Mid Bedfordshire (HQ: Ampthill) 114 900; North Bedfordshire (HQ: Bedford) 136 800; South Bedfordshire (HQ: Leighton Buzzard) 111 500.

Road lengths	km	miles
motorway	25	15.5
trunk	113	70.2
principal	203	126.1
other	2012	1250.2

Schools and colleges nursery 12; lower/primary 218; middle 43; upper/secondary 30; sixth-form college 1; special 15; colleges of FE and HE 3.

BERKSHIRE

First recorded use of the name AD 860 – Anglo-Saxon *Bearucscir*, probably meaning 'the shire of the wooded hill'.

Area 1256 km² (485 miles²).

Population 747 100.

Density 595 per km² (1540 per mile²).

Administrative HQ Shire Hall, Shinfield Park, Reading.

Highest point above sea level Walbury Hill 297 m (974 ft).

Districts Bracknell Forest (HQ: Bracknell) 98 200; Newbury 138 700; Reading 132 400; Slough 100 300; Windsor and Maidenhead (HQ: Maidenhead) 127 400; Wokingham 150 000.

Road lengths	km	miles
motorway	127	78.9
trunk	51	31.7
principal	323	200.7
other	2770	1720.2

Schools and colleges nursery 18; primary 271; secondary 55; special 12; colleges of FE and HE 10.

BUCKINGHAMSHIRE

First recorded use of the name 1016 – Anglo-Saxon *Buccingahamscir*, meaning 'the shire of the hamm or water meadow of Bucca'.

Area 1883 km² (727 miles²).

Population 627 300.

Density 333 per km² (863 per mile²).

Administrative HQ County Hall, Aylesbury.

Highest point above sea level Nr. Aston Hill 267 m (876 ft).

Districts Aylesbury Vale (HQ: Aylesbury) 145 400; Chiltern (HQ: Amersham) 87 900; Milton Keynes 177 600; South Bucks (HQ: Slough, i.e. outside the district) 60 000; Wycombe (HQ: High Wycombe) 156 300.

Road lengths	km	miles
motorway	69	42.8
trunk	61	37.9
principal	409	254.0
other	3431	2130.6

Schools and colleges nursery 5; first 127; middle 67; combined 100; secondary 47; special 20; colleges of FE and HE 3.

CAMBRIDGESHIRE

First recorded use of the name 1010 – Anglo-Saxon *Grantabricscir*, from a corruption of *Grantabrice*, meaning 'the shire of the bridge over the River Granta'.

Area 3409 km² (1316 miles²).

Population 651 600.

Density 191 per km² (495 per mile²).

Administrative HQ Shire Hall, Castle Hill, Cambridge.

Highest point above sea level 275 m (300 yd) south of the Hall, Great Chishill, 145 m (478 ft).

Districts Cambridge (city) 97 800; East Cambridgeshire (HQ: Ely) 60 600; Fenland (HQ: Wisbech) 73 200; Huntingdonshire (HQ: Huntingdon) 147 700; Peterborough (city) 152 900; South Cambridgeshire (HQ: Cambridge, i.e. outside the district) 119 300.

Road lengths	km	miles
motorway	24	38.7
trunk	288	178.8
other	4583	2846.0

Schools and colleges nursery 5; primary 27; secondary 46; special 17; colleges of FE and HE 5.

CHESHIRE

First recorded use of the name AD 980 – Anglo-Saxon *Legaeceastersir*, meaning 'the shire of the camp (*castra*) of the legions (*legiones*)'.

Area 2328 km² (899 miles²).

Population 955 800.

Density 411 per km² (1063 per mile²).

Administrative HQ County Hall, Chester.

Highest point above sea level Shining Tor 559 m (1834 ft)

Districts Chester (city) 117 100; Congleton 86 600; Crewe and Nantwich (HQ: Crewe) 96 800; Ellesmere Port and Neston (HQ: Ellesmere Port) 79 700; Halton (HQ: Widnes) 124 000; Macclesfield 152 300; Vale Royal (HQ: Frodsham) 113 300; Warrington 186 000.

Road lengths	km	miles
motorway	207.5	129.7
trunk	212	131.6
principal	684	424.8
other	4604	2859

Schools and colleges nursery 8; primary 472; secondary 75; special 21; colleges of FE and HE 7.

CLEVELAND

First recorded use of the name 1110 – Anglo-Saxon *Clivelanda*, meaning 'the hilly district'.

Area 590 km² (228 miles²).

Population 553 100.

Density 937 per km² (2426 per mile²).

Administrative HQ Municipal Buildings, Middlesbrough.

Highest point above sea level Hob on the Hill 328 m (1078 ft).

Districts Hartlepool 88 400; Langbaurgh-on-Tees (HQ: South Bank) 144 800; Middlesbrough 143 200; Stockton-on-Tees 176 800.

Road lengths	km	miles
trunk	70	43.5
principal	277	172.0
other	1882	1169.0

Schools and colleges nursery 2; primary 209; secondary 46; special 16; colleges of FE and HE 5; polytechnic 1.

CORNWALL (and the Isles of Scilly)

First recorded use of the name AD 884 – Anglo-Saxon *Cornubia*, possibly meaning the territory of

the Welsh tribe the Cornovii.

Area 3548 km² (1370 miles²).

Population 460 600.

Density 130 per km² (336 per mile²).

Administrative HQ County Hall, Truro.

Highest point above sea level Brown Willy 419 m (1375 ft).

Districts Caradon (HQ: Liskeard) 74 900; Carrick (HQ: Truro) 80 300; Kerrier (HQ: Camborne) 86 800; North Cornwall (HQ: Bodmin) 71 600; Penwith (HQ: Penzance) 59 300; Restormel (HQ: St Austell) 85 700.

Road lengths	km	miles
trunk	238.1	148
principal	490.7	305
classified	3084.4	1917
unclassified	3737.7	2323

Schools and colleges nursery 2; primary 265; secondary 33; special 4; colleges of FE and HE 3.

Isles of Scilly The Isles of Scilly are administered by the Council of the Isles of Scilly. This unique local-government body – which was set up by an Order made under the Local Government Act (1974) – combines the powers of an English county council and district council. For some purposes the Isles are included with Cornwall, whose county council provides services on an agency basis.
Area: 16·35 km² (6·31 sq mi).
Population: 2006 (1981 estimate).
Centre of administration: Hugh Town (St Mary's).

There are five populated islands (1981 estimates): Bryher (pop. 155), St Agnes (pop. 60), St Martin's (pop. 80), St Mary's (pop. 1650) and Tresco (pop. 155). There are 19 other islands and numerous rocks and islets.

CUMBRIA

First recorded use of the name AD 935 – Anglo-Saxon *Cumbra land* meaning 'the land of the Cumbrians', which was derived from the Welsh *Cymri*.

Area 6810 km² (2629 miles²).

Population 489 200.

Density 72 per km² (186 per mile²).

Administrative HQ The Courts, Carlisle.

Highest point above sea level Scafell Pike 978 m (3210 ft).

Districts Allerdale (HQs: Wigton and Workington) 96 600; Barrow-in-Furness 72 400; Carlisle (city) 102 000; Copeland (HQ: Whitehaven) 71 600; Eden (HQ: Penrith) 46 200; South Lakeland (HQ: Kendal) 100 200.

Road lengths	km	miles
motorway	97	60.2
trunk	349	216.7
principal	642	398.7
other	6407	3978.7

Schools and colleges nursery 8; primary 318; secondary 44; special 12; colleges of FE and HE 10.

DERBYSHIRE

First recorded use of the name 1049 – Anglo-Saxon *Deorbyscir* meaning 'the shire of the village with a deer park'.

Area 2631 km² (1016 miles²).

Population 924 200.

Density 351 per km² (910 per mile²).

Administrative HQ County Offices, Matlock.

Highest point above sea level Kinder Scout 636 m (2088 ft).

Districts Amber Valley (HQ: Ripley) 111 900; Bolsover (HQ: Chesterfield, i.e. outside the district) 69 900; Chesterfield 99 700; Derby (city) 215 400; Derbyshire Dales (HQ: Matlock) 66 800; Erewash (HQ: Ilkeston) 107 900; High Peak (HQ: Chapel-en-le-Frith) 84 300; North East Derbyshire (HQ: Chesterfield, i.e. outside the district) 96 800; South Derbyshire (HQ: Burton upon Trent, i.e. outside the district) 71 600.

Road lengths	km	miles
motorway	40	24.8
trunk	249	154.6
principal	523	324.8
other	4952	3075.2

Schools and colleges nursery 15; primary 452; secondary 77; special 33; colleges of FE and HE 6.

DEVON

First recorded use of the name AD 851 – Anglo-Saxon *Defenascir* meaning 'the shire of the Dumonii', an aboriginal Celtic tribal name adopted by the Saxons.

Area 6711 km² (2590 miles²).

Population 1 021 100.

Density 152 per km² (394 per mile²).

Administrative HQ County Hall, Exeter.

Highest point above sea level High Willhays 621 m (2038 ft).

Districts East Devon (HQ: Sidmouth) 118 100; Exeter (city) 99 600; Mid Devon (HQ: Tiverton) 63 200; North Devon (HQ: Barnstaple) 84 400; Plymouth (city) 258 100; South Hams (HQ: Totnes) 75 700; Teignbridge (HQ: Newton Abbot) 108 000; Torbay (HQ: Torquay) 118 900; Torridge (HQ: Bideford) 51 200; West Devon (HQ: Tavistock) 43 900.

Road lengths	km	miles
motorway	38.0	23.6
trunk	310	192.5
principal	944	586.2
classified	5146.7	3196.1
unclassified	6770.4	4204.4

Schools and colleges nursery 3; primary 446; secondary 75; special 23; colleges of FE and HE 10; polytechnic 1.

DORSET

First recorded use of the name AD 940 – Anglo-Saxon *Dorseteschire*, which is thought to mean 'the shire of the dwellers (*saete*) of the place of fist-play (*dorn-gweir*)'.

Area 2654 km² (1024 miles²).

Population 655 700.

Density 247 per km² (640 per mile²).

Administrative HQ County Hall, Dorchester.

Highest point above sea level Pilsdon Pen 277 m (909 ft).

Districts Bournemouth 154 800; Christchurch 40 300; East Dorset (HQ: Wimborne) 79 600; North Dorset (HQ: Blandford Forum) 54 700; Poole 130 700; Purbeck (HQ: Wareham) 46 200; West Dorset (HQ: Dorchester) 85 200; Weymouth and Portland (HQ: Weymouth) 64 000.

Road lengths	km	miles
trunk	94.9	59
principal	465	289
classified	1583.5	984
unclassified	2569.6	1597

Schools and colleges primary/first 191; middle 26; secondary/upper 41; special 14; colleges of FE and HE 4, polytechnic 1.

DURHAM

First recorded use of the name c. AD 1000 – Anglo-Saxon *Dunholme* meaning 'the hill (*dun*) crowning a holm or island'.

Area 2436 km² (940 miles²).

Population 596 800.

Density 245 per km² (635 per mile²).

Administrative HQ County Hall, Durham.

Highest point above sea level Mickle Fell 798 m (2591 ft).

Districts Chester-le-Street 53 100; Darlington 99 700; Derwentside (HQ: Consett) 85 900; Durham (city) 85 800; Easington (HQ: Peterlee) 95 000; Sedgefield (HQ: Spennymoor) 88 400; Teesdale (HQ: Barnard Castle) 24 900; Wear Valley (HQ: Crook) 64 100.

Road lengths	km	miles
motorway	45.40	28.2
trunk	92.17	57.2
principal	377.66	234.5
classified	1568.83	974.2
unclassified	2173.29	1349.6

Schools and colleges nursery 27; primary 301; secondary 46; special 17; colleges of FE and HE 4.

EAST SUSSEX

First recorded use of the name AD 722 – Anglo-Saxon *Suth Seaxe* meaning 'the territory of the southern Saxons'.

Area 1795 km² (693 miles²).

Population 712 800.

Density 397 per km² (1029 per mile²).

Administrative HQ Pelham House, St Andrew's Lane, Lewes.

Highest point above sea level Ditchling Beacon, 248 m (813 ft).

Districts Brighton 149 200; Eastbourne 80 300; Hastings 83 100; Hove 90 700; Lewes 90 800; Rother (HQ: Bexhill) 84 700; Wealden (HQs: Crowborough and Hailsham) 133 900.

Road lengths	km	miles
trunk	100.1	62.2
principal	395.2	245.6
classified	1036.8	644.3
unclassified	2048.0	1273.1

Schools and colleges nursery 3; primary and junior/middle 442; secondary 35; sixth form colleges 4; special 20; colleges of FE and HE 5, polytechnic 1.

ESSEX

First recorded use of the name AD 604 – Anglo-Saxon *East Seaxe* meaning 'the territory of the eastern Saxons'.

Area 3672 km² (1417 miles²).

Population 1 529 500.

Density 416 per km² (1079 per mile²).

Administrative HQ County Hall, Chelmsford.

Highest point above sea level In High Wood, Langley 146 m (480 ft).

Districts Basildon 157 500; Braintree 117 200; Brentwood 70 000; Castle Point (HQ: South Benfleet) 85 500; Chelmsford 151 700; Colchester

150 200; Epping Forest (HQ: Epping) 111 800; Harlow 72 000; Maldon 53 600; Rochford 74 400; Southend-on-Sea 165 400; Tendring (HQ: Clacton) 129 600; Thurrock (HQ: Grays Thurrock) 124 400; Uttlesford (HQ: Saffron Walden) 66 100.

Road lengths	km	miles
motorway/trunk	257	159.6
principal	665	412.9
classified	2410	1496.6
unclassified	4273	2653.5

Schools and colleges nursery 2; primary 583; secondary 107; sixth form colleges 3; special 38; colleges of FE and HE 4, polytechnic 1.

GLOUCESTERSHIRE

First recorded use of the name AD 1016 – Anglo-Saxon *Gleawcestrescir* meaning 'the shire around the fort (*ceaster*) at the splendid place (Old Welsh *gloiu*)'.

Area 2643 km² (1020 miles²).

Population 527 500.

Density 199 per km² (517 per mile²).

Administrative HQ Shire Hall, Gloucester.

Highest point above sea level Cleeve Cloud 330 m (1083 ft).

Districts Cheltenham 86 400; Cotswold (HQ: Cirencester) 75 100; Forest of Dean (HQ: Coleford) 77 900; Gloucester (city) 90 500; Stroud 110 500; Tewkesbury 87 200.

Road lengths	km	miles
motorway	48	29.8
trunk	163	101.2
principal	506	314.2
other	4519	2806.3

Schools and colleges primary 262; secondary 48; special 16; colleges of FE and HE 4.

GREATER LONDON*

First recorded use of the name AD 115 – Latin *Londinium*, possibly derived from the Celtic word *Londo* meaning 'a wild or bold man'.

Area 1580 km² (610 miles²).

Population 6 731 000.

Density 4260 per km² (11 034 per mile²).

Administrative HQ No central authority. Functions rest with individual Boroughs and the City of London.

Highest point above sea level 246 m (809 ft); 30 m (33 yd) southeast of Westerham Heights (a house) on the Kent-Greater London boundary.

London boroughs Barking and Dagenham (HQ: Dagenham) 147 600; Barnet (HQ: Hendon) 301 400; Bexley (HQ: Bexleyheath) 220 400; Brent (HQ: Wembley) 257 200; Bromley 298 200; Camden 182 600; Croydon 317 200; Ealing 297 300; Enfield 260 900; Greenwich (HQ: Woolwich) 214 500; Hackney 188 900; Hammersmith and Fulham (HQ: Hammersmith) 149 600; Haringey (HQ: Wood Green) 192 300; Harrow 197 100; Havering (HQ: Romford) 235 600; Hillingdon (HQ: Uxbridge) 231 900; Hounslow 190 800; Islington 169 200; Kensington and Chelsea (HQ: Kensington) 125 600; Kingston-upon-Thames 134 500; Lambeth (HQ: Brixton) 239 500; Lewisham (HQ: Catford) 228 900; Merton (HQ: Morden) 164 100; Newham (HQ: East Ham) 207 000; Redbridge (HQ: Ilford) 230 800; Richmond-upon-Thames (HQ: Twickenham) 160 800; Southwark (HQ: Camberwell) 217 000; Sutton 168 200; Tower Hamlets (HQ: Bethnal Green) 161 800; Waltham Forest (HQ: Walthamstow) 213 300; Wandsworth 257 100; Westminster (city) 169 700.

The City of London – population 4400 – is not a London borough. The local government of the historic 'square mile' is the responsibility of the Corporation of the City of London whose boundaries, powers and customs were unaffected by the reform of local government in the 1960s and 1970s.

Road lengths (1987)	km	miles
motorway	47	29.2
trunk	279.2	173.5
principal	2367.7	1471.3
classified	1843.7	1145.2
unclassified	9150.3	5685.4

Schools and colleges nursery 128; primary and middle 1914; secondary and middle (including sixth form colleges) 508; special 101; colleges of FE and HE 63; polytechnics 8.

GREATER MANCHESTER*

First recorded use of the name AD 923 – Anglo-Saxon *Mameceaster* meaning 'the camp (*ceaster*) of Mamucion (an Old British word of uncertain origin).

Area 1286 km² (496 miles²).

Population 2 577 500.

Density 2004 per km² (5196 per mile²).

Administrative HQ No central authority. Functions rest with individual districts.

Highest point above sea level Featherbed Moss 540 m (1774 ft).

Districts Bolton 263 000; Bury 175 000; Manchester (city) 445 900; Oldham 219 500; Rochdale 206 800; Salford (city) 235 600; Stockport 290 900; Tameside (HQ: Ashton-under-Lyne) 216 800; Trafford (HQ: Stretford) 215 800; Wigan 307 600.

Road lengths (1986)	km	miles
motorway	169.0	105.0
trunk	43.0	26.7
principal	815.0	506.4
classified	809.0	502.6
unclassified	6008.0	3733.1

Schools and colleges nursery 46; primary 925; middle and secondary 209; special 92; colleges of FE and HE 35; polytechnic 1.

HAMPSHIRE

First recorded use of the name AD 866 – Anglo-Saxon *Hamtunscir* meaning 'the shire dependent on Hamtun (*hamm* 'a meadow'; *tun* 'a homestead').

Area 3777 km² (1458 miles²).

Population 1 542 900.

Density 408 per km² (1058 per mile²).

Administrative HQ The Castle, Winchester.

Highest point above sea level Pilot Hill 285 m (937 ft).

Districts Basingstoke and Deane (HQ: Basingstoke) 139 700; East Hampshire (HQ: Petersfield) 102 500; Eastleigh 101 000; Fareham 100 300; Gosport 76 900; Hart (HQ: Fleet) 85 900; Havant 117 500; New Forest (HQ: Lyndhurst) 163 300; Portsmouth (city) 183 800; Rushmoor (HQ: Farnborough) 77 000; Southampton (city) 196 700; Test Valley (HQ: Andover) 102 300; Winchester (city) 96 000.

Road lengths	km	miles
motorway	144.8	90
trunk	199.5	124
principal	756.2	470
classified	2476.2	1539
unclassified	5562.3	3457

Schools and colleges nursery 3; primary 577; secondary and sixth form colleges 117; special 47; colleges of FE and HE 14; polytechnic 1.

HEREFORD AND WORCESTER

First recorded use of name Hereford c. 1038 – from Anglo-Saxon *herepaeth* and *ford*, meaning 'the military road river crossing', and Worcester AD 889 – Anglo-Saxon *Uuegorna ceastre* meaning 'the fort (*caester*) of the Weogoran tribe' (probably named from the Wyre Forest).

Area 3927 km² (1516 miles²).

Population 671 000.

Density 171 per km² (443 per mile²).

Administrative HQ County Hall, Worcester.

Highest point above sea level In the Black Mountains 702 m (2306 ft).

Districts Bromsgrove 89 600; Hereford (city) 49 000; Leominster 39 300; Malvern Hills (HQ: Malvern) 87 900; Redditch 77 500; South Herefordshire (HQ: Hereford, i.e. outside the district) 51 100; Worcester (city) 81 200; Wychavon (HQ: Pershore) 101 000; Wyre Forest (HQ: Stourport-on-Severn) 94 400.

Road lengths	km	miles
motorway	83.2	51.7
trunk	179.8	111.7
principal	762.6	473.6
other	5955	3698.5

Schools and colleges primary 284; middle 42; secondary 46; sixth form colleges 2; special 15; colleges of FE and HE 11.

HERTFORDSHIRE

First recorded use of the name AD 866 – Anglo-Saxon *Heortfordscir* meaning 'the shire of the ford or river crossing of the harts or stags'.

Area 1634 km² (631 miles²).

Population 985 900.

Density 603 per km (1562 per mile²).

Administrative HQ County Hall, Hertford.

Highest point above sea level Hastoe 244 m (802 ft).

Districts Broxbourne (HQ: Cheshunt) 82 500; Dacorum (HQ: Hemel Hempstead) 133 100; East Hertfordshire (HQ: Hertford and Bishop's Stortford) 118 700; Hertsmere (HQ: Borehamwood) 88 600; North Hertfordshire (HQ: Letchworth) 112 300; St Albans (city) 128 500; Stevenage 73 700; Three Rivers (HQ: Rickmansworth) 80 000; Watford 75 200; Welwyn Hatfield (HQ: Welwyn Garden City) 93 400.

Road lengths	km	miles
motorway	168.9	104.9
trunk	140.1	87.0
principal	349.2	216.8
other	3667.5	2277.5

Schools and colleges nursery 16; primary 448; secondary 117; colleges of FE and HE 12; polytechnic 1.

HUMBERSIDE

First recorded use of the name c. AD 730 – Celtic *humbri* a river name of uncertain meaning.

Area 3512 km² (1356 miles²).

Population 850 500.

Density 242 per km² (627 per mile²).

Administrative HQ County Hall, Beverley, N. Humberside.

Highest point above sea level Cot Nab 246 m (808 ft).

Districts East Yorkshire Borough of Beverley (HQ: Beverley) 114 000; Boothferry (HQ: Goole) 64 100; Cleethorpes 68 400; East Yorkshire (HQ: Bridlington) 84 800; Glanford (HQ: Brigg) 72 100; Great Grimsby (HQ: Grimsby) 89 100; Holderness (HQ: Hornsea) 50 600; Kingston-upon-Hull (city; HQ: Hull) 247 000; Scunthorpe 60 500.

Road lengths	km	miles
motorway	109	67.7
trunk	128	79.5
principal	497	308.6
other	4919	3054.7

Schools and colleges nursery 9; primary 343; middle 23; secondary 60; special 16; colleges of FE and HE 6, polytechnic 1.

In 1990 a report of the Local Government Commission recommended that the districts of Humberside south of the Humber should be transferred back to Lincolnshire. Any measures to effect this recommendation would – if approved – take several years. If such measures were to be taken the reduced county of Humberside would probably be renamed East Yorkshire.

The new county of East Yorkshire would have an area of 2706 km² (1025 sq mi) and a population of 560 500. Its administrative headquarters would be in Beverley (see above). The county would comprise the districts of Beverley, Boothferry, East Yorkshire, Holderness and Kingston-upon-Hull.

ISLE OF WIGHT

First recorded use of the name Pre-Roman – Celtic *Ynys-yr-Wyth* from which the Romans derived the name *Vectis*.

Area 381 km² (147 miles²).

Population 129 800.

Density 341 per km² (883 per mile²).

Administrative HQ County Hall, Newport.

Highest point above sea level St Boniface Down 240 m (787 ft).

Districts Medina (HQ: Newport) 72 900; South Wight (HQs: Newport, i.e. outside the district, and Sandown and Ventnor) 56 900.

Road lengths	km	miles
trunk	nil	nil
principal	122	75.7
classified	269	167
unclassified	351	218

Schools and colleges primary 46; middle 16; secondary 5; special 2; College of FE 1.

KENT

First recorded use of the name c. 308 BC – Celtic *canto* meaning 'a rim or coastal area'.

Area 3732 km² (1441 miles²).

Population 1 520 400.

Density 407 per km² (1055 per mile²).

Administrative HQ County Hall, Maidstone.

Highest point above sea level Betsom's Hill,

Westerham 251 m (824 ft).

Districts Ashford 95 100; Canterbury (city) 131 900; Dartford 78 400; Dover 106 300; Gillingham 95 300; Gravesham (HQ: Gravesend) 90 200; Maidstone 136 000; Rochester upon Medway (city; HQ: Strood) 146 600; Sevenoaks 107 300; Shepway (HQ: Folkestone) 87 600; Swale (HQ: Sittingbourne) 115 300; Thanet (HQ: Margate) 129 700; Tonbridge and Malling (HQ: West Malling) 101 200; Tunbridge Wells 99 300.

Road lengths	km	miles
motorway	175	108.7
trunk	219	136
principal	774	480.6
other	7653	4752.5

Schools and colleges nursery and primary 588; middle 10; secondary 139; special 38; colleges of FE and HE 8.

LANCASHIRE

First recorded use of the name 1087 – Anglo-Saxon *Lancastre* meaning 'the camp (*ceaster*) on the River Lune'.

Area 3069 km² (1185 miles²).

Population 1 381 900.

Density 450 per km² (1166 per mile²).

Administrative HQ County Hall, Preston.

Highest point above sea level Gragareth 627 m (2058 ft).

Districts Blackburn 134 400; Blackpool 143 800; Burnley 85 400; Chorley 96 700; Fylde (HQ: St Annes) 73 200; Hyndburn (HQ: Accrington) 78 900; Lancaster (city) 131 100; Pendle (HQ: Nelson) 84 400; Preston 128 100; Ribble Valley (HQ: Clitheroe) 52 800; Rossendale (HQ: Rawtenstall) 64 600; South Ribble (HQ: Leyland) 100 200; West Lancashire (HQ: Ormskirk) 105 400; Wyre (HQ: Poulton-le-Fylde) 103 000.

Road lengths	km	miles
motorway	168	104.3
trunk	157	97.5
principal	625	388.1
other	6 322	3925.9

Schools and colleges nursery 38; primary 600; secondary 110; special 45; colleges of FE and HE 9, polytechnic 1.

LEICESTERSHIRE

First recorded use of the name 1086 (in the Domesday Book) – Anglo-Saxon *Ledecestrescire* meaning 'the shire of the camp (*ceaster*) of the Ligore, the dwellers on the River Legra (now the River Soar)'.

Area 2553 km² (985 miles²).

Population 885 500.

Density 347 per km² (899 per mile²).

Administrative HQ County Hall, Glenfield, Leicester.

Highest point above sea level Bardon Hill 277 m (912 ft).

Districts Blaby (HQ: Narborough) 84 200; Charnwood (HQ: Loughborough) 148 500; Harborough (HQ: Market Harborough) 66 900; Hinckley and Bosworth (HQ: Hinckley) 96 300; Leicester (city) 278 500; Melton (HQ: Melton Mowbray) 43 500; North West Leicestershire (HQ: Coalville) 79 500; Oadby and Wigston (HQ: Wigston) 51 500; Rutland (HQ: Oakham) 36 400.

Road lengths	km	miles
motorway	98	60
trunk	240.4	149.3
principal	427.03	265.2
classified	1716.8	1066.1
unclassified	2781.2	1727.1

Schools and colleges nursery 1; primary 333; high 37; upper 17; secondary (11–16) 16; secondary (11–18) 7; special 19; community colleges 3; sixth form colleges 4; colleges of FE and HE 10, polytechnic 1.

LINCOLNSHIRE

First recorded use of the name 1016 – Anglo-Saxon *Lincolnescire* meaning 'the shire of the colony (Latin *colonia*) by the *lindum* (a widening in the river, i.e. the River Witham)'.

Area 5918 km² (2285 miles²).

Population 582 600.

Density 98 per km² (255 per mile²).

Administrative HQ County Offices, Lincoln.

Highest point above sea level Normanby-le-Wold 167 m (548 ft).

Districts Boston 52 200; East Lindsey (HQ: Louth) 117 700; Lincoln (city) 80 400; North Kesteven (HQ: Sleaford) 84 000; South Holland (HQ: Spalding) 66 300; South Kesteven (HQ: Grantham) 105 200; West Lindsey (HQ: Gainsborough) 76 800.

Road lengths	km	miles
trunk	354	219.8
principal	771	478.8
other	7540	4682.3

Schools and colleges nursery 3; primary 296; secondary 67; special 19; colleges of FE and HE 7.

In 1990 a report of the Local Government Commission recommended that the districts of Cleethorpes, Glanford, Great Grimsby and Scunthorpe should be transferred from Humberside to Lincolnshire. This would increase the area of Lincolnshire to 6724 km² (2616 sq mi) and its population to 872 600. (See also Humberside above.)

MERSEYSIDE*

First recorded use of the name 1002 – Anglo-Saxon *Maerse* meaning 'the boundary river (between Mercia and Northumbria)'.

Area 652 km² (252 miles²).

Population 1 448 000.

Density 2221 per km² (5746 per mile²).

Administrative HQ No central authority. Functions rest with individual districts.

Highest point above sea level Billinge Hill 179 m (588 ft).

Districts Knowsley (HQ: Kirkby) 158 400; Liverpool (city) 469 600; St Helens 187 600; Sefton (HQ: Bootle) 297 600; Wirral (HQ: Wallasey) 334 800.

Road lengths (1987)	km	miles
motorway	47.1	29.3
trunk	91.1	56.6
principal	362.2	225.1
classified	484.7	301.2
unclassified	3573.3	2220.4

Schools and colleges nursery 8; primary (inc. middle) 526; secondary 115; special 63; colleges of FE and HE 24; polytechnic 1.

NORFOLK

First recorded use of the name AD 1043 – meaning 'the territory of the *nor* (northern) *folk* (people) of East Anglia'.

Area 5369 km² (2072 miles²).

Population 744 300.

Density 139 per km² (359 per mile²).

Administrative HQ County Hall, Martineau Lane, Norwich.

Highest point above sea level Sandy Lane, east of Sheringham 102 m (335 ft).

Districts Breckland (HQ: Attleborough) 104 300; Broadland (HQ: Norwich, i.e. outside the district) 104 400; Great Yarmouth 88 900; King's Lynn and West Norfolk (HQ: King's Lynn) 134 100; North Norfolk (HQ: Cromer) 94 700; Norwich (city) 117 300; South Norfolk (HQ: Long Stratton) 100 700.

Road lengths	km	miles
trunk	247	153.4
principal	674	418.5
classified	3860	2397.0
unclassified	4617	2867.2

Schools and colleges nursery 4; primary and middle 408; secondary 58; special 13; colleges of FE and HE 6.

NORTHAMPTONSHIRE

First recorded use of the name c. AD 1011 – Anglo-Saxon *Hamtunscir* (see Hampshire above). In time Northampton was distinguished from Southampton, but initially both were referred to as 'Hamptun'.

Area 2367 km² (914 miles²).

Population 570 300.

Density 241 per km² (624 per mile²).

Administrative HQ County Hall, Northampton.

Highest point above sea level Arbury Hill 223 m (734 ft).

Districts Corby 51 000; Daventry 63 000; East Northamptonshire (HQ: Thrapston) 66 500; Kettering 74 600; Northampton 182 100; South Northamptonshire (HQ: Towcester) 66 900; Wellingborough 66 200.

Road lengths	km	miles
motorway	45	27.9
trunk	226	140.3
principal	425	263.9
other	3122	1938.8

Schools and colleges nursery 38; primary 273; middle and secondary 66; special 18; colleges of FE and HE 5.

NORTHUMBERLAND

First recorded use of the name AD 895 – Anglo-Saxon *Norohymbraland* meaning 'the land to the north of the Humber'.

Area 5032 km² (1943 miles²).

Population 301 400.

Density 60 per km² (155 per mile²).

Administrative HQ County Hall, Morpeth.

Highest point above sea level The Cheviot 815 m (2676 ft).

Districts Alnwick 30 400; Berwick-upon-Tweed 26 800; Blyth Valley (HQ: Seaton Delaval) 78 500; Castle Morpeth (HQ: Morpeth) 50 400; Tynedale (HQ: Hexham) 56 300; Wansbeck (HQ: Ashington) 59 000.

Road lengths	km	miles
trunk	274.1	170.2
primary	322.0	199.9

other	4542.0	2820.6

Schools and colleges first 144; middle 45; secondary (high) 16; special 10; colleges of FE and HE 2.

NORTH YORKSHIRE

First recorded use of the name c. AD 150 – Greek *Ebórakon* (mentioned in Ptolemy) – and 1050 – Anglo-Saxon *Eoferwicscir* (derived from the above), meaning 'the land possessed by Eburos'.

Area 8312 km² (3209 miles²).

Population 713 100.

Density 86 per km² (222 per mile²).

Administrative HQ County Hall, Northallerton.

Highest point above sea level Whernside 737 m (2419 ft).

Districts Craven (HQ: Skipton) 49 500; Hambleton (HQ: Northallerton) 77 300; Harrogate 147 000; Richmondshire (HQ: Richmond) 51 600; Ryedale (HQ: Malton) 90 800; Scarborough 105 400; Selby 90 900; York (city); 100 600.

Road lengths	km	miles
motorway	21.7	13.5
trunk	394.4	245.1
principal	750.9	466.6
classified	3570.6	2217.3
unclassified	4665.5	2897.3

Schools and colleges nursery 5; primary 402; secondary (various) 61; special 17; colleges of FE and HE 7.

NOTTINGHAMSHIRE

First recorded use of the name 1016 – Anglo-Saxon *Snotingahamscir*, meaning 'the shire around the dwelling (ham) of the followers of Snot (a Norseman)'.

Area 2164 km² (835 miles²).

Population 1 007 700.

Density 466 per km² (1207 per mile²).

Administrative HQ County Hall, West Bridgford.

Highest point above sea level Herrod's Hill 198 m (652 ft).

Districts Ashfield (HQ: Kirkby-in-Ashfield) 107 700; Bassetlaw (HQ: Worksop) 104 800; Broxtowe (HQ: Beeston) 108 300; Gedling (HQ: Arnold) 110 300; Mansfield 100 000; Newark and Sherwood (HQ: Kelham) 103 800; Nottingham (city) 273 500; Rushcliffe (HQ: West Bridgford) 99 300.

Road lengths	km	miles
motorway	15.0	9.3
trunk	238.0	147.8
other	4428.25	2749.9

Schools and colleges nursery and primary 430; secondary 88; special 28; colleges of FE and HE 10; polytechnic 1.

OXFORDSHIRE

First recorded use of the name 1010 – Anglo-Saxon *Oxnfordscir*, meaning 'the shire around the river ford for oxen'. The city was first recorded (as Osnaforda) in AD 912.

Area 2608 km² (1007 miles²).

Population 579 000.

Density 222 per km² (575 per mile²).

Administrative HQ County Hall, New Road, Oxford.

Highest point above sea level White Horse Hill 260 m (856 ft).

Districts Cherwell (HQ: Bodicote) 122 400; Oxford (city) 115 400; South Oxfordshire (HQ: Crowmarsh Gifford) 131 100; Vale of White Horse (HQ: Abingdon) 112 300; West Oxfordshire (HQ: Witney) 97 800.

Road lengths	km	miles
motorway	15	9.3
trunk	279	173.3
principal	378	234.7
classified	1546	960.0
unclassified	1767	1097.3

Schools and colleges nursery 13; first/primary 239; middle and secondary 47; special 15; colleges of FE and HE 6, polytechnic 1.

SHROPSHIRE

First recorded use of the name 1006 – Anglo-Saxon *Scrobbesbyrigscir*, derived from *Scrobbesbyrig*, the early name of Shrewsbury.

Area 3490 km² (1347 miles²).

Population 400 800.

Density 115 per km² (297 per mile²).

Administrative HQ Shirehall, Abbey Foregate, Shrewsbury.

Highest point above sea level Brown Clee Hill 545 m (1790 ft).

Districts Bridgnorth 51 000; North Shropshire (HQ: Wem) 56 200; Oswestry 32 500; Shrewsbury and Atcham (HQ: Shrewsbury) 90 900; South Shropshire (HQ: Ludlow) 36 000; The Wrekin (HQ: Telford) 134 200.

Road lengths	km	miles
motorway	37.5	23.3
trunk	225.4	140.1
principal	432.5	268.8
classified	2525.3	1569.5
unclassified	2595.3	1613.0

Schools and colleges nursery 2; primary 219; secondary (various) 39; special 10; colleges of FE and HE 8.

SOMERSET

First recorded use of the name AD 845 – Anglo-Saxon *Sumorsaete*, meaning 'the people who looked to Somerton as the tribal capital of the land of summer (Welsh *gwlad yr haf*)'.

Area 3451 km² (1332 miles²).

Population 457 700.

Density 133 per km² (344 per mile²).

Administrative HQ County Hall, Taunton.

Highest point above sea level Dunkery Beacon 519 m (170 ft).

Districts Mendip (HQ: Shepton Mallet) 94 000; Sedgemoor (HQ: Bridgwater) 96 400; Taunton Deane (HQ: Taunton) 94 100; South Somerset (HQ: Yeovil) 141 700; West Somerset (HQ: Williton) 31 500.

Road lengths	km	miles
motorway	53	32.9
trunk	96	59.6
principal	631	391.8
classified	2557	1587.9
unclassified	3074	1908.9

Schools and colleges primary 234; middle 9; secondary 29; special 8; colleges of FE and HE 8.

SOUTH YORKSHIRE*

First recorded use of the name See North Yorkshire above.

Area 1560 km² (602 miles²).

Population 1 292 600.

Density 828 per km² (2147 per mile²).

Administrative HQ No central authority. Functions rest with individual boroughs.

Highest point above sea level Margery Hill 546 m (1793 ft).

Districts Barnsley 220 900; Doncaster 291 600; Rotherham 251 800; Sheffield (city) 528 300.

Road lengths	km	miles
motorway	113.6	70.5
trunk	112.79	70.0
classified	1483.2	921.0
unclassified	3593.9	2231.8

Schools and colleges nursery 10; primary 523; secondary 134; special 39; colleges of FE and HE 12; polytechnic 1.

STAFFORDSHIRE

First recorded use of the name 1016 – Anglo-Saxon *Staeffordscir*, meaning 'the shire around a ford by a *staeth* or landing place'.

Area 2716 km² (1048 miles²).

Population 1 032 900.

Density 380 per km² (986 per mile²).

Administrative HQ County Buildings, Stafford.

Highest point above sea-level Oliver Hill, near Flash 513 m (1684 ft).

Districts Cannock Chase (HQ: Cannock) 87 700; East Staffordshire (HQ: Burton-upon-Trent) 95 700; Lichfield 93 800; Newcastle-under-Lyme 117 500; South Staffordshire (HQ: Codsall) 108 100; Stafford 117 900; Staffordshire Moorlands (HQ: Leek) 97 100; Stoke-on-Trent (city) 246 800; Tamworth 68 100.

Road lengths	km	miles
motorway	70.5	43.8
trunk	239.2	148.5
principal	598.4	371.6
classified	1734.2	1076.9
unclassified	3541.9	2199.5

Schools and colleges nursery 27; primary 423; middle and secondary 85; special 30; sixth-form college 1; colleges of FE and HE 12; polytechnic 1.

SUFFOLK

First recorded use of the name 895 – Anglo-Saxon *Suthfolchi*, meaning 'the territory of the southern folk (of East Anglia).

Area 3797 km² (1466 miles²).

Population 638 600.

Density 168 per km² (436 per mile²).

Administrative HQ County Hall, Ipswich.

Highest point above sea level Rede 128 m (420 ft).

Districts Babergh (HQ: Hadleigh) 78 500; Forest Heath (HQ: Mildenhall) 57 600; Ipswich 114 900; Mid Suffolk (HQ: Needham Market) 77 600; St Edmundsbury (Bury St Edmunds) 92 300; Suffolk Coastal (HQ: Woodbridge) 111 300; Waveney (HQ: Lowestoft) 106 500.

Road lengths	km	miles
trunk	248.9	154.7
principal	492.3	306.0

classified 2499.3 | 1553.3
unclassified 3059.5 | 1901.5
Schools and colleges nursery 1; primary 259; middle 39; high 39; special 10; colleges of FE and HE 4.

SURREY
First recorded use of the name 722 – Anglo-Saxon *Suthrige*, meaning 'the southern district'.
Area 1679 km² (648 miles²).
Population 999 800.
Density 595 per km² (1543 per mile²).
Administrative HQ County Hall, Kingston-upon-Thames (i.e. outside the county). The traditional county town is Guildford.
Highest point above sea level Leith Hill 294 m (965 ft).
Districts Elmbridge (HQ: Walton-on-Thames) 107 100; Epsom and Ewell (HQ: Epsom) 67 500; Guildford 123 200; Mole Valley (HQ: Dorking) 76 200; Reigate and Banstead (HQ: Reigate) 113 600; Runnymede (HQ: Weybridge) 71 300; Spelthorne (HQ: Staines) 85 800; Surrey Heath (HQ: Camberley) 83 600; Tandridge (HQ: Caterham) 75 600; Waverley (HQ: Godalming) 109 700; Woking 86 100.

Road lengths	km	miles
motorway	135.2	84
trunk	125.5	78
principal	949.3	590
classified	1580.0	982
unclassified	4635.5	2791

Schools and colleges nursery 6; primary and middle 390; secondary 69; special 70; colleges of FE and HE 7.

TYNE AND WEAR*
First recorded use of the name c. AD 150 – Latin *Tina* (River Tyne), mentioned by Ptolemy – and c. AD 720 – 'Church Latin' *Wirus* (River Wear), mentioned by Bede.
Area 540 km² (208 miles²).
Population 1 130 500.
Density 2093 per km² (5435 per mile²).
Administrative HQ No central authority. Functions rest with individual boroughs.
Highest point above sea level Leadgate near Chopwell 259 m (851 ft).
Districts Gateshead 206 200; Newcastle upon Tyne (city) 279 600; North Tyneside (HQ: North Shields) 192 900; South Tyneside (HQ: South Shields) 155 700; Sunderland 296 100.

Road lengths	km	miles
motorway	9.0	5.5
trunk	63.0	39.1
principal	320.0	198.8
classified	456.0	283.3
unclassified	3190.0	1982.1

Schools and colleges nursery 31; primary 408; secondary 100; special 38; colleges of FE and HE 5; polytechnics 2.

WARWICKSHIRE
First recorded use of the name 1001 – meaning 'the shire of the dwellings by the weir'.
Area 1981 km² (765 miles²).
Population 484 600.
Density 245 per km² (633 per mile²).

Administrative HQ Shire Hall, Warwick.
Highest point above sea level Ilmington Downs 260 m (854 ft).
Districts North Warwickshire (HQ: Atherstone) 59 100; Nuneaton and Bedworth (HQ: Nuneaton) 116 000; Rugby 86 300; Stratford-on-Avon 106 800; Warwick (HQ: Leamington Spa) 116 400.

Road lengths	km	miles
motorway	100	62.1
trunk	240	149.0
principal	295	183.2
classified	1206	748.9
unclassified	1697	1053.8

Schools and colleges nursery 9; primary 244; secondary 40; special 15; colleges of FE and HE 5.

WEST MIDLANDS*
First recorded use of the name 1555 – *mydlande*, meaning 'the mid lands or middle counties of England'.
Area 899 km² (347 miles²).
Population 2 662 200.
Density 2961 per km² (7672 per mile²).
Administrative HQ No central authority. Functions rest with individual boroughs.
Highest point above sea level Turner's Hill 267 m (876 ft).
Districts Birmingham (city) 993 700; Coventry (city) 306 200; Dudley 304 300; Sandwell (HQ: West Bromwich) 296 300; Solihull 205 000; Walsall 262 300; Wolverhampton 294 400.

Road lengths	km	miles
motorway	70.0	43.5
trunk	68.5	42.6
principal	596.9	370.9
classified	733.0	455.5
unclassified	5045.8	3135.4

Schools and colleges nursery 52; primary (inc. middle) 970; secondary 201; special 76; colleges of FE and HE 20; polytechnics 3.

WEST SUSSEX
First recorded use of the name See East Sussex above.
Area 1989 km² (768 miles²).
Population 703 400.
Density 354 per km² (916 per mile²).
Administrative HQ County Hall, West Street, Chichester.
Highest point above sea level Blackdown Hill 280 m (919 ft).
Districts Adur (HQ: Shoreham) 56 800; Arun (HQ: Littlehampton) 130 200; Chichester 105 900; Crawley 84 300; Horsham 107 900; Mid Sussex (HQ: Haywards Heath) 120 000; Worthing 98 200.

Road lengths	km	miles
trunk	90.7	56.4
principal	490.8	305.0
classified	1248.8	776.0
unclassified	1907.0	1185.0

Schools and colleges nursery 4; primary 241; secondary 44; sixth-form colleges 3; special 14; colleges of FE and HE 5.

WEST YORKSHIRE*
First recorded use of the name See South Yorkshire above.

COMPARATIVE DENSITIES/AREAS/POPULATIONS OF UK COUNTIES

Counties	Density (per km²)	Area (km²)	Population
Greater London*	4260	1580	6 731 000
West Midlands*	2961	899	2 662 200
Merseyside*	2221	652	1 448 000
Tyne and Wear*	2093	540	1 130 500
Greater Manchester*	2004	1286	2 577 500
West Yorkshire*	1019	2039	2 056 500
South Glamorgan	970	416	403 400
Cleveland	937	590	553 100
South Yorkshire*	828	1560	1 292 600
Avon	709	1345	954 300
Hertfordshire	603	1634	985 900
Berkshire	595	1256	747 100
Surrey	595	1679	999 800
Mid-Glamorgan	526	1019	535 900
Nottinghamshire	466	2164	1 007 700
Lancashire	450	3069	1 381 900
West Glamorgan	444	818	362 900
Bedfordshire	430	1235	530 700
Lothian	424	1755	743 700
Essex	416	3672	1 529 500
Cheshire	411	2328	955 800
Hampshire	408	3777	1 542 900
Kent	407	3732	1 520 400
East Sussex	397	1795	712 800
Staffordshire	380	2716	1 032 900
West Sussex	354	1989	703 400
Derbyshire	351	2631	924 200
Leicestershire	347	2553	885 500
Isle of Wight	341	381	129 800
Buckinghamshire	333	1883	627 300
Gwent	324	1374	445 500
Fife	263	1308	344 590
Dorset	247	2654	655 700
Durham	245	2436	596 800
Warwickshire	245	1981	484 600
Humberside	242	3512	850 500
Northamptonshire	241	2367	570 300
Oxfordshire	222	2608	579 000
Gloucestershire	199	2643	527 500
Cambridgeshire	191	3409	651 600
Hereford and Worcester	171	3927	671 000
Clwyd	168	2428	407 000
Suffolk	168	3797	638 600
Strathclyde	167	13 857	2 316 000
Devon	152	6711	1 021 100
Norfolk	139	5369	744 300
Somerset	133	3451	457 700
Cornwall (inc. Isles of Scilly)	130	3548	460 600
Shropshire	115	3490	400 800
Central	103	2637	272 077
Lincolnshire	98	5918	582 600
North Yorkshire	86	8312	713 100
Cumbria	72	6810	489 200
Gwynedd	62	3865	239 000
Dyfed	60	5773	348 400
Northumberland	60	5032	301 400
Grampian Region	58	8704	502 863
Tayside	53	7503	393 748
Dumfries and Galloway	23	6364	147 036
Powys	23	5077	114 900
Borders	22	4705	102 592
Orkney	20	975	19 338
Shetland	16	1408	22 913
Western Isles	11	2901	31 048
Highland Region	8	25 391	201 866

* Counties that are no longer administrative units.

Area 2039 km² (787 miles²).

Population 2 056 500.

Density 1019 per km² (2613 per mile²).

Administrative HQ County Hall, Wakefield.

Highest point above sea level Black Hill 581 m (1908 ft).

Districts Bradford (city) 464 100; Calderdale (HQ: Halifax) 195 900; Kirklees (HQ: Huddersfield) 375 300; Leeds (city) 709 600; Wakefield (city) 311 600.

Road lengths	km	miles
motorway	63.0	39.1
trunk	100.0	62.1
principal	499.0	310.0
classified	607.8	377.7
unclassified	3550.7	2206.4

Schools and colleges nursery 90; primary 791; middle and secondary (various) 316 (inc. sixth-form colleges); special 70; colleges of FE and HE 15; polytechnics 2.

WILTSHIRE

First recorded use of the name AD 878 – Anglo-Saxon *Wiltunscire*, meaning 'the shire around Wilton' (the town on the River Wylye).

Area 3481 km² (1344 miles²).

Population 557 000.

Density 160 per km² (414 per mile²).

Administrative HQ County Hall, Trowbridge.

Highest point above sea level Milk Hill and Tan Hill (or St Anne's Hill) 293 m (964 ft).

Districts Kennet (HQ: Devizes) 67 700; North Wiltshire (HQ: Chippenham) 113 300; Salisbury 101 000; Thamesdown (HQ: Swindon) 166 800; West Wiltshire (HQ: Trowbridge) 106 200.

Road lengths	km	miles
motorway	53.1	33.0
trunk	144.6	89.8
principal	631.0	3918
classified	2043.2	1268.8
unclassified	2139.8	1328.8

Schools and colleges primary 295; middle and secondary 44; special 13; colleges of FE and HE 7.

COUNTY TOWNS

Each of the traditional counties of England (see the map on p. 684) was originally administered from a county town. In time, many county towns were replaced by new, more convenient, administrative centres – thus Matlock replaced Derby as the administrative centre of Derbyshire. However, Derby remained the nominal county town of Derbyshire. The traditional county towns of England were as follows:

Bedfordshire Bedford. **Berkshire** Reading. **Buckinghamshire** Aylesbury. **Cambridgeshire** Cambridge. **Cheshire** Chester. **Cornwall** Bodmin. **Cumberland** Carlisle. **Devon** Exeter. **Dorset** Dorchester. **Durham** Durham. **Essex** Chelmsford. **Gloucestershire** Gloucester. **Hampshire** Winchester. **Herefordshire** Hereford. **Hertfordshire** Hertford. **Huntingdonshire** Huntingdon. **Kent** Maidstone. **Lancashire** Lancaster. **Leicestershire** Leicester. **Lincolnshire** Lincoln. **London** London. **Middlesex** Brentford. **Norfolk** Norwich. **Northamptonshire** Northampton. **Northumberland** Newcastle. **Nottinghamshire** Notting-

ham. **Oxfordshire** Oxford. **Rutland** Oakham. **Shropshire** Shrewsbury. **Somerset** Taunton. **Staffordshire** Stafford. **Suffolk** Ipswich. **Surrey** Guildford. **Sussex** Lewes. **Warwickshire** Warwick. **Westmoreland** Appleby. **Wiltshire** Salisbury. **Worcestershire** Worcester. **Yorkshire** York.

REGIONS AND ISLAND AUTHORITIES OF SCOTLAND

BORDERS

First recorded use of the name 1580 in an Act of the English Parliament – Middle English *bordure* meaning the 'district bordering on the boundary between England and Scotland'.

Area 4705 km² (1817 miles²).

Population 102 592.

Density 22 per km² (56 per mile²).

Administrative HQ Regional Headquarters, Newtown St Boswells.

Highest point above sea level Broad Law (southern summit) 840 m (2756 ft).

Districts Berwickshire (HQ: Duns) 18 800; Ettrick and Lauderdale (HQ: Galashiels) 33 400; Roxburgh (HQ: Hawick) 35 100; Tweeddale (HQ: Peebles) 14 600.

Road lengths	km	miles
trunk	294.4	183
classified	2875.3	1787
unclassified	1720.0	1069

Schools and colleges nursery 7; primary 85; secondary 9; special 13; college of FE and HE 1.

CENTRAL

First recorded use of the name Pertaining to the centre – the word 'central' was first recorded in this sense in 1647.

Area 2637 km² (1018 miles²).

Population 272 077.

Density 103 per km² (267 per mile²).

Administrative HQ Central Regional Council, Viewforth, Stirling.

Highest point above sea level Ben More 1174 m (3852 ft).

Districts Clackmannan (HQ: Alloa) 47 400; Falkirk 143 200; Stirling 81 400.

Road lengths	km	miles
motorway	69.0	42.9
trunk	112.8	70.1
principal	336.6	209.2
classified	611.5	380.0
unclassified	942.2	585.5

Schools and colleges nursery 11; primary 120; secondary 21; colleges of FE and HE 2.

DUMFRIES AND GALLOWAY

First recorded use of the name c. 1183 – *Dum prys* meaning 'the fort of the copse' – and c. 990 – *Gall-Gaidheal* meaning 'the foreign Gael'.

Area 6364 km² (2456 miles²).

Population 147 036.

Density 23 per km² (60 per mile²).

Administrative HQ Regional Council Offices, Dumfries.

Highest point above sea level Merrick 844 m (2770 ft).

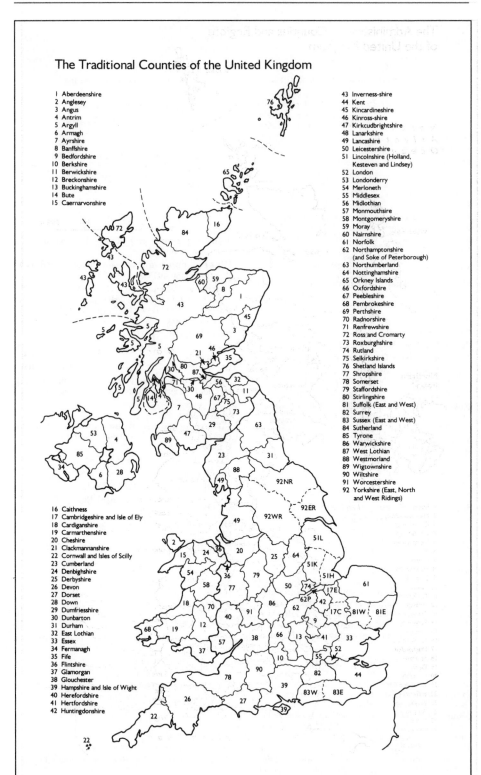

The Traditional Counties of the United Kingdom

The Administrative Counties and Regions
of the United Kingdom

Shetland

North
Atlantic
Ocean

Orkney

Western Isles

Scotland

Highland

Grampian

0   50   100   150 km

Tayside

Strathclyde

Central

Fife

North Sea

Lothian

Northern
Ireland

Strathclyde

Borders

Dumfries and
Galloway

Northumberland

Tyne and Wear

Cumbria

Durham

Cleveland

North Yorkshire

North Channel

Humberside

Lancashire

West
Yorkshire

Irish Sea

G. Manch.

South
Yorks.

England

Merseyside

Cheshire

Derby—
shire

Lincolnshire

Gwyn.

Clwyd

Notts.

Staffs.

Wales

Shrop-
shire

W.
Mid.

Leicester—
shire

Norfolk

Powys

Hereford and
Worcester

War.

Northants.

Cambs.

Dyfed

Beds.

Suffolk

Glos.

Herts.

Essex

W.
Glam.

Mid
Glam.

Gwent

Oxford—
shire

Bucks.

S. Glam.

Greater
London

Bristol Channel

Avon

Wiltshire

Berkshire

Surrey

Kent

Somerset

Hampshire

West
Sussex

East
Sussex

Strait of Dover

Devon

Dorset

Isle of Wight

Cornwall

English Channel

Isles of Scilly

1 Belfast
2 Newtownabbey
3 Carrickfergus
4 Castlereagh
5 North Down
6 Ards
7 Down
8 Newry & Mourne
9 Banbridge
10 Lisburn
11 Craigavon
12 Armagh
13 Dungannon
14 Fermanagh
15 Omagh
16 Cookstown
17 Magherafelt
18 Strabane
19 Derry
20 Limavady
21 Coleraine
22 Ballymoney
23 Moyle
24 Ballymena
25 Larne
26 Antrim

Districts Annandale and Eskdale (HQ: Annan) 35 900; Nithsdale (HQ: Dumfries) 57 300; Stewartry (HQ: Kirkcudbright) 23 100; Wigtown (HQ: Stranraer) 30 400.

Road lengths	km	miles
trunk	345	214.2
principal	500	310.5
classified	1826	1133.9
unclassified	1662	1032.1

Schools and colleges nursery 9; primary 116; secondary 16; special 12; colleges of FE 5.

FIFE

First recorded use of the name c. AD 590 – possibly from Fibh, who was thought to be one of the seven sons of the ancient British leader Cruithne.

Area 1308 km² (505 miles²).

Population 344 590.

Density 263 per km² (682 per mile²).

Administrative HQ Fife House, North Street, Glenrothes.

Highest point above sea level West Lomond 522 m (1713 ft).

Districts Dunfermline 129 000, Kirkcaldy 148 000, North East Fife 66 700 (HQ: Cupar).

Road lengths	km	miles
motorway/trunk	160.6	99.7
principal	339.4	210.9
classified	575.0	357.3
unclassified	1206.4	749.6

Schools and colleges nursery 90; primary 147; secondary 19; colleges of FE 4.

GRAMPIAN

First recorded use of the name 1526 – derivation uncertain, but possibly from the Gaelic *greannich* meaning 'gloomy' or 'rugged'.

Area 8704 km² (3359 miles²).

Population 502 863.

Density 58 per km² (150 per mile²).

Administrative HQ Woodhill House, Westburn Road, Aberdeen.

Highest point above sea level Ben Macdhui 1310 m (4300 ft).

Districts Aberdeen (city) 215 300; Banff and Buchan (HQ: Banff) 83 200; Gordon (HQ: Inverurie) 70 800; Kincardine and Deeside (HQ: Stonehaven) 47 900; Moray (HQ: Elgin) 85 900.

Road lengths	km	miles
trunk	344.3	214
principal	849.5	528
classified	3134.3	1948
unclassified	3399.8	2113

Schools and colleges nursery 55; primary 274; secondary 39; special 13; colleges of FE and HE 5.

HIGHLAND

First recorded use of the name c. 1425 – from the adjective 'high', and the noun 'land'.

Area 25 391 km² (9 800 miles²).

Population 201 866.

Density 8 per km² (20 per mile²).

Administrative HQ Regional Buildings, Glenurquhart Road, Inverness. The Regional Council meets at County Buildings, Dingwall.

Highest point above sea level Ben Nevis 1342 m (4406 ft).

Districts Badenoch and Strathspey (HQ: Kingussie) 10 000; Caithness (HQ: Wick) 27 000; Inverness 61 100; Lochaber (HQ: Fort William) 19 400; Nairn 10 300; Ross and Cromarty (HQ: Dingwall) 48 400; Skye and Lochalsh (HQ: Portree) 11 500; Sutherland (HQ: Golspie) 13 200.

Road lengths	km	miles
trunk	759	471.3
principal	1642	1019.7
classified	2401	1491
other	2632	1634.4

Schools and colleges primary 210; secondary 54; special 7; colleges of FE and HE 3.

LOTHIAN

First recorded use of the name c. AD 970 – from a personal name, possible a Welsh derivative of Laudinus.

Area 1755 km² (677 miles²).

Population 743 700.

Density 424 per km² (1098 per mile²).

Administrative HQ Regional Headquarters, George IV Bridge, Edinburgh.

Highest point above sea level Blackhope Scar 651 m (2137 ft).

Districts East Lothian (HQ: Haddington) 82 800; Edinburgh (city) 438 200; Midlothian (HQ: Edinburgh, i.e. outside the district) 81 400; West Lothian (HQ: Linlithgow) 143 000.

Road lengths	km	miles
motorway	48.3	30
trunk	104.6	65
principal	457	284
other	2996	1862

Schools and colleges nursery 47; primary 244; secondary 51; special 23; colleges of FE and HE 5.

ORKNEY

First recorded use of the name c. 308 BC – Celtic *Innse Orc* meaning 'the islands of the Boars' (a Pictish tribe) – but later altered to the Norse *Orkneyjar* meaning 'the islands of the young seals'.

Area 975 km² (376 miles²).

Population 19 338.

Density 20 per km² (51 per mile²).

Administrative HQ Council Offices, Kirkwall.

Highest point above sea level Ward Hill, Hoy 478 m (1570 ft).

Road lengths	km	miles
principal	2565	159.4
classified	584.5	363.3
unclassified	675.1	419.6

Schools and colleges primary 20; secondary 6; special 1.

SHETLAND

First recorded use of the name 1289 – meaning 'the land of Hjalto' (an Old Norse personal name).

Area 1408 km² (543 miles²).

Population 22 918.

Density 16 per km² (42 per mile²).

Administrative HQ Town Hall, Lerwick.

Highest point above sea level Ronas Hill, Mainland 450 m (1477 ft).

Road lengths

	km	miles
principal	199.5	124
other	690.3	429

Schools and colleges primary 35; secondary 8.

STRATHCLYDE

First recorded use of the name c. AD 875 – *Straecled* meaning 'the valley of the Clyde'.

Area 13 857 km² (5348 mile²).

Population 2 316 000.

Density 167 per km² (433 per mile²)

Administrative HQ Strathclyde House, 20 India Street, Glasgow G2 4PF.

Highest point above sea level Bidean nam Bian 1147 m (3766 ft).

Districts Argyll and Bute (HQ: Lochgilphead) 65 700; Bearsden and Milngavie (HQ: Milngavie) 40 400; Clydebank 49 000; Clydesdale (HQ: Lanark) 58 400; Cumbernauld and Kilsyth (HQ: Cumbernauld) 62 500; Cumnock and Doon Valley (HQ: Ayr, i.e. outside the district) 43 400; Cunninghame (HQ: Irvine) 137 300; Dumbarton 79 200; East Kilbride 81 800; Eastwood (HQ: Paisley, i.e. outside the district); Glasgow (City) 715 600; Hamilton 107 000; Inverclyde (HQ: Greenock) 96 400; Kilmarnock and Loudon (HQ: Kilmarnock) 81 200; Kyle and Carrick (HQ: Ayr) 113 100; Monklands (HQ: Coatbridge); Motherwell 147 500; Renfrew (HQ: Paisley) 201 300; Strathkelvin (HQ: Kirkintilloch) 89 800.

Road lengths

	km	miles
motorway	144	89.4
trunk	728	452
principal	1700	1056
other	10 483	6514

Schools and colleges nursery 274; primary 903; secondary 190; special 150; colleges of FE and HE 20.

TAYSIDE

First recorded use of the name c. AD 85 – *Taus* or *Tanaus* (the River Tay), mentioned by Tacitus.

Area 7503 km² (2896 miles²).

Population 393 748.

Density 53 per km² (136 per mile²).

Administrative HQ Tayside House, Dundee.

Highest point above sea level Ben Lawers 1214 m (3984 ft).

Districts Angus (HQ: Forfar) 94 400; Dundee (city) 175 700; Perth and Kinross (HQ: Perth) 123 600.

Road lengths

	km	miles
motorway	55	34.2
trunk	231	143.4
principal	712	422.2
classified	1844	1145.1
unclassified	1994	1238.3

Schools and colleges nursery 27; primary 191; secondary 32; special 28; colleges of FE and HE 3.

WESTERN ISLES

First recorded use of the name possibly 14th century – during the reign of David II the style 'Lord of the Isles' appears for the first time. The Western Isles were known up to the 13th century by the Norse name *Sudreys*.

Area 2901 km² (1120 miles²).

Population 31 048.

Density 11 per km² (28 per mile²).

Administrative HQ Council Offices, Stornoway, Isle of Lewis.

Highest point above sea level Clisham, Harris 799 m (2622 ft).

Road lengths

	km	miles
classified	426	265
unclassified	299	186

Schools and colleges primary 43; secondary 15; college of FE 1.

WELSH COUNTIES

CLWYD

First recorded use of the name 1973 – from the river of that name.

Area 2428 km² (937 miles²).

Population 407 000.

Density 168 per km² (434 per mile²).

Administrative HQ Shire Hall, Mold.

Highest point above sea level Moel Sych 826 m (2713 ft).

Districts Alyn and Deeside (HQ: Hawarden) 72 600; Colwyn (HQ: Colwyn Bay) 54 800; Delyn (HQ: Flint) 65 100; Glyndwr (HQ: Ruthin) 41 500; Rhuddlan (HQ: Rhyl) 56 100; Wrexham Maelor (HQ: Wrexham) 117 000.

Road lengths

	km	miles
trunk	199.5	124
principal	440.9	274
classified	4316.9	2683

Schools and colleges nursery 5; primary 253; secondary 33; special 11; colleges of FE and HE 7.

DYFED

First recorded use of the name Dyfed was the name of a kingdom dating from the 5th century AD.

Area 5773 km² (2228 miles²).

Population 348 400.

Density 60 per km² (156 per mile²).

Administrative HQ County Hall, Carmarthen.

Highest point above sea level Carmarthen Fan Foel 762 m (2500 ft).

Districts Carmarthen 55 800; Ceredigion (HQ: Aberystwyth) 67 000; Dinefwr (HQ: Llandeilo) 38 900; Llanelli 74 100; Preseli Pembrokeshire (HQ: Haverfordwest) 70 700; South Pembrokeshire (HQ: Pembroke) 41 900.

Road lengths

	km	miles
trunk	377.9	234.7
principal	554.5	344.3
classified	3918.0	2433.0
unclassified	3273.8	2033.0

Schools and colleges nursery 3; primary 320; secondary 32; special 5; colleges of FE and HE 5.

GWENT

First recorded use of the name Gwent was the name of an ancient kingdom dating from the 5th century AD.

Area 1374 km² (530 miles²).

Population 445 500.

Density 324 per km² (841 per mile²).

Administrative HQ County Hall, Cwmbran.

Highest point above sea level Chwarel-y-Fan 679 m (2228 ft).

Districts Blaenau Gwent (HQ: Ebbw Vale) 77 300; Islwyn (HQ: Pontllanfraith) 66 400; Monmouth (HQ: Pontypool, i.e. outside the district) 81 300; Newport 128 100; Torfaen (HQ: Pontypool) 92 400.

Road lengths	km	miles
motorway	51.2	31.8
trunk	133.2	82.7
principal	219.3	136.2
classified	1003.9	623.4
unclassified	2079.8	1291.5

Schools and colleges nursery 13; primary 226; secondary 34; special 7; colleges of FE and HE 6.

GWYNEDD

First recorded use of the name Gwynedd was the name of an ancient kingdom dating from the 5th century AD.

Area 3865 km² (1493 miles²).

Population 239 000.

Density 62 per km² (160 per mile²).

Administrative HQ County Offices, Caernarfon.

Highest point above sea level Snowdon 1085 m (3560 ft).

Districts Aberconwy (HQ: Llandudno) 54 100; Arfon (HQ: Bangor) 55 200; Dwyfor (HQ: Pwllheli) 27 000; Meirionnydd (HQ: Dolgellau) 31 600; Ynys Môn-Isle of Anglesey (HQ: Llangefni) 71 000.

Road lengths	km	miles
trunk	336	208.6
principal	446	277.0
classified	1826	1133.9
unclassified	2193	1361.8

Schools and colleges primary 195; secondary 23; special 6; colleges of FE and HE 4.

MID-GLAMORGAN

First recorded use of the name 1242 – *Gwlad Morgan*, meaning 'the land of Morgan', a 10th-century Welsh prince.

Area 1019 km² (393 miles²).

Population 535 900.

Density 526 per km² (1364 per mile²).

Administrative HQ County Hall, Cathays Park, Cardiff (i.e. outside the county).

Highest point above sea level Near Craig-y-Llyn 585 m (1919 ft).

Districts Cynon Valley (HQ: Aberdare) 64 300; Merthyr Tydfil 58 100; Ogwr (HQ: Bridgend) 137 500; Rhondda (HQ: Pentre) 76 600; Rhymney Valley (HQ: Ystrad Mynach) 104 500; Taff-Ely (HQ: Pontypridd) 94 900.

Road lengths	km	miles
motorway and trunk	88.7	55.1
principal	340.2	211.3
classified	475.8	295.5
unclassified	1845.4	1146.0

Schools and colleges nursery 23; primary 150; infants 93; junior 69; comprehensive 42; special 10; colleges of FE and HE 7; polytechnic 1.

POWYS

First recorded use of the name Powys was the name of an ancient kingdom dating from c. 5th century AD.

Area 5077 km² (1960 miles²).

Population 114 900.

Density 23 per km² (59 per mile²).

Administrative HQ County Hall, Llandrindod Wells.

Highest point above sea level Pen-y-Fan (Cadet Arthur) 886 m (2906 ft).

Districts Brecknock (HQ: Brecon) 41 100; Montgomeryshire (HQ: Welshpool) 51 200; Radnor (HQ: Llandrindod Wells) 22 600.

Road lengths	km	miles
trunk	425.6	264.3
principal	237.7	147.6
classified	2613.0	1622.7
unclassified	2390.0	1484.2

Schools and colleges primary 114; secondary 13; special 4; college of FE 1.

SOUTH GLAMORGAN

First recorded use of the name See Mid-Glamorgan above.

Area 416 km² (161 miles²).

Population 403 400.

Density 970 per km² (2506 per mile²).

Administrative HQ County Hall, Atlantic Wharf, Cardiff.

Highest point above sea level near Lisvane 264 m (866 ft).

Districts Cardiff (city) 283 900; Vale of Glamorgan (HQ: Barry) 119 500.

Road lengths	km	miles
motorway and trunk	64	39.7
principal	103	64.0
other	1579	980.6

Schools and colleges nursery 10; primary 156; secondary 28; special 15; colleges of FE and HE 4.

WEST GLAMORGAN

First recorded use of the name See Mid-Glamorgan above.

Area 818 km² (316 miles²).

Population 362 900.

Density 444 per km² (1148 per mile²).

Administrative HQ County Hall, Swansea.

Highest point above sea level Cefnffordd 600 m (1969 ft).

Districts Lliw Valley (HQ: Penllergaer) 61 800; Neath 65 200; Port Talbot 49 000; Swansea (city) 186 900.

Road lengths	km	miles
motorway	37.0	23.0
trunk	36.9	22.9
principal	217.2	134.9
classified	335.5	208.3
unclassified	1389.8	863.1

Schools and colleges nursery 2; primary 168; secondary 27; senior 26; special 6; colleges of FE and HE 5.

NORTHERN IRELAND

Area 14 120 km² (5450 miles²).

Population 1 566 800 (1986 estimate).

Density 111 per km² (287 per mile²).

Administrative HQ Belfast.

Districts The province is now divided into 26 districts, whose councils have responsibility for a wide range of local services including leisure, environmental, regulatory, etc. The six geographical counties no longer exist as administrative units. Northern Ireland is divided into nine areas: five education and library areas plus four health and social services areas (other functions such as police, planning, roads, water, housing, fire services, etc., are run centrally from Stormont). The area boards are not directly elected: about a third of their members are district councillors while the rest are persons appointed by the appropriate United Kingdom minister. The six traditional geographic counties of Northern Ireland in order of size are:

COUNTY TYRONE

First recorded name and derivation from Tir Eoghan, land of Eoghan (Owen son of Niall).
Area 3400 km² (1313 miles²).
Former capital Omagh on the river Strule.
Highest point Sawel (in Sperrin Mts) 683 m (2240 ft).
Coastline length nil.

COUNTY ANTRIM

First recorded name and derivation from the 5th-century monastery of Aentrebh.
Area 3046 km² (1176 miles²).
Former capital City of Belfast on the river Lagan.
Highest point Trostan 544 m (1817 ft).
Coastline length 145 km (90 miles).

COUNTY DOWN

First recorded name and derivation From Dun, Irish gaelic for fort (i.e. St Patrick's fort).
Area 2466 km² (952 miles²).
Former capital Downpatrick on the river Quoile.
Highest point Slieve Donard 852 m (2796 ft).
Coastline length 201 km (125 miles).

COUNTY LONDONDERRY

First recorded name and derivation From the charter granted by James I in 1613 to the City of London (England) livery companies. Known as Derry prior to charter. 'Derry' is a corruption of the celtic *doire*, an oak grove c. AD 500.
Area 2075 km² (801 miles²).
Former capital City of Londonderry on the river Foyle.
Highest point Sawel 683 m (2240 ft).
Coastline length 29 km (18 miles).

COUNTY FERMANAGH

First recorded name and derivation from Fir Mhanach, territory of the men of Managh.
Area 1851 km² (715 miles²).
Former capital Enniskillen.
Highest point Cuilcagh 667 m (2188 ft).
Coastline length nil.

COUNTY ARMAGH

First recorded name and derivation from Queen Macha c. 3rd century BC.
Area 1326 km² (512 miles²).
Former capital Armagh on the Blackwater tributary Callan.

Highest point Slieve Gullion 577 m (1894 ft).
Coastline length 3.2 km (2 miles).

DISTRICTS OF NORTHERN IRELAND

Antrim Population: 48 100.
Ards (HQ: Newtownards) Population: 64 500.
Armagh Population: 49 000.
Ballymena Population: 57 200.
Ballymoney Population: 23 900.
Banbridge Population: 31 900.
Belfast (City) Population: 296 900.
Carrickfergus Population: 30 400.
Castlereagh (HQ: Belfast, i.e. outside the district) Population: 58 000.
Coleraine Population: 48 500.
Cookstown Population: 27 600.
Craigavon (HQ: Portadown) 77 700.
Derry (HQ: Londonderry/Derry) Population: 99 500.
Down (HQ: Downpatrick) Population: 57 200.
Dungannon Population: 43 700.
Fermanagh (HQ: Enniskillen) Population: 50 400.
Larne Population: 29 100.
Limavady Population: 29 800.
Lisburn Population: 97 400.
Magherafelt Population: 32 900.
Moyle (HQ: Ballycastle) Population: 15 100.
Newry and Mourne (HQ: Newry) Population: 88 900.
Newtownabbey (HQ: Ballyclare) Population: 72 900.
North Down (HQ: Bangor) Population: 71 900.
Omagh Population: 44 900.
Strabane Population: 35 600.

PRINCIPAL CITIES, TOWNS AND DISTRICTS

Since the reform of local government in 1974–75 the definition of many towns has been difficult. A few new districts show an improved delineation of towns, but many new districts have borough status, although the towns from which they take their name may represent but a fraction of their population. Also, some urban districts, usually with Borough status, do not bear the name of the principal town; e.g. the Borough in which West Bromwich is the main town is called Sandwell. The list below shows local-government districts with a population of over a quarter of a million (mid-1988 estimates).

1.	London	Greater London	6 731 000
2.	Birmingham	West Midlands	993 700
3.	Glasgow	Strathclyde	715 600
4.	Leeds	West Yorkshire	709 600
5.	Sheffield	South Yorkshire	528 300
6.	Liverpool	Merseyside	469 600
7.	Bradford	West Yorkshire	464 100
8.	Manchester	Greater Manchester	445 900
9.	Edinburgh	Lothian	438 200
10.	Bristol	Avon	377 700
11.	Kirklees	West Yorkshire	375 300
12.	Wirral	Merseyside	334 800
13.	Wakefield	West Yorkshire	311 600
14.	Wigan	Greater Manchester	307 600

15. Coventry	West Midlands	306 200
16. Dudley	West Midlands	304 300
17. Sefton	Merseyside	297 600
18. Belfast	N. Ireland	296 900
19. Sandwell	West Midlands	296 300
20. Sunderland	Tyne and Wear	296 100
21. Wolverhampton	West Midlands	294 400
22. Doncaster	South Yorkshire	291 600
23. Stockport	Greater Manchester	290 900
24. Cardiff	South Glamorgan	283 900
25. Newcastle-upon-Tyne	Tyne and Wear	279 600
26. Leicester	Leicestershire	278 500
27. Nottingham	Nottinghamshire	273 500
28. Bolton	Greater Manchester	263 600
29. Walsall	West Midlands	262 300
30. Plymouth	Devon	258 100
31. Rotherham	South Yorkshire	251 800

URBAN AREAS

Recognizing the difficulty of defining the population of towns, the Office of Population Censuses and Surveys has defined a number of conurbations and urban areas.

Many of the districts shown in the list above do not meet the ordinary concepts of a town, e.g. Kirklees, Wirral and Sefton. In some cases, e.g. Newcastle and Nottingham, the local government boundary has been drawn so close to the city centre that most of the suburbs have been excluded from the total. In yet other cases, the figures given in the list above include large areas of countryside, e.g. Doncaster. The existing local government boundaries in the majority of cases do not reflect the true extent of cities.

The urban areas listed here give a more accurate impression of the size of the major centres in the United Kingdom and have been defined in a manner similar to the urban areas whose population figures are recorded under the heading 'Major cities' in the vast majority of cases in the Countries of the World section of Chapter 12.

The figures given here are estimates based upon the 1981 census figures for urban areas and the mid-1988 estimates for local-government districts.

1. **London**   7 680 000
   Greater London Urban Area, of which Greater London 6 731 000
2. **Birmingham**   2 355 000
   West Midlands Urban Area, of which Birmingham (City) 993 700
3. **Manchester**   2 340 000
   Greater Manchester Urban Area, of which Manchester (City) 445 900
4. **Glasgow**   1 660 000
   Central Clydesdale Urban Area, of which Glasgow (City) 715 600
5. **Leeds**   1 480 000
   West Yorkshire Urban Area, of which Leeds (City) 709 600, Bradford (City) 464 100
6. **Newcastle-upon-Tyne**   780 000
   Tyneside Urban Area, of which Newcastle-upon-Tyne (City) 279 600
7. **Liverpool**   750 000
   Liverpool Urban Area, of which Liverpool (City) 469 600
8. **Sheffield**   645 000
   Sheffield Urban Area, of which Sheffield (City) 528 300
9. **Nottingham**   600 000

Nottingham Urban Area, of which Nottingham (City) 273 500
10. **Bristol**   525 000
    Bristol Urban Area, of which Bristol (City) 377 700
11. **Edinburgh**   460 000
    Edinburgh Urban Area, of which Edinburgh (City) 438 200
12. **Brighton**   440 000
    Brighton–Worthing–Littlehampton, of which Brighton (Borough) 149 200
13. **Belfast**   435 000
    Belfast Urban Area, of which Belfast (City) 296 900
14. **Portsmouth**   415 000
    Portsmouth Urban Area, of which Portsmouth (City) 183 800
15. **Leicester**   410 000
    Leicester Urban Area, of which Leicester (City) 278 500
16. **Middlesbrough**   380 000
    Teesside Urban Area, of which Middlesbrough (Borough) 143 200
17. **Stoke-on-Trent**   375 000
    The Potteries Urban Area, of which Stoke-on-Trent (City) 246 800
18. **Coventry**   350 000
    Coventry–Bedworth Urban Area, of which Coventry (City) 306 200
19. **Bournemouth**   335 000
    Bournemouth Urban Area, of which Bournemouth (Borough) 154 800
20. **Hull**   325 000
    Kingston-upon-Hull Urban Area, of which Kingston-upon-Hull (City) 247 000
21. **Cardiff**   284 000
    Cardiff Urban Area, coterminous with Cardiff (City) 283 900
22. =**Swansea**   280 000
    Swansea Urban Area, of which Swansea (City) 186 900
22. =**Birkenhead**   280 000
    Birkenhead Urban Area, which is part of Wirral District, of which Birkenhead (former Borough) 99 000
24. **Southend**   275 000
    Southend Urban Area, of which Southend-on-Sea (Borough) 165 400
25. **Southampton**   270 000
    Southampton–Eastleigh Urban Area, of which Southampton (City) 196 700
26. **Blackpool**   265 000
    Blackpool Urban Area, of which Blackpool (Borough) 143 800
27. **Plymouth**   258 000
    Plymouth Urban Area, of which Plymouth (City) 258 000
28. **Preston**   250 000
    Preston Urban Area, of which Preston (Borough) 128 100
29. **Rochester**   243 000
    The Medway Towns Urban Area, of which Rochester-upon-Medway (City) 146 600
30. **Aldershot**   230 000
    Aldershot Urban Area, of which Aldershot (former Borough) 55 000
31. **Luton**   217 000
    Luton–Dunstable Urban Area, of which Luton (Borough) 167 600
32. **Derby**   215 000

Derby Urban Area, coterminous with
Derby (City) 215 400

33. **Aberdeen** 214 000
Aberdeen Urban Area, coterminous
with Aberdeen (City) 214 100

34. **Reading** 210 000
Reading Urban Area, of which
Reading (Borough) 132 400

35. **Sunderland** 200 000
Sunderland–Whitburn Urban Area,
which is part of Sunderland
Metropolitan Borough

36. **Norwich** 190 000
Norwich Urban Area, of which
Norwich (City) 117 300

THE 58 CITIES OF THE UNITED KINGDOM

The term 'City' as used in the United Kingdom is a title of dignity applied to 58 towns of varying local government status by virtue of their importance as either archiepiscopal or episcopal sees or former sees, or as commercial or industrial centres. The right has been acquired in the past by (1) traditional usage – for example, the Domesday Book describes Coventry, Exeter and Norwich as *civitas*; by (2) statute; or by (3) royal prerogative, and in more recent times solely by royal charter and letters patent – the most recent examples are Lancaster (1937), Cambridge (1951). Southampton (1964), Swansea (1969), and Derby (1977). St David's (Dyfed), Armagh and a number of other towns are cities only by repute; although they have a cathedral they do not have the right to use the title 'City'.

Name of City with geographical county or region	First recorded charter	Title of civic head
Aberdeen, Grampian, Scotland	1179	Lord Provost
Bangor, Gwynedd, Wales	1883	Mayor
Bath, Avon	1590	Mayor
Belfast, Antrim, Northern Ireland	1613	Lord Mayor*
Birmingham, West Midlands	1838	Lord Mayor
Bradford, W. Yorkshire	1847	Lord Mayor
Bristol, Avon	1188	Lord Mayor
Cambridge, Cambridgeshire	1207	Mayor
Canterbury, Kent	1448	Mayor
Cardiff, South Glamorgan, Wales	1608	Lord Mayor
Carlisle, Cumbria	1158	Mayor
Chester, Cheshire	1506	Mayor
Chichester, W. Sussex	1135–54	Mayor
Coventry, W. Midlands	1345	Lord Mayor
Derby, Derbyshire	1154 (present charter 1977)	Mayor
Dundee, Tayside, Scotland	c. 1179	Lord Provost
Durham, Durham	1602	Mayor
Edinburgh, Lothian, Scotland	c. 1124	Lord Provost
Elgin, Grampian, Scotland	1234	Lord Provost
Ely, Cambridgeshire	1974**	Mayor
Exeter, Devon	1156	Mayor
Glasgow, Strathclyde, Scotland	1690	Lord Provost*
Gloucester, Gloucestershire	1483	Mayor
Hereford, Hereford and Worcester	1189	Mayor
Kingston upon Hull, Humberside	1440	Lord Mayor
Lancaster, Lancashire	1193	Mayor
Leeds, W. Yorkshire	1626	Lord Mayor
Leicester, Leicestershire	1589	Lord Mayor
Lichfield, Staffordshire	1549	Mayor
Lincoln, Lincolnshire	1154	Mayor
Liverpool, Merseyside	1207	Lord Mayor
London, Greater London	1066–87	Lord Mayor*
Londonderry, Londonderry, Northern Ireland	1604	Mayor
Manchester, Greater Manchester	1838	Lord Mayor
Newcastle upon Tyne, Tyne and Wear	1157	Lord Mayor
Norwich, Norfolk	1194	Lord Mayor
Nottingham, Nottinghamshire	1155	Lord Mayor
Oxford, Oxfordshire	1154–87	Lord Mayor
Perth, Tayside, Scotland	1210	Lord Provost
Peterborough, Cambridgeshire	1874	Mayor
Plymouth, Devon	1439	Lord Mayor
Portsmouth, Hampshire	1194	Lord Mayor
Ripon, N. Yorkshire	886	Mayor
Rochester, Kent	1189	Mayor
St Albans, Hertfordshire	1553	Mayor
Salford, Greater Manchester	1835	Mayor
Salisbury, Wiltshire	1227	Mayor
Sheffield, S. Yorkshire	1843	Lord Mayor
Southampton, Hampshire	1447	Mayor
Stoke-on-Trent, Staffordshire	1874 (present charter 1910)	Lord Mayor
Swansea, West Glamorgan, Wales	1169 (present charter 1969)	Mayor
Truro, Cornwall	1589	Mayor
Wakefield, W. Yorkshire	1848	Mayor
Wells, Somerset	1201	Mayor
Westminster, Greater London	1256 (present charter 1965)	Lord Mayor
Winchester, Hampshire	1155	Mayor
Worcester, Hereford and Worcester	1189	Mayor
York, N. Yorkshire	1396	Lord Mayor*

* Is styled 'Rt Hon.'. ** present status.

NEW TOWNS

There are 29 New Towns built by government-appointed Development Corporations in England (21), Wales (2), Scotland (5) and Northern Ireland (1). When development of a New Town in England and Wales is substantially completed its Development Corporation is wound up. This stage has been reached by those towns indicated with an asterisk below. The Development Corporations for Telford and Milton Keynes will be wound up in 1991 and 1992 respectively.

New towns in order of designation:
*Stevenage, Hertfordshire, 1946.
*Crawley, West Sussex, January 1947.
*Hemel Hempstead, Hertfordshire, February 1947.
*Harlow, Essex, May 1947.
*Aycliffe, Durham, July 1947.
East Kilbride, Strathclyde, August 1947.
*Peterlee, Durham, March 1948.

*Welwyn Garden City, Hertfordshire, June 1948.
*Hatfield, Hertfordshire, June 1948.
Glenrothes, Fife, October 1948.
*Basildon, Essex, February 1949.
*Bracknell, Berkshire, October 1949.
*Cwmbran, Gwent, November 1949.
*Corby, Northamptonshire, 1950.
Cumbernauld, Strathclyde, 1956.
*Skelmersdale, Lancashire, 1962.
Livingston, Lothian, 1962.
Telford, Shropshire, 1963.
*Runcorn, Cheshire, 1964.
*Redditch, Hereford and Worcester, 1964.
*Washington, Tyne and Wear, 1964.
Craigavon, Northern Ireland, 1965.
Irvine, Strathclyde, 1966.
Milton Keynes, Buckinghamshire, 1967.
*Newtown, Powys, 1967.
*Northampton, Northamptonshire, 1968.
*Peterborough, Cambridgeshire, 1968.
*Warrington, Cheshire, 1968.
*Central Lancashire New Town (Preston-Leyland-Chorley), 1970.
Stonehouse, Strathclyde, was scheduled in 1973 but development plans were abandoned in 1976.

BRITISH HISTORY

Significant dates in British history are also recorded in the time charts in the History chapter beginning on p. 407.

DATES IN BRITISH PREHISTORY

c. 400 000 BC
Disputed evidence (hand axes?) for *Homo erectus*, predecessor of *Homo sapiens*, found in 1975 near Westbury-sub-Mendip, Somerset.

?285 000–240 000 BC
Coarse hand-axe culture, evidence of which has been found at Fordwich in Kent and Kent's Cavern, near Torquay (Devon).

?240 000–130 000 BC
The earliest British human remains (discovered at Swanscombe in Kent in 1935–6) date from this period. The Swanscombe site also yielded flake assemblages and evidence of a hand-axe industry. Human settlement in Britain may have been discontinuous until c. 59 000 BC.

c. 59 000 BC
Evidence of settlement in England during a warmer period. No further evidence of human population in Britain until c. 40 000–36 000 BC.

c. 26 700 BC
Earliest radiocarbon dating of human artefacts from the Upper Palaeolithic period from a site at Kent's Cavern near Torquay (Devon).

6100 BC
Earliest dated habitation in Scotland, at Morton in Fife.

c. 4600 BC
Earliest dated habitation in Northern Ireland – Neolithic site at Ballynagilly, Tyrone.

c. 4400 BC
Mesolithic man probably began to herd animals.

c. 4300 BC
Earliest Neolithic sites in England – at Broome Heath (Norfolk), Findon (West Sussex) and Lambourn (Berkshire).

4210–3990 BC
Earliest dated British farming site – at Hembury, Devon (first excavated 1934–5).

3795 BC
Earliest dated pottery in UK – at Ballynagilly, Tyrone (Northern Ireland).

3650–3400 BC
Avebury stone circle (Wiltshire) constructed.

2930–2560 BC
The giant round barrow Silbury Hill constructed at Avebury (Wiltshire).

2760 BC
Earliest dated Bronze Age Beaker pottery – at Ballynagilly, Tyrone (Northern Ireland).

c. 2350 BC
Earliest English Bronze Age Beaker pottery – found at Chippenham (Wiltshire), Cambridge (Cambridgeshire) and Mildenhall (Suffolk).

2285–2075 BC
Phase I (ditch construction) of Stonehenge (Wiltshire).

1260 BC
Earliest dated hill-fort – Ivinghoe (Buckinghamshire).

c. 750 BC
Introduction of iron into Britain from Germany by the Celts. Hill-forts proliferate.

c. 525 BC
Britain's recorded history begins with the earliest known references to the island by Himilco of Carthage.

c. 308 BC
Britain visited, and possibly circumnavigated, by Pytheas, a Greek from Massilia (Marseille).

c. 300 BC
Provisional date from palaeobotanical evidence of 'Lindow Man', a victim of ritual sacrifice whose remarkably preserved remains have been found in the bog of Lindow Moss, near Wilmslow (Cheshire).

c. 125 BC
Introduction of Gallo-Belgic gold coinage into Kent from the Beauvais region of France.

c. 90
Earliest British coinage – the gold staters found at Westerham (Kent) in 1927.

DATES IN ROMAN BRITAIN

55 (26 August) BC
Julius Caesar's exploratory expedition with the 7th and 10th legions and 98 ships from Boulogne and Ambleteuse. He landed against opposition from the local tribe, the Cantii, between Deal and Walmer. Repeated skirmishing prevented the reconnaissance being a success and Caesar withdrew.

54 (18 or 21 July) BC
Julius Caesar led the second Roman invasion with

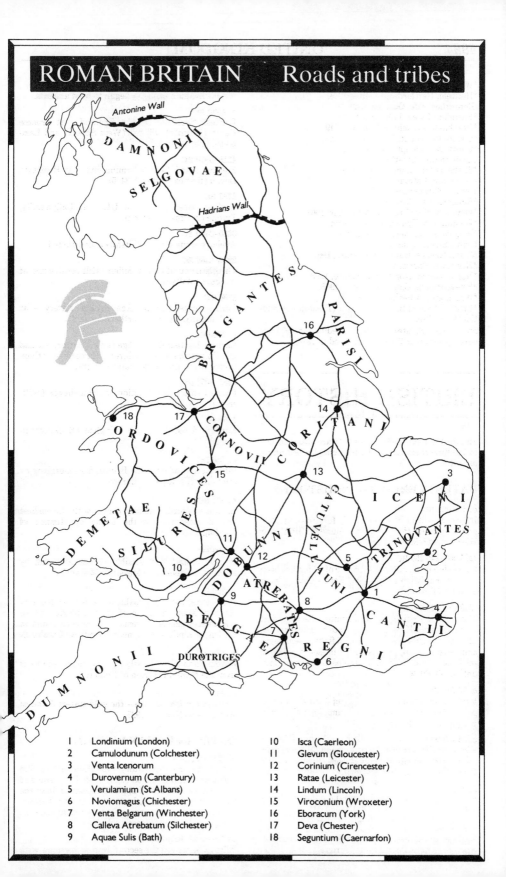

ROMAN BRITAIN   Roads and tribes

Antonine Wall

DAMNONII

SELGOVAE

Hadrians Wall

BRIGANTES

PARISI

16

CORNOVII

CORITANI

14

ORDOVICES

18   17

15   13   CATUVELLAUNI   ICENI   I

DEMETAE   3

SILURES   11   DOBUNNI   TRINOVANTES

10   12   5   2

ATREBATES   1

9   8   CANTII

BELGAE   REGNI   4

7

DUROTRIGES   6

DUMNONII

1	Londinium (London)	10	Isca (Caerleon)
2	Camulodunum (Colchester)	11	Glevum (Gloucester)
3	Venta Icenorum	12	Corinium (Cirencester)
4	Durovernum (Canterbury)	13	Ratae (Leicester)
5	Verulamium (St.Albans)	14	Lindum (Lincoln)
6	Noviomagus (Chichester)	15	Viroconium (Wroxeter)
7	Venta Belgarum (Winchester)	16	Eboracum (York)
8	Calleva Atrebatum (Silchester)	17	Deva (Chester)
9	Aquae Sulis (Bath)	18	Seguntium (Caernarfon)

five legions and 2000 cavalry. He encamped on the Kentish shore and crossed the Thames near Brentford. He was much harried by the British leader, Cassivellaunus, who was based at the old Belgic capital of St Albans (*Verulamium*). The attempt to conquer Britain was not successful.

AD 43
Third (Claudian) Roman invasion in three waves under Plautius with some 2000 men is successful. The start of the Roman Occupation.

AD 61
The revolt of the Iceni tribe under Queen Boudicca (Boadicea) in East Anglia. Boudicca sacked Colchester (*Camulodunum*), London (*Londinium*) and St Albans, but was defeated by Suetonius' 14th and 20th Legions on a battlefield perhaps near Hampstead Heath, North London, when for the loss of only about 400 of the fully armed Romans, 70 000 Britons were claimed to have been killed.

AD 83
Subjugation of Britain completed when Agricola, the Roman Governor, won the Battle of Mons Graupius, suggested by some to be the Pass of Killiecrankie, Tayside. Locally recruited troops were then garrisoned at Chester, Caerleon-on-Usk, York.

AD 122
Emperor Hadrian arrived in Britain after the annihilation of the 9th Legion by the Picts. He ordered the 120 km (74.5 mile) long wall to be built between the Tyne and the Solway. Hadrian's Wall was completed by AD 129.

c. AD 150
The 59·5 km (37 mile) long Forth–Clyde or Antonine Wall was built, but was abandoned within 40 years.

c. AD 208–11
Emperor Severus re-established military order in Britain.

c. AD 287–93
Raids by the Saxons from the Schleswig-Holstein area became increasingly troublesome.

AD 402
Theodosius was forced to recall the majority of Roman garrisons from Britain to help resist the incursions of the Visigoths in northern Italy.

AD 410
The Britons were effectively abandoned by the Romans to defend themselves against increasing raids from the Saxons, Picts, and Scots.

ANGLO-SAXON ENGLAND

By 449 a Jutish Kingdom had been set up in Kent, traditionally by Hengist and Horsa. The 5th and 6th centuries were a period of confusion with conflict between the invading Germanic tribes (principally Jutes, Angles and Saxons, collectively known as Anglo-Saxons) and the remaining Britons, whose last champion was reputedly King Arthur. Some time between 493 and 503 the Britons fought the Battle of Mountbadon against the Saxon invaders on an uncertain site, often ascribed to Liddington Camp, Badbury, near Swindon (Wiltshire).

England (excluding Cumbria) did not again become a unified state before AD 954, when Athelstan united the country. Until then England was divided between a number of small kingdoms, traditionally said to be seven (the Heptarchy), but for most of the period more existed. Some early kings exercised direct rule

over all England for intermittent periods during their reigns. Edward the Elder (899–924 or 925) – son of Alfred (871–99), the most famous of the Kings of the West Saxons – had suzerainty over the whole of England, though he did not directly rule the Danish kingdom of York, which was not finally extinguished until 954.

By the end of the 7th century most of southern Britain was divided between eight main kingdoms and a smaller number of 'sub-kingdoms', which were at times independent.

The map on p. 695 shows the situation as it existed in the early 8th century.

PRINCIPAL KINGDOMS

Kingdom	Principal seat of king
Northumbria	York

558–654 Northumbria was divided into

Bernicia founded 547	Bamburgh
Deira founded 558	York

The kingdom of Northumbria was finally overthrown by the invading Danes in 878.

Lindsey — *Lincoln*
Founded after 550; dependent on Mercia after c. 715; absorbed by Mercia between 790 and 795.

Mercia — *Tamworth*
Founded c. 595; acknowledged overlordship of Wessex 829; divided between Wessex and the Danes from 880.

Two 'sub-kingdoms' briefly enjoyed independence but were more usually dependent upon the kings of Mercia.

Kingdom of the Hwicce	Winchcombe

Founded 628; finally absorbed by Mercia 788.

Kingdom of the Magonsaetan	Leominster

(Sometimes known as the Kingdom of the West Angles or West Anglia) Founded c. 645; finally absorbed by Mercia 725.

East Anglia — *Elmham*
Founded c. 600; dependent on Mercia c. 740–835; a Danish kingdom 876–917.

Essex — *London*
(*London* until c. 730 when Middlesex and Hertfordshire were lost to Mercia; *Colchester* after c. 730.) Founded before 604; dependent on Mercia after c. 730; absorbed by Wessex c. 825.

Kent — *Canterbury*
Founded c. 455; dependent on Mercia from c. 786; absorbed by Wessex 825.

Sussex — *Chichester*
Founded 477; absorbed by Mercia c. 774.

Wessex — *Winchester*
Founded – as the principality of the Gewissae – 519; unified England 954.

In the late 9th and early 10th century much of England was occupied by the Danes. By the end of the 9th century the map of 'England' would have been divided between the following 'kingdoms'.

ANGLO-SAXON KINGDOMS

NORTHUMBRIA

Yeavering

BERNICIA

DEIRA

York

LINDSEY

Lincoln

MERCIA

Tamworth

Elmham

EAST
ANGLIA

TERRITORY OF
THE MAGANSAETAN

Leominster

TERRITORY OF
THE HWICCE

Winchcombe

ESSEX

London

Canterbury

KENT

WESSEX

Winchester

SUSSEX

Chichester

Saxon Earldom of Bamburgh   *Bamburgh*
A remnant of the kingdom of Northumbria; absorbed by the Danish kingdom of York before 920.

Danish Kingdom of York   *York*
Founded c. 875; overthrown by Wessex 954.

'The Five Boroughs'

Borough of Lincoln

Borough of Nottingham

Borough of Leicester

Borough of Derby

Borough of Stamford

Five autonomous Danish communities, each based upon a stronghold.

Danish Kingdom in East Anglia   *Bury St Edmunds*
Founded 876; overthrown by Wessex 916.

Saxon Kingdom of Wessex   *Winchester*
See above.

Earldom of Mercia   *Tamworth*
Taken from the Danes by Mercia 886; dependent on Wessex 886 onwards; fully absorbed by Wessex by 920.

KINGS OF ALL ENGLAND

The West Saxon King Egbert (802–39), grandfather of King Alfred, is often quoted as the first king of all England from AD 829, although he never conquered the kingdom of Northumbria ruled by Eanred (808 or 810 to 840 or 841).

Athelstan eldest son of the eldest son of King Alfred of the West Saxons, acceded 924 or 925. The first to establish rule over all England (excluding Cumbria) in 927; d. 27 Oct 939 aged over 40 years.

Edmund younger half-brother of Athelstan; acceded 939 but did not regain control of all England until 944–45. Murdered 26 May 946 by Leofa at Pucklechurch, near Bristol (Avon).

Edred younger brother of Edmund; acceded May 946. Effectively king of all England 946–48, and from 954 to his death on 23 Nov 955. Also intermittently during the intervening period.

Edwy son of Edmund, b. c. 941; acceded November 955 (crowned at Kingston, Greater London); lost control of the Mercians and Northumbrians in 957; d. 1 Oct 959, aged about 18.

Edgar son of Edmund, b. 943; acceded October 959 as king of all England (crowned at Bath, 11 May 973); d. 8 July 975, aged c. 32.

Edward the Martyr son of Edgar by Aethelflaed, b. c. 962; acceded 975; d. 18 Mar 978 or 979, aged 16 or 17.

Ethelred the Unready (*unraed*, i.e. ill-counselled), second son of Edgar by Aelfthryth, b. ?968–69; acceded 978 or 979 (crowned at Kingston, 14 Apr 978 or 4 May 979); dispossessed by the Danish king, Swegn Forkbeard, 1013–14; d. 23 Apr 1016, aged c. 47 or 48.

Swegn Forkbeard king of Denmark 987–1014, acknowledged as king of all England from about September 1013 to his death on 3 Feb 1014.

Edmund Ironside probably the third son of Ethelred, b. c. 992; chosen as king in London, April 1016. In the summer of 1016 he made an agreement with Cnut whereby he retained dominion only over Wessex; d. 30 Nov 1016.

Cnut younger son of King Swegn Forkbeard of Denmark, b. c. 995. Secured Mercia and Danelaw in the summer 1016; assumed dominion over all England December 1016; king of Denmark 1019–35; king of Norway 1028–1035; overlord of the king of the Scots and probably ruler of the Norse-Irish kingdom of Dublin; d. 12 Nov 1035, aged c. 40 years.

Harold Harefoot natural son of Cnut by Aelfgifu of Northampton, b. ?c. 1016–17; chosen as regent for his half-brother, Harthacnut, late 1035 or early 1036; sole King 1037; d. 17 Mar 1040, aged c. 23 or 24 years.

Harthacnut son of Cnut by Emma, widow of King Ethelred (d. 1016) b. ?c. 1018; titular king of Denmark from 1028; effectively king of England from June 1040; d. 8 June 1042, aged c. 24 years.

Edward the Confessor elder half-brother of Harthacnut and son of King Ethelred and Emma, b. 1002–5; acceded 1042; crowned 3 Apr 1043; d. 5 Jan 1066, aged between 60 and 64. Declared a saint by the Church.

Harold Godwinson brother-in-law of Edward the Confessor and brother of his Queen Edith, son of Godwin, Earl of Wessex, b. ?c. 1020; acceded 6 Jan 1066; killed 14 Oct 1066.

Edgar Etheling grandson of Edmund Ironside; chosen by Londoners as king after the Battle of Hastings, October 1066, but apparently not crowned; he submitted to William I before 25 Dec 1066; believed to be still living c. 1125.

RULERS IN WALES (547–1289)

Wales was divided into half a dozen small kingdoms and principalities, which by the start of the 8th century numbered:

Kingdom/ Principality	
Gwynedd	Northwest Wales
Powys	Northeast and central Wales
Ceredigion	Cardiganshire
Ystrad Towy	West Glamorgan/ Carmarthenshire

(Ceredigion and Ystrad Towy were united as the Kingdom of **Seisyllwg** from the 9th century)

Buellt	North Brecknock/ Radnorshire
Gwent	Gwent
Brycheiniog	South Brecknock
Glywising	Mid and South Glamorgan
Dyfed	Pembrokeshire

By c. 1170 these had been reduced to the three kingdoms listed below.

Kingdom	Principal seat of king

Gwynedd   *Deganwy*
Founded before 547 by Maelgwn Hir. In 1152 Owain Gwynedd submitted to Henry II as his overlord and changed his title to Prince of Gwynedd. Llywelyn II of Gwynedd united all of north Wales and assumed the title Prince of Wales (1258), but Edward I of England overran Gwynedd except for Anglesey (1277). Llywelyn was killed trying to retake his principality

(1282) and English rule was extended over the whole of Gwynedd in 1283.

Powys
Powys was ruled by the kings of Gwynedd (855–1063) and then ruled by independent princes (1075–1160). In 1160 it was divided into two lordships – South Powys (Powys Wenwynwyn) – which lasted until 1208 when the area passed under English rule – and North Powys (Powys Fadog) – which came under English rule in 1269.

Deheubarth *Dinefor*
Deheubarth was founded as a personal union of the territories of Hywel Dda, king of Dyfed 904–950, king of Seisyllwg 909–50. The other territories of south Wales were usually dependent on Deheubarth from this time. The last king, Rhys ap Tewdwr, was murdered in 1093. A smaller principality of Deheubarth lasted from 1135 to 1201, during which time south Wales was gradually absorbed by the English.

KINGS OF SCOTLAND

The formation of Scotland began in 843 when Kenneth I (MacAlpin), King of Dalriada (the kingdom of the Scots), became King of Caledonia (the kingdom of the Picts).

From the 6th to the 9th centuries, Scotland was divided into a number of smaller kingdoms whose names and boundaries were constantly changing. About the year 950 four kingdoms existed (see the accompanying map on p. 698).

Kingdom	*Principal seat of king*

Kingdom of the Isles
Covered the Western Isles, Orkney and Shetland. A Norse kingdom ruled from Scandinavia, it reached its greatest extent in the middle of the 11th century.

Strathclyde *Alclyde* (Dumbarton)
A British kingdom, which included the sub-kingdom of Galloway; annexed by Scotland c. 1016.

Caledonia *Scone*
The Pictish kingdom – from 843 united with Dalriada as Alba.

Dalriada *Dunstaffnage*
The Scottish kingdom – from 843 united with Caledonia as Alba.

KINGS OF ALBA

Kenneth I (MacAlpin; 843–858/9), King of Dalriada from 841.

Donald I (858/9–862/3), brother of Kenneth I.

Constantine I (862/3–877), son of Kenneth I. Killed in battle by the Danes.

Aedh (877–78), son of Kenneth I. Murdered by King Giric of Strathclyde.

Eochaid (878–89), nephew of Aedh. Deposed by Donald II.

Donald II (889–900), son of Constantine I.

Constantine II (900–42), son of Aedh. Abdicated to become Abbot of St Andrews; d. 952.

Malcolm I (942–54), son of Donald II. Murdered.

Indulf (954–62), son of Constantine II. Killed by the Vikings.

Dubh (962–966/7), son of Malcolm I. Murdered.

Culen (966/7–971), son of Indulf. Murdered.

KINGS OF SCOTS

Kenneth II (971–95), son of Malcolm I. Took the title King of Scots – Alba was from this time known as Scotland. Received Lothian from King Edgar of England.

Constantine III (995–97), son of Culen. Killed by Kenneth III.

Kenneth III (997–1005), son of Dubh. Killed by Malcolm II.

Malcolm II (1005–34), b. c. 954; d. 25 Nov 1034, aged c. 80 years. Consolidated the kingdom of Scotland by annexing Strathclyde, c. 1016.

Duncan I (1034–40), son of Malcolm II's daughter, Bethoc.

Macbeth (1040–57), probably son of Malcolm II's daughter, Donada; d. aged c. 52 years.

Lulach (1057–8), stepson of Macbeth; d. aged c. 26.

Malcolm III (Canmore; 1058–93), son of Duncan I; d. aged c. 62.

Donald Bane (1093–4 and 1094–7), son of Duncan I, twice deposed.

Duncan II (May–Oct 1094), son of Malcolm III; d. aged c. 34.

Edgar (1097–1107), son of Malcolm III, half-brother of Duncan II; d. aged c. 33.

Alexander I (1107–24), son of Malcolm III and brother of Edgar; d. aged c. 47.

David I (1124–53), son of Malcolm III and brother of Edgar; d. aged c. 68.

Malcolm IV (1153–65), son of Henry, Earl of Northumberland, and grandson of David I; d. aged c. 24.

William I (the Lion; 1165–1214), brother of Malcolm IV; d. aged c. 72 (from 1174 to 1189 the king of England was acknowledged as overlord of Scotland).

Alexander II (1214–49), son of William I; d. aged 48.

Alexander III (1249–86), son of Alexander II; d. aged 44.

Margaret (Maid of Norway; 1286–90), daughter of Margaret (daughter of Alexander III) by King Eric II of Norway. Queen Margaret never visited her realm; d. aged 7.

First Interregnum 1290–2.

John (Balliol; 1292–96), son of Dervorguilla, a great-great-granddaughter of David I. He was awarded the throne from 13 contestants by the adjudication of King Edward I of England. He was overthrown by an English invasion and abdicated; d. in 1313 aged 63.

Second Interregnum 1296–1306.

Robert I (the Bruce; 1306–29), grandson of Robert de Bruce (one of the 13 claimants to the Scottish throne in 1291) and a descendant of David I; d. aged c. 55.

David II (1329–71; deposed September–December 1332 and not in effective control of most of Scotland

SCOTLAND c.820

BEGINNINGS OF NORSE SETTLEMENTS

PICTLAND

OR

ALBA

DÁLRIADA

Dúnstaffnage

Scone

Alclyde

STRATHCLYDE

NORTHUMBRIA

1333–56), son of Robert I; d. aged 46.

Edward (1332 and 1333–56), son of John; he acknowledged Edward III of England as his overlord in 1333 and surrendered all claims to the Scottish crown to him in 1356; d. 1364 aged over 60.

Robert II (1371–90), founder of the Stewart dynasty, son of Walter the Steward and Marjorie Bruce (daughter of Robert I); d. aged 74.

Robert III (1390–1406), legitimate natural son of Robert II; d. aged c. 69.

James I (1406–37), son of Robert III, captured by the English 13 days before his accession and kept prisoner in England till March 1424; d. aged 42.

James II (1437–60), son of James I; d. aged 29.

James III (1460–88), son of James II; d. aged 36.

James IV (1488–1513), son of James III and Margaret of Denmark, married Margaret Tudor; d. aged 40.

James V (1513–42), son of James IV and Margaret Tudor; d. aged 30.

Mary (*Queen of Scots*; 1542–67), daughter of James V and Mary of Lorraine, acceded aged 6 or 7 days, abdicated 24 July 1567 and was succeeded by her son, James VI (by her second husband, Henry Stuart, Lord Darnley). She was executed 8 Feb 1587, aged 44.

James VI (1567–1625), son of Mary and Lord Darnley (see above), succeeded to the English throne as James I on 24 Mar 1603, so effecting a personal union of the two realms; d. aged 58.

THE ELEVEN ROYAL HOUSES OF ENGLAND (since 1066)

A royal dynasty normally takes its house name from the family's patronymic. The name does not change upon the occasion of a Queen Regnant's marriage – for example, Queen Victoria, a member of the House of Hanover and Brunswick, did not become a member of the House of Saxe-Coburg and Gotha (her husband's family). However, her son, Edward VII, and (from 1910 until 1917) her grandson, George V, were members of the House of Saxe-Coburg and Gotha.

The House of Normandy

The House of Normandy assumed the throne by right of conquest and reigned for 69 years.

The name derives from the fact that William I was the 7th Duke of Normandy with the style William II.

Sovereigns: William I, William II, Henry I and Matilda.

The House of Blois

The House of Blois reigned for 19 years. The name

derives from the fact that the father of King Stephen was Stephen (sometimes called Henry), Count of Blois.

Sovereign: Stephen.

The House of Anjou

The House of Anjou reigned for 331 years. The name derives from the fact that the father of King Henry II was Geoffrey V, 10th Count of Anjou and Maine. This family was alternatively referred to as the Angevins, the name deriving from Angers, the chief town of Anjou.

Sovereigns: Henry II and the next 13 kings down to and including Richard III.

Since the mid-15th century (and, in fact, less than 50 years before its male line became extinct) this house has also been referred to as the House of Plantagenet. This name originates from Count Geoffrey's nickname 'Plantagenet', which is said to derive from his habit of wearing a sprig of broom (*Planta genista*) in his cap during a Crusade.

After the deposition of Richard II, in 1399, the House of Anjou is subdivided into the House of Lancaster (Henry IV, Henry V and Henry VI) and the House of York (Edward IV, Edward V and Richard III). The names Lancaster and York derived respectively from the titles of the 4th and 5th sons of Edward III – John of Gaunt (1340–99) was 1st Duke of Lancaster (of the second creation), and the father of Henry IV, and Edmund of Langley (1341–1402) was 1st Duke of York and a great-grandfather of Edward IV.

The House of Tudor

The House of Tudor reigned for 118 years. The name derives from the surname of Henry VII's father, Edmund Tudor, Earl of Richmond. (Edmund Tudor was the son of Sir Owen Tudor, by Catherine, widow of King Henry V.)

Sovereigns: Henry VII, Henry VIII, Edward VI, Mary I and Elizabeth I.

The House of Grey or Suffolk

The House of Grey reigned for 14 days. The name derives from the family and surname of the 3rd Marquess of Dorset, the father of Lady Guilford Dudley (Jane Grey), who reigned as Queen Jane from 6 July 1553 for 14 days until 19 July when the House of Tudor regained the throne.

The House of Stuart and the House of Stuart and Orange

The House of Stuart reigned in England for 98 years, including 5 years jointly with the House of Orange. The name is derived from the family and surnames of both Henry Stuart, Lord Darnley and Duke of Albany, and his cousin and wife Mary, Queen of Scots – the parents of James VI of Scotland and I of England. Spelt 'Stewart' until the reign of Mary, Queen of Scots, the name derives from a distant ancestor who was steward to the count of Dol in Brittany.

Sovereigns: James I, Charles I, Charles II, James II, Mary II and Anne.

The house name became the House of Stuart and Orange when, in 1689, William III, son of William II, Prince of Orange, became the sovereign conjointly with his wife, Mary II, the 5th Stuart monarch.

William III reigned alone during his widowerhood from 1694 to 1702, but exercised the sole regal power during his entire reign from 1689.

The House of Hanover and Brunswick-Lüneburg

The House of Hanover and Brunswick reigned for 187 years. The name derives from the fact that George I's father, Ernest Augustus, was the Elector of Hanover and a duke of the House of Brunswick-Lüneburg.

Sovereigns: George I, George II, George III, George IV, William IV and Victoria.

The House of Saxe-Coburg and Gotha

The House of Saxe-Coburg and Gotha reigned for 16 years. The name derives from the princely title of Queen Victoria's husband, Prince Albert, later Prince Consort.

Sovereigns: Edward VII and George V until 17 July 1917 when King George V declared by Royal Proclamation that he had changed the name of the royal house to the House of Windsor.

The House of Windsor

Sovereigns: George V, Edward VIII, George VI and Elizabeth II.

In the normal course of events Prince Charles, Prince of Wales, on inheriting the throne would become the first monarch of the House of Mountbatten, but by further Proclamations the Queen first declared (in 1952) that her children and descendants would belong to the House of Windsor, and later (in 1960) that this Declaration would only affect her descendants in the male line who will bear a royal style and title. Descendants outside this class will bear the surname 'Mountbatten-Windsor'.

TITLES OF THE ROYAL HOUSE

Husbands of Queens Regnant

The husband of a queen regnant derives no title from his marriage. Philip II of Spain, husband of Queen Mary I, was termed 'King Consort'. Prince George of Denmark, husband of Queen Anne, was created Duke of Cumberland. Prince Albert of Saxe-Coburg-Gotha, husband of Queen Victoria, was created 'Royal Highness' upon his marriage in February 1840 and granted the title 'Prince Consort' in 1857. Prince Philip, husband of Queen Elizabeth II, was born a prince of Greece and Denmark. He renounced those titles in February 1947 and assumed his mother's surname, Mountbatten. He was created Duke of Edinburgh with the style 'Royal Highness' upon his marriage in November 1947 and a prince of the United Kingdom of Great Britain and Northern Ireland in 1957.

Queens Consort

A queen consort ranks with and shares the king's titles. In the event of her being widowed she cannot continue to use the title 'The Queen'. She must add to it her Christian name or use the style additionally, or by itself, of 'Queen Mother' (if she has children), or, as in the case of Queen Adelaide, the widow of King William IV, 'Queen Dowager'.

In the event of her remarriage, which can only be with the consent of the Sovereign, she does not forfeit her royal status. The last such example was when Queen Catherine (Parr) married, as her fourth husband, Lord Seymour of Sudeley, KG, in 1547.

The Heir to the Throne

The Heir Apparent to the throne can only be the son or grandson (as in the case of the Prince of Wales from 1751 to 1760) of the reigning Sovereign. Should the first person in the order of succession bear any relationship other than in the direct male line, they are the Heir (or Heiress) Presumptive. The last

Heiress Presumptive to the Throne was HRH the Princess Elizabeth (1936–52). A female could be an Heiress Apparent if she were the only or eldest daughter of a deceased Heir Apparent who had no male issue.

The eldest surviving son of a reigning Sovereign inherits at birth the titles The Duke of Cornwall, The Duke of Rothesay, The Earl of Carrick and The Baron Renfrew, together with the styles of Lord of the Isles, Prince and Great Steward (or Seneschal) of Scotland. The titles Prince of Wales and Earl of Chester are a matter of creation and not of birthright. If, however, a Prince of Wales dies, his eldest son automatically succeeds to that title and the Earldom of Chester but not to the Dukedom of Cornwall and the other honours because they are expressly reserved for the son (and not the grandson) of a Sovereign. This situation happened in 1751 when Frederick Lewis, Prince of Wales, the eldest son of George II, died.

Princes, Princesses and Royal Highnesses
Since 1917 the style HRH Prince or Princess has been limited to the children of the Monarch and the children of the sons of the Monarch and their wives. Grandchildren of a Prince of Wales also would enjoy this style. Sons and daughters of the Sovereign are additionally distinguished by the use of the article 'The' – for example HRH The Prince Edward and HRH The Princess Margaret (cf. HRH Princess Alexandra of Kent).

In practice the sons of a Sovereign have a dukedom bestowed upon them either upon marriage or after they become of age. Such royal dukedoms only enjoy their special precedence (i.e. senior to the two English archbishops and other dukes) for the next generation. A third duke would take his seniority among the non-royal dukes according to the date of the original creation.

The title 'Princess Royal' is conferred (if vacant) for life on the eldest daughter of the Sovereign. HRH The Princess Anne was created Princess Royal in 1987.

THE ORDER OF SUCCESSION

The order of succession is determined according to ancient common-law rules, but these may be upset by an enactment of the Crown in Parliament under powers taken in the Succession to the Crown Act of 1707, provided always (since 1931) that the parliaments of all the members of the Commonwealth assent. At common law the Crown descends lineally to the legitimate issue of the sovereign, males being preferred to females, in their respective orders of age. In the event of failure of such issue (e.g. King Edward VIII in 1936) the Crown passes to the nearest collateral being an heir at law. The common law of descent of the Crown specifically departs from the normal feudal rules of land descent at two points. First, in the event of two or more sisters being next in succession the eldest alone (e.g. The Princess Elizabeth from 1936 to 1952) shall be the heiress and shall not be merely a coparcener (coheir) with her sister or sisters. Secondly, male issue by a second or subsequent marriage takes precedence over half sisters (e.g. King Edward VI, son of King Henry VIII's third wife, took precedence over Queen Mary I, daughter of his first marriage, and Queen Elizabeth I, daughter of his second marriage).

The following is the Order of Succession to the Crown.

1 The heir apparent is HRH The Prince CHARLES Philip Arthur George, KG, KT, The Prince of Wales, The Duke of Cornwall, The Duke of Rothesay, The Earl of Carrick, and The Baron Renfrew, Lord of the Isles and Great Steward of Scotland, b. 14 Nov 1948. (He m. 29 Jul 1981, Lady DIANA Frances Spencer – HRH The Princess of Wales – who was b. 1 Jul 1961.)

2 HRH Prince WILLIAM Arthur Philip Louis, b. 21 June 1982 – elder son of The Prince Charles.

3 HRH Prince HENRY Charles Albert David, b. 15 Sept 1984 – younger son of The Prince Charles.

4 HRH The Prince ANDREW Albert Christian Edward, The Duke of York, The Earl of Inverness, and The Baron Killyleagh, b. 19 Feb 1960 – second son of HM Queen Elizabeth II. (He m. 23 Jul 1986, Miss SARAH Margaret Ferguson – HRH The Duchess of York – who was b. 15 Oct 1959.)

5 HRH Princess BEATRICE Elizabeth Mary of York, b. 8 Aug 1988 – elder daughter of The Prince Andrew.

6 HRH Princess EUGENIE Victoria Helena of York, b. 23 Mar 1990 – younger daughter of The Prince Andrew.

7 HRH The Prince EDWARD Antony Richard Louis, b. 10 Mar 1964 – youngest son of HM Queen Elizabeth II.

8 HRH The Princess ANNE Elizabeth Alice Louise, The Princess Royal, Mrs Mark Phillips, b. 15 Aug 1950 – only daughter of HM Queen Elizabeth II. (She m. 14 Nov 1973 Captain MARK Anthony Peter Phillips, who was b. 22 Sep 1948. Separated Aug 1989.)

9 PETER Mark Andrew Phillips, b. 15 Nov 1977 – son of The Princess Anne.

10 ZARA Anne Elizabeth Phillips, b. 15 May 1981 – daughter of The Princess Anne.

11 HRH The Princess MARGARET Rose, CI, GCVO, The Countess of Snowdon, b. 21 Aug 1930 – younger daughter of HM King George VI. (She m. 6 May 1960 ANTHONY Charles Robert Armstrong-Jones, created Earl of Snowdon, who was b. 7 Mar 1930. Divorced 1978.)

12 DAVID Albert Charles Armstrong-Jones, Viscount Linley, b. 3 Nov 1961 – son of The Princess Margaret.

13 The Lady SARAH Frances Elizabeth Armstrong-Jones, b. 1 May 1964 – daughter of The Princess Margaret.

14 HRH Prince RICHARD Alexander Walter George, the (2nd) Duke of Gloucester, b. 26 Aug 1944 – surviving son of HRH The Prince Henry, Duke of Gloucester, who was the third son of HM King George V. (He m. 8 Jul 1972 BIRGITTE Eva van Deurs – HRH The Duchess of Gloucester.)

15 Lord ALEXANDER Patrick George Richard, Earl of Ulster, b. 24 Oct 1974 – son of HRH The Duke of Gloucester.

16 The Lady DAVINA Elizabeth Alice Benedikte Windsor, b. 19 Nov 1977 – elder daughter of HRH The Duke of Gloucester.

17 The Lady ROSE Victoria Birgitte Louise Windsor, b. 1 Mar 1980 – younger daughter of HRH The Duke of Gloucester.

18 HRH Prince EDWARD George Nicholas Paul Patrick, GCVO, the (2nd) Duke of Kent, the Earl of St

Andrews and the Baron Downpatrick, b. 9 Oct 1935 – elder son of HRH The Prince George, Duke of Kent, who was the fourth son of HM King George V. (He m. 8 Jun 1961 KATHARINE Lucy Mary Worsley – HRH The Duchess of Kent.)

(GEORGE Philip Nicholas Windsor, Earl of St Andrews, b. 26 Jun 1962 – elder son of HRH The Duke of Kent – forfeited his claim to the throne by his marriage, on 16 Jan 1988, to a Roman Catholic, SYLVANA Tomaselli – the Countess of St Andrews.)

19 EDWARD Edmund Maximilian George Windsor, Baron Downpatrick, b. 10 Dec 1988 – son of George, Earl of St Andrews.

20 Lord NICHOLAS Charles Edward Jonathan Windsor, b. 25 July 1970 – younger son of HRH The Duke of Kent.

21 The Lady HELEN Marina Lucy Windsor, b. 28 Apr 1964 – daughter of HRH The Duke of Kent. (HRH Prince MICHAEL George Charles Franklin, b. 4 Jul 1942 – younger son of HRH The Prince George, Duke of Kent – forfeited his claim to the throne by his marriage, on 30 Jun 1978, to a Roman Catholic, Baroness MARIE-CHRISTINE Agnes Hedwig Ida von Reibnitz – HRH Princess Michael of Kent.)

22 Lord FREDERICK Michael George David Louis Windsor, b. 6 Apr 1979 – son of HRH Prince Michael of Kent.

23 The Lady GABRIELA Marina Alexandra Ophelia Windsor, b. 23 Apr 1981 – daughter of HRH Prince Michael of Kent.

24 HRH Princess ALEXANDRA Helen Elizabeth Olga Christabel of Kent, GCVO, the Lady Ogilvy, b. 25 Dec 1936 – daughter of HRH The Prince George, Duke of Kent. (She m. 24 Apr 1936 Hon. – now Sir – Angus Ogilvy.)

25 JAMES Robert Bruce Ogilvy, b. 29 Feb 1964 – son of HRH Princess Alexandra of Kent. (He m. 30 Jul 1988 JULIA Rawlinson.)

Next in line to succession is Marina Mowatt (the daughter of HRH Princess Alexandra of Kent) and her daughter Zenouska, followed by George, Earl of Harewood (the elder son of HRH Princess Mary, the only daughter of HM King George V) and his descendants, and Hon. Gerald Lascelles (the younger son of HRH Princess Mary) and his descendants.

FACTORS AFFECTING THE ORDER

Three further factors determine the order of succession.

No person may unilaterally renounce their right to succeed. Only an Act of Parliament can undo what another Act of Parliament (the Act of Settlement, 1701) has done.

Some marriages among the descendants of George II are null and void and hence the descendants are not heirs at law, by failure to obtain the consent to marry as required by the Royal Marriage Act of 1772. In some cases this failure, prior to 1956, may have been inadvertent because it was only then confirmed by the House of Lords that every such descendant, born before 1948, is by a statute of 1705 deemed a British subject. So the escape from the requirements of the Royal Marriage Act accorded to all female descendants of George II who apparently married into foreign families is not so readily available as was once thought.

The Act of Settlement – which came into force on 6 February 1701 – laid down that failing issue from HRH The Princess George of Denmark (later Queen Anne) and/or secondly from any subsequent marriage by her first cousin and brother-in-law, the widower King William III, the crown would pass to Princess Sophia, Dowager Electress of Hanover (1630–1714), the granddaughter of King James I, and the heirs of her body, with the proviso that all Roman Catholics, or persons marrying Roman Catholics, were for ever to be excluded, as if they 'were naturally dead'. This proviso excludes both the Earl of St Andrews and Prince Michael of Kent from the present order of succession.

The only subsequent change in statute law was on 11 December 1936 by His Majesty's Declaration of Abdication Act, 1936, by which the late HRH The Prince Edward, MC (later HRH The Duke of Windsor), and any issue he might subsequently have had were expressly excluded from the succession.

CONDITIONS OF TENURE

On succeeding to the Crown the Sovereign must (1) join in Communion with the established Church of England; (2) declare that he or she is a Protestant; (3) swear the oaths for the preservation of both the Established Church of England and the Presbyterian Church of Scotland, and (4), and most importantly, take the coronation oath, which may be said to form the basis of the contract between Sovereign and subject, last considered to have been broken, on the Royal side, by King James II in 1688.

'THE KING NEVER DIES'

The Sovereign can never be legally a minor, but in fact a regency is provided until he or she attains the age of 18.

There is never an interregnum on the death of a Sovereign. In pursuance of the common law maxim 'the King never dies' the new Sovereign succeeds to full prerogative rights instantly on the death of his or her predecessor.

THE CIVIL LIST (1990)

The Civil List is the annuities paid by Parliament for the upkeep of both the Royal Family and the Royal Household.

The Queen[1]	£5 090 000
The Queen Mother	439 500
The Duke of Edinburgh	245 000
Duke of York	169 000
Prince Edward	20 000
Princess Royal	154 400
Princess Margaret	148 500
Princess Alice	60 500
Duke of Gloucester	119 500
Duke of Kent	161 500
Princess Alexandra	154 000

[1] The Queen's expenses come from three sources: various government departments (85%), the grant from the Civil List, and revenue of her own.
The Prince of Wales does not receive an income from the Civil List, but receives revenue from the Duchy of Cornwall.

Kings and Queens of England and Great Britain

The precise dates of all the main events in the lives of the earlier monarchs are not known, and probably now never will be. Where recognized authorities are in dispute, as quite frequently occurs in the first twenty or so reigns, we have adhered to the dates given by the Royal Historical Society's *Handbook of British Chronology* (second edition, 1961). This work includes the fruits of recent researches.

King or Queen Regnant / Date of Accession and / Final Year of Reign; Style	Date and Place of Birth and Parentage	Marriages and No. of Children	Date, Cause and Place of Death, and Place of Burial	Notes and Succession
1. WILLIAM I / 25 Dec 1066–87 / 'The Bastard' / 'The Conqueror' / *Style*: 'Willielmus Rex Anglorum'.	1027 or 1028 at Falaise, north France; illegitimate son of Robert I, 6th Duke of Normandy, and Herleva, d of Fulbert the Tanner.	m. at Eu in 1050 or 1051 MATILDA (d. 1083), d of Baldwin V, Count of Flanders. 4s 5d.	d., aged 59 or 60, 9 Sept 1087 of an abdominal injury from his saddle pommel at the Priory of St Gervais, nr. Rouen. The Abbey of St Stephen at Caen (remains lost during French Revolution).	William I succeeded by right of conquest by winning the Battle of Hastings, 14 Oct 1066, from Harold II, the nominated heir of Edward III ('The Confessor'). Succeeded as King of England, by his third, but second surviving, son, William.
2. WILLIAM II / 26 Sept 1087–1100 / 'Rufus' / *Style*: 'Dei Gratia Rex Anglorum'.	between 1056 and 1060 in Normandy; third son of William I and Matilda.	unmarried. Had illegitimate issue.	d., aged between 40 and 44, 2 Aug 1100 (according to tradition), of impalement by a stray arrow while hunting in the New Forest nr. Brockenhurst, Hampshire. Winchester Cathedral.	Succeeded by his younger brother, Henry.
3. HENRY I / 5 Aug 1100–35 / 'Beauclerc' / *Style*: As No. 2 but also Duke of Normandy from 1106.	in the latter half of 1068 at Selby, Yorks; fourth son of William I and Matilda.	m. (1) at Westminster Abbey, 11 Nov 1100 EADGYTH (Edith), known as MATILDA (d. 1118), d of Malcolm III, King of the Scots, and Margaret (grand-d of Edmund 'Ironside') 1s, 1d and a child who died young. m. (2) 29 Jan 1121 ADELA (d. 1151), d of Godfrey VII, Count of Louvain. No issue.	d., aged 67, 1 Dec 1135, from a feverish illness at St Denis-le-Ferment, nr. Grisors. Reading Abbey.	Succeeded by his nephew, Stephen (the third, but second surviving, son of Adela, the fifth d of William I) who usurped the throne from Henry's only surviving legitimate child and d Matilda (1102–67).
4. STEPHEN / 22 Dec 1135–54 / *Style*: As No. 2.	between 1096 and 1100 at Blois, France; third son of Stephen (sometimes called Henry), Count of Blois, and Adela, d. of William I.	m. 1125, MATILDA (d. 1151), d of Eustace II, Count of Boulogne, and Mary, sister of Queen Matilda, wife of Henry I. 3s 2d.	d., age between 54 and 58, 25 Oct 1154, from a heart attack at St Martin's Priory, Dover. Faversham Abbey.	Succeeded by his first cousin once removed downwards, Henry. Between April and November 1141 he was not *de facto* King and was imprisoned in Bristol Castle.

King or Queen Regnant / Date of Accession and / Final Year of Reign; Style	Date and Place of Birth and Parentage	Marriages and No. of Children	Date, Cause and Place of Death, and Place of Burial	Notes and Succession
5. MATILDA / April–November 1141 / 'Empress Maud' / Style: 'Imperatrix Henrici Regis filia et Anglorum domina'.	Feb 1102 in London, only legitimate d of Henry I.	m. (1) 1114 Henry V, Emperor of Germany (d. 1125). No issue. m. (2) 1130 GEOFFREY V, Count of Anjou (d. 1151). 3s.	d., aged 65, 10 Sept 1167 of uncertain cause, nr. Rouen in Normandy. Fontevraud, France.	Succeeded by her cousin, Stephen, whom she had deposed.
6. HENRY II / 19 Dec 1154–1189 / Style: 'Rex Angliae, Dux Normaniae et Aquitaniae et Comes Andigaviae'.	5 Mar 1133 at Le Mans, France; eldest son of Geoffrey V, Count of Anjou (surnamed Plantagenet), and Matilda (only d of Henry I).	m. at Bordeaux, 18 May 1152, ELEANOR (c. 1122–1204), d of William X, Duke of Aquitaine, and divorced wife of Louis, VII, King of France, 5s 3d.	d., aged 56, 6 July 1189, of a fever at the Castle of Chinon, nr. Tours, France. Fontevraud abbey church in Anjou. Reburied Westminster Abbey.	Succeeded by his third surviving son, Richard. On 14 June 1170, Henry II's second and eldest surviving son Henry was crowned and three years later re-crowned with his wife at Winchester as King of England. Contemporaneously he was called King Henry III. He pre-deceased his father, 11 June 1183.
7. RICHARD I / 3 Sept 1189–99 / 'Coeur de Lion' / Style: As No. 6.	8 Sept 1157 at Oxford; third son of Henry II and Eleanor.	m. at Limassol, Cyprus, 12 May 1191, BERENGARIA (d. soon after 1230), d of Sancho VI of Navarre. No issue.	d., aged 41, 6 Apr 1199 from a mortal arrow wound while besieging the Castle of Châlus in Limousin, France. Fontevraud abbey church in Anjou. Reburied Westminster Abbey.	Succeeded by his younger brother, John, who usurped the throne from his nephew Arthur, the only son of Geoffrey, Duke of Brittany (1158–86); and from his niece, Eleanor (1184–1241). Arthur (b. posthumously 1187) was murdered (unmarried) 3 Apr 1203 in his 17th year.
8. JOHN / 27 May 1199–1216 / 'Lackland' / Style: 'Joannes Rex Angliae et Dominus Hiberniae', etc.	24 Dec 1167 at Beaumont Palace, Oxford; fifth son of Henry II and Eleanor.	m. (1) at Marlborough, Wilts, 29 Aug 1189, ISABEL (d. 1217). No issue. m. (2) at Angoulême, 24 Aug 1200, ISABELLA (d. 1246), d of Aimir, Count of Angoulême. 2s 3d.	d., aged 48, 18–19 Oct 1216, of dysentery at Newark Castle, Nottinghamshire. Worcester Cathedral.	In late 1215 the Crown was offered to Louis, son of Philip II of France, but despite a visit in 1216 the claim was abandoned in September 1217. Succeeded by his elder son, Henry.

Kings and Queens of England and Great Britain (continued)

King or Queen Regnant / Date of Accession and / Final Year of Reign; Style	Date and Place of Birth and Parentage	Marriages and No. of Children	Date, Cause and Place of Death, and Place of Burial	Notes and Succession
9. HENRY III 28 Oct 1216–72 *Style:* 'Rex Angliae, Dominus Hiberniae et Dux Aquitaniae'.	1 Oct 1207 at Winchester; elder son of John and Isabella.	m. at Canterbury, 20 Jan 1236, ELEANOR (d. 1291), d of Raymond Berengar IV, Count of Provence. 2s 3d and at least 4 other children who died in infancy.	d., aged 65, 16 Nov 1272, at Westminster. Westminster Abbey church.	The style 'Dux Normaniae' and Count Anjou was omitted from 1259. Succeeded by Edward, his first son to survive infancy (probably his third son).
10. EDWARD I 20 Nov 1272–1307 'Longshanks' *Style:* As the final style of No. 8.	17/18 June 1239 at Westminster; eldest son to survive infancy (probably third son) of Henry III and Eleanor.	m. (1) at the monastery of Las Huelgas, Spain, 13–31 Oct 1254, ELEANOR (d. 1290), d of Ferdinand III, King of Castile 4s 7d. m. (2) at Canterbury, 10 Sept 1299, MARGARET (1282–1317), d of Philip III, King of France. 2s 1d.	d., aged 68, 7 July 1307, at Burgh-upon-the-Sands, nr. Carlisle. Westminster Abbey.	Succeeded by the fourth, and only surviving, son of his first marriage, Edward (created Prince of Wales, 7 Feb 1301).
11. EDWARD II 8 July 1307 (deposed 20 Jan 1327) 'of Caernarfon' *Style:* As the final style of No. 8.	25 Apr 1284 at Caernarfon Castle; fourth and only surviving son of Edward I and Eleanor.	m. at Boulogne, c. 25 Jan 1308, ISABELLA (1292–1358), d of Philip IV, King of France, 2s 2d.	murdered, aged 43, 21 Sept 1327 (traditionally by disembowelling with red-hot iron) at Berkeley Castle. The abbey of St Peter (now the cathedral), Gloucester.	Succeeded by his elder son, Edward of Windsor. Edward II was deposed by Parliament on 20 Jan 1327, having been imprisoned on 16 Nov 1326.
12. EDWARD III 25 Jan 1327–77 *Style:* As No. 10, until 13th year when 'Dei Gratia, Rex Angliae, et Franciae et Dominus Hiberniae'.	13 Nov 1312 at Windsor Castle; elder son of Edward II and Isabella.	m. at York, 24 June 1328, PHILIPPA (c. 1314–69), d of William I, Count of Holland and Hainault. 7s 5d.	d. peacefully, aged 64, 21 June 1377 at Sheen (now in Greater London). Westminster Abbey	Succeeded by his grandson Richard, the second and only surviving son of his eldest son Edward, the Black Prince.

King or Queen Regnant Date of Accession and Final Year of Reign; Style	Date and Place of Birth and Parentage	Marriages and No. of Children	Date, Cause and Place of Death, and Place of Burial	Notes and Succession
13. **RICHARD II** 22 June 1377–99 *Style:* As the final style of No. 12.	6 Jan 1367 at Bordeaux; second, but only surviving, son of Edward, the Black Prince, and Joane, commonly called The Fair Maid of Kent (grand-d of Edward I).	m. (1) at St Stephen's Chapel, Westminster, 20 Jan 1382, ANNE of Bohemia (1366–94), d of Emperor Charles IV. No issue. m. (2) at St Nicholas' Church, Calais, probably 4 Nov 1396, ISABELLE (1389–1409), d of Charles VI of France. No issue.	d., aged 33, probably 14 Feb 1400, possibly murdered at Pontefract Castle, Yorks. Westminster Abbey.	He was a prisoner of Henry, Duke of Lancaster, later Henry IV, from 19 Aug 1399 until death. He was deposed 30 Sept 1399. Henry usurped the throne from the prior claims of the issue of his father John of Gaunt's deceased elder brother, Lionel of Antwerp.
14. **HENRY IV** 30 Sept 1399–1413 *Style:* As No. 12.	probably April 1366 at Bolingbroke Castle, nr. Spilsby, Lincolnshire; eldest son of John of Gaunt, 4th son of Edward III, and Blanche, great-great-grand-d of Henry III.	m. (1) at Rochford, Essex, between 1380 and March 1381, Lady MARY de Bohun (?1368/70–94), younger d of Humphrey, Earl of Hereford. 5s 2d. m. (2) at Winchester, 7 Feb 1403, JOAN (c. 1370–1437), second d of Charles II, King of Navarre. No issue.	d., aged probably 46, 20 Mar 1413, of pustulated eczema and gout in the Jerusalem Chamber, Westminster. Canterbury Cathedral.	Succeeded by his second, but eldest surviving, son, Henry of Monmouth.
15. **HENRY V** 21 Mar 1413–22 *Style:* As No. 13, until 8th year when 'Rex Angliae, Haeres, et Regens Franciae, et Dominus Hiberniae'.	probably 16 Sept 1387 at Monmouth; second and eldest surviving son of Henry IV and the Lady Mary de Bohun.	m. at the church of St. John, Troyes, 2 June 1420, CATHERINE of Valois (1401–37), youngest d of Charles VI of France. 1s.	d., aged probably 34, 31 Aug/ Sept 1422, of dysentery at Bois de Vincennes, France. Chapel of the Confessor, Westminster Abbey.	Succeeded by his only child Henry.
16. **HENRY VI** 1 Sept 1422–61 and 6 Oct 1470–1 *Style:* 'Dei Gratiâ Rex Angliae et Franciae et Dominus Hiberniae'.	6 Dec 1421 at Windsor; only son of Henry V and Catherine.	m. at Tichfield Abbey, 23 Apr 1445, MARGARET (1430–82), d of René, Duke of Anjou, 1s.	murdered by stabbing, aged 49, 21 May 1471 at Tower of London. Windsor.	Succeeded by the usurpation of his third cousin, Edward IV.

Kings and Queens of England and Great Britain (continued)

King or Queen Regnant / Date of Accession and / Final Year of Reign; Style	Date and Place of Birth and Parentage	Marriages and No. of Children	Date, Cause and Place of Death, and Place of Burial	Notes and Succession
17. EDWARD IV 4 Mar 1461–70 and 11 Apr 1471–83 Style: As No. 16.	28 Apr 1442 at Rouen; eldest son of Richard, 3rd Duke of York ('The Protector') and the Lady Cecily Nevill.	m. at Grafton, Northampton-shire, 1 May 1464, ELIZABETH (c. 1437–92), eldest d of Sir Richard Woodville. 3s 7d.	d., aged 40, 9 Apr 1483, of pneumonia at Westminster. Windsor.	Edward IV was a prisoner of the Earl of Warwick in Aug and Sept of 1469; he fled to the Netherlands 3 Oct 1470; returned to England 14 Mar 1471, and was restored to kingship 11 Apr 1471. Succeeded by his eldest son, Edward.
18. EDWARD V 9 Apr–25 June 1483 Style: As No. 16.	2 Nov 1470 in the Sanctuary at Westminster; eldest son of Edward IV and Elizabeth Woodville.	unmarried.	d. (traditionally murdered), possibly in 1483 or in 1486, at the Tower of London. A body with the stature and dentition of a 12-year-old male was discovered at the Tower on 6 July 1933.	Edward V was deposed 25 June 1483, when the throne was usurped by his uncle, Richard III (the only surviving brother of his father).
19. RICHARD III 26 June 1483–5 Style: As No. 16.	2 Oct 1452 at Fotheringay Northamptonshire; fourth and only surviving, son of Richard, 3rd Duke of York ('The Protector'), and the Lady Cecily Nevill.	m. 12 July 1472, the Lady ANNE (1456–85), younger d of Richard Nevill, Earl of Warwick ('The King Maker') and widow of Edward, Prince of Wales, only child of Henry VI. 1s.	killed aged 32, 22 Aug 1485, at the battle of Bosworth Field. The Abbey of the Grey Friars, Leicester.	Richard III was succeeded by his third cousin once removed downwards, Henry Tudor, 2nd Earl of Richmond.
20. HENRY VII 22 Aug 1485–1509 Style: As No. 16.	27 Jan 1457 at Pembroke Castle; only child of Edmund Tudor, 1st Earl of Richmond, and Margaret Beaufort, great-great-grand-d of Edward III.	m. at Westminster, 18 Jan 1486, ELIZABETH (1466–1503) d of Edward IV. 3s and 4d, of whom 2 died in infancy.	d., aged 52, 21 Apr 1509, at Richmond suffering from rheumatoid arthritis and gout. In his own chapel at Westminster.	Succeeded by his second and only surviving son, Henry.

King or Queen Regnant, Date of Accession and Final Year of Reign; Style	Date and Place of Birth and Parentage	Marriages and No. of Children	Date, Cause and Place of Death, and Place of Burial	Notes and Succession
21. HENRY VIII 22 Apr 1509–47 *Style:* (from 35th year) 'Henry the eighth, by the Grace of God, King of England, France, and Ireland, Defender of the Faith and of the Church of England, and also of Ireland, on earth the Supreme Head'.	28 June 1491 at Greenwich; second and only surviving son of Henry VII and Elizabeth.	m. (1) secretly at the chapel of the Observant Friars, 11 June 1509, CATHERINE of Aragon (1485–1536), d of Ferdinand II, King of Spain, and widow of Arthur, Prince of Wales. 2s 2d (one of whom died young). *Subsequent marriages of HENRY VIII:* m. (2) secretly 25 Jan 1533, ANNE Marchioness of Pembroke (b. 1507, beheaded 1536), d of Sir Thomas Boleyn, the Viscount Rochford. A daughter and possibly another child m. (3) in the Queen's Closet, York Place, London, 30 May 1536, JANE Seymour. 1s m. (4) at Greenwich, 6 Jan 1540, ANNE (1515–57), second d of John, Duke of Cleves. No issue m. (5) at Oatlands, 28 July 1540, CATHERINE (beheaded 1542), d of Lord Edmund Howard. No issue m. (6) at Hampton Court, 12 July 1543, CATHERINE (c. 1512–48), d of Sir Thomas Parr and widow of 1. Sir Edward Borough and 2. John Neville, 3rd Lord Latimer. No issue.	d., aged 55, 28 Jan 1547, at the Palace of Westminster suffering from chronic sinusitis and periostitis of the leg. Windsor.	Henry was the first King to be formally styled with a post-nominal number in his own life time, i.e. VIII. Succeeded by his only surviving son, Edward.
22. EDWARD VI 28 Jan 1547–53 *Style:* As No. 21.	12 Oct 1537 at Hampton Court; only surviving son of Henry VIII, by Jane Seymour.	unmarried.	d., aged 15, 6 July 1553, of pulmonary tuberculosis at Greenwich. Henry VII's Chapel, Westminster Abbey.	Succeeded briefly by Lady Guilford Dudley (Lady Jane Grey), his first cousin once removed.
23. JANE 6 July (proclaimed 10 July) 1553 (deposed 19 July).	October 1537 at Bradgate Park, Leicestershire; eldest d of Henry Grey, 3rd Marquess of Dorset, and Frances (d of Mary Tudor, sister of Henry VIII).	m. at Durham House, London, 21 May 1553, Lord GUILFORD DUDLEY (beheaded 1554) 4th son of John Dudley, Duke of Northumberland. No issue.	beheaded, aged 16, 12 Feb 1554, in the Tower of London. St Peter ad Vincula, within the Tower.	Succeeded by her second cousin once removed upwards, Mary.
24. MARY I 19 July 1553–8 *Style:* As No. 21 (but supremacy title was dropped) until marriage.	18 Feb 1516 at Greenwich Palace; only surviving child of Henry VIII and Catherine of Aragon.	m. at Winchester Cathedral, 25 July 1554, PHILIP (1527–98), King of Spain, Naples and Jerusalem, son of Emperor Charles V and widower of Maria, d of John III of Portugal. No issue.	d., aged 42, 17 Nov 1558 of endemic influenza at London. Westminster Abbey.	Philip was styled, but not crowned, king. Mary was succeeded by her half sister, Elizabeth, the only surviving child of Henry VIII.

Kings and Queens of England and Great Britain (continued)

King or Queen Regnant Date of Accession and Final Year of Reign; Style	Date and Place of Birth and Parentage	Marriages and No. of Children	Date, Cause and Place of Death, and Place of Burial	Notes and Succession
25. ELIZABETH I 17 Nov 1558–1603 *Style*: 'Queen of England, France and Ireland, Defender of the Faith' etc.	7 Sept 1533 at Greenwich; d of Henry VIII and Anne Boleyn.	unmarried.	d., aged 69, 24 Mar 1603, of sepsis from tonsillar abscess at Richmond. Westminster Abbey.	Succeeded by her first cousin twice removed, James.
26. JAMES I 26 Mar 1603–25 and VI of Scotland from 24 July 1567 *Style*: 'King of England, Scotland, France and Ireland, Defender of the Faith', etc.	19 June 1566 at Edinburgh Castle; only son of Henry Stuart, Lord Darnley, and Mary, Queen of Scots (d of James V of Scotland, son of Margaret Tudor, sister of Henry VIII).	m. 20 Aug 1589 (by proxy) ANNE (1574–1619), d of Frederick II, King of Denmark and Norway. 3s 4d.	d., aged 58, 27 Mar 1625, of Bright's disease at Theobalds Park, Hertfordshire. Westminster Abbey.	Succeeded by his second and only surviving son, Charles.
27. CHARLES I 27 Mar 1625–49 *Style*: As No. 26.	19 Nov 1600 at Dunfermline Palace, second and only surviving son of James I and Anne.	m. in Paris, 1 May 1625 (by proxy) HENRIETTA MARIA (1609–69) d of Henry IV of France. 4s 5d.	beheaded, aged 48, 30 Jan 1649, in Whitehall. Windsor.	The Kingship was *de facto* declared abolished 17 Mar 1649.
28. CHARLES II 29 May 1660 (but *de jure* 30 Jan 1649) to 1685 *Style*: As No. 26.	29 May 1630 at St James's Palace, London; eldest surviving son of Charles I and Henrietta Maria.	m. at Portsmouth, 21 May 1662, CATHERINE (1638–1705), d of John, Duke of Braganza. No legitimate issue.	d., aged 54, 6 Feb 1685, of uraemia and mercurial poisoning at Whitehall. Henry VII's Chapel, Westminster Abbey.	Succeeded by his younger and only surviving brother, James.
29. JAMES II 6 Feb 1685–8 *Style*: As No. 26.	14 Oct 1633 at St James's Palace, London; only surviving son of Charles I and Henrietta Maria.	m. (1) at Worcester House, The Strand, London, 3 Sept 1660, ANNE (1637–71), eldest d of Edward Hyde. 4s 4d. m. (2) at Modena (by proxy), 30 Sept 1673, MARY D'Este (1658–1718), only d of Alfonso IV, Duke of Modena. 2s 5d.	d., aged 67, 6 Sept 1701, of a cerebral haemorrhage at St Germain, France. His remains were divided and interred at five different venues in France. All are now lost except for those at the parish church of St Germain.	James II was deemed by legal fiction to have ended his reign 11 Dec 1688 by flight. A Convention Parliament offered the Crown of England and Ireland 13 Feb 1689 to Mary, his eldest surviving d., and her husband, his nephew, William Henry of Orange.

King or Queen Regnant Date of Accession and Final Year of Reign; Style	Date and Place of Birth and Parentage	Marriages and No. of Children	Date, Cause and Place of Death, and Place of Burial	Notes and Succession
30. WILLIAM III 13 Feb 1689–1702.	4 Nov 1650 at The Hague; only son of William II, Prince of Orange, and Mary (Stuart), d of Charles I		d., aged 51, 8 Mar 1702, of pleuro-pneumonia following fracture of right collarbone, in Kensington	
MARY II 13 Feb 1689–94 *Style:* 'King and Queen of England, Scotland, France and Ireland, Defenders of the Faith', etc.	30 Apr 1662 at St James's Palace, London; elder surviving d of James II and Anne Hyde.	They were married at St James's Palace, London, 4 Nov 1677. No issue.	d., aged 32, 28 Dec 1694, of confluent haemorrhagic small-pox with pneumonia, at Kensington. They were buried in Henry VII's Chapel, Westminster Abbey.	The widower, King William III, was succeeded by his sister-in-law, Anne, who was also his first cousin.
31. ANNE 8 Mar 1702–14 *Style:* Firstly as No. 25; secondly (after Union with Scotland 6 Mar 1707) 'Queen of Great Britain, France and Ireland, Defender of the Faith', etc.	6 Feb 1665 at St James's Palace, London; only surviving d of James II and Anne Hyde.	m. at the Chapel Royal, St James's Palace, 28 July 1683, GEORGE (1653–1708), second son of Frederick III, King of Denmark. 2s 3d from 17 confinements.	d., aged 49, 1 Aug 1714, of a cerebral haemorrhage and possibly chronic Bright's disease at Kensington. Henry VII's Chapel, Westminster Abbey.	Succeeded in the terms of the Act of Settlement (which excluded all Roman Catholics and their spouses) by her second cousin, George Lewis, Elector of Hanover.
32. GEORGE I 1 Aug 1714–27 *Style:* 'King of Great Britain, France, Ireland, Duke of Brunswick-Lüneburg, etc., Defender of the Faith'.	28 May 1660 at Osnabrück; eldest son of Ernest Augustus, Duke of Brunswick-Lüneburg and Elector of Hanover, and Princess Sophia, 5th and youngest d and 10th child of Elizabeth, Queen of Bohemia, eldest d of James I.	m. 21 Nov 1682 (div. 1694), SOPHIA Dorothea (1666–1726), only d of George William, Duke of Lüneburg-Celle. 1s 1d.	d., aged 67, 11 June 1727, of coronary thrombosis, at Ibbenbüren or Osnabrück. Hanover.	The Kings of England were Electors of Hanover from 1714 to 1814. Succeeded by his only son, George Augustus.
33. GEORGE II 11 June 1727–60 *Style:* As No. 32.	30 Oct 1683 at Hanover; only son of George I and Sophia Dorothea.	m. 22 Aug (O.S.), 2 Sept (N.S.), 1705, Wilhelmina Charlotte CAROLINE (1683–1737), d of John Frederick, Margrave of Brandenburg-Ansbach. 3s 5d.	d., aged 76, 25 Oct 1760, of coronary thrombosis at the Palace of Westminster. Henry VII's Chapel, Westminster Abbey.	Succeeded by his elder son's eldest son, George William Frederick.

Kings and Queens of England and Great Britain (continued)

King or Queen Regnant / Date of Accession and / Final Year of Reign; Style	Date and Place of Birth and Parentage	Marriages and No. of Children	Date, Cause and Place of Death, and Place of Burial	Notes and Succession
34. GEORGE III 25 Oct 1760–1820 *Style:* As No. 31 (until Union of Great Britain and Ireland, 1 Jan 1801), whereafter 'By the Grace of God, of the United Kingdom of Great Britain and Ireland, King, Defender of the Faith'.	24 May (O.S.) 1738 at Norfolk House, St James's Square, London; eldest son of Frederick Lewis, Prince of Wales (d. 20 Mar 1751) and Princess Augusta of Saxe-Gotha.	m. at St James's Palace, London, 8 Sept 1761, CHARLOTTE Sophia (1744–1818), youngest d of Charles Louis Frederick. Duke of Mecklenburg-Strelitz. 9s 6d.	d., aged 81 years 239 days, 29 Jan 1820, of old age at Windsor. St George's Chapel, Windsor.	His eldest son became Regent owing to his insanity 5 Feb 1811. Hanover was made a kingdom in 1814. Succeeded by his eldest son, George Augustus Frederick.
35. GEORGE IV 29 Jan 1820–30 *Style:* As later style of No. 34.	12 Aug 1762 at St James's Palace, London; eldest son of George III and Charlotte.	m. (1) in a ceremony not recognized under English law 15 Dec 1785 Maria FitzHerbert m. (2) at the Chapel Royal, St James's Palace, 8 Apr 1795, CAROLINE Amelia Elizabeth (1768–1821), his first cousin, second d of Charles, Duke of Brunswick-Wolfenbüttel. 1d.	d., aged 67, 26 June 1830, of rupture of the stomach blood vessels, alcoholic cirrhosis, and dropsy at Windsor. St George's Chapel, Windsor.	Succeeded by his eldest surviving brother, William Henry (George's only child, Princess Charlotte, having died in childbirth 6 Nov 1817).
36. WILLIAM IV 26 June 1830–7 *Style:* As No. 34.	21 Aug 1765 at Buckingham Palace; third and oldest surviving son of George III and Charlotte.	m. at Kew, 11 July 1818, ADELAIDE Louisa Theresa Caroline Amelia (1792–1849), eldest d of George, Duke of Saxe-Meiningen. 2d.	d., aged 71, 20 June 1837, of pleuro-pneumonia and alcoholic cirrhosis at Windsor. St George's Chapel, Windsor.	On William's death the crown of Hanover passed by Salic law to his brother, Ernest, Duke of Cumberland. Succeeded by his niece, Alexandrina Victoria.
37. VICTORIA 20 June 1837–1901 *Style:* As (except for 'Queen') No. 34 until 1 May 1876, whereafter 'Empress of India' was added.	24 May 1819 at Kensington Palace, London; only child of Edward, Duke of Kent and Strathearn, 4th son of George III, and Victoria, widow of Emich Charles, Prince of Leiningen, and d of Francis, Duke of Saxe-Coburg-Saafeld.	m. at St James's Palace, London, 10 Feb 1840, her first cousin Francis ALBERT Augustus Charles Emmanuel (1819–61), second son of Ernest I, Duke of Saxe-Coburg-Gotha. 4s 5d.	d., aged 81 years 243 days, 22 Jan 1901 of old age at Osborne, I.o.W. Frogmore.	Assumed title Empress of India 1 May 1876. Succeeded by her elder surviving son, Albert Edward.
38. EDWARD VII 22 Jan 1901–10 *Style:* 'By the Grace of God, of the United Kingdom of Great Britain and Ireland and the British Dominions beyond the Seas, King, Defender of the Faith, Emperor of India'	9 Nov 1841 at Buckingham Palace, London; elder surviving son of Victoria and Albert.	m. at St George's Chapel, Windsor, 10 Mar 1863, ALEXANDRA Caroline Maria Charlotte Louisa Julia (1844–1925), d of Christian IX of Denmark. 3s 3d.	d., aged 68, 6 May 1910, of bronchitis at Buckingham Palace. St George's Chapel, Windsor.	Succeeded by his only surviving son, George Frederick Ernest Albert.

King or Queen Regnant, Date of Accession and Final Year of Reign; Style	Date and Place of Birth and Parentage	Marriages and No. of Children	Date, Cause and Place of Death, and Place of Burial	Notes and Succession
39. GEORGE V 6 May 1910–36 *Style:* As for No. 37 until 12 May 1927, whereafter 'By the Grace of God, of Great Britain, Ireland, and of the British Dominions beyond the Seas, King, Defender of the Faith, Emperor of India'.	3 June 1865 at Marlborough House, London; second and only surviving son of Edward VII and Alexandra.	m. at St James's Palace, London, 6 July 1893, Victoria MARY Augusta Louise Olga Pauline Claudine Agnes (1867–1953), eldest d of Francis, Duke of Teck. 5s 1d.	d., aged 70, 20 Jan 1936, of bronchitis at Sandringham House, Norfolk. St George's Chapel, Windsor.	Succeeded by his eldest son, Edward Albert Christian George Andrew Patrick David.
40. EDWARD VIII 20 Jan–11 Dec 1936 *Style:* As for No. 39.	23 June 1894 at the White Lodge, Richmond Park; eldest son of George V and Mary.	m. at the Château de Candé, Monts, France, 3 June 1937, Bessie Wallis Warfield (1896–1986), previous wife of Lt. Earl Winfield Spencer, USN (div. 1927) and Ernest Simpson (div. 1936). No issue.	d., aged 77, 28 May 1972, of cancer of the throat at 4, Route du Champ, D'Entraînement, Paris, XVIᵉ, France.	Edward VIII abdicated for himself and his heirs and was succeeded by his eldest brother, Albert Frederick Arthur George.
41. GEORGE VI 11 Dec 1936–52 *Style:* As for No. 39 until the Indian title was dropped 22 June 1947.	14 Dec 1895 at York Cottage, Sandringham; second son of George V and Mary.	m. at Westminster Abbey, 26 Apr 1923, Lady ELIZABETH Angela Marguerite Bowes-Lyon (b. 1900), youngest d of 14th Earl of Strathmore and Kinghorne. 2d.	d., aged 56, 6 Feb 1952, of lung cancer at Sandringham House, Norfolk. St George's Chapel, Windsor.	Succeeded by his elder d Elizabeth Alexandra Mary.
42. ELIZABETH II Since 6 Feb 1952 *Style:* (from 29 May 1953) 'By the Grace of God, of the United Kingdom of Great Britain and Northern Ireland and of Her other Realms and Territories, Queen, Head of the Commonwealth, Defender of the Faith'.	21 Apr 1926 at 17 Bruton Street, London, W1: elder d of George VI and Elizabeth.	m. at Westminster Abbey, 20 Nov 1947, her third cousin PHILIP (b. Corfu, Greece, 10 June 1921), only son of Prince Andrea (Andrew) of Greece and Princess Alice (great-grand-d of Queen Victoria). 3s 1d.	—	The Heir Apparent is Charles Philip Arthur George, Prince of Wales, b. 14 Nov 1948.

GOVERNMENT

The UK is a constitutional monarchy without a written constitution. Parliament comprises two houses – the House of Lords (the upper house) and the House of Commons (the lower house). The Lords is made up of over 750 hereditary peers and peeresses, over 20 Lords of Appeal (the Law Lords; non-hereditary peers), over 370 life peers, and 2 arch-bishops and 24 bishops of the Church of England. All members of the Lords are non-elected. The House of Commons consists of 650 members elected for five years by universal adult suffrage. (The division of the Milton Keynes constituency will increase the membership of the House of Commons to 651 at the first general election after 1990.)

THE EVOLUTION OF PARLIAMENT
Unlike most modern parliaments, the British parliament is not the conscious creation of constitution-framers, but has evolved from a feudal relationship between monarch and subjects.

The term 'House of Lords' was not in use until the 16th century. However, from the Middle Ages the great magnates and prelates had a feudal obligation to attend the sovereign's Great Council to judge pleas and to advise the monarch on matters of state, as well as to grant aid when necessary. The Commons emerged in the 13th century when the financial support of the shires and boroughs was needed by the king and the nobility for assistance in their disputes with each other and with the Scots, Welsh and French. Originally there was no intention that the Commons should play any part in the deliberation of policy, but gradual changes over centuries in the concepts of law and representation, together with the formalization of procedures, gave the Commons a clear corporate identity. A change in the relative economic strength of king, Lords and Commons – and civil wars – helped confirm the clear constitutional concept (defined in 1869) that sovereignty lay with the monarch in Parliament of Lords *and* Commons.

THE ROLE OF THE MONARCH
These antecedents are clearly visible and important in the procedures and rituals of Parliament today. In theory, the role of the Lords and Commons is to advise the monarch's servants on the formulation of policy and to consent to the necessary financial assistance. However, in practice the development of democratic ideology, the extention of the franchise to almost the entire adult population, combined with the growth of modern political parties have significantly changed the functions and relative power of monarch, Lords and Commons. Sovereignty has gradually shifted from the monarch to 'the monarch in Parliament', and power has moved from the Lords to the Commons.

The monarch's power has been largely eroded by convention and statute, and most of the functions she carries out, or prerogatives she possesses, are exercised on the advice of the Prime Minister. Nonetheless, she retains an important formal role within Parliament. Public measures are proposed and enacted in the name of her government, and it is her assent that converts bills passed by both Houses into statutes. The Royal Prerogative, which enables action to be taken without the formal consent of Parliament, is seldom used but is a potential force within the system. Some of these powers, such as the dissolution of Parliament before the end of its statutory maximum of five years, the appointment of the Prime Minister, the creation of peers, and the distribution of honours, facilitate the smooth operation of the wider political system, although they are mostly mere formal powers often taken 'on advice' from the prime minister. Other powers, such as the power to make an Order in Council, enables the government to take swift executive action. The monarch also retains a less formal role in providing advice for her Prime Minister.

THE ROLE OF THE HOUSE OF LORDS
The House of Lords has also seen its power gradually diminish over the past two centuries. Since 1911 the Lords have had no right to amend bills concerning taxation, and subsequently, their right to delay bills passed by the Commons has been reduced from two to one year. Nevertheless, the Lords carries out significant functions. The House retains one of its original roles as the supreme civil and criminal court in United Kingdom. It scrutinizes bills passed by House of Commons, and proposes amendments. It provides a means of introducing minor public bills, allows additional opportunities for the debate of private member's bills, bears the burden of debate concerning powers under delegated legislation, and debates private bills.

The composition and procedures of the House of Lords give a different emphasis from that of the Commons. Scrutiny is usually less detailed, but procedures more flexible, and the debate less partisan than in the Commons.

THE HOUSE OF COMMONS
The House of Commons is, undoubtedly, the dominant element within Parliament today. Its 650 Members of Parliament are the basis of British parliamentary democracy. Finance remains at the centre of the Commons' power. The House has the sole right to deliberate issues of taxation – or 'supply' as it is known – without which government would be impossible.

THE PRIME MINISTER
The post of Prime Minister was not officially recognized until this century, but it had long been accepted that the monarch's treasurer had to be able to command a majority in the Commons. The power of the premier is still ill-defined, but ultimately it depends upon maintaining a majority in the Commons. The Prime Minister can exercise the prerogative powers of the monarch, and choose, transfer and dismiss Cabinet ministers and junior members of the government. The Prime Minister is also the First Lord of the Treasury, the political head of the Civil Service. He chairs the Cabinet, and the major Cabinet committees, with all the possibilities for coordination, supervision and control of policy and individuals that this entails.

THE CABINET
The Cabinet was originally a meeting of the monarch's personal advisers. It is now the major policy-making body of the government. Members of the Cabinet are chosen by the Prime Minister from the Commons or Lords – in modern times overwhelmingly from the Commons. They attend Cabinet meetings either as heads of government departments

or 'without portfolio' (without the responsibility of a department). Because modern governments have such a great workload, the Cabinet increasingly works through a system of committees. Some are permanent committees dealing with tasks such as managing the economy, while others are formed to deal with particular problems. The Cabinet are collectively responsible to Parliament for the actions of the government, and if defeated in a motion of confidence must either resign or seek a dissolution of Parliament and a renewed mandate from the electorate.

The Cabinet works under the convention of collective responsibility. This means that even if not all Cabinet ministers agree on a subject, the Cabinet must act unanimously. Departmental policies must be generally consistent with government policies. If a departmental minister fails to follow this principle he or she is expected to resign.

THE PRIVY COUNCIL

The Privy Council was the chief source of executive power until the development of cabinet government. Its main purpose now is to advise the sovereign on the approval of Orders in Council and on the issue of royal proclamations. All cabinet ministers must be Privy counsellors and are sworn in on first assuming office. Membership is for life and is awarded by the monarch, on the recommendation of the prime minister. It is awarded to eminent citizens of the UK and of Commonwealth countries with independent monarchs.

THE SPEAKER AND LEADER OF THE HOUSE

The workload of the House of Commons has increased greatly since 1945, as the quantity and complexity of government measures have increased. This has put an increasing burden upon the Speaker, the Leader of the House and the party whips who, together, do much to ensure that matters on the floor of the House proceed smoothly. The Speaker's function as spokesman for the House remains important, but his duties to regulate debate, decide points of order and interpret the rules of the House, are vital day-to-day functions that require tact and the confidence of all parties in the selection of one of their number as Speaker. Once selected, the Speaker is extremely careful to betray no hint of his former party allegiance.

The working of the Commons is also facilitated by the work of the Leader of the House, who is chosen by the Prime Minister to organize government business going through the Commons. This entails working with the chief whips of the major parties to ensure that adequate scrutiny is given to measures, whilst preserving the government's legislative timetable.

THE OPPOSITION

The evolutionary nature of Parliament has meant that the Commons has adapted itself over centuries to the changing conditions within which scrutiny of government must take place. The Opposition is now formalized under a Leader of the Opposition, who since 1937 has been paid by the Crown. The Leader of the Opposition – the leader of the second biggest party in the House – creates a 'Shadow Cabinet', so the actions of all ministers can be effectively examined.

COMMITTEES

Perhaps the most effective scrutiny takes place not on the floor of the House but in committees. There are many types of committee. Select Committees usually report on specific matters, such as Public Accounts, Privileges and Members' Interests. In 1978 the select-committee system was reorganized to provide a committee to examine each of the government departments, although that on Scottish Affairs has not sat since 1987. All bills before Parliament, many statutory instruments and European Community documents, must pass through a Standing, or Legislative Committee, appointed to examine their clauses in detail. Similar committees exist in the House of Lords, and on some issues Joint Committees of both Houses are held.

THE ELECTORAL SYSTEM

The United Kingdom uses a 'first-past-the-post' system for electing Members of Parliament. Each constituency elects one MP, the person gaining the most votes being elected. In a contest between four parties, it would be possible for an MP to be elected with less than a third of the total vote. At a national level, it is possible for the party that obtains the largest number of votes not to win the election. The British system tends to produce majority governments that do not have to rely on coalition partners to govern.

LOCAL GOVERNMENT

Much of the work of governing Britain is done by local government. Local authorities (county councils and district councils in England and Wales, regional, island and district councils in Scotland) are responsible for services such as education, social services, policing, local authority housing, and the fire brigade. There has been some loss of responsibility by local government in the 1980s and their role is still a matter of political debate. (For more information on local government see listing of counties on pp. 673–89.)

PARLIAMENTARY GLOSSARY

act a bill that has completed its passage through both Houses of Paliament and received royal assent. Once a bill receives royal assent, it is law.

adjournment debate the discussion – for about half an hour – at the end of each Parliamentary day of an issue raised by a backbencher. The issue is selected by ballot.

amendments changes to bills and motions put before either House. Amendments may be proposed by any member.

backbencher an MP who has neither government nor shadow-ministerial responsibilities.

bill any proposed legislation before Parliament, which has not proceeded as far as royal assent. Bills may be:
Public – a draft statute of general application, affecting the nation at large. The majority of public bills are sponsored by the government and are put through both Houses during government time.
Private Member's – a public bill which is introduced into the House by a private member (backbencher) on one of ten Fridays set aside for this purpose in each Parliamentary session. Bills are selected by ballot.
Private – individuals or groups of people may petition Parliament for legislation for their own benefit.
Hybrid – public bills containing clauses that affect

specific individuals in a similar manner to private bills.

bills, passage of

Public and Private Member's Bills (general procedures):

i) First Reading: usually a brief statement of the intent of the bill, after which the bill is circulated.

ii) Second Reading: the general principles of the bill are debated in the Chamber, or, if uncontentious, in the Second Reading Committee.

iii) Committee Stage: most bills are committed to a standing committee that examines the bill clause by clause. Some particularly important bills may be debated in the chamber of the House. It is in committee that bills receive the most detailed scrutiny and amendment.

iv) Report Stage: the committee's report is considered by the House and the bill is given its final form.

v) Third Reading: the bill is presented for the last time for debate on the amended bill, after which it is sent up to the House of Lords.

vi) The bill in the House of Lords goes through similar stages to those outlined above, except that the committee stage is usually carried out on the floor of the chamber. If the bill is accepted by the Lords without amendment, it proceeds to its final stage, the royal assent. If amendments are proposed, the bill is sent back to the Commons. If the Commons accepts the amendments, the bill proceeds to royal assent. If the Commons refuses to accept the amendments, a compromise has to be reached or the bill is defeated.

vii) Royal Assent: the monarch's assent to the bill converts it into an Act of Parliament.

Most public bills originate in the Commons, but some uncontentious bills are introduced in the Lords, in which case the procedure outlined above is reversed. Other bills may be introduced in either house.

Private bills The general procedures are the same as those for public bills except that they are initiated by petitions from those desiring the legislation, and at the committee stage witnesses for and against the bill are heard.

Chiltern Hundreds, stewardship of a nominal office of profit to which an MP must apply in order to resign from the House. The holder of the stewardship of the Chiltern Hundreds, or of the Manor of Northstead, is disqualified from sitting as an MP.

closure the method by which a debate in the House is closed. Any member may move to close a debate in the House or in committee by moving 'that the question may now be put'. If the chair accepts, this motion is put. If it receives the support of 100 or more members in the House, or 20 in committee, the motion is passed. Debate is then terminated and the original question is put.

Consolidated Fund bill the Consolidated Fund is the money received by the Exchequer from taxation and elsewhere. Consolidated Fund bills authorize the government to withdraw money from this fund.

convention any parliamentary procedure that is not sanctioned by standing order. Although standing orders provide a framework for the work of Parliament, most of the daily routine is based upon less formal conventions.

dissolution Parliament is dissolved five years after the date of its first meeting, and a general election must be called. Within this five years, a prime minister may request the monarch to dissolve Parliament and summon a new one.

Dod's Parliamentary Companion an annual publication giving current details of the personnel and procedures of Parliament.

early day motion a procedure by which MPs who wish to raise an issue in the Commons may table a motion for it to be debated at an 'early day', i.e. an indeterminate date in the future.

emergency debate a debate initiated as a result of a member's request for an adjournment debate to discuss a specific, urgent matter. If the Speaker agrees, the matter is debated that evening or the following day.

'Erskine May' the popular name for *A Treatise upon the Law, Privileges, Proceedings and Usage of Parliament* by Thomas Erskine May (1815–86). It is kept up to date and remains the main reference work on Parliament.

Father of the House the MP who has served longest without a break.

General Synod Measure any statute that relates to the Church of England, passed by special procedures. Measures submitted by the General Synod are considered by the Ecclesiastical Committee before being placed before both Houses. They may not be amended, but are seldom controversial. Once passed, Measures receive royal assent in the same manner as bills.

guillotine a form of closure motion used to speed government legislation through the Commons. It imposes a strict timetable on each of the bill's following stages. This does not operate in the House of Lords.

Hansard since 1909, the official report of proceedings in Parliament.

Joint Committees Select Committees of the Lords and Commons that sit together to consider matters of common interest.

Lord Chancellor the head of the United Kingdom judiciary and Speaker of the House of Lords. As a member of the government, he plays an important part in debates and a major role in carrying out the monarch's parliamentary functions in her absence.

maiden speech the first speech of a new MP.

naming the procedure by which an MP who is considered to have abused the rules of the House and refuses to leave the chamber may be 'named' by the Speaker. After 'naming' the member is suspended for a period dependent upon the number of previous occasions he or she has been named.

Opposition Day one of 20 days set aside each Parliamentary session for debates initiated by the opposition.

Parliamentary session a sub-division of the period in which Parliament is sitting. Each session lasts from about early November in one year until mid-October in the next.

Prime Minister's Questions the parliamentary time set aside during which MPs may ask the Prime Minister questions about general issues raised by government policy. Oral questions are answered by the Prime Minister in the House for about 15 minutes on Tuesdays and Thursdays.

private notice question a question of particular urgency put by the Speaker in the Commons or the Leader of the Lords – on behalf of a member – for oral answer on the same day.

privileges the special rights and exemptions from

the law enjoyed by members. The most significant privileges are freedom of speech within the chamber (for example, an MP may not be sued for slander if he names names in the House), the right of MPs to decide their own procedures, and the right to punish those who breach the privileges of the House.

prorogation the ending of a session of Parliament. After prorogation almost all business that has not been completed is deemed lost.

Queen's Speech a statement delivered by the Queen at the opening of each session outlining the government's legislative programme for that session.

Question Time the period between 2.35 and 3.00 pm from Monday to Thursday that is set aside for the Prime Minister or ministers to answer oral questions. If an MP requires an oral answer for a question it is identified by an asterisk. Members can table up to two questions in a sitting and are usually allowed to ask a 'supplementary question' in response to the minister's answer.

Select Committees committees of either the Commons or Lords that report on specific issues to the whole House. Select Committees are provided to examine the 14 major government departments. Other Select Committees may be appointed on an ad hoc basis.

Standing Committees usually committees established to examine bills in their Committee Stage. Members are nominated by the Committee of Selection based upon their previous experience or interest.

standing orders orders regulating the proceedings of Parliament. They may be modified or repealed by the House, and in exceptional circumstances they may be suspended.

State Opening the annual opening of a new session of Parliament, usually in November. The monarch summons the Commons to attend her in the House of Lords. The new session is opened by the reading of the Queen's Speech (see above).

strangers anyone who is not a member of either House or an official of Parliament. Strangers may be ordered out of Parliament by the passage of a motion put by the Speaker if a member declares 'I spy strangers'.

talking out the attempt by opponents of a bill to force it to fall behind its timetable by prolonging debate or scrutiny (it is also known as filibustering). The guillotine (see above) was introduced to counter this tactic in the reading of government bills. However, talking out can still be an effective tactic against private member's bills.

ten minute rule the procedure by which backbenchers may introduce a private member's bill on Tuesdays and Wednesdays in a speech lasting no more than 10 minutes. An opponent is also given 10 minutes, after which a motion to introduce the bill is put. It is usually used by members to test parliamentary opinion.

three line whip the number of times that a printed request to a member to attend a debate is underlined by the party whips. The request is circulated to members in the weekly order of business. The number of lines indicates the relative importance of attending – three lines indicates that attendance is imperative.

whips the members responsible for ensuring the discipline of their own parties. They circulate the weekly order of business, also known as the whip.

written answer an answer to an MP's question

printed in Hansard. MPs may request any number of written answers from ministers, so long as the substance of the question is within the minister's departmental responsibility. Answers are usually printed within ten working days.

MINISTRIES AND DEPARTMENTS

Prime Minister's Office the office of the Prime Minister, who is also the First Lord of the Treasury and Minister for the Civil Service.

Ministry of Agriculture, Fisheries and Food is responsible for all matters concerning agriculture, fishing and food production, safety and standards, including these industries' interests in Europe and abroad.

Ministry of Defence has overall responsibility for the Army, the Royal Navy, the Royal Air Force and the Meteorological Office.

Department of Education and Science is responsible for all levels of education, for recruiting and training teachers, and the promotion of science and technology.

Department of Employment is responsible for encouraging employment, training, safety at work, and the Advisory Conciliation and Arbitration Service (ACAS).

Department of Energy is accountable for government functions in the coal, electricity, and atomic-energy industries, and the oil and gas resources.

Department of the Environment includes ministries for Housing and Planning, Local Government, and the Environment and Countryside. In addition there is a Minister for Sport.

Foreign and Commonwealth Office deals with international relations, and protects British interests and citizens abroad.

Department of Health is responsible for the administration of the National Health Service (in England), local social services, food hygiene and emergency services.

Home Office administers criminal law, the prison and probation service, the police, and immigration.

Lord Advocate's Department is the office of the Solicitor-General for Scotland. It is responsible for drawing up Scottish legislation and advising other departments on points of Scottish law.

Lord Chancellor's Department is responsible for general reforms in civil law and the administration of civil courts, the supreme court, county courts and legal aid.

Northern Ireland Office has overall responsibility for the government of the province and is directly accountable for law and order, constitutional changes, security, and electoral matters.

Privy Council Office is the office of the Leader of the House of Commons. It makes preparations for Royal Proclamations and aspects of ministerial changes. In addition there is a Minister for Arts.

Scottish Office has various statutory functions that are divided between the Scottish departments of Agriculture and Fisheries, Education, Development, Home and Health, and Industry. In addition the Secretary has some responsibility for the Scottish Courts Administration.

Department of Social Security is responsible for the social-security services in England, Wales and Scotland.

Department of Trade and Industry is responsible for promoting UK exports, domestic industry, international trade, publicly owned industries, competition policy, consumer protection, research policy, and the administration of company legislation.

Department of Transport has overall responsibility for all transport, particularly British Rail and London Regional Transport, but also the construction and maintenance of motorways and trunk roads, transport planning, shipping and ports, and international and domestic aviation policy.

Treasury is the office of the Chancellor of the Exchequer. It has overall responsibility for the control of public expenditure, overseas aid, export credit, Inland Revenue duties and taxes, privatization policy, monetary policy, the financial system, international finance, and Customs and Excise.

Welsh Office has areas of responsibility including health and social services and some areas of education in Wales, Welsh culture, local government, sport, agriculture, fisheries, forestry, regional industrial development, and conservation.

PRINCIPAL BRITISH POLITICAL PARTIES

The following political parties are either represented in Parliament or contest the majority of seats in Northern Ireland, Wales or Scotland or a considerable number of seats in England.

Alliance Party
88 University Street, Belfast BT7 1HE. Membership: 12 000. Leader: Dr John Alderdice.

Communist Party of Great Britain
16 St John Street, London EC1M 4AL. Membership: 8 500. Secretary: Nina Temple.

Conservative Party
32 Smith Square, London SW1P 3HH. Membership: approx. 1 500 000. Parliamentary Leader: John Major.

Co-operative Party
158 Buckingham Palace Road, London SW1W 9UB. Membership: 12 000 Secretary: David Wise. (Under an agreement with the Labour Party, the Co-operative Party sponsors Labour and Co-operative candidates at general and local elections.)

Democratic Unionist Party
296 Albertbridge Road, Belfast BT5 4GX. Membership: not published. Parliamentary Leader: Rev Ian Paisley.

Green Party
10 Station Parade, Balham High Road, London SW12 9AZ. Membership: 17 000. Co-Chairs: Nick Anderson, David Batchelor, Caroline Lucas.

Labour Party
144-152 Walworth Road, London SE17 1JT. Membership: 288 000 (5 564 000 affiliated members). Parliamentary Leader: Neil Kinnock.

Liberal Democratic Party
4 Cowley Street, London SW1P 3NB. Membership: 83 000. Parliamentary Leader: Paddy Ashdown.

Plaid Cymru (Welsh Nationalist Party)
51 Cathedral Road, Cardiff CF1 9HD. Membership: 10 000. Parliamentary Leader: Dafydd Elis Thomas.

Scottish National Party 6 North Charlotte Street, Edinburgh EH2 4JH. Membership: not published. Parliamentary Leader: Margaret Ewing.

Social Democratic and Labour Party
24 Mount Charles, Belfast BT7 1NZ. Membership: not published. Parliamentary Leader: John Hume.

Socialist Party of Great Britain
52 Clapham High Street, London SW4 7UN. Membership: 700. General Secretary: Paul Hope.

Socialist Workers' Party
PO Box 82, London E3 3LH. Membership: 5 000. Chair: Duncan Hallas.

Ulster Popular Unionist Party
Eastonville, Donaghadee Road, Millisle, Newtownards, Co Down, Northern Ireland, BT22 2BZ. Membership: not published. Parliamentary Leader: James Kilfedder.

Ulster Unionist Party
3 Glengall Street, Belfast BT12 5AE. Membership: not published. Parliamentary Leader: James Molyneaux.

THE BRITISH PEERAGE

There are five ranks in the British temporal peerage. In ascending order they are:
  baron or baroness;
  viscount or viscountess;
  earl or countess;
  marquess (sometimes referred to as marquis) or marchioness;
  duke or duchess.

The British spiritual peerage is of two ranks. Archbishops (of Canterbury and of York) rank in precedence between Royal Dukes and dukes. Twenty-four of the bishops (always including the Bishops of London, Durham and Winchester and excluding the Bishop of Sodor and Man) rank between viscounts and barons, based on their seniority of appointment.

A few women hold peerages in their own right and since the Peerage Act, 1963, have become peers of Parliament. The remaining category of membership of the House of Lords is life peers. These are of two sorts:
– the Lords of Appeal in Ordinary, who are appointed by virtue of the Appellate Jurisdiction Act, 1876. Their number has been increased from the original four to six in 1913, to seven in 1929, and to nine since 1947;
– life peers created by virtue of the Life Peerages Act, 1958, by which both men and women may be appointed for life membership of the House of Lords. Such creations so far have been confined to the rank of baron or baroness.

There are five types of hereditary peerage:
  peerages of England, i.e. those created prior to the union with Scotland on 1 May 1707;
  peerages of Scotland, i.e. those created before the union with England;
  peerages of Ireland (the last creation was in 1898);
  peerages of Great Britain, i.e. those created between the union with Scotland (1707) and the union with Ireland (2 July 1800);
  peerages of the United Kingdom of Great Britain and (Northern) Ireland, i.e. those created since 2 July 1800.

All holders of peerages of England, Great Britain and the United Kingdom, and (only since the Peerage Act, 1963) also of Scotland, are also peers of Parliament provided they are over 21 and are not unpardoned major felons, bankrupts, lunatics or of foreign nationality. Peers who are civil servants may sit but neither speak nor vote.

The single exception to the rule concerning minors is that The Duke of Cornwall (HRH The Prince of Wales) has been technically entitled to a seat from the moment of his mother's accession, when he was only three years of age.

The peers (and peeresses in their own right) of Ireland are not peers of Parliament but they are entitled to stand for election to the House of Commons for any seat in the United Kingdom.

Life peers The Crown in the past has occasionally granted life peerages, both to men and women. The Wensleydale peerage case of 1856 acknowledged the Crown's right to do this but denied the consequent right of a seat in the House of Lords to such a peer. The two current categories of life peers are treated above. It should be noted that there is no provision for these non-hereditary peers or peeresses to disclaim their peerages.

Widows of peers The only correct style for the widow of a peer is 'The Dowager' prefixed to her peerage title of duchess, marchioness, countess, viscountess, or lady ('baroness' is only normally used by a peeress in her own right). But as most widowed peeresses dislike this title because of its association with advanced age, they prefix their Christian name to their title. In the event of a widow remarrying, she should forfeit her previous title but some, quite unjustifiably, retain it.

Divorced peeresses Some peeresses who divorce their husbands or have been divorced by them continue to bear their former husband's style, though in strict English law they are probably no longer peeresses. If a new wife appears they adopt the practice of most widows and prefix their Christian name to their title. With Scottish peerages, however, the position of a divorced peeress is exactly the same as if her husband were dead and hence she takes her legal rights as a widow.

Courtesy titles Only the holder of a peerage can be described as noble. In the eyes of the law the holder of a courtesy title is a commoner. For example, the Duke of Marlborough's son is known by courtesy as Marquess of Blandford – note the omission of the definite article 'the' because the Duke of Marlborough is also *the* Marquess of Blandford and his secondary peerage style is merely *lent* to this son.

According to the preamble of the Peerage Act, 1963, 'Courtesy titles are, by definition, not matters of law.' They are governed by custom and fall into two categories – those borne by all the children of a peer and those reserved for the heir. The children (except the eldest son) of a duke or marquess take the title 'Lord' or 'Lady' before their Christian name and the family name (e.g. Lord Charles Cavendish). The same applies to the daughters of an earl but not, oddly enough, to the younger sons who take the style 'Honourable'. Honourable is also the style for *all* the children of a viscount or of a baron. When male holders of this title marry, their wives also become 'The Honourable'. The heir to a dukedom is given the courtesy style 'Marquess', provided, of course, his father has a marquessate, which failing he takes the title 'Earl' but enjoys the precedence of a duke's eldest son. Likewise, the heir to a marquessate takes the courtesy style of 'Earl' (if available) and similarly the heir of an earldom takes the title of his father's viscountcy (if any) or barony.

In the Scottish peerage the term 'Master of' is used by the male heir to many peerages as of right. If he is

married, his wife is styled 'The Hon. Mrs'.

Courtesy titles in the second generation extend only to the grandchildren who are the children of an elder son.

DUKES

ROYAL DUKES

Created	Title
1947	*Edinburgh*, The Prince Philip, Duke of Edinburgh, b. 1921
1337	*Cornwall*, Charles, Prince of Wales, Duke of Cornwall (Scottish duke, Rothesay), b. 1948
1986	*York*, The Prince Andrew, Duke of York, b. 1960
1928	*Gloucester (2nd)*, Richard, Duke of Gloucester, b. 1944
1934	*Kent (2nd)*, Edward, Duke of Kent, b. 1945

DUKES

1868	*Abercorn (5th)*
1701	*Argyll (12th)*
1703	*Atholl (10th)*
1682	*Beaufort (11th)*
1694	*Bedford (13th)*
1663	*Buccleuch (9th) and Queensberry (11th)*
1694	*Devonshire (11th)*
1900	*Fife (3rd)*
1675	*Grafton (11th)*
1643	*Hamilton (15th) and Brandon (12th)*
1766	*Leinster (8th)*
1719	*Manchester (12th)*
1702	*Marlborough (11th)*
1707	*Montrose (7th)*
1483	*Norfolk (17th)*
1766	*Northumberland (11th)*
1675	*Richmond (9th) and Gordon (5th) and Lennox (10th)*
1707	*Roxburghe (10th)*
1703	*Rutland (10th)*
1684	*St. Albans (14th)*
1547	*Somerset (19th)*
1833	*Sutherland (6th)*
1814	*Wellington (8th)*
1874	*Westminster (6th)*

The signature of peers A peer's signature, whether on a formal or informal document, is simply his title without any qualification of rank or the use of a Christian name. This also applies to peeresses in their own right. Members of the Royal Family who hold peerages, however, sign with their principal Christian name.

The prefix 'Lady' This title causes more confusion than any other, simply because of the wide range of its use. It can be used as a less formal alternative by marchionesses, countesses, viscountesses and the wives of barons. It is never used by duchesses. It is used, but only with the addition of their Christian names, by the daughters of dukes, marquesses and earls. It is also used by the wives of the younger sons of dukes and marquesses, e.g. Lady Charles Cavendish. It is used, but never with the definite article, by the wives of baronets and knights. There is one baronetess.

Special remainders The Crown has power to create what are termed 'special remainders' so that a peerage can, for example, pass to an elder brother or some other relative. An example is that the earldom of Mountbatten of Burma passed to the first earl's elder daughter and her male issue.

Dormant peerages A peerage is deemed dormant when there is no discoverable heir but there is a reasonable presumption that there may be an heir if he or she could be found. The Crown will not permit the use of a name of a peerage for a subsequent creation unless there is absolute certainty that the former creation is truly extinguished.

The descent of peerages A peerage usually descends in the male line. Illegitimate offspring are, of course, excluded, although under Scottish law an illegitimate child is legitimated by the subsequent marriage of his or her parents. If the direct male line fails, then the succession may go back to the male line in an earlier cadet branch of the family.

AUTHORIZED POST-NOMINAL LETTERS

There are 72 Orders, Decorations, and Medals that have been bestowed by the Sovereign that carry the entitlement to a group of letters after the name. Of these, 54 are currently awardable. The order (*vide London Gazette*, supplement 27 Oct 1964) is as follows:

1	VC	Victoria Cross.
2	GC	George Cross.
3	KG	(but *not* for Ladies of the Order), Knight of the Most Noble Order of the Garter.
4	KT	(but *not* for Ladies of the Order), Knight of the Most Ancient and Most Noble Order of the Thistle.
5	GCB	Knight Grand Cross of the Most Honourable Order of the Bath.
6	OM	Member of the Order of Merit.
7*	GCSI	Knight Grand Commander of the Most Excellent Order of the Star of India.
8	GCMG	Knight (or Dame) Grand Cross of the Most Distinguished Order of St Michael and St George.
9*	GCIE	Knight Grand Commander of the Most Eminent Order of the Indian Empire.
10*	CI	Lady of The Imperial Order of the Crown of India.
11	GCVO	Knight (or Dame) Grand Cross of the Royal Victorian Order.
12	GBE	Knight (or Dame) Grand Cross of the Most Excellent Order of the British Empire.
13	CH	Member of the Order of Companions of Honour.
14	KCB	(but *not* if also a GCB) Knight Commander of the Most Honourable Order of the Bath.
15	DCB	(but *not* if also a GCB) Dame Commander of the Most Honourable Order of the Bath.
16*	KCSI	(but *not* if also a GCSI), Knight

		Commander of the Most Excellent Order of the Star of India.
17	KCMG	(but *not* if also a GCMG), Knight Commander of the Most Distinguished Order of St Michael and St George.
18	DCMG	(but *not* if also a GCMG) Dame Commander of the Most Distinguished Order of St Michael and St George.
19*	KCIE	(but *not* if also a GCIE), Knight Commander of the Most Eminent Order of the Indian Empire.
20	KCVO	(but *not* if also a GCVO), Knight Commander of the Royal Victorian Order.
21	DCVO	(but *not* if also a GCVO), Dame Commander of the Royal Victorian Order.
22	KBE	(but *not* if also a GBE), Knight Commander of the Most Excellent Order of the British Empire.
23	DBE	(but *not* if also a GBE), Dame Commander of the Most Excellent Order of the British Empire.
24	CB	(but *not* if also a GCB and/or a KCB), Companion of the Most Honourable Order of the Bath.
25*	CSI	(but *not* if also a GCSI and/or a KCSI), Companion of the Most Excellent Order of the Star of India.
26	CMG	(but *not* if also a GCMG and/or a KCMG or DCMG), Companion of the Most Distinguished Order of St Michael and St George.
27*	CIE	(but *not* if also a GCIE and/or a KCIE), Companion of the Most Eminent Order of the Indian Empire.
28	CVO	(but *not* if also a GCVO and/or a KCVO or DCVO), Commander of the Royal Victorian Order.
29	CBE	(but *not* if also a GBE and/or a KBE or DBE), Commander of the Most Excellent Order of the British Empire.
30	DSO	Companion of the Distinguished Service Order.
31	MVO	(but *not* if also either a GCVO and/or a KCVO a DCVO, and/or a CVO), Lieutenant of the Royal Victorian Order.
32	OBE	(but *not* if also either a GBE and/or a KBE or DBE and/or a CBE), Officer of the Most Excellent Order of the British Empire.
33	QSO	Queen's Service Order (NZ only).
34	ISO	Companion of the Imperial Service Order.
	MVO	(but *not* if also either a GCVO and/or a KCVO or a DCVO, and/or a CVO and/or an LVO), Member of the Royal Victorian Order.
35	MBE	(but *not* if also a GBE and/or a KBE or DBE and/or a CBE and/or an OBE), Member of the Most Excellent Order of the British Empire.
36*	IOM	(if in Military Division), Indian Order of Merit.
37*	OB	Order of Burma (when for gallantry).
38	RRC	Member of the Royal Red Cross.
39	DSC	Distinguished Service Cross.

40	MC	Military Cross.
41	DFC	Distinguished Flying Cross.
42	AFC	Air Force Cross.
43	ARRC	(but *not* if also an RRC), Associate of the Royal Red Cross.
44*	OBI	Order of British India.
*	OB	Order of Burma (when for distinguished service).
45	DCM	Distinguished Conduct Medal.
46	CGM	(both the Naval and the Flying decorations), Conspicuous Gallantry Medal.
47	GM	George Medal.
48*	KPM	King's Police Medal
49*	KPFSM	or King's Police & Fire Services Medal for Gallantry.
50	QPM	Queen's Police Medal
51	QFSM	Queen's Fire Service Medal for Gallantry
*	DCM	(if for Royal West African Frontier Force), Distinguished Conduct Medal.
*	DCM	(if for the King's African Rifles), Distinguished Conduct Medal.
52*	IDSM	Indian Distinguished Service Medal.
53*	BGM	Burma Gallantry Medal.
54	DSM	Distinguished Service Medal.
55	MM	Military Medal.
56	DFM	Distinguished Flying Medal.
57	AFM	Air Force Medal.
58	SGM	Medal for Saving Life at Sea (Sea Gallantry Medal).
*	IOM	(if in Civil Division), Indian Order of Merit.
59*	EGM	Empire Gallantry Medal (usable only in reference to pre-1940 honorary awards unexchangeable for the GC).
60	CPM	Colonial Police Medal for Gallantry.
61	QGM	Queen's Gallantry Medal.
62	QSM	Queen's Service Medal (NZ only).
63	BEM	British Empire Medal, for Gallantry, or the British Empire Medal.
64*	CM	(or for French speakers M du C, Medaille du Canada), Canada Medal.
*	KPM	
*	KPFSM	See 48–51 above, but for distinguished or good service.
	QPM	
	QFSM	
65*	MSM	(but only if awarded for Naval service prior to 20 July 1928), Medal for Meritorious Service.
66	ERD	Emergency Reserve Decoration (Army).
67*	VD	Volunteer Officers' Decoration (1892–1908); for India and the Colonies (1894–1930) and the Colonial Auxiliary Forces Officers' Decoration (1899–1930).
68	TD	(for either the obsolescent Territorial Decoration (1908–30) or for the current Efficiency Decoration (inst. 1930) when awarded to an officer of the (*Home*) Auxiliary Military Forces and the TAVR (inst. 1969)).
69	ED	(if for the current Efficiency Decoration (inst. 1930) when awarded to an officer of Common-

		wealth or Colonial Auxiliary Military Forces).
70	RD	Decoration for Officers of the Royal Naval Reserve.
71*	VRD	Decoration for Officers of the Royal Naval Volunteer Reserve.
72	CD	Canadian Forces Decoration.

* This distinction is no longer awarded, but there are surviving recipients.

Any of the above post-nominal letters precede any others which may relate to academic honours or professional qualifications. The single exception is that the abbreviation 'Bt.' (or less favoured 'Bart.'), indicating a Baronetcy, should be put before *all* other letters, e.g. The Rt Hon. Sir John Smyth, Bt., VC, MC.

The abbreviation PC (indicating membership of the Privy Council), which used to be placed after KG, is now not to be used, except possibly with peers, because in their case the style 'Rt Hon.' cannot be used to indicate membership of the Privy Council, since Barons, Viscounts and Earls already enjoy this style *ipso facto* and Marquesses and Dukes have the superior styles 'Most Hon.' and 'Most Noble' respectively.

Obsolete post-nominal letters include: KP Knight of St Patrick; KB Knight of the Bath (prior to its division into 3 classes in 1815); GCH, KCH and KH Knight Grand Cross, Knight Commander or Knight of the Order of the Guelphs (1815–37); KSI Knight of the Star of India (1861–6); CSC Conspicuous Service Cross (1901–14); AM Albert Medal; EM Edward Medal; VD Volunteer Decoration.

ORDERS OF CHIVALRY

The Most Noble Order of the Garter was established in 1348 by King Edward III. It is considered the highest British civil and military honour obtainable. The number of knights companions is restricted to 24 and always includes the Sovereign and the Prince of Wales. While women can be made ladies of the Order, they are not ranked among the 24 knights companions. An appointment to the Order is bestowed solely at the discretion of the British monarch. Members of European royal families are admitted as extra knights and ladies.

The Most Ancient and Most Noble Order of the Thistle is an exclusively Scottish order. Its modern foundation by James II of Great Britain (James VII of Scotland) dates from 1687 (but it is probably older). Membership comprises the Sovereign and no more than 16 knights.

The Most Honourable Order of the Bath was established in 1725 by King George I. It is awarded for either military service or outstanding civilian merit. The Order has been remodelled over the years, and divided into civil and military divisions. At present the Order comprises the Sovereign, members of the royal family, 'honorary members' (foreigners), and classes of knights; 115 knights or dames grand cross, 328 knights or dames commanders, and 1815 companions. Women are admitted to all classes of the order.

The Order of Merit was established in 1902 by King Edward VII to reward especially eminent military service or for work in science, art, literature or the promotion of culture. The Order has a limit of 24 members – which includes women – although the Queen can appoint foreign 'honorary members'. The

Order is entirely in the gift of the Sovereign.

The Most Distinguished Order of St. Michael and St. George was established by the Prince Regent, later George IV, in 1818 to commemorate the British protectorate over the Ionian islands and Malta. Originally conferred on inhabitants of, or British citizens in, the Ionian Islands and Malta, since 1879 any UK citizen has been eligible. However, it has usually been conferred for work in colonial affairs or the foreign service.

The Royal Victorian Order was founded by Queen Victoria in 1896. It is bestowed for personal services rendered to the monarch and as such is conferred solely at the discretion of the British sovereign. There is no limit to the number of members and since 1936 the Order has admitted women.

The Most Excellent Order of the British Empire was instituted in 1917 by George V. Originally rewarded for both civilian and military service, it is now bestowed for commendable service to the government in times of peace and war. A separate

military division was created in 1918. There are five classes of civil and military divisions, all of which can be conferred on women. An associated award is the British Empire Medal (BEM).

The Order of the Companions of Honour was founded in 1917 by King George V. It is awarded for notable national services, most usually artists and those who work for the advancement of culture. Membership is limited to 65, although there are foreign 'honorary members'.

The Distinguished Service Order was instituted by Queen Victoria in 1886 and is awarded for commendable service in action to officers of the Royal Navy, the Army, the Royal Air Force, and, since 1942, the Mercantile Marine.

The Imperial Service Order was established in 1902. It is bestowed upon members of British and foreign civil services. The Order comprises the Sovereign and up to 1700 companions, including women.

The Royal Victorian Chain was founded by Edward VII in 1902.

THE RESULTS OF THE GENERAL ELECTIONS since 1945

Election and Date	Total Seats	Conservatives	Result (and % share of Total Poll) Liberals	Labour	Others	% Turn-out of Electorate
1945 (5 July)	640	213 (39·8)	12 (9·0)	393 (47·8)	22 (2·8)	72·7 of 33 240 391
1950 (23 Feb)	625	298 (43·5)	9 (9·1)	315 (46·4)	3 (1·3)	84·0 of 33 269 770
1951 (25 Oct)	625	321 (48·0)	6 (2·5)	295 (48·7)	3 (0·7)	82·5 of 34 465 573
1955 (25 May)	630	344 (49·8)	6 (2·7)	277 (46·3)	3 (1·2)	76·7 of 34 858 263
1959 (8 Oct)	630	365 (49·4)	6 (5·9)	258 (43·8)	1 (0·9)	78·8 of 35 397 080
1964 (15 Oct)	630	303 (43·4)	9 (11·1)	317 (44·2)	1 (1·3)	77·1 of 35 894 307
1966 (31 Mar)	630	253 (41·9)	12 (8·5)	363 (47·9)	2 (1·7)	75·9 of 35 965 127
1970 (18 June)	630	330 (46·4)	6 (7·5)	288 (43·0)	6 (3·1)	72·0 of 39 247 683
1974 (28 Feb)	635	297 (38·2)	14 (19·3)	301 (37·2)	23 (5·3)	78·8 of 39 752 317
1974 (10 Oct)	635	277 (35·8)	13 (18·3)	319 (39·3)	26 (6·6)	72·8 of 40 083 286
1979 (3 May)	635	339 (43·9)	11 (13·8)	268 (36·9)	17 (5·4)	75·9 of 41 093 262
1983 (9 June)	650	397 (42·4)	17 (25·4) (Alliance)	209 (27·6)	21 (4·6)	72·7 of 42 197 344
1987 (11 June)	650	375 (42·3)	17 (12·8)	229 (30·8)	24 (3·4)	75·4 of 43 181 321

PRIME MINISTERS OF GREAT BRITAIN AND THE UNITED KINGDOM

The biographical detail for each of 52 prime ministers of Great Britain and the United Kingdom includes:
- the final style as prime minister (with earlier or later styles);
- the date or dates as prime minister with party affiliation;
- the date and place of birth, and death and place of burial;
- marriage or marriages with the number of children;
- education and membership of Parliament with the constituency and dates.

1. The Rt Hon., Sir Robert **WALPOLE**, KG (1726) KB (1725, resigned 1726), (PC 1714), cr. 1st Earl of Orford (of the 2nd creation) in the week of his retirement; ministry, 3 Apr 1721 to 8 Feb 1742, (i) reappointed on the accession of George II on 11 June 1727, (ii) Walpole's absolute control of the Cabinet can only be said to have dated from 15 May 1730; Whig; b. 26 Aug 1676 at Houghton, Norfolk; d. 18 Mar 1745 at 5 Arlington St, Piccadilly, London; bur. Houghton, Norfolk; m. 1 (1700) Catherine Shorter (d. 1717), m. 2 (1738) Maria Skerrett (d. 1738); children, 1st, 3s and

2d; 2nd, 2d (born prior to the marriage); ed. Eton and King's, Cambridge (scholar); MP (Whig) for Castle Rising (1701–2); King's Lynn (1702–42) (expelled from the House for a short period 1712–13).

2. The Rt Hon., the Hon. Sir Spencer Compton, 1st and last Earl of **WILMINGTON**, KG (1733), KB (1725, resigned 1733), (PC 1716), cr. Baron Wilmington 1728; cr. Earl 1730; ministry, 16 Feb 1742 to 2 July 1743; Whig; b. 1673 or 1674; d. 2 July 1743; bur. Compton Wynyates, Warwickshire; unmarried; no legitimate issue; ed. St Paul's School, London, and Trinity, Oxford; MP (originally Tory until about 1704) for Eye (1698–1710); East Grinstead (1713–15); Sussex (Whig) (1715–28); Speaker 1715–27.

3. The Rt Hon., the Hon. Henry **PELHAM** (PC 1725); prior to 1706 was Henry Pelham, Esq.; ministry 27 Aug 1743 to 6 Mar 1754 (with an interval 10–12 Feb 1746); Whig; b. c. 1695; d. 6 Mar 1754 at Arlington St, Piccadilly, London; bur. Laughton Church, nr. Lewes, E. Sussex; m. (1726) Lady Catherine Manners; children, 2s and 6d; ed. Westminster School and Hart Hall, Oxford; MP Seaford (1717–22); Sussex (1722–54).

4. The Rt Hon. Sir William Pulteney, 1st and last Earl of **BATH** (cr. 1742) (PC 1716) (struck off 1731);

kissed hands 10 Feb 1746 but unable to form a ministry; Whig; b. 22 Mar 1684 in London; d. 7 July 1764; bur. Westminster Abbey; m. Anna Maria Gumley; ed. Westminster School and Christ Church, Oxford; MP Hedon (or Heydon) 1705–34; Middlesex 1734–42.

5. His Grace the 1st Duke of **NEWCASTLE** upon Tyne and 1st Duke of Newcastle-under-Lyme (The Rt Hon., the Hon. Sir Thomas Pelham-Holles), Bt, KG (1718). (PC 1717); added the surname Holles in July 1711; known as Lord Pelham of Laughton (1711–14); Earl of Claire (1714–15); cr. Duke of Newcastle upon Tyne 1715 and cr. Duke of Newcastle-under-Lyme 1756; ministry, (a) 16 Mar 1754 to 26 Oct 1756, (b) 2 July 1757 to 25 Oct 1760, (c) 25 Oct 1760 to 25 May 1762; Whig; b. 21 July 1693; d. 17 Nov 1768 at Lincoln's Inn Field, London; bur. Laughton Church, nr. Lewes, E. Sussex; m. (1717) Lady Henrietta Godolphin (d. 1776); no issue; ed. Westminster School and Claire Hall, Cambridge.

6. His Grace the 4th Duke of **DEVONSHIRE** (Sir William Cavendish), KG (1756), (PC 1751, but struck off roll 1762); known as Lord Cavendish of Hardwick until 1729 and Marquess of Hartington until 1755; ministry, 16 Nov 1756 to May 1757; Whig; b. 1720; d. 2 Oct 1764 at Spa, Belgium; bur. Derby Cathedral; m. (1748) Charlotte Elizabeth, Baroness Clifford (d. 1754); children, 3s and 1d; ed. privately; MP (Whig) for Derbyshire (1741–51). Summoned to Lords (1751) in father's Barony Cavendish of Hardwick.

7. The Rt Hon. James **WALDEGRAVE**, 2nd Earl of Waldegrave (pronounced 'Wallgrave') from 1741, (PC 1752), KG (1757); kissed hands 8 June 1757 but returned seals 12 June being unable to form Ministry; b. 14 Mar 1715; d. 28 Apr 1763; m. Marion Walpole (niece of No. 1); children 3d; ed. Eton; took seat in House of Lords, 1741.

8. The 3rd Earl of **BUTE** (The Rt Hon., the Hon. Sir John Stuart, KG (1762), KT (1738, resigned 1762), (PC 1760)); until 1723 was The Hon. John Stuart; ministry, 26 May 1762 to 8 Apr 1763; Tory; b. 25 May 1713 at Parliament Square, Edinburgh; d. 10 Mar 1792 at South Audley St, Grosvenor Square, London; bur. Rothesay, Bute; m. (1736) Mary Wortley-Montagu later (1761) Baroness Mount Stuart (d. 1794); children, 4s and 4d (with other issue); ed. Eton.

9. The Rt Hon., the Hon. George **GRENVILLE** (PC 1754); prior to 1749 was G. Grenville Esq; ministry, 16 Apr 1763 to 10 July 1765; Whig; b. 14 Oct 1712 at? Wotton, Bucks; d. 13 Nov 1770 at Bolton St, Piccadilly, London; bur. Wotton, Bucks; m. (1749) Elizabeth Wyndham (d. 1769); children, 4s and 5d; ed. Eton and Christ Church, Oxford; MP for Buckingham (1741–70).

10. The Most Hon. The 2nd Marquess of **ROCK-INGHAM** (The Rt Hon. Lord Charles Watson-Wentworth, KG (1760), (PC 1765); known as Hon. Charles Watson-Wentworth until 1739; Viscount Higham (1739–46); Earl of Malton (1746–50); succeeded to Marquessate 14 Dec 1750; ministry, (a) 13 July 1765 to July 1766, (b) 27 March 1782 to his death on 1 July 1782; Whig; b. 13 May 1730; d. 1 July 1782; bur. York Minster; m. (1752) Mary Bright (her father was formerly called Liddell) (d. 1804); no issue; ed. Westminster School (and possibly St John's, Cambridge). Took his seat in House of Lords 21 May 1751.

11. The 1st Earl of **CHATHAM** (The Rt Hon. William Pitt (PC 1746)); cr. Earl 4 Aug 1766; ministry, 30 July 1766 to 14 Oct 1768; Whig; his health in 1767 prevented his being PM in other than name; b. 15 Nov 1708 at St James's, Westminster, London; d. 11 May 1788 at Hayes, Kent; bur. Westminster Abbey; m. (1754) Hon. Hester Grenville*, later (1761) cr. Baroness Chatham in her own right (d. 1803); children, 3s and 2d; ed. Eton, Trinity, Oxford (took no degree owing to gout), and Utrecht; MP (Whig) Old Sarum (1735–47); Seaford (1747–54); Aldborough (1754–6); Okehampton (1756–7) (also Buckingham (1756), Bath (1757–66)).

---

*This lady had the extraordinary distinction of being the wife, the mother, the sister and the aunt of four British Prime Ministers. They were Nos. 11, 16, 9, and 18 respectively.

---

12. His Grace the 3rd Duke of **GRAFTON** (The Rt Hon. Sir Augustus Henry FitzRoy) KG (1769), (PC 1765); prior to 1747 known as the Hon. Augustus H. FitzRoy; 1747–57 as Earl of Euston; succeeded dukedom in 1757; ministry, 14 Oct 1768 to 28 Jan 1770; Whig; he was virtually PM in 1767 when Lord Chatham's ministry broke down; b. 28 Sept 1735 at St Marylebone, London; d. 14 Mar 1811 at Euston Hall, Suffolk; bur. Euston, Suffolk; m. 1 (1765) Hon. Anne Liddell (sep. 1765, mar. dis. by Act of Parl. 1769) (d. 1804), m. 2 (1769) Elizabeth Wrottesley (d. 1822); children, 1st, 2s and 1d; 2nd, 6s and 6d (possibly also another d who died young; ed. private school at Hackney, Westminster School, and Peterhouse, Cambridge; MP (Whig) Bury St Edmunds (1756–7).

13. Lord **NORTH** (The Rt Hon., the Hon. Sir Frederick North), KG (1772), (PC 1766); succ. (Aug 1790) as 2nd Earl of Guilford; ministry 28 Jan 1770 to 20 Mar 1782; Tory; b. 13 Apr 1732 at Albermarle St, Piccadilly, London; d. 5 Aug 1792 at Lower Grosvenor St, London; bur. All Saints' Church, Wroxton, Oxfordshire; m. (1756) Anne Speke (d. 1797); children, 4s and 3d; ed. Eton; Trinity, Oxford, and Leipzig; MP (Tory) for Banbury (1754–90) (can be regarded as a Whig from 1783). Took his seat in the House of Lords 25 Nov 1790.

14. The 2nd Earl of **SHELBURNE** (Rt Hon., the Hon. Sir William Petty, KG (1782), (PC 1763); formerly, until 1751, William Fitz-Maurice; Viscount Fitz-Maurice (1753–61); succeeded to Earldom 10 May 1761; cr. the 1st Marquess of Lansdowne (6 Dec 1784); Col. 1760; Maj. Gen. 1765; Lt. Gen. 1772, and Gen. 1783; ministry, 4 July 1782 to 24 Feb 1783; Whig; b. 20 May 1737 at Dublin, Ireland; d. 7 May 1805 at Berkeley Square, London; bur. High Wycombe, Bucks; m. 1 (1765) Lady Sophia Carerett (d. 1771), m. 2 (1779) Lady Louisa FitzPatrick (d. 1789); children, 1st, 2s; 2nd, 1s and 1d; ed. local school in S. Ireland, private tutor, and Christ Church, Oxford; MP Chipping Wycombe (1760–1). Took seat in House of Lords (as Baron Wycombe) 3 Nov 1761.

15. His Grace the 3rd Duke of **PORTLAND** (The Most Noble Sir William Henry Cavendish Bentinck, KG (1794), (PC 1765)); assumed additional name of Bentinck in 1775; assumed by Royal Licence surname of Cavendish-Bentinck in 1801; Marquess of Titchfield from birth until he succeeded to the dukedom on 1 May 1762; ministry (a) 2 Apr 1783 to Dec 1783, (b) 31 Mar 1807 to Oct 1809; (a) coalition and (b) Tory; b. 14th Apr 1738; d. 30 Oct 1809 at

Bulstrode, Bucks; bur. St Marylebone, London; m. (1766) Lady Dorothy Cavendish (d. 1794); children, 4s and 1d; ed. Westminster or Eton and Christ Church, Oxford; MP (Whig) Weobley, Herefordshire (1761–2).

16. The Rt Hon., the Hon. William **PITT** (PC 1782) prior August 1766 was William Pitt, Esq.; ministry (a) 19 Dec 1783 to 14 Mar 1801, (b) 10 May 1804 to his death on 23 Jan 1806; Tory; b. 28 May 1759 at Hayes, nr. Bromley, Kent; d. 23 Jan 1806 at Bowling Green House, Putney, Surrey; bur. Westminster Abbey; unmarried; ed. privately and Pembroke Hall, Cambridge; MP (Tory) Appleby.

17. The Rt Hon. Henry **ADDINGTON** (PC 1789); cr. 1st Viscount Sidmouth 1805; ministry, 17 Mar 1801 to 30 April 1804; Tory; b. 30 May 1757 at Bedford Row, London; d. 15 Feb 1844 at White Lodge, Richmond Park, Surrey; bur. Mortlake; m. 1 (1781) Ursula Mary Hammond (d. 1811), m. 2 (1823) Hon. Mrs Marianne Townshend (*née* Scott) (d. 1842); children, 1st, 3s and 4d; 2nd, no issue; ed. Cheam, Winchester Col., Lincoln's Inn, and Brasenose, Oxford (Chancellor's Medal for English Essay); MP (Tory) Devizes (1783–1805). Speaker 1789–1801. As a peer he supported the Whigs in 1807 and 1812 administration.

18. The Rt Hon. the 1st Baron **GRENVILLE** of Wotton-under-Bernewood (William Wyndham Grenville (PC(I) 1782; PC 1783); cr. Baron 25 Nov 1790; ministry, 10 Feb 1806 to Mar 1807; b. (the son of No. 9) 25 Oct 1759; d. 12 Jan 1834 at Dropmore Lodge, Bucks; bur. Burnham, Bucks; m. (1792) Hon. Anne Pitt (d. 1864 aged 91); no issue; ed. Eton, Christ Church, Oxford (Chancellor's prize for Latin Verse), and Lincoln's Inn; MP Buckingham (1782–4), Buckinghamshire (1784–90). Speaker January–June 1789.

19. The Rt Hon., the Hon. Spencer **PERCEVAL** (PC 1807), KC (1796); ministry, 4 Oct 1809 to 11 May 1812; b. 1 Nov 1762 at Audley Sq., London; murdered 11 May 1812 in lobby of the House; bur. Charlton; m. (1790) Jane Spencer-Wilson (later Lady Carr) (d. 1844); children, 6s and 6d; ed. Harrow, Trinity, Cambridge, and Lincoln's Inn; MP (Tory) Northampton (1796–7).

20. The Rt Hon. the 2nd Earl of **LIVERPOOL** (Sir Robert Banks Jenkinson, KG (1814) (PC 1799)); from birth to 1786 R. B. Jenkinson, Esq.; from 1786–96 The Hon. R. B. Jenkinson; from 1796–1808 (when he succeeded to the earldom) Lord Hawkesbury; ministry, (a) 8 June 1812 to 29 Jan 1820, (b) 29 Jan 1820 to 17 Feb 1827; Tory; b. 7 June 1770; d. 4 Dec 1828 at Coombe Wood, near Kingston-on-Thames; bur. at Hawkesbury; m. 1 (1795) Lady Louisa Theodosia Hervey (d. 1821), m. 2 (1822) Mary Chester (d. 1846); no issue; ed. Charterhouse and Christ Church, Oxford; summoned to House of Lords in his father's barony of Hawkesbury 15 Nov 1803 (elected MP (Tory) for Appleby (1790) but did not sit as he was under age); Rye (1796–1803).

21. The Rt Hon. George **CANNING** (PC 1800); ministry, 10 Apr 1827 to his death; Tory; b. 11 Apr 1770 in London; d. 8 Aug 1827 at Chiswick Villa, London; m. (1800) Joan Scott (later, 1828, cr. Viscountess) (d. 1837); children, 3s and 1d; ed. in London; Hyde Abbey (nr. Winchester); Eton; Christ Church, Oxford (Chancellor's prize, Latin Verse), and Lincoln's Inn; MP (Tory) Newtown, I.o.W. (1793–6); Wendover

(1796–1802); Tralee (1802–6); Newton (1806–7); Hastings (1807–12); Liverpool (1812–23); Harwich (1823–6); Newport (1826–7), and Seaford (1827).

22. The Viscount **GODERICH** (Rt Hon., the Hon. Frederick John Robinson (PC 1812, PC (I) c. 1833); cr. Earl of Ripon 1833; ministry 31 Aug 1827 to 8 Jan 1828; Tory; b. 1 Nov 1782 in London; d. 28 Jan 1859 at Putney Heath, London; bur. Nocton, Lincolnshire; m. (1814) Lady Sarah Albinia Louisa Hobart (d. 1867); children, 2s and 1d; ed. Harrow; St John's, Cambridge, and Lincoln's Inn; MP Carlow (1806–7); Ripon (1807–27).

23. His Grace The 1st Duke of **WELLINGTON** (The Most Noble, The Hon. Sir Arthur Wellesley, KG (1813), GCB (1815), GCH (1816), (PC 1807, PC (I) 1807)); known as The Hon. Arthur Wesley until 1804; then as The Hon. Sir Arthur Wellesley, KB, until 1809 when cr. the Viscount Wellington; cr. Earl of Wellington February 1812; Marquess of Wellington October 1812 and Duke May 1814. Ensign (1787); Lieut. (1787); Capt. (1791); Major (1793); Lt.-Col. (1793); Col. (1796); Maj. Gen. (1802); Lt. Gen. (1808); Gen. (1811); Field Marshal (1813); ministry, (a) 22 Jan 1828 to 26 June 1830, (b) 26 June 1830 to 21 Nov 1830, (c) 17 Nov to 9 Dec 1834; Tory; b. 1 May 1769 at Mornington House, Upper Merrion St, Dublin; d. 14 Sept 1852 at Walmer Castle, Kent; bur. St Paul's Cathedral; m. (1806) the Hon. Catherine Sarah Dorothea Pakenham (d. 1831); children, 2s; ed. Browns Seminary, King's Rd, Chelsea, London; Eton; Brussels, and The Academy at Angiers; MP Rye (1806); St Michael (1807); Newport, IoW (1807–9). Took seat in House of Lords as Viscount, Earl, Marquess, and Duke 28 June 1814. Physical height: 1·76 m (5 ft 9½ in).

24. The 2nd Earl **GREY** (The Rt Hon., the Hon. Sir Charles Grey, Bt (1808), KG (1831), (PC 1806)); styled Viscount Howick 1806–7 and previously The Hon. Charles Grey; ministry, 22 Nov 1830 to July 1834; Whig; b. 13 Mar 1764 at Fallodon, Northumberland; d. 17 July 1845 and bur. at Howick House, Northumberland; m. (1794) Hon. Mary Elizabeth Ponsonby (d. 1861); children, 8s and 5d; ed. at a private school in Marylebone, London; Eton; Trinity, Cambridge, and Middle Temple; MP (Whig) Northumberland (1786–1807); Appleby (1807); Tavistock (1807).

25. The 3rd Viscount **MELBOURNE** (The Rt Hon., The Hon. Sir William Lamb, Bt (PC (UK & I) 1827)); ministry, (a) 17 July 1834 to November 1834, (b) 18 Apr 1835 to 20 June 1837, (c) 20 June 1837 to August 1841; Whig; b. (of disputed paternity) 15 Mar 1779 Melbourne House, Piccadilly, London; d. 24 Nov 1848 at Brocket; bur. Hatfield; m. (1805) Lady Caroline Ponsonby, separated 1824 (d. 1828); only 1s survived infancy; ed. Eton; Trinity, Cambridge; Glasgow University, and Lincoln's Inn; MP (Whig) Leominster (1806); Haddington Borough (1806–7); Portarlington (1807–12); Peterborough (1816–19); Hertfordshire (1819–26); Newport, IoW (1827); Bletchingley (1827–8). Took his seat in House of Lords 1 Feb 1829.

26. The Rt Hon. Sir Robert **PEEL**, Bt (PC 1812); prior to May 1830 he was Robert Peel, Esq., MP, when he succeeded as 2nd Baronet; ministry, (a) 10 Dec 1834 to 8 Apr 1835, (b) 30 Aug 1841 to 29 June 1846; Conservative; b. 5 Feb 1788 prob. at Chamber Hall, nr. Bury, Lancashire; d. 2 July 1850 after fall from horse; bur. Drayton Bassett; m. (1820) Julia Floyd (d. 1859); children, 5s and 2d; ed. Harrow; Christ

Church, Oxford (Double First in Classics and Mathematics), and Lincoln's Inn; MP (Tory) Cashel (Tipperary) (1809–12); Chippenham (1812–17); Univ. of Oxford (1817–29); Westbury (1829–30); Tamworth (1830–50).

27. The Rt Hon. Lord John **RUSSELL** (PC 1830), and after 30 July 1861 1st Earl **RUSSELL**, KG (1862), GCMG (1869); ministry, (a) 30 June 1846 to February 1852, (b) 29 Oct 1865 to June 1866; (a) Whig and (b) Liberal; b. 18 Aug 1792 in Hertford St, Mayfair; d. 28 May 1878 at Pembroke Lodge, Richmond Park, Surrey; bur. Chenies, Bucks; m. 1 (1835) Adelaide (*née* Lister), Dowager Baroness Ribblesdale (d. 1838), m. 2 (1841) Lady Frances Anna Maria Elliot-Murray-Kynynmound (d. 1898); children, 1st, 2d; 2nd, 3s and 3d; ed. Westminster School and Edinburgh University; MP (Whig) Tavistock (1813–17, 1818–20 and 1830–1); Hunts (1820–6); Bandon (1826–30); Devon (1831–2); S. Devon (1832–5); Stroud (1835–41); City of London (1841–61). Took seat in the House of Lords on 30 July 1861.

28. The 14th Earl of **DERBY**, Rt Hon. Sir Edward Geoffrey Smith-Stanley, Bt, KG (1859), GCMG (1869), PC 1830, PC (I) (1831); prior to 1834 known as the Hon. E. G. Stanley, MP; then known as Lord Stanley MP until 1844; ministry, (a) 23 Feb 1852 to 18 Dec 1852, (b) 20 Feb 1858 to 11 June 1859, (c) 28 June 1866 to 26 Feb 1868; Tory and Conservative; b. 19 Mar 1799 Knowsley, Lancs; d. 23 Oct 1869; and bur. Knowsley, Lancs; m. (1825) Hon. Emma Caroline Wilbraham-Bootle (d. 1876); 2s, 1d; ed. Eton; Christ Church, Oxford (Chancellor's prize for Latin Verse); MP (Whig) Stockbridge (1822–6); Preston (1826–30); Windsor (1831–2); North Lancs (1832–44). Summoned 1844 to House of Lords as Lord Stanley (of Bickerstaffe); succeeded to Earldom 1851; became a Tory in 1835.

29. The Rt Hon. Sir George Hamilton Gordon, Bt, 4th Earl of **ABERDEEN**, KG (1855), KT (1808), (PC 1814); prior to October 1791 known as the Hon. G. Gordon; from 1791 to Aug 1801 known as Lord Haddo; assumed additional name of Hamilton November 1818; ministry, 19 Dec 1852 to 5 Feb 1855; Peelite; b. 28 Jan 1784 in Edinburgh; d. 14 Dec 1860 at Argyll House, St James's, London; bur. at Stanmore, Mddx.; m. 1 (1805) Lady Catherine Elizabeth Hamilton (d. 1812), m. 2 (1815) her sister-in-law Harriet (*née* Douglas), Dowager Viscountess Hamilton (d. 1833); children, 1st, 1s and 3d; 2nd, 4s and 1d; ed. Harrow and St John's, Cambridge. Took seat in House of Lords 1814.

30. The Rt Hon. Sir Henry John Temple, 3rd and last Viscount **PALMERSTON** (a non-representative peer of Ireland), KG (1856), CGB (1832), (PC 1809); known (1784–1802) as the Hon. H. J. Temple; ministry, (a) 6 Feb 1855 to 19 Feb 1858, (b) 12 June 1859 to 18 Oct 1865; Liberal; b. 20 Oct 1784 at Broadlands, nr. Romsey, Hants (or possibly in Park St, London); d. 18 Oct 1865 at Brocket Hall, Hertfordshire; bur. Westminster Abbey; m. (1839) Hon. Emily Mary (*née* Lamb), the Dowager Countess Cowper (d. 1869); no issue; ed. Harrow; Univ. of Edinburgh, and St John's, Cambridge; MP (Tory) Newport, IoW (1807–11); Cambridge Univ. (1811–31); Bletchingley (1831–2); S. Hampshire (1832–4); Tiverton (1835–65); from 1829 a Whig and latterly a Liberal.

31. The Rt Hon. Benjamin **DISRAELI**, 1st and last Earl of **BEACONSFIELD**, KG (1878), (PC 1852);

prior to 12 Aug 1876 Benjamin Disraeli (except that until 1838 he was known as Benjamin D'Israeli); ministry, (a) 27 Feb 1868 to Nov 1868, (b) 20 Feb 1874 to Apr 1880; Conservative; b. 21 Dec 1804 at either the Adelphi, Westminster, or at 22 Theobald's Rd, or St Mary Axe; d. 19 Apr 1881 at 19 Curzon St, Mayfair, London; bur. Hughenden Manor, Bucks (monument in Westminster Abbey); m. (1839) Mrs Mary Anne Lewis (*née* Evans) later (1868) Viscountess (in her own right) Beaconsfield; no issue; ed. Lincoln's Inn; MP (Con.) Maidstone (1837–41); Shrewsbury (1841–7); Buckinghamshire (1847–76), when he became a peer.

32. The Rt Hon. William Ewart **GLADSTONE** (PC 1841); ministry, (a) 3 Dec 1868 to February 1874, (b) 23 Apr 1880 to 12 June 1885, (c) 1 Feb 1886 to 20 July 1886, (d) 15 Aug 1892 to 3 Mar 1894; Liberal; b. 29 Dec 1809 at 62 Rodney St, Liverpool; d. 19 May 1898 (aged 88 yrs 142 days) at Hawarden Castle, Clwyd; bur. Westminster Abbey; m. (1839) Catherine Glynne (d. 1900); children, 4s and 4d; ed. Seaforth Vicarage; Eton and Christ Church, Oxford (Double First in Classics and Mathematics); MP Tory, Newark (1832–45); Univ. of Oxford (1847–65) (Peelite to 1859, thereafter a Liberal); S. Lancashire (1865–8); Greenwich (1868–80); Midlothian (1880–95).

33. The Rt Hon. Robert Arthur Talbot Gascoyne-Cecil, the 3rd Marquess of **SALISBURY**, KG (1878), GCVO (1902), (PC 1866); known as Lord Robert Cecil till 1865; and as Viscount Cranbourne, MP, from 1865 to 1868; ministry, (a) 23 June 1885 to 28 Jan 1886, (b) 25 July 1886 to August 1892, (c) 25 June 1895 to 22 Jan 1901, (d) 23 Jan 1901 to 11 July 1902; Conservative; b. 3 Feb 1830 at Hatfield House, Hertfordshire; d. 22 Aug 1903 at Hatfield House; bur. Hatfield; m. (1857) Georgiana Charlotte (*née* Alderson), Lady of the Royal Order of Victoria and Albert and C.I. (1899) (d. 1899); children, 4s and 3d; ed. Eton and Christ Church, Oxford (Hon. 4th Cl. Maths.); MP (Con.) for Stamford (1853–68).

34. The Rt Hon. Sir Archibald Philip Primrose, Bt, 5th Earl of **ROSEBERY**, KG (1892), KT (1895), VD (PC 1881); b. the Hon. A. P. Primrose; known as Lord Dalmeny (1851–68); Earl of Midlothian from 1911 although he did not adopt the style; ministry, 5 Mar 1894 to 21 June 1895; Liberal; b. 7 May 1847 at Charles St, Berkeley Square, London; d. 21 May 1929 at 'The Durdans', Epsom, Surrey; bur. Dalmeny; m. (1878) Hannah de Rothschild (d. 1890); children, 2s and 2d; ed. Eton and Christ Church, Oxford.

35. The Rt Hon. Arthur James **BALFOUR** (PC 1885, PC (I) 1887); KG (1922), later (1922) the 1st Earl of Balfour, OM (1916); ministry, 12 July 1902 to 4 Dec 1905; Conservative; b. 25 July 1848 at Whittinge-hame, E. Lothian, Scotland; d. 19 Mar 1930 at Fisher's Hill, Woking, Surrey; bur. Whittingehame; unmarried; ed. Eton and Trinity, Camb.; MP (Con.) Hertford (1874–85); E. Manchester (1885–1906); City of London (1906–22).

36. The Rt Hon. Sir Henry **CAMPBELL-BANNERMAN**, GCB (1895), (PC 1894); known as Henry Campbell until 1872; ministry, 5 Dec 1905 to 5 Apr 1908; Liberal; b. 7 Sept 1836 at Kelvinside House, Glasgow; d. 22 Apr 1908 at 10 Downing Street, London; bur. Meigle, Scotland; m. (1860) Sarah Charlotte Bruce (d. 1906); no issue; ed. Glasgow High School; Glasgow Univ. (Gold Medal for Greek); Trinity, Camb. (22nd Sen. Optime in Maths Tripos; 3rd Cl. in Classical Tripos); MP (Lib.) Stirling District (1868–1908).

37. The Rt Hon. Herbert Henry **ASQUITH** (PC 1892, PC (I) 1916); later (1925) 1st Earl of **OXFORD AND ASQUITH**, KG (1925); ministry, (a) 7 Apr 1908 to 7 May 1910, (b) 8 May 1910 to 5 Dec 1916 (coalition from 25 May 1915); Liberal; b. 12 Sept 1852 at Morley, W. Yorks; d. 15 Feb 1928 at 'The Wharf', Sutton Courtney, Berks; bur. Sutton Courtney Church; m. 1 (1877) Helen Kelsall Melland (d. 1891), 2 (1894) Emma Alice Margaret Tennant; children, 1st, 4s and 1d; 2nd, 1s and 1d; ed. City of London School; Balliol, Oxford (Scholar, 1st Class Lit. Hum.); MP (Lib.) East Fife (1886–1918); Paisley (1920–4).

38. The Rt Hon. David **LLOYD GEORGE**, OM (1919), (PC 1905); later (1945) 1st Earl Lloyd-George of Dwyfor; ministry, 7 Dec 1916 to 19 Oct 1922; Coalition; b. 17 Jan 1863 Manchester; d. 26 Mar 1945 Ty Newydd, nr. Llanystumdwy; bur. on the bank of the river Dwyfor; m. 1 (1888) Margaret Owen, GBE (1920) (d. 1941), m. 2 (1943) Frances Louise Stevenson, CBE; children, 1st, 2s and 3d; 2nd, no issue; ed. Llanystumdwy Church School and privately; MP Caernarvon Boroughs (1890–1945) (Lib. 1890–1931 and 1935–45; Ind. Lib. 1931– 5). Physical height: 1·67 m (5 ft 6 in).

39. The Rt Hon. (Andrew) Bonar **LAW** (PC 1911); ministry, 23 Oct 1922 to 20 May 1923; Conservative; b. 16 Sept 1858 at Kingston, nr. Richibucto, New Brunswick, Canada; d. 30 Oct 1923 at 24 Onslow Gardens, London; bur. Westminster Abbey; m. (1891) Annie Pitcairn (d. 1909); children, 4s and 2d; ed. Gilbertfield School, Hamilton; Glasgow High School; MP (Con.) Blackfriars Div. of Glasgow (1900–6); Dulwich Div. of Camberwell (1906–10); MP Bootle Div. of Lancashire (1911–18); Central Div. of Glasgow (1918–23). Physical height: 1·83 m (6 ft 0 in).

40. The Rt Hon. Stanley **BALDWIN** (PC 1920, PC (Can.) 1927); later (1937) 1st Earl Baldwin of Bewdley, KG (1937); ministry, (a) 22 May 1923 to 22 Jan 1924 (Con.), (b) 4 Nov 1924 to 4 June 1929 (Con.), (c) 7 June 1935 to 20 Jan 1936 (Nat.), (d) 21 Jan 1936 to 11 Dec 1936 (Nat.), (e) 12 Dec 1936 to 28 May 1937 (Nat.); b. 3 Aug 1867 at Bewdley; d. Astley, 14 Dec 1947; bur. Worcester Cathedral; m. (1892) Lucy Ridsdale, GBE (1937) (d. 1945); children, 2s and 3d; ed. Harrow and Trinity, Camb.; MP (Con.) Bewdley Div. of Worcestershire (1908–37). Physical height: 1·74 m (5 ft 8½ in).

41. The Rt Hon. (James) Ramsay **MACDONALD** (PC 1924, PC (Can.) (1929); ministry (a) 22 Jan 1924 to 4 Nov 1924 (Lab.), (b) 5 June 1929 to 7 June 1935 (Lab. and from 1931 National Coalition); b. 12 Oct 1866 at Lossiemouth, Grampian; d. 9 Nov 1937 at sea, mid-Atlantic; bur. Spynie Churchyard, nr. Lossiemouth, Scotland; m. (1896) Margaret Ethel Gladstone (d. 1911); children, 3s and 3d; ed. Drainie Parish Board School; MP (Lab.) Leicester (1906–18); (Lab.) Aberavon (1922–9); (Lab.) Seaham Div. Co. Durham (1929–31); (Nat. Lab.) (1931–5); MP for Scottish Univs. (1936–7). Physical height: 1·79 m (5 ft 10½ in).

42. The Rt Hon. (Arthur) Neville **CHAMBERLAIN** (PC 1922); ministry, 28 May 1937 to 10 May 1940; National; b. 18 Mar 1869 at Edgbaston, Birmingham; d. 9 Nov 1940 at High Field Park, Hickfield, nr. Reading; ashes interred Westminster Abbey; m. (1911) Annie Vere Cole (d. 12 Feb 1967); children, 1s and 1d; ed. Rugby School; Mason College (later Birmingham Univ.) (Metallurgy & Engineering Design); MP (Con.) Ladywood Div. of Birmingham

(1918–29); Edgbaston Div. of Birmingham (1929–40). Physical height: 1·77 m (5 ft 10 in).

43. The Rt Hon. Sir Winston (Leonard Spencer) **CHURCHILL**, KG (1953), OM (1946), CH (1922), TD (PC 1907); ministry, (a) 10 May 1940 to 26 July 1945 (Coalition but from 23 May 1945 Con.), (b) 26 Oct 1951 to 6 Feb 1952 (Con.), (c) 7 Feb 1952 to 5 Apr 1955 (Con.); b. 30 Nov 1874 at Blenheim Palace, Woodstock, Oxfordshire; d. 24 Jan 1965 Hyde Park Gate, London; bur. Bladon, Oxfordshire; m. (1908) Clementine Ogilvy Hozier, GBE (1946), cr. 1965 (Life) Baroness Spencer-Churchill (d. 13 Dec 1977); children, 1s and 4d; ed. Harrow School and Royal Military College; MP (Con. until 1904, then Lib.) Oldham (1900–6); (Lib.) N.-W. Manchester (1906–8); (Lib.) Dundee (1908–18 and (Coalition Lib.) until 1922; Epping Div. of Essex (1924–45); Woodford Div. of Essex (1945–64). Physical height: 1·74 m (5 ft 8½ in).

44. The Rt Hon. Clement (Richard) **ATTLEE**, CH (1945), (PC 1935); cr. 1955 1st Earl Attlee, KG (1956), OM (1951); ministry, 26 July 1945 to 26 Oct 1951; Labour; b. 3 Jan 1883 at Putney, London; d. Westminster Hospital, 8 Oct 1967; m. (1922) Violet Helen Millar; children, 1s and 3d; ed. Haileybury College and Univ. College, Oxford (2nd Cl. Hons. (Mod. Hist.)); MP Limehouse Div. of Stepney (1922–50); West Walthamstow (1950–5). Physical height: 1·73 m (5 ft 8 in).

45. The Rt Hon. Sir (Robert) Anthony **EDEN**, KG (1954), MC (1917), (PC 1934); cr. 1961 1st Earl of Avon; ministry, 6 Apr 1955 to 9 Jan 1957; Conservative; b. 12 June 1897, Windlestone, Durham; d. Alvediston, Wiltshire, 14 Jan 1977; m. 1 (1923) Beatrice Helen Beckett (m. dis. 1950) (d. 1957), m. 2 (1952) Anne Clarissa Spencer-Churchill; children, 1st, 2s; 2nd, no issue; ed. Eton and Christ Church, Oxford (1st Cl. Hons (Oriental Langs)); MP Warwick and Leamington (1923–57). Physical height; 1·83 m (6 ft 0 in).

46. The Rt Hon. (Maurice) Harold **MACMILLAN**, OM (1976) (PC 1942); cr. 1984 1st Earl of Stockton; ministry, 10 Jan 1957 to 18 Oct 1963; Conservative; b. 10 Feb 1894, 52 Cadogan Place, London; d. 29 Dec 1986; m. (1920) Lady Dorothy Evelyn Cavendish, GBE; children, 1s and 3d; ed. Eton (Scholar); Balliol, Oxford ((Exhibitioner) 1st Class Hon. Mods.); MP Stockton-on-Tees (1924–9 and 1931–45); Bromley (1945–64). Physical height: 1·83 m (6 ft 0 in).

47. The Rt Hon. Sir Alexander (Frederick) **DOUGLAS-HOME**, KT (1962), (PC 1951); known until 30 Apr 1918 as the Hon. A. F. Douglas-Home; thence until 11 July 1951 as Lord Dunglass; thence until his disclaimer of 23 Oct 1963 as the (14th) Earl of Home, Lord Home of the Hirsel; cr. 1974 Baron Home of the Hirsel (Life Peer); ministry, 19 Oct 1963 to 16 Oct 1964; Conservative; b. 2 July 1903, 28 South St, London; m. (1936) Elizabeth Hester Alington (d. 1990); children, 1s and 3d; ed. Eton; Christ Church, Oxford; MP South Lanark (1931–45); Lanark (1950–1); Kinross and West Perthshire (1963–74). Physical height: 1·80 m (5 ft 11 in).

48. The Rt Hon. Sir (James) Harold **WILSON**, KG (1976), OBE (civ.) (1945) (PC 1947); cr. 1983 Baron Wilson of Rievaulx (Life Peer); ministry, (a) 16 Oct 1964 to 30 Mar 1966, (b) 31 Mar 1966 to 17 June 1970, (c) 4 Mar 1974 to 10 Oct 1974, (d) 10 Oct 1974 to 5 Apr 1976; Labour; b. Linthwaite, W. Yorkshire, 11 Mar

1916; m. (1940) Gladys Mary Baldwin; children, 2s; ed. Milnsbridge C.S.; Royds Hall S.; Wirral G.S.; Jesus College, Oxford (1st Cl. Philosophy, Politics and Economics); MP Ormskirk (1945–50); Huyton (1950–?). Physical height: 1·74 m (5 ft 8½ in).

49. The Rt Hon. Edward (Richard George) **HEATH**, MBE (mil.) (1946), (PC 1955); ministry, 18 June 1970 to 3 Mar 1974; Conservative; b. 9 July 1916 at Broadstairs, Kent; unmarried; ed. Chatham House School, Ramsgate, and Balliol College, Oxford; MP Bexley (1950–74); Bexley-Sidcup from 1974. Physical height: 1·80 m (5 ft 11 in).

50. The Rt Hon. (Leonard) James **CALLAGHAN** (PC 1964); cr. 1987 Baron Callaghan of Cardiff (Life Peer); ministry 5 Apr 1976 to 4 May 1979; Labour; b. 27 Mar 1912 at 38 Funtingdon Rd, Portsmouth, Hampshire; m. (1938) Audrey Elizabeth Moulton; children 1s and 2d; ed. Portsmouth Northern Secondary Sch.; MP South Cardiff (1945–50); Southeast Cardiff (1950 to date). Physical height: 1·87 m (6 ft 1½ in).

51. The Rt Hon. Mrs Margaret (Hilda) **THATCHER** OM *née* Roberts (from Nov 1990 Lady Thatcher although she did not use the style) (PC 1970); ministry (a) 4 May 1979 to 9 June 1983, (b) 10 June 1983 to 4 May 1987, (c) 12 June 1987 to 28 Nov 1990; Conservative; b. 13 Oct 1925, Grantham, Lincolnshire; m. (13 Dec 1951) Denis Thatcher MBE cr. Bt. 1990 (b. 10 May 1915, he prev. m. Margaret D. Kempson, who in 1948 m. Sir Howard Hickman 3rd Bt.); 1s 1d (twins); ed. Kesteven & Grantham Girls' Sch.; Somerville Coll., Oxford (MA, BSc); MP Finchley (1959–74); Barnet, Finchley (1974 to date). Physical height: 1·65 m (5 ft 5 in).

52. The Rt Hon. John **MAJOR** (PC 1987); ministry from Nov 1990; Conservative; b. 29 Mar 1943, London; m. (1970) Norma Christina Elizabeth Johnson; children 1s and 1d; ed. Rutlish Grammar Sch.; MP for Huntingdonshire (1979–83) and MP for Huntingdon (1983–).

ECONOMY

NATIONAL EMPLOYMENT AND UNEMPLOYMENT

	Working Population (Thousands)	Unemployment* (excluding school leavers and students)	Percentage Rate
1965	25 504	338 200	1·4%
1970	25 293	602 000	2·6%
1975	25 665	929 000	3·6%
1980	26 324	1 667 600	6·3%
1985	24 204	3 146 600	13·0%
1990	26 960	1 610 000	8·3%

* the basis upon which the government calculates unemployment figures has undergone numerous revisions, making the series discontinuous

THE NATIONAL DEBT

The National Debt is the nominal amount of outstanding debt chargeable on the Consolidated Fund of the United Kingdom Exchequer (excluding the debt created by the separate Northern Ireland Exchequer).

The National Debt became a permanent feature of the country's economy as early as 1692. The table below shows how the net total Debt has increased over the years (the figure shown is for 31 March of each year listed):

Year	National Debt (£ million)	Year	National Debt (£ million)
1697	14	1945	21 365·9
1727	52	1946	23 636·5
1756	75	1947	25 630·6
1763	133	1948	25 620·8
1775	127	1949	25 167·6
1781	187	1950	25 802·3
1784	243	1951	25 921·6
1793	245	1952	25 890·5
1802	523	1953	26 051·2
1815	834	1954	26 538
1828	800	1955	26 933
1836	832	1956	27 038
1840	827	1957	27 007
1854	802	1958	27 232
1855	789	1959	27 376
1857	837	1960	27 732
1860	799	1961	28 251
1899	635	1962	28 674
1900	628·9	1963	29 847
1903	770·8	1964	30 226
1909	702·7	1965	30 440
1910	713·2	1966	31 340
1914	649·8	1967	31 985
1915	1 105·0	1968	34 193
1916	2 133·1	1969	33 984
1917	4 011·4	1970	33 079
1918	5 871·9	1971	33 441
1919	7 434·9	1972	35 839
1920[1]	7 828·8	1973	36 884
1921	7 574·4	1974	40 124
1923	7 742·2	1975	45 886
1931	7 413·3	1976	56 557
1934	7 822·3	1977	54 041
1935[2]	6 763·9	1978	79 000
1936	6 759·3	1979	82 597
1937	6 764·7	1980	91 245
1938	6 993·7	1981	112 780
1939	7 130·8	1982	117 959
1940	7 899·2	1983	127 072
1941	10 366·4	1984	142 545
1942	13 041·1	1985	158 101
1943	15 822·6	1986	162 191
1944	18 562·2	1987	186 000
		1988	197 500

[1] Beginning 1920, total excludes bonds tendered for death duties and held by the National Debt Commissioner.
[2] Beginning 1935, total excludes external debt, then £1036·5 million, arising out of the 1914–18 war.

DISTRIBUTION OF WORKFORCE 1987

Agriculture, forestry and fishing	592 000
Mining and quarrying	208 000
Manufacturing	5 398 000
Electricity, gas and water	285 000
Construction	1 559 000
Trade, restaurants and hotels	5 061 000
Transport, storage and communications	1 502 000

Financing, insurance, real estate and business services	2 610 000
Community, social and personal services	7 455 000
Armed Forces	319 000
Total	**24 989 000**
Males	14 335 000
Females	10 653 000

IMPORTS

Principal Imports into the UK (1988)	£ millions c.i.f.*
Vegetables and fruit	2 462.4
Petroleum, petroleum products, etc.	3 495.2
Organic chemicals	2 352.9
Artificial resins, plastic materials, etc.	2 846.0
Paper, paperboard and manufactures	3 622.7
Textile yarn, fabrics, etc.	3 635.6
Non-metallic mineral manufactures	3 301.0
Iron and steel	2 367.4
Non-ferrous metals	2 504.2
Other metal manufactures	2 146.4
Power-generating machinery and equipment	3 047.0
Machinery specialized for particular industries	3 476.1
General industrial machinery, equipment and parts	3 544.9
Office machines and automatic data-processing equipment	6 278.6
Telecommunications and sound equipment	3 176.7
Other electrical machinery apparatus, etc.	5 813.5
Road vehicles and parts†	11 247.9
Other transport equipment	2 657.7
Clothing and accessories (excl. footwear)	3 108.1
Professional, scientific and controlling instruments, etc.	2 024.6

* Cost, insurance and freight.
† Excluding tyres, engines and electrical parts.

EXPORTS

Principal Exports from the UK (1988)	f.o.b.*
Petroleum, petroleum products, etc.	5 575.9
Organic chemicals	3 138.3
Non-metallic mineral manufactures	2 971.1
Iron and steel	2 391.2
Power-generating machinery and equipment	3 884.8
Machinery specialized for particular industries	3 288.4
General industrial machinery, equipment and parts	3 577.5
Office machines and automatic data-processing equipment	5 296.6
Other electrical machinery apparatus, etc.	4 343.4
Road vehicles and parts†	4 992.3
Other transport equipment	3 964.9
Professional, scientific and controlling instruments, etc.	2 531.6

* Free on board.
† Excluding tyres, engines and electrical parts.

PRINCIPAL IMPORTING NATIONS INTO UK (1988)

	£ million	% of total UK imports
West Germany	17 667.1	16.6%
USA	10 767.8	10.1%
France	9 390.2	8.8%
Netherlands	8 279.7	7.78%
Japan	6 509.1	6.1%
Italy	5 817.4	5.46%
Belgium & Luxembourg	4 956.0	4.65%
Irish Republic	3 878.6	3.6%
Switzerland	3 840.6	3.6%
Sweden	3 366.5	3.16%
Norway	3 074.3	2.88%
Spain	2 482.4	2.3%
Canada	2 038.2	1.91%
Denmark	2 028.1	1.90%
Finland	1 813.0	1.7%
Hong Kong	1 788.6	1.68%
Taiwan	1 150.4	1%
Korea (Republic)	1 135.1	1%
Portugal	928.0	0.87%
Austria	874.4	0.82%

UK EXPORTS (TO PRINCIPAL NATIONS) 1988

	£ million	% of total UK exports
USA	10 544.1	12.9%
West Germany	9 521.9	11.6%
France	8 270.4	10%
Netherlands	5 583.3	6.8%
Belgium/Luxembourg	4 252.0	5.2%
Italy	4 106.4	5.0%
Irish Republic	4 057.0	4.9%
Spain	2 691.7	3.3%
Sweden	2 195.0	2.69%
Canada	2 038.4	2.5%
Switzerland	1 854.9	2.27%
Japan	1 742.7	2.1%
Saudi Arabia	1 713.4	2.1%
Australia	1 378.0	1.6%
Denmark	1 170.9	1.4%
India	1 111.7	1.3%
South Africa	1 074.8	1.3%
Norway	1 053.6	1.29%
Hong Kong	1 030.7	1.26%

BALANCE OF PAYMENTS (£s million)

	Visible Exports	Visible Imports	Visible Balance	Invisible Balance	Current Balance (− deficit + surplus)
1965	4 848	5 071	− 223	+ 198	− 27
1970	8 121	8 163	− 42	+ 818	+ 776
1971	9 060	8 799	+ 261	+ 889	+ 1150
1972	9 450	10 172	− 722	+ 930	+ 208
1973	12 115	14 498	− 2383	+ 1508	− 875
1974	16 538	21 773	− 5235	+ 1928	− 3307
1975	19 463	22 699	− 3236	+ 1615	− 1621
1976	25 441	29 012	− 3601	+ 2759	− 842
1977	32 148	33 892	− 1744	+ 2037	+ 293
1978	35 432	36 607	− 1175	+ 2207	+ 1032
1979	40 678	44 136	− 3458	+ 2595	− 863
1980	47 389	46 211	+ 1178	+ 2028	+ 3206
1981	50 977	47 325	+ 3652	+ 3620	+ 7272
1982	55 565	53 181	+ 2384	+ 3167	+ 5551
1983	60 658	61 158	− 500	+ 2549	+ 2049
1984	70 367	74 751	− 4384	+ 5858	+ 1474
1985	78 111	80 289	− 2178	+ 5097	+ 2919
1986	72 843	81 306	− 8463	+ 7483	− 980
1987	79 421	90 350	− 10 929	+ 7106	− 3822
1988	80 602	101 428	− 20 826	+ 6154	− 14 762
1989	92 526	115 638	− 23 112	+ 2261	− 20 851

STERLING – US DOLLAR EXCHANGE RATES

$4·50–$5·00	War of Independence	1776
$12·00	All-time Peak (Civil War)	1864
$4·86 21/32	Fixed parity	1880–1914
$4·76 7/16	Pegged rate World War I	December 1916
$3·40	Low point after £ floated, 19 May 1919	February 1920
$4·86 21/32	Britain's return to Gold Standard	28 Apr 1925
$3·14$^1/_2$	Low point after Britain forced off Gold Standard (20 Sept 1931 [$3·43])	November 1932
$5·20	High point during floating period	March 1934
$4·03	Fixed rate World War II	4 Sept 1939
$2·80	First post-war devaluation	18 Sept 1949
$2·40	Second post-war devaluation	20 Nov 1967
$2·42	Convertibility of US dollar into gold was suspended on	15 Aug 1971
$2·58	£ refloated	22 June 1972
$1·99	£ broke $2 barrier	5 Mar 1976
$1·56	£ at new all-time low	28 Oct 1976
$1·76	Bank of England buying pounds	10 Oct 1977
$2·00	£ breaks back to $2 level (1978 av. $1·91)	15 Aug 1978
$2·26	Dollar weakens	June 1979
$2·19	Iranian crisis unresolved	8 Dec 1979
$1·99	£ again falls below $2	3 June 1981
$1·90	One year of 'Reaganomics'	20 Jan 1982
$1·04	Strength of dollar against all currencies	6 Mar 1985
$1·21	Recovery after Ohio Bank anxiety	11 Apr 1985
$1·47	1986 Budget	March 1986
$1·55	Pound strengthens	June 1986
$1·40	Dollar strong against other currencies – 'Big Bang'	October 1986
$1·60	Pound strong against other currencies	March 1987
$1·75	Beginning of Bush presidency	February 1989
$1.85	Iraqi invasion of Kuwait	2 Aug 1990
$1.97	Resignation of Margaret Thatcher as PM	22 Nov 1990
$1.91	End of Second Gulf War	28 Feb 1991

THE TRADES UNION CONGRESS

The Trades Union Congress (TUC) is a voluntary association of trade unions, founded in 1868. Its aims are to keep watch on all industrial movements and legislation affecting labour and trade unions, to promote common action on general issues, and to assist all trade unions in their organization.

There is an annual Congress comprising delegates of the affiliated unions on the basis of one delegate for every 5000 members (or fraction thereof). Congress elects 48 representatives of the TUC to the General Council – the executive of the Congress. The Congress also elects a General Secretary who holds office until retirement at 65 (subject to the decision of Congress or the General Council). Systematic contact between the TUC and the government, the Confederation of British Industry and other bodies is maintained through the General Council and its standing committees.

PRINCIPAL UK TRADE UNIONS (affiliated to the TUC)

Amalgamated Engineering Union (AEU) f. 1920; 793 610 members.

Associated Society of Locomotive Engineers and Firemen (ASLEF), f. 1880; 19 065 members.

Association of University Teachers f. 1919; 30 000 members.

Bakers, Food and Allied Workers' Union f. 1861; 34 032 members.

Banking, Insurance and Finance Union f. 1918 (until 1979 known as the Bank Officers' Guild); 168 408 members.

British Actors' Equity Association f. 1929; 42 000 members.

Civil and Public Services Association f. 1919; 143 062 members.

Confederation of Health Service Employees (COHSE), f. 1910; 220 000 members.

Engineers' and Managers' Association f. 1913; 42 000 members.

Fire Brigades Union f. 1918; 45 683 members.

Furniture, Timber and Allied Trades Union f. 1971; 46 096 members.

GMB (formerly General, Municipal, Boilermakers and Allied Trades Union and amalgamated with APEX 1988), f. 1982; 800 000 members.

Graphical, Paper and Media Union f. 1991; 305 000 members. (An amalgamation of the National Graphical Association – f. 1963 – which merged with Society of Lithographic Artists, Designers, Engravers and Process Workers in 1982, and the Society of Graphical and Allied Trades (SOGAT), f. 1786.)

Inland Revenue Staff Federation f. 1892; 52 972 members.

Institution of Professional Civil Servants f. 1919; 90 820 members.

Iron and Steel Trades Confederation f. 1917; 41 679 members.

Manufacturing, Science and Finance Union (amalgamation of TASS and ASTMS), f. 1968; 653 000 members.

Musicians' Union f. 1921; 41 150 members.

National and Local Government Officers' Association (NALGO), f. 1905; 754 701 members.

National Association of Schoolmasters/

Union of Women Teachers (NAS/UWT), f. 1919, merged with UWT in 1976; 82 000 members.

National Association of Teachers in Further and Higher Education f. 1976; 82 000 members.

National Communications Union f. 1985, 152 000 members.

National Union of Civil and Public Servants f. 1988; 120 000 members.

National Union of Hosiery and Knitwear Workers f. 1945; 43 526 members.

National Union of Journalists (NUJ), f. 1907; 32 206 members.

National Union of Maritime and Transport Workers (merger of National Union of Railwaymen and National Union of Seamen), f. 1990; approx. 130 000 members.

National Union of Mineworkers (NUM), f. 1945; 70 000 members.

National Union of Public Employees (NUPE), f. 1888; 635 000 members.

National Union of Tailors and Garment Workers f. 1920; 76 000 members.

National Union of Teachers (NUT), f. 1870; 216 614 members.

Transport and General Workers' Union (TGWU), f. 1897; 1 312 853 members.

Transport Salaried Staffs' Association f. 1897; 40 000 members.

Union of Communication Workers f. 1920; 204 834 members.

Union of Construction, Allied Trades and Technicians (UCATT), f. 1921; 250 000 members.

Union of Shop, Distributive and Allied Workers (USDAW), f. 1947; 400 000 members.

PRINCIPAL TRADE UNIONS (not affiliated to the TUC)

Electrical, Electronic, Telecommunication and Plumbing Union (EETPU), f. 1968, expelled from the TUC in Dec 1988; 330 000 members.

Union of Democratic Mineworkers f. 1986 after breaking away from the National Union of Mineworkers; 21 568 members.

LAW AND LAW ENFORCEMENT

THE LAW IN ENGLAND AND WALES

The law of England and Wales is divided into two distinct areas; civil law – disputes between individuals – and criminal law – acts harmful to the community. The law and structure of the judicial procedure is arranged along these two lines. The judicial system of Northern Ireland is very similar to that in England and Wales – it differs only in some of the laws enacted.

CIVIL LAW

Civil law governs rights and duties between citizens. As it includes the law of contract civil law deals with important business matters such as trade, credit and insurance, but also governs more commonplace agreements. In civil cases the person injured – known in England and Wales as 'the plaintiff' – will use the law to bring an action against the defendant in a civil court, probably seeking damages (financial compensation). Another civil remedy is an injunction. In such cases the plaintiff does not seek compensation but a court order to stop the offending behaviour.

CRIMINAL LAW

Criminal law governs those situations where the accused person is said to have broken a law that has caused an injury not just to another individual, but also to the state. This law covers offences that range from murder, manslaughter, assault and sexual crimes, to offences against property such as theft, burglary and criminal damage. The purpose of the criminal law is quite different from that of civil law; the state prosecutes accused persons in a criminal court not to obtain compensation, but to punish them for what they have done.

Serious criminal cases are tried on indictment by a judge and jury, but most cases – summary offences – can be decided by magistrates, or justices of the peace, who are not lawyers and are usually unpaid. With the exception of some libel cases, a jury is never used in a civil case in Britain. In England and Wales a jury is composed of 12 impartial people, aged between 18 and 70. At the end of the case they decide if the accused is guilty or not guilty and a majority verdict, with up to two dissenters, is allowed. If the jury cannot agree, there may be a retrial.

THE COURTS

Most minor civil cases are dealt with in the County Courts. Such cases include those where the sum in dispute is less than £5000, cases where the two parties consent to County Court jurisdiction, uncontested divorces, and some bankruptcy proceedings (outside London). Civil cases pertaining to the family are dealt with in a Magistrates' Court.

The High Court of Justice is the superior civil court and is divided into three Divisions: the Chancery Division, the Queen's Bench, and the Family Division. The Chancery Division deals mainly with equity, bankruptcy and contentious probate business; the Queen's Bench is concerned with commercial and maritime law, civil cases not assigned to other courts, and appeals from the lower courts; and the Family Division deals with family law. High Court judges sit alone to hear cases at first instance. Appeals from lower courts are heard by two or three judges, or by a single judge of the appropriate division.

Further appeals for civil cases can be made to the Courts of Appeal (Civil Division) presided over by the Master of the Rolls, and may go on to the House of Lords (see diagram).

Most minor criminal offences are dealt with in a Magistrates' Court, which usually consists of three lay magistrates (Justices of the Peace) sitting without a jury and advised by a legally qualified clerk of the justices. A full-time legally qualified magistrate presides over the busier courts. These courts also deal with the preliminary proceedings of some serious cases in order to decide whether or not evidence justifies a Crown Court trial. For cases involving people under 17 there are separate juvenile courts composed of specially qualified justices.

The Crown Court deals with serious criminal offences, the sentencing of offenders from a Magistrates' Court in cases where its sentencing powers are inadequate, and appeals from the lower courts.

Appeals upon a point of law, however, are made to the High Court, and may go on to the House of Lords. They are presided over by a High Court or Circuit judge, always sitting with a 12-member jury.

Further appeals from the Crown Court, either against sentence or conviction, are made to the Court of Appeal (Criminal Division), presided over by the Lord Chief Justice. The next level of appeal is to the House of Lords if a point of law of general public importance is considered to be involved.

The House of Lords is the supreme judicial court for the United Kingdom. It is the ultimate court of appeal from all courts, except the Scottish criminal courts. Leave to appeal to it is not as of right and is usually reserved for important points of law. The work is executed by the Lord High Chancellor and nine Lords of Appeal. Only one case in 40 000 ever reaches them.

CROWN COURTS (England and Wales)

The Crown Courts in England and Wales are organized into six circuits and three tiers.

First tier courts are served by both High Court and Circuit judges, and are able to hear civil and criminal cases.

Second tier courts are also served by both High Court and Circuit judges but hear only criminal cases.

Third tier courts are served by Circuit judges and only hear criminal cases.

The six circuits are:

Midland and Oxford Circuit

First tier courts: Birmingham, Lincoln, Nottingham, Oxford, Stafford, Warwick.
Second tier courts: Leicester, Northampton, Shrewsbury.
Third tier courts: Coventry, Derby, Grimsby, Hereford, Peterborough, Stoke-on-Trent, Wolverhampton.

North Eastern Circuit

First tier courts: Leeds, Newcastle-upon-Tyne, Sheffield, Teesside (Middlesbrough).
Second tier courts: York.
Third tier courts: Beverley, Doncaster, Durham, Huddersfield, Wakefield.

Northern Circuit

First tier courts: Carlisle, Liverpool, Manchester, Preston.
Second tier courts: none.
Third tier courts: Barrow-in-Furness, Bolton, Burnley, Lancaster.

South Eastern Circuit

First tier courts: Chelmsford, Lewes, London (Royal Courts of Justice – High Court), Norwich.
Second tier courts: Ipswich, London (Central Criminal Court), Maidstone, Reading, St Albans.
Third tier courts: Aylesbury, Bury St Edmunds, Cambridge, Canterbury, Chichester, Guildford, King's Lynn, London (Acton, Croydon, Inner London, Isleworth, Kingston-upon-Thames, Knightsbridge, Middlesex Guildhall, Snaresbrook, Southwark, Wood Green), Southend.

Wales and Chester Circuit

First tier courts: Caernarfon, Cardiff, Chester, Mold, Swansea.
Second tier courts: Carmarthen, Newport, Welshpool.
Third tier courts: Dolgellau, Haverfordwest, Knutsford, Merthyr Tydfil, Warrington.

Western Circuit
First tier courts: Bristol, Exeter, Truro, Winchester.
Second tier courts: Dorchester, Gloucester, Plymouth.
Third tier courts: Barnstaple, Bournemouth, Devizes, Newport (IoW), Portsmouth, Salisbury, Southampton, Swindon, Taunton.

SCOTTISH LAW

Scotland's judicial system and laws are quite different from those in England and Wales. It is characterized by the system of public prosecution – independent of the police – and headed by the Lord Advocate. The Lord Advocate – through the Crown Office – is responsible for bringing prosecutions in the High Court, sheriff courts and district courts.

The High Court of Justiciary is the senior court for criminal cases, and tries all serious crimes such as murder, rape, treason, etc. It is also the final appeal court for any indictment trial. Prosecutions are conducted in court by a law officer or an advocate-depute. No appeal from the High Court of Justiciary can be made to the House of Lords.

District courts deal with minor summary offences and are administered by local government authorities. Prosecution is carried out by procurators-fiscals – lawyers and full-time civil servants – and presided over by lay justices (in Glasgow by stipendiary magistrates).

Most civil cases are tried in the sheriff courts. Sheriffs principals head the six sheriffdoms of Scotland, which are divided into sheriff court districts and administered by sheriffs. Sheriffs principals and sheriffs have equal powers in criminal cases, and in serious cases they sit with a 15-member jury, who may return a third verdict of 'not proven'. An appeal from the decision of a sheriff court can be made to the Court of Session.

The Court of Session in Edinburgh is divided into two Houses, the Inner House and the Outer House. The Outer House hears more serious civil cases in the first instance. The Inner House is divided into two, and hears appeals from both the sheriff courts and the Outer House. Further appeals from the Inner House can be made to the House of Lords.

SCOTTISH SHERIFFDOMS

Grampian, Highland and Islands
Court districts: Aberdeen and Stonehaven; Banff and Peterhead; Elgin; Fort William; Inverness, Lochmaddy, Portree, Stornoway, Dingwall, Tain, Wick and Dornoch; Kirkwall and Lerwick.

Lothian and Borders
Court districts: Edinburgh; Haddington; Jedburgh and Duns; Linlithgow; Peebles; Selkirk.

North Strathclyde
Court districts: Dumbarton; Dunoon; Greenock; Kilmarnock; Oban and Campbeltown; Paisley.

Glasgow and Strathkelvin
Court districts: Glasgow.

South Strathclyde, Dumfries and Galloway
Court districts: Airdrie; Ayr; Hamilton; Lanark; Stranraer and Kirkcudbright.

THE LEGAL PROFESSION

In Britain the legal profession is divided into two groups: solicitors and barristers (the latter are known as advocates in Scotland). Solicitors have a general knowledge of most of the law, and it is to a solicitor that a client would go with a legal problem. In many cases the solicitor is able to deal with the matter alone. If, however, the problem involves a complex issue in a specialized area of law, or there is likely to be a case in a higher court, the solicitor briefs a barrister. A barrister is not allowed to deal directly with the public. Senior barristers are awarded the title of Queen's Council (QC).

Solicitors are governed by the Law Society of England and Wales, the Law Society of Northern Ireland and the Law Society of Scotland. Barristers are similarly governed by the General Council for the Bar, the General Council for the Bar in Northern Ireland, the Executive Council of the Inn of Court of Northern Ireland, and, in Scotland, by the Faculty of Advocates.

Judges are almost always appointed from the ranks of senior barristers, though it is possible for solicitors to become judges. Judges are appointed by the Queen on the advice of the prime minister, and may be promoted to sit in the appeal courts. Once appointed, judges hold office until their retirement, unless they resign or are removed from office by a complex procedure involving resolution by both Houses of Parliament. In Scotland dismissal of a judge is not possible.

THE POLICE

The 52 police forces of the UK have responsibility for law enforcement in their own area. These areas are usually defined along the borders of English and Welsh counties or Scottish regions, although there are exceptions (see map on p. 736). The Metropolitan Police Force and the City of London Police are responsible for London's law enforcement. The Royal Ulster Constabulary cover law enforcement for Northern Ireland; and the Isle of Man, States of Jersey and Guernsey Forces are responsible for their respective islands.

Each force is maintained by a police authority, which in England and Wales is composed of a committee of local councillors and magistrates. In Scotland the regional and island councils are the authorities. However, the Home Secretary has responsibility for the Metropolitan Force, while the authority for the Royal Ulster Constabulary is appointed by the Secretary of State for Northern Ireland.

Central and local government finance the authorities, who appoint the chief constable, decide the size of the force, and provide buildings and equipment. The overall organization and administration of the police service – covering the areas of police ranks, pay, discipline and hours of duty – is the responsibility of the Home Secretary, and, in Northern Ireland, of the Secretary of State. In England and Wales the investigation of a serious complaint against an officer is supervised by the Police Complaints Authority. In Scotland complaints are investigated by independent public prosecutors.

POLICE HIERARCHY

(from the highest rank downwards)
  Chief Constable
  Deputy Chief Constable
  Assistant Chief Constable
  Chief Superintendent
  Superintendent
  Chief Inspector

Inspector
Sergeant
Constable

METROPOLITAN POLICE

(from the highest rank downwards)
Metropolitan Commissioner
Deputy Commissioner
Assistant Commissioner
Deputy Assistant Commissioner
Commander
Chief Superintendent
Superintendent
Chief Inspector
Inspector
Sergeant
Constable

CRIMINAL STATISTICS

ENGLAND AND WALES (Crimes and Offences recorded by the Police 1989)

Offence	No. of Offences 1989
Violence against the person	177 000
Sexual offences	29 700
Burglary	826 000
Robbery	33 100
Theft and handling stolen goods	2 012 700
Fraud and forgery	134 400
Criminal damage	630 100
Other offences	27 700

SCOTLAND (crimes and offences recorded by the Police 1989)

Crime	No. of crimes 1989
Non-sexual crimes of violence	18 500
Crimes of indecency	5700
Crimes of dishonesty	354 200
Fire-raising, vandalism, etc.	78 700
Other crimes	34 000
Offence	No. of offences 1989
Miscellaneous offences	124 800
Motor-vehicle offences	277 700

SENTENCING AND PRISONS

Most criminal and civil offences are punished by a system of fines; prison sentences are imposed in a minority of cases. Sentenced offenders make up the bulk of the prison population, but a small minority is made up by:
– those who have been refused bail and are awaiting trial (on remand; 19%);
– those awaiting sentence from a higher court (3%);
– non-criminals, such as people in default of court orders and immigrants.

Once sentenced, prisoners are categorized according to the risk they pose to the public:

Category A 'Those whose escape would be highly dangerous to the public, the police or the security of the State'. These offenders are kept in prisons especially equipped to accommodate dangerous prisoners. No more than 15% of a prison's total population must be category A prisoners.

Category B 'Those for whom the highest conditions of security are not required but for whom escape must be made very difficult.'

Category C 'Those who cannot be trusted in open

conditions but who do not have the ability or resources to make a determined escape attempt.' The majority of prisoners come under this category.

Category D 'Those who can reasonably be trusted to serve their sentences in open conditions.' These prisoners pose the least risk to the public and are trusted to serve their sentence in open prisons without making an attempt at escape.

THE COURTS OF ENGLAND AND WALES

The arrows indicate where a right of appeal lies from one court to another. The more serious criminal cases start off in the Crown Court and more complicated civil cases in the High Court.

Three judges sit in the Court of Appeal. They are known as Lord Justices of Appeal. Five judges sit in the House of Lords. They are known as Lords of Appeal in Ordinary, or the Law Lords.

The head of the Civil Division of the Court of Appeal is the Master of the Rolls. This title derives from his historical custodianship of the court record, or rolls. The head of the Criminal Division of the Court of Appeal is the Lord Chief Justice. The head of the House of Lords is the Lord Chancellor. The Lord Chancellor is the only judge who is also a member of the Government.

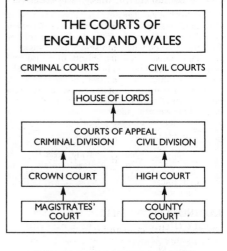

THE COURTS OF ENGLAND AND WALES

UK DEFENCE

The Sovereign, as the head of state, is technically in charge of all the Armed Forces. In reality Parliament is the decision-making body for defence. The Cabinet, and in particular the Secretary of State for Defence, is responsible to Parliament for these matters.

The day-to-day running of the Armed Forces – in both peacetime and wartime – is the responsibility of the Defence Council. This consists of the Ministers of State for the Armed Forces and for Defence Procurement (and their undersecretaries), the Secretary for State, the Chief Scientific Adviser, the Chief of Defence Procurement, and professional members of the Armed Forces. The detailed administration of the Army, Navy and Air Force is carried out by the Army Board, the Admiralty Board and the Air Force Board respectively.

PRINCIPAL SERVICE BASES, UK

Army The Army is based at the following places in the UK: Aldermaston, Aldershot, Andover, Arborfield, Ballymena, Belfast, Benbecula, Blandford, Bordon, Beaconsfield, Ballykinler, Blackdown, Bulford, Camberley, Catterick, Chatham, Chattenden, Chichester, Chilwell, Chester, Colchester, Devizes, Donnington, Deepcut, Edinburgh, Exeter, Eltham, Glasgow, Hereford, Inverness (Fort George), Kirton, Kneller Hall, Larkhill, Lisburn, Lichfield, Liverpool, London, Londonderry, Lulworth, Lurgan, Middle Wallop, Ouston (Newcastle), Pirbright, Preston, Ripon, Royston, Shrewsbury, Shrivenham, South Cerney, Stirling, Strensall (York), Tern Hill, Tidworth, Warminster, Woolwich, Worthy Down, Winchester, York. Bases are also maintained abroad, mainly in Germany, the Falkland Islands and Cyprus.

Royal Navy/Royal Marines The Royal Navy and the Royal Marines are based at the following places in the UK: Coulport, Devonport, Dartmouth, Deal (RM), Faslane, Greenock, Greenwich, Gosport, Lympstone (RM), Portsmouth, Portland, Poole (RM), Rosyth, South Queensferry, Weymouth.

Royal Air Force The Royal Air Force are based at the following places in the UK: Abingdon, Aberporth, Aldergrove, Benson, Bentley Priory, Biggin Hill, Boddington, Binbrook, Bracknell, Brawdy, Buchan, Brize Norton, Cranwell, Cardington, Church Fenton, Coltishall, Coningsby, Cosford, Cottesmore, Culdrose, Digby, Dishforth, Fairford, Farnborough, Finningley, Fylingdales, Hendon, Halton, High Wycombe, Honington, Leeming, Lossiemouth, Llanbedr, Linton, Lyneham, Kemble, Kinloss, Manston, Marham, Netheravon, Nocton Hall, Northolt, Newton (Notts), Odiham, Stanmore Park, Scampton, Swinderby, St. Mawgan, Waddington, Wattisham, Woodvale, West Drayton, Wittering, Valley, Yeovilton. Bases are also maintained abroad, mainly in Germany, the Falkland Islands and Cyprus.

COMPOSITION OF THE BRITISH ARMY (Principal Regular Units only)

Household Cavalry
The Life Guards
The Blues and Royals (Royal Horse Guard and 1st Dragoons)

Royal Armoured Corps
1st The Queen's Dragoon Guards
The Royal Scots Dragoon Guards (Carabiniers and Greys)
4th/7th Royal Dragoon Guards
5th Royal Inniskilling Dragoon Guards
The Queen's Own Hussars
The Queen's Royal Irish Hussars
9th/12th Royal Lancers (Prince of Wales's)
The Royal Hussars (Prince of Wales's Own)
13th/18th Royal Hussars (Queen Mary's Own)
14th/20th King's Hussars
15th/19th The King's Royal Hussars
16th/5th The Queen's Royal Lancers
17th/21st Lancers
Royal Tank Regiment (4 regiments)
Royal Regiment of Artillery

Royal Horse Artillery
Corps of Royal Engineers
Royal Corps of Signals

The Guards Division
Grenadier Guards (2 battalions)
Coldstream Guards (2 battalions)
Scots Guards (2 battalions)
Irish Guards
Welsh Guards

The Scottish Division
The Royal Scots
The Royal Highland Fusiliers
The King's Own Scottish Borderers
The Black Watch
Queen's Own Highlanders
The Gordon Highlanders
The Argyll and Sutherland Highlanders

The Queen's Division
The Queen's Regiment (3 battalions)
The Royal Regiment of Fusiliers (3 battalions)
The Royal Anglian Regiment (3 battalions)

The King's Division
The King's Own Royal Border Regiment
The King's Regiment
The Prince of Wales' Own Regiment of Yorkshire
The Green Howards
The Royal Irish Rangers (2 battalions)
The Queen's Lancashire Regiment
The Duke of Wellington's Regiment

The Prince of Wales' Division
The Devonshire and Dorset Regiment
The Cheshire Regiment
The Royal Welsh Fusiliers
The Royal Regiment of Wales
The Gloucestershire Regiment
The Worcestershire and Sherwood Foresters
The Royal Hampshire Regiment
The Staffordshire Regiment
The Duke of Edinburgh's Royal Regiment

The Light Division
The Light Infantry (3 battalions)
The Royal Green Jackets (3 battalions)

The Brigade of Gurkhas
2nd King Edward VII's Own Gurkha (Goorkha) Rifles
6th Queen Elizabeth's Own Gurkha Rifles (2 battalions)
7th Duke of Edinburgh's Own Gurkha Rifles
10th Princess Mary's Own Gurkha Rifles
Gurkha Engineers
Gurkha Signals
Gurkha Transport Regiment

Others
The Parachute Regiment (3 battalions)
The Special Air Service Regiment
The Army Air Corps
The Ulster Defence Regiment

Royal Army Chaplain's Department
Royal Corps of Transport
Royal Army Medical Corps
Royal Army Ordnance Corps
Corps of Royal Electrical and Mechanical Engineers
Corps of Royal Military Police
Royal Army Pay Corps
Royal Army Veterinary Corps
Small Arms School Corps
Military Provost Staff Corps
Royal Army Educational Corps
Royal Army Dental Corps

Royal Pioneer Corps	Women's Royal Army Corps
Intelligence Corps	Army Legal Services
Army Physical Training Corps	The Gibraltar Regiment
Army Catering Corps	The Royal Military Academy Sandhurst
Queen Alexandra's Royal Army Nursing Corps	The Royal Military School of Music

COMPARATIVE TABLE OF RANKS, HM FORCES

Royal Navy	*Army*	*Royal Air Force*
Admiral of the Fleet	Field Marshal	Marshal of the RAF
Admiral	General	Air Chief Marshal
Vice Admiral	Lieutenant-General	Air Marshal
Rear Admiral	Major-General	Air Vice Marshal
Commodore	Brigadier	Air Commodore
Captain	Colonel	Group Captain
Commander	Lieutenant-Colonel	Wing Commander
Lieutenant-Commander	Major	Squadron Leader
Lieutenant	Captain	Flight Lieutenant
Sub-Lieutenant	Lieutenant	Flying Officer
Acting Sub-Lieutenant	Second Lieutenant	Pilot Officer

NB: Royal Marine ranks are the same as those of the Army, but progress as far as Lieutenant-General only

SHIPS OF THE LINE

Submarines

Polaris SSBNs	(4)	*Resolution, Repulse, Renown, Revenge*
Fleet	(15)	*Churchill, Courageous, Sceptre, Spartan, Splendid, Sovereign, Superb, Swiftsure, Tireless, Torbay, Trafalgar, Trenchant, Turbulent, Valiant, Warspite*
Type 2400	(1)	*Upholder*
Oberon Class	(8)	*Ocelot, Oynx, Opportune, Opossum, Oracle, Osiris, Otter, Otus*

ASW Carriers

	(3)	*Ark Royal, Invincible, Illustrious*

Destroyers (Guided Missile)

Type 82	(1)	*Bristol*
Type 42	(12)	*Birmingham, Newcastle, Glasgow, Exeter, Southampton, Nottingham, Liverpool, Manchester, Gloucester, Edinburgh, York, Cardiff*

Frigates

Type 23	(1)	*Norfolk*
Type 22	(14)	*Battleaxe, Beaver, Boxer, Brave, Brazen, Brilliant, Broadsword, Campbeltown, Chatham, Cornwall, Coventry, Cumberland, London, Sheffield*
Type 21	(6)	*Active, Alacrity, Amazon, Ambuscade, Arrow, Avenger*
Leander	(12)	*Andromeda, Argonaut, Ariadne, Charybdis, Cleopatra, Danae, Hermione, Jupiter, Minerva, Penelope, Scylla, Sirius*

Assault Ships

	(2)	*Fearless, Intrepid*

Other ships of the line include 42 patrol and coastal combatants, 36 mine-countermeasures vessels, 5 LSTs, 32 LCU/LCVPs, 37 support and miscellaneous (29 of them manned by Royal Fleet Auxiliary or Royal Maritime Auxiliary).

NB: On 1 August 1990 the MoD announced that one Fleet Submarine (*Conqueror*), two Oberon Class submarines (*Odin* and *Onslaught*), and one Leander Class frigate (*Phoebe*) and five support vessels would be paid off; they are not included in the above list.

PERSONNEL IN HM FORCES

Total, all Services:	Regular	311 600
	Reserve	324 700
Regulars	Royal Navy male:	53 500
	female:	3450
	Royal Marines:	7700
	Army, male:	149 000
	female:	6500
	RAF, male:	85 150
	female:	6300
Regular Reserves	Royal Navy:	24 700
	Royal Marines:	2400
	Army:	173 100
	RAF:	34 100
Volunteer Reserves/ Auxiliary Forces	Royal Navy:	8800
	Royal Marines:	1300
	Territorial Army:	72 800
	Ulster Defence Regiment:	*2900
	Home Service Force:	3000
	RAF:	1600

* (part time)

TRANSPORT

GOODS TRANSPORT (1987)

Tonne kilometres (thousand millions)
Road	113·3
Rail (British Rail only)	17·3
Water (coastwise oil products)*	31·8
Water (other)*	22·4
Pipelines (excluding gases)	10·5
Total	195·3

Tonnes (million tonnes)
Road	1542
Rail (British Rail only)	141
Water (coastwise oil products)*	43
Water (other coastwise products)*	100
Pipelines (excluding gases)	83
Total	1909

* coastwise includes all sea traffic within the British Isles. 'Other' means coastwise traffic plus inland waterways and one-port traffic.

PASSENGER TRANSPORT 1961–88 (1000 million passenger miles)

	1961	1971	1981	1988
Air	0.6	1.2	1.9	3.1
Rail	24.2	22.4	21.1	25.5
Road	136	210.7	283.4	353.5
buses and coaches	41.6	31.7	26.1	25.5
cars, taxis and motorcycles	88.2	176.5	254.8	324.9
bicycles	6.2	2.5	2.5	3.1

MAJOR BRITISH AIRPORTS

Airport	Terminal passengers handled per annum (1988)
London Heathrow	37 000 000
London Gatwick	20 800 000
Manchester	9 700 000
Glasgow	3 700 000
Birmingham	2 900 000
Luton	2 800 000
Belfast (Aldergrove)	2 200 000
Edinburgh	2 100 000
Jersey	1 800 000
Aberdeen	1 600 000
Newcastle	1 400 000
East Midlands	1 300 000
London Stansted	1 000 000
Guernsey	800 000
Cardiff	700 000
Bristol	700 000
Leeds/Bradford	700 000

The following airports are also served by scheduled passenger flights and have been designated as Customs airports:

Blackpool, Bournemouth (Hurn), Cambridge, Coventry, Exeter, Humberside, Kent International (Manston), Liverpool, London City (available only to aircraft with short landing and take-off characteristics), Norwich, Plymouth (Roborough), Prestwick, Ronaldsway (Isle of Man), Southampton (Eastleigh), Southend, Sumburgh (Shetland), Teesside. Customs facilities are also available at the following airports: Alderney, Biggin Hill, Lydd and Shoreham.

UK–OVERSEAS AIR TRAFFIC (thousands)

	1982	1984	1986	1988
Flights				
UK scheduled flights	143.5	151.3	177.5	216.9
UK non-scheduled flights	176.3	214.0	198.8	225.5
Overseas airlines scheduled flights	154.3	160.9	195.8	249.8
Overseas airlines non-scheduled flights	37.3	40.2	43.6	43.0
Total	511.4	566.4	615.7	735.2
Passengers				
UK airlines scheduled services	12 214.7	13 174.2	15 082.9	19 237.6
UK airlines non-scheduled services	13 216.6	16 643.7	12 929.7	23 062.1
Overseas airlines scheduled services	15 520.5	17 623.0	19 409.5	25 029.3
Overseas airlines non-scheduled services	3 180.1	3 713.9	4 186.0	40 886.5
Total	44 131.9	51 154.8	51 608.1	108 215.5

ROAD LENGTHS IN APRIL 1988

Road	England	Wales	Scotland	N. Ireland	UK total
Public roads	167 935 mi	20 407 mi	31 818 mi	14 812 mi	234 972 mi
	(270 258 km)	(32 841 km)	(51 205 km)	(23 837 km)	(378 140 km)
Trunk roads (incl. motorways)	6 602 mi	1 057 mi	1 953 mi	1 433 mi	11 045 mi
	(10 625 km)	(1 701 km)	(3 143 km)	(2 306 km)	(17 775 km)
Trunk motorways*	1 576 mi	74 mi	145 mi	70 mi	1 865 mi
	(2 536 km)	(119 km)	(233 km)	(113 km)	(3 001 km)

* Additionally there are 48 miles (77 km) of local-authority motorway in England and 15 miles (24 km) in Scotland

NUMBER OF LICENSED VEHICLES (thousands)

	1986	1987	1988
Private motor cars	16 981	17 421	18 432
Motor cycles, scooters/mopeds	1 065	978	912
Goods vehicles	593	609	647
Public passenger vehicles	125	129	132

figures taken on 31 December of the above years

BREAKDOWN OF ROAD ACCIDENTS 1988

Total casualties	
Pedestrians	58 843
Vehicle users	263 462
Killed	
Pedestrians	1753
Pedal cycles	227
Two-wheeled motor vehicles	670
Cars and taxis	2142
Others	260
Vehicles involved	
Pedal cycles	26 561
Motor vehicles	404 571

ROAD ACCIDENTS 1965–88

Year	Killed	Injured
1965	7952	389 985
1970	7499	355 869
1975	6366	318 584
1980	6010	323 000
1988	5052	317 253

CHANNEL TUNNEL

The idea of a Channel Tunnel – an undersea tunnel link between mainland Britain and France – has been proposed many times since the early 19th century. The latest project began in February 1986 with the signing of the Channel Tunnel Treaty by Britain and France.

The private-sector Anglo-French consortium, Eurotunnel, was awarded the concession (until 2042) to build and operate a cross-Channel rail link. The building of the tunnel has been subcontracted to a consortium of 10 British and French construction firms – TransManche Ltd. They are responsible for completing work by 15 June 1993. Although £5000 million was raised for the project in 1987, the total cost is now projected at an estimated £7500 million.

The cross-Channel link will have three tunnels: two tunnels for the running of high-speed trains, and a third, between them, for ventilation and maintenance. Waterloo Station (London) and Gare du Nord (Paris) and Gare Centrale (Brussels) will be the main terminals – journey times to continental destinations will be cut to three hours and two hours 40 minutes respectively.

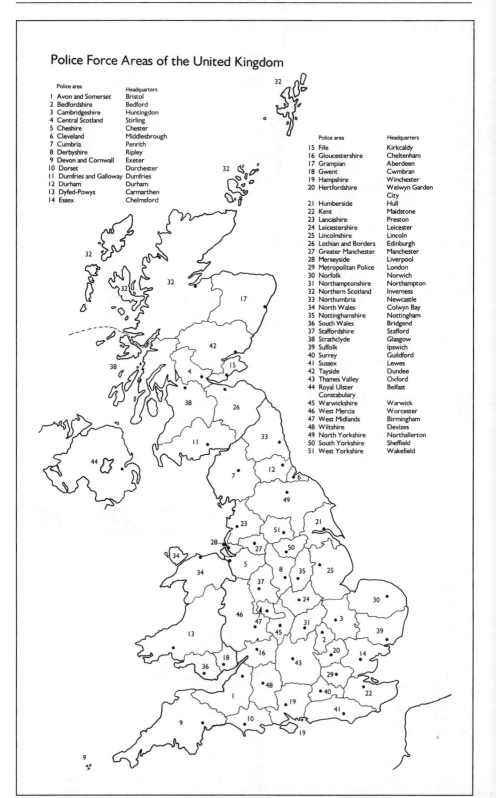

Police Force Areas of the United Kingdom

Police area	Headquarters
1 Avon and Somerset	Bristol
2 Bedfordshire	Bedford
3 Cambridgeshire	Huntingdon
4 Central Scotland	Stirling
5 Cheshire	Chester
6 Cleveland	Middlesbrough
7 Cumbria	Penrith
8 Derbyshire	Ripley
9 Devon and Cornwall	Exeter
10 Dorset	Dorchester
11 Dumfries and Galloway	Dumfries
12 Durham	Durham
13 Dyfed-Powys	Carmarthen
14 Essex	Chelmsford

Police area	Headquarters
15 Fife	Kirkcaldy
16 Gloucestershire	Cheltenham
17 Grampian	Aberdeen
18 Gwent	Cwmbran
19 Hampshire	Winchester
20 Hertfordshire	Welwyn Garden City
21 Humberside	Hull
22 Kent	Maidstone
23 Lancashire	Preston
24 Leicestershire	Leicester
25 Lincolnshire	Lincoln
26 Lothian and Borders	Edinburgh
27 Greater Manchester	Manchester
28 Merseyside	Liverpool
29 Metropolitan Police	London
30 Norfolk	Norwich
31 Northamptonshire	Northampton
32 Northern Scotland	Inverness
33 Northumbria	Newcastle
34 North Wales	Colwyn Bay
35 Nottinghamshire	Nottingham
36 South Wales	Bridgend
37 Staffordshire	Stafford
38 Strathclyde	Glasgow
39 Suffolk	Ipswich
40 Surrey	Guildford
41 Sussex	Lewes
42 Tayside	Dundee
43 Thames Valley	Oxford
44 Royal Ulster Constabulary	Belfast
45 Warwickshire	Warwick
46 West Mercia	Worcester
47 West Midlands	Birmingham
48 Wiltshire	Devizes
49 North Yorkshire	Northallerton
50 South Yorkshire	Sheffield
51 West Yorkshire	Wakefield

EDUCATION

PRE-SCHOOL AND PRIMARY EDUCATION

Nursery school, whether private or state funded, is usually the first experience of school for most children. Under-5s learn mainly through play activities, with more formal learning introduced as the time for full-time school approaches.

Primary school follows nursery school. Children attend primary (sometimes called 'first') schools from the age of 5 to the age of 11. The first two years are spent in the 'infants' and the remainder as 'juniors', although some areas have *middle schools* attended by children from 8 or 9 to 12 or 13.

SECONDARY EDUCATION

Secondary education is provided for children from the age of 11 to the age of 16 (or 18 if pupils choose). In those areas with middle schools, secondary education begins at 12 or 13. The vast majority of local education authorities provide secondary education in the form of *comprehensive schools*, accepting children of all abilities. A smaller number of educational authorities divide education facilities between *grammar* and *secondary modern schools*. A selective exam – usually still known as the eleven-plus – decides which type of school children will attend (children that pass their eleven-plus may go to grammar school). Grammar schools provide a more academic education, while secondary moderns offer a general education with a practical bias. The percentage breakdown of children in each of these types of schools are: comprehensive 85.8% in England, 98.5% Wales; secondary modern 4.1% England, 0.6% Wales; grammar 3.1% England, 0.5% Wales.

Schools are either wholly funded by local education authorities (LEAs), grant maintained, or voluntary/voluntary aided/voluntary controlled. Funding for the latter comes from various sources, depending on the school's exact status: usually a combination of LEA funding, grants from central government, governing bodies and other sources. The majority of church schools, for example, receive funds from local parishes.

Grant-maintained schools came into being as a result of the 1988 Education Act, which permits schools with more than 300 pupils to 'opt out' of local-authority control if the majority of parents wish to do so. Governing bodies of such schools receive all their funding direct from central government and are responsible for all administration, staffing and maintenance.

Independent or *public schools* receive no LEA or central-government money, but are dependent on fee income, trusts and investment.

City Technology Colleges were set up in the 1980s in an attempt to widen the choice of secondary education in disadvantaged urban areas. They are state-aided but independent of the LEAs. Although they teach a broad curriculum, their emphasis is on science, technology, business understanding and art technologies. There are presently seven such colleges, but plans for further colleges are in some doubt owing to a lack of independent sponsorship.

Education is compulsory until the age of 16. Pupils staying in full-time education after this age have the choice (always depending on local provision) of opting for academic education – usually leading to A levels (Highers in Scotland), often offered in sixth form colleges – or choosing a more vocationally slanted course leading to a qualification in, for example, agriculture, business, engineering, hairdressing, catering, secretarial work, etc. Some business courses are available in sixth form colleges; the majority of vocational or career-directed courses, however, are provided by further education, technical or tertiary colleges – which in some towns teach A level and vocational courses, acting as sixth form and technical college under one roof.

SCOTTISH SECONDARY EDUCATION

Scottish secondary schools are divided into three types. The most common is the *education authority school* which is funded and managed by the regional and islands councils. Secondly, there are *grant-aided schools* financed by direct grants from the Scottish Education Department and administered by voluntary managers. Thirdly, there are independent schools which run on similar lines to the English independent schools.

THE NATIONAL CURRICULUM

A key element of the 1988 Education Act is the *national curriculum*. It consists of *core* and *foundation subjects* to be studied by all pupils in state schools. Core subjects are English (or Welsh), mathematics, and science. Foundation subjects comprise history, geography, music, art, technology, a modern language (at secondary level), and physical education. Education under the national curriculum divides a pupil's time at school into *four key stages*, 5–7 years old, 8–11, 12–14, and 15–16. Attainment targets are set for each age group and pupils will be tested at the end of each stage.

The main changes brought about by the introduction of the national curriculum are that science and technology will be taught to all children from the age of 5 and that all pupils must study a foreign language from 11 to 16.

It is expected that national-curriculum subjects will occupy 70% of the timetable, with wider educational topics such as social education, political and economic awareness and careers education also being studied. Religious education must be taught, and schools may also offer extra languages, business studies, classics, and home economics.

The introduction of the national curriculum is being phased in over a period. Key stages 1–3 have already begun; stage 4 will begin in 1992–3. State schools must follow the new national curriculum. Independent schools need not do so, but many are choosing to follow it fairly closely.

THE EXAMINATION SYSTEM

Since 1988 the main examination for 16-year-olds in England, Wales and Northern Ireland has been the General Certificate of Secondary Education (GCSE). Unlike its predecessors the GSE (O levels) and the CSE, the GCSE syllabuses are based on national criteria and cover course objectives, content and assessment objectives, and use differentiated assessment. The GCSE is awarded on an A–G seven-point basis; grades A–C are equivalent to an O level, and grades D–G reflect the CSE 2–5 grade scale.

NUMBER OF PUBLIC-SECTOR EDUCATIONAL ESTABLISHMENTS 1988

	United Kingdom	England	Wales	Scotland	N. Ireland
Nursery	1 298	558	58	596	86
Primary	24 482	19 319	1 753	2 418	992
Secondary	5 020	4 153	233	438	196
Non-maintained	2 546	2 273	67	118	88
Special	1 900	1 443	65	346	46
Universities*	48	37	1	8	2
Polytechnics, other					
major establishments†	724	475[1]	41[2]	180	28

* including Open University
† including maintained, assisted and grant-aided institutions
[1] 31 were polytechnics
[2] 1 is a polytechnic

PUPILS AND TEACHERS IN UK, PLUS PUPIL/TEACHER RATIO 1988

	Pupils	Teachers	Ratio
Nursery	57 600	2 700	21/3
Primary	4 598 900	210 100	21/9
Secondary	3 701 500	244 900	15/1
Special schools	120 900	19 300	6/3
Total	9 100 700	531 100	17/1

After GCSE pupils may sit an examination for the Certificate of Extended Education (CEE) or the more traditional A levels. The CEE comprise single-subject examinations in English, mathematics and more unusual subjects like social, environmental, technological, business and health studies. A-level courses last two years and traditionally provide the qualifications for entry into higher education. Pupils normally take up to three subjects. A levels are graded on an A-to-E basis with an additional N class for narrow failure and U for unclassified. There is an alternative or complement to A levels in AS levels – introduced in 1987 – which cover half the A-level syllabus in two years but with half the teaching time. Two AS levels correspond to one A level. An additional complementary qualification is the S level, short for special (or scholarship) level. These are additional papers of greater difficulty, usually taken with A levels.

Alternative qualifications that can be taken by the 16-plus age group are vocational diplomas/certificates awarded by the City and Guilds of London Institute (CGLI), the Royal Society of Arts (RSA), the Business and Technician Education Council (BTEC), and the Scottish Vocational Education Council (SCOTVEC).

THE SCOTTISH EXAMINATION SYSTEM

Scottish public examinations – which are taken by pupils at 16 (during their 4th year) – are divided between the Ordinary grade and the Standard grade of the Scottish Certificate of Education. As with the all-encompassing GCSE, the Ordinary grade is gradually being replaced by a new Standard-grade examination suited to every level of ability.

At the age of 17 Scottish pupils who have passed their Ordinary/ Standard grades may sit the Higher-grade examination. The one-year Higher courses are normally studied to a lesser depth than A levels

although pupils often sit four or more subjects. A further year of education is often used to gain a Certificate of Sixth Year Studies (CSYS), during which pupils study up to three of their Higher subjects in depth. Alternatively a sixth year of further education can be spent gaining improved or additional Ordinary/Standard or Higher grades.

HIGHER AND TERTIARY EDUCATION

At 18 (sometimes 17) students again have the option of following academic or vocational courses. The main academic qualification in England and Wales is the first degree. First-degree courses last three or four years (longer in the case of professional qualifications such as medicine and architecture), and are studied in universities, polytechnics and a variety of colleges and institutes of higher education. First degrees in England and Wales are known as Bachelor degrees (Bachelor of Arts, Bachelor of Science, Bachelor of Education, etc.). Higher degrees, awarded for postgraduate or advanced study, may be Master of Arts or Master of Science, while the highest level is a doctorate – namely a PhD or DPhil. In Scotland first degrees are usually called MAs, and courses normally last three or four years, in the case of ordinary and honours courses respectively; ordinary degrees involve the study of a wider range of subjects.

The Diploma of Higher Education (Dip. H.E.) is a two-year diploma and is often studied for entry into university or other further education. The BTEC Higher National Certificate (HNC) is gained after two years part-time study, while the Diploma (HND) is awarded after two years full-time study and is rated just below degree level.

HIGHER-EDUCATION INSTITUTIONS

Universities. These self-governing institutions have

control of their own academic appointments, curricula and student admissions although they are funded by the government through the University Funding Council and the payment of course fees from each student (paid by local education authorities). They offer mostly academic and some vocational courses.

Polytechnics offer a growing number of academic courses but still provide vocational courses.

Scottish Central Institutions are more vocational but offer some academic courses.

Other tertiary-stage institutions include colleges of agriculture, art, drama, music, professions related to medicine, etc.

THE UNIVERSITIES

There are 48 institutions of degree-giving status in the United Kingdom. The list below is given in order of seniority of date of foundation, and the data run as follows: name, year of foundation, location and full-time student population as at 1990.

1. University of Oxford (1249*) Oxford OX1 2JD. Student nos: 13 800

Colleges, Halls and Societies: University (1249), Balliol (1263), Merton (1264), St Edmund Hall (1278), Exeter (1314), Oriel (1326), Queen's (1341), New College (1379), Lincoln (1427), Magdalen (1428), All Souls (1438), Brasenose (1509), Corpus Christi (1517), Christ Church (1546), Trinity (1554), St John's (1555), Jesus (1571), Wadham (1610), Pembroke (1624), Worcester (1714), Hertford (1740), Manchester (1786), Regent's Park (1810), Keble (1870), Lady Margaret Hall (1878), Somerville (1879), Mansfield (1886), St Hugh's (1886), St Hilda's (1893), St Anne's (1893), Campion (1896), St Benet's (1897), Greyfriars (1910), St Peter's (1929), St Antony's (1953), Nuffield (1958), Linacre House (1962), St Cross (1965), Wolfson (1965), Green (1979), Rewley House (1990).

2. The University of Cambridge (1284*) Cambridge CB2 1QJ. Student nos: 13 150

Peterhouse (1284), Clare (1326), Pembroke (1347), Gonville and Caius (1348), Trinity Hall (1350), Corpus Christi (1352), King's (1441), Queens' (1448), St Catherine's (1473), Jesus (1496), Christ's (1505), St John's (1511), Magdalene (1542), Trinity (1546), Emmanuel (1584), Sidney Sussex (1596), Downing (1800), Fitzwilliam (1869), Girton (1869), Newnham (1871), Selwyn (1882), Hughes Hall (1885), Homerton (1894), St Edmund's (1896), New Hall (1954), Churchill (1959), Wolfson (1965), Lucy Cavendish (1965), Robinson (1977).

3. University of St. Andrews (1411) College Gate, St Andrews, Scotland, KY16 9AJ. Student nos: 4045

Colleges: United College of St Salvator and St Leonard; College of St Mary.

4. University of Glasgow (1451) Glasgow, Scotland, G12 8QQ. Student nos: 11 562

5. University of Aberdeen (1495) Aberdeen, Scotland, AB9 1FX. Student nos: 6050

6. University of Edinburgh (1583) Old College, South Bridge, Edinburgh, Scotland, EH8 9YL. Student nos: 10 795

7. University of Durham (1832) Old Shire Hall, Durham, DH1 3HP. Student nos: 5299

Colleges and Schools: University, Hatfield, Grey, St Chad's, St John's, St Mary's, St Aidan's, St Hild and St Bede, Neville's Cross, St Cuthbert's Society, Van

Mildert, Trevelyan, Collingwood, Ushaw, Graduate Society.

8. University of London (1836) Senate House, Malet Street, London, WC1E 7HU. Student nos: 48 707

Colleges and Schools: Birbeck College, Heythrop College, Goldsmith's College, Imperial College of Science, Technology and Medicine, King's College, London School of Economics and Political Science, Queen Mary and Westfield College, Royal Academy of Music, Royal College of Music, Royal Holloway and Bedford New College, Royal Veterinary College, School of Oriental and African Studies, School of Pharmacy, School of Slavonic and East European Studies, Trinity College of Music, University College, Wye College.

Medical Schools: Charing Cross and Westminster Medical School, King's College of Medicine and Dentistry, London Hospital Medical School, Royal Free Hospital School of Medicine, St Bartholomew's Hospital Medical College, St George's Hospital Medical School, St Mary's Hospital Medical School, United Medical and Dental Schools of Guy's and St Thomas's Hospitals, University College and Middlesex School of Medicine.

Institutes: Courtauld Institute of Art, Institute of Commonwealth Studies, Institute of Education, Institute of Germanic Studies, Institute of United States Studies, Warburg Institute.

9. University of Manchester Institute of Science and Technology(1824) PO Box 88, Manchester, M60 1QD. Student nos: 4634

10. University of Manchester (1851) Manchester, M13 9PL. Student nos: 12 238

11. University of Newcastle upon Tyne (1852) Newcastle upon Tyne, NE1 7RU. Student nos: 8368

12. University of Wales (1893) Cathays Park, Cardiff, CF1 3NS. Student nos: 21 781

Colleges: Aberystwyth, Bangor, Cardiff, Lampeter, Swansea, University of Wales College of Medicine.

13. University of Birmingham (1900) PO Box 363, Birmingham B15 2TT. Student nos: 9724

14. University of Liverpool (1903) PO Box 147, Liverpool, L69 3BX. Student nos: 9143

15. University of Leeds (1904) Leeds, Yorkshire, LS2 9JT. Student nos: 11 454

16. University of Sheffield (1905) Sheffield, S10 2TN. Student nos: 8937

17. The Queen's University of Belfast (1908) Belfast, Northen Ireland, BT7 1NN. Student nos: 7826

18. University of Bristol (1909) Senate House, Bristol, BS8 1TH. Student nos: 7744

19. University of Reading (1926) Reading, Berkshire, RG6 2AH. Student nos: 7393

20. University of Nottingham (1948) University Park, Nottingham, NG7 2RD. Student nos: 8074

21. University of Southampton (1952) Highfield, Southampton, SO9 5NH. Student nos: 6983

22. University of Hull (1954) Hull, HU6 7RX. Student nos: 5815.

23. University of Exeter (1955) Exeter, EX4 4QJ. Student nos: 5572

24. University of Leicester (1957) University Road, Leicester, LE1 7RH. Student nos: 5461

25. **University of Sussex** (1961) Sussex House, Falmer, Brighton, BN1 9RH. Student nos: 4708

26. **University of Keele** (1962) Keele, Staffordshire, ST5 5BG. Student nos: 3092

27. **University of East Anglia** (1963) Norwich, NR4 7TJ. Student nos: 4680

28. **University of York** (1963) Heslington, York, YO1 5DD. Student nos: 4139

29. **University of Lancaster** (1964) University House, Lancaster, LA1 4YW. Student nos: 5125

30. **University of Essex** (1964) Wivenhoe Park, Colchester, CO4 3SQ. Student nos: 3453

31. **University of Strathclyde** (1964) 16 Richmond Street, Glasgow, Scotland, G1 1XQ. Student nos: 8304

32. **University of Warwick** (1965) Coventry, CV4 7AL. Student nos: 6901

33. **University of Kent at Canterbury** (1965) Canterbury, Kent, CT2 7NZ. Student nos: 4621

34. **University of Ulster** (1965) Coleraine, County Londonderry, Northern Ireland, BT52 1SA. Student nos: 8717

35. **Heriot-Watt University** (1966) Riccarton, Edinburgh, Scotland, EH14 4AS. Student nos: 4471

36. **Loughborough University of Technology** (1966) Loughborough, Leicestershire, LE11 3TU. Student nos: 5510

37. **Aston University** (1966) Aston Triangle, Birmingham, B4 7ET. Student nos: 3637

38. **City University** (1966) Northampton Square, London, EC1V 0HB. Student nos: 3276

39. **Brunel University** (1966) Uxbridge, Middlesex, UB8 3PH. Student nos: 3043

40. **University of Bath** (1966) Claverton Down, Bath, BA2 7AY. Student nos: 4067

41. **University of Bradford** (1966) Bradford, West Yorkshire, BD7 1DP. Student nos: 4780

42. **University of Surrey** (1966) Guildford, Surrey, GU2 5XH. Student nos: 3840

43. **University of Salford** (1967) Salford, M5 4WT. Student nos: 4105

44. **University of Dundee** (1967) Dundee, Scotland, DD1 4HN. Student nos: 4069

45. **University of Stirling** (1967) Stirling, Scotland, FK9 4LA. Student nos: 3300

46. **Cranfield Institute of Technology** (1969) Cranfield, Bedford, MK43 1EG. Student nos: 700 *Includes:* Silsoe College (Bedford) and Royal Military College of Science at Shrivenham.

47. **The Open University** (1969) Walton Hall, Milton Keynes, Buckinghamshire, MK7 6AA. Student nos: 71 018

48. **University of Buckingham** (1976) Buckingham, MK18 1EG. Student nos: 724. Independent of state finance.

* *date of foundation of oldest college*

THE 33 POLYTECHNICS OF ENGLAND AND WALES

Bristol Polytechnic (1969) Coldharbour Lane, Frenchay, Bristol, BS16 1QY

Leicester Polytechnic (1969) PO Box 143, Leicester, LE1 9BH

Newcastle upon Tyne Polytechnic (1969) Ellison Road, Newcastle upon Tyne, NE1 8ST

Portsmouth Polytechnic (1969) Museum Road, Portsmouth, PO1 2QQ

Sheffield City Polytechnic (1969) Pond Street, Sheffield, S1 1WB

Sunderland Polytechnic (1969) Langham Tower, Ryhope Road, Sunderland, Tyne and Wear, SR2 7EE

Wolverhampton Polytechnic (1969) Wulfruna Street, Wolverhampton, WV1 1SB

Brighton Polytechnic (1970) Lewes Road, Brighton, BN2 4AT

Polytechnic of Central London (1970) 309 Regent Street, London, W1R 8AL

City of London Polytechnic (1970) India House, 139 Minories, London, EC3N 2EY

Coventry Polytechnic (1970; founded as Lanchester Polytechnic) Priory Street, Coventry, CV1 5FB

Polytechnic of East London (1970; founded as North East London Polytechnic) Romford Road, London, E15 4LZ

Hatfield Polytechnic (1970) College Lane, Hatfield, Hertfordshire, AL10 9AB

Huddersfield Polytechnic (1970) Queensgsate, Huddersfield, HD1 3DH

Kingston Polytechnic (1970) Penryhn Road, Kingston upon Thames, Surrey, KT1 2EE

Leeds Polytechnic (1970) Calverley Street, Leeds, LS1 3HE

Liverpool Polytechnic (1970) 70 Mount Pleasant, Liverpool, L3 5UX

Manchester Polytechnic (1970) All Saints, Manchester, M15 6BH

Nottingham Polytechnic (1971; founded as Trent Polytechnic) Burton Street, Nottingham, NG1 4BU

Oxford Polytechnic (1970) Headington, Oxford, OX3 0BP

Polytechnic South West (1970; founded as Plymouth Polytechnic) Drake Circus, Plymouth, PL4 8AA

South Bank Polytechnic (1970) Borough Road, London, SE1 0AA

Staffordshire Polytechnic (1970; founded as North Staffordshire Polytechnic) College Road, Stoke-on-Trent, ST4 2DE

Teesside Polytechnic (1970) Borough Road, Middlesbrough, Cleveland, TS1 3BA

Thames Polytechnic (1970) Wellington Street, Woolwich, London, SE18 6PF

Polytechnic of Wales (1970) Pontypridd, Mid Glamorgan, CF37 1DL

Birmingham Polytechnic (1971) Perry Barr, Birmingham, B42 2SU

The Polytechnic of North London (1971) Holloway Road, London, N7 8DB

Lancashire Polytechnic (1972; founded as Preston Polytechnic) Preston, Lancashire, PR1 2TQ

Middlesex Polytechnic (1973) Bramley Road, Oakwood, London, N14 4XS

Bournemouth Polytechnic (1990; formerly

Dorset Institute) Poole House, Fern Barrow, Dorset, BH12 5BB

Humberside Polytechnic (1990; formerly Humberside College of Higher Education) Cottingham Road, Hull, HU6 7RT

Anglia Polytechnic (1991) Victoria Road South, Chelmsford, Essex, CM1 1LL

CENTRAL INSTITUTIONS IN SCOTLAND

In Scotland, degree-level and other advanced work outside the universities is provided by the fifteen constituent colleges of the Central Institutions. The five largest, with the dates of foundation of their current status, are:

Dundee Institute of Technology (1888) Bell Street, Dundee, DD1 1HG

Paisley College of Technology (1897) High Street, Paisley, Scotland, PA1 2BE

Robert Gordon's Institute of Technology (1965) Schoolhill, Aberdeen, Scotland, AB9 1FR

Glasgow College (1971) 70 Cowcaddens Road, Glasgow, G4 0BA

Napier Polytechnic of Edinburgh (1985) 219 Colinton Road, Edinburgh, EH10 1DJ

RELIGION

The doctrines and histories of the major religions are described in the Beliefs and Ideas chapter, beginning on p. 304.

The Anglican Communion About 55% of the population of the United Kingdom nominally belongs to the Churches of the Anglican Communion (the Church of England, the Church in Wales, the Episcopal Church in Scotland and the Church of Ireland) – see p. 322. However, only 4% of the population are practising Anglicans. The organization of the Anglican Churches in the United Kingdom is shown on the map on p. 742.

The Roman Catholic Church About 9% of the population of the United Kingdom belongs to the Roman Catholic Church. The organization of the Church in the UK is shown in the map on p. 743. (See also p. 305.)

Presbyterian Churches Some 3% of the population belongs to the Presbyterian Churches including the Church of Scotland (see p. 314 and below). Other major Presbyterian Churches in the United Kingdom include the Presbyterian Church of Wales (the only Church of Welsh origin, it includes most of the Welsh-speaking population in its membership), and the Presbyterian Church in Ireland.

The Church of Scotland – the Established Church in Scotland – is governed by kirk sessions, presbyteries, 12 synods and the General Assembly. A kirk session consists of the minister and the elected elders of each of the 1700 churches. Churches are grouped into 46 presbyteries, which in turn are grouped into the 12 regional synods. The annual General Assembly – composed of equal numbers of ministers and elders – is presided over by the Moderator, who holds office for one year.

Methodist Churches Some 2% of the population belongs to Methodist Churches. Most Methodist congregations in the UK belong to the Methodist Church in Great Britain, which was formed in 1932 from the union of the Wesleyan Methodist Church, the Primitive Methodist Church and the United Methodist Church. It is governed by the annual Conference, by district synods, and by local circuit meetings. Other Methodist Churches include the Independent Methodist Church (which is Congregationalist in character) and the Wesleyan Reform Union (which is Methodist in doctrine and Congregationalist in its organization).

Other groups Other major Christian organizations combined in the United Kingdom account for less than 4% of the population. They include:
The Baptist Union of Great Britain (see p. 312). There are also separate Baptist Unions in Scotland, Ireland and Wales.
The Congregational Federation, which includes those congregations in England and Wales who did not join the United Reformed Church in 1972 (see below and p. 312).
The Salvation Army – founded by William Booth in 1865 – is characterized by a military-style organization. It is administered locally by colonels and over larger areas by commissioners and territorial commissioners who elect the world leader of the Army, the General.
The United Reformed Church was formed by the union of the Congregational Church in England and Wales and the Presbyterian Church of England. It is divided into 12 provinces. (See also pp. 313–14.)

Islam About 2% of the population follows Islam, overwhelmingly Sunni Islam (see pp. 315–18).

Judaism Less than 1% of the population of the United Kingdom practises Judaism (see pp. 321–23). The representative body of British Judaism is the Board of Deputies of British Jews, established in 1760, and the leader is the Chief Rabbi. The Court of Judgement (the *Beth Din*) is a rabbinic body that arbitrates and gives religious judgements, e.g. in matters of marriage and dietary laws.

ARCHBISHOPS OF CANTERBURY

(since the Reformation)

Thomas Cranmer (1532–1555)
Reginald Pole (under whom allegiance to Rome was briefly restored; 1555–1558)
Matthew Parker (1559–1575)
Edmund Grindal (1575–1583)
John Whitgift (1583–1604)
Richard Bancroft (1604–1610)
George Abbot (1611–1633)
William Laud (1633–1645)
Interregnum (1645–1660)
William Juxon (1660–1663)
Gilbert Sheldon (1663–1677)
William Sancroft (1677–1690)
John Tillotson (1691–1694)
Thomas Tenison (1694–1715)
William Wake (1715–1737)
John Potter (1737–1747)
Thomas Herring (1747–1757)
Matthew Hutton (1757–1758)
Thomas Secker (1758–1768)
Frederick Cornwallis (1768–1783)

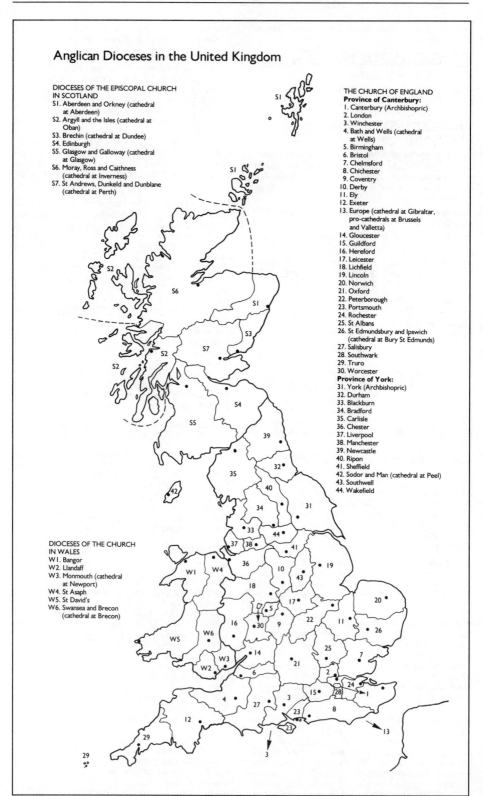

Anglican Dioceses in the United Kingdom

DIOCESES OF THE EPISCOPAL CHURCH IN SCOTLAND
S1. Aberdeen and Orkney (cathedral at Aberdeen)
S2. Argyll and the Isles (cathedral at Oban)
S3. Brechin (cathedral at Dundee)
S4. Edinburgh
S5. Glasgow and Galloway (cathedral at Glasgow)
S6. Moray, Ross and Caithness (cathedral at Inverness)
S7. St Andrews, Dunkeld and Dunblane (cathedral at Perth)

THE CHURCH OF ENGLAND
Province of Canterbury:
1. Canterbury (Archbishopric)
2. London
3. Winchester
4. Bath and Wells (cathedral at Wells)
5. Birmingham
6. Bristol
7. Chelmsford
8. Chichester
9. Coventry
10. Derby
11. Ely
12. Exeter
13. Europe (cathedral at Gibraltar, pro-cathedrals at Brussels and Valletta)
14. Gloucester
15. Guildford
16. Hereford
17. Leicester
18. Lichfield
19. Lincoln
20. Norwich
21. Oxford
22. Peterborough
23. Portsmouth
24. Rochester
25. St Albans
26. St Edmundsbury and Ipswich (cathedral at Bury St Edmunds)
27. Salisbury
28. Southwark
29. Truro
30. Worcester
Province of York:
31. York (Archbishopric)
32. Durham
33. Blackburn
34. Bradford
35. Carlisle
36. Chester
37. Liverpool
38. Manchester
39. Newcastle
40. Ripon
41. Sheffield
42. Sodor and Man (cathedral at Peel)
43. Southwell
44. Wakefield

DIOCESES OF THE CHURCH IN WALES
W1. Bangor
W2. Llandaff
W3. Monmouth (cathedral at Newport)
W4. St Asaph
W5. St David's
W6. Swansea and Brecon (cathedral at Brecon)

Roman Catholic Dioceses in the United Kingdom

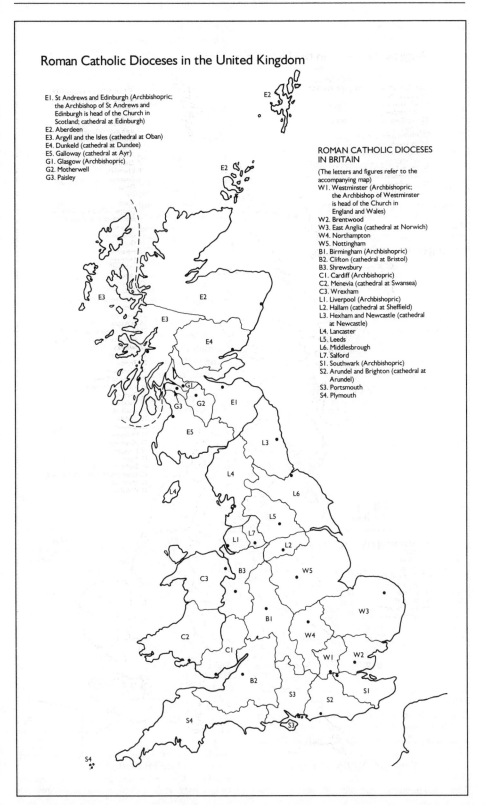

E1. St Andrews and Edinburgh (Archbishopric;
the Archbishop of St Andrews and
Edinburgh is head of the Church in
Scotland; cathedral at Edinburgh)
E2. Aberdeen
E3. Argyll and the Isles (cathedral at Oban)
E4. Dunkeld (cathedral at Dundee)
E5. Galloway (cathedral at Ayr)
G1. Glasgow (Archbishopric)
G2. Motherwell
G3. Paisley

ROMAN CATHOLIC DIOCESES
IN BRITAIN

(The letters and figures refer to the
accompanying map)

W1. Westminster (Archbishopric;
the Archbishop of Westminster
is head of the Church in
England and Wales)
W2. Brentwood
W3. East Anglia (cathedral at Norwich)
W4. Northampton
W5. Nottingham
B1. Birmingham (Archbishopric)
B2. Clifton (cathedral at Bristol)
B3. Shrewsbury
C1. Cardiff (Archbishopric)
C2. Menevia (cathedral at Swansea)
C3. Wrexham
L1. Liverpool (Archbishopric)
L2. Hallam (cathedral at Sheffield)
L3. Hexham and Newcastle (cathedral
at Newcastle)
L4. Lancaster
L5. Leeds
L6. Middlesbrough
L7. Salford
S1. Southwark (Archbishopric)
S2. Arundel and Brighton (cathedral at
Arundel)
S3. Portsmouth
S4. Plymouth

John Moore (1783–1805)
Charles Manners Sutton (1805–1828)
William Howley (1828–1848)
John Bird Sumner (1848–1862)
Charles Thomas Longley (1862–1868)
Archibald Campbell Tait (1868–1882)
Edward White Benson (1883–1896)
Frederick Temple (1896–1902)
Randall Thomas Davidson (1903–1928)
Cosmo Gordon Lang (1928–1942)
William Temple (1942–1944)
Geoffrey Francis Fisher (1945–1961)
Arthur Michael Ramsay (1961–1974)
Frederick Donald Coggan (1974–1980)
Robert Alexander Kennedy Runcie (1980–1991)
George Leonard Carey (1991–)

DIOCESES IN NORTHERN IRELAND

Dioceses in Northern Ireland extend across the political boundary with the Republic of Ireland.

CHURCH OF IRELAND DIOCESES

Armagh (Archbishopric; the Archbishop of Armagh is Primate of All Ireland)
Clogher (cathedral at Clogher and Enniskillen)
Connor (cathedral at Lisburn, plus a cathedral jointly maintained by the dioceses of Connor and Down and Dromore at Belfast)
Derry and Raphoe (cathedrals at Londonderry and at Raphoe in the Republic of Ireland)
Down and Dromore (cathedrals at Downpatrick and Dromore)

ROMAN CATHOLIC DIOCESES

Armagh (Archbishopric; the Archbishop of Armagh is head of the Church in Ireland)
Derry (cathedral at Londonderry)
Connor (cathedral at Belfast)
Dromore (cathedral at Newry)
Clogher (cathedral at Monaghan in the Republic of Ireland)
Kilmore (cathedral at Cavan in the Republic of Ireland)

MEDIA

PRINCIPAL DAILY NATIONAL NEWSPAPERS

(and circulation figures)

Daily Express circ. 1 570 365; part of Express Newspapers Ltd.

Daily Mail circ. 1,739 756; part of Associated Newspapers Group (Holdings) PLC.

Daily Mirror circ. 3 171 720; part of Mirror Group Newspapers Ltd.

Daily Star circ. 891 016; part of Express Newspapers Ltd.

Daily Telegraph circ. 1 105 366; part of Daily Telegraph PLC.

Evening Standard circ. 464 141; part of Associated Newspapers Groups (Holdings) PLC.

Financial Times circ. 285 854; part of Pearson PLC.

The Guardian circ. 431 716; part of Guardian Newspapers Ltd.

The Independent circ. 422 679; part of News-

paper Publishing PLC.

Morning Star circ. 28 544.

The Sun circ. 4 195 056; part of News International PLC.

The Times circ. 450 626; part of News International PLC.

Today circ. 601 871; part of News International PLC.

WEEKLY NEWSPAPERS (and circulation figures)

The European circ. figs. unavailable; published Friday; part of Mirror Group Newspapers Ltd.

The Independent on Sunday circ. 395 000; part of Newspaper Publishing PLC.

The Mail on Sunday circ. 1 932 799; part of Associated Newspapers Group (Holdings) PLC.

News of the World circ. 4 549 291; Sunday newspaper; part of News International PLC.

The Observer circ. 749 644; Sunday newspaper; controlled by Lonhro International.

The People circ. 2 932 472; Sunday newspaper; part of Mirror Group Newspapers Ltd.

Sunday Express circ. 2 143 374; part of Express Newspapers PLC.

Sunday Mirror circ. 2 991 030; part of Mirror Group Newspapers Ltd.

Sunday Post (Glasgow) circ. 1 432 645.

Sunday Sport circ. 463 714.

Sunday Telegraph circ. 648 317; part of Daily Telegraph PLC.

The Sunday Times circ. 1 272 591; part of News International PLC.

THE PRESS COMPLAINTS COMMISSION

The Press Complaints Commission was established in January 1990, superseding the Press Council (founded in 1953). The Press Complaints Commission is a more streamlined body than its predeceser with 15 members compared with 37 in the Press Council. It is, however, still a voluntary, self-regulating body, and like the Press Council acts as the watchdog for the press. The main points of the PCC code are: accuracy; respecting others' privacy (intrusion is acceptable only in the public interest); avoid misrepresentation, subterfuge and harassment; sympathetic handling of those in grief or shock; payment of witnesses only in the public interest; no interviewing or photographing of children without parental consent and no naming of children in sex cases; no discrimination; no use of financial information for personal gain; and the protection of confidential sources.

RADIO BROADCASTING

There are five national BBC radio services for the UK, plus national regional services in Wales, Scotland and Northern Ireland. BBC local radio services extend over England and the Channel Islands. The five national BBC stations are:

Radio 1 Pop and rock network; frequencies: VHF-FM 97.6–99.8 MHz and MW 1053 kHz and 1089 kHz.

Radio 2 Light music, entertainment and sport; frequencies VHF-FM 88–90.2 MHz.

Radio 3 Classical music, drama and documentaries, poetry and cricket in season; frequencies

VHF-FM 90.2–92.4 MHz and MW 1215 kHz.

Radio 4 News, documentaries, drama and entertainment; frequencies VHF-FM 92.4–94.6 MHz and LW 198 kHz.

Radio 5 Educational and children's programmes, and sport; frequencies MW 693, 909.

Local radio is also served by 80 independent radio stations. This figure includes some two dozen community stations, that serve communities of interest or offer a service for particular ethnic groups or cover a very small area.

THE RADIO AUTHORITY

The Radio Authority was established 1 January 1991, replacing the former Independent Broadcasting Authority's in its regulating role over radio. The purpose of the Authority is to assign frequencies, to grant licences to provide independent radio services, and to regulate the output of services to ensure they meet programming, advertising and sponsorship standards. The Authority has the right to impose fines on radio stations if complaints are upheld.

TELEVISION

There are four national television stations:

BBC 1 part of the British Broadcasting Corporation; founded in 1929 (with high-definition TV in 1936; see below). Colour service began in 1969; breakfast-time service began 1983.

BBC 2 part of the British Broadcasting Corporation. Colour service began in 1967.

ITV (Channel 3) an independent station made up of (regional) programme contractors picked by the IBA. The service was founded in 1954 and is financed by advertising.

Channel 4 an independent station set up by the IBA and financed by advertising. It was founded in 1982.

S4C Welsh Fourth Channel available only in Wales (instead of Channel Four), broadcasting in Welsh and financed by advertising.

BBC

The British Broadcasting Corporation (BBC) was founded in 1922 under a Royal charter. It is financed by licence fees and a governmental grant (for external services).

INDEPENDENT TELEVISION COMMISSION

The Independent Television Commission was established at the end of 1990, replacing the Independent Broadcasting Authority (IBA; formerly known as the Independent Television Authority). The ITC is responsible for licensing and regulating all commercially funded UK television services.

THE BROADCASTING COMPLAINTS COMMISSION

The Commission was established in 1981 to consider complaints against sound, television and cable programmes broadcast by both the BBC and the IBA. Members of the Commission are appointed by the Home Secretary.

SATELLITE BROADCASTING

British Sky Broadcasting PLC founded in 1990 from the merger of British Satellite Broadcasting (BSB) and Sky TV PLC. It offers sport, film, music and news channels.

ITV PROGRAMME CONTRACTORS

Anglia Television Ltd serves eastern England.

Border Television PLC serves the Borders, Cumbria and the Isle of Man.

Central Independent Television PLC serves the East and West Midlands.

Channel Television serves the Channel Islands.

Grampian Television PLC serves the north of Scotland.

Granada Television Ltd serves northwest England.

HTV Ltd serves Wales and the west of England.

London Weekend Television Ltd serves the London region (5.15 pm Friday to closedown on Monday morning).

Scottish Television PLC serves central Scotland.

TV-am PLC is a nationwide breakfast-time service.

Television South Ltd. (TVS) serves south and southeast England.

TSW (Television South West Ltd.) serves southwest England.

Thames Television Ltd. serves the London area (Monday to Thursday, Friday up to 5.15 pm).

Tyne Tees Television Ltd. serves northeast England.

Ulster Television PLC serves Northern Ireland.

Yorkshire Television Ltd. serves Yorkshire.

Independent Television News (ITN) a non-profit-making organization owned by the ITV companies. It supplies news information to Channel Four and ITV.

The franchises that allow independent programme contractors to operate will expire at the end of 1992. Contractors will compete with other independent contractors for the renewal of their franchises.

THE WORLD SERVICE

The BBC World Service broadcasts 24 hours a day in English and is directed to almost all countries of the world. Special Broadcasts in foreign languages include:

African Service, broadcast in Swahili, Somali and Hausa.

Arabic Service, broadcast to the Middle East and North Africa (on air 9 hours a day) in Arabic, French, Persian, and Pashto.

Eastern Service, broadcast in Bengali, Burmese, Hindi, Nepali, Pashto, Persian, Tamil and Urdu.

Far Eastern Service, broadcast in Cantonese, Mandarin, Indonesian, Japanese, Malay, Thai and Vietnamese.

Latin American Service, broadcast in Spanish and Portuguese.

German Service, broadcast to Germany (formerly both East and West), Austria, and German-speaking Switzerland.

Central European Service, broadcast in Czech and Slovak, Hungarian, Polish and Finnish.

Russian Service, broadcast in Russian (on air for 6 ½ hours a day).

Southeast European Service, broadcast in Bulgarian, Romanian, Serbo-Croat, Slovene, Greek and Turkish.

INDEX

An emboldened page reference indicates a major entry.

A

a priori probability 253, 300
Aalto, Alvar 368
Aargau (Argovie) 609
Abacus 243
Abbado, Claudio 383
Abelard, Peter 302
Aberdeen 691
Aberdeen, Sir George Hamilton-Gordon, Earl 723
Abisko National Park 130
Abruzzi 555
Abruzzi National Park 130
absolute magnitude, of a star 11
absolute zero 199
Abstract Expressionism 357
Abstraction (art) 355–56
Abu-Dhabi 620
Abu Nuwas 333
acceleration 191, 193, 194, 197
accidents, road (UK) 735
ace inhibitors 159
acid rain 109, 226
acids 224
Acoelomata 131
acoustics 202–03
Action Painting 357
active volcanoes 72
actors 396–403
  film 396–99
  stage 401–03
acupuncture 166
Adam, Robert 366
adding machine 284
Addington, Henry 722
addition 240
Adélie Land 638
adiabatic system 200
Adlerian psychology 162
Adorno, Theodor 303
Adrastea 19
adrenal glands 148
Advent Sunday 50–51
aepyornis 140
aerodynes 274
aerostats 274
Aeschylus 332
aestivation 139
affective disorder 150
Afghanistan 46, 449, 465, 493–94
Africa 55–56
  history 411, 429, 431, 433, 435
African art 349
African churches 313
African traditional religions 320–21
Agnatha 134
Agni 319
agricultural crops
  in the EC 127
  in Europe 126–27
agricultural products 472–73
Ahimsa 319, 323
AIDS 150–51
ailerons 274
air 95–97
air pollution 108, 109
air traffic 735
airbrush technique 346
aircraft 274–75, 294
airlines (major) 296
airports (major) 293, 295, 734
Ajman 620
Al Khwarizmi 230
Alabama 626
Aland Islands 533
Alaska 626
Alba, kings of 697
Albania 46, 449, 465, 494
Albéniz, Isaac 380

Alberta 514
Albinoni, Tommaso 378
Alder, Alfred 163
Alderney 668
Aldershot 690
Alexander of Miletus 301
Alexander Technique 166
algae, blue-green 123
algebra 240, 241, 244–48
  arithmetic and 240, 244–48
Algeria 46, 449, 465, 494–95
alimentary system 148
alkalis 224
All African Games 665
All Saints' Day 50
All Souls Day 50
allemande 386
allergies 17
almsgiving (Islamic) 316
Alpha decay 205
Alpha particles 205
Alpine World Cup Champions 657
Altdorfer, Albrecht 351
Alternating current (AC) 209
altocumulus cloud 98
altruism 300
aluminium 473
Amalthea 19
American 19th-century writers 339
American art, native 349
American football 641
American notation (music) 373
American Samoa 464, 629
Americas, history of the 422, 423, 429, 431, 433, 435
amino acids 123, 228
ammonia 226
amnesia 159
amoebic dysentery 151
ampere 188, 207
Amphybia 133, 134
amplitude 196
  modulation (AM) 196, 287
  of an earthquake wave 90
anaesthetics 148
analytical philosophy 300
analytical psychology 162
Ananke 19
anatomy 144–48
Ancient Near East art 348
Ancient World, history 408–09
Andalusia 604
Andaman and Nicobar Islands 548
Andean America, history 422
Andersen, Hans Christian 342
Andhra Pradesh 548
Andorra 46, 449, 465, 495–96
Andrew (apostle) 305
Angelico, Fra 350
Angiospermopsida 126
Anglican Churches 312, 741
Anglican dioceses (UK) 742
Anglicans 304
Anglo-Latin language 330
Anglo-Saxon architecture 363
Anglo-Saxon England 694, 696
Angola 46, 449, 465, 496
Anguilla 463, 624
angular acceleration 197
animal kingdom 133
animal stature 191
Animalia 125, 131–44
animals 131–44
  collective nouns of 137–39
  domesticated 142–44
  endangered species 141–42
  gestation periods of 136–37
  longevity of 135–36
  prehistoric 139–41
  velocity of movement of the 135
Anjou, House of 699
ankylosaurus 140
Anne, Queen 709

anniversaries, wedding 53
anode 208
anorexia 159
Anselm 302
antacids 159
Antarctica 56, 638
anthrax 151
anthroposophical medicine 166
Antigua and Barbuda 46, 449, 465, 496–97
antiphons 376
Antisthenes 301
Antrim 689
aorta 148
apatosaurus 140
aphelion 13
Apocrypha 315
apogee 16
apostles (of the Christian Church) 305
Apothecaries' system 188
apparent magnitude 10
Appenzell Ausser Rhoden 609
Appenzell Inner Rhoden 609
apples, annual production 190
applied mathematics 230
apse 363
aquatint 347
Aquinas, St Thomas 302
Arabic language 327
Arabic numerals 243
Arabic writers 333
Arachnida 132, 133
Aragon 604
ARC-AIDS 150
arcades 362
archaeopteryx 140
archery 641
Archimedes 230
Archimedes' principle 198
architects (major) 362, 364, 365, 366, 367, 368
architecture 361–69
  20th-century 367–68
  Age of Revival 366–67
  Anglo-Saxon 363
  Baroque 365
  Byzantine 362–63
  Carolingian 363
  Egyptian 361
  glossary of terms 368–69
  Gothic 363–64
  Greek 361–62
  Mannerism 365
  medieval (early) 363
  Modernism (international) 367–68
  Near Eastern 361
  Neoclassicism 366
  Palladianism 365, 366
  Post-Impressionism 354
  Post-Modernism 368
  Renaissance 364
  Rococo 365
  Roman 362
  Romanesque 363
Ards 689
area, units of 189, 191, 192
Argentina 44, 46, 436, 449, 465, 497–98
Argentinian Antarctic Territory 638
Ariel (moon) 22
Ariosto, Lodovico 334
Aristophanes 332
Aristotle 301, 332
arithmetic 244–48
  and algebra 240, 244–48
  natural numbers and 240
Arizona 626
Arkansas 626
armadillo 141
Armagh 689
Armenia 617
arms control 488–89
Arnold, Matthew 338
aromatherapy 166
ars antiqua 376